Collins

COBUILD
Learner's
American English
Dictionary

Published by Collins
An imprint of HarperCollins Publishers
Westerhill Road
Bishopbriggs
Glasgow G64 2QT

Third Edition 2016

10 9 8 7 6 5 4 3 2 1

© HarperCollins Publishers 2016

ISBN 978-0-00-813578-2

Collins® and COBUILD® are registered
trademarks of HarperCollins Publishers Limited

Copyright © HarperCollins Publishers Ltd 2016:
Dictionary text, Thesaurus text, About COBUILD
dictionaries, Guide to dictionary entries,
Pronunciation, Parts of speech used in the
dictionary, Parts of speech quick reference,
Irregular verbs list, Prefixes and suffixes list,
Subject vocabulary, and Key words.

Copyright © 2016 National Geographic Learning,
a part of Cengage Learning:
In-text features including: Picture Dictionary,
Thesaurus, Usage, Word Web, Word Link, and
Word Partnership, and supplements including:
Grammar reference, Activity guide, Writer's
handbook, Speaker's handbook, and Visual
thesaurus design.

www.collinsdictionary.com/cobuild
www.collinselt.com

Typeset by Davidson Publishing Solutions,
Glasgow

Printed and bound by Manipal Technologies
Ltd., Manipal

Contents

Acknowledgments

The publishers would like to thank the following reviewers:

Yospa Abin
Tropical Elementary
Miami, FL

Maria Victoria Aguirre
Houston Independent School
District
Houston, TX

Sandra Ahmad
Miami Dade County P.S. D.A.
Dorsey Educational Center
Miami, FL

Antoinette Alitto
Harrisburg Area Community
College
Harrisburg, PA

Michele Ameno
Action, Inc.
Gloucester, MA

Erika Anderson
Sauk Valley Community
College
Dixon, IL

Priscilla Arbuckle
Mendon-Upton Regional
School District
Mendon-Upton, MA

Teresa Arvizu
McFarland Unified School
District
McFarland, CA

Gohar Atamian
Q752, NYC
Jamaica, NY

Barbara Auris
Montgomery County
Community College
Blue Bell, PA

Saba Baptiste
New Alternative Education
High School of Hillsborough
County
Tampa, FL

Barbara Biba
Cape Fear Literacy Council
Wilmington, NC

Rosario Bickert
Taylor Business Institute
Chicago, IL

Alexander Bochkov
Seattle WA

Carol Brady
Miami Senior Adult
Educational Center
Miami, FL

Geri Brehm
Brandeis International
Business School
Waltham, MA

Karmen Buck
Pampa Jr. High School
Pampa, TX

Sr. Eileen Burns
Sisters of Notre Dame de
Namur
Notre Dame Education Center–
Lawrence
Lawrence, MA

Debra Butt
West Briar Middle School
Houston, TX

Richard Ciriello
Lower East Side Preparatory
High School
New York, NY

Suann Claunch
Fort Worth Independent
School District
Fort Worth, TX

Christina Chavez
Elk Grove Adult and
Community Education
Sacramento, CA

Judy Cole
Randolph County Schools
Asheboro, NC

Kevin Davidson
Perth Amboy Board of
Education
Eatontown, NJ

Charmaine Della Bella
Norwood Public School
Norwood, NJ

Gwendolyn Dickens
Huntington Park-Bell CAS
Huntington Park, CA

Kim Oanh Tran Dinh
Lone Star College System
Houston,TX

Gregory Dobie
Van Nuys Community Adult
School
Van Nuys, CA

Eddie Dominguez
Woodlake Union High School
Woodlake CA

Phyllis Doty
Suwannee/Hamilton
Vocational Tech Center
Live Oak, FL

Gayle Earley
Worcester Public Schools
Worcester, MA

Julie Elmore
Barrow County School System
Winder, GA

Heidi Enck
Cornerstone University
Grand Rapids, MI

Mary Endress
Katy Independent School
District
Katy, TX

Elizabeth Farris
Dallas Independent School
District
Dallas, TX

Maida Feliciano
Houston Independent School
District
Houston, TX

Ashley Fenelus
World Relief
Chicago, IL

Daisy Flores
Blanton Elementary
Arlington Independent School
District
Arlington,TX

Martin Flores, Jr.
Houston Community College
Houston, TX

Sandra Fourzan
North Hills Preparatory
Irving, TX

Beverly Gandall
Coastline Community College
Westminster, CA

Louis G. Giancola
Vermont Adult Learning
Colchester, VT

Carol Glickman
Chattahoochee Technical
College
Marietta, GA

Sumru Gokcen
Myers Park High School
Charlotte, NC

Evelyn Gomez
Academy for New Americans
Astoria, NY

Karen Grimwood
Carl Hayden Community High
School
Phoenix, AZ

Sara Hamerla, Ed.D.
Framingham Public Schools
Framingham, MA

Sharon Hahnlen
Liberty University
Lynchburg, VA

Laurie Hartwick
Health and Human Services
High School
Lawrence Public Schools
Lawrence, MA

Colleen Henriquez
Central Islip High School
Central Islip, NY

Leah Hinkle
Greater Albany Public Schools
Albany, OR

Carolyn Hirsch
West Adult Basic Education
Monticello, MN

Linda Hively
Santa Clara Adult Education
Santa Clara, CA

Debra Homan
Millville Public Schools
Millville, NJ

Diane Hunter
Georgia Piedmont Technical
College
Clarkston, GA

Mario Marlon J. Ibao
Houston Independent
School District
Houston, TX

Christina Jones
Pittsburg Jr. High
Pittsburg, TX

Karen Kapeluck
Transitional ESOL High School
Fairfax County Public Schools
Falls Church, VA

Robert Kelso
Miami Dade College
Miami, FL

Judith Knox
Cypress Lakes High School
Katy, TX

Mira Krolikowska
Polish American Association
Chicago, IL

Susan Kuhn
Mt. Hood Community College
Portland, PA

Karin Linn-Nieves
San Joaquin County Office of
Education
Stockton, CA

Gabriela Lo Coco Hector
Department of Education
West Hawaii District
Kamuela, HI

Reyna Lopez
MidCity Learning Center
Los Angeles, CA

Cara Lovell
Will Rogers College Junior
High
Tulsa, OK

Robin Mackie
Valadez Middle School
Academy
Placentia, CA

Susan Marion
Denver Center for
International Studies
Denver, CO

Mary Martin
Keller Independent School
District
Keller, TX

Erlinda Mauricio
Pahoa High & Intermediate
School
Pahoa, HI

Alesha McCauley
Wake County Public Schools
Cary, NC

Dominika McPartland
I.S. 93 Ridgewood
Queens, NY

Suzanne Meador
Waltrip High School
Houston, TX

Monica Merry-Mason
Madison Area Technical
College
Madison, WI

Karen Neal
Fort Worth Independent
School District
Fort Worth, TX

Debbie Noorda
Lee Antonello Elementary
North Las Vegas, NV

Hilda Nuñez
Los Angeles Unified School
District
Los Angeles, CA

Linda Pabon
Alief Independent School
District
Houston, TX

Sonja Pantry
Robert Morgan Educational
Center
Miami, FL

Melchor Perez
Gilbert High School
Anaheim, CA

Ryan Phinisee
Pioneer Academy of Science
Clifton, NJ

Reine Price
Miami Dade College
Miami, FL

Mary Elaine Priester
Westview High School
Portland, OR

Sharon Pritzos
Huntington Beach Adult
School
Huntington Beach, CA

Caroline Purcell
Mount St. Mary's University
Seminary
Emmitsburg, MD

Zarina Qadir
Kilmer Elementary School
Chicago, IL, 60626

Jesus Ranero
Miami Dade College
Hialeah, FL

Teresa Reen
Overfelt Adult Center
San Jose, CA

Catherine Rifkin
Florida State College at
Jacksonville
Jacksonville, FL

Danette Roe
Evans Community Adult
School
Los Angeles, CA

Patricia Saenz
Northside Independent School
District
San Antonio, TX

Katharine Sims
Fremont High School
Sunnyvale, CA

Sonia Solla
Darwin Elementary School
Chicago Public Schools
Chicago, IL

Graciela Somoza
Lorezo Walker Institute of
Technology
Naples, FL

Sharon Staples
Columbia County Schools
Evans, GA

Ilza Sterling
Falcon Cove Middle School
Weston, FL

Paula Stewart
Benito Juarez Community
Academy
Chicago, IL

Teri Suzuki
Amelia Earhart Elementary
Alameda, CA

Monica Teles-Carr
YWCA of Greater Harrisburg
Harrisburg, PA

Joseph S. Terzo
Capital Regional Education
Council
Hartford, CT

Gwen Thornburgh
Blue Ridge Community College
Flat Rock, NC

Sigrun Utash
Simi Valley Adult School
Glendale Community College
Simi Valley, CA

Rolando Vergara
Miami Dade County Public
Schools
Miami, FL

Sonia Walmsley
Attleboro Public Schools
Attleboro, MA

Heather Wilson
Alhambra High School
Phoenix, AZ

Jill Wright
Project Literacy of Greater
Bergen County
Hackensack, NJ

Becky Young
Dayton City School
Dayton, TN

Dolores Zawadzki
Wilbur Wright College
Chicago, IL

Acknowledgments

The publishers would also like to acknowledge the following for their invaluable contribution to the original COBUILD concept:

John Sinclair
Patrick Hanks
Gwyneth Fox
Richard Thomas

David Brazil, Stephen Bullon, Jeremy Clear, Rosalind Combley,
Susan Hunston, Ramesh Krishnamurthy, Rosamund Moon, Elizabeth Potter

Jane Bradbury, Joanna Channell, Alice Deignan, Andrew Delahunty,
Sheila Dignen, Gill Francis, Helen Liebeck, Elizabeth Manning,
Carole Murphy, Michael Murphy, Jonathan Payne, Elaine Pollard,
Christina Rammell, Penny Stock, John Todd, Jenny Watson,
Laura Wedgeworth, John Williams

We would also like to thank the following for their contribution to the first edition of this dictionary:

Sandra Anderson, Katharine Coates, Helen Forrest, Robert Grossmith,
Lucy Hollingworth, Alison Macaulay, Enid Pearsons, Anne Robertson

Finally, we would like to acknowledge the assistance of the many hundreds of individuals and companies who have kindly given permission for copyright material to be used in the Collins Corpus. The written sources include many national and regional newspapers, magazines and periodicals, and books published in the United States, Britain, and Australia. Extensive spoken data has been provided by radio and television broadcasting companies; research workers at many universities and other institutions; and numerous individual contributors. We are grateful to them all.

Consultant
Paul Nation

About COBUILD dictionaries

When the first COBUILD dictionary was published in 1987, it revolutionized dictionaries for learners. It was the first of a new generation of dictionaries that were based on actual evidence of how English was used, rather than lexicographer intuition.

Collins and the University of Birmingham, led by the outstanding linguist John Sinclair, developed an electronic corpus in the 1980s, called the Collins Birmingham University International Language Database (COBUILD). This corpus, which is also known as the Collins Corpus, became the largest collection of English data in the world, and COBUILD dictionary editors use the corpus to analyze the way that people really use the language.

The Collins Corpus contains 4.5 billion words taken from websites, newspapers, magazines, and books published around the world, and from spoken material from radio, TV, and everyday conversations. New data is added to the corpus every month, to help COBUILD editors identify new words and meanings from the moment they are first used.

All COBUILD dictionaries are based on the information our editors find in the Collins Corpus. Because the corpus is so large, our editors can look at lots of examples of how people really use words. The data tells us how words are used; what they mean; which words are used together; and how often words are used.

This information helps us decide which words to include in COBUILD dictionaries. Did you know, for example, that around 90% of English speech and writing is made up of approximately 3,500 words? The corpus tells us which words these are, and helps us ensure that when you use a COBUILD dictionary, you can be sure that you are learning the words you really want to know.

All of the examples in COBUILD dictionaries are examples of real English, taken from the Collins Corpus. The examples have been carefully chosen to demonstrate typical grammatical patterns, typical vocabulary, and typical contexts for each word.

The corpus lies at the heart of COBUILD and you can be confident that COBUILD will show you what you need to know to be able to communicate easily and accurately in English.

Guide to key features

Vocabulary builders

The vocabulary-building features within the *Collins COBUILD Learner's American English Dictionary* encourage users to explore and enjoy the English language. In turn, these features help the learner to build both their active and passive vocabulary. These 'vocabulary builders' aim to increase language fluency and improve the user's ability to communicate accurately, whilst providing the learner with a greater depth and breadth of knowledge of English.

Picture Dictionary boxes present vocabulary, concepts, and processes in an eye-catching and memorable way. The vocabulary has been selected from key topics and is particularly relevant for users studying other subjects in English.

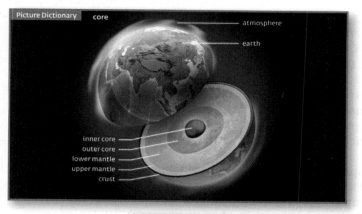

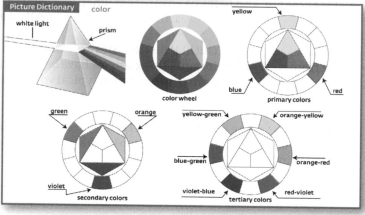

Word Webs present topic-related vocabulary in illustrated encyclopedic panels. These features encourage language exploration and provide learners with the opportunity to gain a deeper understanding of the language and concepts. The key words from the texts (in bold) are defined in the dictionary and when users look up one word, they discover other related words that will draw them further into the dictionary. The longer the learner spends exploring vocabulary, the greater and richer their language acquisition will be.

Word Web   spice

While studying the use of **spices** in cooking, scientists found that many spices can help prevent disease. Bacteria can grow quickly on food and cause serious illnesses in humans. The researchers found that many spices kill bacteria. For example, **garlic**, **onion**, allspice, and oregano kill almost all common **germs**. **Cinnamon**, tarragon, cumin, and chili **peppers** also stop about 75% of bacteria. And even common, everyday **black pepper** kills about 25% of all germs. The scientists also found that food is connected to climate. Spicy food is common in hot climates. Bland food is common in cold climates.

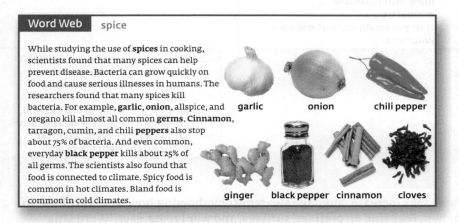

garlic   onion   chili pepper

ginger   black pepper   cinnamon   cloves

Word Web   wave

THE ELECTROMAGNETIC SPECTRUM

As **wind** blows across water, it makes **waves**. It does this by transferring energy to the water. If the waves meet an object, they bounce off it. Light also moves in waves and acts the same way. We can see an object only if light waves bounce off it. Light waves differ in **frequency**. Wave frequency is usually the measure of the number of waves per second. **Radio waves** and **microwaves** are examples of low-frequency light waves. **Visible light** is made of medium-frequency light waves. **Ultraviolet radiation** and **X-rays** are high-frequency light waves.

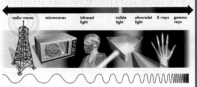

Word Partnerships highlight the most important collocations of words with the highest frequency in the Collins Corpus. For each collocation, the headword is repeated and the collocate is shown in bold. The numbers refer the student to the correct meaning of the headword.

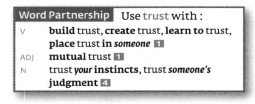

Word Links increase language awareness by showing how words are built in English. Focusing on prefixes, suffixes, and word roots, each 'Word Link' provides a simple definition of the building block and then shows three examples of it appearing in a word. Providing three examples encourages learners to look up these words to develop and consolidate their understanding.

| Word Link | *port ≈ carrying* : *export, import, portable* |

| Word Link | *geo ≈ earth* : *geography, geology, geologist* |

Thesaurus boxes provide both synonyms and antonyms for high-frequency words. These features offer an excellent way for learners to expand their knowledge of vocabulary and usage by directing them to other words they can research in the dictionary. The numbers refer the student to the correct meaning within the headword's entry.

Thesaurus talk Also look up :
N   argument, conversation, dialogue, discussion, interview, negotiation; (ant.) silence **1**
V   chat, discuss, gossip, say, share, speak, tell; (ant.) listen **1**

Thesaurus difficult Also look up :
ADJ   challenging, demanding, hard, tough; (ant.) easy, simple, uncomplicated **1** disagreeable, irritable; (ant.) accommodating, cooperative **2**

Usage notes explain shades of meaning, clarify cultural references, and highlight important grammatical information.

Usage   **less** and **fewer**
Less is used to describe general amounts (or noncount nouns). *Less snow fell in December than in January. Fewer* is used to describe amounts of countable items. *Maria is working fewer hours this semester.*

Usage   **one** and **you**
Sometimes *one* is used to refer to any person or to people in general, but it sounds formal: *One has to be smart about buying a computer.* In everyday English, use *you* instead of *one*: *You should only call 911 in an emergency.*

The **Visual thesaurus** on pages 1046–1077 focuses on offering alternatives to the 50 most over-used words in English, helping learners to develop fluency and creativity in their use of English

Guide to dictionary entries

Over 3,000 of the most common English words are highlighted in pink.

Definitions are written in full sentences using simple words and show the common ways in which the headword is used.

Subject-area labels

Examples of real English, taken from the Collins Corpus, demonstrate how the word is used.

Cross-references direct the user to other relevant entries and to illustrated features.

Phrasal verbs are shown at the end of the entry.

Menus help users to navigate entries.

Pronunciation

Verb forms are shown.

When there is more than one meaning, the different meanings are numbered.

Word origin

---

ac|count /əkaʊnt/ (**accounts, accounting, accounted**)

1 N-COUNT If you have an **account** with a bank, you leave your money there and take some out when you need it. ❑ *I have $3,000 in my bank account.*

2 N-COUNT BUSINESS **Accounts** are records of all the money that a person or a business receives and spends. ❑ *He kept detailed accounts of all the money he spent.*

3 N-COUNT TECHNOLOGY An **account** is an arrangement you have with a company to use a service they provide. ❑ *...an email account.*

4 N-COUNT An **account** is a report of something that has happened. ❑ *He gave a detailed account of the events.*

5 → see also **accounting, checking account**

6 PHRASE If you **take** something **into account**, or **take account of** something, you consider it when you are thinking about a situation. ❑ *You have to take everyone into account before making a decision.* [from Old French]
→ look at Word Web: **history**

▶ **account for** If you can **account for** something, you can explain it or give the reason for it. ❑ *How do you account for these differences?*

```
              bow
  ❶ BENDING
  ❷ OBJECTS
```

❶ bow /baʊ/ (**bows, bowing, bowed**)

1 V-I When you **bow to** someone, you bend your head or body toward them as a formal way of greeting them or showing respect. ❑ *They bowed low to the king.*

2 N-COUNT Bow is also a noun. ❑ *I gave a theatrical bow and waved.*

3 V-T If you **bow** your head, you bend it downward so that you are looking toward the ground. ❑ *The colonel bowed his head and whispered a prayer.* [from Old English]

xii

❷ bow /b<u>oʊ</u>/ (**bows**) ⎯⎯⎯⎯⎯⎯⎯⎯⎯

 1 N-COUNT A **bow** is a knot with two round parts and two loose ends that is used in tying laces and ribbons. ❑ *Add some ribbon tied in a bow.*

 2 N-COUNT A **bow** is a weapon for shooting arrows. ❑ *Some of the men were armed with bows and arrows.*

 3 N-COUNT MUSIC The **bow** of a violin or other similar instrument is a long thin piece of wood with threads stretched along it that you move across the strings. [from Old English]

fore|cast /f<u>ɔ</u>rkæst/ (**forecasts, forecasting, forecast** or **forecasted**)

> **LANGUAGE HELP**
> The forms **forecast** and **forecasted** can both be used for the past tense and past participle.

 1 N-COUNT A **forecast** is what someone expects will happen in the future. ❑ *Did you see the weather forecast?*

 2 V-T If you **forecast** events, you say what you think is going to happen in the future. ❑ *Economists were forecasting higher oil prices.*

 ● **fore|cast|er** (**forecasters**) **N-COUNT** ❑ *David worked for 34 years as a weather forecaster.*

 → look at Word Webs: **forecast, tsunami**

per|mit (**permits, permitting, permitted**)

> **PRONUNCIATION HELP**
> Pronounce the verb /pərm<u>ɪ</u>t/. Pronounce the noun /p<u>ɜ</u>rmɪt/.

 1 V-T If someone **permits** you **to** do something, they allow you to do it. [FORMAL] ❑ *The guards permitted me to bring my camera.*

 2 N-COUNT A **permit** is an official document that allows you to do something. ❑ *She hasn't got a work permit.* [from Latin]

smoky /sm<u>oʊ</u>ki/ (**smokier, smokiest**) also **smokey** **ADJ** If a place is **smoky**, there is a lot of smoke in the air. ❑ *The bar was dark, noisy, and smoky.* [from Old English]

wa|ter va|por **N-NONCOUNT** SCIENCE **Water vapor** is water in the form of gas in the air.

Plural forms of nouns are shown.

Part of speech

The | symbol shows where a word may be split across lines.

Language Help notes advise the user on how to use words correctly.

Related word

Pronunciation Help notes advise the user on how to correctly pronounce words.

Set structures are shown in bold within definitions.

Labels indicate words that are restricted to formal, informal, written, spoken, or literary language.

Comparative and superlative forms of adjectives and adverbs are shown.

Alternative spellings of headwords are shown.

Stress at compounds is shown by underlining.

Pronunciation

IPA Symbols

Vowel	Sounds		Consonant	Sounds
ɑ	bar, calm		b	bed, rub
æ	act, mass		d	done, red
ɑɪ	dive, cry		f	fit, if
ɑɪər	fire, tire		g	good, dog
ɑʊ	out, down		h	hat, horse
ɑʊər	flour, sour		k	king, pick
ɛ	met, lend, pen		l	lip, bill
eɪ	say, weight		ᵊl	handle, panel
ɛər	fair, care		m	mat, ram
ɪ	fit, win		n	not, tin
i	seem, me		ᵊn	hidden, written
ɪər	near, beard		p	pay, lip
ɒ	lot, spot		r	run, read
oʊ	note, coat		s	soon, bus
ɔ	claw, more		t	talk, bet
ɔɪ	boy, joint		v	van, love
ʊ	could, stood		w	win, wool
u	you, use		y	yellow, you
ʊər	lure, endure		z	zoo, buzz
ɜr	turn, third		ʃ	ship, wish
ʌ	fund, must		ʒ	measure, leisure
ə	about		ŋ	sing, working
i	very		tʃ	cheap, witch
u	actual		θ	thin, myth
			ð	then, bathe
			dʒ	joy, bridge

Stress

Stress is shown by underlining the vowel in the stressed syllable:

two /tu̱/
result /rɪ zʌlt/
disappoint /dɪ̱səpɔ̱ɪnt/

If two syllables are underlined, the first will have secondary stress, and the second will have primary stress.

In the case of compound words, where the pronunciation of each part is given separately, the stress pattern is shown by underlining the headword: "fu̱ll-ti̱me", "fi̱rst-cla̱ss", but "be̱ll pepper".

Stressed syllables

When words are used in context, the way in which they are pronounced depends upon the information units that are constructed by the speaker. For example, a speaker could say:

1 "the reSULT was disapPOINTing"
2 "it was a DISappointing reSULT"
3 "it was VERy disappointing inDEED"

In (3), neither of the two underlined syllables in disappointing receives either primary or secondary stress. This shows that it is not possible for a dictionary to predict whether a particular syllable will be stressed in context.

It should be noted, however, that in the case of adjectives with two stressed syllables, the second syllable often loses its stress when it is used before a noun:

"a FIRST-class SEAT"
"AIR-conditioned TRAINS"

Two things should be noted about the marked syllables:

1 They can take primary or secondary stress in a way that is not shared by the other syllables.
2 Whether they are stressed or not, the vowel must be pronounced distinctly; it cannot be weakened to /ə/, /ɪ/ , or /ʊ/.

These features are shared by most of the one-syllable words in English, which are therefore transcribed in this dictionary as stressed syllables:

two /tu̱/
inn /ɪ̱n/
tree /tri̱/

Unstressed syllables

It is an important characteristic of English that vowels in unstressed syllables tend not to be pronounced clearly. Many unstressed syllables contain the vowel /ə/, a neutral vowel which is not found in stressed syllables. The vowels /ɪ/ , or /ʊ/, which are relatively neutral in quality, are also common in unstressed syllables.

Single-syllable grammatical words such as "shall" and "at" are often pronounced with a weak vowel such as /ə/. However, some of them are pronounced with a more distinct vowel under certain circumstances, for example when they occur at the end of a sentence. This distinct pronunciation is generally referred to as the strong form, and is given in this dictionary after the word STRONG.

shall /ʃəl, STRONG ʃæl/
at /ət, STRONG æt/

Parts of speech used in the dictionary

Nearly all the words that are explained in this dictionary have grammar information given about them. For each word or meaning, its part of speech is shown in capital letters, just before the definition. Examples of parts of speech are ADJ, N-COUNT, PRON, and V-T.

The sections below contain further information about each part of speech.

Verbs

A verb is a word that is used to say what someone or something does or what happens to them, or to give information about them.

V-I

An intransitive verb is one that does not take an object, e.g.:

> **collapse:** *The bridge collapsed last October.*

V-T

A transitive verb is one that takes an object, e.g.:

> **mail:** *He mailed me the contract.*

V-LINK

V-LINK means link verb. A link verb is a verb such as *be, feel*, or *seem*. These verbs connect the subject of a sentence to a complement. Most link verbs do not occur in the passive, e.g.:

> **be:** *The sky was black.*
>
> **feel:** *It feels good to finish a piece of work.*
>
> **seem:** *The thunder seemed quite close.*

AUX

AUX means an auxiliary verb. An auxiliary verb is used with another verb to add particular meanings to that verb, for example, to form the continuous or the passive, or to form negatives and questions. The verbs *be, do, get*, and *have* are used as auxiliary verbs in some meanings, e.g.:

> **be:** *She was driving to work when the accident happened.*
>
> **do:** *They don't work very hard.*
>
> **get:** *A pane of glass got broken.*
>
> **have:** *What have you found?*

MODAL

A modal is a modal verb such as *may*, *must*, or *would*. A modal is used before the infinitive form of a verb, e.g., *I must go home now*. In questions, it comes before the subject, e.g., *May we come in?* In negatives, it comes before the negative word, e.g., *She wouldn't say where she bought her shoes*. It does not inflect; for example, it does not take an *-s* in the third person singular, e.g., *I can take care of myself*.

Nouns

N-COUNT

N-COUNT means a count noun. Count nouns refer to a thing that can be counted, and count nouns have both a singular and a plural form. When a count noun is used in the singular, it must normally have a word such as *a*, *an*, *the*, or *her* in front of it, e.g.:

> **aunt:** *She wrote to her aunt in Alabama.*

> **room:** *A minute later he left the room.*

N-NONCOUNT

N-NONCOUNT means a noncount noun. Noncount nouns refer to things that are not normally counted or which we do not think of as individual items. Noncount nouns do not have a plural form and are used with a singular verb, e.g.:

> **help:** *Thanks very much for your help.*

> **rain:** *We got very wet in the rain.*

> **bread:** *She bought a loaf of bread at the store.*

N-SING

N-SING means a singular noun. A singular noun is always singular and must have a word such as *a*, *an*, *the*, or *my* in front of it, e.g.:

> **sun:** *The sun was now high in the sky.*

> **fault:** *The accident was my fault.*

N-PLURAL

N-PLURAL means a plural noun. A plural noun is always plural and is used with plural verbs, e.g.:

> **clothes:** *Milly went upstairs to change her clothes.*

> **feelings:** *I'm really sorry if I hurt your feelings.*

N-PROPER

N-PROPER means a proper noun. A proper noun refers to one person, place, thing, or institution, and begins with a capital letter, e.g.:

> **Earth:** *The space shuttle Atlantis returned safely to Earth today.*

> **Pentagon:** *There was a news conference at the Pentagon.*

Other parts of speech

ADJ

ADJ means an adjective. An adjective is a word that is used to tell you more about a person or thing, such as its appearance, color, size, or other qualities, e.g.:

> **angry:** *An angry crowd gathered.*
>
> **wet:** *He dried his wet hair with a towel.*
>
> **white:** *He had nice white teeth.*

ADV

ADV means an adverb. An adverb is a word that gives more information about when, how, or where something happens, e.g.:

> **tomorrow:** *Bye, see you tomorrow.*
>
> **slowly:** *He spoke slowly and clearly.*
>
> **home:** *She wasn't feeling well and she wanted to go home.*

CONJ

CONJ means a conjunction. Conjunctions are words such as *and*, *but*, *although*, or *since*, which are used to link two words or two clauses in a sentence, e.g.:

> **although:** *They all play basketball, although on different teams.*
>
> **but:** *I've enjoyed my vacation, but now it's time to get back to work.*
>
> **since:** *I've lived here since I was six years old.*

DET

DET means a determiner. A determiner is a word such as *a*, *the*, *my*, or *every* which is used at the beginning of a noun group, e.g.:

> **an:** *He started eating an apple.*
>
> **the:** *The doctor's on his way.*
>
> **every:** *Every room has a window facing the ocean.*

INTERJ

INTERJ means an interjection. An interjection is a word or phrase that is used to express strong emotion or, for example, to greet someone or to apologize, e.g.:

> **hello:** *Hello , Trish. How are you?*
>
> **oh:** *"Oh!" Kenny said. "Has everyone gone?"*
>
> **sorry:** *Sorry I took so long.*
>
> **wow:** *I thought, "Wow , what a good idea."*

NUM

NUM means number, e.g.:

> **one:** *They have one daughter.*
>
> **billion:** *The country's debt has risen to 3 billion dollars.*

PHRASE

A phrase is a group of words that have a particular meaning when they are used together. This meaning is not always understandable from the separate parts, e.g.:

by heart: *Mike knew this song by heart.*

shake hands: *Michael shook hands with Burke.*

PREDET

PREDET means a predeterminer. A predeterminer is a word such as *all* or *half* which can come before a determiner, e.g.:

all: *Hugh and all his friends came to the party.*

half: *We sat and talked for half an hour.*

PREP

PREP means a preposition. A preposition is a word such as *by*, *with*, or *from* which is always followed by a noun group or the *-ing* form of a verb, e.g.:

near: *The café is near the station in Edmonton.*

of: *The boy was drinking a glass of milk.*

PRON

PRON means a pronoun. A pronoun is used to refer to someone or something that has already been mentioned or whose identity is already known, e.g.:

he: *John was my boss, but he couldn't remember my name.*

they: *She said goodbye to the children as they left for school.*

this: *I have seen many movies, but never one like this.*

Some meanings in entries have more than one part of speech, for example,

celebrate: V-T/V-I

This means that **celebrate** is both a transitive verb and an intransitive verb.

I passed my test and wanted to celebrate.

Dick celebrated his 60th birthday on Monday.

Activity guide

Activity guide

1. GOING IN CIRCLES

Grammar Activities Picture Dictionary Activities	Word Link Activities

1. **Grammar Activities**
    Many different words are based on the word *circle*. Write the part of
    speech of each underlined word—noun, verb, or adjective. Use your
    dictionary to check your answers.
    a. The moon was perfectly <u>circular</u> last night.   _____
    b. The students arranged the chairs in a <u>circle</u>.   _____
    c. Vitamin E improves the <u>circulation</u> of the blood.   _____
    d. Airplanes sometimes <u>circle</u> several times
        before landing.   _____
    e. Please open the window so the air can <u>circulate</u>.   _____
    f. What is the <u>circulation</u> of *The Times*?   _____
    g. Did the teacher <u>circle</u> your mistakes?   _____
    h. I like <u>circular</u> eyeglasses, not square ones.   _____

2. **Picture Dictionary Activities—A**
    a. How many other shapes can you think of besides the circle? Write
        your list below.

        _____
        Look at the Picture Dictionary feature *shapes* and check your answers.
    b. Which two shapes most closely resemble the circle?

        _____   _____

3. **Picture Dictionary Activities—B**
    Look at the Picture Dictionary feature entitled *area*. Pay special
    attention to how to find the area of a circle.
    a. What do you call the distance from the center
        of the circle to the outside edge?   _____
    b. What do you call the line that runs around the
        outside of the circle?   _____
    c. What do you call the line that runs across the
        circle from one side to the other?   _____
    d. What is the formula for finding the area of
        a circle?   _____
    e. If a circle has a radius of 3 inches, what is
        its area? Use $\pi = 3.14$.   _____

4. **Word Link Activities**

   a. The first four letters of the word *circle* form a Word Link. What is that link? _____

   b. Look up the words *circle*, *circuit*, and *circulate*. Notice the Word Link *circ-* in those words. Write each word below.
   Then look it up in the dictionary and identify it as *verb, noun, or both*.

   _____, _____

   (word)   (part of speech)

   _____, _____

   (word)   (part of speech)

   _____, _____

   (word)   (part of speech)

   c. Complete each sentence below with the correct word from item **b.**
   1. Blood _____ around the body.
   2. A _____ is a shape with all points the same distance from the center.
   3. A tree fell on the power lines and broke the electrical _____.

ANSWER KEY:

1. **a.** adjective; **b.** noun; **c.** noun; **d.** verb; **e.** verb; **f.** noun; **g.** verb; **h.** adjective
2. **a.** Answers will vary; **b.** ellipse, oval
3. **a.** radius; **b.** circumference; **c.** diameter; **d.** πr^2; **e.** 28.26 inches
4. **a.** circ; **b.** circle, both; circuit, noun; circulate, verb; **c1.** circulates; **c2.** circle; **c3.** circuit

2. TRANSPORTATION

Choosing the Right Definition Word Web Activities	Dictionary Research Word Link Activities

1. **Choosing the Right Definition**

   Study the numbered definitions for *transportation*. Then write the number of the definition that relates to each sentence below.

   a. _____ The <u>transportation</u> of nuclear waste through large cities can be dangerous.

   b. _____ Using mass <u>transportation</u> helps the environment.

   c. _____ Many schools provide <u>transportation</u> for children in the form of school buses.

   d. _____ Subways provide rapid <u>transportation</u>.

   e. _____ Bad weather slows down most forms of <u>transportation</u>.

2. **Word Web Activities**

   Use the Word Web feature entitled *ship* to answer the following questions.

   Look up these words in the dictionary to check your answers.

   a. What do you call things other than people that are carried on ships? _____

   b. What do you call the place where a ship stops? _____

   c. What do you call the large ships that carry tourists? _____

3. **Dictionary Research**
   a. Reread the definition of *transportation*. Write your own definition of the word *goods* as it is used in the definition.

   _____

   b. Look up the word *goods* in the dictionary and complete the following sentence.

   Goods are things that people _____.

4. **Word Link Activities**
   The first five letters of the word *transportation* form a Word Link.
   a. What is the Word Link? _____
   b. What does the Word Link *trans* mean? _____
   c. Look up the words *transfer*, *transition*, and *translate*. Notice the Word Link *trans* in those words. Read the definitions.
   d. Complete each sentence below with the correct word from item **c.** Check your answers by looking up each word in the dictionary.
   1. I don't know how to read Chinese. Can you _____ this letter for me?
   2. After the president of the college left, there was a period of _____ before a new one was appointed.
   3. You'll have to take two buses to get there. You can _____ from the 101 to the 145 at Main Street.

ANSWER KEY:

1. **a.** 2; **b.** 1; **c.** 1; **d.** 2; **e.** 2
2. **a.** cargo; **b.** port; **c.** ocean liner, cruise ship
3. **a.** Answers will vary; **b.** buy or sell
4. **a.** trans; **b.** across; **d1.** translate; **d2.** transition; **d3.** transfer

3. ORCHESTRA

Word Web Activities Word Partnership Activities	Choosing the Right Definition

1. **Word Web Activities**

   Study the information in the Word Web feature entitled *orchestra*. Then answer the questions below. Write T for *true* or F for *false*.

   _____ **a.** A symphony orchestra usually has more than 100 players.

   _____ **b.** The largest section of the orchestra is the string section.

   _____ **c.** The double bass plays in the string section.

   _____ **d.** The brass section needs to play very loud.

   _____ **e.** The timpani is part of the brass section.

2. **Word Partnership Activities**

   The job of a symphony orchestra is to *perform* for the public. Look up the word *perform* in the dictionary.

   a. Write the number of the definition that applies to music. _____

   Study the Word Partnership feature for *perform*. Then complete the four sentences below using the word *perform* before or after one of these words or phrases: *tasks, able to, miracles, well*. Use each of these words or phrases one time.

   b. Some people believe that people can _____ _____.

   c. The violinist felt ill and was not _____ _____.

   d. The new tires _____ _____ on icy roads.

   e. Doctors believe the brains of adults and children _____ _____ in different ways.

3. **Choosing the Right Definition**

   Reread the Word Web feature for *orchestra*. Several of the bold words in this feature have multiple meanings.

   Study the numbered definitions for *composition*. Then write the number of the definition that relates to each sentence below.

   _____ **a.** The <u>composition</u> of water is hydrogen and oxygen.

   _____ **b.** Have you written any new <u>compositions</u> lately?

   Study the numbered definitions for *instrument*. Then write the number of the definition that relates to each sentence below.

   _____ **c.** The piano is my favorite <u>instrument.</u>

   _____ **d.** The dentist placed the <u>instruments</u> on the shelf.

ANSWER KEY:

1. **a.** F; **b.** T; **c.** T; **d.** F; **e.** F
2. **a.** 2; **b.** perform miracles; **c.** able to perform; **d.** perform well; **e.** perform tasks
3. **a.** 2; **b.** 1; **c.** 2; **d.** 1

4. COOKING

Word Web Activities	Thesaurus Activities
Picture Dictionary Activities	Grammar Activities
	Dictionary Research

1. **Word Web Activities**

   As you complete this activity, look up any words you aren't sure of.

   Read the definitions for *cook* and *cooking*. Then use the Word Web feature entitled *cooking* to answer the following questions.

   a. Which bold word means the opposite of *tough*? _____

   b. Which bold word means *absorb food into your body*? _____

   Now use the Word Web feature entitled *spice* to answer the following questions.

   c. Which spice is the least effective in killing germs? _____

   d. What kind of food do people in cold climates usually like? _____

   Now use the Word Web feature entitled *pan* to answer the following questions.

   e. Cooking pans are very heavy when made of what material? _____

   f. Copper pans are usually covered with a thin layer of what metal? _____

2. **Picture Dictionary Activities—A**

   Look at the Picture Dictionary feature for *cook*. Then complete the sentences correctly.

   a. If you want to make tea, you have to _____ the water.

   b. You need an oven if you want to _____, _____, or _____ food.

   c. When you put food in a wire container with boiling water under it, you _____ the food.

   d. When you make a slice of bread brown by cooking it you _____ it.

   e. When you cook food in an oven very close to the flame, you _____ it.

3. **Picture Dictionary Activities—B**

   Look at the Picture Dictionary feature for *egg*. Then answer the questions below. Look up any words you aren't sure of. Write T for *true* or F for *false*.

   _____ **a.** The scrambled eggs have peppers in them.

   _____ **b.** The hard-boiled egg has a round yolk.

   _____ **c.** The fried egg is in a frying pan.

4. **Thesaurus Activities**

Find the Thesaurus feature with the word *cook*. Then complete the sentences using words from the feature. Look up any words you aren't sure of.

a. A _____ works in a restaurant.

b. Yeast is the ingredient that _____ bread rise.

c. If the meal was cooked but it has gotten cold, you might _____ _____ the food.

d. Busy people tend to eat meals that are simple to _____.

5. **Grammar Activities**

Write the part of speech of each underlined word—noun or verb.

a. I don't like <u>cooking</u> vegetables. _____

b. My sister's <u>cooking</u> is fantastic. _____

c. Which do you prefer, <u>cooking</u> or baking? _____

d. On Sunday I <u>cooked</u> dinner for my family. _____

e. My husband is a very good <u>cook</u>. _____

6. **Dictionary Research**

Look at other words and phrases that follow the word *cook* in the dictionary.

a. Which one describes a collection of recipes? _____

b. Which one describes something you eat? _____

ANSWER KEY:

1. **a.** tender; **b.** digest; **c.** black pepper; **d.** bland; **e.** cast iron; **f.** tin
2. **a.** boil; **b.** roast, bake, broil; **c.** steam; **d.** toast; **e.** broil
3. **a.** F; **b.** T; **c.** T
4. **a.** chef; **b.** makes; **c.** heat up; **d.** prepare
5. **a.** verb; **b.** noun; **c.** verb; **d.** verb; **e.** noun
6. **a.** cookbook; **b.** cookie

5. ENERGY

Choosing the Right Definition Word Web Activities	Word Link Activities Grammar Activities

1. **Choosing the Right Definition**
   Study the numbered definitions for *energy*. Then write the number of the definition that relates to each sentence below.
   a. _____ She's putting all her <u>energy</u> into her performance.
   b. _____ My children have more <u>energy</u> than I do.
   c. _____ One problem with nuclear <u>energy</u> is that it produces radioactive waste.
   d. _____ You should save your <u>energy</u> for tomorrow's match.
   e. _____ Which <u>energy</u> source do you think is the cleanest?
   f. _____ Conserve your <u>energy</u>. Go to bed early.

2. **Word Web Activities**
   Use the Word Web feature entitled *energy* to answer the following questions. Answer each question with one of the bold words in the Word Web feature.
   a. What kind of power plants were built in the 1970s? _____
   b. What kind of gas is still used for home heating? _____
   c. What was the primary energy source for American settlers? _____
   d. What was the source of electrical power in the early 1900s? _____

3. **Word Link Activities**
   Look up the words below to find the Word Link in the word. Write the Word Link on the line.
   a. hydropower _____   d. complicate _____
   b. carefree _____   e. seller _____
   c. electricity _____

   Match the Word Link with the correct definition.

Word Link	Definition
_____ f. hydr	1. without
_____ g. free	2. causing to be
_____ h. electr	3. one who acts as
_____ i. ate	4. water
_____ j. er	5. electric

Now look back at the Word Web feature for *energy*. Write the three words from this feature that are formed from these Word Links.

k. g_____   **l.** h_____   **m.** e_____

4. **Grammar Activities**
   Review the dictionary entries for *energetic* and *energy*. Then complete each sentence with the correct form of a word starting with the letters *energ-*. Identify the part of speech of each word you use—noun, verb, adjective, or adverb.

		Part of Speech
a.	Celia is very _____ today.	_____
b.	I don't know what happened to all my _____. I'm really tired.	_____
c.	Clothes dryers use a lot of _____.	_____

ANSWER KEY:

1. **a.** 1; **b.** 1; **c.** 2; **d.** 1; **e.** 2; **f.** 1
2. **a.** nuclear; **b.** natural; **c.** wood; **d.** coal
3. **a.** hydr; **b.** free; **c.** electr; **d.** ate; **e.** er; **f.** 4; **g.** 1; **h.** 5; **i.** 2; **j.** 3; **k.** generate; **l.** hydroelectric ; **m.** electrical *or* electricity
4. **a.** energetic, adjective; **b.** energy, noun; **c.** energy, noun

6. STARS AND ASTRONOMERS

Word Web Activities Choosing the Right Definition	Word Partnership Activities Thesaurus Activities Word Link Activities

1. **Word Web Activities**
   Use the Word Web feature entitled *star* to answer the following questions.
   a. What is the scientific study of the stars called? _____
   b. What do people call the idea that the stars control our lives? _____
   c. What is a group of stars called? _____
   d. Which star is used to guide ships on the sea? the _____

   Use the Word Web feature entitled *astronomer* to answer this question:
   e. Copernicus was an astronomer who thought that the center of the universe was the _____.

2. **Choosing the Right Definition**
   Study the five numbered definitions for *star*. Then write the number of the definition that relates to each sentence below.
   a. _____ Eric is starring in a new TV comedy called *Just for You*.
   b. _____ It was cloudy last night, and we couldn't see any stars.
   c. _____ Madonna is my favorite singing star.
   d. _____ The flag of the United States has 50 stars on it.

3. **Word Partnership Activities**
   Reread the Word Web feature for *star*. Find the word *object* in the second sentence. Look up the word *object* in the dictionary and read the definitions.
   a. The first meaning of *object* is *a thing that has a* _____, *and that is not*
      _____.
   b. The second meaning of *object* is *The object of what someone is doing is their*
      _____.

   Study the Word Partnership feature for the noun form of *object*. Then complete the three sentences below using the word *object* and one of these words: *foreign, moving, solid*. Use each of these words one time. Look up any words you aren't sure of.
   c. We watched as the magician passed a _____ _____ through a mirror.
   d. A fast-_____ _____ has a high speed.
   e. If a child swallows a _____ _____ call a doctor for advice.

4. **Thesaurus Activities**

Reread the Word Web feature entitled *astronomer*. Notice the word *study* in the second sentence of the feature. A synonym for *study* is *observe*. Look up *observe* in the dictionary and study the Thesaurus entry that accompanies it. Which of the words in the box goes with each sentence below?

| notice   watch   study |

a. I'll show you how to do it. _____ me.

b. I checked the level of the water every hour, but I didn't _____ any change.

c. Jane Goodall would _____ the chimps carefully for hours without moving.

5. **Word Link Activities**

The first five letters of the word *astronomer* form a Word Link. Look at the information in the Word Link for *aster, astro*.

a. What does the Word Link *aster, astro* mean? _____

b. What are the three Word Links for *aster, astro*?

_____   _____   _____

c. Complete each sentence below with the correct word from item b. Check your answers by looking up each word in the dictionary.

1. This symbol (*) is called the _____.

2. You need a telescope to study _____.

3. You have to know how to fly a plane before you can study to become an _____.

ANSWER KEY:

1. **a.** astronomy; **b.** astrology; **c.** constellation; **d.** North Star; **e.** sun

2. **a.** 4; **b.** 1; **c.** 3; **d.** 2

3. **a.** shape, alive; **b.** purpose; **c.** solid object; **d.** moving object; **e.** foreign object

4. **a.** watch; **b.** notice; **c.** study

5. **a.** star; **b.** asterisk, astronaut, astronomy; **c.** **1.** asterisk; **2.** astronomy; **3.** astronaut

7.   ART

Word Web Activities Thesaurus Activities	Word Link Activities Choosing the Right Definition

1. **Word Web Activities**
    Use the Word Web feature entitled *art* to answer the following questions.
    a. What inspired the term "impressionist"?   a painting by _____
    b. In what part of the world did impressionism start?   in _____
    c. What did the impressionists usually paint?   _____
    d. What elements did they emphasize in their paintings?
    _____ and color
    e. The art of what country influenced the impressionists?   _____

2. **Thesaurus Activities**
    The Word Web feature for *art* says that the impressionists were interested in light and color. Find the Thesaurus feature with the word *light*. Then complete the sentences using words from the feature. Look up any words you aren't sure of.
    a. The noun synonyms for *light* are _____, _____, _____, and _____.
    b. Which noun meaning best describes the soft light of a fire when there are no flames?   _____
    c. Which noun meaning describes the happiness on a person's face?   _____
    d. Which adjective describes a room with a lot of windows facing south?   _____

3. **Word Link Activities**
    Review the Word Web feature for *art* noting the word *realistic*. Look up the word *reality* and study the Word Link. Then answer the questions.
    a. What does the Word Link *real* mean?   _____
    b. Which word in this link means to become aware of or understand something?   _____
    c. Which word in this link can be used for emphasis?   _____

Look up *biologist, dramatist, pharmacist*. Look at the Word Link for -*ist*.

d. What does *ist* mean? _____

e. Which word in this link means someone who
writes plays? _____

f. Which word describes someone who works in a
drugstore? _____

4. **Choosing the Right Definition**
The Word Web feature for *art* says that the impressionists stopped
painting in their *studios*. Study the numbered definitions for *studio*. Then
write the number of the definition that relates to each sentence below.

a. _____ The TV show originated in a studio in New York City.

b. _____ The photographer has a large studio with large windows.

ANSWER KEY:

1. **a.** Monet; **b.** Europe; **c.** landscapes; **d.** light; **e.** Japan
2. **a.** brightness, glow, radiance, shine; **b.** glow; **c.** radiance/glow;
   d. sunny
3. **a.** actual; **b.** realize; **c.** really; **d.** one who practices; **e.** dramatist;
   f. pharmacist
4. **a.** 2; **b.** 1

8. MONEY

Word Web Activities Word Partnership Activities Thesaurus Activities	Choosing the Right Definition

1. **Word Web Activities**
   Use the Word Web feature entitled *money* to answer the following questions.
   a. Which word in the feature means the same as *trade*? _____
   b. What form of ocean life was used as money at one time? _____
   c. Were the first coins round? _____
   d. What country had the first circular coins? _____
   e. Which two metals were used by the Lydians to make coins? _____ and _____

2. **Word Partnership Activities**
   Look up the word *buy* in the dictionary.
   a. What is the past tense of the verb *buy*? _____

   Study the Word Partnership feature for *buy*. Then complete the four sentences below using the word *buy* before or after one of these words or phrases: *online, and sell, tickets, afford to*. Use each of these items once.
   b. I can't _____ _____ a flat screen TV. I don't have enough money.
   c. If you _____ _____ stocks at the right time, you can get rich.
   d. Is it safe to _____ _____ ?
   e. Let's _____ _____ to the concert.

3. **Thesaurus Activities**
   Find the Thesaurus feature with the word *money*. Then complete the sentences using words from the feature. Look up any words you aren't sure of.
   a. A single _____ is now in use in many European Union countries.
   b. I never use _____. I prefer to pay by credit card or check.
   c. I don't have the amount of _____ I need to start my own business.
   d. The group decided to raise _____ to help people with AIDS.
   e. The discovery of oil brought great _____ to the Middle East.

4. **Choosing the Right Definition**

Study the numbered definitions for *bill*. Then write the number of the definition that relates to each sentence below.

_____ **a.** Please ask the waiter to bring the <u>bill</u>.

_____ **b.** My electric <u>bill</u> this month was over $100.

_____ **c.** He handed me three crisp dollar <u>bills</u>.

_____ **d.** Congress passed a <u>bill</u> that prohibited smoking in hospitals.

ANSWER KEY:

1. **a.** barter; **b.** cowrie shells; **c.** no; **d.** China; **e.** gold, silver
2. **a.** bought; **b.** afford to buy; **c.** buy and sell; **d.** buy online; **e.** buy tickets
3. **a.** currency; **b.** cash; **c.** capital; **d.** funds; **e.** wealth
4. **a.** 1; **b.** 1; **c.** 2; **d.** 3

Parts of speech quick reference

For a complete explanation of the parts of speech, see pages xviii–xxi.

ADJ	adjective
ADV	adverb
AUX	auxiliary verb
CONJ	conjunction
DET	determiner
INTERJ	interjection
MODAL	modal verb
N-COUNT	count noun
N-NONCOUNT	noncount noun
N-SING	singular noun
N-PLURAL	plural noun
N-PROPER	proper noun
NUM	number
PHRASE	phrase
PREDET	predeterminer
PREP	preposition
PRON	pronoun
V-I	intransitive verb
V-LINK	link verb
V-T	transitive verb

Aa

a /ə, STRONG eɪ/ or **an** /ən, STRONG æn/

> **LANGUAGE HELP**
> Use **an** before words that begin with the sound of **a, e, i, o,** or **u.**

1 DET You use **a** or **an** before a noun when people may not know which particular person or thing you are talking about. ❑ *A waiter came in with a glass of water.* ❑ *He started eating an apple.*
2 DET You use **a** or **an** when you are talking about any person or thing of a particular type. ❑ *You should leave it to an expert.* ❑ *Bring a sleeping bag.*
3 DET You use **a** or **an** instead of the number "one" before some numbers or measurements. ❑ *...a hundred miles.*
4 DET A or **an** means "each" or "for each." ❑ *Cheryl goes to London three times a month.*

AB /eɪ bi/ **N-NONCOUNT** MUSIC A piece of music or a poem that has an **AB** form or structure consists of two separate parts.

ABA /eɪ bi eɪ/ **N-NONCOUNT** MUSIC A piece of music or a poem that has an **ABA** form or structure consists of three separate parts. The second part contrasts with the first part, and the third part repeats the first part in a different form.

aban|don /əbændən/ (**abandons, abandoning, abandoned**)
1 V-T If you **abandon** a place, a thing, or a person, you leave them, especially when you should not. ❑ *His parents abandoned him when he was a baby.* ● **aban|doned ADJ** ❑ *They found an abandoned car.*
2 V-T If you **abandon** an activity or a piece of work, you stop doing it before it is finished. ❑ *After several hours they abandoned their search.* [from Old French]

> **Thesaurus** abandon Also look up :
> V   desert, leave, quit; (*ant.*) stay **1**
>   break off, give up, quit, stop;
>   (*ant.*) continue **2**

abate /əbeɪt/ (**abates, abating, abated**) **V-I** If something bad **abates**, it becomes much less strong or severe. [FORMAL] ❑ *The rain showed no sign of abating.* [from Old French]

ab|bey /æbi/ (**abbeys**) **N-COUNT** An **abbey** is a church with buildings attached to it in which monks or nuns live or used to live. [from Old French]

ab|bre|vi|ate /əbrivieɪt/ (**abbreviates, abbreviating, abbreviated**) **V-T** If you **abbreviate** something, especially a word or a piece of writing, you make it shorter. ❑ *"Compact disc" is often abbreviated to "CD."* [from Late Latin]

ab|bre|via|tion /əbrivieɪʃən/ (**abbreviations**) **N-COUNT** LANGUAGE ARTS An **abbreviation** is a short form of a word or phrase. ❑ *The abbreviation for Kansas is KS.* [from Late Latin]

ab|do|men /æbdəmən/ (**abdomens**)
1 N-COUNT SCIENCE Your **abdomen** is the part of your body below your chest. ❑ *The pain in my abdomen is getting worse.*
● **ab|domi|nal** /æbdɒmɪnəl/ **ADJ** ❑ *...the abdominal muscles.*
2 N-COUNT SCIENCE An insect's **abdomen** is the back part of the three parts that its body is divided into. [from Latin]
→ look at Picture Dictionary: **insect**

abil|ity /əbɪlɪti/ (**abilities**)
N-COUNT/N-NONCOUNT An **ability** is a quality or a skill that makes it possible for you to do something. ❑ *Her drama teacher noticed her acting ability.* ❑ *His mother had strong musical abilities.* [from Old French]

> **Thesaurus** ability Also look up :
> N   capability, competence, skill

> **Word Partnership** Use ability with :
> V   ability **to handle, have the** ability, **lack the** ability
> N   **lack of** ability
> ADJ   **natural** ability

abiot|ic /eɪbaɪɒtɪk/ **ADJ** SCIENCE **Abiotic** factors in the environment are things such

A

as the climate and the quality of the soil, which affect the ability of organisms to survive. [from Greek]

able /ˈeɪbᵊl/ (**abler** /ˈeɪblər/, **ablest** /ˈeɪblɪst/)
1 PHRASE If you **are able to** do something, you have skills or qualities that make it possible for you to do it. ❑ *A 10-year-old should be able to prepare a simple meal.* ❑ *The company says they're able to keep prices low.*
2 PHRASE If you **are able to** do something, you have enough freedom, power, time, or money to do it. ❑ *Are you able to help me?* ❑ *If I get this job, I'll be able to buy a new car.*
3 ADJ Someone who is **able** is very intelligent or very good at doing something. ❑ *Mr. Nicholas was one of the most able men in the industry.* [from Latin]

Usage   be able to and could
Could is used to refer to ability in the past: *When I was younger I could swim very fast.* When referring to single events in the past, use *be able to* instead: *I was able to finish my essay last night.* In negative sentences or when referring to things that happened frequently or over a period of time, you can use either *be able to* or *could*: *I wasn't able to/couldn't finish my essay last night.* When you were in college could you usually/were you usually able to get your work done on time?

ab|nor|mal /æbˈnɔrmᵊl/ **ADJ** Someone or something that is **abnormal** is unusual, especially in a way that is a problem. ❑ *She has an abnormal heartbeat.* [from Latin]

aboard /əˈbɔrd/
1 PREP If you are **aboard** a ship or a plane, you are on it or in it. ❑ *He invited us aboard his boat.*
2 ADV **Aboard** is also an adverb. ❑ *It took two hours to get all the people aboard.*

abol|ish /əˈbɒlɪʃ/ (**abolishes, abolishing, abolished**) **V-T** If someone in authority **abolishes** a system or a practice, they officially end it. ❑ *The committee voted Thursday to abolish the death penalty.*
● **abo|li|tion** /æbəˈlɪʃᵊn/ **N-NONCOUNT** ❑ *I support the total abolition of slavery.* [from Old French]

Thesaurus   abolish Also look up :
v   eliminate, end; (*ant.*) continue

abo|li|tion|ist /æbəˈlɪʃᵊnɪst/ (**abolitionists**)
N-COUNT SOCIAL STUDIES An **abolitionist** is someone who tries to stop people from being allowed to buy and sell slaves.

❑ *He was a national leader in the abolitionist movement.* [from Latin]

abor|tion /əˈbɔrʃᵊn/ (**abortions**)
N-COUNT/N-NONCOUNT If a woman has an **abortion**, she ends her pregnancy deliberately so that the baby is not born alive. ❑ *This drug is not used as a method of abortion in the U.S.* [from Latin]

about /əˈbaʊt/
1 PREP You use **about** to introduce a particular subject. ❑ *She knew a lot about food.* ❑ *He never complains about his work.*
2 PREP If there is a particular quality **about** someone, they have that quality. ❑ *There was something special about her.*
3 ADV **About** is used in front of a number to show that the number is not exact. ❑ *The child was about eight years old.* ❑ *It got dark at about six o'clock.*
4 ADJ If you are **about to** do something, you are going to do it very soon. ❑ *I think he's about to leave.* [from Old English]

Usage   about to
About to is used to say that something is going to happen very soon without specifying exactly when. A time expression is not necessary and should be avoided: *The concert is about to start.* means that it is imminent; *The concert starts in five minutes.* tells us exactly when.

above /əˈbʌv/
1 PREP If one thing is **above** another, it is over it or higher than it. ❑ *He lifted his hands above his head.* ❑ *Their apartment was above a clothing store.*
2 ADV **Above** is also an adverb. ❑ *A long scream sounded from somewhere above.*
3 PREP If an amount or a measurement is **above** a particular level, it is greater than that level. ❑ *The temperature rose to just above 40 degrees.*
4 ADV **Above** is also an adverb. ❑ *Banks have been charging 25 percent and above for loans.*
5 PREP If someone is **above** you, they are in a higher position than you at work. ❑ *You have people above you making decisions.*
6 ADV **Above** is also an adverb. ❑ *The policemen were acting on orders from above.*
7 ADV In writing, you use **above** to refer to something that has already been mentioned or discussed. ❑ *Several conclusions can be drawn from the results described above.*

[from Old English]
→ look at Picture Dictionary: **location**

abra|sion /əbreɪʒ°n/ **N-NONCOUNT** Abrasion is the gradual wearing away of the surface of rock as a result of other rock or sand particles rubbing against it. [from Medieval Latin]

abroad /əbrɔd/ **ADV** If you go **abroad**, you go to a foreign country. ❑ *Many students go abroad to work for the summer.*

ab|rupt /əbrʌpt/
■ **ADJ** An **abrupt** change or action is very sudden, often in a way that is unpleasant. ❑ *His career came to an abrupt end last week.* ● **ab|rupt|ly ADV** ❑ *The horses stopped abruptly.* ■ **ADJ** Someone who is **abrupt** speaks or acts in a rude, unfriendly way. ❑ *His voice was abrupt.* ● **ab|rupt|ly ADV** ❑ *"Good night, then," she said abruptly.* [from Latin]

ab|sence /æbs°ns/ (**absences**)
■ **N-COUNT/N-NONCOUNT** Someone's **absence** from a place is the fact that they are not there. ❑ *Her absence from work is becoming a problem.* ■ **N-SING** The **absence** of something from a place is the fact that it is not there or does not exist. ❑ *The presence or absence of clouds can have an important impact on temperature.* [from Old French]

ab|sent /æbs°nt/ **ADJ** If someone or something is **absent from** a place, they are not there. ❑ *Anna was absent from the meeting.* [from Latin]

ab|sen|tee /æbs°nti/ (**absentees**)
■ **N-COUNT** An **absentee** is a person who should be in a particular place but who is not there. ❑ *Two of the absentees had good reasons for being away.* ■ **ADJ** SOCIAL STUDIES In elections in the United States, if you vote by **absentee** ballot or if you are an **absentee** voter, you vote in advance because you will be unable to go to the polling place. ❑ *He voted by absentee ballot.* [from Latin]
→ look at Word Web: **election**

absent-mind|ed ADJ Someone who is **absent-minded** forgets things or does not pay attention to what they are doing. ❑ *She looked around the room in an absent-minded dream.* ● **ab|sent-mind|ed|ly ADV** ❑ *Elliot absent-mindedly scratched his head.*

ab|so|lute /æbsəlut/ **ADJ** Absolute means total and complete. ❑ *No one knows anything with absolute certainty.* [from Latin]

ab|so|lute da|ting N-NONCOUNT SCIENCE In archeology, **absolute dating** is a method of estimating the age of something such as a building or a tool by examining its physical or chemical properties.

ab|so|lute|ly /æbsəlutli/
■ **ADV** Absolutely means totally and completely. ❑ *Joan is absolutely right.* ❑ *I absolutely refuse to get married.* ■ **ADV** Absolutely is a way of saying yes or of agreeing with someone strongly. ❑ *"Do you think I should call him?"—"Absolutely."* [from Latin]

ab|so|lute mag|ni|tude (**absolute magnitudes**) **N-COUNT** SCIENCE The **absolute magnitude** of a star or galaxy is a measure of its actual brightness, after its distance from the Earth has been taken into account.

ab|so|lute val|ue (**absolute values**) **N-COUNT** MATH The **absolute value** of a number is the difference between that number and zero. The absolute value of -4 is 4, and the absolute value of +4 is 4.

ab|so|lute zero N-NONCOUNT SCIENCE **Absolute zero** is a theoretical temperature that is thought to be the lowest possible temperature.

ab|sorb /əbsɔrb, -zɔrb/ (**absorbs, absorbing, absorbed**)
■ **V-T** SCIENCE To **absorb** a substance means to take it in. ❑ *Cook the rice until it absorbs the water.* ● **ab|sorb|ent** /əbsɔrbənt, -zɔrb-/ **ADJ** ❑ *A real sponge is softer and more absorbent.* ■ **V-T** If you **absorb** information, you learn and understand it. ❑ *He has a quick mind, and he can absorb a lot of information in a short time.* [from Old French]

ab|sorb|ing /əbsɔrbɪŋ, -zɔrb-/ **ADJ** An **absorbing** activity is very interesting and uses all your attention and energy. ❑ *This is a very absorbing game.* [from Old French]

ab|stract /æbstrækt/
■ **ADJ** Abstract thoughts are based on general ideas rather than on real things. ❑ *The students are intelligent and good at abstract thought.* ■ **ADJ** ARTS **Abstract** art uses shapes and patterns rather than showing people or

things. ❑ *...Mondrian's abstract paintings, with their heavy black lines and bright blocks of color.* [from Latin]

ab|surd /æbsɜrd, -zɜrd/

1 **ADJ** If you say that something is **absurd**, you are criticizing it because you think that it is ridiculous or that it does not make sense. ❑ *That's absurd.* ❑ *It's absurd to suggest that they knew what was going on but did nothing.* ● **ab|surd|ly** **ADV** ❑ *Prices were still absurdly low.* ● **ab|surd|ity** /æbsɜrdɪti, -zɜrd-/ (absurdities) **N-COUNT/N-NONCOUNT** ❑ *...the absurdity of the situation.* **2** **N-SING** The absurd is something that is absurd. [FORMAL] ❑ *She has a strong sense of the absurd.* [from French]

Thesaurus	absurd	Also look up :
ADJ	crazy, foolish	

abuse (abuses, abusing, abused)

PRONUNCIATION HELP
Pronounce the noun /əbyus/. Pronounce the verb /əbyuz/.

1 **N-COUNT/N-NONCOUNT** Abuse of someone or something is cruel treatment of them. ❑ *There were reports of child abuse.* **2** **N-NONCOUNT** Abuse is very rude things that people say when they are angry. ❑ *I shouted abuse as the car drove away.* **3** **N-COUNT/N-NONCOUNT** Abuse of something is the use of it in a wrong way or for a bad purpose. ❑ *He wrote about his experience of drug abuse.* **4** **V-T** If someone **is abused**, they are treated cruelly. ❑ *The film is about her daughter, who was abused as a child.* **5** **V-T** If you **abuse** something, you use it in a wrong way or for a bad purpose. ❑ *The rich and powerful sometimes abuse their position.* [from Old French]

Thesaurus	abuse	Also look up :
N	damage, harm, injury, violation **1** blame, injury, insult; (*ant.*) compliment **2**	
V	damage, harm, injure, insult, mistreat, offend, pick on, put down; (*ant.*) care for, compliment, flatter, praise, protect, respect **4**	

abyss /əbɪs/ (abysses)

1 **N-COUNT** An **abyss** is a very deep hole in the ground. [LITERARY] ❑ *They could see the river disappearing into a black abyss.*

2 **N-COUNT** If someone is on the edge or brink of an **abyss**, they are about to enter into a very frightening or threatening situation. [LITERARY] ❑ *...a warning that the nation was on the brink of an abyss.* [from Late Latin]

abys|sal plain /əbɪsəl pleɪn/ (abyssal plains) **N-COUNT** SCIENCE An **abyssal plain** is a wide, flat area at the bottom of an ocean.

a/c /eɪ si/ also A/C **N-NONCOUNT** a/c is short for **air-conditioning**. ❑ *Keep your windows closed and the a/c on high.* ❑ *60 Motel Units. All Units A/C, Heat, Cable TV.*

aca|dem|ic /ækədɛmɪk/ **ADJ** Academic means relating to the work done in schools, colleges, and universities. ❑ *Their academic standards are high.* [from Latin]

acad|emy /əkædəmi/ (academies)

1 **N-COUNT** Academy is sometimes used in the names of schools. ❑ *He is an English teacher at the Seattle Academy for Arts and Sciences.* **2** **N-COUNT** Academy appears in the names of some societies that are formed to improve standards in a particular field. ❑ *...the National Academy of Sciences.* [from Latin]

ac|cel|er|ate /æksɛləreɪt/ (accelerates, accelerating, accelerated)

1 **V-T/V-I** If the rate of something **accelerates** or if something **accelerates** it, it gets faster. ❑ *Her heartbeat accelerated when she saw him in the crowd.* **2** **V-I** When a moving vehicle **accelerates**, it goes faster. ❑ *Suddenly the car accelerated.* [from Latin]

ac|cel|era|tion /æksɛləreɪʃⁿn/ **N-NONCOUNT** SCIENCE **Acceleration** is the rate at which the speed of an object increases. [from Latin]
→ look at Word Web: **motion**

ac|cent /æksɛnt/ (accents)

1 **N-COUNT** Someone who speaks with a particular **accent** pronounces words in a way that shows where they come from. ❑ *He had a slight Southern accent.* **2** **N-COUNT** LANGUAGE ARTS An **accent** is a mark written above a letter to show how it is pronounced. ❑ *The word "café" has an accent on the "e."* [from Old French]

ADJ	**regional** accent, **thick** accent **1**
ADV	**heavily** accented **1**
V	**do an** accent, **have an** accent **1**
	put the accent **on 2**

ac|cen|tu|ate /æksɛntʃueɪt/ (**accentuates, accentuating, accentuated**) **v-t** To **accentuate** something means to emphasize it or make it more noticeable. ❑ *His bald head accentuates his large round face.* [from Medieval Latin]

ac|cept /æksɛpt/ (**accepts, accepting, accepted**)

1 **v-t/v-i** If you **accept** something that someone offers you, you say yes to it or agree to take it. ❑ *She accepted his offer of marriage.* ❑ *All those invited to next week's peace conference have accepted.* ❑ *Doctors may not accept gifts.*
● **ac|cept|ance** /æksɛptəns/ **N-NONCOUNT** ❑ *We listened to his acceptance speech for the Nobel Peace Prize.*

2 **v-t** If you **accept** an unpleasant fact or situation, you recognize that it cannot be changed. ❑ *People often accept noise as part of city life.*

3 **v-t** If an organization or group **accepts** you, you are allowed to join it or use its services. ❑ *He's been accepted into a PhD program at the Massachusetts Institute of Technology.*

4 **v-t** If you **accept** responsibility for something, you recognize that you are responsible for it. ❑ *The company accepted responsibility for the damage.* [from Latin]

| **Usage** | accept and except |

Accept and *except* sound similar but have different meanings. *Accept* means "to receive." *Monique accepted her diploma.* *Except* means "other than." *Everyone in the class knew the answer except John.*

| **Thesaurus** | accept | Also look up : |

V	receive, take; (*ant.*) refuse, reject **2**
	endure, live with, tolerate;
	(*ant.*) disallow, reject **2**

| **Word Link** | able ≈ able to be : accept*able*, download*able*, honor*able* |

ac|cept|able /æksɛptəb°l/

1 **ADJ Acceptable** activities and situations are ones that most people consider to be normal. ❑ *Asking people for money is not acceptable behavior.* ● **ac|cept|ably ADV** ❑ *They try to teach children to behave acceptably.*

2 **ADJ** If something is **acceptable**, it is good enough. ❑ *There was one restaurant that looked acceptable.* [from Latin]

ac|cept|ed /æksɛptɪd/ **ADJ Accepted** ideas are agreed by most people to be correct or reasonable. ❑ *It was not a widely accepted idea.* [from Latin]

ac|cess /æksɛs/ (**accesses, accessing, accessed**)

1 **N-NONCOUNT** If you have **access to** a building or other place, you are allowed to go into it. ❑ *The general public does not have access to the White House.*

2 **N-NONCOUNT** If you have **access to** information or equipment, you are allowed to see it or use it. ❑ *Patients have access to their medical records.*

3 **v-t** If you **access** information on a computer, you find it. ❑ *Parents can see which sites their children have accessed.*

ac|ces|sible /æksɛsɪb°l/

1 **ADJ** If a place or building is **accessible**, it is easy for people to reach it or enter it. ❑ *The city center is easily accessible to the general public.* ❑ *Most of the bedrooms and bathrooms are accessible for wheelchairs.*

2 **ADJ** If something is **accessible to** people, they can easily use it or obtain it. ❑ *The computer system is accessible to all our workers.* [from Old French]
→ look at Word Web: **disability**

ac|ces|so|ry /æksɛsəri/ (**accessories**)

1 **N-COUNT Accessories** are small things such as belts and scarves that you wear with your clothes. ❑ *We shopped for handbags, scarves and other accessories.*

2 **N-COUNT Accessories** are items that can be added to something else in order to make it more useful or attractive. ❑ *...bathroom accessories.* [from Late Latin]

ac|ci|dent /æksɪdənt/ (**accidents**)

1 **N-COUNT** An **accident** happens when a vehicle hits something and causes injury or damage. ❑ *There were 14 highway accidents yesterday afternoon.*

accident

2 **N-COUNT** If someone has an **accident**, something bad happens to them by chance, sometimes causing injury or death. ❑ *She died in a car accident.*

3 **PHRASE** If something happens **by**

accident, it happens by chance. ❑ *We met by accident at a party in Los Angeles.* [from Old French]

Word Partnership	Use accident with :
N	**car** accident **1**
	the cause of an accident **1** **2**
ADJ	**bad** accident, **a tragic** accident **1** **2**
V	**cause an** accident, **insure against** accident, accident, **report an** accident **1** **2**
PREP	**without** accident **2**
	by accident **3**

ac|ci|den|tal /ˌæksɪdɛntᵊl/ **ADJ** An **accidental** event happens by chance or as the result of an accident. ❑ *He witnessed the accidental death of his younger brother.* ● **ac|ci|den|tal|ly** /ˌæksɪdɛntli/ **ADV** ❑ *They accidentally removed the names from the computer.* [from Old French]

Word Link	claim, clam ≈ shouting : acclaim, clamor, exclaim

ac|claim /əkleɪm/ (**acclaims, acclaiming, acclaimed**)
1 **V-T** If someone or something **is acclaimed**, they are praised enthusiastically. [FORMAL] ❑ *The restaurant has been widely acclaimed for its excellent French food.* ❑ *He was acclaimed as America's greatest filmmaker.* ● **ac|claimed** **ADJ** ❑ *She has published six highly acclaimed novels.*
2 **N-NONCOUNT** **Acclaim** is public praise for someone or something. [FORMAL] ❑ *Angela Bassett has won acclaim for her excellent performance.* [from Latin]

ac|com|mo|da|tions /əkɒmədeɪʃᵊns/ **N-PLURAL** **Accommodations** are buildings or rooms where people live or stay. ❑ *Some people paid extra for luxury accommodations.* [from Latin]

ac|com|pa|ny /əkʌmpəni/ (**accompanies, accompanying, accompanied**)
1 **V-T** If you **accompany** someone, you go somewhere with them. [FORMAL] ❑ *Ken agreed to accompany me on a trip to Africa.*
2 **V-T** If one thing **accompanies** another, the two things happen or exist at the same time. [FORMAL] ❑ *Stress often accompanies change of any sort.*
3 **V-T** MUSIC If you **accompany** a singer or a musician, you play one part of a piece of music while they sing or play the main tune. ❑ *Her singing teacher accompanied her on the piano.* [from Old French]

ac|com|plish /əkɒmplɪʃ/ (**accomplishes, accomplishing, accomplished**) **V-T** If you **accomplish** something, you succeed in doing it. ❑ *If we all work together, I think we can accomplish our goal.* [from Old French]

Thesaurus	accomplish Also look up :
V	achieve, complete, gain, realize, succeed

ac|com|plished /əkɒmplɪʃt/ **ADJ** If someone is **accomplished** at something, they are very good at it. [FORMAL] ❑ *He is an accomplished painter.* [from Old French]

ac|com|plish|ment /əkɒmplɪʃmənt/ (**accomplishments**) **N-COUNT** An **accomplishment** is something unusual or special that someone has made or achieved. ❑ *This book is an amazing accomplishment.* [from Old French]

ac|cord /əkɔrd/ (**accords, according, accorded**)
1 **N-COUNT** An **accord** between countries or groups of people is a formal agreement, for example to end a war. ❑ *...the 1991 peace accords.*
2 **V-T** If you **are accorded** a particular kind of treatment, people act toward you or treat you in that way. [FORMAL] ❑ *He was accorded the very highest status.* ❑ *The government accorded him the rank of Colonel.*
3 **PHRASE** If something happens **of its own accord**, it seems to happen by itself, without anyone making it happen. ❑ *In many cases the disease will clear up of its own accord.*
4 **PHRASE** If you do something **of your own accord**, you do it because you want to, without being asked or forced. ❑ *He left his job of his own accord.* [from Old French]

ac|cord|ing|ly /əkɔrdɪŋli/ **ADV** You use **accordingly** to say that one thing happens as a result of another. ❑ *It is a difficult job and we should pay them accordingly.* [from Old French]

ac|cord|ing to
1 **PHRASE** If something is true **according to** a particular person, that is where the information comes from. ❑ *They drove away in a white van, according to police reports.*
2 **PHRASE** If something is done **according to** a particular set of rules, these rules say how it should be done. ❑ *They played the game according to the British rules.*
3 **PHRASE** If something happens **according to plan**, it happens in exactly the way that it

was intended to happen. ❏ *Everything is going according to plan.*

ac|cor|di|on /əkɔːʳdiən/ (**accordions**)
N-COUNT MUSIC An **accordion** is a musical instrument in the shape of a box, which you hold in your hands. You play it by pressing keys and buttons on the side, while moving the two ends in and out. [from German]

ac|count /əkaʊnt/ (**accounts, accounting, accounted**)
1 **N-COUNT** If you have an **account** with a bank, you leave your money there and take some out when you need it. ❏ *I have $3,000 in my bank account.*
2 **N-COUNT** BUSINESS **Accounts** are records of all the money that a person or a business receives and spends. ❏ *He kept detailed accounts of all the money he spent.*
3 **N-COUNT** TECHNOLOGY An **account** is an arrangement you have with a company to use a service they provide. ❏ *...an email account.*
4 **N-COUNT** An **account** is a report of something that has happened. ❏ *He gave a detailed account of the events.*
5 → see also **accounting, checking account**
6 **PHRASE** If you **take** something **into account**, or **take account of** something, you consider it when you are thinking about a situation. ❏ *You have to take everyone into account before making a decision.* [from Old French]
→ look at Word Web: **history**
▶ **account for** If you can **account for** something, you can explain it or give the reason for it. ❏ *How do you account for these differences?*

ac|count|able /əkaʊntəbªl/ **ADJ** If you are **accountable for** something that you do, you are responsible for it. ❏ *We are accountable to taxpayers.* ● **ac|count|abil|ity** /əkaʊntəbɪliti/ **N-NONCOUNT** ❏ *There's too much waste and too little accountability.* [from Old French]

ac|count|ant /əkaʊntənt/ (**accountants**)
N-COUNT An **accountant** is a person whose job is to keep financial accounts. [from Old French]

ac|count|ing /əkaʊntɪŋ/
1 **N-NONCOUNT** **Accounting** is the theory or practice of keeping financial accounts. [from Old French]
2 → see also **account**

ac|cre|tion /əkriʃªn/ (**accretions**)
1 **N-COUNT** An **accretion** is an addition to something, usually one that has been added over a period of time. [FORMAL] ❏ *The script has been gathering editorial accretions for years.*
2 **N-NONCOUNT** **Accretion** is when new layers or parts are added to something so that it increases in size. [FORMAL] ❏ *A coral reef is built by the accretion of tiny, identical organisms.* [from Latin]

ac|cu|rate /ækyərɪt/
1 **ADJ** **Accurate** information is correct. ❏ *I can't give an accurate description of the man because it was too dark.* ● **ac|cu|ra|cy** **N-NONCOUNT** ❏ *Don't trust the accuracy of weather reports.* ● **ac|cu|rate|ly** **ADV** ❏ *He described it quite accurately.*
2 **ADJ** A person or machine that is **accurate** is able to work without making a mistake. ❏ *The car's steering is accurate, and the brakes are powerful.* ● **ac|cu|ra|cy** **N-NONCOUNT** ❏ *He questioned the accuracy of the story.*
● **ac|cu|rate|ly** **ADV** ❏ *He hit the golf ball powerfully and accurately.* [from Latin]

Thesaurus	accurate	Also look up :
ADJ	right, true; (ant.) inaccurate **1**	
	correct, precise, rigorous **2**	

ac|cu|sa|tion /ækyuzeɪʃªn/ (**accusations**)
N-COUNT/N-NONCOUNT If you make an **accusation** against someone, you criticize them or express the belief that they have done something wrong. ❏ *...an accusation of murder.* [from Old French]

ac|cuse /əkyuz/ (**accuses, accusing, accused**) **V-T** If you **accuse** someone **of** something, you say that they did something wrong or dishonest. ❏ *They accused her of lying.* [from Old French]

Thesaurus	accuse	Also look up :
V	blame, charge, implicate	

ace /eɪs/ (**aces**)
1 **N-COUNT** If you describe someone as an **ace**, you mean that they are very good at what they do. ❏ *...former tennis ace John McEnroe.*
2 **ADJ** **Ace** is also an adjective. ❏ *...an ace movie producer.*
3 **N-COUNT** An **ace** is a playing card with a single symbol on it. ❏ *...the ace of hearts.*
4 **N-COUNT** SPORTS In tennis, an **ace** is a serve that is so fast that the other player

cannot return the ball. ❏ *Federer served three aces in the final set of the tennis match.* [from Old French]

ache /eɪk/ (**aches, aching, ached**)
1 **V-I** If you **ache**, or a part of your body **aches**, you feel a steady pain. ❏ *Her head was hurting and she ached all over (= in every part of her body).* ❏ *My leg still aches when I stand for a long time.*
2 **N-COUNT** An **ache** is a steady pain in a part of your body. ❏ *A hot bath will take away all your aches and pains.* [from Old English]
3 → see also **heartache**

Thesaurus	ache Also look up :
V	throb **1**
N	hurt, pain **2**
ADJ	sore **2**

achieve /ətʃiv/ (**achieves, achieving, achieved**) **V-T** If you **achieve** something, you succeed in doing it, usually after a lot of effort. ❏ *He worked hard to achieve his goals.* [from Old French]

Thesaurus	achieve Also look up :
V	accomplish, bring about; (*ant.*) fail, lose, miss

achieve|ment /ətʃivmənt/ (**achievements**)
1 **N-COUNT** An **achievement** is something that you have succeeded in doing, especially after a lot of effort. ❏ *Being chosen for the team was a great achievement.*
2 **N-NONCOUNT** Achievement is the process of achieving something. ❏ *Only the achievement of these goals will bring peace.* [from Old French]

acid /æsɪd/ (**acids**) **N-COUNT/N-NONCOUNT**
SCIENCE An **acid** is a chemical, usually a liquid, that can burn your skin and cause damage to other substances. ❏ *As you can see, the acid damaged the metal bowl.* [from French]

acid rain **N-NONCOUNT** Acid rain is rain that contains acid that can harm the environment. The acid comes from pollution in the air.
→ look at Word Web: **pollution**

ac|knowl|edge /æknɒlɪdʒ/ (**acknowledges, acknowledging, acknowledged**)
1 **V-T** If you **acknowledge** a fact or a situation, you agree that it is true or that it exists. [FORMAL] ❏ *He acknowledged that he was wrong.* ❏ *At last, the government has acknowledged the problem.*
2 **V-T** If you **acknowledge** a message or a letter, you write to the person who sent it in

order to say that you have received it. ❏ *The army sent me a postcard acknowledging my request.* [from Old English]

ac|knowl|edg|ment /æknɒlɪdʒmənt/ (**acknowledgments**) also **acknowledgement** **N-PLURAL**
LANGUAGE ARTS The **acknowledgments** in a book are the names of all the people who helped the writer. ❏ *There are two pages of acknowledgments at the beginning of the book.* [from Old English]

acous|tic /əkustɪk/ (**acoustics**)
1 **ADJ** An **acoustic** guitar or other instrument is one whose sound is produced without any electrical equipment.
2 **N-PLURAL** The **acoustics** of a space are the structural features which determine how well you can hear music or speech in it. ❏ *The theater's acoustics are very clear.*
3 **N-NONCOUNT** SCIENCE **Acoustics** is the scientific study of sound. ❏ *...his work in acoustics.* [from Greek]
→ look at Picture Dictionary: **strings**

ac|quaint|ance /əkweɪntəns/ (**acquaintances**) **N-COUNT** An **acquaintance** is someone you have met, but don't know well. ❏ *He spoke to the owner, who was an old acquaintance of his.* [from Old French]

ac|qui|esce /ækwiɛs/ (**acquiesces, acquiescing, acquiesced**) **V-I** If you **acquiesce**, you agree to do what someone wants or you accept what they do. [FORMAL] ❏ *Steve seemed to acquiesce in the decision.* ❏ *When her mother suggested that she stay, Alice willingly acquiesced.* [from Latin]

ac|quire /əkwaɪər/ (**acquires, acquiring, acquired**)
1 **V-T** If you **acquire** something, you obtain it. [FORMAL] ❏ *The club wants to acquire new sports equipment.*
2 **V-T** If you **acquire** a skill or a habit, you learn it or develop it. ❏ *Students on this program will acquire a wide range of skills.* [from Old French]

ac|qui|si|tion /ækwɪzɪʃ°n/ (**acquisitions**)
1 **N-COUNT/N-NONCOUNT** BUSINESS If a company or a business person makes an **acquisition**, they buy another company or part of a company. ❏ *...AT&T's acquisition of TCI.*
2 **N-COUNT** If you make an **acquisition**, you buy or obtain something, often to add to things that you already have. ❏ *Her acquisition*

of a computer music program helped her to start writing music.

3 **N-NONCOUNT** The **acquisition** of a skill or a particular type of knowledge is the process of learning it or developing it. ❏ ...language acquisition. [from Latin]

acre /**eɪ**kər/ (**acres**) **N-COUNT** An **acre** is a unit for measuring an area of land. ❏ He rented three acres of land. [from Old English]

across /əkr**ɔ**s/
1 **PREP** If someone or something goes **across** a place, they go from one side of it to the other. ❏ She walked across the floor and sat down. ❏ He watched Karl run across the street.
2 **ADV** **Across** is also an adverb. ❏ Richard stood up and walked across to the window.
3 **PREP** If something is **across** something else, it goes from one side of it to the other. ❏ The bridge across the river was closed. ❏ He wrote his name across the check. [from Old French]

acryl|ic /əkr**ɪ**lɪk/ (**acrylics**)
1 **ADJ** ARTS **Acrylic** paint is a type of artist's paint that dries very quickly. ❏ Most people prefer acrylic paint because it dries faster.
2 **N-PLURAL** ARTS **Acrylics** are acrylic paints. ❏ This book is a great introduction to painting with acrylics.

act /**æ**kt/ (**acts, acting, acted**)
1 **V-I** When you **act**, you do something for a particular purpose. ❏ The police acted to stop the fight.
2 **V-I** If someone **acts** in a particular way, they behave in that way. ❏ The youths were acting suspiciously. ❏ He acts as if I'm not there.
3 **V-I** If someone or something **acts as** a particular thing, they have that role or function. ❏ He acted as the ship's doctor.
4 **V-I** ARTS If you **act** in a play or film, you have a part in it. ❏ He acted in many films, including "Reds."
5 **N-COUNT** An **act** is a single thing that someone does. [FORMAL] ❏ As a child I loved the act of writing.
6 **N-COUNT** SOCIAL STUDIES An **Act** is a law passed by the government. ❏ The organization was set up by an Act of Congress in 1998.
7 **N-COUNT** An **act** in a play is one of the main parts it is divided into. ❏ Act two has a really funny scene.
8 **N-COUNT** An **act** in a show is a short performance that is one of several in the show. ❏ This year, several bands are playing, as well as comedy acts.

9 **N-SING** If you say that someone's behavior is an **act**, you mean that it does not express their real feelings. ❏ His anger was real. It wasn't an act. [from Latin]

act|ing /**æ**ktɪŋ/
1 **N-NONCOUNT** ARTS **Acting** is the activity or profession of performing in plays or films. ❏ I'd like to do some acting some day.
2 **ADJ** You use **acting** before the title of a job to say that someone is doing that job for a short time only. ❏ She is the new acting president. [from Latin]

act|ing area (**acting areas**) **N-COUNT** ARTS In a theater, the **acting areas** are the different parts of the stage such as the front or back of the stage.

ac|tion /**æ**kʃ°n/ (**actions**)
1 **N-NONCOUNT** **Action** is doing something for a particular purpose. ❏ The government is taking emergency action.
2 **N-COUNT** An **action** is something that you do on a particular occasion. ❏ Peter could not explain his actions.
3 **N-SING** SCIENCE In physics, **action** is the force that is applied to an object.
4 **N-NONCOUNT** SCIENCE The **action** of a chemical is the way that it works, or the effect that it has.
5 **PHRASE** If someone is **out of action**, they are injured and cannot work. ❏ He's been out of action for 16 months with a knee injury. [from Latin]
→ look at Word Webs: **genre, motion**

Word Partnership	Use **action** with :
N	**course of** action, **plan of** action **1**
V	**take** action **1**
ADJ	**disciplinary** action **1**

ac|ti|va|tion en|er|gy /**æ**ktɪve**ɪ**ʃ°n **ɛ**nərdʒi/ **N-SING** SCIENCE In chemistry and biology, the **activation energy** is the minimum amount of energy that is needed in order for a chemical reaction to occur.

ac|tive /**æ**ktɪv/
1 **ADJ** Someone who is **active** moves around a lot. ❏ We've got three very active little kids.
2 **ADJ** If someone is **active** in an organized activity, they do things for it rather than just giving it their support. ❏ We should play an active role in politics.
3 **N-SING** LANGUAGE ARTS In grammar, **the active** is the form of a verb that you use to show that the subject performs the action.

For example, in "I saw him," the verb "see" is in the active. Compare with **passive**. [from Latin]

ac|tive so|lar heat|ing **N-NONCOUNT** SCIENCE **Active solar heating** is a method of heating a building by using solar collectors and pipes to distribute energy from the sun throughout the building.

ac|tive trans|port **N-NONCOUNT** SCIENCE In biology, **active transport** is the movement of chemicals and other substances through the membranes of cells, which requires the cells to use energy.

ac|tive voice **N-SING** LANGUAGE ARTS In grammar, **the active voice** means the forms of a verb which are used when the subject of the sentence refers to a person or thing that does something. For example, in "I saw her yesterday," the verb is in the active voice.

ac|tiv|ist /ˈæktɪvɪst/ (**activists**) **N-COUNT** An **activist** is a person who works to bring about political or social changes. ❑ ...*animal rights activists.* [from Latin]

ac|tiv|ity /ækˈtɪvɪti/ (**activities**)
❶ **N-NONCOUNT** **Activity** is when people do a lot of things. ❑ *Children are supposed to get physical activity every day.*
❷ **N-COUNT** An **activity** is something that you spend time doing. ❑ *There were no activities for small children.* [from Latin]

ac|tor /ˈæktər/ (**actors**) **N-COUNT** ARTS An **actor** is someone whose job is acting in plays or movies. ❑ *His father was an actor.* [from Latin]
→ look at Picture Dictionary: **drama**
→ look at Word Web: **theater**

ac|tor's po|si|tion (**actor's positions** or **actors' positions**) **N-COUNT** ARTS In the theater, an **actor's position** is the position that an actor occupies in relation to the audience, for example facing toward the audience or facing away from the audience.

ac|tress /ˈæktrɪs/ (**actresses**) **N-COUNT** ARTS An **actress** is a woman whose job is acting in plays or movies. ❑ *She's a really good actress.* [from Latin]

ac|tual /ˈæktʃuəl/ **ADJ** You use **actual** to show that you are talking about something real, exact, or genuine. ❑ *The stories in this book are based on actual people.* [from Late Latin]

ac|tu|al|ly /ˈæktʃuəli/
❶ **ADV** You use **actually** to show that

something really is true. ❑ *The judge actually fell asleep for a few minutes.*
❷ **ADV** You use **actually** when you are correcting someone, or to introduce a new topic into a conversation. ❑ *No, I'm not a student. I'm a doctor, actually.* [from Late Latin]

acute /əˈkyut/
❶ **ADJ** An **acute** situation or feeling is very severe or serious. ❑ *He was in acute pain.*
❷ **ADJ** If a person's or animal's senses are **acute**, they are sensitive and powerful. ❑ *When she lost her sight, her other senses grew more acute.* [from Latin]

acute ac|cent (**acute accents**) **N-COUNT** LANGUAGE ARTS An **acute accent** is a symbol that you put over vowels in some languages to show how to pronounce that vowel. For example, there is an acute accent over the letter "e" in the French word "café."

acute an|gle /əˈkyut ˈæŋɡəl/ (**acute angles**) **N-COUNT** MATH An **acute angle** is an angle of less than 90°.

ad /æd/ (**ads**) **N-COUNT** An **ad** is an advertisement. [INFORMAL] ❑ *It costs $175.00 to place an ad in the newspaper for 30 days.*

AD /ˈeɪ ˈdi/ also **A.D.** SOCIAL STUDIES You can use **AD** in dates to show the number of years that have passed since the year in which Jesus Christ was born. Compare with **BC**. ❑ *The church was built in 600 AD.* [from Latin]

a|dapt /əˈdæpt/ (**adapts, adapting, adapted**)
❶ **V-I** If you **adapt to** a new situation, you change your ideas or behavior in order to deal with it. ❑ *The world will be different in the future, and we will have to adapt to the change.*
❷ **V-T** If you **adapt** something, you change it so that you can use it in a different way. ❑ *They adapted the library for use as an office.* [from Latin]

Usage   adapt and adopt

Adapt and *adopt* sound similar and have similar meanings, but be careful not to confuse them. When you *adapt* something, you change it to make it fit your purpose: *Gilberto tried to adapt the recipe to cook a fish instead of a chicken—what a mistake!* When you *adopt* something, you use it unchanged: *Lucas adopted his boss' technique for dealing with rude customers—he ignored them!*

Thesaurus   adapt   Also look up :

V	acclimate, adjust, conform ❶
	modify, revise ❷

a

adapt|able /ədæptəbəl/ **ADJ** Someone or something that is **adaptable** is able to deal with new situations. ❑ *Dogs and cats are easily adaptable to new homes.* [from Latin]

add /æd/ (**adds, adding, added**)

1 **V-T** If you **add** one thing **to** another, you put it with the other thing. ❑ *Add the grated cheese to the sauce.*

2 **V-T** MATH If you **add** numbers or amounts **together**, you calculate their total. ❑ *Add all the numbers together, and divide by three.*

3 **V-I** If one thing **adds to** another, it makes the other thing greater in degree or amount. ❑ *The cozy look of the fireplace adds to the room.*

4 **V-T** If you **add** something when you are speaking, you say something more. ❑ *"He's very angry," Mr. Smith added.*

5 **V-I** MATH If you can **add**, you are able to calculate the total of numbers or amounts. ❑ *Many seven-year-olds cannot add properly.* [from Latin]

→ look at Picture Dictionary: **fraction**

▶ **add up** **1** MATH If you **add up** numbers or amounts, you calculate their total. ❑ *Add up the number of hours you spent on the task.*

2 If facts or events do not **add up**, they do not seem to match what you already know. ❑ *His story did not add up.*

▶ **add up to** If amounts **add up to** a particular total, they result in that total when they are put together. ❑ *Profits can add up to millions of dollars.*

Thesaurus add Also look up :
v put on, throw in **1**
calculate, tally, total; *(ant.)* reduce, subtract **2**
augment, increase; *(ant.)* lessen, reduce **3**

ad|dict /ædɪkt/ (**addicts**)

1 **N-COUNT** An **addict** is someone who cannot stop doing something harmful or dangerous, such as using drugs. ❑ *His girlfriend is a former drug addict.*

2 **N-COUNT** You can say that someone is an **addict** when they like a particular activity very much. ❑ *She is a TV addict.* [from Latin]

ad|dict|ed /ədɪktɪd/ **ADJ** Someone who is **addicted to** a harmful drug cannot stop taking it. ❑ *Many of the women are addicted to heroin.* [from Latin]

ad|dic|tion /ədɪkʃən/ (**addictions**)

1 **N-COUNT/N-NONCOUNT** Addiction is the condition of not being able to stop taking drugs, alcohol, or some other substance. ❑ *She helped him fight his drug addiction.*

2 **N-COUNT/N-NONCOUNT** An **addiction** is a strong need to do a particular activity for as much time as possible. ❑ *...children's addiction to computer games.* [from Latin]

ad|di|tion /ədɪʃən/ (**additions**)

1 **N-NONCOUNT** MATH Addition is the process of calculating the total of two or more numbers. ❑ *She can count to 100, and do simple addition problems.*

2 **N-COUNT** An **addition to** something is a thing that is added to it. ❑ *This is a great book; a fine addition to the series.* ● **ad|di|tion|al** /ədɪʃənəl/ **ADJ** ❑ *Add the garlic and cook for an additional three minutes.*

3 **PHRASE** You use **in addition** when you want to mention another thing relating to the subject you are discussing. ❑ *In addition to meals, drinks will be provided.* [from Latin]

→ look at Word Web: **mathematics**

ad|di|tive /ædɪtɪv/ (**additives**)

1 **N-COUNT** An **additive** is a substance that is added to foods in order to improve them or to make them last longer. ❑ *...food additives.*

2 **ADJ** ARTS Additive sculpture is sculpture that is created by adding material such as clay or wax until the sculpture is complete. [from Late Latin]

ad|dress (**addresses, addressing, addressed**)

PRONUNCIATION HELP
Pronounce the noun /ədrɛs/ or /ædrɛs/. Pronounce the verb /ədrɛs/.

1 **N-COUNT** Your **address** is the number of the building, the name of the street, and the town or city and state where you live or work. ❑ *The address is 2025 M Street NW, Washington, DC 20036.*

2 **N-COUNT** TECHNOLOGY The **address** of a website is its location on the Internet, for example http://www.collinsdictionary.com. ❑ *Our website address is at the bottom of this page.*

3 **V-T** If something **is addressed to** you, your name and address have been written on it. ❑ *One of the letters was addressed to her.*

4 **V-T** If you **address** a group of people, you speak to them formally. ❑ *He addressed the crowd of 17,000 people.*

5 **N-COUNT** Address is also a noun. ❑ *Judge Richardson began his address to the jury.* [from Old French]

A

Thesaurus address Also look up :
N lecture, speech, talk **4**

Word Partnership Use address with :
N **name and** address, **street** address **1**
address **remarks to 4**
ADJ **permanent** address **1**
inaugural address, **public** address **4**

ad|dress book (**address books**)
1 N-COUNT An **address book** is a book in which you write people's names and addresses.
2 N-COUNT TECHNOLOGY An **address book** is a computer program that you use to record people's email addresses and telephone numbers.

ad|enine /ǽdᵊnin, -nɪn/ (**adenines**)
N-COUNT/N-NONCOUNT SCIENCE Adenine is an organic molecule that forms an important part of the structure of DNA. [from German]

adept /ædέpt/ ADJ Someone who is **adept at** something can do it skillfully. □ He is adept at avoiding difficult questions. [from Medieval Latin]

ad|equate /ǽdɪkwɪt/ ADJ If something is **adequate**, there is enough of it or it is good enough. □ One in four people worldwide do not have adequate homes. [from Latin]

ad|here /ædhɪ́ər/ (**adheres, adhering, adhered**)
1 V-I If you **adhere to** a rule or an agreement, you act in the way that it says you should. □ Different churches adhere to different teachings. ● **ad|her|ence** /ædhɪ́ərəns/ **N-NONCOUNT** □ ...strict adherence to the constitution.
2 V-I If something **adheres to** something else, it sticks firmly to it. □ The self-stick backing adheres to metal and plastic. [from Medieval Latin]

ad|he|sive /ædhísɪv/ (**adhesives**) **N-COUNT/N-NONCOUNT** An **adhesive** is a substance used for making things stick together. □ Attach the mirror to the wall with a strong adhesive. [from Medieval Latin]

ad ho|mi|nem /ǽd hɒ́mɪnɛm, -nəm/ ADJ/ ADV In logic, an **ad hominem** argument is an argument which attacks the motives or character of the person presenting a claim rather than the claim itself.

ad|ja|cent /ədʒéɪsᵊnt/ ADJ If two things are **adjacent**, they are next to each other. □ He sat in an adjacent room and waited. □ The schools were adjacent but there were separate doors. [from Latin]

ad|jec|tive /ǽdʒɪktɪv/ (**adjectives**) **N-COUNT** LANGUAGE ARTS An **adjective** is a word such as "big" or "beautiful" that describes a person or a thing. Adjectives usually come before nouns or after verbs like "be" or "feel." [from Late Latin]

ad|just /ədʒʌ́st/ (**adjusts, adjusting, adjusted**)
1 V-T If you **adjust** something, you make a small change to it. □ The company adjusts gas prices once a year. □ You can adjust the height of the table. ● **ad|just|ment N-COUNT** □ ...a large workshop for repairs and adjustments.
2 V-T/V-I When you **adjust to** a new situation, you get used to it by changing your behavior or your ideas. □ She has adjusted to the idea of being a mother very well. [from Old French]

ad|min|is|ter /ædmɪ́nɪstər/ (**administers, administering, administered**)
1 V-T If someone **administers** something such as a country, the law, or a test, they take responsibility for organizing and supervising it. □ Who will administer these accounts and what will it cost?
2 V-T If a doctor or a nurse **administers** a drug, they give it to a patient. [FORMAL] □ The tests will focus on how to administer the drug safely. [from Old French]

ad|min|is|trate /ædmɪ́nɪstreɪt/ (**administrates, administrating, administrated**) **V-T** If you **administrate** an organization's business activities, you manage or direct them. □ The Internet opens up new ways of administrating the tax system. [from Latin]

ad|min|is|tra|tion /ædmɪnɪstréɪʃᵊn/ (**administrations**)
1 N-NONCOUNT Administration is the job of managing a business or an organization. □ A private company took over the administration of the local jail.
2 N-COUNT The administration is the government of a country. □ Three officials in the Bush administration have resigned. [from Old French]

ad|min|is|tra|tive /ædmɪ́nɪstreɪtɪv/ ADJ Administrative work involves managing a business or an organization. ❏ *Administrative costs were high.* [from Old French]

ad|min|is|tra|tor /ædmɪnɪstreɪtər/ (**administrators**) **N-COUNT** An **administrator** is a person whose job is to help manage a business or an organization. ❏ *Students and parents met with school administrators to discuss the problem.* [from Old French]

ad|mi|rable /ædmɪrəbəl/ **ADJ** An **admirable** quality or action is one that deserves to be praised and admired. ❏ *She did an admirable job of holding their attention.* ● **ad|mi|rably** /ædmɪrəbli/ **ADV** ❏ *Peter dealt admirably with the questions.* [from Latin]

ad|mi|ral /ædmərəl/ (**admirals**) **N-COUNT** An **admiral** is a very senior officer who commands a navy. ❏ *...Admiral Hodges.* [from Old French]

ad|mi|ra|tion /ædmɪreɪʃən/ **N-NONCOUNT** **Admiration** is a strong feeling of liking and respect. ❏ *I have great admiration for him.* [from Latin]

ad|mire /ədmaɪər/ (**admires, admiring, admired**)
1 **V-T** If you **admire** someone or something, you like and respect them. ❏ *I admired her when I first met her.* ● **ad|mir|er** (**admirers**) **N-COUNT** ❏ *He was an admirer of her paintings.*
2 **V-T** If you **admire** someone or something, you look at them with pleasure. ❏ *We took time to stop and admire the view.* [from Latin]

Thesaurus admire Also look up :
V	adore, esteem, honor, look up to, respect **1**

ad|mis|sion /ædmɪʃən/ (**admissions**)
1 **N-COUNT/N-NONCOUNT** **Admission** is permission given to a person to enter a place. ❏ *One man was refused admission to the restaurant.*
2 **N-COUNT/N-NONCOUNT** An **admission** is when you admit that you have done something wrong. ❏ *By his own admission, he is not playing well.*
3 **N-NONCOUNT** **Admission** at a park, museum, or other place is the amount of money that you pay to enter it. ❏ *Gates open at 10:30 a.m. and admission is free.* [from Latin]

ad|mit /ædmɪt/ (**admits, admitting, admitted**)
1 **V-T/V-I** If you **admit** that you have done something wrong, you agree that you did it. ❏ *I am willing to admit that I made a mistake.* ❏ *They didn't admit to doing anything wrong.*

2 **V-T** If someone **is admitted to** a place or an organization, they are allowed to enter it or join it. ❏ *She was admitted to law school.* ❏ *Security officers refused to admit him.* [from Latin]

Word Partnership Use admit with :
V	ashamed to admit, **be the first to** admit, **must** admit, **willing to** admit **1**
N	admit **defeat 1**
CONJ	admit **that 1**

ad|mon|ish /ædmɒnɪʃ/ (**admonishes, admonishing, admonished**) **V-T** If you **admonish** someone, you tell them that they have done something wrong. [FORMAL] ❏ *They admonished me for taking risks with my health.* ● **ad|mon|ish|ment** (**admonishments**) **N-COUNT/N-NONCOUNT** ❏ *Sometimes he gave them a severe admonishment.* [from Old French]

ado|les|cent /ædəlɛsənt/ (**adolescents**)
1 **ADJ** **Adolescent** describes young people who are no longer children but who have not yet become adults. ❏ *Her music is popular with adolescent girls.* ● **ado|les|cence** /ædəlɛsəns/ **N-NONCOUNT** ❏ *Adolescence is often a difficult period for young people.*
2 **N-COUNT** An **adolescent** is an adolescent boy or girl. ❏ *Adolescents don't like being treated like children.* [from Old French]
→ look at Picture Dictionary: **age**
→ look at Word Web: **child**

Word Link opt ≈ choosing : ad*opt*, *opt*ion, *opt*ional

adopt /ədɒpt/ (**adopts, adopting, adopted**)
1 **V-T** If you **adopt** a new attitude, plan, or way of behaving, you begin to have it. ❏ *You need to adopt a more positive attitude.*
2 **V-T/V-I** If you **adopt** someone else's child, you take it into your own family and make it legally your son or daughter. ❏ *There are hundreds of people who want to adopt a child.* ❏ *They really want to adopt.* ● **adop|tion** (**adoptions**) **N-COUNT/N-NONCOUNT** ❏ *They gave their babies up for adoption.* [from Latin]
→ look at Usage note at **adapt**

Thesaurus adopt Also look up :
V	approve, endorse, support; (ant.) refuse, reject **1** care for, raise, take in **2**

adore /ədɔr/ (**adores, adoring, adored**)
1 **V-T** If you **adore** someone, you feel strong love and admiration for them. ❏ *She adored*

her parents and would do anything to please them.
2 **V-T** If you **adore** something, you like it very much. [INFORMAL] ❑ *Robyn adores university life.* [from French]

adult /əd**ʌ**lt/ (adults)

1 **N-COUNT** An **adult** is a fully grown person or animal. ❑ *Tickets cost $20 for adults and $10 for children.*
2 **ADJ** Adult is also an adjective. ❑ *I am the mother of two adult sons.* [from Latin]
→ look at Picture Dictionary: **age**

Thesaurus	adult	Also look up :
ADJ	full-grown	
N	grown-up, man, woman	

ad|vance /ædv**æ**ns/ (advances, advancing, advanced)

1 **V-I** To **advance** means to move forward, often in order to attack someone. ❑ *Soldiers are advancing toward the capital.*
2 **V-I** To **advance** means to make progress, especially in your knowledge of something. ❑ *Science has advanced greatly in the last 100 years.*
3 **N-COUNT** An **advance** is money that is lent or paid to someone before they would normally receive it. ❑ *She was paid a $100,000 advance for her next two novels.*
4 **N-COUNT/N-NONCOUNT** An **advance** is a movement forward, usually as part of a military operation. ❑ *Hitler's army began its advance on Moscow in June 1941.*
5 **N-COUNT/N-NONCOUNT** An **advance** in a subject or activity is progress in understanding it. ❑ *There have been many advances in medicine and public health.*
6 **ADJ** **Advance** notice or warning is done or given before an event happens. ❑ *You must give 30 days' advance notice.*
7 **PHRASE** If you do something **in advance**, you do it before a particular date or event. ❑ *The theater sells tickets in advance.* [from Latin]

ad|vanced /ædv**æ**nst/

1 **ADJ** Something that is **advanced** is modern. ❑ *This is one of the most advanced phones available.*
2 **ADJ** An **advanced** student has already learned the basic facts of a subject and is doing more difficult work. ❑ *This course is for advanced students only.* [from Latin]

Thesaurus	advanced	Also look up :
ADJ	cutting-edge, foremost, latest, sophisticated **1**	

ad|van|tage /ædv**æ**ntɪdʒ/ (advantages)

1 **N-COUNT** An **advantage** is something that puts you in a better position than other people. ❑ *Being small gives our company an advantage.*
2 **N-COUNT** An **advantage** is a way in which one thing is better than another. ❑ *The advantage of home-grown vegetables is their great flavor.*
3 **PHRASE** If you **take advantage of** something, you make good use of it while you can. ❑ *People are taking advantage of lower prices.*
4 **PHRASE** If someone **takes advantage of** you, they unfairly get what they want from you, especially when you are trying to be kind to them. ❑ *She took advantage of him, borrowing money and not paying it back.* [from Latin]

Word Partnership	Use advantage with :
ADJ	**competitive** advantage, **unfair** advantage **1**
V	**have an** advantage **1**
	take advantage **of** *something* **3**

ad|vent /**æ**dvɛnt/ **N-NONCOUNT** The advent

of something is the fact of it starting or coming into existence. [FORMAL] ❑ *...the advent of the computer.* [from Latin]

ad|ven|ture /ædv**ɛ**ntʃər/ (adventures)

1 **N-COUNT/N-NONCOUNT** An **adventure** is an experience that is unusual, exciting, and perhaps dangerous. ❑ *I'm planning a new adventure in Alaska.*
2 **N-COUNT** An **adventure** story is a story about exciting, unusual, and dangerous events. [from Latin]

ad|verb /**æ**dvɜrb/ (adverbs) **N-COUNT**

LANGUAGE ARTS An **adverb** is a word such as "slowly," "now," "very," or "happily" that adds information about an action, event, or situation. [from Latin]

ad|verse /**æ**dvɜrs/ **ADJ** **Adverse** decisions,

conditions, or effects cause problems for you. ❑ *There may be adverse effects as a result of this treatment.* ● **ad|verse|ly** **ADV** ❑ *The change didn't adversely affect him.* [from Latin]

ad|ver|tise /**æ**dvərtaɪz/ (advertises, advertising, advertised) **V-T/V-I** If you

advertise something, you tell people about it in newspapers, on television, on signs, or on the Internet. ❑ *The house is being advertised for sale.* ❑ *We advertise on radio stations.* [from Old French]

ad|ver|tise|ment /ˈædvərtaɪzmənt/
(**advertisements**) **N-COUNT** An
advertisement is information that tells
you about a product, an event, or a job.
[WRITTEN] ❑ *They saw an advertisement for a job
on a farm.* ❑ *...an advertisement for a new movie.*
[from Old French]

ad|ver|tis|ing /ˈædvərtaɪzɪŋ/ **N-NONCOUNT**
Advertising is the business of creating
information that tells people about a
product or an event. ❑ *I work in advertising.*
[from Old French]

ad|vice /ædvaɪs/ **N-NONCOUNT** If you give
someone **advice**, you tell them what you
think they should do. ❑ *Take my advice and stay
away from him!* ❑ *I'd like to ask you for some advice.*
[from Old French]

Usage   advice and advise

Be careful not to confuse *advice* and *advise*.
Advice is a noun, and the *c* is pronounced like
the *ss* in *less*; *advise* is a verb, and the *s* is
pronounced like the *z* in *size*: *Quang advised Tuyet
not to give people advice!*

Thesaurus   advice   Also look up :

N   counsel, encouragement, guidance,
     help, information, input, opinion,
     recommendation, suggestion

Word Partnership   Use advice with :

PREP   **against** advice
V   **ask for** advice, **give** advice, **need some**
     advice, **take** advice
ADJ   **good/bad** advice, **expert** advice

ad|vise /ædvaɪz/ (**advises, advising, advised**)
■ **V-T** If you **advise** someone **to** do
something, you tell them what you think
they should do. ❑ *Passengers are advised to
check in two hours before their flight.*
❷ **V-T** If an expert **advises** people **on** a
particular subject, he or she gives them
help and information on that subject.
❑ *My job is to advise students on money matters.*
[from Old French]

ad|vis|er /ædvaɪzər/ (**advisers**) also **advisor**
N-COUNT An **adviser** is an expert whose job
is to give advice. ❑ *Your college adviser will
be happy to help you choose your classes.*
[from Old French]

ad|vi|so|ry /ædvaɪzəri/ (**advisories**)
■ **N-COUNT** An **advisory** is an official
announcement or report that warns people

about bad weather, diseases, or other dangers
or problems. ❑ *...public health advisories.*
❷ **ADJ** An **advisory** group regularly gives
suggestions and help to people or
organizations, especially about a particular
subject or area of activity. [FORMAL] ❑ *...an
advisory group on oil and gas.* [from Old French]

Word Link   *aer ≈ air : aerial, aerobics, aerosol*

aer|ial /ɛəriəl/ **ADJ** **Aerial** means from an
airplane. ❑ *The aerial attacks may continue for
weeks more.* ❑ *...an aerial photograph.* [from Latin]

aer|ial per|spec|tive (**aerial perspectives**)
N-COUNT/N-NONCOUNT ARTS In a painting or
drawing, **aerial perspective** is a method of
representing more distant objects by using
lighter or duller colors.

aero|bics /ɛəroʊbɪks/ **N-NONCOUNT** SPORTS
Aerobics is a form of exercise that makes
your heart and lungs stronger. ❑ *I'd like to
join an aerobics class to improve my fitness.*
[from Greek]

aero|phone /ɛərəfoʊn/ (**aerophones**)
N-COUNT MUSIC An **aerophone** is a musical
instrument such as a trumpet or flute which
produces sound by causing the air to vibrate.

aero|sol /ɛərəsɔl/ (**aerosols**) **N-COUNT** An
aerosol is a metal container with liquid in
it. When you press a button, the liquid
comes out strongly in a lot of very small
drops. ❑ *...an aerosol spray can.*

aes|thet|ic /ɛsθɛtɪk/ also **esthetic** **ADJ** ARTS
Aesthetic qualities relate to beauty and art.
❑ *In this restaurant, eating is a truly aesthetic
experience.* ● **aes|theti|cal|ly** /ɛsθɛtɪkli/ **ADV**
❑ *We want our product to be aesthetically pleasing.*
[from Greek]

aes|thet|ic cri|teria **N-PLURAL** ARTS
Aesthetic criteria are standards that are
used in making judgments about the
artistic value of a work of art.

aes|thet|ics /ɛsθɛtɪks/ also **esthetics**
N-NONCOUNT ARTS **Aesthetics** is a branch of
philosophy concerned with the study of the
idea of beauty. [from Greek]

af|fable /ˈæfəbᵊl/ **ADJ** Someone who is
affable is pleasant and friendly. ❑ *Mr. Brooke
is an affable and friendly man.* [from Latin]

af|fair /əfɛər/ (**affairs**)
■ **N-SING** An **affair** is an event or a group of
related events. ❑ *She has handled the whole
affair badly.*

2 **N-COUNT** If two people who are not married to each other have an **affair**, they have a sexual relationship. ❑ *He was having an affair with the woman next door.*

3 **N-PLURAL** Your **affairs** are things in your life that you consider to be private. ❑ *Why are we so interested in the private affairs of famous people?* [from Old French]

af|fect /əfɛkt/ (**affects, affecting, affected**) **V-T** If something **affects** a person or a thing, it causes them to change in some way. ❑ *This problem affects all of us.* ❑ *This area was badly affected by the earthquake.* [from Latin]
→ look at Usage note at **effect**

af|fec|tion /əfɛkʃ°n/ **N-NONCOUNT** If you feel **affection** for someone, you love or like them a lot. ❑ *She thought of him with affection.* [from Latin]
→ look at Word Web: **love**

af|fec|tion|ate /əfɛkʃənɪt/ **ADJ** If you are **affectionate**, you show that you like someone very much. ❑ *She's very affectionate, and she's always hugging the kids.*
● **af|fec|tion|ate|ly** **ADV** ❑ *He looked affectionately at his niece.* [from Latin]

af|firm /əfɜrm/ (**affirms, affirming, affirmed**)
1 **V-T** If you **affirm** that something is true, you state firmly and publicly that it is true. [FORMAL] ❑ *The newspaper report affirmed that the story was true.* ● **af|fir|ma|tion** /æfərmeɪʃ°n/ (**affirmations**) **N-COUNT/N-NONCOUNT** ❑ *...an affirmation of support.*
2 **V-T** If an event **affirms** something, it shows that it is true or exists. [FORMAL] ❑ *Everything I did seemed to affirm that opinion.* ● **af|fir|ma|tion** **N-NONCOUNT/N-SING** ❑ *Maguire's performance is an affirmation of his talent.* [from Old French]

af|fix /æfɪks/ (**affixes**) **N-COUNT** LANGUAGE ARTS An **affix** is a letter or group of letters, for example "un-" or "-y," which is added to either the beginning or the end of a word to form a different word with a different meaning. For example, "un-" is added to "kind" to form "unkind." Compare with **prefix** and **suffix**. [from Medieval Latin]

> **Word Link** *flict ≈ striking : affliction, conflict, inflict*

af|flic|tion /əflɪkʃ°n/ (**afflictions**) **N-COUNT/N-NONCOUNT** An **affliction** is something that causes physical or mental suffering.

[FORMAL] ❑ *Not one of them was willing to talk about their affliction.* [from Latin]

af|flu|ent /æfluənt/
1 **ADJ** If you are **affluent**, you have a lot of money. ❑ *It is one of the most affluent areas in the country.* ● **af|flu|ence** **N-NONCOUNT** ❑ *They enjoyed a lifetime of affluence.*
2 **N-PLURAL** The **affluent** are people who are affluent. ❑ *These tax changes let the affluent keep more of their money.* [from Latin]

af|ford /əfɔrd/ (**affords, affording, afforded**)
1 **V-T** If you **can afford** something, you have enough money to pay for it. ❑ *Some people can't even afford a new refrigerator.*
2 **V-T** If you cannot **afford to** do something or allow it to happen, you must not do it or must prevent it from happening. ❑ *We can't afford to wait.* [from Old English]

Word Partnership	Use **afford** with :
V	afford **to buy/pay** **1**
	can/could afford, **can't/couldn't** afford **1** **2**
	afford **to lose** **2**
ADJ	**able/unable to** afford **1** **2**

af|ford|able /əfɔrdəb°l/ **ADJ** If something is **affordable**, most people have enough money to buy it. ❑ *...affordable housing.*
● **af|ford|abil|ity** /əfɔrdəbɪlɪti/ **N-NONCOUNT** ❑ *Affordability is a problem for students going to college.* [from Old English]

afloat /əfloʊt/ **ADV** Someone or something that is **afloat** is floating. ❑ *They tried to keep the ship afloat.*

afraid /əfreɪd/
1 **ADJ** If you are **afraid** that something unpleasant will happen, you are worried that it may happen. ❑ *I was afraid that nobody would believe me.*
2 **ADJ** If you are **afraid of** someone or **afraid to** do something, you are frightened because you think that something very unpleasant is going to happen to you. ❑ *I was afraid of the other boys.*

Thesaurus	**afraid** Also look up :
ADJ	alarmed, fearful, frightened, petrified, scared, terrified, worried **2**

Af|ri|can-Amer|i|can /æfrɪkən əmɛrɪkən/ (**African-Americans**)
1 **N-COUNT** SOCIAL STUDIES African-Americans are people living in the United States who are descended from families that

originally came from Africa. ❑ *Today African-Americans is 12 percent of the population.*
2 ADJ SOCIAL STUDIES **African-American** is also an adjective. ❑ *She is the daughter of an African-American father and an East Indian mother.*

af|ter /ǽftər/
1 PREP If something happens **after** a particular date or event, it happens later than that date or event. ❑ *He died after a long illness.* ❑ *After breakfast Amy took a taxi to the station.*
2 CONJ After is also a conjunction. ❑ *The phone rang two seconds after we arrived.*
3 PREP If something goes or comes **after** something else, it follows it in position or order. ❑ *What number comes after 99?*
4 PREP If you go **after** someone, you follow or chase them. ❑ *Why don't you go after him? He's your son.*
5 PREP To be named **after** someone means to be given the same name as them. ❑ *He wanted us to name the baby after him.*
6 PREP After is used when you are telling the time. If it is **ten after six**, for example, the time is ten minutes past six. [from Old English]

after|math /ǽftərmæθ/ **N-SING** The **aftermath of** an important event, especially a harmful one, is the situation that results from it. ❑ *The team worked closely together in the aftermath of the fire.* [from Old English]

after|noon /ǽftərnún/ (**afternoons**) **N-COUNT/N-NONCOUNT** The **afternoon** is the part of each day that begins at lunchtime and ends at about six o'clock. ❑ *He's arriving in the afternoon.* ❑ *He stayed in his room all afternoon.*
→ look at Picture Dictionary: **time**

after|ward /ǽftərwərd/ also **afterwards**
ADV If something happens **afterward**, it happens after a particular event or time that you have already mentioned. ❑ *Shortly afterward, the police arrived.* [from Old English]

again /əgɛ́n, əgéɪn/
1 ADV You use **again** to say that something happens another time. ❑ *He kissed her again.* ❑ *Again there was a short silence.*
2 ADV You use **again** to say that something is now in the same state it was in before. ❑ *He opened his case, took out a folder, then closed it again.* [from Old English]

against /əgɛ́nst, əgéɪnst/
1 PREP If one thing is leaning or pressing

against another thing, it is touching it. ❑ *She leaned against him.* ❑ *The rain was beating against the window panes.*
2 PREP If you are **against** something, you think it is wrong or bad. ❑ *He was against the war.*
3 ADV Against is also an adverb. ❑ *66 people voted in favor of the decision and 34 voted against.*
4 PREP If you compete **against** someone, you try to beat them. ❑ *This is the first of two games against Denver.*
5 PREP If you do something **against** someone or something, you try to harm them. ❑ *Security forces are still using violence against opponents of the government.*
6 PREP If you do something **against** someone's wishes or advice, you do not obey them. ❑ *She left the hospital against the doctors' advice.*
7 PREP If something is **against** the law or **against** the rules, there is a law or a rule that says you must not do that thing. ❑ *It is against the law to help other people to kill themselves.*

age /eɪdʒ/ (**ages, aging** or **ageing, aged**)
1 N-COUNT/N-NONCOUNT Your **age** is the number of years that you have lived. ❑ *Diana left school at the age of 16.* ❑ *They have two children: Julia, age 8, and Jackie, age 10.*
2 N-NONCOUNT Age is the state of being old. ❑ *He refuses to let age slow him down.*
3 V-T/V-I When someone **ages**, or when something **ages** them, they seem much older. ❑ *Worry has aged him.* ❑ *Both parents said they have aged in the past six months.*
4 N-COUNT An **age** is a period in history. ❑ *...the age of silent films.* [from Old French]
5 → see also **middle age**
→ look at Picture Dictionary: **age**

aged

PRONUNCIATION HELP
Pronounce meaning **1** /eɪdʒd/. Pronounce meanings **2** and **3** /éɪdʒɪd/.

1 ADJ You use **aged** followed by a number to say how old someone is. ❑ *Alan has two children, aged eleven and nine.*
2 ADJ Aged means very old. ❑ *She has an aged parent who can be very difficult.*
3 N-PLURAL You can refer to all people who are very old as **the aged**. ❑ *...daycare centers and homes for the aged.* [from Old French]
4 → see also **middle-aged**

Picture Dictionary   age

infant   toddler   teenager / adolescent   woman   man   senior citizen

CHILD	ADULT

YOUNG	MIDDLE–AGED	ELDERLY

agen|cy /ˈeɪdʒənsi/ (**agencies**)

1 **N-COUNT** BUSINESS An **agency** is a business that provides a service. ❑ *I work in an advertising agency.*

2 **N-COUNT** An **agency** is a government organization that is responsible for a certain area of administration. ❑ *...local, state, and federal agencies.* [from Medieval Latin]

agen|da /əˈdʒɛndə/ (**agendas**)

1 **N-COUNT** Someone's **agenda** is a set of things they want to do. ❑ *They support the president's education agenda.*

2 **N-COUNT** An **agenda** is a list of things to be discussed at a meeting. ❑ *I'll add it to the agenda for Monday's meeting.* [from Latin]

Word Partnership	Use agenda with :
ADJ	**domestic/legislative/political** agenda, **hidden** agenda **1**
PREP	**on the** agenda **2**
V	**set the** agenda **2**

agent /ˈeɪdʒənt/ (**agents**)

1 **N-COUNT** BUSINESS An **agent** is a person whose job is to do business for another person or company. ❑ *I am buying direct, not through an agent.*

2 **N-COUNT** An **agent** is a person who works for a particular government department. ❑ *He was arrested by FBI agents at his home in*

Hawaii. [from Latin]
→ look at Word Web: **concert**

ag|gre|gate /ˈæɡrɪɡɪt/ **ADJ** An **aggregate** amount is made up of several smaller amounts added together. ❑ *The rate of growth of GNP will depend upon the rate of growth of aggregate demand.* [from Latin]

ag|gres|sion /əˈɡrɛʃ°n/ **N-NONCOUNT** **Aggression** is violent and attacking behavior. ❑ *They are using aggression and violence against their neighbors.* [from Latin]
→ look at Word Web: **anger**

Word Partnership	Use aggression with :
N	**act of** aggression
PREP	aggression **against**
ADJ	**military** aggression, **physical** aggression

ag|gres|sive /əˈɡrɛsɪv/

1 **ADJ** An **aggressive** person or animal behaves angrily or violently toward other people. ❑ *Some children are much more aggressive than others.* ● **ag|gres|sive|ly** **ADV** ❑ *They'll react aggressively.*

2 **ADJ** People who are **aggressive** in their work or other activities behave in a forceful way because they are very eager to succeed. ❑ *He was an aggressive manager.*
● **ag|gres|sive|ly** **ADV** ❑ *They want to play aggressively and do what is necessary to be successful.* [from Latin]

ag|ile /ˈædʒ°l/

1 **ADJ** Someone who is **agile** can move quickly and easily. ❑ *At 20 years old he was not as agile as he is now.* ● **agil|ity** /ədʒɪlɪti/ **N-NONCOUNT** ❑ *She was surprised at his agility.*

2 **ADJ** If you have an **agile** mind, you think quickly and intelligently. ❑ *She had a very agile mind.* ● **agil|ity** **N-NONCOUNT** ❑ *His mental agility has never been in doubt.* [from Latin]

agi|tate /ˈædʒɪteɪt/ (**agitates, agitating, agitated**) **V-I** If people **agitate for** something, they protest or take part in political activity in order to get it. ❑ *The workers were agitating for better conditions.* ● **agi|ta|tion** /ædʒɪteɪʃ°n/ **N-NONCOUNT** ❑ *...continuing agitation against the decision.* [from Latin]

ag|nos|tic /ægnɒstɪk/ **N-COUNT** An **agnostic** believes that it is not possible to know whether God exists or not. ❑ *For the last twenty-three or twenty-four years I have been an agnostic.*

ago /əgoʊ/ **ADV** You use **ago** to talk about past time. For example, if something happened one year **ago**, one year has passed since it happened. ❑ *I got your letter a few days ago.* [from Old English]

ago|ny /ˈægəni/ **N-NONCOUNT** Agony is great physical or mental pain. ❑ *He tried to move, but screamed in agony.* [from Late Latin]

ago|ra|pho|bia /ægərəfoʊbiə/ **N-NONCOUNT** Agoraphobia is the fear of open or public places.

agree /əgri/ (**agrees, agreeing, agreed**)

1 **V-T/V-I** If people **agree with** each other about something, they have the same opinion about it. ❑ *I agree with you.* ❑ *Do we agree that there's a problem?*

2 **V-T/V-I** If people **agree on** something, they all decide to accept or do that thing. ❑ *They agreed on a price of $85,000.*

3 **V-T/V-I** If you **agree to** do something, you say that you will do it. If you **agree to** a proposal, you accept it.

4 **V-I** If you **agree with** an action or suggestion, you approve of it. ❑ *Most people agreed with what we did.* [from Old French]

Word Link *ment ≈ state, condition : agreement, management, movement*

agree|ment /əgrimənt/ (**agreements**)

1 **N-COUNT** An **agreement** is a plan or a decision that two or more people have made.
❑ *After two hours' discussion, they finally reached an agreement.*

2 **N-NONCOUNT** If people are **in agreement**, they both have the same opinion. ❑ *The doctors were in agreement.* [from Old French]

Word Partnership	Use **agreement** with :	
N	**peace** agreement, **terms of an** agreement, **trade** agreement **1**	
V	**enter into an** agreement, **sign an** agreement **1**	
	reach an agreement **1**	

ag|ri|cul|ture /ˈægrɪkʌltʃər/ **N-NONCOUNT** **Agriculture** is the business or activity of taking care of crops and farm animals.
● **ag|ri|cul|tur|al** /ægrɪkʌltʃərəl/ **ADJ** ❑ *...agricultural land.* [from Latin]
→ look at Word Webs: **farm, industry**

ahead
❶ ADVERB USES
❷ PREPOSITION USES

❶ ahead /əhɛd/

1 **ADV** Someone or something that is **ahead** is in front of you. ❑ *The road ahead was blocked.*

2 **ADV** If you look **ahead**, you look directly in front of you. ❑ *Brett looked straight ahead.*

3 **ADV** If a person or a team is **ahead** in a competition, they are winning. ❑ *Dallas was ahead all through the game.*

4 **ADV** **Ahead** means in the future. ❑ *There are exciting times ahead.*

5 **PHRASE** You say **Go ahead** when you are giving someone permission to do something. ❑ *"Can I borrow your dictionary?"— "Sure, go ahead."*

Word Partnership	Use **ahead** with :	
ADV	**straight** ahead **❶ 1**	
V	**get** ahead **❶ 1**	
	look ahead **❶ 2**	
	go ahead **❶ 5**	
PREP	ahead **of schedule/time ❷ 3**	

❷ ahead of

1 **PHRASE** If someone is **ahead of** you, they are in front of you. ❑ *I saw a man thirty yards ahead of me.*

2 **PHRASE** If an event or period of time lies **ahead of** you, it is going to happen or take place soon or in the future. ❑ *Heather was thinking about the future that lay ahead of her.*

3 **PHRASE** If something happens **ahead of** a planned time, it happens earlier than you

A

expected. ❑ *We were a week ahead of schedule.*
4 **PHRASE** If someone is **ahead of** someone else, they have made more progress and are more advanced in what they are doing. ❑ *Henry was ahead of the others in most subjects.*

aid /eɪd/ (**aids, aiding, aided**)
1 **N-NONCOUNT** **Aid** is money, equipment, or services that are given to people who do not have enough money. ❑ *They have promised billions of dollars in aid.*
2 **V-T** To **aid** people means to provide them with money, equipment, or services that they need. ❑ *...a $1 billion fund to aid storm victims.*
3 → see also **first aid**
4 **N-COUNT** An **aid** is an object that makes something easier to do. ❑ *The book is a valuable aid to teachers of literature.* [from Old French]

aide /eɪd/ (**aides**) **N-COUNT** An **aide** is an assistant to someone who has an important job, especially in government or in the armed forces. ❑ *An aide to the president described the meeting as very useful.* [from Old French]

AIDS /eɪdz/ **N-NONCOUNT** **AIDS** is a disease that destroys the body's system of protection against other diseases. ❑ *Twenty-five percent of adults here have AIDS.*

Word Partnership Use AIDS with :

N	AIDS **activists**, AIDS **epidemic**, AIDS **patient**, AIDS **research**, **spread of** AIDS, AIDS **victims**
V	**infected with** AIDS

aim /eɪm/ (**aims, aiming, aimed**)
1 **V-T/V-I** If you **aim for** something or **aim to** do something, you plan or hope to do it. ❑ *He is aiming for the 100 meter world record.* ❑ *The appeal aims to raise money for children with special needs.*
2 **V-T** If your actions or remarks **are aimed at** a particular person or group, you want that person or group to be influenced by them. ❑ *Most of their advertisements are aimed at women.*
3 **V-T** If you **aim** a weapon or object **at** something or someone, you point it toward them. ❑ *He was aiming the rifle at Wright.*
4 **N-COUNT** The **aim** of something that you do is the purpose of it. ❑ *The aim of the event is to bring parents and children together.* [from Old French]

air /ɛər/ (**airs, airing, aired**)
1 **N-NONCOUNT** SCIENCE **Air** is the mixture of gases all around us that we breathe. ❑ *Keith opened the window and felt the cold air on his face.*
2 **N-NONCOUNT** **Air** is used for talking about travel in aircraft. ❑ *Air travel will continue to grow at around 6% per year.*
3 **N-NONCOUNT** **The air** is the space around things or above the ground. ❑ *He was waving his arms in the air.*
4 **V-T** If you **air** a room or building, you let fresh air into it. ❑ *One day a week her mother cleaned and aired each room.* [from Old French]
→ look at Word Webs: **air, erosion, respiratory system, wind**

air-con|di|tioned /ɛər kəndɪʃᵊnd/ **ADJ** If a room or a vehicle is **air-conditioned**, a special piece of equipment makes the air in it colder. ❑ *All the rooms are air-conditioned, with private bathrooms and satellite TV.*

air-condition|ing /ɛər kəndɪʃᵊnɪŋ/ **N-NONCOUNT** **Air-conditioning** is a system for keeping the air cool and dry in a building or a vehicle.

Word Web air

The **air** we breathe has seventeen different **gases**. It is made up mostly of **nitrogen**, not **oxygen**. Recently, human activities have changed the balance in the earth's **atmosphere**. The widespread burning of coal and oil increases the levels of **carbon dioxide** gas. Some scientists believe this air **pollution** may depelete the **ozone layer**. With less protection from the sun, the air temperature rises and makes the earth warmer. This leads to harmful effects on people, farming, animals, and the natural environment.

Composition of Air

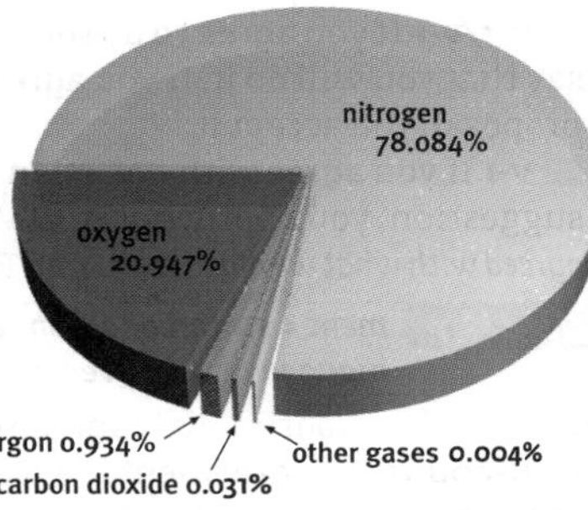
nitrogen 78.084%
oxygen 20.947%
argon 0.934%
carbon dioxide 0.031%
other gases 0.004%

air|craft /ˈɛərkræft/ (aircraft) **N-COUNT**
An **aircraft** is an airplane or a helicopter.
❑ *The aircraft landed safely.*
→ look at Word Webs: **fly, ship**

air|field /ˈɛərfild/ (airfields) **N-COUNT**
An **airfield** is an area of ground where
aircraft take off and land. It is smaller than
an airport.

air force (air forces) **N-COUNT** An **air force**
is a military force that uses airplanes.
❑ *...the United States Air Force.*

air|lift /ˈɛərlɪft/ (airlifts, airlifting, airlifted)
■ **N-COUNT** An **airlift** is an operation to
move people, troops, or goods by air,
especially in a war or when land routes are
closed. ❑ *...an airlift of food, medicines, and
blankets.*
■ **V-T** If people, troops, or goods **are airlifted**
somewhere, they are carried by air,
especially in a war or when land routes are
closed. ❑ *The injured were airlifted to a hospital in
Dayton.*

air|line /ˈɛərlaɪn/ (airlines) **N-COUNT**
An **airline** is a company that carries people
or goods in airplanes. ❑ *Most low-cost airlines
do not serve food.*

air mass (air masses) **N-COUNT** SCIENCE
An **air mass** is a large area of air that has
the same temperature and amount of
moisture throughout.

air|plane /ˈɛərpleɪn/ (airplanes) **N-COUNT**
An **airplane** is a vehicle with wings that can
fly through the air.
→ look at Word Web: **fly**

air pol|lu|tion **N-NONCOUNT** SCIENCE Air
pollution is chemicals or other substances
that have a harmful effect on the air. ❑ *We
think that air pollution may be the cause of the illness.*

air|port /ˈɛərpɔrt/ (airports) **N-COUNT**
An **airport** is a place
where airplanes
come and go, with
buildings and
services for
passengers.
❑ *Heathrow Airport is
the busiest international
airport in the world.*

airport

air pres|sure **N-NONCOUNT** SCIENCE Air
pressure is a measure of the force with
which air presses against a surface.

air sac /ˈɛər sæk/ (air sacs) **N-NONCOUNT**
SCIENCE An **air sac** is a very small, round
structure in the lungs of some animals
that helps them to breathe.

aisle /aɪl/ (aisles) **N-COUNT** An **aisle** is a long
narrow passage
where people can
walk between rows
of seats or shelves.
❑ *You'll find the peas in
the frozen food aisle.*
[from Old French]

aisle

alarm /əˈlɑrm/ (alarms, alarming, alarmed)
■ **N-COUNT** An **alarm** is a piece of
equipment that warns you of danger, for
example by making a noise. ❑ *The fire alarm
woke us at 5 a.m.*
■ **N-COUNT** An **alarm** is the same as an
alarm clock. ❑ *Dad set the alarm for eight the
next day.*
■ **N-NONCOUNT** **Alarm** is a feeling of fear
that something unpleasant or dangerous
might happen. ❑ *She greeted the news with
alarm.*
■ **V-T** If something **alarms** you, it makes
you afraid that something unpleasant or
dangerous might happen. ❑ *I don't know
what alarmed him.* [from Old French]

Word Partnership	Use **alarm** with :
N	**alarm** system ■
V	**set** the alarm ■ ■
	cause alarm ■

alarm clock (alarm clocks) **N-COUNT** An
alarm clock is a clock that makes a noise to
wake you up. ❑ *I set my alarm clock for 4:30.*

al|be|it /ɔlˈbiɪt/ **ADV** You use **albeit** to
introduce a fact or a comment that reduces
the force or significance of what you have
just said. [FORMAL] ❑ *It was just another work
day, albeit a quieter one.*

al|bum /ˈælbəm/ (albums)
■ **N-COUNT** An **album** is a collection of
songs. ❑ *They released their new album on
July 1.*
■ **N-COUNT** An **album** is a book in which
you keep things that you have collected.
❑ *Theresa showed me her photo album.*
[from Latin]

al|co|hol /ˈælkəhɔl/
■ **N-NONCOUNT** Drinks that can make
people drunk are sometimes called **alcohol.**

A

❏ *It is not legal to drink alcohol until you are 21.*
2 N-NONCOUNT Alcohol is a liquid that is found in drinks such as beer and wine. It is also used as a chemical for cleaning things. ❏ *Clean the wound with alcohol.* [from New Latin]

al|co|hol|ic /ælkəhɔlɪk/ (**alcoholics**)
1 N-COUNT An **alcoholic** is someone who drinks alcohol too often and cannot stop. ❏ *He admitted that he is an alcoholic.*
2 ADJ Alcoholic drinks are drinks that contain alcohol. ❏ *Wine and beer are alcoholic drinks.* [from New Latin]

alert /əlɜrt/ (**alerts, alerting, alerted**)
1 ADJ If you are **alert**, you are paying attention and are ready to deal with anything that might happen. ❏ *We all have to stay alert.*
2 N-COUNT An **alert** is a situation in which people prepare themselves for something dangerous that might happen soon. ❏ *The incident sparked a major security alert.*
3 V-T If you **alert** someone **to** a dangerous situation, you tell them about it. ❏ *He wanted to alert people to the danger.* [from Italian]

al|gae /ældʒi/ **N-PLURAL** SCIENCE **Algae** are plants with no stems or leaves that grow in water or on damp surfaces. ❏ *...an effort to control algae in Green Lake.* [from Latin]

al|ge|bra /ældʒɪbrə/ **N-NONCOUNT** MATH **Algebra** is a type of mathematics in which letters and signs are used to represent numbers. [from Medieval Latin]
→ look at Word Web: **mathematics**

al|ge|bra|ic /ældʒɪbreɪɪk/ **ADJ** MATH **Algebraic** equations, expressions, and principles are based on or use algebra.

al|go|rithm /ælgərɪðəm/ (**algorithms**)
N-COUNT MATH An **algorithm** is a series of mathematical steps, especially in a computer program, which will give you the answer to a particular kind of problem or question. [from Greek]

al|ien /eɪliən/ (**aliens**)
1 ADJ If something is **alien to** you, it is not the way you would normally feel or behave. [FORMAL] ❏ *Such behavior is alien to most people.*
2 N-COUNT An **alien** is someone who lives in a country where they are not a legal citizen. ❏ *He's an illegal alien.*
3 N-COUNT An **alien** is a creature from another planet. ❏ *Robin Williams plays the part of an alien from the planet "Ork."*

4 N-COUNT SCIENCE An **alien** is a plant or an animal that lives in a different geographical area from the place where it originally lived. [from Latin]

al|ien|ate /eɪliəneɪt/ (**alienates, alienating, alienated**)
1 V-T If you **alienate** someone, you make them become unfriendly or unsympathetic toward you. ❏ *We do not want to alienate anybody.*
2 V-T To **alienate** a person **from** someone or something that they are normally linked with means to cause them to be emotionally or intellectually separated from them. ❏ *His second wife, Alice, alienated him from his two boys.* • **alien|at|ed ADJ** ❏ *Most of these students feel alienated from their parents.* • **alien|ation N-NONCOUNT** ❏ *...her sense of alienation from the world.* [from Latin]

align|ment /əlaɪnmənt/ **N-NONCOUNT** The **alignment** of a person's body is the relationship between the position of their spine and their feet when they are standing or sitting. [from Old French]

Word Link | like ≈ similar : a*like*, *like*ness, un*like*

alike /əlaɪk/
1 ADJ If two or more things are **alike**, they are similar in some way. ❏ *They all look alike to me.*
2 ADV Alike means in a similar way. ❏ *They even dressed alike.* [from Old English]

Thesaurus | alike | Also look up :

| ADJ | comparable, equal, equivalent, matching, parallel, similar; (ant.) different |

alive /əlaɪv/
1 ADJ If people or animals are **alive**, they are not dead. ❏ *Is your father still alive?*
2 ADJ If an activity, organization, or situation is **alive**, it continues to exist or function. ❏ *The big factories are trying to stay alive by cutting costs.* [from Old English]

Word Partnership | Use **alive** with :

ADJ	**dead or** alive **1**
ADV	alive **and well 1**
	still alive **1 2**
V	**found** alive, **keep** *someone/something* alive **1**
	stay alive **1 2**

al|ka|li /ælkəlaɪ/ (**alkalis**)
N-COUNT/N-NONCOUNT SCIENCE An **alkali** is a substance that is the opposite of an acid.

It can burn your skin. [from Medieval Latin]

al|ka|li met|al (**alkali metals**) **N-COUNT**
SCIENCE **Alkali metals** are a group of metallic
elements that includes sodium.

al|ka|line /ǽlkəlaɪn/ **ADJ** SCIENCE
Something that is **alkaline** contains an
alkali or has a pH value of more than 7.
❑ *Some soils are actually too alkaline for certain
plant life.*

alkaline-earth met|al (**alkaline-earth
metals**) or **alkaline earth** **N-COUNT** SCIENCE
Alkaline-earth metals are a group of
metallic elements that includes calcium.

all /ɔl/
1 **PREDET** You use **all** or **all of** to talk about
the whole of something. ❑ *Did you eat all of it?*
❑ *He watches TV all day.*
2 **PREDET** You use **all** or **all of** to talk about
everyone or everything of a particular type.
❑ *Hugh and all his friends came to the party.*
3 **DET** **All** is also an adjective. ❑ *He loves all
literature.*
4 **ADV** **All** means completely. ❑ *I went away
and left her all alone.*
5 **PHRASE** You use **all in all** to introduce
a summary or general statement.
❑ *We thought that all in all it wasn't a bad idea.*
6 **PHRASE** You use **at all** to make negative
sentences stronger. ❑ *I never really liked him
at all.* [from Old English]

> **Usage**   **all**
> As a determiner or quantifier, *all* can often be
> followed by *of* with no change in meaning:
> *All (of) her friends are here. Please put all (of) the paper
> back in the drawer. Of* is required after *all* when a
> pronoun follows: *Harry took all of us to the movies.*

Allah /ɑlə, ǽlə, ɑlɑ/ **N-PROPER** **Allah** is the
name of God in Islam. ❑ *We thank Allah that
the boy is safe.* [from Arabic]

al|le|ga|tion /ǽlɪgeɪʃ°n/ (**allegations**)
N-COUNT An **allegation** is a statement saying
that someone has done something wrong.
❑ *The company denied the allegations.* [from Latin]

al|lege /əlɛdʒ/ (**alleges, alleging, alleged**) **V-T**
If you **allege that** something bad is true, you
say it but do not prove it. [FORMAL] ❑ *They
alleged that the murder resulted from a quarrel
between the two men.* ❑ *The accused is alleged to
have killed a man.* ● **al|leg|ed|ly** /əlɛdʒɪdli/ **ADV**
❑ *His van allegedly hit them as they were crossing
the street.* [from Latin]

al|lele /əlil/ (**alleles**) **N-COUNT** SCIENCE
Alleles are different forms of a particular
gene within an organism. [from German]

al|ler|gic /əlɜrdʒɪk/ **ADJ** If you are **allergic to**
something, you become sick when you eat it
or touch it, or breathe it in. ❑ *I'm allergic to
cats.* [from German]
→ look at Word Web: **peanut**

al|ler|gy /ǽlərdʒi/ (**allergies**)
N-COUNT/N-NONCOUNT If you have an
allergy to something, you become sick, or
red marks appear on your skin when you
eat it or touch it. ❑ *He has an allergy to nuts.*
[from German]

al|le|vi|ate /əliviːeɪt/ (**alleviates, alleviating,
alleviated**) **V-T** If you **alleviate** pain,
suffering, or an unpleasant condition, you
make it less intense or severe. [FORMAL]
❑ *Nowadays, a lot can be done to alleviate back
pain.* ● **al|le|via|tion** /əliviéɪʃ°n/ **N-NONCOUNT**
❑ *Yoga can help in the alleviation of illness.*
[from Late Latin]

al|ley /ǽli/ (**alleys**) **N-COUNT** An **alley** is a
narrow street between the backs of
buildings. [from Old French]

al|li|ance /əláɪəns/ (**alliances**) **N-COUNT**
An **alliance** is a group of people, countries,
organizations, or political parties that work
together. ❑ *The two parties formed an alliance.*
[from Old French]

al|lied /əláɪd/
1 **ADJ** SOCIAL STUDIES **Allied** countries,
troops, or political parties are united by a
political or military agreement. ❑ *...forces
from three allied nations.*
2 **ADJ** If one thing or group is **allied to**
another, it is related to it because the two
things have particular qualities or
characteristics in common. ❑ *...books on
subjects allied to health, beauty, and fitness.*
[from Old French]

al|li|ga|tor
/ǽlɪgeɪtər/
(**alligators**)
N-COUNT An
alligator is a
long animal
with rough
skin, big teeth,
and short legs. ❑ *Do not feed the alligators.*
[from Spanish]

alligator

A

Word Link liter ≈ letter : al*liter*ation, *liter*acy,
*liter*ature

al|lit|era|tion /əlɪtəreɪʃən/ (**alliterations**)
N-COUNT/N-NONCOUNT LANGUAGE ARTS
Alliteration is the use in speech or writing of
several words close together that all begin
with the same letter or sound. [from
Medieval Latin]

al|lo|cate /æləkeɪt/ (**allocates, allocating,
allocated**)
1 V-T If something **is allocated to** a person,
it is given to them. ❑ *Some of the tickets will be
allocated to students.*
2 V-T If something **is allocated for** a
purpose, it is used for that purpose. ❑ *They
allocated one billion dollars for malaria research.*
[from Medieval Latin]

al|low /əlaʊ/ (**allows, allowing, allowed**)
1 V-T If someone **is allowed to** do
something, they have permission to do it.
❑ *The children are allowed to watch TV after school.*
2 V-T If something is **allowed**, you have
permission to do it, have it, or use it.
❑ *Dogs are not allowed in the park.*
3 V-T If you **allow** something **to** happen,
you give permission for it to happen.
❑ *Cellphone use is not allowed.*
4 V-T If you **allow** a length of time **for** a
particular purpose, you include it in your
planning. ❑ *Please allow 28 days for delivery.*
[from Old French]

Thesaurus allow Also look up :
V   approve, consent, tolerate;
      (ant.) disallow, forbid, prohibit,
      prevent **3**

al|low|ance /əlaʊəns/ (**allowances**)
1 N-COUNT An **allowance** is money that is
given regularly to someone. ❑ *She gets an
allowance for taking care of Amy.*
2 N-COUNT A child's **allowance** is money
that is given to him or her every week or
every month by his or her parents. ❑ *When you
give kids an allowance make sure they save some of it.*
3 PHRASE If you **make allowances for**
something, you take it into account in your
decisions, plans, or actions. ❑ *She tried to
make allowances for his age.*
4 PHRASE If you **make allowances for**
someone, you accept behavior from them
that you would not normally accept, because
of a problem that they have. ❑ *He's tired so I'll
make allowances for him.* [from Old French]

al|loy /ælɔɪ/ (**alloys**) **N-COUNT/N-NONCOUNT**
SCIENCE An **alloy** is a metal that is made by
mixing two or more types of metal together.
[from Old French]

all right
1 ADJ If you say that someone or something
is **all right**, you mean that they are
satisfactory or acceptable. ❑ *I'll do that if it's
all right with you.*
2 ADJ If someone or something is **all right**,
they are well or safe. ❑ *Are you all right?*
3 PHRASE You say **all right** when you are
agreeing to something. ❑ *"I think you should go
now."—"All right."*

al|lu|vial fan /əluviəl fæn/ (**alluvial fans**)
or **alluvial cone** **N-COUNT** GEOGRAPHY An
alluvial fan is material such as sand and
gravel, shaped like a fan, that is deposited
on the land by a fast-flowing river.

al|lu|vium /əluviəm/ **N-NONCOUNT**
GEOGRAPHY **Alluvium** is soil or rock that has
been deposited by a river. [from Latin]

all-weath|er **ADJ** In sports, an **all-weather**
surface is made from an artificial material
instead of grass or earth. ❑ *...an all-weather
tennis court.*

al|ly /ælaɪ/ (**allies**)
1 N-COUNT A country's **ally** is another
country that supports it, especially in war.
❑ *...the Western allies.*
2 N-COUNT An **ally** is someone who helps
and supports another person. ❑ *He is a close
ally of the president.* [from Old French]

al|mond /ɑmənd, æm-, ælm-/ (**almonds**)
N-COUNT/N-NONCOUNT **Almonds** are nuts
that you can eat or use in cooking.
❑ *She made a cake flavored with almonds.*
[from Old French]

al|most /ɔlmoʊst/ **ADV** **Almost** means
nearly but not completely. ❑ *We have been
married for almost three years.* ❑ *He caught flu,
which almost killed him.*

Usage almost and most
Be sure to use *almost*, not *most*, before such
words as *all, any, anyone, every,* and *everyone*:
*Almost all people like chocolate. Almost anyone can
learn to ride a bike. Strangely, almost every student in
the class is left-handed.*

Thesaurus almost Also look up :
ADV   about, most, practically, virtually

a

alone /əloʊn/

1 **ADJ** When you, or you and another person are **alone**, you are not with any other people. ❏ *She wanted to be alone.* ❏ *We were alone together.*

2 **ADV** Alone is also an adverb. ❏ *He lived alone in this house for almost five years.*

3 **ADV** When someone does something **alone**, they do it without help from other people. ❏ *Raising a child alone is very difficult.* [from Old English]

> **Thesaurus** **alone** Also look up :
> ADJ solitary; *(ant.)* crowded, together

along /əlɔŋ/

1 **PREP** If you move **along** a road or other place, you move toward one end of it. ❏ *Pedro walked along the street.*

2 **PREP** If something is **along** a road or other long narrow place, it is in it or beside it. ❏ *There were traffic jams all along the roads.*

3 **ADV** When someone or something moves **along**, they keep moving. ❏ *He was talking as they walked along.*

4 **ADV** If you bring someone or something **along** when you go somewhere, you take them with you. ❏ *Bring along your friends and family.*

5 **PHRASE** You use **along with** to mention someone or something else that is also involved in a situation. ❏ *She escaped from the fire along with her two children.*

6 **PHRASE** If something has been true **all along**, it has been true throughout a period of time. ❏ *I was right all along.* [from Old English]

along|side /əlɔŋsaɪd/

1 **PREP** If one thing is **alongside** another thing, the first thing is next to the second. ❏ *He crossed the street and walked alongside Central Park.*

2 **ADV** Alongside is also an adverb. ❏ *He waited for a car to stop alongside.*

3 **PREP** If you work **alongside** other people, you all work together in the same place. ❏ *He worked alongside Frank and Mark.*

aloud /əlaʊd/ **ADV** When you speak, read, or laugh **aloud**, you speak, read, or laugh so that other people can hear you. ❏ *When we were children, our father read aloud to us.*

al|pha|bet /ælfəbɛt, -bɪt/ (**alphabets**)
N-COUNT LANGUAGE ARTS An **alphabet** is a set of letters that is used for writing words. ❏ *The modern Russian alphabet has 31 letters.* [from Late Latin]

al|pha|beti|cal /ælfəbɛtɪkəl/ **ADJ** **Alphabetical** means in the normal order of the letters in the alphabet. ❏ *The books are arranged in alphabetical order.* [from Late Latin]

al|pha|bet|ic prin|ci|ple /ælfəbɛtɪk prɪnsɪpəl/ **N-SING** LANGUAGE ARTS The **alphabetic principle** is the idea that each of the letters of an alphabet represents a particular sound in the language.

al|pha par|ti|cle /ælfə pɑrtɪkəl/ (**alpha particles**) **N-COUNT** SCIENCE **Alpha particles** are subatomic particles that are emitted by radioactive substances such as uranium.

al|ready /ɔlrɛdi/

1 **ADV** You use **already** to show that one thing happened before another thing. ❏ *The meeting had already finished when we arrived.*

2 **ADV** You use **already** to show that a situation exists now or that it started earlier than expected. ❏ *We've already spent most of the money.* ❏ *Most of the guests have already left.* [from Middle English]

> **Usage** **already** and **all ready**
> Its easy to confuse *already* and *all ready. Already* means "before now": *Have you finished eating already? Akiko had already heard the good news. All ready* means "completely prepared": *Jacob is all ready to leave, but Michelle still has to get dressed.*

also /ɔlsoʊ/ **ADV** You can use **also** to give more information about something. ❏ *The book also includes an index of all U.S. presidents.* ❏ *We've got a big table and also some stools and benches.* [from Old English]

> **Thesaurus** **also** Also look up :
> ADV additionally, furthermore, plus, still **1**

al|ter /ɔltər/ (**alters, altering, altered**) **V-T/V-I** If something **alters**, it changes. ❏ *World War II altered American life in many ways.* ❏ *She has altered over the years.* [from Old French]

al|ter|nate (**alternates, alternating, alternated**)

> **PRONUNCIATION HELP**
> Pronounce the verb /ɔltərneɪt/. Pronounce the adjective /ɔltɜrnɪt/.

1 **V-T/V-I** When you **alternate** between two things, you do one and then the other. ❏ *Alternate between walking and running.*

2 **V-T/V-I** When one thing **alternates** **with** another, the first thing happens, then the second thing, then the first thing again. ❑ *Rain alternated with snow.*

3 **ADJ** **Alternate** actions, events, or processes regularly occur after each other. ❑ *...alternate bands of color.* ● **al|ter|nate|ly** **ADV** ❑ *He lived alternately in New York and Seattle.*

4 **ADJ** If something happens on **alternate** days, weeks, or years, for example, it happens on one, then it happens on every second one after that. ❑ *We go skiing on alternate years.*

5 **ADJ** **Alternate** describes a plan or system that is different from the one that is being used now. ❑ *They were forced to turn back and take an alternate route.* [from Latin]
→ look at Usage note at **alternatively**

al|ter|na|tive /ɔltɜrnətɪv/ (**alternatives**)
1 **N-COUNT** If one thing is an **alternative to** another, the first can be used or done instead of the second. ❑ *The new treatment may provide an alternative to painkillers.*
2 **ADJ** An **alternative** plan or offer is different from the one that you already have. ❑ *Alternative methods of travel were available.*
3 **ADJ** **Alternative** describes something that is different from the usual thing. ❑ *Have you considered alternative health care?* [from Latin]

al|ter|na|tive|ly /ɔltɜrnətɪvli/ **ADV** You use **alternatively** to introduce a suggestion or to mention something different from what has just been stated. ❑ *Hotels are not too expensive. Alternatively you could stay in an apartment.* [from Latin]

Usage	alternatively and alternately

Alternatively and *alternately* are often confused. *Alternatively* is used to talk about a choice between different things: *Sheila might go to the beach tomorrow; alternatively, she could go to the museum. Alternately* is used to talk about things that regularly occur after each other: *The traffic light was alternately green, yellow, and red. The days have been alternately sunny and rainy.*

al|though /ɔlðoʊ/
1 **CONJ** You use **although** to introduce an idea that may seem surprising. ❑ *Their system worked, although no one knew how.* ❑ *Although I was only six, I can remember seeing it on TV.*
2 **CONJ** You use **although** to introduce information that slightly changes what you have already said. ❑ *They all play basketball, although on different teams.* [from Middle English]

al|ti|tude /æltɪtud/ (**altitudes**)
N-COUNT/N-NONCOUNT GEOGRAPHY **Altitude**

is a measurement of height above the level of the ocean. ❑ *The aircraft reached an altitude of about 39,000 feet.* ❑ *The illness does not occur in areas of high altitude.* [from Latin]

al|to|geth|er /ɔltəgɛðər/
1 **ADV** If several amounts add up to a particular amount **altogether**, that amount is the total. ❑ *There were eleven of us altogether.*
2 **ADV** You use **altogether** to emphasize a quality that someone or something has. ❑ *That's an altogether different story.*

Usage	altogether and all together

Altogether and *all together* are easily confused. *Altogether* means "in all": *Altogether, I saw four movies at the film festival last week. All together* means "together in a group": *It was the first time we were all together in four years and it meant a lot to me.*

al|tri|cial /æltrɪʃəl/ **ADJ** SCIENCE An **altricial** chick is a young bird that is weak and blind when it is born and is dependent on its parents for food and care. [from New Latin]

alu|mi|num /əluˈmɪnəm/ **N-NONCOUNT** **Aluminum** is a light metal used for making things such as cooking equipment and cans for food and drink. ❑ *We recycle aluminum cans.* [from Latin]
→ look at Word Web: **metal**

al|veo|lus /ælˈviələs/ (**alveoli**) **N-COUNT** SCIENCE **Alveoli** are hollow structures in the lungs of mammals that carry oxygen to the bloodstream. [from Latin]

al|ways /ɔlweɪz/
1 **ADV** If you **always** do something, you do it whenever a particular situation happens. ❑ *She's always late for school.* ❑ *She always gave me socks for my birthday.*
2 **ADV** If you say that you will **always** do something, you mean that you will do it for ever. ❑ *I'll always love him.*
3 **ADV** If someone is **always** doing something, they do it a lot, and it annoys you. ❑ *Why are you always interrupting me?* [from Old English]

Thesaurus	always Also look up :
ADV	consistently, constantly **1** **3** continuously, endlessly, repeatedly; (*ant.*) never, rarely **1**–**3**

am /əm, STRONG æm/ **Am** is the first person singular of the present tense of **be**. [from Old English]

a.m. /eɪ ɛm/ also **am** **ADV** You use **a.m.** after a number when you are talking about a time between midnight and noon. Compare with **p.m.** ❑ *The program starts at 9 a.m.* [from Latin]

ama|teur /ˈæmətʃər, -tʃʊər/ (**amateurs**) **N-COUNT** An **amateur** is someone who does something as a hobby and not as a job. ❑ *...an amateur golfer.* [from French]

amaze /əˈmeɪz/ (**amazes, amazing, amazed**) **V-T/V-I** If something **amazes** you, it surprises you very much. ❑ *He amazed us with his knowledge of Colorado history.* ❑ *14-year-old Michelle Wie continued to amaze.* ● **amazed** **ADJ** ❑ *I was amazed at how difficult it was.* [from Old English]

amaze|ment /əˈmeɪzmənt/ **N-NONCOUNT** **Amazement** is the feeling you have when something surprises you very much. ❑ *I looked at her in amazement.* [from Old English]

amaz|ing /əˈmeɪzɪŋ/ **ADJ** You say that something is **amazing** when it is very surprising and you like it. ❑ *It's amazing what we can remember if we try.* ● **amaz|ing|ly** **ADV** ❑ *She was an amazingly good cook.* [from Old English]

am|bas|sa|dor /æmˈbæsədər/ (**ambassadors**) **N-COUNT** An **ambassador** is an important official person who lives in a foreign country and represents his or her own country there. ❑ *We met the ambassador to Poland.* [from Old French]

am|bigu|ous /æmˈbɪgyuəs/ **ADJ** If you describe something as **ambiguous**, you mean that it is unclear or confusing because it can be understood in more than one way. ❑ *This agreement is very ambiguous.* ● **am|bigu|ous|ly** **ADV** ❑ *...an ambiguously worded statement.* [from Latin]

am|bi|tion /æmˈbɪʃən/ (**ambitions**) **1** **N-COUNT** If you have an **ambition** to do something, you want very much to do it. ❑ *His ambition is to sail around the world.* **2** **N-NONCOUNT** **Ambition** is the desire to be successful, rich, or powerful. ❑ *These young people have hopes for the future and great ambition.* [from Old French]

am|bi|tious /æmˈbɪʃəs/ **1** **ADJ** Someone who is **ambitious** has a strong feeling that they want to be successful, rich, or powerful. ❑ *Chris is very ambitious.* **2** **ADJ** An **ambitious** idea or plan needs a lot of work or money. ❑ *He has ambitious plans for the firm.* [from Old French]

am|bu|lance /ˈæmbyələns/ (**ambulances**) **N-COUNT** An **ambulance** is a vehicle for taking people to the hospital. [from French]

am|bush /ˈæmbʊʃ/ (**ambushes, ambushing, ambushed**) **1** **V-T** If a group of people **ambush** their enemies, they attack them after hiding and waiting for them. ❑ *Gunmen ambushed and killed 10 soldiers.* **2** **N-COUNT/N-NONCOUNT** An **ambush** is an attack on someone by people who have been hiding and waiting for them. ❑ *Three civilians were killed in an ambush.* [from Old French]

amend|ment /əˈmɛndmənt/ (**amendments**) **N-COUNT/N-NONCOUNT** SOCIAL STUDIES An **amendment** is a change that is added to a law. ❑ *Do you know anything about the Fifth Amendment?* ❑ *They suggested an amendment to the defense bill.* [from Old French]

amen|ity /əˈmɛniti/ (**amenities**) **N-COUNT** **Amenities** are things such as shopping centers or sports facilities that are provided for people's convenience, enjoyment, or comfort. ❑ *Amenities include a heated swimming pool.* [from Latin]

Ameri|can /əˈmɛrɪkən/ (**Americans**) **1** **ADJ** SOCIAL STUDIES **American** means belonging to or coming from the United States of America. ❑ *We spoke with the American ambassador at the United Nations.* **2** **ADJ** SOCIAL STUDIES You can call someone **American** when they come from North America, South America, or the Caribbean. **3** **N-COUNT** SOCIAL STUDIES An **American** is someone who is from the United States of America. ❑ *He's an American living in Israel.* **4** **N-COUNT** SOCIAL STUDIES You can call someone an **American** when they come from North America, South America, or the Caribbean. [from Latin]

5 → see also **Latin American**

ami|able /ˈeɪmiəbəl/ **ADJ** Someone who is **amiable** is friendly and pleasant to be with. [WRITTEN] ❏ *She was surprised at how amiable and polite he was.* ● **ami|ab|ly ADV** ❏ *We chatted amiably about old friends.* [from Old French]

ami|cable /ˈæmɪkəbəl/ **ADJ** When people have an **amicable** relationship, they are pleasant to each other and solve their problems without quarreling. ❏ *The meeting ended on amicable terms.* ● **ami|cably** /ˈæmɪkəbli/ **ADV** ❏ *He and his partner separated amicably earlier this year.* [from Late Latin]

am|mu|ni|tion /ˌæmyʊˈnɪʃən/

1 **N-NONCOUNT** **Ammunition** is bullets and rockets that are made to be fired from weapons. ❏ *He had only seven rounds of ammunition.*

2 **N-NONCOUNT** You can describe information that you can use against someone in an argument or a discussion as **ammunition.** ❏ *The data in the study might be used as ammunition.* [from French]

am|nes|ty /ˈæmnɪsti/ (**amnesties**)

1 **N-COUNT/N-NONCOUNT** SOCIAL STUDIES An **amnesty** is an official pardon granted to a group of prisoners by the state. ❏ *...an amnesty for political prisoners.*

2 **N-COUNT** SOCIAL STUDIES An **amnesty** is a period of time during which people can admit to a crime or give up weapons without being punished. ❏ *The government announced an immediate amnesty.* [from Latin]

am|ni|on /ˈæmniɒn, -ən/ (**amnions**) **N-COUNT** SCIENCE The **amnion** is a thin covering that surrounds and protects an embryo in reptiles, birds, and mammals. [from New Latin]

amoe|ba /əˈmiːbə/ (**amoebae** /əˈmiːbi/ or **amoebas**) **N-COUNT** SCIENCE An **amoeba** is the smallest kind of living creature. Amoebae consist of only one cell, and are found in water or soil. [from New Latin]

among /əˈmʌŋ/

1 **PREP** Someone or something that is **among** a group of things or people is surrounded by them. ❏ *There were teenagers sitting among adults.*

2 **PREP** If something happens **among**

a group of people, it happens within that group. ❏ *We discussed it among ourselves.*

3 **PREP** If something exists **among** a group of people, most of them have it or experience it. ❏ *There is concern among parents about teaching standards.*

4 **PREP** If something is shared **among** a number of people, some of it is given to all of them. ❏ *The money will be shared among family members.* [from Old English]

→ look at Usage note at **between**

amo|rous /ˈæmərəs/ **ADJ** If you describe someone's feelings or actions as **amorous,** you mean that they involve sexual desire. [from Old French]

amount /əˈmaʊnt/ (**amounts, amounting, amounted**)

1 **N-COUNT/N-NONCOUNT** The **amount of** something is how much of it there is, or how much you have, need, or get. ❏ *He needs that amount of money to live.* ❏ *I still do a certain amount of work for them.*

2 **V-I** If something **amounts to** a particular total, all the parts of it add up to that total. ❏ *The payment amounted to $42 billion.* [from Old French]

Usage   amount and number

Number is used to talk about how many there are of something: *Madhu was surprised at the large number of students in the class.* Amount is used to talk about how much there is of something: *There is only a small amount of water in the glass.*

am|phib|ian /æmˈfɪbiən/ (**amphibians**) **N-COUNT** SCIENCE **Amphibians** are animals such as frogs and toads that can live both on land and in water. [from Latin]

→ look at Word Web: **amphibian**

Word Link   ampl ≈ large : ample, amplifier, amplify

am|ple /ˈæmpəl/ (**ampler, amplest**) **ADJ** If there is an **ample** amount of something, there is enough of it and usually some extra. ❏ *There'll be ample opportunity to relax.* ● **am|ply ADV** ❏ *He has amply shown his ability.* [from Old French]

am|pli|fi|er /ˈæmplɪfaɪər/ (**amplifiers**) **N-COUNT** An **amplifier** is a piece of electric equipment that makes sounds louder. [from Old French]

am|pli|fy /ˈæmplɪfaɪ/ (**amplifies, amplifying, amplified**) **V-T** If you **amplify** a sound, you make it louder, usually by using electronic

Word Web   amphibian

Amphibians were the first four-legged animals to develop **lungs**. Amphibians lay eggs in water. The **larvae** use **gills** to breathe. During **metamorphosis**, the larvae begin to breathe with lungs and move on to land. **Frogs** follow this cycle, going from egg to **tadpole** to adult. Amphibians have **permeable** skin. They are extremely sensitive to changes in their **environment**. This makes them a bellwether **species**. Scientists use the disappearance of amphibians as an early warning sign of damage to the local **ecology**.

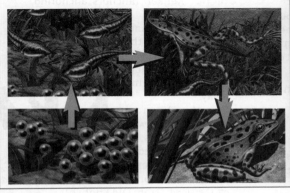

equipment. ❑ *The band amplified the music with microphones.* ● **am|pli|fi|ca|tion** /ˌæmplɪfɪˈkeɪʃ°n/ **N-NONCOUNT** ❑ *Her voice did not need any amplification.* [from Old French]

am|pli|tude /ˈæmplɪtud/ (**amplitudes**) **N-COUNT/N-NONCOUNT** SCIENCE In physics, the **amplitude** of a sound wave or electrical signal is its strength. [from Latin]

amu /ˌeɪ ɛm ˈyu/ (**amu**) SCIENCE **amu** is short for **atomic mass unit**.

amuse /əˈmyuz/ (**amuses, amusing, amused**)
■ **V-T** If something **amuses** you, it makes you laugh or smile. ❑ *The thought amused him.*
■ **V-T** If you **amuse yourself**, you do something in order to not become bored. ❑ *I expect you'll find a way to amuse yourselves for another hour.* [from Old French]
■ → see also **amusing**

amused /əˈmyuzd/ **ADJ** If you are **amused**, something makes you laugh or smile.
❑ *For a moment, Jackson looked amused.*
❑ *Alex looked at me with an amused expression on his face.* [from Old French]

amuse|ment /əˈmyuzmənt/ (**amusements**)
■ **N-NONCOUNT** Amusement is the feeling that you have when you think that something is funny. ❑ *Tom watched them with amusement.*
■ **N-COUNT** Amusements are ways of passing the time pleasantly. ❑ *People did not have many amusements to choose from in those days.* [from Old French]

amuse|ment park (**amusement parks**)
N-COUNT An **amusement park** is a place where people pay to ride on machines for fun or to try to win prizes in games.

amus|ing /əˈmyuzɪŋ/
■ **ADJ** Someone or something that is **amusing** makes you laugh or smile. ❑ *It's an amusing program that the whole family can enjoy.* [from Old French]
■ → see also **amuse**

an /ən, STRONG æn/ **DET** An is used instead of "a" before words that begin with vowel sounds. [from Old English]

an|aero|bic /ænərou̇bɪk/ **ADJ** SCIENCE
Anaerobic creatures or processes do not need
oxygen in order to function or survive.

analog /ænəlɔg/ **ADJ** TECHNOLOGY An **analog**
clock or watch shows the time using hands
instead of numbers. Compare with **digital**.
[from Latin]

analo|gous /ənæləgəs/
1 **ADJ** If two things are **analogous**, they are
similar in some way. [FORMAL] ❑ *Swimming
has no event that is analogous to the 100 meters in
track and field.*
2 **ADJ** ARTS **Analogous** colors are colors
that are similar or related to one another
such as yellow and green. [from Latin]

anal|ogy /ənælədʒi/ (**analogies**) **N-COUNT**
If you make or draw an **analogy between**
two things, you show that they are similar
in some way. ❑ *The analogy between light and
sound is clear.* [from Greek]

Word Partnership	Use **analogy** with :
PREP	analogy **between**
V	**draw an** analogy, **make an** analogy
ADJ	**false** analogy

analy|sis /ənælɪsɪs/ (**analyses** /ənælɪsiz/)
1 **N-COUNT/N-NONCOUNT** **Analysis** is the
process of considering something
carefully in order to understand it or
explain it. ❑ *Our analysis shows that the
treatment was successful.*
2 **N-COUNT/N-NONCOUNT** **Analysis** is the
scientific process of finding out what is in
something. ❑ *They collect blood samples for
analysis.* [from New Latin]

ana|lyst /ænəlɪst/ (**analysts**)
1 **N-COUNT** An **analyst** is a person whose job
is to analyze a subject and give opinions
about it. ❑ *...a political analyst.*
2 **N-COUNT** An **analyst** is someone who
examines and treats people who have
emotional problems. ❑ *My analyst helped me to
feel better about myself.*

ana|lyze /ænəlaɪz/ (**analyzes, analyzing,
analyzed**) **V-T** If you **analyze** something,
you consider it carefully in order to fully
understand it or to find out what is in it.
❑ *We need more time to analyze the decision.*
❑ *They haven't analyzed those samples yet.*

Thesaurus	analyze Also look up :
V	consider, examine, inspect

ana|phase /ænəfeɪz/ **N-NONCOUNT** SCIENCE
Anaphase is a stage in the process of cell
division that takes place within animals
and plants.

anato|my /ənætəmi/ **N-NONCOUNT** SCIENCE
Anatomy is the study of the structure of the
bodies of people or animals. ❑ *...a course in
anatomy.* [from Latin]
→ look at Word Web: **medicine**

an|ces|tor /ænsɛstər/ (**ancestors**) **N-COUNT**
SOCIAL STUDIES Your **ancestors** are the people
in your family who lived before you.
❑ *Our daily lives are so different from those of
our ancestors.* [from Old French]

an|chor /æŋkər/ (**anchors, anchoring,
anchored**)
1 **N-COUNT** An **anchor**
is a heavy object that
you drop into the
water from a boat to
stop it from moving
away.
2 **V-T/V-I** When a
boat **anchors** or when
you **anchor** it, its
anchor is dropped into
the water in order to
make it stay in one place. ❑ *The boat anchored
off the island.* [from Old English]

anchor

an|cient /eɪnʃənt/ **ADJ** **Ancient** means very
old, or from a long time ago. ❑ *...ancient Jewish
traditions.* [from Old French]
→ look at Word Web: **history**

and /ənd, STRONG ænd/
1 **CONJ** You use **and** to connect two or more
words or phrases. ❑ *She and Simon have already
gone.* ❑ *I'm 53 and I'm very happy.*
2 **CONJ** You use **and** to connect two words
that are the same, in order to make the
meaning stronger. ❑ *Learning becomes more
and more difficult as we get older.* ❑ *We talked for
hours and hours.*
3 **CONJ** You use **and** when one event
happens after another. ❑ *I waved goodbye and
went down the steps.*
4 **CONJ** You use **and** to show that two
numbers are added together. ❑ *Two and two
makes four.* [from Old English]

an|ec|do|tal script|ing /ænəkdoutᵊl
skrɪptɪŋ/ **N-NONCOUNT** LANGUAGE ARTS
Anecdotal scripting is a method of recording
and organizing information about a text

such as a play or a novel by writing notes in the margins of the text.

ane|mia /əni̱miə/ **N-NONCOUNT** Anemia is a condition in your blood that makes you feel tired and look pale. ❑ *She suffered from anemia.* [from New Latin]

ane|mic /əni̱mɪk/ **ADJ** Someone who is **anemic** suffers from anemia. ❑ *Tests showed that she was anemic.* [from New Latin]

an|emom|eter /æ̱nɪmɒ̱mɪtər/ (**anemometers**) **N-COUNT** **SCIENCE** An **anemometer** is an instrument that is used to measure wind speeds.

an|es|thet|ic /æ̱nɪsθe̱tɪk/ (**anesthetics**) **N-COUNT/N-NONCOUNT** An **anesthetic** is a substance that doctors use to stop you feeling pain. ❑ *The operation was performed under a general anesthetic.* [from New Latin]

an|gel /e̱ɪndʒəl/ (**angels**)
■ **N-COUNT** Angels are beings that some people believe can bring messages from God. In pictures, angels often have wings.
■ **N-COUNT** An **angel** is someone who is very kind and good. ❑ *Thank you so much, you're an angel.* [from Old English]

an|ger /æ̱ŋgər/ (**angers, angering, angered**)
■ **N-NONCOUNT** Anger is the strong emotion that you feel when you think that someone has behaved badly or has treated you unfairly. ❑ *He cried with anger.*
■ **V-T** If something **angers** you, it makes you feel angry. ❑ *The decision angered some Californians.* [from Old Norse]
→ look at Word Webs: **anger, emotion**

anger man|age|ment **N-NONCOUNT** Anger management is a way of helping people control their anger. ❑ *...an anger management program.*

an|gio|sperm /æ̱ndʒiəspɜrm/ (**angiosperms**)
N-COUNT **SCIENCE** An **angiosperm** is a plant that produces seeds within its flowers.

an|gle /æ̱ŋgəl/ (**angles**)
■ **N-COUNT** **MATH** An **angle** is the space between two lines or surfaces that meet in one place. Angles are measured in degrees. ❑ *...a 30 degree angle.*

angle

■ → see also **right angle**
■ **N-COUNT** An **angle** is the direction from which you look at something. ❑ *From this angle, he looks young.*
■ **N-COUNT** You can refer to a way of thinking about something as a particular **angle.** ❑ *He was considering the idea from all angles.*
■ **PHRASE** If something is **at an angle**, it is leaning so that it is not straight. ❑ *He wore his hat at an angle.* [from Old English]
→ look at Word Web: **mathematics**

an|gry /æ̱ŋgri/ (**angrier, angriest**) **ADJ** When you are **angry**, you feel strong annoyance or resentment about something. ❑ *We are very angry about the decision to close the school.* ❑ *An angry crowd gathered.* ● **an|gri|ly** /æ̱ŋgrɪli/ **ADV** ❑ *"Do you know what this means?" she said angrily.* [from Middle English]

Thesaurus angry Also look up :
ADJ bitter, enraged, mad; (ant.) content, happy, pleased

Word Link anim ≈ alive, mind : animal, animation, unanimously

ani|mal /æ̱nɪm°l/ (**animals**)
■ **N-COUNT** **SCIENCE** An **animal** is a creature such as a dog or a cat, but not a bird, fish,

Word Web   anger

Anger can be a positive thing. Until we feel anger, we may not know how **upset** we are about a situation. Anger can give us a sense of our own power. Showing someone how **annoyed** we are with them may lead them to change. Anger also helps us to let go of **tension** in **frustrating** situations. This allows us to move on with our lives. But anger has its downside. It's hard to think clearly when we're **furious**. We may use bad judgment. **Rage** can also keep us from seeing the truth about ourselves. And when anger turns into **aggression**, people get hurt.

A

insect, or human. ❑ *He was attacked by wild animals.*

2 **N-COUNT** SCIENCE Any living creature, including a human, can be called an **animal.** [from Latin]

→ look at Picture Dictionary: **barn**

→ look at Word Webs: **earth, pet**

Word Partnership	Use animal with :
N	**cruelty to** animals, animal **hide,** animal **kingdom,** animal **noises, plant and** animal, animal **shelter** **1**
ADJ	**domestic** animal, **stuffed** animal, **wild** animal **1**

Ani|ma|lia /ænɪmeɪlyə, -liə/ **N-PLURAL** SCIENCE All the animals, birds, and insects in the world can be referred to together as **Animalia.**

ani|mate /ænɪmət/ **ADJ** Something that is **animate** has life, in contrast to things like stones and machines which do not. ❑ *...animate beings.* [from Latin]

ani|ma|tion /ænɪmeɪʃ°n/ **N-NONCOUNT** ARTS **Animation** is the process of making films in which drawings appear to move. ❑ *...computer animation.* [from Latin]

→ look at Word Web: **animation**

ani|mos|ity /ænɪmɒsɪti/ (**animosities**) **N-COUNT/N-NONCOUNT** **Animosity** is a strong feeling of dislike and anger. ❑ *The animosity between the two men grew.* [from Late Latin]

an|kle /æŋk°l/ (**ankles**) **N-COUNT** Your **ankle** is the joint where your foot joins your leg. ❑ *John twisted his ankle badly.* [from Old Norse]

→ look at Picture Dictionaries: **body, foot**

an|nals /æn°lz/ **N-PLURAL** If something is **in the annals of** a nation or area of activity, it is recorded as part of its history. ❑ *He has become a legend in the annals of military history.* [from Latin]

an|nex (**annexes, annexing, annexed**)

PRONUNCIATION HELP
Pronounce the verb /ænɛks/. Pronounce the noun /æneks/.

1 **V-T** If a country **annexes** another country or an area of land, it seizes it and takes control of it. ❑ *Chicago annexed Pullman in 1889.* ● **an|nexa|tion** /ænɛkseɪʃ°n/ (**annexations**) **N-COUNT** ❑ *...the annexation of Texas in 1845.* **2** **N-COUNT** An **annex** is a building joined to or next to a larger main building. ❑ *There is a museum in an annex to the theater.* [from Medieval Latin]

Word Link	**ann ≈ year** : *anniversary,* **annual,** *annuity*

an|ni|ver|sa|ry /ænɪvɜrsəri/ (**anniversaries**) **N-COUNT** An **anniversary** is a date that is remembered because something special happened on that date in an earlier year. ❑ *They just celebrated their fiftieth wedding anniversary.* [from Latin]

an|no|ta|ted bib|li|og|ra|phy /ænəteɪtɪd bɪblɪɒgrəfi/ (**annotated bibliographies**) **N-COUNT** LANGUAGE ARTS An **annotated bibliography** is a list of books or articles on a particular subject that contains additional comments such as a summary of each book or article.

Word Link	**nounce ≈ reporting** : *announce,* *denounce,* **pronounce**

an|nounce /ənaʊns/ (**announces, announcing, announced**) **V-T** If you **announce** something, you tell people about it officially. ❑ *He will announce tonight that he is resigning.* ❑ *She was planning to announce her engagement.* [from Old French]

Thesaurus	announce	Also look up :
V	advertise, declare, make public, reveal; *(ant.)* withhold	

Word Web   animation

TV **cartoons** are one of the most popular forms of **animation.** Each **episode,** or show, begins with a storyline. Once the **script** is final, cartoonists make up storyboards. The director uses them to plan how the **artists** will **illustrate** the episode. First the illustrators **draw** some **sketches.** Next they draw a few important **frames** for each **scene. Animators** turn these into moving storyboards. This form of the cartoon looks unfinished. The producers then look at the storyboard and suggest changes. After they make these changes, the artists fill in the missing frames. This makes the movements of the characters look smooth and natural.

an|nounce|ment /ənaʊnsmənt/
(**announcements**) **N-COUNT** An **announcement** is information that someone tells to a lot of people. ❑ *The president is expected to make an announcement about his future today.* ❑ *An announcement told us that the train was going to be late.* [from Old French]

Word Partnership	Use announcement with :
V	**make an** announcement
ADJ	**formal** announcement, **public** announcement, **surprise** announcement, **official** announcement

an|nounc|er /ənaʊnsər/ (**announcers**)
N-COUNT An **announcer** is someone whose job is to talk between programs on radio or television. ❑ *The radio announcer said it was nine o'clock.* [from Old French]

an|noy /ənɔɪ/ (**annoys, annoying, annoyed**)
V-T If someone or something **annoys** you, they make you angry and upset. ❑ *Rosie said she didn't mean to annoy anyone.* ❑ *It annoyed me that she believed him.* [from Old French]
→ look at Word Web: **anger**

an|noyed /ənɔɪd/ **ADJ** If you are **annoyed**, you are angry about something. ❑ *She was annoyed that Sasha was there.* [from Old French]

an|noy|ing /ənɔɪɪŋ/ **ADJ** Someone or something that is **annoying** makes you feel angry and upset. ❑ *It's very annoying when this happens.* [from Old French]

an|nual /ænyuəl/
1 **ADJ** **Annual** events happen once every year. ❑ *They held their annual meeting May 20.* ● **an|nual|ly** **ADV** ❑ *The prize is awarded annually.*
2 **ADJ** **Annual** amounts or rates are for a period of one year. ❑ *The company has annual sales of about $80 million.* ● **an|nual|ly** **ADV** ❑ *El Salvador produces 100,000 tons of copper annually.* [from Late Latin]

an|nual ring (**annual rings**) **N-COUNT** **SCIENCE** An **annual ring** is the layer of wood that forms during a single year in a plant such as a tree. Annual rings can be used to measure the age of plants.

an|nu|ity /ənuɪti/ (**annuities**) **N-COUNT** **BUSINESS** An **annuity** is an investment or an insurance policy that pays someone a fixed amount of money each year. ❑ *He received a small annuity of $100.* [from French]

an|nu|lar eclipse /ænyələr ɪklɪps/ (**annular eclipses**) **N-COUNT** **SCIENCE** An **annular eclipse** is a solar eclipse in which the edge of the sun can be seen around the moon.

anony|mous /ənɒnɪməs/ **ADJ** If you remain **anonymous** when you do something, you do not tell people that you were the person who did it. ❑ *You can speak to a police officer at any time, and you can choose to remain anonymous.*
● **anony|mous|ly** **ADV** ❑ *The photographs were sent anonymously to the magazine's offices.* [from Late Latin]

an|oth|er /ənʌðər/
1 **DET** **Another** person or thing means one more person or thing of the same type. ❑ *We're going to have another baby.*
2 **PRON** **Another** is also a pronoun. ❑ *"These cookies are delicious."—"Would you like another?"*
3 **DET** **Another** person or thing is a different person or thing. ❑ *I'll deal with this problem another time.*
4 **PRON** **Another** is also a pronoun. ❑ *He said one thing and did another.*
5 **PRON** You use **one another** to show that each member of a group does something to or for the other members. ❑ *These women are learning to help one another.*

Word Partnership	Use another with :
ADV	**yet** another **1**
N	another **chance**, another **day**, another **one** **1**
	another **man/woman**, another **thing** **2**
V	**tell one from** another **2**
PRON	**one** another **3**

an|swer /ænsər/ (**answers, answering, answered**)
1 **V-T/V-I** When you **answer** someone, you say something back to them. ❑ *I asked him but he didn't answer.* ❑ *Williams answered that he didn't know.*
2 **N-COUNT** **Answer** is also a noun. ❑ *Without waiting for an answer, he turned and walked away.*
3 **V-T/V-I** If you **answer** a letter or an email, you write back to the person who wrote it. ❑ *I emailed him but he didn't answer.* ❑ *Did he answer your letter?*
4 **V-T/V-I** When you **answer** the telephone, you pick it up when it rings. ❑ *Why didn't you answer when I called?* ❑ *She answered her phone on the first ring.*
5 **V-T/V-I** When you **answer** the door, you open it when you hear a knock or the bell. ❑ *I rang the doorbell but no one answered.*

Picture Dictionary   answer

Check

Check the correct answer.

"Small" is a/an ___.

  ___ noun
  ✓ adjective
  ___ verb

Choose

Choose the correct answer.

_b_ Q: Is he a waiter?
   A: Yes, he ___.
   a. am
   b. is
   c. are

Circle

Circle the best answer.

She isn't tall. She's
(thin / short / little).

Cross out

Cross out the word
that doesn't belong.

chicken
dog
table
cow

Match

Match the words
that go together.

savings   dispenser
cash   guard
security   account

Fill in the circle

Fill in the circle.

Ann ___ with her family.
○ live
○ living
◉ lives

Fill in the blank

Fill in the blank.

Q: Have you met Bill?
A: Yes, I _have_ .

Underline

Underline the adjectives.

The young woman was talking
with a tall man.

Unscramble

Unscramble the words.

(been / you / where / have)
Where have you been?

❏ A middle-aged woman answered the door. **6** N-COUNT **Answer** is also a noun. ❏ I knocked at the front door but there was no answer. **7** V-T When you **answer** a question in a test, you write or say what you think is correct. ❏ Before you start to answer the questions, read the whole exam carefully. **8** N-COUNT An **answer to** a problem is a way to solve it. ❏ There are no easy answers to this problem. **9** N-COUNT An **answer to** a question in a test is the information that you give when you are doing it. ❏ I got three answers wrong. [from Old English]
→ look at Picture Dictionary: **answer**

Thesaurus	**answer** Also look up :
V	reply, respond **1** **2**

Word Partnership	Use **answer** with :
V	**refuse to** answer **1** **2** **have an** answer, **wait for an** answer, **find the** answer **6**
N	answer **a question** **1** answer **the door/telephone** **3** **4**
DET	**no** answer **3**
ADJ	**correct/right** answer, **straight** answer, **wrong** answer **7**

an|swer|ing ma|chine (answering machines) N-COUNT An **answering machine** is a small machine that records telephone messages.

ant /ænt/ (ants) N-COUNT **Ants** are small crawling insects that live in large groups. [from Old English]
→ look at Picture Dictionary: **insect**
→ look at Usage note at **aunt**

an|tago|nist /æntægənɪst/ (antagonists) **1** N-COUNT Your **antagonist** is your opponent or enemy. ❏ He expected his antagonist to lose. **2** N-COUNT LANGUAGE ARTS In literature, a character's **antagonist** is another person or a situation that makes it harder for the character to achieve what they want. [from Greek]

ante|ced|ent /æntɪsiːdᵊnt/ (antecedents) N-COUNT LANGUAGE ARTS In grammar, an **antecedent** is a word, phrase, or clause to which a pronoun that occurs later in the sentence refers. For example, in the sentence "Mary tried but she failed," "Mary" is the antecedent of "she." [from Latin]

an|ten|na /æntɛnə/ (**antennae** /æntɛni/ or **antennas**)

> **LANGUAGE HELP**
>
> **Antennae** is the usual plural for meaning **1**. **Antennas** is the usual plural for meaning **2**.

1 **N-COUNT** SCIENCE The **antennae** of an insect are the two long, thin parts attached to its head that it uses to feel things with.
2 **N-COUNT** An **antenna** is a piece of equipment that sends and receives television or radio signals. [from Latin]
→ look at Picture Dictionary: **insect**

antenna

ante|ri|or /æntɪəriər/ **ADJ** SCIENCE **Anterior** describes a part of the body that is at the front of another part. ❑ ...the left anterior descending artery. [from Latin]

an|ther /ænθər/ (**anthers**) **N-COUNT** SCIENCE The **anther** is the male part of a flower, which produces pollen. [from New Latin]

> Word Link   **logy, ology ≈ study of** : anthropo*logy*, bio*logy*, geo*logy*

an|thro|pol|ogy /ænθrəpɒlədʒi/ **N-NONCOUNT Anthropology** is the scientific study of people, society, and culture.
● **an|thro|polo|gist** (**anthropologists**) **N-COUNT** ❑ ...an anthropologist who worked in the South Pacific. [from Greek]
→ look at Word Web: **evolution**

> Word Link   **anti ≈ against** : *anti*biotic, *anti*body, *anti*social

> Word Link   **otic ≈ affecting, causing** : antibi*otic*, bi*otic*, patri*otic*

anti|bi|ot|ic /æntibaɪɒtɪk, æntaɪ-/ (**antibiotics**) **N-COUNT Antibiotics** are drugs that are used for killing bacteria and treating infections. ❑ Your doctor may prescribe antibiotics. [from Greek]
→ look at Word Web: **medicine**

anti|body /æntibɒdi, æntaɪ-/ (**antibodies**) **N-COUNT Antibodies** are substances that your body produces in order to fight diseases. ❑ Your body produces antibodies to fight disease. [from Old English]

an|tici|pate /æntɪsɪpeɪt/ (**anticipates, anticipating, anticipated**) **V-T** If you **anticipate** an event, you think about it and prepare for it before it happens. ❑ Organizers anticipate an even bigger crowd this year. [from Latin]

an|tici|pa|tion /æntɪsɪpeɪʃⁿn/
1 **N-NONCOUNT Anticipation** is a feeling of excitement about something that you know is going to happen. ❑ The days before Christmas were filled with anticipation and excitement.
2 **PHRASE** If you do something **in anticipation of** an event, you do it because you believe that event is going to happen. ❑ Some schools were closed in anticipation of the bad weather. [from Latin]

> Word Link   **clin ≈ leaning** : *anti*cline, de*cline*, in*cline*

anti|cline /æntɪklaɪn/ (**anticlines**) **N-COUNT** SCIENCE An **anticline** is a rock formation in which layers of rock are folded so that they resemble an arch.

an|tipa|thy /æntɪpəθi/ **N-NONCOUNT** If you feel **antipathy**, you feel a strong feeling of dislike toward someone or something. [FORMAL] ❑ ...the voting public's antipathy toward the president. [from Latin]

an|ti|per|spi|rant /æntipɜrspɪrənt, æntaɪ-/ (**antiperspirants**) **N-COUNT/N-NONCOUNT Antiperspirant** is a substance that you use under your arms to keep that area dry. ❑ Try using an antiperspirant for sensitive skin.

anti|quat|ed /æntɪkweɪtɪd/ **ADJ** If you describe something as **antiquated**, you are criticizing it because it is very old or old-fashioned. ❑ Many factories are so antiquated they are not worth saving. [from Latin]

an|tique /æntik/ (**antiques**) **N-COUNT** An **antique** is an old object that is valuable because of its beauty or because of the way it was made. ❑ Jill started collecting antiques as a hobby about a year ago. [from Latin]

anti|so|cial /æntisoʊʃⁿl, æntaɪ-/ **ADJ** Someone who is **antisocial** is not friendly toward other people. ❑ ...antisocial behavior. [from Latin]

anti-vi|rus /æntivaɪrəs, æntaɪ-/ also **antivirus** **ADJ** TECHNOLOGY **Anti-virus** software is software that protects a computer from attack by viruses (= programs that enter your computer and stop it from working properly).

ant|ler /ˈæntlər/ (**antlers**) **N-COUNT Antlers** are the horns that are shaped like branches on the head of a male deer. [from Old French]

an|to|nym /ˈæntənɪm/ (**antonyms**) **N-COUNT** LANGUAGE ARTS An **antonym** is a word that means the opposite of another word. [from Greek]

anus /ˈeɪnəs/ (**anuses**) **N-COUNT** SCIENCE A person's **anus** is the hole from which solid waste matter leaves their body. [from Latin]

anxi|ety /æŋˈzaɪɪti/ (**anxieties**) **N-COUNT/N-NONCOUNT Anxiety** is a feeling of being nervous and worried. ❑ *Her voice was full of anxiety.* [from Latin]

anx|ious /ˈæŋkʃəs/
1 **ADJ** If you are **anxious**, you are nervous or worried about something. ❑ *She became very anxious when he didn't come home.*
● **anx|ious|ly** **ADV** ❑ *They are waiting anxiously for news.*
2 **ADJ** If you are **anxious to** do something, you very much want to do it. ❑ *He is anxious to go back to work.* [from Latin]

any /ˈɛni/
1 **DET** You use **any** in negative sentences to show that no person or thing is involved. ❑ *I don't have any plans for the summer vacation yet.* ❑ *We made this without any help.*
2 **PRON Any** is also a pronoun. ❑ *The children needed new clothes and we couldn't afford any.*
3 **DET** You use **any** in questions to ask if there is some of a particular thing. ❑ *Do you speak any foreign languages?*
4 **PRON Any** is also a pronoun. ❑ *I will stay and answer questions if there are any.*
5 **DET** You use **any** in positive sentences when you want to say that it does not matter which person or thing you choose. ❑ *I'll take any advice.*
6 **PRON Any** is also a pronoun. ❑ *We looked at several programs but didn't find any that were good enough.*
7 **PHRASE** If something does not happen **any longer**, it has stopped happening or is no longer true. ❑ *I couldn't hide the tears any longer.* [from Old English]

any|body /ˈɛnibɒdi, -bʌdi/ **PRON Anybody** means the same as **anyone**.

any|how /ˈɛnihaʊ/ **ADV Anyhow** means the same as **anyway**.

any|more /ɛnɪˈmɔr/ also **any more** **ADV** If something does not happen or is not true **anymore**, it has stopped happening or is no longer true. ❑ *I couldn't trust him anymore.*

Usage **anymore and any more**
Anymore and *any more* are different. *Anymore* means "from now on": *Jacqueline doesn't wear glasses anymore, so she won't have to worry anymore about losing them. Any more* means "an additional quantity of something": *Please don't give me any more cookies—I don't have any more room in my stomach!*

any|one /ˈɛniwʌn/ or **anybody**
1 **PRON** You use **anyone** or **anybody** in negative statements and questions instead of "someone" or "somebody." ❑ *I won't tell anyone I saw you here.* ❑ *Why would anyone want that job?*
2 **PRON** You use **anyone** or **anybody** to talk about someone when the exact person is not important. ❑ *It's not a job for anyone who is slow with numbers.*
3 **PRON** You use **anyone** or **anybody** to talk about all types of people. ❑ *Anyone could do what I'm doing.*

Usage **anyone and any one**
Anyone and *any one* are different. *Anyone* can refer to an unspecified person: *Does anyone know the answer? Any one* refers to an unspecified individual person or thing in a group: *Any one of the players is capable of winning. All those desserts look good—please give me any one with strawberries on it.*

any|thing /ˈɛnɪθɪŋ/
1 **PRON** You use **anything** in negative statements and questions instead of "something." ❑ *We can't do anything.* ❑ *She couldn't see or hear anything at all.* ❑ *Did you find anything?*
2 **PRON** You use **anything** to talk about something when the exact thing is not important. ❑ *More than anything else, he wanted to become a teacher.*
3 **PRON** You use **anything** to show that you are talking about a very large number of things. ❑ *He is young and ready for anything.*

any|time /ˈɛnitaɪm/ **ADV** You use **anytime** to mean a point in time that is not fixed. ❑ *The college admits students anytime during the year.* ❑ *He can leave anytime he wants.*

any|way /ˈɛniweɪ/ or **anyhow**
1 **ADV** You use **anyway** or **anyhow** to

suggest that something is true despite other things that have been said. ❑ *I'm not very good at golf, but I play anyway.*

2 ADV You use **anyway** or **anyhow** to show that a statement explains or supports a previous point. ❑ *I'm sure David told you. Anyway, everyone knows that he owes money.*

3 ADV You use **anyway** or **anyhow** to change the topic or return to a previous topic. ❑ *Anyway, as I was saying, I met Anne the other day.* [from Old English]

> **Usage** anyway and any way
>
> Be sure to use *anyway* and *any way* correctly. *Anyway* can mean "in any situation, no matter what": *It's raining, but let's go for a walk anyway. Any way* means "by any method": *It's not far to Tom's house, so we can walk, drive, or ride our bikes—any way you want.*

any|where /ɛniwɛər/

1 ADV You use **anywhere** in negative statements and questions instead of "somewhere." ❑ *Did you try to get help from anywhere?* ❑ *I haven't got anywhere to live.*

2 ADV You use **anywhere** to talk about a place when the exact place is not important. ❑ *I can meet you anywhere you want.*

apart /əpɑrt/

1 ADV When people or things are **apart**, they are some distance from each other. ❑ *Ray and his sister lived just 25 miles apart.* ❑ *Jane and I live apart now.*

2 ADV If you take something **apart**, you separate it into parts. ❑ *He likes taking bikes apart and putting them together again.* [from Old French]

> **Word Partnership** Use **apart** with :
>
> | | |
> |---|---|
> | ADV | **far** apart **1** |
> | N | **miles** apart **1** |
> | V | **take** apart **2** |

apart|heid /əpɑrthaɪt/ **N-NONCOUNT** SOCIAL STUDIES **Apartheid** was a political system in South Africa in which people were divided into racial groups and kept apart by law. ❑ *...the struggle against apartheid.* [from Afrikaans]

apart|ment /əpɑrtmənt/ (**apartments**) **N-COUNT** An **apartment** is a group of rooms where someone lives in a large building. ❑ *Christina has her own apartment at the top of the building.* [from French]
→ look at Word Web: **city**

> **Word Link** path ≈ feeling : a*path*y, em*path*y, sym*path*y

apa|thy /æpəθi/ **N-NONCOUNT** You can use **apathy** to talk about someone's state of mind if you are criticizing them because they do not seem to be interested in or enthusiastic about anything. ❑ *...political apathy.* ● **apa|thet|ic** /æpəθɛtɪk/ **ADJ** ❑ *Even the most apathetic students are beginning to listen.* [from Latin]

ape /eɪp/ (**apes**) **N-COUNT** An **ape** is a type of animal like a monkey that lives among trees in hot countries and has long, strong arms and no tail. ❑ *...wild animals such as monkeys and apes.* [from Old English]
→ look at Word Web: **primate**

aphe|li|on /əfilyən, -liən, æphɪl-/ (**aphelia**) **N-SING** SCIENCE The **aphelion** of a planet is the point in its orbit at which it is furthest from the sun. [from New Latin]

apolo|gize /əpɒlədʒaɪz/ (**apologizes, apologizing, apologized**)

1 V-I When you **apologize**, you say that you are sorry. ❑ *He apologized to everyone.*

2 V-I You can say **I apologize** as a formal or polite way of saying sorry. ❑ *I apologize for being late.* [from Old French]

> **Word Link** log ≈ reason, speech : apo*log*y, dia*log*ue, *log*ic

apol|ogy /əpɒlədʒi/ (**apologies**) **N-COUNT/ N-NONCOUNT** An **apology** is something that you say or write in order to tell someone that you are sorry. ❑ *I didn't get an apology.* ❑ *We received a letter of apology.* [from Old French]

> **Word Partnership** Use **apology** with :
>
> | | |
> |---|---|
> | V | **demand an** apology, **make an** apology, **owe** *someone* **an** apology |
> | ADJ | **formal/public** apology |
> | N | **letter of** apology |

apos|tro|phe /əpɒstrəfi/ (**apostrophes**) **N-COUNT** LANGUAGE ARTS An **apostrophe** is the mark ' that shows that one or more letters have been removed from a word, as in "isn't" and "we'll." It is also added to nouns to show possession, as in "Mike's car." [from Latin]
→ look at Picture Dictionary: **punctuation**

app /æp/ (**apps**)

1 N-COUNT TECHNOLOGY An **app** is a computer program that is written and designed for a specific purpose. ❑ *...a basic picture-editing app.*

2 N-COUNT TECHNOLOGY An **app** is a

computer program that is designed for use on a mobile digital device. ❑ *The company recently launched a free phone app that translates conversations while you speak.*

ap|pal|ling /əpɔlɪŋ/ **ADJ** Something that is **appalling** is so bad that it shocks you. ❑ *They have been living under the most appalling conditions.* ● ap|pal|ling|ly **ADV** ❑ *...an appallingly bad speech.* [from Old French]

ap|par|el /əpærəl/ **N-NONCOUNT** **Apparel** is clothes. [FORMAL] ❑ *Women's apparel is offered in petite, regular, and tall sizes.* [from Old French]

ap|par|ent /əpærənt/
1 **ADJ** An **apparent** situation or quality seems to exist, although you cannot be certain that it does exist. ❑ *I was worried by our apparent lack of progress.*
2 **ADJ** If something is **apparent**, it is clear and obvious. ❑ *It's apparent that standards have improved.* [from Latin]

ap|par|ent|ly /əpærəntli/ **ADV** You use **apparently** to talk about something that seems to be true, although you are not sure whether it is true. ❑ *Apparently the girls are not at all talented.* [from Latin]

ap|par|ent mag|ni|tude (**apparent magnitudes**) **N-COUNT** SCIENCE The **apparent magnitude** of a star or a galaxy is a measure of how bright it appears to an observer on Earth.

ap|peal /əpil/ (**appeals, appealing, appealed**)
1 **V-I** If something **appeals to** you, you find it attractive or interesting. ❑ *The idea appealed to him.*
2 **V-I** If you **appeal to** someone, you make a serious and urgent request to them. ❑ *Police appealed to the public for help.* ❑ *The president appealed for calm.*
3 **N-COUNT** An **appeal** is a serious and urgent request. ❑ *The police made an urgent appeal for help.*
4 **N-NONCOUNT** The **appeal** of something is a quality that people find attractive or interesting. ❑ *...tiny dolls with great appeal to young girls.* [from Old French]
→ look at Word Web: **trial**

Word Partnership	Use **appeal** with :
PREP	appeal **to *someone*** **1** **2**
	appeal **to a court**, appeal **for *something*** **2**
V	**make an** appeal **3**

ap|peal|ing /əpilɪŋ/ **ADJ** Something that is **appealing** is pleasant and attractive. ❑ *The restaurant serves an appealing mix of Asian dishes.* [from Old French]

ap|peal to author|ity (**appeals to authority**) **N-COUNT/N-NONCOUNT** In logic, an **appeal to authority** is a type of argument in which someone tries to support their view by referring to an expert on the subject who shares their view.

ap|peal to emo|tion (**appeals to emotion**) **N-COUNT/N-NONCOUNT** In logic, an **appeal to emotion** is a type of argument in which someone tries to support their view by using emotional language that is intended to arouse feelings such as excitement, anger, or hatred.

ap|peal to pa|thos (**appeals to pathos**) or appeal to pity **N-COUNT/N-NONCOUNT** In logic, an **appeal to pathos** is a type of argument in which someone tries to support their view by using language that is intended to arouse feelings of pity or mercy.

ap|peal to rea|son (**appeals to reason**) **N-COUNT/N-NONCOUNT** In logic, an **appeal to reason** is a type of argument in which someone tries to support their view by showing that it is based on good reasoning.

ap|pear /əpɪər/ (**appears, appearing, appeared**)
1 **V-I** When someone or something **appears**, it becomes possible to see them. ❑ *A woman appeared at the far end of the street.* ❑ *These small white flowers appear in early summer.*
2 **V-LINK** If something **appears to** be the way you describe it, it seems that way. ❑ *The boy appeared to be asleep.*
3 **V-I** When someone **appears in** a play, a show, or a television program, they take part in it. ❑ *Jill Bennett appeared in several of Osborne's plays.*
4 **V-I** When someone **appears before** a court of law they go there in order to answer questions. ❑ *They will appear in federal court today.* [from Old French]

Thesaurus	appear	Also look up :
V	arrive, show up, turn up; (*ant.*) disappear, vanish **1**
	seem **2**

ap|pear|ance /əpɪərəns/ (**appearances**)
1 **N-SING** Someone's or something's

appearance is the way that they look. □ *She hates it when people make remarks about her appearance.*

2 **N-COUNT** When someone makes an **appearance** at a public event or in a broadcast, they take part in it. □ *It was the president's second public appearance.*

3 **N-SING** The **appearance of** someone or something in a place is the fact of their arriving or becoming visible there. □ *Flowering plants were making their first appearance.* [from Old French]

Word Partnership	Use **appearance** with :
N	**court** appearance **2**
ADJ	**physical** appearance **1**
	public appearance, **sudden** appearance **2**
V	**change** *your* appearance **1**
	make an appearance **2**

ap|pend /əpɛnd/ (**appends, appending, appended**) **V-T** When you **append** something **to** a piece of writing, you attach it or add it to the end of it. [FORMAL] □ *She appended a note at the end of the letter.* □ *It was a relief that his real name hadn't been appended to the manuscript.* [from Late Latin]

ap|pen|dix /əpɛndɪks/ (**appendixes** or **appendices**)

> **LANGUAGE HELP**
>
> **Appendixes** is the plural for meaning **1**. **Appendices** /əpɛndɪsiz/ is the usual plural for meaning **2**.

1 **N-COUNT** SCIENCE Your **appendix** is a small closed tube in the right side of your body. □ *They had to remove his appendix.*

2 **N-COUNT** LANGUAGE ARTS An **appendix to** a book or document is extra information that is placed after the end of the main text. □ *...an appendix to the main document.* [from Latin]

ap|pe|tite /æpɪtaɪt/ (**appetites**) **N-COUNT/ N-NONCOUNT** Your **appetite** is the feeling that you want to eat. □ *He has a healthy appetite, so I cooked huge meals.* [from Old French]

ap|plaud /əplɔd/ (**applauds, applauding, applauded**) **V-T/V-I** When people **applaud**, they clap their hands together to show that they like something. □ *The audience laughed and applauded.* □ *We applauded him for his bravery.* [from Latin]

ap|plause /əplɔz/ **N-NONCOUNT** Applause is the noise that a group of people make when they all clap their hands together to show that they like something. □ *The crowd greeted the couple with loud applause.* [from Latin]

ap|ple /æpᵊl/ (**apples**) **N-COUNT/N-NONCOUNT** An **apple** is a firm round fruit with green, red, or yellow skin. □ *I always have an apple in my packed lunch.* [from Old English]
→ look at Picture Dictionary: **fruit**

ap|pli|ance /əplaɪəns/ (**appliances**) **N-COUNT** An **appliance** is a machine that you use to do a job in your home. [FORMAL] □ *You can buy a DVD player from any electronic appliance store.* [from Old French]

ap|pli|cant /æplɪkənt/ (**applicants**) **N-COUNT** An **applicant for** a job or a course is someone who formally asks to be considered for it. □ *The company keeps records on every job applicant.* [from Latin]

ap|pli|ca|tion /æplɪkeɪʃᵊn/ (**applications**) **1** **N-COUNT** An **application for** a job or a course is a written request to be considered for it. □ *We have not yet received your application form.*

2 **N-COUNT** TECHNOLOGY In computing, an **application** is a piece of software that is designed to do a particular task. □ *This is a software application that you can access via the Internet.*

3 **N-COUNT/N-NONCOUNT** The **application of** a rule or a piece of knowledge is the use of it in a particular situation. □ *...the practical application of the theory.* [from Old French]

Word Partnership	Use **application** with :
V	**accept/reject an** application, **file/ submit an** application, **fill out an** application **1**
N	**college** application, application **form**, **grant/loan** application, **job** application, **membership** application **1** application **software** **2**
ADJ	**practical** application **3**

ap|plied /əplaɪd/ **ADJ** An **applied** subject of study has a practical use, rather than being concerned only with theory. □ *...Applied Physics.* [from Old French]
→ look at Word Web: **science**

ap|ply /əplaɪ/ (**applies, applying, applied**) **1** **V-T/V-I** If you **apply for** a job, you write a letter or write on a form in order to ask for it.

A

❏ *I am applying for a new job.* ❏ *They applied to join the organization.*

2 **v-I** If a rule or a statement **applies to** a person or a situation, it is about them.
❏ *This rule does not apply to you.*

3 **v-T** If you **apply** something **to** a surface, you put it on or rub it into the surface.
❏ *Apply direct pressure to the wound.* [from Old French]

→ look at Word Web: **makeup**

Word Partnership	Use **apply** with :
PREP	apply **for admission**, apply **for a job** **1**
N	**laws/restrictions/rules** apply **2**
	apply **makeup**, apply **pressure 3**

ap|point /əpɔ́ɪnt/ (**appoints, appointing, appointed**) **v-T** If you **appoint** someone **to** a job or a position, you choose them for it.
❏ *The bank appointed Kenneth Conley as manager of its office in Aurora.* [from Old French]

ap|point|ment /əpɔ́ɪntmənt/ (**appointments**)

1 **N-COUNT** An **appointment with** someone is an arrangement to see them at a particular time. ❏ *She has an appointment with her doctor.*

2 **N-COUNT** An **appointment** is a job or a position of responsibility. ❏ *I decided to accept the appointment as music director.* [from Old French]

Thesaurus	appointment Also look up :
N	date, engagement, meeting **1**

ap|posi|tive /əpɒ́zɪtɪv/ (**appositives**)

1 **ADJ** LANGUAGE ARTS In grammar, an **appositive** word or phrase is a word or phrase that modifies the meaning of the noun that comes before it. For example, in the sentence "My son David got married," "David" is appositive.

2 **N-COUNT** LANGUAGE ARTS **Appositive** is also a noun. [from Latin]

ap|pre|ci|ate /əprɪ́ʃieɪt/ (**appreciates, appreciating, appreciated**)

1 **v-T** If you **appreciate** something, you like it. ❏ *Everyone can appreciate this kind of art.*

2 **v-T** If you **appreciate** something that someone has done for you, you are grateful.
❏ *Peter helped me so much. I really appreciate that.*

● **ap|pre|cia|tion** **N-NONCOUNT** ❏ *He wants to show his appreciation for her support.*

3 **v-T** If you **appreciate** a situation or a problem, you understand it and know what

it involves. ❏ *I don't think we appreciated how much time it would take.* [from Medieval Latin]

ap|pre|hen|sive /æprɪhɛ́nsɪv/ **ADJ** Someone who is **apprehensive** is afraid that something bad may happen. ❏ *People are still terribly apprehensive about the future.* [from Latin]

ap|pren|tice /əprɛ́ntɪs/ (**apprentices**) **N-COUNT** An **apprentice** is a young person who works for someone in order to learn their skill. ❏ *Their son Dominic is an apprentice woodworker.* [from Old French]

ap|proach /əpróʊtʃ/ (**approaches, approaching, approached**)

1 **v-T/v-I** When you **approach** something, you move closer to it. ❏ *He approached the front door.* ❏ *We waited while the woman approached.* ❏ *When I approached, the girls stopped talking.*

2 **v-T** If you **approach** someone **about** something, you speak to them about it for the first time, often making an offer or a request. ❏ *Robinson first approached him about the job in late September.*

3 **v-T** When you **approach** a task, a problem, or a situation in a particular way, you deal with it or think about it in that way. ❏ *The bank has approached the situation in a practical way.*

4 **N-COUNT** Your **approach to** a task or problem is the way you deal with it or think about it. ❏ *There are two approaches: spend less money or find a new job.*

5 **v-I** As a future time or event **approaches**, it gradually gets nearer as time passes.
❏ *As autumn approached, the plants and colors in the garden changed.*

6 **v-T** As you **approach** a future time or event, time passes so that you get gradually nearer to it. ❏ *We are approaching the end of the year.*

7 **v-T** If something **approaches** a particular level or state, it almost reaches that level or state. ❏ *They drove at speeds approaching 200 mph.* [from Old French]

Thesaurus	approach Also look up :
V	close in, near; (*ant.*) go away, leave **1**
N	attitude, method, technique **4**

ap|pro|pri|ate /əpróʊpriɪt/ **ADJ** Something that is **appropriate** is correct for a particular situation. ❏ *Is it appropriate that they pay for it?* ❏ *Wear clothes that are appropriate to the job.*

● **ap|pro|pri|ate|ly** **ADV** ❏ *Try to behave*

appropriately and ask intelligent questions.
[from Late Latin]

ap|prov|al /əpr**uː**vᵊl/

1 **N-NONCOUNT** If you get someone's
approval for something, they agree to it.
❏ The chairman gave his approval for an investigation.
2 **N-NONCOUNT** If someone or something
has your **approval**, you like and admire
them. ❏ She wanted her father's approval.
[from Old French]

ap|prove /əpr**uː**v/ (**approves, approving,
approved**)

1 **V-I** If you **approve of** someone or
something, you like them or think they are
good. ❏ My father approves of you.
2 **V-T** If someone in a position of authority
approves a plan, they formally agree to it.
❏ The directors have approved the change.
[from Old French]

ap|proxi|mate /əpr**ɒ**ksɪmət/ **ADJ** An
approximate number, time, or position is
near the correct number, time, or position,
but is not exact. ❏ The approximate value of the
apartment is $300,000. ● **ap|proxi|mate|ly**
ADV ❏ They've spent approximately $150 million.
[from Late Latin]

apri|cot /**æ**prɪkɒt, **eɪ**p-/ (**apricots**) **N-COUNT/
N-NONCOUNT** An **apricot** is a small, soft,
round fruit with yellow flesh and a large
seed inside. ❏ ...a bag of dried apricots. [from
Portuguese]

April /**eɪ**prɪl/ (**Aprils**) **N-COUNT/N-NONCOUNT**
April is the fourth month of the year.
❏ I'm getting married in April. [from Latin]

apron /**eɪ**prən/ (**aprons**) **N-COUNT** An **apron**
is a piece of clothing that you wear over the
front of your normal clothes, especially
when you are cooking, in order to prevent
your clothes from getting dirty. [from
Old French]

apt /**æ**pt/

1 **ADJ** An **apt** remark, description, or choice
is especially suitable. ❏ "Happy" is an apt
description of Maggie. ● **apt|ly** **ADV** ❏ ...the aptly
named town of Oceanside.
2 **ADJ** If someone is **apt to** do something,
they often do it and so it is likely that they
will do it again. ❏ She was apt to raise her voice.
[from Latin]

aquar|ium /əkw**ɛə**riəm/ (**aquariums**)

1 **N-COUNT** An **aquarium** is a building
where fish and ocean animals live.
2 **N-COUNT** An **aquarium** is a glass box filled
with water, in which people keep fish.
[from Latin]
→ look at Word Web: **aquarium**

aque|ous /**eɪ**kwiəs, **æ**kwi-/ **ADJ** SCIENCE
In chemistry, an **aqueous** solution or cream
has a base that consists of water. ❏ ...an
aqueous solution containing various sodium salts.
[from Medieval Latin]

aqui|fer /**æ**kwɪfər/ (**aquifers**) **N-COUNT**
SCIENCE In geology, an **aquifer** is an area of
rock underneath the surface of the earth
which absorbs and holds water.
[from New Latin]

arach|nid /ər**æ**knɪd/ (**arachnids**)
N-COUNT SCIENCE **Arachnids** are a group
of small animals such as spiders that
have eight legs and no antennae.
[from New Latin]

Word Web   **aquarium**

People started to keep **fish** in **glass** bowls in 17th-century
China. Two hundred years later, Europeans started to use
rectangular glass **tanks**. Early aquariums were simple.
Sunlight heated the water and live plants provided
aeration. These aquariums contained only local fish or
goldfish. Then **air pumps** and **heaters** became available.
These controlled temperature and oxygen. This allowed
people to have a variety of fish species, including **tropical**
fish. Today, large public aquariums are popular.
Thousands of people visit them each week. Sea World
in San Diego is one famous example.

A

ar|bi|ter /ɑrbɪtər/ (**arbiters**)

1 N-COUNT An **arbiter** is a person or an institution that judges and settles an argument between two other people or groups. [FORMAL] ❑ *He was the ultimate arbiter on both theological and political matters.*

2 N-COUNT An **arbiter of** taste or style is someone who has a lot of influence in deciding what is fashionable. [from Latin] [FORMAL]

ar|bi|trary /ɑrbɪtrɛri/ ADJ An **arbitrary** action, rule, or decision is not based on any principle, plan, or system. It often seems unfair because of this. ❑ *This arbitrary arrangement often fails to work.* ● **ar|bi|trari|ly** /ɑrbɪtrɛərɪli/ ADV ❑ *The victims were not chosen arbitrarily.* [from Latin]

ar|bi|trary col|or (**arbitrary colors**)

N-COUNT/N-NONCOUNT ARTS An artist who uses **arbitrary colors** paints things in colors that do not naturally belong to the object being painted, for example a blue horse, in order to express their feelings about the object.

arc /ɑrk/ (**arcs**) N-COUNT An **arc** is a smoothly curving line or movement. ❑ *...the rainbow's arc.* [from Old French]

arch /ɑrtʃ/ (**arches**)

N-COUNT An **arch** is a structure that is curved at the top and is supported on either side. ❑ *The bridge is 65 feet at the top of the main arch.* [from Old French] → look at Picture Dictionary: **foot** → look at Word Web: **architecture**

arch

Ar|chae|bac|te|ria /ɑrkibæktɪəriə/

N-PLURAL SCIENCE **Archaebacteria** are a type of bacteria that can live in extreme environments such as volcanoes. Compare with **Eubacteria**.

ar|cha|ic /ɑrkeɪɪk/ ADJ **Archaic** means extremely old or extremely old-fashioned. ❑ *...archaic laws.* [from French]

ar|che|ol|ogy /ɑrkiɒlədʒi/ N-NONCOUNT

SOCIAL STUDIES **Archeology** is the study of the past by examining the things that remain, such as buildings and tools. ● **ar|cheo|logi|cal** /ɑrkiəlɒdʒɪkᵊl/ ADJ ❑ *This is one of the region's most important archeological sites.* ● **ar|che|olo|gist** /ɑrkiɒlədʒɪst/ (**archeologists**) N-COUNT ❑ *Archeologists discovered buildings from an ancient culture in Mexico City.* [from Late Latin] → look at Word Web: **history**

ar|che|typ|al criti|cism N-NONCOUNT

LANGUAGE ARTS **Archetypal criticism** is a type of literary criticism that interprets a literary work by emphasizing its use of archetypes such as ancient myths and symbols.

ar|che|type /ɑrkɪtaɪp/ (**archetypes**)

N-COUNT An **archetype** is something that is considered to be a perfect or typical example of a particular kind of person or thing, because it has all their most important characteristics. [FORMAL] ❑ *He is the archetype of the successful businessman.* ● **ar|che|typ|al** /ɑrkɪtaɪpᵊl/ ADJ ❑ *...the archetypal American middle-class family.* [from Latin]

Archimedes' prin|ci|ple /ɑrkɪmidiz prɪnsɪpᵊl/ N-NONCOUNT SCIENCE **Archimedes' principle** is a law of physics which states that, when an object is in a fluid such as water, its apparent loss of weight is equal to the weight of the fluid that the object has displaced.

archi|tect /ɑrkɪtɛkt/ (**architects**) N-COUNT An **architect** is a person whose job is to design buildings. [from French]

archi|tec|ture /ɑrkɪtɛktʃər/

1 N-NONCOUNT **Architecture** is the art of designing buildings. ❑ *He studied architecture in Rome.* ● **archi|tec|tur|al** /ɑrkɪtɛktʃərəl/ ADJ ❑ *...architectural drawings.*

2 N-NONCOUNT The **architecture** of a building is the style of its design. ❑ *...modern architecture.* [from French] → look at Word Web: **architecture**

ar|chive /ɑrkaɪv/ (**archives**) N-COUNT **Archives** are a collection of documents and records that contain historical information. ❑ *...the State Library's archives.* [from Late Latin]

ar|du|ous /ɑrdʒuəs/ ADJ Something that is **arduous** is difficult and tiring, and involves a lot of effort. ❑ *...a long, hot, and arduous trip.* [from Latin]

are /ər, STRONG ɑr/ **Are** is the plural and the second person singular of the present tense of **be**. [from Old English]

Word Web   architecture

The Colosseum (sometimes spelled Coliseum) in Rome is a great **architectural** success of the ancient world. This amphitheater, built in the first century BC, could hold 50,000 people. It was used for animal fights, human executions, and staged battles. The oval shape allowed people to be closer to the action. It also prevented participants from hiding in the corners. The **arches** are an important part of the **building**. They are an example of a Roman improvement to the simple arch. Each arch is supported by a **keystone** in the top center. The **design** of the Colosseum has influenced the design of thousands of other public places. Many modern day sports stadiums are the same shape.

area /ɛəriə/ (**areas**)

1 N-COUNT An **area** is a particular part of a town, a country, a region, or the world. ❑ *There are 11,000 people living in the area.* ❑ *The survey was carried out in both urban and rural areas.*

2 N-COUNT A particular **area** is a piece of land or a part of a building that is used for a particular activity. ❑ *We had lunch in the picnic area.*

3 N-COUNT An **area** is a particular subject. ❑ *Let's discuss the area of child care.*

4 N-COUNT/N-NONCOUNT MATH The **area** of a surface is the amount of flat space that it covers, measured in square units. ❑ *What's the area of this triangle?* ❑ *The islands cover a total area of 400 square miles.* [from Latin]
→ look at Picture Dictionary: **area**

Word Partnership   Use **area** with :

N	**downtown** area **1**
	tourist area **2**
ADJ	**local** area, **metropolitan** area, **remote** area, area, **surrounding** area **1**
	residential area, **restricted** area **2**
PREP	**throughout the** area **1 2**
	area **of expertise 3**

area code (**area codes**) N-COUNT The **area code** for a particular city or area is the set of numbers at the beginning of a telephone number that represent that city or area. ❑ *The area code for western Pennsylvania is 412.*

are|na /ərinə/ (**arenas**) N-COUNT An **arena** is a place where sports or entertainments take

Picture Dictionary   area

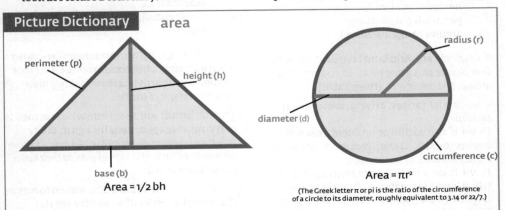

perimeter (p)   height (h)   base (b)
Area = 1/2 bh

radius (r)   diameter (d)   circumference (c)
Area = πr²
(The Greek letter π or pi is the ratio of the circumference of a circle to its diameter, roughly equivalent to 3.14 or 22/7.)

place. ❑ *This is the largest indoor sports arena in the world.* [from Latin]

aren't /ɑrnt, ɑrənt/
① **Aren't** is short for "are not."
② **Aren't** is the form of "am not" that is used in questions. ❑ *I'm invited, aren't I?*

arête /əreɪt/ (**arêtes**) **N-COUNT** SCIENCE
An **arête** is a thin ridge of rock separating two valleys in mountainous regions. [from French]

ar|gue /ɑrgyu/ (**argues, arguing, argued**)
① **V-T/V-I** If you **argue with** someone, you disagree with them about something.
❑ *He was arguing with his wife about money.*
❑ *They are arguing over details.*
② **V-T** If you **argue that** something is true, you give the reasons why you think it is true. ❑ *Employers argue that the law should be changed.* [from Old French]

Thesaurus	argue Also look up :
v	bicker, disagree, fight, quarrel; (*ant.*) agree ① claim ②

ar|gu|ment /ɑrgyəmənt/ (**arguments**)
① **N-COUNT** An **argument** is a conversation in which people disagree with each other. ❑ *Annie had an argument with one of the other girls.*
② **N-COUNT/N-NONCOUNT** An **argument** is what you say in order to try to convince people that your opinion is correct. ❑ *This is a strong argument against nuclear power.* [from Old French]

Word Partnership	Use argument with :
v	**get into an** argument, **have an** argument ①
	support an argument ②
ADJ	**heated** argument ①
	persuasive argument ②
PREP	argument **against/for** ②

arid /ærɪd/ **ADJ Arid** land is so dry that very few plants can grow on it. ❑ *...crops that can grow in arid conditions.* [from Latin]

arise /əraɪz/ (**arises, arising, arose, arisen** /ərɪzən/)
① **V-I** If a situation or problem **arises**, it begins to exist. ❑ *When the opportunity finally arose, thousands of workers left.*
② **V-I** If something **arises from** a particular situation, it is created by that situation.
❑ *The idea arose from discussions held last year.* [from Old English]

arith|me|tic /ərɪθmɪtɪk/ **N-NONCOUNT** MATH
Arithmetic is basic number work, for example adding or multiplying. ❑ *We teach the young children reading, writing, and arithmetic.* [from Latin]
→ look at Word Web: **mathematics**

ar|ith|met|ic se|quence /ærɪθmɛtɪk sikwəns/ (**arithmetic sequences**) or **arithmetic progression N-COUNT** MATH
An **arithmetic sequence** is a series of numbers in which each number differs from the one before it by the same amount, for example the sequence 3, 6, 9, 12.

arm /ɑrm/ (**arms, arming, armed**)
① **N-COUNT** Your **arms** are the two parts of your body between your shoulders and your hands. ❑ *She stretched her arms out.*
② **N-COUNT** The **arm** of a chair is the part on which you rest your arm when you are sitting down. ❑ *Mack held the arms of the chair.*
③ **N-COUNT** The **arm** of a piece of clothing is the part of it that covers your arm. ❑ *The coat was short in the arms.*
④ **N-PLURAL Arms** are weapons, especially bombs and guns. ❑ *Soldiers searched their house for illegal arms.*
⑤ **V-T** If you **arm** someone **with** a weapon, you provide them with a weapon. ❑ *She was so frightened that she armed herself with a rifle.* [Senses 1, 2, and 3 from Old English. Senses 4 and 5 from Old French.]
→ look at Picture Dictionary: **body**

Word Partnership	Use arms with :
PREP	arms **around** ①
v	arms **crossed/folded; hold/take in your** arms, **join/link** arms ①
ADJ	**open/outstretched** arms ①
v	**bear** arms ④
N	arms **control**, arms **embargo**, arms **sales** ④

arm|chair /ɑrmtʃɛər/ (**armchairs**) **N-COUNT**
An **armchair** is a big comfortable chair that supports your arms. ❑ *She was sitting in an armchair in front of the TV.*

armed /ɑrmd/ **ADJ** Someone who is **armed** is carrying a weapon, usually a gun. ❑ *City police said the man was armed with a gun.* ❑ *There were armed guards in the street outside their house.* [from Old French]

armed forces N-PLURAL The **armed forces** or the **armed services** of a country are its military forces, usually the army, navy, marines, and air force. ❑ ...*members of the armed forces.*

ar|mor /ɑrmər/ **N-NONCOUNT** In the past, **armor** was special metal clothing that soldiers wore for protection in battles. ❑ ...*a suit of armor.* [from Old French]
→ look at Word Web: **army**

ar|mored /ɑrmərd/ **ADJ Armored** vehicles are equipped with a hard metal covering in order to protect them from gunfire and other missiles. ❑ *More than forty armored vehicles have gone into the area.* [from Old French]

arm|pit /ɑrmpɪt/ (**armpits**) **N-COUNT** Your **armpits** are the areas of your body under your arms where your arms join your shoulders. ❑ *The water came up to my armpits.*

army /ɑrmi/ (**armies**)
1 **N-COUNT** An **army** is a large group of soldiers who are trained to fight battles on land. ❑ *Perkins joined the Army in 1990.*
2 **N-COUNT** An **army of** people is a large number of them, especially when they are regarded as a force. ❑ *We have an army of volunteers.* [from Old French]
→ look at Word Web: **army**

aro|ma /əroʊmə/ (**aromas**) **N-COUNT** An **aroma** is a strong, pleasant smell. ❑ ...*the wonderful aroma of fresh bread.* [from Latin]

arose /əroʊz/ **Arose** is the past tense of **arise.**

around /əraʊnd/
1 **PREP** Things or people that are **around** a place or an object surround it or are on all sides of it. ❑ *She looked at the people around her.*
2 **PREP** If you move **around** a place, you go along its edge, and back to the point where

you started. ❑ *We went for a walk around the lake.*
3 **ADV Around** is also an adverb. ❑ *They live in a little village with hills all around.* ❑ *They celebrated their win by running around on the football field.*
4 **PREP** If you move **around** something, you move to the other side of it. ❑ *The man turned back and hurried around the corner.*
5 **PREP** If you look **around** something, you look to see what is on the other side. ❑ *I looked around the door but the hall was empty.*
6 **PREP** You use **around** to say that something happens in different parts of a place or area. ❑ *Police say ten people have been arrested around the country.*
7 **ADV Around** is also an adverb. ❑ *Why are you following me around?*
8 **ADV** If you move things **around**, you move them so that they are in different places. ❑ *She moved things around so the table was under the window.*
9 **ADV** If someone or something is **around**, they are present in a place. ❑ *Have you seen my wife anywhere around?*
10 **ADV Around** means approximately. ❑ *My salary was around $45,000.*
11 **PREP Around** is also a preposition. ❑ *We're leaving around May 15.*

arouse /əraʊz/ (**arouses, arousing, aroused**) **V-T** If something **arouses** a particular reaction or feeling in you, it causes you to have that reaction or feeling. ❑ *Our presence aroused his curiosity.*

ar|range /əreɪndʒ/ (**arranges, arranging, arranged**)
1 **V-T** If you **arrange** an event, you make plans for it to happen. ❑ *She arranged an appointment for Friday afternoon.* ❑ *I've arranged to see him Thursday.*

Word Web   army

The first Roman **army** was a poorly organized militia band. Its members had no **weapons** such as **swords** or **spears**. Things changed after the Etruscans, an advanced society from west-central Italy, **conquered** Rome. Then the Roman army became more powerful. They learned how to prepare their **troops** to **fight** better in **battles**. By the first century BC, the Roman army learned the importance of protective equipment. They started wearing bronze **helmets**, **armor**, and carrying wooden **shields**. They fought many **military campaigns** and won many **wars**.

A

2 **V-T** If you **arrange** things somewhere, you carefully place them in a particular position. ❑ *She enjoys arranging dried flowers.* [from Old French]

ar|range|ment /əreɪndʒmənt/ (**arrangements**)

1 **N-COUNT Arrangements** are plans that you make so that something can happen. ❑ *They're working on final arrangements for the meeting.*
2 **N-COUNT** An **arrangement** of things is a group of them that have been placed in a particular position. ❑ *...a flower arrangement.* [from Old French]

ar|ray /əreɪ/ (**arrays**) **N-COUNT** An **array of** different things or people is a large number or wide range of them. ❑ *...a wide array of products.* [from Old French]

ar|rest /ərɛst/ (**arrests, arresting, arrested**)
1 **V-T** If the police **arrest** you, they take you to a police station, because they believe you may have broken the law. ❑ *Police arrested five young men in the city.*
2 **N-COUNT/N-NONCOUNT Arrest** is also a noun. ❑ *Police later made two arrests.* [from Old French]

ar|ri|val /əraɪvəl/ (**arrivals**)
N-COUNT/N-NONCOUNT Your **arrival** is when you arrive somewhere. ❑ *It was the day after his arrival in Wichita.* [from Old French]

ar|rive /əraɪv/ (**arrives, arriving, arrived**)
1 **V-I** When a person or vehicle **arrives** at a place, they come to it from somewhere else. ❑ *Their train arrived on time.* ❑ *After a couple of hours, we arrived at the airport.*
2 **V-I** When something **arrives**, it is brought to you or becomes available. ❑ *The movie will finally arrive in the stores this month.* [from Old French]

Thesaurus arrive Also look up :
v   enter, land, pull in, reach; *(ant.)* depart **1**

ar|ro|gant /ærəgənt/ **ADJ** Someone who is **arrogant** behaves in an unpleasant way toward other people because they believe that they are more important than others. ❑ *Some rather arrogant people think they know everything.* ● **ar|ro|gance** **N-NONCOUNT** ❑ *...the arrogance of powerful people.* [from Latin]

ar|row /æroʊ/ (**arrows**)
1 **N-COUNT** An **arrow** is a long thin weapon that is sharp and pointed at one end. ❑ *They were armed with bows and arrows.*
2 **N-COUNT** An **arrow** is a written sign that points in a particular direction. ❑ *The arrow pointed down to the bottom of the page.* [from Old English]

art /ɑrt/ (**arts**)
1 **N-NONCOUNT** ARTS **Art** is pictures or objects that are created for people to look at. ❑ *...modern American art.*
2 **N-NONCOUNT** ARTS **Art** is the activity of creating pictures or objects for people to look at. ❑ *She decided she wanted to study art.* ❑ *...Savannah College of Art and Design.*
3 **N-PLURAL** ARTS **The arts** are activities such as music, painting, literature, film, theater, and dance. ❑ *She knew she wanted a career in the arts.*
4 **N-COUNT** If you describe an activity as an **art**, you mean that it requires skill ❑ *...the art of public speaking.* [from Old French]
5 → see also **fine art**
→ look at Word Webs: **art, culture**

art criti|cism **N-NONCOUNT** LANGUAGE ARTS **Art criticism** is the study and evaluation of the visual arts, especially painting.

Word Web   art

The Impressionist movement in **painting** began in Europe during the second half of the 19th century. Until then, traditional portraits and **realistic** paintings of objects were done in **studios**. The Impressionists often painted **landscapes** outdoors. They used more light and color in

their **interpretations** of everyday life. Among these painters were French artists Paul Cézanne, Pierre Renoir, and Claude Monet. The word "Impressionist" comes from the name of a Monet painting, "Impression, Sunrise." Japanese prints also influenced the Impressionist movement. The Impressionists liked the use of contrasting dark and bright colors found in these prints.

art el|ement (art elements) **N-COUNT** ARTS **Art elements** are the basic parts that a painting or drawing consists of, such as lines, colors, and shapes.

ar|tery /ɑrtəri/ (arteries) **N-COUNT** SCIENCE **Arteries** are the tubes in your body that carry blood from your heart to the rest of your body. Compare with **vein**. □ *Many patients suffer from blocked arteries.* [from Latin] → look at Word Web: **cardiovascular system**

ar|te|sian spring /ɑrtiʒən sprɪŋ/ (artesian springs) **N-COUNT** SCIENCE An **artesian spring** is a place where water rises naturally through holes or cracks in the ground.

ar|thri|tis /ɑrθraɪtɪs/ **N-NONCOUNT** **Arthritis** is a medical condition in which the joints in your body swell and become painful. □ *I have arthritis in my wrist.* [from Latin]

ar|ti|choke /ɑrtɪtʃoʊk/ (artichokes) **N-COUNT/N-NONCOUNT** **Artichokes** or **globe artichokes** are round green vegetables that have thick leaves and look like flowers. [from Italian]

Word Link	cle ≈ small : article, cubicle, particle

ar|ti|cle /ɑrtɪkəl/ (articles)
■ **N-COUNT** An **article** is a piece of writing in a newspaper or magazine. □ *I read about it in a newspaper article.*
■ **N-COUNT** You can refer to objects as **articles** of a particular kind. □ *...articles of clothing.*
■ **N-COUNT** LANGUAGE ARTS In grammar, an **article** is a word like "a," "an," or "the," which shows whether you are talking about a particular thing or things in general. [from Old French]

ar|ticu|late (articulates, articulating, articulated)

> **PRONUNCIATION HELP**
> Pronounce the adjective /ɑrtɪkyəlɪt/.
> Pronounce the verb /ɑrtɪkyəleɪt/.

■ **ADJ** If you describe someone as **articulate**, you mean that they are able to express their thoughts and ideas easily and well. □ *She is an articulate young woman.*
■ **V-T** When you **articulate** your ideas or feelings, you express them clearly in words. [FORMAL] □ *She articulated her views.* [from Latin]

ar|ticu|la|tion /ɑrtɪkyəleɪʃən/ **N-NONCOUNT** ARTS **Articulation** is the action of producing a sound or a word clearly in speech or music. [from Latin] [FORMAL]

ar|ti|fact /ɑrtɪfækt/ (artifacts) **N-COUNT** SOCIAL STUDIES An **artifact** is an ornament, tool, or other object that is made by a human being, especially one that is historically or culturally interesting. □ *They repair broken religious artifacts.* [from Latin] → look at Word Web: **history**

Word Link	fact, fic ≈ making : artificial, factor, fiction

ar|ti|fi|cial /ɑrtɪfɪʃəl/ **ADJ** **Artificial** objects or materials are made by people, instead of nature. □ *The city has many small lakes, natural and artificial.* □ *Try to follow a diet that is free from artificial additives.* ● **ar|ti|fi|cial|ly** **ADV** □ *...artificially sweetened lemonade.* [from Latin]

Thesaurus	artificial Also look up :
ADJ	manmade, manufactured, synthetic, unnatural; (ant.) natural

ar|ti|fi|cial in|tel|li|gence **N-NONCOUNT** TECHNOLOGY **Artificial intelligence** is the way in which computers can work in a similar way to the human mind.

ar|ti|fi|cial light (artificial lights) **N-COUNT/N-NONCOUNT** **Artificial light** is light from a source such as an electric light or a gas lamp rather than from the sun.

ar|til|lery /ɑrtɪləri/
■ **N-NONCOUNT** **Artillery** consists of large, powerful guns that are transported on wheels. □ *...tanks and heavy artillery.*
■ **N-SING** The **artillery** is the section of an army that is trained to use large, powerful guns. □ *From 1935 to 1937 he was in the artillery.* [from Old French]

art|ist /ɑrtɪst/ (artists)
■ **N-COUNT** ARTS An **artist** is someone who draws, paints, or creates other works of art. □ *Each painting is signed by the artist.*
■ **N-COUNT** ARTS An **artist** is a performer such as a musician, an actor, or a dancer. □ *The song has been performed by many artists over the years.* [from Old French] → look at Word Webs: **animation, genre, painting**

ar|tis|tic /ɑrtɪstɪk/ **ADJ** Someone who is **artistic** is good at drawing or painting. □ *The boys are sensitive and artistic.* [from Old French]

as /əz, STRONG æz/
■ **CONJ** If one thing happens **as** something else happens, it happens at the same time. □ *We shut the door behind us as we entered.*

A

2 **CONJ** You use **as** to say how something happens or is done. ❑ *Today, as usual, he was wearing a suit.* ❑ *Please do as you're asked first time.*

3 **CONJ** You can use **as** to mean "because." ❑ *As I was so young, I didn't have to pay.*

4 **PREP** You use **as** when you are talking about someone's job. ❑ *She works as a nurse.*

5 **PREP** You use **as** when you are talking about the purpose of something. ❑ *The fourth bedroom is used as a study.*

6 **PHRASE** You use **as...as...** when you are comparing things, or saying how large or small something is. ❑ *It's not as easy as I expected.* ❑ *I'm nearly as big as you.*

7 **PREP** You use **as** when you are saying what someone or something is or is thought to be. ❑ *The news came as a complete surprise.*

8 **PHRASE** You use **as if** when you are saying that something appears to be the case. ❑ *Anne stopped, as if she didn't know what to say next.* [from Old English]

Word Link	*scend ≈ climbing : a*scend, *de*scend, *tran*scend

as|cend /əsɛnd/ (**ascends, ascending, ascended**)

1 **V-T** If you **ascend** a hill or a staircase, you go up it. [WRITTEN] ❑ *Mrs. Clayton held Lizzie's hand as they ascended the steps.*

2 **V-I** If a staircase or path **ascends**, it leads up to a higher position. [WRITTEN] ❑ *A number of staircases ascend from the streets.* [from Latin]

Word Link	*cert ≈ determined, true : a*scer*tain, cert*ifi*cate, cert*ify

as|cer|tain /æsərteɪn/ (**ascertains, ascertaining, ascertained**) **V-T** If you **ascertain** the truth about something, you find out what it is. [FORMAL] ❑ *We'll call him and ascertain the facts.* ❑ *They ascertained that he was telling the truth.* [from Old French]

asexu|al re|pro|duc|tion /eɪsɛksyuəl riprədʌkʃⁿn/ **N-NONCOUNT** SCIENCE **Asexual reproduction** is a form of reproduction that involves no sexual activity.

ash /æʃ/ (**ashes**) **N-COUNT/N-NONCOUNT** **Ash** is the gray powder that remains after something is burned. You can also call this substance **ashes**. ❑ *...the cold ashes of a log fire.* [from Old English]

→ look at Word Webs: **fire, glass, volcano**

ashamed /əʃeɪmd/ **ADJ** If you are **ashamed** of someone or something, you feel embarrassed or guilty because of them. ❑ *I was ashamed of myself for getting so angry.* [from Old English]

ashore /əʃɔr/ **ADV** Someone or something that comes **ashore** comes from the ocean onto the shore. ❑ *The hurricane came ashore south of Miami.*

ash|tray /æʃtreɪ/ (**ashtrays**) **N-COUNT** An **ashtray** is a small dish for cigarette ash.

aside /əsaɪd/

1 **ADV** If you move something **aside**, you move it to one side of you. ❑ *Sarah closed the book and put it aside.*

2 **ADV** If you move **aside**, you move so that someone can pass you. ❑ *She stepped aside to let them pass.*

3 **PHRASE** You use **aside from** when you are making an exception to a general statement. ❑ *The room was empty aside from one man seated beside the fire.*

ask /æsk/ (**asks, asking, asked**)

1 **V-T/V-I** If you **ask** someone something, you say something to them in the form of a question. ❑ *"How is Frank?" he asked.* ❑ *I asked him his name.* ❑ *She asked me if I was enjoying my dinner.* ❑ *All you have to do is ask.*

2 **V-T** If you **ask** someone **to** do something, you tell them that you want them to do it. ❑ *We politely asked him to leave.*

3 **V-I** If you **ask for** something, you say that you would like to know it or have it. ❑ *She asked for my address.*

4 **V-T** If you **ask** someone's permission, opinion, or forgiveness, you try to obtain it. ❑ *He asked permission to leave.*

5 **V-T** If you **ask** someone **to** an event or place, you invite them to go there. ❑ *I asked Juan to the party.* [from Old English]

Thesaurus	ask	Also look up :
v	demand, interrogate, question, quiz; *(ant.)* answer, reply, respond **1**	
	beg, plead, request; *(ant.)* command, insist **4**	

Word Partnership	Use **ask** with :
ADJ	**afraid to** ask **1**
V	**come to** ask, **have to** ask **1**
DET	ask **how/what/when/where/who/why 1**
CONJ	ask **if/whether 1**
PREP	ask **about** *someone/something* **1**
	ask **to 2 5**
	ask **for** *someone/something* **3**
N	ask **a question 1**
	ask **for help 3**
	ask **forgiveness**, ask *someone's* **opinion**, ask **permission 4**

asleep /əsliːp/
■ **ADJ** Someone who is **asleep** is sleeping. □ *My daughter was asleep on the sofa.*
■ **PHRASE** When you **fall asleep**, you start sleeping. □ *Sam soon fell asleep.*
■ **PHRASE** Someone who is **fast asleep** or **sound asleep** is sleeping deeply. □ *They were both fast asleep in their beds.*
→ look at Word Web: **sleep**

as|para|gus /əspærəgəs/ **N-NONCOUNT**
Asparagus is a long, thin, green vegetable. [from Latin]
→ look at Picture Dictionary: **vegetable**

as|pect /æspɛkt/ (**aspects**) **N-COUNT**
An **aspect** of something is a quality or a part of it. □ *He was interested in all aspects of the work here.* [from Latin]

as|pi|ra|tion /æspɪreɪʃ°n/ (**aspirations**)
N-COUNT/N-NONCOUNT Someone's **aspirations** are their desire to achieve things. □ *The girl had aspirations to a movie career.* [from Latin]

as|pi|rin /æspərɪn, -prɪn/ (**aspirin** or **aspirins**)
N-COUNT/N-NONCOUNT Aspirin is a mild drug that reduces pain and fever. [from German]

as|sas|si|nate /əsæsɪneɪt/ (**assassinates, assassinating, assassinated**) **V-T**
SOCIAL STUDIES When someone important **is assassinated**, they are murdered for political reasons. □ *Robert Kennedy was assassinated in 1968.* ● **as|sas|si|na|tion** /əsæsɪneɪʃ°n/ (**assassinations**) **N-COUNT/N-NONCOUNT**
□ *Pope John Paul survived an assassination attempt in 1981.* [from Medieval Latin]

as|sault /əsɔːlt/ (**assaults, assaulting, assaulted**)
■ **N-COUNT/N-NONCOUNT** An **assault** is a physical attack on a person. □ *There has been a series of assaults in the university area.*
■ **V-T** To **assault** someone means to physically attack them. □ *The gang assaulted him with baseball bats.* [from Old French]

as|sem|blage /əsɛmblɪdʒ/ (**assemblages**)
N-COUNT ARTS An **assemblage** is a piece of sculpture that combines a number of different objects. [from Old French]

as|sem|ble /əsɛmb°l/ (**assembles, assembling, assembled**)
■ **V-T/V-I** When people **assemble** or when someone **assembles** them, they come or are brought together in a group. □ *There was nowhere for students to assemble between classes.*

□ *The teacher assembled the children together in the room.*
■ **V-T** To **assemble** something means to collect it together or to fit the different parts of it together. □ *Workers were assembling airplanes.* [from Old French]
→ look at Word Web: **industry**

as|sem|bly /əsɛmbli/ (**assemblies**)
■ **N-COUNT** An **assembly** is a group of people gathered together for a particular purpose. □ *She made the announcement during a school assembly.*
■ **N-NONCOUNT** The **assembly** of something is the process of fitting its different parts together. □ *...an automobile assembly line.* [from Old French]

as|sert /əsɜːrt/ (**asserts, asserting, asserted**)
■ **V-T** If you **assert** a fact or belief, you state it firmly. [FORMAL] □ *He asserted that he had a right to go anywhere.* □ *He asserted his innocence.* ● **as|ser|tion** /əsɜːrʃ°n/ (**assertions**)
N-COUNT/N-NONCOUNT □ *There is nothing to support these assertions.*
■ **V-T** If you **assert yourself** or **assert** your authority, you speak and act in a forceful way. □ *He's speaking up and asserting himself.* ● **as|ser|tion** **N-NONCOUNT** □ *The decision is an assertion of his authority.* [from Latin]

as|sess /əsɛs/ (**assesses, assessing, assessed**) **V-T** When you **assess** a person, thing, or situation, you consider them in order to make a judgment about them. □ *I looked around and assessed the situation.* □ *The doctor is assessing whether I am well enough to travel.* ● **as|sess|ment** (**assessments**)
N-COUNT/N-NONCOUNT □ *We carry out an annual assessment of senior managers.* [from Old French]

as|set /æsɛt/ (**assets**)
■ **N-COUNT** An **asset** is something or someone that is considered to be useful or valuable. □ *He is a great asset to the company.*
■ **N-PLURAL** BUSINESS The **assets** of a company or a person are all the things that they own. □ *In 2009, the group had assets of $3.5 billion.*

as|sign|ment /əsaɪnmənt/ (**assignments**)
N-COUNT An **assignment** is a task that you are given to do, especially as part of your studies. □ *We give written assignments as well as practical tests.* [from Old French]

Thesaurus	assignment	Also look up :
N		chore, duty, job, task

A

as|simi|late /əsɪmɪleɪt/ (**assimilates, assimilating, assimilated**)

1 v-t/v-i When people such as immigrants **assimilate into** a community or when that community **assimilates** them, they become an accepted part of it. ❑ *School should help assimilate immigrants.* ❑ *It's important for us to assimilate into the American way of life.* ● **as|simi|la|tion** /əsɪmɪleɪʃ°n/ **N-NONCOUNT** ❑ *...the assimilation of minority groups.*

2 v-t If you **assimilate** new ideas, customs, or techniques, you learn them or adopt them. ❑ *You need to relax and assimilate the changes in your life.* ● **as|simi|la|tion** **N-NONCOUNT** ❑ *...assimilation of knowledge.* [from Latin]

as|sist /əsɪst/ (**assists, assisting, assisted**)
v-t/v-i If someone or something **assists** you, they help you. ❑ *He was assisting elderly passengers with their baggage.* ❑ *They assisted with serving meals.* [from French]

as|sis|tance /əsɪstəns/ **N-NONCOUNT** If you give someone **assistance**, you help them. ❑ *Please let us know if you need any assistance.* [from French]

Word Partnership	Use **assistance** with :
ADJ	**emergency** assistance, **financial** assistance, **technical** assistance **1**
V	**need/require** assistance, **provide** assistance **1**

as|sis|tant /əsɪstənt/ (**assistants**) **N-COUNT** Someone's **assistant** is a person who helps them in their work. ❑ *Kalan asked his assistant to answer the phone while he went out.* [from French]

Word Link	soci ≈ companion : as**soci**ate, **soci**al, **soci**ology

as|so|ci|ate (**associates, associating, associated**)

> **PRONUNCIATION HELP**
> Pronounce the verb /əsoʊʃieɪt, -sieɪt/.
> Pronounce the noun /əsoʊʃiɪt, -siɪt/.

1 v-t If you **associate** someone or something **with** another thing, you connect them in some way. ❑ *Some people associate money with happiness.*

2 v-i If someone **is associating with** another person or group, they are spending a lot of time with them. ❑ *I think she's associating with a bad crowd.*

3 N-COUNT Your **associates** are the people you are closely connected with, especially at work. ❑ *...business associates.* [from Latin]

as|so|ci|ate de|gree (**associate degrees**)
N-COUNT An **associate degree** is a college degree that is given to a student who has completed a two-year course of study. ❑ *She has an associate degree in accounting.*

as|so|cia|tion /əsoʊʃieɪʃ°n, -sieɪ-/ (**associations**) **N-COUNT** An **association** is an official group of people who have the same job, aim, or interest. ❑ *We're all members of the National Basketball Association.* [from Latin]

as|sort|ed /əsɔrtɪd/ **ADJ** A group of **assorted** things is a group of things that are different from each other in some way. ❑ *We have a selection of cotton sweaters in assorted colors.* [from Old French]

as|sort|ment /əsɔrtmənt/ (**assortments**) **N-COUNT** An **assortment** is a group of things that are different from each other in some way. ❑ *There was an assortment of books on the shelf.* [from Old French]

Word Link	sume ≈ taking : as**sume**, con**sume**, pre**sume**

as|sume /əsum/ (**assumes, assuming, assumed**)

1 v-t If you **assume that** something is true, you suppose that it is true. ❑ *I assumed it was an accident.*

2 v-t If someone **assumes** power or responsibility, they take power or responsibility. ❑ *Mr. Lopez will assume the role of CEO.* [from Latin]

Word Partnership	Use **assume** with :
V	**tend to** assume, **let's** assume **that** **1**
ADV	assume **so** **1** **automatically** assume **1** **2**
N	assume **the worst** **1** assume **power/control**, assume **responsibility**, assume **a role** **2**

as|sum|ing /əsumɪŋ/ **CONJ** You use **assuming** or **assuming that** when you are considering a possible situation or event, so that you can think about the consequences. ❑ *"Assuming you're right," he said, "there's not much I can do about it, is there?"* [from Latin]

as|sump|tion /əsʌmpʃ°n/ (**assumptions**) **N-COUNT** If you make an **assumption that** something is true or will happen, you suppose that it is true or will happen, often wrongly. ❏ *You are making an assumption that I agree with you.* [from Latin]

as|sur|ance /əʃʊ̯ərəns/ (**assurances**)
1 **N-COUNT/N-NONCOUNT** If you give someone an **assurance that** something is true or will happen, you say that it is definitely true or will definitely happen, in order to make them feel less worried. ❏ *I gave him an assurance that it wouldn't happen again.*
2 **N-NONCOUNT** If you do something **with assurance**, you do it with a feeling of confidence and certainty. ❏ *Masur led the orchestra with assurance.* [from Old French]

as|sure /əʃʊ̯ər/ (**assures, assuring, assured**)
V-T If you **assure** someone **that** something is true or will happen, you tell them that it is true or will happen. ❏ *He assured me that there was nothing wrong.* ❏ *"Are you sure it's safe?" she asked anxiously. "It couldn't be safer," Max assured her.* [from Old French]

as|sured /əʃʊ̯ərd/ **ADJ** Someone who is **assured** is very confident and relaxed. ❏ *He gave an assured performance.* [from Old French]

> **Word Link** *aster, astro* ≈ *star : asterisk, astronaut, astronomy*

as|ter|isk /æstərɪsk/ (**asterisks**) **N-COUNT** An **asterisk** is the sign *. [from Late Latin]

as|ter|oid /æstərɔɪd/ (**asteroids**) **N-COUNT** **SCIENCE** An **asteroid** is one of the very small planets that move around the sun between Mars and Jupiter. [from Greek]
→ look at Picture Dictionary: **solar system**

as|ter|oid belt (**asteroid belts**) **N-COUNT** **SCIENCE** The **asteroid belt** is the region of the solar system between Mars and Jupiter where most asteroids occur.

as|theno|sphere /æsθɛnəsfɪər/ **N-SING** **SCIENCE** The **asthenosphere** is the region of the Earth which lies between approximately 70 and 120 miles below the surface. [from Greek]

asth|ma /æzmə/ **N-NONCOUNT** **Asthma** is a lung condition that causes difficulty in breathing. [from Greek]

as|ton|ish /əstɒnɪʃ/ (**astonishes, astonishing, astonished**) **V-T** If something or someone **astonishes** you, they surprise you very much. ❏ *The news astonished them.*
● **aston|ished** **ADJ** ❏ *They were astonished to find the driver was a six-year-old boy.* [from Old French]

aston|ish|ing /əstɒnɪʃɪŋ/ **ADJ** Something that is **astonishing** is very surprising. ❏ *She found that fact astonishing.*
● **aston|ish|ing|ly** **ADV** ❏ *Andrea was an astonishingly beautiful young woman.* [from Old French]

aston|ish|ment /əstɒnɪʃmənt/ **N-NONCOUNT** **Astonishment** is a feeling of great surprise. ❏ *He looked at her in astonishment.* [from Old French]

as|tro|naut /æstrənɔt/ (**astronauts**) **N-COUNT** **SCIENCE** An **astronaut** is a person who is trained for traveling in space. [from Greek]

as|tro|nomi|cal unit /æstrənɒmɪkᵊl yunɪt/ (**astronomical units**) **N-COUNT** **SCIENCE** An **astronomical unit** is a unit for measuring distance used in astronomy. It is equal to the average distance between the Earth and the sun. The short form **AU** is also used.

> **Word Link** *er, or* ≈ *one who does, that which does : astronomer, author, writer*

as|trono|my /əstrɒnəmi/ **N-NONCOUNT** **SCIENCE** **Astronomy** is the scientific study of the stars, planets, and other natural objects in space. ● **as|trono|mer** (**astronomers**) **N-COUNT** ❏ *...an amateur astronomer.* [from Old French]
→ look at Word Webs: **astronomer, galaxy, star, telescope**

as|tute /əstut/ **ADJ** Someone who is **astute** shows understanding of behavior and situations, and is skillful at using this knowledge to their own advantage. ❏ *He's an astute businessman.* [from Latin]

asy|lum /əsaɪləm/ (**asylums**) **N-NONCOUNT** **SOCIAL STUDIES** If a government gives a person from another country **asylum**, they allow them to stay, usually because they are unable to return home safely for political reasons. ❏ *He applied for asylum the following year.* [from Latin]

asym|met|ri|cal /eɪsɪmɛtrɪkᵊl/ **ADJ** **MATH** Something that is **asymmetrical** has two sides or halves that are different in shape, size, or style.

asym|me|try /eɪsɪmətri/ (**asymmetries**) **N-COUNT/N-NONCOUNT** **SCIENCE** **Asymmetry** is the appearance that something has when its two sides or halves are different in shape, size, or style.

A

Word Web astronomer

The Italian **astronomer** Galileo Galilei did not invent the telescope. However, he was the first person to use it to study **celestial** bodies. He recorded his findings. What Galileo saw through the telescope supported the theory that the **planet** Earth is not the center of the universe. This theory was written by the Polish astronomer Nicolaus Copernicus in 1530. Copernicus said that all of the planets in the universe revolve around the **sun**. In 1609, Galileo used a telescope to see the **craters** on Earth's **moon**. He also discovered the four largest **satellites** of the planet Jupiter. These four bodies are called the Galilean moons.

as|ymp|tote /ǽsɪmtoʊt, -ɪmp-/ (**asymptotes**) **N-COUNT** MATH An **asymptote** is a straight line to which a curved line approaches closer and closer as one moves along it. [from Greek]

at /ət, STRONG ǽt/
1 **PREP** You use **at** to say where something happens or is situated. ❑ *He will be at the airport to meet her.* ❑ *I didn't like being alone at home.* ❑ *They agreed to meet at a restaurant.*
2 **PREP** You use **at** to say when something happens. ❑ *The funeral will take place this afternoon at 3:00.* ❑ *Zachary started playing violin at age 4.*
3 **PREP** You use **at** to say how fast, how far, or how much. ❑ *I drove back down the highway at normal speed.* ❑ *There were only two apartments at that price.*
4 **PREP** You use **at** when you direct an action toward someone. ❑ *He looked at Michael and laughed.*
5 **PREP** If you work **at** something, you try hard to make it successful. ❑ *She has worked hard at her marriage.*
6 **PREP** If something is done **at** your request, it is done as a result of it. ❑ *She closed the window at his request.*
7 **PREP** You use **at** to say that someone or something is in a particular state or condition. ❑ *The two nations are at war.*
8 **PREP** You are good **at** something if you do it well. ❑ *I'm good at my work.*
9 **PREP** You use **at** to say what someone is reacting to. ❑ *Mom was annoyed at the mess.* [from Old English]

ate /eɪt/ **Ate** is the past tense of **eat**.

ath|lete /ǽθlit/ (**athletes**) **N-COUNT** SPORTS An **athlete** is a person who is good at any type of physical sports, exercise, or games, especially in competitions. ❑ *Jesse Owens was one of the greatest athletes of the twentieth century.* [from Latin]

ath|let|ic /æθlέtɪk/ **ADJ** **Athletic** means relating to athletes and athletics. ❑ *He comes from an athletic family.* [from Latin]

ath|let|ics /æθlέtɪks/ **N-NONCOUNT** SPORTS **Athletics** refers to any kind of physical sports, exercise, or games. ❑ *...college athletics.* [from Latin]

at|las /ǽtləs/ (**atlases**) **N-COUNT** GEOGRAPHY An **atlas** is a book of maps. [from Latin]

ATM /eɪ ti: ɛm/ (**ATMs**) **N-COUNT** An **ATM** is a machine that allows people to take money from their bank account, using a special card. **ATM** is short for "automated teller machine."

Word Link sphere ≈ ball : atmo*sphere*, blogo*sphere*, hemi*sphere*

at|mos|phere /ǽtməsfɪər/ (**atmospheres**)
1 **N-COUNT** SCIENCE A planet's **atmosphere** is the layer of air or other gases around it. ❑ *The shuttle Columbia will re-enter the Earth's atmosphere tomorrow morning.*
● **at|mos|pher|ic** /ǽtməsfέrɪk/ **ADJ** ❑ *...atmospheric gases.*
2 **N-SING** The **atmosphere** of a place is the general feeling that you get about it. ❑ *The rooms are warm and the atmosphere is welcoming.* [from New Latin]
→ look at Picture Dictionary: **core**
→ look at Word Webs: **air, biosphere, earth, greenhouse effect, moon, ozone, water**

at|mos|pher|ic per|spec|tive
(atmospheric perspectives)
N-COUNT/N-NONCOUNT SCIENCE Atmospheric perspective is the same as **aerial perspective**.

atmos|pher|ic pres|sure (atmospheric pressures) **N-COUNT/N-NONCOUNT** SCIENCE Atmospheric pressure is the amount of pressure that is produced by the weight of the Earth's atmosphere.

atom /ˈætəm/ (atoms) **N-COUNT** SCIENCE An **atom** is the very smallest part of something. [from Old French]
→ look at Word Web: **element**

atom|ic /əˈtɒmɪk/ **ADJ** SCIENCE Atomic means relating to atoms or to power that is produced by splitting atoms. ❑ ...atomic energy. ❑ ...the atomic number of an element. [from Old French]

atom|ic mass (atomic masses)
N-COUNT/N-NONCOUNT SCIENCE The **atomic mass** of a chemical element is the weight of one atom of that element, usually expressed in atomic mass units.
→ look at Word Web: **periodic table**

atom|ic mass unit (atomic mass units)
N-COUNT SCIENCE An **atomic mass unit** is a unit for measuring the atomic mass of chemical elements. The abbreviation **amu** is also used.

atom|ic num|ber (atomic numbers)
N-COUNT MATH The **atomic number** of a chemical element is the number of protons in the nucleus of one atom of the element.

aton|al /eɪˈtoʊnªl/ **ADJ** MUSIC Atonal music is music that is not written or played in any key or system of scales.

atone /əˈtoʊn/ (atones, atoning, atoned) **V-I** If you **atone for** something that you have done, you do something to show that you are sorry. [FORMAL] ❑ He felt he had atoned for his past mistakes.

ATP /ˌeɪ ti ˈpi/ **N-NONCOUNT** SCIENCE ATP is a molecule that is found in all plant and animals cells and provides the cells with their main source of energy. **ATP** is short for "adenosine triphosphate."

atri|um /ˈeɪtriəm/ (atria) **N-COUNT** SCIENCE The **left atrium** and the **right atrium** are the two upper chambers of the heart. [from Latin]

atroc|ity /əˈtrɒsɪti/ (atrocities)
N-COUNT/N-NONCOUNT An **atrocity** is a very cruel, shocking action. ❑ The people who committed this atrocity should be punished. [from Latin]

at|tach /əˈtætʃ/ (attaches, attaching, attached)
1 V-T If something is **attached to** an object, it is fastened to it. ❑ There is usually a label with instructions attached to the plant. ❑ Please use the form attached to this letter.
2 V-T If you **attach** a file **to** an email, you send it with the message. ❑ I'm attaching the document to this email. [from Old French]

at|tached /əˈtætʃt/ **ADJ** If you are **attached to** someone or something, you like them very much. ❑ She is very attached to her family and friends. [from Old French]

at|tach|ment /əˈtætʃmənt/ (attachments)
N-COUNT TECHNOLOGY An **attachment** is a file that is attached to an email message and sent with it. ❑ You can send your resume as an attachment to an email. [from Old French]

at|tack /əˈtæk/ (attacks, attacking, attacked)
1 V-T/V-I To **attack** a person or a place means to try to hurt or damage them. ❑ I thought he was going to attack me. ❑ He was in the yard when the dog attacked.
2 N-COUNT/N-NONCOUNT Attack is also a noun. ❑ There have been several attacks on police officers.
3 V-T If you **attack** a person or their ideas, you criticize them strongly. ❑ He attacked bosses for giving themselves big pay raises.
4 N-COUNT/N-NONCOUNT Attack is also a noun. ❑ He responded to attacks on his work.
5 V-T If you **attack** a job or a problem, you start to deal with it in an energetic way. ❑ Parents shouldn't attack the problem on their own.
6 N-COUNT An **attack of** an illness is a time when you suffer badly from it. ❑ ...an asthma attack. [from French]
7 → see also **heart attack**

Word Link	*tempt* ≈ *trying* : at**tempt**, **tempt**ation, **tempt**ed

at|tempt /əˈtɛmpt/ (attempts, attempting, attempted)
1 V-T If you **attempt to** do something, you try to do it. ❑ He attempted to enter law school.
2 N-COUNT If you make an **attempt to** do

something, you try to do it, often without success. ❑ *He made three attempts to rescue his injured colleague.* [from Old French]

Thesaurus attempt Also look up :

V	strive, tackle, take on, try **1**
N	effort, try, venture **2**

Word Partnership Use attempt with :

N	attempt **suicide 1**
ADJ	**any** attempt, **desperate** attempt, **failed/successful** attempt **2**
V	attempt **to control/find/prevent/solve**, **make an** attempt **2**

at|tend /ətɛnd/ (**attends, attending, attended**)

1 **V-T/V-I** If you **attend** an event, you are present at it. ❑ *Thousands of people attended the wedding.* ❑ *I was invited but was unable to attend.*

2 **V-T** If you **attend** a school, a college, or a church, you go there regularly. ❑ *They attended college together.*

3 **V-I** If you **attend to** someone or something, you deal with them. ❑ *The staff will attend to your needs.* [from Old French]

at|ten|dance /ətɛndəns/ (**attendances**)

1 **N-COUNT/N-NONCOUNT** The **attendance** at an event is the number of people who are present at it. ❑ *People had a good time, and attendance was high.*

2 **N-NONCOUNT** **Attendance** at a school, college, or church is the fact of going there regularly. ❑ *Attendance at the school is above average.* [from Old French]

at|tend|ant /ətɛndənt/ (**attendants**)

N-COUNT An **attendant** is someone whose job is to serve people in a public place. ❑ *Tony Williams was working as a parking lot attendant in Los Angeles.* [from Old French]

at|ten|tion /ətɛnʃ°n/

1 **N-NONCOUNT** If you give someone or something your **attention**, you look at them, listen to them, or think about them carefully. ❑ *Can I have your attention?*

2 **N-NONCOUNT** If someone or something is getting **attention**, someone is dealing with them or caring for them. ❑ *Each year more than two million people need medical attention.*

3 **PHRASE** If you **pay attention**, you watch and listen carefully. ❑ *Are you paying attention to what I'm saying?* [from Latin]

Word Partnership Use attention with :

PREP	attention **to detail 1**
ADJ	**careful/close/undivided** attention **1** **special** attention **1 2** **unwanted** attention **2**
V	**attract** attention, **call/direct** *someone's* attention, **catch** *someone's* attention, **draw** attention, **focus** attention, **turn** attention **to** *something/someone* **1** **pay** attention **3**
N	**center of** attention **2**

at|test /ətɛst/ (**attests, attesting, attested**)

V-T/V-I To **attest** something or **attest to** something means to say, show, or prove that it is true. [FORMAL] ❑ *Police records attest to his history of violence.* [from Latin]

at|tic /ætɪk/ (**attics**) **N-COUNT** An **attic** is a room at the top of a house just under the roof.

→ look at Picture Dictionary: **house**

at|ti|tude /ætɪtud/ (**attitudes**)

N-COUNT/N-NONCOUNT Your **attitude to** something is the way that you think and feel about it. ❑ *You need to change your attitude to life.* [from French]

Word Partnership Use attitude with :

PREP	attitude **toward/about**
ADJ	**bad** attitude, **new** attitude, **positive/negative** attitude, **progressive** attitude
V	**change your** attitude

at|tor|ney /ətɜrni/ (**attorneys**) **N-COUNT** In the United States, an **attorney** or **attorney-at-law** is a lawyer. ❑ *...a prosecuting attorney.* ❑ *At the hearing, her attorney did not enter a plea.* [from Old French]

→ look at Word Web: **trial**

at|tract /ətrækt/ (**attracts, attracting, attracted**)

1 **V-T** If you are **attracted to** someone or something, you like them, and you are interested in knowing more about them. ❑ *I was attracted to her immediately.*

2 **V-T** If something **attracts** people or animals, they want to see or visit it. ❑ *The museum is attracting many visitors.*

3 **V-T** **SCIENCE** If one object **attracts** another object, it causes the second object to move towards it. ❑ *Opposite ends of a magnet attract each other.* [from Latin]

→ look at Word Web: **magnet**

at|trac|tion /ətrǽkʃªn/ (**attractions**)

1 **N-NONCOUNT** **Attraction** is a feeling of liking someone. ❑ *His attraction to her was growing.*

2 **N-COUNT** An **attraction** is something that people can visit for interest or enjoyment. ❑ *Disney World is an important tourist attraction.*

3 **N-NONCOUNT** SCIENCE **Attraction** is the force that exists between two objects when they are pulled toward one another, for example by magnetism or gravity. [from Latin]

at|trac|tive /ətrǽktɪv/

1 **ADJ** An **attractive** person or thing is pleasant to look at. ❑ *She's a very attractive woman.* ❑ *The apartment was small but attractive.*

2 **ADJ** You can describe something as **attractive** when it seems worth having or doing. ❑ *Younger players are more attractive to major-league teams.* [from Latin]

> **Thesaurus** attractive Also look up :
>
> ADJ   appealing, charming, good-looking, pleasant; (ant.) repulsive, ugly, unattractive **1**

AU /éɪ yú/ (**AU**) SCIENCE **AU** is short for **astronomical unit.**

auc|tion /ɔ́kʃªn/ (**auctions, auctioning, auctioned**)

1 **N-COUNT/N-NONCOUNT** An **auction** is a public sale where items are sold to the person who offers the most money. ❑ *The painting sold for $400,000 at auction.*

2 **V-T** If something **is auctioned**, it is sold in an auction. ❑ *Eight drawings by French artist Jean Cocteau will be auctioned next week.* [from Latin]

auda|cious /ɔdéɪʃəs/ **ADJ** Someone who is **audacious** takes risks in order to achieve something. ❑ *...an audacious plan to win the presidency.* ● **audac|ity** /ɔdǽsɪti/ **N-NONCOUNT** ❑ *I was shocked at his audacity.* [from Latin]

> **Word Link** *ible ≈ able to be :* au**dible**, flex**ible**, poss**ible**

au|di|ble /ɔ́dɪbªl/ **ADJ** A sound that is **audible** is loud enough to be heard. ❑ *Her voice was barely audible.* ● **au|di|bly** /ɔ́dɪbli/ **ADV** ❑ *Frank sighed audibly.* [from Late Latin]

> **Word Link** *audi ≈ hearing :* **audi**ence, **audi**tion, **audi**torium

audi|ence /ɔ́diəns/ (**audiences**)

1 **N-COUNT** The **audience** of a performance, movie, or television program is all the people who are watching or listening to it. ❑ *There was a TV audience of 35 million.*

2 **N-COUNT** The **audience** of a writer or artist is the people who read their books or look at their work. ❑ *His books reached a wide audience during his lifetime.* [from Old French] → look at Word Web: **concert**

> **Word Partnership** Use audience with :
>
> | | |
> |---|---|
> | PREP | **before/in front of an** audience **1** |
> | N | audience **participation, studio** audience **1** |
> | ADJ | **captive** audience, **general** audience, **live** audience, **wide** audience **1** **large** audience **1** **2** |
> | V | **reach an** audience **2** |

au|dio /ɔ́dioʊ/ **ADJ** **Audio** equipment is used for recording and producing sound. ❑ *...audio and video files.*

au|dit /ɔ́dɪt/ (**audits, auditing, audited**)

1 **V-T** When an accountant **audits** an organization's accounts, he or she examines the financial records officially in order to make sure that they are correct. ❑ *Each year they audit our financial records.* ● **audi|tor** (**auditors**) **N-COUNT** ❑ *...the group's internal auditors.*

2 **N-COUNT** **Audit** is also a noun. ❑ *The bank learned of the problem when it carried out an internal audit.* [from Latin]

audi|tion /ɔdɪ́ʃªn/ (**auditions**) **N-COUNT** An **audition** is a short performance that an actor, dancer, or musician gives so that someone can decide if they are good enough to be in a play, film, or orchestra. ❑ *She went to an audition for a Broadway musical.* [from Latin] → look at Word Web: **theater**

audi|to|rium /ɔdɪtɔ́riəm/ (**auditoriums** or **auditoria** /ɔdɪtɔ́riə/)

1 **N-COUNT** An **auditorium** is the part of a theater or concert hall where the audience sits. ❑ *...a 250-seat auditorium.*

2 **N-COUNT** An **auditorium** is a large room, hall, or building that is used for events such as meetings and concerts. ❑ *...a high school auditorium.* [from Latin]

aug|ment /ɔgmɛ́nt/ (**augments, augmenting, augmented**) **V-T** To **augment** something means to make it larger, stronger, or more effective by adding something to it. [FORMAL] ❑ *She was looking for a way to augment the family income.* [from Late Latin]

A

aug|ment|ed in|ter|val (augmented intervals) **N-COUNT** MUSIC An **augmented interval** is an interval that is increased by half a step or half a tone.

Au|gust /ɔɡəst/ (Augusts) **N-COUNT/N-NONCOUNT** August is the eighth month of the year. ❏ *The movie comes out in August.* [from Old English]

aunt /ænt, ɑnt/ (aunts) **N-COUNT** Your **aunt** is the sister of your mother or father, or the wife of your uncle. ❏ *She wrote to her aunt in Alabama.* ❏ *Aunt Margaret is coming to visit next week.* [from Old French]
→ look at Picture Dictionary: **family**

> **Usage**　aunt and ant
> Be sure not to confuse *aunt* and *ant*, which many English speakers pronounce the same way. Your *aunt* is a sister of your parent; an *ant* is an insect: *Linh's aunt has an unusual fear—she's terrified of stepping on ants.*

aus|pi|cious /ɔspɪʃəs/ **ADJ** An **auspicious** sign, or an **auspicious** start to a relationship or a period of activity, is one that indicates that success is likely. [FORMAL] ❏ *His career as a playwright had an auspicious start.* [from Latin]

Aus|tra|lo|pithe|cine /ɔstreɪloʊpɪθəsin, -saɪn, ɔstrə-/ (Australopithecines) also **australopithecine** **N-COUNT** SOCIAL STUDIES **Austalopithecines** were a species of primates, resembling early human beings, that lived over 3 million years ago. [from New Latin]

authen|tic /ɔθɛntɪk/ **ADJ** An **authentic** person, object, or emotion is real. ❏ *They serve authentic Italian food.* [from Late Latin]

> **Word Link**　er, or ≈ one who does, that which does : astronom**er**, auth**or**, writ**er**

au|thor /ɔθər/ (authors)
　1 **N-COUNT** LANGUAGE ARTS The **author** of a piece of writing is the person who wrote it. ❏ *Jill Phillips is the author of the book "Give Your Child Music."*
　2 **N-COUNT** LANGUAGE ARTS An **author** is a person whose job is writing books. ❏ *Haruki Murakami is Japan's best-selling author.* [from Old French]

author|ity /əθɔrɪti/ (authorities)
　1 **N-NONCOUNT** Authority is the power to control other people. ❏ *Only the police have the authority to close roads.* ❏ *He is now in a position of authority.*

　2 **N-PLURAL** The **authorities** are the people who are in charge of everyone else. ❏ *The authorities are investigating the attack.*
　3 **N-COUNT** Someone who is an **authority** on a particular subject knows a lot about it. ❏ *He's an authority on Russian music.*
　4 **N-NONCOUNT** Authority is official permission to do something. ❏ *They acted without authority.*
　5 **N-COUNT** An **authority** is an official organization or government department. ❏ *...the Philadelphia Parking Authority.* [from French]

author|ize /ɔθəraɪz/ (authorizes, authorizing, authorized) **V-T** If someone **authorizes** something, they give their permission for it to happen. ❏ *Only the president could authorize its use.*
　● **authori|za|tion** /ɔθərɪzeɪʃᵊn/ (authorizations) **N-COUNT/N-NONCOUNT** ❏ *We didn't have authorization from the general to leave.* [from Old French]

auto|bi|og|ra|phy /ɔtəbaɪɒgrəfi/ (autobiographies) **N-COUNT** LANGUAGE ARTS Your **autobiography** is the story of your life, that you write yourself. ❏ *He published his autobiography last fall.* ● **auto|bio|graphi|cal** /ɔtoʊbaɪəgræfɪkᵊl/ **ADJ** ❏ *...an autobiographical novel.*

> **Word Link**　graph ≈ writing : auto**graph**, bio**graph**y, seismo**graph**

auto|graph /ɔtəgræf/ (autographs) **N-COUNT** An **autograph** is the signature of someone famous. ❏ *He asked for her autograph.* [from Late Latin]

auto|mate /ɔtəmeɪt/ (automates, automating, automated) **V-T** To **automate** a factory, office, or industrial process means to provide machines that can do the work instead of people. ❏ *He wanted to use computers to automate the process.* ● **auto|ma|tion** /ɔtəmeɪʃᵊn/ **N-NONCOUNT** ❏ *In the last ten years automation has reduced the work force here by half.* [from Greek]

> **Word Link**　auto ≈ self : **auto**matic, **auto**mobile, **auto**nomy

auto|mat|ic /ɔtəmætɪk/
　1 **ADJ** An **automatic** machine can continue to work when no one is operating it. ❏ *Modern trains have automatic doors.*
　2 **ADJ** An **automatic** action is one that you do without thinking about it. ❏ *All of the*

automatic body functions, even breathing, are affected. ● **auto|mati|cal|ly** /ˌɔtəmætɪkli/ **ADV** ❑ *You will automatically wake up after 30 minutes.* [from Greek]

Word Link	mobil ≈ moving : auto**mobil**e, **mobil**e, **mobil**ize

auto|mo|bile /ˈɔtəməbil/ (**automobiles**) **N-COUNT** An **automobile** is a car. ❑ *...the automobile industry.*
→ look at Word Web: **car**

autono|my /ɔtɒnəmi/
1 **N-NONCOUNT** SOCIAL STUDIES **Autonomy** is the control or government of a country, organization, or group by itself rather than by others. ❑ *Reagan spoke about his idea of greater autonomy for individual states.* ● **autono|mous** **ADJ** ❑ *...the autonomous region of Andalucia.*
2 **N-NONCOUNT** **Autonomy** is the ability to make your own decisions about what to do rather than being influenced by someone else or told what to do. [FORMAL] ❑ *Each of the area managers has a great deal of autonomy in the running of his own area.* ● **autono|mous** **ADJ** ❑ *...autonomous business managers.* [from Greek]

au|tumn /ˈɔtəm/ (**autumns**)
1 **N-COUNT/N-NONCOUNT** **Autumn** is the season between summer and winter when the weather becomes cooler and the leaves fall off the trees. [from Latin]
2 → see also **fall**

aux|ilia|ry /ɔgzɪlyəri, -zɪləri/ (**auxiliaries**) **N-COUNT** LANGUAGE ARTS In grammar, an **auxiliary** or **auxiliary verb** is a verb that you can combine with another verb to change its meaning slightly. In English, "be," "have," and "do" are auxiliary verbs. [from Latin]

avail /əveɪl/ **PHRASE** If you do something **to no avail** or **to little avail**, what you do fails to achieve what you want. [WRITTEN] ❑ *His efforts were to no avail.* [from Old French]

avail|able /əveɪləbᵊl/
1 **ADJ** If something you want or need is **available**, you can find it or get it. ❑ *Breakfast is available from 6 a.m.*
2 **ADJ** Someone who is **available** is not busy and is free to do something. ❑ *Mr. Leach is not available for interviews today.* [from Old French]

Thesaurus	**available** Also look up :
ADJ	accessible, free, handy, obtainable, usable **1**

ava|lanche /ˈævəlæntʃ/ (**avalanches**) **N-COUNT** SCIENCE An **avalanche** is a large amount of snow that falls down the side of a mountain. [from French]
→ look at Word Web: **snow**

ava|rice /ˈævərɪs/ **N-NONCOUNT** **Avarice** is a strong desire for money and possessions. ❑ *He paid a month's rent in advance, just enough to satisfy the landlord's avarice.* [from Old French]

av|a|tar /ˈævətɑr/ (**avatars**) **N-COUNT** TECHNOLOGY An **avatar** is an image that you can use to represent yourself on the Internet. ❑ *This site will create your avatar from any photo.* [from Sanskrit]

av|enue /ˈævɪnyu, -nu/ (**avenues**)
1 **N-COUNT** **Avenue** is sometimes used in the names of streets. The written short form **Ave.** is also used. ❑ *They live on Park Avenue.*
2 **N-COUNT** An **avenue** is a straight road, especially one with trees on either side. [from French]

av|er|age /ˈævərɪdʒ, ˈævrɪdʒ/ (**averages, averaging, averaged**)
1 **N-COUNT** MATH An **average** is the result that you get when you add two or more amounts together and divide the total by the number of amounts you added together. ❑ *The average age was 63.*
2 **ADJ** MATH **Average** is also an adjective. ❑ *The average price of goods went up by just 2.2%.*
3 **N-SING** An amount or quality that is **the average** is the normal amount or quality for a particular group. ❑ *Rainfall was twice the average for this time of year.*
4 **ADJ** **Average** is also an adjective. ❑ *The average adult man burns 1,500 to 2,000 calories per day.*
5 **V-T** To **average** a particular amount means to get or produce that amount as an average over a period of time. ❑ *We averaged 42 miles per hour.*
6 **ADJ** **Average** means ordinary. ❑ *He seemed like a pleasant, average guy.* [from Old Italian]

av|er|age speed (**average speeds**) **N-COUNT** SCIENCE The **average speed** of a moving object is the overall rate at which it moves, which you calculate by dividing the distance that the object travels by the time it takes to travel that distance.

avert /əvɜrt/ (**averts, averting, averted**)
1 **V-T** If you **avert** something unpleasant,

you prevent it from happening. ❏ *They managed to avert war.*

2 **v-T** If you **avert** your eyes or gaze **from** someone or something, you look away from them. ❏ *I saw her but I averted my eyes.* [from Old French]

avia|tion /eɪviˈeɪʃⁿn/ **N-NONCOUNT** Aviation is the operation and production of aircraft. ❏ *...the aviation industry.* [from French]

avo|ca|do /ˌævəkɑdoʊ/ (avocados) **N-COUNT/ N-NONCOUNT** An **avocado** is a fruit with dark green skin and a large seed in the middle. ❏ *...crab and avocado salad.* [from Spanish]

avoid /əvɔɪd/ (avoids, avoiding, avoided)
1 **v-T** If you **avoid** something unpleasant, you do something to stop it from happening. ❏ *It was a last-minute attempt to avoid a disaster.*

2 **v-T** If you **avoid** doing something, you choose not to do it. ❏ *I avoid working in public places.*

3 **v-T** If you **avoid** a person or thing, you keep away from them. ❏ *She went to the women's restroom to avoid him.* [from Old French]

await /əweɪt/ (awaits, awaiting, awaited)
1 **v-T** If you **await** someone or something, you wait for them. [FORMAL] ❏ *We awaited the arrival of the chairman.*

2 **v-T** Something that **awaits** you is going to happen or come to you in the future. [FORMAL] ❏ *A surprise awaited them inside the store.*

awake /əweɪk/
1 **ADJ** Someone who is **awake** is not sleeping. ❏ *I stayed awake until midnight.*

2 **PHRASE** Someone who is **wide awake** is fully awake and unable to sleep. ❏ *I could not relax and still felt wide awake.* [from Old English]
→ look at Word Web: **sleep**

Word Partnership	Use awake with :	
v	keep *someone* awake, lie awake, stay awake **1**	
ADV	fully awake, half awake **1** wide awake **2**	

award /əwɔrd/ (awards, awarding, awarded)
1 **N-COUNT** An **award** is a prize that a person is given for doing something well. ❏ *He again won the National Book Award for fiction.*

2 **v-T** If someone **is awarded** a prize, it is given to them. ❏ *She was awarded the prize for both films.*

3 **v-T** To **award** something **to** someone means to decide that it will be given to that person. ❏ *We have awarded the contract to a company in New York.* [from Old Northern French]

Usage   award and reward
Be careful not to confuse *award* and *reward*. You get an *award* for doing something well, and you get a *reward* for doing a good deed or service: *Tuka got an award for writing the best short story, and Gina got a $50 reward for giving a lost wallet back to the owner—so they went out and had a fancy dinner at a fine restaurant.*

Word Link	war ≈ watchful : a**war**e, be**war**e, **war**ning

Word Link	ness ≈ state, condition : aware**ness**, conscious**ness**, kind**ness**

aware /əwɛər/
1 **ADJ** If you are **aware of** something, you know about it. ❏ *They are well aware of the danger.* ● aware|ness **N-NONCOUNT** ❏ *We are trying to raise awareness of the pollution problem.*

2 **ADJ** If you are **aware of** something, you realize that it is there. ❏ *She was very aware of the noise of the city.* [from Old English]

Word Partnership	Use aware with :	
ADV	painfully aware, well aware **1** **2** acutely/vaguely aware, fully aware **1** **2**	
PREP	aware of *something/someone*, aware that **1** **2**	
V	become aware **1** **2**	

away /əweɪ/
1 **ADV** If someone or something moves **away from** a place, they move so that they are no longer there. ❏ *He walked away from his car.*

2 **ADV** If you are **away from** a place, you are not in the place where people expect you to be. ❏ *Jason was working away from home for a while.*

3 **ADV** When a sports team plays **away**, it goes to its opponents' ground to play. Compare with **home**. ❏ *Canada's Davis Cup team will play away against the Netherlands in February.*

4 **ADJ** **Away** is also an adjective. ❏ *The team is about to play an important away game.*

5 **ADV** If you put something **away**, you put it where it should be. ❏ *I put my book away and went to bed.*

6 **ADV** If an event is a week **away**, it will happen after a week. ❏ *Christmas is now only two weeks away.*

7 **ADV** You use **away** with certain verbs when something slowly disappears or becomes less important. ❏ *The snow has already melted away.*

8 **PHRASE** If something is a particular distance **away from** a person or place, it is not near that person or place. ❏ *Remember to stay a safe distance away from the car in front.* [from Old English]

Word Partnership	Use **away** with :
N	**away from home** **1**
V	**back** away, **blow** away, **break** away, **chase** *someone* away, **drive** away, **get** away, **go** away, **hide** away, **move** away, **pull/take** *something* away, **walk** away **1** **put** away **3**
ADJ	**far** away **1** **6**

Word Link	*some* ≈ *causing* : *awe*some, *bother*some, *lone*some

awe|some /ɔsəm/

1 **ADJ** An **awesome** person or thing is very powerful or frightening. ❏ *I love the awesome power of the ocean waves.*

2 **ADJ** If something is **awesome**, it is very good or special. [INFORMAL] ❏ *We all agreed the game was awesome.* [from Old Norse]

aw|ful /ɔfəl/

1 **ADJ** If someone or something is **awful**, they are very bad. ❏ *I thought he was an awful actor.* ❏ *There was an awful smell of paint.*

2 **ADJ** You can use **awful** to emphasize how large an amount is. ❏ *I have an awful lot of work to do.*

Thesaurus	awful Also look up :
ADJ	bad, dreadful, horrible, terrible; (*ant.*) good, nice, pleasing **1**

awhile /əwaɪl/ **ADV** **Awhile** means for a short time. ❏ *I waited awhile.*

awk|ward /ɔkwərd/

1 **ADJ** An **awkward** situation is embarrassing and difficult to deal with. ❏ *He kept asking awkward questions.* ● **awk|ward|ly** **ADV** ❏ *There was an awkwardly long silence.*

2 **ADJ** Someone who is **awkward** is uncomfortable in social situations. ❏ *When I was younger, I was shy and awkward, especially with girls.*

3 **ADJ** Something that is **awkward to** use or carry is difficult to use or carry because of its design. ❏ *The bicycle was small but awkward to carry.*

4 **ADJ** An **awkward** movement or position

looks strange or uncomfortable. ❏ *Amy made an awkward movement with her hands.*

● **awk|ward|ly** **ADV** ❏ *He fell awkwardly.* [from Old Norse]

Thesaurus	awkward Also look up :
ADJ	embarrassing, delicate, sticky, uncomfortable **1** uncoordinated **2**

awoke /əwoʊk/ **Awoke** is the past tense of **awake**.

awok|en /əwoʊkən/ **Awoken** is the past participle of **awake**.

ax /æks/ (**axes**) **N-COUNT** An **ax** is a tool used for cutting wood. It has a heavy metal blade and a long handle. [from Old English]

ax|ial move|ment /æksiəl muvmənt/ (**axial movements**) **N-COUNT/N-NONCOUNT** SCIENCE **Axial movement** is movement such as bending or stretching, which does not involve moving from one place to another.

axi|om /æksiəm/ (**axioms**) **N-COUNT** An **axiom** is a statement or an idea that people accept as being true. [from Latin] [FORMAL]

axis /æksɪs/ (**axes**)

1 **N-COUNT** SCIENCE An **axis** is an imaginary line through the middle of something. ❏ *The Earth spins around its axis.*

2 **N-COUNT** MATH An **axis** is one of the two lines that you mark points on to show measurements or amounts. ❏ *We can label the axes: time is on the vertical axis and money is on the horizontal one.* [from Latin]

→ look at Word Webs: **graph, moon**

axle /æksəl/ (**axles**) **N-COUNT** An **axle** is a rod connecting a pair of wheels on a car or other vehicle. [from Old Norse]

→ look at Word Web: **wheel**

axon /æksɒn/ (**axons**) **N-COUNT** SCIENCE **Axons** are the long, thin parts of a nerve cell that carry electrical impulses to other parts of the nervous system. [from New Latin]

azi|muth|al pro|jec|tion /æzɪmʌθəl prədʒɛkʃən/ (**azimuthal projections**) **N-COUNT/N-NONCOUNT** GEOGRAPHY An **azimuthal projection** is an image of a map that is made by projecting the map on a globe onto a flat surface.

Bb

baby /beɪbi/ (**babies**) **N-COUNT** A **baby** is a very young child. ❑ *He bathed the baby and put her to bed.* ❑ *My wife just had a baby.*
→ look at Word Web: **child**

Word Partnership	Use **baby** with :
N	baby **boy/girl/sister**, baby **clothes**, baby **food**, baby **names**, baby **talk**
V	**deliver a** baby, **have a** baby
ADJ	**new/newborn** baby, **unborn** baby

baby|sit /beɪbisɪt/ (**babysits, babysitting, babysat**) **V-T/V-I** If you **babysit for** someone, you look after their children while they are not at home. ❑ *I promised to babysit for Mrs. Plunkett.* ❑ *She was babysitting him and his little sister.*

bach|elor /bætʃələr/ (**bachelors**) **N-COUNT** A **bachelor** is a man who has never married. [from Old French]

---
back
❶ ADVERB USES
❷ OPPOSITE OF FRONT; NOUN AND ADJECTIVE USES
❸ VERB USES

---

❶ back /bæk/
1 **ADV** If you move **back**, you move in the opposite direction to the one in which you are looking. ❑ *She stepped back from the door.*
2 **ADV** If you go **back** somewhere, you return to where you were before. ❑ *I went back to bed.* ❑ *I'll be back as soon as I can.*
3 **ADV** If someone or something is **back** in a particular state, they were in that state before and are now in it again. ❑ *The bus company expects service to get slowly back to normal.*
4 **ADV** If you put or give something **back**, you return it to the place where it was before. ❑ *Put the meat back in the freezer.*
5 **ADV** If you write or call **back**, you write to or call someone after they have written to or telephoned you. ❑ *I'll call you back after dinner.*
6 **ADV** Something that happened **back** in the past or several years **back** happened a

long time ago. ❑ *The story starts back in 1950.*
7 **PHRASE** If someone moves **back and forth**, they move in one direction and then in the opposite direction. ❑ *He paced back and forth.* [from Old English]

❷ back /bæk/ (**backs**)
1 **N-COUNT** Your **back** is the part of your body from your neck to your waist that is on the opposite side to your chest. ❑ *Her son was lying on his back.*
2 **N-COUNT** The **back of** something is the side or part of it that is farthest from the front. ❑ *She was in a room at the back of the store.*
3 **ADJ** **Back** describes the side or part of something that is farthest from the front. ❑ *She opened the back door.* ❑ *Ann sat in the back seat of their car.*
4 **PHRASE** If you say or do something **behind** someone's **back**, you do it without them knowing about it. ❑ *You shouldn't criticize her behind her back.* [from Old English]
→ look at Picture Dictionaries: **body, horse**

❸ back /bæk/ (**backs, backing, backed**)
1 **V-T/V-I** When you **back** a vehicle somewhere, you move it backward. ❑ *He backed his car out of the driveway.* ❑ *She backed quickly out of the room.*
2 **V-T** If you **back** someone, you support them. ❑ *We told them what we wanted to do, and they agreed to back us.* [from Dutch]
3 → see also **backing**
▶ **back away** If you **back away**, you move away, often because you are frightened. ❑ *James stood up, but the girl backed away.*
▶ **back down** If you **back down**, you withdraw something that you said or promised earlier. ❑ *It's too late to back down now.*
▶ **back off** If you **back off**, you move away in order to avoid problems. ❑ *When she saw me she backed off, looking worried.*
▶ **back out** If you **back out**, you decide not to do something that you agreed to do. ❑ *They've backed out of the project.*
▶ **back up** **1** To **back up** a statement means to show evidence to suggest that it is true.

❑ *He didn't have any proof to back up his story.*
2 TECHNOLOGY If you **back up** a computer file, you make a copy of it that you can use if the original file is lost. ❑ *Make sure you back up your files every day.*
3 If you **back** someone **up**, you show your support for them. ❑ *His employers backed him up.*
4 If you **back** someone **up**, you help them by confirming that what they are saying is true. ❑ *The girl denied being there, and the man backed her up.*
5 → see also **backup**

back|bone /bǽkboʊn/ (**backbones**)
N-COUNT SCIENCE Your **backbone** is the line of bones down the middle of your back.

Word Link	ground ≈ bottom : back*ground*, *ground*water, under*ground*

back|ground /bǽkgraʊnd/ (**backgrounds**)
1 **N-COUNT** Your **background** is the type of family you come from and the type of education and experiences you have had. ❑ *He came from a very poor background.*
2 **N-SING** The **background** is sounds, such as music, that you can hear but that you are not listening to with your full attention. ❑ *I heard the sound of music in the background.*
3 **N-COUNT** ARTS The **background** of a picture is the part that is behind the main things or people in it. Compare with **foreground**. ❑ *I looked at the man in the background of the photograph.*

Word Partnership	Use **background** with :
N	background **check**, background **information/knowledge** **1** background **music/noise** **2**
ADJ	**cultural/ethnic/family** background, **educational** background **1**
PREP	**in the** background **2** **3** **against a** background **3**
V	**blend into the** background **3**

back|ing /bǽkɪŋ/ (**backings**)
1 **N-NONCOUNT** **Backing** is money, resources, or support given to a person or organization. ❑ *He said the president had the full backing of his government.*
2 **N-COUNT/N-NONCOUNT** A **backing** is a layer of something such as cloth that is put onto the back of something in order to strengthen or protect it. ❑ *The placemats have a non-slip backing.* [from Old English]
3 → see also **back** **3**

back|pack /bǽkpæk/ (**backpacks**) **N-COUNT**
A **backpack** is a bag that you carry on your back.

back|stab|bing /bǽkstæbɪŋ/
1 **N-NONCOUNT** **Backstabbing** is behaviour that is unkind and that harms a friend or colleague. ❑ *She accused her colleagues of bullying and backstabbing.*
2 **ADJ** **Backstabbing** is also an adjective. ❑ *He was not prepared to deal with his backstabbing boss.*

back|stroke /bǽkstroʊk/ **N-NONCOUNT**
SPORTS **Backstroke** is a way of swimming on your back. ❑ *Linda swam backstroke and Isabelle swam breaststroke.*

back|up /bǽkʌp/ (**backups**) also **back-up**
1 **N-COUNT/N-NONCOUNT** **Backup** is extra help that you can get if you need it. ❑ *If you need backup, just call me.*
2 **N-COUNT** TECHNOLOGY A **backup** is a copy of a computer file that you can use if the original file is lost or damaged. ❑ *It is very important to make backups of your data.*

Word Link	ward ≈ in the direction of : back*ward*, down*ward*, for*ward*

back|ward /bǽkwərd/
1 **ADJ** A **backward** movement or look is in the direction that your back is facing. ❑ *He walked away without a backward glance.*
2 **ADV** If you move **backward**, you move in the direction that your back is facing. ❑ *He took two steps backward.*
3 **ADV** If you do something **backward**, you do it in the opposite way to the usual way. ❑ *Kate counted backward from ten to zero.*
4 **PHRASE** If something moves **backward and forward**, it keeps moving in one direction and then in the opposite direction. ❑ *Jennifer moved backward and forward in time with the music.*
5 **ADJ** A **backward** country does not have modern industries and machines. ❑ *...backward nations.* [from Old English]

back|yard /bǽkyɑrd/ (**backyards**) also **back yard** **N-COUNT** A **backyard** is the land at the back of a house. ❑ *The house has a large backyard.* [from Old English]

ba|con /béɪkən/ **N-NONCOUNT** **Bacon** is strips of meat that come from a pig and that are treated with salt or smoke. ❑ *...cafes offering bacon and eggs for breakfast.* [from Old French]

B

bac|te|ria /bæktɪəriə/ **N-PLURAL** SCIENCE
Bacteria are very, very small living things
that can make people sick. ❏ There were high
levels of dangerous bacteria in the water.
● **bac|te|rial** **ADJ** ❏ Tuberculosis is a bacterial
disease. [from New Latin]

bad /bæd/ (**worse, worst**)
1 **ADJ** Something that is **bad** is unpleasant
or harmful. ❏ When the weather was bad,
I stayed indoors. ❏ When Ross and Judy heard
the bad news, they were very upset. ❏ Too much
coffee is bad for you.
2 **ADJ** Something that is **bad** is of a very low
standard, quality, or amount. ❏ ...bad
housing. ❏ The school's main problem is that
teachers' pay is so bad.
3 **ADJ** Someone who is **bad at** doing
something is not good at doing it. ❏ He's a
bad driver.
4 **ADJ** Something that is **not bad** is good or
acceptable. ❏ "How much is he paying you?"—
"Oh, five thousand."—"Not bad." ❏ That's not
a bad idea.
5 **ADJ** If you are in a **bad** mood, you are
angry and you behave unpleasantly to
people. ❏ She is in a bad mood because she is tired.
6 **ADJ** If you **feel bad about** something, you
feel sorry or guilty about it. ❏ I feel bad that
he's doing most of the work.
7 **ADJ** If you have a **bad** back, heart, or leg,
for example, there is something wrong with
it. ❏ Joe has to be careful because of his bad back.
8 **ADJ** **Bad** language is language that
contains rude or offensive words. ❏ I don't
like to hear bad language in the street. [from
Old English]
9 → see also **worse, worst**

Thesaurus	bad Also look up :
ADJ	damaging, dangerous, harmful; (ant.) good **1** inferior, poor, unsatisfactory; (ant.) acceptable, good, satisfactory **2** **3**

badge /bædʒ/ (**badges**) **N-COUNT** A **badge** is
a small piece of metal or plastic that you
wear on your clothes to show people who
you are. ❏ I showed him my police badge.
[from Norman French]

badg|er /bædʒər/ (**badgers**) **N-COUNT**
A **badger** is a wild animal that has a white
head with two wide black stripes on it.
Badgers live beneath the ground and come
out to feed at night.

bad|ly /bædli/ (**worse, worst**)
1 **ADV** If something is done **badly** or goes
badly, it is not very successful or effective.
❏ I was angry because I played so badly.
❏ The whole project was badly managed.
2 **ADV** If someone or something is **badly**
hurt or **badly** affected, they are seriously
hurt or affected. ❏ The fire badly damaged
a church. ❏ One man was killed and another
was badly injured.
3 **ADV** If you want or need something
badly, you want or need it very much.
❏ Why do you want to go so badly? [from
Old English]
4 → see also **worse, worst**

bad|min|ton /bædmɪntən/ **N-NONCOUNT**
SPORTS **Badminton** is a game played by two
or four players. The players get points by
hitting a small object called a shuttlecock
across a high net using a racket.

bad-tem|pered /bæd tɛmpərd/ **ADJ**
Someone who is **bad-tempered** is not very
cheerful and gets angry easily. ❏ I usually feel
tired and bad-tempered on Friday evening.

baf|fle /bæfᵊl/ (**baffles, baffling, baffled**) **V-T**
If something **baffles** you, you cannot
understand it or explain it. ❏ These ancient
markings in the desert have baffled experts for many
years. ● **baf|fling** **ADJ** ❏ I was ill, with a baffling
set of symptoms.

bag /bæg/ (**bags**)
1 **N-COUNT** A **bag** is a container made of
paper, plastic, or leather, used for carrying
things. ❏ He ate a whole bag of candy. ❏ The old
lady was carrying a heavy shopping bag.
[from Old Norse]
2 → see also **sleeping bag**
→ look at Picture Dictionary: **container**

bag|gage /bægɪdʒ/ **N-NONCOUNT** Your
baggage is all the bags that you take with
you when you travel. ❏ He collected his baggage
and left the airport. [from Old French]

bag|gy /bægi/ (**baggier, baggiest**) **ADJ** Baggy
clothes are big and loose. ❏ He wore baggy
pants and no shirt.

bail /beɪl/ (**bails, bailing, bailed**)

> **LANGUAGE HELP**
> The spelling **bale** is also used for meaning
> **2**, and for the phrasal verb.

1 **N-NONCOUNT** **Bail** is money that is paid to
get a prisoner out of prison while he or she

is waiting to go to court. ❑ *He was held without bail after a court appearance in Detroit.*

2 **V-T/V-I** If you **bail** water from a boat, you use a container to take water out of it. ❑ *We kept the boat afloat by bailing with a cup.* ❑ *We started to bail the water out of the boat.*

3 **PHRASE** If a prisoner **is freed on bail**, or **released on bail**, or **makes bail**, he or she is let out of prison until they go to court, because someone has paid their bail. ❑ *When Guerrero made bail, he escaped to Colombia.* [from Old French]

▶ **bail out** BUSINESS If you **bail** someone **out**, you help them out of a difficult situation, often by giving them money. ❑ *They will discuss how to bail out the country's banking system.*

bait /beɪt/ **N-NONCOUNT** Bait is food that you put on a hook or in a trap to catch fish or animals. ❑ *This shop sells fishing bait.* [from Old Norse]

bake /beɪk/ (**bakes, baking, baked**)

1 **V-T/V-I** When you **bake** food, you cook it in an oven. ❑ *Bake the cake in the oven for 20 minutes.* ❑ *The batter rises as it bakes.* [from Old English]

bake

2 → see also **baking**
→ look at Picture Dictionary: **cook**

bak|er /beɪkər/ (**bakers**) **N-COUNT** A **baker** is a person whose job is to make and sell bread and cakes. [from Old English]

bak|ery /beɪkəri, beɪkri/ (**bakeries**) **N-COUNT** A **bakery** is a place where bread and cakes are baked or sold. ❑ *The town has two bakeries.* [from Old English]

bak|ing /beɪkɪŋ/

1 **N-NONCOUNT** Baking is the activity of cooking bread or cakes in an oven. ❑ *The children want to do some baking.* [from Old English]

2 → see also **bake**

bal|ance /bæləns/ (**balances, balancing, balanced**)

1 **V-T/V-I** If someone **balances**, they stay steady and they do not fall. ❑ *I balanced on Mark's shoulders.* ❑ *She balanced the chair on top of the table.*

2 **N-NONCOUNT** Balance is the ability to stay steady and not to fall over or to the side when you are standing or walking. ❑ *Dan lost his balance and started to fall.*

3 **V-T/V-I** If you **balance** one thing **with** something different, each of the things has the same importance. ❑ *Bob has difficulty balancing the demands of his work with the needs of his family.*

4 **N-SING** A **balance** is when all the different parts of something have the same importance. ❑ *It is important to have a balance between work and play.*

5 **N-COUNT** The **balance** in your bank account is the amount of money you have in it. ❑ *I'll need to check my bank balance first.*

6 **N-SING** The **balance** of an amount of money is what remains to be paid for something. ❑ *You sign the final agreement and pay the balance.*

7 **N-NONCOUNT** ARTS In a painting or drawing, **balance** is a sense of harmony in the arrangement of the different parts of the painting or drawing.

8 **N-NONCOUNT** SCIENCE If two or more physical objects are in a state of **balance**, their weight is evenly distributed around a central point.

9 **N-COUNT** SCIENCE A **balance** is a scientific instrument that is used for weighing things. [from Old French]
→ look at Word Web: **brain**

bal|anced /bælənst/

1 **ADJ** A **balanced** way of considering things is fair and reasonable. ❑ *Journalists should present balanced reports.*

2 **ADJ** A **balanced** diet has the right amounts of different foods to keep your body healthy. ❑ *Eat a healthy, balanced diet and get regular exercise.* [from Old French]

bal|anced forces **N-PLURAL** SCIENCE In physics, **balanced forces** are forces that are equal and opposite to each other, so that an object to which the forces are applied does not move.

b

bal|co|ny /bǽlkəni/ (**balconies**)

1 **N-COUNT** A **balcony** is a place where you can stand or sit on the outside of a building, above the ground.

2 **N-SING** In a theater, the **balcony** is the seats upstairs. [from Italian]

bald /bɔld/ (**balder, baldest**) **ADJ** Someone who is **bald** has no hair, or very little hair, on the top of their head. ❑ He rubbed his hand across his bald head. [from Danish]

ball /bɔl/ (**balls**)

1 **N-COUNT** SPORTS A **ball** is a round object that is used in games such as tennis and soccer. ❑ Michael was kicking a soccer ball against the wall.

2 **N-COUNT** A **ball** is something that has a round shape. ❑ Form the butter into small balls.

3 **N-COUNT** A **ball** is a large formal party where people dance. ❑ My parents go to a New Year's ball every year. [Senses 1 and 2 from Old Norse. Sense 3 from French.]

→ look at Picture Dictionaries: **foot, golf, soccer**

Word Partnership	Use **ball** with :
V	**bounce/catch/hit/kick/throw a** ball **1**
	roll into a ball **2**
N	**bowling/golf/soccer/tennis** ball, ball **field**, ball **game 1**
	snow ball **2**
PREP	ball **of** *something* **2**

bal|let /bælé͟ɪ/ (**ballets**)

1 **N-NONCOUNT** ARTS **Ballet** is a type of dancing with carefully planned movements. ❑ We saw a film about a boy who becomes a ballet dancer.

2 **N-COUNT** ARTS A **ballet** is a performance of this type of dancing that tells a story. ❑ Many people's favorite ballet is "Swan Lake." [from French]

→ look at Picture Dictionary: **dance**

ball game (**ball games**) also **ballgame**

N-COUNT SPORTS A **ball game** is a baseball match. ❑ They were listening to the ball game on the radio.

→ look at Picture Dictionary: **baseball**

bal|loon /bəlún/ (**balloons**)

1 **N-COUNT** A **balloon** is a small, thin, brightly-colored rubber bag that you blow air into so that it becomes larger. **Balloons** are used as decorations at parties. ❑ Large balloons floated above the crowd.

2 **N-COUNT** A **balloon** is a large, strong bag filled with gas or hot air, which can carry passengers in a container that hangs under it. ❑ They will attempt to circle the Earth by balloon. [from Italian]

→ look at Word Web: **fly**

bal|lot /bǽlət/ (**ballots**) **N-COUNT** A **ballot** is a secret vote in which people select a candidate in an election, or express their opinion about something. ❑ The result of the ballot will not be known for two weeks. [from Italian]

→ look at Word Webs: **election, vote**

ball|park /bɔ́lpɑrk/ (**ballparks**) also **ball park**

1 **N-COUNT** SPORTS A **ballpark** is a field where baseball is played. ❑ He has watched baseball games in nearly every major-league ballpark.

2 **ADJ** A **ballpark** figure is an approximate figure. ❑ I can't tell you the exact cost, but $500 is a ballpark figure.

bam|boo /bæmbú/ (**bamboos**) **N-COUNT/ N-NONCOUNT** **Bamboo** is a tall plant that grows in hot countries. It has hard, hollow stems that are sometimes used for making furniture. ❑ The family lived in a bamboo hut. [from Malay]

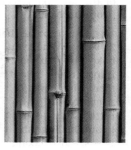
bamboo

ban /bǽn/ (**bans, banning, banned**)

1 **V-T** If someone **bans** something, they say that it must not be done, shown, or used. ❑ Ireland was the first country to ban smoking in all workplaces.

2 **N-COUNT** A **ban** is an official order that something must not be done, shown, or used. ❑ The report proposes a ban on plastic bags.

3 **V-T** If you **are banned from** doing something, you are officially prevented from doing it. ❑ He was banned from driving for three years. [from Old English]

ba|na|na /bənǽnə/ (**bananas**)

N-COUNT/N-NONCOUNT **Bananas** are long curved fruit with yellow skins. ❑ I bought milk, bread and a bunch of bananas. [from Spanish]

→ look at Picture Dictionary: **fruit**

band /bǽnd/ (**bands**)

1 **N-COUNT** MUSIC A **band** is a group of people who play music together. ❑ Matt's a drummer in a rock band.

2 N-COUNT A **band** is a flat, narrow strip of material that you wear around your head or wrists, or that is part of a piece of clothing. ❑ *Before treatment, doctors and nurses should always check the patient's wristband.*

3 N-COUNT A **band** is a strip or circle of metal or another strong material that makes something stronger, or that holds several things together. ❑ *He took out a white envelope with a rubber band around it.* [Sense 1 from French. Senses 2 and 3 from Old French.]
→ look at Word Webs: **concert, theater**

band|age /bændɪdʒ/ (**bandages, bandaging, bandaged**)

1 N-COUNT A **bandage** is a long strip of cloth that is wrapped around an injured part of your body to protect or support it. ❑ *We put a bandage on John's knee.*

2 V-T If you **bandage** a wound or part of someone's body, you tie a bandage around it. ❑ *Mary finished bandaging her sister's hand.* [from French]

ban|dit /bændɪt/ (**bandits**) N-COUNT A **bandit** is a person who robs people who are traveling. ❑ *The family was attacked by a gang of armed bandits.* [from Italian]

bang /bæŋ/ (**bangs, banging, banged**)

1 N-COUNT A **bang** is a sudden loud noise. ❑ *I heard four or five loud bangs.*

2 V-T/V-I If you **bang on** something, or if you **bang** it, you hit it hard, making a loud noise. ❑ *Lucy banged on the table with her fist.*

3 V-T If you **bang** a part of your body, you accidentally knock it against something and hurt yourself. ❑ *She fainted and banged her head.*

4 N-PLURAL **Bangs** are hair that is cut so that it hangs down above your eyes. ❑ *Both of them had blond bangs.* [from Old Norse]
→ look at Picture Dictionary: **hair**

bank /bæŋk/ (**banks, banking, banked**)

1 N-COUNT A **bank** is a place where people can keep their money. ❑ *He had just $14 in the bank when he died.*

2 N-COUNT A **bank** is a store of something. ❑ *...a national data bank.*

3 N-COUNT The **banks of** a river are the raised areas of ground along its edge. ❑ *We walked along the east bank of the river.* [Senses 1 and 2 from Italian. Sense 3 of Scandinavian origin.]

4 → see also **banking**

▶ **bank on** If you **bank on** someone or something, you rely on them. ❑ *Everyone is banking on his recovery.*

bank card (**bank cards**) or **ATM card**
N-COUNT A **bank card** is a plastic card that your bank gives you so that you can get money from your bank account using a cash machine.

bank|er /bæŋkər/ (**bankers**) N-COUNT A **banker** is someone who works in banking at a senior level. ❑ *...an investment banker.* [from Italian]

bank|ing /bæŋkɪŋ/

1 N-NONCOUNT **Banking** is the business activity of banks and similar institutions. ❑ *...online banking.* [from Italian]

2 → see also **bank**
→ look at Word Web: **industry**

bank|note /bæŋknoʊt/ (**banknotes**) also **bank note** N-COUNT **Banknotes** are pieces of paper money. ❑ *...a shopping bag full of banknotes.*

bank|rupt /bæŋkrʌpt/ ADJ BUSINESS People or organizations that go **bankrupt** do not have enough money to pay their debts. ❑ *If the company cannot sell its products, it will go bankrupt.* [from Old French]

bank|rupt|cy /bæŋkrʌptsi/ (**bankruptcies**)

1 N-NONCOUNT BUSINESS **Bankruptcy** is the state of being bankrupt. ❑ *He was brought in to rescue the company from bankruptcy.*

2 N-COUNT BUSINESS A **bankruptcy** is an instance of an organization or a person going bankrupt. ❑ *The number of corporate bankruptcies climbed in August.* [from Old French]

Word Partnership	Use **bankruptcy** with :
V	**force into** bankruptcy **1**
	avoid bankruptcy **1 2**
	declare bankruptcy, **file for** bankruptcy **2**
N	bankruptcy **law**, bankruptcy **protection 1 2**

ban|ner /bænər/ (**banners**) N-COUNT A **banner** is a long strip of cloth or plastic with something written on it. ❑ *The crowd danced and sang, and waved banners.* [from Old French]

bap|tism /bæptɪzəm/ (**baptisms**) N-COUNT/
N-NONCOUNT A **baptism** is a Christian ceremony in which a person is baptized. ❑ *Father Wright regularly performs weddings and baptisms.* [from Late Latin]

bap|tize /bæptaɪz/ (**baptizes, baptizing, baptized**) **v-T** When someone **is baptized**, they are touched or covered with water, to show that they have become a member of the Christian church. ❑ *Mary decided to become a Christian and was baptized.* [from Late Latin]

bar /bɑr/ (**bars**)

1 **N-COUNT** A **bar** is a long, straight piece of metal. ❑ *The building had bars on all of the windows.*

2 **N-COUNT** A **bar of** something is a small block of it. ❑ *What is your favorite chocolate bar?*

3 **N-COUNT** A **bar** is a place where you can buy and drink alcoholic drinks. ❑ *Lyndsay met her boyfriend at a local bar.*

4 **N-COUNT** MUSIC In music, a **bar** is one of the several short parts of the same length into which a piece of music is divided. ❑ *The opening bars of a waltz filled the room.*

5 **PHRASE** If someone is **behind bars**, they are in prison. ❑ *Fisher was behind bars last night, charged with attempted murder.* [from Old French]
→ look at Picture Dictionary: **chart**
→ look at Word Web: **soap**

bar|becue /bɑrbɪkyu/ (**barbecues, barbecuing, barbecued**) also **barbeque, BBQ**

1 **N-COUNT** A **barbecue** is a piece of equipment that you use for cooking outdoors.

2 **N-COUNT** If someone has a **barbecue**, they cook food on a barbecue outdoors. ❑ *On Saturday we had a barbecue on the beach.*

3 **V-T** If you **barbecue** food, you cook it on a barbecue. ❑ *Tuna can be grilled, fried or barbecued.* [from American Spanish]
→ look at Picture Dictionary: **cook**

bar|ber /bɑrbər/ (**barbers**) **N-COUNT** A **barber** is a person whose job is to cut men's hair. [from Old French]

bare /bɛər/ (**barer, barest**)

1 **ADJ** If a part of your body is **bare**, it is not covered by any clothing. ❑ *Jane's feet were bare.*

2 **ADJ** A **bare** surface is not covered or decorated with anything. ❑ *The apartment has bare wooden floors.*

3 **ADJ** If a room, a cupboard, or a shelf is **bare**, it is empty. ❑ *His refrigerator was bare.* [from Old English]

bare|foot /bɛərfʊt/ **ADV** If you do something **barefoot**, you do it without wearing shoes or socks. ❑ *He walked 10 miles barefoot to find help.*

bare|ly /bɛərli/

1 **ADV** You use **barely** to say that something is only just true or possible ❑ *Anastasia could barely remember the ride to the hospital.* ❑ *It was 90 degrees and the air conditioning barely cooled the room.*

2 **ADV** If you say that one thing had **barely** happened when something else happened, you mean that the first event was followed immediately by the second. ❑ *She had barely sat down at the awards ceremony when she was called on stage.* [from Old English]

bar|gain /bɑrgɪn/ (**bargains, bargaining, bargained**)

1 **N-COUNT** Something that is a **bargain** is being sold at a lower price than usual. ❑ *At this price the dress is a bargain.*

2 **V-I** When two or more people **bargain**, they discuss what each of them will do, pay, or receive. ❑ *The workers have the right to bargain for better pay.* [from Old French]
→ look at Word Web: **union**

Thesaurus	bargain	Also look up :
N	deal, discount, markdown **1**	
	agreement, deal, understanding **2**	
V	barter, haggle, negotiate **3**	

Word Partnership	Use bargain with :
V	find/get a bargain **1**
	make/strike a bargain **2**
N	bargain **hunter**, bargain **price**, bargain **rates 1**
PREP	bargain **with someone 2**

barge /bɑrdʒ/ (**barges, barging, barged**)

1 **N-COUNT** A **barge** is a long, narrow boat with a flat bottom, used for carrying heavy loads. ❑ *The barges carried water, food, and medicines.*

2 **V-I** If you **barge into** a place, you rush into it in a rough and rude way. [INFORMAL] ❑ *Please knock before you barge into my room.* [from Old French]

bar graph (**bar graphs**) **N-COUNT** A **bar graph** is a graph that uses parallel rectangular shapes to represent changes in the size, value, or rate of something.

bark /bɑrk/ (**barks, barking, barked**)

1 **V-I** When a dog **barks**, it makes a short, loud noise. ❑ *Don't let the dogs bark.*

2 **N-COUNT Bark** is also a noun. ❑ *Your child may be afraid of a dog's bark, or its size.*

3 **N-NONCOUNT** SCIENCE **Bark** is the rough surface of a tree. [Senses 1 and 2 from Old English. Sense 3 from Old Norse.]

Picture Dictionary   barn

hay

barn

field

greenhouse   orchard

tractor   plow   animals   graze

barn /bɑrn/ (**barns**) **N-COUNT** A **barn** is a building on a farm where animals and crops are kept. [from Old English]
→ look at Picture Dictionary: **barn**

ba|rom|eter /bərɒmɪtər/ (**barometers**) **N-COUNT** SCIENCE A **barometer** is an instrument that measures air pressure and shows when the weather is changing.

bar|racks /bærəks/ (**barracks**) **N-COUNT** A **barracks** is a building where soldiers or policemen live and work. ❑ ...an army barracks. [from French]

bar|rel /bærəl/ (**barrels**)
1 N-COUNT A **barrel** is a large container, with curved sides and flat ends, for storing liquids. ❑ The U.S. uses about 20 million barrels of oil a day.
2 N-COUNT The **barrel** of a gun is the long metal part. [from Old French]

barrel

bar|rette /bərɛt/ (**barrettes**) **N-COUNT** A **barrette** is a small metal or plastic device that a woman uses to hold her hair in position. ❑ Sarah's hair was held back by a barrette. [from French]

bar|ri|cade /bærɪkeɪd/ (**barricades, barricading, barricaded**)
1 N-COUNT A **barricade** is a line of things that have been put across a road to stop people from passing. ❑ The street was blocked by a barricade.
2 V-T If you **barricade** a road or an entrance, you put a barricade across it, to stop people from entering. ❑ Police barricaded all entrances to the square. [from Old French]

bar|ri|er /bæriər/ (**barriers**)
1 N-COUNT A **barrier** is a fence or a wall that prevents people or things from moving from one area to another. ❑ A police barrier blocked the road.
2 N-COUNT A **barrier** is a rule that makes it difficult or impossible for something to happen. ❑ Taxes are the most obvious barrier to free trade. [from Old French]

Word Partnership	Use **barrier** with :
N	**police** barrier **1**
	language barrier **2**
PREP	barrier **between** **1** **2**
V	**break down a** barrier, **cross a** barrier **1** **2**
ADJ	**psychological** barrier, **racial** barrier **2**

bar|ris|ter /bærɪstər/ (**barristers**) **N-COUNT** In England and Wales, a **barrister** is a lawyer who represents clients in the higher courts of law.

B

bar|tender /bɑrtɛndər/ (**bartenders**)
N-COUNT A **bartender** is a person who makes and serves drinks in a bar.

bar|ter /bɑrtər/ (**barters, bartering, bartered**)
1 **V-T/V-I** If you **barter** goods, you exchange them for other goods, rather than selling them for money. ❑ *They have been bartering wheat for cotton and timber.* ❑ *The men were trading animal skins, bartering for jewellery.*
2 **N-NONCOUNT** **Barter** is also a noun. ❑ *Overall, barter is a very inefficient means of organizing transactions.* [from Old French]
→ look at Word Web: **money**

bas|alt /bəsɔlt, beɪsɔlt/ **N-NONCOUNT**
SCIENCE **Basalt** is a type of black rock that is produced by volcanoes. [from Late Latin]

base /beɪs/ (**bases, basing, based**)
1 **N-COUNT** The **base** of something is its lowest part, or the part that it stands on. ❑ *They planted flowers around the base of the tree.* ❑ *The base of the statue weighs four tons.*
2 **V-T** If you **base** one thing **on** another thing, the first thing develops from the second thing. ❑ *The film is based on a novel by Alexander Trocchi.*
3 **N-COUNT** A military **base** is a place where soldiers live and work. ❑ *The army base is close to the airport.*
4 **N-COUNT** Your **base** is the main place where you work or live. ❑ *In the summer her base is her home in Connecticut.*
5 **N-COUNT** SPORTS A **base** is one of the four squares on a baseball field that runners touch. ❑ *The first runner to reach second base was John Flaherty.*
6 **N-COUNT** SCIENCE In chemistry, a **base** is a substance that has the opposite effect to an acid. Bases react with acids to form salts. [from Old French]
→ look at Picture Dictionaries: **area, baseball**

Word Partnership	Use **base** with :
ADJ	**military/naval** base **3**
	stolen base **5**
N	base **camp, home** base, base **of operation 4**
	base **hit/run 5**

base|ball /beɪsbɔl/ **N-NONCOUNT** SPORTS
Baseball is a game that is played with a bat and a ball on a large field by two teams of nine players. Players must hit the ball and run around four bases to score.

→ look at Picture Dictionary: **baseball**
→ look at Word Web: **park**

base|ball cap (**baseball caps**) **N-COUNT**
A **baseball cap** is a cap with a curved part at the front that sticks out above your eyes. ❑ *Joe often wears a baseball cap.*

base|ment /beɪsmənt/ (**basements**)
N-COUNT The **basement** of a building is a floor that is built below ground level. ❑ *They put the old toys in the basement.* [from Old French]
→ look at Picture Dictionary: **house**

bases

PRONUNCIATION HELP
Pronounce meaning **1** /beɪsɪz/.
Pronounce meaning **2** /beɪsiz/.

1 **Bases** is the plural of **base**.
2 **Bases** is the plural of **basis**.

base word (**base words**) **N-COUNT**
LANGUAGE ARTS A **base word** is a word that you can add a prefix or suffix to in order to create other related words.

bash /bæʃ/ (**bashes, bashing, bashed**) **V-T**
If you **bash** someone or something, you hit them very hard. [INFORMAL] ❑ *I bashed him on the head.*

ba|sic /beɪsɪk/
1 **ADJ** **Basic** describes the simplest and most important part of something. ❑ *Everyone needs the basic skills of reading and writing.*
2 **ADJ** **Basic** goods and services are very simple ones that every person needs. ❑ *There were shortages of the most basic foods.* [from Old French]

Thesaurus	basic	Also look up :
ADJ	essential, fundamental, key, main, necessary, principal, vital; *(ant.)* nonessential, secondary **1** **2**	

Word Partnership	Use **basic** with :
N	basic **idea**, basic **principles/values**, basic **problem**, basic **questions**, basic **right**, basic **skills**, basic **understanding 1** basic **(health) care**, basic **needs 2**
ADJ	**most** basic, basic **types of something 1 2**

ba|si|cal|ly /beɪsɪkli/ **ADV** You can use **basically** when you are talking about a situation in a general way. ❑ *Basically, he is a nice boy.* [from Old French]

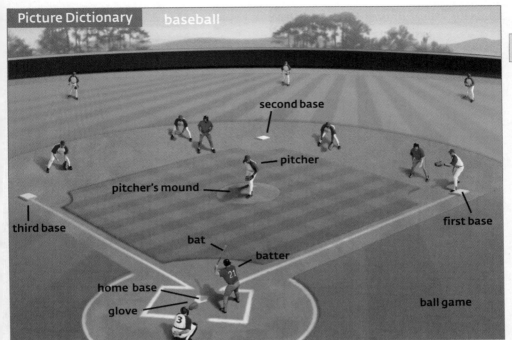

Picture Dictionary **baseball**

second base

pitcher

pitcher's mound

third base

first base

bat

batter

home base

glove

ball game

ba|sin /beɪsᵊn/ (basins)
■ **N-COUNT** A **basin** is a deep bowl that you use for holding liquids.
■ **GEOGRAPHY** The **basin** of a large river is the area of land around it from which streams run down into it. [from Old French]
→ look at Word Web: **lake**

ba|sis /beɪsɪs/ (bases /beɪsiz/)
■ **N-SING** If something is done **on** a particular **basis**, that is the way that it is done. ❏ *We meet here for lunch on a regular basis.*
■ **N-COUNT** The **basis** of something is the most important part of it that other things can develop from. ❏ *The UN plan is a possible basis for peace talks.* [from Latin]

Word Partnership	Use **basis** with :
ADJ	**equal** basis, **on a daily/regular/weekly** basis ■
PREP	basis **for** *something* ■
V	**provide** a basis, **serve as** a basis ■

bas|ket /bæskɪt/ (baskets)
■ **N-COUNT** A **basket** is a container made from thin strips of wood, plastic, or metal, that is used for carrying or storing objects. ❏ *The picnic basket was filled with sandwiches and fruit.*
■ **N-COUNT** SPORTS A **basket** is the net that you throw the ball through in basketball.

■ **N-COUNT** SPORTS In basketball, if you **shoot** a **basket** you manage to throw the ball through the net. [from Old Northern French]
→ look at Picture Dictionary: **basketball**

basket|ball /bæskɪtbɔl/ **N-NONCOUNT**
SPORTS **Basketball** is a game in which two teams of five players each try to throw a large ball through a round net hanging from a high metal ring.
→ look at Picture Dictionary: **basketball**

bas|ket sponge (basket sponges) **N-COUNT**
SCIENCE A **basket sponge** is a type of primitive sea creature with a hollow body that is open at the top.

bass /beɪs/ (basses)
■ **N-COUNT** A **bass** is a man with a very deep singing voice. ❏ *...the great Russian bass Chaliapin.*
■ **ADJ** MUSIC A **bass** drum or guitar makes a very deep sound. [from Italian]

bass clef (bass clefs) **N-COUNT** MUSIC A **bass clef** is a symbol that you use when writing music in order to show that the notes on the staff are below middle C.

bas|soon /bəsun/ (bassoons)
N-COUNT/N-NONCOUNT MUSIC A **bassoon** is a large musical instrument that is shaped like a tube. You play it by blowing into a curved metal pipe. [from French]

b

Picture Dictionary   basketball

- basketball
- basket
- sideline
- referee
- free throw line
- uniform
- player

bat /bæt/ (**bats, batting, batted**)

1 N-COUNT SPORTS A **bat** is a long piece of wood that is used for hitting the ball in games such as baseball. ❑ ...a baseball bat.

2 V-I SPORTS When you **bat**, you hit the ball with a bat in a game such as baseball. ❑ Paxton hurt his elbow while he was batting.

3 N-COUNT A **bat** is a small flying animal that looks like a mouse with wings. Bats hang upside down when they sleep during the day, and come out to fly at night. [Senses 1 and 2 from Old English. Sense 3 of Scandinavian origin.]

→ look at Word Web: **bat**

→ look at Picture Dictionary: **baseball**

batch /bætʃ/ (**batches**) N-COUNT A **batch** is a group of things or people of the same type. ❑ I baked a batch of cookies. [from Old English]

Word Web   bat

Bats fly like birds, but they are **mammals**. Female bats give birth to their young and produce milk to feed them. Bats are nocturnal. They search for food at night and sleep during the day. They **roost** upside down in dark, quiet places such as caves and attics. People think that bats drink blood, but only vampire bats do this. Most bats eat fruit or insects. As bats fly they make high-pitched sounds that bounce off objects. This echolocation is a kind of **radar** that guides them as they fly.

bath /bæθ/ (baths) **N-COUNT** When you take a **bath**, you sit or lie in a bathtub filled with water, and wash your body. ❑ *He took a bath before he went to bed.* [from Old English]
→ look at Picture Dictionary: **bathroom**

bathe /beɪð/ (bathes, bathing, bathed)
1 **V-I** When you **bathe**, you take a bath. ❑ *Most people bathe or shower once a day.*
2 **V-T** If you **bathe** a child, you wash them in a bathtub. ❑ *Back home, Shirley fed and bathed the baby.* [from Old English]
3 → see also **sunbathe**

bath|ing suit (bathing suits) **N-COUNT** A **bathing suit** is a piece of clothing that you wear for swimming. ❑ *The children changed into their bathing suits.*

bath|room /bæθrum/ (bathrooms)
1 **N-SING** A **bathroom** is a room that contains a toilet. ❑ *She asked if she could use the bathroom.*
2 **PHRASE** When someone **goes to the bathroom**, they use the toilet. ❑ *She got up in the middle of the night to go to the bathroom.*
→ look at Picture Dictionaries: **bathroom, house**

Thesaurus	bathroom	Also look up :
N	lavatory, boys'/girls'/ladies'/men's/ women's room, restroom, toilet, washroom **1**	

bath|tub /bæθtʌb/ (bathtubs) **N-COUNT** A **bathtub** is a long container that you fill with water and sit or lie in to wash your body. ❑ *She was lying in a huge pink bathtub.*

ba|ton /bətɑ:n/ (batons)
1 **N-COUNT** MUSIC A **baton** is a light, thin stick that is used by a conductor.
2 **N-COUNT** SPORTS A **baton** is a short stick that one runner passes to another in a race. [from French]

bat|tal|ion /bətælyən/ (battalions)
N-COUNT A **battalion** is a large group of soldiers that consists of three or more companies. [from French]

bat|ter /bætər/ (batters)
1 **N-NONCOUNT** **Batter** is a mixture of flour, eggs, and milk, that is used for making cakes. ❑ *Pour the cake batter into a round pan.*
2 **N-COUNT** SPORTS In some sports, a **batter** is a person who hits the ball. ❑ *The batter hit the ball toward second base.*
→ look at Picture Dictionary: **baseball**

bat|tery /bætəri/ (batteries)
1 **N-COUNT** **Batteries** are small objects that provide electricity for things such as radios. ❑ *The game requires two AA batteries.*
2 **N-COUNT** A car **battery** is a box containing acid. It provides the electricity that is needed to start the car. ❑ *Wendy can't take us because her car's battery is dead.* [from Old French]
→ look at Word Web: **cellphone**

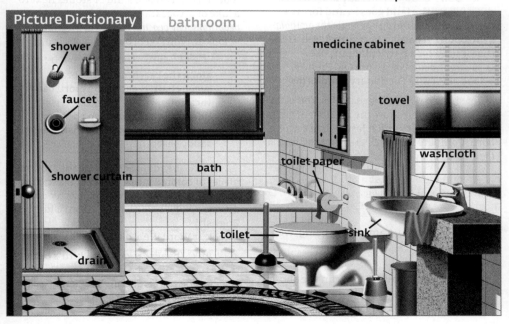

Picture Dictionary bathroom

shower
faucet
shower curtain
drain
bath
medicine cabinet
towel
toilet paper
washcloth
toilet
sink

bat|tle /bæt³l/ (**battles, battling, battled**)

■ **N-COUNT/N-NONCOUNT** A **battle** is a violent fight between groups of people, especially between armies during a war. ❑ *The battle of Gettysburg took place in July 1863.*

■ **N-COUNT** A **battle** is a struggle for success or control over something. ❑ *Lance Armstrong won his battle against cancer.*

■ **V-T/V-I** If you **battle**, you try very hard to do something although it is extremely difficult ❑ *Doctors battled all night to save her life.* ❑ *Firefighters are still battling the two fires.* [from Old French]

→ look at Word Web: **army**

Word Partnership	Use battle with :
ADJ	**bloody** battle, **major** battle ■
	constant battle, **legal** battle, **losing** battle, **uphill** battle ■
V	**prepare for** battle ■
	fight a battle, **win/lose a** battle ■ ■

battle|field /bæt³lfild/ (**battlefields**)

■ **N-COUNT** A **battlefield** is a place where a battle is fought. ❑ *...the struggle to save America's Civil War battlefields.*

■ **N-COUNT** You can refer to an issue or field of activity over which people disagree or compete as a **battlefield**. ❑ *...the battlefield of family life.*

bay /beɪ/ (**bays**)

■ **N-COUNT** GEOGRAPHY A **bay** is a part of a coast where the land goes in and forms a curve. ❑ *We sailed across the bay in the morning.*

■ **N-COUNT** A **bay** is a partly enclosed area that is used for a particular purpose. ❑ *...a cargo loading bay.* [from Old French]

→ look at Picture Dictionary: **landforms**

BC /bi si/ also **B.C.** SOCIAL STUDIES You can use **BC** in dates to show the number of years before the year in which Jesus Christ was born. Compare with **AD**. ❑ *He probably lived in the fourth century BC.*

---

be
❶ AUXILIARY VERB USES
❷ OTHER VERB USES

---

❶ **be** /bi, STRONG bi/ (**am, are, is, being, was, were, been**)

LANGUAGE HELP

When you are speaking, you can use short forms of **be**. For example "I am" becomes "I'm" and "was not" becomes "wasn't."

■ **AUX** You use **be** with another verb to form the past or present continuous. ❑ *This is happening everywhere in the country.* ❑ *She was driving to work when the accident happened.*

■ **AUX** You use **be** with another verb to form the passive. ❑ *Her husband was killed in a car crash.*

■ **AUX** You use **be** with an infinitive to show that something is planned to happen. ❑ *The talks are to begin tomorrow.* ❑ *It was to be Johnson's first meeting with the board.*

❷ **be** /bi, STRONG bi/ (**am, are, is, being, was, were, been**)

■ **V-LINK** You use **be** to describe someone or something. ❑ *She's my mother.* ❑ *He is a very kind man.* ❑ *He is fifty years old.* ❑ *The sky was black.*

■ **V-LINK** You use **be** to say where someone or something is. ❑ *Dad's in the yard.* ❑ *The car is in the garage.*

■ **V-LINK** You use **be** with "it" when you are giving your opinion on a situation. ❑ *It was too cold for swimming.* ❑ *Sometimes it is necessary to say no.* ❑ *It's nice having friends to talk to.*

■ **V-LINK** You use **be** in expressions like **there is** and **there are** to say that something exists. ❑ *There are very few cars on this street.* [from Old English]

■ → see also **being**

beach /bitʃ/ (**beaches**) **N-COUNT** SCIENCE A **beach** is an area of sand or stones next to a lake or an ocean. ❑ *The children played on the beautiful sandy beach.* [from Old English]

→ look at Word Web: **beach**

Word Partnership	Use beach with :
PREP	**along the** beach, **at/on the** beach
N	beach **chair**, beach **club/resort**, beach **vacation**
V	**lie on the** beach, **walk on the** beach
ADJ	**nude** beach, **private** beach, **rocky** beach, **sandy** beach

bead /bid/ (**beads**) **N-COUNT** **Beads** are small pieces of colored glass, wood, or plastic that are used for making jewelry. ❑ *Victoria was wearing a purple bead necklace.* [from Old English]

→ look at Word Web: **glass**

beak /bik/ (**beaks**) **N-COUNT** A bird's **beak** is the hard, pointed part of its mouth. ❑ *She pointed to a black bird with a yellow beak.* [from Old French]

→ look at Word Web: **bird**

b

Word Web   beach

Beaches have a natural cycle of build-up and **erosion**. **Ocean currents**, **wind**, and **waves** move **sand** along the **coast**. In certain spots, some of the sand gets left behind. The **surf** deposits it on the beach. Then the wind blows it into **dunes**. As currents change, they **erode** sand from the beach. High waves carry beach sand out to **sea**. This process raises the **seafloor**. As the water gets shallower, the waves become smaller. Then they begin depositing sand on the beach. At the same time, small **pebbles** smash into each other. They break up and form new sand.

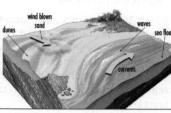

beak|er /bíkər/ (**beakers**) **N-COUNT** SCIENCE A **beaker** is a glass cup with straight sides used in a laboratory. [from Old Norse]
→ look at Picture Dictionary: **laboratory**

beam /bím/ (**beams, beaming, beamed**)
1 **V-T/V-I** If someone **is beaming**, they have a big happy smile on their face. [WRITTEN] ❏ Frances beamed at her friend. ❏ "Welcome back," she beamed.
2 **N-COUNT** SCIENCE A **beam** of light is a line of light that shines from something bright.
3 **N-COUNT** A **beam** is a long thick bar of wood or metal that supports the roof of a building. ❏ The ceilings are supported by oak beams. [from Old English]
→ look at Word Web: **laser**

bean /bín/ (**beans**)
1 **N-COUNT** **Beans** are the seeds of some plants that you can eat as a vegetable. ❏ "More green beans, anyone?" Sheila asked.
2 **N-COUNT** Coffee **beans** or cocoa **beans** are the seeds of
plants that are used to make coffee, cocoa, and chocolate. [from Old English]

bean

bear /béər/ (**bears, bearing, bore, borne**)
1 **V-T** If you **bear** an unpleasant experience, you accept it. ❏ The loneliness was hard to bear.
2 **V-T** If you can't **bear** someone or something, you dislike them very much. ❏ I can't bear people being late.

bear

3 **V-T** If something **bears** your weight, it is able to support it. ❏ The ice was not thick enough to bear their weight.
4 **N-COUNT** A **bear** is a large, strong wild animal with thick fur and sharp claws. [from Old English]
5 → see also **bearing, bore**
→ look at Word Web: **carnivore**
▶ **bear with** If you ask someone to **bear with** you, you are asking them to be patient. ❏ If you'll bear with me, Frank, just let me try to explain.

Thesaurus	bear	Also look up :
V		endure, put up with, stand, tolerate **1**

bear|able /béərəbəl/ **ADJ** If something is **bearable**, you feel that you can deal with it without too much difficulty. ❏ A cool breeze made the heat bearable. [from Old English]

beard /bíərd/ (**beards**) **N-COUNT** A man's **beard** is the hair that grows on his chin and cheeks. ❏ He's 60 years old, with a long white beard. [from Old English]
→ look at Picture Dictionary: **hair**

bear|ing /béərɪŋ/ (**bearings**)
1 **PHRASE** If something **has a bearing on** a situation or an event, it is relevant to it. ❏ The food you eat has an important bearing on your general health.
2 **PHRASE** If you **get** your **bearings** or **find** your **bearings**, you find out where you are or what you should do next. If you **lose** your **bearings**, you do not know where you are or what you should do next. ❏ A bus tour of the city will help you get your bearings. [from Old English]
3 → see also **bear**

beast /bíst/ (**beasts**) **N-COUNT** A **beast** is a large and dangerous animal. [LITERARY] ❏ He told the children that there were wild beasts in the woods. [from Old French]

beat

beat /bit/ (**beats, beating, beat, beaten**)

> **LANGUAGE HELP**
> The form **beat** is used in the present tense and is the past tense.

1 **v-t** To **beat** someone or something means to hit them very hard. ❑ *They beat him, and left him on the ground.* ❑ *We could hear the rain beating against the windows.*

2 **v-i** When your heart **beats**, it makes a regular sound and movement. ❑ *I felt my heart beating faster.*

3 **N-COUNT** **Beat** is also a noun. ❑ *He could hear the beat of his heart.*

4 **N-COUNT** MUSIC The **beat** of a piece of music is the rhythm that it has. ❑ *Play some music with a steady beat.*

5 **v-t** If you **beat** eggs, cream, or butter, you mix them quickly. ❑ *Beat the eggs and sugar together.*

6 **v-t** SPORTS If you **beat** someone in a competition or election, you defeat them. ❑ *The Red Sox beat the Yankees 5-2 last night.* [from Old English]

▶ **beat up** If someone **beats** a person **up**, they hit or kick the person many times. ❑ *Then they beat her up as well.*

> **Usage** beat
> As a verb, *beat* is commonly used to talk about fighting an illness or addiction: *Together we will beat cancer. She just can't beat her addiction to cocaine.*

> **Thesaurus** beat Also look up :
> V   hit, pound, punch; (*ant.*) caress, pat, pet **1**
>   mix, stir, whip **5**

> **Word Partnership** Use beat with :
> N   beat **a rug** **1**
>   **heart** beat **2**
>   beat **eggs** **5**
> PREP beat **against**, beat **on** **1**
>   **on/to** a beat **4**

> **Word Link** ful ≈ filled with : beautiful, careful, dreadful

beau|ti|ful /byutɪfəl/

1 **ADJ** A **beautiful** person is very attractive to look at. ❑ *She was a very beautiful woman.*

2 **ADJ** Something that is **beautiful** is very attractive to look at or listen to. ❑ *New England is beautiful in the fall.* ❑ *It was a beautiful morning.* ● **beau|ti|ful|ly** /byutɪfli/ **ADV** ❑ *Karin sings beautifully.* [from Old French]

> **Thesaurus** beautiful Also look up :
> ADJ   gorgeous, lovely, pretty, ravishing, stunning; (*ant.*) grotesque, hideous, homely, ugly **1**

beau|ty /byuti/ **N-NONCOUNT** Beauty is the quality of being beautiful. ❑ *The hotel is in an area of natural beauty.* [from Old French]

bea|ver /bivər/ (**beavers**) **N-COUNT** A beaver is an animal with thick fur, a big flat tail, and large teeth. [from Old English]

be|came /bɪkeɪm/ **Became** is the past tense of **become**.

be|cause /bɪkɔz, -kʌz/

1 **CONJ** You use **because** when you are giving the reason for something. ❑ *He is called Mitch because his name is Mitchell.* ❑ *I'm sad because he didn't ask me to his birthday party.*

2 **PHRASE** If an event or situation happens **because of** something, that thing is the reason or cause. ❑ *He's retiring because of ill health.*

be|come /bɪkʌm/ (**becomes, becoming, became, become**)

> **LANGUAGE HELP**
> The form **become** is used in the present tense and is the past participle.

v-LINK If someone or something **becomes** a particular thing, they start to be that thing. ❑ *The weather became cold and wet in October.* ❑ *Teresa wants to become a teacher.* [from Old English]

> **Usage** become
> Become is a linking verb and may be followed by a noun: *I'd like to become a teacher.* or by an adjective: *In the summer the weather becomes hot.*

bed /bɛd/ (**beds**)

1 **N-COUNT** A **bed** is a piece of furniture that you lie on when you sleep. ❑ *We went to bed at about 10 p.m.* ❑ *Nina was already in bed.*

2 **N-COUNT** A **bed** in a garden or a park is an area of ground that has been specially prepared so that plants can be grown in it. ❑ *...beds of strawberries.*

3 **N-COUNT** The ocean **bed** or a river **bed** is the ground at the bottom of the ocean or of a river. [from Old English]

→ look at Picture Dictionary: **bed**
→ look at Word Webs: **lake, sleep**

b

Picture Dictionary bed

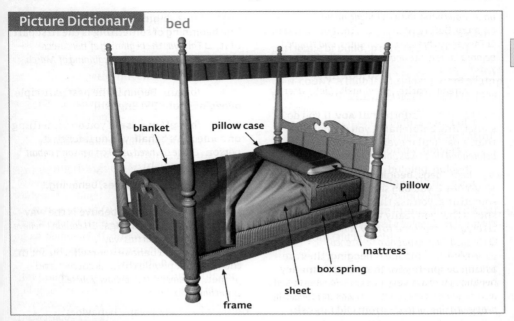

blanket pillow case pillow mattress box spring sheet frame

Word Partnership Use **bed** with :

ADJ	**asleep in** bed, **double/single/twin** bed, **ready for** bed **1**
V	**be sick in** bed, **get into** bed, **go to** bed, **lie (down) in** bed, **put** *someone* **to** bed **1**
PREP	**in/out of** bed, **under the** bed **1** bed **of** *something* **2**

bed|room /bɛdrum/ (**bedrooms**) **N-COUNT**
A **bedroom** is a room that is used for
sleeping in. ❑ *Emma, please clean your bedroom.*
→ look at Picture Dictionary: **house**

bee /bi/ (**bees**) **N-COUNT** A **bee** is a flying
insect with a yellow-and-black striped
body. Bees make honey, and they can
sting you. ❑ *Bees buzzed in the flowers.*
[from Old English]

beef /bif/ **N-NONCOUNT** Beef is meat from
a cow. ❑ *...roast beef and mashed potatoes.* [from
Old French]
→ look at Word Web: **meat**

been /bɪn/
1 **Been** is the past participle of **be**.
2 **V-I** If you have **been** to a place, you have
gone to it or visited it. ❑ *Have you ever been
to Paris?* [from Old English]

beer /bɪər/ (**beers**) **N-COUNT/N-NONCOUNT**
Beer is an alcoholic drink made from grain.
❑ *He sat in the kitchen drinking beer.* [from Old
English]

beet /bit/ (**beets**) **N-COUNT/N-NONCOUNT**
Beets are dark red roots that are eaten as a
vegetable. They are often preserved in
vinegar. ❑ *The duck was served with potato slices,
beets and carrots.* [from Old English]
→ look at Word Web: **sugar**

bee|tle /bitᵊl/ (**beetles**) **N-COUNT** A **beetle** is
an insect with a hard, shiny black body.
[from Old English]

be|fore /bɪfɔr/
1 **PREP** If something happens **before** a
particular date, time, or event, it happens
earlier than that date, time, or event.
❑ *Annie was born a few weeks before Christmas.*
2 **CONJ** Before is also a conjunction.
❑ *Brush your teeth before you go to bed.*
3 **ADV** You use **before** when you are talking
about something that happened earlier.
❑ *Carlton's girlfriend had moved to Denver a month
before.*
4 **ADV** If someone has done something
before, they have done it in the past.
❑ *I've never been here before.* ❑ *I have met Professor
Lown before.*
5 **CONJ** You use **before** when you are trying
to warn someone that something bad might
happen if they do not act quickly. ❑ *Clean up
that mess before someone slips and gets hurt.*
6 **CONJ** You use **before** when you are talking
about the time it took you until something
happened. ❑ *It took me a minute before I*

understood what she was talking about.

7 **PREP** **Before** means "in front of." [FORMAL]
❏ They drove through the tall gates, and stopped before a large white house. [from Old English]

Thesaurus before Also look up :
ADV already, earlier, previously; (ant.) after **3**

before|hand /bɪfɔ̱rhænd/ **ADV** If you do something **beforehand**, you do it earlier than a particular event. ❏ How did she know beforehand that I was going to go out?

beg /bɛ̱g/ (**begs, begging, begged**)
1 **V-T/V-I** If you **beg** someone **to** do something, you ask them in a way that shows that you really want them to do it. ❏ I begged him to come to New York with me. ❏ I begged for help but no one listened.
2 **V-T/V-I** If someone **is begging**, they are asking people to give them food or money because they are very poor. ❏ Homeless people were begging on the streets. ❏ I was surrounded by people begging for food. [from Old English]

be|gan /bɪgæ̱n/ **Began** is the past tense of **begin**. [from Old English]

beg|gar /bɛ̱gər/ (**beggars**) **N-COUNT** A **beggar** is someone who lives by asking people for money or food. ❏ There are no beggars on the streets in Vienna. [from Old English]

be|gin /bɪgɪ̱n/ (**begins, beginning, began, begun**)
1 **V-T** To **begin to** do something means to start doing it. ❏ Jack stood up and began to move around the room. ❏ David began to look angry.
2 **V-T/V-I** When something **begins** or when you **begin** it, it starts to happen. ❏ The problems began last November. ❏ He has just begun his second year at college.
3 **PHRASE** You use **to begin with** when you are talking about the first stage of a situation, event, or process. ❏ It was great to begin with, but now it's difficult. ❏ "What do scientists think about that?"—"Well, to begin with, they doubt it's going to work." [from Old English]

Thesaurus begin Also look up :
V commence, kick off, start; (ant.) end, stop **2**

be|gin|ner /bɪgɪ̱nər/ (**beginners**) **N-COUNT** A **beginner** is someone who has just started learning to do something. ❏ The course is for both beginners and advanced students. [from Old English]

be|gin|ning /bɪgɪ̱nɪŋ/ (**beginnings**) **N-COUNT** The **beginning of** something is the first part of it. ❏ This was the beginning of her career. ❏ The wedding will be at the beginning of March. [from Old English]

be|gun /bɪgʌ̱n/ **Begun** is the past participle of **begin**. [from Old English]

be|half /bɪhæ̱f/ **PHRASE** If you do something **on** someone's **behalf**, you do it for that person. ❏ She thanked us all on her son's behalf. [from Old English]

be|have /bɪhe̱ɪv/ (**behaves, behaving, behaved**)
1 **V-I** The way that you **behave** is the way that you do and say things. ❏ I couldn't believe Molly was behaving in this way.
2 **V-T/V-I** If you **behave yourself**, you act in the way that people think is correct and proper. ❏ Remember to behave yourself. ❏ You have to behave.

be|hav|ior /bɪhe̱ɪvyər/ (**behaviors**)
1 **N-COUNT/N-NONCOUNT** A person's or an animal's **behavior** is the way that they behave. ❏ You should always reward good behavior.
2 **N-NONCOUNT** SCIENCE The **behavior** of something is the way that it behaves. [from Middle English]

Word Partnership Use behavior with :		
ADJ	**aggressive/criminal** behavior, **bad/good** behavior, **learned** behavior	
V	**change** *someone's* behavior	
N	**human** behavior, behavior **pattern**, behavior **problems**	

be|hind /bɪha̱ɪnd/
1 **PREP** If something is **behind** a thing or person, it is at the back of it. ❏ I put a cushion behind his head. ❏ They were parked behind the truck.
2 **PREP** If you are walking or traveling **behind** someone or something, you are following them. ❏ Keith walked along behind them.
3 **ADV** **Behind** is also an adverb. ❏ The other police officers followed behind in a second vehicle.
4 **PREP** If people or things are **behind**, or **behind** schedule, they are slower than they should be. ❏ The work is 22 weeks behind schedule.
5 **ADV** If you leave something or someone **behind**, you do not take them with you when you go. ❏ The soldiers escaped into the

mountains, leaving behind their weapons.
[from Old English]
→ look at Picture Dictionary: **location**

beige /beɪʒ/ (**beiges**)
■ **ADJ** Something that is **beige** is pale
brown in color. ❑ *The walls are beige.*
■ **N-NONCOUNT** Beige is also a noun. ❑ *I like
beige more than dark brown.* [from Old French]

be|ing /biɪŋ/ (**beings**)
■ **Being** is the present participle of **be**.
■ **N-COUNT** A **being** is a person or a living
thing. ❑ *Remember you are dealing with a living
being—consider the horse's feelings too.* [from
Old English]
■ → see also **human being, well-being**

be|lief /bɪlif/ (**beliefs**) **N-COUNT/N-NONCOUNT**
Belief is a powerful feeling that something
is real or true. ❑ *Benedict has a deep belief
in God.* [from Old English]

be|liev|able /bɪliɪvəbʰl/ **ADJ** If something is
believable, you feel that it could be true or
real. ❑ *Mark's excuse was believable.* [from
Old English]

be|lieve /bɪliv/ (**believes, believing,
believed**)
■ **V-T** If you **believe** that something is true,
you think that it is true. [FORMAL] ❑ *Scientists
believe that life began around 4 billion years ago.*
❑ *We believe that the money is hidden here in this
apartment.*
■ **V-T** If you **believe** someone, you feel sure
that they are telling the truth. ❑ *Never believe
what you read in the newspapers.*
■ **V-I** If you **believe in** something, you feel
sure that it exists. ❑ *I don't believe in ghosts.*
■ **PHRASE** You say **believe it or not** if you are
saying something that is surprising is true.
[INFORMAL] ❑ *Believe it or not, I won the race.*
■ **PHRASE** If you **cannot believe your eyes**
you have seen something that surprises you.
If you **cannot believe your ears** you have
heard something that surprises you.
[INFORMAL] ❑ *I couldn't believe my eyes when
I saw the price.* [from Old English]

bell /bɛl/ (**bells**)
■ **N-COUNT** A **bell** is a metal object that
makes a ringing sound. ❑ *I was eating my
lunch when the bell rang.*
■ **N-COUNT** A **bell** is a
hollow metal object
with a loose piece
hanging inside it that
hits the sides and
makes a pleasant
sound. ❑ *It was a
Sunday, and all the church
bells were ringing.* [from
Old English]

bell

bel|li|cose /bɛlɪkoʊs/ **ADJ** Bellicose behavior
is aggressive, and is likely to cause an
argument or a fight. ❑ *He expressed alarm
about the government's increasingly bellicose
statements.* [from Latin]

bell pep|per (**bell peppers**) **N-COUNT** A **bell
pepper** is a hollow green, red, or yellow
vegetable with seeds.

bel|ly /bɛli/ (**bellies**) **N-COUNT** The **belly** of a
person or animal is their stomach. ❑ *She put
her hands on her swollen belly.* [from Old English]
→ look at Picture Dictionary: **horse**

be|long /bɪlɔŋ/ (**belongs, belonging,
belonged**)
■ **V-I** If something **belongs to** you, you own
it. ❑ *The house has belonged to her family for three
generations.*
■ **V-I** If someone or something **belongs to** a
group or an organization, they are a
member of that group or organization.
❑ *I used to belong to the tennis club.*
■ **V-I** If something or someone **belongs**
somewhere, that is the right place for them
to be. ❑ *After ten years in New York, I really feel
that I belong here.* [from Old High German]

be|long|ings /bɪlɔŋɪŋz/ **N-PLURAL** Your
belongings are the things that you own.
❑ *I gathered my belongings and left.* [from Old
High German]

be|low /bɪloʊ/
■ **PREP** If something is **below** something
else, it is in a lower position. ❑ *He came out of
the apartment below Leonard's.* ❑ *We watched the
sun sink below the horizon.*

b

2 ADV Below is also an adverb. ❑ *I could see the street below.*

3 PREP If something is **below** an amount, rate, or level, it is less than that amount, rate, or level. ❑ *Night temperatures can drop below 15 degrees.*

4 ADV Below is also an adverb. ❑ *Daytime temperatures were at zero or below.*

Word Partnership	Use **below** with :
ADV	**directly** below, **far/significantly/substantially/well** below, **just/slightly** below **1**
N	below **the surface 1** below **cost**, below **freezing**, below **ground** below **the poverty level/line**, below **zero 2**
V	**dip/drop/fall** below **1 2**
ADJ	below **average**, below **normal 2**

belt /bɛlt/ (**belts**)

1 N-COUNT A **belt** is a strip of leather or cloth that you wear around your waist. ❑ *He wore a belt with a large brass buckle.* [from Old English]
2 → see also **seat belt**
→ look at Picture Dictionary: **button**

belt

bench /bɛntʃ/ (**benches**) **N-COUNT**
A **bench** is a long seat made of wood or metal. ❑ *Tom sat down on a park bench.* [from Old English]

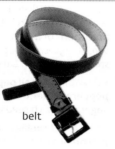
bench

bend /bɛnd/ (**bends, bending, bent**)

1 V-I When you **bend**, you move the top part of your body down and forward. ❑ *I bent over and kissed her cheek.* ❑ *She bent down and picked up the toy.*

2 V-T/V-I When you **bend** a part of your body, or when it **bends**, you change its position so that it is no longer straight. ❑ *Remember to bend your legs when you do this exercise.*

3 V-T/V-I When something straight **bends**, or when something **bends** it, it changes direction to form a curve. ❑ *The road bends slightly to the right.*

4 V-T If you **bend** something that is flat or straight, you use force to make it curved. ❑ *Bend the bar into a horseshoe.*

5 N-COUNT A **bend** in a road or a pipe is a curve or angle in it. ❑ *The accident happened on a sharp bend in the road.* [from Old English]
6 → see also **bent**

Thesaurus	bend	Also look up :
v	arch, bow, hunch, lean; (*ant.*) straighten **1** contort, curl, twist **4**
N	angle, curve, deviation, turn **5**

be|neath /bɪniθ/ **PREP** Something that is **beneath** another thing is under it. ❑ *She could see the muscles of his shoulders beneath his T-shirt.* ❑ *There are four levels of parking beneath the mall.* [from Old English]

ben|efi|cial /bɛnɪfɪʃəl/ **ADJ** Something that is **beneficial** helps people or improves their lives. ❑ *...vitamins that are beneficial to our health.* [from Late Latin]

ben|efit /bɛnɪfɪt/ (**benefits, benefiting, benefited**)

1 N-COUNT/N-NONCOUNT The **benefit** of something is the help that you get from it or the advantage that comes from it. ❑ *Parents need to educate their children about the benefits of exercise.*

2 V-T/V-I If you **benefit from** something or if it **benefits** you, it helps you or improves your life. ❑ *You would benefit from a change in your diet.*

3 N-PLURAL Benefits are money or other advantages which come from your job, the government, or an insurance company. ❑ *He will receive about $921,000 in retirement benefits.* ❑ *The article talked about the rising cost of health care and medical benefits.* [from Latin]

be|nevo|lent /bɪnɛvələnt/ **ADJ** A **benevolent** person is kind and fair. ❑ *The company has proved to be a most benevolent employer.*
● **be|nevo|lence N-NONCOUNT** ❑ *He tried to help with his small acts of benevolence.* [from Latin]

be|nign /bɪnaɪn/

1 ADJ You use **benign** to describe someone who is kind, gentle, and harmless. ❑ *They are normally a more benign audience.* ● **be|nign|ly ADV** ❑ *I just smiled benignly.*

2 ADJ A **benign** substance or process does not have any harmful effects. ❑ *This is a relatively benign medicine.*

3 ADJ SCIENCE A **benign** tumor will not cause death or serious harm. ❑ *It wasn't cancer, only a benign tumor.* [from Old French]

bent /bɛnt/
1 **Bent** is the past tense and past participle of **bend**.
2 **ADJ** Something that is **bent** is not straight. ❑ *Keep your knees slightly bent.* ❑ *He found a bent nail on the ground.* [from Old English]

ben|thic en|vir|on|ment /bɛnθɪk ɪnvaɪərənmənt, -vaɪərn-/ or **benthic zone**
N-SING SCIENCE The **benthic environment** or **benthic zone** is the area on or near the bottom of seas, rivers, and lakes, and all the organisms that live there. Compare with **pelagic environment**.

ben|thos /bɛnθɒs/ **N-PLURAL** SCIENCE **Benthos** are plants and animals that live in or near the bottom of seas, rivers, and lakes. You can also use **benthos** to mean the areas at the bottom of seas, rivers, and lakes. [from Greek]

Bernoulli's prin|ci|ple /bərnuliz prɪnsɪpᵊl/ **N-NONCOUNT** SCIENCE **Bernoulli's principle** is a law in physics which states that the pressure of a moving fluid decreases as its speed increases. [after David Bernoulli (1700-82), a Swiss mathematician and physicist]

ber|ry /bɛri/ (**berries**) **N-COUNT** Berries are small, round fruit that grow on a bush or a tree. [from Old English]

be|side /bɪsaɪd/ **PREP** Something that is **beside** something else is next to it. ❑ *Can I sit beside you?* [from Old English]

be|sides /bɪsaɪdz/
1 **PREP** **Besides** something means in addition to it. ❑ *She has many good qualities besides being very beautiful.*
2 **ADV** You use **besides** when you want to give another reason for something. ❑ *The house is far too expensive. Besides, I don't want to leave our little apartment.* [from Old English]
→ look at Usage note at **except**

Usage besides and beside
Besides and beside are often confused. Besides means "in addition (to)": *What are you doing today besides working?* Beside means "next to": *Come sit beside me.*

be|siege /bɪsidʒ/ (**besieges, besieging, besieged**)
1 **V-T** If you **are besieged by** people, many people want something from you and

people continually bother you. ❑ *She was besieged by journalists and the public.*
2 **V-T** If soldiers **besiege** a place, they surround it and wait for the people in it to stop fighting or resisting. ❑ *The main part of the army moved to Sevastopol to besiege the town.* [from Middle English]

best /bɛst/
1 **Best** is the superlative of **good**. ❑ *Who is your best friend?* ❑ *Drink regularly through the day—water is best.*
2 **Best** is the superlative of **well**. ❑ *I did best in physics in my class.* ❑ *J. R. R. Tolkien is best known as the author of "The Hobbit."*
3 **N-SING** If someone or something is **the best**, they are better than all other people or things. ❑ *We offer only the best to our clients.*
4 **PHRASE** If you say **All the best** to someone, you are telling them that you hope they will be happy.
5 **PHRASE** If you **do your best**, you try very hard to do something as well as possible. ❑ *If you do your best, no one can criticize you.*
6 **PHRASE** If you **like** something **the best**, you like it more than anything else. ❑ *Amy chose the color she liked the best.* [from Old English]

bet /bɛt/ (**bets, betting, bet**)

LANGUAGE HELP
The form **bet** is used in the present tense and is the past tense and past participle.

1 **V-T/V-I** If you **bet on** a race or a sports game, you give someone some money and say what you think that the result of the race or game will be. If you are correct, they give you your money back with some extra money, but if you are wrong they keep your money. ❑ *Jockeys are forbidden to bet.* ❑ *I bet $20 on a horse called Bright Boy.* ● **bet|ting** **N-NONCOUNT** ❑ *Betting is illegal in many countries.*
2 **N-COUNT** **Bet** is also a noun. ❑ *Did you make a bet on the horse race?*
3 **PHRASE** You say **I bet** to show that you are sure something is true. [INFORMAL] ❑ *I bet you were good at sports when you were at school.*

beta par|ti|cle /beɪtə pɑrtɪkᵊl/ (**beta particles**) **N-COUNT** SCIENCE **Beta particles** are atomic particles that are released by the nuclei of certain radioactive substances. Compare with **alpha particle** and **gamma rays**.

be|tray /bɪtreɪ/ (**betrays, betraying, betrayed**)

1 **v-T** If you **betray** someone who loves or trusts you, your actions hurt and disappoint them. ❑ *She betrayed him by starting a relationship with another writer.*

2 **v-T** If someone **betrays** their country or their friends, they give information to an enemy, putting their country's security or their friends' safety at risk. ❑ *They offered me money if I would betray my friends.*

3 **v-T** If you **betray** a feeling or quality, you show it without intending to. ❑ *She studied his face, but it betrayed nothing.* [from Old French]

bet|ter /bɛtər/

1 **Better** is the comparative of **good**.

2 **Better** is the comparative of **well**.

3 **ADV** If you like one thing **better than** another, you like it more. ❑ *I like your poem better than mine.*

4 **ADJ** If you are **better** after an illness or injury, you have recovered from it. ❑ *When I'm better, I'll talk to him.*

5 **ADJ** If you feel **better**, you no longer feel so ill. ❑ *He is feeling much better today.*

6 **PHRASE** You use **had better** when you are saying what should happen. ❑ *I think we had better go home.* [from Old English]

Word Partnership	Use **better** with :
N	better **idea**, **nothing** better **1**
ADV	**any** better, **even** better, better **than** **1** **2** **much** better **1** **4**
V	**look** better **4** **feel** better, **get** better **2** **4**

be|tween /bɪtwin/

1 **PREP** If something is **between** two people or things, it has one of them on one side of it and the other on the other side. ❑ *Nicole was standing between the two men.*

2 **PREP** If you travel **between** two places, you travel from one place to the other and back again. ❑ *I spend a lot of time traveling between Waco and El Paso.*

3 **PREP** A relationship, discussion, or difference **between** two people, groups, or things is one that involves them both. ❑ *There's a lot of trust between patients and doctors.*

4 **PREP** If something is **between** two amounts, it is greater than the first amount and smaller than the second amount. ❑ *Try to exercise between 15 and 20 minutes every day.*

5 **PREP** If something happens **between** two times, it happens after the first time and before the second time. ❑ *The house was built between 1793 and 1797.*

6 **PREP** If you choose **between** two or more things, you choose one of them. ❑ *Students will be able to choose between English, French, and Russian as their first foreign language.*

7 **PREP** When something is divided or shared **between** two people, they each have a part of it. ❑ *There is only one bathroom shared between eight people.* [from Old English]

→ look at Picture Dictionary: **location**

Usage	**between** and among

Between can be used to refer to two or more persons or things, but *among* can only be used to refer to three or more persons or things, or to a group. *Mr. Elliot's estate was divided between his two children. Mrs. Elliot's estate was divided between/ among her three grandchildren.*

Word Partnership	Use **between** with :
N	**line** between, **link** between **1** between **countries/nations**, **difference** between, **relationship** between **3** **choice** between **6**
ADV	**somewhere** in between **1** **5**
V	**caught** between **1** **choose/decide/distinguish** between **6**

bev|er|age /bɛvərɪdʒ, bɛvrɪdʒ/ (**beverages**)

N-COUNT **Beverages** are drinks. [WRITTEN] ❑ *Try to avoid beverages that contain a lot of sugar.* [from Old French]

→ look at Word Web: **sugar**

Word Link	war ≈ watchful : a*ware*, be*ware*, *war*ning

be|ware /bɪwɛər/

LANGUAGE HELP

Beware is only used as an imperative or infinitive. It does not have any other forms.

V-I If you tell someone to **beware** of a person or thing, you are telling them to be careful because the person or thing is dangerous. ❑ *Beware of the dangers of swimming in the ocean at night.*

be|wil|dered /bɪwɪldərd/ **ADJ** If you are **bewildered**, you are very confused and cannot decide what you should do. ❑ *The shoppers looked bewildered by the huge variety of goods for sale.*

be|yond /bɪyɒnd/

1 **PREP** Something that is **beyond** a place is on the other side of it, or further away than it. ❑ *On his right was a garden and beyond it a large house.*

2 **ADV** **Beyond** is also an adverb. ❑ *The house had a fabulous view out to the ocean beyond.*

3 **PREP** If something happens **beyond** a particular time, it continues after that time has passed. ❑ *Few jockeys continue riding beyond the age of 40.*

4 **ADV** **Beyond** is also an adverb. ❑ *The actor was popular through the 1990s and beyond.* [from Old English]

bi|ased /baɪəst/ **ADJ** If someone is **biased**, they prefer one group of people to another, and behave unfairly as a result. ❑ *He seemed a bit biased against women in my opinion.* [from Old French]

Bi|ble /baɪbəl/ **N-PROPER** The **Bible** is the holy book of the Christian and Jewish religions. [from Old French]

bib|li|og|ra|phy /bɪbliɒɡrəfi/ (**bibliographies**)

1 **N-COUNT** A **bibliography** is a list of books on a particular subject. ❑ *At the end of this chapter there is a bibliography of useful books.*

2 **N-COUNT** LANGUAGE ARTS A **bibliography** is a list of the books and articles that are referred to in a particular book. ❑ *The full bibliography is printed at the end of the second volume.* [from French]

bi|ceps /baɪsɛps/ **N-PLURAL** SCIENCE Your **biceps** are the large muscles at the front of the upper part of your arms. [from Latin]

| Word Link | bi ≈ two : bicycle, bilingual, bisect |

| Word Link | cycl ≈ circle : bicycle, cycle, recycle |

bi|cy|cle /baɪsɪkəl/ (**bicycles**) **N-COUNT** SPORTS A **bicycle** is a vehicle with two wheels. You ride it by sitting on it and using your legs to make the wheels turn. [from Late Latin]

→ look at Word Web: **bicycle**

bid /bɪd/ (**bids, bidding, bid**)

> **LANGUAGE HELP**
>
> The form **bid** is used in the present tense and is the past tense and past participle.

1 **N-COUNT** A **bid for** something or a **bid to** do something is an attempt to obtain it or do it. ❑ *Chicago's Olympic bid was unsuccessful.*

2 **N-COUNT** If you make a **bid** for something that is being sold, you say that you will pay a certain amount of money for it. ❑ *Bill made the winning $620 bid for the statue.*

3 **V-T/V-I** If you **bid** for something that is being sold, you say that you will pay a certain amount of money for it. ❑ *Lily wanted to bid for the painting.* ❑ *The manager is prepared to bid $2 million for the soccer player.* [from Old English]

| Word Link | er ≈ more : bigger, louder, taller |

big /bɪɡ/ (**bigger, biggest**)

1 **ADJ** Someone or something that is **big** is large in size. ❑ *Australia is a big country.* ❑ *Her husband was a big man.* ❑ *The crowd included a big group from Cleveland.*

2 **ADJ** Someone or something that is **big** is important or serious. ❑ *Mandy's problem was too big for her to solve alone.* ❑ *He owns one of the biggest companies in Italy.*

3 **ADJ** Children often call their older brother or sister their **big** brother or sister. ❑ *I live with my dad and my big brother, John.* [of Scandinavian origin]

Thesaurus	big	Also look up :
ADJ	enormous, huge, large, massive; *(ant.)* little, small, tiny **1**	

Word Web   bicycle

A Scotsman named Kirkpatrick MacMillan invented the first **bicycle** with **pedals** around 1840. Early bicycles had wooden or metal **wheels**. However, by the mid-1800s **tires** with tubes appeared. Modern **racing bikes** are very lightweight and aerodynamic. The wheels have fewer **spokes** and the tires are very thin and smooth. **Mountain bikes** allow riders to ride up and down steep hills on dirt trails. The **tandem** is a bicycle for two people. It has about the same **wind resistance** as a one-person bike. But with twice the power, it goes faster.

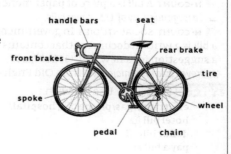

handle bars   seat

front brakes   rear brake

   tire

spoke   wheel

pedal   chain

B

big bang theo|ry **N-SING** SCIENCE The **big bang theory** is a theory that states that the universe was created after an extremely large explosion.

big da|ta **N-NONCOUNT** TECHNOLOGY **Big data** is extremely large amounts of information that can only be managed using special computing tools. ❑ ...*valuable analysis of big data.*

big gov|ern|ment **N-NONCOUNT** SOCIAL STUDIES **Big government** is a way that some people refer to government that supports high taxation, public spending, and the centralization of political power. ❑ *Republicans tried to portray Democrats as favoring big government over individuals' rights.*

bike /baɪk/ (**bikes**) **N-COUNT** SPORTS A **bike** is a bicycle or a motorcycle. [INFORMAL] ❑ *When you ride a bike, you exercise all your leg muscles.*

bi|ki|ni /bɪkini/ (**bikinis**) **N-COUNT** A **bikini** is a piece of clothing with two parts that women wear for swimming.

bi|lat|er|al sym|met|ry /baɪlætərəl sɪmətri/ **N-NONCOUNT** SCIENCE An organism that has **bilateral symmetry** has a body that consists of two halves which are exactly the same, except that one half is the mirror image of the other. Compare with **radial symmetry**.

bi|lin|gual /baɪlɪŋgwəl/
1 **ADJ** Someone who is **bilingual** can speak two languages equally well. ❑ *He is bilingual in French and English.*
2 **ADJ** Something that is **bilingual** is written or spoken in two languages. ❑ *The company specializes in bilingual dictionaries.*

bill /bɪl/ (**bills**)
1 **N-COUNT** A **bill** is a piece of paper that shows how much money you must pay for something. ❑ *They couldn't afford to pay their bills.*
2 **N-COUNT** A **bill** is a piece of paper money. ❑ *... a large quantity of U.S. dollar bills.*
3 **N-COUNT** SOCIAL STUDIES In government, a **bill** is a written document that contains a suggestion for a new law. ❑ *The bill was approved by a large majority.* [from Old English]

Word Partnership	Use **bill** with :	
N	electricity/gas/phone bill, hospital/ hotel bill **1**	
	dollar bill **2**	
V	pay a bill **1**	
	pass a bill, sign a bill, vote on a bill **3**	

bill|board /bɪlbɔrd/ (**billboards**) **N-COUNT** A **billboard** is a very large board for advertisements at the side of the road.

bil|lion /bɪlyən/ (**billions**)

> **LANGUAGE HELP**
> The plural is **billion** after a number.

1 **NUM** MATH A **billion** or **one billion** is the number 1,000,000,000. ❑ *The country's debt has risen to 3 billion dollars.*
2 **NUM** **Billions of** people or things means a very large number of them. ❑ *The Universe is billions of years old.* [from French]

bil|lion|aire /bɪlyənɛər/ (**billionaires**) **N-COUNT** A **billionaire** is an extremely rich person who has money or property worth at least a billion dollars. [from French]

Bill of Rights **N-SING** SOCIAL STUDIES A **Bill of Rights** is a written list of the rights of people living in a particular country.

bi|me|tal|lic strip /baɪmətælɪk strɪp/ (**bimetallic strips**) **N-COUNT** SCIENCE A **bimetallic strip** is a long thin piece of material containing two different metals that expand at different rates when heated.

bin /bɪn/ (**bins**) **N-COUNT** A **bin** is a container that you keep things in. ❑ *...a plastic storage bin.* [from Old English]

bi|na|ry fis|sion /baɪnəri fɪʃ°n/ **N-NONCOUNT** SCIENCE **Binary fission** is the biological process by which a single cell divides to form two new cells.

bind /baɪnd/ (**binds, binding, bound**)
1 **V-T** If you **bind** something, you tie rope or string around it to hold it firmly. ❑ *Bind the ends of the rope with thread.* ❑ *They bound his hands behind his back.* [from Old English]
2 → see also **bound**

bind|ing /baɪndɪŋ/ (**bindings**)
1 **ADJ** A **binding** promise, agreement, or decision must be obeyed or carried out. ❑ *It can take months to enter into a legally binding contract to buy a house.*
2 **N-COUNT/N-NONCOUNT** The **binding** of a book is its cover. ❑ *Its books are noted for the quality of their paper and bindings.* [from Old English]

bin|ocu|lars /bɪnɒkyələrz/ **N-PLURAL** **Binoculars** are special glasses that you use to look at things that are a long distance away. [from Latin]

bi|no|mial /baɪnoʊmiəl/ (binomials)

1 **N-COUNT** MATH A **binomial** is an expression in algebra that consists of two terms, for example "3x + 2y." Compare with **monomial** and **polynomial**.

2 **ADJ** MATH **Binomial** means relating to binomials. [from Medieval Latin]

bi|no|mial dis|tri|bu|tion (binomial distributions) **N-COUNT** MATH A **binomial distribution** is a calculation that measures the probability of a particular outcome resulting from an event that has two possible outcomes.

bi|no|mial no|men|cla|ture /baɪnoʊmiəl noʊmənkleɪtʃər/ **N-NONCOUNT** SCIENCE **Binomial nomenclature** is a system of classifying plants and animals by giving them a name consisting of two parts, first the genus and then the species.

bi|no|mial theo|rem (binomial theorems) **N-COUNT** MATH The **binomial theorem** is a mathematical formula that is used to calculate the value of a binomial that has been multiplied by itself a particular number of times.

Word Link	chem ≈ chemical : biochemical, chemical, chemistry

bio|chemi|cal /baɪoʊkɛmɪkəl/ (biochemicals)

1 **ADJ** SCIENCE **Biochemical** changes, reactions, and mechanisms relate to the chemical processes that happen in living things. ❑ *Starvation causes biochemical changes in the body.*

2 **N-COUNT** SCIENCE **Biochemicals** are chemicals that are made by living things, for example hormones and enzymes.

bio|degrad|able /baɪoʊdɪgreɪdəbəl/ **ADJ** Something that is **biodegradable** decays naturally without any special scientific treatment, and can therefore be thrown away without causing pollution.

bio|di|ver|sity /baɪoʊdaɪvɜrsɪti/ **N-NONCOUNT** SCIENCE **Biodiversity** is the existence of a wide variety of plant and animal species living in their natural environment.

bio|ge|net|ics /baɪoʊdʒɪnɛtɪks/ **N-NONCOUNT** SCIENCE **Biogenetics** is the branch of biology concerned with altering the genomes of living organisms.

Word Link	bio ≈ life : biography, biology, biotechnology

Word Link	graph ≈ writing : autograph, biography, seismograph

bi|og|ra|phy /baɪɒgrəfi/ (biographies) **N-COUNT** LANGUAGE ARTS A **biography** of someone is the story of their life that is written by someone else. ❑ *I am reading a biography of Franklin D. Roosevelt.* [from Late Greek]

→ look at Word Web: **library**

bio|logi|cal /baɪəlɒdʒɪkəl/ **ADJ** SCIENCE **Biological** processes happen in the bodies and cells of living things. ❑ *...biological processes such as reproduction and growth.* [from French]

→ look at Word Web: **zoo**

bio|logi|cal clock (biological clocks) **N-COUNT** Your **biological clock** is your body's way of registering time. It does not rely on events such as day or night, but on factors such as your habits, your age, and chemical changes taking place in your body.

Word Link	logy, ology ≈ study of : anthropology, biology, geology

Word Link	ist ≈ one who practices : biologist, dramatist, pharmacist

bi|ol|ogy /baɪɒlədʒi/ **N-NONCOUNT** SCIENCE **Biology** is the scientific study of living things. ●**bi|olo|gist** /baɪɒlədʒɪst/ (biologists) **N-COUNT** ❑ *The marine biologist was killed by a shark while diving.* [from French]

bio|mass /baɪoʊmæs/

1 **N-NONCOUNT** SCIENCE The **biomass** of a particular area is the total number of organisms that live there.

2 **N-NONCOUNT** SCIENCE **Biomass** is biological material such as dead plants that is used to provide fuel or energy.

bi|ome /baɪoʊm/ (biomes) **N-COUNT** SCIENCE A **biome** is a group of plants and animals that live in a particular region because they are suited to its physical environment.

→ look at Word Web: **habitat**

bio|sphere /baɪəsfɪər/ **N-SING** SCIENCE The **biosphere** is the part of the Earth's surface and atmosphere where there are living things.

→ look at Word Web: **biosphere**

Word Web biosphere

Earth is the only place in the **universe** where we are sure that **life** exists. A **geologist,** Eduard Suess*, invented the term **biosphere** in 1875. For him it included the **land, water,** and **atmosphere** in which all life occurs. Later scientists studied the relationships among living things and the biosphere. They created the term **ecosystem** to describe these interactions.

Eduard Suess (1831-1914): an Austrian geologist.

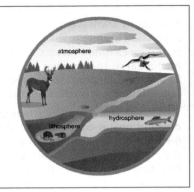

bio|tech|nol|ogy /baɪoʊtɛknɒlədʒi/
N-NONCOUNT SCIENCE **Biotechnology** is the use of living parts such as cells or bacteria in industry and technology. ❏ ...the Scottish biotechnology company that developed Dolly the cloned sheep.
→ look at Word Web: **technology**

Word Link otic ≈ affecting, causing : antibiotic, biotic, patriotic

bi|ot|ic /baɪɒtɪk/ **ADJ** SCIENCE **Biotic** means relating to plants, animals, and other living organisms. [from Greek]

bio|weap|on /baɪoʊwɛpən/ (**bioweapons**)
N-COUNT **Bioweapons** are biological weapons.

bird /bɜrd/ (**birds**) **N-COUNT** A **bird** is an animal with feathers and wings. ❏ ...a bird's nest. ❏ The bird flew away as I came near. [from Old English]
→ look at Word Webs: **bird, pet**

birth /bɜrθ/ (**births**)
1 **N-COUNT/N-NONCOUNT** When a baby is born, you call this moment his or her **birth**. ❏ They are celebrating the birth of their first child. ❏ Alice weighed 5 lbs 7 oz at birth.
2 **N-NONCOUNT** You can call the beginning of something its **birth**.

❏ ...the birth of democracy.
3 **PHRASE** When a woman **gives birth,** a baby comes out of her body. ❏ She's just given birth to a baby girl. [from Old Norse]
→ look at Word Web: **reproduction**

Word Partnership	Use birth with :	
PREP	**at** birth, **before** birth **1**	
ADJ	**premature** birth **1**	
N	birth **of a baby/child**, birth **certificate**, birth **control**, birth **and death**, birth **defect**, birth **rate 1** date of birth **1 3** birth **of a** nation **2**	
V	**give** birth **3**	

birth con|trol **N-NONCOUNT** **Birth control** means planning whether to have children, and using contraception to prevent unwanted pregnancy. ❏ ...today's methods of birth control.

birth|day /bɜrθdeɪ, -di/ (**birthdays**)
N-COUNT Your **birthday** is the day of the year that you were born. ❏ Mom always sends David a present on his birthday.

bi|sect /baɪsɛkt/ (**bisects, bisecting, bisected**) **V-T** If a line **bisects** an area or another line, it divides the area or line in half. ❏ The main street bisects the town from end to end.

Word Web bird

Many scientists today believe that birds evolved from **avian** dinosaurs. Recently many links have been found. Like birds, these dinosaurs laid their **eggs** in **nests.** Some had **wings, beaks,** and **claws** similar to modern birds. But perhaps the most dramatic link was found in 2001. Scientists in China discovered a well-preserved *Sinornithosaurus*, a bird-like dinosaur with **feathers.** This dinosaur is believed to be related to a prehistoric bird, the *Archaeopteryx*.

Sinornithosaurus

bi|sex|ual /baɪsɛkʃuəl/ **ADJ** Someone who is **bisexual** is sexually attracted to both men and women.

bish|op /bɪʃəp/ (**bishops**)
■ **N-COUNT** A **bishop** is a leader in the Christian church whose job is to look after all the churches in an area.
■ **N-COUNT** In chess, a **bishop** is a piece that can be moved diagonally across the board on squares that are the same color. [from Old English]
→ look at Word Web: **chess**

bit /bɪt/ (**bits**)
■ **N-COUNT** TECHNOLOGY A **bit** is a unit of information that can be stored on a computer.
■ **Bit** is the past tense of **bite**.
■ **PHRASE** A **bit of** something is a small amount of it, or a small part or section of it. ❑ I do a bit of work at my children's school sometimes. ❑ Only a bit of the cake was left.
■ **PHRASE** A **bit** means a little. ❑ This girl was a bit strange. ❑ I think people feel a bit happier now.
■ **PHRASE** If you do something **a bit** or **for a bit**, you do it for a short time. ❑ Let's wait a bit.
■ **PHRASE** Quite a bit means quite a lot. [INFORMAL] ❑ Things have changed quite a bit. [from Old English]

bitch /bɪtʃ/ (**bitches**) **N-COUNT** A **bitch** is a female dog. [from Old English]

bite /baɪt/ (**bites, biting, bit, bitten**)
■ **V-T/V-I** If you **bite** something, you use your teeth to cut into it or through it. ❑ William bit into his sandwich. ❑ She bit the end off the chocolate bar.
■ **N-COUNT** A **bite** of food is a small piece of it that you cut into with your teeth. ❑ Dan took another bite of apple.
■ **V-T/V-I** If a snake or an insect **bites**, it makes a mark or a hole in your skin with a sharp part of its body. ❑ Do these flies bite?
■ **N-COUNT** A **bite** is a painful mark on your body where an animal, a snake, or an insect has bitten you. ❑ A dog bite needs immediate medical attention. [from Old English]

bit|ten /bɪtⁿn/ **Bitten** is the past participle of **bite**. [from Old English]

bit|ter /bɪtər/ (**bitterest**)
■ **ADJ** A **bitter** taste is unpleasantly sharp and sour. ❑ The medicine tasted bitter.
■ **ADJ** If someone is **bitter**, they feel very angry and upset about something that has happened to them. ❑ She is very bitter about the way she lost her job. ● **bit|ter|ly** **ADV** ❑ "And he didn't even try to help us," Grant said bitterly. ● **bit|ter|ness** **N-NONCOUNT** ❑ I still feel bitterness toward the person who stole my purse.
■ **ADJ** In a **bitter** argument or conflict, people argue very angrily or fight very fiercely. ❑ ...the scene of bitter fighting. ❑ ...a bitter attack on the government.
■ **ADJ** **Bitter** weather is extremely cold. ❑ A bitter east wind was blowing. ● **bit|ter|ly** **ADV** ❑ It's bitterly cold here in Moscow. [from Old English]
→ look at Word Web: **taste**

bi|zarre /bɪzɑr/ **ADJ** Something that is **bizarre** is very strange. ❑ They were all surprised by their manager's bizarre behavior. ● **bi|zarre|ly** **ADV** ❑ She dresses bizarrely. [from French]

black /blæk/ (**blacker, blackest, blacks, blacking, blacked**)
■ **ADJ** Something that is **black** is the color of the sky at night. ❑ She was wearing a black coat with a white collar. ❑ He had thick black hair.
■ **N-NONCOUNT** **Black** is also a noun. ❑ She was wearing black.
■ **ADJ** A **black** person belongs to a race of people with dark skins, especially a race originally from Africa. ❑ He worked for the rights of black people.
■ **N-COUNT** Black people are sometimes called **blacks**, especially when comparing different groups of people. Other uses of the word could cause offense. ❑ There are about 31 million blacks in the U.S.
■ **ADJ** **Black** coffee has no milk in it. ❑ A cup of black coffee contains no calories.
■ **ADJ** If you describe a situation as **black**, you are saying that it is very bad. ❑ It was one of the blackest days of his political career. [from Old English]
→ look at Picture Dictionary: **hair**
→ look at Word Web: **spice**
▶ **black out** If you **black out**, you suddenly become unconscious for a short time. ❑ I felt as if I was going to black out.

black and white also black-and-white **ADJ** In a **black and white** photograph or film, everything is shown in black, white, and gray. ❑ ...*old black and white films.* ❑ *...a black-and-white photo.*

black|berry /blǽkbɛri/ (**blackberries**)
N-COUNT A **blackberry** is a small, soft black or dark purple fruit.

black|board /blǽkbɔrd/ (**blackboards**)
N-COUNT A **blackboard** is a big, dark-colored board for writing on in a classroom. [from Old English]

black eye (**black eyes**) **N-COUNT** If someone has a **black eye**, they have a dark-colored mark around their eye because they have been hit there by someone or something. ❑ *Jan arrived at the hospital with a broken nose and a black eye.*

black hole (**black holes**) **N-COUNT** SCIENCE **Black holes** are areas in space where gravity is so strong that nothing, not even light, can escape from them. Black holes are thought to be formed by collapsed stars.

black|mail /blǽkmeɪl/ (**blackmails, blackmailing, blackmailed**)
1 N-NONCOUNT **Blackmail** is saying that you will say something bad about someone if they do not do what you tell them to do or give you money. ❑ *Mr. Stanley was accused of blackmail.*
2 V-T If one person **blackmails** another person, they use blackmail against them. ❑ *Jeff suddenly realized that Linda was blackmailing him.*

black rhi|no (**black rhinos**) or black rhinoceros **N-COUNT** A **black rhino** is a type of rhinoceros with gray skin and two horns on its nose, that lives in Africa.

black|smith /blǽksmɪθ/ (**blacksmiths**)
N-COUNT A **blacksmith** is a person whose job is making things out of metal.

blad|der /blǽdər/ (**bladders**) **N-COUNT**
SCIENCE Your **bladder** is the part of your body where liquid waste is stored until it leaves your body. [from Old English]

blade /bleɪd/ (**blades**)
N-COUNT The **blade** of a knife is the flat, sharp edge that is used for cutting. ❑ *The ax blade cut deep into the log.* [from Old English]
→ look at Word Web: **silverware**

blade

blame /bleɪm/ (**blames, blaming, blamed**)
1 V-T If you **blame** someone or something **for** something bad, you say that they caused it. ❑ *Police blamed the bus driver for the accident.*
2 N-NONCOUNT If you get the **blame for** something bad that has happened, people say that you caused it. ❑ *I'm not going to take the blame for a mistake he made.*
3 V-T If you say that you do not **blame** someone **for** doing something, you mean that you consider it was a reasonable thing to do. ❑ *I don't blame them for trying to make some money.*
4 PHRASE If someone is **to blame for** something bad that has happened, they are responsible for causing it. ❑ *You are not to blame for your illness.* [from Old French]

Word Partnership	Use blame with :
N	blame **the victim** **1**
V	**tend to** blame **1**
	lay blame, **share the** blame **2**
	can hardly blame *someone* **3**

bland /blænd/ (**blander, blandest**)
1 ADJ Someone or something that is **bland** is dull and not interesting. ❑ *Their music is bland and boring.*
2 ADJ Food that is **bland** has very little flavor. ❑ *The pizza tasted bland, like warm cardboard.* [from Latin]
→ look at Word Web: **spice**

blank /blæŋk/
1 ADJ Something that is **blank** has nothing on it. ❑ *He tore a blank page from his notebook.*
2 ADJ If you look **blank**, your face shows no reaction. ❑ *Albert looked blank. "I don't know him, sir."* ● **blank|ly** **ADV** ❑ *Ellie stared at him blankly.* [from Old French]
→ look at Picture Dictionary: **answer**

blan|ket /blǽŋkɪt/ (**blankets**)
1 N-COUNT A **blanket** is a large, thick piece of cloth that you put on a bed to keep you warm.
2 N-COUNT A **blanket of** snow is a thick layer of it that hides what is below it. ❑ *The mud disappeared under a blanket of snow.* [from Old French]
→ look at Picture Dictionary: **bed**

blast /blæst/ (**blasts**) **N-COUNT** A **blast** is a big explosion, especially one caused by a bomb. ❑ *250 people were killed in the blast.* [from Old English]

blaze /bleɪz/ (blazes, blazing, blazed)

1 **V-I** When a fire **blazes**, it burns strongly and brightly. ❑ *Three people died as the building blazed.*

2 **N-COUNT** A **blaze** is a large fire that destroys a lot of things. ❑ *More than 4,000 firefighters are battling the blaze.* [from Old English]

blaz|er /bleɪzər/ (blazers) **N-COUNT** A **blazer** is a type of light jacket for men or women. [from Old English]

bleach /blitʃ/ (bleaches, bleaching, bleached)

1 **V-T** If you **bleach** something, you use a chemical to make it white or lighter in color. ❑ *These products don't bleach the hair.*

2 **N-NONCOUNT** **Bleach** is a chemical that is used for making cloth white, or for making things very clean. [from Old English]

bleak /blik/ (bleaker, bleakest)

1 **ADJ** If a situation is **bleak**, people do not expect it to be happy or successful. ❑ *The future looks bleak.*

2 **ADJ** When the weather is **bleak**, it is cold and unpleasant. ❑ *The weather can be very bleak here.*

3 **ADJ** If you describe a place as **bleak**, you mean that it looks cold, empty, and unattractive. ❑ *The island's bleak landscape allows few plants to grow.* [from Old English]

bleed /blid/ (bleeds, bleeding, bled) **V-I** When part of your body **bleeds**, you lose blood from it. ❑ *Ian's lip was bleeding.*

● **bleed|ing** **N-NONCOUNT** ❑ *We tried to stop the bleeding from the cut on his arm.* [from Old English]

blend /blɛnd/ (blends, blending, blended)

1 **V-T/V-I** If you **blend** substances together, you mix them together. ❑ *Blend the butter with the sugar.*

2 **N-COUNT** A **blend** of things is a mixture of them. ❑ *Their music is a blend of jazz and rock'n'roll.*

3 **V-T/V-I** When different things **blend**, they combine well. ❑ *All the colors blend perfectly together.*

4 **N-COUNT** LANGUAGE ARTS A **blend** is a combination of sounds that are represented by letters, for example the sound "spl" in "splash." [from Old English]

bless /blɛs/ (blesses, blessing, blessed)

1 **V-T** When a priest **blesses** people or things, he or she asks for God's protection for them. ❑ *The pope blessed the crowd.*

2 **INTERJ** You can say **Bless you** to someone when they sneeze. [from Old English] [SPOKEN]

bless|ing /blɛsɪŋ/ (blessings)

1 **N-COUNT** A **blessing** is something good that you are grateful for. ❑ *Rivers are a blessing for an agricultural country.*

2 **N-COUNT** If something is done with your **blessing**, it is done with your approval and support. ❑ *Hailey quit school with the blessing of her parents.* [from Old English]

blew /blu/ **Blew** is the past tense of **blow**. [from Old English]

blind /blaɪnd/ (blinds, blinding, blinded)

1 **ADJ** Someone who is **blind** is unable to see. ❑ *My grandfather is going blind.*

● **blind|ness** **N-NONCOUNT** ❑ *Early treatment can usually prevent blindness.*

2 **N-PLURAL** The **blind** are people who are blind. ❑ *He's a teacher of the blind.*

3 **V-T** If something **blinds** you, it makes you unable to see, either for a short time or permanently. ❑ *The sun hit the windshield, momentarily blinding him.*

4 **N-COUNT** **Blinds** are a piece of cloth or other material that you can pull down over a window to cover it. ❑ *Susan pulled the blinds up to let the bright sunlight into the room.* [from Old English]

→ look at Word Web: **disability**

Word Partnership	Use **blind** with :	
ADJ	blind **and deaf** **1**	
ADV	**legally** blind, **partially** blind **1**	
N	blind **person** **1**	

blind|fold /blaɪndfoʊld/ (blindfolds, blindfolding, blindfolded)

1 **N-COUNT** A **blindfold** is a strip of cloth that is tied over your eyes so that you cannot see.

2 **V-T** If you **blindfold** someone, you tie a blindfold over their eyes. ❑ *Mr. Li was handcuffed and blindfolded.* [from Old English]

bling /blɪŋ/ or **bling-bling** **N-NONCOUNT** **Bling** is expensive or fancy jewelry. [INFORMAL] ❑ *Famous jewelers want celebrities to wear their bling.*

blink /blɪŋk/ (blinks, blinking, blinked)

1 **V-T/V-I** When you **blink**, you shut your

eyes and very quickly open them again. ❑ *I stood blinking in bright light.* ❑ *She was blinking her eyes rapidly.*

2 N-COUNT Blink is also a noun. ❑ *She gave a couple of blinks and her eyes cleared.* [from Middle Dutch]

blis|ter /blɪstər/ (**blisters**) **N-COUNT** A **blister** is a raised area of skin filled with a clear liquid. ❑ *I get blisters when I wear these shoes.* [from Old French]

bliz|zard /blɪzərd/ (**blizzards**) **N-COUNT** A **blizzard** is a very bad storm with snow and strong winds.
→ look at Word Webs: **snow, storm, weather**

blob /blɒb/ (**blobs**) **N-COUNT** A **blob** of thick liquid is a small amount of it. [INFORMAL] ❑ *Denise wiped a blob of jelly off Edgar's chin.*

bloc /blɒk/ (**blocs**) **N-COUNT** SOCIAL STUDIES A **bloc** is a group of countries that have similar political aims and interests and that act together over some issues. ❑ *...the former Soviet bloc.* [from French]

block /blɒk/ (**blocks, blocking, blocked**)
1 N-COUNT A **block of** a substance is a large, solid piece of it with straight sides. ❑ *Elizabeth carves animals from blocks of wood.*
2 N-COUNT A **block** in a town or a city is a group of buildings with streets on all sides, or the distance between each group of buildings. ❑ *He walked around the block three times.* ❑ *She walked four blocks down Main Street.*
3 V-T If someone or something **blocks** a road, there is something on it so that nothing can pass along it. ❑ *The police blocked a highway through the center of the city.* ❑ *A tree blocked the road.* [from Old French]
4 → see also **blocked, blocking**
▸ **block out** If you **block out** a thought, you try not to think about it. ❑ *She accused me of blocking out the past.*

block|ade /blɒkeɪd/ (**blockades, blockading, blockaded**)
1 N-COUNT A **blockade** of a place is an action that is taken to prevent goods or people from entering or leaving it. ❑ *It's not yet clear who will enforce the blockade.*
2 V-T If a group of people **blockade** a place, they stop goods or people from reaching that place. If they **blockade** a road or a port, they stop people from using that road or port. ❑ *The town has been blockaded for 40 days.*

block and tack|le (**block and tackles** or **blocks and tackles**) **N-COUNT** A **block and tackle** is a device consisting of two or more pulleys connected by a rope or cable, which is used for lifting heavy objects.

blocked /blɒkt/ or **blocked up**
1 ADJ If something is **blocked**, it is completely closed so that nothing can get through it. ❑ *The pipes are blocked and the water can't get through.* [from Old French]
2 → see also **block**

block|ing /blɒkɪŋ/
1 N-NONCOUNT ARTS In the theater, **blocking** is the process of planning the movements that the actors will make on the stage during the performance of a play.
2 → see also **block**

blog /blɒg/ (**blogs, blogging, blogged**)
1 N-COUNT TECHNOLOGY A **blog** is a website that describes the daily life of the person who writes it, and also their thoughts and ideas. ❑ *His blog was later published as a book.*
● **blog|ger** (**bloggers**) **N-COUNT** ❑ *Loewenstein is a freelance author, blogger and journalist.*
● **blog|ging N-NONCOUNT** ❑ *Blogging is very popular.*
2 V-I TECHNOLOGY Someone who **blogs** regularly writes a blog. ❑ *She blogs about US politics.*
→ look at Word Web: **blog**

Word Web blog

The word **blog** is a combination of the words **web** and **log**. It is a **website** that has many dated **entries**. A blog can focus on one subject of interest. Most blogs are written by one person. Many blogs ask readers to leave comments on the site. This often results in a group of readers who write back and forth to each other. The total group of web logs is the **blogosphere**. A blogstorm occurs when there are many people are **blogging** or reading about the same topic.

Word Link *sphere ≈ ball : atmo*sphere, *blogo*sphere, *hemi*sphere

blogo|sphere /blɒgəsfɪər/ or **blogsphere** /blɒgsfɪər/ **N-SING** TECHNOLOGY The **blogosphere** is all the blogs on the Internet. ❑ *The blogosphere continues to expand.*
→ look at Word Web: **blog**

blog|post /blɒgpoʊst/ (**blogposts**) **N-COUNT** TECHNOLOGY A **blogpost** is a piece of writing that forms part of a regular blog. ❑ *His latest blogpost describes the journey.*

blonde /blɒnd/ (**blonder, blondest**)
 1 **ADJ** Someone who has **blonde** hair has pale-colored hair. ❑ *My sister has blonde hair.*
 2 **ADJ** Someone who is **blonde** has blonde hair. ❑ *He's blonder than his brother.* [from Old French]
→ look at Picture Dictionary: **hair**

blood /blʌd/ **N-NONCOUNT** SCIENCE **Blood** is the red liquid that flows inside your body. ❑ *His shirt was covered in blood.* [from Old English]
→ look at Word Webs: **cardiovascular system, donor**

Word Partnership Use blood with :

N	**(red/white)** blood **cells**, blood **clot**, blood **disease**, blood **loss**, **pool of** blood, blood **sample**, blood **stream**, blood **supply**, blood **test**, blood **transfusion**
ADJ	**covered in** blood, blood **stained**
V	**donate/give** blood

blood pres|sure **N-NONCOUNT** Your **blood pressure** is the amount of force with which your blood flows around your body. ❑ *Your doctor will take your blood pressure.* ❑ *What are the causes of high blood pressure?*
→ look at Word Web: **diagnosis**

blood|stream /blʌdstrim/ (**bloodstreams**) **N-COUNT** Your **bloodstream** is the blood that flows around your body. ❑ *The virus stays in the bloodstream for only a short time.*

blood ves|sel (**blood vessels**) **N-COUNT** SCIENCE **Blood vessels** are the narrow tubes that your blood flows through.

bloody /blʌdi/ (**bloodier, bloodiest**)
 1 **ADJ** Something that is **bloody** is covered in blood. ❑ *...a bloody nose.*
 2 **ADJ** A situation or event that is **bloody** is one in which there is a lot of violence and people are killed. ❑ *...a long and bloody battle.* [from Old English]

bloom /blum/ (**blooms, blooming, bloomed**)
 V-I When a plant or tree **blooms**, it grows flowers on it. When a flower **blooms**, it opens. ❑ *This plant blooms between May and June.* [from Old English]

blos|som /blɒsəm/ (**blossoms, blossoming, blossomed**)
 1 **N-COUNT/N-NONCOUNT** **Blossoms** are the flowers that appear on trees and plants. ❑ *The apple blossoms were in full bloom last week.*
 2 **V-I** When a tree **blossoms**, it produces blossoms. ❑ *The peach trees will blossom soon.*
 3 **V-I** If someone or something **blossoms**, they develop good, attractive, or successful qualities. ❑ *We give them a contract and hope they blossom into superstars.* [from Old English]

blot /blɒt/ (**blots**) **N-COUNT** A **blot** is a drop of liquid on a surface. ❑ *The page was covered with ink blots.* [of Germanic origin]

blouse /blaʊs/ (**blouses**) **N-COUNT** A **blouse** is a shirt for a girl or woman. [from French]
→ look at Picture Dictionary: **clothing**
→ look at Usage note at **shirt**

blow /bloʊ/ (**blows, blowing, blew, blown**)
 1 **V-I** When a wind or breeze **blows**, the air moves. ❑ *A cold wind was blowing.*
 2 **V-T/V-I** If the wind **blows** something somewhere, it moves it there. ❑ *The wind blew her hair back.* ❑ *Sand blew in our eyes.*
 3 **V-I** If you **blow**, you send out air from your mouth. ❑ *Danny blew on his fingers.*
 4 **V-T/V-I** When someone **blows** a whistle or a musical instrument, they make a sound by blowing into it. ❑ *When the referee blows his whistle, the game begins.* ❑ *The whistle blew and the train moved forward.*
 5 **V-T** When you **blow** your nose, you force air out of it in order to clear it. ❑ *He took out a handkerchief and blew his nose.*
 6 **N-COUNT** If someone receives a **blow**, they are hit hard with something. ❑ *He went to the hospital after a blow to the face.*
 7 **N-COUNT** If something that happens is a **blow to** someone, it is very disappointing to them. ❑ *The increase in tax was a blow to the industry.* [from Old English]
→ look at Word Webs: **glass, wind**
 ▶ **blow out** If you **blow out** a flame, you blow at it so that it stops burning. ❑ *I blew out the candle.*
 ▶ **blow up** **1** If someone **blows** something **up** or if it **blows up**, it is destroyed by an explosion. ❑ *He was jailed for trying to blow up a plane.*

B

2 If you **blow** something **up**, you fill it with air. ❑ *Can you help me blow up the balloons?*

Word Partnership	Use blow with :
ADV	blow **away** **2**
N	blow **bubbles**, blow **smoke** **3**
	blow **a whistle** **4**
	blow *your* **nose** **5**
V	**deliver/strike** a blow **6**
	cushion/soften a blow, **suffer a**
	blow **6** **7**
ADJ	**crushing/devastating/heavy**
	blow **6** **7**
PREP	blow **to the head** **6**
	blow **to** *someone* **6** **7**

blown /bloʊn/ **Blown** is the past participle of **blow**. [from Old English]

blue /blu/ (**bluer, bluest, blues**)
1 **ADJ** Something that is **blue** is the color of the sky on a sunny day. ❑ *We looked up at the cloudless blue sky.* ❑ *She has pale blue eyes.*
2 **N-NONCOUNT** **Blue** is also a noun. ❑ *Julie and Angela wore blue.*
3 **N-PLURAL** MUSIC **The blues** is a type of slow, sad music that developed among African American musicians in the southern United States. ❑ *I grew up singing the blues at home with my mom.* [from Old French]
→ look at Picture Dictionary: **color**
→ look at Word Web: **rainbow**

blu|ish /bluɪʃ/ also **blueish** **ADJ** Something that is **bluish** is slightly blue in color. ❑ *...bluish-gray eyes.*

blunt /blʌnt/ (**blunter, bluntest**)
1 **ADJ** If you are **blunt**, you say exactly what you think and you do not try to be polite.
2 **ADJ** A **blunt** object is not sharp or pointed. ❑ *...a blunt pencil.* ❑ *The edge of his sword was as blunt as a butter knife.* [of Scandinavian origin]

blur /blɜr/ (**blurs, blurring, blurred**)
1 **N-COUNT** A **blur** is a shape or area which you cannot see clearly because it has no distinct outline or because it is moving very fast. ❑ *I saw a blur of movement on the other side of the glass door.*
2 **V-T/V-I** When a thing **blurs** or when something **blurs** it, you cannot see it clearly because its edges are no longer distinct. ❑ *Removing your eyeglasses blurs the image.*
3 **V-T** If something **blurs** an idea or a distinction between things, that idea or distinction no longer seems clear.

❑ *She constantly blurs the line between work, personal life, and love.*

blurred /blɜrd/
1 **ADJ** When a picture is **blurred**, it is not clear. ❑ *She showed me a blurred black and white photograph.*
2 **ADJ** If an idea or a distinction between things is **blurred**, that idea or distinction no longer seems clear. ❑ *The line between fact and fiction is becoming blurred.*

blush /blʌʃ/ (**blushes, blushing, blushed**)
V-I When you **blush**, your face becomes red because you are ashamed or embarrassed. ❑ *"Hello, Maria," he said, and she blushed again.* [from Old English]

board /bɔrd/ (**boards, boarding, boarded**)
1 **N-COUNT** A **board** is a flat, thin piece of wood. ❑ *There were wooden boards over the doors and windows.*
2 **N-COUNT** A **board** is a flat piece of wood or plastic that you use for a special purpose. ❑ *The picture was on the staff bulletin board.* ❑ *A wooden chopping board can be very heavy.*
3 **N-COUNT** The **board** of a company is the group of people who organize it and make decisions about it. ❑ *The board meets today, and it will announce its decision tomorrow.*
4 **V-T** When you **board** a train, a ship, or an aircraft, you get into it to travel somewhere. [FORMAL] ❑ *I boarded the plane to Boston.*
5 **PHRASE** When you are **on board** a train, a ship, or an aircraft, you are on it. ❑ *All 25 people on board the plane were killed.*
6 **PHRASE** If you **take on board** an idea or a problem, you begin to accept it or understand it. ❑ *We hope that they will take on board some of what you have said.* [from Old English]

Word Partnership	Use board with :
N	**cutting** board, **diving** board **2**
	bulletin board, **message** board **2**
	chair/member of the board, board **of**
	directors, board **meeting** **3**
	board **a flight/plane/ship** **4**

board|ing pass (**boarding passes**) **N-COUNT** A **boarding pass** is a card that a passenger must show when they are entering an aircraft or a boat.

boast /boʊst/ (**boasts, boasting, boasted**)
V-I If someone **boasts** about something that they have done or that they own, they talk about it too proudly, in a way that annoys

b

→ look at Picture Dictionary: **body**

Word Web   boat

People once used **boats** only for transportation. But today millions of people enjoy boating as a form of recreation. Weekend **captains** enjoy quietly **sailing** their **sailboats** along the shore. Other boaters like to ride around in **motorboats**. Any **rowboat** can become a motorboat just by attaching **motor** to the back. Fishermen usually like to use a rowboat with **oars**. That way they won't scare the fish away. For an even more peaceful ride, some people **paddle** around in **canoes**.

---

other people. ❏ *He boasted that the police would never catch him.* ❏ *Carol boasted about her new job.* [from French]

boat /boʊt/ (boats) **N-COUNT** A **boat** is a small ship. ❏ *One of the best ways to see the area is in a small boat.* ❏ *...a fishing boat.* [from Old English]
→ look at Word Webs: **boat, ship**

bob /bɒb/ (bobs, bobbing, bobbed) **V-I** If something **bobs**, it moves up and down, like something does when it is floating on water. ❏ *Huge balloons bobbed about in the sky above.*

body /bɒdi/ (bodies)
1 **N-COUNT** A person's or animal's **body** is all their physical parts. ❏ *Yoga creates a healthy mind in a healthy body.*
2 **N-COUNT** A person's or animal's **body** is the main part of them, but not their arms, head, and legs. ❏ *Lying flat on your back, twist your body onto one side.*
3 **N-COUNT** A **body** is a dead person or animal. ❏ *Two days later, her body was found in a wood.*
4 **N-COUNT** A **body** is an organized group of people who deal with something officially.

❏ *...the oldest governing body of amateur athletes in America.* [from Old English]
→ look at Picture Dictionary: **body**

body|guard /bɒdigɑrd/ (bodyguards) **N-COUNT** A **bodyguard** is a person whose job is to protect someone important. ❏ *Three of his bodyguards were injured in the attack.*

body image (body images) **N-COUNT/N-NONCOUNT** A person's **body image** is their perception of their physical appearance. Someone with a good body image thinks they are attractive, while someone with a poor body image thinks they are unattractive.

body position (body positions) **N-COUNT/N-NONCOUNT** ARTS An actor's **body position** is their posture at a particular point in a play or other theatrical production, for example whether they are sitting or standing.

bog /bɒg/ (bogs) **N-COUNT** A **bog** is an area of land that is very wet and muddy. [from Gaelic]

Picture Dictionary   body

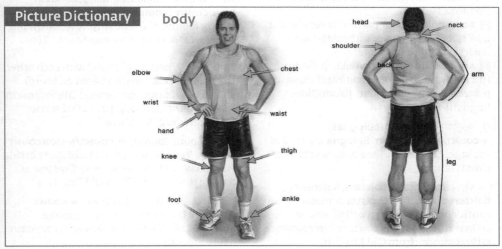

B

boil /bɔɪl/ (boils, boiling, boiled)

1 **V-T/V-I** When a hot liquid **boils**, bubbles appear in it and it starts to change into steam. ❑ *I stood in the kitchen, waiting for the water to boil.* ❑ *Boil the water in the saucepan and add the salt.*

boil

2 **V-T/V-I** When you **boil** food, you cook it in boiling water. ❑ *Wash and boil the rice.* ❑ *I peeled potatoes and put them in a pot to boil.*

3 **PHRASE** When you **bring** a liquid **to a boil**, you heat it until it boils. When it **comes to a boil**, it begins to boil. ❑ *Put the milk into a saucepan and bring it slowly to a boil.* [from Old French]

→ look at Picture Dictionaries: **cook, egg**

→ look at Word Webs: **tea, thermometer**

boiler|plate /bɔɪlərpleɪt/ (boilerplates)
N-COUNT/N-NONCOUNT A **boilerplate** is a basic written contract that can be used to make many different kinds of contracts. ❑ *...a predictable boilerplate of tax-relief proposals.*

boil|ing /bɔɪlɪŋ/ **ADJ** Something that is **boiling** or **boiling hot** is very hot. ❑ *"It's boiling in here," complained Miriam.* [from Old French]

boil|ing point **N-NONCOUNT** **SCIENCE** The **boiling point** of a liquid is the temperature at which it starts to change into steam.

bold /boʊld/ (bolder, boldest)

1 **ADJ** A **bold** action shows that you are not afraid to do dangerous things. ❑ *Their bold plan almost worked.*

2 **ADJ** A **bold** color or pattern is very bright. ❑ *Jill's dress was patterned with bold flowers in shades of red, blue, and white.*

3 **ADJ** **Bold** lines are printed in a darker, thicker way. ❑ *Find the definitions of the words printed in bold type in the text.* [from Old English]

bo|lo|gna /bəloʊni/ (bolognas)
N-COUNT/N-NONCOUNT **Bologna** is a type of sausage. ❑ *Would you like a bologna sandwich?* [from Italian]

bol|ster /boʊlstər/ (bolsters, bolstering, bolstered) **V-T** If you **bolster** someone's confidence or courage, you increase it. ❑ *The president is attempting to bolster confidence in the economy.* [from Old English]

bolt /boʊlt/ (bolts, bolting, bolted)

1 **N-COUNT** A **bolt** is a long piece of metal that you use with another small piece of metal with a hole in it called a nut to fasten things together. ❑ *Tighten any loose bolts and screws on your bicycle.*

2 **N-COUNT** A **bolt** on a door is a piece of metal that you move across to lock it.

3 **V-T** When you **bolt** a door, you move the bolt across to lock it. ❑ *He locked and bolted the kitchen door.* [from Old English]

→ look at Word Web: **lightning**

bomb /bɒm/ (bombs, bombing, bombed)

1 **N-COUNT** A **bomb** is a weapon that explodes and damages things nearby. ❑ *Bombs went off at two London train stations.* ❑ *The police do not know who planted the bomb.*

2 **V-T** When people **bomb** a place, they attack it with bombs. ❑ *Military airplanes bombed the airport.* ● **bomb|ing** (bombings) **N-COUNT/N-NONCOUNT** ❑ *The bombing of Pearl Harbor started World War II.* [from French]

Word Partnership	Use **bomb** with :	
ADJ	**atomic/nuclear** bomb, **live** bomb **1**	
N	bomb **blast, car** bomb, **pipe** bomb, bomb **shelter**, bomb **squad**, bomb **threat** **1**	
V	**drop/plant** a bomb, **set off** a bomb **1**	

bomb|er /bɒmər/ (bombers)

1 **N-COUNT** **Bombers** are people who cause bombs to explode in public places. ❑ *Detectives hunting the bombers will be eager to interview him.*

2 **N-COUNT** A **bomber** is a military aircraft which drops bombs. ❑ *...a high-speed bomber with twin engines.* [from French]

bond /bɒnd/ (bonds, bonding, bonded)

1 **N-COUNT** A **bond between** people is a strong feeling of friendship, love, or shared beliefs. ❑ *The experience created a special bond between us.*

2 **V-T/V-I** When people **bond with** each other, they form a relationship based on love or shared beliefs and experiences. ❑ *Belinda quickly bonded with her new baby.* [from Old Norse]

→ look at Word Web: **love**

bone /boʊn/ (bones) **N-COUNT/N-NONCOUNT** **SCIENCE** Your **bones** are the hard parts inside your body. ❑ *Many passengers suffered broken bones in the accident.* [from Old English]

bon|fire /bɒnfaɪər/ (bonfires) **N-COUNT** A **bonfire** is a large fire that you make outside. ❑ *Bonfires are not allowed in many areas.* [from French]

bo|nus /bo͟ʊnəs/ (**bonuses**)

1 **N-COUNT** A **bonus** is an extra amount of money that you earn, usually because you have worked very hard. ❑ *Each member of staff received a $100 bonus.*

2 **N-COUNT** A **bonus** is something good that you would not usually expect to get. ❑ *As a bonus you will also receive two free e-books.* [from Latin]

book /bʊ͟k/ (**books, booking, booked**)

1 **N-COUNT** LANGUAGE ARTS A **book** is a number of pieces of paper, usually with words printed on them, that are fastened together and fixed inside a cover. ❑ *Her second book was an immediate success.* ❑ *I just read a new book by Rosella Brown.*

2 **V-T** When you **book** a hotel room or a ticket, you arrange to have it or use it at a particular time. ❑ *Laurie booked a flight home.*

3 **N-PLURAL** BUSINESS An organization's **books** are its records of money that has been spent and earned. ❑ *He left the books to his accountant.* [from Old English]

→ look at Word Webs: **concert, library**

Word Partnership	Use **book** with :
N	**address** book, book **award, children's** book, book **club, comic** book, **copy of a** book, book **cover, phone** book, book **review, subject of a** book, **title of a** book **1**
ADJ	**latest/new/recent** book **1**
V	**publish** a book, **read** a book, **write** a book **1**

book|case /bʊ͟kkeɪs/ (**bookcases**) **N-COUNT** A **bookcase** is a piece of furniture with shelves that you keep books on.

Word Link	*let* ≈ *little* : book**let**, leaf**let**, pamph**let**

book|let /bʊ͟klɪt/ (**booklets**) **N-COUNT** A **booklet** is a very thin book that has a paper cover and that gives you information about something. ❑ *The travel office gave us a booklet about places to visit in Venice.*

Word Link	*mark* ≈ *boundary, sign* : book**mark**, land**mark**, trade**mark**

book|mark /bʊ͟kmɑrk/ (**bookmarks, bookmarking, bookmarked**)

1 **N-COUNT** TECHNOLOGY In computing, a **bookmark** is the address of a website that you add to a list on your computer so that you can return to it easily. ❑ *Use bookmarks to give you quick links to your favorite websites.*

2 **V-T** TECHNOLOGY **Bookmark** is also a verb. ❑ *Do you want to bookmark this page?*

book|store /bʊ͟kstɔr/ (**bookstores**) **N-COUNT** A **bookstore** is a store where books are sold.

boom /bu͟m/ (**booms, booming, boomed**)

1 **N-COUNT** If there is a **boom** in the economy, there is an increase in the number of things that people are buying. ❑ *...an economic boom.*

2 **V-T/V-I** When something **booms**, it makes a loud, deep sound. ❑ *"Ladies," boomed Helena, "we all know why we're here tonight."* ❑ *Thunder boomed over Crooked Mountain.*

3 **N-COUNT** **Boom** is also a noun. ❑ *We heard the boom of an explosion.* [from Dutch]

Thesaurus	**boom** Also look up :
V	flourish, prosper, succeed, thrive; (*ant.*) fail **1**
N	explosion, roar **2**

boor|ish /bʊ͟ərɪʃ/ **ADJ** **Boorish** behavior is rough and rude. ❑ *Karl's rude, boorish behavior was making their life unbearable.* [from Old English]

boost /bu͟st/ (**boosts, boosting, boosted**)

1 **V-T** If one thing **boosts** another, it causes it to increase, improve, or be more successful. ❑ *Lower prices will boost sales.*

2 **N-COUNT** **Boost** is also a noun. ❑ *The event would give the economy the boost that it needs.*

3 **V-T** If something **boosts** your confidence, it improves it. ❑ *If the team wins, it will boost their confidence.*

4 **N-COUNT** **Boost** is also a noun. ❑ *Scoring that goal gave me a real boost.*

boot /bu͟t/ (**boots, booting, booted**)

1 **N-COUNT** **Boots** are shoes that cover your whole foot and the lower part of your leg. ❑ *He sat down and took off his boots.*

2 **V-T/V-I** TECHNOLOGY If you **boot** a computer, you make it ready to start working. ❑ *Put the CD into the drive and boot the machine.* ❑ *The computer won't boot.*

boot

3 TECHNOLOGY **Boot up** means the same as **boot.** ❑ *Go over to your computer and boot it up.* [from Old French]

→ look at Picture Dictionaries: **clothing, shoe**

bor|der /bɔrdər/ (**borders, bordering, bordered**)

■ **N-COUNT** SOCIAL STUDIES The **border** between two countries is an imaginary line that divides them. ❑ *They drove across the border.* ❑ *Soldiers closed the border between the two countries.*

■ **V-T** A country that **borders** another country or a sea is next to it. ❑ *...the countries bordering the Mediterranean Sea.*

■ **N-COUNT** A **border** is a decoration around the edge of something. ❑ *The curtains were white with a red border.* [from Old French]

Thesaurus	border Also look up :
N	boundary, end, extremity, perimeter; *(ant.)* center, inside, middle ■

bore /bɔr/ (**bores, boring, bored**)

■ **V-T** Someone or something that **bores** you is not at all interesting. ❑ *Dick bored me with stories of his vacation.*

■ **Bore** is the past tense of **bear**.

bored /bɔrd/ **ADJ** If you are **bored**, you are not interested in something or you have nothing to do. ❑ *I am getting very bored with this television program.*

Word Link	dom ≈ state of being : bore**dom**, free**dom**, wis**dom**

bore|dom /bɔrdəm/ **N-NONCOUNT** Boredom is the state of being bored. ❑ *Students never complain of boredom when great teachers are teaching.* [from Old English]

bor|ing /bɔrɪŋ/ **ADJ** Someone or something that is **boring** is not at all interesting. ❑ *Washing dishes is boring work.*

Thesaurus	boring Also look up :
ADJ	dull, tedious; *(ant.)* exciting, fun, interesting, lively

born /bɔrn/

■ **V-T** When a baby **is born**, it comes out of its mother's body and begins life. ❑ *She was born in Milan on April 29, 1923.*

■ **ADJ** **Born** describes someone who has a natural ability to do a particular activity or job. ❑ *Jack was a born teacher.* [from Old English]

■ → see also **newborn**

borne /bɔrn/ **Borne** is the past participle of **bear**. [from Old English]

bor|ough /bɜrou/ (**boroughs**) **N-COUNT** A **borough** is a town, or a district within a large city, which has its own council, government, or local services. ❑ *...the New York City borough of Brooklyn.* [from Old English]

bor|row /bɒrou/ (**borrows, borrowing, borrowed**) **V-T** If you **borrow** something that belongs to someone else, you use it for a period of time and then return it. ❑ *Can I borrow a pen please?* [from Old English]

→ look at Word Web: **library**

Usage	borrow and lend

Borrow means "to take something while intending to give it back later": *Jiao borrowed Terry's cell phone and then lost it!* Lend means "to give something to someone while expecting to get it back later": *Terry will never lend anything to Jiao again!*

bor|row|er /bɒrouər/ (**borrowers**) **N-COUNT** A **borrower** is a person or an organization that borrows money. ❑ *Borrowers of more than $100,000 pay less interest.* [from Old English]

boss /bɒs/ (**bosses, bossing, bossed**) **N-COUNT** Your **boss** is the person in charge of you at the place where you work. ❑ *He likes his new boss.* [from Dutch]

▶ **boss around** If someone **bosses** you **around,** they keep telling you what to do in a way that is annoying. ❑ *No-one like to be bossed around or told what to do.*

Thesaurus	boss Also look up :
N	chief, director, employer, foreman, manager; *(ant.)* owner, superintendent, supervisor

bossy /bɒsi/ (**bossier, bossiest**) **ADJ** If someone is **bossy**, they enjoy telling people what to do. ❑ *Susan is a bossy little girl.* [from Dutch]

bota|ny /bɒtəni/ **N-NONCOUNT** SCIENCE **Botany** is the scientific study of plants. ● **bo|tani|cal** /bətænɪkᵊl/ **ADJ** ❑ *The area is of great botanical interest.*

both /bouθ/

■ **DET** You use **both** when you are saying that something is true about two people or things. ❑ *Stand up straight with both arms at your sides.* ❑ *Both men were taken to hospital.*

■ **PRON** **Both** is also a pronoun. ❑ *Miss Brown and her friend are both from Brooklyn.* ❑ *They both worked at Harvard University.* ❑ *Both of these women have strong memories of the war.* ❑ *Both of them have to go to London regularly.*

■ **CONJ** You use **both...and...** to show that each of two facts is true. ❑ *Now women work both before and after having their children.* [from Old Norse]

b

Usage both...and...

In sentences with *both...and...* use a plural verb: *Both the president and the vice president are Texans.*

both|er /bɒðər/ (**bothers, bothering, bothered**)

■ **V-T/V-I** If you do not **bother to** do something, you do not do it because you think it is not necessary. □ *Lots of people don't bother to get married these days.* □ *Nothing I do makes a difference, so why bother?*

■ **V-T** If something **bothers** you, it makes you feel worried or angry. □ *Is something bothering you?*

■ **V-T** If someone **bothers** you, they try to talk to you when you are busy. □ *I'm sorry to bother you, but there's someone here to speak to you.*

■ **PHRASE** If you **can't be bothered to** do something, you are not going to do it because you are feeling lazy. □ *I can't be bothered to clean the house.* [from Irish]

Word Link *some ≈ causing : awe*some, *bother*some, *lone*some

both|er|some /bɒðərsəm/ **ADJ** Someone or something that is **bothersome** is annoying or irritating. [OLD-FASHIONED] □ *...bothersome day-to-day problems.* [from Irish]

bot|tle /bɒtᵊl/ (**bottles**) **N-COUNT** A **bottle** is a glass or plastic container in which drinks and other liquids are kept. □ *There were two empty water bottles on the table.* □ *She drank half a bottle of apple juice.* [from Old French]
→ look at Picture Dictionary: **container**
→ look at Word Web: **glass**

bot|tom /bɒtəm/ (**bottoms**)

■ **N-COUNT** The **bottom of** something is the lowest or deepest part of it. □ *He sat at the bottom of the stairs.* □ *Answers can be found at the bottom of page 8.*

■ **ADJ** The **bottom** thing is the lowest one. □ *There are pencils in the bottom drawer of the desk.*

■ **N-SING** If someone is at **the bottom** in a class, a test, or a league, their performance is worse than that of all the other people involved. □ *He was always at the bottom of the class in school.*

■ **N-SING** The **bottom** of a river, a lake, or a sea is the ground under the water. □ *I leaned over the edge of my boat and looked down to the bottom of the sea.* [from Old English]

Thesaurus bottom Also look up :

N base, floor, foundation, ground; (*ant.*) peak, top ■

Word Partnership Use **bottom** with :

N bottom **of a hill**, bottom **of the page/ screen** ■
bottom **drawer**, bottom **of the pool**, bottom **of the sea** ■ ■
bottom **lip**, bottom **rung** ■

PREP **along the** bottom, **on the** bottom ■ ■
at/near the bottom ■–■

V **reach the** bottom, **sink to the** bottom ■ ■

bought /bɔt/ **Bought** is the past tense and past participle of **buy**. [from Old English]

boul|der /boʊldər/ (**boulders**) **N-COUNT** A **boulder** is a large round rock. □ *A passenger said that the train hit a boulder.* [of Scandinavian origin]

boule|vard /bʊləvɑrd/ (**boulevards**) **N-COUNT** A **boulevard** is a wide street in a city. □ *The shop was on Lenton Boulevard.* [from French]

bounce /baʊns/ (**bounces, bouncing, bounced**)

■ **V-T/V-I** When an object such as a ball **bounces**, it hits a surface and immediately moves away from it again. □ *The ball bounced across the floor.* □ *Matthew came into the kitchen bouncing a rubber ball.*

■ **V-I** If you **bounce** on a soft surface, you jump up and down on it. □ *Some children were playing soccer; others were riding scooters or bouncing on the trampoline.*

■ **V-I** If an email **bounces**, it is returned to the person who sent it because the address was wrong, or because of a problem with one of the computers involved in sending it.

■ **V-T/V-I** If a check **bounces** or if someone **bounces** it, the bank refuses to pay out the money, because the person who wrote it does not have enough money in their account. □ *Our only complaint would be if the check bounced.* [from Low German]

bound /baʊnd/ (**bounds, bounding, bounded**)

■ **Bound** is the past tense and past participle of **bind**.

■ **PHRASE** If something **is bound to** happen, it is certain to happen. □ *There are bound to be price increases next year.*

■ **V-I** If a person or animal **bounds** somewhere, they move quickly with large steps or jumps. □ *He bounded up the steps.*

■ **ADJ** If a vehicle or a person is **bound for** a

B

particular place, they are traveling toward it. ❑ *The ship was bound for Italy.* [Senses 1, 2, and 4 from Old Norse. Sense 3 from Old French.]

Word Partnership	Use **bound** with :
N	bound **by duty** **1**
ADV	**legally** bound, **tightly** bound **1**
V	bound **and gagged** **1**
	bound **to fail** **2**
N	**feet/hands/wrists** bound, **leather** bound, bound **with tape** **1**
	a flight/plane/ship/train bound **for** **3**

bounda|ry /ba͞undəri, -dri/ (**boundaries**)
1 N-COUNT The **boundary of** an area of land is an imaginary line that separates it from other areas. ❑ *The river forms the western boundary of my farm.*
2 N-COUNT LANGUAGE ARTS A **boundary** is a division between one word and another or between the different parts of a word. [from Old French]

Word Partnership	Use **boundary** with :
PREP	boundary **around places/things**, boundary **between places/things**, **beyond a** boundary, boundary **of** *someplace/something*
V	**cross a** boundary, **mark/set a** boundary
N	boundary **dispute**, boundary **line**

bou|quet /bo͞ukeɪ, bu-/ (**bouquets**) **N-COUNT**
A **bouquet** is a bunch of flowers that have been cut. ❑ *The woman carried a bouquet of roses.* [from French]

bout /ba͞ut/ (**bouts**)
1 N-COUNT If you have a **bout of** an illness, you have it for a short period. ❑ *He was recovering from a severe bout of flu.*
2 N-COUNT A **bout of** something that is unpleasant is a short time during which it occurs a great deal. ❑ *...the latest bout of violence.* [from German]

bou|tique /buti͞k/ (**boutiques**) **N-COUNT**
A **boutique** is a small store that sells fashionable clothes, shoes, or jewelry. [from French]

bow
❶ BENDING
❷ OBJECTS

❶ **bow** /ba͞u/ (**bows, bowing, bowed**)
1 V-I When you **bow to** someone, you bend your head or body toward them as a formal

way of greeting them or showing respect. ❑ *They bowed low to the king.*
2 N-COUNT Bow is also a noun. ❑ *I gave a theatrical bow and waved.*
3 V-T If you **bow** your head, you bend it downward so that you are looking toward the ground. ❑ *The colonel bowed his head and whispered a prayer.* [from Old English]

❷ **bow** /bo͞u/ (**bows**)
1 N-COUNT A **bow** is a knot with two round parts and two loose ends that is used in tying laces and ribbons. ❑ *Add some ribbon tied in a bow.*
2 N-COUNT A **bow** is a weapon for shooting arrows. ❑ *Some of the men were armed with bows and arrows.*
3 N-COUNT MUSIC The **bow** of a violin or other similar instrument is a long thin piece of wood with threads stretched along it that you move across the strings. [from Old English]

bow|el /ba͞uəl/ (**bowels**) **N-COUNT** SCIENCE
Your **bowels** are the tubes in your body where digested food from your stomach is stored before you pass it from your body. ❑ *Eating fruit and vegetables can help to keep your bowels healthy.* [from Old French]

bowl /bo͞ul/ (**bowls, bowling, bowled**)
1 N-COUNT A **bowl** is a round container that is used for mixing and serving food. ❑ *Put the soup in a bowl.*

bowl

2 V-T/V-I In a sport such as bowling, when a person **bowls**, or **bowls** a ball, he or she rolls the ball down a narrow track. [Sense 1 from Old English. Sense 2 from French.]
→ look at Picture Dictionaries: **dish, utensil**

bowl|ing /bo͞ulɪŋ/ **N-NONCOUNT Bowling** is a game in which you roll a heavy ball down a narrow track toward a group of wooden objects and try to knock down as many of them as possible. ❑ *We go bowling every Saturday afternoon.* [from French]

box /bɒks/ (**boxes, boxing, boxed**)
1 N-COUNT A **box** is a container with a hard bottom, hard sides, and usually a lid. ❑ *He packed his books into the cardboard box beside him.* ❑ *They sat on wooden boxes.*
2 N-COUNT A **box** is a square shape that is printed on paper. ❑ *For more information, just check the box and send us the form.*

3 **V-I** SPORTS To **box** means to fight someone according to the rules of boxing. ❑ *At school I boxed and played baseball.* ● **box|er** (**boxers**) **N-COUNT** ❑ *He wants to be a professional boxer.* [from Old English]

box|ing /bɒksɪŋ/ **N-NONCOUNT** SPORTS **Boxing** is a sport in which two people fight following special rules. [from Old English]

box of|fice (**box offices**) also **box-office** **N-COUNT** The **box office** in a theater or a concert hall is the place where the tickets are sold. ❑ *There was a long line of people outside the box office.*

box plot (**box plots**) or **box-and-whisker plot**, **box-and-whisker chart** **N-COUNT** SCIENCE A **box plot** is a graph that shows the distribution of a set of data by using the middle fifty percent of the data.

boy /bɔɪ/ (**boys**)
1 **N-COUNT** A **boy** is a male child. ❑ *Did you have any pets when you were a little boy?*
2 **N-COUNT** You can refer to a young man as a **boy**, especially when talking about relationships between men and women. ❑ *Our guide was a nice Canadian boy.* [from Latin]

boy|cott /bɔɪkɒt/ (**boycotts, boycotting, boycotted**)
1 **V-T** SOCIAL STUDIES If you **boycott** a country, an organization, or an activity, you refuse to be involved with it, because you disapprove of it. ❑ *Some groups threatened to boycott the meeting.*
2 **N-COUNT** SOCIAL STUDIES **Boycott** is also a noun. ❑ *The boycott of British beef was finally lifted in June.* [from Irish]

boy|friend /bɔɪfrɛnd/ (**boyfriends**) **N-COUNT** A **boyfriend** of a woman or a girl is a man or a boy that she is having a romantic relationship with. ❑ *Brenda came with her boyfriend, Anthony.*

Boyle's law /bɔɪlz lɔ/ **N-NONCOUNT** SCIENCE **Boyle's law** is a law in physics which describes the relationship between the pressure of a gas and its volume. [from Irish]

bra /brɑ/ (**bras**) **N-COUNT** A **bra** is a piece of underwear that women wear to support their breasts. [from French]

brace /breɪs/ (**braces, bracing, braced**)
1 **V-T** If you **brace yourself for** something unpleasant or difficult, you prepare yourself for it. ❑ *He braced himself for the icy dive into the black water.*
2 **V-T** If you **brace yourself against** something or **brace** part of your body **against** it, you press against something in order to steady your body or to avoid falling. ❑ *Elaine braced herself against the table.*
3 **N-COUNT** A **brace** is a device attached to a part of a person's body to strengthen or support it. ❑ *They make wheelchairs and leg braces for children.*
4 **N-PLURAL** **Braces** are a metal device that can be fastened to a person's teeth in order to help them grow straight. ❑ *I used to have to wear braces.* [from Old French]
→ look at Word Web: **teeth**

brace|let /breɪslɪt/ (**bracelets**) **N-COUNT** A **bracelet** is a piece of jewelry that you wear around your wrist. [from Old French]
→ look at Picture Dictionary: **jewelry**

brack|et /brækɪt/ (**brackets**) **N-COUNT** LANGUAGE ARTS **Brackets** are curved ( ) or square [ ] marks that you can place around words, letters, or numbers when you are writing. ❑ *There's a telephone number in brackets under his name.* [from Old French]

brag /bræg/ (**brags, bragging, bragged**) **V-T/V-I** If you **brag**, you annoy people by proudly saying that you have something or have done something. ❑ *He's always bragging about winning the gold medal.* ❑ *He's always bragging that he's a great artist.*

braid /breɪd/ (**braids, braiding, braided**)
1 **V-T** You **braid** hair when you twist three lengths of it together. ❑ *She braided Louisa's hair with a red ribbon.*
2 **N-COUNT** A **braid** is a length of hair that has been twisted in this way. ❑ *Kelly wore her hair in two braids.* [from Old English]
→ look at Picture Dictionary: **hair**

brain /breɪn/ (**brains**)
1 **N-COUNT** SCIENCE Your **brain** is the organ inside your head that controls your body's activities and allows you to think and to feel things.
2 **N-COUNT** Your **brain** is your mind and the way that you think. ❑ *Sports are good for your brain as well as your body.*
3 **N-COUNT** If someone has **brains**, they have the ability to learn and understand things quickly. ❑ *Scientists need brains and imagination.* [from Old English]
→ look at Word Webs: **brain, nervous system**

B

Word Web   brain

The human **brain** weighs about three pounds. It has seven different parts. The largest are the cerebrum, the cerebellum, and the medulla oblongata. The cerebrum wraps around the outside of the brain. It handles **learning**, **communication**, and voluntary **movement**. The cerebellum controls **balance**, **posture**, and movement. The medulla oblongata joins the **spinal cord** with other parts of the brain. This part of the brain controls those actions that happen without us knowing, such as breathing, heartbeat, and swallowing. It also tells us when we are hungry and when we need to sleep.

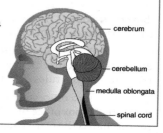

cerebrum

cerebellum

medulla oblongata

spinal cord

brake /breɪk/ (**brakes, braking, braked**)

1 **N-COUNT** **Brakes** are the parts in a vehicle that make it go slower or stop. ❑ *He stepped on the brakes as the light turned red.*

2 **V-T/V-I** When the driver of a vehicle **brakes**, he or she makes it slow down or stop. ❑ *The driver braked to avoid an accident.* ❑ *He braked the car slightly.* [from Middle Dutch]

Usage   brake and break

Brake and *break* sound the same, but they have very different meanings. You step on the *brake* to make your car slow down or stop: *Sometimes, Nayana steps on the accelerator when she means to step on the brake.* If you *break* something, you damage it: *I learned something today—if your laptop falls off your desk, it will probably break!*

branch /bræntʃ/ (**branches, branching, branched**)

1 **N-COUNT** The **branches** of a tree are the parts that have leaves, flowers, and fruit. ❑ *We picked apples from the upper branches of a tree.*

2 **N-COUNT** A **branch of** a business or an organization is one of the offices, stores, or groups that belong to it. ❑ *The local branch of the bank is handling the accounts.*

3 **N-COUNT** A **branch of** a subject is a part of it. ❑ *Astronomy is a branch of science.* [from Old French]

▶ **branch out** If a person or an organization **branches out**, they do something that is different from their normal activities. ❑ *They started as the leading maker of TVs, and then branched out into various other electrical goods.*

brand /brænd/ (**brands**) **N-COUNT** A **brand** is the name of a product that a particular company makes. ❑ *The store did not sell my favorite brand of cookies.* [from Old English]

brand-new **ADJ** A **brand-new** object is completely new. ❑ *Yesterday he bought a brand-new car.*

bran|dy /brændi/ (**brandies**) **N-COUNT/ N-NONCOUNT** **Brandy** is a strong alcoholic drink that is made from wine. [from Dutch]

brass /bræs/

1 **N-NONCOUNT** **Brass** is a yellow-colored metal. ❑ *Ritchie lifted the shiny brass door knocker.*

2 **N-NONCOUNT** MUSIC **Brass** is musical instruments that are made of brass. ❑ *...a piece of music for brass.*

3 **N-NONCOUNT** MUSIC The **brass** is all the musical instruments in an orchestra that are made of brass. ❑ *Suddenly the brass comes in with great power and intensity.* [from Old English]

→ look at Word Web: **orchestra**

brave /breɪv/ (**braver, bravest, braves, braving, braved**)

1 **ADJ** Someone who is **brave** is willing to do things that are dangerous, and does not show fear in dangerous situations. ❑ *A brave 12-year-old boy tried to help his friends.* ● **brave|ly** **ADV** ❑ *The army fought bravely.*

2 **V-T** If you **brave** unpleasant conditions, you deal with them in order to achieve something. [WRITTEN] ❑ *Thousands have braved icy rain to show their support.* [from French]

→ look at Word Web: **hero**

brav|ery /breɪvəri, breɪvri/ **N-NONCOUNT** **Bravery** is the ability to do things that are dangerous without showing fear. ❑ *He received an award for his bravery.* [from French]

breach /briːtʃ/ (**breaches, breaching, breached**)

1 **V-T** If you **breach** an agreement, a law, or a promise, you break it. ❑ *The newspaper breached the rules on privacy.*

2 **N-COUNT/N-NONCOUNT** A **breach of** an agreement, a law, or a promise is an act of breaking it. ❑ *Their actions are a breach of contract.*

3 **N-COUNT** A **breach in** a relationship is a serious disagreement which often results in the relationship ending. [FORMAL] ❑ *...a serious breach in relations between the two countries.*

4 **v-t** If someone or something **breaches** a barrier, they make an opening in it, usually leaving it weakened or destroyed. [FORMAL] ❑ *Tree roots have breached the roof of the cave.*

5 **v-t** If you **breach** security, you manage to get through and attack an area that is heavily guarded and protected. ❑ *The bomber breached security by hurling his dynamite from a roof.*

6 **N-COUNT** Breach is also a noun. ❑ *...serious breaches of security.* [from Old English]

bread /brɛd/ **N-NONCOUNT** Bread is a food made mostly from flour and water. ❑ *She bought a loaf of bread at the store.* ❑ *I usually just have bread and butter for breakfast.* [from Old English]
→ look at Picture Dictionary: **bread**

break /breɪk/ (**breaks, breaking, broke, broken**)

1 **v-i** When something **breaks**, it suddenly separates into pieces, often because someone has hit it or dropped it. ❑ *The plate broke.* ❑ *The plane broke into three pieces.*

2 **v-t** When you **break** something, you make it separate into two or more pieces, often because you have dropped it or hit it. ❑ *I'm sorry. I've broken a glass.*

3 **v-t/v-i** If you **break** a part of your body, or a part of your body **breaks**, a bone cracks in it. ❑ *She broke her leg in a skiing accident.* ❑ *Old bones break easily.*

4 **N-COUNT** Break is also a noun. ❑ *Gabriella had a bad break in her leg.*

5 **v-t/v-i** When a machine **breaks**, it no longer works. ❑ *The cable on the elevator broke, and it crashed to the ground.* ❑ *My cell phone broke last night.*

6 **N-COUNT** A **break** is a short period of time when you have a rest. ❑ *We get a 15-minute break for coffee.*

7 **N-COUNT** A **break** is a short vacation from school or work. ❑ *His college friends went to Miami for their spring break.*

8 **v-i** If someone **breaks for** a short period of time, they rest for a that period. ❑ *They broke for lunch.*

9 **v-t** If you **break** a rule, a promise, or the law, you do something that you should not do. ❑ *We didn't know we were breaking the law.* ❑ *No more lies and broken promises.*

10 **v-t** When you **break** a piece of bad news to someone, you tell it to them. ❑ *Then Louise broke the news that she was leaving me.*

11 **v-t** If you **break** a record, you beat the previous record for a particular achievement. ❑ *Lewis has broken the world record in the 100 meters.* [from Old English]
→ look at Usage notes at **brake, tear**
→ look at Word Webs: **crash, factory**

▶ **break down** **1** If a machine or a vehicle **breaks down**, it stops working. ❑ *Their car broke down.*

2 If someone **breaks down**, they start crying. ❑ *I broke down and cried.*

3 → see also **breakdown**

▶ **break in** **1** If someone **breaks in**, they get into a building by force. ❑ *The robbers broke in and stole $8,000.*

2 → see also **break-in**

▶ **break into** If someone **breaks into** a building, they get into it by force. ❑ *There was someone trying to break into the house.*

▶ **break off** If you **break** a part of something **off**, you remove it by breaking it.

Picture Dictionary   bread

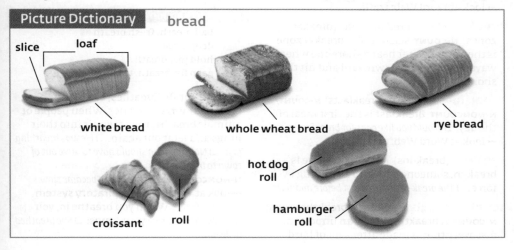

slice

loaf

white bread

whole wheat bread

rye bread

hot dog roll

croissant   roll

hamburger roll

b

❏ *Grace broke off a large piece of bread.*
▶ **break out** ◼ If something **breaks out**, it begins suddenly. ❏ *He was 29 when war broke out.*
◻ If your face **breaks out**, red spots appear on your skin. ❏ *I tend to break out when I get nervous.*
▶ **break through** If you **break through** something, you succeed in forcing your way through it. ❏ *Protesters tried to break through a police barricade.*
▶ **break up** If you **break up with** someone, your relationship with that person ends. ❏ *My girlfriend has broken up with me.*

Word Partnership	Use **break** with :
N	break **a bone**, break **your arm/leg/ neck** ◼ **coffee/lunch** break ◻ break **the law**, break **a promise**, break **a rule** ◻
V	break **a record** ◻ **need a** break, **take a** break ◻

break|down /brˈeɪkdaʊn/ (**breakdowns**)
◼ **N-COUNT** The **breakdown of** a relationship, a plan, or a discussion is its failure. ❏ *Newspapers reported the breakdown of talks between the U.S. and European Union officials.* ❏ *Arguments about money led to the breakdown of their marriage.*
◻ **N-COUNT** If you have a **breakdown**, you become extremely unhappy, so that you are unable to cope with your life. ❏ *My mother died, and a couple of years later I had a nervous breakdown.*
◻ **N-COUNT** If a car or a piece of machinery has a **breakdown**, it stops working. ❏ *You should be prepared for breakdowns and accidents.*
→ look at Word Web: **traffic**

break|er zone /brˈeɪkər zoʊn/ (**breaker zones**) **N-COUNT** SCIENCE The **breaker zone** is the area of water near a shoreline where waves begin to fall downward and hit the shore.

break|fast /brˈɛkfəst/ (**breakfasts**) **N-COUNT/ N-NONCOUNT** Breakfast is the first meal of the day. ❏ *Would you like eggs for breakfast?*
→ look at Word Web: **meal**

break-in (**break-ins**) **N-COUNT** If there is a **break-in**, someone gets into a building by force. ❏ *The break-in occurred just before midnight.*

break|through /brˈeɪkθru/ (**breakthroughs**) **N-COUNT** A **breakthrough** is an important discovery that is made after a lot of hard

work. ❏ *The scientist described a medical breakthrough in cancer treatment.*

break|up /brˈeɪkʌp/ (**breakups**) **N-COUNT** The **breakup of** a marriage, a relationship, or an association is its end. ❏ *...the sudden breakup of the meeting.*

breast /brˈɛst/ (**breasts**)
◼ **N-COUNT** SCIENCE A woman's **breasts** are the two soft, round parts on her chest that can produce milk to feed a baby.
◻ **N-COUNT/N-NONCOUNT** A **breast** is a piece of meat that is cut from the front of a bird. ❏ *For dinner I cooked chicken breast with vegetables.* [from Old English]

breast|stroke /brˈɛststroʊk/ **N-NONCOUNT** SPORTS **Breaststroke** is a way of swimming in which you pull both of your arms back at the same time, and kick your legs with your knees bent. ❏ *I'm learning to swim breaststroke.*

breath /brˈɛθ/ (**breaths**)
◼ **N-COUNT/N-NONCOUNT** Your **breath** is the air that you let out through your mouth when you breathe. ❏ *His breath smelled of onion.*
◻ **N-COUNT/N-NONCOUNT** When you take a **breath**, you breathe in once. ❏ *He took a deep breath, and began to climb the stairs.*
◻ **PHRASE** If you are **out of breath**, you are breathing very quickly because your body has been working hard. ❏ *She was out of breath from running.*
◻ **PHRASE** If you **hold your breath**, you breathe air into your lungs and you do not let it out for a period of time. ❏ *Hold your breath for a moment and then exhale.* [from Old English]

Word Partnership	Use **breath** with :
ADJ	**bad** breath, **fresh** breath ◼ **deep** breath ◻
V	**hold** *your* breath ◻ **gasp for** breath, **take a** breath ◻

breathe /brˈið/ (**breathes, breathing, breathed**) **V-T/V-I** SCIENCE When people or animals **breathe**, they take air into their lungs and let it out again. ❏ *He was breathing fast.* ❏ *No American should have to drive out of town to breathe clean air.* ● **breath|ing** **N-NONCOUNT** ❏ *Her breathing became slow.*
→ look at Word Web: **respiratory system**
▶ **breathe in** When you **breathe in**, you take some air into your lungs. ❏ *She breathed in deeply.*

▶ **breathe out** When you **breathe out**, you send air out of your lungs through your nose or mouth. ❏ *Breathe out and bring your knees in toward your chest.*

breath|less /brɛθlɪs/ **ADJ** If you are **breathless**, you have difficulty in breathing properly, because you have been running, for example. ❏ *I was breathless after the race.* [from Old English]

breed /brid/ (**breeds, breeding, bred**)
■ **N-COUNT** SCIENCE A **breed** of animal is a particular type of it. ❏ *There are about 300 breeds of horse.*
■ **V-T** SCIENCE If you **breed** animals or plants, you produce more animals or plants with the same qualities. ❏ *He breeds dogs for the police.* ● **breed|ing** **N-NONCOUNT** ❏ *They are involved in the breeding of guide dogs for blind people.*
■ **V-I** SCIENCE When animals **breed**, they produce babies. ❏ *Birds usually breed in the spring.* ● **breed|ing** **N-NONCOUNT** ❏ *During the breeding season the birds come ashore.* [from Old English]
→ look at Word Web: **zoo**

breeze /briz/ (**breezes**) **N-COUNT** A **breeze** is a gentle wind. ❏ *We enjoyed the cool summer breeze.* [from Old Spanish]
→ look at Word Web: **wind**

brev|ity /brɛvɪti/ **N-NONCOUNT** The **brevity** of something is the fact that it is short or lasts for only a short time. [FORMAL] ❏ *...the brevity of human existence.* [from Latin]

brew /bru/ (**brews, brewing, brewed**)
■ **V-T** If you **brew** tea or coffee, you make it by pouring hot water over tea leaves or ground coffee. ❏ *He brewed a pot of coffee.*
■ **N-COUNT** A **brew** is a particular kind of tea or coffee. It can also be a pot of tea or coffee.

❏ *She swallowed a mouthful of the hot strong brew.*
■ **V-T** If someone **brews** beer, they make it. ❏ *I brew my own beer.*
■ **V-I** If an unpleasant or difficult situation **is brewing**, it is starting to develop. ❏ *At home a crisis was brewing.* [from Old English]
→ look at Word Web: **tea**

bribe /braɪb/ (**bribes, bribing, bribed**)
■ **N-COUNT** A **bribe** is money or something valuable that one person offers to another in order to persuade them to do something. ❏ *The police took bribes from criminals.*
■ **V-T** If one person **bribes** another, they offer them money or something valuable in order to persuade them to do something. ❏ *He was accused of bribing a bank official.* [from Old French]

brib|ery /braɪbəri/ **N-NONCOUNT** **Bribery** is the act of offering someone money or something valuable in order to persuade them to do something for you. ❏ *He was arrested for bribery.* [from Old French]

brick /brɪk/ (**bricks**) **N-COUNT/N-NONCOUNT** **Bricks** are rectangular blocks used for building walls. ❏ *...a brick wall.* [from Old French]

bride /braɪd/ (**brides**) **N-COUNT** A **bride** is a woman who is getting married. [from Old English]
→ look at Word Web: **wedding**

brides|maid /braɪdzmeɪd/ (**bridesmaids**) **N-COUNT** A **bridesmaid** is a woman or a girl who helps the bride on her wedding day. [from Old English]
→ look at Word Web: **wedding**

bridge /brɪdʒ/ (**bridges, bridging, bridged**)
■ **N-COUNT** A **bridge** is a structure that is built over a river or a road so that people or vehicles can cross from one side to the other.

Word Web   bridge

The world's longest **suspension bridge** is the Akashi Kaikyo Bridge. It is 6,570 feet long and over 900 feet tall. It can withstand an 8.5 magnitude earthquake. Another famous **span**, the Brooklyn Bridge in New York City, dates from 1883. It was the first suspension bridge to use **steel** for its **cable** wire. More than 120,000 vehicles still use the bridge every day. The Evergreen Point Floating Bridge near Seattle, Washington, floats on **pontoons**. It's over a mile long. During windy weather the **drawbridge** in the middle must stay open to protect the bridge from damage.

B

❑ *He walked over the bridge to get to school.*

2 **v-t** To **bridge** the gap between two people or things means to reduce the difference between them. ❑ *These colleges can bridge the gap between high school and university.* [from Old English]

→ look at Word Web: **bridge**

brief /brif/ (**briefer, briefest, briefs**)

1 **ADJ** Something that is **brief** lasts for only a short time. ❑ *She once made a brief appearance on television.*

2 **ADJ** A **brief** speech or piece of writing does not contain many words or details. ❑ *The book begins with a brief description of his career.*

3 **N-PLURAL** Men's or women's underpants are sometimes called **briefs.** ❑ *...a pair of briefs.* [from Old French]

Word Partnership	Use brief with :
N	brief **appearance**, brief **conversation**, brief **pause** **1**
	brief **description**, brief **explanation**, brief **history**, brief **speech**, brief **statement** **2**

brief|case /brifkeɪs/ (**briefcases**) **N-COUNT** A **briefcase** is a small suitcase for carrying business papers in.

brief|ing /brifɪŋ/ (**briefings**) **N-COUNT/N-NONCOUNT** A **briefing** is a meeting at which information or instructions are given to people. ❑ *They're holding a press briefing tomorrow.* [from Old French]

brief|ly /brifli/
1 **ADV** Something that happens **briefly** happens for a very short period of time. ❑ *He smiled briefly.*

2 **ADV** If you say or write something **briefly**, you use very few words or give very few details. ❑ *There are four basic choices; they are described briefly below.* [from Old French]

bri|gade /brɪgeɪd/ (**brigades**) **N-COUNT** A **brigade** is one of the groups that an army is divided into. ❑ *...the soldiers of the 173rd Airborne Brigade.* [from Old French]

bright /braɪt/ (**brighter, brightest**)
1 **ADJ** A **bright** color is strong and noticeable. ❑ *She wore a bright red dress.*

2 **ADJ** A **bright** light is shining strongly. ❑ *He looked pale and tired under the bright lights of the TV studio.* ● **bright|ly** **ADV** ❑ *The sun shone brightly in the sky.* ● **bright|ness** **N-NONCOUNT**

❑ *An astronomer can determine the brightness of each star.*

3 **ADJ** A **bright** place is full of light. ❑ *There was a bright room where patients could sit with their visitors.*

4 **ADJ** If someone is **bright**, they learn things quickly. ❑ *He seems brighter than most boys.*

5 **ADJ** If the future is **bright**, it is likely to be pleasant or successful. ❑ *Both had successful careers and the future looked bright.* [from Old English]

bright|en /braɪtᵊn/ (**brightens, brightening, brightened**)
1 **v-i** If someone **brightens**, they suddenly look happier. ❑ *Seeing him, she seemed to brighten a little.*

2 **v-t** If someone or something **brightens** a place, they make it more colorful and attractive. ❑ *Pots planted with flowers brightened the area outside the door.* [from Old English]

bril|liant /brɪlyənt/
1 **ADJ** A **brilliant** person, idea, or performance is very clever or skillful. ❑ *She had a brilliant mind.* ● **bril|liant|ly** **ADV** ❑ *The movie was brilliantly written and acted.* ● **bril|liance** **N-NONCOUNT** ❑ *Mozart showed his brilliance at an early age.*

2 **ADJ** A **brilliant** light or color is extremely bright. ❑ *The woman had brilliant green eyes.* [from French]

brim /brɪm/ (**brims**) **N-COUNT** The **brim** of a hat is the part that sticks out around the bottom. ❑ *Rain dripped from the brim of his old hat.* [from Middle High German]

bring /brɪŋ/ (**brings, bringing, brought**)
1 **v-t** If you **bring** someone or something **with** you when you come to a place, you have them with you. ❑ *Remember to bring an old shirt to wear when we paint.* ❑ *Can I bring Susie to the party?*

2 **v-t** If you **bring** something that someone wants, you get it for them. ❑ *He poured a glass of milk for Dena and brought it to her.*

3 **v-t** If something **brings** a particular feeling, situation, or quality, it makes people experience it or have it. ❑ *Her three children brought her much joy.*

4 **v-t** If you cannot **bring yourself to** do something, you cannot do it because you find it too upsetting, embarrassing, or disgusting. ❑ *It is all very sad and I just cannot bring myself to talk about it.* [from Old English]

b

▶ **bring along** If you **bring** someone or something **along**, you bring them with you when you come to a place. ❑ *They brought baby Michael along in a stroller.*

▶ **bring back** When you **bring** something **back**, you return it. ❑ *Please could you bring back those books that I lent you?*

▶ **bring in** ■ When a government or an organization **brings in** a new law or system, they introduce it. ❑ *The government brought in a law under which it could take any land it wanted.* ■ Someone or something that **brings in** money earns it. ❑ *My job brings in about $24,000 a year.*

▶ **bring out** When a person or a company **brings out** a new product, they produce it and put it on sale. ❑ *He's just brought out a new book.*

▶ **bring up** ■ When someone **brings up** a child, they take care of it until it is an adult. ❑ *She brought up four children.* ❑ *He was brought up in Nebraska.* ■ If you **bring up** a particular subject, you introduce it into a conversation. ❑ *Her mother brought up the subject of going back to work.*

Thesaurus	**bring** Also look up :
V	accompany, bear, carry, take; *(ant.)* drop, leave ■

Word Partnership	Use **bring** with :
N	bring **bad/good luck**, bring *something/ someone* **home** ■

brink /brɪŋk/ **N-SING** If you are **on the brink of** something important, terrible, or exciting, you are just about to do it or experience it. ❑ *Their economy is on the brink of collapse.* [from Middle Dutch]

brisk /brɪsk/ (**brisker, briskest**) **ADJ** A **brisk** activity or action is done quickly and with energy. ❑ *He gave me a brisk handshake.* ● **brisk|ly** **ADV** ❑ *Eve walked briskly through the park.*

bris|tle /brɪsəl/ (**bristles**) ■ **N-COUNT** **Bristles** are the short hairs that grow on a man's face. ■ **N-COUNT** The **bristles** of a brush are the thick hairs on it. [from Old English]

brit|tle /brɪtəl/ **ADJ** Something that is **brittle** is hard but easily broken. ❑ *I have very brittle finger nails.* [from Old English]

broad /brɔd/ (**broader, broadest**) ■ **ADJ** Something that is **broad** is wide. ❑ *His shoulders were broad and his waist was narrow.*

■ **ADJ** A **broad** smile is a big, happy smile. ❑ *He greeted them with a wave and a broad smile.* ■ **ADJ** **Broad** means including a large number of different things. ❑ *The library had a broad range of books.* [from Old English]

Word Partnership	Use **broad** with :
N	broad **expanse**, broad **shoulders** ■ broad **smile** ■ broad **range**, broad **spectrum** ■

broad|band /brɔdbænd/ **N-NONCOUNT** TECHNOLOGY **Broadband** is a method of sending many electronic messages at the same time over the Internet. ❑ *They've announced big price cuts for broadband customers.*

broad|cast /brɔdkæst/ (**broadcasts, broadcasting, broadcast**)

> LANGUAGE HELP
> The form **broadcast** is used in the present tense and is the past tense and past participle of the verb.

■ **N-COUNT** A **broadcast** is a program, a performance, or a speech on the radio or on television. ❑ *We saw a live television broadcast of Saturday's football game.* ■ **V-T/V-I** To **broadcast** a program means to send it out so that it can be heard on the radio or seen on television. ❑ *The concert will be broadcast live on television and radio.* ❑ *CNN also broadcasts in Europe.*

broad|cast|er /brɔdkæstər/ (**broadcasters**) **N-COUNT** A **broadcaster** is someone who gives talks or takes part in interviews and discussions on radio or television programs. ❑ *...the naturalist and broadcaster, Sir David Attenborough.*

broad|en /brɔdən/ (**broadens, broadening, broadened**) ■ **V-I** When something **broadens**, it becomes wider. ❑ *The trails broadened into roads.* ■ **V-T/V-I** When you **broaden** something or when it **broadens**, the number of things or people that it includes becomes greater. ❑ *We must broaden our appeal.* ❑ *Gradually the fair has broadened to include big London dealers.* [from Old English]

broad|ly /brɔdli/ **ADV** You can use **broadly** to indicate that something is generally true. ❑ *The president broadly got what he wanted out of his meeting.* [from Old English]

broc|co|li /brɒkəli, brɒkli/ **N-NONCOUNT** **Broccoli** is a vegetable with thick green stems

and small green flowers on top. [from Italian]
→ look at Picture Dictionary: **vegetable**

bro|chure /broʊʃʊər/ (brochures) **N-COUNT**
A **brochure** is a thin magazine with pictures
that gives you information about a product
or a service. ❑ *The city looked beautiful in the*
travel brochures. [from French]

broil /brɔɪl/ (broils, broiling, broiled) **V-T**
When you **broil** food, you cook it using very
strong heat directly above it. ❑ *I'll broil the*
hamburgers. [from Old French]

broke /broʊk/
■ **Broke** is the past tense of **break**.
■ **ADJ** If you are **broke**, you have no money.
[INFORMAL] ❑ *I don't have a job, and I'm broke.*
[from Old English]

bro|ken /broʊkən/
■ **Broken** is the past participle of **break**.
■ **ADJ** Something that is **broken** is in pieces.
❑ *She was taken to hospital with a broken leg.*
❑ *...a broken window.* [from Old English]

bro|ker /broʊkər/ (brokers, brokering,
brokered)
■ **N-COUNT** BUSINESS A **broker** is a person
whose job is to buy and sell securities,
foreign money, real estate, or goods for
other people.
■ **V-T** If a country or a government **brokers**
an agreement, a ceasefire, or a round of talks,
they try to negotiate or arrange it. ❑ *The UN*
brokered a peace agreement in March. [from Old
Northern French]

bro|mance /broʊmæns/ (bromances)
N-COUNT A **bromance** is a very close
friendship between two men. ❑ *The two men*
continued their bromance with a trip to the theater.

bron|chi /brɒŋki, -kaɪ/ **N-PLURAL** SCIENCE
The **bronchi** are the two large tubes in your
body that connect your windpipe to your
lungs. [from New Latin]

bronze /brɒnz/
■ **N-NONCOUNT** **Bronze** is a yellowish-
brown metal that is a mixture of copper and
tin. ❑ *...a bronze statue of a ballet dancer.*
■ **ADJ** Something that is **bronze** is
yellowish-brown in color. ❑ *The sky began to*
fill with bronze light.
■ **N-NONCOUNT** **Bronze** is also a noun. ❑ *...the*
bronze of the hair on his forearms. [from French]

bronze med|al (bronze medals) **N-COUNT**
A **bronze medal** is an award made of brown

metal that you get as third prize in a
competition.

brooch /broʊtʃ/ (brooches) **N-COUNT**
A **brooch** is a piece of jewelry that has a pin
on the back so that it can be fastened on to
your clothes. [from Old French]
→ look at Picture Dictionary: **jewelry**

brood /bruːd/ (broods, brooding, brooded)
V-I If someone **broods** over something, they
feel sad about it or they worry about it a lot.
❑ *She constantly broods about having no friends.*
[from Old English]

brood|ing /bruːdɪŋ/ (broodings)
■ **ADJ** **Brooding** is used to describe an
atmosphere or feeling that makes you feel
anxious or slightly afraid. [LITERARY]
❑ *...a heavy, brooding silence.*
■ **N-COUNT** SCIENCE **Brooding** is the
process by which birds help their
eggs to hatch by sitting on them.
[from Old English]

broom /bruːm/ (brooms) **N-COUNT**
A **broom** is a type of brush with
a long handle. You use
a broom for sweeping
the floor.
[from Old English]   broom

broth|er /brʌðər/ (brothers)
N-COUNT Your **brother** is a boy or a man
who has the same parents as you.
❑ *Are you Peter's brother?* [from Old English]
→ look at Picture Dictionary: **family**

broth|er-in-law (brothers-in-law) **N-COUNT**
Someone's **brother-in-law** is the brother of
their husband or wife, or the man who is
married to their sister.
→ look at Picture Dictionary: **family**

brought /brɔt/ **Brought** is the past
tense and past participle of **bring**.
[from Old English]

brow /braʊ/ (brows)
■ **N-COUNT** Your **brow** is your forehead.
❑ *He wiped his brow with the back of his hand.*
■ **N-COUNT** Your **brows** are your eyebrows.
❑ *His glasses covered his thick dark brows.*
[from Old English]

brown /braʊn/ (browner, brownest, browns,
browning, browned)
■ **ADJ** Something that is **brown** is the
color of earth or wood. ❑ *He looked into her*
brown eyes.

2 **N-NONCOUNT** **Brown** is also a noun. ❑ *Colors such as dark brown and green will be popular in the fashion world this fall.*

3 **V-T/V-I** When food **browns** or when you **brown** it, you cook it until it becomes brown. ❑ *Cook for ten minutes until the sugar browns.* [from Old English]
→ look at Picture Dictionary: **hair**

browse /br**au**z/ (**browses, browsing, browsed**)
1 **V-I** If you **browse** in a store, you look at things in it. ❑ *I stopped in several bookstores to browse.*
2 **V-I** If you **browse through** a book or a magazine, you look through it in a relaxed way. ❑ *She was sitting on the sofa browsing through the TV magazine.*
3 **V-T/V-I** TECHNOLOGY If you **browse** the Internet, you search for information there. ❑ *The software allows you to browse the Internet on your cellphone.* ❑ *...an Internet café where they can browse during their free time.* [from French]

brows|er /br**au**zər/ (**browsers**) **N-COUNT** TECHNOLOGY A **browser** is a piece of computer software that allows you to search for information on the Internet. ❑ *You need an up-to-date Web browser.* [from French]

bruise /br**u**z/ (**bruises, bruising, bruised**)
1 **N-COUNT** A **bruise** is an injury that appears as a purple mark on your body. ❑ *How did you get that bruise on your arm?*
2 **V-T/V-I** If you **bruise** a part of your body, or a part of your body **bruises**, a bruise appears on it because you injured it. ❑ *I bruised my knee on a desk drawer.* ❑ *I bruise easily.* ● **bruised** **ADJ** ❑ *...a bruised knee.* [from Old English]

brush /br**ʌ**ʃ/ (**brushes, brushing, brushed**)
1 **N-COUNT** A **brush** is an object that has a lot of bristles or hairs attached to it. You use a brush for painting, for cleaning things, and for making your hair neat. ❑ *We gave him paint and brushes.* ❑ *He brought buckets of soapy water and scrubbing brushes to clean the floor.*

brush

2 **V-T** If you **brush** something, you clean it or make it neat using a brush. ❑ *Have you brushed your teeth?* ❑ *She brushed the sand out of her hair.*
3 **V-T** If you **brush** something away, you remove it with movements of your hands.

❑ *He brushed the snow off his suit.*

4 **V-T/V-I** If one thing **brushes against** another, the first thing touches the second thing lightly. ❑ *Something brushed against her leg.* ❑ *I felt her dark hair brushing the back of my shoulder.* [from Old French]
→ look at Word Web: **teeth**

▶ **brush aside** If you **brush** a remark or suggestion **aside**, you refuse to consider it. ❑ *He brushed aside any suggestion that he might retire.*

▶ **brush up on** If you **brush up on** something, you practice it or improve your knowledge of it. ❑ *I'm hoping to brush up on my Spanish when I'm away.*

brus|sels sprout /br**ʌ**səlz spr**au**t/ (**brussels sprouts**) **N-COUNT** **Brussels sprouts** are small round vegetables made of many leaves.

bru|tal /br**u**t°l/ **ADJ** A **brutal** act or person is cruel and violent. ❑ *...a brutal military dictator.* ❑ *...brutal punishment.* ● **bru|tal|ly** **ADV** ❑ *Her parents were brutally murdered.* [from Latin]

BTW **BTW** is short for "by the way," and is often used in email. ❑ *BTW, the machine is simply amazing.*

bub|ble /b**ʌ**b°l/ (**bubbles, bubbling, bubbled**)
1 **N-COUNT** **Bubbles** are small balls of air or gas in a liquid. ❑ *Air bubbles rise to the surface.*
2 **N-COUNT** A **bubble** is a hollow ball of liquid that is floating in the air or standing on a surface. ❑ *With soap and lots of bubbles children love bathtime.*
3 **V-I** When a liquid **bubbles**, bubbles move in it, for example because it is boiling. ❑ *Heat the soup until it is bubbling.* [of Scandinavian origin]
→ look at Word Web: **soap**

bub|bly /b**ʌ**bli/ (**bubblier, bubbliest**)
1 **ADJ** Someone who is **bubbly** is very lively and cheerful. ❑ *Sue is a bubbly girl who loves to laugh.*
2 **ADJ** If something is **bubbly**, it has a lot of bubbles in it. ❑ *When the butter is melted and bubbly, put in the flour.* [of Scandinavian origin]

buck /b**ʌ**k/ (**bucks, bucking, bucked**)
1 **N-COUNT** A **buck** is a U.S. or Australian dollar. [INFORMAL] ❑ *The food cost about fifty bucks.* ❑ *Why don't you spend a few bucks on a warm coat?*
2 **V-I** If a horse **bucks**, it kicks both of its back legs or jumps into the air in an

B

uncontrolled way. ❑ *The horse bucked and kicked.* [from Old English]

buck|et /bʌkɪt/ (**buckets**) **N-COUNT** A **bucket** is a round metal or plastic container with a handle. Buckets are often used for holding and carrying water. ❑ *She threw a bucket of water on the fire.* [from Old English]

buck|le /bʌkəl/ (**buckles, buckling, buckled**)
1 **N-COUNT** A **buckle** is a piece of metal or plastic on one end of a belt or a strap that is used for fastening it. ❑ *He wore a belt with a large silver buckle.*
2 **V-T** When you **buckle** a belt or a strap, you fasten it with a buckle. ❑ *The girl sat down to buckle her shoes.* [from Old French]
→ look at Picture Dictionary: **button**

bud /bʌd/ (**buds**) **N-COUNT** **SCIENCE** A **bud** is a new growth on a tree or a plant that develops into a leaf or a flower. ❑ *Small pink buds were beginning to form on the bushes.* [from Middle English]
→ look at Picture Dictionary: **flowers**
→ look at Word Web: **taste**

Bud|dhism /bʊdɪzəm, bʌd-/ **N-NONCOUNT** **Buddhism** is a religion that teaches that the way to end suffering is by controlling your desires. [from Sanskrit]

Bud|dhist /bʊdɪst, bʌd-/ (**Buddhists**)
1 **N-COUNT** A **Buddhist** is a person whose religion is Buddhism.
2 **ADJ** **Buddhist** means relating or referring to Buddhism. ❑ *...Buddhist monks.* [from Sanskrit]

bud|ding /bʌdɪŋ/
1 **ADJ** If you describe someone as, for example, a **budding** businessman or a **budding** artist, you mean that they are starting to succeed or become interested in business or art. ❑ *...budding writers.*
2 **ADJ** You use **budding** to describe a situation that is just beginning. ❑ *Our budding romance was over.*
3 **N-NONCOUNT** **SCIENCE** **Budding** is a type of reproductive process in which a new cell or organism grows on the surface of its parent's body and then separates from it. [from Germanic]

bud|dy /bʌdi/ (**buddies**) **N-COUNT** A **buddy** is a close friend, usually a male friend of a man. ❑ *We became great buddies.*

budge /bʌdʒ/ (**budges, budging, budged**)
1 **V-T/V-I** If someone will not **budge**, or

if nothing **budges** them, they refuse to change their mind. ❑ *The British will not budge on this point.*
2 **V-T/V-I** If someone or something will not **budge**, they refuse to move. If you cannot **budge** them, you cannot make them move. ❑ *I tried to open the window, but it wouldn't budge.* [from Old French]

budg|et /bʌdʒɪt/ (**budgets, budgeting, budgeted**)
1 **N-COUNT** **BUSINESS** Your **budget** is the amount of money that you have available to spend. ❑ *She will design a new kitchen for you within your budget.* ❑ *The actress will star in a low budget film.*
2 **V-T/V-I** If you **budget** a certain amount of money for something, you decide that you can afford to spend that amount. ❑ *The company has budgeted $10 million for advertising.* ❑ *I'm learning how to budget.*
3 **N-COUNT** **SOCIAL STUDIES** The **budget** is a statement from the government about a country's financial situation. It gives details about changes to taxes, and the amount of money that will be spent on public services. [from Old French]

Word Partnership	Use budget with :	
V	**balance a** budget **1**	
N	budget **crisis**, budget **crunch**, budget **cuts**, budget **deficit** **1**	
PREP	**over** budget, **under** budget **1**	
ADJ	**federal** budget, **tight** budget **1** **3**	

buf|fa|lo /bʌfəloʊ/ (**buffalo** or **buffaloes**) **N-COUNT** A **buffalo** is a wild animal like a large cow with horns that curve upward. [from Italian]

buf|fet /bʊfeɪ/ (**buffets**) **N-COUNT** A **buffet** is a meal that is arranged on a long table at a party or public occasion. Guests usually serve themselves. ❑ *After the event, there will be a buffet.* [from Old French]

bug /bʌg/ (**bugs, bugging, bugged**)
1 **N-COUNT** A **bug** is an insect. [INFORMAL]
2 **N-COUNT** A **bug** is an illness. [INFORMAL] ❑ *I think I have a stomach bug.*
3 **N-COUNT** **TECHNOLOGY** If there is a **bug** in a computer program, there is a mistake in it. ❑ *There is a bug in the software.*
4 **V-T** If someone **bugs** a place, they hide recording equipment in it so they can hear what people are saying. ❑ *He heard that they were planning to bug his office.*

5 **V-T** If someone or something **bugs** you, they worry or annoy you. [INFORMAL] ❏ *It really bugs me when people arrive late.*

Thesaurus	bug Also look up :
N	disease, germ, infection, microorganism, virus **2** breakdown, defect, error, glitch, hitch, malfunction **3**

build /bɪld/ (**builds, building, built**)
1 **V-T** If you **build** something, you make it by joining things together. ❏ *They are going to build a hotel here.* ❏ *The house was built in the early 19th century.*
2 **N-NONCOUNT/N-SING** Someone's **build** is the shape of their body. ❏ *He's six feet tall and of medium build.* [from Old English]
→ look at Word Web: **muscle**
▶ **build up** **1** If you **build up** something or if it **builds up**, it gradually becomes bigger. ❏ *The collection has been built up over the last seventeen years.* ❏ *Pressure is building up inside the volcano.*
2 → see also **build-up**

Thesaurus	build Also look up :
v	assemble, make, manufacture, produce, put together, set up; (*ant.*) demolish, destroy, knock down **1**

Word Partnership	Use build with :
N	build **bridges**, build **roads**, build **schools** **1**
V	**plan to** build **1**
ADJ	**athletic** build, **slender** build, **strong** build **2**

build|er /bɪldər/ (**builders**) **N-COUNT** A **builder** is a person whose job is to build or repair houses and other buildings. ❏ *The builders have finished the roof.* [from Old English]

build|ing /bɪldɪŋ/ (**buildings**) **N-COUNT** A **building** is a structure that has a roof and walls. ❏ *They lived on the upper floor of the building.* [from Old English]
→ look at Word Web: **architecture**

build-up (**build-ups**) also **buildup, build up**
1 **N-COUNT** A **build-up** is a gradual increase in something. ❏ *There will be a slight build-up of cloud later on this afternoon.*
2 **N-COUNT** The **build-up** to an event is the way that journalists or other people talk about it a lot in the period of time immediately before it, and try to make it seem important and exciting. ❏ *...the*

excitement of the build-up to Christmas.

built /bɪlt/ **Built** is the past tense and past participle of **build**. [from Old English]

bulb /bʌlb/ (**bulbs**)
1 **N-COUNT** A **bulb** is the glass part of a lamp that gives out light. ❏ *A single bulb hangs from the ceiling.*
2 **N-COUNT** SCIENCE A **bulb** is a root of a flower or plant. ❏ *...tulip bulbs.* [from Latin]
→ look at Picture Dictionary: **flowers**

bulge /bʌldʒ/ (**bulges, bulging, bulged**)
1 **V-I** If something **bulges**, it sticks out. ❏ *His pockets were bulging with coins.*
2 **N-COUNT** **Bulges** are lumps that stick out. ❏ *The police officer noticed a bulge under the man's coat.* [from Old French]

bulk /bʌlk/
1 **N-SING** The **bulk of** something is most of it. ❏ *The bulk of the money will go to the children's hospital in Dublin.*
2 **PHRASE** If you buy or sell something **in bulk**, you buy or sell it in large amounts. ❏ *It is cheaper to buy supplies in bulk.* [from Old Norse]

bulky /bʌlki/ (**bulkier, bulkiest**) **ADJ** Something that is **bulky** is large and heavy. ❏ *The store can deliver bulky items like lawn mowers.* [from Old Norse]

bull /bʊl/ (**bulls**) **N-COUNT** A **bull** is a male animal of the cow family, and some other animals. [from Old English]

bull|dog /bʊldɔg/ (**bulldogs**) **N-COUNT** A **bulldog** is a short dog with a large square head.

bull|doz|er /bʊldoʊzər/ (**bulldozers**) **N-COUNT** A **bulldozer** is a large vehicle with a broad metal blade at the front that is used for moving large amounts of earth.

bul|let /bʊlɪt/ (**bullets**) **N-COUNT** A **bullet** is a small piece of metal that is shot out of a gun. ❏ *Police fired rubber bullets at the crowd.* [from French]

bul|letin /bʊlɪtɪn/ (**bulletins**) **N-COUNT** A **bulletin** is a short news report on the radio or television. ❏ *We heard the early morning news bulletin.* [from French]

bul|letin board (**bulletin boards**)
1 **N-COUNT** A **bulletin board** is a board on a wall for notices giving information. ❏ *Her telephone number was pinned to the bulletin board.*

B

2 **N-COUNT** TECHNOLOGY In computing, a **bulletin board** is a system that allows users to send and receive messages. ❑ *The Internet is the largest computer bulletin board in the world.*

bul|ly /bʊli/ (**bullies, bullying, bullied**)

1 **N-COUNT** A **bully** is someone who uses their strength or power to frighten other people. ❑ *He was the class bully.*

2 **V-T** If someone **bullies** you, they use their strength or power to frighten you. ❑ *I wasn't going to let him bully me.* [from Middle Dutch]

bump /bʌmp/ (**bumps, bumping, bumped**)

1 **V-T/V-I** If you **bump** into something or someone, you accidentally hit them while you are moving. ❑ *They stopped walking and I almost bumped into them.* ❑ *She bumped her head on a low branch.*

2 **N-COUNT** A **bump** is an injury that you get if you hit something or if something hits you. ❑ *She fell over and got a large bump on her head.*

bump|er /bʌmpər/ (**bumpers**) **N-COUNT** **Bumpers** are heavy bars at the front and back of a vehicle that protect the vehicle if it hits something. ❑ *I felt something hit the rear bumper of my car.*

bumpy /bʌmpi/ (**bumpier, bumpiest**) **ADJ** A **bumpy** road or path is not smooth or flat. ❑ *We rode our bicycles down the bumpy streets.*

bun /bʌn/ (**buns**)

1 **N-COUNT** A **bun** is bread in a small round shape. ❑ *He had a cinnamon bun and a glass of milk.*

2 **N-COUNT** If you have your hair in a **bun**, you have attached it tightly at the back of your head in the shape of a ball.

→ look at Picture Dictionary: **bread**

bunch /bʌntʃ/ (**bunches**)

1 **N-COUNT** A **bunch of** people is a group of them. [INFORMAL] ❑ *They're a great bunch of kids.*

2 **N-COUNT** A **bunch of** flowers is a number of flowers with their stems held together. ❑ *He left a huge bunch of flowers in her hotel room.*

3 **N-COUNT** A **bunch of** bananas or grapes is a group of them growing together.

4 **N-SING** A **bunch of** things is a number of things. [INFORMAL] ❑ *We recorded a bunch of songs together.*

bun|dle /bʌndəl/ (**bundles**) **N-COUNT** A **bundle of** things is a number of things that are tied or wrapped together so that they can be carried or stored. ❑ *He left a bundle of papers on the floor.* [from Middle Dutch]

bunk /bʌŋk/ (**bunks**) **N-COUNT** A **bunk** is a narrow bed that is usually attached to a wall, especially in a ship. ❑ *Sally was lying on her narrow wooden bunk.*

bunk bed (**bunk beds**) **N-COUNT** **Bunk beds** are two single beds that are built one on top of the other. ❑ *The children slept in bunk beds.*

bun|ker /bʌŋkər/ (**bunkers**)

1 **N-COUNT** A **bunker** is a place, usually underground, that has been built with strong walls to protect it against heavy gunfire and bombing. ❑ *...an extensive network of underground bunkers.*

2 **N-COUNT** A **bunker** is a container for coal or other fuel.

3 **N-COUNT** On a golf course, a **bunker** is a large area filled with sand that is deliberately put there as an obstacle that golfers must try to avoid.

bun|ny /bʌni/ (**bunnies**) **N-COUNT** **Bunny** is a child's word for a rabbit. [INFORMAL] [from Scottish Gaelic]

buoy /buːi/ (**buoys**) **N-COUNT** A **buoy** is an object floating in a lake or an ocean that shows ships and boats where they can go. [from Middle Dutch]

→ look at Word Web: **tsunami**

buoy|ant force /buːyənt fɔrs/ (**buoyant forces**) **N-COUNT** SCIENCE The **buoyant force** of an object that is completely covered in a fluid is the physical force that causes the object to float or to rise upward.

bur|den /bɜrdən/ (**burdens, burdening, burdened**)

1 **N-COUNT** A **burden** is something that causes people a lot of worry or hard work. ❑ *I don't want to become a burden on my family when I get old.*

2 **V-T** If someone **burdens** you **with** a problem, they cause you to have it, often by telling you some bad news. ❑ *We decided not to burden him with the news.* [from Old English]

bu|reau /byʊəroʊ/ (**bureaus**)

1 **N-COUNT** A **bureau** is an office, an organization, or a government department. ❑ *The Federal Bureau of Investigation has an office in Washington, D.C.*

2 **N-COUNT** A **bureau** is a piece of furniture with drawers in which you keep clothes or other things. [from French]

bu|reau|cra|cy /byʊrɒkrəsi/ (**bureaucracies**)

■ **N-COUNT** A **bureaucracy** is a management system controlled by a large number of officials. ❑ *It's hard for a bureaucracy to accept new ideas.*

■ **N-NONCOUNT Bureaucracy** means all the rules and procedures of government departments or other large organizations, especially when people think that these rules and procedures are complicated and cause long delays. ❑ *People complain about too much bureaucracy.* [from French]

bu|reau|crat /byʊərəkræt/ (**bureaucrats**)

N-COUNT Bureaucrats are officials who work in a large administrative system, especially ones who seem to follow rules and procedures too strictly. ❑ *The economy is still controlled by bureaucrats.* [from French]

bu|reau|crat|ic /byʊərəkrætɪk/ **ADJ Bureaucratic** means involving complicated rules and procedures which can cause long delays. ❑ *...bureaucratic delays.* [from French]

bur|geon /bɜrdʒ³n/ (**burgeons, burgeoning, burgeoned**) **V-I** If something **burgeons**, it grows or develops rapidly. [LITERARY] ❑ *Plants burgeon from every available space.* ❑ *My confidence began to burgeon later in life.* [from Old French]

burg|er /bɜrgər/ (**burgers**) **N-COUNT** A **burger** is meat that is cut into very small pieces and pressed into a flat round shape. Burgers are often eaten between two pieces of bread. **Burger** is short for **hamburger.** ❑ *I ordered a burger for lunch.* [after Hamburg, a city in Germany]

bur|glar /bɜrglər/ (**burglars**) **N-COUNT** A **burglar** is someone who enters a building by force in order to steal things. ❑ *Dogs often help the police to catch burglars.* [from Medieval Latin]

bur|glar|ize /bɜrglərɑɪz/ (**burglarizes, burglarizing, burglarized**) **V-T** If a building **is burglarized**, a thief enters it by force and steals things. ❑ *Her home was burglarized last week.* [from Medieval Latin]

bur|gla|ry /bɜrgləri/ (**burglaries**) **N-COUNT/ N-NONCOUNT** If someone commits a **burglary**, they enter a building by force and steal things. ❑ *An 11-year-old boy committed a burglary.* [from Medieval Latin]
→ look at Picture Dictionary: **crime**

bur|ial /bɛriəl/ (**burials**)

N-COUNT/N-NONCOUNT A **burial** is the act or ceremony of putting a dead body into a grave in the ground. ❑ *Charles and his two sons attended the burial.* [from Old English]

burn /bɜrn/ (**burns, burning, burned** or **burnt**)

■ **V-T** If you **burn** something, you destroy or damage it with fire. ❑ *She burned her old love letters.*

■ **V-T** If you **burn** part of your body, or **burn yourself**, you are injured by fire or by something very hot. ❑ *Take care not to burn your fingers.*

■ **N-COUNT Burn** is also a noun. ❑ *She suffered burns to her back.*

■ **V-I** If there is a fire somewhere, you say that a fire is **burning** there. ❑ *Forty forest fires were burning in Alberta yesterday.*

■ **V-I** If something **is burning**, it is on fire. ❑ *When I arrived, one of the vehicles was still burning.*

■ **V-T** To **burn** a CD means to copy something onto it. ❑ *I have the equipment to burn CDs.*

■ **V-T** SCIENCE If a substance **burns**, it produces flames or smoke when heated. [from Old English]
→ look at Word Webs: **calorie, fire**

▶ **burn down** If a building **burns down** or if someone **burns** it **down**, it is completely destroyed by fire. ❑ *Six months after Bud died, the house burned down.*

Thesaurus	burn	Also look up :
v	ignite, incinerate, kindle, scorch, singe; *(ant.)* extinguish, put out ■–■	

Word Partnership	Use **burn** with :
v	watch *something* burn ■
N	fires burn ■
	burn victim ■
	burn a CD ■
ADJ	first/second/third degree burn ■

burn|er /bɜrnər/ (**burners**) **N-COUNT** A **burner** is a device that produces heat or a flame, especially as part of a stove or heater. ❑ *He put the frying pan on the gas burner.* [from Old English]
→ look at Picture Dictionary: **laboratory**

burn|ing /bɜrnɪŋ/

■ **ADJ** You use **burning** to describe something that is extremely hot. ❑ *...the burning desert of central Asia.*

■ **ADV Burning** is also an adverb.

❑ *He touched the boy's forehead. It was burning hot.* [from Old English]

burnt /bɜrnt/ **Burnt** is the past tense and past participle of **burn**. [from Old English]

burqa /bɜrkə/ (**burqas**) also **burka** N-COUNT A **burqa** is a long dress that covers the head and body and is traditionally worn by some women in Islamic countries. [from Arabic]

burst /bɜrst/ (**bursts, bursting, burst**)

> **LANGUAGE HELP**
>
> The form **burst** is used in the present tense and is the past tense and past participle.

1 V-T/V-I If something **bursts**, it suddenly breaks open and the air or other substance inside it comes out. ❑ *The driver lost control of his car when a tire burst.* ❑ *It's not a good idea to burst a blister.*

2 N-COUNT A **burst of** something is a sudden short period of it. ❑ *...a burst of energy.* [from Old English]

→ look at Word Web: **crash**

▶ **burst into** If you **burst into** tears, laughter, or song, you suddenly begin to cry, laugh, or sing. ❑ *She burst into tears and ran from the kitchen.*

▶ **burst out** If someone **bursts out** laughing, crying, or making another noise, they suddenly start making that noise. ❑ *The class burst out laughing.*

→ look at Word Web: **cry**

Thesaurus	burst	Also look up :
V	blow, explode, pop, rupture **1**	

Word Partnership	Use **burst** with :
N	burst **appendix, bubble** burst, **pipe** burst **1**
	burst **of air**, burst **of energy**, burst **of laughter 3**
ADJ	**ready to** burst **1**
	sudden burst **3**

bury /bɛri/ (**buries, burying, buried**)
1 V-T To **bury** something means to put it into a hole in the ground and cover it up. ❑ *Some animals bury nuts and seeds.*
2 V-T To **bury** a dead person means to put their body into a grave and cover it with earth. ❑ *Soldiers helped to bury the dead.* [from Old English]

bus /bʌs/ (**buses**) N-COUNT A **bus** is a large motor vehicle that carries passengers. ❑ *He missed his last bus home.*
→ look at Word Web: **transportation**

bush /bʊʃ/ (**bushes**)
1 N-COUNT The **bush** is an area in a hot country that is far from cities. Not many people live there. ❑ *...the Australian bush.*
2 N-COUNT A **bush** is a plant with leaves and branches that is smaller than a tree. ❑ *...a rose bush.* [of Germanic origin]
→ look at Picture Dictionary: **plant**

busi|ly /bɪzɪli/ ADV If you do something **busily**, you do it in a very active way. ❑ *Workers were busily trying to repair the damage.* [from Old English]

busi|ness /bɪznɪs/ (**businesses**)
1 N-NONCOUNT **Business** is work that is related to producing, buying, and selling things. ❑ *He had a successful career in business.* ❑ *She attended Harvard Business School.*
2 N-COUNT A **business** is an organization that produces and sells goods or that provides a service. ❑ *The bakery is a family business.*
3 ADJ If you go on a **business** trip or go out for a **business** lunch, you are working while you are away or at lunch. ❑ *They went on a combined business trip and honeymoon.*
4 → see also **show business**
5 PHRASE If you say that someone **means business**, you mean they are serious and determined about what they are doing. [INFORMAL] ❑ *Now people are starting to realize that he means business.*
6 PHRASE If you say to someone **mind your own business** or **it's none of your business**, you are rudely telling them not to ask about something that is private. [INFORMAL] ❑ *I asked Laura what was wrong and she told me to mind my own business.* [from Old English]
→ look at Word Web: **city**

Thesaurus	business	Also look up :
N	company, corporation, firm, organization **2**	

Word Partnership	Use **business** with :
N	**close of** business, business **opportunity**, business **school 1**
	business **administration**, business **decision**, business **hours**, business **owner**, business **practices 1 2**
ADJ	**family** business, **online** business, **small** business **2**
V	**go out of** business, **run a** business **2**

business|man /bɪznɪsmæn/ (**businessmen**)
N-COUNT A **businessman** is a man who works in business. ❑ *He's a rich businessman.*

business|woman /bɪznɪswʊmən/ (**businesswomen**) **N-COUNT** A **businesswoman** is a woman who works in business. ❑ *She's a successful businesswoman who manages her own company.*

bust /bʌst/ (**busts, busting, busted** or **bust**)

> **LANGUAGE HELP**
>
> The form **bust** is used as the present tense of the verb, and can also be used as the past tense and past participle.

1 **V-T** If you **bust** something, you break it or damage it so badly that it cannot be used. [INFORMAL] ❑ *They will have to bust the door to get him out.*

2 **PHRASE** If a company **goes bust**, it loses so much money that it is forced to close down. [INFORMAL] ❑ *...a Swiss company which went bust last May.*

3 **N-COUNT** A **bust** is a statue of the head and shoulders of a person. ❑ *...a bronze bust of Thomas Jefferson.* [from French]

busy /bɪzi/ (**busier, busiest**)
1 **ADJ** When you are **busy**, you are working hard, so that you are not free to do anything else. ❑ *What is it? I'm busy.* ❑ *They are busy preparing for a party on Saturday.*

2 **ADJ** A **busy** place is full of people who are doing things. ❑ *We walked along a busy city street.*

3 **ADJ** When a telephone line is **busy**, you cannot make your call because the line is already being used by someone else. ❑ *I tried to reach him, but the line was busy.* [from Old English]

4 → see also **busily**

but /bət, STRONG bʌt/
1 **CONJ** You use **but** to introduce something that is different than what you have just said. ❑ *I've enjoyed my vacation, but now it's time to get back to work.* ❑ *Heat the milk until it is very hot but not boiling.*

2 **PREP** **But** means "except." ❑ *You've done nothing but complain all day.* [from Old English]

> **Usage** **but** and **yet**
>
> But is used to add something to what has been said: *Lisa tried to bake cookies, but she didn't have enough sugar.* Yet is used to indicate an element of surprise: *He doesn't eat much, yet he is gaining weight.*

butch|er /bʊtʃər/ (**butchers**) **N-COUNT**
A **butcher** is someone who cuts up and sells meat. [from Old French]

but|ter /bʌtər/ (**butters, buttering, buttered**)
1 **N-NONCOUNT** **Butter** is a soft yellow food made from cream. You spread it on bread or use it in cooking. ❑ *The waitress brought us bread and butter.*

2 **V-T** If you **butter** bread or toast, you spread butter on it. ❑ *She put two pieces of bread on a plate and buttered them.* [from Old English]

butter|fly /bʌtərflaɪ/ (**butterflies**) **N-COUNT**
A **butterfly** is an insect with large colored wings. ❑ *Butterflies are attracted to the wild flowers.* [from Old English]
→ look at Picture Dictionary: **insect**

butterfly

but|ton /bʌtᵊn/ (**buttons, buttoning, buttoned**)
1 **N-COUNT** **Buttons** are small hard objects that you push through buttonholes to fasten your clothes. ❑ *I bought a blue jacket with silver buttons.*

2 **V-T** If you **button** a shirt, a coat, or another piece of clothing, you fasten it by pushing its buttons through the buttonholes. ❑ *Ferguson stood up and buttoned his coat.*

3 **N-COUNT** A **button** is a small object on a piece of equipment that you press to operate it. ❑ *He put in a DVD and pressed the "play" button.* [from Old French]
→ look at Word Webs: **buttons and fasteners, photography**

> **Word Partnership** Use **button** with :
>
> | N | **shirt** button **1** |
> |---|---|
> | V | **sew on a** button **1** |
> | | **press a** button, **push a** button **3** |
> | PREP | button **up something 2** |

button|hole /bʌtᵊnhoʊl/ (**buttonholes**)
N-COUNT A **buttonhole** is a hole that you push a button through in order to fasten a shirt, a coat, or another piece of clothing. [from Old French]

> **Word Link** *ar, er ≈ one who acts as : buyer, liar, seller*

buy /baɪ/ (**buys, buying, bought**) **V-T** If you **buy** something, you get it by paying money for it. ❑ *He could not afford to buy a house.* ❑ *Lizzie bought herself a bike.* ● **buy|er** (**buyers**)

Picture Dictionary · buttons and fasteners

button, buttonhole | zipper | hook and loop tape

snap | belt, buckle | shoelace

N-COUNT ❑ *Car buyers are more interested in safety than speed.* [from Old English]

Thesaurus	buy	Also look up :
V	acquire, bargain, barter, get, obtain, pay, purchase	

Word Partnership	Use **buy** with :
V	**afford to** buy, buy **and/or sell**
N	buy **in bulk**, buy **clothes**, buy **a condo/ house**, buy **food**, buy **shares/stocks**, buy **tickets**
ADV	buy **direct**, buy **online**, buy **retail**, buy **secondhand**, buy **wholesale**

buzz /bʌz/ (**buzzes, buzzing, buzzed**)

1 **V-I** If something **buzzes**, it makes a sound like a bee. ❑ *There was a fly buzzing around my head.*

2 **N-COUNT** **Buzz** is also a noun. ❑ *The annoying buzz of an insect kept us awake.*

3 **V-I** If a place **is buzzing with** activity, there is a lot of activity there. ❑ *Suddenly the place was buzzing with excitement.*

by

> **PRONUNCIATION HELP**
> Pronounce the preposition /baɪ/.
> Pronounce the adverb /baɪ/.

1 **PREP** If something is done **by** a person or thing, that person or thing does it. ❑ *The dinner was served by his mother and sisters.* ❑ *She was woken by a loud noise in the street.*

2 **PREP** If a book or a painting is **by** a particular person, they wrote it or painted it. ❑ *Here's a painting by Van Gogh.*

3 **PREP** **By** is used to say how something

is done. ❑ *We usually travel by car.*

4 **PHRASE** If you are **by yourself**, you are alone. ❑ *A man was sitting by himself in a corner.*

5 **PHRASE** If you do something **by yourself**, you do it without any help. ❑ *I can do it by myself.*

6 **PREP** Someone or something that is **by** something else is beside it. ❑ *Judith was sitting in a chair by the window.* ❑ *Jack stood by the door, ready to leave.*

7 **PREP** If a person or vehicle goes **by** you, they move past you without stopping. ❑ *A few cars passed close by me.*

8 **ADV** **By** is also an adverb. ❑ *People waved and smiled as she went by.*

9 **PREP** If something happens **by** a particular time, it happens at or before that time. ❑ *I'll be home by eight o'clock.*

10 **PREP** If something increases or decreases **by** a particular amount, that amount is gained or lost. ❑ *Violent crime has increased by 10 percent since last year.* [from Old English]

bye /baɪ/ or **bye-bye** **INTERJ** **Bye** and **bye-bye** are informal ways of saying goodbye. ❑ *Bye, Daddy.*

by|pass /baɪpæs/ (**bypasses, bypassing, bypassed**)

1 **V-T** If you **bypass** someone or something that you would normally have to get involved with, you ignore them, often because you want to achieve something more quickly. ❑ *The president gives radio interviews to bypass the newspapers.*

2 **N-COUNT** A **bypass** is a surgical operation performed on or near the heart, in which the flow of blood is directed so that it does not flow through a part of the heart that is blocked or affected by disease. ❑ ...*heart bypass surgery.*

3 **N-COUNT** A **bypass** is a main road that takes traffic around the edge of a town or a city rather than through its center. ❑ *A new bypass around the city is being built.*

4 **V-T** If you **bypass** a place when you are traveling, you avoid going through it. ❑ *His bus trip to the Midwest bypassed all the big cities.*

byte /baɪt/ (**bytes**) **N-COUNT** TECHNOLOGY In computing, a **byte** is a unit for measuring information. ❑ ...*two million bytes of data.*

Cc

cab /kæb/ (cabs) **N-COUNT** A **cab** is a car that you can hire with its driver, to take you where you want to go. ❑ *Can I call a cab?* [from French]

cab|bage /kæbɪdʒ/ (cabbages) **N-COUNT/N-NONCOUNT** A **cabbage** is a round vegetable with white, green, or purple leaves. [from Old French]

cab|in /kæbɪn/ (cabins)
◼ **N-COUNT** A **cabin** is a small wooden house in the woods or mountains. ❑ *We stayed in a log cabin.*
◼ **N-COUNT** A **cabin** is a small room on a boat. ❑ *He showed her to a small cabin.*
◼ **N-COUNT** The **cabin** is the part of a plane where people sit. ❑ *He sat in the first-class cabin.* [from Old French]

cabi|net /kæbɪnɪt/ (cabinets)
◼ **N-COUNT** A **cabinet** is a piece of furniture with shelves, used for storing things in. ❑ *I looked in the medicine cabinet.*
◼ **N-COUNT** SOCIAL STUDIES The **cabinet** is a group of members of the government who give advice to the president, and who are responsible for its policies. [from Old French]
→ look at Picture Dictionary: **bathroom**

ca|ble /keɪbᵊl/ (cables)
◼ **N-COUNT/N-NONCOUNT** A **cable** is a very strong, thick rope, made of metal. ❑ *They used a cable made of steel wire.*
◼ **N-COUNT/N-NONCOUNT** A **cable** is a thick wire that carries electricity. ❑ *The island gets its electricity from underground power cables.* [from Old Norman French]
→ look at Picture Dictionary: **computer**
→ look at Word Webs: **bridge, laser, television**

ca|ble tele|vi|sion **N-NONCOUNT** Cable television is a television system in which signals travel along wires. ❑ *We don't have cable television.*

cac|tus /kæktəs/ (cacti /kæktaɪ/) **N-COUNT** A **cactus** is a plant with lots of sharp points that grows in hot, dry places. [from Latin]
→ look at Picture Dictionary: **desert**

café /kæfeɪ/ (cafés) also **cafe** **N-COUNT** A **café** is a place where you can buy drinks and small meals. [from French]

caf|eteria /kæfɪtɪəriə/ (cafeterias) **N-COUNT** A **cafeteria** is a restaurant where you buy a meal and carry it to the table yourself. Places like hospitals, schools, and offices have **cafeterias**. [from American Spanish]

caf|feine /kæfin/ **N-NONCOUNT** Caffeine is a chemical in coffee and tea that makes you more active. [from German]

cage /keɪdʒ/ (cages) **N-COUNT** A **cage** is a structure made of metal bars where you keep birds or animals. ❑ *I hate to see birds in cages.* [from Old French]

cake /keɪk/ (cakes)
◼ **N-COUNT/N-NONCOUNT** A **cake** is a sweet food that you make from flour, eggs, sugar, and butter. ❑ *He ate a piece of chocolate cake.* ❑ *We made her a birthday cake.*
◼ **N-COUNT** Food that is formed into flat, round shapes before it is cooked can be referred to as **cakes**. ❑ *...fish cakes.* [from Old Norse]
→ look at Picture Dictionary: **dessert**

cal|cium /kælsiəm/ **N-NONCOUNT** SCIENCE Calcium is a soft white chemical element that is found in bones and teeth, and also chalk and marble. [from New Latin]

cal|cu|late /kælkyəleɪt/ (calculates, calculating, calculated) **V-T** MATH If you **calculate** an amount, you find it out by using numbers. ❑ *Have you calculated the cost of your trip?* [from Late Latin]

cal|cu|la|tion /kælkyəleɪʃᵊn/ (calculations) **N-COUNT/N-NONCOUNT** MATH You make a **calculation** when you find out a number or amount by using mathematics. ❑ *Ryan made a quick calculation in his head.*
→ look at Word Web: **mathematics**

cal|cu|la|tor /kælkyəleɪtər/ (calculators) **N-COUNT** A **calculator** is a small electronic machine that you use to calculate numbers.

❑ *He takes a pocket calculator to school.*
[from Late Latin]
→ look at Picture Dictionary: **office**

cal|de|ra /kældɛərə/ (**calderas**) **N-COUNT**
SCIENCE A **caldera** is a large crater at the top
of a volcano that is formed when a volcano
collapses. [from Spanish]

cal|en|dar /kælɪndər/ (**calendars**) **N-COUNT**
A **calendar** is a list of days, weeks, and
months for a particular year. ❑ *There was a
calendar on the wall.* [from Norman French]
→ look at Word Web: **year**

calf /kæf/ (**calves** /kævz/)
1 **N-COUNT** A **calf** is a young cow.
2 **N-COUNT** Your **calf** is the thick part at the
back of your leg, between your ankle and the
back of your knee. [from Old Norse]

cali|ber /kælɪbər/
1 **N-NONCOUNT** The **caliber of** someone or
something is their qualities, abilities, or
high standards. ❑ *The caliber of the teaching
was very high.* ❑ *I was impressed by the high caliber
of the researchers.*
2 **N-COUNT** The **caliber** of a gun is the width
of the inside of its barrel. ❑ *...a small-caliber
rifle.*
3 **N-COUNT** The **caliber** of a bullet is its
diameter. ❑ *...a .22-caliber bullet.* [from Old
French]

cal|is|then|ics /kælɪsθɛnɪks/ **N-PLURAL**
Calisthenics are simple exercises that you
can do to keep fit and healthy. [from Greek]

```
───────── call ─────────
❶ VERB USES
❷ NOUN USES
❸ PHRASAL VERBS
```

❶ **call** /kɔl/ (**calls, calling, called**)
1 **V-T** If you **call** a person or an animal a
particular name, you give them that name.
❑ *I wanted to call the dog Mufty.* ❑ *Her daughter is
called Charlotte.*
2 **V-T** If you **call** a person or a situation
something, that is how you describe them.
❑ *She calls me lazy.*
3 → see also **so-called**
4 **V-T** If you **call** a meeting, you arrange for
it to take place. ❑ *We're going to call a meeting
for next week.*
5 **V-T** If you **call** something, you say it in
a loud voice. ❑ *Someone called his name.*
6 **V-T** If you **call** someone, you telephone

them. ❑ *Would you call me as soon as you find out?*
❑ *I think we should call the doctor.*
7 **V-I** If you **call** somewhere, you make
a short visit there. ❑ *A salesman called at
the house.*
8 **N-COUNT** Call is also a noun. ❑ *The doctor
was out on a call.*
9 **V-T** If you **call** someone somewhere, you
order them to come there. ❑ *He called me into
the garden.* [from Old English]

❷ **call** /kɔl/ (**calls**)
1 **N-COUNT** When you make a telephone
call, you telephone someone. ❑ *I made a phone
call to my grandmother.*
2 **N-COUNT** The **call** of a bird or an animal
is the loud sound that it makes. ❑ *...the call of
a mockingbird.*
3 **N-COUNT** If there is a **call for** something,
someone asks for it to happen. ❑ *There have
been calls for new security arrangements.* [from
Old English]

❸ **call** /kɔl/ (**calls, calling, called**)
▶ **call back** If you **call** someone **back**, you
telephone them in return for a call they
made to you. ❑ *I'll call you back.*
▶ **call off** If you **call off** an event that has
been planned, you cancel it. ❑ *He called off
the trip.*
▶ **call on 1** If you **call on** someone **to do**
something, you say publicly that you want
them to do it. ❑ *He called on the government
to resign.*
2 If you **call on** someone, you visit them
for a short time. ❑ *Sofia was intending to call
on Miss Kitts.*
▶ **call up** If you **call** someone **up**, you
telephone them. ❑ *When I'm in Pittsburgh,
I'll call him up.*

call|er /kɔlər/ (**callers**) **N-COUNT** A **caller** is
a person who is making a telephone call.
❑ *A caller told police what happened.*

cal|lous /kæləs/ **ADJ** A **callous** person or
action is cruel and shows no concern for
other people. ❑ *...the callous treatment he
received.* ● **cal|lous|ness** **N-NONCOUNT**
❑ *...the callousness of the sick woman's family.*
● **cal|lous|ly** **ADV** ❑ *I did not want to abandon
my parents callously.* [from Latin]

calm /kɑm/ (**calmer, calmest, calms,
calming, calmed**)
1 **ADJ** A **calm** person is not worried, angry,
or excited. ❑ *She is a calm, patient woman.*
❑ *Try to keep calm.* ● **calm|ly** **ADV** ❑ *Alan said*

C

calmly, "I don't believe you."

2 **N-NONCOUNT/N-SING** **Calm** is also a noun. ❏ *He felt a sudden sense of calm.*

3 **ADJ** If water is **calm**, it is not moving much. ❏ *The ocean was very calm and the stars were bright.*

4 **ADJ** If the weather is **calm**, there is not much wind. ❏ *It was a fine, calm day.*

5 **V-T** If you **calm** someone, or if you **calm** their feelings, you do something to make them less upset or excited. ❏ *Isabella helped calm her fears.* [from Old French]

▶ **calm down** If you **calm down**, you become less upset or excited. ❏ *Calm down and listen to me.* ❏ *I'll try to calm him down.*

Thesaurus	**calm**	Also look up :
ADJ	laid-back, relaxed; *(ant.)* excited, upset **1**	
	mild, peaceful, placid, serene, tranquil; *(ant.)* rough **1**–**3**	

---

calo|rie /kǽləri/ (**calories**)

1 **N-COUNT** SCIENCE **Calories** are units for measuring the amount of energy in food. ❏ *These sweet drinks have a lot of calories in them.*

2 **N-COUNT** SCIENCE In physics, a **calorie** is the amount of heat that is needed to increase the temperature of one gram of water by one degree Celsius. **Calorie** is also sometimes used to mean a **kilocalorie**. [from French]

→ look at Word Webs: **calories, diet**

calo|rim|eter /kǽlərɪmɪtər/ (**calorimeters**) **N-COUNT** SCIENCE A **calorimeter** is a scientific instrument that measures the amount of heat given off or absorbed in a chemical reaction.

came /keɪm/ **Came** is the past tense of **come**.

cam|el /kǽməl/ (**camels**) **N-COUNT** A **camel** is an animal with one or two large lumps on its back. **Camels** live in hot, dry places and are used for carrying people or things. [from Old English]

cam|era /kǽmrə/ (**cameras**) **N-COUNT** A **camera** is a piece of equipment for taking photographs or making movies. ❏ *...a digital camera.* [from Latin]

→ look at Word Web: **photography**

cam|era phone (**camera phones**) **N-COUNT** TECHNOLOGY A **camera phone** is a cellphone that can take photographs.

camp /kæmp/ (**camps, camping, camped**)

1 **N-COUNT** A **camp** is a place where people live or stay in tents. ❏ *...an army camp.*

2 **N-COUNT** A **camp** is a place in the countryside where care and activities are provided for children during the summer. ❏ *She's working with children on a summer camp.*

3 **V-I** If you **camp** somewhere, you stay there in a tent. ❏ *We camped near the beach.*

● **camp|ing** **N-NONCOUNT** ❏ *They went camping in Colorado.* [from Old French]

cam|paign /kæmpeɪn/ (**campaigns, campaigning, campaigned**)

1 **N-COUNT** A **campaign** is a number of things that you do over a period of time in order to get a particular result. ❏ *January marks the start of the election campaign.*

2 **V-I** If you **campaign**, you do certain things over a period of time in order to get a particular result. ❏ *We are campaigning for better health services.* ● **cam|paign|er** (**campaigners**) **N-COUNT** ❏ *...anti-war campaigners.* [from French]

→ look at Word Webs: **army, election**

camp|er /kǽmpər/ (**campers**) **N-COUNT** A **camper** is a person who is staying in a

---

Word Web   calories

Calories are a measure of **energy**. One calorie of heat raises the **temperature** of 1 gram of water by 1°C*. However, we usually think of calories in relation to food and exercise. A person eating a cup of vanilla ice cream **takes in** 270 calories. Walking a mile **burns** 66 calories. Different types of foods store different amounts of energy. **Proteins** and **carbohydrates** contain 4 calories per gram. However **fat** contains 9 calories per gram. Our bodies store extra calories in the form of fat. For every 3,500 extra calories we take in, we gain a pound of fat.

0°Celsius = 32° Fahrenheit

tent, for example on vacation. ❏ *The campers packed up their tents.* [from Old French]

Word Link	site, situ ≈ position, location :
	campsite, situ**ation**, web**site**

camp|site /kǽmpsaɪt/ (**campsites**)
N-COUNT A **campsite** is a place where you can stay in a tent.

cam|pus /kǽmpəs/ (**campuses**) **N-COUNT**
A **campus** is an area of land that contains the main buildings of a university or college. [from Latin]

can
❶ MODAL USES
❷ CONTAINER

❶ **can** /kən, STRONG kæn/

LANGUAGE HELP
Use the form **cannot** in negative statements. When you are speaking, you can use the short form **can't**, pronounced /kænt/.

1 **MODAL** If you **can** do something, you have the ability to do it. ❏ *I can take care of myself.* ❏ *Can you swim yet?*
2 **MODAL** You use **can** to show that something is sometimes true. ❏ *Exercising alone can be boring.*
3 **MODAL** You use **can** with words like "smell," "see," and "hear." ❏ *I can smell smoke.*
4 **MODAL** If you **can** do something, you are allowed to do it. ❏ *Can I go to the party at the weekend?* ❏ *Sorry. We can't answer any questions.*
5 **MODAL** You use **cannot** and **can't** to state that you are certain that something is not the case or will not happen. ❏ *Things can't be that bad.*
6 **MODAL** You use **can** to make requests or offers. ❏ *Can I have a look at that book?* ❏ *Can I help you?* [from Old English]

Usage | **can** and **may**
Both *can* and *may* are used to talk about possibility and permission: *Highway traffic can/may be heavier in the summer than in the winter. Can/May I interrupt you for a moment?* To talk about ability, use *can* but not *may*: *Kazuo can run a mile in five minutes.*

❷ **can** /kæn/ (**cans**) **N-COUNT** A **can** is a metal container for food, drink, or paint. ❏ *...a can of tomato soup.* [from Old English]
→ look at Picture Dictionary: **containers**

ca|nal /kənǽl/ (**canals**) **N-COUNT** GEOGRAPHY
A **canal** is a long narrow path filled with water that boats travel along. ❏ *The Erie Canal connects the Great Lakes with the Atlantic Ocean.* [from Latin]

can|cel /kǽnsəl/ (**cancels, canceling** or **cancelling, canceled** or **cancelled**)
1 **V-T/V-I** If you **cancel** something that has been planned, you stop it from happening. ❏ *We canceled our trip to Washington.* ❏ *The customer called to cancel.* ● **can|cel|la|tion** /kænsəléɪʃⁿn/ (**cancellations**) **N-COUNT/N-NONCOUNT** ❏ *The cancellation of his visit upset many people.*
2 **V-T** If someone **cancels** a document or a debt, they declare that it no longer legally exists. ❏ *...a government order canceling his passport.* ● **can|cel|la|tion** **N-NONCOUNT** ❏ *...cancellation of Third World debt.* [from Old French]

Thesaurus | **cancel** Also look up :
v | break, call off, scrap, undo **1**

can|cer /kǽnsər/ (**cancers**)
N-COUNT/N-NONCOUNT **Cancer** is a serious disease that makes groups of cells in the body grow when they should not. ❏ *Jane had cancer when she was 25.* [from Latin]
→ look at Word Web: **cancer**

Word Web | cancer

The traditional **treatments** for **cancer** are **surgery**, **radiation therapy**, and **chemotherapy**. However, there is a new type of treatment called targeted therapy. This treatment uses drugs that target specific types of cancer cells. Targeted therapy does not have many of the **toxic** effects on healthy **tissue** that traditional chemotherapy can have. One of these drugs helps stop blood vessels that feed a **tumor** from growing. Another drug kills cancer cells.

can|did /kǽndɪd/ **ADJ** If you are **candid** about something or with someone, you speak honestly. ❑ *Natalie is candid about the problems she is having with Steve.* ❑ *I haven't been completely candid with him.* [from Latin]

can|di|date /kǽndɪdeɪt/ (**candidates**) **N-COUNT** A **candidate** is someone who is trying to get a particular job, or trying to win a political position. ❑ *He is a candidate for governor of Illinois.* [from Latin]
→ look at Word Webs: **election, vote**

can|dle /kǽndəl/ (**candles**) **N-COUNT** A **candle** is a long stick of wax with a piece of string through the middle, that you burn to give you light. ❑ *The only light in the bedroom came from a candle.* [from Old English]

can|dy /kǽndi/ (**candies**) **N-COUNT/N-NONCOUNT** **Candy** is sweet food such as chocolate or taffy. ❑ *I gave him a piece of candy.* [from Old French]

can|dy bar (**candy bars**) **N-COUNT** A **candy bar** is a long, thin, sweet food, usually covered in chocolate.

cane /keɪn/ (**canes**) **N-COUNT** A **cane** is a long stick that people use to help them walk. ❑ *He has used a cane for the last five years.* [from Old French]
→ look at Word Webs: **disability, sugar**

can|non /kǽnən/ (**cannons**) **N-COUNT** A **cannon** is a large heavy gun on wheels that was used in battles in the past. ❑ *The soldiers stood beside the cannons.* [from Old French]

can|not /kǽnɒt, kənɒt/ **Cannot** is the negative form of **can**.

ca|noe /kənúː/ (**canoes**) **N-COUNT** A **canoe** is a small, narrow boat that you move through the water using a paddle. [from Spanish]
→ look at Word Web: **boat**

canoe

can|on /kǽnən/ (**canons**) **1 N-COUNT** A **canon** is a member of the clergy on the staff of a cathedral. **2 N-COUNT** MUSIC A **canon** is a piece of music in which several voices or instruments perform the same melody but start at different times. A **canon** is also a dance form in which the dancers perform the same movements but start at different

times. [Sense 1 from Anglo-French. Sense 2 from Old English.]

can't /kǽnt/ **Can't** is short for **cannot**.

can|vas /kǽnvəs/ (**canvases**) **1 N-NONCOUNT** **Canvas** is a strong, heavy cloth that is used for making tents and bags. ❑ *...a canvas bag.* **2 N-COUNT/N-NONCOUNT** ARTS A **canvas** is a piece of this cloth that you paint on. ❑ *...an artist's canvas.* [from Norman French]
→ look at Word Web: **painting**

can|yon /kǽnyən/ (**canyons**) **N-COUNT** SCIENCE A **canyon** is a long, narrow valley with very steep sides. ❑ *...the Grand Canyon.* [from Spanish]

cap /kǽp/ (**caps**) **1 N-COUNT** A **cap** is a soft, flat hat with a curved part at the front. ❑ *He wore a dark blue baseball cap.* **2 N-COUNT** The **cap** of a bottle is its lid. ❑ *She took the cap off her water bottle and drank.* [from Old English]
→ look at Picture Dictionaries: **clothing, hats**

ca|pable /kéɪpəbəl/ **1 ADJ** If you are **capable of** doing something, you are able to do it. ❑ *He was not even capable of standing up.* **2 ADJ** Someone who is **capable** is able to do something well. ❑ *She's a very capable teacher.* [from French]

Thesaurus	capable	Also look up :
ADJ	able, competent, skillful, talented;	
	(ant.) incapable, incompetent **2**	

Word Link	*cap ≈ head* : *capacity, capital,*
	captain

ca|pac|ity /kəpǽsɪti/ (**capacities**) **1 N-COUNT/N-NONCOUNT** Your **capacity for** something is your ability to do it. ❑ *Every human being has the capacity for love.* **2 N-COUNT/N-NONCOUNT** The **capacity** of something is the maximum amount that it can hold. ❑ *The stadium has a capacity of 50,000.* **3 N-COUNT** If you do something in a particular **capacity**, you do it as part of your job. [WRITTEN] ❑ *She was there in her capacity as U.S. ambassador.* **4 ADJ** A **capacity** crowd or audience completely fills a theater or other place. ❑ *A capacity crowd of 76,000 people was at the stadium for the event.* [from Old French]

cape /keɪp/ (**capes**)

■ **N-COUNT** SCIENCE A **cape** is a large piece of land that sticks out into the ocean. ❑ *...the Cape of Good Hope.* [from Old French]

■ **N-COUNT** A **cape** is a long coat without sleeves, that covers your body and arms. [from French.]

ca|pil|lary /kæpəleri/ (**capillaries**) **N-COUNT** **Capillaries** are tiny blood vessels in your body. [from Latin]

capi|tal /kæpɪtᵊl/ (**capitals**)

■ **N-COUNT** GEOGRAPHY The **capital** of a country is the city where its government meets. ❑ *Berlin is the capital of Germany.*

■ **N-COUNT** LANGUAGE ARTS A **capital** or a **capital letter** is the large letter that you use at the beginning of sentences and names. ❑ *He wrote his name in capitals.*

■ **N-NONCOUNT** BUSINESS **Capital** is money that you use to start a business. ❑ *They provide capital for small businesses.* [from Latin] → look at Word Webs: **city, country**

capi|tal|ism /kæpɪtᵊlɪzəm/ **N-NONCOUNT** SOCIAL STUDIES **Capitalism** is an economic and political system in which property, business, and industry are privately owned and not owned by the state. [from Latin]

capi|tal|ist /kæpɪtᵊlɪst/ (**capitalists**)

■ **ADJ** SOCIAL STUDIES In a **capitalist** system, industry is owned by private companies rather than by the government. ❑ *Banks play an important part in the capitalist system.*

■ **N-COUNT** SOCIAL STUDIES A **capitalist** is someone who believes in a system where industry is owned by private companies rather than by the government.

capi|tal pun|ish|ment **N-NONCOUNT** **Capital punishment** is when a criminal is killed legally as a punishment. ❑ *Capital punishment is not used in some countries.*

cap|i|tol /kæpɪtᵊl/ (**capitols**) also **Capitol**

■ **N-COUNT** SOCIAL STUDIES A **capitol** is a building where a state's government meets. ❑ *The state capitol was built in 1908.*

■ **N-PROPER** SOCIAL STUDIES The **Capitol** is the government building in Washington, D.C., where the U.S. Congress meets. ❑ *Thousands of people waited in front of the Capitol.* [from Latin]

cap|sule /kæpsᵊl/ (**capsules**) **N-COUNT** A **capsule** is a very small closed tube with medicine inside it, that you swallow. [from French]

cap|tain /kæptɪn/ (**captains**)

■ **N-COUNT** In the army or navy, a **captain** is an officer of middle rank. ❑ *... a captain in the army.*

■ **N-COUNT** SPORTS The **captain of** a sports team is its leader. ❑ *Mickey Thomas is the captain of the tennis team.*

■ **N-COUNT** The **captain** of an airplane or a ship is the person who is in charge of it. ❑ *Who is the captain of this boat?* [from Old French] → look at Word Webs: **boat, ship**

cap|tcha /kæptʃə/ (**captchas**) **N-COUNT** TECHNOLOGY A **captcha** is a set of numbers and letters in unusual shapes that a user must type in order to access certain services. ❑ *We use captchas to screen for spam.*

cap|tion /kæpʃᵊn/ (**captions**) **N-COUNT** A **caption** is a piece of writing next to a picture, that tells you something about the picture. ❑ *The photo had the caption "John, aged 6 years."* [from Latin]

Word Link cap ≈ seize : *cap*tive, *cap*tivity, *cap*ture

---

cap|tive /kæptɪv/ (**captives**)

■ **ADJ** A **captive** animal or person is being kept in a place and is not allowed to leave. [LITERARY] ❑ *Scientists are studying the behavior of the captive birds.*

■ **N-COUNT** A **captive** is a prisoner. [LITERARY]

■ **PHRASE** If you **take** someone **captive**, you keep them as a prisoner. ❑ *The kidnappers held Richard captive for a year.* [from Latin]

cap|tiv|ity /kæptɪvɪti/ **N-NONCOUNT** **Captivity** is when you are kept in a place and you cannot leave. ❑ *The birds were kept in captivity.* [from Latin]

cap|ture /kæptʃər/ (**captures, capturing, captured**)

■ **V-T** If you **capture** someone or something, you catch them and keep them somewhere. ❑ *The enemy shot down the airplane and captured the pilot.*

■ **N-NONCOUNT** **Capture** is also a noun. ❑ *The battles led to the army's capture of the town.*

■ **V-T** If someone or something **captures** a quality or a feeling, they represent or express it successfully. ❑ *...food that captures the spirit of the Mediterranean.* [from Latin]

Word Partnership Use **capture** with :

V	**avoid** capture, **escape** capture, **fail to** capture ■
N	capture **territory** ■
	capture **your attention**, capture **your imagination** ■

C

Word Web   car

The first mass-produced **automobile** in the U.S. was the Model T. In 1909, Ford sold over 10,000 of these **vehicles**. They all had the same basic **engine** and **chassis**. For years the only color choice was black. Three different bodies were available—**roadster**, **sedan**, and **coupe**. Today car makers offer many more choices. These include **convertibles**, **sports cars**, **station wagons**, **vans**, **pick-up trucks**, and **SUVs**. Laws now require **seat belts** and **airbags** to make **driving** safer. Some car makers now offer **hybrid** vehicles. They combine an electrical engine with an **internal combustion engine** to improve **fuel** economy.

car /kɑr/ (**cars**)
 1 **N-COUNT** A **car** is a motor vehicle with space for about 5 people. ❑ *They arrived by car.*
 2 **N-COUNT** A **car** is one of the long parts of a train. ❑ *He stood up and walked to the dining car.* [from Latin]
 → look at Word Webs: **car**, **train**

cara|mel /kærəmɛl, -məl, kɑrməl/
 N-NONCOUNT Caramel is a type of sweet food made from burnt sugar, butter, and milk. [from French]

carb /kɑrb/ (**carbs**) **N-COUNT** Carbs are foods such as potatoes, pasta, and bread that contain a lot of carbohydrates. ❑ *Eat a wide variety of carbs, fruit, and vegetables.*

> **Word Link**   hydr ≈ water : carbo**hydr**ate, de**hydr**ate, **hydr**opower

car|bo|hy|drate /kɑrboʊhaɪdreɪt/
 (**carbohydrates**) **N-COUNT/N-NONCOUNT**
 SCIENCE Carbohydrates are substances in foods that provide the body with energy.
 ❑ *You need to eat more carbohydrates such as bread, pasta, or potatoes.*
 → look at Word Webs: **calorie**, **diet**

car|bon /kɑrbən/ **N-NONCOUNT** SCIENCE
 Carbon is a chemical element that diamonds and coal are made of. [from French]
 → look at Word Web: **fossil**

car|bon di|ox|ide /kɑrbən daɪɒksaɪd/
 N-NONCOUNT SCIENCE Carbon dioxide is a gas that animals and people produce when they breathe out.
 → look at Word Webs: **air**, **greenhouse effect**, **ozone**, **photosynthesis**, **respiratory system**

car|bon foot|print (**carbon footprints**)
 N-COUNT Your **carbon footprint** is a measure of the amount of carbon dioxide released

into the atmosphere by your activities over a particular period. ❑ *We all need to look for ways to reduce our carbon footprint.*

car|bon mon|ox|ide /kɑrbən mənɒksaɪd/
 N-NONCOUNT SCIENCE Carbon monoxide is a poisonous gas that is produced by engines that use gasoline.
 → look at Word Web: **ozone**

car|bon neu|tral **ADJ** A **carbon neutral** lifestyle, company, or activity does not increase the amount of carbon dioxide in the atmosphere. ❑ *You can make your flights carbon neutral by planting trees to make up for the greenhouse gas emissions.*

car|bon trad|ing **N-NONCOUNT** Carbon trading is the practice of buying the right to produce carbon dioxide from countries or organizations that do not use much fuel or electricity.

card /kɑrd/ (**cards**)
 1 **N-COUNT** A **card** is a piece of stiff paper with a picture and a message, that you send to someone on a special occasion. ❑ *She sends me a card on my birthday.*
 2 **N-COUNT** A **card** is a small piece of cardboard or plastic that has information about you written on it. ❑ *Please remember to bring your membership card.*
 3 **N-COUNT** A **card** is a small piece of plastic that you use to pay for things. ❑ *He paid the bill with a credit card.*
 4 **N-COUNT** Cards are pieces of stiff paper with numbers or pictures on them that you use for playing games. ❑ *They enjoy playing cards.* [from Old French]
 5 → see also **bank card**, **credit card**, **debit card**, **playing card**

card|board /kɑrdbɔrd/ **N-NONCOUNT**
Cardboard is thick, stiff paper that is used
for making boxes. ❏ ...a cardboard box. [from
Old French]

card|holder /kɑrdhoʊldər/ (**cardholders**)
N-COUNT A **cardholder** is someone who
has a credit card or a bank card. ❏ The average
cardholder today carries three to four bank cards.

car|di|ac mus|cle (**cardiac muscles**)
N-COUNT/N-NONCOUNT SCIENCE The **cardiac**
muscle is the muscle in the heart that pumps
blood around the body by contracting.
→ look at Word Web: **muscle**

car|di|gan /kɑrdɪgən/ (**cardigans**) **N-COUNT**
A **cardigan** is a sweater that opens at the
front. [after James Thomas Brudenell,
7th Earl of Cardigan (1797-1868), a British
cavalry officer]

car|di|nal /kɑrdᵊnᵊl/ (**cardinals**)
1 **N-COUNT** A **cardinal** is a high-ranking
priest in the Catholic church. ❏ In 1448,
Nicholas became a cardinal.
2 **ADJ** A **cardinal** rule or quality is extremely
important. [FORMAL] ❏ As a salesman, your
cardinal rule is to do everything you can to satisfy
a customer.
3 **N-COUNT** A **cardinal** is a common North
American bird. The male has bright red
feathers. [from Latin]

car|di|nal di|rec|tion (**cardinal directions**)
N-COUNT The **cardinal directions** are the four
main points of the compass, north, south,
east, and west.

cardio- /kɑrdioʊ/ SCIENCE When **cardio-**
begins a word, it means something to do
with the heart. [from Greek]

car|dio|vas|cu|lar sys|tem
/kɑrdioʊvæskyʊlər sɪstəm/
(**cardiovascular systems**) **N-COUNT** SCIENCE
The **cardiovascular system** carries blood to
and from the body's cells. The organs in this
system include the heart, the arteries, and
the veins.
→ look at Word Web: **cardiovascular system**

care /kɛər/ (**cares, caring, cared**)
1 **V-T/V-I** If you **care** about someone or
something, you are interested in them, or
you think they are very important. ❏ We care
about the environment. ❏ These young men did not
care whether they lived or died.
2 **V-I** If you **care for** someone or something,
you look after them. ❏ A nurse cares for David in
his home.
3 **N-NONCOUNT** Care is also a noun.
❏ Sensitive teeth need special care.
4 **V-I** If you **care for** someone or **care about**
someone, you feel a lot of affection for them.
❏ He still cared for me.
5 **N-NONCOUNT** If you do something with
care, you do it very carefully so that you do
not make any mistakes. ❏ He chose his words
with care.
6 **N-COUNT** Your **cares** are your worries or
fears. ❏ Lean back in a hot bath and forget all the
cares of the day.
7 → see also **caring**
8 **PHRASE** If you **take care of** someone, you
look after them. ❏ There was no one to take care
of the children. [from Old English]

Word Partnership	Use **care** with :
ADJ	**good** care, **loving** care **2**
V	**provide** care, **receive** care **2**

ca|reer /kərɪər/ (**careers**) **N-COUNT** A **career**
is a job, or the years of your life that you
spend working. ❏ She had a long career as a
teacher. [from French]

Word Web cardiovascular system

The **cardiovascular system** carries **oxygen** and **nutrients** to **cells** in
all parts of the human body. It also removes waste from these cells.
The **heart** pumps the **blood** through the more than 100,000 kilometers
of **veins** and **arteries**. The blood follows two main routes. **Pulmonary**
circulation carries blood through the **lungs** where it absorbs oxygen.
The **systemic route** carries the oxygen-rich blood from the lungs to
the rest of the body. Blood contains three types of cells. **Red blood cells**
carry oxygen. **White blood cells** help fight disease. **Platelets** help
the blood clot when there is an injury.

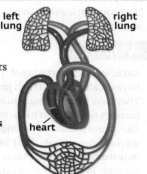

Thesaurus career Also look up :

N	field, job, profession, specialty, vocation, work

Word Partnership Use career with :

N	career **advancement**, career **goals**, career **opportunities**, career **path**
ADJ	**political** career, **professional** career
V	**pursue a** career

Word Link free ≈ without : carefree, duty-free, hands-free

care|free /kɛərfri/ **ADJ** A **carefree** person or period of time is without problems or responsibilities. ❑ Chantal remembered carefree summers at the beach.

Word Link ful ≈ filled with : beautiful, careful, dreadful

care|ful /kɛərfəl/

1 **ADJ** If you are **careful**, you think a lot about what you are doing so that you do not make any mistakes. ❑ Be very careful with this liquid, it can be dangerous.
● **care|ful|ly** **ADV** ❑ Have a nice time, and drive carefully.
2 **ADJ** **Careful** work, thought, or examination is thorough and shows a concern for details. ❑ The trip needs careful planning. ● **care|ful|ly** **ADV** ❑ All her letters were carefully filed away. [from Old English]

Word Partnership Use careful with :

ADV	**better be** careful **1**
	extremely careful, **very** careful **1** **2**
N	careful **attention**, careful **consideration**, careful **planning** **2**

care|giver /kɛərgɪvər/ (**caregivers**) **N-COUNT** A **caregiver** is someone who takes care of a sick person or young children in their home. ❑ We have employed the same caregiver for seventeen years.

care|less /kɛərlɪs/ **ADJ** If you are **careless**, you do not give enough attention to what you are doing, and so you make mistakes. ❑ Some of my students were very careless with homework. [from Old English]

Thesaurus careless Also look up :

ADJ	absent-minded, forgetful, irresponsible, reckless, sloppy; (ant.) attentive, careful, cautious **1**

care|taker /kɛərteɪkər/ (**caretakers**)
1 **N-COUNT** A **caretaker** is someone who looks after a building and the area around it.
2 **N-COUNT** A **caretaker** is the same as a **caregiver**.

car|go /kɑrgoʊ/ (**cargoes**)
N-COUNT/N-NONCOUNT The **cargo** of a ship or a plane is the goods that it is carrying. ❑ The ship was carrying a cargo of bananas. [from Spanish]
→ look at Word Webs: **ship**, **train**

car|ing /kɛərɪŋ/
1 **ADJ** A **caring** person is affectionate, helpful, and sympathetic. ❑ He is a lovely boy, very gentle and caring. [from Old English]
2 → see also **care**

car|na|tion /kɑrneɪʃən/ (**carnations**)
N-COUNT A **carnation** is a plant with white, pink, or red flowers. [from French]

car|ni|val /kɑrnɪvəl/ (**carnivals**) **N-COUNT**
A **carnival** is a celebration in the street, with music and dancing. [from Italian]

car|ni|vore /kɑrnɪvɔr/ (**carnivores**)
1 **N-COUNT** SCIENCE A **carnivore** is an animal that eats mainly meat. Compare with **herbivore** and **omnivore**.
2 **N-COUNT** If you describe someone as a **carnivore**, you are saying, especially in a humorous way, that they eat meat.
→ look at Word Web: **carnivore**

Word Web carnivore

Carnivores are at the top of the **food chain**. These **predators** have to catch and kill their **prey**, so they must be fast and agile. They have large, strong canine teeth to **stab** their prey. Sharp **incisors** work almost like scissors to tear into animal **flesh**. Carnivores include large **wild** animals such as **lions** and **wolves**. Many people think **bears** are carnivorous, but they are **omnivorous**. They eat plants and berries as well as **meat**. There are more **herbivores** than carnivores in the world.

car|ol /kærəl/ (carols) **N-COUNT** MUSIC Carols are religious songs that Christians sing usually at Christmas. ❑ *The children all sang carols as loudly as they could.* [from Old French]

car|pen|ter /kɑrpɪntər/ (carpenters) **N-COUNT** A **carpenter** is a person whose job is to make and repair wooden things. [from Latin]

car|pet /kɑrpɪt/ (carpets) **N-COUNT/N-NONCOUNT** A **carpet** is a thick, soft covering for the floor. ❑ *He picked up the clothes and vacuumed the carpets.* [from Old French]

carpet|bag|ger /kɑrpɪtbægər/ (carpetbaggers) **N-COUNT** SOCIAL STUDIES A **carpetbagger** is someone who is trying to become a politician in an area that is not their home. ❑ *He was called a carpetbagger because he lived outside the district.*

car|riage /kærɪdʒ/ (carriages) **N-COUNT** A **carriage** is an old-fashioned vehicle pulled by horses. ❑ *...an open carriage pulled by six beautiful gray horses.* [from Old Northern French]

car|ri|er /kæriər/ (carriers)
1 **N-COUNT** A **carrier** is a vehicle that is used for carrying people, especially soldiers, or things. ❑ *...a helicopter carrier.*
2 **N-COUNT** A **carrier** is a company that provides telecommunications services, such as telephone and Internet services. ❑ *The company is Japan's top wireless carrier.*
3 **N-COUNT** A **carrier** is a passenger airline. ❑ *The airline is the third-largest carrier at Denver International Airport.* [from Old Northern French]
→ look at Word Web: **ship**

car|rot /kærət/ (carrots) **N-COUNT/N-NONCOUNT** **Carrots** are long, thin, orange-colored vegetables. ❑ *We had chicken with potatoes, peas, and carrots.* [from Old French]
→ look at Picture Dictionary: **vegetables**

car|ry /kæri/ (carries, carrying, carried)
1 **V-T** If you **carry** something, you hold it in your hand and take it with you. ❑ *He was carrying a briefcase.*
2 **V-T** If you **carry** something, you always have it with you. ❑ *You have to carry a passport.*
3 **V-T** To **carry** someone or something means to take them somewhere. ❑ *Trucks carrying food and medicine left the capital city yesterday.*

4 **V-T** If someone **is carrying** a disease, they have it and can pass it on to others. ❑ *...people carrying the virus.*
5 **V-T** If something **carries** a particular risk or result, it causes that risk or has that result. ❑ *The medication carries no risk for your baby.* ❑ *It was a crime that carried the death penalty.*
6 **V-T** If a newspaper **carries** a picture or an article, it contains it. ❑ *Several papers carry the photograph of Mr. Anderson.*
7 **V-T** In a debate, if a proposal **is carried**, a majority of people vote for it. ❑ *The motion was carried by 322 votes to 296.*
8 **V-T** If a store **carries** a product, it has it and can sell it to you. ❑ *The store carries many different styles of shirts.*
9 **PHRASE** If you **get carried away**, you are so excited about something that you do something foolish. ❑ *I got completely carried away and almost cried.* [from Old Northern French]
▶ **carry on** **1** If you **carry on** doing something, you continue to do it. ❑ *The teacher carried on talking.*
2 If you **carry on** an activity, you do it for a period of time. ❑ *They carried on a conversation all morning.*
▶ **carry out** If you **carry** something **out**, you do it. ❑ *They carried out tests in the laboratory.*

Thesaurus	carry	Also look up :
v	bear, bring, cart, haul, move **1**	

car|ry|ing ca|pac|ity (carrying capacities) **N-COUNT** SCIENCE The **carrying capacity** of a particular area is the maximum number of people or animals that can live there on a long-term basis.

car|ry-on **ADJ** **Carry-on** baggage or luggage are the bags that you take inside an airplane with you. ❑ *Passengers who have only carry-on luggage may go directly to the departure gate.*

cart /kɑrt/ (carts)
1 **N-COUNT** A **cart** is an old-fashioned wooden vehicle that is usually pulled by a horse.
2 **N-COUNT** A **cart** or a **shopping cart** is a large plastic or metal basket on wheels that customers use in supermarkets. [from Old Norse]
→ look at Picture Dictionary: **golf**

car|tel /kɑrtɛl/ (cartels) **N-COUNT** BUSINESS A **cartel** is an association of similar companies or businesses that have grouped together in order to prevent competition and to control prices. ❏ ...the OPEC oil cartel. [from German]

car|ti|lage /kɑrtɪlɪdʒ/ (cartilages) **N-COUNT/ N-NONCOUNT** SCIENCE Cartilage is a strong, flexible substance that surrounds joints in your body. ❏ The player tore cartilage in his chest. [from Latin]
→ look at Word Web: **shark**

car|ton /kɑrtᵊn/ (cartons) **N-COUNT** A **carton** is a plastic or cardboard container for food or drink. ❏ ...a quart carton of milk. [from French]
→ look at Picture Dictionary: **containers**

car|toon /kɑrtun/ (cartoons)
1 N-COUNT A **cartoon** is a funny drawing, often in a magazine or a newspaper. ❏ ...cartoon characters.
2 N-COUNT A **cartoon** is a film that uses drawings for all the characters and scenes instead of real people or objects. ❏ We watched children's cartoons on TV. [from Italian]
→ look at Word Web: **animation**

car|tridge /kɑrtrɪdʒ/ (cartridges) **N-COUNT** A **cartridge** is a part of a machine you can easily remove when it is empty. ❏ You need to change the ink cartridge in your printer.

carve /kɑrv/ (carves, carving, carved)
1 V-T/V-I ARTS If you **carve** an object, you cut it out of wood or stone. ❏ He carved the statue from one piece of rock. ❏ He picked up the piece of wood and started carving.
2 V-T If you **carve** writing or a design **on** an object, you cut it into the surface. ❏ He carved his name on his desk.
3 V-T If you **carve** meat, you cut slices from it. ❏ Andrew began to carve the chicken. [from Old English]

case /keɪs/ (cases)
1 N-COUNT A **case** is a particular situation, especially one that you are using as an example. ❏ In some cases, it can be very difficult.
2 N-COUNT A **case** is a legal matter that will be brought to a court of law. ❏ ...a murder case.
3 N-COUNT A **case** is a container that is designed to hold or protect something. ❏ He uses a black case for his glasses.
4 → see also **bookcase, briefcase**
5 PHRASE You say **in any case** when you are adding another reason for something.

❏ The concert was sold out, and in any case most of us could not afford a ticket.
6 PHRASE If you do something **in case** a particular thing happens, you do it because that thing might happen. ❏ I've brought some food in case we get hungry. ❏ Many stores along the route are closed in case of trouble.
7 PHRASE In that case means if that is the situation. ❏ "It's raining."—"Oh, in that case we'll have to stay in." [from Old French]

cash /kæʃ/ (cashes, cashing, cashed)
1 N-NONCOUNT Cash is money in the form of bills and coins. ❏ ...two thousand dollars in cash.
2 V-T If you **cash** a check, you take it to a bank and get money for it. [from Old Italian]

cash|ier /kæʃɪər/ (cashiers) **N-COUNT** A **cashier** is a person whose job is to take customers' money in stores or banks. [from Middle Dutch]

cash|less /kæʃləs/ **ADJ** Cashless payments are made using cards or electronic methods rather than actual money. ❏ The school cafeteria uses a cashless system.

ca|si|no /kəsinoʊ/ (casinos) **N-COUNT** A **casino** is a place where people gamble by playing games. [from Italian]

cast /kæst/ (casts, casting, cast)

> **LANGUAGE HELP**
> The form **cast** is used in the present tense and is the past tense and past participle.

1 N-COUNT The **cast** of a play or a movie is all the people who act in it. ❏ The show is very amusing and the cast is very good.
2 N-COUNT A **cast** is a hard cover for protecting a broken arm or leg. ❏ His arm is in a cast.
3 V-T To **cast** an actor means to choose them to act a particular role. ❏ He was cast as a college professor.
4 V-T If something **casts** a light or a shadow somewhere, it causes it to appear there. [WRITTEN] ❏ The moon cast a bright light over the yard.
5 V-T To **cast** doubt **on** something means to cause people to be unsure about it. ❏ A criminal psychologist cast doubt on the theory.
6 V-T When you **cast** your vote in an election, you vote. ❏ The people will cast their votes in the country's first elections. [from Old Norse]
→ look at Word Webs: **election, theater, vote**

caste /kæst/ (castes) **N-COUNT/N-NONCOUNT**
SOCIAL STUDIES A **caste** is one of the social
classes into which people are divided in a
Hindu society. ❑ *Most of the upper castes
worship the goddess Kali.* [from Portuguese]

cas|tle /kæsᵊl/
(castles) **N-COUNT**
A **castle** is a large
building with thick,
high walls that was
built in the past to
protect people
during wars and
battles. [from Latin]

castle

cas|ual /kæʒuəl/
■ **ADJ** If you are **casual**, you are relaxed and
not worried about what is happening.
❑ *She tried to sound casual, but she was frightened.*
● **casu|al|ly** **ADV** ❑ *"No need to hurry," Ben
said casually.*
■ **ADJ** **Casual** clothes are clothes that you
normally wear at home or on vacation, and
not on formal occasions. ❑ *I also bought some
casual clothes for the weekend.* ● **casu|al|ly** **ADV**
❑ *They were casually dressed.*
■ **ADJ** A **casual** event or situation happens
without planning. ❑ *...a casual remark.*
[from Late Latin]

casu|al|ty /kæʒuəlti/ (casualties) **N-COUNT**
A **casualty** is a person who is injured or
killed in a war or in an accident. ❑ *Helicopters
bombed the town, causing many casualties.* [from
Late Middle English]

cat /kæt/ (cats) **N-COUNT**
A **cat** is a small animal
covered with fur that
people often keep as a
pet. ❑ *The cat sat on my lap,
purring.* [from Old
English]
→ look at Word Web: **pets**

cat

cata|log /kætᵊlɒg/ (catalogs) also
catalogue **N-COUNT** A **catalog** is a list of
things you can buy from a particular
company. ❑ *The website has an on-line catalog of
products.* [from Late Latin]
→ look at Word Web: **library**

ca|tas|tro|phe /kətæstrəfi/ (catastrophes)
N-COUNT A **catastrophe** is an unexpected
event that causes a lot of suffering or damage.
❑ *They learn how to deal with major catastrophes,
including earthquakes.* [from Greek]

cata|stroph|ic /kætəstrɒfɪk/ **ADJ**
Catastrophic means extremely bad or
serious, often causing a lot of damage.
❑ *A storm caused catastrophic damage to the
houses.* [from Greek]

catch
❶ HOLD OR TOUCH
❷ MANAGE TO GET, SEE,
   HEAR
❸ OTHER USES AND
   PHRASAL VERBS

❶ **catch** /kætʃ/ (catches, catching, caught)
■ **V-T** If you **catch** a person or an animal,
you find them and hold them. ❑ *Police say
they are confident of catching the man.* ❑ *Where did
you catch the fish?*
■ **V-T** SPORTS If you **catch** an object that is
moving through the air, you take hold of it
with your hands. ❑ *I jumped up to catch the ball.*
■ **N-COUNT** SPORTS **Catch** is also a noun.
❑ *That was a great catch.*
■ **V-T** If you **catch** part of your body
somewhere, it accidentally gets stuck there.
❑ *I caught my finger in the car door.* [from Old
Northern French]

Thesaurus	catch	Also look up :
v	arrest, capture, grab, seize, snatch, trap;	
	(ant.) free, let go, let off, release ❶ ■	

❷ **catch** /kætʃ/ (catches, catching, caught)
■ **V-T** When you **catch** a bus, a train, or a
plane, you get on it in order to travel
somewhere. ❑ *We caught the bus on the corner
of the street.*
■ **V-T** If you **catch** someone doing
something wrong, you see or find them
doing it. ❑ *They caught him with $30,000 cash in
a briefcase.*
■ **V-T** If you do not **catch** something that
someone has said, you do not hear it.
❑ *I'm sorry; I didn't catch your name.*
■ **V-T** If something **catches** your attention
or your eye, you notice it. ❑ *My shoes caught
his attention.* [from Old Northern French]

❸ **catch** /kætʃ/ (catches, catching, caught)
■ **V-T** If you **catch** an illness, you become ill
with it. ❑ *Keep warm, or you'll catch a cold.*
■ **V-T** If you **are caught** in an unpleasant
situation, it happens when you cannot
avoid it. ❑ *He was caught in a storm and
almost drowned.*
■ **N-COUNT** A **catch** is a hidden problem or
difficulty in a plan or an offer. ❑ *The catch is*

that some of the students in need of help do not ask for it. [from Old Northern French]

▶ **catch on** If something **catches on**, it becomes popular. ❑ *The idea has been around for years without catching on.*

▶ **catch up** **1** If you **catch up with** someone, you reach them by walking faster than they are walking. ❑ *I stopped and waited for her to catch up.*

2 To **catch up** means to reach the same level as someone else. ❑ *You'll have to work hard to catch up.*

catch|er /kǽtʃər/ (**catchers**) **N-COUNT** SPORTS In baseball, the **catcher** is the player who stands behind the batter. The catcher has a special glove for catching the ball. [from Old Northern French]
→ look at Picture Dictionary: **baseball**

catch|ment area (**catchment areas**) **N-COUNT** GEOGRAPHY The **catchment area** of a river is the area of land from which water flows into the river.

cat|ego|rize /kǽtɪgəraɪz/ (**categorizes, categorizing, categorized**) **V-T** If you **categorize** people or things, you say which group or type they belong to. ❑ *Their music is usually categorized as jazz.* [from Late Latin]

cat|ego|ry /kǽtɪgɔri/ (**categories**) **N-COUNT** If people or things are divided into **categories**, they are divided into similar groups. ❑ *Their music falls into the category of "jazz."* [from Late Latin]

Thesaurus	category	Also look up :
N	class, grouping, kind, rank, sort, type	

ca|ter /kéɪtər/ (**caters, catering, catered**) **V-I** If someone **caters for** a party, they provide the food for it. ❑ *We can cater for birthday parties of any size.* [from Latin]

ca|ter|ing /kéɪtərɪŋ/ **N-NONCOUNT** **Catering** is the activity or business of providing food for large numbers of people. ❑ *His catering business made him a millionaire at 41.* [from Latin]

cat|er|pil|lar /kǽtərpɪlər/ (**caterpillars**) **N-COUNT** A **caterpillar** is a small animal with a long body that develops into a butterfly. [from Old Northern French]

ca|thar|sis /kəθɑ́rsɪs/ **N-NONCOUNT** **Catharsis** is getting rid of unhappy memories or strong emotions such as anger or sadness by expressing them in some way. [from New Latin]

ca|thedral /kəθi̱drəl/ (**cathedrals**) **N-COUNT** A **cathedral** is a large and important church. ❑ *We visited some of the great cathedrals of Madrid.* [from Late Latin]

Catho|lic /kǽθəlɪk/ (**Catholics**)
1 **ADJ** The **Catholic** Church is a section of the Christian Church. ❑ *...a Catholic priest.*
2 **N-COUNT** A **Catholic** is a member of the Catholic Church. ❑ *His parents are Catholics.* [from Latin]

cat|tle /kǽtᵊl/ **N-PLURAL** **Cattle** are cows that are kept for their milk or meat. [from Old Northern French]
→ look at Word Webs: **dairy, herbivore**

caught /kɔ́t/ **Caught** is the past tense and past participle of **catch**.

cau|li|flow|er /kɔ́liflaʊər/ (**cauliflowers**) **N-COUNT/N-NONCOUNT** A **cauliflower** is a large, round, white vegetable surrounded by green leaves. [from Italian]
→ look at Picture Dictionary: **vegetables**

cause /kɔ́z/ (**causes, causing, caused**)
1 **N-COUNT** The **cause of** an event is what makes it happen. ❑ *We still don't know the exact cause of the accident.*
2 **N-COUNT** A **cause** is an aim that some people support or fight for. ❑ *A strong leader will help our cause.*
3 **N-NONCOUNT** If you have **cause for** a particular feeling or action, you have reasons for feeling it or doing it. ❑ *Only a few people can find any cause for celebration.*
4 **V-T** To **cause** something means to make it happen. ❑ *Stress can cause headaches.* [from Latin]

Thesaurus	cause	Also look up :
V	generate, make, produce, provoke; *(ant.)* deter, prevent, stop **4**	

Word Partnership		Use cause with :
V	determine the cause **1**	
	support a cause **2**	
N	cause of death **1**	
	cause for concern **3**	
	cause an accident, cause cancer, cause problems, cause a reaction **4**	

Word Link	*caut ≈ taking care : caution, cautious, precaution*

cau|tion /kɔ́ʃᵊn/ **N-NONCOUNT** **Caution** is great care to avoid danger or problems. ❑ *Always cross the street with caution.* [from Old French]

cau|tious /kɔʃəs/ **ADJ** A **cautious** person is very careful to try to avoid danger. ❑ *Doctors are cautious about using this new medication.* ● **cau|tious|ly** **ADV** ❑ *David moved cautiously forward and looked down into the water.* [from Old French]

cav|al|ry /kævəlri/ **N-SING** SOCIAL STUDIES In the past, **the cavalry** was the group of soldiers in an army who rode horses. ❑ *He was a young cavalry officer.* [from French]

cave /keɪv/ (**caves, caving, caved**) **N-COUNT** SCIENCE A **cave** is a large hole in the side of a hill or under the ground. [from Old French]
▶ **cave in** If a roof or a wall **caves in**, it collapses. ❑ *Part of the roof caved in.*

cc /si si/ BUSINESS **cc** is used at the beginning of emails or at the end of a business letter to show that a copy is being sent to another person. ❑ *...cc g.gray@harpercollins.com.*

CCTV /si si ti vi/ **N-NONCOUNT** CCTV is short for **closed-circuit television**. ❑ *We saw him on the CCTV camera.*

CD /si di/ (**CDs**) **N-COUNT** TECHNOLOGY A **CD** is a disk for storing music or computer information. **CD** is short for **compact disc**. ❑ *You can buy a CD of all her songs.*
→ look at Word Web: **laser**

CD burn|er /si di bɜrnər/ (**CD burners**) **N-COUNT** TECHNOLOGY A **CD burner** is a piece of computer equipment that you use for copying information or music from a computer onto a CD.

CD play|er (**CD players**) **N-COUNT** TECHNOLOGY A **CD player** is a machine that plays CDs.

CD-ROM /si di rɒm/ (**CD-ROMs**) **N-COUNT** TECHNOLOGY A **CD-ROM** is a CD that stores a very large amount of information that you can read using a computer.
→ look at Picture Dictionary: **computer**

cease /sis/ (**ceases, ceasing, ceased**)
1 **V-I** When something **ceases**, it stops. [FORMAL] ❑ *At one o'clock the rain ceased.*
2 **V-T** If you **cease** something, or **cease to** do something, you stop doing it. [FORMAL] ❑ *The newspaper ceased publication this week.* [from Old French]

cease|fire /sisfaɪər/ (**ceasefires**) **N-COUNT** SOCIAL STUDIES A **ceasefire** is an agreement to stop fighting a war. ❑ *They have agreed to a ceasefire after three years of conflict.*

ceil|ing /silɪŋ/ (**ceilings**) **N-COUNT** A **ceiling** is the top inside part of a room. ❑ *The rooms all had high ceilings.*

cel|ebrate /sɛlɪbreɪt/ (**celebrates, celebrating, celebrated**) **V-T/V-I** If you **celebrate**, you do something enjoyable for a special reason. ❑ *I passed my test and wanted to celebrate.* ❑ *Dick celebrated his 60th birthday on Monday.* ● **cel|ebra|tion** /sɛlɪbreɪʃən/ (**celebrations**) **N-COUNT/N-NONCOUNT** ❑ *There was a celebration in our house that night.* [from Latin]

cel|ebrat|ed /sɛlɪbreɪtɪd/ **ADJ** A **celebrated** person or thing is famous and much admired. ❑ *...one of the most celebrated young painters in England.* [from Latin]

ce|leb|rity /sɪlɛbrɪti/ (**celebrities**) **N-COUNT** A **celebrity** is someone who is famous. ❑ *Kylie Minogue will be our celebrity guest.* [from Latin]

cel|ery /sɛləri/ **N-NONCOUNT** Celery is a vegetable that consists of long, pale-green sticks. ❑ *Cut a stick of celery into small pieces.* [from French]

cell /sɛl/ (**cells**)
1 **N-COUNT** SCIENCE A **cell** is the smallest part of an animal or a plant. ❑ *We are studying blood cells.*
2 **N-COUNT** A **cell** is a small room with a lock in a prison or a police station. ❑ *How many prisoners were in the cell?*
3 **N-COUNT** SCIENCE A **cell** is a device that produces electricity as the result of a chemical reaction. [from Medieval Latin]
→ look at Word Webs: **cardiovascular system, cellphone, clone, skin**

cel|lar /sɛlər/ (**cellars**) **N-COUNT** A **cellar** is a large space under a building. ❑ *He kept the boxes in the cellar.* [from Latin]

cell cy|cle (**cell cycles**) **N-COUNT** SCIENCE A **cell cycle** is the series of changes that a biological cell goes through from the beginning of its life until its death.

C

cell di|vi|sion **N-NONCOUNT** SCIENCE **Cell division** is the biological process by which a cell inside an animal or a plant divides into two new cells during growth or reproduction.

cell mem|brane (cell membranes) **N-COUNT** SCIENCE **Cell membranes** are the thin outer layers of the cells inside an animal.

cel|lo /tʃɛloʊ/ (cellos) **N-COUNT/N-NONCOUNT** MUSIC A **cello** is a musical instrument that is like a large violin. You sit behind it and rest it on the floor. ● **cel|list** /tʃɛlɪst/ (cellists) **N-COUNT** ❑ *He is a great cellist.*
→ look at Picture Dictionary: **strings**
→ look at Word Web: **orchestra**

cell|phone /sɛlfoʊn/ (cellphones) **N-COUNT** TECHNOLOGY A **cellphone** is a telephone that you can carry wherever you go. ❑ *The woman called the police on her cellphone.*
→ look at Word Web: **cellphone**

cell theo|ry **N-SING** SCIENCE The **cell theory** is a set of basic principles relating to biological cells, such as the principle that all living creatures are composed of cells and that all cells come from other cells.

cel|lu|lar /sɛlyələr/ **ADJ** SCIENCE **Cellular** means relating to the cells of animals or plants. ❑ *...cellular growth.* [from Medieval Latin]
→ look at Word Web: **cellphone**

cel|lu|lar res|pi|ra|tion /sɛlyʊlər rɛspəreɪʃ°n/ **N-NONCOUNT** SCIENCE **Cellular respiration** is the biological process by which cells convert substances such as sugar into energy.

cell wall (cell walls) **N-COUNT** SCIENCE **Cell walls** are the thin outer layers of the cells inside plants and bacteria.

Celsius /sɛlsiəs/ **ADJ** SCIENCE **Celsius** is a way of measuring temperature. Water freezes at 0° Celsius and boils at 100° Celsius. ❑ *11° Celsius is 52° Fahrenheit.* [from Swedish]
→ look at Word Web: **thermometer**

ce|ment /sɪmɛnt/ (cements, cementing, cemented)
1 **N-NONCOUNT** **Cement** is a gray powder that you mix with sand and water to make concrete.
2 **V-T** Something that **cements** a relationship makes it stronger. ❑ *Nothing cements a friendship between countries so much as trade.* [from Old French]

Word Link   *ery ≈ place where something happens : bakery, cemetery, surgery*

cem|etery /sɛmətɛri/ (cemeteries) **N-COUNT** A **cemetery** is a place where dead people are buried. [from Late Latin]

Ce|no|zo|ic era /sinəzoʊɪk, sɛn-/ **N-SING** SCIENCE The **Cenozoic era** is the most recent period in the history of the Earth, from 65 million years ago up to the present day.

cen|sus /sɛnsəs/ (censuses) **N-COUNT** SOCIAL STUDIES A **census** is when a government counts all the people in a country. ❑ *That census counted a quarter of a billion Americans.* [from Latin]

cent /sɛnt/ (cents) **N-COUNT** A **cent** is a coin. There are one hundred cents in a dollar. ❑ *The book cost six dollars and fifty cents.* [from Latin]

Word Web   cellphone

The word **"cell"** is not something inside the **cellular phone** itself. It describes the area around the **wireless transmitter** that your phone uses to make a call. The electrical system and **battery** in today's **mobile** phones are tiny. This makes their electronic **signals** weak. They can't travel very far. Therefore today's **cellular** phone systems need a lot of cells close together. When you make a call, your phone connects to the wireless transmitter with the strongest signal. Then it chooses a radio **channel** and connects you to the number you dialed. If you are riding in a car, **stations** in several different cells may handle your call.

cen|ter /sɛntər/ (**centers, centering, centered**)

1 **N-COUNT** The **center** of something is the middle of it. ❑ *We sat in the center of the room.*

2 **N-COUNT** A **center** is a place where people can take part in a particular activity, or get help. ❑ *The building is now a health center.*

3 **N-COUNT** If someone or something is the **center of** attention, people are giving them a lot of attention. ❑ *She was used to being the center of attention.*

4 **V-T/V-I** If a discussion, a plan, or an idea **centers on** a particular thing or person, that thing or person is the main subject of attention. ❑ *...a plan which centered on academic achievement.* [from Latin]

→ look at Picture Dictionary: **soccer**

Word Partnership	Use **center** with :
N	**center of** a circle **1**
	convention center, **research** center **2**
	center **of attention 3**

cen|ter stage **N-NONCOUNT** ARTS In a theater, **center stage** is the middle part of the stage.

cen|ti|li|ter /sɛntɪlitər/ (**centiliters**)
N-COUNT A **centiliter** is ten milliliters or one-hundredth of a liter.

Word Link	*cent ≈ hundred : centimeter, century, percentage*

cen|ti|me|ter /sɛntɪmitər/ (**centimeters**)
N-COUNT MATH A **centimeter** is a unit for measuring length. There are ten millimeters in a centimeter. ❑ *This tiny plant is only a few centimeters high.*

→ look at Picture Dictionary: **measurement**

cen|ti|pede /sɛntɪpid/ (**centipedes**)
N-COUNT A **centipede** is a long, thin creature with a lot of legs.

cen|tral /sɛntrəl/

1 **ADJ** Something that is **central** is in the middle part of a place. ❑ *They live in Central America.*

2 **ADJ** The **central** person or thing in a situation is the most important one. ❑ *Black dance music has been central to pop since the early '60s.* [from Latin]

cen|tral heat|ing **N-NONCOUNT** Central heating is a heating system that uses hot air or water to heat every part of a building.

cen|tral|ize /sɛntrəlaɪz/ (**centralizes, centralizing, centralized**) **V-T** SOCIAL STUDIES

To **centralize** a country or organization means to create a system in which one central group of people gives instructions to regional groups. ❑ *Very large firms usually centralize their operations.* ● **cen|trali|za|tion** /sɛntrəlɪzeɪʃən/ **N-NONCOUNT** ❑ *...the centralization of power.* [from Latin]

cen|tral nerv|ous sys|tem (**central nervous systems**) **N-COUNT** SCIENCE Your **central nervous system** is the part of your nervous system that consists of the brain and spinal cord.

→ look at Word Web: **nervous system**

cen|trifu|gal force /sɛntrɪfyəgəl fɔrs, -trɪfəgəl/ **N-NONCOUNT** SCIENCE **Centrifugal force** is the force that makes objects move away from the center when they are moving around a central point. ❑ *The juice is removed by centrifugal force.*

cen|trip|etal ac|cel|era|tion /sɛntrɪpɪtəl æksɛləreɪʃən/ **N-NONCOUNT** SCIENCE **Centripetal acceleration** is the acceleration that is required to keep an object traveling at a constant speed when it is moving in a circle.

cen|tro|mere /sɛntrəmɪər/ (**centromeres**)
N-COUNT SCIENCE The **centromere** is the central part of a chromosome where the two ends of the chromosome are connected. [from Latin]

cen|tu|ry /sɛntʃəri/ (**centuries**)

1 **N-COUNT** A **century** is one hundred years. ❑ *The story started a century ago.* ❑ *She was one of the most important painters of the nineteenth century.*

2 **N-COUNT** A **century** is any period of a hundred years. ❑ *The winter was the worst in a century.* [from Latin]

cephalo|tho|rax /sɛfələθɔræks/ (**cephalothoraces** or **cephalothoraxes**)
N-COUNT SCIENCE In animals such as spiders and crabs, the **cephalothorax** is the front part of the body consisting of the head and thorax.

ce|ram|ic /sɪræmɪk/ (**ceramics**)

1 **N-NONCOUNT** ARTS **Ceramic** is clay that has been heated to a very high temperature so that it becomes hard. ❑ *The wall is covered with ceramic tiles.*

2 **N-PLURAL** ARTS **Ceramics** are ceramic objects. ❑ *The museum has a huge collection of Chinese ceramics.* [from Greek]

→ look at Word Web: **pottery**

C

ce|real /sɪəriəl/ (**cereals**)
■ **N-COUNT/N-NONCOUNT** Cereal is a food made from grain, that you can mix with milk and eat for breakfast. ❑ *I have a bowl of cereal every morning.*
■ **N-COUNT** Cereals are plants that produce grain for food. ❑ *Rice is similar to other cereal grains such as corn and wheat.* [from Latin]

cer|ebel|lum /sɛrəbɛləm/ (**cerebellums** or **cerebella**) **N-COUNT** SCIENCE The **cerebellum** is a part of the brain in humans and other mammals that controls the body's movements and balance. [from Latin]

cer|ebrum /sərɪbrəm, sɛrə-/ (**cerebrums** or **cerebra**) **N-COUNT** SCIENCE The **cerebrum** is the large, front part of the brain, which is divided into two halves and controls activities such as thinking and memory. [from Latin]

cer|emo|nial /sɛrɪmoʊniəl/ **ADJ** Something that is **ceremonial** is used or done at a ceremony. ❑ *The children watched the ceremonial dances.* [from Medieval Latin]

cer|emo|ny /sɛrɪmoʊni/ (**ceremonies**)
■ **N-COUNT** A ceremony is a formal event. ❑ *...a wedding ceremony.*
■ **N-NONCOUNT** Ceremony consists of the special things that are said and done on very formal occasions. ❑ *The historic meeting took place with great ceremony.* [from Medieval Latin]
→ look at Word Webs: **graduation, wedding**

cer|tain /sɜrtən/
■ **ADJ** If you are **certain** about something or if it is **certain**, you strongly believe it is true. ❑ *She's absolutely certain that she's going to recover.* ❑ *One thing is certain, both players are great sportsmen.*
■ **ADJ** You use **certain** when you are referring to one particular thing or person, although you are not saying exactly which it is. ❑ *There will be certain people who'll say "I told you so!"*
■ **PHRASE** If you know something **for certain**, you have no doubt at all about it. ❑ *She didn't know for certain if he was at home.*
■ **PHRASE** If you **make certain that** something is the way you want it to be, you check it so that you are sure. ❑ *Parents should make certain that children do their homework.* [from Old French]

Thesaurus	certain	Also look up :
ADJ	definite, known, positive, sure, true; (ant.) unmistakable ■	

cer|tain|ly /sɜrtənli/
■ **ADV** You use **certainly** to show that you are sure about what you are saying. ❑ *The meeting will almost certainly last an hour.*
■ **ADV** You use **certainly** when you are agreeing or disagreeing strongly with what someone has said. ❑ *"Are you still friends?"—"Certainly." ❑ "Perhaps I should go now."—"Certainly not!"* [from Old French]

cer|tain|ty /sɜrtənti/ **N-NONCOUNT** Certainty is when you have no doubts at all about something. ❑ *I can tell you this with absolute certainty.* [from Old French]

Word Link	cert ≈ determined, true : ascertain,
	certificate, certify

cer|tifi|cate /sərtɪfɪkɪt/ (**certificates**) **N-COUNT** A **certificate** is an official document that proves that the facts on it are true. ❑ *You must show your birth certificate.*
❑ *I have a certificate signed by my teacher.* [from Old French]
→ look at Word Web: **wedding**

cer|ti|fy /sɜrtɪfaɪ/ (**certifies, certifying, certified**) **V-T** If someone **certifies** something, they officially say that it is true. ❑ *The doctor certified that I was suffering from a chest infection.* [from Old French]

chain /tʃeɪn/ (**chains, chaining, chained**)
■ **N-COUNT** A **chain** is a line of metal rings that are connected together. ❑ *He wore a gold chain around his neck.*
■ **N-COUNT** A **chain of** stores is a number of them owned by the same company. ❑ *...a large supermarket chain.*
■ **N-SING** A **chain of** events is a series of them happening one after another. ❑ *...the chain of events that led to his departure.*
■ **V-T** If a person or thing **is chained to** something, they are attached to it with a chain. ❑ *The dogs were chained to a fence.* [from Old French]
→ look at Word Web: **food**

chair /tʃɛər/ (**chairs, chairing, chaired**)
■ **N-COUNT** A **chair** is a piece of furniture for one person to sit on, with a back and four legs. ❑ *He suddenly got up from his chair.*
■ **N-COUNT** The **chair of** a committee or meeting is the person in charge of it. ❑ *She is the chair of the Defense Advisory Committee on Women in the Military.*
■ **V-T** If you **chair** a meeting, you are the

person who controls it. ❑ *They asked him to chair the committee meeting.* [from Old French]

chair|man /tʃɛərmən/ (**chairmen**) **N-COUNT** The **chairman** of a meeting or an organization is the person who controls it. ❑ *He is chairman of the committee that wrote the report.*

chair|person /tʃɛərpɜrsən/ (**chairpersons**) **N-COUNT** The **chairperson** of a meeting or organization is the person who controls it. ❑ *She's the chairperson of the planning committee.*

chair|woman /tʃɛərwʊmən/ (**chairwomen**) **N-COUNT** The **chairwoman** of a meeting or organization is the woman who controls it. ❑ *The chairwoman welcomed us and opened the meeting.*

chalk /tʃɔk/ (**chalks**)
■ **N-NONCOUNT** **Chalk** is a soft white rock.
■ **N-COUNT/N-NONCOUNT** ARTS **Chalk** is small sticks of chalk that you use for writing or drawing. ❑ *Now use a piece of colored chalk.* [from Old English]

chalk|board /tʃɔkbɔrd/ (**chalkboards**) **N-COUNT** A **chalkboard** is a dark-colored board that you write on with chalk. [from Old English]

chal|lenge /tʃælɪndʒ/ (**challenges, challenging, challenged**)
■ **N-COUNT/N-NONCOUNT** A **challenge** is something difficult to do. ❑ *His first challenge was learning the rules of the game.*
■ **V-T** If you **challenge** someone, you invite them to fight or play a game with you. ❑ *Jackson challenged O'Meara to another game.*
■ **N-COUNT** **Challenge** is also a noun. ❑ *Both the Swiss and the German team will provide a serious challenge for the gold medals.*
■ **V-T** If you **challenge** ideas or people, you question their truth or authority. ❑ *They challenged the laws and tried to change them.*
■ **N-COUNT** **Challenge** is also a noun. ❑ *...a challenge to his authority.* [from Old French]

Word Partnership	Use **challenge** with :
ADJ	**biggest** challenge, **new** challenge ■ **legal** challenge ■
V	**accept a** challenge, **present a** challenge ■ ■ **dare to** challenge ■

chal|leng|er /tʃælɪndʒər/ (**challengers**) **N-COUNT** A **challenger** is someone who competes for a position or title. ❑ *...a*

challenger for the America's Cup. [from Old French]

chal|leng|ing /tʃælɪndʒɪŋ/
■ **ADJ** A **challenging** task or job requires great effort and determination. ❑ *Mike found a challenging job as a computer programmer.*
■ **ADJ** **Challenging** behavior seems to be inviting people to argue or compete. ❑ *Mona gave him a challenging look.* [from Old French]

cham|ber /tʃeɪmbər/ (**chambers**)
■ **N-COUNT** A **chamber** is a large room that is designed and equipped for a particular purpose, for example for formal meetings. ❑ *...the council chamber.* ❑ *...a burial chamber.*
■ **N-COUNT** SOCIAL STUDIES You can refer to a country's legislature or to one section of it as a **chamber**. ❑ *...a two-chamber parliament.* [from Old French]

cham|pagne /ʃæmpeɪn/ (**champagnes**) **N-COUNT/N-NONCOUNT** **Champagne** is an expensive French white wine with bubbles in it.

cham|pi|on /tʃæmpiən/ (**champions**)
■ **N-COUNT** SPORTS A **champion** is the winner of a competition. ❑ *He was an Olympic champion twice.* ❑ *Kasparov became the world champion.*
■ **N-COUNT** If you are a **champion of** a person or a principle, you support or defend them. ❑ *...a champion of freedom.* [from Old French]

cham|pi|on|ship /tʃæmpiənʃɪp/ (**championships**) **N-COUNT** SPORTS A **championship** is a competition to find the best player or team in a particular sport. ❑ *The world chess championship was on TV last night.* [from Old French]

chance /tʃæns/ (**chances**)
■ **N-COUNT/N-NONCOUNT** If there is a **chance** that something will happen, it is possible that it will happen. ❑ *There is a good chance that we can win the game against Australia.*
■ **N-SING** If you have a **chance to** do something, there is a time when you can do it. ❑ *Everyone gets a chance to vote.* ❑ *Millions of children never get the chance to go to school.*
■ **PHRASE** Something that happens **by chance** was not planned by anyone. ❑ *He met Justin by chance in the street.*
■ **PHRASE** When you **take a chance**, you try to do something although there is a risk of danger or failure. ❑ *You take a chance on the*

weather if you vacation in Maine. [from Old French]

Word Partnership	Use **chance** with :
ADJ	**fair** chance, **good** chance, **slight** chance **1**
N	chance **of success**, chance **of survival 1**
V	**get a** chance, **give** *someone/something* **a** chance, **have a** chance, **miss a** chance **2**

chan|cel|lor /tʃænsələr, -slər/ (**chancellors**)
1 **N-COUNT** SOCIAL STUDIES **Chancellor** is the title of the head of government in Germany and Austria. ❑ *...Chancellor Angela Merkel of Germany.*
2 **N-COUNT** The head of some American universities is called **the chancellor**.
3 **N-COUNT** In Britain, the **Chancellor** or **Chancellor of the Exchequer** is the minister in charge of finance and taxes. [from Late Latin]

change /tʃeɪndʒ/ (**changes, changing, changed**)
1 **N-COUNT/N-NONCOUNT** If there is a **change**, something becomes different. ❑ *There will soon be some big changes in our company.*
2 **V-T/V-I** When something **changes** or when you **change** it, it becomes different. ❑ *The color of the sky changed from pink to blue.* ❑ *She changed into a happy woman.* ❑ *They should change the law.*
3 **V-T/V-I** To **change** something means to replace it with something new or different. ❑ *They decided to change the name of the band.* ❑ *He changed to a different medication.*
4 **N-COUNT** **Change** is also a noun. ❑ *A change of leadership alone will not be enough.*
5 **V-T/V-I** When you **change** your clothes, you put on different ones. ❑ *Ben changed his shirt.* ❑ *They let her shower and change.*
6 **V-T/V-I** When you **change** buses or planes, or **change**, you get off one bus or plane and get on to another in order to continue your trip. ❑ *I changed planes in Chicago.*
7 **N-NONCOUNT** Your **change** is the money that you get back when you pay with more money than something costs. ❑ *"There's your change."—"Thanks very much."*
8 **N-NONCOUNT** **Change** is coins. ❑ *I need 36 cents. Do you have any change?*
9 **PHRASE** If you say that something is happening **for a change**, you mean that it is

unusual but you are happy about it. ❑ *Now let me ask you a question, for a change.*
10 **PHRASE** SCIENCE When a substance undergoes a **change of state**, it changes from one form to another, for example from a solid to a liquid. [from Old French]

Thesaurus	change	Also look up :
N	adjustment, alteration **1**	
V	adapt, modify, transform, vary **2 3**	

Word Partnership	Use **change** with :
V	**adapt to** change, **resist** change **1** **make a** change **1**
ADJ	**gradual** change, **social** change, **sudden** change **1** **loose** change, **spare** change **7**
N	change **of pace, policy** change **1** change **of address**, change **clothes,** change **color**, change **direction**, change **the subject 2-4**

chan|nel /tʃænəl/ (**channels**)
1 **N-COUNT** A **channel** is a television station. ❑ *There is a huge number of television channels in America.*
2 **N-COUNT** GEOGRAPHY A **channel** is a narrow passage that water can flow along. ❑ *...a shipping channel.* [from Old French]
→ look at Word Web: **cellphone**

chant /tʃænt/ (**chants, chanting, chanted**)
1 **N-COUNT** A **chant** is a word or group of words that is repeated again and again. ❑ *Then the crowd started the chant of "U-S-A!"*
2 **V-T/V-I** If you **chant** something, or if you **chant**, you repeat the same words again and again. ❑ *The people chanted his name.* ❑ *The crowd chanted, "We are with you."* [from Old French]

cha|os /keɪɒs/ **N-NONCOUNT** **Chaos** is when there is no order or organization. ❑ *The race ended in chaos.* [from Latin]

Word Partnership	Use **chaos** with :
V	**bring** chaos, **cause** chaos
ADJ	**complete** chaos, **total** chaos
N	chaos **and confusion**

cha|ot|ic /keɪɒtɪk/ **ADJ** Something that is **chaotic** is completely confused and without order. ❑ *The city seemed to be a chaotic place to me.* [from Latin]

chap|el /tʃæpəl/ (**chapels**) **N-COUNT** A **chapel** is a small church or a part of a church that people pray in. ❑ *She went to the chapel on the hillside to pray.* [from Old French]

chap|ter /tʃǽptər/ (**chapters**) **N-COUNT**
LANGUAGE ARTS A **chapter** is a part of a book. ❑ *For more information, see Chapter 4.* [from Old French]

char|ac|ter /kǽrɪktər/ (**characters**)
1 **N-COUNT** The **character** of a person or a place is all the things that make them different from other people or places. ❑ *It's difficult to understand the change in her character.*
2 **N-COUNT** LANGUAGE ARTS The **characters** in a story are the people in it. ❑ *Collard himself plays the main character.*
3 **N-COUNT** A **character** is a letter or another symbol that is written or printed. ❑ *...a shopping list written in Chinese characters.*
4 **N-COUNT/N-NONCOUNT** Your **character** is your reputation. ❑ *...a series of personal attacks on my character.* [from Latin]
→ look at Word Web: **printing**

Word Partnership	Use character with :
N	character **flaw**, character **trait** **1**
	character **development** **1** **2**
	character **in a book/movie**, **cartoon** character **2**
ADJ	**moral** character **1**
	fictional character, **main** character, **minor** character **2**

char|ac|ter|is|tic /kǽrɪktərɪ́stɪk/ (**characteristics**)
1 **N-COUNT** A **characteristic** is a quality that is typical of someone or something. ❑ *The twins already had their own characteristics.*
2 **ADJ** If something is **characteristic of** a person or a thing, it is typical of them. ❑ *Refusal to admit defeat was characteristic of Davis.* ❑ *Churches are a characteristic feature of the English countryside.* [from Latin]

char|ac|ter|is|tic prop|er|ty (**characteristic properties**) **N-COUNT** SCIENCE
A **characteristic property** of a substance is a quality of the substance that distinguishes it from other substances, for example the fact that it melts at a particular temperature.

char|ac|teri|za|tion /kǽrɪktərɪzéɪʃən/ (**characterizations**)
1 **N-COUNT/N-NONCOUNT** Characterization is the description of someone or something as a particular thing or a particular type of thing. ❑ *...his characterization of other designers as "thieves."*
2 **N-COUNT/N-NONCOUNT** Characterization is the way an author or an actor describes or shows what a character is like. [from Latin]

char|ac|ter|ize /kǽrɪktəraɪz/ (**characterizes, characterizing, characterized**)
1 **V-T** If something **is characterized by** a particular feature or quality, that feature or quality is an obvious part of it. [FORMAL] ❑ *This election campaign has been characterized by violence.*
2 **V-T** If you **characterize** someone or something **as** a particular thing, you describe them in that way. [FORMAL] ❑ *Both companies characterized the relationship as "friendly."* [from Latin]

char|coal /tʃɑ́rkoʊl/ **N-NONCOUNT** ARTS
Charcoal is burnt wood that you can use for drawing. ❑ *We all did charcoal drawings of the building.*
→ look at Word Web: **firework**

charge /tʃɑ́rdʒ/ (**charges, charging, charged**)
1 **V-T/V-I** If you **charge** someone, you ask them to pay money for something. ❑ *The driver only charged us $2 each.* ❑ *How much do you charge for printing photos?*
2 **V-T** If you **charge** something you are buying to your credit card, you use a credit card to buy it. ❑ *I'll charge it to my Visa.*
3 **V-T** When the police **charge** someone, they formally tell them that they have done something wrong. ❑ *They have enough evidence to charge him.*
4 **V-I** If you **charge** toward someone or something, you move quickly toward them. ❑ *He charged through the door to my mother's office.* ❑ *Our captain ordered us to charge.*
5 **V-T** SCIENCE To **charge** a battery means to put electricity into it. ❑ *Alex forgot to charge his cellphone.*
6 **N-COUNT** SCIENCE An electrical **charge** is the amount or type of electrical force that something has.
7 **N-COUNT** A **charge** is an amount of money that you have to pay for a service. ❑ *We can arrange this for a small charge.*
8 **N-COUNT** A **charge** is a formal statement from the police that someone has done something wrong. ❑ *He may still face criminal charges.*
9 **PHRASE** If you are **in charge of** someone or

C

something, you are responsible for them.
❑ *Who is in charge here?* [from Old French]
→ look at Word Webs: **lightning, magnet, trial**

Word Partnership	Use **charge** with :	
N	charge **a fee** 1	
	charge **a battery** 5	
ADJ	**criminal** charge, **guilty of a** charge 3	
V	**deny a** charge 3	
	lead a charge 4	

cha|ris|ma /kərɪzmə/ **N-NONCOUNT** You say that someone has **charisma** when they can attract, influence, and inspire people by their personal qualities. ❑ *He doesn't have the personal charisma to inspire people.* ● **char|is|mat|ic** /kærɪzmætɪk/ **ADJ** ❑ *...her charismatic personality.* [from Church Latin]

chari|table /tʃærɪtəbəl/
1 **ADJ** A **charitable** organization or activity helps and supports people who are ill, disabled, or very poor. ❑ *...charitable work.*
2 **ADJ** Someone who is **charitable** is kind and tolerant. ❑ *They were not very charitable toward the referee.* [from Old French]

char|ity /tʃærɪti/ (**charities**)
N-COUNT/N-NONCOUNT A **charity** is an organization that collects money for people who need help. ❑ *Michael is working for a children's charity.* [from Old French]

Word Partnership	Use **charity** with :	
V	**collect for** charity, **donate to** charity, **give to** charity	
N	**donation to** charity, charity **event**, **money for** charity, charity **organization**, charity **work**	
ADJ	**local** charity, **private** charity	

Charles's law /tʃɑrlzɪz lɔ/ also **Charles' law** **N-NONCOUNT** **SCIENCE** **Charles's law** is a principle in physics which states that the volume of a gas increases when the gas gets hotter.

charm /tʃɑrm/ (**charms, charming, charmed**)
1 **N-NONCOUNT** **Charm** is the quality of being pleasant and attractive. ❑ *This hotel has real charm.*
2 **V-T** If you **charm** someone, you please them by being pleasant and attractive. ❑ *He charmed all of us.*
3 **N-COUNT** A **charm** is an act, a saying, or an object that is believed to have magic powers. ❑ *...a good luck charm.* [from Old French]
→ look at Picture Dictionary: **jewelry**

charm|ing /tʃɑrmɪŋ/ **ADJ** If someone is **charming**, they are very pleasant and attractive. ❑ *He seemed to be a charming young man.* [from Old French]

chart /tʃɑrt/ (**charts**) **N-COUNT** A **chart** is a diagram or a graph that shows information. ❑ *See the chart on next page for more details.* [from Latin]
→ look at Picture Dictionary: **chart**

char|ter /tʃɑrtər/ (**charters, chartering, chartered**)
1 **N-COUNT** **SOCIAL STUDIES** A **charter** is a formal document that describes the rights or principles of an organization. ❑ *...the United Nations Charter.*
2 **V-T** If someone **charters** a plane or a boat, they rent it for their own use. ❑ *He chartered a jet to fly her home.* [from Old French]

chase /tʃeɪs/ (**chases, chasing, chased**)
1 **V-T** If you **chase** someone, you run after them in order to catch them. ❑ *She chased the boys for 100 yards.*
2 **N-COUNT** **Chase** is also a noun. ❑ *The chase ended at about 10:30 p.m. on Highway 522.* [from Old French]

Picture Dictionary
chart

bar graph

35 students in class				
Monday	28	30	29	34
Tuesday	30	35	29	28
Wednesday	29	31	29	33
Thursday	28	34	33	29
Friday	30	33	35	31
	1	2	3	4

chart

line graph

92%
8%

pie chart

chat /tʃæt/ (**chats, chatting, chatted**)

1 **V-T/V-I** When people **chat**, they talk in an informal, friendly way. ❑ *The women sit and chat at coffee time.* ❑ *I was chatting to him the other day.*

2 **N-COUNT** Chat is also a noun. ❑ *I had a chat with John.*

3 **V-I** TECHNOLOGY In computing, when you **chat**, you exchange written messages with someone using the Internet. ❑ *The problem of cyberbullying appears to be growing, as more kids chat on the Internet.*

4 **N-COUNT** TECHNOLOGY Chat is also a noun. ❑ *After the program, the minister took questions from the public in an online chat session.*

chat room (**chat rooms**) also **chatroom**

N-COUNT TECHNOLOGY A **chat room** is a website where people can exchange messages.

chat|ter /tʃætər/ (**chatters, chattering, chattered**)

1 **V-I** If you **chatter**, you talk quickly about unimportant things. ❑ *Erica chattered about her grandchildren.*

2 **N-NONCOUNT** Chatter is also a noun. ❑ *The students stopped their noisy chatter.*

3 **V-I** If your teeth **chatter**, they keep knocking together because you are cold. ❑ *She was so cold her teeth chattered.*

Word Link	*eur ≈ one who does : amateur, chauffeur, entrepreneur*

chauf|feur /ʃoufər, ʃoufɜr/ (**chauffeurs**)

N-COUNT A **chauffeur** is a person whose job is to drive for another person. [from French]

cheap /tʃip/ (**cheaper, cheapest**)

1 **ADJ** Goods or services that are **cheap** cost little money or less than you expected. ❑ *I'm going to rent a room if I can find somewhere cheap enough.* ❑ *People who own cars are calling for cheaper oil.* ● **cheap|ly** **ADV** ❑ *You can deliver more food more cheaply by ship.*

2 **ADJ** Cheap goods cost less money than similar products but their quality is often bad. ❑ *Don't buy any of those cheap watches.*

3 **ADJ** If you describe someone as **cheap**, you are criticizing them for not wanting to spend money. ❑ *He's too cheap to take a cab.* [from Old English]

Thesaurus	cheap Also look up :
ADJ	budget, economical, low-cost, reasonable; (ant.) costly, expensive **1** second-rate **2**

cheat /tʃit/ (**cheats, cheating, cheated**)

1 **V-I** If someone **cheats**, they do not obey the rules in a game or exam. ❑ *Students sometimes cheated in order to get into top schools.* ● **cheat|ing** **N-NONCOUNT** ❑ *He was accused of cheating.*

2 **N-COUNT** Cheat is also a noun. ❑ *Are you calling me a cheat?*

3 **V-T** If someone **cheats** you **out of** something, they get it from you by behaving dishonestly. ❑ *It was a deliberate effort to cheat them out of their money.*

▶ **cheat on** If someone **cheats on** their husband, wife, or partner, they have a sexual relationship with another person. [INFORMAL]

check /tʃɛk/ (**checks, checking, checked**)

1 **V-T/V-I** If you **check** something, you make sure that it is correct. ❑ *Check the meanings of the words in a dictionary.* ❑ *I think there is an age limit, but I'll check.* ❑ *He checked whether he had a clean shirt.*

2 **N-COUNT** Check is also a noun. ❑ *We need to do some quick checks before the plane leaves.*

3 **V-T** If you **check** something that is written on a piece of paper, you put a mark like this ✔ next to it. ❑ *Please check the box below.*

4 **V-T** When you **check** your luggage at an airport, you give it to the airline so that it can go on your plane. ❑ *We checked our luggage early and walked around the airport.*

5 **N-COUNT** The **check** in a restaurant is a piece of paper with the cost of your meal on it.

6 **N-COUNT** Checks or a check is a pattern of squares, usually of two colors. ❑ *Styles include stripes and checks.*

7 **N-COUNT** A **check** is a printed form from a bank that you write on and use to pay for things. ❑ *He handed me a check for $1,500.* [from Old French]

→ look at Picture Dictionary: **answer**

▶ **check in** **1** When you **check in** at an airport or a hotel, you tell the person at the desk that you have arrived. ❑ *He checked in at Amsterdam's Schiphol airport for a flight to Atlanta.*

2 → see also **check-in**

→ look at Word Web: **hotel**

▶ **check out** **1** When you **check out of** a hotel, you pay the bill and leave. ❑ *They packed and checked out of the hotel.* ❑ *They checked out yesterday morning.*

2 When you **check out** a book, you borrow it from a library. ❑ *He checked out books on architecture.*

3 If you **check out** in a store, you pay for the

things you are buying. ❏ *He headed to the cash register to check out.*

4 If you **check out** something or someone, you find out information about them. ❏ *We ought to check him out on the computer.*

▶ **check up** If you **check up on** something or someone, you find out information about them. ❏ *Are you asking me to check up on my colleagues?*

Thesaurus check Also look up :	
v	confirm, find out, make sure, verify; (*ant.*) ignore, overlook **1**

Word Partnership Use check with :	
PREP	check **for/that** *something*, check **with** *someone* **1**
N	**background** check, **credit** check, **security** check **1**
	check **your baggage/luggage** **3**
V	**cash** a check, **deposit** a check, **pay with** a check **6**

checked /tʃɛkt/ **ADJ** Something that is **checked** has a pattern of small squares, usually of two colors. ❏ *The waiter had a checked shirt on.* [from Old French]

check|ers /tʃɛkərz/ **N-NONCOUNT** Checkers is a game for two people, that you play with 24 round pieces on a board.

check-in (**check-ins**) **N-COUNT** At an airport, a **check-in** is the counter or desk where you check in.

check|ing ac|count (**checking accounts**) **N-COUNT** A **checking account** is a personal bank account that you can take money out of by writing a check.

check mark (**check marks**) **N-COUNT** A **check mark** is a written mark like this ✔. You use it to show that something is correct or done.

check|out /tʃɛkaʊt/ (**checkouts**) **N-COUNT** In a supermarket or other store, a **checkout** is where you pay for the things you are buying.

check-up (**check-ups**) **N-COUNT** A **check-up** is an examination by your doctor or dentist.

cheek /tʃik/ (**cheeks**) **N-COUNT** Your **cheeks** are the sides of your face below your eyes. ❏ *The tears started rolling down my cheeks.* [from Old English]
→ look at Picture Dictionary: **face**

cheer /tʃɪər/ (**cheers, cheering, cheered**)
1 **V-T/V-I** When people **cheer**, they shout loudly to show they are pleased or to encourage someone. ❏ *We cheered as she went up the steps to the stage.* ❏ *Thousands of Americans cheered him on his return.*

2 **N-COUNT** Cheer is also a noun. ❏ *The audience gave him a loud cheer.* [from Old French]

▶ **cheer up** When you **cheer up** you become happier. When you **cheer** someone **up**, you make them feel happier. ❏ *Cheer up. Life could be worse.* ❏ *Stop trying to cheer me up.*

cheer|ful /tʃɪərfəl/
1 **ADJ** Someone who is **cheerful** seems to be happy. ❏ *Paddy was always smiling and cheerful.*
● **cheer|ful|ly** **ADV** ❏ *"We've got good news," Pat said cheerfully.* ● **cheer|ful|ness** **N-NONCOUNT** ❏ *I liked his natural cheerfulness.*
2 **ADJ** Something that is **cheerful** is pleasant and makes you feel happy. ❏ *The nursery is bright and cheerful.* [from Old French]

cheer|leader /tʃɪərlidər/ (**cheerleaders**)
N-COUNT SPORTS A **cheerleader** is one of a group of people who encourage the crowd to shout support for their team at a sports event.

cheese /tʃiz/ (**cheeses**)
N-COUNT/N-NONCOUNT Cheese is a solid food made from milk. It is usually white or yellow. ❏ *We had bread and cheese for lunch.* ❏ *This shop sells delicious French cheeses.* [from Old English]

chef /ʃɛf/ (**chefs**) **N-COUNT** A **chef** is a cook in a restaurant. [from French]

Word Link chem ≈ chemical : biochemical, chemical, chemistry

chemi|cal /kɛmɪkəl/ (**chemicals**)
1 **ADJ** SCIENCE **Chemical** means relating to chemicals or chemistry. ❏ *Do you know what caused the chemical reaction?* ❏ *Almost all of the natural chemical elements are found in the ocean.*
● **chemi|cal|ly** /kɛmɪkli/ **ADV** ❏ *...chemically-related drugs.*
2 **N-COUNT** SCIENCE **Chemicals** are substances that are used in a chemical process or made by a chemical process. ❏ *The program was about the use of chemicals in farming.* [from French]
→ look at Word Webs: **farm, fireworks, periodic table**

chemi|cal bond (**chemical bonds**) **N-COUNT** SCIENCE A **chemical bond** is the force that holds atoms together to make molecules.

chemi|cal bond|ing **N-NONCOUNT** SCIENCE **Chemical bonding** is the joining together of atoms to make molecules.

chem|i|cal change (**chemical changes**)
N-COUNT SCIENCE A **chemical change** is a
change in a substance that results in a new
or different substance. For example, when
wood is burned it changes to smoke and ash.

chem|i|cal en|er|gy **N-NONCOUNT** SCIENCE
Chemical energy is the energy that is
released during a chemical reaction or a
chemical change.

chem|i|cal equa|tion (**chemical equations**)
N-COUNT SCIENCE A **chemical equation** is an
equation that describes a chemical reaction.

chem|i|cal for|mu|la (**chemical formulas** or
chemical formulae) **N-COUNT** SCIENCE
A **chemical formula** is the scientific name
for a substance, based on the number and
type of atoms in one molecule of the
substance. For example, H_2O is the chemical
formula for water.

chem|i|cal prop|er|ty (**chemical properties**)
N-COUNT SCIENCE The **chemical properties** of
a substance are the physical qualities that
determine how it will react with other
substances.

chem|i|cal re|ac|tion (**chemical reactions**)
N-COUNT SCIENCE A **chemical reaction** is the
change that happens when two or more
substances are mixed and a new substance
is formed.

chem|i|cal weath|er|ing **N-NONCOUNT**
SCIENCE **Chemical weathering** is the change
that takes place in the structure of rocks and
minerals as a result of their exposure to
water and the atmosphere.

chem|ist /kɛmɪst/ (**chemists**) **N-COUNT**
SCIENCE A **chemist** is a scientist who studies
chemistry. [from New Latin]

chem|is|try /kɛmɪstri/ **N-NONCOUNT**
SCIENCE **Chemistry** is the science of gases,
liquids, and solids, their structure, and how
they change.

cher|ry /tʃɛri/ (**cherries**) **N-COUNT** **Cherries**
are small, round fruit with red skins.
[from Old English]

chess /tʃɛs/ **N-NONCOUNT** **Chess** is a game for
two people, played on a board using
different shaped pieces. ❑ *He was playing
chess with his uncle.* [from Old French]
→ look at Word Web: **chess**

chest /tʃɛst/ (**chests**)
1 **N-COUNT** Your **chest** is the top part of the
front of your body from your neck to your
stomach. ❑ *He folded his arms across his broad
chest.* ❑ *He was shot in the chest.*
2 **N-COUNT** A **chest** is a large, strong box for
storing things. ❑ *We know she has money locked
in a chest somewhere.* [from Old English]
→ look at Picture Dictionary: **body**

chew /tʃu/ (**chews, chewing, chewed**) **V-T/V-I**
When you **chew** food, you break it up with
your teeth in your mouth. ❑ *Always chew
your food well.* ❑ *He chewed on his toast.*
[from Old English]

chick /tʃɪk/ (**chicks**) **N-COUNT** A **chick** is a
baby bird.

chick|en /tʃɪkɪn/ (**chickens, chickening,
chickened**)
1 **N-COUNT** **Chickens** are birds that are kept
on farms for their eggs and for their meat.
2 **N-NONCOUNT** **Chicken** is the meat of
this bird. ❑ *We had chicken sandwiches.*
[from Old English]
→ look at Word Web: **meat**
▶ **chicken out** If someone **chickens out**,
they do not do something because they are
afraid. [INFORMAL] ❑ *I wanted to ask Mom but
I chickened out.*

Word Web   chess

Some scholars believe the game of **chess** is more than
2,500 years old. In early versions of the **game**, the **king**
was the most powerful **chess piece**. But when the game
was brought to Europe in the Middle Ages, a new form
appeared. It was called Queen's Chess. Modern chess
is based on this game. The king is the most important
piece, but the **queen** is the most powerful. Chess **players**
use **rooks, bishops, knights,** and **pawns** to protect their
king and to put their **opponent** in checkmate.

chief /tʃif/ (**chiefs**)

1 **N-COUNT** The **chief** of a group is its leader. ❑ *The police chief has said very little.*

2 **ADJ** The **chief** thing is the most important one. ❑ *Sunburn is the chief cause of skin cancer.* [from Old French]

Thesaurus	chief	Also look up :
N	boss, director, head, leader **1**	
ADJ	key, main, major; *(ant.)* minor, unimportant **2**	

chief|ly /tʃifli/ **ADV** You use **chiefly** to mean not completely, but especially or mostly. ❑ *Rhodes is chiefly known for her fashion designs.* [from Old French]

child /tʃaɪld/ (**children**)

1 **N-COUNT** A **child** is a young boy or girl. ❑ *When I was a child I lived in a village.* ❑ *The show is free for children age 6 and under.*

2 **N-COUNT** Someone's **children** are their sons and daughters. ❑ *They have three young children.* [from Old English]

→ look at Word Web: **child**
→ look at Picture Dictionary: **age**

Word Partnership	Use child with :
N	child **abuse**, child **care 1**
V	**adopt a** child, **have a** child, **raise a** child **1**
ADJ	**difficult** child, **happy** child, **small/ young** child **1**

Word Link	hood ≈ state, condition : child*hood*, mother*hood*, neighbor*hood*

child|hood /tʃaɪldhʊd/ (**childhoods**)
N-COUNT/N-NONCOUNT A person's **childhood** is the period when they are a child. ❑ *She had a happy childhood.* [from Old English]
→ look at Word Web: **child**

child|ish /tʃaɪldɪʃ/ **ADJ** An adult who is **childish** behaves like a child. ❑ *Paco got up with a childish smile on his face.* [from Old English]

chil|dren /tʃɪldrən/ **Children** is the plural of **child**. [from Old English]

chili /tʃɪli/ (**chilies** or **chilis**) **N-COUNT/ N-NONCOUNT** Chilies are small red or green peppers that taste very hot. [from Spanish]
→ look at Word Web: **spice**

chill /tʃɪl/ (**chills, chilling, chilled**)

1 **V-T/V-I** To **chill** something means to make it cold. ❑ *Chill the fruit salad in the fridge.* ❑ *Put the pastry in the fridge to chill.*

2 **N-COUNT** If something sends a **chill** through you, it gives you a sudden feeling of fear. ❑ *He felt a chill of fear.* [from Old English]
→ look at Word Web: **illness**

▶ **chill out** To **chill out** means to relax. [INFORMAL] ❑ *We often chill out and watch TV.*

chil|lax /tʃɪlæks/ (**chillaxes, chillaxing, chillaxed**) **V-I** If you **chillax**, you stop working for a period of time and relax. [INFORMAL] ❑ *He spent time chillaxing at this beach house.*

chil|ly /tʃɪli/ (**chillier, chilliest**) **ADJ** Chilly means rather cold. ❑ *It was a chilly afternoon.* [from Old English]

chimes /tʃaɪmz/ **N-PLURAL** MUSIC Chimes are a set of small objects that make a ringing sound when they are struck or blown by the wind. ❑ *...the sound of the wind chimes.* [from Latin]
→ look at Picture Dictionary: **percussion**

chim|ney /tʃɪmni/ (**chimneys**) **N-COUNT**
A **chimney** is a pipe above a fire that lets the smoke travel up and out of the building. ❑ *Smoke from chimneys polluted the skies.* [from Old French]

chimney

Word Web   child

In the Middle Ages, only **infants** and **toddlers** enjoyed the freedoms of **childhood**. A **child** of seven or eight helped the family by working. In the countryside, **sons** started working on the family's farm. **Daughters** did important housework. In cities, children became laborers and worked along with adults. Today **parents** treat children with special care. **Babies** play with toys to help them learn. There are educational programs for preschoolers. The idea of **adolescence** as a separate stage of life appeared about 100 years ago. Today **teenagers** often have part-time jobs while they go to school.

chim|pan|zee /tʃɪmpænzi/ (chimpanzees)
N-COUNT A **chimpanzee** is a type of small African ape. [from Kongo]
→ look at Word Webs: **primate, zoo**

chin /tʃɪn/ (chins) **N-COUNT** Your **chin** is the part of your face below your mouth. [from Old English]

chi|na /tʃaɪnə/
1 **N-NONCOUNT** **China** is a hard white substance that is used for making expensive cups and plates. □ *He ate from a small bowl made of china.*
2 **N-NONCOUNT** Cups, plates, and objects made of china are called **china**. □ *Judy collects blue and white china.* [from Persian]
→ look at Word Web: **pottery**

chip /tʃɪp/ (chips, chipping, chipped)
1 **N-COUNT** **Chips** or **potato chips** are very thin slices of fried potato. □ *My snack was a bag of potato chips.*
2 **N-COUNT** A **chip** is a very small part that controls a piece of electronic equipment. □ *...a computer chip.*
3 **N-COUNT** A **chip** is a small piece that has been broken off something. □ *It contains real chocolate chips.*
4 **V-T** If you **chip** something, you break a small piece off it. □ *The candy chipped the woman's tooth.* ● **chipped** **ADJ** □ *The paint on the door was badly chipped.* [from Old English]
▶ **chip in** When a group of people **chip in**, each person gives some money so that they can pay for something together. [INFORMAL] □ *They all chipped in for the gas.*

chlo|rine /klɔrin/ **N-NONCOUNT** **Chlorine** is a gas that is used to disinfect water and to make cleaning products.

chlo|ro|phyll /klɔrəfɪl/ **N-NONCOUNT**
SCIENCE **Chlorophyll** is a green substance in plants which enables them to use the energy from sunlight in order to grow.
→ look at Word Web: **photosynthesis**

chlo|ro|plast /klɔrəplæst/ (chloroplasts)
N-COUNT SCIENCE **Chloroplasts** are the parts of cells in plants and algae where photosynthesis takes place.

choco|late /tʃɔkəlɪt, tʃɔklɪt/ (chocolates)
1 **N-NONCOUNT** **Chocolate** is a sweet brown food that you eat as a sweet, or that is used to give flavor to other food. □ *We shared a bar of chocolate.*

2 **N-COUNT/N-NONCOUNT** **Chocolate** or **hot chocolate** is a hot drink made from chocolate. □ *The visitors can buy tea, coffee, and chocolate.*
3 **N-COUNT** **Chocolates** are small candies or nuts covered with chocolate. □ *The class gave the teacher a box of chocolates.* [from Spanish]

choice /tʃɔɪs/ (choices)
1 **N-COUNT** If there is a **choice of** things, there are several of them and you can choose the one you want. □ *It comes in a choice of colors.* □ *There's a choice between meat or fish.*
2 **N-COUNT** Your **choice** is the thing or things that you choose. □ *Her husband didn't really agree with her choice.*
3 **PHRASE** If you **have no choice**, you cannot choose to do something else. □ *We had to agree—we had no choice.* [from Old French]

Word Partnership	Use **choice** with :
ADJ	**best/good** choice, **wide** choice **1**
N	**freedom of** choice, choice **of** *something* **1**
V	**given a** choice, **have a** choice, **make a** choice **1** **2**

choir /kwaɪər/ (choirs) **N-COUNT** MUSIC
A **choir** is a group of people who sing together. □ *He sang in his church choir for years.* [from Old French]

choke /tʃoʊk/ (chokes, choking, choked)
1 **V-T/V-I** If you **choke**, you cannot breathe because there is not enough air, or because something is blocking your throat. □ *A small child may choke on the toy.* □ *The smoke was choking her.*
2 **V-T** To **choke** someone means to squeeze their neck until they are dead. □ *They choked him with his tie.* [from Old English]

cho|les|ter|ol /kəlɛstərɔl/ **N-NONCOUNT**
SCIENCE **Cholesterol** is a substance that exists in your blood. Too much cholesterol in the blood can cause heart disease. □ *He has a dangerously high cholesterol level.* [from Greek]

choose /tʃuz/ (chooses, choosing, chose, chosen)
1 **V-T/V-I** If you **choose** someone or something, you decide to have that person or thing. □ *Each group will choose its own leader.* □ *You can choose from several different patterns.*
2 **V-T/V-I** If you **choose to** do something, you do it because you want to. □ *A few families chose to educate their children at home.* □ *You can remain silent if you choose.* [from Old English]
→ look at Picture Dictionary: **answer**

Thesaurus	**choose** Also look up :
v	decide on, opt, prefer, settle on; (ant.) pass over, refuse, reject ◼

chop /tʃɒp/ (**chops, chopping, chopped**)
◼ **V-T** If you **chop** something, you cut it into pieces with a knife. ❑ *Chop the butter into small pieces.* ❑ *We started chopping wood for a fire.*
◼ **N-COUNT** A **chop** is a piece of meat cut from the ribs of a sheep or pig. ❑ *...lamb chops.* [of Germanic origin]
→ look at Picture Dictionary: **cut**
▸ **chop down** If you **chop down** a tree, you cut through its trunk. ❑ *Sometimes they chop down a tree for firewood.*
▸ **chop off** To **chop** something **off** means to cut it off. ❑ *Chop off the fish's heads and tails.*

chop|stick /tʃɒpstɪk/
(**chopsticks**) **N-COUNT**
Chopsticks are thin
sticks that people in
East Asia use for
eating food.

chopsticks

chord /kɔrd/ (**chords**) **N-COUNT** MUSIC
A **chord** is a number of musical notes played or sung at the same time. ❑ *I can play a few chords on the guitar.* [from Latin]

chor|do|phone /kɔrdəfoʊn/
(**chordophones**) **N-COUNT** MUSIC
A **chordophone** is any musical instrument which produces its sound by means of vibrating strings, for example a harp or a guitar.

chore /tʃɔr/ (**chores**) **N-COUNT** A **chore** is a job that you have to do, for example cleaning the house. ❑ *After I finished my chores, I could go outside and play.* [from Middle English]

cho|rus /kɔrəs/ (**choruses**)
◼ **N-COUNT** MUSIC A **chorus** is the part of a song that you repeat several times. ❑ *Caroline sang two verses and the chorus of her song.*
◼ **N-COUNT** MUSIC A **chorus** is a large group of people who sing together. ❑ *The Harvard orchestra and chorus performed Beethoven's Ninth Symphony.* [from Latin]

chose /tʃoʊz/ **Chose** is the past tense of **choose**. [from Old English]

cho|sen /tʃoʊzⁿn/ **Chosen** is the past participle of **choose**. [from Old English]

chris|ten /krɪsⁿn/ (**christens, christening, christened**) **V-T** When a baby **is christened**, he or she is given a name during a Christian ceremony. ❑ *She was born in March and christened in June.* [from Old English]

chris|ten|ing /krɪsⁿnɪŋ/ (**christenings**)
N-COUNT A **christening** is a ceremony in which members of a church welcome a baby and it is officially given its name. ❑ *I cried at my granddaughter's christening.* [from Old English]

Word Link	*an, ian ≈ one of, relating to :* Christ*ian*, European, pedestr*ian*

Chris|tian /krɪstʃən/ (**Christians**)
◼ **N-COUNT** A **Christian** is someone who believes in Jesus Christ, and follows what he taught.
◼ **ADJ Christian** means to do with Christians. ❑ *...the Christian Church.* [from Old English]

Chris|ti|an|ity /krɪstʃiænɪti/ **N-NONCOUNT**
Christianity is a religion that believes in Jesus Christ and follows what he taught. [from Old English]

Christ|mas /krɪsməs/ (**Christmases**)
N-COUNT/N-NONCOUNT Christmas is the period around the 25th of December, when Christians celebrate the birth of Jesus Christ. ❑ *Merry Christmas!* ❑ *We're staying at home for the Christmas holidays.* [from Old English]

chro|ma|tid /kroʊmətɪd/ (**chromatids**)
N-COUNT SCIENCE A **chromatid** is one of the two identical halves of a chromosome. [from Greek]

chro|mo|some /kroʊməsoʊm/
(**chromosomes**) **N-COUNT** SCIENCE
A **chromosome** is a part of a cell in an animal or a plant. ❑ *Each cell of our bodies contains 46 chromosomes.*

chro|mo|sphere /kroʊməsfɪər/ **N-SING**
SCIENCE The **chromosphere** is the thin, middle layer of the sun's atmosphere.

Word Link	*chron ≈ time :* chron*ic*, chron*icle*, chron*ological*

chron|ic /krɒnɪk/
◼ **ADJ** A **chronic** illness lasts for a very long time. ❑ *...chronic back pain.* ● **chroni|cal|ly** /krɒnɪkli/ **ADV** ❑ *Most of them were chronically ill.*
◼ **ADJ** A **chronic** situation is very severe and unpleasant. ❑ *...chronic poverty.* ● **chroni|cal|ly** **ADV** ❑ *His wife is chronically ill.* [from Latin]

chroni|cle /krɒnɪkⁿl/ (**chronicles, chronicling, chronicled**)
◼ **V-T** To **chronicle** a series of events means to describe them in the order in which they

happened. ❑ *The series chronicles the adventures of two friends.*

2 **N-COUNT** A **chronicle** is an account or a record of a series of events. ❑ *...a chronicle of the civil rights movement.* [from Latin]
→ look at Word Web: **diary**

chrono|logi|cal /krɒnˈlɒdʒɪkˈl/ **ADJ** If things are described or shown in **chronological** order, they are described or shown in the order in which they happened. ❑ *I have arranged these stories in chronological order.* ● **chrono|logi|cal|ly** **ADV** ❑ *The exhibition is organized chronologically.*

chrysa|lis /krɪsəlɪs/ (**chrysalises**)
1 **N-COUNT** SCIENCE A **chrysalis** is a butterfly or a moth in the stage between being a larva and an adult.
2 **N-COUNT** SCIENCE A **chrysalis** is the hard, protective covering that a chrysalis has. [from Latin]

chub|by /tʃʌbi/ (**chubbier, chubbiest**) **ADJ** A **chubby** person is slightly fat. ❑ *Do you think I'm too chubby?*

chuck /tʃʌk/ (**chucks, chucking, chucked**)
V-T When you **chuck** something somewhere, you throw it there in a casual or careless way. [INFORMAL] ❑ *I chucked the clock in the trash.* [from Chinook Jargon]

chuck|le /tʃʌkˈl/ (**chuckles, chuckling, chuckled**)
1 **V-I** When you **chuckle**, you laugh quietly. ❑ *He chuckled and said, "Of course not."*
2 **N-COUNT** Chuckle is also a noun. ❑ *He gave a little chuckle.*

chunk /tʃʌŋk/ (**chunks**) **N-COUNT** Chunks of something are thick, solid pieces of it. ❑ *Large chunks of ice floated past us.*

chunky /tʃʌŋki/ (**chunkier, chunkiest**) **ADJ** Something that is **chunky** is large and heavy. ❑ *She was wearing a chunky gold necklace.*

church /tʃɜrtʃ/ (**churches**)
1 **N-COUNT/N-NONCOUNT** A **church** is a building where Christians go to pray. ❑ *We got married in Coburn United Methodist Church.* ❑ *The family has gone to church.*
2 **N-COUNT** A **Church** is one of the groups of people within the Christian religion that have their own beliefs and forms of worship. ❑ *...the Catholic Church.* [from Old English]

ci|der /saɪdər/ (**ciders**)
N-COUNT/N-NONCOUNT Cider is a drink made

from apples. ❑ *He ordered a glass of cider.* [from Old French]

ci|gar /sɪɡɑr/ (**cigars**) **N-COUNT** A **cigar** is a roll of dried tobacco leaves that some people smoke. [from Spanish]

ciga|rette /sɪɡərɛt/ (**cigarettes**) **N-COUNT** A **cigarette** is a small tube of paper containing tobacco that some people smoke. [from French]

cilia /sɪliə/ **N-PLURAL** SCIENCE **Cilia** are short thin structures, resembling hairs, on the surfaces of some types of cells and organisms.

cin|der cone /sɪndər koʊn/ (**cinder cones**) or **cinder cone volcano** **N-COUNT** SCIENCE A **cinder cone** or a **cinder cone volcano** is a small volcano with steep sides, made from pieces of rock and ash.

cin|ema /sɪnɪmə/ (**cinemas**) **N-COUNT** A **cinema** is a building where people go to watch movies. ❑ *There is a mall with a multiplex cinema.*

cin|na|mon /sɪnəmən/ **N-NONCOUNT** **Cinnamon** is a sweet spice used for adding flavor to food. [from Old French]
→ look at Word Web: **spice**

cir|ca|dian rhythm /sɜrkeɪdiən rɪðəm/ (**circadian rhythms**) **N-COUNT** SCIENCE **Circadian rhythms** are patterns in the function or behavior of living organisms that are repeated every 24 hours.

Word Link	circ ≈ around : circle, circuit, circulate

cir|cle /sɜrkˈl/ (**circles, circling, circled**)
1 **N-COUNT** MATH A **circle** is a round shape. ❑ *The Japanese flag is white, with a red circle in the center.* ❑ *She drew a mouth, a nose, and two circles for eyes.*
2 **V-T/V-I** To **circle** someone or something means to move around them in a circle. ❑ *The plane circled above the airport, waiting to land.* [from Latin]
→ look at Word Web: **circle**
→ look at Picture Dictionaries: **answer, shapes**

Word Partnership	Use circle with :	
V	draw a circle **1**	
	form a circle, make a circle **1**	
ADJ	big/large/small circle **1**	
PREP	inside/outside/within a circle **1**	

Word Web circle

During the 1970s crop **circles** began to appear in England and the U.S. Something creates these mysterious **rings** in fields of crops such as wheat or corn. Are they messages left by visitors from other worlds? Most people think they are made by humans. The **diameter** of each crop circle ranges from a few inches to a few hundred feet. Sometimes the patterns have **shapes** that are not **circular**, such as **ovals**, **triangles**, and **spirals**. Occasionally the shapes seem to represent something, such as a face or a flower. One pattern even had a written message: *We are not alone.*

Word Link circ ≈ around : circle, circuit, circulate

cir|cuit /sɜrkɪt/ (circuits)
1 N-COUNT A **circuit** is a track that cars race around. □ *...the grand prix circuit.*
2 N-COUNT SCIENCE An electrical **circuit** is a complete path that electricity can flow around. □ *The electrical circuit was broken.* [from Latin]

cir|cu|lar /sɜrkyələr/ ADJ Something that is **circular** is shaped like a circle. □ *The house has a large garage and a circular driveway.* [from Latin]
→ look at Word Web: **circle**

cir|cu|late /sɜrkyəleɪt/ (circulates, circulating, circulated)
1 V-I When something **circulates**, it moves easily and freely in a place. □ *The blood circulates through the body.*
2 V-T/V-I When information, ideas, or messages **circulate** or **are circulated**, they are passed around among a group of people. □ *Rumors were beginning to circulate.* [from Latin]

cir|cu|la|tion /sɜrkyəleɪʃən/
1 N-NONCOUNT SCIENCE Your **circulation** is the movement of blood through your body. □ *Regular exercise is good for the circulation.*
2 N-NONCOUNT The **circulation** of a liquid or a gas is its easy and free movement in a place. □ *...the circulation of air.*
3 N-NONCOUNT The **circulation** of information or ideas is the process by which they are passed from one group of people to another. □ *...the free circulation of ideas.* [from Latin]
→ look at Word Web: **cardiovascular system**

Word Link circum ≈ around : circumference, circumnavigate, circumstances

cir|cum|fer|ence /sərkʌmfrəns/
N-NONCOUNT MATH The **circumference** of a circle is the distance around its edge. □ *Think*

of a way to calculate the Earth's circumference. [from Old French]
→ look at Picture Dictionary: **area**

cir|cum|navi|gate /sɜrkəmnævɪgeɪt/ (circumnavigates, circumnavigating, circumnavigated) V-T SOCIAL STUDIES If someone **circumnavigates** the world, they sail or fly all the way around it. [FORMAL] □ *Sir Francis Drake was the first Englishman to circumnavigate the world.* [from Latin]

cir|cum|stan|ces /sɜrkəmstænsɪz/
N-PLURAL **Circumstances** are the facts about a particular situation. □ *You're doing really well, considering the circumstances.* □ *Under normal circumstances, this trip would only take about 20 minutes.* [from Old French]

Word Partnership Use **circumstances** with :

ADJ **certain** circumstances, **different/similar** circumstances, **difficult** circumstances, **exceptional** circumstances
PREP **under the** circumstances

cir|cus /sɜrkəs/ (circuses) N-COUNT A **circus** is a group of people and animals that travels around to different places and performs shows. □ *I always wanted to work as a clown in a circus.* [from Latin]

citi|zen /sɪtɪzən/ (citizens)
1 N-COUNT SOCIAL STUDIES Someone who is a **citizen** of a particular country legally belongs to that country. □ *We are proud to be American citizens.*
2 N-COUNT The **citizens of** a town or a city are the people who live there. □ *He traveled to Argentina to meet the citizens of Buenos Aires.* [from Old French]
3 → see also **senior citizen**
→ look at Word Webs: **citizenship, election**

Word Web   citizenship

Citizenship gives people important **rights**. In most countries **citizens** have the right to vote in **elections**. Citizens can hold government jobs and travel with a **passport**. They are also free to **demonstrate** to show disagreement with the government. In addition, citizens have **duties** and **responsibilities**. Two main duties of citizens are obeying the law and paying **taxes**. They may also be asked to be a **juror** in a court case. In some countries citizens have to do military service.

Word Link   ship ≈ condition or state :   citizen**ship**, dictator**ship**, friend**ship**

citi|zen|ship /sɪtɪzᵊnʃɪp/ **N-NONCOUNT**
If you have **citizenship** of a country, you are legally accepted as belonging to it. ❏ He decided to apply for American citizenship. [from Old French]
→ look at Word Web: **citizenship**

cit|rus /sɪtrəs/ **ADJ** A **citrus** fruit is a juicy fruit with a sharp taste, such as an orange or a lemon. ❏ Citrus fruits are a good source of vitamin C. [from Latin]

city /sɪti/ (**cities**) **N-COUNT** A **city** is a large town. ❏ We visited the city of Los Angeles. [from Old French]
→ look at Word Web: **city**

Word Link   civ ≈ citizen : civic, civil, civilian

civ|ic /sɪvɪk/
1 ADJ You use **civic** to describe people or things that have an official status in a city or a town. ❏ Civic leaders say they want the city to look its best.
2 ADJ You use **civic** to describe the duties or feelings that people have because they belong to a particular community. ❏ ...a sense of civic pride. [from Latin]

civ|il /sɪvᵊl/
1 ADJ You use **civil** to talk about the people of a country and their activities. ❏ The American Civil War is also called the War Between the States. ❏ ...civil rights.
2 ADJ You use **civil** to talk about people or things that are connected with the state, and not with the army or the church. ❏ We had a civil wedding in the town hall.
3 ADJ Someone who is **civil** is polite, but not very friendly. [FORMAL] ❏ Please try to be a little more civil to people. [from Old French]

Word Partnership   Use civil with :

N   civil **disobedience**, civil **liberties/rights**, civil **unrest** **1**

ci|vil|ian /sɪvɪlyən/ (**civilians**)
1 N-COUNT A **civilian** is a person who is not a member of a military organization. ❏ The soldiers were not shooting at civilians.
2 ADJ **Civilian** describes people or things that are not military. ❏ The men were wearing civilian clothes. [from Latin]

Word Web   city

For the past 6,000 years people have been moving from the **countryside** to **urban** centers. The world's oldest **capital** is Damascus, Syria. People have lived there for over 2,500 years. Cities are usually economic, commercial, cultural, political, social, and transportation centers. **Tourists** travel to cities for shopping and **sightseeing**. In some big cities, **skyscrapers** have **apartments**, **businesses**, **restaurants**, **theaters**, and **retail stores** all in one. People never have to leave their building. Sometimes cities become overpopulated and **crime rates** soar. Then people move to the **suburbs**. In recent decades this trend has been reversed in some places and **inner cities** are being rebuilt.

civi|li|za|tion /sɪvɪlɪzeɪʃᵊn/ (**civilizations**)

1 **N-COUNT/N-NONCOUNT** SOCIAL STUDIES A **civilization** is a group of people with their own social organization and culture. ❑ *We learned about the ancient civilizations of Greece.*

2 **N-NONCOUNT** Civilization is the state of having a high level of social organization. ❑ *...our advanced state of civilization.* [from Old French]

→ look at Word Web: **history**

civi|lized /sɪvɪlaɪzd/

1 **ADJ** A **civilized** social group has a high level of organization. ❑ *Boxing should be illegal in a civilized society.*

2 **ADJ** A **civilized** person is polite and reasonable. ❑ *She was very civilized about it.* [from Old French]

civ|il rights **N-PLURAL** SOCIAL STUDIES **Civil rights** are the legal rights that all people have to fair treatment. ❑ *She never stopped fighting for civil rights.*

civ|il serv|ant (**civil servants**) **N-COUNT** A **civil servant** is a person who works for the civil service. ❑ *...two senior civil servants.*

civ|il ser|vice **N-SING** The **civil service** of a country consists of its government departments and all the people who work in them. ❑ *...a job in the civil service.*

civ|il war (**civil wars**) **N-COUNT** SOCIAL STUDIES A **civil war** is a war between different groups of people who live in the same country. ❑ *When did the American Civil War begin?*

claim /kleɪm/ (**claims, claiming, claimed**)

1 **V-T** If someone **claims** something, they say that it is true. ❑ *She claimed that she was not responsible for the mistake.* ❑ *The man claimed to be very rich.*

2 **N-COUNT** A **claim** is something that someone says, which may or may not be true. ❑ *Most people just don't believe their claims.*

3 **V-T** If you **claim** something, you say that it belongs to you. ❑ *If nobody claims the money, you can keep it.*

4 **N-COUNT** A **claim** is something that you ask for because you think you should have it. ❑ *...an insurance claim.* [from Old French]

clam /klæm/ (**clams**) **N-COUNT** **Clams** are a type of shellfish. [from Old English]

→ look at Picture Dictionary: **shellfish**

Word Link *claim, clam ≈ shouting : ac*claim, clamor, ex*claim*

clam|or /klæmər/ (**clamors, clamoring, clamored**) **V-I** If people **are clamoring for** something, they are demanding it in a noisy or angry way. ❑ *Both parties are clamoring for the attention of the voter.* [from Old French]

clamp /klæmp/ (**clamps, clamping, clamped**)

1 **N-COUNT** A **clamp** is a piece of equipment that holds two things together.

2 **V-T** When you **clamp** one thing **to** another, you fasten the two things together with a clamp. ❑ *Clamp the microphone to the stand.* [from Dutch or Low German]

→ look at Picture Dictionary: **laboratory**

clan /klæn/ (**clans**) **N-COUNT** A **clan** is a group which consists of families that are related to each other. ❑ *...enemy clans.* [from Scottish Gaelic]

clap /klæp/ (**claps, clapping, clapped**) **V-T/V-I** When you **clap**, you hit your hands together, usually to show that you like something. ❑ *The men danced and the women clapped.* ❑ *Margaret clapped her hands.* [from Old English]

Word Link *clar ≈ clear : clarify, clarity, declare*

Word Link *ify ≈ making : clarify, diversify, intensify*

clari|fy /klærɪfaɪ/ (**clarifies, clarifying, clarified**) **V-T** To **clarify** something means to make it easier to understand, usually by explaining it. [FORMAL] ❑ *I would like to clarify those remarks I made.* [from Old French]

clari|net /klærɪnɛt/ (**clarinets**) **N-COUNT/N-NONCOUNT** MUSIC A **clarinet** is a musical instrument that you blow. It is a long black wooden tube with keys on it that you press, and a single reed (= small flat part that moves and makes a sound when you blow). [from French]

→ look at Word Web: **orchestra**

clar|ity /klærɪti/ **N-NONCOUNT** **Clarity** is the quality of being clear and easy to understand. ❑ *This new law will bring some clarity to the situation.* [from Latin]

clash /klæʃ/ (**clashes, clashing, clashed**)

1 **V-T/V-I** When people **clash**, they fight or argue with each other. ❑ *He often clashed with his staff.*

2 **N-COUNT** **Clash** is also a noun. ❑ *There have*

been a number of clashes between police and students.

3 **V-T/V-I** If one color **clashes with** another, they do not look nice together. ❑ *His pink shirt clashed with his red hair.*

clasp /klæsp/ (**clasps, clasping, clasped**)

1 **V-T** If you **clasp** someone or something, you hold them tightly. ❑ *She clasped the children to her.*

2 **N-COUNT** A **clasp** is a small object that fastens something. ❑ *Kathryn undid the metal clasp of her handbag.* [from Old English]

class /klæs/ (**classes**)

1 **N-COUNT** A **class** is a group of students who learn at school together. ❑ *He spent six months in a class with younger students.*

2 **N-COUNT** A **class** is a time when you learn something at school. ❑ *Classes start at 9 o'clock.* ❑ *We do lots of reading in class.*

3 **N-COUNT** A **class** is a group of students who are taught together. ❑ *He spent six months in a class with younger students.*

4 **N-COUNT** A **class of** things is a group of them that are the same in some way. ❑ *These vegetables all belong to the same class of plants.*

5 **N-COUNT/N-NONCOUNT** A **class** is one of the social groups into which people are divided. ❑ *These programs only help the middle class.* [from Latin]

6 → see also **middle class, upper class, working class**

Word Partnership	Use **class** with :
N	**class for beginners**, class **size**, **students in a class 1**
	leisure class, class **struggle**, **working** class **5**
V	**take a** class, **teach a** class **1** **3**
ADJ	**social** class **5**

clas|sic /klæsɪk/ (**classics**)

1 **ADJ** A **classic** movie or piece of writing is very good, and has been popular for a long time. ❑ *Fleming directed the classic movie "The Wizard of Oz."*

2 **N-COUNT** **Classic** is also a noun. ❑ *"Jailhouse Rock" is one of the classics of modern popular music.*

3 **N-NONCOUNT** ARTS SOCIAL STUDIES **Classics** is the study of the languages, literature, and cultures of ancient Greece and Rome.

4 **ADJ** A **classic** example of something has all the features which you expect such a thing to have. ❑ *It's a classic example of racism in our country.* [from Latin]

clas|si|cal /klæsɪkᵊl/ **ADJ** MUSIC **Classical** describes music that is traditional in form, style, or content. ❑ *I like listening to classical music and reading.* [from Latin]

→ look at Word Web: **genre**

clas|si|fy /klæsɪfaɪ/ (**classifies, classifying, classified**) **V-T** To **classify** things means to divide them into groups or types. ❑ *Vitamins can be classified into two categories.*

class|mate /klæsmeɪt/ (**classmates**) **N-COUNT** Your **classmates** are students who are in the same class as you at school.

class|room /klæsrum/ (**classrooms**) **N-COUNT** A **classroom** is a room in a school where lessons take place.

classy /klæsi/ (**classier, classiest**) **ADJ** If someone or something is **classy**, they are fashionable and attractive, or of very good quality. [INFORMAL] ❑ *We had dinner at a classy restaurant.* [from Latin]

clause /klɔz/ (**clauses**)

1 **N-COUNT** LANGUAGE ARTS In grammar, a **clause** is a group of words that contains a verb.

2 **N-COUNT** A **clause** is a section of a legal document. ❑ *There is a clause in his contract about company cars.* [from Old French]

claw /klɔ/ (**claws**)

N-COUNT The **claws** of a bird or an animal are the thin, hard, pointed parts at the end of its feet. ❑ *Kittens have very sharp claws and teeth.* [from Old English]

→ look at Picture Dictionary: **shellfish**

→ look at Word Web: **bird**

claw

clay /kleɪ/ **N-NONCOUNT** ARTS **Clay** is a type of earth that is soft when it is wet and hard when it is dry. Clay is used for making things such as pots and bricks. ❑ *...a clay pot.* [from Old English]

→ look at Word Web: **pottery**

clean /klin/ (**cleaner, cleanest, cleans, cleaning, cleaned**)

1 **ADJ** Something that is **clean** is not dirty. ❑ *Make sure the children's hands are clean before they eat.* ❑ *This floor is easy to keep clean.*

2 **V-T/V-I** If you **clean**, or **clean** something, you remove the dirt from it. ❑ *He fell from*

a ladder while he was cleaning the windows.
[from Old English]
→ look at Word Web: **soap**

▶ **clean up** **1** If you **clean up** a place, you clean it completely. ❑ *Hundreds of workers are cleaning up the beaches.*

2 If you **clean up** dirt, you remove it from a place. ❑ *Who is going to clean up this mess?*

Thesaurus clean Also look up :

| ADJ | neat, pure; *(ant.)* dirty, filthy **1** |
| V | rinse, wash; *(ant.)* dirty, soil, stain **2** |

clean|er /klínər/ (**cleaners**)
1 **N-COUNT** A **cleaner** is a substance or a piece of equipment used for cleaning things. ❑ *Wear gloves when you use oven cleaner.*
2 **N-COUNT** A **cleaner** is someone whose job is to clean rooms and furniture. ❑ *...the hospital where Sid worked as a cleaner.*
3 **N-COUNT** The **cleaners** is a place where you pay for your clothes to be dry-cleaned. ❑ *Did you pick up my suit from the cleaners?* [from Old English]
4 → see also **vacuum cleaner**

cleanse /klɛnz/ (**cleanses, cleansing, cleansed**)
1 **V-T** To **cleanse** a place, a person, or an organization **of** something dirty, unpleasant, or evil means to make them free from it. ❑ *He tried to cleanse the house of bad memories.*
2 **V-T** If you **cleanse** your skin or a wound, you clean it. ❑ *Catherine demonstrated the proper way to cleanse the face.* [from Old English]

```
                    clear
        ❶ FREE FROM CONFUSION
        ❷ FREE FROM OBSTACLES
           OR GUILT
        ❸ PHRASAL VERBS
```

❶ **clear** /klíər/ (**clearer, clearest**)
1 **ADJ** Something that is **clear** is easy to understand, see, or hear. ❑ *The instructions are clear and readable.* ❑ *It is clear that things will have to change.* ❑ *This camera takes very clear pictures.*
● **clear|ly** **ADV** ❑ *Clearly, the police cannot break the law.*
2 **ADJ** If your mind or thinking is **clear**, you are not confused. ❑ *She needed a clear head to carry out her instructions.* ● **clear|ly** **ADV**
❑ *The only time I can think clearly is when I'm alone.* [from Old French]
❷ **clear** /klíər/ (**clearer, clearest, clears, clearing, cleared**)
1 **ADJ** If a substance is **clear**, it has no color

and you can see through it. ❑ *...a clear plastic bag.*
2 **ADJ** If a place is **clear**, it does not have anything blocking the way. ❑ *The runway is clear—you can land.*
3 **ADJ** If the sky is **clear**, there are no clouds. ❑ *It was a beautiful day with a clear blue sky.*
4 **V-T** When you **clear** a place, you remove things from it because you do not want or need them there. ❑ *Can someone clear the table, please?*
5 **V-I** When the sky **clears**, it stops raining. ❑ *The sky cleared and the sun came out.*
6 **V-T** If someone **is cleared**, they are proved to be not guilty of a crime. ❑ *She was cleared of the murder.* [from Old French]

Thesaurus clear Also look up :

| ADJ | obvious, plain, straightforward ❶ **1** |
| | bright, cloudless, sunny ❷ **3** |

Word Partnership Use **clear** with :

N	clear **goals/purpose**, clear **picture** ❶ **1**
	clear **idea**, clear **understanding** ❶ **1** **2**
	clear **the way** ❷ **4**
V	be clear, **seem** clear ❶ **1** **2**
	make it clear ❶ **1** **2**
ADJ	**crystal** clear ❶ **1** ❷ **1**

❸ **clear** /klíər/ (**clears, clearing, cleared**)
▶ **clear away** When you **clear** things **away**, you put away the things that you have been using. ❑ *The waitress cleared away the plates.*
▶ **clear out** If you **clear out** a closet or a place, you make it neat and throw away the things in it that you no longer want. ❑ *I cleared out my desk before I left.*
▶ **clear up** **1** When you **clear up**, you make things neat and put them away. ❑ *The children played while I cleared up.*
2 To **clear up** something means to deal with something or find a good explanation for it. ❑ *The purpose of the meeting is to clear up these disagreements.*
3 When the weather **clears up**, it stops raining or being cloudy. ❑ *It all depends on the weather clearing up.*

clear|ing /klíərɪŋ/ (**clearings**) **N-COUNT**
A **clearing** is a small area in a forest where there are no trees or bushes. ❑ *The helicopter landed in a clearing in the dense jungle.* [from Old French]

cleav|age /klívɪdʒ/ (**cleavages**) **N-COUNT**
SCIENCE **Cleavage** is the tendency of a mineral to split along smooth, regular surfaces. [from Old English]

clef /klɛf/ (clefs)

1 **N-COUNT** MUSIC A **clef** is a symbol at the beginning of a line of music that indicates the pitch of the written notes. [from French]

2 → see also **bass clef, treble clef**

cler|gy /klɜrdʒi/ **N-PLURAL** The **clergy** are the official religious leaders of a particular group of believers. □ ...Catholic clergy. [from Old French]

clerk /klɜrk/ (clerks)

1 **N-COUNT** A **clerk** is a person whose job is to work with numbers or documents in an office. □ She works as a clerk in a travel agency.

2 **N-COUNT** A **clerk** is someone who sells things to customers in a store, or who works behind the main desk in a hotel. □ Thomas was working as a clerk in a shoe store. [from Old English]

→ look at Word Web: **hotel**

clev|er /klɛvər/ (cleverer, cleverest)

1 **ADJ** Someone who is **clever** is intelligent and can think and understand quickly. □ He's a very clever man. ● **clev|er|ly ADV** □ She cleverly concealed this fact.

2 **ADJ** A **clever** idea or invention is very effective and shows great skill. □ It is a clever novel. ● **clev|er|ly ADV** □ The garden has been cleverly designed.

Thesaurus	clever Also look up :
ADJ	bright, ingenious, smart; (ant.) dumb, stupid **1** **2**

click /klɪk/ (clicks, clicking, clicked)

1 **V-T/V-I** If something **clicks**, or if you **click** it, it makes a short, sharp sound. □ Hundreds of cameras clicked as she stepped out of the car.

2 **N-COUNT** **Click** is also a noun. □ I heard a click and then her recorded voice.

3 **V-T/V-I** TECHNOLOGY If you **click** on a part of a computer screen, you press one of the buttons on the mouse in order to make something happen on the screen. □ I clicked on a link.

4 **N-COUNT** TECHNOLOGY **Click** is also a noun. □ You can check your email with a click of your mouse.

cli|ent /klaɪənt/ (clients) **N-COUNT** BUSINESS A **client** is a person who pays someone for a service. □ A lawyer and his client were sitting at the next table. [from Latin]

→ look at Usage note at **customer**

→ look at Word Web: **trial**

cliff /klɪf/ (cliffs) **N-COUNT** SCIENCE A **cliff** is a high area of land with a very steep side. □ The car rolled over the edge of a cliff. [from Old English]

→ look at Picture Dictionaries: **landforms, mountain**

cli|mate /klaɪmɪt/ **N-COUNT/N-NONCOUNT** SCIENCE The **climate** of a place is the normal weather there. □ She loves the hot and humid climate of Florida. [from Late Latin]

→ look at Word Web: **climate**

cli|max /klaɪmæks/ (climaxes) **N-COUNT** The **climax of** something is the most exciting or important moment, near the end. □ The climax of the story is when Romeo and Juliet die. [from Late Latin]

Word Web   climate

During the past 100 years, the air **temperature** of the earth has increased by about 1° Fahrenheit (F). Alaska has warmed by about 4° F. At the same time, **precipitation** over the northern hemisphere increased by around 10%. This suggests that the increase in rain and snow has caused the sea level to rise 4-8 inches around the world. The years 2005, 2010, and 2014 were the three hottest ever recorded. This warm period followed what some scientists call the "Little Ice Age."

Researchers found that from the 1400s to the 1800s the Earth cooled by about 6° F. Air and water temperatures were lower, **glaciers** grew quickly, and **ice floes** came further south than usual.

St. Mark's Square in Venice flooded 111 times in 2002.

climb /klaɪm/ (**climbs, climbing, climbed**)

1 **V-T/V-I** If you **climb** or **climb up** something, you move toward the top of it. ❑ *Climbing the hill took half an hour.* ❑ *Climb up the steps onto the bridge.* ❑ *The steps are steep, are you able to climb up?*

2 **N-COUNT** **Climb** is also a noun. ❑ *It was a hard climb to the top of the mountain.*

3 **V-I** If you **climb** somewhere, you move into or out of a small space. ❑ *The girls climbed into the car and drove off.* ❑ *He climbed out of his bed.*

4 **V-I** When something **climbs**, it increases in value or amount. ❑ *The price of gas has been climbing steadily.* [from Old English]

Word Partnership	Use **climb** with :
PREP	climb **in/on**, climb **up/down** **1**
N	climb **the stairs** **1**
	prices climb **3**
V	**begin/continue to** climb **3**

climb|er /klaɪmər/ (**climbers**) **N-COUNT** SPORTS A **climber** is a person who climbs rocks or mountains. ❑ *A climber was rescued yesterday after falling 300 feet.* [from Old English]

climb|ing /klaɪmɪŋ/ **N-NONCOUNT** SPORTS **Climbing** is the activity of climbing rocks or mountains. [from Old English]

clinch /klɪntʃ/ (**clinches, clinching, clinched**) **V-T** If you **clinch** something you are trying to achieve, you succeed in getting it. ❑ *The Lakers scored the next ten points to clinch the victory.*

cling /klɪŋ/ (**clings, clinging, clung**)

1 **V-I** If you **cling to** someone or something, you hold them tightly. ❑ *The man was rescued as he clung to the boat.*

2 **V-I** If you **cling to** a position or a way of behaving, you try very hard to keep it or continue doing it. ❑ *He appears determined to cling to power.* ❑ *Parents of the missing teenagers were still clinging to hope yesterday.* [from Old English]

clin|ic /klɪnɪk/ (**clinics**) **N-COUNT** A **clinic** is a place where people receive medical advice or treatment. [from Latin]

clini|cal /klɪnɪkᵊl/ **ADJ** **Clinical** means involving medical treatment or testing people for illnesses. ❑ *She received her clinical training in Chicago.* [from Latin]

clip /klɪp/ (**clips, clipping, clipped**)

1 **N-COUNT** A **clip** is a small object for holding things together. ❑ *She took the clip out of her hair.*

2 **N-COUNT** A **clip** from a movie is a short piece of it that is broadcast separately. ❑ *They showed a film clip of the Apollo moon landing.*

3 **V-T/V-I** When you **clip** things together, or when things **clip** together, you fasten them using a clip. ❑ *Clip the rope onto the ring.*

4 **V-T** If you **clip** something, you cut small pieces from it. ❑ *I saw an old man clipping his bushes.* [Senses 1 and 3 from Old English. Senses 2 and 4 from Old Norse.]

clock /klɒk/ (**clocks**)

1 **N-COUNT** A **clock** is a device that shows what time of day it is. ❑ *He could hear a clock ticking.*

2 → see also **alarm clock, o'clock**

3 **PHRASE** If you do something **around the clock**, you do it all day and all night without stopping. ❑ *Firemen have been working around the clock.* [from Middle Dutch]

→ look at Picture Dictionary: **time**

Word Partnership	Use **clock** with :
N	**hands of a** clock, clock **radio** **1**
V	**look at a** clock, **put/turn the** clock **forward/back**, **set a** clock, clock **strikes**, clock **ticks** **1**

Word Link	wise ≈ in the direction or manner of :
	clock**wise**, like**wise**, other**wise**

clock|wise /klɒkwaɪz/

1 **ADV** When something is moving **clockwise**, it is moving in a circle in the same direction as the hands on a clock. ❑ *The children started moving clockwise around the room.*

2 **ADJ** **Clockwise** is also an adjective. ❑ *Move your right arm around in a clockwise direction.* [from Middle Dutch]

close
❶ SHUTTING
❷ NEARNESS

❶ close /kloʊz/ (**closes, closing, closed**)

1 **V-T/V-I** When you **close** a door or a window, you shut it. ❑ *If you are cold, close the window.* ❑ *Zac heard the door close quietly.*

2 **V-T/V-I** When a store **closes**, people cannot use it. ❑ *The store closes on public holidays.* ❑ *They closed the store early because of the flood.*

▶ **close down** If a business **closes down**, all work stops there, usually forever. ❑ *That store closed down years ago.*

Thesaurus	close Also look up :
v	fasten, seal, shut, slam; (ant.) open ❶ 🔳

❷ **close** /kloʊs/ (**closer, closest**)

🔳 **ADJ** Something that is **close to** something else is near to it. ❑ *The apartment is close to the beach.* ❑ *The man moved closer.* ● **close|ly ADV** ❑ *They crowded closely around the fire.*

🔳 **ADJ** People who are **close** like each other very much and know each other well. ❑ *She was close to her sister, Gail.* ❑ *We were close friends at school.*

🔳 **ADJ** A **close** look at something is careful and complete. ❑ *Let's have a closer look.*

🔳 **ADJ** Your **close** relatives are the members of your family who are directly related to you, for example your parents. ❑ *...the death of a close relative.*

🔳 **ADJ Close** contact or cooperation involves seeing or working with someone often. ❑ *Both nations are seeking closer links with the West.* ● **close|ly ADV** ❑ *We work closely with local groups.*

🔳 **ADJ** If there is a **close** connection or resemblance between two things, they are strongly connected or are very similar. ❑ *There is a close connection between income and education.* ● **close|ly ADV** ❑ *The two problems are closely linked.*

🔳 **ADJ** A **close** competition is won by only a small amount. ❑ *It was a close contest for a Senate seat.*

🔳 **ADJ** If you are **close to** something, or if it is **close**, it is likely to happen soon. ❑ *She sounded close to tears.*

🔳 **PHRASE** Something that is **close by** is near to you. ❑ *Did a new hair salon open close by?*

🔟 **PHRASE** If you look at something **close up**, you look at it when you are very near to it. ❑ *The airplane looked much bigger close up.* [from Old French]

Word Partnership	Use close with :
N	close **a door** ❶ 🔳
	close **friend**, close **to** *someone* ❷ 🔳
	close **family/relative** ❷ 🔳 🔳
	close **election**, close **race** ❷ 🔳
ADV	close **enough**, **so/too/very** close ❷ 🔳 🔳

closed /kloʊzd/ **ADJ** When a store or business is **closed**, it is not open and you cannot buy or do anything there. ❑ *The supermarket was closed when we got there.* [from Old French]

closed-cir|cuit ADJ Closed-circuit television is a television system used to film people within a limited area such as a building. ❑ *There's a closed-circuit television camera in the reception area.*

closed cir|cu|la|tory sys|tem /kloʊzd sɜrkyələtɔri sɪstəm/ (**closed circulatory systems**) **N-COUNT SCIENCE** In animals that have a **closed circulatory system**, their blood flows through vessels such as veins and arteries and never flows through other parts of their body.

closed sys|tem (**closed systems**) **N-COUNT SCIENCE** In a **closed system**, matter cannot enter or leave the system and the system cannot be affected by anything outside it.

clos|et /klɒzɪt/ (**closets**) **N-COUNT** A **closet** is a very small room for storing things, especially clothes. ❑ *My closet is full of clothes that I never wear.* [from Old French]
→ look at Picture Dictionary: **house**

clo|sure /kloʊʒər/ (**closures**)

🔳 **N-COUNT/N-NONCOUNT** The **closure** of a place such as a business or a factory is the permanent ending of work or activity there. ❑ *...the closure of the steel mill.*

🔳 **N-COUNT** The **closure** of a road or a border is the blocking of it in order to prevent people from using it. ❑ *Storms forced the closure of many roads.* [from Old French]

cloth /klɔθ/ (**cloths**)

🔳 **N-NONCOUNT Cloth** is material that is used for making clothing. ❑ *You need two yards of cloth.*

🔳 **N-COUNT** A **cloth** is a piece of cloth that you use for cleaning, drying, or protecting things. ❑ *Clean the surface with a damp cloth.* [from Old English]

clothes /kloʊz, kloʊðz/ **N-PLURAL Clothes** are the things that people wear, such as shirts, coats, pants, and dresses. ❑ *Milly went upstairs to change her clothes.* [from Old English]

cloth|ing /kloʊðɪŋ/ **N-NONCOUNT Clothing** is the things that people wear. ❑ *She works in a women's clothing store.* [from Old English]
→ look at Picture Dictionary: **clothing**

cloud /klaʊd/ (**clouds, clouding, clouded**)

🔳 **N-COUNT/N-NONCOUNT** A **cloud** is a white or gray mass in the sky that contains drops of water. ❑ *Clouds began to form in the sky.*

Picture Dictionary

clothing

jacket

shawl

sweatshirt

blouse

T-shirt

skirt

jeans

sock

sweatpants

sneakers

shoes

high heels

baseball cap

shirt

tie

sweater

coat

pants

suit

boots

2 N-COUNT A **cloud of** smoke or dust is an amount of it floating in the air. ❑ *A cloud of black smoke spread across the sky.*

cloud

3 V-T If you say that something **clouds** your thinking, you mean that it affects you so that you are less able to understand or remember things. ❑ *The man claimed that the drug clouded his judgment.* [from Old English]
→ look at Word Webs: **precipitation, water**

cloud com|put|ing N-NONCOUNT
TECHNOLOGY **Cloud computing** is a model of computer use in which services that are available on the Internet are provided to users on a temporary basis.

cloudy /klaʊdi/ (**cloudier, cloudiest**) ADJ If it is **cloudy**, there are a lot of clouds in the sky. ❑ *It was a windy, cloudy day.* [from Old English]

clown /klaʊn/ (**clowns**) N-COUNT A **clown** is a performer who wears funny clothes and does silly things to make people laugh. [from Low German]

club /klʌb/ (**clubs**)
1 N-COUNT A **club** is an organization of people who all like doing a particular activity. ❑ *He joined the local golf club.*

2 N-COUNT A **club** is a place where the members of a club meet. ❑ *I stopped at the club for a drink.*

3 N-COUNT A **club** is the same as a **nightclub**. ❑ *The streets are full of bars, clubs, and restaurants.*

4 N-COUNT A **club** is a long, thin, metal stick that you use to hit the ball in the game of golf.

5 N-COUNT A **club** is a thick, heavy stick that can be used as a weapon. ❑ *The men were carrying knives and clubs.*

6 N-NONCOUNT **Clubs** is one of the four suits in a deck of playing cards. Each card in the suit is marked with one or more black symbols: ♣. ❑ *...the ace of clubs.*

7 N-COUNT A **club** is a playing card of this suit. ❑ *The next player put down a club.* [from Old Norse]
→ look at Picture Dictionary: **golf**

clue /klu/ (**clues**)
1 N-COUNT A **clue** is information that helps you to find an answer. ❑ *I'll give you a clue; the answer begins with the letter "p."*

2 PHRASE If you **don't have a clue** about something, you do not know anything about it. [INFORMAL] ❑ *I don't have a clue what I'll give Carl for his birthday.*

clum|sy /klʌmzi/ (**clumsier, clumsiest**)
1 ADJ A **clumsy** person does not move in a

very easy way and often breaks things.
❑ *As a child she was very clumsy.* ❑ *Dad was rather clumsy on his skates.* ●**clum|si|ly** /klʌ́mzɪli/ **ADV** ❑ *He fell clumsily onto the bed.*

2 **ADJ** A **clumsy** action or statement is not skillful and is likely to fail or to upset people. ❑ *...a clumsy attempt to bring down the government.* ●**clum|si|ly** **ADV** ❑ *The matter was handled clumsily.* [of Scandinavian origin]

clung /klʌ́ŋ/ **Clung** is the past tense and past participle of **cling**.

clus|ter /klʌ́stər/ (**clusters**) **N-COUNT** A **cluster of** people or things is a small group of them close together. ❑ *There was a cluster of houses near the river.* [from Old English]

clus|ter|ing /klʌ́stərɪŋ/ **N-NONCOUNT** **Clustering** is a teaching method in which information is presented as a group of ideas in order to help students to remember it better. [from Old English]

clutch /klʌ́tʃ/ (**clutches, clutching, clutched**)
1 **V-T/V-I** If you **clutch** something, you hold it very tightly. ❑ *Michelle clutched my arm.* ❑ *I clutched at a chair for support.*
2 **N-COUNT** In a vehicle, the **clutch** is the part that you press with your foot before you change gears. [from Northern English]

clut|ter /klʌ́tər/ (**clutters, cluttering, cluttered**)
1 **N-NONCOUNT** **Clutter** is a lot of things that you do not need in a messy state. ❑ *I'm a very tidy person, and I hate clutter.*
2 **V-T** If things or people **clutter** a place, they fill it in a messy way. ❑ *Empty cans clutter the desks.*

cm **cm** is short for **centimeter** or **centimeters**.

coach /koʊtʃ/ (**coaches, coaching, coached**)
1 **N-COUNT** SPORTS A **coach** is someone who is in charge of teaching a person or a sports team. ❑ *She's the women's soccer coach at Rowan University.*
2 **V-T** SPORTS If you **coach** someone, you help them to become better at a particular sport or skill. ❑ *She coached a golf team in San José.*
3 **N-COUNT** A **coach** is a vehicle with four wheels that is pulled by horses. [from French]

coal /koʊl/ **N-NONCOUNT** **Coal** is a hard black substance that comes from under the ground and is burned to give heat. ❑ *Put some more coal on the fire.* [from Old English]
→ look at Word Web: **energy**

| Word Link | co ≈ together : *co*alition, *co*llaborate, *co*llect |

coa|li|tion /koʊəlɪ́ʃ°n/ (**coalitions**)
1 **N-COUNT** SOCIAL STUDIES A **coalition** is a government consisting of people from two or more political parties. ❑ *The country has a coalition government.*
2 **N-COUNT** A **coalition** is a group consisting of people from different political or social groups. ❑ *...a coalition of women's organizations.* [from Medieval Latin]

coarse /kɔ́rs/ (**coarser, coarsest**) **ADJ** **Coarse** things feel dry and rough. ❑ *His skin was coarse and dry.* ●**coarse|ly** **ADV** ❑ *...coarsely-ground black pepper.*

coarse ad|just|ment **N-NONCOUNT** SCIENCE The part of a microscope that controls the **coarse adjustment** is the part that allows you to obtain the correct general focus for the object you are looking at.

coast /koʊst/ (**coasts**) **N-COUNT** GEOGRAPHY The **coast** is the land that is next to the ocean. ❑ *We stayed at a campsite on the coast.* ●**coast|al** /koʊst°l/ **ADJ** ❑ *Coastal areas have been flooded.* [from Old French]
→ look at Word Web: **beach**

coast|line /koʊstlaɪn/ (**coastlines**) **N-COUNT/N-NONCOUNT** GEOGRAPHY A country's **coastline** is the edge of its coast.

coat /koʊt/ (**coats, coating, coated**)
1 **N-COUNT** A **coat** is a piece of clothing with long sleeves that you wear over other clothes when you go outside. ❑ *He put on his coat and walked out.*
2 **N-COUNT** An animal's **coat** is its fur or hair.
3 **N-COUNT** A **coat of** paint is a thin layer of it. ❑ *The front door needs a new coat of paint.*
4 **V-T** If you **coat** something **with** a substance, you cover it with a thin layer of it. ❑ *Coat the fish with flour.* [from Old French]
→ look at Picture Dictionary: **clothing**
→ look at Word Web: **painting**

cob|web /kɒ́bwɛb/ (**cobwebs**) **N-COUNT** A **cobweb** is the fine net that a spider makes for catching insects. ❑ *The windows are cracked and covered in cobwebs.* [from Old English]

co|caine /koʊkeɪn/ **N-NONCOUNT** **Cocaine** is an illegal drug which some people choose to take.

C

coch|lea /kɒkliə, koʊ-/ (**cochleae**) **N-COUNT** SCIENCE The **cochlea** is the spiral-shaped part of the inner ear. [from Latin]

cock|pit /kɒkpɪt/ (**cockpits**) **N-COUNT** In an airplane or racing car, the **cockpit** is the part where the pilot or driver sits.

cock|roach /kɒkroʊtʃ/ (**cockroaches**) **N-COUNT** A **cockroach** is a large brown insect that likes to live in places where food is kept. [from Spanish]
→ look at Picture Dictionary: **insect**

cock|tail /kɒkteɪl/ (**cocktails**)
1 **N-COUNT** A **cocktail** is an alcoholic drink which contains several ingredients.
❑ Guests are offered a champagne cocktail.
2 **N-COUNT** A **cocktail** is a mixture of a number of different things. ❑ ...a cocktail of chemicals.

co|coa /koʊkoʊ/
1 **N-NONCOUNT** Cocoa is a brown powder used for making chocolate.
2 **N-NONCOUNT** Cocoa is a hot drink made from cocoa powder and milk or water.
❑ Let's have a cup of cocoa.

coco|nut /koʊkənʌt/ (**coconuts**)
1 **N-COUNT** A **coconut** is a very large nut with a hairy shell that grows on trees in warm countries.
2 **N-NONCOUNT** Coconut is the white flesh of a coconut. ❑ Add two cups of grated coconut.

co|coon /kəkun/ (**cocoons**) **N-COUNT** SCIENCE A **cocoon** is a case that some insects make around themselves before they grow into adults. ❑ The butterfly slowly breaks out of its cocoon. [from French]

cod /kɒd/ (**cod**)
1 **N-COUNT/N-NONCOUNT** A **cod** is a large ocean fish with white flesh.
2 **N-NONCOUNT** Cod is this fish eaten as food. [of Germanic origin]

code /koʊd/ (**codes**)
1 **N-COUNT** A **code** is a set of rules for people to follow. ❑ We keep a strict dress code (= people must wear particular clothes).
2 **N-COUNT** A **code** is a secret way to replace the words in a message with other words or symbols, so that some people will not understand the message. ❑ They sent messages using codes.
3 **N-NONCOUNT** TECHNOLOGY Computer

code is a set of instructions that a computer can understand.
4 **N-COUNT** A **code** is a group of numbers or letters that gives information about something. ❑ The area code for western Pennsylvania is 412. [from French]
5 → see also **zip code**

co|ef|fi|cient /koʊɪfɪʃənt/ (**coefficients**) **N-COUNT** SCIENCE A **coefficient** is a number that expresses a measurement of a particular quality of a substance or object under specified conditions. [from New Latin]

coe|lom /siləm/ (**coeloms**) **N-COUNT** SCIENCE The **coelom** is a hollow space in the body of an animal which contains organs such as the heart and kidneys. [from Greek]

co|evo|lu|tion /koʊɛvəluʃ°n/ **N-NONCOUNT** SCIENCE **Coevolution** is a process in which different species of animals or plants evolve in a particular way because of their close interaction with each other.

cof|fee /kɔfi/ (**coffees**)
1 **N-NONCOUNT** Coffee is the beans of the coffee plant, made into a powder. ❑ The island produces plenty of coffee.
2 **N-COUNT/N-NONCOUNT** Coffee is a drink made from boiling water and coffee beans. ❑ Would you like some coffee? [from Italian]

cof|fin /kɔfɪn/ (**coffins**) **N-COUNT** A **coffin** is a box that you put a dead person in when you bury them. [from Old French]

co|her|ent /koʊhɪərənt, -hɛrənt/
1 **ADJ** If something is **coherent**, it is well planned, so that it is clear and sensible. ❑ We need a coherent policy. ● **co|her|ence** /koʊhɪərəns, -hɛrəns/ **N-NONCOUNT** ❑ I thought the speech lacked coherence.
2 **ADJ** If someone is **coherent**, they express their thoughts in a clear and calm way. ❑ He wasn't capable of holding a coherent conversation. ● **co|her|ent|ly** **ADV** ❑ Many young people are unable to express themselves coherently. [from Latin]

coil /kɔɪl/ (**coils**) **N-COUNT** A **coil** is a piece of rope or wire that forms a series of rings. ❑ He was carrying a coil of rope. [from Old French]

coin /kɔɪn/ (**coins**) **N-COUNT** A **coin** is a small round piece of metal money. ❑ She put the coins in her pocket. [from Old French]
→ look at Word Webs: **English, money**

co|in|ci|dence /koʊɪnsɪdəns/ (**coincidences**) **N-COUNT/N-NONCOUNT**
A **coincidence** is when similar or related events happen at the same time without planning. ❏ *It is a coincidence that they arrived at the same time.* ❏ *We met by coincidence several years later.* [from Medieval Latin]

cola /koʊlə/ (**colas**) **N-COUNT/N-NONCOUNT**
Cola is a sweet brown drink containing small bubbles of carbon dioxide. ❏ *...a can of cola.*

cold /koʊld/ (**colder, coldest, colds**)
■ **ADJ** If someone is **cold**, they feel uncomfortable because they are not warm enough. ❏ *I was freezing cold.* ❏ *Put on a sweater if you're cold.*
■ **ADJ** If something is **cold**, it does not have any warmth in it. ❏ *He washed his face with cold water.* ❏ *We went out into the cold, dark night.*
■ **ADJ** A **cold** person does not show emotion and is not friendly. ❏ *Her mother was an angry, cold woman.*
■ **N-NONCOUNT** You can call cold weather or low temperatures **the cold**. ❏ *He must have come inside to get out of the cold.*
■ **N-COUNT** If you have a **cold**, you have an illness that makes liquid flow from your nose, and makes you cough. ❏ *I have a bad cold.*
■ **PHRASE** If you **catch cold**, or **catch a cold**, you become ill with a cold. ❏ *Dry your hair so you don't catch cold.* [from Old English]

Thesaurus	cold	Also look up :
ADJ	bitter, chilly, cool, freezing, frozen, raw; (*ant.*) hot, warm ■	
	cool, distant; (*ant.*) friendly, warm ■	

Word Partnership	Use **cold** with :
ADV	**bitterly** cold ■
	freezing cold ■ ■
V	**feel** cold, **get** cold ■
	catch/get a cold ■
N	cold **air**, **dark and** cold, cold **night**, cold **rain**, cold **water**, cold **weather**, cold **wind** ■ ■

cold-blood|ed /koʊld blʌdɪd/ **ADJ Cold-blooded** animals have a body temperature that changes according to the surrounding temperature. Reptiles, for example, are cold-blooded.

cold read|ing (**cold readings**) **N-COUNT** ARTS
A **cold reading** is a reading of the script of a play, read aloud for the first time by actors who are going to perform the play.

Cold War N-PROPER SOCIAL STUDIES **The Cold War** was the difficult relationship between the Soviet Union and the Western powers after the Second World War. ❏ *This was the first major crisis of the post-Cold War era.*

Word Link	co ≈ together : coalition, collaborate, collect

col|labo|rate /kəlæbəreɪt/ (**collaborates, collaborating, collaborated**)
■ **V-T/V-I** When people **collaborate**, they work together on a particular project. ❏ *He collaborated with his son Michael on the English translation.* ❏ *Students collaborate in group exercises.* ● **col|labo|ra|tion** /kəlæbəreɪʃⁿn/ (**collaborations**) **N-COUNT/N-NONCOUNT** ❏ *...collaboration between parents and schools.* ❏ *...scientific collaborations.* ● **col|labo|ra|tor** /kəlæbəreɪtər/ (**collaborators**) **N-COUNT** ❏ *He and his collaborator completed the book in two years.*
■ **V-I** If someone **collaborates with** an enemy that is occupying their country during a war, they help them. ❏ *He was accused of collaborating with the secret police.* ● **col|labo|ra|tion** **N-NONCOUNT** ❏ *...collaboration with the enemy.* ● **col|labo|ra|tor** **N-COUNT** ❏ *He was suspected of being a collaborator.* [from Late Latin]

col|lage /kəlɑʒ/ (**collages**) **N-COUNT** ARTS
A **collage** is a picture that you make by sticking pieces of paper or cloth on a surface. ❏ *The children made a collage of words and pictures from magazines.* [from French]

col|lapse /kəlæps/ (**collapses, collapsing, collapsed**)
■ **V-I** If a structure or a person **collapses**, they fall very suddenly. ❏ *The bridge collapsed last October.* ❏ *He collapsed at his home last night.*
■ **N-NONCOUNT** **Collapse** is also a noun. ❏ *A few days after his collapse he was sitting up in bed.* [from Latin]

col|lar /kɒlər/ (**collars**)
■ **N-COUNT** The **collar** of a shirt or a coat is the part that goes around your neck. ❏ *He pulled up his jacket collar in the cold wind.*
■ **N-COUNT** A **collar** is a band of leather or plastic that you put around the neck of a dog or cat. [from Latin]

collar|bone /kɒlərboʊn/ (**collarbones**) **N-COUNT** SCIENCE Your **collarbones** are the two long bones between your throat and your shoulders. ❏ *Harold had a broken collarbone.*

col|lat|er|al /kəlætərəl/ **N-NONCOUNT**
Collateral is money or property which is
used as a guarantee that someone will repay
a loan. [FORMAL] ❑ *They used their house as
collateral for the loan.* [from Medieval Latin]

col|league /kɒlig/ (**colleagues**) **N-COUNT**
Your **colleagues** are the people you work
with. ❑ *She's busy talking to a colleague.*
[from French]

| Word Link | co ≈ together : coalition, collaborate, collect |

col|lect /kəlɛkt/ (**collects, collecting,
collected**)
■ **V-T** If you **collect** things, you bring them
together from several places or several
people. ❑ *Two young girls collected wood for the
fire.*
■ **V-T** If you **collect** things, you get them
and save them over a period of time because
you like them. ❑ *I collect stamps.*
■ **V-T/V-I** If a substance **collects**
somewhere, it keeps arriving and is held in
that place or thing. ❑ *Gas collects in the mines
around here.* ❑ *...tanks that collect rainwater.*
[from Medieval Latin]

| Thesaurus | collect Also look up : |
| v | accumulate, compile, gather; (ant.) scatter ■ |

col|lec|tion /kəlɛkʃ°n/ (**collections**)
■ **N-COUNT** A **collection of** things is a group
of similar or related things. ❑ *He has a large
collection of paintings.*
■ **N-NONCOUNT** The **collection** of ideas or
things is the process of bringing them
together from several places or several
people. ❑ *Computers can help with the collection
of information.* [from Latin]

col|lec|tive /kəlɛktɪv/ (**collectives**)
■ **ADJ** **Collective** means shared by every
member of a group. ❑ *It was a collective
decision.* ● **col|lec|tive|ly ADV** ❑ *They
collectively decided to move on.*
■ **N-COUNT** BUSINESS A **collective** is a
business or a farm that is run, and often
owned, by a group of people. ❑ *He participates
in all the decisions of the collective.* [from Latin]

col|lec|tor /kəlɛktər/ (**collectors**) **N-COUNT**
A **collector** is someone who collects things
that they like, such as stamps or old
furniture. ❑ *Her parents were both art collectors.*
[from Latin]
→ look at Word Web: **solar**

col|lege /kɒlɪdʒ/ (**colleges**)
N-COUNT/N-NONCOUNT College is a place
where students study after they leave high
school. ❑ *I have one son in college.* ❑ *Joan is
attending a local college.* [from Latin]
→ look at Word Web: **graduation**

col|lide /kəlaɪd/ (**collides, colliding, collided**)
V-T/V-I If people or vehicles **collide**, they
crash into each other. ❑ *The two cars collided.*
❑ *He ran up the stairs and collided with Susan.*
[from Latin]

| Thesaurus | collide Also look up : |
| v | bump, clash, crash, hit, smash; (ant.) avoid |

col|li|sion /kəlɪʒ°n/ (**collisions**)
N-COUNT/N-NONCOUNT A **collision** happens
when two moving objects hit each other.
❑ *Many passengers were killed in the collision.*
[from Late Latin]
→ look at Word Web: **crash**

col|loid /kɒlɔɪd/ (**colloids**) **N-COUNT** SCIENCE
A **colloid** is a mixture containing tiny particles
of a substance that do not dissolve or settle
at the bottom of the mixture. [from Greek]

col|lo|quial /kəloʊkwiəl/ **ADJ** LANGUAGE ARTS
Colloquial words and phrases are informal
and are used mainly in conversation.
❑ *...a colloquial expression.* [from Latin]

co|lon /koʊlən/ (**colons**)
■ **N-COUNT** LANGUAGE ARTS A **colon** is the
punctuation mark : that you can use to join
parts of a sentence.
■ **N-COUNT** SCIENCE Your **colon** is the lower
part of the tube that takes waste out of your
body. ❑ *...colon cancer.* [from Latin]
→ look at Picture Dictionary: **punctuation**

colo|nel /kɜrn°l/ (**colonels**) **N-COUNT**
SOCIAL STUDIES A **colonel** is a senior officer in
an army, air force, or the marines. ❑ *...an
ex-army colonel.* [from Old French]

co|lo|nial /kəloʊniəl/
■ **ADJ** SOCIAL STUDIES **Colonial** means relating
to countries that are colonies. ❑ *...Jamaica's
independence from British colonial rule.*
■ **ADJ** A **colonial** building or piece of furniture
was built or made in a style that was popular
in America in the 17th and 18th centuries.
❑ *...big white colonial houses.* [from Latin]

colo|nist /kɒlənɪst/ (**colonists**) **N-COUNT**
SOCIAL STUDIES **Colonists** are the people who
start a colony or the people who are among

the first to live in a particular colony.
❑ ...*the early American colonists.* [from Latin]

colo|nize /kɒlənaɪz/ (**colonizes, colonizing, colonized**) **v-t** SOCIAL STUDIES If people **colonize** a foreign country, they go to live there and take control of it. ❑ ...*the first British attempt to colonize Ireland.* [from Latin]

colo|ny /kɒləni/ (**colonies**)
1 **N-COUNT** SOCIAL STUDIES A **colony** is an area or a group of people that is controlled by another country. ❑ *Massachusetts was a British colony.*
2 **N-COUNT** A **colony** is a group of people or animals of a particular kind living together. ❑ ...*an artists' colony.* ❑ ...*colonies of sea birds.* [from Latin]

col|or /kʌlər/ (**colors, coloring, colored**)
1 **N-COUNT** The **color** of something is the way it looks in the light. Red, blue, and green are colors. ❑ *"What color is the car?"—"It's red."* ❑ *Judy's favorite color is pink.*
2 **N-COUNT** Someone's **color** is the color of their skin, when it shows their race. ❑ *I don't care what color she is.*
3 **ADJ** A **color** television or photograph is one that shows things in all their colors, and not just in black, white, and gray. ❑ *The book is illustrated with color photos.*
4 **V-T** If you **color** something or **color** it **in,**

you use pens or pencils to add color to a picture. ❑ *The children colored in their pictures.* [from Old French]
→ look at Picture Dictionary: **color**
→ look at Word Web: **painting**

Word Partnership	Use **color** with :
ADJ	**bright** color, **favorite** color **1**
N	color **blind**, **eye/hair** color **1**
	skin color **2**
	color **film/photograph**, color **television 3**

col|ored /kʌlərd/ **ADJ Colored** means having a particular color or colors. ❑ *They wore brightly colored hats.* [from Old French]

col|or|ful /kʌlərfəl/
1 **ADJ** Something that is **colorful** has bright colors or a lot of different colors. ❑ *The people wore colorful clothes.*
2 **ADJ Colorful** means interesting and exciting. ❑ *The story she told was certainly colorful.* [from Old French]

Thesaurus	**colorful** Also look up :
ADV	bright, lively, vibrant, vivid; (*ant.*) bland, colorless, dull **1**
	animated, dramatic, interesting **2**

col|or|less /kʌlərlɪs/ **ADJ** Something that is **colorless** has no color at all. ❑ ...*a colorless liquid.* [from Old French]

C

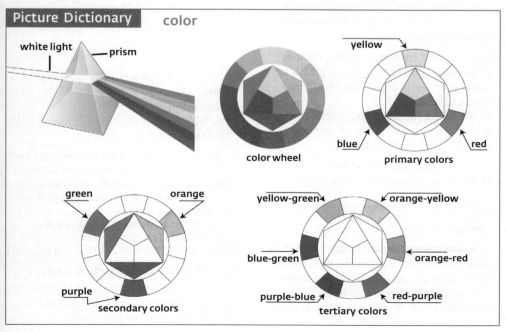

Picture Dictionary   color

white light — prism

color wheel

yellow

blue   red

primary colors

green   orange

purple

secondary colors

yellow-green   orange-yellow

blue-green   orange-red

purple-blue   red-purple

tertiary colors

col|or re|la|tion|ship (**color relationships**) or **color harmony**, **color scheme** **N-COUNT** **ARTS** **Color relationships** are pleasing combinations of colors that are based on the position of colors on the color wheel.

col|or the|ory (**color theories**) **N-COUNT/N-NONCOUNT** **ARTS** **Color theory** is a set of rules for mixing colors in order to achieve a particular result in a painting.

col|umn /kɒləm/ (**columns**)
1 **N-COUNT** A **column** is a tall, solid structure that supports part of a building. ❑ *The house has six white columns across the front.*
2 **N-COUNT** A **column** is a separate group of words that go straight up and down on a page. ❑ *The left column contains a list of names.*
3 **N-COUNT** A **column** is something that has a tall, narrow shape. ❑ *...a column of smoke.*
4 **N-COUNT** A **column** is a group of people or animals that moves in a long line. ❑ *...columns of military vehicles.* [from Latin]

col|um|nist /kɒləmnɪst, -əmɪst/ (**columnists**) **N-COUNT** A **columnist** is a journalist who writes a regular article in a newspaper or magazine. ❑ *...a columnist for the Chicago Tribune.* [from Latin]

coma /koʊmə/ (**comas**) **N-COUNT** If someone is in a **coma**, they are not conscious for a long time. ❑ *She was in a coma for seven weeks.* [from medical Latin]

comb /koʊm/ (**combs, combing, combed**)
1 **N-COUNT** A **comb** is a piece of plastic or metal with teeth. You use a comb to make your hair neat.
2 **V-T** When you **comb** your hair, you make it neat using a comb. ❑ *He combed his hair carefully.* [from Old English]

com|bat (**combats, combating** or **combatting, combated** or **combatted**)

> **PRONUNCIATION HELP**
> Pronounce the noun /kɒmbæt/.
> Pronounce the verb /kəmbæt/.

1 **N-NONCOUNT** **Combat** is fighting during a war. ❑ *More than 16 million men died in combat.*
2 **V-T** If people in authority try to **combat** something, they try to stop it from happening. ❑ *They've introduced new laws to combat crime.* [from French]

> **Word Partnership** Use **combat** with :
>
> | ADJ | **hand-to-hand** combat, **heavy** combat **1** |
> |---|---|
> | N | combat **forces/troops/units**, combat **gear 1** |
> | | combat **crime**, combat **disease**, combat **terrorism 2** |

com|bi|na|tion /kɒmbɪneɪʃ°n/ (**combinations**) **N-COUNT** A **combination** of things is a mixture of them. ❑ *That is an interesting combination of colors.* [from Late Latin]

> **Word Link** com ≈ with, together : combine, compact, companion

com|bine /kəmbaɪn/ (**combines, combining, combined**) **V-T/V-I** If you **combine** two or more things, or if they **combine**, they join or exist together. ❑ *Combine the flour with 3 tablespoons of water.* ❑ *Disease and hunger combine to kill thousands of people.* [from Late Latin]

> **Thesaurus** combine Also look up :
>
> | V | blend, fuse, incorporate, join, mix, unite; *(ant.)* detach, disconnect, divide, separate |
> |---|---|

com|bus|tion /kəmbʌstʃən/ **N-NONCOUNT** **SCIENCE** **Combustion** is the act of burning something or the process of burning. ❑ *The energy is released by combustion.* [from Old French]
→ look at Word Web: **engine**

> **come**
> **1** ARRIVE
> **2** OTHER USES
> **3** PHRASAL VERBS

1 come /kʌm/ (**comes, coming, came, come**)

> **LANGUAGE HELP**
> The form **come** is used in the present tense and is the past participle.

1 **V-I** You use **come** to say that someone or something arrives somewhere, or moves toward you. ❑ *Two police officers came into the hall.* ❑ *He came to a door.* ❑ *Eleanor came to see her.* ❑ *Come here, Tom.*
2 **V-I** When an event or a time **comes**, it happens. ❑ *The announcement came after a meeting at the White House.* [from Old English]

2 come /kʌm/ (**comes, coming, came**)

> **LANGUAGE HELP**
> The form **come** is used in the present tense and is the past participle.

1 **V-LINK** If something that you wish for or dream about **comes** true, it actually happens. ❑ *My life-long dream has just come true.*

2 **V-I** If someone or something **comes from** a particular place, that place is where they started. ❑ *Nearly half the students come from other countries.* ❑ *Most of Germany's oil comes from the North Sea.*

3 **V-T** If someone or something **comes** first, next, or last, they are first, next, or last. ❑ *I came last in the race.*

4 **V-I** If something **comes in** a range of colors, forms, or sizes, it can have any of those colors, forms, or sizes. ❑ *Flowers come in all shapes and sizes.*

5 You say **how come**... to someone when you want them to explain something that has happened. ❑ *How come the books are so popular?* [from Old English]

6 → see also **coming**

❸ **come** /kʌm/ (**comes, coming, came**)

> **LANGUAGE HELP**
> The form **come** is used in the present tense and is the past participle.

▶ **come across** **1** If you **come across** something or someone, you find them or meet them by chance. ❑ *I came across a photo of my grandparents when I was looking for my diary.*

2 The way that someone **comes across** is the impression that they make on other people. ❑ *He comes across as a very pleasant young man.*

▶ **come along** To **come along** is to go somewhere with someone. ❑ *There's a party tonight and you're welcome to come along.*

▶ **come around** **1** If you **come around to** an idea, you change your mind and accept it. ❑ *It looks like they're coming around to our way of thinking.*

2 When someone who is unconscious **comes around**, they become conscious again. ❑ *When I came around I was on the kitchen floor.*

▶ **come back** **1** If someone **comes back** to a place, they return to it. ❑ *He wants to come back to Washington.*

2 When something **comes back**, it becomes fashionable again. ❑ *I'm glad hats are coming back.*

3 → see also **comeback**

▶ **come down** **1** If an amount **comes down**, it becomes less than it was before. ❑ *Interest rates should come down.*

2 If something **comes down**, it falls to the ground. ❑ *The rain came down for hours.*

▶ **come in** **1** If someone **comes in**, they enter a place. ❑ *Come in and sit down.*

2 If you have money **coming in**, you receive it regularly as your income. ❑ *She had no money coming in and no savings.*

▶ **come off** If something **comes off**, it is removed. ❑ *This lid won't come off.*

▶ **come on** You say **Come on** to someone to encourage them to do something or to be quicker. [SPOKEN] ❑ *Come on, or we'll be late.*

▶ **come out** **1** When the sun **comes out**, it appears in the sky because the clouds have moved away. ❑ *Oh, look! The sun's coming out!*

2 When a new product **comes out**, it becomes available to the public. ❑ *The book comes out this week.*

▶ **come round** → look up **come around**

▶ **come to** **1** If something **comes to** a particular amount, it adds up to it. ❑ *Lunch came to $80.*

2 If a thought or a memory **comes to** you, you suddenly think of it or remember it. ❑ *He was about to shut the door when an idea came to him.*

▶ **come up** **1** If something **comes up** in a conversation, someone mentions it. ❑ *The subject came up at work.*

2 When the sun **comes up**, it rises. ❑ *It will be so great watching the sun come up.*

3 If a person or animal **comes up** or **comes up to** you, they approach you. ❑ *Her cat came up and rubbed itself against their legs.*

4 If something **comes up** in a conversation, it is mentioned. ❑ *The subject came up at work.*

▶ **come up with** If you **come up with** something that is useful or needed, you think of it or get it. ❑ *We came up with a plan.*

come|back (**comebacks**)

1 **N-COUNT** If a well-known person makes a **comeback**, they return to their profession or sport after a period away. ❑ *At the age of 65 he's trying to make a comeback.*

2 **N-COUNT** If something makes a **comeback**, it becomes fashionable again. ❑ *Tight fitting T-shirts are making a comeback.*

co|median /kəmiːdiən/ (**comedians**)
N-COUNT A **comedian** is a person whose job is to make people laugh. ❑ *Who is your favorite comedian?* [from Old French]

com|edy /kɒmədi/ (**comedies**) **N-COUNT**
LANGUAGE ARTS A **comedy** is a play, a movie, or a television program that is intended to make people laugh. ❑ *The movie is a romantic comedy.* [from Old French]
→ look at Word Web: **genre**

com|et /kɒmɪt/ (**comets**) **N-COUNT** SCIENCE
A **comet** is a bright object that has a long tail and travels around the sun. [from Old French]
→ look at Picture Dictionary: **solar system**

com|fort /kʌmfərt/ (**comforts, comforting, comforted**)
1 **N-NONCOUNT** Comfort is being relaxed, and having no pain or worry. ❑ *You can sit in comfort while you are watching the show.*
2 **N-NONCOUNT** If you live in **comfort**, you have a pleasant life in which you have everything you need. ❑ *He lived in comfort for the rest of his life.*
3 **V-T** If you **comfort** someone, you make them feel less worried or unhappy. ❑ *Ned tried to comfort her.* [from Old French]

com|fort|able /kʌmftəbᵊl, -fərtəbᵊl/
1 **ADJ** If furniture is **comfortable**, it makes you feel physically relaxed. ❑ *This is a really comfortable chair.* ❑ *A home should be comfortable.*
2 **ADJ** If a person is **comfortable**, they feel physically relaxed. ❑ *Lie down on your bed and make yourself comfortable.* ● **com|fort|ably**
ADV ❑ *Are you sitting comfortably?* [from Old French]

Thesaurus comfortable Also look up :
ADV comfy, cozy, soft; (*ant.*) uncomfortable **1**

com|fort food **N-NONCOUNT** Comfort food is a type of food that you eat to make you feel happier or warmer. ❑ *Here are some recipes for heart-warming comfort food.*

com|ic /kɒmɪk/ (**comics**)
1 **ADJ** A **comic** movie or actor makes you laugh. ❑ *It is one of the greatest comic films.*
2 **N-PLURAL** The **comics** are cartoon drawings in a newspaper that tell a story. ❑ *Fortunately they don't carry comics in the Times.* [from Latin]

comi|cal /kɒmɪkᵊl/ **ADJ** If something is **comical**, it makes you want to laugh because it is funny or silly. ❑ *They had slightly comical smiles on their faces.* [from Latin]

com|ic book /kɒmɪk bʊk/ (**comic books**)
N-COUNT A **comic book** is a magazine that contains stories told in drawings.

com|ing /kʌmɪŋ/
1 **ADJ** A **coming** event or time is an event or a time that will happen soon. ❑ *...the weather in the coming months.* [from Old English]
2 → see also **come**

com|ma /kɒmə/ (**commas**) **N-COUNT**
LANGUAGE ARTS A **comma** is the punctuation mark ,. [from Latin]
→ look at Picture Dictionary: **punctuation**

com|mand /kəmænd/ (**commands, commanding, commanded**)
1 **N-COUNT** A **command** is an official instruction to do something. ❑ *He shouted a command at his soldiers.* ❑ *He obeyed the command.*
2 **N-COUNT** TECHNOLOGY A **command** is an instruction that you give to a computer. ❑ *The keyboard command "Ctrl+S" saves your document.*
3 **V-T** If someone **commands** you to do something, they tell you that you must do it. [mainly WRITTEN] ❑ *He commanded his soldiers to attack.*
4 **V-T** An officer who **commands** part of an army is responsible for controlling and organizing it. ❑ *...the French general who commands the U.N. troops.*
5 **N-NONCOUNT** Command is also a noun. ❑ *The force will be under the command of an American general.* [from Old French]

com|mand|er /kəmændər/ (**commanders**)
1 **N-COUNT** SOCIAL STUDIES A **commander** is an officer in charge of a military operation or organization. ❑ *The commander and some of the men were released.*
2 **N-COUNT** SOCIAL STUDIES A **commander** is an officer in the U.S. Navy or the Royal Navy. [from Old French]

com|mand mod|ule (**command modules**)
N-COUNT SCIENCE The **command module** is the part of a spacecraft in which the astronauts live and operate the controls.

com|media dell'ar|te /kəmeɪdiə dɛlɑrti, -teɪ/ **N-NONCOUNT** ARTS **Commedia dell'arte** was a form of improvised theater that began in Italy in the sixteenth century and used well-known characters and stories. [from Italian]

Word Link *memor ≈ memory : com*memor*ate, memor*ial, *memor*y

com|memo|rate /kəmɛməreɪt/ (**commemorates, commemorating, commemorated**) **V-T** To **commemorate** an important event or person means to remember them by means of a special action or ceremony, or a specially-created object. ❑ *...paintings commemorating great moments in baseball history.*

● **com|memo|ra|tion** /kəmɛməreɪʃ°n/ (**commemorations**) **N-COUNT/N-NONCOUNT** ❑ *...a commemoration of victory.* [from Latin]

com|mence /kəmɛns/ (**commences, commencing, commenced**) **V-T/V-I** When something **commences** or you **commence** it, it begins. [FORMAL] ❑ *The school year commences in the fall.* ❑ *They commenced a thorough search.* [from Old French]

com|men|sal|ism /kəmɛnsəlɪzəm/ (**commensalisms**) **N-COUNT/N-NONCOUNT** SCIENCE A **commensalism** between two species of plants or animals is a relationship which benefits one of the species and does not harm the other species. [from Middle English]

com|ment /kɒmɛnt/ (**comments, commenting, commented**)
◼ **V-T/V-I** If you **comment on** something, you give your opinion or say something about it. ❑ *Mr. Cooke has not commented on these reports.* ❑ *You really can't comment until you know the facts.*
◼ **N-COUNT/N-NONCOUNT** A **comment** is something that you say about a person or a situation. ❑ *It is difficult to make a comment about the situation.* [from Latin]

com|men|tary /kɒməntɛri/ (**commentaries**)
◼ **N-COUNT/N-NONCOUNT** A **commentary** is a description of an event that is broadcast on radio or television while the event is taking place. ❑ *He turned on his car radio to listen to the commentary.*
◼ **N-COUNT** A **commentary** is an article or a book which explains or discusses something. ❑ *...a commentary on American society and culture.* [from Latin]

com|men|ta|tor /kɒmənteɪtər/ (**commentators**)
◼ **N-COUNT** A **commentator** is a broadcaster who gives a commentary on an event. ❑ *...a sports commentator.*
◼ **N-COUNT** A **commentator** is someone who often writes or broadcasts about a particular subject. ❑ *...a political commentator.* [from Latin]

Word Link	merc ≈ trading : commerce, merchandise, merchant

com|merce /kɒmɜrs/ **N-NONCOUNT** **Commerce** is the buying and selling of large amounts of goods. ❑ *There are rules for international commerce.* [from Latin]

com|mer|cial /kəmɜrʃ°l/ (**commercials**)
◼ **ADJ** **Commercial** means relating to the buying and selling of goods. ❑ *New York is a center of commercial activity.*
◼ **ADJ** **Commercial** organizations and activities are concerned with making profits. ❑ *The company has become more commercial over the past few years.*
● **com|mer|cial|ly** **ADV** ❑ *...a commercially successful movie.*
◼ **N-COUNT** A **commercial** is an advertisement on television or radio. ❑ *There are too many commercials on TV these days.* [from Latin]

com|mis|sion|er /kəmɪʃənər/ (**commissioners**) also **Commissioner**
N-COUNT A **commissioner** is an important official in a government department or other organization. ❑ *...Alaska's commissioner of education.* [from Old French]

com|mit /kəmɪt/ (**commits, committing, committed**)
◼ **V-T** If someone **commits** a crime or a sin, they do something illegal or bad. ❑ *I have never committed a crime.*
◼ **V-T** If you **commit yourself to** something, you say that you will do it. ❑ *People should think carefully about committing themselves to working Sundays.* [from Latin]

com|mit|ment /kəmɪtmənt/ (**commitments**)
◼ **N-NONCOUNT** **Commitment** is when you work hard at something that you think is important. ❑ *They praised him for his commitment to peace.*
◼ **N-COUNT** If you make a **commitment to** do something, you promise to do it. ❑ *We made a commitment to work together.*
◼ **N-COUNT** A **commitment** is a regular activity that takes up some of your time. ❑ *I've got a lot of commitments.* [from Latin]

Word Partnership	Use commitment with :
ADJ	**deep/firm/strong** commitment ◼ **long-term** commitment, **prior** commitment ◼ ◼
N	*someone's* commitment ◼–◼
PREP	commitment **to** *someone/ something* ◼ ◼
V	**make a** commitment ◼

com|mit|tee /kəmɪti/ (**committees**)
N-COUNT A **committee** is a group of people who meet to make decisions or plans for a

larger group. ❏ *I was on the tennis club committee for 20 years.*

com|mon /kɒmən/

1 **ADJ** If something is **common**, it is found in large numbers or it happens often. ❏ *Hansen is a common name in Norway.* ❏ *What is the most common cause of road accidents?* ● **com|mon|ly** **ADV** ❏ *Parsley is a commonly used herb.*

2 **ADJ** A **common** language, culture, or interest is shared by two or more people or groups. ❏ *The United States and Canada share a common language.*

3 **PHRASE** If people or things have something **in common**, they have similar qualities or interests. ❏ *He had nothing in common with his sister.* [from Old French]

Thesaurus	common	Also look up :
ADJ	frequent, typical, usual **1**	

Word Partnership	Use common with :	
N	common **belief**, common **language**, common **practice**, common **problem** **1**	
ADV	**fairly/increasingly/more/most** common **1**	
V	**have something in** common **3**	

com|mon an|ces|tor (**common ancestors**)
N-COUNT SOCIAL STUDIES The **common ancestor** of a group of human beings or animals is the individual who is an ancestor of all of them.

common|place /kɒmənpleɪs/ **ADJ** If something is **commonplace**, it happens often or is often found. ❏ *Home computers have become commonplace.* [from Latin]

com|mon sense also **commonsense**
N-NONCOUNT **Common sense** is the ability to make good judgments and to be sensible. ❏ *Use common sense: don't leave valuable items in your car.*

common|wealth /kɒmənwɛlθ/

1 **N-COUNT** SOCIAL STUDIES A **commonwealth** is a group of countries that have the same political or economic interests.

2 SOCIAL STUDIES **Commonwealth** is used in the official names of some countries and of several states in the U.S. ❏ *...the Commonwealth of Australia.* ❏ *...the Commonwealth of Massachusetts.*

com|mu|nal /kəmyuⁿl/

1 **ADJ** **Communal** means relating to particular groups in a country or a society.

❏ *These groups developed strong communal ties.*

2 **ADJ** You use **communal** to describe something that is shared by a group of people. ❏ *They ate in a communal dining room.*

Word Link	commun ≈ sharing : communicate, communism, community

com|mu|ni|cate /kəmyunɪkeɪt/ (**communicates, communicating, communicated**)

1 **V-T/V-I** If you **communicate with** other people, you share information with them, for example by speaking or writing. ❏ *They communicate with their friends by cellphone.* ❏ *They use email to communicate with each other.*

2 **V-T/V-I** If people are able to **communicate**, they are able to let each other know what they are feeling. ❏ *We had to learn how to communicate with each other.*

3 **V-T** If you **communicate** something **to** someone, you let them know about it. ❏ *They successfully communicate their knowledge to others.* [from Latin]

com|mu|ni|ca|tion /kəmyunɪkeɪʃⁿn/ (**communications**)

1 **N-PLURAL** **Communications** are ways of sending or receiving information. ❏ *...a communications satellite.*

2 **N-NONCOUNT** **Communication** is the act of sharing information with other people, for example by speaking or writing. ❏ *Good communication is important in business.*

3 **N-NONCOUNT** If there is **communication** between people, they are able to let each other know what they are feeling. ❏ *There was a lack of communication between us.* [from Latin] → look at Word Webs: **brain, radio**

Com|mun|ion /kəmyunyən/ (**Communions**) **N-COUNT/N-NONCOUNT** **Communion** is the Christian ceremony in which people eat bread and drink wine in memory of Christ's death. [from Latin]

Word Link	ism ≈ action or state : communism, optimism, pessimism

com|mun|ism /kɒmyənɪzəm/ also **Communism** **N-NONCOUNT** SOCIAL STUDIES **Communism** is the political idea that people should not own private property and workers should control how things are produced. ❏ *Walesa campaigned to end communism in his homeland, Poland.* [from French]

com|mun|ist /kɒmyənɪst/ (**communists**) also **Communist** **N-COUNT** SOCIAL STUDIES

A **communist** is someone who believes in communism. ❑ *He was a committed communist and an economics student at the University of Gdansk.* ❑ *She is a member of the Communist Party.*

com|mu|nity /kəmyu̱niti/ (**communities**)
■ **N-SING** A **community** is a group of people who live in a particular area. ❑ *When you live in a small community, everyone knows you.*
② **N-SING** A **community** is a group of people who are similar in some way, or who have similar interests. ❑ *...the black community.*
③ **N-COUNT** SCIENCE A **community** is a group of plants and animals that live in the same region and interact with one another. [from Latin]

Thesaurus	community	Also look up :
N	neighborhood, public, society ■	

com|mute /kəmyu̱t/ (**commutes, commuting, commuted**) **V-I** If you **commute**, you travel to work or school. ❑ *Mike commutes to Miami every day.*
● **com|mut|er** (**commuters**) **N-COUNT** ❑ *In Tokyo, most commuters travel to work on trains.* [from Latin]
→ look at Word Webs: **traffic, transportation**

Word Link	com ≈ with, together : combine, compact, companion

com|pact /kəmpæ̱kt/ **ADJ Compact** things are small, or take up very little space. ❑ *The garden is compact and easy to manage.* [from Latin]

com|pact bone **N-NONCOUNT** SCIENCE **Compact bone** is very hard, dense bone that exists in the arms and legs and forms the outer layer of other bones.

com|pact disc /kəmpæ̱kt dɪ̱sk/ (**compact discs**) **N-COUNT** TECHNOLOGY A **compact disc** is a small shiny disk that contains music or information. The short form **CD** is also used.

com|pact|ed /kəmpæ̱ktɪd/ **ADJ** SCIENCE **Compacted** rock is rock that is formed when layers of material such as clay or sand press against each other over a long period of time. [from Latin]

com|pan|ion /kəmpæ̱nyən/ (**companions**) **N-COUNT** A **companion** is someone who you spend time with or who you travel with. ❑ *Her traveling companion was her father.* [from Late Latin]
→ look at Word Web: **pet**

com|pa|ny /kʌ̱mpəni/ (**companies**)
■ **N-COUNT** A **company** is a business that

sells goods or services. ❑ *Her mother works for an insurance company.*
② **N-COUNT** A **company** is a group of singers, dancers, or actors who work together. ❑ *...the Phoenix Dance Company.*
③ **N-NONCOUNT Company** is having another person or other people with you. ❑ *I always enjoy Nick's company.*
④ **PHRASE** If you **keep** someone **company**, you spend time with them and stop them from feeling lonely or bored. ❑ *I'll stay here and keep Emma company.* [from Old French]
→ look at Word Web: **electricity**

Word Partnership	Use **company** with :
ADJ	**foreign** company, **parent** company ■
V	**buy/own/sell/start a** company, company **employs**, company **makes** ■ **have** company, **keep** company, **part** company ③

com|pa|rable /kɒ̱mpərəbəl/
■ **ADJ** If two or more things are **comparable**, they are similar. ❑ *House prices here are comparable to prices in Paris and Tokyo.*
② **ADJ** If two or more things are **comparable**, they are similar and so they can be compared. ❑ *In comparable countries wages increased much more rapidly.* [from Old French]

Word Link	para ≈ beside : comparative, paradox, parallel

com|para|tive /kəmpæ̱rətɪv/ (**comparatives**)
■ **N-COUNT** LANGUAGE ARTS In grammar, the **comparative** is the form of an adjective or an adverb that shows that one thing has more of a particular quality than something else has. For example, "bigger" is the comparative form of "big." Compare with **superlative**.
② **ADJ** You use **comparative** to show that you are judging something in comparison to a different or previous situation. ❑ *...a life of comparative ease.* ● **com|para|tive|ly** **ADV** ❑ *...a comparatively small nation.* [from Old French]

Word Link	par ≈ equal : compare, disparate, part

com|pare /kəmpɛ̱ər/ (**compares, comparing, compared**)
■ **V-T** When you **compare** things, you consider how they are different and how they are similar. ❑ *I use the Internet to compare prices.*
② **V-T** If you **compare** one person or thing **to** another, you say that they are like the other person or thing. ❑ *Some critics compared his work to that of James Joyce.* [from Old French]

Thesaurus   compare   Also look up :

v   analyze, consider, contrast, examine **1**
     equate, match **2**

com|pared /kəmpɛ̱ərd/ **PHRASE** If you say,
for example, that one thing is large or small
compared with another or **compared to**
another, you mean that it is larger or
smaller than the other thing. ❑ *Your bag is
light compared to mine.* [from Old French]

com|pari|son /kəmpæ̱rɪsən/ (**comparisons**)
1 N-COUNT/N-NONCOUNT When you make
a **comparison**, you study the differences
between two things. ❑ *The information helps
parents to make comparisons between schools.*
2 N-COUNT When you make a **comparison**,
you say that one thing is like another.
❑ *...the comparison of her life to a journey.*
[from Old French]

com|part|ment /kəmpɑ̱rtmənt/
(**compartments**)
1 N-COUNT A **compartment** is a separate
part inside a box or a bag where you keep
things. ❑ *The case has a separate compartment
for camera accessories.*
2 N-COUNT A **compartment** is one of the
separate spaces of a railroad car. ❑ *The family
always sat in the first-class compartment.*
[from French]

com|pass /kʌ̱mpəs/ (**compasses**) **N-COUNT**
GEOGRAPHY A **compass** is an instrument that
people use for finding directions (north,
south, east, and west). ❑ *You'll need a map and
a compass.* [from Old French]
→ look at Word Webs: **magnet, navigation**

com|pas|sion /kəmpæ̱ʃⁿn/ **N-NONCOUNT**
Compassion is a feeling of pity, sympathy,
and understanding for someone who is
suffering. ❑ *Elderly people need compassion from
their doctors.* [from Old French]

com|pat|ible /kəmpæ̱tɪbᵊl/
1 ADJ If things are **compatible**, they work
well together. ❑ *The software program should be
compatible with your computer system.*
2 ADJ If you are **compatible** with someone,
you have a good relationship with them
because you have similar opinions and
interests. ❑ *Hannah and I are very compatible.*
[from Medieval Latin]

Word Link   *pel* ≈ *driving, forcing : com*pel*, ex*pel*,
      pro*pel*

com|pel /kəmpɛ̱l/ (**compels, compelling,
compelled**) **V-T** If a situation, a rule, or a

person **compels** you **to** do something, they
force you to do it. ❑ *...a law to compel cyclists to
wear a helmet.* [from Latin]

com|pel|ling /kəmpɛ̱lɪŋ/ **ADJ** A **compelling**
argument or reason is one that convinces
you that something is true or that
something should be done. ❑ *...a compelling
reason to spend money.* [from Latin]

com|pen|sa|tion /kɒ̱mpənseɪ̱ʃⁿn/
N-NONCOUNT Compensation is money that
someone who has had a bad experience
claims from the person or organization who
caused it. ❑ *He has to pay $6,960 compensation
for the damage he caused.* [from Latin]

com|pete /kəmpiːt/ (**competes, competing,
competed**)
1 V-I If you **compete** in a contest or a game,
you participate in it. ❑ *He will compete in the
10k road race again this year.*
2 V-T/V-I When one company or country
competes with another **for** something, it
tries to get that thing for themselves.
❑ *Hardware stores are competing for business.*
[from Late Latin]

com|pe|tence /kɒ̱mpɪtəns/ **N-NONCOUNT**
Competence is the ability to do something
well. ❑ *No one doubts his competence.* [from Latin]

com|pe|tent /kɒ̱mpɪtənt/ **ADJ** Someone
who is **competent** is able to do something
well. ❑ *He is a confident, competent driver.*
[from Latin]

com|pe|ti|tion /kɒ̱mpɪtɪ̱ʃⁿn/ (**competitions**)
1 N-COUNT/N-NONCOUNT A **competition** is
an event in which people try to show that
they are best at an activity. ❑ *The two boys
entered a surfing competition.*
2 N-NONCOUNT Competition is when two or
more people are trying to get something
that not everyone can have. ❑ *There's been a
lot of competition for the prize.* [from Late Latin]

com|peti|tive /kəmpɛ̱tɪtɪv/
1 ADJ A **competitive** person wants to be
more successful than other people. ❑ *He has
always been very competitive.*
2 ADJ Competitive situations are ones in
which people are trying to be the most
successful. ❑ *Japan is a highly competitive
market system.*
3 ADJ Goods that are **competitive** are likely
to be bought because they are less expensive
than others of the same quality. ❑ *...homes for
sale at competitive prices.* [from Late Latin]

Word Partnership Use **competitive** with :

N	competitive **person** **1**
	competitive **sport** **2**
ADV	**fiercely** competitive, **highly** competitive, **more** competitive **1** **2**

com|peti|tor /kəmpɛtɪtər/ (**competitors**)

1 **N-COUNT** A **competitor** is a person who takes part in a competition. ❑ *One of the oldest competitors won the silver medal.*

2 **N-COUNT** A company's **competitors** are companies that are trying to sell similar goods or services. ❑ *The bank isn't performing as well as some of its competitors.* [from Late Latin]

com|plain /kəmpleɪn/ (**complains, complaining, complained**)

1 **V-T/V-I** If you **complain**, you say that you are not satisfied with someone or something. ❑ *Voters complained about the election result.* ❑ *I shouldn't complain; I've got a good job.* ❑ *"Someone should do something about it," he complained.*

2 **V-I** If you **complain of** a pain or an illness, you say that you have it. ❑ *He went to the hospital, complaining of a sore neck.* [from Old French]

com|plaint /kəmpleɪnt/ (**complaints**)

N-COUNT/N-NONCOUNT You make a **complaint** when you say that you are not satisfied. ❑ *The police received several complaints about the noise.* [from Old French]

Word Link ple ≈ filling : complement, complete, deplete

com|ple|ment (**complements, complementing, complemented**)

PRONUNCIATION HELP
Pronounce the verb /kɒmplɪmɛnt/.
Pronounce the noun /kɒmplɪmənt/.

1 **V-T** If people or things **complement** each other, they have different qualities that go together well. ❑ *There will be a written examination to complement the listening test.*

2 **N-COUNT** Something that is a **complement to** something else complements it. ❑ *Our sauces are the perfect complement to your favorite dishes.*

3 **N-COUNT** LANGUAGE ARTS In grammar, the **complement** of a link verb is an adjective group or a noun group which comes after the verb and describes or identifies the subject. For example, in the sentence "They felt very tired," "very tired" is the complement. In "They were students,"

"students" is the complement. [from Latin]
→ look at Usage note at **compliment**

com|ple|men|tary /kɒmplɪmɛntəri, -mɛntri/

1 **ADJ Complementary** things are different from each other but make a good combination. [FORMAL] ❑ *Their complementary talents make them a good team.*

2 **ADJ Complementary** medicine refers to ways of treating patients that are different from the ones used by most Western doctors, for example homeopathy. ❑ *...a wide range of complementary therapies.*

3 **ADJ** ARTS **Complementary colors** are colors that are directly opposite each other on the color wheel, such as red and green. [from Latin]

com|plete /kəmplit/ (**completes, completing, completed**)

1 **ADJ Complete** means in every way. ❑ *His birthday party was a complete surprise.*

● **com|plete|ly** **ADV** ❑ *Thousands of homes have been completely destroyed.*

2 **ADJ** If something is **complete**, it contains all the parts that it should contain. ❑ *The list may not be complete.*

3 **ADJ** If a job is **complete**, it is finished. ❑ *The project is not yet complete.*

4 **V-T** If you **complete** a task, you finish it. ❑ *We hope to complete the project by January.*

5 **V-T** To **complete** something means to provide the last part that is needed. ❑ *Children don't complete their set of 20 baby teeth until they are two to three years old.*

6 **V-T** If you **complete** a form, you write the necessary information on it. ❑ *Complete the first part of the application form.* [from Latin]

Thesaurus complete Also look up :

ADJ	total, utter **1**
	entire, whole; (ant.) partial **2**

com|plex (**complexes**)

PRONUNCIATION HELP
Pronounce the adjective /kəmplɛks/ or sometimes /kɒmplɛks/. Pronounce the noun /kɒmplɛks/.

1 **ADJ** Something that is **complex** has many parts and is difficult to understand. ❑ *Crime is a complex problem.*

2 **N-COUNT** A **complex** is a group of buildings used for a particular purpose. ❑ *The family moved to a new apartment complex.* [from Latin]

com|plex|ion /kəmplɛkʃ°n/ (**complexions**)
N-COUNT Your **complexion** is the natural color of the skin on your face. ❑ *She had a pale complexion.* [from Latin]
→ look at Word Web: **makeup**

com|plex|ity /kəmplɛksɪti/ (**complexities**)
N-COUNT/N-NONCOUNT **Complexity** is the state of having many different parts connected or related to each other in a complicated way. ❑ *...the complexity of the problem.* ❑ *...the legal complexities of the issue.* [from Latin]

com|plex num|ber (**complex numbers**)
N-COUNT MATH **Complex numbers** are numbers of the form a+bi, where a and b are real numbers and i is the square root of -1.

> **Word Link** *ate ≈ causing to be : complicate, motivate, pollinate*

com|pli|cate /kɒmplɪkeɪt/ (**complicates, complicating, complicated**) **V-T** To **complicate** something means to make it more difficult to understand or deal with. ❑ *Please don't complicate the situation.* [from Latin]

com|pli|cat|ed /kɒmplɪkeɪtɪd/ **ADJ** Something that is **complicated** has many parts, and is difficult to understand. ❑ *The situation is very complicated.* [from Latin]

com|pli|ca|tion /kɒmplɪkeɪʃ°n/ (**complications**) **N-COUNT** A **complication** is a problem or a difficulty. ❑ *There were a number of complications.* [from Latin]

com|pli|ment (**compliments, complimenting, complimented**)

> **PRONUNCIATION HELP**
> Pronounce the verb /kɒmplɪmɛnt/.
> Pronounce the noun /kɒmplɪmənt/.

1 **N-COUNT** A **compliment** is something nice that you say to someone, for example about their appearance. ❑ *He was very nice to me and paid me several compliments.*
2 **V-T** If you **compliment** someone, you say something nice to them, for example about their appearance. ❑ *They complimented me on the way I looked.* [from French]

> **Usage** **compliment** and **complement**
> *Compliment* and *complement* are easily confused. *Compliment* means to say something nice to or about someone. *Jack complimented Rita on her pronunciation. Complement* means to go well together or to make something good seem even better. *The wine complemented the meal.*

com|ply /kəmplaɪ/ (**complies, complying, complied**) **V-I** If you **comply with** a demand or a rule, you do what is required. ❑ *Our changes comply with the new law.* [from Italian]

com|po|nent /kəmpoʊnənt/ (**components**) **N-COUNT** The **components** of something are its parts. ❑ *The plan has four main components.* [from Latin]

com|pose /kəmpoʊz/ (**composes, composing, composed**)
1 **V-T** The things that something **is composed of** are its parts or members. ❑ *Water is composed of oxygen and hydrogen.*
2 **V-T/V-I** MUSIC When someone **composes** a piece of music, a speech, or a letter, they write it. ❑ *Vivaldi composed a large number of concertos.* [from Old French]
→ look at Word Web: **music**

com|pos|er /kəmpoʊzər/ (**composers**) **N-COUNT** MUSIC A **composer** is a person who writes music. ❑ *Mozart and Beethoven were great composers.* [from Old French]
→ look at Word Web: **music**

com|po|site /kəmpɒzɪt/ (**composites**)
1 **ADJ** A **composite** object or item is made up of several different things, parts, or substances. ❑ *...skis made from layers of different composite materials.*
2 **N-COUNT** **Composite** is also a noun. ❑ *The book is a composite of two real-life stories.* [from Latin]

com|pos|ite vol|ca|no (**composite volcanoes**) **N-COUNT** SCIENCE A **composite volcano** is a volcano with steep sides composed of layers of lava and rock.

com|po|si|tion /kɒmpəzɪʃ°n/ (**compositions**)
1 **N-COUNT** ARTS A **composition** is a piece of music or writing.
2 **N-NONCOUNT** The **composition** of something is its parts or members. ❑ *They study the chemical composition of the food we eat.*
3 **N-NONCOUNT** ARTS **Composition** is the technique or skill involved in composing something such as a piece of music or a poem. [from Old French]
→ look at Word Web: **orchestra**

> **Word Link** *post ≈ after : compost, postscript, postwar*

com|post /kɒmpoʊst/ **N-NONCOUNT** **Compost** is a mixture of decayed plants that is used to improve soil. ❑ *...a small*

compost pile. [from Old French]
→ look at Word Web: **dump**

com|pound (**compounds, compounding, compounded**)

> **PRONUNCIATION HELP**
> Pronounce the noun and adjective
> /kɒmpaʊnd/. Pronounce the verb
> /kəmpaʊnd/.

1 **N-COUNT** SCIENCE In chemistry, a **compound** is a substance that is made from two or more elements. ❑ *Dioxins are chemical compounds that are produced when material is burned.*

2 **V-T** To **compound** a problem means to make it worse by adding to it. ❑ *Additional loss of life will only compound the tragedy.*

3 **ADJ** LANGUAGE ARTS In grammar, a **compound** is a word that is made from two or more other words, for example "fire truck."

4 **ADJ** LANGUAGE ARTS In grammar, a **compound** sentence is one that is made up of two or more main clauses. [from Old French.]
→ look at Word Webs: **element, rock**

com|pound eye (**compound eyes**) **N-COUNT** SCIENCE A **compound eye** is a type of eye found in some creatures that is made up of many identical elements that work together.

com|pound light micro|scope (**compound light microscopes**) **N-COUNT** SCIENCE A **compound light microscope** is a microscope that uses glass lenses and light to produce an image.

com|pound ma|chine (**compound machines**) **N-COUNT** SCIENCE A **compound machine** is a machine that consists of two or more smaller machines working together. Compare with **simple machine**.

com|pound me|ter (**compound meters**) **N-COUNT/N-NONCOUNT** MUSIC In a piece of music written in **compound meter**, the beat is divided into three parts.

com|pre|hend /kɒmprɪhɛnd/ (**comprehends, comprehending, comprehended**) **V-T/V-I** If you do not **comprehend** something or do not **comprehend**, you do not understand it. [FORMAL] ❑ *I don't think you fully comprehend what's happening.* [from Latin]

com|pre|hen|sion /kɒmprɪhɛnʃⁿn/ **N-NONCOUNT** **Comprehension** is the ability to understand something. [FORMAL] ❑ *...a reading comprehension test.* [from Latin]

com|press /kəmprɛs/ (**compresses, compressing, compressed**) **V-T/V-I** When you **compress** something or when it **compresses**, it is pressed or squeezed so that it takes up less space. ❑ *Compressing a gas heats it up.*

com|pro|mise /kɒmprəmaɪz/ (**compromises, compromising, compromised**)

1 **N-COUNT/N-NONCOUNT** A **compromise** is a situation in which people accept something slightly different from what they really want. ❑ *Try to reach a compromise between the demands of work and family life.*

2 **V-T/V-I** If people **compromise**, they both agree to give up something that they want. ❑ *"Nine," I said. "Nine thirty," he replied. We compromised on 9.15.* [from Old French]

> **Word Link** **puls ≈ driving, pushing : com**puls**ory, ex**puls**ion, im**puls**e**

com|pul|so|ry /kəmpʌlsəri/ **ADJ** If something is **compulsory**, you must do it. ❑ *In Australia, voting is compulsory.* [from Old French]

com|pute /kəmpyut/ (**computes, computing, computed**) **V-T** MATH To **compute** a quantity or a number means to calculate it. ❑ *To compute your score, simply add up your scores for each item.* [from Latin]

> **Word Link** **put ≈ thinking : com**put**er, dis**put**e, in**put**

com|put|er /kəmpyutər/ (**computers**)

1 **N-COUNT** TECHNOLOGY A **computer** is an electronic machine that can store and deal with large amounts of information. ❑ *He watched the concert on his computer via the Internet.* ❑ *The company installed a $650,000 computer system.* [from Latin]

2 → see also **personal computer**
→ look at Picture Dictionaries: **computer, office**

com|put|er|ize /kəmpyutəraɪz/ (**computerizes, computerizing, computerized**) **V-T** To **computerize** a system or a type of work means to arrange for a lot of the work to be done by computer. ❑ *I'm trying to computerize everything.*
● **com|put|er|ized** **ADJ** ❑ *...a computerized system.* [from Latin]

com|pu|ting /kəmpyutɪŋ/

1 **N-NONCOUNT** **Computing** is the activity of using a computer and writing programs for

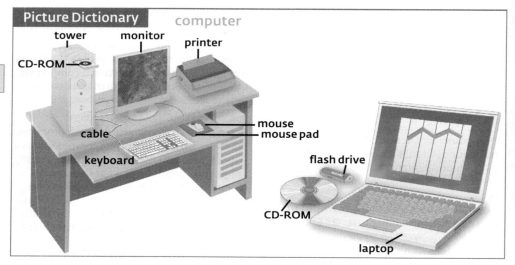

Picture Dictionary — computer

tower — monitor — printer — CD-ROM — cable — keyboard — mouse — mouse pad — flash drive — CD-ROM — laptop

it. ❑ *They offer a course in business and computing.* [from Latin]

2 → see also **compute**

con /kɒn/ (**cons, conning, conned**)

1 **v-t** If someone **cons** you, they persuade you to do something or believe something by telling you things that are not true. [INFORMAL] ❑ *He claimed that the businessman conned him of $10,000.* ❑ *White conned his way into a job.*

2 **N-COUNT** A **con** is a trick in which someone deceives you by telling you something that is not true. [INFORMAL] ❑ *It was all a con.*

con|cave lens /kɒnkeɪv lɛnz/ (**concave lenses**) **N-COUNT** **SCIENCE** A **concave lens** is a lens that is thinner in the middle than at the edges. Compare with **convex lens**.

con|ceal /kənsiːl/ (**conceals, concealing, concealed**) **v-t** To **conceal** something means to hide it or keep it secret. ❑ *The hat concealed her hair.* ❑ *Robert could not conceal his happiness.* [from Old French]

con|cede /kənsiːd/ (**concedes, conceding, conceded**) **v-t** If you **concede** something, you admit, often unwillingly, that it is true or correct. ❑ *Bess finally conceded that Nancy was right.* ❑ *"Well," he conceded, "there have been a few problems."* [from Latin]

con|ceive /kənsiːv/ (**conceives, conceiving, conceived**)

1 **v-t/v-i** If you cannot **conceive of** something, you cannot imagine it or believe

it. ❑ *I can't even conceive of that amount of money.* ❑ *We could not conceive that he might soon be dead.*

2 **v-t** If you **conceive** a plan or idea, you think of it and work out how it can be done. ❑ *She conceived the idea of a series of novels.*

3 **v-t/v-i** When a woman or a couple **conceives**, the woman becomes pregnant. ❑ *They have been trying to conceive for three years now.* ❑ *The baby was conceived naturally, and is due in October.* [from Old French]

con|cen|trate /kɒnsəntreɪt/ (**concentrates, concentrating, concentrated**)

1 **v-i** You **concentrate on** something when you give it all your attention. ❑ *He should concentrate on his studies.* ❑ *She had to concentrate hard to win the race.*

2 **v-t** If something **is concentrated in** one place, it is all there. ❑ *Italy's industrial cities are concentrated in the north.* [from Latin]

con|cen|trat|ed /kɒnsəntreɪtɪd/

1 **ADJ** A **concentrated** liquid has been increased in strength by having water removed from it. ❑ *...concentrated apple juice.*

2 **ADJ** A **concentrated** activity is done with great intensity in one place. ❑ *...a concentrated effort to control his temper.* [from Latin]

con|cen|tra|tion /kɒnsəntreɪʃən/ (**concentrations**)

1 **N-NONCOUNT** **Concentration** on something means giving it all your attention. ❑ *At first there is greater concentration on speaking skills.*

2 **N-COUNT/N-NONCOUNT** **SCIENCE** The **concentration of** a substance is the proportion of essential ingredients or substances in it. [from Latin]

con|cept /kɒnsɛpt/ (**concepts**) **N-COUNT** A **concept** is an idea about something. ❑ *Our laws are based on the concept of fairness.* [from Latin]

con|cep|tion /kənsɛpʃⁿn/ (**conceptions**) **N-COUNT/N-NONCOUNT** A **conception of** something is an idea that you have of it in your mind. ❑ *...my conception of a garden.* [from Latin]

con|cern /kənsɜrn/ (**concerns, concerning, concerned**)
■ **N-NONCOUNT** **Concern** is worry about something. ❑ *She expressed concern about my grandfather's health.*
■ **V-T** If something **concerns** you, it worries you. ❑ *It concerns me that she hasn't telephoned.* ● **con|cerned** **ADJ** ❑ *I've been concerned about you lately.*
■ **V-T** If a book or a piece of information **concerns** a particular subject, it is about that subject. ❑ *The book concerns Sandy's two children.* ● **con|cerned** **ADJ** ❑ *Randolph's work is concerned with the effects of pollution.*
■ **V-T** If a situation or activity **concerns** you, it affects or involves you. ❑ *It doesn't concern you at all.* ● **con|cerned** **ADJ** ❑ *It's a very stressful situation for everyone concerned.*
■ **N-COUNT** A **concern** is a fact or situation that worries you. ❑ *His concern was that people would know that he was responsible.* [from Late Latin]

con|cern|ing /kənsɜrnɪŋ/ **PREP** You use **concerning** to show what subject is being talked or written about. [FORMAL] ❑ *Contact Mr. Coldwell for more information concerning the class.* [from Late Latin]

con|cert /kɒnsərt/ (**concerts**) **N-COUNT** MUSIC A **concert** is a performance of music. ❑ *We attended a concert by the great jazz pianist Harold Maburn.* ❑ *The weekend began with an outdoor rock concert.* [from French]
→ look at Word Web: **concert**

con|cer|to /kəntʃɛərtoʊ/ (**concertos**) **N-COUNT** MUSIC A **concerto** is a piece of music for one or more solo instruments and an orchestra. ❑ *...Tchaikovsky's First Piano Concerto.* [from Italian]
→ look at Word Web: **music**

con|ces|sion /kənsɛʃⁿn/ (**concessions**)
■ **N-COUNT** If you make a **concession to** someone, you agree to let them do or have something, especially in order to end an argument or a conflict. ❑ *We made too many concessions to the workers and we got too little in return.*
■ **N-COUNT** BUSINESS A **concession** is an arrangement where someone is given the right to sell a product or to run a business, especially in a building belonging to another business. ❑ *Concession sales at the airport are up 15%.* [from Latin]

con|clude /kənkluːd/ (**concludes, concluding, concluded**)
■ **V-T** If you **conclude** something, you make a decision after thinking about it carefully. ❑ *We've concluded that it's best to tell her the truth.* ❑ *So what can we conclude from this experiment?*
■ **V-T/V-I** When something **concludes** or if you **conclude** it, it ends. [FORMAL] ❑ *The evening concluded with dinner and speeches.* ❑ *He politely, if not abruptly, concluded the conversation.* [from Latin]

con|clu|sion /kənkluːʒⁿn/ (**conclusions**)
■ **N-COUNT** A **conclusion** is a decision that

Word Web concert

A **rock concert** is much more than a group of **musicians** playing **music** on a **stage**. It is a full-scale **performance**. Each **band** must have a **manager** and an **agent** who **books** the **venue** and **promotes** the **show** in each new location. The band's assistants, called roadies, set up the stage, test the **microphones**, and tune the **instruments**. **Sound engineers** make sure the band sounds as good as possible. There's always **lighting** to **spotlight** the **lead singer** and **backup** singers. The bright, moving lights help to build excitement. The **fans** scream and yell when they hear their favorite **songs**. The **audience** never wants the show to end.

you make after thinking carefully about something. ❏ *I've come to the conclusion that she's a great musician.*

2 **N-SING** LANGUAGE ARTS The **conclusion** of a story is its ending. ❏ *What do you understand from the conclusion of the story?*

3 **PHRASE** You say **in conclusion** to show that what you are about to say will be the last thing you say. ❏ *In conclusion, walking is cheap, safe, and enjoyable.* [from Old French]

Word Partnership	Use **conclusion** with :
V	**come to a** conclusion, **draw a** conclusion, **reach a** conclusion **1**
N	conclusion **of** *something* **2**
PREP	**in** conclusion **3**

con|coct /kənk**ɒ**kt/ (**concocts, concocting, concocted**)

1 **V-T** If you **concoct** an excuse, you invent one. ❏ *The prisoner concocted the story.*

2 **V-T** If you **concoct** something, especially something unusual, you make it by mixing several things together. ❏ *Eugene was concocting a new pudding.* [from Latin]

con|crete /k**ɒ**ŋkrit/

1 **N-NONCOUNT** **Concrete** is a hard substance made by mixing a gray powder with sand and water. It is used for building. ❏ *The hotel is constructed from steel and concrete.* ❏ *We sat on the concrete floor.*

2 **ADJ** Something that is **concrete** is definite and specific. ❏ *I had no concrete evidence.*

3 **ADJ** A **concrete** object is a real, physical object. A **concrete** image is an image of a real, physical object. [from Latin]

con|demn /kənd**ɛ**m/ (**condemns, condemning, condemned**)

1 **V-T** If you **condemn** something, you say that it is not acceptable. ❏ *Police condemned the recent violence.*

2 **V-T** If someone **is condemned to** a punishment, they are given that punishment. ❏ *He was condemned to life in prison.* [from Old French]

con|den|sa|tion /k**ɒ**ndɛnseɪʃᵊn/

N-NONCOUNT SCIENCE **Condensation** consists of small drops of water which form when warm water vapor or steam touches a cold surface such as a window. [from Latin]

con|den|sa|tion point (**condensation points**) **N-COUNT/N-NONCOUNT** SCIENCE The **condensation point** of a gas or vapor is the temperature at which it becomes a liquid.

con|dense /kənd**ɛ**ns/ (**condenses, condensing, condensed**)

1 **V-T** If you **condense** something, especially a piece of writing or a speech, you make it shorter. ❏ *To save time, teachers condense lesson plans.*

2 **V-I** SCIENCE When a gas or vapor **condenses**, or **is condensed**, it changes into a liquid. ❏ *Water vapor condenses to form clouds.* [from Latin]

→ look at Word Webs: **matter, water**

con|di|ment /k**ɒ**ndɪmənt/ (**condiments**)

N-COUNT A **condiment** is a substance such as salt, pepper, or mustard that you add to food when you eat it in order to improve the flavor. [from Latin]

→ look at Word Web: **ketchup**

con|di|tion /kənd**ɪ**ʃᵊn/ (**conditions**)

1 **N-SING** The **condition** of someone or something is the state that they are in. ❏ *Doctors expect his condition to improve.* ❏ *The old house is in terrible condition.*

2 **N-PLURAL** The **conditions** in which people live or work are the things that affect their comfort and safety. ❏ *People are living in terrible conditions with little food or water.*

3 **N-COUNT** A **condition** is something which must happen in order for something else to be possible. ❏ *...terms and conditions of employment.*

4 **N-COUNT** Someone who has a particular **condition** has a medical problem. ❏ *Doctors think he may have a heart condition.* [from Latin]

→ look at Word Web: **factory**

con|di|tion|al /kənd**ɪ**ʃənᵊl/ (**conditionals**)

N-COUNT LANGUAGE ARTS In grammar, you use the **conditional** for talking about a situation that may exist or happen. Most conditionals begin with "if." For example "If you work hard, you'll pass your exams." [from Latin]

con|dom /k**ɒ**ndəm/ (**condoms**) **N-COUNT** A **condom** is a rubber covering that a man wears on his penis during sex as a method of contraception or as protection against disease.

con|do|min|ium /k**ɒ**ndəm**ɪ**niəm/ (**condominiums**)

1 **N-COUNT** A **condominium** is an apartment building in which each apartment is owned by the person who lives there.

2 **N-COUNT** A **condominium** is an apartment in a condominium. [from New Latin]

con|du|cive /kənd<u>u</u>sɪv/ **ADJ** If one thing is **conducive to** another thing, it makes the other thing likely to happen. ❑ *Make your bedroom as conducive to sleep as possible.* [from Latin]

con|duct (**conducts, conducting, conducted**)

> PRONUNCIATION HELP
> Pronounce the verb /kənd<u>ʌ</u>kt/. Pronounce the noun /k<u>ɒ</u>ndʌkt/.

■ **V-T** When you **conduct** an activity or a task, you organize it and do it. ❑ *I decided to conduct an experiment.*
■ **V-T** If you **conduct** yourself in a particular way, you behave in that way. ❑ *The way he conducts himself embarrasses the family.*
■ **V-T** SCIENCE If something **conducts** heat or electricity, heat or electricity can pass through it.
■ **V-T/V-I** MUSIC When someone **conducts** musicians, they stand in front and direct the performance. ❑ *The new musical work was composed and conducted by Leonard Bernstein.* ❑ *Solti continued to conduct here and abroad.*
■ **N-NONCOUNT** Someone's **conduct** is the way they behave. ❑ *She won a prize for good conduct in school.* [from Medieval Latin]

Thesaurus	conduct	Also look up :
v	control, direct, manage ■	
N	attitude, behavior, manner ■	

Word Partnership	Use conduct with :
N	conduct **business**, conduct an **experiment** ■ code of conduct ■

con|duc|tion /kənd<u>ʌ</u>kʃ°n/ **N-NONCOUNT** SCIENCE **Conduction** is the process by which heat or electricity passes through or along something. [from Medieval Latin]

con|duc|tor /kənd<u>ʌ</u>ktər/ (**conductors**)
■ **N-COUNT** MUSIC A **conductor** is a person who stands in front of a group of musicians and directs their performance.
■ **N-COUNT** On a train, a **conductor** is a person whose job is to help passengers and check tickets.
■ **N-COUNT** SCIENCE A **conductor** is a substance that heat or electricity can pass through. ❑ *Water is an excellent conductor of electricity.* [from Medieval Latin]
→ look at Word Web: **metal**

cone /k<u>oʊ</u>n/ (**cones**)
■ **N-COUNT** MATH A **cone** is a solid shape with one flat round end and one pointed end. ❑ *Bright-orange traffic cones stop people from parking on the bridge.*
■ **N-COUNT** A **cone** is a thin cookie in the shape of a cone that you put ice cream into and eat. ❑ *...an ice-cream cone.*
■ **N-COUNT** A **cone** is the fruit of a tree such as a pine or a fir. ❑ *...a pine cone.*
■ **N-COUNT** SCIENCE **Cones** are cells in the eye that detect bright light and help you to see colors. [from Latin]
→ look at Picture Dictionaries: **solid, volume**
→ look at Word Web: **volcano**

con|fed|era|tion /kənfɛdəreɪʃ°n/ (**confederations**) **N-COUNT** SOCIAL STUDIES A **confederation** is an organization or a group consisting of smaller groups or states, especially one that exists for business or political purposes. ❑ *...the Confederation of Indian Industry.* [from Late Latin]

con|fer|ence /k<u>ɒ</u>nfərəns, -frəns/ (**conferences**) **N-COUNT** A **conference** is a long meeting about a particular subject. ❑ *We attended a conference on education last month.* [from Medieval Latin]

con|fess /kənf<u>ɛ</u>s/ (**confesses, confessing, confessed**) **V-T/V-I** When you **confess**, you admit that you did something wrong. ❑ *He confessed to seventeen murders.* ❑ *Ed confessed that he broke the window.* [from Old French]

con|fes|sion /kənf<u>ɛ</u>ʃ°n/ (**confessions**) **N-COUNT** If you make a **confession**, you admit that you have done something wrong. ❑ *I have a confession to make. I lied about my age.* [from Old French]

con|fide /kənf<u>aɪ</u>d/ (**confides, confiding, confided**) **V-T/V-I** If you **confide in** someone, you tell them a secret. ❑ *She confided in me earlier.* ❑ *He confided to me that he felt lonely.* [from Latin]

con|fi|dence /k<u>ɒ</u>nfɪdəns/
■ **N-NONCOUNT** If you have **confidence in** someone, you feel that you can trust them. ❑ *I have great confidence in you.*
■ **N-NONCOUNT** If you have **confidence**, you feel sure about your own abilities and ideas. ❑ *The team is full of confidence.*
■ **N-NONCOUNT** If you tell someone something **in confidence**, you tell them a secret. ❑ *We told you all these things in confidence.* [from Latin]

con|fi|dent /kɒnfɪdənt/

1 **ADJ** If you are **confident** about something, you are certain that the result will be good. ❑ *I am confident that I'll get the job.*
2 **ADJ** People who are **confident** feel sure about their own abilities and ideas. ❑ *In time he became more confident and relaxed.*
● **con|fi|dent|ly** **ADV** ❑ *She walked confidently into the boss's office.* [from Latin]

con|fi|den|tial /kɒnfɪdɛnʃᵊl/ **ADJ**
Information that is **confidential** must be kept secret. ❑ *After her death, some newspapers printed confidential information about her private life.* ● **con|fi|den|tial|ly** **ADV** ❑ *Any information they give will be treated confidentially.* [from Latin]

Thesaurus	confidential	Also look up :
ADJ	private, restricted; *(ant.)* public	

con|fine /kənfaɪn/ (**confines, confining, confined**) **V-T** If a person or an animal **is confined** in a particular place, they cannot leave it. ❑ *The animals are confined in tiny cages.*
● **con|fine|ment** /kənfaɪnmənt/
N-NONCOUNT ❑ *He read a lot during his two-year confinement in prison.* [from Medieval Latin]

con|fined /kənfaɪnd/
1 **ADJ** If something is **confined to** a particular place, it exists only in that place. If it is **confined to** a particular group, only members of that group have it. ❑ *The problem is not confined to Georgia.*
2 **ADJ** A **confined** space or area is small and enclosed by walls. ❑ *I don't like confined spaces.* [from Medieval Latin]

con|firm /kənfɜrm/ (**confirms, confirming, confirmed**)
1 **V-T** When someone **confirms** something, they say that it is true. ❑ *The doctor confirmed that my nose was broken.*
2 **V-T** If you **confirm** a meeting or an arrangement, you say that it will definitely happen. ❑ *He called at seven to confirm our appointment.* ● **con|fir|ma|tion** **N-NONCOUNT** ❑ *You will receive confirmation of your order by email.* [from Old French]

Word Link	*flict* ≈ striking : af*flict*ion, con*flict*, in*flict*

con|flict (**conflicts, conflicting, conflicted**)

PRONUNCIATION HELP
Pronounce the noun /kɒnflɪkt/. Pronounce the verb /kənflɪkt/.

1 **N-COUNT/N-NONCOUNT** A **conflict** is a fight or an argument between people or countries. [WRITTEN] ❑ *The military conflict lasted many years.*
2 **V-T/V-I** If ideas or plans **conflict**, they are very different from each other. ❑ *His opinions usually conflicted with mine.* [from Latin]

con|form /kənfɔrm/ (**conforms, conforming, conformed**)
1 **V-I** If something **conforms to** a rule or a law, it follows it. ❑ *The lamp conforms to new safety standards.*
2 **V-I** If you **conform**, you behave in a way that most people think is correct or normal. ❑ *At her age, it is important to conform.* [from Old French]

con|front /kənfrʌnt/ (**confronts, confronting, confronted**)
1 **V-T** If you **are confronted with** a problem or a task, you have to deal with it. ❑ *She was confronted with serious money problems.* ❑ *We are learning how to confront death.*
2 **V-T** If you **confront** someone, you stand or sit in front of them, especially when you are going to fight or argue with them. ❑ *She confronted him face to face.*
3 **V-T** If you **confront** someone **with** evidence, you present it to them in order to accuse them of something. ❑ *She decided to confront Kathryn with the truth.* ❑ *I could not bring myself to confront him about it.* [from Medieval Latin]

con|fron|ta|tion /kɒnfrʌnteɪʃᵊn/ (**confrontations**) **N-COUNT/N-NONCOUNT** A **confrontation** is a dispute, a fight, or a battle. ❑ *...confrontation with the enemy.*
● **con|fron|ta|tion|al** /kɒnfrʌnteɪʃənᵊl/ **ADJ** ❑ *...his confrontational style.* [from Medieval Latin]

con|fuse /kənfyuz/ (**confuses, confusing, confused**)
1 **V-T** If you **confuse** two things, you think one of them is the other one. ❑ *I always confuse my left with my right.*
2 **V-T** To **confuse** someone means to make it difficult for them to understand something. ❑ *My words confused him.* [from Latin]

con|fused /kənfyuzd/
1 **ADJ** If you are **confused**, you do not understand what is happening, or you do not know what to do. ❑ *People are confused about what's going to happen.*
2 **ADJ** Something that is **confused** does not

have any order and is difficult to understand. ❏ *The situation remains confused.* [from Latin]

con|fus|ing /kənfyuzɪŋ/ **ADJ** Something that is **confusing** is difficult to understand, and makes it difficult for people to know what to do. ❏ *The directions are really confusing.* [from Latin]

con|fu|sion /kənfyuʒᵊn/ (**confusions**)
1 **N-COUNT/N-NONCOUNT** If there is **confusion** about something, the facts are not clear. ❏ *There's still confusion about the number of students.*
2 **N-NONCOUNT** **Confusion** is a situation in which a lot of things are happening in a badly organized way. ❏ *People were pushing and shouting, and there was confusion everywhere.*
3 **N-NONCOUNT** **Confusion** is a situation in which you think that one thing is another thing. ❏ *Use different colors to avoid confusion.* [from Latin]

con|gratu|late /kəngrætʃəleɪt/ (**congratulates, congratulating, congratulated**) **V-T** If you **congratulate** someone, you express pleasure about something good that has happened to them. ❏ *She congratulated him on the birth of his son.* ● **con|gratu|la|tion** /kəngrætʃəleɪʃᵊn/ **N-NONCOUNT** ❏ *We received several letters of congratulation.* [from Latin]

con|gratu|la|tions /kəngrætʃəleɪʃᵊnz/ **INTERJ** You say **Congratulations** to someone in order to congratulate them. ❏ *Congratulations on your new job.* [from Latin]

Con|gress /kɒŋgrɪs/ **N-PROPER** SOCIAL STUDIES **Congress** is the part of the government that makes laws in the United States. ❏ *Members of Congress are elected by the people.* [from Latin]

congress|man /kɒŋgrɪsmən/ (**congressmen**) **N-COUNT** SOCIAL STUDIES A **congressman** is a male member of the U.S. Congress, especially of the House of Representatives.

congress|woman /kɒŋgrɪswʊmən/ (**congresswomen**) **N-COUNT** SOCIAL STUDIES A **congresswoman** is a female member of the U.S. Congress, especially of the House of Representatives.

con|gru|ent /kɒŋgruənt, kəngru-/ **ADJ** MATH In geometry, two shapes are **congruent** if they are the same size

and shape but in different positions. [from Latin]

con|ic pro|jec|tion /kɒnɪk prədʒɛkʃən/ (**conic projections**) **N-COUNT/N-NONCOUNT** SCIENCE A **conic projection** is an image of a map that is made by projecting the map on a globe onto a cone. Compare with **azimuthal projection** and **Mercator projection**.

co|ni|fer /kɒnɪfər/ (**conifers**) **N-COUNT** SCIENCE **Conifers** are a type of trees and shrubs such as pine trees and fir trees. They have fruit called cones, and very thin leaves called needles which they do not normally lose in winter. [from Latin]

con|junc|tion /kəndʒʌŋkʃᵊn/ (**conjunctions**) **N-COUNT** LANGUAGE ARTS A **conjunction** is a word that joins together parts of sentences. For example, "and" and "or" are conjunctions. [from Latin]

con|jure /kɒndʒər/ (**conjures, conjuring, conjured**)
1 **V-T** If you **conjure** something out of nothing, you make it appear as if by magic. ❏ *She found herself having to conjure a career from thin air.*
2 **Conjure up** means the same as **conjure**. ❏ *Phyllis conjured up a delicious dinner.* [from Old French]
▶ **conjure up** **1** If you **conjure up** a memory, a picture, or an idea, you create it in your mind. ❏ *Try to conjure up that pleasant thought again.*
2 → look up **conjure**

con|nect /kənɛkt/ (**connects, connecting, connected**)
1 **V-T/V-I** If you **connect** one thing **to** another, the two things are joined together. ❏ *Next, connect the printer to your computer.*
2 **V-T** If a piece of equipment or a place **is connected to** a supply of power or water, it is joined to that supply. ❏ *The house is not yet connected to the water supply.*
3 **V-I** If one train, plane, or boat **connects with** another, passengers can change to the other one and continue their trip. ❏ *The train connects with a plane to Ireland.* [from Latin]

con|nect|ed /kənɛktɪd/ **ADJ** If one thing is **connected with** another, there is a relationship between them. ❏ *She described the problems connected with a high-fat diet.* [from Latin] con|nec|tion /kənɛkʃ°n/ (connections)

1 **N-COUNT/N-NONCOUNT** A **connection** is a relationship between two things, people, or groups. ❑ *I felt a strong connection between us.* ❑ *Children need to understand the connection between energy and the environment.*

2 **N-COUNT** A **connection** is a place where two wires or pipes are joined together. ❑ *The fire was cause by a faulty electrical connection.*

3 **N-COUNT** A **connection** is a way of communicating using the telephone or a computer. ❑ *You'll need a fast Internet connection to view this site.*

4 **N-COUNT** A **connection** is a train, a bus, or a plane that allows you continue your trip by changing from one to another. ❑ *My flight was late and I missed the connection.*

5 **PHRASE** **In connection with** something means relating to or involving it. ❑ *No arrests have been made in connection with Murphy's murder.* [from Latin]

con|nec|tive tis|sue /kənɛktɪv tɪʃu/

N-NONCOUNT SCIENCE **Connective tissue** is the substance in the bodies of animals and people which fills in the spaces between organs and connects muscles and bones.

con|quer /kɒŋkər/ (conquers, conquering, conquered)

1 **V-T** SOCIAL STUDIES If one country or group of people **conquers** another, they take complete control of their land. ❑ *Germany conquered France in 1940.*

2 **V-T** If you **conquer** a problem, you manage to deal with it. ❑ *I've conquered my fear of spiders.* [from Old French]
→ look at Word Webs: **army, empire**

con|science /kɒnʃ°ns/ (consciences)

1 **N-COUNT** Your **conscience** is the part of your mind that tells you if what you are doing is wrong. ❑ *My conscience is clear about everything I have done (= I do not feel that I have done anything wrong).*

2 **PHRASE** If you have a **guilty conscience,** you feel bad because you know you did something wrong. ❑ *She has a guilty conscience about downloading music from the Internet without paying.* [from Old French]

con|sci|en|tious /kɒnʃiɛnʃəs/ **ADJ** Someone who is **conscientious** is careful to follow rules and do things correctly. ❑ *She is very conscientious about doing her homework.*
● con|sci|en|tious|ly **ADV** ❑ *He conscientiously exercised every night.* [from Old French]

Word Link	sci ≈ knowing : *con*sci*ous, *sci*ence, *un*con*sci*ous*

con|scious /kɒnʃəs/

1 **ADJ** If you are **conscious of** something, you notice it. ❑ *She was conscious of Nick watching her across the room.*

2 **ADJ** If you are **conscious of** something, you think about it a lot because you think it is important. ❑ *I'm very conscious of my weight.*

3 **ADJ** Someone who is **conscious** is awake, and is not asleep or unconscious. ❑ *She was fully conscious soon after the operation.* [from Latin]

Thesaurus	conscious Also look up :
ADJ	awake, aware, responsive; *(ant.)* unaware, unconscious **3**

Word Link	ness ≈ state, condition : *aware*ness*, *conscious*ness*, *kind*ness*

con|scious|ness /kɒnʃəsnɪs/ (consciousnesses)

1 **N-COUNT** Your **consciousness** is your mind, thoughts, beliefs, and attitudes. ❑ *...ideas about the nature of consciousness.*

2 **N-NONCOUNT** If you **lose consciousness,** you become unconscious, and if you **regain consciousness,** you become conscious again. ❑ *She banged her head and lost consciousness.* [from Latin]

con|secu|tive /kənsɛkyətɪv/ **ADJ** **Consecutive** periods of time or events happen one after the other without interruption. ❑ *The Cup was won for the third consecutive year by the Toronto Maple Leafs.* [from French]

Word Link	con ≈ together, with : *con*sensus, *con*struct, *con*vene

con|sen|sus /kənsɛnsəs/ **N-SING** A **consensus** is general agreement among a group of people. ❑ *The consensus among scientists is that the world is likely to warm up.* [from Latin]

con|sent /kənsɛnt/ (consents, consenting, consented)

1 **N-NONCOUNT** If you give your **consent to** something, you allow someone to do it. [FORMAL] ❑ *Pollard finally gave his consent to the police search.*

2 **V-T/V-I** If you **consent to** something, you agree to do it or to allow it to happen. [FORMAL] ❑ *She consented to marry him.* ❑ *He consented to the idea.* [from Old French]

Word Link *sequ ≈ following : con*sequ*ence, sequ*ence, sub*sequ*ent*

con|se|quence /kɒnsɪkwɛns, -kwəns/ (**consequences**) **N-COUNT Consequences** are the results or effects of something that has happened. ❑ *She understood the consequences of her actions.* [from Latin]

con|se|quent|ly /kɒnsɪkwɛntli, -kwəntli/ **ADV** You use **consequently** to talk about the result of something. [FORMAL] ❑ *He worked all night, and consequently he slept during the day.* [from Latin]

con|ser|va|tion /kɒnsərveɪʃⁿn/
1 **N-NONCOUNT** SCIENCE **Conservation** is taking care of the environment. ❑ *...wildlife conservation.*
2 **N-NONCOUNT** The **conservation** of a supply of something is the careful use of it so that it lasts for a long time. [from Latin]

con|ser|va|tion of en|er|gy **N-NONCOUNT** SCIENCE The law of **conservation of energy** is a principle in physics which states that energy cannot be created or destroyed.

con|ser|va|tion of mass or **conservation of matter** **N-NONCOUNT** SCIENCE The law of **conservation of mass** is a principle in physics which states that matter cannot be created or destroyed.

con|serva|tive /kənsɜrvətɪv/ (**conservatives**)
1 **ADJ** Someone who is **conservative** does not like changes and new ideas. ❑ *People often become more conservative as they get older.*
2 **ADJ** SOCIAL STUDIES In politics, someone who is **conservative** does not want sudden or great changes in society. ❑ *...the most conservative candidate.*
3 **N-COUNT** SOCIAL STUDIES **Conservative** is also a noun. ❑ *The new judge is a conservative.* [from Latin]

Thesaurus conservative Also look up :
ADJ conventional, right-wing, traditional; *(ant.)* left-wing, liberal, radical **2**

Word Link *serv ≈ keeping : con*serv*e, ob*serv*e, pre*serv*e*

con|serve /kənsɜrv/ (**conserves, conserving, conserved**)
1 **V-T** If you **conserve** energy or water, you use it carefully so that it lasts for a long time. ❑ *The factories have closed for the weekend to conserve energy.*

2 **V-T** If you **conserve** the environment, you take care of it. ❑ *World leaders agreed to work together to conserve forests.* [from Latin]

con|sid|er /kənsɪdər/ (**considers, considering, considered**)
1 **V-T** If you **consider** a person or a thing **to** be a particular way, that is your opinion of them. ❑ *The police consider him to be dangerous.*
2 **V-T** If you **consider** something, you think about it carefully. ❑ *The president says he's still considering the situation.* ❑ *You should consider the feelings of other people.* [from Latin]
3 → see also **considering**

Thesaurus consider Also look up :
V contemplate, examine, study, think about, think over; *(ant.)* dismiss, forget, ignore **2**

con|sid|er|able /kənsɪdərəbⁿl/ **ADJ** **Considerable** means great or large. [FORMAL] ❑ *The land cost a considerable amount of money.* ● **con|sid|er|ably** **ADV** ❑ *The king's wife was considerably taller and larger than he was.* [from Latin]

con|sid|er|ate /kənsɪdərɪt/ **ADJ** Someone who is **considerate** thinks about and cares about the feelings of other people. ❑ *He's the most considerate man I know.* [from Latin]

con|sid|era|tion /kənsɪdəreɪʃⁿn/ (**considerations**)
1 **N-NONCOUNT** If you show **consideration**, you think about and care about the feelings of other people. ❑ *Show consideration for your neighbors.*
2 **N-COUNT** A **consideration** is something that you should think about when you are deciding something. ❑ *Price has become a more important consideration for shoppers.*
3 **N-NONCOUNT** **Consideration** is the act or process of thinking about something carefully. ❑ *After careful consideration, we've decided that a change is necessary.*
4 **PHRASE** If you **take** something **into consideration**, you think about it because it is important to what you are doing. ❑ *Safe driving takes into consideration the lives of other people.* [from Latin]

con|sid|er|ing /kənsɪdərɪŋ/
1 **PREP** You use **considering** to indicate that you are thinking about a particular fact when making a judgment or giving an

opinion. ❏ *Considering the current situation, he may be hoping for too much.* ❏ *Graham did very well considering that he hasn't been playing regularly.* [from Latin]

2 → see also **consider**

con|sist /kənsɪst/ (**consists, consisting, consisted**) **V-I** Something that **consists of** particular things or people is made up of them. ❏ *My diet consisted of cookies and milk.* [from Latin]

con|sist|ent /kənsɪstənt/

1 **ADJ** Someone who is **consistent** always behaves in the same way. ❏ *Oakley is one of the team's most consistent players.*

● **con|sist|en|cy** **N-NONCOUNT** ❏ *She scores goals with great consistency.* ● **con|sist|ent|ly** **ADV** ❏ *The airline consistently wins awards for its service.*

2 **ADJ** If one fact or idea is **consistent with** another, they agree with each other. ❏ *This result is consistent with the theory.* [from Latin]

con|sole (**consoles, consoling, consoled**)

PRONUNCIATION HELP

Pronounce the verb /kənsoʊl/. Pronounce the noun /kɒnsoʊl/.

---

1 **V-T** If you **console** someone who is unhappy, you try to make them feel more cheerful. ❏ *She started to cry and I tried to console her.*

2 **N-COUNT** A **console** is a part of a machine that has many switches and lights. You use these switches to operate the machine. ❏ *A light flashed on the console.* [Sense 1 from Latin. Sense 2 from French.]

con|soli|date /kənsɒlɪdeɪt/ (**consolidates, consolidating, consolidated**) **V-T** If you **consolidate** something such as your power or success, you strengthen it so that it becomes more effective or secure. ❏ *The government consolidated its power by force.* [from Latin]

con|so|nant /kɒnsənənt/ (**consonants**) **N-COUNT** LANGUAGE ARTS A **consonant** is one of the letters of the alphabet that is not a, e, i, o, or u. ❏ *The word "book" contains two consonants and two vowels.* [from Latin]

con|so|nant dou|bling **N-NONCOUNT** LANGUAGE ARTS In grammar, **consonant doubling** is the repetition of the final consonant in certain words when a suffix is added, for example the repetition of the "r" in "occur" to make "occurred."

con|sor|tium /kənsɔrʃiəm, -ti-/ (**consortia** /kənsɔrʃiə, -ti-/ or **consortiums**) **N-COUNT** BUSINESS SOCIAL STUDIES A **consortium** is a group of people or companies who have agreed to work together. [FORMAL] ❏ *The consortium includes some of the biggest firms in North America.* [from Latin]

con|spira|cy /kənspɪrəsi/ (**conspiracies**) **N-COUNT/N-NONCOUNT** **Conspiracy** is secret planning by a group of people to do something wrong or illegal. ❏ *Seven men admitted conspiracy to commit murder.* [from Old French]

con|stant /kɒnstənt/

1 **ADJ** Something that is **constant** happens all the time or is always there. ❏ *Doctors say she is in constant pain.* ● **con|stant|ly** **ADV** ❏ *The direction of the wind is constantly changing.*

2 **ADJ** If an amount or level is **constant**, it stays the same over a particular period of time. ❏ *The temperature remains more or less constant.* [from Old French]

con|stitu|en|cy /kənstɪtʃuənsi/ (**constituencies**)

1 **N-COUNT** SOCIAL STUDIES A **constituency** is an area that elects its own representative to serve in the government. ❏ *The two senators represent very different constituencies.*

2 **N-COUNT** SOCIAL STUDIES A **constituency** is a group of people that may give political support to a particular party or politician. ❏ *In Iowa, farmers are a powerful political constituency.* [from Latin]

con|stitu|ent /kənstɪtʃuənt/ (**constituents**) **N-COUNT** SOCIAL STUDIES A **constituent** is someone who lives in a particular constituency. ❏ *He told his constituents that he would continue to support them.* [from Latin]

con|sti|tu|tion /kɒnstɪtuʃən/ (**constitutions**) **N-COUNT** SOCIAL STUDIES The **constitution** is the laws of a country or of an organization. ❏ *The government has to write a new constitution this year.* [from Latin]

con|straint /kənstreɪnt/ (**constraints**)

1 **N-COUNT** A **constraint** is something that limits or controls what you can do. ❏ *...financial constraints.*

2 **N-NONCOUNT** **Constraint** is control over the way you behave which prevents you from doing what you want to do. ❏ *Journalists must be free to report without constraint.* [from Old French]

con|strict /kənstrɪkt/ (**constricts, constricting, constricted**)

1 **V-T/V-I** If a part of your body, especially your throat, **constricts** or is **constricted**, something causes it to become narrower. ❏ *Don't scream as this constricts the throat.* ● **con|stric|tion** /kənstrɪkʃ°n/ **N-NONCOUNT** ❏ *...constriction of air passages in the lungs.*

2 **V-T** If something **constricts** you, it limits your actions so that you cannot do what you want to do. ❏ *The constant testing constricts her teaching style.* ● **con|stric|tion** (**constrictions**) **N-COUNT** [FORMAL] ❏ *I hated the constrictions of school.* [from Latin]

Word Link	*con* ≈ *together, with* : *con*sensus, *con*struct, *con*vene

Word Link	*struct* ≈ *building* : *con*struct, *de*struct*ive*, *in*struct

con|struct /kənstrʌkt/ (**constructs, constructing, constructed**) **V-T** If you **construct** something, you build it. ❏ *His company constructed an office building in Denver.* [from Latin]

con|struc|tion /kənstrʌkʃ°n/ (**constructions**)

1 **N-NONCOUNT** **Construction** is building something. ❏ *He has started construction on a swimming pool.*

2 **N-COUNT** A **construction** is something that has been built. ❏ *The new theater is an impressive steel and glass construction.* [from Latin]

con|struc|tive /kənstrʌktɪv/ **ADJ** A **constructive** discussion, comment, or approach is useful and helpful. ❏ *She welcomes constructive criticism.* [from Latin]

con|strue /kənstru/ (**construes, construing, construed**) **V-T** If something is **construed** in a particular way, its nature or meaning is interpreted in that way. [FORMAL] ❏ *Her attempts to be helpful were construed as interference.* [from Latin]

con|sult /kənsʌlt/ (**consults, consulting, consulted**) **V-T/V-I** If you **consult** someone you ask them for their advice. ❏ *Perhaps you should consult an attorney.* ❏ *He told him to wait to answer each question until after they consulted.* [from French]

con|sult|ant /kənsʌltənt/ (**consultants**) **N-COUNT** A **consultant** is someone who gives expert advice on a subject. ❏ *Alex is a young management consultant from San Francisco.* [from French]

con|sul|ta|tion /kɒnsəlteɪʃ°n/ (**consultations**)

1 **N-COUNT/N-NONCOUNT** A **consultation** is a meeting to discuss something. ❏ *The unions want consultations with the employers.*

2 **N-COUNT/N-NONCOUNT** A **consultation** is a meeting with a person who gives you expert advice. ❏ *I had a consultation with a doctor.* [from French]

Word Link	*sume* ≈ *taking* : *as*sume, *con*sume, *pre*sume

con|sume /kənsum/ (**consumes, consuming, consumed**)

1 **V-T** If you **consume** something, you eat or drink it. [FORMAL] ❏ *Martha consumed a box of cookies every day.*

2 **V-T** Something that **consumes** fuel, energy, or time uses it. ❏ *Airlines consume huge amounts of fuel every day.* [from Latin]

con|sum|er /kənsumər/ (**consumers**)

1 **N-COUNT** A **consumer** is a person who buys something or uses a service. ❏ *What are my consumer rights?*

2 **N-COUNT** SCIENCE A **consumer** is a plant or animal that obtains energy by eating other plants or animals. [from Latin]

con|sump|tion /kənsʌmpʃ°n/

1 **N-NONCOUNT** The **consumption** of fuel or energy is the act of using it or the amount that is used. ❏ *...a reduction in fuel consumption.*

2 **N-NONCOUNT** The **consumption** of food or drink is the act of eating or drinking something. [FORMAL] ❏ *Most of the meat was unfit for human consumption.*

3 **N-NONCOUNT** **Consumption** is the act of buying and using things. ❏ *...the production and consumption of goods and services.* [from Latin]

con|tact /kɒntækt/ (**contacts, contacting, contacted**)

1 **N-NONCOUNT** **Contact** is meeting or communicating with someone. ❏ *I don't have much contact with teenagers.* ❏ *Anita has not been in contact with us since last year.* ❏ *We are trying to make contact with the soldiers' families..*

2 **N-NONCOUNT** If people or things are in **contact**, they often meet or communicate by telephone or email. ❏ *I'm still in contact with my classmates from fifth grade.*

3 **V-T** If you **contact** someone, you telephone them or send them a message or a letter. ❏ *The girl's parents contacted the police.*

4 **N-NONCOUNT** If you come **into contact with** something, you have some experience of it. ❑ *The college has brought me into contact with western ideas.*

5 **N-NONCOUNT** If people or things are in **contact**, they are touching each other. ❑ *There was no physical contact.*

6 **N-COUNT** A **contact** is someone you know in an organization who helps you. ❑ *Their contact at the United States embassy was Phil.* [from Latin]

con|tact lens (**contact lenses**) **N-COUNT** **Contact lenses** are small, very thin pieces of plastic that you put on your eyes to help you see better.
→ look at Word Web: **eye**

con|ta|gious /kənteɪdʒəs/ **ADJ** A **contagious** disease passes easily from one person to another. Compare with **infectious**. ❑ *The disease is highly contagious.* [from Latin]

con|tain /kənteɪn/ (**contains, containing, contained**)
1 **V-T** If one thing **contains** other things, those things are inside it. ❑ *The envelope contained a Christmas card.*
2 **V-T** If something **contains** a substance, that substance is a part of it. ❑ *Apples contain vitamins.* [from Old French]

con|tain|er /kənteɪnər/ (**containers**)
N-COUNT A **container** is a box that is used for holding or storing things. ❑ *Store the food in a plastic container.* [from Old French]
→ look at Picture Dictionary: **containers**
→ look at Word Web: **ship**

con|tami|nate /kəntæmɪneɪt/
(**contaminates, contaminating, contaminated**) **V-T** If something **is contaminated by** dirt, chemicals, or

radiation, they make it dirty or harmful. ❑ *Have any fish been contaminated?*
● **con|tami|na|tion** /kəntæmɪneɪʃᵊn/
N-NONCOUNT ❑ *...the contamination of the ocean.* [from Latin]

con|tem|plate /kɒntəmpleɪt/
(**contemplates, contemplating, contemplated**)
1 **V-T** If you **contemplate** an action, you consider it as a possibility. ❑ *For a time he contemplated a career as a doctor.*
2 **V-T** If you **contemplate** an idea or a subject, you think about it carefully for a long time. ❑ *He cried as he contemplated his future.* ● **con|tem|pla|tion** /kɒntəmpleɪʃᵊn/
N-NONCOUNT ❑ *It is a place of quiet contemplation.*
3 **V-T** If you **contemplate** something or someone, you look at them for a long time. ❑ *He contemplated his hands.* [from Latin]

Word Link	*tempo ≈ time : contemporary, temporary, temporarily*

con|tem|po|rary /kəntɛmpərɛri/
(**contemporaries**)
1 **ADJ** **Contemporary** means existing now or at the time you are talking about. ❑ *...contemporary art.*
2 **N-COUNT** Someone's **contemporary** is a person who is, or was, alive at the same time as them. [from Medieval Latin]

con|tempt /kəntɛmpt/ **N-NONCOUNT** If you have **contempt for** someone or something, you have no respect for them. ❑ *He has contempt for politicians of all parties.* [from Latin]

con|tend /kəntɛnd/ (**contends, contending, contended**)
1 **V-I** If you have to **contend with** a problem

Picture Dictionary   containers

bag

packet

carton

container

tube

package   **bottle**   **jar**   **can**   **carton**

or difficulty, you have to deal with it or overcome it. ❏ *It is time, once again, to contend with racism.*

2 **V-T** If you **contend that** something is true, you state or argue that it is true. [FORMAL] ❏ *Evans contends that he has been falsely accused.*

3 **V-T/V-I** If you **contend with** someone **for** something, you compete with them to try to get it. ❏ *...the two main groups contending for power.* ❏ *Clubs such as the Kansas City Royals have had trouble contending with richer teams.*

● **con|tend|er** /kəntɛndər/ (**contenders**) **N-COUNT** ❏ *...a strong contender for a place on the Olympic team.* [from Latin]

---
content
❶ NOUN USES
❷ ADJECTIVE USES
---

❶ **con|tent** /kɒntɛnt/ (**contents**)

1 **N-PLURAL** The **contents** of a container are the things inside it. ❏ *Empty the contents of the can into a bowl.*

2 **N-PLURAL** The **contents** of a book are its different chapters and sections. ❏ *There is no table of contents.*

3 **N-COUNT/N-NONCOUNT** The **content** of a book or television program is its subject and the ideas in it. ❏ *She refused to discuss the content of the letter.* [from Latin]

❷ **con|tent** /kəntɛnt/ **ADJ** If you are **content**, you are happy or satisfied. ❏ *He says his daughter is quite content.* [from Old French]

con|tent|ed /kəntɛntɪd/ **ADJ** If you are **contented**, you are happy and satisfied. ❏ *Richard was a very contented baby.* [from Latin]

con|ten|tion /kəntɛnʃ°n/ (**contentions**)

1 **N-COUNT** Someone's **contention** is the opinion that they are expressing. ❏ *It is my contention that everyone wants to be loved.*

2 **N-NONCOUNT** If something is a cause **of contention**, it is a cause of disagreement or argument. ❏ *What happened next is a matter of contention.* [from Latin]

con|tent|ment /kəntɛntmənt/ **N-NONCOUNT** **Contentment** is a feeling of happiness and satisfaction. ❏ *...a feeling of contentment.* [from Latin]

con|test (**contests, contesting, contested**)

PRONUNCIATION HELP
Pronounce the noun /kɒntɛst/. Pronounce the verb /kəntɛst/.
---

1 **N-COUNT** A **contest** is a competition or a game. ❏ *It was an exciting contest.*

2 **V-T** If you **contest** a statement or a decision, you object to it formally. ❏ *He has to reply within 14 days in order to contest the case.* [from Latin]

Thesaurus contest Also look up :
N competition, game, match **1**
---

con|test|ant /kəntɛstənt/ (**contestants**) **N-COUNT** A **contestant** is a person who takes part in a competition or a game. ❏ *Contestants on the TV show have to answer six questions correctly.* [from Latin]

con|text /kɒntɛkst/ (**contexts**)

1 **N-COUNT/N-NONCOUNT** The **context of** an event is the situation in which it happens. ❏ *Don't use this sort of language in a business context.*

2 **N-COUNT/N-NONCOUNT** The **context of** a word or a sentence is the words and sentences that come before and after it, that help you to understand its meaning. [from Latin]

con|text clue (**context clues**) **N-COUNT** LANGUAGE ARTS **Context clues** are words or phrases that surround a particular word and help the reader to understand the word's meaning or pronunciation.

con|ti|nent /kɒntɪnənt/ (**continents**) **N-COUNT** GEOGRAPHY A **continent** is a very large area of land, such as Africa or Asia. [from Latin]
→ look at Word Web: **continents, earth**

con|ti|nen|tal /kɒntɪnɛnt°l/ **ADJ** The **continental** United States is all the states that are on the main continent of North America, and not Hawaii or the Virgin Islands. ❏ *Pikes Peak is the highest mountain in the continental United States.*

con|ti|nen|tal drift **N-NONCOUNT** SCIENCE **Continental drift** is the slow movement of the Earth's continents toward and away from each other.

con|ti|nen|tal mar|gin (**continental margins**) **N-COUNT** SCIENCE The **continental margin** is the part of the ocean floor between the edge of a continent and the deepest part of the ocean.

con|ti|nen|tal rise (**continental rises**) **N-COUNT** SCIENCE The **continental rise** is the part of the ocean floor that lies at the base of a continental slope.

C

C

Word Web   continents

In 1912, Alfred Wegener* made an important discovery. The shapes of the various **continents** seemed to fit together like the pieces of a puzzle. He decided they had once been a single **land mass**, which he called Pangea. He thought the continents had slowly moved apart. Wegener called this theory **continental drift**. He said the earth's **crust** is not a single, solid piece. It's full of cracks which allow huge pieces to move around on the earth's mantle. The movement of these **tectonic plates** increases the distance between Europe and North America by about 20 millimeters every year.

Major Plates of the Earth's Crust

Alfred Wegener (1880-1930): a German scientist.

---

con|ti|nen|tal shelf N-NONCOUNT SCIENCE
The **continental shelf** is the area which forms the edge of a continent, ending in a steep slope to the depths of the ocean.

con|ti|nen|tal slope (**continental slopes**)
N-COUNT SCIENCE The **continental slope** is the steepest part of the continental margin.

con|tin|gent /kəntɪndʒ°nt/ (**contingents**)
N-COUNT A **contingent** is a group of people representing a country or an organization at a meeting or another event. [FORMAL]
❑ *The American contingent will stay overnight in London.* [from Latin]

con|tin|ual /kəntɪnyuəl/ ADJ Something that is **continual** happens without stopping, or happens repeatedly. ❑ *The team has had almost continual success since last year.*
● **con|tin|al|ly** ADV ❑ *Gemma cried almost continually when she was a baby.* ❑ *Malcolm was continually changing his mind.* [from Old French]

Thesaurus   continual   Also look up :
ADJ   ongoing, constant, repeated, unending

con|tinu|ation /kəntɪnyueɪʃ°n/
(**continuations**) N-COUNT/N-NONCOUNT
The **continuation of** something is the fact that it continues to happen or to exist.
❑ *We do not support the continuation of the war.* [from Old French]

con|tinue /kəntɪnyu/ (**continues, continuing, continued**)
1 V-I If something **continues**, it does not stop. ❑ *The war continued for another four years.*
2 V-T If you **continue to** do something, you do not stop doing it. ❑ *They continue to fight for*

justice. ❑ *Outside the building people continue their protest.*
3 V-I If something **continues**, it starts again. ❑ *The trial continues today.*
4 V-T/V-I If you **continue** doing something, you start doing it again. ❑ *She looked up for a minute and then continued drawing.* ❑ *Tony drank some coffee before he continued.*
5 V-I If you **continue** in a particular direction, you keep going in that direction. ❑ *He continued rapidly up the path.* [from Old French]

Thesaurus   continue   Also look up :
V   go on, persist; (ant.) stop **1**
     carry on, resume **3** **4**

con|tinu|ous /kəntɪnyuəs/
1 ADJ A **continuous** event happens over a long time without stopping. ❑ *They heard continuous gunfire.* ● **con|tinu|ous|ly** ADV
❑ *The police are working continuously on the case.*
2 ADJ A **continuous** line has no spaces in it.
❑ *There was a continuous line of cars outside in the street.*
3 ADJ LANGUAGE ARTS In English grammar, the **continuous** form is made using the auxiliary "be" and the present participle of a verb, as in "I'm going on vacation." [from Latin]

con|tort /kəntɔrt/ (**contorts, contorting, contorted**) V-T/V-I If something **contorts**, it moves into an unnatural or unusual shape. ❑ *His face contorted with pain.* ● **con|tor|tion** /kəntɔrʃ°n/ (**contortions**) N-COUNT ❑ *...the contortions of the gymnasts.* [from Latin]

con|tour /kɒntʊər/ (**contours**)
1 N-COUNT You can refer to the general

shape or outline of an object as its **contours**. [LITERARY] ❑ ...*the contours of the body.*
2 **N-COUNT** SCIENCE A **contour** on a map is a line joining points of equal height. ❑ ...*a contour map showing two hills.* [from French]

con|tour draw|ing (contour drawings)
N-COUNT/N-NONCOUNT ARTS Contour **drawing** is a method of drawing in which you draw the outline of an object in a single, continuous line without looking at the drawing as a whole. A **contour drawing** is a drawing that is made using this method.

con|tour feath|er (contour feathers)
N-COUNT SCIENCE Contour **feathers** are the outermost feathers on the body of an adult bird.

con|tour in|ter|val (contour intervals)
N-COUNT GEOGRAPHY A **contour interval** on a map is the difference in height between one contour line and the contour line next to it.

con|tour line (contour lines) **N-COUNT**
GEOGRAPHY **Contour lines** on a map are the same as **contours**.

contra|cep|tion /kɒntrəsɛpʃ°n/
N-NONCOUNT **Contraception** refers to methods of preventing pregnancy. ❑ *Use a reliable method of contraception.*

con|tract (contracts, contracting, contracted)

> **PRONUNCIATION HELP**
> Pronounce the noun /kɒntrækt/.
> Pronounce the verb /kəntrækt/.

1 **N-COUNT** A **contract** is an official agreement between two companies or two people. ❑ *He signed a contract to play for the team for two years.*
2 **V-I** When something **contracts**, it becomes smaller or shorter. ❑ *When you are anxious, your muscles contract.* [from Latin]
→ look at Word Web: **muscle**

Word Partnership	Use **contract** with :
v	**sign** a contract **1**
N	**terms of** a contract **1**

con|trac|tion /kəntrækʃ°n/ (contractions)
1 **N-COUNT/N-NONCOUNT** **Contraction** is the process of becoming smaller. ❑ ...*the contraction and expansion of blood vessels.*
2 **N-COUNT** LANGUAGE ARTS A **contraction** is a short form of a word or words. ❑ *"It's" (with an apostrophe) can be used as a contraction for "it is."* [from French]

con|trac|tor /kɒntræktər, kəntræk-/
(contractors) **N-COUNT** BUSINESS A **contractor** is a person or company that does work for other people or organizations.
❑ ...*a building contractor.* [from Latin]

Word Link	contra ≈ against : contra**dict**, contra**ry**, contra**st**

Word Link	dict ≈ speaking : contra**dict**, **dict**ate, pre**dict**

contra|dict /kɒntrədɪkt/ (contradicts, contradicting, contradicted) **V-T** If you **contradict** someone, you say that what they have just said is wrong. ❑ *She looked surprised, but she did not contradict him.* [from Latin]

contra|dic|tion /kɒntrədɪkʃ°n/
(contradictions) **N-COUNT** A **contradiction** is an aspect of a situation that appears to conflict with other aspects, so that they cannot all exist or be true. ❑ ...*the contradiction between her private life and her public image.* [from Latin]

contra|dic|tory /kɒntrədɪktəri/ **ADJ** If two or more facts, ideas, or statements are **contradictory**, they state or suggest that opposite things are true. ❑ ...*a series of contradictory statements.* [from Latin]

con|tra|ry /kɒntrɛri/
1 **ADJ** **Contrary** ideas or opinions are completely different from each other. ❑ *Contrary to what people think, light exercise makes you less hungry.*
2 **PHRASE** You use **on the contrary** when you disagree with something and you are going to say that the opposite is true. ❑ *"People just don't do things like that."—"On the contrary, they do them all the time."* [from Latin]

con|trast (contrasts, contrasting, contrasted)

> **PRONUNCIATION HELP**
> Pronounce the noun /kɒntræst/.
> Pronounce the verb /kəntræst/.

1 **N-COUNT/N-NONCOUNT** A **contrast** is a clear difference between two or more people or things. ❑ *There is a clear contrast between the two men.*
2 **V-T** If you **contrast** things, you show the differences between them. ❑ *In this section we contrast four different ideas.*
3 **N-NONCOUNT** **Contrast** is the degree of difference between the darker and lighter parts of a photograph, a television picture, or a painting. [from French]

C

con|trib|ute /kəntrɪbyut/ (**contributes, contributing, contributed**)

■ **V-T/V-I** If you **contribute** money **to** something, you help to pay for it. ❑ *The U.S. is contributing $4 billion to the project.* ❑ *Local businesses have agreed to contribute.*

■ **V-I** If you **contribute to** something, you do something to help make it successful. ❑ *The three sons also contribute to the family business.*

■ **V-I** If something **contributes to** something, it is one of the causes of it. ❑ *The wet road contributed to the accident.* [from Latin]

Thesaurus	contribute Also look up :
V	aid, assist, chip in, commit, donate, give, grant, help, support; (*ant.*) neglect, take away ■

con|tri|bu|tion /kɒntrɪbyuʃ°n/ (**contributions**)

■ **N-COUNT** If you make a **contribution**, you give money to help to pay for something. ❑ *He made a $5,000 contribution to the charity.*

■ **N-COUNT** If you make a **contribution to** something, you do something to help make it successful or to produce it. ❑ *He received an award for his contribution to world peace.* [from Latin]

Word Partnership	Use contribution with :
ADJ	**important** contribution, **significant** contribution ■ ■
V	**make a** contribution, **send a** contribution ■ ■

con|tribu|tor /kəntrɪbyətər/ (**contributors**)

■ **N-COUNT** A **contributor** is someone who helps to pay for something or helps to make it successful. ❑ *The financial services industry is a major contributor to the economy.*

■ **N-COUNT** You can use **contributor** to refer to one of the causes of an event or situation, especially if that event or situation is an unpleasant one. ❑ *Old buses are major contributors to pollution in cities.*

con|trol /kəntroʊl/ (**controls, controlling, controlled**)

■ **N-NONCOUNT** **Control of** something is the power to make all the important decisions about it. ❑ *He took control of every situation.*

■ **PHRASE** If you are **in control of** something, you have the power to make all the important decisions about it. ❑ *She feels that she's in control of her life again.*

■ **V-T** If someone **controls** something, they

have the power to make all the important decisions about it. ❑ *He controls the largest company in California.*

■ **V-T** If you **control** a person or a machine, you are able to make them do what you want them to do. ❑ *There was a computer system to control the gates.* ❑ *My parents couldn't control me.*

■ **N-NONCOUNT** **Control** is also a noun. ❑ *He lost control of his car.*

■ **V-T** To **control** something means to limit it to an acceptable level. ❑ *The government tried to control rising health-care costs.*

■ **PHRASE** If something or someone is **out of control**, people cannot deal with them successfully. ❑ *The fire was out of control.*

■ **PHRASE** If something is **under control**, people can deal with it. ❑ *The situation is under control.*

■ **V-T** If you **control yourself** or your feelings, you behave calmly even though you are angry, excited, or upset. ❑ *Jo should learn to control herself.*

■ **N-NONCOUNT** **Control** is also a noun. ❑ *Sometimes he would completely lose control.*

■ **N-COUNT** A **control** is a switch you use in order to operate a machine. ❑ *You operate the controls without looking at them.*

■ **N-COUNT** SCIENCE In a test of a new drug, a **control** is the use of a group of people or animals that do not receive the drug, so that the two groups can be compared to see if the drug works.

■ **V-I** SCIENCE In a scientific experiment, to **control for** a particular variable means to carry out a second experiment in which the variable does not occur, so that the results of the two experiments can be compared and the effect of the variable seen. [from Old French]

■ → see also **birth control, remote control**
→ look at Word Web: **experiment**

con|trolled ex|peri|ment (**controlled experiments**) **N-COUNT** SCIENCE A **controlled experiment** is a scientific experiment which examines the effect of a single variable by keeping all the other variables fixed.

con|tro|ver|sial /kɒntrəvɜrʃ°l/ **ADJ** A **controversial** subject is one that people argue about. ❑ *In business, I try to stay away from controversial subjects.* [from Latin]

con|tro|ver|sy /kɒntrəvɜrsi/ (**controversies**) **N-COUNT/N-NONCOUNT** **Controversy** is when people argue about something, or disapprove of it. ❑ *The TV show*

caused controversy when it was shown last year.
[from Latin]

con|vec|tion /kənvɛkʃ°n/ **N-NONCOUNT**
SCIENCE **Convection** is the process by which
heat travels through air, water, and other
gases and liquids. [from Late Latin]

con|vec|tion cur|rent (**convection
currents**) **N-COUNT** SCIENCE A **convection
current** is a circular current within a
substance such as air or water resulting
from a difference in density between warm
and cool parts of the substance.

con|vec|tive zone /kənvɛktɪv zoʊn/
(**convective zones**) **N-COUNT** SCIENCE
The **convective zone** is the area of the sun
where energy is carried toward the surface
by convection currents.

> **Word Link** con ≈ together, with : consensus,
> construct, convene

con|vene /kənvin/ (**convenes, convening,
convened**) **V-T/V-I** If you **convene** a meeting,
you arrange for it to take place. You can also
say that people **convene** at a meeting.
[FORMAL] ❑ He convened a meeting of his closest
advisers. [from Latin]

con|veni|ence /kənvinyəns/
(**conveniences**)
1 **N-NONCOUNT** If something is done for
your **convenience**, it is done in a way that is
helpful for you. ❑ We include an envelope for your
convenience.
2 **N-COUNT** **Conveniences** are pieces of
equipment designed to make your life
easier. ❑ This apartment includes all the
modern conveniences.
3 **N-NONCOUNT** **Convenience** is a situation
in which something is easier to do.
❑ They may use a credit card for convenience.
[from Latin]

con|veni|ent /kənvinyənt/
1 **ADJ** Something that is **convenient** is easy
or useful for a particular purpose. ❑ ...a
convenient way of paying. ● **con|veni|ent|ly**
ADV ❑ ...conveniently placed cupholders.
2 **ADJ** A place that is **convenient** is near
where you are, or near a place where you
want to go. ❑ The town is convenient to Dulles
Airport. ● **con|veni|ent|ly** **ADV** ❑ The house is
conveniently located close to the railroad station.
3 **ADJ** A **convenient** time is a time when you
are available to do something. ❑ She will try to
arrange a convenient time. [from Latin]

con|ven|tion /kənvɛnʃ°n/ (**conventions**)
1 **N-COUNT/N-NONCOUNT** A **convention** is an
accepted way of behaving or of doing
something. ❑ It's a social convention that men
don't wear skirts.
2 **N-COUNT** A **convention** is an official
agreement between countries or
organizations. ❑ ...the U.N. convention on
climate change.
3 **N-COUNT** A **convention** is a large meeting
of an organization or a group. ❑ ...the annual
convention of the Society of Professional Journalists.
4 **N-COUNT** In art, literature, or the theater,
a **convention** is a traditional method or
style. [from Latin]

con|ven|tion|al /kənvɛnʃən°l/
1 **ADJ** **Conventional** people behave in a way
that is considered to be normal by most
people. ❑ I've always been quite conventional;
I work hard and behave properly.
2 **ADJ** A **conventional** method or product is
one that is usually used. ❑ In a conventional
oven, bake at 350°F for 30 minutes. [from Latin]

> **Word Link** verg, vert ≈ turning : converge,
> diverge, subvert

con|verge /kənvɜrdʒ/ (**converges,
converging, converged**)
1 **V-I** If people or vehicles **converge on** a
place, they move toward it from different
directions. ❑ Thousands of protesters will
converge on the capital.
2 **V-I** If roads or lines **converge**, they meet
or join. [FORMAL] ❑ As they flow south, the five
rivers converge. [from Late Latin]

con|ver|gent bounda|ry /kənvɜrdʒənt
baʊndəri, -dri/ (**convergent boundaries**)
N-COUNT SCIENCE A **convergent boundary** is
an area in the Earth's crust where two tectonic
plates are moving toward each other.

con|ver|sa|tion /kɒnvərseɪʃ°n/
(**conversations**) **N-COUNT** If you have a
conversation with someone, you talk to each
other about something. ❑ I had an interesting
conversation with him. [from Old French]

con|vert /kənvɜrt/ (**converts, converting,
converted**) **V-T** To **convert** one thing **into**
another means to change it into a different
form. ❑ The signal will be converted into electronic
form. ❑ He wants to convert the building into a
hotel. [from Old French]

> **Thesaurus** convert Also look up :
> v   adapt, alter, change, modify, transform

con|vex lens /kɒnvɛks lɛnz/ (**convex lenses**) **N-COUNT SCIENCE** A **convex lens** is a lens that is thicker in the middle than at the edges. Compare with **concave lens**.

con|vey /kənveɪ/ (**conveys, conveying, conveyed**) **V-T** To **convey** information or feelings means to cause them to be known or understood. ❑ *I tried to convey the wonder of this machine to my husband.* [from Old French]

> **Word Link** *vict, vinc ≈ conquering : con*vict*, *con*vince*, *victory*

con|vict /kənvɪkt/ (**convicts, convicting, convicted**) **V-T** If someone is **convicted of** a crime, they are found guilty of it in a court of law. ❑ *He was convicted of murder.* [from Latin]

con|vic|tion /kənvɪkʃən/ (**convictions**)
1 N-COUNT A **conviction** is a strong belief or opinion. ❑ *It is our firm conviction that a step forward has been taken.*
2 N-COUNT If someone has a **conviction**, they have been found guilty of a crime in a court of law. ❑ *He will appeal against his conviction.* [from Latin]

con|vince /kənvɪns/ (**convinces, convincing, convinced**)
1 V-T If someone or something **convinces** you **to** do something, they persuade you to do it. ❑ *He convinced her to marry Tom.*
2 V-T If someone or something **convinces** you **of** something, they make you believe that it is true or that it exists. ❑ *The new players have convinced me of their ability.* ● **con|vinced** /kənvɪnst/ **ADJ** ❑ *She was convinced that the diamonds were real.* [from Latin]

> **Thesaurus** convince Also look up :
> v   persuade, sell, talk into, win over;
>   (ant.) discourage **1 2**

con|vinc|ing /kənvɪnsɪŋ/ **ADJ** If someone or something is **convincing**, you believe them. ❑ *There is no convincing evidence that power lines cause cancer.* ● **con|vinc|ing|ly ADV** ❑ *He argued convincingly.* [from Latin]

con|voy /kɒnvɔɪ/ (**convoys**) **N-COUNT** A **convoy** is a group of vehicles or ships traveling together. ❑ *...a U.N. convoy carrying food and medical supplies.* [from Old French]

cook /kʊk/ (**cooks, cooking, cooked**)
1 V-T/V-I When you **cook**, or **cook** a meal, you prepare and heat food. ❑ *I have to go and cook dinner.*
2 V-I When food **cooks**, it is heated until it is ready to eat. ❑ *Let the vegetables cook for about 10 minutes.*
3 N-COUNT A **cook** is a person who prepares and cooks food. ❑ *I'm a terrible cook.* [from Old English]
4 → see also **cooking**
→ look at Picture Dictionary: **cook**

> **Usage** cook and make
> *Cook* is used when referring to the preparation of food using a process involving heat. If preparation only involves assembling ingredients which may have previously been cooked, then *make* is used. *"Who made this salad? It's delicious!"—"Oh, I just threw it together while I was cooking/making the rest of the dinner."*

> **Thesaurus** cook Also look up :
> v   heat up, make, prepare **1**
> N   chef **3**

Picture Dictionary cook

bake

microwave

roast

toast

fry

barbecue

stir fry

broil

boil
steam

cook|book /kʊkbʊk/ (**cookbooks**) **N-COUNT**
A **cookbook** is a book that tells you how to prepare different meals.

cook|ie /kʊki/ (**cookies**) **N-COUNT** A cookie is a small, flat, sweet cake. ❏ *She brought us a plate of warm chocolate chip cookies.* [from Dutch] → look at Picture Dictionary: **dessert**

cook|ing /kʊkɪŋ/
■ **N-NONCOUNT** Cooking is the activity of preparing food. ❏ *He did the cooking and cleaning.*
■ **N-NONCOUNT** Cooking is food that is cooked in a particular way. ❏ *The restaurant specializes in Italian cooking.* [from Old English]
■ → see also **cook**
→ look at Word Web: **cooking**

cool /kul/ (**cooler, coolest, cools, cooling, cooled**)
■ **ADJ** Something that is **cool** has a low temperature, but is not cold. ❏ *I felt the cool air on my neck.* ❏ *The water was cool.*
■ **ADJ** When you stay **cool** in a difficult situation, you remain calm. ❏ *You have to remain cool in very difficult situations.*
■ **ADJ** If a person or thing is **cool**, they are fashionable and interesting. [INFORMAL] ❏ *I met some really cool people last night.* ❏ *She had really cool boots.*
■ **V-T/V-I** When something **cools**, it becomes lower in temperature. ❏ *Drain the meat and allow it to cool.* ❏ *Huge fans cool the room.*
■ **Cool down** means the same as **cool**. ❏ *Once it cools down, you'll be able to touch it.*
■ **ADJ Cool** colors have blue, green, or violet in them, rather than red, orange, or yellow. [from Old English]
▶ **cool down** ■ → look up **cool** ■
■ If someone **cools down**, they become less angry. ❏ *He has had time to cool down.*

Thesaurus cool Also look up:
ADJ   chilly, cold, nippy; *(ant.)* warm ■

C

Word Partnership Use **cool** with:
N   cool **air**, cool **breeze** ■

Word Link *oper ≈ work : coop*er*ate, op*er*a, *oper*ation*

co|oper|ate /koʊɒpəreɪt/ (**cooperates, cooperating, cooperated**) **V-T/V-I** If you **cooperate with** someone, you work with them or help them. ❏ *He finally agreed to cooperate with the police.* ● **co|op|er|a|tive** /koʊɒpərətɪv/ **ADJ** ❏ *I made an effort to be cooperative.* ● **co|opera|tion** /koʊɒpəreɪʃ³n/ **N-NONCOUNT** ❏ *Thank you for your cooperation.* [from Late Latin]

Word Partnership Use **cooperate** with:
V   **agree to** cooperate, **continue to** cooperate, **fail to** cooperate, **refuse to** cooperate
ADV   cooperate **fully**
N   **willingness to** cooperate

co|or|di|nate /koʊɔrd³neɪt/ (**coordinates, coordinating, coordinated**)
■ **V-T** When you **coordinate** an activity, you organize it. ❏ *She coordinates the weekend activities.*
■ **V-T** If you **coordinate** the parts of your body, you make them work together well. ❏ *You need to coordinate legs, arms, and breathing.* ● **co|or|di|na|tion** **N-NONCOUNT** ❏ *You need great hand-eye coordination to hit the ball.*

Thesaurus coordinate Also look up:
V   direct, manage, organize ■

co|or|di|nate sys|tem (**coordinate systems**) **N-COUNT SCIENCE** A **coordinate system** is a system that uses coordinates to describe the position of objects on a map or graph.

cop /kɒp/ (**cops**) **N-COUNT** A **cop** is a policeman or a policewoman. [INFORMAL] ❏ *The cops know where to find him.* [from Old French]

Word Web   cooking

Scientists believe humans began to experiment with **cooking** about 1.5 million years ago. Cooking made some poisonous plants safe to **eat**. It made tough meat **tender** and easier for our bodies to **digest**. It also improved the flavor of the food they ate. **Heating up food** to a high **temperature** killed dangerous bacteria. **Cooked** food could be stored longer. This all helped increase the amount of food available.

C

cope /koʊp/ (**copes, coping, coped**) **v-ɪ** If you **cope with** a problem or a task, you deal with it in a successful way. ❑ *The group has helped her cope with a serious illness.* [from Old French]

Word Partnership	Use **cope** with :
N	**ability to** cope, cope **with loss**
ADV	**how to** cope
V	**learn to** cope, **manage to** cope
ADJ	**unable to** cope

cop|per /kɒpər/ **N-NONCOUNT** Copper is a soft reddish-brown metal. ❑ *Chile produces much of the world's copper.* [from Old English] → look at Word Webs: **metal, mineral, pan**

cop|per wire (**copper wires**) **N-COUNT/N-NONCOUNT** SCIENCE Copper wire is a type of cable made of copper that is good at conducting heat and electricity.

copy /kɒpi/ (**copies, copying, copied**)
1 N-COUNT If you make a **copy of** something, you produce something that looks like the original thing. ❑ *I made a copy of Steve's letter.*
2 N-COUNT A **copy of** a book or a newspaper is one of many that are exactly the same. ❑ *Did you get a copy of "USA Today"?*
3 V-T If you **copy** something, you make or write something that is exactly like the original thing. ❑ *Copy files from your old computer to your new one.*
4 V-T If you **copy** a person, you try to behave as they do. ❑ *Children try to copy the behavior of*

people they admire. [from Medieval Latin] → look at Picture Dictionary: **draw**

Thesaurus	**copy** Also look up :
N	likeness, photocopy, replica, reprint; *(ant.)* master, original **1**
V	reproduce; *(ant.)* originate **3** imitate, mimic **4**

copy|right /kɒpiraɪt/ (**copyrights**) **N-COUNT/N-NONCOUNT** If someone has the **copyright** on a piece of writing or music, it is illegal to reproduce or perform it without their permission. ❑ *Who owns the copyright on this movie?*

cor|al /kɔrəl/ (**corals**)
1 N-COUNT/N-NONCOUNT Coral is a hard substance formed from the bones of very small ocean animals. ❑ *She was wearing a coral necklace.*
2 N-COUNT Corals are very small sea animals formed from coral. [from Old French]

cord /kɔrd/ (**cords**)
1 N-COUNT/N-NONCOUNT Cord is strong, thick string. ❑ *She was carrying a package tied with heavy cord.*
2 N-COUNT/N-NONCOUNT A **cord** is an electrical wire covered in rubber or plastic. ❑ *Place all electrical cords out of children's reach.* [from Old French]

core /kɔr/ (**cores**)
1 N-COUNT The **core** is the central part of a fruit that contains the seeds. ❑ *Annie put her apple core in the garbage.*

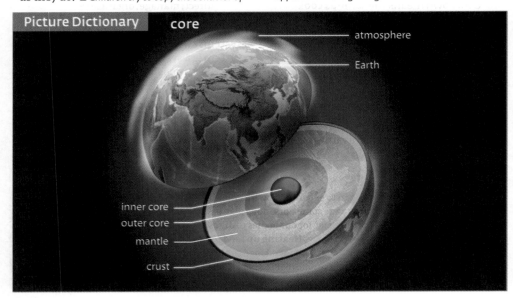

Picture Dictionary   **core**

atmosphere
Earth
inner core
outer core
mantle
crust

2 **N-COUNT** SCIENCE The Earth's **core** is its central part. ❑ *What is the temperature in the Earth's core?*
→ look at Picture Dictionary: **core**

> **Word Partnership**   Use **core** with :
>
> N   **apple** core **1**
>   core **curriculum**, **Earth's** core, core **group 2**

Coriolis ef|fect /kɔrioulɪs ɪfɛkt/ (**Coriolis effects**) **N-COUNT** SCIENCE The **Coriolis effect** is the tendency of moving objects to turn to the right in the northern hemisphere and to the left in the southern hemisphere, because of the Earth's rotation.

cork /kɔrk/ (**corks**) **N-COUNT** A **cork** is an object that you push into the top of a bottle to close it. ❑ *He took the cork out of the bottle.* [from Arabic]

cork|screw /kɔrkskru/ (**corkscrews**) **N-COUNT** A **corkscrew** is a tool for pulling corks out of bottles.

corn /kɔrn/
1 **N-NONCOUNT** Corn is a tall plant that produces long vegetables covered with yellow seeds, or the seeds of this plant. [from Old English]
2 → see also **popcorn**
→ look at Picture Dictionary: **vegetables**
→ look at Word Web: **grain**

cor|ner /kɔrnər/ (**corners**) **N-COUNT** A **corner** is a point where two sides of something meet, or where a road meets another road. ❑ *There was a table in the corner of the room.* ❑ *He stood on the street corner, waiting for a taxi.* [from Old French]

> **Word Partnership**   Use **corner** with :
>
> ADJ   **far** corner, **sharp** corner
> V   **round/turn** a corner, **sit in** a corner
> N   **street** corner
> PREP   **in** a corner, **around** the corner

corn|row /kɔrnroʊ/ (**cornrows**) also **corn row** **N-COUNT** If someone wears their hair in **cornrows**, they braid their hair in parallel rows that lie flat upon their head. ❑ *...a tall woman in cornrows.*
→ look at Picture Dictionary: **hair**

co|ro|na /kərounə/ **N-SING** SCIENCE The sun's **corona** is its outer atmosphere. [from Latin]

cor|po|rate /kɔrpərɪt, -prɪt/ **ADJ** BUSINESS **Corporate** means relating to large companies. ❑ *Our city apartments are popular with private and corporate customers.* [from Latin]

> **Word Partnership**   Use **corporate** with :
>
> N   corporate **clients**, corporate **culture**, corporate **hospitality**, corporate **image**, corporate **lawyer**, corporate **sector**, corporate **structure**

cor|po|ra|tion /kɔrpəreɪʃ°n/ (**corporations**) **N-COUNT** BUSINESS A **corporation** is a large business or company. ❑ *Her father works for a big corporation.* [from Latin]

corps /kɔr/ (**corps**)
1 **N-COUNT** A **corps** is a part of the army which has special duties. ❑ *...the Army Medical Corps.*
2 **N-COUNT** A **corps** is a small group of people who do a special job. ❑ *...the U.S. diplomatic corps.* [from French]

corpse /kɔrps/ (**corpses**) **N-COUNT** A **corpse** is a dead body. ❑ *Police found the corpse in a nearby river.* [from Old French]

> **Word Link**   rect ≈ right, straight : correct, direct, rectangle

cor|rect /kərɛkt/ (**corrects, correcting, corrected**)
1 **ADJ** Something is **correct** when it is right or true. ❑ *The correct answers can be found on page 8.* ● **cor|rect|ly** **ADV** ❑ *Did I pronounce your name correctly?*
2 **ADJ** If you are **correct**, what you have said or thought is true. [FORMAL] ❑ *You are absolutely correct.*
3 **ADJ** The **correct** thing is the one that is most suitable in a particular situation. ❑ *The use of the correct materials was essential.*
4 **V-T** If you **correct** a problem or a mistake you make it right. ❑ *There is another way you can correct the problem.* ❑ *Students are given a chance to correct mistakes.*
5 **V-T** If you **correct** someone, you say something that is more accurate than what they have just said. ❑ *"Actually, that isn't what happened," George corrected me.*
6 **V-T** When someone **corrects** a piece of writing, they look at it and mark the mistakes in it. ❑ *He was correcting his students' work.* [from Latin]

C

C

Thesaurus correct Also look up :

| ADJ | accurate, legitimate, precise, right, true; (ant.) false, inaccurate, incorrect, wrong **1** |
| V | fix, repair; (ant.) damage, hurt **4** |

Word Partnership Use correct with :

| N | correct **answer**, correct **response** **1** **4** correct **a mistake**, correct **a situation** **5** correct *someone* **5** |

cor|rec|tion /kərɛkʃᵊn/ (**corrections**)
1 **N-COUNT/N-NONCOUNT** A **correction** is a change that you make to something in order to make it right or better. **Correction** is the act of making a change like this. ❑ ...the correction of factual errors.
2 **N-COUNT** **Corrections** are marks or comments made on a piece of written work which indicate where there are mistakes and what are the right answers. ❑ ...corrections to the text.
3 **N-NONCOUNT** **Correction** is the punishment of criminals. ❑ ...jails and other parts of the correction system. ● **cor|rec|tion|al** /kərɛkʃənᵊl/ **ADJ** ❑ He is currently in a city correctional center. [from Latin]

cor|re|la|tion|al de|sign /kɔrəleɪʃənᵊl dɪzaɪn/ (**correlational designs**)
N-COUNT/N-NONCOUNT SCIENCE Research that has a **correlational design** involves studying the relationship between two or more things.

cor|re|spond /kɔrɪspɒnd/ (**corresponds, corresponding, corresponded**)
1 **V-T/V-I** If one thing **corresponds to** another, or if two things **correspond**, there is a close similarity or connection between them. ❑ The rise in food prices corresponds closely to rises in oil prices. ❑ The two maps correspond closely.
2 **V-T/V-I** If you **correspond with** someone, you write letters to them. ❑ She still corresponds with her American friends. ❑ We corresponded regularly. [from Medieval Latin]

cor|re|spond|ence /kɔrɪspɒndəns/
N-NONCOUNT Someone's **correspondence** is the letters that they receive or send. ❑ The website contains copies of Einstein's personal correspondence. [from Medieval Latin]

cor|re|spond|ent /kɔrɪspɒndənt/
(**correspondents**) **N-COUNT** A **correspondent** is a person who writes news reports.

❑ He's the White House correspondent for The Times. [from Medieval Latin]

cor|rupt /kərʌpt/ (**corrupts, corrupting, corrupted**)
1 **ADJ** Someone who is **corrupt** behaves in a dishonest way in order to gain money or power. ❑ We know that there are some officials who are corrupt.
2 **V-T** TECHNOLOGY If a computer file or program **is corrupted**, it no longer works properly, and it may not be safe to use. ❑ The files were corrupted by a virus. [from Latin]

cor|rup|tion /kərʌpʃᵊn/ **N-NONCOUNT** **Corruption** is dishonesty and illegal behavior by people in positions of power. ❑ The president faces charges of corruption. [from Latin]

co|sine /koʊsaɪn/ (**cosines**) **N-COUNT** MATH A **cosine** is a mathematical calculation that is used especially in the study of triangles. The abbreviation **cos** is also used. [from New Latin]

cos|met|ics /kɒzmɛtɪks/ **N-PLURAL** **Cosmetics** are makeup products. ❑ She wears nail polish and cosmetics. [from Greek]
→ look at Word Web: **makeup**

cos|mic back|ground ra|dia|tion /kɒzmɪk bækgraʊnd reɪdieɪʃᵊn/ **N-NONCOUNT** SCIENCE **Cosmic background radiation** is the heat that is present throughout the universe as a result of the original explosion which started the universe.

cos|mol|ogy /kɒzmɒlədʒi/ **N-NONCOUNT** SCIENCE **Cosmology** is the study of the origin and nature of the universe. [from Greek]

cost /kɔst/ (**costs, costing, cost**)
1 **N-COUNT** The **cost of** something is the amount of money you need in order to buy, do, or make it. ❑ The cost of a loaf of bread has gone up. ❑ There will be an increase in the cost of mailing a letter.
2 **V-T** If something **costs** an amount of money, you have to pay that amount in order to buy, do, or make it. ❑ This course costs $150 per person. ❑ It will cost us over $100,000 to buy new trucks.
3 **V-T** If an event **costs** you something, you lose that thing as the result of it. ❑ ...an operation that cost him his sight.
4 **PHRASE** If you say that something must be avoided **at all costs**, you mean that it

must not be allowed to happen. ❑ *A world trade war must be avoided at all costs.* [from Old French]

Thesaurus	cost	Also look up :
N	fee, price **1**	
	harm, loss, sacrifice **3**	

Word Partnership	Use **cost** with :
ADJ	**additional** costs **1**
V	**cover the** cost, **cut** costs, **keep** costs **down 1**
N	cost **of living 1**

cost|ly /kɔstli/ (**costlier, costliest**) **ADJ**
Something that is **costly** is very expensive.
❑ *We must try to avoid such costly mistakes.*
[from Old French]

cos|tume /kɒstum/ (**costumes**)
1 **N-COUNT/N-NONCOUNT** ARTS A **costume** is a set of clothes that someone wears in a performance. ❑ *The costumes and scenery were designed by Robert Rauschenberg.*
2 **N-NONCOUNT** **Costume** is the type of clothes that people wear at a particular time in history or in a particular country. ❑ *...men and women in eighteenth-century costume.* [from French]
→ look at Picture Dictionary: **drama**
→ look at Word Web: **theater**

cot /kɒt/ (**cots**) **N-COUNT** A **cot** is a narrow bed that you can fold and store in a small space. [from Old English]

cot|tage /kɒtɪdʒ/ (**cottages**) **N-COUNT**
A **cottage** is a small house, usually in the country. ❑ *She lived in a little white cottage in the woods.*

cot|ton /kɒtᵊn/ (**cottons**)
1 **N-COUNT/N-NONCOUNT** **Cotton** is cloth or thread that is made from the cotton plant.
❑ *He's wearing a cotton shirt.* ❑ *...a reel of cotton.*
2 **N-NONCOUNT** **Cotton** is a plant that is used for making cloth. ❑ *They own a large cotton plantation in Tennessee.*
3 **N-NONCOUNT** **Cotton** is a soft mass of this substance that you use for cleaning your skin. ❑ *Then take the cream off with cotton balls.*
[from Old French]

coty|ledon /kɒtᵊlidᵊn/ (**cotyledons**)
N-COUNT SCIENCE A **cotyledon** is the first leaf to grow after a seed germinates, before the proper leaves grow. [from Latin]

couch /kaʊtʃ/ (**couches**) **N-COUNT** A **couch** is a long, comfortable seat for two or three

people. [from Old French]

cough /kɔf/ (**coughs, coughing, coughed**)
1 **V-I** When you **cough**, you suddenly force air out of your throat with a noise. ❑ *James began to cough violently.* ● **cough|ing**
N-NONCOUNT ❑ *We could hear loud coughing in the background.*
2 **N-COUNT** **Cough** is also a noun. ❑ *Do you have any cough medicine?*
3 **N-COUNT** A **cough** is an illness that makes you cough. ❑ *I had a cough for over a month.*
[from Old English]
→ look at Word Web: **illness**

could /kəd, STRONG kʊd/
1 **MODAL** If you **could** do something, you were able to do it. ❑ *I could see that something was wrong.* ❑ *It was so dark that I couldn't see where I was going.*
2 **MODAL** You use **could have** to show that something was possible, although it did not happen. ❑ *He could have made a lot of money as a lawyer.*
3 **MODAL** You use **could** to show that something is possibly true, or that it may possibly happen. ❑ *It could snow again tonight.*
❑ *"Where's Jack?"—"I'm not sure; he could be in the bathroom."*
4 **MODAL** You use **could** after "if" when you are imagining what would happen if something was true. ❑ *If I could afford it I'd have four television sets.*
5 **MODAL** You use **could** when you are making offers and suggestions. ❑ *I could call the doctor.*
6 **MODAL** You use **could** in questions to make polite requests. ❑ *Could I stay tonight?*
❑ *He asked if he could have a cup of coffee.* [from Old English]
→ look at Usage note at **able**

couldn't /kʊdᵊnt/ **Couldn't** is short for "could not."

could've /kʊdəv/ **Could've** is short for "could have."

coun|cil /kaʊnsᵊl/ (**councils**) **N-COUNT**
SOCIAL STUDIES A **council** is a group of people who are chosen to control a particular area.
❑ *The city council has decided to build a new school.*
[from Old French]

coun|ci|lor /kaʊnsələr/ (**councilors**)
N-COUNT SOCIAL STUDIES A **councilor** is a member of a local council. ❑ *...Councilor Michael Poulter.* [from Old French]

C

coun|sel /kaʊnsᵊl/ (**counsels, counseling** or **counselling, counseled** or **counselled**)
1 **N-NONCOUNT** Counsel is advice. [FORMAL] ❑ If you have a problem, it is a good idea to ask for help and counsel.
2 **V-T** If you **counsel** someone **to** do something, you advise them to do it. [FORMAL] ❑ My advisers counseled me to do nothing.
3 **V-T** If you **counsel** people, you listen to them talk about their problems and help them to resolve them. ❑ She counsels people with eating disorders.
4 **N-COUNT** Someone's **counsel** is the lawyer who gives advice on a legal case and speaks for them in court. ❑ Singleton's counsel said that he would appeal. [from Old French]

coun|sel|ing /kaʊnsəlɪŋ/ also **counselling**
N-NONCOUNT Counseling is advice that a therapist or another expert gives to someone about a particular problem. ❑ She will need counseling to overcome the tragedy.

coun|se|lor /kaʊnsələr/ (**counselors**)
1 **N-COUNT** A counselor is a young person who takes care of children at a summer camp. ❑ Hicks worked as a camp counselor in the summer vacation.
2 **N-COUNT** A counselor is someone whose job is to give people advice and help them with problems. ❑ My husband and I went to see a marriage counselor. [from Old French]

count /kaʊnt/ (**counts, counting, counted**)
1 **V-I** When you **count**, you say all the numbers in order. ❑ Nancy counted slowly to five.
2 **V-T** If you **count** all the things in a group, you see how many there are. ❑ I counted the dollar bills. ❑ I counted 34 sheep on the hillside.
3 **Count up** means the same as **count**. ❑ They counted up all the hours the villagers work.
4 **V-I** If someone or something **counts** or **counts for** something, they are important. ❑ Every penny counts if you want to be a millionaire.
5 **N-COUNT** A count is the action of counting, or the number that you get after counting. ❑ The final count showed 56.7 percent in favor.
6 **ADJ** LANGUAGE ARTS A count noun is a noun that has a plural.
7 **PHRASE** If you **keep count of** a number of things, you know how many have occurred. ❑ Keep count of the number of hours you work.
8 **PHRASE** If you **lose count of** a number of things, you cannot remember how many there have been. ❑ I lost count of the number of times she called. [from Anglo-French]
→ look at Word Webs: **mathematics, zero**
▶ **count on** If you **count on** someone or something, you feel sure they will help you. ❑ You can count on us to keep your secret. ❑ Can we count on your support for Ms. Ryan?

coun|ter /kaʊntər/ (**counters**)
1 **N-COUNT** In a store or café, a **counter** is a long, flat surface where customers are served. ❑ That guy works behind the counter at the DVD rental store.
2 **N-COUNT** In a kitchen, a **counter** is a long, flat surface where you prepare your meals. ❑ There are marble counters in the kitchen.
3 **N-COUNT** A **counter** is a very small object that you use in board games. ❑ Move your counter one square for each spot on the dice. [from Old French]

counter|bal|ance /kaʊntərbæləns/ (**counterbalances**) **N-COUNT** A **counterbalance** is a weight that balances another weight.

counter|clockwise /kaʊntərklɒkwaɪz/
1 **ADV** Something that moves **counterclockwise** moves in the opposite direction to the way the hands of a clock move. ❑ Now turn the wheel counterclockwise.
2 **ADJ** Counterclockwise is also an adjective. ❑ Each group moves around the room in a counterclockwise direction.

counter|feit /kaʊntərfɪt/ **ADJ** Counterfeit money, goods, or documents are not real, but they look exactly like real ones. ❑ He admitted using counterfeit bills. [from Old French]

counter|part /kaʊntərpɑrt/ (**counterparts**)
N-COUNT Someone's or something's **counterpart** is another person or thing that has a similar function in a different place. ❑ The Foreign Secretary telephoned his German and Italian counterparts.

coun|ter|ter|ror|ism /kaʊntərterərɪzəm/
N-NONCOUNT SOCIAL STUDIES
Counterterrorism refers to activities that are intended to prevent terrorist acts or to get rid of terrorist groups.
● **coun|ter|ter|ror|ist** **ADJ** ❑ There were gaps in their counterterrorist strategy.

count|less /kaʊntlɪs/ **ADJ** Countless means very many. ❑ She made countless people happy through her music. [from Old French]

count noun (count nouns) **N-COUNT**
LANGUAGE ARTS A **count noun** is a noun such
as "bird," "chair," or "year" that has a
singular and a plural form.

coun|try /kʌntri/ (countries)
1 **N-COUNT** GEOGRAPHY SOCIAL STUDIES
A **country** is an area of the world with its
own government and people. ❑ *This is the
greatest country in the world.* ❑ *We crossed the
border between the two countries.*
2 **N-SING** The **country** is land that is away
from cities and towns. ❑ *You can live a healthy
life in the country.* ❑ *She was cycling along a
country road.* ❑ *She lived alone in a small house in
the country.*
3 **N-NONCOUNT** A particular kind of **country**
is an area of land that has particular
characteristics. ❑ *...mountainous country.*
4 **N-NONCOUNT** **Country** music is a style of
popular music from the southern United
States. ❑ *I always wanted to play country music.*
[from Old French]
→ look at Word Web: **country**

country|side /kʌntrisaɪd/ **N-NONCOUNT**
The **countryside** is land that is away from
cities and towns. ❑ *I've always loved the English
countryside.*
→ look at Word Web: **city**

coun|ty /kaʊnti/ (counties) **N-COUNT**
A **county** is a part of a state or a country.
❑ *...Palm Beach County.* [from Old French]

coup /ku/ (coups)
1 **N-COUNT** SOCIAL STUDIES When there is
a **coup**, a group of people seize power in
a country. ❑ *...a military coup.*
2 **N-COUNT** A **coup** is an achievement
which is thought to be especially good

because it was very difficult. ❑ *The sale is a big
coup for them.* [from French]

cou|ple /kʌpᵊl/ (couples)
1 **N-COUNT** A **couple** means two people or
things, or a small number of people or
things. ❑ *Out of 750 customers, there may be a
couple that are unhappy.* ❑ *There are a couple of
police officers outside.* ❑ *Things should get better in
a couple of days.*
2 **DET** In spoken English, you can use **a
couple** as a determiner. ❑ *...a couple weeks
before the election.*
3 **N-COUNT** A **couple** is two people who are
married or who are having a romantic
relationship. ❑ *The couple have no children.*
[from Old French]

cou|pon /kupɒn, kyu-/ (coupons) **N-COUNT**
A **coupon** is a piece of paper that allows you
to pay less money than usual for a product,
or to get it free. ❑ *Cut out the coupon on page 2
and take it to your local supermarket.* [from
French]

Word Link	age ≈ state of, related to : *courage*, *marriage*, *percentage*

cour|age /kɜrɪdʒ/ **N-NONCOUNT** **Courage** is
the quality someone shows when they are
not afraid. ❑ *The girl had the courage to tell the
police.* [from Old French]

cou|ra|geous /kəreɪdʒəs/ **ADJ** Someone
who is **courageous** shows courage.
❑ *The courageous girl saved her baby sister from
a house fire.* [from Old French]

cou|ri|er /kuəriər, kɜr-/ (couriers,
couriering, couriered)
1 **N-COUNT** A **courier** is a person who is paid
to take letters and packages direct from one

Word Web   country

The largest **country** in the world
geographically is Russia. It has an area of six
million square miles and a **population** of
more than 142 million people. Russia is a
federal **state** with a republican form of
government. The government is based in
Russia's **capital** city, Moscow.

One of the smallest countries in the world is
Nauru. This tiny island **nation** in the South
Pacific Ocean is 8.1 square miles in size. Many of Nauru's more than 9,000 **residents** live in
Yaren, which is the largest city, but not the capital. The Republic of Nauru is the only nation
in the world without an official capital.

place to another. ❑ ...a motorcycle courier.
2 **V-T** If you **courier** something somewhere, you send it there by courier. ❑ I couriered it to Darren in New York. [from Old French]

course /kɔrs/ (**courses**)
1 **N-COUNT** A **course** is a series of lessons on a particular subject. ❑ I'm taking a course in business administration.
2 **N-COUNT** A **course** is one part of a meal. ❑ Lunch was excellent, especially the first course.
3 **N-COUNT** SPORTS In sports, a **course** is an area of land for racing, or for playing golf. ❑ The hotel complex has a swimming pool, tennis courts, and a golf course.
4 **N-NONCOUNT/N-SING** The **course** of a vehicle is the route along which it is traveling. ❑ The pilot changed course to land in Chicago.
5 **N-NONCOUNT/N-SING** The **course** of something is the way that something develops over time. ❑ Meeting him changed the course of her life. [from Old French]

court /kɔrt/ (**courts**)
1 **N-COUNT** A **court** is a place where a judge and a jury decide if someone has done something wrong. ❑ The man will appear in court later this month.
2 **N-COUNT** SPORTS A **court** is an area for playing a game such as tennis. ❑ The hotel has several tennis courts. [from Old French]
→ look at Word Web: **park**

cour|teous /kɜrtiəs/ **ADJ** Someone who is **courteous** is polite. ❑ He was a kind and courteous man. ● **cour|teous|ly** **ADV** ❑ He nodded courteously to me. [from Old French]

cour|tesy /kɜrtɪsi/ **N-NONCOUNT** **Courtesy** is polite behavior that shows that you consider other people's feelings. [FORMAL] ❑ Showing courtesy to other drivers costs nothing. [from Old French]

court|yard /kɔrtyɑrd/ (**courtyards**)
N-COUNT A **courtyard** is an open area that is surrounded by buildings or walls. ❑ The second bedroom overlooked the courtyard. [from Old French]

cous|in /kʌzªn/ (**cousins**) **N-COUNT** Your **cousin** is the child of your uncle or your aunt. ❑ Do you know my cousin Alex? [from Old French]

co|va|lent bond /koʊveɪlənt bɒnd/ (**covalent bonds**) **N-COUNT** SCIENCE A **covalent**

bond is the force that holds together two atoms that share a pair of electrons.

co|va|lent com|pound /koʊveɪlənt kɒmpaʊnd/ (**covalent compounds**) **N-COUNT** SCIENCE A **covalent compound** is a chemical compound made of molecules in which the atoms are held together by covalent bonds.

cov|er /kʌvər/ (**covers, covering, covered**)
1 **V-T** If you **cover** something, you put something over it to protect it. ❑ Cover the dish with a heavy lid.
2 **V-T** If one thing **covers** another, it forms a layer over its surface. ❑ Snow covered the city. ❑ The desk was covered with papers.
3 **V-T** If you **cover** a particular distance, you travel that distance. ❑ It would not be easy to cover ten miles on that amount of gas.
4 **V-T** If an insurance policy **covers** a person or a thing, money will be paid by the insurance company. ❑ Our insurance does not cover damage caused by floods.
5 **V-T** If you **cover** a particular topic, you discuss it in a lecture or book. ❑ Introduction to Chemistry aims to cover the main topics in chemistry.
6 **N-COUNT** A **cover** is something that is put over an object to protect it. ❑ Keep a plastic cover on your computer when you are not using it.
7 **N-COUNT** The **cover** of a book or a magazine is the outside part of it. ❑ She appeared on the cover of last week's "Zoo" magazine.
8 **N-PLURAL** Bed **covers** are sheets and blankets. ❑ She slid under the covers. [from Old French]
▶ **cover up** If you **cover** something or someone **up**, you put something over them in order to protect or hide them. ❑ I covered him up with a blanket.

Thesaurus cover Also look up :		
v	conceal, drape, hide, screen; (ant.) uncover **1** **2** guard, insure, protect **4**	

Word Partnership Use cover with :		
N	cover *your face* **1** **2** covered *in something* **2**	

cov|er|age /kʌvərɪdʒ/
1 **N-NONCOUNT** The **coverage** of something in the news is the reporting of it. ❑ A special TV network gives live coverage of most races.
2 **N-NONCOUNT** **Coverage** is a guarantee from an insurance company that money will be paid by them in particular

situations. ❑ *Make sure that your insurance coverage is adequate.* [from Old French]

cov|er|ing /kˈʌvərɪŋ/ (**coverings**) **N-COUNT** A **covering** is a layer of something that protects or hides something else. ❑ *...a light covering of snow.* [from Old French]

cow /kaʊ/ (**cows**) **N-COUNT** A **cow** is a large female animal that is kept on farms for its milk. ❑ *Dad went out to milk the cows.* [from Old English]
→ look at Word Webs: **dairy, meat**

cow|ard /kaʊərd/ (**cowards**) **N-COUNT** A **coward** is someone who has no courage. ❑ *They called him a coward because he refused to fight.* [from Old French]

cow|ard|ly /kaʊərdli/ **ADJ** A **cowardly** person is not brave and is easily frightened. ❑ *I was too cowardly to complain.* [from Old French]

cow|boy /kaʊbɔɪ/ (**cowboys**) **N-COUNT** A **cowboy** is a man who rides a horse and takes care of cows in North America.
→ look at Picture Dictionary: **hat**

cozy /koʊzi/ (**cozier, coziest**) **ADJ** A **cozy** place is comfortable and warm. ❑ *You can relax in the cozy hotel lounge.* [from Scots]

crab /kræb/ (**crabs**)
■ **N-COUNT** A **crab** is an ocean animal with a shell and five pairs of legs. Crabs usually move sideways.
■ **N-NONCOUNT** **Crab** is the meat of this animal. ❑ *I'll have the crab salad, please.* [from Old English]
→ look at Picture Dictionary: **shellfish**

crack /kræk/ (**cracks, cracking, cracked**)
■ **V-T/V-I** If something hard **cracks**, it becomes slightly broken, with lines appearing on its surface. ❑ *The plane's windshield cracked.* ❑ *She cracked the mirror.*
■ **V-T** When you **crack** something hard, you hit it and it breaks or is damaged. ❑ *Crack the eggs into a bowl.*
■ **N-COUNT** A **crack** is a very narrow gap between two things. ❑ *Kathryn saw him through a crack in the curtains.*
■ **N-COUNT** A **crack** is a line that appears on a surface when it is slightly broken. ❑ *The plate had a crack in it.*
■ **N-COUNT** A **crack** is a sharp sound, like the sound of a piece of wood breaking. ❑ *Suddenly there was a loud crack.*
■ **V-T** If you **crack** a joke, you tell it.

❑ *He cracked jokes, and talked about girls.* [from Old English]
→ look at Word Web: **crash**

Word Partnership	Use **crack** with :
ADJ	crack **open** ■ ■
ADJ	**deep** crack ■
V	**have a** crack ■ ■
N	crack **jokes** ■

crack|down /krækdaʊn/ (**crackdowns**) **N-COUNT** A **crackdown** is strong official action that is taken to punish people who break laws. ❑ *The unrest ended with a violent crackdown.*

crack|er /krækər/ (**crackers**) **N-COUNT** A **cracker** is a thin, hard piece of baked bread that people sometimes eat with cheese. [from Old English]

crack|le /krækəl/ (**crackles, crackling, crackled**) **V-I** Something that **crackles** makes a lot of short, sharp noises. ❑ *The radio crackled again.* [from Old English]

cra|dle /kreɪdəl/ (**cradles**) **N-COUNT** A **cradle** is a baby's bed that you can move from side to side. [from Old English]

craft /kræft/ (**craft** or **crafts**)

LANGUAGE HELP
Craft is the plural for meaning ■. **Crafts** is the plural for meaning ■.

■ **N-COUNT** You can call a boat a **craft**. ❑ *The fisherman guided his small craft close to the shore.*
■ **N-COUNT** A **craft** is an activity that involves making things skillfully with your hands. ❑ *We want to teach our children about native crafts and culture.* [from Old English]

crafty /kræfti/ (**craftier, craftiest**) **ADJ** Someone who is **crafty** gets what they want in a clever way, perhaps by being dishonest. ❑ *She was so crafty, nobody ever suspected her.* [from Old English]

cramp /kræmp/ (**cramps**) **N-COUNT/N-NONCOUNT** A **cramp** is a sudden strong pain in a muscle. ❑ *Mike was complaining of stomach cramps.* [from Middle Dutch]

crane /kreɪn/ (**cranes**)
■ **N-COUNT** A **crane** is a large machine with a long arm that can lift very heavy things.
■ **N-COUNT** A **crane** is a large water bird with a long neck and long legs. [from Old English]

C

crash /kræʃ/ (crashes, crashing, crashed)

1 **N-COUNT** A **crash** is an accident in which a vehicle hits something. ❑ *His son was killed in a car crash.*

2 **N-COUNT** A **crash** is a sudden loud noise. ❑ *They heard a loud crash at about 1:30 a.m.*

3 **V-T/V-I** If a vehicle **crashes**, or if a driver **crashes** it, it hits something. ❑ *The plane crashed into a nearby field.* ❑ *Her car crashed into the back of a truck.*

4 **V-I** To **crash** means to move or fall, making a loud noise. ❑ *The walls above us crashed down.*

5 **V-I** BUSINESS If a business **crashes**, it fails suddenly. ❑ *When the market crashed, the deal was canceled.*

6 **N-COUNT** BUSINESS **Crash** is also a noun. ❑ *...a stock market crash.*

7 **V-I** TECHNOLOGY If a computer or a computer program **crashes**, it suddenly stops working. ❑ *My computer crashed for the second time that day.*

→ look at Word Web: **crash**

Thesaurus	crash	Also look up :
N	collision, wreck **1**	
	bang **2**	
V	collide, hit, smash **3**	

crate /kreɪt/ (crates) **N-COUNT** A **crate** is a large box for moving or storing things. ❑ *The pictures are packed in wooden crates.* [from Latin]

cra|ter /kreɪtər/ (craters) **N-COUNT** SCIENCE A **crater** is a very large hole in the top of a volcano. ❑ *Rocks shot up three miles from the volcano's crater.* [from Latin]

→ look at Word Webs: **astronomer, lake, moon, solar system**

crawl /krɔl/ (crawls, crawling, crawled)

1 **V-I** When you **crawl**, you move on your hands and knees. ❑ *I began to crawl toward the door.*

2 **V-I** If something **crawls** somewhere, it moves there slowly. ❑ *Yellow cabs crawl up Fifth Avenue.*

3 **N-SING** **Crawl** is also a noun. ❑ *The traffic slowed to a crawl.*

4 **N-NONCOUNT** SPORTS **Crawl** is a way of swimming in which you lie on your front and move one arm over your head, and then the other, while kicking your legs. ❑ *Neil is learning to swim crawl.* [from Old Norse]

cray|on /kreɪɒn/ (crayons) **N-COUNT** A **crayon** is a small colored stick that you use for drawing. [from French]

cra|zy /kreɪzi/ (crazier, craziest)

1 **ADJ** Someone who is **crazy** is very strange or not at all sensible. [INFORMAL] ❑ *People obviously thought we were crazy.* ● **cra|zi|ly** **ADV** ❑ *He ran crazily around in circles.*

2 **ADJ** Someone who is going **crazy** is extremely bored or upset, or feels they cannot wait for something any longer. [INFORMAL] ❑ *Annie thought she might go crazy if she didn't find out soon.*

3 **ADJ** If you are **crazy about** someone or something, you like them very much. [INFORMAL] ❑ *He's still crazy about his job.* ❑ *We're crazy about each other.* [of Scandinavian origin]

creak /krik/ (creaks, creaking, creaked)

1 **V-I** If something **creaks**, it makes a short, high sound when you move it. ❑ *The stairs creaked under his feet.* ❑ *The door creaked open.*

Word Web   crash

Every year the National Highway Traffic Safety Administration* conducts crash tests on new cars. They evaluate exactly what happens during an accident. How fast do you have to be going to **dent** a bumper during a **collision?** Does the gas tank **rupture?** Do the tires **burst?** What happens when the windshield **breaks?** Does it **crack**, or does it **shatter** into a thousand pieces?

Does the force of the **impact crush** the front of the car completely? This is actually a good thing. It means that the engine and hood would protect the passengers during the crash.

National Highway Traffic Safety Administration: a U.S. government agency that sets safety standards.

2 N-COUNT Creak is also a noun. ❏ *The door opened with a creak.*

cream /kri̱m/ (creams)

1 N-NONCOUNT Cream is a thick liquid that is made from milk. ❏ *She went to the store to buy some cream.*

2 N-COUNT/N-NONCOUNT A cream is a substance that you rub into your skin. ❏ *...hand cream.*

3 ADJ Something that is cream is yellowish-white in color. ❏ *She wore a cream silk shirt.*

4 N-NONCOUNT Cream is also a noun. ❏ *Many women say they can't wear cream.* [from Old French]

5 → see also **ice cream**

cream|er /kri̱mər/ **N-COUNT** A creamer is a small pitcher used for pouring cream or milk. [from Old French]
→ look at Picture Dictionary: **dish**

creamy /kri̱mi/ (creamier, creamiest)

1 ADJ Food or drink that is creamy has a lot of cream or milk in it. ❏ *I like rich, creamy coffee.*

2 ADJ Food that is creamy is soft and smooth. ❏ *We had pasta in a rich, creamy sauce.* [from Old French]

crease /kri̱s/ (creases, creasing, creased)

1 N-COUNT Creases are the lines that appear in cloth or paper when it has been folded. ❏ *Dad always wears pants with sharp creases.*

2 V-T/V-I If cloth creases, lines form in it when it is pressed or folded. ❏ *Most clothes crease a bit when you are traveling.* ❏ *I creased my skirt.* ● **creased ADJ** ❏ *His clothes were terribly creased.* [from Old French]

> **Word Link** ator ≈ one who does : creator, narrator, translator

cre|ate /krie̱ɪt/ (creates, creating, created)
V-T To create something means to make it happen or exist. ❏ *It's great for a group of schoolchildren to create a show like this.* ❏ *Could this solution create problems for us in the future?* ● **crea|tor** /krie̱ɪtər/ (creators) **N-COUNT** ❏ *...Matt Groening, creator of The Simpsons.* [from Latin]

> **Thesaurus** create Also look up :
> v   produce, make; *(ant.)* destroy

> **Word Link** creat ≈ making : creation, creature, recreation

crea|tion /krie̱ɪʃ°n/ (creations) **N-COUNT**
You can call something that someone has made a **creation**. ❏ *The new bathroom is my own creation.* [from Latin]

crea|tive /krie̱ɪtɪv/

1 ADJ A creative person is good at having new ideas. ❏ *When you don't have much money, you have to be creative.*

2 ADJ If you use something in a **creative** way, you use it in a new way. ❏ *He is famous for his creative use of words.* [from Latin]

crea|tive dra|ma (creative dramas)
N-COUNT/N-NONCOUNT ARTS Creative drama is a form of improvised drama that is often used in teaching.

crea|ture /kri̱tʃər/ (creatures) **N-COUNT**
A **creature** is a living thing that is not a plant. ❏ *Like all living creatures, birds need plenty of water.* [from Church Latin]

> **Word Link** cred ≈ to believe : discredit, credibility, incredible

cred|ible /kre̱dɪb°l/

1 ADJ Credible means able to be trusted or believed. ❏ *Her claims seem credible to many.* ● **cred|ibil|ity** /kre̱dɪbɪlɪti/ **N-NONCOUNT** ❏ *The police have lost their credibility.*

2 ADJ A credible candidate, policy, or system is one that appears to have a chance of being successful. ❏ *Mr. Robertson is a credible candidate.* [from Latin]

cred|it /kre̱dɪt/ (credits, crediting, credited)

1 N-NONCOUNT If you buy something on **credit**, you are allowed to have it and pay for it later. ❏ *We buy everything on credit.*

2 N-NONCOUNT If you get **the credit for** something, people praise you because they think you are responsible for it. ❏ *I can't take all the credit myself.*

3 V-T If people **credit** someone **with** an achievement, people say that they were responsible for it. ❏ *The staff is crediting him with saving Hythe's life.*

4 N-COUNT A **credit** is one part of a course at a school or a college. ❏ *He doesn't have enough credits to graduate.*

5 N-PLURAL The credits is the list of all the people who made a movie or a television program. ❏ *It was great to see my name in the credits.* [from Old French]

> **Word Partnership** Use **credit** with :
>
> | | |
> |---|---|
> | N | credit **history, letter of** credit **1** |
> | V | **provide** credit **1** |
> | | **deserve** credit, **take** credit **2** |
> | ADJ | **personal** credit **1 2** |

cred|it card (**credit cards**) **N-COUNT** A **credit card** is a card that you use to buy something and pay for it later. ❑ *Call this number to order by credit card.*

credi|tor /krɛdɪtər/ (**creditors**) **N-COUNT** Your **creditors** are the people who you owe money to. ❑ *The company said it would pay all its creditors.* [from Old French]

creed /krid/ (**creeds**)
1 **N-COUNT** A **creed** is a set of beliefs or principles that influence the way people live or work. [FORMAL] ❑ *...their creed of self-help.*
2 **N-COUNT** A **creed** is a religion. [FORMAL] ❑ *The center is open to all, of every race or creed.* [from Old English]

creek /krik/ (**creeks**) **N-COUNT** A **creek** is a stream or a small river. ❑ *The road follows Austin Creek for a few miles.* [from Old Norse]

creep /krip/ (**creeps, creeping, crept**)
1 **V-I** If you **creep** somewhere, you move there quietly and slowly. ❑ *He crept up the stairs.*
2 **V-I** If something **creeps** in or **creeps** back, it gradually starts happening or returning. ❑ *The inflation rate has been creeping up.*
3 **N-NONCOUNT** SCIENCE In geology, **creep** is the very slow downhill movement of rocks and soil as a result of gravity. [from Old English]

Word Partnership	Use **creep** with :
PREP	creep **into**, creep **toward**, creep **up** **1** creep **in** **2**

creepy /kripi/ (**creepier, creepiest**) **ADJ** Something or someone that is **creepy** makes you feel nervous or frightened. [INFORMAL] ❑ *This place is really creepy at night.* [from Old English]

cre|mate /krimeɪt/ (**cremates, cremating, cremated**) **V-T** When someone **is cremated**, their dead body is burned, usually as part of a funeral service. ❑ *She wants Chris to be cremated.* ● **cre|ma|tion** /krɪmeɪʃ°n/ (**cremations**) **N-COUNT/N-NONCOUNT** ❑ *There was a cremation after a private ceremony.* [from Latin]

crept /krɛpt/ **Crept** is the past tense and past participle of **creep**. [from old English]

Word Link	cresc, creas ≈ growing : crescent, decrease, increase

cres|cent /krɛs°nt/ (**crescents**) **N-COUNT** A **crescent** is a curved shape like the shape of a new moon. [from Latin]

crest /krɛst/ (**crests**) **N-COUNT** The **crest of** a hill or a wave is the top of it. [from Old French]
→ look at Word Web: **sound**

cre|vasse /krɪvæs/ (**crevasses**) **N-COUNT** GEOGRAPHY A **crevasse** is a large, deep crack in thick ice or rock. [from French]

crew /kru/ (**crews**)
1 **N-COUNT** The **crew** of a ship or aircraft is the people who work on it. ❑ *He was new on the crew of the space shuttle.* ❑ *These ships carry small crews of about twenty men.*
2 **N-COUNT** A **crew** is a group of people with special skills who work together on a project. ❑ *...a two-man film crew.* [from Old French]
→ look at Word Web: **theater**

crib /krɪb/ (**cribs**) **N-COUNT** A **crib** is a bed with high sides for a baby. [from Old English]

crick|et /krɪkɪt/ (**crickets**)
1 **N-NONCOUNT** SPORTS **Cricket** is an outdoor game played between two teams who try to score points, called runs, by hitting a ball with a wooden bat. ❑ *During the summer term we played cricket.*
2 **N-COUNT** A **cricket** is a small jumping insect that produces short, loud sounds by rubbing its wings together. [from Old French]
→ look at Picture Dictionary: **insect**

crime /kraɪm/ (**crimes**)
N-COUNT/N-NONCOUNT A **crime** is an illegal act. ❑ *The police are searching the scene of the crime.* [from Old French]
→ look at Picture Dictionary: **crime**
→ look at Word Web: **city**

Word Partnership	Use **crime** with :
V	**commit a** crime, **fight against** crime
ADJ	**organized** crime, **terrible** crime, **violent** crime
N	**partner in** crime, crime **prevention**, crime **scene**, crime **wave**

crimi|nal /krɪmɪn°l/ (**criminals**) **N-COUNT** A **criminal** is a person who does something illegal. ❑ *We want to protect ourselves against dangerous criminals.* [from Late Latin]

Picture Dictionary

crime

graffiti   **mugging**   **theft**   **burglary**

crip|ple /krɪpᵊl/ (**cripples, crippling, crippled**) **V-T** Someone who **is crippled** by an injury can never move their body normally again. ❑ *Mr. Easton was crippled in an accident.* [from Old English]

cri|sis /kraɪsɪs/ (**crises** /kraɪsiz/)
1 N-COUNT/N-NONCOUNT A **crisis** is a situation that is very serious or dangerous. ❑ *This is a worldwide crisis that affects us all.*
2 N-COUNT ARTS The **crisis** is the most dramatic part of a play or a movie, or the most important part of its plot. [from Latin]

crisp /krɪsp/ (**crisper, crispest**) **ADJ** Food that is **crisp** is pleasantly hard. ❑ *Bake the potatoes for 15 minutes, until they're nice and crisp.* ❑ *...crisp bacon.* [from Old English]

cri|teri|on /kraɪtɪəriən/ (**criteria** /kraɪtɪəriə/) **N-COUNT** A **criterion** is a factor on which you judge or decide something. ❑ *The bank is reviewing its criteria for lending money.* [from Greek]

Word Link *crit ≈ to judge : critic, critical, criticize*

crit|ic /krɪtɪk/ (**critics**)
1 N-COUNT A **critic** is a person who writes and gives their opinion about books, movies, music, or art. ❑ *Mather was a film critic for many years.*
2 N-COUNT Someone who is a **critic** of a person or system criticizes them publicly. ❑ *He has been one of the critics of the government.* [from Latin]

criti|cal /krɪtɪkᵊl/
1 ADJ A **critical** situation is very serious and dangerous. ❑ *The economic situation may soon become critical.* ● **criti|cal|ly** ADV ❑ *Food supplies are critically low.*
2 ADJ A **critical** time or situation is very important. ❑ *The incident happened at a critical point in the campaign.*
3 ADJ To be **critical** means to criticize a person or a thing. ❑ *His report is critical of the*

judges. ● **criti|cal|ly** ADV ❑ *She spoke critically about Lara.* [from Latin]

Word Partnership	Use **critical** with :
N	critical **condition** **1**
	critical **state** **1** **2**
	critical **issue**, critical **role** **2**
V	**become** critical **1** **2**
PREP	critical **of** *someone/something* **3**

criti|cism /krɪtɪsɪzəm/ (**criticisms**)
1 N-NONCOUNT **Criticism** is when someone expresses disapproval of someone or something. ❑ *The president faced strong criticism for his remarks.*
2 N-COUNT A **criticism** is a statement that expresses disapproval. ❑ *Teachers should say something positive before making a criticism.* [from Latin]

Thesaurus	**criticism** Also look up :
N	disapproval, judgment; *(ant.)* approval, flattery, praise **1** **2**

Word Partnership	Use **criticism** with :
PREP	criticism **against** *something*, criticism **from** *something*, criticism **of** *something* **1** **2**
ADJ	**constructive** criticism, **open to** criticism **2**

criti|cize /krɪtɪsaɪz/ (**criticizes, criticizing, criticized**) **V-T** If you **criticize** someone or something, you express your disapproval of them. ❑ *His mother rarely criticized him.* [from Latin]

croco|dile /krɒkədaɪl/ (**crocodiles**) **N-COUNT** A **crocodile** is a large animal with a long body, a long mouth and sharp teeth. Crocodiles live in rivers. [from Old French]

crois|sant /krwɑsɒn, krəsɒnt/ (**croissants**) **N-COUNT/N-NONCOUNT** **Croissants** are bread rolls in the shape of a crescent that are eaten

for breakfast. [from French]
→ look at Picture Dictionary: **bread**

Cro-Mag|non /kroʊ mǽgnən, mǽnyən/
(**Cro-Magnons**)
1 **N-COUNT** SOCIAL STUDIES **Cro-Magnons**
were a species of early human being who
lived between 50,000 and 100,000 years ago.
2 **ADJ** SOCIAL STUDIES **Cro-Magnon** is also an
adjective. ❑ ...*Cro-Magnon man.*

crook /krʊk/ (**crooks**) **N-COUNT** A **crook** is a
dishonest person or a criminal. [INFORMAL]
❑ *The man is a crook and a liar.* [from Old Norse]

crook|ed /krʊkɪd/ **ADJ** Something that is
crooked is not straight. ❑ *I looked at his crooked
broken nose.* [from Old Norse]

crop /krɒp/ (**crops**) **N-COUNT** **Crops** are plants
that people grow for food. ❑ *Rice farmers here
still plant their crops by hand.* [from Old English]
→ look at Picture Dictionary: **plant**
→ look at Word Webs: **farm, grain**

---

cross
❶ MOVING ACROSS
❷ ANGRY

---

❶ cross /krɒs/ (**crosses, crossing, crossed**)
1 **V-T/V-I** If you **cross** a place, you move to
the other side of it. ❑ *She crossed the road.*
❑ *Egan crossed to the window and looked out.*
2 **V-T** A road or bridge that **crosses** an area
of land or water passes over it. ❑ *The road
crosses the river half a mile outside the town.*
3 **V-T/V-I** SPORTS In sports, if you **cross** the
ball, you hit it or kick it from one side of the
field to a person on the other side.
❑ *Ronaldinho crossed the ball into the penalty area.*
4 **N-COUNT** SPORTS In sports, a **cross** is the
act of hitting or kicking the ball from one
side of the field to a person on the other side.
5 **V-T** If you **cross** your arms, legs, or
fingers, you put one of them on top of the
other. ❑ *Jill crossed her legs.*
6 **V-T/V-I** Lines or roads that **cross** meet and
go across each other. ❑ ...*the place where Main
and Center Streets cross.*
7 **N-COUNT** A **cross** is a shape like ✝. It is the
most important Christian symbol. ❑ *She
wore a cross around her neck.*
8 **N-COUNT** A **cross** is a written mark in the
shape of an X. ❑ *Put a cross next to those
activities you like.*
9 **N-SING** Something that is **a cross
between** two things is a mixture of both
things. ❑ *"Ha!" It was a cross between a laugh and*

a bark. [from Old English]
10 → see also **crossing**
▶ **cross out** If you **cross out** words, you
draw a line through them. ❑ *He crossed out
her name and added his own.*

❷ cross /krɒs/ (**crosser, crossest**) **ADJ**
Someone who is **cross** is angry. ❑ *I'm terribly
cross with him.* ● **cross|ly** **ADV** ❑ *"No, no, no,"
Morris said crossly.* [from Old English]

cross-coun|try
1 **N-NONCOUNT** SPORTS **Cross-country** is the
sport of running, riding, or skiing across
open countryside. ❑ *She finished third in the
world cross-country championships.*
2 **ADJ** A **cross-country** trip takes you from
one side of a country to the other. ❑ ...*cross-
country rail services.*
3 **ADV** **Cross-country** is also an adverb.
❑ *I drove cross-country in his van.*

cross|ing /krɒsɪŋ/ (**crossings**)
1 **N-COUNT** A **crossing** is a boat journey to
a place on the other side of an ocean, a river,
or a lake. ❑ *He made the crossing to Sydney.*
2 **N-COUNT** A **crossing** is a place where you
can cross something such as a road or a
border. [from Old English]
3 → see also **cross**

cross|ing over **N-NONCOUNT** SCIENCE In
biology, **crossing over** is a process in which
genetic material is exchanged between two
chromosomes, resulting in new
combinations of genes.

cross-par|ty **ADJ** SOCIAL STUDIES **Cross-party**
activities involve two or more political
parties. A **cross-party** group consists of
members from two or more political parties.
❑ *Special election procedures allow cross-party
voting.* ❑ ...*cross-party committees.*

cross|roads /krɒsroʊdz/ (**crossroads**)
N-COUNT A **crossroads** is a place where two
roads cross each other. ❑ *Turn right at the first
crossroads.*

cross|walk /krɒswɔk/
(**crosswalks**) **N-COUNT**
A **crosswalk** is a place
where drivers must
stop to let people
walk across a street.

crosswalk

cross|word /krɒswɜrd/ (**crosswords**)
N-COUNT A **crossword** or a **crossword puzzle**
is a printed word game that consists of a

pattern of black and white squares. You write the answers down or across on the white squares. ❑ *He could do the New York Times crossword puzzle in 15 minutes.*

crouch /kraʊtʃ/ (**crouches, crouching, crouched**) **v-ı** If you **crouch**, you bend your legs so that you are close to the ground. ❑ *We crouched in the bushes to hide.* [from Old French]

crow /kroʊ/ (**crows, crowing, crowed**)
1 **N-COUNT** A **crow** is a large black bird that makes a loud noise.
2 **v-ı** When a rooster **crows**, it makes a loud sound, often early in the morning. ❑ *We got up when the rooster crowed.* [from Old English]

crowd /kraʊd/ (**crowds, crowding, crowded**)
1 **N-COUNT** A **crowd** is a large group of people who have gathered together. ❑ *A huge crowd gathered in the town square.*
2 **v-ı** When people **crowd around** someone or something, they move closely together around them. ❑ *The children crowded around him.*
3 **v-T/v-ı** If a lot of people **crowd into** a place, they enter it so that it becomes very full. ❑ *Thousands of people crowded into the city center to see the president.* ❑ *One group of journalists were crowded into a bus.* [from Old English]

crowd|ed /kraʊdɪd/ **ADJ** A **crowded** place is full of people. ❑ *He looked slowly around the small crowded room.* ❑ *This is a crowded city of 2 million.* [from Old English]

crowd|fund|ing /kraʊdfʌndɪŋ/
N-NONCOUNT TECHNOLOGY **Crowdfunding** is a method of raising money by asking for small amounts from a lot of people, usually through a website. ❑ *The project was financed through crowdfunding.*

crowd|sourc|ing /kraʊdsɔrsɪŋ/
N-NONCOUNT TECHNOLOGY **Crowdsourcing** is the act of using the Internet to send an open request to a large number of people in order to get help with a task.

crown /kraʊn/ (**crowns, crowning, crowned**)
1 **N-COUNT** A **crown** is a gold or silver circle that a king or a queen wears on their head.
2 **v-T** SOCIAL STUDIES When a king or a queen **is crowned**, they officially become king or queen, and a crown is put on their

crown

head. ❑ *Two days later, Juan Carlos was crowned king.* [from Old French]

cru|cial /kruʃ³l/ **ADJ** Something that is **crucial** is extremely important. ❑ *He made all the crucial decisions himself.* ● **cru|cial|ly** **ADV** ❑ *Chewing properly is crucially important.* [from French]

crude /krud/ (**cruder, crudest**)
1 **ADJ** Something that is **crude** is simple and rough. ❑ *We sat on crude wooden boxes.* ● **crude|ly** **ADV** ❑ *Someone has crudely painted over the original sign.*
2 **ADJ** A **crude** person or joke is rude or offensive. ❑ *The boys sang loudly and told crude jokes.* ❑ *Please don't be so crude.* ● **crude|ly** **ADV** ❑ *He hated it when she spoke so crudely.* [from Latin]

cru|el /kruəl/ (**crueler, cruelest**) **ADJ** Someone who is **cruel** deliberately makes people suffer. ❑ *Children can be very cruel.* ● **cru|el|ly** **ADV** ❑ *Douglas was often treated cruelly by his sisters.* ● **cru|el|ty** /kruəlti/ (**cruelties**) **N-COUNT/N-NONCOUNT** ❑ *There are laws against cruelty to animals.* [from Old French]

Thesaurus	**cruel**	Also look up :
ADJ	harsh, mean, nasty, unkind; (*ant.*) gentle, kind **1**	

cruise /kruz/ (**cruises, cruising, cruised**)
1 **N-COUNT** A **cruise** is a vacation that you spend on a ship or boat. ❑ *...a world cruise.*
2 **v-ı** If a car, a ship, or an aircraft **cruises** somewhere, it moves at a steady comfortable speed. ❑ *A black and white police car cruised past.* [from Dutch]
→ look at Word Web: **ship**

cruise ship (**cruise ships**) **N-COUNT** A **cruise ship** is a large ship that takes people to several places on a vacation. ❑ *He got a job as a singer on a cruise ship.*

crumb /krʌm/ (**crumbs**) **N-COUNT** **Crumbs** are small pieces that fall from bread when you break it. ❑ *I stood up, brushing crumbs from my pants.* [from Old English]

crum|ble /krʌmb³l/ (**crumbles, crumbling, crumbled**)
1 **v-ı** If a building or a wall is **crumbling**, pieces are breaking off it. ❑ *The stone wall was crumbling away in places.*
2 **v-T** If you **crumble** something, you break it into a lot of small pieces. ❑ *Crumble the goat cheese into a salad bowl.*
3 **v-ı** If a system, a relationship, or a hope

C

crumbles, it comes to an end. ❑ *Their economy crumbled as a result of the war.* [from Old English]

crum|ple /krʌmpᵊl/ (**crumples, crumpling, crumpled**)

1 **V-T/V-I** If you **crumple** paper or cloth, or if it **crumples**, it is squashed, making a lot of lines and folds in it. ❑ *She crumpled the paper in her hand.* ● **crum|pled** **ADJ** ❑ *His uniform was crumpled and dirty.*

2 **Crumple up** means the same as **crumple**. ❑ *She crumpled up the note.* [from Old High German]

crunch /krʌntʃ/ (**crunches, crunching, crunched**)

1 **V-I** When a lot of small stones **crunch**, they make a loud noise when you walk or drive over them. ❑ *The gravel crunched under his boots.*

2 **N-COUNT Crunch** is also a noun. ❑ *We heard the crunch of tires on the road up to the house.*

3 **V-T/V-I** If you **crunch** something, or if it **crunches**, you noisily break it into small pieces between your teeth. ❑ *She crunched an ice cube loudly.*

crunchy /krʌntʃi/ (**crunchier, crunchiest**)

ADJ Food that is **crunchy** is pleasantly hard, so that it makes a noise when you eat it. ❑ *We enjoyed the fresh, crunchy vegetables.*

crush /krʌʃ/ (**crushes, crushing, crushed**)

1 **V-T** If you **crush** something, you press it very hard so that it breaks or loses its shape. ❑ *Andrew crushed his empty can.* ❑ *The drinks were full of crushed ice.*

2 **V-T** To **crush** a group of opponents means to defeat it completely. ❑ *...a plan to crush the protests.* [from Old French]

→ look at Word Web: **crash**

crust /krʌst/ (**crusts**)

1 **N-COUNT** The **crust** on a loaf of bread is the hard outer part. ❑ *Cut the crusts off the bread.*

2 **N-COUNT** The Earth's **crust** is its outer layer. ❑ *Earthquakes damage the Earth's crust.* [from Latin]

→ look at Picture Dictionary: **core**

→ look at Word Webs: **continents, earthquake**

crutch /krʌtʃ/ (**crutches**) **N-COUNT** A **crutch** is a long stick that you use to support yourself when you walk. ❑ *I can walk without crutches now.* [from Old English]

cry /kraɪ/ (**cries, crying, cried**)

1 **V-I** When you **cry**, tears come from your eyes. ❑ *I hung up the phone and started to cry.*

2 **V-T** If you **cry** something, you say it very loudly. ❑ *"Nancy Drew," she cried, "you're under arrest!"*

3 **Cry out** means the same as **cry**. ❑ *"You're wrong, you're all wrong!" Henry cried out.*

4 **N-COUNT** A **cry** is a loud, high sound that you make when you feel a strong emotion. ❑ *She saw the spider and let out a cry of horror.*

5 **N-COUNT** A bird's or an animal's **cry** is the loud, high sound that it makes. ❑ *The cry of a strange bird sounded like a whistle.* [from Old French]

→ look at Word Web: **cry**

Thesaurus	cry	Also look up :
v	sob, weep **1**	
	call, shout, yell **2**	
	howl, moan, shriek **3**	

Word Partnership	Use **cry** with :
v	**begin to** cry, **start to** cry **1**
N	cry **with anger** **1** **2**
	cry **for help**, cry **with joy**, cry **of horror**, cry **of pain** **3**

crys|tal /krɪstᵊl/ (**crystals**)

1 **N-COUNT** A **crystal** is a small, hard piece of a natural substance such as salt or ice. ❑ *...salt crystals.* ❑ *...ice crystals.*

Word Web cry

Have you ever seen someone **burst into tears** when something wonderful happened to them? We expect people to **cry** when they are **sad** or upset. But why do people sometimes **weep** when they are happy? Scientists have found there are three different types of **tears**. Basal tears keep the **eyes** moist. Reflex tears clear the eyes of dirt or smoke. The third type, **emotional** tears, occur when people experience strong feelings, either good or bad. These tears have high levels of chemicals called manganese and prolactin. Decreasing the amount of these chemicals in the body helps us feel better. When people experience strong feelings, **shedding tears** may help restore emotional balance.

Word Web crystal

The outsides of **crystals** have smooth flat planes. These surfaces form because of the repeating patterns of atoms, molecules, or ions inside the crystal. Evaporation, temperature changes, and pressure can all help to form crystals. Crystals grow when sea water evaporates and leaves behind **salt**. When water freezes, **ice** crystals form. When melted rock cools, it becomes **rock** with a crystalline structure. Pressure can create one of the hardest, most beautiful crystals—the **diamond**.

---

2 N-COUNT/N-NONCOUNT SCIENCE **Crystal** is a transparent rock used in jewelry. ❑ *Liza wore a crystal necklace at her wedding.*
3 N-NONCOUNT Crystal is high-quality glass. ❑ *Their drinking glasses were made from crystal.* [from Old English]
→ look at Word Webs : **crystal, precipitation, rock, sugar**

crys|tal lat|tice /krɪstəl lætɪs/ (**crystal lattices**) **N-COUNT** SCIENCE A **crystal lattice** is a symmetrical arrangement of atoms within a crystal.

cub /kʌb/ (**cubs**) **N-COUNT** A **cub** is a young wild animal such as a bear. ❑ *...young lion cubs.* [from Old Norse]

cube /kyub/ (**cubes**) **N-COUNT** MATH A **cube** is a solid object with six square surfaces.
❑ *She took a tray of ice cubes from the freezer.*
❑ *He dropped two sugar cubes into his coffee.*
[from Latin]
→ look at Picture Dictionaries: **solids, volume**

cu|bic /kyubɪk/ **ADJ** MATH You use **cubic** to talk about units of volume. ❑ *They moved 3 billion cubic meters of earth.* [from Latin]

> **Word Link** cle ≈ small : article, cubicle, particle

cu|bi|cle /kyubɪkəl/ (**cubicles**) **N-COUNT** A **cubicle** is a very small enclosed area, for example, one where you can take a shower or change your clothes. ❑ *...a separate shower cubicle.* [from Latin]

cuck|oo /kuku, kuku/ (**cuckoos**) **N-COUNT** A **cuckoo** is a bird that has a call that sounds like "cuck-oo," and lays its eggs in other birds' nests. [from Old French]

cu|cum|ber /kyukʌmbər/ (**cucumbers**) **N-COUNT/N-NONCOUNT** A **cucumber** is a long dark-green vegetable that you eat raw. ❑ *We had cheese and cucumber sandwiches for lunch.* [from Latin]
→ look at Picture Dictionary: **vegetables**

cud|dle /kʌdəl/ (**cuddles, cuddling, cuddled**)
1 V-T/V-I If you **cuddle** someone, you put your arms around them and hold them close. ❑ *Everybody wanted to cuddle the baby.*
2 N-COUNT Cuddle is also a noun. ❑ *I just wanted to give him a cuddle.*

cud|dly /kʌdli/ (**cuddlier, cuddliest**) **ADJ** A **cuddly** person or animal looks soft and pleasant, and makes you want to put your arms around them. ❑ *...a big, cuddly teddy bear.*

cue /kyu/ (**cues**)
1 N-COUNT A **cue** is something that a performer says or does that is a signal for another performer to say or do something. ❑ *The actors sit at the side of the stage, waiting for their cues.*
2 N-COUNT A **cue** is an action or a statement that tells someone that they should do something. ❑ *The church bell struck eleven. That was my cue to leave.*
3 N-COUNT A **cue** is a long, thin wooden stick that you use to hit the ball across the table in some games. [from Latin]

cuff /kʌf/ (**cuffs**)
1 N-COUNT The **cuffs** of a shirt are the ends of the sleeves. ❑ *He was wearing a blue shirt with a white collar and white cuffs.*
2 N-COUNT The **cuffs** on a pair of pants are the ends of the legs that are folded up.

cult /kʌlt/ (**cults**)
1 N-COUNT A **cult** is a fairly small religious group, especially one which is considered strange.
2 ADJ Cult is used to describe things that are very popular or fashionable among a particular group. ❑ *The movie became a cult classic.* [from Latin]

cul|ti|vate /kʌltɪveɪt/ (**cultivates, cultivating, cultivated**) **V-T** If you **cultivate** land, you grow plants on it. ❑ *She cultivated a*

small garden of her own. [from Medieval Latin]
→ look at Word Webs: **farm, grain**

cul|tur|al /kʌltʃərəl/ **ADJ Cultural** means relating to the arts. ❏ *We've organized a range of sports and cultural events.* [from Old French]

cul|ture /kʌltʃər/ (**cultures**)

1 **N-NONCOUNT** ARTS **Culture** is activities such as art, music, literature, and theater. ❏ *Movies are part of our popular culture.*

2 **N-COUNT** SOCIAL STUDIES A **culture** is the way of life, and the traditions and beliefs of a particular group of people. ❏ *I live in the city among people from different cultures.* [from Old French]
→ look at Word Webs: **culture, myth**

Word Partnership	Use culture with :
ADJ	**ancient** culture, **popular** culture **1**
N	culture **and religion, richness of** culture, culture **shock, society and** culture **2**

cu|mu|lo|nim|bus /kyuːmyəlouˈnɪmbəs/ (**cumulonimbi** /kyuːmyəlouˈnɪmbaɪ/) also **cumulo-nimbus** **N-COUNT/N-NONCOUNT** SCIENCE **Cumulonimbus** is a type of cloud, similar to cumulus, that extends to a great height and is associated with thunderstorms.

cu|mu|lus /kyuːmyələs/ (**cumuli** /kyuːmyəlaɪ/) **N-COUNT/N-NONCOUNT** SCIENCE **Cumulus** is a type of thick white cloud formed when hot air rises very quickly. [from Latin]

cun|ning /kʌnɪŋ/ **ADJ** A **cunning** person is clever and possibly dishonest. ❏ *Police described the man as cunning and dangerous.* [from Old English]

cup /kʌp/ (**cups**)

1 **N-COUNT** A **cup** is a small round container that you drink from. ❏ *Let's have a cup of coffee.*

2 **N-COUNT** A **cup** is a measure of 16 tablespoons or 8 fluid ounces. ❏ *Gradually add 1 cup of milk.* ❏ *Add half a cup of sugar, and mix.*

3 **N-COUNT** A **cup** is a large round metal container that is given as a prize to the winner of a competition. ❏ *I think New Zealand will win the cup.*

4 **N-COUNT** **Cup** is used in the names of some competitions that have a cup as a prize. ❏ *...the Ryder Cup.* [from Old English]
→ look at Picture Dictionaries: **dish, kitchen utensils**
→ look at Word Web: **tea**

cup|board /kʌbərd/ (**cupboards**) **N-COUNT** A **cupboard** is a piece of furniture with doors, and shelves for storing food or dishes. ❏ *The kitchen cupboard was full of cans of soup.* [from Old English]

curb /kɜrb/ (**curbs, curbing, curbed**)

1 **N-COUNT** The **curb** is the edge of a sidewalk next to the road. ❏ *I pulled over to the curb.*

2 **V-T** If you **curb** something, you keep it within limits. ❏ *...advertisements aimed at curbing the spread of AIDS.* [from Old French]

cure /kyʊər/ (**cures, curing, cured**)

1 **V-T** If a doctor or a treatment **cures** someone or their illness, the person becomes well again. ❏ *The new medicine cured her headaches.* ❏ *Almost overnight I was cured.*

2 **V-T** If someone or something **cures** a problem, they bring it to an end. ❏ *We need to cure our economic problems.*

3 **N-COUNT** A **cure for** an illness is a treatment that makes the person well again. ❏ *There is still no cure for a cold.* [from Old French]

cur|few /kɜrfyu/ (**curfews**)
N-COUNT/N-NONCOUNT A **curfew** is a law stating that people must stay inside their houses after a particular time at night. ❑ *The village was placed under curfew.* [from Old French]

cu|ri|os|ity /kyuərɪɒsɪti/ **N-NONCOUNT**
Curiosity is a desire to know about something. ❑ *The children show a lot of curiosity about the past.* [from Latin]

cu|ri|ous /kyuəriəs/ **ADJ** If you are **curious about** something, you want to know more about it. ❑ *Steve was curious about the place I came from.* ● **cu|ri|ous|ly** **ADV** ❑ *The woman in the shop looked at them curiously.* [from Latin]

curl /kɜrl/ (**curls, curling, curled**)
1 **N-COUNT** If you have **curls**, your hair is shaped in curves. ❑ *She was talking to a little girl with blonde curls.*
2 **V-T/V-I** If your hair **curls** or if you **curl** it, it forms curved shapes. ❑ *Her hair curled around her shoulders.* ❑ *Maria curled her hair for the party.*
3 **V-T/V-I** If you **curl** something or it **curls**, it forms a round or curved shape. ❑ *Cook the prawns in a big pot until the tails curl.* [from Middle Dutch]
▶ **curl up** If you **curl up**, you move your head, arms, and legs close to your body. ❑ *She curled up next to him.*

curly /kɜrli/ (**curlier, curliest**) **ADJ** **Curly** hair is shaped in curves. ❑ *I've got naturally curly hair.* [from Middle Dutch]
→ look at Picture Dictionary: **hair**

cur|ren|cy /kɜrənsi/ (**currencies**) **N-COUNT/ N-NONCOUNT** SOCIAL STUDIES The money that is used in a particular country is its **currency**. ❑ *The plans were for a single European currency.* [from Medieval Latin]
→ look at Word Web: **money**

Word Link   curr, curs ≈ running, flowing : current, curriculum, excursion

cur|rent /kɜrənt/ (**currents**)
1 **N-COUNT** SCIENCE A **current** is a steady flow of water, air, or energy. ❑ *The fish move with the ocean currents.* ❑ *I felt a current of cool air.* ❑ *The wires carry a powerful electric current.*
2 **ADJ** **Current** events are happening now. ❑ *The current situation is different than the one in 1990.* ● **cur|rent|ly** **ADV** ❑ *He is currently unmarried.* [from Old French]
→ look at Word Webs: **beach, erosion, ocean, tide**

cur|rent elec|tric|ity **N-NONCOUNT** SCIENCE
Current electricity is electricity that is flowing through a circuit. Compare with **static**.

cur|ricu|lum /kərɪkyələm/ (**curriculums** or **curricula** /kərɪkyələ/)
1 **N-COUNT** A **curriculum** is all the courses of study that are taught in a school or college. ❑ *Business skills should be part of the school curriculum.*
2 **N-COUNT** A particular **curriculum** is one particular course of study. ❑ *...the history curriculum.* [from Latin]

cur|ry /kɜri/ (**curries**) **N-COUNT/N-NONCOUNT**
Curry is a dish, originally from Asia, that is cooked with hot spices. ❑ *Our favorite dish is the vegetable curry.* [from Tamil]

curse /kɜrs/ (**curses, cursing, cursed**)
1 **V-I** If you **curse**, you use very rude or offensive language. [WRITTEN] ❑ *Jake nodded, but he was cursing silently.*
2 **N-COUNT** **Curse** is also a noun. [FORMAL] ❑ *Shouts and curses came from all directions.*
3 **N-COUNT** A **curse** is a strange power that seems to cause unpleasant things to happen to someone. ❑ *He believed that an evil spirit put a curse on his business.* [from Old English]

cur|sor /kɜrsər/ (**cursors**) **N-COUNT**
TECHNOLOGY On a computer screen, the **cursor** is a small line that shows where you are working. ❑ *He moved the cursor and clicked the mouse.* [from Old English]

cur|tain /kɜrtⁿn/ (**curtains**)
1 **N-COUNT** **Curtains** are pieces of material that hang from the top of a window. ❑ *She closed her bedroom curtains.*
2 **N-SING** In a theater, **the curtain** is the large piece of material that hangs at the front of the stage until a performance begins. ❑ *The curtain fell, and the audience stood and applauded.* [from Old French]

cur|va|ture /kɜrvətʃər, -tʃuər/ **N-NONCOUNT**
SCIENCE The **curvature of** something is its curved shape, especially when this shape is part of the circumference of a circle. [from Latin]

curve /kɜrv/ (**curves, curving, curved**)
1 **N-COUNT** A **curve** is a smooth, bent line. ❑ *She carefully drew the curve of his lips.*
2 **V-I** If something **curves**, it has the shape of a curve or moves in a curve. ❑ *Her spine*

curved forward. ❑ *The ball curved through the air.* [from Latin]

curved /kɜrvd/ **ADJ** A **curved** object has the shape of a curve or has a smoothly bending surface. ❑ *...the curved lines of the chairs.*

cur|vi|lin|ear /kɜrvɪlɪliər/ **ADJ** MATH A **curvilinear** shape has curving lines. Compare with **rectilinear**.

cush|ion /kʊʃⁿn/ (**cushions**) **N-COUNT** A **cushion** is a bag of soft material that you put on a seat to make it more comfortable. ❑ *The cat lay on a velvet cushion.* [from Latin]

cus|tard /kʌstərd/ (**custards**) **N-COUNT/N-NONCOUNT Custard** is a sweet yellow dish made of milk, eggs, and sugar. ❑ *We had frozen custard for dessert.* [from Middle English] → look at Picture Dictionary: **dessert**

cus|to|dian /kʌstoʊdiən/ (**custodians**) **N-COUNT** The **custodian** of an office or a school is the person whose job is to take care of the building and the ground around it. ❑ *He worked as a school custodian for 20 years.* [from Latin]

cus|to|dy /kʌstədi/
1 N-NONCOUNT Custody is the legal right to keep and take care of a child, especially the right given to a child's mother or father when they get divorced. ❑ *I'm going to court to get custody of the children.*
2 PHRASE Someone who is **in custody** has been arrested and is being kept in prison. [from Latin]

cus|tom /kʌstəm/ (**customs**)
1 N-COUNT/N-NONCOUNT A **custom** is something that is usual or traditional among a particular group of people. ❑ *This is an ancient Japanese custom.* ❑ *It was the custom to give presents.*
2 ADJ A **custom** product is produced for a particular person. ❑ *...a supplier of custom cabinets for kitchens and bathrooms.* [from Old French]
3 → see also **customs**
→ look at Word Web: **culture**

cus|tom|er /kʌstəmər/ (**customers**) **N-COUNT** A **customer** is someone who buys something. ❑ *I was a very satisfied customer.* [from Old French]

Word Partnership	Use customer with :
N	customer **account**, customer **loyalty**, customer **satisfaction**
V	**greet** customers, **satisfy a** customer

cus|tom|er ser|vice **N-NONCOUNT** BUSINESS **Customer service** refers to the way that companies behave toward their customers, for example how well they treat them. ❑ *...a business with a strong reputation for customer service.*

cus|toms /kʌstəmz/
1 N-NONCOUNT Customs is the place at an airport, for example, where people have to show certain goods that they have bought abroad. ❑ *He walked through customs.* [from Old French]
2 → see also **custom**

cut /kʌt/ (**cuts, cutting, cut**)

LANGUAGE HELP
The form **cut** is used in the present tense and is the past tense and past participle.

1 V-T/V-I If you **cut** something, you use something sharp to remove part of it, or to break it. ❑ *Mrs. Haines cut the ribbon.* ❑ *Cut the tomatoes in half.* ❑ *You had your hair cut; it looks great.*
2 N-COUNT Cut is also a noun. ❑ *Carefully make a cut in the fabric.*
3 V-T If you **cut yourself**, you accidentally injure yourself on a sharp object so that you bleed. ❑ *I started to cry because I cut my finger.*
4 N-COUNT Cut is also a noun. ❑ *He had a cut on his left eyebrow.*
5 V-T If you **cut** something, you reduce it. ❑ *We need to cut costs.*
6 N-COUNT Cut is also a noun. ❑ *The government announced a 2% cut in interest rates.*
7 V-T If you **cut** part of a piece of writing or a performance, you do not publish or perform that part of it. ❑ *Branagh has cut the play a little.*

8 N-COUNT Cut is also a noun. ❑ *It was necessary to make some cuts in the text.*

9 V-I If you **cut across** or **through** a place, you go through it because it is the shortest route. ❑ *Jesse cut across the parking lot.*

10 V-T To **cut** a supply of something means to stop providing it. ❑ *Winds have knocked down power lines, cutting electricity to thousands of people.* [of Scandinavian origin]

11 → see also **cutting**

→ look at Picture Dictionary: **cut**

▶ **cut back** If you **cut back** something or **cut back on** it, you reduce it. ❑ *Customers have cut back spending.*

▶ **cut down 1** If you **cut down on** something, you use or do less of it. ❑ *He cut down on coffee.*

2 If you **cut down** a tree, you cut through it so that it falls to the ground. ❑ *They cut down several trees.*

▶ **cut off 1** If you **cut** something **off**, you remove it using scissors or a knife. ❑ *Mrs. Johnson cut off a large piece of meat.*

2 To **cut off** a supply of something means to stop providing it. ❑ *They have cut off the electricity.*

▶ **cut out** If you **cut** something **out**, you remove it using scissors or a knife. ❑ *I cut the picture out and stuck it on my wall.*

▶ **cut up** If you **cut** something **up**, you cut it into several pieces. ❑ *Cut up the tomatoes.*

Thesaurus	cut	Also look up :
v	carve, slice, trim **1**	
	graze, nick, stab **2**	
	decrease, lower, reduce;	
	(ant.) increase **1 3**	
N	gash, incision, slit **1**	
	gash, nick, wound **2**	

cut and paste (**cuts and pastes, cutting and pasting, cut and pasted**) **V-T** TECHNOLOGY When you **cut and paste** words or pictures on a computer, you remove them from one place and copy them to another place. ❑ *You can cut and paste words, phrases, sentences, or even paragraphs from one part of your document to another.*

cute /kyut/ (**cuter, cutest**) **ADJ** A **cute** person or thing is pretty or attractive. [INFORMAL] ❑ *Oh, look at that dog! He's so cute.* ❑ *I thought that girl was really cute.*

Thesaurus	cute	Also look up :
ADJ	adorable, charming, pretty;	
	(ant.) homely, ugly **1**	

cu|ti|cle /kyutɪkəl/ (**cuticles**) **N-COUNT/N-NONCOUNT** SCIENCE **Cuticle** is a protective covering on the surface of leaves and other parts of a plant. [from Latin]

cut|lery /kʌtləri/ **N-NONCOUNT Cutlery** is knives, forks, and spoons. ❑ *We had to eat our breakfast with plastic cutlery.* [from French]

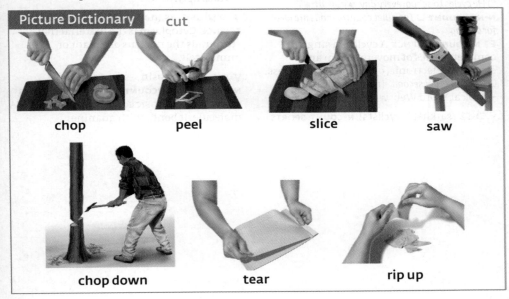

Picture Dictionary cut

chop   peel   slice   saw

chop down   tear   rip up

cut|ting /kʌtɪŋ/ (**cuttings**)

■ **N-COUNT** A **cutting** is a part of a plant that you have cut off so that you can grow a new plant from it. ❑ *Take cuttings from garden tomatoes in late summer.*

■ **ADJ** A **cutting** remark is unkind and hurts your feelings. ❑ *People make cutting remarks to help themselves feel superior.* [of Scandinavian origin]

■ → see also **cut**

cyano|bac|te|ria /saɪənoʊbæktɪəriə/ **N-PLURAL** SCIENCE **Cyanobacteria** are bacteria that obtain their energy through photosynthesis.

cy|ber|bul|ly|ing /saɪbərbʊliɪŋ/ **N-NONCOUNT** TECHNOLOGY **Cyberbullying** is a way of frightening or upsetting someone by sending them unpleasant messages using the Internet. ❑ *More than half of the children said that they had experienced cyberbullying at some point.*

cy|ber|space /saɪbərspeɪs/ **N-NONCOUNT** TECHNOLOGY **Cyberspace** is the imaginary place where electronic communications take place. ❑ *Our cyberspace communications started in an Internet chat room.*

Word Link	cycl ≈ circle : bicycle, cycle, recycle

cy|cle /saɪkəl/ (**cycles, cycling, cycled**)

■ **N-COUNT** SCIENCE A **cycle** is a process that is repeated again and again. ❑ *We are studying the life cycle of the plant.*

■ **V-I** SPORTS If you **cycle**, you ride a bicycle. ❑ *He cycles to school every day.* ● **cy|cling** **N-NONCOUNT** ❑ *The quiet country roads are ideal for cycling.*

■ **N-COUNT** SCIENCE A **cycle** is a single complete series of movements in an electrical, electronic, or mechanical process. ❑ *...10 cycles per second.* [from Late Latin]

→ look at Word Web: **water**

cy|clist /saɪklɪst/ (**cyclists**) **N-COUNT** SPORTS A **cyclist** is someone who rides a bicycle. ❑ *We must have better protection for cyclists.* [from Late Latin]

→ look at Word Web: **park**

cy|clone /saɪkloʊn/ (**cyclones**) **N-COUNT** SCIENCE A **cyclone** is a violent tropical storm in which the air goes around and around. ❑ *The race was called off as a cyclone struck.* [from Greek]

→ look at Word Web: **hurricane**

cyl|in|der /sɪlɪndər/ (**cylinders**) **N-COUNT** MATH A **cylinder** is a shape or a container with circular ends and long straight sides. ❑ *Never store or change gas cylinders near a flame.* [from Latin]

→ look at Picture Dictionaries: **solid, volume**

→ look at Word Web: **engine**

cym|bal /sɪmbəl/ (**cymbals**) **N-COUNT** MUSIC A **cymbal** is a flat, round, metal musical instrument that makes a loud noise when you hit it, or when you hit two of them together. [from Old English]

cyni|cal /sɪnɪkəl/ **ADJ** A **cynical** person believes that people are usually bad or dishonest. ❑ *He has a cynical view of the world.* ● **cyni|cal|ly** **ADV** ❑ *He laughed cynically.* [from Latin]

cy|to|ki|nesis /saɪtoʊkɪnisɪs/ **N-NONCOUNT** SCIENCE **Cytokinesis** is the stage in cell division at which the cytoplasm of the cell divides in two.

cyto|plasm /saɪtəplæzəm/ **N-NONCOUNT** SCIENCE **Cytoplasm** is the material that surrounds the nucleus of a plant or animal cell.

cyto|sine /saɪtəsin, -sɪn/ (**cytosines**) **N-COUNT/N-NONCOUNT** SCIENCE **Cytosine** is one of the four basic components of the DNA molecule. It bonds with guanine.

Dd

dad /dæd/ (**dads**) **N-COUNT** Your **dad** is your father. [INFORMAL] ❑ *Don't tell my mom and dad about this!* [from Greek]

dad|dy /dædi/ (**daddies**) **N-COUNT** Children often call their father **daddy**. [INFORMAL] ❑ *Look at me, Daddy!* ❑ *My daddy always reads me stories and helps me with my homework.* [from Greek]

daf|fo|dil /dæfədɪl/ (**daffodils**) **N-COUNT** A **daffodil** is a yellow flower with a long stem that appears in spring. [from Dutch]

dai|ly /deɪli/
1 **ADV** Something that happens **daily** happens every day. ❑ *The students use this dictionary almost daily.*
2 **ADJ** **Daily** is also an adjective. ❑ *The French daily newspaper "Le Monde" was first to report the story.*
3 **PHRASE** Your **daily life** is the things that you do every day as part of your normal life. ❑ *Laughter was part of their daily life then.* [from Old English]

dain|ty /deɪnti/ (**daintier, daintiest**) **ADJ** A **dainty** movement, person, or object is small, delicate, and pretty. ❑ *Did she walk here in her dainty little shoes?* ● **dain|ti|ly** **ADV** ❑ *She walked daintily down the steps.* [from Old French]

dairy /dɛəri/ (**dairies**)
1 **N-COUNT** A **dairy** is a place where milk, and food made from milk, such as butter, cream, and cheese are produced.
2 **ADJ** **Dairy** is used for talking about foods such as butter and cheese that are made from milk. ❑ *He can't eat dairy products.* [from Old English]
→ look at Word Web: **dairy**

dai|sy /deɪzi/ (**daisies**) **N-COUNT** A **daisy** is a small wild flower with a yellow center and white petals. [from Old English]

dam /dæm/ (**dams**) **N-COUNT** A **dam** is a wall that is built across a river in order to make a lake. ❑ *Before the dam was built, the Campbell River often flooded.* [from Middle Low German]
→ look at Word Web: **dam**

dam|age /dæmɪdʒ/ (**damages, damaging, damaged**)
1 **V-T** To **damage** something means to break it or harm it. ❑ *He damaged a car with a baseball bat.* ❑ *The new tax will badly damage Australian industries.* ● **dam|ag|ing** **ADJ** ❑ *We can see the damaging effects of pollution in cities.*
2 **N-NONCOUNT** **Damage** is physical harm that happens to an object. ❑ *The explosion caused a lot of damage to the house.*
3 **N-PLURAL** If a court of law awards **damages** to someone, it orders money to be paid to them by a person who has damaged their property, or who has injured them. ❑ *She won more than $75,000 in damages.* [from Old French]
→ look at Word Web: **disaster**

Word Web   dairy

Farmers no longer **milk** one **cow** at a time. Today most dairy **farms** use machines instead. The **milk** is taken from the cow by a vacuum-powered **milking machine**. Then it travels through a pipeline to be stored in a **refrigerated** storage tank. From there it goes to the factory for pasteurization and packaging. The largest such dairy farm in the world is the Modern Dairy Company in China with around 40,000 head of **cattle**. An even bigger dairy farm, with possibly 100,000 cows, is currently being built in China.

Word Web   dam

The Egyptians built the world's first **dam** in about 2900 BC. The dam sent water into a **reservoir** near the capital city of Memphis*. Later they built another dam to prevent **flooding** south of Cairo*. Today, dams are used with **irrigation** systems to prevent **droughts**. Modern **hydroelectric** dams also provide more than 20% of the world's electricity. The world's largest hydroelectric power station is the Three Gorges Dam in China. It took 18 years to build! Hydroelectric power is non-polluting. However, the dams endanger some species of fish and sometimes destroy valuable forest lands.

Memphis: an ancient city in Egypt.
Cairo: the capital of Egypt.

Thesaurus   damage   Also look up :

V	break, harm, hurt, ruin, wreck **1**
N	harm, loss **2**

damn /dæm/ (**damns, damning, damned**)
V-T To **damn** someone or something means to criticize them severely. ❑ *His report damns the proposed law.* [from Old French]

damp /dæmp/ (**damper, dampest**) **ADJ**
Something that is **damp** is slightly wet. ❑ *Her hair was still damp.* ❑ *We went out into the damp, cold air.* [from Middle Low German]
→ look at Word Web: **weather**

dance /dæns/ (**dances, dancing, danced**)
1 **V-I** ARTS When you **dance**, you move your body to music. ❑ *She turned on the radio and danced around the room.* ● **danc|ing**
N-NONCOUNT ❑ *Let's go dancing tonight.*
2 **N-COUNT** ARTS A **dance** is a particular series of movements that you usually do in time to music. ❑ *...a traditional Scottish dance.*
3 **N-NONCOUNT** ARTS **Dance** is the activity of performing dances. ❑ *...international dance and music.*
4 **N-COUNT** A **dance** is a party where people dance with each other. ❑ *At the school dance he talked to her all evening.*
5 **V-T/V-I** ARTS When you **dance with** someone, you take part in a dance together. You can also say that two people **dance**. ❑ *Nobody wanted to dance with him.* ❑ *Shall we dance?* [from Old French]
→ look at Picture Dictionary: **dance**

Picture Dictionary   dance

dancing

folk dancing

tap dancing

ballroom dancing

modern dance

ballet

dance form (**dance forms**) **N-COUNT** ARTS
A **dance form** is a type of dancing, such as
ballet or tap dancing.

dance phrase (**dance phrases**) **N-COUNT**
ARTS A **dance phrase** is a short section of a
dance consisting of a series of
interconnected movements.

danc|er /dǽnsər/ (**dancers**) **N-COUNT** ARTS
A **dancer** is a person who earns money by
dancing, or a person who is dancing.
❑ She's a dancer with the New York City Ballet.
[from Old French]

dance se|quence (**dance sequences**)
N-COUNT ARTS A **dance sequence** is a section
of a dance that develops a particular theme
or idea.

dance struc|ture (**dance structures**)
N-COUNT/N-NONCOUNT ARTS Dance **structure**
is the general way in which a dance is
organized and the way that the parts of the
dance relate to one another.

dance study (**dance studies**)
N-COUNT/N-NONCOUNT ARTS A **dance study** is
a series of movements that a dance teacher
or student performs in order to develop an
idea for a dance.

dan|de|lion /dǽndɪlaɪən/ (**dandelions**)
N-COUNT A **dandelion** is a wild plant with
yellow flowers that turn into balls of soft
white seeds. [from Old French]

dan|ger /déɪndʒər/ (**dangers**)
1 **N-NONCOUNT** If you are **in danger**, it is
possible that something unpleasant will
happen, or that you may be harmed or
killed. ❑ I'm worried. I think Mary's in danger.
2 **N-COUNT** A **danger** is something or
someone that can hurt or harm you. ❑ They
warned us about the dangers of driving too fast.
3 **N-SING** If there is a **danger that**
something unpleasant will happen, it is
possible that it will happen. ❑ There is a real
danger that this crisis will spread across the country.
[from Old French]
→ look at Word Web: **hero**

dan|ger|ous /déɪndʒərəs, déɪndʒrəs/ **ADJ** If
something is **dangerous**, it may harm you.
❑ We are in a very dangerous situation. ❑ He owns a
dangerous dog. ● **dan|ger|ous|ly** **ADV** ❑ He is
dangerously ill. [from Old French]

dan|gle /dǽŋgəl/ (**dangles, dangling,
dangled**) **V-T/V-I** If something **dangles from**
somewhere or if you **dangle** it somewhere, it
hangs or swings loosely. ❑ A gold bracelet
dangled from his left wrist. [from Danish]

dare /déər/ (**dares, daring, dared**)
1 **V-T** If you **dare to** do something, you are
brave enough to do it. ❑ Most people don't dare
to disagree with Harry.
2 **MODAL** Dare is also a modal verb. ❑ She
dare not leave the house.
3 **V-T** If you **dare** someone **to** do something,
you ask them if they will do it in order to see
if they are brave enough. ❑ His friends dared
him to ask Mr. Roberts for the money.
4 **N-COUNT** A **dare** is a challenge that one
person gives to another to do something
dangerous or frightening. ❑ Jones stole the car
on a dare.
5 **PHRASE** You say **How dare you** to someone
when you are very angry about something
that they have done. [SPOKEN] ❑ How dare you
say that about my mother! [from Old English]

dar|ing /déərɪŋ/ **ADJ** A **daring** person is
willing to do things that might be
dangerous or shocking. ❑ He made a daring
escape from the island in a small boat. [from
Old English]

dark /dɑ́rk/ (**darker, darkest**)
1 **ADJ** When it is **dark**, there is not much
light. ❑ It was too dark to see much. ● **dark|ness**
N-NONCOUNT ❑ The light went out, and we were in
total darkness. ● **dark|ly** **ADV** ❑ ...a darkly lit hall.
2 **ADJ** When it gets **dark**, night comes.
❑ People shut the curtains when it gets dark.
3 **ADJ** Something **dark** is black or a color
close to black. ❑ He wore a dark suit. ❑ ...a dark

D

blue dress. ● **dark|ly ADV** ❏ *His skin was darkly tanned.*

4 ADJ If someone has **dark** hair, eyes, or skin, they have brown or black hair, eyes, or skin. ❏ *He had dark, curly hair.*

5 N-SING The **dark** is the lack of light in a place. ❏ *Children are often afraid of the dark.* [from Old English]

Word Partnership	Use **dark** with :
V	**get** dark **1**
	afraid of the dark, **scared of the** dark **5**
N	dark **clouds**, dark **suit 2**

dar|ling /dɑrlɪŋ/

1 You call someone **darling** if you love them or like them very much. ❏ *Thank you, darling.*

2 ADJ Darling describes someone or something that you like very much. [INFORMAL] ❏ *They have a darling baby boy.* [from Old English]

dart /dɑrt/ (**darts, darting, darted**)

1 V-I If a person or animal **darts** somewhere, they move there suddenly and quickly. [WRITTEN] ❏ *Ingrid darted across the street.*

2 N-COUNT A **dart** is a small, narrow object with a sharp point that you can throw or shoot.

3 N-NONCOUNT SPORTS **Darts** is a game in which you throw darts at a round board that has numbers on it. ❏ *I enjoy playing darts.* [from Old French]

dash /dæʃ/ (**dashes, dashing, dashed**)

1 V-I If you **dash** somewhere, you go there quickly and suddenly. ❏ *She dashed downstairs when the doorbell rang.*

2 N-SING If you **make** a **dash** for a place, you go there quickly and suddenly. ❏ *She screamed and made a dash for the door.*

3 N-COUNT LANGUAGE ARTS A **dash** is a short, straight, horizontal line that you use in writing. ❏ *Sometimes people use a dash (—) where they could use a colon (:).*

4 V-T If an event or person **dashes** your hopes, it destroys them by making something impossible. [LITERARY] ❏ *The fighting dashed hopes for a return to peace.* [from Middle English]

dash|board /dæʃbɔrd/ (**dashboards**)
N-COUNT The **dashboard** in a car is the area in front of the driver where most of the controls are. ❏ *The clock on the dashboard showed two o'clock.*

da|ta /deɪtə, dætə/

1 N-PLURAL You can talk about information as **data**, especially when it is in the form of facts or numbers. ❏ *Government data shows that unemployment is going up.*

2 N-NONCOUNT TECHNOLOGY **Data** is information that can be used by a computer program. ❏ *These hard drives can hold huge amounts of data.* [from Latin]
→ look at Word Web: **forecast**

Thesaurus	data	Also look up :
N	facts, figures, information, results, statistics **1**	

data|base /deɪtəbeɪs, dætə-/ (**databases**)
also **data base N-COUNT** TECHNOLOGY A **database** is a collection of data that is stored in a computer and that can easily be used and added to. ❏ *There is a database of names of people who are allowed to vote.*

da|ta ta|ble (**data tables**) **N-COUNT** SCIENCE A **data table** is a chart containing a set of data.

date /deɪt/ (**dates, dating, dated**)

1 N-COUNT A **date** is a particular day and month or a particular year. ❏ *"What's the date today?"—"July 23."*

2 N-COUNT A **date** is an arrangement to meet a boyfriend or a girlfriend. ❏ *I have a date with Bob tonight.*

3 V-T/V-I If you **are dating** someone, you go out with them regularly because you are having a romantic relationship with them. ❏ *I dated a woman who was a teacher.*

4 N-COUNT Your **date** is someone that you have arranged to meet as part of a romantic relationship ❏ *His date was one of the girls in the show.*

5 V-T When you **date** a letter or an agreement, you write that day's date on it. ❏ *Please sign and date the agreement, and send one copy back to us.*

6 N-COUNT A **date** is a small, dark-brown, sticky fruit with a pit inside. [from Old French]
→ look at Word Web: **fossil**

▶ **date back** If something **dates back to** a particular time, it started at that time. ❏ *The problem is not a new one. It dates back to the* 1930s.

daugh|ter /dɔtər/ (**daughters**) **N-COUNT**
Someone's **daughter** is their female child. ❏ *We met Flora and her daughter Catherine.*

❑ She's the daughter of a university professor. [from Old English]
→ look at Word Web: **child**

daugh|ter cell (daughter cells) **N-COUNT**
SCIENCE A **daughter cell** is one of the two cells that are formed when a single cell divides.

daught|er-in-law (daughters-in-law)
N-COUNT Someone's **daughter-in-law** is the wife of their son.

dawn /dɔn/ (dawns, dawning, dawned)
1 **N-COUNT/N-NONCOUNT** Dawn is the time of day when the sky becomes light in the morning. ❑ Nancy woke at dawn.
2 **N-SING** The dawn of a period of time is the beginning of it. [LITERARY] ❑ ...the dawn of a new age in computing. [from Old English]
▶ **dawn on** or **dawn upon** If a fact or an idea **dawns on** you, you become aware of it. ❑ It slowly dawned on me that I was trapped.

day /deɪ/ (days)
1 **N-COUNT** A **day** is one period of twenty-four hours. There are seven days in a week. ❑ They'll be back in three days. ❑ It snowed every day last week.
2 **N-COUNT/N-NONCOUNT** The **day** is the time when it is light outside. ❑ We spent the day watching tennis. ❑ The streets are busy during the day.
3 **N-COUNT** You can call a particular period in history or in the future a **day**. ❑ ...the most famous artist of his day. ❑ I look forward to the day when I can buy my own apartment.
4 **PHRASE** One day or some day means at some time in the future. ❑ I dream of living in Dallas some day. ❑ I hope one day you will find someone who will make you happy. [from Old English]
→ look at Word Web: **year**

day|dream /deɪdrim/ (daydreams, daydreaming, daydreamed)
1 **V-I** If you **daydream**, you think about pleasant things for a period of time. ❑ I was daydreaming about a job in France.
2 **N-COUNT** A **daydream** is a series of pleasant thoughts, usually about things that you would like to happen. ❑ She was looking out the window in a daydream.

Word Link	light ≈ shining : day**light**, moon**light**, sun**light**

day|light /deɪlaɪt/ **N-NONCOUNT** Daylight is the natural light that there is during the day. ❑ A little daylight came through a crack in the wall.

day|time /deɪtaɪm/ **N-SING** The **daytime** is the part of a day between the time when it gets light and the time when it gets dark. ❑ He rarely went anywhere in the daytime; he was always out at night.

day-to-day **ADJ** Day-to-day things or activities exist or happen every day as part of ordinary life. ❑ I pay our day-to-day expenses in cash.

dead /dɛd/
1 **ADJ** A person, animal, or plant that is **dead** has stopped living. ❑ She told me her husband was dead. ❑ They put the dead body into the ambulance.
2 **N-PLURAL** The dead are people who have died. ❑ Two soldiers were among the dead.
3 **ADJ** A piece of electrical equipment that is **dead** has stopped working. ❑ I answered the phone and the line went dead.
4 **ADJ** Dead means "complete," especially before the words "center," "silence," and "stop." ❑ They watched in dead silence. [from Old English]

Thesaurus	dead	Also look up :
ADJ	deceased, lifeless; (ant.) alive, living **1**	

dead|line /dɛdlaɪn/ (deadlines) **N-COUNT**
A **deadline** is a time or a date before which a piece of work must be finished. ❑ We missed the deadline because of several problems.

dead|ly /dɛdli/ (deadlier, deadliest) **ADJ** If something is **deadly**, it can kill a person or animal. ❑ This deadly disease killed 70 people in Malaysia last year. [from Old English]

deaf /dɛf/ (deafer, deafest)
1 **ADJ** Someone who is **deaf** is unable to hear anything, or is unable to hear very well. ❑ She is now totally deaf.
2 **N-PLURAL** The deaf are people who are deaf. ❑ Marianne works as a part-time teacher for the deaf. [from Old English]
→ look at Word Web: **disability**

deaf|en /dɛfən/ (deafens, deafening, deafened) **V-T** If a noise **deafens** you, it is so loud that you cannot hear anything else. ❑ The noise of the engine deafened her. [from Old English]

deaf|en|ing /dɛfənɪŋ/ **ADJ** A **deafening** noise is a very loud noise. ❑ All we could hear was the deafening sound of gunfire. [from Old English]

deal /diːl/ (**deals, dealing, dealt**)

1 **N-COUNT** BUSINESS If you **make** a **deal**, you make an agreement with someone, especially in business. ❑ *They made a deal to share the money between them.*

2 **V-I** BUSINESS If a company **deals in** a type of goods, it buys or sells those goods. ❑ *They deal in antiques.* ● **deal|er** (**dealers**) **N-COUNT** ❑ *...an antique dealer.*

3 **V-T** If you **deal** playing cards, you give them out to the players in a game of cards. ❑ *She dealt each player a card.*

4 **Deal out** means the same as **deal**. ❑ *Dalton dealt out five cards to each player.*

5 **PHRASE** If you have **a great deal of** a particular thing, you have a lot of it. ❑ *You can earn a great deal of money in this job.* [from Old English]

▶ **deal with** **1** When you **deal with** something or someone, you give your attention to them. ❑ *Could you deal with this customer, please?*

2 If you **deal with** a particular person or organization, you have business relations with them. ❑ *When I worked in Florida I dealt with tourists all the time.*

3 If a book, a speech, or a movie **deals with** a particular thing, it has that thing as its subject. ❑ *This is a sad story dealing with love and grief.*

deal|ings /diːlɪŋz/ **N-PLURAL** Someone's **dealings with** a person or an organization are the relations that they have with them or the business that they do with them. ❑ *He has learned little in his dealings with the community.* [from Old English]

dear /dɪər/ (**dearer, dearest**)

1 **ADJ** **Dear** describes someone that you love. ❑ *Mrs. Cavendish is a dear friend of mine.*

2 **ADJ** You write **Dear** at the beginning of a letter or an email, followed by the name of the person you are writing to. ❑ *Dear Peter, How are you?* ❑ *Dear Sir or Madam...* [from Old English]

death /dɛθ/ (**deaths**)

1 **N-COUNT/N-NONCOUNT** **Death** is the end of the life of a person or an animal. ❑ *1.5 million people are in danger of death from hunger.* ❑ *It's the thirtieth anniversary of her death.*

2 **PHRASE** If you say that something is a **matter of life and death**, you mean that it is very important, and people should act immediately. ❑ *Never mind, John, it's not a matter of life and death.*

3 **PHRASE** You use **to death** after adjectives such as "scared" and "bored" to show that the feeling is very strong. ❑ *I was scared to death watching him climbing the cliff.* [from Old English]

Word Partnership	Use **death** with :
ADJ	**accidental** death, **sudden** death, **violent** death **1**
N	**brush with** death, **cause of** death, death **threat**, *someone's* death **1**

de|bate /dɪbeɪt/ (**debates, debating, debated**)

1 **N-COUNT/N-NONCOUNT** A **debate** is a long discussion or argument. ❑ *The debate will continue until they vote on Thursday.* ❑ *There has been a lot of debate among teachers about this subject.*

2 **V-T/V-I** If people **debate** a topic, they discuss it. ❑ *The committee will debate the issue today.* ❑ *They were debating which team would win.* [from Old French]

→ look at Word Web: **election**

Word Partnership	Use **debate** with :
V	**open to** debate **1**
ADJ	**major** debate, **ongoing** debate, **televised** debate **2** **political** debate, **presidential** debate **2**
N	debate **over** *something*, debate **the issue 2**

deb|it card /dɛbɪt kɑrd/ (**debit cards**) **N-COUNT** A **debit card** is a bank card that you can use to pay for things.

de|bris /dəbriː, deɪ-/ **N-NONCOUNT** **Debris** is pieces from something that has been destroyed. ❑ *Debris from the plane was found over an area the size of a soccer field.* [from French]

debt /dɛt/ (**debts**)

1 **N-COUNT/N-NONCOUNT** A **debt** is an amount of money that you owe someone. ❑ *He is still paying off his debts.*

2 **PHRASE** If you are **in debt**, or if you get **into debt**, you owe money. ❑ *Many students get into debt.* [from Old French]

Word Partnership	Use **debt** with :
V	**incur** debt, **pay off** a debt, **reduce** debt, **repay** a debt **1**
ADV	**deeply in** debt **2**

de|but /deɪbyuː/ (**debuts**) **N-COUNT** The **debut** of a performer or a sports player is their first public performance, appearance, or recording. ❑ *She made her debut in a 1937 production of "Hamlet."* [from French]

dec|ade /dɛkeɪd/ (**decades**) **N-COUNT**
A **decade** is a period of ten years. ❑ *She spent a decade studying in San Francisco.* [from Old French]

de|cay /dɪkeɪ/ (**decays, decaying, decayed**)
1 **V-I** When something **decays**, it is gradually destroyed by a natural process. ❑ *The bodies slowly decayed.*
2 **N-NONCOUNT** Decay is also a noun. ❑ *Eating too much candy causes tooth decay.* [from Old Northern French]
→ look at Word Web: **teeth**

de|ceased /dɪsist/ (**deceased**)
1 **N-SING/N-PLURAL** The deceased is used to refer to a particular person or to particular people who have recently died. [FORMAL] ❑ *Police will inform the families of the deceased.*
2 **ADJ** A **deceased** person is one who has recently died. [FORMAL] ❑ *...his recently deceased mother.* [from Old French]

de|ceive /dɪsiv/ (**deceives, deceiving, deceived**) **V-T** If you **deceive** someone, you make them believe something that is not true. ❑ *She accused the government of trying to deceive the public.* [from Old French]

De|cem|ber /dɪsɛmbər/ (**Decembers**) **N-COUNT/N-NONCOUNT** December is the twelfth and last month of the year. ❑ *I arrived on a bright morning in December.* [from Old French]

de|cent /disənt/
1 **ADJ** Decent describes something that is acceptable or good enough. ❑ *He didn't get a decent explanation.* ● **de|cent|ly** **ADV** ❑ *They treated their prisoners decently.*
2 **ADJ** Decent describes something that is morally right or polite. ❑ *It was very decent of him to call and explain.* [from Latin]

de|cep|tion /dɪsɛpʃən/ **N-NONCOUNT** Deception is when someone deliberately makes you believe something that is not true. ❑ *Lies and deception are not a good way to start a marriage.* [from Old French]

de|cep|tive /dɪsɛptɪv/ **ADJ** If something is **deceptive**, it makes you believe something that is not true. ❑ *The ocean looked warm, but appearances can be deceptive.* ● **de|cep|tive|ly** **ADV** ❑ *The atmosphere in the hall was deceptively peaceful.* [from Old French]

de|cide /dɪsaɪd/ (**decides, deciding, decided**)
1 **V-T/V-I** If you **decide** to do something, you choose to do it after thinking about it. ❑ *She decided to take a course in philosophy.* ❑ *Think about it very carefully before you decide.*
2 **V-T** If a person or a group of people **decides** something, they choose what something should be like. ❑ *Schools need to decide the best way of testing students.*
3 **V-T** If an event or a fact **decides** a particular result, it makes it certain that there will be a particular result. ❑ *This goal decided the game.*
4 **V-T** If you **decide** that something is true, you form that opinion about it. ❑ *He decided Franklin was suffering from a bad cold.* [from Old French]
▶ **decide on** If you **decide on** something, you choose it from two or more possibilities. ❑ *Have you decided on a name for the baby?*

Thesaurus	decide	Also look up :
V	choose, elect, pick, select **1** **2**	

Word Partnership	Use decide with :
V	**help (to)** decide, **let** *someone* decide, **try to** decide **1** **2**
ADJ	**unable to** decide **1** **2** **4**

de|cidu|ous /dɪsɪdʒuəs/ **ADJ** **SCIENCE** A **deciduous** tree or bush is one that loses its leaves in the fall every year. [from Latin]
→ look at Picture Dictionary: **plants**
→ look at Word Web: **tree**

deci|mal /dɛsɪməl/ (**decimals**)
1 **N-COUNT** **MATH** A **decimal** is part of a number that is written in the form of a dot followed by one or more numbers. ❑ *The interest rate is shown as a decimal, such as 0.10, which means 10%.*
2 **ADJ** **MATH** A **decimal** system involves counting in units of ten. ❑ *The mathematics of ancient Egypt used a decimal system.* [from Medieval Latin]
→ look at Picture Dictionary: **fractions**

deci|mal point (**decimal points**) **N-COUNT** **MATH** A **decimal point** is the dot that you use when you write a number as a decimal. ❑ *A waiter forgot to put the decimal point in the $13.09 bill.*

de|ci|sion /dɪsɪʒən/ (**decisions**) **N-COUNT** When you make a **decision**, you choose what to do. ❑ *I don't want to make the wrong decision and regret it later.* [from Old French]

d

Word Partnership Use **decision** with :

V   **arrive at a** decision, **make a** decision, **postpone a** decision, **reach a** decision

ADJ   **difficult** decision, **final** decision, **important** decision, **right** decision, **wise** decision, **wrong** decision

D

de|ci|sive /dɪsaɪsɪv/
1 ADJ If a fact, action, or event is **decisive**, it makes certain a particular result. □ ...his decisive victory in the presidential elections. ● **de|ci|sive|ly ADV** □ The plan was decisively rejected by Congress.
2 ADJ If someone is **decisive**, they have or show an ability to make quick decisions in a difficult or complicated situation. □ He was a decisive leader. ● **de|ci|sive|ly ADV** □ "I'll call you at ten," she said decisively. ● **de|ci|sive|ness N-NONCOUNT** □ His supporters admire his decisiveness. [from Old French]

deck /dɛk/ (**decks**)
1 N-COUNT A **deck** on a vehicle such as a bus or a ship is a lower or upper level in it. □ We went on a luxury ship with five passenger decks.
2 N-COUNT A **deck** is a flat wooden area attached to a house, where people can sit. □ A deck leads into the main room of the home.
3 N-COUNT A **deck** of cards is a complete set of playing cards. □ Matt picked up the cards and shuffled the deck. [from Middle Dutch]
→ look at Word Web: **ship**

dec|la|ra|tion /dɛkləreɪʃⁿn/ (**declarations**)
N-COUNT A **declaration** is something that is said officially. □ We consider these attacks to be a declaration of war. [from Latin]

Dec|la|ra|tion of In|de|pend|ence
N-PROPER SOCIAL STUDIES The **Declaration of Independence** is the official document of July 4, 1776, that stated that thirteen American colonies (= areas where British people went to live) were no longer ruled by Great Britain.

de|clara|tive /dɪklɛərətɪv/ **ADJ**
LANGUAGE ARTS A **declarative** sentence is a sentence that expresses a statement, for example "My car is blue." [from Latin]

Word Link clar ≈ clear : clarify, clarity, declare

de|clare /dɪklɛər/ (**declares, declaring, declared**)
1 V-T If you **declare** that something is true, you say that it is true in a firm, clear way.

[WRITTEN] □ Melinda declared that she was leaving home.
2 V-T If you **declare** something, you officially state that it is the case. □ The president finally declared an end to the war. □ The judges declared Mr. Stevens innocent.
3 V-T If you **declare** goods that you have bought in another country, you say how much you have bought so that you can pay tax on it. □ Please declare all food, plants, and animal products. [from Latin]

Word Link clin ≈ leaning : anticline, decline, incline

de|cline /dɪklaɪn/ (**declines, declining, declined**)
1 V-I If something **declines**, it becomes less in amount, importance, or strength. □ The local population is declining.
2 V-T/V-I If you **decline** something, you politely refuse to accept it. [FORMAL] □ He declined their invitation. □ He offered the boys some coffee. They declined politely.
3 N-COUNT/N-NONCOUNT If there is a **decline in** something, it becomes less in quantity, importance, or quality. □ Official records show a sharp decline in the number of foreign tourists. [from Old French]

de|cod|ing /dikoʊdɪŋ/ **N-NONCOUNT**
LANGUAGE ARTS **Decoding** is the process that is involved in understanding the meaning of a written word.

de|com|pose /dikəmpoʊz/ (**decomposes, decomposing, decomposed**) **V-T/V-I** SCIENCE When things such as dead plants or animals **decompose**, or when something **decomposes** them, they change chemically and begin to decay. □ The waste slowly decomposes into compost. ● **de|com|po|si|tion** /dikɒmpəzɪʃⁿn/ **N-NONCOUNT** □ The body was in an advanced stage of decomposition. [from French]

de|com|pos|er /dikəmpoʊzər/ (**decomposers**) **N-COUNT** SCIENCE **Decomposers** are organisms such as bacteria, fungi, and earthworms that feed on dead plants and animals and convert them into soil. [from French]

de|com|po|si|tion re|ac|tion (**decomposition reactions**) **N-COUNT** SCIENCE A **decomposition reaction** is a chemical reaction in which a compound is broken down into two or more simpler substances.

de|cor /deɪkɔr/ **N-NONCOUNT** The **decor** of a house or room is the style of its furniture and the way it is decorated. ❑ *The decor is simple—white walls.* [from French]

deco|rate /dɛkəreɪt/ (**decorates, decorating, decorated**)

■ **V-T** If you **decorate** something, you make it more attractive by adding things to it. ❑ *He decorated his room with pictures of sports stars.*

② **V-T/V-I** If you **decorate** a room or the inside of a building, you put new paint or paper on the walls and the ceiling. ❑ *They were decorating Jemma's bedroom.* ❑ *They are planning to decorate when they get the time.*

● **deco|rat|ing N-NONCOUNT** ❑ *I did a lot of the decorating myself.* [from Latin]

deco|ra|tion /dɛkəreɪʃ°n/ (**decorations**) **N-COUNT/N-NONCOUNT** **Decorations** are things that are used for making something look more attractive. ❑ *Colorful paper decorations were hanging from the ceiling.* [from Latin]

deco|ra|tive /dɛkərətɪv, -əreɪtɪv/ **ADJ** Something **decorative** is intended to look pretty or attractive. ❑ *The drapes are only decorative—they do not open or close.* [from Latin]

Word Link	cresc, creas ≈ growing : crescent, decrease, increase

Word Link	de ≈ from, down, away : decrease, deflate, descend

de|crease (**decreases, decreasing, decreased**)

> **PRONUNCIATION HELP**
> Pronounce the verb /dɪkris/. Pronounce the noun /dikris/ or /dɪkris/.

■ **V-T/V-I** When something **decreases** or when you **decrease** it, it becomes less in amount, size, or strength. ❑ *The average price decreased from $134,000 to $126,000.* ❑ *Property may start to decrease in value.*

② **N-COUNT** A **decrease in** the amount, size, or strength of something is when it becomes less. ❑ *There has been a decrease in the number of people without a job.* [from Old French]

Thesaurus	decrease Also look up :
v	decline, diminish, go down; (*ant.*) increase ■

de|cree /dɪkri/ (**decrees, decreeing, decreed**)

■ **N-COUNT** SOCIAL STUDIES A **decree** is an official order or decision, especially one made by the ruler of a country. ❑ *The decree banned all meetings, strikes, parades, and protests.*

② **N-COUNT** SOCIAL STUDIES A **decree** is a judgment made by a law court. ❑ *...court decrees.*

③ **V-T** SOCIAL STUDIES If someone in authority **decrees** that something must happen, they decide or state this officially. ❑ *The government decreed that all children should have an education.* [from Old French]

dedi|cate /dɛdɪkeɪt/ (**dedicates, dedicating, dedicated**)

■ **V-T** If someone **dedicates** themselves **to** something, they give a lot of time and effort to it. ❑ *For the next few years, she dedicated herself to her work.* ● **dedi|cat|ed ADJ** ❑ *He's dedicated to his students.* ● **dedi|ca|tion** /dɛdɪkeɪʃ°n/ **N-NONCOUNT** ❑ *We admire her dedication to achieving peace.*

② **V-T** If someone **dedicates** a book, a play, or a piece of music **to** you, they say on the first page that they have written it for you. ❑ *She dedicated her first book to her sons.* ● **dedi|ca|tion** (**dedications**) **N-COUNT** ❑ *I read the dedication at the beginning of the book.* [from Latin]

de|duce /dɪdus/ (**deduces, deducing, deduced**) **V-T** If you **deduce** something or **deduce** that something is true, you reach that conclusion because of other things that you know to be true. ❑ *Alison cleverly deduced that I was the author of the letter.* ❑ *The date of the document can be deduced from references to the Civil War.* [from Latin]

de|duct /dɪdʌkt/ (**deducts, deducting, deducted**) **V-T** When you **deduct** an amount from a total, you make the total smaller by that amount. ❑ *The company deducted the money from his wages.* [from Latin]

de|duc|tion /dɪdʌkʃ°n/ (**deductions**)

■ **N-COUNT** A **deduction** is an amount that has been subtracted from a total. ❑ *...an income tax deduction.*

② **N-COUNT** A **deduction** is a conclusion that you have reached about something because of other things that you know to be true. ❑ *It was a pretty clever deduction.* [from Latin]
→ look at Word Web: **science**

deed /did/ (**deeds**) **N-COUNT** A **deed** is something that is done, especially something that is very good or very bad.

D

deep [LITERARY] ❑ *The people who did this evil deed must be punished.* [from Old English]

deep /diːp/ (**deeper, deepest**)

1 ADJ If something is **deep**, it goes down a long way. ❑ *The water is very deep.* ❑ *The kids dug a deep hole in the middle of the yard.*

2 ADV **Deep** is also an adverb. ❑ *She put her hands deep into her pockets.*

3 ADJ A **deep** container, such as a closet, extends or measures a long distance from front to back. ❑ *...a deep cupboard.*

4 ADJ You use **deep** to talk about the seriousness or strength of something. ❑ *He expressed his deep sympathy to the family.* ● **deep|ly ADV** ❑ *He loved his brother deeply.*

5 ADJ A **deep** sound is low and usually strong. ❑ *He spoke in a deep, warm voice.*

6 ADJ **Deep** describes colors that are strong and dark. ❑ *The sky was deep blue and starry.*

7 ADJ If you are in a **deep** sleep, it is difficult for someone to wake you. ❑ *Una fell into a deep sleep.* ● **deep|ly ADV** ❑ *She slept deeply, but woke early.*

8 ADJ A **deep** breath fills the whole of your lungs. ❑ *Cal took a long, deep breath, as he tried to control his emotions.* ● **deep|ly ADV** ❑ *She sighed deeply.*

9 ADJ If you describe a piece of writing as **deep**, you mean that it is important, serious, or complicated. ❑ *They're adventure stories. They're not supposed to be deep.* [from Old English]

deep cur|rent (**deep currents**) **N-COUNT** SCIENCE A **deep current** is a current of water that flows far below the surface of an ocean.

deep|en /diːpən/ (**deepens, deepening, deepened**) **V-T/V-I** If a situation or an emotion **deepens**, or if something **deepens** it, it becomes stronger. ❑ *These friendships will probably deepen in your teenage years.* [from Old English]

deep ocean ba|sin (**deep ocean basins**) **N-COUNT** SCIENCE The **deep ocean basin** is the part of the Earth's surface that lies beneath the ocean.

deep-wa|ter zone (**deep-water zones**) **N-COUNT** SCIENCE The **deep-water zone** of a lake or a pond is the area furthest from the surface, where no sunlight reaches.

deer /dɪər/ (**deer**) **N-COUNT** A **deer** is a large wild animal that eats grass and leaves. A male deer usually has large horns that are like branches. [from Old English]

de|fault /dɪfɔlt/ (**defaults, defaulting, defaulted**)

1 N-NONCOUNT The **default** is the way that something will be done if you do not give any other instruction. ❑ *The default setting on the printer is for color.*

2 V-I If a person or organization **defaults on** an agreement, they do not respect it. ❑ *More borrowers are defaulting on loan repayments.*

3 PHRASE If something happens **by default**, it happens only because something else has not happened. [FORMAL] ❑ *He kept his title by default because no one else wanted it.* [from Old French]

de|feat /dɪfiːt/ (**defeats, defeating, defeated**)

1 V-T If you **defeat** someone, you beat them in a battle, a game, or a competition. ❑ *They defeated the French army in 1954.*

2 N-COUNT/N-NONCOUNT **Defeat** is the experience of being beaten in a battle, a game, or a competition. ❑ *He didn't want to accept defeat.* ❑ *...the team's defeat at Sacramento.* [from Old French]

de|fect (**defects, defecting, defected**)

> **PRONUNCIATION HELP**
> Pronounce the noun /diːfɛkt/. Pronounce the verb /dɪfɛkt/.

1 N-COUNT A **defect** is a fault in a person or a thing. ❑ *He was born with a hearing defect.* ❑ *The report shows the defects of the present system.*

2 V-I SOCIAL STUDIES If you **defect**, you leave your country, political party, or other group, and join an opposing country, party, or group. ❑ *...a Democrat who defected in 2004.* ● **de|fec|tion** /dɪfɛkʃən/ (**defections**) **N-COUNT/N-NONCOUNT** ❑ *...the defection of ten Republicans.* ● **de|fec|tor** /dɪfɛktər/ (**defectors**) **N-COUNT** ❑ *The government has attracted defectors from other parties.* [from Latin]

de|fec|tive /dɪfɛktɪv/ **ADJ** If something is **defective**, it does not work properly. ❑ *We returned the defective equipment.* [from Latin]

> Word Link   **fend ≈ striking : de*fend*, *fend*er, of*fend***

de|fend /dɪfɛnd/ (**defends, defending, defended**)

1 V-T If you **defend** someone or something, you take action in order to protect them. ❑ *The army must be able to defend its own country against attack.*

2 **V-T** SPORTS In sports, if you are **defending**, you are trying to stop the other team from getting points.

3 **V-T** If you **defend** a decision, you argue in support of it. ❑ *The president defended his decision to go to war.*

4 **V-T** SOCIAL STUDIES When a lawyer **defends** a person in a court, they argue that the person is not guilty of a particular crime. ❑ *He has hired a lawyer to defend him in court.* [from Old French]

→ look at Word Web: **hero**

> **Word Link** **ant ≈ one who does, has : defend**ant, **occup**ant, **pollut**ant

de|fend|ant /dɪfɛndənt/ (**defendants**)
N-COUNT SOCIAL STUDIES A **defendant** is a person who has been accused of breaking the law and is being tried in court. ❑ *The defendant pleaded guilty and was fined $500.* [from Old French]

→ look at Word Web: **trial**

de|fend|er /dɪfɛndər/ (**defenders**) **N-COUNT** SPORTS A **defender** in a game is a player whose main task is to try and stop the other side from scoring. ❑ *Lewis was the team's top defender.* [from Old French]

de|fense

> **PRONUNCIATION HELP**
> Pronounce meanings **1** to **4** /dɪfɛns/.
> Pronounce meaning **5** /dɪfɛns/.

1 **N-NONCOUNT** Defense is action to protect someone or something against attack. ❑ *The land was flat, which made defense difficult.*

2 **N-NONCOUNT** Defense is the organization of a country's armies and weapons, and their use to protect the country. ❑ *Twenty-eight percent of the country's money is spent on defense.* ❑ *...the U.S. Defense Secretary.*

3 **N-COUNT** A **defense** is something that you say or write that supports ideas or actions that have been criticized. ❑ *...his defense of the government's performance.*

4 **N-SING** The **defense** is the case that is presented by a lawyer in a court of law for the person who has been accused of a crime. ❑ *The defense was that the police had not kept full records of the interviews.*

5 **N-SING** SPORTS In games such as soccer or football, the **defense** is the group of players in a team who try to stop the opposing players from scoring a goal or a point. ❑ *Their defense was weak and allowed 35 points.* [from Old French]

de|fen|sive /dɪfɛnsɪv/
1 **ADJ** You use **defensive** to describe things that are intended to protect someone or something. ❑ *The Government organized defensive measures to protect the city.*

2 **ADJ** If someone or their behavior is **defensive** they are behaving in a way that shows that they feel they have been criticized. ❑ *She heard the defensive note in his voice.*

3 **ADJ** SPORTS In sports such as football or soccer, **defensive** players try to stop the other team from scoring points or goals. ❑ *He spent four years as a defensive back in the National Football League.* [from Old French]

de|fi|ance /dɪfaɪəns/ **N-NONCOUNT** Defiance is behavior or an attitude which shows that you are not willing to obey someone. ❑ *...his brave defiance of the government.* [from Old English]

de|fi|ant /dɪfaɪənt/ **ADJ** A **defiant** person refuses to obey someone. ❑ *She stood looking at her father with a defiant expression on her face.*
●**de|fi|ant|ly** **ADV** ❑ *They defiantly refused to accept the plan.* [from Old French]

de|fi|cien|cy /dɪfɪʃ°nsi/ (**deficiencies**)
1 **N-COUNT/N-NONCOUNT** Deficiency in something, especially something that your body needs, is not having enough of it. ❑ *He had blood tests for signs of vitamin deficiency.*

2 **N-COUNT/N-NONCOUNT** A **deficiency** that someone or something has is a weakness or an imperfection in them. [FORMAL] ❑ *The company failed to correct deficiencies in the system.* [from Latin]

defi|cit /dɛfəsɪt/ (**deficits**) **N-COUNT** A **deficit** is the amount by which something is less than the amount that is needed. ❑ *The state budget showed a deficit of five billion dollars.* [from Latin]

de|fine /dɪfaɪn/ (**defines, defining, defined**) **V-T** If you **define** something, you say clearly what it is and what it means. ❑ *The government defines a household as "a group of people who live in the same house."* [from Old French]

defi|nite /dɛfɪnɪt/
1 **ADJ** A **definite** decision or arrangement is firm and clear, and will probably not be changed. ❑ *I need a definite answer soon.* ❑ *I want to make some definite plans for the future.*

2 **ADJ** Definite information is true, rather

than being an opinion or a guess. ❑ *We didn't have any definite proof.* [from Latin]

Thesaurus	definite Also look up :
ADJ	clear-cut, distinct, precise, specific; (*ant.*) ambiguous, vague **1**

defi|nite ar|ti|cle (**definite articles**)
N-COUNT LANGUAGE ARTS **The definite article** is the word "the." ❑ *Placenames often have a definite article, as in "the Alps."*

defi|nite|ly /dɛfɪnɪtli/ **ADV** You use **definitely** to show that you are certain about something. ❑ *The extra money will definitely help.* [from Latin]

defi|ni|tion /dɛfɪnɪʃⁿn/ (**definitions**)
N-COUNT LANGUAGE ARTS A **definition** gives the meaning of a word or an expression, especially in a dictionary. ❑ *The definition of marriage has changed over time.* [from Latin]

de|fini|tive /dɪfɪnɪtɪv/
1 **ADJ** Something that is **definitive** provides a firm conclusion that cannot be questioned. ❑ *The study provides definitive proof that the drug is safe.* ● **de|fini|tive|ly** **ADV** ❑ *He wasn't able to answer the question definitively.*
2 **ADJ** A **definitive** book or performance is thought to be the best of its kind that has ever been done or that will ever be done. ❑ *...a definitive book on Spanish history.* [from Latin]

Word Link	*de ≈ from, down, away* : *de*crease, *de*flate, *de*scend

de|flate /dɪfleɪt/ (**deflates, deflating, deflated**)
1 **V-T** If you **deflate** someone or something, you take away their confidence or make them seem less important. ❑ *The mention of her name seemed to deflate him.* ● **de|flat|ed** **ADJ** ❑ *When she refused I felt deflated.*
2 **V-T/V-I** When something such as a tire or a balloon **deflates**, or when you **deflate** it, all the air comes out of it. ❑ *We drove a few miles until the tire deflated.*

de|fla|tion /dɪfleɪʃⁿn/ **N-NONCOUNT** SCIENCE In geology, **deflation** is the removal of soil and other material from the surface of the Earth by wind.

de|for|esta|tion /difɔrɪsteɪʃⁿn/
N-NONCOUNT GEOGRAPHY **Deforestation** is the cutting down of trees over a large area. ❑ *...the deforestation of the Amazon.*
→ look at Word Web: **greenhouse effect**

de|form /dɪfɔrm/ (**deforms, deforming, deformed**) **V-T/V-I** If something **deforms** a person's body, it causes it to have an unnatural shape. In technical English, you can also say that the second thing **deforms** when it changes to an unnatural shape. ❑ *The disease deforms the arms and the legs.* ● **de|formed** **ADJ** ❑ *He had a deformed right leg.* [from Latin]

de|for|ma|tion /difɔrmeɪʃⁿn/ (**deformations**) **N-COUNT/N-NONCOUNT** SCIENCE **Deformation** is a change in the shape of a rock as a result of pressure, for example in an earthquake. [from Latin]

defy /dɪfaɪ/ (**defies, defying, defied**) **V-T** If you **defy** someone or something, you refuse to obey them. ❑ *This was the first time I defied my mother.* [from Old French]

de|gen|er|ate (**degenerates, degenerating, degenerated**)

PRONUNCIATION HELP
Pronounce the verb /dɪdʒɛnəreɪt/. Pronounce the adjective /dɪdʒɛnərɪt/.

1 **V-I** If you say that someone or something **degenerates**, you mean that they become worse in some way, for example weaker, lower in quality, or more dangerous. ❑ *Your bones may begin to degenerate if you are too inactive.* ● **de|gen|era|tion** /dɪdʒɛnəreɪʃⁿn/ **N-NONCOUNT** ❑ *...various forms of physical and mental degeneration.*
2 **ADJ** If you describe a person or their behavior as **degenerate**, you disapprove of them because you think they have low standards of behavior or morality. ❑ *...the effects of a degenerate lifestyle.* [from Latin]

de|gree /dɪgri/ (**degrees**)
1 **N-COUNT** You use **degree** to talk about how much something happens or is felt. ❑ *He treated her with a high degree of respect.*
2 **N-COUNT** SCIENCE A **degree** is a unit for measuring temperatures. It is often written as °, for example 70°. ❑ *It's over 80 degrees outside.*
3 **N-COUNT** MATH A **degree** is a unit for measuring angles. It is often written as °, for example 90°. ❑ *It was pointing outward at an angle of 45 degrees.*
4 **N-COUNT** A **degree** is a qualification that you receive when you have successfully completed a course of study at a college or a university. ❑ *He has an engineering degree.* [from Old French]

→ look at Word Webs: **graduation**, **thermometer**

Word Partnership	Use **degree** with :
N	degree **of certainty**, degree **of difficulty** 🔟
	45/90 degree **angle** 🔢
	bachelor's/master's degree, **college** degree, degree **program** 🔢
ADJ	**high** degree 🔟
	honorary degree 🔢

Word Link	**hydr ≈ water : carbo**hydr**ate,** de**hydr**ate, **hydr**opower

Word Link	**ation ≈ state of : dehydr**ation**,** elev**ation, preserv**ation

de|hy|drate /dihaɪdreɪt/ (**dehydrates, dehydrating, dehydrated**)

🔟 **V-T** When something such as food **is dehydrated**, all the water is removed from it, often in order to preserve it. ❑ The food was dehydrated.

🔢 **V-T/V-I** If you **dehydrate** or if something **dehydrates** you, you lose too much water from your body so that you feel weak or ill. ❑ People can dehydrate in hot weather like this.

● **de|hy|dra|tion** /dihaɪdreɪʃ°n/ **N-NONCOUNT** ❑ The child is suffering from dehydration.

de|lay /dɪleɪ/ (**delays, delaying, delayed**)

🔟 **V-T/V-I** If you **delay** doing something, you do not do it immediately or at the planned time, but you leave it until later. ❑ Many women delay motherhood because they want to have a career. ❑ There was no time to delay.

🔢 **V-T** To **delay** someone or something means to make them late. ❑ Passengers were delayed at the airport for five hours.

🔢 **N-COUNT/N-NONCOUNT** If there is a **delay**, something does not happen until later than planned. ❑ He apologized for the delay. [from Old French]

Thesaurus	**delay** Also look up :
V	hold up, postpone, stall; (ant.) hurry, rush 🔟
N	interruption, lag; (ant.) rush 🔢

del|egate (**delegating, delegated**)

PRONUNCIATION HELP
Pronounce the noun /dɛlɪgɪt/. Pronounce the verb /dɛlɪgeɪt/.

🔟 **N-COUNT** SOCIAL STUDIES A **delegate** is a person who represents a group of other people at a meeting, for example. ❑ About 750

delegates attended the conference.

🔢 **V-T/V-I** If you **delegate** duties or responsibilities **to** someone, you give them those duties or responsibilities so that they can act for you. ❑ He wants to delegate more tasks to his assistant. ❑ As a team leader, you must delegate effectively. [from Latin]

del|ega|tion /dɛlɪgeɪʃ°n/ (**delegations**)
N-COUNT SOCIAL STUDIES A **delegation** is a group of people who have been sent somewhere to have talks with other people on behalf of a larger group of people. ❑ ...the Chinese delegation to the UN talks in New York. [from Latin]

de|lete /dɪlit/ (**deletes, deleting, deleted**)
V-T TECHNOLOGY If you **delete** something that has been written down or stored in a computer, you put a line through it or remove it. ❑ He deleted files from the computer. [from Old Latin]

Thesaurus	**delete** Also look up :
V	cut out, erase, remove

de|lib|er|ate (**deliberates, deliberating, deliberated**)

PRONUNCIATION HELP
Pronounce the adjective /dɪlɪbərɪt/. Pronounce the verb /dɪlɪbəreɪt/.

🔟 **ADJ** A **deliberate** action is one that you intended. ❑ They told deliberate lies in order to sell newspapers. ● **de|lib|er|ate|ly** **ADV** ❑ He started the fire deliberately.

🔢 **V-I** If you **deliberate**, you think about something carefully. ❑ She deliberated over the decision before she made up her mind. [from Latin]

→ look at Word Web: **trial**

deli|cate /dɛlɪkɪt/
🔟 **ADJ** Something that is **delicate** is small and beautifully shaped. ❑ He had delicate hands.

🔢 **ADJ** Something that is **delicate** can break or become damaged easily. ❑ The machine even washes delicate glassware. ❑ Do not rub the delicate skin around the eyes.

🔢 **ADJ** A **delicate** color, taste, or smell is pleasant and light. ❑ The beans have a delicate flavor.

🔢 **ADJ** You use **delicate** to describe a situation that needs to be dealt with in a careful and sensitive manner. ❑ ...the delicate issue of money. [from Latin]

deli|ca|tes|sen /dɛlɪkətɛsᵊn/
(**delicatessens**) **N-COUNT** A **delicatessen** is a
store that sells food such as cold meats and
cheeses. [from German]

de|li|cious /dɪlɪʃəs/ **ADJ** Food that is
delicious tastes very good. □ *There was a wide
choice of delicious meals.* ● **de|li|cious|ly** **ADV**
□ *This yogurt has a deliciously creamy flavor.*
[from Old French]

de|light /dɪlaɪt/ (**delights, delighting,
delighted**)
■ **N-NONCOUNT** **Delight** is a feeling of great
pleasure. □ *He expressed delight at the news.*
□ *Andrew laughed with delight.*
■ **V-T** If something **delights** you, it gives
you a lot of pleasure. □ *Her style of music
delighted audiences everywhere.* [from Old French]

de|light|ed /dɪlaɪtɪd/ **ADJ** If you are
delighted, you are extremely pleased about
something. □ *Frank was delighted to see her.*
[from Old French]

de|light|ful /dɪlaɪtfəl/ **ADJ** If you describe
something or someone as **delightful**, you
mean they are very pleasant. □ *...a delightful
garden.* ● **de|light|ful|ly** **ADV** □ *...a delightfully
refreshing perfume.* [from Old French]

de|liv|er /dɪlɪvər/ (**delivers, delivering,
delivered**)
■ **V-T** If you **deliver** something somewhere,
you take it there. □ *Only 90% of first-class mail
is delivered on time.* □ *The Canadians plan to deliver
more food to Somalia.*
■ **V-T** If you **deliver** a speech, you give it in
public. [FORMAL] □ *The president will deliver a
speech about schools.*
■ **V-T** When someone **delivers** a baby, they
help the woman who is giving birth to the
baby. □ *He didn't expect to deliver his own baby!*
[from Old French]

Word Partnership	Use **deliver** with :
N	deliver **a letter**, deliver **mail**, deliver **a message**, deliver **news**, deliver **a package** ■
	deliver **a lecture**, deliver **a speech** ■
	deliver **a baby** ■

de|liv|ery /dɪlɪvəri/ (**deliveries**)
■ **N-COUNT/N-NONCOUNT** **Delivery** is when
someone brings letters, packages, or other
goods to an arranged place. □ *Please allow
28 days for delivery.*
■ **N-COUNT** A **delivery** of something is the

goods that are delivered. □ *I got a delivery of
fresh eggs this morning.* [from Old French]

del|ta /dɛltə/ (**deltas**) **N-COUNT** GEOGRAPHY
A **delta** is an area of low, flat land shaped
like a triangle, where a river splits and
spreads out into several branches before
entering the sea. □ *...the Mississippi delta.*
[from Latin]
→ look at Picture Dictionary: **landforms**

del|uge /dɛlyudʒ/ (**deluges, deluging,
deluged**)
■ **N-COUNT** A **deluge of** things is a large
number of them which arrive or happen at
the same time. □ *There was a deluge of requests
for interviews.*
■ **V-T** If a place or person **is deluged with**
things, a large number of them arrive or
happen at the same time. □ *The office was
deluged with complaints.*
■ **N-COUNT** A **deluge** of rain is a very heavy
fall of rain. □ *The deluge was too much for the
drains.* [from Old French]

de|luxe /dɪlʌks/ **ADJ** **Deluxe** goods or
services are better and more expensive than
ordinary ones. □ *She only stays in deluxe hotel
suites.* [from French]

de|mand /dɪmænd/ (**demands, demanding,
demanded**)
■ **V-T** If you **demand** information or action,
you ask for it in a very firm way. □ *The victim's
family is demanding an investigation into the
shooting.* □ *He demanded that I give him an answer.*
■ **N-COUNT** A **demand** is a firm request for
something. □ *There were demands for better
services.*
■ **N-NONCOUNT** If you talk about the
demand for something, you are referring to
how many people want to have it or do it.
□ *Demand for the product has increased.*
■ **N-PLURAL** The **demands of** something
are the things that you have to do for it.
□ *...the demands of a new job.*
■ **PHRASE** If someone or something is **in
demand** or **in great demand**, they are very
popular and a lot of people want them.
□ *Math teachers are always in demand.*
■ **PHRASE** If something is available **on
demand**, you can have it whenever you want
it. □ *The package delivers 24-hour entertainment
and movies on demand.* [from Medieval Latin]

Thesaurus demand Also look up :

v   command, insist on, order; *(ant.)* give, grant, offer **1**

de|moc|ra|cy /dɪmɒkrəsi/ (**democracies**)
1 **N-NONCOUNT** SOCIAL STUDIES **Democracy** is a system of government in which people choose their leaders by voting for them in elections. ❑ *We're studying democracy in Eastern Europe.*
2 **N-COUNT** SOCIAL STUDIES A **democracy** is a country in which the people choose their government by voting for it. ❑ *...the new democracies of Eastern Europe.* [from French]
→ look at Word Web: **vote**

demo|crat /dɛməkræt/ (**democrats**)
1 **N-COUNT** SOCIAL STUDIES A **Democrat** is a supporter of a political party that has the word "democrat" or "democratic" in its title, for example the Democratic Party in the United States. ❑ *Democrats voted against the plan.*
2 **N-COUNT** SOCIAL STUDIES A **democrat** is a person who believes in and wants democracy. ❑ *This is the time for democrats and not dictators.* [from French]

demo|crat|ic /dɛməkrætɪk/
1 **ADJ** SOCIAL STUDIES A **democratic** country, government, or political system has leaders who are elected by the people that they govern. ❑ *Bolivia returned to democratic rule in 1982.*
2 **ADJ** SOCIAL STUDIES Something that is **democratic** is based on the idea that everyone has equal rights and should be involved in making important decisions. ❑ *Education is the basis of a democratic society.* [from French]

de|mol|ish /dɪmɒlɪʃ/ (**demolishes, demolishing, demolished**) **V-T** To **demolish** a building means to destroy it completely. ❑ *The storm demolished buildings and flooded streets.* ● **demo|li|tion** /dɛməlɪʃⁿn/ **N-NONCOUNT** ❑ *The bomb caused the total demolition of the old bridge.* [from French]

dem|on|strate /dɛmənstreɪt/ (**demonstrates, demonstrating, demonstrated**)
1 **V-T** If you **demonstrate** something, you show people how it works or how to do it. ❑ *Several companies were demonstrating their new products.* ● **dem|on|stra|tion** (**demonstrations**) **N-COUNT** ❑ *We watched a cooking demonstration.*

2 **V-T** To **demonstrate** a fact means to make it clear to people. ❑ *Studies have demonstrated the link between certain foods and heart disease.*
3 **V-T** If you **demonstrate** a particular skill or quality, you show that you have it. ❑ *They have demonstrated their ability to work together.*
4 **V-I** When people **demonstrate**, they march or gather somewhere to show that they oppose or support something. ❑ *200,000 people demonstrated against the war.* ● **dem|on|stra|tion** (**demonstrations**) **N-COUNT** ❑ *Soldiers broke up an anti-government demonstration.* ● **de|mon|stra|tor** (**demonstrators**) **N-COUNT** ❑ *Police were dealing with a crowd of demonstrators.* [from Latin]
→ look at Word Web: **citizenship**

Thesaurus demonstrate Also look up :

v   describe, illustrate, prove, show **1** **2** march, picket, protest **4**

de|mure /dɪmyʊər/
1 **ADJ** If you describe a girl or young woman as **demure**, you mean that she is quiet and shy, and that she behaves well. ❑ *She's very demure and sweet.* ● **de|mure|ly** **ADV** ❑ *She smiled demurely.*
2 **ADJ** **Demure** clothes do not reveal your body and they give the impression that you are shy and well-behaved. [WRITTEN] ❑ *...a demure high-necked white blouse.* ● **de|mure|ly** **ADV** ❑ *She was demurely dressed in a black wool suit.*

den /dɛn/ (**dens**)
1 **N-COUNT** A **den** is the home of some types of wild animal.
2 **N-COUNT** Your **den** is a quiet room in your house where you can go to study, work, or relax. [from Old English]

den|drite /dɛndraɪt/ (**dendrites**) **N-COUNT** SCIENCE **Dendrites** are thin fibers with which nerve cells receive messages from other nerve cells. [from Greek]

de|ni|al /dɪnaɪəl/ (**denials**) **N-COUNT/N-NONCOUNT** A **denial** of something is when you say that it is not true, or that it does not exist. ❑ *There have been many official denials of the government's involvement.* [from Old French]

den|im /dɛnɪm/ **N-NONCOUNT** **Denim** is a thick cotton cloth, usually blue, which is used for making clothes. ❑ *...a denim jacket.* [from French]

de|noue|ment /deɪnumɑ̃n/
(**denouements**) also **dénouement** **N-COUNT**
ARTS In a book, a play, or a series of events,
the **denouement** is the sequence of events at
the end, when things come to a conclusion.
[from French]

de|noue|ment de|sign (**denouement
designs**) **N-COUNT** ARTS In a book or a play,
the **denouement design** is the way that the
main theme of the book or play is resolved.

Word Link	nounce ≈ reporting : announce, denounce, pronounce

de|nounce /dɪnaʊns/ (**denounces,
denouncing, denounced**) **V-T** If you
denounce a person or an action, you criticize
them severely and publicly because you
feel strongly that they are wrong or evil.
□ German leaders denounced the attacks.
[from Old French]

dense /dɛns/ (**denser, densest**)
1 **ADJ** Something that is **dense** contains
a lot of things or people in a small area.
□ The road runs through a dense forest. ● **dense|ly**
ADV □ Java is a densely populated island.
2 **ADJ** **Dense** fog or smoke is very thick.
□ The planes came close to each other in dense fog.
3 **ADJ** SCIENCE In science, a **dense** substance
is very heavy for its size. □ Ice is less dense than
water, and so it floats. [from Latin]

den|sity /dɛnsɪti/ (**densities**)
N-COUNT/N-NONCOUNT SCIENCE In science,
the **density** of a substance or an object is
how heavy it is for its size. □ Jupiter's moon Io
has a density of 3.5 grams per cubic centimeter.
[from Latin]

dent /dɛnt/ (**dents, denting, dented**)
1 **V-T** If you **dent** the surface of something,
you make a hollow area in it by hitting it.
□ The stone dented the car's fender.
2 **N-COUNT** A **dent** is a hollow in the surface
of something that has been hit or pressed
too hard. □ There was a dent in the car door.
[from Old English]

Word Link	dent, dont ≈ tooth : dental, dentist, dentistry

den|tal /dɛntəl/ **ADJ** SCIENCE **Dental** means
relating to teeth. □ Regular dental care is
important. [from Medieval Latin]

den|tist /dɛntɪst/ (**dentists**)
1 **N-COUNT** A **dentist** is a person whose job
is to examine and treat people's teeth.
□ Visit your dentist twice a year for a check-up.

2 **N-SING** The **dentist** or the **dentist's** is the
place where a dentist works. □ I'm going to the
dentist's after school. [from French]
→ look at Word Web: **teeth**

den|tis|try /dɛntɪstri/ **N-NONCOUNT**
Dentistry is the work done by a dentist.
[from French]

deny /dɪnaɪ/ (**denies, denying, denied**)
1 **V-T** When you **deny** something, you
state that it is not true. □ Robby denied
stealing the bike. □ He denied that he was involved
in the crime.
2 **V-T** If you **deny** someone something, you
refuse to let them have it. □ Many of these
young people were denied access to higher
education. [from Old French]

Word Partnership	Use deny with :
N	deny **a charge, officials** deny **1** deny **access,** deny **entry,** deny **a request 2**
V	**confirm or** deny **1**

de|odor|ant /dioʊdərənt/ (**deodorants**)
N-COUNT/N-NONCOUNT **Deodorant** is a
substance that you can put on your skin
to hide or prevent bad smells.

de|part /dɪpɑrt/ (**departs, departing,
departed**) **V-T/V-I** When something or
someone **departs**, they leave. You can also
say that someone **departs** a place. □ Flight 43
will depart from Denver at 11:45 a.m. □ In the
morning, Mr. McDonald departed for Sydney.
[from Old French]

de|part|ment /dɪpɑrtmənt/ (**departments**)
1 **N-COUNT** A **department** is one of the
sections in an organization such as a
government, a business, or a university.
□ She works for the U.S. Department of Health and
Human Services.
2 **N-COUNT** A **department** is one of the
sections in a large store. □ He works in the shoe
department. [from French]

de|part|ment store (**department stores**)
N-COUNT A **department store** is a large store
that sells many different types of goods.

de|par|ture /dɪpɑrtʃər/ (**departures**)
N-COUNT/N-NONCOUNT **Departure** is the act
of going away from somewhere. □ Illness
delayed the president's departure for Helsinki.
[from Old French]

de|par|tures /dɪpɑrtʃərz/ **N-SING** In an
airport, **departures** is the place where

passengers wait before they get onto their plane. [from Old French]

de|pend /dɪpɛnd/ (**depends, depending, depended**)

1 **V-I** If one thing **depends on** another, the first thing will be affected by the second thing. ❑ *The cooking time depends on the size of the potato.*

2 **V-I** If you **depend on** someone or something, you need them in order to do something. ❑ *He depended on his writing for his income.*

3 **V-I** If you can **depend on** someone or something, you know that they will support you or help you when you need them. ❑ *"You can depend on me," I assured him.*

4 **PHRASE** You use **depending on** when you are saying that something can change according to the situation mentioned. ❑ *The trip takes between two and three hours, depending on the traffic.*

5 **PHRASE** You use **It depends** to show that you cannot give a clear answer to a question because the answer will be affected by other factors. ❑ *"How long can you stay?"—"I don't know. It depends."* [from Old French]

de|pend|able /dɪpɛndəbəl/ **ADJ** You say that someone is **dependable** when you feel that they will always be helpful and sensible. ❑ *He was a dependable friend.* [from Old French]

| Word Link | *ent* ≈ one who does, has : depend*ent*, resid*ent*, superintend*ent* |

| Word Link | *ence* ≈ state, condition : depend*ence*, excell*ence*, independ*ence* |

de|pend|ent /dɪpɛndənt/ (**dependents**) also **dependant**

1 **ADJ** If you are **dependent on** something or someone, you need them in order to succeed or to be able to survive. ❑ *The young gorillas are completely dependent on their mothers.*
● **de|pend|ence** **N-NONCOUNT** ❑ *We discussed the city's dependence on tourism.*

2 **N-COUNT** Your **dependents** are the people you support financially, such as your children. ❑ *He's a single man with no dependents.* [from Old French]

de|pict /dɪpɪkt/ (**depicts, depicting, depicted**) **V-T** To **depict** someone or something means to show or represent them in a work of art such as a drawing or a painting. ❑ *...pictures depicting Lee's most*

famous battles. ● **de|pic|tion** (**depictions**) **N-COUNT/N-NONCOUNT** ❑ *...their depiction in the book as thieves.* [from Latin]

de|plete /dɪplit/ (**depletes, depleting, depleted**) **V-T** To **deplete** a stock or amount of something means to reduce it. [FORMAL] ❑ *...substances that deplete the ozone layer.* ● **de|plet|ed** **ADJ** ❑ *...Lee's tired and depleted army.* ● **de|ple|tion** /dɪpliʃən/ **N-NONCOUNT** ❑ *...the depletion of water supplies.* [from Latin]

de|ploy /dɪplɔɪ/ (**deploys, deploying, deployed**) **V-T** SOCIAL STUDIES To **deploy** troops or military resources means to organize or position them so that they are ready to be used. ❑ *The president has no intention of deploying troops.* ● **de|ploy|ment** (**deployments**) **N-COUNT/N-NONCOUNT** ❑ *...the deployment of soldiers.* [from French]

de|port /dɪpɔrt/ (**deports, deporting, deported**) **V-T** SOCIAL STUDIES If a government **deports** someone, usually someone who is not a citizen of that country, it sends them out of the country because they have committed a crime or because it believes they do not have the right to be there. ❑ *...a government decision to deport all illegal immigrants.* ● **de|por|ta|tion** /dɪpɔrteɪʃən/ (**deportations**) **N-COUNT/N-NONCOUNT** ❑ *Thousands of people face deportation.* [from French]

| Word Link | *pos* ≈ placing : de*pos*it, pre*pos*ition, *pos*ition |

de|pos|it /dɪpɒzɪt/ (**deposits, depositing, deposited**)

1 **N-COUNT** A **deposit** is a sum of money that is part of the full price of something, and that you pay when you agree to buy it. ❑ *He paid a $500 deposit for the car.*

2 **N-COUNT** A **deposit** is an amount of a substance that has been left somewhere as a result of a chemical or geological process. ❑ *...underground deposits of gold.*

3 **N-COUNT** A **deposit** is an amount of money that you put into a bank account. ❑ *I made a deposit every week.*

4 **V-T** If you **deposit** a sum of money, you put it into a bank account or a savings account. ❑ *The customer has to deposit a minimum of $100 monthly.* [from Medieval Latin]

depo|si|tion /dɛpəzɪʃən/ **N-NONCOUNT** SCIENCE **Deposition** is a geological process in

d

which material that has been carried by the wind or water from one area is left on the surface of another area. [from Late Latin]

de|pot /dípoʊ/ (**depots**) **N-COUNT** A **depot** is a place where goods or vehicles are kept until they are needed. ❑ *The food is stored in a depot at the airport.* ❑ *...a bus depot.* [from French]

de|pre|ci|ate /dɪpríʃieɪt/ (**depreciates, depreciating, depreciated**) **V-T/V-I** BUSINESS If something such as a currency **depreciates** or if something **depreciates** it, it loses some of its original value. ❑ *Inflation is rising rapidly; the yuan is depreciating.* ❑ *The demand for foreign currency depreciates the real value of local currencies.* ● **de|pre|cia|tion** /dɪpríʃieɪʃᵊn/ (**depreciations**) **N-COUNT/N-NONCOUNT** ❑ *...various costs, including machinery depreciation.* [from Late Latin]

de|press /dɪprɛs/ (**depresses, depressing, depressed**) **V-T** If someone or something **depresses** you, they make you feel sad. ❑ *This time of year always depresses me.* [from Old French]

de|pressed /dɪprɛst/
1 **ADJ** If you are **depressed**, you are sad, and you feel that you cannot enjoy anything. ❑ *She was very depressed after her husband died.*
2 **ADJ** A **depressed** area does not have enough business or employment to be successful. ❑ *They plan to encourage more business in depressed areas.* [from Old French]

de|press|ing /dɪprɛsɪŋ/ **ADJ** Something that is **depressing** makes you feel sad. ❑ *The view from the window was gray and depressing.* [from Old French]

de|pres|sion /dɪprɛʃᵊn/ (**depressions**)
1 **N-COUNT/N-NONCOUNT** Depression is a state of mind in which you are sad and you feel that you cannot enjoy anything. ❑ *Mr. Thomas was suffering from depression.*
2 **N-COUNT** SOCIAL STUDIES A depression is a time when there is very little economic activity, which causes a lot of unemployment and social problems.
3 **N-PROPER** SOCIAL STUDIES The Depression or The Great Depression was a period in the U.S. during the 1920s and 1930s when there were very few jobs because the economy was in a bad state. ❑ *...the Great Depression of the 1930s.* [from Old French]

de|prive /dɪpraɪv/ (**deprives, depriving, deprived**) **V-T** If you **deprive** someone **of** something, you take it away from them,

or you prevent them from having it. ❑ *They were deprived of fuel to heat their homes.*
● **dep|ri|va|tion** /dɛprɪveɪʃᵊn/ (**deprivations**) **N-COUNT/N-NONCOUNT** ❑ *Many new mothers were suffering from sleep deprivation.* ● **de|prived** **ADJ** ❑ *These are some of the most deprived children in the country.* [from Old French]

depth /dɛpθ/ (**depths**)
1 **N-COUNT/N-NONCOUNT** The **depth** of something is how deep it is. ❑ *The average depth of the ocean is 4000 meters.* ❑ *The depth of the hole is 520 yards.*
2 **N-COUNT/N-NONCOUNT** The **depth** of something such as a closet or a drawer is the distance between its front surface and its back.
3 **N-COUNT/N-NONCOUNT** If an emotion is very strongly or intensely felt, you can talk about its **depth**. ❑ *...the depth of feeling on the subject.*
4 **N-NONCOUNT** The **depth** of someone's knowledge is the great amount that they know. ❑ *We were impressed with the depth of her knowledge.*
5 **PHRASE** If you deal with a subject **in depth**, you deal with it in a very detailed way. ❑ *We will discuss these three areas in depth.*

depu|ty /dɛpyəti/ (**deputies**)
1 **N-COUNT** A **deputy** is the second most important person in an organization. ❑ *Dr. Thomas is a former deputy director of NASA's astronaut office.*
2 **N-COUNT** A **deputy** is a police officer. ❑ *Robyn asked the deputy if she could speak with Sheriff Adkins.* [from Old French]

der|mis /dɜrmɪs/ **N-SING** SCIENCE The **dermis** is the layer of skin beneath the epidermis. [from New Latin]

de|sali|na|tion /diːsælɪneɪʃᵊn/ **N-NONCOUNT** SCIENCE **Desalination** is the process of removing salt from sea water so that it can be used for drinking, or for watering crops.

des|cant /dɛskænt/ (**descants**) **N-COUNT** MUSIC A **descant** is a tune which is played or sung above the main tune in a piece of music. [from Old Northern French]

Word Link	de ≈ from, down, away : *de*crease, *de*flate, *de*scend

Word Link	scend ≈ climbing : a*scend*, de*scend*, tran*scend*

de|scend /dɪsɛnd/ (**descends, descending, descended**)

1 **v-t/v-i** If you **descend**, or if you **descend** a staircase, you move down from a higher level to a lower level. [FORMAL] ❑ *We descended to the basement.*

2 **v-i** If a situation **descends into** a particular state, it becomes bad. ❑ *The country descended into chaos.* [from Old French]

de|scend|ant /dɪsɛndənt/ (**descendants**)
N-COUNT SOCIAL STUDIES Someone's **descendants** are their children, their grandchildren, and all their family that live after them. ❑ *He says that he is a descendant of King David.* [from Old French]

de|scribe /dɪskraɪb/ (**describes, describing, described**)
1 **v-t** If you **describe** something, you say what it is like. ❑ *She described what she did in her spare time.* ❑ *The poem describes their life together.*
2 **v-t** If you **describe** someone or something **as** a particular thing, you say that they are like that thing. ❑ *He described it as the worst job in the world.* [from Latin]

de|scrip|tion /dɪskrɪpʃ°n/ (**descriptions**)
N-COUNT/N-NONCOUNT A description is an explanation of what someone looks like, or what something is. ❑ *Police have given a description of the man.* ❑ *He gave a detailed description of how the new system will work.* [from Latin]

de|scrip|tive de|sign /dɪskrɪptɪv dɪzaɪn/ (**descriptive designs**) **N-COUNT/N-NONCOUNT** SCIENCE Research that has a **descriptive design** involves studying the similarities and differences between two or more things.

des|ert (**deserts, deserting, deserted**)

PRONUNCIATION HELP
Pronounce the noun /dɛzərt/. The verb is pronounced /dɪzɜrt/ and is hyphenated de|sert.

1 **N-COUNT/N-NONCOUNT** GEOGRAPHY A **desert** is a large area of land where there is almost no water, trees, or plants. ❑ *They traveled through the Sahara Desert.*
2 **v-t** If people **desert** a place, they leave it and it becomes empty. ❑ *Poor farmers are deserting their fields and coming to the cities to find jobs.* ● **de|sert|ed** **ADJ** ❑ *She led them into a deserted street.*

Picture Dictionary   desert

cactus

palm tree

oasis

sand dune

lizard

sand

snake

D

3 **V-T** If someone **deserts** you, they go away and leave you, and no longer help or support you. □ *Sadly, most of her friends have deserted her.* [Sense 1 from Old French. Senses 2 and 3 from French.]
→ look at Picture Dictionary: **desert**
→ look at Word Web: **habitat**

de|serve /dɪzɜrv/ (**deserves, deserving, deserved**) **V-T** If a person or thing **deserves** something, they should receive it because of their actions or qualities. □ *These people deserve to get more money.* [from Old French]

Word Partnership	Use deserve with :
N	deserve **a chance**, deserve **credit**, deserve **recognition**, deserve **respect**
V	**don't** deserve, deserve **to know**
PRON	deserve **nothing**

des|ic|ca|ted /dɛsɪkeɪtɪd/
1 **ADJ** If something is **desiccated**, it has lost all the moisture that was in it. [FORMAL] □ *...desiccated flowers and leaves.*
2 **ADJ** If food has been **desiccated**, it has been dried in order to preserve it. □ *...desiccated coconut.* [from Latin]

de|sign /dɪzaɪn/ (**designs, designing, designed**)
1 **V-T** When you **design** something new, you plan what it should be like. □ *They wanted to design a machine that was both attractive and practical.*
2 **N-NONCOUNT** ARTS **Design** is the process of planning and drawing things. □ *He had a talent for design.*
3 **N-NONCOUNT** The **design** of something is the way in which it has been planned and made. □ *The design of the window is typically Victorian.*
4 **N-COUNT** ARTS A **design** is a drawing that shows how something should be built or made. □ *They drew the design for the house.*
5 **N-COUNT** ARTS A **design** is a pattern of lines, flowers, or shapes that is used for decorating something. □ *The tablecloths come in three different designs.*
6 **N-NONCOUNT** ARTS In the theater, **design** is the planning and making of things such as the costumes, sets, and lighting for a play or other production. [from Latin]
→ look at Word Webs: **architecture, quilt**

des|ig|nate (**designates, designating, designated**)

PRONUNCIATION HELP
Pronounce the verb /dɛzɪgneɪt/. Pronounce the adjective /dɛzɪgnɪt/.

1 **V-T** When you **designate** someone or something **as** a particular thing, you formally give them that description or name. □ *The president designated Sunday, February 3rd, as a national day of prayer for peace.* □ *...plans to designate the hotel a historic building.*
● **des|ig|na|tion** /dɛzɪgneɪʃ°n/ (**designations**) **N-COUNT/N-NONCOUNT** □ *The NC-17 designation for motion pictures stands for no children under 17 admitted.*
2 **V-T** If something **is designated for** a particular purpose, it is set aside for that purpose. □ *Some of the rooms were designated as offices.*
3 **ADJ** **Designate** is used to describe someone who has been formally chosen to do a particular job, but has not yet started doing it. □ *...Japan's prime minister-designate.* [from Latin]

de|sign|er /dɪzaɪnər/ (**designers**)
1 **N-COUNT** ARTS A **designer** is a person whose job is to design things by making drawings of them. □ *Carolyne is a fashion designer.*
2 **ADJ** **Designer** clothes are expensive, fashionable clothes made by a famous designer. □ *He drives fast cars and wears designer clothes.* [from Latin]

de|sir|able /dɪzaɪərəb°l/ **ADJ** If something is **desirable**, you want to have it or do it because it is useful or attractive. □ *The house is in a desirable neighborhood, close to schools.* [from Old French]

de|sire /dɪzaɪər/ (**desires, desiring, desired**)
1 **N-COUNT** A **desire** is a strong wish to do or have something. □ *I had a strong desire to help people.*
2 **V-T** If you **desire** something, you want it. [FORMAL] □ *This house is ideal for someone who desires a bit of peace.* ● **de|sired** **ADJ** □ *This will produce the desired effect.* [from Old French]

Word Partnership	Use desire with :
N	**heart's** desire **1**
V	**have no** desire, **satisfy a** desire **1** desire **to change** **1** **2**

desk /dɛsk/ (**desks**)

1 **N-COUNT** A **desk** is a table that you sit at to write or work.

2 **N-SING** A **desk** is a place in a public building where you can get information. ❑ *They asked for Miss Minton at the reception desk.* [from Medieval Latin]

→ look at Picture Dictionary: **office**

desk|top /dɛsktɒp/ (**desktops**) also **desk-top**

1 **ADJ** TECHNOLOGY **Desktop** computers are a convenient size for using on a desk or a table.

2 **N-COUNT** TECHNOLOGY The **desktop** of a computer is the images that you see on the screen when the computer is ready to use. ❑ *You can rearrange the icons on the desktop.*

des|pair /dɪspɛər/ (**despairs, despairing, despaired**)

1 **N-NONCOUNT** **Despair** is the feeling that everything is wrong and that nothing will improve. ❑ *I looked at my wife in despair.*

2 **V-I** If you **despair**, you feel that everything is wrong and that nothing will improve. ❑ *"Oh, I despair sometimes," she said, looking at the mess.* [from Old French]

des|per|ate /dɛspərɪt/

1 **ADJ** If you are **desperate**, you are willing to try anything to change your situation. ❑ *He was desperate to get back to the city.* ❑ *There were hundreds of patients desperate for his help.*

● **des|per|ate|ly** **ADV** ❑ *Thousands of people are desperately trying to leave the country.*

2 **ADJ** If you are **desperate for** something or **desperate to** do something, you want or need it very much. ❑ *Amy was desperate to have a baby.* ● **des|per|ate|ly** **ADV** ❑ *He was a boy who desperately needed affection.*

3 **ADJ** A **desperate** situation is very difficult, serious, or dangerous. ❑ *Conditions in the hospitals are desperate.* [from Latin]

Word Partnership	Use **desperate** with :
N	desperate **act**, desperate **attempt**, desperate **measures**, desperate **need**, desperate **struggle** **1** desperate **situation** **3**
V	**sound** desperate **1** **grow** desperate **1**–**3**

des|pera|tion /dɛspəreɪʃᵊn/ **N-NONCOUNT** **Desperation** is the feeling that you have when you are in such a bad situation that you will try anything to change it. ❑ *There was a look of desperation in her eyes.* [from Latin]

des|pise /dɪspaɪz/ (**despises, despising, despised**) **V-T** If you **despise** something or someone, you dislike them very much. ❑ *She despises dishonesty, and she hated lying to Dave.* [from Old French]

de|spite /dɪspaɪt/ **PREP** You use **despite** to introduce a fact that makes something surprising. ❑ *The event was a success, despite the rain.* [from Old French]

des|sert /dɪzɜrt/ (**desserts**) **N-COUNT/N-NONCOUNT** **Dessert** is something sweet that you eat at the end of a meal. ❑ *She had ice cream for dessert.* [from French]

→ look at Picture Dictionary: **dessert**

des|ti|na|tion /dɛstɪneɪʃᵊn/ (**destinations**) **N-COUNT** Your **destination** is the place you are going to. ❑ *He wanted to arrive at his destination before dark.* ❑ *Ellis Island is one of America's most popular tourist destinations.* [from Old French]

des|tined /dɛstɪnd/ **ADJ** If something is **destined to** happen or if someone is **destined to** behave in a particular way, that thing seems certain to happen or be done. ❑ *The plan is destined to fail.* [from Old French]

d

Picture Dictionary   dessert

ice cream | cake | pie | cookies | cheesecake
custard | brownie | chocolate mousse | rice pudding | fruit salad

des|ti|ny /dɛstɪni/ (**destinies**) **N-COUNT**
A person's **destiny** is everything that happens to them during their life, including what will happen in the future. ❑ *Do we control our own destiny?* [from Old French]

de|stroy /dɪstrɔɪ/ (**destroys, destroying, destroyed**) **V-T** To **destroy** something means to cause so much damage to it that it cannot be used any longer, or it does not exist any longer. ❑ *The original house was destroyed by fire.* ● **de|struc|tion** /dɪstrʌkʃ°n/ **N-NONCOUNT** ❑ *We must stop the destruction of our forests.* [from Old French]

Thesaurus destroy Also look up :
v crush, demolish, ruin, wipe out;
 (*ant.*) build, construct, create, repair

Word Link *struct ≈ building : con*struct*, de*struct*ive, in*struct*

de|struc|tive /dɪstrʌktɪv/ **ADJ** Something that is **destructive** can cause great damage. ❑ *...a destructive storm.* [from Old French]

de|tach /dɪtætʃ/ (**detaches, detaching, detached**) **V-T/V-I** If you **detach** something, you remove it. If one thing **detaches from** another, it becomes separated from it. [FORMAL] ❑ *Detach the card and mail it to this address.* ❑ *They tried to detach the kite from the tree.* [from Old French]

de|tached /dɪtætʃt/ **ADJ** A **detached** building is one that is not joined to any other building. ❑ *We have a house with a detached garage.* [from Old French]

de|tail /diteɪl/ (**details**)
1 N-COUNT The **details of** something are its small, individual parts. ❑ *We discussed the details of the letter.*
2 N-PLURAL **Details** about someone or something are facts about them. ❑ *See the bottom of this page for details of how to apply for this offer.*
3 PHRASE If you discuss a situation or examine something **in detail**, you talk about many different facts or parts of it. ❑ *Examine the contract in detail before signing it.* [from French]

Thesaurus detail Also look up :
N component, element, feature, point **1** **2**
 fact, information **2**
v depict, describe, specify;
 (*ant.*) approximate, generalize **3**

de|tailed /diteɪld/ **ADJ** A **detailed** report or plan contains a lot of details. ❑ *She gave us a detailed description of the man.* [from French]

Word Partnership Use detailed with :
N detailed **account**, detailed **analysis**, detailed **description**, detailed **instructions**, detailed **plan**, detailed **record**

de|tain /dɪteɪn/ (**detains, detaining, detained**)
1 V-T When people such as the police **detain** someone, they keep them in a place under their control. [FORMAL] ❑ *Police have detained two people in connection with the attack.*
2 V-T To **detain** someone means to delay them, for example by talking to them. [FORMAL] ❑ *Could I ask just one more question—if I'm not detaining you?* [from Old French]

Word Link *tect ≈ covering : de*tect*, pro*tect*, pro*tect*ive*

de|tect /dɪtɛkt/ (**detects, detecting, detected**) **V-T** If you **detect** something, you find it or notice it. ❑ *One of the hotel guests detected the smell of smoke.* ❑ *Arnold could detect a sadness in the old man's face.* ● **de|tec|tion** **N-NONCOUNT** ❑ *The process is used in the detection of cancer.* [from Latin]

de|tec|tive /dɪtɛktɪv/ (**detectives**) **N-COUNT** A **detective** is someone whose job is to discover what has happened in a crime, and to find the people who did it. ❑ *Detectives are still searching for the four men.* [from Latin]

de|ten|tion /dɪtɛnʃ°n/ (**detentions**)
1 N-NONCOUNT **Detention** is when someone is arrested or put into prison. ❑ *...the detention of people involved in crime.*
2 N-COUNT/N-NONCOUNT **Detention** is a punishment for students who behave badly. They are made to stay at school after the other students have gone home. ❑ *He kept most of the class after school for detention.* [from Latin]

de|ter /dɪtɜr/ (**deters, deterring, deterred**) **V-T** To **deter** someone **from** doing something means to make them not want to do it or continue doing it. ❑ *High prices deter people from buying.* [from Latin]

de|ter|gent /dɪtɜrdʒ°nt/ (**detergents**) **N-COUNT/N-NONCOUNT** **Detergent** is a chemical substance that is used for washing things such as clothes or dishes. ❑ *Hand-*

wash the gloves in warm water, using a mild detergent. [from Latin]
→ look at Word Web: **soap**

de|terio|rate /dɪtɪəriəreɪt/ (**deteriorates, deteriorating, deteriorated**) **v-I** If something **deteriorates**, it becomes worse. ❑ Her eyesight is rapidly deteriorating. ● **de|terio|ra|tion** /dɪtɪəriəreɪʃ°n/ **N-NONCOUNT** ❑ Too little sleep can cause a deterioration in your health. [from Late Latin]

de|ter|mi|na|tion /dɪtɜrmɪneɪʃ°n/ **N-NONCOUNT Determination** is the feeling you have when you have firmly decided to do something. ❑ Everyone behaved with courage and determination. [from Old French]

Word Link	term, termin ≈ limit, end : determine, terminal, terminate

de|ter|mine /dɪtɜrmɪn/ (**determines, determining, determined**)
1 v-T If something **determines** what will happen, it controls it. [FORMAL] ❑ The size of the chicken pieces will determine the cooking time.
2 v-T To **determine** a fact means to discover it. [FORMAL] ❑ The investigation will determine what really happened. [from Old French]

de|ter|mined /dɪtɜrmɪnd/ **ADJ** If you are **determined to** do something, you have made a firm decision to do it. ❑ He is determined to win gold at the Olympics. [from Old French]

de|ter|min|er /dɪtɜrmɪnər/ (**determiners**)
N-COUNT LANGUAGE ARTS In grammar, a **determiner** is a word that is used at the beginning of a noun group to indicate, for example, which thing you are referring to or whether you are referring to one thing or several. Common English determiners are "a," "the," "some," "this," and "each." [from Old French]

de|test /dɪtɛst/ (**detests, detesting, detested**) **v-T** If you **detest** someone or something, you dislike them very much. ❑ You are probably aware that I detest smoking. [from Latin]

de|value /divælyu/ (**devalues, devaluing, devalued**)
1 v-T To **devalue** something means to cause it to be thought less impressive or less deserving of respect. ❑ They tried to devalue her work.
2 v-T BUSINESS To **devalue** the currency of a country means to reduce its value in relation to other currencies. ❑ India has devalued the rupee by about eleven percent.
● **de|valua|tion** /divælyueɪʃ°n/ (**devaluations**) **N-COUNT/N-NONCOUNT** ❑ It resulted in the devaluation of several currencies.

dev|as|tate /dɛvəsteɪt/ (**devastates, devastating, devastated**) **v-T** If something **devastates** an area or a place, it damages it very badly or destroys it completely. ❑ The earthquake devastated parts of Indonesia.
● **dev|as|ta|tion** /dɛvəsteɪʃ°n/ **N-NONCOUNT** ❑ The war brought massive devastation to the area. [from Latin]

dev|as|tat|ing /dɛvəsteɪtɪŋ/ **ADJ** If you describe something as **devastating**, you are emphasizing that it is very harmful or upsetting. ❑ We must find a cure for this devastating disease. ❑ When I heard about my dad's illness, it was devastating. [from Latin]

de|vel|op /dɪvɛləp/ (**develops, developing, developed**)
1 v-I When something **develops**, it grows or changes over a period of time. ❑ Children need time to develop. ❑ Over the years, their friendship developed into love. ● **de|vel|oped ADJ** ❑ Their bodies were well developed and very fit.
2 v-I If a problem or difficulty **develops**, it begins to occur. ❑ A problem developed aboard the space shuttle.
3 v-I If a country **develops**, it changes from being a poor country to being a rich country. ❑ All of these countries developed fast.
● **de|vel|oped ADJ** ❑ Family size is smaller in more developed countries.
4 v-T If someone **develops** a new product, they design it and produce it. ❑ Scientists have developed a car paint that changes color.
● **de|vel|op|er** (**developers**) **N-COUNT** ❑ ...a developer of computer software.
5 v-T To **develop** land or property means to build houses or factories on it. ❑ Local business people developed fashionable restaurants in the area. ● **de|vel|op|er** (**developers**) **N-COUNT** ❑ The land has a high value if it is sold to developers. [from Old French]

de|vel|op|ing /dɪvɛləpɪŋ/ **ADJ** SOCIAL STUDIES If you talk about **developing** countries or the **developing** world, you mean the countries or the parts of the world that are poor and have few industries. ❑ In the developing world pollution is increasing. [from Old French]

d

D

de|vel|op|ment /dɪvɛləpmənt/
(**developments**)
■ **N-NONCOUNT Development** is the process of growing or changing over a period of time. ❑ *We've been studying the development of language.*
■ **N-NONCOUNT** BUSINESS **Development** is the growth of a business or an industry. ❑ *Our business is the development of new technology.*
■ **N-COUNT** A **development** is an event or an incident that has recently happened and has an effect on an existing situation. ❑ *Police say this is an important development in the investigation.*
■ **N-COUNT** A **development** is a group of buildings that have been built together on a piece of land. ❑ *...a 16-house development.* [from Old French]

de|vi|ate /diːvieɪt/ (**deviates, deviating, deviated**) **V-I** To **deviate from** something means to start doing something different or not planned, especially in a way that causes problems for others. ❑ *The message deviated from the government's policy.* ● **de|via|tion** /diːvieɪʃⁿn/ (**deviations**) **N-COUNT/N-NONCOUNT** ❑ *...a deviation from your daily routine.* [from Late Latin]

de|vice /dɪvaɪs/ (**devices**) **N-COUNT** A **device** is an object that has been invented for a particular purpose. ❑ *He used an electronic device to measure the rooms.* [from Old French]

dev|il /dɛvⁿl/ **N-PROPER** Some people believe that **the devil** is an evil spirit that makes bad things happen. [from Old English]

de|vise /dɪvaɪz/ (**devises, devising, devised**) **V-T** If you **devise** a plan, you have the idea for it. ❑ *We devised a plan to help him.* [from Old French]

de|vote /dɪvoʊt/ (**devotes, devoting, devoted**) **V-T** If you **devote** yourself, your time, or your energy **to** something, you spend all or most of your time or energy on it. ❑ *He devoted the rest of his life to science.* [from Latin]

de|vot|ed /dɪvoʊtɪd/ **ADJ** Someone who is **devoted to** a person loves that person very much. ❑ *He was devoted to his wife.* [from Latin]

dew /du/ **N-NONCOUNT Dew** is small drops of water that form on the ground during the night. ❑ *The dew formed on the leaves.* [from Old English]

dew point (**dew points**) **N-COUNT** SCIENCE The **dew point** is the temperature at which water vapor in the air becomes liquid and dew begins to form.

dia|be|tes /daɪəbitɪs, -tiz/ **N-NONCOUNT Diabetes** is a medical condition in which someone has too much sugar in their blood. [from Latin]
→ look at Word Web: **sugar**

| Word Link | *dia* ≈ *across, through* : *diagnose, diagonal, dialogue* |

di|ag|nose /daɪəgnoʊs/ (**diagnoses, diagnosing, diagnosed**) **V-T** If someone is **diagnosed as** having a particular illness, a doctor discovers what is wrong with them. ❑ *His wife was diagnosed with diabetes.* [from New Latin]
→ look at Word Webs: **diagnosis, illness**

| Word Link | *osis* ≈ *state or condition* : *diagnosis, hypnosis, symbiosis* |

di|ag|no|sis /daɪəgnoʊsɪs/ (**diagnoses**) **N-COUNT/N-NONCOUNT Diagnosis** is when a doctor discovers what is wrong with someone who is ill. ❑ *I had a second test to confirm the diagnosis.* [from New Latin]
→ look at Word Web: **diagnosis**

di|ago|nal /daɪægənⁿl, -ægnⁿl/ **ADJ** MATH A **diagonal** line goes from one corner of

---

Word Web diagnosis

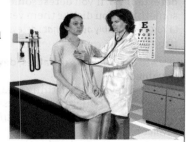

Many doctors suggest that their **patients** get a routine **physical examination** once a year—even if they're feeling healthy. This enables the **physician** to see any **symptoms** early and **diagnose** possible **diseases** at an early stage. The doctor may begin by looking down the patient's throat for possible **infections**. Then he or she may use a **stethoscope** to listen to subtle sounds in the heart, lungs, and stomach. A **blood pressure** reading is always part of the physical exam.

a square across to the opposite corner.
❑ *The screen showed a pattern of diagonal lines.*
● **di|ago|nal|ly** **ADV** ❑ *He ran diagonally across the field.* [from Latin]

> **Word Link**   gram ≈ writing : *dia*gram, *pro*gram, *tele*gram

dia|gram /daɪəgræm/ (**diagrams**) **N-COUNT**
A **diagram** is a simple drawing of lines that is used, for example, to explain how a machine works. ❑ *He showed us a diagram of the inside of a computer.* [from Latin]

dial /daɪəl/ (**dials, dialing, dialed**)
■ **N-COUNT** A **dial** is the part of a machine or a piece of equipment that shows you the time or a measurement. ❑ *The dial on the clock showed five minutes to seven.*
◗ **N-COUNT** A **dial** is a small wheel on a piece of equipment that you can move in order to control the way it works. ❑ *He turned the dial on the radio.*
■ **V-T/V-I** If you **dial** or if you **dial** a number, you press the buttons on a telephone in order to call someone. ❑ *Dial the number, followed by the "#" sign.* [from Medieval Latin]

dia|lect /daɪəlɛkt/ (**dialects**) **N-COUNT**
A **dialect** is a form of a language that people speak in a particular area. ❑ *They were speaking in the local dialect.* [from Latin]
→ look at Word Web: **English**

dia|log box /daɪəlɔg bɒks/ (**dialog boxes**)
N-COUNT TECHNOLOGY A **dialog box** is a small area that appears on a computer screen, containing information or questions.
❑ *Clicking here brings up another dialog box.*

> **Word Link**   log ≈ reason, speech : *apo*log*y*, *dia*log*ue*, *lo*gic

dia|logue /daɪəlɔg/ (**dialogues**) also **dialog**
N-COUNT/N-NONCOUNT LANGUAGE ARTS
A **dialogue** is a conversation between two people in a book, a movie, or a play.
❑ *He writes great dialogues.* ❑ *The movie contains some very funny dialogue.* [from Old French]

dial-up **ADJ** TECHNOLOGY A **dial-up** connection to the Internet uses a normal telephone line. ❑ *This website takes a few minutes to load over a dial-up connection.*

di|am|eter /daɪæmɪtər/ (**diameters**)
N-COUNT MATH The **diameter** of a round object is the length of a straight line that can be drawn across it, passing through the middle of it. ❑ *The tube is much smaller than*

the diameter of a human hair. [from Medieval Latin]
→ look at Picture Dictionary: **area**
→ look at Word Web: **circle**

dia|mond /daɪmənd, daɪə-/ (**diamonds**)
■ **N-COUNT/N-NONCOUNT** A **diamond** is a hard, clear, stone that is very expensive, and is used for making jewelry. ❑ *...a pair of diamond earrings.*
◗ **N-COUNT** A **diamond** is the shape ♦.
❑ *A baseball field is in the shape of a diamond.*
■ **N-NONCOUNT** **Diamonds** is one of the four suits in a deck of playing cards. Each card is marked with one or more red symbols: ♦.
❑ *He picked the seven of diamonds.*
◖ **N-COUNT** A **diamond** is a playing card of this suit. ❑ *He played a diamond.* [from Old French]
→ look at Word Web: **crystal**

dia|per /daɪpər, daɪə-/ (**diapers**) **N-COUNT**
A **diaper** is a piece of soft cloth or paper that you fasten around a baby's bottom and between its legs. ❑ *She fed the baby and changed its diaper.* [from Old French]

dia|phragm /daɪəfræm/ (**diaphragms**)
N-COUNT SCIENCE Your **diaphragm** is a muscle between your lungs and your stomach. It is used when you breathe.
❑ *...the skill of breathing from the diaphragm.* [from Late Latin]
→ look at Word Web: **respiratory system**

di|ar|rhea /daɪəriə/ **N-NONCOUNT** If someone has **diarrhea**, all the waste products come out of their body as liquid because they are sick. ❑ *Many team members suffered from diarrhea.* [from Late Latin]

dia|ry /daɪəri/ (**diaries**) **N-COUNT** A **diary** is a book that has a separate space for each day of the year. You use a diary to write down things that you plan to do, or to record what happens in your life. ❑ *I read the entry from his diary for July 10, 1940.* [from Latin]
→ look at Word Webs: **diary, history**

dia|ton|ic scale /daɪətɒnɪk skeɪl/ (**diatonic scales**) **N-COUNT** SCIENCE A **diatonic scale** is the sequence of musical notes that make up a major or minor scale.

dice /daɪs/ (**dice**) **N-COUNT** A **dice** is a small block of wood or plastic with spots on its sides, used for playing games. ❑ *I threw both dice and got a double 6.*

d

Word Web   diary

Someone writes in a **diary** to tell about the things that happen in their daily life. Most diaries are private **documents** and are not shared with others. But sometimes an important diary is published as a book. One such example is *The Diary of a Young Girl*. This is Anne Frank's World War II **chronicle** of her family's experience as they hid from the Nazis. They were found and arrested, and later Anne died in a concentration camp. This **primary source** document tells Anne's story in her own words. It is full of rich details that are often missing from other historical **texts**. The book is now available in 60 different languages.

---

di|choto|mous key /daɪkɒtəməs kiː/ (**dichotomous keys**) **N-COUNT** SCIENCE
A **dichotomous key** is a system for identifying species of plants or animals based on pairs of questions.

di|choto|my /daɪkɒtəmi/ (**dichotomies**) **N-COUNT** If there is a **dichotomy** between two things or ideas, there is a great difference between them. [FORMAL] ❑ *There is a dichotomy between the academic world and the industrial world.* [from Greek]

> **Word Link**   dict ≈ speaking : contradict, dictate, predict

dic|tate /dɪkteɪt, dɪkteɪt/ (**dictates, dictating, dictated**)
1 **V-T** If you **dictate** something, you say it or record it onto a machine, so that someone else can write it down. ❑ *He dictated his life story to his grandson.*
2 **V-T** If you **dictate to** someone, you tell them what they must do. ❑ *Why should they dictate to us what we should eat?* [from Latin]

dic|ta|tion /dɪkteɪʃᵊn/ **N-NONCOUNT**
Dictation is when one person speaks and someone else writes down what they are saying. ❑ *She was taking dictation from the dean of the graduate school.* [from Latin]

dic|ta|tor /dɪkteɪtər/ (**dictators**) **N-COUNT**
SOCIAL STUDIES A **dictator** is a ruler who has complete power in a country. ❑ *The country was ruled by a dictator for more than twenty years.* [from Latin]

> **Word Link**   ship ≈ condition or state : citizenship, dictatorship, friendship

dic|ta|tor|ship /dɪkteɪtərʃɪp/ (**dictatorships**)
1 **N-COUNT/N-NONCOUNT** SOCIAL STUDIES
Dictatorship is government by a dictator.

❑ *...a long period of military dictatorship in the country.*
2 **N-COUNT** SOCIAL STUDIES A **dictatorship** is a country that is ruled by a dictator or by a very strict and harsh government. ❑ *Every country in the region was a military dictatorship.* [from Latin]

dic|tion /dɪkʃᵊn/ **N-NONCOUNT** Someone's **diction** is how clearly they speak or sing. [from Latin]

dic|tion|ary /dɪkʃəneri/ (**dictionaries**)
N-COUNT LANGUAGE ARTS A **dictionary** is a book in which the words and phrases of a language are listed, together with their meanings. ❑ *We checked the spelling in the dictionary.* [from Medieval Latin]

did /dɪd/ **Did** is the past tense of **do**. [from Old English]

didn't /dɪdᵊnt/ **Didn't** is short for "did not."

die /daɪ/ (**dies, dying, died**)
1 **V-I** When people, animals, and plants **die**, they stop living. ❑ *My dog died last week.* ❑ *Sadly, my mother died of cancer.*
2 **V-I** You can say that you **are dying of** thirst, hunger, or curiosity if you are very thirsty, hungry, or curious. [INFORMAL] ❑ *I need a drink—I'm dying of thirst.*
3 **V-I** You can say that you **are dying for** something if you want it very much. [INFORMAL] ❑ *I'm dying for some fresh air.*
4 **V-T** You can say that you **are dying to** do something if you want to do it very much. [INFORMAL] ❑ *I was dying to read the news.*
5 **V-I** When something **dies**, or when it **dies down**, it gradually becomes weaker, until it no longer exists. ❑ *My love for you will never die.* ❑ *The wind died down.* [from Old English]
6 → see also **dying**
▶ **die out** If something **dies out**, it becomes

less and less common and eventually disappears completely. ❑ *The old customs are dying out.*

Word Partnership	Use **die** with :
v	**deserve to** die, **going to** die, **live or** die, **sentenced to** die, **want to** die, **would rather** die **1**
N	**right to** die **1**

die\|sel /díz^əl/ **N-NONCOUNT** Diesel or diesel oil is a fuel that is used in some vehicles' engines. [after Rudolf Diesel (1858-1913), a German inventor and mechanical engineer]

diet /dáɪɪt/ (**diets, dieting, dieted**)
1 **N-COUNT/N-NONCOUNT** Your **diet** is the type of food that you regularly eat. ❑ *It's never too late to improve your diet.*
2 **N-COUNT/N-NONCOUNT** If you are on a **diet**, you eat special types of food, or you eat less food than usual. ❑ *Have you been on a diet? You've lost a lot of weight.*
3 **V-I** If you **are dieting**, you eat special types of food or you eat less food than usual. ❑ *I've been dieting since the birth of my child.* [from Old French]
→ look at Word Webs: **diet, vegetarian**

Word Partnership	Use **diet** with :
ADJ	**balanced** diet, **healthy** diet, **proper** diet, **vegetarian** diet **1** strict diet **2**
N	diet **and exercise**, diet **supplements 1 2** diet **pills 2**
PREP	**on a** diet **2**

dif\|fer /dífər/ (**differs, differing, differed**)
V-T/V-I If two or more things **differ**, they are different from each other. ❑ *The story he told police differed from the one he told his mother.* [from Latin]

Usage	differ

Be sure to use the correct preposition after *differ*. *Differ from* means "are different from" or "are unlike": *Bicycles differ from tricycles in having two wheels instead of three.* *Differ with* means "disagree with": *Milagros differed with Armando about where to go this summer, to the beach or to the mountains.*

dif\|fer\|ence /dífərəns, dífrəns/ (**differences**)
1 **N-COUNT** The **difference** between two things is the way in which they are different from each other. ❑ *The main difference between the two computers is the price.*
2 **N-SING** A **difference** between two quantities is the amount by which one quantity is more or less than the other. ❑ *The difference between 8532 and 8522 is 10.*
3 **PHRASE** If something **makes** a **difference** or **makes** a lot of **difference**, it has an important effect on you. ❑ *Where you live makes such a difference to the way you feel.*
4 **PHRASE** If something **makes** no **difference**, it does not have any effect on what you are doing. ❑ *The weather makes no difference to me in my job.* [from Latin]

Word Partnership	Use **difference** with :
ADJ	**big/major** difference **1**
V	**know the** difference, **notice a** difference, **tell the** difference **1** **pay the** difference **2** **make a** difference **3**
N	difference **in age**, difference **in price 2**

dif\|fer\|ent /dífərənt, dífrənt/
1 **ADJ** If two people or things are **different**, they are not like each other. ❑ *London was different from most European capital cities.*
● **dif\|fer\|ent\|ly** **ADV** ❑ *Every person learns differently.*
2 **ADJ** You use **different** to show that you are

Word Web   diet

Recent U.S. government reports show that about 66% of American adults are **overweight** or **obese**. The number of people on **weight-loss diets** is the highest ever. Many people are trying **fad** diets to lose weight. One diet tells people to eat mostly **protein**—meat, fish, and cheese—and very few **carbohydrates**. However, another diet tells people to eat at least 40% carbohydrates. A weight-loss diet works when you burn more **calories** than you eat. Most doctors agree that a balanced diet with plenty of exercise is the best way to lose weight.

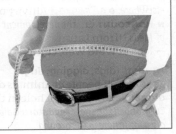

D

talking about two or more separate things of the same type. ❑ *Different countries export different products.*

❸ **ADJ** You say something is **different** when it is unusual. ❑ *Her taste in clothes is interesting and different.* [from Latin]

dif|fi|cult /dɪfɪkʌlt, -kəlt/

❶ **ADJ** Something that is **difficult** is not easy to do, understand, or deal with. ❑ *The homework was too difficult for us.* ❑ *It was a very difficult decision to make.*

❷ **ADJ** Someone who is **difficult** behaves in a way that is not reasonable or helpful. ❑ *My son is 10 years old and a very difficult child.*

Thesaurus difficult Also look up :
ADJ challenging, demanding, hard, tough; (ant.) easy, simple, uncomplicated ❶ disagreeable, irritable; (ant.) accommodating, cooperative ❷

dif|fi|cul|ty /dɪfɪkʌlti, -kəlti/ (**difficulties**)

❶ **N-COUNT** A **difficulty** is a problem. ❑ *There's always the difficulty of getting information.*

❷ **N-NONCOUNT** If you have **difficulty** doing something, you are not able to do it easily. ❑ *Do you have difficulty walking?*

❸ **PHRASE** If someone or something is **in difficulty**, they are having a lot of problems. ❑ *The city's movie industry is in difficulty.* [from Latin]

dif|fi|dent /dɪfɪdənt/ **ADJ** Someone who is **diffident** is rather shy and lacks confidence. ❑ *Helen was diffident.* ● **dif|fi|dence** /dɪfɪdəns/ **N-NONCOUNT** ❑ *My initial diffidence has given way to confidence over the years.* [from Latin]

dif|fuse /dɪfyuz/ (**diffuses, diffusing, diffused**) **V-T/V-I** If something such as knowledge or information **is diffused**, or if it **diffuses** somewhere, it is made known over a wide area or to a lot of people. [WRITTEN] ❑ *The technology is diffused and used by other countries.* ❑ *...to diffuse new ideas obtained from elsewhere.* ● **dif|fu|sion** /dɪfyuʒən/ **N-NONCOUNT** ❑ *...the development and diffusion of ideas.* [from Latin]

→ look at Word Web: **culture**

dig /dɪg/ (**digs, digging, dug**)

❶ **V-T/V-I** If people or animals **dig**, or if they **dig** a hole, they make a hole in the ground. ❑ *I grabbed the shovel and started digging.* ❑ *First, dig a large hole in the ground.*

❷ **V-T/V-I** If you **dig** one thing **into** another, of if one thing **digs into** another, you push the first thing hard into the second. ❑ *She dug her spoon into the chocolate pudding.*

→ look at Word Web: **tunnel**

▶ **dig up** If you **dig** something **up**, you remove it from under the ground. ❑ *They made tools for digging up roots.*

dig

di|gest (**digests, digesting, digested**) **V-T/V-I** SCIENCE When you **digest** food, it passes through your body to your stomach. ❑ *Do not swim for an hour after a meal to allow time to digest your food.* ❑ *Give him time for his food to digest.* ● **di|ges|tion** /daɪdʒɛstʃən/ **N-NONCOUNT** ❑ *Peppermint helps digestion.* [from Late Latin]

→ look at Word Web: **cooking**

dig|it /dɪdʒɪt/ (**digits**) **N-COUNT** MATH A **digit** is a written symbol for any of the ten numbers from 0 to 9. ❑ *Her telephone number differs from mine by one digit.* [from Latin]

digi|tal /dɪdʒɪtəl/

❶ **ADJ** TECHNOLOGY **Digital** systems record or send information in the form of thousands of very small signals. ❑ *Most people now have digital television.*

❷ **ADJ** TECHNOLOGY **Digital** equipment gives information in the form of numbers. Compare with **analog**. ❑ *I've got a new digital watch.* [from Latin]

→ look at Picture Dictionary: **time**

→ look at Word Webs: **technology, television**

Word Link dign ≈ proper, worthy : dignified, dignitary, dignity

dig|ni|fied /dɪgnɪfaɪd/ **ADJ** Someone or something that is **dignified** is calm and serious, and deserves respect. ❑ *He was a very dignified and charming man.* [from Old French]

dig|ni|tary /dɪgnɪtɛri/ (**dignitaries**) **N-COUNT** **Dignitaries** are people who have a high rank in government or in a church. ❑ *...money used for entertaining visiting dignitaries.* [from Old French]

dig|nity /dɪgnɪti/ **N-NONCOUNT** If someone behaves or moves with **dignity**, they are serious, calm, and controlled. ❑ *She received the news with quiet dignity.* [from Old French]

Word Link *di ≈ two : digraph, dilemma, diverge*

di|graph /daɪgræf/ (digraphs) N-COUNT
LANGUAGE ARTS A **digraph** is a combination of two letters that represents a single speech sound, such as "ea" in "bread."

di|la|tion /daɪleɪʃ³n/ (dilations)
N-COUNT/N-NONCOUNT MATH In mathematics, a **dilation** is a procedure in which a figure such as a triangle is made bigger or smaller but its shape stays the same. [from Latin]

di|lem|ma /dɪlɛmə/ (dilemmas) N-COUNT
A **dilemma** is a difficult situation in which you have to make a choice between two things. ❑ *He was facing a dilemma: should he return to his country or stay in Europe?* [from Latin]

dili|gent /dɪlɪdʒ³nt/ ADJ Someone who is **diligent** works hard in a careful and thorough way. ❑ *She's a diligent student.*
● **dili|gence** /dɪlɪdʒ³ns/ N-NONCOUNT
❑ *He performed his duties with diligence.*
● **dili|gent|ly** ADV ❑ *He was diligently searching the house.* [from Old French]

di|lute /daɪlut/ (dilutes, diluting, diluted) V-T
SCIENCE If you **dilute** a liquid, you add water or another liquid to it. ❑ *This juice is quite strong, but you can dilute it with water.* ❑ *The liquid is then diluted.* [from Latin]

dim /dɪm/ (dimmer, dimmest, dims, dimming, dimmed)
■ ADJ **Dim** light is not bright. ❑ *She waited in the dim light.* ● **dim|ly** ADV ❑ *Two lamps burned dimly.*
■ V-T/V-I If you **dim** a light or if it **dims**, it becomes less bright. ❑ *Could someone dim the lights, please?* [from Old English]

dime /daɪm/ (dimes) N-COUNT A **dime** is a U.S. coin worth ten cents. [from Old French]

di|men|sion /dɪmɛnʃ³n, daɪ-/ (dimensions)
■ N-COUNT A particular **dimension** of something is an aspect of it. ❑ *He could bring the moral dimension back to politics.*
■ N-PLURAL MATH The **dimensions** of something are its measurements. ❑ *We do not yet know the exact dimensions of the room.* [from Old French]

di|men|sion|al analy|sis /dɪmɛnʃən³l ənælɪsɪs, daɪ-/ (dimensional analyses)
N-COUNT/N-NONCOUNT SCIENCE **Dimensional analysis** is a method used by scientists to understand the relationships between things that are measured in different sorts of units.

Word Link *min ≈ small, lessen : diminish, minus, minute*

di|min|ish /dɪmɪnɪʃ/ (diminishes, diminishing, diminished) V-T/V-I When something **diminishes**, or when something **diminishes** it, it becomes reduced in size, importance, or intensity. ❑ *The threat of war has diminished.* ❑ *This doesn't diminish what he has achieved.* [from Latin]

di|min|ished in|ter|val (diminished intervals) N-COUNT MUSIC In music, a **diminished interval** is an interval that is reduced by half a step or half a tone.

di|minu|tive /dɪmɪnyətɪv/ ADJ A **diminutive** person or object is very small. ❑ *A diminutive figure stood at the entrance.* [from Latin]

dine /daɪn/ (dines, dining, dined) V-I When you **dine**, you have dinner. [FORMAL] ❑ *He drives a nice car and dines at the best restaurants.* [from Old French]

din|er /daɪnər/ (diners) N-COUNT A **diner** is a small cheap restaurant that is often open all day. ❑ *...an all-night diner.* [from Old French]

din|ing room (dining rooms) N-COUNT
A **dining room** is a room where people eat their meals.
→ look at Picture Dictionary: **house**

din|ner /dɪnər/ (dinners)
■ N-COUNT/N-NONCOUNT **Dinner** is the main meal of the day, usually served in the evening. ❑ *She invited us for dinner.* ❑ *Would you like to stay and have dinner?*
■ N-COUNT A **dinner** is a formal social event in the evening at which a meal is served. ❑ *...a series of official dinners.* [from Old French]
→ look at Word Web: **meal**

dino|flag|el|late /daɪnoʊflædʒəlɪt, -leɪt/ (dinoflagellates) N-COUNT SCIENCE
Dinoflagellates are tiny organisms that live in sea water and fresh water and are found in plankton. [from New Latin]

di|no|saur /daɪnəsɔr/ (dinosaurs) N-COUNT
Dinosaurs were large animals that lived millions of years ago. [from New Latin]

dip /dɪp/ (dips, dipping, dipped)
■ V-T If you **dip** something **in** a liquid, you put it in and then quickly take it out again. ❑ *Dip each apple in the syrup.*
■ N-COUNT A **dip** is a thick sauce that you

dip pieces of food into before eating them. ❑ *We sat and watched the Super Bowl with a huge plate of chips and dips.*

❸ v-i If something **dips**, it makes a downward movement. ❑ *The boat dipped slightly as he got in.*

❹ v-i If a road or a path **dips**, it goes down suddenly to a lower level. ❑ *The road dipped and rose again.* [from Old English]

di|plo|ma /dɪploʊmə/ (**diplomas**) **N-COUNT** A **diploma** is a qualification that a student who has completed a course of study may receive. ❑ *He was awarded a diploma in social work.* [from Latin]

→ look at Word Web: **graduation**

di|plo|ma|cy /dɪploʊməsi/ **N-NONCOUNT** **Diplomacy** is the activity or profession of managing relations between the governments of different countries. ❑ *If diplomacy fails, there could be a war.* [from French]

dip|lo|mat /dɪpləmæt/ (**diplomats**) **N-COUNT** A **diplomat** is a senior official whose job is to discuss international affairs with officials from other countries. ❑ *Sir Harold is a Western diplomat with experience in Asia.* [from French]

dip|lo|mat|ic /dɪpləmætɪk/

❶ ADJ **Diplomatic** means relating to diplomacy and diplomats. ❑ *The two countries enjoy good diplomatic relations.*

● **dip|lo|mati|cal|ly** /dɪpləmætɪkli/ **ADV** ❑ *The conflict was resolved diplomatically.*

❷ ADJ Someone who is **diplomatic** is careful to say or do things without offending people. ❑ *She is very direct, but I prefer a more diplomatic approach.* ● **dip|lo|mati|cal|ly ADV** ❑ *"Of course," agreed Sloan diplomatically.* [from French]

Word Link	*rect ≈ right, straight : cor*rect, *di*rect, *rect*angle

di|rect /dɪrɛkt, daɪ-/ (**directs, directing, directed**)

❶ ADJ **Direct** means moving toward a place or an object, without changing direction and without stopping. ❑ *They took a direct flight to Athens.*

❷ ADV **Direct** is also an adverb. ❑ *You can fly direct from Seattle to London.*

❸ ADJ **Direct** means with nothing else in between. ❑ *Protect your plants from direct sunlight.*

❹ ADV **Direct** is also an adverb. ❑ *More farms*

are selling direct to consumers.

❺ ADJ Someone whose behavior is **direct** is honest and open, and says exactly what they mean. ❑ *He avoided giving a direct answer.*

● **di|rect|ness N-NONCOUNT** ❑ *He spoke with rare directness.*

❻ v-t If something **is directed at** a particular person or thing, it is aimed at them. ❑ *The question was directed toward her.* ❑ *The abuse was directed at the manager.*

❼ v-t If you **direct** someone to a place, you tell them how to get there. ❑ *Could you direct our visitors to Dr. Lamont's office, please?*

❽ v-t When someone **directs** a project or a group of people, they are responsible for organizing them. ❑ *Christopher will direct everyday operations.*

❾ v-t/v-i When someone **directs** a movie, a play, or a television program, they are responsible for the way in which it is performed. ❑ *He directed several TV shows.* ❑ *Branagh himself will star and direct.* [from Latin]

Thesaurus	direct Also look up :
ADJ	nonstop, straight **❶**
	firsthand, personal **❷**
	candid, frank, plain **❸**

di|rect|ing /dɪrɛkt, daɪ-/ **N-NONCOUNT** **Directing** is the work that the director of a movie, a play, or a television program does. [from Latin]

di|rec|tion /dɪrɛkʃən, daɪ-/ (**directions**)

❶ N-COUNT/N-NONCOUNT A **direction** is the general line that someone or something is moving or pointing in. ❑ *The nearest town was ten miles in the opposite direction.* ❑ *He started walking in the direction of Larry's shop.*

❷ N-PLURAL **Directions** are instructions that tell you what to do, how to do something, or how to get somewhere. ❑ *She stopped the car to ask for directions.*

❸ N-NONCOUNT **Direction** is the control and management of a project or a group of people. ❑ *Organizations need clear direction.* [from Latin]

Word Partnership	Use direction with :
ADJ	**general** direction, **opposite** direction, **right** direction, **wrong** direction **❶**
N	**sense of** direction **❶**
V	**change** direction, **move in a** direction **❶**
	lack direction, **take** direction **❸**

di|rec|tive /dɪrɛktɪv, daɪ-/ (**directives**)
N-COUNT A **directive** is an official instruction that is given by someone in authority. ❏ *The new directive means that food labeling will be more specific.* [from Latin]

di|rect|ly /dɪrɛktli, daɪ-/
1 ADV If one thing is **directly** above, below, or in front of another thing, there is nothing between them. ❏ *They live in the apartment directly above us.*
2 ADV **Directly** means in a way that involves two people or things, with no one or nothing else in between. ❏ *Never look directly at the sun.*
3 ADV If you say something **directly**, you are honest and open, and you say exactly what you mean. ❏ *Explain simply and directly what you hope to achieve.*
4 ADV If you move **directly** toward a place or an object, you do not stop or change direction on your way. ❏ *On arriving in New York, Dylan went directly to Greenwich Village.* [from Latin]

di|rect ob|ject (**direct objects**) **N-COUNT** In grammar, the **direct object** of a verb is the noun or pronoun that is directly affected by the action of the subject. For example, in "I saw him yesterday," "him" is the direct object. Compare with **indirect object**.

di|rec|tor /dɪrɛktər, daɪ-/ (**directors**)
1 N-COUNT BUSINESS The **directors** of a company or an organization are the people who control it. ❏ *We wrote to the directors of the bank.*
2 N-COUNT ARTS The **director** of a play, a movie, or a television program is the person who tells the actors and technical staff what to do. [from Latin]
→ look at Word Web: **theater**

di|rec|tory /dɪrɛktəri, daɪ-/ (**directories**)
N-COUNT A **directory** is a book containing lists of people's names, addresses, and telephone numbers. ❏ *You'll find our number in the telephone directory.* [from Latin]

dirt /dɜrt/
1 N-NONCOUNT If there is **dirt** on something, there is dust or mud on it. ❏ *I started to clean the dirt off my hands.*
2 N-NONCOUNT You can call the earth on the ground **dirt**. ❏ *They all sat on the dirt under a tree.* [from Old Norse]
→ look at Word Web: **erosion**

dirty /dɜrti/ (**dirtier, dirtiest**) **ADJ** If something is **dirty**, it needs to be cleaned. ❏ *She collected the dirty plates from the table.* [from Old Norse]

dis|abil|ity /dɪsəbɪliti/ (**disabilities**)
N-COUNT A **disability** is a permanent injury or condition that makes it difficult for someone to work or live normally. ❏ *We're building a new classroom for people with disabilities.* [from Old French]
→ look at Word Web: **disability**

dis|abled /dɪseɪbᵊld/ **ADJ** Someone who is **disabled** has an injury or a condition that makes it difficult for them to move around. ❏ *...parents of disabled children.* [from Latin]

dis|ad|vant|age /dɪsədvæntɪdʒ/ (**disadvantages**)
1 N-COUNT A **disadvantage** is something that makes things more difficult for you. ❏ *The big disadvantage of this computer is its size.*
2 PHRASE If you are **at a disadvantage**, you have a difficulty that many other people do not have. ❏ *Children from poor families were at a disadvantage.* [from Latin]

Word Web   disability

Careful planning is making public places more **accessible** for people with **disabilities**. For hundreds of years **wheelchairs** have helped **paralyzed** people move around their homes. Today, **ramps** help people cross the street, enter buildings, and get to work. Extra-wide doorways make it easier to use public restrooms. **Blind** people are also more active and independent. Seeing Eye dogs, **canes**, and beeping crosswalks all help them get around safely. Some movie theaters rent headsets for people who have a hearing impairment. **Hearing dogs** help **deaf** people stay connected. And sign language allows people who are deaf to communicate.

Word Link dis ≈ negative, not : dis**agree**, dis**comfort**, dis**connect**

dis|agree /dɪsəgriː/ (**disagrees, disagreeing, disagreed**)

1 **V-T/V-I** If you **disagree with** someone, you have a different opinion from theirs. ❑ *I really have to disagree with you here.* ❑ *O'Brien disagreed with the suggestion that his team played badly.*

2 **V-I** If you **disagree with** an action or a decision, you disapprove of it. ❑ *I respect the president but I disagree with his decision.* [from Old French]

dis|agree|ment /dɪsəgriːmənt/ (**disagreements**)

1 **N-NONCOUNT** **Disagreement** is when people do not agree with a plan or an idea. ❑ *Britain and France have expressed disagreement with the plan.*

2 **N-COUNT/N-NONCOUNT** When there is **disagreement** about something, people disagree with each other about it. ❑ *Congress and the president are still in disagreement over the plans.* [from Old French]

dis|ap|pear /dɪsəpɪər/ (**disappears, disappearing, disappeared**)

1 **V-I** If someone or something **disappears**, they go away and you cannot see them. ❑ *His daughter disappeared thirteen years ago.* ❑ *The sun disappeared and it started raining again.*

● **dis|ap|pear|ance** (**disappearances**) **N-COUNT/N-NONCOUNT** ❑ *Her disappearance is a mystery.*

2 **V-I** If something **disappears**, it stops existing. ❑ *The immediate threat has disappeared.* [from Old French]

dis|ap|point /dɪsəpɔɪnt/ (**disappoints, disappointing, disappointed**) **V-T** If something **disappoints** you, it is not as good as you hoped. ❑ *The team did not disappoint the crowd.* ● **dis|ap|point|ing** **ADJ** ❑ *The restaurant looked great, but the food was disappointing.* [from Old French]

dis|ap|point|ed /dɪsəpɔɪntɪd/ **ADJ** If you are **disappointed**, you are sad because something has not happened or because something is not as good as you hoped. ❑ *I was disappointed that John was not there.* [from Old French]

dis|ap|point|ment /dɪsəpɔɪntmənt/ (**disappointments**)

1 **N-NONCOUNT** **Disappointment** is the feeling you have when you are disappointed. ❑ *She couldn't hide the disappointment in her voice.*

2 **N-COUNT** Something or someone that is a **disappointment** is not as good as you hoped. ❑ *The loss was a huge disappointment for the fans.* [from Old French]

dis|ap|prov|al /dɪsəpruːvəl/ **N-NONCOUNT** If you show **disapproval**, you show that you do not approve of someone or something. ❑ *He stared at Marina with disapproval.* [from Old French]

dis|ap|prove /dɪsəpruːv/ (**disapproves, disapproving, disapproved**) **V-I** If you **disapprove of** something or someone, you do not like them, or do not approve of them. ❑ *Most people disapprove of violence.* [from Old French]

dis|as|ter /dɪzæstər/ (**disasters**)

1 **N-COUNT** A **disaster** is a very bad accident or event that may hurt many people. ❑ *It was the second air disaster (= plane crash) that month.*

2 **N-COUNT** If something is a **disaster**, it is not at all successful. ❑ *The concert was a total disaster.* [from Italian]

→ look at Word Web: **disaster**

dis|as|trous /dɪzæstrəs/ **ADJ** A **disastrous** event causes a lot of problems for many people. ❑ *The country suffered a disastrous earthquake in July.* [from Italian]

Word Web disaster

We are learning more about nature's cycles. But natural **disasters** remain a big challenge. We can predict some disasters, such as **hurricanes** and **floods**. However, we still can't avoid the **damage** they do. Each year **monsoons** strike southern Asia. Monsoons are a combination of **typhoons**, **tropical storms**, and heavy **rains**. In addition to the damage caused by floods, **landslides** and **mudslides** add to the problem.

dis|be|lief /dɪsbɪliːf/ N-NONCOUNT Disbelief is when you do not believe that something is true or real. ❑ *She looked at him in disbelief.*

disc /dɪsk/ → look up **disk**

dis|card /dɪskɑrd/ (discards, discarding, discarded) V-T If you discard something, you get rid of it. ❑ *Do not discard your receipt.* [from Old French]

dis|cern|ible /dɪsɜrnəbᵊl/ ADJ If something is discernible, you can see it or recognize that it exists. [FORMAL] ❑ *The outline of the island is just discernible.* [from Old French]

dis|charge (discharges, discharging, discharged)

> **PRONUNCIATION HELP**
> Pronounce the verb /dɪstʃɑrdʒ/. Pronounce the noun /dɪstʃɑrdʒ/.

1 V-T When someone is discharged from a hospital, a prison, or one of the armed services, they are officially allowed to leave, or told that they must leave. ❑ *He was discharged from hospital today.*
2 N-COUNT/N-NONCOUNT Discharge is also a noun. ❑ *...his discharge from the army.*
3 V-T If someone discharges their duties or responsibilities, they do everything that needs to be done in order to complete them. [FORMAL] ❑ *...the quiet skill with which he discharged his duties.*
4 V-T If something is discharged from inside a place, it comes out. [FORMAL] ❑ *The salty water was discharged at sea.*
5 N-COUNT/N-NONCOUNT When there is a discharge of a substance, the substance comes out from inside somewhere. [FORMAL] ❑ *The disease causes a discharge from the eyes.*
6 N-COUNT SCIENCE The discharge of a river is the amount of water that it carries from one place to another in a particular period of time. [from Old French]
→ look at Word Web: **lightning**

dis|ci|pline /dɪsɪplɪn/ (disciplines, disciplining, disciplined)
1 N-NONCOUNT Discipline is the practice of making people obey rules. ❑ *Children need discipline in order to feel secure and safe.*
2 N-NONCOUNT Discipline is the quality of being able to obey particular rules and standards. ❑ *He was impressed by the team's speed and discipline.*
3 V-T If someone is disciplined for something that they have done wrong,

they are punished for it. ❑ *The workman was disciplined by his company, but not dismissed.*
4 N-COUNT A discipline is a particular area of study. [FORMAL] ❑ *We're looking for people from a wide range of disciplines.* [from Latin]

disc jock|ey /dɪsk dʒɒki/ (disc jockeys) also **disk jockey** N-COUNT A disc jockey is someone whose job is to play music and talk on the radio.

dis|close /dɪskloʊz/ (discloses, disclosing, disclosed) V-T If you disclose information, you tell people about it. ❑ *They refused to disclose details of the deal.* [from Old French]

dis|clo|sure /dɪskloʊʒər/ (disclosures) N-COUNT/N-NONCOUNT Disclosure is the act of giving people new or secret information. ❑ *...disclosure of negative information about the company.* [from Old French]

dis|co /dɪskoʊ/ (discos) N-COUNT A disco is a place or an event where people dance to pop music. ❑ *Fridays and Saturdays are regular disco nights.*

dis|com|fort /dɪskʌmfərt/ N-NONCOUNT Discomfort is an unpleasant feeling in part of your body. ❑ *Steve had some discomfort, but no real pain.* [from Old French]

dis|con|nect /dɪskənɛkt/ (disconnects, disconnecting, disconnected) V-T If you disconnect a piece of equipment, you stop electricity or water from going into it. ❑ *Try disconnecting the telephone for a while.* [from Latin]

dis|count /dɪskaʊnt/ (discounts) N-COUNT A discount is a reduction in the usual price of something. ❑ *All staff get a 20% discount.* [from Old French]

dis|cour|age /dɪskɜrɪdʒ/ (discourages, discouraging, discouraged) V-T If someone or something discourages you, you do not want to do a particular activity any more. ❑ *Learning a language may be difficult at first. Don't let this discourage you.* ❑ *He discouraged her from accepting the invitation.* ● **dis|cour|aged** ADJ ❑ *He felt discouraged by his lack of progress.* [from Old French]

dis|course /dɪskɔrs/ N-NONCOUNT Discourse is spoken or written communication between people. ❑ *...political discourse.* [from Medieval Latin]

dis|cov|er /dɪskʌvər/ (discovers, discovering, discovered)
1 V-T If you discover something that you

D

did not know about before, you become aware of it. ❏ *She discovered that her daughter was earning $40 a day.*

2 V-T If something **is discovered**, someone finds it. ❏ *The car was discovered on a roadside outside the city.*

3 V-T When someone **discovers** a new place, substance, or method, they are the first person to find it or use it. ❏ *Who was the first European to discover America?* [from Old French]

Thesaurus discover Also look up :

v detect, find out, learn, uncover; (*ant.*) ignore, miss, overlook **1**
---

dis|cov|ery /dɪskʌvəri/ (**discoveries**)

1 N-COUNT/N-NONCOUNT If someone makes a **discovery**, they become aware of something that they did not know about before. ❏ *I made a surprising discovery.*

2 N-COUNT/N-NONCOUNT If someone makes a **discovery**, they are the first person to find or become aware of something that no one knew about before. ❏ *In that year, two important discoveries were made.* [from Old French]

Word Link cred ≈ to believe : discredit, credibility, incredible
---

dis|cred|it /dɪskrɛdɪt/ (**discredits, discrediting, discredited**) **V-T** To **discredit** someone or something means to cause them to lose people's respect or trust. ❏ *...research which discredits the theory.*
● **dis|cred|it|ed ADJ** ❏ *The government is thoroughly discredited.* [from Old French]

dis|cred|it|able /dɪskrɛdɪtəbᵊl/ **ADJ** Discreditable behavior is shameful and wrong. [FORMAL] ❏ *She had been suspended from her job for discreditable behavior.* [from Old French]

dis|creet /dɪskrit/ **ADJ** If you are **discreet**, you are polite and careful in what you do or say. ❏ *He was a real gentleman, and he was always very discreet.* [from Old French]

dis|crete /dɪskrit/ **ADJ** Discrete ideas or things are separate and distinct from each other. [FORMAL] ❏ *The instruction manual breaks the job down into several discrete steps.* [from Latin]

dis|cre|tion /dɪskrɛʃᵊn/

1 N-NONCOUNT Discretion is the quality of behaving in a quiet and controlled way

without drawing attention to yourself or giving away personal or private information. [FORMAL] ❏ *Angela was a model of discretion and didn't ask what had been in the letter.*

2 N-NONCOUNT If someone in a position of authority uses their **discretion** or has **the discretion** to do something in a particular situation, they have the freedom and authority to decide what to do. [FORMAL] ❏ *City departments have wide discretion on the contracts.* ❏ *We may change the rate at our discretion and will notify you of any change.* [from Old French]

dis|crimi|nate /dɪskrɪmɪneɪt/ (**discriminates, discriminating, discriminated**) **V-I** SOCIAL STUDIES To **discriminate against** a group of people means to treat them unfairly. ❏ *They believe the law discriminates against women.* [from Latin]

dis|crimi|na|tion /dɪskrɪmɪneɪʃᵊn/ **N-NONCOUNT** SOCIAL STUDIES Discrimination is the practice of treating one person or group unfairly. ❏ *Many companies are breaking age discrimination laws.* [from Latin]

dis|cus /dɪskəs/ (**discuses**) **N-COUNT** SPORTS The **discus** is the sport of throwing a heavy round object. ❏ *He won the discus at the Montreal Olympics.* [from Latin]

dis|cuss /dɪskʌs/ (**discusses, discussing, discussed**) **V-T** If people **discuss** something, they talk about it. ❏ *We are meeting next week to discuss plans for the future.* [from Late Latin]

Word Partnership Use discuss with :

v meet to discuss, refuse to discuss

n discuss options, discuss problems discuss an issue, discuss a matter, discuss plans
---

dis|cus|sion /dɪskʌʃᵊn/ (**discussions**) **N-COUNT/N-NONCOUNT** A discussion is a conversation about a subject. ❏ *Managers are having informal discussions later today.* [from Late Latin]

Thesaurus discussion Also look up :

n conference, conversation, debate, talk
---

dis|ease /dɪziz/ (**diseases**) **N-COUNT/N-NONCOUNT** A disease is an illness that affects people, animals, or plants. ❏ *There are no drugs available to treat this disease.* ❏ *...heart disease.* [from Old French]
→ look at Word Webs: **diagnosis, illness, medicine**

Word Link	grac ≈ pleasing : dis*grace*, *grace*, *grace*ful

dis|grace /dɪsgreɪs/ **N-SING** If something is **a disgrace**, it is very bad or wrong. ❑ *His behavior was a disgrace.* [from Old French]

dis|grace|ful /dɪsgreɪsfəl/ **ADJ** If you say that something is **disgraceful**, you strongly disapprove of it. ❑ *The way they treated him was disgraceful.* ● **dis|grace|ful|ly** **ADV** ❑ *His brother behaved disgracefully.* [from Old French]

dis|guise /dɪsgaɪz/ (**disguises, disguising, disguised**)
1 **N-COUNT/N-NONCOUNT** If you are **in disguise**, you have changed the way you look so that people will not recognize you. ❑ *He traveled in disguise.*
2 **V-T** To **disguise** something means to hide it or make it appear different so that people will not recognize it. ❑ *I tried to disguise the fact that I was ill.* ● **dis|guised** **ADJ** ❑ *The robber was disguised as a medical worker.* [from Old French]

dis|gust /dɪsgʌst/ (**disgusts, disgusting, disgusted**)
1 **N-NONCOUNT** **Disgust** is a feeling of very strong dislike or disapproval. ❑ *George watched in disgust.*
2 **V-T** To **disgust** someone means to make them feel a strong sense of dislike and disapproval. ❑ *He disgusted many people with his behavior.* [from Old French]

dis|gust|ed /dɪsgʌstɪd/ **ADJ** If you are **disgusted**, you feel a strong sense of dislike and disapproval. ❑ *I'm disgusted by the way that he was treated.* [from Old French]

dis|gust|ing /dɪsgʌstɪŋ/ **ADJ** If something is **disgusting**, it is extremely unpleasant or unacceptable. ❑ *The food tasted disgusting.* [from Old French]

dish /dɪʃ/ (**dishes, dishing, dished**)
1 **N-COUNT** A **dish** is a shallow container for cooking or serving food. ❑ *Pour the mixture into a square glass dish.*
2 **N-COUNT** A **dish** is food that is prepared in a particular way. ❑ *There are plenty of delicious dishes to choose from.*
3 **N-COUNT** You can use **dish** to talk about anything that is round and hollow in shape with a wide uncovered top. ❑ *...a dish used to receive satellite broadcasts.* [from Old English]
4 → see also **satellite dish**
→ look at Picture Dictionary: **dish**
→ look at Word Web: **pottery**
▶ **dish out** If you **dish out** something, you give it to a number of people. [INFORMAL] ❑ *...dishing out money.*
▶ **dish up** If you **dish up** food, you serve it. [INFORMAL] ❑ *They dished up a lovely meal.*

dis|hon|est /dɪsɒnɪst/ **ADJ** If someone is **dishonest**, they are not honest, and you cannot trust them. ❑ *I admit that I was dishonest with him.* ● **dis|hon|est|ly** **ADV** ❑ *He dishonestly received $500,000.* [from Old French]

dis|hon|es|ty /dɪsɒnɪsti/ **N-NONCOUNT** **Dishonesty** is dishonest behavior. ❑ *She accused the government of dishonesty.*

dish|washer /dɪʃwɒʃər/ (**dishwashers**) **N-COUNT** A **dishwasher** is a machine that washes and dries dishes.

dish|washing liq|uid /dɪʃwɒʃɪŋ lɪkwɪd/ (**dishwashing liquids**) **N-COUNT/N-NONCOUNT**

d

Picture Dictionary   dish

salt & pepper shakers
butter dish
gravy boat
cup & saucer
creamer
sugar bowl
mug
dinner plate
salad plate
bread plate
bowl
platter

D

Dishwashing liquid is liquid soap that you add to hot water to clean dirty dishes.

dis|in|fect /dɪsɪnfɛkt/ (**disinfects, disinfecting, disinfected**) **v-t** If you **disinfect** something, you clean it using a substance that kills bacteria. ❑ *Chlorine is used for disinfecting water.* [from Latin]

dis|in|fect|ant /dɪsɪnfɛktənt/ (**disinfectants**) **N-COUNT/N-NONCOUNT Disinfectant** is a substance that kills bacteria. ❑ *They washed their hands with disinfectant.* [from Latin]

dis|in|te|grate /dɪsɪntɪgreɪt/ (**disintegrates, disintegrating, disintegrated**)
1 **v-i** If something **disintegrates**, it becomes seriously weakened, and is divided or destroyed. ❑ *The empire began to disintegrate.*
● **dis|in|te|gra|tion** /dɪsɪntɪgreɪʃ°n/ **N-NONCOUNT** ❑ *...the violent disintegration of Yugoslavia.*
2 **v-i** If an object or substance **disintegrates**, it breaks into many small pieces or parts and is destroyed. ❑ *At 420 mph the windshield disintegrated.* [from Latin]

disk /dɪsk/ (**disks**) also **disc**
1 **N-COUNT** A **disk** is a flat, circular object. ❑ *The food processor has three slicing disks.*
2 **N-COUNT** TECHNOLOGY In a computer, the **disk** is the part where information is stored. ❑ *The program uses 2.5 megabytes of disk space.* [from Latin]
3 → see also **hard disk**

disk drive (**disk drives**) **N-COUNT**
TECHNOLOGY The **disk drive** on a computer is the part that holds a disk.

dis|like /dɪslaɪk/ (**dislikes, disliking, disliked**)
1 **v-t** If you **dislike** someone or something, you think they are unpleasant and you do not like them. ❑ *Many children dislike the taste of green vegetables.*
2 **N-NONCOUNT Dislike** is the feeling that you do not like someone or something. ❑ *...his dislike of publicity.*
3 **N-COUNT** Your **dislikes** are the things that you do not like. ❑ *Make a list of your likes and dislikes about your job.* [from Old English]

dis|man|tle /dɪsmænt°l/ (**dismantles, dismantling, dismantled**) **v-t** If you **dismantle** a machine or structure, you carefully separate it into its different parts. ❑ *Expertly he dismantled the gun.* [from Old French]

dis|may /dɪsmeɪ/ **N-NONCOUNT Dismay** is a strong feeling of fear, worry, or sadness. [FORMAL] ❑ *Local people reacted with dismay.*
● **dis|mayed** **ADJ** ❑ *Glen was shocked and dismayed at her reaction.* [from Old French]

Word Link	miss ≈ sending : dismiss, missile, missionary

dis|miss /dɪsmɪs/ (**dismisses, dismissing, dismissed**)
1 **v-t** If you **dismiss** something, you say that it is not important enough for you to consider. ❑ *Perry dismissed the suggestion as nonsense.*
2 **v-t** When an employer **dismisses** an employee, the employee has to leave their job. ❑ *Locke was dismissed from the team after admitting to stealing the money.*
3 **v-t** If you **are dismissed** by someone in authority, they tell you that you can leave. ❑ *Two more witnesses were heard, and dismissed.* [from Medieval Latin]

Word Partnership	Use dismiss with :
ADJ	**easy to** dismiss **1**
N	dismiss **an idea**, dismiss **a possibility 1**
	dismiss **an employee 2**
	dismiss **a case 3**

dis|mis|sal /dɪsmɪs°l/ (**dismissals**)
1 **N-COUNT/N-NONCOUNT** When an employee is dismissed from their job, you call this their **dismissal**. ❑ *...Mr. Low's dismissal from his job.*
2 **N-NONCOUNT Dismissal of** something means deciding or saying that it is not important. ❑ *...dismissal of public opinion.* [from Medieval Latin]

dis|obey /dɪsəbeɪ/ (**disobeys, disobeying, disobeyed**) **v-t/v-i** When someone **disobeys** a person or an order, they do not do what they have been told to do. ❑ *He often disobeyed his mother and father.* ❑ *He will not dare disobey.* [from Old French]

dis|or|der /dɪsɔrdər/ (**disorders**)
1 **N-COUNT/N-NONCOUNT** A **disorder** is a problem or an illness which affects your mind or body. ❑ *...a rare blood disorder.*
2 **N-NONCOUNT Disorder** is violence or rioting in public. ❑ *America's worst civil disorder erupted in the city of Los Angeles.*
3 **N-NONCOUNT Disorder** is a situation in which things are not neat or organized. ❑ *The emergency room was in disorder.* [from Old French]

dis|or|gan|ized /dɪsɔrgənaɪzd/
1 **ADJ** Something that is **disorganized** is badly arranged, planned or managed.

❏ *He walked into the large, disorganized office.*
2 **ADJ** Someone who is **disorganized** is very bad at organizing things in their life. ❏ *My boss is completely disorganized.*

dis|ori|ent /dɪsɔriɛnt/ (**disorients, disorienting, disoriented**) **V-T** If something **disorients** you, you lose your sense of direction, or you feel lost and uncertain. ❏ *An overnight stay at a friend's house disorients me.*
● **dis|ori|ent|ed** **ADJ** ❏ *I feel dizzy and disoriented.*
● **dis|ori|en|ta|tion** /dɪsɔriənteɪʃ°n/ **N-NONCOUNT** ❏ *Morris was so stunned by the news that he experienced a moment of total disorientation.* [from French]

> **Word Link** *par ≈ equal : compare, disparate, part*

dis|par|ate /dɪspərɪt/ **ADJ Disparate** things are clearly different from each other in quality or type. [FORMAL] ❏ *...disparate ideas.* [from Latin]

dis|par|ity /dɪspærɪti/ (**disparities**) **N-COUNT/N-NONCOUNT** A **disparity** between two or more things is a noticeable difference between them. [FORMAL] ❏ *...the health disparities between different ethnic groups in the U.S.* [from Late Latin]

dis|patch /dɪspætʃ/ (**dispatches, dispatching, dispatched**)
1 **V-T** If you **dispatch** someone or something to a place, you send them there. [FORMAL] ❏ *He dispatched another letter to his cousin.*
2 **N-NONCOUNT** **Dispatch** is also a noun. [FORMAL] ❏ *We have 125 cases ready for dispatch.* [from Italian]

dis|pens|er /dɪspɛnsər/ (**dispensers**) **N-COUNT** A **dispenser** is a machine or a container from which you can get something. ❏ *...a soap dispenser.* [from Medieval Latin]

dis|perse /dɪspɜrs/ (**disperses, dispersing, dispersed**)
1 **V-T/V-I** When something **disperses** or when you **disperse** it, it spreads over a wide area. ❏ *When the sandbags open, the sand is dispersed on the ocean floor.*
2 **V-T/V-I** When a group of people **disperses** or when someone **disperses** them, the group splits up and the people leave in different directions. ❏ *Police used tear gas to disperse the demonstrators.* [from Latin]

dis|place /dɪspleɪs/ (**displaces, displacing, displaced**) **V-T** If one thing **displaces** another, it forces the other thing out and then occupies its position. ❏ *These factories have displaced tourism as the country's main source of income.*

dis|play /dɪspleɪ/ (**displays, displaying, displayed**)
1 **V-T** If you **display** something, you put it in a place where people can see it. ❏ *Old soldiers proudly displayed their medals.*
2 **N-NONCOUNT** **Display** is also a noun. ❏ *The artist's work is on display in New York next month.*
3 **V-T** If you **display** an emotion, you behave in a way that shows that you are feeling it. ❏ *Gordon didn't often display his feelings.*
4 **N-COUNT** A **display** is an arrangement of things that have been put in a particular place, so that people can see them easily. ❏ *In the second gallery, there was a display of World War II aircraft.*
5 **N-COUNT** A **display** is a public event that is intended to entertain people. ❏ *...a fireworks display.* [from Late Latin]

dis|pos|able /dɪspoʊzəb°l/ **ADJ** A **disposable** product is designed to be thrown away after it has been used. ❏ *...disposable diapers.* [from Old French]

dis|pos|al /dɪspoʊz°l/
1 **N-NONCOUNT** **Disposal** is when you get rid of something that you no longer want or need. ❏ *...waste disposal.*
2 **PHRASE** If you have something at your **disposal**, you are able to use it whenever you want. ❏ *Do you have this information at your disposal?* [from Old French]

dis|pose /dɪspoʊz/ (**disposes, disposing, disposed**)
▶ **dispose of** If you **dispose of** something, you get rid of it. ❏ *How do they dispose of nuclear waste?*

dis|prove /dɪspruv/ (**disproves, disproving, disproved, disproven**) **V-T** To **disprove** an idea, a belief, or a theory means to show that it is not true. ❏ *The research disproved his theory.* [from Old French]
→ look at Word Web: **science**

> **Word Link** *put ≈ thinking : computer, dispute, input*

dis|pute /dɪspyut/ (**disputes, disputing, disputed**)
1 **N-COUNT/N-NONCOUNT** A **dispute** happens when two people or groups cannot agree about something. ❏ *The government had to do something to end the dispute.*
2 **V-T** If you **dispute** a fact or statement,

d

D

you say that it is incorrect or untrue.
❏ *He disputed the idea that he had made
a mistake.* [from Late Latin]

dis|quali|fy /dɪskwɒlɪfaɪ/ (**disqualifies,
disqualifying, disqualified**) **v-t** When
someone **is disqualified**, they are stopped
from taking part in a competition.
❏ *Thomson was disqualified from the race.*
[from Old French]

dis|re|gard /dɪsrɪgɑrd/ (**disregards,
disregarding, disregarded**)
1 v-t If you **disregard** something, you
ignore it or do not take account of it.
❏ *He disregarded the advice of his parents.*
2 N-NONCOUNT Disregard is also a noun.
❏ *These terrorists had a total disregard for human
life.* [from Old French]

dis|robe /dɪsroʊb/ (**disrobes, disrobing,
disrobed**) **v-i** When someone **disrobes**, they
remove their clothes. [FORMAL] ❏ *She stood up
and began to disrobe, folding each garment neatly.*
[from Old French]

| Word Link | *rupt ≈ breaking : dis**rupt**, e**rupt**,
inter**rupt*** |

dis|rupt /dɪsrʌpt/ (**disrupts, disrupting,
disrupted**) **v-t** If someone or something
disrupts an event, they cause difficulties
that prevent it from continuing. ❏ *Several
injuries disrupted preparations this week.*
● **dis|rup|tion** (**disruptions**)
N-COUNT/N-NONCOUNT ❏ *The bad weather
caused disruption at many airports.* [from Latin]

dis|rup|tive /dɪsrʌptɪv/ **adj** If someone is
disruptive, they prevent something from
continuing in a normal way. ❏ *We have a lot
of difficult, disruptive children.* [from Latin]

| Word Link | *sat, satis ≈ enough : dis**sat**isfied,
satisfy, un**sat**isfactory* |

dis|sat|is|fied /dɪssætɪsfaɪd/ **adj** If you are
dissatisfied, you are not happy about
something. ❏ *Thousands of dissatisfied
customers called the company to complain.*

| Word Link | *sect ≈ cutting : bi**sect**, dis**sect**,
section* |

dis|sect /dɪsɛkt, daɪ-/ (**dissects, dissecting,
dissected**) **v-t** SCIENCE If someone **dissects**
a dead body, they cut it open in order to
examine it. ❏ *We dissected a frog in biology class.*
● **dis|sec|tion** /dɪsɛkʃᵊn, daɪ-/ (**dissections**)
N-COUNT/N-NONCOUNT ❏ *The dissection of
the tiny insect took place under a microscope.*
[from Latin]

dis|sent /dɪsɛnt/ (**dissents, dissenting,
dissented**)
1 N-NONCOUNT Dissent is strong
disagreement with a decision or opinion,
especially one that is supported by most
people or by people in authority.
❏ *...political dissent.*
2 v-i If you **dissent**, you express
disagreement with a decision or opinion,
especially one that is supported by most
people or by people in authority. [FORMAL]
❏ *Just one of the 10 members dissented.* ❏ *No one
dissents from the decision.* ● **dis|sent|er**
(**dissenters**) **N-COUNT** ❏ *The party does not
tolerate dissenters.* ● **dis|sent|ing adj** ❏ *He
ignored dissenting views.* [from Latin]

dis|si|dent /dɪsɪdənt/ (**dissidents**) **N-COUNT**
SOCIAL STUDIES **Dissidents** are people who
disagree with and criticize their
government, especially because it is
not democratic. ❏ *...political dissidents.*
[from Latin]

dis|simi|lar /dɪsɪmɪlər/ **adj** If one thing is
dissimilar to another, or if two things are
dissimilar, they are very different from each
other. ❏ *His methods were not dissimilar to those
used by Freud.* ❏ *It would be difficult to find two men
who were more dissimilar.* [from Old French]

dis|so|ci|ate /dɪsoʊʃieɪt, -sieɪt/ (**dissociates,
dissociating, dissociated**) **v-t** If you
dissociate yourself from something or
someone, you say or show that you are not
connected with them. ❏ *The president is unable
to dissociate himself from the scandals.*

dis|solve /dɪzɒlv/ (**dissolves, dissolving,
dissolved**) **v-t/v-i** SCIENCE If a substance
dissolves in liquid, or if you **dissolve** it, it
becomes mixed with the liquid and
disappears. ❏ *Heat the mixture gently until the
sugar dissolves.* [from Latin]

dis|suade /dɪsweɪd/ (**dissuades, dissuading,
dissuaded**) **v-t** If you **dissuade** someone
from doing or believing something, you
persuade them not to do or believe it.
[FORMAL] ❏ *Nothing can dissuade him from that
decision.* [from Latin]

dis|tance /dɪstəns/ (**distances**)
1 N-COUNT/N-NONCOUNT The **distance**
between two places is the amount of space
between them. ❏ *Measure the distance between
the wall and the table.*
2 PHRASE Something that is **in the distance**

is a long way away from you. ❑ *We had a beautiful view of the countryside with the mountains in the distance.*
3 **PHRASE** If you see something **from a distance**, you see it from a long way away. ❑ *From a distance, the lake looked beautiful.* [from Latin]

Word Partnership	Use distance with :
ADJ	**safe** distance, **short** distance **1**
PREP	**within walking** distance **1**
	from a distance **3**

dis|tant /dɪstənt/
1 **ADJ** **Distant** means very far away. ❑ *The mountains were on the distant horizon.*
2 **ADJ** You use **distant** to describe a time that is far away in the future or in the past. ❑ *Things will improve in the not too distant future.*
3 **ADJ** A **distant** relative is one who you are not closely related to. ❑ *I received a letter from a distant cousin.* [from Latin]

Thesaurus	distant	Also look up :
ADJ	faraway, remote; *(ant.)* close, near **1**	

dis|tinct /dɪstɪŋkt/
1 **ADJ** If something is **distinct from** something else, it is different from it. ❑ *Quebec is quite distinct from the rest of Canada.*
2 **ADJ** If something is **distinct**, you can hear, see, or taste it clearly. ❑ *Each vegetable has its own distinct flavor.* [from Latin]

Usage   distinct and distinctive
Distinct and *distinctive* are easy to confuse. You use *distinct* to say that something is separate, different, clear, or noticeable; you use *distinctive* to say that something is special and easily recognized: *The distinct taste of lemon gave Elenas cake a distinctive and delicious flavor.*

dis|tinc|tion /dɪstɪŋkʃ°n/ (**distinctions**)
PHRASE If you **draw a distinction** or **make a distinction**, you say that two things are different. ❑ *He makes a distinction between art and culture.* [from Latin]

dis|tinc|tive /dɪstɪŋktɪv/ **ADJ** Something that is **distinctive** has a special quality or feature that makes it easy to recognize. ❑ *...the distinctive smell of gas.*
● **dis|tinc|tive|ly** **ADV** ❑ *...distinctively American music.* [from Latin]

dis|tin|guish /dɪstɪŋgwɪʃ/ (**distinguishes, distinguishing, distinguished**)
1 **V-T/V-I** If you can **distinguish** one thing

from another, or **between** two things, you can see or understand how they are different. ❑ *Could he distinguish right from wrong?* ❑ *When do babies learn to distinguish between men and women?*
2 **V-T** If you can **distinguish** something, you can just see, hear, or taste it. [FORMAL] ❑ *He could distinguish voices.* [from Latin]

dis|tin|guished /dɪstɪŋgwɪʃt/ **ADJ** Someone who is **distinguished** is very successful and has a good reputation. ❑ *He came from a distinguished academic family.* [from Latin]

dis|tort /dɪstɔrt/ (**distorts, distorting, distorted**)
1 **V-T** If you **distort** a statement, a fact, or an idea, you report or represent it in an untrue way. ❑ *The media distorts reality.*
● **dis|tort|ed** **ADJ** ❑ *These figures give a distorted view of the situation.* ● **dis|tor|tion** (**distortions**) **N-COUNT/N-NONCOUNT** ❑ *...a gross distortion of reality.*
2 **V-T/V-I** If something you can see or hear **is distorted** or **distorts**, its appearance or sound is changed so that it seems unclear. ❑ *An artist may distort shapes in a painting.*
● **dis|tort|ed** **ADJ** ❑ *The sound was becoming distorted.* ● **dis|tor|tion** (**distortions**) **N-COUNT/N-NONCOUNT** ❑ *Audio signals can travel along cables without distortion.* [from Latin]

dis|tract /dɪstrækt/ (**distracts, distracting, distracted**) **V-T** If something **distracts** you, it takes your attention away from what you are doing. ❑ *I'm easily distracted by noise.* [from Latin]

dis|trac|tion /dɪstrækʃ°n/ (**distractions**) **N-COUNT/N-NONCOUNT** A **distraction** is something that turns your attention away from something you want to concentrate on. ❑ *DVD players in cars are a dangerous distraction for drivers.* [from Latin]

dis|tress /dɪstrɛs/ **N-NONCOUNT** **Distress** is a strong feeling of sadness or pain. ❑ *The condition can cause great distress in young people.*
● **dis|tressed** **ADJ** ❑ *I feel very distressed about this problem.* ● **dis|tress|ing** **ADJ** ❑ *It is very distressing when your baby is sick.* [from Old French]

dis|trib|ute /dɪstrɪbyut/ (**distributes, distributing, distributed**)
1 **V-T** If you **distribute** things, you give

them to a number of people. ❑ *They distributed free tickets to young people.*
2 V-T BUSINESS When a company **distributes** goods, it supplies them to the stores or businesses that sell them. ❑ *The company manufactures and distributes skin care products.* ● **dis|tribu|tor** (**distributors**) **N-COUNT** ❑ *...Spain's largest distributor of food products.* [from Latin]

dis|tri|bu|tion /dɪstrɪbyuʃ^ən/ (**distributions**) **1 N-NONCOUNT** The **distribution** of things is the act of giving them to a number of people. ❑ *They are trying to stop the illegal distribution of music over the Internet.* **2 N-NONCOUNT** The **distribution** of goods is the act of supplying them to the stores or businesses that sell them. ❑ *...the distribution of goods and services.* **3 N-COUNT/N-NONCOUNT** The **distribution** of something is how much of it there is in each place or at each time, or how much of it each person has. ❑ *...a fairer distribution of wealth.* [from Latin]

dis|trict /dɪstrɪkt/ (**districts**) **N-COUNT** A **district** is a particular area of a city or country. ❑ *I drove around the business district.* [from Medieval Latin]

dis|turb /dɪstɜrb/ (**disturbs, disturbing, disturbed**)
1 V-T If you **disturb** someone, you interrupt and upset them. ❑ *Sorry, am I disturbing you?*
2 V-T If something **disturbs** you, it makes you feel upset or worried. ❑ *He was disturbed by the news of the attack.* [from Latin]
3 → see also **disturbing**

Word Partnership	Use **disturb** with :
V	**do not** disturb **1**
	be sorry to disturb **1 2**
	be careful not to disturb **1 3**
N	disturb **the neighbors 2**

dis|turb|ance /dɪstɜrbəns/ (**disturbances**) **N-COUNT** A **disturbance** is an event in which people behave violently in public. ❑ *During the disturbance, three men were hurt.* [from Latin]

dis|turbed /dɪstɜrbd/ **ADJ** A **disturbed** person is very upset emotionally, and often needs special care or treatment. ❑ *...emotionally disturbed children.* [from Latin]

dis|turb|ing /dɪstɜrbɪŋ/
1 ADJ Something that is **disturbing** makes

you feel worried or upset. ❑ *We've received some disturbing news.* [from Latin]
2 → see also **disturb**

dis|used /dɪsyuzd/ **ADJ** A **disused** place or building is empty and is no longer used. ❑ *...a disused gas station.*

ditch /dɪtʃ/ (**ditches, ditching, ditched**)
1 N-COUNT A **ditch** is a deep, long, narrow hole that carries water away from a road or a field. ❑ *Both vehicles landed in a ditch.*
2 V-T If you **ditch** something, you get rid of it. [INFORMAL] ❑ *He has ditched plans to make a movie about Formula 1 racing.* [from Old English]

dive /daɪv/ (**dives, diving, dived** or **dove, dived**)
1 V-I SPORTS If you **dive into** water, you jump in so that your arms and your head go in first. ❑ *Ben dove into the river.* ● **div|ing** **N-NONCOUNT** ❑ *Shaun won medals in diving and swimming.*
2 N-COUNT SPORTS **Dive** is also a noun. ❑ *Pam walked out and did another perfect dive.*
3 V-I SPORTS If you **dive**, you go under the surface of the ocean or a lake, using special equipment for breathing. ❑ *We were diving to look at fish.* ● **div|er** (**divers**) **N-COUNT** ❑ *...a deep-sea diver.* ● **div|ing** **N-NONCOUNT** ❑ *...equipment for diving.*
4 N-COUNT SPORTS **Dive** is also a noun. ❑ *He is already planning the next dive.* [from Old English]
5 → see also **dove**

Word Link	di ≈ two : digraph, dilemma, diverge

Word Link	verg, vert ≈ turning : converge, diverge, subvert

di|verge /dɪvɜrdʒ, daɪ-/ (**diverges, diverging, diverged**)
1 V-T/V-I When two things **diverge**, they are different or become different. ❑ *His interests diverged from those of his colleagues.*
2 V-T/V-I If roads or lines **diverge**, they separate and go in different directions. [from Medieval Latin]

di|ver|gent bounda|ry /dɪvɜrdʒənt baʊnd^əri, daɪ-/ (**divergent boundaries**) **N-COUNT** SCIENCE A **divergent boundary** is an area in the Earth's crust where two tectonic plates are moving away from each other.

di|verse /dɪvɜrs, daɪ-/ **ADJ** If a group of people or things is **diverse**, it is made up of many different people or things. ❑ *We have a very diverse group of students this year.* [from Latin]

> **Word Link** *ify ≈ making : claify, diversify, intensify*

di|ver|si|fy /dɪvɜrsɪfaɪ, daɪ-/ (**diversifies, diversifying, diversified**) **v-t/v-i** When an organization or a person **diversifies** into other things, or **diversifies** their product line, they increase the variety of things that they do or make. ❑ *The company's troubles started when it diversified into new products.* ❑ *Manufacturers need to diversify and improve quality.* • **di|ver|si|fi|ca|tion** /dɪvɜrsɪfɪkeɪʃ°n, daɪ-/ (**diversifications**) **N-COUNT/N-NONCOUNT** ❑ *...diversification of teaching methods.* [from Old French]

di|ver|sion /dɪvɜrʒ°n, daɪ-/ (**diversions**) **N-COUNT** A **diversion** is an activity that takes your attention away from what you are doing. ❑ *The trip was a welcome diversion from their troubles at home.* [from Latin]

di|ver|sity /dɪvɜrsɪti, daɪ-/ (**diversities**)
1 **N-COUNT/N-NONCOUNT** The **diversity** of something is the fact that it contains many very different elements. ❑ *...the cultural diversity of Latin America.*
2 **N-SING** A **diversity** of things is a range of things which are very different from each other. ❑ *There was a diversity of attitudes about race.* [from Latin]
→ look at Word Web: **zoo**

di|vert /dɪvɜrt, daɪ-/ (**diverts, diverting, diverted**)
1 **v-t** To **divert** vehicles or travelers means to make them go a different route. ❑ *The plane was diverted to Boston's Logan International Airport.*
2 **v-t** If someone **diverts** your attention from something, they do something that stops you thinking about it. ❑ *I don't want to divert attention from the project.* [from French]

di|vide /dɪvaɪd/ (**divides, dividing, divided**)
1 **v-t/v-i** When people or things **are divided** or **divide into** smaller groups or parts, they become separated into smaller parts. ❑ *Divide the pastry in half.* ❑ *The class was divided into two groups of six.*
2 **v-t** MATH If you **divide** one number **by** another number, you find out how many times the second number can fit into the first number. ❑ *Measure the floor area and divide it by six.*
3 **v-t** If a line **divides** two areas, it makes

the two areas separate. ❑ *A 1969-mile border divides Mexico from the United States.*
4 **v-t/v-i** If people **divide** over something or something **divides** people, they cannot agree about it. ❑ *Several major issues divided the country.*
5 **N-COUNT** GEOGRAPHY A **divide** is a line of high ground between areas that are drained by different rivers. [from Latin]
▶ **divide up** If you **divide** something **up**, you separate it into smaller or more useful groups. ❑ *They divided the country up into four areas.*

> **Thesaurus** divide Also look up :
> v   categorize, group, separate, split **1**
>   part, separate, split; *(ant.)* unite **4**

divi|dend /dɪvɪdɛnd/ (**dividends**)
1 **N-COUNT** BUSINESS A **dividend** is the part of a company's profits which is paid to people who own shares in the company. ❑ *The dividend has increased by 4 percent.*
2 **PHRASE** If something **pays dividends**, it brings advantages at a later date. ❑ *Things you do now to improve your health will pay dividends later on.* [from Latin]

di|vine /dɪvaɪn/ **ADJ** You use **divine** to describe something that is provided by or relates to a god or goddess. ❑ *...a divine punishment.*
• **di|vine|ly** **ADV** ❑ *The work was divinely inspired.* • **di|vin|ity** /dɪvɪnɪti/ **N-NONCOUNT** ❑ *...the divinity of Christ's word.* [from Latin]

div|ing board (**diving boards**) **N-COUNT** SPORTS A **diving board** is a board at the edge of a swimming pool from which people can jump into the water.

di|vi|sion /dɪvɪʒ°n/ (**divisions**)
1 **N-NONCOUNT** The **division** of something is when someone or something separates it into parts. ❑ *...the division of land after the war.*
2 **N-NONCOUNT** MATH **Division** is the process of dividing one number by another number. ❑ *I taught my daughter how to do division.*
3 **N-COUNT/N-NONCOUNT** A **division** is an important distinction or argument between two groups. ❑ *The division between the rich and the poor is growing.*
4 **N-COUNT** In a large organization, a **division** is a group of departments with similar tasks. ❑ *She manages the bank's Latin American division.* [from Latin]
→ look at Word Web: **mathematics**

di|vorce /dɪvɔrs/ (**divorces, divorcing, divorced**)
1 **N-COUNT/N-NONCOUNT** A **divorce** is the

legal ending of a marriage. ❑ *Many marriages end in divorce.*

2 v-T/v-I If a man and woman **get divorced** or if one of them **divorces** the other, their marriage is legally ended. ❑ *Jack and Lillian got divorced in 2006.* ❑ *He divorced me and married my friend.* [from Old French]

di|vorced /dɪvɔrst/ **ADJ** Someone who **is divorced** from their former husband or wife is no longer legally married to them. ❑ *He is divorced, with a young son.* [from Old French]

DIY /di aɪ waɪ/ **N-NONCOUNT** DIY is the activity of making or repairing things yourself, especially in your home. **DIY** is short for **do-it-yourself**. ❑ *...a DIY project.*

diz|zy /dɪzi/ (**dizzier, dizziest**) **ADJ** If you feel **dizzy**, you feel that you are losing your balance and that you are going to fall. ❑ *Her head hurt, and she felt slightly dizzy.*
● **diz|zi|ness N-NONCOUNT** ❑ *His head injury caused dizziness.* [from Old English]

DJ /di dʒeɪ/ (**DJs**) also D.J., dj **N-COUNT** A DJ is the same as a **disc jockey**.

DNA /di ɛn eɪ/ **N-NONCOUNT** SCIENCE DNA is an acid in the chromosomes in the center of the cells of living things. DNA determines the particular structure and functions of every cell and is responsible for characteristics being passed on from parents to their children. **DNA** is short for "deoxyribonucleic acid." ❑ *A DNA sample was taken.*

DNA finger|print|ing /di ɛn eɪ fɪŋɡərprɪntɪŋ/ **N-NONCOUNT** SCIENCE DNA **fingerprinting** is the same as **genetic fingerprinting**.

DNA se|quenc|ing /di ɛn eɪ sikwənsɪŋ/ **N-NONCOUNT** SCIENCE DNA **sequencing** is the process of determining the order of base pairs in a section of DNA.

do
❶ AUXILIARY VERB USES
❷ OTHER VERB USES

❶ **do** /də, STRONG du/ (**does, doing, did, done**)

> **LANGUAGE HELP**
>
> When you are speaking, you can use the negative short forms **don't** for **do not** and **didn't** for **did not**.

1 AUX You use **do** with "not" to form the negative of main verbs. ❑ *They don't work very*

hard. ❑ *I did not know Jamie had a car.*

2 AUX You use **do** with another verb to form questions. ❑ *Do you like music?* ❑ *What did he say?*

3 AUX You use **do** instead of repeating a verb when you are answering a question. ❑ *"Do you think he is telling the truth?"—"Yes, I do."*

4 AUX You use **do** after "so" and "neither" to say that the same statement is true for two people or groups. ❑ *You know that's true, and so do I.* [from Old English]

❷ **do** /du/ (**does, doing, did, done**)

1 v-T When you **do** something, you take some action or perform an activity or task. ❑ *I was trying to do some work.* ❑ *After lunch Elizabeth and I did the dishes.*

2 v-T If you **do** something **about** a problem, you take action to try to solve it. ❑ *They refuse to do anything about the real cause of crime: poverty.*

3 v-T If an action or event **does** good or harm, it has a good or a bad effect. ❑ *A few bombs can do a lot of damage.*

4 v-T If you ask someone what they **do**, you want to know what their job is. ❑ *"What does your father do?"—"He's a doctor."*

5 v-T If you ask someone if they **are doing** anything at a particular time, you want to know if they have planned an activity for that time. ❑ *Are you doing anything tomorrow night?*

6 v-I If someone or something **does** well or badly, they are successful or unsuccessful. ❑ *Connie did well at school and graduated with honors.*

7 v-T/v-I If something **will do**, it is good enough. ❑ *It doesn't matter what you wear— anything warm will do.* ❑ *Twenty dollars will do me fine, thanks.*

8 → see also **done**

9 PHRASE If you say that you **could do with** something, you mean that you need it or want it. ❑ *I could do with a hot shower.*

10 PHRASE If you ask **what** someone or something **is doing** in a particular place, you are asking why they are there. ❑ *"What are you doing here?" he said, clearly surprised.*

11 PHRASE If one thing **has** or **is** something **to do with** another thing, the two things are connected. ❑ *Clarke insists all this has nothing to do with him.* [from Old English]

▶ **do over** If you **do** a task **over**, you perform it again from the beginning. ❑ *He made me do it over twice.*

▶ **do up** If you **do** something **up**, you fasten it. ❑ *Mari did up the buttons.*

▶ **do without** If you **do without** something, you are able to continue, although you do not have it. ❑ *We can do without their help.*

doc|ile /dɑsᵊl/ **ADJ** A person or animal that is **docile** is quiet, not aggressive, and easily controlled. ❑ *...docile, obedient children.* ●**do|cil|ity** /dɒsɪlɪti/ **N-NONCOUNT** ❑ *Her docility had surprised him.* ●**doc|ile|ly** **ADV** ❑ *She stood there, docilely awaiting my decision.* [from Latin]

dock /dɒk/ (**docks, docking, docked**)
1 **N-COUNT** A **dock** is an area of water beside land where ships go so that people can get on or off them.
2 **N-COUNT** A **dock** is a small structure at the edge of water where boats can be tied up. ❑ *He had a house, a private dock, and a little boat.*

dock

3 **V-T/V-I** When a ship **docks** or **is docked**, it is brought into a dock. ❑ *The crash happened as the ferry tried to dock on Staten Island.* [from Middle Dutch]

doc|tor /dɒktər/ (**doctors**)
1 **N-COUNT** A **doctor** is a person whose job is to treat people who are sick or injured. ❑ *Be sure to speak to your doctor before planning your trip.*
2 **N-COUNT** A **doctor** is someone who has been awarded the highest academic degree by a university. ❑ *He is a doctor of philosophy.* [from Latin]

doc|trine /dɒktrɪn/ (**doctrines**)
1 **N-COUNT/N-NONCOUNT** A **doctrine** is a set of principles or beliefs. ❑ *...Christian doctrine.*
2 **N-COUNT** SOCIAL STUDIES A **doctrine** is a statement of official government policy, especially foreign policy. ❑ *...Bush's doctrine on terrorism.* [from Old French]

docu|ment /dɒkyəmənt/ (**documents**)
1 **N-COUNT** A **document** is an official piece of paper with important information on it. ❑ *Always read legal documents carefully before you sign them.*
2 **N-COUNT** TECHNOLOGY A **document** is a piece of text that is stored on a computer. ❑ *Remember to save your document before you send it.* [from Latin]
→ look at Word Webs: **diary, history, printing**

docu|men|tary /dɒkyəmɛntəri, -tri/ (**documentaries**) **N-COUNT** A **documentary** is a television program or a movie that provides information about a particular subject. ❑ *Did you see that documentary on TV last night?* [from Latin]

dodge /dɒdʒ/ (**dodges, dodging, dodged**)
1 **V-I** If you **dodge**, you move suddenly, especially to avoid something. ❑ *I dodged back behind the tree and waited.*
2 **V-T** If you **dodge** something, you avoid it by moving. ❑ *He dodged a speeding car.*
3 **V-T** If you **dodge** something, you deliberately avoid doing it. ❑ *He dodged military service by pretending to be sick.*

dodo /doʊdoʊ/ (**dodos** or **dodoes**) **N-COUNT** A **dodo** was a very large bird that was unable to fly. Dodos are now extinct. [from Portuguese]

does /dəz, STRONG dʌz/ **Does** is the third person singular of the present tense of **do**. [from Old English]

doesn't /dʌzᵊnt/ **Doesn't** is short for "does not."

dog /dɔg/ (**dogs**) **N-COUNT** A **dog** is an animal that is often kept by people as a pet. ❑ *He was walking his dog.* [from Old English]
→ look at Word Webs: **disability, pet**

dog

dog|ma /dɔgmə/ (**dogmas**) **N-COUNT/N-NONCOUNT** If you refer to a belief or a system of beliefs as a **dogma**, you disapprove of it because people are expected to accept that it is true, without questioning it. ❑ *Practical action is more important than political dogma.* [from Latin]

dole|ful /doʊlfəl/ **ADJ** A **doleful** expression, manner, or voice is sad. ❑ *He gave me a long, doleful look.* ●**dole|ful|ly** **ADV** ❑ *"I don't know why they left," he said dolefully.* [from Old French]

doll /dɒl/ (**dolls**) **N-COUNT** A **doll** is a child's toy that looks like a small person or a baby.

dol|lar /dɒlər/ (**dollars**) **N-COUNT** The **dollar** ($) is the unit of money that is used in the U.S., Canada, and some other countries.

There are 100 cents in a **dollar**. ❏ *She earns seven dollars an hour.* [from Low German]

dol|phin /dɒlfɪn/ (**dolphins**) **N-COUNT**
A **dolphin** is a large gray or black and white intelligent animal that lives in the ocean. [from Old French]
→ look at Word Web: **whale**

dolphin

> **Word Link** **dom ≈ home** : *domain name*, *dome*, *domestic*

do|main name /doʊmeɪn neɪm/ (**domain names**) **N-COUNT** **TECHNOLOGY** A **domain name** is the main part of a website address that tells you who the website belongs to. ❏ *I've just bought the domain name "AdamWilson.com."*

dome /doʊm/
(**domes**) **N-COUNT**
A **dome** is a round roof. ❏ *Kiev is known as "the city of golden domes."* [from French]

dome

do|mes|tic /dəmɛstɪk/
1 **ADJ** **Domestic** means happening or existing within one particular country. ❏ *The airline offers over 100 domestic flights a day.*
2 **ADJ** **Domestic** means relating to the home and family. ❏ *We eat together and share domestic chores.*
3 **ADJ** A **domestic** animal is one that is not wild and is kept on a farm or as a pet. ❏ *...a domestic cat.* [from Old French]

domi|nant /dɒmɪnənt/
1 **ADJ** Someone or something that is **dominant** is more powerful, successful, influential, or noticeable than other people or things. ❏ *...his party's dominant position in politics.* ● **domi|nance** **N-NONCOUNT** ❏ *By 1942 Hitler had achieved dominance in all of Europe except Britain.*
2 **ADJ** **SCIENCE** A **dominant** gene is one that produces a particular characteristic, whether a person has only one of these genes from one parent, or two genes, one from each parent. Compare with **recessive**. [from Latin]

domi|nate /dɒmɪneɪt/ (**dominates, dominating, dominated**)
1 **V-T/V-I** To **dominate** a situation means to

be the most powerful or important person or thing in it. ❏ *...countries where life is dominated by war.* ● **domi|na|tion** /dɒmɪneɪʃ°n/ **N-NONCOUNT** ❏ *...the domination of the market by a small number of organizations.*
2 **V-T** If one country or person **dominates** another, they have power over them. ❏ *Women are no longer dominated by men.* ● **domi|na|tion** **N-NONCOUNT** ❏ *...domination by a foreign country.* [from Latin]

domi|no /dɒmɪnoʊ/ (**dominoes**) **N-COUNT/ N-NONCOUNT** **Dominoes** is a game that uses small rectangular blocks, called dominoes, that are marked with spots. [from French]

> **Word Link** **don ≈ giving** : *donate*, *donor*, *pardon*

do|nate /doʊneɪt, doʊneɪt/ (**donates, donating, donated**)
1 **V-T** If you **donate** something **to** an organization, you give it to them. ❏ *He often donates large amounts of money to charity.* ● **do|na|tion** /doʊneɪʃ°n/ (**donations**) **N-COUNT/N-NONCOUNT** ❏ *Employees make regular donations to charity.*
2 **V-T** If you **donate** your blood or a part of your body, you allow doctors to use it to help someone who is sick. ❏ *If you are able to donate blood, you should do it.* [from Latin]
→ look at Word Web: **donor**

done /dʌn/
1 **Done** is the past participle of **do**.
2 **ADJ** When something that you are cooking is **done**, it has been cooked long enough and is ready. ❏ *As soon as the cake is done, remove it from the oven.* [from Old English]

don|key /dɒŋki/ (**donkeys**) **N-COUNT**
A **donkey** is an animal like a small horse with long ears.

do|nor /doʊnər/ (**donors**)
1 **N-COUNT** A **donor** is a person who gives a part of their body or some of their blood so that doctors can use them to help someone who is sick. ❏ *...a blood donor.*
2 **N-COUNT** A **donor** is a person who gives something, especially money, to an organization that needs it. ❏ *The money was provided by a wealthy donor.* [from Old French]
→ look at Word Web: **donor**

don't /doʊnt/ **Don't** is short for "do not."

doomed /dumd/
1 **ADJ** If something **is doomed to** happen, or if you **are doomed to** a particular state, something unpleasant is certain to happen,

---

Word Web   donor

Many people **give donations**. They like to **help** others. They **donate money,** clothes, food, or volunteer their time. Some people even give parts of their bodies. Doctors performed the first successful human **organ transplants** in the 1950s. Today this type of operation is very common. The problem now is finding enough **donors** to meet the needs of potential **recipients**. Organs such as the **kidney** often come from a living donor. **Hearts, lungs,** and other vital organs come from donors who have died. Of course our health care system relies on **blood** donors. They help save lives every day.

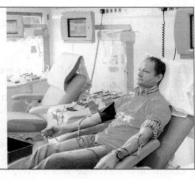

d

---

and you can do nothing to prevent it. ❑ *Their plans seemed doomed to failure.*

2 **ADJ** Someone or something that is **doomed** is certain to fail or be destroyed. ❑ *The project was doomed from the start.* [from Old English]

door /dɔr/ (**doors**)

1 **N-COUNT** A **door** is a piece of wood, glass, or metal that fills an entrance. ❑ *I knocked at the front door, but there was no answer.*

2 **N-COUNT** A **door** is the space in a wall when a door is open. ❑ *She looked through the door of the kitchen.*

3 **PHRASE** When you **answer the door,** you open a door because someone has knocked on it or rung the bell. ❑ *Carol answered the door as soon as I knocked.*

4 **PHRASE** If someone goes **door to door,** they go along a street stopping at each house. ❑ *They are going from door to door collecting money.* [from Old English]

door|step /dɔrstɛp/ (**doorsteps**) **N-COUNT** A **doorstep** is a step in front of a door outside a building. ❑ *I went and sat on the doorstep.*

door|way /dɔrweɪ/ (**doorways**) **N-COUNT** A **doorway** is a space in a wall where a door opens and closes. ❑ *David was standing in the doorway.* [from Old English]

dorm /dɔrm/ (**dorms**) **N-COUNT** A **dorm** is the same as a **dormitory.** [INFORMAL] ❑ *...a university dorm.* [from Latin]

dor|mant /dɔrmənt/ **ADJ** Something that is **dormant** has not been active or used for a long time. ❑ *The dormant volcano of Mount St. Helens erupted in 1980.* [from Old French]

Word Link   *ory ≈ place where something happens : dormit*ory*, laborat*ory*, territ*ory

dor|mi|tory /dɔrmɪtɔri/ (**dormitories**) **N-COUNT** A **dormitory** is a building at a

school or a university where students live. ❑ *She lived in a college dormitory.* [from Latin]

dose /doʊs/ (**doses**) **N-COUNT** A **dose of** medicine or a drug is an amount you take at one time. ❑ *You can treat the infection with one big dose of antibiotics.* [from French]

dot /dɒt/ (**dots**) **N-COUNT** A **dot** is a very small round mark, like the one on the letter "i," or in the names of websites. ❑ *He makes paintings with little tiny dots of color.* [from Old English]

dot|ted /dɒtɪd/ **ADJ** A **dotted** line is a line made of a row of dots. ❑ *Cut along the dotted line.* [from Old English]

dou|ble /dʌbəl/ (**doubles, doubling, doubled**)

1 **ADJ** You use **double** to show that something has two parts. ❑ *This room has double doors opening on to a balcony.*

2 **ADJ** **Double** means twice the normal size. ❑ *I gave him a double portion of ice cream.*

3 **ADJ** A **double** room or bed is intended for two people, usually a couple. ❑ *The hotel charges $180 for a double room.* ❑ *One of the bedrooms has a double bed.*

4 **V-T/V-I** When something **doubles** or when you **double** it, it becomes twice as big. ❑ *The number of students has doubled from 50 to 100.*

5 **N-NONCOUNT** In tennis or badminton, when people play **doubles,** each team consists of two players. ❑ *In the doubles, they beat the Williams sisters.* [from Old French] → look at Picture Dictionary: **tennis**

dou|ble bass /dʌbəl beɪs/ (**double basses**) **N-COUNT/N-NONCOUNT** MUSIC A **double bass** is a very big wooden musical instrument with four strings.

dou|ble-click (**double-clicks, double-clicking, double-clicked**) **V-T** TECHNOLOGY If you **double-click on** an area of a computer

D

screen, you press one of the buttons on the mouse twice quickly in order to make something happen. ❑ *Double-click on a file to start the application.*

dou|ble he|lix /dʌbᵊl hiliks/ **N-SING** **SCIENCE** The **double helix** is a term used to describe the shape of the DNA molecule, which resembles a long ladder twisted into a coil.

dou|ble-re|place|ment re|ac|tion (**double-replacement reactions**) **N-COUNT** **SCIENCE** A **double-replacement reaction** is a chemical reaction between two compounds in which some of the atoms in each compound switch places and form two new compounds.

doubt /daʊt/ (**doubts, doubting, doubted**)
1 **N-COUNT/N-NONCOUNT** If you have a **doubt** or **doubts** about something, you do not feel certain about it. ❑ *Rendell had doubts about the plan.* ❑ *There is no doubt that the Earth's climate is changing.*
2 **V-T** If you **doubt** something, you think that it is probably not true or likely. ❑ *I doubt if I'll learn anything new from this lesson.*
3 **V-T** If you **doubt** someone, you think that they may be saying something that is not true. ❑ *No one doubted him.*
4 **PHRASE** If you are **in doubt** about something, you are not sure about it. ❑ *He is in no doubt about what to do.*
5 **PHRASE** If you say that something is **in doubt**, you consider it to be uncertain. ❑ *The future of the business was still in doubt.*
6 **PHRASE** You use **no doubt** to show that you feel certain about something. ❑ *She will no doubt be here soon.*
7 **PHRASE** If you say that something is true **without doubt** or **without a doubt**, you mean that it is definitely true. ❑ *This was without doubt the best day of Amanda's life.* [from Old French]

doubt|ful /daʊtfəl/
1 **ADJ** If it is **doubtful that** something will happen, it seems that it will probably not happen. ❑ *It is doubtful that he will marry again.*
2 **ADJ** If you are **doubtful about** something, you do not feel sure about it. ❑ *Sophie sounded doubtful about the idea.* [from Old French]

dough /doʊ/ **N-NONCOUNT** **Dough** is a mixture of flour, water, and other things that can be cooked to make bread and cakes. ❑ *Leave the cookie dough in a cool place overnight.* [from Old English]

dough|nut /doʊnʌt, -nət/ (**doughnuts**) also **donut** **N-COUNT** A **doughnut** is a sweet round cake with a hole in the middle.

dove /dʌv/ (**doves**)

PRONUNCIATION HELP
Pronounce meaning **1** /dʌv/. Pronounce meaning **2** /doʊv/.

1 **N-COUNT** A **dove** is a bird that is used as a symbol of peace.
2 **Dove** is sometimes used as the past tense of **dive**. [from Old English]

down /daʊn/
1 **PREP** **Down** means toward a lower level, or in a lower place. ❑ *A man came down the stairs to meet them.* ❑ *He was halfway down the hill.*
2 **ADV** **Down** is also an adverb. ❑ *She went down to the kitchen.*
3 **PREP** If you go **down** a road or a river, you go along it. ❑ *They walked quickly down the street.*
4 **ADV** If you put something **down**, you put it onto a surface. ❑ *Danny put down his glass.*
5 **ADV** If an amount goes **down**, it decreases. ❑ *Prices went down today.*
6 **ADJ** If you are feeling **down**, you are feeling unhappy or depressed. [INFORMAL] ❑ *The man sounded really down.*
7 **ADJ** **TECHNOLOGY** If a computer system is **down**, it is not working. ❑ *The computers are down again.*
8 **N-NONCOUNT** **Down** is the small, soft feathers on young birds. **Down** is used to make bed-covers and pillows. ❑ *...goose down.* [Senses 1 to 7 from Old English. Sense 8 of Scandinavian origin.]

down|draft /daʊndræft/ (**downdrafts**) **N-COUNT** **SCIENCE** A **downdraft** is a downward current of air, usually accompanied by rain.

down feath|er (**down feathers**) **N-COUNT** **SCIENCE** **Down feathers** are the soft feathers on the bodies of young birds.

Word Link	down ≈ below, lower : downhill, downstairs, downturn

down|hill /daʊnhɪl/
1 **ADV** If something or someone is moving **downhill**, they are moving down a slope. ❑ *He walked downhill toward the river.*
2 **ADJ** **Downhill** is also an adjective. ❑ *...downhill ski runs.*

down|load /daʊnloʊd/ (**downloads, downloading, downloaded**) **V-T** TECHNOLOGY
If you **download** information, you move it to your computer from a bigger computer or network. ❑ *You can download the software from the Internet.*

Word Link	able ≈ able to be : accept*able*,
	download*able*, honor*able*

down|load|able /daʊnloʊdəbªl/ **ADJ**
TECHNOLOGY If a computer file is **downloadable**, you can copy it to another computer. ❑ *More information is available in the downloadable files below.*

down|pour /daʊnpɔr/ (**downpours**)
N-COUNT A **downpour** is a sudden heavy fall of rain. ❑ *The heavy downpours caused problems for motorists last night.*

down|scale /daʊnskeɪl/ **ADJ** If you describe a product or service as **downscale**, you think that it is cheap and not very good in quality. ❑ *...downscale stores.*

down|stage /daʊnsteɪdʒ/
1 ADV ARTS When an actor is **downstage** or moves **downstage**, he or she is or moves toward the front part of the stage.
2 ADJ ARTS **Downstage** is also an adjective. ❑ *...downstage members of the cast.*

down|stairs /daʊnstɛərz/
1 ADV If you go **downstairs** in a building, you walk down the stairs toward the ground floor. ❑ *Denise went downstairs and made some tea.*
2 ADV If someone or something is **downstairs** in a building, they are on a lower floor than you. ❑ *The telephone was downstairs in the kitchen.*
3 ADJ **Downstairs** rooms are on the first floor of a building. ❑ *She painted the downstairs rooms.*

down|town /daʊntaʊn/
1 ADJ The **downtown** part of a city is where the large stores and businesses are. ❑ *He works in an office in downtown Chicago.*
2 ADV **Downtown** is also an adverb. ❑ *He worked downtown for an insurance firm.*

down|turn /daʊntɜrn/ (**downturns**)
N-COUNT BUSINESS If there is a **downturn** in the economy or in a company or an industry, it becomes worse or less successful than it had been. ❑ *They predicted a severe economic downturn.*

Word Link	ward ≈ in the direction of :
	back*ward*, down*ward*, for*ward*

down|ward /daʊnwərd/

> **LANGUAGE HELP**
> The form **downwards** is also used for the adverb.

1 ADJ A **downward** movement or look goes to a lower place or a lower level. ❑ *John waved his hand in a downward motion.*
2 ADV If you move or look **downward**, you move or look toward the ground or a lower level. ❑ *Ben pointed downward with his stick.*
3 ADV If an amount or rate moves **downward**, it decreases. ❑ *Inflation is moving downward.* [from Old English]

doze /doʊz/ (**dozes, dozing, dozed**) **V-I**
When you **doze**, you sleep lightly or for a short period. ❑ *She dozed for a while in the cabin.* [from Old Norse]
→ look at Word Web: **sleep**
▸ **doze off** If you **doze off**, you fall into a light sleep. ❑ *I closed my eyes and dozed off.*

doz|en /dʌzªn/ (**dozens**)

> **LANGUAGE HELP**
> The plural is **dozen** after a number.

1 NUM A **dozen** means twelve. ❑ *Will you buy a loaf of bread and a dozen eggs please?*
2 N-PLURAL **Dozens of** things or people means a lot of them. ❑ *The storm destroyed dozens of buildings.* [from Old French]

Dr. (**Drs.**) You use **Dr.** before the name of a person who is a qualified doctor. ❑ *...Dr. John Hardy of Vanderbilt Hospital.*

drab /dræb/ (**drabber, drabbest**) **ADJ**
Something that is **drab** is dull and boring. ❑ *He was living in a small, drab apartment in Tokyo.* [from Old French]

draft /dræft/ (**drafts, drafting, drafted**)
1 N-COUNT LANGUAGE ARTS A **draft** is a piece of writing that you have not finished working on. ❑ *I emailed a first draft of the article to him.*
2 N-COUNT A **draft** is cold air that comes into a room. ❑ *Block drafts around doors and windows.*
3 V-T If you **are drafted**, you are ordered to serve in the armed forces, usually for a limited period of time. ❑ *He was drafted into the U.S. Army.* [from Old Norse]

d

D

Word Partnership	Use draft with :
ADJ	**final** draft, **rough** draft **1**
V	**revise a** draft, **write a** draft **1**
	feel a draft **2**
	dodge the draft **3**

drag /dræg/ (**drags, dragging, dragged**)

1 **V-T** If you **drag** something, you pull it along the ground. ❏ *He dragged his chair toward the table.*

2 **V-T** If you **drag** a computer image, you use the mouse to move it on the screen. ❏ *Simply drag and drop the file into the desired folder.*

3 **V-T** If someone **drags** you somewhere, they pull you there. ❏ *They dragged the men out of the car.*

4 **V-T** If you **drag** someone somewhere they do not want to go, you make them go there. ❏ *He's very friendly, when you can drag him away from his work!* ❏ *I find it really hard to drag myself out and exercise regularly.*

5 **V-I** If a period of time or an event **drags**, it seems to last a long time. ❏ *The minutes dragged past.*

6 **N-NONCOUNT** SCIENCE **Drag** is the resistance to movement that is experienced by something that is moving through air or through a fluid. [from Old English]

▶ **drag out** If you **drag** something **out**, you make it last for longer than is necessary. ❏ *They did everything they could to drag out the process.*

drag and drop (**drags and drops, dragging and dropping, dragged and dropped**) also **drag-and-drop**

1 **V-T** TECHNOLOGY If you **drag and drop** computer files or images, you move them from one place to another on the computer screen. ❏ *Drag and drop the folder to the hard drive.*

2 **N-NONCOUNT** TECHNOLOGY **Drag and drop** is also a noun. ❏ *Copying software onto an iPod is as easy as drag and drop.*

drag|on /drægən/ (**dragons**) **N-COUNT** In stories, a **dragon** is an animal with rough skin that has wings and breathes out fire. [from Old French]
→ look at Word Web: **fantasy**

drain /dreɪn/ (**drains, draining, drained**)

1 **N-COUNT** A **drain** is a pipe or an opening that carries a liquid away from a place. ❏ *A piece of soap was clogging the drain.*

2 **V-T/V-I** If you **drain** a liquid, you remove it by making it flow somewhere else. If a liquid **drains** somewhere, it flows there. ❏ *They*

built the tunnel to drain water out of the mines.

3 **V-T/V-I** If you **drain** food or if food **drains**, you remove the liquid that it has been in. ❏ *Drain the pasta well.*

4 **V-T** If something **drains** you, it makes you feel exhausted. ❏ *All that worrying drained me.*

● **drained** **ADJ** ❏ *I suffer from headaches, which make me feel completely drained.*

5 **N-SING** If something is **a drain on** resources, it costs a lot of money. ❏ *The fuel bills were a constant drain on our cash.*

6 **PHRASE** If something **is going down the drain**, it is being destroyed or wasted. [INFORMAL] ❏ *All her dreams were soon down the drain.* [from Old English]
→ look at Picture Dictionary: **bathroom**

drain|age /dreɪnɪdʒ/ **N-NONCOUNT** **Drainage** is the system or process by which water or other liquids are drained from a place. ❏ *Plant pots need good drainage.* [from Old English]
→ look at Word Web: **farm**

drain|age ba|sin (**drainage basins**) **N-COUNT** SCIENCE A **drainage basin** is the same as a **catchment area**.

dra|ma /drɑmə, dræmə/ (**dramas**)

1 **N-COUNT** ARTS LANGUAGE ARTS A **drama** is a serious play or movie. ❏ *The movie is a drama about a woman searching for her children.*

2 **N-NONCOUNT** ARTS **Drama** is plays and the theater in general. ❏ *He knew nothing about Greek drama.*

3 **N-COUNT/N-NONCOUNT** A real situation that is exciting can be called a **drama**. ❏ *This novel is full of drama.* [from Late Latin]
→ look at Picture Dictionary: **drama**
→ look at Word Web: **genre**

dra|mat|ic /drəmætɪk/

1 **ADJ** A **dramatic** change or event is a big change that happens suddenly. ❏ *There's been a dramatic change in the way we shop.*

● **dra|mati|cal|ly** /drəmætɪkli/ **ADV** ❏ *The climate has changed dramatically.*

2 **ADJ** A **dramatic** action or event is exciting and impressive. ❏ *His dramatic escape involved a helicopter and a large rescue team.* [from Late Latin]

dra|mat|ic play **N-NONCOUNT** ARTS **Dramatic play** is children's play that involves imagined characters and situations.

dra|mat|ic struc|ture (**dramatic structures**) **N-COUNT/N-NONCOUNT** ARTS The **dramatic structure** of a play or other

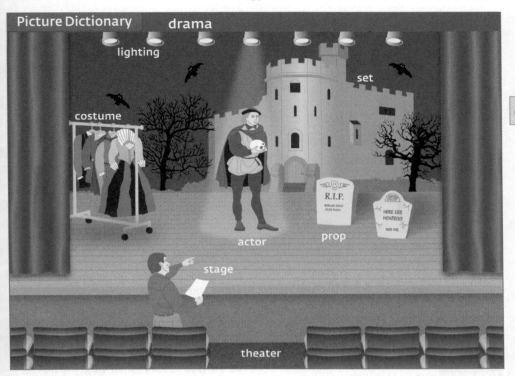

Picture Dictionary   drama

lighting

set

costume

actor

prop

R.I.P.

HERE LIES MONTECCHI

stage

theater

story is the different parts into which it can be divided, such as the climax and the denouement.

Word Link | ist ≈ one who practices : biologist, dramatist, pharmacist

drama|tist /drǽmətɪst/ (**dramatists**)
N-COUNT ARTS A **dramatist** is a person who writes plays. [from Late Latin]

drama|turg /drǽmətɜrdʒ/ (**dramaturgs**)
N-COUNT ARTS A **dramaturg** is a person who works with writers and theaters to help them to develop and produce plays. [from French]

drank /dræŋk/ **Drank** is the past tense of **drink**. [from Old English]

drape /dreɪp/ (**drapes, draping, draped**)
1 **V-T** If you **drape** a piece of cloth somewhere, you put it there so that it hangs down. ❑ He draped the damp towel over a chair.
2 **N-COUNT** **Drapes** are pieces of heavy fabric that you hang from the top of a window. ❑ He pulled the drapes shut. [from Old French]

dras|tic /drǽstɪk/
1 **ADJ** A **drastic** action has a very big effect. ❑ Drastic measures are needed to improve the situation.

2 **ADJ** A **drastic** change is a very great change. ❑ ...drastic alterations to the company's products.
● **dras|ti|cal|ly** **ADV** ❑ As a result, services have been drastically reduced. [from Greek]

draw /drɔ/ (**draws, drawing, drew, drawn**)
1 **V-T/V-I** ARTS When you **draw**, or when you **draw** something, you use a pencil or a pen to make a picture. ❑ She was drawing with a pencil. ❑ I've drawn a picture of you.
2 **V-T** If you **draw** something or someone somewhere, you move them there. [WRITTEN] ❑ He drew his chair nearer the fire. ❑ He drew Caroline close to him.
3 **V-T** When you **draw** the curtains or the drapes, you pull them across a window. ❑ He went to the window and drew the drapes.
4 **V-T** If someone **draws** a gun, a knife, or another weapon, they pull it out of its container so that it is ready to use. ❑ He drew his knife and turned to face them.
5 **V-T** If you **draw** money out of a bank account, you get it from the account so that you can use it. ❑ A few months ago he drew out nearly all his savings.
6 **V-T** If you **draw** someone's attention to something, you make them think about it. ❑ He was waving his arms to draw their attention.

D

Picture Dictionary   draw

draw   trace   sketch

erase   paint   copy

[from Old English]

7 → see also **drawing**

→ look at Picture Dictionary: **draw**

→ look at Word Web: **animation**

▶ **draw up** If you **draw up** a list or a plan, you write it or type it. ❑ *They drew up a formal agreement.*

Thesaurus draw Also look up :
v   illustrate, sketch, trace **1**
bring out, pull out, take out **4**

draw|back /drɔbæk/ (**drawbacks**) **N-COUNT** A **drawback** is a part of something that makes it less useful than you would like. ❑ *The apartment's only drawback was that it was too small.*

draw|bridge /drɔbrɪdʒ/ (**drawbridges**) **N-COUNT** A **drawbridge** is a bridge that can be pulled up, for example, to allow ships to pass underneath it or to prevent people from getting into a castle.

→ look at Word Web: **bridge**

draw|er /drɔr/ (**drawers**) **N-COUNT** A **drawer** is part of a desk, for example, that you can pull out and put things in. ❑ *She opened her desk drawer and took out the book.* [from Old English]

drawer

draw|ing /drɔɪŋ/ (**drawings**)

1 **N-COUNT** ARTS A **drawing** is a picture made with a pencil or a pen. ❑ *She did a drawing of me.*

2 **N-NONCOUNT** ARTS **Drawing** is the activity of making pictures with a pencil or a pen.

❑ *I like dancing, singing, and drawing.*

[from Old English]

3 → see also **draw**

drawn /drɔn/ **Drawn** is the past participle of **draw**. [from Old English]

dread /drɛd/ (**dreads, dreading, dreaded**)

1 **V-T** If you **dread** something, you feel very anxious because you think it will be unpleasant or upsetting. ❑ *I've been dreading this moment for a long time.*

2 **N-NONCOUNT** **Dread** is a feeling of great anxiety and fear about something that may happen. ❑ *She thought with dread of the cold winters.* [from Old English]

Word Link   ful ≈ filled with : beautiful, careful, dreadful

dread|ful /drɛdfəl/ **ADJ Dreadful** means very unpleasant, or very poor in quality. ❑ *They told us the dreadful news.* ❑ *I didn't enjoy the movie; the acting was dreadful.* [from Old English]

dream /drim/ (**dreams, dreaming, dreamed** or **dreamt**)

1 **N-COUNT** A **dream** is a series of events that you see in your mind while you are asleep. ❑ *He had a dream about Claire.*

2 **N-COUNT** A **dream** is something that you often think about because you would like it to happen. ❑ *After all these years, my dream has finally come true.*

3 **V-T/V-I** When you **dream**, you see events in your mind while you are asleep. ❑ *Richard dreamed that he was on a bus.* ❑ *She dreamed about her baby.*

4 **V-T/V-I** If you often think about

something that you would like, you can say that you **dream of** it. ❑ *She dreamed of becoming an actress.* ❑ *I dream that my son will attend college.*

5 **V-I** If you say that you **would not dream of** doing something, you mean that you would never do it because you think it is wrong. ❑ *I wouldn't dream of laughing at you.* [from Old English]

Thesaurus	dream Also look up :
N	nightmare, vision **1**
	ambition, aspiration, design, hope, wish **2**
V	hope, long for, wish **4**

Word Partnership	Use dream with :
V	**have a** dream **1**
	fulfill a dream, **pursue a** dream, **realize a** dream **2**
N	dream **interpretation** **1**

dress /drɛs/ (dresses, dressing, dressed)
1 **N-COUNT** A **dress** is a piece of woman's or girl's clothing that covers the body and part of the legs. ❑ *She was wearing a short black dress.*
2 **N-NONCOUNT** Particular types of clothing are sometimes called **dress**. ❑ *He wore formal evening dress.*
3 **V-T/V-I** When you **dress** or **dress yourself**, you put on clothes. ❑ *Sarah waited while he dressed.* [from Old French]
▶ **dress up** **1** If you **dress up**, you put on formal clothes. ❑ *You do not need to dress up for dinner.*
2 If you **dress up**, you put on clothes that make you look like someone else for fun. ❑ *He was dressed up like a cowboy.*

Word Partnership	Use dress with :
V	**put on a** dress, **wear a** dress **1**
ADJ	**casual** dress, **formal** dress, **traditional** dress **2**
ADV	dress **appropriately**, dress **casually**, dress **well** **3**

dressed /drɛst/
1 **ADJ** If you are **dressed**, you are wearing clothes. ❑ *He threw her into a swimming pool, fully dressed.*
2 **ADJ** If you are **dressed** in a particular way, you are wearing clothes of a particular color or type. ❑ *...a tall woman dressed in black.* [from Old French]

dress|er /drɛsər/ (dressers) **N-COUNT**
A **dresser** is a piece of furniture with several drawers in it, usually for holding clothes. [from Old French]

dress re|hears|al (dress rehearsals)
N-COUNT ARTS The **dress rehearsal** of a play, an opera, or a show is the final rehearsal before it is performed, in which the performers wear their costumes and the lights and scenery are all used as they will be in the performance.

drew /dru/ **Drew** is the past tense of **draw**. [from Old English]

drib|ble /drɪbᵊl/ (dribbles, dribbling, dribbled)
1 **V-T/V-I** If a liquid **dribbles** somewhere, or if you **dribble** it, it flows there in a thin stream. ❑ *Blood dribbled down Harry's face.*
2 **V-T/V-I** When players **dribble** the ball in a game, they keep it moving by using their hand or foot. ❑ *He dribbled the ball toward Ferris.* ❑ *He dribbled past four players.*

dried /draɪd/
1 **ADJ** **Dried** food has had all the water removed from it so that it will last for a long time. ❑ *...dried herbs.* [from Old English]
2 → see also **dry**

dri|er /draɪər/ → look up **dry** → look up **dryer**

drift /drɪft/ (drifts, drifting, drifted)
1 **V-I** When something **drifts** somewhere, it is carried there by wind or water. ❑ *We drifted up the river.*
2 **V-I** To **drift** somewhere means to move there slowly or gradually. ❑ *The show ended, and the crowds drifted away.*
3 **N-COUNT** A **drift** is a movement away or toward something different. ❑ *Our first task is to stop the drift of farm workers toward the cities.*
4 **N-COUNT** A **drift** is a mass of snow that has formed a pile as a result of the movement of wind. ❑ *A boy was trapped in a snow drift.* [from Old Norse]
→ look at Word Webs: **continents, snow**
▶ **drift off** If you **drift off** to sleep, you gradually fall asleep. ❑ *He finally drifted off to sleep.*

drill /drɪl/ (drills, drilling, drilled)
1 **N-COUNT** A **drill** is a tool for making holes. ❑ *...an electric drill.*
2 **V-T/V-I** When you **drill into** something or **drill** a hole in something, you make a hole in it using a drill. ❑ *You'll need to drill a hole in the wall.*
3 **N-COUNT/N-NONCOUNT** A **drill** is repeated training for a group of people, especially

soldiers, so that they can do something quickly and efficiently. ❏ *...a drill that included 18 ships and 90 planes.* [from Middle Dutch]
→ look at Picture Dictionary: **tool**
→ look at Word Web: **oil**

drink /drɪŋk/ (**drinks, drinking, drank, drunk**)
1 **V-T/V-I** When you **drink** a liquid, you take it into your mouth and swallow it. ❏ *He drank his cup of coffee.* ❏ *He drank thirstily.*
● **drink|er** (**drinkers**) **N-COUNT** ❏ *We're all coffee drinkers.*
2 **V-I** To **drink** means to drink alcohol. ❏ *He drinks too much.* ● **drink|er** (**drinkers**) **N-COUNT** ❏ *I'm not a heavy drinker.* ● **drink|ing** **N-NONCOUNT** ❏ *She left him because of his drinking.*
3 **N-COUNT** A **drink** is an amount of a liquid that you drink. ❏ *I'll get you a drink of water.*
4 **N-COUNT** A **drink** is an alcoholic drink. ❏ *They invited us to drop by for coffee or for a drink anytime.* [from Old English]
5 → see also **drunk**

drip /drɪp/ (**drips, dripping, dripped**)
1 **V-T/V-I** When liquid **drips** somewhere, or you **drip** it somewhere, it falls in drops. ❏ *The rain dripped down my face.*
2 **V-I** When something that contains a liquid **drips**, drops of liquid escape from it. ❏ *A faucet in the kitchen was dripping.*
3 **N-COUNT** A **drip** is a piece of medical equipment used for slowly putting liquid through a tube into a patient's blood. ❏ *He was put on a drip to treat his dehydration.* [from Old English]

drive /draɪv/ (**drives, driving, drove, driven**)
1 **V-T/V-I** When you **drive**, you control the movement and direction of a car or other vehicle. ❏ *I drove into town.* ❏ *She never learned to drive.* ❏ *We drove the car to Richmond.*
● **driv|ing** **N-NONCOUNT** ❏ *...a driving instructor.*
2 **V-T** If you **drive** someone somewhere, you take them there in a car. ❏ *She drove him to the train station.*
3 **V-T** The feeling that **drives** a person **to** do something is the feeling that causes them to do it. ❏ *His unhappiness drove him to ask for help.*
4 **N-COUNT** A **drive** is a trip in a car. ❏ *Let's go for a drive on Sunday.*
5 **N-COUNT** The **drive** is the part of a computer that reads and stores information. ❏ *Save your work on the C drive.*
6 **N-COUNT** A **drive** is a small road that leads from the main road to a person's

house. ❏ *The boys followed Eleanor up the drive.*
7 **N-NONCOUNT** **Drive** is energy and determination. ❏ *John has a lot of drive and enthusiasm.*
8 **N-SING** A **drive** is a special effort made by a group of people for a particular purpose. ❏ *He helped to organize a fund-raising drive for children with cancer.* [from Old English]
9 → see also **disk drive**
→ look at Word Web: **car**
▶ **drive away** To **drive** people **away** means to make them go away. ❏ *Patrick's rudeness drove Monica's friends away.*

driven /drɪvᵊn/ **Driven** is the past participle of **drive**.

driv|er /draɪvər/ (**drivers**) **N-COUNT** A **driver** is a person who drives a bus, a car, or a train, for example. ❏ *The driver got out of his truck.* ❏ *...a taxi driver.* [from Old English]

driv|er's li|cense (**driver's licenses**) **N-COUNT** A **driver's license** is a card that shows that you have passed a driving test and that you are allowed to drive.

drive-through (**drive-throughs**) also **drive-thru** **N-COUNT** A **drive-through** is a place with a window at a bank, a restaurant or a store where you can be served without leaving your car. ❏ *...a fast-food drive-through.*

drive|way /draɪvweɪ/ (**driveways**) **N-COUNT** A **driveway** is a small road that leads from the street to the front of a building. ❏ *There is a driveway at the front of the house.* [from Old English]

driveway

driz|zle /drɪzᵊl/ **N-NONCOUNT/N-SING** **Drizzle** is light rain falling in fine drops. ❏ *Finally the drizzle stopped.* [from Old English]
→ look at Word Web: **precipitation**

drone /droʊn/ (**drones**) **N-COUNT** A **drone** is a type of aircraft that does not have a pilot and is controlled by someone on the ground. ❏ *Drones frequently pass over this region.*

droop /druːp/ (**droops, drooping, drooped**) **V-I** If something **droops**, it hangs or leans downward. ❏ *His eyelids drooped and he yawned.* [from Old Norse]

drop /drɒp/ (**drops, dropping, dropped**)
1 **V-T/V-I** If a level or an amount **drops**, or if someone or something **drops** it, it quickly

becomes less. ❑ *Temperatures can drop to freezing at night.* ❑ *His blood pressure had dropped severely.*
2 **N-COUNT** Drop is also a noun. ❑ *There was a sudden drop in the number of visitors to the site.*
3 **V-T/V-I** If you **drop** something, or if it **drops**, you let it fall, or it falls. ❑ *I dropped my glasses and broke them.* ❑ *Tears were dropping onto his book.* ❑ *He felt tears dropping onto his fingers.*
4 **V-T** If you **drop** someone somewhere, you take them there in a car and leave them there. ❑ *He dropped me outside the hotel.*
5 **Drop off** means the same as **drop**. ❑ *Dad dropped me off at school on his way to work.*
6 **V-T** If you **drop** an idea or course of action, you do not continue with it. ❑ *He decided to drop the idea.*
7 **N-COUNT** A **drop of** a liquid is a very small amount of it shaped like a little ball. ❑ *...a drop of water.* [from Old English]
▶ **drop by** If you **drop by**, you visit someone informally. ❑ *She will drop by later.*
▶ **drop in** If you **drop in**, or **drop in on** someone, you visit them informally. ❑ *Why not drop in for a chat?*
▶ **drop off** If you **drop off** to sleep, you go to sleep. [INFORMAL] ❑ *I lay on the bed and dropped off to sleep.*
▶ **drop out** If someone **drops out of** school or a race, for example, they leave it without finishing. ❑ *He dropped out of high school at the age of 16.*

Word Partnership	Use **drop** with :
ADJ	**sudden** drop **1**
N	drop **in sales 1**
	drop **a ball 2**
	drop **of blood**, **tear** drop, drop **of water 5**

drop-down menu (**drop-down menus**)
N-COUNT TECHNOLOGY On a computer screen, a **drop-down menu** is a list of choices that appears, usually when you click on a small arrow. ❑ *If you click on the search box, a drop-down menu appears.*

drought /dra͟ʊt/ (**droughts**)
N-COUNT/N-NONCOUNT A **drought** is a long period of time with no rain. ❑ *The drought has killed all their crops.* [from Old English]
→ look at Word Web: **dam**

drove /dro͟ʊv/ **Drove** is the past tense of **drive**. [from Old English]

drown /dra͟ʊn/ (**drowns, drowning, drowned**) **V-T/V-I** When someone **drowns** or

is **drowned**, they die under water because they cannot breathe. ❑ *A child can drown in only a few inches of water.* ❑ *Last night a boy was drowned in the river.* [from Old English]

drowsy /dra͟ʊzi/ (**drowsier, drowsiest**) ADJ
If you feel **drowsy**, you feel tired and you cannot think clearly. ❑ *He felt pleasantly drowsy.* [from Old English]

drug /drʌ͟g/ (**drugs, drugging, drugged**)
1 **N-COUNT** SCIENCE A **drug** is a chemical that is used as a medicine. ❑ *The new drug is too expensive for most African countries.*
2 **N-COUNT** **Drugs** are illegal substances that some people take because they enjoy their effects. ❑ *She was sure Leo was taking drugs.*
3 **V-T** To **drug** a person or an animal means to give them a chemical substance in order to make them sleepy or unconscious. ❑ *She was drugged and robbed.* [from Old French]

drug ad|dict (**drug addicts**) **N-COUNT** A **drug addict** is someone who cannot stop using illegal drugs.

drug|store /drʌ͟gstɔr/ (**drugstores**) **N-COUNT**
A **drugstore** is a store where medicines, makeup, and some other things are sold.

drum /drʌ͟m/ (**drums, drumming, drummed**)
1 **N-COUNT** MUSIC A **drum** is a simple musical instrument that you hit with sticks or with your hands. ● **drum|mer** (**drummers**)
N-COUNT ❑ *He was a drummer in a band.*
2 **N-COUNT** A **drum** is a large container that is used to store fuel or other substances. ❑ *...an oil drum.*
3 **V-T/V-I** If something **drums on** a surface, it hits it regularly, making a continuous beating sound. ❑ *He drummed his fingers on the top of his desk.* [from Middle Dutch]
→ look at Picture Dictionary: **percussion**

drunk /drʌ͟ŋk/
1 ADJ Someone who is **drunk** has drunk too much alcohol. ❑ *He got drunk and fell down the stairs.*
2 **Drunk** is the past participle of **drink**. [from Old English]

dry /dra͟ɪ/ (**drier** or **dryer, driest, dries, drying, dried**)
1 ADJ If something is **dry**, there is no water on it or in it. ❑ *Clean the metal with a soft dry cloth.* ● **dry|ness** **N-NONCOUNT** ❑ *...the dryness of the air.*
2 ADJ If the weather is **dry**, there is no rain. ❑ *The Sahara is one of the driest places in Africa.*

d

3 ADJ If your skin or hair is **dry**, it is not soft. ❑ *She had dry, cracked lips.*

4 V-I When something **dries**, it becomes dry. ❑ *Let your hair dry naturally if possible.*

5 V-T When you **dry** something, you remove the water from it. ❑ *Mrs. Madrigal picked up a towel and began drying dishes.* [from Old English]

6 → see also **dried**

→ look at Word Web: **weather**

▶ **dry out** If something **dries out**, it loses all the water that was in it and becomes hard. ❑ *If the soil dries out, the tree could die.*

▶ **dry up** If something **dries up**, it becomes completely dry. ❑ *The river dried up.*

dry-clean (**dry-cleans, dry-cleaning, dry-cleaned**) **V-T** When clothes **are dry-cleaned**, they are cleaned with a chemical rather than with water. ❑ *The suit must be dry-cleaned.*

dry|er /dra͟ɪər/ (**dryers**) also **drier N-COUNT** A **dryer** is a machine for drying things. ❑ *Put the clothes in the dryer for a few minutes.*

dual /du͟əl/ **ADJ Dual** means having two parts, functions, or aspects. ❑ *...his dual role as head of the party and head of state.* [from Latin]

dub /dʌ͟b/ (**dubs, dubbing, dubbed**)

1 V-T If someone or something **is dubbed** a particular thing, they are given that description or name. ❑ *...a man dubbed as the "biggest nuisance in the U.S."*

2 V-T If a movie or soundtrack in a foreign language **is dubbed**, a new soundtrack is added with actors giving a translation. ❑ *It was dubbed into Spanish for Mexican audiences.* [from Old English]

du|bi|ous /du͟biəs/

1 ADJ If you describe something as **dubious**, you think it is not completely honest, safe, or reliable. ❑ *This claim seems to be rather dubious.* ● **du|bi|ous|ly ADV** ❑ *The government was dubiously re-elected.*

2 ADJ If you are **dubious about** something, you are not completely sure about it and have not yet made up your mind about it. ❑ *Hayes was originally dubious about becoming involved with the project.* ● **du|bi|ous|ly ADV** ❑ *He looked at Coyne dubiously.* [from Latin]

duck /dʌ͟k/ (**ducks, ducking, ducked**)

1 N-COUNT A **duck** is a bird that lives near water. ❑ *A few ducks were swimming around in the shallow water.*

2 N-NONCOUNT Duck is meat from this bird. ❑ *...roasted duck.*

3 V-T/V-I If you **duck**, you move your head quickly downward so that something does not hit you, or so that someone does not see you. ❑ *There was a loud noise and I ducked.* ❑ *Hans deftly ducked their blows.* [Senses 1 and 2 from Old English. Sense 3 from Old High German.]

duc|til|ity /dʌktɪ͟lɪti/ **N-NONCOUNT** SCIENCE The **ductility** of a metal is its ability to be stretched without breaking. [from Old French]

dude /du͟d/ (**dudes**) **N-COUNT** A **dude** is a man. **Dude** is sometimes used as an informal greeting for a man. [INFORMAL] ❑ *He's a real cool dude.* ❑ *Hey, dude, how're you doing?*

due /du͟/

1 ADJ If something is **due** at a particular time, it is expected to happen or arrive at that time. ❑ *The results are due at the end of the month.*

2 ADJ Money that is **due** is owed to someone. ❑ *When is the next payment due?*

3 PHRASE If a situation is **due to** something, it exists as a result of that thing. ❑ *She couldn't do the job, due to pain in her hands.*

4 PHRASE If something happens **in due course**, it happens when the time is right. ❑ *In due course the baby was born.* [from Old French]

duet /du͟ɛt/ (**duets**) **N-COUNT** MUSIC A **duet** is a piece of music performed by two people. ❑ *She sang a duet with Maurice Gibb.* [from Italian]

dug /dʌ͟g/ **Dug** is the past tense and past participle of **dig**.

duke /du͟k/ (**dukes**) **N-COUNT** A **duke** is a man with a very high social rank in some countries. ❑ *...the Duke of Edinburgh.* [from Old French]

dull /dʌ͟l/ (**duller, dullest**)

1 ADJ Dull means not interesting or exciting. ❑ *I thought he was boring and dull.*

2 ADJ A **dull** knife is not sharp.

3 ADJ A **dull** color or light is not bright. ❑ *...the dull gray sky of London.*

4 ADJ A **dull** pain is weak, but it continues for a long time. ❑ *The pain was a dull ache.* [from Old English]

Thesaurus	dull	Also look up :
ADJ	drab, faded, plain **2**	

dumb /dʌm/ (**dumber, dumbest**)

1 **ADJ** Someone who is **dumb** is completely unable to speak. [OFFENSIVE] ❑ *He was born deaf and dumb.*

2 **ADJ** If you call a person **dumb**, you mean that they are stupid. [INFORMAL] ❑ *He was a brilliant guy. He made me feel dumb.*

3 **ADJ** If something is **dumb**, it is silly and annoying. [INFORMAL] ❑ *He had this dumb idea.* [from Old English]

→ look at Word Web: **disability**

dumb|found /dʌmfaʊnd/ (**dumbfounds, dumbfounding, dumbfounded**) **V-T** If someone or something **dumbfounds** you, they surprise you so much that you do not know what to say. ❑ *This suggestion dumbfounded Joe.*

dum|my /dʌmi/ (**dummies**)

1 **N-COUNT** A **dummy** is a model of a person, often used in safety tests. ❑ *...a crash-test dummy.*

2 **N-COUNT** If you call a person a **dummy**, you are rudely saying that they are stupid. [INFORMAL]

dump /dʌmp/ (**dumps, dumping, dumped**)

1 **V-T** If you **dump** something somewhere, you leave it there quickly and without being careful. [INFORMAL] ❑ *We dumped our bags at the hotel and went to the market.*

2 **V-T** If something **is dumped** somewhere, it is put or left there because it is no longer wanted. [INFORMAL] ❑ *The robbers' car was dumped near the freeway.*

3 **V-T** If someone **dumps** their girlfriend or boyfriend, they end their relationship. [INFORMAL] ❑ *My boyfriend dumped me last night.*

4 **N-COUNT** A **dump** is a place where you can take garbage. ❑ *He took his trash to the dump.*

5 **N-COUNT** If a place is a **dump**, it is ugly and unpleasant. [INFORMAL] ❑ *"What a dump!"* Christabel said, looking at the house.

→ look at Word Web: **dump**

dune /dun/ (**dunes**) **N-COUNT** SCIENCE A **dune** is a hill of sand near the ocean or in a desert. ❑ *Behind the beach is an area of sand dunes and grass.* [from Old French]

→ look at Picture Dictionary: **desert**
→ look at Word Web: **beach**

duo /duoʊ/ (**duos**) **N-COUNT** MUSIC A **duo** is a pair of musicians, singers, or other performers. ❑ *...a famous singing duo.* [from Italian]

du|ple me|ter /dupᵊl mitər/ (**duple meters**) **N-COUNT/N-NONCOUNT** MUSIC Music that is written in **duple meter** has a beat that is repeated in groups of two.

du|rable /dʊərəbᵊl/ **ADJ** Something that is **durable** is strong and lasts a long time. ❑ *It's one of the most durable tennis shoes on the market.* [from Old French]

dur|ing /dʊərɪŋ/

1 **PREP** If something happens **during** a period of time, it happens between the beginning and the end of that period. ❑ *Storms are common during the winter.* ❑ *I fell asleep during the performance.*

2 **PREP** An event that happens **during** a period of time happens at some point in that period. ❑ *During his stay, the president will visit the new hospital.* [from Latin]

Usage	during and for

During and *for* are often confused. *During* answers the question "When?": *Bats hibernate during the winter.* *For* answers the question "How long?": *Carla talks on the phone to her boyfriend for an hour every night.*

Word Web   dump

Most communities used to dispose of **solid waste** in **dumps**. Today there are more **environmentally friendly** methods as alternatives to dumping **garbage** in a **landfill**.
Reduction means creating less waste. For example, using washable napkins instead of paper napkins. **Reuse** involves finding a second use for something without processing it. For instance, reusing a shopping bag. **Recycling** and **composting** involve finding a new use for something by processing it—using food scraps to fertilize a garden. **Incineration** involves burning solid waste and using the heat for another useful purpose.

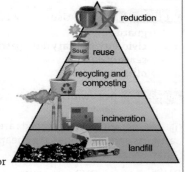

D

dusk /dʌsk/ **N-NONCOUNT** Dusk is the time just before night when it is not completely dark. ❑ *We arrived home at dusk.* [from Old English]

dust /dʌst/ (dusts, dusting, dusted)
1 **N-NONCOUNT** Dust is a fine powder of dry earth or dirt. ❑ *I could see a thick layer of dust on the stairs.*
2 **V-T/V-I** When you dust furniture, you remove dust from it with a cloth. ❑ *I dusted and polished the furniture in the living room.* ❑ *I was dusting in his study.* [from Old English]

dust mite /dʌst maɪt/ (dust mites) **N-COUNT** Dust mites are very small creatures that cause allergies. ❑ *It's not easy to remove the dust mites from soft toys.*

dusty /dʌsti/ (dustier, dustiest) **ADJ** If something is dusty, it is covered with dust. ❑ *...a dusty room.* [from Old English]

duty /duti/ (duties)
1 **N-COUNT/N-NONCOUNT** Duty or a duty is work that you have to do. ❑ *Staff must report for duty at 8 a.m.* ❑ *I did my duties without complaining.*
2 **N-SING** If something is your duty, you feel that you have to do it. ❑ *I consider it my duty to warn you of the dangers.*
3 **N-COUNT/N-NONCOUNT** Duties are taxes that you pay to the government on goods that you buy. ❑ *Import duties are around 30%.*
4 **PHRASE** If someone is off duty, they are not working. If someone is on duty, they are working. ❑ *The two police officers were off duty when the accident happened.* [from Old French]
→ look at Word Web: **citizenship**

Thesaurus	duty	Also look up :
N	assignment, responsibility, task **1** **2** obligation **2**	

Word Partnership	Use duty with :
N	**guard** duty **1**
ADJ	**civic** duty, **military** duty, **patriotic** duty, **sense of** duty **2**
PREP	**off** duty, **on** duty **4**

Word Link	free ≈ without : care*free*, duty-*free*, hands-*free*

duty-free **ADJ** Duty-free goods are sold at airports or on airplanes at a cheaper price than usual. ❑ *...duty-free perfume.*

DVD /di vi di/ (DVDs) **N-COUNT** **TECHNOLOGY** A DVD is a disk on which a movie or music is recorded. DVD is short for "digital video disk." ❑ *...a DVD player.*
→ look at Word Web: **laser**

DVD burn|er /di vi di bɜrnər/ (DVD burners) or DVD writer **N-COUNT** **TECHNOLOGY** A DVD burner is a piece of computer equipment that you use for putting information onto a DVD.

DVD play|er (DVD players) **N-COUNT** **TECHNOLOGY** A DVD player is a machine for showing movies that are stored on a DVD. ❑ *We got a portable DVD player for the kids to watch in the car.*

dwarf /dwɔrf/ (dwarves, dwarfs)
1 **N-COUNT** A dwarf is a very short person with short arms and legs. [OFFENSIVE]
2 **N-COUNT** In children's stories, a dwarf is a small man who sometimes has magical powers. [from Old English]

dwarf plan|et (dwarf planets) **N-COUNT** **SCIENCE** A dwarf planet is a round object that orbits the sun and is larger than an asteroid but smaller than a planet.

dwell|er /dwɛlər/ (dwellers) **N-COUNT** A city dweller or slum dweller, for example, is a person who lives in the kind of place or house indicated. ❑ *The number of city dwellers is growing.* [from Old English]

dwell|ing /dwɛlɪŋ/ (dwellings) **N-COUNT** A dwelling or a dwelling place is a place where someone lives. [FORMAL] ❑ *3,500 new dwellings are planned for the area.* [from Old English]

dwin|dle /dwɪndəl/ (dwindles, dwindling, dwindled) **V-I** If something dwindles, it becomes smaller, weaker, or less in number. ❑ *The factory's workforce dwindled from over 4,000 to a few hundred.* [from Old English]

dye /daɪ/ (dyes, dyeing, dyed)
1 **V-T** If you dye something, you change its color by putting it in a special liquid. ❑ *He had to dye his hair for the movie.*
2 **N-COUNT/N-NONCOUNT** Dye is a substance that is used for changing the color of cloth or hair. ❑ *...a bottle of hair dye.* [from Old English]

dy|ing /daɪɪŋ/
1 Dying is the present participle of **die**.
2 **ADJ** A dying person or animal is very ill and likely to die soon. ❑ *...a dying man.*
3 **N-PLURAL** The dying are people who are dying. ❑ *By the time our officers arrived,*

the dead and the dying were everywhere.
4 **ADJ** A **dying** tradition or industry is becoming less important and is likely to disappear completely. ❑ *Shipbuilding is a dying business.* [from Old English]

dy|nam|ic /daɪnæmɪk/
1 **ADJ** Someone who is **dynamic** is full of energy, or has new and exciting ideas. ❑ *He was a dynamic and energetic leader.*
2 **N-PLURAL** SCIENCE **Dynamics** are forces that produce power or movement.
3 **N-NONCOUNT** SCIENCE **Dynamics** is the scientific study of motion, energy, and forces.
4 **N-PLURAL** ARTS The **dynamics** of a piece of music are how softly or loudly it is being played. [from French]

dy|nam|ic mark|ing (**dynamic markings**)
N-COUNT MUSIC **Dynamic markings** are words and symbols in a musical score which show how softly or loudly the music should be played.

dys|en|tery /dɪsənteri/ **N-NONCOUNT**
SCIENCE **Dysentery** is an infection in a person's intestines. ❑ *Starvation, typhus, and dysentery killed about 300,000 people.* [from Latin]

dys|func|tion /dɪsfʌŋkʃən/ (**dysfunctions**)
1 **N-COUNT** If you refer to a **dysfunction** in a relationship or in someone's behavior, you mean that it does not work well, or that it is not normal. [FORMAL] ❑ *...his severe emotional dysfunction was very apparent.*
2 **N-COUNT/N-NONCOUNT** SCIENCE If someone has a physical **dysfunction**, part of their body is not working properly. ❑ *...kidney and liver dysfunction.* [from Latin]

dys|lexia /dɪslɛksiə/ **N-NONCOUNT** **Dyslexia** is a condition that affects the brain, making it difficult for someone to read and write. [from Greek]

dys|pep|sia /dɪspɛpʃə, -siə/ **N-NONCOUNT** SCIENCE **Dyspepsia** is the same as **indigestion**. [from Latin] [OLD-FASHIONED]

dys|tro|phy /dɪstrəfi/ → look up **muscular dystrophy** [from New Latin]

d

Ee

each /itʃ/

1 **DET** **Each** person or thing is every person or thing. ❏ *Each book is beautifully illustrated.* ❏ *The library buys 2,000 new books each year.*

2 **PRON** **Each** is also a pronoun. ❏ *We each have different needs and interests.* ❏ *He gave each of them a book.* ❏ *Each of these exercises takes one or two minutes to do.*

3 **ADV** **Each** is also an adverb. ❏ *Tickets are six dollars each.*

4 **PRON** You use **each other** to show that each member of a group does something to or for the other members. ❏ *We looked at each other in silence.* [from Old English]

> **Usage**   **each**
>
> Sentences that begin with *each* take a singular verb. *Each of the drivers has a license.*

ea|ger /igər/ **ADJ** If you are **eager to** do something, you want to do it very much. ❏ *The children are all very eager to learn.*
● **eager|ly** **ADV** ❏ *"So what do you think will happen?" he asked eagerly.* [from Old French]

ea|gle /igəl/ (**eagles**) **N-COUNT** An **eagle** is a large bird that eats small animals. [from Old French]

ear /ɪər/ (**ears**) **N-COUNT** Your **ears** are the two parts of your body that you hear sounds with. ❏ *He whispered something in her ear.* [from Old English]

→ look at Picture Dictionary: **face**
→ look at Word Web: **ear**

ear|ache /ɪəreɪk/ **N-NONCOUNT** If you have **earache**, you have a pain inside your ear. ❏ *I woke up in the morning with terrible earache.*

ear|bud /ɪərbʌd/ (**earbuds**) **N-COUNT** **Earbuds** are small headphones that you wear in your ears to listen to audio equipment.

ear ca|nal (**ear canals**) **N-COUNT** Your **ear canal** is the tube that opens in your outer ear and leads inside your ear. ❏ *Your hearing can be affected by ear wax blocking the ear canal.*
→ look at Word Web: **ear**

ear|drum /ɪərdrʌm/ (**eardrums**) also **ear drum** **N-COUNT** **SCIENCE** Your **eardrums** are the parts inside your ears that react when sound waves reach them. ❏ *The explosion burst Ollie Williams' eardrum.*
→ look at Word Web: **ear**

ear|li|er /ɜrliər/

1 **Earlier** is the comparative of **early.**

2 **ADV** **Earlier** is used to refer to a point or period in time before the present or before the one you are talking about. ❏ *They finished making the movie earlier this year.*

3 **ADJ** **Earlier** is also an adjective. ❏ *Earlier reports suggested that the fire started accidentally.* [from Old English]

Word Web   ear

The **ear** collects **sound waves** and sends them to the brain. First the **external ear** picks up sound waves. Then these sound **vibrations** travel along the **ear canal** and strike the **eardrum**. The eardrum pushes against a series of tiny bones. These bones carry the vibrations into the **inner ear**. There they are picked up by the hair cells in the cochlea. At that point, the vibrations turn into electric impulses. The cochlea is connected to the hearing **nerve**. It sends the electric impulses to the brain.

inner ear
hearing nerve
eardrum
cochlea
ear canal
outer ear

ear|li|est /ˈɜrliɪst/
■ **Earliest** is the superlative of **early**.
■ **PHRASE** At the earliest means not before the date or time mentioned. ❑ *The official results are not expected until Tuesday at the earliest.* [from Old English]

ear|lobe /ˈɪərloʊb/ (**earlobes**) also **ear lobe**
N-COUNT Your **earlobes** are the soft parts at the bottom of your ears. ❑ *...the holes in her earlobes.*
→ look at Picture Dictionary: **face**

ear|ly /ˈɜrli/ (**earlier, earliest**)
■ **ADV** **Early** means before the usual time. ❑ *I had to get up early this morning.* ❑ *She arrived early to get a place at the front.*
■ **ADJ** **Early** is also an adjective. ❑ *I want to get an early start in the morning.*
■ **ADJ** **Early** means near the beginning of an activity, process, or period of time. ❑ *...the early 1980s.*
■ **ADV** **Early** is also an adverb. ❑ *We'll see you some time early next week.* [from Old English]

ear|ly adopt|er /ˈɜrli əˈdɒptər/ (**early adopters**) **N-COUNT** TECHNOLOGY **Early adopters** are the first people or organizations to make use of a new technology. ❑ *The market has been shaped by the demands of early adopters.*

earn /ˈɜrn/ (**earns, earning, earned**)
■ **V-T** If you **earn** money, you receive money for work that you do. ❑ *She earns $37,000 a year.* ❑ *What a great way to earn a living (= get the money you need to buy things).*
■ **V-T** If you **earn** something, you get it because you deserve it. ❑ *A good manager earns the respect of his team.* [from Old English]

ear|nest /ˈɜrnɪst/
■ **PHRASE** If something is done or happens **in earnest**, it happens to a much greater extent and more seriously than before. ❑ *He'll start work in earnest next week.*

■ **ADJ** **Earnest** people are very serious and sincere. ❑ *Catherine was an earnest woman.*
● **ear|nest|ly** **ADV** ❑ *She always listened earnestly.* [from Old English]

earn|ings /ˈɜrnɪŋz/ **N-PLURAL** Your **earnings** are the sums of money that you earn by working. ❑ *Average weekly earnings rose by 1.5% in July.* [from Old English]

ear|phone /ˈɪərfoʊn/ (**earphones**) **N-COUNT** **Earphones** are things that you wear on or in your ears so that you can listen to music or the radio without anyone else hearing.

ear|ring /ˈɪərɪŋ/ (**earrings**) **N-COUNT** **Earrings** are jewelry that you wear on your ears. ❑ *The woman wore large, gold earrings.* [from Old English]
→ look at Picture Dictionary: **jewelry**

earth /ˈɜrθ/
■ **N-PROPER** SCIENCE **Earth** or **the Earth** is the planet that we live on. ❑ *The space shuttle Atlantis returned safely to Earth today.*
■ **N-SING** The **earth** is the land surface that we live on. ❑ *The earth shook and the walls fell around them.*
■ **N-NONCOUNT** SCIENCE **Earth** is the substance in which plants grow. ❑ *...a huge pile of earth.*
■ **PHRASE** You use **on earth** in questions that begin with "how," "why," "what," or "where," to show that you are very surprised. ❑ *How on earth did that happen?* [from Old English]
→ look at Picture Dictionary: **core**
→ look at Word Webs: **earth, eclipse, erosion**

earth|quake /ˈɜrθkweɪk/ (**earthquakes**) **N-COUNT** SCIENCE An **earthquake** is when the ground shakes because the Earth's surface is moving. ❑ *...the San Francisco earthquake of 1906.*
→ look at Word Webs: **earthquake, tsunami**

e

Word Web **earth**

The **earth** is made of material left over after the **sun** formed. In the beginning, about 4 billion years ago, the earth was made of liquid **rock**. During its first million years, it cooled into solid rock. **Life**, in the form of bacteria, began in the **oceans** about 3.5 billion years ago. During the next billion years, the **continents** formed. At the same time, the level of **oxygen** in the **atmosphere** increased. **Life forms evolved**, and some of them began to use oxygen. **Evolution** allowed **plants** and **animals** to move from the oceans onto the **land**.

E

Word Web earthquake

Earthquakes occur when two **tectonic plates** meet and start to move past each other. This meeting point is called the **focus**. It may be located anywhere from a few hundred meters to a few hundred kilometers below the surface of the earth. The resulting pressure causes a split in the earth's **crust** called a **fault**. Vibrations move out from the focus in all directions. These **seismic waves** cause little damage until they reach the surface. The **epicenter**, directly above the focus, receives the greatest damage. Seismologists use **seismographs** to measure the amount of ground movement during an earthquake.

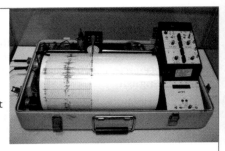

A seismograph recording a major earthquake.

earth|worm /ɜrθwɜrm/ (**earthworms**)
N-COUNT An **earthworm** is a kind of worm that lives in the ground.

ease /iz/ (**eases, easing, eased**)
1 PHRASE If you do something **with ease**, you do it without difficulty or effort. ❏ *Anne passed her exams with ease.*
2 V-T/V-I If something unpleasant **eases** or if you **ease** it, it is reduced in degree or speed. ❏ *I gave him some aspirin to ease the pain.*
3 PHRASE If you are **at ease**, you are feeling confident and relaxed. ❏ *It is important that you feel at ease with your doctor.* [from Old French]

ea|sel /izᵊl/ (**easels**) **N-COUNT** ARTS An **easel** is a stand that supports a picture while an artist is working on it. [from Dutch]
→ look at Word Web: **painting**

easi|ly /izɪli/
1 ADV If you can do a task **easily**, you can do it without difficulty. ❏ *Most students were easily able to find jobs at the end of the course.*
2 ADV You use **easily** to emphasize that something is very likely to happen, or is very likely to be true. ❏ *It could easily be another year before things improve.*
3 ADV You use **easily** to say that something happens more quickly or more often than is usual or normal. ❏ *He has always cried very easily.* [from Old French]

east /ist/ also East
1 N-NONCOUNT GEOGRAPHY The **east** is the direction that is in front of you when you look at the sun in the morning. ❏ *In the east, the sun was rising.* ❏ *The city lies to the east of the river.*
2 ADJ GEOGRAPHY **East** is also an adjective. ❏ *There is a line of hills along the east coast.*
3 N-SING GEOGRAPHY The **east of** a place or

a country is the part that is in the east.
❏ *...a village in the east of the country.*
4 ADV GEOGRAPHY If you go **east**, you travel toward the east. ❏ *Go east on Route 9.*
5 ADV GEOGRAPHY Something that is **east** of a place is located to the east of it.
❏ *The airport is about twenty miles east of the city.*
6 ADJ An **east** wind blows from the east. ❏ *A cold east wind was blowing.*
7 N-SING GEOGRAPHY The **East** is the southern and eastern part of Asia, including India, China, and Japan. [from Old English]
8 → see also **Middle East**

East|er /istər/ (**Easters**) **N-COUNT/N-NONCOUNT**
Easter is a Christian festival in March or April when Jesus Christ's return to life is celebrated. [from Old English]

east|er|ly /istərli/
1 ADJ GEOGRAPHY **Easterly** means to the east or toward the east. ❏ *We sailed slowly along the coast in an easterly direction.*
2 ADJ An **easterly** wind is a wind that blows from the east. ❏ *It was a beautiful September day, with cool easterly winds.* [from Old English]

east|ern /istərn/
1 ADJ GEOGRAPHY **Eastern** means in or from the east of a place. ❏ *...Eastern Europe.*
2 ADJ SOCIAL STUDIES **Eastern** describes things, people, or ideas that come from the countries of the East, such as India, China, or Japan. ❏ *Exports to Eastern countries have gone down.* [from Old English]

easy /izi/ (**easier, easiest**)
1 ADJ If a task is **easy**, you can do it without difficulty. ❏ *Losing weight is not an easy task.* ❏ *The software is easy to use.*
2 PHRASE If someone tells you to **take it easy,**

they mean that you should relax and that you should not worry. [INFORMAL] ❑ I suggest you take it easy for a week or two. [from Old French]

Thesaurus	easy Also look up :
ADJ	basic, elementary, simple, uncomplicated; (ant.) complicated, difficult, hard ■

eat /it/ (eats, eating, ate, eaten) **V-T/V-I** When you **eat** something, you put it into your mouth and swallow it. ❑ I ate spaghetti with tomato sauce. ❑ I ate slowly and without speaking. [from Old English]
→ look at Word Webs: **cooking, food**
▶ **eat out** If you **eat out**, you eat a meal in a restaurant. ❑ We usually eat out.
▶ **eat up** If you **eat up** something, you eat all of it. ❑ Both of you, eat up these potatoes.

e-bank|ing **N-NONCOUNT** TECHNOLOGY E-banking is a system that allows you to access banking services using the Internet. **E-banking** is short for **electronic banking**. ❑ How do I sign onto e-banking?

e-book (e-books) **N-COUNT** TECHNOLOGY An **e-book** is a digital book that you can read on a screen. **E-book** is short for **electronic book**. ❑ ...a successful e-book series.

e-card (e-cards) **N-COUNT** TECHNOLOGY An **e-card** is a digital version of a card that you send to someone over the Internet. **E-card** is short for **electronic card**. ❑ She sent me an e-card for my birthday.

ec|cen|tric /ɪksɛntrɪk/ **ADJ** Someone who is **eccentric** is unusual, and has habits that are different from those of most people. ❑ He is an eccentric character. [from Medieval Latin]

echo /ɛkoʊ/ (echoes, echoing, echoed)
■ **N-COUNT** SCIENCE An **echo** is a sound that you hear again because it hits a surface and then comes back. ❑ I heard the echo of

someone laughing across the hall.
❷ **V-I** If a sound **echoes**, you hear it again because it hits a surface and then comes back. ❑ His feet echoed on the stone floor. [from Latin]
→ look at Word Webs: **echo, sound**

e-ciga|rette (e-cigarettes) **N-COUNT** An **e-cigarette** is an object that is shaped like a cigarette and that produces the same effect as smoking. **E-cigarette** is short for **electronic cigarette**.

eclipse /ɪklɪps/ (eclipses) **N-COUNT** SCIENCE An **eclipse** happens when the light from the sun or the moon is blocked for a short time because of the position of the sun, the moon, and the Earth. [from Old English]
→ look at Word Web: **eclipse**

eco-friend|ly /ɛkoʊfrɛndli, ik-/ **ADJ** **Eco-friendly** products or services are less harmful to the environment than other similar products or services. ❑ ...eco-friendly laundry detergent.

eco|logi|cal suc|ces|sion **N-NONCOUNT** SCIENCE **Ecological succession** is the process in which one population of plants and animals gradually replaces another population in a particular area as a result of changing environmental conditions.

ecol|ogy /ɪkɒlədʒi/ **N-NONCOUNT** SCIENCE **Ecology** is the study of the relationships between living things and their environment. ❑ He is professor of ecology at the university. ● **ecolo|gist** (ecologists) **N-COUNT** ❑ Ecologists are concerned that these chemicals will pollute lakes. ● **eco|logi|cal** /ɛkəlɒdʒɪkᵊl, ik-/ **ADJ** ❑ How can we save the Earth from ecological disaster? [from German]

eco|nom|ic /ɛkənɒmɪk, ik-/ **ADJ** **Economic** means connected with the organization of the money and industry of a country.

Word Web echo

We can learn a lot from studying **echoes**. Geologists use **sound reflection** to predict how earthquake waves will travel through the earth. They also use echolocation to find underground oil reservoirs. Oceanographers use sonar to explore the ocean. Marine mammals, bats, and humans also use sonar for navigation. Architects study building materials and surfaces to understand how they absorb or **reflect** sound **waves**. They may use hard reflective surfaces to help create a noisy, exciting atmosphere in a restaurant. They may suggest soft drapes and carpeting to create a quiet, calm library.

E

There is more than one kind of eclipse. When the **earth** passes between the **sun** and the **moon**, we see a **lunar eclipse**. When the moon passes between the sun and the earth, we see a **solar eclipse**. A total eclipse of the sun happens when the moon covers the sun completely. In the past, people were frightened of eclipses. Some civilizations understood eclipses. Their leaders pretended to control the sun in order to gain the respect of their people. On August 21, 2017, a total eclipse of the sun will be visible in North America.

Sun
Moon
Earth
orbit of the Moon

❑ *The economic situation is very bad.* [from Latin]

eco|nomi|cal /ɛkənɒmɪkəl, ik-/ **ADJ**
Something that is **economical** does not need a lot of money to make it work. ❑ *People are driving smaller and more economical cars.*
● **eco|nomi|cal|ly** **ADV** ❑ *Services could be operated more economically.* [from Latin]

eco|nom|ics /ɛkənɒmɪks, ik-/ **N-NONCOUNT**
SOCIAL STUDIES **Economics** is the study of the way in which money and industry are organized in a society. ❑ *His sister is studying economics.* [from Latin]

econo|mist /ikɒnəmɪst/ (**economists**)
N-COUNT SOCIAL STUDIES An **economist** is a person who studies economics. [from Latin]

econo|my /ikɒnəmi/ (**economies**) **N-COUNT**
SOCIAL STUDIES An **economy** is the system for organizing the money and industry of the world, a country, or local government. ❑ *The Indian economy is changing fast.* [from Latin]

eco|sys|tem /ɛkoʊsɪstəm, ik-/ (**ecosystems**)
N-COUNT SCIENCE An **ecosystem** is the relationship between all the living things in a particular area together. ❑ *These industries are destroying whole ecosystems.*
→ look at Word Web: **biosphere**

eco|tar|i|an /ɛkoʊtɛəriən, ik-/ (**ecotarians**)
N-COUNT An **ecotarian** is a person who eats only food that has been produced in a way that does not harm the environment.
❑ *Strictly speaking, you don't have to be a vegetarian or a vegan to be an ecotarian.*

eco|tec|ture /ɛkoʊtɛktʃər, ik-/ **N-NONCOUNT**
Ecotecture is a type of architecture with designs based on ecological principles such as sustainability and environmental impact.

ec|to|therm /ɛktəθɜrm/ (**ectotherms**)
N-COUNT SCIENCE An **ectotherm** is a cold-blooded animal, such as a reptile, whose body temperature depends on the temperature of the environment around it. Compare with **endotherm**.

edge /ɛdʒ/ (**edges**)
1 **N-COUNT** The **edge** of something is the part of it that is farthest from the middle. ❑ *We lived in an apartment block on the edge of town.*
❑ *She was standing at the water's edge.*

edge

2 **N-COUNT** The **edge** of a knife is its sharp side. ❑ *His hand touched the edge of the sword.*
3 **PHRASE** If you or your nerves are **on edge**, you are tense and nervous. ❑ *My nerves were constantly on edge.* [from Old English]

ed|ible /ɛdɪbəl/ **ADJ** If something is **edible**, it is safe to eat. ❑ *The flowers are edible, and they look wonderful in salads.* [from Late Latin]

edit /ɛdɪt/ (**edits, editing, edited**) **V-T** If you **edit** a text, you check it and correct the mistakes in it. ❑ *She helped him edit his paper.*

edi|tion /ɪdɪʃən/ (**editions**) **N-COUNT** An **edition** is one of a number of books, magazines, or newspapers that is printed at one time. ❑ *The second edition was published in Canada.* [from Latin]

N	**collector's** edition, **paperback** edition
ADJ	**limited** edition, **new** edition, **revised** edition, **special** edition

edi|tor /ɛdɪtər/ (**editors**)
1 **N-COUNT** An **editor** is a person who checks and corrects texts. ❑ *He works as an editor of children's books.*
2 **N-COUNT** An **editor** is the person who is in charge of a newspaper or magazine, or a

section of a newspaper or magazine.
❑ *Her father was the editor of the Saturday Review.*
[from Late Latin]

edi|to|rial /ɛdɪtɔriəl/ (**editorials**)
1 **ADJ** **Editorial** means involved in preparing a newspaper, a magazine, or a book for publication. ❑ *I went to the editorial meetings when I had time.*
2 **ADJ** **Editorial** means involving the attitudes, opinions, and contents of something such as a newspaper, a magazine, or a television program. ❑ *The editorial standpoint of the magazine is right-wing.*
3 **N-COUNT** An **editorial** is an article in a newspaper, or an item on television or radio, that gives the opinion of the newspaper, network, or radio station. ❑ *...an editorial in The New York Times.* [from Late Latin]

edu|cate /ɛdʒʊkeɪt/ (**educates, educating, educated**)
1 **V-T** When someone **is educated**, he or she is taught at a school or college. ❑ *He was educated at Yale and Stanford.*
2 **V-T** To **educate** people means to teach them better ways of doing something. ❑ *We want to educate people about healthy eating.* [from Latin]

edu|cat|ed /ɛdʒʊkeɪtɪd/ **ADJ** Someone who is **educated** has a lot of knowledge. ❑ *He was an educated and honest man.* [from Latin]

edu|ca|tion /ɛdʒʊkeɪʃⁿn/
1 **N-NONCOUNT** **Education** involves teaching and learning. ❑ *My children's education is important to me.* ❑ *We need better health education.*
● **edu|ca|tion|al** /ɛdʒʊkeɪʃənⁿl/ **ADJ** ❑ *...the American educational system.* [from Latin]
2 → see also **higher education**
→ look at Word Web: **industry**

eel /il/ (**eels**) **N-COUNT/N-NONCOUNT** An **eel** is a long, thin fish that looks like a snake. [from Old English]

ef|face /ɪfeɪs/ (**effaces, effacing, effaced**) **V-T** If you **efface** something, you destroy or remove it so that it cannot be seen anymore. [FORMAL] ❑ *...an event that has helped efface the country's traditional image.* [from French]

ef|fect /ɪfɛkt/ (**effects**)
1 **N-COUNT/N-NONCOUNT** An **effect** is a change or a reaction that is the result of something. ❑ *Parents worry about the effect of junk food on their child's health.*
2 → see also **greenhouse effect, side effect**

3 **PHRASE** When something **takes effect**, it begins to apply or starts to have results. ❑ *The second injection should be given once the first drug takes effect.* [from Latin]

Word Partnership Use **effect** with :

| ADJ | **adverse** effect, **desired** effect, **immediate** effect, **lasting** effect, **negative/positive** effect **1** |
| V | **have an** effect **1** **produce an** effect, **take** effect **5** |

ef|fec|tive /ɪfɛktɪv/
1 **ADJ** Something that is **effective** produces the results that you wanted. ❑ *No drugs are effective against this disease.*
2 **ADJ** When a law or an agreement becomes **effective**, it begins officially to apply. ❑ *The new rules will become effective in the next few days.* [from Latin]

Word Partnership Use **effective** with :

| N | effective **means**, effective **method**, effective **treatment**, effective **use** **1** |
| ADV | **highly** effective **1** effective **immediately** **2** |

ef|fec|tive|ly /ɪfɛktɪvli/
1 **ADV** If you do something **effectively**, you do it in a way that produces the results that you wanted. ❑ *We need to use water more effectively.*
2 **ADV** You use **effectively** with a statement to show that it is not accurate in every detail, but that you feel it is a reasonable description of a particular situation. ❑ *The region was effectively independent.* [from Latin]

ef|fi|cient /ɪfɪʃⁿnt/ **ADJ** If something or someone is **efficient**, they are able to do tasks successfully, without wasting time or energy. ❑ *The engine is efficient and powerful.*
● **ef|fi|cien|cy** /ɪfɪʃⁿnsi/ **N-NONCOUNT** ❑ *We must think of ways to improve efficiency.*
● **ef|fi|cient|ly** **ADV** ❑ *We want people to use energy more efficiently.* [from Latin]

Word Partnership	Use efficient with :
N	energy efficient, **fuel** efficient, efficient **method**, efficient **system**, efficient **use** of *something*
ADV	**highly** efficient

ef|fi|gy /ɛfɪdʒi/ (effigies)

1 N-COUNT An **effigy** is an ugly or amusing image of someone that is often destroyed as part of a protest.

2 N-COUNT An **effigy** is a statue or a carving of a famous person. [FORMAL] ❏ *The monument contains a white marble effigy.* [from Latin]

ef|fort /ɛfərt/ (efforts)

1 N-COUNT/N-NONCOUNT If you make an **effort to** do something, you try very hard to do it. ❏ *You should make an effort to speak the local language when you go abroad.*

2 N-NONCOUNT/N-SING If you do something **with effort**, or if it is **an effort**, you mean it is difficult to do. [WRITTEN] ❏ *She sat up slowly and with great effort.* [from Old French]

Thesaurus	effort Also look up :
N	attempt **1**
	exertion, labor, work **2**

ef|fort force **N-NONCOUNT** **SCIENCE** In physics, **effort force** is force that is used to move an object.

e.g. /i dʒi/ **e.g.** means "for example." ❏ *We need professionals of all types, e.g. teachers.* [from Latin]

egg /ɛg/ (eggs)

1 N-COUNT An **egg** is a round object that is produced by a female bird and contains a baby bird. Other animals such as insects and fish also lay eggs.

2 N-COUNT/N-NONCOUNT In many countries, an **egg** means a hen's egg, that people eat as food. ❏ *Break the eggs into a bowl.*

3 N-COUNT **SCIENCE** An **egg** is a cell that is produced in the bodies of female animals and humans. If it combines with a sperm, a baby develops from it. ❏ *It only takes one sperm to fertilize an egg.* [from Old Norse]

→ look at Picture Dictionary: **egg**
→ look at Word Webs: **bird, reproduction**

egg|plant /ɛgplænt/ (eggplants) **N-COUNT/ N-NONCOUNT** An **eggplant** is a vegetable with a smooth, dark purple skin.

→ look at Picture Dictionary: **vegetables**

ego /igoʊ, ɛgoʊ/ (egos)

N-COUNT/N-NONCOUNT Someone's **ego** is their sense of their own worth. ❏ *He had a big ego and never admitted that he was wrong.* [from Latin]

egre|gious /ɪgridʒəs/ **ADJ** **Egregious** means very bad and offensive. [FORMAL] ❏ *...the most egregious abuses of human rights.* [from Latin]

eight /eɪt/ **NUM** **MATH** **Eight** is the number 8. [from Old English]

Word Link	teen ≈ plus ten, from 13-19 : **eight**teen, **seven**teen, **teen**ager

eight|een /eɪtin/ **NUM** **MATH** **Eighteen** is the number 18. [from Old English]

eight|eenth /eɪtinθ/ **ADJ/ADV** **MATH** The **eighteenth** item in a series is the one that you count as number eighteen. ❏ *The talks are now in their eighteenth day.* [from Old English]

eighth /eɪtθ/ (eighths)

1 ADJ/ADV **MATH** The **eighth** item in a series is the one that you count as number eight. ❏ *Shekhar was the eighth prime minister of India.*

2 N-COUNT **MATH** An **eighth** is one of eight equal parts of something (⅛). ❏ *The ring was an eighth of an inch thick.* [from Old English]

eighti|eth /eɪtiəθ/ **ADJ/ADV** **MATH** The **eightieth** item in a series is the one that you count as number eighty. ❏ *Mr. Stevens recently celebrated his eightieth birthday.* [from Old English]

eighty /eɪti/ (eighties)

1 NUM **MATH** **Eighty** is the number 80.

2 N-PLURAL The **eighties** are the years between 1980 and 1989. ❏ *He ran his own business in the eighties.*

3 N-PLURAL When you talk about the

Picture Dictionary   egg

| fried egg | scrambled eggs | hard-boiled egg | soft-boiled egg | omelet |

eighties, you mean the numbers between 80 and 89. For example, if you are **in** your **eighties**, you are aged between 80 and 89. ❑ *The temperature went up to the mid eighties.* [from Old English]

either /iðər, aɪðər/

1 CONJ You use **either...or...** to show that there are two possibilities to choose from. ❑ *Either she goes or I go.* ❑ *I will either walk or take the bus.* ❑ *You can contact him either by phone or by email.*

2 PRON **Either** is also a pronoun. ❑ *She wants a husband and children. I don't want either.* ❑ *There are no simple answers to either of those questions.*

3 DET **Either** means each. ❑ *The teams waited at either end of the gym.* ❑ *He couldn't remember either man's name.*

4 DET **Either** means one of two things or people. ❑ *You can choose either date.*

5 ADV You use **either** in negative sentences to mean also. ❑ *He said nothing, and she did not speak either.* [from Old English]

> Word Link e ≈ away, out : **e**ject, **e**migrate, **e**mit

eject /ɪdʒɛkt/ (**ejects, ejecting, ejected**) V-T To **eject** something means to remove it or push it out. ❑ *Click on 'OK' and the drive automatically ejects the disc.* [from Latin]

elabo|rate (**elaborates, elaborating, elaborated**)

> **PRONUNCIATION HELP**
> Pronounce the adjective /ɪlæbərɪt/.
> Pronounce the verb /ɪlæbəreɪt/.

1 ADJ You use **elaborate** to describe something that is very complex because it has a lot of different parts. ❑ *...an elaborate research project.* ● **elabo|rate|ly** ADV ❑ *It was an elaborately planned operation.*

2 V-I If you **elaborate on** something that

has been said, you say more about it, or give more details. ❑ *A spokesman declined to elaborate on yesterday's statement.* [from Latin]

elas|tic /ɪlæstɪk/ N-NONCOUNT **Elastic** is a rubber material that stretches when you pull it, and returns to its original size and shape when you let it go. ❑ *The hat has a piece of elastic that goes under the chin.* [from New Latin]

elas|tic re|bound (**elastic rebounds**) N-COUNT/N-NONCOUNT SCIENCE **Elastic rebound** is a geological process associated with earthquakes, in which rock is stretched and then contracts as a result of energy stored within it.

el|bow /ɛlboʊ/ (**elbows**) N-COUNT Your **elbow** is the joint in the middle of your arm where it bends. ❑ *She leaned forward, with her elbows on the table.* [from Old English]
→ look at Picture Dictionary: **body**

el|der /ɛldər/ (**elders**)

1 ADJ The **elder of** two people is the one who was born first. ❑ *...his elder brother.*

2 N-COUNT A person's **elder** is someone who is older than them, especially someone quite a lot older. [FORMAL] ❑ *They have no respect for their elders.*

3 N-COUNT In some societies, an **elder** is one of the respected older people who have influence and authority. ❑ *...a meeting of tribal elders.* [from Old English]

el|der|ly /ɛldərli/

1 ADJ You use **elderly** as a polite way of saying that someone is old. ❑ *An elderly couple lived in the house next door.*

2 N-PLURAL The **elderly** are people who are old. ❑ *It's a lovely home for the elderly.* [from Old English]
→ look at Picture Dictionary: **age**

e

> ## Word Web   election
>
> **Presidential candidates** spend millions of dollars on their **campaigns**. They give **speeches**. They appear on TV and **debate**. On election day, **voters cast** their **votes** at local **polling places**. **Citizens** living outside of the US mail in **absentee ballots**. But voters don't **elect** the **president** directly. States send representatives to the **electoral college**. There, representatives from all but two states must cast all their votes for one candidate—even if 49% of the people wanted the other
>
>
>
> candidate. Four times a candidate has **won** the popular vote and lost the election. This happened when George W. Bush won in 2000.

elect /ɪlɛkt/ (**elects, electing, elected**) **v-T**
SOCIAL STUDIES When people **elect** someone, they choose that person to represent them, by voting for them. ❑ *The people have elected a new president.* [from Latin]
→ look at Word Web: **election**

elec|tion /ɪlɛkʃ°n/ (**elections**) **N-COUNT/ N-NONCOUNT** SOCIAL STUDIES An **election** is a process in which people vote to choose a person who will hold an official position. ❑ *She won her first election in 2000.* [from Latin]
→ look at Word Webs: **election, citizenship**

Word Partnership	Use **election** with :
N	election **campaign**, election **day**, election **official**, election **results**
V	**hold an** election, **lose an** election, election, **win an** election

elec|tor|al /ɪlɛktərəl/ **ADJ Electoral** is used to describe things that are connected with elections. ❑ *...electoral reform.* ● **elec|tor|al|ly ADV** ❑ *The government's tax increases were electorally unpopular.* [from Latin]

Elec|toral College /ɪlɛktərəl kɒlɪdʒ/ **N-PROPER** SOCIAL STUDIES In the United States, the **Electoral College** consists of the representatives in each state who elect the president of the United States. ❑ *He won enough Electoral College votes to win the election.*
→ look at Word Web: **election**

elec|toral vote /ɪlɛktərəl voʊt/ (**electoral votes**) **N-COUNT/N-NONCOUNT** SOCIAL STUDIES In the United States, the **electoral vote** is the number of votes that each state has that its representatives can use to elect a new president. ❑ *California's 55 electoral votes are the most of any state.*

elec|tor|ate /ɪlɛktərɪt/ (**electorates**) **N-COUNT** SOCIAL STUDIES The **electorate** of a country or an area is all the people in it who have the right to vote in an election. ❑ *He has the support of almost a quarter of the electorate.* [from Latin]

elec|tric /ɪlɛktrɪk/
1 ADJ SCIENCE An **electric** machine or piece of equipment works using electricity. ❑ *Kelly loves to play the electric guitar.*
2 ADJ Electric plugs, sockets, or power lines carry electricity. [from New Latin]
→ look at Picture Dictionary: **keyboard**

elec|tri|cal /ɪlɛktrɪk°l/
1 ADJ Electrical equipment works using electricity. ❑ *...an electrical appliance.*
2 ADJ Electrical industries or workers are involved in the supply of electricity or electrical products. ❑ *He had to work as an electrical engineer.* [from New Latin]
→ look at Word Webs: **electricity, energy**

elec|tri|cal charge N-SING SCIENCE The law of **electrical charges** is a principle in physics which states that two electrical charges will attract one another if they are opposite and repel one another if they are the same.

elec|tri|cal en|er|gy N-NONCOUNT SCIENCE **Electrical energy** is the form of energy that is produced by electricity.

elec|tric force (**electric forces**) **N-COUNT/N-NONCOUNT** SCIENCE An **electric force** is the force that exists between two objects with an electric charge.

elec|tric gen|era|tor (**electric generators**) **N-COUNT** An **electric generator** is a machine which produces electricity.

Word Link	**electr** ≈ electric : **electr**ician, **electr**icity, **electr**on

Word Link	**ician** ≈ person who works at : electr**ician**, mus**ician**, phys**ician**

elec|tri|cian /ɪlɛktrɪʃ°n, ɪlɛk-/ (**electricians**) **N-COUNT** An **electrician** is a person whose job is to repair electrical equipment. [from New Latin]

elec|tric|ity /ɪlɛktrɪsɪti, ɪlɛk-/ **N-NONCOUNT** SCIENCE **Electricity** is energy that is used for heating and lighting, and to provide power for machines. [from New Latin]
→ look at Word Webs: **electricity, energy, light bulb**

elec|tric pow|er N-NONCOUNT **Electric power** is the same as **electricity**.

elec|tric shock (**electric shocks**) **N-COUNT** If you get an **electric shock**, you get a sudden painful feeling when electricity goes through your body.

elec|tro|mag|net /ɪlɛktroʊmægnɪt/ (**electromagnets**) **N-COUNT** SCIENCE An **electromagnet** is a magnet that consists of a piece of iron or steel surrounded by a coil. The metal becomes magnetic when an electric current is passed through the coil.

elec|tro|mag|net|ic /ɪlɛktroʊmægnɛtɪk/ **ADJ** SCIENCE **Electromagnetic** is used to

Word Web	electricity

The need for **electrical** power in the U.S. may rise by 35 percent over the next 20 years. **Power companies** are working hard to meet this need. At the center of every **power station** are electrical **generators**. Traditionally, they ran on **hydroelectric** power or **fossil fuel**. However, today new sources of **energy** are available. On **wind farms**, wind **turbines** use the power of moving air to run generators. Seaside tidal power stations make use of the forces of rising and falling tides to turn turbines. And in sunny climates, photovoltaic **cells** produce electrical power from the sun's rays.

describe the electrical and magnetic forces or effects produced by an electric current.
❏ ...*electromagnetic fields*.

elec|tro|mag|net|ic spec|trum **N-SING** **SCIENCE** The **electromagnetic spectrum** is the complete range of electromagnetic radiation, from the longest radio waves to the shortest gamma rays.

elec|tro|mag|net|ic wave (**electromagnetic waves**) **N-COUNT** **SCIENCE** **Electromagnetic waves** are waves of energy inside an electromagnetic field.

elec|tron /ɪlɛktrɒn/ (**electrons**) **N-COUNT** **SCIENCE** An **electron** is a tiny particle of matter that is smaller than an atom and has a negative electrical charge.
→ look at Word Web: **television**

elec|tron cloud (**electron clouds**) **N-COUNT** **SCIENCE** An **electron cloud** is an area inside an atom where electrons are likely to exist.

elec|tron|ic /ɪlɛktrɒnɪk, i-/
1 **ADJ** **Electronic** equipment has small electrical parts that make it work. ❏ *Please do not use electronic equipment on the plane.*
● **elec|troni|cal|ly** **ADV** ❏ *The gates are operated electronically.*
2 **ADJ** An **electronic** process or activity involves the use of electronic equipment, especially computers. ❏ *...electronic music.*

elec|tron|ic me|dia **N-PLURAL** **TECHNOLOGY** **Electronic media** are means of communication such as radio, television, and the Internet, which use technology to produce information.

Word Link	ics ≈ system, knowledge : economics, electronics, genetics

elec|tron|ics /ɪlɛktrɒnɪks, i-/ **N-NONCOUNT** **Electronics** is the technology of using

transistors and silicon chips, especially in devices such as radios, televisions, and computers. ❏ *...Ohio's three main electronics companies.*

elec|tron micro|scope (**electron microscopes**) **N-COUNT** **SCIENCE** An **electron microscope** is a type of very powerful microscope that uses electrons instead of light to produce a magnified image of something.

elec|tro|stat|ic dis|charge /ɪlɛktrəstætɪk dɪstʃɑrdʒ/ (**electrostatic discharges**) **N-COUNT/N-NONCOUNT** **SCIENCE** An **electrostatic discharge** is the sudden release of static electricity that can occur when two objects with different electrical charges are brought close together.

el|egant /ɛlɪgənt/ **ADJ** An **elegant** person or thing is beautiful in a simple way. ❏ *Our room was elegant, with high ceilings and tall, narrow windows.* [from Latin]

el|ement /ɛlɪmənt/ (**elements**)
1 **N-COUNT** The different **elements** of something are the different parts of it. ❏ *Good health is an important element in our lives.*
2 **N-COUNT** If something has an **element of** a particular quality, it has a certain amount of it. ❏ *Many of the complaints contain an element of truth.*
3 **N-COUNT** **SCIENCE** An **element** is a basic chemical substance such as gold, oxygen, or carbon. [from Latin]
→ look at Word Webs: **element, periodic table, rock**

el|emen|ta|ry /ɛlɪmɛntəri, -tri/ **ADJ** Something that is **elementary** is very easy and basic. ❏ *It's a simple system that uses elementary mathematics.* [from Latin]

Word Web element

Elements—like copper, sodium, and oxygen—are made from only one type of **atom**. Each element has its own unique **properties**. For example, oxygen is a gas at room temperature and copper is a solid. Often elements come together with other types of elements to make **compounds**. When the atoms in a compound bind together, they form a **molecule**. One of the best known molecules is H_2O. It is made up of two hydrogen atoms and one oxygen atom. This molecule is also known as water. The **periodic table** is a complete listing of all the elements.

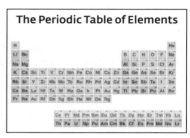

The Periodic Table of Elements

el|emen|ta|ry school (**elementary schools**) **N-COUNT/N-NONCOUNT** An **elementary school** is a school where children go from the ages of six to eleven.

el|ements of art N-PLURAL ARTS The **elements of art** are the basic components of a painting or a drawing, such as line, color, and shape.

el|ements of mu|sic N-PLURAL MUSIC The **elements of music** are the basic components of a piece of music, such as melody, harmony, and rhythm.

el|ephant /ɛlɪfənt/ (**elephants**) **N-COUNT** An **elephant** is a very large animal with a long nose called a trunk. [from Latin] → look at Word Web: **herbivore**

Word Link *ation ≈ state of: dehydration, elevation, preservation*

el|evate /ɛlɪveɪt/ (**elevates, elevating, elevated**)
1 **V-T** When someone or something is **elevated to** a more important rank or status, they achieve it. [FORMAL] ❑ *He was elevated to the post of president.* ● **el|eva|tion** /ɛlɪveɪʃ°n/ **N-NONCOUNT** ❑ *...the elevation of the assistant coach to the head coaching position.*
2 **V-T** To **elevate** something means to increase it in amount or intensity. [FORMAL] ❑ *Emotional stress can elevate blood pressure.*
3 **V-T** If you **elevate** something, you raise it higher. ❑ *I built a platform to elevate the bed.* [from Latin]

el|eva|tor /ɛlɪveɪtər/ (**elevators**) **N-COUNT** An **elevator** is a machine that carries people or things up and down inside tall buildings. ❑ *We took the elevator to the fourteenth floor.* [from Latin]

elev|en /ɪlɛv°n/ **NUM** MATH **Eleven** is the number 11. [from Old English]

elev|enth /ɪlɛv°nθ/ **ADJ/ADV** MATH The **eleventh** item in a series is the one that you count as number eleven. ❑ *We were working on the eleventh floor.* [from Old English]

elic|it /ɪlɪsɪt/ (**elicits, eliciting, elicited**)
1 **V-T** If you **elicit** a response or a reaction, you do or say something that makes other people respond or react. ❑ *He was hopeful that his request would elicit a positive response.*
2 **V-T** If you **elicit** a piece of information, you get it by asking the right questions. [FORMAL] ❑ *Several phone calls elicited no further information.* [from Latin]

eli|gible /ɛlɪdʒɪb°l/ **ADJ** Someone who is **eligible to** do something is allowed to do it. ❑ *Almost half the population are eligible to vote.* [from Late Latin]

elimi|nate /ɪlɪmɪneɪt/ (**eliminates, eliminating, eliminated**) **V-T** To **eliminate** something means to remove it completely. [FORMAL] ❑ *The touch screen eliminates the need for a keyboard.* [from Latin]

elite /ɪlit, eɪ-/ (**elites**)
1 **N-COUNT** You can refer to the most powerful, rich, or talented people within a particular group, place, or society as the **elite**. ❑ *...the political elite.*
2 **ADJ** **Elite** is also an adjective. ❑ *...the elite troops of the president's bodyguard.* [from French]

Eliza|bethan thea|ter /ɪlɪzəbiθ°n θiətər/ **N-NONCOUNT** ARTS **Elizabethan theater** is the plays that were written or performed in England during the reign of Queen Elizabeth I.

el|lipse /ɪlɪps/ (**ellipses**) **N-COUNT** MATH
An **ellipse** is an oval shape similar to a circle but longer and flatter.

el|lip|ti|cal /ɪlɪptɪkəl/ **ADJ** Something that is **elliptical** has the shape of an ellipse. [FORMAL] ❑ ...the moon's elliptical orbit.

el|lip|ti|cal gal|axy (**elliptical galaxies**) **N-COUNT** SCIENCE An **elliptical galaxy** is a galaxy containing mainly older stars, which are distributed in an elliptical pattern.

El Niño /ɛl ninyoʊ/ **N-PROPER** SCIENCE
El Niño is a current of warm water that occurs every few years in the Pacific Ocean and can affect the weather throughout the world. [from Spanish]

else /ɛls/
1 **ADJ** You use **else** after words such as "someone" and "everyone," and after question words like "what" to talk about another person, place, or thing. ❑ She is much taller than everyone else. ❑ What else did you get for your birthday?
2 **PHRASE** You use **or else** to introduce another possibility, usually something bad. ❑ Hold on tight or else you will fall out. [from Old English]

else|where /ɛlswɛər/ **ADV** Elsewhere means in other places or to another place. ❑ 80 percent of the state's residents were born elsewhere. [from Old English]

elu|ci|date /ɪluːsɪdeɪt/ (**elucidates, elucidating, elucidated**) **V-T/V-I** If you **elucidate** something, you make it clear and easy to understand. [FORMAL] ❑ Haig went on to elucidate his personal principle of war. ❑ There was no need for him to elucidate. ● **elu|ci|da|tion** /ɪluːsɪdeɪʃən/ **N-NONCOUNT** ❑ He made several attempts at elucidation. [from Latin]

elude /ɪluːd/ (**eludes, eluding, eluded**)
1 **V-T** If something that you want **eludes** you, you fail to obtain it. ❑ Sleep eluded her. ❑ The appropriate word eluded him.
2 **V-T** If you **elude** someone or something, you avoid them or escape from them. ❑ He eluded the police for 13 years. [from Latin]

email /imeɪl/ (**emails, emailing, emailed**) also **e-mail**
1 **N-COUNT/N-NONCOUNT** TECHNOLOGY **Email** is a system of sending written messages from one computer to another. **Email** is short for **electronic mail**. ❑ You can contact us by email.

2 **V-T** If you **email** someone, you send them an email. ❑ Jamie emailed me to say he couldn't come.
→ look at Word Web: **Internet**

Word Link	man ≈ hand : emancipate, manicure, manual

eman|ci|pate /ɪmænsɪpeɪt/ (**emancipates, emancipating, emancipated**) **V-T** SOCIAL STUDIES If people **are emancipated**, they are freed from unpleasant or unfair social, political, or legal restrictions. [FORMAL] ❑ Catholics were emancipated in 1792. ❑ The war preserved the Union and emancipated the slaves. ● **eman|ci|pa|tion** /ɪmænsɪpeɪʃən/ **N-NONCOUNT** ❑ ...the emancipation of women in the 20th century. [from Latin]

em|bar|go /ɪmbɑːrgoʊ/ (**embargoes**) **N-COUNT** SOCIAL STUDIES If one country or group of countries imposes an **embargo** against another, it forbids trade with that country. ❑ The United Nations imposed an embargo. [from Spanish]

em|bark /ɪmbɑːrk/ (**embarks, embarking, embarked**)
1 **V-I** If you **embark on** something new, difficult, or exciting, you start doing it. ❑ He's embarking on a new career as a writer.
2 **V-I** When you **embark on** a ship, you go on board before the start of a journey. ❑ They embarked on a ship bound for Europe. [from French]

em|bar|rass /ɪmbærəs/ (**embarrasses, embarrassing, embarrassed**) **V-T** If something or someone **embarrasses** you, they make you feel shy or ashamed. ❑ His mother's behavior embarrassed him. ● **em|bar|rass|ing** **ADJ** ❑ He always found Judith a bit embarrassing. [from French]

em|bar|rassed /ɪmbærəst/ **ADJ** A person who is **embarrassed** feels shy, ashamed, or guilty about something. ❑ He looked a bit embarrassed when he noticed his mistake. [from French]

em|bar|rass|ment /ɪmbærəsmənt/ **N-NONCOUNT** Embarrassment is the feeling you have when you are embarrassed. ❑ I feel no embarrassment at making mistakes or failing. [from French]

em|bas|sy /ɛmbəsi/ (**embassies**) **N-COUNT** An **embassy** is a group of people who represent their government in a foreign country. The building in which they work is also called an **embassy**. ❏ *The embassy advised British nationals to leave the country immediately.* ❏ *The embassy was surrounded by the FBI.* [from Old French]

em|bel|lish|ment /ɪmbɛlɪʃmənt/ (embellishments) **N-COUNT** MUSIC In music, **embellishments** are extra notes that are added to a melody or a rhythm to make it more pleasing. [from Old French]

em|brace /ɪmbreɪs/ (embraces, embracing, embraced)
■ **V-T/V-I** If you **embrace** someone, you put your arms around them to show that you love or like them. ❏ *Penelope came forward and embraced her sister.* ❏ *People were crying with joy and embracing.* [from Old French]
■ **N-COUNT Embrace** is also a noun. ❏ *...a young couple locked in an embrace.*

em|broi|der /ɪmbrɔɪdər/ (embroiders, embroidering, embroidered) **V-T** If clothing or cloth **is embroidered with** a design, the design is sewn on it. ❏ *The dress was embroidered with flowers.* [from Old French]

em|broi|dery /ɪmbrɔɪdəri/ **N-NONCOUNT** **Embroidery** is a pattern of threads that is sewn onto cloth. ❏ *The shorts had blue embroidery over the pockets.* [from Old French]
→ look at Word Web: **quilt**

em|bryo /ɛmbriou/ (embryos) **N-COUNT** SCIENCE An **embryo** is an animal or a human in the very early stages of development before it is born. [from Late Latin]
→ look at Word Web: **reproduction**

em|er|ald /ɛmərəld, ɛmrəld/ (emeralds) **N-COUNT** An **emerald** is a bright green stone that is used in jewelry. [from Old French]

Word Link	merg ≈ sinking : emerge, merge, submerge

emerge /ɪmɜrdʒ/ (emerges, emerging, emerged) **V-I** To **emerge** means to come out from a place. ❏ *Richard was waiting outside the door as she emerged from her house.* [from Latin]

emer|gen|cy /ɪmɜrdʒ°nsi/ (emergencies)
■ **N-COUNT** An **emergency** is a serious situation, such as an accident, when people need help quickly. ❏ *Come quickly. This is an emergency!*
■ **ADJ** An **emergency** action is one that is done or arranged quickly, because an emergency has happened. ❏ *The board held an emergency meeting.*

■ **ADJ Emergency** equipment or supplies are to be used in an emergency. ❏ *The plane is carrying emergency supplies for refugees.* [from Latin]

Word Partnership	Use emergency with :
ADJ	**major** emergency, **medical** emergency, **minor** emergency ■
N	**state of** emergency ■ emergency **care**, emergency **surgery** ■ emergency **supplies**, emergency **vehicle** ■

emer|gen|cy room (emergency rooms) **N-COUNT** The **emergency room** is the part of a hospital where people who have serious injuries or sudden illnesses can get treatment. The short form **ER** is often used.

Word Link	migr ≈ moving, changing : emigrate, immigrant, migration

emi|grate /ɛmɪgreɪt/ (emigrates, emigrating, emigrated) **V-I** If you **emigrate**, you leave your own country and go to live in another country. ❏ *His parents emigrated to the U.S. in 1954.* [from Latin]

emis|sion /ɪmɪʃ°n/ (emissions) **N-COUNT/N-NONCOUNT** SCIENCE An **emission** of something such as gas or radiation is the release of it into the atmosphere. [FORMAL] ❏ *...the emission of gases such as carbon dioxide.* [from Latin]
→ look at Word Web: **pollution**

emit /ɪmɪt/ (emits, emitting, emitted) **V-T** To **emit** a sound, a smell, or a substance means to produce it or send it out. [FORMAL] ❏ *Whitney emitted a long, low whistle.* [from Latin]

emo|ji /ɪmoudʒiː/ (emojis) **N-COUNT** TECHNOLOGY An **emoji** is a digital image that is used to express an emotion in an email or text message. ❏ *He added a 'wink' emoji at the end.*

emo|tion /ɪmouʃ°n/ (emotions) **N-COUNT/N-NONCOUNT** An **emotion** is a feeling such as joy or love. ❏ *He never shows his emotions in public.* ❏ *Jill's voice was full of emotion.* [from French]
→ look at Word Web: **emotion**

emo|tion|al /ɪmouʃən°l/
■ **ADJ Emotional** means concerned with feelings. ❏ *After my wife's death, I needed some emotional support.* ● **emo|tion|al|ly ADV** ❏ *By the end of the show, I was physically and emotionally exhausted.*
■ **ADJ** If someone is **emotional**, they often show their feelings, especially when they

e

Word Web   emotion

Scientists believe that animals experience **emotions** such as **happiness** and **sadness** just like humans do. Research shows animals also feel **anger, fear, love**, and **hate**. Biochemical changes in mammals' brains cause these emotions. When an elephant gives birth, a **hormone** goes through her bloodstream. This causes feelings of **adoration** for her baby. The same thing happens to human mothers. When a dog chews on a bone, a chemical increases in its brain to produce feelings of **joy**. The same chemical produces **elation** in humans. Scientists aren't sure whether animals experience **shame**. However, they do know that animals experience **stress**.

are upset. ❑ *He is a very emotional man.* [from French]
→ look at Word Web: **cry**

Word Link   path ≈ feeling : apathy, empathy, sympathy

em|pa|thy /ɛmpəθi/ **N-NONCOUNT** Empathy is the ability to share another person's feelings and emotions as if they were your own. ❑ *Very young children are capable of empathy.* [from Greek]

em|per|or /ɛmpərər/ (**emperors**) **N-COUNT** SOCIAL STUDIES An **emperor** is a man who rules an empire. ❑ *...the emperor of Japan.* [from Old French]
→ look at Word Web: **empire**

em|pha|sis /ɛmfəsɪs/ (**emphases** /ɛmfəsiz/)
1 N-COUNT/N-NONCOUNT Emphasis is special importance that is given to something. ❑ *Schools should place more emphasis on health education.*
2 N-COUNT/N-NONCOUNT LANGUAGE ARTS Emphasis is extra force that you put on a word or a part of a word when you are speaking. ❑ *The emphasis is on the first syllable of the word "elephant."* [from Latin]

em|pha|size /ɛmfəsaɪz/ (**emphasizes, emphasizing, emphasized**) **V-T** To emphasize something means to show that it is especially important. ❑ *He emphasizes the importance of reading to young children.* [from Latin]

em|pire /ɛmpaɪər/ (**empires**) **N-COUNT** SOCIAL STUDIES An **empire** is a number of separate nations that are all controlled by the ruler of one particular country. ❑ *...the Roman Empire.* [from Old French]
→ look at Word Webs: **empire, history**

em|ploy /ɪmplɔɪ/ (**employs, employing, employed**)
1 V-T If a person or a company **employs** you, they pay you to work for them. ❑ *The company employs 18 workers.*
2 V-T If you **employ** things, you use them. ❑ *All good teachers employ a variety of methods to teach reading.* [from Old French]

Word Web   empire

An **empire** is formed when a strong nation-state **conquers** other states and creates a larger **political union**. An early example is the Roman Empire which began in 31 BC. The Roman **emperor** Augustus Caesar* ruled a large area from the Mediterranean Sea* to Western Europe. Later, the British Empire ruled from about 1600 to 1900 AD. Queen Victoria's* empire spread across oceans and continents. One of her many titles was **Empress** of India. Both of these empires spread their political influence as well as their language and culture over large areas.

- British Empire (1900 AD)
- Roman Empire (117 AD)
- British and Roman Empires

Augustus Caesar: the first emperor of Rome.
Mediterranean Sea: between Europe and Africa.
Queen Victoria (1819-1901): queen of Great Britain and Ireland.

em|ploy|ee /ɪmplɔɪi/ (**employees**) **N-COUNT**
An **employee** is a person who is paid to work for another person or a company. ❏ *The police believe that airport employees were involved.* [from Old French]
→ look at Word Webs: **factory, union**

em|ploy|er /ɪmplɔɪər/ (**employers**) **N-COUNT**
Your **employer** is the person or the company that you work for. ❏ *Your employer should agree to pay you for this work.* [from Old French]

em|ploy|ment /ɪmplɔɪmənt/ **N-NONCOUNT**
Employment is work that you are paid for. ❏ *She was unable to find employment.* [from Old French]

em|press /ɛmprɪs/ (**empresses**) **N-COUNT**
An **empress** is a woman who rules an empire or who is the wife of an emperor. ❏ *...Catherine II, Empress of Russia.* [from Old French]

emp|ty /ɛmpti/ (**emptier, emptiest, empties, emptying, emptied**)
1 **ADJ** An **empty** place or container has no people or things in it. ❏ *The room was cold and empty.* ❏ *There were empty beer cans all over the floor.*
2 **V-T** If you **empty** a container, you remove its contents. ❏ *I emptied the garbage can.* ❏ *Empty the noodles into a bowl.* [from Old English]

Word Partnership	Use **empty** with :
N	empty **bottle**, empty **box**, empty **building**, empty **seat**, empty **space**, empty **stomach 1** empty **the trash 2**

emu|late /ɛmyʊleɪt/ (**emulates, emulating, emulated**) **V-T** If you **emulate** something or someone, you imitate them because you admire them a great deal. [FORMAL] ❏ *Sons are traditionally expected to emulate their fathers.* [from Latin]

Word Link	*en* ≈ *making, putting* : *en*able, *en*act, *en*danger

en|able /ɪneɪbəl/ (**enables, enabling, enabled**) **V-T** If someone or something **enables** you **to** do something, they make it possible for you to do it. ❏ *The new test will enable doctors to treat the disease early.*

en|act /ɪnækt/ (**enacts, enacting, enacted**)
1 **V-T** SOCIAL STUDIES When a government or authority **enacts** a proposal, they make it into a law. ❏ *President Johnson led the battle to enact civil-rights laws.* ● **en|act|ment** (**enactments**) **N-COUNT/N-NONCOUNT** ❏ *...the enactment of a Bill of Rights.*
2 **V-T** ARTS If people **enact** a story or a play, they perform it by acting. ❏ *She often enacted the stories told to her by her father.*

en|chant /ɪntʃænt/ (**enchants, enchanting, enchanted**)
1 **V-T** If you **are enchanted by** someone or something, they cause you to have feelings of great delight or pleasure. ❏ *Dena was enchanted by the house.* ● **en|chant|ing** **ADJ** ❏ *She's an absolutely enchanting child.*
2 **V-T** In fairy tales and legends, to **enchant** someone or something means to put a magic spell on them. ❏ *...stories of enchanted princesses.* [from Old French]

en|cir|cle /ɪnsɜrkəl/ (**encircles, encircling, encircled**) **V-T** To **encircle** something or someone means to surround or enclose them, or to go around them. ❏ *A forty-foot-high concrete wall encircles the jail.*

en|close /ɪnkloʊz/ (**encloses, enclosing, enclosed**)
1 **V-T** If a place or an object **is enclosed** by something, the place or object is completely surrounded by it. ❏ *The park is enclosed by a wooden fence.*
2 **V-T** If you **enclose** something with a letter, you put it in the same envelope as the letter. ❏ *I have enclosed a check for $100.*

en|com|pass /ɪnkʌmpəs/ (**encompasses, encompassing, encompassed**) **V-T** If something **encompasses** particular things, it includes them. ❏ *The western region encompasses nine states.*

en|core /ɒŋkɔr, -kɔr/ (**encores**) **N-COUNT**
An **encore** is a short extra performance at the end of a show that a musician gives because the audience has asked for it. ❏ *Lang's final encore last night was "Barefoot."* [from French]

en|coun|ter /ɪnkaʊntər/ (**encounters, encountering, encountered**)
1 **V-T** If you **encounter** problems or difficulties, you experience them. ❏ *Every day of our lives we encounter stress.*
2 **V-T** If you **encounter** someone, you meet them, usually unexpectedly. [FORMAL] ❏ *Did you encounter anyone in the building?*
3 **N-COUNT** **Encounter** is also a noun. [FORMAL] ❏ *Rachel had a romantic encounter with a guy called Richard.* [from Old French]

E

en|cour|age /ɪnkɜrɪdʒ/ (**encourages, encouraging, encouraged**)

■ **V-T** If you **encourage** someone, you give them hope or confidence. ❑ *When things aren't going well, he encourages me.*

■ **V-T** If you **encourage** someone **to** do something, you try to persuade them to do it. ❑ *We want to encourage people to take more exercise.*

■ **V-T** If something **encourages** a particular activity or state, it causes it to happen or increase. ❑ *...a drug that encourages cell growth.*

en|cour|age|ment /ɪnkɜrɪdʒmənt/

N-NONCOUNT Encouragement is the act of encouraging someone. ❑ *Friends gave me a lot of encouragement.*

en|cour|ag|ing /ɪnkɜrɪdʒɪŋ/ **ADJ**

Something that is **encouraging** gives people hope or confidence. ❑ *The results have been encouraging.*

en|cy|clo|pedia /ɪnsaɪkləpidiə/

(**encyclopedias**) **N-COUNT** An **encyclopedia** is a book or a CD-ROM containing facts about many different subjects. [from New Latin]

end /ɛnd/ (**ends, ending, ended**)

■ **N-SING** The **end of** a period of time or a story is the final point in it. ❑ *Work will start before the end of the year.* ❑ *Don't tell me the end of the story!*

■ **N-COUNT** The **end of** a long object is the farthest part of it. ❑ *Both ends of the tunnel were blocked.*

■ **N-COUNT** An **end to** something or the **end of** it is the fact that it finishes and stops. ❑ *The government today called for an end to the violence.*

■ **V-T/V-I** When an activity **ends**, it reaches its final point and stops. ❑ *The meeting quickly ended.* ❑ *I ended the conversation.*

■ → see also **ending**

■ **PHRASE** If you cannot **make ends meet**, you do not have enough money for the things you need. ❑ *With Betty's salary they couldn't make ends meet.*

■ **PHRASE** When something happens for hours, days, weeks, or years **on end**, it happens continuously and without stopping for that amount of time. ❑ *We can talk for hours on end.* [from Old English]

▶ **end up** If you **end up** in a particular place or situation, you are in that place or situation after a series of events. ❑ *We ended up back at the house again.*

Thesaurus	end Also look up :
N	close, conclusion, finish, stop; (*ant.*) beginning ■
V	conclude, finish, wrap up ■

en|dan|ger /ɪndeɪndʒər/ (**endangers, endangering, endangered**) **V-T** To **endanger** something or someone means to put them in a situation where they might be harmed or destroyed completely. ❑ *The debate could endanger the peace talks.*

en|dan|gered spe|cies (**endangered species**) **N-COUNT** SCIENCE An **endangered species** is a type of animal that may soon disappear from the world. ❑ *These African beetles are on the list of endangered species.*

en|deav|or /ɪndɛvər/ (**endeavors, endeavoring, endeavored**)

■ **V-T** If you **endeavor to** do something, you try very hard to do it. [FORMAL] ❑ *They are endeavoring to protect labor union rights.*

■ **N-COUNT/N-NONCOUNT** An **endeavor** is an attempt to do something, especially something new or original. [FORMAL] ❑ *...the company's creative endeavors.* [from Old French]

end|ing /ɛndɪŋ/ (**endings**)

■ **N-COUNT** You can call the last part of a book or a movie the **ending**. ❑ *The film has a happy ending.* [from Old English]

■ → see also **end**

Word Link	*less ≈ without : endless, hopeless, wireless*

end|less /ɛndlɪs/ **ADJ** Something that is **endless** lasts for a very long time. ❑ *The morning classes seemed endless.* ● **end|less|ly ADV** ❑ *They talk about it endlessly.* [from Old English]

endo|crine /ɛndəkrɪn, -kraɪn/ **ADJ** SCIENCE The **endocrine** system is the system of glands that produce hormones for the bloodstream. [from Greek]

endo|cy|to|sis /ɛndoʊsaɪtoʊsɪs/

N-NONCOUNT SCIENCE **Endocytosis** is a process in which a cell absorbs material from outside itself by enclosing the material within a part of the cell membrane. Compare with **exocytosis**.

endo|plas|mic re|ticu|lum

/ɛndoʊplæzmɪk rɪtɪkyələm/ (**endoplasmic reticulums** or **endoplasmic reticula**)

N-COUNT SCIENCE The **endoplasmic reticulum** is a network of tubes and

E

membranes within cells that is involved in the making and movement of proteins.

en|dorse /ɪndɔrs/ (**endorses, endorsing, endorsed**)

■ **v-T** If you **endorse** someone or something, you say publicly that you support or approve of them. ❑ *I can endorse their opinion wholeheartedly.* ● **en|dorse|ment** (**endorsements**) **N-COUNT** ❑ *This is a powerful endorsement for his softer style of government.*

■ **v-T** If you **endorse** a product or a company, you appear in advertisements for it. ❑ *The twins endorsed a line of household cleaning products.* ● **en|dorse|ment** **N-COUNT** ❑ *...his commercial endorsements for breakfast cereals.* [from Old French]

endo|skel|eton /ɛndoʊskɛlɪtᵊn/ (**endoskeletons**) **N-COUNT** SCIENCE Animals with an **endoskeleton** have their skeleton inside their body, like humans.

endo|therm /ɛndəθɜrm/ (**endotherms**) **N-COUNT** SCIENCE An **endotherm** is a warm-blooded animal, such as a bird or a mammal, that can keep its body temperature above or below that of the surrounding environment. Compare with **ectotherm**.

endo|ther|mic /ɛndoʊθɜrmɪk/ **ADJ** SCIENCE An **endothermic** chemical reaction or process is one that takes in heat from its surroundings, such as when ice melts.

en|dur|ance /ɪndʊərəns/ **N-NONCOUNT** **Endurance** is the ability to continue with a difficult activity over a long period of time. ❑ *The exercise will improve strength and endurance.* [from Old French]

en|dure /ɪndʊər/ (**endures, enduring, endured**)

■ **v-T** If a person or an organization **endures** a difficult situation, they experience it. ❑ *The company endured heavy financial losses.*

■ **v-I** If something **endures**, it continues to exist. ❑ *Somehow the language endures and continues to survive.* [from Old French]

en|emy /ɛnəmi/ (**enemies**)

■ **N-COUNT** If someone is your **enemy**, they hate you, and want to harm you. ❑ *His enemies hated and feared him.*

■ **N-SING** The **enemy** is an army that is fighting against you in a war. ❑ *We are going to attack the enemy tomorrow morning.* [from Old French]

en|er|get|ic /ɛnərdʒɛtɪk/ **ADJ** An **energetic** person has a lot of energy. ❑ *Young children are very energetic.* [from Late Latin]

en|er|gy /ɛnərdʒi/

■ **N-NONCOUNT** **Energy** is the ability and strength to do active physical things. ❑ *He's saving his energy for next week's race.*

■ **N-NONCOUNT** SCIENCE **Energy** is the power from electricity or the sun, for example, that makes machines work or provides heat. ❑ *These machines are powered with energy from the sun.* [from Late Latin] → look at Word Webs: **energy, calorie, electricity, food, petroleum, photosynthesis, solar**

Word Partnership	Use **energy** with :
V	**focus** energy ■
	conserve/save energy ■
ADJ	**full of** energy, **physical** energy, **sexual** energy ■
	atomic energy, **nuclear** energy, **solar** energy ■

en|er|gy con|ver|sion **N-NONCOUNT** SCIENCE **Energy conversion** is the changing of energy from one form to another, for example from mechanical energy to electrical energy.

en|er|gy ef|fi|cien|cy **N-NONCOUNT** SCIENCE **Energy efficiency** is the careful use of resources

Word Web energy

Wood was the most important **energy** source for American settlers. Then, as industry developed, factories began to use **coal**. Coal was also used to **generate** most of the **electrical power** in the early 1900s. However, the popularity of automobile use soon made **oil** the most important **fuel**. **Natural gas** remains popular for home heating and industrial use. Hydroelectric power isn't a major source of energy in the U.S. It requires too much land and water to produce. Some companies built **nuclear** power plants to make **electricity** in the 1970s. Today **solar** panels and giant wind farms convert sunlight and wind into electricity.

such as electricity or fuel in order to reduce the amount of energy that is wasted.

en|er|gy-ef|fi|cient also energy efficient
ADJ A device or building that is **energy-efficient** uses relatively little energy to provide the power it needs. ❑ *...energy-efficient light bulbs.*

en|er|gy pyra|mid (energy pyramids)
N-COUNT SCIENCE An **energy pyramid** is a diagram that shows the amount of energy that is available at each level of a food chain.

en|er|gy re|source (energy resources)
N-COUNT SCIENCE An **energy resource** is a source of energy such as oil, coal, and wind.

en|er|gy source (energy sources) **N-COUNT**
SCIENCE An **energy source** is any substance or system from which energy can be obtained, such as coal, gas, water, or sunlight.

en|force /ɪnfɔ̱rs/ (enforces, enforcing, enforced) **V-T** If people in authority **enforce** a law or a rule, they make sure that it is obeyed, usually by punishing people who do not obey it. ❑ *Many states enforce drug laws.*
● **en|force|ment** /ɪnfɔ̱rsmənt/ **N-NONCOUNT**
❑ *The doctors want stricter enforcement of existing laws.*

en|gage /ɪngeɪdʒ/ (engages, engaging, engaged)
1 **V-I** If you **engage in** an activity, you do it. [FORMAL] ❑ *Many of these young people engage in criminal activities.*
2 **V-T** If something **engages** you, it keeps you interested in it. ❑ *He has an amazing ability to engage an audience.* [from Old French]

en|gaged /ɪngeɪdʒd/ **ADJ** When two people are **engaged**, they have agreed to marry

each other. ❑ *We got engaged on my 26th birthday.* [from Old French]

en|gage|ment /ɪngeɪdʒmənt/ (engagements)
1 **N-COUNT** An **engagement** is an agreement that two people have made with each other to get married. ❑ *We announced our engagement in November.*
2 **N-COUNT** An **engagement** is an arrangement that you have made to do something at a particular time. [FORMAL] ❑ *He had an engagement at a restaurant at eight.* [from Old French]

en|gine /ɛ̱ndʒɪn/ (engines)
1 **N-COUNT** The **engine** of a car is the part that produces the power to make it move. ❑ *He got into the driving seat and started the engine.*
2 **N-COUNT** An **engine** is the front part of a train that pulls it. ❑ *In 1941, trains were pulled by steam engines.* [from Old French]
→ look at Word Webs: **engine, car**

Word Link	eer ≈ one who does : engin**eer**, mountain**eer**, volunt**eer**

en|gi|neer /ɛ̱ndʒɪnɪ̱ər/ (engineers)
1 **N-COUNT** An **engineer** is a person who designs, builds, and repairs machines, or structures such as roads, railroads, and bridges.
2 **N-COUNT** An **engineer** is a person who repairs mechanical or electrical machines. ❑ *They sent an engineer to fix the computer.* [from Old French]

en|gi|neer|ing /ɛ̱ndʒɪnɪ̱ərɪŋ/
1 **N-NONCOUNT** **Engineering** is the work of designing and constructing machines or structures such as roads and bridges. ❑ *She studies science and engineering at college.*

Word Web   engine

In the **internal combustion engine** found in most cars, there are four, six, or eight **cylinders**. To start an engine, the **intake valve** opens and a small amount of **fuel** enters the **combustion** chamber of the cylinder. A **spark plug** ignites the fuel and air mixture, causing it to explode. This **combustion** moves the **cylinder head**, which causes the crankshaft to turn and the car to move. Next, the **exhaust valve** opens and the burned gases are drawn out. As the cylinder head returns to its original position, it compresses the new gas and air mixture and the process repeats itself.

internal combustion engine

[from Old French]
2 → see also **genetic engineering**

Eng|lish /ˈɪŋglɪʃ/
1 **N-NONCOUNT** LANGUAGE ARTS **English** is the language spoken by people who live in Great Britain and Ireland, the United States, Canada, Australia, and many other countries. ❑ *Do you speak English?*
2 **ADJ** **English** means belonging to or relating to England. ❑ *He began to enjoy the English way of life.* [from Old English]
→ look at Word Web: **English**

en|hance /ɪnˈhæns/ (**enhances, enhancing, enhanced**) **V-T** To **enhance** something means to improve its quality. ❑ *A little sugar enhances the natural sweet flavor of the peas.* [from Old French]

| Word Link | joy ≈ being glad : en*joy*, *joy*ful, *joy*fully |

en|joy /ɪnˈdʒɔɪ/ (**enjoys, enjoying, enjoyed**)
1 **V-T** If you **enjoy** something, you like doing it. ❑ *I enjoyed playing basketball.*
2 **V-T** If you **enjoy yourself**, you have a good time doing something. ❑ *I am really enjoying myself at the moment.* [from Old French]

en|joy|able /ɪnˈdʒɔɪəbəl/ **ADJ** Something that is **enjoyable** gives you pleasure. ❑ *The movie was much more enjoyable than I expected.* [from Old French]

en|joy|ment /ɪnˈdʒɔɪmənt/ **N-NONCOUNT** **Enjoyment** is the feeling of pleasure that you have when you do something that you like. ❑ *We get a lot of enjoyment from our garden.* [from Old French]

en|large /ɪnˈlɑrdʒ/ (**enlarges, enlarging, enlarged**) **V-T/V-I** When you **enlarge** something or when it **enlarges**, it becomes bigger. ❑ *You can enlarge these photographs.*
→ look at Word Web: **photography**

enor|mous /ɪnˈɔrməs/ **ADJ** Something that is **enormous** is extremely large in size or degree. ❑ *The main bedroom is enormous.* ❑ *It was an enormous disappointment.*
● **enor|mous|ly** **ADV** ❑ *I admired him enormously.* [from Latin]

enough /ɪˈnʌf/
1 **DET** **Enough** means as much as you need. ❑ *They had enough cash for a one-way ticket.*
2 **ADV** **Enough** is also an adverb. ❑ *I was old enough to work and earn money.*
3 **PRON** **Enough** is also a pronoun. ❑ *They are not doing enough.* ❑ *Is your child getting enough of the right foods?*
4 **ADV** You use **enough** in expressions such as **strangely enough** and **interestingly enough** when you think a fact is strange or interesting. ❑ *Strangely enough, the last person he mentioned was Tanya.* [from Old English]

Thesaurus	enough	Also look up :
ADJ		adequate, complete, satisfactory, sufficient; (*ant.*) inadequate, insufficient **1**

en|rich /ɪnˈrɪtʃ/ (**enriches, enriching, enriched**) **V-T** To **enrich** something means to improve its quality, usually by adding something to it. ❑ *It is important to enrich the soil before planting.* ● **en|rich|ment** **N-NONCOUNT** ❑ *...spiritual enrichment.*

en|roll /ɪnˈroʊl/ (**enrolls, enrolling, enrolled**) **V-T/V-I** If you **enroll** or **enroll in** a class, you officially join it. ❑ *He has already enrolled to study at medical college.* ❑ *Already, 46 students are enrolled in the two classes.*

en|sem|ble /ɑnˈsɑmbəl/ (**ensembles**) **N-COUNT** MUSIC An **ensemble** is a group of musicians, actors, or dancers who regularly perform together. [from French]

Word Web   **English**

The **English language** has more **words** than any other language. Early English grew out of a Germanic language.

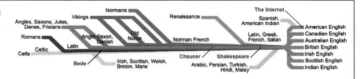

Much of its **grammar** and basic **vocabulary** came from that language. But in 1066, England was conquered by the Normans. Norman French became the language of the rulers. Therefore many French and Latin words came into the English language. The playwright Shakespeare* **coined** over 1,600 new words in his plays. English has become an international language with many regional **dialects**.
William Shakespeare (1564-1616): an English playwright and poet.

en|sue /ɪnsu̱/ (**ensues, ensuing, ensued**) **v-ɪ** If something **ensues**, it happens immediately after another event, usually as a result of it. ❑ *A brief but embarrassing silence ensued.* [from Old French]

en|sure /ɪnʃʊ̱ər/ (**ensures, ensuring, ensured**) **v-ᴛ** To **ensure** something means to make sure that it happens. [FORMAL] ❑ *The school ensures the safety of all students.* ❑ *We will work hard to ensure that this doesn't happen again.*

Usage	ensure and insure

Ensure and *insure* both mean "to make certain." *Automobile inspections ensure that a car is safe to drive. Insure* can also mean "to protect against loss." *Drivers should insure their cars against theft.*

en|ter /ɛ̱ntər/ (**enters, entering, entered**)
1 **v-ᴛ/v-ɪ** When you **enter** a place such as a room or a building, you go into it. [FORMAL] ❑ *He entered the room and stood near the door.* ❑ *When Spinks entered they all turned to look at him.*
2 **v-ᴛ** If you **enter** a competition or a race, you state that you will be a part of it. ❑ *To enter the competition, simply go to our website and fill in the details.*
3 **v-ᴛ** If you **enter** information, you write or type it in a form or a book, or into a computer. ❑ *They enter the addresses into the computer.* [from Old French]
▶ **enter into** If you **enter into** an agreement, a discussion, or a relationship, you become involved in it. [FORMAL] ❑ *I have not entered into any agreements with them.*

en|ter|prise /ɛ̱ntərpraɪz/ (**enterprises**) **N-COUNT** BUSINESS An **enterprise** is a company or a business. ❑ *We provide help for small and medium-sized enterprises.* [from Old French]

en|ter|tain /ɛ̱ntərteɪn/ (**entertains, entertaining, entertained**)
1 **v-ᴛ** If you **entertain** people, you do something that amuses or interests them. ❑ *They were entertained by singers and dancers.*
● **en|ter|tain|ing** **ADJ** ❑ *His show is entertaining, intelligent, and funny.*
2 **v-ᴛ/v-ɪ** If you **entertain** guests, you invite them to your home and give them food and drink. ❑ *This is the season for entertaining.* ❑ *I don't like to entertain guests anymore.* [from Old French]

en|ter|tain|er /ɛ̱ntərteɪnər/ (**entertainers**) **N-COUNT** An **entertainer** is a person whose job is to entertain audiences, for example by telling jokes, singing, or dancing. ❑ *Chaplin was possibly the greatest entertainer of the twentieth century.* [from Old French]

en|ter|tain|ment /ɛ̱ntərteɪnmənt/ (**entertainments**) **N-COUNT/N-NONCOUNT** **Entertainment** is performances of plays and movies, and activities such as reading and watching television, that give people pleasure. ❑ *At the party, there was children's entertainment and a swimming competition.* [from Old French]
→ look at Word Web: **radio**

en|thrall /ɪnθrɔ̱l/ (**enthralls, enthralling, enthralled**) **v-ᴛ** If you **are enthralled by** something, you enjoy it and give it your complete attention and interest. ❑ *The passengers were enthralled by the scenery.*

en|thuse /ɪnθu̱z/ (**enthuses, enthusing, enthused**)
1 **v-ɪ** If you **enthuse about** something, you talk about it in a way that shows how excited you are about it. ❑ *"We had a fantastic time!" she enthused.*
2 **v-ᴛ** If you **are enthused** by something, it makes you feel excited and enthusiastic. ❑ *I was immediately enthused.* [from Late Latin]

en|thu|si|asm /ɪnθu̱ziæzəm/ **N-NONCOUNT** **Enthusiasm** is the feeling that you have when you really enjoy something or want to do something. ❑ *Does your girlfriend share your enthusiasm for sports?* [from Late Latin]

Thesaurus	enthusiasm Also look up :
N	eagerness, energy, excitement, passion, zest; (*ant.*) apathy, indifference

en|thu|si|ast /ɪnθu̱ziæst/ (**enthusiasts**) **N-COUNT** An **enthusiast** is a person who is very interested in a particular activity, and who spends a lot of time on it. ❑ *Ryan is a sports car enthusiast.* [from Late Latin]

en|thu|si|as|tic /ɪnθu̱ziæstɪk/ **ADJ** If you are **enthusiastic about** something, you show how much you like or enjoy it. ❑ *Tom was not very enthusiastic about the idea.*
● **en|thu|si|as|ti|cal|ly** /ɪnθu̱ziæstɪkli/ **ADV** ❑ *The announcement was greeted enthusiastically.* [from Late Latin]

en|tire /ɪntaɪ̱ər/ **ADJ** You use **entire** when you want to make it clear that you are talking about all of something. ❑ *He spent his entire life in China.* [from Old French]

e

Thesaurus	entire Also look up :
ADJ	absolute, complete, total, whole; (ant.) incomplete, limited, partial

en|tire|ly /ɪntaɪərli/ **ADV** Entirely means completely and not just partly. ❑ *I agree entirely.* ❑ *I'm not entirely sure what I'm supposed to do.* [from Old French]

en|ti|tle /ɪntaɪtᵊl/ (**entitles, entitling, entitled**)
1 **V-T** If you **are entitled to** something, you are allowed to have it or do it. ❑ *They are entitled to first class travel.*
2 **V-T** You say that a book, a movie, or a painting **is entitled** a particular thing when you are mentioning its title. ❑ *...a performance entitled "The Lovers."* [from Old French]

en|trance /ɛntrəns/ (**entrances**)
1 **N-COUNT** The **entrance to** a place is the door or gate where you go into it. ❑ *He came out of a side entrance.*
2 **N-COUNT** Someone's **entrance** is when they arrive in a room. ❑ *She didn't notice her father's entrance.*
3 **N-NONCOUNT** **Entrance** is the right to go into a place. ❑ *We tried to go in, but we were refused entrance.*
4 **N-NONCOUNT** If you gain **entrance to** an institution, you are accepted as a member of it. ❑ *Many students fail to gain entrance to the university of their choice.* [from French]

Word Link	eur ≈ one who does : amateur, chauffeur, entrepreneur

en|tre|pre|neur /ɒntrəprənɜr, -nʊər/ (**entrepreneurs**) **N-COUNT** BUSINESS An **entrepreneur** is a person who starts a business. [from French]

en|try /ɛntri/ (**entries**)
1 **N-NONCOUNT** **Entry to** a particular place is when you go into it. ❑ *Entry to the museum is free.*
2 **PHRASE** **No Entry** is used on signs to show that you are not allowed to go into a particular area.
3 **N-NONCOUNT** A person's or an organization's **entry into** a group is their joining of it. ❑ *...China's entry into the World Trade Organization.*
4 **N-COUNT** An **entry** in a book or a computer file is a short piece of writing in it. ❑ *...Valerie's diary entry for April 20, 1917.*
5 **N-COUNT** An **entry for** a competition is

something that you complete in order to take part. ❑ *The closing date for entries is December 31.*
6 **N-COUNT** The **entry to** a place is the way into it, for example a door or gate. ❑ *The entry was blocked.* [from Old French]
→ look at Word Web: **blog**

en|velope /ɛnvəloʊp, ɒn-/ (**envelopes**) **N-COUNT** An **envelope** is the paper cover in which you put a letter before you send it to someone. ❑ *She put the letter back into the envelope and handed it to me.* [from French]
→ look at Picture Dictionary: **office**

en|vi|ous /ɛnviəs/ **ADJ** If you are **envious of** someone, you want something that they have. ❑ *I'm envious of your success.*
● **en|vi|ous|ly** **ADV** ❑ *People talked enviously about his good luck.* [from Latin]

en|vi|ron|ment /ɪnvaɪrənmənt, -vaɪərn-/ (**environments**)
1 **N-COUNT/N-NONCOUNT** Someone's **environment** is the conditions in which they live or work. ❑ *The children are taught in a safe and happy environment.*
2 **N-SING** SCIENCE The **environment** is the natural world of land, the oceans, the air, plants, and animals. ❑ *Please respect the environment by recycling.* ● **en|vi|ron|men|tal** /ɪnvaɪrənmɛntᵊl, -vaɪərn-/ **ADJ** ❑ *Environmental groups protested loudly during the conference.* ● **en|vi|ron|men|tal|ly** **ADV** ❑ *...environmentally friendly cleaning products.* [from Old French]
→ look at Word Webs: **amphibian, dump, habitat, pollution**

Word Partnership	Use environment
with :	
ADJ	**hostile** environment, **safe** environment, **supportive** environment, **unhealthy** environment **1** **natural** environment **2**
V	**damage the** environment, **protect the** environment **2**

en|vi|ron|men|tal|ist /ɪnvaɪrənmɛntəlɪst, -vaɪərn-/ (**environmentalists**) **N-COUNT** SCIENCE An **environmentalist** is a person who is concerned with protecting and preserving the natural environment. [from Old French]

en|vis|age /ɪnvɪzɪdʒ/ (**envisages, envisaging, envisaged**) **V-T** If you **envisage** something, you imagine that it is true, real, or likely to happen. ❑ *I don't envisage spending my whole life in this job.* [from French]

en|vi|sion /ɪnvɪʒ³n/ (**envisions, envisioning, envisioned**) **v-T** If you **envision** something, you envisage it. ❑ *We can envision a better future.*

en|voy /ɛnvɔɪ, ɒn-/ (**envoys**)
1 **N-COUNT** SOCIAL STUDIES An **envoy** is someone who is sent as a representative from one government or political group to another. ❑ *A U.S. envoy is expected in the region this month.*
2 **N-COUNT** SOCIAL STUDIES An **envoy** is a diplomat in an embassy who is immediately below the ambassador in rank. [from French]

envy /ɛnvi/ (**envies, envying, envied**)
1 **v-T** If you **envy** someone, you wish that you had the same things that they have. ❑ *I don't envy young people these days.*
2 **N-NONCOUNT** **Envy** is also a noun. ❑ *She was full of envy when she heard their news.* [from Old French]

en|zyme /ɛnzaɪm/ (**enzymes**) **N-COUNT** SCIENCE An **enzyme** is a chemical substance found in living creatures that produces changes in other substances without being changed itself. [from Medieval Greek]

epic /ɛpɪk/ (**epics**)
1 **N-COUNT** LANGUAGE ARTS An **epic** is a long book, poem, or movie about important events. ❑ *We read Homer's epics about the Trojan war.*
2 **ADJ** LANGUAGE ARTS **Epic** is also an adjective. ❑ *This is an epic story of love and war.* [from Latin]
→ look at Word Web: **hero**

epic thea|ter **N-NONCOUNT** ARTS **Epic theater** is a style of theater that uses non-realistic devices such as songs and captions to illustrate social or political ideas.

epi|dem|ic /ɛpɪdɛmɪk/ (**epidemics**) **N-COUNT** If there is an **epidemic of** a particular disease, it affects a large number of people. ❑ *...a flu epidemic.* [from French]
→ look at Word Web: **illness**

epi|der|mis /ɛpɪdɜrmɪs/ **N-SING** SCIENCE Your **epidermis** is the thin protective outer layer of your skin. [from Late Latin]

epi|di|dy|mis /ɛpɪdɪdəmɪs/ (**epididymes**) **N-COUNT** SCIENCE The **epididymis** is a long, narrow tube behind the testicles of male animals, where sperm is stored. [from Greek]

epi|logue /ɛpɪlɔg/ (**epilogues**) also **epilog**
N-COUNT LANGUAGE ARTS An **epilogue** is an extra part that is added at the end of a piece of writing. [from Latin]

epi|sode /ɛpɪsoʊd/ (**episodes**)
1 **N-COUNT** An **episode** is one of the parts of a story on television or radio. ❑ *The final episode will be shown next Sunday.*
2 **N-COUNT** An **episode** is an event or a short period of time that is important or unusual, or has a particular quality. ❑ *This episode is deeply embarrassing for Washington.* [from Greek]
→ look at Word Web: **animation**

epi|thelial tis|sue /ɛpɪθiliəl tɪʃu/ (**epithelial tissues**) **N-COUNT/N-NONCOUNT** SCIENCE **Epithelial tissue** is a layer of cells in animals that covers the skin and other surfaces of the body.

equal /ikwəl/ (**equals, equaling, equaled**)
1 **ADJ** If two things are **equal**, they are the same in size, number, or value. ❑ *There are equal numbers of men and women.*
2 **ADJ** If different groups of people are given **equal** treatment, they have the same rights or are treated in the same way. ❑ *We want equal rights at work.*
3 **N-COUNT** Someone who is your **equal** has the same ability or rights as you have. ❑ *You and I are equals.*
4 **V-LINK** MATH If something **equals** a particular number or amount, it is the same as that amount. ❑ *9 minus 7 equals 2.* [from Latin]

Word Partnership	Use **equal** with :
N	equal **importance**, equal **number**, equal **parts**, equal **pay**, equal **share** **1** equal **rights**, equal **treatment** **2**

equal|i|ty /ikwɒliti/ **N-NONCOUNT** **Equality** is the fair treatment of all the people in a group. ❑ *Few people really believed in racial equality in the 1800s.* [from Latin]

equal|ly /ikwəli/
1 **ADV** If something is divided **equally**, the parts are the same in size, number, or value. ❑ *The money will be divided equally among his three children.*
2 **ADV** If different people or groups of people are treated **equally**, they have the same rights or are treated in the same way. ❑ *The system should treat everyone equally.*
3 **ADV** **Equally** is used to introduce another

E

comment on the same topic, that balances or contrasts with the previous comment. ❑ *I think it is a serious issue, but equally I don't think it is a matter of life and death.* [from Latin]

equal op|por|tu|nity N-NONCOUNT
BUSINESS **Equal opportunity** means giving everyone the same opportunities for employment and pay. ❑ *We believe in equal opportunity for women.*

equal sign (**equal signs**) N-COUNT MATH
An **equal sign** is the sign =, which is used in mathematics to show that two numbers are equal.

equa|tion /ɪkweɪʒ³n/ (**equations**) N-COUNT
MATH An **equation** is a mathematical statement that two amounts or values are the same. [from Latin]

equa|tor /ɪkweɪtər/ N-SING GEOGRAPHY
The **equator** is a line that is shown on maps around the middle of the world. [from Medieval Latin]
→ look at Picture Dictionary: **globe**

equa|to|rial /ikwətɔriəl, ɛk-/ ADJ
GEOGRAPHY **Equatorial** regions are at or near the equator. ❑ *The cassava plant grows in most equatorial regions.* [from Medieval Latin]

equip /ɪkwɪp/ (**equips, equipping, equipped**)
V-T If a person or a thing **is equipped with** something, they have the things that they need to do a particular job. ❑ *The army is equipped with 5,000 tanks.* ❑ *Each classroom is equipped with educational toys and books.* [from Old French]

equip|ment /ɪkwɪpmənt/ N-NONCOUNT
Equipment is all the things that are used for a particular purpose. ❑ *...tractors and other farm equipment.* [from Old French]

Thesaurus	equipment Also look up :
N	accessories, facilities, gear, machinery, supplies; (*ant.*) tools, utensils

equi|ty /ɛkwɪti/ N-NONCOUNT BUSINESS

In finance, your **equity** is the sum of your assets, for example the value of your house, once your debts have been subtracted from it. ❑ *To raise equity, Murphy must either sell or refinance.* [from Old French]

equiva|lent /ɪkwɪvələnt/ (**equivalents**)
1 N-SING If one thing is **the equivalent of** another, they are the same, or they are used in the same way. ❑ *The Internet has become the modern equivalent of the phone.*
2 ADJ **Equivalent** is also an adjective. ❑ *...an equivalent amount.* [from Late Latin]

ER /i ɑr/ (**ERs**) N-COUNT The **ER** is the part of a hospital where people go when they have seriously hurt themselves or when they suddenly become sick. **ER** is short for **emergency room**.

era /ɪərə/ (**eras**) N-COUNT An **era** is a period of time that is considered as a single unit. ❑ *...a new era of peace.* [from Latin]

erase /ɪreɪs/ (**erases, erasing, erased**) V-T
If you **erase** writing or a mark, you remove it. ❑ *She erased his name from her address book.* [from Latin]
→ look at Picture Dictionary: **draw**

eras|er /ɪreɪsər/ (**erasers**) N-COUNT
An **eraser** is an object that is used for removing marks that have been written using a pencil. [from Latin]

e-reader (**e-readers**) N-COUNT TECHNOLOGY
An **e-reader** is a small device with a screen that you use for reading digital texts.

erect /ɪrɛkt/ (**erects, erecting, erected**)
1 V-T If people **erect** a building or a bridge, they build it. [FORMAL] ❑ *The building was erected in 1900.*
2 ADJ People or things that are **erect** are straight and upright. ❑ *Stand erect, with your arms hanging naturally.* [from Latin]

erode /ɪroʊd/ (**erodes, eroding, eroded**)
1 V-T/V-I If rock or soil **erodes** or **is eroded** by the weather, sea, or wind, it cracks and

---

Word Web erosion

There are two main causes of **soil erosion—water** and **wind. Rainfall,** especially heavy **thunderstorms,** breaks down **dirt.** Small particles of **earth, sand,** and silt are then carried away by the water. When the soil contains too much water, **mudslides** occur. Strong **currents** of **air** cause wind erosion. Trees and other permanent **vegetation** anchor the soil and prevent this damage.

breaks so that it is gradually destroyed. ❑ *The sea is gradually eroding the coastline.*

● **ero|sion** /ɪroʊʒ³n/ **N-NONCOUNT** ❑ *The storms caused soil erosion and flooding.*

2 **V-T/V-I** If something **is eroded**, it gradually weakens or loses value. ❑ *Profits have been eroded by competition.* ❑ *They say that television continues to erode moral standards.* [from Latin]

→ look at Word Webs: **erosion, beach, rock**

erot|ic /ɪrɒtɪk/ **ADJ** If you describe something as **erotic**, you mean that it involves sexual feelings or arouses sexual desire. ❑ *It wasn't an erotic experience at all.* [from Greek]

er|rand /ɛrənd/ (**errands**) **N-COUNT** An **errand** is a short trip to do a job, for example when you go to a store to buy something. ❑ *We ran errands and took her meals when she was sick.* [from Old English]

er|rat|ic /ɪrætɪk/ **ADJ** Something that is **erratic** happens at unexpected times or moves in an irregular way. ❑ *...Argentina's erratic inflation rate.* ● **er|rati|cal|ly** /ɪrætɪkli/ **ADV** ❑ *Police stopped him for driving erratically.* [from Latin]

er|ror /ɛrər/ (**errors**) **N-COUNT/N-NONCOUNT** An **error** is a mistake. ❑ *You should check your work for errors in grammar or spelling.* [from Latin]

Word Partnership	Use **error** with :
ADJ	**common** error, **fatal** error, **human** error
V	**commit an** error, **correct an** error, **make an** error

Word Link	*rupt* ≈ *breaking : dis*rupt*, e*rupt*, inter*rupt*

erupt /ɪrʌpt/ (**erupts, erupting, erupted**)
1 **V-I** SCIENCE When a volcano **erupts**, it throws out a lot of lava. ❑ *Krakatoa erupted in 1883.* ● **erup|tion** /ɪrʌpʃ³n/ (**eruptions**) **N-COUNT/N-NONCOUNT** ❑ *The country's last volcanic eruption was 600 years ago.*
2 **V-I** If something such as violence **erupts**, it suddenly begins or gets more intense. ❑ *Heavy fighting erupted there today.* [from Latin]

→ look at Word Webs: **rock, volcano**

Word Link	*scal, scala* ≈ *ladder, stairs : e*scal*ate, e*scal*ator, *scale

es|ca|late /ɛskəleɪt/ (**escalates, escalating, escalated**) **V-T/V-I** If a bad situation

escalates or if someone **escalates** it, it becomes worse. ❑ *Nobody wants the situation to escalate.*

es|ca|la|tor /ɛskəleɪtər/ (**escalators**)
N-COUNT An **escalator** is a set of moving stairs. ❑ *Take the escalator to the third floor.*

es|cape /ɪskeɪp/ (**escapes, escaping, escaped**)
1 **V-I** If you **escape from** a place, you manage to get away from it. ❑ *A prisoner has escaped from a jail in northern Texas.*
2 **N-COUNT** **Escape** is also a noun. ❑ *He made his escape at night.*
3 **V-T/V-I** You **escape** when you avoid an accident. ❑ *The man's girlfriend escaped unhurt.* ❑ *The two officers escaped serious injury.*
4 **N-COUNT** **Escape** is also a noun. ❑ *I had a narrow escape on the bridge.*
5 **V-T** If something **escapes** you or **escapes** your attention, you do not remember it, or you do not notice it. ❑ *His name escapes me for the moment.* [from Old Northern French]

Word Partnership	Use **escape** with :
N	**chance to** escape, escape **from prison** **1**
V	**try to** escape **1**
	manage to escape **1** **2**
	make an escape **2**

es|cort (**escorts, escorting, escorted**)

> **PRONUNCIATION HELP**
> Pronounce the noun /ɛskɔrt/. Pronounce the verb /ɪskɔrt/.

1 **V-T** If you **escort** someone somewhere, you accompany them there, usually in order to make sure that they go. ❑ *I escorted him to the door.*
2 **N-COUNT** An **escort** is a person who travels with someone in order to protect or guard them. ❑ *He arrived with a police escort.*
3 **PHRASE** If someone is taken somewhere **under escort**, they are accompanied by guards, either because they have been arrested or because they need to be protected.
4 **N-COUNT** An **escort** is a person who accompanies another person of the opposite sex to a social event. Sometimes people are paid to be escorts. ❑ *My sister needed an escort for a company dinner.* [from French]

esopha|gus /ɪsɒfəgəs/ (**esophaguses**)
N-COUNT SCIENCE Your **esophagus** is the tube in your body that carries the food from

E

your throat to your stomach. ❑ *He has cancer of the esophagus.* [from New Latin]

es|pe|cial|ly /ɪspɛʃ°li/

1 **ADV** You use **especially** to show that what you are saying applies more to one person or thing than to any others. ❑ *Millions of wild flowers grow in the valleys, especially in April and May.*

2 **ADV** You use **especially** to emphasize a characteristic or a quality. ❑ *The brain and the heart are especially sensitive to lack of oxygen.* [from Old French]

Thesaurus	especially	Also look up :
ADV	exclusively, only, solely **1**	
	extraordinarily, particularly **2**	

es|pio|nage /ɛspiənɑʒ/ **N-NONCOUNT**
SOCIAL STUDIES **Espionage** is the activity of finding out the political, military, or industrial secrets of your enemies or rivals by using spies. [FORMAL] ❑ *The authorities have arrested several people suspected of espionage.* [from French]

es|say /ɛseɪ/ (**essays**) **N-COUNT**
LANGUAGE ARTS An **essay** is a short piece of writing on a subject. ❑ *We asked Jason to write an essay about his hometown.* [from Old French]

es|sence /ɛs°ns/ (**essences**)

1 **N-NONCOUNT** The **essence of** something is its basic and most important characteristic that gives it its individual identity. ❑ *The essence of being a customer is having a choice.*

2 **PHRASE** You use **in essence** to emphasize that you are talking about the most important or central aspect of an idea, a situation, or an event. [FORMAL] ❑ *Local taxes are in essence simple.*

3 **PHRASE** If you say that something **is of the essence,** you mean that it is absolutely necessary in order for a particular action to be successful. [FORMAL] ❑ *Speed was of the essence in a project of this type.* [from Medieval Latin]

es|sen|tial /ɪsɛnʃ°l/ **ADJ** Something that is **essential** is necessary. ❑ *Play is an essential part of a child's development.* [from Medieval Latin]

Word Partnership	Use **essential** with :
N	essential **element**, essential **function**, essential **information**, essential **ingredients**, essential **nutrients**, essential **personnel**, essential **services**

es|sen|tial|ly /ɪsɛnʃəli/

1 **ADV** You use **essentially** to emphasize a quality that someone or something has, and to say that it is their most important or basic quality. [FORMAL] ❑ *He was essentially a simple man.*

2 **ADV** You use **essentially** to indicate that what you are saying is mainly true, although some parts of it are wrong or more complicated than has been stated. [FORMAL] ❑ *His analysis proved essentially correct.* [from Medieval Latin]

Word Link	stab ≈ steady : e*stab*lish, in*stab*ility, *stab*ilize

es|tab|lish /ɪstæblɪʃ/ (**establishes, establishing, established**)

1 **V-T** If someone **establishes** an organization, they create it. ❑ *He established the business in 1990.*

2 **V-T/V-I** If you **establish** contact with someone, you start to have contact with them. [FORMAL] ❑ *He wants to establish contact with his family.*

3 **V-T** If you **establish that** something is true, you discover facts that show that it is true. [FORMAL] ❑ *Medical tests established that she had a heart defect.* [from Old French]

Word Partnership	Use **establish** with :
N	establish **control**, establish **independence**, establish **rules 1** establish **contact**, establish **relations 2** establish *someone's* **identity 3**

es|tab|lished /ɪstæblɪʃt/ **ADJ** If you use **established** to describe something such as an organization, you mean that it is well known because it has existed for a long time. ❑ *...old established companies.* [from Old French]

es|tab|lish|ment /ɪstæblɪʃmənt/ (**establishments**)

1 **N-COUNT** An **establishment** is an organization in a building in a particular place. [FORMAL] ❑ *...an educational establishment.*

2 **N-SING** The **establishment** is the people who have power in a country. ❑ *...the American establishment.* [from Old French]

es|tate /ɪsteɪt/ (**estates**)

1 **N-COUNT** An **estate** is a large house in a large area of land in the country, owned by a person or an organization. ❑ *He spent the holidays at his aunt's 300-acre estate.*

2 N-COUNT Someone's **estate** is all the money and property that they leave when they die. ❑ *His estate was valued at $150,000.* [from Old French]

3 → see also **real estate**

es|teem /ɪstim/

1 N-NONCOUNT **Esteem** is admiration and respect. [FORMAL] ❑ *He is held in high esteem by colleagues.* [from Old French]

2 → see also **self-esteem**

es|ti|mate (estimates, estimating, estimated)

PRONUNCIATION HELP
Pronounce the verb /ɛstɪmeɪt/. Pronounce the noun /ɛstɪmɪt/.
---

1 V-T If you **estimate** an amount or a value, you say how much you think there is of it. ❑ *It's difficult to estimate how much money is involved.*

2 N-COUNT **Estimate** is also a noun. ❑ *She made an estimate of the truck's speed.* [from Latin]

Thesaurus	estimate	Also look up :
V	appraise, guess, judge **1**	
N	appraisal, evaluation, guessing, valuation **2**	

Word Partnership	Use estimate with :
ADJ	**best** estimate, **conservative** estimate, **original** estimate, **rough** estimate **2**
V	**make an** estimate **2**

es|ti|va|tion /ɛstɪveɪʃ°n/ also aestivation
N-NONCOUNT SCIENCE **Estivation** is a period during which some animals become inactive because the weather is very hot or dry. [from Latin]

etc. /ɛt sɛtərə, -sɛtrə/ **etc.** is used at the end of a list to show that you have not given a full list. **etc.** is short for "etcetera." ❑ *She knew all about my schoolwork, my hospital work, etc.*

et|cet|era /ɛtsɛtərə, -sɛtrə/ also et cetera
→ look up **etc.**

eter|nal /ɪtɜrn°l/ **ADJ** Something that is **eternal** lasts forever. ❑ *What's the secret of eternal happiness?* [from Late Latin]

ethi|cal /ɛθɪk°l/
1 ADJ **Ethical** means relating to beliefs about right and wrong. ❑ *Heather is now a vegetarian for ethical reasons.*

2 ADJ If something is **ethical**, it is morally right or morally acceptable. ❑ *...ethical business practices.* [from Latin]

eth|nic /ɛθnɪk/ **ADJ** SOCIAL STUDIES **Ethnic** means relating to groups of people that have the same culture or belong to the same race. ❑ *Most of their friends come from other ethnic groups.* [from Late Latin]

ety|mol|ogy /ɛtɪmɒlədʒi/ (etymologies)
1 N-NONCOUNT LANGUAGE ARTS **Etymology** is the study of the origins and historical development of words.

2 N-COUNT LANGUAGE ARTS The **etymology** of a particular word is its history. [from Latin]

Eu|bac|te|ria /yubæktɪəriə/ **N-PLURAL**
SCIENCE **Eubacteria** are bacteria that have a rigid cell wall. Compare with **Archaebacteria**. [from New Latin]

eugen|ics /yudʒɛnɪks/ **N-NONCOUNT**
SCIENCE **Eugenics** is the theory that people should be allowed to become parents only if there is a strong chance that they will have healthy, intelligent children. ❑ *The eugenics movement glorified the blond and blue-eyed Nordic ideal.* [from Greek]

eu|glena /yuglinə/ (euglena) **N-COUNT**
SCIENCE **Euglena** is a type of single-celled organism that lives mainly in fresh water. [from New Latin]

eu|karyot|ic cell /yukæriɒtɪk sɛl/
(eukaryotic cells) **N-COUNT** SCIENCE
Eukaryotic cells are cells that have a nucleus, such as the cells in animals and plants. Compare with **prokaryotic cell**.

eulo|gize /yulədʒaɪz/ (eulogizes, eulogizing, eulogized) **V-T** If you **eulogize** someone who has died, you make a speech praising them. ❑ *Leaders from around the world eulogized the president.* [from Late Latin]

eu|phe|mism /yufəmɪzəm/ (euphemisms)
N-COUNT A **euphemism** is a polite word or expression that is used to talk about something unpleasant or embarrassing, for example death or sex. ❑ *He prefers the word "chubby" as a euphemism for fat.* [from Greek]

euro /yuərou/ (euros) **N-COUNT** The **euro** (€) is a unit of money that is used by many countries in the European Union (= an organization that encourages trade). ❑ *He gets paid in euros.*

Word Link	*an, ian ≈ one of, relating to :*
	Christ*ian*, Europe*an*, pedestr*ian*

Euro|pean /yʊərəpiən/ (**Europeans**)

1 **ADJ** SOCIAL STUDIES **European** means belonging to or coming from Europe. ❑ ...*European countries.*

2 **N-COUNT** SOCIAL STUDIES A **European** is a person who comes from Europe. [from French]

eutha|na|sia /yuθəneɪʒə/ **N-NONCOUNT**
Euthanasia is the practice of killing a dying person in order to end their suffering. ❑ ...*those in favor of voluntary euthanasia.* [from New Latin]

evacu|ate /ɪvækyueɪt/ (**evacuates, evacuating, evacuated**) **V-T** If people are **evacuated from** a place, they move out of it because it is dangerous. ❑ *Families were evacuated from the area because of the fighting.* [from Latin]

evade /ɪveɪd/ (**evades, evading, evaded**) **V-T**
If you **evade** something unpleasant or difficult, you avoid it. ❑ *He admits he evaded taxes.* [from French]

evalu|ate /ɪvælyueɪt/ (**evaluates, evaluating, evaluated**) **V-T** If you **evaluate** something or someone, you consider them in order to decide how good or bad they are. ❑ *We need to evaluate the situation very carefully.* ● **evalu|ation** /ɪvælyueɪʃən/ (**evaluations**) **N-COUNT/N-NONCOUNT** ❑ *The program includes an evaluation of students' writing skills.* [from French]

evapo|rate /ɪvæpəreɪt/ (**evaporates, evaporating, evaporated**) **V-I** SCIENCE When a liquid **evaporates**, it changes into a gas. ❑ *Boil the sauce until most of the liquid evaporates.* [from Late Latin]
→ look at Word Webs: **matter, water**

eve /iv/ (**eves**) **N-COUNT** The **eve of** a particular event or occasion is the day before it, or the period of time just before it. ❑ *The story begins on the eve of her birthday.*

---
even
  ❶ ADJECTIVE USES
  ❷ DISCOURSE USES
---

❶ even /ivən/

1 **ADJ** MATH An **even** number can be divided exactly by two.

2 **ADJ** An **even** surface is smooth and flat. ❑ *You will need a table with an even surface.*

3 **ADJ** An **even** measurement stays at about the same level. ❑ *How important is it to have an even temperature?*

4 **ADJ** If there is an **even** division of something, each person, group, or area involved has an equal amount. ❑ *Divide the dough into 12 even pieces.* ● **even|ly** **ADV** ❑ *The money was divided evenly.*

5 **ADJ** An **even** competition is equally balanced between the two sides. ❑ *It was an even game.* [from Old English]

❷ even /ivən/

1 **ADV** You use **even** to say that something is rather surprising. ❑ *Rob still seems happy, even after the bad news.*

2 **ADV** You use **even** to make another word stronger. ❑ *Our car is big, but theirs is even bigger.*

3 **PHRASE** You use **even if** or **even though** to show that a particular fact does not change anything. ❑ *She wasn't embarrassed, even though she made a mistake.*

4 **PHRASE** You use **even so** to add a surprising fact. ❑ *The bus was nearly empty. Even so, the man sat down next to her.* [from Old English]

Usage	even

Even is used for emphasis or to say that something is surprising. *He didn't even try. How can you even think about that?*

eve|ning /ivnɪŋ/ (**evenings**)
N-COUNT/N-NONCOUNT The **evening** is the part of each day between the end of the afternoon and midnight. ❑ *That evening he went to see a movie.* ❑ *We usually have dinner at seven in the evening.* [from Old English]
→ look at Picture Dictionary: **time**

event /ɪvɛnt/ (**events**)

1 **N-COUNT** An **event** is something that happens. ❑ *This terrible event caused death and injury to many.*

2 **N-COUNT** An **event** is an organized activity or celebration. ❑ *Several cultural and sports events were canceled.*

3 **PHRASE** You use **in the event of** when you are talking about a possible future situation, especially when you are planning what to do if it happens. ❑ *The bank will give an immediate refund in the event of an error.* [from Latin]
→ look at Word Webs: **graduation, history**

even|tual /ɪvɛntʃuəl/ **ADJ** The **eventual** result of something is what happens at the end of it. ❑ *The eventual winner will receive* $200,000. [from Latin]

even|tu|al|ly /ɪvɛntʃuəli/ **ADV** Eventually means at some later time, especially after a lot of delays or problems. ❑ *They eventually married in America.* ❑ *Eventually your child will leave home.* [from Latin]

ever /ɛvər/
1 **ADV** Ever means at any time. It is usually used in questions and negative sentences. ❑ *I don't think I'll ever trust people again.* ❑ *Have you ever seen anything like it?* ❑ *Japan is more powerful than ever before.*
2 **ADV** You use **ever** to show the degree to which something is true. ❑ *She is singing better than ever.*
3 → see also **forever**
4 **PHRASE** If something has been the situation **ever since** a particular time, it has been the situation all the time from then until now. ❑ *He's been there ever since you left!* [from Old English]

ever|green /ɛvərgrin/ (**evergreens**)
1 **N-COUNT** SCIENCE An **evergreen** is a tree or bush that has green leaves all year long.
2 **ADJ** SCIENCE **Evergreen** is also an adjective. ❑ *Plant evergreen shrubs around the end of the month.*
→ look at Picture Dictionary: **plants**

ev|ery /ɛvri/
1 **DET** You use **every** to show that you are talking about all the members of a group. ❑ *Every room has a window facing the ocean.* ❑ *Every child gets a free piece of fruit.*
2 **DET** You use **every** to say how often something happens. ❑ *We had to attend meetings every day.* ❑ *He saw his family once every two weeks.*
3 **PHRASE** You use **every now and then** and **every so often** to say that something happens occasionally. ❑ *Stir the mixture every now and then.*
4 **PHRASE** If something happens **every other day**, it happens one day, then it does not happen the next day, and continues in this way. ❑ *I called my mother every other day.* [from Old English]

every|body /ɛvribɒdi, -bʌdi/ **Everybody** means the same as **everyone**.

every|day /ɛvrideɪ/ **ADJ** **Everyday** describes something that is a regular part of your life. ❑ *They were doing everyday activities around the house.* ❑ *Computers are a central part of everyday life.*

every|one /ɛvriwʌn/ or **everybody** **PRON** **Everyone** or **everybody** means all people, or all the people in a particular group. ❑ *Everyone on the street was shocked when they heard the news.* ❑ *Not everyone thinks that the government is acting fairly.*

every|thing /ɛvriθɪŋ/
1 **PRON** You use **everything** when you are talking about all the objects, actions, or facts in a situation. ❑ *Everything in his life has changed.* ❑ *Susan and I do everything together.*
2 **PRON** You use **everything** when you are talking about all the important things in your life. ❑ *Is everything all right?*

every|where /ɛvriwɛər/ or **everyplace** **ADV** You use **everywhere** when you are talking about a whole area or all the places in a particular area. ❑ *People everywhere want the same things.* ❑ *We went everywhere together.*

evi|dence /ɛvɪdəns/ **N-NONCOUNT** **Evidence** is an object or a piece of information that makes you believe that something is true or has really happened. ❑ *There is no evidence that he stole the money.* ❑ *Evidence shows that most of us are happy with our lives.* [from Latin]
→ look at Word Webs: **experiment, trial**

Word Partnership	Use evidence with :
ADJ	**new** evidence, **physical** evidence
V	**find** evidence, **gather** evidence, **present** evidence, evidence **to support** *something*

evi|dent /ɛvɪdənt/ **ADJ** If something is **evident**, you notice it easily. ❏ *Changes are evident across the country.* ❏ *It was evident that she was not feeling well.* [from Latin]

evi|dent|ly /ɛvɪdəntli, -dɛnt-/ **ADV** You use **evidently** to say that something is clearly true. ❏ *The two men evidently knew each other.* [from Latin]

evil /iv°l/ (**evils**)

1 **ADJ** If an act or a person is **evil**, they are morally very bad. ❏ *Who's the most evil person in all of history?*

2 **N-NONCOUNT** **Evil** is all the wicked and bad things that happen in the world. ❏ *...a conflict between good and evil.*

3 **N-COUNT** An **evil** is a very unpleasant or harmful situation or activity. ❏ *...the evils of prejudice.* [from Old English]

evoke /ɪvoʊk/ (**evokes, evoking, evoked**) **V-T** To **evoke** a particular memory, idea, emotion, or response means to cause it to occur. [FORMAL] ❏ *The scene evoked memories of those old movies.* [from Latin]

evo|lu|tion /ɛvəluʃ°n, iv-/ (**evolutions**)

1 **N-NONCOUNT** SCIENCE **Evolution** is a process in which animals or plants slowly change over many years. ❏ *The evolution of mammals involved many changes in the body.*

2 **N-COUNT/N-NONCOUNT** **Evolution** is a process of gradual development in a particular situation or thing over a period of time. [FORMAL] ❏ *This was an important period in the evolution of modern science.* [from Latin] → look at Word Webs: **evolution, earth**

evolve /ɪvɒlv/ (**evolves, evolving, evolved**)

1 **V-I** SCIENCE When animals or plants **evolve**, they gradually change and develop into different forms. ❏ *The theory is that humans evolved from apes.*

2 **V-T/V-I** If something **evolves** or you **evolve** it, it gradually develops over a period of time into something different. ❏ *Popular music evolved from folk songs.* [from Latin] → look at Word Web: **earth**

ex|act /ɪgzækt/

1 **ADJ** **Exact** means correct and complete in every way. ❏ *I don't remember the exact words.* ❏ *Can you tell me the exact date of the incident?*

2 **ADJ** You use **exact** before a noun to show that you are referring to that particular thing and no other. ❏ *...the exact moment when he realized the truth.* [from Latin]

Thesaurus	**exact** Also look up :
ADJ	accurate, clear, precise, true; (ant.) wrong **1**

Word Partnership	Use **exact** with :
N	exact **change**, exact **duplicate**, exact **number**, exact **replica**, exact **science**, exact **words 1**
	exact **cause**, exact **location**, exact **moment 2**

ex|act|ly /ɪgzæktli/

1 **ADV** If you give facts or amounts **exactly**, you give them correctly and completely. ❏ *The tower was exactly a hundred meters in height.*

2 **ADV** **Exactly** means in every way, or with all the details. ❏ *Both drugs will be exactly the same.*

3 **ADV** You can say **Exactly** when you are agreeing with someone. ❏ *Eve nodded. "Exactly."*

4 **ADV** You use **not exactly** to say that a meaning or situation is slightly different from what people think. ❏ *He's not exactly homeless, he just hangs out in this park.* [from Latin]

Word Web   **evolution**

The **theory** of **human evolution** states that humans **evolved** from an ape-like ancestor. In 1856 the **fossils** of a Neanderthal were found. This was the first time that **scientists** realized that there were earlier forms of humans. **Anthropologists** have found other fossils that show how hominids changed over time. One of the earliest ancestors that has been found is called Australopithecus. This **species** lived about 4 million years ago in Africa. The oldest fossils of Homo sapiens date back to approximately 130,000 years ago.

ex|ag|ger|ate /ɪgzǽdʒəreɪt/ (**exaggerates, exaggerating, exaggerated**) **v-T/v-I** If you **exaggerate**, you say that something is bigger, worse, or more important than it really is. ❑ *He thinks I'm exaggerating.* ❑ *Try not to exaggerate the risks of traveling alone.*
● **ex|ag|gera|tion** /ɪgzǽdʒəreɪʃ³n/ (**exaggerations**) **N-COUNT/N-NONCOUNT** ❑ *It's not an exaggeration, it's a fact.* [from Latin]

ex|ag|ger|at|ed /ɪgzǽdʒəreɪtɪd/ **ADJ** Something that is **exaggerated** is or seems larger, better, worse, or more important than it actually needs to be. ❑ *Western fears, he insists, are greatly exaggerated.* [from Latin]

ex|am /ɪgzǽm/ (**exams**) **N-COUNT** An **exam** is a formal test that you take to show your knowledge of a subject. ❑ *I don't want to take any more exams.*

ex|ami|na|tion /ɪgzǽmɪneɪʃ³n/ (**examinations**)
1 **N-COUNT** An **examination** is the same as an **exam**. [FORMAL]
2 **N-COUNT** If you have a medical **examination**, a doctor looks at your body in order to check how healthy you are. ❑ *She is waiting for the results of a medical examination.*
3 **N-COUNT/N-NONCOUNT** **Examination** is the act of looking at someone or something carefully. ❑ *The government said the plan needed careful examination.* [from Old French]
→ look at Word Web: **diagnosis**

ex|am|ine /ɪgzǽmɪn/ (**examines, examining, examined**) **v-T** If you **examine** something or someone, you look at them carefully. ❑ *He examined her documents.* ❑ *A doctor examined her and could find nothing wrong.* [from Old French]

Thesaurus **examine** Also look up :
V   analyze, go over, inspect, investigate, research; (ant.) scrutinize

ex|am|in|er /ɪgzǽmɪnər/ (**examiners**) **N-COUNT** An **examiner** is a person who conducts an examination. ❑ *They have asked a judge to appoint an independent examiner.* [from Old French]

ex|am|ple /ɪgzǽmp³l/ (**examples**)
1 **N-COUNT** An **example** is something that shows what other things in a particular group are like. ❑ *The building is a fine example of 19th-century architecture.*
2 **PHRASE** You use **for example** to introduce

an example of something. ❑ *The technique can be used for treating diseases like cancer, for example.*
3 **PHRASE** If you **follow** someone's **example**, you copy their behavior, especially because you admire them. ❑ *Following the example set by her father, she has done her duty.*
4 **PHRASE** If you **set an example**, you encourage people by your behavior to act in a similar way. ❑ *An officer's job is to set an example.* [from Old French]

Thesaurus **example** Also look up :
N   model, representation, sample **1**

Word Partnership Use **example** with :
ADJ   **classic** example, **good** example, **obvious** example, **typical** example **1**
V   **give an** example **1**
      follow an example **3**

Word Link *ex ≈ away, from, out : exceed, exit, explode*

ex|ceed /ɪksíd/ (**exceeds, exceeding, exceeded**)
1 **v-T** If something **exceeds** a particular amount, it is greater than that amount. [FORMAL] ❑ *The cost of a new boat exceeded $100,000.*
2 **v-T** If you **exceed** a limit, you go beyond it. [FORMAL] ❑ *He accepts that he was exceeding the speed limit.* [from Latin]

ex|ceed|ing|ly /ɪksídɪŋli/ **ADV** **Exceedingly** means very or very much. [OLD-FASHIONED] ❑ *We had an exceedingly good lunch.* [from Latin]

Word Link *ence ≈ state, condition : dependence, excellence, independence*

ex|cel|lence /ɛksələns/ **N-NONCOUNT** **Excellence** is the quality of being extremely good in some way. ❑ *She won an award for excellence in teaching.* [from Latin]

ex|cel|lent /ɛksələnt/ **ADJ** Something that is **excellent** is extremely good. ❑ *The printing quality is excellent.* [from Latin]

ex|cept /ɪksɛpt/
1 **PREP** You use **except** or **except for** to show that you are not including a particular thing or person. ❑ *The shops are open every day except Sunday.* ❑ *The room was empty except for a television.*
2 **CONJ** **Except** is also a conjunction. ❑ *I'm much better now, except that I still have a headache.* [from Old French]
→ look at Usage note at **accept**

Usage   **except** and **besides**

Except and *besides* are often confused. *Except* refers to someone or something that is not included: *I've taken all my required courses except psychology. I'm going to take it next term. Besides* means "in addition to." *What courses should I take next term besides psychology?*

ex|cep|tion /ɪksɛpʃᵊn/ (**exceptions**)
  N-COUNT An **exception** is a particular thing, person, or situation that is not included in what you say. ❑ *Not many musicians can sing well and play well, but Eddie is an exception.* [from Old French]

ex|cep|tion|al /ɪksɛpʃənᵊl/ **ADJ Exceptional** describes someone or something that is better than others in some way. ❑ *He is a player with exceptional ability.*
  ● **ex|cep|tion|al|ly ADV** ❑ *She's an exceptionally talented dancer.* [from Old French]

ex|cess (**excesses**)

> **PRONUNCIATION HELP**
> Pronounce the noun /ɪksɛs/ or /ɛksɛs/.
> Pronounce the adjective /ɛksɛs/.

  1 N-COUNT/N-NONCOUNT An **excess of** something is a larger amount than is needed or usual. ❑ *...the problems created by an excess of wealth.*
  2 ADJ Excess is also an adjective. ❑ *After cooking the fish, pour off any excess fat.* [from Latin]

ex|ces|sive /ɪksɛsɪv/ **ADJ** If the amount or level of something is **excessive**, it is more than is necessary. ❑ *Their spending on clothes is excessive.* [from Latin]

ex|change /ɪkstʃeɪndʒ/ (**exchanges, exchanging, exchanged**)
  1 V-T/V-I If two or more people **exchange** things, they give them to each other at the same time. ❑ *We exchanged addresses.* ❑ *The two men exchanged glances.*
  2 N-COUNT Exchange is also a noun. ❑ *There will be a meal, followed by the exchange of gifts.*
  3 V-T If you **exchange** something, you take it back to a store and get a different thing. ❑ *If you are unhappy with the product, we will exchange it.*
  4 → see also **foreign exchange, stock exchange**
  5 PHRASE If you do or give something **in exchange for** something else, you do it or give it in order to get that thing. ❑ *It is illegal* for public officials to receive money in exchange for favors. [from Vulgar Latin]

Word Partnership   Use **exchange** with :

N	**currency** exchange, exchange **gifts**, exchange **greetings** **1**
ADJ	**cultural** exchange **1**

ex|change rate (**exchange rates**) **N-COUNT** The **exchange rate** of one country's money is the amount of another country's money that you can buy with it. ❑ *The exchange rate is around 3.7 pesos to the dollar.*

ex|cite /ɪksaɪt/ (**excites, exciting, excited**)
  1 V-T If something **excites** you, it makes you feel very happy or enthusiastic. ❑ *Scientists are excited by the discovery of a new type of whale.* [from Latin]
  2 → see also **exciting**

ex|cit|ed /ɪksaɪtɪd/ **ADJ** If you are **excited**, you are very happy or enthusiastic. ❑ *I was excited about playing football again.* [from Latin]

ex|cite|ment /ɪksaɪtmənt/ **N-NONCOUNT Excitement** is the feeling you have when you are excited. ❑ *He shouted with excitement.* [from Latin]

ex|cit|ing /ɪksaɪtɪŋ/
  1 ADJ If something is **exciting**, it makes you feel very happy or enthusiastic. ❑ *The movie is exciting, and also very scary.* [from Latin]
  2 → see also **excite**

Word Link   *claim, clam ≈ shouting : ac*claim, *clam*or, ex*claim*

ex|claim /ɪkskleɪm/ (**exclaims, exclaiming, exclaimed**) **V-T LANGUAGE ARTS** Writers sometimes use **exclaim** to show that someone is speaking suddenly or loudly, often because they are excited, shocked, or angry. ❑ *"There!" Jackson exclaimed delightedly.* [from Latin]

ex|cla|ma|tion /ɛkskləmeɪʃᵊn/ (**exclamations**) **N-COUNT** An **exclamation** is something that you say suddenly and loudly, showing that you are excited or angry. ❑ *Sue gave an exclamation when she saw the house.* [from Latin]

ex|cla|ma|tion point (**exclamation points**) or **exclamation mark N-COUNT LANGUAGE ARTS** An **exclamation point** is the punctuation mark ! that is used in writing to show that a word or a sentence is an exclamation.
  → look at Picture Dictionary: **punctuation**

ex|cla|ma|tory /ɪksklæmətɔri/ **ADJ**
An **exclamatory** sentence is a sentence that
is spoken suddenly or loudly, for example
"We won!" [from Latin]

ex|clude /ɪksklud/ (**excludes, excluding,
excluded**)
■ **V-T** If you **exclude** someone **from** a place
or an activity, you prevent them from
entering it or doing it. ❑ *The public was
excluded from both meetings.*
■ **V-T** If you **exclude** something, you
deliberately do not use it or consider it.
❑ *The price excludes taxes.* [from Latin]

ex|clu|sive /ɪksklusɪv/ **ADJ** Something that
is **exclusive** is available only to people who
are rich or powerful. ❑ *It was a private, exclusive
club.* [from Latin]

ex|clu|sive|ly /ɪksklusɪvli/ **ADV** Exclusively
is used for talking about situations that
involve only the place or thing mentioned,
and nothing else. ❑ *This perfume is available
exclusively from selected David Jones stores.* [from
Latin]

Word Link *curr, curs ≈ running, flowing :*
current, curriculum, excursion

ex|cur|sion /ɪkskɜrʒən/ (**excursions**)
N-COUNT An **excursion** is a short trip,
especially one taken for pleasure. ❑ *Sam's
father took him on an excursion.* [from Latin]

ex|cuse (**excuses, excusing, excused**)

PRONUNCIATION HELP
Pronounce the noun /ɪkskyus/. Pronounce
the verb /ɪkskyuz/.

■ **N-COUNT** An **excuse** is a reason that you
give in order to explain why you did
something. ❑ *They are trying to find excuses for
their failure.*
■ **V-T** If you **excuse** someone **for** doing
something, you forgive them for it. ❑ *I'm not
excusing him for what he did.*
■ **V-T** To **excuse** someone or to **excuse** their
behavior means to give reasons for their
actions. ❑ *He excused himself by saying that his
English was not good enough.*
■ **V-T** If someone **is excused from** a duty,
they do not have to do it. ❑ *She is usually
excused from her duties during summer vacation.*
■ **PHRASE** You say **Excuse me** when you
want to politely get someone's attention.
❑ *Excuse me, but are you Mr. Hess?*
■ **PHRASE** You say **Excuse me** when you
want to say you are sorry for doing

something. ❑ *Oh, excuse me, I didn't know you
were busy.* [from Latin]

Thesaurus excuse Also look up :
N   apology, explanation, reason ■
V   forgive, pardon, spare; (*ant.*) accuse,
     blame, punish ■

ex|ecute /ɛksɪkyut/ (**executes, executing,
executed**)
■ **V-T** To **execute** someone means to kill
them as a punishment. ❑ *These soldiers were
executed by the army in World War I.*
● **ex|ecu|tion** /ɛksɪkyuʃən/ (**executions**)
N-COUNT/N-NONCOUNT ❑ *He wrote the story
a week before his execution for murder.*
■ **V-T** If you **execute** a difficult action or
movement, you successfully perform it.
❑ *The landing was skillfully executed.* [from
Old French]

ex|ecu|tive /ɪgzɛkyətɪv/ (**executives**)
N-COUNT An **executive** is someone who
has an important job at a company.
❑ *She loved her job as an advertising executive.*
[from Old French]

exec|utive branch **N-SING** SOCIAL STUDIES
The **executive branch** of a government is all
the people and departments that run the
country. ❑ *The president is the head of the
executive branch of our government.*

ex|em|pli|fy /ɪgzɛmplɪfaɪ/ (**exemplifies,
exemplifying, exemplified**) **V-T** If a person or
a thing **exemplifies** something, they are a
typical example of it. [FORMAL] ❑ *The room's
style exemplifies their ideal of "beauty and
practicality."* [from Old French]

ex|empt /ɪgzɛmpt/ **ADJ** If someone is
exempt from a rule or a duty, they do not
have to obey it or perform it. ❑ *Men in college
were exempt from military service.* [from Latin]

ex|er|cise /ɛksərsaɪz/ (**exercises, exercising,
exercised**)
■ **N-PLURAL** SPORTS **Exercises** are a series of
movements that you do in order to stay
healthy and strong. ❑ *I do special neck and
shoulder exercises every morning.*
■ **N-COUNT** An **exercise** is an activity that
you do in order to practice a skill. ❑ *Dennis
said that the writing exercise was very useful.*
■ **V-I** SPORTS When you **exercise**, you move
your body in order to stay healthy and
strong. ❑ *You should exercise at least two or
three times a week.*

e

E

4 **N-NONCOUNT** SPORTS **Exercise** is also a noun. ❑ *Lack of exercise can cause sleep problems.*
5 **V-T** If you **exercise** your authority or your rights, you use it or put it into effect. [FORMAL] ❑ *They are merely exercising their right to free speech.* [from Old French]
→ look at Word Web: **muscle**

ex|ert /ɪgzɜrt/ (**exerts, exerting, exerted**)
1 **V-T** If someone or something **exerts** influence or pressure, they use their influence or put pressure on someone else in order to produce a particular effect. [FORMAL] ❑ *Parents exert a huge influence over their children when it comes to diet and exercise.*
2 **V-T** If you **exert yourself**, you make a physical or mental effort to do something. ❑ *Do not exert yourself unnecessarily.* ● **ex|er|tion** **N-NONCOUNT** ❑ *...the stress of physical exertion.* [from Latin]
→ look at Word Web: **motion**

ex|hale /ɛksheɪl/ (**exhales, exhaling, exhaled**)
V-I When you **exhale**, you breathe air out of your body. [FORMAL] ❑ *Hold your breath for a moment and then exhale.* [from Latin]
→ look at Word Web: **respiratory system**

ex|haust /ɪgzɔst/ (**exhausts, exhausting, exhausted**)
1 **V-T** If something **exhausts** you, it makes you very tired. ❑ *We were worried that the trip would exhaust him.* ● **ex|haust|ed** **ADJ** ❑ *She was too exhausted to talk.* ● **ex|haust|ing** **ADJ** ❑ *It was an exhausting climb to the top of the hill.* ● **ex|haus|tion** /ɪgzɔstʃ°n/ **N-NONCOUNT** ❑ *He fainted from exhaustion.*
2 **N-NONCOUNT** **Exhaust** is the gas or steam that the engine of a vehicle produces. ❑ *The vehicle's exhaust fumes began to fill the yard.* [from Latin]
→ look at Word Webs: **engine, pollution**

ex|hib|it /ɪgzɪbɪt/ (**exhibits, exhibiting, exhibited**)
1 **V-T** ARTS When an object **is exhibited**, it is put in a public place such as a museum so that people can come to look at it. ❑ *The paintings were exhibited in Paris in 1874.*
2 **N-COUNT** ARTS An **exhibit** is an object of interest that is displayed to the public in a museum or an art gallery. ❑ *Shona showed me some of the exhibits.*
3 **N-COUNT** ARTS An **exhibit** is a public display of art or interesting objects. ❑ *These objects are part of an exhibit at the Museum of Modern Art.*

4 **V-T** To **exhibit** a quality, a feeling, or a behavior means to show it. [FORMAL] ❑ *He exhibited symptoms of anxiety.* [from Latin]

ex|hi|bi|tion /ɛksɪbɪʃ°n/ (**exhibitions**)
N-COUNT ARTS An **exhibition** is a public event where art or interesting objects are shown. ❑ *The Museum of the City of New York has an exhibition of photographs.* [from Latin]

ex|ile /ɛksaɪl, ɛgz-/ (**exiles, exiling, exiled**)
1 **V-T** SOCIAL STUDIES If someone **is exiled**, they are living in a foreign country because they cannot live in their own country, usually for political reasons. ❑ *His wife, Hilary, was exiled from South Africa.* ❑ *They threatened to exile her in southern Spain.*
2 **N-NONCOUNT** SOCIAL STUDIES **Exile** is also a noun. ❑ *He is now living in exile in Egypt.* ❑ *He returned from exile earlier this year.*
3 **N-COUNT** SOCIAL STUDIES An **exile** is someone who has been exiled. ❑ *He is an exile who has given up the idea of going home.* [from Latin]

Word Partnership	Use **exile** with :
V	**force into** exile, **go into** exile, **live in** exile, **return from** exile, **send into** exile **1**
ADJ	**political** exile **1** **2**

ex|ist /ɪgzɪst/ (**exists, existing, existed**) **V-I**
If something **exists**, it is a real thing or situation. ❑ *It is clear that a serious problem exists.* [from Latin]

ex|ist|ence /ɪgzɪstəns/ **N-NONCOUNT** The **existence** of something is the fact that it is a real thing or situation. ❑ *We can understand the existence of stars and planets.* ❑ *The club is still in existence.* [from Latin]

Word Partnership	Use **existence** with :
V	**come into** existence, **deny the** existence
ADJ	**continued** existence, **daily** existence, **everyday** existence

ex|ist|ing /ɪgzɪstɪŋ/ **ADJ** **Existing** describes something that is in this world or available now. ❑ *There is a need to improve existing products.* [from Latin]

Word Link	ex ≈ away, from, out : exceed, exit, explode

exit /ɛgzɪt, ɛksɪt/ (**exits, exiting, exited**)
1 **N-COUNT** The **exit** is the door that you use to leave a public building. ❑ *He walked toward the exit.*
2 **N-COUNT** An **exit** on a highway is a place

where cars can leave it. ❏ *She continued to the next exit.*

3 **v-t** If you **exit** a place, you leave it. ❏ *Exit the freeway at 128th Street Southwest.*

4 **v-t** TECHNOLOGY If you **exit** a computer program, you stop running it. ❏ *Do you want to exit this program?* [from Latin]

exo|cy|to|sis /ɛksoʊsaɪtoʊsɪs/ **N-NONCOUNT** SCIENCE **Exocytosis** is a process in which a cell releases material from inside itself by sending the material to the surface of the cell. Compare with **endocytosis.**

exo|skel|eton /ɛksoʊskɛlɪtⁿn/ (**exoskeletons**) **N-COUNT** SCIENCE Animals with an **exoskeleton** have their skeleton on the outside of their body, like insects.

exo|sphere /ɛksəsfɪər/ **N-SING** SCIENCE The **exosphere** is the highest layer of the Earth's atmosphere.

exo|ther|mic /ɛksoʊθɜrmɪk/ **ADJ** SCIENCE An **exothermic** chemical reaction or process is one that releases heat.

ex|ot|ic /ɪgzɒtɪk/ **ADJ** Something that is **exotic** is unusual and interesting, usually because it comes from another country. ❏ *The house has a garden with exotic plants.* [from Latin]

ex|pand /ɪkspænd/ (**expands, expanding, expanded**) **v-t/v-i** If something **expands** or is **expanded**, it becomes larger. ❏ *The industry expanded in the 19th century.* ❏ *We want to expand children's knowledge of the world.* ● **ex|pan|sion** /ɪkspænʃⁿn/ (**expansions**) **N-COUNT/N-NONCOUNT** ❏ *Local people are against the expansion of the airport.* [from Latin]

ex|pand|ed form (**expanded forms**) **N-COUNT** SCIENCE In mathematics, the **expanded form** of an expression is a version of the expression that is written in full, for example without any brackets.

ex|pect /ɪkspɛkt/ (**expects, expecting, expected**)

1 **v-t** If you **expect** something **to** happen, you believe that it will happen. ❏ *He expects to lose his job.* ❏ *We expect the price of bananas to rise.*

2 **v-t** If you **are expecting** something or someone, you believe that they will arrive soon. ❏ *I wasn't expecting a visitor.*

3 **v-t** If you **expect** a person **to** do something, you believe that it is the person's duty to do it. ❏ *I expect you to help around the house.*

4 **v-t/v-i** If a woman **is expecting** a baby, she has a baby growing inside her. ❏ *She announced that she was expecting another child.* ❏ *I hear Dawn's expecting.* [from Latin]

ex|pec|ta|tion /ɛkspɛkteɪʃⁿn/ (**expectations**) **N-COUNT** A person's **expectations** are beliefs they have about how something should happen. ❏ *Young people have high expectations for the future.* [from Latin]

ex|pedi|tion /ɛkspɪdɪʃⁿn/ (**expeditions**) **N-COUNT** An **expedition** is an organized trip made for a particular purpose such as exploration. ❏ *...an expedition to Antarctica.* [from Latin]

> **Word Link** *pel* ≈ *driving, forcing : compel, expel, propel*

ex|pel /ɪkspɛl/ (**expels, expelling, expelled**)

1 **v-t** If someone **is expelled from** a school or an organization, they are officially told to leave. ❏ *Two students were expelled for cheating.*

2 **v-t** If people **are expelled from** a place, they are forced to leave it. ❏ *An American was expelled from the country yesterday.* [from Latin]

ex|pendi|ture /ɪkspɛndɪtʃər/ (**expenditures**) **N-COUNT/N-NONCOUNT** **Expenditure** is the spending of money on something, or the money that is spent on something. [FORMAL] ❏ *The total expenditure of the administration was $11.4 billion.* [from Latin]

ex|pense /ɪkspɛns/ (**expenses**)

1 **N-COUNT/N-NONCOUNT** **Expense** is the cost or price of something. ❏ *He bought a big television at great expense.*

2 **N-PLURAL** **Expenses** are amounts of money that you spend on things. ❏ *Her hotel expenses were paid by the company.* [from Late Latin]

ex|pen|sive /ɪkspɛnsɪv/ **ADJ** If something is **expensive**, it costs a lot of money. ❏ *People thought that healthy food was more expensive than fast food.* [from Late Latin]

> **Thesaurus** expensive Also look up :
> ADJ   costly, pricey, upscale; (ant.) cheap, economical, inexpensive

ex|peri|ence /ɪkspɪəriəns/ (**experiences, experiencing, experienced**)

1 **N-NONCOUNT** **Experience** is knowledge or skill in a job or an activity that you have done for a long time. ❏ *No teaching experience*

e

E

is necessary. ● **ex|pe|ri|enced** **ADJ** ❑ *He is an experienced pilot.*

2 **N-NONCOUNT** **Experience** is the past events, knowledge, and feelings that make up your life or character. ❑ *Experience has taught me caution.*

3 **N-COUNT** An **experience** is something important that happens to you. ❑ *What has been your most enjoyable experience?*

4 **V-T** If you **experience** something, it happens to you. ❑ *I have never experienced true love.* [from Latin]

Thesaurus	**experience** Also look up :
N	know-how, knowledge, wisdom; *(ant.)* inexperience **1**

Word Partnership	Use **experience** with :
ADJ	**professional** experience **1**
	valuable experience **1**–**3**
	past experience, **shared** experience **2** **3**
	learning experience, **religious** experience, **traumatic** experience **3**
N	**work** experience **1**
	life experience **2**
	experience **a loss**, experience **symptoms** **4**

ex|peri|ment (**experiments, experimenting, experimented**)

PRONUNCIATION HELP
Pronounce the noun /ɪkspɛ́rɪmənt/. Pronounce the verb /ɪkspɛ́rɪmɛnt/.

1 **N-COUNT/N-NONCOUNT** SCIENCE An **experiment** is a scientific test that you do in order to discover what happens to something. ❑ *Laboratory experiments show that vitamin D slows cancer growth.*

2 **V-I** SCIENCE If you **experiment with** something or **experiment on** it, you do a scientific test on it. ❑ *The scientists have experimented on mice.*

3 **N-COUNT/N-NONCOUNT** An **experiment** is when you test a new idea or method. ❑ *They started the magazine as an experiment.*

4 **V-I** To **experiment** means to test a new idea or method. ❑ *I like cooking, and I have the time to experiment.* [from Latin]

→ look at Word Webs: **experiment, laboratory, science**

Word Partnership	Use **experiment** with :
V	**conduct an** experiment **1**
	perform an experiment, **try an** experiment **1** **3**
ADJ	**scientific** experiment **1**
	simple experiment **1** **3**

ex|peri|men|tal /ɪkspɛrɪmɛntᵊl/ **ADJ** Something that is **experimental** is new, or uses new ideas or methods. ❑ *...an experimental musician.* [from Latin]

ex|peri|men|tal de|sign (**experimental designs**) **N-COUNT/N-NONCOUNT** SCIENCE Research that has an **experimental design** involves carrying out scientific experiments.

ex|pert /ɛ́kspɜrt/ (**experts**)

1 **N-COUNT** An **expert** is a person who knows a lot about a particular subject. ❑ *His brother is a computer expert.*

2 **ADJ** **Expert** is also an adjective. ❑ *...an expert gardener.* [from Latin]

Word Partnership	Use **expert** with :
ADJ	**leading** expert **1**
N	expert **advice**, expert **opinion**, expert **witness** **2**

ex|per|tise /ɛ́kspɜrtíz/ **N-NONCOUNT** **Expertise** is special skill or knowledge. ❑ *We're looking for someone with expertise in foreign languages.* [from French]

ex|pire /ɪkspáɪər/ (**expires, expiring, expired**) **V-I** When a document **expires**, it cannot be

---

Word Web   **experiment**

Scientists learn much of what they know through **controlled experiments**. The **scientific method** provides a dependable way to understand natural **phenomena**. The first step in any experiment is **observation**. During this stage researchers examine the situation and ask a question about it. They may also read what others have discovered about it. Next, they state a **hypothesis**. Then they use the hypothesis to design an experiment and **predict** what will happen. Next comes the **testing** phase. Often researchers do several experiments using different **variables**. If all of the **evidence** supports the hypothesis, it becomes a new **theory**.

used any more. ❑ *My contract expires in July.* [from Old French]

ex|plain /ɪkspl<u>eɪ</u>n/ (**explains, explaining, explained**)

1 **V-T/V-I** If you **explain** something to someone, you describe it so that they can understand it. ❑ *He explained the law in simple language.* ❑ *Don't worry, you don't need to explain.*
2 **V-T/V-I** If you **explain** something that happened, you give reasons for it. ❑ *She left a note explaining her actions.* ❑ *Can you explain why you didn't telephone?* [from Latin]

ex|pla|na|tion /<u>ɛ</u>ksplən<u>eɪ</u>ʃ°n/ (**explanations**) **N-COUNT** An **explanation** is information that you give someone to help them to understand something. ❑ *There was no explanation for the car accident.* [from Latin]

Word Partnership	Use **explanation** with :
ADJ	**brief** explanation, **detailed** explanation, **logical** explanation, **only** explanation, **possible** explanation
V	**give an** explanation, **offer an** explanation, **provide** explanation

ex|plic|it /ɪkspl<u>ɪ</u>sɪt/ **ADJ** Something that is **explicit** is expressed or shown clearly, without hiding anything. ❑ *Many parents worry about explicit violence on television.* [from Latin]

Word Link	ex ≈ away, from, out : ex*ceed*, ex*it*, ex*plode*

ex|plode /ɪkspl<u>oʊ</u>d/ (**explodes, exploding, exploded**) **V-T/V-I** If an object such as a bomb **explodes**, it bursts with great force. ❑ *A second bomb exploded in the capital yesterday.* ❑ *...gunfire which exploded the fuel tank.* [from Latin]
→ look at Word Web: **fireworks**

Thesaurus	explode Also look up :
V	blow up, erupt, go off

Word Partnership	Use **explode** with :
N	**bombs** explode, **missiles** explode
ADJ	**about to** explode, **ready to** explode

ex|ploit /ɪkspl<u>ɔɪ</u>t/ (**exploits, exploiting, exploited**)

1 **V-T** If someone **exploits** you, they treat you unfairly by using your work or ideas. ❑ *They said that he exploited other musicians.*
2 **V-T** To **exploit** a situation means to use it to get an advantage for yourself. ❑ *They*

exploit the troubles to their advantage.
3 **V-T** To **exploit** resources means to develop them and use them for industry. ❑ *We're being very short-sighted in not exploiting our own coal.* ● **ex|ploi|ta|tion** **N-NONCOUNT** ❑ *...the exploitation of oil and natural gas reserves.* [from Old French]

ex|plore /ɪkspl<u>ɔ</u>r/ (**explores, exploring, explored**)

1 **V-T/V-I** If you **explore**, or **explore** a place, you travel around it to find out what it is like. ❑ *The best way to explore the area is in a boat.* ❑ *I just wanted to explore on my own.* ● **ex|plo|ra|tion** /<u>ɛ</u>ksplər<u>eɪ</u>ʃ°n/ (**explorations**) **N-COUNT/N-NONCOUNT** ❑ *He led the first English exploration of North America.* ● **ex|plor|er** (**explorers**) **N-COUNT** ❑ *Who was the US explorer who discovered the Titanic shipwreck?*
2 **V-T** If you **explore** an idea, you carefully think about or discuss it. ❑ *The movie explores the relationship between artist and model.* [from Latin]

ex|plo|sion /ɪkspl<u>oʊ</u>ʒ°n/ (**explosions**) **N-COUNT** An **explosion** is when something suddenly bursts with a loud sound. ❑ *Six soldiers were injured in the explosion.* [from Latin]

ex|plo|sive /ɪkspl<u>oʊ</u>sɪv/ (**explosives**)

1 **N-COUNT/N-NONCOUNT** An **explosive** is a substance or an object that can cause an explosion. ❑ *The 400 pounds of explosives were packaged in yellow bags.*
2 **ADJ** **Explosive** is also an adjective. ❑ *No explosive device was found.* [from Latin]
→ look at Word Web: **tunnel**

ex|po|nent /ɪksp<u>oʊ</u>nənt/ (**exponents**)

1 **N-COUNT** An **exponent of** an idea, a theory, or a plan is a person who supports and explains it. [FORMAL] ❑ *...an exponent of free speech.*
2 **N-COUNT** An **exponent of** a particular skill or activity is a person who is good at it. ❑ *...a leading exponent of modern dance.*
3 **N-COUNT** MATH An **exponent** is a number that indicates how many times a particular quantity should be multiplied by itself. For example, the exponent of 2^3 is 3. [from Latin]

ex|po|nen|tial func|tion /<u>ɛ</u>kspən<u>ɛ</u>nʃ°l f<u>ʌ</u>ŋkʃ°n/ (**exponential functions**) **N-COUNT** MATH An **exponential function** is a mathematical calculation that is used to study processes that increase at a constant rate, such as population growth or compound interest.

> **Word Link** *port ≈ carrying : ex*port*, im*port*, port*able*

ex|port (exports, exporting, exported)

> **PRONUNCIATION HELP**
> Pronounce the verb /ɪkspɔrt/. Pronounce the noun /ɛksport/.

1 **V-T/V-I** SOCIAL STUDIES To **export** products means to sell them to another country. ❑ *They also export beef.* ❑ *The company now exports to Japan.* ● **ex|port|er** /ɛksportər, ɪksportər/ (exporters) **N-COUNT** ❑ *Brazil is a big exporter of coffee.*
2 **N-NONCOUNT** SOCIAL STUDIES **Export** is also a noun. ❑ *A lot of our land is used for growing crops for export.*
3 **N-COUNT** **Exports** are goods that one country sells to another country. ❑ *Spain's main export is oil.* [from Latin]

ex|pose /ɪkspouz/ (exposes, exposing, exposed)

1 **V-T** To **expose** something means to show it so that people can see it. ❑ *Vitamin D is made when the skin is exposed to sunlight.*
2 **V-T** To **expose** a person or a situation means to reveal the truth about them. ❑ *Officials exposed him as a fake.*
3 **V-T** If someone **is exposed to** something unpleasant, they are in a situation in which it might affect them. ❑ *They have not been exposed to these diseases.* [from Old French]

ex|po|si|tion /ɛkspəzɪʃⁿn/ (expositions)
1 **N-COUNT** An **exposition of** an idea or a theory is a detailed explanation or account of it. [FORMAL] ❑ *...a clear exposition of the problem.*
2 **N-COUNT/N-NONCOUNT** LANGUAGE ARTS In a story or a play, the **exposition** is the part, usually near the beginning, where important information about the characters and the situation is given. [from Latin]

ex|po|sure /ɪkspouʒər/ (exposures)
1 **N-NONCOUNT** **Exposure to** something dangerous means being in a situation where it might affect you. ❑ *Exposure to the sun can damage your skin.*
2 **N-NONCOUNT** **Exposure** is the harmful effect on your body caused by very cold weather. ❑ *He was suffering from exposure and shock.*

3 **N-NONCOUNT** The **exposure** of a well-known person is the revealing of the fact that they are bad or immoral in some way. ❑ *...his exposure as a spy.*
4 **N-NONCOUNT** **Exposure** is publicity that a person, a company, or a product receives. ❑ *All the candidates have been getting an enormous amount of exposure on television.*
5 **N-COUNT** In photography, an **exposure** is a single photograph. [from Old French]

ex|press /ɪksprɛs/ (expresses, expressing, expressed)
1 **V-T** When you **express** an idea or a feeling, you show what you think or feel. ❑ *Only one company expressed an interest in his plan.*
2 **ADJ** You use an **express** service when you want to send or receive things faster than usual. ❑ *An express mail service is available.*
3 **N-COUNT** An **express** or an **express train** is a fast train that stops at only a few stations. ❑ *The express to Kuala Lumpur has just left Singapore station.* [from Latin]

> **Word Partnership** Use **express** with :
>
> N express **appreciation**, express **your emotions**, express **gratitude**, express **sympathy**, **words to** express **something** **1**
> express **mail**, express **service** **2**

ex|pres|sion /ɪksprɛʃⁿn/ (expressions)
1 **N-COUNT/N-NONCOUNT** The **expression of** ideas or feelings is the act of showing them through words or actions. ❑ *Your baby's smiles are expressions of happiness.* ❑ *...the rights of the individual to freedom of expression.*
2 **N-COUNT/N-NONCOUNT** Your **expression** is the way that your face looks at a particular moment. ❑ *There was an expression of sadness on his face.*
3 **N-COUNT** An **expression** is a word or a phrase. ❑ *Try to learn a few words and expressions in the language.* [from Latin]

ex|pres|sive /ɪksprɛsɪv/ **ADJ** Something that is **expressive** clearly shows a person's feelings. ❑ *He has a very expressive little face, so you always know what he's thinking.* [from Latin]

ex|pres|sive con|tent **N-NONCOUNT** LANGUAGE ARTS **Expressive content** is writing, speech, or another form of communication which expresses someone's feelings about a particular subject.

ex|pres|sive writ|ing N-NONCOUNT
LANGUAGE ARTS **Expressive writing** is writing
such as diaries and letters that describes the
writer's feelings, ideas, or beliefs.

ex|press|way /ɪksprɛsweɪ/ (**expressways**)
N-COUNT An **expressway** is a wide road that
allows cars to travel very fast over a long
distance. ❑ *The E11 expressway connects Paris and
Barcelona.*

> **Word Link** *puls ≈ driving, pushing : compulsion,*
> *expulsion, impulse*

ex|pul|sion /ɪkspʌlʃⁿn/ (**expulsions**)
1 N-COUNT/N-NONCOUNT **Expulsion** is
when someone is forced to leave a school,
a university, or an organization. ❑ *...her
expulsion from high school.*
2 N-COUNT/N-NONCOUNT **Expulsion** is when
someone is forced to leave a place. [FORMAL]
❑ *...the expulsion of foreign workers.* [from Latin]

ex|quis|ite /ɪkskwɪzɪt, ɛkskwɪzɪt/ ADJ
Exquisite means extremely beautiful.
❑ *The Indians brought in exquisite things to sell.*
● **ex|quis|ite|ly** ADV ❑ *...exquisitely made
dollhouses.* [from Latin]

ex|tend /ɪkstɛnd/ (**extends, extending,
extended**)
1 V-T If you **extend** something, you make it
longer or bigger. ❑ *These treatments have
extended the lives of people with cancer.*
2 V-I If you say that something **extends**
for a particular distance, you are giving
its size. ❑ *The caves extend for 12 miles.*
[from Latin]

ex|ten|sion /ɪkstɛnʃⁿn/ (**extensions**)
1 N-COUNT An **extension** is an extra period
of time for which something lasts. ❑ *He was
given a six-month extension to his visa.*
2 N-COUNT An **extension** is a part that is
added to something to make it longer or
bigger. ❑ *They built an extension to the house.*
3 N-COUNT An **extension** is a telephone that
connects to the main telephone line in a
building. ❑ *She can talk to me on extension 308.*
[from Late Latin]

ex|ten|sive /ɪkstɛnsɪv/
1 ADJ If something is **extensive**, it covers a
wide area. ❑ *It is a four-bedroom house with
extensive gardens.*
2 ADJ Something that is **extensive** covers
a wide range of details, ideas, or items.
❑ *She recently completed an extensive study of
elected officials.* [from Late Latin]

ex|ten|sor /ɪkstɛnsər/ (**extensors**) N-COUNT
SCIENCE **Extensors** are muscles that extend
or straighten a part of your body. [from
New Latin]

ex|tent /ɪkstɛnt/
1 N-SING When you talk about **the extent
of** a situation, you are talking about how
important or serious it is. ❑ *The government
has information on the extent of industrial pollution.*
❑ *He soon discovered the extent of the damage.*
2 N-SING **The extent of** something is its
length, area, or size. ❑ *Their commitment was
to maintain the extent of forests.*
3 PHRASE You use expressions such as **to a
large extent** or **to some extent** in order to say
how far something is true. ❑ *To some extent
this was the truth.* [from Old French]

> **Word Partnership** Use **extent** with :
>
> | N | **extent of the damage** 1 |
> |---|---|
> | V | **determine the** extent, **know the** extent 1 |
> | ADJ | **lesser** extent 1 |
> | | **full** extent 1 2 |
> | | **a certain** extent 3 |

ex|te|ri|or /ɪkstɪəriər/ (**exteriors**)
1 N-COUNT The **exterior** of something is its
outside surface. ❑ *They are going to paint the
exterior of the building.*
2 ADJ You use **exterior** to talk about the
outside parts of something. ❑ *...exterior walls.*
[from Latin]

> **Thesaurus** exterior Also look up :
>
> | N | coating, cover, shell, skin 1 |
> |---|---|
> | ADJ | external, outer, surface 2 |

ex|ter|mi|nate /ɪkstɜrmɪneɪt/
(**exterminates, exterminating,
exterminated**) V-T To **exterminate** a group
of people or animals means to kill all of
them. ❑ *A huge effort was made to exterminate
the rats.* ● **ex|ter|mi|na|tion** /ɪkstɜrmɪneɪʃⁿn/
N-NONCOUNT ❑ *...the extermination of wild dogs.*
[from Latin]

ex|ter|nal /ɪkstɜrnⁿl/ ADJ Something that is
external happens or exists outside a place, a
person, or an area. ❑ *You lose a lot of heat
through external walls.* [from Latin]

ex|ter|nal com|bus|tion en|gine
(**external combustion engines**) N-COUNT
SCIENCE An **external combustion engine** is
an engine that burns fuel outside the
engine.

e

ex|ter|nal fer|ti|li|za|tion **N-NONCOUNT**
SCIENCE **External fertilization** is a method of
reproduction in some animals in which the
egg and sperm join together outside the
female's body, for example in water.
Compare with **internal fertilization**.

ex|ter|nal fuel tank (**external fuel tanks**)
N-COUNT SCIENCE An **external fuel tank** is a
container for fuel that is fitted to the
outside of a spacecraft.

ex|tinct /ɪkstɪŋkt/ **ADJ** SCIENCE A type of
animal or plant that is **extinct** does not exist
any more. ❑ *Many animals could become extinct
in less than 10 years.* [from Latin]

ex|tinc|tion /ɪkstɪŋkʃⁿn/ **N-NONCOUNT**
The **extinction** of a species of animal or
plant is the death of all its living members.
❑ *We are trying to save these animals from
extinction.* [from Latin]

ex|tin|guish /ɪkstɪŋgwɪʃ/ (**extinguishes,
extinguishing, extinguished**) **V-T** If you
extinguish a fire, you stop it from burning.
[FORMAL] ❑ *It took about 50 minutes to extinguish
the fire.* [from Latin]

ex|tol /ɪkstoʊl/ (**extols, extolling, extolled**)
also **extoll** **V-T** If you **extol** something, you
praise it enthusiastically. ❑ *The book extols the
joys of living in the country.* [from Latin]

ex|tra /ɛkstrə/ (**extras**)
1 **ADJ** An **extra** person, thing, or amount is
another one or amount that is added.
❑ *He used the extra time to check his work.*
2 **ADV** **Extra** is also an adverb. ❑ *You may be
charged $10 extra for this service.*
3 **PRON** **Extra** is also a pronoun. ❑ *She won't
pay any extra.*
4 **N-COUNT** **Extras** are things that are not
necessary, but that make something more
comfortable, useful, or enjoyable. ❑ *Optional
extras include cooking classes.*

Word Link	extra ≈ outside of : extract, extradite,
	extraordinary

ex|tract (**extracts, extracting, extracted**)

> **PRONUNCIATION HELP**
> Pronounce the verb /ɪkstrækt/. Pronounce
> the noun /ɛkstrækt/.

1 **V-T** If you **extract** something, you take it
out or pull it out. ❑ *A dentist may decide to
extract the tooth.*
2 **N-COUNT** An **extract from** a piece of
writing is a small part of it that is printed

separately. ❑ *Read this extract from an
information booklet.* [from Latin]
→ look at Word Web: **industry**

ex|tra|dite /ɛkstrədaɪt/ (**extradites,
extraditing, extradited**) **V-T** If someone **is
extradited**, they are officially sent back to
their own or another country or state to be
tried for a crime. [FORMAL] ❑ *A judge agreed to
extradite him to Texas.* ● **ex|tra|di|tion**
/ɛkstrədɪʃⁿn/ (**extraditions**) **N-COUNT/
N-NONCOUNT** ❑ *A New York court turned down
the British government's request for his extradition.*

extraor|di|nary /ɪkstrɔrdⁿnɛri/
1 **ADJ** If something or someone is
extraordinary, they have an extremely
good or special quality. ❑ *He's an
extraordinary musician.*
2 **ADJ** If something is **extraordinary**, it is
very unusual or surprising. ❑ *An extraordinary
thing just happened.* [from Latin]

ex|trava|gant /ɪkstrævəgənt/
1 **ADJ** Someone who is **extravagant** spends
too much money. ❑ *He was extravagant in all
things—his clothing and his partying.*
2 **ADJ** Something that is **extravagant**
costs too much money. ❑ *He came home
with extravagant gifts for everyone.*
[from Medieval Latin]

ex|treme /ɪkstrim/
1 **ADJ** **Extreme** means very great in degree.
❑ *You should use any drug with extreme care.*
● **ex|treme|ly** **ADV** ❑ *My cellphone is
extremely useful.*
2 **ADJ** You use **extreme** to describe
situations and behavior that are much more
severe or unusual than you would expect.
❑ *It is hard to imagine Jesse capable of anything
so extreme.*
3 **ADJ** The **extreme** end of something is its
farthest end. ❑ *...the room at the extreme end of
the corridor.* [from Latin]

Word Partnership	Use extreme with :	
N	extreme **caution**, extreme **difficulty** **1**	
	extreme **case**, extreme **left**, extreme **right**, extreme **sports**, extreme **views** **2**	
ADJ	**the opposite** extreme **3**	

ex|trem|ist /ɪkstrimɪst/ (**extremists**)
N-COUNT SOCIAL STUDIES If you describe
someone as an **extremist**, you disapprove of
them because they try to bring about
political change by using violent or extreme
methods. ❑ *...foreign extremists.* ● **ex|trem|ism**

N-NONCOUNT ❑ ...*left and right-wing extremism.*
[from Latin]

ex|tru|sive /ɪkstru̱sɪv/ **ADJ** SCIENCE
Extrusive rock is rock that forms on the
surface of the Earth after lava has been
released and has cooled. Compare with
intrusive. [from Latin]

---

eye
❶ PART OF THE BODY,
    ABILITY TO SEE
❷ PART OF SOMETHING
❸ PHRASES

---

❶ **eye** /a̱ɪ/ (**eyes, eyeing** or **eying, eyed**)
   ◼ **N-COUNT** Your **eyes** are the parts of your
body with which you see. ❑ *I opened my eyes
and looked.* ❑ *Mrs. Brooke was a tall lady with dark
brown eyes.*
   ◼ **V-T** If you **eye** someone or something in a
particular way, you look at them carefully in
that way. ❑ *Sally eyed James with interest.*
   ◼ **N-COUNT** You use **eye** to talk about a
person's abilities or their way of thinking
about things. ❑ *...a man with an eye for quality.*
❑ *Conrad had recovered sufficiently in the eyes of his
doctors.* [from Old English]
   ◼ → see also **black eye**
   → look at Picture Dictionary: **face**
   → look at Word Webs: **eye, cry**

❷ **eye** /a̱ɪ/ (**eyes**)
   ◼ **N-SING** The **eye of** a storm, a tornado, or a
hurricane is the center of it. ❑ *The eye of the
hurricane hit Florida just south of Miami.*
   ◼ **N-COUNT** The **eye** of a needle is the small
hole at one end that the thread passes
through. ❑ *The difficult part was threading the
thread through the eye of the needle.* [from
Old English]
   → look at Word Web: **hurricane**

❸ **eye** /a̱ɪ/ (**eyes**)
   ◼ **PHRASE** If something **catches** your **eye**,
you suddenly notice it. ❑ *A movement*

across the garden caught her eye.
   ◼ **PHRASE** If you **catch** someone's **eye**, you
do something to attract their attention, so
that you can speak to them. ❑ *He tried to catch
Annie's eye.*
   ◼ **PHRASE** If you **have** your **eye on**
something, you want to have it. [INFORMAL]
❑ *I've had my eye on that dress for a while now.*
   ◼ **PHRASE** If you **keep** your **eye on**
something, you watch it or take care of it.
[INFORMAL] ❑ *Keep your eye on the road at all
times.* [from Old English]

eye|ball /a̱ɪbɔl/ (**eyeballs**) **N-COUNT** SCIENCE
Your **eyeballs** are the parts of your eyes that
are like white balls.

eye|brow /a̱ɪbraʊ/ (**eyebrows**) **N-COUNT**
Your **eyebrows** are the lines of hair that
grow above your eyes.
   → look at Picture Dictionary: **face**

eye|glasses /a̱ɪglæsɪz/ **N-PLURAL** **Eyeglasses**
are two glass or plastic lenses in a frame,
that some people wear in front of their eyes
to help them to see better. ❑ *...a pair of
eyeglasses.*

eye|lash /a̱ɪlæʃ/ (**eyelashes**) **N-COUNT**
Your **eyelashes** are the hairs that grow on
the edges of your eyes.
   → look at Picture Dictionary: **face**

eye|lid /a̱ɪlɪd/ (**eyelids**) **N-COUNT** Your
eyelids are the pieces of skin that cover
your eyes when they are closed.
   → look at Picture Dictionary: **face**

eye|piece /a̱ɪpis/ (**eyepieces**) **N-COUNT**
SCIENCE The **eyepiece** of a microscope or
a telescope is the piece of glass at one end,
where you put your eye in order to look
through the instrument.

eye|sight /a̱ɪsaɪt/ **N-NONCOUNT** Your
eyesight is your ability to see. ❑ *He cannot
get a driver's license because he has poor eyesight.*

Word Web   eye

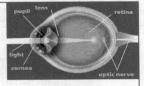

Light enters the eye through the **cornea**. The cornea bends the light and
directs it through the **pupil**. The colored **iris** opens and closes the **retina**.
This helps focus the **image** clearly on the **retina**. Nerve cells in the retina
change the light into electrical signals. The **optic nerve** then carries
these signals to the brain. In a **nearsighted** person the light rays focus in front of the retina. The image
comes into focus in the back of the retina in a **farsighted** person. **Glasses** or **contact lenses** can correct
these problems.

Ff

fa|ble /fˈeɪbəl/ (fables) **N-COUNT/N-NONCOUNT**
LANGUAGE ARTS A **fable** is a type of story,
usually about animals, that teaches a lesson
about human behavior. ❑ *Here is a children's
fable about love and honesty.* [from Latin]

fab|ric /fˈæbrɪk/ (fabrics)
N-COUNT/N-NONCOUNT Fabric is cloth that
you use for making things like clothes and
bags. ❑ *The shirt is made from beautiful soft fabric.*
[from Latin]
→ look at Word Web: **quilt**

fab|ri|cate /fˈæbrɪkeɪt/ (fabricates,
fabricating, fabricated) **V-T** If someone
fabricates information, they invent it in
order to deceive people. ❑ *Jones fabricated
details about his education to get the job.*
● **fab|ri|ca|tion** /fˈæbrɪkeɪʃən/ (fabrications)
N-COUNT/N-NONCOUNT ❑ *She described the
interview as a "complete fabrication."* [from Latin]

Word Link	ous ≈ having the qualities of :
	dangerous, fabulous, poisonous

fabu|lous /fˈæbyələs/ **ADJ** Something that
is **fabulous** is very good. [INFORMAL]
❑ *The apartment offers fabulous views of the city.*
[from Latin]

---
face
❶ NOUN USES AND PHRASES
❷ VERB USES
---

❶ face /fˈeɪs/ (faces)
1 **N-COUNT** Your **face** is the front part of
your head. ❑ *She had a beautiful face.*
2 **N-COUNT** The **face** of something is the
front or a vertical side of it. ❑ *...the south face
of Mount Everest.* ❑ *...a clock face.*
3 **N-NONCOUNT** If you lose **face**, you do
something that makes people respect or
admire you less. ❑ *They don't want a war, but
they don't want to lose face.*
4 **PHRASE** If you are **face to face** with
someone, you can look at them directly.
❑ *I got off the bus and came face to face with
my teacher.*

Picture Dictionary face

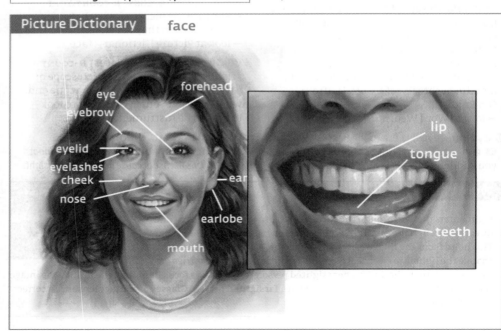

eye
eyebrow
forehead
eyelid
eyelashes
cheek
nose
ear
earlobe
mouth
lip
tongue
teeth

5 **PHRASE** If you **make a face**, you change your face into an ugly expression. ❑ *She made a face at the horrible smell.*

6 **PHRASE** If you manage to keep **a straight face**, you manage to look serious, although you want to laugh. [from Old French]

→ look at Picture Dictionary: **face**
→ look at Word Web: **makeup**

② face /feɪs/ (**faces, facing, faced**)
1 **V-T/V-I** To **face** a particular direction means to look in that direction. ❑ *They faced away from each other.* ❑ *Our house faces south.*
2 **V-T** If you **face** something difficult or unpleasant, you have to deal with it. ❑ *Williams faces life in prison.*
3 **V-T** If you **cannot face** something, you do not feel able to do it because it seems so difficult or unpleasant. ❑ *I can't face telling my girlfriend.* [from Old French]

fac|et /fǽsɪt/ (**facets**) **N-COUNT** A **facet** of something is a single part or aspect of it. ❑ *...every facet of American life.* [from French]

fac|et /fǽsɪt/ (**facets**) **N-COUNT** A **facet** of something is a single part or aspect of it. ❑ *...every facet of American life.* [from French]

face time **N-NONCOUNT** **Face time** is time that you spend talking directly to someone, rather than talking by phone or email. ❑ *I'd love the opportunity to have some face time with you.*

fa|cili|tate /fəsɪlɪteɪt/ (**facilitates, facilitating, facilitated**) **V-T** If you **facilitate** an action, you help it to happen. [FORMAL] ❑ *The discussion will be facilitated by two professional counselors.* [from Latin]

fa|cil|ity /fəsɪlɪti/ (**facilities**)
1 **N-COUNT** **Facilities** are rooms, buildings, or pieces of equipment that are used for a particular purpose. ❑ *The hotel has excellent sports facilities, including a golf course.*
2 **N-COUNT** A **facility** is a useful service or feature provided by an organization or a machine. ❑ *...a website's search facility.* [from Latin]

fac|simi|le /fæksɪmɪli/ (**facsimiles**) **N-COUNT** A **facsimile** of something is a copy or an imitation of it. [FORMAL] ❑ *...a facsimile edition of Beethoven's manuscripts.*

fact /fækt/ (**facts**)
1 **N-COUNT** A **fact** is a piece of information that is true. ❑ *He doesn't hide the fact that he wants to win.*

2 **PHRASE** You use **the fact that** after some verbs or prepositions, such as **despite the fact that**, to link the verb or preposition with a clause. ❑ *My family now accepts the fact that I don't eat sugar or bread.*
3 **PHRASE** You use **in fact** when you are giving more information about something that you have just said. ❑ *I don't watch television; in fact, I no longer own a TV.* [from Latin]

→ look at Word Web: **history**

Word Partnership	Use **fact** with :
V	**accept a** fact, **check the** facts, **face a** fact **1**
N	fact **and fiction 1**
ADJ	**hard** fact, **historical** fact, **important** fact, **obvious** fact, **random** fact, **simple** fact **1**

fac|tion /fǽkʃ°n/ (**factions**) **N-COUNT** A **faction** is an organized group of people within a larger group, that opposes some of the ideas of the larger group and fights for its own ideas. ❑ *...the leaders of the country's warring factions.* ●**fac|tion|al** **ADJ** ❑ *...factional disputes.* [from Latin]

Word Link	*fact, fic ≈ making : artificial, factor, fiction*

fac|tor /fǽktər/ (**factors, factoring, factored**)
1 **N-COUNT** A **factor** is something that helps to produce a result. ❑ *Exercise is an important factor in a healthy lifestyle.*
2 **N-COUNT** **MATH** A **factor** is one of the numbers that you multiply when you multiply two or more numbers together. [from Latin]

▶ **factor in** or **factor into** If you **factor** a particular cost or element **into** a calculation you are making, or if you **factor** it **in**, you include it. ❑ *You'd better consider this and factor it into your decision making.*

fac|to|ry /fǽktəri, -tri/ (**factories**) **N-COUNT** A **factory** is a large building where people use machines to make goods. [from Late Latin]
→ look at Word Web: **factory**

fac|ul|ty /fǽk°lti/ (**faculties**)
1 **N-COUNT** Your **faculties** are your physical and mental abilities. ❑ *Despite the fractures in my skull, I was in full control of my faculties.*
2 **N-COUNT/N-NONCOUNT** **Faculty** is all the teaching staff of a school, a university, or a college, or of one department. ❑ *The new program creates more work for faculty.* [from Latin]

f

Word Web   factory

Life in a 19th-century **factory** was very difficult. **Employees** often **worked** twelve hours a day, six days a week. **Wages** were low and **child labor** was common. Many **workers** were not allowed to take **breaks**. Some even had to eat while working. As early as 1832, doctors started warning about the dangers of **air pollution**. The 20th century brought some big changes. Workers began to join **unions**. During World War I, **government regulations** set standards for **minimum wages** and better **working conditions**. In addition, **automation** took over some of the most difficult and dangerous jobs.

F

fade /feɪd/ (**fades, fading, faded**)

1 **v-t/v-i** When a colored object **fades** or when the light **fades** it, it gradually becomes lighter in color. ❑ *The color suddenly faded from her cheeks.* ❑ *Sunlight has faded the carpets and curtains.* ● **fad|ed** **ADJ** ❑ *Michael was wearing faded jeans and a green cotton shirt.*

2 **v-i** If memories, feelings, or possibilities **fade**, they slowly become less intense or less strong. ❑ *My wish to live here has started to fade.* [from Old French]

Fahr|en|heit /færənhaɪt/ **ADJ** SCIENCE **Fahrenheit** is a way of measuring how hot something is. It is shown by the symbol °F. Water freezes at 32°F (0°C) and boils at 212°F (100°C). ❑ *The temperature was above 100 °F.* [from German]
→ look at Word Webs: **climate, thermometer**

Usage   Fahrenheit and Celsius
The Fahrenheit scale is commonly used to express temperature in the U.S. rather than the Celsius (or centigrade) scale.

fail /feɪl/ (**fails, failing, failed**)

1 **v-t** If you **fail** an exam or a test, you do not pass it. ❑ *75 percent of high school students failed the exam.*

2 **v-t/v-i** If you **fail** to do something, you do not succeed when you try to do it. ❑ *The Republicans failed to get the 60 votes they needed.* ❑ *He failed in his attempt to take control of the company.*

3 **v-t** If someone or something **fails** to do a particular thing that they should have done, they do not do it. [FORMAL] ❑ *Sometimes he failed to appear for meals.*

4 **PHRASE** If you do something **without fail**, you always do it. ❑ *Andrew attended every board meeting without fail.* [from Old French]

fail|ure /feɪlyər/ (**failures**)

1 **N-NONCOUNT** Failure is when you do not

succeed in doing something. ❑ *Brian was depressed after the failure of his marriage.* ❑ *The project ended in failure in late 2001.*

2 **N-NONCOUNT** Your **failure to** do something is the fact that you do not do it. ❑ *They were upset by his failure to tell the truth.*

3 **N-COUNT** If something is **a failure**, it is not a success. ❑ *His first novel was a failure.* [from Old French]

faint /feɪnt/ (**fainter, faintest, faints, fainting, fainted**)

1 **ADJ** Something that is **faint** is not strong or clear. ❑ *I could hear the faint sound of traffic far in the distance.* ❑ *There was still the faint hope that Kimberly might return.* ● **faint|ly** **ADV** ❑ *The room smelled faintly of paint.*

2 **ADJ** Someone who is **faint** feels that they are going to fall, usually because they are sick or very tired. ❑ *Ryan was unsteady on his feet and felt faint.*

3 **v-i** If you **faint**, you become unconscious for a short time. ❑ *She suddenly fell forward and fainted.* [from Old French]

fair /fɛər/ (**fairer, fairest, fairs**)

1 **ADJ** Something or someone that is **fair** is reasonable and right. ❑ *It's not fair; she's got more than me!* ❑ *I wanted everyone to get fair treatment.* ❑ *Do you feel they're paying their fair share?* ● **fair|ness** **N-NONCOUNT** ❑ *There were concerns about the fairness of the election campaign.*

2 **ADJ** A **fair** amount, degree, size, or distance is quite a large amount, degree, size, or distance. ❑ *My neighbors travel a fair amount.*

3 **ADJ** If something is **fair**, it is not bad, but it is not very good. ❑ *"What did you think of the movie?"—"Hmm. Fair."*

4 **ADJ** Someone who is **fair** has light-colored hair or skin. ❑ *My mother is very fair.* ❑ *Eric had thick fair hair.*

5 **N-COUNT** A **fair** is a place where you can play games to win prizes, and you can ride on special, big machines for fun.

6 **N-COUNT** A **fair** is an event where people show, buy, and sell goods, or share information. ❑ *US Airways is organizing a job fair to hire new workers.* [Senses 1 to 3 from Old English. Senses 4 and 6 from Old French.]

Usage   fair and fare

Avoid confusing *fair* and *fare*, which sound exactly the same. The adjective *fair* means reasonable, or attractive, or light in color; the noun *fare* refers to the price of a bus, train, ferry, or airplane ticket, while the verb *fare* refers to how well someone is doing in a particular situation: *Was it fair that all the fair-haired people on the boat fared well, while all the dark-haired people got seasick? After all, everyone had paid the same fare.*

---

fair|ly /fɛ̯ərli/

1 **ADV** **Fairly** means quite. ❑ *The team has been playing fairly well lately.* ❑ *She's fairly good at math and science.*

2 **ADV** If you do something **fairly**, you do it in a way that is reasonable and right. ❑ *We solved the problem quickly and fairly.* [from Old English]

fairy /fɛ̯əri/ (**fairies**) **N-COUNT** A **fairy** is a very small creature with wings, that can do magic. Fairies appear in children's stories, and they are not real. [from Old French] → look at Word Web: **fantasy**

fairy tale (**fairy tales**) also **fairytale** **N-COUNT** LANGUAGE ARTS A **fairy tale** is a story for children about magic and fairies.

faith /feɪθ/ (**faiths**)

1 **N-NONCOUNT** If you have **faith in** someone or something, you feel sure that they are able to do something, or that they will behave honestly. ❑ *I have faith in the honesty of my employees.*

2 **N-NONCOUNT** **Faith** is strong religious belief in a particular god. ❑ *They respect his faith.*

3 **N-COUNT** A **faith** is a particular religion. ❑ *The children will learn about a variety of faiths such as Islam and Judaism.*

4 **PHRASE** If you do something **in good faith**, you believe that what you are doing is right, even though it may not be. [from Latin]

faith|ful /feɪθfəl/

1 **ADJ** If you are **faithful**, you always support your family and friends. ❑ *Help your brothers and sisters, and be faithful to your friends.*

2 **ADJ** Someone who is **faithful to** their husband, wife, or lover does not have a sexual relationship with anyone else. [from Latin]

faith|ful|ly /feɪθfəli/

1 **ADV** If you do something **faithfully**, you show firm support or loyalty. ❑ *Mary has worked faithfully for the company for many years.*

2 **PHRASE** When you start a formal or business letter with "Dear Sir" or "Dear Madam," you can write **Yours faithfully** before your signature at the end. [from Latin]

fake /feɪk/ (**fakes**)

1 **ADJ** A **fake** thing is a copy of something, especially of something that is valuable. ❑ *The men used fake passports to get into the country.*

2 **N-COUNT** A **fake** is something that is fake. ❑ *Art experts think that the painting is a fake.* [from Italian]

fall /fɔl/ (**falls, falling, fell, fallen**)

1 **V-I** If someone or something **falls**, they move quickly toward the ground by accident. ❑ *Tyler fell from his horse and broke his arm.* ❑ *Jacob lost his balance and fell backwards.* ❑ *There was a huge crash as a large painting fell off the wall.*

2 **N-COUNT** A **fall** is when you fall to the ground. ❑ *Grandpa broke his right leg in a bad fall.*

3 **Fall down** means the same as **fall**. ❑ *The wind hit Chris so hard, he fell down.*

4 **V-I** When rain or snow **falls**, it comes down from the sky. ❑ *More than 30 inches of rain fell in 6 days.*

5 **N-COUNT/N-NONCOUNT** **Fall** is the season between summer and winter, when the weather becomes cooler and the leaves start to fall off the trees. ❑ *They got married in the fall of 1991.* ❑ *I'm going to a new school next fall.*

6 **V-I** If something **falls**, it decreases in amount, value, or strength. ❑ *Unemployment fell to 4.6 percent in May.* ❑ *Here, temperatures at night can fall below freezing.*

7 **N-COUNT** A **fall** is when something decreases in amount, value, or strength. ❑ *There has been a sharp fall in the value of the dollar.*

8 **N-SING** The **fall** of a powerful or successful person is when they suddenly lose their power or position. ❏ ...*the fall of the military dictator.*

9 **V-I** If something or someone **falls into** a particular group or category, they belong in that group or category. ❏ *The problems fall into two categories.*

10 **V-LINK** If you **fall** asleep or if you **fall** ill, you start to sleep or you become sick. ❏ *Emily suddenly fell ill and was rushed to the hospital.* [from Old English]

▶ **fall apart** **1** If something **falls apart**, it breaks into pieces because it is old or badly made. ❏ *Gradually, the old building fell apart.* **2** If an organization or a system **falls apart**, it becomes disorganized and stops working well. ❏ *Europe's monetary system is falling apart.*

▶ **fall back on** If you **fall back on** something, you use it after other things have failed. ❏ *When things get tricky, you fall back on your experience.*

▶ **fall behind** If you **fall behind**, you do not make progress or move forward as fast as other people. ❏ *Some of the students fell behind in their work.*

▶ **fall for** **1** If you **fall for** someone, you start loving them. ❏ *I just fell for him right away.* **2** If you **fall for** a lie or a trick, you believe it or are deceived by it. ❏ *He pretended he was famous, but none of us fell for it.*

▶ **fall off** If something **falls off**, it separates from the thing it was attached to. ❏ *An engine fell off the wing of the airplane.*

▶ **fall out** **1** If a person's hair or tooth **falls out**, it comes out. **2** If you **fall out** with someone, you have an argument and stop being friendly with them. You can also say that two people **fall out**. ❏ *Ashley has fallen out with her boyfriend.*

▶ **fall through** If an arrangement, a plan, or a deal **falls through**, it fails to happen. ❏ *They wanted to turn the estate into a private golf course, but the deal fell through.*

Thesaurus	**fall** Also look up :
V	fall down, plunge, topple **1** **2** come down **3** drop, plunge; (*ant.*) increase, rise **5**

fal|la|cy /fǽləsi/ (**fallacies**) **N-COUNT/N-NONCOUNT** A **fallacy** is an idea that many people believe to be true, but that is in fact false. ❏ *It's a fallacy that you can't earn money by doing what you really like.* [from Latin]

fall|en /fɔ́lən/ **Fallen** is the past participle of **fall**. [from Old English]

fal|lo|pian tube /fəlóupiən tub/ (**fallopian tubes**) **N-COUNT** **SCIENCE** A woman's **fallopian tubes** are the two tubes in her body along which eggs pass from her ovaries to her womb.

false /fɔls/

1 **ADJ** If something is **false**, it is wrong or not true. ❏ *The president received false information from his advisers.* ❏ *You do not know whether the information is true or false.* ● **false|ly** **ADV** ❏ *She was falsely accused of stealing.*

2 **ADJ** You use **false** to describe objects that are artificial but that are intended to look real. ❏ *My grandma has false teeth.*

3 **ADJ** If you describe a person or their behavior as **false**, you mean that they are behaving in a way that does not show their real feelings. ❏ *"Thank you," she said with false enthusiasm.* ● **false|ly** **ADV** ❏ *They smiled at one another, somewhat falsely.* [from Old English]

false cau|sal|ity **N-NONCOUNT** In logic, **false causality** is an error that occurs when one event is wrongly considered to be the cause of another event.

fame /feɪm/ **N-NONCOUNT** **Fame** is when you are very well known by a lot of people. ❏ *Connery gained fame as Agent 007 in the Bond movies.* [from Latin]

Word Partnership	Use **fame** with :
V	bring fame, gain fame, rise to fame
N	claim to fame, fame and fortune, hall of fame
ADJ	international fame

fa|mili|ar /fəmɪ́lyər/

1 **ADJ** If someone or something is **familiar**, you have seem them or heard of them before. ❏ *That boy's face looks familiar.* ❏ *Her name sounds familiar to me.* ● **fa|mili|ar|ity** /fəmɪliǽrɪti/ **N-NONCOUNT** ❏ ...*the comforting familiarity of her face.*

2 **ADJ** If you are **familiar with** something, you know or understand it well. ❏ *Are you familiar with the region?* ● **fa|mili|ar|ity** **N-NONCOUNT** ❏ ...*familiarity with advanced technology.* [from Latin]

fami|ly /fǽmɪli, fǽmli/ (**families**)

1 **N-COUNT** A **family** is a group of people who are related to each other, especially parents and their children. ❏ *William and his family live in Hawaii.* ❏ *A ticket for a family of four costs $68.*

2 **N-COUNT** When people talk about their **family**, they sometimes mean the people who they are related to who lived before them.

Picture Dictionary   family

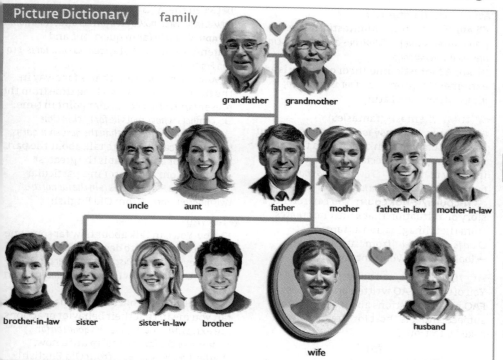

grandfather   grandmother

uncle   aunt   father   mother   father-in-law   mother-in-law

brother-in-law   sister   sister-in-law   brother   husband

wife

f

for example their great-grandparents.
❑ *My father's family came from Ireland.*
3 **N-COUNT** SCIENCE A **family** of animals
or plants is a group of related species.
→ look at Picture Dictionary: **family**

fam|ine /fǽmɪn/ (famines)
N-COUNT/N-NONCOUNT A **famine** is a time
when there is not enough food for people to
eat, and many people die. ❑ *Their country is
suffering from famine and war.* [from Old French]

fa|mous /féɪməs/ ADJ Someone or
something that is **famous** is very well
known. ❑ *Edvard Munch's "The Scream" is one of
the world's most famous paintings.* [from Latin]

Thesaurus   **famous**   Also look up :

ADJ   acclaimed, celebrated, prominent,
renowned; *(ant.)* anonymous, obscure,
unknown

fan /fæn/ (fans, fanning, fanned)
1 **N-COUNT** If you are a **fan** of someone or
something, you like them very much.
❑ *If you're a Johnny Depp fan, you'll love this movie.*
2 **N-COUNT** A **fan** is a piece of electrical
equipment that moves the air around a
room to make you cooler.

3 **N-COUNT** A **fan** is a flat object that you
move in front of your face to make you cooler.
4 **V-T** If you **fan** yourself when you are hot,
you move a fan or another flat object around
in front of yourself, to make yourself feel
cooler. ❑ *Jessica fanned herself with a newspaper.*
→ look at Word Web: **concert**

fa|nat|ic /fənǽtɪk/ (fanatics) **N-COUNT**
A **fanatic** is someone whose behavior or
opinions are very extreme. ❑ *I am not a
religious fanatic but I am a Christian.* [from Latin]

fan|boy /fǽnbɔɪ/ (fanboys) **N-COUNT**
A **fanboy** is a boy or young man who is very
enthusiastic about a particular movie,
entertainer, or type of music. ❑ *StarWars
fanboys will love this new game.*

fan|cy /fǽnsi/ (fancier, fanciest) **ADJ**
If you describe something as **fancy**, you
mean that it is special or unusual, for
example because it has a lot of decoration.
❑ *...fancy jewelry*

fan|girl /fǽngɜːrl/ (fangirls) **N-COUNT**
A **fangirl** is a girl or young woman who is
very enthusiastic about a particular movie,
entertainer, or type of music. ❑ *This new
version of the phone will be popular with fangirls.*

fan|tas|tic /fæntæstɪk/

1 **ADJ** If something is **fantastic**, it is very good. [INFORMAL] ❑ *Sarah has a fantastic social life—she's always out.*

2 **ADJ** A **fantastic** amount or quantity is an extremely large one. ❑ *...fantastic sums of money.* [from Late Latin]

fan|ta|sy /fæntəsi/ (fantasies)

1 **N-COUNT** A **fantasy** is a pleasant situation or event that you think about and that you want to happen, especially one that is unlikely to happen. ❑ *Everyone has had a fantasy about winning the lottery.*

2 **N-COUNT/N-NONCOUNT** You can refer to a story or a situation that someone creates from their imagination as **fantasy**.
❑ *...a fantasy novel.* [from Latin]
→ look at Word Web: **fantasy**

FAQ /fæk/ (FAQs) **N-COUNT** TECHNOLOGY
You often see **FAQ** written on websites. **FAQ** means questions about a particular subject, and it is short for "frequently asked questions."

far

1 DISTANT IN SPACE OR TIME
2 THE EXTENT TO WHICH SOMETHING HAPPENS
3 EMPHATIC USES

❶ far /fɑr/

LANGUAGE HELP

Far has two comparatives, **farther** and **further**, and two superlatives, **farthest** and **furthest**. **Farther** and **farthest** are used mainly in sense **1**, and are dealt with here. **Further** and **furthest** are dealt with in separate entries.

1 **ADV** If one place, thing, or person is **far** away from another, there is a great distance between them. ❑ *We've gone too far to go back now.* ❑ *My sister moved even farther away from home.*

2 **ADV** You use **far** in questions and statements about distances. ❑ *How far is it to San Francisco?*

3 **ADV** A time or event that is **far** away in the future or the past is a long time from the present or from a particular point in time. ❑ *...conflicts whose roots lie far back in time.* ❑ *I can't plan any farther than the next six months.*

4 **ADJ** You can use **far** to talk about the part of an area or object that is the greatest distance from the center in a particular direction. ❑ *Port Angeles is in the far north of Washington State.* [from Old English]

❷ far /fɑr/

1 **ADV** You can talk about how **far** someone or something gets to describe the progress that they make. ❑ *Discussions never progressed very far.* ❑ *Think of how far we have come in a short time.*

2 **ADV** If you say that someone has gone **too far**, you mean that their behavior or actions are extreme. ❑ *This time he's gone too far.*

3 **PHRASE** **So far** means up until now. ❑ *So far, they have failed.* [from Old English]

❸ far /fɑr/

1 **ADV** You can use **far** to mean "very much" when you are comparing two things and emphasizing the difference between them. ❑ *Your essay is far better than mine.*

2 **PHRASE** You use the expression **by far** when you are comparing something or someone with others of the same kind, in order to emphasize how great the difference is between them. ❑ *Unemployment is by far the most important issue.*

3 **PHRASE** If you say that something is **far from** a particular thing or **far from** being true, you are emphasizing that it is not that

---

Word Web   fantasy

All **fictional** writing involves the use of **imaginary** situations and characters. However, **fantasy** goes even further. This **genre** uses more **imagination** than **reality**. Authors create new creatures, **myths**, and **legends**. A **novelist** may use **realistic** people and settings. But a fantasy writer is free to create a whole different world. Contemporary movies have found a rich source of stories in the genre. Today you can see many different films about **fairies**, **wizards**, and **dragons**.

particular thing or not true at all. ❑ *What they said was far from the truth.* [from Old English]

fare /fɛər/ (**fares**) **N-COUNT** A **fare** is the money that you pay for a trip that you make, for example, in a bus, a train, an airplane, or a taxi. ❑ *The fare is $11 one way.* [from Old English]
→ look at Usage note at **fair**

fare|well /fɛərwɛl/ (**farewells**)
■ **N-COUNT** If you **say farewell** to someone, or **say your farewells**, you say goodbye to them. ❑ *We said our farewells and got in the car.*
■ **ADJ** You organize a **farewell** event in order to say goodbye to people. ❑ *Before she left, she organized a farewell party for family and friends.*

farm /fɑrm/ (**farms, farming, farmed**)
■ **N-COUNT** A **farm** is a piece of land where people grow crops and raise animals, and the buildings on it. ❑ *Both boys like to work on the farm.*
■ **V-T/V-I** If you **farm** an area of land, you grow crops or keep animals on it. ❑ *They farmed some of the best land in the country.* ❑ *Bease has been farming for 30 years.* [from Old French]
■ → see also **farming**
→ look at Word Webs: **farm, dairy**

farm|er /fɑrmər/ (**farmers**) **N-COUNT** A **farmer** is a person who owns or works on a farm. [from Old French]
→ look at Word Web: **farm**

farm|house /fɑrmhaʊs/ (**farmhouses**) **N-COUNT** A **farmhouse** is the house on a farm where the farmer lives.

farm|ing /fɑrmɪŋ/
■ **N-NONCOUNT** **Farming** is the job of growing crops or keeping animals on a farm. [from Old French]
■ → see also **farm**

farm|land /fɑrmlænd/ **N-NONCOUNT** **Farmland** is land that is farmed, or that is suitable for farming.

far|ther /fɑrðər/ **Farther** is a comparative of **far**.

far|thest /fɑrðɪst/ **Farthest** is a superlative of **far**.

fas|ci|nate /fæsɪneɪt/ (**fascinates, fascinating, fascinated**) **V-T** If something **fascinates** you, you find it extremely interesting. ❑ *American history fascinates me.* [from Latin]

fas|ci|nat|ed /fæsɪneɪtɪd/ **ADJ** If you are **fascinated by** something, you think it is very interesting. ❑ *My brother is fascinated by racing cars.* [from Latin]

fas|ci|nat|ing /fæsɪneɪtɪŋ/ **ADJ** If something is **fascinating**, it is very interesting. ❑ *Madagascar is a fascinating place.* [from Latin]

fas|cist /fæʃɪst/ (**fascists**)
■ **ADJ** SOCIAL STUDIES Someone with **fascist** views has right-wing political beliefs that include strong control by the state and a powerful role for the armed forces. ❑ *...extreme fascist organizations.* ● **fas|cism** **N-NONCOUNT** ❑ *...the rise of fascism in the 1930s.*
■ **N-COUNT** SOCIAL STUDIES A **fascist** is someone who has fascist views. [from Italian]

fash|ion /fæʃⁿn/ (**fashions**)
■ **N-NONCOUNT** **Fashion** is the activity or business that involves styles of clothing and appearance. ❑ *The magazine contains 20 full-color pages of fashion.*
■ **N-COUNT** A **fashion** is a style of clothing that is popular at a particular time. ❑ *Long dresses were the fashion when I was a child.*
■ → see also **old-fashioned**

Word Web   farm

Farmers no longer simply plant a **crop** and **harvest** it. Today's **farmer** uses engineering and technology to make a living. Careful **irrigation** and **drainage** control the amount of water **plants** receive. **Insecticides** protect plants from insects. **Fertilizers** make things grow. High-tech **agricultural** methods may increase the world's **food** supply. Using hydroponic methods, farmers use **chemical** solutions to **cultivate** plants. This has several advantages. **Soil** can contain **pests** and diseases not present in water alone. Growing plants hydroponically also requires less water and less labor than conventional growing methods.

F

4 **PHRASE** If something is **in fashion**, it is popular at a particular time. If it is **out of fashion**, it is not popular. ❑ *Long dresses were in fashion back then.* [from Old French]

fash|ion|able /fǽʃənəbᵊl/
1 **ADJ** Something or someone that is **fashionable** is popular at a particular time. ❑ *Long dresses will be very fashionable this year.*
2 **ADJ** Someone who is **fashionable** wears fashionable clothes. ● **fash|ion|ably** **ADV** ❑ *Brianna is always fashionably dressed.* [from Old French]

fast /fǽst/ (**faster, fastest, fasts, fasting, fasted**)
1 **ADJ** Something or someone that is **fast** is quick. ❑ *Jane has always loved fast cars.* ❑ *I'm a fast reader.* ❑ *The subway is the fastest way to get around New York.*
2 **ADV** If something moves **fast**, it moves quickly. ❑ *James drives too fast.* ❑ *Can't you run any faster?*
3 **ADJ** If a watch or a clock is **fast**, it is showing a time that is later than the real time. ❑ *That clock's an hour fast.*
4 **ADV** If something happens **fast**, it happens without any delay. ❑ *You need to see a doctor—fast!*
5 **V-I** If you **fast**, you do not eat any food for a period of time.
6 **N-COUNT** A **fast** is when you do not eat food for a period of time. ❑ *The fast ends at sunset.*
7 **PHRASE** Someone who is **fast asleep** is deeply asleep. ❑ *Anna climbed into bed and five minutes later she was fast asleep.* [from Old English]

Thesaurus	fast Also look up :
ADJ	hasty, quick, rapid, speedy, swift; (*ant.*) slow **1**
ADV	quickly, rapidly, soon, swiftly; (*ant.*) leisurely, slowly **4**

fas|ten /fǽsᵊn/ (**fastens, fastening, fastened**)
1 **V-T/V-I** When you **fasten** something, you join the two sides of it together so that it is closed. If something **fastens** with buttons or straps, you can close it in this way. ❑ *Heather got quickly into her car and fastened the seat-belt.* ❑ *Her long hair was fastened at her neck by an elastic band.*
2 **V-T** If you **fasten** one thing **to** another, you attach the first thing to the second. ❑ *There was a notice fastened to the gate.* [from Old English]

fast food **N-NONCOUNT** **Fast food** is hot food that is served quickly in a restaurant. ❑ *He likes fast food like hamburgers, pizzas, and hot dogs.*
→ look at Word Web: **meal**

fat /fǽt/ (**fatter, fattest, fats**)
1 **ADJ** A **fat** person weighs too much. ❑ *I ate too much and I began to get fat.*
2 **ADJ** A **fat** object is very thick or wide. ❑ *Emily picked up a fat book and handed it to me.*
3 **N-COUNT/N-NONCOUNT** **Fat** is a substance containing oil that is found in some foods. ❑ *Cream contains a lot of fat.*
4 **N-NONCOUNT** **Fat** is the soft substance that people and animals have under their skin. [from Old English]
→ look at Word Web: **calorie**

Thesaurus	fat Also look up :
ADJ	big, heavy, obese, overweight, thick; (*ant.*) lean, skinny, slim, thin **1**

fa|tal /féɪtᵊl/
1 **ADJ** A **fatal** action has very bad results. ❑ *Justin made the fatal mistake of lending her some money.*
2 **ADJ** A **fatal** accident or illness causes someone's death. ❑ *The TV star was attacked in a fatal stabbing.* ● **fa|tal|ly** **ADV** ❑ *The soldier was fatally wounded in the chest.* [from Old French]

fa|tal|ity /fətǽlɪti/ (**fatalities**) **N-COUNT** A **fatality** is a death that is caused by an accident or by violence. [FORMAL] ❑ *Yesterday's fatality is the 36th this year.* [from Old French]

fate /féɪt/ (**fates**)
1 **N-NONCOUNT** **Fate** is a power that some people believe controls everything that happens in the world. ❑ *I think it was fate that Andy and I met.*
2 **N-COUNT** Someone's or something's **fate** is what happens to them. ❑ *Frank was never seen again, and we never knew his fate.* [from Latin]

fa|ther /fɑ́ðər/ (**fathers**)
1 **N-COUNT** Your **father** is your male parent. ❑ *His father was an artist.* ❑ *He is a father of three boys.*
2 **N-COUNT** The man who invented or started something is sometimes referred to as the **father of** that thing. ❑ *...Max Dupain, the father of modern photography.* [from Old English]
→ look at Picture Dictionary: **family**

fa|ther-in-law (fathers-in-law) **N-COUNT**
Someone's **father-in-law** is the father of
their husband or wife.
→ look at Picture Dictionary: **family**

fath|om /fǽðəm/ (fathoms, fathoming,
fathomed)
1 **N-COUNT** A **fathom** is a measurement of
6 feet or 1.8 meters, used when referring to
the depth of water. ◻ *They found the wrecked
boat in only fifteen fathoms of water.*
2 **V-T** If you cannot **fathom** something, you
are unable to understand it, although you
think carefully about it. ◻ *I really couldn't
fathom what Steiner was talking about.*
3 **Fathom out** means the same as **fathom**.
◻ *We're trying to fathom out what's going on.*
[from Old English]

fa|tigue /fətíg/ **N-NONCOUNT** Fatigue is a
feeling of being extremely tired. ◻ *He was
taken to hospital suffering from extreme fatigue.*
[from French]

fat|ty /fǽti/ (fattier, fattiest)
1 **ADJ** Fatty food contains a lot of fat.
◻ *Don't eat fatty food or chocolates.*
2 **ADJ** Fatty acids or **fatty** tissues contain a
lot of fat. [from Old English]

fau|cet /fɔ́sɪt/ (faucets) **N-COUNT** A **faucet** is
an object that controls the flow of a liquid or
a gas from a pipe. Sinks and baths have
faucets. ◻ *Tina turned off the faucet and dried her
hands.* [from Old French]
→ look at Picture Dictionary: **bathroom**

fault /fɔ́lt/ (faults, faulting, faulted)
1 **N-SING** If a bad situation is your **fault**, you
made it happen. ◻ *The accident was my fault.*
2 **N-COUNT** A **fault** in someone or
something is a weakness in them.
◻ *Brandon's worst fault is his temper.*
3 **N-COUNT** SCIENCE A **fault** is a large crack
in the surface of the Earth. ◻ *The San Andreas
Fault is in the San Francisco area.*
4 **V-T** If you **cannot fault** someone, you
cannot find any reason for criticizing them
or the things that they are doing. ◻ *You can't
fault their determination.*
5 **PHRASE** If someone or something is **at
fault**, they are responsible for something
that has gone wrong. ◻ *He could not accept
that he was at fault.* [from Old French]
→ look at Word Web: **earthquake**

Thesaurus	**fault** Also look up :
N	blunder, error, mistake **1**
	defect, flaw, imperfection, weakness **2**

fault block (fault blocks) **N-COUNT** SCIENCE
A **fault block** is a large area of rock that is
separated from other rock by faults in the
Earth's surface.

fault-block moun|tain (fault-block
mountains) **N-COUNT** SCIENCE A **fault-block
mountain** is a mountain that is formed when
the land between two fault lines rises up or
the land outside the fault lines drops down.

faulty /fɔ́lti/ **ADJ** Faulty equipment is not
working well. ◻ *The car had worn tires and faulty
brakes.* [from Old French]

fa|vor /féɪvər/ (favors, favoring, favored)
1 **N-COUNT** If you **do** someone **a favor**, you
do something to help them. ◻ *Please would
you do me a favor and give David a message for me?*
2 **V-T** If you **favor** something, you prefer it
to the other choices available. ◻ *The majority
of Americans favor raising taxes on the rich.*
3 **V-T** If you **favor** someone, you treat them
better than you treat other people. ◻ *The
company favors U.S. citizens.*
4 **PHRASE** If you are **in favor of** something,
you think that it is a good thing. ◻ *I'm in favor
of income tax cuts.*
5 **PHRASE** If someone makes a judgment **in
your favor**, they say that you are right about
something. ◻ *The Supreme Court ruled in
Fitzgerald's favor.*
6 **PHRASE** If something is **in your favor**, it
helps you or gives you an advantage.
◻ *This is a career where age works in your favor.*
7 **PHRASE** If one thing is rejected **in favor of**
another, the second thing is done or chosen
instead of the first. ◻ *The writing program is
being rejected in favor of computer classes.*
[from Latin]

fa|vor|able /féɪvərəbəl/
1 **ADJ** If your opinion of something is
favorable, you agree with it or approve of it.
◻ *The president's speech received favorable reviews.*
2 **ADJ** Favorable conditions are good.
◻ *We hope that the weather will be favorable.*
[from Latin]

fa|vor|ite /féɪvərɪt, féɪvrɪt/ (favorites)
1 **ADJ** Your **favorite** thing or person is the
one that you like more than all the others.
◻ *What is your favorite movie?*

2 N-COUNT Your **favorite** is the person or thing that you like more than all the others. ❏ *Of all the seasons, fall is my favorite.* [from Italian]

fax /fæks/ (**faxes, faxing, faxed**)
1 N-COUNT A **fax** or a **fax machine** is a machine that is joined to a telephone line. It is no longer in use as much. You would use a **fax** to send and receive documents.
2 N-COUNT A **fax** is a copy of a document that you would send or receive using a fax machine. ❏ *I sent Daniel a long fax this morning.*
3 V-T If you **faxed** a document to someone, you would send it to their fax machine. ❏ *I faxed a copy of the letter to my boss.*

fear /fɪər/ (**fears, fearing, feared**)
1 N-COUNT/N-NONCOUNT **Fear** is the unpleasant feeling you have when you think that you are in danger. ❏ *My whole body was shaking with fear.*
2 N-COUNT/N-NONCOUNT A **fear** is a thought that something unpleasant might happen. ❏ *Sara has a fear of spiders.*
3 V-I If you **fear** someone or something, you are very afraid of them. ❏ *Many people fear flying.* [from Old English]
→ look at Word Web: **emotion**

Thesaurus	fear Also look up :
N	alarm, dread, panic, terror **1** concern, worry **2**

Word Partnership	Use fear with :
ADJ	constant fear **1** irrational fear **1 2** worst fear **2**
V	face *your* fear, hide *your* fear, live in fear, overcome *your* fear **1 2**
N	fear of failure, fear of rejection, fear of the unknown **2** fear change, nothing to fear, fear the worst **3**

fear|ful /fɪərfəl/ ADJ If you are **fearful of** something, you are afraid of it. [FORMAL] ❏ *They were all fearful of losing their jobs.* [from Old English]

fear|less /fɪərlɪs/ ADJ If someone is **fearless,** they are not afraid of anything. ❏ *He was brave and fearless—a true hero.* [from Old English]

fea|sible /fiːzəbəl/ ADJ If something is **feasible,** it can be done. ❏ *She questioned whether it was feasible to travel to these regions.*

● **fea|sibil|ity** /fiːzəbɪlɪti/ N-NONCOUNT ❏ *They discussed the feasibility of building a stadium in downtown Los Angeles.* [from Latin]

feast /fiːst/ (**feasts, feasting, feasted**)
1 N-COUNT A **feast** is a large and special meal for a lot of people. ❏ *On Friday night, they had a wedding feast for 1,000 guests.*
2 V-I If you **feast on** a particular food, you eat a large amount of it with great enjoyment. ❏ *They feasted on Indian food.* [from Anglo-French]

feat /fiːt/ (**feats**) N-COUNT A **feat** is a very brave or difficult act. ❏ *The men performed feats of physical bravery.* [from Anglo-French]

feath|er /fɛðər/ (**feathers**) N-COUNT A bird's **feathers** are the light soft things that cover its body. ❏ *...peacock feathers.* [from Old English]
→ look at Word Web: **bird**

fea|ture /fiːtʃər/ (**features, featuring, featured**)
1 N-COUNT A **feature of** something is an interesting or important part of it. ❏ *The house has many attractive features, including a swimming pool.*
2 N-COUNT A **feature** is a special story in a newspaper or a magazine, or a special program on radio or television. ❏ *There was a feature on Tom Cruise in the New York Times.*
3 N-COUNT A **feature** or a **feature** film or movie is a full-length film about a fictional situation.
4 N-PLURAL Your **features** are your eyes, nose, mouth, and other parts of your face. ❏ *Emily's best feature is her dark eyes.*
5 V-T When a program, a movie, or an exhibition **features** a particular person or thing, they are an important part of it. ❏ *The program will feature highlights from recent games.* [from Latin]

Word Partnership	Use feature with :
ADJ	key feature **1** special feature **1 2** best feature, striking feature **1 4** animated feature, double feature, full-length feature **3** facial feature **4**

Feb|ru|ary /fɛbyuɛri, fɛbru-/ (**Februaries**) N-COUNT/N-NONCOUNT **February** is the second month of the year. ❏ *The band's U.S. tour starts in February.* [from Latin]

fe|ces /físiz/ **N-NONCOUNT** Feces is the solid waste substance that leaves the body through the anus. [FORMAL] [from Latin]

fed /fɛd/
■ Fed is the past tense and past participle of **feed**. [from Old English]
■ → see also **fed up**

fed|er|al /fɛdərəl/
■ **ADJ** SOCIAL STUDIES In a **federal** country or system, a group of states is controlled by a central government.
■ **ADJ** SOCIAL STUDIES **Federal** means relating to the national government of a federal country. ❑ *The federal government moved to Washington in the fall of 1800.* [from Latin]

fed|er|al govern|ment (**federal governments**) **N-COUNT** SOCIAL STUDIES A **federal government** controls all the states of a country as a group.

fed|er|al|ism /fɛdərəlɪzəm/ **N-NONCOUNT** SOCIAL STUDIES **Federalism** is a political system in which a central government controls separate states. ❑ *The basic principle of American federalism is fixed in the tenth amendment.* [from Latin]

fed|era|tion /fɛdəreɪʃən/ (**federations**)
■ **N-COUNT** SOCIAL STUDIES A **federation** is a federal country. ❑ *...the Russian Federation.*
■ **N-COUNT** A **federation** is a group of organizations that have joined together for a common purpose. ❑ *...the American Federation of Government Employees.* [from Latin]

fed up **ADJ** If you are **fed up**, you are unhappy or bored. [INFORMAL] ❑ *My brother soon became fed up with city life.*

fee /fí/ (**fees**)
■ **N-COUNT** A **fee** is the money that you pay to be allowed to do something. ❑ *We paid the small entrance fee and drove inside.*
■ **N-COUNT** A **fee** is the money that you pay a person or an organization for advice or for a service. ❑ *We had to pay the lawyer fees ourselves.* [from Old French]

fee|ble /fíbᵊl/ (**feebler, feeblest**) **ADJ** If someone or something is **feeble**, they are weak. ❑ *My uncle was old and feeble, and was not able to walk far.* ● **fee|bly** **ADV** ❑ *Her left hand moved feebly at her side.* [from Old French]

feed /fíd/ (**feeds, feeding, fed**)
■ **V-T** If you **feed** a person or an animal, you give them food. ❑ *It's time to feed the baby.* ❑ *It's usually best to feed a small dog twice a day.*
■ **V-T** To **feed** a family or a community means to supply food for them. ❑ *Feeding a hungry family can be expensive.* [from Old English]

Word Partnership	Use **feed** with :
N	feed **the baby**, feed **the cat**, feed **the children**, feed *your* **family**, feed **the hungry** ■
V	feed **and clothe** ■

feed|back /fídbæk/ **N-NONCOUNT** If you get **feedback on** your work, someone tells you how well or badly you are doing. ❑ *Ask your teacher for feedback on your work.*

feed|back con|trol **N-NONCOUNT** TECHNOLOGY **Feedback control** is a system that regulates a process by using the output of the system in order to make changes to the input of the system.

feel /fíl/ (**feels, feeling, felt**)
■ **V-LINK** If you **feel** a particular emotion or a physical feeling, you experience it. ❑ *I am feeling really happy today.* ❑ *I felt a sharp pain in my shoulder.* ❑ *How do you feel?*
■ **V-LINK** If you talk about how an experience or an event **feels**, you talk about the emotions and sensations connected with it. ❑ *It feels good to finish a piece of work.* ❑ *The speed at which everything moved felt strange.*
■ **V-LINK** The way that something **feels** is the way it seems when you touch it or experience it. ❑ *The blanket feels soft.* ❑ *The sun felt hot on my back.* ❑ *The room felt rather cold.*
■ **V-T/V-I** If you **feel** something, you touch it with your hand, so that you can find out what it is like. ❑ *The doctor felt my pulse.* ❑ *Feel how soft this leather is.* ❑ *I felt gently with my hand.*
■ **V-T** If you can **feel** something, you are aware of it because you touch it or it touches you. ❑ *Anna felt something touching her face.*
■ **V-T** If you **feel** the presence of someone or something, you become aware of them. ❑ *He felt her eyes on him.* ❑ *I could feel that a man was watching me.*
■ **V-T** If you **feel** that something is true, you have a strong idea in your mind that it is true. ❑ *I feel that not enough is being done.* ❑ *She felt certain that it wasn't the same guy.*
■ **V-I** If you talk about how you **feel about** something, you tell someone your opinion about it. ❑ *She felt guilty about spending so much money on clothes.*
■ **V-I** If you **feel like** doing something or

having something, you want to do it or have it. □ *"I just don't feel like going out tonight,"* Rose said quietly. [from Old English]

10 → see also **felt**

▶ **feel for** **1** If you **feel for** something, you try to find it using your hands and not your eyes. □ *I felt for my keys in my pocket.*

2 If you **feel for** someone, you have sympathy for them. □ *Nicole was crying, and I really felt for her.*

feel|ing /fíːlɪŋ/ (**feelings**)
1 **N-COUNT** A **feeling** is an emotion. □ *I had feelings of sadness and loneliness.*
2 **N-COUNT** If you have **a feeling that** something is going to happen, you think that it is probably the case or that it is probably going to happen. □ *I have a feeling that everything will be all right.*
3 **N-PLURAL** Your **feelings** about something are what you think and feel about it. □ *They have strong feelings about politics.*
4 **N-PLURAL** If you hurt someone's **feelings**, you say or do something that makes them upset. □ *I'm really sorry if I hurt your feelings.*
5 **N-NONCOUNT** **Feeling** in part of your body is the ability to experience the sense of touch there. □ *After the accident, Jason had no feeling in his legs.*
6 **N-SING** If you have a **feeling of** being in a particular situation, you feel that you are in that situation. □ *I had the terrible feeling of being left behind to bring up the baby on my own.* [from Old English]

feet /fíːt/ **Feet** is the plural of **foot**. [from Old English]

feign /féɪn/ (**feigns, feigning, feigned**) **V-T** If someone **feigns** a particular feeling or attitude, they try to make other people think that they have it or are experiencing it, although this is not true. [FORMAL] □ *I didn't want to go to school, and decided to feign illness.* [from Old French]

feld|spar /féldspɑr, fɛl-/ (**feldspars**) **N-COUNT/N-NONCOUNT** SCIENCE **Feldspar** is a mineral that forms rocks and makes up most of the Earth's crust. [from German]

fell /fɛl/ **Fell** is the past tense of **fall**. [from Old English]

fel|low /félːoʊ/ (**fellows**)
1 **N-COUNT** A **fellow** is a man. □ *Chris was a cheerful fellow.*
2 **ADJ** **Fellow** describes people who are like

you or from the same place as you. □ *Richard was just 18 when he married fellow student Barbara.* [from Old English]

felo|ny /félɑni/ (**felonies**) **N-COUNT** A **felony** is a very serious crime. □ *The judge found him guilty of six felonies.* [from Medieval Latin]

fel|sic /félsɪk/ **ADJ** SCIENCE **Felsic** rocks are igneous rocks that contain a lot of lighter elements such as silicon, aluminum, and sodium. Compare with **mafic**.

felt /fɛlt/
1 **Felt** is the past tense and past participle of **feel**.
2 **N-NONCOUNT** **Felt** is a type of soft thick cloth. □ *Amy was wearing an old felt hat.* [from Old English]

| **Word Link** | **fem, femin ≈ woman** : **female, feminine, feminist** |

fe|male /fíːmeɪl/ (**females**)
1 **N-COUNT** SCIENCE A **female** is any animal, including humans, that can give birth to babies or lay eggs. □ *Each female will lay just one egg.*
2 **ADJ** SCIENCE **Female** is also an adjective. □ *...female gorillas.*
3 **N-COUNT** A **female** is a woman or a girl. □ *This disease affects males more than females.*
4 **ADJ** **Female** is also an adjective. □ *Who is your favorite female singer?* [from Latin]
→ look at Word Web: **reproduction**

| **Usage** | **female** and **woman** |

In everyday situations, you should avoid using *female* to refer to women, because that can sound offensive. When used as a noun, *female* is mainly used in scientific or medical contexts. *The leader of the herd of elephants is usually the oldest female.*

femi|nine /fémɪnɪn/
1 **ADJ** **Feminine** qualities and things are considered to be typical of women. □ *I love feminine clothes, so I wear skirts a lot.* □ *His voice was strangely feminine.*
2 **ADJ** LANGUAGE ARTS In some languages, a **feminine** noun, pronoun, or adjective has a different form from other forms (such as "masculine" forms). Compare with **masculine** [from Latin]

femi|nism /fémɪnɪzəm/ **N-NONCOUNT** SOCIAL STUDIES **Feminism** is the belief that women should have the same rights and opportunities as men. [from Latin]

femi|nist /fɛmɪnɪst/ (**feminists**)

1 **N-COUNT** SOCIAL STUDIES A **feminist** is a person who believes in feminism.
❑ *Feminists argue that women should not have to choose between children and a career.*

2 **ADJ** **Feminist** groups, ideas, and activities are involved in feminism. ❑ *...feminist writer Simone de Beauvoir.* [from Latin]

fence /fɛns/ (**fences**)

1 **N-COUNT** A **fence** is a wooden or metal wall around a piece of land.

2 **PHRASE** If you are **on the fence**, you avoid supporting a particular side in a discussion or argument. ❑ *I'm still on the fence. I may vote Democratic next time, but I'm not sure.*

Word Link	fend ≈ striking : defend, fender, offend

fend|er /fɛndər/ (**fenders**) **N-COUNT** The **fender** of a car is the area above the wheels.

fer|ment (**ferments, fermenting, fermented**)
V-T/V-I If a food, drink, or other natural substance **ferments**, or if it **is fermented**, a chemical change takes place in it so that alcohol is produced. ❑ *The dried grapes are allowed to ferment until there is no sugar left.* [from Latin]
→ look at Word Web: **fungus**

fern /fɜrn/ (**ferns**) **N-COUNT/N-NONCOUNT** A **fern** is a plant that has long stems with leaves that look like feathers. [from Old English]

fer|ry /fɛri/ (**ferries, ferrying, ferried**)

1 **N-COUNT** A **ferry** is a boat that takes people and sometimes also vehicles a short distance across water. ❑ *They crossed the River Gambia by ferry.*

2 **V-T** If a vehicle **ferries** people or goods, it transports them by means of regular trips between the same two places. ❑ *A truck arrived to ferry guests to and from the camp.* [from Old English]
→ look at Word Web: **ship**

fer|tile /fɜrtəl/

1 **ADJ** SCIENCE If land or soil is **fertile**, plants grow very well in it. ● **fer|til|ity** /fɜrtɪlɪti/ **N-NONCOUNT** ❑ *...the fertility of the soil.*

2 **ADJ** SCIENCE A person or an animal that is **fertile** is able to have babies. ● **fer|til|ity** **N-NONCOUNT** ❑ *Smoking and drinking alcohol affect fertility.* [from Latin]

fer|ti|lize /fɜrtəlaɪz/ (**fertilizes, fertilizing, fertilized**) **V-T** SCIENCE When an egg from the ovary of a woman or female animal **is fertilized**, a sperm from the male joins with the egg, causing a baby or young animal to begin forming. A female plant **is fertilized** when its reproductive parts come into contact with pollen from the male plant. ❑ *...the normal sperm levels needed to fertilize the egg.* ● **fer|ti|li|za|tion** /fɜrtəlɪzeɪʃən/ **N-NONCOUNT** ❑ *From fertilization until birth is about 266 days.*
→ look at Word Web: **reproduction**

fer|ti|liz|er /fɜrtəlaɪzər/ (**fertilizers**)
N-NONCOUNT **Fertilizer** is a substance that you put on soil to make plants grow better. [from Latin]
→ look at Word Webs: **farm, pollution**

fes|ti|val /fɛstɪvəl/ (**festivals**)

1 **N-COUNT** ARTS A **festival** is a series of special events such as concerts or plays. ❑ *The actress was in Rome for the city's film festival.*

2 **N-COUNT** A **festival** is a time when people celebrate a special event. ❑ *Shavuot is a two-day festival for Jews.* [from Church Latin]

fetch /fɛtʃ/ (**fetches, fetching, fetched**)

1 **V-T** If you **fetch** something or someone, you go and get them from the place where they are. ❑ *Sylvia fetched a towel from the bathroom.* ❑ *Please could you fetch me a glass of water?*

2 **V-T** If something **fetches** a particular sum of money, it is sold for that amount. ❑ *The painting fetched three million dollars.* [from Old English]

fe|tus /fitəs/ (**fetuses**) **N-COUNT** SCIENCE A **fetus** is an animal or a human being before it is born. [from Latin]
→ look at Word Web: **reproduction**

fe|ver /fivər/ (**fevers**) **N-COUNT/N-NONCOUNT** If you have a **fever** when you are sick, your body temperature is higher than usual. ❑ *Jim had a high fever.* [from Old English]
→ look at Word Web: **illness**

fe|ver|ish /fivərɪʃ/ **ADJ** If you are **feverish**, you have a fever. ❑ *Joshua was feverish and wouldn't eat anything.* [from Old English]

few /fyu/ (**fewer, fewest**)

1 **DET** A **few** means some, but not many. ❑ *I'm having a dinner party for a few close friends.* ❑ *Here are a few ideas that might help you.*

2 **PRON** A **few** is also a pronoun. ❑ *Most were Americans but a few were British.* ❑ *I met a few of her friends at the party.*

f

3 **DET** Few means not many. ❑ *She had few friends.*

4 **PRON** Few is also a pronoun. ❑ *Few can survive more than a week without water.* ❑ *Few of the houses still had lights on.*

5 **PHRASE** You use **as few as** before a number to suggest that it is surprisingly small. ❑ *Some people put on weight eating as few as 800 calories a day.*

6 **PHRASE** Things that are **few and far between** are very rare or do not happen very often. ❑ *Kelly's trips to the hairdresser were few and far between.*

7 **PHRASE** You use **no fewer than** to emphasize that a number is surprisingly large. ❑ *No fewer than thirteen foreign ministers attended the session.* [from Old English]
→ look at Usage note at **less**

> **Usage**   few and a few
>
> Be careful to use *few* and *a few* correctly. *Few* means "not many," and is used to emphasize that the number is very small: *He had few complaints about his workload.* A *few* means "more than one or two," and is used when we wish to imply a small but significant number: *He had a few complaints about his workload.*

fi|an|cé /fianseɪ, fiɑnseɪ/ (**fiancés**) **N-COUNT** A woman's **fiancé** is the man that she is going to marry. [from French]

fi|an|cée /fianseɪ, fiɑnseɪ/ (**fiancées**) **N-COUNT** A man's **fiancée** is the woman that he is going to marry. [from French]

fi|ber /faɪbər/ (**fibers**)
1 **N-COUNT** A **fiber** is a thin thread that is used for making cloth or rope. ❑ *We only sell clothing made from natural fibers.*
2 **N-NONCOUNT** **Fiber** is the part of a fruit or a vegetable that helps all the food you eat to move through your body. ❑ *Most vegetables contain fiber.* [from Latin]
→ look at Word Web: **paper**

fi|brous root /faɪbrəs rut/ (**fibrous roots**)
N-COUNT **SCIENCE** Plants with **fibrous roots** have a series of thin roots that branch out from the stem of the plant.

> **Word Link**   *fact, fic ≈ making : artificial, factor, fiction*

fic|tion /fɪkʃən/
1 **N-NONCOUNT** LANGUAGE ARTS **Fiction** is books and stories about imaginary people and events. ● **fic|tion|al** **ADJ** ❑ *...Harry Potter, the fictional hero of J. K. Rowling's books.*

2 **N-NONCOUNT** A statement or an account that is **fiction** is not true. ❑ *The truth or fiction of this story has never really been determined.* [from Latin]
→ look at Word Webs: **fantasy, genre, library**

fi|del|ity /fɪdɛlɪti/ **N-NONCOUNT** **Fidelity** is loyalty to a person, an organization, or a set of beliefs. [FORMAL] ❑ *Your lawyer will serve you with total fidelity.* [from Latin]

fidg|et /fɪdʒɪt/ (**fidgets, fidgeting, fidgeted**)
V-I If you **fidget**, you keep moving slightly, because you are nervous or bored. ❑ *Brenda fidgeted in her seat.* [from Old Norse]

field /fild/ (**fields, fielding, fielded**)
1 **N-COUNT** A **field** is a piece of land where crops are grown, or where animals are kept. ❑ *We drove past fields of sunflowers.*
2 **N-COUNT** SPORTS A sports **field** is a piece of land where sports are played. ❑ *...a football field.*
3 **V-I** SPORTS In a game of baseball, the team that **is fielding** is trying to catch the ball, while the other team is trying to hit it. ❑ *The Tigers were pitching and fielding superbly.*
4 **N-COUNT** A **field** is a subject that someone knows a lot about. ❑ *Professor Greenwood is an expert in the field of international law.* [from Norwegian]
→ look at Picture Dictionary: **barn**

> **Word Partnership**   Use **field** with :
>
> | ADJ | **open** field **1** |
> | V | **work in a** field **1** |
> | N | **ball** field, field **hockey, track and field 2** |
> | | **expert in a** field **4** |

field|er /fildər/ (**fielders**) **N-COUNT** A **fielder** is a player in some sports who has to pick up or catch the ball after a player from the other team has hit it. ❑ *He hit 10 home runs and he's also a good fielder.*

fierce /fɪərs/ (**fiercer, fiercest**)
1 **ADJ** A **fierce** animal or person is very angry and is likely to attack you. ● **fierce|ly** **ADV** ❑ *"Go away!" she said fiercely.*
2 **ADJ** **Fierce** feelings or actions are very strong or enthusiastic. ❑ *There's fierce competition for places in the team.* ● **fierce|ly** **ADV** ❑ *Amanda is fiercely ambitious.* [from Old French]

fif|teen /fɪftin/ **NUM** MATH **Fifteen** is the number 15. [from Old English]

fif|teenth /fɪftiːnθ/ **ADJ/ADV** MATH The **fifteenth** item in a series is the one that you count as number fifteen. ❑ ...the fifteenth century. [from Old English]

fifth /fɪfθ/ (**fifths**)
1 **ADJ/ADV** MATH The **fifth** item in a series is the one that you count as number five. ❑ This is his fifth trip to Australia.
2 **N-COUNT** MATH A **fifth** is one of five equal parts of something (⅕). ❑ The machine allows us to do the job in a fifth of the usual time. [from Old English]

fif|ti|eth /fɪftiəθ/ **ADJ/ADV** MATH The **fiftieth** item in a series is the one that you count as number fifty. ❑ ...his fiftieth birthday. [from Old English]

fif|ty /fɪfti/ (**fifties**)
1 **NUM** MATH **Fifty** is the number 50.
2 **N-COUNT** A **fifty** is a fifty-dollar bill. ❑ Judy opened her wallet, took out a fifty, and handed it to him.
3 **N-PLURAL** The **fifties** are the years between 1950 and 1959. ❑ Her parents were born in the fifties.
4 **N-PLURAL** When you talk about the **fifties**, you mean the numbers between 50 and 59. For example, if you are in your **fifties**, you are aged between 50 and 59. ❑ Some people find they gain weight when they get into their fifties. [from Old English]

fig /fɪg/ (**figs**) **N-COUNT** A **fig** is a soft sweet fruit full of tiny seeds. Figs grow on trees in hot countries. [from Old French]
→ look at Picture Dictionary: **fruit**

fight /faɪt/ (**fights, fighting, fought**)
1 **V-T/V-I** If people **fight**, they hit or kick each other because they want to hurt each other. ❑ "Stop fighting!" Mom shouted. ❑ Susan fought a lot with her younger sister.
2 **N-COUNT** **Fight** is also a noun. ❑ He had a fight with Smith.
3 **V-T/V-I** If you **fight** something unpleasant, you try very hard to prevent it or stop it from happening. ❑ It is very hard to fight forest fires. ❑ I've spent a lifetime fighting against racism and prejudice.
4 **N-COUNT** **Fight** is also a noun. ❑ ...the fight against crime.
5 **V-I** If you **fight** for something, you try very hard to get it. ❑ Lee had to fight hard for his place on the team.
6 **N-COUNT** **Fight** is also a noun. ❑ ...the fight for justice.
7 **V-T/V-I** If a person or army **fights** in a

battle or a war, they take part in it. ❑ He fought in the war and was taken prisoner. ❑ I would rather go to prison than fight for this country.
● **fight|ing** **N-NONCOUNT** ❑ More than nine hundred people have died in the fighting.
8 **V-T/V-I** When people **fight**, they argue. [INFORMAL] ❑ Robert and Lorene fight all the time.
9 **N-COUNT** **Fight** is also a noun. [INFORMAL] ❑ He had a big fight with his mum. [from Old English]
→ look at Word Web: **army**
▶ **fight back** If you **fight back**, you defend yourself by taking action against someone who is attacking you. ❑ The passengers and crew chose to fight back against the hijackers.
▶ **fight off** **1** If you **fight off** an illness, you succeed in getting rid of it. ❑ ...the body's ability to fight off infection.
2 If you **fight off** someone who has attacked you, you fight with them, and succeed in making them stop attacking you. ❑ She fought off three armed robbers.

Thesaurus	fight Also look up :
V	argue, quarrel **5**
N	fist fight **1**
	argument, disagreement **5**

Word Partnership	Use fight with :
V	**join a** fight, **lose a** fight, **win a** fight **1** **2** **5**
	stay and fight **1** **4** **5**
	break up a fight, **have a** fight, **pick a** fight, **start a** fight **1** **5**
N	fight **crime**, fight **fire** **2**
	fight **a battle/war**, fight **an enemy** **4**

fight|er /faɪtər/ (**fighters**)
1 **N-COUNT** SPORTS A **fighter** is a person who fights another person, especially as a sport. ❑ He was a professional fighter for 17 years. [from Old English]
2 → see also **firefighter**

fig|ment /fɪgmənt/ **PHRASE** If you say that something is a **figment of** someone's **imagination**, you mean that it does not really exist and that they are imagining it. ❑ The attack wasn't just a figment of my imagination. [from Late Latin]

fig|ura|tive /fɪgyərətɪv/
1 **ADJ** LANGUAGE ARTS If you use a word or expression in a **figurative** sense, you use it with a more abstract or imaginative meaning than its ordinary one. Compare with **literal**. ❑ "Like I said before, I'm in a different

figure   318   fill

place." His statement was both literal and figurative. ● **fig|ura|tive|ly** **ADV** ❑ *Figuratively, the world is standing still, waiting to see what will happen.*

2 **ADJ** ARTS **Figurative** art is a style of art in which people and things are shown in a realistic way. [from Latin]

fig|ure /fɪɡyər/ (figures, figuring, figured)
1 **N-COUNT** MATH A **figure** is one of the symbols from o to 9 that you use to write numbers. ❑ *They've put the figures in the wrong column.* ❑ *John earns a seven-figure salary—$1,000,000 at least.*

2 **N-COUNT** MATH A **figure** is an amount expressed as a number. ❑ *Can I see your latest sales figures?*

3 **N-COUNT** A **figure** is the shape of a person you cannot see clearly. ❑ *Two figures moved behind the thin curtain.*

4 **N-COUNT** Your **figure** is the shape of your body. ❑ *Lauren has a very good figure.*

5 **N-COUNT** A well-known or important **figure** is a person who is well-known and important. ❑ *...key figures in the three main political parties.*

6 **N-PLURAL** MATH An amount or a number that is in single **figures** is between zero and nine. An amount or a number that is in double **figures** is between ten and ninety-nine.

7 **V-T** If you **figure** that something is true, you think or guess that it is true. [INFORMAL] ❑ *She figured that she had learned a lot from the experience.* [from Latin]

▶ **figure out** If you **figure out** a solution to a problem, you succeed in solving it. [INFORMAL] ❑ *We couldn't figure out how to use the equipment.*

file /faɪl/ (files, filing, filed)
1 **N-COUNT** A **file** is a box or a folder that you keep papers in. ❑ *The file contained letters and reports.*

2 **N-COUNT** A **file** is a collection of information about a particular person or thing. ❑ *We have files on people's tax details.*

3 **N-COUNT** TECHNOLOGY A **file** is a collection of related information on a computer. ❑ *I deleted the files by mistake.*

4 **N-COUNT** A **file** is a tool that is used for rubbing rough objects to make them smooth. ❑ *...a nail file.*

5 **V-T** If you **file** a document, you put it in the correct file. ❑ *The letters are all filed alphabetically.*

6 **V-T** If you **file** something, you make it

smooth. ❑ *Mom was filing her nails.*

7 **V-I** If people **file** somewhere, they walk there in a line, one behind the other. ❑ *More than 10,000 people filed past the dead woman's coffin.*

8 **PHRASE** A group of people who are walking or standing **in single file** are in a line, one behind the other. [Senses 1, 2, 3, 5, and 7 from Old French. Senses 4 and 6 from Old English.]
→ look at Picture Dictionary: **tool**

file|name /faɪlneɪm/ (filenames) **N-COUNT** TECHNOLOGY A **filename** is the name that you give to a particular computer file.

file-shar|ing also file sharing **N-NONCOUNT** TECHNOLOGY **File-sharing** is a way of sharing computer files among a large number of users.

fil|ing cabi|net (filing cabinets) **N-COUNT** A **filing cabinet** is a piece of office furniture, usually made of metal, that has drawers in which files are kept.
→ look at Picture Dictionary: **office**

fill /fɪl/ (fills, filling, filled)
1 **V-T/V-I** If you **fill** something, or if it **fills**, a liquid or a substance enters it and makes it full. ❑ *Rachel went to the bathroom and filled a glass with water.* ❑ *The boy's eyes filled with tears.*

2 **V-T** If something **fills** a space, the space is full of it. ❑ *Rows of desks filled the office.* ● **filled** **ADJ** ❑ *The museum is filled with historical objects.*

3 **Fill up** means the same as **fill**. ❑ *Filling up your car's gas tank these days is very expensive.*

4 **V-T** If you **fill** a crack or a hole, you put a substance into it to make the surface smooth again. ❑ *Fill the cracks between walls and window frames.*

5 **Fill in** means the same as **fill**. ❑ *Start by filling in any cracks.*

6 **V-T** If something **fills** you **with** an emotion, you experience this emotion strongly. ❑ *My father's work filled me with awe.* [from Old English]

▶ **fill in** **1** If you **fill in** a form, you write information in the spaces. ❑ *When you have filled in the form, send it to your employer.*

2 If you **fill in** for someone, you do the work that they normally do because they are unable to do it.
→ look at Word Web: **answer**

▶ **fill out** If you **fill out** a form, you write information in the spaces. ❑ *Fill out the application carefully.*

▶ **fill up** ■ If a place **fills up**, it becomes full. ❑ *The theater was filling up quickly.*

■ → look up **fill** ■

fill|ing /fɪlɪŋ/ (**fillings**)

■ **N-COUNT** A **filling** is a small amount of metal that fills a hole in a tooth. ❑ *The dentist said I needed two fillings.*

■ **N-COUNT/N-NONCOUNT** The **filling** in a cake, a pie, or a sandwich is what is inside it. ❑ *Next, make the pie filling.* [from Old English]
→ look at Word Web: **teeth**

film /fɪlm/ (**films, filming, filmed**)

■ **N-COUNT** ARTS A **film** is a movie. ❑ *I'm going to see a film tonight.*

■ **N-COUNT** A **film of** liquid is a very thin layer of it. ❑ *The sea is coated with a film of oil.*

■ **V-T** ARTS If you **film** something, you use a camera to take moving pictures of it. ❑ *He filmed her life story.*

■ **N-COUNT/N-NONCOUNT** A **film** is the roll of plastic that is used for taking photographs in some older cameras. ❑ *Emily put a new roll of film into the camera.* [from Old English]
→ look at Word Web: **genre**

Word Partnership	Use **film** with :
N	film **clip**, film **critic**, film **director**, film **producer**, film **studio** ■ roll of film ■
V	**direct** a film, **edit** film, **watch** a film ■ **develop** film ■

fil|ter /fɪltər/ (**filters, filtering, filtered**)

■ **N-COUNT** SCIENCE A **filter** is an object that only allows liquid or air to pass through it, and that holds back solid parts such as dirt or dust. ❑ *The water filters are available in different styles, colors, and designs.*

■ **V-T** SCIENCE If you **filter** a liquid or air, you clean it by passing it through a filter. ❑ *The device cleans and filters the air.*

■ **V-I** If light or sound **filters into** a place, it can be seen or heard, but it is not very strong. ❑ *Light filtered into my kitchen through the tree.* [from Medieval Latin]

filthy /fɪlθi/ (**filthier, filthiest**) **ADJ** Something that is **filthy** is very dirty. ❑ *He never washed and always wore a filthy old*

jacket. [from Old English]

fin /fɪn/ (**fins**) **N-COUNT** SCIENCE A fish's **fins** are the flat parts like wings that help it to swim. [from Old English]
→ look at Picture Dictionary: **fish**

Word Link	fin ≈ end : final, finalist, finish

fi|nal /faɪnᵊl/ (**finals**)

■ **ADJ** In a series of things, the **final** one is the last one. ❑ *The team's final game of the season will be tomorrow.*

■ **ADJ** If a decision is **final**, it cannot be changed. ❑ *The judges' decision is final.*

■ **N-COUNT** SPORTS The **final** is the last game or race in a series, that decides who is the winner. ❑ *Williams played in the final of the US Open in 1997.*

■ → see also **quarterfinal, semifinal**

■ **N-PLURAL** When you take your **finals** or your **final exams**, you take the last and most important exams in a class. ❑ *Anna took her finals in the summer.* ❑ *I'm studying for my final exams.* [from Latin]

Thesaurus	final Also look up :
ADJ	last, ultimate ■ absolute, decisive, definite, settled ■

fi|nal|ist /faɪnᵊlɪst/ (**finalists**) **N-COUNT** A **finalist** is someone who reaches the final of a competition. ❑ *Thompson was an Olympic finalist in 1996.* [from Italian]

fi|nal|ly /faɪnᵊli/

■ **ADV** If something **finally** happens, it happens after a long time. ❑ *The letter finally arrived at the end of last week.*

■ **ADV** You use **finally** before you say the last thing in a list. ❑ *Combine the flour and the cheese, and finally, add the cream.* [from Latin]

fi|nance /faɪnæns, fɪnæns/ (**finances, financing, financed**)

■ **V-T** When someone **finances** something, they provide the money to pay for it. ❑ *The government used the money to finance the war.*

■ **N-NONCOUNT** **Finance** is when people manage large amounts of money. ❑ *Professor Buckley teaches finance and law at Princeton University.*

■ **N-PLURAL** Your **finances** are the money that you have. ❑ *Take control of your finances now and save thousands of dollars.* [from Old French]

fi|nan|cial /faɪnænʃᵊl, fɪn-/ **ADJ** **Financial** means relating to money. ❑ *The company is* *in financial difficulties.* ● **fi|nan|cial|ly ADV** ❑ *She would like to be more financially independent.* [from Old French]

find /faɪnd/ (**finds, finding, found**)

1 **V-T** If you **find** someone or something, you see them or learn where they are after you have been looking for them. ❑ *The police searched the house and found a gun.*

2 **V-T** If you **find** something that you need or want, you succeed in getting it. ❑ *Many people here cannot find work.* ❑ *We have to find him an apartment.*

3 **V-T** If you **find** something, you see something by chance. ❑ *If you find my purse, can you let me know?*

4 **V-T** If you **find yourself** doing something, you are doing it without deciding or intending to do it. ❑ *I found myself having a good time.*

5 **V-T** When a court **finds** someone guilty or not guilty, it says that they are guilty or not guilty of a crime. ❑ *The woman was found guilty of murdering her husband.*

6 **V-T** You can use **find** to express your opinion about something. ❑ *I find his behavior extremely rude.* ❑ *We all found the movie very funny.*

7 **V-T** If something **is found** in a particular place or thing, it exists in that place. ❑ *Many different types of plant are found in the park.*

8 → see also **found**

9 **PHRASE** If you **find** your **way** somewhere, you get there by choosing the right way to go. ❑ *We lost our dog, but he found his way home.* [from Old English]

▶ **find out** If you **find** something **out**, you learn the facts about it. ❑ *I'll watch the next episode to find out what happens.*

find|ing /faɪndɪŋ/ (**findings**) **N-COUNT** Someone's **findings** are the information they get as the result of an investigation or some research. ❑ *...one of the main findings of the survey.* [from Old English]

→ look at Word Webs: **laboratory, science**

fine /faɪn/ (**finer, finest, fines, fining, fined**)

1 **ADJ** Something that is **fine** is very good. ❑ *There is a fine view of the countryside.*

2 **ADJ** If you are **fine**, you are in good health or you are happy. ❑ *Lina is fine and sends you her love.*

3 **ADJ** If something is **fine**, it is satisfactory or acceptable. ❑ *Everything is going to be just fine.*

4 **ADV** **Fine** is also an adverb. ❑ *All the instruments are working fine.*

5 **ADJ** Something that is **fine** is very thin or small. ❑ *...fine hairs.* ● **fine|ly ADV** ❑ *Chop the onions finely.*

6 **ADJ** When the weather is **fine**, the sun is shining.

7 **N-COUNT** A **fine** is money that someone has to pay because they have done something illegal or broken a rule.

8 **V-T** If someone **is fined**, they have to pay some money because they have done something illegal or broken a rule. ❑ *She was fined $300 for driving dangerously.* [Senses 1 to 6 from Italian. Senses 7 to 8 from Old French.]

fine ad|just|ment N-NONCOUNT SCIENCE The part of a microscope that controls the **fine adjustment** is the part that allows you to obtain the best possible focus for the object you are looking at.

fine art (**fine arts**) **N-COUNT/N-NONCOUNT ARTS** **Fine art** is the paintings and objects that artists produce for other people's pleasure, rather than for a particular use. ❑ *...the Santa Fe Museum of Fine Arts.*

fin|ger /fɪŋgər/ (**fingers**)

1 **N-COUNT** Your **fingers** are the long thin parts at the end of each hand. ❑ *Amber had a huge diamond ring on her finger.*

2 **PHRASE** If you **cross** your **fingers**, you put one finger on top of another and hope for good luck.

3 **PHRASE** If you **put** your **finger on** a reason or a problem, you see or say exactly what it is. ❑ *We couldn't put our finger on what went wrong.* [from Old English]

→ look at Picture Dictionary: **hand**

finger|nail /fɪŋgərneɪl/ (**fingernails**) **N-COUNT** Your **fingernails** are the thin hard parts at the end of each of your fingers.

→ look at Picture Dictionary: **hand**

finger|print /fɪŋgərprɪnt/ (**fingerprints**) **N-COUNT** **Fingerprints** are the marks that your fingers make when they touch something. ❑ *His fingerprints were found on the gun.*

finger|tip /fɪŋgərtɪp/ (**fingertips**) also **finger-tip N-COUNT** Your **fingertips** are the ends of your fingers. ❑ *He plays the drum very lightly with his fingertips.*

Word Link *fin ≈ end : final, finalist, finish*

fin|ish /fɪnɪʃ/ (**finishes, finishing, finished**)

1 **V-T** When you **finish** doing something, you do the last part of it, so that there is no more for you to do. ❑ *Dad finished eating, and left the room.*

2 **Finish up** means the same as **finish**. ❑ *We waited outside while Nick finished up his meeting.*

3 **V-I** When something **finishes**, it ends, especially at a planned time. ❑ *The concert finished just after midnight.*

4 **N-SING** The **finish** of something is the end of it or the last part of it. ❑ *There was an exciting finish to the women's 800-meter race.*

5 **N-COUNT** If the surface of something that has been made has a particular type of **finish**, it has a particular type of appearance or texture. ❑ *Each bowl is made by hand, and has a silky smooth finish.*

6 **PHRASE** If you add **the finishing touches** to something, you do the last things that are necessary to complete it. ❑ *She was adding the finishing touches to her novel.* [from Old French]

▶ **finish off** or **finish up** If you **finish off** or **finish up** food or drink, you eat or drink the last part of it. ❑ *Kelly finished off her coffee.* ❑ *Finish up your soup now, please.*

Thesaurus   finish   Also look up :

v   conclude, end, wrap up; *(ant.)* begin, start **1** **2**

Word Partnership   Use **finish** with :

N   finish **a conversation**, finish **school**, finish **work** **1**
finish **a job**, **time to** finish **1** **2**

fin|ished /fɪnɪʃt/ **ADJ** Someone who is **finished with** something is no longer using it or dealing with it. ❑ *When you have finished with the book, please give it back to your teacher.* [from Old French]

fi|nite /faɪnaɪt/ **ADJ** Something that is **finite** has a definite fixed size or extent. [FORMAL] ❑ *...the realization that life is finite.* [from Latin]

fir /fɜr/ (**firs**) **N-COUNT/N-NONCOUNT** SCIENCE A **fir** or a **fir tree** is a tall tree with needles that do not fall in winter. [from Old English]

---

fire

1 BURNING, HEAT
2 VERB USES
3 PHRASES

1 fire /faɪər/ (**fires**)

1 **N-NONCOUNT** Fire is the hot, bright flames that come from things that are burning. ❑ *We learned how to make fire and hunt for fish.*

2 **N-COUNT/N-NONCOUNT** Fire or a **fire** is flames that destroy things, such as buildings or forests. ❑ *87 people died in a fire at the theater.* ❑ *...a forest fire.*

3 **N-COUNT** A **fire** is a burning pile of wood, coal, or other fuel that you make. ❑ *There was a fire in the fireplace.* [from Old English]
→ look at Word Web: **fire**

2 fire /faɪər/ (**fires, firing, fired**)

1 **V-T/V-I** If someone **fires** a gun or a bullet, or if they **fire**, a bullet is sent from a gun that they are using. ❑ *Have you ever fired a gun before?* ❑ *The policeman fired at the gangsters.*

2 **V-T** If an employer **fires** you, he or she tells you to leave your job. ❑ *She was fired from that job in August.* [from Old English]

3 fire /faɪər/

1 **PHRASE** If something **catches fire**, it starts burning. ❑ *Several buildings caught fire in the explosion.*

2 **PHRASE** If something is **on fire**, it is burning and being damaged by a fire. ❑ *Quick! My car's on fire!*

3 **PHRASE** If you **set fire to** something, or if you **set it on fire**, you make it start to burn. [from Old English]

fire alarm (**fire alarms**) **N-COUNT** A **fire alarm** is a piece of equipment that makes a loud noise to warn people when there is a fire.

fire|arm /faɪərɑrm/ (**firearms**) **N-COUNT** Firearms are guns. [FORMAL] ❑ *The guards were carrying firearms.*

f

Word Web   fire

A single **match**, a **campfire**, or even a bolt of lightning can **spark** a **wild fire**. Wild fires can **burn down** forests. But there are some ecosystems that depend on fire. Once the fire passes, the **smoke** clears and the **ash** settles, then the cycle of life begins again. Humans have learned to use fire. The **heat** cooks our food. People build fires in **fireplaces** and **wood** stoves. The **flames** warm our hands. And before electricity, the **glow** of **candlelight** lit our homes.

fire blan|ket (fire blankets) **N-COUNT** A fire blanket is a thick cloth made from fire-resistant material that is designed to put out small fires.

fire de|part|ment (fire departments) **N-COUNT** The fire department is the organization whose job is to stop fires.

fire en|gine (fire engines) **N-COUNT** A fire engine is a large vehicle that carries people and equipment for putting out fires.

fire ex|tin|guish|er /faɪər ɪkstɪŋgwɪʃər/ (fire extinguishers) **N-COUNT** A fire extinguisher is a metal container with water or chemicals inside for stopping fires.

fire|fight|er /faɪərfaɪtər/ (firefighters) **N-COUNT** A firefighter is a person whose job is to put out fires.

fire|place /faɪərpleɪs/ (fireplaces) **N-COUNT** In a room, the fireplace is the place made out of brick or stone where you can light a fire. → look at Word Web: **fire**

fire|work /faɪərwɜrk/ (fireworks) **N-COUNT** Fireworks are things that fly up into the air and explode, making bright colors in the sky. ❑ We watched the fireworks from the balcony. → look at Word Web: **fireworks**

firm /fɜrm/ (firmer, firmest, firms) **❶ N-COUNT** A firm is an organization that sells or produces something, or that provides a service that people pay for. ❑ Kevin works for a Chicago law firm. **❷ ADJ** If something is firm, it is not soft. ❑ When you buy fruit, make sure it is firm. **❸ ADJ** A firm physical action is strong. ❑ His handshake was firm. ● **firm|ly ADV** ❑ She held me firmly by the elbow. **❹ ADJ** A firm person behaves in a way that shows that they are not going to change their mind. ❑ She was firm with him. "I don't want to see you again." ● **firm|ly ADV** ❑ "You must

go to bed now, kids," he said firmly. **❺ ADJ** A firm decision or opinion is not likely to change. ❑ He made a firm decision to leave. [from Spanish]

Thesaurus	firm	Also look up :
N	business, company, enterprise, organization **❶**	
ADJ	dense, hard, sturdy **❷**	

first /fɜrst/ **❶ ADJ** The first thing, person, event, or period of time is the one that happens or comes before all the others. ❑ January is the first month of the year. **❷ ADV** First is also an adverb. ❑ Aaron and Steve came first in the junior competition. **❸ PRON** First is also a pronoun. ❑ I've seen the movie twice and the second time I liked it even better than the first. **❹ ADV** If you do something first, you do it before you do anything else. ❑ First, I went to the police and told them what happened. **❺ ADV** If you do something first, you do it before anyone else. ❑ The people who lived nearby arrived first. **❻ PHRASE** You use first of all to introduce the first thing that you want to say. ❑ First of all, I'd like to thank you for coming. **❼ PHRASE** You use at first when you are talking about what happened at the beginning of an event. ❑ At first, he seemed surprised by my questions. [from Old English]

first aid N-NONCOUNT First aid is simple medical treatment that you give to a sick or injured person. ❑ Each group leader must do a course in basic first aid.

first aid kit (first aid kits) **N-COUNT** A first aid kit is a bag or a case containing basic medical supplies that are designed to be used on someone who is injured or who suddenly becomes ill.

Word Web   **fireworks**

Fireworks were created in China more than a thousand years ago. Historians believe that the discovery was made by **alchemists**. They heated sulfur, potassium nitrate, **charcoal**, and arsenic together and the mixture **exploded**. It made a very hot, bright fire. Later they mixed these **chemicals** in a hollow bamboo tube and threw it in the fire. The **firecracker** was born. Marco Polo brought firecrackers to Europe from the Orient in 1292. Soon the Italians began experimenting with ways of producing elaborate, colorful fireworks displays. This launched the era of modern pyrotechnics.

first-class also **first class**

1 **ADJ** First-class describes something that people consider to be of the highest standard. ❑ *The Altea is a newly built first-class hotel.*

2 **ADJ** First-class seats on a train or an airplane are the best and most expensive seats. ❑ *He won two first-class tickets to fly to Dublin.*

3 **ADV** First class is also an adverb. ❑ *We never fly first class.*

4 **ADJ** First-class mail is used for sending letters and cards. ❑ *...a first-class letter.*

first floor (**first floors**) **N-COUNT** The first floor of a building is the floor that is on the same level as the ground.

First Lady (**First Ladies**) **N-COUNT** SOCIAL STUDIES The First Lady in a country or a state is the wife of the president or the governor.

first name (**first names**) **N-COUNT** Your first name is the name that comes before your family name. ❑ *"What's Dr. Garcia's first name?"—"It's Maria. Maria Garcia."*

fis|cal /fɪskəl/ **ADJ** BUSINESS Fiscal is used to describe something that relates to government money or public money, especially taxes. ❑ *...fiscal policy.* [from Latin]

fish /fɪʃ/ (**fish** or **fishes, fishes, fishing, fished**)

1 **N-COUNT** A fish is a creature that lives in water and has a tail and fins. ❑ *Dave caught a 3-pound fish this morning.*

2 **N-NONCOUNT** Fish is the flesh of a fish eaten as food. ❑ *This fish is delicious.*

3 **V-I** SPORTS If you fish, you try to catch fish. ❑ *Brian learned to fish in the Colorado River.* [from Old English]

→ look at Picture Dictionary: **fish**
→ look at Word Webs: **aquarium, pet, shark**

fisher|man /fɪʃərmən/ (**fishermen**) **N-COUNT** A fisherman is a person who catches fish as a job or for sport.

fish|ing /fɪʃɪŋ/ **N-NONCOUNT** SPORTS Fishing is the sport or business of catching fish. [from Old English]

fish|ing rod (**fishing rods**) **N-COUNT** SPORTS A fishing rod is a long thin pole with a thread and a hook, that is used for catching fish.

fis|sion /fɪʃən/ **N-NONCOUNT** SCIENCE Nuclear fission is the splitting of the nucleus of an atom to produce a large amount of energy or cause a large explosion.

fist /fɪst/ (**fists**) **N-COUNT** Your fist is your hand with your fingers closed tightly together. ❑ *Steve stood up and shook an angry fist at Patrick.* [from Old English]

---

fit

① BEING RIGHT OR GOING IN THE RIGHT PLACE
② HEALTHY
③ UNCONTROLLABLE MOVEMENTS

---

① fit /fɪt/ (**fits, fitting, fitted** or **fit**)

1 **V-T/V-I** If something fits, it is the right size and shape for someone or something. ❑ *The costume fit the child perfectly.* ❑ *The game is small enough to fit into your pocket.*

2 **V-T** If you fit something somewhere, you attach it there. ❑ *He fits locks on the doors.*

3 **N-SING** If something is a good fit, it fits well. ❑ *He was happy that the doors were a reasonably good fit.*

4 **ADJ** If something is fit for a particular purpose, it is suitable for that purpose. ❑ *Only two of the bicycles were fit for the road.* [from Middle Dutch]

5 → see also **fitting**

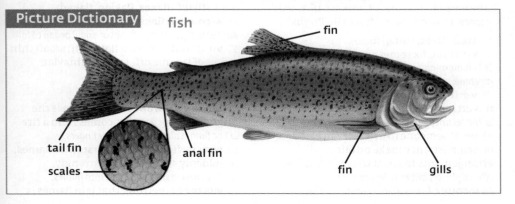

Picture Dictionary   fish

fin

tail fin

anal fin

scales

fin

gills

▶ **fit in** **1** If you manage to **fit** someone or something **in**, you find time or space for them. ❑ *The dentist can fit you in just after lunch.* ❑ *We can't fit any more children in the car.*
2 If you **fit in** as part of a group, you feel happy there because you are similar to the other people in it. ❑ *She was great with the children and fitted in beautifully.*

❷ **fit** /fɪt/ (**fitter, fittest**) **ADJ** Someone who is **fit** is healthy and strong. ❑ *You look very fit. I can tell you exercise regularly.* ● **fit|ness** **N-NONCOUNT** ❑ *Sophie is a fitness instructor.* [from Middle Dutch]

❸ **fit** /fɪt/ (**fits**)
1 **N-COUNT** If you have a **fit of** anger, laughter, or coughing, you suddenly become very angry or start laughing or coughing. ❑ *I went into a coughing fit.*
2 **N-COUNT** If someone has a **fit**, they suddenly become unconscious and their body makes violent and uncontrollable movements. [from Old English]

fit|ting /fɪtɪŋ/ (**fittings**)
1 **ADJ** Something that is **fitting** is right or suitable. ❑ *A solitary man, it was perhaps fitting that he died alone.* ● **fit|ting|ly** **ADV** ❑ *He ended his baseball career, fittingly, by hitting a home run.*
2 **N-COUNT** A **fitting** is one of the smaller parts on the outside of a piece of equipment or furniture, for example a handle or a faucet. ❑ *...brass light fittings.*
3 **N-PLURAL** **Fittings** are things such as ovens or heaters, that are fitted inside a building, but can be removed if necessary. [from Middle Dutch]
4 → see also **fit** ❶

five /faɪv/
1 **NUM** **MATH** **Five** is the number 5.
2 **N-COUNT** A **five** is a five-dollar bill. ❑ *He reached into his pocket, took out a five, and slapped it on the counter.* [from Old English]

fix /fɪks/ (**fixes, fixing, fixed**)
1 **V-T** If you **fix** something, you repair it. ❑ *This morning, a man came to fix my washing machine.*
2 **V-T** If something **is fixed** somewhere, it is attached there firmly or securely. ❑ *The security camera is fixed on the wall.*
3 **V-T** If someone **fixes** a race, an election, or a contest, they make unfair arrangements to affect the result. ❑ *They offered players bribes to fix the game.*
4 **N-COUNT** **Fix** is also a noun. ❑ *It's all*

a fix, a deal they've made.
5 **V-T** If you **fix** a meal, you prepare it. ❑ *Everyone helped to fix dinner.*
6 **V-T** If you **fix** a problem, you find a way of dealing with it. ❑ *Getting married does not fix problems.* [from Medieval Latin]
▶ **fix up** If you **fix** someone **up with** someone else, or if you **fix** two people **up**, you introduce them to each other so that they might start a romantic relationship.

fixed /fɪkst/ **ADJ** You use **fixed** to describe something that stays the same and does not or cannot vary. ❑ *The company issues a fixed number of shares.* ❑ *...fixed-price menus.* [from Medieval Latin]

fixed pul|ley (**fixed pulleys**) **N-COUNT** A **fixed pulley** is a pulley that is attached to something that does not move.

| **Word Link** | *fix ≈ fastening : fixture, prefix, suffix* |

fix|ture /fɪkstʃər/ (**fixtures**) **N-COUNT** **Fixtures** are fittings or furniture that belong to a building and are legally part of it, for example a bathtub or a toilet. ❑ *...fixtures and fittings are included in the purchase price.* [from Late Latin]

flag /flæg/ (**flags**)
N-COUNT A **flag** is a piece of colored cloth with a pattern on it that is used as a symbol for a country or an organization. ❑ *The crowd was shouting and waving American flags.*

flag

fla|gella /flədʒɛlə/ **N-PLURAL** **SCIENCE** **Flagella** are the long, thin extensions of cells in some microorganisms that help them move.

flake /fleɪk/ (**flakes, flaking, flaked**)
1 **N-COUNT** A **flake** is a small thin piece of something. ❑ *Large flakes of snow began to fall.*
2 **V-I** If paint **flakes** or **flakes off**, small thin pieces of it come off. [of Scandinavian origin]

flame /fleɪm/ (**flames**)
1 **N-COUNT/N-NONCOUNT** A **flame** is the bright burning gas that comes from a fire. ❑ *The flames almost burned her fingers.*
2 **PHRASE** If something **bursts into flames**, it suddenly starts burning strongly. ❑ *The plane crashed and burst into flames.*
3 **PHRASE** Something that is **in flames** is

burning. ❑ *When we arrived, the house was in flames.* [from Old French]
→ look at Picture Dictionary: **laboratory**
→ look at Word Web: **fire**

fla|min|go /fləmɪŋgoʊ/ (**flamingos** or **flamingoes**) **N-COUNT** A **flamingo** is a bird with pink feathers, long thin legs, a long neck, and a curved beak. Flamingos live near water in warm areas. [from Portuguese]

flam|mable /flæməbªl/ **ADJ Flammable** things burn easily. ❑ *Always store flammable liquids away from the house.* [from Latin]

flank /flæŋk/ (**flanks, flanking, flanked**)
1 N-COUNT An animal's **flank** is its side, between the ribs and the hip.
2 N-COUNT A **flank** of an army or navy force is one side of it when it is organized for battle.
3 V-T If something **is flanked by** things, it has them on both sides of it, or sometimes on one side of it. ❑ *The altar was flanked by two Christmas trees.* [from Old French]
→ look at Picture Dictionary: **horse**

flap /flæp/ (**flaps, flapping, flapped**)
1 V-T/V-I If something **flaps** or if you **flap** it, it moves quickly up and down or from side to side. ❑ *Sheets flapped on the clothes line.*
2 V-T/V-I If a bird **flaps** its wings or if its wings **flap**, its wings move up and down quickly. ❑ *The birds flapped their wings.*
3 N-COUNT A **flap** of something is a flat piece that can move up and down or from side to side. ❑ *I opened the flap of the envelope and took out the letter.*

flare /flɛər/ (**flares, flaring, flared**)
1 N-COUNT A **flare** is a small device that produces a bright flame. Flares are used as distress signals, for example on ships.
2 V-I If a fire **flares**, the flames suddenly become larger.
3 Flare up means the same as **flare**. ❑ *Don't spill too much fat on the barbecue as it could flare up.*
4 V-I If something such as trouble, violence, or conflict **flares**, it starts or becomes more violent. ❑ *Trouble flared in several American cities.*
5 Flare up means the same as **flare**.
❑ *Dozens of people were injured as fighting flared up.*

flash /flæʃ/ (**flashes, flashing, flashed**)
1 N-COUNT A **flash** is a sudden bright light. ❑ *There was a flash of lightning.*
2 V-T/V-I If a light **flashes** or if you **flash** a

light, it shines on and off very quickly.
❑ *They saw a lighthouse flashing through the fog.*
3 PHRASE If something happens **in a flash**, it happens suddenly and lasts only a very short time. ❑ *The answer came to him in a flash.*

flash drive (**flash drives**) **N-COUNT** TECHNOLOGY A **flash drive** is a small object for storing computer information that you can carry with you and use in different computers.
→ look at Picture Dictionary: **computer**

flash flood (**flash floods**) **N-COUNT** SCIENCE A **flash flood** is a sudden rush of water over dry land, usually caused by a lot of rain.

flash|light /flæʃlaɪt/ (**flashlights**) **N-COUNT** A **flashlight** is a small electric light that you can carry in your hand. ❑ *Adam shone a flashlight into the backyard but he couldn't see anyone.*

flash mob (**flash mobs**) **N-COUNT** A **flash mob** is a group of people who arrange to meet in a public place to put on a short, surprise performance. ❑ *...a flash mob performing a song and dance routine.*

flask /flæsk/ (**flasks**) **N-COUNT** A **flask** is a bottle that you use for carrying alcoholic or hot drinks around with you. ❑ *...a flask of coffee.* [from Old French]
→ look at Picture Dictionary: **laboratory**

flat /flæt/ (**flatter, flattest**)
1 ADJ Something that is **flat** is level, smooth, or even. ❑ *Tiles can be fixed to any flat surface.* ❑ *...a flat roof.*
2 ADJ A **flat** object is not very tall or deep in relation to its length and width. ❑ *...a square flat box.*
3 ADJ A **flat** tire or ball does not have enough air in it.
4 ADJ If something happened, for example, in ten seconds **flat**, it happened very quickly, and only took ten seconds. ❑ *The engine will take you from 0 to 60 mph in six seconds flat.*
5 ADJ MUSIC A B **flat** or an E **flat**, for example, is a note that is slightly lower than B or E. Compare with **sharp**.
6 ADV MUSIC If someone sings **flat**, their singing is slightly lower than it should be.
7 ADJ MUSIC **Flat** is also an adjective. ❑ *His singing was flat.* [from Old Norse]
8 → see also **flatter**

Thesaurus	flat	Also look up :
ADJ		even, horizontal, level, smooth **1**

flat|screen /ˈflætskrin/ (flatscreens)

1 **ADJ** A **flatscreen** television or computer monitor has a flat screen. ❑ *They finally replaced their 40-year-old television with a flatscreen TV.*

2 **N-COUNT** **Flatscreen** is also a noun. ❑ *...a 42" digital flatscreen.*

flat|ten /ˈflætᵊn/ (flattens, flattening, flattened) **V-T/V-I** If you **flatten** something, or if it **flattens**, you make it flat. ❑ *Flatten the bread dough with your hands.* ❑ *The dog's ears flattened slightly as Chris spoke his name.* [from Old Norse]

flat|ter /ˈflætər/ (flatters, flattering, flattered)

1 **V-T** If you **flatter** someone, you say nice things to them because you want them to like you. ❑ *Everyone likes to be flattered, to be told that they're beautiful.* [from Old French]

2 → see also **flat**

flat|ter|ing /ˈflætərɪŋ/ **ADJ** Something that is **flattering** makes you look or seem attractive or important. ❑ *It was a very flattering photograph—he looked like a movie star.* [from Old French]

flat|ware /ˈflætwɛər/ **N-NONCOUNT** You can refer to knives, forks, and spoons that you eat food with as **flatware**.

fla|vor /ˈfleɪvər/ (flavors, flavoring, flavored)

1 **N-COUNT/N-NONCOUNT** The **flavor** of a food or a drink is its taste. ❑ *I added some pepper for extra flavor.*

2 **V-T** If you **flavor** food or drink, you add something to it to give it a particular taste. ❑ *Flavor your favorite dishes with herbs and spices.* [from Old French]

fla|vor|ing /ˈfleɪvərɪŋ/ (flavorings) **N-COUNT/N-NONCOUNT** **Flavorings** are substances that you add to food or drink to give it a particular taste. [from Old French]

flaw /flɔ/ (flaws) **N-COUNT** A **flaw** in something is something that is wrong with it. ❑ *There are a number of flaws in his theory.* [from Old Norse]

flea /fli/ (fleas) **N-COUNT** A **flea** is a very small insect that jumps. Fleas live on the bodies of humans or animals, and drink their blood as food. ❑ *Our dog has fleas.* [from Old English]

fled /flɛd/ **Fled** is the past tense and past participle of **flee**. [from Old English]

flee /fli/ (flees, fleeing, fled) **V-T/V-I** If you **flee** from something or someone, or **flee** a person or a thing, you run away from them. [WRITTEN] ❑ *He slammed the door behind him and fled.* ❑ *...refugees fleeing torture.* [from Old English]

fleece /flis/ (fleeces)

1 **N-COUNT** A sheep's **fleece** is the coat of wool that covers it.

2 **N-COUNT** A **fleece** is a jacket or a sweater made from a soft warm cloth called fleece. ❑ *He was wearing track pants and a dark blue fleece.* [from Old English]

fleet /flit/ (fleets) **N-COUNT** A **fleet** is a large group of boats, aircraft, or cars. ❑ *The fleet sailed out to the ocean.* [from Old English]

flesh /flɛʃ/

1 **N-NONCOUNT** **Flesh** is the soft part of a person's or an animal's body between the bones and the skin. ❑ *The bullet went straight through the flesh of his arm.*

2 **N-NONCOUNT** The **flesh** of a fruit or a vegetable is the soft part that is inside it.

3 **PHRASE** If someone is your **own flesh and blood**, they are a member of your family.

4 **PHRASE** If you meet or see someone **in the flesh**, you actually meet or see them in person. ❑ *When people see me in the flesh, they say, "You're smaller than you look on TV."* [from Old English]

→ look at Word Web: **carnivore**

flew /flu/ **Flew** is the past tense of **fly**. [from Old English]

Word Link	flex ≈ bending : flexible, flexor, reflexive verb

Word Link	ible ≈ able to be : audible, flexible, possible

flex|ible /ˈflɛksɪbᵊl/

1 **ADJ** If something is **flexible**, it bends easily without breaking. ❑ *These children's books have flexible plastic covers.*

2 **ADJ** If something or someone is **flexible**, they are able to change easily. ❑ *I'm very lucky to have flexible working hours.* ● **flexi|bil|ity** **N-NONCOUNT** ❑ *It's possible to go there by bus, but a car gives more flexibility.* [from Latin]

flex|or /ˈflɛksər/ (flexors) **N-COUNT** **SCIENCE** A **flexor** is a muscle that bends a part of your body. [from New Latin]

flick /flɪk/ (flicks, flicking, flicked)

1 **N-COUNT** A **flick** is a quick, sharp movement. ❑ *The pony gave a quick flick of its tail.*

F

2 **v-t/v-i** If you **flick** something, you move it using a quick, sharp movement. ❑ *He shook his head to flick hair out of his eyes.* ❑ *His tongue flicked across his lips.*

3 **v-t** If you **flick** a switch, you press it quickly. ❑ *Sam was flicking a flashlight on and off.*

4 **v-i** If you **flick through** a book or a magazine, you turn its pages quickly. ❑ *I picked up a magazine and flicked through it.*

flick|er /flɪkər/ (**flickers, flickering, flickered**)

1 **v-i** If a light or a flame **flickers**, it shines in a way that is not steady. ❑ *The lights flickered, and suddenly it was dark.*

2 **N-COUNT** A **flicker** is an unsteady flame. ❑ *He could see the flicker of flames.* [from Old English]

flight /flaɪt/ (**flights**)

1 **N-COUNT** A **flight** is a trip in an aircraft. ❑ *The flight to New York will take four hours.* ❑ *Our flight was two hours late.*

2 **N-COUNT** An airplane carrying passengers on a particular trip is a particular **flight**. ❑ *BA flight 286 was two hours late.*

3 **N-COUNT** A **flight of** stairs or steps is a set of stairs that go from one level to another. ❑ *Ashley walked up the short flight of steps.*

4 **N-NONCOUNT** **Flight** is the action of flying, or the ability to fly. ❑ *The photograph showed an eagle in flight.* [from Old English]
→ look at Word Web: **fly**

flim|sy /flɪmzi/ (**flimsier, flimsiest**)

1 **ADJ** A **flimsy** object is easily damaged because it is made of a weak material, or is badly made. ❑ *...a flimsy wooden door.*

2 **ADJ** **Flimsy** cloth or clothing is thin and does not give much protection. ❑ *...a flimsy pink nightgown.*

3 **ADJ** If you describe something such as evidence or an excuse as **flimsy**, you mean that it is not very good or convincing.

fling /flɪŋ/ (**flings, flinging, flung**)

1 **v-t** If you **fling** something somewhere, you throw it there using a lot of force. ❑ *She flung down the magazine and ran from the room.*

2 **N-COUNT** If two people have **a fling**, they have a brief romantic relationship. [INFORMAL] ❑ *She had a brief fling with him 30 years ago.* [of Scandinavian origin]

flip /flɪp/ (**flips, flipping, flipped**)

1 **v-i** If you **flip** through the pages of a book, you turn the pages quickly. ❑ *He was flipping through a magazine in the living room.*

2 **v-t/v-i** If something **flips** over, or if you **flip** it over or into a different position, it moves or is moved into a different position. ❑ *The car flipped over and burst into flames.*

flirt /flɜrt/ (**flirts, flirting, flirted**)

1 **v-t/v-i** If you **flirt**, you behave toward someone in a way that shows that you think they are attractive. ❑ *My brother was flirting with all the girls.*

2 **N-COUNT** Someone who is a **flirt** likes to flirt a lot. ❑ *I'm not a flirt. I'm only interested in my boyfriend.*

float /floʊt/ (**floats, floating, floated**)

1 **v-t/v-i** If something or someone **floats**, they stay on the surface of a liquid, and do not sink. You can also **float** something on a liquid. ❑ *A plastic bottle was floating in the water.* ❑ *It's below freezing and small icebergs are floating by.*

2 **v-i** If something **floats** in the air, it moves slowly and gently through it. ❑ *A yellow balloon floated past.*

3 **N-COUNT** A **float** is an object that stays on the surface of the water and supports your body while you are learning to swim. [from Old English]

flock /flɒk/ (**flocks, flocking, flocked**)

1 **N-COUNT** A **flock of** birds, sheep, or goats is a group of them. ❑ *A flock of birds flew overhead.*

2 **v-i** If people **flock to** a particular place or event, a lot of them go there. ❑ *The public has flocked to the show.* ❑ *People are flocking to see the film.* [from Old English]

flood /flʌd/ (**floods, flooding, flooded**)

1 **N-COUNT/N-NONCOUNT** If there is a **flood**, a lot of water covers an area that is usually dry. ❑ *More than 70 people died in the floods.*

2 **v-t/v-i** If water **floods** an area, or if an area **floods**, the area becomes covered with water. ❑ *The water tank burst and flooded the house.* ❑ *The whole town flooded.* ● **flood|ing** **N-NONCOUNT** ❑ *The flooding is the worst in sixty-five years.*

3 **v-i** If people or things **flood** into a place, they arrive there in large numbers. ❑ *Thousands of refugees flooded into the area.* [from Old English]
→ look at Word Webs: **dam, disaster, storm**

flood|light /flʌdlaɪt/ (**floodlights**) **N-COUNT** **Floodlights** are very powerful lights that are used outside for lighting public buildings and sports grounds at night.

f

flood plain (**flood plains**) also **floodplain**
N-COUNT SCIENCE A **flood plain** is a flat area on the edge of a river, where the ground consists of soil, sand, and rock left by the river when it floods.

floor /flɔr/ (**floors**)
1 **N-COUNT** The **floor** of a room is the part of it that you walk on. ◻ *There were no seats, so we sat on the floor.*
2 **N-COUNT** A **floor** of a building is all the rooms that are on a particular level. ◻ *The café was on the seventh floor.*
3 → see also **first floor**
4 **N-COUNT** The ocean **floor** is the ground at the bottom of an ocean. [from Old English]

Word Partnership	Use **floor** with :
V	**fall on the** floor, **sit on the** floor, **sweep the** floor **1**
N	floor **to ceiling,** floor **space 1** floor **plan 2** **forest** floor, **ocean** floor **3**

flop /flɒp/ (**flops, flopping, flopped**)
1 **V-I** If you **flop** down, you sit down suddenly and heavily because you are so tired. ◻ *Ben flopped down on the bed and fell asleep at once.*
2 **N-COUNT** If something is a **flop**, it is completely unsuccessful. [INFORMAL] ◻ *It is the public who decides whether a film is a hit or a flop.*

flop|py /flɒpi/ (**floppier, floppiest**) ADJ
Floppy things are loose, and hang down. ◻ *Stephanie was wearing a blue floppy hat.*

flo|rist /flɔrɪst/ (**florists**)
1 **N-COUNT** A **florist** is a person who works in a store that sells flowers.
2 **N-COUNT** A **florist** or a **florist's** is a store where you can buy flowers. [from New Latin]

floun|der /flaʊndər/ (**flounders, floundering, floundered**)
1 **V-I** If something **is floundering**, it has many problems and may soon fail completely. ◻ *What a pity that his career was left to flounder.*
2 **V-I** If you say that someone **is floundering**, you are criticizing them for not making decisions or for not knowing what to say or do. ◻ *Right now, you've got a president who's floundering.*

flour /flaʊər/ **N-NONCOUNT** Flour is a fine powder that is used for making bread,

cakes, and pastry.
→ look at Word Web: **grain**

flour|ish /flɜrɪʃ/ (**flourishes, flourishing, flourished**) **V-I** If something **flourishes**, it is successful or active, and is developing quickly and strongly. ◻ *This plant flourishes in warm climates.* ◻ *Heckart's career really flourished in the 1950s.* [from Old French]

flow /floʊ/ (**flows, flowing, flowed**)
1 **V-I** If a liquid, a gas, or an electrical current **flows** somewhere, it moves there in a steady and continuous way. ◻ *A stream flowed gently down into the valley.*
2 **N-COUNT/N-NONCOUNT** A **flow** is a steady, continuous movement in a particular direction. ◻ *Vicky tried to stop the flow of blood.* ◻ *The new tunnel will speed up traffic flow.* [from Old English]
→ look at Word Web: **traffic**

flow chart (**flow charts**) **N-COUNT** SCIENCE A **flow chart** or a **flow diagram** is a diagram that represents the sequence of actions in a particular process or activity.

flow|er /flaʊər/ (**flowers, flowering, flowered**)
1 **N-COUNT** A **flower** is the brightly colored part of a plant that grows at the end of a stem. ◻ *Dad gave Mom a huge bunch of flowers.*
2 **V-I** When a plant or a tree **flowers**, its flowers appear and open. ◻ *These plants will flower soon.* [from Old French]
→ look at Picture Dictionaries: **flowers, plants**

Word Partnership	Use **flower** with :
N	flower **arrangement,** flower **garden,** flower **shop,** flower **show 1**
ADJ	**dried** flower, **fresh** flower **1**
V	**pick a** flower **1**

flow|er|ing /flaʊərɪŋ/ ADJ **Flowering** shrubs, trees, or plants are those that produce noticeable flowers. [from Old French]

flown /floʊn/ **Flown** is the past participle of **fly**.

flu /flu/ **N-NONCOUNT** Flu is an illness that is like a very bad cold. **Flu** is short for "influenza." ◻ *I've got the flu and I ache all over.*

fluc|tu|ate /flʌktʃueɪt/ (**fluctuates, fluctuating, fluctuated**) **V-I** If something **fluctuates**, it changes a lot in an irregular way. ◻ *Body temperature can fluctuate if you are ill.* ● **fluc|tua|tion** /flʌktʃueɪʃ°n/

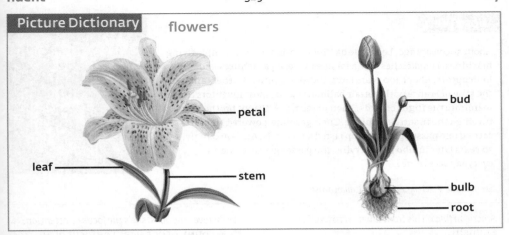

petal

bud

leaf

stem

bulb

root

f

(fluctuations) **N-COUNT/N-NONCOUNT** ❑ *Don't worry about tiny fluctuations in your weight.* [from Latin]

flu|ent /flu̱ənt/ **ADJ** If you are **fluent in** a particular language, you can speak it easily and correctly. ❑ *Jose is fluent in Spanish and English.* ● **flu|ent|ly ADV** ❑ *He spoke three languages fluently.* [from Latin]

fluffy /flʌ̱fi/ (**fluffier, fluffiest**) **ADJ** If something is **fluffy**, it is very soft. ❑ *I dried myself with a big fluffy towel.*

flu|id /flu̱ɪd/ (**fluids**)
1 **N-COUNT/N-NONCOUNT** A **fluid** is a liquid. [FORMAL] ❑ *Make sure that you drink plenty of fluids.*
2 **ADJ** **Fluid** movements, lines, or designs are smooth and graceful. ❑ *His painting became more fluid.* [from Latin]

flung /flʌ̱ŋ/ **Flung** is the past tense and past participle of **fling**. [of Scandinavian origin]

flunk /flʌ̱ŋk/ (**flunks, flunking, flunked**) **V-T** If you **flunk** an exam or a course, you do not pass it. [INFORMAL] ❑ *Three of the students flunked the math test.*

fluo|res|cent /flʊrɛ̱sᵊnt/
1 **ADJ** A **fluorescent** surface, substance, or color has a very bright appearance when light is directed onto it. ❑ *...a piece of fluorescent tape.*
2 **ADJ** A **fluorescent** light shines with a very hard, bright light and is usually in the form of a long strip.
→ look at Word Web: **light bulb**

flush /flʌ̱ʃ/ (**flushes, flushing, flushed**)
1 **V-I** If you **flush**, your face becomes red because you are hot, ill, embarrassed, or angry. ● **flushed ADJ** ❑ *Amanda was flushed with embarrassment.*
2 **V-T/V-I** When someone **flushes** a toilet, they press a handle and water flows into the toilet bowl, cleaning it. ❑ *I heard the toilet flush.*
3 **N-COUNT** **Flush** is also a noun. ❑ *He heard the flush of a toilet.*

flute /flu̱t/ (**flutes**) **N-COUNT/N-NONCOUNT** MUSIC A **flute** is a musical instrument that you play by blowing. You hold it sideways to your mouth. [from Old French]
→ look at Word Web: **orchestra**

flut|ter /flʌ̱tər/ (**flutters, fluttering, fluttered**) **V-T/V-I** If something **flutters**, or if you **flutter** it, it makes a lot of quick, light movements. ❑ *The butterfly fluttered its wings.* ❑ *Her silk skirt was fluttering in the breeze.* [from Old English]

fly /fla̱ɪ/ (**flies, flying, flew, flown**)
1 **N-COUNT** A **fly** is a small insect with two wings.
2 **N-COUNT** The front opening on a pair of pants is called the **fly**.
3 **V-I** When a bird, an insect, or an aircraft **flies**, it moves through the air. ❑ *The planes flew through the clouds.* ● **fly|ing ADJ** ❑ *...flying insects.*
4 **V-I** If you **fly** somewhere, you travel there in an aircraft. ❑ *Jerry flew to Los Angeles this morning.*
5 **V-T/V-I** When someone **flies** an aircraft, they control its movement in the air. ❑ *He flew a small plane to Cuba.* ❑ *I learned to fly in Vietnam.*
6 **V-T/V-I** If you **fly** a flag or if it **is flying**, it is displayed at the top of a pole. ❑ *He flies the*

F

> ## Word Web   fly
>
> About 500 years ago, Leonardo da Vinci* designed some simple flying machines. His sketches look a lot like modern **parachutes** and **helicopters**. About 300 years later, the Montgolfier Brothers amazed the king of France with hot-air **balloon** flights. Most inventors tried to imitate the **flight** of birds. Then in 1903, the Wright brothers invented the first true **airplane**. Their gasoline-powered air **craft** carried one **passenger**. The trip lasted 59 seconds. And amazingly, 70 years later **jumbo jets** carrying 400 passengers became an everyday occurrence.
>
>
>
> *Leonardo da Vinci (1452–1519): an Italian artist.*

American flag on his front lawn. [from Old English]

→ look at Picture Dictionary: **insects**

→ look at Word Web: **fly**

fly|er /flaɪər/ (**flyers**) also **flier** **N-COUNT**
A **flyer** is a small printed notice that advertises something. ❑ *A tall girl gave us a flyer for the concert.* [from Old English]

foam /foʊm/ **N-NONCOUNT** Foam is the mass of small bubbles that you sometimes see on the surface of a liquid. ❑ *He drank his cappuccino, and wiped the foam off his mustache.* [from Old English]

fo|cal point /foʊkəl pɔɪnt/ (**focal points**)
1 **N-COUNT** The **focal point** of something is the thing that people concentrate on or pay most attention to. ❑ *The focal point for the town's many visitors is the museum.*
2 **N-COUNT** ARTS The **focal point** of a painting or a drawing is the part of the picture that the viewer spends most time looking at.

fo|cus /foʊkəs/ (**focuses** or **foci** /foʊsaɪ/, **focuses, focusing, focused**)
1 **V-T/V-I** If you **focus on** something, or if your attention **is focused on** it, you give all your attention to it. ❑ *Voters' attention is now focused on the war.*
2 **V-T/V-I** If you **focus** your eyes, or if your eyes **focus**, you try to see clearly. ❑ *He sat up in bed and tried to focus his eyes in the darkness.* ❑ *His eyes focused on the large chocolate cake.*
3 **V-T** If you **focus** a camera, you make changes to it so that you can see clearly through it. ❑ *The camera was focused on his terrified face.*
4 **N-COUNT** The **focus** of something is the thing that receives most attention.

❑ *Wherever she goes, she's the focus of attention.*
5 **N-COUNT** GEOGRAPHY The **focus** of an earthquake is the point within the Earth where the earthquake starts.
6 **PHRASE** If an image or a camera is **out of focus**, the edges of what you see are unclear. [from New Latin]

→ look at Word Webs: **earthquake, photography, telescope**

fog /fɒg/ **N-NONCOUNT** Fog is thick cloud that is close to the ground. ❑ *The car crash happened in thick fog.*

fog|gy /fɒgi/ (**foggier, foggiest**) **ADJ** When it is **foggy**, there is fog.

foil /fɔɪl/ (**foils, foiling, foiled**)
1 **N-NONCOUNT** Foil is very thin metal sheets that you use for wrapping food in. It is often called **tin foil** or **aluminum foil**. ❑ *Cover the turkey with foil and cook it for another 20 minutes.*
2 **V-T** If someone **foils** your plan or attempt to do something, they succeed in stopping you from doing what you want. ❑ *A brave police chief foiled an armed robbery.* [from Old French]

fold /foʊld/ (**folds, folding, folded**)
1 **V-T** If you **fold** a piece of paper or cloth, you bend it so that one part covers another part. ❑ *He folded the paper carefully.* ❑ *I folded the towels and put them in the closet.*
2 **V-T/V-I** If a piece of furniture **folds**, or if you can **fold** it, you can make it smaller by bending or closing parts of it. ❑ *The rear seats of the car fold.* ❑ *She folded the pushchair.*
3 **Fold up** means the same as **fold**. ❑ *When you don't need to use it, the table folds up.*
4 **V-T** When you **fold** your arms, you put one arm under the other and hold them over

your chest. ❏ *Jack stood with his arms folded.*

5 **N-COUNT** A **fold** in a piece of paper or cloth is a bend that you make in it when you put one part of it over another part and press the edge. ❏ *Make another fold down the middle of the paper.*

6 **N-COUNT** GEOGRAPHY A **fold** is a bend in a layer of rock that occurs when the rock is compressed. ● **fold|ing** **N-NONCOUNT** ❏ *...where the fracturing has resulted from folding of the rock.* [from Old English]

▶ **fold up** **1** If you **fold** something **up**, you make it into a smaller, neater shape by folding it several times. ❏ *I folded up the map and put it away.*

2 → see also **fold** **3**

Word Partnership	Use **fold** with :
ADV	fold **carefully**, fold **gently**, fold **neatly** **1**
N	fold **clothes**, fold **paper** **1** fold *your* **arms/hands** **3**

fold|ed moun|tain (**folded mountains**)
N-COUNT SCIENCE A **folded mountain** is a mountain that forms when rock is bent or folded because of stresses in the Earth's crust.

fold|er /foʊldər/ (**folders**)
1 **N-COUNT** A **folder** is a folded piece of cardboard or plastic that you keep papers in. ❏ *Liz carried her work folders into the study.*
2 **N-COUNT** TECHNOLOGY A **folder** is a group of files that are stored together on a computer. ❏ *I deleted the folder by mistake.* [from Old English]
→ look at Picture Dictionary: **office**

fo|li|at|ed /foʊlieɪtɪd/ **ADJ** SCIENCE **Foliated** rock is rock that consists of lots of thin layers. [from Old French]

folk /foʊk/ (**folk** or **folks**)

LANGUAGE HELP
Folks is always the plural for meaning **2**.

1 **N-PLURAL** You can call people **folk** or **folks**. ❏ *Most folks around here think she's a bit crazy.*
2 **N-PLURAL** Your **folks** are your mother and father. [INFORMAL] ❏ *I'll introduce you to my folks.*
3 **ADJ** ARTS SOCIAL STUDIES **Folk** art and customs belong to a particular group of people or country. ❏ *...South American folk art.* [from Old English]
→ look at Picture Dictionary: **dance**

folk|lore /foʊklɔr/ **N-NONCOUNT**
LANGUAGE ARTS **Folklore** consists of the traditional stories, customs, and habits of a particular community or nation. ❏ *In Chinese folklore the bat is a symbol of good fortune.*

folk mu|sic /foʊk myuzɪk/ **N-NONCOUNT**
MUSIC **Folk music** or **folk** is music that is traditional or typical of a particular community or nation. ❏ *I listen to a variety of music including classical and folk.*

fol|li|cle /fɒlɪkəl/ (**follicles**) **N-COUNT**
SCIENCE A **follicle** is one of the small hollows in the skin that hairs grow from. [from Latin]

fol|low /fɒloʊ/ (**follows, following, followed**)
1 **V-T/V-I** If you **follow** someone who is going somewhere, you move along behind them. ❏ *We followed him up the steps.* ❏ *They took him into a small room and I followed.*
2 **V-T/V-I** An event that **follows** a particular thing happens after that thing. ❏ *Great celebrations followed the announcement.* ❏ *Other problems may follow.*
3 **V-T** If you **follow** someone, you secretly move along behind them, in order to catch them or find out where they are going. ❏ *She realized that the car was following her.*
4 **V-T** If you **follow** one thing **with** another, you do or say the second thing after you have done or said the first thing. ❏ *Warm up first then follow this with a series of simple stretching exercises.*
5 **Follow up** means the same as **follow**. ❏ *The Phillies followed up a five-game winning streak with three straight losses.*
6 **V-T** If you **follow** a path, aa route, or a sign, you go somewhere using it to direct you. ❏ *All we had to do was follow the map.*
7 **V-T** If you **follow** advice or instructions, you do something in the way that it says. ❏ *Follow the recipe carefully.*
8 **V-T/V-I** If you are able to **follow** an explanation or a movie, you understand it. ❏ *Can you follow the story so far?* ❏ *I'm sorry, I don't follow.*
9 **PHRASE** You use **as follows** to introduce a list or an explanation. ❏ *The winners are as follows: E. Walker; R. Foster; R. Gates.*
10 **PHRASE** You use **followed by** to say what comes after something in a list. ❏ *Potatoes are still the most popular food, followed by white bread.* [from Old English]

f

Word Partnership Use **follow** with :

ADV	**closely** follow **1** **3**
N	follow **a road**, follow **signs**, follow a **trail** **5**
	follow **orders**, follow **rules** **6**
	follow **advice**, follow **directions**, follow **instructions**, follow **a story** **6** **7**

fol|low|er /fɒloʊər/ (**followers**) **N-COUNT**
A **follower** of a particular person, group, or belief is someone who supports or admires this person, group, or belief. ❑ ...*followers of Judaism.* [from Old English]

fol|low|ing /fɒloʊɪŋ/
1 **PREP** **Following** a particular event means after that event. ❑ *He took four months off work following the birth of his first child.*
2 **ADJ** The **following** day, week, or year is the day, week, or year after the one you have just mentioned. ❑ *We had dinner together on Friday and then met for lunch the following day.*
3 **ADJ** You use **following** to refer to something that you are about to mention. ❑ *Write down the following information: name of product, date purchased, and price.* [from Old English]

fond /fɒnd/ (**fonder, fondest**)
1 **ADJ** If you are **fond of** someone, you like them very much. ❑ *I am very fond of Michael.*
● **fond|ness** **N-NONCOUNT** ❑ ...*a great fondness for children.*
2 **ADJ** If you are **fond of** something, you like it or you like doing it very much. ❑ *Dad's fond of singing.* ● **fond|ness** **N-NONCOUNT** ❑ ...*a fondness for chocolate cake.*

font /fɒnt/ (**fonts**) **N-COUNT** In printing, a **font** is a set of letters of the same style and size. ❑ *You can change the font so that it's easier to read.*

food /fud/ (**foods**)
1 **N-COUNT/N-NONCOUNT** Food is what

people and animals eat. ❑ *The waitress brought our meal and said, "Enjoy your food!"* ❑ ...*frozen foods.* [from Old English]
2 → see also **fast food**
→ look at Word Webs: **food, cooking, farm, habitat, rice, sugar, vegetarian**

food chain (**food chains**) **N-COUNT** **SCIENCE**
The **food chain** is the natural process by which one living thing is eaten by another, which is then eaten by another, and so on.
→ look at Word Web: **carnivore**

food web (**food webs**) **N-COUNT** **SCIENCE**
A **food web** is a network of interconnected food chains.

fool /ful/ (**fools, fooling, fooled**)
1 **N-COUNT** A **fool** is a stupid or silly person. ❑ *I didn't understand anything. I felt like a fool.*
2 **V-T** If you **fool** someone, you make them believe something that is not true. ❑ *Harris fooled people into believing she was a doctor.*
3 **PHRASE** If you **make a fool of** someone, you make them seem silly by telling people about something stupid that they have done, or by tricking them. ❑ *Your brother is making a fool of you.* [from Old French]
▶ **fool around** If you **fool around**, you behave in a silly way. ❑ *They fool around and get into trouble at school.*

fool|ish /fulɪʃ/ **ADJ** **Foolish** behavior is stupid or silly. ❑ *It would be foolish to ignore the risks.*
● **fool|ish|ly** **ADV** ❑ *He knows that he acted foolishly.* [from Old French]

foot /fʊt/ (**feet**)
1 **N-COUNT** Your **feet** are the parts of your body at the ends of your legs that you stand on. ❑ *We danced until our feet were sore.* ❑ *He's suffering from a foot injury.*
2 **N-COUNT** **MATH** A **foot** is a unit for measuring length. A foot is equal to 12 inches or 30.48 centimeters. The plural

---

Word Web food

The **food chain** begins with sunlight. Green **plants** absorb and store **energy** from the sun through **photosynthesis**. This energy is passed on to an **herbivore** (such as a mouse) that **eats** these plants. The mouse is then eaten by a **carnivore** (such as a snake). The snake may be eaten by a **top predator** (such as a hawk). When the hawk dies, its body is broken down by bacteria. Soon its **nutrients** become food for plants and the cycle begins again.

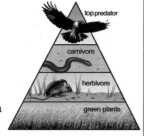

Food chain

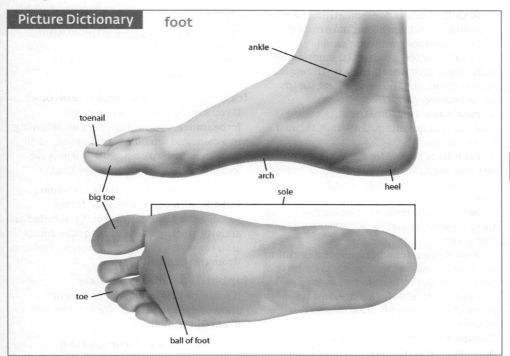

Picture Dictionary   foot

ankle

toenail

big toe

arch

sole

heel

toe

ball of foot

form is **feet** or **foot**. ❏ *We were six thousand feet above sea level.* ❏ *The room is 10 foot long and 6 foot wide.*

3 **N-SING** The **foot of** something is the part that is farthest from its top. ❏ *He was waiting at the foot of the stairs.*

4 **PHRASE** If you go somewhere **on foot**, you walk there. ❏ *We explored the island on foot.*

5 **PHRASE** If you are **on** your **feet**, you are standing up. ❏ *Everyone was on their feet shouting and clapping.*

6 **PHRASE** If someone is **on** their **feet** again after an illness, they have recovered. ❏ *You need someone to help you get back on your feet.*

7 **PHRASE** If someone **puts** their **foot down**, they use their authority in order to stop something from happening. ❏ *He wanted to go skiing in March but his wife put her foot down.*

8 **PHRASE** If you **put** your **feet up**, you take a rest. ❏ *I'll do the chores, so you can put your feet up.* [from Old English]

→ look at Picture Dictionaries: **foot, body, measurement**

foot|age /f**ʊ**tɪdʒ/ **N-NONCOUNT** Footage of a particular event is a film of it or the part of a film that shows this event. ❏ *...footage from this summer's festivals.* [from Old English]

foot|ball /f**ʊ**tbɔl/ (**footballs**)

1 **N-NONCOUNT** SPORTS Football is a game for two teams of eleven players. Each team tries to win points by kicking, carrying, or throwing the ball into an area at the other end of the field. ❏ *Paul loves playing football.*

2 **N-COUNT** SPORTS A football is a ball that is used for playing football. ❏ *Antonio kicked the football off the field.*

foot|print /f**ʊ**tprɪnt/ (**footprints**) **N-COUNT** Your **footprint** is the mark that your foot makes on the ground.

→ look at Word Web: **fossil**

foot|step /f**ʊ**tstɛp/ (**footsteps**) **N-COUNT** A **footstep** is the sound that you make each time your foot touches the ground when you are walking. ❏ *I heard footsteps outside.*

foot|wall /f**ʊ**twɔl/ (**footwalls**) **N-COUNT** SCIENCE A **footwall** is the rock beneath a geological fault. Compare with **hanging wall**.

for /fər, STRONG fɔr/

1 **PREP** If something is **for** someone, they are intended to have it or use it. ❏ *These flowers are for you.* ❏ *I reserved a table for two at the restaurant.*

2 **PREP** If you work **for** a person or a company, they employ you. ❏ *He works for a bank.*

f

F

3 PREP If someone does something **for** you, they do it so that you do not have to do it. ❑ *I held the door open for the next person.*

4 PREP If you feel a particular emotion **for** someone or something, they are the object of that emotion. ❑ *I'm sorry for Steve, but I think you've made the right decision.*

5 PREP A word **for** something, is a word that has that meaning. ❑ *In French, the word for "love" is "amour."*

6 PREP To be named **for** someone means to be given the same name as them. ❑ *The Brady Bill is named for former White House Press Secretary James Brady.*

7 PREP You use **for** when you are describing the purpose of something. ❑ *This knife is for slicing bread.*

8 PREP You use **for** when you are describing a reason. ❑ *...his reasons for going.* ❑ *The hospital could find no physical cause for my problems.*

9 PREP If you leave **for** a place, you are going there. ❑ *They left for Rio early the next morning.*

10 PREP You use **for** when you are saying how long something lasts. ❑ *We talked for about half an hour.*

11 PREP You use **for** to say how far someone or something goes. ❑ *We continued to drive for a few miles.*

12 PREP If you buy, sell, or do something **for** a particular amount of money, that is its price. ❑ *The Martins sold their house for 1.4 million dollars.*

13 PREP If something is planned **for** a particular time, it is planned to happen then. ❑ *The Boat Show is planned for January 21–29.*

14 PHRASE You use expressions such as **for the first time** and **for the last time** when you are talking about how often something has happened before. ❑ *He was married for the second time.*

15 PREP You use **for** when you say that a quality of something or someone is surprising. ❑ *He was tall for an eight-year-old.*

16 PREP If you are **for** someone or something, you agree with them or support them. ❑ *Well, are you for us or against us?*

17 PREP SPORTS If you play **for** a particular team, you are in that team. ❑ *Kristy plays hockey for the high school team.* [from Old English]

→ look at Usage note at **during**

Usage **for**

Use *for* to describe a length of time. *Noriko has studied English for seven years. She lived in Japan for the first fifteen years of her life and has lived in the U. S. for two years.*

for|bear|ance /fɔrbɛərəns/ **N-NONCOUNT** If you say that someone has shown **forbearance**, you admire them for behaving in a calm and sensible way. [FORMAL] ❑ *All the Greenpeace people behaved with impressive forbearance and dignity.* [from Old English]

for|bid /fərbɪd, fɔr-/ (**forbids, forbidding, forbade, forbidden**) **V-T** If you **forbid** someone **to** do something or if you **forbid** an activity, you say that it must not be done. ❑ *My parents have forbidden me to see my boyfriend.* [from Old English]

for|bid|den /fərbɪdⁿn, fɔr-/ **ADJ** If something is **forbidden**, you are not allowed to do it. ❑ *Smoking is forbidden here.* [from Old English]

force /fɔrs/ (**forces, forcing, forced**)

1 V-T If someone **forces** you **to** do something, they make you do it when you do not want to. ❑ *They forced him to give them the money.*

2 V-T If someone **forces** a lock, a door, or a window, they break the lock. ❑ *Police forced the door of the apartment and arrested Mr. Roberts.*

3 V-T If you **force** something into a particular position, you use a lot of strength to make it move there. ❑ *She forced her key into the lock.*

4 N-NONCOUNT If someone uses **force** to do something, they use their strength to do it. ❑ *Police used force to break up the fight.*

5 N-NONCOUNT SCIENCE **Force** is the power or strength that something has. ❑ *The force of the explosion destroyed the building.*

6 N-COUNT **Forces** are groups of people, for example soldiers or police officers, who do a particular job. ❑ *Rioters threw rocks at security forces.* [from Old French]

7 → see also **air force, armed forces, workforce**

8 N-COUNT/N-NONCOUNT SCIENCE In physics, a **force** is the pulling or pushing effect that something has on something else. ❑ *...the Earth's gravitational force.*

→ look at Word Web: **motion**

Word Partnership	Use force with :
V	force **to resign** **1**
N	force **a smile** **3**
	use of force **4**
	force **of gravity** **7**
ADJ	**excessive** force, **necessary** force **4**
	enemy forces, **military** forces **6**

force|ful /fɔrsfəl/ **ADJ** Someone who is **forceful** expresses their opinions and wishes in a strong and confident way. ❑ *He was a man of forceful character.* ● **force|ful|ly ADV** ❑ *He argued forcefully against this course of action.* [from Old French]

Word Link	fore ≈ before : forecast, foreground, foresee

fore|cast /fɔrkæst/ (**forecasts, forecasting, forecast** or **forecasted**)

> **LANGUAGE HELP**
>
> The forms **forecast** and **forecasted** can both be used for the past tense and past participle.

1 **N-COUNT** A **forecast** is what someone expects will happen in the future. ❑ *Did you see the weather forecast?*
2 **V-T** If you **forecast** events, you say what you think is going to happen in the future. ❑ *Economists were forecasting higher oil prices.* ● **fore|cast|er** (**forecasters**) **N-COUNT** ❑ *David worked for 34 years as a weather forecaster.*
→ look at Word Webs: **forecast, tsunami**

fore|clo|sure /fɔrkloʊʒər/ (**foreclosures**) **N-COUNT/N-NONCOUNT** BUSINESS **Foreclosure** takes place when a person or organization who has lent someone money for property takes possession of the property because the money has not been paid back. ❑ *If homeowners can't keep up the payments, they face foreclosure.*

fore|ground /fɔrgraʊnd/ (**foregrounds**) **N-COUNT/N-NONCOUNT** ARTS The **foreground** of a picture is the part that seems nearest to you. Compare with **background**. ❑ *There are five people and a dog in the foreground of the painting.*

fore|head /fɔrhɛd, fɔrɪd/ (**foreheads**) **N-COUNT** Your **forehead** is the front part of your head between your eyebrows and your hair. [from Old English] → look at Picture Dictionary: **face**

for|eign /fɔrɪn/
1 **ADJ** Someone or something that is **foreign** comes from a country that is not your own. ❑ *It's good to learn a foreign language.*
2 **ADJ** In politics, **foreign** describes people and activities that deal with other countries. ❑ *...the German foreign minister.* ❑ *...American foreign policy.* [from Old French]

Thesaurus	foreign	Also look up :
ADJ	alien, exotic, strange; (ant.) domestic, native **1** **3**	

for|eign|er /fɔrɪnər/ (**foreigners**) **N-COUNT** A **foreigner** is someone who comes from a different country. [from Old French]

for|eign ex|change (**foreign exchanges**)
1 **N-PLURAL** BUSINESS **Foreign exchanges** are the institutions or systems involved with changing one currency into another. ❑ *On the foreign exchanges, the U.S. dollar is up point forty-five.*
2 **N-NONCOUNT** BUSINESS **Foreign exchange** is used to refer to foreign currency that is obtained through the foreign exchange system. ❑ *...an important source of foreign exchange.*

fore|see /fɔrsi/ (**foresees, foreseeing, foresaw, foreseen**) **V-T** If you **foresee**

Word Web   forecast

Weather forecasters depend on good information. They make **observations**. They gather **data** about barometric **pressure**, **temperature**, and **humidity**. They track **storms** with **radar** and **satellites**. They track cold **fronts** and warm fronts. They put all of this information into their computers and **model** possible weather patterns. Today scientists are trying to make better **weather forecasts**. They are installing thousands of small, inexpensive **radar** units on rooftops and cellphone towers. They will gather information near the Earth's surface and high in the sky. This will give meteorologists more information to help them **predict** tomorrow's weather.

something, you expect and believe that it will happen. ❑ *He did not foresee any problems.*

for|est /fɔrɪst/ (**forests**)
N-COUNT/N-NONCOUNT GEOGRAPHY A **forest** is a large area where trees grow close together. ❑ *...a forest fire.* [from Old French]
→ look at Word Webs: **forest, habitat**

for|ever /fɔrɛvər, fər-/
1 ADV Something that will continue **forever** will always continue. ❑ *I think that we will live together forever.*
2 ADV Something that has gone or changed **forever** will never come back or return to the way it was. ❑ *His pain was gone forever.*

fore|word /fɔrwɜrd/ (**forewords**) **N-COUNT**
LANGUAGE ARTS A **foreword** is an introduction to a book. ❑ *She has written the foreword to a cookbook.* [from Old English]

for|feit /fɔrfɪt/ (**forfeits, forfeiting, forfeited**)
1 V-T If you **forfeit** a right, a privilege, or a possession, you have to give it up because you have done something wrong. ❑ *He was ordered to forfeit more than 1.5 million dollars.*
2 N-COUNT A **forfeit** is something that you have to give up because you have done something wrong. ❑ *That is the forfeit he must pay.* [from Old French]

for|gave /fərgeɪv/ **Forgave** is the past tense of **forgive**. [from Old English]

forge /fɔrdʒ/ (**forges, forging, forged**) V-T
If someone **forges** paper money, a document, or a painting, they make false copies of it in order to deceive people. ❑ *He admitted to forging passports.* ❑ *They used forged documents to leave the country.* ● **forg|er** (**forgers**) **N-COUNT** ❑ *He's an expert art forger.* [from Old French]
▶ **forge ahead** If you **forge ahead** with something, you continue with it and make a lot of progress with it. ❑ *He forged ahead with his plans for reform.*

Word Partnership	Use **forge** with :
N	forge **documents**, forge **an identity**, forge **a signature** **1** forge **a bond**, forge **a friendship**, forge **links**, forge **ties** **2**

for|gery /fɔrdʒəri/ (**forgeries**)
1 N-COUNT A **forgery** is something that has been forged. ❑ *The letter was a forgery.*
2 N-NONCOUNT **Forgery** is the crime of forging money, documents, or paintings. [from Old French]

for|get /fərgɛt/ (**forgets, forgetting, forgot, forgotten**)
1 V-T If you **forget** something, or **forget** how to do something, you cannot think of it or think how to do it, although you knew in the past. ❑ *She forgot where she left the car.*
2 V-T/V-I If you **forget** something or **forget** to do it, you do not remember it or remember to do it. ❑ *He never forgets his dad's birthday.* ❑ *I forgot to lock the door.* ❑ *I meant to ask you about it but I forgot.*
3 V-T If you **forget** something that you intended to bring with you, you do not remember to bring it. ❑ *Once, when we were going to Paris, I forgot my passport.* [from Old English]

Word Partnership	Use **forget** with :
ADV	**never** forget, **quickly** forget, **soon** forget **1** **almost** forget **1**–**3**
ADJ	**easy/hard** to forget **1**–**3**

for|get|ful /fərgɛtfəl/ ADJ Someone who is **forgetful** often does not remember things. ❑ *My mother became very forgetful and confused when she got old.* [from Old English]

Word Web   forest

Four hundred years ago, settlers in North America found endless **forests**. This large supply of **wood** helped them. They used **timber** to build homes and make furniture. They burned wood for cooking and heat. They cut down the **woods** to create farmland. By the late 1800s, most of the old growth forests on the East Coast had disappeared. The **lumber** industry has also destroyed millions of trees. Reforestation has replaced some of them. However, **logging** companies usually plant single species forests. Some people say these are not really forests at all—just **tree** farms.

for|give /fərgɪv/ (**forgives, forgiving, forgave, forgiven**) **v-t** If you **forgive** someone who has done something bad or wrong, you stop being angry with them. ❑ *Hopefully Jane will understand and forgive you.* ❑ *Irene forgave Terry for stealing her money.* ● **for|give|ness N-NONCOUNT** ❑ *...a spirit of forgiveness.* [from Old English]

for|got /fərgɒt/ **Forgot** is the past tense of **forget.** [from Old English]

for|got|ten /fərgɒtᵊn/ **Forgotten** is the past participle of **forget.** [from Old English]

fork /fɔrk/ (**forks, forking, forked**)
1 N-COUNT A **fork** is a tool with long metal points, used for eating food. ❑ *Please use your knife and fork.*
2 N-COUNT A **fork** in a road, a path, or a river is where it divides into two parts and forms a "Y" shape. ❑ *We arrived at a fork in the road.*
3 V-I If a road, a path, or a river **forks**, it divides into two. [from Old English]
→ look at Word Web: **silverware**
▶ **fork over** or **fork out** If you **fork over** or **fork out for** something, you spend a lot of money on it. [INFORMAL] ❑ *I forked over $530 on a ticket for a month's train travel in Europe.* ❑ *Visitors to the castle had to fork out for a guidebook.*

form /fɔrm/ (**forms, forming, formed**)
1 N-COUNT A **form of** something is a type of it. ❑ *She has a rare form of the disease.* ❑ *I am against violence in any form.*
2 N-COUNT The **form** of something is its shape or the way it appears. ❑ *The dress fits the form of the body exactly.*
3 N-COUNT A **form** is a piece of paper with questions on it and spaces where you should write the answers. ❑ *Please fill in this form and sign it at the bottom.*
4 V-T/V-I When a particular shape **forms** or **is formed,** people or things move so that this shape is made. ❑ *A line formed to use the bathroom.* ❑ *The 12 students formed a circle with their arms around each other.* ❑ *Form a diamond shape with your legs.*
5 V-T If something consists of particular things or features, you can say that they **form** that thing. ❑ *These articles formed the basis of Randolph's book.*
6 V-T If you **form** an organization, you start it. ❑ *They formed a study group on human rights.*
7 V-T/V-I When something natural **forms**

or **is formed,** it begins to exist and develop. ❑ *The stars formed 10 to 15 billion years ago.*
8 N-COUNT LANGUAGE ARTS In grammar, the **form** of a noun or a verb is the way that it is spelled or spoken when it is used to talk about the plural, the past, or the present, for example. [from French]

Thesaurus form Also look up :		
N	class, description, kind **1**	
	body, figure, frame, shape **2**	
	application, document, sheet **3**	

for|mal /fɔrmᵊl/
1 ADJ Formal speech or behavior is very correct and serious rather than relaxed and friendly. ❑ *We received a very formal letter of apology.* ● **for|mal|ly ADV** ❑ *He spoke formally, and without expression.* ● **for|mal|ity N-NONCOUNT** ❑ *Lilly's formality and seriousness amused him.*
2 ADJ A **formal** statement or request is an official one. ❑ *No formal announcement has been made.* ● **for|mal|ly ADV** ❑ *Officials haven't formally agreed to Anderson's plan.* [from Latin]
→ look at Usage note at **formerly**

for|mal thea|ter N-NONCOUNT ARTS Formal theater is entertainment consisting of plays performed before an audience in a theater.

for|mat /fɔrmæt/ (**formats, formatting, formatted**)
1 N-COUNT TECHNOLOGY The **format** of a computer document is the way in which the text is arranged. ❑ *You can change the format of your document from two columns to three.*
2 V-T TECHNOLOGY You **format** a document when you arrange the design of the text in it. ❑ *The software can automatically format the text in a document as you type it.* [from French]

for|ma|tion /fɔrmeɪʃᵊn/ (**formations**)
1 N-NONCOUNT The **formation of** something is the beginning of its existence. ❑ *The vitamin is essential for the formation of red blood cells.*
2 N-COUNT SCIENCE A rock or cloud **formation** is rock or cloud of a particular shape or structure. [from French]

for|mer /fɔrmər/
1 ADJ You use **former** when you are talking about someone's or something's position in the past. ❑ *There was an interview with the former president, Richard Nixon.*
2 PRON When two people or things have just been mentioned, you can talk about the

first of them as **the former**. ❏ *Both the seeds and the leaves are useful—the former for soups, and the latter for salads.*

Thesaurus former Also look up :
ADJ prior **1**
past, previous **1 2**

for|mer|ly /fɔrmərli/ ADV If something happened **formerly**, it happened in the past. ❏ *He was formerly in the navy.* [from Old French]

Usage formerly and formally
Formerly and *formally* sound very similar but have very different meanings. *Formerly* is used to talk about something that used to be true but isn't true now; *formally* means "in a formal manner": *Jacques was formerly the president of our club, but he formally resigned last week by sending a letter to the club secretary.*

for|mi|dable /fɔrmɪdəbᵊl, fərmɪd-/ ADJ Something or someone that is **formidable** makes you feel slightly frightened. ❏ *We have a formidable task ahead of us.* [from Latin]

for|mu|la /fɔrmyələ/ (**formulae** /fɔrmyəli/ or **formulas**)
1 N-COUNT A **formula** is a plan for dealing with a particular problem. ❏ *...a formula for peace.*
2 N-COUNT MATH SCIENCE A **formula** is a group of letters, numbers, or other symbols that represents a scientific or mathematical rule. ❏ *This mathematical formula describes the distances of the planets from the Sun.*
3 N-COUNT SCIENCE The **formula** for a substance is a description of the chemical elements that it contains. ❏ *Glucose and fructose have the same chemical formula.* [from Latin]

for|mu|late /fɔrmyəleɪt/ (**formulates, formulating, formulated**) V-T If you **formulate** a plan, you invent it, thinking about the details carefully. ❏ *Little by little, he formulated his plan for escape.* ● **for|mu|la|tion** N-NONCOUNT ❏ *...the formulation of U.S. environmental policies.* [from Latin]

fort /fɔrt/ (**forts**) N-COUNT A **fort** is a strong building that is used as a military base. [from Old French]

forth /fɔrθ/
1 ADV When someone goes **forth** from a place, they leave it. [LITERARY] ❏ *Go forth into the desert.*

2 ADV If one thing brings **forth** another, the first thing produces the second. [LITERARY] ❏ *My reflections brought forth no conclusion.* [from Old English]

for|ti|eth /fɔrtiəθ/ ADJ/ADV MATH The **fortieth** item in a series is the one that you count as number forty. ❏ *It was the fortieth anniversary of the death of the composer.* [from Old English]

for|ti|fy /fɔrtɪfaɪ/ (**fortifies, fortifying, fortified**)
1 V-T To **fortify** a place means to make it stronger and more difficult to attack, often by building a wall or a ditch around it. ❏ *Soldiers worked to fortify the airbase.*
2 V-T If food or drink **is fortified**, another substance is added to it to make it healthier or stronger. ❏ *...margarine fortified with vitamin D.* [from Old French]

for|tress /fɔrtrɪs/ (**fortresses**) N-COUNT A **fortress** is a castle or other large strong building that is difficult for enemies to enter. [from Old French]

for|tu|nate /fɔrtʃənɪt/ ADJ If someone or something is **fortunate**, they are lucky. ❏ *He was extremely fortunate to survive.* ❏ *She is in the fortunate position of having plenty of choice.* [from Old French]

for|tu|nate|ly /fɔrtʃənɪtli/ ADV You can say **fortunately** when you start to talk about an event or a situation that is good. ❏ *Fortunately, the weather last winter was good.* [from Old French]

for|tune /fɔrtʃən/ (**fortunes**)
1 N-COUNT A **fortune** is a very large amount of money. ❏ *He made a fortune buying and selling houses.*
2 N-COUNT Someone who has a **fortune** has a very large amount of money. ❏ *He made his fortune in car sales.*
3 N-NONCOUNT Fortune or good **fortune** is good luck. ❏ *Patrick still can't believe his good fortune.* [from Old French]

for|ty /fɔrti/ (**forties**)
1 NUM MATH **Forty** is the number 40.
2 N-PLURAL The **forties** are the years between 1940 and 1949. ❏ *They met in New York in the forties.*
3 N-PLURAL When you talk about the **forties**, you mean the numbers between 40 and 49. For example, if you are in your **forties**, you are aged between 40 and 49.

❑ *The temperature was in the low forties.*
[from Old English]

fo|rum /fɔrəm/ (forums) **N-COUNT** A forum
is a place, a situation, or a group in which
people exchange ideas and discuss issues.
❑ *The discussion groups are an open forum for
listening.* [from Latin]

> **Word Link**   *ward ≈ in the direction of :*
>   back*ward*, down*ward*, for*ward*

for|ward /fɔrwərd/ (forwards, forwarding,
forwarded)
1 **ADV** If you move or look **forward**, you
move or look in a direction that is in front
of you. ❑ *He came forward and asked for help.*
❑ *She fell forward on to her face.*
2 **ADV** **Forward** means in a position near
the front of something. ❑ *Try to get a seat as
far forward as possible.*
3 **ADJ** **Forward** is also an adjective.
❑ *The troops moved to forward positions.*
4 **V-T** If you **forward** a letter or an email **to**
someone, you send it to them after you have
received it. ❑ *He asks each person to forward the
email to 10 other people.* [from Old English]

for|ward slash (forward slashes) **N-COUNT**
TECHNOLOGY A **forward slash** is the sloping
line / that separates letters, words, or
numbers.

fos|sil /fɒsəl/ (fossils) **N-COUNT** SCIENCE
A **fossil** is the part of a plant or an animal
that died a long time ago and has turned
into rock. [from Latin]
→ look at Word Webs: **fossil, evolution**

fos|sil fu|el (fossil fuels)
N-COUNT/N-NONCOUNT SCIENCE A **fossil fuel**
is a substance such as coal or oil that is
found in the ground and used for producing
power. ❑ *When we burn fossil fuels, we use oxygen
and produce carbon dioxide.*
→ look at Word Webs: **electricity, greenhouse
effect**

fos|sil rec|ord (fossil records) **N-COUNT**
SCIENCE The **fossil record** is the history of life
on Earth that is recorded in fossils found in
rocks.

fos|ter /fɒstər/ (fosters, fostering, fostered)
1 **ADJ** **Foster** parents are people who are
paid by the government to take care of
someone else's child for a period of time.
2 **V-T** If you **foster** a child, you take it into
your family for a period of time, without
becoming its legal parent.
3 **V-T** If you **foster** a feeling or an idea, you
help it to develop. ❑ *These organizations
fostered a strong sense of pride within the black
community.* [from Old English]

fought /fɔt/ **Fought** is the past tense and
past participle of **fight**. [from Old English]

foul /faʊl/ (fouler, foulest, fouls)
1 **ADJ** Something that is **foul** is dirty, and
smells or tastes unpleasant. ❑ *...foul,
polluted water.*
2 **ADJ** **Foul** language is offensive and
contains rude words.
3 **N-COUNT** SPORTS In a game or a sport,
a **foul** is an act that is not allowed according
to the rules. ❑ *Why did the referee not call a foul?*
[from Old English]

found /faʊnd/ (founds, founding, founded)
1 **Found** is the past tense and past
participle of the verb **find**.
2 **V-T** When an organization **is founded** by
someone, that person starts it. ❑ *The New
York Free-Loan Society was founded in 1892.*
[Sense 1 from Old English. Sense 2 from
Old French.]

foun|da|tion /faʊndeɪʃˀn/ (foundations)
1 **N-SING** The **foundation** of an
organization is the process of starting it.
❑ *...the foundation of the National Association of
Evangelicals in 1942.*
2 **N-PLURAL** The **foundations** of a building

f

There are two types of animal **fossils**—body fossils and **trace** fossils. Body fossils
help us understand how the animal looked when it was alive. Trace fossils, such as
tracks and **footprints**, show us how the animal moved. Since we don't find tracks
of dinosaurs' tails, we know they lifted them up as they
walked. Footprints tell us about the weight of the dinosaur
and how fast it moved. Scientists use two methods to
calculate the date of a fossil. They sometimes count the
number of **rock** layers covering it. They also use **carbon** dating.

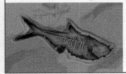

are the layer of bricks, stones, or concrete that it is built on.

3 **N-COUNT** A **foundation** is an organization that provides money for a special purpose. ❑ *We applied to the National Foundation for Educational Research.* [from Old French]

found|er /faʊndər/ (**founders, foundering, foundered**)

1 **N-COUNT** The **founder** of an organization is the person who started it. ❑ *...the founder of the modern Olympic movement.*

2 **V-I** If something such as a plan or a project **founders**, it fails. ❑ *The talks foundered, without agreement.* [from Old French]

foun|tain /faʊntɪn/ (**fountains**)

1 **N-COUNT** A **fountain** is a structure in a pool or a lake where water is forced up into the air and falls down again.

2 **N-COUNT** A **fountain** is a piece of equipment that you can drink water from in a public place. [from Old French]

four /fɔr/ (**fours**)

1 **NUM** **MATH** **Four** is the number 4.

2 **PHRASE** If you are **on all fours**, your knees, feet, and hands are on the ground. ❑ *She crawled over on all fours.* [from Old English]

four|teen /fɔrtin/ **NUM** **MATH** **Fourteen** is the number 14. [from Old English]

four|teenth /fɔrtinθ/ **ADJ/ADV** **MATH** The **fourteenth** item in a series is the one that you count as number fourteen. ❑ *The festival is now in its fourteenth year.* [from Old English]

fourth /fɔrθ/ (**fourths**)

1 **ADJ/ADV** **MATH** The **fourth** item in a series is the one that you count as number four.

❑ *Last year's winner is in fourth place in the race.*

2 **N-COUNT** **MATH** A **fourth** is one of four equal parts of something (¼). ❑ *A fourth of the public want a national vote on the new tax.* [from Old English]

fowl /faʊl/ (**fowl** or **fowls**) **N-COUNT** **Fowl** are birds that can be eaten as food, such as a chickens. [from Old English]

fox /fɒks/ (**foxes**) **N-COUNT** A **fox** is a wild animal that looks like a dog, has red fur and a thick tail. [from Old English]

frack|ing /frækɪŋ/ **N-NONCOUNT** **SCIENCE** **Fracking** is a way of getting oil or gas from under the ground by forcing liquid and sand into the rock. ❑ *Local people are against fracking in the area.*

Word Link	fract, frag ≈ breaking : fraction, fracture, fragile

frac|tion /frækʃ°n/ (**fractions**)

1 **N-COUNT** **MATH** A **fraction** is a part of a whole number. For example, ½ and ⅓ are both fractions.

2 **N-COUNT** A **fraction of** something is a very small amount of it. ❑ *She hesitated for a fraction of a second.* [from Late Latin]

→ look at Picture Dictionary: **fractions**

frac|ture /fræktʃər/ (**fractures, fracturing, fractured**)

1 **N-COUNT** A **fracture** is a break in something, especially a bone. ❑ *She suffered a hip fracture.*

2 **V-T/V-I** If something such as a bone **is fractured**, or **fractures**, it has a crack or a break in it. ❑ *Several of his ribs were fractured in the fall.* ❑ *She fractured her arm in two places.*

Picture Dictionary   fractions

fraction	decimal	percentage
1/4	0.25	25%

fraction	decimal	percentage
1/3	0.33	33%

fraction	decimal	percentage
1/2	0.50	50%

adding fractions	
problem:	solution:
1 1/4	1 1/4
+2 1/2	+2 2/4
?	3 3/4

subtracting fractions	
problem:	solution:
5 2/3	5 4/6
- 1 1/6	- 1 1/6
?	4 3/6 = 4 1/2

frag|ile /frǽdʒ^əl/ **ADJ** Something that is **fragile** is easily broken or damaged. ❑ ...*fine, fragile crystal.* ● **fra|gil|ity** **N-NONCOUNT** ❑ ...*the fragility of their bones.* [from Latin]

> Thesaurus **fragile** Also look up :
> ADJ   unstable, weak, breakable, delicate; *(ant.)* sturdy

frag|ment /frǽgmənt/ (**fragments**) **N-COUNT** A **fragment of** something is a small piece of it. ❑ *We tried to pick up the tiny fragments of glass.* [from Latin]

frag|men|ta|tion /frǽgmɛnteɪʃ^ən/ **N-NONCOUNT** SCIENCE **Fragmentation** is a type of reproduction in some worms and other organisms, in which the organism breaks into several parts and each part grows into a new individual. [from Latin]

fra|grance /fréɪgrəns/ (**fragrances**) **N-COUNT/N-NONCOUNT** A **fragrance** is a pleasant or sweet smell. ❑ *The cream is easy to apply and has a pleasant fragrance.* [from Latin]

frail /freɪl/ (**frailer, frailest**) **ADJ** Someone who is **frail** is not very strong or healthy. ❑ *He looked very frail in his hospital bed.* [from Old French]

frame /freɪm/ (**frames, framing, framed**)
1 **N-COUNT** The **frame** of a picture is the wood, metal, or plastic that is fitted around it. ❑ *She had a photograph of her mother in a silver frame.*
2 **N-COUNT** The **frame** of an object is the part that gives it its strength and shape. ❑ *He supplies builders with door frames and window frames.*
3 **V-T** When a picture **is framed**, it is put in a frame. ❑ *The picture has already been framed and hung on the wall.* [from Old English]
→ look at Picture Dictionary: **bed**
→ look at Word Webs: **animation, painting**

frame|work /fréɪmwɜrk/ (**frameworks**)
1 **N-COUNT** A **framework** is a set of rules, ideas, or beliefs that you use in order to decide what to do. ❑ ...*the framework of federal regulations.*
2 **N-COUNT** A **framework** is a structure that forms a support for something. ❑ *The wooden shelves sit on a steel framework.*

fran|chise /frǽntʃaɪz/ (**franchises**)
1 **N-COUNT** BUSINESS A **franchise** is an authority that is given by an organization to someone, allowing them to sell its goods or services or to take part in an activity that the organization controls. ❑ ...*a franchise to develop Hong Kong's first cable TV system.*
2 **N-NONCOUNT** SOCIAL STUDIES **Franchise** is the right to vote in an election. ❑ ...*the introduction of universal franchise.* [from Old French]

frank /frǽŋk/ (**franker, frankest, franks**)
1 **ADJ** Someone who is **frank** says things in an open and honest way. ❑ *My husband has not been frank with me.*
2 **N-COUNT** A **frank** is a long thin piece of sausage. ❑ *I really enjoy eating franks and beans.* [from Old French]

frank|ly /frǽŋkli/
1 **ADV** You use **frankly** when you are going to say something that may be surprising or direct. ❑ *Frankly, this whole thing is getting boring.*
2 **ADV** If you speak **frankly**, you say things in an open and honest way. ❑ *You can talk frankly to me.* [from Old French]

fran|tic /frǽntɪk/ **ADJ** A person who is **frantic** is very frightened or worried, and does not know what to do. ❑ *They became frantic when their 4-year-old son did not return.* ● **fran|ti|cal|ly** /frǽntɪkli/ **ADV** ❑ *Two people were waving frantically from the boat.* [from Old French]

fraud /frɔd/ (**frauds**)
1 **N-NONCOUNT** **Fraud** is the crime of getting money by tricking people or by lying. ❑ *He was jailed for two years for fraud.*
2 **N-COUNT** A **fraud** is someone who deceives people, often in a way that is illegal. ❑ *He's a fraud and a cheat.* [from Old French]

freak /frik/ (**freaks**)
1 **ADJ** A **freak** event or action is one that is very unusual. ❑ *James broke his leg in a freak accident playing golf.*
2 **N-COUNT** People are sometimes called **freaks** when their behavior or appearance is very different or unusual. ❑ *I'm not a freak—I'm just like you guys.*

freck|le /frɛk^əl/ (**freckles**) **N-COUNT** **Freckles** are small light brown spots on your skin, especially on your face. ❑ *He had short red hair and freckles.* [from Old Norse]

free /fri/ (**freer, freest, frees, freeing, freed**)
1 **ADJ** If something is **free**, you do not have to pay for it. ❑ *The classes are free, with lunch provided.*
2 **ADJ** Someone or something that is **free** is not controlled or limited, for example by

f

rules or other people. ❑ *They are free to bring their friends home at any time.*

3 **ADJ** Someone who is **free** is no longer a prisoner. ❑ *He walked from the court house a free man.*

4 **ADJ** If you have **free** time, or if you are **free** at a particular time, you are not working or busy then. ❑ *She spent her free time shopping.* ❑ *Are you free tonight?*

5 **ADJ** If a seat or a table is **free**, it is not being used by anyone.

6 **V-T** To **free** a prisoner means to let them go.

7 **V-T** If you **free** someone or something, you remove them from the place in which they have been trapped. ❑ *Rescue workers freed him by cutting away part of the car.*

8 **PHRASE** You say **Feel free** when you want to give someone permission to do something, in a very willing way. [INFORMAL] ❑ *If you have any questions at all, please feel free to ask me.* [from Old English]

Thesaurus	free Also look up :
ADJ	complimentary **1**
	independent, unrestricted **2**
	available, vacant **5**
V	emancipate, let go, liberate **6** **7**

Word Link	*dom ≈ state of being : bore*dom, *free*dom, *wis*dom

free|dom /frídəm/ (**freedoms**)

1 **N-COUNT/N-NONCOUNT** Freedom is the state of being allowed to do what you want to do. ❑ *They enjoy the freedom to spend their money as they wish.* ❑ *We are fighting for freedom of choice.*

2 **N-NONCOUNT** When a prisoner is set free, they gain their **freedom**. ❑ *The agreement led to all hostages gaining their freedom.* [from Old English]

Word Partnership	Use freedom with :
ADJ	**artistic** freedom, **political** freedom, **religious** freedom **1**
N	freedom **of choice, feeling/sense of** freedom, freedom **of the press,** freedom **of speech 1**
	struggle for freedom **1** **2**

free fall also **free-fall** **N-NONCOUNT** SCIENCE An object that is **in free fall** is falling through the air because of gravity, and no other forces are affecting it.

free|ly /fríli/

1 **ADV** Freely means many times or in large quantities. ❑ *We have referred freely to his ideas.* ❑ *George was spending very freely.*

2 **ADV** If you can do something **freely**, you are not controlled or limited, for example by rules or other people. ❑ *They cast their votes freely in the election.*

3 **ADV** If you can talk **freely**, you can talk without needing to be careful about what you say. ❑ *They all express their opinions freely in class.*

4 **ADV** If someone gives or does something **freely**, they give or do it willingly, without being ordered or forced to do it. ❑ *Danny shared his knowledge freely with anyone interested.*

5 **ADV** If something or someone moves **freely**, they move easily and smoothly, without any obstacles or resistance. ❑ *Traffic is flowing freely.* [from Old English]

free|way /fríweɪ/ (**freeways**) **N-COUNT** A **freeway** is a main road that has been specially built for fast travel over long distances. [from Old English]

freeze /fríz/ (**freezes, freezing, froze, frozen**)

1 **V-I** SCIENCE If a liquid **freezes**, it becomes solid because the temperature is low. ❑ *If the temperature drops below 32 °F, water freezes.* ❑ *The ground froze solid.*

2 **V-T** If you **freeze** food or drink, you make it very cold in order to preserve it.

3 **V-I** If you **freeze**, you feel extremely cold. ❑ *The window would not close so we froze.*

4 **V-I** If someone who is moving **freezes**, they suddenly stop and become completely still and quiet. ❑ *"Freeze," shouted the police officer.* [from Old English]

5 → see also **frozen**
→ look at Word Webs: **thermometer, water**

freez|er /frízər/ (**freezers**) **N-COUNT** A **freezer** is a large container or part of a refrigerator used for freezing food. [from Old English]

freez|ing /frízɪŋ/

1 **ADJ** Something that is **freezing** is very cold. ❑ *The movie theater was freezing.*

2 **ADJ** If you are **freezing**, you feel very cold. ❑ *"You must be freezing,"* she said.

3 **N-NONCOUNT** SCIENCE Freezing is when a liquid becomes solid because the temperature is low. ❑ *The damage was caused by freezing and thawing.* [from Old English]
→ look at Word Web: **precipitation**

freez|ing point (**freezing points**) also **freezing-point**

1 **N-NONCOUNT** SCIENCE Freezing point is

32° Fahrenheit or o° Celsius, the temperature at which water freezes. Freezing point is often used when talking about the weather.

2 **N-COUNT** SCIENCE The **freezing point** of a particular substance is the temperature at which it freezes.

freight /freɪt/ **N-NONCOUNT** Freight is goods that are moved by trucks, trains, ships, or airplanes. ❑ ...a freight train. [from Middle Dutch]
→ look at Word Web: **train**

French fries /frɛntʃ fraɪz/ **N-PLURAL** French fries are long, thin pieces of potato that are fried.
→ look at Word Web: **ketchup**

French horn /frɛntʃ hɔrn/ (**French horns**) **N-COUNT/N-NONCOUNT** MUSIC A French horn is a musical instrument shaped like a long round metal tube with one wide end, that is played by blowing into it.
→ look at Word Web: **orchestra**

fre|quen|cy /frikwənsi/ (**frequencies**)
1 **N-NONCOUNT** The **frequency** of an event is the number of times it happens.
❑ The frequency of Kara's phone calls increased rapidly.
2 **N-COUNT/N-NONCOUNT** SCIENCE The **frequency** of a sound wave or a radio wave is the number of times it vibrates within a period of time. ❑ You can't hear waves of such a high frequency. [from Latin]
→ look at Word Web: **sound**

fre|quent /frikwənt/ **ADJ** If something is **frequent**, it happens often. ❑ Bordeaux is on the main Paris-Madrid line so there are frequent trains. ● **fre|quent|ly** **ADV** ❑ He was frequently unhappy. [from Latin]

fresh /frɛʃ/ (**fresher, freshest**)
1 **ADJ** Fresh food has been picked or produced recently. ❑ We only sell fresh fish that has been caught locally.
2 **ADJ** Something that is **fresh** has been done, made, or experienced recently. ❑ There were fresh car tracks in the snow. ● **fresh|ly** **ADV** ❑ We bought some freshly-baked bread.
3 **ADJ** Something that smells, tastes, or feels **fresh**, is clean or cool. ❑ The air was fresh and she immediately felt better.
4 **ADJ** A **fresh** thing or amount replaces or is added to an existing thing or amount. ❑ The waiter placed a fresh glass on the table.

5 **ADJ** Fresh paint is not yet dry. ❑ There was fresh paint on the walls.
6 **ADJ** A child who is **fresh** is rude and disrespectful. [from Old English] [INFORMAL]
→ look at Word Web: **glacier**

fresh|man /frɛʃmən/ (**freshmen**) **N-COUNT** In the United States, a **freshman** is a student who is in their first year at a high school or college.

fric|tion /frɪkʃən/ **N-NONCOUNT** SCIENCE Friction is the force that makes it difficult for things to move freely when they are touching each other. [from French]

Fri|day /fraɪdeɪ, -di/ (**Fridays**)
N-COUNT/N-NONCOUNT Friday is the day after Thursday and before Saturday. ❑ He is going home on Friday. ❑ We hope to finish the work by Friday. [from Old English]

fridge /frɪdʒ/ (**fridges**) **N-COUNT** A fridge is the same as a **refrigerator**. [INFORMAL]

friend /frɛnd/ (**friends**)
1 **N-COUNT** A **friend** is someone who you like and know well, but who is not related to you. ❑ She's my best friend. ❑ She was never a close friend of mine.
2 **N-PLURAL** If you are **friends with** someone, you are their friend and they are yours. ❑ I still wanted to be friends with Alison. ❑ We remained good friends.
3 **PHRASE** If you **make friends with** someone, you meet them and become their friend. ❑ He has made friends with the kids on the street. ❑ Dennis made friends easily. [from Old English]

Word Partnership	Use **friend** with :
ADJ	**best** friend, **close** friend, **dear** friend, **faithful** friend, friend, **good** friend, **loyal** friend, **mutual** friend, **old** friend, **personal** friend, **trusted** friend **1**
N	**childhood** friend, friend **of the family**, friend **1**
	friend **or foe** **1** **2**
V	**tell** a friend **1**
	make a friend **1** **3**

friend|ly /frɛndli/ (**friendlier, friendliest**)
1 **ADJ** If someone is **friendly**, they behave in a pleasant, kind way. ❑ Godfrey was friendly to me. ❑ The man had a pleasant, friendly face.
● **friend|li|ness** **N-NONCOUNT** ❑ She loves the friendliness of the people there.
2 **ADJ** If you are **friendly with** someone,

f

you like each other and enjoy spending time together. ❑ *I'm friendly with his mother.* [from Old English]

Word Partnership	Use **friendly** with :
N	friendly **atmosphere**, friendly **face**, friendly **neighbors**, friendly **service**, friendly **voice** 1 friendly **relationship** 2
V	**become** friendly 2

Word Link	*ship ≈ condition or state :*
	citizenship, dictatorship, friendship

friend|ship /frɛndʃɪp/ (**friendships**)
N-COUNT/N-NONCOUNT A **friendship** is a relationship between two or more friends. ❑ *Their friendship has lasted more than sixty years.* [from Old English]

fries /fraɪz/
1 N-PLURAL **Fries** are the same as **French fries**. [from Old French]
2 → see also **fry**

fright /fraɪt/ (**frights**)
1 N-NONCOUNT **Fright** is a sudden feeling of fear. ❑ *There was a loud noise, and Franklin jumped with fright.*
2 N-COUNT A **fright** is an experience that makes you suddenly afraid. ❑ *The snake raised its head, which gave everyone a fright.* [from Old English]

fright|en /fraɪt³n/ (**frightens, frightening, frightened**) V-T Something or someone that **frightens** you makes you suddenly feel afraid, anxious, or nervous. ❑ *He knew that Soli was trying to frighten him.* [from Old English]
▶ **frighten away** If you **frighten** a person or animal **away**, you make them afraid so that they run away or stay some distance away from you. ❑ *The boats were frightening away the fish.*

fright|ened /fraɪt³nd/ ADJ A **frightened** person or animal is anxious or afraid. ❑ *She was frightened of making a mistake.* [from Old English]

fright|en|ing /fraɪt³nɪŋ/ ADJ If something is **frightening**, it makes you feel afraid, anxious, or nervous. ❑ *It was a very frightening experience.* [from Old English]

frig|id /frɪdʒɪd/ ADJ **Frigid** means extremely cold. [FORMAL] ❑ *A snowstorm hit the West today, bringing with it frigid temperatures.* [from Latin]

frill /frɪl/ (**frills**) N-COUNT A **frill** is a long narrow strip of cloth or paper with a lot

of folds in it, used as a decoration. ❑ *She loves party dresses with ribbons and frills.* [from Flemish]

fringe /frɪndʒ/ (**fringes**)
1 N-COUNT A **fringe** is a decoration attached to clothes or curtains, for example, consisting of a row of hanging threads. ❑ *The jacket had leather fringes on the sleeves.*
2 N-COUNT To be **on the fringe** or **on the fringes of** a place means to be on the outside edge of it. ❑ *...a small town on the fringes of the city.* [from Old French]

frog /frɒg/ (**frogs**) N-COUNT A **frog** is a small animal with smooth skin, big eyes, and long back legs that it uses for jumping. [from Old English]
→ look at Word Web: **amphibian**

from /frəm, STRONG frʌm/
1 PREP If something comes **from** a particular person or thing, or if you get something **from** them, they give it to you or send it to you. ❑ *I received a letter from Mary yesterday.* ❑ *The watch was a present from his wife.*
2 PREP Someone who comes **from** a particular place lives there or was born there. ❑ *I come from New Zealand.*
3 PREP If someone or something moves **from** a place, they leave it. ❑ *Everyone watched as she ran from the room.* ❑ *Mr. Baker traveled from Washington to London for the meeting.*
4 PREP If you take something **from** a person or a thing, you remove it from them. ❑ *Bone can be taken from other parts of the patient's body.*
5 PREP If you take something **from** an amount, you reduce the amount by that much. ❑ *The $103 was deducted from Mrs. Adams' salary.*
6 PREP If you return **from** a place, you return after being there. ❑ *My son has just returned from Amsterdam.*
7 PREP You can use **from** when you are talking about how far away something is. ❑ *The park is only a hundred yards from the center of town.* ❑ *How far is the hotel from here?*
8 PREP If a road goes **from** one place to another, you can travel along it between those two places. ❑ *...the road from St. Petersburg to Tallinn.*
9 PREP You use **from** to say what was used to make something. ❑ *This bread is made from white flour.* ❑ *The cans are made from steel.*
10 PREP If something changes **from** one thing **to** another, it stops being the first

thing and becomes the second thing. ❏ *The expression on his face changed from sympathy to surprise.* ❏ *Unemployment fell from 7.5 to 7.2%.*
11 **PREP** You can use **from** to talk about the beginning of a period of time. ❏ *Breakfast is available from 6 a.m.* [from Old English]

front /frʌnt/ (**fronts**)
1 **N-COUNT** The **front of** something is the part of it that faces you, or that faces forward. ❏ *Stand at the front of the line.*
2 **PHRASE** A person or a thing that is **in front** is ahead of others in a moving group. ❏ *Don't drive too close to the car in front.*
3 **PHRASE** Someone who is **in front** in a competition is winning. ❏ *Richard Dunwoody is in front in the race.*
4 **PHRASE** Someone or something that is **in front of** a particular thing is facing it, ahead of it, or close to the front part of it. ❏ *She sat down in front of her mirror.* ❏ *A child ran in front of my car.*
5 **PHRASE** If you do or say something **in front of** someone else, you do or say it when they are present. ❏ *They never argued in front of their children.*
6 **N-COUNT** GEOGRAPHY In relation to the weather, a **front** is a line where a mass of cold air meets a mass of warm air. [from Latin]
→ look at Word Web: **forecast**

fron|tier /frʌntɪər, frɒn-/ (**frontiers**)
1 **N-COUNT** A **frontier** is an area of land where people are just starting to live. ❏ *...a frontier town.*
2 **N-COUNT** SOCIAL STUDIES In the western part of America before the twentieth century, the **frontier** was the part that Europeans had reached. ❏ *The family moved west to the frontier, and took up land in Dixon County.* [from Old French]

front line (**front lines**) also **front-line**
N-COUNT SOCIAL STUDIES The **front line** is the place where two opposing armies are fighting each other. ❏ *...taking supplies to soldiers on the front line.*

front-page **ADJ** A **front-page** article or picture appears on the front page of a newspaper because it is very important or interesting.

front-run|ner (**front-runners**) **N-COUNT** In a competition or a contest, the **front-runner** is the person who seems most likely to win it. ❏ *Neither of the front-runners in the presidential*

election is a mainstream politician.

frost /frɒst/ (**frosts, frosting, frosted**)
1 **N-COUNT/N-NONCOUNT** **Frost** is ice like white powder that forms outside when the weather is very cold. ❏ *There was frost on my windshield this morning.*
2 **V-T** If you **frost** a cake, you cover and decorate it with frosting. [from Old English]
→ look at Word Web: **snow**

frost|ing /frɒstɪŋ/ **N-NONCOUNT** **Frosting** is a sweet substance that is used for decorating cakes. [from Old English]

frown /fraʊn/ (**frowns, frowning, frowned**)
1 **V-I** When someone **frowns**, their eyebrows move together because they are annoyed, worried, or confused, or because they are concentrating. ❏ *Nancy shook her head, frowning.* ❏ *He frowned at her anxiously.*
2 **N-COUNT** **Frown** is also a noun. ❏ *There was a deep frown on the boy's face.* [from Old French]
▶ **frown upon** or **frown on** If something **is frowned upon** or **is frowned on**, people disapprove of it. ❏ *This practice is frowned upon as being wasteful.*

froze /froʊz/ **Froze** is the past tense of **freeze**. [from Old English]

fro|zen /froʊzᵊn/
1 **Frozen** is the past participle of **freeze**.
2 **ADJ** If the ground is **frozen** it has become hard because the weather is very cold. ❏ *It was extremely cold and the ground was frozen hard.*
3 **ADJ** **Frozen** food has been stored at a very low temperature. ❏ *Frozen fish is a healthy convenience food.*
4 **ADJ** If you are **frozen**, you are very cold. ❏ *I'm frozen out here.* [from Old English]
→ look at Word Web: **glacier**

fruit /fruːt/ (**fruit** or **fruits**)
N-COUNT/N-NONCOUNT **Fruit** is the part of a tree that contains seeds, covered with a substance that you can eat. ❏ *Fresh fruit and vegetables provide fiber and vitamins.* ❏ *We grow bananas and other tropical fruits here.* [from Old French]
→ look at Picture Dictionaries: **fruit, dessert**
→ look at Word Web: **grain**

frus|trate /frʌstreɪt/ (**frustrates, frustrating, frustrated**) **V-T** If a problem **frustrates** you, it upsets or makes you angry because you cannot do anything about it.

Picture Dictionary   fruit

peel | skin | figs | kiwi | grapes | apple | banana | lemon | seeds | segment | orange | pear | pineapple | watermelon

❑ *His lack of ambition frustrated me.*
● **frus|trat|ed** **ADJ** ❑ *Roberta felt frustrated and angry.* ● **frus|trat|ing** **ADJ** ❑ *This situation is very frustrating for us.* ● **frus|tra|tion** /frʌstreɪʃᵊn/ (**frustrations**) **N-COUNT/N-NONCOUNT** ❑ *The team was beginning to show signs of frustration.* [from Latin]
→ look at Word Web: **anger**

fry /fraɪ/ (**fries, frying, fried**)
1 **V-T** When you **fry** food, you cook it in hot fat or oil. ❑ *Fry the onions until brown.*
2 **N-PLURAL** Fries are the same as **French fries**. [from Old French]
→ look at Picture Dictionaries: **cook, egg**
→ look at Word Web: **pan**

fudge /fʌdʒ/ **N-NONCOUNT** Fudge is soft candy made from butter, sugar, and milk, and sometimes chocolate. ❑ *For dessert, we had coffee served with home-made fudge.*

fuel /fyuəl/ **N-NONCOUNT** Fuel is a substance such as coal or oil that is burned to provide heat or power. ❑ *They bought some fuel on the freeway.* [from Old French]
→ look at Word Webs: **car, energy, engine, oil, petroleum, solar**

Word Partnership Use **fuel** with :

N	**cost of** fuel, fuel **oil**, fuel **pump**, fuel **shortage**, fuel **supply**, fuel **tank**
ADJ	**unleaded** fuel

fugue /fyug/ (**fugues**) **N-COUNT** MUSIC
A **fugue** is a piece of music that begins with a simple tune which is then repeated by other voices or instrumental parts with small variations. [from French]

ful|crum /fʊlkrəm/ **N-SING** SCIENCE In physics, **the fulcrum** is the central point on which a lever balances when it is lifting or moving something. [from Latin]

ful|fill /fʊlfɪl/ (**fulfills, fulfilling, fulfilled**)
1 **V-T** If you **fulfill** a promise or a dream, you manage to do what you said or hoped you would do. ❑ *She fulfilled her dream of starting law school.*
2 **V-T** If something **fulfills** you, you feel happy and satisfied with what you are doing. ❑ *Rachel knew that a life of luxury could not fulfill her.* ● **ful|filled** **ADJ** ❑ *...a fulfilled life.* ● **ful|fill|ing** **ADJ** ❑ *...a fulfilling career.* ● **ful|fill|ment** **N-NONCOUNT** ❑ *...professional fulfillment.* [from Old English]

full /fʊl/ (**fuller, fullest**)
1 **ADJ** If something is **full**, it contains as much of a substance or as many objects as it can. ❑ *The gas tank was full.*
2 **ADJ** If a place or a thing **is full of** things or people, it contains a large number of them. ❑ *The case was full of clothes.* ❑ *The streets were full of tourists.*
3 **ADJ** If you feel **full**, you have eaten or drunk so much that you do not want anything else. ❑ *You should stop eating when you're full.*
4 **ADJ** Your **full** name is your first name, other names that you may have, and your family name. ❑ *"May I have your full name?"—"Yes, it's Amy Anne Gray."*
5 **ADJ** A **full** description is complete, with nothing missing. ❑ *For full details of the event, visit our website.*
6 **ADJ** You use **full** when you are saying that something is as big, loud, strong, fast, etc.

as possible. ❑ *The car crashed into the wall at full speed.* ❑ *...the sound of Mozart, playing at full volume.*

7 **ADJ** When there is a **full** moon, the moon is a bright, complete circle.

8 **PHRASE** If you do something **in full**, you do it completely, giving every detail. ❑ *Mr. Thompson signed his name in full.* [from Old English]

Thesaurus	full Also look up :
ADJ	brimming; *(ant.)* empty **1**
	loaded **1** **2**
	bursting **2**

full-time also **full time**

1 **ADJ** **Full-time** work or study involves working or studying for all of each normal working week. ❑ *I'm looking for a full-time job.*
2 **ADV** **Full-time** is also an adverb. ❑ *Deirdre works full-time.*

ful|ly /fʊli/

1 **ADV** **Fully** means completely. ❑ *We are fully aware of the problem.*
2 **ADV** If you deal with something **fully**, you deal with every detail of it. ❑ *He promised to answer fully and truthfully.* [from Old English]

Word Partnership	Use fully with :
ADJ	fully **adjustable**, fully **aware**, fully **clothed**, fully **functional**, fully **operational**, fully **prepared** **1**
V	fully **agree**, fully **expect**, fully **extend**, fully **understand** **1**
	fully **explain** **2**

fun /fʌn/

1 **N-NONCOUNT** **Fun** is pleasure and enjoyment. ❑ *It's interesting and it's also fun.* ❑ *It could be fun to watch them.*
2 **N-NONCOUNT** Someone who is **fun** is interesting or amusing. ❑ *Liz was always so much fun.*
3 **PHRASE** If you do something **for fun**, you do it as a joke, without wanting to cause any harm. ❑ *Don't say such things, even for fun.*
4 **PHRASE** If you **make fun of** someone or something, you laugh at them or make jokes about them. ❑ *Don't make fun of me.*

Thesaurus	fun Also look up :
N	amusement, enjoyment, play; *(ant.)* misery **1**
ADJ	amusing, enjoyable, entertaining, happy, pleasant; *(ant.)* boring **2**

func|tion /fʌŋkʃən/ (**functions, functioning, functioned**)

1 **N-COUNT** The **function** of something or someone is the useful thing that they do or are intended to do. ❑ *One of the main functions of the skin is protection.*
2 **N-COUNT** A **function** is a large formal dinner or party. ❑ *He attended a private function hosted by one of his students.*
3 **V-I** If a machine or a system **is functioning**, it is working well. ❑ *Your heart is functioning normally.*
4 **N-COUNT** If you say that one thing is a **function** of another, you mean that its amount or nature depends on the other thing. [from Latin] [FORMAL]

func|tion|al /fʌŋkʃənəl/

1 **ADJ** **Functional** things are useful rather than decorative. ❑ *I like modern, functional furniture.*
2 **ADJ** **Functional** equipment works in the way that it is supposed to. ❑ *We have fully functional smoke alarms on all staircases.* [from Latin]

fund /fʌnd/ (**funds, funding, funded**)

1 **N-PLURAL** **Funds** are amounts of money that are available to be spent. ❑ *We're having a concert to raise funds for cancer research.*
2 → see also **fund-raising**
3 **N-COUNT** A **fund** is an amount of money that people save for a particular purpose. ❑ *There is a scholarship fund for engineering students.*
4 **V-T** When a person or an organization **funds** something, they provide money for it. ❑ *The Foundation has funded a variety of programs.* [from Latin]
5 → see also **funding**

fun|da|men|tal /fʌndəmɛntəl/ **ADJ** **Fundamental** things are very important and necessary. ❑ *I'll give you five fundamental steps for a healthy lifestyle.* ❑ *We all have a fundamental right to protect ourselves.* ● **fun|da|men|tal|ly** **ADV** ❑ *He is fundamentally a good man.* [from Latin]

fun|da|men|tal|ism /fʌndəmɛntəlɪzəm/ **N-NONCOUNT** **Fundamentalism** is the belief in the original form of a religion or theory, without accepting any later ideas. ❑ *...religious fundamentalism.* ● **fun|da|men|tal|ist** (**fundamentalists**) **N-COUNT** ❑ *...Christian fundamentalists.* [from Latin]

fund|ing /fʌndɪŋ/

1 **N-NONCOUNT** **Funding** is money that a

f

government or organization provides for a particular purpose. ❑ *They are hoping to get government funding for the program.* [from Latin] **2** → see also **fund**

fund·rais·ing also fundraising
N-NONCOUNT Fund-raising is the activity of collecting money for a particular use.

fu·ner·al /fyuunərəl/ (**funerals**) **N-COUNT**
A **funeral** is a ceremony that takes place when the body of someone who has died is buried or cremated. ❑ *The funeral will be in Joplin, Missouri.* [from Medieval Latin]

fun·gus /fʌŋgəs/ (**fungi** /fʌndʒaɪ, -ŋgaɪ/ or **funguses**) **N-COUNT/N-NONCOUNT** SCIENCE
Fungi are organisms that are similar to plants but they do not have flowers or leaves and they are not green in color. Fungi grow in wet places. ❑ *This fungus likes living in warm, wet places.* ❑ *There were mushrooms and other fungi growing out of the wall.* [from Latin]
→ look at Word Web: **fungus**

fun·nel /fʌnᵊl/ (**funnels**)
1 **N-COUNT** A **funnel** is a tube with a wide, round top, used for pouring liquids into a container such as a bottle.
2 **N-COUNT** A **funnel** is a tube on the top of a ship or a railroad engine where steam can escape.
3 **N-COUNT** SCIENCE A **funnel** is an organ on the bodies of some animals such as octopuses, that is used for breathing, laying eggs, and getting rid of waste.
4 **N-COUNT** GEOGRAPHY A **funnel** or **funnel cloud** is a rotating column of air below a cumulonimbus cloud, that can become part of a tornado. [from Old Provençal]

fun·ny /fʌni/ (**funnier, funniest**)
1 **ADJ** Someone or something that is **funny**
is amusing and likely to make you smile or laugh. ❑ *I'll tell you a funny story.*
2 **ADJ** A **funny** thing or person is strange, surprising, or confusing. ❑ *Children get some very funny ideas sometimes!* ❑ *There's something funny about him.*
3 **ADJ** If you feel **funny**, you feel slightly ill. [INFORMAL] ❑ *My head began to ache and my stomach felt funny.*

Thesaurus funny Also look up :
ADJ amusing, comical, entertaining; (*ant.*) serious **1** bizarre, odd, peculiar **2**

fur /fɜr/ **N-NONCOUNT** Fur is the thick hair that grows on the bodies of many animals. ❑ *This creature's fur is short, dense, and silky.* [from Old French]

fu·ri·ous /fyuəriəs/ **ADJ** Someone who is **furious** is extremely angry. ❑ *He is furious at the way he has been treated.* ● **fu·ri·ous·ly ADV** ❑ *Workers have reacted furiously to the management decision.* [from Latin]
→ look at Word Web: **anger**

fur·nace /fɜrnɪs/ (**furnaces**) **N-COUNT**
A **furnace** is a container with a very hot fire inside it. ❑ *The iron bars glow in the red hot furnace.* [from Old French]

fur·ni·ture /fɜrnɪtʃər/ **N-NONCOUNT**
Furniture is large objects such as tables, chairs, or beds. ❑ *Each piece of furniture matched the style of the house.* [from French]

fur·ry /fɜri/ (**furrier, furriest**)
1 **ADJ** A **furry** animal is covered with thick, soft hair.
2 **ADJ** Something that is **furry** feels similar to fur. ❑ *The leaves are soft and furry.* [from Old French]

Word Web fungus

Fungi can be both harmful and helpful. For example, **mold** and **mildew** destroy crops, ruin clothing, cause diseases, and can even lead to death. But many fungi are useful. For instance, a single-cell fungus called **yeast** makes bread rise. Another form of yeast makes wine ferment. It turns the sugar in grape juice into alcohol. And **mushrooms** are a part of the diet of people all over the world. Cheese makers use a specific fungus to produce the creamy white skin on brie. A different **microorganism** gives blue cheese its characteristic color. **Truffles**, the most expensive fungi, cost more than $100 an ounce.

fur|ther /fɜ́rðər/ (**furthers, furthering, furthered**)

> **LANGUAGE HELP**
> **Further** is a comparative of **far**. It is also a verb.

1 **ADV** **Further** means to a greater extent or degree. ❑ *Inflation is below 5% and set to fall further.* ❑ *The rebellion further damaged the country's image.*

2 **ADV** If you go or get **further with** something, or take something **further**, you make some progress. ❑ *We've got a great chance of going further in this competition.*

3 **ADV** **Further** means a greater distance than before or than something else. ❑ *People are living further away from their jobs.* ❑ *...a main road fifty yards further on.*

4 **ADV** **Further** is used in expressions such as **further back** and **further ahead** to refer to a point in time that is earlier or later than the time you are talking about. ❑ *Looking still further ahead, by the end of the next century world population is expected to be about ten billion.*

5 **ADJ** A **further** thing, number of things, or amount of something is an additional thing, number of things, or amount. ❑ *...further evidence of slowing economic growth.*

6 **V-T** If you **further** something, you help it to progress, to be successful, or to be achieved. ❑ *Education isn't only about furthering your career.* [from Old English]

fur|thest /fɜ́rðɪst/

> **LANGUAGE HELP**
> **Furthest** is a superlative form of **far**.

1 **ADV** **Furthest** means to a greater extent or degree than ever before or than anything or anyone else. ❑ *Prices have fallen furthest in the south.*

2 **ADV** **Furthest** means at a greater distance from a particular point than anyone or anything else, or for a greater distance than anyone or anything else. ❑ *...those areas furthest from the coast.*

3 **ADJ** **Furthest** is also an adjective. ❑ *...the furthest point from Earth that any spacecraft has ever been.* [from Old English]

fury /fyʊ́əri/ **N-NONCOUNT** **Fury** is violent or very strong anger. ❑ *Her eyes were full of fury.* [from Latin]

fuse /fyuz/ (**fuses**) **N-COUNT** A **fuse** is a small wire in a piece of electrical equipment that melts when too much electricity passes through it. ❑ *The fuse blew as he pressed the* button to start the motor. [from Latin]

fu|sion /fyúʒən/ (**fusions**)

1 **N-COUNT/N-NONCOUNT** The **fusion** of two or more things involves joining them together to form one thing. ❑ *...a delicate fusion of Eastern and Western art.*

2 **N-NONCOUNT** SCIENCE In physics, **fusion** is the process in which atomic particles combine and produce a large amount of nuclear energy. ❑ *...research into nuclear fusion.* [from Latin] → look at Word Web: **sun**

fuss /fʌs/ (**fusses, fussing, fussed**)

1 **N-SING** **Fuss** is anxious or excited behavior that is not useful. ❑ *I don't know what all the fuss is about.*

2 **V-I** If you **fuss**, you worry or behave in a nervous, anxious way about things that are not important. ❑ *Carol fussed about getting me a drink.*

3 **V-I** If you **fuss over** someone, you pay them a lot of attention and do things to make them happy or comfortable. ❑ *Aunt Laura fussed over him all afternoon.*

fussy /fʌ́si/ (**fussier, fussiest**) **ADJ** Someone who is **fussy** is very difficult to please and is interested in small details. ❑ *She is very fussy about her food.*

fu|ture /fyútʃər/ (**futures**)

1 **N-SING** The **future** is the time that will come after now. ❑ *He was making plans for the future.*

2 **ADJ** **Future** things will happen or exist after the present time. ❑ *The lives of future generations will be affected by our decisions.*

3 **N-COUNT** Someone's **future** is what will happen to them after the present time. ❑ *His future depends on the result of the election.*

4 **PHRASE** You say **in the future** when you are talking about what will happen after now. ❑ *I asked her to be more careful in the future.* [from Latin]

Word Partnership	Use **future** with :
ADJ	**bright** future, **distant** future, **immediate** future, **near** future, **uncertain** future **1**
V	**discuss the** future, **have a** future, **plan for the** future, **predict/see the** future **1**
N	future **date**, future **events**, future **generations**, future **plans**, **for** future **reference 2**

fu|ture tense (**future tenses**) **N-COUNT** LANGUAGE ARTS In grammar, **the future tense** is the form that is used for talking about the time that will come after the present.

Gg

gadg|et /gǽdʒɪt/ (**gadgets**) **N-COUNT**
A **gadget** is a small machine or useful object. ❑ *The store sells computers and other electronic gadgets.* [from French]
→ look at Word Web: **technology**

gain /geɪn/ (**gains, gaining, gained**)
1 **V-T** If you **gain** something, you get it. ❑ *You can gain access to the website for $14 a month.* ❑ *Students can gain valuable experience by working during their vacations.*
2 **V-T/V-I** If you **gain from** something, you get an advantage from it. ❑ *Everybody is going to gain from working together.* ❑ *The company expects to gain billions from the deal.*
3 **V-T** To **gain** something means to have more of it. ❑ *Some women gain weight after they have a baby.* ❑ *The car was gaining speed as it came toward us.*
4 **N-COUNT/N-NONCOUNT** Gain is also a noun. ❑ *Sales showed a gain of nearly 8% last month.* [from Old French]

gal|axy /gǽləksi/ (**galaxies**) also Galaxy **N-COUNT** SCIENCE A **galaxy** is a very large group of stars and planets. ❑ *Astronomers have discovered a distant galaxy.* [from Medieval Latin]
→ look at Word Webs: **galaxy, star**

gale /geɪl/ (**gales**) **N-COUNT** A **gale** is a very strong wind. ❑ *A strong gale was blowing.*
→ look at Word Web: **wind**

gal|lery /gǽləri/ (**galleries**) **N-COUNT** ARTS A **gallery** is a place where people go to look at art. ❑ *We visited an art gallery.* [from Old French]

gal|lon /gǽlən/ (**gallons**) **N-COUNT** MATH A **gallon** is a unit for measuring liquids. A **gallon** is equal to 3.785 liters. There are eight pints in a gallon. ❑ *The tank holds 1,000 gallons of water.* [from Old Northern French]
→ look at Picture Dictionary: **measurements**

gal|lop /gǽləp/ (**gallops, galloping, galloped**) **V-T/V-I** When a horse **gallops**, it runs very fast. If you **gallop** a horse, you make it gallop. ❑ *The horses galloped away.* [from Old French]

gam|ble /gǽmbəl/ (**gambles, gambling, gambled**)
1 **N-COUNT** A **gamble** is a risk that you take because you hope that something good will happen. ❑ *She took a gamble and started up her own business.*
2 **V-T/V-I** If you **gamble on** something, you take a risk because you hope that something good will happen. ❑ *Companies sometimes have to gamble on new products.* ❑ *He gambled his career on this movie.*
3 **V-T/V-I** If you **gamble**, you risk money in a game or on the result of a race or a competition. ❑ *John gambled heavily on horse racing.* ❑ *Most people visit Las Vegas to gamble their money.*

gam|bler /gǽmblər/ (**gamblers**) **N-COUNT** A **gambler** is someone who risks money regularly, for example in card games or

---

Word Web   galaxy

The word **galaxy** with a small *g* refers to an extremely large group of **stars** and **planets**. It measures billions of **light years** wide. There are about 100 billion galaxies in the **universe**. **Astronomers** classify galaxies into four different types. Irregular galaxies have no particular shape. Elliptical galaxies look like flattened spheres. Spiral galaxies have long curving arms. A barred spiral galaxy has straight lines of stars extending from its nucleus. Galaxy with a capital G refers to our own **solar system**. The name of this galaxy is the **Milky Way**. It is about 100,000 light years wide.

horse racing. ❑ *Her husband was a heavy gambler.*

gam|bling /gǽmblɪŋ/ **N-NONCOUNT**
Gambling is the act or activity of risking money, for example in card games or horse racing. ❑ *The gambling laws are quite tough.*

game /geɪm/ (**games**)
 1 **N-COUNT** SPORTS A **game** is an activity or a sport in which you try to win against someone. ❑ *Football is a popular game.*
❑ *We played a game of cards.*
 2 **N-COUNT** SPORTS A **game** is one particular occasion when you play a game. ❑ *It was the first game of the season.*
 3 **N-COUNT** You can describe a way of behaving as a **game** when a person uses it to gain an advantage. ❑ *The Americans are playing a very delicate political game.*
 4 **N-NONCOUNT** **Game** is wild animals or birds that are hunted for sport or food.
❑ *The men shot game for food.*
 5 **PHRASE** If someone or something **gives the game away**, they reveal a secret or reveal their feelings, and this puts them at a disadvantage. ❑ *Their faces gave the game away.*
[from Old English]
→ look at Word Webs: **chess, mammal**

game con|sole (**game consoles**) or **games console** **N-COUNT** TECHNOLOGY A **game console** is a piece of electronic equipment that is used for playing computer games on a television screen. ❑ *More than half of six- to ten-year-olds have a game console.*

gamer /geɪmər/ (**gamers**) **N-COUNT** A **gamer** is someone who plays computer games.

ga|meto|phyte /gəmiːtəfaɪt/
(**gametophytes**) **N-COUNT** SCIENCE
A **gametophyte** is a stage in the life of a plant when it produces eggs and sperm, or a plant during this stage of its life.

gam|ma rays /gǽmə reɪz/ **N-PLURAL**
SCIENCE **Gamma rays** are a type of electromagnetic radiation that has a shorter wavelength and higher energy than X-rays.

gang /gǽŋ/ (**gangs, ganging, ganged**)
 1 **N-COUNT** A **gang** is a group of people, especially young people, who go around together and often deliberately cause trouble. ❑ *They had a fight with another gang.*
 2 **N-COUNT** A **gang** is an organized group of criminals. ❑ *Police are hunting for a gang that has stolen several cars.* [from Old English]

▶ **gang up** If people **gang up on** someone, they join together in a group against that person. [INFORMAL] ❑ *Harrison complained that his colleagues ganged up on him.*

gan|gli|on /gǽŋgliən/ (**ganglia**) **N-COUNT**
SCIENCE **Ganglia** are groups of nerve cells, usually outside the central nervous system. [from Late Latin]

gap /gǽp/ (**gaps**)
 1 **N-COUNT** A **gap** is a space between two things. ❑ *There was a narrow gap between the curtains.*
 2 **N-COUNT** A **gap** is a hole in something.
❑ *His horse escaped through a gap in the fence.*
 3 **N-COUNT** A **gap** is a period of time between two events, or when you stop doing something that you normally do.
❑ *There was a gap of five years between the birth of her two children.*
 4 **N-COUNT** A **gap between** two groups of people is a big difference between them.
❑ *...the gap between rich and poor.* [from Old Norse]

gap hy|poth|esis **N-SING** SCIENCE The **gap hypothesis** is a theory in geology that states that strong earthquakes are more likely to occur close to fault lines that have had few earthquakes in the past.

gar|age /gərɑ́ʒ/ (**garages**)
 1 **N-COUNT** A **garage** is a building where you keep a car. ❑ *The house has a large garage.*
 2 **N-COUNT** A **garage** is a place where you can have your car repaired. ❑ *Nancy took her car to a local garage.* [from French]

gar|bage /gɑ́rbɪdʒ/
 1 **N-NONCOUNT** **Garbage** is things such as old papers, empty cans, and old food that you do not want anymore. ❑ *They took the trash to a garbage dump.*
 2 **N-NONCOUNT** If you say that an idea or an opinion is **garbage**, you mean that you think it is not true or not important. [INFORMAL]
❑ *I think this theory is garbage.* [from Old Italian]
→ look at Word Web: **pollution**

gar|bage can (**garbage cans**) **N-COUNT**
A **garbage can** is a container for garbage.

gar|bage man (**garbage men**) **N-COUNT**
A **garbage man** is a person whose job is to take people's garbage away.

gar|den /gɑ́rdᵊn/ (**gardens, gardening, gardened**)
 1 **N-COUNT** A **garden** is the part of a yard

g

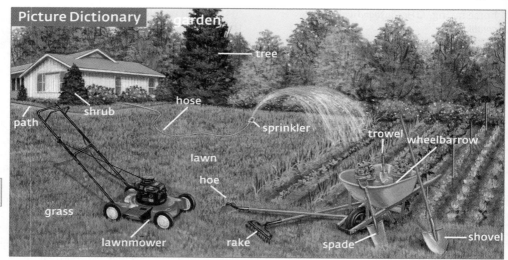

Picture Dictionary garden

tree
hose
shrub
path
sprinkler
trowel
wheelbarrow
lawn
hoe
grass
lawnmower
rake
spade
shovel

G

where you grow flowers and vegetables.
❑ *She had a beautiful garden.*
2 **v-i** If you **garden**, you do work in your
garden. ❑ *Jim gardened on weekends.*
● **gar|den|ing** **N-NONCOUNT** ❑ *My favorite
hobby is gardening.*
3 **N-PLURAL** **Gardens** are places with plants,
trees, and grass, that people can visit.
❑ *The gardens are open from 10:30 a.m. until
5:00 p.m.* [from Old French]
→ look at Picture Dictionary: **garden**
→ look at Word Web: **park**

gar|den|er /gɑrdᵊnər/ (**gardeners**) **N-COUNT**
A **gardener** is a person who works in a
garden. ❑ *She employed a gardener.*

gar|lic /gɑrlɪk/ **N-NONCOUNT** **Garlic** is a plant
like a small onion with a strong flavor,
which you use in cooking. ❑ *When the oil is
hot, add a clove of garlic.* [from Old English]
→ look at Word Web: **spice**

gar|ment /gɑrmənt/ (**garments**) **N-COUNT**
A **garment** is a piece of clothing. ❑ *Exports of
garments to the U.S. fell 3%.* [from Old French]

gas /gæs/ (**gases**)
1 **N-COUNT/N-NONCOUNT** **SCIENCE** A **gas** is
any substance that is not a liquid or a solid.
❑ *Hydrogen is a gas, not a metal.*
2 **N-NONCOUNT** **Gas** is a liquid that you put
into a car or other vehicle to make it work.
Gas is short for **gasoline**. ❑ *The car had a full
tank of gas.*
3 → see also **greenhouse gas**
4 **PHRASE** If you **step on the gas** when you
are driving a vehicle, you go faster.

[INFORMAL] [from Flemish]
→ look at Word Webs: **air, energy,
greenhouse effect, matter, petroleum,
solar system**

gas ex|change **N-NONCOUNT** SCIENCE
Gas exchange is the same as **respiration**.

gas gi|ant (**gas giants**) **N-COUNT** SCIENCE
A **gas giant** is a large planet that is composed
mainly of gas, such as Neptune or Jupiter.

gaso|hol /gæsəhɔl/ **N-NONCOUNT** **Gasohol** is
a mixture of gasoline and alcohol that can
be used instead of gasoline in cars.

gaso|line /gæsəlin/ **N-NONCOUNT** **Gasoline**
is a liquid that you put into a car or other
vehicle to make it work.
→ look at Word Webs: **oil, petroleum**

gasp /gæsp/ (**gasps, gasping, gasped**)
1 **N-COUNT** A **gasp** is a short, quick breath
of air that you take in through your mouth.
❑ *There was a gasp from the crowd.*
2 **v-i** When you **gasp**, you take a short,
quick breath through your mouth. ❑ *She
gasped for air.* [from Old Norse]

gas sta|tion (**gas stations**) **N-COUNT** A **gas
station** is a place where you can buy gas for
your car.

gate /geɪt/ (**gates**)
1 **N-COUNT** A **gate**
is a structure like a
door that you use to
enter a field, or the
area around a
building. ❑ *He opened*

gate

the gate and walked up to the house.
2 **N-COUNT** In an airport, a **gate** is a place where passengers leave the airport and get on an airplane. ❏ *Please go to gate 15.* [from Old English]

gath|er /gǽðər/ (**gathers, gathering, gathered**)
1 **V-T/V-I** If people **gather** somewhere, or if someone **gathers** them, they come together in a group. ❏ *We gathered around the fireplace and talked.* ❏ *The teacher gathered the children onto the bus.*
2 **V-T** If you **gather** things, you collect them together so that you can use them. ❏ *They gathered enough firewood to make a fire.* ❏ *Attending a college fair is the best way to gather information.*
3 **V-T** If something **gathers** speed or force, it gradually becomes faster or more powerful. ❏ *The train slowly gathered speed.*
4 **V-T** You use **gather** in expressions such as **I gather** and **as far as I can gather** to introduce information that you have found out. ❏ *I gather he didn't enjoy the show.* ❏ *"He speaks English."—"I gathered that."* [from Old English]

gath|er|ing /gǽðərɪŋ/ (**gatherings**)
N-COUNT A **gathering** is a group of people meeting together for a particular purpose. ❏ *They held a large family gathering.* [from Old English]

gaudy /gɔ́di/ (**gaudier, gaudiest**) **ADJ** If something is **gaudy**, it is very brightly colored in a way you find unattractive. ❏ *...a gaudy orange and purple hat.* [from Old French]

gauge /geɪdʒ/ (**gauges, gauging, gauged**)
1 **V-T** If you **gauge** something, you measure it or judge it. ❏ *She found it hard to gauge his mood.*
2 **N-COUNT** A **gauge** is a piece of equipment that measures the amount or level of something. ❏ *The temperature gauge showed that the water was boiling.* [from Old Northern French]

gave /geɪv/ **Gave** is the past tense of **give.** [from Old English]

gay /geɪ/ **ADJ** A **gay** man or woman is attracted to people of the same sex. ❏ *The quality of life for gay men has improved.* [from Old French]

gaze /geɪz/ (**gazes, gazing, gazed**)
1 **V-I** If you **gaze at** someone or something, you look steadily at them for a long time.

❏ *She was gazing at herself in the mirror.* ❏ *He gazed into the fire.*
2 **N-COUNT** You can talk about someone's **gaze** as a way of describing how they are looking at something. [WRITTEN] ❏ *She felt uncomfortable under the woman's steady gaze.* [from Swedish]

gear /gɪər/ (**gears, gearing, geared**)
1 **N-COUNT** **Gears** are the part of an engine that changes engine power into movement. ❏ *On a hill, use low gears.* ❏ *The car was in fourth gear.*
2 **N-NONCOUNT** The **gear** involved in a particular activity is the equipment or special clothing that you use. ❏ *He took his fishing gear with him.* ❏ *...camping gear.*
3 **V-T** If someone or something **is geared to** or **toward** a particular purpose, they are organized or designed in order to achieve that purpose. ❏ *Colleges are not always geared to the needs of part-time students.* ❏ *My training was geared toward winning the gold medal.* [from Old Norse]

gear|shift /gɪərʃɪft/ (**gearshifts**) **N-COUNT** The **gearshift** is the handle that you use to change gear in a car or other vehicle.

GED /dʒi i di/ **N-COUNT** The **GED** is a test in basic subject areas such as math and English for adults who did not finish high school. The test shows that they have the same academic skills as a high school graduate. **GED** is short for **General Educational Development.** ❏ *We help students who did not complete high school to obtain their GED certificate.* ❏ *...the GED Test.*

geese /gis/ **Geese** is the plural of **goose.** [from Old English]

gel /dʒɛl/ **N-NONCOUNT Gel** is a thick substance like jelly, especially one that you use to keep your hair in a particular style.

gem /dʒɛm/ (**gems**) **N-COUNT** A **gem** is a valuable stone that is used in jewelry. ❏ *...precious gems.* [from Old French]

gen|der /dʒɛndər/ (**genders**)
1 **N-COUNT/N-NONCOUNT** A person's **gender** is the fact that they are male or female. ❏ *We do not know the children's ages and genders.*
2 **N-COUNT/N-NONCOUNT** LANGUAGE ARTS In grammar, the **gender** of a noun, a pronoun, or an adjective is whether it is masculine or feminine. In English, only personal pronouns such as "she," reflexive pronouns such as "himself," and possessive

g

determiners such as "her" have gender.
❑ *In French, all nouns have gender: they are either masculine of feminine.* [from Old French]

gene /dʒin/ (**genes**) **N-COUNT** SCIENCE
A **gene** is the part of a cell that controls a person's, an animal's, or a plant's physical characteristics, growth, and development. ❑ *He carries the gene for red hair.* [from German]

gen|er|al /dʒɛnərəl/ (**generals**)
1 **ADJ** **General** describes something that involves most people and things. ❑ *There is not enough general understanding of this problem.*
2 **ADJ** If you talk about the **general** situation, you are describing the situation as a whole rather than considering its details. ❑ *There has been a general fall in unemployment.* ❑ *In general terms life has gotten better.*
3 **ADJ** You use **general** to describe something that involves or affects most people. ❑ *There is not enough general awareness of this problem.*
4 **PHRASE** You use **in general** to talk about something as a whole, rather than part of it. ❑ *We need to improve our educational system in general.*
5 **N-COUNT** A **general** is an officer with a high rank in the army. ❑ *The troops received a visit from the general.* [from Latin]

gen|er|al elec|tion (**general elections**)
N-COUNT SOCIAL STUDIES A **general election** is a time when people choose a new government. Compare with **primary**.

gen|er|al|ize /dʒɛnrəlaɪz/ (**generalizes, generalizing, generalized**) **V-I** If you **generalize**, you say something that is usually, but not always, true. ❑ *You shouldn't generalize and say that all men are the same.* [from Latin]

gen|er|al|ly /dʒɛnrəli/
1 **ADV** **Generally** describes something without giving any particular details. ❑ *He was generally a good man.*
2 **ADV** You use **generally** to say that something usually happens, but not always. ❑ *It is generally true that darker fruits contain more iron.* [from Latin]

gen|er|ate /dʒɛnəreɪt/ (**generates, generating, generated**)
1 **V-T** To **generate** something means to cause it to exist. ❑ *The reforms will generate new jobs.*

2 **V-T** To **generate** a form of energy or power means to produce it. ❑ *We use oil to generate electricity.* [from Latin]
→ look at Word Web: **energy**

gen|era|tion /dʒɛnəreɪʃⁿn/ (**generations**)
1 **N-COUNT** A **generation** is all the people in a group or a country who are of a similar age. ❑ *The current generation of teens are the richest in history.*
2 **N-COUNT** A **generation** is the period of time that it takes for children to grow up and become adults. ❑ *Within a generation, flying has become a very common method of travel.*
3 **N-COUNT** A **generation** is a stage of development in the design and manufacture of machines. ❑ *...a new generation of computers.* [from Latin]

gen|era|tion time (**generation times**)
N-COUNT/N-NONCOUNT SCIENCE The **generation time** of an organism is the average time between the birth of one generation of the organism and the birth of the next generation.

gen|era|tor /dʒɛnəreɪtər/ (**generators**)
N-COUNT A **generator** is a machine that produces electricity. ❑ *The house has its own power generators.* [from Latin]
→ look at Word Web: **electricity**

gen|er|ous /dʒɛnərəs/
1 **ADJ** A **generous** person gives you more than you expect of something. ❑ *He is generous with his money.* ● **gen|er|os|ity** /dʒɛnərɒsɪti/ **N-NONCOUNT** ❑ *Diana was surprised by his kindness and generosity.*
● **gen|er|ous|ly** **ADV** ❑ *We would like to thank everyone who generously gave their time.*
2 **ADJ** A **generous** person is friendly, helpful, and willing to see the good qualities in someone or something. ❑ *He was always generous in sharing his knowledge.* ● **gen|er|ous|ly** **ADV** ❑ *He generously offered some advice.*
3 **ADJ** A **generous** amount of something is much larger than is usual. ❑ *The house has a generous amount of storage space.*
● **gen|er|ous|ly** **ADV** ❑ *Season the steaks generously with salt and pepper.* [from Old French]

Thesaurus	generous Also look up :
ADJ	charitable, kind; (*ant.*) mean, selfish, stingy **1** **2**
	abundant, overflowing **3**

ge|net|ic /dʒɪnɛtɪk/ **ADJ** SCIENCE **Genetic** describes something that is related to genetics or genes. ❑ ...a rare genetic disease.

ge|neti|cal|ly modi|fied /dʒɪnɛtɪkli mɒdɪfaɪd/ **ADJ** SCIENCE **Genetically modified** plants and animals have had their genetic structure (= pattern of chemicals in cells) changed in order to make them more suitable for a particular purpose. The short form **GM** is also used.

ge|net|ic en|gi|neer|ing **N-NONCOUNT** SCIENCE **Genetic engineering** is the science or activity of changing the genetic structure of an animal, a plant, or other organism in order to make it stronger or more suitable for a particular purpose.

ge|net|ic finger|print|ing /dʒɪnɛtɪk fɪŋgərprɪntɪŋ/ **N-NONCOUNT** SCIENCE **Genetic fingerprinting** is a method of identifying people using the genetic material in their bodies.

| Word Link | ics ≈ system, knowledge : economics, electronics, genetics |

ge|net|ics /dʒɪnɛtɪks/ **N-NONCOUNT** SCIENCE **Genetics** is the study of how qualities are passed on from parents to children. ❑ Genetics is changing our understanding of cancer.

ge|ni|us /dʒinyəs/ (geniuses)
1 **N-COUNT** A **genius** is a very skilled or intelligent person. ❑ Chaplin was a comic genius.
2 **N-NONCOUNT** **Genius** is very great ability or skill in a particular subject or activity. ❑ ...her genius as a designer. [from Latin]

ge|nome /dʒinoʊm/ (genomes) **N-COUNT** SCIENCE A **genome** is the particular number and arrangement of chromosomes within the cells of an organism that distinguishes

it from other types of organism. ❑ ...the mapping of the human genome.

geno|type /dʒinətaɪp, dʒɛn-/ (genotypes) **N-COUNT/N-NONCOUNT** SCIENCE A **genotype** is the particular set of genes possessed by an individual organism. Compare with **phenotype**.

gen|re /ʒɒnrə/ (genres) **N-COUNT** ARTS A **genre** is a particular type of literature, painting, music, film, or other art form that people consider as a class because it has special characteristics. [FORMAL] ❑ ...novels in the romance genre. [from French]
→ look at Word Webs: **genre, fantasy**

gen|tle /dʒɛntᵊl/ (gentler, gentlest)
1 **ADJ** Someone who is **gentle** is kind, mild, and calm. ❑ My husband was a quiet and gentle man. ● **gen|tle|ness** **N-NONCOUNT** ❑ She treated her mother with great gentleness.
● **gen|tly** **ADV** ❑ She smiled gently at him.
2 **ADJ** **Gentle** actions or movements are calm, slow, or soft. ❑ Rest and gentle exercise will make you feel better. ● **gen|tly** **ADV** ❑ Patrick took her gently by the arm.
3 **ADJ** If you describe the wind as **gentle**, you mean that it is pleasant and calm. ❑ ...a gentle breeze. [from Old French]

gentle|man /dʒɛntᵊlmən/ (gentlemen)
1 **N-COUNT** A **gentleman** is a man who is polite, educated, and kind to other people. ❑ He was always such a gentleman.
2 **N-PLURAL** You can use **gentlemen** to talk to men or to talk about them in a polite way. ❑ This way, please, ladies and gentlemen.

genu|ine /dʒɛnyuɪn/ **ADJ** If a person, a thing, or an emotion is **genuine**, they are true and real. ❑ He's a genuine American hero. ❑ We have a genuine friendship. ● **genu|ine|ly** **ADV** ❑ He was genuinely surprised. [from Latin]

g

| Word Web | genre |

Each of the arts includes several different types called **genres**. The four basic types of **literature** are **fiction, nonfiction, poetry**, and **drama**. In painting, some of the special areas are **realism**, expressionism, and Cubism. In music, they include **classical, jazz**, and **popular** forms. Each genre contains several parts. For example, popular music takes in **country and western, rap music**, and **rock**. Modern movie-making has produced a wide variety of genres. These include **horror films, comedies, action movies**, and **westerns**. Some **artists** work within more than one genre.

Thesaurus genuine Also look up :
ADJ actual, original, real, true; *(ant.)* bogus, fake

ge|nus /dʒinəs/ (**genera** /dʒɛnərə/) **N-COUNT**
SCIENCE A **genus** is a type of animal or plant.
❑ ...*a genus of plants called "Lonas."* [from Latin]

geo|graphi|cal /dʒiəgræfɪkəl/ or
geographic /dʒiəgræfɪk/ **ADJ Geographical**
or **geographic** means concerned with or
relating to geography. ❑ ...*a vast geographical
area.* ● **geo|graphi|cal|ly** /dʒiəgræfɪkli/ **ADV**
❑ *It is geographically a very diverse continent.*
[from French]

Word Link geo ≈ earth : geography, geology,
geothermal

ge|og|ra|phy /dʒiɒgrəfi/
1 **N-NONCOUNT** GEOGRAPHY **Geography** is
the study of the countries of the world and
of things such as the land, oceans, weather,
towns, and population.
2 **N-NONCOUNT** The **geography** of a place is
the way that rivers, mountains, or towns are
arranged within it. ❑ ...*police officers who knew
the local geography.* [from French]

geo|logi|cal time scale (**geological time
scales**) also geological timescale **N-COUNT**
SCIENCE The **geological time scale** is an
arrangement of the main geological and
biological events in the history of the Earth.

Word Link logy, ology ≈ study of : anthropology,
biology, geology

ge|ol|ogy /dʒiɒlədʒi/ **N-NONCOUNT** SCIENCE
Geology is the study of the Earth's structure,
surface, and origins. ❑ *He was professor of
geology at the University of Georgia.*
● **geo|logi|cal** /dʒiəlɒdʒɪkəl/ **ADJ** ❑ ...*a
geological survey.* ● **ge|olo|gist** (**geologists**)
N-COUNT ❑ *Geologists have studied the way that
heat flows from the Earth.* [from Latin]
→ look at Word Web: **biosphere**

geo|met|ric /dʒiəmɛtrɪk/ or geometrical
/dʒiəmɛtrɪkəl/
1 **ADJ Geometric** or **geometrical** patterns or
shapes consist of regular shapes or lines.
❑ ...*geometric designs.*
2 **ADJ** MATH **Geometric** or **geometrical** means
relating to or involving the principles of
geometry. ❑ ...*geometric laws.* [from Latin]

geo|met|ric se|quence (**geometric
sequences**) or geometric progression
N-COUNT MATH A **geometric sequence** is a

series of numbers in which there is the
same ratio between each number and the
next one, for example the series 1, 2, 4, 8, 16.

ge|om|etry /dʒiɒmɪtri/ **N-NONCOUNT** MATH
Geometry is the branch of mathematics
relating to lines, angles, curves, and shapes.
❑ *They're studying basic geometry.* [from Latin]
→ look at Word Web: **mathematics**

geo|sta|tion|ary /dʒioʊsteɪʃənɛri/ or
geosynchronous /dʒioʊsɪŋkrənəs/ **ADJ**
SCIENCE A satellite that is in **geostationary**
orbit is positioned directly above the equator
and moves at the same speed as the Earth's
rotation, so that it appears to be stationary.

geo|ther|mal en|er|gy /dʒioʊθɜrməl
ɛnərdʒi/ **ADJ** MATH **Geothermal** energy is
heat that comes from hot water and steam
beneath the Earth's surface. ❑ *The house is
heated and cooled with geothermal energy.*

germ /dʒɜrm/ (**germs**) **N-COUNT** A **germ** is a
very small living thing that can cause
disease or illness. ❑ *This chemical is used for
killing germs.* [from French]
→ look at Word Webs: **medicine, spice**

ger|mi|nate /dʒɜrmɪneɪt/ (**germinates,
germinating, germinated**) **V-T/V-I** If a seed
germinates, or if it **is germinated**, it starts to
grow. ❑ *Some seeds germinate in just a few days.*

ges|ta|tion pe|ri|od /dʒɛsteɪʃən pɪəriəd/
(**gestation periods**) **N-COUNT** MATH The
gestation period of a particular species of
animal is the length of time that animals
belonging to that species are pregnant for.

ges|ture /dʒɛstʃər/ (**gestures, gesturing,
gestured**)
1 **N-COUNT** A **gesture** is a movement that
you make with a part of your body, especially
your hands, to express emotion or
information. ❑ *Sarah made a gesture with her fist.*
2 **N-COUNT** A **gesture** is something that you
say or do in order to express your attitude.
❑ *In a typically generous gesture, he donated the
prize to the local youth group.*
3 **V-I** If you **gesture**, you use movements of
your hands or head to tell someone
something. ❑ *I gestured toward the house.*
[from Medieval Latin]

ges|ture draw|ing (**gesture drawings**)
N-COUNT ARTS A **gesture drawing** is a quick,
simple drawing that aims to represent the
movements or gestures of a body.

---
get
- ❶ CHANGING, CAUSING, MOVING, OR REACHING
- ❷ OBTAINING, RECEIVING, OR CATCHING
- ❸ PHRASAL VERBS
---

❶ **get** /gɛt/ (**gets, getting, got, gotten** or **got**)

> **LANGUAGE HELP**
> In most of its uses **get** is a fairly informal word.

1 **V-LINK** You use **get** with adjectives to mean "become." ❑ *The boys were getting bored.* ❑ *Don't worry. Things will get better.*

2 **V-T** If you **get** someone **to** do something, you make them do it. ❑ *They got him to give them a lift in his car.*

3 **V-T** If you **get** something done, someone does it for you. ❑ *Why don't you get your car fixed?*

4 **V-I** If you **get** somewhere, you arrive there. ❑ *He got home at 4 a.m.* ❑ *How do I get to your place from here?*

5 **AUX** You sometimes use **get** with another verb when you are talking about something that happens to someone. [INFORMAL] ❑ *He got arrested for possession of drugs.* [from Old English]

> **Usage**   **get**
> In conversation *get* is often used instead of *become*. *We're getting worried about her.*

❷ **get** /gɛt/ (**gets, getting, got, gotten** or **got**)

1 **V-T** If you **get** something, you buy it or obtain it. ❑ *Dad needs to get a birthday present for Mom.* ❑ *I got a job at the store.*

2 **V-T** If you **get** something, you receive it. ❑ *I'm getting a bike for my birthday.* ❑ *He gets a lot of letters from fans.*

3 **V-T** If you **get** someone or something, you go and bring them to a particular place. ❑ *I went downstairs to get the mail.* ❑ *It's time to get the kids from school.*

4 **V-T** If you **get** a joke, you understand it. ❑ *Dad laughed, but I didn't get the joke.*

5 **V-T** If you **get** an illness or a disease, you become sick with it. ❑ *I've got flu.*

6 **V-T** When you **get** a train, a bus, an airplane, or a boat, you leave a place on a particular train, bus, airplane, or boat. ❑ *I got the train home at 10.45 p.m.*

7 **V-T** If you **get** a particular price **for** something that you sell, you obtain that amount of money by selling it. ❑ *He can't get a good price for his crops.*

8 **V-T** If you **get** an idea or a feeling, you begin to have that idea or feeling. ❑ *I get the feeling that you're an honest man.* [from Old English]

9 → see also **got**

❸ **get** /gɛt/ (**gets, getting, got, gotten** or **got**)

▶ **get along** If you **get along with** someone, you have a friendly relationship with them. You can also say that two people **get along.** ❑ *He's always complaining. I can't get along with him.* ❑ *We all get along well.*

▶ **get around** **1** The way that someone **gets around** is the way that they go from one place to another. ❑ *It is difficult for Gail to get around since she broke her leg.*

2 If you **get around**, you visit a lot of different places as part of your life. ❑ *He was a journalist, and he got around.*

3 To **get around** a problem or a difficulty means to overcome it. ❑ *We need to find a way to get around this problem.*

▶ **get around to** When you **get around to** doing something, you finally do it. ❑ *I said I would write you, but I never got around to it.*

▶ **get away** **1** If you **get away**, you leave a place or a person's company. ❑ *She wanted to get away from the city for a while.*

2 If you **get away**, you go away for a period of time in order to have a vacation. ❑ *He is too busy to get away.*

3 When someone or something **gets away**, they escape. ❑ *The thieves got away through an upstairs window.*

▶ **get away with** If you **get away with** something, you are not punished for it. ❑ *These criminals know how to steal and get away with it.*

▶ **get back** If you **get back** somewhere, you return there. ❑ *I'll call you when we get back from Scotland.*

▶ **get by** If you can **get by**, you have just enough of something. ❑ *We have enough money to get by.*

▶ **get down** If you **get down**, you make your body lower until you are sitting, resting on your knees, or lying on the ground. ❑ *Everybody got down on the ground and started looking for my earring.*

▶ **get in** When a train, a bus, or an airplane **gets in**, it arrives. ❑ *Our flight got in two hours late.*

▶ **get into** **1** If you **get into** a car, you climb into it. ❑ *We said goodbye and I got into the cab.*

2 If you **get into** a school, a college, or a

university, you are accepted there as a student. ❑ *I was working hard to get into Yale.*

▶ **get off** If you **get off** a bus, a train, or a bicycle, you leave it. ❑ *He got off the train at Central Station.*

▶ **get on** If you **get on with** something, you continue doing it or start doing it. ❑ *Jane got on with her work.*

▶ **get out** ■ If you **get out**, you leave a place because you want to escape from it. ❑ *They got out of the country just in time.* ■ If you **get out** of a car, you leave it. ❑ *A man got out of the van and ran away.* ■ If news or information **gets out**, it becomes known. ❑ *News got out about their relationship.*

▶ **get over** If you **get over** an unhappy experience or an illness, you become happy or well again. ❑ *It took me a long time to get over her death.*

▶ **get through** If you **get through** a task or an amount of work, you complete it. ❑ *We got through plenty of work today.*

▶ **get together** ■ When people **get together**, they meet in order to talk about something or to spend time together. ❑ *Thanksgiving is a time for families to get together.* ■ If you **get** something **together**, you organize it. ❑ *Paul and I got a band together.*

▶ **get up** ■ When someone who is sitting or lying down **gets up**, they move their body so that they are standing. ❑ *I got up and walked over to the window.* ■ When you **get up**, you get out of bed. ❑ *They have to get up early in the morning.*

ghast|ly /ɡǽstli/ **ADJ** If you describe someone or something as **ghastly**, you mean that you find them very unpleasant or shocking. [INFORMAL] ❑ *It was the worst week of my life. It was ghastly.* [from Old English]

ghet|to /ɡɛtoʊ/ (**ghettos** or **ghettoes**) **N-COUNT** A **ghetto** is a part of a city where many poor people live. ❑ *They came from the inner-city ghettos.* [from Italian]

ghost /ɡoʊst/ (**ghosts**) **N-COUNT** A **ghost** is the spirit of a dead person that someone believes they can see or feel. ❑ *He saw the ghost of a dead man.* [from Old English]

gi|ant /dʒáɪənt/ (**giants**) ■ **ADJ** Something that is **giant** is very large or important. ❑ *America's giant car makers are located in Detroit.* ❑ *They watched the concert on a giant TV screen.*

■ **N-COUNT** A **giant** is an imaginary person who is very big and strong, especially one that appears in children's stories. [from Old French]

<table>
<tr><td>**Thesaurus**</td><td>giant</td><td>Also look up :</td></tr>
<tr><td>ADJ</td><td colspan="2">enormous, gigantic, huge, immense; (ant.) miniature ■</td></tr>
</table>

gi|ant pan|da (**giant pandas**) **N-COUNT** A **giant panda** is the same as a **panda**.

gift /ɡɪft/ (**gifts**) ■ **N-COUNT** A **gift** is something that you give to someone as a present. ❑ *We gave her a birthday gift.* ■ **N-COUNT** If someone has a **gift for** doing something, they have a natural ability to do it. ❑ *He found he had a gift for teaching.* [from Old English]

gig /ɡɪɡ/ (**gigs**) **N-COUNT** A **gig** is a live performance by someone such as a musician or a comedian. [INFORMAL] ❑ *We went to a gig at Madison Square Garden.*

gi|ga|byte /ɡɪ́ɡəbaɪt/ (**gigabytes**) **N-COUNT** TECHNOLOGY In computing, a **gigabyte** is a unit for measuring information. One gigabyte is one thousand and twenty-four megabytes.

gi|gan|tic /dʒaɪɡǽntɪk/ **ADJ** If something is **gigantic**, it is extremely large. ❑ *There are gigantic rocks along the roadside.* [from Greek]

gig|gle /ɡɪ́ɡəl/ (**giggles, giggling, giggled**) ■ **V-T/V-I** If you **giggle**, you laugh in a silly way, like a child. ❑ *The girls began to giggle.* ❑ *"I beg your pardon?" she giggled.* ■ **N-COUNT** **Giggle** is also a noun. ❑ *He gave a little giggle.*
→ look at Word Web: **laugh**

gill /ɡɪl/ (**gills**) **N-COUNT** SCIENCE **Gills** are the organs on the sides of fish and other water creatures through which they breathe. [of Scandinavian origin]
→ look at Picture Dictionary: **fish**
→ look at Word Web: **amphibian**

gin|ger /dʒɪ́ndʒər/ **N-NONCOUNT** **Ginger** is a plant with a sweet, spicy flavor that you use in cooking. [from Old French]

gin|ger|ly /dʒɪ́ndʒərli/ **ADV** If you do something **gingerly**, you do it in a careful manner, usually because you expect it to be dangerous, unpleasant, or painful. [WRITTEN] ❑ *He stepped gingerly into the elevator.* [from Old French]

G

gi|raffe /dʒɪræf/ (**giraffes**) **N-COUNT** A **giraffe** is a large animal with a very long neck, long legs, and dark spots on its body. [from Italian]

girl /gɜrl/ (**girls**) **N-COUNT** A **girl** is a female child. ❑ *They have two girls and a boy.* [from Low German]

Usage	girl

Don't refer to an adult female as a *girl*. This may cause offense. Use *woman*. *I'm studying with Diana. She's a woman from my English class.*

girl|friend /gɜrlfrɛnd/ (**girlfriends**)
1 **N-COUNT** A **girlfriend** is a girl or a woman who someone is having a romantic relationship with. ❑ *Does he have a girlfriend?*
2 **N-COUNT** A **girlfriend** is a female friend. ❑ *I had lunch with my girlfriends.*

give
❶ TRANSFERRING
❷ USED WITH NOUNS DESCRIBING ACTIONS
❸ OTHER USES AND PHRASAL VERBS

❶ **give** /gɪv/ (**gives, giving, gave, given**)
1 **V-T/V-I** If you **give** someone something, you let them have it. ❑ *My parents gave me a watch for my birthday.* ❑ *They gave him the job.* ❑ *I gave him my phone number.* ❑ *How much money have you been given?*
2 **V-T** If you **give** someone an object, you pass it to them, so that they can take it. ❑ *Give me that pencil.* ❑ *Please give me your bag to carry.*
3 **V-T** You use **give** with some nouns when you are talking about how information or opinions are communicated. ❑ *He gave no details.* ❑ *Would you please give me your name?* [from Old English]
→ look at Word Web: **donor**

❷ **give** /gɪv/ (**gives, giving, gave, given**)
1 **V-T** You can use **give** with nouns when you are talking about physical actions. For example, "She gave a smile" means "She smiled." ❑ *She gave me a big kiss.* ❑ *He gave her a friendly smile.*
2 **V-T** If you **give** a party, you organize it. ❑ *I gave a dinner party for a few friends.*
3 **V-T** If you **give** a performance or a speech, you perform or speak in public. ❑ *She gives a wonderful performance in her new movie.*
4 **V-T** If you **give** something thought or attention, you think about it or deal with it.

❑ *I've given the matter some thought.* [from Old English]

❸ **give** /gɪv/ (**gives, giving, gave, given**) **V-I** If something **gives**, it can no longer support someone or something. ❑ *My knees gave under me.* [from Old English]
▶ **give away** If you **give away** something that you own, you give it to someone. ❑ *She likes to give away plants from her garden.*
▶ **give back** If you **give** something **back**, you return it to the person who gave it to you. ❑ *I gave the book back to him.* ❑ *Give me back my camera.*
▶ **give in** **1** If you **give in**, you admit that you cannot do something. ❑ *It was tough, but we were determined not to give in.*
2 If you **give in**, you agree to do something although you do not really want to do it. ❑ *After saying "no" a hundred times, I finally gave in and said "yes."*
▶ **give out** If you **give out** a number of things, you give one to each person in a group of people. ❑ *Our teacher gave out papers, pencils, and calculators for the math test.*
▶ **give up** **1** If you **give up** something, you stop doing it or having it. ❑ *We gave up hope of finding the fishermen.*
2 If you **give up**, you decide that you cannot do something and you stop trying to do it. ❑ *I give up. I'll never understand this.*

giv|en /gɪvᵊn/
1 **Given** is the past participle of **give**.
2 **ADJ** If you talk about any **given** time, you mean any particular time. ❑ *There are usually about 250 students in the building at any given time.*
3 **PHRASE** **Given the opportunity** or **given the chance** means "if I had the opportunity." ❑ *Given the opportunity, I'd like to travel more.* [from Old English]

gla|cial /gleɪʃᵊl/ **ADJ** GEOGRAPHY **Glacial** means relating to or produced by glaciers or ice. ❑ *...a glacial landscape.* [from French]
→ look at Word Web: **lake**

gla|cial drift **N-NONCOUNT** GEOGRAPHY **Glacial drift** is rocks that have been carried and left by a glacier.

glaci|er /gleɪʃər/ (**glaciers**) **N-COUNT** GEOGRAPHY A **glacier** is a very large amount of ice that moves very slowly, usually down a mountain. [from French Savoy]
→ look at Picture Dictionary: **mountain**
→ look at Word Webs: **glacier, climate**

g

G

Two-thirds of all **fresh water** on Earth is frozen. The largest **glaciers** in the world are the **polar ice caps** of Antarctica and Greenland. They cover more than six million square miles. Their average depth is almost one mile. If all the glaciers **melted**, the average **sea level** would rise by more than 250 feet. Glaciologists have noted that the Antarctic is about 1° C* warmer than it was 50 years ago. Some of them are worried. Continued warming might cause floating **ice** shelves there to begin to fall apart. This, in turn, could cause disastrous coastal flooding around the world.

1° Celsius = 1.8° Fahrenheit

glad /glæd/
■ **ADJ** If you are **glad** about something, you are happy and pleased about it. ❑ *They seemed glad to see me.* ❑ *I'm glad you like the present.*
● **glad|ly ADV** ❑ *Malcolm gladly accepted the invitation.*
■ **ADJ** If you say that you will be **glad to** do something, you mean that you are willing and happy to do it for someone. ❑ *I'll be glad to show you everything.* [from Old English]

glam|or /glæmər/ **N-NONCOUNT** → look up **glamour**

glam|or|ous /glæmərəs/ **ADJ** If someone or something is **glamorous**, they are very attractive, exciting, or interesting. ❑ *She looked glamorous in a white dress.*

glam|our /glæmər/ also **glamor**
N-NONCOUNT Glamour is the quality of being more attractive, exciting, or interesting than ordinary people or things. ❑ *...the glamour of show biz.*

glance /glæns/ (**glances, glancing, glanced**)
■ **V-I** If you **glance at** something or

someone, you look at them very quickly. ❑ *He glanced at his watch.*
■ **N-COUNT** A **glance** is a quick look at someone or something. ❑ *Trevor and I exchanged a glance.* [from Old French]

gland /glænd/ (**glands**) **N-COUNT SCIENCE** A **gland** is an organ in the body that produces chemical substances for the body to use or get rid of. ❑ *...sweat glands.* [from Latin]

glare /glɛər/ (**glares, glaring, glared**)
■ **V-I** If you **glare at** someone, you look at them with an angry expression on your face. ❑ *The old woman glared at him.*
■ **N-COUNT** A **glare** is an angry look. ❑ *She gave him a furious glare.*
■ **V-I** If the sun or a light **glares**, it shines with a very bright light. ❑ *The sun glared down on us.*
■ **N-NONCOUNT Glare** is very bright light that is difficult to look at. ❑ *...the glare from a car's lights.* [from Middle Low German]

glass /glɑs, glæs/ (**glasses**)
■ **N-NONCOUNT Glass** is a hard, transparent substance that is used for making things

The basic ingredients for **glass** are **silica** (found in **sand**) and **ash** (left over from burning wood). The earliest glass objects are glass **beads** made in Egypt around 3500 BC. By 14 AD, the Syrians had learned how to **blow** glass to form hollow containers. These included primitive **bottles** and **vases**. By 100 AD, the Romans were making clear glass for **windows**. Modern factories now produce **safety glass** which doesn't **shatter** when it breaks. It includes a layer of cellulose between two **sheets** of glass.

such as windows and bottles. ❑ *He served the salad in a glass bowl.*

2 **N-COUNT** A **glass** is a container made from glass, which you can drink from. ❑ *He picked up his glass and drank.* ❑ *I drink a glass of milk every day.*

3 **N-NONCOUNT** Glass is objects made of glass. ❑ *They sell beautiful silver and glass.*

4 **N-PLURAL** Glasses are two glass or plastic lenses in a frame, that some people wear in front of their eyes to help them to see better. ❑ *He took off his glasses.* [from Old English]
→ look at Word Webs: **glass, aquarium, light bulb**

glass slide (glass slides) → look up **slide** **5**

glaze /gleɪz/ (glazes) **N-COUNT** A **glaze** is a thin layer of a hard shiny substance that is put on a piece of pottery. ❑ *...tiles with decorative glazes.*
→ look at Word Web: **pottery**

gleam /glim/ (gleams, gleaming, gleamed)
1 **V-I** If an object or a surface **gleams**, it shines with a soft light. ❑ *His black hair gleamed in the sun.*
2 **N-COUNT** A **gleam of** something is a faint sign of it. ❑ *There was a gleam of hope for peace.* [from Old English]

glide /glaɪd/ (glides, gliding, glided)
1 **V-I** If you **glide** somewhere, you move quietly and easily. ❑ *Waiters glide between the tables carrying trays.*
2 **V-I** When birds or airplanes **glide**, they move along by floating in the air. ❑ *Geese glide over the lake.* [from Old English]

glim|mer /glɪmər/ (glimmers, glimmering, glimmered)
1 **V-I** If something **glimmers**, it shines with a weak light. ❑ *The moon glimmered through the mist.*
2 **N-COUNT** A **glimmer** is a weak light. ❑ *In the east there was a glimmer of light.*
3 **N-COUNT** A **glimmer of** something is a small sign of it. ❑ *The new drug offers a glimmer of hope for patients.* [from Middle High German]

glimpse /glɪmps/ (glimpses, glimpsing, glimpsed)
1 **N-COUNT** If you get a **glimpse of** someone or something, you see or experience it very briefly. ❑ *Fans waited outside the hotel to catch a glimpse of the star.*
2 **V-T** If you **glimpse** someone or

something, you see them for a very short amount of time. ❑ *She glimpsed a poster through the car window.* [from Old English]

glis|ten /glɪsᵊn/ (glistens, glistening, glistened) **V-I** If something **glistens**, it shines, usually because it is wet. ❑ *The ocean glistened in the sunlight.* ❑ *David's face was glistening with sweat.* [from Old English]

glit|ter /glɪtər/ (glitters, glittering, glittered) **V-I** If something **glitters**, small flashes of light shine from different parts of it. ❑ *The ring glittered on Andrea's finger.* [from Old Norse]

glob|al /gloʊbᵊl/ **ADJ** **Global** means relating to the whole world. ❑ *American businesses compete in a global economy.* ● **glob|al|ly** **ADV** ❑ *The company employs 5,800 people globally, including 2,000 in Colorado.* [from Old French]

glob|al econo|my **N-SING** SOCIAL STUDIES The **global economy** is the way in which the nations of the world work together through international trade and financial matters. ❑ *We will soon see the effect of rising oil prices on the global economy.*

glo|bal|iza|tion /gloʊʌbᵊlaɪzeɪʃᵊn/ **N-NONCOUNT** SOCIAL STUDIES **Globalization** is the idea that the world is developing a single economy as a result of improved technology and communications. ❑ *The report focuses on the globalization of business activities around the world.* [from Old French]

glob|al warm|ing **N-NONCOUNT** SCIENCE **Global warming** is the gradual rise in the Earth's temperature caused by high levels of certain gases. ❑ *If we use less energy we can help to reduce global warming.*
→ look at Word Webs: **greenhouse effect, ozone**

globe /gloʊb/ (globes)
1 **N-COUNT** GEOGRAPHY A **globe** is an object shaped like a ball with a map of the world on it. ❑ *A large globe stood on his desk.*
2 **N-SING** You can call the world **the globe** when you want to say how big it is or that something happens in many different parts of it. ❑ *Thousands of people across the globe took part in the survey.* [from Old French]

globu|lar clus|ter /glɒbyʊlər klʌstər/ (globular clusters) **N-COUNT** SCIENCE A **globular cluster** is a dense group of older stars that is roughly the shape of a sphere.

g

gloom /glu̱m/

1 **N-SING** **The gloom** is a state of near darkness. ❑ ...the gloom of a foggy November morning.

2 **N-NONCOUNT** Gloom is a feeling of sadness and lack of hope. ❑ There is increasing gloom over the economy. [from Norwegian]

gloomy /glu̱mi/ (**gloomier, gloomiest**)

1 **ADJ** If a place is **gloomy**, it is almost dark so that you cannot see very well. ❑ Inside it's gloomy after all that sunshine.

2 **ADJ** If people are **gloomy**, they are unhappy and they do not think that the situation will get better. ❑ He is gloomy about the future of the country.

3 **ADJ** If a situation is **gloomy**, it does not give you much hope of success or happiness. ❑ The economic prospects for next year are gloomy. [from Norwegian]

→ look at Word Web: **weather**

glo|ri|ous /glɔ̱riəs/

1 **ADJ** Something that is **glorious** is very beautiful. ❑ We saw a glorious rainbow.

● **glo|ri|ous|ly** **ADV** ❑ The trees are gloriously colored in the fall.

2 **ADJ** If something is **glorious**, it makes you feel very happy. ❑ He has glorious memories of his days as a champion. ● **glo|ri|ous|ly** **ADV** ❑ It was a gloriously sunny morning.

3 **ADJ** A **glorious** experience or occasion involves great fame or success. ❑ He had a glorious career as a broadcaster and writer.

● **glo|ri|ous|ly** **ADV** ❑ The mission was gloriously successful. [from Old French]

glo|ry /glɔ̱ri/ **N-NONCOUNT** Glory is the fame and admiration from other people that you gain by doing something great. ❑ He had his moment of glory when he won the cycling race. [from Old French]

Word Partnership	Use glory with :
V	**bask in the** glory
N	**blaze of** glory, glory **days, hope and glory**

glos|sa|ry /glɔ̱səri/ (**glossaries**) **N-COUNT** LANGUAGE ARTS A **glossary** is a list of difficult words that are used in a book or special subject, with explanations of their meanings. [from Late Latin]

glossy /glɔ̱si/ (**glossier, glossiest**) **ADJ** Glossy means smooth and shiny. ❑ She had glossy black hair. [of Scandinavian origin]

glove /glʌ̱v/ (**gloves**) **N-COUNT** Gloves are pieces of clothing that you wear on your hands, with a separate part for each finger. ❑ He put his gloves in his pocket. [from Old English]

→ look at Picture Dictionaries: **baseball**

glow /glo̱ʊ/ (**glows, glowing, glowed**)

1 **N-COUNT** A **glow** is a soft, steady light, for example the light from a fire when there are no flames. ❑ She saw the red glow of a fire.

2 **V-I** If something **glows**, it makes a soft, steady light. ❑ The lantern glowed softly in the darkness.

3 **N-SING** A **glow** is a pink color on a person's face, usually because they are healthy or have been exercising. ❑ The moisturizer gave my face a healthy glow.

4 **V-I** If someone's skin **glows**, it looks pink because they are healthy or have been exercising. ❑ Her skin glowed with health.

5 **V-I** If someone **glows with** an emotion such as pride or pleasure, the expression on their face shows how they feel. ❑ Her mother glowed with pride. [from Old English] [from Old English]

→ look at Word Webs: **fire, light bulb**

Thesaurus	glow	Also look up :
N	beam, glimmer, light **1**
	blush, flush, radiance **3**
V	gleam, radiate, shine **2** **5**

glue /glu̱/ (**glues, glueing** or **gluing, glued**)

1 **N-COUNT/N-NONCOUNT** Glue is a sticky substance used for joining things together. ❑ You will need scissors and a tube of glue.

2 **V-T** If you **glue** one object to another, you stick them together with glue. ❑ She glued the pieces of newspaper together. [from Old French]

GM /dʒi̱ ɛ̱m/ **ADJ** GM crops have had one or more genes changed to make them stronger or to help them grow. **GM** is short for **genetically modified**. ❑ They are growing large-scale GM food crops, like soybeans.

GMT /dʒi̱ ɛm ti̱/ **GMT** is the standard time in Great Britain which is used to calculate the time in the rest of the world. **GMT** is short for **Greenwich Mean Time**. ❑ New Mexico is seven hours behind GMT.

go
① MOVING OR LEAVING
② LINK VERB USE
③ OTHER VERB USES AND PHRASES
④ PHRASAL VERBS

① **go** /goʊ/ (**goes, going, went, gone**)

> **LANGUAGE HELP**
> In most cases the past participle of **go** is **gone**, but occasionally you use **been**. See **been**.

1 **v-t/v-i** When you **go** somewhere, you move or travel there. ❑ *We went to Rome on vacation.* ❑ *I went home for the weekend.* ❑ *It took an hour to go three miles.*

2 **v-i** When you **go**, you leave the place where you are. ❑ *It's time for me to go.*

3 **v-t/v-i** You use **go** to say that you leave a place in order to do something. ❑ *We went early this morning.* ❑ *They've gone shopping.* ❑ *He went for a walk.* ❑ *I'll go and make breakfast.*

4 **v-i** If you **go to** school, work, or church, you visit it regularly. ❑ *Does your daughter go to school yet?*

5 **v-i** If you say that something **goes to** someone, you mean that it is given to them. ❑ *A lot of credit should go to his father.*

6 **v-i** When you say where a road or a path **goes**, you are saying where it leads to. ❑ *This road goes from Blairstown to Millbrook Village.*

7 **v-i** If something **goes** in a particular place, that is the place where you normally keep it. ❑ *The shoes go on the shoe shelf.*

8 **v-i** If something such as a light bulb or a part of an engine **goes**, it is no longer working and needs to be replaced. ❑ *A light bulb has gone in the bathroom.* [from Old English]

> **Usage** **go**
> *Go* is often used to mean *visit*. *Sarah has gone to London twice this year, and Tony went three times last year. It's their favorite city.*

② **go** /goʊ/ (**goes, going, went, gone**) **v-link** **Go** means become. ❑ *I'm going crazy.* ❑ *The meat has gone bad.* [from Old English]

③ **go** /goʊ/ (**goes, going, went, gone**)

1 **v-i** You use **go** to talk about the way that something happens. ❑ *How's your job going?* ❑ *Everything is going wrong.*

2 **v-i** If a machine **is going**, it is working. ❑ *Can you get my car going again?*

3 **v-t/v-i** If something **goes with** something else, or if two things **go together**, they look or taste good together. ❑ *Those pants would go with my blue shirt.* ❑ *Cheese and tomato go together well.*

4 → see also **going, gone**

5 **PHRASE** If someone **is making a go of** something, they are trying to have some success with it. ❑ *She's determined to make a go of her music career.*

6 **PHRASE** If someone is always **on the go**, they are always busy and active. [INFORMAL] ❑ *In my job I am on the go all the time.*

7 **PHRASE** In a restaurant, you ask for food **to go** when you want to take it with you and eat it somewhere else. ❑ *She ordered coffee to go.*

8 **PHRASE** If there is a certain amount of time **to go**, there is that amount of time left before something happens or ends. ❑ *There is a week to go until the party.* [from Old English]

④ **go** /goʊ/ (**goes, going, went, gone**)

▸ **go about** When you **are going about** your normal activities, you are doing them. ❑ *People were going about their business when they heard an explosion.*

▸ **go ahead** If an event **goes ahead**, it takes place. ❑ *The wedding went ahead as planned, about 14 hours after the accident.*

▸ **go around** If there is enough of something **to go around**, there is enough of it to be shared among a group of people ❑ *In the future we may not have enough water to go around.*

▸ **go away** **1** If you **go away**, you leave a place or a person. ❑ *Just go away and leave me alone!*

2 If you **go away**, you leave a place and spend time somewhere else, especially as a vacation. ❑ *Why don't we go away this weekend?*

▸ **go back** If you **go back** somewhere, you return there. ❑ *He'll be going back to college soon.*

▸ **go by** When time **goes by**, it passes. ❑ *The week went by so quickly.*

▸ **go down** **1** If an amount **goes down**, it becomes less. ❑ *House prices went down last month.*

2 When the sun **goes down**, it goes below the line between the land and the sky. ❑ *It gets cold after the sun goes down.*

3 If a ship **goes down**, it sinks. If a plane **goes down**, it crashes. ❑ *The aircraft went down during a training exercise.*

▸ **go off** **1** If a bomb **goes off**, it explodes.

g

❏ *A bomb went off, destroying the vehicle.*

2 If an alarm bell **goes off**, it makes a sudden loud noise. ❏ *The fire alarm went off and everybody ran out.*

3 If food **goes off**, it is no longer good to eat or drink. ❏ *This fish has gone off.*

▶ **go on 1** If you **go on** doing something, you continue to do it. ❏ *She just went on laughing.*

2 If something **is going on**, it is happening. ❏ *While this conversation was going on, I just listened.*

▶ **go out 1** If you **go out**, you leave your home to do something enjoyable. ❏ *I'm going out tonight.*

2 If you **go out with** someone, you have a romantic relationship with them. ❏ *I've been going out with my girlfriend for three months.*

3 If a light **goes out**, it stops shining. ❏ *The bedroom light went out after a moment.*

4 If a fire **goes out**, it stops burning. ❏ *The fire went out and the room became cold.*

▶ **go over** If you **go over** something, you look at it or think about it very carefully. ❏ *We went over the details again.*

▶ **go through** If you **go through** a difficult experience, you experience it. ❏ *He went through a difficult time when his wife died.*

▶ **go up** If an amount **goes up**, it becomes greater. ❏ *The cost of calls went up to $1.95 a minute.*

go-ahead

1 **N-SING** If you give someone or something **the go-ahead**, you give them permission to start doing something. ❏ *He got the go-ahead to start the project.*

2 **ADJ** A **go-ahead** person or organization tries hard to succeed, often by using new methods.

goal /goʊl/ (goals)

1 **N-COUNT** SPORTS In games such as soccer, the **goal** is the place where the players try to get the ball in order to win a point for their team. ❏ *The ball went straight into the goal.*

2 **N-COUNT** SPORTS In games such as soccer, a **goal** is a point that is scored when the ball goes into the goal. ❏ *He scored five goals in one playoff game.*

3 **N-COUNT** Your **goal** is the aim or purpose that you have when you do something. ❏ *Our goal is to make patients comfortable.* [from Middle English]

→ look at Picture Dictionary: **soccer**

Word Partnership	Use **goal** with :	
V	**shoot at a** goal **1**	
	score a goal **2**	
	accomplish a goal, **share a** goal **3**	
ADJ	**winning** goal **2**	
	main goal **3**	

goal|keeper /goʊlkipər/ (**goalkeepers**) **N-COUNT** SPORTS A **goalkeeper** is the player on a sports team whose job is to guard the goal.

goal|less /goʊllɪs/ **ADJ** SPORTS In soccer, a **goalless** game ends with no goals scored. ❏ *Goalkeeper Antonin Kinsky played his first goalless game this season.*

goal|post /goʊlpoʊst/ (**goalposts**) **N-COUNT** SPORTS A **goalpost** is one of the two wooden posts that form the goal in games such as soccer.

goat /goʊt/ (**goats**) **N-COUNT** A **goat** is an animal that is about the size of a sheep. Goats have horns, and hairs on their chin that look like a beard. [from Old English]

gob|ble /gɒbəl/ (**gobbles, gobbling, gobbled**) **V-T** If you **gobble** food, or **gobble** it **up**, you eat it very quickly. ❏ *Pete hungrily gobbled up the rest of the sandwiches.*

god /gɒd/ (**gods**)

1 **N-PROPER** In many religions, **God** is the name given to the spirit that people believe created the world. ❏ *He believes in God.*

2 **INTERJ** People sometimes use **God** in exclamations. This use could cause offense. ❏ *Oh my God, look what they've done!*

3 **N-COUNT** In many religions, **gods** are spirits that people believe have power over a particular part of the world or nature. ❏ *Poseidon was the Greek god of the sea.* [from Old English]

god|dess /gɒdɪs/ (**goddesses**) **N-COUNT** In many religions, a **goddess** is a female spirit that people believe to have power over a particular part of the world or nature. ❏ *There was a statue of a goddess in the temple.* [from Old English]

gog|gles /gɒgəlz/ **N-PLURAL** **Goggles** are large glasses that fit closely to your face around your eyes to protect them. ❏ *...a pair of swimming goggles.*

going /goʊɪŋ/

1 **PHRASE** If something **is going to** happen,

it will happen in the future. ❑ *I think it's going to be successful.* ❑ *You're going to enjoy this.*

2 **PHRASE** You say that you **are going to** do something when you intend to do it. ❑ *I'm going to go to bed.* ❑ *He announced that he's going to resign.*

3 **ADJ** The **going** rate for something is the usual amount of money that you expect to pay or receive for it. ❑ *What is the going rate for a room in a five-star hotel?*

4 → see also **go**

5 **PHRASE** When you **get going**, you start doing something or start a journey. ❑ *The plane leaves in two hours so I've got to get going.*

6 **PHRASE** If you **keep going**, you continue doing things or doing a particular thing. ❑ *She kept going even when she was sick.* [from Old English]

> **Usage**   **going to**
>
> *Going to* and the present continuous are both used to talk about the future. *Going to* is used to describe things that you intend to do: *I'm going to call my sister tonight.* The present continuous is used to talk about things that are already planned or decided: *We are meeting for lunch on Saturday at noon.*

gold /goʊld/

1 **N-NONCOUNT** Gold is a valuable, yellow-colored metal that is used for making jewelry, ornaments, and coins. ❑ *...a ring made of gold.* ❑ *The price of gold was going up.*

2 **N-NONCOUNT** Gold is jewelry and other things that are made of gold. ❑ *We handed over all our gold and money.*

3 **ADJ** Something that is **gold** is bright-yellow in color, and is often shiny. ❑ *He wore a black and gold shirt.*

4 **N-NONCOUNT** Gold is also a noun.

❑ *She decorated the room in shades of blue and gold.* [from Old English]

→ look at Word Webs: **metal, mineral, money**

gold|en /goʊldⁿn/

1 **ADJ** Something that is **golden** has a bright yellow color. ❑ *She combed her golden hair.*

2 **ADJ** Golden things are made of gold. ❑ *He wore a golden chain.*

3 **ADJ** A **golden** opportunity is likely to be very successful and rewarding. ❑ *This is a golden opportunity for peace.*

4 **ADJ** A **golden** age or era is a period in the past when something was very successful. ❑ *...the golden age of Hollywood.* [from Old English]

gold|fish /goʊldfɪʃ/ (**goldfish**) **N-COUNT** Goldfish are small orange fish that people often keep as pets.

→ look at Word Web: **aquarium**

gold med|al (**gold medals**) **N-COUNT** A **gold medal** is an award made of gold metal that you get as first prize in a competition. ❑ *Her dream is to win a gold medal at the Winter Olympics.*

golf /gɒlf/ **N-NONCOUNT** SPORTS Golf is a game in which you use golf clubs to hit a small, hard ball into holes. ❑ *Do you play golf?* ● **golf|er** (**golfers**) **N-COUNT** ❑ *He is one of the world's best golfers.* ● **golf|ing** **N-NONCOUNT** ❑ *You can play tennis or go golfing.* [from Middle Dutch]

→ look at Picture Dictionary: **golf**

golf club (**golf clubs**) **N-COUNT** SPORTS A **golf club** is a long, thin, metal stick with a piece of wood or metal at one end that you use to hit the ball when you play golf.

Picture Dictionary   **golf**

clubhouse
cart path
sand trap
green
golfer
sand trap
golf cart
golf club
golf ball
hole
green

golf course (**golf courses**) N-COUNT SPORTS
A **golf course** is a large area of grass where people play golf.

Golgi com|plex /gɔldʒi kɒmplɛks, goʊl-/ (**Golgi complexes**) or **Golgi body, Golgi apparatus** N-COUNT SCIENCE The **Golgi complex** is a structure inside the cells of animals and plants that controls the production and secretion of substances such as proteins. [from Italian]

gone /gɔn/
1 **Gone** is the past participle of **go**.
2 ADJ When someone is **gone**, they have left the place where you are and are no longer there. ❑ *Things were hard for her while he was gone.* ❑ *He's already been gone four hours!* [from Old English]

gong /gɔŋ/ (**gongs**) N-COUNT MUSIC A **gong** is a large, flat, circular piece of metal that you hit with a hammer to make a sound like a loud bell. Gongs are sometimes used as musical instruments, or to give a signal that it is time to do something. [from Malay]
→ look at Picture Dictionary: **percussion**

---
good
❶ DESCRIBING QUALITY, EXPRESSING APPROVAL
❷ SUITABLE, USEFUL
❸ OTHER USES
---

❶ **good** /goʊd/ (**better, best**)
1 ADJ **Good** means pleasant or enjoyable. ❑ *We had a really good time.* ❑ *These people want a better life for their children.*
2 ADJ **Good** means of a high quality or level. ❑ *Good food is important for your health.* ❑ *Our customers want the best possible quality at a low price.*
3 ADJ If you are **good at** something, you are skillful at doing it. ❑ *I'm not very good at singing.*
4 ADJ A child who is **good** behaves well. ❑ *The children were very good.* [from Old English]

Thesaurus	**good** Also look up :
ADJ	agreeable, enjoyable, nice, pleasant; *(ant.)* unpleasant **1**
	able, capable, skilled; *(ant.)* unqualified, unskilled **7**

❷ **good** /goʊd/ (**better, best**)
1 ADJ A **good** place or time for an activity is a suitable place or time for it. ❑ *This room is*

a good place for relaxing and reading.
2 ADJ A **good** idea, reason, or decision is a sensible one. ❑ *It's a good idea to keep your desk neat.* ❑ *There was a good reason for his strange behavior.*
3 PHRASE If something is **no good**, it will not bring any success. ❑ *I asked her to repeat the question, but it was no good—I couldn't understand her.* ❑ *It's no good worrying about it now.* [from Old English]

❸ **good** /goʊd/ (**better, best**)
1 ADJ Someone who is in a **good** mood is feeling cheerful. ❑ *She woke up in a good mood.*
2 ADJ A **good** twenty minutes or a **good** three miles, for example, means more than twenty minutes, or more than three miles. ❑ *We waited a good fifteen minutes.*
3 ADJ Someone who is **good** is kind and thoughtful. ❑ *You are good to me.*
4 N-NONCOUNT **Good** is what people consider to be morally right. ❑ *They should know the difference between good and bad, right and wrong.*
5 → see also **better, best**
6 PHRASE **As good as** means "almost." ❑ *His career is as good as finished.*
7 PHRASE If something disappears **for good**, it never comes back. ❑ *These forests may be gone for good.* [from Old English]

good after|noon INTERJ You say **Good afternoon** when you see or speak to someone in the afternoon. [FORMAL]

good|bye /goʊdbaɪ/ also **good-bye** INTERJ You say **Goodbye** to someone when you or they are leaving a place, or at the end of a telephone conversation.

good eve|ning INTERJ You say **Good evening** the first time you see or speak to someone in the evening. [FORMAL]

good guy (**good guys**) N-COUNT You can call the good characters in a movie or a story the **good guys**. You can also talk about the **good guys** in a situation in real life. [INFORMAL] ❑ *We're the good guys in this situation.*

good-look|ing (**better-looking, best-looking**) ADJ Someone who is **good-looking** has an attractive face. ❑ *Katy noticed him because he was good-looking.*

good morn|ing INTERJ You say **Good morning** the first time you see or speak to someone in the morning. [FORMAL]

good|ness /gʊdnɪs/

1 **N-NONCOUNT** **Goodness** is the quality of being kind, helpful, and honest. ❏ *He believes in human goodness.*

2 **INTERJ** People sometimes say **Goodness** or **My goodness** to express surprise. ❏ *Goodness, I wonder how that happened?* [from Old English]

good night **INTERJ** You say **Good night** to someone late in the evening before you go home or go to bed.

goods /gʊdz/ **N-PLURAL** **Goods** are things that you can buy or sell. ❏ *Companies sell goods or services.* [from Old English]

Word Partnership	Use **goods** with :
V	**buy** goods, **sell** goods, **transport** goods
N	**consumer** goods, **delivery of** goods, **exchange of** goods, **variety of** goods
ADJ	**sporting** goods, **stolen** goods

good|will /gʊdwɪl/ **N-NONCOUNT** **Goodwill** is a friendly or helpful attitude toward other people, countries, or organizations. ❏ *I invited them to dinner to show my goodwill.*

goof /guf/ (**goofs, goofing, goofed**) **N-COUNT** A **goof** is a small mistake. [INFORMAL] ❏ *There were a few minor technical goofs.* [from Old French]
▶ **goof off** If someone **goofs off**, they waste time and do nothing. [INFORMAL] ❏ *I goofed off all day.*

goose /gus/ (**geese**) **N-COUNT** A **goose** is a large bird that has a long neck. ❏ *The Canada Goose is a beautiful bird.* [from Old English]

gore /gɔr/ (**gores, goring, gored**)

1 **V-T** If someone **is gored** by an animal, they are badly wounded by its horns or tusks. ❏ *The farmer was gored by a bull.*

2 **N-NONCOUNT** **Gore** is blood from a wound that has become thick. ❏ *There was blood and gore on the sidewalk.* [from Old English]

gor|geous /gɔrdʒəs/ **ADJ** Someone or something that is **gorgeous** is very pleasant or attractive. [INFORMAL] ❏ *It's a gorgeous day.* ❏ *You look gorgeous.* [from Old French]

go|ril|la /gərɪlə/ (**gorillas**) **N-COUNT** A **gorilla** is a very large animal with long arms, black fur, and a black face. [from New Latin]
→ look at Word Web: **primate**

gos|pel /gɒspəl/ **N-NONCOUNT** MUSIC **Gospel** or **gospel music** is a style of religious music. ❏ *I used to sing gospel.* [from Old English]

gos|sip /gɒsɪp/ (**gossips, gossiping, gossiped**)

1 **N-NONCOUNT/N-SING** **Gossip** is informal conversation about other people. ❏ *There has been gossip about the reasons for his absence.*

2 **V-T/V-I** If you **gossip**, you talk in an informal way, especially about other people or local events. ❏ *They sat at the kitchen table gossiping.* [from Old English]

got /gɒt/

1 **Got** is the past tense and sometimes the past participle of **get**.

2 **PHRASE** You use **have got** to say that you have a particular thing. [SPOKEN] ❏ *I've got a coat just like this.*

3 **PHRASE** You use **have got to** when you are saying that something must happen. [SPOKEN] ❏ *I'm not happy with the situation, but I've got to accept it.*

4 **PHRASE** If you say that something **has got to** be true, you think it must be true. [SPOKEN] ❏ *"You've got to be joking!" he replied.* [from Old English]

got|ten /gɒtən/ **Gotten** is a past participle of **get**.

gov|ern /gʌvərn/ (**governs, governing, governed**) **V-T** SOCIAL STUDIES To **govern** a country means to officially control and organize it. ❏ *The people choose who they want to govern their country.* [from Old French]

Thesaurus	**govern** Also look up :
V	administer, command, control, direct, guide, head up; *(ant.)* lead, manage, reign

gov|ern|ment /gʌvərnmənt/ (**governments**)

1 **N-COUNT** SOCIAL STUDIES The **government** is the group of people who control and organize a country, a state, or a city. ❏ *The government has decided to make changes.*
● **gov|ern|men|tal** /gʌvərnmɛntəl/ **ADJ** ❏ *She works for a governmental agency.*

2 **N-COUNT** **Government** also refers to the activities and principles involved in controlling and organizing a country. ❏ *...our system of government.* [from Old French]
→ look at Word Web: **country**

gov|er|nor /gʌvərnər/ (**governors**)

1 **N-COUNT** SOCIAL STUDIES A **governor** is a person who is in charge of part of a country. ❏ *He was governor of Iowa.*

2 **N-COUNT** A **governor** is a member of a

g

committee that controls an organization such as a university or a hospital. ❑ ...*the board of governors at City University, Bellevue.* [from Old French]

gown /ga͡ʊn/ (**gowns**)

◻ **N-COUNT** A **gown** is a long dress that women wear on formal occasions. ❑ *She was wearing a ball gown.*

◻ **N-COUNT** A **gown** is a loose black piece of clothing that students wear at their graduation ceremony (= the ceremony where they receive their degree). ❑ *He was wearing a university graduation gown.* [from Old French]

GP /dʒi pi/ (**GPs**) also **G.P.** **N-COUNT** A **GP** is a doctor who does not specialize in any particular area of medicine, but who has a medical practice in which he or she treats all types of illness. **GP** is short for "general practitioner." ❑ *Her husband called their local GP.*

GPA /dʒi pi eɪ/ (**GPAs**) **N-COUNT** **GPA** is short for **grade point average**. ❑ *You need a good GPA to get into graduate school.*

grab /græb/ (**grabs, grabbing, grabbed**) **V-T** If you **grab** something, you take something suddenly and roughly. ❑ *I grabbed her hand.* [from Middle Low German]

Thesaurus	grab	Also look up :
v	capture, catch, seize; (*ant.*) release	

Word Link	*grac* ≈ *pleasing* : dis*grac*e, *grac*e, *grac*eful

grace /greɪs/ (**graces, gracing, graced**)

◻ **N-NONCOUNT** If someone moves with **grace**, they move in a smooth, controlled, and attractive way. ❑ *He moved with the grace of a dancer.*

◻ **V-T** If you say that something **graces** a place or a person, you mean that it makes them more attractive. [FORMAL] ❑ *Beautiful antique furniture graces their home.*

◻ **N-COUNT/N-NONCOUNT** When someone says **grace** before or after a meal, they say a prayer in which they thank God for the food and ask Him to bless it. ❑ *Will you say grace?* [from Old French]

graceful /greɪsfəl/ **ADJ** Someone or something that is **graceful** moves in a smooth and attractive way. ❑ *His movements were smooth and graceful.* ● **gracefully** **ADV** ❑ *She stepped gracefully onto the stage.* [from Old French]

grad /græd/ (**grads**) **N-COUNT** A **grad** is a **graduate**. [INFORMAL]

grade /greɪd/ (**grades, grading, graded**)

◻ **N-COUNT** A **grade** is a group of classes in a school where all the children are a similar age. ❑ *Mr. White teaches first grade.*

◻ **N-COUNT** Your **grade** is the mark that a teacher gives you to show how good your work is. ❑ *The best grade you can get is an A.*

◻ **V-T** If you **grade** something, you judge its quality. ❑ *Restaurants are graded according to the quality of the food and service.* ❑ *Teachers grade the students' work from A to F.*

◻ **N-COUNT** The **grade** of a product is its level of quality. ❑ *The price of all grades of gasoline has gone up.*

◻ **PHRASE** If someone **makes the grade,** they succeed. ❑ *She wanted to be a dancer but failed to make the grade.* [from French]

grade point av|er|age (**grade point averages**) also **grade-point average** **N-COUNT** A student's **grade point average** is a measure of how good their work is, based on an average of all the grades they receive. ❑ *She had the highest grade point average in the class.*

gradual /grædʒuəl/ **ADJ** A **gradual** change or process happens slowly, over a long period of time. ❑ *Losing weight is a gradual process.* ● **gradually** /grædʒuəli/ **ADV** ❑ *We are gradually learning to use the new computer system.* [from Medieval Latin]

graduate (**graduates, graduating, graduated**)

> **PRONUNCIATION HELP**
> Pronounce the noun /grædʒuɪt/.
> Pronounce the verb /grædʒueɪt/.

◻ **N-COUNT** A **graduate** is a student who has completed a course at a high school, a college, or a university. ❑ *His parents are both college graduates.*

◻ **V-I** When a student **graduates,** they complete their studies at school or university. ❑ *Her son just graduated from high school.* [from Medieval Latin]
→ look at Word Web: **graduation**

graduated /grædʒueɪtɪd/ **ADJ** **Graduated** jars are marked with lines and numbers that show particular measurements. [from Medieval Latin]

graduation /grædʒueɪʃ°n/ (**graduations**) **N-COUNT** A **graduation** is a special ceremony

Word Web graduation

High school and **college graduations** are important **events** for students. This **ceremony** tells the world that the **student** is educated. In college, **graduates** receive different types of **diplomas** depending on their subject and level of study. After four years of study, students earn a Bachelor of Arts or Bachelor of Science **degree**. A Master of Arts or Master of Science usually takes one or two more years. The PhD, or doctor of philosophy degree, may require several more years. In addition, a PhD student must write a **thesis** and defend it in front of a group of **professors**.

for students when they have completed their studies at a university, a college, or a school. ❑ *Her parents came to her graduation.* [from Medieval Latin]
→ look at Word Web: **graduation**

graf|fi|ti /ɡrəfiːti/ **N-NONCOUNT Graffiti** is words or pictures that people write or draw on walls or in public places. ❑ *There was graffiti all over the walls.* [from Italian]
→ look at Picture Dictionary: **crime**

grain /ɡreɪn/ (**grains**)
■ **N-COUNT** A **grain of** a particular crop is a single seed from it. ❑ *He was grateful for every single grain of rice.*
■ **N-COUNT** A **grain of** sand or salt is a tiny, hard piece of it. ❑ *How many grains of sand are there in the desert?*
■ **N-SING** A **grain of** a quality is a very small amount of it. ❑ *There's a grain of truth in what he says.*
■ **PHRASE** If an idea or an action **goes against the grain**, it is very difficult for you to accept it. ❑ *Paying more taxes goes against the grain for him.* [from Old French]
→ look at Picture Dictionary: **vegetarian**
→ look at Word Webs: **grain, rice**

gram /ɡræm/ (**grams**) **N-COUNT MATH SCIENCE** A **gram** is a unit for measuring weight. There are one thousand grams in a kilogram. ❑ *A soccer ball weighs about 400 grams.* [from French]

gram|mar /ɡræmər/
■ **N-NONCOUNT** LANGUAGE ARTS **Grammar** is a set of rules for a language that describes how words go together to form sentences ❑ *You need to know the basic rules of grammar.*
■ **N-NONCOUNT** LANGUAGE ARTS Someone's **grammar** is the way in which they obey or do not obey the rules of grammar when they write or speak. ❑ *His grammar is excellent.* [from Old French]
→ look at Word Web: **English**

gram|mati|cal /ɡrəmætɪkəl/
■ **ADJ** LANGUAGE ARTS **Grammatical** describes something that relates to grammar. ❑ *He studied a book of grammatical rules.*
■ **ADJ** LANGUAGE ARTS If language is **grammatical**, it is correct because it obeys the rules of grammar. ❑ *We want to see if students can write grammatical English.* [from Old French]

grand /ɡrænd/ (**grander, grandest**)
■ **ADJ** If a building or a place is **grand**, its size or appearance is very impressive. ❑ *The courthouse is a grand building in the center of town.*
■ **ADJ** **Grand** plans or actions are intended to achieve important results. ❑ *He had a grand design to change the entire future of the United States.*
■ **ADJ** A **grand** total is the final result of a calculation. ❑ *We collected a grand total of $220,329.* [from Old French]

Word Web grain

People first began **cultivating grain** about 10,000 years ago in Asia. Working in groups made growing and **harvesting** the **crop** easier. This probably led Stone Age people to live in communities. Today grain is still the principal food source for humans and domestic animals. Half of all the farmland in the world is used to produce grain. The most popular are **wheat, rice, corn**, and **oats**. Grain is often **ground** into **flour** or meal.

grand|child /grǽntʃaɪld/ (**grandchildren**)
N-COUNT Someone's **grandchild** is the child
of their son or daughter. ❑ *You're grandma's
favorite grandchild.*

grand|daughter /grǽndɔtər/
(**granddaughters**) **N-COUNT** Someone's
granddaughter is the daughter of their son
or daughter. ❑ *This is my granddaughter, Amelia.*

grand|father /grǽnfɑðər/ (**grandfathers**)
N-COUNT Your **grandfather** is the father of
your father or mother. ❑ *His grandfather was a
professor.*
→ look at Picture Dictionary: **family**

grand|ma /grǽnmɑ/ (**grandmas**) **N-COUNT**
Your **grandma** is your grandmother.
[INFORMAL] ❑ *Grandma was from Scotland.*

grand|mother /grǽnmʌðər/
(**grandmothers**) **N-COUNT** Your **grandmother**
is the mother of your father or mother.
❑ *My grandmothers were both teachers.*
→ look at Picture Dictionary: **family**

grand|pa /grǽnpɑ/ (**grandpas**) **N-COUNT**
Your **grandpa** is your grandfather.
[INFORMAL] ❑ *Grandpa was sitting in the yard.*

grand|parent /grǽnpɛərənt, -pær-/
(**grandparents**) **N-COUNT** Your **grandparents**
are the parents of your father or mother.
❑ *Tammy lives with her grandparents.*

grand|son /grǽnsʌn/ (**grandsons**) **N-COUNT**
Someone's **grandson** is the son of their son
or daughter. ❑ *My grandson's birthday was on
Tuesday.*

gran|ny /grǽni/ (**grannies**) **N-COUNT** Granny
is an informal word for grandmother.
[INFORMAL] ❑ *I hugged my granny.*

gra|no|la /grənoʊlə/ **N-NONCOUNT** Granola
is a breakfast food that contains fruit and
nuts. ❑ *I usually have granola for breakfast.*

grant /grǽnt/ (**grants, granting, granted**)
1 **N-COUNT** A **grant** is an amount of money
that a government gives to a person or to an
organization for a special purpose. ❑ *They got
a grant to research the disease.*
2 **V-T** If someone **grants** you something,
you are allowed to have it. [FORMAL] ❑ *France
granted him political asylum.*
3 **PHRASE** If someone **takes** you **for granted,**
they do not show that they are grateful for
anything that you do. ❑ *She feels that her family
takes her for granted.*
4 **PHRASE** If you **take** something **for**

granted, you accept it as normal without
thinking about it. ❑ *We take things like
electricity and running water for granted.* [from
Old French]

grape /greɪp/ (**grapes**)
1 **N-COUNT** Grapes are small green or
purple fruit that grow in bunches. ❑ *I bought
six oranges and a small bunch of grapes.*
2 **PHRASE** If you describe someone's
attitude as **sour grapes,** you mean that they
are criticizing something because they
want it themselves but cannot have it.
❑ *These accusations are just sour grapes.*
[from Old French]
→ look at Picture Dictionary: **fruit**

grape|fruit /greɪpfrut/ (**grapefruit** or
grapefruits) **N-COUNT/N-NONCOUNT**
A **grapefruit** is a large, round, yellow fruit
that has a slightly sour taste.

graph /grǽf/ (**graphs**) **N-COUNT** MATH
A **graph** is a picture that shows the
relationship between sets of numbers or
measurements. ❑ *The graph shows that prices
went up about 20 percent last year.*
→ look at Picture Dictionary: **chart**
→ look at Word Web: **graph**

graph|ic /grǽfɪk/ **ADJ** If you say that a
description or an account of something
unpleasant is **graphic,** you are emphasizing
that it is clear and detailed. ❑ *...graphic
descriptions of violence.* ● **graphi|cal|ly**
/grǽfɪkli/ **ADV** ❑ *War was very graphically
depicted in the movie.* [from Latin]

graph|ics /grǽfɪks/
1 **N-PLURAL** ARTS TECHNOLOGY Graphics are
drawings, pictures, or symbols, especially
when they are produced by a computer.
❑ *The game's graphics are very good, so you can see
things clearly.*
2 **N-NONCOUNT** ARTS TECHNOLOGY Graphics
is the activity of drawing or making
pictures, especially in publishing, industry,
or computing. ❑ *...a computer manufacturer that
specializes in graphics.*

grasp /grǽsp/ (**grasps, grasping, grasped**)
1 **V-T** If you **grasp** something, you take it in
your hand and hold it very firmly. ❑ *He
grasped both my hands.*
2 **N-SING** A **grasp** is a very firm hold or grip.
❑ *He took her hand in a firm grasp.*
3 **V-T** If you **grasp** something that is
complicated, you understand it. ❑ *I don't*

Word Web   graph

There are three main elements in a **line** or **bar graph**:
- a **vertical axis** (the y-axis)
- a **horizontal axis** (the x-axis)
- at least one line or set of bars.

To understand a **graph**, do the following:
1. Read the **title** of the graph.
2. Read the **labels** and the **range** of numbers along the side (the **scale** or vertical axis).
3. Read the information along the bottom (horizontal axis) of the graph.
4. Determine what **units** the graph uses. This information can be found on the axis or in the **key**.
5. Look for patterns, groups, and differences.

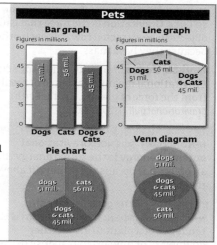

g

---

think you have grasped how serious this problem is.

4 **N-SING** A **grasp of** a subject is an understanding of it. ❑ *She has a good grasp of geometry.* [from Low German]

grass /græs/ **N-NONCOUNT** Grass is a plant with thin, green leaves that cover the surface of the ground. ❑ *We sat on the grass and ate our picnic.* [from Old English]
→ look at Picture Dictionaries: **garden, plants**
→ look at Word Webs: **habitat, herbivore**

grass|hopper /græshɒpər/ (**grasshoppers**) **N-COUNT** A **grasshopper** is an insect that jumps high into the air and makes a sound with its long back legs.

grassy /græsi/ (**grassier, grassiest**) **ADJ** A **grassy** area of land is covered in grass. ❑ *...a grassy hillside.* [from Old English]

grate /greɪt/ (**grates, grating, grated**)
1 **N-COUNT** A **grate** is a framework of metal bars in a fireplace that holds the wood or coal. ❑ *A fire burned in the grate.*
2 **V-T** If you **grate** food such as cheese or carrots, you rub it over a metal tool called a grater so that the food is cut into very small pieces. ❑ *Grate the cheese into a bowl.*
3 **V-I** When something **grates**, it rubs against something else, making a harsh, unpleasant sound. ❑ *His chair grated as he stood up.*
4 **V-I** If something such as someone's behavior **grates on** you or **grates**, it makes you feel annoyed. ❑ *His voice grates on me.* [from Old French]

grate|ful /greɪtfəl/ **ADJ** If you are **grateful for** something that someone gives you or does for you, you feel glad and you want to thank them. ❑ *She was grateful to him for being so helpful.* ● **grate|ful|ly** **ADV** ❑ *He said that any help would be gratefully received.* [from Latin]

grati|tude /grætɪtud/ **N-NONCOUNT** **Gratitude** is the feeling you have when you want to thank someone. ❑ *He expressed gratitude to everyone for their help.* [from Medieval Latin]

grave /greɪv/ (**graver, gravest, graves**)
1 **N-COUNT** A **grave** is a place where a dead person is buried. ❑ *They visit her grave twice a year.*
2 **ADJ** A **grave** event or situation is very serious and important. ❑ *These weapons are a grave danger to the world.* ● **grave|ly** **ADV** ❑ *They have gravely damaged the government's reputation.*
3 **ADJ** A **grave** person is quiet and serious in their appearance or behavior. ❑ *He looked grave and worried.* ● **grave|ly** **ADV** ❑ *"Shall I get a priest?" she asked. He nodded gravely.* [Sense 1 from Old English. Senses 2 and 3 from Old French.]

grav|el /grævəl/ **N-NONCOUNT** Gravel consists of very small stones. It is often used to make paths. ❑ *...a gravel path.* [from Old French]

grave|yard /greɪvyɑrd/ (**graveyards**) **N-COUNT** A **graveyard** is an area of land where dead people are buried. ❑ *They went to the graveyard to put flowers on her grave.* [from Old English]

gravi|ta|tion /grævɪteɪʃ°n/ **N-NONCOUNT**
SCIENCE **Gravitation** is the force that causes
objects to be attracted towards each other
because they have mass.

gravi|ta|tion|al /grævɪteɪʃənᵊl/ **ADJ** SCIENCE
Gravitational means relating to or resulting
from the force of gravity. ❑ ...the Earth's
gravitational pull. [from Latin]

gravi|ta|tion|al po|ten|tial en|er|gy
N-NONCOUNT SCIENCE **Gravitational
potential energy** is the stored energy that
an object has because of its height above
the Earth.

gra|vit|ro|pism /grævɪtrəpɪzəm/
N-NONCOUNT SCIENCE **Gravitropism** is the
tendency of a plant to grow either
downward or upward in response to the
force of gravity.

grav|ity /grævɪti/
1 **N-NONCOUNT** SCIENCE **Gravity** is the force
that makes things fall to the ground.
❑ The force of gravity pulls everything down.
2 **N-NONCOUNT** The **gravity of** a situation is
its extreme importance or seriousness.
❑ We didn't understand the gravity of the situation.
[from Latin]
→ look at Word Webs: **moon, tide**

gra|vy /greɪvi/ **N-NONCOUNT** **Gravy** is a sauce
made from the juices that come from meat
when it cooks. [from Old French]

gray /greɪ/ (**grayer, grayest**)
1 **ADJ** Something that is **gray** is a mixture
of black and white, like the color of clouds
on a rainy day. ❑ ...a gray suit.
2 **N-NONCOUNT** **Gray** is also a noun. ❑ Expect
to see more grays and browns this fall. [from
Old English]
→ look at Picture Dictionary: **hair**

Word Partnership	Use **gray** with :
N	gray **eyes**, gray **hair**, **shades of** gray, gray **sky**, gray **suit**

graze /greɪz/ (**grazes, grazing, grazed**)
1 **V-T/V-I** When animals **graze** or **are
grazed**, they eat the grass or other plants
that are growing in a particular place. You
can also say that a field **is grazed** by animals.
❑ Cows were grazing peacefully in the field.
❑ Horses grazed the meadow.
2 **V-T** If you **graze** a part of your body,
you injure your skin by scraping against
something. ❑ I fell and grazed my knees.

3 **N-COUNT** A **graze** is a small wound caused
by scraping against something. ❑ Cuts and
grazes can be quite painful.
4 **V-T** If something **grazes** another thing,
it touches that thing lightly as it passes by.
❑ The ball grazed the hitter's face. [from
Old English]
→ look at Picture Dictionary: **barn**
→ look at Word Web: **herbivore**

grease /gris/
1 **N-NONCOUNT** **Grease** is a thick substance
like oil. ❑ His hands were covered in grease.
2 **N-NONCOUNT** **Grease** is animal fat that is
produced when you cook meat. ❑ I could smell
bacon grease. [from Old French]

greasy /grisi, -zi/ (**greasier, greasiest**) **ADJ**
Something that is **greasy** has grease on it
or in it. ❑ He wiped the greasy counter. [from
Old French]

Word Link	est ≈ most : great**est**, kind**est**, loud**est**

great /greɪt/ (**greater, greatest**)
1 **ADJ** **Great** or **great big** describes
something that is very large. ❑ She had a great
big smile on her face.
2 **ADJ** **Great** means large in amount or
degree. ❑ She lived to a great age.
3 **ADJ** **Great** describes someone or
something that is important, famous, or
exciting. ❑ They made great scientific discoveries.
❑ He has the ability to be a great player.
● **great|ness** **N-NONCOUNT** ❑ She dreamed of
achieving greatness.
4 **ADJ** If something is **great**, it is very good.
❑ I thought it was a great idea.
5 **INTERJ** **Great** is also an interjection.
❑ Oh, great! You made a cake. [from Old
English]

Thesaurus	great Also look up :
ADJ	enormous, immense, vast; (ant.) small **1** **2** distinguished, famous, important, remarkable **3**

great|ly /greɪtli/ **ADV** You use **greatly** to
emphasize the degree or extent of
something. [FORMAL] ❑ He will be greatly
missed.

Great Red Spot **N-SING** SCIENCE The **Great
Red Spot** is a large area in the atmosphere
of the planet Jupiter where a powerful
storm has been taking place for hundreds
of years.

greed /griːd/ **N-NONCOUNT** Greed is the feeling that you want to have more of something than you need. ❑ *People say that the world economy is based on greed.*

greedy /griːdi/ (greedier, greediest) **ADJ** If someone is **greedy**, they want to have more of something than they need. ❑ *They still want more money? I think that's a bit greedy.*
● **greedi|ly ADV** ❑ *He raised the bottle to his lips and drank greedily.* [from Old English]

Greek thea|ter N-NONCOUNT ARTS Greek theater is the style of theater associated with ancient Greece.

green /griːn/ (greener, greenest)
1 ADJ Something that is **green** is the color of grass or leaves. ❑ *She wore a green dress.*
2 N-NONCOUNT Green is also a noun. ❑ *I've never looked good in green.*
3 ADJ A place that is **green** is covered with grass, plants, and trees. ❑ *The city has lots of parks and green spaces.*
4 ADJ Green ideas and organizations relate to the protection of the environment. ❑ *...the Green Party.* [from Old English]
→ look at Picture Dictionaries: **color, golf**
→ look at Word Web: **rainbow**

green|house /griːnhaʊs/ (greenhouses) **N-COUNT** A **greenhouse** is a glass building where you grow plants to protect them from bad weather.
→ look at Picture Dictionary: **barn**

green|house ef|fect N-SING SCIENCE The greenhouse effect is the problem of the Earth's temperature getting higher because of the gases that go into the air. ❑ *Carbon dioxide is one of the gases that contribute to the greenhouse effect.*
→ look at Word Webs: **greenhouse effect, ozone**

green|house gas (greenhouse gases) N-COUNT/N-NONCOUNT SCIENCE Greenhouse **gases** are the gases that cause a gradual rise in the Earth's temperature. The main greenhouse gas is carbon dioxide. ❑ *They signed an international agreement to limit greenhouse gases.*
→ look at Word Web: **biosphere**

green|ish /griːnɪʃ/ **ADJ** Greenish means slightly green in color. ❑ *...his cold greenish eyes.*

green plant (green plants) N-COUNT SCIENCE Green plants are plants that get their energy by means of photosynthesis.

greet /griːt/ (greets, greeting, greeted)
1 V-T When you **greet** someone, you say "Hello" or shake hands with them. ❑ *She greeted him when he came in from school.*
2 V-T If information or opinions **are greeted** in a particular way, people react to it in that way. ❑ *His comments were greeted with anger.* [from Old English]

greet|ing /griːtɪŋ/ (greetings) **N-COUNT/N-NONCOUNT** A greeting is something friendly that you say or do when you meet someone. ❑ *We exchanged friendly greetings.* [from Old English]

grew /gruː/ **Grew** is the past tense of **grow**. [from Old English]

grid /grɪd/ (grids) **N-COUNT** A **grid** is a pattern of straight lines that cross over each other to make squares. On maps, you can use the grid to help you find a particular thing or place. ❑ *The number puzzle uses a grid of nine squares.*

grief /griːf/ **N-NONCOUNT** Grief is a feeling of great sadness. ❑ *We all experience grief at some point in our lives.*

g

Word Web   greenhouse effect

Over the past 100 years, the global average **temperature** has risen dramatically. Researchers believe that this **global warming** comes from added **carbon dioxide** and other **gases** in the **atmosphere**. With **water vapor**, they form a layer that holds in heat. It acts like the glass in a greenhouse. Scientists call this the **greenhouse effect**. Some natural causes of this warming may include increased **solar radiation** and tiny changes in the earth's orbit. However, human activities, such as deforestation, and the use of **fossil fuels**, seem to be an important cause.

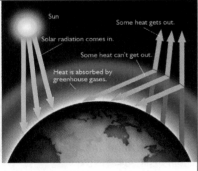

grieve /griːv/ (**grieves, grieving, grieved**) **v-ı**
If you **grieve over** something, especially
someone's death, you feel very sad about it.
❏ *He's grieving over his dead wife.* [from Old
French]

grill /grɪl/ (**grills, grilling, grilled**)
■ **N-COUNT** A **grill** is a flat frame of metal
bars that you can use to cook food over a fire.
❏ *We cooked the fish on a grill over the fire.*
■ **v-T** When you **grill** food, or when it **grills**,
you cook it on metal bars above a fire or a
barbecue. ❏ *Grill the steaks for about 5 minutes
each side.* [from French]
→ look at Picture Dictionary: **cook**

grim /grɪm/ (**grimmer, grimmest**)
■ **ADJ** A situation or a piece of information
that is **grim** is unpleasant, depressing, and
difficult to accept. ❏ *There was grim news about
the economy yesterday.* ❏ *With rising crime and
violence, the situation is grim.*
■ **ADJ** A place that is **grim** is unattractive
and depressing. ❏ *...a grim, industrial city.*
[from Old English]

gri|mace /grɪməs, grɪmeɪs/ (**grimaces,
grimacing, grimaced**)
■ **v-ı** If you **grimace**, you twist your face in
an ugly way because you are annoyed,
disgusted, or in pain. [WRITTEN] ❏ *When she
tried to get up she grimaced.*
■ **N-COUNT** **Grimace** is also a noun.
a grimace. [from French]

grin /grɪn/ (**grins, grinning, grinned**)
■ **v-ı** When you **grin**, you have a big smile
on your face. ❏ *He grinned with pleasure.*
❏ *Phillip grinned at her.*
■ **N-COUNT** A **grin** is a broad smile. ❏ *She had
a big grin on her face.* [from Old English]

grind /graɪnd/ (**grinds, grinding, ground**)
■ **v-T** If you **grind** a substance, you rub it
against something hard until it becomes
a fine powder. ❏ *Grind some pepper into
the sauce.*
■ → see also **ground**
■ **PHRASE** If a vehicle **grinds to a halt**, it
stops slowly and noisily. ❏ *The truck ground to
a halt after a hundred yards.* [from Old English]
→ look at Word Web: **grain**

grip /grɪp/ (**grips, gripping, gripped**)
■ **v-T** If you **grip** something, you take it
with your hand and hold it firmly. ❏ *She
gripped the rope.*
■ **N-COUNT** A **grip** is a firm, strong hold on

something. ❏ *Keep a tight grip on your purse.*
■ **v-T** If you **are gripped by** something, it
affects you strongly and your attention
is concentrated on it. ❏ *The audience was
gripped by the dramatic story.* [from Old
English]

groan /groʊn/ (**groans, groaning, groaned**)
■ **v-ı** If you **groan**, you make a long, low
sound because you are feeling pain, or
because you are unhappy about something.
❏ *He began to groan with pain.* ❏ *The man on the
floor was groaning.*
■ **N-COUNT** **Groan** is also a noun. ❏ *I heard
a groan from the crowd.* [from Old English]

gro|cery /groʊsəri, groʊsri/ (**groceries**)
■ **N-COUNT** A **grocery** or a **grocery store** is
a store that sells food. ❏ *I went to the grocery
store to buy some milk.*
■ **N-PLURAL** **Groceries** are the things that
you buy at a grocery or at a supermarket.
❏ *...a small bag of groceries.* [from Old French]

groom /gruːm/ (**grooms, grooming,
groomed**)
■ **N-COUNT** A **groom** is a person whose job is
to look after horses.
■ **v-T** If you **groom** an animal, you clean its
fur, usually by brushing it. ❏ *She groomed the
horses regularly.* [from Old English]

groove /gruːv/ (**grooves**) **N-COUNT** A **groove**
is a deep line that is cut into a surface.
❏ *He used a knife to cut a groove in the stick.*
[from Dutch]

gross /groʊs/ (**grosser, grossest**)
■ **ADJ** Someone or something that is **gross**
is very unpleasant. [INFORMAL] ❏ *Some scenes
in the movie were really gross.*
■ **ADJ** You use **gross** to describe something
that is totally unacceptable. ❏ *...gross abuse of
human rights.* ● **gross|ly** **ADV** ❏ *He was
sentenced to nine years in prison after a grossly
unfair trial.* [from Old French]

Word Partnership	Use **gross** with :
v	**feel** gross ■
N	**act of** gross **injustice**, gross **mismanagement**, gross **negligence** ■

gross na|tion|al prod|uct (**gross national
products**) **N-COUNT/N-NONCOUNT**
SOCIAL STUDIES A country's **gross national
product** is the total value of all its income
in a particular year.

ground
1. NOUN USES
2. ADJECTIVE AND VERB USES
3. PHRASES

① ground /graʊnd/ (grounds)

1 **N-SING** The **ground** is the surface of the Earth or the floor of a room. ❑ *They are sitting on the ground.* ❑ *Jack fell to the ground.*

2 **N-COUNT** You can use **ground** to refer to an area of land, sea, or air that is used for a particular activity. ❑ *There are great fishing grounds around the islands.*

3 **N-PLURAL** The **grounds** of a large building are the area of land that surrounds it. ❑ *...the palace grounds.*

4 **N-COUNT/N-NONCOUNT** If something is **grounds for** a feeling or action, it is a reason for it. If you do something **on the grounds** of a particular thing, that thing is the reason for your action. ❑ *There are some grounds for optimism.* ❑ *They denied his request on the grounds that it would cost too much money.*

5 **N-COUNT** The **ground** in a piece of electrical equipment is the wire through which electricity passes into the ground and which makes the equipment safe. [from Old English]

② ground /graʊnd/

1 **ADJ** **Ground** meat has been cut into very small pieces in a machine. ❑ *The sausages are made of ground pork.*

2 **Ground** is the past tense and past participle of **grind**. [from Old English]

③ ground /graʊnd/

1 **PHRASE** If something such as a project gets **off the ground**, it begins or starts functioning. ❑ *We help small companies to get off the ground.*

2 **PHRASE** If you **stand** your **ground** or **hold** your **ground**, you do not run away from a situation, but face it bravely. ❑ *He was angry, but she stood her ground.*

3 **PHRASE** ARTS In a painting, the **middle ground** is the area between the foreground and the background. [from Old English]

Word Link ground ≈ bottom : back**ground**, **ground**water, under**ground**

ground|water /graʊndwɔtər/ **N-NONCOUNT** SCIENCE **Groundwater** is water that is found under the ground. Groundwater has usually passed down through the soil and become trapped by rocks.

group /grup/ (groups, grouping, grouped)

1 **N-COUNT** A **group of** people or things is a number of them that are together. ❑ *A small group of people stood on the street corner.*

2 **N-COUNT** A **group** is a set of people who have the same interests or aims, and who organize themselves to work or act together. ❑ *...members of an environmental group.*

3 **N-COUNT** A **group** is a number of people who play music together. ❑ *He played guitar in a rock group.*

4 **N-COUNT** SCIENCE In chemistry, a **group** of elements is a number of them that are in the same column in the periodic table of elements.

5 **V-T/V-I** If a number of things or people **are grouped together** or if they **group together**, they are together in one place or within one system. ❑ *Plants are grouped into botanical "families."* ❑ *We group the students together according to ability.* [from French]

→ look at Word Web: **periodic table**

Thesaurus	group Also look up :
N	collection, crowd, gang, organization, society **1**
V	arrange, categorize, class, order, rank, sort **5**

grove /groʊv/ (groves) **N-COUNT** A **grove** is a group of trees that are close together. ❑ *...an olive grove.* [from Old English]

→ look at Word Web: **tree**

grow /groʊ/ (grows, growing, grew, grown)

1 **V-I** When someone or something **grows**, they gradually become bigger. ❑ *All children grow at different rates.*

2 **V-I** If a plant or a tree **grows** in a particular place, it lives there. ❑ *There were roses growing by the side of the door.*

3 **V-T** If you **grow** a particular type of plant, you put seeds or young plants in the ground and take care of them. ❑ *I always grow a few red onions.* ● **grow|er** (growers) **N-COUNT** ❑ *...apple growers.*

4 **V-T/V-I** When your hair or nails **grow**, they gradually become longer. If you **grow** your hair or nails, you stop cutting them so that they become longer. ❑ *My hair grows really fast.* ❑ *He's growing a beard.*

5 **V-LINK** **Grow** means "become." ❑ *I grew a little afraid of him.* ❑ *He's growing old.*

6 **V-I** If something **grows**, it becomes bigger or more intense. ❑ *The number of unemployed people grew to 4 million.* ❑ *The public's*

g

anger is growing. ❏ The economy continues to grow. [from Old English]

▶ **grow apart** If two people **grow apart**, they gradually lose interest in each other. ❏ He and his wife grew apart.

▶ **grow out of** ■ If you **grow out of** a type of behavior, you stop behaving in that way as you get older. ❏ Most children who bite their nails grow out of it.

■ When a child **grows out of** a piece of clothing, they become too big to wear it. ❏ You've grown out of your shoes again.

▶ **grow up** ■ When someone **grows up**, they gradually change from being a child into being an adult. ❏ She grew up in Tokyo.

■ → see also **grown-up**

Word Partnership	Use grow with :
V	continue to grow ■–■
	try to grow ■
ADJ	grow older ■
N	grow food ■

growl /gra͟ʊl/ (**growls, growling, growled**)
■ **V-I** When a dog or other animal **growls**, it makes a low noise in its throat, usually because it is angry. ❏ The dog was growling and showing its teeth.

■ **N-COUNT Growl** is also a noun. ❏ The animal gave a growl. [from Old French]

grown /gro͟ʊn/ **ADJ** A **grown** man or woman is one who is fully developed. ❏ Why do grown men love games so much? [from Old English]

grown-up (**grown-ups**) also **grownup**

LANGUAGE HELP
Stress both syllables when **grown-up** is an adjective.

■ **N-COUNT Grown-up** is a child's word for an adult ❏ Jan's almost a grown-up now.

■ **ADJ** Someone who is **grown-up** is an adult and no longer depends on their parents or another adult. ❏ She has two grown-up children who both live nearby.

growth /gro͟ʊθ/ (**growths**)
■ **N-NONCOUNT** The **growth of** something is its development. ❏ The city's population growth slowed to 1.6% last year. ❏ The government expects strong economic growth.

■ **N-NONCOUNT** The **growth** of a person, an animal, or a plant is the process of getting bigger. ❏ Milk is important for a baby's growth and development.

■ **N-COUNT** A **growth** is a lump caused by

a disease. ❏ He had a growth on his back. [from Old English]

grudge /grʌ͟dʒ/ (**grudges**) **N-COUNT** If you have a **grudge against** someone, you feel angry with them because of something they did in the past. ❏ He seems to have a grudge against me. [from Old French]

grum|ble /grʌ͟mbᵊl/ (**grumbles, grumbling, grumbled**)
■ **V-T/V-I** If someone **grumbles**, they complain about something. ❏ They grumble about how hard they have to work. ❏ Dad grumbled that we never cleaned our rooms.

■ **N-COUNT Grumble** is also a noun. ❏ The high prices have brought grumbles from some customers. [from Middle Low German]

grumpy /grʌ͟mpi/ (**grumpier, grumpiest**)
ADJ If someone is **grumpy**, they are a little angry. ❏ He's getting grumpy and depressed.

● **grumpi|ly ADV** ❏ "Go away, I'm busy," said Ken grumpily.

grunt /grʌ͟nt/ (**grunts, grunting, grunted**)
■ **V-T/V-I** If you **grunt**, you make a low sound, especially because you are annoyed or not interested in something. ❏ When I said hello he just grunted. ❏ "Huh," he grunted.

■ **N-COUNT Grunt** is also a noun. ❏ Barbara replied with a grunt. [from Old English]

gua|nine /gwɑ͟nin, -nin/ (**guanines**)
N-COUNT/N-NONCOUNT SCIENCE **Guanine** is one of the four basic components of the DNA molecule. It bonds with cytosine.

guar|an|tee /gæ̱rənti͟/ (**guarantees, guaranteeing, guaranteed**)
■ **V-T** If you **guarantee** something, you promise that it will happen. ❏ We guarantee the safety of our products. ❏ I guarantee that you will enjoy this movie.

■ **N-COUNT Guarantee** is also a noun. ❏ He gave me a guarantee he would finish the job.

■ **N-COUNT** If one thing is a **guarantee of** another, the first thing makes it certain that the second will happen or be true. ❏ A famous company name is not a guarantee of quality.

■ **N-COUNT** A **guarantee** is a written promise by a company to repair a product or give you a new one if it has anything wrong with it. ❏ Keep the guarantee in case something goes wrong.

■ **V-T** If a company **guarantees** its product or work, they provide a guarantee for it.

❏ *All our computers are guaranteed for 12 months.* [from Spanish]

guard /gɑrd/ (**guards, guarding, guarded**)

1 **V-T** If you **guard** a place, a person, or an object, you stand near them to watch and protect them. ❏ *Armed police guarded the court.*

2 **V-T** If you **guard** someone, you watch them and keep them in a particular place to stop them from escaping. ❏ *Marines with rifles guarded them.*

3 **N-COUNT** A **guard** is a soldier, or a police officer, who is guarding a particular place or person. ❏ *The prisoners attacked their guards.*

4 **N-COUNT** A **guard** is an object that protects people from danger. ❏ *...the chin guard of my helmet.* ❏ *...a fire guard.*

5 **PHRASE** If you are **on** your **guard**, you are being very careful because you think a situation might become difficult or dangerous. ❏ *He was on his guard because the police were asking questions.* [from Old French]

Word Partnership	Use guard with :
N	guard **a door/house/prisoner 1 2**
	prison guard, **security** guard **3**
V	**be on** guard **5**

guard cell (**guard cells**) **N-COUNT** SCIENCE **Guard cells** are pairs of cells on the leaves of plants that control things such as how much air a plant takes in and how much water it releases.

guard|ian /gɑrdiən/ (**guardians**) **N-COUNT** A **guardian** is a person who is legally responsible for another person, often a child. ❏ *Diana's grandmother was her legal guardian.* [from Old French]

guer|ril|la /gərɪlə/ (**guerrillas**) also **guerilla** **N-COUNT** A **guerrilla** is a person who fights for a military group that does not form part of the regular military. ❏ *Five soldiers were killed in a guerrilla attack.* [from Spanish]

guess /gɛs/ (**guesses, guessing, guessed**)

1 **V-T/V-I** If you **guess** something, you give an answer or provide an opinion when you do not know if it is true. ❏ *Yvonne guessed that he was around 40 years old.* ❏ *He didn't know the answer, so I asked him to guess.*

2 **V-T** If you **guess that** something is the case, you correctly form the opinion that it is the case. ❏ *I guessed that he was American.* ❏ *He should have guessed what would happen.*

3 **N-COUNT** A **guess** is an attempt to give an answer or provide an opinion when you do

not know if it is true. ❏ *He made a guess at her age.* ❏ *If you don't know, just have a guess.*

4 **PHRASE** You say **I guess** to show that you are slightly uncertain about what you are saying. [INFORMAL] ❏ *I guess he's right.* ❏ *"I think we should stop."—"Yeah. I guess so."* [of Scandinavian origin]

Thesaurus	guess	Also look up :
V	estimate, predict, suspect **1**	
N	assumption, prediction, theory **3**	

Word Partnership	Use guess with :
N	guess **a secret 2**
V	**make a** guess **3**
ADJ	**educated** guess, **good** guess, **wild** guess **3**

guest /gɛst/ (**guests**)

1 **N-COUNT** A **guest** is someone who you invite to your home or to an event. ❏ *She was a guest at the wedding.*

2 **N-COUNT** A **guest** is someone who is staying in a hotel. ❏ *A few guests were having breakfast.*

3 **N-COUNT** A **guest** is someone who visits a place or an organization, or who has been invited to a radio or television show. ❏ *Dr. Gerald Jeffers is the guest speaker.* ❏ *...a frequent talk show guest.* [from Old English] → look at Word Web: **hotel**

Word Partnership	Use guest with :
ADJ	**unwelcome** guest **1**
V	**accommodate a** guest **1**–**3**
	be *someone's* guest, **entertain a** guest **1 3**
N	**hotel** guest **2**
	guest **appearance**, guest **list**, guest **speaker 3**

guid|ance /gaɪdᵊns/ **N-NONCOUNT** Guidance is help and advice. ❏ *My tennis game improved under his guidance.* [from Old French]

guide /gaɪd/ (**guides, guiding, guided**)

1 **N-COUNT** A **guide** is a book or a website that gives you information to help you do or understand something. ❏ *He found a step-by-step guide to building your own home.*

2 **N-COUNT** A **guide** is a book or a website that gives tourists information about a town, an area, or a country. ❏ *The guide to Paris lists hotel rooms for as little as $35 a night.*

3 **N-COUNT** A **guide** is someone who shows tourists around places such as museums or cities. ❏ *A guide will take you on a tour of the city.*

g

G

4 **v-t** If you **guide** someone somewhere, you go there with them to show them the way. ❏ *He took her by the arm and guided her toward the door.*

5 **v-t** If you **guide** a vehicle somewhere, you control it carefully to make sure that it goes in the right direction. ❏ *Captain Shelton guided his plane along the runway.* [from Old French]

Thesaurus	**guide** Also look up :
N	directory, handbook, information **1** **2**
V	accompany, direct, instruct, lead, navigate; *(ant.)* follow **4**

guild /gɪld/ (**guilds**) **N-COUNT** A **guild** is an organization of people who do the same job. ❏ *...the Writers' Guild of America.* [of Scandinavian origin]

guilt /gɪlt/

1 **N-NONCOUNT** **Guilt** is an unhappy feeling that you have when you think that you have done something wrong. ❏ *She felt a lot of guilt about her children's unhappiness.*

2 **N-NONCOUNT** **Guilt** is the fact that you have done something wrong or illegal. ❏ *The jury was convinced of his guilt.* [from Old English]

Word Partnership	Use **guilt** with :
N	**burden of** guilt, **feelings of** guilt, **sense of** guilt, guilt **trip** **1**
V	**admit** guilt **2**

guilty /gɪlti/ (**guiltier, guiltiest**)

1 **ADJ** If you feel **guilty**, you feel unhappy because you think that you have done something wrong. ❏ *I feel so guilty, leaving all this work to you.* ● **guiltily** **ADV** ❏ *He looked up guiltily when I walked in.*

2 **ADJ** A **guilty** secret is one that you feel guilty about. ❏ *He discovered her guilty secret.*

3 **ADJ** If someone is **guilty of** a crime or offense, they have done it. ❏ *They were found guilty of murder.* [from Old English]

→ look at Word Web: **trial**

Word Partnership	Use **guilty** with :
V	**feel** guilty, **look** guilty **1**
	find someone guilty, **plead (not)** guilty, **prove someone** guilty **3**
N	guilty **conscience**, guilty **secret** **2**
	guilty **party**, guilty **plea**, guilty **verdict** **3**
PREP	guilty **of something** **3**

guinea pig /gɪni pɪg/ (**guinea pigs**)

1 **N-COUNT** A **guinea pig** is a person who is used in an experiment. ❏ *The doctor used himself as a guinea pig in his research.*

2 **N-COUNT** A **guinea pig** is a small animal with fur and no tail. People often keep guinea pigs as pets.

guitar /gɪtɑr/ (**guitars**) **N-COUNT/N-NONCOUNT** MUSIC A **guitar** is a musical instrument with strings. [from Spanish]

→ look at Picture Dictionary: **strings**

guitarist /gɪtɑrɪst/ (**guitarists**) **N-COUNT** MUSIC A **guitarist** is a person who plays the guitar. ❏ *He's one of the world's best jazz guitarists.*

gulf /gʌlf/ (**gulfs**) **N-COUNT** GEOGRAPHY A **gulf** is a large area of ocean that has land almost all the way around it. ❏ *A storm is crossing the Gulf of Mexico.* [from Old French]

gully /gʌli/ (**gullies**) also **gulley** **N-COUNT** GEOGRAPHY A **gully** is a long, narrow valley with steep sides. ❏ *They fell down a steep gully.* [from French]

→ look at Word Web: **erosion**

gulp /gʌlp/ (**gulps, gulping, gulped**)

1 **v-t** If you **gulp** something, you eat or drink it very quickly. ❏ *She gulped her soda.*

2 **N-COUNT** A **gulp of** air, food, or drink is a large amount of it that you swallow. ❏ *She took a gulp of fresh air.* [from Middle Dutch]

gum /gʌm/ (**gums**)

1 **N-NONCOUNT** **Gum** is a sweet sticky substance that you keep in your mouth for a long time but do not swallow. ❏ *I do not chew gum in public.*

2 **N-COUNT** SCIENCE Your **gums** are the areas of firm, pink flesh inside your mouth, where your teeth grow. ❏ *Gently brush your teeth and gums.* [Sense 1 from Old French. Sense 2 from Old English.]

→ look at Word Web: **teeth**

gun /gʌn/ (**guns**) **N-COUNT** A **gun** is a weapon that shoots bullets. ❏ *He pointed the gun at the police officer.* [of Scandinavian origin]

gunfire /gʌnfaɪr/ **N-NONCOUNT** **Gunfire** is the repeated shooting of guns. ❏ *We heard the sound of gunfire.*

gunman /gʌnmən/ (**gunmen**) **N-COUNT** A **gunman** is a criminal who uses a gun. ❏ *A gunman fired at police.*

gush /gʌʃ/ (**gushes, gushing, gushed**)

1 **v-t/v-i** When liquid **gushes**, or when something **gushes** liquid, it flows very quickly and strongly. ❑ *Gallons of water gushed out of the tank.*

2 **N-SING** A **gush of** liquid is an amount of it that suddenly flows out of a place. ❑ *I heard a gush of water.* [from Old Norse]

gust /gʌst/ (**gusts**) **N-COUNT** A **gust** is a short, strong, sudden rush of wind. ❑ *A gust of wind came down the valley.* [from Old Norse]

gut /gʌt/ (**guts**)

1 **N-SING** SCIENCE The **gut** is the tube inside the body of a person or animal that food passes through after it has been in the stomach. ❑ *The food then passes into the gut.*

2 **N-PLURAL** If you have the **guts** to do something that is difficult or unpleasant, you have the courage to do it. [INFORMAL] ❑ *She has the guts to say what she thinks.* [from Old English]

gut|ter /gʌtər/ (**gutters**)

1 **N-COUNT** The **gutter** is the edge of a road, where water collects and flows away when it rains. ❑ *His hat fell into the gutter.*

2 **N-COUNT** A **gutter** is a pipe under the edge of a roof that carries water away when it rains. ❑ *We need to fix the gutters.* [from Old French]

guy /gaɪ/ (**guys**)

1 **N-COUNT** A **guy** is a man. [INFORMAL] ❑ *I was working with a guy from Milwaukee.*

2 **N-PLURAL** You can address a group of people, whether they are male or female, as **guys** or **you guys**. [INFORMAL] ❑ *Hi, guys. How are you doing?* [after Guy Fawkes (1570-1606), an English conspirator in the Gunpowder Plot]

gym /dʒɪm/ (**gyms**)

1 **N-COUNT** SPORTS A **gym** is a club, a building, or a large room with equipment for doing physical exercises. ❑ *I go to the gym twice a week.*

2 **N-NONCOUNT** **Gym** is the activity of doing physical exercises in a gym, especially at school. ❑ *...gym classes.*

gym|na|sium /dʒɪmneɪziəm/ (**gymnasiums** or **gymnasia** /dʒɪmneɪziə/) **N-COUNT** SPORTS A **gymnasium** is the same as a **gym**. [from Latin] [FORMAL]

gym|nas|tics /dʒɪmnæstɪks/ **N-NONCOUNT** SPORTS **Gymnastics** is a sport that consists of physical exercises that develop your strength and your ability to move easily. ❑ *The women's gymnastics team won a silver medal.* [from Latin]

gym|no|sperm /dʒɪmnəspɜrm/ (**gymnosperms**) **N-COUNT** SCIENCE A **gymnosperm** is a plant that produces seeds but does not produce flowers.

g

Hh

a and an with the letter h

Before a word beginning with *h*: *a* is used if the *h* is pronounced and the first syllable is stressed at all: *Paul has a hidden agenda. That is a harmonica. I'm staying at a hotel.* A or *an* is used if the *h* is pronounced by the speaker: *This is a/an historic moment. He is making a/an habitual mistake.* (If *an* is used, the *h* isnt pronounced.) *An* is used if the *h* is never pronounced: *It is an honor to meet you.*

hab|it /hǽbɪt/ (**habits**)

1 **N-COUNT/N-NONCOUNT** A **habit** is something that you do often or regularly. ❑ *He has many bad habits, such as biting his nails.*

2 **PHRASE** If you **are in the habit of** doing something, you do it regularly. ❑ *They were in the habit of watching TV every night.* [from Latin]

habi|tat /hǽbɪtæt/ (**habitats**)

N-COUNT/N-NONCOUNT SCIENCE The **habitat** of an animal or a plant is the environment in which it lives or grows. ❑ *In its natural habitat, the plant will grow up to 25 feet.* [from Latin]

→ look at Word Web: **habitat**

hack /hǽk/ (**hacks, hacking, hacked**)

1 **V-T/V-I** If you **hack** something or **hack away at** it, you cut it with strong, rough strokes using a sharp tool such as an ax or a knife. ❑ *He hacked the wood with an ax.* ❑ *He started to hack away at the tree bark.*

2 **V-I** TECHNOLOGY If someone **hacks into** a computer system, they break into the system, especially in order to get secret information. ❑ *Criminals hacked into websites owned by the bank.* ● **hack|er** (**hackers**) **N-COUNT** ❑ *...a hacker who steals credit card numbers.* ● **hack|ing** **N-NONCOUNT** ❑ *...the common crime of computer hacking.*

3 **N-COUNT** If you refer to a professional writer, such as a journalist, as a **hack**, you disapprove of them because they write for money and do not worry very much about the quality of their writing. [Senses 1 and 2 from Old English.]

→ look at Word Web: **Internet**

had

> **PRONUNCIATION HELP**
>
> Pronounce the auxiliary verb /həd/, STRONG hǽd/. Pronounce the main verb /hǽd/.

Had is the past tense and past participle of **have**. [from Old English]

hadn't /hǽdᵊnt/ **Hadn't** is short for "had not." [from Old English]

ha ha INTERJ You write **ha ha** to show the sound that people make when they laugh. ❑ *"Ha ha!" he laughed.*

hail /héɪl/ **N-NONCOUNT** SCIENCE **Hail** is small

Word Web   habitat

The **environment** where a plant or animal lives is its **habitat**. The habitat provides **food, water,** and **shelter**. Each habitat has different **temperatures, rainfall,** and amounts of **sunlight**. A **desert** is a sunny, dry habitat where few plants and animals can live. The **tropical rainforest** gets heavy rain every day and has many types of **vegetation** and animal life. **Prairies** get little rain but are home to many **grass**-eating animals. The boreal **forest** is the largest **biome** in the world. Its winters are cold and snowy, and summers are warm, rainy, and humid.

desert

boreal forest

rain forest

prairie

balls of ice that fall like rain from the sky.
❑ *There will be storms with heavy rain and hail.*
[from Old English]
→ look at Word Webs: **precipitation, storm**

hair /hɛər/ (**hairs**)
■ **N-COUNT/N-NONCOUNT** Your **hair** is the fine threads that grow on your head. ❑ *I wash my hair every night.*
■ **N-COUNT/N-NONCOUNT** Hair is the short threads that grow on the bodies of humans and animals. ❑ *Most men have hair on their chest.* ❑ *There were dog hairs all over the sofa.*
[from Old English]
→ look at Picture Dictionary: **hair**

Word Partnership	Use **hair** with :
ADJ	**black/blonde/brown/gray** hair, **curly/ straight/ wavy** hair ■
V	**bleach your** hair, **brush/comb your** hair, **color your** hair, **cut your** hair, **do your** hair, **dry your** hair, **fix your** hair, **lose your** hair, **pull** *someone's* hair, **wash your** hair ■
N	**lock of** hair ■

hair|cut /hɛərkʌt/ (**haircuts**) **N-COUNT** If you get a **haircut**, someone cuts your hair for

you. ❑ *You need a haircut.*

hair|dresser /hɛərdrɛsər/ (**hairdressers**)
N-COUNT A **hairdresser** is a person whose job is to cut and style people's hair. ❑ *She works as a hairdresser.*

hair|style /hɛərstaɪl/ (**hairstyles**) **N-COUNT** Your **hairstyle** is the style in which your hair has been cut or arranged. ❑ *I think her new hairstyle looks great.*

hairy /hɛəri/ (**hairier, hairiest**) **ADJ** Someone or something that is **hairy** is covered with hairs. ❑ *He was wearing shorts that showed his hairy legs.* [from Old English]

half /hæf/ (**halves** /hævz/)
■ **N-COUNT** MATH **Half of** a number, an amount, or an object is one of two equal parts (½). ❑ *More than half of all U.S. houses are heated with gas.*
■ **PREDET** MATH You use **half a**, **half an**, or **half the** to talk about one of two equal parts of the thing mentioned. ❑ *We sat and talked for half an hour.* ❑ *They only received half the money.*
■ **ADJ** MATH **Half** is also an adjective. ❑ *...a half century.*
■ **ADV** You use **half** to say that something is

h

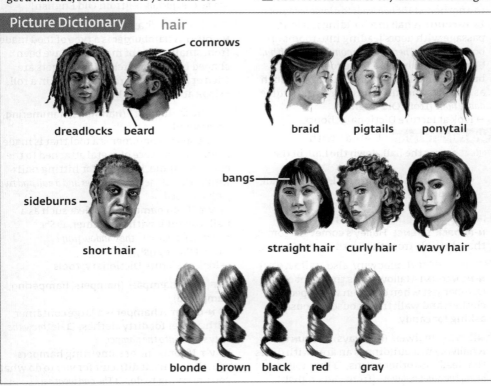

Picture Dictionary hair

cornrows

dreadlocks beard

braid pigtails ponytail

sideburns —

bangs—

short hair

straight hair curly hair wavy hair

blonde brown black red gray

only partly in the state that you are describing. ❑ *The glass was half empty.* [from Old English]

half-hour (half-hours) **N-COUNT** A **half-hour** is a period of thirty minutes. ❑ *The talk was followed by a half-hour of discussion.*

half-life (half-lives) also half life **N-COUNT** SCIENCE The **half-life** of a radioactive substance is the amount of time that it takes to lose half its radioactivity.

half|time /hæftaɪm/ **N-NONCOUNT** SPORTS **Halftime** is the period between the two parts of a sports event, when the players take a short rest. ❑ *We bought something to eat during halftime.*

half|way /hæfweɪ/
1 ADV Halfway means in the middle of a place or between two points. ❑ *He was halfway up the ladder.*
2 ADV Halfway means in the middle of an event or a period of time. ❑ *We were more than halfway through our tour.* [from Old English]

hall /hɔl/ (halls)
1 N-COUNT The **hall** in a house or an apartment is the area that connects one room to another. ❑ *The hall leads to a large living room.*
2 N-COUNT A **hall** in a building is a long passage with doors leading into rooms on both sides. ❑ *There are ten rooms along each hall.*
3 N-COUNT A **hall** is a large room or a building that is used for public events such as concerts and meetings. ❑ *We went into the dance hall.* [from Old English]
→ look at Picture Dictionary: **house**

Word Partnership	Use hall with :
PREP	**across the** hall, **down the** hall, **in the** hall **1 2**
N	**concert** hall, **lecture** hall, **meeting** hall, **pool** hall **3**

Hal|ley's com|et /hæliz kɒmɪt, heɪ-/ **N-PROPER** SCIENCE **Halley's comet** is a comet that is visible from the Earth every 76 years.

Hal|low|een /hæloʊwin/ also Hallowe'en **N-NONCOUNT** **Halloween** is the night of October 31st when children wear special clothes, and walk from house to house asking for candy.

hall|way /hɔlweɪ/ (hallways) **N-COUNT** A **hallway** in a building is an area with doors that lead into other rooms. ❑ *They walked along the quiet hallway.* [from Old English]

halo|phile /hæləfaɪl/ (halophiles) **N-COUNT** SCIENCE **Halophiles** are bacteria that need salt in order to grow.

halt /hɔlt/ (halts, halting, halted)
1 V-T/V-I When a person or a thing **halts**, or when someone or something **halts** them, they stop completely. ❑ *Officials halted the race at 5:30 p.m. yesterday.*
2 PHRASE If someone or something **comes to a halt**, they stop moving. ❑ *The elevator came to a halt at the first floor.* [from Old English]

halve /hæv/ (halves, halving, halved)
1 V-T/V-I When you **halve** something or when it **halves**, it is reduced to half its previous size or amount. ❑ *People who exercise may halve their risk of getting heart disease.*
2 V-T If you **halve** something, you divide it into two equal parts. ❑ *Halve the peppers and remove the seeds.*
3 Halves is the plural of **half**. [from Old English]

ham /hæm/ (hams) **N-COUNT/N-NONCOUNT** **Ham** is meat from a pig that has been prepared with salt and spices. ❑ *We had ham sandwiches for lunch.* [from Old English]

ham|burg|er /hæmbɜrgər/ (hamburgers) **N-COUNT** A **hamburger** is a type of food made from small pieces of meat that have been shaped into a flat circle. Hamburgers are fried or grilled and are often eaten in a roll.
→ look at Word Web: **ketchup**

ham|mer /hæmər/ (hammers, hammering, hammered)
1 N-COUNT A **hammer** is a tool that is made from a heavy piece of metal attached to the end of a handle. It is used for hitting nails into wood. ❑ *She got a hammer and a nail and two pieces of wood.*
2 V-T If you **hammer** an object such as a nail, you hit it with a hammer. ❑ *She hammered a nail into the window frame.* [from Old English]
→ look at Picture Dictionary: **tools**

ham|per /hæmpər/ (hampers, hampering, hampered)
1 N-COUNT A **hamper** is a large container with a cover for dirty clothes. ❑ *He threw the dirty sheets into the hamper.*
2 V-T If someone or something **hampers** you, they make it difficult for you to do what you are trying to do. ❑ *The bad weather*

hampered the rescue operation. [Sense 1 from Old French. Sense 2 from Old English.]

---
hand
- ❶ NOUN USES
- ❷ PHRASES
- ❸ VERB USE AND PHRASAL VERBS
---

❶ **hand** /hænd/ (**hands**)

1 **N-COUNT** Your **hands** are the parts of your body at the end of your arms that you use for holding things. ❑ *I put my hand into my pocket and took out the letter.*

2 **N-SING** If you ask someone for **a hand** with something, you are asking them to help you. ❑ *Come and give me a hand in the kitchen.*

3 **N-COUNT** The **hands** of a clock or a watch are the long thin parts that move to show the time. [from Old English]

→ look at Picture Dictionaries: **hand, body, time**

❷ **hand** /hænd/

1 **PHRASE** If you make something **by hand**, you do it using your hands rather than a machine. ❑ *The dress was made by hand.*

2 **PHRASE** If two people are **walking hand in hand**, they are holding each other by the hand. ❑ *They go everywhere hand in hand.*

3 **PHRASE** If someone or something is on **hand**, they are near and ready to be used. ❑ *There are experts on hand to give you all the help you need.*

4 **PHRASE** You use **on the one hand** to talk about the first of two different ways of looking at something. ❑ *On the one hand, the body cannot survive without fat. On the other hand, if the body has too much fat, our health starts to suffer.*

5 **PHRASE** You use **on the other hand** to introduce the second of two opposite ways of looking at something. ❑ *The movie lost money. Reviews, on the other hand, were mostly favorable.*

6 **PHRASE** If a person or a situation gets **out of hand**, you are no longer able to control them. ❑ *The argument got out of hand when her boyfriend hit her.* [from Old English]

❸ **hand** /hænd/ (**hands, handing, handed**)
V-T If you **hand** something **to** someone, you put it into their hand. ❑ *He handed me a piece of paper.* [from Old English]

▶ **hand in** If you **hand in** something, you take it to someone and give it to them. ❑ *I need to hand in my homework today.* ❑ *They found $7,500 in cash on the street and handed it in to police.*

▶ **hand out** **1** If you **hand** things **out**, you give one to each person in a group. ❑ *My job was to hand out the prizes.*

2 → see also **handout**

Picture Dictionary   hand

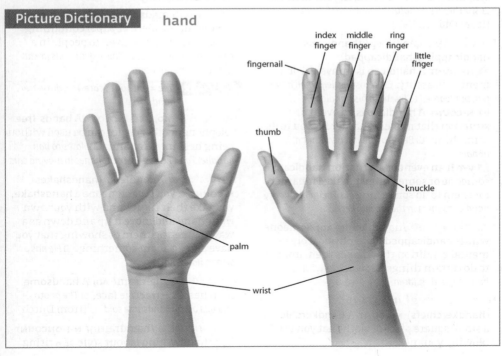

index finger
middle finger
ring finger
little finger
fingernail
thumb
knuckle
palm
wrist

▶ **hand over** If you **hand over to** someone or **hand** something **over to** them, you give them the responsibility for dealing with a particular situation. ❑ *The chairman handed over control to someone younger.*

hand|bag /hǽndbæg/ (**handbags**) **N-COUNT** A **handbag** is a small bag that a woman uses for carrying things such as money and keys.

hand|book /hǽndbʊk/ (**handbooks**) **N-COUNT** A **handbook** is a book that gives you advice and instructions about a particular subject. ❑ *The staff handbook says we get two weeks of vacation.*

hand|cuff /hǽndkʌf/ (**handcuffs, handcuffing, handcuffed**)
1 N-PLURAL **Handcuffs** are two connected metal rings that can be locked around someone's wrists. ❑ *He was taken to prison in handcuffs.*
2 V-T If you **handcuff** someone, you put handcuffs around their wrists. ❑ *Police tried to handcuff him but he ran away.*

hand|ful /hǽndfʊl/ (**handfuls**)
1 N-SING A **handful of** people or things is a small number of them. ❑ *Only a handful of people knew his secret.*
2 N-COUNT A **handful of** something is the amount that you can hold in your hand. ❑ *She threw a handful of sand into the water.* [from Old English]

handi|cap /hǽndikæp/ (**handicaps, handicapping, handicapped**)
1 N-COUNT A **handicap** is a physical or mental disability. ❑ *He lost his leg when he was ten, but learned to live with his handicap.*
2 N-COUNT A **handicap** is an event or a situation that makes it harder for you to do something. ❑ *Being a foreigner was not a handicap.*
3 V-T If an event or a situation **handicaps** someone or something, it makes it harder for them to do something. ❑ *Their nationality handicaps them in the job market.*

handi|capped /hǽndikæpt/ **ADJ** Someone who is **handicapped** has a physical or mental condition that makes them unable to do certain things. ❑ *She works with handicapped children.*

hand|ker|chief /hǽŋkərtʃɪf/ (**handkerchiefs**) **N-COUNT** A **handkerchief** is a small square piece of cloth that you use for blowing your nose.

han|dle /hǽndᵊl/ (**handles, handling, handled**)
1 N-COUNT A **handle** is an object that is attached to a door or a drawer, used for opening and closing it. ❑ *I turned the handle and the door opened.*
2 N-COUNT A **handle** is the part of a tool, a bag, or a cup, that you hold. ❑ *I held the knife handle tightly.*
3 V-T If you **handle** a situation, you deal with it. ❑ *I think I handled the meeting very badly.*
4 V-T If you **handle** a particular area of work, you have responsibility for it. ❑ *She handles travel plans for the company's managers.*
5 V-T When you **handle** something, you hold it or move it with your hands. ❑ *Wash your hands before handling food.* [from Old English]
→ look at Word Web: **silverware**

Word Partnership	Use **handle** with :
N	handle **a job/problem/situation**, handle **pressure/responsibility** **3** **4** **ability to** handle *something* **3** **4**
ADJ	**difficult/easy/hard to** handle **3** **5**

hand|made /hǽndmeɪd/ also **hand-made** **ADJ** **Handmade** objects have been made by someone without using machines. ❑ *The store sells beautiful handmade jewelry.*

hand|out /hǽndaʊt/ (**handouts**) **N-COUNT** A **handout** is a piece of paper containing information that is given to people in a meeting or a class. ❑ *The instructions are all written in the handout.*

Word Link	free ≈ without : care*free*, duty-*free*, hands-*free*

hands-free **ADJ** TECHNOLOGY A **hands-free** telephone or other device can be used without being held in your hand. ❑ *...laws to ban handheld and hands-free cellphones in moving cars.*

hand|shake /hǽndʃeɪk/ (**handshakes**) **N-COUNT** If you give someone a **handshake**, you take their right hand with your own right hand and move it up and down as a way of greeting them or showing that you have agreed about something. ❑ *He has a strong handshake.*

hand|some /hǽnsəm/ **ADJ** A **handsome** man has an attractive face. ❑ *The photo showed a tall, handsome soldier.* [from Dutch]

hand|writing /hǽndraɪtɪŋ/ **N-NONCOUNT** Your **handwriting** is your style of writing with a pen or a pencil. ❑ *The address was in Anna's handwriting.*

hand|written /hǽndrɪtᵊn/ **ADJ** A piece of writing that is **handwritten** is one that someone has written using a pen or pencil rather than by typing it. ❑ *...a handwritten note.*

handy /hǽndi/ (**handier, handiest**)
  1 **ADJ** Something that is **handy** is useful. ❑ *The book gives handy ideas on growing plants.*
  2 **ADJ** A thing or a place that is **handy** is nearby and easy to reach. ❑ *Make sure you have a pencil and paper handy.* [from Old English]

hang /hǽŋ/ (**hangs, hanging, hung** or **hanged**)

> **LANGUAGE HELP**
> Use **hanged** as the past tense and past participle for meaning **4** only.

  1 **V-T/V-I** If something **hangs** somewhere, it is attached there so that it does not touch the ground. ❑ *Flags hang at every entrance.*
  2 **V-T/V-I** If you **hang** something somewhere, you attach it there so that it does not touch the ground. ❑ *She hung her clothes outside to dry.*
  3 **V-I** If something **hangs** in a particular way, that is how it is worn or arranged. ❑ *...a coat that hung down to her ankles.*
  4 **V-T/V-I** If someone **is hanged**, they are killed by having a rope tied around their neck. ❑ *The five men were hanged on Tuesday.*
  5 **PHRASE** If you **get the hang of** a skill or activity, you begin to understand how to do it. [INFORMAL] ❑ *Driving is difficult at first until you get the hang of it.* [from Old English]
  ▶ **hang on** **1** If you ask someone to **hang on**, you want them to wait. [INFORMAL] ❑ *Can you hang on for a minute?*
  2 If you **hang on to** or **hang onto** something, you hold it very tightly. ❑ *He hung on to the rail as he went downstairs.*
  ▶ **hang out** If you **hang out** in a particular place or area, you spend a lot of time there. [INFORMAL] ❑ *I often hang out at the mall.*
  ▶ **hang up** If you **hang up**, you end a phone call. ❑ *Don't hang up on me!*

hang|ing val|ley (**hanging valleys**) **N-COUNT** SCIENCE A **hanging valley** is a type of valley associated with glaciers. It is connected to another valley that is larger and lower than it.

hang|ing wall (**hanging walls**) **N-COUNT** SCIENCE A **hanging wall** is the rock above a geological fault. Compare with **footwall**.

hap|pen /hǽpən/ (**happens, happening, happened**)
  1 **V-I** Something that **happens** takes place without being planned. ❑ *We don't know what will happen.*
  2 **V-I** When something **happens to** you, it takes place and affects you. ❑ *What's the worst thing that has ever happened to you?*
  3 **V-T** If you **happen to** do something, you do it by chance. ❑ *I happened to be at the library at the same time as Jim.*

hap|pi|ly /hǽpɪli/
  1 **ADV** If you add **happily** to something you say, it shows that you are glad that something happened. ❑ *Happily, this situation will soon get much easier.*
  2 **ADV** If you are doing something **happily**, you feel pleased and satisfied with what you are doing. ❑ *The children played happily together all day.*

hap|py /hǽpi/ (**happier, happiest**)
  1 **ADJ** Someone who is **happy** feels pleased and satisfied. ❑ *Marina was a happy child.*
  ● **hap|pi|ness** **N-NONCOUNT** ❑ *I think she was looking for happiness.*
  2 **ADJ** A **happy** time, place, or relationship is full of happy feelings and pleasant experiences. ❑ *She had a very happy childhood.* ❑ *Grandma's house was always a happy place.*
  3 **ADJ** If you are **happy about** or **with** a situation or an arrangement, you are satisfied with it. ❑ *I'm not happy with what I've written.*
  4 **ADJ** If you are **happy to** do something, you are very willing to do it. ❑ *I'm happy to answer any questions.*
  5 **ADJ** **Happy** is used in some expressions to say that you hope someone will enjoy a special occasion. ❑ *Happy Birthday!*
  → look at Word Web: **emotion**

Thesaurus	happy	Also look up :
ADJ	cheerful, content, delighted, glad, pleased, upbeat; (*ant.*) sad, unhappy **1**	

Word Partnership	Use **happy** with :
ADV	**extremely/perfectly/very** happy **1**
V	**feel** happy, **make** *someone* happy, **seem** happy **1**
N	happy **ending**, happy **family**, happy **marriage 2**

h

har|ass /həræs, hærəs/ (**harasses,
harassing, harassed**) **v-t** If someone
harasses you, they trouble or annoy you.
❑ *Players harassed the referee throughout the game.*
● **har|ass|ment** /həræsmənt, hærəs-/
N-NONCOUNT ❑ *...rules to prevent harassment at
work.* [from French]

har|bor /hɑrbər/ (**harbors**) **N-COUNT**
A **harbor** is an area of water next to the land
where boats can safely stay. ❑ *The fishing
boats left the harbor and went out to sea.* [from
Old English]

hard /hɑrd/ (**harder, hardest**)
1 **ADJ** Something that is **hard** feels very
firm, and is not easily bent, cut, or broken.
❑ *The glass hit the hard wooden floor.*
2 **ADJ** Something that is **hard** is very
difficult to do or deal with. ❑ *That's a very hard
question.* ❑ *She's had a hard life.*
3 **ADV** If you work **hard**, you work with a lot
of effort. ❑ *If I work hard, I'll finish the job tomorrow.*
4 **ADJ** **Hard** is also an adjective. ❑ *I admire him
because he's a hard worker.*
5 **ADV** If you strike something **hard**, you
strike it with a lot of force. ❑ *I kicked a trash
can very hard and broke my toe.* [from Old
English]
→ look at Usage note at **hardly**

Thesaurus	**hard** Also look up :
ADJ	firm, solid, tough; *(ant.)* gentle, soft **1**
complicated, difficult, tough;
(ant.) easy **2**

hard disk (**hard disks**) **N-COUNT** TECHNOLOGY
A computer's **hard disk** is the part inside it
where information and programs are
stored.

hard drive (**hard drives**) **N-COUNT**
TECHNOLOGY The **hard drive** on a computer is
the part that contains the computer's hard
disk. ❑ *You can download music to your hard drive.*

hard|en /hɑrdən/ (**hardens, hardening,
hardened**)
1 **v-t/v-i** When something **hardens** or
when you **harden** it, it becomes stiff or firm.
❑ *Mold the mixture before it hardens.*
2 **v-t/v-i** When an attitude or an opinion
hardens or **is hardened**, it becomes harsher,
stronger, or fixed. ❑ *Their actions will harden the
government's attitude.* ● **hard|en|ing** **N-SING**
❑ *...a hardening of public opinion.*
3 **v-t/v-i** When events **harden** people or
when people **harden**, they become less

easily affected emotionally and less
sympathetic and gentle than they were
before. ❑ *Nina's heart hardened against her father.*
[from Old English]

hard-line also **hardline** **ADJ** If you describe
someone's policy or attitude as **hard-line**,
you mean that it is strict or extreme, and
they refuse to change it. ❑ *...the country's
hard-line government.*

hard|ly /hɑrdli/
1 **ADV** You use **hardly** to say that something
is almost, or only just true. ❑ *I hardly know
you.* ❑ *I've hardly slept for three days.*
2 **ADV** You use **hardly** in expressions such
as **hardly ever** and **hardly any** to mean
almost never or almost none. ❑ *We hardly ever
eat fish.* ❑ *They hire young workers with hardly any
experience.* [from Old English]

Usage	**hardly** and **hard**

Hardly is not the adverb form of *hard*. *Hard* is
used for both the adjective: *The test was very
hard.* and the adverb: *The staff worked hard.*
However, to say: "*The staff hardly worked.*" means
that they did not work hard. The adverbs
hardly and *hard* means just about the opposite
of each other.

hard|ship /hɑrdʃɪp/ (**hardships**) **N-COUNT/
N-NONCOUNT** Hardship is a situation in
which your life is difficult or unpleasant.
❑ *Higher bus fares are a hardship on elderly people.*
[from Old English]

| **Word Link** | *ware* ≈ *merchandise* : hard*ware*,
soft*ware*, *ware*house |
|---|---|

hard|ware /hɑrdwɛər/
1 **N-NONCOUNT** TECHNOLOGY In computer
systems, **hardware** is things such as the
computer, the keyboard, and the screen,
rather than the software programs that tell
the computer what to do. Compare with
software. ❑ *The hardware costs about $200.*
2 **N-NONCOUNT** Hardware is tools and
equipment that are used in the home and
garden. ❑ *He bought a hammer and some nails at
a hardware store.*

har|dy /hɑrdi/ (**hardier, hardiest**) **ADJ**
People, animals and plants that are **hardy**
are strong and able to survive difficult
conditions. ❑ *The plant is hardy and easy to grow.*
[from Old French]

harm /hɑrm/ (**harms, harming, harmed**)
1 **v-t** To **harm** someone or something

means to injure or damage them. ❑ *The boys didn't mean to harm anyone.* ❑ *This product may harm the environment.*

2 **N-NONCOUNT** **Harm** is injury or damage to a person or thing. ❑ *Don't worry. He won't do you any harm.* [from Old English]

Thesaurus	harm Also look up :
v	abuse, damage, hurt, injure, ruin, wreck; (*ant.*) benefit **1**
n	abuse, damage, hurt, injury, ruin, violence **2**

Word Partnership	Use harm with :
ADJ	**bodily** harm **2**
v	**cause** harm, **not mean any** harm **2**
N	harm **the environment** **1**

harm|ful /hɑrmfəl/ **ADJ** Something that is **harmful** has a bad effect on someone or something. ❑ *People should know about the harmful effects of the sun.* [from Old English]

harm|less /hɑrmlɪs/ **ADJ** Something that is **harmless** does not have any bad effects. ❑ *These insects are harmless.* [from Old English]

har|mon|ic pro|gres|sion (**harmonic progressions**) **N-COUNT** MUSIC A **harmonic progression** is a series of chords or harmonies within a piece of music.

har|mo|ny /hɑrməni/ (**harmonies**)
1 **N-NONCOUNT** If people are living **in harmony**, they are living together without harming anyone or anything. ❑ *People have lived in harmony with nature for centuries.*
2 **N-COUNT/N-NONCOUNT** MUSIC **Harmony** is the pleasant combination of different notes of music played at the same time. ❑ *The children were singing in harmony.* [from Latin]

harp /hɑrp/ (**harps**) **N-COUNT/N-NONCOUNT** MUSIC A **harp** is a large musical instrument that has strings stretched from the top to the bottom of a frame. You play the harp with your fingers. [from Old English]
→ look at Picture Dictionary: **strings**

harsh /hɑrʃ/ (**harsher, harshest**)
1 **ADJ** If something is **harsh**, it is hard and unpleasant. ❑ *We met during the first harsh winter after the war.*
2 **ADJ** **Harsh** actions or speech are unkind. ❑ *She said many harsh things about her brother.* ● **harsh|ly** **ADV** ❑ *He was harshly treated in prison.*
3 **ADJ** Something that is **harsh** is unpleasant because it is too hard, bright, or

rough. ❑ *The leaves can burn badly in harsh sunlight.* [of Scandinavian origin]

har|vest /hɑrvɪst/ (**harvests, harvesting, harvested**)
1 **N-SING** The **harvest** is the gathering of a farm crop. ❑ *Wheat harvests were poor in both Europe and America last year.*
2 **N-COUNT** A **harvest** is the crop that is gathered in. ❑ *...the potato harvest.*
3 **V-T** When you **harvest** a crop, you gather it in. ❑ *Farmers here still plant and harvest their crops by hand.* [from Old English]
→ look at Word Webs: **farm, grain**

has

> **PRONUNCIATION HELP**
> Pronounce the auxiliary verb /həz, STRONG hæz/. Pronounce the main verb /hæz/.

Has is the third person singular of the present tense of **have**. [from Old English]

hasn't /hæzᵊnt/ **Hasn't** is short for "has not." [from Old English]

haste /heɪst/ **N-NONCOUNT** **Haste** is when you do things too quickly. ❑ *He almost fell down the stairs in his haste to get to the phone.* [from Old French]

has|ten /heɪsᵊn/ (**hastens, hastening, hastened**)
1 **V-T** If you **hasten** an event or a process, you make it happen faster or sooner. ❑ *It was part of a plan to hasten his departure.*
2 **V-T** If you **hasten to** do something, you are quick to do it. ❑ *She hastened to sign the contract.* [from Old French]

has|ty /heɪsti/ (**hastier, hastiest**) **ADJ** A **hasty** action is done suddenly or quickly. ❑ *Perhaps I was too hasty when I said she couldn't come.* ● **hasti|ly** /heɪstɪli/ **ADV** ❑ *A meeting was hastily arranged to discuss the problem.* [from Old French]

hat /hæt/ (**hats**) **N-COUNT** A **hat** is a thing that you wear on your head. ❑ *Look for a woman in a red hat.* [from Old English]
→ look at Picture Dictionary: **hats**

hatch /hætʃ/ (**hatches, hatching, hatched**)
V-T/V-I When a baby bird, an insect, or another animal **hatches**, it comes out of its egg by breaking the shell. You can also say that an egg **hatches**. ❑ *The young birds died soon after they hatched.* ❑ *The eggs hatch after a week.* [of Germanic origin]

h

Picture Dictionary   hats

cowboy hat   top hat   beret   baseball cap

cycle helmet   fedora   balaclava   stocking cap

hard hat   Panama hat   bonnet   mortarboard

hate /heɪt/ (**hates, hating, hated**)
1 **v-т** If you **hate** someone or something, you have a strong feeling of dislike for them. ❑ *She thinks that everyone hates her.* ❑ *He hates losing.*
2 **N-NONCOUNT** Hate is also a noun.
❑ *He spoke of the hate that he felt for some people.* [from Old English]
→ look at Word Web: **emotion**

ha|tred /heɪtrɪd/ **N-NONCOUNT** Hatred is an extremely strong feeling of dislike for someone or something. ❑ *...her hatred of her daughter's killer.* [from Old English]

haul /hɔl/ (**hauls, hauling, hauled**) **v-т** If you **haul** something somewhere, you move it using a lot of effort. ❑ *They hauled the car out of the water.* [from Old French]

haunt /hɔnt/ (**haunts, haunting, haunted**)
1 **v-т** If something unpleasant **haunts** you, you keep thinking or worrying about it over a long period of time. ❑ *The memory of the accident haunted him for a long time.*
2 **N-COUNT** A place that is the **haunt** of a particular person is one that they often visit because they enjoy going there. ❑ *The islands are a favorite summer haunt for tourists.*

3 **v-т** A ghost or a spirit that **haunts** a place or a person regularly appears in the place, or is seen by the person and frightens them. ❑ *His ghost is believed to haunt the room.* [from Old French]

haunt|ed /hɔntɪd/ **ADJ** A **haunted** building is a place where people believe ghosts appear. ❑ *Tracy said the house was haunted.* [from Old French]

---

have
1. AUXILIARY VERB USES
2. USED WITH NOUNS DESCRIBING ACTIONS
3. OTHER VERB USES AND PHRASES
4. MODAL PHRASES

---

① have /həv, STRONG hæv/ (**has, having, had**)

LANGUAGE HELP
When you are speaking, you can use the short forms **I've** for **I have** and **hasn't** for **has not**.

AUX You use **have** and **has** with another verb to form the present or past perfect. ❑ *Alex hasn't left yet.* ❑ *What have you found?* ❑ *Frankie hadn't been feeling well that day.* [from Old English]

In speech, when *have* follows verbs such as *could, should, would, might,* and *must,* contracting *have* makes it sound like *of:* could've sounds like "could of"; might've sounds like "might of"; and so on. Be sure to say (and write) *have* when you don't use contractions: *could have; might have;* and so on.

❷ **have** /hæv/ (**has, having, had**) **v-т** You can use **have** with a noun to talk about an action or an event. ❑ *Come and have a look at this!* ❑ *We had a long talk last night.* ❑ *Come and have a meal with us tonight.* ❑ *We are having a meeting to decide what to do.* ❑ *I had an accident and broke my wrist.* [from Old English]

❸ **have** /hæv/ (**has, having, had**)
■ **v-т** You use **have** to say that someone or something owns something. ❑ *Billy has a new bicycle.*
■ **v-т** You use **have** to talk about people's relationships. ❑ *Do you have any brothers or sisters?*
■ **v-т** You use **have** when you are talking about a person's appearance or character. ❑ *You have beautiful eyes.* ❑ *George has a terrible temper.*
■ **v-т** If you **have** something in a particular position or state, it is in that position or state. ❑ *Mary had her eyes closed.*
■ **v-т** If you **have** something done, someone does it for you. ❑ *He had his hair cut yesterday.*
■ **v-т** If someone **has** something unpleasant happen to them, it happens to them. ❑ *We had our money stolen.*
■ **v-т** If a woman **has** a baby, she gives birth to it. If she **is having** a baby, she is pregnant. ❑ *My wife has just had a baby.* [from Old English]

❹ **have** /hæv, hæf/ (**has, having, had**) **PHRASE** You use **have to** when you are saying that someone must do something, or that something must happen. If you do not **have to** do something, it is not necessary for you to do it. ❑ *I have to go home soon.* ❑ *You have to tell me the truth.* ❑ *"You don't have to explain."* [from Old English]

ha|ven /heɪvᵊn/ (**havens**) **N-COUNT** A **haven** is a place where people or animals feel safe, secure, and happy. ❑ *...Lake Baringo, a haven for birds.* [from Old English]

haven't /hævᵊnt/ **Haven't** is short for "have not." [from Old English]

hawk /hɔk/ (**hawks**) **N-COUNT** A **hawk** is a large bird that catches and eats small birds and animals. [from Old English]

hay /heɪ/ **N-NONCOUNT** Hay is grass that has been cut and dried so that it can be used for feeding animals. [from Old English] → look at Picture Dictionary: **barn**

haz|ard /hæzərd/ (**hazards**) **N-COUNT** A **hazard** is something that could be dangerous. ❑ *Too much salt may be a health hazard.* [from Old French]

haz|ard|ous /hæzərdəs/ **ADJ** Something that is **hazardous** is dangerous, especially to people's health or safety. ❑ *Some people think cell phones are hazardous to health.* [from Old French]

haze /heɪz/ (**hazes**)
■ **N-COUNT/N-NONCOUNT** Haze is light mist, caused by particles of water or dust in the air. ❑ *...a heat haze.*
■ **N-SING** If there is a **haze of** something such as smoke or steam, you cannot see clearly through it. [LITERARY] ❑ *...a haze of smoke.*

HDTV /eɪtʃ di ti vi/ **N-NONCOUNT** TECHNOLOGY **HDTV** is a television system that provides a very clear image. **HDTV** is short for "high-definition television." ❑ *The quality of digital TV is better, especially HDTV.*

he /hi, i, STRONG hi/

PRON You use **he** to talk about a man, a boy, or a male animal. ❑ *John was my boss, but he couldn't remember my name.* [from Old English]

head
❶ NOUN USES
❷ VERB USES
❸ PHRASES

❶ **head** /hɛd/ (**heads**)
■ **N-COUNT** Your **head** is the top part of your body that has your eyes, mouth, and brain in it. ❑ *The ball came down and hit him on the head.*
■ **N-COUNT** Your **head** is your mind. ❑ *I just said the first thing that came into my head.*
■ **N-COUNT** The **head** of a company or an organization is the person who is in charge of it. ❑ *I spoke to the head of the department.*

4 N-COUNT The **head** of something is the top, the start, or the most important end of it. ❑ *She sat at the head of the table.* [from Old English]
→ look at Picture Dictionary: **body**

❷ **head** /hɛd/ (**heads, heading, headed**)
1 V-T If you **head** a department, a company, or an organization, you are the person who is in charge of it. ❑ *Michael Williams heads the department's Office of Civil Rights.*
2 V-T If someone or something **heads** a list or a group, they are at the top or the front of it. ❑ *She heads the list of the most popular actors in the U.S.*
3 V-T If you **are heading** for a particular place, you are going toward that place. ❑ *We're heading back to Washington tomorrow.*
4 V-T/V-I If something or someone is **heading for** a particular result, that result is very likely. ❑ *The talks seem to be heading for failure.* [from Old English]
5 → see also **heading**

❸ **head** /hɛd/
1 PHRASE The cost or amount **a head** or **per head** is the cost or amount for one person. ❑ *This simple meal costs less than $3 a head.*
2 PHRASE If a problem **comes to a head** it becomes so bad that something must be done about it. ❑ *Things came to a head on Saturday when they had a fight.*
3 PHRASE If an idea or a joke goes **over** your **head**, it is too difficult for you to understand. ❑ *A lot of the ideas at the meeting went over my head.* [from Old English]

head|ache /hɛdeɪk/ (**headaches**) N-COUNT
If you have a **headache**, you have a pain in your head. ❑ *I have a terrible headache.*

head|first /hɛdfɜrst/ also **head-first** ADV
If you fall or jump **headfirst**, your head is in front of your body when you are moving. ❑ *He fell headfirst down the stairs.*

head|ing /hɛdɪŋ/ (**headings**)
1 N-COUNT A **heading** is a title that is written at the top of a page. ❑ *When you read the book, notice the chapter headings.* [from Old English]
2 → see also **head** ❷

head|light /hɛdlaɪt/ (**headlights**) N-COUNT
A vehicle's **headlights** are the large lights at the front. ❑ *He turned on the car's headlights when the rain started.*

head|line /hɛdlaɪn/ (**headlines**)
1 N-COUNT A **headline** is the title of a newspaper story, printed in large letters. ❑ *The headline said: "New Government Plans."*
2 N-PLURAL The **headlines** are the important parts of the news that you hear first on radio or television news reports. ❑ *Claudia Polley read the news headlines.*

head of state (**heads of state**) N-COUNT
SOCIAL STUDIES A **head of state** is the leader of a country, for example a president, a king, or a queen. ❑ *More than 200 heads of state attended the meeting.*

head-on
1 ADV If two vehicles hit each other **head-on**, they hit each other with their fronts pointing toward each other. ❑ *The car crashed head-on into a truck.*
2 ADJ **Head-on** is also an adjective. ❑ *There was a serious head-on crash.*
3 ADJ A **head-on** conflict or approach is direct, without any attempt to compromise or avoid the issue. ❑ *...a head-on clash between the president and the government.*
4 ADV **Head-on** is also an adverb. ❑ *I dealt with the issue head-on.*

head|phones /hɛdfoʊnz/ N-PLURAL
Headphones are things that you wear on your ears so that you can listen to music or the radio without anyone else hearing. ❑ *I listened to the program on headphones.*

head|quarters /hɛdkwɔrtərz/ N-SING
The **headquarters** of an organization are its main offices. ❑ *The news broadcast came from Chicago's police headquarters.*

heal /hil/ (**heals, healing, healed**)
1 V-I When a broken bone or other injury **heals**, it becomes healthy again. ❑ *It took six months for her injuries to heal.*
2 V-T/V-I If you **heal** a bad situation, or if it **heals**, the situation is made better so that people are happy again. ❑ *When you remember the other person is your friend, you can begin to heal the disagreement.* [from Old English]

health /hɛlθ/
1 N-NONCOUNT A person's **health** is the condition of their body. ❑ *Too much fatty food is bad for your health.*
2 N-NONCOUNT **Health** is a state in which a person is fit and well. ❑ *In the hospital they nursed me back to health.*
3 N-NONCOUNT The **health** of an

organization or a system is its level of success. ❏ ...*the health of the banking industry.* [from Old English]

health care also **healthcare** **N-NONCOUNT** **Health care** is services for preventing and treating illnesses and injuries. ❏ *Nobody wants to pay more money for health care.*
→ look at Word Web: **hospital**

healthy /hɛlθi/ (**healthier, healthiest**)
1 **ADJ** Someone who is **healthy** is well and is not often sick. ❏ *People need to exercise to be healthy.*
2 **ADJ** Something that is **healthy** is good for your health. ❏ *Try to eat a healthy diet.*
3 **ADJ** A **healthy** organization or system is successful. ❏ ...*an economically healthy country.* [from Old English]

Word Partnership	Use **healthy** with :
N	healthy **baby** **1**
	healthy **diet/food**, healthy **lifestyle** **2**

heap /hip/ (**heaps, heaping, heaped**)
1 **N-COUNT** A **heap of** things is a messy pile of them. ❏ *There was a heap of clothes in the corner of the room.*
2 **V-T** If you **heap** things in a pile, you put them in a large pile. ❏ *His mother heaped more carrots onto Michael's plate.* [from Old English]

hear /hɪər/ (**hears, hearing, heard** /hɜrd/)
1 **V-T/V-I** When you **hear** a sound, you become aware of it through your ears. ❏ *She could hear music in the distance.* ❏ *I heard him say "Thanks."* ❏ *He doesn't hear very well.*
2 **V-T** When a judge or a court of law **hears** a case, they listen to it in order to make a decision about it. [FORMAL] ❏ *The court will hear the case next week.*
3 **V-I** If you **hear from** someone, you receive a letter, an email or a telephone call from them. ❏ *It's always great to hear from you.*
4 **V-T/V-I** If you **hear** information about something, you find out about it by someone telling you, or from the radio or television. ❏ *My mother heard about the school from Karen.* ❏ *I hear that Bruce Springsteen is playing at Madison Square Garden tomorrow evening.*
5 **V-I** If you **have heard of** something or someone, you know about them. ❏ *I've heard of him, but I've never met him.* [from Old English]

Thesaurus hear Also look up :
v   detect, listen, pick up **4**

hear|ing /hɪərɪŋ/ (**hearings**)
1 **N-NONCOUNT** **Hearing** is the sense that makes it possible for you to be aware of sounds. ❏ *His hearing was excellent.*
2 **N-COUNT** A **hearing** is an official meeting that is held in order to collect facts about something bad that has happened. ❏ *The hearing will last about two weeks.* [from Old English]
→ look at Word Web: **disability**

Word Partnership	Use **hearing** with :
N	hearing **impairment/loss** **1**
	court hearing **2**
V	**hold a** hearing, **testify at/before a** hearing **2**

hear|ing aid (**hearing aids**) **N-COUNT** A **hearing aid** is a small piece of equipment that people wear in their ear to help them to hear better.

hear|ing-im|paired /hɪərɪŋ ɪmpɛərd/
1 **ADJ** A **hearing-impaired** person cannot hear as well as most people. ❏ *We apologize to our hearing-impaired viewers for the temporary loss of subtitles.*
2 **N-PLURAL** The **hearing-impaired** are people who are hearing-impaired. ❏ *The hearing-impaired say digital phones interfere with hearing aids.*

heart
❶ NOUN USES
❷ PHRASES

❶ **heart** /hɑrt/ (**hearts**)
1 **N-COUNT** SCIENCE Your **heart** is the organ inside your chest that makes the blood move around your body. ❏ *His heart was beating fast.*
2 **N-COUNT** Your **heart** is your deep feelings. [LITERARY] ❏ *Anne's words filled her heart with joy.*
3 **N-COUNT/N-NONCOUNT** You use **heart** when you are talking about someone's good character. ❏ *She has a good heart.*
4 **N-SING** The **heart of** something is the central and most important part of it. ❏ *The heart of the problem is money.*
5 **N-SING** The **heart of** a place is the middle part of it. ❏ *They own a busy hotel in the heart of the city.*
6 **N-COUNT** A **heart** is the shape ♥.
7 **N-NONCOUNT** **Hearts** is one of the four suits in a deck of playing cards. Each card in

h

the suit is marked with one or more red symbols: ♥. ❑ *...the queen of hearts.*

8 **N-COUNT** A **heart** is a playing card of this suit. ❑ *West had to decide whether to play a heart.* [from Old English]

→ look at Word Webs: **cardiovascular system, donor**

❷ **heart** /hɑrt/

1 **PHRASE** If someone **breaks** your **heart**, they make you very unhappy. ❑ *I fell in love on vacation but the girl broke my heart.*

2 **PHRASE** If you know a poem or a song **by heart**, you can remember every word of it. ❑ *Mike knew this song by heart.*

3 **PHRASE** If you **take** something **to heart**, you are deeply affected and upset by it. ❑ *If someone says something unpleasant, I take it to heart.*

4 **PHRASE** If you feel or believe something **with all** your **heart**, you feel or believe it very strongly. ❑ *I loved him with all my heart.* [from Old English]

heart at|tack (**heart attacks**) **N-COUNT** If someone has a **heart attack**, they suddenly have a lot of pain in their chest and their heart stops working. ❑ *He died of a heart attack.*

heart|beat /hɑrtbit/ (**heartbeats**) **N-SING** SCIENCE Your **heartbeat** is the regular movement of your heart as it pushes blood through your body. ❑ *The doctor listened to her heartbeat.*

heart|worm /hɑrtwɜrm/ (**heartworms**) **N-COUNT/N-NONCOUNT** SCIENCE **Heartworms** are parasitic worms that are spread through mosquito bites and affect cats, dogs, foxes and some other animals. You can also use **heartworm** to mean the disease caused by heartworms.

heat /hit/ (**heats, heating, heated**)

1 **V-T** When you **heat** something, you make it hot. ❑ *Heat the tomatoes and oil in a pan.*

2 **N-NONCOUNT** **Heat** is the feeling of being hot. ❑ *Our clothes dried quickly in the heat of the sun.*

3 **N-NONCOUNT** The **heat** of something is its temperature. ❑ *Check the heat of the oven.*

4 **N-SING** In cooking, you use **heat** to talk about a source of heat, for example on the top of a stove. ❑ *Remove the pan from the heat.* [from Old English]

→ look at Word Webs: **cooking, fire, petroleum, weather**

▶ **heat up** **1** When you **heat** something

up, especially food which has already been cooked and allowed to go cold, you make it hot. ❑ *Freda heated up a pie for me.*

2 When something **heats up**, it gradually becomes hotter. ❑ *In the summer her house heats up like an oven.*

→ look at Word Web: **pan**

heat|ed /hitɪd/

1 **ADJ** A **heated** discussion or quarrel is one where the people involved are angry and excited. ❑ *It was a heated argument.*

2 **ADJ** If someone gets **heated about** something, they get angry and excited about it. ❑ *People get heated about issues such as these.* ● **heat|ed|ly** **ADV** ❑ *The crowd continued to argue heatedly.* [from Old English]

heat en|gine (**heat engines**) **N-COUNT** SCIENCE A **heat engine** is a machine that uses energy from heat to do work.

heat|er /hitər/ (**heaters**) **N-COUNT** A **heater** is a piece of equipment that is used for making a room warm. ❑ *There's an electric heater in the bedroom.* [from Old English]

→ look at Word Web: **aquarium**

heave /hiv/ (**heaves, heaving, heaved**)

1 **V-T** If you **heave** something heavy or difficult to move somewhere, you push, pull, or lift it using a lot of effort. ❑ *Five strong men heaved it up the hill.*

2 **N-COUNT** **Heave** is also a noun. ❑ *It took one heave to throw him into the river.*

3 **V-I** If something **heaves**, it moves up and down with large regular movements. ❑ *His chest heaved as he took a deep breath.* [from Old English]

heav|en /hɛvən/ (**heavens**) **N-PROPER** **Heaven** is the place where some people believe good people go when they die. ❑ *I believe that when I die I will go to heaven.* [from Old English]

heavy /hɛvi/ (**heavier, heaviest**)

1 **ADJ** Something that is **heavy** weighs a lot. ❑ *This bag is very heavy. What's in it?*

2 **ADJ** You use **heavy** to talk about how much someone or something weighs. ❑ *How heavy is your suitcase?*

3 **ADJ** **Heavy** means great in amount. ❑ *We drove through heavy traffic for two hours.* ● **heavi|ly** **ADV** ❑ *It rained heavily all day.* [from Old English]

heavy|weight /hɛviweɪt/ (**heavyweights**)

1 **N-COUNT** SPORTS A **heavyweight** is a boxer

weighing more than 175 pounds and therefore in the heaviest class.

2 **N-COUNT** If you refer to a person or an organization as a **heavyweight**, you mean that they have a lot of influence, experience, and importance in a particular field. ❑ *He was a political heavyweight.*

hec|tic /hɛktɪk/ **ADJ** A **hectic** situation is very busy and involves a lot of activity. ❑ *Ben had a hectic work schedule.* [from Late Latin]

he'd /hid, id, STRONG hid/
1 **He'd** is short for "he had." ❑ *He'd seen her before.*
2 **He'd** is short for "he would." ❑ *He'd like to come with us.*

hedge /hɛdʒ/ (**hedges, hedging, hedged**)
1 **N-COUNT** A **hedge** is a row of bushes or small trees, usually along the edge of a lawn, a garden, a field, or a road.
2 **V-I** If you **hedge against** something unpleasant or unwanted that might affect you, especially losing money, you do something which will protect you from it. ❑ *You can hedge against illness with insurance.*
3 **PHRASE** If you **hedge** your **bets**, you reduce your chances of losing by supporting more than one person or thing. ❑ *The organization may support one candidate, or hedge its bets by supporting several candidates.* [from Old English]

hedge|hog cac|tus (**hedgehog cacti**)
N-COUNT/N-NONCOUNT SCIENCE Hedgehog cactus is a name given to several types of cactus with short, sharp points, especially a type that has edible fruit.

heel /hil/ (**heels**)
1 **N-COUNT** Your **heel** is the back part of your foot, just below your ankle.
2 **N-COUNT** The **heel** of a shoe is the raised part on the bottom at the back. ❑ *She always wears shoes with high heels.* [from Old English]
→ look at Picture Dictionary: **foot**

height /haɪt/ (**heights**)
1 **N-COUNT/N-NONCOUNT** The **height** of a person or a thing is their size from the bottom to the top. ❑ *Her weight is normal for her height.* ❑ *I am five feet six inches in height.*
2 **N-COUNT/N-NONCOUNT** A particular **height** is the distance that something is above the ground. ❑ *It's very easy to change the height of the seat.*

3 **N-SING** If something is **the height of** a particular quality, it has that quality to the greatest degree. ❑ *The dress was the height of fashion.* [from Old English]
→ look at Picture Dictionary: **area**

Word Partnership	Use **height** with :
ADJ	**average** height, **medium** height, **the right** height **1**
V	**reach a** height **1**
N	height **and weight**, height **and width 1** **the** height **of fashion/popularity/ style 3**

height|en /haɪt³n/ (**heightens, heightening, heightened**) **V-T/V-I** If something **heightens** a feeling or if the feeling **heightens**, the feeling increases in degree or intensity. ❑ *It heightened awareness of the differences between them.* ❑ *Chris's interest in her heightened.* [from Old English]

heir /ɛər/ (**heirs**) **N-COUNT** An **heir** is someone who will receive a person's money or property when that person dies. ❑ *Elizabeth was her father's heir.* [from Old French]

held /hɛld/ **Held** is the past tense and past participle of **hold**. [from Old English]

heli|cop|ter /hɛlɪkɒptər/ (**helicopters**) **N-COUNT** A **helicopter** is an aircraft with long blades on top that go around very fast. It is able to stay still in the air and to move straight upward or downward. [from French]
→ look at Word Web: **fly**

helicopter

he|lium /hiliəm/ **N-NONCOUNT** SCIENCE Helium is a very light gas that is colorless and has no smell.

hell /hɛl/
1 **N-PROPER** **Hell** is the place where some people believe bad people go when they die. ❑ *My mother says I'll go to hell if I lie.*
2 **N-NONCOUNT** If you say that a particular situation or place is **hell**, you mean that it is very unpleasant. ❑ *...the hell of prison.* [from Old English]

h

he'll /hɪl, il, STRONG hil/ **He'll** is short for "he will." ❏ *He'll be very successful, I'm sure.*

hel|lo /hɛloʊ/ also **hullo**

1 INTERJ You say **Hello** to someone when you meet them. ❏ *Hello, Margaret. How are you?*

2 INTERJ You say **Hello** when you answer the phone. ❏ *Cohen picked up the phone and said, "Hello?"*

hel|met /hɛlmɪt/ (**helmets**) N-COUNT

A **helmet** is a hat made of a hard material, that you wear to protect your head. [from Old French] → look at Picture Dictionary: **hats** → look at Word Web: **army**

helmet

help /hɛlp/ (**helps, helping, helped**)

1 V-T/V-I If you **help** someone, you make it easier for them to do something. ❏ *Can somebody help me, please?* ❏ *You can help by giving them some money.*

2 N-NONCOUNT **Help** is also a noun. ❏ *Thanks very much for your help.*

3 V-T/V-I If something **helps**, it improves a situation. ❏ *Thanks for your advice. That helps.* ❏ *He helped to raise money.*

4 N-SING **Help** is also a noun. ❏ *Thank you. You've been a great help.*

5 INTERJ You shout **Help!** when you are in danger in order to attract someone's attention. ❏ *Help! I'm drowning!*

6 V-T If you **help yourself to** something, you take what you want. ❏ *There's bread on the table. Help yourself.*

7 PHRASE If you **can't help** the way you feel or behave, you cannot stop it from happening. ❏ *I couldn't help laughing when I saw her face.* [from Old English] → look at Word Web: **donor**

Usage help

After *help*, you can use the infinitive with or without *to*: *Budi helped Lastri study for the exam; then he asked her to help him to write an email to the professor.*

Thesaurus help Also look up :

V	aid, assist, support; (*ant.*) hinder **1**
N	aid, assistance, guidance, support **1**

Word Partnership Use **help** with :

ADJ	**financial** help, **professional** help **1**
V	**ask for** help, **get** help, **need** help, **want to** help **1**
	try to help **1 3**
	cry/scream/shout for help **3**
	cant help **thinking/feeling** *something* **5**

help|ful /hɛlpfəl/

1 ADJ If someone is **helpful**, they help you by being useful or willing to work for you. ❏ *The staff in the hotel are very helpful.*

2 ADJ Something that is **helpful** makes a situation easier. ❏ *It is helpful to have someone with you when you go to the doctor.* [from Old English]

help|less /hɛlpləs/ ADJ If you are **helpless**, you do not have the strength or ability to do anything useful. ❏ *Parents often feel helpless when their children are sick.* ● **help|less|ly** ADV ❏ *They watched helplessly as the house burned to the ground.* [from Old English]

Word Link *sphere ≈ ball : atmo*sphere, *blogo*sphere, *hemi*sphere

---

hemi|sphere /hɛmɪsfɪər/ (**hemispheres**)

1 N-COUNT GEOGRAPHY A **hemisphere** is one half of the Earth. ❏ *These animals live in the northern hemisphere.*

2 N-NONCOUNT MATH A **hemisphere** is one half of a sphere. → look at Picture Dictionaries: **globe, solids**

hen /hɛn/ (**hens**) N-COUNT A **hen** is a female chicken. [from Old English]

hence|forth /hɛnsfɔrθ/ ADV **Henceforth** means from this or that time onward. [FORMAL] ❏ *Henceforth all groups were equal to one another.*

her /hər, ər, STRONG hɜr/

LANGUAGE HELP

Her is a third person singular pronoun. **Her** is used as the object of a verb or a preposition. **Her** is also a possessive determiner.

---

1 PRON You use **her** to talk about a woman, a girl, or a female animal. ❏ *I told her that dinner was ready.*

2 DET You use **her** to show that something belongs to or relates to a girl or a woman. ❏ *She took her coat off and sat down.* ❏ *She traveled around the world with her husband.* [from Old English]

her|ald /hɛrəld/ (**heralds, heralding, heralded**)

1 **V-T** Something that **heralds** a future event or situation is a sign that it is going to happen or appear. [FORMAL] ❑ *This discovery could herald a cure for cancer.*

2 **N-COUNT** Something that is a **herald of** a future event or situation is a sign that it is going to happen or appear. [FORMAL] ❑ *These cool mornings are a herald of fall.* [from Old French]

herb /ɜrb/ (**herbs**) **N-COUNT** An **herb** is a plant whose leaves are used in cooking to add flavor to food, or as a medicine. ❑ *Fry the mushrooms in a little olive oil and add the chopped herbs.* ● **herb|al** **ADJ** ❑ *Do you know any herbal remedies for colds?* [from Old French]

her|bi|vore /hɜrbɪvɔr, ɜr-/ (**herbivores**) **N-COUNT** **SCIENCE** A **herbivore** is an animal that eats only plants. Compare with **carnivore** and **omnivore**. [from New Latin]
→ look at Word Webs: **herbivore, carnivore**

herb|i|vor|ous /hɜrbɪvərəs, ɜr-/ **ADJ** **Herbivorous** animals only eat plants. [from New Latin]

herd /hɜrd/ (**herds, herding, herded**)

1 **N-COUNT** A **herd** is a large group of one type of animal that lives together. ❑ *Herds of elephants crossed the river each day.*

2 **V-T** If you **herd** people or animals somewhere, you make them move there in a group. ❑ *He began to herd the prisoners out.* ❑ *Stefano used a dog to herd the sheep.* [from Old English]

here /hɪər/

1 **ADV** You use **here** when you are talking about the place where you are. ❑ *I can't stay here all day.* ❑ *Come and sit here.*

2 **ADV** You use **here** to draw attention to something or someone who has just arrived. ❑ *"Here's the taxi," she said.*

3 **ADV** You use **here** to refer to a particular point in time that you have come to. ❑ *It's here that our problems started.*

4 **ADV** You use **here** when you are offering or giving something to someone. ❑ *Here's your coffee.* [from Old English]

he|red|ity /hɪrɛdɪti/ **N-NONCOUNT** **Heredity** is the process by which features and characteristics are passed on from parents to their children before the children are born. [from Old French]

her|etic /hɛrɪtɪk/ (**heretics**)

1 **N-COUNT** A **heretic** is someone whose beliefs or actions are considered wrong by most people, because they conflict with beliefs that are generally accepted. ❑ *He was considered a heretic and was ridiculed for his ideas.*

2 **N-COUNT** A **heretic** is a person who belongs to a particular religion, but whose beliefs or actions seriously conflict with the principles of that religion. ❑ *These so-called Christians were classified as heretics by the Church.* [from Old French]

her|it|age /hɛrɪtɪdʒ/ (**heritages**) **N-COUNT/ N-NONCOUNT** A country's **heritage** is all the qualities, traditions, or features of life there that have continued over many years and have been passed on from one generation to another. ❑ *Old buildings are part of our heritage.* [from Old French]

hero /hɪəroʊ/ (**heroes**)

1 **N-COUNT** **LANGUAGE ARTS** The **hero** of a story is the main male character. ❑ *The actor Daniel Radcliffe plays the hero in the Harry Potter movies.*

2 **N-COUNT** A **hero** is someone who has done something brave or good. ❑ *Mr. Mandela is a hero who has inspired millions.* [from Latin]
→ look at Word Webs: **hero, myth**

he|ro|ic /hɪroʊɪk/ **ADJ** If a person or their actions are **heroic**, you admire them because they have been very brave. ❑ *He made a heroic*

h

---

herbivore

Herbivores come in all shapes and sizes. The tiny aphid lives on the juices found in **plants**. The **elephant** eats 100 to 1,000 pounds of **vegetation** a day. Some herbivores prefer a single plant. For example, the **koala** eats only eucalyptus **leaves**. **Cattle graze** on **grass** all day long. In the evening they regurgitate food from their stomachs and chew it again. **Rabbits** have two pairs of long teeth in the front of their mouths. These teeth never stop growing. They use them to gnaw on hard **seeds**.

Word Web   hero

Odysseus is a **hero** from Greek **mythology**. He is a warrior. He is brave in battle. He faces many **dangers**. However, he knows he must return home after the Trojan War*. During his **epic** journey home, Odysseus faces many difficulties. He must survive wild storms at sea and fight a monster. At home Penelope, Odysseus' wife, **defends** their home and **protects** their son. She remains **loyal** and **brave** through many trials. She is the **heroine** of the story.

Trojan War: a legendary war between Greece and Troy. Odysseus saves his men from the Cyclops.

effort to save the boy from the fire. [from Latin]

hero|in /hɛroʊɪn/ **N-NONCOUNT** Heroin is a strong illegal drug. [from German]

hero|ine /hɛroʊɪn/ (**heroines**)
■ **N-COUNT** LANGUAGE ARTS The **heroine** of a story is the main female character. ❑ *The heroine of the book is a young doctor.*
■ **N-COUNT** A **heroine** is a woman who has done something brave or good. ❑ *China's first gold medal winner became a national heroine.* [from Latin]
→ look at Word Web: **hero**

hers /hɜrz/

> **LANGUAGE HELP**
> **Hers** is a third person possessive pronoun.

PRON You use **hers** to show that something belongs to a woman, a girl, or a female animal. ❑ *She admitted that the bag was hers.*

her|self /hərsɛlf/

> **LANGUAGE HELP**
> **Herself** is a third person singular reflexive pronoun. **Herself** is used when the object of a verb or preposition refers to the same person as the subject of the verb.

■ **PRON** You use **herself** to talk about a woman, a girl, or a female animal that you have just mentioned. ❑ *She looked at herself in the mirror.* ❑ *If she's not careful, she'll hurt herself.*
■ **PRON** If a woman or a girl does something **herself**, she, and not anyone else, does it. ❑ *She doesn't go to the hairdresser's. She cuts it herself.*

Hertz|sprung-Rus|sell dia|gram /hɛərtsprʊŋrʌsᵊl daɪəgræm/ (**Hertzsprung-Russell diagrams**) **N-COUNT** SCIENCE The **Hertzsprung-Russell diagram** is a chart used in astronomy to show the relationships between different types of stars. The abbreviations **H-R diagram** and **HRD** are also used. [after Ejnar Hertzsprung (1873-1967), a Danish astronomer, and Henry Norris Russell (1877-1957), a U.S. astronomer and astrophysicist]

he's /hiz, ɪz, STRONG hiz/ **He's** is short for "he is" or "he has." ❑ *He's coming home tomorrow.*

hesi|tate /hɛzɪteɪt/ (**hesitates, hesitating, hesitated**)
■ **V-I** If you **hesitate**, you do not act quickly, usually because you are not sure about what to say or do. ❑ *Catherine hesitated before answering.* ● **hesi|ta|tion** /hɛzɪteɪʃᵊn/ (**hesitations**) **N-COUNT/N-NONCOUNT** ❑ *After some hesitation, she replied, "I'll have to think about that."*
■ **V-T** If you **hesitate to** do something, you are unwilling to do it. ❑ *Don't hesitate to ask if you have any questions.* [from Latin]

hetero|geneous /hɛtərədʒiniəs, -dʒinyəs/ **ADJ** A **heterogeneous** group consists of many different types of things or people. [from Medieval Latin] [FORMAL]

hetero|geneous mix|ture (**heterogeneous mixtures**) **N-COUNT** SCIENCE In chemistry, a **heterogeneous mixture** is a mixture of two or more substances that remain separate, for example oil and water.

hetero|sex|ual /hɛtəroʊsɛkʃuəl/ (**heterosexuals**)
■ **ADJ** Someone who is **heterosexual** is sexually attracted to people of the opposite sex. ❑ *...heterosexual couples.*
● **hetero|sexu|al|ity** /hɛtəroʊsɛkʃuælɪti/ **N-NONCOUNT** ❑ *He is proud of his heterosexuality.*

2 **N-COUNT** **Heterosexual** is also a noun. ☐ ...unmarried heterosexuals.

hexa|gon /hɛksəgɒn/ (**hexagons**) **N-COUNT** MATH A **hexagon** is a shape with six straight sides. [from Late Latin]

hey /heɪ/
1 **INTERJ** In informal situations, you say or shout **Hey** to attract someone's attention. ☐ "Hey! Be careful!" shouted Patty.
2 **INTERJ** In informal situations, you can say **Hey** to greet someone. ☐ He smiled and said "Hey, Kate." [from Old French]

hi /haɪ/ **INTERJ** In informal situations, you say **Hi** to greet someone. ☐ "Hi, Liz," she said.

hi|ber|nate /haɪbərneɪt/ (**hibernates, hibernating, hibernated**) **V-I** SCIENCE Animals that **hibernate** spend the winter in a state like a deep sleep. [from Latin]

hi|ber|na|tion /haɪbərneɪʃ°n/ **N-NONCOUNT** SCIENCE **Hibernation** is when some animals sleep through the winter. ☐ The animals consume three times more calories to prepare for hibernation. [from Latin]

hic|cup /hɪkʌp/ (**hiccups, hiccuping** or **hiccupping, hiccuped** or **hiccupped**)
1 **N-PLURAL** When you have **hiccups**, you make repeated short sounds in your throat, often because you have been eating or drinking too quickly. ☐ Do you know how to cure hiccups?
2 **V-I** When you **hiccup**, you make repeated short sounds in your throat. ☐ He laughed so hard he started hiccuping.

hid /hɪd/ **Hid** is the past tense of **hide**. [from Old English]

hid|den /hɪd°n/
1 **Hidden** is the past participle of **hide**.
2 **ADJ Hidden** things are not easy to see or know about. ☐ There are hidden dangers on the beach. [from Old English]

hide /haɪd/ (**hides, hiding, hid, hidden**)
1 **V-T** If you **hide** something or someone, you put them in a place where they cannot easily be seen or found. ☐ He hid the bicycle behind the wall.
2 **V-T/V-I** If you **hide**, or if you **hide yourself**, you go somewhere where people cannot easily find you. ☐ The little boy hid in the closet.
3 **V-T** To **hide** something means to cover it so that people cannot see it. ☐ She hid her face in her hands.

4 **V-T** If you **hide** what you feel or know, you do not let people know about it. ☐ Lee tried to hide his excitement. [from Old English]

Word Partnership	Use **hide** with :
ADV	**nowhere to** hide **1** **2**
V	**attempt/try to** hide **1** **4**
	run and hide **2**
N	hide **your face** **3**
	hide **a fact/secret**, hide **your fear/feelings/tears/** **4**

hid|eous /hɪdiəs/ **ADJ** If someone or something is **hideous**, they are very ugly or unpleasant. ☐ She saw a hideous face at the window. ☐ He was injured in a hideous knife attack. ● **hid|eous|ly** **ADV** ☐ I was convinced that I was hideously ugly. [from Old French]

hid|ing /haɪdɪŋ/ **N-NONCOUNT** If someone is **in hiding**, they have secretly gone somewhere where they cannot be seen or found. ☐ Cohen is in hiding with his wife. [from Old English]

high /haɪ/ (**higher, highest**)
1 **ADJ** Something that is **high** extends a long way from the bottom to the top. ☐ They lived in a house with a high wall around it. ☐ Mount Marcy is the highest mountain in the Adirondacks.
2 **ADJ** You use **high** to talk or ask about how much something measures from the bottom to the top. ☐ The grass in the yard was a foot high.
3 **ADJ** If something is **high**, it is a long way above the ground. ☐ I looked down from the high window. ☐ The sun was high in the sky.
4 **ADV High** is also an adverb. ☐ She can jump higher than other people.
5 **ADJ High** means great in amount or strength. ☐ High winds destroyed many trees and buildings. ☐ The number of people injured was high.
6 **ADJ** A **high** sound or voice is not deep. ☐ She spoke in a high voice.
7 **ADJ** If something is a **high** priority, it is very important for you to do. ☐ The government made education a high priority.
8 **ADJ** Someone who is **high in** a particular organization has an important position. ☐ He was very high in the administration.
9 **ADJ** If the quality of something is **high**, it is very good. ☐ This is high quality stuff. [from Old English]

high-defi|ni|tion also **high definition**
1 **ADJ High-definition** television or technology is a digital system that gives a

h

clearer picture than traditional television systems. ❑ ...*high-definition TV, with its sharper images and improved sound.*

2 **N-NONCOUNT** **High definition** is also a noun. ❑ *These games are more popular now that they are available in high definition.*

high|er edu|ca|tion **N-NONCOUNT** **Higher education** is education at universities and colleges. ❑ ...*students in higher education.*

high-fre|quen|cy word (**high-frequency words**) **N-COUNT** LANGUAGE ARTS **High-frequency words** are words that occur much more often than most other words in written or spoken language.

high jump **N-SING** SPORTS The **high jump** is a sports event that involves jumping over a bar that can be raised higher after each jump.

high|light /haɪlaɪt/ (**highlights, highlighting, highlighted**)

1 **V-T** If someone or something **highlights** a point or a problem, they show that it is important. ❑ *Her talk highlighted the problems of homeless people.*

2 **N-COUNT** The **highlights of** an event are the most interesting parts of it. ❑ *That tennis game was one of the highlights of the tournament.*

high|ly /haɪli/

1 **ADV** **Highly** is used before some adjectives to mean "very." ❑ *Mr. Singh was a highly successful salesman.*

2 **ADV** If you think **highly** of something or someone, you think they are very good. ❑ *Michael thought highly of the school.* [from Old English]

Word Partnership	Use **highly** with :
ADJ	highly **addictive**, highly **competitive**, highly **controversial**, highly **critical**, highly **educated**, highly **intelligent**, highly **qualified**, highly **skilled**, highly **successful**, highly **technical**, highly **trained**, highly **unlikely**, highly **visible 1**
V	highly **recommended**, highly **respected 1**

high-main|te|nance also **high maintenance** **ADJ** If you describe something or someone as **high-maintenance**, you mean that they require a lot of time, money, or effort. ❑ *Small gardens*

can be high maintenance. ❑ *She is particularly good at dealing with some of the hotel's more high-maintenance guests.*

high power lens (**high power lenses**) **N-COUNT** SCIENCE A **high power lens** is a very powerful lens on an instrument such as a microscope.

high school (**high schools**) **N-COUNT/ N-NONCOUNT** A **high school** is a school for children usually aged between fourteen and eighteen. ❑ *My daughter has just started high school.*
→ look at Word Web: **graduation**

high-tech /haɪ tɛk/ also **high tech, hi tech** **ADJ** TECHNOLOGY **High-tech** equipment uses modern methods and computers. ❑ ...*high-tech camera equipment.*

high tide **N-NONCOUNT** At the coast, **high tide** is the time when the sea is at its highest level because the tide is in.
→ look at Word Web: **tide**

high|way /haɪweɪ/ (**highways**) **N-COUNT** A **highway** is a main road that connects towns or cities. ❑ *The accident happened on the highway between Chicago and Madison.* [from Old English]
→ look at Word Web: **traffic**

hi|jack /haɪdʒæk/ (**hijacks, hijacking, hijacked**)

1 **V-T** If someone **hijacks** a plane or other vehicle, they illegally take control of it while it is traveling from one place to another. ❑ *Two men hijacked the plane.*

2 **N-COUNT** **Hijack** is also a noun. ❑ *Finally, six months after the hijack, he was arrested.*

hike /haɪk/ (**hikes, hiking, hiked**)

1 **N-COUNT** A **hike** is a long walk, especially outside of a city. ❑ *We went for a hike up Mount Desmond.*

2 **V-I** If you **hike**, you go for a long walk. ❑ *We hiked through the Fish River Canyon.* ● **hik|er** (**hikers**) **N-COUNT** ❑ *The hikers spent the night in the mountains.* ● **hik|ing** **N-NONCOUNT** ❑ *I love hiking in the mountains.*

3 **V-T** To **hike** prices or taxes means to increase them suddenly or by a large amount. [INFORMAL] ❑ *The company hiked its prices by 5 percent.*
→ look at Picture Dictionary: **shoe**

hi|lari|ous /hɪlɛəriəs/ **ADJ** If something is **hilarious**, it is very funny. ❑ *He told me a hilarious story.* [from Latin]

hill /hɪl/ (hills) **N-COUNT** GEOGRAPHY A **hill** is an area of land that is higher than the land around it. ❑ *The castle is on a hill above the old town.* [from Old English]

hilly /ˈhɪli/ (hillier, hilliest) **ADJ** A **hilly** area has a lot of hills. ❑ *The countryside in this area is quite hilly.* [from Old English]

him /hɪm/

> **LANGUAGE HELP**
>
> **Him** is a third person singular pronoun. **Him** is used as the object of a verb or a preposition.

PRON You use **him** to talk about a man, a boy, or a male animal. ❑ *Elaine met him at the railroad station.* ❑ *Is Sam there? Let me talk to him.* [from Old English]

him|self /hɪmˈsɛlf/

> **LANGUAGE HELP**
>
> **Himself** is a third person singular reflexive pronoun. **Himself** is used when the object of a verb or preposition refers to the same person as the subject of the verb.

1 **PRON** You use **himself** to talk about a man, a boy, or a male animal that you have just mentioned. ❑ *He poured himself a cup of coffee.* ❑ *He was talking to himself.*
2 **PRON** If a man or a boy does something **himself**, he, and not anyone else, does it. ❑ *He made your card himself.* ❑ *He'll probably tell you about it himself.* [from Old English]

Hin|du /ˈhɪndu/ (Hindus)
1 **N-COUNT** A **Hindu** is a person who believes in Hinduism.
2 **ADJ** **Hindu** describes things that belong or relate to Hinduism. ❑ *We visited a Hindu temple.* [from Persian]

Hin|du|ism /ˈhɪnduɪzəm/ **N-NONCOUNT** **Hinduism** is an Indian religion. It has many gods and teaches that people have another life on Earth after they die. [from Persian]

hinge /hɪndʒ/ (hinges) **N-COUNT** A **hinge** is a piece of metal that is used for joining two pieces of wood together so that they open and shut. ❑ *The hinge is broken and the door won't shut.* [from Old English]

hint /hɪnt/ (hints, hinting, hinted)
1 **N-COUNT** A **hint** is a suggestion that is not made directly. ❑ *Has he given you any hints about what he wants for his birthday?*
2 **V-I** If you **hint** at something, you suggest it in a way that is not direct. ❑ *She has hinted at the possibility of having a baby.*
3 **N-COUNT** A **hint** is a helpful piece of advice. ❑ *Here are some helpful hints to make your trip easier.*
4 **N-SING** A **hint of** something is a very small amount of it. ❑ *...pancakes with a hint of vanilla.* ❑ *...a hint of a smile.*

Word Partnership	Use **hint** with :
V	take a hint **1**
	drop a hint, give a hint **1** **3**
ADJ	helpful hint **3**
	slight hint **4**

hip /hɪp/ (hips) **N-COUNT** Your **hips** are the two areas or bones at the sides of your body between the tops of your legs and your waist. ❑ *Tracey put her hands on her hips and laughed.* [from Old English]

hip-hop **N-NONCOUNT** MUSIC **Hip-hop** is a type of music and dance that developed among African-American people in the United States in the 1970s and 1980s.

hippo|pota|mus /hɪpəˈpɒtəməs/ (hippopotamuses) **N-COUNT** A **hippopotamus** is a very large animal with short legs and thick skin that lives in and near rivers. [from Latin]

hire /haɪər/ (hires, hiring, hired) **V-T** If you **hire** someone, you pay them to do a job for you. ❑ *He just hired a new secretary.* [from Old English]

his

> **PRONUNCIATION HELP**
>
> Pronounce the determiner /hɪz/. Pronounce the pronoun /hɪz/.

> **LANGUAGE HELP**
>
> **His** is a third person singular possessive determiner. **His** is also a possessive pronoun.

1 **DET** You use **his** to show that something belongs or relates to a man, a boy, or a male animal. ❑ *He spent part of his career in Hollywood.* ❑ *He went to the party with his girlfriend.*
2 **PRON** **His** is also a pronoun. ❑ *Henry said the decision was his.* [from Old English]

His|pan|ic /hɪˈspænɪk/ (Hispanics)
1 **ADJ** SOCIAL STUDIES A **Hispanic** person is a citizen of the United States of America who originally came from Latin America, or

whose family originally came from Latin America. ❑ ...a group of Hispanic doctors.

2 **N-COUNT** SOCIAL STUDIES A **Hispanic** is someone who is Hispanic. ❑ About 80 percent of Hispanics here are U.S. citizens. [from Latin]

hiss /hɪs/ (**hisses, hissing, hissed**)
1 **V-I** To **hiss** means to make a sound like a long "s." ❑ My cat hisses when I step on its tail.
2 **N-COUNT** Hiss is also a noun. ❑ The hiss of steam came from the kitchen.

his|to|gram /hɪstəgræm/ (**histograms**)
N-COUNT SCIENCE A **histogram** is a graph that uses vertical bars with no spaces between them to represent the distribution of a set of data.

his|to|rian /hɪstɔriən/ (**historians**)
N-COUNT SOCIAL STUDIES A **historian** is a person who specializes in the study of history, and who writes books and articles about it. [from Latin]
→ look at Word Web: **history**

his|tor|ic /hɪstɔrɪk/ **ADJ** Something that is **historic** is important in history, or likely to be considered important at some time in the future. ❑ ...the historic changes in Eastern Europe. [from Latin]

his|tori|cal /hɪstɔrɪkəl/
1 **ADJ** **Historical** people, situations, or things existed in the past and are considered to be a part of history. ❑ ...an important historical figure.
● **his|tori|cal|ly** **ADV** ❑ Historically, royal marriages have been unhappy.
2 **ADJ** **Historical** books, works of art, or

studies are concerned with people, situations, or things that existed in the past. ❑ ...a historical novel about nineteenth-century France. ❑ ...historical records. [from Latin]

his|to|ry /hɪstəri, -tri/ (**histories**)
1 **N-NONCOUNT** SOCIAL STUDIES **History** is events that happened in the past. ❑ The film showed great moments in football history.
2 **N-NONCOUNT** SOCIAL STUDIES **History** is the study of events that happened in the past. ❑ He studied history at Indiana University.
3 **N-COUNT** If a person or a place has **a history of** something, that thing has been common in their past. ❑ He had a history of health problems.
4 **N-COUNT** Someone's **history** is the facts that are known about their past. ❑ He couldn't get a new job because of his medical history. [from Latin]
→ look at Word Web: **history**

Word Web   history

 3800 BC The wheel is invented.

 31 BC Roman Empire founded.

1200 AD Incan empire is founded.

 1969 Humans land on the Moon.

 2600 BC The Pyramid of Giza is built.

 700 AD The Great Wall of China is started.

 1492 Columbus sails for America.

Open any history textbook and you will find **timelines**. They show important dates for **ancient civilizations**—when **empires** appeared and disappeared, and when **wars** were fought. But, how much of what we read in **history** books is **fact**? **Accounts** of the **past** are often based on how **archaeologists** interpret the **artifacts** they find. **Scholars** often rely on the **records** of the people who were in power. These **historians** included certain facts and left out others. Historians today look beyond official records. They research **documents** such as **diaries**. They describe **events** from different **points of view**.

hit /hɪt/ (hits, hitting, hit)

> **LANGUAGE HELP**
>
> The form **hit** is used in the present tense and is the past tense and past participle.

1 **V-T** If you **hit** someone or something, you touch them with a lot of force. ❑ *She hit the ball hard.*

2 **V-T** When one thing **hits** another, it touches it with a lot of force. ❑ *The car hit a traffic sign.*

3 **N-COUNT** **Hit** is also a noun. ❑ *The building took a direct hit from the bomb.*

4 **V-T** If something **hits** a person, a place, or a thing, it affects them very badly. ❑ *The earthquake hit northern Peru.*

5 **N-COUNT** If a song, a movie, or a play is a **hit**, it is very popular and successful. ❑ *The song was a big hit in Japan.*

6 **N-COUNT** A **hit** is a single visit to a web page. ❑ *The company has had 78,000 hits on its website.*

7 **N-COUNT** If someone who is searching for information on the Internet gets a **hit**, they find a website that contains that information.

8 **PHRASE** If two people **hit it off**, they become friendly. [INFORMAL] ❑ *Dad and Walter hit it off right away.* [from Old English]

> **Thesaurus** hit Also look up :
> V   bang, beat, knock, pound, slap, smack, strike **1**
> N   smash, success, triumph; (ant.) failure **5**

> **Word Partnership** Use hit with :
> N   hit **a ball**, hit **a button**, hit **the brakes 1**
>   earthquakes/famine/storms hit *someplace* **3**
>   a hit **movie/show/song 4**

hitch|hike /hɪtʃhaɪk/ (hitchhikes, hitchhiking, hitchhiked) V-I If you **hitchhike**, you travel by getting rides from passing vehicles without paying. ❑ *Neil hitchhiked to New York during his vacation.* ● **hitch|hiker** (hitchhikers) **N-COUNT** ❑ *On my way to Vancouver I picked up a hitchhiker.*

HIV /eɪtʃ aɪ viː/

1 **N-NONCOUNT** **HIV** is a virus that reduces the ability of people's bodies to fight illness and that can cause AIDS.

2 **PHRASE** If someone is **HIV positive**, they are infected with the HIV virus, and may develop AIDS. If someone is **HIV negative**, they are not infected with the virus.

hive /haɪv/ (hives) N-COUNT A **hive** is a structure in which bees live. [from Old English]

hoax /hoʊks/ (hoaxes) N-COUNT A **hoax** is when someone says that something bad is going to happen, when this is not true. ❑ *Police say that the bomb alert was a hoax.*

hob|by /hɒbi/ (hobbies) N-COUNT A **hobby** is an activity that you enjoy doing in your free time. ❑ *My hobbies are music and tennis.*

> **Thesaurus** hobby Also look up :
> N   activity, craft, interest, pastime

hock|ey /hɒki/ N-NONCOUNT SPORTS **Hockey** is a game that is played on ice between two teams who try to score goals using long curved sticks to hit a small rubber disk. ❑ *The Australian men's hockey team finished second.*

hock|ey stick (hockey sticks) N-COUNT SPORTS A **hockey stick** is a long curved stick that is used for hitting a small rubber disk in the game of hockey.

> ──────────── **hold** ────────────
> **1** PHYSICALLY TOUCHING, SUPPORTING, OR CONTAINING
> **2** HAVING OR DOING
> **3** CONTROLLING OR REMAINING
> **4** PHRASES AND PHRASAL VERBS

1 hold /hoʊld/ (holds, holding, held)

1 **V-T** When you **hold** something, you have it in your hands or your arms. ❑ *She held his hand tightly.* ❑ *I held the baby in my arms.*

2 **N-COUNT** **Hold** is also a noun. ❑ *Cooper took hold of the rope and pulled on it.*

3 **V-T** When you **hold** something in a particular position, you put it into that position and keep it there. ❑ *Hold your hands up.* ❑ *Try to hold the camera steady.*

4 **N-COUNT** In a ship or an airplane, the **hold** is the place where goods or luggage are stored.

5 **V-T** If something **holds** a particular amount of something, it can contain that amount. ❑ *The stadium is massive and can hold over 70,000 people.* [from Old English]

② hold /hoʊld/ (**holds, holding, held**)

1 **v-т** If you **hold** an opinion or a belief, that is your opinion or belief. ❑ *He held opinions which were usually different from mine.*

2 **v-т** If people **hold** an event, they plan and organize it. ❑ *The country will hold elections within a year.*

3 **v-т** If someone **holds** office or power, they have a particular position of power or authority. ❑ *She has never held an elected office.* [from Old English]

③ hold /hoʊld/ (**holds, holding, held**)

1 **v-т** If you **hold** someone's attention or interest, you do or say things that keep them interested. ❑ *If you want to hold someone's attention, look straight into their eyes.*

2 **v-т** If someone **holds** you in a place, they do not allow you to leave. ❑ *Two angry drivers held a man prisoner in his own car.*

3 **v-т/v-i** If someone asks you to **hold**, or to **hold the line**, when you are making a telephone call, they are asking you to wait for a short time. ❑ *Please can you hold, sir?* [from Old English]

④ hold /hoʊld/ (**holds, holding, held**)

1 **PHRASE** If you **get hold of** something, you find it, usually after some difficulty. ❑ *It is hard to get hold of medicines in some areas of the country.*

2 **PHRASE** If you **get hold of** someone, you succeed in speaking to them. ❑ *I've called him several times but I can't get hold of him.*

3 **PHRASE** If you say **Hold it**, you are telling someone to stop what they are doing and to wait. ❑ *Hold it! Don't move!*

4 **PHRASE** If you put something **on hold**, you decide not to do it now, but to leave it until later. ❑ *He put his retirement on hold to help to find a solution.* [from Old English]

▸ **hold back** When you **hold** someone or something **back**, you stop them from moving forwards or from doing something. ❑ *The police held back the crowd.*

▸ **hold on** or **hold onto** If you **hold on** or **hold onto** something, you keep your hand on it or around it. ❑ *The thief pulled me to the ground but I held onto my purse.*

▸ **hold up** **1** If someone or something **holds** you **up**, they make you late. ❑ *I won't hold you up—I just have one quick question.*

2 If someone **holds up** a bank or a store, they point a weapon at someone there to get money or goods. ❑ *He held up a gas station with a toy gun.*

hold|er /hoʊldər/ (**holders**) **N-COUNT** A **holder** is a container in which you put an object. ❑ *...a toothbrush holder.* [from Old English]

hold|up /hoʊldʌp/ (**holdups**) also **hold-up** **N-COUNT** A **holdup** is when someone uses a weapon to make someone give them money or other valuable things. ❑ *Police are looking for a man after a hold-up in a local bank.*

hole /hoʊl/ (**holes**) **N-COUNT** A **hole** is an opening or an empty space in something. ❑ *He dug a hole 45 feet wide and 15 feet deep.* ❑ *I've got a hole in my jeans.* [from Old English] → look at Picture Dictionary: **golf**

Word Partnership	Use **hole** with :
ADJ	**big/huge/small** hole, **deep** hole, hole
V	**cut/punch a** hole **in something, dig a** hole, hole **in *something*, fill/plug a** hole

holi|day /hɒlɪdeɪ/ (**holidays**) **N-COUNT** A **holiday** is a day when people do not go to work or school because of a religious or national celebration. ❑ *...the Jewish holiday of Passover.* [from Old English]

hol|ler /hɒlər/ (**hollers, hollering, hollered**) **v-т/v-i** If you **holler**, you shout loudly. [INFORMAL] ❑ *"Watch out!" he hollered.* ❑ *He'll be hollering at me for being late.* [from French]

hol|low /hɒloʊ/ (**hollows**)

1 **ADJ** Something that is **hollow** has an empty space inside it. ❑ *...a hollow tree.*

2 **N-COUNT** A **hollow** is an area that is lower than the surrounding surface. ❑ *Below him the town lay in the hollow of the hill.* [from Old English]

hol|ly /hɒli/ (**hollies**) **N-COUNT/N-NONCOUNT** **Holly** is a plant that has hard, shiny leaves with sharp points, and red berries in winter. [from Old English]

holo|caust /hɒləkɔst, hoʊlə-/ **N-SING** SOCIAL STUDIES The **Holocaust** is the organized killing by the Nazis of millions of Jews during the Second World War. [from Late Latin]

holy /hoʊli/ (**holier, holiest**) **ADJ** Something that is **holy** is connected with God or a particular religion. ❑ *This is a holy place.* [from Old English]

home /hoʊm/ (**homes**)

1 **N-COUNT** Someone's **home** is the house or apartment where they live. ❑ *He died from* *a fall at his home in London.* ❑ *Hi, Mom, I'm home!*

2 **ADV** **Home** means to or at the place where you live. ❑ *She wasn't feeling well and she wanted to go home.*

3 **N-NONCOUNT** You can use **home** to talk generally about the house, town, or country where someone lives now or where they were born. ❑ *Ms. Highsmith has made Switzerland her home.* ❑ *His father worked away from home most of the time.*

4 **N-COUNT** A **home** is a building where people who cannot care for themselves live and are cared for. ❑ *It's a home for elderly people.*

5 **N-SING** If you refer to the **home of** something, you mean the place where it began or where it is usually found. ❑ *Greece is the home of the Olympics.*

6 **ADV** When a sports team plays **at home**, it plays on its own ground. Compare with **away**. ❑ *The Red Sox are playing at home tonight.*

7 **ADJ** **Home** is also an adjective. ❑ *Nolan may return for Saturday's home game against the New York Rangers.*

8 **PHRASE** If you feel **at home**, you feel comfortable in the place or situation that you are in. ❑ *We soon felt at home.* [from Old English]

Thesaurus	home	Also look up :
N	dwelling, house, residence **1**	
	birthplace **3** **5**	

Word Partnership	Use **home** with :
V	**bring/take** *someone/something* home, **build a buy a** home, **buy a** home, **call/phone** home, **come** home, **drive** home, **feel at** home, **fly** home, **get** home, **go** home, **head for** home, **leave** home, **return** home, **ride** home, **sit** *at* home, **stay** *at* home, **walk** home, **work at** home **1**–**3**
ADJ	**new home 1 3**
	close to home **1**–**3**

home|land /hoʊmlænd/ (**homelands**) **N-COUNT** SOCIAL STUDIES Your **homeland** is your native country. [mainly WRITTEN] ❑ *Many people are planning to return to their homeland.*

home|less /hoʊmlɪs/

1 **ADJ** **Homeless** people have nowhere to live. ❑ *There are a lot of homeless families in the city.*

2 **N-PLURAL** The **homeless** are people who are homeless. ❑ *We're collecting money for the homeless.* [from Old English]

home|ly /hoʊmli/ **ADJ** If someone is **homely**, they are not very attractive. ❑ *John was homely and overweight.* [from Old English]

home|made /hoʊmmeɪd/ **ADJ** Something that is **homemade** has been made in someone's home, rather than in a store or factory. ❑ *I miss my mother's homemade bread.*

homeopa|thy /hoʊmiɒpəθi/ **N-NONCOUNT** SCIENCE **Homeopathy** is a way of treating an illness in which the patient is given very small amounts of a drug that produces signs of the illness in healthy people.
● **homeo|path|ic** /hoʊmioʊpæθɪk/ **ADJ** ❑ *...homeopathic remedies.*

homeo|sta|sis /hoʊmiəsteɪsɪs/ **N-NONCOUNT** SCIENCE An organism or a system that is capable of **homeostasis** is able to regulate processes such as its temperature so that it can function normally when external conditions change.
● **homeo|stat|ic** /hoʊmiəstætɪk/ **ADJ** ❑ *...a homeostatic mechanism.*

home page (**home pages**) **N-COUNT** TECHNOLOGY On the Internet, a person's or an organization's **home page** is the main page of their website. ❑ *The company offers a number of services on its home page.*

home|sick /hoʊmsɪk/ **ADJ** If you are **homesick**, you feel unhappy because you are away from home and you are missing your family and friends. ❑ *He was homesick for his family.*

home|work /hoʊmwɜrk/ **N-NONCOUNT** **Homework** is work for school that teachers give to students to do at home. ❑ *Have you done your homework, Gemma?*

homi|nid /hɒmɪnɪm/ (**hominids**) **N-COUNT** SOCIAL STUDIES **Hominids** are members of a group of animals that includes human beings and early ancestors of human beings. [from New Latin]

homo|geneous mixture /hɒmədʒiniəs mɪkstʃər, hoʊ-/ (**homogeneous mixtures**) **N-COUNT** SCIENCE In chemistry, a **homogeneous mixture** is a mixture of two or more substances that have mixed completely, for example salt and water.

homo|graph /hɒməgræf/ (**homographs**) **N-COUNT** LANGUAGE ARTS **Homographs** are words that are spelled the same but have different meanings and are sometimes

h

pronounced differently. For example, "bow" (in the sense of a weapon) and "bow" (meaning the front of a ship) are homographs.

ho|molo|gous /həmɒ͟pləgəs/ **ADJ** SCIENCE **Homologous** chromosomes are pairs of chromosomes that contain the same genetic information but come from different parents.

homo|phone /hɒ͟məfoʊn/ (**homophones**) **N-COUNT** LANGUAGE ARTS **Homophones** are words with different meanings that are pronounced in the same way but are spelled differently. For example, "write" and "right" are homophones.

homo|sex|ual /ho͟ʊmoʊsɛ͟kʃuəl/ (**homosexuals**)
■ **ADJ** Someone who is **homosexual** is sexually attracted to people of the same sex. ❑ The study found that 4 to 10 percent of American men are homosexual.
■ **N-COUNT Homosexual** is also a noun. ❑ The organization wants equal treatment for homosexuals.

hon|est /ɒ͟nɪst/
■ **ADJ** If someone is **honest**, they always tell the truth and they do not steal or cheat. ❑ She's honest, and I trust her.
■ **ADJ** If you are **honest** in a particular situation, you tell the complete truth. ❑ I was honest about what I was doing.
■ **ADV** You say **honest** before or after a statement to show that you want people to believe you. [INFORMAL] ❑ I'm not sure, honest. [from Old French]

Thesaurus	honest Also look up :
ADJ	fair, genuine, sincere, true, truthful, upright ■
	candid, frank, straight, truthful ■

hon|est|ly /ɒ͟nɪstli/
■ **ADV** If you describe someone as acting **honestly**, you mean that they always tell the truth and they do not steal or cheat. ❑ Lawrence acts fairly and honestly.
■ **ADV** If you act **honestly** in a particular situation, you tell the complete truth. ❑ She answered the question honestly.
■ **ADV** You say **honestly** before or after a statement to show that you want people to believe you. ❑ Honestly, I don't know anything about it.
■ **ADV** You use **honestly** to indicate that you

are annoyed or impatient. [SPOKEN] ❑ Honestly, Brian! I wish you weren't so rude to him. [from Old French]

hon|es|ty /ɒ͟nɪsti/ **N-NONCOUNT Honesty** is the quality of being honest. ❑ I admire his courage and honesty. [from Old French]

hon|ey /hʌ͟ni/
■ **N-NONCOUNT Honey** is a sweet, sticky food that is made by bees.
■ You call someone **honey** as a sign of affection. ❑ Honey, I don't think that's a good idea. [from Old English]

honey|moon /hʌ͟nimun/ (**honeymoons**) **N-COUNT** A **honeymoon** is a vacation taken by a man and a woman who have just gotten married. ❑ We went to Florida on our honeymoon.
→ look at Word Web: **wedding**

hon|or /ɒ͟nər/ (**honors, honoring, honored**)
■ **N-COUNT** An **honor** is a special award that is given to someone. ❑ He won many honors—among them an award for his movie performance.
■ **N-NONCOUNT Honor** means doing what you believe to be right. ❑ He behaved with honor.
■ **N-SING** If you describe an experience as an **honor**, you think it is something special. ❑ He had the honor of hosting the Olympic Games.
■ **V-T** If you **honor** a promise, you do what you said you would do. ❑ He was ready to honor the agreement.
■ **V-T** If someone **is honored**, they are given public praise for something they have done. ❑ Maradona was honored with an award from Argentina's soccer association. [from Old French]

Thesaurus	honor Also look up :
N	award, distinction, recognition ■
V	commend, praise, recognize ■

Word Partnership	Use honor with :
ADJ	great/highest honor ■ ■
N	code of honor, sense of honor ■

Word Link	able ≈ able to be : acceptable, downloadable, honorable

hon|or|able /ɒ͟nərəbəl/ **ADJ** If people or actions are **honorable**, they are good, and the person has a right to be respected. ❑ I'm sure his intentions were perfectly honorable. [from Old French]

hood /hʊ͟d/ (**hoods**)
■ **N-COUNT** A **hood** is the part of a coat that you can pull up to cover your head. ❑ Put up your hood—it's starting to rain.

hoof

2 N-COUNT The **hood** of a car is the metal cover over the engine. ❏ *Dad raised the hood of the truck.* [from Old English]

hoof /hʊf, huf/ (**hoofs** or **hooves**) **N-COUNT** **Hooves** are the hard parts of the feet of horses, cows and some other animals. ❏ *He heard the sound of horses' hooves behind him.* [from Old English]
→ look at Picture Dictionary: **horse**

hook /hʊk/ (**hooks, hooking, hooked**)
1 N-COUNT A **hook** is a curved piece of metal or plastic that you use for hanging things on. ❏ *His jacket hung from a hook.*
2 N-COUNT A **hook** is a curved piece of metal with a sharp point that you tie to the end of a fishing line to catch fish with. ❏ *Mr. Kruger removed the hook from the fish's mouth.*
3 V-T/V-I If you **hook** one thing **to** another, you attach it there using a hook. ❏ *Paul hooked his tractor to the car.* [from Old English]
▶ **hook up** When someone **hooks up** an electronic machine, they connect it to other machines or to a power supply. ❏ *...technicians who hook up computer systems.*

hoop /hup/ (**hoops**)
1 N-COUNT A **hoop** is a ring made of wood, metal, or plastic. ❏ *Jessica was wearing jeans, sneakers and gold hoop earrings.*
2 N-COUNT A basketball **hoop** is the ring that players try to throw the ball into in order to score points for their team. [from Old English]

hoot /hut/ (**hoots, hooting, hooted**)
1 V-I If an owl **hoots**, it makes a loud noise. ❏ *An owl hooted in the distance.*
2 N-COUNT **Hoot** is also a noun. ❏ *Suddenly, he heard the loud hoot of a train.* [from Maori]

hooves /huvz/ **Hooves** is a plural of **hoof**. [from Old English]

hop /hɒp/ (**hops, hopping, hopped**)
1 V-I If you **hop**, you move by jumping on one foot.
2 V-I When birds and animals **hop**, they move by jumping on both of their feet or all four of their feet together. ❏ *A small brown bird hopped in front of them.*
3 N-COUNT A **hop** is a short jump.
4 V-I If you **hop** somewhere, you move there quickly or suddenly. [INFORMAL] ❏ *We hopped on the train.* [from Old English]

hope /hoʊp/ (**hopes, hoping, hoped**)
1 V-T/V-I If you **hope** that something is true, or if you **hope** for something, you want it to be true or you want it to happen. ❏ *The team are hoping to win a medal at the Olympic Games.* ❏ *I hope that you get better soon.* ❏ *We're all hoping for some good weather.* ❏ *"I hope we'll meet again soon."—"I hope so, too."*
2 N-COUNT/N-NONCOUNT **Hope** is the feeling of wanting something good to happen, and believing that it will happen. ❏ *What are your hopes for the future?* ❏ *This medicine will give new hope to millions of people around the world.* ❏ *As time passes, the police are losing hope of finding the men alive.*
3 PHRASE If you do one thing **in the hope that** another thing will happen, you do it to help the other thing to happen. ❏ *He was studying hard in the hope that he would get a place at college.* [from Old English]

Thesaurus hope Also look up:
V aspire, desire, dream, wish **1**
N ambition, aspiration, desire, dream, wish **2**

Word Partnership Use hope with:
ADJ **faint** hope, **false** hope, **little** hope **2**
V **give** *someone* hope, **give up** *all* hope, **hold out** hope, **lose** *all* hope **2**
N **glimmer of** hope **2**

hope|ful /hoʊpfəl/
1 ADJ If you are **hopeful**, you think that something that you want will probably happen. ❏ *The doctors are hopeful that Grandma will get better soon.*
2 ADJ A **hopeful** sign makes you feel that what something will happen in the way that you would like. ❏ *He welcomed the news as a hopeful sign.* [from Old English]

hope|ful|ly /hoʊpfəli/
1 ADV You say **hopefully** when you are talking about something that you hope will happen. ❏ *Hopefully, you won't have any more problems.*
2 ADV If you do something **hopefully**, you do it hoping that something good will happen. ❏ *David looked hopefully at the coffee pot.* [from Old English]

Word Link less ≈ without : end**less**, hope**less**, wire**less**

hope|less /hoʊplɪs/
1 ADJ Someone or something that is **hopeless** has no chance of success. ❏ *I don't believe the situation is hopeless.*
2 ADJ If you feel **hopeless**, you feel unhappy because there seems to be no chance of a

H

better situation. ❑ *He had not heard her cry before in this hopeless way.*
3 **ADJ** If someone or something is **hopeless**, they are very bad. ❑ *I'm hopeless at sports.*
● **hope|less|ly** **ADV** ❑ *Harry realized that he was hopelessly lost.* [from Old English]

ho|ri|zon /həra͟ɪzᵊn/ (**horizons**)
1 **N-SING** The **horizon** is the line that appears between the sky and the land or the ocean. ❑ *A small boat appeared on the horizon.*
2 **N-COUNT** Your **horizons** are the limits of what you want to do or of what you are interested in. ❑ *Children's horizons open up when they start school.*
3 **PHRASE** If something is **on the horizon**, it is almost certainly going to happen or be done quite soon. ❑ *There is more bad news on the horizon.* [from Latin]

hori|zon|tal /hɔ͟rɪzɒntᵊl/ **ADJ** Something that is **horizontal** is flat and level with the ground. ❑ *She was wearing a gray sweater with black horizontal stripes.* [from Latin]
→ look at Word Web: **graph**

hor|mone /hɔ͟rmoʊn/ (**hormones**) **N-COUNT**
SCIENCE A **hormone** is a chemical substance in your body that affects the way your body works. ❑ *This hormone is present in both sexes.* [from Greek]
→ look at Word Web: **emotion**

horn /hɔ͟rn/ (**horns**)
1 **N-COUNT** An animal's **horns** are the hard pointed things that grow from its head.
2 **N-COUNT** A **horn** is the part in a car or another vehicle that makes a loud noise, and that you use as a warning of danger. ❑ *I could hear the sound of a car horn outside.*
3 **N-COUNT** **MUSIC** A **horn** is a musical instrument with a long metal tube that you play by blowing into it. ❑ *Joshua started playing the horn when he was eight.*
4 **N-COUNT** **SCIENCE** In geology, a **horn** is a sharp peak that forms when the sides of a mountain are eroded. [from Old English]

| Word Link | scope ≈ looking : horo*scope*, micro*scope*, tele*scope* |

horo|scope /hɔ͟rəskoʊp/ (**horoscopes**)
N-COUNT Your **horoscope** is what some people believe will happen to you in the future, using the position of the stars when you were born. ❑ *I always read my horoscope in the newspaper.* [from Old English]

hor|ri|ble /hɔ͟rɪbᵊl, hɒr-/ **ADJ** If someone or something is **horrible**, they are very unpleasant. [INFORMAL] ❑ *The smell was horrible.* ❑ *It was a horrible experience.* ❑ *Stop being horrible to me!* ● **hor|ri|bly** /hɔ͟rɪbli, hɒr-/ **ADV** ❑ *Sam was feeling horribly ill.* [from Old French]

hor|ri|fy /hɔ͟rɪfaɪ, hɒr-/ (**horrifies, horrifying, horrified**) **V-T** If someone is **horrified**, they are very shocked. ❑ *His family was horrified by the news.* ● **hor|ri|fy|ing** **ADJ** ❑ *It was a horrifying sight.* [from Latin]

hor|ror /hɔ͟rər, hɒr-/ (**horrors**)
1 **N-NONCOUNT** **Horror** is a feeling of great shock and fear when you see or experience something very unpleasant. ❑ *I felt sick with horror.*
2 **N-COUNT** You can refer to very unpleasant or frightening experiences as **horrors**. ❑ *...the horrors of war.*
3 **ADJ** A **horror** movie is a very frightening movie that you watch for entertainment. ❑ *I'm not a fan of horror movies.* [from Latin]
→ look at Word Web: **genre**

horse /hɔ͟rs/ (**horses**) **N-COUNT** A **horse** is a large animal that people can ride. ❑ *Have you ever ridden a horse?* [from Old English]
→ look at Picture Dictionary: **horse**

horse|back /hɔ͟rsbæk/
1 **N-NONCOUNT** If you do something on **horseback**, you do it while riding a horse. ❑ *Many people traveled on horseback.*
2 **ADJ** A **horseback** ride is a ride on a horse. ❑ *...a horseback ride into the mountains.*
3 **ADV** **Horseback** is also an adverb. ❑ *Many people here ride horseback.*

horse|back rid|ing /hɔ͟rsbæk raɪdɪŋ/
N-NONCOUNT **SPORTS** **Horseback riding** is the activity of riding a horse.

horse rac|ing **N-NONCOUNT** **SPORTS** **Horse racing** is a sport in which people ride horses in races.

horse|shoe /hɔ͟rsʃu/ (**horseshoes**) **N-COUNT** A **horseshoe** is a piece of metal in the shape of a U, that is fixed to a horse's foot. People sometimes hang a **horseshoe** on the wall as a sign of good luck.

hose /ho͟ʊz/ (**hoses**) **N-COUNT** A **hose** is a long rubber or plastic pipe that you use to put water on plants or on a fire. [from Old English]
→ look at Picture Dictionary: **garden**

Picture Dictionary horse

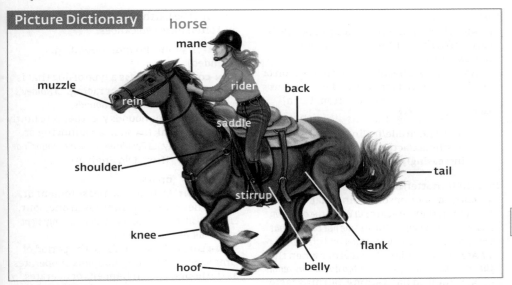

mane
muzzle
rein
rider
back
saddle
shoulder
tail
stirrup
knee
flank
hoof
belly

h

hos|pi|tal /hɒspɪtᵊl/ (**hospitals**)
N-COUNT/N-NONCOUNT A **hospital** is a place where doctors and nurses care for people who are sick or injured. ❑ *The two men were taken to the hospital after the car crash.* [from Medieval Latin]
→ look at Word Web: **hospital**

host /hoʊst/ (**hosts, hosting, hosted**)
1 **N-COUNT** The **host** at a party is the person who has invited the guests. ❑ *I didn't know anyone at the party, except the host.*
2 **N-COUNT** SCIENCE The **host** of a parasite is the plant or animal which it lives on or inside and from which it gets its food.
3 **N-COUNT** The **host** of a radio or television show is the person who talks to the people who appear on it. ❑ *I am the host of a live radio program.*
4 **V-T** If someone **hosts** a party, they have invited the guests. ❑ *She hosted a party for 300 guests.* [from French]

hos|tage /hɒstɪdʒ/ (**hostages**)
1 **N-COUNT** A **hostage** is someone who is kept as a prisoner by people until the people get what they want. ❑ *The two hostages were freed yesterday.*
2 **PHRASE** If someone **is taken hostage,** they are taken and kept as a hostage. ❑ *He was taken hostage on his first trip to the country.* [from Old French]

host|ess /hoʊstɪs/ (**hostesses**) **N-COUNT**
The **hostess** at a party is the woman who has invited the guests. ❑ *She's the perfect hostess, making sure that all her guests are relaxed and happy.* [from French]

Word Web hospital

Children's **Hospital** in Boston has one of the best pediatric **health care** centers in the country. The hospital records about 25,000 **admissions** every year. In addition to **physicians,** the staff includes **residents** and **fellows,** who are studying to be **doctors.** The hospital also has excellent **researchers.** Their work helped find **vaccines** for **polio** and **measles.** The hospital has also led the way in liver, heart, and lung **transplants** in children.

hos|tile /hɒstəl/

1 ADJ A **hostile** person or group of people is very unfriendly. ❑ *A large, hostile crowd surrounded him.*

2 ADJ If you are **hostile to** another person or an idea, you do not approve of them. ❑ *He was hostile to the idea of democracy.* [from Latin]

Word Partnership	Use hostile with :
N	hostile **attitude/feelings/intentions** **1** hostile **act/action**
ADV	**increasingly** hostile **1** **2**

hot /hɒt/ (**hotter, hottest**)

1 ADJ Someone or something that is **hot** has a high temperature. ❑ *When the oil is hot, add the sliced onion.* ❑ *Have some hot coffee. That will warm you up.* ❑ *I was too hot and tired to eat.*

2 ADJ **Hot** describes the weather when the temperature is high. ❑ *It's too hot to play tennis.*

3 ADJ **Hot** food has a strong, burning taste. ❑ *I love eating hot curries.* [from Old English]
→ look at Word Web: **weather**

hot dog (**hot dogs**) **N-COUNT** A **hot dog** is a long piece of bread with a hot sausage inside it. ❑ *The children ate hot dogs and ice cream at Melissa's birthday party.*
→ look at Word Web: **ketchup**

ho|tel /hoʊtɛl/ (**hotels**) **N-COUNT** A **hotel** is a building where people pay to sleep and eat meals. ❑ *Janet stayed the night in a small hotel near the harbor.* [from French]
→ look at Word Web: **hotel**

Word Partnership	Use hotel with :
V	**check into a** hotel, **check out of a** hotel, **stay at a** hotel
N	hotel **guest**, hotel **reservation**, hotel **room**
ADJ	**luxury** hotel, **new** hotel

hot spot (**hot spots**) also **hotspot** **N-COUNT** **SCIENCE** In geology, **hot spots** are areas beneath the Earth's surface where lava rises and often forms volcanoes.

hound /haʊnd/ (**hounds, hounding, hounded**)

1 N-COUNT A **hound** is a type of dog that is often used for hunting or racing. ❑ *Rainey's main interest is hunting with hounds.*

2 V-T If someone **hounds** you, they constantly disturb or speak to you in an annoying or upsetting way. ❑ *People were always hounding him for advice.* [from Old English]

hour /aʊər/ (**hours**)

1 N-COUNT An **hour** is a measurement of time. There are sixty minutes in one hour. ❑ *They waited for about two hours.* ❑ *I only slept about half an hour last night.*

2 N-PLURAL You can refer to the period of time when something happens or operates as the **hours** when it happens or operates. ❑ *Call us at this number during office hours.* [from Old French]
→ look at Picture Dictionary: **time**

hour|ly /aʊərli/

1 ADJ An **hourly** event happens once every hour. ❑ *He listened to the hourly news program on the radio.*

2 ADV Something that happens **hourly**, happens once every hour. ❑ *The buses run hourly between the two cities.* [from Old French]

house (**houses, housing, housed**)

PRONUNCIATION HELP
Pronounce the noun /haʊs/. Pronounce the verb /haʊz/. The form **houses** is pronounced /haʊzɪz/.

1 N-COUNT A **house** is a building where people live. ❑ *Amy's invited me to her house for dinner.* ❑ *Grandma has moved to a small house in the country.*

2 N-SING You can refer to all the people who live together in a house as **the house.**

Word Web **hotel**

When making **reservations** at a **hotel**, most people request a **single** or a **double** room. Sometimes the **clerk** invites the person to **upgrade** to a **suite**. When arriving at the hotel, the first person to greet the **guest** is the **porter**. He will put the person's suitcases on a **luggage cart** and later deliver them to their room. The guest then goes to the **front desk** and **checks in**. The clerk often describes **amenities** such as a **fitness club** or **spa**. Most hotels provide **room service** for late night snacks.

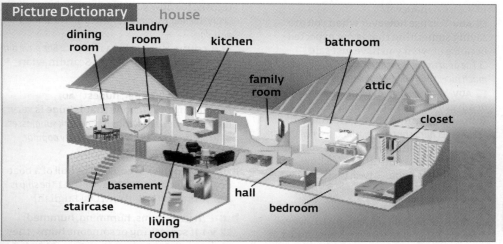

dining room · laundry room · kitchen · bathroom · family room · attic · closet · basement · hall · staircase · living room · bedroom

h

❑ *He set his alarm clock for midnight, and it woke the whole house.*

3 **N-COUNT** SOCIAL STUDIES You can call one of the two parts of the U.S. Congress a **House**. The House of Representatives is sometimes called **the House**. ❑ *Some members of the House and Senate worked all day yesterday.*

4 **V-T** To **house** someone means to provide a house or an apartment for them to live in. ❑ *The building was used to house refugees.*
[from Old English]

5 → see also **White House, housing**
→ look at Picture Dictionary: **house**

house|hold /haʊshoʊld/ (**households**)
N-COUNT A **household** is all the people who live together in a house. ❑ *I grew up in a large household, with three brothers and three sisters.*

house|wife /haʊswaɪf/ (**housewives**)
N-COUNT A **housewife** is a woman who does not have a paid job, but spends most of her time looking after her house and family. ❑ *Sarah's a housewife and mother of four children.*

house|work /haʊswɜrk/ **N-NONCOUNT**
Housework is the work that you do to keep a house clean and neat. ❑ *Men are doing more housework nowadays.*

hous|ing /haʊzɪŋ/
1 **N-NONCOUNT** **Housing** is the buildings that people live in. ❑ *...a housing shortage.*
[from Old English]
2 → see also **house**

hov|er /hʌvər/ (**hovers, hovering, hovered**)
V-I If something **hovers**, it stays in one place in the air, and does not move forward or backward. ❑ *Helicopters hovered over the scene of the accident.*

how /haʊ/
1 **ADV** You use **how** to ask about the way that something happens or is done. ❑ *How do you spell his name?* ❑ *"How do you get to work?"—"By bus."* ❑ *How does a cellphone work?*
2 **ADV** You use **how** to ask questions about time, or the amount or age of something. ❑ *How much money do you have?* ❑ *How many people will be at the dinner?* ❑ *How long will you stay?* ❑ *How old is your son?*
3 **ADV** You use **how** when you are asking someone whether something was good. ❑ *How was your trip to Orlando?*
4 **ADV** You use **how** to ask if someone is well. ❑ *Hi! How are you doing?* ❑ *How's Rosie?*
5 **ADV** You say **how about...** when you are suggesting something to someone. ❑ *How about a cup of coffee?* ❑ *How about meeting tonight?*
6 **PHRASE** It is polite to say **How do you do?** when you meet someone for the first time. They answer by saying **How do you do?** also.
[from Old English]

how|ever /haʊɛvər/

1 **ADV** You use **however** when you are saying something that is not expected because of what you have just said. ❑ *The apartment is rather small. It is, however, much nicer than our old apartment.*

2 **ADV** You use **however** before an adjective or adverb to say that the degree of something cannot change a situation. ❑ *However hard she tried, nothing seemed to work.*

3 **CONJ** You use **however** when you want to say that it makes no difference how something is done. ❑ *Wear your hair however you want.*

Usage **however**

Be sure to punctuate sentences with *however* correctly. When *however* expresses contrast, it is followed by a comma (and preceded by a period or a semicolon): *Dae's parents sent her a new computer; however, she can't figure out how to set it up.* In other uses, *however* isn't followed by a comma: *I'm surprised—Dae can usually figure anything out, however difficult it seems to be.*

howl /haʊl/ (howls, howling, howled)

1 **V-I** If a person or an animal **howls**, they make a long, loud, crying sound. ❑ *A dog suddenly howled.* ❑ *Daniel fell to the ground, howling with pain.*

2 **N-COUNT** Howl is also a noun. ❑ *The dog gave a long howl.* [from Middle High German] → look at Word Web: **laugh**

H-R dia|gram /eɪtʃ ɑr daɪəgræm/ (H-R diagrams) or HRD N-COUNT SCIENCE

An **H-R diagram** or HRD is the same as a **Hertzsprung-Russell diagram.**

HTML /eɪtʃ ti ɛm ɛl/ N-NONCOUNT

TECHNOLOGY **HTML** is the standard way of preparing documents so that people can read them on the Internet. **HTML** is short for "hypertext markup language." ❑ *I'm teaching myself HTML.*

hub /hʌb/ (hubs) N-COUNT If a place is the

hub of an activity, it is a very important center for that activity. ❑ *They say that New York is the hub of the art world.*

hue /hyu/ (hues) N-COUNT A hue is a color.

[LITERARY] ❑ *The same hue will look different in different light.* [from Old English]

hug /hʌg/ (hugs, hugging, hugged)

1 **V-T** When you **hug** someone, you put your arms around them and hold them

tightly, to show your love or friendship. ❑ *Crystal hugged him and invited him to dinner the next day.*

2 **N-COUNT** Hug is also a noun. ❑ *She gave him a hug and said, "Well done."* [of Scandinavian origin]

huge /hyudʒ/ (huger, hugest) ADJ

Something or someone that is **huge** is very large. ❑ *Emily was wearing huge dark sunglasses.* ● **huge|ly** ADV ❑ *This hotel is hugely popular.* [from Old French]

hull /hʌl/ (hulls) N-COUNT The hull of a boat

or a tank is the main body of it. ❑ *The ship is new, with a steel hull.* [from Old English]

hum /hʌm/ (hums, humming, hummed)

1 **V-I** If something or someone **hums**, they make a low continuous noise. ❑ *The birds sang and the bees hummed.*

2 **N-SING** Hum is also a noun. ❑ *I could hear the distant hum of traffic.*

3 **V-T/V-I** When you **hum**, or **hum** a tune, you sing a tune with your lips closed. ❑ *Barbara began humming a song.* [from Dutch]

hu|man /hyumən/ (humans)

1 **ADJ** **Human** means relating to people, and not animals or machines. ❑ *What is the smallest bone in the human body?*

2 **N-COUNT** A **human** is a person, rather than an animal or a machine. ❑ *Humans are capable of some terrible crimes.* [from Latin] → look at Word Webs: **evolution, primate**

Word Partnership Use **human** with :

N   human **behavior**, human **body**, human **brain**, human **dignity**, human **life** **1**

hu|man be|ing (human beings) N-COUNT

SCIENCE A **human being** is a man, a woman, or a child. ❑ *Every human being has the right to freedom.*

Word Link *man ≈ human being : humane, mankind, woman*

hu|mane /hyumeɪn/ ADJ Humane people

act in a kind, sympathetic way toward other people and animals. ❑ *...a humane society.* ● **hu|mane|ly** ADV ❑ *We should treat all animals humanely.*

Hu|man Ge|nome Proj|ect N-SING

SCIENCE The **Human Genome Project** is an international research program that is designed to provide a complete set of information about human DNA.

Word Link | *arian ≈ believing in, having :*
*humanit*arian, **totalit**arian,
vegetarian

hu|mani|tar|ian /hyumǽnɪtɛəriən/ **ADJ**
SOCIAL STUDIES If a person or a society has
humanitarian ideas or behavior, they try to
avoid making people suffer or they help
people who are suffering. ❏ *The soldiers were
there for humanitarian reasons, to give out food and
medicines.* [from Latin]

hu|man|ity /hyumǽnɪti/
1 **N-NONCOUNT** **Humanity** is all the people
in the world. ❏ *Can humanity survive the future?*
2 **N-NONCOUNT** **Humanity** is the quality of
being kind and thoughtful. ❏ *Her speech
showed great humanity.*

hu|man na|ture **N-NONCOUNT** **Human
nature** is the way that most people behave.
❏ *It is human nature to worry about your children.*

hu|man race **N-SING** The **human race**
means all the people living in the world.
❏ *Some people believe that the human race is
destroying the Earth.*

hu|man rights **N-PLURAL** SOCIAL STUDIES
Human rights are basic rights that all people
should have. ❏ *Both armies promised to respect
human rights.*

hum|ble /hʌ́mbəl/ (**humbler, humblest**)
1 **ADJ** A **humble** person does not believe
that they are better than other people.
❏ *He remains humble about his achievements.*
2 **ADJ** A **humble** person or thing is ordinary
and not special in any way. ❏ *Ms. Cruz comes
from a humble background.* [from Old French]

hu|mid /hyúmɪd/ **ADJ** **Humid** weather is wet
and warm. ❏ *Tomorrow, we can expect hot and
humid conditions.* [from Latin]
→ look at Word Web: **weather**

hu|mid|ity /hyumɪ́dɪti/ **N-NONCOUNT**
Humidity is the amount of water in the air.
❏ *The humidity is relatively low at the moment.*
[from Latin]
→ look at Word Web: **forecast**

hu|milia|tion /hyumɪlieɪʃən/ (**humiliations**)
1 **N-NONCOUNT** **Humiliation** is the
embarrassment and shame you feel when
someone makes you appear stupid, or when
you make a mistake in public. ❏ *He faced the
humiliation of forgetting his wife's birthday.*
2 **N-COUNT** A **humiliation** is an occasion or
a situation in which you feel embarrassed

and ashamed. ❏ *The result is a humiliation for
the president.* [from Late Latin]

hu|mor /hyúmər/
1 **N-NONCOUNT** **Humor** is the quality of
being funny. ❏ *I laughed when I saw the humor
of the situation.*
2 **N-NONCOUNT** **Humor** is the amusing
things that people say. ❏ *He told his story with
humor.* [from Latin]
→ look at Word Web: **laugh**

hu|mor|ous /hyúmərəs/ **ADJ** If someone or
something is **humorous**, they make you
laugh or smile. ❏ *He usually likes to write
humorous poems.* ● **hu|mor|ous|ly** **ADV**
❏ *Mr. Stevenson smiled humorously.* [from Latin]

hump /hʌ́mp/ (**humps**)
1 **N-COUNT** A **hump** is a small hill or raised
area.
2 **N-COUNT** A camel's **hump** is the large lump
on its back. ❏ *Camels store water in their hump.*

hump|back whale /hʌ́mpbæk weɪl/
(**humpback whales**) **N-COUNT** A **humpback
whale** is a large whale with long front fins.

hu|mus /hyúməs/ **N-NONCOUNT** SCIENCE
Humus is the part of soil that consists of
dead plants that have begun to decay.
[from Latin]

hun|dred /hʌ́ndrɪd/ (**hundreds**)

> **LANGUAGE HELP**
> The plural is **hundred** after a number.

1 **NUM** MATH A **hundred** or **one hundred** is
the number 100. ❏ *More than a hundred people
were there.*
2 **NUM** **Hundreds of** things or people means
a lot of them. ❏ *He received hundreds of letters.*
3 **PRON** You can also use **hundreds** as a
pronoun. ❏ *Hundreds were killed in the fighting.*
[from Old English]

hun|dredth /hʌ́ndrɪdθ, -drɪtθ/
(**hundredths**)
1 **ADJ/ADV** MATH The **hundredth** item in
a series is the one that you count as number
one hundred. ❏ *The bank's hundredth
anniversary is in December.*
2 **N-COUNT** MATH A **hundredth** is one of
a hundred equal parts of something.
❏ *Mitchell beat Lewis by three-hundredths of
a second.* [from Old English]

hung /hʌ́ŋ/ **Hung** is the past tense and past
participle of most of the senses of **hang**.
[from Old English]

h

hun|ger /hʌŋgər/

■ **1** **N-NONCOUNT** **Hunger** is the feeling that you get when you need something to eat. ❑ *Hunger is the body's signal that you need to eat.*

■ **2** **N-NONCOUNT** **Hunger** is a lack of food that causes suffering or death. ❑ *Three hundred people in this town are dying of hunger every day.* [from Old English]

hun|gry /hʌŋgri/ (hungrier, hungriest) **ADJ** When you are **hungry**, you want to eat. ❑ *My friend was hungry, so we drove to a shopping mall to get some food.* ● **hun|gri|ly** /hʌŋgrɪli/ **ADV** ❑ *James ate hungrily.* [from Old English]

hunt /hʌnt/ (hunts, hunting, hunted)

■ **1** **V-T/V-I** When people or animals **hunt**, or **hunt** something, they chase and kill wild animals for food or as a sport. ❑ *I learned to hunt and fish when I was a child.*

■ **2** **N-COUNT** A **hunt** is when people chase and kill wild animals for food or as a sport. ❑ *Dad went on a moose hunt last year.* ● **hunt|ing** **N-NONCOUNT** ❑ *He went deer hunting with his cousins.*

■ **3** **V-I** If you **hunt for** something or someone, you try to find them by searching carefully. ❑ *Police are still hunting for clues at the victim's apartment.*

■ **4** **N-COUNT** A **hunt** is a careful search for something. ❑ *Many people helped in the hunt for the missing children.* ● **hunt|ing** **N-NONCOUNT** ❑ *Job hunting is not easy.* [from Old English]

hunt|er /hʌntər/ (hunters) **N-COUNT** A **hunter** is a person who hunts wild animals for food or as a sport. ❑ *Hundreds of deer hunters will visit the area this season.* [from Old English]

hur|dle /hɜrdəl/ (hurdles)

■ **1** **N-COUNT** A **hurdle** is a difficulty that may stop you from doing something. ❑ *Writing a résumé is the first hurdle in a job search.*

■ **2** **N-COUNT** **SPORTS** **Hurdles** is a race in which people have to jump over a series of frames. ❑ *Davis won the 400 meter hurdles.* [from Old English]

hurl /hɜrl/ (hurls, hurling, hurled)

■ **1** **V-T** If you **hurl** something, you throw it violently and with a lot of force. ❑ *Groups of boys hurled stones at police.* ❑ *Simon caught the book and hurled it back.*

■ **2** **V-T** If you **hurl** abuse or insults **at** someone, you shout insults at them aggressively. ❑ *The driver of the other car hurled abuse at him.*

hur|ri|cane /hɜrɪkeɪn, hʌr-/ (hurricanes) **N-COUNT** **SCIENCE** A **hurricane** is a storm with very strong winds and rain. [from Spanish]

→ look at Word Webs: **hurricane, disaster**

hur|ry /hɜri, hʌr-/ (hurries, hurrying, hurried)

■ **1** **V-T/V-I** If you **hurry**, you move or do something as quickly as you can. ❑ *Claire hurried along the road.* ❑ *Everyone hurried to find a seat.*

■ **2** **N-SING** If you are **in a hurry**, you need or want to do something quickly. ❑ *I'm sorry, I'm in a hurry and I have to go!*

■ **3** **V-T** To **hurry** someone means to try to make them do something more quickly. ❑ *Sorry to hurry you, John.* [from Middle High German]

▶ **hurry up** If you tell someone to **hurry up**, you are telling them to do something more quickly. ❑ *Hurry up and get ready, or you'll miss the school bus!*

Thesaurus	**hurry** Also look up :
v	rush, run; *(ant.)* slow down, relax ■

hurt /hɜrt/ (hurts, hurting, hurt)

■ **1** **V-T** If you **hurt** someone or something, you make them feel pain. ❑ *Yasin hurt himself while he was playing baseball.* ❑ *I fell over and hurt my leg yesterday.*

Word Web	hurricane

A **hurricane** is a violent **storm** or tropical **cyclone** that develops in the Atlantic Ocean or Caribbean Sea. When a hurricane develops in the Pacific Ocean it is known as a typhoon. A hurricane begins as a **tropical depression**. It becomes a **tropical storm** when its winds reach 39 miles per hour (mph). When wind speeds reach 74 mph, a distinct **eye** forms in the center. Then the storm is officially a hurricane. It has heavy **rains** and very high **winds**.

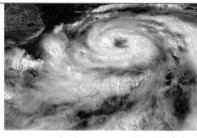

2 **v-i** If a part of your body **hurts**, you feel pain there. ❑ *His arm hurt.*

3 **ADJ** If you are **hurt**, you have been injured. ❑ *How badly are you hurt?*

4 **v-t/v-i** If you **hurt** someone, you say or do something that makes them unhappy. ❑ *I'm really sorry if I hurt your feelings.* ❑ *What hurts most is that I had to find out for myself.*

5 **v-t** To **hurt** someone or something means to have a bad effect on them. ❑ *The hot weather is hurting many businesses.*

6 **ADJ** If you are **hurt**, you are upset because of something that someone has said or done. ❑ *She was deeply hurt by what Smith said.* [from Old French]

Thesaurus	hurt Also look up :
V	ache, smart, sting **2**
	harm, injure, wound **5**
ADJ	injured, wounded **3**
	saddened, upset **4** **6**

Word Partnership	Use hurt with :
ADV	**badly/seriously** hurt **1** **3**
V	**get** hurt **3**
	feel hurt **6**
N	hurt *someone's* **chances**, hurt **the economy**, hurt *someone's* **feelings**, hurt **sales 5**

hus|band /hʌzbənd/ (**husbands**) **N-COUNT** A woman's **husband** is the man she is married to. ❑ *Eva married her husband in 1957.* [from Old English]
→ look at Picture Dictionary: **family**
→ look at Word Web: **love**

hush /hʌʃ/
1 **INTERJ** You say **Hush** when you are telling someone to be quiet. ❑ *Hush! The teacher's talking.*
2 **N-SING** There is a **hush** in a place when everything is quiet. ❑ *There was a sudden hush in the room.*

hut /hʌt/ (**huts**) **N-COUNT** A **hut** is a small simple building, especially one made of wood. [from French]

hy|brid /haɪbrɪd/ (**hybrids**)
1 **N-COUNT** SCIENCE A **hybrid** is an animal or a plant that is made from two different types of animal or plant. ❑ *A mule is a hybrid of a horse and a donkey.*
2 **ADJ** SCIENCE **Hybrid** is also an adjective. ❑ *The hybrid seed produces larger flowers.*
3 **N-COUNT** TECHNOLOGY A **hybrid** or a **hybrid**

car is a car that can use either gasoline or electricity as its power. ❑ *Hybrid cars can go almost 600 miles between refueling.* [from Latin]
→ look at Word Web: **car**

hydro|car|bon /haɪdroʊkɑrbən/ (**hydrocarbons**) **N-COUNT** SCIENCE A **hydrocarbon** is a chemical compound that is a mixture of hydrogen and carbon.

hydro|elec|tric /haɪdroʊɪlɛktrɪk/ also **hydro-electric** **ADJ** SCIENCE **Hydroelectric** means relating to or involving electricity made from the energy of running water.

hydro|elec|tric|ity /haɪdroʊɪlɛktrɪsɪti/ **N-NONCOUNT** SCIENCE **Hydroelectricity** is electricity made from the energy of running water.

hydro|gen /haɪdrədʒən/ **N-NONCOUNT** SCIENCE **Hydrogen** is a colorless gas that is the lightest and most common element in the universe. [from French]
→ look at Word Web: **sun**

Word Link	hydr ≈ water : carbohydrate, dehydrate, hydropower

hydro|power /haɪdrəpoʊər/ **N-NONCOUNT** SCIENCE **Hydropower** is the use of energy from running water, especially in hydroelectricity.

hy|giene /haɪdʒin/ **N-NONCOUNT** **Hygiene** is the practice of keeping yourself and the things you use clean. ❑ *The key to good hygiene is washing your hands before touching food.*
● **hy|gien|ic** /haɪdʒɛnɪk/ **ADJ** ❑ *This kitchen is easy to keep clean and hygienic.* [from New Latin]

hymn /hɪm/ (**hymns**) **N-COUNT** MUSIC A **hymn** is a religious song that Christians sing in church. ❑ *I like singing hymns.* [from Latin]

hype /haɪp/ (**hypes, hyping, hyped**)
1 **N-NONCOUNT** **Hype** is the use of a lot of publicity and advertising to make people interested in something such as a product. ❑ *There's been a lot of hype about her new book.*
2 **v-t** To **hype** a product means to advertise or praise it a lot. ❑ *We hyped the film to raise money.*
3 **Hype up** means the same as **hype**. ❑ *...hyping up famous people.*

hyper|ac|tive /haɪpəræktɪv/ **ADJ** Someone who is **hyperactive** is unable to relax, and finds it difficult to stop themselves from moving around. ❑ *His research was used in planning treatments for hyperactive children.*

hyper|bo|le /haɪpɜrbəli/ **N-NONCOUNT**
LANGUAGE ARTS **Hyperbole** is speech or writing that makes something sound much more impressive than it really is. [FORMAL]
❑ *...the hyperbole that portrays him as one of the greatest artists in the world.* [from Greek]

hyper|link /haɪpərlɪŋk/ (**hyperlinks**)
N-COUNT TECHNOLOGY In a document on a computer, a **hyperlink** is a link to another part of the document or to another document. ❑ *Web pages are full of hyperlinks.*

hyper|sen|si|tive /haɪpərsɛnsɪtɪv/
1 ADJ If you say that someone is **hypersensitive**, you mean that they become annoyed or offended very easily. ❑ *Student teachers were hypersensitive to any criticism of their performance.*
2 ADJ SCIENCE A **hypersensitive** reaction is a strong reaction that indicates that someone is extremely sensitive to certain drugs or chemicals. ❑ *Hypersensitive reactions also occur with inhaled chemicals.* [from Medieval Latin]

hyper|ten|sion /haɪpərtɛnʃən/
N-NONCOUNT SCIENCE **Hypertension** is a medical condition in which a person has very high blood pressure. ❑ *Vegetarians are less likely to suffer from hypertension or obesity.*

hy|phen /haɪfən/ (**hyphens**) **N-COUNT**
LANGUAGE ARTS A **hyphen** is the punctuation mark - that you use to join two words together, as in "left-handed." You also use a hyphen to show that a word continues on the next line. [from Late Latin]
→ look at Picture Dictionary: **punctuation**

| Word Link | *osis ≈ state or condition : diagnosis, hypnosis, symbiosis* |

hyp|no|sis /hɪpnoʊsɪs/ **N-NONCOUNT**
Hypnosis is when someone is in a sort of deep sleep, but they can still see, hear, and speak. ❑ *Ms. Chorley uses hypnosis to help her clients relax.* [from Late Latin]

hyp|no|tize /hɪpnətaɪz/ (**hypnotizes, hypnotizing, hypnotized**) **V-T** If someone **hypnotizes** you, they put you into a sort of deep sleep, but you can still see, hear, or speak to them. ● **hyp|no|tism** /hɪpnətɪzəm/ **N-NONCOUNT** ❑ *The doctor used hypnotism to help her deal with her fear of flying.* ● **hyp|no|tist** (**hypnotists**) **N-COUNT** ❑ *My sister-in-law makes regular visits to a hypnotist.* [from Late Latin]

hy|pot|enuse /haɪpɒtənus/ (**hypotenuses**)
N-COUNT MATH The **hypotenuse** of a right-angled triangle is the side opposite its right angle.

hy|poth|esis /haɪpɒθɪsɪs/ (**hypotheses**)
N-COUNT/N-NONCOUNT A **hypothesis** is an idea that is suggested as a possible explanation for a particular situation or condition, but which has not yet been proved to be correct. [FORMAL] ❑ *Work will now begin to test the hypothesis in rats.* [from Greek]
→ look at Word Webs: **experiment, science**

hys|teri|cal /hɪstɛrɪkəl/
1 ADJ If you are **hysterical**, you are so excited or upset that you cannot control your feelings. ❑ *Calm down. Don't get hysterical.* ● **hys|teri|cal|ly** /hɪstɛrɪkli/ ADV ❑ *One young girl screamed hysterically and fell to the ground.*
2 ADJ **Hysterical** laughter is loud and cannot be controlled. [INFORMAL] ❑ *We could hear hysterical laughter coming from the kitchen.* ● **hys|teri|cal|ly** ADV ❑ *Everyone was laughing hysterically.*
3 ADJ If something or someone is **hysterical**, they are very funny. [INFORMAL] ❑ *Robert's stories are always hysterical.* ● **hys|teri|cal|ly** ADV ❑ *His new movie is hysterically funny.* [from Latin]

Ii

I /aɪ/ **PRON** You use **I** to talk about yourself. You use **I** as the subject of a verb. ❑ *I live in Arizona.* ❑ *Jim and I are getting married.* [from Latin]

ice /aɪs/
1 **N-NONCOUNT** **Ice** is frozen water. ❑ *The ground was covered with ice.* ❑ *Do you want ice in your soda?*
2 **PHRASE** If you **break the ice** in a situation, you do something to make people feel relaxed and comfortable. ❑ *Her friendly manner helped break the ice.* [from Old English]
→ look at Word Webs: **climate, crystal, glacier, precipitation, snow**

Ice Age **N-PROPER** SCIENCE The **Ice Age** was a period of time lasting many thousands of years, during which a lot of the Earth's surface was covered with ice.

ice|berg /aɪsbɜrg/ (**icebergs**) **N-COUNT** SCIENCE An **iceberg** is a very large piece of ice that floats in the ocean. [from Middle Dutch]

ice cream (**ice creams**)
1 **N-COUNT/N-NONCOUNT** **Ice cream** is a very cold sweet food that is made from frozen cream. ❑ *Serve the pie warm with vanilla ice cream.*
2 **N-COUNT** An **ice cream** is a portion of ice cream. ❑ *Do you want an ice cream?*
→ look at Picture Dictionary: **dessert**

ice cream

ice hock|ey **N-NONCOUNT** SPORTS **Ice hockey** is a game that is played on ice by two teams. They use long curved sticks to try to hit a small rubber disk called a puck into a goal.

ice skate (**ice skates, ice skating, ice skated**)
1 **N-COUNT** **Ice skates** are boots with a thin metal blade underneath that people wear to move quickly on ice.
2 **V-I** If you **ice skate**, you move around on ice wearing ice skates. ❑ *We never learned to ice*

skate or ski. ● **ice skat|ing** **N-NONCOUNT** ❑ *I love watching ice skating on television.*

ice wedg|ing /aɪs wɛdʒɪŋ/ **N-NONCOUNT** SCIENCE **Ice wedging** is a geological process in which rocks are broken because water freezes in gaps or cracks in the rocks.

ici|cle /aɪsɪkᵊl/ (**icicles**) **N-COUNT** An **icicle** is a long pointed piece of ice that hangs down from a surface. [from Old English]

icon /aɪkɒn/ (**icons**) **N-COUNT** TECHNOLOGY An **icon** is a picture on a computer screen that you can choose using a mouse, in order to open a particular program. ❑ *Kate clicked on the mail icon on her computer screen.* [from Latin]

icy /aɪsi/ (**icier, iciest**)
1 **ADJ** Something that is **icy** is extremely cold. ❑ *An icy wind was blowing.*
2 **ADJ** An **icy** road has ice on it. [from Old English]

ID /aɪ di/ (**IDs**) **N-COUNT/N-NONCOUNT** If you have **ID**, you are carrying a document that shows who you are. ❑ *I had no ID so I couldn't prove that it was my car.*

I'd /aɪd/
1 **I'd** is short for "I had." ❑ *I was sure I'd seen her before.*
2 **I'd** is short for "I would." ❑ *There are some questions I'd like to ask.*

idea /aɪdiə/ (**ideas**)
1 **N-COUNT** An **idea** is a thought, especially a new one. ❑ *These people have a lot of great ideas.* ❑ *"Let's have something to eat."—"Good idea."*
2 **N-COUNT** An **idea** is an opinion or a belief about what something is like or should be like. ❑ *Everyone has different ideas about how to raise children.*
3 **N-SING** If you have an **idea** of something, you know something about it. ❑ *We had no idea what was happening.*
4 **N-SING** The **idea** of something is its aim or purpose. ❑ *The idea is to have fun.* [from Late Latin]

Word Partnership	Use idea with :
ADJ	**bad** idea, **bright** idea, **brilliant** idea, **great** idea **1**
	crazy idea, **different** idea, **dumb** idea, **interesting** idea, **new** idea, **original** idea **1 2**
	the main idea, **the whole** idea **4**
V	**get an** idea, **have an** idea **1 3**

ideal /aɪdiəl/ (**ideals**)

1 **ADJ** The **ideal** person or thing for a particular purpose is the best possible person or thing for it. ❑ *You are the ideal person to do the job.*

2 **ADJ** An **ideal** situation is a perfect one. ❑ *Imagine for a moment that you're living in an ideal world.*

3 **N-COUNT** An **ideal** is a principle or an idea that people try to achieve. ❑ *We must defend the ideals of liberty and freedom.* [from Late Middle English]

ideal|ly /aɪdiəli/ **ADV** If you say that **ideally** a particular thing should happen or be done, you mean that this is what you would like to happen or be done, but you know that it may not be possible or practical. ❑ *Ideally, you should drink every 10–15 minutes during exercise.* [from Late Middle English]

ideal ma|chine (**ideal machines**) **N-COUNT**
SCIENCE An **ideal machine** is a machine that is a hundred percent efficient but cannot exist in reality because of forces such as friction.

Word Link	ident ≈ same : identical, identification, unidentified

iden|ti|cal /aɪdɛntɪkəl/ **ADJ** Things that are **identical** are exactly the same. ❑ *The houses were almost identical.* [from Late Latin]

iden|ti|fi|ca|tion /aɪdɛntɪfɪkeɪʃən/ (**identifications**)

1 **N-NONCOUNT** If someone asks you for some **identification**, they want to see a document that proves who you are. ❑ *The police asked him to show some identification.*

2 **N-COUNT/N-NONCOUNT** **Identification** is the act of recognizing someone or something. ❑ *Early identification of the disease is important.*

3 **N-COUNT/N-NONCOUNT** The **identification** of one person or thing **with** another, is the idea or feeling that they are closely related in some way. ❑ *...the identification of Spain with Catholicism.* [from Late Latin]

iden|ti|fy /aɪdɛntɪfaɪ/ (**identifies, identifying, identified**)

1 **V-T** If you can **identify** someone or something, you are able to say who or what they are. ❑ *Now we have identified the problem, we must decide how to fix it.* ❑ *The handbook tells you how to identify the different birds.*

2 **V-T** If you **identify** something, you discover or notice its existence. ❑ *Scientists have identified foods that are able to fight cancer.*

3 **V-T** If a particular thing **identifies** someone or something, it makes them easy to recognize, by making them different in some way. ❑ *She wore a nurse's hat to identify her.*

4 **V-T** If you **identify** one person or thing **with** another, you think that they are closely related in some way. ❑ *He identified himself with modern Russian composers.* [from Late Latin]

iden|tity /aɪdɛntɪti/ (**identities**)

1 **N-COUNT** Your **identity** is who you are. ❑ *He uses the name Abu to hide his identity.*

2 **N-COUNT/N-NONCOUNT** The **identity** of a person or a place is the characteristics that make them different from others. ❑ *I wanted a sense of my own identity.* [from Late Latin]

Word Partnership	Use identity with :
N	identity **theft** **1**
	identity **crisis, sense of** identity **2**
ADJ	**ethnic** identity, **national** identity, **personal** identity **2**

iden|tity theft **N-NONCOUNT** **Identity theft** is the crime of stealing someone's personal information, making it possible to use their bank account. ❑ *Cases of criminal identity theft are going to increase.*

idi|om /ɪdiəm/ (**idioms**) **N-COUNT**
LANGUAGE ARTS An **idiom** is a group of words that have a particular meaning when you use them together. For example, "to hit the roof" is an idiom that means to become very angry. [from Latin]

idio|phone /ɪdiəfoʊn/ (**idiophones**)
N-COUNT MUSIC An **idiophone** is any musical instrument that produces its sound by being hit or shaken.

id|iot /ɪdiət/ (**idiots**) **N-COUNT** An **idiot** is someone who is very stupid. ❑ *I felt like an idiot.* [from Latin]

idle /aɪdəl/

1 **ADJ** If people who were working are **idle**, they have no jobs or work. ❑ *4,000 workers* *have been idle for 12 weeks.*

2 **ADJ** If machines or factories are **idle**, they are not working or being used. ❑ *The machine is lying idle.*

3 **ADJ** If you say that someone is **idle**, you disapprove of them because they are not doing anything and you think they should be. ❑ *...idle men who spent the day reading.* ● **idly** **ADV** ❑ *We were idly sitting around.*

4 **ADJ** **Idle** is used to describe something that you do for no particular reason. ❑ *We filled the time with idle talk.* ● **idly** **ADV** ❑ *We talked idly about baseball.* [from Old English]

idol /ˈaɪdəl/ (**idols**) **N-COUNT** An **idol** is a famous person who is greatly admired or loved. ❑ *The crowd cheered when their idol waved to the cameras.* [from Late Latin]

IED /ˈaɪ iː diː/ (**IEDs**) **N-COUNT** An **IED** is a simple bomb, especially one that is used by people who are not in the army. ❑ *...a roadside IED.*

if /ɪf/

PRONUNCIATION HELP

If is often pronounced /ɪf/ at the beginning of a sentence.

---

1 **CONJ** You use **if** to talk about things that might happen. ❑ *You can go if you want.* ❑ *He might win—if he's lucky.*

2 **CONJ** You use **if** when you are talking about a question that someone has asked. ❑ *He asked if I wanted some water.*

3 **CONJ** You use **if** to suggest that something might be slightly different from what you are stating in the main part of the sentence. ❑ *That standard is quite difficult, if not impossible, to achieve.* ❑ *What one quality, if any, do you dislike about your partner?*

4 **PHRASE** You use **if only** to express a strong wish. ❑ *If only I had a car.*

5 **PHRASE** You use **as if** to compare one thing with another. ❑ *He moved his hand as if*

he was writing something. [from Old English]
→ look at Usage note at **whether**

ig|ne|ous /ˈɪɡniəs/ **ADJ** **SCIENCE** In geology, **igneous** rocks are rocks that were once so hot that they were liquid. [from Latin]

ig|no|rant /ˈɪɡnərənt/ **ADJ** An **ignorant** person does not know things. ❑ *People don't want to appear ignorant.* ❑ *Most people are ignorant of these facts.* ● **ig|no|rance** /ˈɪɡnərəns/ **N-NONCOUNT** ❑ *I feel embarrassed by my ignorance of world history.* [from Latin]
→ look at Usage note at **stupid**

ig|nore /ɪɡˈnɔːr/ (**ignores, ignoring, ignored**) **V-T** If you **ignore** someone or something, you do not pay any attention to them. ❑ *Her husband ignored her.* [from Latin]

ill /ɪl/ (**ills**)

1 **ADJ** Someone who is **ill** is not in good health. ❑ *He is seriously ill with cancer.*

2 **N-COUNT** Problems are sometimes referred to as **ills**. [FORMAL] ❑ *He's responsible for many of the country's ills.*

3 **ADJ** You can use **ill** in front of some nouns to show that you are referring to something harmful or unpleasant. [FORMAL] ❑ *Fortunately, no one suffered any ill effects.*

Word Partnership	Use **ill** with :
V	become ill, feel ill, look ill **1**
ADV	critically ill, mentally ill, physically ill, seriously ill, very ill **1**

I'll /aɪl/ **I'll** is short for "I will" or "I shall." ❑ *I'll go there tomorrow.*

il|legal /ɪˈliːɡəl/ **ADJ** If something is **illegal**, it is not allowed by law. ❑ *It is illegal for the interviewer to ask your age.* ❑ *I have done nothing illegal.* ● **il|legal|ly** **ADV** ❑ *He was parked illegally.*

ill|ness /ˈɪlnɪs/ (**illnesses**)

1 **N-COUNT** An **illness** is a particular disease

Word Web   illness

Most **infectious diseases** pass from person to person. However, some people have caught **viruses** from animals. During the 2002 SARS **epidemic,** doctors discovered that the disease came from birds. In 2014, the Ebola virus caused more than 11,000 deaths, mainly in a few West African nations. Medical workers used **symptoms** such as **fever, vomiting,** and a **rash** to help **diagnose** the disease. **Treatment** was not easy. By the time the symptoms appeared, the disease had already caused a lot of damage.

or a period of bad health. ❑ *She is recovering from a serious illness.*

2 **N-NONCOUNT** Illness is the fact or experience of being ill. ❑ *He was away from school because of illness.* [from Old Norse]

→ look at Word Web: **illness**

Thesaurus	illness	Also look up :
N	ailment, disease **1**	
	sickness; *(ant.)* health **2**	

Word Partnership	Use illness with :
N	**signs/symptoms of** *an* illness **1**
ADJ	**serious** illness, **long/short** illness, **mental** illness, **mysterious** illness, **sudden** illness, **terminal** illness **2**
V	**diagnose an** illness, **have an** illness, **suffer from** *an* illness, **treat** *an* illness **1**

il|lu|mi|nate /ɪlúmɪneɪt/ (**illuminates, illuminating, illuminated**)

1 **V-T** To **illuminate** something means to shine light on it and to make it brighter. [FORMAL] ❑ *Streetlights illuminated the street.*

● **il|lu|mi|na|tion** /ɪlúmɪneɪʃ°n/ **N-NONCOUNT** ❑ *The only illumination came from a small window.*

2 **V-T** If you **illuminate** something that is unclear or difficult to understand, you make it clearer by explaining it carefully or giving information about it. [FORMAL] ❑ *They use games and drawings to illuminate their subject.*

● **il|lu|mi|nat|ing** **ADJ** ❑ *This is a very illuminating book.* [from Latin]

il|lu|sion /ɪlúʒ°n/ (**illusions**)

1 **N-COUNT/N-NONCOUNT** An **illusion** is a false idea or belief. ❑ *He's under the illusion that money makes people happy.*

2 **N-COUNT** An **illusion** is something that seems to exist. ❑ *Large windows can give the illusion of more space.* [from Latin]

Word Partnership	Use illusion with :
PREP	**be under an** illusion **1**
V	**create an** illusion, **give an** illusion **about/of/that** *something* **1** **2**

il|lus|trate /ɪləstreɪt/ (**illustrates, illustrating, illustrated**)

1 **V-T** If you **illustrate** a book, you put pictures into it. ❑ *She illustrates children's books.* ● **il|lus|tra|tion** (**illustrations**) **N-COUNT/N-NONCOUNT** ❑ *It's a book with beautiful illustrations.*

2 **V-T** If something **illustrates** a point, it makes it clearer or proves it. ❑ *Let me give an example to illustrate my point.* ❑ *The accident*

illustrates how difficult it is to design a safe system.

● **il|lus|tra|tion** /ɪləstreɪʃ°n/ (**illustrations**) **N-COUNT/N-NONCOUNT** ❑ *This is a good illustration of how an essay should be written.* [from Latin]

→ look at Word Web: **animation**

IM /aɪ ɛm/ (**IMs**) **N-COUNT/N-NONCOUNT** TECHNOLOGY **IM** is short for **instant messaging**. ❑ *The device lets you chat via IM.*

I'm /aɪm/ **I'm** is short for "I am." ❑ *I'm sorry.*

im|age /ɪmɪdʒ/ (**images**)

1 **N-COUNT** An **image** is a picture of someone or something. [FORMAL] ❑ *The image on screen changes every 10 seconds.*

2 **N-COUNT** If you have an **image** of something or someone, you have a picture or an idea of them in your mind. ❑ *If you talk about California, people have an image of sunny blue skies.*

3 **N-COUNT** The **image** of a person, a group, or an organization is the way that they appear to other people. ❑ *The government does not have a good public image.* [from Old French]

→ look at Word Webs: **eye, photography, telescope, television**

Word Partnership	Use image with :
N	image **on a screen** **1** **body** image, **self-**image **2**
ADJ	**corporate** image, **negative/positive** image, **public** image **3**
V	**display an** image **1** **project an** image **2** **3**

im|agi|nary /ɪmædʒɪnɛri/ **ADJ** An **imaginary** person, place, or thing exists only in your mind or in a story, and not in real life. ❑ *Lots of children have imaginary friends.* [from Latin]

→ look at Word Web: **fantasy**

im|agi|na|tion /ɪmædʒɪneɪʃ°n/ (**imaginations**) **N-COUNT/N-NONCOUNT** Your **imagination** is your ability to invent pictures or ideas in your mind. ❑ *You must use your imagination to find an answer to this problem.* [from Latin]

→ look at Word Web: **fantasy**

Word Partnership	Use imagination with :
ADJ	**active** imagination, **lively** imagination, **vivid** imagination
PREP	**beyond** (*someone's*) imagination
N	**lack of** imagination

im|agi|na|tive /ɪmædʒɪnətɪv/ **ADJ** If you describe someone or their ideas as **imaginative**, you are praising them because they are easily able to think of or create new or exciting things. ❑ ...an imaginative writer. ● **im|agi|na|tive|ly ADV** ❑ The hotel is decorated imaginatively. [from Latin]

im|ag|ine /ɪmædʒɪn/ (**imagines, imagining, imagined**)
1 **V-T** If you **imagine** something, you form a picture or an idea of it in your mind. ❑ He could not imagine a more peaceful scene.
2 **V-T** If you **imagine** that something is true, you think that it is true. ❑ I imagine you're hungry.
3 **V-T** If you **imagine** something, you think that you have seen, heard, or experienced that thing, but in fact you have not. ❑ I realize that I imagined the whole thing. [from Latin]

Thesaurus imagine Also look up :
V   picture, see, visualize **1**
     believe, guess, think **2**

Word Partnership Use imagine with :
V   can/can't/could/couldn't imagine something, try to imagine **1 2**
ADJ difficult/easy/hard/impossible to imagine **1 2**

imi|tate /ɪmɪteɪt/ (**imitates, imitating, imitated**) **V-T** If you **imitate** someone, you copy what they do or produce. ❑ I didn't like the way he imitated my voice. [from Latin]

imi|ta|tion /ɪmɪteɪʃⁿn/ (**imitations**)
1 **N-COUNT** An **imitation** of something is a copy of it. ❑ He tried to do an imitation of an English accent. ❑ Make sure you get the real thing—don't buy an imitation.
2 **ADJ** **Imitation** things are made to look like other, more expensive products. ❑ The books are covered in imitation leather. [from Latin]

Word Link im ≈ not : immature, immortal, impossible

im|ma|ture /ɪmətʃʊər, -tʊər/ **ADJ** Someone who is **immature** behaves in a silly way that is more typical of young people. ❑ His parents thought he was too immature to get married. [from Latin]

Thesaurus immature Also look up :
ADJ childish, foolish, juvenile

im|medi|ate /ɪmidiɪt/
1 **ADJ** Something that is **immediate** happens next or very soon. ❑ There is no immediate solution to the problem.
2 **ADJ** A result or an action that is **immediate** happens or is done without any delay. ❑ The changes in the law had an immediate effect. ● **im|medi|ate|ly ADV** ❑ He immediately fell to the floor.
3 **ADJ** Someone who is in an **immediate** relationship to you is directly related to you in that relationship. ❑ Her immediate boss refused to help, so she went to his boss.
4 **ADJ** The **immediate** period before or after an event is directly before or after it. ❑ This is not likely to happen in the immediate future. ● **im|medi|ate|ly ADV** ❑ ...the weeks immediately before the war. [from Medieval Latin]

Word Partnership Use immediate with :
N   immediate **action**, immediate **plans**, immediate **reaction**, immediate **response**, immediate **results 2** immediate **future 4**

im|mense /ɪmɛns/ **ADJ** Something that is **immense** is extremely large. ❑ We still need to do an immense amount of work. [from Latin]

im|mense|ly /ɪmɛnsli/ **ADV** **Immensely** means very much. ❑ I enjoyed the movie immensely. [from Latin]

Word Link migr ≈ moving, changing : emigrant, immigrant, migrate

im|mi|grant /ɪmɪgrənt/ (**immigrants**)
N-COUNT SOCIAL STUDIES An **immigrant** is a person who comes to live in a country from another country. ❑ The company employs several immigrant workers. [from Latin]
→ look at Word Web: **culture**

im|mi|grate /ɪmɪgreɪt/ (**immigrates, immigrating, immigrated**) **V-I** If someone **immigrates** to a particular country, they come to live or work in that country, after leaving the country where they were born. ❑ ...a Russian-born professor who had immigrated to the United States. ❑ He immigrated from India at age 18. ❑ 10,000 people are expected to immigrate in the next two years. [from Latin]

im|mi|gra|tion /ɪmɪgreɪʃⁿn/
1 **N-NONCOUNT** **Immigration** is when people come into a country to live and work there. ❑ The government is changing the immigration laws.
2 **N-NONCOUNT** **Immigration** or

immigration control is the place at an international border where officials check people's passports. ❑ *You have to go through immigration and customs when you enter the country.* [from Latin]

im|mi|nent /ɪmɪnənt/ **ADJ** If something is **imminent**, it is almost certain to happen very soon. ❑ *We are not in any imminent danger.* [from Latin]

> **Word Link** im ≈ not : im**mature**, im**mortal**, im**possible**

im|mor|al /ɪmɔrəl/ **ADJ** Someone or something that is **immoral** is bad or wrong. ❑ *Some people think that it's immoral to earn a lot of money.* [from Latin]

im|mor|tal /ɪmɔrtəl/ **ADJ** Someone or something that is **immortal** will live or last forever. ❑ *They prayed to their immortal gods.* ❑ *When you're young, you think you're immortal.* [from Latin]

im|mune /ɪmyun/
1 **ADJ** If you are **immune to** a particular disease, it cannot affect you. ❑ *Some people are naturally immune to measles.*
2 **ADJ** If you are **immune to** something that happens or is done, you are not affected by it. ❑ *She is immune to criticism.* [from Latin]

im|mune sys|tem (immune systems) **N-COUNT** SCIENCE Your **immune system** consists of all the organs and processes in your body that protect you from illness and infection. ❑ *The disease affects the immune system.*

im|pact /ɪmpækt/ (impacts)
1 **N-COUNT** If someone or something has an **impact**, they have a strong effect. ❑ *The experience had a huge impact on her.*
2 **N-COUNT/N-NONCOUNT** An **impact** is the action of one object hitting another. ❑ *The impact of the crash turned the truck over.* [from Latin]
→ look at Word Web: **crash**

> **Word Partnership** Use **impact** with :
>
> | | |
> |---|---|
> | ADJ | **historical** impact, **important** impact **1** |
> | V | **have an** impact, **make an** impact **1** |
> | | **die on** impact **2** |
> | PREP | **on** impact **2** |

im|pa|tient /ɪmpeɪʃənt/
1 **ADJ** If you are **impatient**, you are annoyed because you have to wait too long for something. ❑ *People are impatient for the war to*

be over. ● **im|pa|tient|ly** **ADV** ❑ *She waited impatiently for the mail to arrive.*
2 **ADJ** If you are **impatient**, things or people annoy you very quickly. ❑ *Try not to be impatient with your kids.* ● **im|pa|tience** **N-NONCOUNT** ❑ *She tried to hide her growing impatience with him.*
3 **ADJ** If you are **impatient to** do something, you want to do it soon, and you do not want to wait. ❑ *He was impatient to get home.*
● **im|pa|tience** **N-NONCOUNT** ❑ *He didn't hide his impatience to leave.*

im|peach /ɪmpitʃ/ (impeaches, impeaching, impeached) **V-T** SOCIAL STUDIES If an official body **impeaches** a president or a government official, it decides that the president or the official has committed a serious crime. ❑ *The Republicans wanted to impeach the president.* [from Old French]

im|pede /ɪmpid/ (impedes, impeding, impeded) **V-T** If you **impede** someone or something, you make their movement, development, or progress difficult. [FORMAL] ❑ *Bad weather conditions are impeding the progress of rescue workers.* [from Latin]

> **Word Link** ped ≈ foot : **ped**al, im**ped**iment, **ped**estrian

im|pedi|ment /ɪmpɛdɪmənt/ (impediments)
1 **N-COUNT** An **impediment to** a person or thing makes their movement, development, or progress difficult. [FORMAL] ❑ *There is no legal impediment to the marriage.*
2 **N-COUNT** Someone who has a speech **impediment** has a disability that makes speaking difficult. ❑ *John's speech impediment made it difficult for people to understand him.* [from Latin]

im|pera|tive /ɪmpɛrətɪv/
1 **N-SING** LANGUAGE ARTS In grammar, **the imperative** consists of the base form of a verb and usually has no subject. The imperative is used for telling someone to do something. Examples are "Go away" and "Please be careful."
2 **ADJ** LANGUAGE ARTS An **imperative** sentence is a sentence that tells someone to do something, for example "Go home." [from Late Latin]

im|per|fect /ɪmpɜrfɪkt/ **ADJ** Something that is **imperfect** has faults. [FORMAL] ❑ *We live in an imperfect world.* [from Latin]

im|perial /ɪmpɪəriəl/

1 **ADJ** SOCIAL STUDIES **Imperial** is used to refer to things or people that are or were connected with an empire. ❑ *...the Imperial Palace in Tokyo.*
2 **ADJ** SCIENCE The **imperial** system of measurement uses inches, feet, yards, and miles to measure length, ounces and pounds to measure weight, and pints, quarts, and gallons to measure volume. [from Late Latin]

im|peri|al|ism /ɪmpɪəriəlɪzəm/

N-NONCOUNT SOCIAL STUDIES **Imperialism** is a system in which a powerful country controls other countries. ❑ *These nations are victims of imperialism.* ● **im|peri|al|ist** (**imperialists**) **N-COUNT** ❑ *She accused me of being a Western imperialist.* [from Late Latin]

im|plant (**implants, implanting, implanted**)

> PRONUNCIATION HELP
> Pronounce the verb /ɪmplænt/. Pronounce the noun /ɪmplænt/.

1 **V-T** SCIENCE To **implant** something into a person's body means to put it there, usually by means of a medical operation. ❑ *Doctors implanted a new heart a year ago.*
2 **N-COUNT** SCIENCE An **implant** is something that is implanted into a person's body. ❑ *We can replace your knee with an artificial implant.*
3 **V-I** SCIENCE When an egg or an embryo **implants in** the womb, it becomes established there and can then develop. ● **im|plan|ta|tion** /ɪmplænteɪʃ°n/ **N-NONCOUNT** ❑ *The hormone may prevent implantation of the embryo.* [from Old English]

im|pli|cate /ɪmplɪkeɪt/ (**implicates, implicating, implicated**) **V-T** To **implicate** someone means to show or claim that they were involved in something wrong or criminal. ❑ *A newspaper article implicated him in the killings.* [from Latin]

im|pli|ca|tion /ɪmplɪkeɪʃ°n/ (**implications**)

1 **N-NONCOUNT** **Implication** is the fact of showing or claiming that someone was involved in a wrong or criminal action. ❑ *...his implication in a murder.*
2 **N-COUNT** The **implications of** something are the things that are likely to happen as a result. ❑ *What are the implications of his decision?* [from Latin]

> **Word Partnership** Use **implication** with :
> ADJ   **clear** implication, **important** implication, **obvious** implication **2**

im|ply /ɪmplaɪ/ (**implies, implying, implied**)

1 **V-T** If you **imply that** something is true, you say something that indicates in an indirect way that it is true. ❑ *Are you implying that this is my fault?*
2 **V-T** If an event or situation **implies** that something is true, it makes you think that it is true. ❑ *The news article implies that he is guilty.* [from Old French]

> **Usage**   **imply** and **infer**
> *Imply* and *infer* are often confused. When you *imply* something, you say or suggest it indirectly, but when you *infer* something, you figure it out: *Xian-li smiled to imply that she thought Dun was nice, but Dun inferred that she thought he was silly.*

> **Word Link**   **port** ≈ *carrying* : ex**port**, im**port**, **port**able

im|port (**imports, importing, imported**)

> PRONUNCIATION HELP
> Pronounce the verb /ɪmpɔrt/ or /ɪmpɔrt/. Pronounce the noun /ɪmpɔrt/.

1 **V-T** SOCIAL STUDIES To **import** goods means to buy them from another country for use in your own country. ❑ *The U.S. imports over half of its oil.* ● **im|port|er** (**importers**) **N-COUNT** ❑ *Japan is the biggest importer of U.S. beef.*
2 **N-COUNT** SOCIAL STUDIES **Import** is also a noun. ❑ *Cheap imports are adding to the problems of our farmers.* [from Latin]

im|por|tant /ɪmpɔrt°nt/

1 **ADJ** If something is **important** to you, you feel that you must do, have, or think about it. ❑ *The most important thing in my life is my career.* ❑ *It's important to answer her questions honestly.* ● **im|por|tance** **N-NONCOUNT** ❑ *The teacher stressed the importance of doing our homework.* ● **im|por|tant|ly** **ADV** ❑ *I was hungry, and, more importantly, my children were hungry.*
2 **ADJ** Someone who is **important** has influence or power. ❑ *She's an important person in the world of television.* [from Old Italian]

> **Thesaurus**   **important**   Also look up :
> ADJ   critical, essential, principal, significant; (*ant.*) unimportant **1**
>   distinguished **2**

im|pose /ɪmpoʊz/ (**imposes, imposing, imposed**) **v-t** If you **impose** something **on** people, you force them to accept it. ❑ *We impose fines on drivers who break the speed limit.*
● **im|po|si|tion** /ɪmpəzɪʃ°n/ **N-NONCOUNT** ❑ ...*the imposition of a new property tax.* [from Old French]

im|pos|ing /ɪmpoʊzɪŋ/ **ADJ** If you describe someone or something as **imposing**, you mean that they have an impressive appearance or manner. ❑ *He was an imposing man.* [from Old French]

im|pos|sible /ɪmpɒsɪb°l/
1 **ADJ** Something that is **impossible** cannot be done or cannot happen. ❑ *It is impossible for me to get another job at my age.* ❑ *The snow made it impossible to play the game.*
2 **ADJ** If you describe someone as **impossible**, you mean that their bad behavior or strong views make them difficult to deal with. ❑ *You are an impossible man!* [from Latin]

im|prac|ti|cal /ɪmpræktɪk°l/ **ADJ** Something that is **impractical** is not sensible or realistic. ❑ *She was wearing impractical high-heeled shoes.* [from French]

im|press /ɪmprɛs/ (**impresses, impressing, impressed**)
1 **v-t** If something **impresses** you, you feel great admiration for it. ❑ *Their speed impressed everyone.* ● **im|pressed** **ADJ** ❑ *I was very impressed by his lecture.*
2 **v-t** If you **impress** something **on**

someone, you make them understand its importance. ❑ *I impressed the importance of hard work on the children.* [from Latin]

im|pres|sion /ɪmprɛʃ°n/ (**impressions**)
1 **N-COUNT** Your **impression** of a person or thing is what you feel or think about them. ❑ *What were your first impressions of college?*
2 **N-SING** If someone or something gives you a particular **impression**, they do or say something that makes you believe that something is true. ❑ *I don't want to give the impression that I'm running away.*
3 **PHRASE** If someone or something **makes an impression**, they have a strong effect on you. ❑ *It's her first day at work and she has already made an impression.*
4 **PHRASE** If you are **under the impression that** something is true, you believe that it is true. ❑ *I was under the impression that you were moving to New York.* [from Latin]

im|pres|sive /ɪmprɛsɪv/ **ADJ** Something that is **impressive** makes you feel strong admiration. ❑ *They collected an impressive amount of cash: $390.8 million.* [from Latin]

im|pris|on /ɪmprɪz°n/ (**imprisons, imprisoning, imprisoned**) **v-t** If someone is **imprisoned**, they are locked up or kept somewhere. ❑ *He was imprisoned for 18 months.*
● **im|pris|on|ment** /ɪmprɪz°nmənt/ **N-NONCOUNT** ❑ *She was sentenced to seven years' imprisonment.* [from Old French]

im|prop|er /ɪmprɒpər/
1 **ADJ** **Improper** activities are illegal or dishonest. [FORMAL] ❑ *The two men were arrested for improper use of a computer.*
● **im|prop|er|ly** **ADV** ❑ *I did not act improperly.*
2 **ADJ** **Improper** conditions or methods of treatment are not suitable or good enough for a particular purpose. [FORMAL] ❑ *The improper use of medicine could be dangerous.*
● **im|prop|er|ly** **ADV** ❑ *Many doctors were improperly trained.*
3 **ADJ** If you describe someone's behavior as **improper**, you mean it is offensive or shocking. ❑ *He considered it improper for a young lady to go out alone.* ● **im|prop|er|ly** **ADV** ❑ *He showed up at his job interview improperly dressed.* [from Old French]

im|prove /ɪmpruːv/ (**improves, improving, improved**)
1 **v-t/v-i** If something **improves**, or if you **improve** it, it gets better. ❑ *Your general health will improve if you drink more water.* ❑ *Their French*

improved during their trip to Paris. ❑ We are trying to improve our services to customers.

● im|prove|ment /ɪmpruvmənt/ (improvements) **N-COUNT/N-NONCOUNT** ❑ There have been some great improvements in technology in recent years.

2 **v-ɪ** If you **improve on** something, you achieve a better standard or result. ❑ We need to improve on our successes.

● im|prove|ment (improvements) **N-COUNT** ❑ The new governor is an improvement on the previous one. [from Late Latin]

Word Partnership	Use improve with :
V	**continue to** improve, **expected to** improve, **try to** improve **1** **2**
ADV	**significantly** improve, improve **slightly** **1** **2**

Word Partnership	Use improvement with :
ADJ	**big** improvement, **dramatic** improvement, **gradual** improvement, **marked** improvement, **significant** improvement, **slight** improvement **1** **2**
N	**home** improvement, **self**-improvement, **signs of** improvement **1** **2**

im|pro|vise /ɪmprəvaɪz/ (improvises, improvising, improvised) **v-T/v-ɪ** When performers **improvise**, they invent music or words as they play, sing, or speak. ❑ The jazz band improvised on well-known tunes. ❑ Richard improvised a prayer. [from French]

Word Link	puls ≈ driving, pushing : compulsion, expulsion, impulse

im|pulse /ɪmpʌls/ (impulses) **1** **N-COUNT/N-NONCOUNT** An **impulse** is a sudden feeling that you must do something. ❑ I felt a sudden impulse to tell her that I loved her.

2 **PHRASE** If you do something **on impulse**, you suddenly decide to do it. ❑ Sean usually acts on impulse. [from Latin]

Word Partnership	Use impulse with :
ADJ	**first** impulse, **strong** impulse, **sudden** impulse **1**
V	**control an** impulse, **resist an** impulse **1** **act on** impulse **2**

im|pul|sive /ɪmpʌlsɪv/ **ADJ** An **impulsive** person does things suddenly, without thinking about them carefully first. ❑ He is too impulsive to be a good leader. [from Latin]

in

① POSITION
② TIME AND NUMBERS
③ OTHER USES AND PHRASES

① **in**

PRONUNCIATION HELP
Pronounce the preposition /ɪn/.
Pronounce the adverb /ɪn/.

1 **PREP** You use **in** when you are saying where someone or something is. ❑ My brother was playing in the backyard. ❑ Mark now lives in Singapore. ❑ Are you still in bed? It's almost lunchtime!

2 **ADV** If you **are in**, you are at your home or the place where you work. ❑ Maria isn't in just now.

3 **PREP** If you are dressed **in** a piece of clothing, you are wearing it. ❑ Who is the woman in the red dress?

4 **ADJ** SPORTS In games such as tennis or basketball, a ball that is **in** is inside the area of play. Compare with **out**. ❑ The line judge signalled that the ball was in. [from Old English]
→ look at Picture Dictionary: **location**

② **in** /ɪn/

1 **PREP** If something happens **in** a particular period of time, it happens during that time. ❑ He was born in 1996. ❑ Sales improved in April.

2 **PREP** If you do something **in** a particular period of time, that is how long it takes. ❑ He walked two hundred and fifty miles in eleven days.

3 **PREP** If something will happen **in** a particular length of time, it will happen after that length of time. ❑ Lunch will be ready in a few minutes.

4 **PREP** You use **in** for saying that a number is within a particular range. ❑ ...young people in their twenties.

5 **PREP** You use **in** to express a relationship between numbers. ❑ One in three children can't find the U.S. on a map. [from Old English]

③ **in** /ɪn/

1 **PREP** You use **in** to talk about a state or situation. ❑ Dave was in a hurry to get back to work. ❑ The kitchen's in a mess.

2 **PREP** You use **in** to talk about the way that something is done or said. ❑ Please do not write in pencil—use a pen. ❑ The men were speaking in Russian. ❑ She always talks in a loud voice.

i

3 **PREP** You use **in** when you are talking about the job that someone does. ❑ *John's son is in the navy.* ❑ *Dad works in the music industry.*

4 **PHRASE** If someone **is in for** a shock or a surprise, they are going to experience it. ❑ *You might be in for a shock when you start high school.*

5 **PHRASE** You use **in that** to introduce an explanation of a statement you have just made. ❑ *I'm lucky in that I've got four sisters.* [from Old English]

Word Link	in ≈ not : **in**ability, **in**accurate, **in**adequate

in|abil|ity /ɪnəbɪlɪti/ **N-NONCOUNT** Someone's **inability to** do something is the fact that they cannot do it. ❑ *Her inability to concentrate could cause an accident.* [from Old French]

in|ac|ces|sible /ɪnəksɛsɪbªl/
1 **ADJ** An **inaccessible** place is very difficult or impossible to reach. ❑ *...people living in inaccessible parts of China.*
2 **ADJ** Someone or something that is **inaccessible** is difficult or impossible to understand or appreciate. ❑ *The language in the book is inaccessible to ordinary people.* [from Old French]

in|ac|cu|rate /ɪnækyərɪt/ **ADJ** Information that is **inaccurate** is not completely correct. ❑ *Her comments are inaccurate and untrue.* [from Latin]

in|ac|tive /ɪnæktɪv/ **ADJ** Someone or something that is **inactive** is not doing anything or is not working. ❑ *He has always been politically inactive.* ● **in|ac|tiv|ity** /ɪnæktɪvɪti/ **N-NONCOUNT** ❑ *Long periods of inactivity are bad for you.* [from Latin]

in|ad|equate /ɪnædɪkwɪt/ **ADJ** If something is **inadequate**, there is not enough of it, or it is not good enough. ❑ *Inadequate sleep was the cause of his headaches.* [from Latin]

in|ap|pro|pri|ate /ɪnəproupriɪt/ **ADJ** Something that is **inappropriate** is wrong or bad in a particular situation. ❑ *The movie is inappropriate for young children.* [from Late Latin]

in|augu|rate /ɪnɔgyʊreɪt/ (**inaugurates, inaugurating, inaugurated**) **V-T** SOCIAL STUDIES When a new leader **is inaugurated**, they are given their new position at an official ceremony. ❑ *The new president will be inaugurated on January 20th.* ● **in|augu|ra|tion**

/ɪnɔgyʊreɪʃªn/ (**inaugurations**) **N-COUNT/N-NONCOUNT** ❑ *...the inauguration of the new governor.* [from Latin]

in|au|then|tic /ɪnɔθɛntɪk/ **ADJ** Something that is **inauthentic** is false or copied, often in a way that does not follow tradition. ❑ *...an inauthentic but tasty paella recipe.* [from Late Latin]

in|box /ɪnbɒks/ (**inboxes**) also **in-box**
N-COUNT TECHNOLOGY Your **inbox** is where your computer stores emails that have arrived for you. ❑ *I went home and checked my inbox.* [from Old English]

Inc. BUSINESS **Inc.** is short for "Incorporated" when it is used after a company's name. ❑ *...BP America Inc.*

in|ca|pable /ɪnkeɪpəbªl/ **ADJ** Someone who is **incapable of** doing something is unable to do it. ❑ *She is incapable of making sensible decisions.* [from French]

in|cen|tive /ɪnsɛntɪv/ (**incentives**)
N-COUNT/N-NONCOUNT An **incentive** is something that makes you want to do something. ❑ *We want to give our employees an incentive to work hard.* [from Late Latin]

inch /ɪntʃ/ (**inches, inching, inched**)
1 **N-COUNT** MATH An **inch** is a unit for measuring length. There are 2.54 centimeters in an inch. There are twelve inches in a foot. ❑ *Dig a hole 18 inches deep.*
2 **V-T/V-I** To **inch** somewhere means to move there very slowly and carefully. ❑ *A climber was inching up the wall of rock.* [from Old English]
→ look at Picture Dictionary: **measurement**

in|ci|dent /ɪnsɪdənt/ (**incidents**) **N-COUNT** An **incident** is something unpleasant that happens. [FORMAL] ❑ *The incident happened in the early hours of Sunday morning.* [from Medieval Latin]

in|ci|den|tal|ly /ɪnsɪdɛntli/ **ADV** You use **incidentally** to introduce a point that is not directly relevant to what you are saying, often a question or extra information that you have just thought of. ❑ *She introduced me to her boyfriend (who, incidentally, doesn't speak a word of English).* [from Medieval Latin]

in|cin|er|ate /ɪnsɪnəreɪt/ (**incinerates, incinerating, incinerated**) **V-T** When authorities **incinerate** garbage or waste material, they burn it completely in a special container. ❑ *They were incinerating* leaves. ● **in|cin|era|tion** /ɪnsɪnəreɪʃ°n/ **N-NONCOUNT** ❑ ...the incineration of the weapons. [from Medieval Latin]

in|ci|sor /ɪnsaɪzər/ (incisors) **N-COUNT** SCIENCE Your **incisors** are the teeth at the front of your mouth that you use for biting into food. [from Latin]
→ look at Word Web: carnivore

Word Link clin ≈ leaning : anticline, decline, incline

in|cline /ɪnklaɪn/ (inclines) **N-COUNT** An **incline** is land that slopes at an angle. [FORMAL] ❑ He stopped at the edge of a steep incline.

in|clined /ɪnklaɪnd/ **ADJ** If you say that you are **inclined to** have a particular opinion, you mean that you have this opinion, but you do not feel strongly about it. ❑ I am inclined to agree with Alan. [from Latin]

in|clined plane (inclined planes) **N-COUNT** MATH An **inclined plane** is a flat surface that is sloping at a particular angle.

in|clude /ɪnklud/ (includes, including, included) **V-T** If something **includes** another thing, it has that thing as one of its parts. ❑ The trip will include a day at the beach. [from Latin]

Usage include

Saying that a group *includes* one or more people or things implies that the group has additional people or things in it also. For instance, the sentence: *Cities in Japan include Tokyo and Kyoto* implies that Japan has additional cities.

in|clud|ing /ɪnkludɪŋ/ **PREP** You use **including** to talk about people or things that are part of a particular group of people or things. ❑ Thousands were killed, including many women and children. [from Latin]

in|come /ɪnkʌm/ (incomes) **N-COUNT/N-NONCOUNT** BUSINESS A person's **income** is the money that they earn or receive. ❑ Many of the families here are on low incomes. [from Old English]

Word Partnership Use income with :

ADJ	**average** income, **fixed** income, **large/ small** income, **a second** income, **steady** income, **taxable** income
V	**earn an** income, **supplement your** income
N	**loss of** income, **source of** income

in|come tax (income taxes) **N-COUNT/N-NONCOUNT** BUSINESS **Income tax** is a part of your income that you have to pay regularly to the government. ❑ You pay income tax every month.

in|com|pe|tent /ɪnkɒmpɪtənt/ **ADJ** Someone who is **incompetent** is unable to do a job properly. ❑ He always fires incompetent employees. [from Latin]

in|com|plete /ɪnkəmplit/ **ADJ** Something that is **incomplete** is not yet finished, or does not have all the parts that it needs. ❑ The data we have is incomplete. [from Latin]

in|con|sid|er|ate /ɪnkənsɪdərɪt/ **ADJ** Someone who is **inconsiderate** does not think enough about how their behavior will affect other people. ❑ It was inconsiderate of her to come without calling. [from Latin]

in|con|ven|ience /ɪnkənvinyəns/ (inconveniences, inconveniencing, inconvenienced)
1 **N-COUNT/N-NONCOUNT** If someone or something causes **inconvenience**, they cause problems or difficulties. ❑ We apologize for any inconvenience caused during the repairs.
2 **V-T** If someone **inconveniences** you, they cause problems or difficulties for you. ❑ He promised not to inconvenience them any further. [from Latin]

in|con|ven|ient /ɪnkənvinyənt/ **ADJ** Something that is **inconvenient** causes difficulties for someone. ❑ I know it's inconvenient, but I have to see you now. [from Latin]

in|cor|po|rate /ɪnkɔrpəreɪt/ (incorporates, incorporating, incorporated) **V-T** If one thing **incorporates** another thing, it includes the other thing. [FORMAL] ❑ The new cars will incorporate a number of major changes. [from Late Latin]

in|cor|rect /ɪnkərɛkt/ **ADJ** Something that is **incorrect** is wrong or untrue. ❑ The answer he gave was incorrect. ● **in|cor|rect|ly** **ADV** ❑ The article suggested, incorrectly, that he was sick. [from Latin]

Word Link cresc, creas ≈ growing : crescent, decrease, increase

in|crease (increases, increasing, increased)

PRONUNCIATION HELP
Pronounce the verb /ɪnkris/. Pronounce the noun /ɪnkris/.

1 **V-T/V-I** If something **increases**, or you

increase it, it gets bigger in some way.
❏ *The population continues to increase.* ❏ *Japanese exports increased by 2% last year.* ❏ *My employers increased my pay when I was promoted.*
2 **N-COUNT** If there is an **increase in** the number, level, or amount of something, it becomes greater. ❏ *There was a sudden increase in the cost of oil.* [from Old French]

Thesaurus	increase Also look up :
V	expand, extend, raise; *(ant.)* decrease, reduce **1**
N	gain, hike, raise, rise; *(ant.)* decrease, reduction **2**

Word Partnership	Use increase with :
ADV	increase **dramatically**, increase **rapidly** **1**
N	**population** increase, **price** increase, **salary** increase **1** increase **in crime**, increase **in demand**, increase **in spending**, increase **in temperature**, increase **in value** **2**
ADJ	**big** increase, **marked** increase, **sharp** increase **1** **2**

in|creas|ing|ly /ɪnkrisɪŋli/ **ADV** You can use **increasingly** to talk about a situation that is happening more and more. ❏ *He was finding it increasingly difficult to make decisions.* [from Old French]

Word Link	cred ≈ to believe : credibility, discredit, incredible

in|cred|ible /ɪnkrɛdɪbəl/
1 **ADJ** You use **incredible** to say how good something is, or to make what you are saying stronger. ❏ *The food was incredible.* ❏ *I work an incredible number of hours.*
● **in|cred|ibly** **ADV** ❏ *It was incredibly hard work.*
2 **ADJ** If you say that something is **incredible**, you mean that you cannot believe it is really true. ❏ *It seems incredible that nobody saw the danger.* [from Latin]

Word Partnership	Use incredible with :
N	incredible **discovery**, incredible **experience**, incredible **prices** **1**

in|cre|du|lity /ɪnkrɪduliti/ **N-NONCOUNT**
If someone reacts with **incredulity**, they are unable to believe something because it is very surprising or shocking. [WRITTEN]
❏ *The announcement has been met with incredulity.* [from French]

in|credu|lous /ɪnkrɛdʒələs/ **ADJ** If someone is **incredulous**, they are unable to believe something because it is very surprising or shocking. ❏ *Her voice was incredulous.*
● **in|credu|lous|ly** **ADV** ❏ *"You told Pete?" Rachel said incredulously.* [from Latin]

in|cum|bent /ɪnkʌmbənt/ (**incumbents**)
1 **N-COUNT** SOCIAL STUDIES An **incumbent** is someone who holds an official post at a particular time. [FORMAL] ❏ *Incumbents usually have a high chance of being re-elected.*
2 **ADJ** SOCIAL STUDIES **Incumbent** is also an adjective. [FORMAL] ❏ *...the only candidate who defeated an incumbent senator.* [from Latin]

in|cur /ɪnkɜr/ (**incurs, incurring, incurred**)
V-T If you **incur** something unpleasant, it happens to you because of something you have done. [WRITTEN] ❏ *The government incurred huge debts.* [from Latin]

in|deed /ɪndid/
1 **ADV** You use **indeed** to make something you have said stronger. ❏ *He admitted that he had indeed paid him.*
2 **ADV** You use **indeed** to make the word "very" stronger ❏ *The results were very strange indeed.*
3 **ADV** You use **indeed** to introduce a statement that makes the point you have already made stronger. ❏ *We have nothing against change; indeed, we encourage it.* [from Old English]

in|defi|nite /ɪndɛfɪnɪt/ **ADJ** If a situation or a period is **indefinite**, people have not decided when it will end. ❏ *He was sent to jail for an indefinite period.* ● **in|defi|nite|ly** **ADV** ❏ *We cannot allow this situation to continue indefinitely.* [from Latin]

in|defi|nite ar|ti|cle (**indefinite articles**)
N-COUNT LANGUAGE ARTS The words "a" and "an" are sometimes called **the indefinite article**.

in|den|tured serv|ant /ɪndɛntʃərd sɜrvənt/ (**indentured servants**) **N-COUNT**
SOCIAL STUDIES In the past, an **indentured servant** was a worker who had to serve another person in exchange for things such as food, clothes, and a place to sleep, for a period of time that was agreed in a contract.

Word Link	ence ≈ state, condition : dependence, excellence, independence

in|de|pend|ence /ɪndɪpɛndəns/
1 **N-NONCOUNT** SOCIAL STUDIES If a country has **independence**, it is not ruled by another

country. ❑ *In 1816, Argentina declared its independence from Spain.*

2 **N-NONCOUNT** Someone's **independence** is the fact that they do not need help from other people. ❑ *He was afraid of losing his independence.*

Word Partnership	Use **independence** with :
ADJ	**economic/financial** independence **1** **2**
V	**fight for** independence, **gain** independence **1** **2**
N	**a struggle for** independence **1** **2**

in|de|pend|ent /ɪndɪpɛndənt/
1 **ADJ** If things or people are **independent**, they are not affected by, or do not need help from, other people. ❑ *We need an independent review.* ● **in|de|pen|dent|ly** **ADV** ❑ *We have groups of people working independently in different parts of the world.*
2 **ADJ** If someone is **independent**, they can take care of themselves without needing help or money from anyone else. ❑ *Children become more independent as they grow.* ● **in|de|pen|dent|ly** **ADV** ❑ *We want to help disabled students to live independently.*
3 **ADJ** **Independent** countries and states are not ruled by other countries, but have their own government. ❑ *Papua New Guinea became independent from Australia in 1975.*

in|dex /ɪndɛks/ (**indexes** or **indices** /ɪndɪsiz/)

> **LANGUAGE HELP**
> **Indexes** or **indices** can be used as the plural for meaning **1**. **Indexes** is the plural for meaning **2**.

1 **N-COUNT** LANGUAGE ARTS An **index** is a list printed at the back of a book that tells you what is included in it and on which pages you can find each item. ❑ *There's a subject index at the back of the book.*
2 **N-COUNT** An **index** is a system that is used for recording or measuring changes. ❑ *Your body mass index (= your height in relation to your weight) should not be more than 30.* [from Latin]

in|dex con|tour (**index contours**) or **index contour line** **N-COUNT** SCIENCE An **index contour** is a thick contour line on a map that shows the height of the area marked by the line.

In|dian /ɪndiən/ (**Indians**) **N-COUNT** SOCIAL STUDIES **Indians** are the people who

lived in America before Europeans arrived. Now, people prefer to call them **Native Americans**.

in|di|cate /ɪndɪkeɪt/ (**indicates, indicating, indicated**)
1 **V-T** One thing **indicates** another when the first thing shows that the second is true. ❑ *The report indicates that most people agree.*
2 **V-T** If you **indicate** something to someone, you show them where it is. [FORMAL] ❑ *He indicated a chair. "Sit down."*
3 **V-T** If you **indicate** an opinion, an intention, or a fact, you mention it in an indirect way. ❑ *Mr. Rivers indicated that he might leave the company.* [from Latin]

Thesaurus	**indicate** Also look up :
V	demonstrate, hint, mean, reveal, show **3**

in|di|ca|tion /ɪndɪkeɪʃⁿn/ (**indications**) **N-COUNT/N-NONCOUNT** An **indication** is a sign that suggests something. ❑ *This statement is a strong indication that the government is changing its mind.* [from Latin]

in|di|ca|tor /ɪndɪkeɪtər/ (**indicators**) **N-COUNT** An **indicator** is a measurement or value that gives you an idea of what something is like. ❑ *The phone has a low battery indicator.* [from Latin]

in|dict|ment /ɪndaɪtmənt/ (**indictments**) **N-COUNT** If you say that one thing is **an indictment of** another thing, you mean that it shows how bad the other thing is. ❑ *The movie is an indictment of Hollywood.*

in|dif|fer|ent /ɪndɪfərənt/ **ADJ** Someone who is **indifferent to** something is not at all interested in it. ❑ *We have become indifferent to the suffering of other people.* [from Latin]

in|dig|enous /ɪndɪdʒɪnəs/ **ADJ** SOCIAL STUDIES **Indigenous** people or things belong to the country in which they are found, rather than coming there or being brought there from another country. [FORMAL] ❑ *...the country's indigenous population.* [from Latin]

in|di|ges|tion /ɪndɪdʒɛstʃn, -daɪ-/ **N-NONCOUNT** If you have **indigestion**, you have pains in your stomach because of something that you have eaten.

in|di|rect /ɪndaɪrɛkt, -dɪr-/
1 **ADJ** An **indirect** result or effect is not caused directly by the person or thing

mentioned, but it does happen because of them. ❑ *Millions could die of hunger as an in direct result of the war.* ● **in|di|rect|ly ADV** ❑ *The government is indirectly responsible for the violence.* **2 ADJ** An **indirect** route or journey is not the shortest route between two places. ❑ *He took an indirect route back home.* **3 ADJ Indirect** remarks suggest something, without stating it clearly. ❑ *It was an indirect criticism of the president.* ● **in|di|rect|ly ADV** ❑ *She indirectly suggested that he should leave.* [from Latin]

in|di|rect ob|ject (indirect objects) **N-COUNT** LANGUAGE ARTS In a sentence, an **indirect object** is the thing or person that something is done to. For example, in "She gave him her address," "him" is the indirect object. Compare with **direct object**.

in|dis|crimi|nate /ɪndɪskrɪmɪnɪt/ **ADJ** If you describe an action as **indiscriminate**, you are critical of it because it does not involve any careful thought or choice. ❑ *Indiscriminate use of chemicals is dangerous.* ● **in|dis|crimi|nate|ly ADV** ❑ *The disease kills indiscriminately.* [from Latin]

in|dis|pen|sable /ɪndɪspɛnsəbəl/ **ADJ** If you say that someone or something is **indispensable**, you mean that they are absolutely essential and other people or things cannot function without them. ❑ *She was indispensable to the company.*

in|di|vid|ual /ɪndɪvɪdʒuəl/ (individuals) **1 ADJ Individual** means relating to one person or thing, rather than to a large group. ❑ *We ask each individual customer for suggestions.* ● **in|di|vid|ual|ly ADV** ❑ *You can remove each seat individually.* **2 N-COUNT** An **individual** is a person. ❑ *We want to reward individuals who do good things.* [from Medieval Latin]

Thesaurus	individual	Also look up :
N	human being, person **2**	
PRON	somebody, someone **2**	

in|di|vis|ible /ɪndɪvɪzɪbəl/ **ADJ** If you say that something is **indivisible**, you mean that it cannot be divided into different parts. ❑ *Far from being separate, the mind and body form an indivisible whole.* [From Latin]

in|door /ɪndɔr/ **ADJ Indoor** activities happen inside a building and not outside. ❑ *The hotel has an indoor pool.* [from Old English]

in|doors /ɪndɔrz/ **ADV** If something happens **indoors**, it happens inside a building. ❑ *They warned us to close the windows and stay indoors.* [from Old English]

in|duce /ɪndus/ (induces, inducing, induced) **1 V-T** To **induce** a state or condition means to cause it. ❑ *Doctors said surgery could induce a heart attack.* **2 V-T** If you **induce** someone **to** do something, you persuade or influence them to do it. ❑ *More than 4,000 teachers were induced to retire early.* [from Latin]

in|duct /ɪndʌkt/ (inducts, inducting, inducted) **V-T** If someone **is inducted into** the army, they are officially made to join the army. ❑ *He was inducted into the army.* [from Latin]

in|duc|tion /ɪndʌkʃən/ (inductions) **1 N-COUNT/N-NONCOUNT Induction** is a procedure or a ceremony for introducing someone to a new job, organization, or way of life. ❑ *...his induction as president.* **2 N-NONCOUNT** SCIENCE **Induction** is the process by which electricity or magnetism is passed between two objects or circuits without them touching each other. [from Latin]

in|dulge /ɪndʌldʒ/ (indulges, indulging, indulged) **1 V-T/V-I** If you **indulge in** something or if you **indulge yourself**, you allow yourself to have or do something that you know you will enjoy. ❑ *She occasionally indulges in a candy bar.* ❑ *In New York you can indulge your passion for art.* **2 V-T** If you **indulge** someone, you let them have or do what they want, even if this is not good for them. ❑ *He did not agree with indulging children.* [from Latin]

in|dus|trial /ɪndʌstriəl/ **1 ADJ** SOCIAL STUDIES **Industrial** describes things that relate to industry. ❑ *The company sells industrial machinery and equipment.* **2 ADJ** SOCIAL STUDIES An **industrial** city or country is one in which industry is very important. ❑ *...Western industrial countries.* [from Latin]

Word Partnership	Use **industrial** with :
N	industrial **machinery**, industrial **production**, industrial **products** **1** industrial **area**, industrial **city**, industrial **country** **2**

in|dus|tri|al|ize /ɪndʌstriəlaɪz/
(**industrializes, industrializing, industrialized**)
v-T/v-I When a country **industrializes** or **is industrialized**, it develops a lot of industries.
❑ *By the late nineteenth century, both Russia and Japan had begun to industrialize.*
● **in|dus|tri|ali|za|tion** /ɪndʌstriəlɪzeɪʃᵊn/
N-NONCOUNT ❑ *Industrialization began early in Spain.* [from Latin]

in|dus|try /ɪndəstri/ (**industries**)
■ **N-NONCOUNT** SOCIAL STUDIES **Industry** is the work of making things in factories.
❑ *The meeting was for leaders in banking and industry.*
◻ **N-COUNT** SOCIAL STUDIES A particular **industry** consists of all the people and activities involved in making a particular product or providing a particular service.
❑ *The country depends on its tourism industry.*
[from Latin]
→ look at Word Web: **industry**

in|ef|fi|cient /ɪnɪfɪʃᵊnt/ **ADJ** Someone or something that is **inefficient**, does not use time or energy in the best way. ❑ *...inefficient work methods.* [from Latin]

in|equal|ity /ɪnɪkwɒliti/ (**inequalities**)
■ **N-COUNT/N-NONCOUNT** **Inequality** is when people do not have the same social position, wealth, or chances. ❑ *Now there is even greater inequality between the rich and the poor.*
◻ **N-COUNT/N-NONCOUNT** MATH In mathematics, **inequality** is the relationship between two quantities that are not equal. Sometimes **inequality** is also used to mean that one quantity is either greater than or equal to another quantity. [from Latin]

Word Partnership Use **inequality** with :

ADJ	**economic** inequality, **growing/ increasing** inequality, **racial** inequality, **social** inequality
N	**gender** inequality, **income** inequality

in|ert /ɪnɜrt/ **ADJ** Someone or something that is **inert** does not move at all. ❑ *He covered the inert body with a blanket.* [from Latin]

in|er|tia /ɪnɜrʃə/
■ **N-NONCOUNT** If you have a feeling of **inertia**, you feel very lazy and unwilling to move or be active. ❑ *He was annoyed by her inertia, her lack of energy.*
◻ **N-NONCOUNT** SCIENCE **Inertia** is the tendency of a physical object to remain still or to continue moving, unless a force is applied to it. [from Latin]

in|evi|table /ɪnɛvɪtəbᵊl/ **ADJ** Something that is **inevitable** cannot be prevented or avoided. ❑ *Suffering is an inevitable part of life.*
● **in|evi|tably** /ɪnɛvɪtəbli/ **ADV** ❑ *Advances in technology will inevitably lead to unemployment.* [from Latin]

in|ex|pe|ri|enced /ɪnɪkspɪəriənst/ **ADJ** If you are **inexperienced**, you have little knowledge or experience of a particular subject. ❑ *She was treated by an inexperienced young doctor.* [from Latin]

in|fan|cy /ɪnfənsi/
■ **N-NONCOUNT** **Infancy** is the period of your life when you are a baby or very young child. ❑ *...the way our brains develop during infancy.*
◻ **N-NONCOUNT** If something is **in its infancy**, it is new and has not developed very much. ❑ *Computing science was still in its infancy.*

Word Web industry

There are three general categories of **industry**. Primary industry means **extracting raw materials** from the environment. Examples include agriculture, forestry, and mining. In secondary industry, people **refine** raw materials to make new **products**. It also includes **assembling** parts made by other **manufacturers**. There are two types of secondary industry—**light industry** (such as **textile weaving**) and **heavy industry** (such as shipbuilding). The third industry, tertiary industry, is **service**, which does not produce a product. Some examples are **banking, tourism,** and **education**. Recently, computers have created millions of jobs in the **information technology** field. Some researchers describe this as a fourth type of industry.

in|fant /ˈɪnfənt/ (**infants**) **N-COUNT** An **infant** is a baby or a very young child. [FORMAL] ❑ *He held the infant in his arms.* [from Latin]
→ look at Picture Dictionary: **age**
→ look at Word Web: **child**

in|fan|try /ˈɪnfəntri/ **N-NONCOUNT Infantry** are soldiers who fight on foot. ❑ *...an infantry division.* [from Italian]

in|fect /ɪnˈfɛkt/ (**infects, infecting, infected**)
1 **V-T** To **infect** people or animals means to give them a disease or an illness. ❑ *A single mosquito can infect a large number of people.*
2 **V-T** TECHNOLOGY If a virus **infects** a computer, it damages or destroys files or programs. ❑ *This virus infected thousands of computers across the world.* [from Latin]

Word Partnership	Use **infect** with :
N	**bacteria** infect, infect **cells**, infect **people** **1**
	viruses infect, infect **with a virus** **1** **2**
PRON	infect **others** **1**

in|fec|tion /ɪnˈfɛkʃən/ (**infections**)
1 **N-COUNT** An **infection** is an illness that is caused by bacteria. ❑ *Ear infections are common in young children.*
2 **N-NONCOUNT Infection** is the process of getting a disease, or giving it to others. ❑ *Even a small cut can lead to infection.* [from Latin]
→ look at Word Web: **diagnosis**

Word Partnership	Use **infection** with :
N	**cases of** infection, **rates of** infection, **risk of** infection, **symptoms of** infection
V	**cause an** infection, **have an** infection, **prevent** infection, **spread an** infection

in|fec|tious /ɪnˈfɛkʃəs/ **ADJ** A disease that is **infectious** can be passed easily from one person to another. Compare with **contagious**. ❑ *The disease is highly infectious.* [from Latin]
→ look at Word Web: **illness**

in|fer /ɪnˈfɜr/ (**infers, inferring, inferred**) **V-T** If you **infer** that something is true, you decide that it is true on the basis of information that you already have. ❑ *I inferred from what she said that you were sick.* [from Latin]
→ look at Usage note at **imply**

in|fe|ri|or /ɪnˈfɪəriər/
1 **ADJ** Something that is **inferior** is not as good as something else. ❑ *If you buy it*

somewhere else, you'll get an inferior product.
2 **ADJ** If you feel **inferior**, you feel as if you are less important or successful than certain other people. ❑ *Successful people made him feel inferior.* [from Latin]

in|fer|tile /ɪnˈfɜrtəl/
1 **ADJ** A person or an animal that is **infertile** is unable to produce babies. ❑ *Ten percent of couples are infertile.*
2 **ADJ Infertile** soil is of poor quality. ❑ *Nothing grew on the land, which was poor and infertile.* [from Latin]

in|fi|nite /ˈɪnfɪnɪt/
1 **ADJ** Something that is **infinite** has no limit, end, or edge. ❑ *There is an infinite number of stars.*
2 **ADJ** If you describe something as **infinite**, you mean that it is extremely great in amount or degree. ❑ *...an infinite variety of plants.* ❑ *With infinite care, John laid down the baby.* ● **in|fi|nite|ly** **ADV** ❑ *His design was infinitely better than anything I could have done.* [from Latin]

in|fini|tive /ɪnˈfɪnɪtɪv/ (**infinitives**) **N-COUNT** LANGUAGE ARTS The **infinitive** of a verb is the basic form, for example "do," "be," "take," and "eat." The infinitive is often used with "to" in front of it. [from Latin]

in|flat|able /ɪnˈfleɪtəbəl/ **ADJ** An **inflatable** object needs to be filled with air when you want to use it. ❑ *The children were playing on the inflatable castle.* [from Latin]

in|flate /ɪnˈfleɪt/ **V-T/V-I** If you **inflate** something, or if it **inflates**, you fill it with air. ❑ *You should inflate tires to the level recommended by the manufacturer.* [from Latin]

in|fla|tion /ɪnˈfleɪʃən/ **N-NONCOUNT** BUSINESS **Inflation** is a general increase in the prices of goods and services in a country. ❑ *The whole world is suffering from rising inflation.* [from Latin]

Word Partnership	Use **inflation** with :
V	**control** inflation, **reduce** inflation
N	inflation **fears**, **increase in** inflation, inflation **rate**
ADJ	**high/low** inflation

Word Link	flict ≈ striking : affliction, conflict, inflict

in|flict /ɪnˈflɪkt/ (**inflicts, inflicting, inflicted**) **V-T** To **inflict** harm or damage **on** someone or something means to make them suffer it. ❑ *...sports which inflict pain on animals.* [from Latin]

in|flu|ence /ɪnfluəns/ (**influences, influencing, influenced**)

1 **N-NONCOUNT** **Influence** is the power to make other people agree with you or do what you want. ❑ *He used his influence to get his son into medical school.*

2 **V-T** If you **influence** someone, you use your power to make them agree with you or do what you want. ❑ *The newspapers tried to influence public opinion.*

3 **N-COUNT** To have an **influence on** people or situations means to affect what they do or what happens. ❑ *Alan had a big influence on my career.*

4 **N-COUNT** Someone or something that is a good or bad **influence on** people has a good or bad effect on them. ❑ *I thought Sonny would be a good influence on you.* [from Medieval Latin]

in|flu|en|tial /ɪnfluɛnʃ°l/ **ADJ** Someone or something that is **influential** has a lot of influence over people or events. ❑ *He was influential in changing the law.* [from Medieval Latin]

info /ɪnfoʊ/ **N-NONCOUNT** **Info** is information. [INFORMAL] ❑ *For more info call 414-3935.*

in|form /ɪnfɔrm/ (**informs, informing, informed**) **V-T** If you **inform** someone **of** something, you tell them about it. ❑ *We will inform you of any changes.* ❑ *My daughter informed me that she was leaving home.* [from Latin]

in|for|mal /ɪnfɔrm°l/ **ADJ** **Informal** means relaxed and friendly, rather than serious or official. ❑ *Her style of writing is very informal.* ❑ *The house has an informal atmosphere.*
● **in|for|mal|ly** **ADV** ❑ *She was chatting informally to the children.* [from Latin]

Thesaurus informal Also look up :

N   casual, natural, relaxed, unofficial; (*ant.*) formal

in|for|mal thea|ter **N-NONCOUNT** **Informal theater** is drama that is performed in somewhere such as a classroom or workshop and is not usually intended to be seen by the general public.

in|for|ma|tion /ɪnfərmeɪʃ°n/

1 **N-NONCOUNT** **Information** about someone or something is facts about them. ❑ *Pat did not give her any information about Sarah.* ❑ *We can provide information on training.*

2 **N-NONCOUNT** **Information** is a service that

you can telephone to find out someone's telephone number. ❑ *He called information, and they gave him the number.* [from French]

Word Partnership Use **information** with :

| ADJ | **additional** information, **background** information, **important** information, **personal** information **1** |
| V | **find** information, **get** information, **have** information, **provide** information, **retrieve** information, **store** information, **want** information **1** |

in|for|ma|tion ar|chi|tec|ture **N-NONCOUNT** **Information architecture** is the practice of organizing information for particular purposes.

in|for|ma|tion tech|nol|ogy **N-NONCOUNT** TECHNOLOGY **Information technology** is the theory and practice of using computers. The short form **I.T.** is often used. ❑ *He works in the information technology industry.*
→ look at Word Web: **industry**

in|forma|tive /ɪnfɔrmətɪv/ **ADJ** Something that is **informative** gives you useful information. ❑ *The meeting was friendly and informative.* [from French]

infra|red /ɪnfrərɛd/ **ADJ** SCIENCE **Infrared** radiation is similar to light but has a longer wavelength, so you cannot see it without special equipment.
→ look at Word Web: **sun**

in|gre|di|ent /ɪngridiənt/ (**ingredients**) **N-COUNT** **Ingredients** are the things that you use to make something, especially when you are cooking. ❑ *Mix together all the ingredients.* [from Latin]

Word Partnership Use **ingredient** with :

| ADJ | **active** ingredient, **a common** ingredient, **important** ingredient, **key** ingredient, **main** ingredient, **secret** ingredient |

in|hab|it /ɪnhæbɪt/ (**inhabits, inhabiting, inhabited**) **V-T** If a place **is inhabited** by a group of people, those people live there. ❑ *The people who inhabit these islands do not use money.* [from Latin]

in|hab|it|ant /ɪnhæbɪtənt/ (**inhabitants**) **N-COUNT** The **inhabitants** of a place are the people who live there. ❑ *The inhabitants of the town wrote a letter to the president.* [from Latin]

in|hale /ɪnheɪl/ (inhales, inhaling, inhaled)
v-т/v-i When you **inhale**, you breathe in. When you **inhale** something such as smoke, you take it into your lungs when you breathe in. ❑ *He took a long slow breath, inhaling deeply.* ❑ *The men inhaled the poisonous gas and began to feel sick.* [from Latin]
→ look at Word Web: **respiratory system**

in|her|it /ɪnhɛrɪt/ (inherits, inheriting, inherited)
1 v-т If you **inherit** money or property, you receive it from someone who has died. ❑ *He has no child to inherit his house.*
2 v-т If you **inherit** a task or a problem, you get it from the people who had it before. ❑ *The government has inherited a difficult situation.*
3 v-т If you **inherit** a personal quality, you are born with it because other members of your family had it. ❑ *Her children have inherited her love of sports.* [from Old French]

in|her|it|ance /ɪnhɛrɪtəns/ (inheritances)
N-COUNT/N-NONCOUNT An **inheritance** is money or property that you receive from someone who has died. ❑ *She used her inheritance to buy a house.* [from Old French]

in|hibi|tor /ɪnhɪbɪtər/ (inhibitors) **N-COUNT**
SCIENCE An **inhibitor** is a substance that slows down or stops a chemical reaction. [from Latin]

ini|tial /ɪnɪʃ°l/ (initials)
1 ADJ Initial means happening at the beginning of a process. ❑ *The initial reaction has been excellent.*
2 N-COUNT Initials are the capital letters that begin each word of a name. ❑ *She drove a silver car with her initials on the side.* [from Latin]

ini|tial con|so|nant (initial consonants) or
initial blend N-COUNT LANGUAGE ARTS Initial consonants are two or more letters that begin a word and are pronounced in their normal way when they are joined, for example the letters "b" and "l" in "blue."

ini|tial|ly /ɪnɪʃəli/ **ADV Initially** means near the beginning of a process or a situation. ❑ *The list initially included 11 players.* [from Latin]

ini|ti|ate /ɪnɪʃieɪt/ (initiates, initiating, initiated)
1 v-т If you **initiate** something, you start it or cause it to happen. ❑ *He wanted to initiate a discussion on education.* ● **ini|tia|tion** /ɪnɪʃieɪʃ°n/ **N-NONCOUNT** ❑ *...the initiation of a program of changes.*

2 v-т If someone **is initiated into** something such as a religion, a secret society, or a social group, they become a member of it during a special ceremony. ❑ *In many societies, young people are formally initiated into their adult roles.* ● **ini|tia|tion** (initiations) **N-COUNT/N-NONCOUNT** ❑ *This was my initiation into the peace movement.* [from Latin]

ini|tia|tive /ɪnɪʃiətɪv, -ʃətɪv/ (initiatives)
1 N-COUNT An **initiative** is an important act or statement that is intended to solve a problem. ❑ *...new initiatives to help young people.*
2 N-SING If you have **the initiative**, you are in a stronger position than your opponents because you are able to do something first. ❑ *We'll make sure we don't lose the initiative.*
3 N-NONCOUNT If you have **initiative**, you have the ability to decide what to do next and to do it, without needing other people to tell you what to do. ❑ *Don't keep asking me for help—use your initiative.*
4 N-COUNT An **initiative** is a political procedure in which a group of citizens propose a new law or a change to the law, that all voters can then vote on. ❑ *The public will vote on the initiative in November.*
5 PHRASE If you **take the initiative** in a situation, you are the first person to act, and are therefore able to control the situation. ❑ *We must take the initiative and end the war.* [from Latin]

in|ject /ɪndʒɛkt/ (injects, injecting, injected)
1 v-т To **inject** a substance into someone means to put it into their body using a special type of needle. ❑ *The drug was injected into patients four times a week.*
2 v-т BUSINESS If you **inject** money or resources **into** a business or an organization, you provide more money or resources for it. ❑ *We need to inject money into the economy.* [from Latin]

in|jec|tion /ɪndʒɛkʃ°n/ (injections)
1 N-COUNT If you have an **injection**, someone puts medicine into your body using a special type of needle ❑ *They gave me an injection to help me sleep.*
2 N-COUNT BUSINESS An **injection of** money into an organization is the act of providing enough money to help the organization become more profitable. ❑ *An injection of cash is needed to fund these projects.* [from Latin]

in|jure /ɪndʒər/ (**injures, injuring, injured**)
v-т If you **injure** a person or an animal, you damage part of their body. ❑ *The bomb seriously injured five people.*

Word Partnership	Use **injure** with :
v	**kill or** injure
ADV	**seriously** injure
PRON	injure *someone*, injure *yourself*

in|jured /ɪndʒərd/
1 **ADJ** An **injured** person or animal has suffered damage to part of their body. ❑ *Nurses helped the injured man.*
2 **N-PLURAL** The **injured** are people who are injured. ❑ *Army helicopters moved the injured.*

Word Partnership	Use **injured** with :
N	injured **in an accident/attack**, injured **people**
ADV	**badly** injured, **critically** injured, **seriously** injured
ADJ	**dead/killed and** injured
V	**get** injured, **rescue the** injured

in|ju|ry /ɪndʒəri/ (**injuries**) **N-COUNT/ N-NONCOUNT** An **injury** is damage to a person's or an animal's body. ❑ *He was suffering from serious head injuries.* [from Latin]

Word Partnership	Use **injury** with :
ADJ	**bodily** injury, **internal** injury, **minor** injury, **personal** injury, **serious** injury, **severe** injury
V	**escape** injury, **suffer an** injury

in|jus|tice /ɪndʒʌstɪs/ (**injustices**) **N-COUNT/ N-NONCOUNT Injustice** is when a situation is not fair or right. ❑ *They have fought injustice all their lives.* [from Old French]

ink /ɪŋk/ (**inks**) **N-COUNT/N-NONCOUNT Ink** is the colored liquid that you use for writing or printing. ❑ *The letter was written in blue ink.* [from Old French]

in|land

PRONUNCIATION HELP
Pronounce the adverb /ɪnlænd, -lənd/. Pronounce the adjective /ɪnlənd/.

1 **ADV Inland** means not beside the ocean, and in or near the middle of a country. ❑ *Most of the population lives inland.* ❑ *The town is about 15 minutes' drive inland from Pensacola.*
2 **ADJ Inland** places are not beside the ocean, but are in or near the middle of a country. ❑ *...inland lakes.* [from Old English]

in-laws N-PLURAL Your **in-laws** are the parents of your husband or wife. ❑ *At Christmas, we had lunch with my in-laws.*

in|mate /ɪnmeɪt/ (**inmates**) **N-COUNT** The **inmates** of a prison or a mental hospital are the prisoners or patients who live there. ❑ *...education for prison inmates.* [from Middle Low German]

inn /ɪn/ (**inns**) **N-COUNT** An **inn** is a hotel, or a restaurant, often one in the country. ❑ *...the Waterside Inn.* [from Old English]

in|ner /ɪnər/
1 **ADJ** The **inner** parts of something are the parts inside it, or the parts closest to the center. ❑ *James has an infection of the inner ear.*
2 **ADJ** Your **inner** feelings are feelings that you have but do not show to other people. ❑ *Loving relationships give a child an inner sense of security.* [from Old English]

in|ner city (**inner cities**) **N-COUNT** The **inner city** is the poor areas near the center of a big city. ❑ *Samuel grew up in an inner-city neighborhood in Houston.*
→ look at Word Web: **city**

in|ner core (**inner cores**) **N-COUNT** SCIENCE The **inner core** of the Earth is the central part of the Earth's interior. It is solid and made of nickel and iron.

in|no|cence /ɪnəsəns/
1 **N-NONCOUNT Innocence** is the quality of having no experience or knowledge of the more difficult aspects of life. ❑ *Ah! The sweet innocence of youth!*
2 **N-NONCOUNT** If someone proves their **innocence**, they prove that they are not guilty of a crime. ❑ *This information could prove your brother's innocence.* [from Latin]

in|no|cent /ɪnəsənt/
1 **ADJ** If you are **innocent**, you are not guilty of a crime. ❑ *The jury found him innocent of murder.*
2 **ADJ** If someone is **innocent**, they have no experience or knowledge of the more difficult aspects of life. ❑ *They seemed so young and innocent.* [from Latin]

Word Partnership	Use **innocent** with :
V	**plead** innocent, **presumed** innocent, **proven** innocent **1**
N	innocent **man/woman 1** innocent **children 2**

in|no|vate /ɪnəveɪt/ (**innovates, innovating, innovated**) **v-ι** If someone **innovates**, they introduce changes and new ideas in the way something is done or made. ❑ *What makes Ross different from most engineers is his constant desire to innovate and experiment.* [from Latin]

Word Link | *nov ≈ new : innovation, novel, novice*

in|no|va|tion /ɪnəveɪʃ°n/ (**innovations**)
1 **N-COUNT** An **innovation** is a new thing or a new way of doing something. ❑ *They showed us some of their latest technological innovations.*
2 **N-NONCOUNT** **Innovation** is the introduction of new ideas, methods, or things. ❑ *Technological innovation is very important to business.* [from Latin]

in|no|va|tive /ɪnəveɪtɪv/
1 **ADJ** Something that is **innovative** is new and different. ❑ *The company produces innovative car designs.*
2 **ADJ** An **innovative** person has new ideas and does different things. ❑ *He is one of America's most innovative film-makers.* [from Latin]
→ look at Word Web: **technology**

in|or|di|nate /ɪnɔrd°nɪt/ **ADJ** If you describe something as **inordinate**, you are emphasizing that it is greater in amount or degree than you would expect or want. [FORMAL] ❑ *They spend an inordinate amount of time talking.* ● **in|or|di|nate|ly** **ADV** ❑ *He is inordinately proud of his wife.* [from Latin]

Word Link | *put ≈ thinking : computer, dispute, input*

in|put /ɪnpʊt/ (**inputs, inputting, input**)
1 **N-COUNT/N-NONCOUNT** **Input** is the help, information, or advice that one person gives to another person. ❑ *There has been a lot of hard work and input from the public.*
2 **N-NONCOUNT** **Input** is information that you type into a computer. ❑ *Who is responsible for data input here?*
3 **V-T** If you **input** information into a computer, you type it using a keyboard. ❑ *We need more staff to input the data.* [from Old English]

in|put force (**input forces**)
N-COUNT/N-NONCOUNT SCIENCE In physics, the **input force** is the effort that is applied to a machine such as a lever or a pulley in order to do work. Compare with **output force**.

in|quire /ɪnkwaɪər/ (**inquires, inquiring, inquired**) **V-T/V-I** If you **inquire** about something, you ask for information about it. [FORMAL] ❑ *"What are you doing here?" she inquired.* ❑ *He called the company to inquire about a job.* [from Latin]

Thesaurus inquire *Also look up :*
v ask, question

in|quiry /ɪnkwaɪəri, ɪŋkwɪri/ (**inquiries**)
1 **N-COUNT** If you make an **inquiry**, you ask a question in order to get some information. ❑ *Dad made some inquiries and found her address.*
2 **N-COUNT** An **inquiry** takes place when people officially try to find out the truth about something. ❑ *Pike is leading the inquiry into the shooting.* [from Latin]

in|quisi|tive /ɪnkwɪzɪtɪv/ **ADJ** An **inquisitive** person likes finding out about things. ❑ *Amy was very inquisitive, always wanting to know how things worked.* [from Latin]

in|sane /ɪnseɪn/
1 **ADJ** Someone who is **insane** is seriously mentally ill. ❑ *For a while, I thought I was going insane.*
2 **ADJ** If an idea or an action is **insane**, it is very foolish. ❑ *I thought the idea was completely insane.* [from Latin]

in|sect /ɪnsɛkt/ (**insects**) **N-COUNT** An **insect** is a very small animal that has six legs. Most insects have wings. [from Latin]
→ look at Picture Dictionary: **insects**

in|secure /ɪnsɪkyʊər/
1 **ADJ** If you are **insecure**, you think that you are not good enough. ❑ *Most people are a little insecure about their looks.* ● **in|secu|rity** /ɪnsɪkyʊərɪti/ (**insecurities**) **N-COUNT/N-NONCOUNT** ❑ *Both men and women can have feelings of shyness and insecurity.*
2 **ADJ** Something that is **insecure** is not safe, or is not firm and steady. ❑ *Don't take risks with an insecure ladder.* [from Latin]

in|sen|si|tive /ɪnsɛnsɪtɪv/ **ADJ** If someone is **insensitive**, they do not think about or care about other people's feelings. ❑ *My husband is very insensitive to my problem.*
● **in|sen|si|tiv|ity** /ɪnsɛnsɪtɪvɪti/ **N-NONCOUNT** ❑ *I'm sorry about my insensitivity toward her.* [from Medieval Latin]

in|sert /ɪnsɜrt/ (**inserts, inserting, inserted**)
1 **V-T** If you **insert** an object **into** something, you put the object inside it. ❑ *Mike took a key from his pocket and inserted it into the lock.*
2 **V-T** If you **insert** text into a piece of writing, you add it. ❑ *He inserted a paragraph about the recent accident.* [from Latin]

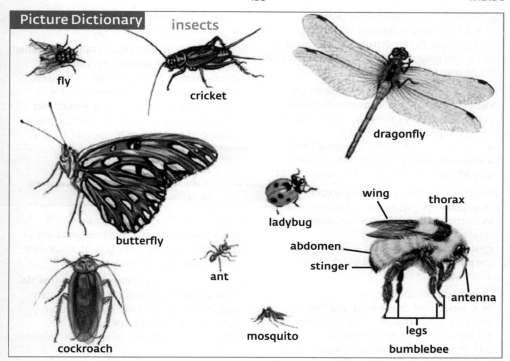

Picture Dictionary — insects

fly

cricket

dragonfly

butterfly

ladybug

wing

thorax

abdomen

stinger

antenna

ant

legs

mosquito

bumblebee

cockroach

in|side

1 PREP Something or someone that is
inside or **inside of** something, is in it.
❏ *Inside the envelope was a photograph.*

2 ADJ Inside is also an adjective. ❏ *Josh
took his cellphone from the inside pocket of his
jacket.*

3 ADV If you go **inside**, you go into a
building. ❏ *The couple chatted on the doorstep
before going inside.*

4 N-COUNT The **inside** of something is the
inner part of it. ❏ *I've painted the inside of the
house.*

5 ADJ Inside information is taken from
someone who is involved in a situation and
therefore knows a lot about it. ❏ *I have no
inside knowledge.*

6 PHRASE If a piece of clothing is **inside
out**, the part that is normally inside is on
the outside. ❏ *I didn't realize that my shirt was
inside out.* [from Old English]

Thesaurus inside Also look up :

PREP	in; (*ant.*) outside **1**
ADV	indoors **3**
N	interior, middle **4**

in|sight /ɪnsaɪt/ (**insights**)

N-COUNT/N-NONCOUNT An **insight into**
something is a good understanding of it.
❏ *This book provides fascinating insights into the
way the mind works.* [from Old English]

in|sig|nifi|cant /ɪnsɪgnɪfɪkənt/ **ADJ**
Something that is **insignificant** is not
important. ❏ *In 1949, Bonn was a small,
insignificant city.* [from Latin]

in|sip|id /ɪnsɪpɪd/

1 ADJ If you describe food or drink as
insipid, you dislike it because it has very
little taste. ❏ *The bread tasted bland and insipid,
like warmed cardboard.*

2 ADJ If you describe someone or
something as **insipid**, you mean that they
are dull and boring. ❏ *On the surface she
seemed meek and insipid.* [from Latin]

in|sist /ɪnsɪst/ (**insists, insisting, insisted**)

1 V-T/V-I If you **insist**, you say firmly that
something must happen. ❏ *Rob insisted on
driving them to the station.* ❏ *He insisted that I stay*

for dinner. ❑ *She insisted on being present.*

2 **V-T/V-I** If you **insist** that something is true, you say so very firmly. ❑ *Clarke insisted that he was telling the truth.* ❑ *They hadn't told any lies, he insisted.* [from Latin]

in|spect /ɪnspɛkt/ (**inspects, inspecting, inspected**) **V-T** If you **inspect** something, you look at it very carefully. ❑ *Dad inspected the car carefully before he bought it.* ● **in|spec|tion** /ɪnspɛkʃ°n/ (**inspections**) **N-COUNT/N-NONCOUNT** ❑ *Dixon still makes weekly inspections of all his stores.* [from Latin]

in|spec|tor /ɪnspɛktər/ (**inspectors**)
1 **N-COUNT** An **inspector** is a person whose job is to check that people do things correctly. ❑ *...a fire inspector.*
2 **N-COUNT** An **inspector** is an officer in the police. ❑ *...Police Inspector John Taylor.* [from Latin]

in|spi|ra|tion /ɪnspɪreɪʃ°n/
1 **N-NONCOUNT** **Inspiration** is a feeling of enthusiasm and new ideas that you get from someone or something.
❑ *My inspiration as a writer comes from poets like Walt Whitman.*
2 **N-SING** If something or someone is **the inspiration for** a particular book, work of art, or action, they are the source of the ideas in it. ❑ *The garden was the inspiration for a series of flower paintings.* [from Latin]

Word Link *spir ≈ breath : in*spire*, per*spir*ation,* re*spiration*

in|spire /ɪnspaɪər/ (**inspires, inspiring, inspired**)
1 **V-T** If someone or something **inspires** you, they give you new ideas and a strong feeling of enthusiasm. ❑ *Singer and songwriter Bob Dylan inspired a generation of young people.*
● **in|spir|ing** **ADJ** ❑ *She was one of the most inspiring people I ever met.*
2 **V-T** If someone or something **inspires** a particular feeling in people, it makes them feel that way. ❑ *A teacher has to inspire confidence in the students.*
3 **V-T** If a book, a work of art, or an action **is inspired by** something, that thing is the source of the idea for it. ❑ *The book was inspired by a real event.* [from Latin]

Word Link *stab ≈ steady : e*stab*lish, in*stab*ility,* stab*ilize*

in|stabil|ity /ɪnstəbɪlɪti/ (**instabilities**)
N-COUNT/N-NONCOUNT **Instability** is a lack of

stability in a place, a situation, or a person. ❑ *...political instability.*

in|stall /ɪnstɔl/ (**installs, installing, installed**)
V-T If you **install** something, you put it somewhere so that it is ready to be used. ❑ *They installed a new telephone line in the apartment.* ● **in|stal|la|tion** **N-NONCOUNT** ❑ *The installation of smoke alarms could save hundreds of lives.* [from Medieval Latin]

Word Partnership	Use **install** with :
ADJ	**easy to** install
N	install **equipment**, install **machines**, install **software**

in|stal|la|tion art **N-NONCOUNT** ARTS **Installation art** is art that uses a variety of materials such as everyday objects, video, and sound to create an artistic work.

in|stall|ment /ɪnstɔlmənt/ (**installments**)
1 **N-COUNT** If you pay for something in **installments**, you make small regular payments for it over a period of time.
❑ *She is repaying the loan in monthly installments of $300.*
2 **N-COUNT** An **installment** is one part of a story in a magazine, or on TV or radio.
❑ *Charles Dickens' fourth novel, The Old Curiosity Shop, was published in 1840-41, in weekly installments.* [from Old French]

in|stance /ɪnstəns/ (**instances**)
1 **N-COUNT** An **instance** is a particular example or occurrence of something.
❑ *This was an instance of bad timing.*
2 **PHRASE** You say **for instance** when you are giving an example of what you are talking about. ❑ *I want to talk about environmental issues, for instance, global warming.* [from Medieval Latin]

in|stant /ɪnstənt/ (**instants**)
1 **N-COUNT** An **instant** is a very short period of time. ❑ *For an instant, I wanted to cry.*
2 **ADJ** **Instant** means immediate. ❑ *Her book was an instant success.* ● **in|stant|ly** **ADV** ❑ *The man was killed instantly.*
3 **ADJ** **Instant** food or drink can be prepared very quickly and easily. ❑ *He stirred instant coffee into a mug of hot water.*
4 **PHRASE** To do something **the instant** something else happens means to do it immediately. ❑ *I knew who he was the instant I saw him.* [from Latin]

Word Partnership Use instant with :

PREP	**for an** instant, **in an** instant ∎
ADJ	**the next** instant ∎
N	instant **access**, instant **messaging**, instant **success** ∎

in|stant mes|sag|ing N-NONCOUNT
TECHNOLOGY **Instant messaging** is the activity of sending written messages from one computer to another. The message appears immediately on the screen of the computer you send it to if this computer is also using the service. ❑ *Instant messaging is my favorite way to communicate with friends.*

in|stead /ɪnstɛd/
∎ **PHRASE** If you do one thing **instead of** another, you do the first thing and not the second thing. ❑ *Why don't you walk to work, instead of driving?*
∎ **ADV** If you do not do something, but do something else **instead**, you do the second thing and not the first thing. ❑ *Robert didn't want to go bowling. He went to the movies instead.*

in|stinct /ɪnstɪŋkt/ (**instincts**)
N-COUNT/N-NONCOUNT Instinct is the natural way that a person or an animal behaves or reacts. ❑ *My first instinct was to laugh.* [from Latin]

Word Partnership Use instinct with :

| ADJ | **basic** instinct, **maternal** instinct, **natural** instinct |
| N | **survival** instinct |

in|stinc|tive /ɪnstɪŋktɪv/ **ADJ** An **instinctive** feeling or action is one that you have or do without stopping to think first. ❑ *Smiling is instinctive to all human beings.* ● **in|stinc|tive|ly ADV** ❑ *When the phone rang, Jane instinctively knew something was wrong.* [from Latin]

in|sti|tute /ɪnstɪtut/ (**institutes, instituting, instituted**)
∎ **N-COUNT** An **institute** is an organization or a place where people study a particular subject in detail in order to discover new facts. ❑ *My uncle works at the National Cancer Institute.*
∎ **V-T** If you **institute** a system, a rule, or a course of action, you start it. [FORMAL] ❑ *We will institute a number of changes to improve public safety.* [from Latin]

in|sti|tu|tion /ɪnstɪtuʃ°n/ (**institutions**)
∎ **N-COUNT** An **institution** is a large organization such as a school, a bank, or a church. ❑ *Most financial institutions offer interest-only loans for home-buyers.*
∎ **N-COUNT** An **institution** is a building where certain people are cared for, such as people who are mentally ill. ❑ *Larry has been in an institution since he was four.* [from Latin]

Word Link struct ≈ building : construct, destructive, instruct

in|struct /ɪnstrʌkt/ (**instructs, instructing, instructed**)
∎ **V-T** If you **instruct** someone **to** do something, you formally tell them to do it. [FORMAL] ❑ *Grandpa's doctor instructed him to get more fresh air.*
∎ **V-T** If you **instruct** someone **in** a subject, you teach it to them. ❑ *Our teachers instruct the children in music, dance, and physical education.* [from Latin]

in|struc|tion /ɪnstrʌkʃ°n/ (**instructions**)
∎ **N-COUNT** An **instruction** is something that someone tells you to do. ❑ *We had instructions from our teacher not to leave the building.*
∎ **N-PLURAL Instructions** are information on how to do something. ❑ *The cook book uses simple instructions and photographs.* [from Latin]

in|struc|tor /ɪnstrʌktər/ (**instructors**)
N-COUNT An **instructor** is someone whose job is to teach a skill or an activity. ❑ *Rachel is a swimming instructor.* [from Latin]

Thesaurus instructor Also look up :

| N | educator, leader, professor, teacher |

in|stru|ment /ɪnstrəmənt/ (**instruments**)
∎ **N-COUNT** An **instrument** is a tool that you use for doing a particular job. ❑ *...scientific instruments.*
∎ **N-COUNT** MUSIC A musical **instrument** is an object that you use for making music. ❑ *Tim plays four musical instruments, including piano and guitar.* [from Latin]
→ look at Word Webs: **concert, orchestra**

in|stru|men|tal /ɪnstrəmɛnt°l/
∎ **ADJ** Someone or something that is **instrumental in** something helps to make it happen. ❑ *Mr. Johnson was instrumental in the company's success.*
∎ **ADJ** MUSIC **Instrumental** music is for musical instruments only, and not for voices. ❑ *We welcomed the visitors with traditional dance and instrumental music.* [from Latin]

in|suf|fi|cient /ɪnsəfɪʃ°nt/ **ADJ** Something that is **insufficient** is not large enough in amount or degree for a particular purpose. [FORMAL] ❑ *There was insufficient evidence to charge him with murder.* ● **in|suf|fi|cient|ly ADV** ❑ *Food that is insufficiently cooked can cause food poisoning.* [from Latin]

| Word Link | insula ≈ island : insulate, insulator, peninsula |

in|su|late /ɪnsəleɪt/ (**insulates, insulating, insulated**) **V-T** SCIENCE If a piece of equipment **is insulated**, it is covered with rubber or plastic to prevent electricity from passing through it. ❑ *...insulated wire.* [from Late Latin]

in|su|la|tor /ɪnsəleɪtər/ (**insulators**) **N-COUNT** An **insulator** is a material that insulates something. [from Late Latin]

in|sult (**insults, insulting, insulted**)

> **PRONUNCIATION HELP**
> Pronounce the verb /ɪnsʌlt/. Pronounce the noun /ɪnsʌlt/.

1 V-T If someone **insults** you, they say or do something to you that is rude or offensive. ❑ *I'm sorry. I didn't mean to insult you.* ● **in|sult|ed ADJ** ❑ *I was really insulted by the way he spoke to me.* ● **in|sult|ing ADJ** ❑ *Don't use insulting language.*
2 N-COUNT An **insult** is something rude that a person says or does. ❑ *The boys shouted insults at each other.* [from Latin]

| Word Link | ance ≈ quality, state : insurance, performance, resistance |

in|sur|ance /ɪnʃʊərəns/ **N-NONCOUNT** **Insurance** is an agreement that you make with a company in which you pay money to them regularly, and they pay you if something bad happens to you or to your property. ❑ *I pay about $100 per month for auto insurance.* [from Old French]

Word Partnership	Use insurance with :
N	insurance **claim**, insurance **company**, insurance **coverage**, insurance **payments**, insurance **policy**
V	**buy/purchase** insurance, **carry** insurance, **sell** insurance

in|sure /ɪnʃʊər/ (**insures, insuring, insured**) **V-T/V-I** If you **insure** yourself or your property, you pay money regularly to a company so that, if you become ill, or if your property is damaged or stolen, the company

will pay you an amount of money. ❑ *It costs a lot of money to insure your car.* ❑ *Many people insure against death or long-term sickness.* [from Old French]
→ look at Usage note at **ensure**

Word Partnership	Use insure with :
N	insure **your car/health/house/property** insure **your safety**
ADJ	**difficult to** insure, **necessary to** insure

in|tact /ɪntækt/ **ADJ** Something that is **intact** is complete and has not been damaged or changed. ❑ *The roof was still intact.* [from Latin]

in|take /ɪnteɪk/ **N-SING** Your **intake** of a particular kind of food or drink is the amount that you eat or drink. ❑ *Your intake of salt should be no more than a few grams per day.* [from Old English]

in|te|ger /ɪntɪdʒər/ (**integers**) **N-COUNT** MATH An **integer** is an exact whole number such as 1, 7, or 24 as opposed to a number with fractions or decimals. [from Latin]

in|tegu|men|tary sys|tem /ɪntɛgyəmɛntəri sɪstəm/ (**integumentary systems**) **N-COUNT** SCIENCE The **integumentary system** of animals and people is a group of body parts that includes the skin, hair, and nails.

intel /ɪntɛl/
1 N-NONCOUNT **Intel** is military intelligence (= information collected about an enemy's secret plans). [INFORMAL] ❑ *What makes this intel credible?*
2 N-NONCOUNT **Intel** is information. [INFORMAL]

in|tel|lec|tual /ɪntɪlɛktʃuəl/ (**intellectuals**)
1 ADJ **Intellectual** means involving a person's ability to think and to understand ideas and information. ❑ *Dr. Miller is an expert on the intellectual development of children.* ● **in|tel|lec|tual|ly ADV** ❑ *...intellectually satisfying work.*
2 N-COUNT An **intellectual** is someone who spends a lot of time studying and thinking about complex ideas. ❑ *...teachers, artists and other intellectuals.*
3 ADJ **Intellectual** is also an adjective. ❑ *...a highly intellectual, intelligent group of people.* [from Latin]

in|tel|li|gence /ɪntɛlɪdʒ°ns/
1 N-NONCOUNT **Intelligence** is the ability to

understand and learn things quickly and well. ❑ *Stephanie's a woman of great intelligence.*
2 **N-NONCOUNT** **Intelligence** is information that is collected by the government or the army about other countries' activities. ❑ *There is a need for better military intelligence.* [from Latin]

Word Partnership	Use intelligence with :
ADJ	**secret** intelligence **2**
N	intelligence **agent**, intelligence **expert**, **military** intelligence **2**

in|tel|li|gent /ɪntɛlɪdʒ³nt/
1 **ADJ** An **intelligent** person or animal is able to think, understand, and learn things quickly and well. ❑ *Susan's a very intelligent woman.* ● **in|tel|li|gent|ly** **ADV** ❑ *William can talk intelligently on many different subjects.*
2 **ADJ** TECHNOLOGY An **intelligent** machine or piece of software can react to changes in the same way that humans do. ❑ *Intelligent computers will soon be an important tool for every doctor.* [from Latin]

Thesaurus	intelligent Also look up :
ADJ	bright, clever, sharp, smart; *(ant.)* dumb, stupid **1**

in|tend /ɪntɛnd/ (**intends, intending, intended**)
1 **V-T** If you **intend** to do something, you have decided to do it. ❑ *We're intending to stay in Philadelphia for four years.*
2 **V-T** If something **is intended** for a particular purpose or person, it has been planned or made for that purpose. ❑ *This money is intended for schools.* ❑ *The big windows were intended to make the room brighter.* [from Latin]

in|tense /ɪntɛns/ **ADJ** Something that is **intense** is very great or strong. ❑ *The intense heat made him sweat.* ● **in|tense|ly** **ADV** ❑ *The fast-food business is intensely competitive.* [from Latin]

Word Link	ify ≈ making : clarify, diversify, intensify

in|ten|si|fy /ɪntɛnsɪfaɪ/ (**intensifies, intensifying, intensified**) **V-T/V-I** If you **intensify** something or if it **intensifies**, it becomes greater in strength, amount, or degree. ❑ *We must intensify our efforts to find a solution.* [from Latin]

in|ten|si|ty /ɪntɛnsɪti/ (**intensities**) **N-COUNT** The **intensity** of a color is how bright or dull it is. [from Latin]

in|ten|sive /ɪntɛnsɪv/ **ADJ** **Intensive** activities involve a lot of effort or many people. ❑ *The program begins with sixteen weeks of intensive training.* ● **in|ten|sive|ly** **ADV** ❑ *Dan is working intensively on his new book.* [from Latin]

in|tent /ɪntɛnt/ (**intents**)
1 **ADJ** If you are **intent on** doing something, you are eager and determined to do it. ❑ *We are intent on winning this competition.*
2 **ADJ** If someone does something in an **intent** way, they pay great attention to what they are doing. [WRITTEN] ❑ *There was an intent expression of concentration on her face.* ● **in|tent|ly** **ADV** ❑ *He listened intently, then slammed down the phone.*
3 **N-NONCOUNT/N-SING** A person's **intent** is their intention to do something. [FORMAL] ❑ *It was our intent to keep the wedding as private as possible.* ❑ *...an intent to frighten us.*
4 **PHRASE** You say **for all intents and purposes** to suggest that a situation is not exactly as you describe it but the effect is the same as if it were. ❑ *He sees me as his second son, which I am, for all intents and purposes.* [from Late Latin]

in|ten|tion /ɪntɛnʃ³n/ (**intentions**)
1 **N-COUNT/N-NONCOUNT** An **intention** is something that you plan to do. ❑ *It is my intention to retire later this year.* ❑ *Karen has no intention of getting married again.*
2 **PHRASE** If you **have no intention of** doing something, you are not planning to do it. ❑ *I have no intention of going without you.* [from Late Latin]

in|ten|tion|al /ɪntɛnʃən³l/ **ADJ** If something is **intentional**, you do it on purpose, and not by mistake. ❑ *I'm sorry if I hurt him—it wasn't intentional.* ● **in|ten|tion|al|ly** **ADV** ❑ *He intentionally crashed his car to collect insurance money.* [from Late Latin]

inter|act /ɪntərækt/ (**interacts, interacting, interacted**)
1 **V-T/V-I** When people **interact with** each other or **interact**, they communicate as they work or spend time together. ❑ *The other children interacted and played together.* ● **inter|ac|tion** /ɪntəræKʃ³n/ (**interactions**) **N-COUNT/N-NONCOUNT** ❑ *...social interactions with other people.*
2 **V-T/V-I** When one thing **interacts with** another or two things **interact**, the two things affect each other's behavior or

condition. ❑ *You have to understand how cells interact.* • **inter|ac|tion** (**interactions**) **N-COUNT/N-NONCOUNT** ❑ *...the interaction between physical and emotional illness.* [from Latin]

inter|ac|tive /ɪntərǽktɪv/ **ADJ** An **interactive** piece of equipment allows direct communication between itself and the user. ❑ *Press the red button on your interactive TV to vote for your favorite singer.* [from Latin]

inter|cept /ɪntərsɛ́pt/ (**intercepts, intercepting, intercepted**) **V-T** If you **intercept** someone or something that is traveling from one place to another, you stop them before they get to their destination. ❑ *We can easily intercept emails on non-secure Web sites.* • **inter|cep|tion** /ɪntərsɛ́pʃ°n/ (**interceptions**) **N-COUNT/N-NONCOUNT** ❑ *...the interception of a ship off the coast of Oregon.* [from Latin]

Word Link	inter ≈ between : inter**changeable**, inter**nal**, inter**view**

inter|change|able /ɪntərtʃéɪndʒəb°l/ **ADJ** Things that are **interchangeable** can be exchanged with each other without it making any difference. ❑ *In most recipes, chicken and turkey are almost interchangeable.* • **inter|change|ably** **ADV** ❑ *These expressions are often used interchangeably, but they have different meanings.* [from Old French]

inter|con|nect /ɪntərkənɛ́kt/ (**interconnects, interconnecting, interconnected**) **V-T/V-I** Things that **interconnect** or **are interconnected** are connected to or with each other. ❑ *The two bedrooms and the bathroom interconnect.* [from Latin]

inter|course /ɪntərkɔ́rs/ **N-NONCOUNT** **Intercourse** is the act of having sex. [from Medieval Latin] [FORMAL]

in|ter|est /ɪntrɪst, -tərɪst/ (**interests, interesting, interested**)

1 N-NONCOUNT/N-SING If you have an **interest** in something, you want to know more about it. ❑ *There is a lot of interest in making the book into a film.* ❑ *She liked Jason at first, but she soon lost interest in him.*

2 N-COUNT Your **interests** are the things that you like doing. ❑ *"What are your interests?"—"I enjoy riding horses and I also play tennis."*

3 V-T If something **interests** you, you want

to know more about it. ❑ *Fashion does not interest her.*

4 N-COUNT If something is in the **interests** of a particular person or group, it will benefit them in some way. ❑ *He has a duty to act in the best interests of the company.*

5 N-NONCOUNT BUSINESS **Interest** is the extra money that you pay if you have borrowed money, or the extra money that you receive if you have money in some types of bank account. ❑ *Do you earn interest on your checking account?* ❑ *How much interest do you have to pay on the loan?* [from Latin]

Word Partnership	Use interest with :
V	**attract** interest, **express** interest, **lose** interest **1**
	earn interest, **pay** interest **5**
ADJ	**great** interest, **little** interest, **strong** interest **1**
N	**level of** interest, **places of** interest, **self**-interest **1**
	conflict of interest **4**
	interest **charges**, interest **expenses**, interest **5**

in|ter|est|ed /ɪntərɪstɪd, -trɪstɪd/ **ADJ** If you are **interested in** something, you want to know more about it. ❑ *I thought you might be interested in this article in the newspaper.* [from Latin]

Word Partnership	Use interested with :
V	**become** interested, interested **in buying**, **get** interested, interested **in getting**, interested **in helping**, interested **in learning**, interested **in making**, **seem** interested
ADV	**really** interested, **very** interested

in|ter|est|ing /ɪntərɛstɪŋ, -trɪstɪŋ/ **ADJ** If you find something **interesting**, you want to know more about it. ❑ *It was interesting to be in a new town.* • **in|ter|est|ing|ly** /ɪntərɛstɪŋli, -trɪstɪŋli/ **ADV** ❑ *Interestingly, there are no British writers on the list.* [from Latin]

Word Partnership	Use interesting with :
ADV	**especially** interesting, **really** interesting, **very** interesting
N	interesting **idea**, interesting **people**, interesting **point**, interesting **question**, interesting **story**, interesting **things**

inter|fere /ɪntərfíər/ (**interferes, interfering, interfered**)

1 V-I If you **interfere**, you get involved in a

situation when other people do not want you to. ❑ *I wish everyone would stop interfering and just leave me alone.*

2 **V-I** Something that **interferes with** an activity stops it from going well. ❑ *Cellphones can interfere with aircraft equipment.* [from Old French]

inter|fer|ence /ɪntərfɪərəns/

1 **N-NONCOUNT** **Interference** is unwanted or unnecessary involvement in something. ❑ *She didn't appreciate her mother's interference in her life.*

2 **N-NONCOUNT** SCIENCE When there is **interference**, a radio signal is affected by other radio waves or electrical activity so that it cannot be received properly. ❑ *There was too much interference and we couldn't hear the broadcast.* [from Old French]

in|te|ri|or /ɪntɪəriər/ (**interiors**)

1 **N-COUNT** The **interior** of something is the inside part of it. ❑ *The interior of the house was dark and old-fashioned.*

2 **ADJ** **Interior** is also an adjective. ❑ *They painted the interior walls of the house white.* [from Latin]

Thesaurus	interior	Also look up :
N	inside; *(ant.)* exterior, outside	

Word Link	med ≈ middle : intermediate, media, medium

inter|medi|ate /ɪntərmidiɪt/ **ADJ** An **intermediate** level is in the middle level, between two other levels. ❑ *We teach beginner, intermediate, and advanced level students.* [from Medieval Latin]

inter|mit|tent /ɪntərmɪtˀnt/ **ADJ** Something that is **intermittent** happens occasionally rather than continuously. ❑ *After three hours of intermittent rain, the game*

was abandoned. ● **inter|mit|tent|ly** **ADV** ❑ *The talks went on intermittently for years.* [from Latin]

in|ter|nal /ɪntɜrnˀl/

1 **ADJ** Something **internal** exists or happens on the inside of something. ❑ *After the accident, Aaron suffered internal bleeding.*

2 **ADJ** **Internal** is used to describe things that exist or happen inside a country or an organization. ❑ *The country improved its internal security.* ❑ *...Russia's Ministry of Internal Affairs.* [from Medieval Latin]
→ look at Word Web: **engine**

in|ter|nal com|bus|tion en|gine /ɪntɜrnˀl kəmbʌstʃən ɛndʒɪn/ (**internal combustion engines**) **N-COUNT** SCIENCE An **internal combustion engine** is an engine that creates its energy by burning fuel inside itself. Most cars have internal combustion engines.

in|ter|nal fer|ti|li|za|tion /ɪntɜrnˀl fɜrtˀlɪzeɪʃˀn/ **N-NONCOUNT** SCIENCE **Internal fertilization** is a method of reproduction in which the egg and sperm join together inside the female's body. Compare with **external fertilization**.

inter|na|tion|al /ɪntərnæʃənˀl/ **ADJ** **International** events or situations involve different countries. ❑ *The best way to end poverty is through international trade.*
● **inter|na|tion|al|ly** **ADV** ❑ *Bruce Lee is an internationally famous movie star.*

In|ter|net /ɪntərnɛt/ also **internet** **N-PROPER** TECHNOLOGY The **Internet** is the network that allows computer users to connect with computers all over the world, and that carries email. ❑ *Do you have Internet access at home?* ❑ *You can pay for your ticket online using Internet banking.*

Word Web	Internet

The **Internet** allows information to be shared by users around the world. The **World Wide Web** allows users to access **servers** anywhere. **User names** and **passwords** give access and protect information. **E-mail** travels through **networks**. **Websites** are created by companies and individuals to share information. **Web pages** can include images, words, sound, and video. **Hackers** can break into computer networks. They sometimes steal information or damage the system. **Webmasters** usually build **firewalls** for protection.

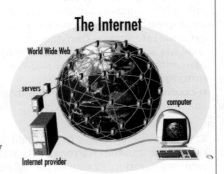

The Internet

in|ter|pret /ɪntɜrprɪt/ (**interprets, interpreting, interpreted**)

1 **V-T** If you **interpret** something in a particular way, you decide what it means. ❑ *You can interpret the data in different ways.*

2 **V-T/V-I** If you **interpret** what someone is saying, you put the words that they are saying into another language. ❑ *She spoke little English, so her husband came with her to interpret.* ❑ *He asked if I could interpret English into French.* ● **in|ter|pret|er** /ɪntɜrprɪtər/ (**interpreters**) **N-COUNT** ❑ *Speaking through an interpreter, he said that he was very happy to be in the United States.* [from Latin]

in|ter|pre|ta|tion /ɪntɜrprɪteɪʃ°n/ (**interpretations**)

1 **N-COUNT/N-NONCOUNT** An **interpretation** of something is an opinion about what it means. ❑ *Professor Wolfgang gives the data a very different interpretation.*

2 **N-COUNT** ARTS A performer's **interpretation** of something such as a piece of music or a role in a play is the particular way in which they choose to perform it. ❑ *...the pianist's interpretation of Chopin.* [from Latin]
→ look at Word Web: **art**

in|ter|re|late /ɪntərrɪleɪt/ (**interrelates, interrelating, interrelated**) **V-T/V-I** If two or more things **interrelate**, there is a connection between them and they have an effect on each other. ❑ *The body and the mind interrelate.* ❑ *Each of these cells have their specific jobs to do, but they also interrelate with each other.* ❑ *...the way in which we communicate and interrelate with others.* ● **in|ter|re|lated** **ADJ** ❑ *All things are interrelated.* [from Latin]

in|ter|ro|gate /ɪntɛrəgeɪt/ (**interrogates, interrogating, interrogated**) **V-T** If a police officer **interrogates** someone, they ask them questions for a long time in order to get some information from them. ❑ *Mr. Wright was interrogated by police for eight hours on Thursday night.* ● **in|ter|ro|ga|tion** /ɪntɛrəgeɪʃ°n/ (**interrogations**) **N-COUNT/N-NONCOUNT** ❑ *He confessed during an interrogation by police.* [from Latin]

in|ter|roga|tive /ɪntərɒgətɪv/

1 **N-SING** LANGUAGE ARTS In grammar, a clause that is in **the interrogative** is in the form of a question. Examples are "When did he get back?" and "Are you all right?"

2 **ADJ** LANGUAGE ARTS An **interrogative** sentence is a sentence that asks a question, for example "Who are you?" [from Latin]

Word Link	*rupt ≈ breaking : dis***rupt**, *e***rupt**, *inter***rupt**

in|ter|rupt /ɪntərʌpt/ (**interrupts, interrupting, interrupted**)

1 **V-T/V-I** If you **interrupt** someone, you say or do something that causes them to stop what they are doing. ❑ *Don't interrupt the teacher when she's speaking.* ❑ *I'm sorry to interrupt, but there's a phone call for you.* ● **in|ter|rup|tion** /ɪntərʌpʃ°n/ (**interruptions**) **N-COUNT/N-NONCOUNT** ❑ *I can't concentrate on my work—there are too many interruptions.*

2 **V-T** If someone or something **interrupts** an activity, they cause it to stop for a period of time. ❑ *Rain interrupted the tennis match for two hours.* ● **in|ter|rup|tion** (**interruptions**) **N-COUNT/N-NONCOUNT** ❑ *The meeting continued with no more interruptions.* [from Latin]

inter|sperse /ɪntərspɜrs/ (**intersperses, interspersing, interspersed**) **V-T** If you **intersperse** one group of things **with** another or **among** another, you put the second things between or among the first things. ❑ *Originally the intention was to intersperse the historical scenes with modern ones.* [from Latin]

in|ter|val /ɪntərv°l/ (**intervals**)

1 **N-COUNT** An **interval** is the period of time between two events. ❑ *We met again after an interval of 12 years.*

2 **N-COUNT** MUSIC An **interval** in music is the distance in pitch between two tones.

3 **PHRASE** If things are placed **at intervals**, there are equal spaces between them. ❑ *White barriers marked the road at intervals of about a mile.* [from Latin]

inter|vene /ɪntərvin/ (**intervenes, intervening, intervened**) **V-I** If you **intervene** in a situation, you become involved in it and try to change it. ❑ *The situation calmed down when police intervened.* ● **inter|ven|tion** /ɪntərvɛnʃ°n/ (**interventions**) **N-COUNT/N-NONCOUNT** ❑ *...the intervention of the U.S. in the affairs of other countries.* [from Latin]

Word Link	*inter ≈ between : inter***changeable**, *inter***nal**, *inter***view**

inter|view /ɪntərvyu/ (**interviews, interviewing, interviewed**)

1 **N-COUNT/N-NONCOUNT** An **interview** is a

formal meeting in which someone asks you questions to find out if you are the right person for a job. ❑ *The interview went well, so I hope that I've got the job.*

2 **V-T** If you **are interviewed** for a particular job, someone asks you questions about yourself to find out if you are the right person for it. ❑ *Anna was interviewed for a job at The New York Times yesterday.* ● **inter|view|er** (**interviewers**) **N-COUNT** ❑ *The interviewer asked me why I wanted the job.*

3 **N-COUNT** An **interview** is a conversation in which a journalist asks someone a series of questions. ❑ *Allan gave an interview to the Chicago Tribune last month.*

4 **V-T** When a journalist **interviews** a famous person, they ask that person a series of questions. ❑ *She has interviewed many famous actors.* [from Old French]

Word Partnership	Use **interview** with :
N	**job** interview **1**
	(tele)phone interview **1** **3**
	radio/magazine/newspaper/television interview **3**
V	**conduct an** interview, **give an** interview, **request an** interview **1** **3**

in|tes|tine /ɪntɛstɪn/ (**intestines**) **N-COUNT** Your **intestines** are the tubes in your body that food passes through when it has left your stomach. [from Latin]

in|ti|mate /ɪntɪmɪt/
1 **ADJ** If you have an **intimate** friendship with someone, you know them very well and you like them a lot. ❑ *I told my intimate friends I wanted to have a baby.* ● **in|ti|mate|ly** **ADV** ❑ *He knows the family fairly well, but not intimately.*

2 **ADJ** If two people are in an **intimate** relationship, they are involved with each other in a loving or sexual way. ❑ *...people in marriages and other intimate relationships.* ● **in|ti|mate|ly** **ADV** ❑ *He was cautious about becoming intimately involved with others.*

3 **ADJ** An **intimate** occasion or place is quiet and pleasant, and is suitable for conversations between friends. ❑ *...an intimate dinner for two.*

4 **ADJ** An **intimate** knowledge of something is a detailed knowledge of it. ❑ *She surprised me with her intimate knowledge of football.* ● **in|ti|mate|ly** **ADV** ❑ *...musicians whose work she knew intimately.* [from Latin]

in|timi|date /ɪntɪmɪdeɪt/ (**intimidates,** **intimidating, intimidated**) **V-T** If you

intimidate someone, you frighten them, in order to make them do what you want. ❑ *Many people feel intimidated by these teenage gangs.* ● **in|timi|da|tion** /ɪntɪmɪdeɪʃən/ **N-NONCOUNT** ❑ *Witnesses are often afraid of intimidation.* [from Medieval Latin]

into

> **PRONUNCIATION HELP**
> Pronounce **into** /ɪntu/ or, particularly before pronouns, /ɪntu/.

1 **PREP** If you put one thing **into** another thing, you put the first thing inside the second thing. ❑ *Put the apples into a dish.*

2 **PREP** If you go **into** a place or a vehicle, you move from being outside it to being inside it. ❑ *Mom got into the car and started the engine.*

3 **PREP** If you crash **into** something, you hit it accidentally. ❑ *A train crashed into the barrier at the end of the track.*

4 **PREP** When you change **into** a piece of clothing, you put it on. ❑ *I'm cold—I'll change into some warmer clothes.*

5 **PREP** If someone or something gets **into** a particular state, they start being in that state. ❑ *He got into a panic.*

6 **PREP** If you talk someone **into** doing something, you persuade them to do it. ❑ *They talked him into selling the farm.*

7 **PREP** If something changes **into** something else, it changes so that it has a new form. ❑ *The book has been made into a movie.*

8 **PREP** You use **into** when you are talking about how something is divided. ❑ *I cut the cake into 12 slices.*

9 **PREP** You use **into** when you are dividing one number by another number. ❑ *5 into 15 is 3.*

in|tol|er|able /ɪntɒlərəbəl/ **ADJ** If something is **intolerable**, it is so bad or extreme that no one can bear it or tolerate it. ❑ *His job put intolerable pressure on him.* ● **in|tol|er|ably** /ɪntɒlərəbli/ **ADV** ❑ *...intolerably crowded conditions.*

in|tol|er|ant /ɪntɒlərənt/ **ADJ** If you are **intolerant**, you do not accept people who behave and think differently to you. ❑ *They are intolerant of the opinions of others.* ● **in|tol|er|ance** **N-NONCOUNT** ❑ *They worry about people's intolerance toward foreigners.*

in|tra|net /ɪntrənɛt/ (**intranets**) **N-COUNT** TECHNOLOGY An **intranet** is a network of computers in a particular organization.

in|tran|si|tive /ɪntrænsɪtɪv/ **ADJ**
LANGUAGE ARTS An **intransitive** verb does not
have an object.

in|trep|id /ɪntrɛpɪd/ **ADJ** An **intrepid** person
acts in a brave way. ❑ ...an intrepid space
traveler. [from Latin]

in|tri|cate /ɪntrɪkɪt/ **ADJ** You use **intricate** to
describe something that has many small
parts or details. ❑ ...carpets with very intricate
patterns. ● **in|tri|ca|cy** /ɪntrɪkəsi/
N-NONCOUNT ❑ The price depends on the intricacy
of the work. ● **in|tri|cate|ly** **ADV** ❑ ...intricately
carved sculptures. [from Latin]

in|trigue (intrigues, intriguing, intrigued)

> PRONUNCIATION HELP
> Pronounce the noun /ɪntrig/. Pronounce
> the verb /ɪntrig/.

◼ **N-COUNT/N-NONCOUNT** Intrigue is the
making of secret plans to harm or deceive
people. ❑ ...political intrigue.
◻ **V-T** If something, especially something
strange, **intrigues** you, it interests you
and you want to know more about it.
❑ Her remark intrigued him. ● **in|trigued** **ADJ**
❑ I would be intrigued to hear his views.
[from French]

in|tri|guing /ɪntrigɪŋ/ **ADJ** If you describe
something as **intriguing**, you mean that
it is interesting or strange. ❑ This is an
intriguing story. ● **in|tri|guing|ly** **ADV**
❑ The results are intriguingly different each time.
[from French]

in|trin|sic /ɪntrɪnsɪk/ **ADJ** If something has
intrinsic value or **intrinsic** interest, it is
valuable or interesting because of its basic
nature or character, and not because of its
connection with other things. [FORMAL]
❑ Diamonds have little intrinsic value.
● **in|trin|si|cal|ly** /ɪntrɪnsɪkli/ **ADV** ❑ The
sounds of speech are intrinsically interesting to
babies. [from Late Latin]

intro|duce /ɪntrədus/ (introduces,
introducing, introduced)
◼ **V-T** If you **introduce** people, you tell them
each other's names
so that they can get
to know each other.
If you **introduce**
yourself to someone,
you tell them your
name. ❑ Tim, may I

introduce

introduce you to my wife, Jennifer? ❑ Before the
meeting, we all introduced ourselves.
◻ **V-T** If you **introduce** someone **to**
something, you cause them to experience it
for the first time. ❑ He introduced us to the
delights of Spanish food.
◼ **V-T** If you **introduce** something new, you
bring it to a place or make it exist for the
first time. ❑ The airline introduced a new direct
service from Houston last month. [from Latin]

> **Word Partnership**   Use **introduce** with :
>
> V   **allow me to** introduce, **let me**
>   introduce, **want to** introduce ◼
> N   introduce **a bill**, introduce **changes**,
>   introduce **legislation**, introduce
>   **reform** ◼

intro|duc|tion /ɪntrədʌkʃ°n/
(**introductions**)
◼ **N-COUNT** LANGUAGE ARTS The **introduction**
to a book is the part at the beginning
that tells you what the book is about.
❑ J.D. Salinger wrote the introduction to the book.
◻ **N-COUNT** A book that is an **introduction to**
a particular subject explains the basic facts
about that subject. ❑ The book is a simple
introduction to physics.
◼ **N-COUNT** If you make the **introductions**,
you tell people each other's names when
they meet for the first time. ❑ Elaine, the
hostess, made the introductions.
◼ **N-SING** Your **introduction to** something is
your first experience of it. ❑ The vacation was
a gentle introduction to camping.
◼ **N-NONCOUNT** The **introduction** of
something new is the process of bringing it
to a place or making it exist for the first
time. ❑ Did the introduction of the euro affect
prices? [from Latin]

in|trude /ɪntrud/ (intrudes, intruding,
intruded) **V-I** If you say that someone is
intruding into a particular place or situation,
you mean that they are not wanted or
welcome there. ❑ The press should not intrude
into people's personal lives. [from Latin]

in|trud|er /ɪntrudər/ (intruders) **N-COUNT**
An **intruder** is a person who goes into a place
without permission. ❑ Mrs. Baker called 911
when an intruder entered her home. [from Latin]

in|tru|sive /ɪntrusɪv/
◼ **ADJ** Something that is **intrusive** disturbs
your mood or your life in a way you do not
like. ❑ The cameras were an intrusive presence.

I

2 **ADJ** SCIENCE **Intrusive** rock is rock that forms when lava from inside the Earth cools and becomes solid just below the Earth's surface. Compare with **extrusive**. [from Latin]

in|tui|tion /ɪntuɪʃən/ **N-NONCOUNT** Intuition is an ability to know or understand something through your feelings. ❑ *My intuition told me that I could trust him.* [from Late Latin]

in|un|date /ɪnʌndeɪt/ (**inundates, inundating, inundated**) **V-T** If you **are inundated with** things such as letters, demands, or requests, you receive so many of them that you cannot deal with them all. ❑ *We were inundated with letters of complaint.* [from Latin]

in|vade /ɪnveɪd/ (**invades, invading, invaded**) **V-T/V-I** If an army **invades**, or **invades** a country, it attacks and enters it. ❑ *In 1944 the Allies invaded the Italian mainland.* ❑ *The enemy had invaded.* [from Latin]

in|va|lid (**invalids**)

> **PRONUNCIATION HELP**
> Pronounce the noun /ɪnvəlɪd/. The adjective is pronunced /ɪnvælɪd/ and is hyphenated in|val|id.

1 **N-COUNT** An **invalid** is someone who needs to be cared for by another person because they are very sick or badly injured. ❑ *Both of Mary's parents were invalids.*
2 **ADJ** If a document is **invalid**, it cannot be accepted, because it breaks an official rule. ❑ *He was trying to board a flight for the Philippines with an invalid passport.* [Sense 1 from Latin. Sense 2 from Medieval Latin.]

in|vari|ably /ɪnvɛəriəbli/ **ADV** If something **invariably** happens or is **invariably** true, it always happens or is always true. ❑ *He is invariably late.*

in|va|sion /ɪnveɪʒən/ (**invasions**)
1 **N-COUNT/N-NONCOUNT** If there is an **invasion** of a country, an army enters it and attacks it. ❑ *Cyprus has been divided since an invasion in 1974.*
2 **PHRASE** An **invasion of privacy** is an occasion where someone finds out information about your personal life without your permission. ❑ *Reading someone's diary is an invasion of privacy.* [from Latin]

in|vent /ɪnvɛnt/ (**invents, inventing, invented**)
1 **V-T** If you **invent** something, you are the first person to think of it or make it.

❑ *The ballpoint pen was invented by the Hungarian, Laszlo Biro.* ● **in|ven|tor** (**inventors**) **N-COUNT** ❑ *Alexander Graham Bell was the inventor of the telephone.*
2 **V-T** If you **invent** a story or an excuse, you try to make other people believe that it is true when it is not. ❑ *Heather invented an excuse not to attend Ryan's birthday party.* [from Latin]

in|ven|tion /ɪnvɛnʃən/ (**inventions**)
1 **N-COUNT** An **invention** is something that has been invented by someone. ❑ *Paper was a Chinese invention.*
2 **N-NONCOUNT** **Invention** is when something that has never been made or used before is invented. ❑ *The invention of the telescope led to the discovery of Uranus in 1781.* [from Latin]

in|ven|tory /ɪnvəntɔri/ (**inventories**)
1 **N-COUNT/N-NONCOUNT** An **inventory** is a supply or stock of something. ❑ *...an inventory of ten items at $15 each.*
2 **N-COUNT** An **inventory** is a written list of all the objects in a particular place such as all the merchandise in a store. ❑ *He made an inventory of everything that was in the apartment.* [from Medieval Latin]

in|ver|te|brate /ɪnvɜrtɪbrɪt/ (**invertebrates**)
1 **N-COUNT** SCIENCE An **invertebrate** is an animal that does not have a spine. Compare with **vertebrate**.
2 **ADJ** SCIENCE **Invertebrate** is also an adjective. ❑ *Ponds contain many invertebrate species.*

in|vest /ɪnvɛst/ (**invests, investing, invested**)
1 **V-T/V-I** If you **invest in** something, or **invest** your money, you put your money into a business or a bank, to try to make a profit from it. ❑ *He invested millions of dollars in the business.*
2 **V-T** If you **invest** time or energy **in** something, you spend a lot of time or energy on it. ❑ *I would rather invest time in my children than in my work.* [from Medieval Latin]

in|ves|ti|gate /ɪnvɛstɪgeɪt/ (**investigates, investigating, investigated**) **V-T/V-I** If you **investigate** something, you try to find out what happened. ❑ *The crime was thoroughly investigated.* ❑ *Officials are still investigating the cause of the explosion.* ● **in|ves|ti|ga|tion** /ɪnvɛstɪgeɪʃən/ (**investigations**) **N-COUNT/N-NONCOUNT** ❑ *We have begun an investigation into the man's death.* [from Latin]

i

in|ves|ti|ga|tor /ɪnvɛstɪɡeɪtər/
(**investigators**) **N-COUNT** An **investigator** is
someone whose job it is to find out about
something. ❑ *Investigators have been
questioning the survivors.* [from Latin]

in|vest|ment /ɪnvɛstmənt/ (**investments**)
1 **N-NONCOUNT** **Investment** is the activity
of investing money. ❑ *John's an investment
advisor in Chicago.*
2 **N-COUNT/N-NONCOUNT** An **investment** is
an amount of money that you invest, or the
thing that you invest it in. ❑ *Anthony made a
$1 million investment in the company.*
3 **N-COUNT** If you describe something you
buy as an **investment**, you mean that it will
help you to do a task more cheaply or
efficiently. ❑ *Buying good quality leather boots is
a wise investment.* [from Medieval Latin]

in|vis|ible /ɪnvɪzɪbəl/ **ADJ** If something is
invisible, you cannot see it. ❑ *In the story,
Matilda becomes invisible after eating blue candy.*
[from Latin]
→ look at Word Web: **sun**

in|vi|ta|tion /ɪnvɪteɪʃən/ (**invitations**)
1 **N-COUNT** If you have an **invitation** to an
event, someone has asked you to go to it.
❑ *I accepted Sarah's invitation to her birthday party.*
2 **N-COUNT** An **invitation** is the card or
paper on which an invitation is written or
printed. ❑ *Hundreds of invitations are being sent
out this week.* [from Latin]

Word Partnership	Use invitation with :
V	**accept an** invitation, **decline an** invitation, **extend an** invitation **1** **get/receive an** invitation **1** **2**

in|vite /ɪnvaɪt/ (**invites, inviting, invited**)
1 **V-T** If you **invite** someone to an event,
you ask them to come to it. ❑ *She invited him to
her 26th birthday party.*
2 **V-T** If you **are invited to** do something,
you are formally asked or given permission
to do it. ❑ *Managers were invited to buy stocks in
the company.* [from Latin]

Word Partnership	Use invite with :
N	invite *someone* to dinner, invite **friends**, invite **people** **1**

in|voice /ɪnvɔɪs/ (**invoices, invoicing, invoiced**)
1 **N-COUNT** An **invoice** is a document that
shows how much money you must pay for
goods you have ordered or the work that
someone has done for you. ❑ *We sent them an
invoice for $11,000 four months ago.*
2 **V-T** If you **invoice** someone, you send
them a bill for the goods you have sent
them or the work you have done for them.
❑ *You will not be invoiced for the work until January.*
[from Old French]

in|vol|un|tary /ɪnvɒləntɛri/ **ADJ** If you
make an **involuntary** movement or sound,
you make it suddenly and without
intending to because you are unable to
control yourself. ❑ *Pain in my ankle caused me to
give an involuntary scream.* [from Latin]
→ look at Word Web: **muscle**

in|volve /ɪnvɒlv/ (**involves, involving,
involved**)
1 **V-T** If an activity **involves** something,
that thing is a necessary part of it. ❑ *Running
a household involves lots of different skills.*
2 **V-T** If an activity **involves** someone, they
are taking part in it. ❑ *The scandal involved
a former senator.*
3 **V-T** If you **involve** someone **in** something,
you get them to take part in it. ❑ *We involve
the children in everything we do.* [from Latin]

in|volved /ɪnvɒlvd/ **ADJ** If you are **involved
in** something, you take part in it. ❑ *All of
their children are involved in the family business.*
[from Latin]

in|volve|ment /ɪnvɒlvmənt/ **N-NONCOUNT**
If you have an **involvement in** something,
you take part in it. ❑ *Edwards has always denied
any involvement in the crime.* [from Latin]

ion /aɪən, aɪɒn/ (**ions**) **N-COUNT** SCIENCE
An **ion** is an atom with an electrical charge.
[from Greek]

ion|ic bond /aɪɒnɪk bɒnd/ (**ionic bonds**)
N-COUNT SCIENCE An **ionic bond** is a force
that holds together two atoms with
opposite electric charges.

ion|ic com|pound (**ionic compounds**)
N-COUNT SCIENCE An **ionic compound** is a
chemical compound, consisting of a metal
and a nonmetal, in which the atoms are
held together by ionic bonds.

irate /aɪreɪt/ **ADJ** If someone is **irate**, they are
very angry about something. ❑ *He was so
irate he started throwing things.* [from Latin]

iris /aɪrɪs/ (**irises**) **N-COUNT** SCIENCE The **iris** is
the round colored part of a person's eye.
[from Latin]
→ look at Word Webs: **eye, muscle**

iron /aɪrɒn/ (**irons, ironing, ironed**)

1 **N-NONCOUNT** **Iron** is a hard, dark gray metal. ❑ *We waited for the iron gates to open.*

2 **N-COUNT** An **iron** is a piece of electrical equipment with a flat metal base that you heat and move over clothes to make them smooth.

3 **V-T** If you **iron** clothes, you make them smooth using an iron. ❑ *I began to iron some shirts.* ● **iron|ing** **N-NONCOUNT** ❑ *I was doing the ironing when she called.* [from Old English] → look at Word Web: **pan**

Word Partnership	Use iron with :
N	iron **bar**, iron **gate** **1**
	iron **a shirt** **3**
ADJ	**a hot** iron **2**

iron|ic /aɪrɒnɪk/ or **ironical** /aɪrɒnɪkᵊl/

1 **ADJ** LANGUAGE ARTS When you make an **ironic** remark, you say the opposite of what you really mean, often as a joke. ❑ *The comment was meant to be ironic.*

2 **ADJ** An **ironic** fact or situation is strange or funny because it is very different from what people expect. ❑ *It is ironic that we lie in the sun to make our skin look more attractive.* ● **ironi|cal|ly** /aɪrɒnɪkli/ **ADV** ❑ *His enormous dog is ironically called "Tiny."* [from Latin]

iro|ny /aɪrəni, aɪər-/

1 **N-NONCOUNT** LANGUAGE ARTS **Irony** is a type of humor where you say the opposite of what you really mean. ❑ *"You're early!" he said, as we arrived two hours late, his voice full of irony.*

2 **N-NONCOUNT** If you talk about the **irony** of a situation, you mean that it is strange or funny because it is different from what people expect. ❑ *The irony is that although we all know we should save money for the future, few of us do.* [from Latin]

Word Link	ir ≈ not : **ir**rational, **ir**regular, **ir**responsible

Word Link	ratio ≈ reasoning : ir**ratio**nal, **ratio**nal, **ratio**nally

ir|ra|tion|al /ɪræʃənᵊl/ **ADJ** **Irrational** behavior is not based on sensible, clear thinking. ❑ *I think hatred is often irrational.* ● **ir|ra|tion|al|ly** **ADV** ❑ *My husband is irrationally jealous of my ex-boyfriends.* [from Latin]

ir|ra|tion|al num|ber (**irrational numbers**) **N-COUNT** MATH An **irrational number** is a number that cannot be written as a simple fraction, for example the square root of 2.

ir|regu|lar /ɪrɛgyələr/

1 **ADJ** If something is **irregular**, the periods of time between it happening are of different lengths. ❑ *The tests showed that his heartbeat was irregular.* ● **ir|regu|lar|ly** **ADV** ❑ *He was eating irregularly and losing weight.*

2 **ADJ** Something that is **irregular** is not smooth or straight, or does not form a regular pattern. ❑ *The irregular surface makes it difficult for plants to grow.*

3 **ADJ** LANGUAGE ARTS An **irregular** noun or verb does not follow the usual rules of grammar. For example, "run" is an irregular verb, because the past form is "ran" (and not "runned.") Compare with **regular**. [from Old French]

ir|regu|lar gal|axy (**irregular galaxies**) **N-COUNT** SCIENCE An **irregular galaxy** is a galaxy with an irregular shape that does not belong to the other main types of galaxy such as spiral or elliptical galaxies.

ir|rel|evant /ɪrɛlɪvᵊnt/ **ADJ** If something is **irrelevant**, it is not connected with what you are talking about or doing. ❑ *Remove any irrelevant details from your essay.* [from Medieval Latin]

ir|re|sist|ible /ɪrɪzɪstɪbᵊl/

1 **ADJ** If a desire or a force is **irresistible**, it is so powerful that it makes you act in a certain way, and there is nothing you can do to prevent this. ❑ *He had an irresistible urge to yawn.* ● **ir|re|sist|ibly** /ɪrɪzɪstɪbli/ **ADV** ❑ *I found myself irresistibly drawn to Steve.*

2 **ADJ** If you describe something or someone as **irresistible**, you mean that they are so good or attractive that you cannot stop yourself from liking them or wanting them. [INFORMAL] ❑ *The music is irresistible.* ● **ir|re|sist|ibly** **ADV** ❑ *She had a charm that men found irresistibly attractive.*

ir|re|spon|sible /ɪrɪspɒnsɪbᵊl/ **ADJ** Someone who is **irresponsible** does not think about the possible results of their actions. ❑ *There are still too many irresponsible drivers who use their cellphones while driving.* [from Latin]

ir|ri|gate /ɪrɪgeɪt/ (**irrigates, irrigating, irrigated**) **V-T** SCIENCE To **irrigate** land means to supply it with water in order to help crops grow. ❑ *Water from Lake Powell is used to irrigate the area.* ● **ir|ri|ga|tion** /ɪrɪgeɪʃᵊn/ **N-NONCOUNT** ❑ *The irrigation of the surrounding agricultural land is poor.* [from Latin] → look at Word Web: **dam**

i

ir|ri|ta|ble /ɪrɪtəbᵊl/ **ADJ** If you are **irritable**, you become angry very easily. ❑ *After waiting for him for over an hour, Amber was beginning to feel irritable.* ● **ir|ri|tably** /ɪrɪtəbli/ **ADV** ❑ *"Why are you talking so loudly?" he asked irritably.* [from Latin]

ir|ri|tate /ɪrɪteɪt/ (**irritates, irritating, irritated**)
1 **V-T** If something **irritates** you, it keeps annoying you. ❑ *His voice really irritates me.* ● **ir|ri|tat|ed** **ADJ** ❑ *He has become increasingly irritated by questions about his retirement.* ● **ir|ri|tat|ing** **ADJ** ❑ *The children have an irritating habit of leaving the door open.* **2** **V-T** If something **irritates** a part of your body, it makes it slightly painful. ❑ *The smoke from the fire irritated his eyes, nose and throat.* [from Latin]

ir|ri|ta|tion /ɪrɪteɪʃᵊn/
1 **N-NONCOUNT** **Irritation** is the feeling you have when you are annoyed. ❑ *David tried not to show his irritation.* **2** **N-NONCOUNT** **Irritation** is a feeling of slight pain in a part of your body. ❑ *These oils may cause irritation to sensitive skins.* [from Latin]

is /ɪz/ **Is** is the third person singular of the present tense of **be**. [from Old English]

Is|lam /ɪslɑm/ **N-NONCOUNT** **Islam** is the religion that was started by Muhammed. ❑ *Michael converted to Islam at the age of 16.* ● **Is|lam|ic** /ɪslæmɪk, -lɑ-/ **ADJ** ❑ *He's an expert in Islamic law.* [from Arabic]

is|land /aɪlənd/ (**islands**) **N-COUNT**
GEOGRAPHY An **island** is a piece of land that is completely surrounded by water. ❑ *They live on the Caribbean island of Barbados.* [from Old English] → look at Picture Dictionary: **landforms**

island

isle /aɪl/ (**isles**) **N-COUNT** An **isle** is an island. ❑ *Ireland is sometimes called "the emerald isle."* [from Old French]

isn't /ɪzᵊnt/ **Isn't** is short for "is not." [from Old English]

iso|bar /aɪsəbɑr/ (**isobars**) **N-COUNT** An **isobar** is a line on a weather map that connects points of equal atmospheric pressure. [from Greek]

iso|late /aɪsəleɪt/ (**isolates, isolating, isolated**) **V-T** If you **isolate** someone, you keep them away from other people. ❑ *Julie was quickly isolated from other patients in the hospital.* [from Italian]

iso|lat|ed /aɪsəleɪtɪd/
1 **ADJ** An **isolated** place is far away from other places. ❑ *Mark and his girlfriend have bought an isolated farmhouse in Spain.* **2** **ADJ** An **isolated** occasion happens only once. ❑ *There was one isolated case of cheating.* [from Italian]

iso|la|tion /aɪsəleɪʃᵊn/ (**isolations**)
1 **N-COUNT/N-NONCOUNT** ARTS In dance, an **isolation** is a movement or an exercise that involves only one part of your body, for example shrugging your shoulders or rolling your head. **2** **PHRASE** If someone does something **in isolation**, they do it without other people present or without their help. ❑ *She is good at working in isolation.* [from Italian]

iso|tope /aɪsətoʊp/ (**isotopes**) **N-COUNT** SCIENCE **Isotopes** are atoms that have the same number of protons and electrons but different numbers of neutrons and therefore have different physical properties. [from Greek]

ISP /aɪ ɛs pi/ (**ISPs**) **N-COUNT** TECHNOLOGY An **ISP** is a company that provides Internet and email services. **ISP** is short for "Internet service provider."

is|sue /ɪʃu/ (**issues, issuing, issued**)
1 **N-COUNT** An **issue** is an important subject that people are talking about. ❑ *Climate change is a major environmental issue.* **2** **N-SING** If something is **the issue**, it is the thing you consider to be the most important part of a situation or a discussion. ❑ *Job satisfaction is the issue for me, not money.* **3** **N-COUNT** An **issue** of a magazine or a newspaper is the copy of it that is published in a particular month or on a particular day. ❑ *Have you read the latest issue of "TIME Magazine"?* **4** **V-T** If you **issue** something, you officially say it or give it. ❑ *The government issued a warning of possible attacks.* ❑ *The embassy has stopped issuing visas to journalists.* [from Old French] → look at Word Web: **philosophy**

I.T. /aɪ ti/ TECHNOLOGY **I.T.** is short for **information technology**. ❑ *The company needs people with I.T. skills.* [from Old English]

it /ɪt/

1 PRON You use **it** when you are talking about an object, an animal, a thing, or a situation that you have already mentioned. ❑ *They live in a beautiful cottage. Here's a photo of it.* ❑ *She has a problem but she's too embarrassed to talk about it.*

2 PRON You use **it** before certain nouns, adjectives, and verbs to talk about your feelings. ❑ *It was nice to see Steve again.* ❑ *It's a pity you can't come to the party, Sarah.*

3 PRON You use **it** in passive clauses that report a situation or an event. ❑ *It is said that stress can cause cancer.*

4 PRON You use **it** when you are talking about the time, the date, the weather, or the distance to a place. ❑ *It's three o'clock.* ❑ *It was Saturday, so she was at home.* ❑ *It was snowing yesterday.* ❑ *It's ten miles to the next gas station.*

5 PRON You use **it** when you are saying who someone is. ❑ *"Who's that on the phone?"—"It's Mrs. Williams."* [from Old English]

ital|ic /ɪtælɪk/ (**italics**)

1 N-PLURAL Italics are letters that slope to the right. The examples in this dictionary are printed in italics.

2 ADJ Italic letters slope to the right. [from Venice]

itch /ɪtʃ/ (**itches, itching, itched**)

1 V-I When a part of your body **itches**, you have an unpleasant feeling on your skin that makes you want to scratch it. ❑ *Her perfume made my eyes itch.* ● **itchy ADJ** ❑ *My eyes feel itchy and sore.*

2 N-COUNT Itch is also a noun. ❑ *Can you scratch my back? I've got an itch.* [from Old English]

it'd /ɪtəd/

1 It'd is short for "it would." ❑ *It'd be better to keep quiet.*

2 It'd is short for "it had." ❑ *Marcie was watching a movie. It'd just started.* [from Old English]

item /aɪtəm/ (**items**)

1 N-COUNT An **item** is one thing in a list or in a group of things. ❑ *The most valuable item in the sale was a Picasso drawing.*

2 N-COUNT An **item** is a piece of news in a newspaper or a magazine, or on television or radio. ❑ *There was an item in the paper about him.* [from Latin]

itin|er|ant /aɪtɪnərənt/ (**itinerants**)

1 ADJ An **itinerant** worker travels around a region, working for short periods in different places. [FORMAL] ❑ *...the author's experiences as an itinerant musician.*

2 N-COUNT An **itinerant** is someone whose way of life involves traveling around, usually someone who is poor and homeless. [from Late Latin] [FORMAL]

it'll /ɪtᵊl/ **It'll** is short for "it will." ❑ *It'll be nice to see them next weekend.* [from Old English]

its /ɪts/

DET You use **its** to show that something belongs or relates to a thing, a place, or an animal that has just been mentioned. ❑ *He held the knife by its handle.* [from Old English]

it's /ɪts/ **It's** is short for "it is" or "it has." [from Old English]

it|self /ɪtsɛlf/

1 PRON You use **itself** as the object of a verb or a preposition when an animal or a thing is both the subject and the object of the verb. ❑ *The kitten washed itself, then lay down by the fire.*

2 PRON You use **itself** to make a word stronger. ❑ *There are lots of good restaurants on the road to Wilmington, and in Wilmington itself.*

3 PRON If an animal or a thing does something **by itself**, it does it without any help. ❑ *The company are working on a car that can drive by itself.*

I've /aɪv/ **I've** is short for "I have." ❑ *I've been invited to a party.* [from Old English]

ivo|ry /aɪvəri/ **N-NONCOUNT Ivory** is a hard cream-colored substance that forms the tusks of elephants. ❑ *...the international ban on the sale of ivory.* [from Old French]

ivy /aɪvi/ (**ivies**) **N-COUNT/N-NONCOUNT Ivy** is a dark-green plant that grows up walls or along the ground. [from Old English]

Jj

jack /dʒæk/ (jacks)

1 **N-COUNT** A **jack** is a tool for lifting a car slightly. ❑ *You'll find the jack under the spare tire in the trunk.*

2 **N-COUNT** A **jack** is a playing card whose value is between a ten and a queen. ❑ *...the jack of spades.*

jack|et /dʒækɪt/ (jackets) **N-COUNT** A **jacket** is a short coat with long sleeves. ❑ *He wore a black leather jacket.* [from Old French]

→ look at Picture Dictionary: **clothing**

jack|pot /dʒækpɒt/ (jackpots) **N-COUNT** The **jackpot** is a large sum of money that is the most valuable prize in a game. ❑ *She won the jackpot of $5 million.*

jag|ged /dʒægɪd/ **ADJ** Something that is **jagged** has a rough shape or edge with lots of sharp points. ❑ *There were sharp jagged rocks just below the surface of the water.*

jail /dʒeɪl/ (jails, jailing, jailed)

1 **N-COUNT/N-NONCOUNT** A **jail** is a place where criminals have to stay as a punishment. ❑ *He went to jail for 15 years.* ❑ *Three prisoners escaped from a jail.*

2 **V-T** If someone **is jailed**, they are put into jail. ❑ *He was jailed for twenty years.* [from Old French]

jam /dʒæm/ (jams, jamming, jammed)

1 **V-T** If you **jam** something into a place, you push it there hard. ❑ *He jammed the key in the lock.*

2 **V-I** If something **jams**, it is unable to move freely or work properly. ❑ *When he tried to open the door, it jammed.*

3 **N-NONCOUNT** **Jam** is a sweet food that contains soft fruit and sugar. ❑ *Kate spread the strawberry jam on her toast.*

4 **N-COUNT** If there is a traffic **jam** on a road, there are so many vehicles there that they cannot move. ❑ *The trucks sat in a traffic jam for ten hours.*

→ look at Word Web: **traffic**

jani|tor /dʒænɪtər/ (janitors) **N-COUNT** A **janitor** is a person whose job is to clean and take care of a building. ❑ *The janitor finished*

cleaning the classrooms, and locked the school for the night. [from Latin]

Janu|ary /dʒænyuɛri/ (Januaries) **N-COUNT/N-NONCOUNT** **January** is the first month of the year. ❑ *We always have snow in January.* [from Latin]

jar /dʒɑr/ (jars) **N-COUNT** A **jar** is a glass container with a lid that is used for storing food. ❑ *There were several glass jars filled with candy.* [from Old French]

→ look at Picture Dictionary: **containers**

jave|lin /dʒævlɪn/ (javelins) **N-COUNT** SPORTS A **javelin** is a long pointed stick that is thrown in sports competitions. [from Old French]

jaw /dʒɔ/ (jaws) **N-COUNT** SCIENCE A person's or an animal's **jaws** are the top and bottom bones of their mouth. ❑ *Andrew broke his jaw.* [from Old French]

jazz /dʒæz/ **N-NONCOUNT** MUSIC **Jazz** is a style of music that has strong rhythms. ❑ *The club plays live jazz on Sundays.*

→ look at Word Web: **genre**

jazz dance **N-NONCOUNT** ARTS **Jazz dance** is a form of dance that developed in America in the twentieth century, based on jazz-influenced music and complex rhythmic movements.

jeal|ous /dʒɛləs/

1 **ADJ** If someone is **jealous**, they feel angry because they think that another person is trying to take away someone or something that they love. ❑ *He got jealous and there was a fight.*

2 **ADJ** If you are **jealous of** another person's possessions or qualities, you feel angry because you do not have them. ❑ *She was jealous of her sister's success.* ● **jeal|ous|ly** **ADV** ❑ *Gloria looked jealously at his new car.* [from Old French]

jeal|ousy /dʒɛləsi/

1 **N-NONCOUNT** **Jealousy** is the unhappy or angry feeling that someone has when they think that another person is trying to take away someone or something that they love.

❑ *He could not control his jealousy when he saw her new husband.*

2 **N-NONCOUNT** **Jealousy** is the unhappy or angry feeling that someone has when they wish that they could have the qualities or possessions that another person has. ❑ *...jealousy of her beauty.* [from Old French]

jeans /dʒiːnz/ **N-PLURAL** **Jeans** are pants that are made of strong cotton cloth. ❑ *We saw a young man in jeans and a T-shirt.*
→ look at Picture Dictionary: **clothing**

jel|ly /dʒɛli/ (**jellies**) **N-COUNT/N-NONCOUNT** **Jelly** is a sweet food made by cooking fruit with a large amount of sugar. **Jelly** is usually spread on bread. ❑ *She loved peanut butter and jelly sandwiches.* [from Old French]

jelly|fish /dʒɛlifɪs/ (**jellyfish**) **N-COUNT** A **jellyfish** is a sea creature that has a clear soft body and can sting you.

jeop|ardy /dʒɛpərdi/ **PHRASE** If someone or something is **in jeopardy**, they are in danger of being harmed or lost. ❑ *His job was in jeopardy.* [from Old French]

jerk /dʒɜːrk/ (**jerks, jerking, jerked**)
1 **V-T/V-I** If you **jerk** something or someone in a particular direction, or they **jerk** in a particular direction, they move a short distance very suddenly and quickly. ❑ *Sam jerked his head in my direction.* ❑ *Mr. Griffin jerked forward in his chair.*
2 **N-COUNT** **Jerk** is also a noun. ❑ *He gave a jerk of his head to the other two men.*
3 **N-COUNT** If you call someone a **jerk**, you are rudely saying that they annoy you. [from Old English] [INFORMAL]

jerky /dʒɜːrki/ (**jerkier, jerkiest**) **ADJ** **Jerky** movements are very sudden and quick. ❑ *Avoid any sudden or jerky movements.* [from Old English]

jer|sey /dʒɜːrzi/ (**jerseys**)
N-COUNT/N-NONCOUNT A **jersey** is a piece of clothing with sleeves that you wear on the top part of your body ❑ *The boys wore baseball caps and sports jerseys.*

Jesus /dʒiːzəs/ **N-PROPER** **Jesus** or **Jesus Christ** is the name of the man who Christians believe was the son of God, and whose teachings are the basis of Christianity. [from Latin]

jet /dʒɛt/ (**jets**)
1 **N-COUNT** A **jet** is an airplane that flies

very fast. ❑ *He arrived from Key West by jet.*

2 **N-COUNT** A **jet** of liquid or gas is a strong, fast, thin stream of it. ❑ *A jet of water poured through the windows.* [from Old French]

jet

→ look at Word Web: **fly**

jet lag /dʒɛt læg/ **N-NONCOUNT** If you have **jet lag**, you feel tired after a long trip by airplane. ❑ *We were tired because we still had jet lag.*

jet stream (**jet streams**) **N-COUNT** SCIENCE The **jet stream** is a very strong wind that blows high in the Earth's atmosphere and has an important influence on the weather.

jet|ti|son /dʒɛtɪsən, -zən/ (**jettisons, jettisoning, jettisoned**) **V-T** If you **jettison** something that is not needed, you throw it away or get rid of it. ❑ *The governor has jettisoned the plan.* [from Old French]

Jew /dʒuː/ (**Jews**) **N-COUNT** A **Jew** is a person who practices the religion of Judaism. [from Old French]

jew|el /dʒuːəl/ (**jewels**) **N-COUNT** A **jewel** is a valuable stone, such as a diamond. ❑ *The box was filled with precious jewels and gold.* [from Old French]

jew|el|ry /dʒuːəlri/ **N-NONCOUNT** **Jewelry** is decorations that you wear on your body, such as a ring that you wear on your finger. ❑ *He sold his wife's gold jewelry.* [from Old French]
→ look at Picture Dictionary: **jewelry**

Jew|ish /dʒuːɪʃ/
1 **ADJ** If something is **Jewish** it belongs or relates to the religion of Judaism. ❑ *We celebrated the Jewish festival of Passover.*
2 **ADJ** A **Jewish** person believes in and practices the religion of Judaism. ❑ *She was from a traditional Jewish family.* [from Old French]

jig|saw /dʒɪgsɔː/ (**jigsaws**) **N-COUNT** A **jigsaw** or **jigsaw puzzle** is a picture on cardboard or wood that has been cut up into different shapes that you have to put back together again. ❑ *The children put the last pieces in the jigsaw puzzle.*

jin|gle /dʒɪŋɡəl/ (**jingles, jingling, jingled**)
V-T/V-I When something **jingles**, it makes a gentle sound like small bells. ❑ *Her bracelets jingled on her thin wrist.* ❑ *Brian put his hands in his pockets and jingled some coins.* [from Dutch]

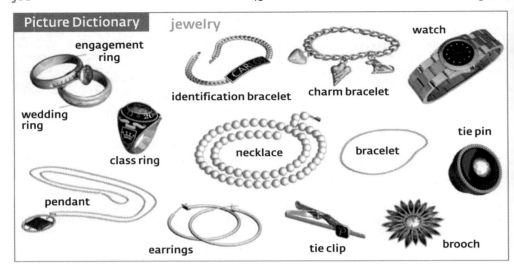

Picture Dictionary — jewelry

engagement ring

wedding ring

class ring

identification bracelet

charm bracelet

watch

tie pin

necklace

bracelet

pendant

earrings

tie clip

brooch

job /dʒɒb/ (**jobs**)

1 **N-COUNT** A **job** is the work that someone does to earn money. ❑ *I want to get a job.* ❑ *Terry was looking for a new job.*

2 **N-COUNT** A **job** is a particular task. ❑ *I have some jobs to do in the house today.*

3 **N-COUNT** The **job** of a particular person or thing is their duty or function. ❑ *Drinking a lot of water helps the kidneys do their job.*

4 **N-SING** If someone is doing a good **job**, they are doing something well. ❑ *Most of our teachers are doing a good job in the classroom.*

Thesaurus	job	Also look up :
N	employment, occupation, profession	

job|less /dʒɒbləs/ **ADJ** Someone who is **jobless** does not have a job. ❑ *The number of jobless people went up last month.*

jock|ey /dʒɒki/ (**jockeys**) **N-COUNT** **SPORTS** A **jockey** is someone who rides a horse in a race.

jog /dʒɒg/ (**jogs, jogging, jogged**)

1 **V-I** **SPORTS** If you **jog**, you run slowly, often as a form of exercise. ❑ *They went jogging every morning.* ● **jog|ger** (**joggers**) **N-COUNT** ❑ *The park was full of joggers.* ● **jog|ging** **N-NONCOUNT** ❑ *The jogging helped him to lose weight.*

2 **N-COUNT** **SPORTS** **Jog** is also a noun. ❑ *He went for an early morning jog.*

join /dʒɔɪn/ (**joins, joining, joined**)

1 **V-T** If you **join** an organization, you become a member of it. ❑ *He joined the Army five years ago.*

2 **V-T** If one person **joins** another, they go together to the same place. ❑ *She joined him in a trip to France.*

3 **V-T** If you **join** a line, you stand at the end of it so that you are part of it. ❑ *He joined the line of people waiting to get on the bus.*

4 **V-T** To **join** two things means to attach or fasten them together. ❑ *"And" is often used for joining two sentences.* ❑ *Join the two squares of fabric to make a bag.*

5 **V-T/V-I** If two roads or rivers **join**, they meet or come together. ❑ *The path joins the nearby road by The Ramblers Hotel.* ❑ *The two rivers joined at the bridge.* [from Old French]

▶ **join in** If you **join in** an activity, you take part in it. ❑ *I hope everyone will join in the fun.*

joint /dʒɔɪnt/ (**joints**)

1 **N-COUNT** **SCIENCE** A **joint** is a part of your body such as your elbow or knee where two bones meet and are able to move together. ❑ *Her joints ache if she exercises.*

2 **ADJ** **Joint** means shared by two or more people. ❑ *We opened a joint bank account.* ● **joint|ly** **ADV** ❑ *They jointly write and direct every film themselves.*

3 **N-COUNT** A **joint** is the place where two things are joined together. ❑ *Water dripped from some of the pipe joints.* [from Old French]

joke /dʒoʊk/ (**jokes, joking, joked**)

1 **N-COUNT** A **joke** is something that someone says to make you laugh. ❑ *He made a joke about it.*

2 **V-I** If you **joke**, you say amusing things, or say something that is not true for fun. ❑ *She often joked about her big feet.* ❑ *I was only joking!*

3 **PHRASE** You say **You're joking** when someone tells you something that you find difficult to believe. [SPOKEN] ❑ *You're joking. Are you serious?* [from Latin]

jok|er /dʒoʊkər/ (**jokers**) **N-COUNT** The **joker** in a deck of playing cards is the card that does not belong to any of the four suits. [from Latin]

jol|ly /dʒɒli/ (**jollier, jolliest**) **ADJ** Someone who is **jolly** is happy and cheerful. ❑ *She was a jolly, kind woman.* [from Old French]

jolt /dʒoʊlt/ (**jolts, jolting, jolted**)
1 **V-T/V-I** If something **jolts**, or if something **jolts** it, it moves suddenly and quite violently. ❑ *An earthquake jolted the Philippines early Wednesday.* ❑ *The train jolted again.*
2 **N-COUNT** **Jolt** is also a noun. ❑ *The plane hit the runway with a jolt.*

jot /dʒɒt/ (**jots, jotting, jotted**) **V-T** If you **jot** something **down**, you write it down. ❑ *David jotted down the address on a notepad.* [from Latin]

joule /dʒul/ (**joules**) **N-COUNT** SCIENCE A **joule** is a unit for measuring energy or work. [after James Prescott Joule (1818-89), an English physicist]

jour|nal /dʒɜrnəl/ (**journals**)
1 **N-COUNT** LANGUAGE ARTS A **journal** is a magazine or a newspaper that deals with a special subject. ❑ *The results were published in scientific journals.*
2 **N-COUNT** LANGUAGE ARTS A **journal** is a notebook or a diary. ❑ *Sara wrote her private thoughts in her journal.* [from Old French]

jour|nal|ist /dʒɜrnəlɪst/ (**journalists**)
N-COUNT A **journalist** is a person whose job is to collect news stories and write about them for newspapers, magazines, television, or radio. ❑ *The president spoke to an audience of two hundred journalists.* ● **jour|nal|ism**
N-NONCOUNT ❑ *He began a career in journalism.* [from Old French]

jour|ney /dʒɜrni/ (**journeys**) **N-COUNT** When you go on a **journey**, you travel from one place to another. ❑ *Their journey took them from New York to San Francisco.* [from Old French]

Thesaurus	journey	Also look up :
N	adventure, trip, visit, voyage	
V	cruise, fly, go, travel	

Word Partnership	Use journey with :
V	begin a journey, complete a journey, make a journey
N	journey of discovery, end of a journey, first/last leg of a journey

joy /dʒɔɪ/ (**joys**)
1 **N-NONCOUNT** **Joy** is a feeling of great happiness. ❑ *She shouted with joy.*
2 **N-COUNT** A **joy** is something or someone that makes you feel happy. ❑ *Spending evenings outside is one of the joys of summer.* [from Old French]
→ look at Word Web: **emotion**

Word Partnership	Use joy with :
V	bring *someone* joy, cry/weep for joy, feel joy **1**
ADJ	filled with joy, great joy, pure joy, sheer joy **1**
N	tears of joy **1**

Word Link	joy ≈ being glad : enjoy, joyful, joyfully

joy|ful /dʒɔɪfəl/ **ADJ** Something that is **joyful** causes happiness and pleasure. [FORMAL] ❑ *A wedding is a joyful occasion.* ● **joy|ful|ly** **ADV** ❑ *The children cheered joyfully.* [from Old French]

Ju|da|ism /dʒudiɪzəm, -deɪ-/ **N-NONCOUNT** **Judaism** is the religion of the Jewish people. [from Late Latin]

judge /dʒʌdʒ/ (**judges, judging, judged**)
1 **N-COUNT** A **judge** is the person in a court of law who decides how criminals should be punished. ❑ *The judge sent him to jail for 100 days.*
2 **N-COUNT** A **judge** is a person who decides who will be the winner of a competition. ❑ *A panel of judges will choose the winner.*
3 **V-T** If you **judge** a competition, you decide who is the winner. ❑ *He will judge the contest and award the prize.*
4 **V-T** If you **judge** something or someone, you form an opinion about them. ❑ *People should wait, and judge the movie when they see it.* [from Old French]
→ look at Word Web: **trial**

judg|ment /dʒʌdʒmənt/ (**judgments**)
1 **N-NONCOUNT** **Judgment** is the ability to make sensible decisions about what to do. ❑ *I respect his judgment, and I'll follow his advice.*
2 **N-COUNT/N-NONCOUNT** A **judgment** is an opinion that you have after thinking

j

carefully about something. ❑ *In your judgment, what has changed?*

3 **N-COUNT/N-NONCOUNT** A **judgment** is a decision made by a judge or by a court of law. ❑ *We are waiting for a judgment from the Supreme Court.* [from Old French]

ju|di|cial /dʒudɪʃ°l/ **ADJ** SOCIAL STUDIES **Judicial** means relating to the legal system and to judgments made in a court of law. ❑ *...our judicial system.* [from Latin]

ju|di|cial branch /dʒudɪʃ°l bræntʃ/ **N-SING** SOCIAL STUDIES The **judicial branch** is the part of the government of the United States that applies laws.

ju|di|ci|ary /dʒudɪʃieri/ **N-SING** SOCIAL STUDIES The **judiciary** is the branch of authority in a country that is concerned with law and the legal system. [FORMAL] ❑ *...the head of the judiciary committee.* [from Latin]

judo /dʒudoʊ/ **N-NONCOUNT** SPORTS **Judo** is a sport in which two people fight without weapons. ❑ *He was also a black belt in judo.* [from Japanese]

jug /dʒʌg/ (**jugs**) **N-COUNT** A **jug** is a container with a handle used for holding and pouring liquids.

jug|gle /dʒʌg°l/ (**juggles, juggling, juggled**) **V-T/V-I** If you **juggle**, you throw and catch several things repeatedly and try to keep them in the air. ❑ *She was juggling five balls.* ❑ *We watched the clown juggle.* ● **jug|gler** (**jugglers**) **N-COUNT** ❑ *He was a professional juggler.* ● **jug|gl|ing** **N-NONCOUNT** ❑ *It's a children's show, with juggling and comedy.* [from Old French]

juice /dʒus/ (**juices**)
1 **N-COUNT/N-NONCOUNT** **Juice** is the liquid from a fruit or a vegetable. ❑ *He had a large glass of fresh orange juice.*
2 **N-PLURAL** The **juices** of a piece of meat are the liquid that comes out of it when you cook it. ❑ *Pour off the juices and put the meat in a frying pan.* [from Old French]

juice

juicy /dʒusi/ (**juicier, juiciest**) **ADJ** If food is **juicy**, it has a lot of juice in it and is very enjoyable to eat. ❑ *The waiter brought a thick, juicy steak to the table.* [from Old French]

July /dʒʊlaɪ/ (**Julys**) **N-COUNT/N-NONCOUNT** **July** is the seventh month of the year. ❑ *In July 1969, Neil Armstrong walked on the moon.* [from Latin]

jum|bo /dʒʌmboʊ/ (**jumbos**)
1 **ADJ** **Jumbo** means very large. ❑ *The jumbo shrimp were fresh and juicy.*
2 **N-COUNT** A **jumbo** or a **jumbo jet** is a very large aircraft. [from Swahili]

jump /dʒʌmp/ (**jumps, jumping, jumped**)
1 **V-T/V-I** If you **jump**, you bend your knees, push against the ground with your feet, and move quickly upward into the air. ❑ *I jumped over the fence.* ❑ *I jumped seventeen feet in the long jump.*
2 **N-COUNT** **Jump** is also a noun. ❑ *She set a world record for the longest jump by a woman.*
3 **V-I** If you **jump** somewhere, you move there quickly and suddenly. ❑ *Adam jumped up when he heard the doorbell.*
4 **V-I** If something **makes** you **jump**, it makes you move suddenly because you are frightened or surprised. ❑ *The phone rang and made her jump.*
5 **V-T/V-I** If an amount or level **jumps**, it suddenly increases by a large amount. ❑ *Sales jumped from $94 million to $101 million.*
6 **V-I** If you **jump at** an offer or an opportunity, you accept it quickly and with enthusiasm. ❑ *She jumped at the chance to be on TV.* [from Swedish]

jump|er /dʒʌmpər/ (**jumpers**) **N-COUNT** A **jumper** is a dress without sleeves that is worn over a blouse or a sweater. ❑ *She wore a blue jumper.* [from Old French]

junc|tion /dʒʌŋkʃ°n/ (**junctions**) **N-COUNT** A **junction** is a place where roads or railroad lines join. ❑ *Corinth was a target because it was a railroad junction.* [from Latin]

June /dʒun/ (**Junes**) **N-COUNT/N-NONCOUNT**
June is the sixth month of the year.
❑ *He spent two weeks with us in June 2006.*
[from Old English]

jun|gle /dʒʌŋɡəl/ (**jungles**)
N-COUNT/N-NONCOUNT A **jungle** is a forest in
a tropical country where large numbers of
tall trees and plants grow very close
together. ❑ *The trail led them deeper into the
jungle.* [from Hindi]

jun|ior /dʒunyər/ (**juniors**)
1 **N-COUNT** A **junior** is a student in the third
year of high school or college. ❑ *Her son is a
junior in high school.*
2 **ADJ** A **junior** official or employee has a
low position in an organization. ❑ *His father
was a junior officer in the army.* [from Latin]

jun|ior high school (**junior high schools**) or
junior high **N-COUNT/N-NONCOUNT** A **junior
high school** or a **junior high** is a school for
students from grade seven through grades
nine or ten. ❑ *I teach junior high school and I love
it.* ❑ *She attended Benjamin Franklin Junior High.*

junk /dʒʌŋk/ **N-NONCOUNT** **Junk** is old and
useless things that you do not want or need.
[INFORMAL] ❑ *What are you going to do with all
that junk, Larry?*

Ju|pi|ter /dʒupɪtər/ **N-PROPER** SCIENCE
Jupiter is the fifth planet from the sun and
the largest in our solar system. [from Latin]

ju|ror /dʒʊərər/ (**jurors**) **N-COUNT** A **juror** is a
member of a jury. ❑ *The jurors reached a verdict.*
[from Old French]
→ look at Word Web: **citizenship**

jury /dʒʊəri/ (**juries**) **N-COUNT** In a court of
law, the **jury** is a group of people who listen
to the facts about a crime and decide if a
person is guilty or not. ❑ *The jury decided she
was not guilty of murder..* [from Old French]
→ look at Word Web: **trial**

Word Partnership	Use **jury** with :
V	jury **convicts**, jury **announces**
N	jury **duty**, **trial by** jury
ADJ	**hung** jury, **unbiased** jury

just
❶ ADVERB USES
❷ ADJECTIVE USE

❶ just /dʒʌst/
1 **ADV** If something **just happened**, it
happened a very short time ago. ❑ *I just had*

the most awful dream. ❑ *I've just bought a new house.*
2 **ADV** If you are **just** doing something, you
are doing it now. ❑ *I'm just making some coffee.*
3 **ADV** **Just** means only. ❑ *It costs just a few
dollars.* ❑ *It's just a thought.*
4 **ADV** You use **just** when something is true,
but only by a small amount. ❑ *I arrived just in
time for my flight.* ❑ *I'd been in the house just under
an hour.*
5 **ADV** You use **just** to make the word that
follows it stronger. ❑ *Just stop talking and listen
to me!*
6 **ADV** **Just** means exactly. ❑ *They are just like
the rest of us.*
7 **PHRASE** **Just about** means almost. ❑ *All our
money is just about gone.*
8 **PHRASE** You say **Just a minute, Just a
moment**, or **Just a second** when you are
asking someone to wait for a short time.
❑ *Just a moment. What did you say?* [from Latin]

❷ just /dʒʌst/ **ADJ** A situation that is **just** is
fair or right. [FORMAL] ❑ *I think he got his just
punishment.* [from Latin]

jus|tice /dʒʌstɪs/ (**justices**)
1 **N-NONCOUNT** **Justice** is the fair treatment
of people. ❑ *We want freedom, justice and equality.*
2 **N-COUNT** A **justice** is a judge. ❑ *He is a
justice on the Supreme Court.*
3 **N-NONCOUNT** **Justice** is the legal system
that deals with people who break the law.
❑ *Many young people feel that the criminal justice
system does not treat them fairly.*
4 **PHRASE** If you **do justice to** someone or
something, you deal with them properly
and completely. ❑ *This article doesn't do the
topic justice.* [from Old French]

Word Partnership	Use **justice** with :
ADJ	**racial** justice, **social** justice **1**
	criminal justice, **equal** justice **3**
V	**seek** justice **1**
N	**obstruction of** justice, justice **system 3**

jus|ti|fi|ca|tion /dʒʌstɪfɪkeɪʃən/
(**justifications**) **N-COUNT/N-NONCOUNT**
A **justification for** something is an
acceptable reason or explanation for it.
❑ *There is no justification for this huge price rise.*
[from Old French]

jus|ti|fied /dʒʌstɪfaɪd/ **ADJ** A decision, an
action, or an idea that is **justified** is
reasonable and acceptable. ❑ *In my opinion,
the decision was justified.* ❑ *I work very hard,*

j

so I feel justified in asking for more money. [from Old French]

jus|ti|fy /dʒʌstɪfaɪ/ (justifies, justifying, justified) **v-t** To **justify** a decision or an action means to show that it is reasonable or necessary. ❑ Is there anything that can

justify a war? [from Old French]

ju|venile /dʒuvənᵊl, -naɪl/ (juveniles) **N-COUNT** A **juvenile** is a child or a young person who is not yet old enough to be treated as an adult. [FORMAL] ❑ ...the number of juveniles in the general population. [from Latin]

J

Kk

Ka|bu|ki /kəbu̱ki/ **N-NONCOUNT** ARTS
Kabuki is a form of traditional Japanese theater that uses dance and music as well as acting.

kan|ga|roo /kæ̱ŋgəru̱/ (kangaroos) **N-COUNT**
A **kangaroo** is a large Australian animal. Female kangaroos carry their babies in a pocket on their stomach. [from a native Australian language]

kangaroo

kan|ga|roo rat (kangaroo rats) **N-COUNT**
SCIENCE A **kangaroo rat** is a small rodent that lives in North and Central America. It has long back legs, which it uses in order to hop.

ka|ra|te /kəra̱ti/ **N-NONCOUNT** SPORTS
Karate is a Japanese sport in which people fight using their hands and feet. [from Japanese]

karst to|pog|r|aphy /ka̱rst təpɒ̱grəfi/
N-NONCOUNT SCIENCE **Karst topography** is land where rainwater has dissolved the rock, and features such as caves and underground streams have formed.

KB or **K** TECHNOLOGY **KB** or **K** is short for **kilobyte** or **kilobytes**.

keen /ki̱n/ (keener, keenest)
 1 **ADJ** If you are **keen**, you want to do something or you are very interested in it. ❑ Charles was keen to show his family the photos. ❑ Father was always a keen golfer.
 2 **ADJ** If you have a **keen** sense of something, you are very interested in it or good at it. ❑ For this job, you need to have a keen sense of adventure.
 3 **ADJ** If you have a **keen** eye or ear, you notice things that others do not. ❑ ...an artist with a keen eye for detail. ● **keen|ly** **ADV** ❑ Charles listened keenly.
 4 **ADJ** If someone has a **keen** mind, they are very clever and aware of what is happening around them. ❑ ...a man of keen intelligence. ● **keen|ly** **ADV** ❑ I am keenly aware of

the things that we share as Americans. [from Old English]

```
        ┌─────── keep ───────┐
        ❶ REMAIN, STAY, OR
          CONTINUE TO HAVE/DO
        ❷ STOP OR PREVENT
        ❸ PHRASAL VERBS
        └────────────────────┘
```

❶ **keep** /ki̱p/ (keeps, keeping, kept)
 1 **V-LINK** If you **keep** in a particular state, or if something **keeps** you in it, you remain in it. ❑ We burned wood to keep warm. ❑ The noise of the traffic kept him awake. ❑ Keep still!
 2 **V-T/V-I** If you **keep** or you **are kept** in a particular position or place, you remain in it. ❑ Keep away from the doors while the train is moving. ❑ Keep out! ❑ He kept his head down, hiding his face.
 3 **V-T** If you **keep** doing something, you do it many times or you continue to do it. ❑ I keep forgetting the password for my computer. ❑ She kept running although she was exhausted.
 4 **Keep on** means the same as **keep**. ❑ He kept on saying it.
 5 **V-T** If you **keep** something, you continue to have it. If you **keep** it somewhere, you store it there. ❑ I want to keep these clothes, and I want to give these away. ❑ She kept her money under the bed.
 6 **V-T** **Keep** is used with some nouns, such as "watch" and "control," to show that someone does something for a period of time. ❑ One of them would keep watch on the road.
 7 **V-T** When you **keep** a promise, you do what you said you would do. ❑ He kept his promise to come to my birthday party.
 8 **V-T** If you **keep** a record of a series of events, you write down details of it. ❑ Eleanor began to keep a diary.
 9 **PHRASE** If you **keep** something **to yourself**, you do not tell anyone else about it. ❑ I have to tell someone. I can't keep it to myself. [from Old English]

❷ **keep** /ki̱p/ (keeps, keeping, kept)
 1 **V-T** If someone or something **keeps** you **from** doing something, they prevent you

k

from doing it. ❏ *Embarrassment has kept me from doing all sorts of things.*

2 V-T If someone or something **keeps** you, they make you late. ❏ *Sorry to keep you, Jack.*

3 V-T If you **keep** something **from** someone, you do not tell them about it. ❏ *She knew that Gabriel was keeping something from her.* [from Old English]

❸ keep /kip/ (keeps, keeping, kept)
▶ **keep up** **1** If you **keep up with** someone or something, you move as fast as they do so that you are moving together. ❏ *Sam walked faster to keep up with his father.*
2 If you **keep** something **up**, you continue to do it. ❏ *I could not keep the diet up for longer than a month.*

keep|er /kipər/ (keepers) **N-COUNT** A **keeper** is a person who takes care of something. For example, a **keeper** at a zoo is a person who takes care of the animals. [from Old English]

ken|nel /kɛn³l/ (kennels) **N-COUNT** A **kennel** is a place where you can leave your dog when you go away somewhere. ❏ *The dogs will stay at the kennel until tomorrow.* [from Old French]

kept /kɛpt/ **Kept** is the past tense and past participle of **keep**. [from Old English]

kero|sene /kɛrəsin/ **N-NONCOUNT** Kerosene is a strong-smelling liquid that is used as a fuel in heaters and lamps. ❏ *...a kerosene lamp.* [from Greek]

ket|chup /kɛtʃʌp/ **N-NONCOUNT** Ketchup is a thick, red sauce made from tomatoes. ❏ *He was eating a burger with ketchup.* [from Chinese]
→ look at Word Web: **ketchup**

ket|tle /kɛt³l/ (kettles) **N-COUNT** A **kettle** is a metal container with a lid and a handle, that you use for boiling water. ❏ *I'll put the kettle on and make us some tea.* [from Old Norse]
→ look at Word Web: **tea**

key /ki/ (keys)
1 N-COUNT A **key** is a specially shaped piece of metal that opens or closes a lock. ❏ *They put the key in the door and entered.*

2 N-COUNT TECHNOLOGY The **keys** on a computer keyboard are the buttons that you press in order to operate it. ❏ *Now press the "Delete" key.*

3 N-COUNT MUSIC The **keys** of a piano are the white and black bars that you press in order to play it.

4 N-COUNT/N-NONCOUNT MUSIC In music, a **key** is a particular scale of musical notes. ❏ *...the key of A minor.*

5 ADJ The **key** person or thing in a group is the most important one. ❏ *He's a key player on the team.*

6 N-COUNT The **key to** something good is the thing that will help you to get it. ❏ *The key to getting good grades is to work hard.* [from Old English]
→ look at Word Web: **graph**

Thesaurus key Also look up:
ADJ   critical, important, major, vital **5**

Word Partnership Use **key** with:
V   turn a key **1**
ADJ   key **component**, key **decision**, key **factor**, key **figure**, key **ingredient**, key **issue**, key **official**, key **player**, key **point**, key **question**, key **role**, key **word 5**
       key **to success 6**

key|board /kibɔrd/ (keyboards)
1 N-COUNT TECHNOLOGY The **keyboard** of a computer is the set of keys that you press in order to operate it.

2 N-COUNT MUSIC The **keyboard** of a piano or an organ is the set of black and white keys that you press when you play it. [from Old English]
→ look at Picture Dictionaries: **keyboard, computer**

Word Web ketchup

There are many different spellings for **ketchup**, including catsup and *catchup*. The Chinese first made this **sauce** using **spices** and fish. They called it "ke-tsiap." In the 1600s, British sailors brought it back to Europe. Later, ketchup appeared in America where colonial cooks added **tomatoes**. Most people put this **condiment** on **hamburgers, hot dogs,** and **French fries**.

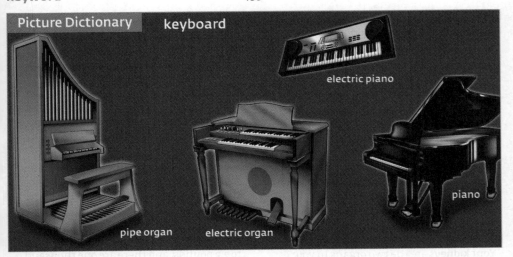

Picture Dictionary keyboard

electric piano

pipe organ   electric organ   piano

key|word /kíwɜrd/ (**keywords**) also **key word** N-COUNT TECHNOLOGY A **keyword** is a word or a phrase that you can use when you are searching for a particular document in an Internet search. ❑ *Users can search by title, by author, by subject, and by keyword.*

kg MATH SCIENCE **kg** is short for **kilogram** or **kilograms**.

kha|ki /kǽki/
1 ADJ Something that is **khaki** is greenish-brown or yellowish-brown in color. ❑ *He was dressed in khaki trousers.*
2 N-NONCOUNT **Khaki** is also a noun. ❑ *The soldiers were all in khaki.* [from Urdu]

kHz SCIENCE In writing, **kHz** is short for **kilohertz**.

kick /kík/ (**kicks, kicking, kicked**)
1 V-T/V-I If you **kick** someone or something, you hit them with your foot. ❑ *He kicked the door hard.* ❑ *He kicked at the ball.*
2 N-COUNT **Kick** is also a noun. ❑ *Johnson scored in the fifth minute with a free kick.*
3 V-T/V-I If you **kick**, or if you **kick** your legs, you move your legs up and down quickly. ❑ *Abby was taken away, kicking and screaming.* ❑ *The baby smiled and kicked her legs.*
4 N-SING A **kick** is a feeling of pleasure or excitement. [INFORMAL] ❑ *I love acting. I get a big kick out of it.*
5 V-T If you **kick** a bad habit, you stop having it. [INFORMAL] ❑ *Nail-biting is*

kick

a difficult habit to kick. [of Scandinavian origin]
▶ **kick in** If something **kicks in**, it begins to have an effect. ❑ *I hoped the aspirin would kick in soon.*
▶ **kick off** If an event, a game, a series, or a discussion **kicks off**, it begins. ❑ *The show kicks off on October 24th.*
▶ **kick out** To **kick** someone **out of** a place or an organization means to force them to leave it. [INFORMAL] ❑ *They kicked five foreign journalists out of the country.*

Thesaurus	kick	Also look up :
N	enjoyment, excitement, fun, thrill **3**	
V	abandon, give up, quit, stop; (ant.) start, take up **5**	

Word Partnership	Use **kick** with :
N	kick **a ball**, kick **a door**, **penalty** kick **1** kick **a habit 5**

kid /kíd/ (**kids, kidding, kidded**)
1 N-COUNT A **kid** is a child. [INFORMAL] ❑ *They have three kids.*
2 V-I If you **are kidding**, you are saying something that is not really true, as a joke. [INFORMAL] ❑ *I thought he was kidding but he was serious.* ❑ *I'm just kidding.*
3 N-COUNT A **kid** is a young goat. [of Scandinavian origin]

Word Partnership	Use **kid** with :
ADJ	**fat** kid, **friendly** kid, **good** kid, **little** kid, **new** kid, **nice** kid, **poor** kid, **skinny** kid, **smart** kid, **tough** kid, **young** kid **1**
N	**school** kid, kid **stuff 1**
V	**raise a** kid **1**

kid|nap /kɪdnæp/ (**kidnaps, kidnapping** or **kidnaping, kidnapped** or **kidnaped**)

1 **V-T** If someone **is kidnapped**, they are taken away by force and kept as a prisoner, often until their friends or family pay a large amount of money. ❑ *The tourists were kidnapped by a group of men with guns.*
● **kid|nap|per** (**kidnappers**) **N-COUNT** ❑ *His kidnappers have threatened to kill him.*
● **kid|nap|ping** (**kidnappings**) **N-COUNT/N-NONCOUNT** ❑ *Williams was jailed for eight years for the kidnapping.*

2 **N-COUNT/N-NONCOUNT** **Kidnap** or a **kidnap** is the crime of taking someone away by force. ❑ *He was charged with the kidnap of a 25-year-old woman.*

kid|ney /kɪdni/ (**kidneys**) **N-COUNT** **SCIENCE** Your **kidneys** are the two organs in your body that remove waste liquid from your blood. ❑ *She urgently needs a kidney transplant.*
→ look at Word Web: **donor**

kill /kɪl/ (**kills, killing, killed**)

1 **V-T/V-I** If a person, an animal, or another living thing **is killed**, something or someone makes them die. ❑ *More than 1,000 people have been killed by the armed forces.* ❑ *Drugs can kill.* ❑ *The hunter killed the rabbit.* ● **kill|ing** **N-NONCOUNT** ❑ *The TV news reported the killing of seven people.*

2 **V-T** If something or someone **kills** an activity, a process, or a feeling, they stop it. ❑ *His objective was to kill the project altogether.* ❑ *She asked for something to kill the pain.*

3 **V-T** If you **are killing** time, you are doing something in order to make the time seem to pass more quickly. ❑ *To kill the hours while she waited, Anna worked in the yard.* [from Old English]

▶ **kill off** If you **kill** things **off**, you destroy or kill all of them. ❑ *She is going to kill off a character in her next book.* ❑ *The radiation is intended to kill off the cancer cells.*

kill|er /kɪlər/ (**killers**)

1 **N-COUNT** A **killer** is a person who has killed someone. ❑ *The police are searching for the killers.*

2 **N-COUNT** You can talk about something that causes death as a **killer**. ❑ *Heart disease is the biggest killer of men in some countries.* [from Old English]

kilo /kiloʊ/ (**kilos**) **N-COUNT** **MATH** **SCIENCE** A **kilo** is the same as a **kilogram**. ❑ *He's lost ten kilos in weight.*

kilo|byte /kɪləbaɪt/ (**kilobytes**) **N-COUNT** **TECHNOLOGY** In computing, a **kilobyte** is a unit for measuring information. There are 1,024 bytes in a kilobyte.

kilo|calo|rie /kɪləkæləri/ (**kilocalories**) **N-COUNT** **SCIENCE** A **kilocalorie** is a unit for measuring energy that is equal to one thousand calories.

kilo|gram /kɪləgræm/ (**kilograms**) **N-COUNT** **MATH** **SCIENCE** A **kilogram** is a unit for measuring weight. One kilogram is equal to 2.2 pounds, and there are one thousand grams in a kilogram. ❑ *The box weighs 4.5 kilograms.*

kilo|hertz /kɪləhɜrts/ (**kilohertz**) **N-COUNT** **SCIENCE** A **kilohertz** is a unit for measuring radio waves. ❑ *The frequency of the radio waves slowly increased to 4 kilohertz.* [after Heinrich Rudolph Hertz (1857-94), a German physicist]

kilo|meter /kɪləmitər, kɪlɒmɪtər/ (**kilometers**) **N-COUNT** **MATH** A **kilometer** is a unit for measuring distance. One kilometer is equal to 0.62 miles, and there are one thousand meters in a kilometer. ❑ *We're now only one kilometer from the border.*
→ look at Picture Dictionary: **measurements**

kilo|watt /kɪləwɒt/ (**kilowatts**) **N-COUNT** **SCIENCE** A **kilowatt** is a unit for measuring electrical power. ❑ *The system produces 25 kilowatts of power.* [after James Watt (1736-1819), a Scottish engineer and inventor]

kind
1 NOUN USE AND PHRASE
2 ADJECTIVE USE

1 kind /kaɪnd/ (**kinds**)

1 **N-COUNT** A particular **kind of** thing is a type of that thing. ❑ *What kind of car do you drive?* ❑ *He travels a lot, and sees all kinds of interesting things.*

2 **PHRASE** **Kind of** means "a little" or "in some way." [SPOKEN] ❑ *When I was new at school, some girls were kind of mean to me.* [from Old English]

❷ **kind** /kaɪnd/ (**kinder, kindest**) **ADJ**
Someone who is **kind** is friendly and helpful.
❑ *Thank you for being so kind to me.* ● **kind|ness**
N-NONCOUNT ❑ *I'll never forget his generosity and*
kindness. [from Old English]

kin|der|gar|ten /kɪndərgɑrtᵊn/
(**kindergartens**) **N-COUNT/N-NONCOUNT**
Kindergarten is a class for children aged
4 to 6 years old. ❑ *She's in kindergarten now.*
[from German]

kind|ly /kaɪndli/
1 **ADJ** **Kindly** means kind and caring.
❑ *He gave her a kindly smile.*
2 **ADV** **Kindly** means in a friendly and
caring way. ❑ *The woman smiled kindly at her.*
[from Old English]

kin|es|thet|ic /kɪnɪsθεtɪk/ also
kinaesthetic **ADJ** SCIENCE **Kinesthetic**
means relating to sensations caused by
movement of the body. [from New Latin]

ki|net|ic en|er|gy **N-NONCOUNT** SCIENCE
In physics, **kinetic energy** is the energy that
is produced when something moves.

king /kɪŋ/ (**kings**)
1 **N-COUNT** SOCIAL STUDIES A **king** is a man
from a royal family, who is the head of state
of that country. ❑ *...the king and queen of Spain.*
2 **N-COUNT** If you describe a man as **the king**
of something, you mean that he is the best
person at doing it. ❑ *He was the king of rock*
and roll.
3 **N-COUNT** A **king** is a playing card with a
picture of a king on it. ❑ *...the king of*
diamonds.
4 **N-COUNT** In chess, the **king** is the piece
which each player must try to capture.
[from Old English]
→ look at Word Web: **chess**

king|dom /kɪŋdəm/ (**kingdoms**)
1 **N-COUNT** SOCIAL STUDIES A **kingdom** is a
country that is ruled by a king or a queen.
❑ *...the Kingdom of Denmark.*
2 **N-SING** The animal **kingdom** is all the
animals, birds, and insects in the world
together. The plant **kingdom** is all the
plants. ❑ *The animal kingdom is full of wonderful*
creatures. [from Old English]

ki|osk /kiɒsk/ (**kiosks**) **N-COUNT** A **kiosk** is a
small building with a window where people
can buy things like newspapers. ❑ *I was*
getting a newspaper at the kiosk. [from French]

kiss /kɪs/ (**kisses, kissing, kissed**)
1 **V-T/V-I** If you **kiss** someone, you touch
them with your lips to show love, or to greet
them. ❑ *She smiled and kissed him on the cheek.*
❑ *The woman gently kissed her baby.* ❑ *We kissed*
goodbye at the airport.
2 **N-COUNT** **Kiss** is also a noun. ❑ *I put my arms*
around her and gave her a kiss. [from Old English]

kit /kɪt/ (**kits**)
1 **N-COUNT** A **kit** is a group of items that are
kept and used together for a particular
purpose. ❑ *...a first aid kit.* ❑ *She just got her first*
drum kit.
2 **N-COUNT** A **kit** is a set of parts that you
can put together in order to make
something. ❑ *...a model airplane kit.*
[from Middle Dutch]

kitch|en /kɪtʃᵊn/ (**kitchens**) **N-COUNT**
A **kitchen** is a room that is used for cooking.
[from Old English]
→ look at Picture Dictionaries: **house,**
kitchen utensils

kite /kaɪt/ (**kites**) **N-COUNT** A **kite** is a toy
that you fly in the wind at the end of a long
string. ❑ *We went to the beach to fly kites.*
[from Old English]

kit|ten /kɪtᵊn/ (**kittens**) **N-COUNT** A **kitten**
is a very young cat. [from Old Northern
French]

kiwi fruit /kiwi frut/ (**kiwi fruit** or **kiwi**
fruits) **N-COUNT/N-NONCOUNT** A **kiwi fruit** is
a small fruit with brown skin, black seeds,
and bright green flesh.
→ look at Picture Dictionary: **fruit**

km (**kms**) MATH **km** is short for **kilometer**.

knead /nid/ (**kneads, kneading, kneaded**)
V-T When you **knead** a mixture for making
bread, you press and stretch it with your
hands to make it smooth. ❑ *Knead the dough*
for a few minutes. [from Old English]

knee /ni/ (**knees**)
1 **N-COUNT** Your **knee** is the joint in the
middle of your leg where it bends. ❑ *Lie down*
and bring your knees up toward your chest.
2 **N-COUNT** If something or someone is **on**
your **knee** or **on** your **knees**, they are resting
or sitting on the top part of your legs when

k

Picture Dictionary: kitchen utensils

bowl, hand mixer, ladle, spatula, colander, measuring cup, grater, measuring cup, whisk, can opener, rolling pin, measuring spoons, wooden spoon

you are sitting down. ❑ *He sat with the package on his knees.*

3 **N-PLURAL** If you are **on** your **knees**, your legs are bent and your knees are on the ground. ❑ *She was on her knees, praying.* [from Old English]

→ look at Picture Dictionaries: **body, horse**

kneel /niːl/ (**kneels, kneeling, kneeled** or **knelt**)

1 **V-I** When you **kneel**, you bend your legs and rest with one or both of your knees on the ground. ❑ *She knelt by the bed and prayed.* ❑ *Other people were kneeling, but she just sat.*
2 **Kneel down** means the same as **kneel**. ❑ *She kneeled down beside him.* [from Old English]

knew /nuː/ **Knew** is the past tense of **know**. [from Old English]

knife /naɪf/ (**knives, knifes, knifing, knifed**)

LANGUAGE HELP

Knives is the plural of the noun. **Knifes** is the third person singular of the present tense of the verb.

1 **N-COUNT** A **knife** is a sharp flat piece of metal with a handle, that you can use to cut things or as a weapon. ❑ *I stopped eating and put down my knife and fork.*
2 **V-T** To **knife** someone means to attack

and injure them with a knife. ❑ *Julius Caesar was knifed to death.* [from Old English]
→ look at Picture Dictionary: **tools**
→ look at Word Webs: **painting, silverware**

knight /naɪt/ (**knights**)

1 **N-COUNT** SOCIAL STUDIES In the past, a **knight** was a special type of soldier who rode a horse. ❑ *...King Arthur's knights.*
2 **N-COUNT** In chess, a **knight** is a piece that is shaped like a horse's head. [from Old English]
→ look at Word Web: **chess**

knit /nɪt/ (**knits, knitting, knitted**) **V-T/V-I** If you **knit** a piece of clothing, you make it from wool by using two long needles. ❑ *I had many hours to knit and sew.* ❑ *I have already started knitting baby clothes.* ● **knit|ting** **N-NONCOUNT** ❑ *My favorite hobbies are knitting and reading.* [from Old English]

knives /naɪvz/ **Knives** is the plural of **knife**. [from Old English]

knob /nɒb/ (**knobs**) **N-COUNT** A **knob** is a round handle or switch. ❑ *He turned the knob and pushed the door.* ❑ *...a volume knob.* [from Middle Low German]

knock /nɒk/ (**knocks, knocking, knocked**)
1 **V-I** If you **knock on** something, you hit it in order to make a noise. ❑ *She went to Simon's apartment and knocked on the door.* ● **knock|ing** **N-SING** ❑ *There was a loud knocking at the door.*
2 **N-COUNT** **Knock** is also a noun. ❑ *They heard a knock at the front door.*
3 **V-T** If you **knock** something, you touch or

hit it roughly. ❑ *She accidentally knocked the glass and it fell off the shelf.* [from Old English]

▶ **knock down** To **knock down** a building or part of a building means to destroy it. ❑ *We're knocking down the wall between the kitchen and the dining room.*

▶ **knock out** **1** To **knock** someone **out** means to hit them hard on the head so that they fall and cannot get up again. ❑ *He was knocked out in a fight.*

2 If a person or a team **is knocked out** of a competition, they are beaten, so that they no longer take part in the competition. ❑ *He got knocked out in the first game.*

▶ **knock over** To **knock** someone or something **over** means to hit them so that they fall over. ❑ *The third wave was so strong it knocked me over.* ❑ *She stood up suddenly, knocking over a glass of milk.*

Word Partnership	Use knock with :
V	**answer a** knock, **hear a** knock **1**
N	knock **on/at a door 1**
ADJ	**loud** knock **1**
	knock *someone* **out cold**, knock *someone* **unconscious 3**

knot /nɒt/ (**knots, knotting, knotted**)

1 **N-COUNT** A **knot** is a point where two pieces of string, rope, or cloth are joined together. ❑ *Tony wore a bright red scarf tied in a knot around his neck.*

knot

2 **V-T** If you **knot** two pieces of string or rope, you tie them together. ❑ *He knotted the laces securely together.* [from Old English]

know /noʊ/ (**knows, knowing, knew, known**)

1 **V-T/V-I** If you **know** a fact or an answer, you have that information in your mind. ❑ *You should know the answer to that question.* ❑ *I don't know his name.* ❑ *"How old is he?"—"I don't know."*

2 **V-T** If you **know** a person or a place, you are familiar with them. ❑ *I've known him for nine years.* ❑ *I know Chicago well. I used to live there.*

3 **V-I** If you **know of** something, you have heard about it but do not have a lot of information about it. ❑ *We know of the accident but have no further details.*

4 **V-T/V-I** If you **know about** something, or **know** it, you understand it. ❑ *My mother knows a lot about antiques.* ❑ *I know how you feel.*

5 **V-T** If someone or something **is known as** a particular name, they are called by that

name. ❑ *Rubella is more commonly known as German measles.* ❑ *Everyone knew him as Dizzy.*

6 → see also **known**

7 **PHRASE** If you **get to know** someone, you find out what they are like by spending time with them. ❑ *The new neighbors were getting to know each other.*

8 **INTERJ** You say **I know** when you are agreeing with what someone has just said. ❑ *"The weather is awful."—"I know."*

9 **PHRASE** You say **You never know** when you think that something good might happen in the future. ❑ *You never know, I might get lucky.*

10 **PHRASE** You use **you know** when you want someone to listen to what you are saying. [SPOKEN] ❑ *I'm doing this for you, you know.*

know-how **N-NONCOUNT** **Know-how** is knowledge of the methods or techniques of doing something. [INFORMAL] ❑ *He doesn't have the know-how to run a farm.*

knowl|edge /nɒlɪdʒ/

1 **N-NONCOUNT** **Knowledge** is information and understanding about a subject. ❑ *She has a wide knowledge of sports.* ❑ *Scientists have very little knowledge of the disease.* ❑ *He has little knowledge about the subject.*

2 **PHRASE** If you say that something is true **to your knowledge** or **to the best of** your **knowledge**, you mean that you believe that it is true, but that you are not sure. ❑ *The president, to my knowledge, hasn't commented on it.* [from Old English]

Word Partnership	Use knowledge with :
V	**acquire** knowledge, **gain** knowledge, **have** knowledge, **require** knowledge, **test** *your* knowledge, **use** *your* knowledge **1**
ADJ	**background** knowledge, **common** knowledge, **prior** knowledge, **scientific** knowledge, **useful** knowledge, **vast** knowledge **1**
N	knowledge **base 1**

knowl|edge|able /nɒlɪdʒəbəl/ also **knowledgable** **ADJ** Someone who is **knowledgeable** knows a lot about a particular subject. ❑ *Our staff are all extremely knowledgeable about our products.* [from Old English]

known /noʊn/

1 **Known** is the past participle of **know**.

2 **ADJ** Someone or something that is **known**

k

is familiar to a particular group of people. ❑ *Hawaii is known for its beautiful beaches.* [from Old English]

knuck|le /nʌkəl/ (knuckles) **N-COUNT** Your **knuckles** are the parts where your fingers join your hands, and where your fingers bend. ❑ *She tapped on the door with her knuckles.* [from Middle High German]
→ look at Picture Dictionary: **hand**

koa|la /kouɑlə/ (koalas) **N-COUNT** A **koala** or a **koala bear** is an Australian animal that looks like a small bear with gray fur and lives in trees. [from a native Australian language]
→ look at Word Web: **herbivore**

Ko|ran /kɔrɑn, -ræn/ **N-PROPER** The **Koran** is the most important book in the religion of Islam. [from Arabic]

Kui|per belt /kaɪpər bɛlt/ **N-SING** SCIENCE The **Kuiper belt** is a region of the solar system beyond Neptune where there are many small, icy comets. [from Dutch American]

kW SCIENCE In writing, **kW** is short for **kilowatt**.

K

L l

lab /lǽb/ (**labs**) **N-COUNT** SCIENCE A **lab** is the same as a **laboratory**.

laba|no|ta|tion /lɑbənoʊteɪʃᵊn, leɪb-/ **N-NONCOUNT** ARTS **Labanotation** is a system for recording dance movements that uses symbols to represent points on the dancer's body.

lab apron (**lab aprons**) **N-COUNT** SCIENCE A **lab apron** is a piece of clothing that you wear when you are working in a laboratory, in order to prevent your clothes from getting dirty.

la|bel /leɪbᵊl/ (**labels, labeling, labeled**)
1 N-COUNT A **label** is a piece of paper or plastic that is attached to an object to give information about it. □ *Always read the label on the bottle.*
2 V-T If something **is labeled**, it has a label on it. □ *All foods must be clearly labeled.*
3 V-T If you say that someone or something **is labeled as** a particular thing, you mean that people generally describe them that way and you think that this is unfair. □ *He was labeled as a difficult child.* [from Old French]
→ look at Word Web: **graph**

Thesaurus	label Also look up :
N	sticker, tag, ticket **1**
V	brand, characterize, classify **3**

la|bor /leɪbər/
1 N-NONCOUNT Labor is very hard work, usually physical work. □ *The punishment for refusing to fight was a year's hard labor.*
2 N-NONCOUNT SOCIAL STUDIES **Labor** is the workers of a country or an industry. □ *Employers want cheap labor.*
3 N-NONCOUNT SCIENCE **Labor** is the last stage of pregnancy, in which the mother gradually pushes the baby out. □ *Her labor was long and difficult.* [from Old French]
→ look at Word Web: **factory**

Word Link	ory ≈ place where something happens : dormit**ory**, laborat**ory**, territ**ory**

la|bora|tory /lǽbrətɔri/ (**laboratories**)
N-COUNT SCIENCE A **laboratory** is a building or a room where scientific work is done. □ *He works in a research laboratory at Columbia University.* [from Medieval Latin]
→ look at Picture Dictionary: **laboratory equipment**
→ look at Word Web: **laboratory**

Word Partnership	Use laboratory with :
N	laboratory **conditions**, laboratory **equipment**, laboratory **experiment**, **research** laboratory, laboratory **technician**, laboratory **test**

la|bor|er /leɪbərər/ (**laborers**) **N-COUNT** A **laborer** is a person who does a job that involves a lot of hard physical work. □ *...a farm laborer.* [from Old French]
→ look at Word Web: **union**

Word Web laboratory

The discovery of the life-saving drug penicillin was a lucky accident. While cleaning his **laboratory**, a **researcher** named Alexander Fleming* noticed that the bacteria in one **Petri dish** had been killed by some kind of **mold**. He took a **sample** and found that it was a form of penicillin. Fleming and others did further **research** and **published** their **findings** in 1928, but few people took notice. However, ten years later a team at Oxford University in England read Fleming's **study** and began animal and human **experiments**. Within ten years, drug companies were manufacturing 650 billion units of penicillin a month!

Alexander Fleming (1881-1955): a Scottish biologist and pharmacologist.

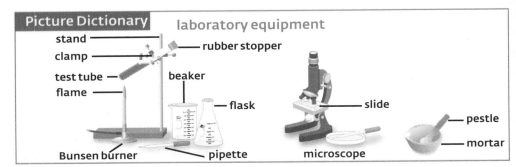

Picture Dictionary laboratory equipment

stand — rubber stopper
clamp
test tube — beaker
flame
— flask
— slide
— pestle
— mortar
Bunsen burner — pipette microscope

lace /leɪs/ (laces, lacing, laced)

1 **N-NONCOUNT**
Lace is a delicate
cloth with a design
made of fine threads.
❑ She wore a blue dress
with a lace collar.
2 **N-COUNT** Laces are

lace

thin pieces of material that are used for
fastening shoes. ❑ Barry put on his shoes and
tied the laces.
3 **V-T** If you lace a pair of shoes, you pull the
laces through the holes and tie them
together. ❑ I laced my shoes tightly.
4 **Lace up** means the same as **lace**. ❑ He sat on
the steps, and laced up his boots. [from Old French]

lach|ry|mose /lækrɪmoʊs/ **ADJ** Someone
who is **lachrymose** is crying, or often cries.
[LITERARY] ❑ ...the tears of lachrymose mourners.
[from Latin]

lack /læk/ (lacks, lacking, lacked)
1 **N-NONCOUNT/N-SING** If there is a **lack of**
something, there is not enough of it or it
does not exist. ❑ I was tired from lack of sleep.
2 **V-T/V-I** If someone or something **lacks** a
particular quality, or a particular quality **is
lacking** in them, they do not have any or
enough of it. ❑ The meat lacked flavor.
3 **PHRASE** If you say there is **no lack of**
something, you are emphasizing that there
is a great deal of it. ❑ There was no lack of things
for them to talk about. [from Middle Dutch]

Word Partnership Use **lack** with :

N   lack of confidence, lack of control, lack
     of enthusiasm, lack of evidence, lack of
     exercise, lack of experience, lack of
     food, lack of information, lack of
     knowledge, lack of money, lack of
     progress, lack of resources, lack of
     skills, lack of sleep, lack of support,
     lack of trust, lack of understanding **1**

lad|der /lædər/ (ladders) **N-COUNT**
A **ladder** is a piece of equipment
used for reaching high places.
It is made of two long pieces of
wood or metal with short steps
between them. ❑ He climbed the
ladder so he could see over the wall.
[from Old English]

lady /leɪdi/ (ladies) **N-COUNT**
You can use **lady** when you
are talking about a woman
in a polite way. ❑ She's a
very sweet old lady.
[from Old English]
ladder

lag /læg/ (lags, lagging, lagged)
1 **V-I** If you **lag behind** someone or
something, you make slower progress than
them. ❑ She's still lagging behind the other
students in her class.
2 **N-COUNT** A time **lag** or a **lag** of a particular
length of time is a period of time between
one event and another related event.
❑ There's a time lag between becoming infected and
getting sick.

laid /leɪd/ **Laid** is the past tense and past
participle of **lay**. [from Old French]

laid-back **ADJ** If someone is **laid-back**, they
behave in a calm, relaxed way. [INFORMAL]
❑ Everyone here is really laid-back.

lain /leɪn/ **Lain** is the past participle of **lie**.
[from Old English]

lake /leɪk/ (lakes) **N-COUNT** GEOGRAPHY A **lake**
is a large area of water with land around it.
❑ They went fishing in the lake. [from Old French]
→ look at Picture Dictionaries: **landforms,
river**
→ look at Word Web: **lake**

lamb /læm/ (lambs)
1 **N-COUNT** A **lamb** is a young sheep.
2 **N-NONCOUNT** **Lamb** is the flesh of a lamb

Word Web lake

Several forces create **lakes**. The movement of a glacier can carve out a deep **basin** in the soil. The Great Lakes between the U.S. and Canada are **glacial** lakes. Very deep lakes appear when large pieces of the earth's crust suddenly shift. Lake Baikal in Russia is more than a mile deep. When a volcano erupts, it creates a **crater**. Crater Lake in Oregon is the perfectly round remains of a volcanic cone. The **water** comes from melted snow and rain. Erosion also creates lakes. When the wind blows away sand, the hole left behind forms a natural lake **bed**.

eaten as food. ❑ *For supper she served lamb and vegetables.* [from Old English]

lame /leɪm/ (**lamer, lamest**)

1 **ADJ** A **lame** animal or person cannot walk very well. ❑ *The horses were lame and the men were tired.*

2 **ADJ** A **lame** excuse is not a very good excuse. ❑ *He gave me some lame excuse about being too busy to call me.* [from Old English]

lamp /læmp/ (**lamps**) **N-COUNT** A **lamp** is a light that works using electricity or by burning oil or gas. ❑ *She switched on the lamp by her bed.* [from Old French]

land /lænd/ (**lands, landing, landed**)

1 **N-NONCOUNT** GEOGRAPHY **Land** is an area of ground, especially one that is used for a particular purpose such as farming or building. ❑ *There is not enough good farm land.*

2 **N-COUNT** You can use **land** to refer to a country. [LITERARY] ❑ *...America, land of opportunity.*

3 **V-I** When someone or something **lands**, they come down to the ground after moving through the air. ❑ *The ball landed 20 feet away.*

4 **V-T/V-I** When someone **lands** a plane, a ship, or a boat, or when it **lands**, it arrives somewhere after a journey. ❑ *The plane landed just after 10 pm.* ❑ *He landed his boat on the western shore.*

5 **V-T/V-I** If you **land in** an unpleasant situation or place, or if something **lands** you **in** it, something causes you to be in that situation or place. [INFORMAL] ❑ *His big ideas have landed him in trouble again.* [from Old English]

→ look at Word Webs: **biosphere, continent, earth**

Thesaurus land Also look up :

N	area, country, real estate **1**
V	arrive, touch down; (*ant.*) take off **3 4**

Word Partnership Use **land** with :

N	**acres of** land, **area of** land, **desert** land, land, land **management**, land **ownership**, **piece of** land, **plot of** land, **strip of** land, **tract of** land, land **use 1**
ADJ	**agricultural** land, **fertile** land, **flat** land, **grazing** land, **private** land, **public** land, **undeveloped** land, **vast** land **1**
V	**buy** land, **own** land, **sell** land **1**

land|fill /lændfɪl/ (**landfills**)

1 **N-NONCOUNT** **Landfill** is a method of getting rid of very large amounts of garbage by burying it in a large deep hole. ❑ *...the high cost of landfill.*

2 **N-COUNT** A **landfill** is a large deep hole in which very large amounts of garbage are buried. ❑ *The trash in modern landfills does not decompose easily.*

→ look at Word Web: **dump**

land|form /lændfɔrm/ (**landforms**) also **land form** **N-COUNT** GEOGRAPHY A **landform** is a natural feature of the Earth's surface, such as a hill, a lake, or a beach. ❑ *This small country has a wide variety of landforms.*

→ look at Picture Dictionary: **landforms**

land|ing /lændɪŋ/ (**landings**)

1 **N-COUNT** In a house or other building, the **landing** is the flat area at the top of the stairs.

2 **N-COUNT/N-NONCOUNT** The **landing** of a plane is the process of moving it down to the ground. ❑ *The pilot made an emergency landing into the ocean.* [from Old English]

land|lady /lændleɪdi/ (**landladies**) **N-COUNT** A **landlady** is a woman who owns a building and allows people to live there in return for rent. ❑ *There was a note under the door from my landlady.*

Picture Dictionary **landforms**

mountain
valley
island
plateau
lake
cliff
river
bay
delta
peninsula

land|lord /lǽndlɔrd/ (**landlords**) **N-COUNT**
A **landlord** is a man who owns a building
and allows people to live there in return for
rent. ❑ *His landlord doubled the rent.*

| Word Link | mark ≈ boundary, sign : book*mark*,
ear*mark*, land*mark* |

land|mark /lǽndmɑrk/ (**landmarks**)
1 **N-COUNT** A **landmark** is a building or
other object that helps people to know
where they are. ❑ *The Empire State Building is a
New York landmark.*
2 **N-COUNT** You can refer to an important
stage in the development of something as a
landmark. ❑ *The baby was a landmark in our lives.*

land|scape /lǽndskeɪp/ (**landscapes**)
1 **N-COUNT/N-NONCOUNT** The **landscape** is
everything you can see when you look across
an area of land. ❑ *We traveled through the
beautiful landscape of eastern Idaho.*
2 **N-COUNT** ARTS A **landscape** is a painting
that shows a scene in the countryside.
❑ *She paints landscapes of hills and river valleys.*
[from Middle Dutch]
→ look at Word Webs: **art, painting**

land|scap|er /lǽndskeɪpər/ (**landscapers**)
N-COUNT A **landscaper** is a person whose job
is to make people's gardens more attractive.
[from Middle Dutch]

land|slide /lǽndslaɪd/ (**landslides**)
1 **N-COUNT** GEOGRAPHY A **landslide** is a large

amount of earth and rocks falling down
a cliff or the side of a mountain. ❑ *The storm
caused landslides and flooding.*
2 **N-COUNT** SOCIAL STUDIES A **landslide** is a
victory in an election in which a person or
political party gets far more votes or seats
than their opponents. ❑ *He won the election
by a landslide.*
→ look at Word Webs: **disaster, tsunami**

lane /leɪn/ (**lanes**)
1 **N-COUNT** A **lane** is a narrow road,
especially in the countryside. ❑ *Our house
was on a quiet country lane.*
2 **N-COUNT** A **lane** is a part of a road that is
marked by a painted line. ❑ *The truck was
traveling at 20 mph in the slow lane.*
3 **N-COUNT** SPORTS At a swimming pool,
a race track, or a bowling alley, a **lane** is a
long narrow section which is separated from
other sections by lines or ropes. ❑ *Who is the
runner in the inside lane?* [from Old English]
→ look at Word Web: **traffic**

lan|guage /lǽŋgwɪdʒ/ (**languages**)
1 **N-COUNT** LANGUAGE ARTS A **language** is a
system of sounds and written symbols that
people of a particular country or region use
in talking or writing. ❑ *The English language
has over 500,000 words.* ❑ *Students must learn to
speak a second language.*
2 **N-NONCOUNT** LANGUAGE ARTS **Language** is
the use of a system of communication that

has a set of sounds or written symbols. ❏ *Some children develop language more quickly than others.*

3 **N-NONCOUNT** You can refer to the words used in connection with a particular subject as **the language of** that subject. ❏ *...the language of business.*

4 **N-NONCOUNT** The **language** of a piece of writing or speech is the style in which it is written or spoken. ❏ *Why can't they explain things in plain language?* ❏ *The tone of his language was polite.* [from Old French]

→ look at Word Webs: **culture, English**

lan|tern /lǽntərn/ (**lanterns**) **N-COUNT** A **lantern** is a light in a metal frame with glass sides. [from Latin]

lap /lǽp/ (**laps, lapping, lapped**)

1 **N-COUNT** Your **lap** is the flat area formed by the tops of your legs when you are sitting down. ❏ *Anthony was sitting on his dad's lap.*

2 **N-COUNT** SPORTS In a race, someone completes a **lap** when they have gone around a course once. ❏ *He was not able to run the last lap of the race.*

3 **V-T** When an animal **laps** a drink, it uses short quick movements of its tongue to take liquid up into its mouth. ❏ *The cat lapped milk from a dish.*

4 **Lap up** means the same as **lap**. ❏ *She poured some water into a bowl and the dog lapped it up eagerly.*

5 **V-T/V-I** When water **laps** against something such as the shore or the side of a boat, it touches it gently and makes a soft

sound. [WRITTEN] ❏ *Water lapped against the shore.* ❏ *...white beaches lapped by warm blue seas.*

● **lap|ping** **N-NONCOUNT** ❏ *The only sound was the lapping of the waves.* [from Old English]

la|pel /ləpɛ́l/ (**lapels**) **N-COUNT** The **lapels** of a jacket or a coat are the folds on the front. ❏ *He wore a flower in his lapel.*

lap|top /lǽptɒp/ (**laptops**) **N-COUNT** TECHNOLOGY A **laptop** is a small computer that you can carry with you. ❏ *She was working at her laptop.*

→ look at Picture Dictionary: **computer**

large /lɑ́rdʒ/ (**larger, largest**)

1 **ADJ** A **large** thing or person is greater in size than most other things of the same type. ❏ *This fish lives mainly in large rivers and lakes.* ❏ *In the largest room a few people were sitting on the floor.*

2 **ADJ** A **large** amount or number is more than the average amount or number. ❏ *The robbers got away with a large amount of cash.* ❏ *A large number of people are still looking for jobs.*

3 **PHRASE** You use **at large** to indicate that you are talking in a general way about most of the people mentioned. ❏ *He wanted to get the public at large interested in modern art.* [from Old French]

large|ly /lɑ́rdʒli/

1 **ADV** You use **largely** to say that something is mostly true. ❏ *The program is largely paid for by taxes.* ❏ *The government is largely to blame for this.*

2 **ADV** **Largely** is used to introduce the main reason for a particular event or situation. ❏ *She failed her exams, largely because she did no work.* [from Old French]

large-scale also **large scale**

1 **ADJ** A **large-scale** action or event happens over a very wide area or involves a lot of people or things. ❏ *...a large-scale military operation.*

2 **ADJ** A **large-scale** map or diagram represents a small area of land, a building, or a machine in a way that allows small details to be shown.

lar|va /lɑ́rvə/ (**larvae** /lɑ́rvi/) **N-COUNT** A **larva** is an insect at the stage of its life after it has developed from an egg and before it changes into its adult form. ❑ *The eggs quickly hatch into larvae.* [from Latin]

→ look at Word Web: **amphibian**

lar|ynx /lǽrɪŋks/ (larynxes) **N-COUNT** SCIENCE Your **larynx** is the top part of the passage that leads from your throat to your lungs and contains your vocal cords. [from New Latin]

la|ser /léɪzər/ (lasers) **N-COUNT** SCIENCE A **laser** is a strong light that is produced by a special machine. ❑ *Doctors are trying new laser technology to help patients.*

→ look at Word Web: **laser**

la|ser print|er (laser printers) **N-COUNT** TECHNOLOGY A **laser printer** is a computer printer that produces clear words and pictures on paper using laser beams (= strong lines of light).

lash /lǽʃ/ (lashes, lashing, lashed)
■ **N-COUNT** Your **lashes** are the hairs that grow on the edge of your eyelids. ❑ *His eyes had very long lashes.*
■ **V-T** If you **lash** two or more things together, you tie one of them firmly to the other. ❑ *He held the boxes tightly while Rita used rope to lash them together.* ❑ *We built the shelter by lashing poles together.*
■ **V-T/V-I** If wind, rain, or water **lashes** someone or something, it hits them violently. [WRITTEN] ❑ *Storms lashed the east coast of North America.* ❑ *Rain lashed against the windows.*
■ **N-COUNT** A **lash** is a blow with a whip, especially a blow on someone's back as a punishment. ❑ *The villagers sentenced one man to five lashes for stealing.* [Sense 2 from Old French.]
▶ **lash out** ■ If you **lash out**, you attempt to hit someone quickly and violently with a weapon or with your hands or feet. ❑ *They held his arms to stop him from lashing out.*

■ If you **lash out at** someone or something, you speak to them or about them very angrily or critically. ❑ *His laughter made her angry and she lashed out at him.*

last /lǽst/ (lasts, lasting, lasted)
■ **DET** You use **last** to talk about the most recent day, night, or year. ❑ *I got married last July.* ❑ *He didn't come home last night.*
■ **ADJ** The **last** event, person, or thing is the most recent one. ❑ *A lot has changed since my last visit.*
■ **PRON** **Last** is also a pronoun. ❑ *Each song was better than the last.*
■ **ADJ** The **last** thing, person, event, or period of time is the one that happens or comes after all the others of the same type. ❑ *I read the last three pages of the chapter.*
■ **ADV** If you do something **last**, you do it at the end, or after everyone else. ❑ *I arrived home last.*
■ **ADV** If something **last** happened on a particular occasion, that is the most recent occasion on which it happened. ❑ *When were you there last?* ❑ *He is a lot taller than when I last saw him.*
■ **PRON** If you are **the last to** do something, everyone else does it before you. ❑ *Rosa was the last to go to bed.*
■ **ADJ** The **last** thing or person is the only one that is left. ❑ *Can I have the last piece of pizza?*
■ **ADJ** You can use **last** to indicate that something is extremely undesirable or unlikely. ❑ *The last thing I wanted to do was teach.*
■ **PRON** **Last** is also a pronoun. ❑ *I'm the last to say that science explains everything.*
■ **V-T/V-I** If a situation **lasts** for a particular length of time, it continues to exist for that length of time. ❑ *The marriage lasted for two years.* ❑ *The games lasted half the normal time.*
■ **V-T/V-I** If something **lasts** for a particular

Word Web   laser

Lasers are an amazing form of technology. Laser **beams** read **CD**s and **DVD**s. They can create three-dimensional holograms. Laser **light shows** add excitement at concerts. **Fiber optic cables** carry intense flashes of laser light. This allows a single cable to transmit thousands of email and phone messages at the same time. Laser **scanners** read prices from bar codes. Lasers are also used in **surgery** to remove hair, birthmarks and tattoos. Dentists use lasers to remove cavities. Laser eye surgery has become very popular. In manufacturing, lasers make precise cuts in everything from fabric to steel.

length of time, it can be used for that time. ❑ *One tube of glue lasts for a long time.* ❑ *This battery lasts twice as long as the smaller size.*

13 **PHRASE** If something happens **at last**, it happens after you have been hoping for it for a long time. ❑ *I'm so glad that we've found you at last!*

14 **PHRASE** You use expressions such as **the night before last**, **the election before last** and **the leader before last** to refer to the period of time, event, or person that came before the most recent one. ❑ *I went out with Helen the night before last.*

15 **PHRASE** You use **the last I heard** to introduce the most recent piece of information that you have on a particular subject. ❑ *The last I heard, Joe and Irene were still happily married.* [from Old English]

Usage   **last** and **latter**

Both *last* and *latter* refer to the final person or thing mentioned. Use *last* when more than two persons or things have been mentioned: *Whales, dolphins, and sharks all have fins and live in the ocean, but only the last is a fish.* Use *latter* when exactly two persons or things have been mentioned: *Jorge and Ana applied for the same scholarship, which was awarded to the latter.*

---

last|ing /lǽstɪŋ/ **ADJ** Lasting describes something that continues to exist for a very long time. ❑ *Everyone wants lasting peace.* [from Old English]

last|ly /lǽstli/ **ADV** You use **lastly** when you want to mention a final item. ❑ *Lastly, can I ask about your future plans?* [from Old English]

last name (last names) **N-COUNT** Your **last name** is the name of your family. In English, your **last** name comes after all your other names. ❑ *"What is your last name?"—"Garcia."*

latch /lǽtʃ/ (latches) **N-COUNT** A **latch** is a metal bar that you use to fasten a door or a gate. You lift the bar to open the door or gate. ❑ *She lifted the latch and pushed the door open.* [from Old English]

late /leɪt/ (later, latest)

1 **ADV** Late means near the end of a period of time. ❑ *It was late in the afternoon.* ❑ *He married late in life.*

2 **ADJ** Late is also an adjective. ❑ *He was in his late 20s.*

3 **ADJ** If it is **late**, it is near the end of the day. ❑ *It was very late and the streets were empty.*
● **late|ness** **N-NONCOUNT** ❑ *A crowd gathered*

despite the lateness of the hour.

4 **ADV** Late means after the time that something should start or happen. ❑ *Steve arrived late for his class.* ● **late|ness** **N-NONCOUNT** ❑ *He apologized for his lateness.*

5 **ADJ** Late is also an adjective. ❑ *The train was 40 minutes late.*

6 **ADJ** You use **late** when you are talking about someone who is dead, especially someone who has died recently. ❑ *...my late husband.*

7 → see also **latest**

8 **PHRASE** If an action or an event is **too late**, it is useless or unsuccessful because it occurs after the best time for it. ❑ *It was too late to change her mind.* [from Old English]

late|ly /leɪtli/ **ADV** You use **lately** to talk about events that happened recently. ❑ *Dad's health hasn't been good lately.* [from Old English]
→ look at Usage note at **recently**

lat|er /leɪtər/

1 **Later** is the comparative of **late**.

2 **ADV** You use **later** to talk about a time that is after the one that you have been talking about. ❑ *He joined the company in 1990 and left his job ten years later.*

3 **PHRASE** You use **later on** to talk about a time that is after the one that you have been talking about. ❑ *Later on I'll be speaking to Patty Davis.*

4 **ADJ** You use **later** to talk about a period of time that comes after the one that you have been talking about. ❑ *The competition was re-scheduled for a later date.*

5 **ADJ** You use **later** to talk about the last part of someone's life or career or the last part of a period of history. ❑ *He found happiness in later life.* ❑ *...the later part of the 20th century.* [from Old English]

lat|er|al line sys|tem /lǽtərəl laɪn sɪstəm/ (lateral line systems) **N-COUNT** SCIENCE A **lateral line system** is a row of sense organs along each side of a fish's body that helps it to detect movement in the water.

lat|est /leɪtɪst/

1 **Latest** is the superlative of **late**.

2 **ADJ** Latest describes something that is the most recent thing of its type. ❑ *I really liked her latest book.*

3 **ADJ** Latest describes something that is new and modern. ❑ *That store sells only the latest fashions.*

4 **PHRASE** You use **at the latest** in order to say that something must happen at or before a particular time and not after that time. ❑ *She'll be back by ten o'clock at the latest.* [from Old English]

Lat|in Ameri|can /lǽtɪn əmɛ́rɪkən/ **ADJ** SOCIAL STUDIES **Latin American** means belonging or relating to the countries of South America, Central America, and Mexico. **Latin American** also means belonging or relating to the people or culture of these countries. ❑ *...Latin American writers.*

lati|tude /lǽtɪtud/ (**latitudes**)
N-COUNT/N-NONCOUNT GEOGRAPHY
The **latitude** of a place is its distance from the equator. Compare with **longitude**. ❑ *The evenings are already long at this northern latitude.* [from Latin]
→ look at Picture Dictionary: **globe**
→ look at Word Web: **navigation**

lat|ter /lǽtər/
1 **PRON** When two people or things have just been mentioned, you can call the second one **the latter**. You can call the first of them **the former**. ❑ *He found his cousin and uncle. The latter was sick.*
2 **ADJ** **Latter** is also an adjective. ❑ *Some people like speaking in public and some don't. Mike belongs in the latter group.*
3 **ADJ** You use **latter** to describe the later part of a period of time or an event. ❑ *...in the latter years of his career.* [from Old English]
→ look at Usage note at **last**

laugh /lǽf/ (**laughs, laughing, laughed**)
1 **V-T/V-I** When you **laugh**, you make a sound while smiling to show that you think something is funny. ❑ *When I saw what he was wearing, I started to laugh.* ❑ *Some of the boys laughed their heads off at his jokes.*
2 **N-COUNT** **Laugh** is also a noun. ❑ *Len gave a loud laugh.*

3 **V-I** If people **laugh at** someone or something, they make jokes about them. ❑ *People used to laugh at me because I was so small.* [from Old English]
→ look at Word Web: **laugh**
▶ **laugh off** If you **laugh off** a difficult or serious situation, you try to suggest that it is funny and unimportant. ❑ *He laughed off reports that he is to be replaced as the team manager.*

Thesaurus laugh Also look up :	
V	chuckle, crack up, giggle, howl; *(ant.)* cry **1**

Word Partnership Use laugh with :	
V	**begin/start to** laugh, **hear** *someone* laugh, **make** *someone* laugh, **try to** laugh **1**
ADJ	**big** laugh, **good** laugh, **hearty** laugh, **little** laugh **1**

laugh|ter /lǽftər/ **N-NONCOUNT** **Laughter** is the sound of people laughing. ❑ *Their laughter filled the room.* [from Old English]
→ look at Word Web: **laugh**

Word Partnership Use laughter with :	
V	**burst into** laughter, **hear** laughter, **roar with** laughter
N	**burst of** laughter, **sound of** laughter
ADJ	**hysterical** laughter, **loud** laughter, **nervous** laughter

launch /lɔ́ntʃ/ (**launches, launching, launched**)
1 **V-T** To **launch** a spacecraft means to send it away from Earth. To launch a ship or a boat means to put it into water. ❑ *NASA plans to launch a new satellite.* ❑ *The Titanic was launched in 1911.*
2 **N-COUNT** **Launch** is also a noun. ❑ *...the launch of the space shuttle Columbia.*
3 **V-T** To **launch** a large and important

Word Web laugh

There is an old saying, "**Laughter** is the best medicine." Scientific research shows that humor really is good for your health. When a person **bursts out laughing,** levels of stress hormones in the bloodstream immediately drop. And laughter is more than just a sound. **Howling with laughter** gives face, stomach, leg, and back muscles a good workout. From polite **giggles** to noisy guffaws, laughter allows the release of anger, sadness, and fear. And that has to be good for you.

activity means to start it. ❑ *The police have launched a search for the missing girl.*
4 **N-COUNT** **Launch** is also a noun. ❑ *...the launch of a campaign for healthy eating.*
5 **V-T** If a company **launches** a new product, it makes it available to the public. ❑ *The company launched a low-cost computer.*
6 **N-COUNT** **Launch** is also a noun. ❑ *...the launch of a new Sunday magazine.* [from Anglo-French]
→ look at Word Web: **satellite**

launch pad (**launch pads**) **N-COUNT** **SCIENCE** A **launch pad** or **launching pad** is a platform from which rockets, missiles, or satellites are launched.

launch ve|hi|cle (**launch vehicles**) **N-COUNT** **SCIENCE** A **launch vehicle** is a rocket that is used to launch a satellite or a spacecraft.

laun|dro|mat /lɔndrəmæt/ (**laundromats**) **N-COUNT** A **laundromat** is a place where people pay to use machines to wash and dry their clothes.

laun|dry /lɔndri/ (**laundries**)
1 **N-NONCOUNT** **Laundry** is clothes and other things that are going to be washed. ❑ *I'll do your laundry.*
2 **N-COUNT** A **laundry** is a business that washes and irons clothes and other things for people. ❑ *He takes his shirts to the laundry.*
→ look at Picture Dictionary: **house**
→ look at Word Web: **soap**

lava /lɑvə, lævə/ **N-NONCOUNT** **SCIENCE** **Lava** is the very hot liquid rock that comes out of a volcano. ❑ *Lava poured from the volcano.* [from Italian Neapolitan]
→ look at Word Webs: **rock, volcano**

lava|tory /lævətɔri/ (**lavatories**) **N-COUNT** A **lavatory** is a room with toilets and sinks in a public building. ❑ *The ladies' lavatory is over there, on the left.* [from Late Latin]

lav|ish /lævɪʃ/ (**lavishes, lavishing, lavished**)
1 **ADJ** If you describe something as **lavish**, you mean that it is very elaborate and impressive and a lot of money has been spent on it. ❑ *...a lavish party.* ● **lav|ish|ly** **ADV** ❑ *The apartment was lavishly decorated.*
2 **ADJ** If you say that spending, praise, or the use of something is **lavish**, you mean that someone spends a lot or that something is praised or used a lot. ❑ *Some people disapprove of his lavish spending.*
3 **V-T** If you **lavish** money, affection, or

praise **on** someone or something, you spend a lot of money on them or give them a lot of affection or praise. ❑ *Walmsley lavished gifts on family and friends.* [from Old French]

law /lɔ/ (**laws**)
1 **N-SING** **SOCIAL STUDIES** **The law** is a system of rules that a society or a government develops to deal with things like crime. ❑ *Driving too fast is against the law.* ❑ *These companies are breaking the law.*
2 **N-COUNT** A **law** is one of the rules in a system of law. ❑ *The government has introduced a new law to protect young people.*
3 **N-COUNT** **SCIENCE** A **law** is a process found in nature in which a particular event or thing always leads to a particular result. ❑ *A falling apple led Isaac Newton to discover the law of gravity.*
4 **N-NONCOUNT** **SOCIAL STUDIES** **Law** or **the law** is all the jobs which deal with giving advice about the law, representing people in court, or giving decisions and punishments. ❑ *He is interested in a career in law.* [from Old English]

law|ful /lɔfəl/ **ADJ** If an activity is **lawful**, it is allowed by law. [FORMAL] ❑ *We want fair and lawful treatment of prisoners.* ● **law|ful|ly** **ADV** ❑ *Did the police act lawfully in shooting him?* [from Old English]

lawn /lɔn/ (**lawns**) **N-COUNT/N-NONCOUNT** A **lawn** is an area of short grass around a house or another building. ❑ *They were sitting on the lawn.* [from Old French]
→ look at Picture Dictionary: **garden**

lawn|mow|er /lɔnmoʊər/ (**lawnmowers**) **N-COUNT** A **lawnmower** is a machine for cutting grass.
→ look at Picture Dictionary: **garden**

law|suit /lɔsut/ (**lawsuits**) **N-COUNT** A **lawsuit** is a case that a court of law deals with. [FORMAL] ❑ *The lawsuit accuses him of theft and kidnapping.*

law|yer /lɔɪər, lɔyər/ (**lawyers**) **N-COUNT** A **lawyer** is a person who advises people about the law and represents them in court. ❑ *His lawyers say that he is not guilty.*
→ look at Word Web: **trial**

lay /leɪ/ (**lays, laying, laid**)
1 **V-T** If you **lay** something somewhere, you put it there carefully. ❑ *He laid the newspaper on the desk.* ❑ *She gently laid the baby in her crib.*
2 **V-T/V-I** When a female bird **lays**, or **lays**

I

an egg, it pushes an egg out of its body.
[from Old English]
3 → see also **lie**

▶ **lay aside** If you **lay aside** a feeling or
belief, you give it up in order to move on
with something. ❏ *We laid aside our differences,
and got on with the job.*

▶ **lay off** BUSINESS If workers **are laid off**,
they are told by their employers to leave
their job, usually because there is no more
work for them to do. ❏ *100,000 employees will
be laid off to cut costs.*

▶ **lay out** **1** If you **lay out** a group of things,
you spread them out and arrange them
neatly. ❏ *We spread the blanket and laid out the
food.*
2 To **lay out** ideas or plans means to explain
or present them clearly. ❏ *Maxwell listened as
Johnson laid out his plan.*

lay|er /leɪər/ (**layers, layering, layered**)
1 N-COUNT A **layer** is a substance or a
material that covers a surface, or that lies
between two other things. ❏ *A fresh layer of
snow covered the street.*
2 N-COUNT If something has many **layers**,
it has many different levels or parts.
❏ *...the layers of meaning in the artist's paintings.*
3 V-T If you **layer** something, you arrange
it in layers. ❏ *Layer the onion slices on top of
the potatoes.*

Word Partnership	Use **layer** with :
ADJ	**bottom/top** layer, **lower/upper** layer, **outer** layer, **protective** layer, **single** layer, **thick/thin** layer **1**
N	layer **cake**, layer **of dust**, layer **of fat**, **ozone** layer, layer **of skin**, **surface** layer **1**

---

lay|man /leɪmən/ (**laymen**) N-COUNT
A **layman** is a person who is not trained,
qualified, or experienced in a particular
subject or activity. ❏ *...information that
a layman can understand.*

lay|out /leɪaʊt/ (**layouts**) N-COUNT The
layout of a place is the way the parts of it
are arranged. ❏ *He tried to remember the layout
of the farmhouse.*

lazy /leɪzi/ (**lazier, laziest**)
1 ADJ If someone is **lazy**, they do not want
to work. ❏ *I'm not lazy; I like to be busy.*
● **la|zi|ness** N-NONCOUNT ❏ *Too much TV
encourages laziness.*
2 ADJ You can use **lazy** to describe an

activity in which you are very relaxed and
which you take part in without making
much effort. ❏ *Her novel is perfect for a lazy
summer's afternoon reading.* ● **la|zi|ly** /leɪzɪli/
ADV ❏ *Liz stretched lazily.*

lb. (**lbs.** or **lb.**) MATH **lb.** is short for **pound**,
when you are talking about weight.
❏ *The baby weighed 8 lbs. 5 oz.* [from Latin]

---

lead
1 BEING AHEAD OR TAKING
SOMEONE SOMEWHERE
2 SUBSTANCES

---

1 lead /liːd/ (**leads, leading, led**)
1 V-T If you **lead** a group of people, you go in
front of them. ❏ *A jazz band led the parade.*
2 V-T If you **lead** someone to a place, you
take them there. ❏ *I took his hand and led him
into the house.*
3 V-I If a road or a path **leads** somewhere, it
goes there. ❏ *This path leads down to the beach.*
4 V-T/V-I If you **are leading** in a race or a
competition, you are winning. ❏ *The Eagles
led by three points at half-time.* ❏ *He's leading the
presidential race.*
5 N-SING If you are **in the lead** in a race or
a competition, you are winning. ❏ *Harvard
were already in the lead after ten minutes.*
6 V-T If you **lead** a group of people, you are
in control of them. ❏ *Chris leads a large team
of salespeople.*
7 V-T You can use **lead** when you are
describing someone's life. ❏ *She led a normal,
happy life.*
8 V-I If something **leads to** a situation, it
causes that situation. ❏ *Every time we talk
about money it leads to an argument.*
9 V-T If something **leads** you **to** do
something, it influences or affects you in
such a way that you do it. ❏ *What led you to
write this book?*
10 V-T You can say that one point in a
discussion or a piece of writing **leads** you
to another in order to introduce a new
point that is linked with the previous one.
❏ *That leads me to the real point.*
11 N-COUNT A **lead** is a piece of information
or an idea which may help people to
discover the facts in a situation where many
facts are not yet known. ❏ *The police are
following up possible leads after receiving 400 calls
from the public.*
12 N-COUNT ARTS **The lead** in a play, a film,
or a show is the most important part in it.

The person who plays this part can also be called the **lead**. ❏ *Neve Campbell is the lead, playing one of the dancers.* [from Old English]

13 → see also **leading**

▶ **lead up to** The events that **lead up to** a particular event happen one after the other until that event occurs. ❏ *...the events that led up to his death.*

Thesaurus | lead Also look up :

v   escort, guide, precede;
    (ant.) follow ❶ **1** **2**
    govern, head, manage ❶ **6**

---

❷ lead /lɛd/ (**leads**)

1 **N-NONCOUNT** **Lead** is a soft, gray, heavy metal. ❏ *In the past, most water pipes were made of lead.*

2 **N-COUNT** The **lead** in a pencil is the gray part in the middle of it that makes a mark on paper. ❏ *He started writing, but his pencil lead immediately broke.* [from Old English]

→ look at Word Web: **mineral**

lead|er /liːdər/ (**leaders**)

1 **N-COUNT** The **leader** of a group of people or an organization is the person who is in charge of it. ❏ *Members today will elect a new leader.*

2 **N-COUNT** The **leader** in a race or a competition is the person who is in front of all the others, or who is winning. ❏ *The leader came in two minutes before the other runners.* [from Old English]

lead|er|ship /liːdərʃɪp/

1 **N-COUNT** You call people who are in control of a group or an organization the **leadership** ❏ *He attended a meeting with the Croatian leadership.*

2 **N-NONCOUNT** Someone's **leadership** is their position of being in control of a group of people. ❏ *The company doubled in size under her leadership.* [from Old English]

lead|ing /liːdɪŋ/

1 **ADJ** A **leading** person or thing in a particular area is the most important or successful one. ❏ *...a leading violin player.*

2 **ADJ** In a race or a competition, the **leading** person or team is the one who is winning. ❏ *It always feels good to be in the leading team.* [from Old English]

3 → see also **lead**

leaf /liːf/ (**leaves** or **leafs**)

1 **N-COUNT** The **leaves** of a tree or a plant are the parts that are flat, thin, and usually green. ❏ *A brown, dry oak leaf fell into the water.*

2 **N-COUNT** A **leaf** in a book or a magazine is a sheet of paper or a page. [from Old English]

→ look at Picture Dictionary: **flowers**

→ look at Word Webs: **herbivore, tea**

▶ **leaf through** If you **leaf through** something such as a book or a magazine, you turn the pages without reading or looking at them very carefully. ❏ *She enjoyed leafing through old photo albums.*

Word Link | let ≈ little : book*let*, leaf*let*, pamph*let*

---

leaf|let /liːflɪt/ (**leaflets**) **N-COUNT** A **leaflet** is a piece of paper containing information about a particular subject. ❏ *My doctor gave me a leaflet about healthy eating.*

league /liːg/ (**leagues**)

1 **N-COUNT** A **league** is a group of people, clubs, or countries that have joined together for a particular purpose. ❏ *The League of Nations was formed after World War I.*

2 **N-COUNT** SPORTS A **league** is a group of teams that play against each other. ❏ *The Boston Red Sox won the American League series.*

3 **N-COUNT** You use **league** to compare different people or things, especially in terms of their quality. ❏ *Her success has taken her out of my league.* [from Old French]

leak /liːk/ (**leaks, leaking, leaked**)

1 **V-I** If a container **leaks**, there is a hole in it that lets liquid or gas escape. ❏ *The roof leaks every time it rains.*

2 **V-I** If liquid or gas **leaks** from a container, it escapes through a hole in it.

leak

❏ *The water is leaking out from the bottom of the bucket.*

3 **N-COUNT** **Leak** is also a noun. ❏ *A gas leak caused the explosion.*

4 **N-COUNT** A **leak** is a crack or a hole that a substance such as a liquid or a gas can pass through. ❏ *...a leak in the radiator.* [of Scandinavian origin]

Thesaurus | leak Also look up :

v   drip, ooze, seep, trickle **1**
N   crack, hole, opening **4**

Word Partnership	Use **leak** with :
V	**cause a** leak, **spring a** leak **1 3**
N	**fuel** leak, **gas** leak, **oil** leak, leak **in the roof, water** leak **1**–**3**

lean /liːn/ (**leaner, leanest, leans, leaning, leaned**)

1 **v-i** When you **lean**, you bend your body from your waist in a particular direction. ❑ *The driver leaned across and opened the passenger door.*

2 **v-t/v-i** If you **lean on** or **against** someone or something, you rest against them so that they partly support your weight. If you **lean** an object **on** or **against** something, you place the object so that it is partly supported by that thing. ❑ *She was feeling tired and leaned against him.*

3 **ADJ** If meat is **lean**, it does not have very much fat.

4 **ADJ** If a person is **lean**, they   lean are thin, and they look fit and healthy. ❑ *He was lean and strong.* [from Old English]

▶ **lean on** or **lean upon** If you **lean on** someone or **lean upon** them, you depend on them for support and encouragement. ❑ *She leaned on him to help her to solve her problems.*

Thesaurus	lean Also look up :
V	bend, incline, prop, tilt **1**
	recline, rest **2**
ADJ	angular, slender, slim, wiry **4**

Word Partnership	Use **lean** with :
ADV	lean **heavily 2**
ADJ	**long and** lean, **tall and** lean **4**
N	lean **beef**, lean **meat 3**
	lean **body 4**

leap /liːp/ (**leaps, leaping, leaped** or **leapt**)

1 **v-i** If you **leap**, you jump high in the air or you jump a long distance. ❑ *He leaped in the air and waved his hands.*

2 **N-COUNT** **Leap** is also a noun. ❑ *Powell won the long jump with a leap of 8 meters 95 centimeters.*

3 **v-i** To **leap** somewhere means to move there suddenly and quickly. ❑ *The two men leaped into the car and drove away.*

4 **N-COUNT** A **leap** is a large and important change, increase, or advance. ❑ *There was a giant leap in productivity at the factory.* ❑ *...a further leap in prices.* [from Old English]

learn /lɜːrn/ (**learns, learning, learned** or **learnt**)

1 **v-t/v-i** If you **learn** something, you get knowledge or a skill by studying, training, or through experience. ❑ *Where did you learn English?* ❑ *He is learning to play the piano.*

● **learn|er** (**learners**) **N-COUNT** ❑ *Clint is a quick learner; he's one of my smarter students.*

● **learn|ing** **N-NONCOUNT** ❑ *...the learning of English.*

2 **v-t/v-i** If you **learn**, or **learn of**, something, you find out about it. ❑ *We first learned of her plans in a newspaper report.* ❑ *She wasn't surprised to learn that he was involved.*

3 **v-t** If you **learn** something such as a poem or a role in a play, you study or repeat the words so that you can remember them. ❑ *He learned this song as a child.* [from Old English]

→ look at Word Web: **brain**

Usage	learn and teach

Learn means "to get information or knowledge about something": *Kim can read English well but hasn't learned to speak it.* *Teach* means "to give someone information or knowledge about something": *Michael enjoys teaching his friends how to drive.*

Thesaurus	learn Also look up :
V	master, pick up, study **1**
	discover, find out, understand **2**

learned be|hav|ior (**learned behaviors**)
N-COUNT/N-NONCOUNT SCIENCE **Learned behavior** is a way of behaving that someone has learned through experience or observation rather than because it is a natural instinct.

lease /liːs/ (**leases, leasing, leased**)

1 **N-COUNT** A **lease** is a legal agreement that allows someone to pay money so that they can use something for a particular period of time. ❑ *She signed a one-year lease on the apartment.*

2 **v-t** If you **lease** something **from** someone, you pay them, and they allow you to use it. ❑ *He leased an apartment in Toronto.*

3 **v-t** If someone **leases** something **to** you, you pay them, and they allow you to use it. ❑ *She's going to lease the building to students.* [from Old French]

least /liːst/

> **LANGUAGE HELP**
>
> **Least** is often considered to be the superlative of **little**.

1 **PHRASE** At **least** means not less than a

particular number or amount. ❑ *Drink at least half a pint of milk each day.*

2 **ADJ** You use **the least** to mean a smaller amount than anyone or anything else, or the smallest amount possible. ❑ *He wants to spend the least amount of money possible on a car.*

3 **PRON** **Least** is also a pronoun. ❑ *The report found that teenage girls exercised the least.*

4 **ADV** **Least** is also an adverb. ❑ *He is one of the least friendly people I have ever met.*

5 **ADJ** You use **least** to say that a particular situation is much less important or serious than other possible or actual ones. ❑ *Getting up at three o'clock every morning was the least of her worries.*

6 **PHRASE** You use **at least** to indicate an advantage that exists in a bad situation. ❑ *At least we know he is still alive.*

7 **PHRASE** You can use **in the least** and **the least bit** to emphasize a negative. ❑ *I'm not like that at all. Not in the least.* ❑ *Alice wasn't the least bit frightened.* [from Old English]

Thesaurus	least	Also look up :
ADJ	fewest, lowest, minimum, smallest **2**

leath|er /lɛðər/ **N-NONCOUNT** **Leather** is animal skin that is used for making shoes, clothes, bags, and furniture. ❑ *She bought a leather jacket.* [from Old English]

```
                    leave
    ❶ NOT USE, TAKE, TOUCH,
       OR INVOLVE
    ❷ OTHER VERB USES AND
       NOUNS
```

❶ leave /liv/ (**leaves, leaving, left**)

1 **V-T** If you **leave** something in a particular place, you do not bring it with you. ❑ *I left my bags in the car.*

2 **V-T** If you **leave** part of something, you do not use it all. ❑ *Please leave some cake for me!*

3 **V-T** To **leave** an amount of something means to keep it available after the rest has been used or taken away. ❑ *He always left a little food for the next day.*

4 **V-T** If you **leave** something in a place, you forget to bring it with you. ❑ *I left my purse in the gas station.*

5 → see also **left**

6 **PHRASE** If you **leave** someone **alone**, you do not speak to them or annoy them. ❑ *Please just leave me alone!*

7 **PHRASE** If you **leave** something **alone**, you do not touch it. ❑ *Leave my purse alone!*

8 **V-T** If you **leave** something **until** a particular time, you delay doing it or dealing with it until then. ❑ *Don't leave it all until the last minute.* [from Old English]

▶ **leave behind** If you **leave behind** an object or a situation, it remains after you have left a place. ❑ *He left his glasses behind in his office.*

▶ **leave out** If you **leave** someone or something **out**, you do not include them. ❑ *Why did they leave her out of the team?*

❷ leave /liv/ (**leaves, leaving, left**)

1 **V-T/V-I** If you **leave** a place or a person, you go away from them. ❑ *He left the country yesterday.* ❑ *My flight leaves in less than an hour.*

2 **V-T** If you **leave** a person with whom you have had a close relationship, you end the relationship. ❑ *He'll never leave you.*

3 **V-T** If an event **leaves** people or things in a particular state, they are in that state when the event has finished. ❑ *An auto accident left him unable to walk.*

4 **V-T** If you **leave** something **to** someone, you give it to them when you die. ❑ *He left everything to his wife when he died.*

5 **N-NONCOUNT** **Leave** is a period of time when you are away from work. ❑ *Why don't you take a few days' leave?*

6 **N-NONCOUNT** If you are **on leave**, you are not working at your job. ❑ *She has gone on leave for a week.* [from Old English]

leaves /livz/

1 **Leaves** is the plural of **leaf**.

2 **Leaves** is the third person singular of the present tense of **leave**. [from Old English]

lec|ture /lɛktʃər/ (**lectures, lecturing, lectured**)

1 **N-COUNT** A **lecture** is a talk that someone gives in order to teach people about a particular subject. ❑ *We attended a lecture by Professor Eric Robinson.*

2 **V-I** If you **lecture on** a particular subject, you give a lecture about it. ❑ *She invited him to Atlanta to lecture on the history of art.*

3 **V-T** If someone **lectures** you about something, they criticize you or tell you how they think you should behave. ❑ *They lectured us about our eating habits.* ❑ *Chuck lectured me about getting a haircut.* [from Medieval Latin]

led /lɛd/ **Led** is the past tense and past participle of **lead**. [from Old English]

ledge /lɛdʒ/ (**ledges**)

1 **N-COUNT** A **ledge** is a narrow shelf of rock on the side of a mountain.

2 **N-COUNT** A **ledge** is a narrow shelf along the bottom edge of a window. ❑ *...a window ledge.*

leek /liːk/ (leeks) **N-COUNT/N-NONCOUNT**
Leeks are long, thin vegetables that are white at one end and have long green leaves. [from Old English]

---
left
❶ REMAINING
❷ DIRECTION AND POLITICAL GROUPINGS
---

❶ **left** /lɛft/
1 **Left** is the past tense and past participle of **leave**.
2 **ADJ** If there is a certain amount of something **left**, it is still there after everything else has gone or been used. ❑ *Is there any milk left?*
3 **PHRASE** If there is a certain amount of something **left over**, or if you have it **left over**, it remains when the rest has gone or been used. ❑ *She spends so much money on clothes, there's never any left over to buy books.* [from Old English]

❷ **left** /lɛft/

LANGUAGE HELP
The spelling **Left** is also used for meaning **4**.

1 **N-SING** You use the **left** to talk about the side or direction that is the same side as your heart. ❑ *The bank is on the left at the end of the road.* ❑ *There is a high brick wall to the left of the building.*
2 **ADV** **Left** is also an adverb. ❑ *Turn left at the corner.*
3 **ADJ** Your **left** arm, hand, or leg is the one that is opposite the side that most people write with. ❑ *I've broken my left leg.*
4 **N-SING** SOCIAL STUDIES In the U.S., **the left** refers to people who want to use laws and the tax system to improve social conditions. In most other countries, **the left** refers to people who support the ideas of socialism. ❑ *...the political parties of the left.* [from Old English]

left-hand **ADJ** If something is on the **left-hand** side of something, it is positioned on the left of it. ❑ *The Japanese drive on the left-hand side of the road.*

left-hand|ed **ADJ** Someone who is **left-handed** uses their left hand rather than their right hand for activities such as writing and sports. ❑ *A left-handed tennis*

player won the tournament.

left|over /lɛftoʊvər/ (leftovers)
1 **N-PLURAL** You can call food that has not been eaten after a meal **leftovers**. ❑ *Put any leftovers in the refrigerator.*
2 **ADJ** **Leftover** describes an amount of something that remains after the rest of it has been used or eaten. ❑ *If you have any leftover chicken, use it to make this delicious pie.*

left-wing

LANGUAGE HELP
The spelling **right wing** is used for meaning **2**.

1 **ADJ** SOCIAL STUDIES **Left-wing** people support the ideas of the political left. ❑ *They will not be voting for him because he is too left-wing.*
2 **N-SING** SOCIAL STUDIES **The left wing** of a group of people, especially a political party, consists of the members of it whose beliefs are closer to those of the political left than are those of its other members. ❑ *She belongs on the left wing of the Democratic Party.*

leg /lɛg/ (legs)
1 **N-COUNT** A person's or animal's **legs** are the long parts of their body that they use for walking and standing. ❑ *He broke his right leg in a motorcycle accident.*
2 **N-COUNT** The **legs** of a pair of pants are the parts that cover your legs. ❑ *Anthony dried his hands on the legs of his jeans.*
3 **N-COUNT** The **legs** of a table or a chair are the long parts that it stands on. ❑ *...a broken chair leg.* [from Old Norse]
→ look at Picture Dictionaries: **body, insects, shellfish**

lega|cy /lɛgəsi/ (legacies)
1 **N-COUNT** A **legacy** is money or property that someone leaves to you when they die. ❑ *His father left him a generous legacy.*
2 **N-COUNT** SOCIAL STUDIES A **legacy of** an event or a period of history is something that is a direct result of it and that continues to exist after it is over. ❑ *...the legacy of slavery.* [from Medieval Latin]

le|gal /liːgəl/
1 **ADJ** **Legal** describes things that relate to the law. ❑ *He promised to take legal action.* ❑ *...the legal system.* ● **le|gal|ly** **ADV** ❑ *It could be difficult, legally speaking.*
2 **ADJ** An action or a situation that is **legal** is allowed by law. ❑ *My actions were completely legal.* [from Latin]

Word Partnership Use **legal** with :

N   legal **action**, legal **advice**, legal **battle**, legal **bills**, legal **costs/expenses**, legal **defense**, legal **department**, legal **documents**, legal **expert**, legal **fees**, legal **guardian**, legal **issue**, legal **liability**, legal **matters**, legal **obligation**, legal **opinion**, legal **problems/troubles**, legal **procedures**, legal **profession**, legal **responsibility**, legal **rights**, legal **services**, legal **status**, legal **system** **1**

ADV   perfectly legal **2**

Word Link   ize ≈ making : legal**ize**, modern**ize**, vandal**ize**

le|gal|ize /líɡəlaɪz/ (**legalizes**, **legalizing**, **legalized**) **v-T** If something **is legalized**, a law is passed that makes it legal. ❑ *Divorce was legalized in 1981.* [from Latin]

leg|end /lέdʒənd/ (**legends**)
1 **N-COUNT/N-NONCOUNT** LANGUAGE ARTS A **legend** is a very old and popular story. ❑ *The play is based on an ancient Greek legend.* **2** **N-COUNT** If you refer to someone as a **legend**, you mean that they are very famous and admired by a lot of people. ❑ *...singing legend Frank Sinatra.* [from Medieval Latin] → look at Word Web: **fantasy**

leg|end|ary /lέdʒənderi/
1 **ADJ** If you describe someone or something as **legendary**, you mean that they are very famous and that many stories are told about them. ❑ *...the legendary jazz singer Adelaide Hall.* **2** **ADJ** LANGUAGE ARTS A **legendary** person, place, or event is mentioned or described in an old legend. ❑ *...the legendary King Arthur.* [from Medieval Latin]

leg|ible /lέdʒɪbəl/ **ADJ** **Legible** writing is clear enough to read. ❑ *My handwriting isn't very legible.* ❑ *...a barely legible sign.* [from Latin]

leg|is|la|tion /lέdʒɪsléɪʃən/ **N-NONCOUNT** SOCIAL STUDIES **Legislation** consists of a law or laws passed by a government. [FORMAL] ❑ *...legislation to protect women's rights.*

Word Partnership Use **legislation** with :

V   **draft** legislation, **enact** legislation, **introduce** legislation, **oppose** legislation, **pass** legislation, legislation, **veto** legislation

ADJ   **federal** legislation, **new** legislation, **proposed** legislation

leg|is|la|tive /lέdʒɪsleɪtɪv/ **ADJ** SOCIAL STUDIES **Legislative** means involving or relating to the process of making and passing laws. [FORMAL] ❑ *Today's hearing was just the first step in the legislative process.*

leg|is|la|tive branch /lέdʒɪsleɪtɪv brǽntʃ/ **N-SING** SOCIAL STUDIES The **legislative branch** is the part of the government of the United States that makes and changes laws.

leg|is|la|ture /lέdʒɪsleɪtʃər/ (**legislatures**) **N-COUNT** SOCIAL STUDIES The **legislature** of a country is the group of people who have the power to make laws. [FORMAL] ❑ *State legislature passed a law forbidding this practice.*

le|giti|mate /lɪdʒítɪmɪt/
1 **ADJ** Something that is **legitimate** is acceptable according to the law. ❑ *...a legitimate driver's license with my picture on it.* ● **le|giti|ma|cy** /lɪdʒítɪməsi/ **N-NONCOUNT** ❑ *...the political legitimacy of his government.* ● **le|giti|mate|ly** **ADV** ❑ *The government was legitimately elected by the people.* **2** **ADJ** If you say that something such as a feeling or a claim is **legitimate**, you think that it is reasonable and justified. ❑ *That's a perfectly legitimate fear.* ● **le|giti|ma|cy** **N-NONCOUNT** ❑ *He refused to accept the legitimacy of Helen's anger.* ● **le|giti|mate|ly** **ADV** ❑ *They argued quite legitimately with some of my choices.* [from Medieval Latin]

lei|sure /líʒər, lέʒ-/
1 **N-NONCOUNT** **Leisure** is the time when you are not working, when you can relax and do things that you enjoy. ❑ *They spend their leisure time painting or drawing.* **2** **PHRASE** If someone does something **at leisure** or **at** their **leisure**, they enjoy themselves by doing it when they want to, without hurrying. ❑ *You can walk at leisure through the gardens.* [from Old French]

lei|sure|ly /líʒərli, lέʒ-/
1 **ADJ** A **leisurely** activity is done in a relaxed way. ❑ *Lunch was a leisurely meal.* **2** **ADV** **Leisurely** is also an adverb. ❑ *We walked leisurely into the hotel.* [from Old French]

lem|on /lέmən/ (**lemons**)
N-COUNT/N-NONCOUNT A **lemon** is a yellow fruit with very sour juice. ❑ *I like a slice of lemon in my tea.* [from Medieval Latin] → look at Picture Dictionary: **fruit**

lem|on|ade /lέmənéɪd/ **N-NONCOUNT** **Lemonade** is a drink that is made from lemons, sugar, and water. ❑ *They ordered two glasses of lemonade.* [from French]

le|mur /límər/ (**lemurs**) **N-COUNT** A **lemur** is an animal that looks like a small monkey and has a long tail and a face similar to that of a fox.

lend /lɛnd/ (**lends, lending, lent**)
1 **V-T/V-I** When a person or an organization such as a bank **lends** you money, they give it to you and you agree to pay it back later. ❑ *The government will lend you money at very good rates.* ❑ *Banks are not the only institutions that lend money.*
2 **V-T** If you **lend** something that you own, you allow someone to use it for a period of time. ❑ *Will you lend me your pen?*
3 **V-T** If something **lends itself to** a particular activity or result, it is easy for it to be used for that activity or to achieve that result. ❑ *The piano lends itself to all styles of music.* [from Old English]
→ look at Usage note at **borrow**

length /lɛŋθ/ (**lengths**)
1 **N-COUNT/N-NONCOUNT** The **length** of something is its measurement from one end to the other. ❑ *The table is about a meter in length.*
2 **N-COUNT/N-NONCOUNT** The **length** of an event is how long it lasts. ❑ *The average length of a patient's stay in the hospital is about 48 hours.*
3 **PHRASE** If someone does something **at length**, they do it for a long time or in great detail. ❑ *They spoke at length about their families.*
4 **PHRASE** If someone **goes to great lengths** to achieve something, they try very hard and perhaps do extreme things in order to do it. ❑ *She went to great lengths to hide from reporters.* [from Old English]

Word Partnership	Use **length** with :	
ADJ	**average** length, **entire** length **1** **2**	
N	length **of your stay**, length **of time 2**	
	length **and width 1**	

length|en /lɛŋθən/ (**lengthens, lengthening, lengthened**) **V-T/V-I** When you **lengthen** something, or when it **lengthen, it** becomes longer. ❑ *This exercise will lengthen the muscles in your legs.* ❑ *The sun went down and the shadows lengthened.* [from Old English]

lengthy /lɛŋθi/ (**lengthier, lengthiest**)
1 **ADJ** **Lengthy** describes an event or a process that lasts for a long time. ❑ *There was a lengthy meeting to decide the company's future.*

2 **ADJ** A **lengthy** piece of writing contains a lot of words. ❑ *The United Nations produced a lengthy report on the subject.* [from Old English]

Word Partnership	Use **lengthy** with :	
N	lengthy **period 1**	
	lengthy **description**, lengthy **discourse**,	
	lengthy **discussion**, lengthy **report 2**	

lens /lɛnz/ (**lenses**)
1 **N-COUNT** SCIENCE A **lens** is a thin, curved piece of glass or plastic that is used in things such as cameras and glasses. A **lens** makes things look larger, smaller, or clearer. ❑ *I bought a powerful lens for my camera.*
2 **N-COUNT** In your eye, the **lens** is the part behind the pupil that focuses light and helps you to see clearly. [from Latin]
3 → see also **contact lens**
→ look at Word Web: **eye**

lent /lɛnt/ **Lent** is the past tense and past participle of **lend**. [from Old English]

len|til /lɛntɪl, -tᵊl/ (**lentils**) **N-COUNT** Lentils are small, round, dried seeds that you use in cooking, for example to make soup. [from Old French]

leop|ard /lɛpərd/ (**leopards**) **N-COUNT** A **leopard** is a large, wild cat. Leopards have yellow fur with black spots, and live in Africa and Asia. [from Old French]

les|bian /lɛzbiən/ (**lesbians**)
1 **N-COUNT** A **lesbian** is a woman who is sexually attracted to other women. ❑ *The main character in the novel is a lesbian.*
2 **ADJ** **Lesbian** is also an adjective. ❑ *The organization supports lesbian and gay members.* [from Greek]

less /lɛs/

LANGUAGE HELP
Less is often considered to be the comparative of **little**.

1 **DET** You use **less** to show that there is a smaller amount of something than before or than is usual. ❑ *People should eat less fat.* ❑ *He earns less money than his brother.*
2 **PRON** **Less** is also a pronoun. ❑ *He thinks people should spend less and save more.* ❑ *She spends less of her time painting now.*
3 **PHRASE** You use **less than** to talk about a smaller amount of something than the amount mentioned. ❑ *The population of the country is less than 12 million.*
4 **PHRASE** You use **less than** to say that

something does not have a particular quality. ❑ *Her greeting was less than welcoming.* [from Old English]

Less is used to describe general amounts (or noncount nouns). *Less snow fell in December than in January.* *Fewer* is used to describe amounts of countable items. *Maria is working fewer hours this semester.*

less|en /lɛsən/ (**lessens, lessening, lessened**)
V-T/V-I If something **lessens** or you **lessen** it, it becomes smaller in size, amount, degree, or importance. ❑ *A change in diet might lessen your risk of heart disease.* [from Old English]

less|er /lɛsər/
1 **ADJ** You use **lesser** in order to indicate that something is smaller in extent, degree, or amount than another thing that has been mentioned. ❑ *He watches sports to a lesser degree than he did five years ago.*
2 **ADV** **Lesser** is also an adverb. ❑ *...lesser-known works by famous artists.* [from Old English]

les|son /lɛsən/ (**lessons**)
1 **N-COUNT** A **lesson** is a time when you learn about a particular subject. ❑ *Johanna has started taking piano lessons.*
2 **PHRASE** If you say that you are going to **teach** someone **a lesson**, you mean that you are going to punish them for something that they have done so that they do not do it again. [from Old French]

Thesaurus lesson Also look up :
N   class, course, instruction, session **1**

Word Partnership Use lesson with :
ADJ   **private** lesson **1**
     hard lesson, **important** lesson, **painful** lesson, **valuable** lesson **2**
V   **get a** lesson, **give a** lesson **1 2**
     learn a lesson, **teach** *someone* **a** lesson **2**

let /lɛt/ (**lets, letting, let**)

LANGUAGE HELP
The form **let** is used in the present tense and is the past tense and past participle.

1 **V-T** If you **let** something happen, you do not try to stop it. ❑ *I just let him sleep.*
2 **V-T** If you **let** someone do something, you give them your permission to do it. ❑ *I love candy but Mom doesn't let me eat it very often.*
3 **V-T** You use **let me** when you are

introducing something you want to say. ❑ *Let me tell you what I saw.* ❑ *Let me explain why.*
4 **V-T** If you **let** someone into or out of a place, you allow them to enter or leave. ❑ *I went down and let them into the building.*
5 **V-T** You use **let me** when you are offering to do something. ❑ *Let me hang up your coat.*
6 **V-T** You say **let's** (short for **let us**) when you are making a suggestion. ❑ *I'm bored. Let's go home.*
7 **PHRASE** If you **let go of** someone or something, you stop holding them. ❑ *She let go of Mona's hand.*
8 **PHRASE** If you **let** someone **know** something, you tell them about it. ❑ *I want to let them know that I'm safe.* [from Old English]
▶ **let down** If you **let** someone **down**, you disappoint them by not doing something that you have said you will do or that they expected you to do. ❑ *I didn't want to let him down by not going out with him.*
▶ **let off** If you **let** someone **off**, you give them a lighter punishment than they expect or no punishment at all. ❑ *He thought that if he said he was sorry, the judge would let him off.*

Thesaurus let Also look up :
V   allow, approve, permit; *(ant.)* prevent, stop **1 2**

le|thal /liθəl/ **ADJ** A substance that is **lethal** can kill people or animals. ❑ *She swallowed a lethal dose of sleeping pills.* [from Latin]

let's /lɛts/ **Let's** is short for "let us." [from Old English]

Be sure to include the apostrophe when you write *let's* (the contraction of *let us*), in order to avoid confusing it with *lets*: *Nisim sometimes lets his workers go home early, and when he does, he always laughs and says, "Let's stop now. We've done enough damage for one day!"*

let|ter /lɛtər/ (**letters**)
1 **N-COUNT** If you write a **letter** to someone, you write a message on paper and send it to them. ❑ *I received a letter from a friend.* ❑ *Mrs. Franklin sent a letter offering me the job.*
2 **N-COUNT** LANGUAGE ARTS **Letters** are written symbols that represent the sounds in a language. ❑ *The children practiced writing the letters of the alphabet.* [from Old French]

let|ter|ing /lɛtərɪŋ/ **N-NONCOUNT** Lettering is writing or printing. ❑ *On the door was a small blue sign with white lettering.* [from Old French]

let|tuce /lɛtɪs/ (**lettuces**)
N-COUNT/N-NONCOUNT A **lettuce** is a plant with large green leaves that is eaten mainly in salads. [from Old French]

lev|el /lɛvəl/ (**levels**)
  1 **N-COUNT** A high or low **level** describes the amount or quality of something. ❑ *We have the lowest level of inflation since 1986.*
  2 **N-SING** The **level** of something is its height. ❑ *The water level is 6.5 feet below normal.*
  3 **N-COUNT** A **level** of a building is one of its different stories, which is situated above or below other stories. ❑ *Thurlow's rooms were on the second level.*
  4 **ADJ** If one thing is **level with** another thing, it is at the same height as it. ❑ *He sat down so his face was level with the boy's.*
  5 **ADJ** When something is **level**, it is completely flat. ❑ *Make sure the ground is level before you start building.*
  6 **ADV** If you draw **level** with someone or something, you get closer to them until you are by their side. ❑ *Courtney walked past me but I drew level with a few quick steps.*
  7 **ADJ** **Level** is also an adjective. ❑ *He waited until they were level with the door.*
  8 **N-COUNT** ARTS In the theater, an actor's **level** is their height above the stage at a particular time, for example when they are sitting or lying down. [from Old French]

Word Partnership	Use **level** with :	
ADJ	**basic** level, **increased** level, **intermediate** level, **top** level, **upper** level **1**	
	high/low level **1** **2**	
N	level **of activity**, level **of awareness**, **cholesterol** level, **college** level, **comfort** level, level **of difficulty**, **energy** level, **noise** level, **reading** level, **skill** level, **stress** level, level **of violence** **1**	
	eye level, **ground** level, **street** level **2**	

lev|er /lɪvər, lɛv-/ (**levers**)
  1 **N-COUNT** A **lever** is a handle that you push or pull to operate a machine. ❑ *Push the lever to switch the machine on.*
  2 **N-COUNT** A **lever** is a bar that you use to lift something heavy. You put one end of it under the heavy object, and then push down on the other end. ❑ *Joseph found a stick to use as a lever and lifted up the stone.* [from Old French]

lev|er|age /lɛvərɪdʒ/ **N-NONCOUNT** Leverage is the ability to influence situations or people so that you can control what happens. ❑ *His senior position gives him leverage to get things done.* [from Old French]

LGBT /ɛl dʒi bi ti/ **LGBT** is short for "lesbian, gay, bisexual, and transgender."

lia|bil|ity /laɪəbɪlɪti/ (**liabilities**)
  1 **N-COUNT** If you say that someone or something is **a liability**, you mean that they cause a lot of problems or embarrassment. ❑ *We want to be an asset to the city, not a liability.*
  2 **N-COUNT** BUSINESS A company's or an organization's **liabilities** are the sums of money that it owes. ❑ *The company had assets of $138 million and liabilities of $120.5 million.* [from Old French]

lia|ble /laɪəbəl/
  1 **PHRASE** If something **is liable to** happen, it is very likely to happen. ❑ *Some of this old equipment is liable to break down.*
  2 **ADJ** If people or things are **liable to** something unpleasant, they are likely to experience it or do it. ❑ *...a woman liable to depression.* [from Old French]

Word Link	ar, er ≈ one who acts as : buyer, liar, seller

liar /laɪər/ (**liars**) **N-COUNT** A **liar** is someone who tells lies. ❑ *He's a liar and a cheat.* [from Old English]

li|bel /laɪbəl/ (**libels, libeling** or **libelling, libeled** or **libelled**)
  1 **N-COUNT/N-NONCOUNT** SOCIAL STUDIES **Libel** is a written statement that wrongly accuses someone of something, and that is therefore against the law. Compare with **slander**. ❑ *Warren sued him for libel over the remarks in the newspaper.*
  2 **V-T** SOCIAL STUDIES To **libel** someone means to write or print something in a book, a newspaper, or a magazine that wrongly damages that person's reputation and is therefore against the law. ❑ *The newspaper which libeled him offered him a large amount of money.* [from Old French]

Word Link	liber ≈ free : liberal, liberate, liberty

lib|er|al /lɪbərəl, lɪbrəl/ (**liberals**)
  1 **ADJ** Someone who has **liberal** ideas understands and accepts that other people have different ideas and beliefs, and may behave differently than them. ❑ *My parents are very liberal and relaxed.*

2 **ADJ** A **liberal** system allows people or organizations a lot of political or economic freedom. ❑ *...a liberal democracy.*
3 **N-COUNT** **Liberal** is also a noun. ❑ *...the free-market liberals.*
4 **ADJ** **Liberal** means giving, using, or taking a lot of something, or existing in large quantities. ❑ *He is liberal with his jokes.*
● **lib|er|al|ly** **ADV** ❑ *Season the steaks liberally with salt and pepper.* [from Latin] [from Latin]

lib|er|ate /lɪbəreɪt/ (**liberates, liberating, liberated**)
1 **V-T** To **liberate** a place or the people in it means to free them from the political or military control of another country, area, or group of people. ❑ *They planned to liberate the city.* ● **lib|era|tion** /lɪbəreɪʃᵊn/ **N-NONCOUNT** ❑ *...a mass liberation movement.*
2 **V-T** To **liberate** someone **from** something means to help them escape from it or overcome it, and lead a better way of life. ❑ *The leadership is committed to liberating its people from poverty.* ● **lib|er|at|ing** **ADJ** ❑ *Talking to a therapist can be a very liberating experience.*
● **lib|era|tion** **N-NONCOUNT** ❑ *...the women's liberation movement.* [from Latin]

lib|er|ty /lɪbərti/ (**liberties**)
N-COUNT/N-NONCOUNT **Liberty** is the freedom to live in the way that you want to. ❑ *We must do all we can to defend liberty and justice.* [from Old French]

li|brar|ian /laɪbrɛəriən/ (**librarians**)
N-COUNT A **librarian** is a person who works in a library. [from Old French]
→ look at Word Web: **library**

li|brary /laɪbreri/ (**libraries**) **N-COUNT**
A public **library** is a building where books, newspapers, DVDs, and music are kept for people to use or borrow. ❑ *I found the book I needed at the local library.* [from Old French]
→ look at Word Web: **library**

lice /laɪs/ **N-PLURAL** **Lice** are small insects that live on the bodies of people or animals. [from Old English]

li|cense /laɪsᵊns/ (**licenses, licensing, licensed**)
1 **N-COUNT** A **license** is an official document that gives you permission to do, use, or own something. ❑ *You need a license to drive a car.*
2 **V-T** To **license** a person or an activity means to give official permission for something to be done. ❑ *...to license songs for films or video games.* [from Old French]

li|cense plate (**license plates**) **N-COUNT**
A **license plate** is a metal sign on the back of a vehicle that shows its official number. ❑ *She drives a car with California license plates.*

lick /lɪk/ (**licks, licking, licked**)
1 **V-T** When you **lick** something, you move your tongue across its surface. ❑ *She licked the stamp and pressed it onto the envelope.*

I

2 **N-COUNT** **Lick** is also a noun. ❑ *Can I have a lick of your ice cream?* [from Old English]

lid /lɪd/ (**lids**) **N-COUNT** A **lid** is the top of a container that can be removed. ❑ *She lifted the lid of the box.* [from Old English]

---
lie
1 POSITION OR SITUATION
2 THINGS THAT ARE NOT TRUE
---

1 lie /laɪ/ (**lies, lying, lay, lain**)

1 **V-I** If you **are lying** somewhere, your body is flat, and you are not standing or sitting. ❑ *There was a man lying on the ground.*

2 **V-I** If an object **lies** in a particular place, it is in a flat position there. ❑ *His clothes were lying on the floor by the bed.*

3 **V-I** If you say that a place **lies** in a particular position or direction, you mean that it is situated there. ❑ *The islands lie at the southern end of Florida.*

4 **V-I** You can talk about where a problem, a solution, or a fault **lies** to say what you think it consists of, involves, or is caused by. ❑ *Some of the blame lies with the president.*

5 **V-I** You use **lie** in expressions such as **lie ahead**, **lie in store**, and **lie in wait** when you are talking about what someone is going to experience in the future, especially when it is something unpleasant. ❑ *She'll need all her strength to cope with what lies ahead.* [from Old English]

6 → see also **lay**

▶ **lie down** When you **lie down**, you move your body so that it is flat on something, usually when you want to rest or sleep. ❑ *Why don't you go upstairs and lie down?*

> Usage   **lie** and **lay**
Lie and lay are often confused. *Lie* is generally used without an object: *Please lie down.* Lay usually requires an object: *Lay your head on the pillow.*

2 lie /laɪ/ (**lies, lying, lied**)

1 **N-COUNT** A **lie** is something that someone says or writes that they know is not true. ❑ *You told me a lie!* ❑ *"How old are you?"—"Eighteen."—"That's a lie."*

2 **V-I** If someone **is lying**, they are saying something that they know is not true. ❑ *I know he's lying.* ❑ *Never lie to me again.* [from Old English]

Thesaurus   **lie** Also look up :
v   recline, rest; *(ant.)* stand **1** **1** **2**
   deceive, distort, fake, falsify, mislead **2** **2**
N   dishonesty **2** **1**
---

lieu|ten|ant /lutɛnənt/ (**lieutenants**) **N-COUNT** A **lieutenant** is an officer in the military or in the U.S. police force. ❑ *Lieutenant Campbell ordered the man to stop.* [from Old French]

life /laɪf/ (**lives** /laɪvz/)

1 **N-COUNT** Someone's **life** is their state of being alive, or the period of time when they are alive. ❑ *Your life is in danger.* ❑ *A nurse tried to save his life.* ❑ *He spent the last fourteen years of his life in France.*

2 **N-NONCOUNT** You can use **life** to refer to things or groups of things that are alive. ❑ *Is there life on Mars?*

3 **N-NONCOUNT** Someone or something that is full of **life** is interesting and full of energy. ❑ *The town was full of life.*

4 **N-COUNT** You can use **life** to refer to particular activities that people regularly do during their lives. ❑ *My personal life has suffered because of my career.*

5 **N-COUNT** The **life** of something such as a machine, an organization, or a project is the period of time that it lasts for. ❑ *The repairs did not increase the value or the life of the equipment.* [from Old English]

→ look at Word Webs: **biosphere, earth**

life|boat /laɪfboʊt/ (**lifeboats**) **N-COUNT** A **lifeboat** is a boat that is used for saving people who are in danger on the ocean.

life cy|cle (**life cycles**) **N-COUNT** SCIENCE The **life cycle** of an animal or a plant is the series of changes that happen to it from the beginning of its life until its death. ❑ *This plant completes its life cycle in a single season.*

life|guard /laɪfgɑrd/ (**lifeguards**) **N-COUNT** A **lifeguard** is a person who works at a beach or a swimming pool and helps people when they are in danger.

life pre|serv|er /laɪf prɪzɜrvər/ (**life preservers**) **N-COUNT** A **life preserver** is a ring or a jacket that helps you float if you fall into deep water.

life sci|ence (**life sciences**) **N-COUNT** SCIENCE The **life sciences** are sciences such as zoology, botany, and anthropology that are

L

concerned with human beings, animals, and plants.

life|style /laɪfstaɪl/ (**lifestyles**) also **life-style, life style** N-COUNT/N-NONCOUNT
The **lifestyle** of a particular person or group is the way they have chosen to live and behave. ❑ *She talked about the benefits of leading a healthier lifestyle.*

life|time /laɪftaɪm/ (**lifetimes**) N-COUNT
A **lifetime** is the length of time that someone is alive. ❑ *He traveled a lot during his lifetime.*

lift /lɪft/ (**lifts, lifting, lifted**)
1 V-T If you **lift** something, you take it and move it upward. ❑ *He lifted the bag onto his shoulder.*
2 **Lift up** means the same as **lift**. ❑ *She lifted the baby up and gave him to me.*
3 V-T If people in authority **lift** a law or a rule that prevents people from doing something, they end it. ❑ *France finally lifted its ban on importing British beef.*
4 N-COUNT If you give someone a **lift** somewhere, you take them there in your car. ❑ *He often gave me a lift home.*
5 N-NONCOUNT **Lift** is the force that makes an aircraft leave the ground and stay in the air. [of Scandinavian origin]

Thesaurus	**lift** Also look up :
V	boost, hoist, pick up; (*ant.*) drop, lower, put down **1**

---
light
❶ BRIGHTNESS
❷ NOT GREAT IN WEIGHT OR AMOUNT
❸ NOT SERIOUS
---

❶ light /laɪt/ (**lighter, lightest, lights, lighting, lit** or **lighted**)
1 N-NONCOUNT SCIENCE **Light** is the energy that comes from the sun that lets you see things. ❑ *He opened the curtains, and suddenly the room was filled with light.*
2 N-COUNT A **light** is an electric lamp that produces light. ❑ *Remember to turn the lights out when you leave.*
3 V-T If a place or an object **is lit** by something, it has light shining on it. ❑ *The room was lit by only one light.*
4 ADJ If it is **light**, the sun is providing light during the day. ❑ *Here it gets light at about 6 a.m.*
5 V-T/V-I If you **light** something such as a

candle or a fire, or if it **lights**, it starts burning. ❑ *Stephen took a match and lit the candle.*
6 N-COUNT If something is presented in a particular **light**, it is presented so that you think about it in a particular way. ❑ *He worked hard to show New York in a better light.*
7 → see also **lighter, lighting**
8 PHRASE If something **comes to light** or is **brought to light**, it becomes obvious or is made known to a lot of people. ❑ *Nothing about this money has come to light.*
9 PHRASE To **shed light on, throw light on**, or **cast light on** something means to make it easier to understand, because more information is known about it. ❑ *No one could shed light on her secret past.* [from Old English]
→ look at Picture Dictionary: **color**
→ look at Word Webs: **eye, laser, light bulb, ozone, telescope**
▶ **light up** If your face or your eyes **light up**, you suddenly look very surprised or happy. ❑ *Sue's face lit up with surprise.*

Thesaurus	**light** Also look up :	
N	brightness, glow, radiance, shine **❶ 1**
ADJ	bright, sunny **❶ 4**

❷ light /laɪt/ (**lighter, lightest**)
1 ADJ Something that is **light** is not heavy, and is easy to lift or move. ❑ *The printer is quite light, so it's easy to move around.*
2 ADJ Something that is **light** is not very great in amount or power. ❑ *She had a light lunch of salad and fruit.* ❑ *There was a light wind that day.* ● **light|ly** ADV ❑ *Cook the onions until they are lightly browned.*
3 ADJ Something that is **light** is pale in color. ❑ *He was wearing jeans and a light-blue T-shirt.*
4 ADJ **Light** work does not involve much physical effort. [from Old English]

❸ light /laɪt/ (**lighter, lightest**) ADJ If you describe things such as books, music, and movies as **light**, you mean that they entertain you without making you think very deeply. ❑ *He doesn't like reading light novels.* ❑ *...light classical music.* [from Old English]

light bulb (**light bulbs**) N-COUNT A **light bulb** is the glass part that you put in an electric light to produce light.
→ look at Word Web: **light bulb**

Word Web   light bulb

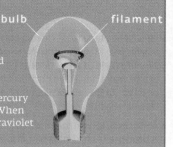

The incandescent **light bulb** has changed little since the 1870s. It consists of a **glass** globe containing an inert gas, such as argon, some wires, and a filament. **Electricity** flows through the wires and the tungsten filament. The filament heats up and **glows**. Light bulbs aren't very efficient. They give off more heat than **light**. **Fluorescent** lights are much more efficient. They contain liquid mercury and argon gas. A layer of phosphorus covers the inside of the tube. When electricity begins to flow, the mercury becomes a gas and **emits** ultraviolet light. This causes the phosphor coating to **shine**.

Word Link   *light ≈ not heavy* : *light**en**, light**er**,*
*light**weight***

light|en /laɪtᵊn/ (**lightens, lightening, lightened**) **v-T/v-I** When something **lightens** or when you **lighten** it, it becomes less dark in color. ❑ *She lightened her hair with a special cream.* [from Old English]
▶ **lighten up** If you say that someone should **lighten up**, you mean that they should be more relaxed or less serious. ❑ *You should lighten up and enjoy yourself a bit more.*

light en|er|gy **N-NONCOUNT** **SCIENCE** Light energy is energy in the form of electromagnetic waves.

light|er /laɪtər/ (**lighters**)
■ **N-COUNT** A **lighter** is a small object that produces a flame. It is used for lighting things such as candles or fires. [from Old English]
■ → see also **light**

light|hearted /laɪthɑrtɪd/
■ **ADJ** Someone who is **lighthearted** is cheerful and happy. ❑ *Kelly was at first lighthearted, but turned serious.*
■ **ADJ** Something that is **lighthearted** is intended to be entertaining or amusing, and not at all serious. ❑ *It was a lighthearted movie.*

light|house /laɪthaʊs/ (**lighthouses**)
N-COUNT A **lighthouse** is a tower that is built near or in the ocean. It has a flashing lamp that warns ships of danger.

light|ing /laɪtɪŋ/
■ **N-NONCOUNT** The **lighting** in a place is the way that it is lit. ❑ *The kitchen had bright overhead lighting.* [from Old English]
■ → see also **light**
→ look at Picture Dictionary: **drama**
→ look at Word Webs: **concert, photography, theater**

light min|ute (**light minutes**) **N-COUNT**
SCIENCE A **light minute** is the distance that light travels in one minute.

light|ning /laɪtnɪŋ/
■ **N-NONCOUNT** **SCIENCE** **Lightning** is the very bright flashes of light in the sky that happen during a storm. ❑ *One man died when he was struck by lightning.*
■ **ADJ** **Lightning** describes things that happen very quickly or last for only a short time. ❑ *He drove off at lightning speed.*
→ look at Word Webs: **lightning, storm**

light source (**light sources**) **N-COUNT**
SCIENCE A **light source** is any object or device that gives off light, such as the sun or an electric light bulb.

Word Web   lightning

Lightning forms in storm clouds. Strong winds cause tiny **particles** within the clouds to rub together violently. This creates **positive charges** on some particles and **negative charges** on others. The negatively charged particles sink to the bottom of the cloud. There they are attracted by the positively charged surface of the earth. Gradually a large negative charge accumulates in a cloud. When it is large enough, a **bolt** of lightning strikes the earth. When a bolt branches out in several directions, the result is called **forked lightning**. Sheet lightning occurs when the bolt **discharges** within a cloud, instead of on the earth.

light|weight /láɪtweɪt/ (**lightweights**) also **light-weight**

1 **ADJ** Something that is **lightweight** weighs less than most other things of the same type. ❑ ...*lightweight denim*.

2 **N-NONCOUNT** SPORTS **Lightweight** is a category in some sports, such as boxing, judo, or rowing, based on the weight of the athlete. ❑ ...*the junior lightweight champion*.

3 **N-COUNT** If you describe someone as a **lightweight**, you are critical of them because you think that they are not very important or skillful in a particular area of activity. ❑ *Critics say that she is an intellectual lightweight*.

4 **ADJ** **Lightweight** is also an adjective. ❑ *Some of the discussion in the book is lightweight and unconvincing*.

lik|able /láɪkəbªl/ also **likeable** **ADJ** Someone or something that is **likable** is pleasant and easy to be with. ❑ *He was a clever and likable guy*. [from Old English]

---
like
❶ PREPOSITION AND CONJUNCTION USES
❷ VERB AND NOUN USES
---

❶ like /laɪk, lǝɪk/

1 **PREP** If one person or thing is **like** another, they are similar to that person or thing. ❑ *He looks like my uncle*. ❑ *His house is just like yours*.

2 **PREP** If you say what something or someone is **like**, you are talking about how they seem to you. ❑ *What does Maria look like?* ❑ *"What was the party like?"—"Great!"*

3 **PREP** You can use **like** to give an example. ❑ ...*large cities like New York and Chicago*.

4 **PREP** If you say that someone is behaving **like** something or someone else, you mean that they are behaving in a way that is typical of that kind of thing or person. ❑ *I was shaking all over, trembling like a leaf*.

5 **CONJ** **Like** is sometimes used in order to indicate that something happens or is done in the same way as something else. Some people consider this use to be incorrect. ❑ *People are walking around the park, just like they do every Sunday*. ❑ *He spoke exactly like I did*. [from Old English]

❷ like /laɪk/ (**likes, liking, liked**)

1 **V-T** If you **like** something or someone, you think they are interesting, enjoyable, or attractive. ❑ *He likes baseball*. ❑ *Do you like swimming?*

2 **V-T** If you say that you **would like** something, you are saying politely that you want it. ❑ *Would you like some coffee?* ❑ *I'd like to ask you a few questions*.

3 **N-PLURAL** Someone's **likes** are the things that they enjoy or find pleasant. ❑ *I knew all Jemma's likes and dislikes*.

4 → see also **liking**

5 **PHRASE** You say **if you like** when you are suggesting something to someone, in an informal way. ❑ *You can stay here if you like*.

6 **PHRASE** You say **like this, like that**, or **like so** when you are showing someone how something is done. ❑ *It opens and closes, like this*. [from Old English]

Thesaurus like Also look up :
| ADJ | alike, comparable, similar **❶** **1** |
| V | admire, appreciate, enjoy; (*ant.*) dislike **❷** **1** |
---

like|able /láɪkəbªl/ → look up **likable**

like|li|hood /láɪklihʊd/ **N-NONCOUNT** The **likelihood of** something happening is how probable it is. ❑ *The likelihood of getting the disease is small*. [from Old Norse]

like|ly /láɪkli/ (**likelier, likeliest**)

1 **ADJ** You use **likely** to say that something is probably true in a particular situation. ❑ *A gas leak was the most likely cause of the explosion*.

2 **ADJ** If someone or something is **likely to** do a particular thing, they will probably do it. ❑ *Eric is a bright young man who is likely to succeed in life*. [from Old Norse]

Word Link like ≈ similar : *alike, likeness, unlike*
---

like|ness /láɪknɪs/ (**likenesses**) **N-COUNT** If a picture of someone is a good **likeness**, it looks just like them. ❑ *The artist's drawing is an excellent likeness of my sister*. [from Old English]

Word Link wise ≈ in the direction or manner of : *clockwise, likewise, otherwise*
---

like|wise /láɪkwaɪz/

1 **ADV** You use **likewise** when you are comparing two people or things and saying that they are similar. ❑ *What is fair for you likewise should be fair to me*.

2 **ADV** If you do something and someone else does **likewise**, you both do the same thing. ❑ *He gave money to charity and encouraged others to do likewise*. [from Old English]

lik|ing /laɪkɪŋ/

1 **PHRASE** If something is **to** your **liking**, it suits you. ❑ *London was more to his liking than Rome.* [from Old English]

2 → see also **like**

li|lac /laɪlək/ (lilac or lilacs)

1 **N-COUNT/N-NONCOUNT** **Lilac** is a purple, pink, or white flower that grows on a small tree. ❑ *Lilac grew against the garden wall.*

2 **ADJ** Something that is **lilac** is pale purple in color. ❑ *The bride wore a lilac dress.*

3 **N-NONCOUNT** **Lilac** is also a noun. ❑ *Would you prefer lilac or yellow for your bedroom?* [from French]

lily /lɪli/ (lilies) **N-COUNT/N-NONCOUNT**

A **lily** is a plant with large sweet-smelling flowers. [from Old English]

limb /lɪm/ (limbs)

1 **N-COUNT** Your **limbs** are your arms and legs. ❑ *She stretched out her aching limbs.*

2 **PHRASE** If someone goes **out on a limb**, they do something they strongly believe in even though it is risky. ❑ *I'm going to go out on a limb here and say this is good news.* [from Old English]

lim|ber /lɪmbər/ (limbers, limbering, limbered) **ADJ** Someone who is **limber** is able to move or bend their body easily. ❑ *Active people stay more limber.*

▶ **limber up** If you **limber up**, you prepare for an energetic physical activity such as a sport by moving and stretching your body. ❑ *Next door, 200 girls are limbering up for their ballet exams.*

lime /laɪm/ (limes) **N-COUNT/N-NONCOUNT**

A **lime** is a round, green fruit that tastes like a lemon. ❑ *Use fresh lime juice and fresh herbs in modern Asian cooking.* [from French]

lim|it /lɪmɪt/ (limits, limiting, limited)

1 **N-COUNT** A **limit** is the greatest amount or degree of something. ❑ *There is no limit to how much fresh fruit you should eat in a day.*

2 **N-COUNT** A **limit** is the largest or smallest amount of something that is allowed. ❑ *He was driving 40 miles per hour over the speed limit.*

3 **V-T** If you **limit** something, you stop it from becoming greater than a particular amount. ❑ *Try to limit the amount of time you spend on the Internet.*

4 **V-T** If you **limit yourself** to something, or if someone or something **limits** you, the number of things that you have or do is reduced. ❑ *Limit yourself to three meals and a snack each day.* ● **lim|it|ing** **ADJ** ❑ *I found the conditions very limiting.*

5 **V-T** If something **is limited to** a particular place or group of people, it exists only in that place, or is had or done only by that group. ❑ *The protests were not limited to New York.*

6 **PHRASE** If an area or a place is **off limits**, you are not allowed to go there. ❑ *Parts of the church are off limits to visitors.* [from Latin]

limi|ta|tion /lɪmɪteɪʃ°n/ (limitations)

1 **N-COUNT/N-NONCOUNT** A **limitation on** something is a rule or a decision which prevents that thing from growing or extending beyond certain limits. ❑ *...a limitation on the amount of tax you pay in a year.*

2 **N-PLURAL** The **limitations** of someone or something are the things that they cannot do, or the things that they do badly. ❑ *Parents often blame schools for the limitations of their children.*

3 **N-COUNT/N-NONCOUNT** A **limitation** is a fact or a situation that allows only some actions and makes others impossible. ❑ *She has ongoing pain and limitation of movement in her arm.* [from Latin]

lim|it|ed /lɪmɪtɪd/ **ADJ** Something that is **limited** is not very great in amount, range, or degree. ❑ *They had only a limited amount of time to talk.* [from Latin]

lim|it|ing fac|tor (limiting factors) **N-COUNT**

SCIENCE A **limiting factor** is a feature of the environment, such as space, sunlight or water, that is only available in small amounts and therefore limits the size of a population of animals or plants.

lim|ou|sine /lɪməzin/ (limousines) **N-COUNT**

A **limousine** is a large and very comfortable car. **Limo** is an informal word for **limousine**. ❑ *As the president's limousine approached, the crowd began to cheer.* [from French]

limp /lɪmp/ (limper, limpest, limps, limping, limped)

1 **V-I** If a person or an animal **limps**, they walk with difficulty because they have hurt one of their legs or feet. ❑ *James limps because of a hip injury.*

2 **N-COUNT** **Limp** is also a noun. ❑ *Anne walks with a limp.*

3 **ADJ** If something is **limp**, it is soft or weak. ❑ *Her body was limp and she was too weak to move.* [Sense 1 from Old English. Sense 2 of Scandinavian origin.]

L

line /laɪn/ (**lines, lining, lined**)

1 **N-COUNT** A **line** is a long, thin mark on something. ❑ *Draw a line at the bottom of the page.*

2 **N-COUNT** A **line** of people or vehicles is a number of them that are waiting one behind the other. ❑ *There was a line of people waiting to go into the movie theater.*

3 **N-COUNT/N-NONCOUNT** A **line** is a long piece of string or rope that you use for a particular purpose. ❑ *Melissa was outside, hanging the clothes on the line.*

4 **N-COUNT** A **line** is a route that trains move along. ❑ *We stayed on the train to the end of the line.*

5 **N-COUNT** A **line** is a very long wire for telephones or electricity. ❑ *Suddenly the telephone line went dead.*

6 **N-COUNT** The **lines** on your skin, especially on your face, are long thin marks that appear there as you grow older. ❑ *He has a large round face with deep lines.*

7 **N-COUNT** A **line** on a page or in a speech is a row of words, usually in the form of a sentence or a phrase. ❑ *He is having trouble memorizing his lines.*

8 **N-COUNT** A state or county **line** is a boundary between two states or counties. ❑ *...the California state line.*

9 **V-T** If people or things **line** a road, they stand in lines along it. ❑ *Thousands of local people lined the streets to welcome the president.*

10 **V-T** If you **line** a container, you cover the inside of it with something. ❑ *Line the box with newspaper.*

11 → see also **lining**

12 **PHRASE** When people **stand in line** or **wait in line**, they stand one behind the other in a line, waiting for something. ❑ *For the homeless, standing in line for meals is part of the daily routine.* [from Latin]

→ look at Picture Dictionary: **chart**
→ look at Word Webs: **graph, mathematics, train**

Thesaurus	line	Also look up :
N	cable, rope, wire **3**	

lin|ear equa|tion (**linear equations**)
N-COUNT **MATH** A **linear equation** is a mathematical equation that contains linear expressions.

lin|ear ex|pres|sion (**linear expressions**)
N-COUNT **MATH** A **linear expression** is a mathematical expression that contains a variable and does not contain any exponents.

lin|ear per|spec|tive (**linear perspectives**)
N-COUNT/N-NONCOUNT **ARTS** Linear perspective is a technique that is used in painting and drawing to create the appearance of three dimensions on a flat surface.

line di|rec|tion (**line directions**) **N-COUNT/N-NONCOUNT** **ARTS** Line direction is the direction in which a line is drawn or painted.

line graph (**line graphs**) **N-COUNT** **SCIENCE** A **line graph** is a graph in which the data are represented by points connected by one or more lines.

lin|en /lɪnɪn/ **N-NONCOUNT** Linen is a type of strong cloth. ❑ *She wore a white linen suit.* [from Old English]

line qual|ity (**line qualities**)
N-COUNT/N-NONCOUNT **ARTS** Line quality is all the characteristics of a drawn or painted line, such as its direction, darkness, and thickness.

lin|er /laɪnər/ (**liners**) **N-COUNT** A **liner** is a large ship in which people travel long distances, especially on vacation. ❑ *...a luxury ocean liner.*
→ look at Word Web: **ship**

lin|ger /lɪŋgər/ (**lingers, lingering, lingered**)
1 **V-I** When something such as an idea, a feeling, or an illness **lingers**, it continues to exist for a long time. ❑ *The scent of her perfume lingered on in the room.* ❑ *He was ashamed. That feeling lingered for some time.*

2 **V-I** If you **linger** somewhere, you stay there for a longer time than is necessary. ❑ *Customers are welcome to linger over coffee until around midnight.* [from Old English]

lin|gerie /lɑnʒəreɪ, læn-/ **N-NONCOUNT** Lingerie is women's underwear. ❑ *The store sells expensive designer lingerie.* [from French]

lin|ing /laɪnɪŋ/ (**linings**)
1 **N-COUNT/N-NONCOUNT** A **lining** is a piece of cloth that is attached to the inside of a piece of clothing or a curtain. ❑ *She wore a black jacket with a red lining.* [from Old French]

2 → see also **line**

link /lɪŋk/ (**links, linking, linked**)
1 **N-COUNT** If there is a **link between** two things, there is a connection between them, often because one of them causes the other. ❑ *Scientists believe there is a link between poor diet and cancer.*

2 V-T Link is also a verb. ❑ *Studies have linked television violence with aggressive behavior.*

3 N-COUNT TECHNOLOGY In computing, a **link** is an area on the screen that allows you to move from one web page or website to another. ❑ *The website has links to other tourism sites.*

4 N-COUNT A **link** is one of the rings in a chain. ❑ *She was wearing a chain of heavy gold links.*

5 V-T If you **link** one person or thing to another, you claim that there is a relationship or connection between them. ❑ *The DNA evidence linked him to the crime.* [of Scandinavian origin]

▶ **link up** If you **link up with** someone, you join them for a particular purpose. ❑ *I linked up with them on the walk.*

	Word Partnership Use **link** with :
ADJ	**direct** link, **possible** link, **vital** link **1** **4**
	strong/weak link **1** **3** **4**
V	**attempt to** link, **establish a** link, **find a** link **1** **4**

lion /ˈlaɪən/ (**lions**) **N-COUNT** A **lion** is a large wild cat that lives in Africa. Lions have yellow fur, and male lions have long hair called a mane on their head and neck. [from Old English]
→ look at Word Web: **carnivore**

lip /lɪp/ (**lips**) **N-COUNT** Your **lips** are the two outer parts of the edge of your mouth. ❑ *He kissed her gently on the lips.* [from Old English]
→ look at Picture Dictionary: **face**

lip|id /ˈlɪpɪd, ˈlaɪp-/ (**lipids**) **N-COUNT** SCIENCE **Lipids** are fatty substances that do not dissolve in water and are found in living cells. [from French]

lip|stick /ˈlɪpstɪk/ (**lipsticks**) **N-COUNT/N-NONCOUNT Lipstick** is a colored substance that women sometimes put on their lips. ❑ *She was wearing red lipstick.*
→ look at Word Web: **makeup**

liq|uid /ˈlɪkwɪd/ (**liquids**) **N-COUNT/N-NONCOUNT** SCIENCE A **liquid** is a substance that is not a solid or a gas. **Liquids** flow and can be poured. Water and oil are **liquids**. ❑ *She took out a small bottle of clear liquid.* ❑ *Drink plenty of liquids while flying and after you land.* [from Old French]
→ look at Word Web: **matter**

liq|uor /ˈlɪkər/ (**liquors**)
N-COUNT/N-NONCOUNT Liquor is strong alcoholic drink. ❑ *She never drinks liquor.* [from Old French]

list /lɪst/ (**lists, listing, listed**)
1 N-COUNT A **list** is a set of names or other things that are written or printed one below the other. ❑ *I added coffee to my shopping list.* ❑ *There were six names on the list.*

2 V-T If you **list** names or other things, you write or say them one after another. ❑ *The students listed the sports they liked best.* [from Old French]

	Word Partnership Use **list** with :
V	**add** *someone/something* **to a** list, list **includes** **1**
N	list **of candidates**, list **of demands**, **guest** list, list **of ingredients**, list **of items**, list **of names**, **price** list, list **of questions**, **reading** list, list **of things**, **wine** list, list **of words** **1**
ADJ	**complete** list, **disabled** list, **injured** list, list, **short** list **1**

lis|ten /ˈlɪsən/ (**listens, listening, listened**)
1 V-I If you **listen to** something or someone, you give your attention to a sound, or to what someone is saying. ❑ *He spends his time listening to the radio.*

2 V-I If you **listen for** a sound, you are ready to hear it if it occurs. ❑ *We listened for footsteps.*

3 V-I If you **listen to** someone, you do what they advise you to do, or you believe them. ❑ *Anne, please listen to me this time.*

4 INTERJ You say **Listen** or **Listen up** when you want someone to pay attention to you because you are going to say something. [SPOKEN] ❑ *Listen, there's something I should warn you about.* ❑ *Okay, listen up, guys. We've got to talk a little about how you look.* [from Old English]

▶ **listen in** If you **listen in** to a private conversation, you secretly listen to it. ❑ *He was sure that someone was listening in on his phone calls.*

	Thesaurus **listen** Also look up :
V	catch, pick up, tune in; *(ant.)* ignore **1** heed, mind **3**

	Word Partnership Use **listen** with :
V	listen **to** *someone's* **voice** **1** **sit** *up* **and** listen, **willing to** listen **1** **3**
ADV	listen **carefully**, listen **closely** **1** **3**

lis|ten|er /lɪsənər, lɪsnər/ (**listeners**) **N-COUNT**
A **listener** is someone who is listening to a speaker. ❑ *When he finished talking, his listeners applauded loudly.* [from Old English]
→ look at Word Web: **radio**

lit /lɪt/ **Lit** is a past tense and past participle of **light**. [from Old English]

li|ter /lɪtər/ (**liters**) **N-COUNT** MATH SCIENCE
A **liter** is a unit for measuring liquids. There are 1,000 milliliters in a liter. ❑ *Adults should drink about two liters of water each day.* [from French]
→ look at Picture Dictionary: **measurements**

lit|era|cy /lɪtərəsi/ **N-NONCOUNT** Literacy is the ability to read and write. ❑ *The library's adult literacy program helps about 2,000 people a year.* [from Latin]

lit|er|al /lɪtərəl/ **ADJ** LANGUAGE ARTS The **literal** sense of a word or phrase is its most basic sense. Compare with **figurative**. ❑ *The people there are fighting, in a literal sense, for their homes.*

lit|er|al|ly /lɪtərəli/
1 **ADV** If you translate something from another language **literally**, you say what each word means in another language. ❑ *Volkswagen literally means "people's car."*
2 **ADV** Some people use **literally** to emphasize what they are saying. ❑ *The view is literally breathtaking.* [from Late Latin]

Word Link	**liter ≈ letter : al**liter**ation,** literacy, literature

lit|er|ary /lɪtərɛri/
1 **ADJ** Literary means connected with literature. ❑ *...literary criticism.* ❑ *She's the literary editor of the "Sunday Review."*
2 **ADJ** Literary words and expressions are often unusual in some way and are used to create a special effect in a piece of writing such as a poem, a speech, or a novel. [from Latin]

lit|er|ary analy|sis **N-NONCOUNT**
LANGUAGE ARTS **Literary analysis** is the academic study of the techniques used in the creation of literature.

lit|er|ary criti|cism **N-NONCOUNT**
LANGUAGE ARTS **Literary criticism** is the analysis and judgment of works of literature.

lit|era|ture /lɪtərətʃər, -tʃʊər/
1 **N-NONCOUNT** LANGUAGE ARTS **Literature** is books, plays, and poetry that most people consider to be of high quality. ❑ *Chris is*

studying English literature at Columbia University.
2 **N-NONCOUNT** **Literature** is written information produced by people who want to sell you something or give you advice. ❑ *I am sending you literature from two other companies.* [from Latin]
→ look at Word Web: **genre**

litho|sphere /lɪθəsfɪər/ **N-SING** SCIENCE
The **lithosphere** is the outer layer of the Earth's surface, consisting of the crust and the outer mantle.

lit|ter /lɪtər/ (**litters, littering, littered**)
1 **N-NONCOUNT** **Litter** is paper or garbage that people leave lying on the ground in public places. ❑ *I hate it when I see people dropping litter.*
2 **V-T** If things **litter** a place, they are lying around it or over it in a messy way. ❑ *Broken glass littered the sidewalk.* ● **lit|tered** **ADJ** ❑ *The room was littered with toys.*
3 **N-COUNT** A **litter** is all the babies that are born to an animal at the same time. ❑ *Our cat has just given birth to a litter of three kittens.* [from Latin]

---
little
❶ DETERMINER, PRONOUN, AND ADVERB USES
❷ ADJECTIVE USES
---

❶ lit|tle /lɪtəl/
1 **DET** You use **little** to show that there is only a very small amount of something. ❑ *I have little money and little free time.* ❑ *I get very little sleep these days.*
2 **PRON** **Little** is also a pronoun. ❑ *He ate little, and drank less.* ❑ *Little of the house has changed since the 1960s.*
3 **ADV** **Little** means not very often or not very much. ❑ *They spoke very little.*
4 **DET** A **little** is a small amount of something. ❑ *I need a little help sometimes.*
5 **PRON** **Little** is also a pronoun. ❑ *They get paid for it. Not much. Just a little.* ❑ *Pour a little of the sauce over the chicken.*
6 **ADV** A **little** or a **little bit** means rather, or to a small degree. ❑ *He was a little bit afraid of the dog.* [from Old English]

❷ lit|tle /lɪtəl/ (**littler, littlest**)

LANGUAGE HELP
The comparative **littler** and the superlative **littlest** are only used in spoken English.

1 **ADJ** **Little** things are small. ❑ *We all sat at a little table.*

2 **ADJ** A **little** distance or period of time is short. ❑ *Go down the road a little way and then turn left.* ❑ *We waited for a little while, and then we went home.* [from Old English]

Thesaurus	little	Also look up :
DET	bit, dab, hint, touch, trace **①** **1** **3**	
ADJ	miniature, petite, slight, small, young; *(ant.)* big **②** **1**	

lit\|to\|ral zone /lɪtərəl zoʊn/ (**littoral zones**)
N-COUNT **SCIENCE** The **littoral zone** is the area along the edge of a pond, lake or sea.

---
live
① VERB USES
② ADJECTIVE AND ADVERB USES

---

① **live** /lɪv/ (**lives, living, lived**)
1 **V-I** If you **live** in a particular place, your home is there. ❑ *She lived in New York for 10 years.* ❑ *Where do you live?*
2 **V-T/V-I** If someone **lives** in a particular way, they have that type of life. ❑ *Nash lives a quiet life in Princeton.* ❑ *We live very well.*
3 **V-T/V-I** To **live** means to be alive. If someone **lives to** a particular age, they stay alive until they are that age. ❑ *We all need water to live.* ❑ *He's very ill and will not live long.*
4 **V-T/V-I** If someone **lives to** a particular age, they stay alive until they are that age. ❑ *He lived to 103.*
5 **V-I** If you say that someone **lives for** a particular thing, you mean that it is the most important thing in their life. ❑ *He lived for his work.* [from Old English]
6 → see also **living**
▶ **live on** or **live off** **1** If an animal **lives on** a particular food, it eats this type of food. ❑ *Sheep live mainly on grass.*
2 If you **live on** or **live off** a particular amount of money, you have that amount of money to buy things. ❑ *They are trying to live on $100 a week.*
▶ **live up to** If someone or something **lives up to** what they were expected to be, they are as good as they were expected to be. ❑ *Sales have not lived up to expectations this year.*
② **live** /laɪv/
1 **ADJ** **SCIENCE** **Live** animals or plants are not dead. ❑ *The local market sells live animals.*
2 **ADJ** A **live** television or radio program is one that you watch at the same time that it happens. ❑ *They watch all the live football games on TV.*

3 **ADV** **Live** is also an adverb. ❑ *The president's speech was broadcast live.*
4 **ADJ** A **live** wire or piece of electrical equipment is directly connected to a source of electricity. ❑ *The plug broke, showing live wires.* [from Old English]

Thesaurus	live	Also look up :
V	dwell, inhabit, occupy, reside **①** **1** manage, subsist, survive **①** **2** exist **①** **3**	
ADJ	active, alive, living, vigorous **②** **1**	

live\|blog /laɪvblɒg/ (**liveblogs, liveblogging, liveblogged**)
1 **N-COUNT** **TECHNOLOGY** A **liveblog** is a blog in which you write about an event as it happens. ❑ *She wrote a liveblog from the conflict area.*
2 **V-T/V-I** **TECHNOLOGY** If you **liveblog** or **liveblog** an event, you write on your blog about an event as it happens. ❑ *Several people were liveblogging from the scene.*

live\|ly /laɪvli/ (**livelier, liveliest**)
1 **ADJ** If you are **lively**, you are cheerful and you have a lot of energy. ❑ *Amy is a lively, sociable little girl.*
2 **ADJ** A **lively** event or discussion has lots of interesting and exciting things happening or being said in it. ❑ *...a lively debate.* [from Old English]

Word Partnership	Use **lively** with :
ADV	**very** lively **1** **2**
N	lively **atmosphere**, lively **conversation**, lively **debate**, lively **discussion**, lively **music**, lively **performance** **2**

liv\|er /lɪvər/ (**livers**)
1 **N-COUNT** **SCIENCE** Your **liver** is the large organ in your body that cleans your blood. ❑ *...liver disease.*
2 **N-COUNT/N-NONCOUNT** **Liver** is the liver of some animals that you can cook and eat. ❑ *...lamb's liver.* [from Old English]
→ look at Word Web: **donor**

liv\|er\|wort /lɪvərwɜrt, -wɔrt/ (**liverworts**)
N-COUNT A **liverwort** is a plant with no leaves or stem that grows in wet places and resembles seaweed or moss. [from Old English]

lives

PRONUNCIATION HELP
Pronounce meaning **1** /laɪvz/. Pronounce meaning **2** /lɪvz/.

1 **Lives** is the plural of **life**.

2 **Lives** is the third person singular of the present tense of **live**. [from Old English]

liv|ing /lɪvɪŋ/

1 **ADJ** A **living** person or animal is alive, and not dead. ❑ *He is perhaps the world's most famous living artist.* ❑ *He has no living relatives.*

2 **N-SING** The work that you do for a **living** is the work that you do to earn money. ❑ *What does she do for a living?* ❑ *Scott earns a living as a lawyer.*

3 **N-NONCOUNT** You use **living** when you are talking about the way that people live. ❑ *Mom believes in healthy living.* [from Old English]

4 → see also **live**

liv|ing room (**living rooms**) also **living-room** **N-COUNT** The **living room** in a house is the room where people sit together and talk or watch television. ❑ *We were sitting in the living room watching TV.*

→ look at Picture Dictionary: **house**

liz|ard /lɪzərd/ (**lizards**) **N-COUNT** A **lizard** is a small animal with a long tail and rough skin. [from Old French]

→ look at Picture Dictionary: **desert**

load /loʊd/ (**loads, loading, loaded**)

1 **V-T** If you **load** a vehicle or a container, you put a large amount of things into it. ❑ *The men finished loading the truck.*

2 **V-T** To **load** data onto a computer or other piece of technology means to put it into it so that it is ready to use. ❑ *You can load the data onto your PC to analyze it later.*

3 **N-COUNT** A **load** is something heavy that is being carried. ❑ *This car can take a big load.*

4 **N-COUNT** SCIENCE A **load** is any electrical device that is connected to a source of electricity such as a generator or circuit.

5 **N-COUNT/N-NONCOUNT** GEOGRAPHY A river's **load** is the sediment and other material that it carries with it.

6 **PHRASE** If you refer to **a load of** people or things or **loads of** them, you are emphasizing that there are a lot of them. [INFORMAL] ❑ *I've got loads of money.* ❑ *...a load of kids.* [from Old English]

Thesaurus	load	Also look up :
V	arrange, fill, pack, pile up, stack **1**	
N	bundle, cargo, freight, haul, shipment **3**	

Word Partnership	Use load with :
N	load **a truck** **1**
ADJ	**big** load, **full** load, **heavy** load **3**
V	**carry a** load, **handle a** load, **lighten a** load, **take on a** load **3**

load|ed /loʊdɪd/

1 **ADJ** A **loaded** question or word has more meaning or purpose than it appears to have, because the person who uses it hopes it will cause people to respond in a particular way. ❑ *That's a loaded question.*

2 **ADJ** If a place or object is **loaded with** things, it has very many of them in it or it is full of them. ❑ *...a tray loaded with cups.* ❑ *The store was loaded with jewelry.*

3 **ADJ** If you say that something is **loaded in favor of** someone, you mean it works unfairly to their advantage. If you say it is **loaded against** them, you mean it works unfairly to their disadvantage. ❑ *The education system is loaded in favor of the rich.* [from Old English]

loaf /loʊf/ (**loaves**) **N-COUNT** A **loaf** of bread is bread that has been shaped and baked in one piece. ❑ *He bought a loaf of bread and some ham and cheese.* [from Old English]

→ look at Picture Dictionary: **bread**

loam /loʊm/ **N-NONCOUNT** SCIENCE **Loam** is soil that is good for growing crops and plants in because it contains a lot of decayed vegetable matter and does not contain too much sand or clay. [from Old English]

loan /loʊn/ (**loans, loaning, loaned**)

1 **N-COUNT** A **loan** is an amount of money that you borrow. ❑ *Right now it's very difficult to get a loan from a bank.*

2 **V-T** If you **loan** something to someone, you lend it to them. ❑ *Brandon loaned his girlfriend $6,000.*

3 **PHRASE** If something is **on loan**, it has been borrowed. ❑ *...paintings on loan from the Metropolitan Museum.* [from Old Norse]

Word Partnership	Use loan with :
N	loan **agreement**, loan **application**, **bank** loan, **interest on a** loan, **mortgage** loan, loan **payment/repayment**, **savings and** loan **1**
V	**apply for a** loan, **get/receive a** loan, **make a** loan, **pay off a** loan, **repay a** loan **1**

loathe /loʊð/ (**loathes, loathing, loathed**)

V-T If you **loathe** something or someone, you

dislike them very much. [FORMAL] ❑ *The two men loathe each other.* [from Old English]

loaves /loʊvz/ **Loaves** is the plural of **loaf.** [from Old English]

lob|by /lɒbi/ (**lobbies, lobbying, lobbied**)

1 **N-COUNT** The **lobby** is the area inside the entrance to a big building. ❑ *I met her in the hotel lobby.*

2 **V-T/V-I** If you **lobby** someone such as a member of a government, you try to convince them that a particular law should be changed or that a particular thing should be done. ❑ *Mr. Bass lobbied city officials for money to build a community center.* ❑ *The group lobbies for women's rights.* [from Medieval Latin]

lob|boto|my /ləbɒtəmi/ (**lobotomies**) **N-COUNT/N-NONCOUNT** SCIENCE A **lobotomy** is a surgical operation in which some of the nerves in the brain are cut in order to treat severe mental illness. [from Late Latin]

lob|ster /lɒbstər/ (**lobsters**) **N-COUNT/N-NONCOUNT** A **lobster** is an ocean animal that has a hard shell and eight legs. ❑ *She sold me two live lobsters.* [from Old English] → look at Picture Dictionary: **shellfish**

lo|cal /loʊkəl/ **ADJ** Something that is **local** is in, or relates to, the area where you live. ❑ *Susan put an advertisement in the local paper.*

● **lo|cal|ly** **ADV** ❑ *I prefer to shop locally.* [from Old French]

Word Partnership	Use **local** with :
N	local **area**, local **artist**, local **business**, local **customs**, local **government**, local **group**, local **hospital**, local **library**, local **news**, local **office**, local **officials**, local **newspaper**, local **people**, local *phone* **call**, local **police**, local **politics**, local **residents**, local **store**

lo|cated /loʊkeɪtɪd/ **ADJ** If something is **located** somewhere, it is in that place. ❑ *The gym and beauty salon are located on the second floor.*

lo|ca|tion /loʊkeɪʃ°n/ (**locations**) **N-COUNT** A **location** is the place where something is. ❑ *For dates and locations of the meetings, call this number.* [from Latin] → look at Picture Dictionary: **location**

Word Partnership	Use **location** with :
ADJ	**central** location, **convenient** location, **exact** location, **geographic** location, **present** location, **secret** location, **specific** location
V	**pinpoint a** location

lock /lɒk/ (**locks, locking, locked**)

1 **V-T** When you **lock** a door or a container, you close it with a key. ❑ *Are you sure you locked the front door?*

Picture Dictionary   location

The squirrel is above/over the bench.

The squirrel is in the tree.

The squirrel is on the bench.

The squirrel is between the bench and the tree.

The squirrel is behind the bench.

The squirrel is under/underneath the bench.

The squirrel is in front of the bench.

2 **N-COUNT** The **lock** on a door or a container is the part that you use to keep it shut and to make sure that no one can open it. You can open a lock with a key. ❑ *She turned the key in the lock and opened the door.*

3 **V-T** If you **lock** something or someone in a place, you put them there and close the door or the lid with a key. ❑ *She locked the case in the closet.*

4 **V-T/V-I** If you **lock** something in a particular position, or if it **locks** there, it is held or fitted firmly in that position. ❑ *He locked his fingers behind his head.* [from Old English]

▶ **lock away** If you **lock** something **away** in a place, you put it there and close it with a key. ❑ *She cleaned her jewelry and locked it away in a case.*

▶ **lock up** If you **lock up**, you lock all the windows and doors of a house or a car. ❑ *Don't forget to lock up before you leave.*

Word Partnership	Use **lock** with :
N	lock **a car**, lock **a door**, lock **a room** **1** **combination** lock, **door** lock, lock **and key**, **key in a** lock **2**
V	**change a** lock, **open a** lock, **pick a** lock **2**

lock|er /lɒkər/ (**lockers**) **N-COUNT** A **locker** is a small cupboard with a lock, that you keep things in at a school or at a sports club. [from Old English]

lo|co|mo|tive /loʊkəmoʊtɪv/ (**locomotives**) **N-COUNT** A **locomotive** is a large vehicle that pulls a train. [from Modern Latin] [FORMAL] → look at Word Web: **train**

lo|co|mo|tor /loʊkəmoʊtər/ **ADJ SCIENCE** **Locomotor** movements are actions such as walking or running, that involve moving from one place to another. [from Latin]

lodge /lɒdʒ/ (**lodges, lodging, lodged**) **1** **N-COUNT** A **lodge** is a small house in the countryside or in the mountains where people stay on vacation. ❑ *We stayed in a lodge about 17 miles north of Paonia, Colorado.*

2 **V-T** If you **lodge** a complaint or a claim, you officially make it. ❑ *The children's parents lodged a formal complaint against the school.*

3 **V-T/V-I** If you **lodge** somewhere such as in someone else's house, or if you **are lodged** there, you live there, usually paying rent. ❑ *She lodged with a farming family when she was a young teacher.* ● **lodg|er** (**lodgers**) **N-COUNT**

❑ *Jennie took in a lodger to help pay the mortgage.*

4 **V-T/V-I** If an object **lodges** or **is lodged** somewhere, it becomes stuck there. ❑ *The bullet lodged in the policeman's leg.* [from Old French]

lo|ess /loʊɪs, lɛs, lɜrs/ **N-NONCOUNT** **SCIENCE** **Loess** is a mixture of sand, soil, and other material that has been deposited by the wind. [from German]

loft /lɒft/ (**lofts**) **1** **N-COUNT** A **loft** is the space directly under the roof of a building. ❑ *The loft was filled with boxes of old photos.*

2 **N-COUNT** A **loft** is an apartment in the upper part of an old factory or a similar building. ❑ *Jack lives in a luxury loft in New York.* [from Late Old English]

log /lɒg/ (**logs, logging, logged**) **1** **N-COUNT** A **log** is a thick piece of wood that has been cut from a tree. ❑ *...a log fire.*

log

2 **N-COUNT** A **log** is a written record of the things that happen each day. ❑ *They examined the three men's telephone logs.*

3 **V-T** If you **log** something that happens, you write it down as a record of the event. ❑ *They log everything that comes in and out of the warehouse.*

→ look at Word Webs: **blog, forest**

▶ **log in** or **log on** **TECHNOLOGY** If you **log in** or **log on**, you type a special secret word so that you can start using a computer or a website. ❑ *She turned on her computer and logged in.*

▶ **log out** or **log off** **TECHNOLOGY** If you **log out** or **log off**, you stop using a computer or a website by clicking on an instruction. ❑ *I logged off and went out for a walk.*

loga|rithm /lɔgərɪðəm/ (**logarithms**) **N-COUNT** **MATH** The **logarithm** of a number is a number that it can be represented by in order to make a difficult multiplication or division sum simpler. [from New Latin]

log|ger|head tur|tle /lɔgərhɛd tɜrtəl/ (**loggerhead turtles**) **N-COUNT** **SCIENCE** A **loggerhead turtle** is a large sea turtle that eats meat.

Word Link | *log ≈ reason, speech : apology,*
dialogue, logic

log|ic /lɒdʒɪk/ **N-NONCOUNT Logic** is a way
of working things out, by saying that one
fact must be true if another fact is true.
❑ *The students study philosophy and logic.*
[from Old French]
→ look at Word Web: **philosophy**

logi|cal /lɒdʒɪkᵊl/
1 ADJ In a **logical** argument or method of
reasoning, each step must be true if the step
before it is true. ❑ *Each logical step is checked by
other mathematicians.* ● **logi|cal|ly** /lɒdʒɪkli/
ADV ❑ *I have learned to think about things logically.*
2 ADJ If something is **logical**, it seems
reasonable or sensible. ❑ *There must be a
logical explanation for his behavior.* [from Old
French]

logo /loʊgoʊ/ (**logos**) **N-COUNT** The **logo** of
an organization is the special design that it
puts on all its products or advertisements.
❑ *The company's logo is a penguin.* [from Greek]

LOL LOL is short for "laughing out loud" or
"lots of love," and is often used in email and
text messages.

lone /loʊn/ **ADJ** A **lone** person or thing is
alone. ❑ *A lone walker disappeared over the top
of the hill.*

lone|ly /loʊnli/ (**lonelier, loneliest**)
1 ADJ If you are **lonely**, you are unhappy
because you are alone. ❑ *Mr. Garcia has been
lonely since his wife died.* ● **lone|li|ness**
N-NONCOUNT ❑ *I have a fear of loneliness.*
2 ADJ A **lonely** place is a place where very
few people go. ❑ *Her car broke down on a lonely
country road.*

Word Link | *some ≈ causing : awesome,*
bothersome, lonesome

lone|some /loʊnsəm/ **ADJ** If you are
lonesome, you are unhappy because you are
alone. ❑ *Her favorite song is "Are You Lonesome
Tonight?" by Elvis Presley.*

─────── **long** ───────
❶ TIME AND DISTANCE USES
❷ VERB USE

❶ long /lɔŋ/ (**longer** /lɔŋgər/, **longest**
/lɔŋgɪst/)
1 ADV Long means a lot of time. ❑ *Cleaning
up didn't take too long.* ❑ *Have you been waiting
long?*
2 ADJ A **long** event lasts for a lot of time.

❑ *We had a long meeting.* ❑ *She is planning a long
vacation in Europe.* ❑ *"How long is the movie?"—
"About two hours."*
3 ADJ Something that is **long** measures
a great distance from one end to the other.
❑ *There was a long table in the middle of the
kitchen.* ❑ *Lucy had long dark hair.*
4 ADJ A **long** distance is a great distance.
❑ *The long trip made him tired.*
5 PHRASE Something that is **no longer** the
case used to be the case but is not the case
now. You can also say that something is not
the case **any longer**. ❑ *Food shortages are no
longer a problem.* ❑ *She couldn't afford to pay the
rent any longer.*
6 PHRASE **As long as** or **so long as** means
"if." ❑ *They can do what they want as long as they
are not breaking the law.* [from Old English]
→ look at Picture Dictionary: **hair**

❷ long /lɔŋ/ (**longs, longing, longed**) **V-T/V-I**
If you **long**, or **long for** something, you want
it very much. ❑ *I'm longing to meet her.* ❑ *Steve
longed for his old life.* ● **long|ing** (**longings**)
N-COUNT/N-NONCOUNT ❑ *She still feels a longing
for her own home and country.* [from Old English]

long-dis|tance ADJ You use **long-distance**
to talk about travel or communication
between places that are a long way from
each other. ❑ *Long-distance travel can be very
tiring.* ❑ *Stacey makes a lot of long-distance calls
on her cellphone.*

lon|gi|tude /lɒndʒɪtud/ (**longitudes**)
N-COUNT/N-NONCOUNT GEOGRAPHY The
longitude of a place is how far it is to the
west or east of an imaginary line that goes
from the North Pole to the South Pole.
Compare with **latitude**. [from Latin]
→ look at Picture Dictionary: **globe**

lon|gi|tu|di|nal wave /lɒndʒɪtudᵊnᵊl weɪv/
(**longitudinal waves**) **N-COUNT** SCIENCE
Longitudinal waves are waves such as sound
waves in which the material that the waves
are passing through moves in the same
direction as the waves. Compare with
transverse wave.

long jump N-SING SPORTS The **long jump** is
a sports event that involves jumping as far
as you can.

long-range ADJ A **long-range** plan or
prediction relates to a period extending
a long time into the future. ❑ *...the need for
long-range planning.*

long|shore cur|rent /lɔŋʃɔr kɜrənt/
(**longshore currents**) **N-COUNT** SCIENCE
A **longshore current** is an ocean current
that flows close to, and parallel to, the shore.

long-stand|ing ADJ A **long-standing**
situation has existed for a long time. ❑ *They
resolved their long-standing dispute over money.*

look /lʊk/ (**looks, looking, looked**)

■ **V-I** If you **look** in a particular direction,
you turn your eyes so that you can see what
is there. ❑ *I looked out of the window.* ❑ *If you
look, you'll see a lake.*

■ **N-SING Look** is also a noun. ❑ *Lucille took
a last look in the mirror.*

■ **N-PLURAL** When you refer to someone's
looks, you are referring to how beautiful or
ugly they are. ❑ *I never chose friends just because
of their looks.*

■ **V-LINK** You use **look** when indicating
what you think will happen in the future or
how a situation seems to you. ❑ *He had lots
of time to think about the future, and it didn't look
good.* ❑ *It looks like we're going to win.* ❑ *The 90
degree heat looks like it will return for the weekend.*

■ **V-I** If you **look for** something or someone,
you try to find them. ❑ *I'm looking for a child.*
❑ *I looked everywhere for my purse.*

■ **V-I** If you **look at** a situation or a subject,
you consider it or judge it. ❑ *Next term we'll be
looking at the Second World War.* ❑ *Anne Holker
looks at ways of making changes to your home.*
❑ *Brian learned to look at her with new respect.*

■ **N-SING Look** is also a noun. ❑ *...a quick look
at the morning newspapers.*

■ **INTERJ** You say **Look** when you want
someone to pay attention to you. ❑ *Look, I'm
sorry. I didn't mean it.*

■ **INTERJ** If you say or shout **Look out** to
someone, you are warning them that they
are in danger. ❑ *"Look out!" somebody shouted,
as the truck started to move toward us.*

■ **V-LINK** You use **look** when you are
describing the way that a person seems to be.
❑ *You look lovely, Marcia!* ❑ *Sheila was looking sad.*

■ **N-SING** If someone or something has a
particular **look**, they have a particular
appearance or expression. ❑ *He saw the look of
surprise on her face.* ❑ *Be very careful. I don't like the
look of those guys.* [from Old English]

▶ **look after** If you **look after** someone or
something, you take care of them. ❑ *Maria
looks after the kids while I'm at work.*

▶ **look back** If you **look back**, you think
about things that happened in the past.

❑ *Looking back, I am surprised how easy it was.*

▶ **look down on** To **look down on** someone
means to consider that person to be inferior
or unimportant, usually when this is not
true. ❑ *They looked down on me because I wasn't
successful.*

▶ **look forward to** If you **look forward to**
something that is going to happen, you
want it to happen because you think you
will enjoy it. ❑ *She's looking forward to her
vacation in Hawaii.*

▶ **look into** If you **look into** something, you
find out about it. ❑ *He once looked into buying
his own island.*

▶ **look on** If you **look on** while something
happens, you watch it happening without
taking part yourself. ❑ *Local people looked on in
silence as he walked past.*

▶ **look out for** If you **look out for** a person or
thing, you pay attention to the people or
things around you so that you find them.
❑ *Officers are looking out for the stolen vehicle.*

▶ **look through** If you **look through** a book,
a magazine, or a group of things, you get an
idea of what is in it by examining items in
it. ❑ *Peter started looking through the mail at once.*

▶ **look up** If you **look up** a fact or a piece of
information, you find it by looking in a book
or on a computer. ❑ *I looked up your number in
my address book.*

▶ **look up to** If you **look up to** someone,
especially someone older than you, you
respect and admire them. ❑ *A lot of the
younger girls look up to you.*

Usage | **look, see,** and **watch**

If you *look* at something, you purposely direct
your eyes at it: *Daniel kept turning around to look at
the big-screen TV—he had never seen one before.* If you
see something, it is visible to you: *Maria couldn't
see the TV because Hector was standing in front of her
and watching it.* If you *watch* something, you pay
attention to it and keep it in sight: *Everyone was
watching TV instead of looking at the photo album.*

---

loom /lum/ (**looms, looming, loomed**)

■ **V-I** If something **looms over** you, it
appears as a large or unclear shape, often in
a frightening way. ❑ *She loomed over me, pale
and gray.*

■ **V-I** If an unpleasant event **is looming**,
it will probably happen soon. ❑ *Another
economic crisis is looming.*

■ **N-COUNT** A **loom** is a machine that is used
for making cloth. [Senses 1 and 2 from East
Frisian. Sense 3 from Old English.]

loop /lup/ (loops, looping, looped)

1 **N-COUNT** A **loop** is a shape like a circle in a piece of string or rope. ❑ *On the ground beside them was a loop of rope.*

2 **V-T** If you **loop** something such as a piece of rope around an object, you tie a length of it in a loop around the object, for example in order to fasten it to the object. ❑ *He looped the rope over the wood.*

3 **PHRASE** If someone is **in the loop**, they are part of a group of people who make decisions about important things, or they know about these decisions. [INFORMAL] ❑ *I think that the vice president was in the loop.*

loose /lus/ (looser, loosest)

1 **ADJ** Something that is **loose** is not firmly fixed to something else. ❑ *One of Hannah's top front teeth is loose.* ● **loose|ly** **ADV** ❑ *He held the gun loosely in his hand.*

2 **ADJ** If people or animals break **loose**, they escape from the place where they are held. ❑ *Our dog got loose and ran away yesterday.*

3 **ADJ** **Loose** clothes do not fit closely. ❑ *Wear loose, comfortable clothing when exercising.* ● **loose|ly** **ADV** ❑ *A scarf hung loosely around his neck.*

4 **PHRASE** If a person or an animal is **on the loose**, they are free because they have escaped from a person or a place. ❑ *A dangerous criminal is on the loose after escaping from jail.* [from Old Norse] → look at Usage note at **lose**

loos|en /lusᵊn/ (loosens, loosening, loosened) V-T/V-I

If your clothing or something that is tied or fastened **loosens**, or you **loosen** it, you undo it slightly so that it is less tight or less firmly held in place. ❑ *He loosened his tie around his neck.*

▸ **loosen up** **1** If a person or a situation **loosens up**, they become more relaxed and less tense. ❑ *Relax, smile; loosen up.*

2 If you **loosen up** your body, or if it **loosens up**, you do simple exercises to get your muscles ready for a difficult physical activity, such as running or playing sports. ❑ *Squeeze your foot with both hands to loosen up tight muscles.*

loot /lut/ (loots, looting, looted) V-T/V-I

If people **loot** stores or houses, or if they **loot** things from them, they steal things from them, for example during a war or riot. ❑ *People started breaking windows and looting shops.* ❑ *The men looted food supplies.* ❑ *People came into the city to look for food and to loot.*

● **loot|ing** **N-NONCOUNT** ❑ *There has been rioting and looting.* ● **loot|er** (**looters**) **N-COUNT** ❑ *Looters took thousands of dollars' worth of food.* [from Hindi]

lord /lɔrd/ (lords)

1 **N-COUNT** A **lord** is a man with a high position in society. ❑ *Kathleen Kennedy married Lord Cavendish in 1944.*

2 **N-PROPER** In some religions, people call God and Jesus Christ the **Lord**. ❑ *She prayed now. "Lord, help me to find courage."* [from Old English]

lose /luz/ (loses, losing, lost)

1 **V-T/V-I** If you **lose** a game, you do not win it. ❑ *Our team lost the game by one point.* ❑ *No one likes to lose.*

2 **V-T** If you **lose** something, you do not know where it is. ❑ *I've lost my keys.*

3 **V-T** If you **lose** something, you do not have it anymore because someone has taken it away from you. ❑ *I lost my job when the company shut down.*

4 **V-T** If someone **loses** a quality or a belief, they no longer have it. ❑ *He lost all sense of reason.*

5 **V-T** If you **lose** weight, you become less heavy. ❑ *His doctor told him to lose weight.*

6 **V-T** If someone **loses** their life, they die. ❑ *192 people lost their lives in the disaster.*

7 **V-T** If you **lose** time, something slows you down so that you do not make as much progress as you hoped. ❑ *Police lost time in the early part of the investigation.*

8 **V-T** If you **lose** an opportunity, you do not take advantage of it. ❑ *If you don't do it soon, you're going to lose your opportunity.* ❑ *They did not lose the opportunity to say what they thought.*

9 **V-T** BUSINESS If a business **loses** money, it earns less money than it spends. ❑ *The company has been losing money for the last three years.*

10 → see also **lost**

11 **PHRASE** If you **lose** your **way**, you become lost when you are trying to go somewhere. ❑ *The men lost their way in a storm.* [from Old English] → look at Usage note at **miss**

Usage   **lose** and **loose**

Be careful not to write *loose* when you mean *lose*. *Lose* means that you no longer have something, and *loose* describes something that is not held firmly or attached. *Loose* rhymes with *goose*, while *lose* rhymes with *shoes*: *You might lose your dog if you let him run loose.*

L

los|er /lúzər/ (losers)

1 **N-COUNT** The **losers** of a game are the people who do not win. ❑ *In any game, there's always a winner and a loser.*

2 **PHRASE** If you are a **good loser**, you accept that you have lost a game without complaining. If you are a **bad loser**, you do not like losing, and you complain about it. ❑ *I try to be a good loser.* [from Old English]

loss /lɔs/ (losses)

1 **N-COUNT/N-NONCOUNT** **Loss** is when you do not have something that you used to have, or when you have less of it than before. ❑ *The first symptoms are a slight fever and a loss of appetite.*

2 **N-NONCOUNT** The **loss** of a relative or a friend is their death. ❑ *He is mourning the loss of his wife and child.*

3 **N-COUNT** A **loss** is the difficulty you suffer when a valuable and useful person or thing leaves or is taken away. ❑ *His death was a great loss to his family.* ❑ *...a terrible loss of human life.*

4 **N-COUNT/N-NONCOUNT** If a business makes a **loss**, it earns less money than it spends. ❑ *The company made a loss again last year.*

5 **PHRASE** If you say that you are **at a loss**, you mean that you do not know what to do in a particular situation. ❑ *I was at a loss for what to do next.* [from Old English]

→ look at Word Webs: **diet, disaster**

Word Partnership	Use **loss** with :
N	loss **of appetite**, **blood** loss, loss **of control**, **hair** loss, **hearing** loss, loss **of income**, loss **of a job**, **memory** loss, **weight** loss **1**
ADJ	**great/huge/substantial** loss **1** **3** **tragic** loss **2** **3** **net** loss **4**

lost /lɔst/

1 **Lost** is the past tense and past participle of **lose**.

2 **ADJ** If you are **lost**, you do not know where you are, and you are unable to find your way. ❑ *I realized I was lost.*

3 **ADJ** If something is **lost**, you cannot find it. ❑ *We complained to the airline about our lost luggage.*

4 **ADJ** If you feel **lost**, you feel very uncomfortable because you are in an unfamiliar situation. ❑ *He remembered feeling very lost at the funeral.* [from Old English]

lost and found

1 **N-SING** **Lost and found** is the area in a public place where they keep things that people have lost.

2 **ADJ** **Lost-and-found** things are things that someone has lost and that someone else has found.

lot /lɒt/ (lots)

1 **PRON** A **lot** or **lots** is a large amount of something. ❑ *I learned a lot from him.* ❑ *A lot of our land is used for growing crops.* ❑ *He drank lots of milk.*

2 **N-COUNT** You can use **lot** to refer to a set or group of things or people. ❑ *He bought two lots of 1,000 shares in the company.*

3 **N-COUNT** A **lot** is a small area of land that belongs to a person or a company. ❑ *Oil was discovered under their lot.*

4 **ADV** A **lot** means very much or often. ❑ *Matthew goes out quite a lot.* ❑ *I like you a lot.* [from Old English]

5 → see also **parking lot**

Usage	lot

Both *a lot* and *lots* mean "very many," "a large number," or "a large amount," and both can be followed by a singular or plural verb, depending on whats being talked about: *Lots/A lot of people are here.* *A lot* is also an adverb: *I like him a lot.*

lo|tion /lóuʃ°n/ (lotions)

N-COUNT/N-NONCOUNT A **lotion** is a liquid that you use to clean or protect your skin. ❑ *Remember to put on some suntan lotion.* [from Old French]

lot|tery /lɒtəri/ (lotteries) **N-COUNT** A

lottery is a type of game where people buy tickets with numbers on them. If the numbers on your ticket are chosen, you win a prize. ❑ *She has won the national lottery twice.* [from Old French]

Word Link	est ≈ most : great**est**, kind**est**, loud**est**

Word Link	er ≈ more : bigg**er**, loud**er**, tall**er**

loud /laʊd/ (louder, loudest)

1 **ADJ** If a noise is **loud**, the level of sound is very high. ❑ *The music was so loud that I couldn't hear what she was saying.* ● **loud|ly** **ADV** ❑ *The cat rolled onto its back, purring loudly.*

2 **PHRASE** If you say something **out loud**, you say it so that other people can hear it. ❑ *Parts of the book made me laugh out loud.* [from Old English]

Word Partnership	Use **loud** with :
N	loud **bang**, loud **crash**, loud **explosion**, loud **music**, loud **noise**, loud **voice** **1**
ADJ	loud **and clear** **1**
V	**laugh out** loud, **read out** loud, **say** *something* out **think out** loud, **think out** loud **2**

lounge /laʊndʒ/ (**lounges, lounging, lounged**)

1 **N-COUNT** A **lounge** is a room in a hotel or an airport where people can sit. ❑ *...an airport lounge.*

2 **V-I** If you **lounge** somewhere, you sit or lie there in a relaxed or lazy way. ❑ *They ate and drank and lounged in the shade.*

louse /laʊs/ (**lice**) **N-COUNT** A **louse** is a small insect that lives on people's and animal's bodies. [from Old English]

lousy /laʊzi/ (**lousier, lousiest**) **ADJ** If something or someone is **lousy**, they are very bad. [INFORMAL] ❑ *The weather was lousy all weekend.* ❑ *I was a lousy secretary.* [from Old English]

lov|able /lʌvəbᵊl/ **ADJ** If someone is **lovable**, they are easy to love. ❑ *He is a sweet, lovable dog.* [from Old English]

love /lʌv/ (**loves, loving, loved**)

1 **V-T** If you **love** someone, you care very much about them, or you have strong romantic feelings for them. ❑ *Oh, Amy, I love you.* ❑ *You will love your baby from the moment she is born.*

2 **N-NONCOUNT** **Love** is the very strong warm feeling that you have when you care very much about someone, or you have strong romantic feelings for them. ❑ *In the four years since we married, our love has grown stronger.* ❑ *...a love story.*

3 **N-NONCOUNT** **Love** is a strong liking for something, or a belief that it is important. ❑ *This is no way to encourage a love of literature.*

4 **V-T** If you **love** something, you like it very much. ❑ *I love food, I love cooking, and I love eating.* ❑ *Sophie loves to play the piano.*

5 **V-T** If you **would love to** have or do something, you very much want to have it or do it. ❑ *I would love to be thinner.* ❑ *I would love a hot bath.*

6 → see also **loving**

7 **PHRASE** You can write **love, love from,** and **all my love,** before your name, at the end of a letter to a friend or a relative. ❑ *The letter ended, "With lots of love from Anna."*

8 **PHRASE** If you **fall in love with** someone, you start to love them in a romantic way. ❑ *Maria fell in love with Danny as soon as she met him.* [from Old English]

→ look at Word Webs: **love, emotion**

Thesaurus	**love** Also look up :
V	adore, cherish, treasure; (*ant.*) dislike, hate **1** **4**
N	adoration, devotion, tenderness; (*ant.*) hate **2** **3**

love|ly /lʌvli/ (**lovelier, loveliest**) **ADJ** If someone or something is **lovely**, they are beautiful, very nice, or very enjoyable. ❑ *You look lovely, Marcia.* ❑ *Sam has a lovely voice.* ❑ *Thank you for a lovely evening!* [from Old English]

lov|er /lʌvər/ (**lovers**)

1 **N-COUNT** People who are **lovers** are having a sexual relationship but they are not married. ❑ *Every Thursday she met her lover Leon.*

2 **N-COUNT** If you are a **lover** of something, you like it very much. ❑ *The website is for music lovers.* [from Old English]

lov|ing /lʌvɪŋ/

1 **ADJ** If you are **loving**, you feel or show love for other people. ❑ *My parents had a loving relationship.* ● **lov|ing|ly** **ADV** ❑ *Brian looked lovingly at Mary.*

2 **ADJ** **Loving** actions are done with great

Word Web   love

Before the Middle Ages, **romance** was not an important part of **marriage**. Parents decided who their children married. The social class and political connections of a future **spouse** were very important. No one expected a couple to **fall in love**. However, during the Middle Ages, poets and musicians began to write about love in a new way. These **romantic** poems and songs describe a new type of courtship. In them, the man **woos** a woman for her **affection**. This is the basis for the modern idea of a romantic **bond** between **husband** and **wife**.

enjoyment and care. ❑ *The house has been decorated with loving care.* ● **lov|ing|ly** ADV ❑ *...lovingly-prepared food.* [from Old English]
❸ → see also **love**

low /loʊ/ (**lower, lowest, lows**)
❶ ADJ If something is **low**, it is close to the ground. ❑ *It was late afternoon and the sun was low in the sky.*
❷ ADV **Low** is also an adverb. ❑ *An airplane flew low over the beach.*
❸ ADJ **Low** is used to describe people who are not considered to be very important because they are near the bottom of a particular scale or system. ❑ *...a soldier of low rank.*
❹ N-COUNT If something reaches a **low** of a particular amount or degree, that is the smallest it has ever been. ❑ *Prices dropped to a low of about $1.12.*
❺ ADJ If something is **low**, it is small in amount. ❑ *House prices are still very low.*
❻ ADJ If you have a **low** opinion of someone or something, you disapprove of them or dislike them. ❑ *...his low opinion of rap music.*
❼ ADJ If the quality of something is **low**, it is very bad. ❑ *The hospital was criticized for its low standards of care.*
❽ ADJ A **low** sound or noise is deep and quiet. ❑ *His voice was so low she couldn't hear him.*
❾ ADJ If you are **low**, you are depressed. [INFORMAL] ❑ *She tried to make him smile when he was feeling low.* [from Old Norse]

low|er /loʊər/ (**lowers, lowering, lowered**)
❶ ADJ The **lower** of two things is the bottom one. ❑ *Emily bit her lower lip nervously.*
❷ V-T If you **lower** something, you move it down. ❑ *They lowered the coffin into the grave.*
❸ V-T If you **lower** something, you make it less. ❑ *The Central Bank lowered interest rates yesterday.* [from Old Norse]

low|er case N-NONCOUNT LANGUAGE ARTS
If you write or type something **in lower case**, you write or type it using small letters, not capital letters. Compare with **upper case**.
❑ *Type your user name and password in lower case.*

low|er man|tle N-SING SCIENCE The **lower mantle** is the part of the Earth's interior that lies between the upper mantle and the outer core.

low-im|pact
❶ ADJ **Low-impact** exercise does not put

a lot of stress on your body. ❑ *The new focus is on gentler forms of exercise, such as low-impact aerobics.*
❷ ADJ **Low-impact** projects, developments, and activities are designed to cause minimum harm to the environment.
❑ *...sensitive, enlightened, low-impact ecotourism.*

low tide (**low tides**) N-COUNT/N-NONCOUNT
SCIENCE At the coast, **low tide** is the time when the sea is at its lowest level because the tide is out.
→ look at Word Web: **tide**

loy|al /lɔɪəl/ ADJ If you are **loyal**, you keep your friends or your beliefs, even in difficult times. ❑ *They have always stayed loyal to the Republican party.* ● **loy|al|ly** ADV ❑ *The staff loyally supported their boss.* [from Old French]
→ look at Word Web: **hero**

loy|al|ty /lɔɪəlti/ (**loyalties**)
❶ N-NONCOUNT **Loyalty** is when you continue to be someone's friend, or to believe in something, even in difficult times. ❑ *I believe in family loyalty.*
❷ N-COUNT **Loyalties** are feelings of friendship, support, or duty toward someone or something. ❑ *She had developed strong loyalties to the Manet family.* [from Old French]

lub|ri|cant /lubrɪkənt/ (**lubricants**) N-COUNT
A **lubricant** is a substance that you put on the surfaces or parts of something, especially something mechanical, to make the parts move smoothly. [from Latin]

luck /lʌk/
❶ N-NONCOUNT **Luck** or **good luck** is the good things that happen to you, that have not been caused by yourself or other people. ❑ *Before the game, we shook hands and wished each other luck.*
❷ N-NONCOUNT **Bad luck** is the bad things that happen to you, that have not been caused by yourself or other people. ❑ *We had a lot of bad luck during the first half of this season.*
❸ PHRASE If you say **Good luck** to someone, you are telling them that you hope they will be successful in something they are trying to do. [INFORMAL]
❹ PHRASE You can say someone **is in luck** when they are in a situation where they can have what they want or need. ❑ *You're in luck. The doctor's still here.* [from Middle Dutch]

Word Partnership	Use luck with :
V	bring *someone* luck, need a little luck, need some luck, push *your* luck, try *your* luck, wish *someone* luck ■1 have any/bad/better/good/no luck ■1 ■2
ADJ	dumb luck, good luck, just luck, pure luck, sheer luck ■1

lucki|ly /lʌkɪli/ **ADV** You use **luckily** when you want to say that it is good that something happened. ❏ *Luckily, nobody was seriously injured in the accident.* [from Middle Dutch]

lucky /lʌki/ (**luckier, luckiest**)

■1 **ADJ** You say that someone is **lucky** when they have good luck. ❏ *I am luckier than most people here. I have a job.* ❏ *Rob is very lucky to be alive after that accident.*

■2 **ADJ** You say that someone is **lucky** when they have something that is very desirable or when they are in a very desirable situation. ❏ *I am luckier than most people round here. I have a job.* ❏ *He is very lucky to be alive.*

■3 **ADJ** A **lucky** object is something that people believe brings them good luck. ❏ *I'm wearing my lucky shirt. How can I lose?* [from Middle Dutch]

Word Partnership	Use lucky with :
V	be lucky, feel lucky, get lucky, lucky to get *something*, lucky to have *something* ■2
ADV	lucky enough, pretty lucky, really lucky, so lucky ■2

lu|cra|tive /lukrətɪv/ **ADJ** A **lucrative** activity, job, or business deal is very profitable. ❏ *...his lucrative career as a filmmaker.* [from Old French]

lug|gage /lʌgɪdʒ/ **N-NONCOUNT** **Luggage** is the bags that you take with you when you travel. ❏ *"Do you have any luggage?"—"Just my briefcase."*

→ look at Word Web: **hotel**

lug|gage rack (**luggage racks**) **N-COUNT** A **luggage rack** is a shelf for putting luggage on in a train or a bus.

luke|warm /lukwɔrm/ **ADJ** If a liquid is **lukewarm**, it is only slightly warm. ❏ *Freddy drank the lukewarm coffee.* [from Old English]

lum|ber /lʌmbər/ **N-NONCOUNT** **Lumber** consists of trees and large pieces of wood that have been roughly cut up. [from Swedish dialect]

→ look at Word Web: **forest**

lump /lʌmp/ (**lumps, lumping, lumped**)

■1 **N-COUNT** A **lump** is a solid piece of something. ❏ *...a lump of coal.*

■2 **N-COUNT** A **lump** on or in your body is a small, hard part. ❏ *I've got a painful lump in my mouth.*

▶ **lump together** If a number of different people or things **are lumped together**, they are considered as a group rather than separately. ❏ *Police officers, bankers and butchers are all lumped together in one group.*

lu|nar eclipse /lunər ɪklɪps/ (**lunar eclipses**) **N-COUNT** SCIENCE A **lunar eclipse** is an occasion when the Earth is between the sun and the moon, so that for a short time you cannot see part or all of the moon. Compare with **solar eclipse**.

→ look at Word Web: **eclipse**

lun|ar mod|ule /lunər mɒdʒul/ (**lunar modules**) **N-COUNT** SCIENCE A **lunar module** is a part of a spacecraft that is designed to separate from the rest of the spacecraft and land on the moon.

lunch /lʌntʃ/ (**lunches**) **N-COUNT/N-NONCOUNT** **Lunch** is the meal that you have in the middle of the day. ❏ *Are you free for lunch?* ❏ *Dad doesn't enjoy business lunches.*

→ look at Word Web: **meal**

Word Partnership	Use lunch with :
V	bring *your* lunch, break for lunch, buy *someone* lunch, eat lunch, go *somewhere* for lunch, go to lunch, have lunch, pack a lunch, serve lunch
ADJ	free lunch, good lunch, hot lunch, late lunch

lunch|room /lʌntʃrum/ (**lunchrooms**) **N-COUNT** A **lunchroom** is the room in a school or at work where you buy or eat your lunch.

lunch|time /lʌntʃtaɪm/ (**lunchtimes**) **N-COUNT/N-NONCOUNT** **Lunchtime** is the time of the day when people have their lunch. ❏ *Could we meet at lunchtime?*

lung /lʌŋ/ (**lungs**) **N-COUNT** SCIENCE Your **lungs** are the two large organs inside your chest that you use for breathing. ❏ *Her father died of lung cancer last year.* [from Old English]

→ look at Word Webs: **amphibian, cardiovascular system, donor, respiratory system**

L

lure /lʊər/ (**lures, luring, lured**)
■ **v-t** To **lure** someone means to trick them into a particular place or to trick them into doing something that they should not do. ❑ *They lured him into a trap.*
■ **n-count** A **lure** is an attractive quality that something has, or something that you find attractive. ❑ *The lure of country life is as strong as ever.* [from Old French]

lush /lʌʃ/ (**lusher, lushest**) **ADJ** Lush fields or gardens have a lot of very healthy grass or plants. ❑ *The lawn was lush and green.* [from Old French]

lus|ter /lʌstər/ **n-noncount** Luster is gentle shining light that is reflected from a surface, for example from polished metal. [from Old French]

lus|trous /lʌstrəs/ **ADJ** Something that is **lustrous** shines brightly and gently, because it has a smooth or shiny surface. ❑ *...a head of thick, lustrous, wavy brown hair.* [from Old French]

luxu|ri|ous /lʌgʒʊəriəs/ **ADJ** If something is **luxurious**, it is very comfortable and expensive. ❑ *My aunt and uncle stayed in a luxurious hotel in Paris.* [from Old French]

luxu|ry /lʌkʃəri, lʌgʒə-/ (**luxuries**)
■ **n-noncount** Luxury is a way of living when you are able to buy all the beautiful and expensive things that you want.
❑ *He leads a life of luxury.*
■ **n-count** A **luxury** is something pleasant and expensive that people want but do not really need. ❑ *Having a vacation is a luxury they can no longer afford.*
■ **n-sing** A **luxury** is a pleasure that you do not often have the opportunity to enjoy. ❑ *Hot baths are my favorite luxury.* [from Old French]

Thesaurus	luxury Also look up :
N	comfort, splendor ■
	extra, nonessential, treat ■ ■

ly|ing /laɪɪŋ/ **Lying** is the present participle of **lie**. [from Old English]

lymph /lɪmf/ **n-noncount** SCIENCE **Lymph** is a liquid that flows through your body and contains cells that help your body to fight infection. [from Latin]

lym|phat|ic sys|tem /lɪmfætɪk sɪstəm/ (**lymphatic systems**) **n-count** SCIENCE The **lymphatic system** is the network of tissues and organs in your body that produces white blood cells and carries lymph.

lym|phat|ic ves|sel /lɪmfætɪk vɛsəl/ (**lymphatic vessels**) **n-count** SCIENCE **Lymphatic vessels** are thin tubes that carry lymph through your body.

lymph ca|pil|lary (**lymph capillaries**) **n-count** SCIENCE **Lymph capillaries** are tiny tubes that join together to form lymphatic vessels.

lymph node /lɪmf noʊd/ (**lymph nodes**) **n-count** SCIENCE **Lymph nodes** are small bean-shaped masses of tissue that help to protect the body against infection by killing bacteria.

lym|pho|cyte /lɪmfəsaɪt/ (**lymphocytes**) **n-count** SCIENCE **Lymphocytes** are white blood cells that are involved in fighting infection and disease. [from Latin]

lynch /lɪntʃ/ (**lynches, lynching, lynched**) **v-t** If an angry crowd of people **lynch** someone, they kill that person by hanging them, without letting them have a trial, because they believe that that person has committed a crime. ❑ *They broke into his house and threatened to lynch him.* [from Virginia]

lyr|ic /lɪrɪk/ (**lyrics**)
■ **n-plural** MUSIC The **lyrics** of a song are its words. ❑ *The music is great, and the lyrics are so funny.*
■ **ADJ** LANGUAGE ARTS **Lyric** poetry is written in a simple and direct style, and usually expresses personal emotions such as love. [from Latin]

lyso|some /laɪsəsoʊm/ (**lysosomes**) **n-count** SCIENCE A **lysosome** is a part of a cell that contains enzymes that can break down many different substances. [from Greek]

Mm

ma'am /mæm/ People sometimes say **ma'am** as a polite way of talking to a woman. ❑ *Would you repeat that please, ma'am?*

ma|chine /məʃin/ (**machines**)
■ **N-COUNT** A **machine** is a piece of equipment that uses electricity or an engine to do a particular job. ❑ *I put the coin in the coffee machine.*
■ **N-COUNT** A **machine** is a computer. ❑ *If there's any programming I'll come home and do it on my machine.* [from French]
→ look at Word Web: **dairy**

Thesaurus	machine Also look up :
N	appliance, computer, gadget, mechanism ■

Word Partnership	Use machine with :
N	**copy** machine, machine **oil**, machine **parts**, machine **shop** ■
V	**design a** machine, **invent a** machine, **use a** machine ■
ADJ	**heavy** machine, **new** machine, machine **washable** ■

ma|chine gun (**machine guns**) **N-COUNT** A **machine gun** is a gun that shoots a lot of bullets very quickly. ❑ *Attackers fired machine guns at the car.*

ma|chin|ery /məʃinəri/ **N-NONCOUNT** **Machinery** means large pieces of electrical equipment that do a particular job. ❑ *We need to invest in new machinery for our factories.* [from French]

macro|cosm /mækrəkɒzəm/ **N-SING** A **macrocosm** is a complex organized system such as the universe or a society, considered as a single unit. [FORMAL] ❑ *The macrocosm of the universe is mirrored in the microcosm of the mind.* [from French]

macro|eco|nom|ics /mækroʊɛkənɒmɪks, -ɪk-/ also **macro-economics** **N-NONCOUNT** SOCIAL STUDIES **Macroeconomics** is the branch of economics that is concerned with the major, general features of a country's economy, such as the level of inflation, employment, or interest rates. ❑ *He teaches macroeconomics.* ● **macro|eco|nom|ic** **ADJ** ❑ *The goal of macroeconomic policy is a growing economy.*

mad /mæd/ (**madder, maddest**)
■ **ADJ** If someone is **mad**, they are very angry. [INFORMAL] ❑ *You're just mad at me because I'm late.*
■ **ADJ** Someone who is **mad** has a medical condition that makes them behave in a strange way. [INFORMAL] ❑ *She was afraid of going mad.*
■ **ADJ** If you are **mad about** someone, you like them very much. [INFORMAL] ❑ *He's mad about you.*
■ **ADJ** **Mad** behavior is not controlled. ❑ *There was a mad rush to get out of the building.*
■ **PHRASE** If you do something **like mad**, you do it with energy and enthusiasm. [INFORMAL] ❑ *He was training for the competition like mad.* [from Old English]

Thesaurus	mad Also look up :
ADJ	angry, furious ■ deranged, insane ■ crazy ■

mad|am /mædəm/ also **Madam**
■ **Madam** is a polite way of talking to a woman. ❑ *Good morning, madam.*
■ **PHRASE** You write **Dear Madam** at the beginning of a formal letter or a business letter when you are writing to a woman. ❑ *Dear Madam, Thank you for your letter.* [from Old French]

made /meɪd/
■ **Made** is the past tense and past participle of **make**.
■ **ADJ** If something is **made of** a particular substance, that substance was used to make it. ❑ *The top of the table is made of glass.* [from Old English]

mad|ly /mædli/
■ **ADV** You can use **madly** to show that one person loves another person very much. ❑ *She is madly in love with him.*

2 ADV If you do something **madly**, you do it in an uncontrolled way. ❑ *People on the streets were waving madly.* [from Old English]

Ma|fia /mɑfiə/ (**Mafias**) also mafia
1 N-PROPER The **Mafia** is a criminal organization that makes money illegally, especially by threatening people and dealing in drugs. ❑ *Italian television does not ignore the Mafia.*
2 N-COUNT You can use **mafia** to refer to an organized group of people who you disapprove of because they use unfair or illegal means in order to get what they want. ❑ *I will not let the fashion mafia tell me what to wear.* [from Sicilian]

maf|ic /mæfɪk/ ADJ SCIENCE **Mafic** rocks are igneous rocks that contain a lot of heavier elements such as iron. Compare with **felsic**.

maga|zine /mægəzin, -zin/ (**magazines**)
N-COUNT A **magazine** is a thin book with stories and pictures that you can buy every week or every month. ❑ *...a fashion magazine.* [from French]
→ look at Word Web: **library**

mag|got /mægət/ (**maggots**) N-COUNT **Maggots** are creatures that look like very small worms and turn into flies. [from Old Norse]

mag|ic /mædʒɪk/
1 N-NONCOUNT **Magic** is a special power that seems to make impossible things happen. ❑ *Most children believe in magic.*
2 ADJ You use **magic** to describe something that appears to do things by magic. ❑ *...the magic ingredient in the face cream that keeps your skin looking smooth.*
3 N-NONCOUNT **Magic** is tricks that a person performs in order to entertain people. ❑ *His stage act combines magic, music, and humor.*
4 ADJ **Magic** is also an adjective. ❑ *He loves performing magic tricks.*

5 N-NONCOUNT The **magic of** something is a special quality that makes it seem wonderful and exciting. ❑ *Children love the magic of the movies.*
6 ADJ **Magic** is also an adjective. ❑ *We had some magic moments together.* [from Old French]

Thesaurus	magic Also look up :
N	enchantment, illusion, sorcery, witchcraft **1**
	appeal, beauty, charm **6**

magi|cal /mædʒɪkəl/
1 ADJ Something that is **magical** seems to use magic. ❑ *I loved the story of a little boy who has magical powers.*
2 ADJ You can say that a place or an object is **magical** when it has a special quality that makes it seem wonderful and exciting. ❑ *Bermuda is a magical place to get married.* [from Old French]

ma|gi|cian /mədʒɪʃən/ (**magicians**) N-COUNT A **magician** is a person who entertains people by doing magic tricks. [from Old French]

mag|net /mægnɪt/ (**magnets**) N-COUNT SCIENCE A **magnet** is a piece of special metal that attracts iron toward it. ❑ *The children used a magnet to find objects made of iron.* [from Latin]
→ look at Word Web: **magnet**

mag|net|ic /mægnɛtɪk/
1 ADJ SCIENCE If something is **magnetic**, it acts like a magnet. ❑ *Because steel is made from iron, it is magnetic.*
2 ADJ TECHNOLOGY **Magnetic** describes objects that use a magnetic substance to hold information that can be read by computers. ❑ *The bank sent him an ID card with a magnetic strip.* [from Latin]

mag|net|ic dec|li|na|tion /mægnɛtɪk dɛklɪneɪʃən/ (**magnetic declinations**)

m

Word Web magnet

Magnets have a north **pole** and a south pole. One side has a **negative charge** and the other side has a **positive** charge. The negative side of a magnet **attracts** the positive side of another magnet. Two sides that have the same charge will **repel** each other. The earth itself is a huge magnet, with a North Pole and a South Pole. A **compass** uses a **magnetized** needle to indicate direction. The "north" end of the needle always points toward the earth's North Pole.

N-COUNT/N-NONCOUNT SCIENCE **Magnetic declination** is the angle between the magnetic North Pole of the Earth and the geographic North Pole.

mag|net|ic field (**magnetic fields**) **N-COUNT** SCIENCE A **magnetic field** is an area around a magnet, or something functioning as a magnet, in which the magnet's power to attract things is felt.

mag|net|ic pole (**magnetic poles**) **N-COUNT** SCIENCE The **magnetic poles** of a magnet are the two areas at opposite ends of the magnet where the magnetic field is strongest. The **magnetic poles** of the Earth are the two areas near the North and South Poles where the Earth's magnetic field is strongest.

mag|net|ic re|ver|sal /mægnɛtɪk rɪvɜrsᵊl/ (**magnetic reversals**) **N-COUNT/N-NONCOUNT** SCIENCE **Magnetic reversal** is the process that causes the Earth's magnetic North Pole and its magnetic South Pole to reverse their positions.

mag|net|ism /mægnɪtɪzəm/ **N-NONCOUNT** SCIENCE **Magnetism** is the natural power of some objects and substances, especially iron, to attract other objects toward them. ❑ ...his research in electricity and magnetism.

mag|nifi|cent /mægnɪfɪsənt/ **ADJ** Something or someone that is **magnificent** is extremely good or beautiful. ❑ They bought a magnificent country house. [from Latin]

mag|ni|fy /mægnɪfaɪ/ (**magnifies, magnifying, magnified**) **V-T** If you **magnify** something, you make it look larger than it really is. ❑ This telescope magnifies objects 11 times. [from Old French]

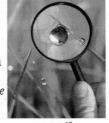

magnify

mag|ni|tude /mægnɪtud/ (**magnitudes**)
1 **N-NONCOUNT** The **magnitude** of something is its great size, scale, or importance. ❑ An operation of this magnitude is going to be difficult.
2 **N-COUNT** A star's **magnitude** is its brightness. [from Latin]
3 → see also **absolute magnitude, apparent magnitude**

maid /meɪd/ (**maids**) **N-COUNT** A **maid** is a woman whose job is to clean rooms in a hotel or a private house. ❑ A maid comes every morning to clean the hotel room.

mail /meɪl/ (**mails, mailing, mailed**)
1 **N-SING** The **mail** is the system that you use for sending and receiving letters and packages. ❑ Your check is in the mail.
2 **N-NONCOUNT** **Mail** is the letters and packages or email that you receive. ❑ There was no mail this morning.
3 **V-T** If you **mail** something to someone, you send it to them by mail. ❑ He mailed the information to a French newspaper. ❑ He mailed me the contract.
4 **N-NONCOUNT** **Mail** is the same as **email**. ❑ With web-based email, you can check your mail from anywhere. [from Old French]

Word Partnership	Use **mail** with :
PREP	**by** mail, **in the** mail, **through the** mail **1**
N	mail **carrier, fan** mail **2**
V	**deliver** mail, **get** mail, **open** mail, **read** mail, **receive** mail, **send** mail **2**

mail|box /meɪlbɒks/ (**mailboxes**)
1 **N-COUNT** A **mailbox** is a box outside your home where your letters are delivered. ❑ The next day there was a letter in her mailbox.
2 **N-COUNT** A **mailbox** is a box in a public place where you put letters that you want to send. ❑ He dropped the letters into the mailbox.
3 **N-COUNT** TECHNOLOGY On a computer, your **mailbox** is the file where your email is stored. ❑ There were 30 new messages in his mailbox.

mail car|ri|er /meɪl kæriər/ (**mail carriers**) **N-COUNT** A **mail carrier** is a person whose job is to collect and deliver letters and packages that you send by mail.

mail|man /meɪlmæn/ (**mailmen**) **N-COUNT** A **mailman** is a man who is a mail carrier.

mail or|der **N-NONCOUNT** **Mail order** is a system of buying goods, in which you order things from a website or a catalog, and the company sends them to you by mail. ❑ The toys are available by mail order.

main /meɪn/ **ADJ** The **main** thing is the most important one of several similar things. ❑ The main reason I came today was to say sorry. [from Old English]

Thesaurus	**main** Also look up :
ADJ	chief, major, primary, principal

M

main clause (main clauses) **N-COUNT**
LANGUAGE ARTS A **main clause** is a part of
a sentence that can stand alone as a
complete sentence.

main idea (main ideas) **N-COUNT**
LANGUAGE ARTS The **main idea** of a piece of
writing is the most important subject or
point of view that it discusses or expresses.

main|land /meɪnlænd/ **N-SING** You can use
the mainland to talk about the largest piece
of land in a country, not including any
smaller islands. ❑ *The island's teenagers go to
school on the mainland.*

main|ly /meɪnli/ **ADV** You use **mainly** to say
that a statement is mostly true. ❑ *The African
people living here are mainly from Senegal.*
[from Old English]

main-se|quence star (main-sequence
stars) **N-COUNT** SCIENCE A **main-sequence
star** is the most common type of star, which
gets its energy by converting hydrogen into
helium.

main|stream /meɪnstrim/ **N-SING** People,
activities, or ideas that are part of the
mainstream are regarded as typical, normal,
and conventional. ❑ *Some people like to live
outside the mainstream.*
→ look at Word Web: **culture**

main|tain /meɪnteɪn/ (maintains,
maintaining, maintained)
1 **V-T** If you **maintain** something, you make
it continue at the same level. ❑ *The army is
trying to maintain order in the country.* ❑ *She
maintained her weight at 150 pounds.*
2 **V-T** If you **maintain** a road, a building,
a vehicle, or a machine, you keep it in good
condition. ❑ *The house costs a lot to maintain.*
[from Old French]

Thesaurus	maintain	Also look up :
v	carry on, continue; *(ant.)* neglect **1**
	keep up, look after, protect, repair **2**

main|te|nance /meɪntɪnəns/ **N-NONCOUNT**
The **maintenance** of something is the
process of keeping it in good condition.
❑ *Maintenance work on the building starts next
week.* [from Old French]

ma|jes|tic /mədʒɛstɪk/ **ADJ** If something or
someone is **majestic**, they are very beautiful
and grand. ❑ *We will miss the majestic mountains
and the emerald green ocean.* [from Old French]

maj|es|ty /mædʒɪsti/ (majesties)
1 **PHRASE** People use **Your Majesty** when
they are talking to a king or a queen, or **Her
Majesty** or **His Majesty** when they are
talking about a king or a queen. ❑ *His Majesty
would like to see you now.*
2 **N-NONCOUNT** **Majesty** is the quality of being
beautiful and grand. ❑ *The poem describes the
majesty of the mountains.* [from Old French]

Word Link	*major* ≈ *larger* : *major, major*
	leagues, *majority*

ma|jor /meɪdʒər/ (majors, majoring, majored)
1 **ADJ** **Major** describes something that is
more important than other things.
❑ *Homelessness is a major problem in some cities.*
2 **N-COUNT** At a university or a college, a
student's **major** is the main subject that
they are studying. ❑ *"What's your major?"—
"Chemistry."*
3 **V-I** If a student at a university or a college
majors in a particular subject, that subject is
the main one they study. ❑ *He majored in
finance at Claremont College.*
4 **N-COUNT** A **major** is an officer of high
rank in the army. ❑ *...Major Wayne Rollings.*
5 **ADJ** MUSIC In music, **major** is used for
talking about a scale with half steps in
sound between the third and fourth and the
seventh and eighth notes. Compare with
minor. ❑ *A C major scale uses only the white keys
on a piano.* [from Latin]

Thesaurus	major	Also look up :
ADJ	chief, critical, crucial, key, main,
	principal; *(ant.)* little, minor,
	unimportant **1**

ma|jor|ity /mədʒɔrɪti/ **N-SING** The **majority**
of people or things in a group is more than
half of them. ❑ *The majority of my patients are
women.* [from Medieval Latin]

Word Partnership	Use majority with :
ADJ	**overwhelming** majority, **vast** majority
N	majority **of people**, majority **of the**
	population, majority **leader**

ma|jor key (major keys) **N-COUNT** MUSIC
In music, the **major key** is based on the
major scale, in which the third note is two
tones higher than the first.

ma|jor leagues **N-PLURAL** SPORTS The **major
leagues** are groups of top baseball teams
that play against each other. ❑ *At 47, he was
the oldest player in the major leagues last season.*

m

make

➊ CREATING OR PRODUCING
➋ CAUSING OR CHANGING
➌ LINK VERB, PHRASE, AND
    PHRASAL VERBS

➊ make /meɪk/ (**makes, making, made**)

1 **V-T** If you **make** something, you produce it, build it, or create it. ❏ *She makes all her own clothes.* ❏ *All our furniture is made from solid wood.*

2 **V-T** If you **make** a note or a list, you write something down in that form. ❏ *Mr. Perry made a note in his book.*

3 **V-T** If you **make** money, you earn it. ❏ *He's good-looking, smart, and makes lots of money.*

4 **N-COUNT** The **make** of something is the name of the company that made it. ❏ *What make of car do you drive?*

5 **V-T** You can use **make** with nouns to show that someone does or says something. ❏ *I'd just like to make a comment.* ❏ *I made a few phone calls.* [from Old English]

6 → see also **made, making**
→ look at Usage note at **cook**

➋ make /meɪk/ (**makes, making, made**)

1 **V-T** If something **makes** you do or feel something, it causes you to do or feel it. ❏ *The smoke made him cough.* ❏ *My boss's behavior makes me so angry!*

2 **V-T** If you **make** someone do something, you force them to do it. ❏ *Mom made me apologize to him.*

3 **V-T Make** means to cause someone or something to be a particular thing or to have a particular quality. ❏ *She made life very difficult for me.*

4 **V-T** If you **make** something **into** something else, you change it. ❏ *They made their apartment into a beautiful home.* [from Old English]

➌ make /meɪk/ (**makes, making, made**)

1 **V-LINK** You can use **make** to say what two numbers add up to. ❏ *Four twos make eight.*

2 **PHRASE** If you **make it**, you achieve something difficult or survive through a difficult period. ❏ *I believe I have the talent to make it.* [from Old English]

▸ **make of** If you ask a person what they **make of** something, you want to know what their impression, opinion, or understanding of it is. ❏ *Nancy wasn't sure what to make of Mick's apology.*

▸ **make out** If you **make** something **out**, you can see, hear or understand it. ❏ *I could just make out a tall figure of a man.* ❏ *I couldn't make out what he was saying.*

▸ **make up 1** If you **make up** a story or an excuse, you invent it. ❏ *It was all lies. I made it all up.*

2 If two people **make up** after an argument, they become friends again. ❏ *You two are always fighting and then making up again.*

mak|er /meɪkər/ (**makers**) **N-COUNT** The **maker** of something is the person or company that makes it. ❏ *Japan's two largest car makers reported increased sales last month.* [from Old English]

make|up /meɪkʌp/ **N-NONCOUNT Makeup** is the creams and powder that people put on their face to make themselves look more attractive. Actors also wear makeup. ❏ *She doesn't usually wear much makeup.*
→ look at Word Webs: **makeup, theater**

mak|ing /meɪkɪŋ/ (**makings**)

1 **N-NONCOUNT** The **making** of something is the act or process of producing or creating it. ❏ *...Salomon's book about the making of the movie.*

2 → see also **make**

The women of ancient Egypt were among the first to **wear makeup.** They **applied** kohl as **eye shadow** to darken their eyelids. Greek women used charcoal as an **eyeliner** and **rouge** on their cheeks. In 14th century Europe, the most popular **cosmetic** was a **powder** made from wheat flour. Women whitened their faces to show their high social class. A light **complexion** meant the woman didn't have to work outdoors. **Cosmetics** containing poisons, such as lead and arsenic, sometimes caused illness and death. Makeup use grew in the early 1900s. For the first time many women could afford to buy mass-produced **lipstick, mascara,** and **face powder.**

M

3 **PHRASE** If you describe a person or a thing as something **in the making,** you mean that they are going to become known or recognized as that thing. ❑ *Her drama teacher thinks Julie is a star in the making.*

4 **PHRASE** If something **is the making of** a person or a thing, it is the reason that they become successful or become very much better than they used to be. ❑ *This new school might be the making of him.*

5 **PHRASE** If you say that a person or a thing **has the makings of** something, you mean it seems possible or likely that they will become that thing, as they have the necessary qualities. ❑ *Godfrey had the makings of a successful journalist.*

6 **PHRASE** If you say that something such as a problem you have is **of** your **own making,** you mean you have caused or created it yourself. ❑ *Some of his problems are of his own making.* [from Old English]

Word Link mal ≈ bad : ma**lar**ia, ma**lign**, ma**lware**

---

ma|lar|ia /məlɛəriə/ **N-NONCOUNT** Malaria is a serious disease that mosquitoes carry. [from Italian]

male /meɪl/ (**males**)
1 **N-COUNT** SCIENCE A **male** is a person or an animal that belongs to the sex that does not have babies. ❑ *Two 17-year-old males were arrested at their high school on Tuesday.*

2 **ADJ** SCIENCE **Male** is also an adjective. ❑ *She reported the unacceptable behavior of her male colleagues.* ❑ *Two male cats were fighting in the street.*

3 **ADJ** **Male** means relating to men rather than women. ❑ *The rate of male unemployment has gone up.* [from Old French]
→ look at Word Web: **reproduction**

ma|li|cious /məlɪʃəs/ **ADJ** Malicious words or actions are intended to harm people or their reputation, or to embarrass or upset them. ❑ *They have been spreading malicious lies about us.* [from Old French]

ma|lign /məlaɪn/ (**maligns, maligning, maligned**) [from Old French]
1 **V-T** If you **malign** someone, you say unpleasant and often untrue things about them. [FORMAL] ❑ *"We have been unfairly maligned," he declared.*

2 **ADJ** A **malign** influence or intention causes harm. [FORMAL] ❑ *...the malign influence that jealousy had on their lives.*

mall /mɔl/ (**malls**) **N-COUNT** A **mall** is a large shopping area. [after The Mall in St. James's Park, London, England]

mal|le|able /mæliəbᵊl/
1 **ADJ** Someone who is **malleable** is easily influenced or controlled by other people. [WRITTEN] ❑ *She was young enough to be malleable.*

2 **ADJ** SCIENCE A substance that is **malleable** is soft and can easily be made into different shapes. ❑ *Silver is the most malleable of all metals.* ● **mal|le|abil|ity** /mæliəbɪliti/ **N-NONCOUNT** ❑ *Red-hot metals rapidly lose their malleability as they cool.* [from Old French]
→ look at Word Web: **metal**

mal|ware /mælwɛər/ **N-NONCOUNT** TECHNOLOGY **Malware** is a type of computer program that is designed to damage or disrupt a computer. ❑ *Hackers conceal malware in pop-up windows.*

mama /mɑmə, məmɑ/ (**mamas**) also **mamma** **N-COUNT** **Mama** means the same as **mother.** [INFORMAL]

mam|mal /mæmᵊl/ (**mammals**) **N-COUNT** SCIENCE **Mammals** are animals that feed their babies with milk. [from New Latin]
→ look at Word Webs: **mammal, bat, pet, whale**

Word Web **mammal**

Elephants, dogs, mice, and humans all belong to the class of animals called **mammals.** Mammals have live babies rather than laying eggs. The females also feed their **young** with milk from their bodies. Mammals are **warm-blooded** and usually have hair on their bodies. Some, such as the brown bear and the raccoon, are omnivorous—they eat meat and plants. Deer and zebras are herbivorous, living mostly on grass and leaves. Lions and tigers are carnivorous—they eat meat. They must have a supply of large **game** to survive.

m

mam|ma|ry /mǽməri/ **ADJ** SCIENCE
Mammary means relating to the breasts.
[from Latin]

mam|ma|ry glands **N-PLURAL** SCIENCE
Mammary glands are milk-producing
glands in mammals.

man /mǽn/ (**men**)
1 **N-COUNT** A **man** is an adult male human.
□ *A handsome man walked into the room.* □ *Both
men and women will enjoy this movie.*
2 **N-COUNT/N-NONCOUNT** People sometimes
use **Man** and **men** to talk about all humans,
including both males and females. Some
people dislike this use, and prefer to say
human beings or **people**. □ *Man first arrived in
the Americas thousands of years ago.* [from Old
Norse]
→ look at Picture Dictionary: **age**

man|age /mǽnɪdʒ/ (**manages, managing,
managed**)
1 **V-T** If you **manage** a business, you control
it. □ *Two years after starting the job, he was
managing the store.*
2 **V-T** If you **manage to** do something,
especially something difficult, you succeed
in doing it. □ *Three girls managed to escape the
fire.* [from Italian]

Word Link	ment ≈ state, condition : agreement, management, movement

man|age|ment /mǽnɪdʒmənt/
(**managements**)
1 **N-NONCOUNT** **Management** is the control
of a business or another organization. □ *The
zoo needed better management, not more money.*
2 **N-COUNT/N-NONCOUNT** BUSINESS The
people who control a business or other
organization are the **management**.
□ *The management is trying hard to keep
employees happy.* [from Italian]

Word Partnership	Use management with :
N	business management, crisis management, management skills, management style, waste management 1 management team, management training 2
ADJ	new management, senior management 2

man|ag|er /mǽnɪdʒər/ (**managers**)
N-COUNT A **manager** is a person who
controls all or part of a business or an

organization. □ *Each department manager is
responsible for staff training.* [from Italian]
→ look at Word Web: **concert**

man|di|ble /mǽndɪbᵊl/ (**mandibles**)
N-COUNT SCIENCE A **mandible** is the bone in
the lower jaw of a person or animal. [from
Old French]

mane /méɪn/ (**manes**) **N-COUNT** The **mane**
on some animals is the long, thick hair
that grows from its neck. □ *You can wash the
horse's mane at the same time as its body.*
[from Old English]
→ look at Picture Dictionary: **horse**

ma|neu|ver /mənúːvər/ (**maneuvers,
maneuvering, maneuvered**)
1 **V-T** If you **maneuver** something into or
out of a difficult position, you skillfully
move it there. □ *He maneuvered the car through
the narrow gate.*
2 **N-COUNT/N-NONCOUNT** **Maneuver** is also
a noun. □ *The airplanes performed some difficult
maneuvers.* [from French]

man|go /mǽŋgoʊ/ (**mangoes** or **mangos**)
N-COUNT/N-NONCOUNT A **mango** is a large,
sweet, yellow or red fruit that grows on trees
in hot countries. [from Portuguese]

man|hood /mǽnhʊd/ **N-NONCOUNT**
Manhood is the state of being a man rather
than a boy. □ *Fathers must help their sons grow
from boyhood to manhood.* [from Old English]

Word Link	man ≈ hand : emancipate, manacle, manicure

mani|cure /mǽnɪkyʊər/ (**manicures,
manicuring, manicured**)
1 **V-T** If you **manicure** your hands or nails,
you care for them by rubbing cream into
your skin and cleaning and cutting your
nails. □ *She carefully manicured her long nails.*
2 **N-COUNT** **Manicure** is also a noun.
□ *I have an appointment for a manicure this
afternoon.* [from French]

mani|fest /mǽnɪfɛst/ (**manifests,
manifesting, manifested**)
1 **ADJ** If you say that something is **manifest**
you mean that it is clearly true and that
nobody would disagree with it if they saw it
or considered it. [FORMAL] □ *...the manifest
power of prayer.* ● **mani|fest|ly ADV** □ *It is
manifestly clear that she hates me.*
2 **V-T** If you **manifest** a particular quality,
feeling, or illness, or if it **manifests itself**, it
becomes visible or obvious. [FORMAL]

❏ *He manifested health problems when he was a child.* ❏ *The virus needs two weeks to manifest itself.*
3 ADJ Manifest is also an adjective. [FORMAL] ❏ *Fear is manifest everywhere.* [from Latin]

mani|fes|to /mænɪfɛstoʊ/ (**manifestos** or **manifestoes**) **N-COUNT** SOCIAL STUDIES A **manifesto** is a statement published by a person or a group of people, especially a political party or a government, in which they say what their aims and policies are. ❏ *The Republicans are preparing their election manifesto.* [from Italian]

ma|nipu|late /mənɪpyəleɪt/ (**manipulates, manipulating, manipulated**)
1 V-T If you **manipulate** people or events, you control them for your own benefit. ❏ *The government is trying to manipulate public opinion.*
2 V-T If you **manipulate** something that requires skill, you operate it or process it. ❏ *The technology uses a pen to manipulate a computer.* [from Latin]

Word Link	man ≈ human being : humane, mankind, woman

man|kind /mænkaɪnd/ **N-NONCOUNT** You can call all humans **mankind** when you are considering them as a group. Some people dislike this use. ❏ *We hope for a better future for all mankind.*

man|ly /mænli/ (**manlier, manliest**) **ADJ** If you describe a man's behavior or appearance as **manly**, you approve of it because it shows qualities that are considered typical of a man, such as strength or courage. ❏ *He had strong manly shoulders.* ● **man|li|ness N-NONCOUNT** ❏ *He has no doubts about his manliness.* [from Old English]

man-made also **manmade** **ADJ** **Man-made** things are made by people. ❏ *Some of the world's problems are man-made.* ❏ *When the dam was built, three man-made lakes were created.*

manned /mænd/ **ADJ** A **manned** vehicle has people in it who are operating its controls. ❏ *The United States have sent a manned spacecraft into space.* [from Old English]

man|ner /mænər/ (**manners**)
1 N-SING The **manner** in which you do something is the way that you do it. ❏ *She smiled in a friendly manner.*
2 N-SING Someone's **manner** is the way in which they behave and talk when they are with other people. ❏ *He has a very confident manner.*

3 N-PLURAL Your **manners** are how polite you are when you are with other people. ❏ *He dressed well and had perfect manners.* ❏ *Is it bad manners to talk on a cellphone on the train?* [from Norman French]

Word Partnership	Use **manner** with :
ADJ	**effective** manner, **efficient** manner **1** **abrasive** manner, **abrupt** manner, **appropriate** manner, **businesslike** manner, **different** manner, **friendly** manner, **usual** manner **1 2**

man|sion /mænʃn/ (**mansions**) **N-COUNT** A **mansion** is a very large, expensive house. ❏ *He bought an eighteenth-century mansion in New Hampshire.* [from Old French]

man|tle /mæntᵊl/ **N-SING** SCIENCE In geology, **the mantle** is the part of the Earth that lies between the crust and the core. It is divided into the upper mantle and the lower mantle. [from Old French]
→ look at Picture Dictionary: **core**

manu|al /mænyuəl/ (**manuals**)
1 ADJ Manual work is work in which you use your hands or your physical strength. ❏ *He began his career as a manual worker.*
2 ADJ Manual means operated by hand, rather than by electricity or a motor. ❏ *We used a manual pump to get the water out of the hole.*
3 N-COUNT A **manual** is a book that tells you how to do something. ❏ *He advised me to read the instruction manual first.* [from Old French]

manu|fac|ture /mænyəfæktʃər/ (**manufactures, manufacturing, manufactured**)
1 V-T BUSINESS To **manufacture** something means to make it in a factory. ❏ *The company manufactures plastics.*
2 N-NONCOUNT BUSINESS **Manufacture** is also a noun. ❏ *Coal is used in the manufacture of steel.* [from Late Latin]

manu|fac|tur|er /mænyəfæktʃərər/ (**manufacturers**) **N-COUNT** A **manufacturer** is a company that makes large amounts of things. ❏ *He works for the world's largest doll manufacturer.* [from Late Latin]
→ look at Word Web: **industry**

manu|fac|turing /mænyəfæktʃərɪŋ/ **N-NONCOUNT** **Manufacturing** is the business of making things in factories. ❏ *During the 1980s, 300,000 workers in the manufacturing industry lost their jobs.*

m

Word Link   *script ≈ writing : manu*script*,*
*post*script*, tran*script

manu|script /mǽnyəskrɪpt/ (**manuscripts**)
N-COUNT LANGUAGE ARTS A **manuscript** is a
handwritten or typed document, especially
a writer's first version of a book before it is
published. ❑ *He has seen a manuscript of the*
book. [from Medieval Latin]

many /mɛ́ni/
1 **DET** You use **many** to talk about a large
number of people or things. ❑ *Many people*
would disagree with that opinion. ❑ *Not many*
stores are open on Sunday.
2 **PRON** **Many** is also a pronoun. ❑ *He made a*
list of his friends. There weren't many. ❑ *Why do*
many of us feel that we need to get married?
3 **ADV** You use **many** when you are asking
or replying to questions about numbers of
things or people. ❑ *"How many of their songs*
were hits?"—"Not very many."
4 **DET** You use **many** after "how" to ask
questions about numbers or amounts.
❑ *How many years have you been here?* [from
Old English]

map /mǽp/ (**maps**)
1 **N-COUNT** GEOGRAPHY A **map** is a drawing
of a particular area such as a city or a
country, that shows things like mountains,
rivers, and roads. ❑ *The detailed map helps*
tourists find their way around the city.
2 **N-COUNT** GEOGRAPHY A **map** is a model or
a representation of the Earth's surface.
[from Medieval Latin]

Word Partnership   Use **map** with :

ADJ	**detailed** map
V	**draw a** map, **look at a** map, **open a** map, **read a** map

map key (**map keys**) **N-COUNT** SOCIAL STUDIES
A **map key** is a list that explains the
meaning of the symbols and abbreviations
used on a map.

ma|ple /mḗɪpəl/ (**maples**)
1 **N-COUNT/N-NONCOUNT** A **maple** or a
maple tree is a tree with leaves that turn
a bright red or gold color in the fall.
2 **N-NONCOUNT** **Maple** is the wood of this
tree. ❑ *Next to the sofa was a solid maple table.*
[from Old English]

ma|quette /mǽkɛt/ (**maquettes**) **N-COUNT**
ARTS A **maquette** is a small model of a
sculpture. Sculptors often use maquettes as

a preparation for a larger sculpture.
[from French]

mar /mɑ́r/ (**mars, marring, marred**) **V-T**
To **mar** something means to spoil or damage
it. ❑ *A number of problems marred the event.*
[from Old English]

mara|thon /mǽrəθɒn/ (**marathons**)
N-COUNT SPORTS A **marathon** is a race in
which people run a distance of 26 miles,
which is about 42 km. ❑ *He is running in his*
first marathon next weekend. [from Greek]

mar|ble /mɑ́rbəl/
1 **N-NONCOUNT** ARTS **Marble** is a type of very
hard rock that people use to make parts of
buildings or statues.
2 **N-NONCOUNT** **Marbles** is a children's
game that you play with small balls made
of colored glass (called marbles). ❑ *Two boys*
were playing marbles. [from Old French]

march /mɑ́rtʃ/ (**marches, marching,**
marched)
1 **V-T/V-I** When soldiers **march** somewhere,
or when a commanding officer **marches**
them somewhere, they walk there with
regular steps, as a group. ❑ *Some soldiers were*
marching down the street. ❑ *Captain Ramirez*
marched them off to the main camp.
2 **N-COUNT** **March** is also a noun. ❑ *After a*
short march, the soldiers entered the village.
3 **V-I** When a large group of people **march**,
they walk through the streets together in
order to show that they disagree with
something. ❑ *Thousands of people marched*
through the city to protest against the war.
4 **N-COUNT** **March** is also a noun.
❑ *Organizers expect 300,000 protesters to join*
the march.
5 **V-I** If someone **marches** somewhere, they
walk there quickly, often because they are
angry. ❑ *He marched into the kitchen without*
knocking. [from Old French]

March /mɑ́rtʃ/ (**Marches**)
N-COUNT/N-NONCOUNT **March** is the third
month of the year. ❑ *I flew to Milwaukee in*
March. [from Old French]

mare /mɛ́ər/ (**mares**) **N-COUNT** A **mare** is an
adult female horse. [from Old English]

mar|ga|rine /mɑ́rdʒərɪn/ **N-NONCOUNT**
Margarine is a yellow substance that is
made from vegetable oil, and is similar
to butter.

mar|gin /mɑrdʒɪn/ (**margins**)

1 **N-COUNT** A **margin** is the difference between two amounts. ❑ *The team won with a 5-point margin.*

2 **N-COUNT** The **margin** of a page is the empty space down the side. ❑ *She wrote comments in the margin.* [from Latin]

Word Partnership	Use **margin** with :
ADJ	**comfortable** margin, **large** margin, **slim** margin **1**
	narrow margin, **wide** margin **1** **2**

mar|gin|al /mɑrdʒɪnᵊl/ **ADJ** If you describe something as **marginal**, you mean that it is small or not very important. ❑ *This is a marginal improvement.* ● **mar|gin|al|ly** /mɑrdʒɪnᵊli/ **ADV** ❑ *Sales last year were marginally higher.* [from Latin]

ma|rine /mərin/ (**marines**)

1 **N-COUNT/N-PROPER** A **marine** is a soldier who is specially trained to fight at sea as well as on land. ❑ *A few Marines were wounded.*

2 **ADJ** **Marine** describes things relating to the ocean. ❑ *The film shows the colorful marine life in the Indian Ocean.* [from Old French] → look at Word Web: **ship**

mari|tal /mærɪtᵊl/ **ADJ** **Marital** means relating to marriage. ❑ *When I was thirteen, my parents started having marital problems.* [from Latin]

mark /mɑrk/ (**marks, marking, marked**)

1 **N-COUNT** A **mark** is a small area of dirt that has accidentally gotten onto a surface or a piece of clothing. ❑ *There was a red paint mark on the wall.*

2 **V-T/V-I** If something **marks** a surface, or if the surface **marks**, the surface is damaged by marks or a mark. ❑ *His shoes marked the carpet.*

3 **N-COUNT** A **mark** is a written or printed symbol. ❑ *...a question mark.*

4 **V-T** If you **mark** something with a particular word, you write that word on it. ❑ *She marked the bill "paid."*

5 **N-COUNT** A **mark** is a number or a letter that indicates how good a student's work is. ❑ *I do all my homework and I get good marks at school.*

6 **V-T** When a teacher **marks** a student's work, the teacher writes a number or a letter on it to show how good it is. ❑ *The teacher was marking essays after class.*

7 **V-T** If something **marks** a place, it shows where a particular thing is. ❑ *A big hole in the road marks the place where the bomb landed.*

8 **V-T** An event that **marks** a particular stage is a sign that something different is about to happen. ❑ *The announcement marks the end of an extraordinary period in European history.* [from Old English]

9 → see also **punctuation mark, question mark**

marked /mɑrkt/ **ADJ** A **marked** change or difference is very obvious and easily noticed. ❑ *There has been a marked increase in traffic on the roads.* ● **mark|ed|ly** /mɑrkɪdli/ **ADV** ❑ *The movie is markedly different from the play.* [from Old English]

mar|ket /mɑrkɪt/ (**markets, marketing, marketed**)

1 **N-COUNT** A **market** is a place where people buy and sell products. ❑ *They usually buy their fruit and vegetables at the market.*

2 **N-COUNT** BUSINESS The **market** for a particular product is the people who want to buy it or the area of the world where it is sold. ❑ *The market for organic wines is growing.*

3 **V-T** BUSINESS If you **market** a product you advertise it and sell it. ❑ *The products were marketed under a different brand name in Europe.*

● **mar|ket|ing** **N-NONCOUNT** ❑ *She works in the marketing department of a large company.*

4 **PHRASE** BUSINESS If something is **on the market**, it is available for people to buy. ❑ *There are many empty offices on the market.* [from Latin]

mar|ma|lade /mɑrməleɪd/ (**marmalades**) **N-COUNT/N-NONCOUNT** **Marmalade** is a food like jelly that is usually made from oranges. [from French]

Word Link	age ≈ state of, related to : courage, marriage, percentage

mar|riage /mærɪdʒ/ (**marriages**)

1 **N-COUNT** A **marriage** is the relationship between a husband and a wife. ❑ *In a good marriage, both husband and wife are happy.*

2 **N-COUNT/N-NONCOUNT** A **marriage** is the time when two people get married. ❑ *...a marriage ceremony.* [from Old French] → look at Word Webs: **love, wedding**

mar|ried /mærɪd/

1 **ADJ** If you are **married**, you have a husband or a wife. ❑ *We have been married for 14 years.* ❑ *She is married to an Englishman.*

2 **ADJ** **Married** means relating to marriage or to people who are married. ❑ *For the first*

m

ten years of our married life we lived in a farmhouse. [from Old French]

mar|ry /mæri/ (**marries, marrying, married**)
v-t/v-i When two people **get married** or **marry**, they legally become husband and wife in a special ceremony. ❑ *I thought he would change after we got married.* ❑ *They married a month after they met.* ❑ *He wants to marry her.* [from Old French]

Mars /mɑrz/ **N-PROPER** SCIENCE **Mars** is the fourth planet from the sun, between the Earth and Jupiter. [from Latin]

marsh /mɑrʃ/ (**marshes**)
N-COUNT/N-NONCOUNT SCIENCE A **marsh** is a soft, wet area of land. [from Old English]

mar|su|pial /mɑrsupiəl/ (**marsupials**)
N-COUNT SCIENCE A **marsupial** is an animal such as a kangaroo or an opossum. Female marsupials carry their babies in a pouch on their stomach.

mar|tial /mɑrʃ°l/ **ADJ Martial** is used to describe things relating to soldiers or war. [FORMAL] ❑ *...a martial court.* [from Latin]

mar|vel /mɑrv°l/ (**marvels, marveling** or **marvelling, marveled** or **marvelled**)
1 v-i If you **marvel** at something, you express your great surprise, wonder, or admiration. ❑ *Her friends marveled at her great energy.* ❑ *Sara and I read the story and marveled.*
2 N-COUNT You can describe something or someone as a **marvel** to indicate that you think that they are wonderful. ❑ *The whale is one of the marvels of nature.* [from Old French]

mar|vel|ous /mɑrvələs/ **ADJ** If someone or something is **marvelous**, they are very good. ❑ *It's a marvelous piece of music.* [from Old French]

Marx|ism /mɑrksɪzəm/ **N-NONCOUNT** SOCIAL STUDIES **Marxism** is a political philosophy based on the writings of Karl Marx and which stresses the importance of the struggle between different social classes. [after Karl Marx (1818-83), a German political philosopher]

Marx|ist /mɑrksɪst/ (**Marxists**)
1 ADJ SOCIAL STUDIES **Marxist** means based on Marxism or relating to Marxism. ❑ *...a Marxist state.*
2 N-COUNT SOCIAL STUDIES A **Marxist** is a person who believes in Marxism or who is a member of a Marxist party. ❑ *...a 78-year-old*

former Marxist. [after Karl Marx (1818-83), a German political philosopher]

mas|cu|line /mæskyəlɪn/
1 ADJ Masculine qualities are typical of men. ❑ *She has a deep, rather masculine voice.*
2 ADJ LANGUAGE ARTS In some languages, a **masculine** noun, pronoun, or adjective has a different form from other forms (such as "feminine" forms). Compare with **feminine**. [from French]

mash /mæʃ/ (**mashes, mashing, mashed**)
v-t If you **mash** food, you press it to make it soft. ❑ *Mash the bananas with a fork.* [from Old English]

mask /mæsk/ (**masks, masking, masked**)
1 N-COUNT A **mask** is something that you wear over your face to protect it or to hide it. ❑ *A man wearing a mask entered the restaurant at about 1:40 p.m. and took out a gun.* ❑ *Wear a mask to protect yourself from the smoke.*
2 v-t If you **mask** your true feelings,

mask

you do not show them in your behavior, so that people cannot know what you really feel. ❑ *She tried to mask her anger by laughing.* [from Italian]

masked /mæskt/ **ADJ** If someone is **masked**, they are wearing a mask. ❑ *Two masked men came through the doors carrying guns.* [from Italian]

mass /mæs/ (**masses**)
1 N-SING A **mass of** something is a large amount of it. ❑ *She had a mass of black hair.*
2 N-PLURAL Masses of something is a large amount of it. [INFORMAL] ❑ *I have masses of work to do.*
3 ADJ Mass describes something that involves or affects a very large number of people. ❑ *Mass unemployment is a big problem.*
4 N-PLURAL The masses are the ordinary people in society. ❑ *His music is aimed at the masses.*
5 N-NONCOUNT SCIENCE **Mass** is the amount of physical matter that something contains. ❑ *Pluto and Triton have nearly the same size, mass, and density.*
6 N-COUNT/N-NONCOUNT Mass is a Christian church ceremony, especially in

a Roman Catholic church. ❑ *She went to Mass each day.* [from Old French]
→ look at Word Web: **continents**

mas|sa|cre /mǽsəkər/ (**massacres, massacring, massacred**)

1 **N-COUNT/N-NONCOUNT** A massacre happens when a large number of people are killed at the same time in a violent and cruel way. ❑ *Her mother died in the massacre.*

2 **V-T** If people **are massacred**, a large number of them are killed in a violent and cruel way. ❑ *Three hundred people were massacred by the soldiers.* [from Old French]

mas|sage /məsɑ́ʒ/ (**massages, massaging, massaged**)

1 **N-COUNT/N-NONCOUNT** Massage is the activity of rubbing someone's body to make them relax or to reduce their pain. ❑ *Alex asked me if I wanted a massage.*

2 **V-T** If you **massage** a part of someone's body, you rub it in order to make them relax or reduce their pain. ❑ *She continued massaging her right foot.* [from French]

mass ex|tinc|tion (**mass extinctions**)
N-COUNT/N-NONCOUNT SCIENCE A mass extinction is a period of time when many different species of animals and plants become extinct.

mas|sive /mǽsɪv/ **ADJ** Something that is massive is very large. ❑ *They borrowed massive amounts of money.* [from French]

mass move|ment (**mass movements**)
N-COUNT/N-NONCOUNT SCIENCE In geology, mass movement is the downhill movement of rocks and soil as a result of gravity. Compare with **creep**.

mass num|ber (**mass numbers**) **N-COUNT/N-NONCOUNT** SCIENCE The mass number of a chemical element is the total number of protons and neutrons in the atomic nucleus of that element.

mass-pro|duce (**mass-produces, mass-producing, mass-produced**) **V-T** BUSINESS To **mass-produce** something means to make it in large amounts, usually by machine. ❑ *Most of the food we eat is mass-produced in large factories.* ● **mass-pro|duced** **ADJ** ❑ *It was cheaper to buy mass-produced food.*

mast /mǽst/ (**masts**) **N-COUNT** The masts of a boat are the tall poles that support its sails. [from Old English]

mas|ter /mǽstər/ (**masters, mastering, mastered**)

1 **N-COUNT** A person's or an animal's **master** is the man who controls that person or animal. ❑ *The dog was listening to its master's voice.*

2 **N-COUNT** If someone is a **master** of a particular activity, they are extremely skilled at it. ❑ *She was a master of the English language.*

3 **V-T** If you **master** something, you learn how to do it well. ❑ *David soon mastered the skills of baseball.* [from Old English]

Thesaurus	master Also look up :
N	owner; *(ant.)* servant, slave **1**
	artist, expert, professional **2**
V	learn, study, understand **3**

master|piece /mǽstərpis/ (**masterpieces**)
N-COUNT ARTS A **masterpiece** is an extremely good painting, novel, movie, or other work of art. ❑ *His book is a masterpiece.* [from Dutch]

mas|ter's de|gree (**master's degrees**)
N-COUNT A **master's degree** is a university qualification that is of a higher level than an ordinary degree.

mat /mǽt/ (**mats**)

1 **N-COUNT** A **mat** is a small piece of cloth, wood, or plastic that you put on a table to protect it. ❑ *...a set of red and white check place mats.*

2 **N-COUNT** A **mat** is a small piece of thick material that you put on the floor. ❑ *There was a letter on the doormat.* [from Old English]

match /mǽtʃ/ (**matches, matching, matched**)

1 **N-COUNT** A **match** is a small wooden or paper stick that produces a flame when you move it along a rough surface. ❑ *Kate lit a match and held it up to the candle.*

2 **N-COUNT** SPORTS A **match** is an organized game of tennis. ❑ *He was watching a tennis match.*

3 **V-T/V-I** If something **matches** another thing, or if they **match**, they have the same color or design, or they look good together. ❑ *Do these shoes match my dress?* ❑ *Your socks don't match.* ● **match|ing** **ADJ** ❑ *She wore a hat and a matching scarf.*

4 **V-T** If you **match** someone or something **to** another, you choose someone or something that goes together with the other person or thing. ❑ *They tried to match*

m

applicants to jobs. [Sense 1 from Old French. Senses 2 to 4 from Old English.]
→ look at Picture Dictionary: **answer**
→ look at Word Web: **fire**

Word Partnership	Use match with :
v	**strike a** match **1**
N	**boxing** match, **chess** match, **tennis** match, **wrestling** match **2**

mate /meɪt/ (**mates, mating, mated**)
1 **N-COUNT** SCIENCE An animal's **mate** is its sexual partner. ❑ *The male bird shows its brightly colored feathers to attract a mate.*
2 **V-T/V-I** SCIENCE When animals **mate**, a male and a female have sex in order to produce babies. ❑ *After mating, the female does not eat.* [from Middle Low German]
3 → see also **classmate, roommate**

ma|terial /mətɪəriəl/ (**materials**)
1 **N-COUNT/N-NONCOUNT** Material is cloth. ❑ *The thick material of her skirt was too warm for summer.*
2 **N-COUNT/N-NONCOUNT** A material is a solid substance. ❑ *...a material such as a metal.*
3 **N-PLURAL** Materials are the things that you need for a particular activity. ❑ *...building materials.* [from French]
→ look at Word Web: **industry**

Word Partnership	Use material with :
ADJ	**new** material, **original** material **1 2** **genetic** material, **hazardous** material **2** **raw** materials **3**

ma|ter|nal /mətɜrnᵊl/ **ADJ** **Maternal** describes feelings or actions that are typical of a mother toward her child. ❑ *No love is stronger than maternal love.* [from Medieval Latin]

ma|ter|nity /mətɜrnɪti/ **ADJ** **Maternity** is used to describe things relating to the help and medical care given to a woman when she is pregnant and when she gives birth. ❑ *Sam was born in the maternity hospital.* [from Medieval Latin]

math /mæθ/ **N-NONCOUNT** MATH **Math** is the same as **mathematics**. ❑ *He studied math in college.*
→ look at Word Web: **mathematics**

math|emati|cal /mæθəmætɪkᵊl/ **ADJ** MATH Something that is **mathematical** involves numbers and calculating. ❑ *He made some quick mathematical calculations.* [from Latin]
→ look at Word Web: **mathematics**

math|emat|ics /mæθəmætɪks/ **N-NONCOUNT** MATH **Mathematics** is the study of numbers, quantities, or shapes. ❑ *Dr. Lewis is a professor of mathematics at Boston College.* [from Latin]
→ look at Word Web: **mathematics**

mati|nee /mætᵊneɪ/ (**matinees**) **N-COUNT** A **matinee** is a performance of a play or a showing of a movie in the afternoon. [from French]

Word Link	arch ≈ rule : matriarch, monarch, patriarch

ma|tri|arch /meɪtriɑrk/ (**matriarchs**)
1 **N-COUNT** A **matriarch** is a woman who rules in a society in which power passes from mother to daughter. ❑ *She is described as the "charismatic matriarch of British politics."*
2 **N-COUNT** A **matriarch** is an old and powerful female member of a family, for example a grandmother. ❑ *She was a warm, smiling matriarch who ruled her domain by kindness.* [from Latin]

M

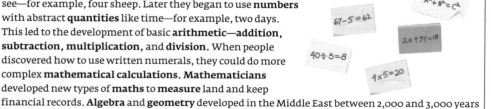

Word Web   mathematics

During prehistoric times people **counted** things they could see—for example, four sheep. Later they began to use **numbers** with abstract **quantities** like time—for example, two days. This led to the development of basic **arithmetic**—**addition**, **subtraction, multiplication,** and **division.** When people discovered how to use written numerals, they could do more complex **mathematical calculations. Mathematicians** developed new types of **maths** to **measure** land and keep financial records. **Algebra** and **geometry** developed in the Middle East between 2,000 and 3,000 years ago. Algebra uses letters to represent possible quantities. Geometry deals with the relationships among **lines, angles,** and **shapes.**

mat|ter /mǽtər/ (**matters, mattering, mattered**)

■ **N-COUNT** A **matter** is something that you must talk about or do. ❑ *She wanted to discuss a private matter with me.*

■ **N-PLURAL** You use **matters** to talk about a situation that someone is involved in. ❑ *If it would make matters easier, I will come to New York.*

■ **N-SING** You say **What's the matter?** when you think that someone has a problem and you want to know what it is. ❑ *Carol, what's the matter? You don't seem happy.*

■ **V-T/V-I** If you say that something does not **matter**, you mean that it is not important to you. ❑ *A lot of the food goes on the floor but that doesn't matter.* ❑ *It does not matter how long your essay is.*

■ **N-NONCOUNT** SCIENCE **Matter** is the physical part of the universe consisting of solids, liquids, and gases. ❑ *The universe is made up of matter and energy.*

■ **N-NONCOUNT Matter** is a type of substance. ❑ *There was a strong smell of rotting vegetable matter.*

■ **PHRASE** You use **no matter** in expressions such as **no matter how** and **no matter what** to say that something is true or happens in all situations. ❑ *Anyone can learn to swim, no matter what their age.* [from Latin]

→ look at Word Web: **matter**

mat|tress /mǽtrɪs/ (**mattresses**) **N-COUNT** On a bed, the **mattress** is the thick, soft part that you lie on. [from Old French]

→ look at Picture Dictionary: **bed**

ma|ture /mətyʊ́ər, -tʊ́ər, -tʃʊ́ər/ (**maturer, maturest, matures, maturing, matured**)

■ **V-I** When a child or a young animal **matures**, it becomes an adult. ❑ *The children will face many challenges as they mature into adulthood.*

■ **ADJ** A **mature** person or animal is fully grown.

■ **ADJ** If someone is **mature**, their behavior is responsible and sensible. ❑ *Fiona was mature for her age.* ● **ma|tur|ity N-NONCOUNT** ❑ *Her speech showed great maturity.*

■ **V-I** When something **matures**, it reaches a state of complete development. ❑ *When the trees matured they cut them down.* [from Latin]

max|im|ize /mǽksɪmaɪz/ (**maximizes, maximizing, maximized**) **V-T** If you **maximize** something, you make it as great in amount or importance as you can. ❑ *In order to maximize profit, the firm produces as many goods as possible.* [from Latin]

maxi|mum /mǽksɪməm/

■ **ADJ** You use **maximum** to describe the largest amount possible. ❑ *Today's maximum temperature in the city will be 80 degrees.*

■ **N-SING Maximum** is also a noun. ❑ *Brett faces a maximum of two years in prison.* [from Latin]

Thesaurus	**maximum** Also look up :
ADJ	biggest, greatest, highest, most; *(ant.)* lowest, minimum

Word Partnership	Use **maximum** with :
N	maximum **benefit**, maximum **charge**, maximum **efficiency**, maximum **fine**, maximum **flexibility**, maximum **height**, maximum **penalty**, maximum **rate**, maximum **sentence**, maximum **speed**

may /meɪ/

■ **MODAL** You use **may** to show that there is a possibility that something will happen or that something is true. ❑ *We may have some*

m

solid   liquid   gas

Matter exists in three states—**solid, liquid,** and **gas**. Changes in the state of matter happen frequently. For example, when a solid becomes hot enough, it **melts** and becomes a liquid. When a liquid is hot enough, it **evaporates** into a gas. The process also works the other way around. A gas which becomes very cool will **condense** into a liquid. And a liquid that is cooled enough will freeze and become a solid. Other changes in **state** are possible. Sublimation describes what happens when a solid, dry ice, turns directly into a gas, carbon dioxide. And did you know that glass is actually a liquid, not a solid?

rain today. ❑ *I may be back next year.*

2 **MODAL** You use **may** to say that someone is allowed to do something. ❑ *You may send a check or pay by credit card.* ❑ *May we come in?* [from Old English]
→ look at Usage note at **can**

May /meɪ/ (**Mays**) **N-COUNT/N-NONCOUNT**
May is the fifth month of the year. ❑ *We went on vacation in May.* [from Old French]

may|be /meɪbi/
1 **ADV** You use **maybe** when you are uncertain about something. ❑ *Maybe she is in love.* ❑ *I do think about having children, maybe when I'm 40.*
2 **ADV** You use **maybe** when you are making suggestions or giving advice. ❑ *Maybe we can go to the movies or something.* ❑ *Maybe you should see a doctor.*

> **Usage**   maybe
>
> *Maybe* is often confused with *may be. Maybe* is an adverb: *Maybe we'll be a little late. May be* is a verb form that means the same thing as *might be: We may be a little late.*

may|on|naise /meɪəneɪz/ **N-NONCOUNT**
Mayonnaise is a cold, thick sauce made from eggs and oil. [from French]

may|or /meɪər, mɛər/ (**mayors**) **N-COUNT**
SOCIAL STUDIES The **mayor** of a city or a town is the person who is responsible for its government. ❑ *The mayor of New York made a speech.* [from Old French]

maze /meɪz/ (**mazes**) **N-COUNT** A **maze** is a place that is difficult to find your way through. ❑ *Only the local people know their way through the town's maze of streets.*

me /mi, STRONG miː/ **PRON** A speaker uses **me** when talking about himself or herself. ❑ *He asked me to go to California with him.* [from Old English]

mead|ow /mɛdoʊ/ (**meadows**) **N-COUNT**
A **meadow** is a field that has grass and flowers growing in it. [from Old English]

meal /miːl/ (**meals**)
1 **N-COUNT** A **meal** is an occasion when people sit down and eat. ❑ *She sat next to him during the meal.*
2 **N-COUNT** A **meal** is the food you eat during a meal. ❑ *Logan finished his meal in silence.* [from Old English]
→ look at Word Web: **meal**

> **Thesaurus**   meal   Also look up :
>
> N   breakfast, dinner, lunch, supper **1**

> **Word Partnership**   Use **meal** with :
>
> V   **enjoy a** meal, **miss a** meal, **skip a** meal **1**
>   **cook a** meal, **eat a** meal, **have a** meal, **order a** meal, **prepare a** meal, **serve a** meal **2**
> ADJ   **big** meal, **delicious** meal, **good** meal, **hot** meal, **large** meal, **simple** meal, **well-balanced** meal **2**

> **mean**
> ❶ VERB USES
> ❷ ADJECTIVE USE
> ❸ NOUN USE

❶ **mean** /miːn/ (**means, meaning, meant**)
1 **V-T** If something **means** something, it has that meaning. ❑ *"Unable" means "not able."* ❑ *What does "software" mean?*
2 **V-T** If something **means** a lot **to** you, it is very important to you. ❑ *Be careful with the photos. They mean a lot to me.*
3 **V-T** If one thing **means** another, the second thing will happen because of the first thing. ❑ *The new factory means more jobs for people.*
4 **V-T** If you **mean** what you are saying, you

> **Word Web**   meal
>
> Customs for eating meals are very different around the world. In the Middle East, popular **breakfast** foods include pita bread, olives and white cheese. In China, favorite **fast food** breakfast items are steamed buns and fried breadsticks. The **continental breakfast** in Europe consists of bread, butter, jam, and a hot drink. In many places **lunch** is a light **meal**, like a **sandwich**. But in Germany, lunch is the main meal of the day. In most places, **dinner** is the name of the meal eaten in the evening. However, some people say they eat dinner at noon and **supper** at night.

M

are serious about it. ❑ *He said he loves her, and I think he meant it.*

5 **V-T** If someone **meant to** do something, they did it deliberately. ❑ *I'm so sorry. I didn't mean to hurt you.*

6 → see also **meaning, means, meant**

7 **PHRASE** You can use **I mean** when you are explaining or correcting something that you have just said. [SPOKEN] ❑ *It was English or Spanish—I mean French or Spanish.* [from Old English]

❷ **mean** /mi̱n/ (**meaner, meanest**) **ADJ** If someone is **mean,** they are unkind or cruel. ❑ *Don't be mean to your brother!* [from Old English]

Thesaurus	mean	Also look up :
V	aim, intend, plan ❶ **5**	
ADJ	nasty, unfriendly, unkind; *(ant.)* kind ❷	

❸ **mean** /mi̱n/ **N-SING** MATH In math, the **mean** is the amount that you get if you add a set of numbers together and divide them by the number of things that you originally added together. For example, the mean of 1, 3, 5, and 7 is 4 (1+3+5+7=16; 16÷4=4). [from Old French]

mean|ing /mi̱nɪŋ/ (**meanings**)

1 **N-COUNT/N-NONCOUNT** The **meaning** of a word or an expression is the idea that it represents. ❑ *Do you know the meaning of the words you're singing?*

2 **N-NONCOUNT** If an activity or an action has **meaning,** it has a good purpose. ❑ *Art has real meaning when it helps people to understand themselves.* [from Old English]

3 → see also **meaning** ❶

Word Partnership	Use meaning with :
N	meaning **of a term,** meaning **of a word** **1**
ADJ	**literal** meaning **1**
	deeper meaning, **new** meaning, **real** meaning, meaning **1** **2**
V	**explain the** meaning **of** *something,* **understand the** meaning **of** *something* **1** **2**

mean|ing|ful /mi̱nɪŋfəl/

1 **ADJ** If you describe something as **meaningful,** you mean that it is serious, important, or useful in some way. ❑ *He does meaningful work, working with children with AIDS.*
● **mean|ing|ful|ly** **ADV** ❑ *We need to talk meaningfully about these problems.*

2 **ADJ** A **meaningful** look or gesture is one

that is intended to express something, usually to a particular person. ❑ *She gave Jane a meaningful look.* ● **mean|ing|ful|ly** **ADV** ❑ *He glanced meaningfully at the other policeman.* [from Old English]

mean|ing|less /mi̱nɪŋlɪs/ **ADJ** Something that is **meaningless** has no meaning or purpose. ❑ *After her death, he felt that his life was meaningless.* [from Old English]

means /mi̱nz/

1 **N-COUNT** A **means** of doing something is a way to do it. **Means** is both the singular and the plural for this use. ❑ *He searched for a door or some other means of escape.* [from Old English]

2 → see also **mean**

meant /me̱nt/

1 **Meant** is the past tense and past participle of **mean.**

2 **ADJ** You use **meant to** to say that something or someone was intended to be or do a particular thing. ❑ *I can't say any more, it's meant to be a big secret.* ❑ *He was meant to arrive an hour ago.*

3 **ADJ** If something **is meant for** particular people or for a particular situation, it is intended for those people or for that situation. ❑ *These stories aren't just meant for children.*

4 **PHRASE** If you say that something **is meant to** have a particular quality, you mean that many people think it is like that. ❑ *They're meant to be one of the best teams in the league.* [from Old English]

mean|time /mi̱ntaɪm/ **PHRASE** You use **in the meantime** or **meantime** to talk about the period of time between two events. ❑ *Elizabeth wants to go to college but in the meantime she has to work.*

mean|while /mi̱nwaɪl/ **ADV** You use **meanwhile** to talk about the period of time between two events or what happens while another thing is happening. ❑ *I'll be ready to meet them tomorrow. Meanwhile, I'm going to talk to Karen.* ❑ *We stayed up late into the night. Meanwhile, the snow was still falling outside.*

mea|sles /mi̱zᵊlz/ **N-NONCOUNT** **Measles** is an illness that gives you a high fever and red spots on your skin. [from Middle Low German]
→ look at Word Web: **hospital**

m

meas|ure /mɛʒər/ (**measures, measuring, measured**)

1 **v-t** If you **measure** something, you find out its size, amount, or speed. ❏ *Measure the length of the table.*

2 **v-t** If something **measures** a particular length or amount, that is its size. ❏ *The football field measures 400 feet.*

3 **n-count** When someone takes **measures** to do something, they act in a particular way to try to do it. [FORMAL] ❏ *The police are taking measures to deal with the problem.* [from Old French]

→ look at Word Webs: **mathematics, thermometer**

Word Partnership	Use measure with :
N	measure **intelligence**, measure **performance**, measure **progress**, **tests** measure **1**

meas|ure|ment /mɛʒərmənt/ (**measurements**)

1 **n-count** A **measurement** is the number that you get when you measure something. ❏ *You'll need to take the measurements of the room when you go to buy the furniture.*

2 **n-plural** Your **measurements** are the size of your waist, chest, hips, and other parts of your body, that you need to know when you are buying clothes. ❏ *I know all her measurements and find it easy to buy clothes she likes.* [from Old French]

→ look at Picture Dictionary: **measurements**

meat /mit/ (**meats**) **n-count/n-noncount** **Meat** is the part of an animal that people cook and eat. ❏ *I don't eat meat or fish.* [from Old English]

→ look at Word Webs: **meat, carnivore, vegetarian**

me|chan|ic /mɪkænɪk/ (**mechanics**) **n-count** A **mechanic** is a person whose job is to repair machines and engines, especially car engines. ❏ *Your mechanic should check the brakes on your car at least once a year.* [from Latin]

me|chani|cal /mɪkænɪkᵊl/ **adj** A **mechanical** object has parts that move when it is working. ❏ *...a mechanical clock.* [from Latin]

me|chani|cal ad|van|tage (**mechanical advantages**) **n-count/n-noncount** SCIENCE The **mechanical advantage** of a machine such as a lever or a pulley is a measure of the difference between the force applied to the machine and the force exerted by the machine.

me|chani|cal en|er|gy **n-noncount** SCIENCE **Mechanical energy** is the energy that an object such as a machine has because of its movement or position.

me|chani|cal weath|er|ing **n-noncount** SCIENCE **Mechanical weathering** is a geological process in which rock is broken down into smaller pieces, for example because of frost.

mecha|nism /mɛkənɪzəm/ (**mechanisms**) **n-count** A **mechanism** is a part of a machine. ❏ *The locking mechanism on the car door was broken.* [from Latin]

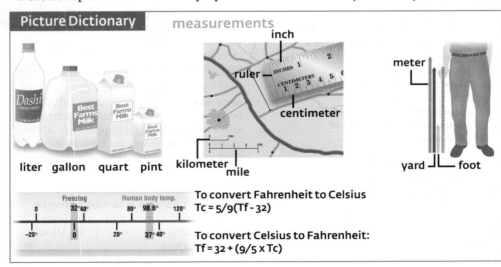

Picture Dictionary   measurements

inch

ruler

centimeter

meter

liter   gallon   quart   pint   kilometer   mile

yard — foot

Freezing   Human body temp.

To convert Fahrenheit to Celsius
Tc = 5/9(Tf - 32)

To convert Celsius to Fahrenheit:
Tf = 32 + (9/5 x Tc)

M

Word Web   **meat**

The English language has different words for animals and the **meat** that comes from those animals. This is because of influences from other languages. In the

year 1066 AD the Anglo-Saxons of England lost a major battle to the French-speaking Normans. As a result, the Normans became the ruling class and the Anglo-Saxons worked on farms. The Anglo-Saxons tended the

animals. They tended **sheep**, **cows**, **chickens**, and **pigs** in the fields. The wealthier Normans, who purchased and ate the meat from these animals, used different words. They bought "mouton," which became the word mutton, "boeuf," which became **beef**, "poulet," which became **poultry**, and "porc," which became **pork**.

---

med|al /mɛdᵊl/ (medals)
N-COUNT A medal is a small metal disk that you receive as a prize for doing something very good. ❑ *He won the Olympic gold medal.* [from French]

medal

med|dle /mɛdᵊl/ (meddles, meddling, meddled) **V-I** If you say that someone **meddles** in something, you are criticizing the fact that they try to influence or change it without being asked. ❑ *Do scientists have any right to meddle in such matters?* ❑ *You should not have meddled.* [from Old French]

Word Link   **med ≈ middle : intermediate, media, medium**

me|dia /midiə/

> **LANGUAGE HELP**
>
> **Media** can take the singular or plural form of the verb.

1 **N-SING** ARTS You can call television, radio, newspapers, and magazines **the media**. ❑ *A lot of people in the media have asked me that question.* ❑ *They told their story to the news media.*
2 → see also **multimedia**
3 ARTS Media is a plural of **medium**. [from Latin]
→ look at Word Web: **library**

me|di|an /midiən/ (medians) **N-COUNT** MATH In math, the **median** is the number that is in the middle of a set of numbers when they are arranged in order. For example, in the numbers 1, 2, 3, 4, 5, the median is 3. [from Latin]

me|dia source (media sources) **N-COUNT** You can refer to television, radio, newspapers, the Internet, and other forms of mass communication as **media sources**.

med|ic /mɛdɪk/ (medics) **N-COUNT** A medic is a doctor who works with the military. ❑ *Jack is an army medic.*

Medi|caid /mɛdɪkeɪd/ **N-PROPER** In the United States, **Medicaid** is a government program that helps to pay medical costs for people who cannot pay them.

medi|cal /mɛdɪkᵊl/ **ADJ** Medical means relating to illness and injuries and how to treat or prevent them. ❑ *Several police officers received medical treatment for their injuries.* [from Medieval Latin]

Word Partnership   Use **medical** with :

> N   medical **advice**, medical **attention**, medical **bills**, medical **care**, medical **center**, medical **doctor**, medical **emergency**, medical **practice**, medical **problems**, medical **research**, medical **science**, medical **supplies**, medical **tests**, medical **treatment** **1**

Medi|care /mɛdɪkɛər/ **N-PROPER** In the United States, **Medicare** is a government program that provides health insurance to pay medical costs for people aged 65 and older.

medi|ca|tion /mɛdɪkeɪʃᵊn/ (medications) **N-COUNT/N-NONCOUNT** Medication is medicine that is used for treating and curing illness. ❑ *Are you taking any medication?*

m

medi|cine /mɛdɪsɪn/ (**medicines**)

1 **N-NONCOUNT** Medicine is the treatment of illness and injuries by doctors and nurses. ❑ *He decided on a career in medicine.*

2 **N-COUNT/N-NONCOUNT** Medicine is a substance that you use to treat or cure an illness. ❑ *The medicine saved his life.* [from Old French]

→ look at Word Web: **medicine**

Word Partnership	Use medicine with :
v	**practice** medicine, **study** medicine **1** **give** *someone* medicine, **take** medicine, **use** medicine **2**

me|di|eval /midiivəl, mɪdivəl/ **ADJ** SOCIAL STUDIES Something that is **medieval** relates to the period of European history between A.D. 476 and about A.D. 1500. ❑ *On our trip we visited a medieval castle.* [from New Latin]

me|dio|cre /midioukər/ **ADJ** If you describe something as **mediocre**, you mean that it is of average quality but you think it should be better. ❑ *His school test results were mediocre.*

● **me|di|oc|rity** /midipkriti/ **N-NONCOUNT** ❑ *...the mediocrity of her work.* [from French]

me|dium /midiəm/ (**mediums** or **media**)

1 **ADJ** If something is of **medium** size, it is neither large nor small. ❑ *Mix the cream and eggs in a medium bowl.* ❑ *For this recipe, you will need one medium-sized onion.*

2 **N-COUNT** ARTS A **medium** is a substance or a material such as paint, wood, or stone that an artist uses. ❑ *...the medium of oil paint.* [from Latin]

3 → see also **media**

me|dul|la /mədʌlə/ (**medullas** or **medullae** /mədʌli/) **N-COUNT** SCIENCE The **medulla** is a part of the brain in humans and other animals that connects the brain to the spinal cord. It controls functions such as breathing and swallowing. The form **medulla oblongata** is also used. [from Latin]

me|du|sa /mədusə/ (**medusas** or **medusae** /mədusi/) **N-COUNT** SCIENCE A **medusa** is a type of jellyfish.

meet /mit/ (**meets, meeting, met**)

1 **V-T/V-I** If you **meet** someone who you know, you see them by chance and you speak to them. ❑ *I met Shona in town today.*

2 **V-T/V-I** If you **meet** someone who you do not know, you see them and speak to them for the first time. ❑ *I have just met an amazing man.*

3 **V-T/V-I** If two or more people **meet**, they go somewhere because they have planned to be there together. ❑ *We could meet for a game of tennis after work.*

4 **V-T** If you **meet** someone at a place, you go there and wait for them to arrive. ❑ *Mom met me at the station.*

5 **V-T/V-I** The place where two lines **meet** is the place where they join together. ❑ *This is the point where the two rivers meet.*

6 **N-COUNT** SPORTS A **meet** is a sports competition. ❑ *He never misses swim meets.*

7 **V-T** If something **meets** a need or requirement, it is good enough. ❑ *This hospital does not meet some patients' needs.*

8 **V-T** If you **meet** the cost of something, you provide the money that is needed for it. ❑ *The government will meet some of the cost of the damage.*

Word Web   medicine

Important Medical Advances

Medicine began in the Western Hemisphere in ancient Greece. The Greek philosopher Hippocrates separated medicine from religion and **disease** from supernatural explanations. He created the Hippocratic **oath** which describes a **physician's** duties. During the Middle Ages, Andreas Vesalius helped to advance medicine through his **research** on **anatomy**. Another major step forward was Friedrich Henle's development of **germ** theory. An understanding of germs led to Joseph Lister's demonstrations of the effective use of **antiseptics,** and Alexander Fleming's discovery of the **antibiotic** penicillin.

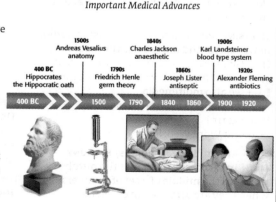

9 **V-T/V-I** If two areas **meet**, they are next to one another. ❑ *We arrived at the place where the desert meets the sea.* [from Old English]

▶ **meet up** If two or more people **meet up**, they go somewhere because they have planned to be there together. ❑ *We meet up for lunch once a week.*

Thesaurus meet Also look up :

V   bump into, encounter, run into **1**
     get together **3**
     comply with, follow, fulfill **7**

meet|ing /míːtɪŋ/ (**meetings**) **N-COUNT**
A **meeting** is an event in which a group of people come together to discuss things or to make decisions. ❑ *Can we have a meeting to discuss that?* [from Old English]

Word Partnership Use **meeting** with :

N   meeting **agenda**, **board** meeting,
     business meeting
V   **attend** a meeting, **call** a meeting, **go to**
     a meeting, **have** a meeting, **hold** a
     meeting, **plan** a meeting, **schedule** a
     meeting

mega|byte /mɛ́gəbaɪt/ (**megabytes**)
N-COUNT TECHNOLOGY In computing, a **megabyte** is a unit for measuring information. There are one million bytes in a **megabyte**. ❑ *...256 megabytes of memory.*

mega|pixel /mɛ́gəpɪksᵊl/ (**megapixels**)
N-COUNT TECHNOLOGY A **megapixel** is a unit for measuring the quality of the picture created by a digital camera, scanner, or other piece of digital equipment. One megapixel is equal to a million pixels.

meio|sis /maɪóʊsɪs/ **N-NONCOUNT** SCIENCE
Meiosis is a type of cell division that results in egg and sperm cells with only half the usual number of chromosomes.
[from New Latin]

mela|nin /mɛ́lənɪn/ **N-NONCOUNT** SCIENCE
Melanin is a dark substance in the skin, eyes, and hair of people and animals, that gives them color and can protect them against strong sunlight. [from Greek]

melo|dy /mɛ́lədi/ (**melodies**) **N-COUNT**
MUSIC A **melody** is a group of musical notes that sound pleasant together. ❑ *He could sing a melody before he could talk.* [from Old French]

mel|on /mɛ́lən/ (**melons**)
N-COUNT/N-NONCOUNT A **melon** is a large fruit with soft, sweet flesh and a hard green or yellow skin. ❑ *For dessert, there were grapes and juicy slices of melon.* [from Old French]

melt /mɛ́lt/ (**melts, melting, melted**) **V-T/V-I**
When a solid substance **melts**, or when you **melt** it, it changes to a liquid because it has become warm. ❑ *The snow melted.* ❑ *Melt the chocolate in a bowl.* [from Old English]
→ look at Word Webs: **glacier, matter**

melt|ing point (**melting points**) **N-COUNT**
SCIENCE The **melting point** of a substance is the temperature at which it melts when you heat it.

mem|ber /mɛ́mbər/ (**members**) **N-COUNT**
A **member** of a group or an organization is someone or something that belongs to that group or organization. ❑ *Joe is a member of the Democratic party.* ❑ *A member of the team saw the accident.* [from Latin]

Mem|ber of Par|lia|ment (**Members of Parliament**) **N-COUNT** SOCIAL STUDIES A **Member of Parliament** is a person who has been elected by the people in a particular area to represent them in a country's parliament. The short form **MP** is often used.

mem|ber|ship /mɛ́mbərʃɪp/ (**memberships**)
1 **N-NONCOUNT** **Membership** in an organization means being a member of it. ❑ *Employees have free membership at the gym.*
2 **N-COUNT/N-NONCOUNT** The **membership** of an organization is the people who belong to it. ❑ *The organization had a membership of 409,000.*

mem|brane /mɛ́mbreɪn/ (**membranes**)
N-COUNT SCIENCE A **membrane** is a thin piece of skin that connects or covers parts of a person's or animal's body. ❑ *...the thin membrane on the edge of the heart.* [from Latin]

mem|bra|no|phone /mɛ́mbreɪnəfoʊn/
(**membranophones**) **N-COUNT** SCIENCE A **membranophone** is any musical instrument that produces its sound by the vibration of a stretched skin, for example a drum. [from Latin]

meme /míːm/ (**memes**) **N-COUNT**
TECHNOLOGY A **meme** is something such as a video, picture, or phrase that a lot of people send to each other on the Internet. ❑ *The image quickly became a meme.*

memo /mɛ́moʊ/ (**memos**) **N-COUNT** A **memo** is a short note that you send to a person who works with you. ❑ *He sent a memo to everyone in his department.* [from Latin]

m

memo|rable /mɛmərəbᵊl/ **ADJ** Something that is **memorable** is easy to remember because it is special or very enjoyable. ❑ *Our wedding was a very memorable day.* [from Latin]

me|mo|rial /mɪmɔriəl/ (**memorials**)
1 **N-COUNT** A **memorial** is something that you build in order to remind people of a famous person or event. ❑ *He wanted to build a memorial to Columbus.*
2 **ADJ** A **memorial** event, object, or prize is in honor of someone who has died. ❑ *A memorial service was held for her at St. Paul's Church.* [from Late Latin]

memo|rize /mɛməraɪz/ (**memorizes, memorizing, memorized**) **V-T** If you **memorize** something, you learn it so that you can remember it exactly. ❑ *He tried to memorize the way to Rose's street.* [from Old French]

memo|ry /mɛməri/ (**memories**)
1 **N-COUNT/N-NONCOUNT** Your **memory** is your ability to remember things. ❑ *All the details of the meeting are clear in my memory.* ❑ *He has a good memory for faces.*
2 **N-COUNT** A **memory** is something that you remember from the past. ❑ *She has happy memories of her childhood.*
3 **N-COUNT** **TECHNOLOGY** A computer's **memory** is the part where it stores information. ❑ *The data is stored in the computer's memory.* [from Old French]

memo|ry card (**memory cards**) **N-COUNT** **TECHNOLOGY** A **memory card** is a small part that stores information inside a piece of electronic equipment such as a camera.

memo|ry stick (**memory sticks**) **N-COUNT** **TECHNOLOGY** A **memory stick** is a small object for storing computer information that you can carry with you and use in different computers.

men /mɛn/ **Men** is the plural of **man**. [from Old English]

mend /mɛnd/ (**mends, mending, mended**) **V-T** If you **mend** a hole in a piece of clothing, you repair it by sewing it. ❑ *He earns money by mending clothes.*

me|nis|cus /mɪnɪskəs/ (**menisci** /mɪnɪsaɪ/) **N-COUNT** **SCIENCE** A **meniscus** is the curved surface of a liquid in a narrow tube. [from New Latin]

men's room (**men's rooms**) **N-COUNT** The **men's room** is a bathroom for men in a public building.

men|tal /mɛntᵊl/
1 **ADJ** **Mental** means relating to the mind. ❑ *...mental illness.* ● **men|tal|ly** **ADV** ❑ *The exam made him mentally tired.*
2 **ADJ** A **mental** act involves only thinking and not physical action. ❑ *Allen did a quick mental calculation.* [from Late Latin]

men|tion /mɛnʃᵊn/ (**mentions, mentioning, mentioned**) **V-T** If you **mention** something, you say something about it, without giving much information. ❑ *She mentioned her mother but not her father.* ❑ *I mentioned that I didn't really like pop music.* [from Old French]

menu /mɛnyu/ (**menus**)
1 **N-COUNT** In a restaurant, the **menu** is a list of the food and drink that you can have there. ❑ *A waiter offered him the menu.*
2 **N-COUNT** **TECHNOLOGY** On a computer screen, a **menu** is a list of choices, showing things that you can do using a particular program. ❑ *Press F7 to show the print menu.* [from French]

Mercator pro|jec|tion /mərkeɪtər prədʒɛkʃᵊn/ (**Mercator projections**) **N-COUNT/N-NONCOUNT** **SCIENCE** A **Mercator projection** is an image of a map that is made by projecting the map on a globe onto the surface of a cylinder. Compare with **azimuthal projection** and **conic projection**. [from Flemish]

mer|chan|dise /mɜrtʃəndaɪz, -daɪs/ **N-NONCOUNT** **Merchandise** is products that you can buy. [FORMAL] ❑ *The company's annual*

soccer merchandise sales are about $1.5 billion.
[from Old French]

mer|chant /mɜrtʃənt/ (**merchants**)
■ **N-COUNT** A **merchant** is a person who
buys or sells goods in large quantities.
❏ *His father was a successful wool merchant.*
■ **N-COUNT** A **merchant** is a person who
owns or runs a store or shop. ❏ *The family buys
most of the things it needs from local merchants.*
■ **ADJ Merchant** seamen or ships are
involved in carrying goods for trade.
❏ *...the merchant navy.* [from Old French]

mer|ci|less /mɜrsɪlɪs/ **ADJ** If you describe
someone as **merciless**, you mean that they
are very cruel or determined and do not
show any concern for the effect their
actions have on other people. ❏ *Their merciless
laughter made her very upset.* ● **mer|ci|less|ly**
ADV ❏ *We teased him mercilessly.* [from Old
French]

mer|cu|ry /mɜrkyəri/ **N-NONCOUNT** SCIENCE
Mercury is a silver-colored liquid metal that
is used in thermometers. [from Latin]
→ look at Word Web: **thermometer**

Mer|cu|ry /mɜrkyəri/ **N-PROPER** SCIENCE
Mercury is the planet that is closest to the
sun. [from Latin]

mer|cy /mɜrsi/ **N-NONCOUNT** If someone
shows **mercy**, they choose not to harm or
punish someone. ❏ *His life was now at the
mercy of a judge.* [from Old French]

mere /mɪər/ (**merest**)

> **LANGUAGE HELP**
>
> **Mere** does not have a comparative form.
> The superlative form **merest** is used to
> emphasize how small something is,
> rather than in comparisons.

ADJ You use **mere** to say that something is
small or not important. ❏ *A mere five percent of
school principals are women.* [from Latin]

mere|ly /mɪərli/ **ADV** You use **merely** to
emphasize that something is only the
thing you are describing and nothing more.
❏ *She said this was merely her own opinion.*
❏ *Dieter merely looked at him, saying nothing.*
[from Latin]

merge /mɜrdʒ/ (**merges, merging, merged**)
V-T/V-I If two things **merge**, they join
together to make one new thing. ❏ *His
company has merged with the advertising firm
Saatchi & Saatchi.* [from Latin]

mer|ger /mɜrdʒər/ (**mergers**) **N-COUNT**
BUSINESS A **merger** is the joining together of
two separate companies or organizations so
that they become one. ❏ *...a merger between
two of America's biggest companies.* [from Latin]

mer|it /mɛrɪt/ (**merits**)
■ **N-NONCOUNT** If something has **merit**, it
has good qualities. ❏ *The drawings have great
artistic merit.*
■ **N-PLURAL** The **merits** of something are its
good points. ❏ *We will consider the merits of all
candidates before making our decision.*
■ **V-T** If someone or something **merits** a
particular action or treatment, they deserve
it. [FORMAL] ❏ *Some of these issues merit urgent
attention.* [from Old French]

mer|maid /mɜrmeɪd/ (**mermaids**) **N-COUNT**
In stories, a **mermaid** is a woman who has a
fish's tail and lives in the ocean.

mer|ry /mɛri/ (**merrier, merriest**) **ADJ Merry**
means happy and cheerful. ❏ *She sang a merry
little tune.* ❏ *Merry Christmas, everyone!* [from
Old English]

meso|sphere /mɛzəsfɪər/
■ **N-SING** SCIENCE The **mesosphere** is the
layer of the Earth's atmosphere that is
directly above the stratosphere.
■ **N-SING** SCIENCE The **mesosphere** is the
part of the Earth's interior that lies between
the upper mantle and the outer core.

Meso|zo|ic era /mɛzəzoʊɪk ɪərə/ **N-SING**
SCIENCE The **Mesozoic era** is a period in the
history of the Earth that began around
250 million years ago and ended around
65 million years ago.

mess /mɛs/ (**messes, messing, messed**)
■ **N-SING** If something is **a mess**, it is not
neat. ❏ *After the party, the house was a mess.*
■ **N-COUNT/N-NONCOUNT** If a situation is **a
mess**, it is full of problems. ❏ *I've made such a
mess of my life.* ❏ *Those are the reasons why the
economy is in such a mess.* [from Old French]
▶ **mess around** If you **mess around**, you
spend time doing things for fun, or for no
particular reason. ❏ *We were just messing
around playing with paint.*
▶ **mess up** ■ If you **mess** something **up**,
you make something go wrong. [INFORMAL]
❏ *This has messed up our plans.*
■ If you **mess up** a place or a thing, you
make it dirty or not neat. [INFORMAL]
❏ *He didn't want to mess up his neat hair.*

m

Word Partnership Use **mess** with :

v **clean up** a mess, **leave a** mess, **make a** mess **1**
  get into a mess **2**

mes|sage /mɛsɪdʒ/ (**messages, messaging, messaged**)

1 **N-COUNT** A **message** is a piece of information that you send to someone. ❏ *I'm getting emails and messages from friends all over the world.*

2 **N-COUNT** Your **message** is the important idea that you are trying to communicate. ❏ *The report's message was clear.*

3 **V-T/V-I** TECHNOLOGY If you **message** someone, you send them an electronic message using a computer. ❏ *I messaged her yesterday but she didn't reply.* ❏ *People who message a lot feel unpopular if they don't get many back.* [from Old French]

Word Partnership Use **message** with :

v **give** *someone* a message, **leave a** message, **read a** message, **take a** message **1**
  deliver a message, **get a** message, **hear a** message **1** **2**
  get a message **across**, **spread a** message **2**

ADJ **clear** message, **important** message, **urgent** message **1** **2**
  powerful message, **simple** message, **strong** message, **wrong** message **2**

mes|sage board (**message boards**)

N-COUNT TECHNOLOGY A **message board** is a system that allows users to send and receive messages on the Internet.

mes|sen|ger /mɛsɪndʒər/ (**messengers**)

N-COUNT A **messenger** is a person whose job is to take messages or packages to people. ❏ *A messenger delivered a large envelope to his office.* [from Old French]

messy /mɛsi/ (**messier, messiest**)

1 **ADJ** A **messy** person or activity makes things dirty or not neat. ❏ *She's a terribly messy cook.*

2 **ADJ** Something that is **messy** is not neat. ❏ *His writing is rather messy.* [from Old French]

met /mɛt/ **Met** is the past tense and past participle of **meet.**

met|al /mɛtᵊl/ (**metals**)

N-COUNT/N-NONCOUNT **Metal** is a hard substance such as iron, steel, or gold. ❏ *All of the houses had metal roofs.* [from Latin]
→ look at Word Webs: **metal, mineral**

me|tal|lic /mətælɪk/ **ADJ** **Metallic** things look or sound like metal. ❏ *The car has heated seats, metallic paint and a sun roof.* [from Latin]

me|tal|lic bond (**metallic bonds**) **N-COUNT** SCIENCE A **metallic bond** is the kind of chemical bond that occurs in metals.

met|al|loid /mɛtᵊlɔɪd/ (**metalloids**)

1 **N-COUNT** SCIENCE **Metalloids** are chemical elements that have some of the properties of metals and some of the properties of nonmetals.

2 **ADJ** SCIENCE **Metalloid** is also an adjective ❏ *...metalloid elements.*

meta|mor|phic /mɛtəmɔrfɪk/ **ADJ** SCIENCE **Metamorphic** rock is rock that is formed from other rock as a result of heat or pressure beneath the surface of the Earth. Compare with **igneous** and **sedimentary.**

meta|mor|pho|sis /mɛtəmɔrfəsɪs/ (**metamorphoses**) **N-COUNT/N-NONCOUNT** When a **metamorphosis** occurs, a person or thing develops and changes into something completely different. [FORMAL] ❏ *...his metamorphosis from a Republican to a Democrat.* ❏ *It undergoes its metamorphosis from a caterpillar to a butterfly.* [from Latin]
→ look at Word Web: **amphibian**

Word Web metal

In their natural state, most **metals** are not pure. They are usually combined with other materials in mixtures known as ores. Almost all metals are **shiny.** Many metals share these special properties. They are ductile, meaning that they can be made into **wire.** They are **malleable** and can be formed into thin, flat sheets. And they are also good **conductors** of heat and electricity. Except for **copper** and **gold**, metals are generally gray or silver in color.

copper

gold

meta|phase /mɛtəfeɪz/ (**metaphases**)
N-COUNT/N-NONCOUNT SCIENCE **Metaphase** is a stage in the process of cell division in which the chromosomes line up before they separate.

meta|phor /mɛtəfɔr/ (**metaphors**)
N-COUNT/N-NONCOUNT LANGUAGE ARTS A **metaphor** is a way of describing someone or something by showing their similarity with something else. For example, the metaphor "a shining light" describes a person who is very skillful or intelligent. ❑ She uses a lot of religious metaphors in her writing. [from Latin]

me|teor /mitiər/ (**meteors**) **N-COUNT** SCIENCE A **meteor** is a piece of rock from space that burns very brightly when it falls to Earth. [from Medieval Latin]
→ look at Word Web: **meteor**

me|teor|oid /mitiərɔɪd/ (**meteoroids**)
N-COUNT SCIENCE A **meteoroid** is a piece of rock or dust that travels around the sun. [from Medieval Latin]

me|teor|ol|ogy /mitiərɒlədʒi/
N-NONCOUNT SCIENCE **Meteorology** is the study of the processes in the Earth's atmosphere that cause particular weather conditions, especially in order to predict the weather. [from Greek]

Word Link	meter ≈ measuring : kilometer, meter, perimeter

me|ter /mitər/ (**meters**)
1 **N-COUNT** MATH A **meter** is an instrument that measures and records something. ❑ A man came to read the electricity meter.
2 **N-COUNT** MATH A **meter** is a unit for measuring length. There are 100 centimeters in a meter. ❑ She's running the 1,500 meter race.

3 **N-COUNT/N-NONCOUNT** MUSIC **Meter** is the rhythmic arrangement of beats according to particular patterns.
4 **PHRASE** SCIENCE **Meters per second** is a unit of speed in physics. An object that is moving at a particular number of **meters per second** travels that number of meters in one second. The abbreviation **m/s** is also used. [Sense 1 from Old English. Sense 2 from French. Sense 3 from Latin.]
→ look at Picture Dictionary: **measurements**

me|thane /mɛθeɪn/ **N-NONCOUNT** SCIENCE **Methane** is a colorless gas that has no smell.

metha|no|gen /məθænədʒən/
(**methanogens**) **N-COUNT** SCIENCE **Methanogens** are bacteria that produce methane.

meth|od /mɛθəd/ (**methods**) **N-COUNT**
A **method** is a particular way of doing something. ❑ Teachers are allowed to try out different teaching methods. [from French]
→ look at Word Webs: **experiment, science**

Thesaurus	method	Also look up :
N	manner, procedure, process, system, technique	

Word Partnership	Use **method** with :
ADJ	**alternative/traditional** method, **best** method, **new** method, **preferred** method
V	**develop** a method, **use a** method
N	method **of payment**, **teaching** method

met|ric /mɛtrɪk/ **ADJ** MATH SCIENCE
A **metric** measurement is given in meters, grams, or liters. ❑ A gram is a unit of weight in the metric system. [from French]

met|ric sys|tem **N-SING** MATH SCIENCE The **metric system** is the system of measurement that uses meters, grams, and liters.

m

Word Web **meteor**

As an **asteroid** flies through **space**, small pieces called **meteoroids** sometimes break off. When a meteoroid enters the earth's **atmosphere**, we call it a meteor. As the earth passes through asteroid belts we see spectacular **meteor showers**. Meteors that reach the earth are called meteorites. Scientists believe a huge meteorite struck the earth about 65 million years ago. It left a pit in Mexico called the Chicxulub **Crater**. It's about 150 miles wide. The crash caused earthquakes and tsunamis. It may also have produced a change in the earth's environment. Some believe this event caused the dinosaurs to die out.

met|ric ton (**metric tons**) **N-COUNT** SCIENCE
A **metric ton** is 1,000 kilograms. ❑ *The Wall Street Journal uses 220,000 metric tons of paper each year.*

| **Word Link** | *poli ≈ city : metropolitan, police, politics* |

met|ro|poli|tan /mɛtrəpɒlɪtən/ **ADJ**
Metropolitan means belonging to or typical of a large, busy city. ❑ *...the metropolitan district of Miami.* ❑ *...major metropolitan hospitals.* [from Late Latin]

met|ro|sex|ual /mɛtroʊsɛkʃuəl/ (**metrosexuals**)
1 **N-COUNT** A **metrosexual** is a man who spends a lot of time and money on his appearance, and often his home. ❑ *A true metrosexual, Brad buys fresh flowers every week to brighten up the apartment.*
2 **ADJ** **Metrosexual** is also an adjective. ❑ *My metrosexual husband has so many shirts that he needs more closet space.*

mg MATH SCIENCE **mg** is short for **milligram** or **milligrams**. ❑ *...300 mg of calcium.*

mice /maɪs/ **Mice** is the plural of **mouse**. [from Old English]

mi|crobe /maɪkroʊb/ (**microbes**) **N-COUNT** SCIENCE A **microbe** is a very small living thing that you cannot see without special equipment. ❑ *We have to kill the microbes that cause food poisoning.* [from French]

| **Word Link** | *micro ≈ small : microchip, microclimate, microscope* |

micro|chip /maɪkroʊtʃɪp/ (**microchips**)
N-COUNT TECHNOLOGY A **microchip** is a very small part inside a computer that makes it work.

micro|cli|mate /maɪkroʊklaɪmɪt/ (**microclimates**) also **micro-climate**
N-COUNT SCIENCE A **microclimate** is the climate that exists in a particular small area, which may be different from the climate of the surrounding area.

micro|cosm /maɪkrəkɒzəm/ (**microcosms**)
N-COUNT A **microcosm** is a small society, place, or activity which has all the typical features of a much larger one and so seems like a smaller version of it. [FORMAL] ❑ *The city was a microcosm of all American culture during the 1960s.* [from Medieval Latin]

micro|eco|nom|ics /maɪkroʊɛkənɒmɪks, -ik-/ also **micro-economics** **N-NONCOUNT**
SOCIAL STUDIES **Microeconomics** is the branch of economics that is concerned with individual areas of economic activity, such as those within a particular company or relating to a particular market.

micro|film /maɪkrəfɪlm/ (**microfilms**)
N-COUNT/N-NONCOUNT **Microfilm** is film that is used for photographing information and storing it in a reduced form. ❑ *...strips of microfilm.*

micro|organism /maɪkroʊɔrgənɪzəm/ (**microorganisms**) **N-COUNT** SCIENCE
A **microorganism** is a very small living thing that you can only see if you use a microscope.
→ look at Word Web: **fungus**

| **Word Link** | *phon ≈ sound : microphone, symphony, telephone* |

micro|phone /maɪkrəfoʊn/ (**microphones**)
N-COUNT A **microphone** is a piece of electronic equipment that you use to make sounds louder or to record them onto a machine.

microphone
→ look at Word Web: **concert**

| **Word Link** | *scope ≈ looking : horoscope, microscope, telescope* |

micro|scope /maɪkrəskoʊp/ (**microscopes**)
N-COUNT SCIENCE A **microscope** is a scientific instrument that makes very small objects look bigger.

micro|scop|ic /maɪkrəskɒpɪk/ **ADJ** SCIENCE
Microscopic objects are extremely small, and usually can be seen only through a microscope. ❑ *...microscopic cells.*

micro|sec|ond /maɪkroʊsɛkənd/ (**microseconds**) **N-COUNT** SCIENCE A **microsecond** is one millionth of a second.

micro|wave /maɪkroʊweɪv/ (**microwaves, microwaving, microwaved**)
1 **N-COUNT** A **microwave** or a **microwave oven** is an oven that cooks food very quickly using electric waves.
2 **V-T** To **microwave** food or drink means to cook or heat it in a microwave oven. ❑ *Microwave the vegetables first.*
→ look at Picture Dictionary: **cook**

| **Word Link** | *mid ≈ middle : midday, midnight, midway* |

mid|day /mɪddeɪ/ **N-NONCOUNT** **Midday** is twelve o'clock in the middle of the day. ❑ *At midday everyone had lunch.*

mid|dle /mɪdəl/ (**middles**)

1 **N-COUNT** The **middle of** something is the part of it that is farthest from its edges. ❑ *Howard stood in the middle of the room.*

2 **ADJ** The **middle** object in a row of objects is the one that has an equal number of objects on each side. ❑ *The middle button of his uniform jacket was missing.*

3 **N-SING** The **middle of** a period of time is the part between the beginning and the end. ❑ *I woke up in the middle of the night and heard a noise outside.*

4 **PHRASE** If you are **in the middle of** doing something, you are busy doing it. ❑ *I'm in the middle of cooking dinner.* [from Old English]

mid|dle age **N-NONCOUNT** **Middle age** is the time in your life when you are between the ages of about 40 and 65. ❑ *Men often gain weight in middle age.*

mid|dle-aged **ADJ** A **middle-aged** person is between the ages of about 40 and 65. ❑ *Most of the men were middle-aged, married businessmen.* → look at Picture Dictionary: **age**

Mid|dle Ages **N-PLURAL** SOCIAL STUDIES In European history, **the Middle Ages** was the period of time between the end of the Roman Empire in 476 AD and about 1500 AD.

mid|dle class (**middle classes**)

1 **N-COUNT** SOCIAL STUDIES The **middle class** or **middle classes** are the people in a society who are not very rich and not very poor, for example business people, doctors, and teachers. ❑ *Most writers come from the middle class.*

2 **ADJ** SOCIAL STUDIES **Middle class** is also an adjective. ❑ *They live in a very middle class area.*

Mid|dle East **N-PROPER** SOCIAL STUDIES The **Middle East** is the area around the eastern Mediterranean that includes Iran and all the countries in Asia to the west and southwest of Iran. ❑ *...the two great rivers of the Middle East.*

mid|dle school (**middle schools**) **N-COUNT** A **middle school** is a school for children between the ages of 10 and 13. ❑ *...Harlem Park Middle School.*

mid|night /mɪdnaɪt/ **N-NONCOUNT** **Midnight** is twelve o'clock in the middle of the night. ❑ *It was well after midnight.* → look at Picture Dictionary: **time**

mid-ocean ridge (**mid-ocean ridges**) or **mid-oceanic ridge** **N-COUNT** SCIENCE A **mid-ocean ridge** is a range of mountains beneath the ocean.

mid|way /mɪdweɪ/

1 **ADV** If something is **midway between** two places, it is the same distance from each of them. ❑ *The studio is midway between his office and his home.*

2 **ADJ** **Midway** is also an adjective. ❑ *Fresno is close to the midway point between Los Angeles and San Francisco.*

3 **ADV** If something happens **midway through** a period of time, it happens during the middle part of it. ❑ *He crashed midway through the race.*

1 **might** /maɪt/ **MODAL** You use **might** when something is possible. ❑ *I might go to study in England.* ❑ *They still hope that he might be alive.* [from Old English]

2 **might** /maɪt/ **N-NONCOUNT** **Might** is power or strength. ❑ *I pulled with all my might.* [from Old English]

mightn't /maɪtənt/ **Mightn't** is short for "might not." [from Old English]

might've /maɪtəv/ **Might've** is short for "might have." [from Old English]

mighty /maɪti/ (**mightier, mightiest**) **ADJ** **Mighty** describes something that is very large or powerful. [LITERARY] ❑ *There was a mighty roar from the crowd as the band came on stage.* [from Old English]

mi|graine /maɪgreɪn/ (**migraines**) **N-COUNT/ N-NONCOUNT** A **migraine** is a severe pain in your head that makes you feel very ill. ❑ *Her mother suffered from migraines.* [from French]

mi|grant /maɪgrənt/ (**migrants**) **N-COUNT** SOCIAL STUDIES A **migrant** is a person who moves from one place to another, especially in order to find work. ❑ *Most of his workers were migrants from the South.* [from Latin]

Word Link	migr ≈ moving, changing : emigrant, immigrant, migration

mi|grate /maɪgreɪt/ (**migrates, migrating, migrated**)

1 **V-I** SOCIAL STUDIES If people **migrate**, they move from one place to another, usually in order to find work. ❑ *People migrate to cities like Jakarta searching for work.* ● **mi|gra|tion** /maɪgreɪʃən/ (**migrations**) **N-COUNT/ N-NONCOUNT** ❑ *There was a large migration of people to the city.*

m

2 **v-i** When birds, fish, or animals **migrate**, they move from one part of the world to another at the same time every year. ❑ *Most birds have to fly long distances to migrate.*
● **mi|gra|tion** (**migrations**)
N-COUNT/N-NONCOUNT ❑ *Scientists are tracking the migration of bears.* [from Latin]

mike /maɪk/ (**mikes**) **N-COUNT** A **mike** is the same as a **microphone**. [INFORMAL]

mild /maɪld/ (**milder, mildest**)
1 **ADJ** **Mild** describes something that is not very strong. ❑ *This cheese has a soft, mild flavor.*
2 **ADJ** **Mild** weather is pleasant because it is not too hot and not too cold. ❑ *We like the area because it has very mild winters.* [from Old English]

mile /maɪl/ (**miles**)
1 **N-COUNT** MATH A **mile** is a unit for measuring distance. One **mile** is equal to 1.6 kilometers and there are 5,280 feet in a mile. ❑ *They drove 600 miles across the desert.*
2 **N-PLURAL** **Miles** is used, especially in the expression **miles away**, to refer to a long distance. ❑ *The gym is miles away from her home.* [from Old English]
→ look at Picture Dictionary: **measurement**

Word Partnership	Use **mile** with :
ADJ	mile **high**, mile **long**, **nautical** mile, **square** mile, mile **wide** **1**

mile|age /maɪlɪdʒ/ (**mileages**)
N-COUNT/N-NONCOUNT **Mileage** is the distance that you have traveled, measured in miles. ❑ *The car has a low mileage.* [from Old English]

mili|tant /mɪlɪtənt/ (**militants**)
1 **ADJ** You use **militant** to describe people who believe in something very strongly and are active in trying to bring about political or social change, often in extreme ways that other people find unacceptable. ❑ *Militant workers voted to go on strike.* ● **mili|tan|cy** **N-NONCOUNT** ❑ *...the rise of militancy in the labor unions.*
2 **N-COUNT** **Militant** is also a noun. ❑ *...terrorist acts committed by militants.* [from Latin]

mili|tary /mɪlɪtɛri/
1 **ADJ** **Military** means relating to the armed forces of a country. ❑ *Military action may become necessary.* ❑ *The president attended a meeting of military leaders.*
2 **N-SING** The **military** are the armed forces of a country. ❑ *The military have said very little*

about the attacks. [from French]
→ look at Word Web: **army**

mi|li|tia /mɪlɪʃə/ (**militias**) **N-COUNT**
SOCIAL STUDIES A **militia** is an organization that operates like an army but whose members are not professional soldiers. ❑ *Young men formed their own militias.* [from Latin]

milk /mɪlk/ (**milks, milking, milked**)
1 **N-NONCOUNT** SCIENCE **Milk** is the white liquid that cows and some other animals produce, which people drink. ❑ *He went out to buy a quart of milk.*
2 **v-t** If someone **milks** a cow or another animal, they take milk from it. ❑ *Farm workers milks the cows in the morning.*
3 **N-NONCOUNT** SCIENCE **Milk** is the white liquid that a mother makes in her body to feed her baby. ❑ *Milk from the mother's breast is a perfect food for the human baby.* [from Old English]
→ look at Word Web: **dairy**

milky /mɪlki/ (**milkier, milkiest**) **ADJ** Drinks or food that are **milky** contain a lot of milk. ❑ *I want a big cup of milky coffee.* [from Old English]

mill /mɪl/ (**mills**)
1 **N-COUNT** A **mill** is a building in which flour is made from grain. ❑ *The old mill is now a restaurant.*
2 **N-COUNT** A **mill** is a factory where materials such as steel, wool, or cotton are made. ❑ *He started work in a cotton mill at the age of ten.* [from Old English]

mil|len|nium /mɪlɛniəm/ (**millenniums** or **millennia**) **N-COUNT** A **millennium** is a period of one thousand years. [FORMAL] ❑ *The year 2000 was the beginning of a new millennium.* [from New Latin]

Word Link	milli ≈ thousandth : **milli**gram, **milli**liter, **milli**meter

mil|li|gram /mɪlɪgræm/ (**milligrams**)
N-COUNT MATH SCIENCE A **milligram** is a unit for measuring weight. There are one thousand milligrams in a gram. ❑ *He added 0.5 milligrams of sodium.* [from French]

mil|li|li|ter /mɪlɪlitər/ (**milliliters**) **N-COUNT**
MATH A **milliliter** is a unit for measuring liquids. There are one thousand milliliters in a liter. ❑ *The nurse measured 100 milliliters of blood.*

mil\|li\|meter /mɪlɪmitər/ (**millimeters**)
N-COUNT MATH A **millimeter** is a unit for measuring length. There are ten millimeters in a centimeter. ❑ *The creature is tiny, just 10 millimeters long.*

mil\|lion /mɪlyən/ (**millions**)

LANGUAGE HELP
The plural is **million** after a number.

1 **NUM** MATH A **million** or **one million** is the number 1,000,000. ❑ *Five million people visit the county each year.*

2 **NUM** **Millions of** people or things means a very large number of them. ❑ *There are millions of people who do not have enough to eat.*

3 **PRON** You can also use **millions** as a pronoun. ❑ *Millions were spent constructing the new building.* [from Old French]

mil\|lion\|aire /mɪlyənɛər/ (**millionaires**)
N-COUNT A **millionaire** is a person who has more than a million dollars. ❑ *By the time he died, he was a millionaire.* [from Old French]

mil\|lionth /mɪlyənθ/ (**millionths**)
1 **ADJ/ADV** The **millionth** item in a series is the one you count as number one million. ❑ *It seemed like the millionth time she asked the question.*

2 **N-COUNT** MATH A **millionth** is one of one million equal parts of something. ❑ *It takes less than one millionth of a second.* [from Old French]

mime /maɪm/ (**mimes, miming, mimed**)
1 **N-COUNT/N-NONCOUNT** ARTS **Mime** is a way of telling a story using your face, hands, and body, but without using speech. ❑ *The story is told through music and mime.*

2 **V-T/V-I** If you **mime**, or **mime** something, you describe it using movements rather than speech. ❑ *He mimed the act of hammering a nail into a piece of wood.* [from Old English]

mim\|ic /mɪmɪk/ (**mimics, mimicking, mimicked**) **V-T** If you **mimic** the way someone moves or speaks, you copy them in an amusing way. ❑ *He could mimic anybody, and often made Olivia laugh.* [from Latin]

mind /maɪnd/ (**minds, minding, minded**)
1 **N-COUNT** Your **mind** is all your thoughts and the way that you think about things. ❑ *She is a bit deaf, but her mind is still sharp.*

2 **N-COUNT** Your **mind** is your ability to think and reason. ❑ *You need a logical mind to solve this problem.*

3 **PHRASE** If you tell someone to **bear** something **in mind**, you are telling them about something important which they should remember. ❑ *Bear in mind that there aren't many gas stations out of town.*

4 **PHRASE** If you **change** your **mind**, you change a decision or an opinion. ❑ *I was going to vote for him, but I changed my mind.*

5 **PHRASE** If you say that an idea never **crossed** your **mind**, you mean that you did not think of it. ❑ *It didn't cross his mind that there might be a problem.*

6 **PHRASE** If you **make up** your **mind**, you decide something. ❑ *He made up his mind to call Kathy.*

7 **PHRASE** If something is **on** your **mind**, you are worried about it and you think about it a lot. ❑ *I don't sleep well. I've got a lot on my mind.*

8 **PHRASE** If you have **an open mind**, you avoid forming an opinion until you know all the facts. ❑ *Try to keep an open mind until you have all the facts.*

9 **PHRASE** If someone is **out of their mind**, they are crazy. [INFORMAL] ❑ *What are you doing? Are you out of your mind?*

10 **PHRASE** If something **takes** your **mind off** a problem, it helps you to stop thinking about it for a while. ❑ *A movie might take your mind off your problems.*

11 **V-T/V-I** If you do not **mind** something, you do not feel annoyed or angry about it. ❑ *Mr. Hernandez, would you mind waiting here a moment?* ❑ *It was hard work but she didn't mind.*

12 **V-T** If you have a choice, and you say that you do not **mind**, you mean that you are happy to do or have either of them. ❑ *"Would you rather play tennis or baseball?"—"I don't mind."*

13 **PHRASE** You say **Never mind** when something is not important. ❑ *"He's going to be late."—"Oh, never mind, we'll start eating without him."*

14 **PHRASE** If you **wouldn't mind** something, you would like it. ❑ *I wouldn't mind a cup of coffee.* [from Old English]

m

mine
❶ PRONOUN USE
❷ NOUN AND VERB USES

❶ **mine** /maɪn/ **PRON** **Mine** means belonging to me. ❑ *Her right hand was close to mine.* ❑ *That isn't your bag, it's mine.* [from Old English]

❷ **mine** /maɪn/ (**mines, mining, mined**)
1 **N-COUNT** A **mine** is a deep hole in the

ground from which people dig coal, diamonds, or gold. ❑ *The company owns gold and silver mines.*

2 **V-T** When people **mine**, they dig deep holes and tunnels into the ground to remove coal, diamonds, or gold. ❑ *Diamonds are mined in South Africa.* ● **min|er** (**miners**) **N-COUNT** ❑ *My father was a miner.*

3 **N-COUNT** A **mine** is a bomb that is hidden under the ground. [from Old French]

min|er|al /mɪnərəl/ (**minerals**) **N-COUNT** SCIENCE A **mineral** is a natural substance such as gold, salt, or coal that comes from the ground. [from Medieval Latin] → look at Word Webs: **mineral, photosynthesis, rock**

min|er|al wa|ter **N-NONCOUNT** Mineral **water** is water that comes from the ground that contains substances that are good for your health.

minia|ture /mɪniətʃər, -tʃʊər/ **ADJ** **Miniature** things are very small, or much smaller than usual. ❑ *The toy house was filled with miniature chairs and tables.* [from Italian]

mini|mal /mɪnɪməl/ **ADJ** If an effect is **minimal**, it is very small. ❑ *The health risk is minimal, so there's no need to worry.* [from Latin]

mini|mal|ism /mɪnɪməlɪzəm/ **N-NONCOUNT** **Minimalism** is a style in which a small number of very simple things are used to create a particular effect. ❑ *...the minimalism of her home.* [from Latin]

min|i|mal|ist /mɪnɪməlɪst/ (**minimalists**) **1** **N-COUNT** A **minimalist** is an artist or designer who uses minimalism. ❑ *...the minimalists in the 1970s.*

2 **ADJ** **Minimalist** is used to describe ideas, artists, or designers that are influenced by minimalism. ❑ *The two designers used a minimalist approach.* [from Latin]

mini|mize /mɪnɪmaɪz/ (**minimizes, minimizing, minimized**) **V-T** If you **minimize** something, you make it as small as possible. ❑ *We have done everything possible to minimize the risk of accidents.* [from Latin]

mini|mum /mɪnɪməm/ **1** **ADJ** You use **minimum** to talk about the smallest amount that is possible. ❑ *Pupils remain at school at least until the minimum age of 16.* ❑ *Many people in the country are still working for less than the minimum wage.*

2 **N-SING** **Minimum** is also a noun. ❑ *Dr. Rayman runs a minimum of three miles every day.* [from Latin]

Word Partnership	Use minimum with :	
N	minimum **age**, minimum **balance**, minimum **purchase**, minimum **salary**	
ADJ	**absolute** minimum, **bare** minimum	

min|is|ter /mɪnɪstər/ (**ministers**) **1** **N-COUNT** A **minister** is a religious leader in some types of church. ❑ *Thirty priests, ministers, and rabbis attended the meeting.*

2 **N-COUNT** In some countries, a **minister** is a senior person in a government. ❑ *Clark became finance minister in 1991.* [from Old French]

min|is|te|rial /mɪnɪstɪəriəl/ **ADJ** SOCIAL STUDIES You use **ministerial** to refer to people, events, or jobs that are connected with government ministers. ❑ *...a series of ministerial meetings in Brussels.* [from Old French]

min|is|try /mɪnɪstri/ (**ministries**) **1** **N-COUNT** In some countries, a **ministry** is

The **extraction** of **minerals** from ore is an ancient process. Neolithic man discovered **copper** around 8000 BC. Using fire and charcoal, they **reduced** the ore to its pure **metal** form. About 4,000 years later, Egyptians learned to pour molten copper into molds. **Silver** ore often contains large amounts of copper and **lead.** Silver refineries often use the **smelting** process to remove these other metals from the silver. Most **gold** does not exist as an ore. Instead, veins of gold run through the earth. Refiners use chemicals such as cyanide to get pure gold.

a government department that deals with one particular thing. ❑ *He has worked for both the ministry of education and the ministry of the interior.*

2 **N-COUNT** The **ministry** of a religious person is the work that they do. ❑ *His ministry is among poor people.* [from Latin]

mi|nor /maɪnər/

1 **ADJ** If something is **minor**, it is not very important or serious. ❑ *The soldier suffered only minor injuries.* ❑ *They both have minor roles in the movie.*

2 **ADJ** MUSIC In music, **minor** is used for talking about a scale in which the third note is one half step lower that the related major scale. Compare with **major**. ❑ *...an A minor scale.* [from Latin]

Thesaurus	minor Also look up :
ADJ	insignificant, lesser, small, unimportant; (*ant.*) important, major, significant **1**

Word Partnership	Use minor with :
N	minor **adjustment**, minor **damage**, minor **detail**, minor **illness**, minor **injury**, minor **operation**, minor **problem**, minor **surgery** **1**
ADV	**relatively** minor **1**

mi|nor|ity /mɪnɔrɪti, maɪ-/ (minorities)

1 **N-SING** A **minority** of people or things is fewer than half of them. ❑ *Only a minority of mothers in this neighborhood go out to work.*

2 **N-COUNT** A **minority** is a group of people of the same race, culture, or religion in a place where most other people are of a different race, culture, or religion. ❑ *...the region's ethnic minorities.* [from Medieval Latin]

Word Partnership	Use minority with :
N	minority **leader**, minority **party** **1** minority **applicants**, minority **community**, minority **group**, minority **population**, minority **students**, minority **voters**, minority **women** **2**

mi|nor key (minor keys) N-COUNT MUSIC
In music, the **minor key** is based on the minor scale, in which the third note is three semitones higher than the first.

min|strel show /mɪnstrəl ʃoʊ/ (minstrel shows) N-COUNT ARTS In the past, a **minstrel show** was a form of entertainment

consisting of songs, dances, and comedy performed by actors wearing black face makeup.

mint /mɪnt/ (mints)

1 **N-NONCOUNT** **Mint** is a plant that has leaves with a fresh, strong taste and smell. ❑ *The waiter brought us two glasses of mint tea.*

2 **N-COUNT** A **mint** is a candy with this flavor. ❑ *Sam offered me a mint.* [from Old English]

Word Link	min ≈ small, lessen : diminish, minus, minute

mi|nus /maɪnəs/ (minuses)

1 **CONJ** MATH You use **minus** when you are taking one number away from another number. ❑ *One minus one is zero.*

2 **ADJ** MATH You use **minus** before a number or an amount to show that it is less than zero. ❑ *The temperature dropped to minus 20 degrees F.* [from Latin]

mi|nus|cule /mɪnɪskyul/ ADJ If you describe something as **minuscule**, you mean that it is very small. ❑ *They filmed the movie in 17 days, a minuscule amount of time.* [from French]

minute
❶ NOUN USES
❷ ADJECTIVE USE

❶ mi|nute /mɪnɪt/ (minutes)

1 **N-COUNT** A **minute** is a measurement of time. There are sixty seconds in one minute, and there are sixty minutes in one hour. ❑ *The pizza will take twenty minutes to cook.*

2 **PHRASE** If you say that something will or may happen **at any minute**, you are saying that it is likely to happen very soon. ❑ *It looked as though it might rain at any minute.*

3 **PHRASE** If something will happen **in a minute**, it will happen very soon. ❑ *The doctor will be with you in a minute.*

4 **PHRASE** A **last-minute** action is one that is done at the latest time possible. ❑ *He made a last-minute decision to stay at home.*

5 **PHRASE** If you ask someone to do something **this minute**, you want them to do it immediately. ❑ *You come back here this minute!*

6 **PHRASE** You say **Just a minute** or **Wait a minute** when you want someone to wait for a short period of time. ❑ *Wait a minute, something is wrong here.* [from Old French]

→ look at Picture Dictionary: **time**

m

②mi|nute /maɪnu̠t/ **ADJ** Something that is **minute** is very small. ❑ *You only need to use a minute amount of glue.* [from Latin]

Minute|man /mɪ̠nɪtmæn/ (**Minutemen**) **N-COUNT** SOCIAL STUDIES In the American Revolution, a **Minuteman** was a soldier who promised to be ready to fight in one minute, if he was needed.

mira|cle /mɪ̠rək³l/ (**miracles**)
■ N-COUNT A **miracle** is a surprising and lucky event that you cannot explain. ❑ *It's a miracle that Chris survived the accident.*
■ N-COUNT A **miracle** is a wonderful and surprising event that is believed to be caused by God. ❑ *...Jesus's ability to perform miracles.* [from Latin]

mir|ror /mɪ̠rər/ (**mirrors**)
■ N-COUNT A **mirror** is a flat piece of special glass that you can see yourself in. ❑ *Dan looked at himself in the mirror.*
■ V-T If something **mirrors** something else, it is similar to it and it seems to be a copy of it. ❑ *The book mirrors the author's own experiences.* [from Old French]
→ look at Word Web: **telescope**

mirror

mirth /mɜ̠rθ/ **N-NONCOUNT** Mirth is happiness and amusement expressed by laughing. [LITERARY] ❑ *That caused considerable mirth among students and coaches alike.* [from Old English]

mis|an|thro|py /mɪsæ̠nθrəpi, mɪz-/ **N-NONCOUNT** Misanthropy is a general dislike of people. [FORMAL] ❑ *He seems consumed by fear, self-loathing, and misanthropy.* [from Greek]

mis|be|hav|ior /mɪ̠sbɪheɪvyər/ **N-NONCOUNT** Misbehavior is bad behavior. [FORMAL] ❑ *Our teachers will not tolerate misbehavior.* [from Middle English]

mis|car|riage /mɪ̠skærɪdʒ, -kær-/ (**miscarriages**) **N-COUNT/N-NONCOUNT** If a pregnant woman has a **miscarriage**, she gives birth to her baby before it is properly formed, and it dies. [from Old Northern French]

mis|chief /mɪ̠stʃɪf/ **N-NONCOUNT** Mischief is bad or silly behavior that is annoying but not too serious. ❑ *Jacob's a typical little boy—full of mischief.* [from Old French]

mis|chie|vous /mɪ̠stʃɪvəs/ **ADJ** A **mischievous** person likes to play tricks on people and behave in a silly, but not very bad way. ❑ *Megan gave me a mischievous smile.*
● **mis|chie|vous|ly** **ADV** ❑ *Thomas grinned mischievously at Anna.* [from Old French]

mis|com|mu|ni|cation /mɪ̠skə myu̠nɪkeɪʃ³n/ (**miscommunications**) **N-COUNT/N-NONCOUNT** A miscommunication is a failure to communicate effectively. ❑ *Don't let your marriage fall apart because of a simple miscommunication.* [from Latin]

mis|con|strue /mɪ̠skənstru̠/ (**misconstrues, misconstruing, misconstrued**) **V-T** If you **misconstrue** something, you understand it wrongly. [FORMAL] ❑ *An outsider might misconstrue the nature of the relationship.* [from Middle English]

mis|er|able /mɪ̠zərəb³l/
■ ADJ If you are **miserable**, you are very unhappy. ❑ *My job was making me miserable.*
● **mis|er|ably** /mɪ̠zərəbli/ **ADV** ❑ *"I feel so guilty," Diane said miserably.*
■ ADJ If something is **miserable**, it makes you feel unhappy. ❑ *It was a gray, wet, miserable day.* [from Old French]

mis|ery /mɪ̠zəri/ (**miseries**) **N-COUNT/N-NONCOUNT** Misery is great unhappiness and suffering. ❑ *People never forget the misery of war.* [from Latin]

mis|for|tune /mɪsfɔ̠rtʃən/ (**misfortunes**) **N-COUNT/N-NONCOUNT** A misfortune is something unpleasant or unlucky that happens to you. ❑ *She seems to enjoy other people's misfortunes.* [from Old French]

M

mis|lead /mɪslid/ (**misleads, misleading, misled**) **V-T** If you **mislead** someone, you make them believe something that is not true. ❑ *The administration has misled the public about this issue.* [from Old English]

mis|lead|ing /mɪslidɪŋ/ **ADJ** If a message is **misleading**, it makes you believe something that is not true. ❑ *Companies must make sure that their advertisements are not misleading.* [from Old English]

mis|led /mɪslɛd/ **Misled** is the past tense and past participle of **mislead**. [from Old English]

mi|sogy|ny /mɪsɒdʒini/ **N-NONCOUNT** **Misogyny** is a strong dislike of women. ❑ *It was not misogyny that discouraged him from writing about women, but the difficulty he found in representing them realistically.* [from Greek]

---
miss
❶ AS PART OF A WOMAN'S NAME
❷ VERB USES
---

❶ **Miss** /mɪs/ (**Misses**) You use **Miss** in front of the name of a girl or a woman who is not married. [FORMAL] ❑ *It was nice talking to you, Miss Ellis.* ❑ *The painting is by Miss Ana Lopez.*

❷ **miss** /mɪs/ (**misses, missing, missed**) **1** **V-T/V-I** If you **miss**, or **miss** something that you are trying to hit or catch, you do not manage to hit or catch it. ❑ *His first shot missed the goal completely.* ❑ *When I'd missed a few times, he suggested I go in goals for a while.* **2** **V-T** If you **miss** something, you do not notice it. ❑ *What did he say? I missed it.* **3** **V-T** If you **miss** someone who is not with you, you feel sad that they are not there. ❑ *I miss my family terribly.* **4** **V-T** If you **miss** something, you feel sad because you no longer have it. ❑ *I love my new apartment, but I miss my garden.* **5** **V-T** If you **miss** an airplane or a train, you arrive too late to get on it. ❑ *He missed the last bus home.* **6** **V-T** If you **miss** a meeting or an activity, you do not take part in it. ❑ *He missed the party because he had to work.* [from Old English]
▶ **miss out** If you **miss out on** something, you do not have the chance take part in it. ❑ *You missed out on all the fun yesterday.*

Usage miss and lose
Miss and *lose* have similar meanings. *Miss* is used to express something you didn't do: *I missed class yesterday.* *Lose* is used when you can't find something you once had. *Cancel your ATM card if you lose your wallet.*

Word Link *miss ≈ sending : dis*miss, *missile, missionary*

mis|sile /mɪsəl/ (**missiles**) **1** **N-COUNT** A **missile** is a weapon that flies through the air and explodes when it hits something. ❑ *The army fired missiles at the building.* **2** **N-COUNT** A **missile** is anything that you can throw as a weapon. ❑ *The youths were throwing missiles at the police.* [from Latin]

miss|ing /mɪsɪŋ/ **1** **ADJ** If someone or something is **missing**, they are not in their usual place, and you cannot find them. ❑ *I discovered that my cellphone was missing.* ❑ *Police are hunting for the missing girl.* **2** **ADJ** If something is **missing**, it is necessary but not included. ❑ *Talking to me gave her something that was missing from her life.* [from Old English]

Word Partnership Use **missing** with :

N	missing **children**, missing **girl**, missing **people**, missing **soldiers** 1 missing **piece** 1 2 missing **information**, missing **ingredient** 2
ADV	**still** missing 1 3

mis|sion /mɪʃən/ (**missions**) **N-COUNT** A **mission** is an important job that someone has to do, especially one that involves traveling. ❑ *His government sent him on a mission to North America.* [from Latin]

Word Partnership Use **mission** with :

V	**accomplish a** mission, **carry out a** mission, **dangerous** mission, **secret** mission, **successful** mission
N	**peacekeeping** mission, **combat** mission, **rescue** mission, **training** mission

mis|sion|ary /mɪʃənɛri/ (**missionaries**) **N-COUNT** A **missionary** is a Christian who has been sent to a foreign country to teach people about Christianity. ❑ *My mother would like me to be a missionary in Africa.*

m

mis|sive /mɪsɪv/ (**missives**) **N-COUNT**
A **missive** is a letter or other message that someone sends. [HUMOROUS or LITERARY] ❑ ...the customary missive from your mother. [from Medieval Latin]

mist /mɪst/ (**mists**) **N-COUNT/N-NONCOUNT**
Mist is a lot of tiny drops of water in the air, that make it difficult to see. ❑ The mist did not lift until midday. ● **mist|y** **ADJ** ❑ Charlie looked across the misty valley. [from Old English]

mis|take /mɪsteɪk/ (**mistakes, mistaking, mistook, mistaken**)
◼ **N-COUNT** A **mistake** is something that is not correct. ❑ Tony made three spelling mistakes in the letter.
◼ **PHRASE** If you do something **by mistake**, you do something that you did not want or plan to do. ❑ I was in a hurry and called the wrong number by mistake.
◼ **V-T** If you **mistake** one person **for** another person, you wrongly think that they are the other person. ❑ People are always mistaking Lauren for her sister because they are so alike.
◼ **V-T** If you **mistake** someone or something, you do not understand them correctly. ❑ He still looked worried, and she mistook the reason. [from Old Norse]

Word Partnership	Use mistake with :
V	admit a mistake, correct a mistake, fix a mistake, make a mistake, realize a mistake ◼
ADJ	fatal mistake, honest mistake, tragic mistake ◼ big mistake, common mistake, costly mistake, huge mistake, serious mistake, terrible mistake ◼

mis|tak|en /mɪsteɪkən/ **ADJ** If you are **mistaken about** something, you are wrong about it. ❑ I think that you must be mistaken—Jackie wouldn't do a thing like that.
● **mis|tak|en|ly** **ADV** ❑ The thieves mistakenly believed there was no one in the house. [from Old Norse]

mis|took /mɪstʊk/ **Mistook** is the past tense of **mistake**. [from Old Norse]

mis|trust /mɪstrʌst/ (**mistrusts, mistrusting, mistrusted**)
◼ **N-NONCOUNT** **Mistrust** is the feeling that you have when you do not trust someone. ❑ There is a deep mistrust of the police around here.
◼ **V-T** If you **mistrust** someone, you do

not trust them. ❑ He mistrusts all journalists. [from Old Norse]

Word Link	mis ≈ bad : misbehavior, misleading, misunderstand

mis|under|stand /mɪsʌndərstænd/ (**misunderstands, misunderstanding, misunderstood**) **V-T/V-I** If you **misunderstand** someone or something, you do not understand them correctly. ❑ I think you've misunderstood me. ❑ They have misunderstood what rock and roll is. ❑ They told me in terms that no one could misunderstand. [from Old English]

mis|under|stand|ing /mɪsʌndərstændɪŋ/ (**misunderstandings**) **N-COUNT/N-NONCOUNT** A **misunderstanding** is a situation where someone does not understand something correctly. ❑ Make your plans clear to avoid misunderstandings. [from Old English]

mis|under|stood /mɪsʌndərstʊd/ **Misunderstood** is the past tense and past participle of **misunderstand**. [from Old English]

mito|chon|drion /maɪtəkɒndriən/ (**mitochondria**) **N-COUNT** **SCIENCE** **Mitochondria** are the parts of a cell that convert nutrients into energy. [from New Latin]

mi|to|sis /maɪtoʊsɪs/ **N-NONCOUNT** **SCIENCE** **Mitosis** is the process by which a cell divides into two identical halves. [from New Latin]

mit|ten /mɪtᵊn/ (**mittens**) **N-COUNT** **Mittens** are gloves that have one part that covers your thumb and another part that covers your four fingers together. ❑ ...a pair of mittens. [from Old French]

mix /mɪks/ (**mixes, mixing, mixed**)
◼ **V-T** If you **mix** things, you put different things together so that they make something new. ❑ Mix the sugar with the butter.
◼ **V-T/V-I** **SCIENCE** If two substances **mix**, they join together and make something new. ❑ Oil and water don't mix.
◼ **N-COUNT** A **mix** of different things or people is two or more of them together. ❑ The story is a mix of fact and fiction.
◼ **V-T/V-I** If you **mix with** other people, you meet them and talk to them. ❑ He loved to mix with the rich and famous. [from Old French]
▶ **mix up** ◼ If you **mix up** two things or people, you think that one of them is the other one. ❑ People often mix me up with my brother. ❑ Children often mix up their words.

M

2 If you **mix up** things, you change the way they are arranged. ❏ *I think the journalist may have mixed up his notes.*

Word Partnership	Use **mix** with :
N	mix **ingredients**, mix **with water** **1**
ADV	mix **thoroughly**, mix **together** **1**

mixed /mɪkst/ **ADJ** If something is **mixed**, it includes different types of things or people. ❏ *There was a very mixed group of people at the party.* ❏ *For lunch we had pasta and a mixed salad.* [from Old French]

mixed me|dia **N-NONCOUNT** ARTS **Mixed media** is the use of more than one medium or material in a work of art, for example the use of both painting and collage.

mixed me|ter (mixed meters) **N-COUNT/N-NONCOUNT** MUSIC Music that is written in **mixed meter** combines two or more meters.

mix|er /mɪksər/ (mixers) **N-COUNT** A **mixer** is a machine that you use for mixing things together. ❏ *Beat the egg yolks and sugar with an electric mixer.* [from Old French]
→ look at Picture Dictionary: **utensil**

mix|ture /mɪkstʃər/ (mixtures)
1 **N-COUNT** A **mixture** is a substance that you make by mixing different substances together. ❏ *The sauce is a mixture of chocolate and cream.*
2 **N-SING** A **mixture of** things consists of several different things together. ❏ *They looked at him with a mixture of horror and surprise.* [from Latin]

ml MATH SCIENCE **ml** is short for **milliliter** or **milliliters**. ❏ *Boil the sugar and 100 ml of water.*

mm MATH **mm** is short for **millimeter** or **millimeters**. ❏ *...a 135 mm lens.*

moan /moʊn/ (moans, moaning, moaned)
1 **V-I** If you **moan**, you make a low sound because you are unhappy or in pain. ❏ *The wounded soldier was moaning in pain.*
2 **N-COUNT** **Moan** is also a noun. ❏ *She gave a soft moan of discomfort.* [from Old English]

mob /mɒb/ (mobs, mobbing, mobbed)
1 **N-COUNT** A **mob** is a large, disorganized, and often violent crowd of people. ❏ *...a mob of angry men.*
2 **V-T** If you say that someone **is being mobbed by** a crowd of people, you mean that the people are trying to talk to them or get near them in an enthusiastic or threatening

way. ❏ *Her car was mobbed by reporters.* [from Latin]

Word Link	mobil ≈ moving : auto**mobil**e, **mobil**e, **mobil**ize

mo|bile /moʊbəl/ **ADJ** Someone or something that is **mobile** can easily move or be moved from place to place. ❏ *The family live in a three-bedroom mobile home near Las Cruces in New Mexico.* ❏ *Grandpa's eighty but he's still very mobile.* [from Old French]
→ look at Word Web: **cellphone**

Word Partnership	Use **mobile** with :
N	mobile **device**, mobile **service**

mo|bi|lize /moʊbɪlaɪz/ (mobilizes, mobilizing, mobilized)
1 **V-T** If you **mobilize** support or **mobilize** people to do something, you succeed in encouraging people to take action. ❏ *The government could not mobilize public support.* ● **mo|bi|li|za|tion** /moʊbɪlɪzeɪʃən/ **N-NONCOUNT** ❏ *...the mobilization of opinion in support of the revolution.*
2 **V-T/V-I** If a country **mobilizes**, or **mobilizes** its armed forces, or if its armed forces **mobilize**, orders are given to prepare for a conflict. ❏ *Sudan threatened to mobilize.* ● **mo|bi|li|za|tion** **N-NONCOUNT** ❏ *...mobilization to defend the republic.* [from Old French]

mock /mɒk/ (mocks, mocking, mocked) **V-T** If you **mock** someone, you laugh at them and try to make them feel foolish. ❏ *My friends mocked me because I didn't have a girlfriend.* [from Old French]

mod|al /moʊdəl/ (modals) **N-COUNT** LANGUAGE ARTS In grammar, a **modal** or a **modal auxiliary** is a word such as "can" or "would" that you use with another verb to express ideas such as possibility, intention, or necessity. [from Latin]

Word Link	mod ≈ measure, manner : **mod**e, **mod**el, **mod**ern

mode /moʊd/ (modes)
1 **N-COUNT** A **mode** of life or behavior is a particular way of living or behaving. [FORMAL] ❏ *He decided to completely change his mode of life.*
2 **N-COUNT** ARTS A **mode** is a particular style in art, literature, or dress. ❏ *...a formal mode of dress.*
3 **N-COUNT** MATH In statistics, the **mode** of a set of numbers is the number that

m

occurs most often.

4 **N-COUNT** MUSIC A **mode** is a scale with a particular arrangement of intervals. [from Latin]

> **Word Link**   mod ≈ measure, manner : mode, model, modern

mod|el /mɒdᵊl/ (**models, modeling, modeled**)

1 **N-COUNT** ARTS A **model** is a small copy of something. ❑ At school, the children are making a model of the solar system. ❑ I made the model using paper and glue.

2 **ADJ** ARTS **Model** is also an adjective. ❑ I spent my childhood building model aircraft.

3 **N-COUNT** A **model** of a vehicle or a machine is a particular design of it. ❑ You don't need an expensive computer, just a basic model.

4 **N-COUNT** ARTS An artist's **model** is a person who sits or stands in front of an artist so that they can draw or paint them. ❑ The model for his painting was his sister.

5 **N-COUNT** A **model** is a person whose job is to wear and show new clothes in photographs and at fashion shows, so that people can see them and buy them. ❑ Kim dreams of becoming a fashion model.

6 **ADJ** You use **model** to express approval of someone when you think that they perform their role or duties extremely well. ❑ She was a model student.

7 **V-T/V-I** If you **model**, you wear clothes as a model. ❑ Nicole began modeling at age 15. ❑ She was modelling a new coat.

8 **V-T** If one thing **is modeled on** another, the first thing is made so that it is like the second thing in some way. ❑ The system was modeled on the one used in Europe. [from Old French]
→ look at Word Web: **forecast**

> **Word Partnership**   Use **model** with :
>
> | V | **build** a model, **make** a model **1** |
> | | **base** *something* **on** a model, **follow** a model, **serve as a** model **1** |
> | ADJ | **basic** model, **current** model, **latest** model, **new** model, **standard** model **2** |

mo|dem /moʊdəm, -dɛm/ (**modems**) **N-COUNT** TECHNOLOGY A **modem** is a piece of equipment that uses a telephone line to connect computers. ❑ ...a cellphone with a built-in modem.

mod|er|ate /mɒdərɪt/

1 **ADJ** If something is **moderate**, it is not too much or too little. ❑ Temperatures are moderate between October and March.
● **mod|er|ate|ly** **ADV** ❑ Heat the oil until it is moderately hot.

2 **ADJ** **Moderate** political opinions or policies are not extreme. ❑ He has very moderate views. [from Latin]

> **Word Partnership**   Use **moderate** with :
>
> | N | moderate **amount**, moderate **exercise**, moderate **growth**, moderate **heat**, moderate **improvement**, moderate **prices**, moderate **speed** **1** |
> | | moderate **approach**, moderate **position**, moderate **view** **2** |

mod|ern /mɒdərn/

1 **ADJ** **Modern** means relating to the time around now, for example the century that we are in. ❑ ...the problems in modern society.

2 **ADJ** If something is **modern**, it is new. ❑ I like antiques, but my husband prefers modern furniture. [from Old French]
→ look at Picture Dictionary: **dance**

> **Thesaurus**   modern   Also look up :
>
> | ADJ | contemporary, current, present **1** state-of-the-art, up-to-date **2** |

> **Word Partnership**   Use **modern** with :
>
> | N | modern **civilization**, modern **culture**, modern **era**, modern **life**, modern **science**, modern **society**, modern **times**, modern **warfare** **1** modern **conveniences**, modern **equipment**, modern **methods**, modern **techniques**, modern **technology** **2** |

mod|ern dance **N-NONCOUNT** ARTS **Modern dance** is a form of dance that developed in the twentieth century and uses movement to express emotion and abstract ideas.

> **Word Link**   ize ≈ making : legalize, modernize, vandalize

mod|ern|ize /mɒdərnaɪz/ (**modernizes, modernizing, modernized**) **V-T** To **modernize** a system or a factory means to change it by introducing new equipment, methods, or ideas. ❑ We need to modernize our schools. [from Old French]

mod|est /mɒdɪst/ **ADJ** If you are **modest**, you do not talk much about your abilities, skills, or successes. ❑ He's modest, as well as being a great player. ● **mod|est|ly ADV** ❑ "I was just lucky," Hughes said modestly. [from Old French]

mod|es|ty /mɒdɪsti/ **N-NONCOUNT** If you show **modesty**, you do not talk much about your abilities, skills or successes. ❑ His humor and gentle modesty won affection and friendships everywhere. [from Old French]

modi|fy /mɒdɪfaɪ/ (**modifies, modifying, modified**) **V-T** If you **modify** something, you change it slightly, usually in order to improve it. ❑ Helen and her husband modified the design of the house to suit their family's needs. ● **modi|fi|ca|tion** /mɒdɪfɪkeɪʃ°n/ (**modifications**) **N-COUNT/N-NONCOUNT** ❑ They made a few small modifications to the plan. [from Old French]

Moho /moʊhoʊ/ or Mohorovicic Discontinuity **N-SING** SCIENCE The Moho is the boundary between the Earth's crust and its mantle.

moist /mɔɪst/ (**moister, moistest**) **ADJ** If something is **moist**, it is slightly wet. ❑ The soil was moist after the rain. [from Old French]

mois|ture /mɔɪstʃər/ **N-NONCOUNT** Moisture is small drops of water in the air, on a surface, or in the ground. ❑ Keep the food covered so that it doesn't lose moisture. [from Old French]

mold /moʊld/ (**molds, molding, molded**)
1 N-COUNT A **mold** is a hollow container that you pour liquid into. When the liquid becomes solid, it takes the same shape as the mold. ❑ Pour the mixture into molds and place them in the refrigerator.
2 V-T If you **mold** a soft substance, you make it into a particular shape. ❑ The mixture is heated then molded.
3 N-NONCOUNT Mold is a soft gray, green, or blue substance that grows on old food or on damp surfaces. ❑ Hannah discovered mold growing in her bedroom closet. [from Old English]
→ look at Word Webs: **fungus, laboratory**

mole /moʊl/ (**moles**)
1 N-COUNT A **mole** is a natural dark spot on your skin. ❑ Rebecca has a mole on the side of her nose.
2 N-COUNT A **mole** is a small animal with black fur that lives under the ground. [Sense 1 from Old English. Sense 2 from Middle Dutch.]

mo|lecu|lar /məlɛkyələr/ **ADJ** SCIENCE **Molecular** means relating to or involving molecules. ❑ ...the molecular structure of oil. [from French]

mol|ecule /mɒlɪkyul/ (**molecules**) **N-COUNT** SCIENCE A **molecule** is the smallest amount of a chemical substance that can exist by itself. ❑ When hydrogen and oxygen molecules combine, the reaction produces heat and water. [from French]
→ look at Word Web: **element**

molt|ing /moʊltɪŋ/ **N-NONCOUNT** SCIENCE **Molting** is a process in which an animal or bird gradually loses its coat or feathers so that a new coat or feathers can grow. [from Old English]

mom /mɒm/ (**moms**) **N-COUNT** Your **mom** is your mother. [INFORMAL] ❑ We waited for my mom and dad to get home. ❑ Bye, Mom. Love you.

mo|ment /moʊmənt/ (**moments**)
1 N-COUNT A **moment** is a very short period of time. ❑ In a moment he was gone.
2 N-COUNT A particular **moment** is the time when something happens. ❑ At that moment a car stopped at the house.
3 PHRASE If something is happening **at the moment**, it is happening at or around the time when you are speaking. ❑ At the moment, the team is playing very well.
4 PHRASE If something is true **for the moment**, it is true now, but it may not be true in the future. ❑ For the moment, everything is fine.
5 PHRASE If something is going to happen **in a moment**, it is going to happen very soon. ❑ Please take a seat. Mr. Garcia will see you in a moment.
6 PHRASE If you say that something happened **the moment** something else happened, you mean that it happened immediately after the first thing. ❑ The moment I closed my eyes, I fell asleep. [from Old French]

Word Partnership	Use **moment** with :
ADV	a moment **ago, just a** moment **1**
N	moment **of silence**, moment **of thought 1**
V	**stop for a** moment, **take a** moment, **think for a** moment, **wait a** moment **1**
ADJ	**an awkward** moment, **a critical** moment, **the right** moment **2**

m

mo|men|tum /moʊmɛntəm/

1 **N-NONCOUNT** If a process or a movement gains **momentum**, it keeps developing or happening more quickly and keeps becoming less likely to stop. ❑ *This campaign is really gaining momentum.*

2 **N-NONCOUNT** SCIENCE In physics, **momentum** is the mass of a moving object multiplied by its speed in a particular direction. [from Latin]

→ look at Word Web: **motion**

Word Partnership	Use **momentum** with :
v	**build** momentum, **gain** momentum, **gather** momentum, **have** momentum, **lose** momentum, **maintain** momentum **1** **2**

mom|my /mɒmi/ (**mommies**) **N-COUNT**
Young children call their mother **Mommy**. [INFORMAL] ❑ *Please can I have a cookie, Mommy?*

Word Link	arch ≈ rule : matriarch, monarch, patriarch

mon|arch /mɒnərk, -ɑrk/ (**monarchs**)
N-COUNT SOCIAL STUDIES The **monarch** of a country is the king, queen, emperor, or empress. [from Late Latin]

mon|ar|chy /mɒnərki/ (**monarchies**)
N-COUNT/N-NONCOUNT SOCIAL STUDIES A **monarchy** is a system in which a country has a king or a queen. ❑ *Greece abolished the monarchy in 1974.* [from Late Latin]

Mon|day /mʌndeɪ, -di/ (**Mondays**)
N-COUNT/N-NONCOUNT **Monday** is the day after Sunday and before Tuesday. ❑ *I went back to work on Monday.* ❑ *The first meeting was last Monday.* [from Old English]

mon|etary /mɒnɪtɛri/ **ADJ** BUSINESS
Monetary means relating to money, especially the total amount of money in a country. ❑ *The U.S. monetary system is a decimal system, with 100 cents in one dollar.* [from Late Latin]

mon|ey /mʌni/ **N-NONCOUNT** **Money** is the coins or bills that you use to buy things. ❑ *Cars cost a lot of money.* ❑ *She spends too much money on clothes and shoes.* ❑ *Companies have to earn money.* [from Old French]

→ look at Word Webs: **money, donor**

Thesaurus	money	Also look up :
N	capital, cash, currency, funds, wealth	

moni|tor /mɒnɪtər/ (**monitors, monitoring, monitored**)

1 **V-T** If you **monitor** something, you watch how it develops or progresses over a period of time. ❑ *Doctors closely monitored her progress.*

2 **N-COUNT** A **monitor** is a machine that is used to check or record things. ❑ *The monitor shows his heartbeat.*

3 **N-COUNT** A **monitor** is a screen that is used to display certain kinds of information. ❑ *He was watching a game of tennis on a television monitor.* [from Latin]

→ look at Picture Dictionary: **computer**
→ look at Word Web: **tsunami**

Word Partnership	Use **monitor** with :
v	monitor **activity**, monitor **elections**, monitor **performance**, monitor **progress**, monitor a **1**
N	**color** monitor, **computer** monitor, **video** monitor **3**
ADV	**carefully** monitor, **closely** monitor **1**

Word Web   money

Early traders used a system of **barter** which didn't involve **money**. For example, a farmer might trade a cow for a

wooden cart. In China, India, and Africa, cowrie shells* became a form of **currency**. The first **coins** were crude lumps of metal. Uniform circular coins appeared in China around 1500 BC. In 1150 AD, the Chinese started using paper bills for money. In 560 BC, the Lydians (living in what is now Turkey) used three types of coins—a **gold** coin, a **silver** coin, and a mixed metal coin. Their use quickly spread through Asia Minor and Greece.

cowrie shell: a small, shiny, oval shell.

monk /mʌŋk/ (monks) **N-COUNT** A **monk** is a member of a group of religious men who live together in a special building. [from Old English]

mon|key /mʌŋki/ (monkeys) **N-COUNT** A **monkey** is an animal that has a long tail and can climb trees. [from Low German]
→ look at Word Web: **primate**

mono /mɒnoʊ/ **ADJ** **Mono** is used to describe a system of playing music in which all the sound is directed through one speaker only. Compare **stereo**. ❏ *This model has a mono soundtrack.*

mono|chro|mat|ic /mɒnəkrəmætɪk/ **ADJ** ARTS **Monochromatic** pictures use only one color in various shades.

mono|cline /mɒnəklaɪn/ (monoclines) **N-COUNT** SCIENCE A **monocline** is a rock formation in which layers of rock are folded so that they are horizontal on both sides of the fold. [from Greek]

> **Word Link** mono ≈ one : monologue, monopoly, monotone

mono|logue /mɒnəlɔg/ (monologues) also monolog
1 **N-COUNT** If you refer to a long speech by one person during a conversation as a **monologue**, you mean it prevents other people from talking or expressing their opinions. ❏ *Morris continued his monologue.*
2 **N-COUNT/N-NONCOUNT** ARTS A **monologue** is a long speech which is spoken by one person as an entertainment, or as part of an entertainment such as a play. [from French]

mo|no|mial /mɒnoʊmiəl/ (monomials)
1 **N-COUNT** MATH A **monomial** is an expression in algebra that consists of just one term, for example "5xy." Compare with **binomial** and **polynomial**.
2 **ADJ** MATH **monomial** is also an adjective ❏ *...monomial expressions.*

mo|nopo|ly /mənɒpəli/ (monopolies)
1 **N-COUNT/N-NONCOUNT** BUSINESS SOCIAL STUDIES If a company or a person has a **monopoly on** an industry, they have complete control over it. ❏ *The East India Company had a monopoly on all trade to Britain from the East.*
2 **N-COUNT** BUSINESS SOCIAL STUDIES A **monopoly** is the only company that provides a particular product. ❏ *The company*

is a state-owned monopoly. [from Late Latin]

mono|tone /mɒnətoʊn/ (monotones)
1 **N-COUNT** If someone speaks in a **monotone**, their voice does not change in tone or volume and so it is not interesting to listen to. ❏ *The evidence was read out to the court in a dull monotone.*
2 **ADJ** A **monotone** voice is not interesting to listen to because it does not change in volume or tone. ❏ *He was seen on TV talking about the crisis in a monotone voice.* [from Greek]

mo|noto|nous /mənɒtᵊnəs/ **ADJ** If something is **monotonous**, it is very boring because it never changes. ❏ *It's monotonous work, like most factory jobs.*

mono|treme /mɒnətrim/ (monotremes) **N-COUNT** SCIENCE A **monotreme** is a mammal that gives birth by laying eggs. [from New Latin]

mon|soon /mɒnsun/ (monsoons) **N-COUNT** SCIENCE In Southern Asia, the **monsoon** is the season when there is a lot of very heavy rain. ❏ *The monsoon season lasts for about four months each year.* [from Dutch]
→ look at Word Web: **disaster**

mon|ster /mɒnstər/ (monsters) **N-COUNT** In stories, a **monster** is a big, ugly, and frightening creature. ❏ *The movie is about a monster in the bedroom closet.* [from Old French]

month /mʌnθ/ (months) **N-COUNT** A **month** is one of the twelve parts that a year is divided into. ❏ *September is the ninth month of the year.* ❏ *We go on vacation next month.* [from Old English]
→ look at Word Web: **year**

month|ly /mʌnθli/
1 **ADJ** A **monthly** event happens every month. ❏ *The monthly rent for his apartment is $1,000.*
2 **ADV** **Monthly** is also an adverb. ❏ *The magazine is published monthly.* [from Old English]

monu|ment /mɒnyəmənt/ (monuments) **N-COUNT** SOCIAL STUDIES A **monument** is something that you build to help people remember an important event or person. ❏ *This monument was built in memory of the soldiers who died in the war.* [from Latin]

monument

mood /mu̱d/ (**moods**)

1 **N-COUNT** Your **mood** is the way you are feeling at a particular time. ❑ *Dad is in a very good mood today.* ❑ *I had an argument with my girlfriend, so I was in a bad mood.*

2 **PHRASE** If you are **in the mood for** something, you feel like having it or doing it. ❑ *He wasn't in the mood for talking.* [from Old English]

Word Partnership	Use **mood** with :
ADJ	**bad/good** mood, **depressed** mood, **foul** mood, **positive** mood, **tense** mood **1**
N	mood **change**, mood **disorder**, mood **swings** **1**

moody /mu̱di/ (**moodier, moodiest**) **ADJ** If you are **moody**, you often become sad or angry without any warning. ❑ *David's mother is very moody.* [from Old English]

moon /mu̱n/ (**moons**)

1 **N-SING** SCIENCE **The moon** is the large object that shines in the sky at night. ❑ *The first man on the moon was an American, Neil Armstrong.*

2 **N-COUNT** A **moon** is an object similar to a small planet that travels around a planet. ❑ *...Neptune's large moon.* [from Old English] → look at Word Webs: **moon, astronomer, eclipse, satellite, solar system, tide**

Word Link	light ≈ shining : day**light**, moon**light**, sun**light**

moon|light /mu̱nlaɪt/ **N-NONCOUNT** **Moonlight** is the light that comes from the moon at night. ❑ *They walked along the road in the moonlight.*

moor /mʊ̱ər/ (**moors, mooring, moored**) **V-T/V-I** If you **moor**, or **moor** a boat somewhere, you stop and tie the boat to the land with a rope or a chain so that it cannot move away. ❑ *She had moored her boat on the right bank of the river.* ❑ *I decided to moor near some small boats.* [of Germanic origin]

moose /mu̱s/ (**moose**) **N-COUNT** A **moose** is the largest member of the deer family. (A **deer** = a large wild animal with horns that are like branches). ❑ *In the fall, they hunt moose and deer.* [from Algonquian]

mop /mɒ̱p/ (**mops, mopping, mopped**)

1 **N-COUNT** A **mop** is a long stick with a lot of thick pieces of string at one end. You use it for washing floors.

2 **V-T** If you **mop** a floor, you clean it with a mop. ❑ *I could see a woman mopping the stairs.* [from Medieval Latin]

mo|raine /məre̱ɪn/ (**moraines**) **N-COUNT** SCIENCE A **moraine** is a pile of rocks and soil left behind by a glacier. [from French]

mor|al /mɔ̱rᵊl/ (**morals**)

1 **N-PLURAL** Your **morals** are your ideas and beliefs about right and wrong behavior. ❑ *Amy has strong morals and high standards.*

2 **ADJ** Something **moral** relates to people's beliefs about what is right or wrong. ❑ *We all have a moral duty to stop racism.* ● **mor|al|ly** **ADV** ❑ *It is morally wrong to kill a person.*

3 **ADJ** A **moral** person behaves in a way that most people believe to be good and right. ❑ *The minister was a deeply moral man.*

4 **N-COUNT** LANGUAGE ARTS **The moral** of a story or event is what you learn from it about how you should or should not behave. ❑ *The moral of this sad story is "do not trust anyone."* [from Latin] → look at Word Web: **philosophy**

mo|rale /mərǽl/ **N-NONCOUNT** **Morale** is the amount of confidence and cheerfulness that a group of people have. ❑ *Many teachers are suffering from low morale.* [from French]

mo|ral|ity /mərǽlɪti/

1 **N-NONCOUNT** **Morality** is the belief that some behavior is right and acceptable and that other behavior is wrong. ❑ *...standards of morality in society.*

Word Web   **moon**

Scientists believe the **moon** is about five billion years old. They think a large **asteroid** hit the earth. A big piece of the earth broke off. It went flying into **space**. However, the earth's **gravity** caught it. It began to circle the earth. This piece became our moon. The moon orbits the earth once a month. It also **rotates** on its **axis** every thirty days. The moon has no **atmosphere**, so **meteoroids** crash into it. When a meteoroid hits the moon, it makes a **crater**. Craters cover the surface of the moon.

2 **N-NONCOUNT** The **morality** of something is how right or acceptable it is. ❑ ...*arguments about the morality of nuclear weapons.* [from French]

more /mɔr/

> **LANGUAGE HELP**
> **More** is often considered to be the comparative of **much** and **many**.

1 **DET** You use **more** to talk about a greater amount of something. ❑ *More people are surviving heart attacks than ever before.* ❑ *I need more time to think about what to do.*

2 **PRON** **More** is also a pronoun. ❑ *As they worked harder, they ate more.* ❑ *We should be doing more to help these people.* ❑ *They're doing more of their own work.*

3 **ADV** **More** shows that something continues to happen. ❑ *You should talk about your problems more.*

4 **DET** You use **more** to talk about an additional thing or amount. ❑ *They needed more time to think about what to do.*

5 **ADJ** **More** is also an adjective. ❑ *We stayed in Danville two more days.*

6 **PHRASE** You use **more than** to talk about a greater amount of something than the amount mentioned. ❑ *The airport had been closed for more than a year.*

7 **PHRASE** You can use **more and more** to show that something is becoming greater all the time. ❑ *She began eating more and more.*

8 **PHRASE** You can use **more or less** to mean not completely or not exactly. ❑ *The fighting had more or less stopped.* [from Old English]

more|over /mɔroʊvər/ **ADV** You use **moreover** when you are adding more information about something. [FORMAL] ❑ *She saw that there was a man behind her. Moreover, he was staring at her.*

morn|ing /mɔrnɪŋ/ (**mornings**)

1 **N-COUNT/N-NONCOUNT** The **morning** is the part of each day between the time that people usually wake up and noon. ❑ *Tomorrow morning we will take a walk around the city.* ❑ *On Sunday morning the telephone woke Bill.*

2 **N-SING** If you talk about a particular time in **the morning,** you mean a time between 12 o'clock midnight and 12 o'clock noon. ❑ *I often stay up until two or three in the morning.*

3 **PHRASE** If you say that something will happen **in the morning,** you mean that it will happen during the morning of the following day. ❑ *I'm flying to St. Louis in the morning.*

→ look at Picture Dictionary: **time**

mor|phol|ogy /mɔrfɒlədʒi/ (**morphologies**)

1 **N-COUNT/N-NONCOUNT** The **morphology** of something is its form and structure. ❑ ...*morphologies of animals and plants.*

2 **N-NONCOUNT** LANGUAGE ARTS **Morphology** is the study of the way in which words are constructed. [from Greek]

mor|tal /mɔrtᵊl/ (**mortals**)

1 **ADJ** If you refer to the fact that people are **mortal,** you mean that they have to die and cannot live forever. ❑ *A man is mortal. He grows, he becomes old, and he dies.* ● **mor|tal|ity** /mɔrtælɪti/ **N-NONCOUNT** ❑ ...*fears about our own mortality.*

2 **N-COUNT** You can describe someone as a **mortal** when you want to say that they are an ordinary person. ❑ *We are all mere mortals and we make mistakes.*

3 **ADJ** You can use **mortal** to show that something is very serious or may cause death. ❑ *The police were defending people against mortal danger.* ● **mor|tal|ly** **ADV** ❑ *He falls, mortally wounded.* [from Latin]

mor|tar /mɔrtər/ (**mortars**)

1 **N-COUNT** A **mortar** is a big gun that fires missiles high into the air over a short distance. ❑ *Mortars were still exploding.*

2 **N-NONCOUNT** **Mortar** is a mixture of sand, water, and cement or lime which is put between bricks to hold them together. ❑ *Bricks and mortar are basic building materials.* [from Latin]

mort|gage /mɔrgɪdʒ/ (**mortgages**)

N-COUNT A **mortgage** is a loan of money that you get from a bank in order to buy a house. ❑ *I had to sell my home because I couldn't afford the mortgage payments.* [from Old French]

mo|sa|ic /moʊzeɪɪk/ (**mosaics**)

N-COUNT/N-NONCOUNT ARTS A **mosaic** is a surface that is made of small pieces of colored glass or stone. ❑ ...*a Roman house with a beautiful mosaic floor.* [from French]

Mos|lem /mʌzlɪm, mʊs-/ → look up **Muslim**

mosque /mɒsk/ (**mosques**) **N-COUNT** A **mosque** is a building where Muslims go to pray. [from Old French]

mos|qui|to /məskitoʊ/ (**mosquitoes** or **mosquitos**) **N-COUNT** **Mosquitos** are small flying insects that bite people and animals. [from Spanish]

→ look at Picture Dictionary: **insect**

m

moss /mɔs/ (**mosses**) **N-COUNT/N-NONCOUNT**
Moss is a very small, soft, green plant that grows on wet soil, or on wood or stone. ❑ *The ground was covered with moss.* [from Old English]

most /moʊst/

> **LANGUAGE HELP**
>
> **Most** is often considered to be the superlative of **much** and **many**.

1 **DET** You use **most** to talk about the largest amount of people or things. ❑ *Most people think he is a great actor.*
2 **PRON** **Most** is also a pronoun. ❑ *Seventeen people were hurt. Most were students.* ❑ *Most of the houses here are very old.* ❑ *I was away from home most of the time.*
3 **ADV** You use **most** to show that something is true or happens more than anything else. ❑ *What do you like most about your job?*
4 **PHRASE** You use **most of all** to show that something happens or is true to a greater extent than anything else. ❑ *It was the moment he had dreaded most of all.*
5 **ADV** You use **most** to show that someone or something has the greatest amount of a particular quality. ❑ *Her children had the most unusual birthday parties in the neighborhood.*
6 **PHRASE** You use **at most** to say that a number or amount is the maximum that is possible. ❑ *Heat the sauce for ten minutes at most.*
7 **PHRASE** If you **make the most of** something, you use it in the best possible way. ❑ *You should make the most of what you have if you want to be happy.* [from Old English]
→ look at Usage note at **almost**

most|ly /moʊstli/ **ADV** If something is **mostly** true, it is almost always true. ❑ *My friends are mostly students.* ❑ *Cars are made mostly of metal.* [from Old English]

mo|tel /moʊtɛl/ (**motels**) **N-COUNT** A **motel** is a hotel for people who are traveling by car.

moth /mɔθ/ (**moths**)
N-COUNT A **moth** is an insect that has large wings and is attracted by lights at night. [from Old English]

moth

moth|er /mʌðər/ (**mothers**) **N-COUNT** Your **mother** is your female parent. ❑ *My mother is a schoolteacher.* ❑ *She's a mother of two children.* [from Old English]
→ look at Picture Dictionary: **family**

> **Word Link** hood ≈ state, condition : child**hood**, mother**hood**, neighbor**hood**

moth|er|hood /mʌðərhʊd/ **N-NONCOUNT**
Motherhood is the state of being a mother. ❑ *I love motherhood. It's just the most extraordinary thing.* [from Old English]

moth|er-in-law (**mothers-in-law**) **N-COUNT**
Someone's **mother-in-law** is the mother of their husband or wife.
→ look at Picture Dictionary: **family**

mo|tif /moʊtif/ (**motifs**)
1 **N-COUNT** A **motif** is a design which is used as a decoration or as part of an artistic pattern. ❑ *...a rose motif.*
2 **N-COUNT** A **motif** is a distinctive idea that is repeated over and over again to create a theme, especially in music or literature. [from French]

> **Word Link** mot ≈ moving : **mot**ion, **mot**ivate, pro**mot**e

mo|tion /moʊʃ°n/ (**motions, motioning, motioned**)
1 **N-NONCOUNT** **Motion** is movement. ❑ *The doors will not open when the elevator is in motion.*
2 **N-COUNT** A **motion** is an action, a gesture,

> ## Word Web   motion
>
> Newton's three laws of **motion** describe how **forces** affect the movement of objects. This is the first law: an object at **rest** won't move unless a force makes it move. Also, a moving object keeps its **momentum** unless something stops it. The second law is about **acceleration**. The **rate** of acceleration depends on two things: how strong the push on the object is, and how much the object weighs. The third law says that for every **action** there is an equal and opposite **reaction**. When one object **exerts** a force on another, the second object pushes back with an equal force.
>
>

or a movement. ❑ *He made a motion toward the door with his hand.*

3 **N-COUNT** A **motion** is a formal proposal in a meeting or a debate, that is discussed and then voted on. ❑ *The committee debated the motion all day.*

4 **V-T/V-I** If you **motion** to someone, you move your hand or head as a way of telling them to do something. ❑ *She motioned for my father to come in.*

5 **PHRASE** If a process or an event is set **in motion**, it is happening or beginning to happen. ❑ *Big changes can be set in motion by small things.* [from Latin]
→ look at Word Web: **motion**

Word Partnership	Use **motion** with :
ADJ	**constant** motion, **full** motion, **perpetual** motion **1** **circular** motion, **smooth** motion **1** **2** **quick** motion **2**
V	**set** *something* in motion **1** **5**

mo|tion|less /moʊʃnlɪs/ **ADJ** If someone or something is **motionless**, they are not moving at all. ❑ *They stood motionless, staring at each other.* [from Latin]

Word Link	ate ≈ causing to be : complicate, motivate, pollinate

mo|ti|vate /moʊtɪveɪt/ (**motivates, motivating, motivated**) **V-T** If someone or something **motivates** you to do something, they make you feel determined to do it. ❑ *How do you motivate people to work hard?*
● **mo|ti|vat|ed** **ADJ** ❑ *We are looking for a highly motivated and hard-working professional.* [from Old French]

mo|ti|va|tion /moʊtɪveɪʃ°n/ (**motivations**)
1 **N-NONCOUNT** Motivation is a feeling that makes you determined to do something. ❑ *His poor performance is caused by lack of motivation.*
2 **N-COUNT** Your **motivation** for doing something is what causes you to want to do it. ❑ *Money is my motivation.* [from Old French]

mo|tive /moʊtɪv/ (**motives**) **N-COUNT** Your **motive** for doing something is your reason for doing it. ❑ *Police do not think robbery was a motive for the killing.* [from Old French]

mo|tor /moʊtər/ (**motors**) **N-COUNT** The **motor** in a machine is the part that makes it move or work. ❑ *She got in the boat and started the motor.* [from Latin]

motor|cycle /moʊtərsaɪk°l/ (**motorcycles**)
N-COUNT A **motorcycle** is a vehicle with two wheels and an engine.

motor|cyclist /moʊtərsaɪklɪst/ (**motorcyclists**) **N-COUNT** A **motorcyclist** is a person who rides a motorcycle.

mo|tor|ist /moʊtərɪst/ (**motorists**) **N-COUNT** A **motorist** is a person who drives a car. ❑ *Motorists should take extra care on the roads when it is raining.* [from Latin]

mo|tor neu|ron (**motor neurons**) **N-COUNT** SCIENCE **Motor neurons** are nerve cells that carry information from the brain and spinal cord to the muscles in your body.

mot|to /mɒtoʊ/ (**mottoes** or **mottos**)
N-COUNT A **motto** is a short sentence or phrase that gives a rule for sensible behavior. ❑ *My motto is "Don't start what you can't finish."* [from Italian]

mound /maʊnd/ (**mounds**)
1 **N-COUNT** A **mound** of something is a large, round pile of it. ❑ *...huge mounds of dirt.*
2 **N-COUNT** In baseball, the **mound** is the raised area where the pitcher stands to throw the ball. ❑ *He went to the mound to talk with the pitcher.* [from Old English]
→ look at Picture Dictionary: **baseball**

mount /maʊnt/ (**mounts, mounting, mounted**)
1 **V-T** If you **mount** a campaign or an event, you organize it and make it take place. ❑ *The police mounted a search of the area.*
2 **V-I** If something **mounts**, it increases in intensity. ❑ *The pressure was mounting.*
3 **V-I** If something **mounts**, it increases in quantity. ❑ *The garbage mounts in city streets.*
4 **Mount up** means the same as **mount**. ❑ *Her medical bills mounted up.*
5 **V-T** If you **mount** the stairs or a platform, you go up the stairs or go up onto the platform. [FORMAL] ❑ *I mounted the steps to my room.*
6 **V-T** If you **mount** a horse or a motorcycle, you climb onto it so that you can ride it. ❑ *A man was mounting a motorcycle.*
7 **V-T** If you **mount** an object **on** something, you fix it there firmly. ❑ *Her husband mounts the work on colored paper.* ● **-mounted** ❑ *...a wall-mounted electric fan.*
8 **N-COUNT** **Mount** is used as part of the name of a mountain. ❑ *...Mount Everest.* [Senses 1 to 6 from Old French. Sense 7 from Old English.]

m

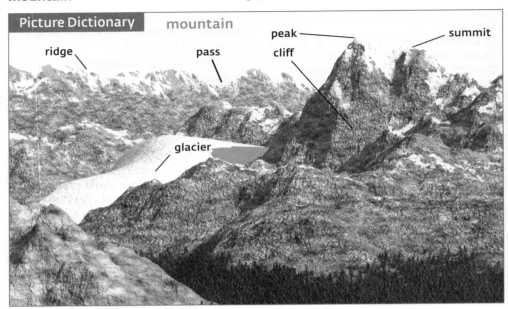

Picture Dictionary — mountain

ridge · pass · peak · cliff · summit · glacier

moun|tain /maʊntᵊn/ (**mountains**)
1 N-COUNT GEOGRAPHY A **mountain** is
a very high area of land with steep sides.
❑ *Mt. McKinley is the highest mountain in North
America.*
2 N-COUNT A **mountain of** something is a
very large amount of it. [INFORMAL] ❑ *He has
a mountain of homework.* [from Old French]
→ look at Picture Dictionary: **mountain**

moun|tain bike (**mountain bikes**) N-COUNT
SPORTS A **mountain bike** is a bicycle with a
strong frame and thick tires.

Word Link   *eer ≈ one who does : engineer,*
mountaineer, volunteer

moun|tain|eer /maʊntᵊnɪər/
(**mountaineers**) N-COUNT A **mountaineer** is a
person who is skillful at climbing the steep
sides of mountains. [from Old French]

moun|tain go|ril|la (**mountain gorillas**)
N-COUNT SCIENCE A **mountain gorilla** is a
type of gorilla that has long, dark hair and
lives in central Africa.

moun|tain|ous /maʊntᵊnəs/ ADJ A
mountainous place has a lot of mountains.
❑ *There were some beautiful shots of the country's
mountainous landscape.* [from Old French]

mourn /mɔrn/ (**mourns, mourning,**
mourned) V-T/V-I If you **mourn** someone
who has died or **mourn for** them, you are
very sad that they have died and show your

sorrow in the way that you behave. ❑ *Joan
still mourns her father.* ❑ *He mourned for his dead
son.* ● **mourn|ing** N-NONCOUNT ❑ *He is still in
mourning for his fiancee.* [from Old English]

mourn|er /mɔrnər/ (**mourners**) N-COUNT
A **mourner** is a person who goes to a funeral.
❑ *Crowds of mourners gathered outside the church.*
[from Old English]

mouse /maʊs/ (**mice**)
1 N-COUNT A **mouse** is a small animal with
a long tail. ❑ *My little sister has three pet mice.*
2 N-COUNT TECHNOLOGY A **mouse** is an
object that you use to do things on a
computer without using the keyboard.
❑ *I clicked the mouse and the message appeared on
the screen.* [from Old English]
→ look at Picture Dictionary: **computer**

mouse pad (**mouse pads**) also **mousepad**
N-COUNT TECHNOLOGY A **mouse pad** is a flat
piece of soft material that you move the
mouse on when you use a computer.
→ look at Picture Dictionary: **computer**

mousse /mus/ N-NONCOUNT **Mousse** is a
sweet, light food made from eggs and
cream. ❑ *His favorite dessert is chocolate mousse.*
[from French]
→ look at Picture Dictionary: **dessert**

mouth /maʊθ/ (**mouths**)
1 N-COUNT SCIENCE Your **mouth** is the part of
your face that you use for eating or speaking.

❑ *When you cough, please cover your mouth.*
2 **N-COUNT** SCIENCE The **mouth** of a cave or a bottle is its entrance or opening. ❑ *He stopped at the mouth of the tunnel.*
3 **N-COUNT** GEOGRAPHY The **mouth** of a river is the place where it goes into the ocean. [from Old English]
→ look at Picture Dictionary: **face**
→ look at Word Web: **respiratory system**

mouth|ful /maʊθfʊl/ (mouthfuls) **N-COUNT**
A **mouthful of** drink or food is the amount that you can put in your mouth at one time. ❑ *She drank a mouthful of coffee.* [from Old English]

mouth|piece /maʊθpis/ (mouthpieces)
1 **N-COUNT** The **mouthpiece** of a telephone is the part that you speak into. ❑ *He shouted into the mouthpiece.*
2 **N-COUNT** MUSIC The **mouthpiece** of a musical instrument or other device is the part that you put into your mouth. ❑ *He showed him how to blow into the trumpet's mouthpiece.*
3 **N-COUNT** The **mouthpiece** of an organization or a person is someone who informs other people of the opinions and policies of that organization or person. ❑ *The organization's mouthpiece is the vice president.*

mov|able /muvəbªl/ also **moveable** **ADJ**
Something that is **movable** can be moved from one place or position to another. ❑ *It's a doll with movable arms and legs.* [from Latin]
→ look at Word Web: **printing**

mov|able pul|ley /muvəbªl pʊli/ (movable pulleys) also **moveable pulley** **N-COUNT**
SCIENCE A **movable pulley** is a pulley that is not attached to anything and can therefore move freely. Compare with **fixed pulley**.

move /muv/ (moves, moving, moved)
1 **V-T/V-I** When you **move** something, or when it **moves**, its position changes. ❑ *A police officer asked him to move his car.* ❑ *The train began to move.*
2 **V-I** When someone or something **moves**, they change their position or go to a different place. ❑ *The train began to move.* ❑ *She waited for him to get up, but he didn't move.*
3 **N-COUNT** Move is also a noun. ❑ *The doctor made a move toward the door.*
4 **N-COUNT** A **move** is something you do in order to achieve something. ❑ *Leaving my job was a good move.*

5 **V-I** If you **move**, you go to live in a different place. ❑ *She's moving to Seattle next month.*
6 **N-COUNT** Move is also a noun. ❑ *After his move to New York, he got a job as an actor.*
7 **V-I** If you **move** toward a particular state or activity, you start to be in that state or do that activity. ❑ *Many countries are now moving toward democracy.*
8 **V-I** If a situation or a process **is moving**, it is developing or progressing. ❑ *Events are moving fast.*
9 **V-T** If something **moves** you, it makes you have strong feelings for another person. ❑ *The story surprised and moved me.* ● **moved** **ADJ** ❑ *We felt quite moved when we heard his story.* [from Latin]
10 → see also **moving**
▶ **move in** When you **move in** somewhere, you begin to live there. ❑ *A new family has moved in next door.*
▶ **move out** If you **move out**, you stop living in a particular place. ❑ *I wasn't happy living there, so I decided to move out.*

Word Link	mov ≈ moving : movement, movie, remove

Word Link	ment ≈ state, condition : agreement, management, movement

move|ment /muvmənt/ (movements)
1 **N-COUNT/N-NONCOUNT** Movement means changing position, or going from one place to another. ❑ *Brian was injured and now has limited movement in his left arm.*
2 **N-COUNT** A **movement** is a group of people who have the same beliefs or ideas. ❑ *It was one of the biggest political movements in the country.*
3 **N-COUNT/N-NONCOUNT** Movement is a gradual development or change. ❑ *...the movement toward democracy in Latin America.* [from Latin]
→ look at Word Web: **brain**

move|ment pat|tern (movement patterns) **N-COUNT** SCIENCE A **movement pattern** is a series of movements that involve a particular part of the body, for example the neck or head.

mov|er /muvər/ (movers) **N-COUNT** Movers are people whose job is to move furniture or equipment from one building to another. [from Latin]

mov|ie /muvi/ (movies)
1 **N-COUNT** A **movie** is a story that is shown in a series of moving pictures. ❑ *Matton made*

m

a movie about the Dutch painter Rembrandt.
2 **N-PLURAL** If you go to **the movies**, you go to see a movie in a movie theater. ❑ *Sam took her to the movies last week.*
→ look at Word Web: **genre**

Word Partnership	Use movie with :
ADJ	**bad/good** movie, **favorite** movie, **new/old** movie, movie **1**
V	**go to a** movie, **see a** movie, **watch a** movie **1**
N	**scene in a** movie, movie **screen**, movie **set**, movie, **television/TV** movie **1**

mov|ie star (**movie stars**) **N-COUNT** A movie star is a famous actor or actress who acts in movies.

mov|ie thea|ter (**movie theaters**) **N-COUNT** A **movie theater** is a place where people go to watch movies.

mov|ing /múvɪŋ/
1 **ADJ** If something is **moving**, it makes you feel a strong emotion such as sadness, pity, or sympathy. ❑ *This is a moving story of the love between a master and his loyal dog.* [from Latin]
2 → see also **move**

mow /móʊ/ (**mows, mowing, mowed, mown**)

> **LANGUAGE HELP**
> The past participle can be either **mowed** or **mown**.

V-T/V-I If you **mow** an area of grass, you cut it using a machine (called a mower). ❑ *Connor was in the backyard, mowing the lawn.* ❑ *It's too wet to start mowing.* [from Old English]

mow|er /móʊər/ (**mowers**) **N-COUNT** A **mower** is a machine that you use to cut grass. ❑ *Clean the mower before and after cutting your lawn.* [from Old English]

moz|za|rel|la /mɑtsərɛlə, moʊt-/ **N-NONCOUNT** Mozzarella is a type of white Italian cheese. ❑ *Maria made a delicious pizza topped with tomato and mozzarella.* [from Italian]

MP3 /ɛm pi θri/ (**MP3s**) **N-COUNT** TECHNOLOGY An **MP3** is a type of computer file that contains music.

MP3 play|er (**MP3 players**) **N-COUNT** TECHNOLOGY An **MP3 player** is a small machine for listening to music that is stored on computer files.

mph also **m.p.h.** MATH **mph** shows the speed of a vehicle. **mph** is short for "miles per hour." ❑ *On this road, you must not drive faster than 20 mph.*

Mr. /mɪstər/ You use **Mr.** before a man's name when you want to be polite or formal. ❑ *Could I please speak to Mr. Robert Johnson?* ❑ *Our teacher this semester is called Mr. Becker.*

Mrs. /mɪsɪz/ You use **Mrs.** before the name of a married woman when you want to be polite or formal. ❑ *Hello, Mrs. Martinez. How are you?* ❑ *Excuse me, does Mrs. Anne Pritchard live here?*

Ms. /mɪz/ You can use **Ms.**, especially in written English, before a woman's name, instead of Mrs. or Miss. ❑ *Ms. Kennedy refused to speak to reporters after the meeting.* ❑ *This is the principal, Ms. Tina Crocker.*

much /mʌtʃ/
1 **ADV** You use **much** to talk about the large amount of something. ❑ *I ate too much food.* ❑ *These plants do not need much water.* ❑ *I don't have much free time these days.*
2 **PRON** **Much** is also a pronoun. ❑ *I ate too much.*
3 **ADV** If something does not happen **much**, it does not happen very often. ❑ *Gwen did not see her father very much.*
4 **ADV** **Much** means a lot. ❑ *His car is much bigger than mine.* ❑ *Thank you very much.* ❑ *He doesn't like jazz much.*
5 **DET** You use **how much** to ask questions about amounts. ❑ *How much money did you spend?* [from Old English]

mud /mʌd/ **N-NONCOUNT** Mud is a sticky mixture of earth and water. ❑ *Andy's clothes were covered with mud.* [from Middle Low German]

mud|dy /mʌdi/ (**muddier, muddiest**) **ADJ** If something is **muddy**, it is covered in mud. ❑ *Philip left his muddy boots at the kitchen door.* [from Middle Low German]

mud|flow /mʌdfloʊ/ (**mudflows**) **N-COUNT** SCIENCE A **mudflow** is the same as a **mudslide**.

mud|slide /mʌdslaɪd/ (**mudslides**) **N-COUNT** A **mudslide** is a large amount of mud sliding down a mountain, usually causing damage or destruction.

muf|fin /mʌfɪn/ (**muffins**) **N-COUNT** Muffins are small, round, sweet cakes that often have fruit inside. People usually eat muffins for breakfast. ❑ *Mrs. Williams handed her a blueberry muffin.* [from Low German]

mug /mʌg/ (**mugs, mugging, mugged**)
1 **N-COUNT** A **mug** is a deep cup with straight sides. ❑ *He poured tea into the mugs.*
2 **V-T** If someone **mugs** you, they attack you and steal your money. ❑ *I was walking to my car when this guy tried to mug me.* ● **mug|ging** (**muggings**) **N-COUNT/N-NONCOUNT** ❑ *Muggings are unusual in this neighborhood.* ● **mug|ger** (**muggers**) **N-COUNT** ❑ *When the mugger grabbed her purse, Ms. Jones fell to the ground.* [of Scandinavian origin]
→ look at Picture Dictionary: **crime**

multi|cel|lu|lar /mʌltisɛlyələr/ **ADJ** **SCIENCE** **Multicellular** organisms are organisms such as animals and plants that consist of more than one cell.

Word Link	multi ≈ many : multicolored, multimedia, multinational

multi|col|ored /mʌltikʌlərd/ **ADJ** A **multicolored** object has many different colors. ❑ *Diego was wearing a new, multicolored shirt.*

multi|media /mʌltimidiə/ **N-NONCOUNT** **ARTS** **Multimedia** computer programs have sound, pictures, and film, as well as text. ❑ *Most of his teachers use multimedia in the classroom.*

multi|na|tion|al /mʌltinæʃənªl/ (**multinationals**)
1 **ADJ** A **multinational** company has offices or businesses in many different countries.
2 **N-COUNT** **Multinational** is also a noun. ❑ *Large multinationals control the industry.*
3 **ADJ** **Multinational** organizations involve people from several different countries. ❑ *The U.S. troops will be part of a multinational force.*

multi|ple /mʌltɪpªl/ **ADJ** You use **multiple** to talk about things that consist of many parts, involve many people, or have many uses. ❑ *He died of multiple injuries.* [from French]

multi|ple scle|ro|sis /mʌltɪpªl sklərousɪs/ **N-NONCOUNT** **SCIENCE** **Multiple sclerosis** is a serious disease of the nervous system that gradually makes a person weaker. The short form **MS** is also used.

multi|plex /mʌltɪplɛks/ (**multiplexes**)
N-COUNT A **multiplex** is a movie theater complex with several screens.

multi|ply /mʌltɪplaɪ/ (**multiplies, multiplying, multiplied**) **V-T** **MATH** If you **multiply** a number, you add it to itself a certain number of times. ❑ *What do you get if you multiply six by nine?* ● **multi|pli|ca|tion** **N-NONCOUNT** ❑ *...a multiplication sum.* [from Old French]
→ look at Word Web: **mathematics**

multi|story /mʌltistɔri/ or **multistoried** **ADJ** A **multistory** building has several floors at different levels above the ground. ❑ *The store is in a big multistory building.*

mum|ble /mʌmbªl/ (**mumbles, mumbling, mumbled**)
1 **V-T/V-I** If you **mumble**, you speak quietly and not clearly. ❑ *The boy blushed and mumbled a few words.* ❑ *Her grandmother mumbled in her sleep.*
2 **N-COUNT** **Mumble** is also a noun. ❑ *His voice fell to a low mumble.*

mum|my /mʌmi/ (**mummies**) **N-COUNT** A **mummy** is a dead body that was preserved long ago by being rubbed with special oils and wrapped in cloth. ❑ *...an Ancient Egyptian mummy.* [from Old French]

mu|nici|pal /myunɪsɪpªl/ **ADJ** **SOCIAL STUDIES** **Municipal** means relating to a city or a town and its local government. ❑ *Her office was in a new municipal building in Flemington, New Jersey.* [from Latin]

mur|der /mɜrdər/ (**murders, murdering, murdered**)
1 **N-COUNT/N-NONCOUNT** **Murder** is the crime of deliberately killing a person. ❑ *The jury found him guilty of murder.* ❑ *The detective has worked on hundreds of murder cases.*
2 **V-T** If someone **murders** another person, they commit the crime of killing them deliberately. ❑ *The movie is about a woman who murders her husband.* ● **mur|der|er** /mɜrdərər/ (**murderers**) **N-COUNT** ❑ *One of these men is the murderer.* [from Old English]

mur|mur /mɜrmər/ (**murmurs, murmuring, murmured**)
1 **V-T** If you **murmur** something, you say it very quietly. ❑ *He turned and murmured something to Karen.* ❑ *"It's lovely," she murmured.*
2 **N-COUNT** A **murmur** is the low, soft sound of a voice or voices. ❑ *They spoke in low murmurs.* [from Latin]

mus|cle /mʌsªl/ (**muscles**)
N-COUNT/N-NONCOUNT **SCIENCE** Your **muscles** are the parts inside your body that

m

Word Web   muscle

There are three types of **muscles** in the body. **Voluntary** or **skeletal** muscles make external movements. **Involuntary** or **smooth** muscles move within the body. For example, the smooth muscles in the **iris** of the eye adjust the size of the pupil. This controls how much light enters the eye. **Cardiac** muscles are in the heart. They work constantly but never get tired. When we **exercise,** voluntary muscles **contract** and then **relax.** Repeated **workouts** can **build** these muscles and increase their **strength.** If we don't exercise, these muscles become **weak.**

connect your bones, and that help you to move. ❏ *Exercise helps to keep your muscles strong.* [from Latin]
→ look at Word Webs: **muscle, nervous system**

Word Partnership   Use muscle with :

N	muscle **aches**, muscle **mass**, muscle **pain**, muscle **tone**
V	**contract** a muscle, **flex** a muscle, **pull** a muscle

mus|cle tis|sue (muscle tissues) **N-COUNT/ N-NONCOUNT** SCIENCE **Muscle tissue** is tissue in animals and plants that is made of cells that can become shorter or longer.

mus|cu|lar /mˈʌskyələr/ **ADJ** If you are **muscular,** you have strong, firm muscles. ❏ *Jordan was tall and muscular.* [from New Latin]

mus|cu|lar dys|tro|phy /mˈʌskyələr dɪstrəfi/ **N-NONCOUNT** SCIENCE **Muscular dystrophy** is a serious disease in which your muscles gradually weaken.

mus|cu|lar sys|tem (muscular systems) **N-COUNT** SCIENCE The **muscular system** is the muscles and other parts of the body that control movement.

mus|cu|lo|skel|e|tal /mˈʌskyələuskˈɛlɪtəl/ **ADJ** SCIENCE **Musculoskeletal** problems

relate to the body's skeleton and muscles. ❏ *...musculoskeletal tension and fatigue.*

muse /myuz/ (muses, musing, mused) **V-T/V-I** If you **muse** on something, you think about it, usually saying or writing what you are thinking at the same time. [WRITTEN] ❏ *Many of the papers muse on what will happen to the president.* ❏ *"I like most of his work," she muses.*
● **mus|ing** (musings) **N-COUNT** ❏ *His mother interrupted his musings.* [from Old French]

mu|seum /myuziəm/ (museums) **N-COUNT** ARTS A **museum** is a building where you can look at interesting and valuable objects. ❏ *Hundreds of people came to the museum to see the exhibition.* [from Latin]

mush|room /mˈʌʃrum/ (mushrooms) **N-COUNT/N-NONCOUNT** A **mushroom** is a fungus with a short stem and a round top that you can eat. ❏ *There are many types of wild mushrooms, and some of them are poisonous.* [from Old French]
→ look at Word Web: **fungus**

mu|sic /myuzɪk/
1 **N-NONCOUNT** MUSIC **Music** is the pleasant sound that you make when you sing or play instruments. ❏ *Diane is studying classical music.* ❏ *What's your favorite music?*
2 **N-NONCOUNT** MUSIC **Music** is the symbols

Word Web   music

Wolfgang Amadeus Mozart lived only 35 years (1756–1791). However, he is one of the most important **musicians** in history. Mozart began playing the **piano** when he was four years old. A year later he

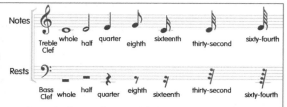

composed his first **song**. Since he hadn't learned musical **notation** yet, his father wrote out the **score** for him. Mozart played for royalty across Europe. Soon Mozart became known as a gifted **composer.** He wrote more than 50 **symphonies.** He also composed **operas, concertos,** and other musical works.

that you write on paper to tell people what to sing or play. ❑ *He can't read music.* [from Old French]

→ look at Word Webs: **music, concert, genre**

Word Partnership	Use music with :
ADJ	**live** music, **loud** music, **new** music, **pop(ular)** music **1**
N	**background** music, music **critic**, music **festival 1** music **business**, music **industry**, music **lesson 2**
V	**download** music, **hear** music, **listen to** music, **play** music **1** **compose** music, **study** music, **write** music **2**

mu|si|cal /myu̱zɪkəl/ (**musicals**)
  1 **ADJ** MUSIC **Musical** means relating to playing or studying music. ❑ *Many of the kids have real musical talent.*
  2 **N-COUNT** MUSIC A **musical** is a play or a movie that uses singing and dancing in the story. ❑ *Have you seen the musical, "Miss Saigon"?*
  3 **ADJ** MUSIC If you are **musical**, you have a natural ability and interest in music. ❑ *I come from a musical family.* [from Old French]
  → look at Word Web: **theater**

mu|si|cal in|stru|ment (**musical instruments**) **N-COUNT** MUSIC A **musical instrument** is an object such as a piano, a guitar, or a violin that you play in order to produce music. ❑ *The drum is one of the oldest musical instruments.*

mu|si|cal|ity /myu̱zɪkæ̱lɪti/ **N-NONCOUNT** ARTS In dance, **musicality** is the ability to interpret music by dancing in a way that is appropriate for the music. [from Old French]

mu|si|cal thea|ter **N-NONCOUNT** ARTS **Musical theater** is a form of entertainment that contains music, song, and dance, as well as spoken dialogue.

Word Link	ician ≈ person who works at :
	electri**cian**, musi**cian**, physi**cian**

mu|si|cian /myuzɪ̱ʃən/ (**musicians**) **N-COUNT** MUSIC A **musician** is a person who plays a musical instrument as their job or hobby. ❑ *Michael is a brilliant musician.* [from Old French]
  → look at Word Webs: **concert, music, orchestra**

Mus|lim /mʊ̱zlɪm, mu̱zlɪm/ (**Muslims**)
  1 **N-COUNT** A **Muslim** is someone who believes in the religion of Islam and lives according to its rules.
  2 **ADJ** **Muslim** means relating to Islam or Muslims. ❑ *...an ancient Muslim mosque.* [from Arabic]

must /məst, STRONG mʌ̱st/
  1 **MODAL** You use **must** to show that you think something is very important or necessary. ❑ *Your clothes must fit well.* ❑ *You must tell me everything you know.*
  2 **MODAL** You use **must** to show that you are almost sure that something is true. ❑ *Claire's car isn't there, so she must be at work.*
  3 **MODAL** You use **must** to express your intention to do something. ❑ *I must go home now.* [from Old English]

mus|tache /mʌ̱stæʃ/ (**mustaches**) **N-COUNT** A man's **mustache** is the hair that grows on his upper lip. ❑ *David has a black mustache and beard.* [from French]

mus|tard /mʌ̱stərd/
  N-NONCOUNT **Mustard** is a spicy yellow or brown sauce that you usually eat with meat. ❑ *I had a cheese and mustard sandwich for lunch.* [from Old French]

mustard

must-have (**must-haves**)
  1 **N-COUNT** A **must-have** is something that many people want to have. ❑ *The cellphone is now a must-have for children.*
  2 **ADJ** **Must-have** is also an adjective. ❑ *...a must-have fashion accessory.*

mustn't /mʌ̱sənt/ **Mustn't** is short for "must not." [from Old English]

must've /mʌ̱stəv/ **Must've** is short for "must have." [from Old English]

mu|ta|gen /myu̱tədʒən, -dʒɛn/ (**mutagens**) **N-COUNT** SCIENCE **Mutagens** are processes or substances, for example X-rays or certain chemicals, that can cause genetic changes in cells.

mute /myu̱t/ (**mutes, muting, muted**)
  1 **ADJ** Someone who is **mute** does not speak. ❑ *Alexander was mute for a few minutes.*
  2 **ADV** **Mute** is also an adverb. ❑ *He could watch her standing mute by the phone.*
  3 **V-T** If someone **mutes** something such as their feelings or their activities, they reduce

m

the strength or intensity of them. ❑ *The problems have not muted the country's economic success.* ● **mut|ed** **ADJ** ❑ *...muted criticism.*
4 **V-T** If you **mute** a noise or sound, you lower its volume or make it less distinct. ❑ *They begin to mute their voices.* ● **mut|ed** **ADJ** ❑ *His voice was so muted that I couldn't hear his reply.* [from Old French]

mut|ter /mʌtər/ (**mutters, muttering, muttered**) **V-T/V-I** If you **mutter**, you speak in a very quiet voice that is difficult to hear, often when you are angry about something. ❑ *"He's crazy," she muttered.* ❑ *She can hear the old woman muttering about politeness.* [from Norwegian]

mut|ton /mʌtᵊn/ **N-NONCOUNT** Mutton is meat from an adult sheep. ❑ *...a leg of mutton.* [from Old French]
→ look at Word Web: **meat**

mu|tu|al /myutʃuəl/ **ADJ** If a feeling or an action is **mutual**, it is felt or done by two people or groups. ❑ *It was a mutual decision by Dean and me.* ❑ *Nick didn't like me, and the feeling was mutual.* [from Old French]

mu|tu|al|ism /myutʃuəlɪzəm/ (**mutualisms**) **N-COUNT/N-NONCOUNT** SCIENCE Mutualism is a relationship between two species of animals or plants from which both species benefit. [from Old French]

my /maɪ/

> **LANGUAGE HELP**
>
> **My** is the first person singular possessive determiner.

DET You use **my** to show that something belongs or relates to yourself. ❑ *We can eat at my apartment tonight.* [from Old English]

my|self /maɪsɛlf/

> **LANGUAGE HELP**
>
> **Myself** is the first person singular reflexive pronoun.

1 **PRON** You use **myself** when the person speaking or writing is both the subject and the object of the verb. ❑ *I asked myself what I should do.*
2 **PRON** You use **myself** to stress that you are speaking about yourself. ❑ *I myself enjoy movies and long walks.*

3 **PRON** You use **myself** or **by myself** to say that you do something without help from anyone else. ❑ *"Where did you get that dress?"—"I made it myself."*

mys|teri|ous /mɪstɪəriəs/ **ADJ** If someone or something is **mysterious**, they are strange, and you do not know about them or understand them. ❑ *A mysterious illness made him sick.* ● **mys|teri|ous|ly** **ADV** ❑ *The evidence mysteriously disappeared.* [from Medieval Latin]

mys|tery /mɪstəri, mɪstri/ (**mysteries**)
1 **N-COUNT** A **mystery** is something that you cannot explain or understand. ❑ *Why he behaved in this way is a mystery.*
2 **ADJ** A **mystery** person or thing is one whose identity is not known. ❑ *The mystery hero immediately called the police after seeing a bomb.*
3 **N-COUNT** LANGUAGE ARTS A **mystery** is a story or a movie about a crime or strange events that are only explained at the end. ❑ *I was alone at home watching a murder mystery on TV.* [from Latin]

Word Partnership	Use **mystery** with :
V	remain a mystery, unravel a mystery **1** solve a mystery **1** **3**
N	murder mystery, mystery **novel**, mystery **readers** **3**

myth /mɪθ/ (**myths**)
1 **N-COUNT/N-NONCOUNT** LANGUAGE ARTS A **myth** is an ancient story about gods and magic. ❑ *...the famous Greek myth of Medusa, the snake-haired monster.*
2 **N-COUNT/N-NONCOUNT** If a belief or an explanation is a **myth**, it is not true. ❑ *This story is a myth.* [from Late Latin]
→ look at Word Webs: **myth, fantasy**

Word Partnership	Use **myth** with :
ADJ	ancient myth, Greek myth **1** popular myth **2**

my|thol|ogy /mɪθɒlədʒi/ (**mythologies**) **N-COUNT/N-NONCOUNT** SOCIAL STUDIES **Mythology** is a group of myths, especially all the myths from a particular country, religion, or culture. ❑ *...Greek mythology.* [from Late Latin]
→ look at Word Web: **hero**

Word Web — myth

The scholar Joseph Campbell* believed that **mythologies** explain how a **culture** understands its world. **Stories, symbols, rituals,** and **myths** explain the **psychological, social,** and **spiritual** parts of life. Campbell also believed that artists and thinkers are a culture's mythmakers. He studied myths from many different cultures. In these myths he saw common **themes**. For example, the **hero's** journey appears in ancient Greece in *The Odyssey*. The hero's journey also appeared later in England in a story about King Arthur's* search for the Holy Grail*. The film *Star Wars* is a 20th century version of the hero's journey.

Joseph Campbell (1904–1987): an American professor and author.

The Odyssey: an epic poem from ancient Greece.

King Arthur: a legendary king of Great Britain.

Holy Grail: a cup that legends say Jesus used.

m

Nn

nag /næg/ (**nags, nagging, nagged**) **V-T/V-I** If someone **nags** you, or if they **nag**, they keep asking you to do something. ❑ *My mom's always nagging me about getting a good job.* ❑ *His nagging never stops.* [of Scandinavian origin]

nail /neɪl/ (**nails, nailing, nailed**)
1 **N-COUNT** A **nail** is a thin piece of metal with one pointed end and one flat end. You hit the flat end with a hammer in order to push the nail into a wall. ❑ *A mirror hung on a nail above the sink.*　　　nail
2 **V-T** If you **nail** something somewhere, you fasten it there using one or more nails. ❑ *The sign was nailed to a tree.*
3 **N-COUNT** Your **nails** are the thin hard parts that grow at the ends of your fingers and toes. ❑ *Try to keep your nails short.* [from Old English]

na|ive /naɪiv/ also **naïve** **ADJ** If someone is **naive**, they do not have a lot of experience, and they expect things to be easy. ❑ *I was naive to think they would agree.* [from French]

na|ked /neɪkɪd/
1 **ADJ** Someone who is **naked** is not wearing any clothes. ❑ *She held the naked baby in her arms.*
2 **PHRASE** If you say that something cannot be seen by **the naked eye**, you mean that it cannot be seen without the help of equipment such as a telescope or microscope. [from Old English]

name /neɪm/ (**names, naming, named**)
1 **N-COUNT** A person's **name** is the word or words that you use to talk to them, or to talk about them. ❑ *"What's his name?"—"Peter."*
2 **N-COUNT** The **name** of a place or a thing is the word or words that you use to talk about them. ❑ *They changed the name of the street.*
3 **N-COUNT** A famous **name** is someone who is well known. ❑ *...some of the most famous names in show business.*
4 **V-T** When you **name** someone or something, you give them a name.

❑ *He named his first child Christopher after his brother.*
5 **V-T** When you **name** someone or something, you say their name. ❑ *Can you name five ethnic groups living in Afghanistan?*
6 → see also **brand name, first name**
7 **PHRASE** If someone **calls** you **names**, they say unpleasant things to you. ❑ *At my last school they called me names because I looked different than everyone else.* [from Old English]
→ look at Word Web: **Internet**

Word Partnership	Use **name** with :	
ADJ	**common** name, **full** name, **real** name **1**	
	familiar name, **famous** name, **well-known** name **3**	
N	name **and address, company** name **1** **2**	

name|ly /neɪmli/ **ADV** You use **namely** to introduce detailed information about the subject you are discussing, or a particular aspect of it. ❑ *...the starting point of business, namely money.* [from Old English]

nan|ny /næni/ (**nannies**) **N-COUNT** A **nanny** is a person whose job is to take care of children.

nap /næp/ (**naps**) **N-COUNT** A **nap** is a short sleep that you have, usually during the day. ❑ *We had a nap after lunch.* [from Old English]
→ look at Word Web: **sleep**

nap|kin /næpkɪn/ (**napkins**) **N-COUNT** A **napkin** is a square of cloth or paper that you use when you are eating to protect your clothes, or to wipe your mouth or hands. ❑ *I ate the sandwich and wiped my face with a paper napkin.* [from Old French]

Word Link	ator ≈ one who does : creator, narrator, translator

nar|rate /næreɪt/ (**narrates, narrating, narrated**) **V-T** LANGUAGE ARTS If you **narrate** a story, you tell it from your own point of view. [FORMAL] ❑ *He narrated the story in his own words.* ● **nar|ra|tion** /næreɪʃ°n/ **N-NONCOUNT** ❑ *...Jim Dale's narration of the Harry Potter books.* ● **nar|ra|tor** /næreɪtər/ (**narrators**) **N-COUNT**

❏ *The story's narrator is a famous actress.*
[from Latin]

nar|ra|tive /nǽrətɪv/ (**narratives**) **N-COUNT**
LANGUAGE ARTS A **narrative** is a story or an
account of a series of events. ❏ *...a fast-moving
narrative.* [from Latin]

nar|row /nǽroʊ/ (**narrower, narrowest**)
■ **ADJ** Something that is **narrow** is a small
distance from one side to the other.
❏ *We walked through the town's narrow streets.*
■ **ADJ** If you have a **narrow** victory, you
succeed in winning but only by a small
amount. ❏ *Mr. Kerry won the debate by a narrow
margin.* ● **nar|row|ly ADV** ❏ *She narrowly failed
to win enough votes.*
■ **ADJ** If you have a **narrow** escape,
something unpleasant nearly happens to
you. ❏ *He had a narrow escape from drowning.*
● **nar|row|ly ADV** ❏ *Five firefighters narrowly
escaped death when a staircase fell on them.*
[from Old English]

Thesaurus narrow Also look up :

| ADJ | close, cramped, restricted, tight; (*ant.*) broad, wide ■ |

Word Partnership Use narrow with :

| N | narrow **band**, narrow **hallway**, narrow **opening**, narrow **path** ■ |
| ADV | **relatively** narrow, **too** narrow ■ |

na|sal /néɪzəl/
■ **ADJ Nasal** is used to describe things
relating to the nose. ❏ *Nasal sprays are
sometimes used to treat asthma.*
■ **ADJ** If someone's voice is **nasal**, it sounds
as if air is passing through their nose
as well as their mouth while they are
speaking. ❏ *He had a high-pitched nasal voice.*
[from French]
→ look at Word Web: **smell**

nas|cent /nǽsənt/ **ADJ Nascent** things or
processes are just beginning, and are expected
to become stronger or bigger. [FORMAL]
❏ *...Kenya's nascent democracy.* ❏ *...the still
nascent science of psychology.* [from Latin]

nas|ty /nǽsti/ (**nastier, nastiest**)
■ **ADJ** Something that is **nasty** is very
unpleasant. ❏ *The tax increase was a nasty
surprise for businesses.*
■ **ADJ** A **nasty** person is unkind or
unpleasant. ❏ *If anyone is nasty to you, you
should tell the teacher.*
■ **ADJ** If you describe an injury or a disease

as **nasty**, you mean that it is serious or looks
unpleasant. ❏ *She had a nasty infection.* [from
Swedish]

na|tion /néɪʃən/ (**nations**) **N-COUNT**
SOCIAL STUDIES A **nation** is an individual
country, its people, and its social and
political structures. ❏ *...the United States and
other nations.* [from Old French]
→ look at Word Web: **country**

Thesaurus nation Also look up :

| N | country, democracy, population, republic, society |

na|tion|al /nǽʃənəl/
■ **ADJ National** means relating to the whole
of a country or a nation. ❏ *He plays for the
Canadian national team.* ❏ *The ad appeared in the
national newspapers.*
■ **ADJ National** means typical of the people
or traditions of a particular country or
nation. ❏ *Baseball is the national pastime.*
[from Old French]

na|tion|al holi|day (**national holidays**)
N-COUNT A **national holiday** is a day when
people do not go to work or to school, in
order to celebrate a special event. ❏ *Today is
a national holiday in Japan.*

na|tion|al|ism /nǽʃənəlɪzəm/
■ **N-NONCOUNT** SOCIAL STUDIES **Nationalism**
is a person's strong love for their nation
and their feeling that it is better than any
other nation. ❏ *Extreme nationalism is common
during wars.*
■ **N-NONCOUNT** SOCIAL STUDIES **Nationalism**
is a group's desire to become a separate
country. ❏ *He gave support to Serbian
nationalism.* [from Old French]

na|tion|al|ist /nǽʃənəlɪst/ (**nationalists**)
■ **ADJ** SOCIAL STUDIES **Nationalist** means
connected with a person's great love for
their nation, or their belief that their nation
is better than others. ❏ *...nationalist beliefs.*
■ **N-COUNT** SOCIAL STUDIES A **nationalist** is
someone who loves and is proud of their
nation, or who believes that their nation is
better than others. ❏ *...the late African-
American nationalist, Malcolm X.*
■ **ADJ** SOCIAL STUDIES **Nationalist** means
connected with the desire of a group of
people within a country for political
independence. ❏ *She has strong nationalist
views.*
■ **N-COUNT** SOCIAL STUDIES A **nationalist** is

n

someone who desires political independence. ❏ ...*demands by nationalists for an independent state.* [from Old French]

na|tion|al|ity /nˌæʃənˈælɪti/ (**nationalities**)
N-COUNT/N-NONCOUNT SOCIAL STUDIES If you have the **nationality** of a particular country, you are a legal citizen of that country. ❏ *I'm not sure of her nationality, but I think she's Canadian.* [from Old French]

nation|wide /ˌneɪʃᵊnˈwaɪd/
1 **ADJ** **Nationwide** activities or situations happen or exist in all parts of a country. ❏ *Car crime is a nationwide problem.*
2 **ADV** **Nationwide** is also an adverb. ❏ *Unemployment fell nationwide last month.*

na|tive /ˈneɪtɪv/ (**natives**)
1 **ADJ** Your **native** country, region, or town is where you were born. ❏ *It was his first visit to his native country since 1948.* ❏ *Joshua Halpern is a native Northern Californian.*
2 **N-COUNT** A **native of** a particular country, region, or town is someone who was born there. ❏ *Dr. Aubin is a native of St. Louis.*
3 **ADJ** Your **native** language is the first language that you learned to speak when you were a child. ❏ *Her native language was Swedish.*
4 **ADJ** Plants or animals that are **native to** a particular region live or grow there naturally and were not brought there. ❏ *Many of the plants are native to Brazil.* [from Latin]

Word Partnership	Use **native** with :
N	native **country**, native **land** **1** native **language**, native **tongue** **3**

Na|tive Ameri|can (**Native Americans**)
1 **N-COUNT** SOCIAL STUDIES **Native Americans** are people from any of the groups who were living in North America before people arrived from Europe. ❏ *Native Americans comprise about 1% of the population of the United States.*
2 **ADJ** SOCIAL STUDIES **Native American** is also an adjective. ❏ *We want to gain a better understanding of Native American culture.*

natu|ral /ˈnætʃərəl, ˈnætʃrəl/
1 **ADJ** If something is **natural**, it is normal. ❏ *It is natural for young people to want excitement.*
2 **ADJ** **Natural** things exist in nature and were not created by people. ❏ *I love the natural beauty of the landscape.*
3 **ADJ** Someone with a **natural** ability was

born with that ability and did not have to learn it. ❏ *Alan is a natural musician.*
4 **ADJ** If someone's behavior is **natural**, they are relaxed and are not hiding anything. ❏ *Mary's sister is as natural as the rest of the family.*
5 **ADJ** **Natural** things exist in nature and were not created by people. ❏ *...a natural harbor.* [from Old French]
→ look at Word Web: **energy**

Thesaurus	natural	Also look up :
ADJ	normal **1** innate, instinctive **2** **3** genuine, sincere, unaffected **5** wild; (*ant.*) artificial **6**	

Word Partnership	Use **natural** with :
N	natural **reaction**, natural **tendency** **1** natural **beauty**, natural **disaster**, natural **food** **2**
ADV	**perfectly** natural **1** **4**

natu|ral gas **N-NONCOUNT** SCIENCE **Natural gas** is gas which is found underground or under the sea. It is collected and stored, and piped into people's homes to be used for cooking and heating.

natu|rali|za|tion /ˌnætʃərəlɪˈzeɪʃᵊn, ˌnætʃrəl-/
N-NONCOUNT SOCIAL STUDIES **Naturalization** is the process by which a person from one country can officially become a citizen of another nation. ❏ *They promised to be loyal to the U.S. and they received their naturalization papers.* [from Middle French]

natu|ral light **N-NONCOUNT** **Natural light** is light from the sun rather than from an artificial source such as an electric light.

natu|ral|ly /ˈnætʃərəli, ˈnætʃrəli/
1 **ADV** You use **naturally** to show that something is very obvious and not surprising. ❏ *When things go wrong, we naturally feel disappointed.*
2 **ADV** If something happens or exists **naturally**, it happens or exists in nature and was not done or created by people. ❏ *Allow your hair to dry naturally in the sun.* ❏ *Gas is naturally odorless.*
3 **ADV** If you are acting **naturally**, you are relaxed and you are not hiding anything. ❏ *It's important to act naturally if you can.* [from Old French]

natu|ral re|sources **N-PLURAL** SCIENCE **Natural resources** are all the land, forests, energy sources, and minerals existing

N

naturally in a place that can be used by people.

natu|ral se|lec|tion **N-NONCOUNT** SCIENCE **Natural selection** is a process by which species of animals and plants that are best adapted to their environment survive and reproduce, while those that are less well adapted die out. ❑ *Natural selection ensures only the fittest survive to pass their genes on to the next generation.*

na|ture /ne͟ɪtʃər/
■ **N-NONCOUNT** SCIENCE **Nature** is all the animals, plants, and other things in the world that are not made by people. ❑ *The essay discusses the relationship between humans and nature.*
■ **N-SING** Someone's **nature** is their character, which they show by the way they behave. ❑ *People called her "Sunny" because of her friendly nature.*
■ **N-SING** The **nature** of something is its basic quality or character. ❑ *The police would not comment on the nature of the investigation.* [from Old French]
■ → see also **human nature**

naugh|ty /nɔ͟ti/ (**naughtier, naughtiest**) **ADJ** A **naughty** child behaves badly or does not do what someone tells them to do. ❑ *When I'm very naughty, my mom sends me to bed early.*

nau|sea /nɔ͟ziə, -ʒə, -siə, -ʃə/ **N-NONCOUNT** **Nausea** is a feeling that you are going to vomit. ❑ *The symptoms include headaches and nausea.* [from Latin]

na|val /ne͟ɪvəl/ **ADJ** **Naval** means relating to a country's navy. ❑ *He was a senior naval officer.* [from Latin]

navi|gate /næ͟vɪgeɪt/ (**navigates, navigating, navigated**)
■ **V-T/V-I** You **navigate** when you find the direction that you need to travel in, using a map or the sun, for example. ❑ *We navigated using the sun by day and the stars by night.* ❑ *Captain Cook navigated his ship without accident for 100 voyages.*
■ **V-T/V-I** TECHNOLOGY If you **navigate** a website, or **navigate to** a website, you find the information that you need by clicking on links that take you from one web page to another. ❑ *A home page gives users information and helps them to navigate the site.* ● **navi|ga|tion** /næ͟vɪge͟ɪʃən/ **N-NONCOUNT** ❑ *The planes had their navigation lights on.* [from Latin]
→ look at Word Webs: **navigation, star**

navy /ne͟ɪvi/ (**navies**) **N-COUNT** A country's **navy** is the military force that can fight at sea, and the ships they use. ❑ *Her son is in the navy.* [from Old French]

navy blue
■ **ADJ** Something that is **navy blue** is very dark blue. ❑ *I wore navy blue pants.*
■ **N-NONCOUNT** **Navy blue** is also a noun. ❑ *She was dressed in navy blue.*

Ne|an|der|thal /niæ͟ndərθɔl, -tɔl/ (**Neanderthals**)
■ **ADJ** SOCIAL STUDIES **Neanderthal** people lived in Europe between 35,000 and 70,000 years ago.
■ **N-COUNT** SOCIAL STUDIES You can refer to people from the Neanderthal period as **Neanderthals**. [after Neandertal, a valley near Düsseldorf, Germany]

n

WordWeb navigation

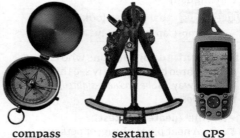

Early explorers used the **sun** and **stars** to navigate the seas. The **sextant** allowed later navigators to use these celestial objects to accurately calculate their **position**. By sighting or measuring their position at noon, sailors could determine their **latitude**. The **compass** helped sailors determine their position at any time of night or day. It also worked in any weather. Today all sorts of travelers use the global positioning system (GPS) to guide their journeys. A GPS **receiver** is connected to a system of **satellites** that can establish a location within a few feet.

compass   sextant   GPS

neap tide /nip taɪd/ (**neap tides**) **N-COUNT**
SCIENCE A **neap tide** is a tide with a smaller rise and fall than normal, which occurs when the moon is halfway between a new moon and a full moon.

near /nɪər/ (**nearer, nearest**)
1 **PREP** If something is **near** a place, a thing, or a person, it is a short distance from them. ❏ *Don't come near me!* ❏ *The café is near the station in Edmonton.*
2 **ADV** Near is also an adverb. ❏ *He stood as near to the door as he could.*
3 **ADJ** Near is also an adjective. ❏ *He sat in the nearest chair.*
4 **PREP** If something happens **near** a particular time, it happens just before or just after that time. ❏ *The group stopped for lunch near midday.*
5 **PREP** You use **near** to say that something is a little more or less than an amount or number stated. ❏ *Temperatures dropped to near zero.*
6 **PHRASE** If something will happen **in the near future**, it will happen very soon. ❏ *I hope I'll be able to meet her sometime in the near future.* [from Old English]

near|by /nɪərbaɪ/
1 **ADV** If something is **nearby**, it is only a short distance away. ❏ *Her sister lives nearby.*
2 **ADJ** Nearby is also an adjective. ❏ *He sat at a nearby table.*

near|ly /nɪərli/
1 **ADV** If something is **nearly** a particular amount, it is very close to that amount but is a little less than it. ❏ *He has worked for the company for nearly 20 years.*
2 **ADV** If something is **nearly** a certain state, it is very close to that state but has not reached it. ❏ *"What time is it?"—"Nearly five o'clock." ❏ I've nearly finished.* [from Old English]

Thesaurus	nearly	Also look up :
ADV	almost, approximately **1**	

near-sight|ed **ADJ** Someone who is **near-sighted** cannot clearly see things that are far away. ❏ *She was near-sighted, so she had to wear glasses.*

neat /nit/ (**neater, neatest**)
1 **ADJ** A **neat** place, thing, or person is organized and clean, and has everything in the correct place. ❏ *She made sure that the apartment was clean and neat before she left.*

● **neat|ly** **ADV** ❏ *He folded his newspaper neatly and put it in his bag.*
2 **ADJ** If you say that someone or something is **neat**, you mean that you like them a lot. [INFORMAL] ❏ *He thought Mike was a really neat guy.* [from Old French]

Thesaurus	neat	Also look up :
ADJ	orderly, tidy **1**	

nebu|la /nɛbyələ/ (**nebulae**) **N-COUNT**
SCIENCE A **nebula** is a cloud of dust and gas in space. New stars are produced from nebulae. [from Latin]

nec|es|sari|ly /nɛsɪsɛərɪli/
1 **ADV** If you say that something is **not necessarily** true, you mean that it may not be true or is not always true. ❏ *Women do not necessarily have to act like men to be successful.*
2 **PHRASE** If you reply **Not necessarily**, you mean that what has just been said or suggested may not be true. ❏ *"He was lying, of course."—"Not necessarily."* [from Latin]

nec|es|sary /nɛsɪsɛri/ **ADJ** Something that is **necessary** is needed to make something happen. ❏ *Experience is necessary for this job.* ❏ *I'm sure I've got the necessary skills for this job.* [from Latin]

Thesaurus	necessary	Also look up :
ADJ	essential, mandatory, obligatory, required; (*ant.*) unnecessary	

ne|ces|sity /nɪsɛsɪti/ (**necessities**)
1 **N-COUNT** **Necessities** are things that you must have to live. ❏ *Water is a basic necessity of life.*
2 **N-NONCOUNT** The **necessity** of something is the fact that it must happen or exist. ❏ *He learned the necessity of hiding his feelings.* [from Latin]

neck /nɛk/ (**necks**)
1 **N-COUNT** Your **neck** is the part of your body between your head and the rest of your body. ❏ *He was wearing a red scarf around his neck.*
2 **N-COUNT** The **neck** of a shirt or a dress is the part that surrounds your neck. ❏ *She wore a dress with a low neck.* [from Old English]
→ look at Picture Dictionary: **body**

Word Partnership	Use neck with :
N	back/nape of the neck, head and neck, neck injury **1**
ADJ	broken neck, long neck, stiff neck, thick neck **1**

neck|lace /nɛklɪs/ (**necklaces**)
N-COUNT A **necklace** is a piece of jewelry that you wear around your neck. ❑ *She was wearing a diamond necklace.*
→ look at Picture Dictionary: **jewelry**

necklace

nec|tar /nɛktər/ **N-NONCOUNT** **Nectar** is a sweet liquid produced by flowers, which bees and other insects collect. [from Latin]

nec|tar|ine /nɛktərin/ (**nectarines**)
N-COUNT A **nectarine** is a red and yellow fruit with a smooth skin.

need /nid/ (**needs, needing, needed**)
■ **V-T** If you **need** something, you must have it. ❑ *He desperately needed money.*
■ **V-T** If you **need to** do something, you must do it. ❑ *I need to make a phone call.*
■ **V-T** If an object or a place **needs** something done to it, that action should be done. ❑ *The building needs quite a few repairs.*
■ **N-SING** If there is a **need for** something, it is necessary to have or to do that thing. ❑ *There is a need for more schools in the area.*
■ **V-T** If you say that someone does not **need to** do something, you are telling them not to do it. ❑ *You don't need to apologize.*
■ **N-COUNT** Your **needs** are the things that are necessary for you to live or to succeed in life. ❑ *Parents have to look after their child's physical and emotional needs.*
■ **PHRASE** If you are **in need of** something, you need it or should have it. ❑ *I was all right but in need of rest.* [from Old English]

nee|dle /nid³l/ (**needles**)
■ **N-COUNT** A **needle** is a small, thin metal tool with a sharp point that you use for sewing. ❑ *If you get me a needle and thread, I'll sew the button on.*

needle

■ **N-COUNT** A **needle** is a thin hollow metal tube with a sharp point that is used for putting a drug into someone's body. ❑ *Dirty needles spread disease.*
■ **N-COUNT** On an instrument that measures speed or weight, the **needle** is the long strip of metal or plastic that moves backward and forward, showing the measurement. ❑ *The needle on the boiler is pointing to 200 degrees.*
■ **N-COUNT** **Needles** are the thin, hard,

pointed parts of some trees that stay green all year. ❑ *There was a thick layer of pine needles on the ground.* [from Old English]

need|less /nidlɪs/ **ADJ** Something that is **needless** is not necessary or can be avoided. ❑ *His death was so needless.* ● **need|less|ly** **ADV** ❑ *Children are dying needlessly.* [from Old English]

needy /nidi/ (**needier, neediest**)
■ **ADJ** **Needy** people do not have enough food, medicine, or clothing. ❑ *They provide housing for needy families.*
■ **N-PLURAL** **The needy** are people who are needy. ❑ *We are trying to get food to the needy.* [from Old English]

nega|tive /nɛgətɪv/
■ **ADJ** A **negative** situation or experience is unpleasant or harmful. ❑ *Patients talked about their negative childhood experiences.*
■ **ADJ** If someone is **negative** they consider only the bad aspects of a situation. ❑ *When someone asks for your opinion, don't be negative.* ● **nega|tive|ly** **ADV** ❑ *Why do so many people think negatively?*
■ **ADJ** A **negative** reply or decision is the answer "no." ❑ *Dr. Velayati gave a negative response.* ● **nega|tive|ly** **ADV** ❑ *Sixty percent of people answered negatively.*
■ **ADJ** MATH A **negative** number is less than zero. Compare with **positive**.
■ **ADJ** LANGUAGE ARTS In grammar, a **negative** form or word expresses the meaning "no" or "not." For example, "don't" and "haven't" are negative forms.
■ **ADJ** ARTS In painting and sculpture, **negative** space is the empty space that surrounds an object or form. [from Latin]
→ look at Word Webs: **lightning, magnet**

Word Partnership	Use **negative** with :
N	negative **effect**, negative **experience**, negative **image**, negative **publicity** ■ negative **attitude**, negative **thoughts** ■ ■ negative **comment**, negative **reaction**, negative **response** ■

nega|tive ac|cel|era|tion **N-NONCOUNT**
SCIENCE **Negative acceleration** is a decrease in speed or velocity.

ne|glect /nɪglɛkt/ (**neglects, neglecting, neglected**)
■ **V-T** If you **neglect** someone or something, you do not take care of them. ❑ *The neighbors*

n

claim that she is *neglecting her children.*
2 **N-NONCOUNT** **Neglect** is also a noun.
❑ *The house is being repaired after years of neglect.*
[from Latin]

neg|li|gence /nɛglɪdʒ°ns/ **N-NONCOUNT**
Negligence is when someone does not do
something that they should do. ❑ *His*
negligence caused the accident. ● **neg|li|gent** **ADJ**
❑ *The jury decided that the airline was negligent.*
● **neg|li|gent|ly** **ADV** ❑ *I believe that the*
physician acted negligently.

neg|li|gible /nɛglɪdʒɪb°l/ **ADJ** An amount
or an effect that is **negligible** is so small
that it is not worth considering or
worrying about. ❑ *The soldiers' pay was*
negligible. [from Latin]

ne|go|ti|ate /nɪgoʊʃieɪt/ (**negotiates,**
negotiating, negotiated) **V-T/V-I** If people
negotiate with each other, they talk about a
problem or a situation in order to reach an
agreement. ❑ *The president is willing to negotiate*
with the Democrats. [from Latin]

ne|go|tia|tion /nɪgoʊʃieɪ°n/ (**negotiations**)
N-COUNT/N-NONCOUNT **Negotiations** are
discussions between people, during
which they try to reach an agreement.
❑ *The negotiations were successful.* [from Latin]

neigh|bor /neɪbər/ (**neighbors**)
1 **N-COUNT** Your **neighbor** is someone who
lives near you. ❑ *Sometimes we invite the*
neighbors over for dinner.
2 **N-COUNT** Something that stands next to
something else is its **neighbor.** ❑ *Consider*
each plant in your garden in relation to its neighbors.
[from Old English]

Word Link	hood ≈ state, condition : child**hood,**
	mother**hood,** neighbor**hood**

neigh|bor|hood /neɪbərhʊd/
(**neighborhoods**) **N-COUNT** A **neighborhood**
is one of the parts of a town where people
live. ❑ *He's from a rich Los Angeles neighborhood.*
[from Old English]

Word Partnership	Use **neighborhood**
with :	
ADJ	**poor** neighborhood, **residential**
	neighborhood, **run-down**
	neighborhood

neigh|bor|ing /neɪbərɪŋ/ **ADJ** **Neighboring**
places or things are near other things of the
same kind. ❑ *...Thailand and its neighboring*
countries. [from Old English]

nei|ther /niðər, naɪ-/
1 **PRON** **Neither** means not one or the other
of two things or people. ❑ *There were two men*
at the desk. Neither was smiling. ❑ *Neither of us*
felt like going out.
2 **CONJ** You use **neither...nor...** when you
are talking about two or more things that
are not true or that do not happen. ❑ *Professor*
Hisamatsu spoke neither English nor German.
3 **ADV** **Neither** means also not. ❑ *I never*
learned to swim and neither did they. [from
Old English]

nek|ton /nɛktɒn/ **N-PLURAL** **SCIENCE** **Nekton**
are animals such as fish and whales that are
capable of swimming against a current.
[from German]

neon /niɒn/ **ADJ** **Neon** lights or signs are
made from glass tubes filled with a special
gas called neon that produces a bright
electric light. ❑ *In the city streets the neon lights*
flashed. [from New Latin]

neph|ew /nɛfyu/ (**nephews**) **N-COUNT** Your
nephew is the son of your sister or your
brother. ❑ *I am planning a birthday party for my*
nephew. [from Old French]

Nep|tune /nɛptun/ **N-PROPER** **SCIENCE**
Neptune is the eighth planet from the sun.
[from Latin]

nerve /nɜrv/ (**nerves**)
1 **N-COUNT** **SCIENCE** **Nerves** are long thin
threads in your body that send messages
between your brain and other parts of your
body. ❑ *...pain from a damaged nerve.*
2 **N-PLURAL** Someone's **nerves** are their
feelings of worry or fear. ❑ *He plays the piano*
to calm his nerves and relax.
3 **N-NONCOUNT** **Nerve** is the courage that
you need to do something difficult or
dangerous. ❑ *I don't know why he lost his nerve.*
4 **PHRASE** If someone or something **gets on**
your **nerves,** they annoy you. [INFORMAL] ❑ *The*
children's noisy games were getting on his nerves.
5 **PHRASE** If you say that someone **has the**
nerve to do something, you feel that they
have no right to do it. [INFORMAL] ❑ *I can't*
believe you have the nerve to sit here and tell unkind
stories about him. [from Latin]
→ look at Word Webs: **ear, eye, nervous**
system, smell

nerv|ous /nɜrvəs/
1 **ADJ** If you are **nervous,** you are frightened
or worried. ❑ *I was very nervous during the job*

Word Web   nervous system

The body's **nervous system** is a two-way road which carries electrochemical messages to and from different parts of the body. **Sensory** neurons carry information from both inside and outside the body to the **central nervous system** (CNS). The CNS is made of both the **brain** and the **spinal cord**. Motor neurons carry impulses from the CNS to **organs** and to **muscles** such as the muscles in the hand, telling them how to move. **Nerves** are made of sensory and motor neurons. **Nerves** run through the whole body.

interview. ● **nerv|ous|ly** ADV ❑ *Beth stood up nervously when the men came into the room.*

● **nerv|ous|ness** N-NONCOUNT ❑ *I smiled warmly so he wouldn't see my nervousness.*

2 ADJ SCIENCE Your **nervous** system consists of all the nerves in your body. ❑ *...a disease of the nervous system.* [from Latin]

Word Partnership   Use nervous with :

PREP	nervous **about** *something* **1**
V	**become** nervous, **feel** nervous, **get** nervous, **look** nervous, **make** *someone* nervous **1**
ADV	**increasingly** nervous, **a little** nervous, **too** nervous, **very** nervous **1**

n̲erv|ous tis|sue (nervous tissues)
N-COUNT/N-NONCOUNT SCIENCE **Nervous tissue** is tissue in the bodies of animals that consists of neurons.

nest /nɛst/ (nests, nesting, nested)
1 N-COUNT A **nest** is the place where a bird, a small animal, or an insect keeps its eggs or its babies. ❑ *The cuckoo leaves its eggs in the nests of other birds.*

2 V-I When a bird **nests** somewhere, it builds a nest and lays its eggs there.

nest

❑ *There are birds nesting on the cliffs.* [from Old English]
→ look at Word Web: **bird**

net /nɛt/ (nets)
1 N-NONCOUNT **Net** is a material made of threads or wire with spaces in between. ❑ *...net curtains.*

2 N-COUNT A **net** is a piece of net that you use for a particular purpose. ❑ *...a fishing net.*

3 N-PROPER TECHNOLOGY **The Net** is the same as the **Internet**. ❑ *We've been on the Net since 1993.*

4 N-COUNT SPORTS In basketball, the **net** is the loose material that hangs down from the metal ring that you put the ball through.

5 N-COUNT SPORTS In tennis, the **net** is the object that you hit the ball over.

6 ADJ A **net** amount is the amount that remains when everything that should be subtracted from it has been subtracted. ❑ *...a rise in sales and net profit.*

7 ADV **Net** is also an adverb. ❑ *Balances of $5,000 and above will earn 8.25 percent net.* ❑ *They pay him around $2 million net.* [Senses 1 to 5 from Old English. Senses 6 and 7 from French.]
→ look at Picture Dictionary: **tennis**

Word Partnership   Use net with :

N	**fishing** net **2** Net **users 3**
V	**access the** Net, **surf the** Net **3**
N	net **earnings**, net **gain**, net **income/loss**, net **increase**, net **proceeds**, net **profit**, net **result**, net **revenue 6**

net|book /nɛtbʊk/ (netbooks) N-COUNT TECHNOLOGY A **netbook** is a type of small computer that you can easily carry around with you.

net force (net forces) N-COUNT SCIENCE A **net force** is the overall force that is acting upon an object, after all the individual forces acting on the object have been added together.

net|work /nɛtwɜrk/ (networks, networking, networked)
1 N-COUNT A radio or a television **network** is a company that broadcasts radio or television programs in a particular area. ❑ *He was a sports presenter on a local TV network.*

2 N-COUNT TECHNOLOGY A **network of** people or things is a large number of them that have a connection with each other and that work together. ❑ *She has a strong network of friends and family to help her.* ❑ *Their computers are connected on a wireless network.*

3 V-I BUSINESS If you **network**, you try to

n

meet people who might be useful to you. ❏ *In business, it is important to network with as many people as possible.*

→ look at Word Web: **Internet**

Word Partnership	Use **network** with :
N	**broadcast** network, **cable** network, **radio** network, network **1**
ADJ	**extensive** network, **vast** network, **worldwide** network **1 2**

neu|rol|ogy /nʊərɒlədʒi/ **N-NONCOUNT**
SCIENCE **Neurology** is the study of the structure, function, and diseases of the nervous system. ❏ *He trained in neurology at the National Hospital for Nervous Diseases.*
● **neu|rolo|gist** (**neurologists**) **N-COUNT**
❏ *Someone with suspected MS (= multiple sclerosis) should see a neurologist who specializes in the disease.* [from Greek]

neu|ron /nʊərɒn/ (**neurons**) **N-COUNT**
SCIENCE A **neuron** is a cell which is part of the nervous system. Neurons send messages to and from the brain. ❏ *Information is transferred along each neuron by means of an electrical impulse.* [from Greek]

neu|tral /nutrəl/
1 **ADJ** SOCIAL STUDIES A **neutral** person or country does not support either side in an argument or a war. ❏ *Let's meet on neutral territory.*
2 **ADJ** If you have a **neutral** expression or a **neutral** voice, you do not show what you are thinking or feeling. ❏ *Isabel said in a neutral voice, "You're very late, darling."*
3 **N-NONCOUNT** **Neutral** is the position between the gears of a vehicle, in which the gears are not connected to the engine. ❏ *She put the truck in neutral and started it again.*
4 **ADJ** **Neutral** colors are colors such as black, white, and gray that are considered to combine well with other colors. [from Latin]

neu|tron /nutrɒn/ (**neutrons**) **N-COUNT**
SCIENCE A **neutron** is an atomic particle that has no electrical charge.

neu|tron star (**neutron stars**) **N-COUNT**
SCIENCE A **neutron star** is a star that has collapsed under the weight of its own gravity.

nev|er /nɛvər/ **ADV** **Never** means at no time in the past, the present, or the future. ❏ *I have never been abroad before.* ❏ *That was a*

mistake. I'll never do it again.* ❏ *Never look directly at the sun.* [from Old English]

never|the|less /nɛvərðəlɛs/ **ADV**
Nevertheless means "although something is true." [FORMAL] ❏ *Leon had problems, but nevertheless managed to finish his most famous painting.*

new /nu/ (**newer, newest**)
1 **ADJ** Something that is **new** has been recently created or invented. ❏ *They've just opened a new hotel.* ❏ *These ideas are not new.*
2 **ADJ** Something that is **new** has not been used or owned by anyone. ❏ *That afternoon she went out and bought a new dress.* ❏ *There are many boats, new and used, for sale.*
3 **ADJ** **New** describes someone or something that has replaced another person or thing. ❏ *I had to find somewhere new to live.* ❏ *Rachel has a new boyfriend.*
4 **ADJ** **New** describes something that has only recently been discovered or noticed. ❏ *The new planet is about ten times the size of the Earth.*
5 **ADJ** If you are **new to** a situation or a place, or if the situation or place is **new to** you, you have not had any experience of it. ❏ *She is new to the company.* [from Old English]
6 → see also **brand-new**

Thesaurus	**new** Also look up :
ADJ	contemporary, current, latest, modern, novel; (*ant.*) existing, old, past **1**

new|born /nubɔrn/ **ADJ** A **newborn** baby or animal is one that has just been born. ❏ *...a mother and her newborn child.*

new|comer /nukʌmər/ (**newcomers**)
N-COUNT A **newcomer** is a person who has recently arrived in a place. ❏ *She's a newcomer to Salt Lake City.*

new|ly /nuli/ **ADV** You can use **newly** to show that an action or a situation is very recent. ❏ *She was young at the time, and newly married.* [from Old English]

news /nuz/
1 **N-NONCOUNT** **News** is information about recent events. ❏ *We waited and waited for news of him.* ❏ *I've just had some bad news.*
2 **N-NONCOUNT** **News** is information about recent events that is reported in newspapers, or on the radio, television, or Internet. ❏ *Here are some of the top stories in the news.*

3 **N-SING** The **news** is a television or radio program that gives information about recent events. ❑ *I heard all about the bombs on the news.* [from Middle English]

Word Partnership	Use **news** with :	
ADJ	**big** news, **grim** news, **latest** news, **sad** news **1**	
V	**spread the** news, **tell** *someone* **the** news **1**	
	hear the news **1 2**	
	listen to the news, **watch the** news **3**	
N	news **headlines**, news **media**, news **report**, news **update** **2**	

news|caster /nuzkæstər/ (**newscasters**)
N-COUNT A **newscaster** is a person who reads the news on the radio or on television. ❑ *...TV newscaster Barbara Walters.*

news|group /nuzgrup/ (**newsgroups**)
N-COUNT TECHNOLOGY A **newsgroup** is an Internet site where people can put information and opinions about a particular subject so they can be read by everyone who looks at the site. ❑ *You can exchange information with others in newsgroups.*

news|letter /nuzlɛtər/ (**newsletters**)
N-COUNT A **newsletter** is a report giving information about an organization that is sent regularly to its members. ❑ *All members receive a free monthly newsletter.*

news|paper /nuzpeɪpər, nus-/ (**newspapers**)
1 **N-COUNT** A **newspaper** is a number of large sheets of folded paper, with news, advertisements, and other information printed on them. ❑ *They read about it in the newspaper.*
2 **N-NONCOUNT** **Newspaper** is pieces of old newspapers. ❑ *He found two pots, each wrapped in newspaper.*

new|ton /nutªn/ (**newtons**) **N-COUNT**
SCIENCE A **newton** is a unit for measuring force. [after Sir Isaac Newton (1642-1727), an English physicist, mathematician, astronomer, and philosopher]

New Year's Day **N-NONCOUNT** **New Year's Day** is the time when people celebrate the start of a year.

next /nɛkst/
1 **ADJ** The **next** thing is the one that comes immediately after this one or after the previous one. ❑ *I got up early the next morning.*

❑ *I took the next available flight.* ❑ *Who will be the next mayor?*
2 **PRON** **Next** is also a pronoun. ❑ *We have several meetings planned. The next is on Wednesday.*
3 **DET** You use **next** to talk about the first day, week, or year that comes after this one or the previous one. ❑ *Let's go see a movie next week.* ❑ *He retires next January.*
4 **PRON** **Next** is also a pronoun. ❑ *John is coming the week after next.*
5 **ADJ** The **next** place is the one that is nearest to you. ❑ *There was a party going on in the next room.*
6 **ADV** The thing that happens **next** is the thing that happens immediately after something else. ❑ *I don't know what to do next.*
7 **PHRASE** If one thing is **next to** another, it is at the side of it. ❑ *She sat down next to him on the sofa.* [from Old English]

Word Partnership	Use **next** with :	
N	next **election**, next **generation**, next **level**, next **move**, next **question**, next **step**, next **time**, next **train** **1** next **day/hour/month/week/year** **1 2**	
V	**come** next, **go** next, **happen** next **4**	

nib|ble /nɪbªl/ (**nibbles, nibbling, nibbled**)
V-T/V-I If you **nibble**, or **nibble** food, you eat it by biting very small pieces of it. ❑ *She nibbled at a piece of bread.* ❑ *He nibbled the apple.* [from Low German]

nice /naɪs/ (**nicer, nicest**)
1 **ADJ** If something is **nice**, it is attractive, pleasant, or enjoyable. ❑ *The chocolate-chip cookies were nice.* ❑ *It's nice to be here together again.*
2 **ADJ** If someone is **nice**, they are friendly and pleasant. ❑ *I've met your father and he's very nice.* ❑ *They were extremely nice to me.*
3 **ADJ** If you say that it is **nice of** someone to do something, you think that they are being kind. ❑ *It's so nice of you to come all this way to see me.* [from Old French]

Thesaurus	**nice** Also look up :	
ADJ	friendly, kind, likable, pleasant, polite; (*ant.*) mean, unpleasant **2 3**	

Word Partnership	Use **nice** with :	
ADJ	nice **and clean** **1**	
V	**look** nice, nice **to see** *someone/ something* **1**	
N	nice **clothes**, nice **guy**, nice **people**, nice **place**, nice **smile** **1 2**	

n

nice|ly /na͟ɪsli/

1 **ADV** If something is **nicely** done, it is attractive, pleasant, or enjoyable. ❑ *The book is nicely illustrated.*

2 **ADV** If someone speaks to you or treats you **nicely**, they are friendly and pleasant. ❑ *He treated you nicely.*

3 **ADV** If something is happening or working **nicely**, it is happening or working in a satisfactory way or in the way that you want it to. ❑ *The computer system is now working nicely.* [from Old French]

niche /nɪtʃ, niʃ/ (**niches**)

1 **N-COUNT** BUSINESS A **niche** in the market is a specific area of marketing that has its own particular requirements, customers, and products. ❑ *I think we have found a niche in the toy market.*

2 **N-COUNT** A **niche** is a hollow area in a wall, that has been made to hold a statue, or a natural hollow part in a hill or a cliff. ❑ *They hid the gold in a niche in a cave.*

3 **N-COUNT** Your **niche** is the job or activity that is exactly suitable for you. ❑ *Steve has found his niche as a Web designer.*

4 **N-COUNT** SCIENCE The **niche** of a species of animal or plant is the particular position that the species occupies in its environment and the way it interacts with that environment. [from French]

nick /nɪk/ (**nicks, nicking, nicked**)

1 **V-T** If you **nick** something or **nick** yourself, you accidentally make a small cut in the surface of the object or your skin. ❑ *A bullet nicked the edge of the wall.* ❑ *He nicked himself on the chin when he was shaving.*

2 **N-COUNT** A **nick** is a small cut made in the surface of something, usually in someone's skin. ❑ *I had a tiny nick just below my right eye.*

3 **PHRASE** If something is achieved **in the nick of time**, it is achieved successfully, at the last possible moment. [INFORMAL] ❑ *It seems we got here just in the nick of time.*

nick|el /nɪkᵊl/ (**nickels**)

1 **N-NONCOUNT** Nickel is a hard, silver-colored metal.

2 **N-COUNT** In the United States and Canada, a **nickel** is a coin that is worth five cents. ❑ *The large glass jar was filled with nickels, dimes, and quarters.* [from German]

nick|name /nɪkneɪm/ (**nicknames, nicknaming, nicknamed**)

1 **N-COUNT** A **nickname** is an informal name for someone or something. ❑ *Red got his nickname for his red hair.*

2 **V-T** If you **nickname** someone or something, you give them an informal name. ❑ *The children nicknamed him "The Giraffe" because he was so tall.*

niece /nis/ (**nieces**) **N-COUNT** Your **niece** is the daughter of your sister or your brother. ❑ *He bought a present for his niece.* [from Old French]

night /na͟ɪt/ (**nights**)

1 **N-COUNT/N-NONCOUNT** The **night** is the time when it is dark outside, and most people sleep. ❑ *The rain continued all night.* ❑ *It was a dark, cold night.* ❑ *It's eleven o'clock at night in Moscow.*

2 **N-COUNT** The **night** is the period of time between the end of the afternoon and the time that you go to bed. ❑ *Did you go to Kelly's party last night?*

3 **PHRASE** If you have **an early night**, you go to bed early. If you have **a late night**, you go to bed late. ❑ *All I want is an early night.* [from Old English]

→ look at Picture Dictionary: **time**
→ look at Word Web: **star**

Word Partnership	Use **night** with :
ADJ	**cold** night, **cool** night, **dark** night, **rainy** night, **warm** night **1**
V	**spend a/the** night **1** **2**
	sleep at night, **stay out at** night, **stay the** night **1** **2**

night|club /na͟ɪtklʌb/ (**nightclubs**) **N-COUNT** A **nightclub** is a place where people go late in the evening to drink and dance.

night|gown /na͟ɪtgaʊn/ (**nightgowns**) **N-COUNT** A **nightgown** is a loose dress that a woman or a girl wears in bed.

night|ly /na͟ɪtli/

1 **ADJ** A **nightly** event happens every night. ❑ *We watched the nightly news.*

2 **ADV** **Nightly** is also an adverb. ❑ *She appears nightly on the television news.* [from Old English]

night|mare /na͟ɪtmɛər/ (**nightmares**)

1 **N-COUNT** A **nightmare** is a very frightening dream. ❑ *She had nightmares for weeks after seeing that movie.*

2 **N-COUNT** If a situation is a **nightmare**, it is very unpleasant. ❑ *New York traffic is a nightmare.* [from Old English]

N

nil /nɪl/ **N-NONCOUNT** If you say that something **is nil**, you mean that it does not exist at all. ❑ *Their legal rights are almost nil.* [from Latin]

nine /naɪn/ **NUM** MATH **Nine** is the number 9. [from Old English]

nine-elev|en also **nine eleven, 9/11** **N-PROPER** You can use **9/11** or **nine-eleven** to talk about the attacks that took place in the United States on September 11, 2001. ❑ *Everything changed after nine-eleven.*

nine|teen /naɪntin/ **NUM** MATH **Nineteen** is the number 19. [from Old English]

nine|teenth /naɪntinθ/ **ADJ/ADV** MATH The **nineteenth** item in a series is the one that you count as number nineteen. ❑ *...my nineteenth birthday.* [from Old English]

nine|ti|eth /naɪntiɪθ/ **ADJ/ADV** MATH The **ninetieth** item in a series is the one that you count as number ninety. ❑ *He celebrates his ninetieth birthday on Friday.* [from Old English]

nine|ty /naɪnti/ (**nineties**)
1 NUM MATH **Ninety** is the number 90.
2 N-PLURAL The **nineties** are the years between 1990 and 1999. ❑ *...British art in the nineties.*
3 N-PLURAL When you talk about the **nineties**, you mean the numbers between 90 and 99. For example, if you are **in** your **nineties**, you are aged between 90 and 99. ❑ *The temperature was up in the nineties.* [from Old English]

ninth /naɪnθ/ (**ninths**)
1 ADJ/ADV MATH The **ninth** item in a series is the one that you count as number nine. ❑ *...January the ninth.* ❑ *...students in the ninth grade.*
2 N-COUNT MATH A **ninth** is one of nine equal parts of something (⅑). ❑ *The area covers one-ninth of the Earth's surface.* [from Old English]

nit|pick /nɪtpɪk/ (**nitpicks, nitpicking, nitpicked**) **V-I** If someone **nitpicks**, they criticize small and unimportant details. [INFORMAL] ❑ *I looked hard for items to nitpick about, and couldn't find any. Altogether a great car.*

ni|trate /naɪtreɪt/ (**nitrates**) **N-COUNT** SCIENCE A **nitrate** is a chemical compound that includes nitrogen and oxygen. Nitrates are used as fertilizers in agriculture. ❑ *...high levels of nitrates.* [from French]
→ look at Word Web: **firework**

ni|tro|gen /naɪtrədʒən/ **N-NONCOUNT** SCIENCE **Nitrogen** is a colorless element that has no smell and is usually found as a gas. It forms about 78 percent of the Earth's atmosphere, and is found in all living things. [from French]
→ look at Word Web: **air**

no /noʊ/
1 INTERJ You use **No** to give a negative response to a question. ❑ *"Are you having any problems?"—"No, I'm okay."* ❑ *"Here, have mine."—"No, thanks; this is fine."* ❑ *"Can I have another cookie?"—"No, you've had enough."*
2 INTERJ You use **No** to show that you accept and understand a negative statement. ❑ *"We're not on the main campus."—"No."*
3 INTERJ You use **No** when you are shocked or disappointed about something. ❑ *Oh no, not again.*
4 DET No means not any or not one person or thing. ❑ *He had no intention of paying.* ❑ *In this game, there are no rules.*
5 DET No is used in notices to say that something is not allowed. ❑ *No parking* ❑ *NO ENTRY* [from Old English]

No. (**Nos.**) **No.** is short for **number**. ❑ *He was named the nation's No.1 college football star.*

no|ble /noʊbəl/ (**nobler, noblest**)
1 ADJ If you say that someone is a **noble** person, you admire and respect them because they are morally good and are not selfish. ❑ *He was a generous and noble man who was always willing to help.* ● **no|bly ADV** ❑ *Eric's sister nobly offered to help with the gardening.*
2 ADJ SOCIAL STUDIES **Noble** means belonging to a high social class and having a title. ❑ *...rich and noble families.* [from Old French]

no|ble gas (**noble gases**) **N-COUNT** SCIENCE The **noble gases** are chemical elements such as helium and neon that do not generally react when mixed with other substances.

no|body /noʊbɒdi, -bʌdi/ **PRON Nobody** means not a single person. ❑ *For a long time nobody spoke.*

noc|tur|nal /nɒktɜrnəl/
1 ADJ Nocturnal means occurring at night. ❑ *...long nocturnal walks.*
2 ADJ SCIENCE **Nocturnal** animals are active mainly at night. ❑ *Rats are nocturnal creatures.* [from Late Latin]
→ look at Word Web: **bat**

n

nod /nɒd/ (**nods, nodding, nodded**)

1 **V-T/V-I** If you **nod**, you move your head downward and upward to show that you are answering "yes" to a question, or to show that you agree. ❑ *"Are you okay?" I asked. She nodded and smiled.* ❑ *Jacques tasted a cookie and nodded his approval.*

2 **N-COUNT** Nod is also a noun. ❑ *She gave a nod and said, "I see."*

▶ **nod off** If you **nod off**, you fall asleep when you did not intend to. [INFORMAL] ❑ *The judge appeared to nod off.*

Noh /noʊ/ **N-NONCOUNT** ARTS Noh is a traditional form of Japanese theater that combines dance, music, and poetry, and in which the actors wear masks. [from Japanese]

noise /nɔɪz/ (**noises**)

1 **N-NONCOUNT** Noise is a loud sound. ❑ *I'll never forget the noise from the crowd at the end of the game.*

2 **N-COUNT** A **noise** is a sound that someone or something makes. ❑ *Suddenly there was a noise like thunder.* [from Old French]

Word Partnership	Use **noise** with :
N	**background** noise, noise **level**, noise **pollution**, **traffic** noise **1**
ADJ	**loud** noise **1** **2**
V	**hear** a noise, **make** a noise **2**

noisy /nɔɪzi/ (**noisier, noisiest**)

1 **ADJ** A **noisy** person or thing makes a lot of loud or unpleasant noise. ❑ *It was a car with a particularly noisy engine.* ● **noisi|ly** **ADV** ❑ *The students cheered noisily.*

2 **ADJ** A **noisy** place is full of a lot of loud or unpleasant noise. ❑ *The airport was crowded and noisy.* [from Old French]

nomi|nal /nɒmɪnᵊl/

1 **ADJ** You use **nominal** to indicate that someone or something is supposed to have a particular identity or status, but in reality does not have it. ❑ *His wife became the nominal head of the company.* ● **nomi|nal|ly** **ADV** ❑ *Both countries are nominally equal.*

2 **ADJ** A **nominal** price or sum of money is very small in comparison with the real cost or value of the thing that is being bought or sold. ❑ *I sold my car at a nominal price.* [from Latin]

nomi|nate /nɒmɪneɪt/ (**nominates, nominating, nominated**) **V-T** If you **nominate** someone, you formally suggest

their name for a job, a position, or a prize. ❑ *He was nominated by the Democratic Party for the presidency of the United States.* [from Latin]

nomi|na|tion /nɒmɪneɪʃᵊn/ (**nominations**)

N-COUNT A **nomination** is an official suggestion that someone should be considered for a job, a position, or a prize. ❑ *He'll probably get a nomination for best actor.* [from Latin]

nomi|nee /nɒmɪni/ (**nominees**) **N-COUNT** A **nominee** is someone who is nominated for a job, a position, or an award. ❑ *...his nominee for vice president.*

non|count noun /nɒnkaʊnt naʊn/ (**noncount nouns**) **N-COUNT** LANGUAGE ARTS A **noncount noun** is a noun that has only one form and that you cannot use with "a" or "one." ❑ *A noncount noun, such as "baggage," "silver," or "advice," does not form a plural.*

none /nʌn/ **PRON** None means not one or not any. ❑ *I searched the Internet for information, but found none.* ❑ *None of us knew her.* [from Old English]

none|the|less /nʌnðəlɛs/ **ADV** Nonetheless means "although something is true." [FORMAL] ❑ *There is still a long way to go. Nonetheless, some progress has been made.*

Word Link	non ≈ not : non**fat**, non**fiction**, non**sense**

non|fat /nɒnfæt/ **ADJ** Nonfat food and drinks have very little or no fat in them. ❑ *A glass of nonfat milk contains about 80 calories.* [from Old English]

non|fic|tion /nɒnfɪkʃᵊn/ **N-NONCOUNT** LANGUAGE ARTS Nonfiction is writing that is about real people and events rather than imaginary ones. ❑ *The school library contains both fiction and nonfiction.* [from Latin] → look at Word Web: **genre**

non|fo|li|at|ed /nɒnfoʊlieɪtɪd/ **ADJ** SCIENCE Nonfoliated rock is rock that does not consist of regular, thin layers.

non|liv|ing /nɒnlɪvɪŋ/ also **non-living** **ADJ** SCIENCE Nonliving objects are objects that are not alive, such as rocks and minerals. [from Old English]

non|met|al /nɒnmɛtᵊl/ (**nonmetals**) also **non-metal** **N-COUNT** SCIENCE Nonmetals are chemical elements that are not metals. [from Latin]

non|objec|tive /nɒnəbdʒɛktɪv/ **ADJ** ARTS
Nonobjective art makes use of shapes
and patterns rather than showing people
or things.

nonpoint-source pol|lu|tion
/nɒnpɔɪntsɔrs pəluʃ°n/ **N-NONCOUNT**
SCIENCE **Nonpoint-source pollution** is
pollution that comes from many different
sources, for example chemicals from
farmland and factories that are carried into
rivers by rain.

non|re|new|able /nɒnrɪnuəb°l/
(**nonrenewables**) also **non-renewable**
1 **ADJ** SCIENCE **Nonrenewable** resources are
natural materials such as coal, oil, and gas
that exist in limited amounts and take a
very long time to replace.
2 **N-PLURAL** You can refer to nonrenewable
resources as **nonrenewables**.

non|sense /nɒnsɛns, -səns/
1 **N-NONCOUNT** If something is **nonsense**,
it is not true or it is silly. ❑ *Most doctors say
that this idea is complete nonsense.* ❑ *Peter said
I was talking nonsense.*
2 **N-NONCOUNT/N-SING Nonsense** is
behavior that you think is foolish. ❑ *I don't
think people can take much more of this nonsense.*
[from Latin]

non|sense syl|la|ble (**nonsense syllables**)
N-COUNT LANGUAGE ARTS A **nonsense syllable**
is a combination of letters, for example
"kak" or "mek," that does not form a proper
word. Nonsense syllables are used in the
teaching of reading skills.

non|sili|cate min|er|al /nɒnsɪlɪkɪt
mɪnərəl/ (**nonsilicate minerals**) **N-COUNT**
SCIENCE A **nonsilicate mineral** is a mineral
that does not contain a compound of silicon
and oxygen.

non|stand|ard unit (**nonstandard units**)
N-COUNT SCIENCE **Nonstandard units** are
units of measurement consisting of objects
that are not normally used to measure
things, for example paper clips.

non|stop /nɒnstɒp/
1 **ADJ** Something that is **nonstop** continues
without stopping. ❑ *A nonstop flight from
London takes you straight to Antigua.*
2 **ADV Nonstop** is also an adverb. ❑ *We drove
nonstop from New York to Miami.* [from Old
English]

non|vas|cu|lar plant /nɒnvæskyələr
plænt/ (**nonvascular plants**) also nonvascular plant **N-COUNT** SCIENCE
Nonvascular plants are plants such as
mosses and algae that are unable to move
water or nutrients through themselves.

non|ver|bal /nɒnvɜrb°l/ **ADJ Nonverbal**
communication consists of things such as
the expression on your face, your arm
movements, or your tone of voice, that show
how you feel about something without
using words.

noo|dle /nud°l/ (**noodles**) **N-COUNT** Noodles
are long, thin strips of pasta. They are used
especially in Chinese and Italian cooking.
[from German]

noon /nun/ **N-NONCOUNT** Noon is twelve
o'clock in the middle of the day. ❑ *The
meeting started at noon.* [from Old English]
→ look at Picture Dictionary: **time**

no one **PRON** No one means not a single
person, or not a single member of a
particular group or set. ❑ *We asked everyone in
the room, but no one wanted to help.*

noon|time /nuntaɪm/ **N-NONCOUNT**
Noontime is the middle part of the day.
❑ *He always came home for a hot meal at noontime.*

nope /noʊp/ **INTERJ** Nope is sometimes used
instead of "no" as a negative response.
[INFORMAL, SPOKEN] ❑ *"Is she supposed to work
today?"—"Nope, tomorrow."*

nor /nɔr/ **CONJ** You use **nor** after "neither"
to introduce the second of two negative
things. ❑ *Neither his friends nor his family knew
how old he was.* [from Old English]

norm /nɔrm/ **N-SING** If a situation is the
norm, it is usual and expected. ❑ *Families of
six or seven are the norm in here.* [from Latin]

nor|mal /nɔrm°l/ **ADJ** Something that is
normal is usual and ordinary. ❑ *Her height
and weight are normal for her age.* [from Latin]

Thesaurus	normal	Also look up :
ADJ	ordinary, regular, typical, usual	

Word Partnership	Use **normal** with :
N	normal **conditions**, normal **development**, normal **routine**
V	**return to** normal
ADV	**back to** normal, **completely** normal, **perfectly** normal

n

nor|mal fault (**normal faults**) **N-COUNT**
SCIENCE A **normal fault** is a fault in the
surface of the Earth where the rock above
the fault has moved down.

nor|mal|ly /nɔ́rməli/
1 ADV If something **normally** happens, it
usually happens. ❑ *Normally the bill is less than
$30 a month.* ❑ *I normally get up at 7 a.m. for work.*
2 ADV If you do something **normally**, you
do it in the usual or ordinary way. ❑ *She's
getting better and beginning to eat normally again.*
[from Latin]

north /nɔ́rθ/ also **North**
1 **N-NONCOUNT** GEOGRAPHY The **north** is the
direction that is on your left when you are
looking at the sun in the morning. ❑ *In the
north, snow and ice cover the ground.* ❑ *The lake is
just a few miles to the north.*
2 ADJ GEOGRAPHY **North** is also an adjective.
❑ *...the north bank of the river.* ❑ *...North America.*
3 **N-SING** GEOGRAPHY The **north of** a place or
country is the part that is in the north.
❑ *He lives in the north of Canada.*
4 ADV GEOGRAPHY If you go **north**, you
travel toward the north. ❑ *Anita drove north up
Pacific Highway.*
5 ADV GEOGRAPHY Something that is **north**
of a place is located to the north of it.
❑ *She lives in a village a few miles north of Portland.*
6 ADJ A **north** wind blows from the north.
❑ *A cold north wind was blowing.* [from Old
English]

north|east /nɔ́rθíst/
1 **N-NONCOUNT** GEOGRAPHY The **northeast**
is the direction that is between north and
east. ❑ *They live in Jerusalem, more than 250 miles
to the northeast.*
2 ADJ GEOGRAPHY **Northeast** is also an
adjective. ❑ *He's from northeast Louisiana.*
3 ADV GEOGRAPHY If you go **northeast**, you
travel toward the northeast. ❑ *They drive
northeast toward the mountains.*
4 ADV GEOGRAPHY Something that is
northeast of a place is located to the
northeast of it. ❑ *Payson is a small town about
70 miles northeast of Phoenix.*

north|eastern /nɔ́rθístərn/ ADJ GEOGRAPHY
Northeastern means in or from the
northeast part of a place. ❑ *Ian comes from
northeastern England.*

nor|ther|ly /nɔ́rðərli/
1 ADJ GEOGRAPHY **Northerly** means to the
north or toward the north. ❑ *The storm is
moving in a northerly direction.*
2 ADJ A **northerly** wind blows from the north.
❑ *...a cold northerly wind.* [from Old English]

north|ern /nɔ́rðərn/ also **Northern** ADJ
GEOGRAPHY **Northern** means in or from
the north of a place. ❑ *...Northern Ireland.*
[from Old English]

north|west /nɔ́rθwɛ́st/
1 **N-NONCOUNT** GEOGRAPHY The **northwest**
is the direction that is between north and
west. ❑ *There are forests to the northwest.*
2 ADJ GEOGRAPHY **Northwest** is also an
adjective. ❑ *The northwest coast is mild and wet.*
3 ADV GEOGRAPHY If you go **northwest**, you
travel toward the northwest. ❑ *We headed
northwest toward the ocean.*
4 ADV GEOGRAPHY Something that is
northwest of a place is located to the
northwest of it. ❑ *It's in the area northwest of
Hudson Bay.*

north|western /nɔ́rθwɛ́stərn/ ADJ
GEOGRAPHY **Northwestern** means in or from
the northwest part of a place. ❑ *There were
floods in northwestern Montana.*

nose /nóʊz/ (**noses**) **N-COUNT** Your **nose** is
the part of your face that sticks out above
your mouth. You use it for smelling and for
breathing. ❑ *She wiped her nose with a tissue.*
[from Old English]
→ look at Picture Dictionary: **face**
→ look at Word Webs: **respiratory system,
smell**

Word Partnership	Use **nose** with :
ADJ	big nose, **bloody** nose, **broken** nose, **long** nose, **red** nose, **runny** nose, **straight** nose

no-show (**no-shows**) **N-COUNT** A **no-show** is
someone who is expected to be at a place,
but who does not arrive. ❑ *Williams was a
no-show at last week's game in Milwaukee.*

nos|tril /nɒ́strɪl/ (**nostrils**) **N-COUNT** SCIENCE
Your **nostrils** are the two holes at the end of
your nose. ❑ *Keeping your mouth closed, breathe
in through your nostrils.* [from Old English]

not /nɒ́t/

LANGUAGE HELP
Use the short form **n't** when you are
speaking English. For example, "didn't"
is short for "did not."

1 ADV You use **not** to form negative

N

sentences. ❏ *Their plan was not working.*
❏ *I don't trust Peter anymore.*

2 **ADV** You use **not** to form questions to which you expect the answer "yes." ❏ *Haven't they got enough problems there already?* ❏ *Didn't I see you at the party last week?*

3 **ADV** You use **not**, usually in the form **n't**, when you want to change a positive statement into a question. ❏ *It's crazy, isn't it?*

4 **ADV** You use **not** when you are giving a negative answer. ❏ *"Have you found Paula?"—"I'm afraid not."*

5 **ADV** You use **not** in expressions such as **not only** and **not just** to emphasize that something is true, but it is not the whole truth. ❏ *These movies were not only making money; they were also very good.*

6 **PHRASE** **Not at all** is a strong way of saying "No" or of agreeing that the answer to a question is "No." ❏ *"Sorry, am I bothering you?"—"No. Not at all."* [from Old English]

no|table /no͟utəbᵊl/ **ADJ** Someone or something that is **notable** is important or interesting. ❏ *The quiet little town is notable for its church.* [from Old French]

no|tably /no͟utəbli/ **ADV** You use **notably** to specify an important or typical example of something that you are talking about. ❏ *He has apologized many times, most notably in the newspapers.* [from Old French]

no|ta|tion /no͟ute͟ɪʃᵊn/ (**notations**) **N-COUNT/N-NONCOUNT** MATH MUSIC A system of **notation** is a set of written symbols that are used to represent something such as music or mathematics. [from Latin]

note /no͟ut/ (**notes, noting, noted**)

1 **N-COUNT** A **note** is a short letter. ❏ *Steven wrote her a note and left it on the table.*

2 **N-COUNT** A **note** is something that you write down to remind yourself of something. ❏ *She didn't take notes on the lecture.*

3 **N-COUNT** In a book or an article, a **note** is a short piece of extra information. ❏ *See Note 16 on p. 223.*

4 **N-COUNT** MUSIC A **note** is one particular sound, or a symbol that represents this sound. ❏ *She has a deep voice and can't sing high notes.*

5 **V-T** If you **note** a fact, you become aware of it. ❏ *We noted his absence an hour ago.*

6 **V-T** When you **note** something, you write it down. ❏ *"He has been very ill," she noted in her diary.* [from Old French]

▶ **note down** If you **note down** something, you write it down quickly. ❏ *She noted down the names.*

Word Partnership	Use **note** with :
v	**leave a** note, **send a** note **1**
	find a note, **read a** note, **scribble a** note, **write a** note **1** **2**
	make a note **2**
	sound a note, **strike a** note **5**
	take note **of** *something* **5**

note|book /no͟utbʊk/ (**notebooks**)

1 **N-COUNT** A **notebook** is a small book for writing notes in. ❏ *He took a notebook and pen from his pocket.*

2 **N-COUNT** TECHNOLOGY A **notebook** computer is a small personal computer that you can carry with you. ❏ *She watched the DVD on her notebook computer.*

not|ed /no͟utɪd/ **ADJ** To be **noted for** something you do or have means to be well known and admired for it. ❏ *Sanders was a man noted for his leadership skills.* [from Old French]

noth|ing /nʌ͟θɪŋ/

1 **PRON** **Nothing** means not a single thing, or not a single part of something. ❏ *There is nothing wrong with the car.* ❏ *There was nothing in the refrigerator except some butter.*

2 **PRON** You use **nothing** to show that something or someone is not important. ❏ *Because he has always had money, it means nothing to him.*

3 **PHRASE** You use **nothing but** in front of a noun to mean "only." ❏ *All that money brought nothing but misery.* [from Old English]

no|tice /no͟utɪs/ (**notices, noticing, noticed**)

1 **V-T/V-I** If you **notice** something or someone, you become aware of them. ❏ *Did you notice anything unusual about him?* ❏ *She noticed he was acting strangely.* ❏ *Did you really think he had put on weight? I hadn't noticed.*

2 **N-COUNT** A **notice** is a piece of writing in a place where everyone can read it. ❏ *She posted a notice on the bulletin board.* ❏ *The notice said "Please close the door."*

3 **N-NONCOUNT** If you give **notice** about something that is going to happen, you give a warning in advance that it is going to happen. ❏ *They moved her to a different office without notice.* ❏ *You must give 30 days' notice if you want to cancel the contract.*

4 **PHRASE** If you **take notice of** something,

n

you show that you are aware of it. ❑ *We want the government to take notice of what we say.* [from Old French]

Thesaurus	notice	Also look up :
V	note, observe, perceive, see **1**
N	advertisement, announcement **2**

Word Partnership	Use notice with :
N	notice **a change**, notice **a difference 1**
V	**begin to** notice, **fail to** notice, **pretend not to** notice **1**
	receive notice, **serve** notice **3**
	give notice **3**

no|tice|able /n<u>ou</u>tɪsəbᵊl/ **ADJ** Something that is **noticeable** is easy to see, hear, or recognize. ❑ *This hotel is slightly more expensive, but the difference is noticeable.* [from Old French]

no|ti|fy /n<u>ou</u>tɪfaɪ/ (**notifies, notifying, notified**) **V-T** If you **notify** someone of something, you officially tell them about it. [FORMAL] ❑ *We have notified the police.* [from Old French]

no|tion /n<u>ou</u>ʃᵊn/ (**notions**)
1 **N-COUNT** A **notion** is an idea or a belief about something. ❑ *We each have a notion of what kind of person we'd like to be.*
2 **N-PLURAL** **Notions** are small articles for sewing, such as buttons, zippers, and thread. [from Latin]

Thesaurus	notion	Also look up :
N	concept, idea, opinion, thought **1**

no|to|ri|ous /noʊt<u>ɔ</u>riəs/ **ADJ** To be **notorious** means to be well known for something bad. ❑ *...an area notorious for crime and violence.*
● **no|to|ri|ous|ly** **ADV** ❑ *Living space in New York City is notoriously expensive.* [from Medieval Latin]

noun /n<u>au</u>n/ (**nouns**)
1 **N-COUNT** LANGUAGE ARTS A **noun** is a word such as "car," "love," or "Anne" that is used for talking about a person or a thing. [from Latin]
2 → see also **count noun, noncount noun, proper noun**

nour|ish /n<u>ɜ</u>rɪʃ/ (**nourishes, nourishing, nourished**) **V-T** To **nourish** a person, an animal, or a plant means to give them the food that they need to live, grow, and be healthy. ❑ *The food she eats nourishes both her and the baby.* ● **nour|ish|ing** **ADJ** ❑ *...nourishing*

home-cooked food.* ● **nour|ish|ment**
N-NONCOUNT ❑ *These delicious drinks will provide sick children with the nourishment they need to recover.* [from Old French]

Word Link	nov ≈ new : in**nov**ation, **nov**el, re**nov**ate

nov|el /n<u>ɒ</u>vᵊl/ (**novels**) **N-COUNT** LANGUAGE ARTS A **novel** is a long written story about imaginary people and events. ❑ *He's reading a novel by Herman Hesse.* [from Old French]

nov|el|ist /n<u>ɒ</u>vəlɪst/ (**novelists**) **N-COUNT** LANGUAGE ARTS A **novelist** is a person who writes novels. ❑ *He was one of America's great novelists.* [from Old French]

nov|el|ty /n<u>ɒ</u>vᵊlti/ (**novelties**) **N-COUNT** A **novelty** is something that is new and interesting. ❑ *Tourists are still a novelty on the island.* [from Old French]

No|vem|ber /noʊv<u>ɛ</u>mbər/ (**Novembers**) **N-COUNT/N-NONCOUNT** **November** is the eleventh month of the year. ❑ *He came to New York in November 1939.* [from Old French]

nov|ice /n<u>ɒ</u>vɪs/ (**novices**) **N-COUNT** A **novice** is someone who has been doing a job or other activity for only a short time and so is not experienced at it. ❑ *I'm a novice at these things. You're the professional.* [from Old French]

now /n<u>au</u>/
1 **ADV** You use **now** to talk about the present time. ❑ *I must go now.* ❑ *She should know that by now.*
2 **PRON** **Now** is also a pronoun. ❑ *Now is your chance to talk to him.*
3 **CONJ** You use **now** or **now that** to show that something has happened, and as a result something else will happen. ❑ *Now that our children are older, I have time to help other people.*
4 **ADV** You use **now** when you talk about the length of time that something has lasted. ❑ *They've been married now for 30 years.*
5 **ADV** You say **Now** or **Now then** when you want to get someone's attention or you want to change the subject. [SPOKEN] ❑ *"Now then," Max said, "to get back to the point."*
6 **PHRASE** If something happens **now and then** or **every now and again**, it happens sometimes but not very often or regularly. ❑ *Now and then they heard the sound of a heavy truck outside.* [from Old English]

nowa|days /ˈnaʊədeɪz/ **ADV** Nowadays means now generally, and not in the past. ❑ *Nowadays almost all children spend some time playing electronic and computer games.* [from Old English]

no|where /ˈnoʊwɛər/
1 **ADV** You use **nowhere** to mean "not in any place" or "not to any place." ❑ *Nowhere is the problem worse than in Asia.* ❑ *I have nowhere else to go.*
2 **PHRASE** If you say that a place is **in the middle of nowhere**, you mean that it is a long way from other places. ❑ *We put up our tent in the middle of nowhere.*

Word Partnership	Use **nowhere** with :
v	nowhere **to be found**, nowhere **to be seen**, *have* nowhere **to go**, *have* nowhere **to hide**, *have* nowhere **to run** **2**

nu|ance /ˈnuɑns/ (**nuances**)
N-COUNT/N-NONCOUNT A **nuance** is a small difference in sound, feeling, appearance, or meaning. ❑ *They talked for hours about him, analyzing every nuance of his behavior.* [from French]

nu|clear /ˈnukliər/ **ADJ** SCIENCE **Nuclear** describes the energy that is released when the nuclei of atoms are split or combined. ❑ *We're building a nuclear power station.* ❑ *They don't have any nuclear weapons.* [from Latin]
→ look at Word Web: **energy**

nu|clear en|er|gy **N-NONCOUNT** SCIENCE **Nuclear energy** is energy that is released when the nuclei of atoms are split or combined.

nu|clear fis|sion **N-NONCOUNT** → look up **fission**

nu|clear fu|sion **N-NONCOUNT** → look up **fusion 2**

nu|clear re|ac|tor (**nuclear reactors**)
N-COUNT SCIENCE A **nuclear reactor** is a machine that is used to produce nuclear energy. ❑ *The nuclear reactor was not damaged in the lightning storm that struck late last night.*

nu|cleic acid /nukliːɪk æsɪd, -kleɪ-/ (**nucleic acids**) **N-COUNT** SCIENCE **Nucleic acids** are complex chemical substances, such as DNA, that are found in living cells.

nu|cleo|tide /ˈnukliətaɪd/ (**nucleotides**)
N-COUNT SCIENCE **Nucleotides** are molecules that join together to form DNA and RNA.

nu|cleus /ˈnukliəs/ (**nuclei** /ˈnukliaɪ/)
N-COUNT SCIENCE The **nucleus** of an atom or cell is the central part of it. [from Latin]

nude /nud/ (**nudes**)
1 **ADJ** A **nude** person is not wearing any clothes. ❑ *She came into the room, almost completely nude.*
2 **N-COUNT** ARTS A **nude** is a painting or a piece of art that shows someone who is not wearing any clothes. [from Latin]

nudge /nʌdʒ/ (**nudges, nudging, nudged**)
1 **V-T** If you **nudge** someone, you push them gently, usually with your elbow. ❑ *I nudged Stan and pointed again.*
2 **N-COUNT** **Nudge** is also a noun. ❑ *She gave him a nudge.* [of Scandinavian origin]

nui|sance /ˈnusᵊns/ (**nuisances**) **N-COUNT** If someone or something is a **nuisance**, they annoy you. ❑ *He can be a bit of a nuisance sometimes.* [from Old French]

numb /nʌm/ (**number, numbest**) **ADJ** If a part of your body is **numb**, you cannot feel anything there. ❑ *It was so cold that his fingers were numb.* [from Old English]

num|ber /ˈnʌmbər/ (**numbers, numbering, numbered**)
1 **N-COUNT** MATH A **number** is a word such as "two," "nine," or "twelve" or a symbol such as 1, 3, or 47 that is used in counting. ❑ *I don't know my room number.* ❑ *What's your phone number?*
2 **N-COUNT** You use **number** with words such as "large" or "small" to say approximately how many things or people there are. ❑ *I received a large number of emails on the subject.*
3 **N-SING** If there are **a number of** things or people, there are several of them. ❑ *Sam told a number of lies.*
4 **N-COUNT** A **number** is the series of numbers that you dial when you are making a telephone call. ❑ *...a list of names and telephone numbers.* ❑ *My number is 555-3925.*
5 **V-T** If you **number** something, you mark it with a number, usually starting at 1. ❑ *He cut the paper up into tiny squares, and he numbered each one.* [from Old French]
→ look at Usage note at **amount**
→ look at Word Webs: **mathematics, zero**

nu|mer|al /ˈnumərəl/ (**numerals**) **N-COUNT** **Numerals** are written symbols used to represent numbers. ❑ *...a flat, square*

n

wristwatch with classic Roman numerals.
❑ *...the numeral 6.*
→ look at Picture Dictionary: **Roman numerals**

nu|mer|ous /n**ʊ**mərəs/ **ADJ** If people or things are **numerous**, they exist in large numbers. ❑ *He made numerous attempts to lose weight.* [from Late Middle English]

nun /n**ʌ**n/ (**nuns**) **N-COUNT** A **nun** is a member of a group of religious women who often live together in a special building. ❑ *When I was seventeen, I decided to become a nun.* [from Old English]

nurse /n**ɜ**rs/ (**nurses, nursing, nursed**)
1 **N-COUNT** A **nurse** is a person whose job is to care for people who are sick. ❑ *She thanked the nurses who cared for her.*
2 **V-T** If you **nurse** someone, you care for them when they are sick. ❑ *My mother has nursed him for the last ten years.* [from Old French]

nurse|ry /n**ɜ**rsəri/ (**nurseries**)
1 **N-COUNT** A **nursery** is a place where people grow and sell plants. ❑ *Buy your plants at the local nursery.*
2 **N-COUNT** A **nursery** is a room in a family home in which the young children of the family sleep or play. ❑ *We painted bright pictures on the walls in the children's nursery.* [from Old French]

nurse|ry rhyme (**nursery rhymes**) **N-COUNT** A **nursery rhyme** is a poem or a song for young children.

nurs|ing home (**nursing homes**) **N-COUNT** A **nursing home** is a place where old or sick people live. ❑ *He died in a nursing home in Florida at the age of 87.*

nur|ture /n**ɜ**rtʃər/ (**nurtures, nurturing, nurtured**)
1 **V-T** If you **nurture** something such as a young child or a young plant, you care for it while it is growing and developing. [FORMAL] ❑ *Parents want to know the best way to*

nurture and raise their child.
2 **V-T** If you **nurture** plans, ideas, or people, you encourage them or help them to develop. [FORMAL] ❑ *She always nurtured the talent of others.* [from Old French]

nut /n**ʌ**t/ (**nuts**)
1 **N-COUNT** A **nut** is a dry fruit with a hard shell. ❑ *Nuts and seeds are very good for you.*
2 **N-COUNT** A **nut** is a thick metal ring that you put onto a bolt. Nuts and bolts are used for holding heavy things together. ❑ *If you want to repair the wheels, you must remove the four nuts.*

nut

3 **N-COUNT** If someone is a baseball **nut** or a health **nut**, for example, they are very enthusiastic about that activity. [INFORMAL] ❑ *It is possible to stay healthy without being a health nut.*
4 **ADJ** If you are **nuts about** something or someone, you like them very much. [INFORMAL] ❑ *She's nuts about you and you're in love with her.*
5 **ADJ** If someone is **nuts**, they are crazy. [INFORMAL] ❑ *You guys are nuts.* [from Old English]
→ look at Word Web: **peanut**

nu|tri|ent /n**ʊ**triənt/ (**nutrients**) **N-COUNT** SCIENCE **Nutrients** are substances that help plants and animals to grow and stay healthy. ❑ *The juice contains vitamins, minerals, and other essential nutrients.* [from Latin]
→ look at Word Webs: **cardiovascular system, food**

nu|tri|tion /n**ʊ**trɪʃ°n/ **N-NONCOUNT** **Nutrition** is the way that the body uses the food that it needs to grow and stay healthy. ❑ *He talked to the children about the importance of good nutrition and exercise.* [from Late Latin]

ny|lon /n**aɪ**lɒn/ **N-NONCOUNT** **Nylon** is a strong artificial cloth. ❑ *I packed a sleeping bag, a pocket knife, and some strong nylon rope.*

N

Oo

oak /oʊk/ (**oaks**)

1 **N-COUNT/N-NONCOUNT** An **oak** or an **oak tree** is a type of large tree.

2 **N-NONCOUNT** Oak is the wood of this tree. ❑ *He sat down at the oak table.* [from Old English]

oar /ɔr/ (**oars**) **N-COUNT** Oars are long poles with one flat end that you use for rowing a boat. [from Old English]
→ look at Word Web: **boat**

oa|sis /oʊeɪsɪs/ (**oases** /oʊeɪsiz/) **N-COUNT** GEOGRAPHY An **oasis** is a small area in a desert where you find water and plants. [from Latin]
→ look at Picture Dictionary: **desert**

oat|meal /oʊtmil/ **N-NONCOUNT** Oatmeal is a hot, thick food that people eat for breakfast. It is made from oats cooked in water or milk.

oats /oʊts/

> **LANGUAGE HELP**
> The form **oat** is used as a modifier.

N-PLURAL Oats are a type of grain that is used in foods. [from Old English]
→ look at Word Web: **grain**

obe|di|ent /oʊbidiənt/ **ADJ** A person or an animal that is **obedient** does what they are told to do. ❑ *As a child, Charlotte was an obedient daughter.* ● **obedi|ence** /oʊbidiəns/ **N-NONCOUNT** ❑ *He expected complete obedience from his sons.* ● **obedi|ent|ly** **ADV** ❑ *The dog sat beside him obediently.* [from Old French]

obese /oʊbis/ **ADJ** If someone is **obese**, they have too much body fat, making them unhealthy. ❑ *Obese people often have more health problems than thinner people.* ● **obesity** /oʊbisɪti/ **N-NONCOUNT** ❑ *Eating too much sugar can lead to obesity.* [from Latin]
→ look at Word Webs: **diet, sugar**

obey /oʊbeɪ/ (**obeys, obeying, obeyed**) **V-T/V-I** If you **obey** a person or a command, you do what you are told to do. ❑ *Most people obey the law.* ❑ *It was his duty to obey.* [from Old French]

Word Partnership	Use **obey** with :
N	obey **a command**, obey **God**, obey **the law**, obey **orders**, obey **the rules**
V	**refuse to** obey

obi|tu|ary /oʊbɪtʃueri/ (**obituaries**) **N-COUNT** Someone's **obituary** is an account of their life and achievements that is published soon after they die. ❑ *I read his obituary in the newspaper.* [from Medieval Latin]

ob|ject (**objects, objecting, objected**)

> **PRONUNCIATION HELP**
> Pronounce the noun /ɒbdʒɪkt/. Pronounce the verb /əbdʒɛkt/.

1 **N-COUNT** An **object** is a thing that has a shape, and that is not alive. ❑ *I have to wear glasses because I can't see distant objects clearly.* ❑ *We could hear someone throwing small, hard objects on to the roof.*

2 **N-COUNT** The **object** of what someone is doing is their purpose. ❑ *The object of the event is to raise money.*

3 **N-COUNT** LANGUAGE ARTS In grammar, the **object** of a verb is the person or thing that is affected by the action.

4 → see also **direct object, indirect object**

5 **V-T/V-I** If you **object** to something, you say that you do not agree with it, or that you do not like it. ❑ *A lot of people objected to the book.* ❑ *Cullen objected that he had too much work.* [Senses 1 to 3 from Late Latin. Sense 5 from Latin.]

Thesaurus	object	Also look up :
N	item, thing **1**	
	aim, goal, intent **2**	
V	argue, disagree, oppose, protest against **4**	

Word Partnership	Use **object** with :
ADJ	**foreign** object, **moving** object, **solid** object **1**
N	object **to** *someone/something* **4**

ob|jec|tion /əbdʒɛkʃ°n/ (**objections**) **N-COUNT/N-NONCOUNT** If you state an

objection, you say that you do not like or agree with something. ❑ *I don't have any objection to people making money.* [from Late Latin]

ob|jec|tive /əbdʒɛktɪv/ (**objectives**)
1 **N-COUNT** Your **objective** is what you are trying to achieve. ❑ *Our main objective was to find the child.*
2 **ADJ** If someone is **objective**, they base their opinions on facts rather than on their personal feelings. ❑ *A journalist should be completely objective.* [from Late Latin]

ob|jec|tive lens (**objective lenses**) **N-COUNT**
SCIENCE The **objective lens** of a microscope is the lens that is closest to the object being observed and furthest from the eyepiece.

ob|li|ga|tion /ɒblɪɡeɪʃ°n/ (**obligations**)
N-COUNT/N-NONCOUNT If you have an **obligation to** do something, you should do it. ❑ *The judge has an obligation to find out the truth.* [from Old French]

Thesaurus	obligation	Also look up :
N	duty, responsibility	

Word Partnership	Use obligation with :
V	obligation **to pay**, **feel an** obligation, **fulfill an** obligation, **meet an** obligation
ADJ	**legal** obligation, **moral** obligation
N	**sense of** obligation

ob|liga|tory /əblɪɡətɔri/ **ADJ** If something is **obligatory**, you must do it because of a rule or a law. ❑ *These medical tests are not obligatory.* [from Old French]

oblige /əblaɪdʒ/ (**obliges, obliging, obliged**)
V-T If you **are obliged to** do something, a situation or a law makes it necessary for you to do it. ❑ *My family needed the money so I was obliged to work.* [from Old French]

ob|long /ɒblɔŋ/ (**oblongs**) **N-COUNT** MATH
An **oblong** is a shape that has two long sides and two short sides. ❑ *Ten people sat around a large oblong table.* [from Latin]

oboe /oʊboʊ/ (**oboes**) **N-COUNT/N-NONCOUNT**
MUSIC An **oboe** is a musical instrument that you blow. It is a long black wooden tube with keys on it that you press, and a double reed (= small flat part that moves and makes a sound when you blow). [from Italian]
→ look at Word Web: **orchestra**

ob|scene /əbsin/ **ADJ** Something that is **obscene** offends you because it relates to sex

or violence in an unpleasant and shocking way. ❑ *...obscene photographs.* [from Latin]

ob|scure /əbskyʊər/ (**obscurer, obscurest, obscures, obscuring, obscured**)
1 **ADJ** If something or someone is **obscure**, they are unknown, or are known by only a few people. ❑ *The origin of the word is obscure.*
● **ob|scu|rity** **N-NONCOUNT** ❑ *She came from obscurity into the world of television.*
2 **ADJ** Something that is **obscure** is difficult to understand or deal with, usually because it involves so many parts or details. ❑ *The contracts are written in obscure language.*
● **ob|scu|rity** **N-NONCOUNT** ❑ *He was irritated by the obscurity of Henry's reply.*
3 **V-T** If one thing **obscures** another, it prevents it from being seen or heard properly. ❑ *Trees obscured his view of the scene.* [from Old French]

ob|ser|va|tion /ɒbzərveɪʃ°n/ (**observations**)
1 **N-NONCOUNT** **Observation** is the action or process of carefully watching someone or something. ❑ *In the hospital she'll be under observation all the time.* ● **ob|ser|va|tion|al** **ADJ** ❑ *...observational studies of children.*
2 **N-COUNT** An **observation** is something that you have learned by seeing or watching something and thinking about it. ❑ *...observations about the causes of heart disease.*
3 **N-COUNT** If a person makes an **observation**, they make a comment about something or someone after watching how they behave. ❑ *He made the observation that life is full of difficulty.*
4 **N-NONCOUNT** **Observation** is the ability to notice things that are not usually noticed. ❑ *She has good powers of observation.* [from Old French]
→ look at Word Webs: **experiment, forecast, science**

Word Partnership	Use observation with :
PREP	**by** observation, **through** observation, **under** observation **1**
ADJ	**careful** observation **1** **direct** observation **1** **2**
V	**make an** observation **3**

Word Link	serv ≈ keeping : conserve, observe, preserve

ob|serve /əbzɜrv/ (**observes, observing, observed**) **V-T** If you **observe** a person or a thing, you watch them carefully in order to learn something about them. ❑ *Olson observed* the behavior of babies. [from Old French]

v study, watch, detect, notice, spot

Word Partnership Use observe with :

N observe **behavior**, **opportunity to** observe, observe **guidelines**, observe **rules**

ob|serv|er /əbzɜrvər/ (**observers**)
■ **N-COUNT** You can refer to someone who sees or notices something as an **observer**. ❑ Observers say the woman stabbed him.
■ **N-COUNT** An **observer** is someone who studies current events and situations. ❑ Observers say the president's decision will affect his popularity. [from Old French]

ob|sess /əbsɛs/ (**obsesses, obsessing, obsessed**) **V-T/V-I** If something **obsesses** you or if you **obsess about** something, you keep thinking about it and find it difficult to think about anything else. ❑ The idea of space travel has obsessed me all my life. ❑ She was obsessing about her weight.
● **ob|sessed** **ADJ** ❑ He was obsessed with crime movies. [from Latin]

ob|ses|sion /əbsɛʃⁿn/ (**obsessions**)
N-COUNT/N-NONCOUNT If someone has an **obsession** with a person or a thing, they spend too much time thinking about them. ❑ She tried to forget her obsession with Christopher. [from Latin]

ob|so|lete /ɒbsəlit/ **ADJ** Something that is **obsolete** is no longer needed because something better has been invented. ❑ A lot of equipment becomes obsolete almost as soon as it's made. [from Latin]

ob|sta|cle /ɒbstəkⁿl/ (**obstacles**) **N-COUNT** An **obstacle** is something that makes it difficult for you to do what you want to do. ❑ We had to overcome two major obstacles. [from Old French]

Word Partnership Use obstacle with :

V **be an** obstacle, **hit an** obstacle, **overcome an** obstacle
ADJ **big/biggest** obstacle, **main** obstacle, **major** obstacle
N obstacle **course**, obstacle **to peace**

ob|sti|nate /ɒbstɪnɪt/ **ADJ** An **obstinate** person is determined to do what they want, and you cannot persuade them to do something else. ❑ When she says "no," nothing

can make her change, and she can be very obstinate. [from Latin]

ob|struct /əbstrʌkt/ (**obstructs, obstructing, obstructed**) **V-T** If someone or something **obstructs** a place, they block it, making it difficult for you to get past. ❑ A group of cars obstructed the road. [from Latin]

ob|struc|tion /əbstrʌkʃⁿn/ (**obstructions**) **N-COUNT** An **obstruction** is something that blocks a road or a path. ❑ The cars outside his house were causing an obstruction. [from Latin]

ob|tain /əbteɪn/ (**obtains, obtaining, obtained**) **V-T** To **obtain** something means to get it. [FORMAL] ❑ Evans tried to obtain a false passport. [from Old French]

Word Partnership Use obtain with :

ADJ **able to** obtain, **difficult to** obtain, **easy to** obtain, **unable to** obtain
N obtain **approval**, obtain **a copy**, obtain **financing**, obtain **help**, obtain **information**, obtain **insurance**, obtain **permission**, obtain **weapons**

ob|vi|ous /ɒbviəs/ **ADJ** If something is **obvious**, it is easy to see or understand. ❑ It's obvious that he's worried about us. [from Latin]

ADJ noticeable, plain, unmistakable ■

Word Partnership Use obvious with :

N obvious **answer**, obvious **choice**, obvious **differences**, obvious **example**, obvious **question**, obvious **reasons**, obvious **solution**
ADV **fairly** obvious, **immediately** obvious, **less** obvious, **painfully** obvious, **quite** obvious

ob|vi|ous|ly /ɒbviəsli/
■ **ADV** You use **obviously** to show that something is easily noticed, seen, or recognized. ❑ He obviously likes you very much.
■ **ADV** You use **obviously** when you are saying something that you expect your listener to know already. ❑ Obviously I'll be disappointed if they don't come, but it wouldn't be a disaster. [from Latin]

oc|ca|sion /əkeɪʒⁿn/ (**occasions**)
■ **N-COUNT** An **occasion** is a time when something happens. ❑ I gave her money on several occasions.
■ **N-COUNT** An **occasion** is an important event, ceremony, or celebration.

O

❏ *The wedding was a happy occasion.* [from Latin]

oc|ca|sion|al /əkeɪʒənᵊl/ **ADJ Occasional** means happening sometimes, but not often. ❏ *I get occasional headaches.*

● **oc|ca|sion|al|ly ADV** ❏ *He misbehaves occasionally.* [from Latin]

oc|cu|pan|cy /ɒkyəpənsi/ **N-NONCOUNT Occupancy** is the act of using a room, a building, or an area of land, usually for a fixed period of time. [FORMAL] ❏ *Hotel occupancy was as low as 40% in winter.* [from Old French]

> **Word Link** *ant ≈ one who does, has : defendant, occupant, pollutant*

oc|cu|pant /ɒkyəpənt/ (**occupants**) **N-COUNT** The **occupants** of a building or a room are the people who live or work there. ❏ *Most of the occupants left the building before the fire spread.* [from Old French]

oc|cu|pa|tion /ɒkyəpeɪʃᵊn/ (**occupations**) **1 N-COUNT** Your **occupation** is your job. ❏ *Please write down your name and occupation.* **2 N-COUNT** An **occupation** is something that you spend time doing, either for fun or because it needs to be done. ❏ *Cooking was his favorite occupation.* **3 N-NONCOUNT** The **occupation** of a country happens when a foreign army enters it and controls it. ❏ *She lived in France during Nazi Germany's occupation.* [from Old French]

oc|cu|py /ɒkyəpaɪ/ (**occupies, occupying, occupied**) **1 V-T** The people who **occupy** a place are the people who live or work there. ❏ *The company occupies the top floor of the building.* **2 V-T** If a room or a seat **is occupied**, someone is using it. ❏ *The chair was occupied by his wife.* **3 V-T** If an army **occupies** a place, they

move into it and use force to control it. ❏ *U.S. forces occupy a part of the country.* **4 V-T** If something **occupies** you or your mind, you are busy doing it or thinking about it. ❏ *Her career occupies all of her time.* ● **oc|cu|pied ADJ** ❏ *Don't get bored. Keep your brain occupied.* [from Old French]

> **Word Partnership** Use **occupy** with :
>
> | N | |
> |---|---|
> | | occupy **a house**, occupy **land** **1** |
> | | occupy **a place** **1** **3** |
> | | occupy **a position** **3** |
> | | occupy **an area**, forces occupy *someplace*, |
> | | occupy **space**, troops occupy *someplace* **3** |

oc|cur /əkɜr/ (**occurs, occurring, occurred**) **1 V-I** When something **occurs**, it happens. ❏ *The car crash occurred at night.* **2 V-I** If a thought or an idea **occurs to** you, you suddenly think of it. ❏ *Suddenly it occurred to her that the door might be open.* [from Latin]

> **Thesaurus** occur Also look up :
>
> | V | come about, develop, happen **1** |
> |---|---|
> | | dawn on, strike **2** |

> **Word Partnership** Use **occur** with :
>
> | N | accidents occur, changes occur, deaths occur, diseases occur, events occur, injuries occur, problems occur **1** |
> |---|---|
> | ADV | frequently occur, naturally occur, normally occur, often occur, usually occur **1** **2** |

oc|cur|rence /əkɜrəns/ (**occurrences**) **N-COUNT** An **occurrence** is something that happens. [FORMAL] ❏ *Complaints against the company were an everyday occurrence.* [from Latin]

ocean /oʊʃᵊn/ (**oceans**) **1 N-SING** GEOGRAPHY The **ocean** is the salty water that covers much of the Earth's surface. ❏ *The house is on a cliff overlooking the ocean.*

> **Word Web** ocean
>
> **Oceans** cover more than seventy-five percent of the earth. These huge bodies of **saltwater** are always moving. On the surface, the wind pushes the **water** into **waves**. At the same time, **currents** under the surface **flow** like **rivers** through the oceans. These currents are affected by the earth's rotation. It shifts them to the right in the northern hemisphere and to the left in the southern hemisphere. Other forces affect the oceans as well. For example, the gravitational pull of the moon and sun affects ocean **tides**.

2 **N-COUNT** GEOGRAPHY An **ocean** is one of the five very large areas of salt water on the Earth's surface. ❑ ...the Pacific Ocean. [from Old French]
→ look at Picture Dictionary: **river**
→ look at Word Webs: **ocean, beach, earth, ship, tide, whale**

ocean|og|ra|phy /oʊʃənɒgrəfi/ **N-NONCOUNT** SCIENCE **Oceanography** is the scientific study of sea currents, the ocean floor, and the fish and animals that live in the sea. [from Old French]

ocean trench /oʊʃ°n trɛntʃ/ (**ocean trenches**) **N-COUNT** SCIENCE An **ocean trench** is a deep crack in the sea floor that forms when one section of the sea floor slides under another section.

o'clock /əklɒk/ **ADV** You use **o'clock** after numbers from one to twelve to say what time it is. ❑ I went to bed at ten o'clock last night.

Usage o'clock

Use *o'clock* for times that are exactly on the hour: "Is it four o'clock yet?"—"Not quite, it's three forty-five."

oc|tave /ɒktɪv/ (**octaves**) **N-COUNT** MUSIC An **octave** is a series of eight notes in music, or the difference between the first and last notes in the series. [from Old French]

Oc|to|ber /ɒktoʊbər/ (**Octobers**) **N-COUNT/ N-NONCOUNT October** is the tenth month of the year. ❑ Her birthday is in October. [from Old English]

oc|to|pus /ɒktəpəs/ (**octopuses**) **N-COUNT/ N-NONCOUNT** An **octopus** is a soft ocean animal with eight long arms. [from New Latin]

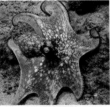
octopus

odd /ɒd/ (**odder, oddest**)
1 **ADJ** If someone or something is **odd**, they are strange or unusual. ❑ His behavior was odd. ● **odd|ly** **ADV** ❑ He dresses rather oddly.
2 **ADJ** MATH **Odd** numbers, such as 3 and 17, are numbers that cannot be divided exactly by the number two.
3 **ADJ** You say that two things are **odd** when they do not belong to the same set or pair. ❑ I'm wearing odd socks. [from Old Norse]

Thesaurus odd Also look up :

ADJ	bizarre, different, eccentric, peculiar, strange, unusual, weird; (ant.) normal, regular **1**

Word Partnership Use **odd** with :

V	**feel** odd, **look** odd, **seem** odd, **sound** odd, **strike** *someone* **as** odd, **think** *something* odd **1**
N	odd **combination**, odd **thing** **1**
ADJ	odd **numbered** **2**

odds /ɒdz/ **N-PLURAL** The **odds** that something will happen are how likely it is to happen. ❑ What are the odds of finding a parking space right outside the door? [from Old Norse]

Word Partnership Use **odds** with :

V	**beat the** odds
N	odds **in** *someone's/something's* **favor**, odds **of winning**
PREP	**the** odds **of** *something*, **against all** odds **3**

odor /oʊdər/ (**odors**) **N-COUNT** An **odor** is a smell. ❑ A bad egg will have an unpleasant odor when you break open the shell. [from Old French]
→ look at Word Webs: **smell, taste**

of /əv, STRONG ʌv/
1 **PREP** You use **of** to say what someone or something is connected with. ❑ Police searched the homes of the criminals. ❑ ...the mayor of Los Angeles.
2 **PREP** You use **of** to say what something relates to. ❑ He was trying to hide his feelings of anger.
3 **PREP** You use **of** to talk about someone or something else who is involved in an action. ❑ He was dreaming of her.
4 **PREP** You use **of** to show that someone or something is part of a larger group. ❑ She is the youngest child of three.
5 **PREP** You use **of** to talk about amounts or contents. ❑ The boy was drinking a glass of milk.
6 **PREP** You use **of** to say what caused a person's or an animal's death. ❑ He died of a heart attack.
7 **PREP Of** describes someone's behavior. ❑ It's very kind of you to help. ❑ It was rude of him to interrupt you. [from Old English]

of course
1 **ADV** You say **of course** to suggest that something is not surprising. [SPOKEN]

❑ *Of course there were lots of interesting things to see.*
2 **PHRASE** You use **Of course** as a polite way of giving permission. [SPOKEN] ❑ *"Can I ask you something?"—"Yes, of course."*
3 **PHRASE** **Of course not** is a strong way of saying no. [SPOKEN] ❑ *"You're not going to go, are you?"—"No, of course not."*

off
① AWAY FROM
② OTHER USES

① off

PRONUNCIATION HELP
Pronounce the preposition /ɔf/.
Pronounce the adverb /ɔf/.

1 **PREP** If you take something **off** another thing, it is no longer on it. ❑ *He took his feet off the desk.*
2 **ADV** **Off** is also an adverb. ❑ *I broke off a piece of chocolate and ate it.*
3 **PREP** When you get **off** a bus, a train, or an airplane, you come out of it. ❑ *Don't get off a moving train!*
4 **ADV** **Off** is also an adverb. ❑ *At the next station, the man got off.*
5 **PREP** If you keep **off** a piece of land, you do not go there. ❑ *The police told visitors to keep off the beach.*
6 **ADV** If you go **off**, you go away. ❑ *He was just about to drive off.*
7 **ADV** If you have time **off**, you do not go to work or school. ❑ *She had the day off.* ❑ *I'm off tomorrow.*
8 **PREP** **Off** is also a preposition. ❑ *He could not get time off work to go on vacation.*
9 **ADV** If something is a long time **off**, it will not happen for a long time. ❑ *An agreement is still a long way off.*

② off /ɔf/
1 **ADV** If an event is **off**, it is canceled. ❑ *The wedding is off.*
2 **ADV** When a piece of electrical equipment is **off**, it is not being used. ❑ *Her bedroom light was off.*
3 **ADV** When a price has an amount **off**, it costs less money than it usually does. ❑ *You will save 50% off the cover price.*

Word Link *fend ≈ striking : defend, fender, offend*

of|fend /əfɛnd/ (**offends, offending, offended**) **V-T/V-I** If you **offend** someone, you say or do something that upsets them. ❑ *I'm sorry if I offended you.* ❑ *Do not use words*

that are likely to offend. ● **of|fend|ed** **ADJ** ❑ *He was deeply offended by her comments.* [from Old French]

of|fense (**offenses**)

PRONUNCIATION HELP
Pronounce meanings **1**, **2**, and **4** /əfɛns/. Pronounce meaning **3** /ɔfɛns/.

1 **N-COUNT** An **offense** is a crime that breaks a law. ❑ *There is a fine of $1,000 for a first offense.*
2 **N-COUNT/N-NONCOUNT** **Offense** is behavior that upsets people. ❑ *He didn't mean to cause offense.*
3 **N-SING** In sports such as football or basketball, **the offense** is the team that has the ball and is trying to score.
4 **PHRASE** If you **take offense**, you are upset by something that someone says or does. ❑ *Many people took offense at his sexist jokes.*

Thesaurus	offense	Also look up :
N	crime, infraction, violation, wrongdoing **1**	
	assault, attack, insult, snub **2**	

Word Partnership	Use **offense** with :
ADJ	**criminal** offense **1**
	serious offense **1** **2**
V	**commit an** offense **1** **2**
	take offense **4**

of|fen|sive /əfɛnsɪv/ **ADJ** Something that is **offensive** upsets people because it is rude or insulting. ❑ *...an offensive remark.*

of|fer /ɔfər/ (**offers, offering, offered**)
1 **V-T** If you **offer** something to someone, you ask them if they would like to have it. ❑ *He offered his seat to the young woman.* ❑ *She offered him a cup of coffee.*
2 **V-T** If you **offer to** do something, you say that you are willing to do it. ❑ *Peter offered to teach me to drive.*
3 **N-COUNT** An **offer** is something that someone says they will give you or do for you. ❑ *I hope you will accept my offer of help.*
4 **N-COUNT** In a store, an **offer** is a specially low price for something, or an extra thing that you get if you buy a certain product. ❑ *There's a special offer on computers.*
5 **V-T** If you **offer** a particular amount of money for something, you say that you will pay that much to buy it. ❑ *He offered $5,000 for the car.* [from Old English]

of|fer|ing /ˈɔfərɪŋ/ (offerings) **N-COUNT**
An **offering** is something that is being sold.
❑ *The meal was much better than offerings in many other restaurants.* [from Old English]

of|fice /ˈɔfɪs/ (offices)
1 **N-COUNT** An **office** is a place where people work sitting at a desk. ❑ *I work in an office with about 25 people.*
2 **N-COUNT** An **office** is a department of an organization, especially the government.
❑ *...the Congressional Budget Office.*
3 **N-COUNT** An **office** is a small building or a room where people can go for information or tickets. ❑ *...a tourist office.*
4 **N-COUNT** A doctor's **office** is a place where a doctor sees patients.
5 **N-NONCOUNT** If someone holds **office** in a government, they have an important job.
❑ *The events marked the president's four years in office.* [from Old French]
6 → see also **box office**, **post office**
→ look at Picture Dictionary: **office**

of|fic|er /ˈɔfɪsər/ (officers)
1 **N-COUNT** In the armed forces, an **officer** is a person who is in charge of other people.
❑ *...an army officer.*
2 **N-COUNT** Members of the police force can be called **officers**. ❑ *The officer saw no sign of a robbery.* ❑ *Officer Montoya was the first on the scene.*
3 **N-COUNT** An **officer** is a person who has a responsible position in a government organization. ❑ *She's the chief executive officer of the company.* [from Old French]
4 → see also **police officer**

of|fi|cial /əˈfɪʃəl/ (officials)
1 **ADJ** **Official** means approved by the government or by someone in power.
❑ *They destroyed all the official documents.*
● **of|fi|cial|ly** **ADV** ❑ *The results have not been officially announced.*

2 **ADJ** **Official** activities are carried out by a person in power as part of their job.
❑ *The president is in Brazil for an official visit.*
3 **N-COUNT** An **official** is a person who holds a position of power in an organization.
❑ *White House officials said that they discussed the matter this morning.* [from Middle English]

Thesaurus	official	Also look up :
ADJ	authentic, formal, legitimate, valid; *(ant.)* unauthorized, unofficial **1**	
N	administrator, director, executive, manager **3**	

Word Partnership	Use **official** with :
N	official **documents**, official **language**, official **report**, official **sources**, official **statement** **1**
	official **duties**, official **visit** **2**
	administration official, **city** official, **government** official **3**
ADJ	**elected** official, **federal** official, **local** official, **military** official, **senior** official, **top** official **3**

off|line /ˈɔflaɪn/
1 **ADJ** TECHNOLOGY If you are **offline**, your computer is not connected to the Internet. Compare with **online**. ❑ *Test your website offline before you put it on the Web.*
2 **ADV** TECHNOLOGY **Offline** is also an adverb. ❑ *Most software programs allow you to write emails offline.*

off|shore /ˈɔfʃɔr/
1 **ADJ** **Offshore** means situated or happening in the ocean, near the coast.
❑ *...the offshore oil industry.*
2 **ADV** **Offshore** is also an adverb. ❑ *A ship anchored offshore.*

off|spring /ˈɔfsprɪŋ/ (offspring) **N-COUNT**
You can refer to a person's children or to an

Picture Dictionary office

paper clips

scissors

stapler

pencil cup

calculator

file folders

animal's young as their **offspring**. [FORMAL]
❑ *Eleanor was worried about her offspring.*

of|ten /ˈɔfən/
1 **ADV** If something **often** happens, it happens many times or much of the time. ❑ *They often spend the weekend together.* ❑ *That doesn't happen very often.*
2 **ADV** You use **how often**... to ask questions about frequency. ❑ *How often do you brush your teeth?*
3 **PHRASE** If something happens **every so often**, it happens sometimes, but not very often. ❑ *She visited every so often.*

Thesaurus	**often** Also look up :
ADV	regularly, repeatedly, usually; (ant.) never, rarely, seldom **1**

oh /oʊ/
1 **INTERJ** You use **Oh** to express a feeling such as surprise, pain, or happiness. [SPOKEN] ❑ *"Oh!" Kenny said. "Has everyone gone?"*
2 **INTERJ** You use **Oh** when you are saying something that you just remembered. [SPOKEN] ❑ *Oh, by the way, I heard you on the radio.*

oil /ɔɪl/ (**oils, oiling, oiled**)
1 **N-COUNT/N-NONCOUNT** **Oil** is a smooth, thick liquid that is used for making machines work. Oil is found underground. ❑ *The company buys and sells 600,000 barrels of oil a day.*
2 **V-T** If you **oil** something, you put oil onto or into it to make it work smoothly or to protect it. ❑ *He oiled the lock on the door.*
3 **N-COUNT/N-NONCOUNT** **Oil** is a smooth, thick liquid made from plants, that is often used for cooking. ❑ *...olive oil.* [from Old French]
→ look at Word Webs: **oil, petroleum, ship**

oil paint|ing (**oil paintings**) **N-COUNT ARTS** An **oil painting** is a picture that is painted using oil paints.

oily /ˈɔɪli/ (**oilier, oiliest**) **ADJ** Something that is **oily** looks, feels, or tastes like oil. ❑ *He wiped his hands on an oily rag.* ❑ *Paul thought the sauce was too oily.* [from Old French]

oint|ment /ˈɔɪntmənt/ (**ointments**)
N-COUNT/N-NONCOUNT An **ointment** is a smooth, thick substance that you put on sore or damaged skin. ❑ *Ointments are available to treat skin problems.* [from Old French]

okay /oʊˈkeɪ/ also OK, O.K., ok
1 **ADJ** If something is **okay**, it is acceptable. [INFORMAL] ❑ *Is it okay if I go by myself?*
2 **ADV** **Okay** is also an adverb. [INFORMAL] ❑ *We seemed to manage okay.*
3 **ADJ** If someone is **okay**, they are safe and well. [INFORMAL] ❑ *Check that the baby's okay.*
4 **INTERJ** You can say **Okay** to show that you agree to something. [INFORMAL] ❑ *"Just tell him I would like to talk to him."—"OK."*
5 **INTERJ** You can say **Okay?** to check whether the person you are talking to understands what you have said and accepts it. [INFORMAL] ❑ *We'll meet next week, OK?*

old /oʊld/ (**older, oldest**)
1 **ADJ** Someone who is **old** has lived for many years and is not young. ❑ *Mr. Kaufmann was a small old man with a beard.*
2 **ADJ** You use **old** to talk or ask about the age of someone or something. ❑ *He is three months old.* ❑ *Her car is less than three years old.*
3 **ADJ** Something that is **old** has existed for a long time. ❑ *We live in a beautiful old house.* ❑ *These books look very old.*
4 **ADJ** Something that is **old** is not in good condition because of its age or because it has been used a lot. ❑ *...his old jeans.*
5 **ADJ** You use **old** to talk about something that used to be part of your life. ❑ *I still remember my old school.*
6 **ADJ** An **old** friend is someone who has been your friend for a long time. ❑ *I called my old friend David Hunter.* [from Old English]

Word Web oil

There is a great demand for **petroleum** in the world today. Companies are always **drilling oil wells** in oilfields on land and on the ocean floor. In the ocean, drilling rigs or **oil platforms** sit on concrete or metal foundations on man-made islands. Others float on ships. The **crude oil** from these wells goes to refineries through **pipelines** or in huge **tanker** ships. At the refinery, the crude oil is processed into a variety of products including **gasoline, aviation fuel**, and **plastics**.

Thesaurus old Also look up :

Thesaurus **old** Also look up :
ADJ   elderly, mature, senior; (*ant.*) young **1**
       ancient, antique, dated, old-fashioned,
       outdated, traditional; (*ant.*) new **3**

old age **N-NONCOUNT** Your **old age** is the part
of your life when you are old. ❑ *They didn't
have much money in their old age.*

old-fash|ioned **ADJ** Something that is
old-fashioned is no longer used, done, or
believed by most people. ❑ *The kitchen was
old-fashioned and in bad condition.*

ol|ive /ɒlɪv/ (**olives**) **N-COUNT/N-NONCOUNT**
Olives are small green or black fruits with a
bitter taste. [from Old French]

ol|ive oil (**olive oils**) **N-COUNT/N-NONCOUNT**
Olive oil is a type of oil that is used in
cooking.

Olym|pic /əlɪmpɪk/ (**Olympics**)
1 **ADJ** SPORTS **Olympic** means relating to
the Olympic Games. ❑ *...the Olympic champion.*
2 **N-PROPER** SPORTS **The Olympics** are the
Olympic Games. [from Latin]

Olym|pic Games /əlɪmpɪk geɪmz/
N-PROPER **The Olympic Games** is an
international sports competition that
takes place every four years, each time in
a different country.

ome|let /ɒmlɪt, ɒməlɪt/ (**omelets**) also
omelette **N-COUNT** An **omelet** is a type of
food made by beating eggs and cooking
them in a frying pan. ❑ *She made a cheese
omelet.* [from French]
→ look at Picture Dictionary: **egg**

omit /oʊmɪt/ (**omits, omitting, omitted**)
1 **V-T** If you **omit** something, you do not
include it. ❑ *Omit the salt in this recipe.*
2 **V-T** If you **omit to** do something, you do
not do it. [FORMAL] ❑ *He omitted to mention his
friend's name.* [from Latin]

Thesaurus **omit** Also look up :
V   forget, leave out, miss; (*ant.*) add,
     include **1**

om|ni|vore /ɒmnɪvɔr/ (**omnivores**)
N-COUNT SCIENCE An **omnivore** is an animal
that eats both meat and plants. Compare
with **carnivore** and **herbivore**. [from Latin]

om|niv|or|ous /ɒmnɪvərəs/ **ADJ** SCIENCE
An **omnivorous** person or animal eats all kinds
of food, including both meat and plants.

❑ *Brown bears are omnivorous, eating anything
that they can get their paws on.* [from Latin]
→ look at Word Web: **carnivore**

on
1 DESCRIBING POSITIONS
   AND LOCATIONS
2 TALKING ABOUT HOW OR
   WHEN SOMETHING
   HAPPENS
3 OTHER USES

① on

PRONUNCIATION HELP
Pronounce the preposition /ɒn/.
Pronounce the adverb /ɒn/.

1 **PREP** If someone or something is **on** a
surface, they are resting on it. ❑ *He was
sitting on the sofa.* ❑ *There was a large box on
the table.*
2 **PREP** If something is **on** a surface, it is
attached to it. ❑ *We hung some paintings on the
walls.* ❑ *You've got dirt on your face.*
3 **PREP** When you are giving directions, if
something is **on** the right or the left, it is to
the right or the left of something else.
❑ *Take the second turn on the right.*
4 **PREP** If something happens **on**
something else, it happens in a particular
place. ❑ *We first met on a beach.* ❑ *Have you read
the article on page five yet?*
5 **ADV** When you **put** a piece of clothing **on**,
you put it on a part of your body. If you **have**
it **on**, you are wearing it. ❑ *He put his coat on.*
❑ *I can't go out. I don't have any shoes on.*
6 **PREP** If you get **on** a bus, a train, or an
airplane, you go into it. If you are **on** it,
you are traveling in it. ❑ *We got on the plane.*
[from Old English]
→ look at Picture Dictionary: **location**

② on

PRONUNCIATION HELP
Pronounce the preposition /ɒn/.
Pronounce the adverb /ɒn/.

1 **PREP** If you do something **on** an
instrument or a machine, you do it using
that instrument or machine. ❑ *I played these
songs on the piano.* ❑ *My dad called me on my
cellphone.*
2 **PREP** If you do something **on** a piece of
equipment, you do it using that piece of
equipment. ❑ *She spends most of the day on the
computer.* ❑ *My dad called me on his cellphone.*
❑ *Let's look it up on the Internet.*

o

3 **PREP** If a television or radio program is being broadcast, you can say that it is **on** television or **on** the radio. ❑ *What's on TV tonight?*

4 **PREP** If something happens **on** a particular day or date, that is when it happens. ❑ *This year's event will be on June 19th.* ❑ *We'll see you on Tuesday.*

5 **ADV** You use **on** to say that someone is continuing to do something. ❑ *They walked on for a while.* [from Old English]

3 on

> **PRONUNCIATION HELP**
> Pronounce the preposition /ɒn/.
> Pronounce the adverb /ɒn/.

1 **PREP** If you spend a particular amount of money **on** something, that is the amount that you pay for it. ❑ *He spent $60 on a pair of shoes.*

2 **PREP** If you spend time **on** something, you spend time doing it. ❑ *Don't waste too much time on it.*

3 **PREP** If something you buy is **on sale**, you pay less money for it. ❑ *I use whichever toothpaste is on sale.*

4 **PREP** Books or ideas **on** a particular subject are about that subject. ❑ *He wrote a book on the history of Russian ballet.*

5 **ADV** When a machine or an electric light is **on**, it is being used. ❑ *The lights were on, but nobody was at home.*

6 **PREP** If you do something **on purpose**, you mean to do it. ❑ *She made a mess on purpose.*

7 **PREP** If you arrive somewhere or do something **on time**, you get somewhere or do something when you are supposed to. ❑ *He always paid his rent on time.* [from Old English]

once /wʌns/

1 **ADV** If something happens **once**, it happens one time only. ❑ *I met Miquela once, at a party.* ❑ *The baby hasn't once slept through the night.*

2 **ADV** If something was **once** true, it was true at some time in the past, but is no longer true. ❑ *Her parents once owned a store.*

3 **CONJ** If something happens **once** another thing has happened, it happens immediately afterward. ❑ *The decision was easy once he read the letter.*

4 **PHRASE** If you do something **at once**, you do it immediately. ❑ *I have to go at once.*

5 **PHRASE** If different things happen **at once** or **all at once**, they all happen at the same time. ❑ *You can't do both things at once.*

6 **PHRASE** **For once** is used for emphasizing that something happens on this particular occasion only. ❑ *For once, Dad is not complaining.*

7 **PHRASE** If you do something **once more**, you do it one more time. ❑ *Jeannie once more explained why she was late.*

8 **PHRASE** **Once upon a time** is used at the beginning of children's stories to show that something happened a very long time ago. ❑ *Once upon a time there was a man who had everything.*

one /wʌn/ (ones)

1 **NUM** **MATH** **One** is the number 1. ❑ *They have one daughter.*

2 **PRON** You can use **one** to talk about one person or thing in a group. ❑ *"Which dress do you prefer?"—"I like the red one."* ❑ *One of their sons survived a car crash.*

3 **PRON** You can use **ones** to talk about several people or things in a group. ❑ *Cut up the large potatoes, but leave the small ones, please.*

4 **DET** You can use **one** when you are talking about a time in the past or in the future. ❑ *Would you like to go out one night?*

5 **PRON** **One** means people in general. [FORMAL] ❑ *One can get very tired on these long flights.*

6 **N-COUNT** A **one** is a dollar bill. ❑ *She opened her purse and counted out five ones.*

7 **PHRASE** **One or two** means a few. ❑ *We made one or two changes.* [from Old English]

> **Usage** **one and you**
> Sometimes *one* is used to refer to any person or to people in general, but it sounds formal: *One has to be smart about buying a computer.* In everyday English, use *you* instead of *one*: *You should only call 911 in an emergency.*

one-point per|spec|tive (one-point perspectives) **N-COUNT** **ARTS** A **one-point perspective** is a method of drawing or painting something in which you create the appearance of three dimensions by using slanting lines that appear to meet at a point on the horizon.

one's /wʌnz/

1 **DET** You use **one's** to show that something belongs to or relates to people in general. [FORMAL] ❑ *It is natural to want to care for one's family and children.*

2 **One's** is a spoken form of "one is" or "one has." ❑ *No one's going to hurt you.* ❑ *This one's been broken too.* [from Old English]

one|self /wʌnsɛlf/

> **LANGUAGE HELP**
> **Oneself** is a third person singular reflexive pronoun.

1 **PRON** Speakers or writers use **oneself** to make statements about themselves and people in general. [FORMAL] ❑ *To work, one must have time to oneself.*
2 **PHRASE** **By oneself** means alone. [FORMAL] ❑ *Traveling by oneself can be an experience.*

one|sie /wʌnzi:/ (**onesies**) **N-COUNT** A **onesie** is a single piece of clothing that covers the whole body. It is often worn for sleeping. ❑ *She came down to breakfast wearing a onesie.*

one-time also **onetime**
1 **ADJ** **One-time** is used to describe something which happened in the past, or something such as a job or a position which someone used to have. ❑ *...Al Gore, the one-time presidential candidate.*
2 **ADJ** A **one-time** thing is made or happens only once. ❑ *...a one-time charge.*

one-way
1 **ADJ** On **one-way** streets, traffic can only move in one direction.
2 **ADJ** A **one-way** ticket is for a trip from one place to another, but not back again. ❑ *...a one-way ticket to New Zealand.*

on|going /ɒngoʊɪŋ/ **ADJ** An **ongoing** situation has been happening for quite a long time and seems likely to continue. ❑ *There is an ongoing debate on the issue.*

on|ion /ʌnyən/ (**onions**) **N-COUNT/N-NONCOUNT** An **onion** is a round vegetable with many layers. It has a strong, sharp smell and taste. [from Old French] → look at Picture Dictionary: **vegetables** → look at Word Web: **spice**

on|line /ɒnlaɪn/
1 **ADJ** BUSINESS An **online** company makes its goods and services available on the Internet. ❑ *...online banking.*
2 **ADJ** TECHNOLOGY If you are **online**, your computer is connected to the Internet. Compare with **offline**. ❑ *You can chat to other people who are online.*
3 **ADV** TECHNOLOGY **Online** is also an adverb. ❑ *I buy most of my clothes online.*

on|looker /ɒnlʊkər/ (**onlookers**) **N-COUNT** An **onlooker** is someone who watches an event but does not take part in it. ❑ *Police cars moved slowly through the crowds of onlookers.*

> **only**
> **①** ADVERB AND ADJECTIVE USES
> **②** CONJUNCTION AND PHRASE USES

① **only** /oʊnli/
1 **ADV** **Only** means "and nobody or nothing else." ❑ *Only one person knew the answer.* ❑ *We have only twelve students in our class.*
2 **ADJ** The **only** person or thing is the one person or thing of a particular type. ❑ *She's the only girl in the class.*
3 **ADJ** An **only** child is a child who has no brothers or sisters. ❑ *I'm an only child.*
4 **ADV** You use **only** when you are saying how small or short something is. ❑ *Their house is only a few miles from here.*
5 **ADV** You use **only** to show that something is not important. ❑ *It's only an idea.*
6 **ADV** You use **only** to say that something is not in any other place. ❑ *The flowers are found only in this part of England.* [from Old English]

> **Thesaurus** only Also look up :
> ADJ alone, individual, single, solitary, unique **2** **3**

② **only** /oʊnli/
1 **CONJ** **Only** means "but." [INFORMAL] ❑ *It's like my house, only it's nicer.*
2 **CONJ** **Only** is used after a clause with "would" to say why something is not done. [SPOKEN] ❑ *I'd ask you to come with me, only it's so far.*
3 **PHRASE** You can say that something has **only just** happened if it happened a very short time ago. ❑ *I've only just arrived.* [from Old English]

ono|mato|poeia /ɒnəmætəpiːə, -mɑtə-/ **N-NONCOUNT** LANGUAGE ARTS **Onomatopoeia** refers to the use of words which sound like the noise they refer to, for example, "hiss," "buzz," and "rat-a-tat-tat". [from Late Latin]

onto /ɒntu/
1 **PREP** If something moves **onto** a surface, it moves to a position on that surface. ❑ *The cat climbed onto her lap.*
2 **PREP** When you get **onto** a bus, a train, or a plane, you enter it. ❑ *He got onto the plane.*

O

oops /ups/ **INTERJ** You say **Oops** when a small mistake or accident has happened. ❑ *Oops! Sorry. Are you all right?*

Oort cloud /ɔrt klaʊd/ (**Oort clouds**) **N-COUNT** **SCIENCE** The **Oort cloud** is a region of rocks, dust, and comets that surrounds our solar system.

ooze /uz/ (**oozes, oozing, oozed**) **V-T/V-I** When a thick liquid **oozes**, it flows out of something slowly and in small amounts. ❑ *They drank the liquid that oozed from the fruit.* ❑ *The house oozes charm.* [from Old English]

---
open
❶ DESCRIBING A POSITION OR MOVEMENT
❷ ACCESSIBLE OR AVAILABLE; NOT HIDDEN, BLOCKED, ETC.
---

❶ **open** /oʊpən/ (**opens, opening, opened**)
1 **V-T/V-I** If you **open** something, or if it **opens**, it has been moved so that is no longer covered or closed. ❑ *He window opened in the wind.* ❑ *After a few seconds, I opened my eyes.*
2 **ADJ** **Open** is also an adjective. ❑ *His eyes were open and he was smiling.*
3 **V-T** If you **open** a container, you remove part of it so that you can take out what is inside. ❑ *Nicole opened the silver box on the table.*
4 **V-T/V-I** If you **open** something such as a book, an umbrella, or your hand, or if it **opens**, the different parts of it move away from each other so that the inside of it can be seen. ❑ *He opened the book and started to read.* [from Old English]

❷ **open** /oʊpən/ (**opens, opening, opened**)
1 **V-T** **TECHNOLOGY** If you **open** a computer file, you give the computer an instruction to show it on the screen. ❑ *To open a file, go to the File menu.*
2 **V-T/V-I** When a store, an office, or a public building **opens**, people can go into it. ❑ *The banks will open again on Monday morning.* ❑ *Are you able to open the shop tomorrow?*
3 **ADJ** **Open** is also an adjective. ❑ *The store is open Monday through Friday, 9 a.m. to 6 p.m.*
4 **V-T/V-I** When a public building, a factory, or a company **opens** or when someone **opens** it, it starts operating for the first time. ❑ *The station opened in 1954.*
5 **ADJ** An **open** area is a large area that does not have many buildings or trees in it. ❑ *Police officers continued their search of open ground.*
6 **ADJ** If a person is **open**, they are honest about their thoughts and feelings. ❑ *He was always open with her.*
7 **ADJ** If you are **open to** suggestions or ideas, you are ready and willing to consider or accept them. ❑ *We are always open to suggestions.* [from Old English]
8 → see also **opening**

open cir|cu|la|tory sys|tem /oʊpən sɜrkyələtɔri sɪstəm/ (**open circulatory systems**) **N-COUNT** **SCIENCE** In animals that have an **open circulatory system**, the heart pumps blood into spaces around the body.

open clus|ter (**open clusters**) **N-COUNT** **SCIENCE** An **open cluster** is a group of stars that were all formed at the same time and are held together by gravity.

open|er /oʊpənər/ (**openers**) **N-COUNT** An **opener** is a tool that is used for opening cans or bottles. ❑ *...a can opener.* [from Old English]
→ look at Picture Dictionary: **utensil**

open|ing /oʊpənɪŋ/ (**openings**)
1 **ADJ** The **opening** event, day, or week in a series is the first one. ❑ *The team lost the opening game.*
2 **N-COUNT** An **opening** is a hole or an empty space that things or people can pass through. ❑ *He managed to get through a narrow opening in the fence.*
3 **N-COUNT** An **opening** is a job that is available. ❑ *We don't have any openings now.* [from Old English]
4 → see also **open**

open|ly /oʊpənli/ **ADV** If you do something **openly**, you do it without hiding any facts or your feelings. ❑ *She openly talked with friends about it.* [from Old English]

open-mind|ed **ADJ** An **open-minded** person is willing to listen to other people's ideas. ❑ *He says that he is open-minded about tomorrow's talks.*

open-source also **open source** **ADJ** **TECHNOLOGY** **Open-source** software is software that anyone is allowed to modify without asking permission from the company that developed it. ❑ *Supporters say open-source software is more secure, cheaper to buy and maintain, and easier to customize.*

open-wa|ter zone (**open-water zones**) **N-COUNT** **SCIENCE** The **open-water zone** of a lake or a pond is the area closest to the surface, where sunlight can reach.

Word Link oper ≈ work : cooperate, opera, operation

op|era /ɒpərə, ɒprə/ (operas)
■ **N-COUNT/N-NONCOUNT** MUSIC An **opera** is a play with music in which all the words are sung. ❑ ...an opera singer. ● **op|er|at|ic** /ɒpərætɪk/ **ADJ** ❑ He was famous for his operatic voice. [from Italian]
■ → see also **opus**, **soap opera**
→ look at Word Web: **music**

op|er|ate /ɒpəreɪt/ (operates, operating, operated)
■ **V-T/V-I** If an organization **operates**, or if you **operate** an organization, it does the work it is supposed to. ❑ The organization has been operating in the area for some time.
■ **V-T/V-I** When you **operate** a machine, you make it work. ❑ Weston showed him how to operate the machine. ❑ Are you able to get this camera to operate?
■ **V-I** When doctors **operate on** a patient, they cut open the patient's body in order to remove or repair a part. ❑ Surgeons operated on Max to remove a brain tumor. [from Latin]

Word Partnership Use operate with :

N	operate a business/company, schools operate ■ forces operate ■
V	be allowed to operate, continue to operate ■–■
ADV	operate efficiently ■ ■

op|er|at|ing sys|tem (operating systems)
N-COUNT TECHNOLOGY The **operating system** of a computer is the main program that controls all the other programs. ❑ Which operating system do you use?

op|era|tion /ɒpəreɪʃⁿn/ (operations)
■ **N-COUNT** An **operation** is an organized activity that involves many people doing different things. ❑ The rescue operation began on Friday.
■ **N-COUNT** BUSINESS People sometimes call a business or a company an **operation**. ❑ ...an electronics operation.
■ **N-COUNT** When a patient has an **operation**, a doctor cuts open their body in order to remove, replace, or repair a part. ❑ Charles had an operation on his arm. [from Latin]

Word Partnership Use operation with :

N	**relief** operation, **rescue** operation ■
V	**carry out an** operation, **plan an** operation ■ **perform an** operation ■ ■
ADJ	**covert** operation, **massive** operation, **military** operation, **undercover** operation ■ **major** operation, **successful** operation ■–■ **emergency** operation ■ ■

op|era|tion|al /ɒpəreɪʃənᵊl/
■ **ADJ** A machine or a piece of equipment that is **operational** is in use or is ready for use. ❑ The new system will be fully operational by December.
■ **ADJ Operational** factors or problems relate to the working of a system, a device, or a plan. ❑ ...high operational costs.
● **op|era|tion|al|ly** **ADV** ❑ Operationally, the company is performing well. [from Latin]

op|era|tive /ɒpərətɪv, -əreɪtɪv/ (operatives)
■ **ADJ** A system or a service that is **operative** is working or having an effect. [FORMAL] ❑ The service was no longer operative.
■ **N-COUNT** An **operative** is a worker, especially one who does work with their hands. [FORMAL] ❑ In an automated car factory, you can't see any human operatives.
■ **N-COUNT** SOCIAL STUDIES An **operative** is someone who works for a government agency such as the intelligence service. ❑ The CIA wants to protect its operatives.
■ **PHRASE** If you describe a word as **the operative word**, you want to draw attention to it because you think it is important or exactly true in a particular situation. ❑ This is a good little company, but the operative word is "little." [from Latin]

op|era|tor /ɒpəreɪtər/ (operators)
■ **N-COUNT** An **operator** is a person who connects telephone calls in a place such as an office or a hotel. ❑ He called the operator.
■ **N-COUNT** An **operator** is a person who is employed to operate or control a machine. ❑ ...a crane operator.
■ **N-COUNT** BUSINESS An **operator** is a person or a company that operates a business. ❑ Several tour operators offer day trips to lakes and castles around the city. [from Latin]

opin|ion /əpɪnyən/ (opinions)
■ **N-COUNT** Your **opinion** about something

is what you think about it. ❏ *I didn't ask for your opinion.*

2 **N-SING** Your **opinion of** someone is what you think about their character or ability. ❏ *I don't have a very high opinion of Thomas.* [from Old French]

Thesaurus	opinion Also look up :
N	feeling, judgment, thought, viewpoint **1** **2**

Word Partnership	Use opinion with :
V	**ask for an** opinion, **express an** opinion, **give an** opinion, **share an** opinion **1** **2**
ADJ	**favorable** opinion **1** **2**

opos|sum /əpɒsəm/ (**opossums**) **N-COUNT/ N-NONCOUNT** SCIENCE An **opossum** is a small animal that lives in America and Australia. It carries its young in a pouch on its body, and has thick fur and a long tail. [from Algonquian]

op|po|nent /əpoʊnənt/ (**opponents**) **N-COUNT** SPORTS In a fight or a sports competition, your **opponent** is the person who is against you. ❏ *She'll face six opponents in today's race.* [from Latin] → look at Word Web: **chess**

op|por|tu|nity /ɒpərtunɪti/ (**opportunities**) **N-COUNT/N-NONCOUNT** An **opportunity** is a situation in which it is possible for you to do something that you want to do. ❏ *I had an opportunity to go to New York and study.* [from Late Middle English]

Word Partnership	Use opportunity with :
N	**business** opportunity, **employment** opportunity
ADJ	**economic** opportunity, **educational** opportunity, **golden** opportunity, **great** opportunity, **lost** opportunity, **rare** opportunity
V	**have an** opportunity, **miss an** opportunity, **see an** opportunity, **seize an** opportunity, opportunity **to speak**, **take advantage of an** opportunity

op|pose /əpoʊz/ (**opposes, opposing, opposed**) **V-T** If you **oppose** something, you disagree with what someone wants to do, and you try to stop them from doing it. ❏ *He said that he would oppose any tax increase.* [from Old French]

op|posed /əpoʊzd/ **ADJ** If you **are opposed to** something, you disagree with it. ❏ *I am opposed to any form of terrorism.* [from Old French]

op|po|site /ɒpəzɪt/ (**opposites**) **1** **PREP** If one person or thing is **opposite** another, it is across from them. ❏ *Jennie sat opposite Sam at breakfast.*

2 **ADV** **Opposite** is also an adverb. ❏ *He looked at the buildings opposite.*

3 **ADJ** **Opposite** describes similar things that are completely different in a particular way. ❏ *We watched the cars driving in the opposite direction.*

4 **N-COUNT** The **opposite of** someone or something is the person or thing that is most different from them. ❏ *Whatever he says, he's probably thinking the opposite.* [from Old French]

Word Partnership	Use opposite with :
ADV	**directly** opposite **1** **exactly (the)** opposite, **precisely (the)** opposite **1** **3** **4**
N	opposite **direction**, opposite **effect** **2**
ADJ	**complete** opposite, **exact** opposite **2**
PREP	**the** opposite **of** *someone/something* **3**

op|po|si|tion /ɒpəzɪʃⁿn/ **N-NONCOUNT** **Opposition** is strong disagreement. ❏ *There is strong opposition to the plan from local people.* [from Old French]

opt /ɒpt/ (**opts, opting, opted**) **V-T/V-I** If you **opt for** something, or **opt to** do something, you choose it or decide to do it in preference to anything else. ❏ *Many students opt for private schools.* [from French]

▶ **opt out** If you **opt out of** something, you choose to be no longer involved in it. ❏ *Rich people can opt out of the public school system.*

op|tic /ɒptɪk/ **ADJ** SCIENCE **Optic** means relating to the eyes or to sight. ❏ *...the optic nerve.* [from Medieval Latin] → look at Word Web: **eye**

op|ti|cian /ɒptɪʃⁿn/ (**opticians**) **N-COUNT** An **optician** is a person whose job is to make and sell glasses. [from Medieval Latin]

op|tic nerve /ɒptɪk nɜrv/ (**optic nerves**) **N-COUNT** SCIENCE The **optic nerve** is the nerve that transfers electrical impulses from the eye to the brain.

Word Link	ism ≈ action or state : commun**ism**, optim**ism**, pessim**ism**

Word Link	optim ≈ the best : **optim**ism, **optim**ist, **optim**istic

op|ti|mism /ɒptɪmɪzəm/ **N-NONCOUNT**
Optimism is a feeling of hope about the success of something. ❑ *There is optimism about the possibility of peace.* ● **op|ti|mist** (optimists) **N-COUNT** ❑ *He is an optimist about the country's future.* [from French]

op|ti|mis|tic /ɒptɪmɪstɪk/ **ADJ** Someone who is **optimistic** has hope about the success of something. ❑ *She is optimistic that they can reach an agreement.* [from French]

Word Link	opt ≈ choosing : ad**opt**, **opt**ion, **opt**ional

op|tion /ɒpʃ°n/ (options)
1 **N-COUNT** An **option** is a choice between two or more things. ❑ *We will consider all options before making a decision.*
2 **N-SING** If you have the **option** of doing something, you can choose whether to do it or not. ❑ *Some criminals are given the option of going to jail or doing a training program.* [from Latin]

Thesaurus	option Also look up :
N	alternative, choice, opportunity, preference; *(ant.)* selection **1** **2**

op|tion|al /ɒpʃən³l/ **ADJ** If something is **optional**, you can choose whether or not you do it or have it. ❑ *All students have to study math, but history and geography are optional.* [from Latin]

opus /oʊpəs/ (opuses or opera)
1 **N-COUNT** MUSIC An **opus** is a piece of classical music by a particular composer. ❑ *...Beethoven's Piano Sonata in E minor, Opus 90.* [from Latin]
2 → see also **opera**

or /ər, STRONG ɔr/
1 **CONJ** You use **or** to show choices or possibilities. ❑ *"Do you want tea or coffee?" John asked.* ❑ *Either you change your behavior, or you will have to leave.*
2 **CONJ** You use **or** after a negative verb to mean not one thing and also not another. ❑ *I don't like hockey or football.*
3 **CONJ** You use **or** between two numbers to show that you are giving an approximate amount. ❑ *You should only drink one or two cups of coffee a day.*

4 **CONJ** You use **or** to introduce a warning that something bad could happen. ❑ *She has to have the operation, or she will die.* [from Old English]

oral /ɔrəl/
1 **ADJ** **Oral** communication is spoken rather than written. ❑ *The English test includes written and oral examinations.*
2 **ADJ** **Oral** means relating to your mouth. ❑ *...good oral hygiene.* [from Late Latin]

oral his|to|ry (oral histories)
N-COUNT/N-NONCOUNT SOCIAL STUDIES
Oral history consists of spoken memories, stories, and songs, and the study of these, as a way of communicating and discovering information about the past.

or|ange /ɔrɪndʒ/ (oranges)
1 **ADJ** Something that is **orange** is of a color between red and yellow.
2 **N-NONCOUNT** **Orange** is also a noun. ❑ *His supporters were dressed in orange.*
3 **N-COUNT/N-NONCOUNT** An **orange** is a round, juicy fruit with a thick, orange-colored skin. [from Old French]
→ look at Picture Dictionaries: **color, fruit**
→ look at Word Web: **rainbow**

ora|to|rio /ɔrətɔrioʊ/ (oratorios) **N-COUNT**
SOCIAL STUDIES An **oratorio** is a long piece of music with a religious theme which is written for singers and an orchestra. [from Italian]

or|bit /ɔrbɪt/ (orbits, orbiting, orbited)
1 **N-COUNT** SCIENCE An **orbit** is the curved path of an object that goes around a planet, a moon, or the sun. ❑ *The Earth has an orbit that changes.*
2 **V-T** SCIENCE If something **orbits** a planet, a moon, or the sun, it moves around it in a curved path. ❑ *The moon orbits the Earth.* [from Latin]
→ look at Word Webs: **satellite, solar system**

or|chard /ɔrtʃərd/ (orchards) **N-COUNT**
An **orchard** is an area of land where fruit trees grow. [from Old English]
→ look at Picture Dictionary: **barn**

or|ches|tra /ɔrkɪstrə/ (orchestras) **N-COUNT**
MUSIC An **orchestra** is a large group of musicians who play different instruments together. ❑ *The orchestra began to play.* [from Latin]
→ look at Word Webs: **orchestra, theater**

o

Word Web   orchestra

The modern **symphony orchestra** usually has between 60 and 100 **musicians**. The largest group of musicians are in the **string** section. It gives the orchestra its rich, flowing sound. String **instruments** include **violins, cellos,** and usually **double basses. Flutes, oboes, clarinets,** and bassoons make up the **woodwind** section. The **brass** section is usually quite small. Too much of this sound could overwhelm the quieter strings. Brass **instruments** include the **French horn, trumpet, trombone** and tuba. The size of the **percussion** section depends on the **composition** being performed.

or|deal /ɔrdil/ (**ordeals**) **N-COUNT** An **ordeal** is a difficult and very unpleasant experience. ❏ *The attack was a terrifying ordeal for both victims.* [from Old English]

---
order
❶ IN ORDER TO
❷ COMMANDS AND REQUESTS
❸ THE WAY THINGS ARE ARRANGED
---

❶ **or|der** /ɔrdər/ **PHRASE** If you do something **in order to** achieve something, you do it because you want to achieve that thing. ❏ *The operation was necessary in order to save the baby's life.* [from Old French]

❷ **or|der** /ɔrdər/ (**orders, ordering, ordered**)
■ **V-T** If you **order** someone **to** do something, you tell them to do it. ❏ *Williams ordered him to leave.*
■ **N-COUNT** If someone gives you an **order,** they tell you to do something. ❏ *The commander gave his men orders to move out of the camp.*
■ **V-T/V-I** When you **order** something from a company, you ask for it to be sent to you. ❏ *They ordered a new washing machine on the Internet.* ❏ *I placed my order on the website.*
■ **V-T/V-I** When you **order** food and drinks in a restaurant, you ask for them to be brought to you. ❏ *The waitress asked, "Are you ready to order?"* ❏ *I ordered eggs for breakfast.*
■ **N-COUNT** Someone's **order** is what they have asked for in return for money. ❏ *He's just placed an order for a new car.* ❏ *The waiter returned with their order.* [from Old French]
■ → see also **mail order**

❸ **or|der** /ɔrdər/ (**orders**)
■ **N-NONCOUNT** If you arrange things **in** a particular **order,** you put one thing first,

another thing second, another thing third, and so on. ❏ *The books are all arranged in alphabetical order.*
■ **N-NONCOUNT Order** is the situation that exists when everything is in the correct place, or happens at the correct time. ❏ *I love rules, and I love order.* ❏ *Everything on the desk is in order.*
■ **N-NONCOUNT Order** is the situation that exists when people obey the law and do not fight or riot. ❏ *The army went to the islands to restore order.*
■ **N-COUNT SCIENCE** In biology, an **order** of animals or plants is a group of related species. Compare with **class** and **family.**
■ **PHRASE** A machine or a piece of equipment that is **in working order** is working properly. ❏ *His old car is still in perfect working order.*
■ **PHRASE** A machine or a piece of equipment that is **out of order** does not work. ❏ *Their phone's out of order.* [from Old French]

or|der|ly /ɔrdərli/ **ADJ** Something that is **orderly** is neat and has everything in the correct place. ❏ *It's a beautiful, clean, and orderly city.* [from Old French]

or|di|nary /ɔrdⁿneri/
■ **ADJ Ordinary** people or things are normal and not special or different. ❏ *These are just ordinary people living ordinary lives.*
■ **PHRASE** Something that is **out of the ordinary** is unusual or different. ❏ *The police asked people to report anything out of the ordinary.* [from Latin]

Thesaurus   ordinary Also look up :
ADJ   common, everyday, normal, regular, standard, typical, usual; (*ant.*) abnormal, unusual ■

| Word Partnership | Use ordinary with : |

Word Partnership	Use ordinary with :
N	ordinary **Americans**, ordinary **circumstances**, ordinary **citizens**, ordinary **day**, ordinary **expenses**, ordinary **folk**, ordinary **life**, ordinary **people**, ordinary **person** 1
PREP	**out of the** ordinary 2

or|gan /ɔrgən/ (**organs**)

1 **N-COUNT** SCIENCE An **organ** is a part of your body that has a particular purpose. ❑ *The brain is the most powerful organ in the body.*

2 **N-COUNT** MUSIC An **organ** is a large musical instrument that is like a piano. ❑ *...a church organ.* [from Old French]

→ look at Picture Dictionary: **keyboard**

→ look at Word Webs: **donor, nervous system**

or|gan|elle /ɔrgənɛl/ (**organelles**) **N-COUNT** SCIENCE **Organelles** are structures within cells that have a specialized function, such as mitochondria or the nucleus. [from New Latin]

or|gan|ic /ɔrgænɪk/

1 **ADJ** SCIENCE **Organic** food is grown without using chemicals. ❑ *We buy only organic fruits and vegetables.*

2 **ADJ** ARTS In art, **organic** shapes or designs use curved lines rather than straight lines and resemble shapes that exist in nature. [from Old French]

or|gan|ic com|pound (**organic compounds**) **N-COUNT** SCIENCE An **organic compound** is a chemical compound that contains carbon.

or|gan|ism /ɔrgənɪzəm/ (**organisms**) **N-COUNT** SCIENCE An **organism** is a living thing. ❑ *We study very small organisms such as bacteria.* [from Old French]

or|gani|za|tion /ɔrgənɪzeɪʃən/ (**organizations**)

1 **N-COUNT** An **organization** is an official group of people such as a business or a club. ❑ *She worked for the same organization for six years.*

2 **N-NONCOUNT** If you help in the **organization** of an activity, you help to plan or arrange it. ❑ *I helped in the organization of the concert.* [from Medieval Latin]

or|gan|ize /ɔrgənaɪz/ (**organizes, organizing, organized**)

1 **V-T** If you **organize** an activity, you plan or arrange it. ❑ *We decided to organize a concert.*

● **or|gan|iz|er** (**organizers**) **N-COUNT** ❑ *Organizers are hoping to raise $65,000 from the concert.*

2 **V-T** If you **organize** things, you plan or arrange them in a neat and effective way. ❑ *He began to organize his papers.* [from Medieval Latin]

→ look at Word Web: **union**

Thesaurus	organize Also look up :
V	coordinate, plan, set up 1 arrange, line up, straighten out 2

or|gan|ized /ɔrgənaɪzd/ **ADJ** Someone who is **organized** plans their work and activities carefully. ❑ *Managers need to be very organized.* [from Medieval Latin]

or|gan sys|tem (**organ systems**) **N-COUNT** SCIENCE An **organ system** is a group of related organs within an organism, for example the nervous system.

ori|en|tal /ɔriɛntəl/ **ADJ** You use **oriental** to talk about things that come from places in eastern Asia. **Oriental** should not be used for talking about people. ❑ *He was an expert in oriental art.* [from French]

ori|ent|ed /ɔriɛntɪd/ or **orientated** **ADJ** If someone **is oriented toward** or **oriented to** a particular thing or person, they are mainly concerned with that thing or person. ❑ *The town has lots of family-oriented things to do.* [from French]

ori|gin /ɔrɪdʒɪn/ (**origins**) **N-COUNT** The **origin** of a thing or a person is the way they started. ❑ *Scientists study the origin of life on Earth.* ❑ *...Americans of Hispanic origin.* [from French]

Word Partnership	Use origin with :
N	origin **of life, point of** origin, origin **of the universe, country of** origin, **family of** origin
ADJ	**unknown** origin, **ethnic** origin, **Hispanic** origin, **national** origin

origi|nal /ərɪdʒɪnəl/ (**originals**)

1 **ADJ** You use **original** when you are talking about something that existed at the beginning. ❑ *The original plan was to go by bus.* ● **origi|nal|ly** **ADV** ❑ *Wright lives in London but he is originally from Melbourne.*

2 **N-COUNT** If something is an **original**, it is not a copy. ❑ *Make a copy of the document and send the original to your employer.*

3 **ADJ** **Original** work shows that the person who did it has imagination and new ideas. ❑ *He is the most original painter of the past 100 years.* [from French]

O

Thesaurus	original Also look up :
ADJ	early, first, initial **1**
	authentic, genuine **2**
	creative, unique **3**
N	master; (ant.) copy **2**

origi|nate /ərɪdʒɪneɪt/ (**originates, originating, originated**) **V-I** If something **originated** at a particular time or in a particular place, it began to happen or exist at that time or in that place. [FORMAL] ❑ *The disease originated in Africa.* [from French]

or|na|ment /ɔrnəmənt/ (**ornaments**) **N-COUNT** An **ornament** is an attractive object that you use to decorate your home. ❑ *There were a few ornaments on the shelf.* [from Latin]

or|phan /ɔrfən/ (**orphans**) **N-COUNT** An **orphan** is a child whose parents are dead. [from Late Latin]

or|phan|age /ɔrfənɪdʒ/ (**orphanages**) **N-COUNT** An **orphanage** is a place where orphans live. [from Late Latin]

ortho|dox /ɔrθədɒks/

> **LANGUAGE HELP**
> The spelling **Orthodox** is also used for meaning **2**.

1 **ADJ** **Orthodox** beliefs, methods, or systems are ones which are accepted or used by most people. ❑ *...orthodox medical treatment.* **2** **ADJ** If you describe someone as **orthodox**, you mean that they hold the older and more traditional ideas of their religion or party. ❑ *...Orthodox Jews.* [from Church Latin]

or|thog|ra|phy /ɔrθɒɡrəfi/ (**orthographies**) **N-COUNT/N-NONCOUNT** LANGUAGE ARTS The **orthography** of a language is the set of rules about how to spell words in the language correctly. [from Late Middle English]

OS /oʊ ɛs/ (**OS's**) **N-COUNT** **OS** is short for **operating system**.

os|ti|na|to /ɒstɪnɑtoʊ/ (**ostinatos**) **N-COUNT** MUSIC An **ostinato** is a short melody or rhythm that is repeated continually throughout a piece of music. [from Italian]

ostrich

os|trich /ɒstrɪtʃ/ (**ostriches**) **N-COUNT** An **ostrich** is a very large bird that cannot fly. [from Old French]

oth|er /ʌðər/ (**others**)

> **LANGUAGE HELP**
> When **other** follows the determiner **an**, it is written as one word. See **another**.

1 **ADJ** You use **other** when you are talking about more things or people that are like the thing or person you have mentioned. ❑ *Mr. Johnson and the other teachers are very worried.* **2** **PRON** **Other** is also a pronoun. ❑ *He had a pen in one hand and a book in the other.* **3** **ADJ** You use **other** when you are talking about a thing or a person that is different from the thing or person you have mentioned. ❑ *He will have to accept it; there is no other way.* **4** **ADJ** You use **the other** to talk about the second of two things or people. ❑ *William was at the other end of the room.* **5** **ADJ** You use **the other** to talk about the rest of the people or things in a group. ❑ *The other kids went to the park but James stayed home.* **6** **PRON** **The others** is also a pronoun. ❑ *Alison is coming here with the others.* **7** **ADJ** You use **the other day** when you are talking about a recent day. ❑ *I called her the other day.* **8** **PHRASE** If something happens, for example, **every other day** or **every other month**, there is a day or a month when it does not happen between each day or month when it happens. ❑ *I wash my hair every other day.* [from Old English]

Word Link	wise ≈ in the direction or manner of :
	clockwise, likewise, otherwise

other|wise /ʌðərwaɪz/ **1** **ADV** You use **otherwise** to say what the result would be if the situation was different. ❑ *I really enjoy this job, otherwise I would not be here.* **2** **ADV** You use **otherwise** when you mention a different condition or way. [WRITTEN] ❑ *He was very tired but otherwise happy.* ❑ *Take one pill three times a day, unless you are told otherwise by a doctor.* [from Old English]

ouch /aʊtʃ/ **INTERJ** People say **Ouch** when they suddenly feel pain. ❑ *The stones cut her feet. "Ouch, ouch!" she cried.*

ought /ɔt/ **1** **PHRASE** If someone **ought to** do something, it is the right thing to do. ❑ *You ought to read this book.*

2 **PHRASE** You use **ought to** when you think something will be true or will happen. ❑ *"This party ought to be fun," he told Alex.* [from Old English]

> **Usage** ought
> Ought is generally used with to: *We ought to go home soon. You ought to tell her the good news right away!*

oughtn't /ɔt°nt/ **Oughtn't** is short for "ought not." [from Old English]

ounce /aʊns/ (ounces) **N-COUNT** **MATH** An **ounce** is a unit for measuring weight. There are sixteen ounces in a pound and one ounce is equal to 28.35 grams. [from Old French]

our /aʊər/

> **LANGUAGE HELP**
> **Our** is the first person plural possessive determiner.

DET You use **our** to show that something belongs or relates both to you and to one or more other people. ❑ *We're expecting our first baby.* [from Old English]

ours /aʊərz/

> **LANGUAGE HELP**
> **Ours** is the first person plural possessive pronoun.

PRON You use **ours** when you are talking about something that belongs to you and one or more other people. ❑ *That car is ours.* [from Old English]

our|selves /aʊərsɛlvz/

> **LANGUAGE HELP**
> **Ourselves** is the first person plural reflexive pronoun.

1 **PRON** You use **ourselves** when you are talking about yourself and one or more other people. ❑ *We sat by the fire to keep ourselves warm.*

2 **PRON** "We did it **ourselves**" means that you and one or more other people did it, and not anyone else. ❑ *We built the house ourselves.*

oust /aʊst/ (ousts, ousting, ousted) **V-T** If someone **is ousted** from a position of power, a job, or a place, they are forced to leave it. ❑ *The leaders were ousted from power.* ❑ *The Republicans may oust him in November.* ● **oust|er** (ousters) **N-COUNT** ❑ *Some groups called for the ouster of the police chief.* ● **oust|ing** **N-NONCOUNT** ❑ *...the ousting of his boss.* [from Latin]

out /aʊt/

1 **ADV** When you take something **out**, you remove it from a place. ❑ *He took out his notebook.*

2 **ADV** If you are **out**, you are not at home. ❑ *I called you yesterday, but you were out.*

3 **ADJ** If a light is **out**, it is no longer shining. ❑ *All the lights were out in the house.*

4 **ADJ** If a fire goes **out**, it is no longer burning. ❑ *Please don't let the fire go out.*

5 **ADJ** If something is **out**, it is in stores and people can buy it. ❑ *The final book in the trilogy is out now.*

6 **ADV** **Out** is also an adverb. ❑ *The book came out in 2006.*

7 **ADJ** In games such as tennis or basketball, a ball that is **out** is outside the area of play. Compare with **in**. ❑ *The referee agreed that the ball was out.*

8 **PHRASE** If you go **out of** a place, you leave it. ❑ *She ran out of the house.*

9 **PHRASE** If you take something **out of** a container, you remove it. ❑ *I took the key out of my purse.*

10 **PHRASE** If you are **out of** something, you no longer have any of it. ❑ *We're out of milk. Can you get some at the supermarket?*

11 **PHRASE** If something is made **out of** a particular material, it has been produced from it. ❑ *The house is made out of wood.*

12 **PHRASE** You use **out of** when you are talking about a smaller group that is part of a larger group. ❑ *Three out of four people say there's too much violence on TV.* [from Old English]

out|break /aʊtbreɪk/ (outbreaks) **N-COUNT** If there is an **outbreak of** violence or a disease, it suddenly starts to happen. ❑ *This is the worst ever outbreak of the disease.*

out|come /aʊtkʌm/ (outcomes) **N-COUNT** The **outcome** of an activity is the situation that exists at the end of it. ❑ *It's too early to know the outcome of the election.*

out|door /aʊtdɔr/ **ADJ** **Outdoor** activities happen outside and not in a building. ❑ *If you enjoy outdoor activities, you should try rock climbing.*

out|doors /aʊtdɔrz/ **ADV** If something happens **outdoors**, it happens outside rather than in a building. ❑ *It was warm enough to play outdoors all afternoon.*

out|er /aʊtər/ **ADJ** The **outer** parts of something are the parts that cover the other

O

parts. ❑ *This material forms the hard outer surface of the tooth.* [from Old English]

out|er core **N-SING** SCIENCE The **outer core** of the Earth is the layer of the Earth's interior between the mantle and the inner core.

outer|most /a͟ʊtərmoʊst/ **ADJ** The **outermost** thing in a group is the one that is farthest from the center. ❑ *...the outermost layer of skin.*

out|fit /a͟ʊtfɪt/ (**outfits**) **N-COUNT** An **outfit** is a set of clothes. ❑ *I need a new outfit for the wedding.*

out|ing /a͟ʊtɪŋ/ (**outings**) **N-COUNT** An **outing** is a short trip, usually with a group of people. ❑ *We went on an outing to the local movie theater.* [from Old English]

out|land|ish /a͟ʊtlæ͟ndɪʃ/ **ADJ** An **outlandish** idea is very unusual, strange, or unreasonable. ❑ *This idea is not as outlandish as it sounds.*

out|law /a͟ʊtlɔ/ (**outlaws, outlawing, outlawed**) **V-T** When you **outlaw** something, or when it **is outlawed**, it is made illegal. ❑ *Should using a cellphone while driving be outlawed?* ❑ *The government has outlawed some political groups.*

out|let /a͟ʊtlɛt, -lɪt/ (**outlets**)
■ **N-COUNT** An **outlet** is a store that sells the goods made by a particular manufacturer at a low price. The goods often come straight from the factory. ❑ *...a factory outlet.*
■ **N-COUNT** If someone has an **outlet for** their feelings or ideas, they have a way to express them. ❑ *He found another outlet for his anger.*
■ **N-COUNT** TECHNOLOGY An **outlet** is a place in a wall where you can connect electrical equipment to the electricity supply. ❑ *Plug the device into an electric outlet.*

out|line /a͟ʊtlaɪn/ (**outlines, outlining, outlined**)
■ **N-COUNT** An **outline** is a general explanation or description of something. ❑ *We are sending you an outline of the plan.*
■ **V-T** **Outline** is also a verb. ❑ *The report outlined some possible changes to the rules.*
■ **N-COUNT** An **outline** of an object or a person is its general shape. ❑ *He could only see the dark outline of the man.*

Word Partnership	Use **outline** with :
ADJ	**broad** outline, **detailed** outline, **general** outline ■
N	**chapter** outline, outline **a paper**, outline **a plan** ■
V	**write an** outline ■

out|look /a͟ʊtlʊk/ (**outlooks**)
■ **N-SING** The **outlook** for something is whether it is going to be successful. ❑ *The economic outlook is not good.*
■ **N-COUNT** Your **outlook** is your general feeling about life. ❑ *He had a positive outlook on life.*

out of date also **out-of-date** **ADJ** Something that is **out of date** is old-fashioned and no longer useful. ❑ *The rules are out of date.* ❑ *They were using an out-of-date map.*

out|put /a͟ʊtpʊt/ (**outputs**)
■ **N-COUNT/N-NONCOUNT** **Output** is used to refer to the amount of something that a person or a thing produces. ❑ *...a large fall in industrial output.*
■ **N-COUNT/N-NONCOUNT** TECHNOLOGY The **output** of a computer is the information that it displays on a screen or prints on paper as a result of a particular program. ❑ *You run the software, then look at the output.*

out|put force (**output forces**) **N-COUNT/ N-NONCOUNT** SCIENCE The **output force** is the force that is applied to an object by a machine.

out|rage (**outrages, outraging, outraged**)

> **PRONUNCIATION HELP**
> Pronounce the verb /a͟ʊtreɪdʒ/. Pronounce the noun /a͟ʊtreɪdʒ/.

■ **V-T** If you **are outraged** by something, it shocks you or makes you very angry. ❑ *Many people were outraged by his comments.*
■ **N-NONCOUNT** **Outrage** is an intense feeling of anger and shock. ❑ *Several teachers wrote to the newspapers to express their outrage.* [from French]

out|ra|geous /a͟ʊtre͟ɪdʒəs/ **ADJ** Something that is **outrageous** shocks you or makes you very angry. ❑ *It was outrageous behavior.* [from French]

out|right

> **PRONUNCIATION HELP**
> Pronounce the adjective /a͟ʊtraɪt/. Pronounce the adverb /a͟ʊtra͟ɪt/.

1 ADJ You use **outright** to describe behavior and actions that are open and direct, rather than indirect. ❑ *He told an outright lie.*

2 ADV **Outright** is also an adverb. ❑ *Why don't you tell me outright?*

3 ADJ **Outright** means complete and total. ❑ *She failed to win an outright victory.*

4 ADV **Outright** is also an adverb. ❑ *The offer wasn't rejected outright.*

5 PHRASE If someone **is killed outright**, they die immediately, for example in an accident.

out|set /ˈaʊtsɛt/ **PHRASE** If something happens **at the outset** of an event, a process, or a period of time, it happens at the beginning of it. If something happens **from the outset**, it happens from the beginning and continues to happen. ❑ *You must decide at the outset which courses you want to take.*

out|side /aʊtˈsaɪd/ (**outsides**)

> **LANGUAGE HELP**
> The form **outside of** can also be used as a preposition.

1 N-COUNT The **outside** of something is the part that surrounds or covers the rest of it. ❑ *The outside of the building was recently painted.*

2 ADJ **Outside** is also an adjective. ❑ *The outside wall is painted white.*

3 ADV If you are **outside**, you are not in a building, but you are very close to it. ❑ *She went outside to look for Sam.*

4 PREP **Outside** is also a preposition. ❑ *She found him standing outside the classroom.*

5 PREP People or things **outside** a country, a city, or a region are not in it. ❑ *...a castle outside Budapest.*

6 PREP If you are **outside** a building or a room, you are not in it. ❑ *She sent him outside the classroom.*

Word Partnership	Use **outside** with :
N	the outside **of a building** 1
	outside **a building**, outside **a car**, outside **a room**, outside **a store** 4
	outside **a city/town**, outside **a country** 3
ADJ	**cold** outside, **dark** outside 2
V	**gather** outside, **go** outside, **park** outside, **sit** outside, **stand** outside, **step** outside, **wait** outside 2 4

out|sid|er /aʊtˈsaɪdər/ (**outsiders**)

1 N-COUNT An **outsider** is someone who does not belong to a particular group or organization. ❑ *A lot of the work went to outsiders.*

2 N-COUNT An **outsider** is someone who is not accepted by a particular group, or who feels that they do not belong in it. ❑ *Malone felt very much an outsider.*

3 N-COUNT In a competition, an **outsider** is a competitor who is unlikely to win. ❑ *He was an outsider in the race.*

out|skirts /ˈaʊtskɜrts/ **N-PLURAL** The **outskirts of** a city or a town are the parts of it that are farthest away from its center. ❑ *I live on the outskirts of the city.*

out|stand|ing /aʊtˈstændɪŋ/ **ADJ** An **outstanding** person or thing is much better than others of a similar type. ❑ *She is an outstanding athlete.*

oval /ˈoʊvəl/

1 N-COUNT MATH An **oval** is a shape like an egg. ❑ *The mirror was an oval about ten inches across.*

2 ADJ **Oval** is also an adjective. ❑ *She had an oval face with large, dark eyes.* [from Medieval Latin]
→ look at Picture Dictionary: **shape**
→ look at Word Web: **circle**

ova|ry /ˈoʊvəri/ (**ovaries**) **N-COUNT SCIENCE** A woman's **ovaries** are the two organs in her body that produce eggs. [from New Latin]

oven /ˈʌvən/ (**ovens**) **N-COUNT** An **oven** is a piece of equipment for cooking that is like a large metal box with a door. [from Old English]

over /ˈoʊvər/

1 PREP If one thing is **over** another thing, the first thing is directly above or higher than the second thing. ❑ *There was a gold mirror over the fireplace.* ❑ *I heard some planes flying over the house.*

2 PREP If one thing is **over** another thing, it covers part or all of it. ❑ *He lay down and pulled the blanket over himself.* ❑ *Pour the sauce over the mushrooms.*

3 PREP If someone or something goes **over** something, they get to the other side of it by going across it to the other side. ❑ *They jumped over the wall.*

4 PREP If something is on the opposite side of a road or river, you can say that it is **over** the road or river. ❑ *...a fashionable neighborhood, just over the river from Manhattan.*

5 ADV You use **over** to talk about a

O

particular position or place a short distance away from you. ❑ *He saw Rolfe standing over by the window.*

6 **ADV** You can use **over** when you are talking about a short distance. ❑ *Come over here!* ❑ *The café is just over there.*

7 **ADV** You use **over** when you are talking about a period of time. ❑ *I broke up with my boyfriend over the summer.*

8 **ADV** If something turns **over**, its position changes so that the part that was facing up is now facing down. ❑ *His car rolled over on an icy road.*

9 **PREP** If something is **over** an amount, it is more than that amount. ❑ *The disease killed over 4 million people last year.* ❑ *The house cost over $1 million.*

10 **ADV** **Over** is also an adverb. ❑ *...people aged 65 and over.*

11 **ADV** If you do something **over**, you do it again. ❑ *If you don't like it, you can just do it over.*

12 **ADJ** If an activity is **over**, it is completely finished. ❑ *The war is over.* ❑ *I am glad it's all over.* [from Old English]
→ look at Picture Dictionary: **location**

over|all (**overalls**)

> **PRONUNCIATION HELP**
> The adjective is pronounced /ouvərɔl/.
> The plural noun is pronounced /ouvərɔlz/.

1 **ADJ** You use **overall** when you are talking about a situation in general or about the whole thing. ❑ *We are very happy with the company's overall performance.*

2 **N-PLURAL** **Overalls** are pants with a piece of cloth that covers your chest. [from Old English]

over|came /ouvərkeɪm/ **Overcame** is the past tense of **overcome**.

over|come /ouvərkʌm/ (**overcomes, overcoming, overcame, overcome**)

> **LANGUAGE HELP**
> The form **overcome** is used in the present tense and is also the past participle.

1 **V-T** If you **overcome** a problem or a feeling, you successfully deal with it and control it. ❑ *Molly finally overcame her fear of flying.*

2 **V-T** If you **are overcome by** a feeling, you feel it very strongly. ❑ *The night before the test I was overcome by fear.*

ADJ	**difficult to** overcome, **hard to** overcome **1**
N	overcome **difficulties**, overcome **a fear**, overcome **an**, overcome **opposition 1** overcome **by emotion**, overcome **by fear 2**

over|crowd|ed /ouvərkraʊdɪd/ **ADJ** An **overcrowded** place has too many people in it. ❑ *We sat on the overcrowded beach.*

overcrowded

over|due /ouvərdu/ **ADJ** If something is **overdue**, it should have happened or arrived before now. ❑ *Your tax payment is overdue.* ❑ *Mr. Giuliano said the changes were long overdue.*

over|flow /ouvərfloʊ/ (**overflows, overflowing, overflowed**)

1 **V-T/V-I** If a container **overflows**, the liquid that is in it flows over the edges. ❑ *The sink overflowed.* ❑ *The bottle overflowed with milk.*

2 **V-T/V-I** If a liquid or a river **overflows**, it flows over the edges of the place it is in. ❑ *During the heavy rains, the river overflowed.* ❑ *The rivers overflowed their banks.*

over|head

> **PRONUNCIATION HELP**
> Pronounce the adjective /ouvərhɛd/.
> Pronounce the adverb /ouvərhɛd/.

1 **ADJ** Something that is **overhead** is above you. ❑ *She turned on the overhead light.*

2 **ADV** **Overhead** is also an adverb. ❑ *Planes passed overhead.*

over|hear /ouvərhɪər/ (**overhears, overhearing, overheard**) **V-T** If you **overhear** someone, you hear what they are saying when they are not talking to you. ❑ *I overheard two doctors discussing me.*

over|heat /ouvərhit/ (**overheats, overheating, overheated**) **V-T/V-I** If something **overheats**, or if you **overheat** it, it becomes too hot. ❑ *The car's engine was overheating.*

over|lap /ouvərlæp/ (**overlaps, overlapping, overlapped**) **V-T/V-I** If two things **overlap**, a part of the first thing covers a part of the other. ❑ *The two circles overlap.*

over|look /oʊvərlʊk/ (**overlooks, overlooking, overlooked**)

1 **V-T** If you **overlook** a fact or a problem, you do not notice it. ❑ *We cannot overlook this important fact.*

2 **V-T** If a building or a window **overlooks** a place, you can see the place clearly from the building or window. ❑ *The hotel's rooms overlook a beautiful garden.*

over|night /oʊvərnaɪt/

1 **ADV** Something that happens **overnight** happens through the whole night or at some point during the night. ❑ *The decision was made overnight.*

2 **ADJ** **Overnight** is also an adjective. ❑ *He decided to take an overnight fishing trip.*

3 **ADV** You can say that something happens **overnight** when it happens very quickly and unexpectedly. ❑ *The rules are not going to change overnight.*

4 **ADJ** **Overnight** is also an adjective. ❑ *He became an overnight success.*

over|popu|la|tion /oʊvərpɒpyəleɪʃ°n/ **N-NONCOUNT** SOCIAL STUDIES If there is a problem of **overpopulation** in an area, there are more people living there than can be supported properly.

over|seas /oʊvərsiz/

1 **ADJ** **Overseas** describes things or people that are in or that come from foreign countries across the ocean. ❑ *He enjoyed his overseas trip.*

2 **ADV** **Overseas** is also an adverb. ❑ *He's now working overseas.*

over|see /oʊvərsi/ (**oversees, overseeing, oversaw, overseen**) **V-T** If someone in authority **oversees** a job or an activity, they make sure that it is done properly. ❑ *As program manager, she oversaw a team of engineers working on a new line of cars.*

over|sleep /oʊvərslip/ (**oversleeps, oversleeping, overslept**) **V-I** If you **oversleep**, you sleep longer than you should. ❑ *I forgot to set my alarm and I overslept.* [from Old English]

over|take /oʊvərteɪk/ (**overtakes, overtaking, overtook, overtaken**) **V-T** If a feeling **overtakes** you, it affects you very strongly. [LITERARY] ❑ *A feeling of panic overtook me.*

over|think /oʊvərθɪŋk/ (**overthinks, overthinking, overthought**) **V-T/V-I** If you

overthink, or if you **overthink** a problem, you spend too much time thinking about something. ❑ *You overthink things and start worrying.* [from Old English]

over|throw (**overthrows, overthrowing, overthrew, overthrown**)

> **PRONUNCIATION HELP**
> Pronounce the verb /oʊvərθroʊ/.
> Pronounce the noun /oʊvərθroʊ/.

1 **V-T** SOCIAL STUDIES When a government or leader **is overthrown,** they are removed from power by force. ❑ *The government was overthrown by the army.*

2 **N-SING** SOCIAL STUDIES **Overthrow** is also a noun. ❑ *...the overthrow of the dictator last April.*

over|time /oʊvərtaɪm/ **N-NONCOUNT** **Overtime** is extra time that you spend doing your job. ❑ *He worked overtime to finish the job.*

over|turn /oʊvərtɜrn/ (**overturns, overturning, overturned**)

1 **V-T/V-I** If something **overturns** or if you **overturn** it, it turns upside down or on its side. ❑ *The car went out of control and overturned.* ❑ *Alex jumped up so quickly that he overturned his glass of water.*

2 **V-T** SOCIAL STUDIES If someone in authority **overturns** a legal decision, they officially decide that that decision is incorrect or not valid. ❑ *The courts overturned his decision.*

over|weight /oʊvərweɪt/ **ADJ** Someone who is **overweight** weighs more than is considered healthy or attractive.
→ look at Word Web: **diet**

over|whelm /oʊvərwɛlm/ (**overwhelms, overwhelming, overwhelmed**)

1 **V-T** If you **are overwhelmed by** a feeling or an event, it affects you very strongly, and you do not know how to deal with it. ❑ *They were overwhelmed by the kindness of the local people.* ● **over|whelmed** **ADJ** ❑ *She felt a little overwhelmed by the crowds.*

2 **V-T** If a group of people **overwhelm** a place or another group, they gain control over them. ❑ *The attack overwhelmed the weakened enemy.*

over|whelm|ing /oʊvərwɛlmɪŋ/ **ADJ** An **overwhelming** feeling affects you very strongly. ❑ *She had an overwhelming feeling of guilt.*

ovule /ɒvyul, oʊv-/ (ovules) **N-COUNT**
SCIENCE An **ovule** is the part of a plant that
develops into a seed. [from French]

owe /oʊ/ (owes, owing, owed)
1 **V-T** If you **owe** money **to** someone, you
have to pay money to them. ❑ *The company
owes money to more than 60 banks.* ❑ *Blake owed
him $50.*
2 **V-T** If you **owe** someone something, you
want to do something for them because you
are grateful. ❑ *She thought Will owed her a favor.*
[from Old English]

Word Partnership	Use **owe** with :
N	owe **a debt**, owe **money**, owe **taxes** **1**
	owe **a great deal to** *someone* **2**

owl /aʊl/ (owls) **N-COUNT** An **owl** is a bird
with large eyes that is active at night.
[from Old English]

own /oʊn/ (owns, owning, owned)
1 **ADJ** You use **own** to say that something
belongs to or is done by a particular person
or thing. ❑ *I wanted to have my own business.*
❑ *They prefer to make their own decisions.*
2 **PRON** **Own** is also a pronoun. ❑ *The man's
face was a few inches from my own.*
3 **ADJ** You use **own** to say that something is
used by only one person or thing. ❑ *Jennifer
wanted her own room.*
4 **V-T** If you **own** something, it belongs to
you. ❑ *His father owns a local computer store.*
5 **PHRASE** When you are **on** your **own**,
you are alone. ❑ *He lives on his own.*
6 **PHRASE** If you do something **on** your **own**,
you do it without any help. ❑ *I work best on my
own.* [from Old English]

own|er /oʊnər/ (owners) **N-COUNT** If you are
the **owner** of something, it belongs to you.
❑ *My brother is the owner of the store.* [from
Old English]

own|er|ship /oʊnərʃɪp/ **N-NONCOUNT**
Ownership of something is when you own
it. ❑ *There has been an increase in home ownership.*
[from Old English]

oxy|gen /ɒksɪdʒən/ **N-NONCOUNT** SCIENCE
Oxygen is a gas in the air that is needed by
all plants and animals. [from French]
→ look at Word Webs: **air, cardiovascular
system, earth, ozone, photosynthesis,
respiratory system**

oys|ter /ɔɪstər/ (oysters) **N-COUNT** An **oyster**
is a small flat ocean animal that has a hard
shell and is eaten as food. Oysters can
produce pearls. [from Old French]
→ look at Picture Dictionary: **shellfish**

oz. **MATH** **Oz.** is short for **ounce**. ❑ *...1 oz. of
butter.*

ozone /oʊzoʊn/ **N-NONCOUNT** SCIENCE
Ozone is a colorless gas that is a form of
oxygen. There is a layer of ozone high
above the Earth's surface that protects us
from harmful radiation from the sun.
[from German]
→ look at Word Web: **ozone**

ozone lay|er /oʊzoʊn leɪər/ **N-SING** SCIENCE
The **ozone layer** is the area high above the
Earth's surface that protects living things
from the harmful effects of the sun.
❑ *Scientists discovered another hole in the ozone
layer last month.*
→ look at Word Webs: **air, ozone**

Word Web   ozone

In the Earth's **atmosphere** there are small
amounts of **ozone**. Ozone is a molecule that is
made up of three **oxygen** atoms. Too much
ozone can cause problems. Near the ground,
it can be a **pollutant.** Cars and factories produce
carbon monoxide and **carbon dioxide**. These
gases mix with ozone and make **smog**. Too little
ozone can also cause problems. The **ozone layer** in the upper **atmosphere** stops harmful **ultraviolet
light** from reaching the Earth. Some scientists say a large hole is opening in the ozone layer. This may
add to the **greenhouse effect** and **global warming**.

Pp

pace /peɪs/ (paces, pacing, paced)

1 **N-SING** The **pace** of something is the speed at which it happens. ❑ *Since her illness, she is taking life at a slower pace.*

2 **N-SING** Your **pace** is the speed at which you walk. ❑ *He moved at a fast pace.*

3 **N-COUNT** A **pace** is the distance that you move when you take one step. ❑ *Peter walked a few paces behind me.*

4 **V-T/V-I** If you **pace** a small area, you keep walking around in it because you are worried. ❑ *As they waited, Kravis paced the room nervously.* ❑ *She was pacing all night.*

5 **PHRASE** If you do something **at your own pace**, you do it at a speed that is comfortable for you. ❑ *The computer will allow students to learn at their own pace.* [from Old French]

Word Partnership	Use **pace** with :
N	pace **of change** **1**
ADJ	**brisk** pace, **fast** pace, **record** pace, **slow** pace **1** **2**
V	**pick up the** pace, **set a** pace **1** **2**

paci|fi|er /ˈpæsɪfaɪər/ (pacifiers) **N-COUNT** A **pacifier** is an object that you put in a baby's mouth to stop it from crying. [from Old French]

pac|ing /ˈpeɪsɪŋ/ **N-NONCOUNT** LANGUAGE ARTS The **pacing** of something such as a play, a movie, or a novel is the speed at which the story develops. [from Old French]

pack /pæk/ (packs, packing, packed)

1 **V-T/V-I** When you **pack**, or **pack** a bag, you put clothes and other things into a bag, because you are going away. ❑ *When I was 17, I packed my bags and left home.* ❑ *I began to pack for the trip.*

pack

● **pack|ing** **N-NONCOUNT** ❑ *She left Fiona to finish her packing.*

2 **V-T/V-I** If people or things **pack into** a place or if they **pack** a place, there are so many of them that the place is full. ❑ *Hundreds of people packed into the temple.*

● **packed** **ADJ** ❑ *The place is packed at lunchtime.* ❑ *...a packed meeting.*

3 **N-COUNT** A **pack of** things is a collection of them together in a container. ❑ *Sanchez took out a pack of gum and offered him a stick.*

4 **N-COUNT** A **pack of** wild dogs or similar animals is a group of them. [from Middle Low German]

pack|age /ˈpækɪdʒ/ (packages)

1 **N-COUNT** A **package** is something wrapped in paper, or put in a box or an envelope. ❑ *I tore open the package.*

2 **N-COUNT** A **package** is a set of proposals that are made by a government or organization. ❑ *Congress passed a package of new rules for the financial markets.* [from Middle Low German]

→ look at Word Web: **containers**

Thesaurus	**package** Also look up :
N	batch, bundle, container, pack **2**

pack|ag|ing /ˈpækɪdʒɪŋ/ **N-NONCOUNT** **Packaging** is the paper or plastic that something is in when you buy it. ❑ *Avoid buying food with plastic packaging.* [from Middle Low German]

pack|et /ˈpækɪt/ (packets)

1 **N-COUNT** A **packet** is a set of information about a particular subject. ❑ *Call us for a free information packet.*

2 **N-COUNT** A **packet** is a small box, bag, or envelope in which an amount of something is sold. ❑ *He bought a packet of cookies.* [from Old French]

→ look at Picture Dictionary: **containers**

pact /pækt/ (pacts) **N-COUNT** SOCIAL STUDIES A **pact** is a formal agreement between two or more people, organizations, or governments. ❑ *He signed a new pact with Germany.* [from Old French]

pad /pæd/ (pads)

1 **N-COUNT** A **pad** is a thick, flat piece of soft material, used for cleaning things or for

P

protection. ❑ *Please wear a helmet and elbow pads.* ❑ *Have you tried using an oven-cleaning pad?*
2 **N-COUNT** A **pad of** paper is a number of pieces of paper attached together along one side. ❑ *Have a pad of paper ready and write down the information.*

pad|ded /pǽdɪd/ **ADJ** Something that is **padded** has soft material in it that makes it softer or warmer, or that protects it. ❑ *...a padded jacket.* ❑ *...a padded envelope.* [from Low German]

pad|ding /pǽdɪŋ/ **N-NONCOUNT** Padding is soft material in something that makes it softer or warmer, or that protects it. ❑ *These headphones have foam rubber padding.* ❑ *Players must wear padding to protect them from injury.* [from Low German]

pad|dle /pǽdᵊl/ (**paddles, paddling, paddled**)
1 **N-COUNT** SPORTS A **paddle** is a short pole with a wide flat part at the end, that you use to move a small boat through water.
2 **V-T/V-I** SPORTS **Paddle** is also a verb.
❑ *He paddled a canoe across the Congo river.*
❑ *She kept paddling against the tide.*
→ look at Word Web: **boat**

pad|lock /pǽdlɒk/ (**padlocks**) **N-COUNT** A **padlock** is a metal lock that is used for fastening two things together. ❑ *They put a padlock on the door of his house.*

pa|gan /péɪgən/ **ADJ** Pagan beliefs are ones that do not belong to any of the main religions of the world, often ancient beliefs that existed before these religions developed. ❑ *...the pagan festival of Yule.* [from Church Latin]

page /péɪdʒ/ (**pages**)
1 **N-COUNT** A **page** is one side of a piece of paper in a book, a magazine, or a newspaper. ❑ *Turn to page 4.* ❑ *The story was on the front page of USA Today.*
2 **N-COUNT** A **page** is one section of a website. [from Old French]
→ look at Word Web: **printing**

paid /péɪd/
1 **Paid** is the past tense and past participle of **pay.**
2 **ADJ** A **paid** worker receives money in exchange for working for an employer.
❑ *A small team of paid staff manages the company.* ❑ *His wife is a well-paid accountant.* [from Old French]

pail /péɪl/ (**pails**) **N-COUNT** A **pail** is a round container with a handle for carrying water. [from Old English]

pain /péɪn/ (**pains**)
1 **N-COUNT/N-NONCOUNT** Pain is the feeling that you have in a part of your body, because of illness or an injury. ❑ *I felt a sharp pain in my lower back.*
2 **N-NONCOUNT** Pain is the sadness that you feel when something upsets you. ❑ *I could see that my words caused him great pain.*
3 **PHRASE** If you call someone or something **a pain** or **a pain in the neck**, you mean that they are very annoying. [INFORMAL] ❑ *I like her work, but she can be a pain in the neck.*
4 **PHRASE** If you are **in pain**, you feel pain. ❑ *My legs are sore and I'm in pain all the time.* [from Old French]

Thesaurus	pain Also look up :
N	ache, agony, discomfort **1** anguish, distress, heartache, suffering **2**
V	bother, distress, grieve, hurt, upset, wound **2**

pain|ful /péɪnfəl/
1 **ADJ** If a part of your body is **painful**, it hurts. ❑ *Her toe was swollen and painful.*
● **pain|ful|ly** **ADV** ❑ *Matt banged his head painfully as he climbed out of the window.*
2 **ADJ** If an injury or a medical condition is **painful**, it causes you a lot of physical pain. ❑ *...a painful back injury.* ● **pain|ful|ly** **ADV** ❑ *He knocked his head painfully against the cupboard.*
3 **ADJ** **Painful** experiences and memories make you feel sad and upset. ❑ *His unkind remarks brought back painful memories.* [from Old French]

Word Partnership	Use **painful** with :
ADV	**extremely** painful, **more/less** painful, **often** painful, **too** painful, **very** painful **1**–**3**
N	painful **death**, painful **process** **2** **3** painful **experience**, painful **feelings**, painful **lesson**, painful **memory** **3**

pain|killer /péɪnkɪlər/ (**painkillers**) **N-COUNT** A **painkiller** is a drug that reduces or stops physical pain.

pain|less /péɪnlɪs/ **ADJ** If a treatment is **painless** it causes no physical pain. ❑ *The operation is a quick, painless procedure.* [from Old French]

paint /peɪnt/ (**paints, painting, painted**)

1 **N-COUNT/N-NONCOUNT** ARTS **Paint** is a colored liquid that you put onto a surface with a brush. ❑ *We'll need about three cans of red paint.*

2 **V-T** If you **paint** a wall or an object, you cover it with paint. ❑ *They started to paint the walls.*

3 **V-T/V-I** ARTS If you **paint** something or **paint** a picture of it, you produce a picture of it using paint. ❑ *He is very good at painting flowers.* ❑ *Monet painted hundreds of pictures of water lilies.* [from Old French]
→ look at Picture Dictionary: **draw**
→ look at Word Webs: **painting, petroleum**

Word Partnership	Use **paint** with :
ADJ	**blue/green/red/white/yellow** paint, **fresh** paint, **peeling** paint **1**
N	**can of** paint, **coat of** paint **1** paint **a picture**, paint **a portrait 3**

paint|brush /peɪntbrʌʃ/ (**paintbrushes**)
N-COUNT A **paintbrush** is a brush that you use for painting.
→ look at Word Web: **painting**

paint|er /peɪntər/ (**painters**)

1 **N-COUNT** ARTS A **painter** is an artist who paints pictures. ❑ *The movie is about the Dutch painter, Vincent van Gogh.*

2 **N-COUNT** A **painter** is a person whose job is to paint walls, doors, or other parts of buildings. ❑ *I worked as a house painter for about five years.* [from Old French]

paint|ing /peɪntɪŋ/ (**paintings**)

1 **N-COUNT** ARTS A **painting** is a picture that someone has painted. ❑ *She hung a large painting on the wall.*

2 **N-NONCOUNT** ARTS **Painting** is the activity of painting pictures or covering surfaces with paint. ❑ *She really enjoys painting and gardening.* [from Old French]

3 → see also **paint**

→ look at Word Webs: **painting, art**

pair /pɛər/ (**pairs**)

1 **N-COUNT** A **pair of** things is two things of the same size and shape that are used together. ❑ *She wore a pair of plain black shoes.* ❑ *...a pair of earrings.*

2 **N-COUNT** You can call some objects that have two main parts of the same size and shape a **pair**. ❑ *He was wearing a pair of old jeans.* ❑ *She took a pair of scissors out of her purse.*

3 **N-SING** A **pair** is two people who are in a romantic relationship together. ❑ *The pair met five years ago at university, and are planning to marry next year.*

4 **N-SING** You can call two people a **pair** when they are standing or walking together. ❑ *...a pair of teenage boys.* [from Old French]

Thesaurus	pair Also look up :
N	combination, couple, duo, match, two **1** **3** **4**

pa|jam|as /pədʒɑməz, -dʒæm-/ **N-PLURAL** **Pajamas** are loose pants and a top that people wear in bed. ❑ *...a pair of blue-and-white striped pajamas.* [from Persian]

pal /pæl/ (**pals**) **N-COUNT** Your **pals** are your friends. [INFORMAL] ❑ *They talked like old pals.* [from Romany]

pal|ace /pælɪs/ (**palaces**) **N-COUNT** A **palace** is a very large impressive house where a king, a queen, or a president lives. ❑ *We visited Buckingham Palace.* [from Old French]

pale /peɪl/ (**paler, palest**)

1 **ADJ** A **pale** color is not strong or bright. ❑ *She's wearing a pale blue dress.*

2 **ADJ** If someone looks **pale**, their face is a lighter color than usual. ❑ *She looked pale and tired.* [from Old French]

P

Word Web   painting

Oil **painting** uses special tools and techniques. First, **artists** stretch a piece of **canvas** over a wooden **frame**. Then they cover the canvas with a **coat** of white **paint**. When it dries, they put it on an **easel**. Most painters mix **colors** together. They paint the canvas with soft bristle **paintbrushes**. Three common oil painting styles are the still life, the **landscape,** and the **portrait.**

pale|on|tol|ogy /peɪliəntɒlədʒi/
N-NONCOUNT SCIENCE **Paleontology** is the
study of fossils as a guide to the history of
life on earth. ● **pale|on|tolo|gist**
(**paleontologists**) **N-COUNT** [from Greek]

Paleo|zo|ic era /peɪliəzoʊɪk ɪərə/ **N-SING**
SCIENCE **The Paleozoic era** is a period in the
history of the Earth that began around
550 million years ago and ended around
230 million years ago.

palm /pɑm/ (**palms**)
1 **N-COUNT/N-NONCOUNT** A **palm** or a **palm
tree** is a tree that grows in hot countries. It
has long leaves at the top, and no branches.
❑ ...white sand and palm trees.
2 **N-COUNT** The **palm of** your hand is the
inside part of your hand, between your
fingers and your wrist. ❑ Dornberg hit the table
with the palm of his hand. [Sense 1 from Old
French. Sense 2 from Old English.]
→ look at Picture Dictionaries: **desert, hand**

> **Word Link** | let ≈ little : book*let*, leaf*let*,
> pamph*let*

pam|phlet /pæmflɪt/ (**pamphlets**) **N-COUNT**
A **pamphlet** is a very thin book with a paper
cover that gives information about
something. ❑ They gave me a pamphlet about
parenting. [from Medieval Latin]

pan /pæn/ (**pans**) **N-COUNT** A **pan** is a
shallow metal container used for cooking or
baking food. ❑ Press the mixture into two 9-inch
cake pans. [from Old English]
→ look at Word Web: **pan**

pan|cake /pænkeɪk/ (**pancakes**) **N-COUNT**
A **pancake** is a thin, flat, round cooked food
made from milk, flour, and eggs. People
often eat pancakes for breakfast, with
butter and syrup.

pan|da /pændə/ (**pandas**) **N-COUNT** A **panda**
is a large animal with black and white fur.
[from French]

→ look at Word Web: **zoo**

pane /peɪn/ (**panes**) **N-COUNT** A **pane** of glass
is a flat sheet of glass in a window or a door.
[from Old French]

pan|el /pænəl/ (**panels**)
1 **N-COUNT** A **panel** is a small group of
people who discuss something in public or
who make a decision. ❑ The government will
take advice from a panel of experts.
2 **N-COUNT** A **panel** is a flat piece of wood or
other material that forms part of a larger
object such as a door. ❑ There was a glass panel
in the center of the door.
3 **N-COUNT** A control **panel** is a board with
switches and controls on it. ❑ You can
switch the lights on or off using a control panel.
[from Old French]

Pan|gaea /pændʒiə/ **N-PROPER** SCIENCE
Pangaea is the name given by scientists to
the huge mass of land that existed on the
Earth millions of years ago, before it split
into separate continents. [from Greek]

pan|ic /pænɪk/ (**panics, panicking, panicked**)
1 **N-COUNT/N-NONCOUNT** **Panic** is a strong
feeling of worry or fear that makes you act
without thinking carefully. ❑ An earthquake
caused panic among the population.
2 **V-T/V-I** If you **panic**, or if someone **panics**
you, you suddenly feel worried or afraid, and
act without thinking carefully. ❑ Guests
panicked and screamed when the bomb exploded.
❑ The sudden memory panicked her. [from French]

> **Thesaurus** **panic** Also look up :
> | N | agitation, alarm, dread, fear, fright;
 (ant.) calm **1** |
> | V | alarm, fear, terrify, unnerve;
 (ant.) relax **2** |

pant /pænt/ (**pants, panting, panted**)
1 **V-I** If a person or an animal **pants**, they
breathe quickly and loudly, because they
have been running or because they are very

> ## Word Web　　pan
>
> No **saucepan** or **frying pan** is perfect. **Copper pans** conduct heat
> well. This makes them good for cooking on the stove. However,
> copper also reacts with the acid in some foods. For this reason, the
> best pans have a thin layer of **tin** covering the copper. **Cast iron**
> pans are very heavy and **heat up** slowly. But they stay hot for a
> long time. Some people like **stainless steel** pans because they
> heat up quickly and don't react with chemicals in food. However,
> the bottom of a stainless pan may not heat up evenly.

P

hot. ❑ *Dogs lose body heat by panting and sweating.* [from Old French]
2 → see also **pants**

pant|ies /pǽntiz/ **N-PLURAL** Panties are underwear for women or girls that covers the lower part of the body, but not the legs.

pan|to|mime /pǽntəmaɪm/ (**pantomimes**) **N-COUNT** ARTS A **pantomime** is a performance involving acting without words through facial expression, gesture, and movement. [from Latin]

pants /pǽnts/
1 **N-PLURAL** Pants are a piece of clothing that covers the lower part of your body and each leg. ❑ *He wore brown corduroy pants and a white cotton shirt.*
2 → see also **pant**
→ look at Picture Dictionary: **clothing**

pant|suit /pǽntsut/ (**pantsuits**) or **pants suit** **N-COUNT** A **pantsuit** is a woman's pants and jacket, made from the same material. ❑ *She wore a white blouse and a gray pantsuit.*

pan|ty|hose /pǽntihoʊz/ also **panty hose** **N-PLURAL** Pantyhose are a piece of thin clothing worn by women, that covers the body from the waist down to the feet.

pa|per /péɪpər/ (**papers**)
1 **N-NONCOUNT** Paper is a material that you write on or wrap things with. ❑ *He wrote his name down on a piece of paper.* ❑ *He carried the groceries in a paper bag.*
2 **N-COUNT** A **paper** is a newspaper. ❑ *I might get a paper when I go downtown.*
3 **N-PLURAL** Papers are sheets of paper with information on them. ❑ *The briefcase also contained important official papers.*
4 **N-PLURAL** Your **papers** are your official documents, such as your passport. ❑ *The young man refused to show his papers to the police.*
5 **N-COUNT** A **paper** is a long piece of writing on an academic subject. ❑ *He just published a paper in the journal "Nature."* ❑ *...the ten errors that appear most frequently in student papers.* [from Latin]
→ look at Word Web: **paper**

Word Partnership	Use **paper** with :
ADJ	**blank** paper, **brown** paper, **colored** paper, **recycled** paper **1**
	daily paper **2**
V	**fold** paper **1**
	read the paper **2**
	present a paper, **publish a** paper **5**
	draft a paper, **write a** paper **5**
N	**morning** paper **2**
	research paper **5**

paper|back /péɪpərbæk/ (**paperbacks**) **N-COUNT** A **paperback** is a book with a thin cardboard or paper cover. ❑ *I'll buy the book when it comes out in paperback.*

pa|per clip (**paper clips**) also **paper-clip**, **paperclip** **N-COUNT** A **paper clip** is a small piece of bent wire that is used to hold papers together.
→ look at Picture Dictionary: **office**

paper|work /péɪpərwɜrk/ **N-NONCOUNT** Paperwork is work that involves dealing with letters, reports, and records. ❑ *There will be paperwork—forms to fill in, letters to write.*

par /pɑr/
1 **PHRASE** If you say that two people or things are **on a par with** each other, you mean that they are equally good or bad, or equally important. ❑ *The coffee was on a par with the one he had in Paris.*
2 **PHRASE** If you say that someone or something is **below par**, they are below the standard you expected. ❑ *Duffy's guitar playing is well below par.* [from Latin]

para|chute /pǽrəʃut/ (**parachutes**) **N-COUNT** A **parachute** is a large piece of thin

---

Word Web   paper

Around 3000 BC, Egyptians began to make **paper** from the papyrus plant. They cut the stems of the plant into thin slices and pressed them into **sheets**. A very different Chinese technique developed about the same time. It was more like today's paper-making process. Chinese paper makers cooked **fiber** made of tree bark. Then they pressed it into molds and let it dry. Around 200 BC, a third paper-making process began in the Middle East. Craftsmen started using animal skins to make parchment. Today, paper manufacturing destroys millions of trees every year. This has led to **recycling** programs and paperless offices.

cloth that a person attaches to their body when they jump from an aircraft to help them float safely to the ground. ❑ *They fell 41,000 feet before opening their parachutes.* [from French]
→ look at Word Web: **fly**

parachute

pa|rade /pər**eı**d/ (**parades, parading, paraded**)

■ **N-COUNT** A **parade** is a line of people or vehicles moving through a public place in order to celebrate an important event. ❑ *A military parade marched down Pennsylvania Avenue.*

■ **V-T** If someone **parades** a person or a thing, they show them in public, often in order to impress people. ❑ *She refused to parade her problems on TV.* ❑ *Prisoners were paraded in front of the television cameras.* [from French]

para|digm /p**æ**rədaım/ (**paradigms**)

N-COUNT/N-NONCOUNT A **paradigm** is a model for something that explains it or shows how it can be produced. [FORMAL] ❑ *...a new paradigm of production.* [from French]

para|dise /p**æ**rədaıs/ (**paradises**)

■ **N-PROPER** In some religions, **paradise** is a beautiful place where good people go after they die.

■ **N-COUNT/N-NONCOUNT** You can call a beautiful or perfect place **paradise** or **a paradise**. ❑ *The island really is a tropical paradise.* [from Old English]

| Word Link | *para* ≈ beside : compara*tive, para*dox, para*llel* |

para|dox /p**æ**rədɒks/ (**paradoxes**)

■ **N-COUNT** You describe a situation as a **paradox** when it involves two or more facts or qualities that seem to contradict each other. ❑ *The paradox is that the more you exercise, the more energy you have.* ● **para|doxi|cal** /p**æ**rədɒksık**ə**l/ **ADJ** ❑ *Low-fat diets have the paradoxical effect of making some people gain weight.* ● **para|doxi|cal|ly ADV** ❑ *The second method is more complicated, but paradoxically, less expensive.*

■ **N-COUNT/N-NONCOUNT** A **paradox** is a statement in which it seems that if one part

of it is true, the other part of it cannot be true. ❑ *The story contains many levels of paradox.* [from Late Latin]

para|graph /p**æ**rəgr**æ**f/ (**paragraphs**)

N-COUNT LANGUAGE ARTS A **paragraph** is a section of a piece of writing. ❑ *The essay begins with a short introductory paragraph.* [from Medieval Latin]

par|al|lax /p**æ**rəl**æ**ks/ (**parallaxes**)

N-COUNT/N-NONCOUNT SCIENCE **Parallax** is when an object appears to change its position because the person or instrument observing it has changed their position. [from French]

par|al|lel /p**æ**rəl**ɛ**l/ (**parallels**)

■ **ADJ** MATH If two lines are **parallel**, they are the same distance apart along their whole length. ❑ *Remsen Street is parallel with Montague Street.*

■ **N-COUNT** If something has a **parallel**, it is similar to something else in some way. ❑ *The author draws parallels between the invention of printing and the development of the Internet.* ❑ *It's a disaster with no parallel anywhere else in the world.* [from French]

par|al|lel cir|cuit (**parallel circuits**) **N-COUNT** SCIENCE A **parallel circuit** is an electrical circuit in which the current travels along more than one path so that it can power several devices at the same time.

par|al|lel|ism /p**æ**rəl**ɛ**lız**ə**m/ **N-NONCOUNT** LANGUAGE ARTS **Parallelism** is the use of similar grammatical structures within a piece of writing so that ideas which are closely related are expressed in a similar way. The phrase "government of the people, by the people, for the people" is an example of parallelism. [from French]

para|lyze /p**æ**rəlaız/ (**paralyzes, paralyzing, paralyzed**) **V-T** If someone **is paralyzed** by an accident or an illness, they are unable to move all or part of their body ❑ *She is paralyzed from the waist down.* [from French]
→ look at Word Web: **disability**

para|mecium /p**æ**rəmiʃıəm, -si-/ (**paramecia**) **N-COUNT** SCIENCE **Paramecia** are a type of protozoa that are found in fresh water. [from New Latin]

para|site /p**æ**rəsaıt/ (**parasites**) **N-COUNT** SCIENCE A **parasite** is a small animal or plant that lives on or inside a larger animal or

P

plant, and gets its food from it. ❑ *Very small parasites live in the stomach of some insects.*
● **para|sit|ic** /pærəsɪtɪk/ **ADJ** ❑ *...tiny parasitic insects.*

para|sit|ism /pærəsaɪtɪzəm/ **N-NONCOUNT**
SCIENCE In biology, **parasitism** is the state of being a parasite. [from Latin]

par|cel /pɑrsəl/ (**parcels**) **N-COUNT** A **parcel** is something that is wrapped in paper so that it can be sent by mail. ❑ *They sent parcels of food and clothing.* [from Old French]

parched /pɑrtʃt/
1 **ADJ** If the ground or a plant is **parched**, it is very dry because there has been no rain. ❑ *Rain poured down on the parched earth.*
2 **ADJ** If your mouth, throat, or lips are **parched**, they are unpleasantly dry. ❑ *Her throat was parched.*
3 **ADJ** If you say that you are **parched**, you mean that you are very thirsty. [INFORMAL]

> Word Link   *don ≈ giving : donate, donor, pardon*

par|don /pɑrdən/ (**pardons, pardoning, pardoned**)
1 **INTERJ** You say **Pardon?** when you want someone to repeat what they have just said. [SPOKEN] ❑ *"Will you let me open it?"—"Pardon?"— "Can I open it?"*
2 **PHRASE** You can also say **I beg your pardon?** or **Pardon me?** when you want someone to repeat what they have just said. [SPOKEN]
3 **PHRASE** You say **I beg your pardon** as a way of apologizing for making a small mistake. [SPOKEN] ❑ *I beg your pardon. I thought*

you were someone else.
4 **V-T** SOCIAL STUDIES If someone who has been found guilty of a crime **is pardoned**, they are allowed to go free and are not punished. ❑ *Hundreds of political prisoners were pardoned and released.*
5 **N-COUNT** SOCIAL STUDIES **Pardon** is also a noun. ❑ *He received a pardon from the president.* [from Old French]

par|ent /pɛərənt, pær-/ (**parents**) **N-COUNT** Your **parents** are your mother and father. ❑ *Children need their parents.* ● **pa|ren|tal** /pərɛntəl/ **ADJ** ❑ *Children must have parental permission to attend the party.* [from Old French] → look at Word Web: **child**

par|ent cell (**parent cells**) **N-COUNT** SCIENCE A **parent cell** is a cell in an organism which divides to produce other cells. Compare with **daughter cell**.

par|ent|hood /pɛərənthʊd, pær-/ **N-NONCOUNT Parenthood** is the state of being a parent. ❑ *They had to deal with the responsibilities of parenthood.* [from Old French]

par|ish /pærɪʃ/ (**parishes**)
1 **N-COUNT** A **parish** is part of a city or town that has its own church and priest.
2 **N-COUNT** SOCIAL STUDIES In some parts of the United States, a **parish** is a small region within a state which has its own local government. [from Old French]

park /pɑrk/ (**parks, parking, parked**)
1 **N-COUNT** A **park** is a public area of land with grass and trees, usually in a town,

P

> ## Word Web   park
>
>
>
> Central Park* was the first planned urban **park** in the United States. When it opened in 1858 only a few wealthy families lived close enough to enjoy it. Today more than 20 million visitors use the park for **recreation** each year. Children enjoy the **playgrounds**, the carousel, and the petting **zoo**. Families have **picnics** on the grass. Couples rent rowboats and row around the lake. Seniors **stroll** through the **gardens**. Players use the **tennis courts** and **baseball diamonds** all summer. **Cyclists** and **runners** use Central Park Drive* on weekends when it is closed to car traffic.
>
> *Central Park: an 843-acre park in New York City.*
> *Central Park Drive: a road in Central Park.*

where people go to relax and enjoy themselves. ❑ ...*Central Park.* ❑ *I took a walk with the dog around the park.*

2 **N-COUNT** A **park** is a place where people play baseball. ❑ *We played baseball in that park every summer.*

3 **V-T/V-I** When you **park** a vehicle or **park** somewhere, you drive a vehicle into a position and you leave it there. ❑ *They parked in the street outside the house.* ❑ *He found a place to park the car.* ● **park|ing** **N-NONCOUNT** ❑ *Parking is allowed only on one side of the street.* [from Old French] → look at Word Web: **park**

park|ing lot (parking lots) **N-COUNT** A **parking lot** is an area of ground where people can leave their cars. ❑ *I found a parking lot one block up the street.*

park|way /pɑrkweɪ/ (parkways) **N-COUNT** A **parkway** is a wide road with trees and grass on both sides. [from Old French]

par|lia|ment /pɑrləmənt/ (parliaments) also Parliament

1 **N-COUNT/N-PROPER** SOCIAL STUDIES The **parliament** of some countries is the group of people who make or change its laws. ❑ *The German Parliament today approved the policy.* [from Old French]

2 → see also **Member of Parliament**

par|lia|men|ta|ry /pɑrləmɛntəri/ **ADJ** SOCIAL STUDIES **Parliamentary** is used to describe things that are connected with a parliament. ❑ *...a parliamentary debate.* [from Old French]

paro|dy /pærədi/ (parodies) **N-COUNT/N-NONCOUNT** LANGUAGE ARTS A **parody** is a piece of writing, drama, or music that copies something in an amusing way. ❑ *The school show was a parody of the "Star Wars" movies.* [from Latin]

pa|role /pəroʊl/ **N-NONCOUNT** A prisoner who is given **parole** may leave prison early if he or she promises to behave well. ❑ *He will soon be able to apply for parole.* [from Old French]

par|rot /pærət/ (parrots) **N-COUNT** A **parrot** is a tropical bird with a curved beak and very bright or gray feathers. [from French]

pars|ley /pɑrsli/ **N-NONCOUNT** Parsley is a type of herb with small green leaves that you use in cooking. [from Old English]

Word Link	par ≈ equal : com**par**e, dis**par**ate, **par**t

part /pɑrt/ (parts, parting, parted)

1 **N-COUNT/N-NONCOUNT** **Part** of something is a piece of it. ❑ *This was a part of Paris he loved.* ❑ *Perry spent part of his childhood in Canada.*

2 **N-COUNT** A **part** is a piece of a machine. ❑ *The company makes small parts for airplanes.*

3 **N-COUNT** A **part** in a play or a movie is one character's words and actions. ❑ *He played the part of Hamlet.*

4 **N-COUNT** A **part** in your hair is a line where your hair lies in different directions on your head.

5 **V-T/V-I** If things that are next to each other **part** or if you **part** them, they move away from each other. ❑ *Her lips parted in a smile.* ❑ *Livy parted the curtains.*

6 **PHRASE** You use **in part** to indicate that something exists or happens to some extent but not completely. [FORMAL] ❑ *They're getting more visitors than before, thanks in part to the weather.*

7 **PHRASE** If something or someone **plays** a large or important **part in** an event or a situation, they are very involved in it and have an important effect on what happens. ❑ *Work plays an important part in our lives.*

8 **PHRASE** If you **take part in** an activity, you do it together with other people. ❑ *Thousands of students took part in the demonstrations.* [from Old French]

▶ **part with** If you **part with** something that you would prefer to keep, you give it or sell it to someone else. ❑ *Think carefully before parting with money.*

Thesaurus	part	Also look up :
N	component, fraction, half, ingredient, piece, portion, section; (ant.) entirety, whole **1**	
	role, share **3**	
V	break up, separate, split **5**	

par|tial /pɑrʃəl/

1 **ADJ** You use **partial** to talk about something that is not complete. ❑ *These plants prefer to grow in partial shade.* ● **par|tial|ly** **ADV** ❑ *Lisa is partially blind.*

2 **ADJ** If you are **partial to** something, you like it. ❑ *Mollie is partial to pink.* [from Old French]

par|tial eclipse (partial eclipses) **N-COUNT** SCIENCE A **partial eclipse of** the sun is an occasion when the moon is between the Earth and the sun, so that for a short time you cannot see part of the sun. A **partial eclipse of** the moon is an occasion when the Earth is between the sun and the moon, so that for a short time you cannot see part of the moon. Compare with **total eclipse**.

par|tici|pant /pɑrtɪsɪpənt/ (**participants**) **N-COUNT** The **participants** in an activity are the people who take part in it. ❑ *Participants in the course will learn techniques to improve their memory.* [from Latin]

par|tici|pate /pɑrtɪsɪpeɪt/ (**participates, participating, participated**) **V-I** If you **participate in** an activity, you take part in it. ❑ *Some of the children participated in sports, or other physical activities.* ● **par|tici|pa|tion** /pɑrtɪsɪpeɪʃⁿn/ **N-NONCOUNT** ❑ *Doctors recommend exercise or participation in sport at least two times a week.* [from Latin]

par|ti|ci|ple /pɑrtɪsɪpᵊl/ (**participles**) **N-COUNT** LANGUAGE ARTS In grammar, a **participle** is a form of the verb that usually ends in "-ed" or "-ing." [from Old French]

Word Link	cle ≈ small : article, cubicle, particle

par|ti|cle /pɑrtɪkᵊl/ (**particles**) **N-COUNT** A **particle of** something is a very small piece or amount of it. ❑ *...a particle of hot metal.* ❑ *There is a particle of truth in his statement.* [from Latin] → look at Word Web: **lightning**

par|ticu|lar /pərtɪkyələr/
1 **ADJ** You use **particular** to show that you are talking about one thing or one type of thing rather than other similar ones. ❑ *Where did you hear that particular story?* ❑ *I have to know exactly why I'm doing a particular job.*
2 **ADJ** You can use **particular** to show that something is greater or stronger than usual. ❑ *We place particular importance on language training.*
3 **ADJ** Someone who is **particular** chooses and does things very carefully. ❑ *Ted is very particular about the clothes he wears.*
4 **PHRASE** You use **in particular** to show that what you are saying applies especially to one thing or person. ❑ *She loves old movies—Hollywood classics in particular.* [from Old French]

par|ticu|lar|ly /pərtɪkyələrli/ **ADV** **Particularly** means more than others. ❑ *Keep your office space looking good, particularly your desk.* ❑ *I particularly liked the wooden chairs.* [from Old French]

par|ti|san /pɑrtɪzən/ (**partisans**) **ADJ** Someone who is **partisan** strongly supports a particular person or cause, often without thinking carefully about the matter. ❑ *It was an extremely partisan crowd, and they were very enthusiastic.* [from French]

part|ly /pɑrtli/ **ADV** **Partly** means not completely, but a little. ❑ *It's partly my fault.* [from Old French]

part|ner /pɑrtnər/ (**partners**)
1 **N-COUNT** Your **partner** is your husband or wife, or your boyfriend or girlfriend. ❑ *Len's partner died four years ago.*
2 **N-COUNT** Your **partner** in an activity such as a game or a dance is the person you are playing or dancing with. ❑ *She needed a new partner for the doubles game.*
3 **N-COUNT** BUSINESS The **partners** in a firm or a business are the people who own it. ❑ *He's a partner in a Chicago law firm.*

part|ner and group skills **N-PLURAL** **Partner and group skills** are skills that require people to work together as a team.

part|ner|ship /pɑrtnərʃɪp/ (**partnerships**) **N-COUNT/N-NONCOUNT** A **partnership** is a relationship in which two or more people or groups work together. ❑ *We want to develop a closer partnership between the government and the auto industry.*

part of speech (**parts of speech**) **N-COUNT** LANGUAGE ARTS In grammar, a **part of speech** is a particular class of word such as noun, adjective, or verb.

part-time

> **LANGUAGE HELP**
> The adverb is spelled **part time**.

1 **ADJ** If someone is a **part-time** worker or has a **part-time** job, they work for only part of each day or week. ❑ *She is trying to get a part-time job in an office.*
2 **ADV** **Part time** is also an adverb. ❑ *I want to work part time.*

par|ty /pɑrti/ (**parties, partying, partied**)
1 **N-COUNT** A **party** is a social event at which people enjoy themselves doing things like eating or dancing. ❑ *The couple met at a party.* ❑ *We organized a huge birthday party.*
2 **N-COUNT** A **party** is a political organization whose members have similar aims and beliefs. ❑ *He is a member*

P

of the Republican Party.

3 **N-COUNT** A **party of** people is a group of them doing something together. ❑ *We passed by a party of tourists.*

4 **v-I** If you **party**, you enjoy yourself doing things such as going out to parties and dancing. ❑ *He partied a little just like all teenagers.* [from Old French]

pas|cal /pæskæl, paskɑl/ (**pascals**) **N-COUNT** SCIENCE A **pascal** is a unit for measuring pressure. [from French]

Pascal's prin|ci|ple or Pascal's law
N-NONCOUNT SCIENCE **Pascal's principle** or **Pascal's law** is a rule in physics which states that, when pressure is applied to a fluid in a container, the pressure is distributed equally throughout all parts of the fluid.

---
pass
❶ VERB USES
❷ NOUN USES
❸ PHRASAL VERBS
---

❶ pass /pæs/ (**passes, passing, passed**)
1 **v-T/v-I** When you **pass** someone or something, you go past them. ❑ *When she passed the library door, the telephone began to ring.* ❑ *Jane stood aside to let her pass.*

2 **v-I** When someone or something **passes** in a particular direction, they move in that direction. ❑ *He passed through the doorway into the kitchen.* ❑ *A helicopter passed overhead.*

3 **v-T** If you **pass** something through, over, or around something else, you move or push it through, over, or around that thing. ❑ *He passed a hand through his hair.*

4 **v-T** If you **pass** an object **to** someone, you give it to them. ❑ *Pam passed the books to Dr. Wong.*

5 **v-T** In sports, if you **pass** the ball **to** someone, you kick or throw it to them. ❑ *Hawkins passed the ball to Payton.*

6 **v-T/v-I** If something **passes** or if you **pass** something **on to** someone, you give them some information. ❑ *Mary Hayes passed the news on to McEvoy.* ❑ *His mother's property passed to him after her death.*

7 **v-I** When time **passes**, it goes by. ❑ *Time passes quickly when you are enjoying yourself.*

8 **v-T** If you **pass** time in a particular way, you spend it in that way. ❑ *The children passed the time watching TV.*

9 **v-T/v-I** If you **pass** an examination, or it is **passed**, you succeed in it. ❑ *Tina passed her driving test last week.*

10 **v-T** SOCIAL STUDIES When a government **passes** a new law, they formally agree to it. ❑ *Congress passed a law that allowed banks to sell insurance.*

11 **v-I** To **pass for** or **pass as** a particular thing means to be accepted as that thing, in spite of not having all the right qualities. ❑ *You could pass for a high school senior.* ❑ *Ted, with his fluent French, passed as one of the locals.* [from Old French]

12 → see also **passing**
→ look at Usage note at **past**

❷ pass /pæs/ (**passes**)
1 **N-COUNT** In sports, a **pass** is an act of throwing or kicking the ball to someone on your team. ❑ *Bryan Randall threw a short pass to Ernest Wilford.*

2 **N-COUNT** A **pass** is a document that allows you to do something. ❑ *He used his journalist's pass to enter the White House.*

3 **N-COUNT** A **pass** is a narrow path or route between mountains. ❑ *The village is in a mountain pass.* [from Old French]
→ look at Picture Dictionary: **mountain**

❸ pass /pæs/ (**passes, passing, passed**)
▶ **pass away** If someone **passes away**, they die. [FORMAL] ❑ *She passed away last year.*
▶ **pass out** If you **pass out**, you suddenly become unconscious. ❑ *He felt sick and then passed out.*

pas|sage /pæsɪdʒ/ (**passages**)
1 **N-COUNT** A **passage** is a long narrow space that connects one place or room with another. ❑ *A dark narrow passage led to the kitchen.*

2 **N-COUNT** LANGUAGE ARTS A **passage** is a short part of a book. ❑ *He read a passage to her from one of Max's books.*

3 **N-SING** The **passage of** a period of time is its passing. ❑ *The painting will increase in value with the passage of time.* [from Old French]

pas|sen|ger /pæsɪndʒər/ (**passengers**)
N-COUNT A **passenger** in a vehicle such as a bus, a boat, or a plane is a person who is traveling in it, but who is not driving it. ❑ *Mr. Smith was a passenger in the car when it crashed.* [from Old French]
→ look at Word Webs: **fly, train**

pass|ing /pæsɪŋ/
1 **ADJ** A **passing** feeling or action is brief and not very serious or important. ❑ *...a passing remark in a television interview.*

2 **N-SING** The **passing** of time is the process

by which it goes by. ❑ ...the passing of time.
3 **N-SING** The **passing** of a person or a thing is the fact of their dying or coming to an end. ❑ We celebrated the passing of the century. ❑ His passing will be mourned by many people.
4 → see also **pass** ❶
5 **PHRASE** If you mention something **in passing**, you mention it briefly while you are talking or writing about something else. ❑ He mentioned the army in passing. [from Old French]

pas|sion /pǽʃ°n/ (passions)
1 **N-NONCOUNT** **Passion** is a very strong feeling of love and sexual attraction for someone. ❑ The message from this movie is that it is good to feel passion, to love people, and to experience pleasure.
2 **N-NONCOUNT** **Passion** is a very strong feeling about something or a strong belief in something. ❑ He spoke with great passion.
3 **N-COUNT** If you have a **passion for** something, you have a very strong interest in it and you like it very much. ❑ She has a passion for music. [from French]

Thesaurus	passion Also look up :
N	affection, desire, love **1** enthusiasm, fondness, interest **2** **3**

pas|sion|ate /pǽʃənɪt/ **ADJ** If you are **passionate about** something, you have very strong feelings about it or a strong belief in it. ❑ He is very passionate about the project. [from French]

pas|sive /pǽsɪv/
1 **ADJ** A **passive** person allows things to happen without taking action. ❑ I disliked his passive attitude. ● **pas|sive|ly** **ADV** ❑ He sat there passively, waiting for me to say something.
2 **N-SING** **LANGUAGE ARTS** In grammar, **the passive** is the form of a verb that you use to show that the subject does not perform the action but is affected by it. For example, in "He's been murdered," the verb "murder" is in the passive. Compare with **active**. [from Latin]

pas|sive so|lar heat|ing **N-NONCOUNT**
SCIENCE **Passive solar heating** is a method of heating a building by using the materials or design of the building to collect sunlight directly, for example by the use of thick walls or large windows.

pas|sive trans|port **N-NONCOUNT** **SCIENCE**
In biology, **passive transport** is the

movement of chemicals and other substances through the membranes of cells by a process called diffusion, which does not require the cells to use energy. Compare with **active transport**.

Pass|over /pǽsouvər/ **N-NONCOUNT**
Passover is a Jewish festival that begins in March or April and lasts for seven or eight days. [from Hebrew]

pass|port /pǽspɔrt/ (passports) **N-COUNT**
Your **passport** is an official document that you have to show when you enter or leave a country. ❑ You should take your passport with you when you change your money. [from French]
→ look at Word Web: **citizenship**

pass|word /pǽswɜrd/ (passwords)
N-COUNT **TECHNOLOGY** A **password** is a secret word or phrase that allows you to enter a place or to use a computer system.
❑ Please contact us for a username and password.
→ look at Word Web: **Internet**

past /pǽst/
1 **N-SING** **The past** is the time before the present, and the things that happened then. ❑ In the past, most babies with the disease died.
2 **ADJ** **Past** events and things happened or existed before the present time. ❑ I knew from past experience that this treatment could help. ❑ ...scenes from life in past centuries.
3 **ADJ** You use **past** to talk about a period of time that has just finished. ❑ Most stores have remained closed for the past three days.
4 **PREP** You use **past** to talk about a time that is thirty minutes or less after a particular hour. ❑ It's ten past eleven.
5 **PREP** If you go **past** someone or something, you pass them. ❑ I walked past him.
6 **ADV** **Past** is also an adverb. ❑ An ambulance drove past.
7 **PREP** If something is **past** a place, it is on the other side of it. ❑ Go north on Route I-15 to the exit just past Barstow.
→ look at Word Web: **history**

Usage	past and passed

The adverb or adjective past and the verb passed (past tense of pass) are often confused. They are pronounced the same and can have similar meanings: Jack passed Jill by rolling past her down the hill.This past week, Shaya passed his history exam and his driving test!

P

pas|ta /pɑstə/

N-NONCOUNT Pasta is a type of food made from a mixture of flour, eggs, and water that is made into different shapes and then boiled. ❑ *Italian pizzas and pasta are the restaurant's specialty.* [from Italian]

pasta

paste /peɪst/ (pastes, pasting, pasted)

1 **V-T** If you **paste** something onto a surface, you put glue on it and stick it on. ❑ *He pasted labels onto the bottles.*

2 **V-T** If you **paste** text or images into a computer document, you copy or move them into it from another part of the document, or from another document. ❑ *The text can be copied and pasted into your email program.* [from Old French]

pas|tel /pæstɛl/ (pastels)

1 **ADJ** **Pastel** colors are pale rather than dark or bright. ❑ *Mother always chooses clothes in delicate pastel shades.* ❑ *...pastel pink, blue, and green.*

2 **N-COUNT** ARTS **Pastels** are sticks of color made of a substance like chalk, and used by artists for drawing. ❑ *This paper is ideal for use with paints, crayons, and pastels.* [from French]

past par|ti|ci|ple (past participles)

N-COUNT LANGUAGE ARTS In grammar, the **past participle** of a verb is a form that is usually the same as the past form and so ends in "-ed." A number of verbs have irregular past participles; for example, the past participle of "break" is "broken." Past participles are used to form perfect tenses and the passive voice.

pas|try /peɪstri/ (pastries)

1 **N-NONCOUNT** Pastry is a food made from flour, fat, and water that is often used for making pies.

2 **N-COUNT** A **pastry** is a small cake made with sweet pastry. ❑ *The bakery sells delicious cakes and pastries.*

past tense (past tenses) **N-COUNT**

LANGUAGE ARTS In grammar, **the past tense** is the form that is used for talking about the time that came before the present. For example, the past tense of the verb "see" is "saw."

pat /pæt/ (pats, patting, patted)

1 **V-T** If you **pat** something or someone, you touch them lightly with your flat hand. ❑ *"Don't you worry," she said, patting me on the knee.* ❑ *The lady patted her hair nervously.*

2 **N-COUNT** **Pat** is also a noun. ❑ *He gave her a friendly pat on the shoulder.*

patch /pætʃ/ (patches, patching, patched)

1 **N-COUNT** A **patch** on a surface is a part that is different in appearance from the area around it. ❑ *She noticed the bald patch on the top of his head.* ❑ *There was a small patch of blue in the gray clouds.*

2 **N-COUNT** A **patch** is a piece of cloth that you use to cover a hole in a piece of clothing. ❑ *Brad was wearing an old jacket with leather patches on the elbows.*

3 **V-T** If you **patch** something that has a hole in it, you repair it by attaching a patch over the hole. ❑ *He and Williams patched the barn roof.*

4 **N-COUNT** TECHNOLOGY A **patch** is a piece of computer program code that is used as a quick solution for dealing with a problem. ❑ *Older machines will need a software patch to correct the problem.*

5 **PHRASE** If you go through **a rough patch**, you have a lot of problems for a period of time. ❑ *He went through a rough patch after he lost his job.* [from French]

▶ **patch up** If you **patch up** something that is damaged, you repair it. ❑ *We can patch up those holes.*

pa|tent /pæt°nt/ (patents, patenting, patented)

1 **N-COUNT** BUSINESS A **patent** is an official right to be the only person or company allowed to make or sell a new product for a certain period of time. ❑ *P&G applied for a patent on its cookies.* ❑ *He held a number of patents for his many inventions.*

2 **V-T** BUSINESS If you **patent** something, you obtain a patent for it. ❑ *He patented the idea that the atom could be split.* ❑ *The invention has been patented by the university.*

3 **ADJ** You use **patent** to emphasize that something, especially something bad, is obvious. ❑ *This was patent nonsense.*

● **pa|tent|ly** **ADV** ❑ *He made his anger patently obvious.* [from Old French]

pa|ter|nal /pətɜrn°l/ **ADJ** Paternal is used to describe feelings or actions that are typical of those of a kind father toward his child. ❑ *...paternal love.* [from Late Latin]

path /pæθ/ (**paths**)

■ **N-COUNT** A **path** is a long, narrow piece of ground that people walk along. ❑ *We followed the path along the cliff.*

■ **N-COUNT** The **path** of someone or something is the line that they move along in a particular direction. ❑ *He stepped into the path of a moving car.* ❑ *A group of reporters blocked his path.*

■ **N-COUNT** A **path** that you take is a particular course of action or way of achieving something. ❑ *He chose the path of rock stardom.* [from Old English]

→ look at Picture Dictionaries: **garden, golf**

pa|thet|ic /pəθɛtɪk/

■ **ADJ** If someone or something is **pathetic**, they are weak or not very good. ❑ *What a pathetic attempt to hide the truth.*

■ **ADJ** If you describe someone or something as **pathetic**, you mean that they make you feel impatient or angry, often because they are weak or not very good. ❑ *What pathetic excuses.* ❑ *"Don't be so pathetic!" she screamed. "Do something!"* ● **pa|theti|cal|ly** **ADV** ❑ *The newspaper has always paid its journalists pathetically low wages.* [from French]

patho|logi|cal /pæθəlɒdʒɪkᵊl/

■ **ADJ** You describe a person as **pathological** when they behave in an extreme and unacceptable way, and have very powerful feelings that they cannot control. ❑ *He experiences almost pathological jealousy.* ❑ *He's a pathological liar.*

■ **ADJ** SCIENCE **Pathological** means relating to pathology or illness. ❑ *...pathological conditions in animals.* [from Latin]

pa|thol|ogy /pəθɒlədʒi/ **N-NONCOUNT** SCIENCE **Pathology** is the study of the way illnesses develop, and the examination of dead bodies in order to find out the cause of death. ● **pa|tholo|gist** /pəθɒlədʒɪst/ (**pathologists**) **N-COUNT** ❑ *The pathologist told the court that Mrs. Snook died of old age.* [from Latin]

path|way /pæθweɪ/ (**pathways**)

■ **N-COUNT** A **pathway** is the same as a **path**. ❑ *Richard was coming up the pathway.* ❑ *...the pathway to success.*

■ **N-COUNT** The **pathway** of something is the line which it moves along in a particular direction. [from Old English]

pa|tience /peɪʃᵊns/ **N-NONCOUNT** If you have **patience**, you are able to stay calm and not get annoyed, for example when something takes a long time. ❑ *He doesn't have the patience to wait.* [from Old French]

pa|tient /peɪʃᵊnt/ (**patients**)

■ **N-COUNT** A **patient** is a person who receives medical treatment from a doctor or a nurse. ❑ *The patient was suffering from heart problems.*

■ **ADJ** If you are **patient**, you stay calm and you do not get annoyed, for example when something takes a long time. ❑ *Please be patient—your check will arrive soon.* ● **pa|tient|ly** **ADV** ❑ *She waited patiently for Frances to finish talking.*

→ look at Usage note at **customer**

→ look at Word Webs: **diagnosis, illness**

pa|tio /pætioʊ/ (**patios**) **N-COUNT** A **patio** is a flat area next to a house, where people can sit and relax or eat. [from Spanish]

> **Word Link** *arch ≈ rule : matriarch, monarch, patriarch*

pa|tri|arch /peɪtriɑrk/ (**patriarchs**)

■ **N-COUNT** A **patriarch** is the male head of a family or tribe. ❑ *The patriarch of the house, Mr. Jawad, rules with a ferocity renowned throughout the neighborhood.*

■ **N-COUNT** A **patriarch** is the head of one of a number of Eastern Christian Churches. [from Old French]

pa|tri|ot /peɪtriət/ (**patriots**)

■ **N-COUNT** A **patriot** is a person who loves their country and feels very loyal toward it. ❑ *He was a true patriot, supporting the government's war effort.*

■ **N-COUNT** SOCIAL STUDIES In America in the 18th century, the **Patriots** were the people who came from Britain, who rejected British rule and fought in the American Revolution. ❑ *The leaders of the Patriots are now called "The Founding Fathers of the United States."* [from French]

> **Word Link** *otic ≈ affecting, causing : antibiotic, biotic, patriotic*

pat|ri|ot|ic /peɪtriɒtɪk/ **ADJ** Someone who is **patriotic** loves their country and feels very loyal toward it. ❑ *They are very patriotic guys who give everything for their country.* [from French]

pa|trol /pətroʊl/ (**patrols, patrolling, patrolled**)

■ **V-T** When soldiers, police, or guards **patrol** an area, they move around it to make

P

sure that there is no trouble there. ❏ *Prison officers continued to patrol the grounds.*

2 **N-COUNT** Patrol is also a noun. ❏ *The army is now on patrol.*

3 **N-COUNT** A **patrol** is a group of soldiers or vehicles that move around an area in order to make sure that there is no trouble there. ❏ *The three men attacked a border patrol last night.* [from French]

pa|tron /peɪtrən/ (**patrons**)

1 **N-COUNT** A **patron** is a person who supports and gives money to artists, writers, or musicians. ❏ *...a patron of the arts.*

2 **N-COUNT** The **patron** of a charity, a group, or a campaign is an important person who allows his or her name to be used for publicity. ❏ *He has now become one of the patrons of the association.*

3 **N-COUNT** The **patrons** of a place such as a restaurant or a hotel are its customers. ❏ *...patrons of a high-priced hotel.* [from Old French]

pat|tern /pætərn/ (**patterns**)

1 **N-COUNT** A **pattern** is the repeated or regular way in which something happens or is done. ❏ *All three attacks followed the same pattern.*

2 **N-COUNT** ARTS A **pattern** is an arrangement of lines or shapes that form a design. ❏ *The carpet had a pattern of light and dark stripes.*

3 **N-COUNT** A **pattern** is a shape that you can use as a guide when you are making something such as a model or a piece of clothing. ❏ *Send for our free knitting patterns.*

[from Medieval Latin]
→ look at Word Web: **quilt**

Word Partnership	Use **pattern** with :
ADJ	**familiar** pattern, **normal** pattern, **typical** pattern **1**
	different pattern, **same** pattern, **similar** pattern **1** **2**
V	**change** a pattern, **fit a** pattern, **see a** pattern **1**
	follow a pattern **1**–**3**

pause /pɔz/ (**pauses, pausing, paused**)

1 **V-I** If you **pause** while you are doing something, you stop for a short time and then continue. ❏ *"It's rather embarrassing,"* he began, and paused. ❏ *She started speaking when I paused for breath.*

2 **N-COUNT** A **pause** is a short period of time when you stop doing something. ❏ *After a pause Al said, "I'm sorry if I upset you."* [from Latin]

Word Partnership	Use **pause** with :
ADJ	**awkward** pause, **brief** pause, **long** pause, **short** pause, **slight** pause **2**

pave|ment /peɪvmənt/ (**pavements**)
N-COUNT The **pavement** is the hard surface of a road. ❏ *It was difficult to control the car on the wet pavement.* [from Latin]

paw /pɔ/ (**paws**) **N-COUNT** The **paws** of an animal such as a cat, a dog, or a bear are its feet. ❏ *The kitten was black with white front paws.* [from Old French]

pawn /pɔn/ (**pawns**) **N-COUNT** In chess, a **pawn** is the smallest and least valuable

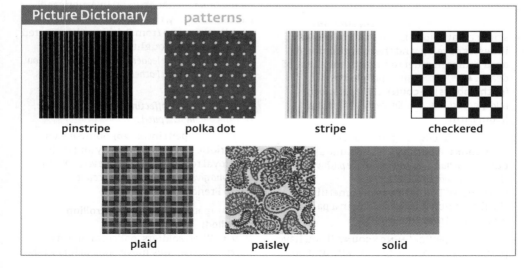

Picture Dictionary patterns

pinstripe   polka dot   stripe   checkered

plaid   paisley   solid

piece. Each player has eight pawns at the start of the game. [from Anglo-Norman] → look at Word Web: **chess**

pawn|broker /pɒnbroʊkər/ (**pawnbrokers**)
N-COUNT A **pawnbroker** is a person who lends people money. People give the pawnbroker something they own, that can be sold if they do not pay back the money before a certain time.

pay /peɪ/ (**pays, paying, paid**)
1 **V-T/V-I** When you **pay for** something, you give someone an amount of money for it. ❑ *Can I pay for my ticket with a credit card?* ❑ *Wealthy people may pay a little more in taxes.*
2 **V-T/V-I** When you **pay** a bill or a debt, you give someone an amount of money for it. ❑ *She paid the hotel bill before she left.* ❑ *The company was given a fine, which they paid.*
3 **V-T** When you **are paid**, you get your salary from your employer. ❑ *The lawyer was paid a huge salary.* ❑ *I get paid monthly.*
4 **N-NONCOUNT** **Pay** is also a noun. ❑ *They complained about their pay and working conditions.*
5 **V-I** If a course of action **pays**, it results in some advantage or benefit for you. ❑ *As always, it pays to do some research.* ❑ *We must show that crime does not pay.*
6 **V-T/V-I** If you **pay for** something that you do or have, you suffer as a result of it. ❑ *Lakoto paid for his beliefs with years in prison.* ❑ *Why should I pay the penalty for somebody else's mistake?*
7 **V-T** You use **pay** with some nouns, such as in the expressions **pay a visit** and **pay attention**, to indicate that something is given or done. ❑ *Pay us a visit next time you're in Portland.* ❑ *He felt a heavy bump, but paid no attention to it.* [from Old French]
8 → see also **paid**
▶ **pay back** If you **pay back** money that you have borrowed from someone, you give them an equal amount at a later time. ❑ *He promised to pay the money back as soon as he could.*
▶ **pay off** **1** If you **pay off** a debt, you give back all the money that you owe. ❑ *It will take him the rest of his life to pay off that loan.*
2 If an action **pays off**, it is successful. ❑ *It looks like all their hard work finally paid off.*

pay|check /peɪtʃɛk/ (**paychecks**) **N-COUNT**
Your **paycheck** is the money that your employer gives you for the work that you have done. ❑ *I get a small paycheck every month.*

pay|ment /peɪmənt/ (**payments**)
1 **N-COUNT** A **payment** is an amount of

money that is paid to someone. ❑ *You will receive 13 monthly payments.*
2 **N-NONCOUNT** **Payment** is the act of paying money or of being paid. ❑ *Players now expect payment for interviews.* [from Old French]

Word Partnership	Use **payment** with :
V	**accept** payment, **make a** payment, **receive** payment **1**
ADJ	**late** payment, **minimum** payment, **monthly** payment **1**
N	payment **in cash**, payment **by check**, **mortgage** payment **1**
	payment **date** **1** **2**
	payment **method**, payment **plan** **2**

pay|wall /peɪwɔːl/ (**paywalls**) **N-COUNT**
TECHNOLOGY A **paywall** is a system that stops the user of a website from seeing other pages on that site if they do not pay. ❑ *Most of their data is behind the paywall.*

PC /pi si/ (**PCs**) **N-COUNT** TECHNOLOGY A **PC** is a computer that people use at school, at home, or in an office. **PC** is short for **personal computer**. ❑ *The price of PCs is falling.*

PDF /pi di ɛf/ **N-NONCOUNT** TECHNOLOGY **PDF** files are computer documents that look exactly like the original documents.

pea /pi/ (**peas**) **N-COUNT** **Peas** are very small, round, green vegetables.

peace /pis/
1 **N-NONCOUNT** When there is **peace** in a country or among a group of people, there is no war or violence. ❑ *The new rulers brought peace to the country.* ❑ *...a peace agreement.*
2 **N-NONCOUNT** **Peace** is the state of being quiet and calm. ❑ *I just want some peace and quiet.* [from Old French]

peace|ful /pisfəl/
1 **ADJ** **Peaceful** means not involving war or violence. ❑ *He has attempted to find a peaceful solution to the conflict.* ● **peace|ful|ly** **ADV** ❑ *The governor asked the protestors to leave peacefully.*
2 **ADJ** A **peaceful** place or time is quiet and calm. ❑ *The backyard looked so peaceful.*
● **peace|ful|ly** **ADV** ❑ *The night passed peacefully.*
3 **ADJ** Someone who feels or looks **peaceful** feels or looks calm and free from worry or pain. ● **peace|ful|ly** **ADV** ❑ *He was sleeping peacefully at her side.* [from Old French]

peach /pitʃ/ (**peaches**)
1 **N-COUNT/N-NONCOUNT** A **peach** is a round fruit with a soft red and orange skin.

2 **ADJ** Something that is **peach** is of a pale color between pink and orange. ❑ *...a peach silk blouse.*

3 **N-NONCOUNT** Peach is also a noun. ❑ *The room was decorated in peach.* [from Old French]

peak /pik/ (**peaks, peaking, peaked**)

1 **N-COUNT** The **peak** of a process or an activity is the point at which it is at its strongest. ❑ *His career was at its peak when he died.*

peak

2 **N-COUNT** A **peak** is a mountain or the top of a mountain. ❑ *They could see the snowy peaks of the Canadian Rockies.*

3 **V-I** When something **peaks**, it reaches its highest value or level. ❑ *Temperatures have peaked at over 90 degrees.* [from Spanish]
→ look at Picture Dictionary: **mountain**

pea|nut /pinʌt, -nət/ (**peanuts**) **N-COUNT** **Peanuts** are small nuts that you can eat.
→ look at Word Web: **peanut**

pear /pɛər/ (**pears**) **N-COUNT/N-NONCOUNT** A **pear** is a juicy fruit that is narrow at the top and wider at the bottom. Pears have white flesh and green, yellow, or brown skin. [from Old English]
→ look at Picture Dictionaries: **fruit, vegetable**

pearl /pɜrl/ (**pearls**) **N-COUNT** A **pearl** is a hard, white, shiny, round object that grows inside the shell of an oyster. **Pearls** are used for making jewelry. ❑ *She wore a string of pearls.* [from Old French]

pearl

peas|ant /pɛzᵊnt/ (**peasants**) **N-COUNT** People call small farmers or farm workers in poor countries **peasants**. ❑ *The film describes the customs and habits of peasants in Peru.* [from Old French]

peb|ble /pɛbᵊl/ (**pebbles**) **N-COUNT** A **pebble** is a small, smooth stone. [from Old English]
→ look at Word Web: **beach**

pe|cu|liar /pɪkyulyər/
1 **ADJ** A **peculiar** person or thing is strange or unusual. ❑ *Mr. Kennet has a rather peculiar sense of humor.*
2 **ADJ** If something is **peculiar to** a particular thing, person, or situation, it belongs or relates only to that thing, person, or situation. ❑ *This expression is peculiar to British English.* ● **pe|cu|liar|ly** **ADV** ❑ *...the peculiarly American business of making Hollywood movies.* [from Latin]

Word Link	**ped ≈ foot** : pedal, impediment, pedestrian

ped|al /pɛdᵊl/ (**pedals, pedaling, pedaled**)
1 **N-COUNT** The **pedals** on a bicycle are the two parts that you push with your feet to make the bicycle move.
2 **V-T/V-I** When you **pedal** a bicycle, you push the pedals around with your feet to make it move. ❑ *We pedaled slowly through the city streets.* ❑ *She pedaled her bike for five miles without stopping.*
3 **N-COUNT** A **pedal** in a car or on a machine is a part that you press with your foot in order to control it. ❑ *...the brake pedal.* [from Latin]
→ look at Word Web: **bicycle**

ped|es|tal /pɛdɪstᵊl/ (**pedestals**) **N-COUNT** A **pedestal** is the base on which something such as a statue stands. ❑ *The statue stood on a stone pedestal.* [from French]

Word Link	**an, ian ≈ one of, relating to** : Christian, European, pedestrian

pe|des|trian /pɪdɛstriən/ (**pedestrians**) **N-COUNT** A **pedestrian** is a person who is walking, especially in a town or city. ❑ *The city's sidewalks were busy with pedestrians.* [from Latin]

Word Web   peanut

The **peanut** is not really a **nut**. Peanuts originated in South America about 3,500 years ago. Explorers took them to Africa. Later, African slaves introduced the peanut into North America. Only poor people ate them at first. But they were a popular **snack** by 1900. You could buy **roasted** peanuts on city streets and at baseball games and circuses. Some scientists believe that roasted peanuts cause more **allergic** reactions than boiled peanuts. George Washington Carver, an African-American scientist, found 325 different uses for peanuts—including **peanut butter**.

pedi|cure /pɛdɪkyʊər/ (pedicures) **N-COUNT**
A **pedicure** is a type of foot treatment in which someone cuts and polishes your toenails and makes the skin soft. ❑ *They celebrated by having a manicure and pedicure at the spa.* [from French]

pe|dom|eter /pɪdɒmɪtər/ (pedometers) **N-COUNT** A **pedometer** is a piece of equipment that measures the distance that someone has walked.

peek /pik/ (peeks, peeking, peeked)
1 V-I If you **peek at** something or someone, you look at them quickly and often secretly. ❑ *She peeked at him through a crack in the wall.*
2 N-COUNT Peek is also a noun. ❑ *I had a peek at his computer screen.* [from Middle Dutch]

peel /pil/ (peels, peeling, peeled)
1 N-COUNT/N-NONCOUNT The **peel** of a fruit such as a lemon or an apple is its skin. ❑ *Add in the grated lemon peel.*
2 V-T When you **peel** fruit or vegetables, you remove their skins. ❑ *She began peeling potatoes.*
3 V-T/V-I If something **peels off** a surface, it comes away from it. ❑ *Paint was peeling off the walls.* ❑ *It took me two days to peel the labels off the books.* [from Old English]
→ look at Picture Dictionaries: **cut, fruit**

peep /pip/ (peeps, peeping, peeped)
1 V-I If you **peep at** something, you take a quick look at it. ❑ *A small child was peeping through the window at him.*
2 N-SING Peep is also a noun. ❑ *She lifted the lid and took a quick peep inside.*

peer /pɪər/ (peers, peering, peered)
1 V-I If you **peer at** something, you look at it very closely, usually because it is difficult to see clearly. ❑ *He found her peering at a computer print-out.*
2 N-COUNT Your **peers** are the people who are the same age as you or who have the same status as you. ❑ *He is popular with his peers.* [Sense 1 from Flemish. Sense 2 from Old French.]

peer pres|sure **N-NONCOUNT** If someone does something because of **peer pressure**, they do it because other people in their social group do it. ❑ *I don't let peer pressure affect me. I think for myself.*

peg /pɛg/ (pegs)
1 N-COUNT A **peg** is a small piece of wood or metal that you use for attaching one thing to another thing. ❑ *He builds furniture using wooden pegs instead of nails.*
2 N-COUNT A **peg** is a small hook on a wall that you hang things on. ❑ *His work jacket hung on the peg in the kitchen.*

pe|lag|ic en|vi|ron|ment /pəlædʒɪk ɛnvaɪrənmənt, -vaɪərn-/ or pelagic zone **N-SING** SCIENCE The **pelagic environment** or **pelagic zone** is the parts of the ocean that are away from the coast and above the ocean floor, and all the organisms that live there. Compare with **benthic environment**.

pel|vis /pɛlvɪs/ (pelvises) **N-COUNT** SCIENCE Your **pelvis** is the wide, curved group of bones between your back and your legs. [from Latin]

pen /pɛn/ (pens, penning, penned)
1 N-COUNT A **pen** is a long thin object that you use for writing with ink.
2 N-COUNT A **pen** is also a small area with a fence around it in which farm animals are kept for a short time. ❑ *...a holding pen for sheep.*
3 V-T If people or animals **are penned** somewhere or **are penned up**, they are forced to remain in a very small area. ❑ *The cattle were penned for the night.* ❑ *The animals were penned up in cages.* [from Old English]
→ look at Picture Dictionary: **office**

pen|al|ty /pɛnəlti/ (penalties)
1 N-COUNT A **penalty** is a punishment for doing something that is against a law or a rule. ❑ *The maximum penalty for dangerous driving is five years in prison.*
2 N-COUNT SPORTS In sports such as football and hockey, a **penalty** is a punishment for the team that breaks a rule, and an advantage for the other team. ❑ *His first goal came on a penalty kick in the fifty-second minute.* [from Medieval Latin]

pen|cil /pɛnsəl/ (pencils) **N-COUNT** ARTS A **pencil** is a thin piece of wood with a black or colored substance through the middle that you use to write or draw with. ❑ *She used a pencil and some blank paper to draw the picture.* [from Old French]
→ look at Picture Dictionary: **office**

pen|dant /pɛndənt/ (pendants) **N-COUNT** A **pendant** is an ornament on a chain that you wear around your neck. [from Old French]
→ look at Picture Dictionary: **jewelry**

P

pend|ing /pɛndɪŋ/

1 **ADJ** If something such as a legal procedure is **pending**, it is waiting to be dealt with or settled. [FORMAL] ❑ *He will not be available while the case is pending.*

2 **PREP** If something is done **pending** a future event, it is not done until that event happens. [FORMAL] ❑ *The police released him pending a further investigation.* [from French]

pen|etrate /pɛnɪtreɪt/ (**penetrates, penetrating, penetrated**)

1 **V-T** If someone or something **penetrates** an object, they get into it or pass through it. ❑ *X-rays can penetrate many objects.*

● **pen|etra|tion** /pɛnɪtreɪʃ°n/ **N-NONCOUNT** ❑ *The thick walls prevented penetration by rainwater.*

2 **V-T** If someone **penetrates** an organization or a group, they succeed in entering it although it is difficult to do so. ❑ *We need people who can speak foreign languages to penetrate these organizations.* [from Latin]

pen|guin /pɛŋgwɪn/ (**penguins**) **N-COUNT** A **penguin** is a black and white bird that lives in very cold places. Penguins can swim but they cannot fly. [from Welsh]

> **Word Link** insula ≈ island : insulate, insulator, peninsula

pen|in|su|la /pənɪnsələ, -nɪnsyə-/ (**peninsulas**) **N-COUNT** GEOGRAPHY A **peninsula** is a long narrow piece of land that sticks out from a larger piece of land and is almost completely surrounded by water. ❑ *...the Alaskan peninsula.* [from Latin]

→ look at Picture Dictionary: **landforms**

pe|nis /pinɪs/ (**penises**) **N-COUNT** SCIENCE A man's **penis** is the part of his body that he uses when he has sex and when he gets rid of urine. [from Latin]

pen|ny /pɛni/ (**pennies**) **N-COUNT** A **penny** is one cent, or a coin worth one cent. [INFORMAL] ❑ *The price of gasoline rose by more than a penny a gallon.* [from Old English]

pen|sion /pɛnʃ°n/ (**pensions**) **N-COUNT** A **pension** is money that you regularly receive from a business or the government after you stop working because of your age. ❑ *He gets a $35,000 a year pension.* [from Old French]

pen|ta|gon /pɛntəgɒn/ (**pentagons**)

1 **N-COUNT** MATH A **pentagon** is a shape with five straight sides.

2 **N-PROPER** SOCIAL STUDIES The **Pentagon** is the main building of the U.S. Defense Department, in Washington DC. ❑ *...a news conference at the Pentagon.* [from Latin]

pen|ta|ton|ic scale /pɛntətɒnɪk skeɪl/ (**pentatonic scales**) **N-COUNT** MUSIC A **pentatonic scale** is a musical scale that has five notes in each octave.

pent|house /pɛnthaʊs/ (**penthouses**) **N-COUNT** A **penthouse** is an expensive apartment at the top of a tall building. ❑ *She lives in an elegant Manhattan penthouse.* [from Old French]

peo|ple /pip°l/

1 **N-PLURAL** **People** are men, women, and children. ❑ *Millions of people have lost their homes.* ❑ *He's reading a book about the people of Angola.*

2 **N-PLURAL** The **people** is sometimes used to refer to ordinary men and women, in contrast to the government or the military. ❑ *...the will of the people.* [from Old French]

3 → see also **person**

peo|ple skills **N-PLURAL** BUSINESS **People skills** refers to the ability to deal with, influence, and communicate effectively with other people. ❑ *She has very good people skills and is able to manage a team.*

pep|per /pɛpər/ (**peppers, peppering, peppered**)

1 **N-NONCOUNT** **Pepper** is a spice with a hot taste that you put on food. ❑ *Season with salt and pepper.*

2 **N-COUNT** A **pepper** is a hollow green, red, or yellow vegetable with seeds inside it. ❑ *Thinly slice two red or green peppers.*

3 **V-T** If something **is peppered with** things, there are a lot of those things in it. ❑ *Readers' letters on the subject were peppered with words like "horrible" and "ugly."* [from Old English]

→ look at Picture Dictionary: **vegetables**

→ look at Word Web: **spice**

pepper|mint /pɛpərmɪnt/ (**peppermints**)

1 **N-NONCOUNT** **Peppermint** is a strong, sharp flavor from the peppermint plant.

2 **N-COUNT** A **peppermint** is a piece of candy with a peppermint flavor.

per /pər, STRONG pɜr/ **PREP** You use **per** to talk about each one of something. For example, if a vehicle is traveling at 40 miles **per** hour, it travels 40 miles each hour. ❑ *They spend $200 per week on groceries.* [from Latin]

per an|num /pər ænəm/ **ADV** A particular amount **per annum** means that amount

P

each year. ❑ *They must pay a fee of $3000 per annum.*

> **Word Link**   *per ≈ through, thoroughly : per*ceive, *per*fect, *per*mit

per|ceive /pərsi̱v/ (**perceives, perceiving, perceived**)

1 **V-T** If you **perceive** something, you notice or realize it, especially when it is not obvious. ❑ *A great artist teaches us to perceive reality in a different way.*

2 **V-T** If you **perceive** something **as** a particular thing, it is your opinion that it is that thing. ❑ *Stress is widely perceived as a cause of heart disease.* [from Old French]

per|cent /pərse̱nt/ (**percent**) **N-COUNT** MATH You use **percent** to talk about amounts as parts of a hundred. One hundred percent (100%) is all of something, and 50 percent (50%) is half. ❑ *Only ten percent of our customers live in this city.* [from Medieval Latin]

> **Word Link**   *age ≈ state of, related to : cour*age, *marri*age, *percent*age

> **Word Link**   *cent ≈ hundred : cent*s, *cent*ury, *per*cent*age*

per|cent|age /pərse̱ntɪdʒ/ (**percentages**) **N-COUNT** MATH A **percentage** is an amount of something. ❑ *He regularly eats foods with a high percentage of protein.* [from Medieval Latin]
→ look at Picture Dictionary: **fraction**

per|cep|tion /pərse̱pʃ³n/ (**perceptions**)

1 **N-COUNT** Your **perception of** something is the way that you think about it or the impression you have of it. ❑ *Our perceptions of death affect the way we live.*

2 **N-NONCOUNT** Someone who has **perception** realizes or notices things that are not obvious. ❑ *It did not require a lot of perception to realize the interview was over.*

3 **N-COUNT** **Perception** is the recognition of things using your senses, especially the sense of sight. [from Latin]

perch /pɜ̱rtʃ/ (**perches, perching, perched**)

1 **V-I** If you **perch on** something, you sit on the edge of it. ❑ *He perched on the corner of the desk.*

2 **V-I** When a bird **perches on** a branch or a wall, it lands on it and stands there. ❑ *Two doves perched on a nearby fence.* [from Old French]

per|cus|sion /pərkʌ̱ʃ³n/ **N-NONCOUNT** MUSIC **Percussion** instruments are musical instruments that you hit, such as drums. ❑ *This is a piece for the orchestra's powerful percussion section.* [from Latin]
→ look at Picture Dictionary: **percussion**
→ look at Word Web: **orchestra**

per|en|nial /pəre̱niəl/ **ADJ** You use **perennial** to describe situations or problems that keep occurring or that seem to exist all the time. ❑ *...the perennial problem of homelessness.* [from Latin]

per|fect (**perfects, perfecting, perfected**)

> **PRONUNCIATION HELP**
> Pronounce the adjective /pɜ̱rfɪkt/.
> Pronounce the verb /pərfe̱kt/.

1 **ADJ** Something that is **perfect** is as good as it could possibly be. ❑ *He spoke perfect English.* ❑ *Nobody is perfect.* ● **per|fect|ly** **ADV** ❑ *The system worked perfectly.*

2 **ADJ** If you say that something is **perfect for** a particular person, thing, or activity, you are emphasizing that it is very suitable for them or for that activity. ❑ *The pool area is*

P

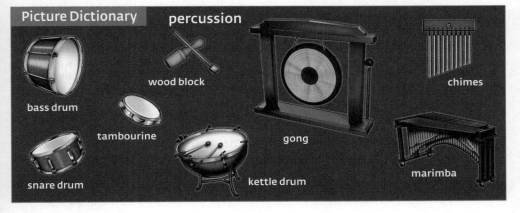

Picture Dictionary   **percussion**

bass drum

wood block

tambourine

snare drum

kettle drum

gong

chimes

marimba

perfect for entertaining.

3 **V-T** If you **perfect** something, you improve it so that it becomes as good as it can possibly be. ❑ *We perfected our recipe for vegetable stew.* [from Latin]

per|fec|tion /pərfɛkʃⁿn/ **N-NONCOUNT**
Perfection is the quality of being as good as possible. ❑ *The meat was cooked to perfection.* [from Latin]

per|fect tense (perfect tenses) **N-COUNT**
LANGUAGE ARTS In grammar, **the perfect tense** is the form that is used for talking about an action that has been completed before the present time. For example, in the sentence: "I have never seen that movie," the verb "see" is in the perfect tense.

per|form /pərfɔrm/ (performs, performing, performed)

1 **V-T** When you **perform** a task or an action, you do it. ❑ *You must perform this exercise correctly to avoid back pain.*

2 **V-T/V-I** If you **perform** a play, a piece of music, or a dance, you do it in front of an audience. ❑ *They will be performing works by Bach and Scarlatti.* ❑ *He began performing regularly in the early fifties.* ● **per|form|er** (**performers**) **N-COUNT** ❑ *She was one of the top jazz performers in New York City.*

3 **V-I** If someone or something **performs well**, they work well or achieve a good result. ❑ *He has not performed well on his exams.* ❑ *The industry has performed poorly this year.* [from Old French]

Word Partnership	Use **perform** with :
N	perform **miracles**, perform **tasks** **1**
ADJ	**able to** perform **1** **2**
V	**continue to** perform **1** **2**
ADV	perform **well** **3**

Word Link	*ance ≈ quality, state : insurance, performance, resistance*

per|for|mance /pərfɔrməns/ (performances)

1 **N-COUNT** If you give a **performance**, you entertain an audience by singing, dancing, or acting. ❑ *They were giving a performance of Bizet's "Carmen."*

2 **N-COUNT/N-NONCOUNT** Someone's or something's **performance** is how successful they are or how well they do something. ❑ *The study looked at the performance of 18 surgeons.* ❑ *He spoke about the poor performance of the economy.* [from Old French]

→ look at Word Web: **concert**

per|for|mance art **N-NONCOUNT** ARTS
Performance art is a theatrical presentation that includes various art forms such as dance, music, painting, and sculpture.

per|fume /pɜrfyum, pərfyum/ (perfumes)
N-COUNT/N-NONCOUNT **Perfume** is a liquid with a pleasant smell that you put on your skin. ❑ *The hall smelled of her mother's perfume.* [from French]

per|haps /pərhæps, præps/ **ADV** You use **perhaps** to show that you are not sure whether something is true, possible, or likely. ❑ *In the end they lost millions, perhaps billions.* ❑ *Perhaps, in time, they will understand.*

peri|he|lion /pɛrɪhiliən, -hilyən/ (perihelia)
N-COUNT SCIENCE The **perihelion** of a planet is the point in its orbit at which it is closest to the sun. Compare with **aphelion**. [from New Latin]

Word Link	*meter ≈ measuring : kilometer, meter, perimeter*

Word Link	*peri ≈ around : perimeter, periodic, peripheral*

pe|rim|eter /pərɪmɪtər/ (perimeters)
N-COUNT MATH The **perimeter** of a flat shape is the total distance around its edge. ❑ *To work out the perimeter of a rectangle, you need to know its length and width.* [from French]
→ look at Picture Dictionary: **area**

pe|ri|od /pɪəriəd/ (periods)

1 **N-COUNT** A **period** is a length of time. ❑ *He couldn't work for a long period of time.*

2 **N-COUNT** LANGUAGE ARTS A **period** is the punctuation mark . that you use at the end of a sentence.

3 **N-COUNT** A woman's **period** is the time when she loses blood from her body each month.

4 **N-COUNT** A **period** during a school day is a section of time when one subject is taught.

5 **N-COUNT** SCIENCE In chemistry, a **period** is one of the horizontal rows of substances in the periodic table of elements.

6 **PHRASE** SCIENCE The **period of revolution** of an object such as a planet is the time it takes to orbit another object such as a star. The Earth's period of revolution is one year.

7 **PHRASE** SCIENCE The **period of rotation** of an object such as a planet is the time it takes to turn once on its axis. The Earth's period of rotation is one day. [from Latin]

P

→ look at Picture Dictionary: **punctuation**
→ look at Word Web: **periodic table**

pe|ri|od|ic /pɪəriɒdɪk/ **ADJ** Periodic events or situations happen occasionally, at fairly regular intervals. ❏ *Periodic checks ensure that high standards are maintained.* [from Latin]

pe|ri|od|ic law **N-SING** **SCIENCE** The periodic law is a law in chemistry which describes the relationship between the chemical properties of elements and their atomic numbers.

pe|ri|od|ic ta|ble **N-SING** **SCIENCE** In chemistry, **the periodic table** is a table showing the chemical elements arranged according to their atomic numbers.
→ look at Word Web: **periodic table**

pe|riph|er|al /pərɪfərəl/ (**peripherals**) **ADJ** A **peripheral** activity or issue is not very important compared with other activities or issues. ❏ *The peripheral events were sometimes even more dramatic.* [from Late Latin]

pe|riph|er|al ner|vous sys|tem (**peripheral nervous systems**) **N-COUNT** **SCIENCE** Your **peripheral nervous system** is all the nerves in your body that are outside your brain and spinal cord. Compare with **central nervous system**.

per|ma|frost /pɜrməfrɔst/ **N-NONCOUNT** **SCIENCE** **Permafrost** is land that is permanently frozen to a great depth.

per|ma|nent /pɜrmənənt/ **ADJ** If something is **permanent** it continues forever or for a very long time. ❏ *Some ear infections can cause permanent damage.* ❏ *He's never had a permanent job.*

● **per|ma|nent|ly** **ADV** ❏ *His confidence has been permanently affected.* [from Latin]

Thesaurus permanent Also look up :		
ADJ	constant, continual, everlasting; (ant.) fleeting, temporary	

per|me|able /pɜrmiəbəl/ **ADJ** If a substance is **permeable**, something such as water or gas can pass through it or soak into it. ● **per|me|a|bil|i|ty** /pɜrmiəbɪləti/ **N-NONCOUNT** ❏ *...the permeability of the rock.* [from Late Latin]
→ look at Word Web: **amphibian**

per|mis|sion /pərmɪʃən/ **N-NONCOUNT** If you give someone **permission to** do something, you allow them to do it. ❏ *He asked permission to leave the room.* ❏ *They cannot leave the country without permission.* [from Latin]

Word Partnership Use permission with :	
V	ask (for) permission, get permission, permission to leave, need permission, obtain permission, receive permission, request permission, seek permission
ADJ	special permission, written permission

Word Link per ≈ through, thoroughly : perceive, perfect, permit

per|mit (**permits, permitting, permitted**)

PRONUNCIATION HELP
Pronounce the verb /pərmɪt/. Pronounce the noun /pɜrmɪt/.

1 **V-T** If someone **permits** you **to** do something, they allow you to do it. [FORMAL] ❏ *The guards permitted me to bring my camera.*

2 **N-COUNT** A **permit** is an official document

P

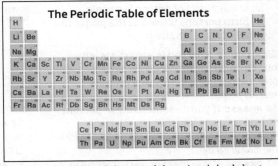

Word Web periodic table

Scientists started finding **elements** thousands of years ago. But it was not until 1869 that anyone understood how one element related to another. In that year, the Russian scientist Dmitri Mendeleyev created the **periodic table**. The vertical columns are called **groups**. Each group contains elements with similar **chemical** and **physical properties**. The horizontal rows are called **periods**. The elements in each row increase in **atomic mass** from left to right. Mendeleyev's original chart had many gaps. He predicted that scientists would find elements to fill these spaces. He was correct. He also predicted the properties of these new elements quite accurately.

that allows you to do something. ❏ *She hasn't got a work permit.* [from Latin]

per|mu|ta|tion /pɜrmyʊteɪʃⁿn/ (**permutations**) **N-COUNT** A permutation is one of the ways in which a number of things can be ordered or arranged. [from Latin]

per|pet|ual mo|tion ma|chine /pərpɛtʃuəl moʊʃⁿn məʃin/ (**perpetual motion machines**) **N-COUNT** SCIENCE A **perpetual motion machine** is an imaginary machine which, if it existed, would be able to continue working forever because it does not need energy from anything else.

per|severe /pɜrsɪvɪər/ (**perseveres, persevering, persevered**) **V-I** If you **persevere with** something difficult, you continue to do it. ❏ *Berman ignored their criticisms, and persevered with his plan.* [from Old French]

per|sis|tent /pərsɪstənt/
1 **ADJ** Something undesirable that is **persistent** continues to exist or happen for a long time. ❏ *...persistent fears.* ❏ *His cough grew more persistent.* ● **per|sis|tence** **N-NONCOUNT** ❏ *...the persistence of the same problems year after year.* ● **per|sis|tent|ly** **ADV** ❏ *...persistently high unemployment.*
2 **ADJ** Someone who is **persistent** continues trying to do something, even though it is difficult or other people are against it. ❏ *...a persistent critic of the president.* ● **per|sis|tence** **N-NONCOUNT** ❏ *Skill comes only with practice, patience, and persistence.* ● **per|sis|tent|ly** **ADV** ❏ *He persistently refused to see a doctor.* [from Latin]

per|son /pɜrsⁿn/ (**people** or **persons**)

LANGUAGE HELP
The usual plural of **person** is **people**. The form **persons** is used as the plural in formal or legal language.

1 **N-COUNT** A **person** is a man, a woman, or a child. ❏ *At least one person died and several others were injured.* ❏ *They were both lovely, friendly people.*
2 **PHRASE** If you do something **in person**, you do it yourself rather than letting someone else do it for you. ❏ *You must pick up the mail in person.*
3 **PHRASE** If you meet or see someone **in person**, you are in the same place as them, and not speaking to them on the telephone or writing to them. ❏ *She saw him in person*

for the first time last night.

4 **N-COUNT** LANGUAGE ARTS In grammar, we use the term **first person** when referring to "I" and "we," **second person** when referring to "you," and **third person** when referring to "he," "she," "it," "they," and all other noun groups. **Person** is also used like this when referring to the verb forms that go with these pronouns and noun groups. [from Old French]
5 → see also **people**

per|son|al /pɜrsən³l/
1 **ADJ** A **personal** opinion or experience relates to a particular person. ❏ *The story is based on his own personal experience.* ❏ *That's my personal opinion.*
2 **ADJ** If you give something **personal** care or attention, you deal with it yourself rather than letting someone else deal with it. ❏ *...a personal letter from the president's secretary.*
3 **ADJ** **Personal** matters relate to your feelings, relationships, and health. ❏ *Did he mention that he has any personal problems?* [from Old French]

per|son|al com|put|er (**personal computers**) **N-COUNT** TECHNOLOGY A **personal computer** is a computer that you use at work, school, or home. The short form **PC** is also used.

per|son|al|ity /pɜrsənælɪti/ (**personalities**)
1 **N-COUNT/N-NONCOUNT** Your **personality** is the qualities that make you different from other people. ❏ *She has such a kind, friendly personality.*
2 **N-COUNT** A famous person, especially in entertainment or sports, is sometimes called a **personality**. ❏ *...the radio and television personality, Johnny Carson.* [from Old French]

Word Partnership	Use **personality** with :
ADJ	**strong** personality, **unique** personality **1**
N	personality **trait** **1** **radio** personality, **television/TV** personality **2**

per|son|al|ly /pɜrsənəli/
1 **ADV** You use **personally** to emphasize that you are giving your own opinion. ❏ *Personally I think it's a waste of time.*
2 **ADV** If you do something **personally**, you do it yourself rather than letting someone else do it. ❏ *He wrote to them personally to explain the situation.*

P

3 **ADV** If you meet or know someone **personally**, you meet or know them in real life, rather than knowing about them. ❏ *He did not know them personally, but he was familiar with their reputation.* [from Old French]

per|son|nel /pɜrsənɛl/ **N-PLURAL** The **personnel** of an organization are the people who work for it. ❏ *The president will give a speech to military personnel at the army base.* [from French]

per|spec|tive /pərspɛktɪv/ (**perspectives**)
1 **N-COUNT** A particular **perspective** is a way of thinking about something. ❏ *The death of his father has given him a new perspective on life.*
2 **N-NONCOUNT** ARTS In art, **perspective** is a way of making some objects or people in a picture seem further away than others.
3 **PHRASE** If you get something **in perspective** or **into perspective**, you judge its real importance by considering it in relation to everything else. If you get something **out of perspective**, you fail to do this. ❏ *Remember to keep things in perspective.* ❏ *I think I've let things get out of perspective.* [from Medieval Latin]

Word Link *spir ≈ breath : inspire, perspiration, respiration*

per|spi|ra|tion /pɜrspɪreɪʃən/ **N-NONCOUNT** **Perspiration** is the liquid that appears on your skin when you are hot. [FORMAL] ❏ *His hands were wet with perspiration.* [from Latin]

Word Link *suad, suas ≈ urging : dissuade, persuade, persuasive*

per|suade /pərsweɪd/ (**persuades, persuading, persuaded**)
1 **V-T** If you **persuade** someone **to** do something, you make them do it by talking to them. ❏ *My husband persuaded me to come.*
2 **V-T** If you **persuade** someone that something is true, you say things that make them believe that it is true. ❏ *He persuaded himself that his actions could do no harm.* [from Latin]

Thesaurus **persuade** Also look up :
V   cajole, convince, influence, sway, talk into, win over; (*ant.*) discourage, dissuade **1** **2**

Word Partnership Use **persuade** with :
V   **attempt to** persuade, **be able to** persuade, **fail to** persuade, **try to** persuade **1** **2**

per|sua|sion /pərsweɪʒən/ **N-NONCOUNT** **Persuasion** is the process of making someone do or think something. ❏ *After much persuasion from Ellis, she agreed to perform.* [from Latin]

per|sua|sive /pərsweɪsɪv/ **ADJ** Someone or something that is **persuasive** is likely to persuade a person to believe or do a particular thing. ❏ *...persuasive arguments.* ❏ *I can be very persuasive.* [from Latin]

per|vade /pərveɪd/ (**pervades, pervading, pervaded**) **V-T** If something **pervades** a place or a thing, it is a noticeable feature throughout it. [FORMAL] ❏ *The smell of glue pervaded the factory.* [from Latin]

Word Link *ism ≈ action or state : communism, optimism, pessimism*

pes|si|mism /pɛsɪmɪzəm/ **N-NONCOUNT** **Pessimism** is the belief that bad things are going to happen. ❏ *There was a general pessimism about the economy.* ● **pes|si|mist** (**pessimists**) **N-COUNT** ❏ *I'm a natural pessimist, so I usually expect the worst.* ● **pes|si|mis|tic** /pɛsɪmɪstɪk/ **ADJ** ❏ *She is so pessimistic about the future.* [from Latin]

pest /pɛst/ (**pests**)
1 **N-COUNT** **Pests** are insects or small animals that damage crops or food. ❏ *They use chemicals to fight pests and diseases.*
2 **N-COUNT** If someone, especially a child, is a **pest**, they are annoying you. [INFORMAL] ❏ *He climbed on the table, pulled my hair, and was generally a pest.* [from Latin]
→ look at Word Web: **farm**

pes|ti|cide /pɛstɪsaɪd/ (**pesticides**) **N-COUNT/N-NONCOUNT** **Pesticides** are chemicals that farmers put on their crops to kill harmful insects. [from Latin]
→ look at Word Web: **pollution**

pet /pɛt/ (**pets, petting, petted**)
1 **N-COUNT** A **pet** is an animal that you keep in your home. ❏ *He loved his pet dog.* ❏ *You should not keep wild animals as pets.*
2 **V-T** If you **pet** an animal, you pat or stroke it in an affectionate way. ❏ *He petted the dog.*
→ look at Word Web: **pet**

P

Word Web   pet

Americans love **pets**. They own more than 70 million **dogs**, 80 million **cats**, and 45 million **birds**. They also have more than 75 million small **mammals** and **reptiles**, and millions of **fish**. Recent studies suggest that adult pet owners are healthier than adults who don't have **companion animals**. One study suggests that pet owners have lower blood pressure. Another study showed that people with pets went to the doctor less often than people without pets.

pet|al /pɛtᵊl/ (**petals**) **N-COUNT** The **petals** of a flower are the thin colored parts that form the flower. ❑ *Her perfume smelled of rose petals.* [from New Latin]
→ look at Picture Dictionary: **flowers**

pe|ti|tion /pətɪʃᵊn/ (**petitions, petitioning, petitioned**)
1 **N-COUNT** SOCIAL STUDIES A **petition** is a document that contains the signatures of a group of people who are asking a government or other official group to do a particular thing. ❑ *People feel so strongly that we recently presented the government with a petition signed by 4,500 people.*
2 **V-T/V-I** If you **petition** someone in authority, you make a formal request to them. ❑ *...couples petitioning for divorce.* ❑ *All the attempts to petition Congress have failed.* [from Latin]

Pe|tri dish /pitri dɪʃ/ (**Petri dishes**) **N-COUNT** SCIENCE A **Petri dish** is a shallow circular dish that is used in laboratories for producing groups of microorganisms. [from German]
→ look at Word Web: **laboratory**

pet|ri|fied /pɛtrɪfaɪd/ **ADJ** If you are **petrified**, you are extremely frightened. ❑ *I've always been petrified of being alone.* [from French]

pe|tro|leum /pətroʊliəm/ **N-NONCOUNT** SCIENCE **Petroleum** is oil that is found under the surface of the Earth or under the sea bed. Gasoline and kerosene are obtained from petroleum. [from Medieval Latin]
→ look at Word Webs: **petroleum, energy, oil**

pet|ty /pɛti/ (**pettier, pettiest**)
1 **ADJ** You can use **petty** to describe things such as problems, rules, or arguments that you think are unimportant. ❑ *Fights would start over petty things.* ❑ *...endless rules and petty regulations.*
2 **ADJ** If you describe someone as **petty**, you disapprove of them because they are willing to be unpleasant to other people because of small, unimportant things. ❑ *Always give your best, never be petty.* ● **pet|ti|ness** **N-NONCOUNT** ❑ *...nasty pettiness.*
3 **ADJ** **Petty** is used of people or actions that are less important, serious, or great than others. ❑ *...petty crime, such as purse-snatching.* [from Old French]

Word Web   petroleum

Most **petroleum** is used as **fuel**. We use **gasoline** to power our cars and **heating oil** to warm our homes. About 20% of **crude oil** becomes **gas** and 10% becomes heating oil. Today 90% of the **energy** used in transportation comes from petroleum. Other petroleum products include household items such as **paint**, **deodorant**, and **shampoo**. Some of our clothes are also made using petroleum. These include **shoes**, **sweaters**, and **polyester shirts** and **dresses**. Petroleum products are also important for building new houses. They are used to make water **pipes**, **shower** doors, and even **toilet** seats.

petu|lant /pɛtʃələnt/ **ADJ** Someone who is **petulant** is angry and upset in an unreasonable, childish way. ❑ *He's just being silly and petulant.* ● **petu|lance** **N-NONCOUNT** ❑ *His petulance made her impatient.* [from Old French]

pH /pi eɪtʃ/ **N-NONCOUNT** SCIENCE The **pH** of a solution indicates how acid or alkaline the solution is. A pH of less than 7 indicates that it is an acid, and a pH of more than 7 indicates that it is an alkali.

phan|tom /fæntəm/ (**phantoms**)
■ **N-COUNT** A **phantom** is a ghost. ❑ *They vanished down the stairs like two phantoms.*
■ **ADJ** You use **phantom** to describe something that does not really exist, but that someone believes or pretends does exist. ❑ *...phantom pain.* ❑ *He invented a phantom life.* [from Old French]

Word Link | *pharma ≈ drug : pharmaceutical, pharmacist, pharmacy*

phar|ma|ceu|ti|cal /fɑrməsutɪkəl/ (**pharmaceuticals**)
■ **ADJ** BUSINESS **Pharmaceutical** means connected with the industrial production of medicines. ❑ *...a Swiss pharmaceutical company.*
■ **N-PLURAL** **Pharmaceuticals** are medicines. [from Late Latin]

Word Link | *ist ≈ one who practices : biologist, dramatist, pharmacist*

phar|ma|cist /fɑrməsɪst/ (**pharmacists**)
N-COUNT A **pharmacist** is a person whose job is to prepare and sell medicines. ❑ *Ask your pharmacist for advice.* [from Medieval Latin]

phar|ma|cy /fɑrməsi/ (**pharmacies**)
N-COUNT A **pharmacy** is a place where you can buy medicines. ❑ *Pick up the medicine from the pharmacy.* [from Medieval Latin]

phar|ynx /færɪŋks/ (**pharynges** /fərɪndʒiz/ or **pharynxes** /færɪŋksɪz/) **N-COUNT** SCIENCE Your **pharynx** is the area at the back of your throat, which connects your mouth and nose to your windpipe. [from New Latin]

phase /feɪz/ (**phases, phasing, phased**)
■ **N-COUNT** A **phase** is a particular stage in a process. ❑ *6000 women will take part in the first phase of the project.*
■ **N-COUNT** SCIENCE The **phases of** the moon are the different stages of the moon's appearance, for example a new moon or a full moon. [from New Latin]
▶ **phase in** If a new way of doing

something **is phased in**, it is introduced gradually. ❑ *The reforms will be phased in over three years.*
▶ **phase out** If something **is phased out**, people gradually stop using it. ❑ *They think that the present system should be phased out.*

Ph.D. /pi eɪtʃ di/ (**Ph.D.s**) also **PhD** **N-COUNT** A **Ph.D.** is a degree awarded to people who have done advanced research into a particular subject. **Ph.D.** is short for **Doctor of Philosophy**. ❑ *He is highly educated and has a Ph.D. in chemistry.*

phe|nom|enon /fɪnɒmɪnɒn/ (**phenomena**) **N-COUNT** A **phenomenon** is something that is observed to happen or exist. [FORMAL] ❑ *...natural phenomena such as thunder and lightning.* [from Late Latin]
→ look at Word Webs: **experiment, science**

phe|no|type /finətaɪp/ (**phenotypes**) **N-COUNT/N-NONCOUNT** SCIENCE The **phenotype** of an animal or plant is all the physical characteristics it has as a result of the interaction between its genes and the environment. [from Greek]

phero|mone /fɛrəmoʊn/ (**pheromones**) **N-COUNT** SCIENCE Some animals and insects produce chemicals called **pheromones** that affect the behavior of other animals and insects of the same type, for example by attracting them sexually. [from Greek]

phil|an|throp|ic /fɪlənθrɒpɪk/ **ADJ** A **philanthropic** person or organization gives money or some other help to people who need it. ❑ *Some of the best services for the seniors are sponsored by philanthropic organizations.* [from Late Latin]

phi|lan|thro|py /fɪlænθrəpi/ **N-NONCOUNT** **Philanthropy** is the practice of giving money to people who need it, without wanting anything in return. ❑ *...a retired banker well known for his philanthropy.* [from Late Latin]

phil|har|mon|ic /fɪlhɑrmɒnɪk, fɪlər-/
■ **ADJ** A **philharmonic** orchestra is a large orchestra that plays classical music. ❑ *The Lithuanian Philharmonic Orchestra played Beethoven's Ninth Symphony.*
■ **N-SING** **Philharmonic** is also a noun. ❑ *He will conduct the Los Angeles Philharmonic in the final concert of the season.* [from French]

phi|lol|ogy /fɪlɒlədʒi/ **N-NONCOUNT** **Philology** is the study of words, especially

P

the history and development of the words in a particular language.

● **phi|lolo|gist** (**philologists**) **N-COUNT** ❏ *He is a philologist, specializing in American poetry.* [from Latin]

phi|loso|pher /fɪlɒsəfər/ (**philosophers**) **N-COUNT** A **philosopher** is a person who studies or writes about philosophy. ❏ *He admired the Greek philosopher Plato.* [from Old French] → look at Word Web: **philosophy**

philo|sophi|cal /fɪləsɒfɪkᵊl/ **1** **ADJ** **Philosophical** means concerned with or relating to philosophy. ❏ *They often had philosophical discussions.* ● **philo|sophi|cal|ly** /fɪləsɒfɪkli/ **ADV** ❏ *He's philosophically opposed to war.* **2** **ADJ** Someone who is **philosophical** remains calm when disappointing or disturbing things happen, and does not get upset. ❏ *Lewis grew philosophical about life.* ● **philo|sophi|cal|ly** **ADV** ❏ *She says philosophically, "It could have been far worse."* [from Old French]

phi|loso|phy /fɪlɒsəfi/ (**philosophies**) **1** **N-NONCOUNT** **Philosophy** is the study of ideas about the meaning of life. ❏ *She is studying traditional Chinese philosophy.* **2** **N-COUNT** A **philosophy** is a particular theory or belief. ❏ *The best philosophy is to change to a low-sugar diet.* [from Old French] → look at Word Web: **philosophy**

phish|ing /fɪʃɪŋ/ **N-NONCOUNT** TECHNOLOGY **Phishing** is the practice of trying to trick people into giving secret financial information by sending them emails that look as if they come from a bank. ❏ *Phishing emails look like genuine emails from your bank.*

phlo|em /floʊɛm/ (**phloems**) **N-COUNT/N-NONCOUNT** SCIENCE **Phloem** is the layer of material in plants that carries food from the leaves to the rest of the plant. Compare with **xylem**. [from German]

pho|bia /foʊbiə/ (**phobias**) **N-COUNT** A **phobia** is a strong irrational fear or hatred of something. ❏ *The man had a phobia about flying.* [from Greek]

phone /foʊn/ (**phones, phoning, phoned**) **1** **N-COUNT** A **phone** is a piece of equipment that you use to talk to someone else in another place. ❏ *Two minutes later the phone rang.* **2** → see also **cellphone** **3** **V-T/V-I** When you **phone** someone, or when you **phone** them **up**, you contact them and speak to them by telephone. ❏ *He phoned Laura up to see if she was better.* ❏ *"Did anybody phone?" asked Alberg.* **4** **PHRASE** If someone is **on the phone**, they are speaking to someone by telephone. ❏ *She's always on the phone.* [from Greek] → look at Picture Dictionary: **office**

phone call (**phone calls**) **N-COUNT** If you make a **phone call**, you enter a number into a telephone and speak to someone who is in another place. ❏ *I have to make a phone call.*

pho|neme /foʊnim/ (**phonemes**) **N-COUNT** LANGUAGE ARTS A **phoneme** is the smallest unit of significant sound in a language. [from French]

Word Web philosophy

Philosophy helps us **understand** ourselves and the purpose of our lives. **Philosophers** have studied the same **issues** for thousands of years. The Chinese philosopher Confucius* wrote about personal and **political morals**. He taught that people should love others and honor their parents. They should do what is right, not what is best for themselves. He thought that a ruler who had to use force had failed. The Greek philosopher Plato* wrote about politics and science. Later, Aristotle* created a system of **logic** and **reasoning**. He wanted to be absolutely sure of what is true and what is not.

Plato   *Aristotle*   *Confucius*

Plato (427-347 BC)
Aristotle (384-322 BC)
Confucius (551-479 BC)

pho|ne|mic aware|ness /fənimɪk/
N-NONCOUNT LANGUAGE ARTS **Phonemic
awareness** is the ability to distinguish the
small, separate sounds that spoken words
consist of.

phon|ics /fɒnɪks/ **N-NONCOUNT**
LANGUAGE ARTS **Phonics** is a method of
teaching people to read by training them to
associate written letters with their sounds.
[from Greek]

pho|no|gram /founəgræm/ (**phonograms**)
N-COUNT LANGUAGE ARTS A **phonogram** is
a written letter or symbol, or a series of
written letters or symbols, that represents
a word or part of a word. For example, the
symbol "@" is a phonogram that represents
the word "at," and the letters "ake" are a
phonogram that appears in words such as
"make" and "take."

pho|ny /founi/ (**phonier, phoniest, phonies**)
also **phoney**
1 **ADJ** Something that is **phony** is not real.
[INFORMAL] ❑ He made some phony excuse.
❑ I answered in a phony British accent.
2 **ADJ** Someone who is **phony** is pretending
to be better or nicer than they really are.
[INFORMAL] ❑ The people there are so phony.

phos|pho|lip|id /fɒsfoulɪpɪd, -laɪp-/
(**phospholipids**) **N-COUNT** SCIENCE
Phospholipids are fats that form an important
part of the structure of cell membranes.

pho|to /foutou/ (**photos**) **N-COUNT** A **photo**
is the same as a **photograph**. [from Greek]
→ look at Word Web: **photography**

photo|bomb /foutoubɒm/ (**photobombs,
photobombing, photobombed**) **V-T** If you
photobomb someone, you jump in front of
the camera just as someone is taking a
photograph of them. ❑ This is the one where my
sister photobombed me.

photo|cell /foutousɛl/ (**photocells**) or
photoelectric cell **N-COUNT** SCIENCE
A **photocell** or a **photoelectric cell** is a device
that measures the amount of light that is
present and converts it into electricity.

photo|copi|er /foutəkɒpiər/ (**photocopiers**)
N-COUNT A **photocopier** is a machine that
copies documents by photographing them.

photo|copy /foutəkɒpi/ (**photocopies,
photocopying, photocopied**)
1 **N-COUNT** A **photocopy** is a copy of a
document that you make using a
photocopier. ❑ He gave me a photocopy of the
letter.
2 **V-T** If you **photocopy** a document, you
make a copy of it using a photocopier. ❑ He
photocopied the documents before sending them off.

photo|graph /foutəgræf/ (**photographs,
photographing, photographed**)
1 **N-COUNT** ARTS A **photograph** is a picture
that you take with a camera. ❑ He wants to
take some photographs of the house.
2 **V-T** ARTS When you **photograph** someone
or something, you use a camera to take a
picture of them. [FORMAL] ❑ She photographed
the children.

pho|tog|ra|pher /fətɒgrəfər/
(**photographers**) **N-COUNT** A **photographer**
is someone who takes photographs as a job
or a hobby. ❑ He's a professional photographer.
→ look at Word Web: **photography**

photo|graph|ic /foutəgræfɪk/ **ADJ**
Photographic means connected with
photographs or photography.
❑ ...photographic equipment.

pho|tog|ra|phy /fətɒgrəfi/ **N-NONCOUNT**
ARTS **Photography** is the skill or process of
producing photographs. ❑ Photography is one
of her hobbies.
→ look at Word Web: **photography**

P

It's easy to **take** a **picture** with a digital **camera**. You just
look through the **viewfinder** and push the **shutter button**.
But professional **photographers** need to produce high
quality **photos**. So their job is harder. They check the
lighting and carefully **focus** the camera. They usually take
several **shots**, one after another. Sometimes a photographer
will **crop** a photo or **enlarge** it to create a more striking
image.

photo|recep|tor /foʊtoʊrɪsɛptər/ (**photoreceptors**) **N-COUNT** SCIENCE **Photoreceptors** are very small structures in the eye which can detect and respond to light.

photo|sphere /foʊtəsfɪər/ (**photospheres**) **N-COUNT** SCIENCE The **photosphere** is the surface of the sun, where the sun's gases appear solid.

photo|syn|the|sis /foʊtoʊsɪnθəsɪs/ **N-NONCOUNT** SCIENCE **Photosynthesis** is the way that green plants make their food using the light of the sun.
→ look at Word Web: **photosynthesis**

pho|tot|ro|pism /foʊtɒtrəpɪzəm/ (**phototropisms**) **N-COUNT/N-NONCOUNT** SCIENCE **Phototropism** is the tendency of a plant to grow in the direction of a light source.

pho|to|vol|ta|ic /foʊtoʊvɒlteɪɪk/ **ADJ** SCIENCE A **photovoltaic** cell or panel is a device that uses sunlight to cause a chemical reaction which produces electricity.

phras|al verb /freɪzəl vɜrb/ (**phrasal verbs**) **N-COUNT** LANGUAGE ARTS A **phrasal verb** is a combination of a verb and an adverb or a preposition, for example "get over" or "give up," which together have a particular meaning.

phrase /freɪz/ (**phrases, phrasing, phrased**)
◼ **N-COUNT** LANGUAGE ARTS A **phrase** is a group of words that you use together as part of a sentence, for example "in the morning." ❑ *At the end of the book, there is a glossary of useful words and phrases.*
◻ **N-COUNT** MUSIC A **phrase** is a short section of a piece of music which expresses a musical idea.
◼ **V-T** If you **phrase** something in a particular way, you say or write it in that way. ❑ *I would have phrased it quite differently.* ❑ *The speech was carefully phrased.* [from Latin]

phras|ing /freɪzɪŋ/ **N-NONCOUNT** LANGUAGE ARTS The **phrasing** of someone who is singing, playing a piece of music, acting, dancing, or reading something aloud is the way in which they divide up the work by pausing slightly in appropriate places. [from Latin]

phy|lum /faɪləm/ (**phyla**) **N-COUNT** SCIENCE A **phylum** is a group of related species of animals or plants. Compare with **kingdom** and **class**. [from New Latin]

phys ed /fɪz ɛd/ **N-NONCOUNT** Phys ed is the same as **physical education**. [INFORMAL] ❑ *Don teaches phys ed.*

Word Link	physi ≈ of nature : physical, physician, physics

physi|cal /fɪzɪkəl/
◼ **ADJ** **Physical** means connected with a person's body, rather than with their mind. ❑ *Physical activity promotes good health.*
● **physi|cal|ly** **ADV** ❑ *Kerry is physically active and in excellent health.*
◻ **ADJ** **Physical** things are real things that can be touched and seen. ❑ *There is no physical barrier to prevent escape.* ❑ *...physical evidence to support the story.* [from Latin]
→ look at Word Webs: **diagnosis, periodic table**

physi|cal change (**physical changes**) **N-COUNT/N-NONCOUNT** SCIENCE When there is a **physical change** to a substance, its form or appearance changes but it does not become a different substance.

physi|cal edu|ca|tion **N-NONCOUNT** SPORTS **Physical education** is the school subject in which students do physical exercises or take part in physical games and sports.

Word Web   photosynthesis

Plants make their own food from **sunlight, water**, and **soil**. They get water and **minerals** from the ground through their roots. They also absorb **carbon dioxide** from the air through tiny holes in their leaves. The green pigment in plant leaves is called **chlorophyll**. It combines **solar energy** with water and carbon dioxide to produce **glucose**. This process is called **photosynthesis**. During the process, the plant releases **oxygen** into the atmosphere. It uses some of the glucose to grow larger. When humans and other animals eat plants, they also make use of this stored **energy**.

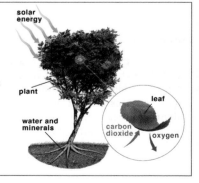

physi|cal prop|er|ty (**physical properties**)
N-COUNT SCIENCE The **physical properties** of
a substance are qualities such as its size and
shape that can be measured without
changing what the substance is.

physi|cal sci|ence (**physical sciences**)
N-COUNT SCIENCE The **physical sciences** are
branches of science such as physics,
chemistry, and geology that are concerned
with natural forces and with things that do
not have life.

physi|cal ther|a|py **N-NONCOUNT** Physical
therapy is medical treatment given to
people who have injured part of their body.
It involves exercise, massage, or heat
treatment.
→ look at Word Web: **illness**

phy|si|cian /fɪzɪʃ³n/ (**physicians**) **N-COUNT**
A **physician** is a medical doctor. [FORMAL]
❑ *Ask your family physician for advice.* [from
Old French]
→ look at Word Webs: **diagnosis, hospital,**
medicine

physi|cist /fɪzɪsɪst/ (**physicists**) **N-COUNT**
A **physicist** is a person who studies physics.
❑ *He was one of the best nuclear physicists in the*
country. [from Latin]

phys|ics /fɪzɪks/ **N-NONCOUNT** SCIENCE
Physics is the scientific study of things
such as heat, light, and sound. ❑ *His favorite*
school subjects were chemistry and physics.
[from Latin]

phyto|plank|ton /faɪtoʊplæŋktən/
N-PLURAL SCIENCE **Phytoplankton** are tiny
plants such as algae that are found in
plankton.

pia|nist /piænɪst, piənɪst/ (**pianists**)
N-COUNT MUSIC A **pianist** is a person who
plays the piano. ❑ *She wants to be a concert*
pianist. [from Italian]

pi|ano /piænoʊ, pyænoʊ/ (**pianos**)
N-COUNT/N-NONCOUNT MUSIC A **piano** is a
large musical instrument that you play by
pressing black and white keys. ❑ *I taught*
myself how to play the piano. [from Italian]
→ look at Picture Dictionary: **keyboard**
→ look at Word Web: **music**

pic|co|lo /pɪkəloʊ/ (**piccolos**)
N-COUNT/N-NONCOUNT MUSIC A **piccolo** is a
musical instrument that is like a small
flute. [from Italian]

pick /pɪk/ (**picks, picking, picked**)
1 **V-T** If you **pick** a particular person or
thing, you choose that one. ❑ *Mr. Nowell*
picked ten people to interview.
2 **V-T** When you **pick** flowers, fruit, or
leaves, you take them from a plant or tree.
❑ *I've picked some flowers from the garden.*
3 **V-T** If you **pick** a fight **with** someone,
you deliberately start one. ❑ *He picked a fight*
with a waiter. [from French]
▶ **pick on** If someone **picks on** you, they
repeatedly criticize you or treat you
unkindly. [INFORMAL] ❑ *Bullies often pick on*
younger children.
▶ **pick out** **1** If you **pick out** someone or
something, you recognize them when it is
difficult to see them. ❑ *I had trouble picking out*
the words, even with my glasses on.
2 If you **pick** someone or something **out**,
you choose them from a group of people or
things. ❑ *They picked me out to represent the*
whole team.
▶ **pick up** **1** When you **pick** something
up, you lift it up. ❑ *He picked his cap up from*
the floor.
2 When you **pick up** someone or
something, you collect them from a place,
often in a car. ❑ *Please could you pick me up at*
5pm? ❑ *She went to her parents' house to pick up*
some clean clothes.
3 If you **pick up** a skill or an idea, you learn
it without really trying over a period of
time. [INFORMAL] ❑ *Her children have picked up*
English really quickly.
4 If you **pick up** an illness, you get it from
somewhere or something. ❑ *They've picked up*
an infection from something they've eaten.

Thesaurus	pick	Also look up :
v	choose, decide on, elect, select **1**	
	collect, gather, harvest, pull **2**	

pick|le /pɪk³l/ (**pickles**)
N-COUNT/N-NONCOUNT **Pickles** are small
cucumbers that are kept in liquid for a long
time to give them a strong, sharp taste.
❑ *We had hamburgers with pickles, ketchup, and*
mustard. [from Middle Dutch]

pic|nic /pɪknɪk/
(**picnics, picnicking,**
picnicked)
1 **N-COUNT** When
people have a **picnic,**
they eat a meal
outdoors, usually in

picnic

a park or a forest, or at the beach.
❑ *We're going on a picnic tomorrow.*
2 **v-I** When people **picnic** somewhere, they have a picnic. ❑ *Afterward, we picnicked by the river.* [from French]
→ look at Word Web: **park**

pic|ture /pɪktʃər/ (**pictures, picturing, pictured**)

1 **N-COUNT** ARTS A **picture** is a drawing or a painting. ❑ *She drew a picture with colored chalk.*

2 **N-COUNT** A **picture** is a photograph. ❑ *I love taking pictures of animals.*

3 **N-COUNT** You can refer to a movie as a **picture.** ❑ *...a director of action pictures.*

4 **v-T** If you **picture** something, you think of it and see it in your mind. ❑ *He pictured her with long black hair.*

5 **v-T** If someone or something **is pictured** in a newspaper or a magazine, they appear in a photograph in it. ❑ *The golfer is pictured on the front page.*

6 **N-COUNT** A **picture** of something is a description of it or an indication of what it is like. ❑ *I'll try and give you a better picture of what the boys do.* [from Latin]
→ look at Word Web: **photography**

Thesaurus	picture	Also look up :
N	drawing, illustration, image, painting **1**	
	photograph **2**	
V	envision, imagine, visualize **4**	

Word Partnership	Use picture with :
ADJ	**pretty as a** picture **1**
	mental picture **4**
	accurate picture, **clear** picture, **complete** picture, **larger** picture, **overall** picture, **whole** picture **4** **6**

pie /paɪ/ (**pies**) **N-COUNT/N-NONCOUNT**

A **pie** is a dish of fruit, meat, or vegetables that is covered with pastry and baked. ❑ *We each had a slice of apple pie.*
→ look at Picture Dictionary: **dessert**

pie

piece /piːs/ (**pieces, piecing, pieced**)

1 **N-COUNT** A **piece of** something is a part of it. ❑ *You must only take one piece of cake.* ❑ *Cut the chicken into pieces.*

2 **N-COUNT** A **piece of** something is an amount of it. ❑ *That's an interesting piece of information.* ❑ *This is his finest piece of work yet.* ❑ *He has composed 1500 pieces of music for TV.*

3 **N-COUNT** A **piece** is something that is written or created, such as an article, a work of art, or a musical composition. [FORMAL] ❑ *She wrote a piece on Gwyneth Paltrow for the "New Yorker."* ❑ *Each piece is painted by an artist according to your design.*

4 **PHRASE** If you **go to pieces**, you are so upset or nervous that you lose control of yourself and cannot do what you should do. [INFORMAL] ❑ *I hope I never have to experience anything like that. I would go to pieces.*

5 **PHRASE** If something is **in pieces**, it is broken. ❑ *The china vase was in pieces on the floor.* [from Old French]
→ look at Word Web: **chess**

▸ **piece together** If you **piece** something **together**, you gradually make it by joining several things or parts together. ❑ *This process is like piecing together a jigsaw puzzle.*

pie chart (**pie charts**) **N-COUNT** MATH SCIENCE A **pie chart** is a circle divided into sections to show the relative proportions of a set of things.

pier /pɪər/ (**piers**) **N-COUNT** A **pier** is a long, flat structure that is built out from the land at the edge of an area of water so that people can get into and out of boats easily. ❑ *The ship was tied up at Chicago's Navy Pier.*

pierce /pɪərs/ (**pierces, piercing, pierced**)

1 **v-T** If you **pierce** something, you make a hole in it with a sharp object. ❑ *Pierce the chicken with a sharp knife to check that it is cooked.*

2 **v-T** If you have your ears **pierced**, small holes are made through them so that you can wear earrings in them. ❑ *I'm having my ears pierced on Saturday.* [from Old French]

pierc|ing /pɪərsɪŋ/ **ADJ** A **piercing** sound is high and clear in a sharp and unpleasant way. ❑ *She let out a piercing scream.* [from Old French]

pig /pɪg/ (**pigs**)

1 **N-COUNT** A **pig** is a farm animal with a fat body and short legs, that is often kept for its meat. ❑ *Kids can help feed the pigs.*

2 → see also **guinea pig**

3 **N-COUNT** **Pig** is a rude way of talking about someone who is unkind or who eats too much. [INFORMAL] ❑ *You've eaten my toast, you greedy pig!*
→ look at Word Web: **meat**

pi|geon /pɪdʒɪn/ (**pigeons**) **N-COUNT** A **pigeon** is a large gray bird that is often seen in cities. [from Old French]

Pi|la|tes /pɪlɑtiz/ **N-NONCOUNT** SPORTS **Pilates** is a type of exercise that helps you to bend more easily, and develops the muscles in your back and abdomen. ❑ *I do Pilates every day before breakfast.* [from German]

pile /paɪl/ (**piles, piling, piled**)
1 **N-COUNT** A **pile of** things is several of them lying on top of each other. ❑ *We searched through the pile of boxes.* ❑ *There was a huge pile of shoes by the door.*
2 **V-T** If you **pile** things somewhere, you put them there so that they form a pile. ❑ *He was piling clothes into the suitcase.* [from Old French]
▶ **pile up** **1** If you **pile** things **up**, you put one on top of another to form a pile. ❑ *They piled up rocks to build a wall.*
2 If you **pile up** work, problems, or losses, or if they **pile up**, you get more and more of them. ❑ *Problems were piling up at work.*

Pil|grim /pɪlgrɪm/ (**Pilgrims**) **N-COUNT** SOCIAL STUDIES The **Pilgrims** were the people who left England and went to live in America in the early seventeenth century. [from Provençal]

pill /pɪl/ (**pills**)
1 **N-COUNT** **Pills** are small solid round pieces of medicine that you swallow. ❑ *Why do I have to take all these pills?*
2 **N-SING** If a woman is **on the pill**, she takes a special pill that keeps her from becoming pregnant. ❑ *She has been on the pill for three years.* [from Middle Flemish]

pil|lage /pɪlɪdʒ/ (**pillages, pillaging, pillaged**)
1 **V-T** If a group of people **pillage** a place, they steal property from it using violent methods. ❑ *Soldiers went on a rampage, pillaging stores and shooting.* ● **pil|lag|ing** **N-NONCOUNT** ❑ *The police were unable to stop the pillaging of the national museum.*
2 **N-NONCOUNT** **Pillage** is also a noun. ❑ *There were no signs of violence or pillage.* [from Old French]

pil|lar /pɪlər/ (**pillars**)
1 **N-COUNT** A **pillar** is a tall solid structure that usually supports part of a building. ❑ *There were eight huge pillars supporting the roof.*
2 **N-COUNT** If you describe someone as a **pillar of** the community, you approve of

them because they play an important and active part in the community. [from Old French]

pil|low /pɪloʊ/ (**pillows**) **N-COUNT** A **pillow** is a soft object that you rest your head on when you are in bed. [from Old English]
→ look at Picture Dictionary: **bed**
→ look at Word Web: **sleep**

pi|lot /paɪlət/ (**pilots, piloting, piloted**)
1 **N-COUNT** A **pilot** is a person who controls an aircraft. ❑ *He spent seventeen years as an airline pilot.*
2 **V-T** If someone **pilots** an aircraft or ship, they act as its pilot. ❑ *He piloted his own plane to Washington.*
3 **ADJ** A **pilot** plan or a **pilot** project is one that is used to test an idea before deciding whether to introduce it on a larger scale. ❑ *We are going to run a pilot study funded by the government.* [from French]

pin /pɪn/ (**pins, pinning, pinned**)
1 **N-COUNT** A **pin** is a very small thin piece of metal with a point at one end. ❑ *She looked in her box of needles and pins.*
2 **V-T** If you **pin** something **on** or **to** something, you fix it there with a pin. ❑ *They pinned a notice to the door.*
3 **V-T** If someone **pins** you in a particular position, they press you against a surface so that you cannot move. ❑ *I pinned him down until the police arrived.*
4 **N-COUNT** A **pin** is any long, narrow piece of metal or wood that is used to fasten two things together. ❑ *...the 18-inch steel pin holding his left leg together.*
5 **N-COUNT** A **pin** is a decorative object that you wear on your clothing that is fastened with a pointed piece of metal. ❑ *We sell all kinds of necklaces, bracelets, and pins.* [from Old English]
→ look at Picture Dictionary: **jewelry**
▶ **pin down** **1** If you try to **pin** something **down**, you try to find out exactly what, where, or when it is. ❑ *We're trying to pin down the exact location of the building.* ❑ *I can pin the event down to some time between 1936 and 1942.*
2 If you **pin** someone **down**, you force them to make a definite statement. ❑ *She couldn't pin him down to a date.*

pinch /pɪntʃ/ (**pinches, pinching, pinched**)
1 **V-T** If you **pinch** someone, you press their skin between your thumb and first finger. ❑ *She pinched his arm as hard as she could.*

P

2 **N-COUNT** Pinch is also a noun. ❑ *She gave him a little pinch.*

3 **N-COUNT** A **pinch of** salt, pepper, or other powder is the amount of it that you can hold between your thumb and your first finger. ❑ *Add a pinch of cinnamon to the apples.* [from Old Norman French]

pine /paɪn/ (**pines, pining, pined**)
1 **N-COUNT/N-NONCOUNT** A **pine** is a tall tree with long thin leaves that it keeps all year. ❑ *The high mountains are covered in pine trees.*
2 **N-NONCOUNT** **Pine** is the wood of this tree. ❑ *There's a big pine table in the kitchen.*
3 **V-I** If you **pine for** something or someone, you feel sad because you cannot have them or cannot be with them. ❑ *I pine for the countryside.* ❑ *Make sure your pet doesn't pine while you're away.* [from Old English]

pine|apple /paɪnæpᵊl/ (**pineapples**)
N-COUNT/N-NONCOUNT A **pineapple** is a large fruit with sweet yellow flesh and thick brown skin.
→ look at Picture Dictionary: **fruit**

pink /pɪŋk/ (**pinker, pinkest, pinks**)
1 **ADJ** Something that is **pink** is of the color between red and white. ❑ *She wore pink lipstick.*
2 **N-NONCOUNT** **Pink** is also a noun. ❑ *I prefer pale pinks and blues.* [from Dutch]

pint /paɪnt/ (**pints**) **N-COUNT** **MATH** A **pint** is a unit for measuring liquids that is equal to 0.57 liters. ❑ *Each carton contains a pint of ice cream.* [from Old French]
→ look at Picture Dictionary: **measurements**

pio|neer /paɪənɪər/ (**pioneers, pioneering, pioneered**)
1 **N-COUNT** A **pioneer** in a particular activity is one of the first people to be involved in it. ❑ *He was one of the leading pioneers of the Internet.*
2 **V-T** Someone who **pioneers** a new activity, invention, or process is one of the first people to do it. ❑ *Professor Alec Jeffreys pioneered DNA tests.*
3 **N-COUNT** **SOCIAL STUDIES** **Pioneers** are people who leave their own country and go and live in a place that has not been lived in before. [from Old French]

pipe /paɪp/ (**pipes, piping, piped**)
1 **N-COUNT** A **pipe** is a long tube through which a liquid or a gas can flow. ❑ *They are going to replace the old water pipes.*
2 **N-COUNT** A **pipe** is an object that is used for smoking tobacco. ❑ *Do you smoke a pipe?*
3 **V-T** If liquid or gas **is piped** somewhere, it is transported from one place to another through a pipe. ❑ *Clean water is piped into our homes.* [from Old English]
→ look at Picture Dictionary: **keyboard**
→ look at Word Web: **petroleum**

pipe|line /paɪplaɪn/ (**pipelines**)
1 **N-COUNT** A **pipeline** is a large pipe that carries oil, gas, or water over a long distance. ❑ *The pipeline provides water for people living in the valley.*
2 **PHRASE** If something is **in the pipeline**, it has been planned or begun. ❑ *A 2.9 percent pay increase is in the pipeline for teachers.*
→ look at Word Web: **oil**

pi|rate /paɪrɪt/ (**pirates, pirating, pirated**)
1 **N-COUNT** **Pirates** are people who attack ships and steal property from them. ❑ *The hero must find the pirates and the hidden gold.*
2 **V-T** Someone who **pirates** CDs, DVDs, books, or computer programs copies them and sells them illegally. ❑ *Computer crimes include stealing data and pirating software.* [from Latin]

pis|til /pɪstᵊl/ (**pistils**) **N-COUNT** **SCIENCE** The **pistil** is the female part of a flower, which produces seeds. [from Latin]

pis|tol /pɪstᵊl/ (**pistols**) **N-COUNT** A **pistol** is a small gun. [from French]

pit /pɪt/ (**pits**)
1 **N-COUNT** A **pit** is a large hole that is dug in the ground. ❑ *The bodies were buried together in a single pit.*
2 **N-COUNT** A **pit** is the part of a coal mine that is under the ground.
3 **N-COUNT** A **pit** is the large hard seed of a fruit. ❑ *I don't always remove the cherry pits.* [Senses 1 and 2 from Old English. Sense 3 from Dutch.]

pitch /pɪtʃ/ (**pitches, pitching, pitched**)
1 **V-T** If you **pitch** something somewhere, you throw it. ❑ *We spent long, hot afternoons pitching a baseball.*
2 **N-NONCOUNT** The **pitch** of a sound is how high or low it is. ❑ *The pitch of a voice falls at the end of a sentence.* [from Old French]
▶ **pitch in** If you **pitch in**, you join in and help with an activity. [INFORMAL] ❑ *International agencies also have pitched in.*

pitch|er /pɪtʃər/ (**pitchers**)

1 **N-COUNT** A **pitcher** is a container with a handle, that is used for holding and pouring liquids. ❑ *We asked for a pitcher of iced water.*

2 **N-COUNT** SPORTS In baseball, the **pitcher** is the person who throws the ball to the batter. [Sense 1 from Old French. Sense 2 from French.]

→ look at Picture Dictionary: **baseball**

pity /pɪti/ (**pities, pitying, pitied**)

1 **V-T** If you **pity** someone, you feel very sorry for them. ❑ *I don't know whether to hate or pity him.*

2 **N-NONCOUNT** **Pity** is also a noun. ❑ *He felt a sudden tender pity for her.*

3 **N-SING** If you say that it is **a pity** that something is true, you mean that you feel disappointed about it. ❑ *It's a pity you arrived so late.*

4 **PHRASE** If you **take pity on** someone, you feel sorry for them and help them. ❑ *Nobody took pity on him.* [from Old French]

pix|el /pɪksəl/ (**pixels**) **N-COUNT** TECHNOLOGY A **pixel** is the smallest area on a computer screen that can be given a separate color by the computer. ❑ *...a display screen that measures one million pixels.*

piz|za /pɪtsə/ (**pizzas**)
N-COUNT/N-NONCOUNT
A **pizza** is a flat, round piece of bread that is covered with tomatoes, cheese, and sometimes other foods, and then baked in an oven. ❑ *I ordered a thin-crust pizza.* [from Italian]

pizza

pjs /pidʒeɪz/ also **pj's** **N-PLURAL** **Pjs** are the same as **pajamas.** [INFORMAL] ❑ *I work from home and live in my pjs most of the time.*

place
❶ NOUN USES
❷ VERB USES
❸ PHRASES

❶ place /pleɪs/ (**places**)

1 **N-COUNT** A **place** is a particular building, area, town, or country. ❑ *Keep your dog on a leash in public places.* ❑ *Please state your date and place of birth.*

2 **N-COUNT** The right or usual position for something is its **place.** ❑ *He returned the photo to its place on the shelf.*

3 **N-COUNT** A **place** is a seat for one person. ❑ *This girl was sitting in my place.*

4 **N-COUNT** Your **place** in a race or a competition is your position. ❑ *Victoria is in third place with 22 points.*

5 **N-COUNT** Your **place** is your home. [INFORMAL] ❑ *Let's all go back to my place!*

6 **N-COUNT** If you get a **place** on a team or in an institution, you are accepted to join the team or to be a part the institution. ❑ *Derek has lost his place on the team.* ❑ *There are no more places available in the school this year.*

7 **N-SING** **Place** can be used after "any," "no," "some," or "every" to mean "anywhere," "nowhere," "somewhere," or "everywhere." [INFORMAL] ❑ *The poor guy didn't have any place to go for Easter.* [from Old French]

→ look at Word Web: **zero**

❷ place /pleɪs/ (**places, placing, placed**)

1 **V-T** If you **place** something somewhere, you put it there. ❑ *Brand placed the letter in his pocket.*

2 **V-T** You can sometimes use **place** instead of "put" or "lay" where the meaning is carried by the following noun. For example, if you **place emphasis on** something, you emphasize it. ❑ *He placed great importance on family life.*

3 **V-T** If you **place an order**, you ask for someone to bring something to you. ❑ *It is a good idea to place your order early.* [from Old French]

❸ place /pleɪs/

1 **PHRASE** If things **fall into place**, events happen naturally to create a situation you want. ❑ *Once the decision was made, things fell into place rapidly.*

2 **PHRASE** If something is **in place**, it is in the correct position. ❑ *A wide band held her hair in place.*

3 **PHRASE** You use **in place of** to mean instead of. ❑ *Try using herbs and spices in place of salt.*

4 **PHRASE** You say **in the first place** when you are talking about the beginning of a situation or about the situation as it was before a series of events. ❑ *What brought you to Washington in the first place?*

5 **PHRASE** If you **put** someone **in their place**, you show them that they are less important or clever than they think they are. ❑ *In a few words she put him in his place.*

6 **PHRASE** When something **takes place**, it happens. ❑ *The discussions took place in Paris.* [from Old French]

P

pla|cen|ta /pləsɛntə/ (**placentas**) **N-COUNT** SCIENCE The **placenta** is the mass of veins and tissue inside the uterus of a pregnant woman or animal that the unborn baby is attached to. [from Latin]

pla|cen|tal mam|mal /pləsɛntᵊl mæməl/ (**placental mammals**) **N-COUNT** SCIENCE A **placental mammal** is an animal that has a placenta.

plac|id /plæsɪd/ **ADJ** A **placid** person or animal is calm and does not easily become excited, angry, or upset. ❑ *She was a placid child who rarely cried.* [from Latin]

pla|gia|rism /pleɪdʒərɪzəm/ **N-NONCOUNT** **Plagiarism** is the practice of using or copying someone else's idea or work and pretending that it is yours. ❑ *Now he's in real trouble. He's accused of plagiarism.* [from Latin]

plague /pleɪg/ (**plagues, plaguing, plagued**) ◼ **N-COUNT** A **plague** is an infectious disease that spreads quickly and kills large numbers of people. ❑ *A cough or a sneeze could spread the plague.* ◻ **N-COUNT** A **plague of** unpleasant things is a large number of them that arrive or happen at the same time. ❑ *...a plague of rats.* ◼ **V-T** If you **are plagued by** unpleasant things, they continually cause you a lot of trouble or suffering. ❑ *She was plagued by weakness and dizziness.* [from Late Latin]

plaid /plæd/ (**plaids**) **N-COUNT/N-NONCOUNT** **Plaid** is material with a pattern of squares on it. **Plaid** is also the pattern itself. ❑ *Eddie wore blue jeans and a plaid shirt.* [from Scottish Gaelic]

plain /pleɪn/ (**plainer, plainest, plains**) ◼ **ADJ** Something that is **plain** is all the same color and has no pattern or writing on it. ❑ *A plain carpet makes a room look bigger.* ❑ *He placed the paper in a plain envelope.* ◻ **ADJ** Something that is **plain** is very simple in style. ❑ *It was a plain, gray stone house.* ◼ **ADJ** If a fact or a situation is **plain**, it is easy to recognize or understand. ❑ *It was plain to him what he had to do.* ◼ **ADJ** Someone who is **plain** looks ordinary and not at all beautiful. ❑ *She was a shy, rather plain girl.* ◼ **N-COUNT** A **plain** is a large flat area of land with very few trees on it. ❑ *She stood alone on the grassy plain.* [from Old French]

Thesaurus plain Also look up :

ADJ	bare, modest, simple; (*ant.*) elaborate, fancy ◻
	common, everyday, modest, ordinary, simple, usual; (*ant.*) elaborate, fancy ◻
	clear, distinct, evident, transparent ◼

Word Partnership Use plain with :

| N | plain **style** ◻ |
| | plain **English**, plain **language**, plain **speech**, plain **truth** ◼ |

plain|ly /pleɪnli/ **ADV** You use **plainly** when something can easily be seen, noticed, or recognized. ❑ *I could plainly see him turning his head.* [from Old French]

plan /plæn/ (**plans, planning, planned**) ◼ **N-COUNT** A **plan** is a method for doing something that you think about in advance. ❑ *They are meeting to discuss the peace plan.* ❑ *She says that everything is going according to plan.* ◻ **V-T/V-I** If you **plan** what you are going to do, you decide in detail what you are going to do. ❑ *Plan what you're going to eat.* ❑ *He plans to leave Baghdad on Monday.* ❑ *They came together to plan for the future.* ◼ **N-PLURAL** If you have **plans**, you are intending to do something. ❑ *We have plans to build a new kitchen at the back of the house.* ◼ **N-COUNT** A **plan of** something is a detailed drawing of it. ❑ *Draw a plan of the garden before you start planting.* [from French] ◼ → see also **planning** ▸ **plan on** If you **plan on** doing something, you intend to do it. ❑ *They were planning on getting married.*

plane /pleɪn/ (**planes**) ◼ **N-COUNT** A **plane** is a vehicle with wings and engines that can fly. ❑ *He had plenty of time to catch his plane.* ◻ **N-COUNT** A **plane** is a flat, level surface that may be sloping at a particular angle. ❑ *...the angled plane of the propeller.* [from Latin.]

Thesaurus plane Also look up :

| N | aircraft, airplane, craft, jet ◼ |
| | horizontal, level, surface ◻ |

plan|et /plænɪt/ (**planets**) **N-COUNT** SCIENCE A **planet** is a large, round object in space that moves around a star. The Earth is a planet. ❑ *We study the planets in the solar system.* [from Old French]

→ look at Word Webs: **astronomer, galaxy, satellite, solar system**

plan|etesi|mal /plænɪtɛsɪməl/ (**planetesimals**) **N-COUNT** SCIENCE **Planetesimals** are small pieces of rock in space that combine to form planets.

plank|ton /plæŋktən/ **N-NONCOUNT** SCIENCE **Plankton** is a mass of tiny animals and plants that live in the surface layer of the sea. [from German]

plan|ner /plænər/ (**planners**) **N-COUNT** **Planners** are people whose job is to make decisions about what is going to be done in the future. ❑ We are waiting for a decision from the city planners. [from French]

plan|ning /plænɪŋ/
1 **N-NONCOUNT** **Planning** is the process of deciding in detail how to do something. ❑ The trip needs careful planning.
2 **N-NONCOUNT** **Planning** is control of the way that land is used in an area and of what new buildings are built there. ❑ He is an architect and a town-planning expert. [from French]
3 → see also **plan**

plant /plænt/ (**plants, planting, planted**)
1 **N-COUNT** SCIENCE A **plant** is a living thing that grows in the earth and has a stem, leaves, and roots. ❑ Water each plant daily.
2 **V-T** When you **plant** something, you put it into the ground so that it will grow. ❑ He plans to plant fruit trees.
3 **N-COUNT** A **plant** is a factory, or a place where power is produced. ❑ We visited one of Ford's car assembly plants.
4 **V-T** If you **plant** something somewhere, you put it there firmly. ❑ She planted her feet wide apart.
5 **V-T** To **plant** something or someone means to hide them somewhere. ❑ So far no one has admitted planting the bomb. [from Old English]
→ look at Picture Dictionary: **plants**
→ look at Word Webs: **earth, farm, food, herbivore, photosynthesis, tree**

Plan|tae /plænti/ **N-PLURAL** SCIENCE All the plants in the world can be referred to together as **Plantae**. [from Latin]

plan|ta|tion /plænteɪʃ°n/ (**plantations**) **N-COUNT** A **plantation** is a large piece of land where crops such as rubber, tea, or sugar are grown. ❑ The fruit comes from the banana plantations in Costa Rica. [from Old English]

plas|ma /plæzmə/ (**plasmas**)
1 **N-NONCOUNT** SCIENCE **Plasma** is the clear liquid part of blood that contains the blood cells.
2 **N-COUNT/N-NONCOUNT** SCIENCE A **plasma** is a very hot substance that is similar to a gas and that contains particles with electrical charge, such as ions and electrons. **Plasma** is often considered to be a fourth state of matter because it is neither a solid nor a liquid nor a gas. [from Late Latin]

plas|ma screen (**plasma screens**) or **plasma display** **N-COUNT** TECHNOLOGY A **plasma screen** is a type of thin television screen or computer screen with good quality images.

Picture Dictionary plants

(deciduous) tree

crop

(evergreen) tree / conifer

flower

grass

weed

bush/shrub

plas|ter /plǽstər/ (**plasters, plastering, plastered**)

◼◼ **N-NONCOUNT** Plaster is a substance that is used for making a smooth surface on the inside of walls and ceilings. ❑ *There were huge cracks in the plaster.*

◼◼ **V-T** If you **plaster** a wall or a ceiling, you cover it with a layer of plaster. ❑ *He has just plastered the ceiling.*

plas|tic /plǽstɪk/ **N-NONCOUNT** Plastic is a light but strong material that is produced by a chemical process. ❑ *The windows are made from sheets of plastic.* ❑ *...a plastic bottle.* ❑ *...a plastic bag.* [from Latin]

→ look at Word Web: **oil**

plas|tic sur|gery **N-NONCOUNT** Plastic surgery is an operation to repair damaged skin, or to improve someone's appearance. ❑ *She had plastic surgery to change the shape of her nose.*

plate /pleɪt/ (**plates**)

◼◼ **N-COUNT** A **plate** is a flat dish that is used for holding food. ❑ *Anita pushed her plate away.* ❑ *He ate a huge plate of spaghetti and meatballs.*

◼◼ **N-COUNT** SCIENCE In geology, a **plate** is a large piece of the Earth's surface, perhaps as large as a continent, that moves very slowly.

◼◼ **N-COUNT** A **plate** is a flat piece of metal, for example on part of a machine. ❑ *He has had a metal plate inserted into his broken jaw.*

◼◼ **N-PLURAL** On a road vehicle, the **plates** are the panels on the front and back that show the license number. ❑ *...cars with New Jersey plates.* [from Old French]

◼◼ → see also **license plate**

→ look at Picture Dictionary: **dish**

→ look at Word Webs: **continent, earthquake, rock**

plat|eau /plætóʊ/ (**plateaus** or **plateaux**) **N-COUNT** GEOGRAPHY A **plateau** is a large area of high and fairly flat land. ❑ *The house is on a wide grassy plateau.* [from French]

→ look at Picture Dictionary: **landforms**

plate bounda|ry (**plate boundaries**) **N-COUNT** SCIENCE A **plate boundary** is a place on the Earth's surface where two or more tectonic plates meet.

plate|let /pleɪtlɪt/ (**platelets**) **N-COUNT** SCIENCE Platelets are a kind of blood cell. If you cut yourself and you are bleeding, platelets help to stop the bleeding.

→ look at Word Web: **cardiovascular system**

plate tec|ton|ics /pleɪt tɛktɒnɪks/ **N-NONCOUNT** SCIENCE Plate tectonics is the way that large pieces of the Earth's surface move slowly around.

plat|form /plǽtfɔrm/ (**platforms**)

◼◼ **N-COUNT** A **platform** is a flat raised structure on which someone or something can stand. ❑ *He walked toward the platform to begin his speech.*

◼◼ **N-COUNT** A **platform** in a train station is the area where you wait for a train. ❑ *...a subway platform.* [from French]

plati|num /plǽtɪnəm, plǽtnəm/ **N-NONCOUNT** Platinum is a very valuable metal that looks like silver. [from New Latin]

plat|ter /plǽtər/ (**platters**) **N-COUNT** A **platter** is a large flat plate used for serving food. ❑ *The food was served on silver platters.* ❑ *...platters of cheese and fruit.* [from Old French]

→ look at Picture Dictionary: **dish**

play /pleɪ/ (**plays, playing, played**)

◼◼ **V-I** When children or animals **play**, they spend time using toys and taking part in games. ❑ *Polly was playing with her dolls.*

◼◼ **N-NONCOUNT** Play is also a noun. ❑ *Children learn mainly through play.*

◼◼ **V-T** SPORTS When you **play** a game or a sport, you take part in it. ❑ *The twins played cards.* ❑ *I used to play basketball.*

◼◼ **V-T/V-I** SPORTS When one person or team **plays** another, or **plays against** them, they compete against each other in a sport or a game. ❑ *Dallas will play Green Bay today.*

◼◼ **V-T** If you **play** a joke or a trick on someone, you deceive them or give them a surprise for fun. ❑ *She wanted to play a trick on her friends.*

◼◼ **N-COUNT** ARTS A **play** is a piece of writing performed in a theater, on the radio, or on television. ❑ *"Hamlet" is my favorite play.*

◼◼ **V-T** ARTS If an actor **plays** a character in a play or a movie, he or she performs the part of that character. ❑ *He played Mr. Hyde in the movie.*

◼◼ **V-T/V-I** MUSIC If you **play** a musical instrument, you produce music from it. ❑ *Nina was playing the piano.* ❑ *He played for me.*

◼◼ **V-T/V-I** If you **play** a DVD, you put it into a machine and watch it. ❑ *It is possible to play the DVD on any PC.* ❑ *An English-language DVD was playing.*

◼◼ **PHRASE** If something or someone **plays a**

part or **plays a role in** a situation, they are involved in it and have an effect on it. ❑ *It appears that the weather played a role in the crash.* [from Old English]
→ look at Word Web: **theater**

▶ **play around** If someone **plays around**, they behave in a silly way to amuse themselves or other people. [INFORMAL] ❑ *Stop playing around and eat!*

▶ **play at** If you say that someone **is playing at** something, you disapprove of the fact that they are not doing it very seriously. ❑ *It was a terrible piece of work; now I see that I was just playing at being a writer.*

▶ **play back** When you **play back** a sound file or a film, you listen to the sounds or watch the pictures after recording them. ❑ *If you press this button, the machine plays back your messages.*

▶ **play on** If you **play on** someone's fears, weaknesses, or faults, you deliberately use them in order to achieve what you want. ❑ *...new laws that play on people's fear of change.*

play|er /pleɪər/ (**players**)
■ **N-COUNT** SPORTS A **player** is a person who takes part in a sport or a game. ❑ *She was a good tennis player.* ❑ *The game is for three players.*
■ **N-COUNT** MUSIC You can use **player** for a musician. ❑ *He's a professional trumpet player.* [from Old English]
■ → see also **CD player, MP3 player**
→ look at Picture Dictionaries: **basketball, soccer**
→ look at Word Web: **chess**

play|ful /pleɪfəl/ **ADJ** A **playful** person or action is not very serious. ❑ *She gave him a playful kiss.* [from Old English]

play|ground /pleɪgraʊnd/ (**playgrounds**)
N-COUNT A **playground** is a piece of land where children can play. ❑ *The park has playground equipment made of wood.*
→ look at Word Web: **park**

play|group /pleɪgrup/ (**playgroups**) also **play group N-COUNT** A **playgroup** is an informal school for very young children.

play|ing card (**playing cards**) **N-COUNT** **Playing cards** are thin pieces of cardboard with numbers or pictures printed on them that are used for playing games. ❑ *He started to shuffle a deck of playing cards.*

play|ing field (**playing fields**) **N-COUNT** A **playing field** is a large area of grass where people play sports. ❑ *The town has three grass playing fields and 18 football teams.*

play|wright /pleɪraɪt/ (**playwrights**)
N-COUNT LANGUAGE ARTS A **playwright** is a person who writes plays.
→ look at Word Web: **theater**

pla|za /plɑzə, plæzə/ (**plazas**)
■ **N-COUNT** A **plaza** is an open square in a city. ❑ *Across the busy plaza, street sellers sell hot dogs.*
■ **N-COUNT** A **plaza** is a group of stores or buildings that are joined together or share common areas. ❑ *...a shopping plaza.* [from Spanish]

plea /pli/ (**pleas**) **N-COUNT** A **plea** is an emotional request for something. ❑ *Their president made a desperate plea for international help.* ❑ *...an emotional plea for help.* [from Old French]

plead /plid/ (**pleads, pleading, pleaded, pled**)
■ **V-I** If you **plead with** someone to do something, you ask them in an emotional way to do it. ❑ *The lady pleaded with her daughter to come back home.*
■ **V-I** When someone **pleads guilty** or **not guilty** in a court of law, they officially say that they are guilty or not guilty of the crime. ❑ *Morris pleaded guilty to robbery.*
■ **V-T** If you **plead the case** or **cause** of someone or something, you speak in their support or defense. ❑ *He appeared before the committee to plead his case.* [from Old French]
→ look at Word Web: **trial**

pleas|ant /plɛzᵊnt/
■ **ADJ** Something that is **pleasant** is enjoyable or attractive. ❑ *It was a very pleasant surprise to receive a free ticket.* ❑ *I have many pleasant memories of this place.* ● **pleas|ant|ly ADV** ❑ *We talked pleasantly of old times.*
■ **ADJ** Someone who is **pleasant** is nice and friendly. ❑ *The doctor was a handsome, pleasant young man.* [from Old French]

Thesaurus	pleasant Also look up :
ADJ	agreeable, cheerful, delightful, likable, friendly, nice; (ant.) unpleasant ■

please /pliz/ (**pleases, pleasing, pleased**)
■ **ADV** You say **please** when you are politely asking someone to do something. ❑ *Can you help us, please?* ❑ *Please come in.* ❑ *Can we have the bill, please?*
■ **ADV** You say **please** when you are

P

accepting something politely. ❑ *"Tea?"—"Yes, please."*

❸ v-t/v-i If someone or something **pleases** you, they make you feel happy and satisfied. ❑ *I just want to please you.* ❑ *He was anxious to please.* [from Old French]

pleased /plizd/
❶ ADJ If you are **pleased**, you are happy about something or satisfied with something. ❑ *I'm so pleased that we solved the problem.* ❑ *I'm pleased with the way things have been going.* ❑ *I am very pleased about the result.*
❷ PHRASE Pleased to meet you is a polite way of saying hello to someone that you are meeting for the first time. [from Old French]

pleas|ing /plizɪŋ/ **ADJ** Something that is **pleasing** gives you pleasure and satisfaction. ❑ *The pleasing smell of fresh coffee came from the kitchen.* [from Old French]

pleas|ure /plɛʒər/ (**pleasures**)
❶ N-NONCOUNT Something that gives you **pleasure** makes you feel happy and satisfied. ❑ *Watching sports gave him great pleasure.* ❑ *Everybody takes pleasure in eating.*
❷ N-COUNT A **pleasure** is an activity or an experience that you find enjoyable. ❑ *Watching TV is our only pleasure.* ❑ *It was a pleasure to see her smiling face.*
❸ PHRASE You can say **It's a pleasure** as a polite way of answering someone who thanks you for doing something. ❑ *"Thanks very much for waiting for me."—"It's a pleasure."* [from Old French]

pledge /plɛdʒ/ (**pledges, pledging, pledged**)
❶ v-t When someone **pledges to** do something, they promise in a serious way to do it. When they **pledge** something, they promise to give it. ❑ *He pledged to support the group.* ❑ *The French president is pledging $150 million in aid next year.*
❷ N-COUNT Pledge is also a noun. ❑ *...a pledge to improve relations between the six states.*
❸ v-t If you **pledge yourself to** something, you commit yourself to following a particular course of action or to supporting a particular person, group, or idea. ❑ *The president pledged himself to protect the poor.* [from Old French]

plen|ti|ful /plɛntɪfəl/ **ADJ** Things that are **plentiful** exist in such large amounts or numbers that there is enough for people's wants or needs. ❑ *Fish are plentiful in the lake.* [from Old French]

plen|ty /plɛnti/ **PRON Plenty** is a large amount of something. ❑ *I don't like long interviews. Fifteen minutes is plenty.* ❑ *Don't worry. There's still plenty of time.* ❑ *Most businesses face plenty of competition.* [from Old French]

Thesaurus plenty Also look up :
N   abundance, capacity, quantity; (ant.) scarcity

pli|ers /plaɪərz/ **N-PLURAL Pliers** are a tool with two handles at one end and two hard, flat, metal parts at the other that are used for holding or pulling things. ❑ *Hold the nail at its base with narrow pointed pliers.*
→ look at Picture Dictionary: **tool**

plight /plaɪt/ (**plights**) **N-COUNT** Someone's **plight** is the difficult or dangerous situation that they are in. ❑ *...the plight of children living in war zones.* [from Old French]

plot /plɒt/ (**plots, plotting, plotted**)
❶ v-t/v-i If people **plot to** do something, or **plot** something illegal or wrong, they plan secretly to do it. ❑ *They plotted to overthrow the government.* ❑ *They were accused of plotting against the state.*
❷ N-COUNT Plot is also a noun. ❑ *We have uncovered a plot to kill the president.*
❸ N-COUNT/N-NONCOUNT LANGUAGE ARTS The **plot** of a movie or a book is a series of events that make up the story. ❑ *He told me the plot of his new book.*
❹ N-COUNT A **plot** is a small piece of land, especially one that is intended for a particular purpose. ❑ *I bought a small plot of land and built a house on it.*
❺ v-t When someone **plots** the position or progress of something, they follow its position or progress and show it on a map. ❑ *We were trying to plot the course of the submarine.* [from Old English]

plow /plaʊ/ (**plows, plowing, plowed**)
❶ N-COUNT A **plow** is a large farming tool that is pulled across the soil to turn it over, usually before seeds are planted.
❷ v-t When someone **plows** an area of land, they turn over the soil using a plow. ❑ *They were using horses to plow their fields.*
❸ v-i If a vehicle **plows into** a person or thing, it hits them with great force. ❑ *The speeding vehicle plowed into a crowd of people.* [from Old English]
❹ → see also **snowplow**
→ look at Picture Dictionary: **barn**

P

pluck /plʌk/ (plucks, plucking, plucked) **v-т**
If you **pluck** a musical instrument, you pull the strings with your fingers, so that they make a sound. ❑ *Nell was plucking a harp.* [from Old English]

plug /plʌg/ (plugs, plugging, plugged)
1 N-COUNT A **plug** on a piece of electrical equipment is the plastic object with metal pins that connects it to the electricity supply. ❑ *Remove the power plug when you have finished.*
2 N-COUNT A **plug** is a round object that you use to block the hole in a bathtub or a sink. ❑ *She put in the plug and filled the sink with cold water.*
3 v-т If you **plug** a hole, you block it with something. ❑ *We are working to plug a major oil leak.*
4 PHRASE If someone in power **pulls the plug on** a project or **on** someone else's activities, they use their power to stop the activities from continuing. ❑ *The banks have the power to pull the plug on the project.* [from Middle Dutch]
▶ **plug in** If you **plug** a piece of electrical equipment **in**, you connect it to the electricity supply. ❑ *I had a TV, but there was no place to plug it in.*

plum /plʌm/ (plums) **N-COUNT/N-NONCOUNT**
A **plum** is a small, sweet fruit with a smooth purple, red, or yellow skin and a large seed in the middle. [from Old English]

plumb|er /plʌmər/ (plumbers) **N-COUNT**
A **plumber** is a person whose job is to put in and repair water and gas pipes. [from Old French]

plump /plʌmp/ (plumper, plumpest) **ADJ**
A **plump** person is round and rather heavy. ❑ *Maria was small and plump.* [from Middle Dutch]

plunge /plʌndʒ/ (plunges, plunging, plunged)
1 v-I If something or someone **plunges** into water, they fall or throw themselves into it. ❑ *The bus plunged into a river.*
2 v-т If you **plunge** an object **into** something, you push it violently into it. ❑ *He plunged a fork into his dinner.*
3 v-т/v-I If a person or thing **is plunged into** a particular state or situation, or if they **plunge into** it, they are suddenly in that state or situation. ❑ *Reforms threaten to plunge the country into violence.* ❑ *...a country plunging*

into poverty. [from Old French]

plu|ral /plʊərəl/ (plurals)
1 N-COUNT LANGUAGE ARTS The **plural** of a noun is the form of it that is used for talking about more than one person or thing. ❑ *"People" is the plural of "person."*
2 ADJ LANGUAGE ARTS **Plural** is also an adjective. ❑ *"Men" is the plural form of "man."* [from Old French]

plus /plʌs/
1 CONJ MATH You say **plus** to show that one number is being added to another. ❑ *Two plus two equals four.*
2 CONJ You can use **plus** when mentioning an additional item or fact. [INFORMAL] ❑ *It's just the original story plus a lot of extra photographs.*
3 ADJ Teachers use **plus** in grading work. "B plus" is a better grade than "B," but it is not as good as "A." [from Latin]

Plu|to /plutoʊ/ **N-PROPER** SCIENCE **Pluto** is the second largest dwarf planet in the solar system. It is farther away from the sun than Neptune. [from Latin]

ply /plaɪ/ (plies, plying, plied) **v-т** If you **ply** someone **with** food or drink, you keep giving them more of it. ❑ *Elsie plied me with food.* [from Old French]

p.m. /pi ɛm/ also **pm** **ADV** You use **p.m.** after a number when you are talking about a particular time between 12 noon and 12 midnight. Compare with **a.m.** ❑ *The pool is open from 7:00 a.m. to 9:00 p.m. every day.* [from Latin]

pneu|mo|nia /nʊmoʊnyə, -moʊniə/ **N-NONCOUNT** **Pneumonia** is a serious disease that affects the lungs. ❑ *She nearly died of pneumonia.* [from New Latin]

pock|et /pɒkɪt/ (pockets, pocketing, pocketed)
1 N-COUNT A **pocket** is a small bag that forms part of a piece of clothing. ❑ *He put the key in his jacket pocket.*
2 ADJ **Pocket** describes something that is small enough to fit into a pocket. ❑ *...a pocket calculator.*
3 v-т If someone

pocket

pockets something that does not belong to them, they keep it or steal it. ❑ *Banks have passed some of the savings on to customers and pocketed the rest.* [from Middle Dutch]

pocket|book /pɒkɪtbʊk/ (**pocketbooks**) **N-COUNT** A **pocketbook** is a small bag in which a woman carries small things such as her money and keys.

pod /pɒd/ (**pods**) **N-COUNT** A **pod** is a seed container that grows on some plants. ❑ *We bought fresh peas in their pods.*

pod|cast /pɒdkæst/ (**podcasts**) **N-COUNT** TECHNOLOGY A **podcast** is a file containing a radio show or something similar, that you can listen to on a computer or an MP3 player. ❑ *There are thousands of new podcasts available every day.*

po|dia|trist /pədaɪətrɪst/ (**podiatrists**) **N-COUNT** A **podiatrist** is a person whose job is to treat and care for people's feet. [from Greek]

po|dium /poʊdiəm/ (**podiums**) **N-COUNT** A **podium** is a small platform on which someone stands in order to give a lecture or conduct an orchestra. ❑ *He stood on the podium and spoke into the microphone.* [from Latin]

po|em /poʊəm/ (**poems**) **N-COUNT** LANGUAGE ARTS A **poem** is a piece of writing in which the words are chosen for their beauty and sound, and are carefully arranged, often in short lines. ❑ *He read to her from a book of love poems.* [from Latin]

poet /poʊɪt/ (**poets**) **N-COUNT** LANGUAGE ARTS A **poet** is a person who writes poems. ❑ *He was a painter and a poet.* [from Latin]

po|et|ry /poʊɪtri/ **N-NONCOUNT** LANGUAGE ARTS **Poetry** is the form of literature that consists of poems. ❑ *We studied Russian poetry last semester.* [from Medieval Latin] → look at Word Web: **genre**

---
point
❶ NOUN USES
❷ VERB USES
❸ PHRASES AND PHRASAL VERB
---

❶ **point** /pɔɪnt/ (**points**)
1 **N-COUNT** A **point** is an idea or a fact. ❑ *We disagreed with every point she made.*
2 **N-SING** The **point of** something is the

purpose of it. ❑ *What is the point of worrying?* ❑ *There's no point in fighting.*
3 **N-COUNT** A **point** is a particular position or time. ❑ *We're all going to die at some point.*
4 **N-COUNT** The **point** of a knife is the thin, sharp end of it. ❑ *Griego felt the cold sharp point of a knife against his neck.*
5 **N-COUNT** A **point** is the small dot that separates whole numbers from parts of numbers. ❑ *The highest temperature today was 98.5° (ninety-eight point five degrees).*
6 **N-COUNT** A **point** is a mark that you win in a game or a sport. ❑ *Chamberlain scored 50 points.*
7 **N-COUNT** The **points of the compass** are directions such as North, South, East, and West. ❑ *People came to visit from all points of the compass.*
8 **N-SING** If you say that someone **has a point**, or if you **take** their **point**, you mean that you accept that what they have said. ❑ *"You have a point there," Dave agreed.*
9 **N-SING** The **point** of what you are saying or discussing is the most important part. ❑ *"Did I ask you to talk to me?"—"That's not the point."* ❑ *He came to the point at once. "You did a splendid job."*
10 **N-COUNT** A **point** is an aspect or a quality of something or someone. ❑ *The most interesting point about the village was the school.* [from Old French]
11 → see also **focal point, point of view**

Thesaurus point Also look up :
N   argument, gist, topic **9**
     location, place, position, spot **3**

❷ **point** /pɔɪnt/ (**points, pointing, pointed**)
1 **V-I** If you **point at** a person or a thing, you use your finger to show where they are. ❑ *I pointed at the boy sitting near me.*
2 **V-T** If you **point** something **at** someone, you hold it toward them. ❑ *She smiled when Laura pointed a camera at her.*
3 **V-I** If something **points to** a place or **points** in a particular direction, it shows where that place is or it faces in that direction. ❑ *An arrow pointed to the restrooms.* [from Old French]

❸ **point** /pɔɪnt/ (**points, pointing, pointed**)
1 **PHRASE** If you **make a point of** doing something, you do it in a deliberate or obvious way. ❑ *She made a point of spending as much time as possible away from him.*
2 **PHRASE** If you are **on the point of** doing

P

something, you are about to do it. ❑ *He was on the point of answering when the phone rang.*

3 PHRASE If you say that something is true **up to a point**, you mean that it is partly but not completely true. ❑ *It worked up to a point.* [from Old French]

▸ **point out** If you **point out** a fact, you tell someone about it or show it to them. ❑ *He pointed out the errors in the book.*

point|ed /pɔɪntɪd/

1 ADJ Something that is **pointed** has a point at one end. ❑ *William was uncomfortable in his new pointed shoes.*

2 ADJ Pointed comments or behavior express criticism in a clear and direct way. ❑ *...her mother's criticisms and pointed remarks.*

● **point|ed|ly ADV** ❑ *They were pointedly absent from the news conference.* [from Old French]

point|less /pɔɪntlɪs/ **ADJ** Something that is **pointless** has no sense or purpose. ❑ *Without an audience the performance is pointless.* [from Old French]

point of view (points of view)

1 N-COUNT Your **point of view** is your opinion on a particular subject. ❑ *Thanks for your point of view, John.*

2 N-COUNT ARTS The **point of view** of someone who is looking at a painting or other object is the angle or position from which they are viewing it.

→ look at Word Web: **history**

point-source pol|lu|tion N-NONCOUNT SCIENCE Point-source pollution is pollution that comes from one particular source, for example from a particular factory.

poised /pɔɪzd/

1 ADJ If a part of your body is **poised**, it is completely still but ready to move at any moment. ❑ *He studied the keyboard carefully, one finger poised.*

2 ADJ If someone is **poised to** do something, they are ready to take action at any moment. ❑ *Foster looked poised to win the match when he won the first game 6–2.*

3 ADJ If you are **poised**, you are calm, dignified, and self-controlled. ❑ *She was self-assured, poised.* [from Old French]

poi|son /pɔɪzᵊn/ (poisons, poisoning, poisoned)

1 N-COUNT/N-NONCOUNT Poison is a substance that harms or kills people or animals if they swallow or touch it. ❑ *Poison from the factory is causing the fish to die.*

2 V-T To **poison** someone or something means to harm them by giving them poison. ❑ *They say that she poisoned her husband.* [from Old French]

Word Link	*ous ≈ having the qualities of :*
	*danger*ous*, fabul*ous*, poison*ous*

poi|son|ous /pɔɪzᵊnəs/

1 ADJ Something that is **poisonous** will kill you or harm you if you swallow or touch it. ❑ *All parts of this tree are poisonous.*

2 ADJ An animal that is **poisonous** produces a substance that will kill you or make you sick if it bites you. ❑ *The zoo keeps a selection of poisonous spiders and snakes.* [from Old French]

poke /poʊk/ (pokes, poking, poked)

1 V-T If you **poke** someone or something, you quickly push them with your finger or with a sharp object. ❑ *Lindy poked him in the ribs.*

2 N-COUNT Poke is also a noun. ❑ *John gave Richard a playful poke.*

3 V-T If you **poke** one thing **into** another, you push the first thing into the second thing. ❑ *He poked his finger into the hole.* [from Low German and Middle Dutch]

pok|er /poʊkər/ **N-NONCOUNT Poker** is a card game, usually played in order to win money. ❑ *Lon and I play in the same weekly poker game.* [from French]

po|lar /poʊlər/ **ADJ GEOGRAPHY Polar** means near the North Pole or South Pole. ❑ *We watched a program about life in the polar regions.* [from Latin]

→ look at Word Web: **glacier**

po|lar co|or|di|nate (polar coordinates)

N-COUNT SCIENCE Polar coordinates are a set of two numbers that are used in mathematics to describe the position of something by measuring its distance and angle from a particular point.

po|lar east|er|lies /poʊlər istərliz/

N-PLURAL SCIENCE The **polar easterlies** are winds that blow from the north and south poles towards the equator.

po|lar equa|tion (polar equations)

N-COUNT SCIENCE A **polar equation** is a mathematical equation that uses polar coordinates.

P

po|lar zone (polar zones) **N-COUNT** SCIENCE
The **polar zones** are the areas of the Earth around the north and south poles.

pole /poʊl/ (poles)
1 **N-COUNT** A **pole** is a long thin piece of wood or metal, used especially for supporting things. ◻ *The car went off the road, knocking down a telephone pole.*
2 **N-COUNT** GEOGRAPHY The Earth's **poles** are its two opposite ends, which are its most northern and southern points. ◻ *For six months of the year, there is very little light at the poles.* [from Latin]
→ look at Picture Dictionary: **globe**
→ look at Word Web: **magnet**

> **Word Link** *poli* ≈ *city* : *metropolitan, police, politics*

po|lice /pəlis/ (polices, policing, policed)
1 **N-PLURAL** The **police** is the organization that is responsible for making sure that people obey the law. ◻ *The police are looking for the car.* ◻ *Police say they have arrested twenty people.*
2 **N-PLURAL** **Police** are men and women who are members of the police. ◻ *More than one hundred police are in the area.*
3 **V-T** To **police** an area, an event, or an activity means to make sure that the law or rules are followed within it. ◻ *...It is difficult to police the border effectively.* ◻ *...the committee that polices senators' behavior.* [from French]

po|lice de|part|ment (police departments) **N-COUNT** A **police department** is an organization that is responsible for making sure that people obey the law. ◻ *They have called in the Los Angeles Police Department.*

po|lice force (police forces) **N-COUNT** A **police force** is the police organization in a particular country or area. ◻ *...the Wichita police force.*

police|man /pəlismən/ (policemen)
N-COUNT A **policeman** is a man who is a member of the police.

po|lice of|fic|er (police officers) **N-COUNT**
A **police officer** is a member of the police. ◻ *...a senior police officer.*

po|lice sta|tion (police stations) **N-COUNT**
A **police station** is the local office of the police in a particular area. ◻ *Two police officers arrested him and took him to the police station.*

police|woman /pəliswʊmən/ (policewomen) **N-COUNT** A **policewoman** is a woman who is a member of the police.

poli|cy /pɒlɪsi/ (policies)
N-COUNT/N-NONCOUNT SOCIAL STUDIES
A **policy** is a set of ideas or plans about a particular subject, especially in politics, economics, or business. ◻ *There will be some important changes in foreign policy.* [from Old French]

po|lio /poʊlioʊ/ **N-NONCOUNT** SCIENCE **Polio** is a serious infectious disease that can cause paralysis. ◻ *Their first child died of polio at the age of 3.*
→ look at Word Web: **hospital**

pol|ish /pɒlɪʃ/ (polishes, polishing, polished)
1 **N-COUNT/N-NONCOUNT** **Polish** is a substance that you put on a surface in order to clean it and make it shine. ◻ *Furniture polish will clean and protect your table.*
2 **V-T** If you **polish** something, you rub it to make it shine. ◻ *He polished his shoes.*
3 **V-T** If you **polish** or **polish up** your skills, you try to improve them. ◻ *They need to polish their technique.* ◻ *Polish up your writing skills.* [from Old French]

po|lite /pəlaɪt/ **ADJ** A **polite** person behaves with respect toward other people. ◻ *He seemed a quiet and very polite young man.*
● **po|lite|ly** **ADV** ◻ *"Your home is beautiful,"* I said politely. ● **po|lite|ness** **N-NONCOUNT** ◻ *She listened to him, but only out of politeness.* [from Latin]

> **Thesaurus** polite Also look up :
> ADJ considerate, courteous, gracious, respectful; (ant.) brash, rude

po|liti|cal /pəlɪtɪkəl/ **ADJ** SOCIAL STUDIES **Political** means relating to politics or the government. ◻ *I am not a member of any political party.* ● **po|liti|cal|ly** /pəlɪtɪkli/ **ADV** ◻ *Politically, this is a very risky move.* [from Old French]
→ look at Word Webs: **empire, philosophy**

po|liti|cal par|ty (political parties) **N-COUNT** SOCIAL STUDIES A **political party** is an organization whose members share similar ideas and beliefs about politics. ◻ *Some members of the main political parties gave interviews to reporters.*

poli|ti|cian /pɒlɪtɪʃən/ (politicians) **N-COUNT** A **politician** is a person who works in politics, especially a member of a government. ◻ *They have arrested a number of politicians.* [from Old French]

P

poli|tics /pɒlɪtɪks/

1 **N-NONCOUNT** SOCIAL STUDIES **Politics** is the activities and ideas that are concerned with government. ❑ *He was involved in local politics.*
2 **N-PLURAL** Your **politics** are your beliefs about how a country should be governed. ❑ *His politics are extreme and often confused.* [from Old French]

poll /poʊl/ (**polls**)

1 **N-COUNT** A **poll** is a way of discovering what people think about something by asking them questions. ❑ *The polls are showing that women are very involved in this campaign.*
2 **N-PLURAL** People **go to the polls** when they vote in an election. ❑ *Voters go to the polls on Sunday to elect a new president.* [from Middle Low German]
→ look at Word Webs: **election, vote**

pol|len /pɒlən/ (**pollens**)

N-COUNT/N-NONCOUNT SCIENCE **Pollen** is a powder that is produced by flowers. ❑ *The male bee carries the pollen from one flower to another.* [from Latin]

Word Link	ate ≈ causing to be : complic*ate*,
	motiv*ate*, pollin*ate*

pol|li|nate /pɒlɪneɪt/ (**pollinates, pollinating, pollinated**) **V-T** SCIENCE To **pollinate** a plant or a tree means to fertilize it with pollen. This is often done by insects. ❑ *Many of the indigenous insects are needed to pollinate the local plants.* ● **pol|li|na|tion** /pɒlɪneɪʃ°n/ **N-NONCOUNT** ❑ *Without sufficient pollination, the growth of the corn is stunted.* [from Latin]

Word Link	ant ≈ defend*ant*, occup*ant*, pollut*ant*

pol|lu|tant /pəlut°nt/ (**pollutants**)

N-COUNT/N-NONCOUNT SCIENCE **Pollutants** are substances that pollute the environment, especially poisonous chemicals produced as waste by vehicles and by industry. [from Latin]
→ look at Word Web: **ozone**

pol|lute /pəlut/ (**pollutes, polluting, polluted**) **V-T** To **pollute** water, air, or land means to make it dirty. ❑ *Industry pollutes our rivers with chemicals.* ● **pol|lut|ed** **ADJ** ❑ *Fish are dying in the polluted rivers.* [from Latin]

pol|lu|tion /pəluʃ°n/

1 **N-NONCOUNT** **Pollution** is the process of making water, air, or land dirty and dangerous. ❑ *The government announced plans for reducing pollution of the air, sea, rivers, and soil.*
2 **N-NONCOUNT** **Pollution** is poisonous substances that pollute water, air, or land. ❑ *The level of pollution in the river was falling.* [from Latin]
→ look at Word Webs: **pollution, air, factory, solar**

poly|es|ter /pɒliɛstər/ **N-NONCOUNT** **Polyester** is a type of artificial cloth that is mainly used for making clothes. ❑ *He wore a green polyester shirt.*
→ look at Word Web: **petroleum**

po|lyga|my /pəlɪgəmi/ **N-NONCOUNT** **Polygamy** is the custom, in some societies, of being legally married to more than one person at the same time.

poly|no|mial /pɒlɪnoʊmiəl/ (**polynomials**)

1 **N-COUNT** MATH A **polynomial** is an expression in algebra that is the sum of several terms. Compare with **binomial** and **monomial**.
2 **ADJ** MATH **Polynomial** is also an adjective. ❑ *...a polynomial expression.*

pol|yp /pɒlɪp/ (**polyps**) **N-COUNT** SCIENCE A **polyp** is a small animal that lives in the sea. It has a hollow body like a tube and long parts called tentacles around its mouth. [from French]

poly|tech|nic /pɒlɪtɛknɪk/ (**polytechnics**)

N-COUNT/N-NONCOUNT A **polytechnic** is the name for a school, a college, or a university that specializes in courses in science and

P

Word Web pollution

Pollution affects the whole **environment. Airborne emissions** from factories and car **exhausts** cause air pollution. These smoky **emissions** combine with fog and make **smog.** Pollutants in the air can travel long distances. **Acid rain** caused by factories in the Midwest falls on states to the east. There it damages trees and kills fish in lakes. Chemicals from factories, **sewage,** and **garbage** pollute the water and land in many areas. Too many **pesticides** and **fertilizers** make the problem worse. These chemicals build up in the soil and poison the earth.

technology. ❑ *He met with his old classmate from the polytechnic.* [from French]

pond /pɒnd/ (ponds) **N-COUNT** A **pond** is a small area of water. ❑ *We sat on a bench beside the duck pond.*

pon|der /pɒndər/ (ponders, pondering, pondered) **V-T** If you **ponder** something, you think about it carefully. ❑ *I found myself constantly pondering the question.* [from Old French]

pon|toon /pɒntun/ (pontoons) **N-COUNT** A **pontoon** is a floating platform, often one used to support a bridge. ❑ *...a pontoon bridge.* → look at Word Web: **bridge**

pony /poʊni/ (ponies) **N-COUNT** A **pony** is a small or young horse.

pony|tail /poʊniteɪl/ (ponytails) **N-COUNT** A **ponytail** is a hairstyle in which your hair is tied up at the back of your head and hangs down like a horse's tail. ❑ *Her long, fine hair was tied back in a ponytail.* → look at Picture Dictionary: **hair**

pool /pul/ (pools, pooling, pooled) **1** **N-COUNT** A **pool** is the same as a **swimming pool**. ❑ *Does the hotel have a heated indoor pool?* **2** **N-COUNT** A **pool of** liquid or light is a small area of it. ❑ *...the pool of light cast from his desk lamp.* **3** **V-T** If people **pool** their money, knowledge, or equipment, they put it together so that it can be used for a particular purpose. ❑ *We pooled ideas and information.* **4** **N-NONCOUNT** **Pool** is a game that is played on a special table. Players use a long stick to hit a white ball so that it knocks colored balls into six holes around the edge of the table. [Senses 1 and 2 from Old English. Senses 3 and 4 from French.]

poor /pʊər/ (poorer, poorest) **1** **ADJ** Someone who is **poor** has very little money and few possessions. ❑ *"We were very poor in those days," he says.* **2** **N-PLURAL** The **poor** are people who are poor. ❑ *There are huge differences between the rich and the poor.* **3** **ADJ** You use **poor** to show that you are sorry for someone. ❑ *I feel sorry for that poor child.* ❑ *Poor Mike. Does he feel better now?* **4** **ADJ** Something that is **poor** is bad. ❑ *The illegal copies are of very poor quality.* ❑ *The actors gave a poor performance.* ● **poor|ly**

ADV ❑ *"We played poorly in the first game,"* Mendez said. **5** **ADJ** If something is **poor in** a particular quality or substance, it contains very little of the quality or substance. ❑ *Fat and sugar are very rich in energy, but poor in vitamins.* [from Old French]

Thesaurus	poor	Also look up :
ADJ	impoverished, penniless; *(ant.)* rich, wealthy **1** inferior **3**	

pop /pɒp/ (pops, popping, popped) **1** **N-NONCOUNT** **Pop** is modern music that usually has a strong rhythm and uses electronic equipment. ❑ *Their music is a combination of Caribbean rhythms and European pop.* ❑ *Her room is covered with posters of pop stars.* **2** **V-I** If something **pops**, it makes a short sharp sound. ❑ *He heard a balloon pop behind his head.* **3** **N-COUNT** **Pop** is also a noun. ❑ *Each piece of corn will make a loud pop when it is cooked.* **4** **V-T** If you **pop** something somewhere, you put it there quickly. [INFORMAL] ❑ *He popped some gum into his mouth.* **5** **N-COUNT** Some people call their father **Pop**. [INFORMAL] ❑ *I looked at Pop and he had big tears in his eyes.* ▶ **pop up** If someone or something **pops up**, they suddenly appear in a place or situation. [INFORMAL] ❑ *She was startled when Lisa popped up.*

pop|corn /pɒpkɔrn/ **N-NONCOUNT** **Popcorn** is a type of food that consists of grains of corn that have been heated until they have burst and become large and light.

Word Link	popul ≈ people : *popular, population, unpopular*

popu|lar /pɒpyələr/ **1** **ADJ** Something or someone that is **popular** is liked by a lot of people. ❑ *He was the most popular politician in Arkansas.* ❑ *Chocolate sauce is always popular with kids.* ● **popu|lar|ity** /pɒpyəlæriti/ **N-NONCOUNT** ❑ *The singer's popularity grew even more with his successful 1999 album.* **2** **ADJ** **Popular** ideas or opinions are held by most people. ❑ *There is a popular belief that unemployment causes crime.* **3** **ADJ** **Popular** is used to describe political activities that involve the ordinary people of a country. ❑ *They are trying to build popular support for military action.* [from Latin] → look at Word Web: **genre**

P

Word Partnership Use **popular** with :

ADV	**extremely** popular, **increasingly** popular, **most** popular, **wildly** popular **1**
N	popular **movie**, popular **restaurant**, popular **show**, popular **song 1**
	popular **culture**, popular **magazine**, popular **music**, popular **novel 1**

popu|la|tion /pɒpyəleɪʃ°n/ (**populations**)

1 N-COUNT SOCIAL STUDIES The **population** of a country or an area is all the people who live in it. ❏ *Bangladesh now has a population of about 150 million.*

2 N-COUNT A particular type of **population** in a country or an area refers to all the people or animals of that type that live there. [FORMAL] ❏ *...75.6 percent of the male population.* [from Medieval Latin]

→ look at Word Web: **country**

pop-up ADJ TECHNOLOGY A **pop-up** window is a message or an advertisement that suddenly appears in front of the text or images on a computer screen. ❏ *...a program for stopping pop-up ads.*

porch /pɔrtʃ/ (**porches**) N-COUNT A **porch** is a raised structure that is built along the outside wall of a house and is often covered with a roof. ❏ *He stood on the porch, waving as we drove away.* [from French]

pore /pɔr/ (**pores**) N-COUNT Your **pores** are the very small holes in your skin. ❏ *Use hot water to clear blocked pores.* [from Late Latin]

pork /pɔrk/ N-NONCOUNT **Pork** is meat from a pig. ❏ *He said he didn't eat pork.* [from Old French]

→ look at Word Web: **meat**

po|ros|ity /pɔrɒsiti/ N-NONCOUNT SCIENCE **Porosity** is the amount of open space between individual rock particles. [from Medieval Latin]

port /pɔrt/ (**ports**)

1 N-COUNT GEOGRAPHY A **port** is a town by the sea where ships arrive and leave. ❏ *We stopped at the Mediterranean port of Marseilles.*

2 N-COUNT A **port** on a computer is a place where you can attach another piece of equipment. ❏ *The scanner plugs into the printer port of your computer.* [from Old English]

→ look at Word Web: **ship**

Word Link *port ≈ carrying : ex**port**, im**port**, **port**able*

port|able /pɔrtəb°l/ ADJ Something that is **portable** is designed to be carried or moved around. ❏ *The iPod can be used as a portable storage device for all types of files.* [from Late Latin]

por|ter /pɔrtər/ (**porters**) N-COUNT A **porter** is a person whose job is to carry things, for example people's baggage. ❏ *Our taxi arrived at the station and a porter came to the door.* [from Old French]

port|fo|lio /pɔrtfoʊlioʊ/ (**portfolios**)

1 N-COUNT ARTS A **portfolio** is a set of pictures or photographs of someone's work, that they show when they are trying to get a job. ❏ *Edith showed them a portfolio of her drawings.*

2 N-COUNT A **portfolio** is an organized collection of student work. [from Italian]

por|tion /pɔrʃ°n/ (**portions**)

1 N-COUNT A **portion of** something is a part of it. ❏ *Only a small portion of the castle was damaged.* ❏ *I have spent a large portion of my life here.*

2 N-COUNT A **portion** is the amount of food that is given to one person at a meal. ❏ *The portions were huge.* [from Old French]

por|trait /pɔrtrɪt, -treɪt/ (**portraits**) N-COUNT A **portrait** is a painting, a drawing, or a photograph of a particular person. ❏ *The wall was covered with family portraits.* [from Old French]

→ look at Word Web: **painting**

por|tray /pɔrtreɪ/ (**portrays, portraying, portrayed**) V-T To **portray** someone or something means to represent them, for example in a book or a movie. ❏ *The film portrays a group of young people who live in lower Manhattan.* [from Old French]

pose /poʊz/ (**poses, posing, posed**)

1 V-T If something **poses** a problem or a danger, it is the cause of that problem or danger. ❏ *New shopping malls pose a threat to independent stores.*

2 V-I If you **pose for** a photograph or a painting, you stay in one position so that someone can photograph you or paint you. ❏ *The six foreign ministers posed for photographs.*

3 N-COUNT A **pose** is a position that you stay in when someone is photographing you or painting you. ❏ *We tried various poses.*

P

4 **v-t** If you **pose** a question, you ask it. [FORMAL] ❏ *I finally posed the question, "Why?"*

5 **v-i** If you **pose as** someone, you pretend to be that person in order to trick people. ❏ *Many shops employ detectives who pose as customers.* [from Old French]

posh /pɒʃ/ (**posher, poshest**) **ADJ** If something is **posh**, it is fashionable and expensive. [INFORMAL] ❏ *We stayed one night in a posh hotel.* [from British slang]

> **Word Link** *pos ≈ placing : deposit, preposition, position*

po|si|tion /pəzɪʃ°n/ (**positions, positioning, positioned**)

1 **N-COUNT** The **position** of someone or something is the place where they are. ❏ *Measure and mark the position of the handle on the door.*

2 **N-COUNT** Your **position** is the way you are sitting, lying, or standing. ❏ *Mr. Dambar raised himself to a sitting position.*

3 **v-t** If you **position** something somewhere, you put it there carefully, so that it is in the right place. ❏ *Position the table in an open area.*

4 **N-COUNT** Your **position** in society is the role and the importance that you have in it. ❏ *...their changing role and position in society.*

5 **N-COUNT** A **position** in a company or an organization is a job. [FORMAL] ❏ *He left a career in teaching to take a position with IBM.*

6 **N-COUNT** Your **position** in a race or a competition is how well you did in relation to the other competitors or how well you are doing. ❏ *The car was running in eighth position.*

7 **N-COUNT** Your **position** at a particular time is the situation you are in. ❏ *He's going to be in a very difficult position if things go badly.* ❏ *The club's financial position is still uncertain.*

8 **N-COUNT** Your **position on** a particular matter is your attitude toward it or your opinion of it. [FORMAL] ❏ *What is your position on this issue?*

9 **N-SING** If you are **in a position to** do something, you are able to do it. ❏ *I am not in a position to comment.* [from Late Latin]
→ look at Word Web: **navigation**

> **Word Partnership** Use **position** with :
> ADJ **better** position **1 2 4–7**
> **fetal** position **2**
> **(un)comfortable** position **2 7**
> **difficult** position, **financial** position **7**
> **official** position **8**

posi|tive /pɒzɪtɪv/

1 **ADJ** If you are **positive**, you are hopeful and confident. ❏ *Be positive about your future.*
● **posi|tive|ly** **ADV** ❏ *You really must try to start thinking positively.*

2 **ADJ** A **positive** experience is pleasant and helpful. ❏ *I want to have a positive effect on my children's lives.*

3 **N-SING** The **positive** in a situation is the good and pleasant aspects of it. ❏ *He prefers to focus on the positive.*

4 **ADJ** If you are **positive** about something, you are completely sure about it. ❏ *"Judith's never late. Are you sure she said eight?"—"Positive."*

5 **ADJ** **Positive** evidence gives definite proof of something. ❏ *There is some positive evidence that the economy is improving.* ● **posi|tive|ly** **ADV** ❏ *She positively identified two men and a woman from the photographs.*

6 **ADJ** If a medical or scientific test is **positive**, it shows that something has happened or is present. ❏ *If the test is positive, treatment will start immediately.*

7 **ADJ** MATH A **positive** number is higher than zero. Compare with **negative**.

8 **ADJ** ARTS In art and sculpture, **positive** space is the parts of a painting that represent solid objects or the parts of a sculpture that are made of solid material. Compare with **negative**. [from Late Latin]
→ look at Word Webs: **lightning, magnet**

posi|tive ac|cel|era|tion **N-NONCOUNT** SCIENCE **Positive acceleration** is an increase in speed or velocity. Compare with **negative acceleration**.

pos|sess /pəzɛs/ (**possesses, possessing, possessed**) **v-t** If you **possess** something, you have it or own it. ❏ *They sold everything they possessed to raise the money.* [from Old French]

pos|ses|sion /pəzɛʃ°n/ (**possessions**)

1 **N-NONCOUNT** If you are **in possession of** something, you have it. [FORMAL] ❏ *Those documents are now in the possession of the Washington Post.*

2 **N-COUNT** Your **possessions** are the things that you own or have with you at a particular time. ❏ *People have lost their homes and all their possessions.* [from Old French]

pos|ses|sive /pəzɛsɪv/ **ADJ** LANGUAGE ARTS In grammar, a **possessive** word is a word such as "my" or "his" that shows who or what something belongs to. [from Old French]

pos|sibil|ity /pɒsɪbɪlɪti/ (**possibilities**)
 1 **N-COUNT** If there is a **possibility that** something will happen, it might happen. ❑ There is a possibility that they jailed the wrong man.
 2 **N-COUNT** A **possibility** is one of several different things that could be done. ❑ There were several possibilities open to us. [from Latin]

> **Word Link** **ible ≈ able to be : au**dible, flex**ible**, poss**ible**

pos|sible /pɒsɪbᵊl/
 1 **ADJ** If it is **possible** to do something, that thing can be done. ❑ If it is possible to find out where your brother is, we will. ❑ Anything is possible if you want it enough.
 2 **ADJ** If it is **possible that** something is true, it might be true, although you do not know for sure. ❑ It is possible that he's telling the truth.
 3 **ADJ** If you do something **as soon as possible**, you do it as soon as you can. ❑ Please make your decision as soon as possible. [from Latin]

> **Thesaurus** **possible** Also look up :
> ADJ feasible, likely; (ant.) impossible, unlikely **1**

pos|sibly /pɒsɪbli/
 1 **ADV** You use **possibly** when you are not sure if something is true or if it will happen. ❑ Exercise will possibly protect against heart attacks.
 2 **ADV** You use **possibly** to show that you are surprised or puzzled. ❑ How could they possibly eat that stuff?
 3 **ADV** You use **possibly** to say that something is possible. ❑ They've done everything they can possibly think of. ❑ I can't possibly answer that! [from Latin]

post /poʊst/ (**posts, posting, posted**)
 1 **V-T** If you **post** signs on a wall, you put them there so that everyone can see them. ❑ Officials began posting warning notices.
 2 **V-T** TECHNOLOGY If you **post** information on the Internet, you put it on a website so that other people can see it. ❑ The statement was posted on the Internet.
 3 **N-COUNT** A **post** is an important job in an organization. [FORMAL] ❑ She accepted the post of the director's assistant.
 4 **N-COUNT** A **post** is a strong piece of wood or metal that is set into in the ground. ❑ The car went through a red light and hit a fence post. [Senses 1, 2, and 4 from Old English. Sense 3 from French.]

post|age /poʊstɪdʒ/ **N-NONCOUNT** Postage is the money that you pay for sending mail. ❑ All prices include postage. [from Old French]

post|card /poʊstkɑrd/ (**postcards**) also **post card** **N-COUNT** A **postcard** is a thin card, often with a picture on one side, that you can write on and mail to someone without using an envelope. [from Old French]

post|er /poʊstər/ (**posters**) **N-COUNT** A **poster** is a large notice or picture that you stick on a wall. ❑ I saw a poster for the jazz festival in Monterey. [from Old English]

post|mod|ern dance /poʊstmɒdərn dæns/ also **post-modern dance** **N-NONCOUNT** ARTS **Postmodern dance** is a form of dance that began in the 1960s as a reaction against modern dance.

post of|fice (**post offices**)
 1 **N-COUNT** A **post office** is a building where you can buy stamps and send mail. ❑ She needed to get to the post office before it closed.
 2 **N-SING** You can use **the post office** to talk about the U.S. Postal Service.

post|pone /poʊstpoʊn, poʊspoʊn/ (**postpones, postponing, postponed**) **V-T** If you **postpone** an event, you arrange for it to happen at a later time. ❑ He decided to postpone the trip until the following day. [from Latin]

> **Word Link** **post ≈ after : com**post, **post**script, **post**war

> **Word Link** **script ≈ writing : manu**script, **post**script, tran**script**

post|script /poʊstskrɪpt/ (**postscripts**)
 1 **N-COUNT** A **postscript** is something that you write at the end of a letter after you have signed your name. You usually write "P.S." in front of it. ❑ A brief, handwritten postscript lay beneath his signature.
 2 **N-COUNT** A **postscript** is an addition to a finished story, account, or statement, that gives further information. ❑ Let me add a postscript to this section on diet. [from Late Latin]

pos|ture /pɒstʃər/ (**postures**)
 1 **N-COUNT/N-NONCOUNT** Your **posture** is the position in which you stand or sit. ❑ You can make your stomach look flatter by improving your posture.
 2 **N-COUNT** A **posture** is an attitude that you have or a way that you behave toward a person or a thing. [FORMAL] ❑ The president's new posture helped open the way

P

for the next proposal. [from French]
→ look at Word Web: **brain**

| Word Link | *post ≈ after : com**post**, **post**script,* |
| | *post**war*** |

post|war /ˈpoʊstwɔr/ **ADJ** Postwar is used to describe things that happened, existed, or were made in the period immediately after a war, especially World War II, 1939–45. ❑ *Bottle feeding babies was popular in the early postwar years.* [from Old Northern French]

pot /pɒt/ (**pots, potting, potted**)
1 **N-COUNT** A **pot** is a deep round container used for cooking food. ❑ *The shelf is full of metal cooking pots.*
2 **N-COUNT** A **pot** is a round container that is used for a particular purpose. ❑ *She asked him to pass the coffee pot.* ❑ *...a pot of paint.*

pot

3 **V-T** If you **pot** a plant, you put it into a container filled with soil. ❑ *Pot the plants individually.* [from Late Old English]

po|ta|to /pəˈteɪtoʊ/ (**potatoes**) **N-COUNT/ N-NONCOUNT** Potatoes are hard round white vegetables with brown or red skins. They grow under the ground. [from Spanish]
→ look at Picture Dictionary: **vegetables**

po|ta|to chip (**potato chips**) **N-COUNT** Potato chips are very thin slices of potato that have been cooked until they are hard, dry, and crisp.

po|tent /ˈpoʊtᵊnt/ **ADJ** Something that is potent is very effective and powerful. ❑ *Their most potent weapon was the Exocet missile.* ● **po|ten|cy** /ˈpoʊtᵊnsi/ **N-NONCOUNT** ❑ *Sunscreen can lose its potency if left over winter in the bathroom cabinet.* [from Latin]

po|ten|tial /pəˈtɛnʃᵊl/
1 **ADJ** You use **potential** to say that someone or something could become a particular type of person or thing. ❑ *The company has identified 60 potential customers.* ❑ *We are aware of the potential problems.* ● **po|ten|tial|ly** **ADV** ❑ *This is a potentially dangerous situation.*
2 **N-NONCOUNT** If someone or something has **potential**, they could become successful or useful in the future. ❑ *The boy has great potential.*
3 **N-NONCOUNT** If you say that someone or something has **potential for** doing a particular thing, you mean that it is possible they may do it. If there is **the potential for** something, it may happen. ❑ *The potential for conflict is great.* [from Old French]

po|ten|tial dif|fer|ence (**potential differences**) **N-COUNT/N-NONCOUNT** SCIENCE **Potential difference** is the difference in voltage between two points on an electrical circuit.

po|ten|tial en|er|gy **N-NONCOUNT** SCIENCE **Potential energy** is the energy that an object has because of its position or condition, for example because it is raised above the ground. Compare with **kinetic energy**.

pot|tery /ˈpɒtəri/ **N-NONCOUNT** ARTS **Pottery** is pots, dishes, and other objects made from clay. ❑ *The store sells a fine range of pottery.* [from Old French]
→ look at Word Web: **pottery**

pouch /paʊtʃ/ (**pouches**) **N-COUNT** SCIENCE The **pouch** of an animal such as a kangaroo is the pocket of skin on its stomach in which its baby grows. ❑ *...a kangaroo with a baby in its pouch.* [from Old Norman French]

| Word Web | pottery |

There are three basic types of **pottery**. Earthenware **dishes** are made from **clay** and **fired** at a relatively low temperature. They are **porous** and must be **glazed** in order to hold water. Potters first created earthenware objects about 15,000 years ago. Stoneware pieces are heavier and are fired at a higher temperature. They are **impermeable** even without a glaze. Porcelain **ceramics** are fragile. They have thin walls and are **translucent**. Stoneware and porcelain are not as old as earthenware. They appeared about 2,000 years ago when the Chinese started building high-temperature kilns. Another name for porcelain is **china**.

clay

stoneware

china

poul|try /ˈpoʊltri/ **N-PLURAL** You can use **poultry** to talk about birds that you keep for their eggs and meat, such as chickens. [from Old French]
→ look at Word Web: **meat**

pounce /paʊns/ (**pounces, pouncing, pounced**) **V-I** If a person or an animal **pounces on** someone or something, they suddenly jump on them. ❑ *He pounced on the photographer and knocked him to the ground.* [from Middle English]

pound /paʊnd/ (**pounds, pounding, pounded**)
1 **N-COUNT** MATH A **pound** is a unit for measuring weight that is used in the U.S., Britain, and some other countries. One pound is equal to 0.454 kilograms. ❑ *Her weight was under ninety pounds.* ❑ *...a pound of cheese.*
2 **N-COUNT** The **pound** (£) is the unit of money used in Britain. ❑ *It cost almost a million pounds.*
3 **V-T/V-I** If you **pound** something or **pound on** it, you hit it with great force, usually loudly and repeatedly. ❑ *He pounded the table with his fist.* ❑ *Somebody began pounding on the front door.* [from Old English]

pour /pɔr/ (**pours, pouring, poured**)
1 **V-T** If you **pour** a liquid or other substance, you make it flow out of a container. ❑ *She poured some water into a bowl.*
2 **V-T** If you **pour** someone a drink, you put some of the drink in a cup or a glass for them. ❑ *She asked Tillie to pour her a cup of coffee.*
3 **V-I** When a liquid **pours** somewhere, it flows there quickly and in large amounts. ❑ *Blood was pouring from his broken nose.* ❑ *Tears poured down our faces.*

pour

4 **V-I** If people **pour** into or out of a place, they go there quickly and in large numbers. ❑ *At six p.m. workers poured from the offices.*
5 **V-I** When it rains very heavily, you can say that **it is pouring.** ❑ *It was still pouring outside.*

▶ **pour out** If you **pour out** a drink, you put some of it in a cup or a glass. ❑ *Larry poured out four glasses of water.*

Word Partnership	Use **pour** with :
N	pour **a liquid**, pour **a mixture**, pour **water** **1**
	pour **coffee**, pour **a drink** **2**

pov|er|ty /ˈpɒvərti/ **N-NONCOUNT** **Poverty** is the state of being very poor. ❑ *Many of these people are living in poverty.* [from Old French]

pow|der /ˈpaʊdər/ (**powders**) **N-COUNT/N-NONCOUNT** **Powder** is a fine dry dust. ❑ *Put a small amount of the powder into a container and mix with water.* ❑ *...cocoa powder.* [from Old French]
→ look at Word Web: **makeup**

pow|er /ˈpaʊər/ (**powers**)
1 **N-NONCOUNT** If someone has **power**, they have control over people. ❑ *When children are young, parents still have a lot of power.*
2 **N-NONCOUNT** Your **power to** do something is your ability to do it. ❑ *She has the power to charm anyone.*
3 **N-NONCOUNT** If someone in authority has the **power** to do something, they have the legal right to do it. ❑ *The police have the power to arrest people who carry knives.*
4 **N-NONCOUNT** If a group of people are **in power**, they are in charge of a country or an organization. ❑ *Idi Amin was in power for eight years.*
5 **N-NONCOUNT** If it is **in** or **within** your **power to** do something, you are able to do it or you have the resources to deal with it. ❑ *It is within your power to change your life if you are not happy.*
6 **N-NONCOUNT** SCIENCE The **power** of something is its physical strength or the ability that it has to affect things. ❑ *This vehicle has more power and better brakes.*
7 **N-NONCOUNT** **Power** is energy that can be used for making electricity or for making machines work. ❑ *Nuclear power is cleaner than coal.* ❑ *The storm left a million homes without electrical power.*
8 **N-COUNT** MATH In math, **power** is used for talking about the number of times that you multiply a number by itself. For example, "5 to the power of 5" means "5×5×5×5×5."
9 **N-NONCOUNT** SCIENCE In physics, **power** is a measure of the amount of work that is done in a particular time. [from Vulgar Latin]
→ look at Word Webs: **electricity, energy, solar**

P

pow|er|ful /paʊərfəl/

1 **ADJ** A **powerful** person or organization is able to control people and events. ❑ *You're a powerful man—people will listen to you.* ❑ *Russia and India are two large, powerful countries.*

2 **ADJ** Someone's body is **powerful** if it is physically strong. ❑ *He lifts weights to maintain his powerful muscles.*

3 **ADJ** A **powerful** machine or substance is very strong. ❑ *We need more and more powerful computer systems.*

4 **ADJ** A **powerful** smell is very strong. ❑ *There was a powerful smell of gasoline in the car.*

5 **ADJ** A **powerful** voice is loud. ❑ *Mrs. Jones's powerful voice interrupted them.*

6 **ADJ** You describe a piece of writing, speech, or work of art as **powerful** when it has a strong effect on people's feelings or beliefs. ❑ *...a powerful drama about the effects of racism.* ● **pow|er|ful|ly** **ADV** ❑ *The play is painful, funny, and powerfully acted.* [from Vulgar Latin]

pow|er|less /paʊrlɪs/ **ADJ** Someone who is **powerless** is unable to do anything to control a situation. ❑ *If you don't have money, you're powerless.* ❑ *Security guards were powerless to stop the crowd.* [from Vulgar Latin]

pow|er line (**power lines**) **N-COUNT** A **power line** is a cable, especially above ground, along which electricity travels to an area or a building.

pow|er sta|tion (**power stations**) **N-COUNT** A **power station** is a place where electricity is produced.

prac|ti|cal /præktɪkəl/

1 **ADJ** **Practical** means involving real situations and events, rather than ideas and theories. ❑ *Our system is the most practical way of preventing crime.*

2 **ADJ** If someone is **practical**, they make sensible decisions and deal effectively with problems. ❑ *We need a practical person to take care of the details.* ❑ *You were always so practical, Maria.*

3 **ADJ** **Practical** ideas and methods are likely to be effective or successful in a real situation. ❑ *Our system is the most practical way of preventing crime.*

4 **ADJ** **Practical** clothes are useful rather than just being fashionable or attractive. ❑ *We'll need plenty of lightweight, practical clothes.* [from French]

Thesaurus	practice Also look up :
ADJ	businesslike, pragmatic, reasonable, sensible, systematic; *(ant.)* impractical **2** **3**

prac|ti|cal|ly /præktɪkli/

1 **ADV** **Practically** means almost. ❑ *He's known the old man practically all his life.*

2 **ADV** You use **practically** to describe something that involves real actions or events rather than ideas or theories. ❑ *The course is practically based.* [from French]

prac|tice /præktɪs/ (**practices, practicing, practiced**)

1 **N-COUNT** A **practice** is something that people do regularly. ❑ *They campaign against the practice of using animals for experiments.*

2 **N-COUNT/N-NONCOUNT** **Practice** is the act of doing something regularly in order to be able to do it better. ❑ *It takes a lot of practice to become a good musician.*

3 **N-COUNT** A doctor's or lawyer's **practice** is his or her business, often shared with other doctors or lawyers. ❑ *The new doctor's practice was miles away from where I lived.*

4 **V-T/V-I** If you **practice** something, you do it regularly in order to do it better. ❑ *She practiced the piano in the school basement.* ❑ *Keep practicing, and maybe next time you'll do better.*

5 **V-T** When people **practice** something such as a custom or a religion, they take part in the activities associated with it. ❑ *...a family that practiced traditional Judaism.*

● **prac|tic|ing** **ADJ** ❑ *He was a practicing Muslim throughout his life.* [from Medieval Latin]

Thesaurus	practice Also look up :
N	custom, habit, method, procedure, system, way **1**
	exercise, rehearsal, training, workout **2**

prai|rie /prɛəri/ (**prairies**)

N-COUNT/N-NONCOUNT GEOGRAPHY A **prairie** is a large area of flat land in North America where very few trees grow. [from French]
→ look at Word Web: **habitat**

praise /preɪz/ (**praises, praising, praised**)

1 **V-T** If you **praise** someone or something, you say that you admire or respect them for something they have done. ❑ *The passengers praised John for saving their lives.*

2 **N-NONCOUNT** **Praise** is also a noun. ❑ *The ladies are full of praise for the staff.* [from Old French]

pray /preɪ/ (**prays, praying, prayed**)

1 **V-T/V-I** When people **pray**, they speak to God or a god. ❑ *We pray that Billy's family will now find peace.* ❑ *He spent his time in prison praying and studying.*

2 **V-T/V-I** If you **are praying** that something will happen, you are hoping for it very much. ❑ *I'm praying for good weather.* ❑ *I'm praying that someone will do something before it's too late.* [from Old French]

prayer /prɛər/ (**prayers**)

1 **N-COUNT** A **prayer** is the words that a person says when they speak to God or a god. ❑ *They should say a prayer for the people on both sides.*

2 **N-NONCOUNT** **Prayer** is the activity of speaking to God or a god. ❑ *The monks give their lives to prayer.*

3 **N-PLURAL** A short religious service at which people gather to pray can be referred to as **prayers**. ❑ *...evening prayers.* [from Old French]

preach /pritʃ/ (**preaches, preaching, preached**)

1 **V-T/V-I** When a member of the clergy **preaches** a sermon, he or she gives a talk on a religious or moral subject during a religious service. ❑ *The priest preached a sermon on the devil.* ❑ *The bishop will preach to a crowd of several hundred people.* ● **preach|er** (**preachers**) **N-COUNT** ❑ *...acceptance of women preachers.*

2 **V-T/V-I** When people **preach**, or **preach** a belief or a course of action, they try to persuade other people to accept the belief or to take the course of action. ❑ *He was trying to preach peace.* ❑ *Experts are preaching that even a little exercise is better than none at all.* [from Old French]

Pre|cam|brian /prɪkæmbriən/ also **Pre-Cambrian** **ADJ** SCIENCE **Precambrian** time is the period of the Earth's history from the time the Earth formed until around 600 million years ago.

pre|cari|ous /prɪkɛəriəs/

1 **ADJ** If your situation is **precarious**, you are not in complete control of events and might fail in what you are doing at any moment. ❑ *Our financial situation has become precarious.* ● **pre|cari|ous|ly** **ADV** ❑ *This left him clinging precariously to his job.*

2 **ADJ** Something that is **precarious** is not securely held in place and seems likely to fall or collapse at any moment. ❑ *They*

crawled up precarious ladders. ● **pre|cari|ous|ly** **ADV** ❑ *One of my grocery bags was precariously balanced on the car trunk.* [from Latin]

Word Link	caut ≈ taking care : caution, cautious, precaution

Word Link	pre ≈ before : precaution, precede, predict

pre|cau|tion /prɪkɔʃⁿn/ (**precautions**)

N-COUNT A **precaution** is an action that is intended to prevent something bad from happening. ❑ *Just as a precaution, he should move to a place of safety.* [from French]

pre|cede /prɪsid/ (**precedes, preceding, preceded**) **V-T** If one event or period of time **precedes** another, it happens before it. [FORMAL] ❑ *Adjectives usually precede the noun they describe.* [from Old French]

prec|edent /prɛsɪdənt/ (**precedents**)

N-COUNT/N-NONCOUNT If there is a **precedent for** an action or an event, it has happened before, and this can be regarded as an argument for doing it again. [FORMAL] ❑ *The trial could set an important precedent for dealing with similar cases.* [from Old French]

pre|cious /prɛʃəs/

1 **ADJ** **Precious** objects are worth a lot of money because they are rare. ❑ *The company mines precious metals throughout North America.*

2 **ADJ** If something is **precious** to you, it is important to you, and you do not want to lose it. ❑ *Her family's support is particularly precious to Josie.* [from Old French]

pre|cipi|ta|tion /prɪsɪpɪteɪʃⁿn/

1 **N-NONCOUNT** SCIENCE **Precipitation** is rain, snow, or hail.

2 **N-NONCOUNT** SCIENCE **Precipitation** is a process in a chemical reaction that causes solid particles to become separated from a liquid. [from Latin]
→ look at Word Webs: **precipitation, climate**

pre|cise /prɪsaɪs/

1 **ADJ** Something that is **precise** is exact and accurate in all its details. ❑ *I can remember the precise moment when I heard the news.*

2 **ADJ** You use **precise** to emphasize that you are referring to an exact thing, rather than something vague. ❑ *I can remember the precise moment when my daughter came to see me.* ❑ *The equipment sent back information on the precise distance between the moon and the Earth.* [from French]

P

Word Web   precipitation

Clouds are made of tiny **droplets** of **water vapor**. When the droplets fall to earth, they are called **precipitation**. Tiny droplets fall as **drizzle**. Larger droplets fall as **rain**. **Snow** is falling **ice crystals**. **Freezing rain** begins as snow. The **snowflakes** melt and then freeze again when they hit an object. **Sleet** is frozen **raindrops** that bounce when they hit the ground. **Hail** is made of frozen raindrops that travel up and down within a cloud. Each time they move downward, more water freezes on their surfaces. Finally they strike the earth as balls of ice.

pre|cise|ly /prɪsaɪsli/
1 **ADV** **Precisely** means accurately and exactly. ❑ *Nobody knows precisely how many people are still living there.*
2 **ADV** You can use **precisely** to show that a reason or a fact is the only important one there is, or that it is obvious. ❑ *Children come to zoos precisely to see captive animals.* [from French]

pre|ci|sion /prɪsɪʒ³n/ **N-NONCOUNT** If you do something **with precision**, you do it exactly as it should be done. ❑ *He hits the ball with precision.* [from Latin]

pre|co|cial /prɪkoʊʃ³l/ **ADJ** SCIENCE A **precocial** chick is a young bird that is relatively well-developed when it is born and requires little parental care. Compare with **altricial**.

pre|con|cep|tion /prikənsɛpʃ³n/ (**preconceptions**) **N-COUNT** Your **preconceptions** about something are beliefs formed about it before you have enough information or experience. ❑ *Did you have any preconceptions about the sort of people who did computing?*

pre|con|di|tion /prikəndɪʃ³n/ (**preconditions**) **N-COUNT** If one thing is a **precondition for** another, it must happen or be done before the second thing can happen or exist. [FORMAL] ❑ *They demanded the release of three prisoners as a precondition for negotiation.*

preda|tor /prɛdətər/ (**predators**) **N-COUNT** SCIENCE A **predator** is an animal that kills and eats other animals. ❑ *With no natural predators on the island, the animals lived happily.* [from Latin]
→ look at Word Webs: **carnivore, food, shark**

pre|de|ces|sor /prɛdɪsɛsər/ (**predecessors**)
1 **N-COUNT** Your **predecessor** is the person who had your job before you. ❑ *He learned everything he knew from his predecessor.*
2 **N-COUNT** The **predecessor** of an object or a machine is the object or machine that came before it in a sequence or process of development. ❑ *The car is 2 inches shorter than its predecessor.* [from Old French]

Word Link *dict ≈ speaking : contradict, dictate, predict*

Word Link *pre ≈ before : precaution, precede, predict*

pre|dict /prɪdɪkt/ (**predicts, predicting, predicted**) **V-T** If you **predict** an event, you say that it will happen. ❑ *The old man correctly predicted the results of fifteen matches.* [from Latin]
→ look at Word Webs: **experiment, forecast**

pre|dict|able /prɪdɪktəb³l/ **ADJ** If an event is **predictable**, it is obvious in advance that it will happen. ❑ *This was a predictable reaction.* [from Latin]

pre|dic|tion /prɪdɪkʃ³n/ (**predictions**) **N-COUNT/N-NONCOUNT** If you make a **prediction**, you say what you think will happen. ❑ *My prediction is that the process will take about 5 years.* [from Latin]
→ look at Word Web: **science**

pre|domi|nant /prɪdɒmɪnənt/ **ADJ** If something is **predominant**, it is more important or noticeable than anything else in a set of people or things. ❑ *Mandy's predominant emotion was confusion.*
● **pre|domi|nance** **N-SING** ❑ *...the predominance of women in teaching.*

P

● **pre|domi|nant|ly** **ADV** ❑ *Scotland is a predominantly rural country.* [from Medieval Latin]

preen /prin/ (**preens, preening, preened**) **V-T** SCIENCE When birds **preen** their feathers, they clean them and arrange them neatly using their beaks. ● **preen|ing** **N-NONCOUNT** ❑ *Preening of the feathers keeps them waterproof and in good condition.* [from Old English]

pref|ace /prɛfɪs/ (**prefaces**) **N-COUNT** LANGUAGE ARTS A **preface** is an introduction at the beginning of a book. ❑ *Have you read the preface to Kelman's novel?* [from Medieval Latin]

pre|fer /prɪfɜr/ (**prefers, preferring, preferred**) **V-T** If you **prefer** someone or something, you like that person or thing better than another. ❑ *Does he prefer a particular sort of music?* ❑ *I preferred books and people to politics.* ❑ *He would prefer to be in Philadelphia.* [from Latin]

pref|er|able /prɛfərəbᵊl, prɛfrə-, prɪfɜrə-/ **ADJ** When one thing is **preferable to** another, it is better or more suitable. ❑ *For me, a trip to the supermarket is preferable to buying food on the Internet.* ● **pref|er|ably** /prɛfərəbli, prɛfrə-, prɪfɜrə-/ **ADV** ❑ *Get exercise, preferably in the fresh air.* [from Latin]

pref|er|ence /prɛfərəns/ (**preferences**)
1 **N-COUNT/N-NONCOUNT** If you have a **preference for** something, you would like to have or do that thing rather than something else. ❑ *Customers have shown a preference for salty snacks.*
2 **N-NONCOUNT** If you **give preference to** someone, you choose them rather than someone else. ❑ *The university will give preference to students from poorer backgrounds.* [from Latin]

Word Link   *fix ≈ fastening : fixture, prefix, suffix*

pre|fix /prifɪks/ (**prefixes**) **N-COUNT** LANGUAGE ARTS A **prefix** is a letter or a group of letters that is added to the beginning of a word in order to form a different word. For example, the prefix "un-" is added to "happy" to form "unhappy." Compare with **suffix**.

preg|nant /prɛgnənt/ **ADJ** If a woman or a female animal is **pregnant**, she has a baby or babies developing in her body. ❑ *I'm seven months pregnant.* ● **preg|nan|cy** /prɛgnənsi/ (**pregnancies**) **N-COUNT/N-NONCOUNT**

❑ *We keep a record of your weight gain during pregnancy.* [from Latin]
→ look at Word Web: **reproduction**

Word Partnership	Use **pregnant** with :
N	**pregnant** with a baby/child, pregnant mother, pregnant wife, pregnant woman
V	be **pregnant**, become pregnant, get pregnant

pre|his|tor|ic /prihɪstɔrɪk/ **ADJ** SOCIAL STUDIES **Prehistoric** people and things existed at a time before information was written down. ❑ *...the prehistoric cave paintings of Lascaux.*

preju|dice /prɛdʒədɪs/ (**prejudices, prejudicing, prejudiced**)
1 **N-COUNT/N-NONCOUNT** SOCIAL STUDIES **Prejudice** is an unreasonable dislike of a particular group of people or things. ❑ *These people have always suffered from racial prejudice.* ❑ *There seems to be some prejudice against workers over 45.*
2 **V-T** If you **prejudice** someone or something, you influence them so that they are unfair in some way. ❑ *Words like "mankind" and "manpower" may prejudice people against women.* ❑ *The report was held back for fear of prejudicing his trial.* [from Old French]

Thesaurus	**prejudice** Also look up :
N	bias, bigotry, disapproval, intolerance; (ant.) tolerance **1**

preju|diced /prɛdʒədɪst/ **ADJ** A person who is **prejudiced** against someone from a different group has an unreasonable dislike of them. ❑ *They complained that the police were racially prejudiced.* [from Old French]

pre|limi|nary /prɪlɪmɪnɛri/ **ADJ** **Preliminary** activities or discussions take place at the beginning of an event, often as a form of preparation. ❑ *Preliminary results show the Republican Party with 11 percent of the vote.* [from New Latin]

prema|ture /primətʃʊər/
1 **ADJ** Something that is **premature** happens earlier than people expect. ❑ *Heart disease is a common cause of premature death.*
2 **ADJ** A **premature** baby is one that was born before the date when it was expected to be born. ❑ *Even very young premature babies respond to their mother's presence.* [from Latin]

prem|ier /prɪmɪər/ (**premiers**)

1 **N-COUNT** A country's **premier** is its leader. ❑ *He will meet the Australian premier John Howard.*

2 **ADJ** **Premier** is used to describe something that is considered to be the best or most important thing of a particular type. ❑ *...the country's premier opera company.* [from Old French]

prem|ise /prɛmɪs/ (**premises**)

1 **N-PLURAL** The **premises** of a business or an institution are all the buildings and land that it occupies. ❑ *There is a kitchen on the premises.*

2 **N-COUNT** A **premise** is something that you suppose is true and that you use as a basis for developing an idea. [FORMAL] ❑ *The premise is that schools will work harder to improve if they must compete.* [from Old French]

pre|mium /priːmiəm/ (**premiums**)

1 **N-COUNT** BUSINESS A **premium** is a sum of money that you pay regularly to an insurance company for an insurance policy. ❑ *...insurance premiums.*

2 **N-COUNT** A **premium** is a sum of money that you have to pay for something in addition to the normal cost. ❑ *People will normally pay a premium for a good house in a good area.*

3 **PHRASE** If something is **at a premium**, it is wanted or needed, but is difficult to get or achieve. ❑ *If space is at a premium, choose furniture that folds away.* [from Latin]

prepa|ra|tion /prɛpəreɪʃən/ (**preparations**)

1 **N-NONCOUNT** **Preparation** is the process of getting something ready for use. ❑ *Todd put the papers in his briefcase in preparation for the meeting.*

2 **N-PLURAL** **Preparations** are all the arrangements that are made for a future event. ❑ *We were making preparations for our wedding.* [from Latin]

pre|pare /prɪpɛər/ (**prepares, preparing, prepared**)

1 **V-T** If you **prepare** something, you make it ready. ❑ *We will need several weeks to prepare the report for publication.*

2 **V-T/V-I** If you **prepare for** an event or an action that will happen soon, you get ready for it. ❑ *You should begin to prepare for the cost of your child's education.* ❑ *He went back to his hotel and prepared to catch a train.*

3 **V-T** When you **prepare** food, you get it ready to be eaten. ❑ *She started preparing dinner.* [from Latin]

Word Partnership	Use prepare with :
N	prepare **a list**, prepare **a plan**, prepare **a report** **1**
	prepare **for battle/war**, prepare **for the future**, prepare **for the worst** **2**
	prepare **dinner**, prepare **food**, prepare **a meal** **3**

pre|pared /prɪpɛərd/

1 **ADJ** If you are **prepared to** do something, you are willing to do it if necessary. ❑ *Are you prepared to help if we need you?*

2 **ADJ** If you are **prepared for** something that you think is going to happen, you are ready for it. ❑ *Police are prepared for large crowds.*

3 **ADJ** You can describe something as **prepared** when it has been done or made beforehand, so that it is ready when it is needed. ❑ *He ended his prepared statement by thanking the police.* [from Latin]

Word Link | pos ≈ placing : de*pos*it, pre*pos*ition, *pos*ition

prepo|si|tion /prɛpəzɪʃən/ (**prepositions**)

N-COUNT LANGUAGE ARTS A **preposition** is a word such as "by," "for," "into," or "with" that usually comes before a noun. [from Latin]

pre|scribe /prɪskraɪb/ (**prescribes, prescribing, prescribed**)

1 **V-T** If a doctor **prescribes** medicine or treatment for you, he or she tells you what medicine or treatment to have. ❑ *The physician examines the patient and prescribes medication.*

2 **V-T** If a person or a set of laws or rules **prescribes** an action or a duty, they state that it must be carried out. [FORMAL] ❑ *...Article II of the Constitution, which prescribes the method of electing a president.* [from Latin]

pre|scrip|tion /prɪskrɪpʃən/ (**prescriptions**)

N-COUNT A **prescription** is a piece of paper on which a doctor writes an order for medicine. ❑ *He gave me a prescription for some cream.* [from Latin]

pres|ence /prɛzəns/

1 **N-SING** Someone's **presence** in a place is the fact that they are there. ❑ *His presence always causes trouble.*

2 **PHRASE** If you are **in** someone's **presence**, you are in the same place as that person. ❑ *Children should do their homework in the presence of their parents.* [from Old French]

---
present
❶ ADJECTIVE AND NOUN
   USES
❷ VERB USES

---

❶ **pres|ent** /prɛzᵊnt/ (**presents**)

1 **ADJ** You use **present** to talk about things and people that exist now. ❑ *The present situation is very difficult for us.*

2 **PHRASE** A situation that exists **at present** exists now. ❑ *At present, we do not know the cause of the disease.*

3 **ADJ** If someone is **present at** an event, they are there. ❑ *Nearly 85 percent of men are present at the birth of their children.*

4 **N-COUNT** A **present** is something that you give to someone, for example on their birthday. ❑ *She bought a birthday present for her mother.*

5 **N-SING** The **present** is the period of time that we are in now and the things that are happening now. ❑ *...the story of my life from my childhood up to the present.*

6 **ADJ** If something, especially a substance or disease, is **present in** something else, it exists in that thing. ❑ *Vitamin D is naturally present in breast milk.* [Senses 1 to 3, 5, and 6 from Latin. Sense 4 from Old French.]

Usage **present**
Make sure you pronounce *present* correctly—the noun or adjective has stress on the first syllable, while the verb has stress on the second syllable: *At the present moment, Timmy has two birthday presents hidden in his closet, ready to present to Abby when she comes home.*

❷ **pres|ent** /prɪzɛnt/ (**presents, presenting, presented**)

1 **V-T** If you **present** something, you formally give it to someone. ❑ *The mayor presented him with a gold medal.* ❑ *Betty will present the prizes to the winners.*

2 **V-T** If you **present** someone or something in a particular way, you describe them in that way. ❑ *Many false statements were presented as facts.* ❑ *...tricks to help him present himself in a more confident way.* [from Old French]

pres|en|ta|tion /prɪzɛnteɪʃᵊn/ (**presentations**)

1 **N-NONCOUNT** Presentation is the appearance of something that someone has worked to create. ❑ *Keep the presentation of food attractive but simple.*

2 **N-NONCOUNT** The **presentation** of

something is the act of formally giving it to someone. ❑ *The evening began with the presentation of awards.*

3 **N-COUNT** A **presentation** is an event at which someone is given an award. ❑ *He received his award at a presentation in Kansas City.*

4 **N-COUNT** When someone gives a **presentation**, they show or explain something to a group of people. ❑ *Philip and I gave a short presentation.* [from Latin]

pres|ent con|tin|uous **N-SING**
LANGUAGE ARTS In grammar, the **present continuous** is the structure that uses "be" and the "-ing" form of a verb. An example of the present continuous is "He is walking down the road."

pres|ent par|ti|ci|ple (**present participles**)
N-COUNT LANGUAGE ARTS In grammar, the **present participle** of a verb is the form that ends in "-ing." Present participles are used to form continuous tenses.

pres|ent per|fect **N-SING** LANGUAGE ARTS In grammar, the **present perfect** is the form of a verb that you use to talk about things that began in the past and are still happening or still important in the present. It is formed with the verb "have" and a past participle. An example of the present perfect is "She has promised to come."

pres|ent tense (**present tenses**) **N-COUNT**
LANGUAGE ARTS In grammar, **the present tense** is the form that is used for talking about things that exist, things that are happening now, or things that happen regularly.

pre|serva|tive /prɪzɜrvətɪv/ (**preservatives**)
N-COUNT/N-NONCOUNT A **preservative** is a chemical that keeps something in good condition. ❑ *The list shows all the preservatives used in food processing.* [from Old French]

Word Link serv ≈ keeping : *conserve, observe, preserve*

Word Link ation ≈ state of : *dehydration, elevation, preservation*

pre|serve /prɪzɜrv/ (**preserves, preserving, preserved**)

1 **V-T** If you **preserve** something, you take action to save it or protect it. ❑ *We need to preserve the forest.* ● **pres|er|va|tion**
N-NONCOUNT ❑ *We're collecting money for the preservation of our historic buildings.*

2 **V-T** If you **preserve** food, you treat it in order to make it last longer. ❑ *Use only*

P

enough sugar to preserve the plums.

3 **N-COUNT** A nature **preserve** is an area of land or water where animals are protected from hunters. ❑ *...Pantanal, one of the world's great wildlife preserves.* [from Old French]

Word Link	sid ≈ sitting : pre**sid**e, pre**sid**ent, re**sid**ence

pre|side /prɪzaɪd/ (**presides, presiding, presided**) **V-I** If you **preside over** a meeting, you are in charge. ❑ *He presided over the weekly meetings of the organization.* [from French]

presi|den|cy /prɛzɪdənsi/ (**presidencies**) **N-COUNT** The **presidency** of a country or an organization is the position of being the president. ❑ *He was offered the presidency of the University of Saskatchewan.* [from Old French]

presi|dent /prɛzɪdənt/ (**presidents**)

1 **N-COUNT** SOCIAL STUDIES The **president** of a country that has no king or queen is the person who is in charge of that country. ❑ *The president must act quickly.*

2 **N-COUNT** The **president** of an organization is the person who has the highest position in it. ❑ *He is the national president of the Screen Actors Guild.* [from Old French]

→ look at Word Web: **election**

presi|den|tial /prɛzɪdɛnʃ°l/ **ADJ** **Presidential** activities or things relate or belong to a president. ❑ *He is reporting on Peru's presidential election.* [from Old French]

press /prɛs/ (**presses, pressing, pressed**)

1 **V-T** If you **press** something somewhere, you push it firmly against something else. ❑ *He pressed his back against the door.*

2 **V-T** If you **press** a button or a switch, you push it with your finger in order to make a machine work. ❑ *David pressed a button and the door closed.*

3 **V-T/V-I** If you **press** something, or **press down on** it, you push hard against it with your foot or hand. ❑ *He pressed the gas pedal hard.*

4 **V-T** If you **press** someone, you try hard to persuade them to do something. ❑ *They pressed him to have something to eat.* ❑ *It is certain they will press Mr. King for more details.*

5 **V-T** If you **press** clothes, you iron them. ❑ *Vera pressed his shirt.*

6 **N-SING** The **press** consists of newspapers and magazines, and the people who write for them. ❑ *She gave several interviews to the local press.*

7 **PHRASE** If you **press charges against** someone, you make an official accusation against them that has to be decided in a court of law. ❑ *I could have pressed charges against him.*

8 **PHRASE** When substances such as sand or gravel **press together** or when they **are pressed together**, they are pushed hard against each other so that they form a single layer. [from Old French]

→ look at Word Web: **printing**

Word Partnership	Use press with :
N	press **a button, at the** press **of a button 2**
	press **accounts,** press **coverage, freedom of the** press, press **reports 6**
	press **charges 7**

pres|sure /prɛʃər/ (**pressures, pressuring, pressured**)

1 **N-NONCOUNT** **Pressure** is force that you produce when you press hard on something. ❑ *The pressure of his fingers on her arm relaxed.*

2 **N-NONCOUNT** SCIENCE The **pressure** in a place or a container is the force produced by the gas or liquid in it. ❑ *If the pressure falls in the cabin, an oxygen mask will drop in front of you.*

3 **N-NONCOUNT** If you are experiencing **pressure**, you feel that you must do a lot of things or make an important decision in very little time. ❑ *Can you work under pressure?*

4 **V-T** If you **pressure** someone **to** do something, you try to persuade them to do it in a forceful way. ❑ *He will never pressure you to get married.* ❑ *He was pressured into making a decision.* ● **pres|sured** **ADJ** ❑ *You're likely to feel anxious and pressured.* [from Late Latin]

5 → see also **blood pressure**

→ look at Word Webs: **forecast, weather**

pres|tige /prɛstiʒ, -stidʒ/ **N-NONCOUNT** If a person, a country, or an organization has **prestige**, they are admired and respected because they are important or successful. ❑ *...efforts to build up the prestige of the United Nations.* ❑ *His position in the company brought him prestige.* [from French]

pres|tig|ious /prɛstɪdʒəs, -stidʒəs/ **ADJ** A **prestigious** institution, job, or activity is respected and admired by people. ❑ *...one of the most prestigious schools in the country.* [from French]

pre|sum|ably /prɪzuməbli/ **ADV** Something that is **presumably** true is probably true. ❑ *He's not going this year, presumably because of his age.* [from Old French]

Word Link	*sume ≈ taking : as*sume, con*sume,* pre*sume*

pre|sume /prɪzu̱m/ (**presumes, presuming, presumed**)

1 **v-t** If you **presume that** something is true, you think that it is true, although you are not sure. ❑ *I presume that you're here on business.* ❑ *"Has he been home all week?"— "I presume so."*

2 **v-t** If you **presume to** do something, you do it even though you have no right to do it. [FORMAL] ❑ *I would not presume to advise you on such matters.* [from Old French]

pre|sump|tu|ous /prɪzʌ̱mptʃuəs/ **ADJ** If you describe someone or their behavior as **presumptuous**, you disapprove of them because they are doing something that they have no right or authority to do. ❑ *It would be presumptuous to guess what the result will be.* [from Old French]

pre|tend /prɪte̱nd/ (**pretends, pretending, pretended**)

1 **v-t** If you **pretend that** something is true, you try to make people believe that it is true, although in fact it is not. ❑ *I pretend that things are really okay when they're not.* ❑ *He pretended to be asleep.*

2 **v-t** If you **pretend that** you are doing something, you imagine that you are doing it, for example, as part of a game. ❑ *She can sunbathe and pretend she's in Cancun.* [from Latin]

pre|tense /prɪte̱ns, pri̱tens/ (**pretenses**)

1 **N-COUNT/N-NONCOUNT** A **pretense** is an action or way of behaving that is intended to make people believe something that is not true. ❑ *He found it difficult to keep up the pretense of happiness.*

2 **PHRASE** If you do something **under false pretenses**, you do it when people do not know the truth about you and your intentions. ❑ *This interview was conducted under false pretenses.* [from Latin]

pret|ty /prɪ̱ti/ (**prettier, prettiest**)

1 **ADJ** Someone, especially a girl, who is **pretty**, looks nice and is attractive in a delicate way. ❑ *She's a very charming and very pretty girl.*

2 **ADJ** A place or a thing that is **pretty** is attractive and pleasant. ❑ *We stayed in a very pretty little town.*

3 **ADV** You can use **pretty** before an adjective or an adverb to mean "fairly."

[INFORMAL] ❑ *I had a pretty good idea what she was going to do.* [from Old English]

Thesaurus	**pretty** Also look up :
ADJ	beautiful, cute, lovely **1**
	beautiful, charming, pleasant **2**

pre|vail /prɪve̱ɪl/ (**prevails, prevailing, prevailed**)

1 **v-i** If a proposal, a principle, or an opinion **prevails**, it gains influence or is accepted. ❑ *We hoped that common sense would prevail.* ❑ *Rick still believes that justice will prevail.*

2 **v-i** If a situation or an attitude **prevails** in a particular place at a particular time, it is normal or most common in that place at that time. ❑ *A similar situation prevails in Canada.* ❑ *...the confusion which prevailed at the time of the revolution.* [from Latin]

pre|vail|ing /prɪve̱ɪlɪŋ/ **ADJ** The **prevailing** wind in an area is the type of wind that blows over that area most of the time. [from Latin]

preva|lent /pre̱vələnt/ **ADJ** A condition, a practice, or a belief that is **prevalent** is common. ❑ *Single-parent households are becoming increasingly prevalent.* ● **preva|lence** **N-NONCOUNT** ❑ *...the prevalence of heart disease in this country.* [from Latin]

pre|vent /prɪve̱nt/ (**prevents, preventing, prevented**) **v-t** To **prevent** something means to make sure that it does not happen. ❑ *The best way to prevent injury is to wear a seat belt.* ❑ *The disease can prevent you from walking properly.* ● **pre|ven|tion** **N-NONCOUNT** ❑ *Scientists are still learning about the prevention of heart disease.* [from Latin]

pre|view /pri̱vyu/ (**previews**) **N-COUNT** A **preview** is an opportunity to see something such as a movie or an invention before it is open or available to the public. ❑ *He went to a preview of the play.*

pre|vi|ous /pri̱viəs/ **ADJ** A **previous** event or thing is one that happened or existed before the one that you are talking about. ❑ *She has a teenage daughter from a previous marriage.* [from Latin]

pre|vi|ous|ly /pri̱viəsli/

1 **ADV** **Previously** means at some time before the period that you are talking about. ❑ *Guyana's railroads were previously owned by private companies.* ❑ *They gave the contract to a previously unknown company.*

2 **ADV** You can use **previously** to say how

P

much earlier one event was than another event. ❏ *Ingrid had moved to San Diego two weeks previously.* [from Latin]

pre|writ|ing /priːraɪtɪŋ/ also **pre-writing**
N-NONCOUNT ARTS **Prewriting** is the thinking and planning that a writer does before beginning to write something.

prey /preɪ/ (**preys, preying, preyed**)
1 **N-NONCOUNT** SCIENCE An animal's **prey** is the birds or other animals that it hunts and eats in order to live. ❏ *These animals can hunt prey in the water or in trees.*
2 **V-I** A creature that **preys on** other creatures lives by catching and eating them. ❏ *...mountain lions and bears that prey on sheep.* [from Old French]
→ look at Word Webs: **carnivore, shark**

price /praɪs/ (**prices**)
1 **N-COUNT** The **price** of something is the amount of money that you have to pay in order to buy it. ❏ *We have seen huge changes in the price of gas.* ❏ *They expect house prices to rise.*
2 **PHRASE** If you want something **at any price**, you are determined to get it. ❏ *They wanted fame at any price.*
3 **N-SING** The **price** that you pay for something that you want is an unpleasant thing that you have to do or suffer in order to get it. ❏ *These stars often pay a high price for their success.* [from Old French]

price|less /praɪsləs/
1 **ADJ** Something that is **priceless** is worth a very large amount of money. ❏ *Several priceless treasures were stolen from the Palace Museum last night.*
2 **ADJ** **Priceless** means extremely useful or valuable. ❏ *Our national parks are priceless treasures.* [from Old French]

pricey /praɪsi/ (**pricier, priciest**) also **pricy**
ADJ If something is **pricey**, it is expensive. [INFORMAL] ❏ *Medical insurance is very pricey.* [from Old French]

prick /prɪk/ (**pricks, pricking, pricked**)
1 **V-T** If you **prick** something, you make small holes in it with a sharp object. ❏ *Prick the potatoes and rub the skins with salt.*
2 **V-T** If something sharp **pricks** you, it presses into your skin and hurts you. ❏ *It felt like a needle pricking me in the foot.* [from Old English]

pride /praɪd/
1 **N-NONCOUNT** **Pride** is a feeling of satisfaction that you have because you have

done something well. ❏ *We all felt the sense of pride when we finished early.* ❏ *We take pride in offering you the highest standards.*
2 **N-NONCOUNT** **Pride** is a sense of dignity and self-respect. ❏ *His pride wouldn't allow him to ask for help.*
3 **N-NONCOUNT** Someone's **pride** is the feeling that they have that they are better or more important than other people. ❏ *His pride may still be his downfall.* [from Old English]

priest /priːst/ (**priests**) **N-COUNT** A **priest** is a person who has religious duties in a place where people worship. ❏ *He trained to be a Catholic priest.* [from Old English]

pri|mari|ly /praɪmɛrɪli/ **ADV** You use **primarily** to say what is mainly true in a particular situation. ❏ *These reports come primarily from passengers on the plane.* [from Latin]

Word Link	*prim ≈ first : primary, prime, primitive*

pri|ma|ry /praɪmɛri, -məri/ (**primaries**)
1 **ADJ** **Primary** describes something that is most important for someone or something. [FORMAL] ❏ *Language difficulties were the primary cause of his problems.*
2 **ADJ** **Primary** education is the first few years of formal education for children. ❏ *Most primary students now have experience with computers.*
3 **N-COUNT** SOCIAL STUDIES A **primary** or a **primary election** is an election in a state in the U.S. in which people vote for someone to represent a political party. Compare with **general election**. ❏ *He won the 1968 New Hampshire primary.* [from Latin]

pri|ma|ry col|or (**primary colors**) **N-COUNT** ARTS **Primary colors** are the three colors (red, yellow, and blue) that can be mixed together to produce other colors. ❏ *The toys come in bright primary colors that kids will love.*
→ look at Picture Dictionary: **color**

pri|ma|ry pol|lu|tant (**primary pollutants**) **N-COUNT** SCIENCE **Primary pollutants** are substances that are released into the atmosphere and cause pollution. Compare with **secondary pollutant**.

pri|mate /praɪmeɪt/ (**primates**) **N-COUNT** A **primate** is a member of the group of mammals that includes humans, monkeys, and apes. ❏ *The woolly spider*

P

Word Web   primate

Monkeys, apes, and **humans** are all primates. Humans and other primates are alike in surprising ways. We used to believe that only humans were right-handed or left-handed. But when researchers studied a group of 66 **chimpanzees,** they found that chimps are also right-handed and left-handed. Other researchers learned that chimpanzee groups have different cultures. In 1972 a female **gorilla** named Koko began to learn sign language from a college student. Today Koko understands about 2,000 words and can sign about 500 of them. She makes up sentences using three to six words.

monkey is the largest primate in the Americas. [from New Latin]
→ look at Word Web: **primate**

prime /praɪm/ (**primes, priming, primed**)
1 **ADJ** You use **prime** to describe something that is most important in a situation. ❑ *Your happiness is my prime concern.* ❑ *It could be a prime target for attack.*
2 **ADJ** You use **prime** to describe something that is of the best possible quality. ❑ *These beaches are prime sites for development.*
3 **ADJ** You use **prime** to describe an example of a particular kind of thing that is absolutely typical. ❑ *Jodie Foster: the prime example of a child actor who became a respected adult star.*
4 **N-NONCOUNT** Your **prime** is the stage in your life when you are strongest, most active, or most successful. ❑ *I'm just coming into my prime now.* ❑ *Some of these athletes are well past their prime.*
5 **V-T** If you **prime** someone **to** do something, you prepare them to do it, for example by giving them information about it beforehand. ❑ *Arnold primed her for her duties.*
6 **N-COUNT** MATH A **prime** is the same as a **prime number.** [from Latin]

prime me|rid|ian /praɪm mərɪdiən/ **N-SING** SCIENCE The **prime meridian** is the line of longitude, corresponding to zero degrees and passing through Greenwich, England, from which all the other lines of longitude are calculated.

prime min|is|ter (**prime ministers**) **N-COUNT** SOCIAL STUDIES The leader of the government in some countries is called the **prime minister.** ❑ *Vaughan Lewis is the former prime minister of St. Lucia.*

prime num|ber (**prime numbers**) **N-COUNT** MATH A **prime number** is a whole number greater than 1 that cannot be divided exactly by any whole number except itself and the number 1, such as 17.

primi|tive /prɪmɪtɪv/
1 **ADJ** **Primitive** means belonging to a society in which people live in a very simple way, usually without industries or a writing system. ❑ *He has traveled the world, visiting many primitive societies.*
2 **ADJ** **Primitive** means belonging to a very early period in the development of an animal or plant. ❑ *...primitive man.*
3 **ADJ** If something is **primitive,** it is very simple in style. ❑ *The conditions in the camp are primitive.* [from Latin]

prince /prɪns/ (**princes**) **N-COUNT** A **prince** is a male member of a royal family, especially the son of the king or queen. [from Old French]

prin|cess /prɪnsɪs, -sɛs/ (**princesses**)
N-COUNT A **princess** is a female member of a royal family, usually the daughter of the king or queen or the wife of a prince. [from Old French]

prin|ci|pal /prɪnsɪpᵊl/ (**principals**)
1 **ADJ** **Principal** means first in order of importance. ❑ *Money was not the principal reason for his action.* ❑ *Newspapers were the principal source of information.*
2 **N-COUNT** The **principal** of a school is the person in charge of the school. ❑ *Donald King is the principal of Dartmouth High School.* [from Old French]

prin|ci|pal parts **N-PLURAL** LANGUAGE ARTS In grammar, the **principal parts** of a verb are the main inflected forms of the verb. The principal parts of the verb "to sing" are "sings," "singing," "sang," and "sung."

p

prin|ci|ple /prɪnsɪpᵊl/ (principles)

1 **N-COUNT/N-NONCOUNT** Your **principles** are the rules and ideas that you have about how you should behave. ❑ *It's against my principles to be dishonest.*

2 **N-COUNT** A **principle** is a rule about how something works or happens. ❑ *The first principle of democracy is that people should have the right to vote.*

3 **PHRASE** If you refuse to do something **on principle**, you refuse to do it because of your beliefs. ❑ *He would vote against the proposal on principle.*

4 **PHRASE** ARTS The **principles of composition** are the rules used to produce good dance, writing, and other art forms.

5 **PHRASE** ARTS The **principles of design** are the rules used by painters and other visual artists to create a work of art, involving concepts such as balance, contrast, and emphasis. [from Latin]

Usage   principle and principal

Principal and *principle* are often confused because they are pronounced exactly alike. A *principle* is a rule, whereas a *principal* is a person in charge of a school: *The principal handed out a list of principles for student behavior in class.* The adjective *principal* means "most important": *The principal reason for going to school is to become educated.*

---

print /prɪnt/ (prints, printing, printed)

1 **V-T** If you **print** something, you use a machine to put words or pictures on paper. ❑ *The publishers have printed 40,000 copies of the novel.* ● **print|ing** **N-NONCOUNT** ❑ *...a printing and publishing company.*

2 **N-NONCOUNT** **Print** is all the letters and numbers in a printed document. ❑ *I can't read this—the print is too small.*

3 **V-T** If you **print** words, you write in letters that are not joined together. ❑ *Please sign here, then print your name and address.*

4 **PHRASE** If you appear **in print**, or get **into print**, what you say or write is published in a book or a newspaper. ❑ *These poets appeared in print long after their deaths.* [from Old French]
→ look at Word Web: **printing**

▶ **print out** **1** If you **print** a computer file **out**, you use a machine to produce a copy of it on paper. ❑ *I printed out a copy of the letter and put it on Mr. Miller's desk.*

2 → see also **printout**

print|er /prɪntər/ (printers)

1 **N-COUNT** A **printer** is a machine for printing copies of computer documents on paper.

2 **N-COUNT** A **printer** is a person or a company whose job is printing things such as books. ❑ *Franklin was a printer, a publisher, and a diplomat.* [from Old French]
→ look at Picture Dictionaries: **computer, office**
→ look at Word Web: **printing**

print|mak|ing /prɪntmeɪkɪŋ/ **N-NONCOUNT** ARTS **Printmaking** is an artistic technique that consists of making a series of pictures from an original, or from a specially prepared surface.

print|out /prɪntaʊt/ (printouts) also **print-out** **N-COUNT** A **printout** is a piece of paper with information from a computer printed on it. ❑ *Maria gave me a printout of the email.*

pri|or /praɪər/

1 **ADJ** You use **prior** to indicate that something has already happened, or must happen, before another event takes place. ❑ *He claimed he had no prior knowledge of the protest.*

2 **PHRASE** If something happens **prior to** a particular time or event, it happens before that time or event. [FORMAL] ❑ *Prior to his trip to Japan, Steven was in New York.* [from Latin]

Word Web   printing

Before **printing** was invented, scribes wrote **documents** by hand. The first **printers** were the Chinese. They used pieces of wood with rows of **characters** carved into them. Later, they started using **movable type** made of baked clay. They created full **pages** by lining up rows of type. A German named Gutenberg made the first metal type. He also invented the **printing press**. The idea came from the wine press, which was hundreds of years old. In the 1500s, printed advertisements were handbills. The earliest newspapers were **published** in the 1600s.

pri|or|ity /praɪɔrɪti/ (**priorities**)

1 **N-COUNT** If something is a **priority**, it is the most important thing, and you have to deal with it before everything else. ❑ *Her children are her first priority.* ❑ *The government's priority is to build more schools.*

2 **PHRASE** If you **give priority to** something or someone, you treat them as more important than anything else. ❑ *The government should give priority to environmental issues.*

3 **PHRASE** If something **takes priority over** other things, it is more important than other things. ❑ *The needs of the poor must take priority over the desires of the rich.* [from Latin]

prism /prɪzəm/ (**prisms**) **N-COUNT** SCIENCE A **prism** is a block of clear glass or plastic that separates the light passing through it into different colors. [from Medieval Latin]
→ look at Picture Dictionary: **color**
→ look at Word Web: **rainbow**

pris|on /prɪzən/ (**prisons**)
N-COUNT/N-NONCOUNT A **prison** is a building where criminals are kept as punishment. ❑ *He was sent to prison for five years.* [from Old French]

	Word Partnership Use **prison** with :
V	**die in** prison, **escape from** prison, **face** prison, **go to** prison, **release** *someone* **from** prison, **send** *someone* **to** prison, **serve/spend time in** prison
N	**life in** prison, prison **officials**, prison **population**, prison **reform**, prison **sentence**, prison **time**

pris|on|er /prɪzənər/ (**prisoners**) **N-COUNT**
A **prisoner** is a person who is not free, usually because they are in prison.
❑ *A prisoner escaped from Arrowhead Correctional Center early Monday.* ❑ *More than 30,000 Australians were taken prisoner in World War II.* [from Old French]

pri|va|cy /praɪvəsi/ **N-NONCOUNT** Privacy is the freedom to do things without people knowing what you are doing. ❑ *What I do in the privacy of my own home is not your business.* ❑ *We have changed the names to protect the privacy of those involved.* [from Latin]

pri|vate /praɪvɪt/

1 **ADJ** BUSINESS **Private** companies are not owned by the government. ❑ *...a private hospital.* ❑ *Their children go to a private school.*

2 **ADJ** If something is **private**, it is only for one particular person or group, and not for everyone. ❑ *The door was marked "Private."* ❑ *It was a private conversation, so I'm not going to talk about it to anyone else.* ● **pri|vate|ly** **ADV** ❑ *We need to talk privately.*

3 **ADJ** Your **private life** is the part of your life that concerns your personal relationships and activities, and not your job. ❑ *I've always kept my private and professional life separate.*

4 **ADJ** A **private** place is quiet, and you can be alone there without being disturbed. ❑ *It was the only private place they could find.*

5 **ADJ** Your **private** thoughts or feelings are ones that you do not talk about to other people. ❑ *...his private grief.* ● **pri|vate|ly** **ADV** ❑ *Privately, she worries about whether she's really good enough.*

6 **PHRASE** If you do something **in private**, you do it without other people being there. ❑ *Mark asked to talk to his boss in private.* [from Latin]

pri|vat|ize /praɪvətaɪz/ (**privatizes, privatizing, privatized**) **V-T** BUSINESS If a company, an industry, or a service that is owned by the state **is privatized**, the government sells it and makes it a private company. ❑ *Many state-owned companies were privatized.* ● **pri|vati|za|tion** /praɪvətɪzeɪʃ³n/ (**privatizations**) **N-COUNT/N-NONCOUNT** ❑ *...the privatization of government services.* [from Latin]

privi|lege /prɪvɪlɪdʒ, prɪvlɪdʒ/ (**privileges**)

1 **N-COUNT** A **privilege** is a special advantage that only one person or group has. ❑ *We are not asking for special privileges, we simply want equal opportunity.*

2 **N-NONCOUNT** **Privilege** is the power and advantages that belong to a small group of people, usually because of their wealth or their connections with powerful people. ❑ *...a life of privilege.* [from Old French]

	Word Partnership Use **privilege** with :
ADJ	**executive** privilege, **special** privilege **1**
N	**attorney-client** privilege **1** **power and** privilege **2**

privi|leged /prɪvɪlɪdʒd, prɪvlɪdʒd/ **ADJ** If you are **privileged**, you have an advantage that most other people do not have, often because you are rich. ❑ *They had a privileged childhood.* [from Old French]

prize /praɪz/ (**prizes, prizing, prized**)

1 **N-COUNT** A **prize** is money or a special object that you give to the person who wins

P

a game, a race, or a competition. ❑ *He won first prize in the golf tournament.*
2 **v-t** Something that **is prized** is wanted and admired because it is considered to be very valuable or very good quality. ❑ *These colorful baskets are prized by collectors.* [from Old French]

Word Partnership	Use **prize** with :
V	**award a** prize, **claim a** prize, **receive a** prize, **win a** prize **1**
ADJ	**first** prize, **grand** prize, **top** prize **1**

pro /proʊ/ (**pros**)
1 **N-COUNT** SPORTS A **pro** is a professional, especially a professional athlete. [INFORMAL] ❑ *Langer was a pro for 29 years, and competed in nearly 80 championships.* ❑ *...a former college and pro basketball player.*
2 **PHRASE** The **pros and cons** of something are its advantages and disadvantages. ❑ *Motherhood has its pros and cons.* [Sense 2 from Latin.]

Word Link	*prob ≈ testing : probability, probably, probe*

prob|abil|ity /prɒbəbɪlɪti/ (**probabilities**)
N-COUNT/N-NONCOUNT MATH The **probability** of something happening is how likely it is to happen. ❑ *We believe there is a high probability of success.* [from Old French]

prob|able /prɒbəbᵊl/ **ADJ** If something is **probable**, it is likely to be true or likely to happen. ❑ *Jess is a great player, and it's highly probable that she will win.* [from Old French]

prob|ably /prɒbəbli/ **ADV** Something that is **probably** true is likely to be true, although you are not sure. ❑ *I will probably go home on Tuesday.* ❑ *Van Gogh is probably the best-known painter in the world.* [from Old French]

pro|ba|tion /proʊbeɪʃᵊn/ **N-NONCOUNT** **Probation** is a period of time during which a person who has committed a crime has to obey the law and be supervised by a probation officer, rather than being sent to prison. ❑ *She admitted theft and was put on probation for two years.* [from Medieval Latin]

probe /proʊb/ (**probes, probing, probed**)
1 **v-i** If you **probe into** something, you ask questions or try to discover facts about it. ❑ *The more they probed into his background, the more suspicious they became.*
2 **N-COUNT** **Probe** is also a noun. ❑ *Officials have opened a probe into Monday's crash.*

3 **v-t** If you **probe** a place, you search it in order to find someone or something that you are looking for. ❑ *A flashlight beam probed the bushes.* [from Medieval Latin]

prob|lem /prɒbləm/ (**problems**)
1 **N-COUNT** A **problem** is something or someone that causes difficulties, or that makes you worry. ❑ *Pollution is a problem in this city.* ❑ *The government has failed to solve the problem of unemployment.*
2 **N-COUNT** A **problem** is a special type of question that you have to think hard about in order to answer. ❑ *...a math problem.* [from Late Latin]
→ look at Picture Dictionary: **fractions**

Thesaurus	**problem** Also look up :
N	complication, difficulty, hitch **1** puzzle, question, riddle **2**

pro|ce|dure /prəsidʒər/ (**procedures**)
N-COUNT/N-NONCOUNT A **procedure** is the usual or correct way of doing something. ❑ *If your car is stolen, the correct procedure is to report the theft to the local police.* [from Latin]

Word Partnership	Use **procedure** with :
V	**follow a** procedure, **perform a** procedure, **use a** procedure
ADJ	**simple** procedure, **standard (operating)** procedure, procedure

Word Link	*pro ≈ in front, before : proceed, produce, prologue*

pro|ceed /prəsid/ (**proceeds, proceeding, proceeded**)
1 **v-t** If you **proceed to** do something, you do it after doing something else. ❑ *He picked up a book, which he proceeded to read.*
2 **v-i** If something **proceeds**, it continues. [FORMAL] ❑ *The building work is proceeding very slowly.* [from Latin]

pro|cess /prɒsɛs/ (**processes, processing, processed**)
1 **N-COUNT** A **process** is a series of actions that have a particular result. ❑ *After the war, the population began the long process of returning to normal life.*
2 **N-COUNT** SCIENCE A **process** is a series of things that happen naturally and result in a biological or chemical change.
3 **v-t** TECHNOLOGY When people **process** information, they put it through a system or into a computer in order to deal with it. ❑ *...facilities to process the data.* ● **pro|cess|ing** **N-NONCOUNT** ❑ *...data processing.*

4 **PHRASE** If you are **in the process of** doing something, you have started to do it and are still doing it. ❑ *We are in the process of working out the details.*

5 **PHRASE** If you are doing something and you do something else **in the process**, you do the second thing as part of doing the first thing. ❑ *We attend the meetings and in the process, we learn new words and phrases.* [from Old French]

pro|ces|sion /prəsɛ́ʃ°n/ (**processions**)
N-COUNT A **procession** is a line of people or vehicles that follow one another as part of a ceremony. ❑ *Sam watched the procession pass him slowly on its way to Fourth Avenue.* [from Old French]

pro|ces|sor /prɒ́sɛsər/ (**processors**)
N-COUNT A **processor** is the part of a computer that performs the tasks that the user has requested. [from Old French]

pro|claim /proʊkléɪm/ (**proclaims, proclaiming, proclaimed**) **V-T** If people **proclaim** something, they formally make it known. ❑ *The new government proclaimed its independence.* ❑ *Britain proudly proclaims that it is a nation of animal lovers.* [from Latin]

pro|duce (**produces, producing, produced**)

> **PRONUNCIATION HELP**
> Pronounce the verb /prədús/. Pronounce the noun /prɒ́dus/ or /proʊdus/.

1 **V-T** If you **produce** something, you make it or grow it. ❑ *The company produces about 2.3 million tons of steel a year.*
2 **V-T** If one thing **produces** another thing, it causes the second thing to happen. ❑ *The talks failed to produce results.*
3 **V-T** If you **produce** an object from somewhere, you show it or bring it out so that it can be seen. ❑ *To rent a car you must produce a passport.*
4 **V-T** If you **produce** a play or a movie, you organize it and decide how it should be made. ❑ *The movie was produced and directed by Johnny White.*
5 **N-NONCOUNT** **Produce** is fruit and vegetables that are grown to be sold. ❑ *The restaurant uses as much local produce as possible.* [from Latin]

pro|duc|er /prədúsər/ (**producers**)
1 **N-COUNT** A **producer** is a person or a company that makes or grows something. ❑ *Saudi Arabia is the world's leading oil producer.*
2 **N-COUNT** A **producer** is a person who

organizes a play or a movie and decides how it should be made. ❑ *The movie was created by producer Alison Millar.*
3 **N-COUNT** **SCIENCE** In biology, **producers** are plants or bacteria that can produce their own food, especially by means of photosynthesis. [from Latin]
→ look at Word Web: **theater**

prod|uct /prɒ́dʌkt/ (**products**)
1 **N-COUNT** A **product** is something that you make or grow, in order to sell it. ❑ *This cellphone is one of the company's most successful products.*
2 **N-COUNT** **SCIENCE** The **product** of a chemical reaction is the substance that is formed as a result of the chemical reaction.
3 **N-COUNT** If you say that someone or something is a **product of** a situation or a process, you mean that the situation or process has had a significant effect in making them what they are. ❑ *We are all products of our time.* [from Latin]
→ look at Word Web: **industry**

pro|duc|tion /prədʌ́kʃ°n/ (**productions**)
1 **N-NONCOUNT** **Production** is the process of making or growing something in large amounts, or the amount of goods that you make or grow. ❑ *This car went into production last year.* ❑ *The factory needs to increase production.*
2 **N-COUNT** A **production** is a play or other show that is performed in a theater. ❑ *Tonight our class is going to see a production of "Othello."*
3 **N-NONCOUNT** **Production** is the process of making a play, a movie, or a program in order to present it to the public. ❑ *She is head of the production company.* [from Latin]
→ look at Word Web: **theater**

pro|duc|tion values **N-PLURAL** **ARTS** The **production values** of a movie or a play are the quality of its technical aspects, such as the lighting, sets, makeup, and special effects.

pro|duc|tive /prədʌ́ktɪv/
1 **ADJ** If someone or something is **productive**, they produce or do a lot. ❑ *Training makes workers more productive.*
2 **ADJ** If you say that a relationship between people is **productive**, you mean that a lot of good or useful things happen as a result of it. ❑ *He was hopeful that the talks would be productive.* [from Latin]

prod|uc|tiv|ity /prɒdʌktɪ́vɪti/ **N-NONCOUNT** **BUSINESS** **Productivity** is the rate at which goods are produced. ❑ *...continued improvements in productivity.* [from Latin]

P

pro|fes|sion /prəfɛʃⁿn/ (**professions**)

1 **N-COUNT** A **profession** is a type of job for which you need special education or training. ❑ *Ava was a doctor by profession.*

2 **N-COUNT** You can use **profession** to talk about all the people who have the same profession. ❑ *...the medical profession.* [from Medieval Latin]

pro|fes|sion|al /prəfɛʃənⁿl/ (**professionals**)

1 **ADJ** **Professional** means relating to a person's work, especially work that requires special training. ❑ *Get professional advice from your accountant first.*

2 **ADJ** **Professional** people have jobs that require advanced education or training. ❑ *...highly qualified professional people like doctors and engineers.*

3 **N-COUNT** **Professional** is also a noun. ❑ *My father wanted me to become a professional.*

4 **ADJ** **Professional** describes people who do a particular activity for money rather than as a hobby. ❑ *My parents were professional musicians.* ● **pro|fes|sion|al|ly** **ADV** ❑ *I've been singing professionally for 10 years.*

5 **N-COUNT** **Professional** is also a noun. ❑ *The competition is open to both professionals and amateurs.*

6 **ADJ** If you say something that someone does or makes is **professional**, you mean that it is of a very high standard. ❑ *They run the business with a truly professional touch.* ● **pro|fes|sion|al|ism** **N-NONCOUNT** ❑ *She did her job with great professionalism.* ● **pro|fes|sion|al|ly** **ADV** ❑ *...very professionally designed invitations.* [from Medieval Latin]

pro|fes|sor /prəfɛsər/ (**professors**) **N-COUNT** A **professor** is a teacher at a university or a college. ❑ *Kate is a professor of history at George Washington University.* [from Medieval Latin] → look at Word Web: **graduation**

pro|fi|cient /prəfɪʃənt/ **ADJ** If you are **proficient in** something, you can do it well. ❑ *Many of them are proficient in foreign languages.* ● **pro|fi|cien|cy** **N-NONCOUNT** ❑ *...basic proficiency in English.* [from Latin]

pro|file /proʊfaɪl/ (**profiles**)

1 **N-COUNT** Your **profile** is the shape of your face when people see it from the side. ❑ *He was slim, with black hair and a handsome profile.*

2 **N-COUNT** A **profile** is a description that explains the qualities of someone or something.

3 **PHRASE** If someone has a **high profile**, people notice them and what they do. If you **keep a low profile**, you avoid doing things that will make people notice you. ❑ *Indians make up only 2% of South Africa's population but they have a high profile.* [from Italian]

prof|it /prɒfɪt/ (**profits, profiting, profited**)

1 **N-COUNT/N-NONCOUNT** A **profit** is the amount of money that you gain when you sell something for more than you paid for it. ❑ *When he sold the house, Chris made a profit of about $50,000.*

2 **V-I** If you **profit from** something, you earn a profit or gain some advantage from it. ❑ *No one was profiting from the war effort.* ❑ *She would profit from a more relaxed lifestyle.* [from Latin]

prof|it|able /prɒfɪtəbⁿl/

1 **ADJ** If something is **profitable**, it makes a profit. ❑ *The business started to be profitable in its second year.*

2 **ADJ** Something that is **profitable** results in some benefit for you. ❑ *...a profitable exchange of ideas.* ● **prof|it|ably** **ADV** ❑ *He could have spent his time more profitably.* [from Latin]

pro|found /prəfaʊnd/ (**profounder, profoundest**)

1 **ADJ** You use **profound** to emphasize that something is very great or intense. ❑ *...discoveries which had a profound effect on many areas of medicine.* ❑ *...profound disagreement.* ● **pro|found|ly** **ADV** ❑ *This has profoundly affected my life.*

2 **ADJ** A **profound** idea, work, or person shows great intellectual depth and understanding. ❑ *...this tender and profound love poem.* [from Old French]

pro|grade ro|ta|tion /proʊgreɪd roʊteɪʃⁿn/ **N-NONCOUNT** **SCIENCE** Planets that have **prograde rotation** spin on their axis in the same direction that they orbit the sun. Compare with **retrograde rotation**.

| **Word Link** | *gram ≈ writing : dia*gram*, pro*gram*, tele*gram |

pro|gram /proʊgræm, -grəm/ (**programs, programming, programmed**)

1 **N-COUNT** A **program** is a plan of things to do. ❑ *The art gallery's education program includes art classes for all ages.*

2 **N-COUNT** A **program** is a television or radio show. ❑ *...a network television program.*

3 **N-COUNT** A theater or concert **program** is a small book or a sheet of paper that tells you about the play or concert. ❑ *When you go to concerts, it's helpful to read the program.*

4 **N-COUNT** TECHNOLOGY A **program** is a set of instructions that a computer uses to do a particular task. ❑ *Ada Lovelace wrote the world's first computer program in 1842.*

5 **V-T** TECHNOLOGY When you **program** a computer or a machine, you give it a set of instructions so that it can do a particular task. ❑ *They can teach you how to program a computer in two weeks.* ● **pro|gram|ming** **N-NONCOUNT** ❑ *Java is a popular programming language.* ● **pro|gram|mer** (**programmers**) **N-COUNT** ❑ *Greg works as a computer programmer.* [from Late Latin]
→ look at Word Web: **radio**

Word Partnership	Use **program** with :
v	**create a** program, **expand a** program, **implement a** program, **launch a** program, **run a** program **1** program **a computer** **5**
N	**computer** program, **software** program **4**

pro|gress (**progresses, progressing, progressed**)

PRONUNCIATION HELP
Pronounce the noun /prɒgrɛs/. Pronounce the verb /prəgrɛs/.

1 **N-NONCOUNT** **Progress** is the process of gradually improving or getting nearer to achieving something. ❑ *We are making progress in the fight against cancer.*

2 **V-I** If you **progress**, you improve or become more advanced or successful. ❑ *All our students are progressing well.*

3 **V-I** If events **progress**, they continue to happen over a period of time. ❑ *As the evening progressed, Leila grew tired.*

4 **PHRASE** If something is **in progress**, it has started and is still happening. ❑ *The game was already in progress when we arrived.* [from Latin]

pro|gres|sive /prəgrɛsɪv/ (**progressives**)

1 **ADJ** SOCIAL STUDIES Someone who is **progressive** has modern ideas about how things should be done, rather than traditional ones. ❑ *...a progressive businessman who fought for the rights of consumers.*

2 **N-COUNT** SOCIAL STUDIES A **progressive** is someone who is progressive. ❑ *The Republicans were split between progressives and conservatives.*

3 **ADJ** A **progressive** change happens gradually over a period of time. ❑ *One symptom of the disease is progressive loss of memory.*

● **pro|gres|sive|ly** **ADV** ❑ *Her symptoms became progressively worse.* [from Latin]

pro|hib|it /proʊhɪbɪt/ (**prohibits, prohibiting, prohibited**) **V-T** If a rule or a law **prohibits** something, it makes it illegal. [FORMAL] ❑ *Smoking is prohibited here.* [from Latin]

pro|hi|bi|tion /proʊɪbɪʃˀn/ (**prohibitions**)

1 **N-COUNT** A **prohibition** is a law that says you must not do something. ❑ *The government intends to remove the prohibition on exporting live horses.*

2 **N-PROPER** SOCIAL STUDIES In the United States, **Prohibition** was the period between 1920 and 1933 when it was illegal to make or sell alcoholic drinks.

proj|ect (**projects, projecting, projected**)

PRONUNCIATION HELP
Pronounce the noun /prɒdʒɛkt/.
Pronounce the verb /prədʒɛkt/.

1 **N-COUNT** A **project** is a plan that takes a lot of time and effort. ❑ *The charity is funding a housing project in India.*

2 **N-COUNT** When a student does a **project** on a subject, they find out a lot of information about the subject and then they write about it. ❑ *Our class has just finished a project on ancient Greece.*

3 **V-T** If something **is projected**, it is planned or expected. ❑ *13% of Americans are over 65; this number is projected to reach 22% by the year 2030.* ❑ *The government has projected a 5% price increase for the year.*

4 **V-T** If you **project** a film or a picture **onto** a screen or a wall, you make it appear there. ❑ *We tried projecting the maps onto the screen.*

5 **V-I** If something **projects**, it sticks out above or beyond a surface or an edge. [FORMAL] ❑ *...a narrow ledge that projected out from the bank of the river.* [from Latin]

Word Partnership	Use **project** with :
V	**approve a** project, **launch a** project **1** **complete a** project, **start a** project **1** **2**
N	**construction** project, **development** project, project **director/manager** **1** **research** project, **writing** project **1** **2** **science** project **1** **2**
ADJ	**involved in a** project, **latest** project, **new** project, **special** project **1** **2**

P

pro|jec|tile mo|tion /prədʒɛktᵊl moʊʃᵊn, -taɪl/ **N-NONCOUNT** SCIENCE **Projectile motion** is the curved path of an object which has been propelled into the air at an angle, for example a ball that is kicked or thrown.

pro|jec|tion /prədʒɛkʃᵊn/ (**projections**)
■ **N-COUNT** A **projection** is an estimate of a future amount. ❑ ...the company's projection of 11 million visitors for the first year.
■ **N-NONCOUNT** The **projection** of a film or a picture is the act of projecting it onto a screen or a wall. ❑ They took me into a projection room to see the picture.
■ **N-NONCOUNT** ARTS A speaker or a performer who has good **projection** is skillful at speaking to an audience or communicating with an audience in a clear and confident way. [from Latin]

pro|jec|tor /prədʒɛktər/ (**projectors**)
N-COUNT A **projector** is a machine that shows movies or pictures on a screen or a wall. [from Latin]

pro|karyo|tic cell /proʊkæriɒtɪk/ (**prokaryotic cells**) or **prokaryote** /proʊkærioʊt/ **N-COUNT** SCIENCE **Prokaryotic cells** or **prokaryotes** are cells or organisms such as bacteria that do not have a nucleus. Compare with **eukaryotic cell**

pro|lif|er|ate /prəlɪfəreɪt/ (**proliferates, proliferating, proliferated**) **V-I** If things **proliferate**, they increase in number very quickly. [FORMAL] ❑ Computerized databases are proliferating fast. ● **pro|lif|era|tion** /prəlɪfəreɪʃᵊn/ **N-NONCOUNT** ❑ ...the proliferation of nuclear weapons. [from Medieval Latin]

> **Word Link** pro ≈ in front, before : pro**ceed,** pro**duce,** pro**logue**

pro|logue /proʊlɔg/ (**prologues**) also **prolog**
N-COUNT LANGUAGE ARTS A **prologue** is a part of a play, a book, or a movie that introduces the story. ❑ She first appears in the prologue to the novel. [from Latin]

pro|long /prəlɔŋ/ (**prolongs, prolonging, prolonged**) **V-T** If you **prolong** something, you make it last longer. ❑ I did not wish to prolong the conversation. [from Late Latin]

pro|longed /prəlɔŋd/ **ADJ** A **prolonged** event or situation continues for a long time, or for longer than expected. ❑ ...a prolonged period of peace. [from Late Latin]

prom /prɒm/ (**proms**) **N-COUNT** A **prom** is a formal dance for high school students to celebrate the end of the school year.
❑ She accepted his invitation to the senior prom.

promi|nent /prɒmɪnənt/
■ **ADJ** A **prominent** person is important and well-known. ❑ Michelle is married to a prominent lawyer in Portland.
■ **ADJ** If something is **prominent**, it is big, and you can see it very easily. ❑ ...a prominent nose. [from Latin]

prom|ise /prɒmɪs/ (**promises, promising, promised**)
■ **V-T/V-I** If you **promise that** you will do something, you say that you will certainly do it. ❑ She promised to write to me soon. ❑ I promise that I'll help you all I can.
■ **N-COUNT Promise** is also a noun. ❑ If you make a promise, you should keep it. ❑ James broke every promise he made.
■ **V-T** If you **promise** someone something, you tell them that you will make sure that they have it or that you will give it to them. ❑ I've promised them a house in the country. [from Latin]

> **Word Partnership** Use **promise** with :
> V **break a** promise, **deliver on a** promise, **keep a** promise, **make a** promise ■
> ADJ **broken** promise, **empty** promise, **false** promise ■
> N **campaign** promise ■

prom|is|ing /prɒmɪsɪŋ/ **ADJ** Someone or something that is **promising** seems likely to be very good or successful. ❑ ...one of the most promising poets of his generation. [from Latin]

prom|on|tory /prɒməntɔri/ (**promontories**) **N-COUNT** GEOGRAPHY A **promontory** is a cliff that stretches out into the sea. ❑ A rocky promontory sticks out from the shore. [from Latin]

> **Word Link** mot ≈ moving : **motion,** mo**tivate,** pro**mote**

pro|mote /prəmoʊt/ (**promotes, promoting, promoted**)
■ **V-T** If you **promote** something, you help to make it successful. ❑ There will be a new TV campaign to promote the products.
■ **V-T** If someone **is promoted**, they are given a more important job in the organization that they work for. ❑ Richard has just been promoted to general manager.
● **pro|mo|tion** (**promotions**)

N-COUNT/N-NONCOUNT ❑ *We went out for dinner to celebrate Dad's promotion.* [from Latin]
→ look at Word Web: **concert**

prompt /pr<u>o</u>mpt/ (**prompts, prompting, prompted**)

■ **ADJ** A **prompt** action is done without waiting. ❑ *These questions require prompt answers from the government.*

■ **V-T** To **prompt** someone **to** do something means to make them decide to do it. ❑ *The article prompted readers to complain.*

■ **V-T** If you **prompt** someone, you encourage or remind them to do something or to continue doing something. ❑ *"Well, Daniel?" Wilson prompted.* ● **prompt|ing** (**promptings**) **N-COUNT/N-NONCOUNT** ❑ *The team needed little prompting from their coach.* [from Latin]

prompt|ly /pr<u>o</u>mptli/

■ **ADV** If you do something **promptly**, you do it immediately. ❑ *Grandma sat down, and promptly fell asleep.*

■ **ADV** If you do something **promptly at** a particular time, you do it at exactly that time. ❑ *Promptly at seven o'clock, we left the hotel.* [from Latin]

prone /pr<u>ou</u>n/

■ **ADJ** To be **prone to** something, usually something bad, means to have a tendency to be affected by it or to do it. ❑ *They are prone to errors and accidents.*

■ **ADJ Prone** combines with nouns to make adjectives that describe people who are frequently affected by something bad. ❑ *...the most injury-prone rider.* [from Latin]

pro|noun /pr<u>ou</u>naun/ (**pronouns**) **N-COUNT** LANGUAGE ARTS A **pronoun** is a word that you use instead of a noun when you are talking about someone or something. "It," "she," "something," and "myself" are pronouns. [from Latin]

| Word Link | nounce ≈ reporting : announce, |
| | denounce, pronounce |

pro|nounce /prən<u>au</u>ns/ (**pronounces, pronouncing, pronounced**)

■ **V-T** When you **pronounce** a word, you make its sound. ❑ *Have I pronounced your name correctly?*

■ **V-T** If you **pronounce** something, you state it formally or publicly. [FORMAL] ❑ *The official pronounced them husband and wife.* [from Latin]
→ look at Word Web: **trial**

pro|nun|cia|tion /prənʌnsieɪʃ°n/ (**pronunciations**) **N-COUNT/N-NONCOUNT** LANGUAGE ARTS The **pronunciation** of a word is the way that you say it. ❑ *We are learning about the differences between Canadian and American pronunciation.* [from Latin]

proof /pr<u>u</u>f/ **N-NONCOUNT** Proof is something that shows that something else is true or exists. ❑ *The scientists hope to find proof that there is water on Mars.* [from Old French]

Word Partnership	Use **proof** with :
ADJ	**convincing** proof, **final** proof, **living** proof, proof **positive**
V	**have** proof, **need** proof, **offer** proof, **provide** proof, **require** proof, **show** proof

prop /pr<u>o</u>p/ (**props, propping, propped**)

■ **V-T** If you **prop** an object **on** or **against** something, you support it by putting something underneath it or by resting it somewhere. ❑ *He propped his feet on the desk.*

■ **Prop up** means the same as **prop**. ❑ *Sam propped his elbows up on the bench behind him.*

■ **N-COUNT** A **prop** is a stick or other object that you use to support something. ❑ *Using the table as a prop, he dragged himself to his feet.*

■ **N-COUNT** ARTS The **props** in a play or a movie are the objects and pieces of furniture that are used in it. ❑ *...the props for a stage show.* [Senses 1 and 2 from Middle Dutch. Sense 3 from Old French.]
→ look at Picture Dictionary: **drama**
→ look at Word Web: **theater**
▶ **prop up** ■ To **prop up** something means to support it or help it to survive. ❑ *Investments in the U.S. money market have propped up the dollar.*
■ → look up **prop** ■

propa|gan|da /pr<u>o</u>pəgændə/ **N-NONCOUNT** SOCIAL STUDIES **Propaganda** is information that a political organization uses in order to influence people. ❑ *The state media began a huge propaganda campaign.* [from Italian]

| Word Link | pel ≈ driving, forcing : compel, expel, |
| | propel |

pro|pel /prəp<u>e</u>l/ (**propels, propelling, propelled**) **V-T** To **propel** something in a particular direction means to cause it to move in that direction. ❑ *The tiny rocket is designed to propel the spacecraft toward Mars.* [from Latin]

pro|pel|ler /prəpɛlər/ (**propellers**) N-COUNT
A **propeller** is a part of a boat or an aircraft that turns around very fast and makes the boat or the aircraft move. ❏ *One of the ship's propellers was damaged in the accident.* [from Latin]

prop|er /prɒpər/
1 ADJ You use **proper** to describe things that you consider to be satisfactory. ❏ *Two out of five people do not have a proper job.* ● **prop|er|ly** ADV ❏ *You're not eating properly.*
2 ADJ The **proper** thing or way is the one that is correct or most suitable. ❏ *The proper procedures have been followed.*
3 ADJ If you say that a way of behaving is **proper**, you mean that it is considered correct. ❏ *The site offers advice on proper online behavior.* ● **prop|er|ly** ADV ❏ *It's about time he learned to behave properly.* [from Old French]

prop|er name (**proper names**) N-COUNT
A **proper name** is the name of a particular person, place, organization, or thing. **Proper names** begin with a capital letter.

prop|er noun (**proper nouns**) N-COUNT
LANGUAGE ARTS A **proper noun** is the name of a particular person, place, organization, or thing. Proper nouns begin with a capital letter.

prop|er|ty /prɒpərti/ (**properties**)
1 N-NONCOUNT Your **property** is anything that belongs to you. [FORMAL] ❏ *That's my property. You can't just take it.*
2 N-COUNT/N-NONCOUNT A **property** is a building and the land around it. [FORMAL] ❏ *Get out of here—this is a private property!*
3 N-COUNT The **properties** of something are the ways in which it behaves in particular situations. ❏ *A radio signal has both electrical and magnetic properties.* [from Old French]
→ look at Word Webs: **element, periodic table**

pro|phase /proʊfeɪz/ (**prophases**) N-COUNT/
N-NONCOUNT SCIENCE **Prophase** is the first stage of cell division, in which the DNA inside a cell forms into chromosomes.

proph|et /prɒfɪt/ (**prophets**) N-COUNT
In some religions, a **prophet** is a person who is sent by God to lead people and to teach them about the religion. ❏ *Muhammad is the Holy Prophet of Islam.* [from Old French]

pro|phet|ic /prəfɛtɪk/ ADJ If something was **prophetic**, it described or suggested something that did actually happen later. ❏ *...George Orwell's prophetic novel, "1984."* [from Greek]

pro|por|tion /prəpɔrʃ°n/ (**proportions**)
1 N-COUNT A **proportion of** an amount is a part of it. [FORMAL] ❏ *A large proportion of the fish in that area have died.*
2 N-COUNT The **proportion of** one type of person or thing in a group is the number of them compared to the total number of people or things in the group. ❏ *The proportion of the population using cellphones is 80-85%.*
3 N-NONCOUNT ARTS **Proportion** is the correct relationship between the size of objects in a piece of art. ❏ *...the symmetry and proportion of classical Greek and Roman architecture.*
4 N-PLURAL ARTS If you refer to the **proportions** in a work of art or a design, you are referring to the relative sizes of its different parts. ❏ *This computer program lets you change the proportions of things in your picture very simply.*
5 PHRASE If something is small or large **in proportion to** something else, it is small or large when compared with that thing. ❏ *His head was large in proportion to the rest of his body.*
6 PHRASE If you say that something is **out of proportion to** something else, you think that it is far greater or more serious than it should be. ❏ *The punishment was out of all proportion to the crime.* [from Latin]

pro|po|sal /prəpoʊz°l/ (**proposals**)
1 N-COUNT A **proposal** is a suggestion or a plan. ❏ *The president has announced new proposals for a peace agreement.*
2 N-COUNT A **proposal** is the act of asking someone to marry you. ❏ *Pam accepted Randy's proposal of marriage.* [from Old French]

Word Partnership	Use **proposal** with :	
ADJ	new proposal, **original** proposal **1**	
V	adopt a proposal, **approve** a proposal, **support** a proposal, **vote on a** proposal **1**	
	accept a proposal, **make a** proposal, **reject a** proposal **1 2**	
N	budget proposal, **peace** proposal **1** marriage proposal **2**	

pro|pose /prəpoʊz/ (**proposes, proposing, proposed**)
1 V-T If you **propose** a plan or an idea, you suggest it. ❏ *The minister has proposed a change in the law.*
2 V-T If you **propose** to do something, you intend to do it. ❏ *Congress is proposing a change to the law.*

3 **v-I** If you **propose to** someone, you ask them to marry you. □ *David proposed to his girlfriend when they were on vacation in Paris.* [from Old French]

> **Word Partnership**   Use propose with :
>
> N   propose **changes**, propose **legislation**, propose **a plan**, propose **a solution**, propose **a tax**, propose **a toast** **1** **2** propose **marriage** **3**

propo|si|tion /prɒpəzɪʃ°n/ (**propositions**)
1 **N-COUNT** If you describe something such as a task or an activity as, for example, a difficult **proposition** or an attractive **proposition**, you mean that it is difficult or pleasant to do. □ *Making money easily has always been an attractive proposition.*
2 **N-COUNT** A **proposition** is a statement or an idea that people can consider or discuss to decide whether it is true. [FORMAL] □ *...the proposition that democracies do not fight each other.*
3 **N-COUNT** A **proposition** is an offer or a suggestion. □ *I went to see him at his office the other day with a business proposition.* [from Latin]

pro|sce|ni|um /proʊsiːniəm, prə-/ (**prosceniums**) **N-COUNT** ARTS A **proscenium** or a **proscenium arch** is an arch in a theater that separates the stage from the audience. [from Latin]

prose /proʊz/ **N-NONCOUNT** LANGUAGE ARTS **Prose** is ordinary written language, not poetry. □ *Hannah writes both poetry and prose.* [from Old French]

pros|ecute /prɒsɪkyut/ (**prosecutes, prosecuting, prosecuted**) **v-T/v-I** If the police **prosecute** a person, they say formally in a law court that the person has committed a crime. □ *The man was prosecuted for a killing at a gas station in Virginia.* □ *Photographs taken by roadside cameras are used to prosecute drivers for speeding.* [from Latin]

pros|ecu|tion /prɒsɪkyuʃ°n/ (**prosecutions**)
1 **N-COUNT/N-NONCOUNT** **Prosecution** is the process of accusing someone of a crime, and asking a law court to judge them. □ *This evidence led to the prosecution of the former leader.*
2 **N-SING** SOCIAL STUDIES The lawyers who try to prove that a person on trial is guilty are called **the prosecution**. □ *...a witness for the prosecution.* [from Latin]

pro|sim|ian /proʊsɪmiən/ (**prosimians**) also pro-simian
1 **N-COUNT** SCIENCE **Prosimians** are animals such as lemurs and other primates who resemble the early ancestors of apes and humans.
2 **ADJ** SCIENCE **prosimian** is also an adjective. □ *...a prosimian species.* [from New Latin]

proslav|ery /proʊsleɪvəri/ **ADJ** SOCIAL STUDIES **Proslavery** ideas support the belief that people can be owned and forced to work with little or no pay. [from Old French]

pro|spec|tive /prəspɛktɪv/ **ADJ** You use **prospective** to describe someone who wants to be the thing mentioned or who is likely to be the thing mentioned. □ *The story should act as a warning to prospective buyers.* [from Latin]

pros|per|ity /prɒspɛriti/ **N-NONCOUNT** **Prosperity** is a condition in which a person or community is doing well financially. □ *...a long period of peace and prosperity.* [from Latin]

pros|per|ous /prɒspərəs/ **ADJ** **Prosperous** people, places, and economies are rich and successful. [FORMAL] □ *...a relatively prosperous family.* [from Latin]

pros|ti|tute /prɒstɪtut/ (**prostitutes**) **N-COUNT** A **prostitute** is a person, usually a woman, who has sex with men in exchange for money. [from Latin]

> **Word Link**   tect ≈ covering : detect, protect, protective

pro|tect /prətɛkt/ (**protects, protecting, protected**) **v-T** If you **protect** someone or something, you keep them safe from harm or damage. □ *Make sure you protect your children from the sun's harmful rays.* [from Latin]
→ look at Word Web: **hero**

> **Word Partnership**   Use protect with :
>
> N   protect **against attacks**, protect **children**, protect **citizens**, **duty to** protect, **efforts to** protect, protect **the environment**, **laws** protect, protect **people**, protect **privacy**, protect **property**, protect **women**, protect **workers**
> ADJ   **designed to** protect, **necessary to** protect, **supposed to** protect

P

pro|tec|tion /prətɛkʃᵊn/ (**protections**)
N-COUNT/N-NONCOUNT If something gives you **protection** against something unpleasant, it stops you from being harmed or damaged by it. ❑ *Long-sleeved t-shirts offer greater protection against the sun.* [from Latin]

Word Link	*tect ≈ covering : detect, protect, protective*

pro|tec|tive /prətɛktɪv/
1 ADJ **Protective** things are intended to protect you from injury or harm. ❑ *You should wear protective gloves when you are gardening.*
2 ADJ If someone is **protective toward** you, they look after you and try to keep you safe. ❑ *Ben is very protective toward his mother.* [from Latin]

pro|tein /proʊtin/ (**proteins**)
N-COUNT/N-NONCOUNT **Protein** is a substance that the body needs. It is found in meat, eggs, fish, and milk. ❑ *Fish is a major source of protein.* [from German]
→ look at Word Webs: **calorie, diet**

pro|test (**protests, protesting, protested**)

> **PRONUNCIATION HELP**
> Pronounce the verb /prətɛst/ and /proʊtɛst/. Pronounce the noun /proʊtɛst/.

1 V-T/V-I If you **protest**, or **protest against** something, you say or show publicly that you do not approve of something. ❑ *The students were protesting against the arrest of one of their teachers.* ❑ *They were protesting high prices.*
2 N-COUNT/N-NONCOUNT A **protest** is the act of showing publicly that you do not approve of something. ❑ *I took part in a protest against the war.*
3 V-T If you **protest** that something is true, you insist that it is true when other people think that it may not be. ❑ *We tried to protest that Mo was beaten up.* ❑ *"I never said any of that to her," he protested.* [from Latin]

Word Partnership	Use **protest** with :
N	**workers** protest **1**
	protest **demonstrations**, protest **groups**, protest **march**, protest **rally 2**
ADJ	**anti-government** protest, **anti-war** protest, **organized** protest, **peaceful** protest, **political** protest **2**

Prot|es|tant /prɒtɪstənt/ (**Protestants**)
N-COUNT A **Protestant** is a Christian who is not a Catholic. [from Latin]

pro|test|er /prətɛstər/ (**protesters**) also
protestor N-COUNT **Protesters** are people who protest publicly about an issue. ❑ *The protesters say that the government is corrupt.*

pro|tist /proʊtɪst/ (**protists**) **N-COUNT**
SCIENCE **Protists** are organisms such as algae and molds that are not animals, plants, or fungi. [from New Latin]

Pro|tis|ta /proʊtɪstə/ **N-NONCOUNT** **SCIENCE**
Protista is the biological group to which organisms called protists belong. [from New Latin]

pro|ton /proʊtɒn/ (**protons**) **N-COUNT**
SCIENCE A **proton** is an atomic particle that has a positive electrical charge. [from Greek]

proto|type /proʊtətaɪp/ (**prototypes**)
N-COUNT A **prototype** is the first model or example of a new type of thing. ❑ *...a prototype of a pollution-free car.* [from Greek]

proto|zoan /proʊtəzoʊən/ (**protozoa** or
protozoans) **N-COUNT** **SCIENCE** **Protozoa** are very small organisms that often live inside larger animals. [from New Latin]

pro|trude /proʊtrud, prə-/ (**protrudes, protruding, protruded**) **V-I** If something **protrudes from** somewhere, it sticks out. [FORMAL] ❑ *...a huge mass of rock protruding from the water.* [from Latin]

proud /praʊd/ (**prouder, proudest**)
1 ADJ If you feel **proud**, you feel pleased and satisfied about something good that you or other people close to you have done. ❑ *The college principal was very proud of her students' success.* ● **proud|ly ADV** ❑ *Nick wears his police uniform proudly.*
2 ADJ Someone who is **proud** has a lot of dignity and self-respect. ❑ *He was too proud to ask his family for help and support.*
3 ADJ If you are **proud**, you think that you are better or more important than other people. ❑ *He described his boss as "proud and selfish."* [from Late Old English]

prove /pruv/ (**proves, proving, proved, proved** or **proven**)

> **LANGUAGE HELP**
> The forms **proved** and **proven** can both be used as the past participle.

1 V-T If you **prove** something, you show that it is true. ❑ *These results prove that we were right.*
2 V-LINK If something **proves to** be true or **to** have a particular quality, it becomes clear

after a period of time that it is true or has that quality. ❑ *All our reports proved to be true.* ❑ *This process has often proven difficult.* [from Old French]
→ look at Word Web: **science**

Word Partnership	Use **prove** with :
v	be able to prove, have to prove, have *something* to prove, try to prove **1**
ADJ	prove **(to be) difficult**, prove **helpful**, prove **useful**, prove **worthy 2** difficult to prove, hard to prove **2**

prov|erb /prɒvɜrb/ (**proverbs**) **N-COUNT** A **proverb** is a short sentence that people often say, because it gives advice or tells you something about life. ❑ *An old Arab proverb says, "The enemy of my enemy is my friend."* [from Old French]

pro|vide /prəvaɪd/ (**provides, providing, provided**)
1 **V-T** If you **provide** something that someone needs or wants, you give it to them. ❑ *The company's website provides lots of useful information.* ❑ *The refugees were provided with food and accommodation.*
2 **V-T** If a law or an agreement **provides that** something will happen, it states that it will happen. [FORMAL] ❑ *The law provides that you can get compensation.* [from Latin]
▸ **provide for** If you **provide for** something that might happen, you make arrangements to deal with it. ❑ *Jim has provided for just such an emergency.*

pro|vid|ed /prəvaɪdɪd/ or **providing CONJ** If something will happen **provided** or **providing** that something else happens, the first thing will happen only if the second thing also happens. ❑ *He can go running at his age, provided that he is sensible.* [from Latin]

pro|vid|ing /prəvaɪdɪŋ/ → look up **provided**

prov|ince /prɒvɪns/ (**provinces**) **N-COUNT** A **province** is a large part of a country that has its own local government. ❑ *...the Canadian province of British Columbia.* [from Old French]

pro|vin|cial /prəvɪnʃəl/
1 **ADJ Provincial** means relating to the parts of a country away from the capital city. ❑ *Victoria is the provincial capital of British Columbia.*
2 **ADJ** If you describe someone or something as **provincial**, you think that they are old-fashioned and boring. ❑ *...the company's provincial image.* [from Old French]

pro|vi|sion /prəvɪʒən/ (**provisions**)
1 **N-COUNT** A **provision** in a law or an agreement is an arrangement that is included in it. ❑ *...a provision that allows the president to decide how to spend the money.*
2 **N-NONCOUNT** The **provision of** something is the act of giving it to people who need or want it. ❑ *This department is responsible for the provision of legal services.* [from Latin]

pro|vi|sion|al /prəvɪʒənəl/ **ADJ** Something that is **provisional** has been arranged or exists now, but it may be changed in the future. ❑ *Your provisional driver's license is valid for 18 months.* ● **pro|vi|sion|al|ly ADV** ❑ *She provisionally accepted the job offer.* [from Latin]

pro|voke /prəvoʊk/ (**provokes, provoking, provoked**)
1 **V-T** If you **provoke** someone, you deliberately annoy them and try to make them angry. ❑ *The demonstrators did not provoke the police and everyone remained calm.*
2 **V-T** If something **provokes** a reaction, it causes it. ❑ *The election result provoked an angry reaction from some students.* [from Latin]

prowl /praʊl/ (**prowls, prowling, prowled**)
V-I If an animal or a person **prowls around**, they move around quietly, waiting to do something. ❑ *She prowled around the living room, unable to sit.*

prox|im|ity /prɒksɪmɪti/ **N-NONCOUNT**
Proximity to a place or a person is the state of being near to that place or person. [FORMAL] ❑ *Part of the attraction of Darwin is its proximity to Asia.* [from Latin]

prune /prun/ (**prunes, pruning, pruned**)
1 **N-COUNT** A **prune** is a dried plum.
2 **V-T** When you **prune** a tree or a bush, you cut off some of the branches so that it will grow better the next year. ❑ *You have to prune a bush if you want fruit.*
3 **Prune back** means the same as **prune**. ❑ *Cherry trees can be pruned back when they have lost their leaves.* [from Old French]

P.S. /pi ɛs/ also **PS** You write **P.S.** when you add something at the end of a letter after you have signed it. ❑ *P.S. Please show your friends this letter.*

pseudo|pod /sudəpɒd/ (**pseudopods** or **pseudopodia**) **N-COUNT SCIENCE Pseudopods** are the tiny extensions of cells within some microorganisms that are used for movement and feeding.

P

Word Link   psych ≈ mind : psychiatrist, psychic, psychologist

psy|chi|a|trist /sɪkaɪətrɪst/ (**psychiatrists**)
N-COUNT A **psychiatrist** is a doctor who takes care of people who have illnesses of the mind. ❑ When Sarah was 16, a psychiatrist treated her for depression.

psy|chic /saɪkɪk/ (**psychics**)
1 **ADJ** If you believe that someone is **psychic**, you believe that they have strange mental powers, such as being able to read the minds of other people or to see into the future. ❑ The woman helped police by using her psychic powers.
2 **N-COUNT** A **psychic** is someone who seems to be psychic. ❑ ...a psychic who can see the future.
3 **ADJ** **Psychic** means relating to ghosts and the spirits of the dead. ❑ ...his total disbelief in psychic phenomena. [from Greek]

psycho|logi|cal /saɪkəlɒdʒɪkᵊl/ **ADJ**
Psychological means concerned with a person's mind and thoughts. ❑ Guilt can lead to psychological illness. [from Modern Latin]
→ look at Word Web: **myth**

psy|chol|ogy /saɪkɒlədʒi/
1 **N-NONCOUNT** SCIENCE **Psychology** is the study of the human mind and the reasons for people's behavior. ❑ Scott is a professor of educational psychology at the University of Connecticut. ● **psy|cholo|gist** (**psychologists**) **N-COUNT** ❑ Amy is seeing a psychologist.
2 **N-NONCOUNT** The **psychology of** a person is the kind of mind that they have, that makes them think or behave in the way that they do. ❑ ...the psychology of murderers. [from Modern Latin]

psycho|path|ic /saɪkəpæθɪk/ **ADJ** Someone who is **psychopathic** has an antisocial personality disorder. ❑ The report labeled him psychopathic. ❑ ...a psychopathic killer. [from Greek]

psycho|thera|py /saɪkoʊθɛrəpi/
N-NONCOUNT **Psychotherapy** is the use of psychological methods in treating people who are mentally ill. ❑ For milder depressions, certain forms of psychotherapy work well.
● **psycho|thera|pist** (**psychotherapists**) **N-COUNT** ❑ He arranged for Jim to see a psychotherapist.

psy|chrom|eter /saɪkrɒmɪtər/
(**psychrometers**) **N-COUNT** SCIENCE

A **psychrometer** is an instrument that is used to measure the amount of water vapor in the air.

pub|lic /pʌblɪk/
1 **N-SING** The **public** is people in general, or everyone. ❑ The exhibition is open to the public from tomorrow.
2 **ADJ** **Public** means relating to all the people in a country or a community. ❑ The government's policies still have strong public support.
3 **ADJ** **Public** buildings and services are for everyone to use. ❑ The New York Public Library was built in 1911. ❑ ...public transportation.
4 **ADJ** **Public** is used to describe statements, actions, and events that are made or done so that the public can be aware of them. ❑ ...a public inquiry. ❑ ...the governor's first public statement on the subject. ● **pub|lic|ly** **ADV** ❑ He never spoke publicly about the incident.
5 **ADJ** If a fact is made **public** or becomes **public**, it becomes known to everyone rather than being kept secret. ❑ The news finally became public.
6 **PHRASE** If you say or do something **in public**, you say or do it when other people are there. ❑ He hasn't performed in public in more than 40 years. [from Latin]
→ look at Word Web: **library**

pub|li|ca|tion /pʌblɪkeɪʃᵊn/ (**publications**)
1 **N-NONCOUNT** The **publication** of a book or a magazine is the act of printing it and sending it to stores to be sold. ❑ The store stayed open late to celebrate the book's publication.
2 **N-COUNT** A **publication** is a book or a magazine. ❑ My uncle has written for several publications. [from Old French]

pub|lic|ity /pʌblɪsɪti/
1 **N-NONCOUNT** **Publicity** means providing people with information about a person or a product. ❑ A lot of publicity was given to the talks. ❑ We are planning a publicity campaign against racism.
2 **N-NONCOUNT** When the news media and the public show a lot of interest in something, you can say that it is receiving **publicity**. ❑ The case has generated enormous publicity in Brazil. [from French]

Word Partnership	Use **publicity** with :
V	**generate** publicity **1 2**
	get publicity, **receive** publicity, publicity **surrounding** *someone/something* **2**
ADJ	**bad** publicity, **negative** publicity **2**

P

pub|li|cize /pʌblɪsaɪz/ (**publicizes, publicizing, publicized**) **v-T** If you **publicize** something, you let people know about it. ❑ *The author appeared on television to publicize her latest book.* [from Latin]

pub|lic of|fice **N-NONCOUNT** SOCIAL STUDIES Someone who is in **public office** has been elected by the public to do a job. ❑ *He held public office for twenty years.*

pub|lic school (**public schools**)
1 **N-COUNT/N-NONCOUNT** In the United States, Australia, and many other countries, a **public school** is a school that is supported financially by the government and usually provides free education. ❑ *...Milwaukee's public school system.*
2 **N-COUNT/N-NONCOUNT** In Britain, a **public school** is a private school that provides secondary education that parents have to pay for. The students often live at the school during the school term. ❑ *He was headmaster of a public school in the West of England.*

pub|lic sec|tor **N-SING** BUSINESS The **public sector** is the part of a country's economy which is controlled or supported financially by the government. ❑ *...Menem's policy of reducing the public sector.*

pub|lish /pʌblɪʃ/ (**publishes, publishing, published**)
1 **v-T** When a company **publishes** a book, a magazine, or a newspaper, it prepares and prints copies of it. ❑ *Harper Collins will publish his new novel on March 4.*
2 **v-T** When someone **publishes** information, they make it known to the public. [from Old French]
→ look at Word Webs: **laboratory, printing**

pub|lish|er /pʌblɪʃər/ (**publishers**) **N-COUNT** A **publisher** is a person or a company that publishes books, newspapers, or magazines. ❑ *She sent the book to a publisher and got a positive response.* [from Old French]

pub|lish|ing /pʌblɪʃɪŋ/ **N-NONCOUNT** **Publishing** is the profession of publishing books. ❑ *I had a job in publishing.* [from Old French]

pud|ding /pʊdɪŋ/ (**puddings**)
N-COUNT/N-NONCOUNT **Pudding** is a soft, sweet dessert made from eggs and milk. ❑ *For dessert, there was chocolate pudding.* [from Old English]
→ look at Picture Dictionary: **dessert**

pud|dle /pʌdəl/ (**puddles**) **N-COUNT** A **puddle** is a small pool of water on the ground. ❑ *Young children love splashing in puddles.* [from Old English]

puff /pʌf/ (**puffs, puffing, puffed**)
1 **N-COUNT** A **puff of** air or smoke is a small amount of it that is blown from somewhere. ❑ *Puffs of steam rose into the air and vanished.*
2 **v-I** If you **are puffing**, you are breathing loudly and quickly, usually because you have been running. ❑ *He puffs and pants if he has to walk up a flight of stairs.* [from Old English]

pull /pʊl/ (**pulls, pulling, pulled**)
1 **v-T/v-I** When you **pull** something, you hold it firmly and use force to move it. ❑ *I helped to pull the boy out of the water.* ❑ *The dentist pulled out all his teeth.* ❑ *Someone pulled her hair.*

pull

2 **N-COUNT** **Pull** is also a noun. ❑ *He felt a pull on the fishing line.*
3 **v-T** When a person or animal **pulls** something, they are attached to it or they hold it so that it moves along behind them when they move forward. ❑ *The beast pulled the cart.*
4 **v-T** If you **pull yourself** or **pull** a part of your body in a particular direction, you move your body with effort or force. ❑ *Hughes pulled himself slowly to his feet.* ❑ *He pulled his arms out of the sleeves.* [from Old English]

▶ **pull away** When a vehicle or a driver **pulls away**, the vehicle starts moving forward. ❑ *I watched the car back out of the driveway and pull away.*

▶ **pull down** If you **pull down** a building, you deliberately destroy it. ❑ *They pulled the offices down, leaving a large open space.*

▶ **pull in** If a vehicle or a driver **pulls in** somewhere, the vehicle stops there. ❑ *The bus pulled in at the side of the road.*

▶ **pull into** When a vehicle or a driver **pulls into** a place, the vehicle moves into the place and stops there. ❑ *David pulled into the driveway in front of her garage.*

▶ **pull off** If you **pull off** something very difficult, you succeed in achieving it. ❑ *The National League for Democracy pulled off a victory.*

▶ **pull out** When a vehicle or a driver **pulls out**, the vehicle moves out into the road or

p

nearer the center of the road. ❑ *I looked in the rear mirror, and pulled out into the street.*

▶ **pull over** When a vehicle or a driver **pulls over**, the vehicle moves closer to the side of the road and stops there. ❑ *I pulled over to let the police car pass.*

▶ **pull yourself together** If someone tells you to **pull yourself together**, they are telling you to control your feelings and be calm again. ❑ *"Now stop crying and pull yourself together!"*

▶ **pull up** When a vehicle or a driver **pulls up**, the vehicle slows down and stops. ❑ *The cab pulled up and the driver jumped out.*

pul|ley /pʊli/ (**pulleys**) **N-COUNT** A **pulley** is a device consisting of a wheel over which a rope or a chain is pulled in order to lift heavy objects. [from Old French]

pull|over /pʊloʊvər/ (**pullovers**) **N-COUNT** A **pullover** is a warm piece of clothing that covers the upper part of your body and your arms.

pul|mo|nary cir|cu|la|tion /pʌlmənɛri sɜrkyəleɪʃ°n/ **N-NONCOUNT** SCIENCE **Pulmonary circulation** is the flow of blood between the heart and lungs.
→ look at Word Web: **cardiovascular system**

pul|sar /pʌlsɑr/ (**pulsars**) **N-COUNT** SCIENCE A **pulsar** is a star that spins very fast and cannot be seen but produces regular radio signals.

pulse /pʌls/ (**pulses**)
■ **N-COUNT** SCIENCE Your **pulse** is the regular beat of your heart that you can feel when you touch your wrist and other parts of your body. ❑ *Dr. Garcia checked her pulse and breathing.*
■ **N-COUNT** A **pulse of** electrical current, light, or sound is a temporary increase in its level. ❑ *...a pulse of radio waves.* [from Latin]

pump /pʌmp/ (**pumps, pumping, pumped**)
■ **N-COUNT** A **pump** is a piece of equipment that makes a liquid or a gas flow in a particular direction. ❑ *A pump brings water directly from the well.* ❑ *There are three water pumps in the village.*
■ **V-T** If something **pumps** a liquid or a gas in a particular direction, it makes it flow in that direction using a pump. ❑ *The heart pumps blood around the body.* [from Middle Dutch]
→ look at Word Web: **aquarium**

▶ **pump up** If you **pump up** something, you fill it with air. ❑ *Pump all the tires up.*

pump|kin /pʌmpkɪn/ (**pumpkins**) **N-COUNT/ N-NONCOUNT** A **pumpkin** is a large, round, orange vegetable with a thick skin. ❑ *...pumpkin pie.* [from Old French]

pun /pʌn/ (**puns**) **N-COUNT** A **pun** is a clever and amusing use of a word or a phrase that has two meanings. For example: "Where do peas have their eyes tested?"— "In an iPod" (= in an "eye pod"). [from Italian]

punch /pʌntʃ/ (**punches, punching, punched**)
■ **V-T** If you **punch** someone or something, you hit them hard with your fist. ❑ *During a concert, the singer punched a photographer.*
■ **N-COUNT** **Punch** is also a noun. ❑ *My brother gave me a punch in the nose.*
■ **V-T** If you **punch** something such as a button on a computer, or **punch in** information using a button, you press it in order to store information or to give a command to do something. ❑ *Lianne punched the button to call the elevator.* ❑ *Punch in your account number on the phone.*
■ **V-T** If you **punch** holes **in** something, you make holes in it by pushing or pressing it with something sharp. ❑ *I took a pen and punched a hole in the box.*
■ **N-COUNT/N-NONCOUNT** **Punch** is a drink made from alcohol or fruit juice, mixed with things such as sugar and spices. ❑ *...a bowl of punch.* [Senses 1 to 4 from Old French. Sense 5 from Hindi.]

punc|tu|al /pʌŋktʃuəl/ **ADJ** If you are **punctual**, you arrive somewhere at the right time. ❑ *He's always very punctual.*
● **punc|tu|al|ly** **ADV** ❑ *The guests all arrived punctually, at eight o'clock.* [from Medieval Latin]

punc|tua|tion /pʌŋktʃueɪʃ°n/ **N-NONCOUNT** LANGUAGE ARTS **Punctuation** is signs such as ( ), !, or ? that you use to divide writing into sentences and phrases. ❑ *You have to give more attention to punctuation and grammar.* [from Medieval Latin]
→ look at Picture Dictionary: **punctuation**

punc|tua|tion mark (**punctuation marks**) **N-COUNT** LANGUAGE ARTS A **punctuation mark** is a symbol such as ( ), !, or ?.

Picture Dictionary — punctuation

A: I want to learn to drive; however, cars scare me.
semi-colon *period*
B: Why not take a driver-training course?
hyphen *question mark*
A: I'm not ready.
apostrophe
B: I know! If you want, I'll teach you to drive.
exclamation mark *comma*
A: OK, but remember this: it was your idea, not mine.
colon

punc|ture /pʌŋktʃər/ (**punctures, puncturing, punctured**)

1 N-COUNT A **puncture** is a small hole that has been made by a sharp object. ❑ *I repaired the puncture in my front tire.*
2 V-T If a sharp object **punctures** something, it makes a hole in it. ❑ *The bullet punctured his left lung.* [from Latin]

pun|gent /pʌndʒ³nt/ **ADJ** Something that is **pungent** has a strong, bitter smell or taste. ❑ *The more herbs you use, the more pungent the sauce will be.* [from Latin]

pun|ish /pʌnɪʃ/ (**punishes, punishing, punished**) **V-T** If you **punish** someone, you make them suffer in some way because they have done something wrong. ❑ *His parents punished him for being rude.* [from Old French]

pun|ish|ment /pʌnɪʃmənt/ (**punishments**)

1 N-NONCOUNT **Punishment** is the act of punishing someone or of being punished. ❑ *They are considering less severe punishment for non-violent crime.*
2 N-COUNT/N-NONCOUNT A **punishment** is a particular way of punishing someone. ❑ *There will be tougher punishments for violent crimes.* [from Old French]
3 → see also **capital punishment**

Pun|nett square /pʌnɪt skwɛər/ (**Punnett squares**) **N-COUNT** SCIENCE A **Punnett square** is a diagram used by biologists to predict the genetic makeup of an organism.

pup /pʌp/ (**pups**)

1 N-COUNT A **pup** is a young dog. ❑ *We've had Pongo since he was a pup.*
2 N-COUNT The babies of some other animals are called **pups**. ❑ *...gray seal pups.*

pu|pil /pyupɪl/ (**pupils**)

1 N-COUNT The **pupils** of an elementary school are the children who go to it. ❑ *Around 270 pupils attend this school.*
2 N-COUNT The **pupil** of your eye is the small, round, black hole in the center of it. ❑ *In low light the pupils are wide open to allow light into the eye.* [from Latin]
→ look at Word Web: **eye**

pup|pet /pʌpɪt/ (**puppets**) **N-COUNT** A **puppet** is a small model of a person or an animal that you can move. [from Old French]

pup|pet|ry /pʌpɪtri/ **N-NONCOUNT** ARTS **Puppetry** is the art of entertaining people with puppets. [from Old French]

pup|py /pʌpi/ (**puppies**) **N-COUNT** A **puppy** is a young dog. [from Old French]

pur|chase /pɜrtʃɪs/ (**purchases, purchasing, purchased**)

1 V-T If you **purchase** something, you buy it. [FORMAL] ❑ *He purchased a ticket for the concert.*
2 N-NONCOUNT The **purchase of** something is the act of buying it. [FORMAL] ❑ *The Canadian company announced the purchase of 1,663 stores in the U.S.*
3 N-COUNT A **purchase** is something that you buy. [FORMAL] ❑ *Her latest purchase is a shiny, black motorcycle.* [from Old French]

pure /pyʊər/ (**purer, purest**)

1 ADJ A **pure** substance is not mixed with anything else. ❑ *I bought a carton of pure orange juice.*
2 ADJ If something is **pure**, it is clean and does not contain any harmful substances. ❑ *The water is so pure that we drink it from the stream.*
3 ADJ **Pure** means complete and total.

P

❑ *There was a look of pure surprise on his face.* [from Old French]

→ look at Word Web: **science**

pure|ly /pyʊ̯ə̯rli/ **ADV** Purely means only or completely. ❑ *This car is designed purely for speed.* [from Old French]

Pu|ri|tan /pyʊ̯ə̯rɪtᵊn/ (**Puritans**) **N-COUNT** SOCIAL STUDIES The **Puritans** were a group of English religious people in the 16th and 17th centuries, who lived in a very strict way. Many of these people moved to the United States. [from Late Latin]

pur|ple /pɜrpᵊl/ (**purples**)
1 ADJ Something that is **purple** is a red-blue color. ❑ *She wore a purple dress.*
2 N-NONCOUNT Purple is also a noun. ❑ *I love the purples and grays of the Scottish mountains.* [from Old English]

pur|pose /pɜrpəs/ (**purposes**)
1 N-COUNT The **purpose** of something is the reason why you do it. ❑ *The purpose of the occasion was to raise money for charity.*
2 N-COUNT Your **purpose** is the thing that you want to achieve. ❑ *They might be prepared to harm you in order to achieve their purpose.*
3 PHRASE If you do something **on purpose**, you do it deliberately. ❑ *I'm sure that Pedro hit me on purpose.* [from Old French]

Word Partnership	Use purpose with :
V	**serve a** purpose **1**
	accomplish a purpose, **achieve a** purpose **2**
ADJ	**main** purpose, **original** purpose, **primary** purpose, **real** purpose, **sole** purpose **1 2**

purr /pɜr/ (**purrs, purring, purred**) **V-I** When a cat **purrs**, it makes a low sound with its throat. ❑ *The little black kitten purred and rubbed against my leg.* [from French]

purse /pɜrs/ (**purses, pursing, pursed**)
1 N-COUNT A **purse** is a small bag that women use to carry money and other things. ❑ *Lauren reached in her purse for her keys.*
2 V-T If you **purse** your **lips**, you move them into a small, rounded shape, often because you disapprove of something. ❑ *She pursed her lips in disapproval.* [from Old English]

pur|sue /pərsu̯/ (**pursues, pursuing, pursued**)
1 V-T If you **pursue** someone or something, you follow them because you want to catch

them. [FORMAL] ❑ *Police pursued the driver for two miles.*
2 V-T If you **pursue** a particular aim or result, you make efforts to achieve it, often over a long period of time. [FORMAL] ❑ *He will pursue a trade policy that protects American workers.* [from Old French]

pur|suit /pərsu̯t/ **N-NONCOUNT** If you are **in pursuit of** something, you are trying to get it. ❑ *He has traveled the world in pursuit of his dream.* [from Old French]

push /pʊʃ/ (**pushes, pushing, pushed**)
1 V-T/V-I If you **push** something, you use force to make it move forward or away from you. ❑ *I pushed back my chair and stood up.* ❑ *The men pushed him into the car and locked the door.* ❑ *Justin put both hands on the door and pushed hard.*

push

2 N-COUNT Push is also a noun. ❑ *Laura gave me a sharp push and I fell to the ground.*
3 V-T If you **push** a button on a machine, you press it with your finger. ❑ *Christina got inside the elevator and pushed the button for the third floor.*
4 V-I If you **push for** something, you try very hard to persuade someone to do it. ❑ *Consumer groups are pushing for health care changes.*
5 N-COUNT Push is also a noun. ❑ *...a push for economic growth.*
6 V-T If you **push** someone **to** do something or **push** them **into** doing it, you encourage or force them to do it. ❑ *She thanked her parents for pushing her to study.* ❑ *Jason did not push her into stealing the money.*
7 N-COUNT Push is also a noun. ❑ *We need a push to take the first step.* [from Old French]
▶ **push ahead** or **push forward** If you **push ahead** or **push forward with** something, you make progress with it. ❑ *The government intends to push ahead with the changes.*
▶ **push over** If you **push** someone or something **over**, you push them so that they fall onto the ground. ❑ *...people damaging hedges, uprooting trees and pushing over walls.*

Thesaurus	push Also look up :
V	drive, force, move, pressure, propel, shove, thrust; *(ant.)* pull **1** encourage, urge **4**

Word Partnership	Use push with :
N	push **a button**, **at the** push **of a button**, push **a door** 1 2 push **prices**, push **an agenda**, push **legislation** 3

push-up (**push-ups**) **N-COUNT** SPORTS
Push-ups are exercises to make your upper body stronger. You do them by lying on your front and pushing your body up with your hands until your arms are straight.

put /pʊt/ (**puts, putting, put**)

> **LANGUAGE HELP**
> The form **put** is used in the present tense and is the past tense and past participle.

1 **V-T** If you **put** something in a particular place or position, you move it into that place or position. ❏ *Steven put the photograph on the desk.* ❏ *She put her hand on Grace's arm.* ❏ *Now, where did I put my purse?*

2 **V-T** If you **put** someone somewhere, you cause them to go there and to stay there for a period of time. ❏ *Rather than put him in the hospital, she is caring for him at home.*

3 **V-T** If you **put** someone or something in a particular state or situation, you cause them to be in that state or situation. ❏ *Your carelessness put the children in danger.*

4 **V-T** If you **put** written information somewhere, you write, type, or print it there. ❏ *They put an announcement in the local paper.* [from Old English]

▸ **put away** If you **put** something **away**, you put it back in the place where it is usually kept. ❏ *Kyle put the milk away in the refrigerator.*

▸ **put back** To **put** something **back** means to delay it or arrange for it to happen later than you previously planned. ❏ *There are always problems that put the opening date back further.*

▸ **put down** **1** If you **put** something **down** somewhere, you stop holding it and place it on a surface. ❏ *The woman put down her newspaper and looked at me.*

2 If someone **puts** you **down**, they treat you in an unpleasant way by criticizing you in front of other people or making you appear foolish. ❏ *I know that I sometimes put people down.*

▸ **put off** If you **put** something **off**, you delay doing it. ❏ *Tony always puts off making difficult decisions.*

▸ **put on** **1** If you **put on** clothing or makeup, you place it on your body in order to wear it. ❏ *Grandma put her coat on and went out.* ❏ *She put on lipstick and combed her hair.*

2 If you **put on** weight, you become heavier. ❏ *I'm lucky—I never put on weight.*

3 If you **put on** a piece of electrical equipment, you make it start working. ❏ *Maria sat up in bed and put on the light.*

4 If you **put** a CD **on**, you place it in a CD player and listen to it.

▸ **put out** **1** If you **put out** an announcement or a story, you make it known to a lot of people. ❏ *Thomson put out a statement saying there was no problem between the two men.*

2 If you **put out** a fire, you make it stop burning. ❏ *All day, firefighters have been trying to put out the blaze.*

3 If you **put out** an electric light, you make it stop shining by pressing a switch. ❏ *He went to the table and put out the light.*

▸ **put through** If someone **puts** you **through** an unpleasant experience, they make you experience it. ❏ *We've put them through a lot. Now it's time we let them have a rest.*

▸ **put together** If you **put together** a group of people or things, you form them into a team or collection. ❏ *I put together a group of 125 volunteers.*

▸ **put up** **1** If you **put up** a wall or a building, you build it. ❏ *The Smiths have put up electric fences on their farm.*

2 If you **put up** a poster or a notice, you attach it to a wall or a board. ❏ *They're putting new street signs up.*

▸ **put up with** If you **put up with** someone or something unpleasant, you accept them without complaining. ❏ *I won't put up with your bad behavior any longer.* ❏ *It was a very bad injury, and he's put up with a lot of pain.*

puz|zle /pʌzᵊl/ (**puzzles, puzzling, puzzled**)
1 **V-T** If something **puzzles** you, you do not understand it and you feel confused. ❏ *My sister's behavior puzzles me.* ● **puz|zled** /pʌzᵊld/ **ADJ** ❏ *Joshua was puzzled by her reaction to the news.* ● **puz|zling** **ADJ** ❏ *Michael's comments are very puzzling.*

2 **V-I** If you **puzzle over** something, you try hard to think of the answer to it. ❏ *In reading Shakespeare, I puzzle over his verse and prose.*

3 **N-COUNT** A **puzzle** is a question, a game, or a toy that is difficult to answer correctly, or to put together properly. ❏ *Mom loves doing word puzzles.*

P

4 **N-SING** Someone or something that is hard to understand is **a puzzle**. ❑ *The rise in the number of accidents on the highway remains a puzzle.*

5 → see also **crossword, jigsaw**

P wave /pi̱ weɪv/ (**P waves**) also **P-wave** **N-COUNT** SCIENCE P waves are rapid waves of energy that are released in an earthquake. P wave is short for "pressure wave" or "primary wave."

pyra|mid /pɪ̱rəmɪd/ (**pyramids**) **N-COUNT** MATH A **pyramid** is a solid shape with a flat base and flat sides that form a point where they meet at the top. ❑ *...the Egyptian Pyramids.* [from Latin]
→ look at Picture Dictionaries: **solids, volume**

pyro|clas|tic ma|terial /pa̱ɪrəklæstɪk məti̱əriəl/ **N-NONCOUNT** SCIENCE Pyroclastic **material** is fragments of rock and other substances that are released into the air when a volcano erupts.

py|thon /pa̱ɪθɒn, -θən/ (**pythons**) **N-COUNT** A **python** is a type of large snake. [from New Latin]

Qq

QR code /kjuːɑːʳ koʊd/ (**QR codes**) **N-COUNT**
TECHNOLOGY A **QR code** is a pattern of black
and white squares that can be read by a
smartphone, allowing the phone user to
get more information about something.
QR code is short for **Quick Response code**
❑ *The ad includes a QR code.*

qt. MATH **qt.** is short for **quart.**

quad|rat|ic func|tion /kwɒdrætɪk fʌŋkʃⁿn/
(**quadratic functions**) **N-COUNT** MATH
A **quadratic function** is a mathematical
expression that is used in calculating the
area within a square.

quag|ga /kwægə/ (**quaggas**) **N-COUNT**
SCIENCE A **quagga** was a type of zebra that is
now extinct. [from Afrikaans]

quali|fi|ca|tion /kwɒlɪfɪkeɪʃⁿn/
(**qualifications**) **N-COUNT** Qualifications are
the skills that you need to be able to do
something. ❑ *I believe I have all the qualifications
to be a good teacher.* ❑ *All our workers have
professional qualifications in engineering or
electronics.* [from Old French]

quali|fied /kwɒlɪfaɪd/ **ADJ** Someone who is
qualified has the right skills or special
training in a particular subject. ❑ *Blake is
qualified in both UK and US law.* [from Old
French]

quali|fi|er /kwɒlɪfaɪər/ (**qualifiers**)
1 **N-COUNT** A **qualifier** is an early round or
stage in some competitions. ❑ *Wang quickly
won her three qualifiers.*
2 **N-COUNT** A **qualifier** in a competition is
someone who is successful in one part of it
and can go on to the next stage. ❑ *Robert was
the fastest qualifier for the 800 meters final.*
[from Old French]

quali|fy /kwɒlɪfaɪ/ (**qualifies, qualifying,
qualified**)
1 **V-I** If you **qualify** in a competition, you
are successful in one part of it and you can
go on to the next stage. ❑ *We qualified for the
final by beating Stanford.*
2 **V-T/V-I** If you **qualify** for something, or if

something **qualifies** you for it, you have the
right to do it or have it. ❑ *This course does not
qualify you for a job in sales.*
3 **V-I** When someone **qualifies**, they
finish their training for a particular job.
❑ *I qualified, and started teaching last year.*
[from Old French]

Word Partnership	Use qualify with :
PREP	qualify **as** *something* **1**
	qualify **for** *something* **2**
V	**chance to** qualify, **fail to** qualify **1** **3**

qual|ity /kwɒlɪti/ (**qualities**)
1 **N-NONCOUNT** The **quality** of something is
how good or bad it is. ❑ *The quality of the food
here is excellent.*
2 **N-COUNT** A **quality** is a particular
characteristic of a person or a thing. ❑ *He
has a childlike quality.* [from Old French]

Word Partnership	Use quality with :
N	**air** quality, quality **of life**, quality **of service**, **water** quality, quality **of work** **1**
ADJ	**best/better/good** quality, **high/higher/highest** quality, **low** quality, **poor** quality, **top** quality **1**

quan|tity /kwɒntɪti/ (**quantities**) **N-COUNT/
N-NONCOUNT** A **quantity** is an amount.
❑ *Pour a small quantity of water into a pan.*
[from Old French]
→ look at Word Web: **mathematics**

quar|rel /kwɔrəl/ (**quarrels, quarreling,
quarreled**)
1 **N-COUNT** A **quarrel** is an angry argument
between two or more people. ❑ *I had a terrible
quarrel with my brothers.*
2 **V-T/V-I** When two or more people
quarrel, they have an angry argument.
❑ *Yes, we quarreled over something silly.*
[from Old French]

quar|ry /kwɔri/ (**quarries**) **N-COUNT**
A **quarry** is an area that is dug out from
a piece of land in order to get stone or
minerals from it. [from Old French]

q

Word Link   *quart ≈ four* : *quart*, *quart***er**, *quart***erback**

quart /kwɔrt/ (**quarts**) **N-COUNT** MATH
A **quart** is a unit for measuring liquids that is equal to two pints. ❏ *Use a quart of milk.* [from Old French]
→ look at Picture Dictionary: **measurements**

Word Link   *quart ≈ four* : *quart*, *quart***er**, *quart***erback**

quar|ter /kwɔrtər/ (**quarters**)
1 **N-COUNT** MATH A **quarter** is one of four equal parts of something (¼). ❏ *A quarter of the residents are over 55 years old.* ❏ *I'll be with you in a quarter of an hour.*
2 **N-COUNT** A **quarter** is an American or Canadian coin that is worth 25 cents.
3 **N-COUNT** A **quarter** is a fixed period of three months. ❏ *We will send you a bill every quarter.*
4 **N-NONCOUNT/N-SING** When you are telling the time, you use **quarter** to talk about the fifteen minutes before or after an hour. ❏ *He came over at quarter after eight in the morning.* ❏ *We arrived at a quarter to nine that night.* [from Old French]

Word Partnership	Use **quarter** with :
N	**quarter (of a) century**, **quarter (of a) pound** **1**
ADJ	**first/fourth/second/third** quarter **3**
PREP	**for the** quarter, **in the** quarter **3** quarter **after**, quarter **of**, quarter **past**, quarter **to** **4**

quarter|back /kwɔrtərbæk/ (**quarterbacks**)
N-COUNT SPORTS In football, a **quarterback** is the player on the attacking team who begins each play, and who decides which play to use.

quarter|final /kwɔrtərfaɪnəl/
(**quarterfinals**) **N-COUNT** SPORTS A **quarterfinal** is one of the four games in a competition that decides which four players or teams will compete in the semifinals.

quar|ter|ly /kwɔrtərli/
1 **ADJ** A **quarterly** event happens four times a year, at intervals of three months. ❏ *...the latest Bank of Japan quarterly report.*
2 **ADV** **Quarterly** is also an adverb. ❏ *Your money can be paid quarterly or annually.* [from Old French]

quar|tet /kwɔrtɛt/ (**quartets**)
1 **N-COUNT** MUSIC A **quartet** is a group of

four people who play musical instruments or sing together.
2 **N-COUNT** MUSIC A **quartet** is a piece of music for four instruments or four singers. [from Italian]

quartz /kwɔrts/ **N-NONCOUNT** **Quartz** is a hard, shiny mineral that is used in making electronic equipment and very accurate watches and clocks. [from German]

qua|sar /kweɪzɑr/ (**quasars**) **N-COUNT**
SCIENCE A **quasar** is an object far away in space that produces bright light and radio waves.

queen /kwin/ (**queens**)
1 **N-COUNT** SOCIAL STUDIES A **queen** is a woman who rules a country. ❏ *...Queen Elizabeth.*
2 **N-COUNT** SOCIAL STUDIES A **queen** is the wife of a king.
3 **N-COUNT** A **queen** is a playing card with a picture of a queen on it. ❏ *...the queen of spades.*
4 **N-COUNT** In chess, the **queen** is the most powerful piece, and can be moved in any direction. [from Old English]
→ look at Word Web: **chess**

que|ry /kwɪəri/ (**queries, querying, queried**)
1 **N-COUNT** A **query** is a question, especially one that you ask an organization, publication, or expert. ❏ *If you have any queries, please do not hesitate to contact us.*
2 **V-T** If you **query** something, you check it by asking about it because you are not sure if it is correct. ❏ *There's a number you can call to query your bill.*
3 **V-T** To **query** means to ask a question. ❏ *"Is there something else?" Ray queried.* [from Latin]

que|sa|dilla /keɪsədiyə/ (**quesadillas**)
N-COUNT A **quesadilla** is a warm, round, flat bread filled with cheese and sometimes other ingredients. ❏ *They ordered two chicken quesadillas.* [from Spanish]

quest /kwɛst/ (**quests**) **N-COUNT** A **quest** is a long and difficult search for something. [LITERARY] ❏ *My quest for a better bank continues.* [from Old French]

ques|tion /kwɛstʃən/ (**questions, questioning, questioned**)
1 **N-COUNT** A **question** is something that you say or write in order to ask a person about something. ❏ *They asked a lot of*

questions about her health.

2 **V-T** If you **question** someone, you ask them a lot of questions about something. ❑ *The doctor questioned Jim about his parents.*

● **ques|tion|ing** **N-NONCOUNT** ❑ *The police want thirty-two people for questioning.*

3 **V-T** If you **question** something, you express doubts about it. ❑ *They never question the doctor's decisions.*

4 **N-SING** If there is no **question** about something, there is no doubt about it. ❑ *There's no question about their success.*

5 **N-COUNT** A **question** is a problem or a subject that needs to be considered. ❑ *The question of nuclear energy is complex.*

6 **N-COUNT** The **questions** on an examination are the problems that test your knowledge. ❑ *Please answer all six questions.*

7 **PHRASE** Something that is **out of the question** is completely impossible. ❑ *An expensive vacation is out of the question for him.* [from Old French]

Word Partnership	Use **question** with :
V	**answer a** question, **ask a** question, **beg the** question, **pose a** question, **raise a** question **1**
N	**answer/response to a** question **1**
ADJ	**difficult** question, **good** question, **important** question **1**

ques|tion mark (**question marks**) **N-COUNT** LANGUAGE ARTS A **question mark** is the punctuation mark **?** that is used in writing at the end of a question.
→ look at Picture Dictionary: **punctuation**

quick /kwɪk/ (**quicker, quickest**)

1 **ADJ** Someone or something that is **quick** moves or does things with great speed. ❑ *You'll have to be quick.* ● **quick|ly** **ADV** ❑ *Cussane worked quickly.*

2 **ADJ** Something that is **quick** takes or lasts only a short time. ❑ *He took a quick look around the room.* ● **quick|ly** **ADV** ❑ *You can get fit quite quickly if you exercise.*

3 **ADJ** **Quick** means happening with very little delay. ❑ *We are hoping for a quick end to the strike.* ● **quick|ly** **ADV** ❑ *We need to get the money back as quickly as possible.* [from Old English]

Thesaurus	**quick** Also look up :
ADJ	brisk, fast, rapid, speedy, swift; (*ant.*) slow **1**

Word Partnership	Use **quick** with :
N	quick **learner** **1** quick **glance**, quick **kiss**, quick **look**, quick **question**, quick **smile** **2** quick **action**, quick **profit**, quick **response**, quick **start**, quick **thinking** **3**

qui|et /kwaɪɪt/ (**quieter, quietest**)

1 **ADJ** Someone or something that is **quiet** makes only a small amount of noise. ❑ *The car has an extremely quiet engine.*

● **qui|et|ly** **ADV** ❑ *She spoke so quietly that we couldn't understand what she said.*

2 **ADJ** If a place is **quiet**, there is no activity or trouble there. ❑ *It's a quiet little village.*

3 **ADJ** If you are **quiet**, you are not saying anything. ❑ *Be quiet and go to sleep.*

● **qui|et|ly** **ADV** ❑ *Amy stood quietly in the doorway.* [from Latin]

Word Partnership	Use **quiet** with :
V	**be** quiet, **keep** quiet **1**
ADV	**really** quiet, **relatively** quiet, **too** quiet, **very** quiet **1**–**3**
N	quiet **day/evening/night**, quiet **life**, quiet **neighborhood/street**, **peace and** quiet, quiet **place/spot** **2**

quilt /kwɪlt/ (**quilts**) **N-COUNT** A **quilt** is a bed cover made by sewing pieces of colored cloth together. ❑ *An old quilt was on the bed.* [from Old French]
→ look at Word Web: **quilt**

quit /kwɪt/ (**quits, quitting, quit**)

LANGUAGE HELP
The form **quit** is used in the present tense and is the past tense and past participle.

1 **V-T/V-I** If you **quit**, or **quit** your job, you choose to stop working. [INFORMAL] ❑ *Christina quit her job last year.* ❑ *That's enough! I quit!*

2 **V-T** If you **quit** doing something, you stop doing it. ❑ *Quit talking now and do some work.* [from Old French]

quite /kwaɪt/

1 **ADV** **Quite** means very but not extremely. ❑ *I felt quite bad about it at the time.* ❑ *I knew her mother quite well.* ❑ *Our house is quite a long way from the city.*

2 **ADV** **Quite** means completely. ❑ *I've not quite finished my project.* ❑ *My position is quite different.*

3 **PREDET** You use **quite a** or **quite an** before

q

Word Web quilt

The Hmong* tribes are famous for their colorful **quilts**. Many people think of a quilt as a bed covering. But these **textiles** feature pictures that tell stories about the people who made them. A favorite story shows how the Hmong fled from China to southeast Asia in the early 1800s. The story sometimes shows the quiltmaker arriving in a new country. The seamstress **sews** small pieces of colorful **fabric** together to make the **design**. The **needlework** is very complicated. It includes cross-stitching, **embroidery,** and appliqué. A common border **pattern** is a design that represents mountains—the Hmong's original home.

Hmong: a group of people who live in the mountains of China, Vietnam, Laos, and Thailand.

a noun to say that a person or thing is very impressive or unusual. ❑ *He's quite a character.* **4** **PHRASE** If there is **quite a bit** or **quite a lot** of something, there is a large amount of it. ❑ *We used to see his wife quite a lot.*

quiz /kwɪz/ (**quizzes**)
1 **N-COUNT** A **quiz** is a game or a competition in which someone tests your knowledge by asking you questions. ❑ *We'll have a quiz after we visit the museum.*
2 **N-COUNT** A **quiz** is a short test that a teacher gives to a class. ❑ *We had a vocabulary quiz today in English class.*

quo|ta /kwoʊtə/ (**quotas**)
1 **N-COUNT** A **quota** is the limited number or quantity of something that is officially allowed. ❑ *There's a quota of four tickets per person.*
2 **N-COUNT** Someone's **quota of** something is their expected or deserved share of it. ❑ *She's had the usual quota of teenage problems.* [from Latin]

quo|ta|tion /kwoʊteɪʃ°n/ (**quotations**)
N-COUNT LANGUAGE ARTS A **quotation** is a sentence or a phrase from a book, a poem, a speech, or a play. ❑ *He used quotations from Martin Luther King Jr. in his lecture.* [from Medieval Latin]

quo|ta|tion mark (**quotation marks**)
N-COUNT LANGUAGE ARTS **Quotation marks** are punctuation marks that are used in writing to show where speech begins and ends. They are usually written or printed as "...".

quote /kwoʊt/ (**quotes, quoting, quoted**)
1 **V-T/V-I** If you **quote** someone as saying something, or **quote** from something, you repeat what someone has written or said. ❑ *I gave the letter to the reporter and he quoted from it.* ❑ *The newspaper article quoted the teacher as saying that the children had disliked reading poetry.*
2 **N-COUNT** LANGUAGE ARTS A **quote from** a book, a poem, a play, or a speech is a section from it. ❑ *He finished with a quote from one of his favorite poems.*
3 **V-T** If someone **quotes** a price **for** something, they say how much money they would charge you for it. ❑ *A travel agent quoted her $260 for a flight from Boston to New Jersey.*
4 **N-PLURAL** LANGUAGE ARTS **Quotes** are the same as **quotation marks**. [INFORMAL] ❑ *The word "remembered" is in quotes here.* [from Medieval Latin]

Thesaurus	quote Also look up :
V	recite, repeat **1** **3**
N	estimate, price **5**

Rr

rab|bi /ˈræbaɪ/ (**rabbis**) **N-COUNT** A **rabbi** is a Jewish religious leader. [from Hebrew]

rab|bit /ˈræbɪt/ (**rabbits**) **N-COUNT** A **rabbit** is a small animal that has long ears and lives in a hole in the ground. [from Flemish]
→ look at Word Web: **herbivore**

race /reɪs/ (**races, racing, raced**)
1 N-COUNT SPORTS A **race** is a competition to see who is the fastest. ❑ *Mark easily won the race.* ❑ *...a horse race.*
2 V-T/V-I If you **race**, you take part in a race. ❑ *Leo started racing in the early 1950s.* ❑ *We raced them to the top of the hill.*
3 N-COUNT A **race** is a situation in which people or organizations compete with each other for power or control. ❑ *He's in the race for the governor of Oregon.*
4 N-COUNT/N-NONCOUNT A **race** is one of the major groups that humans can be divided into according to their physical features, such as the color of their skin. ❑ *The college welcomes students of all races.*
5 → see also **human race**
6 V-I If you **race** somewhere, you go there as quickly as possible. ❑ *He raced across town to the hospital.* [Senses 1, 2, 3, and 6 from Old Norse. Sense 4 from French]
7 → see also **racing**

race|track /ˈreɪstræk/ (**racetracks**) also race track **N-COUNT** SPORTS A **racetrack** is a track for races between runners, horses, dogs, cars, or motorcycles. ❑ *...a horse racetrack.*

ra|cial /ˈreɪʃ°l/ **ADJ** **Racial** describes things relating to people's race. ❑ *The new law promotes racial equality.* ● **ra|cial|ly** **ADV** ❑ *...a racially mixed school.* [from French]

	Word Partnership Use **racial** with :
N	racial **differences**, racial **discrimination**, racial **diversity**, racial **equality**, racial **groups**, racial **minorities**, racial **prejudice**, racial **tensions**

racial pro|fil|ing /ˈreɪʃ°l ˈproʊfaɪlɪŋ/ **N-NONCOUNT** **Racial profiling** is government or police activity that involves using people's racial and cultural characteristics to identify people to investigate. ❑ *...controversies involving racial profiling and corruption.*

rac|ing /ˈreɪsɪŋ/
1 N-NONCOUNT SPORTS **Racing** is the sport of competing in races. ❑ *...a racing car.* [from Old Norse]
2 → see also **race**
→ look at Word Web: **bicycle**

rac|ism /ˈreɪsɪzəm/ **N-NONCOUNT** SOCIAL STUDIES **Racism** is the belief that people of some races are not as good as others. ❑ *Many of these children experienced racism in their daily lives.*

rac|ist /ˈreɪsɪst/ (**racists**)
1 ADJ **Racist** people, things, opinions, or behavior are influenced by the belief that some people are better than others because they belong to a particular race. ❑ *We live in a racist society.*
2 N-COUNT A **racist** is someone who is racist. ❑ *He was attacked by a gang of white racists.* [from Old Norse]

rack /ræk/ (**racks**) **N-COUNT** A **rack** is a frame or a shelf, usually with bars, that is used for holding things. ❑ *Put all your bags in the luggage rack.* [from Middle Dutch]

rack|et /ˈrækɪt/ (**rackets**)

LANGUAGE HELP
The spelling **racquet** is also used for meaning **1**.

1 N-COUNT SPORTS A **racket** is a bat with strings across it, that is used in some ball games. ❑ *I got a tennis racket for my birthday.*
2 N-SING A **racket** is a loud, unpleasant noise. ❑ *The children were making a racket upstairs.*

Word Link	rad ≈ ray : radar, radiant, radiation

ra|dar /ˈreɪdɑr/ **N-NONCOUNT** SCIENCE **Radar** is a way of discovering the position of objects when they cannot be seen, by using

r

radio signals. ❑ *They saw the submarine on the ship's radar screen.*

→ look at Word Webs: **bat, forecast**

ra|dial sym|me|try /reɪdiəl sɪmɪtri/
N-NONCOUNT SCIENCE An organism that has **radial symmetry** has a body that resembles the pattern you get when straight lines are drawn from the center of a circle to a number of points around the edge. Compare with **bilateral symmetry**.

Word Link   *rad ≈ ray : radar, radiant, radiation*
---

ra|di|ant /reɪdiənt/
1 **ADJ** Someone who is **radiant** is so happy that their happiness shows in their face. ❑ *The bride looked radiant.*
● **ra|di|ance** **N-NONCOUNT** ❑ *She had started to lose her radiance.*
2 **ADJ** Something that is **radiant** glows brightly. ❑ *...the radiant glow of the fire.*
● **ra|di|ance** **N-NONCOUNT** ❑ *...the radiance of the candles.* [from Latin]

ra|dia|tion /reɪdieɪʃ°n/ **N-NONCOUNT**
SCIENCE **Radiation** is a type of energy that comes from some substances. Too much **radiation** is harmful to living things. ❑ *The gas protects the Earth against radiation from the sun.* [from Latin]

→ look at Word Webs: **cancer, greenhouse effect**

Word Partnership   Use **radiation** with :

ADJ	**nuclear** radiation
N	radiation **damage, effects of** radiation, **exposure** radiation, radiation **levels,** radiation **therapy/treatment**
---

ra|dia|tive zone /reɪdieɪtɪv zoʊn/
(**radiative zones**) **N-COUNT** SCIENCE The **radiative zone** is the area of the sun around the core, where energy travels in the form of radiation.

ra|dia|tor /reɪdieɪtər/ (**radiators**)
1 **N-COUNT** A **radiator** is a metal object that is full of hot water or steam, and is used for heating a room.
2 **N-COUNT** The **radiator** in a car is the part of the engine that is filled with water in order to cool the engine. [from Latin]

ra|dio /reɪdioʊ/ (**radios, radioing, radioed**)
1 **N-NONCOUNT** **Radio** is the broadcasting of programs for the public to listen to, by sending out signals. ❑ *The event was broadcast on local radio.*
2 **N-COUNT** A **radio** is a piece of equipment that you use in order to listen to radio programs. ❑ *He turned on the radio.*
3 **N-NONCOUNT** **Radio** is a system of sending and receiving sound using electronic signals. ❑ *They are in radio contact with the leader.*
4 **N-COUNT** A **radio** is a piece of equipment that is used for sending and receiving spoken messages. ❑ *The police officer called for extra help on his radio.*
5 **V-T/V-I** If you **radio** someone, you send a spoken message to them by radio. ❑ *The officer radioed for advice.* ❑ *Martin radioed his team to tell them he was OK.*

→ look at Word Webs: **radio, telescope**

radio|ac|tive /reɪdioʊæktɪv/ **ADJ** SCIENCE Something that is **radioactive** contains a substance that produces a type of energy that can be harmful to living things. ❑ *Germany forbids the import of radioactive waste products.* ● **radio|ac|tiv|ity** /reɪdioʊæktɪvɪti/ **N-NONCOUNT** ❑ *...a harmful release of radioactivity.*

radio|act|ive sym|bol (**radioactive symbols**) **N-COUNT** SCIENCE A **radioactive symbol** is a printed sign which shows that a place or an object contains dangerous amounts of radiation.

Word Web   radio

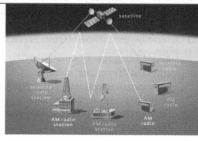

Radio's first use was for **communication** between ships. Ships also radioed **stations** on land. In 1912, the *Titanic* sank in the North Atlantic with more than 2,000 people on board. A radio call to a nearby ship helped save a third of the passengers. What we call a radio is actually a **receiver**. The **waves** it receives come from a **transmitter**. Radio is an important source of **entertainment**. AM radio carries all kinds of radio **programs. Listeners** often prefer musical programs on the FM wave band or from **satellites** because the sound quality is better.

ra|dio tele|scope (radio telescopes)
N-COUNT SCIENCE A **radio telescope** is an instrument that receives radio waves from space and finds the position of stars and other objects in space.

ra|dio wave (radio waves) **N-COUNT** SCIENCE **Radio waves** are the form in which radio signals travel.

ra|dius /reɪdiəs/ (radii /reɪdiaɪ/) **N-COUNT** MATH The **radius** of a circle is the distance from its center to its outside edge. ❑ We offer free delivery within a 5-mile radius of our store. [from Latin]
→ look at Picture Dictionary: **area**

raf|fle /ræf°l/ (raffles) **N-COUNT** A **raffle** is a competition in which you buy tickets with numbers on them. If your number is chosen, you win a prize. ❑ ...raffle tickets. [from Old French]

raft /ræft/ (rafts) **N-COUNT** A **raft** is a floating structure that is made from large pieces of wood that are tied together. [from Old Norse]
→ look at Word Web: **boat**

rag /ræg/ (rags)
1 N-COUNT/N-NONCOUNT A **rag** is a piece of old cloth. ❑ He was wiping his hands on an oily rag.
2 N-PLURAL Rags are old torn clothes. ❑ The streets were full of children dressed in rags. [from Old English]

rage /reɪdʒ/ (rages, raging, raged)
1 N-NONCOUNT Rage is strong anger that is difficult to control. ❑ His face was red with rage.
2 V-I Something powerful such as a fire or a storm **rages** when it continues with great force. ❑ The fire raged for four hours. [from Old French]
→ look at Word Web: **anger**

Thesaurus	rage	Also look up :
N	anger, madness, tantrum **1**	

rag|ged /rægɪd/
1 ADJ Someone who is **ragged** is wearing clothes that are old and torn. ❑ A thin ragged man sat on the park bench.
2 ADJ Ragged clothes are old and torn.

raid /reɪd/ (raids, raiding, raided)
1 V-T If police officers or soldiers **raid** a building, they enter it suddenly in order to look for someone or something. ❑ Police raided the company's offices.

2 N-COUNT Raid is also a noun. ❑ They were arrested after a raid on a house by police. [from Scots]

rail /reɪl/ (rails)
1 N-COUNT A **rail** is a horizontal bar that you hold for support. ❑ She held the hand rail tightly.
2 N-COUNT A **rail** is a horizontal bar that you hang things on. ❑ ...a curtain rail.
3 N-COUNT Rails are the steel bars that trains run on. ❑ The train left the rails.
4 N-NONCOUNT If you travel **by rail**, you travel on a train. ❑ The president arrived by rail. [from Old French]
→ look at Word Webs: **train, transportation**

rail|ing /reɪlɪŋ/ (railings) **N-COUNT** A **railing** is a fence that is made from metal bars. ❑ He jumped over the railing to shake hands with the fans. [from Old French]

rail|road /reɪlroʊd/ (railroads)
1 N-COUNT A **railroad** is a route between two places that trains travel along on metal rails. ❑ ...railroad tracks.
2 N-COUNT A **railroad** is a company or an organization that operates railroad routes. ❑ They send goods on the Chicago and Northwestern Railroad.

rain /reɪn/ (rains, raining, rained)
1 N-NONCOUNT SCIENCE **Rain** is water that falls from the clouds in small drops. ❑ We got very wet in the rain.
2 V-I When rain falls, you can say that **it is raining**. ❑ It was raining hard. [from Old English]
→ look at Word Webs: **disaster, hurricane, precipitation, storm, water**

Thesaurus	rain	Also look up :
N	drizzle, shower, sleet **1**	

rain|bow /reɪnboʊ/ (rainbows) **N-COUNT** SCIENCE A **rainbow** is a half circle of different colors that you can sometimes see in the sky when it rains.
→ look at Word Web: **rainbow**

rain|coat /reɪnkoʊt/ (raincoats) **N-COUNT** A **raincoat** is a coat that you can wear to keep dry when it rains.

rain|drop /reɪndrɒp/ (raindrops) **N-COUNT** A **raindrop** is a single drop of rain.
→ look at Word Web: **precipitation**

rain|fall /reɪnfɔl/ **N-NONCOUNT** SCIENCE **Rainfall** is the amount of rain that falls in a

r

Sunlight contains all colors. When a **ray** of sunlight passes through a **prism**, it splits into different colors. This is also what happens when light passes through the drops of **water** in the air. The light is refracted, and we see a **rainbow**. The colors of the rainbow are **red, orange, yellow, green, blue,** indigo, and **violet**. One tradition says that there is a pot of gold at the end of the rainbow. Other myths say that the rainbow is a bridge between Earth and the land of the gods.

place during a particular period. ❏ *This month we have recorded below average rainfall.*
→ look at Word Webs: **erosion, habitat, storm**

rainfor|est /reɪnfɔrɪst/ (**rainforests**)
N-COUNT/N-NONCOUNT GEOGRAPHY A **rainforest** is a thick forest of tall trees that grows in areas where there is a lot of rain. ❏ *We watched a program about the destruction of the Amazon Rainforest.*
→ look at Word Web: **habitat**

rain|water /reɪnwɔtər/ **N-NONCOUNT**
Rainwater is water that has fallen as rain.

rainy /reɪni/ (**rainier, rainiest**) **ADJ** If it is **rainy**, it is raining a lot. ❏ *Here are some fun things to do on a rainy day.* [from Old English]

raise /reɪz/ (**raises, raising, raised**)
1 **V-T** If you **raise** something, you move it upward. ❏ *He raised his hand to wave.* ❏ *Milton raised the glass to his lips.*
2 **V-T** If you **raise** the rate or level of something, you increase it. ❏ *Many stores have raised their prices.*
3 **V-T** If you **raise** your **voice**, you speak more loudly.
4 **N-COUNT** A **raise** is an increase in the amount of money that you are paid for your work. ❏ *Kelly got a raise of $100.*
5 **V-T** If you **raise** money **for** a particular purpose, you ask people for money for it. ❏ *The purpose of the event is to raise money for the school.*
6 **V-T** If you **raise** a subject, you start to talk about it. ❏ *The matter will be raised at our annual meeting.*
7 **V-T** To **raise** children means to take care of them until they are grown up. ❏ *She raised four children on her own.*
8 **V-T** To **raise** a particular type of animal or

crop means to keep that animal or to grow that crop on a farm. [from Old Norse]
→ look at Word Web: **union**

Raise is often confused with *rise*, but it has a different meaning. *Raise* means "to move something to a higher position": *Students raise their hand when they want to speak in class.*
Rise means that something moves upward: *When steam rises from the pot, add the pasta.*

rai|sin /reɪzᵊn/ (**raisins**) **N-COUNT** Raisins are dried grapes. [from Old French]

rake /reɪk/ (**rakes, raking, raked**)
1 **N-COUNT** A **rake** is a garden tool with a long handle, used for collecting loose grass or leaves.
2 **V-T** If you **rake** leaves, you move them using a rake. ❏ *We raked the leaves into piles.* [from Old English]
→ look at Picture Dictionary: **garden**

ral|ly /ræli/ (**rallies**)
1 **N-COUNT** SOCIAL STUDIES A **rally** is a large public meeting that is held in order to show support for something. ❏ *They organized a rally to demand better working conditions.*
2 **N-COUNT** A **rally** is a competition in which vehicles are driven over public roads. ❏ *Rally driver John Crawford won titles from 1982 to 1987.* [from Old French]

ram /ræm/ (**rams, ramming, rammed**)
1 **V-T** If a vehicle **rams** something, it crashes into it. ❏ *The truck rammed a car.*
2 **N-COUNT** A **ram** is an adult male sheep. [from Old English]

RAM /ræm/ **N-NONCOUNT** TECHNOLOGY **RAM** is the part of a computer where information is stored while you are using it. **RAM** is short for "Random Access Memory." ❑ ...*a PC with 512 MB RAM.*

ramp /ræmp/ (**ramps**) **N-COUNT** A **ramp** is a surface with a slope between two places that are at different levels. ❑ *There's a wheelchair ramp at the front entrance of the school.* [from Old French]
→ look at Word Web: **traffic**

ramp

ran /ræn/ **Ran** is the past tense of **run**. [from Old English]

ranch /ræntʃ/ (**ranches**) **N-COUNT** A **ranch** is a large farm used for keeping animals. ❑ *He owns a cattle ranch in Texas.* [from Mexican Spanish]

ran|dom /rændəm/
1 **ADJ** A **random** process is one in which all the people or things involved have an equal chance of being chosen. ❑ *The survey used a random sample of two thousand people.*
2 **ADJ** If events are **random**, they do not follow a plan or pattern. ❑ *We have seen random violence against innocent victims.*
3 **PHRASE** If something happens **at random**, it happens without a plan or pattern. ❑ *The gunman fired at random.* [from Old French]

ran|dom vari|able (**random variables**) **N-COUNT** SCIENCE In statistics, a **random variable** is a quantity whose value depends on a set of probabilities.

rang /ræŋ/ **Rang** is the past tense of **ring**. [from Old English]

range /reɪndʒ/ (**ranges, ranging, ranged**)
1 **N-COUNT** A **range of** things is a number of different things of the same type. ❑ *These products come in a wide range of colors.*
2 **N-COUNT** A **range** is the complete group that is included between two points on a scale. ❑ *The average age range is between 35 and 55.*
3 **N-COUNT** The **range of** something is the largest area in which it can reach things. ❑ *This electric car has a range of 100 miles.*
4 **V-I** If things **range between** two points on a scale, they are between these two fixed

points. ❑ *The children range in age from five to fourteen.*
5 **N-COUNT** GEOGRAPHY A **range** of mountains or hills is a group of them. ❑ *...snowy mountain ranges.*
6 **N-COUNT** MATH The **range** of a set of numbers is the difference between the biggest number and the smallest number. [from Old French]
→ look at Word Web: **graph**

Word Partnership	Use **range** with :
ADJ	**broad** range, **limited** range, **narrow** range, **wide** range **1**
	full range, **normal** range, **whole** range **2**
N	range **of emotions**, range **of possibilities 1**
	age range, **price** range, **temperature** range **2**

rang|er /reɪndʒər/ (**rangers**) **N-COUNT** A **ranger** is a person whose job is to take care of a forest or a large park. ❑ *He's a park ranger at the National Park.* [from Old French]

rank /ræŋk/ (**ranks, ranking, ranked**)
1 **N-COUNT/N-NONCOUNT** SOCIAL STUDIES Someone's **rank** is the position that they have in an organization. ❑ *He holds the rank of colonel in the U.S. Army.*
2 **V-T/V-I** If an organization **ranks** someone or something 1st or 50th, for example, they calculate that the person or thing has that position on a scale. ❑ *The report ranks the U.S. 20th out of 22 countries.* [from Old French]

Word Partnership	Use **rank** with :
ADJ	**high** rank, **top** rank **1**
PREP	rank **above**, rank **below 2**

ran|som /rænsəm/ (**ransoms**)
N-COUNT/N-NONCOUNT A **ransom** is the money that has to be paid to someone so that they will set a person free. ❑ *Her kidnapper asked for a $250,000 ransom.* [from Old French]

rap /ræp/ (**raps, rapping, rapped**)
1 **N-NONCOUNT** MUSIC **Rap** is a type of popular music in which the words are spoken. ❑ *He performs with a rap group.*
● **rap|per** (**rappers**) **N-COUNT** ❑ *He's a singer and a talented rapper.*
2 **V-I** MUSIC Someone who **raps** performs rap music. [of Scandinavian origin]

r

rape /reɪp/ (**rapes, raping, raped**)

1 **V-T** If someone **is raped**, they are forced to have sex when they do not want to. ❑ *Many women were raped during the war.* ● **rap|ist** (**rapists**) **N-COUNT** ❑ *The information led to the rapist's arrest.*

2 **N-COUNT/N-NONCOUNT** Rape is the crime of forcing someone to have sex. [from Latin]

rap|id /ræpɪd/

1 **ADJ** A **rapid** change happens very quickly. ❑ *This is the end of the country's rapid economic growth.* ● **rap|id|ly** **ADV** ❑ *The firm continues to grow rapidly.*

2 **ADJ** A **rapid** movement is very fast. ❑ *He walked at a rapid pace.* ● **rap|id|ly** **ADV** ❑ *He was moving rapidly around the room.* [from Latin]

Thesaurus	**rapid** Also look up :
ADJ	fast, speedy, swift; (*ant.*) slow **1** **2**

Word Partnership	Use **rapid** with :
N	rapid **change**, rapid **decline**, rapid **development** rapid **expansion**, rapid **growth**, rapid **increase**, rapid **progress** **1**
	rapid **pace**, rapid **pulse** **2**

rare /rɛər/ (**rarer, rarest**)

1 **ADJ** Something that is **rare** is not seen or heard very often. ❑ *This is one of the rarest birds in the world.*

2 **ADJ** An event or situation that is **rare** does not happen very often. ❑ *They have dinner together on the rare occasions when they are both at home.*

3 **ADJ** Meat that is **rare** is cooked very lightly so that the inside is still red. [from Old English]

rar|efac|tion /rɛərɪfækʃ°n/ **N-NONCOUNT** SCIENCE Rarefaction is a reduction in the density of something, especially the density of the atmosphere. [from Old French]

rare|ly /rɛərli/ **ADV** If something **rarely** happens, it does not happen very often. [from Latin]

rash /ræʃ/ (**rashes**)

1 **ADJ** If someone is **rash**, they act without thinking carefully first. ❑ *Don't make any rash decisions.*

2 **N-COUNT** A **rash** is an area of red spots that appears on your skin. ❑ *I always get a rash when I eat nuts.* [Sense 1 from Old High German. Sense 2 from Old French.]

rasp|berry /ræzbɛri/ (**raspberries**) **N-COUNT** Raspberries are small, soft, red fruits that grow on bushes.

rat /ræt/ (**rats**) **N-COUNT** A **rat** is an animal that has a long tail and looks like a large mouse. [from Old English]

rate /reɪt/ (**rates, rating, rated**)

1 **N-COUNT** The **rate** at which something happens is how fast or how often it happens. ❑ *An adult's heart rate is about 72 beats per minute.* ❑ *Spain has the lowest birth rate in Europe.*

2 **N-COUNT** A **rate** is the amount of money that goods or services cost. ❑ *The hotel offers a special weekend rate.*

3 → see also **exchange rate**

4 **N-COUNT** BUSINESS The **rate** of taxation or interest is the amount of tax or interest that needs to be paid, expressed as a percentage. ❑ *...interest rate cuts.*

5 **V-T/V-I** If you **rate** someone or something as good or bad, you consider them to be good or bad. ❑ *We rate him as one of the best.* ❑ *This small shop rated well in our survey.*

6 → see also **rating**

7 **PHRASE** At any rate means "anyway." ❑ *His friends liked her—well, most of them at any rate.* [from Old French]

→ look at Word Web: **motion**

Word Partnership	Use **rate** with :
ADJ	**average** rate, **faster** rate, **slow** rate, **steady** rate **1**
	high rate, **low** rate **1** **3**
N	**birth** rate, rate **of change**, **crime** rate, **dropout** rate, **heart** rate, **pulse** rate, **survival** rate, **unemployment** rate **1**
	interest rate **3**

ra|ther /ræðər/

1 **PHRASE** You use **rather than** to mention a thing or a situation that is not done. ❑ *I prefer to use the bike rather than the car.*

2 **CONJ** Rather than is also a conjunction. ❑ *Use plastic bags again rather than throw them away.*

3 **ADV** You use **rather** when you are correcting something that you have just said. ❑ *This is not a solution, but rather will create new problems.*

4 **PHRASE** If you **would rather** do something, you would prefer to do it. ❑ *Kids would rather play than study.*

5 **ADV** You use **rather** to mean "more than a little." ❑ *I thought the movie was rather boring.* [from Old English]

R

rati|fy /rǽtɪfaɪ/ (**ratifies, ratifying, ratified**)
V-T SOCIAL STUDIES When national leaders or organizations **ratify** a treaty or a written agreement, they make it official by giving their formal approval to it, usually by signing it or voting for it. ● **rati|fi|ca|tion** /rǽtɪfɪkeɪʃ°n/ (**ratifications**)
N-COUNT/N-NONCOUNT ❑ We hope for early ratification of the treaty. [from Old French]

rat|ing /reɪtɪŋ/ (**ratings**)
1 **N-COUNT** A **rating** is a measurement of how good or popular something is. ❑ The president's popularity rating is at its lowest point. [from Old French]
2 → see also **rate**

> | **Word Partnership** | Use **rating** with : |
> |---|---|
> | N | **approval** rating |
> | ADJ | **high** rating, **low** rating, **poor** rating, **top** rating |

ra|tio /reɪʃoʊ, -ʃioʊ/ (**ratios**) **N-COUNT** MATH A **ratio** is a relationship between two things when it is expressed in numbers or amounts. ❑ The adult to child ratio is one to six. [from Latin]

ra|tion /rǽʃ°n, reɪ-/ (**rations, rationing, rationed**)
1 **N-COUNT** Your **ration** of something is a small amount that you are allowed to have when there is not much of it available. ❑ The meat ration was 250 grams per month.
2 **V-T** When something **is rationed**, you are only allowed to have a small amount of it. ❑ Food such as bread and rice was rationed.
3 **N-PLURAL** **Rations** are the food that is given to soldiers or to people who do not have enough food. [from French]

> | **Word Link** | ratio ≈ reasoning : ir**ratio**nal, **ratio**nal, **ratio**nally |
> |---|---|

ra|tion|al /rǽʃən°l/ **ADJ** **Rational** decisions and thoughts are based on reason rather than on emotion. ❑ They discussed it in a rational manner. ● **ra|tion|al|ly** **ADV** ❑ It is difficult to think rationally when you're worried. [from Latin]

> | **Word Partnership** | Use **rational** with : |
> |---|---|
> | N | rational **approach**, rational **choice**, rational **decision**, rational **explanation**, rational **human being**, rational **person** |

ra|tion|al num|ber (**rational numbers**)
N-COUNT MATH **Rational numbers** are numbers that can be expressed as whole numbers, fractions, or decimals.

rat|tle /rǽt°l/ (**rattles, rattling, rattled**)
1 **V-T/V-I** When something **rattles**, or when you **rattle** it, it makes short, sharp, knocking sounds because it is hitting against something hard. ❑ The windows rattled in the wind.
2 **N-COUNT** **Rattle** is also a noun. ❑ I heard the rattle of the door handle.
3 **N-COUNT** A **rattle** is a baby's toy with small, loose objects inside that make a noise when the baby shakes it. [from Middle Dutch]

rattle|snake /rǽt°lsneɪk/ (**rattlesnakes**)
N-COUNT A **rattlesnake** is a snake that lives in America. When it is afraid or angry, it shakes the hard skin at the end of its body and makes a rattling sound. **Rattlesnakes** are dangerous because their bite contains a strong poison.

rave /reɪv/ (**raves, raving, raved**) **V-T/V-I** If you **rave about** something, you speak or write about it with great enthusiasm. ❑ Rachel raved about the movie. ❑ "I didn't know Italy was so beautiful!" she raved. [from Old French]

raw /rɔ/ (**rawer, rawest**)
1 **ADJ** **Raw** materials or substances are in their natural state. ❑ ...raw sugar.
2 **ADJ** **Raw** food has not been cooked. ❑ This is a Japanese dish made of raw fish. [from Old English]

ray /reɪ/ (**rays**) **N-COUNT** SCIENCE A **ray** of light is a narrow line of light. ❑ Protect your eyes against the sun's rays. [from Old French]
→ look at Word Webs: **rainbow, telescope**

ra|zor /reɪzər/ (**razors**)
N-COUNT A **razor** is a tool that people use for shaving. [from Old French]

razor

r-con|trolled sound
/ɑrkəntroʊld saʊnd/ (**r-controlled sounds**)
N-COUNT LANGUAGE ARTS In language teaching, an **r-controlled sound** is a vowel that is pronounced differently when it comes before the letter "r," such as the vowel sound represented by the letters "ai" in "air."

r

reach /riːtʃ/ (**reaches, reaching, reached**)

■ **v-t** When someone or something **reaches** a place, they arrive there. ❑ *He did not stop until he reached the door.*

■ **v-t** If someone or something has **reached** a certain level or amount, they are at that level or amount. ❑ *The number of unemployed could reach 3 million next year.*

■ **v-i** If you **reach** somewhere, you move your arm and hand to take or touch something. ❑ *Judy reached into her bag.*

■ **v-t/v-i** If you can **reach** something, you are able to touch it by stretching out your arm or leg. ❑ *Can you reach your toes with your fingertips?* ❑ *No, I can't reach.*

■ **v-t** If you try to **reach** someone, you try to contact them, usually by telephone. ❑ *You can reach me at this phone number.*

■ **v-t** When people **reach** an agreement or a decision, they succeed in achieving it. ❑ *They failed to reach agreement over the issue.*

■ **phrase** If something is **within reach of** something, it is close to it. ❑ *You leave a notepad and pencil within reach of your bed.* [from Old English]

	Word Partnership Use **reach** with :
N	reach a **destination** ■
	reach a **goal**, reach *one's* **potential** ■
	reach **(an) agreement**, reach a **compromise**, reach a **consensus**, reach a **decision** ■

re|act /riˈækt/ (**reacts, reacting, reacted**)

■ **v-i** When you **react to** something that has happened, you behave in a particular way because of it. ❑ *They reacted violently to the news.*

■ **v-t/v-i** SCIENCE When one chemical substance **reacts with** another, or when two chemical substances **react**, they combine chemically to form another substance. ❑ *Calcium reacts with water.* [from Late Latin]

	Word Partnership Use **react** with :
ADJ	**slow to** react ■
N	react **to news**, react **to a situation** ■
ADV	react **differently**, react **emotionally**, **how to** react, react **negatively**, react **positively**, react **quickly** ■
	react **strongly**, react **violently** ■ ■

re|ac|tant /riˈæktənt/ (**reactants**) **N-COUNT** SCIENCE In a chemical reaction, the **reactants** are the substances that are present at the start of the reaction. [from Late Latin]

re|ac|tion /riˈækʃ°n/ (**reactions**)

■ **N-COUNT/N-NONCOUNT** Your **reaction to** something is what you feel, say, or do because of it. ❑ *He showed no reaction when I told him the result.*

■ **N-COUNT** SCIENCE A chemical **reaction** is a process in which two substances combine together chemically to form another substance. ❑ *...a chemical reaction between oxygen and hydrogen.*

■ **N-PLURAL** Your **reactions** are your ability to move quickly in response to something. ❑ *The sport requires very fast reactions.*

■ **N-COUNT** SCIENCE If you have a **reaction to** a drug or **to** something you have touched, you are affected unpleasantly or made ill by it. ❑ *He suffered a serious reaction to the drug.* [from Latin]

→ look at Word Web: **motion**

	Word Partnership Use **reaction** with :
ADJ	**emotional** reaction, **initial** reaction, **mixed** reaction, **negative** reaction, **positive** reaction ■
	chemical reaction ■
	allergic reaction ■

re|ac|tor /riˈæktər/ (**reactors**) **N-COUNT** SCIENCE A **reactor** is the same as a **nuclear reactor**. [from Late Latin]

read (**reads, reading, read**)

> **PRONUNCIATION HELP**
> Pronounce the present tense /riːd/.
> Pronounce the past tense and the past participle /rɛd/.

■ **v-t/v-i** LANGUAGE ARTS When you **read** a book or a story, you look at the written words and understand them. ❑ *Have you read this book?* ❑ *I read about it in the paper.* ❑ *She spends all her time reading.*

■ **v-t** When you **read** words that you can see, you say them. ❑ *Kevin always read a story to the twins when he got home.*

■ **v-t** If someone **reads** your mind or thoughts, he or she knows exactly what you are thinking.

■ **v-t** MUSIC If you can **read** music, you understand the symbols that are used in written music to represent musical sounds.

■ **v-t** SCIENCE When you **read** a measuring device, you look at it to see the information on it. ❑ *He was able to read a thermometer.* [from Old English]

■ → see also **reading**

▶ **read out** If you **read out** a piece of writing, you look at the words and say them. ❑ *The evidence was read out in court.*

Thesaurus read Also look up :

V   scan, skim, study **1**
     comprehend; (ant.) sense **1** **4**

Word Partnership Use **read** with :

N   **ability to** read, read **a book/magazine/ (news)paper**, read **a sentence**, read **a sign**, read **a statement 1**
ADV read **carefully**, read **silently 1**
V   **learn (how)** to read, **like to** read, **want to** read **1**

read|er /rídər/ (**readers**) **N-COUNT** LANGUAGE ARTS The **readers** of a newspaper, a magazine, or a book are the people who read it. ❑ *The article gives readers an interesting view of life in Spain.* [from Old English]

read|er's thea|ter **N-NONCOUNT** ARTS **Reader's theater** is a form of theater, used especially in teaching, in which the performers read from scripts and which does not involve costumes, stage sets, or special lighting.

read|ily /rédɪli/
1 **ADV** If you do something **readily**, you do it in a way that shows that you are very willing to do it. ❑ *I asked her to help, and she readily agreed.*
2 **ADV** You use **readily** to say that something can be done or obtained quickly and easily. ❑ *The parts are readily available in hardware stores.* [from Old English]

Word Partnership Use **readily** with :

V   readily **accept**, readily **admit**, readily **agree 1**
ADJ readily **apparent 1**
     be readily **available**, **make** readily **available 2**

read|ing /rídɪŋ/ (**readings**)
1 **N-NONCOUNT** LANGUAGE ARTS **Reading** is the activity of reading books. ❑ *I love reading.*
2 **N-COUNT** SCIENCE The **reading** on a measuring device is information that it shows. ❑ *The thermometer gave a faulty reading.* [from Old English]
3 → see also **read**

ready /rédi/ (**readier, readiest**)
1 **ADJ** If someone is **ready**, they are completely prepared for something. ❑ *It takes her a long time to get ready for school.*

2 **ADJ** If something is **ready**, it has been prepared and is now able to be used. ❑ *Go and tell your sister that lunch is ready.*
3 **ADJ** If you are **ready to** do something, you are willing to do it. ❑ *They were ready to help.*
4 **ADJ** To be **ready to** do something means to be about to do it or likely to do it. ❑ *She looked ready to cry.* [from Old English]

Word Partnership Use **ready** with :

N   ready **for bed**, ready **for dinner 1**
ADV **always** ready, **not quite** ready, **not** ready **yet 1–3**
V   **get** ready **1**
     ready **to begin**, ready **to fight**, ready **to go/leave**, ready **to play**, ready **to start 1 3**
     ready **to burst 4**

real /ríl/
1 **ADJ** Something that is **real** actually exists. ❑ *No, it wasn't a dream. It was real.*
2 **ADJ** A material or an object that is **real** is natural, and not a copy. ❑ *I love the smell of real leather.*
3 **ADJ** You can use **real** to describe something that is true, rather than what someone wants you to believe. ❑ *This was the real reason for her call.*
4 **ADV** You can use **real** to mean very. [INFORMAL] ❑ *He is finding prison life real tough.*
5 **ADJ** You can use **real** to mean very great or important. [INFORMAL] ❑ *Shyness can be a real problem.* [from Old French]

real es|tate **N-NONCOUNT** BUSINESS **Real estate** is property in the form of land and buildings. ❑ *We are thinking of investing in real estate.*

re|al|ism /ríəlɪzəm/ **N-NONCOUNT** If things and people are presented with **realism** in paintings, stories, or movies, they are presented in a way that is like real life.
● **realist** **ADJ** ❑ *...a realist painter.* [from Old French]
→ look at Word Web: **genre**

re|al|is|tic /ríəlɪstɪk/
1 **ADJ** If you are **realistic** about a situation, you recognize and accept its true nature. ❑ *Police must be realistic about violent crime.*
2 **ADJ** You say that a picture, a story, or a movie is **realistic** when the people and things in it are like people and things in real life. [from Old French]
→ look at Word Webs: **art, fantasy**

r

Word Partnership	Use **realistic** with :
N	realistic **assessment**, realistic **expectations**, realistic **goals**, realistic **view** **1**
V	**be** realistic **1**
ADV	**more** realistic, **very** realistic **1** **2**

Word Link *real ≈ actual* : *reality, realize, really*

re|al|ity /riǽlɪti/ (**realities**)

1 **N-NONCOUNT** You use **reality** to talk about real things rather than imagined or invented ideas. ❑ *Her dream ended and she had to return to reality.*

2 → see also **virtual reality**

3 **N-COUNT** The **reality of** a situation is the truth about it, especially when it is unpleasant. ❑ *Politicians do not understand the realities of war.*

4 **PHRASE** You can use **in reality** to introduce a statement about the real nature of something. ❑ *He promised a lot, but in reality nothing changed.* [from Old French]

→ look at Word Web: **fantasy**

Word Partnership	Use **reality** with :
ADJ	**virtual** reality **1**
V	**distort** reality **1**
	become a reality **2**
N	reality **of life**, reality **of war** **2**
PREP	**in** reality **3**

re|al|ize /ríəlaɪz/ (**realizes, realizing, realized**) **V-T/V-I** If you **realize** that something is true, you become aware of that fact or you understand it. ❑ *As soon as we realized something was wrong, we rushed to help.* ❑ *People don't realize that he was so ill.*

● **re|a|li|za|tion** **N-NONCOUNT** ❑ *The realization suddenly came to me; I was going to die.* [from Old French]

Word Partnership	Use **realize** with :
ADV	**finally** realize, **fully** realize, **suddenly** realize
V	**begin to** realize, **come to** realize, **fail to** realize, **make** *someone* realize

re|al|ly /ríəli/

1 **ADV** You can use **really** to give a sentence a stronger meaning. [SPOKEN] ❑ *I'm very sorry. I really am.*

2 **ADV** You use **really** when you are discussing the real facts about something. ❑ *You're not really leaving, are you?*

3 **ADV** People sometimes use **really** to reduce the force of a negative statement.

[SPOKEN] ❑ *I'm not really surprised.*

4 **INTERJ** You can say **Really?** to express surprise at what someone has said. [SPOKEN] ❑ *"I once met the president."—"Really?"* [from Old French]

realm /rɛlm/ (**realms**) **N-COUNT** You can use **realm** to refer to any area of activity, interest, or thought. [FORMAL] ❑ *...the realm of politics.* [from Old French]

real num|ber (**real numbers**) **N-COUNT** MATH Rational numbers and irrational numbers can be referred to collectively as **real** numbers.

re|appear /riəpíər/ (**reappears, reappearing, reappeared**) **V-I** When people or things **reappear**, they return again after they have been away or out of sight. [from Old French]

rear /rɪər/ (**rears, rearing, reared**)

1 **N-SING** The **rear** of something is the back part of it. ❑ *Mr. Forbes was sitting in the rear of the vehicle.* ❑ *The car hit the rear of the truck.*

2 **ADJ** **Rear** is also an adjective. ❑ *You must fasten all rear seat belts.*

3 **V-T** If you **rear** children, you take care of them until they are old enough to take care of themselves. ❑ *I was reared in Texas.*

4 **V-T** If you **rear** a young animal, you keep and take care of it until it is old enough to be used for work or food. ❑ *She spends a lot of time rearing animals.*

5 **V-I** When a horse **rears**, it moves the front part of its body upward, so that it is standing on its back legs. ❑ *The horse reared and threw off its rider.* [from Old English]

re|arrange /riəréɪndʒ/ (**rearranges, rearranging, rearranged**) **V-T** If you **rearrange** things, you change the way that they are organized. ❑ *Malcolm rearranged all the furniture.* [from Old French]

rea|son /ríz³n/ (**reasons, reasoning, reasoned**)

1 **N-COUNT** The **reason for** something is a fact or a situation that explains why it happens. ❑ *There is a reason for every important thing that happens.*

2 **N-NONCOUNT** **Reason** is the ability that people have to think and to make sensible judgments. ❑ *He was more interested in emotion than reason.*

3 **N-NONCOUNT** If you have a **reason to** believe or feel something, you have a definite cause for your belief or feeling.

R

❑ *They had reason to believe that he was not telling the truth.* [from Old French]

→ look at Word Web: **philosophy**

▶ **reason with** If you **reason with** someone, you try to persuade them to accept something by using sensible arguments. ❑ *He never listens. I can't reason with him.*

Word Partnership	Use reason with :
ADJ	**main** reason, **major** reason, **obvious** reason, **only** reason, **primary** reason, **real** reason, **same** reason, **simple** reason **1**
	compelling reason, **good** reason, **sufficient** reason **1 3**

rea|son|able /ríːzənəbᵊl/

1 **ADJ** A **reasonable** person is someone who is fair and sensible. ❑ *She seems to be a reasonable person.*

2 **ADJ** If a decision or an action is **reasonable**, it is fair and sensible. ❑ *That's a perfectly reasonable decision.*

3 **ADJ** If you say that an expectation or an explanation is **reasonable**, you mean that there are reasons why it may be correct. ❑ *It seems reasonable to think that cities will increase in size.*

4 **ADJ** If you say that the price of something is **reasonable**, you mean that it is not too high.

5 **ADJ** If something is **reasonable**, it is fairly good, but not very good. ❑ *The boy spoke reasonable French.* ● **rea|son|ably** **ADV** ❑ *I can dance reasonably well.* [from Old French]

Thesaurus	reasonable	Also look up :
ADJ	rational **1**	
	acceptable, fair, sensible; (ant.) unreasonable **2**	
	likely, probable, right **3**	
	fair, inexpensive **4**	

Word Partnership	Use reasonable with :
N	reasonable **person 1**
	beyond a reasonable **doubt**, reasonable **expectation**, reasonable **explanation 3**
	reasonable **cost**, reasonable **price**, reasonable **rates 4**

re|assure /ríːəʃʊ́ər/ (**reassures, reassuring, reassured**) **V-T** If you **reassure** someone, you say or do things to make them stop worrying about something. ● **re|assur|ance** **N-NONCOUNT** ❑ *He needed reassurance that she loved him.* [from Old French]

Word Partnership	Use reassure with :
N	reassure **citizens**, reassure **customers**, reassure **investors**, reassure **the public**
V	**seek to** reassure, **try to** reassure

re|assur|ing /ríːəʃʊ́ərɪŋ/ **ADJ** If someone is **reassuring**, they make you feel less worried about something. ❑ *It was reassuring to hear Jane's voice.* [from Old French]

re|bel (**rebels, rebelling, rebelled**)

> **PRONUNCIATION HELP**
> Pronounce the noun /rɛ́bəl/. Pronounce the verb /rɪbɛ́l/.

1 **N-COUNT** SOCIAL STUDIES **Rebels** are people who are fighting against the people who are in charge somewhere, for example the government. ❑ *There is still heavy fighting between rebels and government forces.*

2 **V-I** When someone **rebels**, they fight against the people who are in charge. ❑ *Teenagers often rebel against their parents.* [from Old French]

re|bel|lion /rɪbɛ́lyən/ (**rebellions**) **N-COUNT/ N-NONCOUNT** SOCIAL STUDIES A **rebellion** is when a large group of people fight against the people who are in charge, for example the government. ❑ *We are awaiting the government's response to the rebellion.* [from Old French]

re|boot /ríːbúːt/ (**reboots, rebooting, rebooted**) **V-T/V-I** TECHNOLOGY If you **reboot** a computer, or if you **reboot**, you shut it down and start it again. ❑ *Now reboot your computer, and the software will be ready to use.* ❑ *Click on ok, then reboot.* [from Old French]

re|bound /rɪbáʊnd/ (**rebounds, rebounding, rebounded**)

1 **V-I** If something **rebounds** from a solid surface, it bounces or springs back from it. ❑ *The ball rebounded from a post.*

2 **V-I** If an action or situation **rebounds on** you, it has an unpleasant effect on you, especially when this effect was intended for someone else. ❑ *Her trick rebounded on her.* [from Old French]

re|build /ríːbɪ́ld/ (**rebuilds, rebuilding, rebuilt**)

1 **V-T** When people **rebuild** something such as a building, they build it again after it has been damaged or destroyed. ❑ *The house must be rebuilt.*

2 **V-T** When people **rebuild** something such as an institution, a system, or an aspect of

r

their lives, they take action to bring it back to its previous condition. ❑ *Everyone worked hard to rebuild the economy.* [from Old English]

re|call /rɪkɔl/ (**recalls, recalling, recalled**) **v-T/v-I** When you **recall** something, you remember it. ❑ *He recalled meeting Pollard during a business trip.* ❑ *"What was his name?"— "I don't recall."* [from Old English]

re|cede /rɪsid/ (**recedes, receding, receded**)
1 **v-I** If something **recedes** from you, it moves away into the distance. ❑ *Luke's footsteps receded.*
2 **v-I** When something such as a quality, a problem, or an illness **recedes**, it becomes weaker, smaller, or less intense.
3 **v-I** If a man's hair starts to **recede**, it no longer grows on the front of his head. [from Latin]

re|ceipt /rɪsit/ (**receipts**) **N-COUNT** BUSINESS A **receipt** is a piece of paper that you get from someone to show that they have received something from you. ❑ *I gave her a receipt for the money.* [from Old Norman French]

re|ceive /rɪsiv/ (**receives, receiving, received**) **v-T** When you **receive** something, you get it after someone gives it to you or sends it to you. ❑ *They received their awards at a ceremony in San Francisco.* [from Old French]

re|ceiv|er /rɪsivər/ (**receivers**) **N-COUNT** TECHNOLOGY A telephone's **receiver** is the part that you hold near to your ear and speak into. ❑ *She picked up the receiver and started to dial.* [from Old French]
→ look at Word Web: **navigation**

re|cent /rɪsᵊnt/ **ADJ** A **recent** event or period of time happened only a short while ago. ❑ *Brad broke his leg on a recent trip to Hawaii.* [from Latin]

re|cent|ly /rɪsᵊntli/ **ADV** If something happened **recently**, it happened only a short time ago. ❑ *The bank recently opened a branch in Miami.* [from Latin]

Usage	recently and lately

Recently and *lately* can both be used to express that something began in the past and continues into the present: *Recently/Lately I've been considering going back to school to get a master's degree. Recently,* but not *lately,* is also used to describe a completed action: *I recently graduated from high school.*

re|cep|tion /rɪsɛpʃᵊn/ (**receptions**)
1 **N-COUNT** A **reception** is a formal party that is given to welcome someone, or to celebrate a special event. ❑ *We were invited to their wedding reception.*
2 **N-NONCOUNT** **Reception** in a hotel or a large building is the desk that you go to when you first arrive. ❑ *She was waiting at reception.*
3 **N-NONCOUNT** If you get good **reception** from your radio or television, the sound or picture is clear because the signal is strong. [from Latin]
→ look at Word Web: **wedding**

re|cep|tion|ist /rɪsɛpʃənɪst/ (**receptionists**) **N-COUNT** A **receptionist** in a hotel or other large building is a person whose job is to answer the telephone and deal with visitors. [from Latin]

re|cep|tor /rɪsɛptər/ (**receptors**) **N-COUNT** SCIENCE **Receptors** are nerve endings in your body which react to changes and stimuli and make your body respond in a particular way. [from Latin]

re|cess /rɪsɛs, risɛs/ **N-NONCOUNT** In a school, **recess** is the period of time between classes when the children are allowed to play. ❑ *She visited the school library during recess.* [from Latin]

re|ces|sion /rɪsɛʃᵊn/ (**recessions**) **N-COUNT/ N-NONCOUNT** SOCIAL STUDIES A **recession** is a period when the economy of a country is not performing well. ❑ *The oil price increases sent Europe into recession.* [from Latin]

re|ces|sive /rɪsɛsɪv/ **ADJ** SCIENCE A **recessive** gene produces a particular characteristic only if a person has two of these genes, one from each parent. Compare with **dominant**. [from Latin]

reci|pe /rɛsɪpi/ (**recipes**) **N-COUNT** A **recipe** is a list of food and a set of instructions telling you how to cook something. ❑ *Do you have a recipe for chocolate cake?* [from Latin]

re|cipi|ent /rɪsɪpiənt/ (**recipients**) **N-COUNT** The **recipient** of something is the person who receives it. [FORMAL] ❑ *...the recipient of the prize.* [from French]
→ look at Word Web: **donor**

re|cip|ro|cal /rɪsɪprəkᵊl/
1 **ADJ** A **reciprocal** action or agreement involves two people or groups who do the

same thing to each other or agree to help each another in a similar way. [FORMAL] ❑ ...*a reciprocal loving relationship between a man and a woman.*

2 **N-COUNT** MATH A **reciprocal** is a pair of numbers whose product is one. For example, the reciprocal of 3 is 1/3. [from Latin]

re|cite /rɪsaɪt/ (**recites, reciting, recited**)
V-T LANGUAGE ARTS When someone **recites** a poem or other piece of writing, they say it aloud after they have learned it. ❑ *We each had to recite a poem in front of the class.* [from Latin]

reck|less /rɛklɪs/ **ADJ** A **reckless** person does not care about danger, or the results of his or her actions. ❑ *He was stopped for reckless driving.* [from Old English]

reck|on /rɛkən/ (**reckons, reckoning, reckoned**)
1 **V-T** If you **reckon** that something is true, you think that it is true. [INFORMAL] ❑ *I reckon it's about three o'clock.*
2 **V-T** If something **is reckoned** to be a particular figure, it is calculated to be roughly that amount. ❑ *The business is reckoned to be worth $1.4 billion.* [from Old English]
▶ **reckon with** **1** If you say that you had not **reckoned with** something, you mean that you had not expected it and so were not prepared for it. ❑ *Gary had not reckoned with the strength of Sally's feelings.*
2 **PHRASE** If you say that there is someone or something **to be reckoned with**, you mean that they must be dealt with and it will be difficult. ❑ *He was someone to be reckoned with.*

rec|la|ma|tion /rɛkləmeɪʃⁿn/ **N-NONCOUNT**
Reclamation is the process of changing land that is unsuitable for farming or building into land that can be used. [from Old French]

rec|og|ni|tion /rɛkəgnɪʃⁿn/
1 **N-NONCOUNT** **Recognition** is the act of knowing who a person is or what something is when you see them. ❑ *There was no sign of recognition on her face.*
2 **N-NONCOUNT** **Recognition of** something is an understanding and acceptance of it. ❑ ...*recognition of the importance of exercise.* [from Latin]

rec|og|nize /rɛkəgnaɪz/ (**recognizes, recognizing, recognized**)
1 **V-T** If you **recognize** someone or something, you know who or what they are because you have seen or heard them before. ❑ *She recognized him immediately.*
2 **V-T** If someone says that they **recognize** something, they know that it exists or that it is true. ❑ *I recognize my own faults.* [from Latin]

rec|ol|lec|tion /rɛkəlɛkʃⁿn/ (**recollections**)
N-COUNT/N-NONCOUNT If you have a **recollection of** something, you remember it. ❑ *Pat has few recollections of the trip.* [from Latin]

re|com|bi|nant DNA /rikɒmbɪnənt di ɛn eɪ/ **N-NONCOUNT** SCIENCE **Recombinant DNA** is DNA that contains genes from different sources, which have been combined using genetic engineering.

rec|om|mend /rɛkəmɛnd/ (**recommends, recommending, recommended**)
1 **V-T** If someone **recommends** a person or a thing to you, they suggest that you would find that person or thing good or useful. ❑ *I recommend Barbados as a place for a vacation.* ❑ *I'll recommend you for the job.*
● **rec|om|men|da|tion** (**recommendations**)
N-COUNT ❑ *The best way of finding a dentist is to get someone else's recommendation.*
2 **V-T** If you **recommend** that something is done, you suggest that it should be done. ❑ *The doctor recommended that I lose some weight.*
● **rec|om|men|da|tion** (**recommendations**)
N-COUNT ❑ *We listened to the committee's recommendations.* [from Medieval Latin]

Word Partnership	Use recommend with :	
N	doctors recommend, **experts** recommend **1** **2** recommend **changes** **2**	
ADV	highly recommend, **strongly** recommend **1** **2**	

rec|on|cile /rɛkənsaɪl/ (**reconciles, reconciling, reconciled**)
1 **V-T** If you **reconcile** two beliefs, facts, or demands that seem to be opposed or completely different, you find a way in which they can both be true or both be successful. ❑ *It's difficult to reconcile the demands of my job and the wish to be a good father.*
2 **V-T/V-I** If you **reconcile** or **are reconciled**

r

with someone, you become friendly with them again after a disagreement. ❑ *I don't think Susan and I will be reconciled.* ❑ *You must reconcile with your partner.* ● **rec|on|cilia|tion** /rɛkənsɪlieɪʃ³n/ (**reconciliations**) **N-COUNT/ N-NONCOUNT** ❑ *...an appeal for reconciliation between the two religious groups.*
3 **V-T** If you **reconcile yourself to** an unpleasant situation, you accept it. ❑ *She reconciled herself to never seeing him again.* ● **rec|on|ciled** **ADJ** ❑ *He seemed reconciled to defeat.* [from Latin]

re|con|fig|ure /rikənfɪgyər/ (**reconfigures, reconfiguring, reconfigured**) **V-T** TECHNOLOGY If you **reconfigure** a system, a device, or a computer application, you rearrange its elements or settings. ❑ *It should be simple to reconfigure the mail servers.* [from Late Latin]

Re|con|struc|tion /rikənstrʌksᵊn/ **N-NONCOUNT** SOCIAL STUDIES **Reconstruction** was the period between 1865 and 1877 when northern and southern American states joined together again after the American Civil War. [from Latin]

rec|ord (**records, recording, recorded**)

> PRONUNCIATION HELP
> Pronounce the noun /rɛkərd/. Pronounce the verb /rɪkɔrd/.

1 **N-COUNT** If you keep a **record of** something, you keep a written account or photographs of it so that it can be looked at later. ❑ *Keep a record of all the payments.*
2 **V-T** If you **record** a piece of information or an event, you write it down or photograph it so that in the future people can look at it. ❑ *Her letters record the details of her life in China.*
3 **V-T** TECHNOLOGY If you **record** a speech or a performance, you store it in a computer file or on a disk so that it can be heard or seen again later. ❑ *Viewers can record the films.*
4 **N-COUNT** MUSIC A **record** is a round, flat piece of black plastic on which sound, especially music, is stored, and that can be played on a record player.
5 **N-COUNT** SPORTS A **record** is the best result ever in a particular sport or activity. ❑ *He set the world record of 12.92 seconds.* [from Old French]
→ look at Word Webs: **diary, history**

re|cord|er /rɪkɔrdər/ (**recorders**) **N-COUNT/ N-NONCOUNT** MUSIC A **recorder** is a wooden or plastic musical instrument in the shape of a pipe. You play it by blowing down one end and covering holes with your fingers.

re|cord|ing /rɪkɔrdɪŋ/ (**recordings**)
1 **N-COUNT** TECHNOLOGY A **recording of** moving pictures and sounds is a computer file or a disk on which they are stored. ❑ *There is a video recording of his police interview.*
2 **N-NONCOUNT** TECHNOLOGY **Recording** is the process of storing moving pictures and sounds on digital files or disks. ❑ *This has been a bad time for the recording industry.* [from Old French]

re|count /rɪkaʊnt/ (**recounts, recounting, recounted**) **V-T** If you **recount** a story or an event, you tell or describe it to people. [FORMAL] ❑ *He recounted the story of his first day at work.* [from Old French]

re|cov|er /rɪkʌvər/ (**recovers, recovering, recovered**)
1 **V-I** When you **recover from** an illness or an injury, you become well again. ❑ *He is recovering from a knee injury.*
2 **V-T** If you **recover** something that has been lost or stolen, you find it or get it back. ❑ *Police searched houses and finally recovered the stolen goods.* [from Old French]

re|cov|ery /rɪkʌvəri/ (**recoveries**) **N-COUNT/ N-NONCOUNT** If a sick person makes a **recovery**, he or she becomes well again. ❑ *Natalie is making an excellent recovery from a serious knee injury.* [from Old French]

> Word Link   **creat ≈ making : creation, creature, recreate**

re|cre|ate /rikrieɪt/ (**recreates, recreating, recreated**) **V-T** If you **recreate** something, you succeed in making it exist or seem to exist again. ❑ *You can't recreate the past.* [from Latin]

rec|rea|tion /rɛkrieɪʃ³n/ **N-NONCOUNT** **Recreation** is things that you do in your spare time to relax. ❑ *Saturday afternoon is for recreation.* [from Latin]
→ look at Word Web: **park**

re|cruit /rɪkrut/ (**recruits, recruiting, recruited**)
1 **V-T** If you **recruit** people for an organization, you ask them to join it. ❑ *We need to recruit and train more teachers.* ● **re|cruit|ment** **N-NONCOUNT** ❑ *There has been a drop in the recruitment of soldiers.*
2 **N-COUNT** A **recruit** is a person who has

R

recently joined an organization or an army. ❏ *He's a new recruit to the police department.* [from French]

Word Link *rect ≈ right, straight : correct, direct, rectangle*
---

rec|tan|gle /rɛktæŋgᵊl/ (rectangles)
N-COUNT MATH A **rectangle** is a shape with four straight sides. ● **rec|tan|gu|lar** /rɛktæŋgyələr/ ADJ ❏ *The room contains a rectangular table.* [from Medieval Latin]
→ look at Picture Dictionaries: **shapes, volume**

rec|ti|lin|ear /rɛktɪlɪniər/ ADJ MATH A **rectilinear** shape has straight lines. Compare with **curvilinear**.

re|cur /rɪkɜr/ (recurs, recurring, recurred) V-I Something that **recurs** happens more than once. ❏ *I have a recurring dream about being late for an important meeting.* [from Latin]

re|cuse /rɪkyuz/ (recuses, recusing, recused) V-T SOCIAL STUDIES If a judge **recuses himself** or **herself from** a legal case, they state that they will not be involved in making decisions about the case, for example because they think they are biased. ❏ *The judge himself must decide which cases to recuse himself from.*

Word Link *cycl ≈ circle : bicycle, cycle, recycle*
---

re|cy|cle /risaɪkᵊl/ (recycles, recycling, recycled) V-T If you **recycle** things such as paper or bottles that have already been used, you put them through a process so that they can be used again. [from Late Latin]
→ look at Word Webs: **dump, paper**

red /rɛd/ (redder, reddest, reds)
1 ADJ Something that is **red** is the color of blood or of a tomato. ❏ *...a bunch of red roses.*
2 N-NONCOUNT Red is also a noun. ❏ *She was dressed in red.*
3 ADJ **Red** hair is between red and brown in color. [from Old English]
→ look at Picture Dictionaries: **color, hair**
→ look at Word Web: **rainbow**

red blood cell (red blood cells) **N-COUNT** SCIENCE Your **red blood cells** are the cells in your blood which carry oxygen around your body. Compare with **white blood cell**.

red|dish /rɛdɪʃ/ ADJ **Reddish** means slightly red in color. ❏ *He had reddish brown hair.*

red gi|ant (red giants) **N-COUNT** SCIENCE A **red giant** is a very large, relatively cool star

that is in the final stages of its life.

red her|ring /rɛd hɛrɪŋ/ (red herrings)
N-COUNT If you say that something is a **red herring**, you mean that it is not important and it takes your attention away from the main subject or problem you are considering.

re|duce /rɪdus/ (reduces, reducing, reduced)
V-T If you **reduce** something, you make it smaller. ❏ *Exercise reduces the risks of heart disease.* [from Latin]
→ look at Word Webs: **dump, mineral**

Word Partnership Use **reduce** with :

N	reduce **anxiety**, reduce **costs**, reduce **crime**, reduce **debt**, reduce **pain**, reduce **spending**, reduce **stress**, reduce **taxes**, reduce **violence**, reduce **waste**
ADV	**dramatically** reduce, **greatly** reduce, **significantly** reduce, **substantially** reduce
V	**help** reduce, **plan to** reduce, **try to** reduce
---

re|duc|tion /rɪdʌkʃᵊn/ (reductions)
N-COUNT/N-NONCOUNT When there is a **reduction in** something, it is made smaller. ❏ *We have noticed a sudden reduction in prices.* [from Latin]

re|dun|dant /rɪdʌndənt/ ADJ Something that is **redundant** is unnecessary, for example, because it has been replaced by something else. ❏ *Changes in technology mean that many skills are now redundant.* [from Latin]

reed /rid/ (reeds)
1 **N-COUNT** **Reeds** are tall plants that grow in large groups in shallow water or on wet ground.
2 **N-COUNT** MUSIC A **reed** is a small piece of cane or metal inserted into the mouthpiece of a woodwind instrument. The reed vibrates when you blow through it and makes a sound. [from Old English]

reef /rif/ (reefs) **N-COUNT** SCIENCE A **reef** is a long line of rocks or sand in the ocean. ❏ *The ship hit coral reefs off the north-eastern coast of Australia.* [from Middle Dutch]

reel /ril/ (reels, reeling, reeled)
1 **N-COUNT** A **reel** is an object that is a cylinder and around which you wrap something such as movie film, magnetic tape, or fishing line. ❏ *...a 30-meter reel of cable.*

r

2 **V-I** If someone **reels**, they move about in an unsteady way as if they are going to fall. ❏ *She was reeling with tiredness.*

3 **V-I** If you **are reeling** from a shock, you are feeling extremely surprised or upset because of it. ❏ *I'm still reeling from the shock of his death.*

4 **V-I** If you say that your brain or your mind **is reeling**, you mean that you are very confused because you have too many things to think about. [from Old English]

▶ **reel off** If you **reel off** information, you repeat it from memory quickly and easily. ❏ *She reeled off a list of things she was going to do.*

re|elect /riːɪlɛkt/ (**reelects, reelecting, reelected**) also re-elect **V-T** SOCIAL STUDIES When someone such as a politician or an official who has been elected **is reelected**, they win another election and are therefore able to continue in their position. ❏ *He was reelected five times.* ● **re|elec|tion** /riːɪlɛkʃⁿn/ **N-NONCOUNT** ❏ *He will run for reelection next year.* [from Latin]

re|fer /rɪfɜr/ (**refers, referring, referred**)
1 **V-I** If you **refer to** a particular subject or person, you mention them. ❏ *He referred to his trip to Canada.*
2 **V-I** LANGUAGE ARTS If a word **refers to** a particular thing, it describes it. ❏ *The word "man" refers to an adult male.*
3 **V-I** If you **refer to** a book or **to** the Internet for information, you look there in order to find something out. ❏ *He referred briefly to his notebook.* [from Latin]

ref|eree /rɛfəri/ (**referees, refereeing, refereed**)
1 **N-COUNT** SPORTS The referee is the person who controls a sports event such as a football game or a boxing match.
2 **V-I** SPORTS When someone **referees** a sports event, they act as referee. ❏ *Vautrot refereed in two soccer games.* [from Latin]

referee

→ look at Picture Dictionary: **basketball**

ref|er|ence /rɛfərəns, rɛfrəns/ (**references**)
1 **ADJ** Reference books are books that you look at when you need information or facts about a subject.
2 **N-COUNT** A reference is a letter that is written by someone who knows you, describing your character and your abilities. ❏ *My boss gave me a good reference.*
3 **N-COUNT/N-NONCOUNT** If you make **reference to** a particular subject or person, you mention them. ❏ *He made no reference to any agreement.*
4 **N-NONCOUNT** Reference is the process of looking at a book or other source of information in order to find something out. ❏ *Keep this book on your desk for easy reference.*
5 **PHRASE** You use **with reference to** or **in reference to** in order to say what something is about. ❏ *I am writing in reference to your advertisement for a personal assistant.* [from Latin]

ref|er|ence point (**reference points**)
N-COUNT SCIENCE A **reference point** is a fixed point, for example on the surface of the Earth, that is used in order to measure the motion of a moving object.

ref|er|en|dum /rɛfərɛndəm/ (**referendums** or **referenda** /rɛfərɛndə/) **N-COUNT** SOCIAL STUDIES A **referendum** is a vote in which all the people in a country are asked whether they agree or disagree with a particular policy. ❏ *The country held a referendum on independence.* [from Latin]

re|fine /rɪfaɪn/ (**refines, refining, refined**)
1 **V-T** SCIENCE When a substance **is refined**, it is made pure by having all other substances removed from it. ❏ *Oil is refined to remove impurities.* ● **re|fin|ing** **N-NONCOUNT** ❏ *...oil refining.*
2 **V-T** If something such as a process, a theory, or a machine **is refined**, it is improved by having small changes made to it. ❏ *Medical techniques are constantly being refined.* ● **re|fine|ment** (**refinements**) **N-COUNT/N-NONCOUNT** ❏ *Older cars lack the latest safety refinements.*
→ look at Word Webs: **industry, sugar**

Word Link	re ≈ back, again : re*flect*, re*fresh*, re*turn*

re|flect /rɪflɛkt/ (**reflects, reflecting, reflected**)
1 **V-T** If something **reflects** an opinion or a situation, it shows that it exists. ❏ *The report reflects the views of both students and teachers.*
2 **V-T/V-I** SCIENCE When light or heat

reflects off a surface, or when a surface **reflects** it, it is sent back from the surface. ❑ *The sun reflected off the snow-covered mountains.*

3 **V-T** When something **is reflected** in a mirror or in water, you can see its image there. ❑ *His face was reflected in the mirror.*

4 **V-I** When you **reflect on** something, you think deeply about it. ❑ *We need some time to reflect.* [from Latin]

→ look at Word Webs: **echo, telescope**

re|flec|tion /rɪflɛkʃ°n/ (**reflections**)

1 **N-COUNT** A **reflection** is an image that you can see in a mirror or in glass or water. ❑ *Meg stared at her reflection in the mirror.*

2 **N-COUNT** If something is a **reflection of** a person's opinion or

reflection

of a situation, it shows that that opinion or situation exists. ❑ *His drawings are a reflection of his own unhappiness.*

3 **N-NONCOUNT** Reflection is careful thought about a particular subject. ❑ *After days of reflection she decided to write to him.*

4 **N-COUNT** SCIENCE A **reflection** produces a mirror image of a geometric figure. For example, a **reflection** of the letter "d" would look like the letter "b."

5 **N-SING** SCIENCE The **law of reflection** is a principle in physics which states that, when a light wave strikes a flat surface, it is returned at the same angle at which it struck the surface. [from Latin]

→ look at Word Web: **echo**

re|flex|ive pro|noun /rɪflɛksɪv proʊnaʊn/ (**reflexive pronouns**) **N-COUNT** LANGUAGE ARTS A **reflexive pronoun** is a word such as "myself" that you use to talk about the subject of a sentence.

Word Link | *flex ≈ bending :* *flexible, flexor,*
| *reflexive verb*

re|flex|ive verb /rɪflɛksɪv vɜrb/ (**reflexive verbs**) **N-COUNT** LANGUAGE ARTS A **reflexive verb** is a verb whose subject and object always refer to the same person or thing. An example is "to enjoy yourself."

re|form /rɪfɔrm/ (**reforms, reforming, reformed**)

1 **N-COUNT/N-NONCOUNT** SOCIAL STUDIES **Reform** consists of changes and improvements to a law or a social system. ❑ *We will introduce a program of economic reform.*

2 **N-COUNT/N-NONCOUNT** A **reform** is a change that is intended to be an improvement. ❑ *The government promised tax reforms.*

3 **V-T** SOCIAL STUDIES Someone who **reforms** a law or a social system changes or improves it. ❑ *He has plans to reform the country's economy.*

4 **V-T/V-I** When someone **reforms**, or when something **reforms** them, they start behaving well. ❑ *After his time in prison, James promised to reform.* ❑ *His time away had reformed him.* [from Old French]

Word Partnership	Use **reform** with :
ADJ	**economic** reform, **political** reform **1**
N	**education** reform, **election** reform, **health care** reform, reform **movement**, **party** reform, **prison** reform, **tax** reform **1**

re|fract /rɪfrækt/ (**refracts, refracting, refracted**) **V-T/V-I** SCIENCE When a ray of light or a sound wave **refracts** or **is refracted**, the path it follows bends at a particular point, for example when it enters water or glass. ❑ *As we age, the lenses of the eyes thicken, and thus refract light differently.* ❑ *...surfaces that cause the light to reflect and refract.* ● **re|frac|tion** /rɪfrækʃ°n/ **N-NONCOUNT** ❑ *...the refraction of the light on the dancing waves.* [from Latin]

→ look at Word Web: **telescope**

re|fract|ing tele|scope (**refracting telescopes**) **N-COUNT** SCIENCE A **refracting telescope** is a telescope that uses lenses to focus light rays and produce a clear image.

re|fresh /rɪfrɛʃ/ (**refreshes, refreshing, refreshed**)

1 **V-T** If something **refreshes** you when you are hot, tired, or thirsty, it makes you feel better. ❑ *The water refreshed them.* ● **re|freshed** **ADJ** ❑ *He awoke feeling completely refreshed.*

2 **V-T** If someone **refreshes** your memory, they tell you something that you had forgotten. ❑ *Can you refresh my memory and tell me what I need to do?* [from Old French]

re|fresh|ing /rɪfrɛʃɪŋ/

1 **ADJ** If something is **refreshing**, it makes you feel less hot, tired, or thirsty. ❑ *They serve refreshing drinks at the poolside.*

2 **ADJ** You say that something is **refreshing** when it is unusual in a pleasant way. ❑ *It's refreshing to hear someone speaking so honestly.* [from Old French]

r

re|fresh|ment /rɪfrɛʃmənt/ (**refreshments**) **N-PLURAL** **Refreshments** are drinks and small amounts of food that are provided, for example, during a meeting or a trip. ❏ *Refreshments will be provided.* [from Old French]

re|frig|er|ate /rɪfrɪdʒəreɪt/ (**refrigerates, refrigerating, refrigerated**) **V-T** If you **refrigerate** food, you make it cold by putting it in a refrigerator. ❏ *Refrigerate the bread dough overnight.* [from Latin] → look at Word Web: **dairy**

re|frig|era|tor /rɪfrɪdʒəreɪtər/ (**refrigerators**) **N-COUNT** A **refrigerator** is a large electric container that is used for keeping food cool. [from Latin]

ref|uge /rɛfyudʒ/ (**refuges**) **1** **N-NONCOUNT** If you take **refuge** somewhere, you go there to try to protect yourself from harm. ❏ *They took refuge in a shelter.* **2** **N-COUNT** A **refuge** is a place where you go for safety and protection. ❏ *He works in a refuge for homeless people.* [from Old French]

refu|gee /rɛfyudʒi/ (**refugees**) **N-COUNT** SOCIAL STUDIES **Refugees** are people who have been forced to leave their homes or their country, because it is too dangerous for them there. ❏ *She grew up in a refugee camp in Pakistan.* [from Old French]

re|fund (**refunds, refunding, refunded**)

> **PRONUNCIATION HELP**
> Pronounce the noun /rifʌnd/. Pronounce the verb /rɪfʌnd/.

1 **N-COUNT** BUSINESS A **refund** is money that is returned to you because you have paid too much, or because you have returned goods to a store. ❏ *He took the boots back to the store and asked for a refund.* **2** **V-T** BUSINESS If someone **refunds** your money, they return what you have paid them. ❏ *We will refund your delivery costs if the items arrive later than 12 noon.* [from Latin]

> **Thesaurus** refund Also look up :
> N   payment, reimbursement **1**
> V   give back, pay back, reimburse **2**

re|fur|bish /rifɜrbɪʃ/ (**refurbishes, refurbishing, refurbished**) **V-T** To **refurbish** a building or a room means to clean it and decorate it and make it more attractive or better equipped. ❏ *We refurbished the offices.*

● **re|fur|bish|ment** (**refurbishments**) **N-COUNT/N-NONCOUNT** ❏ *The restaurant is closed for refurbishment.*

re|fus|al /rɪfyuzəl/ (**refusals**) **N-COUNT/N-NONCOUNT** A **refusal to** do something is when someone says that they will not do it. ❏ *The workers have repeated their refusal to take part in the program.* [from Old French]

re|fuse (**refuses, refusing, refused**)

> **PRONUNCIATION HELP**
> Pronounce the verb /rɪfyuz/. The noun is pronounced /rɛfyus/ and is hyphenated ref|use.

1 **V-I** If you **refuse to** do something, you say strongly that you will not do it. ❏ *He refused to comment.* **2** **V-T** If someone **refuses** you something, they say that they will not give it to you. ❏ *The United States has refused him a visa.* **3** **V-T** If you **refuse** something that is offered to you, you do not accept it. ❏ *The patient has the right to refuse treatment.* **4** **N-NONCOUNT** **Refuse** consists of the trash and all the things that are not wanted and that are regularly thrown away. ❏ *...a weekly collection of refuse.* [from Old French] → look at Word Web: **dump**

> **Thesaurus** refuse Also look up :
> V   decline, reject, turn down; (ant.) accept **1** **3**
> N   garbage, rubbish, trash **4**

> **Word Partnership** Use refuse with :
> V   refuse **to answer**, refuse **to cooperate**, refuse **to go**, refuse **to participate**, refuse **to pay** **1**
>   refuse **to allow**, refuse **to give** **1** **2**
>   refuse **to accept** **1** **3**

re|gain /rɪgeɪn/ (**regains, regaining, regained**) **V-T** If you **regain** something that you have lost, you get it back again. ❏ *Troops have regained control of the city.* [from Old French]

re|gard /rɪgɑrd/ (**regards, regarding, regarded**) **1** **V-T** If you **regard** someone or something **as** being a particular thing, you believe that they are that thing. ❏ *He was regarded as the most successful president of modern times.* **2** **V-T** If you **regard** something or someone **with** a feeling, you have that feeling about

R

them. ❑ *He regarded her with suspicion.*

3 **N-NONCOUNT** If you have **regard for** someone or something, you respect them. ❑ *I have a very high regard for him and his achievements.*

4 **N-PLURAL** **Regards** are greetings. ❑ *Give my regards to your family.*

5 **PHRASE** You can use **in regard to** to say which subject is being talked or written about. ❑ *...his opinions in regard to the law.* [from Old French]

re|gard|ing /rɪgɑrdɪŋ/ **PREP** You use **regarding** to say what subject is being talked or written about. ❑ *He refused to give any information regarding the man's financial situation.* [from Old French]

re|gard|less /rɪgɑrdlɪs/
1 **PHRASE** If something happens **regardless of** something else, the first thing is not affected or influenced at all by the second thing. ❑ *The organization helps anyone regardless of their age.*
2 **ADV** If you say that someone did something **regardless**, you mean that they did it, even though there were problems. ❑ *Her knee was painful but she continued walking regardless.* [from Old French]

reg|gae /rɛgeɪ/ **N-NONCOUNT** MUSIC **Reggae** is a type of West Indian popular music with a very strong beat. [from West Indian]

regi|ment /rɛdʒɪmənt/ (**regiments**) **N-COUNT** A **regiment** is a part of an army. [from Old French]

re|gion /ridʒⁿn/ (**regions**) **N-COUNT** GEOGRAPHY A **region** is an area of a country or of the world. ❑ *Do you have a map of the coastal region of South Carolina?* ● **re|gion|al** **ADJ** ❑ *...Hawaiian regional cooking.* [from Latin]

reg|is|ter /rɛdʒɪstər/ (**registers, registering, registered**)
1 **N-COUNT** A **register** is an official list of people or things. ❑ *We'll check the register of births, deaths, and marriages.*
2 **V-T/V-I** If you **register**, or **register** to do something, you put your name on an official list, in order to be able to do that thing. ❑ *Thousands of people registered to vote.* ❑ *Have your children been registered at the school?*
3 **V-T** If you **register** something, you have it recorded on an official list. ❑ *The boy's mother never registered his birth.*
4 **V-T/V-I** When something **registers on** a

scale or a measuring instrument, it shows a particular value. You can also say that something **registers** a certain amount **on** a scale or measuring instrument. ❑ *The earthquake registered 5.7 on the Richter scale.* ❑ *It will only register in very sophisticated equipment.* [from Medieval Latin]

reg|is|tra|tion /rɛdʒɪstreɪʃⁿn/
1 **N-NONCOUNT** **Registration** is the act of putting your name on an official list, in order to be able to do something. ❑ *The website is free, but it asks for registration from users.*
2 **N-NONCOUNT** The **registration** of something is the recording of it on an official list. ❑ *...voter registration.* [from Medieval Latin]

re|gret /rɪgrɛt/ (**regrets, regretting, regretted**)
1 **V-T** If you **regret** something that you did, you feel sorry that you did it. ❑ *I regret my decision to leave my job.* ❑ *I regret breaking up with my boyfriend.*
2 **N-COUNT/N-NONCOUNT** **Regret** is a feeling of sadness or disappointment, caused by something that you have done or not done. ❑ *He had no regrets about leaving.*
3 **V-T** You use **regret** in expressions such as **I regret to say** or **I regret to inform you** to show that you are sorry about something. [from Old French]

Word Partnership	Use **regret** with :
N	regret **a decision**, regret **a loss** **1**
V	**come to** regret **1**
	express regret **2**

regu|lar /rɛgyələr/
1 **ADJ** **Regular** events have equal amounts of time between them, so that they happen, for example, at the same time each day or each week. ❑ *Get regular exercise.*
2 **ADJ** **Regular** events happen often. ❑ *We meet on a regular basis.* ● **regu|lar|ly** **ADV** ❑ *He writes regularly for the magazine.*
3 **ADJ** If you are a **regular** customer at a store or a **regular** visitor to a place, you go there often. ❑ *She was a regular visitor to the museum.*
4 **ADJ** **Regular** means normal or ordinary. ❑ *Fred is just a regular guy.*
5 **ADJ** If something has a **regular** shape, both halves are the same and it has straight or smooth edges. ❑ *He's a man of average height with regular features.*

r

6 **ADJ** LANGUAGE ARTS A **regular** noun or verb follows the usual rules of grammar. For example, "work" is a regular verb, because the past is formed with "-ed." Compare with **irregular**. ❑ *The past tense of English regular verbs ends in -ed.* [from Old French]

Word Partnership	Use regular with :
N	regular **basis**, regular **checkups**, regular **exercise**, regular **meetings**, regular **schedule**, regular **visits** **1** **2** regular **customer**, regular **visitor** **3** regular **coffee**, regular **guy**, regular **hours**, regular **season** **4** regular **verbs** **6**

regu|late /rɛɡyəleɪt/ (regulates, regulating, regulated) v-T SOCIAL STUDIES To **regulate** an activity means to control it with rules. ❑ *The government introduced new laws to regulate the food industry.* [from Late Latin]

regu|la|tion /rɛɡyəleɪʃ°n/ (regulations) N-COUNT **Regulations** are rules for controlling the way something is done or the way people behave. ❑ *Here are the new safety regulations.* [from Late Latin] → look at Word Web: **factory**

re|ha|bili|tate /rɪhæbɪlɪteɪt/ (rehabilitates, rehabilitating, rehabilitated) v-T SOCIAL STUDIES To **rehabilitate** someone who has been ill or in prison means to help them to live a normal life again. ● re|ha|bili|ta|tion /rɪhəbɪlɪteɪʃ°n/ N-NONCOUNT ❑ *...the rehabilitation of prisoners.* [from Medieval Latin]

re|hears|al /rɪhɜrs°l/ (rehearsals) N-COUNT/ N-NONCOUNT ARTS A **rehearsal** of a performance is a practice of it. ❑ *Tomorrow we start rehearsals for the concert.* [from Old French] → look at Word Web: **theater**

re|hearse /rɪhɜrs/ (rehearses, rehearsing, rehearsed) v-T/v-I ARTS When people **rehearse** a play, a dance, or a piece of music, they practice it. ❑ *The actors are rehearsing a play.* ❑ *Thousands of people are rehearsing for the ceremony.* [from Old French]

reign /reɪn/ (reigns, reigning, reigned) **1** V-I SOCIAL STUDIES When a king or a queen **reigns**, he or she rules a country. ❑ *Henry II reigned in England from 1154 to 1189.* **2** N-COUNT SOCIAL STUDIES **Reign** is also a noun. ❑ *...Queen Victoria's reign.* [from Old French]

rein /reɪn/ (reins) N-PLURAL **Reins** are the long thin pieces of leather that fit around a horse's neck, and that are used for controlling the horse. ❑ *She held the reins while the horse pulled.* [from Old French] → look at Picture Dictionary: **horse**

rein|deer /reɪndɪər/ (reindeer) N-COUNT A **reindeer** is a big animal with large horns that lives in northern areas of Europe, Asia, and America. [from Old Norse]

re|ject (rejects, rejecting, rejected)

PRONUNCIATION HELP
Pronounce the verb /rɪdʒɛkt/. Pronounce the noun /rɪdʒɛkt/.

1 V-T If you **reject** something, you do not accept it or agree to it. ❑ *The president rejected the offer.*
2 V-T If someone **is rejected** for a job or a course of study, it is not offered to them. ❑ *He was rejected by several universities.* ● re|jec|tion (rejections) N-COUNT ❑ *Be prepared for lots of rejections before you get a job.*
3 V-T If someone **rejects** you, they are unfriendly and do not show affection for you. ❑ *...people who were rejected by their parents.* ● re|jec|tion (rejections) N-COUNT/ N-NONCOUNT ❑ *...feelings of rejection and hurt.*
4 N-COUNT A **reject** is a product that has something wrong with it. ❑ *The shirt is a reject—all the buttons are missing.* [from Latin]

Word Partnership	Use reject with :
N	reject **an application**, reject **an idea**, reject **an offer**, reject **a plan**, reject **a proposal**, voters reject **1**
V	vote to reject **1**

re|joice /rɪdʒɔɪs/ (rejoices, rejoicing, rejoiced) v-I If you **rejoice**, you are very happy about something and you show this in the way that you behave. ❑ *We rejoiced in the victory.* ● re|joic|ing N-NONCOUNT ❑ *There was much rejoicing at the news.* [from Old French]

re|late /rɪleɪt/ (relates, relating, related) **1** V-I If something **relates to** a particular subject, it is about that subject. ❑ *We are collecting all the information relating to the crime.* **2** V-T/v-I The way that two things **relate**, or the way that one thing **relates to** another, is the connection that exists between them. ❑ *There is new thinking about how the two sciences relate.* **3** V-T/v-I If you can **relate to** someone, you can understand how they feel or behave. ❑ *He is unable to relate to other people.* [from Latin]

re|lat|ed /rɪleɪtɪd/

1 **ADJ** If two things are **related**, they are connected in some way. ❑ *Crime and poverty are closely related.*

2 **ADJ** People who are **related** belong to the same family. ❑ *The boys have the same last name but they are not related.* [from Latin]

re|la|tion /rɪleɪʃ°n/ (**relations**)

1 **N-PLURAL** **Relations** between people, groups, or countries are the way in which they behave toward each other. ❑ *The country has good relations with Israel.*

2 **N-COUNT** The **relation of** one thing **to** another is the connection between them. ❑ *He has spent years studying the relation between exercise and health.*

3 **N-COUNT** Your **relations** are the members of your family. ❑ *We make frequent visits to friends and relations.*

4 **PHRASE** You can talk about something **in relation to** something else when you want to compare the two things. ❑ *The cost was small in relation to his salary.* [from Latin]

re|la|tion|ship /rɪleɪʃ°nʃɪp/ (**relationships**)

1 **N-COUNT** The **relationship** between two people or groups is the way in which they feel and behave toward each other. ❑ *The ministers want to maintain the friendly relationship between the two countries.*

2 **N-COUNT** A **relationship** is a close friendship between two people, especially involving romantic or sexual feelings. ❑ *She could not accept that their relationship was over.*

3 **N-COUNT** The **relationship** between two things is the way in which they are connected. ❑ *Is there a relationship between diet and cancer?*

4 **N-COUNT** **SCIENCE** The **relationship** between an organism and its environment is the way that the organism and its environment interact and the effect they have on each other. [from Latin]

rela|tive /rɛlətɪv/ (**relatives**)

1 **N-COUNT** Your **relatives** are the members of your family. ❑ *Ask a relative to look after the children.*

2 **ADJ** You use **relative** when you are comparing two things. ❑ *...the relative advantages of New York and Washington as places to live.* ● **rela|tive|ly** **ADV** ❑ *The amount*

of money that you need is relatively small. [from Late Latin]

rela|tive da|ting **N-NONCOUNT** **SCIENCE** **Relative dating** is a technique used by archeologists to determine whether an object such as a fossil is older or younger than other objects.

rela|tive hu|mid|ity (**relative humidities**) **N-COUNT/N-NONCOUNT** **SCIENCE** **Relative humidity** is a measure of the amount of water vapor contained in the air, compared with the maximum amount of water vapor that the air is able to hold.

re|lax /rɪlæks/ (**relaxes, relaxing, relaxed**)

1 **V-T/V-I** If you **relax**, or if something **relaxes** you, you feel more calm and less worried. ❑ *You should relax and stop worrying.* ● **re|laxa|tion** /rɪlækseɪʃ°n/ **N-NONCOUNT** ❑ *Try learning some relaxation techniques.* ● **re|laxed** **ADJ** ❑ *The atmosphere at lunch was relaxed.* ● **re|lax|ing** **ADJ** ❑ *I find cooking very relaxing.*

2 **V-T/V-I** When you **relax** a part of your body, or when it **relaxes**, it becomes less stiff or tight. ❑ *Have a massage to relax your muscles.* [from Latin]

→ look at Word Web: **muscle**

re|lay (**relaying, relayed**)

PRONUNCIATION HELP
Pronounce the noun /rɪleɪ/. Pronounce the verb /rɪleɪ/.

1 **N-COUNT** **SPORTS** A **relay** or a **relay race** is a race between two or more teams in which each member of the team runs or swims one section of the race. ❑ *Britain's chances of winning the relay are good.*

2 **V-T** **TECHNOLOGY** To **relay** television or radio signals means to send them or broadcast them. ❑ *The satellite relays television programs.* [from Old French]

re|lease /rɪliːs/ (**releases, releasing, released**)
1 **v-t** If a person or an animal **is released**, they are allowed to go free. ❑ *He was released from prison the next day.*
2 **v-t** If you **release** someone or something, you stop holding them. [FORMAL] ❑ *He released her hand.*
3 **v-t** If someone in authority **releases** a document or information, they make it available. ❑ *Police are not releasing any more details yet.*
4 **v-t** When an entertainer or a company **releases** a new CD, DVD, or movie, it becomes available so that people can buy it or see it. ❑ *He is releasing his sixth album.*
5 **N-COUNT** A new **release** is a new CD, DVD, or movie that has just become available for people to buy or see. [from Old French]

rel|egate /rɛlɪgeɪt/ (**relegates, relegating, relegated**) **v-t** If you **relegate** someone or something **to** a less important position, you give them this position. ❑ *The coach relegated him to a place on the second team.* [from Latin]

re|lent|less /rɪlɛntlɪs/ **ADJ** Something bad that is **relentless** never stops or never becomes less intense. ❑ *The pressure was relentless.* ● **re|lent|less|ly** **ADV** ❑ *It rained relentlessly.* [from Latin]

rel|evant /rɛləvᵊnt/ **ADJ** Something that is **relevant to** a situation or person is important in that situation or to that person. ❑ *They are trying to make politics more relevant to younger people.* [from Medieval Latin]

re|li|able /rɪlaɪəbᵊl/
1 **ADJ** People or things that are **reliable** can be trusted to work well. ❑ *She was efficient and reliable.*
2 **ADJ** Information that is **reliable** is probably correct. ❑ *There is no reliable information about how many people have died.* ● **re|li|ably** **ADV** ❑ *We are reliably informed that he is here.* ● **re|li|a|bil|i|ty** **N-NONCOUNT** ❑ *We have serious doubts about the reliability of this information.* [from Old French]

	Word Partnership Use **reliable** with :
N	reliable **service** **1**
	reliable **data**, reliable **information**, reliable **source** **2**
ADV	**highly** reliable, **less/more/most** reliable, **usually** reliable, **very** reliable **1** **2**

re|lief /rɪliːf/ (**reliefs**)
1 **N-NONCOUNT** If you feel **relief**, you feel happy because something unpleasant has not happened or is no longer happening. ❑ *I breathed a sigh of relief.*
2 **N-NONCOUNT** **Relief from** pain or worry is when it stops. ❑ *These drugs will give relief from pain.*
3 **N-NONCOUNT** SOCIAL STUDIES **Relief** is money, food, or clothing that is provided for people who suddenly need it. ❑ *Relief agencies are hoping to provide food and shelter in the flooded area.*
4 **N-COUNT** ARTS A **relief** is a piece of art that consists of a raised surface on a flat background.
5 **N-NONCOUNT** GEOGRAPHY The **relief** on a map is the difference in height between the highest area on the map and the lowest area. [from Old French]

	Word Partnership Use **relief** with :
V	**express** relief **1**
	feel relief, **seek** relief **1** **2**
	bring relief, **get** relief, **provide** relief **1**–**3**
	supply relief **2** **3**
N	**sense of** relief, **sigh of** relief **1**
	pain relief, relief **from symptoms**, relief **from** **2**
	disaster relief, **emergency** relief **3**

re|lieve /rɪliːv/ (**relieves, relieving, relieved**)
1 **v-t** If something **relieves** an unpleasant feeling or situation, it makes it less unpleasant or causes it to disappear completely. ❑ *Drugs can relieve the pain.*
2 **v-t** If someone or something **relieves** you **of** an unpleasant feeling or difficult task, they take it from you. ❑ *Receiving the check relieved me of a lot of worry.*
3 **v-t** If you **relieve** someone, you take their place and continue to do the job or duty that they have been doing. ❑ *At seven o'clock another nurse arrived to relieve her.* [from Old French]

re|lieved /rɪliːvd/ **ADJ** If you are **relieved**, you feel happy because something unpleasant has not happened or is no longer happening. ❑ *We are relieved to be back home.* [from Old French]

re|li|gion /rɪlɪdʒᵊn/ (**religions**)
1 **N-NONCOUNT** **Religion** is belief in a god or gods and the activities that are connected with this belief. ❑ *There's little interest in*

organized religion.

2 **N-COUNT** A **religion** is a particular system of belief in a god or gods and the activities that are connected with this system. ❑ *...the Christian religion.* [from Old French]

re|li|gious /rɪlɪdʒəs/

1 **ADJ** **Religious** means connected with religion. ❑ *Religious groups are able to meet quite freely.*

2 **ADJ** Someone who is **religious** has a strong belief in a god or gods. [from Old French]

re|li|gious free|dom **N-NONCOUNT**
SOCIAL STUDIES People who have **religious freedom** may choose to follow any religion that they wish. ❑ *We believe that religious freedom should be treated as a human right.*

re|lin|quish /rɪlɪŋkwɪʃ/ (**relinquishes, relinquishing, relinquished**) **V-T** If you **relinquish** something such as power or control, you give it up. [from French] [FORMAL]

re|luc|tant /rɪlʌktənt/ **ADJ** If you are **reluctant to** do something, you are unwilling to do it. ❑ *Mr. Spero was reluctant to ask for help.* ● **re|luc|tant|ly** **ADV** ❑ *We have reluctantly agreed to let him go.* ● **re|luc|tance** **N-NONCOUNT** ❑ *Frank boarded his train with great reluctance.* [from Latin]

rely /rɪlaɪ/ (**relies, relying, relied**)

1 **V-I** If you **rely on** someone or something, you need them in order to live or work properly. ❑ *They relied heavily on our advice.*

2 **V-I** If you can **rely on** someone to work well or to behave as you want them to, you can trust them to do this. ❑ *I know I can rely on you to deal with the problem.* [from Old French]

re|main /rɪmeɪn/ (**remains, remaining, remained**)

1 **V-LINK** To **remain** in a particular state or condition means to stay in that state or condition. ❑ *The men remained silent.* ❑ *The government remained in control.*

2 **V-I** If you **remain** in a place, you stay there and do not move away. ❑ *Police asked people to remain in their homes.*

3 **V-I** You can say that something **remains** when it still exists. ❑ *The wider problem remains.*

4 **N-PLURAL** The **remains of** something are the parts of it that are left after most of it has been taken away or destroyed. ❑ *They*

were cleaning up the remains of their picnic.

5 **N-PLURAL** The **remains** of a person or animal are the parts of their body that are left after they have been dead for a long time. ❑ *...human remains.* [from Old French]

re|main|der /rɪmeɪndər/ **N-SING** The **remainder of** something is the part that is still there after the first part has gone. ❑ *He drank the remainder of his coffee.* [from Old French]

re|main|ing /rɪmeɪnɪŋ/ **ADJ** The **remaining** things or people out of a group are the things or people that still exist, or that are still present. ❑ *He spoke to his few remaining supporters.* [from Old French]

re|mark /rɪmɑrk/ (**remarks, remarking, remarked**)

1 **V-T/V-I** If you **remark** that something is true, you say that it is true. ❑ *He remarked that it was very cold.* ❑ *She remarked on how tired I looked.*

2 **N-COUNT** If you make a **remark** about something, you say something about it. ❑ *She made rude remarks about his weight.* [from French]

Word Partnership	Use **remark** with :
ADJ	**casual** remark, **offhand** remark **2**
V	**hear** a remark, **make** a remark **2**

re|mark|able /rɪmɑrkəbəl/ **ADJ** Someone or something that is **remarkable** is very unusual or surprising in a good way. ❑ *He was a remarkable man.* ● **re|mark|ably** /rɪmɑrkəbli/ **ADV** ❑ *The book was remarkably successful.* [from Old French]

rem|edy /rɛmədi/ (**remedies**)

1 **N-COUNT** A **remedy** is a successful way of dealing with a problem. ❑ *The government's remedy involved tax increases.*

2 **N-COUNT** A **remedy** is something that is intended to cure you when you are ill. ❑ *...natural remedies for infections.* [from Latin]

re|mem|ber /rɪmɛmbər/ (**remembers, remembering, remembered**)

1 **V-T/V-I** If you **remember** people or events from the past, you still have an idea of them in your mind. ❑ *I remember the first time I met him.* ❑ *I remember that we went to his wedding.* ❑ *The weather was terrible; do you remember?*

2 **V-T** If you **remember** that something is true, you become aware of it again after a time when you did not think about it. ❑ *She*

r

remembered that she was going to the club that evening.

3 **V-T** If you **remember to** do something, you do it when you intend to. ❑ *Please remember to mail the letter.* [from Old French]

Thesaurus	remember Also look up :
V	look back, recall, think back; (ant.) forget **1** **3**

Word Partnership	Use remember with :
ADV	remember **clearly**, remember **correctly**, **still** remember, remember **vividly** **1** remember **1**–**3**
ADJ	**easy to** remember, **important to** remember **1** **3**
CONJ	remember **what**, remember **when**, remember **where**, remember **why** **1**–**3**

re|mind /rɪmaɪnd/ (**reminds, reminding, reminded**)

1 **V-T** If someone **reminds** you **of** a fact or an event that you already know about, they say something that makes you think about it. ❑ *She reminded Tim of the last time they met.*

2 **V-T** If someone **reminds** you **to** do a particular thing, they say something that makes you remember to do it. ❑ *Can you remind me to buy some milk?*

3 **V-T** If someone or something **reminds** you **of** another person or thing, they are similar to them and they make you think about them. ❑ *She reminds me of your sister.* [from Old English]

Word Partnership	Use remind with :
PREP	remind *someone* of *something* **1** remind *you* of *someone/something* **3**

re|mind|er /rɪmaɪndər/ (**reminders**) **N-COUNT** A **reminder of** something makes you think about it again. [WRITTEN] ❑ *The scar on her hand was a constant reminder of the accident.* [from Old English]

remi|nisce /rɛmɪnɪs/ (**reminisces, reminiscing, reminisced**) **V-I** If you **reminisce** about something from your past, you write or talk about it, often with pleasure. [FORMAL] ❑ *I don't like reminiscing because it makes me feel old.* [from Latin]

remi|nis|cent /rɛmɪnɪsənt/ **ADJ** If you say that one thing is **reminiscent of** another, you mean that it reminds you of it. [FORMAL] ❑ *His voice was reminiscent of her son's.* [from Latin]

re|morse /rɪmɔrs/ **N-NONCOUNT** Remorse is a strong feeling of sadness and regret about something wrong that you have done. ❑ *He was filled with remorse.* [from Medieval Latin]

re|mote /rɪmoʊt/ (**remoter, remotest**) **ADJ** **Remote** areas are far away from cities and places where most people live. ❑ *They came from distant villages in remote areas.* [from Latin]

re|mote con|trol (**remote controls**) **N-COUNT** TECHNOLOGY The **remote control** for a television or other piece of equipment is the piece of equipment that you use to control the machine from a distance. ❑ *Rachel picked up the remote control and turned on the television.*

re|mote|ly /rɪmoʊtli/ **ADV** You use **remotely** to emphasize the negative meaning of a sentence. ❑ *He wasn't remotely interested in her.* [from Latin]

re|mote sens|ing **N-NONCOUNT** SCIENCE **Remote sensing** is the gathering of information about something by observing it from space or from the air.

re|mov|al /rɪmuvᵊl/ **N-NONCOUNT** The **removal** of something is the act of removing it. ❑ *She had surgery for the removal of a tumor.* [from Old French]

Word Link	mov ≈ moving : movement, movie, remove

re|move /rɪmuv/ (**removes, removing, removed**)

1 **V-T** If you **remove** something from a place, you take it away. [WRITTEN] ❑ *Remove the cake from the oven when it is cooked.*

2 **V-T** If you **remove** clothing, you take it off. [WRITTEN] ❑ *He removed his jacket.* [from Old French]

Thesaurus	remove Also look up :
V	take away, take out **1** take off, undress **2**

re|nais|sance /rɛnɪsɑns/ **N-SING** If something experiences a **renaissance**, it becomes popular or successful again after a time when people were not interested in it. ❑ *The jazz trumpet is experiencing a renaissance.* [from French]

re|new /rɪnu/ (**renews, renewing, renewed**)

1 **V-T** When you **renew** something, you get a new one to replace the old one, or you arrange for the old one to continue.

❏ *Larry's landlord refused to renew his lease.*

2 **v-T** If you **renew** an activity, you begin it again. ❏ *He renewed his attack on government policy.*

3 **v-T** If you **renew** a relationship **with** someone, you start it again after it has ended. ❏ *When the men met again after the war they renewed their friendship.* [from Old English]

Thesaurus	renew	Also look up :
v	continue, resume, revive **1**–**3**	

re|new|able /rɪnu̯əbəl/

1 **ADJ** **Renewable** resources are natural ones such as wind, water, and sunlight that are always available. ❏ *...renewable energy sources.*

2 **N-PLURAL** You can refer to renewable resources as **renewables**. [from Old English]

Word Link	nov ≈ new : in**nov**ation, **nov**el, re**nov**ate

reno|vate /rɛnəveɪt/ (**renovates, renovating, renovated**) **v-T** If someone **renovates** an old building, they repair and improve it and get it back into good condition. ❏ *They spent a lot of money renovating the house.* [from Latin]

re|nown /rɪnaʊn/ **N-NONCOUNT** A person **of renown** is well-known, usually because they do or have done something good. ❏ *She used to be a singer of some renown.* [from Old French]

re|nowned /rɪnaʊnd/ **ADJ** A person or place that is **renowned for** something, usually something good, is well known because of it. ❏ *The area is renowned for its beautiful churches.* [from Old French]

rent /rɛnt/ (**rents, renting, rented**)

1 **v-T** If you **rent** something, you pay its owner in order to be able to use it yourself. ❏ *She rents a house with three other women.*

2 **v-T** If you **rent** something **to** someone, you let them have it and use it in exchange for money. ❏ *She rented rooms to university students.*

3 **N-COUNT/N-NONCOUNT** **Rent** is the amount of money that you pay to use something that belongs to someone else. ❏ *She worked hard to pay the rent on the apartment.* [from Old French]

▶ **rent out** If you **rent** something **out**, you let someone have it and use it in exchange for money. ❏ *Last summer Brian rented out his house and went camping.*

rent|al /rɛntəl/ (**rentals**)

1 **N-NONCOUNT** The **rental** of something such as a car or a piece of equipment is the activity or process of renting it. ❏ *We can arrange car rental from the airport.*

2 **N-COUNT** The **rental** is the amount of money that you pay when you rent something such as a car, a property, or a piece of equipment. ❏ *We pay a yearly rental of $393,000.*

3 **ADJ** You use **rental** to describe things that are connected with the renting of goods, properties, and services. ❏ *...a rental car.* [from Old French]

re|or|gan|ize /riɔrgənaɪz/ (**reorganizes, reorganizing, reorganized**) **v-T/v-I** To **reorganize** something means to change the way in which it is organized, arranged, or done. ❏ *She wanted to reorganize her life.*

● **re|or|gani|za|tion** /riɔrgənɪzeɪʃən/ (**reorganizations**) **N-COUNT/N-NONCOUNT** ❏ *...the reorganization of the legal system.* [from Medieval Latin]

re|pair /rɪpɛər/ (**repairs, repairing, repaired**)

1 **v-T** If you **repair** something that has been damaged or is not working properly, you fix it. ❏ *Goldman has repaired the roof.*

2 **N-COUNT/N-NONCOUNT** A **repair** is something that you do to fix something that has been damaged or that is not working properly. ❏ *Repairs were made to the roof.* [from Old French]

Word Partnership	Use repair with :
N	repair **a chimney**, repair **damage**, repair **equipment**, repair **a roof** **1**
	auto repair, **car** repair, **home** repair, repair **parts**, **road** repair, repair **service**, repair **shop** **2**

re|pair|man /rɪpɛərmæn/ (**repairmen**) **N-COUNT** A **repairman** is a man whose job is to fix broken machines.

re|pay /rɪpeɪ/ (**repays, repaying, repaid**)

1 **v-T** If you **repay** a debt, you pay back the money that you borrowed from someone.

2 **v-T** If you **repay** a favor that someone did for you, you do something for them. ❏ *It was very kind. I don't know how I can ever repay you.* [from Old French]

re|pay|ment /rɪpeɪmənt/ (**repayments**)

1 **N-NONCOUNT** The **repayment of** money is the act or process of paying it back to the person you borrowed it from. ❏ *The bank will*

r

expect the repayment of the $114 million loan.

2 **N-COUNT** A **repayment** is money that you pay back to the person you borrowed it from. ❑ He took a loan with small, frequent repayments. [from Old French]

re|peat /rɪpit/ (**repeats, repeating, repeated**)

1 **V-T** If you **repeat** something, you say it or write it again. ❑ She repeated her request for more money. ❑ He repeated that he was innocent.

2 **V-T** If you **repeat** something that someone else has said or written, you say or write the same thing. ❑ She had a habit of repeating everything I said to her.

3 **V-T** If you **repeat** an action, you do it again. ❑ Repeat this exercise five times a week.

4 **N-COUNT** A **repeat** is a television or radio program that has been shown before. [from Old French]

re|peat|ed /rɪpitɪd/ **ADJ** Repeated actions are ones that happen many times. ❑ He did not return the money, despite repeated reminders. ● **re|peat|ed|ly** **ADV** ❑ I asked him repeatedly to help me. [from Old French]

re|pel /rɪpɛl/ (**repels, repelling, repelled**)

1 **V-T** SOCIAL STUDIES When an army **repels** an attack, they successfully fight and drive back soldiers from another army who have attacked them. [FORMAL]

2 **V-T** If something **repels** you, you find it horrible and disgusting. ❑ Politics both fascinated and repelled him. ● **re|pelled** **ADJ** ❑ She was very beautiful but in some way I felt repelled. [from Latin]

→ look at Word Web: **magnet**

rep|eti|tion /rɛpɪtɪʃ°n/ (**repetitions**)

1 **N-COUNT/N-NONCOUNT** If there is a **repetition of** an event, it happens again. ❑ The city government wants to prevent a repetition of last year's violence.

2 **N-COUNT/N-NONCOUNT** ARTS In dance, **repetition** means performing the same movement again or doing it several times. [from Latin]

re|peti|tive /rɪpɛtɪtɪv/ **ADJ** Something that is **repetitive** involves repeating an action many times. ❑ They are factory workers who do repetitive jobs. [from Latin]

re|place /rɪpleɪs/ (**replaces, replacing, replaced**)

1 **V-T** If one person or thing **replaces** another, they do the job of the other person

or thing. ❑ During the war, many women replaced male workers.

2 **V-T** If you **replace** something that is damaged or lost, you get a new one. ❑ The shower broke so we have to replace it.

3 **V-T** If you **replace** something, you put it back where it was before. ❑ Replace the caps on the bottles. [from Old French]

re|place|ment /rɪpleɪsmənt/ (**replacements**) **N-COUNT** You can call a person or thing that replaces another a **replacement**. ❑ It won't be easy to find a replacement for Grace. [from Old French]

re|play /rɪpleɪ/ (**replays**) **N-COUNT** A **replay** of an action on television is when it is broadcast again. ❑ We watched the replay of the game. [from Old English]

re|ply /rɪplaɪ/ (**replies, replying, replied**)

1 **V-T/V-I** When you **reply to** something that someone says or writes to you, you say or write an answer to them. ❑ "That's a nice dress," said Michael. "Thanks," she replied. ❑ He replied that this was impossible. ❑ He never replied to my letters.

2 **N-COUNT** A **reply** is something that you say or write when you answer someone. ❑ I called his name, but there was no reply. [from Old French]

Thesaurus	reply Also look up :
V	acknowledge, answer, respond, return **1**
N	acknowledgement, answer, response **2**

Word Partnership	Use reply with :
N	reply **card**, reply **envelope**, reply **form 2**
V	**make a** reply, **receive a** reply **2**

re|port /rɪpɔrt/ (**reports, reporting, reported**)

1 **V-T** If you **report** something that happened, you tell people about it. ❑ I reported the crime to the police. ❑ Officials reported that four people were killed.

2 **N-COUNT** A **report** is a newspaper article or a broadcast that gives information about something that happened. ❑ According to a newspaper report, they are getting married next month.

3 **N-COUNT** A **report** is a piece of work that a student writes on a particular subject. ❑ We had to do a book report on "Huckleberry Finn."

4 **N-COUNT** If you give someone a **report** on

R

something, you tell them what has been happening. ❑ *She gave us a progress report on the project.*

5 **V-T** If someone **reports** you **to** an official person or organization, they tell them about something wrong that you have done. ❑ *His boss reported him to the police.* [from Old French]

re|port card (report cards) **N-COUNT** A report card is an official document that shows how well or how badly a student worked in school. ❑ *I got all "A"s on my report card.*

re|port|ed|ly /rɪpɔrtɪdli/ **ADV** If you say that something is **reportedly** true, you mean that someone has said that it is true, but you have no direct evidence of it. [FORMAL] ❑ *More than two hundred people were reportedly killed.* [from Old French]

re|port|er /rɪpɔrtər/ (reporters) **N-COUNT** A **reporter** is someone who writes newspaper articles or broadcasts the news. ❑ *My dad is a TV reporter.* [from Old French]

rep|re|sent /rɛprɪzɛnt/ (represents, representing, represented)
1 **V-T** SOCIAL STUDIES If a lawyer or a politician **represents** a person or a group, they act or make decisions for them. ❑ *We vote for politicians to represent us.*
2 **V-T** If a sign **represents** something, it means that thing. ❑ *The red line on the map represents a wall.* [from Latin]

rep|re|sen|ta|tion /rɛprɪzɛnteɪʃ°n/ **N-NONCOUNT** SOCIAL STUDIES If you have **representation** on a committee, someone on the committee supports you. ❑ *These people have no representation in Congress.* [from Latin]

rep|re|senta|tive /rɛprɪzɛntətɪv/ (representatives) **N-COUNT** SOCIAL STUDIES A **representative** is a person who acts or makes decisions for another person or group. ❑ *Michael is our class representative.* [from Latin]

rep|re|senta|tive gov|ern|ment **N-NONCOUNT** SOCIAL STUDIES **Representative government** is a system in which the people of a country elect particular people to represent them in their government.

re|pro|duce /riprədus/ (reproduces, reproducing, reproduced)
1 **V-T** If you try to **reproduce** something, you copy it. ❑ *The effect was hard to reproduce.*
2 **V-I** SCIENCE When people, animals, or plants **reproduce**, they produce babies, eggs, or seeds. ● **re|pro|duc|tion** /riprədʌkʃ°n/ **N-NONCOUNT** ❑ *...human reproduction.* [from Latin]
→ look at Word Web: **reproduction**

re|pro|duc|tive /riprədʌktɪv/ **ADJ** SCIENCE **Reproductive** processes and organs are concerned with the reproduction of living things. ❑ *...the female reproductive system.* [from Latin]

rep|tile /rɛptaɪl, -tɪl/ (reptiles) **N-COUNT** **Reptiles** are a group of animals that lay eggs and have cold blood. Snakes are reptiles. [from Late Latin]
→ look at Word Web: **pet**

re|pub|lic /rɪpʌblɪk/ (republics) **N-COUNT** SOCIAL STUDIES A **republic** is a country that does not have a king or a queen and in which the people choose their government. ❑ *In 1918, Austria became a republic.* [from French]

r

Word Web   reproduction

Human **reproduction** requires a **sperm** from the **male** and an **egg** from the **female**. These two cells come together to begin the new life. This process is called **fertilization**. It is the beginning of the woman's **pregnancy**. From fertilization to eight weeks of development, we call the fertilized egg a **zygote**. From eight to twelve weeks, it is called an **embryo**. After three months of development, we call it a **fetus**. **Birth** usually takes place after nine months of pregnancy.

egg and sperm   zygote   embryo   fetus   mother, father, and baby

Re|pub|li|can /rɪpʌblɪkən/ (**Republicans**)

1 **ADJ** SOCIAL STUDIES **Republican** is used for talking about people who belong to or support the Republican Party (= one of the two main political parties in the U.S.). ❑ *Lower taxes made Republican voters happy.*

2 **N-COUNT** SOCIAL STUDIES A **Republican** is someone who belongs to or supports the Republican Party. ❑ *What made you decide to become a Republican?*

re|pul|sive /rɪpʌlsɪv/ **ADJ** If a person or a thing is **repulsive**, they are so unpleasant that people do not want to see them. ❑ *Some people found the movie repulsive.* [from Latin]

repu|ta|tion /rɛpyəteɪʃⁿn/ (**reputations**)

N-COUNT Your **reputation** is the opinion that people have about you. ❑ *This college has a good reputation.* ❑ *He has a reputation for honesty.* [from Latin]

Word Partnership	Use **reputation** with :
ADJ	**bad** reputation, **good** reputation
V	**acquire a** reputation, **build a** reputation, **damage** *someone's* reputation, **earn a** reputation, **establish a** reputation, **gain a** reputation, **have a** reputation, **ruin** *someone's* reputation

re|quest /rɪkwɛst/ (**requests, requesting, requested**)

1 **V-T** If you **request** something, you ask for it politely or formally. [FORMAL] ❑ *To request more information, please check this box.*

2 **N-COUNT** If you **make a request**, you politely or formally ask someone to do something. ❑ *They agreed to his request for more money.* [from Old French]

re|quire /rɪkwaɪər/ (**requires, requiring, required**)

1 **V-T** If you **require** something, you need it. [FORMAL] ❑ *If you require more information, please write to this address.*

2 **V-T** If a law or a rule **requires** you **to** do something, you have to do it. [FORMAL] ❑ *The rules require employers to provide safety training.* [from Old French]

re|quire|ment /rɪkwaɪərmənt/ (**requirements**) **N-COUNT** A **requirement** is something that you must have. ❑ *Our products meet all legal requirements.* [from Old French]

Word Partnership	Use **requirement** with :
ADJ	**legal** requirement, **minimum** requirement
V	**meet a** requirement

requi|site /rɛkwɪzɪt/ **ADJ** **Requisite** means necessary for a particular purpose. [FORMAL] ❑ *He lacked the requisite knowledge for the job.* [from Latin]

res|cue /rɛskyu/ (**rescues, rescuing, rescued**)

1 **V-T** If you **rescue** someone, you save them from a dangerous situation. ❑ *They rescued 20 people from the roof of the building.*

2 **N-COUNT/N-NONCOUNT** A **rescue** is an attempt to save someone from a dangerous situation. ❑ *He helped in the rescue of a bus driver from the river.* ❑ *...a big rescue operation.*

3 **PHRASE** If someone **comes to** your **rescue**, they help you when you are in danger. ❑ *A neighbor came to her rescue.* [from Old French]

Word Partnership	Use **rescue** with :
N	**firefighters** rescue, rescue **a hostage**, rescue **miners**, rescue **people, police** rescue, **volunteers** rescue, rescue **wildlife** **1**
	rescue **attempt**, rescue **crews**, rescue **effort**, rescue **mission**, rescue **operation**, rescue **teams**, rescue **workers** **2**

re|search /rɪsɜrtʃ, rɪsɜrtʃ/ (**researches, researching, researched**)

1 **N-NONCOUNT** **Research** involves studying something and trying to discover facts about it. ❑ *My brother does scientific research.*

2 **V-T** If you **research** something, you try to discover facts about it. ❑ *She spent two years researching the subject.* [from Old French]

● **re|search|er** (**researchers**) **N-COUNT** ❑ *...a market researcher.*

→ look at Word Webs: **hospital, laboratory, medicine, science, zoo**

Word Partnership	Use **research** with :
ADJ	**biological** research, **clinical** research, **current** research, **experimental** research, **medical** research, **recent** research, **scientific** research **1**
N	**animal** research, **cancer** research, research **facility**, research **findings**, **laboratory** research, research **methods**, research **paper**, research **project**, research **report**, research **results**, research **scientist** **1**

R

re|sem|blance /rɪzɛmbləns/ (**resemblances**) **N-COUNT/N-NONCOUNT** If there is a **resemblance** between two people or things, they are similar to each other. ❑ *There was a strong resemblance between the two girls.* [from Old French]

re|sem|ble /rɪzɛmbᵊl/ (**resembles, resembling, resembled**) **V-T** If one person or thing **resembles** another, they look similar to each other. ❑ *She resembles her mother.* [from Old French]

re|sent /rɪzɛnt/ (**resents, resenting, resented**) **V-T** If you **resent** something, you feel angry about it because you think it is not fair. ❑ *Certain people resented my success.* [from French]

re|sent|ment /rɪzɛntmənt/ **N-NONCOUNT** **Resentment** is anger that someone feels about something because they think it is not fair. ❑ *Too many rules can cause resentment.* [from French]

res|er|va|tion /rɛzərveɪʃᵊn/ (**reservations**)
1 **N-COUNT** If you **make a reservation**, you ask a hotel or a restaurant to keep a room or a table for you. ❑ *Have you canceled our reservation?*
2 **N-COUNT/N-NONCOUNT** If you have **reservations about** something, you are not sure that it is entirely good or right. ❑ *He had no reservations at all about leaving home.* [from Old French]
→ look at Word Web: **hotel**

re|serve /rɪzɜrv/ (**reserves, reserving, reserved**)
1 **V-T** If something **is reserved for** a particular person or purpose, it is kept for them. ❑ *A room was reserved for him.*
2 **N-COUNT** A **reserve** is a supply of something that you can use when you need it. ❑ *Saudi Arabia has the world's largest oil reserves.*
3 **PHRASE** If you have something **in reserve**, you have a supply of it that you can use when you need it. ❑ *I always try to keep a little money in reserve.* [from Old French]

re|served /rɪzɜrvd/ **ADJ** Someone who is **reserved** hides their feelings. ❑ *He was quiet and reserved.* [from Old French]

res|er|voir /rɛzərvwɑr/ (**reservoirs**)
N-COUNT GEOGRAPHY A **reservoir** is a lake that is used for storing water before people use it. ❑ *The reservoir provides drinking water for the city of Utica, NY.* [from French]
→ look at Word Web: **dam**

| Word Link | *sid* ≈ *sitting* : *preside, president, residence* |

resi|dence /rɛzɪdəns/ (**residences**)
1 **N-COUNT** A **residence** is a large house where an important person lives. [FORMAL] ❑ *...the president's official residence.*
2 **N-NONCOUNT** Your place of **residence** is the place where you live. [from Latin] [FORMAL]

| Word Link | *ent* ≈ *one who does, has* : *dependent, resident, superintendent* |

resi|dent /rɛzɪdənt/ (**residents**) **N-COUNT** The **residents** of a house or an area are the people who live there. ❑ *Local residents complained that the road was dangerous.* [from Latin]
→ look at Word Web: **country**

resi|den|tial /rɛzɪdɛnʃᵊl/ **ADJ** A **residential** area contains houses rather than offices or stores. ❑ *We drove through a residential area of Maryland.* [from Latin]

re|sign /rɪzaɪn/ (**resigns, resigning, resigned**)
1 **V-T/V-I** If you **resign** from a job, you tell your employer that you are leaving it. ❑ *He was forced to resign.* ❑ *Mr. Robb resigned his position last month.*
2 **V-T** If you **resign yourself to** an unpleasant situation, you accept it because you cannot change it. ❑ *We resigned ourselves to another summer without a boat.* [from Old French]

| Thesaurus | **resign** Also look up : |
| v | leave, quit, step down **1** |

res|ig|na|tion /rɛzɪgneɪʃᵊn/ (**resignations**)
N-COUNT/N-NONCOUNT Your **resignation** is when you tell your employer that you are leaving your job. ❑ *Barbara offered her resignation this morning.* [from Old French]

re|signed /rɪzaɪnd/ **ADJ** If you are **resigned to** an unpleasant situation or fact, you accept it without complaining because you realize that you cannot change it. ❑ *He is resigned to the noise and the mess.* [from Old French]

re|sili|ent /rɪzɪlyənt/ **ADJ** People and things that are **resilient** are able to recover easily and quickly from unpleasant or damaging events. ❑ *The Japanese stock market was the most resilient.* ● **re|sili|ence** **N-NONCOUNT/N-SING** ❑ *...the resilience of human beings.* [from Old French]

r

re|sist /rɪzɪst/ (**resists, resisting, resisted**)

1 **v-t** If you **resist** a force or a change, you fight against it. ❑ *There are people in the organization who resist change.*

2 **v-t** If you **resist** a feeling that you want to do something, you stop yourself from doing it although you would like to do it. ❑ *Resist the temptation to help your child too much.* [from Latin]

> | Word Link | *ance ≈ quality, state : insurance, performance, resistance* |

re|sist|ance /rɪzɪstəns/ (**resistances**)

1 **N-NONCOUNT** **Resistance** to a force or a change is when you fight back against it. ❑ *I am aware of his resistance to anything new.* ❑ *The soldiers are facing strong resistance.*

2 **N-COUNT/N-NONCOUNT** SCIENCE In electrical engineering or physics, **resistance** is the ability of a substance or an electrical circuit to stop the flow of an electrical current through it. [from Latin]
→ look at Word Web: **bicycle**

re|sist|ant /rɪzɪstənt/

1 **ADJ** Someone who is **resistant to** something is opposed to it and wants to prevent it. ❑ *Some people are very resistant to the idea of exercise.*

2 **ADJ** If something is **resistant to** a particular thing, it is not harmed by it. ❑ *...how to make plants more resistant to disease.* [from Latin]

reso|lu|tion /rɛzəluʃ°n/ (**resolutions**)

1 **N-COUNT** If you make a **resolution**, you decide to try very hard to do something. ❑ *They made a resolution to get more exercise.*

2 **N-COUNT** SOCIAL STUDIES A **resolution** is a formal decision made at a meeting by means of a vote. ❑ *...a United Nations resolution authorizing the use of force.* [from Latin]

re|solve /rɪzɒlv/ (**resolves, resolving, resolved**)

1 **v-t** If you **resolve** a problem, an argument, or a difficulty, you find a solution to it. [FORMAL] ❑ *We must resolve these problems.*

2 **v-t** If you **resolve to** do something, you make a decision to do it. [FORMAL] ❑ *Judy resolved to be a better friend.*

3 **N-COUNT/N-NONCOUNT** If you show **resolve**, you are trying very hard to do what you have decided to do. [FORMAL] ❑ *She spoke of the government's resolve to go to war if necessary.* [from Latin]

reso|nance /rɛzənəns/ (**resonances**)

N-COUNT/N-NONCOUNT SCIENCE A **resonance** is the sound that is produced by an object when it vibrates at the same rate as the sound waves from another object. [from Latin]

re|sort /rɪzɔrt/ (**resorts**)

1 **N-COUNT** A **resort** is a place that provides activities for people who stay there during their vacation. ❑ *The ski resorts are busy.*

2 **PHRASE** If you do something **as a last resort**, you do it because you can find no other solution to a problem. ❑ *As a last resort, we hired an expert.* [from Old French]

re|source /risɔrs/ (**resources**) **N-COUNT** SOCIAL STUDIES The **resources** of a country, an organization, or a person are the money and other things that they have and can use. ❑ *We must protect the country's natural resources, including water.* [from Old French]

re|source re|cov|ery **N-NONCOUNT** SCIENCE **Resource recovery** is the process of obtaining useful materials or energy from things that are thrown away, such as paper or glass.

re|spect /rɪspɛkt/ (**respects, respecting, respected**)

1 **v-t** If you **respect** someone, you have a good opinion of them. ❑ *I want people to respect me for my work.*

2 **N-NONCOUNT** If you have **respect for** someone or something, you have a good opinion of them, and you consider them to be important. ❑ *I have great respect for Tom.* ❑ *You should show respect for people's rights.*

3 → see also **self-respect**

4 **v-t** If someone **respects** your wishes, rights, or customs, they avoid doing things that you would dislike. ❑ *I tried to respect her wishes.*

5 **PHRASE** You use **in this respect** and **in many respects** when what you are saying applies to the thing or things you have mentioned. ❑ *The brothers were different from each other in many respects.*

6 **PHRASE** You use **with respect to** to say what something relates to. [FORMAL] ❑ *The decision was legal with respect to Swiss law.* [from Latin]

> | Thesaurus | respect | Also look up : |
> |---|---|---|
> | v | admire **1** | |
> | N | consideration, courtesy, esteem **3** | |

re|spect|able /rɪspɛktəbᵊl/ **ADJ** If someone or something is **respectable**, people have a good opinion of them, and think they are morally correct. ❑ *He comes from a respectable family.* [from Latin]

re|spect|ed /rɪspɛktɪd/ **ADJ** Someone or something that is **respected** is admired and considered important by many people. ❑ *He is highly respected for his art.* [from Latin]

re|spect|ful /rɪspɛktfəl/ **ADJ** If you are **respectful,** you are polite to people. ❑ *The children were always respectful to older people.* [from Latin]

re|spec|tive|ly /rɪspɛktɪvli/ **ADV** **Respectively** means in the same order as the items that you have just mentioned. ❑ *Their sons, Ben and Jonathan, were three and six respectively.* [from Latin]

Word Link *spir ≈ breath : inspire, perspiration, respiration*

res|pi|ra|tion /rɛspɪreɪʃᵊn/ **N-NONCOUNT** **SCIENCE** In humans and animals, **respiration** is the process of breathing. [from Latin]

res|pira|tory sys|tem /rɛspərətɔri sɪstəm/ (**respiratory systems**) **N-COUNT** **SCIENCE** Your body's **respiratory system** is the group of organs that are involved in breathing, including the nose, the mouth, and the lungs.
→ look at Word Web: **respiratory system**

re|spond /rɪspɒnd/ (**responds, responding, responded**) **V-T/V-I** When you **respond** to something that someone does or says, you react to it by doing or saying something. ❑ *The army responded with bombs.* ❑ *They responded positively to the president's request for financial help.* [from Old French]

re|sponse /rɪspɒns/ (**responses**)
1 **N-COUNT** Your **response** to something that someone does or says is your reply or your reaction to it. ❑ *There was no response to his remarks.*
2 **N-COUNT** **SCIENCE** The **response** of an organism to a stimulus is the way that the organism reacts to it. [from Latin]

Word Partnership Use **response** with :

ADJ **correct** response, **enthusiastic** response, **immediate** response, **military** response, **negative/positive** response, **overwhelming** response, **quick** response, **written** response

re|spon|sibil|ity /rɪspɒnsɪbɪlɪti/ (**responsibilities**)
1 **N-NONCOUNT** If you have **responsibility** for something or someone, it is your job to deal with them. ❑ *Each manager had responsibility for ten people.*
2 **N-NONCOUNT** If you accept **responsibility** for something that happened, you agree that it was your fault. ❑ *No one admitted responsibility for the attacks.*
3 **N-PLURAL** Your **responsibilities** are your duties. ❑ *He is busy with work and family responsibilities.* [from Latin]
→ look at Word Web: **citizenship**

Word Partnership Use **responsibility** with :

V **be given** responsibility, **have (a)** responsibility **1**
assume responsibility, **bear** responsibility, responsibility, **take** responsibility **1 2**
accept responsibility, **claim** responsibility **2**
ADJ **financial** responsibility, **moral** responsibility, **personal** responsibility **1 2**

Word Web respiratory system

Respiration moves **air** into and out of the **lungs**. Air enters through the **nose** or **mouth**. Then it travels down the windpipe and into the **lungs**. In the lungs **oxygen** absorbs into the bloodstream. Blood carries oxygen to the heart and other organs. The lungs also remove **carbon dioxide** from the blood. This gas is then **exhaled** through the mouth. During **inhalation** the **diaphragm** moves downward and the lungs fill with air. During exhalation the diaphragm relaxes and air flows out. Adult humans **breathe** about six liters of air each minute.

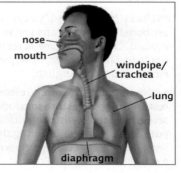

nose
mouth
windpipe/ trachea
lung
diaphragm

r

re|spon|sible /rɪspɒnsɪbᵊl/

■ **ADJ** If you are **responsible for** something, it is your job or duty to deal with it. ❑ *I met the people who are responsible for sales and advertising.*

■ **ADJ** If someone or something is **responsible for** a particular event or situation, it is their fault. ❑ *He still felt responsible for her death.*

■ **ADJ Responsible** people behave in a proper and sensible way. ❑ *She's a responsible child who often helps around the house.* [from Latin]

rest /rɛst/ (**rests, resting, rested**)

■ **V-T/V-I** If you **rest**, or if you **rest** your body, you spend some time relaxing after doing something tiring. ❑ *He's tired, and the doctor advised him to rest.*

■ **N-COUNT/N-NONCOUNT** If you get some **rest**, you spend some time relaxing after doing something tiring. ❑ *You're exhausted— go home and get some rest.*

■ **V-T** If you **rest** something somewhere, you put it on another thing. ❑ *He rested his arms on the table.*

■ **V-I** If a theory or your success **rests on** a particular thing, it depends on that thing. [FORMAL] ❑ *My whole future rests on his decision.*

■ **N-SING The rest** is the parts of something that are left. ❑ *I ate two cakes and saved the rest.* ❑ *It was an experience I will remember for the rest of my life.* [Senses 1 to 4 from Old English. Sense 5 from Old French.]

→ look at Word Webs: **motion, sleep**

Thesaurus	rest	Also look up :
v	lie down, relax ■	

res|tau|rant /rɛstərənt, -tərɑnt, -trɑnt/ (**restaurants**) **N-COUNT** A **restaurant** is a place where you can buy and eat a meal. ❑ *We ate at an Italian restaurant.* [from French]

→ look at Word Web: **city**

rest|less /rɛstlɪs/ **ADJ** If you are **restless**, you are bored or nervous, and you want to move around. ❑ *I got restless and moved to San Francisco.* ❑ *My father seemed very restless and excited.* [from Old English]

re|store /rɪstɔr/ (**restores, restoring, restored**) **V-T** To **restore** someone or something **to** a former condition means to put them in that condition again. ❑ *We will restore her to health.* ❑ *They are experts in restoring old buildings.* [from Old French]

re|strain /rɪstreɪn/ (**restrains, restraining, restrained**)

■ **V-T** If you **restrain** someone, you use force to stop them from doing something. ❑ *Wally held my arm to restrain me.*

■ **V-T** If you **restrain** an emotion, you prevent yourself from showing it. ❑ *She was unable to restrain her anger.* [from Old French]

re|straint /rɪstreɪnt/ (**restraints**)

■ **N-COUNT/N-NONCOUNT Restraints** are rules or conditions that limit or restrict someone or something. ❑ *...the need for spending restraints in some areas.*

■ **N-NONCOUNT Restraint** is calm, controlled behavior. ❑ *They behaved with great restraint.* [from Old French]

re|strict /rɪstrɪkt/ (**restricts, restricting, restricted**)

■ **V-T** If you **restrict** something, you prevent it from becoming too great. ❑ *The school is restricting the number of students it accepts this year.*

■ **V-T** To **restrict** the actions of someone or something means to prevent them from acting freely. ❑ *The bandage restricts the movement in my right arm.* ● **re|stric|tion** /rɪstrɪkʃᵊn/ (**restrictions**) **N-COUNT/N-NONCOUNT** ❑ *Are there any parking restrictions in this street?*

■ **V-T** If you **restrict** someone **to** one thing, they can do or have only that thing. ❑ *She has restricted herself to driving familiar routes in daylight.* [from Latin]

rest|room /rɛstrum/ (**restrooms**) also **rest room N-COUNT** In a public place, a **restroom** is a room with toilets for people to use.

re|sult /rɪzʌlt/ (**results, resulting, resulted**)

■ **N-COUNT** A **result** is something that happens or exists because something else has happened. ❑ *People developed the disease as a direct result of their work.*

■ **V-I** If something **results in** a particular situation or event, it causes that situation or event. ❑ *Half of all road accidents result in head injuries.*

■ **V-I** If something **results from** a particular event or action, it is caused by that event or action. ❑ *Many health problems result from a poor diet.*

■ **N-COUNT Results** are facts such as a score that you get at the end of a competition or a test. ❑ *Are you happy with the election results?* [from Latin]

R

re|sult|ant ve|loc|ity /rɪzʌltənt vəlɒsɪti/ (**resultant velocities**) **N-COUNT** SCIENCE The **resultant velocity** of a moving object is its total speed in a particular direction once all the different forces acting on it have been taken into account.

re|sume /rɪzum/ (**resumes, resuming, resumed**) **V-T/V-I** If you **resume** an activity, you begin it again. [FORMAL] ❑ *After the war he resumed his job at Wellesley College.* ❑ *The talks will resume on Tuesday.* [from Latin]

ré|su|mé /rɛzʊmeɪ/ (**résumés**) also **resume** **N-COUNT** Your **résumé** is a short description of your education and the jobs you have had. [from French]

re|tail /riteɪl/ (**retails, retailing, retailed**)
◼ **N-NONCOUNT** BUSINESS **Retail** is when a business sells goods directly to the public. ❑ *My sister works in retail, in a clothing store.*
◼ **V-I** BUSINESS If an item in a store **retails at** or **for** a particular price, it is for sale at that price. ❑ *The game originally retailed for $23.50.* [from Old French]

re|tail|er /riteɪlər/ (**retailers**) **N-COUNT** BUSINESS A **retailer** is a business that sells goods directly to the public. ❑ *...a furniture retailer.* [from Old French]

re|tain /rɪteɪn/ (**retains, retaining, retained**) **V-T** To **retain** something means to continue to have it. [FORMAL] ❑ *He was looking for a way to retain control of his company.* [from Old French]

Thesaurus	retain Also look up :
v	hold, keep, maintain, remember, save; (*ant.*) give up, lose

re|tali|ate /rɪtælieɪt/ (**retaliates, retaliating, retaliated**) **V-I** If you **retaliate** when someone harms or annoys you, you do something that harms or annoys them in return. ❑ *I was tempted to retaliate.* ❑ *...actions designed to retaliate against the government.*
● **re|talia|tion** /rɪtælieɪʃⁿn/ **N-NONCOUNT** ❑ *The attack was in retaliation for his death.* [from Late Latin]

re|think /riθɪŋk/ (**rethinks, rethinking, rethought**) **V-T** If you **rethink** a problem or a plan, you think about it again and change it. ❑ *Both political parties are rethinking their programs.* [from Old English]

reti|cent /rɛtɪsənt/ **ADJ** Someone who is **reticent** does not tell people about things.

❑ *She is so reticent about her achievements.*
● **reti|cence** **N-NONCOUNT** ❑ *Pauline liked his reticence.* [from Latin]

reti|na /rɛtɪnə/ (**retinas**) **N-COUNT** SCIENCE Your **retina** is the area at the back of your eye that sends images to your brain. [from Medieval Latin]
→ look at Word Web: **eye**

re|tire /rɪtaɪər/ (**retires, retiring, retired**) **V-I** When people **retire**, they leave their job and usually stop working completely. ❑ *He planned to retire at age 65.* ● **re|tired** **ADJ** ❑ *I am a retired teacher.* [from French]

re|tire|ment /rɪtaɪərmənt/ **N-NONCOUNT** A person's **retirement** is the period in their life after they retire. ❑ *What do you plan to do during retirement?* [from French]

re|tort /rɪtɔrt/ (**retorts, retorting, retorted**)
◼ **V-T** To **retort** means to reply angrily to someone. [WRITTEN] ❑ *"I did not!" Sherrie retorted.*
◼ **N-COUNT** **Retort** is also a noun. [WRITTEN] ❑ *She was trying to think of some smart retort.* [from Latin]

re|treat /rɪtrit/ (**retreats, retreating, retreated**)
◼ **V-I** If you **retreat**, you move away from something or someone. ❑ *I retreated from the room.* ❑ *The French soldiers were forced to retreat.*
◼ **N-COUNT/N-NONCOUNT** **Retreat** is also a noun. ❑ *The British Army was in full retreat.* [from Old French]

re|trieve /rɪtriv/ (**retrieves, retrieving, retrieved**) **V-T** If you **retrieve** something, you get it back from the place where you left it. ❑ *Alexander went into the bedroom to retrieve his hat.* [from Old French]

retro|grade /rɛtrəgreɪd/ (**retrogrades**) **N-COUNT/N-NONCOUNT** ARTS A **retrograde** is a section of dance or music in which the usual order is reversed, by beginning at the end and ending at the beginning. [from Latin]

retro|grade or|bit (**retrograde orbits**) **N-COUNT/N-NONCOUNT** SCIENCE Planets that have a **retrograde orbit** move around the sun in the opposite direction to the direction in which they spin on their own axis.

retro|grade ro|ta|tion **N-NONCOUNT** SCIENCE Planets that have **retrograde rotation** spin on their axis in the opposite direction to the direction that they move around the sun. Compare with **prograde rotation**.

retro|spect /rɛtrəspɛkt/ **PHRASE** When you consider something **in retrospect**, you think about it afterward, and often have a different opinion about it from the one that you had at the time. ❏ *The decision was not a very good one in retrospect.* [from Latin]

> **Word Link**   re ≈ back, again : re**flect**, re**fresh**, re**turn**

re|turn /rɪtɜrn/ (**returns, returning, returned**)
1 V-I When you **return to** a place, you go back there. ❏ *He will return to Moscow tomorrow.*
2 N-SING Your **return** is when you arrive back at a place where you were before. ❏ *Dan explained the reason for his return to Dallas.*
3 V-T If you **return** something that you borrowed or took, you give it back or put it back. ❏ *They will return the money later.*
4 N-SING Return is also a noun. ❏ *Marie demanded the return of the stolen money.*
5 V-I If something **returns**, it comes back or happens again. ❏ *Recently, my symptoms have returned.*
6 V-I If you **return to** a state that you were in before, you start being in that state again. ❏ *Life has improved and returned to normal.*
7 V-I If you **return to** a subject that you have mentioned before, you begin talking about it again. ❏ *Reporters returned to the subject of baseball.*
8 V-I If you **return to** an activity that you were doing before, you start doing it again. ❏ *At 52, he is young enough to return to politics.*
9 N-SING Return is also a noun. ❏ *He has not ruled out the possibility of a return to football.*
10 PHRASE If you do something **in return for** what someone did for you, you do it because they did that thing for you. ❏ *I smiled at her and she smiled in return.* [from Old French]
→ look at Word Web: **library**

> **Thesaurus**   return   Also look up :
>
> V   come back, go back, reappear **1**
>   give back, hand back, pay back;
>   (*ant.*) keep **3**
> N   arrival, homecoming; (*ant.*) departure **2**

retweet /riːtwiːt/ (**retweets, retweeting, retweeted**) **V-T** TECHNOLOGY If you **retweet** something, you copy another user's comment on the Twitter® website for your own followers to read. ❏ *His comments were retweeted by hundreds of people.*

re|union /riyuniən/ (**reunions**)
N-COUNT/N-NONCOUNT A **reunion** is a meeting between people who have not seen each other for a long time. ❏ *I am planning a family reunion.* [from Church Latin]

re|unite /riyunaɪt/ (**reunites, reuniting, reunited**) **V-T** If people **are reunited**, they see each other again after a long time. ❏ *She was finally reunited with her family.* [from Late Latin]

re|use (**reuses, reusing, reused**)

> **PRONUNCIATION HELP**
> Pronounce the verb /riyuz/. Pronounce the noun /riyus/.

1 V-T When you **reuse** something, you use it again instead of throwing it away. ❏ *Try where possible to reuse paper.*
2 N-NONCOUNT Reuse is also a noun. ❏ *Copper, brass, and aluminum are separated and remelted for reuse.* [from Old French]
→ look at Word Web: **dump**

re|veal /rɪvil/ (**reveals, revealing, revealed**)
1 V-T To **reveal** something means to tell people something that they do not know already. ❏ *She has refused to reveal any details.*
2 V-T If you **reveal** something, you show it by removing the thing that was covering it. ❏ *She smiled, revealing small white teeth.* [from Old French]

re|veal|ing /rɪvilɪŋ/ **ADJ** A **revealing** statement, account, or action tells you something that you did not know, especially about the person doing it or making it. ❏ *...a revealing interview.* [from Old French]

rev|ela|tion /rɛvəleɪʃən/ (**revelations**)
1 N-COUNT A **revelation** is a surprising or interesting fact that is made known to people. ❏ *...revelations about his private life.*
2 N-COUNT/N-NONCOUNT The **revelation of** something is the act of making it known. ❏ *...the revelation of his true identity.*
3 N-SING If you say that something you experienced was **a revelation**, you are saying that it was very surprising or very good. ❏ *Degas's work was a revelation to her.* [from Church Latin]

re|venge /rɪvɛndʒ/ **N-NONCOUNT Revenge** involves hurting or punishing someone who has hurt or harmed you. ❏ *He wanted revenge for the way they treated his mother.* ❏ *He was afraid that Benny Hall would take revenge on him.* [from Old French]

rev|enue /rɛvənyu/ (**revenues**) **N-COUNT/ N-NONCOUNT** BUSINESS SOCIAL STUDIES **Revenue** is money that a company, an organization, or a government receives from people. ❑ *The company gets 98% of its revenue from Internet advertising.* [from Old French]

re|ver|ber|ate /rɪvɜrbəreɪt/ (**reverberates, reverberating, reverberated**) **v-i** When a loud sound **reverberates** through a place, it echoes through it. ❑ *The noise reverberated through the house.* [from Latin]

Rev|er|end /rɛvərənd/ **Reverend** is a title used before the name of a church leader. ❑ *The Reverend Jim Simons led the service.*

re|verse /rɪvɜrs/ (**reverses, reversing, reversed**)
1 **v-t** To **reverse** a decision or a situation means to change it to the opposite decision or situation. ❑ *They will not reverse the decision to increase prices.*
2 **v-t** If you **reverse** the order of a group of things, you arrange them in the opposite order. ❑ *You've made a spelling mistake. You need to reverse the "i" and the "e."*
3 **N-NONCOUNT** If your car is **in reverse**, you can drive it backward. [from Old French]

re|verse fault (**reverse faults**) **N-COUNT** SCIENCE A **reverse fault** is a fault in the surface of the Earth where the rock above the fault has moved up. Compare with **normal fault**.

re|vert /rɪvɜrt/ (**reverts, reverting, reverted**)
v-i When people or things **revert to** a previous state, system, or type of behavior, they go back to it. ❑ *He made a few comments and then reverted to silence.* [from Latin]

re|view /rɪvyu/ (**reviews, reviewing, reviewed**)
1 **N-COUNT** A **review of** something is when you examine it to see if it needs changes. ❑ *The president ordered a review of the situation.*
2 **v-t** If you **review** something, you consider it carefully to see if it needs changes. ❑ *The new plan will be reviewed by the city council.*
3 **N-COUNT** A **review** is a report that gives your opinion of a book or a movie. ❑ *The movie got a good review in the magazine.*
4 **v-t** If someone **reviews** a book or a movie, they write a report that gives their opinion of it. ❑ *She reviews all the new DVDs.*
● **re|view|er** (**reviewers**) **N-COUNT** ❑ *He's a reviewer for the New York Times.*

5 **v-t/v-i** When you **review for** an exam, or when you **review**, you study all the information about the subject again. ❑ *Review all your notes for each class.* ❑ *I sat in the library all day reviewing for exams.* [from French]

Word Partnership	Use **review** with :
N	**performance** review **1**
	book review, **film/movie** review, **restaurant** review **3**
	review **questions** **5**

re|vise /rɪvaɪz/ (**revises, revising, revised**)
v-t If you **revise** something, you change it in order to make it better or more correct. ❑ *We are revising the rules.* [from Latin]

Word Link	*viv ≈ living : revival, survive, vivid*

re|viv|al /rɪvaɪvᵊl/ (**revivals**)
1 **N-COUNT** When there is a **revival of** something, it becomes active or popular again. ❑ *...a revival of interest in a number of artists.*
2 **N-COUNT** ARTS A **revival** is a new production of a play, an opera, or a ballet. ❑ *...a revival of Chekhov's "The Seagull."* [from Old French]

re|vive /rɪvaɪv/ (**revives, reviving, revived**)
1 **v-t/v-i** If you **revive** someone who has fainted, or they **revive**, they become conscious again. ❑ *A doctor revived the patient.*
2 **v-t/v-i** When a business, a trend, or a feeling **is revived** or when it **revives**, it becomes active or successful again. ❑ *...an attempt to revive the economy.* [from Old French]

re|voke /rɪvouk/ (**revokes, revoking, revoked**) **v-t** SOCIAL STUDIES When people in authority **revoke** something such as a license, a law, or an agreement, they cancel it. [FORMAL] ❑ *Police revoked his driver's license.* [from Latin]

re|volt /rɪvoult/ (**revolts, revolting, revolted**)
1 **N-COUNT/N-NONCOUNT** SOCIAL STUDIES A **revolt** is when a group of people fight against a person or an organization that has control. ❑ *It was a revolt by ordinary people against their leaders.*
2 **v-i** SOCIAL STUDIES When people **revolt**, they fight against a person or an organization that has control. ❑ *Californian citizens revolted against higher taxes.* [from French]

re|volt|ing /rɪvoultɪŋ/ **ADJ** **Revolting** means extremely unpleasant. ❑ *The smell was revolting.* [from French]

revo|lu|tion /rɛvəluʃ°n/ (revolutions)

◾ **N-COUNT** SOCIAL STUDIES A **revolution** is an attempt by a group of people to change their country's government by using force. ❑ *The period since the revolution has been peaceful.*

◾ **N-COUNT** A **revolution** in a particular area of activity is an important change in that area. ❑ *There was a revolution in ship design in the nineteenth century.*

◾ **N-COUNT** SCIENCE A **revolution** of an object such as a planet is one complete circle that it makes around a central point such as a star. [from Old French]

revo|lu|tion|ary /rɛvəluʃənɛri/

◾ **ADJ** SOCIAL STUDIES **Revolutionary** activities, organizations, or people try to cause a revolution. ❑ *Do you know anything about the revolutionary movement?*

◾ **ADJ** Something that is **revolutionary** changes the way that something is done or made. ❑ *It is a revolutionary new product.* [from Old French]

re|volve /rɪvɒlv/ (revolves, revolving, revolved)

◾ **V-I** If your life **revolves around** a particular thing, that thing is the most important part of your life. ❑ *Her life has revolved around sports.*

◾ **V-T/V-I** When something **revolves**, or when you **revolve** it, it moves or turns in a circle. ❑ *The Earth revolves around the sun.* [from Latin]

re|volv|er /rɪvɒlvər/ (revolvers) **N-COUNT** A **revolver** is a type of small gun. [from Latin]

re|ward /rɪwɔrd/ (rewards, rewarding, rewarded)

◾ **N-COUNT** A **reward** is something that someone gives you because you have done something good. ❑ *The school gives rewards for good behavior.*

◾ **N-COUNT** A **reward** is money that a person gets for helping to find lost property or a criminal. ❑ *The firm offered a $10,000 reward for information leading to the arrest of the killer.*

◾ **V-T** If someone **rewards** you, they give you something because you have done something good. ❑ *She was rewarded for her years of hard work.* [from Old Norman French] → look at Usage note at **award**

re|ward|ing /rɪwɔrdɪŋ/ **ADJ** An experience or an action that is **rewarding** gives you satisfaction or brings you benefits. ❑ *I have a job that is very rewarding.* [from Old Norman French]

re|write /riraɪt/ (rewrites, rewriting, rewrote, rewritten) **V-T** LANGUAGE ARTS If someone **rewrites** a text, they write it in a different way in order to improve it. ❑ *She decided to rewrite her article.* [from Old English]

rheto|ric /rɛtərɪk/ **N-NONCOUNT** If you refer to speech or writing as **rhetoric**, you disapprove of it because it is intended to convince and impress people but may not be sincere or honest. ❑ *...political rhetoric rather than reality.* [from Latin]

rhe|tori|cal strat|egy /rɪtɔrɪkəl strætədʒi/ (rhetorical strategies) **N-COUNT** LANGUAGE ARTS A **rhetorical strategy** is one of the traditional methods used to communicate meaning in a speech or a piece of writing, for example exposition or description.

rhi|noc|er|os /raɪnɒsərəs/ (rhinoceroses) **N-COUNT** A **rhinoceros** is a large animal from Asia or Africa with a horn on its nose. [from Latin]

rhi|zoid /raɪzɔɪd/ (rhizoids) **N-COUNT** SCIENCE **Rhizoids** are thin structures that grow downward from plants such as mosses and fungi and have a similar function to roots. [from Greek]

rhi|zome /raɪzoʊm/ (rhizomes) **N-COUNT** SCIENCE **Rhizomes** are the horizontal stems from which some plants, such as irises, grow. Rhizomes are found on or just under the surface of the earth. [from New Latin]

rhyme /raɪm/ (rhymes, rhyming, rhymed)

◾ **V-T/V-I** LANGUAGE ARTS If one word **rhymes with** another, or if two words **rhyme**, they have a very similar sound. ❑ *June rhymes with moon.*

◾ **N-COUNT** LANGUAGE ARTS A **rhyme** is a poem that has words that rhyme at the ends of its lines. ❑ *He was teaching Helen a rhyme.* [from Old French]

rhythm /rɪðəm/ (rhythms)

◾ **N-COUNT/N-NONCOUNT** MUSIC A **rhythm** is a regular pattern of sounds or movements. ❑ *Listen to the rhythms of jazz.*

◾ **N-COUNT** A **rhythm** is a regular pattern of changes, for example changes in your body, in the seasons, or in the tides.

◾ **N-COUNT** ARTS A **rhythm** is a regular repetition of lines or shapes to achieve a specific effect or pattern. [from Latin]

R

rhyth|mic /rɪðmɪk/ or **rhythmical**
/rɪðmɪkᵊl/ **ADJ** A **rhythmic** movement or
sound is repeated in a regular pattern.
❑ *Good breathing is slow and rhythmic.*
[from Latin]

rib /rɪb/ (ribs) **N-COUNT** SCIENCE Your **ribs** are
the 12 pairs of curved bones that surround
your chest. ❑ *Her heart was beating hard against
her ribs.* [from Old English]

rib|bon /rɪbən/ (ribbons)
N-COUNT/N-NONCOUNT A **ribbon** is a long,
narrow piece of cloth that you use to tie
things together, or as a decoration.
❑ *She tied her hair with a ribbon.* [from
Old French]

rib cage (rib cages) **N-COUNT** SCIENCE
Your **rib cage** is the structure of bones in
your chest that protects your lungs and
other organs.

ribo|some /raɪbəsoʊm/ (ribosomes)
N-COUNT SCIENCE **Ribosomes** are structures
within the cells of an organism that
produce proteins.

rice /raɪs/ **N-NONCOUNT** Rice is white or
brown grains from a plant that grows in wet
areas. ❑ *The meal consisted of chicken, rice, and
vegetables.* [from French]
→ look at Word Webs: **rice, grain**

rich /rɪtʃ/ (richer, richest)
1 **ADJ** A **rich** person has a lot of money
or valuable possessions. ❑ *He was a very
rich man.*
2 **N-PLURAL** The **rich** are rich people.
❑ *Only the rich can afford to live there.*
3 **ADJ** If something is **rich in** a useful or
valuable substance, it contains a lot of it.
❑ *Oranges are rich in vitamin C.*
4 **ADJ** Rich food contains a lot of fat or oil.
❑ *More cream would make it too rich.* [from
Old English]

Thesaurus   rich   Also look up :

ADJ	affluent, wealthy; (ant.) poor **1**

Word Partnership   Use **rich** with :

ADJ	rich **and beautiful**, rich **and famous 1**
V	**become** rich, **get** rich **(quick) 1**
N	rich **kids**, rich **man/people**, rich **and poor 1**
	rich **in natural resources 2**
	rich **diet**, rich **food 3**

Richter scale /rɪktər skeɪl/ **N-SING** The
Richter scale is a scale that is used for
measuring how severe an earthquake is.
❑ *An earthquake measuring 6.1 on the Richter Scale
struck California yesterday.* [after Charles
Richter (1900-85), an American
seismologist]
→ look at Word Web: **tsunami**

rid /rɪd/ **PHRASE** When you **get rid of**
something or someone, you remove them
completely or make them leave. ❑ *We had to
get rid of our old car because it was too small.*
[from Old Norse]

rid|den /rɪdᵊn/ **Ridden** is the past participle
of **ride**. [from Old English]

rid|dle /rɪdᵊl/ (riddles) **N-COUNT** A **riddle** is a
question that seems to be nonsense, but
that has a clever answer. [from Old English]

ride /raɪd/ (rides, riding, rode, ridden)
1 **V-T/V-I** SPORTS When you **ride** a bicycle or
a horse, you sit on it, control it, and travel on
it. ❑ *Riding a bike is great exercise.* ❑ *We passed
three men riding on motorcycles.*
2 **V-I** When you **ride in** a vehicle, you travel
in it. ❑ *He rode in the bus to the hotel.*
3 **N-COUNT** A **ride** is a trip on a horse or a
bicycle, or in a vehicle. ❑ *She took some friends
for a ride in the car.* [from Old English]
4 → see also **riding**

r

Word Web   rice

An old Chinese myth says that an animal gave **rice** to
humans. A large flood destroyed all the crops. When the
people returned from the hills, they saw a dog. It had rice
seeds in its tail. They planted this new **grain** and were
never hungry again. In many Asian countries the words for
rice and **food** are the same. Rice has many other uses. It is
the main ingredient in some kinds of laundry **starch**. In
Thailand, rice **straw** is made into hats and shoes.

	Word Partnership	Use ride with :
N	bus/car/train/subway ride 🔳	
V	give *someone* a ride, go for a ride, offer *someone* a ride 🔳	
ADV	ride **home** 🔳	
ADJ	**long** ride, **scenic** ride, **short** ride, **smooth** ride 🔳	

rid|er /raɪdər/ (riders) **N-COUNT** SPORTS
A **rider** is someone who rides a horse, a bicycle, or a motorcycle. ❑ *She is a very good rider.* [from Old English]
→ look at Picture Dictionary: **horse**

ridge /rɪdʒ/ (ridges)
🔳 **N-COUNT** GEOGRAPHY A **ridge** is a long, narrow piece of raised land. ❑ *It's a high road along a mountain ridge.*
🔳 **N-COUNT** A **ridge** is a raised line on a flat surface. ❑ *...the bony ridge above his eyes.* [from Old English]
→ look at Picture Dictionary: **mountain**

ri|dicu|lous /rɪdɪkyələs/ **ADJ** If something or someone is **ridiculous**, they are very silly or not serious. ❑ *They thought it was a ridiculous idea.* [from Latin]

rid|ing /raɪdɪŋ/
🔳 **N-NONCOUNT** SPORTS **Riding** is the activity or sport of riding horses. ❑ *The next morning we went riding.* [from Old English]
🔳 → see also **ride**

ri|fle /raɪfºl/ (rifles) **N-COUNT** A **rifle** is a long gun. ❑ *They shot him with a rifle.* [from Old French]

rift /rɪft/ (rifts)
🔳 **N-COUNT** A **rift** between people or countries is a serious quarrel or disagreement that stops them from having a good relationship. ❑ *...a growing rift between the president and congress.*
🔳 **N-COUNT** A **rift** is a split that appears in something solid, especially in the ground.
🔳 **N-COUNT** SCIENCE In geology, a **rift** occurs when the tectonic plates of the Earth separate. [from Old Norse]

rift val|ley (rift valleys) **N-COUNT** SCIENCE
A **rift valley** is a valley formed as the result of a crack in the Earth's surface.

rig /rɪg/ (rigs, rigging, rigged)
🔳 **V-T** If someone **rigs** an election, a job appointment, or a game, they dishonestly arrange it to get the result they want or to give someone an unfair advantage.

❑ *She accused her opponents of rigging the vote.*
● **rig|ging** **N-NONCOUNT** ❑ *...vote rigging.*
🔳 **N-COUNT** A **rig** is a large structure that is used for looking for oil or gas and for taking it out of the ground or the bottom of the ocean. ❑ *...oil rigs.*
🔳 **N-COUNT** A **rig** is a truck that is made in two or more sections that are connected by metal bars, so that the vehicle can turn more easily. [of Scandinavian origin]

	right
❶	CORRECT
❷	DIRECTION AND POLITICAL GROUPINGS
❸	LAW
❹	EXACTLY OR IMMEDIATELY

❶ **right** /raɪt/
🔳 **ADJ** If someone or something is **right**, they are correct. ❑ *Ron was right about the result of the election.* ❑ *"C" is the right answer.*
🔳 **ADV** **Right** is also an adverb. ❑ *If I'm going to do something, I want to do it right.*
🔳 **INTERJ** You can use **right** to check whether you are correct. [SPOKEN] ❑ *You're coming to the party, right?*
🔳 **ADJ** The **right** action is the best one.
❑ *You made the right choice in moving to New York.*
🔳 **N-NONCOUNT** SOCIAL STUDIES You use **right** to talk about actions that are morally good and acceptable. ❑ *He knew right from wrong.*
🔳 **ADJ** **Right** is also an adjective. ❑ *It's not right to leave the children here alone.* [from Old English]

❷ **right** /raɪt/

LANGUAGE HELP
The spelling **Right** is also used for meaning 🔳.

🔳 **N-SING** The **right** is the side that is toward the east when you look north ❑ *On the right is a vegetable garden.*
🔳 **ADV** **Right** is also an adverb. ❑ *Turn right into the street.*
🔳 **ADJ** Your **right** arm or leg is the one that is on the right side of your body.
🔳 **N-SING** SOCIAL STUDIES You can refer to people who support the political ideals of capitalism and conservatism as **the right**.
❑ *This man is the best hope of the Republican Right.* [from Old English]

❸ **right** /raɪt/ (rights)
🔳 **N-PLURAL** Your **rights** are the things that

you are allowed to do morally, or by law. ❑ *Make sure you know your rights.*

2 **N-SING** If you have a **right to** do or have something, you are morally or legally allowed to do it or have it. ❑ *We have the right to protest.* [from Old English]

→ look at Word Web: **citizenship**

❹ **right** /raɪt/

1 **ADV** You can use **right** to say that something happens exactly in a particular place or at a particular time. ❑ *A car appeared right in front of him.* ❑ *Liz arrived right on time.*

2 **PHRASE** **I'll be right back** means that you will get back to a place in a very short time. ❑ *I'm going to get some water. I'll be right back.*

3 **PHRASE** If you do something **right away**, you do it immediately. [INFORMAL] ❑ *He wants to see you right away.*

4 **PHRASE** You can use **right now** to talk about the present moment. [INFORMAL] ❑ *Right now I'm feeling very excited.* [from Old English]

right an|gle (right angles) **N-COUNT** MATH A **right angle** is an angle that looks like a letter "L" and equals 90 degrees.

right-hand **ADJ** If something is on the **right-hand** side of something, it is positioned on the right of it. ❑ *...a church on the right-hand side of the road.*

right-hand|ed **ADJ** Someone who is **right-handed** uses their right hand rather than their left hand for activities such as writing and sports.

right-wing

> **LANGUAGE HELP**
>
> The spelling **right wing** is used for meaning **2**.

1 **ADJ** SOCIAL STUDIES A **right-wing** person or group has conservative or capitalist views. ❑ *...a right-wing government.* ● **right-wing|er** (right-wingers) **N-COUNT** ❑ *Across Europe, right-wingers are gaining power.*

2 **N-SING** SOCIAL STUDIES The **right wing** of a political party consists of the members who have the most conservative or the most capitalist views. ❑ *...the right wing of the Republican Party.*

rig|id /rɪdʒɪd/

1 **ADJ** Laws or systems that are **rigid** cannot be changed. ❑ *We have rigid rules about student behavior.*

2 **ADJ** A **rigid** substance or object is stiff and does not bend, stretch, or twist easily. ❑ *Use rigid plastic containers.* [from Latin]

rig|id mo|tion (rigid motions)

N-COUNT/N-NONCOUNT MATH **Rigid motion** is a change to the position of a geometric figure such as a triangle in which the distances and angles between points in the figure remain the same.

rig|or /rɪgər/ (rigors)

1 **N-PLURAL** The **rigors of** an activity or job are the difficult or unpleasant things that are associated with it. ❑ *...the rigors of army life.*

2 **N-NONCOUNT** If something is done with **rigor**, it is done in a strict, thorough way. ❑ *The prince behaved with professional rigor.* [from Latin]

rig|or|ous /rɪgərəs/ **ADJ** A test, a system, or a procedure that is **rigorous** is very thorough and strict. ❑ *...rigorous tests.* ● **rig|or|ous|ly** **ADV** ❑ *...rigorously conducted research.*

rim /rɪm/ (rims) **N-COUNT** The **rim** of a curved object is its edge. ❑ *She looked at him over the rim of her glass.* [from Old English]

rind /raɪnd/ (rinds)

1 **N-COUNT/N-NONCOUNT** The **rind** of a fruit such as a lemon or an orange is its thick outside skin.

2 **N-COUNT/N-NONCOUNT** The **rind** of cheese is the hard outside edge that you do not eat. [from Old English]

ring /rɪŋ/ (rings, ringing, rang, rung)

1 **V-T/V-I** When a bell **rings**, it makes its sound. ❑ *The school bell rang.* ❑ *They rang the bell but nobody came to the door.*

2 **N-COUNT** **Ring** is also a noun. ❑ *There was a ring at the door.*

3 **N-COUNT** A **ring** is a small circle of metal that you wear on your finger. ❑ *She was wearing a gold wedding ring.*

ring

4 **N-COUNT** A **ring** is something in the shape of a circle. ❑ *They built the fire in a ring of stones.*

5 **N-COUNT** SPORTS At a boxing match or a circus, the **ring** is the place where the match or performance takes place. ❑ *...a boxing ring.* [from Old English]

6 → see also **rung**

→ look at Picture Dictionary: **jewelry**

→ look at Word Web: **circle**

r

ring|tone /rɪŋtoʊn/ (**ringtones**) **N-COUNT**
TECHNOLOGY The **ringtone** is the sound
made by your cellphone when someone
calls you.

rink /rɪŋk/ (**rinks**) **N-COUNT** SPORTS A **rink** is a
large area of ice where people go to ice skate.
❏ There were hundreds of skaters on the rink.
[from Scots]

rinse /rɪns/ (**rinses, rinsing, rinsed**)
■ **V-T** When you **rinse** something, you wash
it in order to remove dirt or soap from it.
❏ Make sure you rinse all the shampoo out of your
hair.
② **N-COUNT** Rinse is also a noun. ❏ Give
your hair a quick rinse with warm water.
[from Old French]

riot /raɪət/ (**riots, rioting, rioted**)
■ **N-COUNT** SOCIAL STUDIES When there is a
riot, a group of people behave violently in a
public place. ❏ Twelve people were injured during
a riot at the prison.
② **V-I** SOCIAL STUDIES If people **riot**, they
behave violently in a public place. ❏ They
rioted against the government. [from Old
French]

rip /rɪp/ (**rips, ripping, ripped**)
■ **V-T/V-I** When you **rip** something, or
when it **rips**, it tears quickly. ❏ I ripped my
pants when I fell.
② **N-COUNT** A **rip** is a long cut or split in
something made of cloth or paper. ❏ ...the rip
in her new dress. [from Flemish]
→ look at Picture Dictionary: **cut**
▶ **rip up** If you **rip** something **up**, you tear it
into small pieces. ❏ He ripped up the letter and
threw it in the fire.

ripe /raɪp/ (**riper, ripest**)
■ **ADJ** Ripe fruit or grain is ready to eat.
❏ Choose firm but ripe fruit.
② **ADJ** If a situation is **ripe for** a particular
development, that development is likely to
happen soon. ❏ The time was ripe for change.
[from Old English]

rip|ple /rɪpᵊl/ (**ripples, rippling, rippled**)
■ **N-COUNT** Ripples are little waves on the
surface of water.
② **V-T/V-I** When the surface of water **ripples**,
or something **ripples** it, little waves appear
on it. ❏ If you throw a stone in a pool, it ripples.
[from Germanic]

rise /raɪz/ (**rises, rising, rose, risen**)
■ **V-I** If something **rises**, it moves upward.

❏ We could see black smoke rising from the chimney.
② **V-I** When you **rise**, you stand up. [FORMAL]
❏ He rose slowly from the chair.
③ **V-I** When you **rise**, you get out of bed.
[FORMAL] ❏ Tony rose early.
④ **V-I** When the sun or the moon **rises**, it
appears in the sky.
⑤ **V-T/V-I** If an amount or a number **rises**, it
increases. ❏ His income rose by $5,000.
❏ Interest rates rose 4% this quarter.
⑥ **N-COUNT** A **rise in** the amount of
something is an increase in it. ❏ There's been
a rise in the price of oil. [from Old English]
⑦ → see also **rose**
→ look at Usage note at **raise**

ris|ing ac|tion **N-NONCOUNT** ARTS The **rising
action** in the plot of a play or story is the
events that lead to the climax of the plot.

risk /rɪsk/ (**risks, risking, risked**)
■ **N-COUNT/N-NONCOUNT** If there is a **risk** of
something bad, there is a possibility that it
will happen. ❏ There is a small risk of damage.
② **N-COUNT** If something that you do is a
risk, it might have bad results. ❏ You're taking
a big risk by showing this to Robert.
③ **N-COUNT** If something or someone is a
risk, they are likely to harm you. ❏ Being very
fat is a health risk.
④ **V-T** If you **risk** something bad, you do
something knowing that the bad thing
might happen as a result. ❏ He risked breaking
his leg when he jumped.
⑤ **V-T** If you **risk** something important,
you behave in a way that might result in it
being lost or harmed. ❏ She risked her own life
to help him.
⑥ **PHRASE** To be **at risk** means to be in a
situation where something bad might
happen. ❏ Our nation is at risk from an attack.
⑦ **PHRASE** If you do something **at your own
risk**, you are responsible for any harm that
you experience from it. ❏ People who wish to
park here do so at their own risk. [from French]

Thesaurus	risk Also look up :
N	accident, danger, gamble, hazard; (ant.) safety ■ ②
V	chance, endanger, gamble, jeopardize ④ ⑤

risky /rɪski/ (**riskier, riskiest**) **ADJ** If an
activity or an action is **risky**, it is dangerous
or likely to fail. ❏ They encourage young people
to avoid risky behavior. [from French]

rite /raɪt/ (rites) **N-COUNT** A **rite** is a traditional ceremony that is carried out by a particular group or society. ❑ ...a religious rite. [from Latin]

ritu|al /rɪtʃuəl/ (rituals) **N-COUNT/N-NONCOUNT** A **ritual** is a series of actions that people perform in a particular order. ❑ Every religion has holy days and rituals such as baptism. [from Latin] → look at Word Web: **myth**

ri|val /raɪvəl/ (rivals) **N-COUNT** If people or groups are **rivals**, they compete against each other. ❑ He was accused of spying on his political rivals. [from Latin]

ri|val|ry /raɪvəlri/ (rivalries) **N-COUNT/N-NONCOUNT** **Rivalry** is competition or conflict between people or groups who want the same things. ❑ What causes rivalry between brothers? [from Latin]

riv|er /rɪvər/ (rivers) **N-COUNT** GEOGRAPHY A **river** is a long line of water that flows into an ocean. [from Old French] → look at Picture Dictionaries: **river**, **landforms**

RNA /ɑr ɛn eɪ/ **N-NONCOUNT** SCIENCE **RNA** is an acid in the chromosomes of the cells of living things that plays an important part in passing information about protein structure between different cells. **RNA** is an abbreviation for "ribonucleic acid."

roach /roʊtʃ/ (roaches) **N-COUNT** A **roach** is the same as a **cockroach**. [from Old French]

road /roʊd/ (roads) **N-COUNT** A **road** is a long piece of hard ground that vehicles travel on. ❑ There was very little traffic on the roads. [from Old English] → look at Word Web: **traffic**

roam /roʊm/ (roams, roaming, roamed) **V-T/V-I** If you **roam** an area, or **roam around** it, you move around it without planning where exactly you are going. ❑ Children roamed the streets in groups.

roar /rɔr/ (roars, roaring, roared) **1** **V-I** If a person, an animal, or a thing **roars**, they make a very loud noise. ❑ The engine roared, and the vehicle moved forward. **2** **N-COUNT** **Roar** is also a noun. ❑ Who could forget the first time they heard the roar of a lion? [from Old English]

roast /roʊst/ (roasts, roasting, roasted) **1** **V-T** When you **roast** meat or other food, you cook it in an oven or over a fire. ❑ He roasted the chicken. **2** **ADJ** **Roast** meat is cooked in an oven or over a fire. ❑ We had roast chicken. [from Old French] → look at Picture Dictionary: **cook** → look at Word Web: **peanut**

rob /rɒb/ (robs, robbing, robbed) **V-T** If a person **is robbed**, someone steals money or property from them. ❑ She was robbed of her watch. ● **rob|ber** (robbers) **N-COUNT** ❑ ...a bank robber. [from Old French]

rob|bery /rɒbəri/ (robberies) **N-COUNT/N-NONCOUNT** **Robbery** is when

Picture Dictionary — river

spring
river
lake
stream
gorge
valley
river
delta
ocean

r

a person steals money or property from a place. ❑ *There have been several robberies in the area.* [from Old French]

robe /roʊb/ (**robes**)

1 **N-COUNT** A **robe** is a special piece of clothing that an important person wears during a ceremony. [FORMAL] ❑ *The judge was wearing a black robe.*

2 **N-COUNT** A **robe** is a piece of clothing that you wear in the house before you get dressed. ❑ *I put on a robe and went down to the kitchen.* [from Old French]

rob|in /rɒbɪn/ (**robins**) **N-COUNT** A **robin** is a brown bird with a red chest.

ro|bot /roʊbɒt, -bɒt/ (**robots**) **N-COUNT** A **robot** is a machine that can move and perform tasks automatically. ❑ *We have robots that we could send to the moon.* [from Czech]

ro|bust /roʊbʌst, roʊbʌst/ **ADJ** Someone or something that is **robust** is very strong or healthy. ❑ *He was young and physically robust.* [from Latin]

rock /rɒk/ (**rocks, rocking, rocked**)

1 **N-NONCOUNT** SCIENCE **Rock** is the hard substance that is in the ground and in mountains. ❑ *We tried to dig, but the ground was solid rock.*

2 **N-COUNT** A **rock** is a large piece of rock. ❑ *She sat on a rock and looked out across the ocean.*

3 **V-T/V-I** When something **rocks**, or is **rocked**, it moves slowly backward and forward. ❑ *His body rocked gently in the chair.* ❑ *She rocked the baby in her arms.*

4 **N-NONCOUNT** MUSIC **Rock** is loud music with a strong beat that you play on electric instruments. ❑ *We went to a rock concert.* [Senses 1 and 2 from Old French. Senses 3 and 4 from Old English.]

→ look at Word Webs: **rock, crystal, earth, fossil, genre**

rock and roll also rock'n'roll **N-NONCOUNT** MUSIC **Rock and roll** is a type of music that was popular in the 1950s. ❑ *Elvis Presley was known as the King of Rock and Roll.*

rock cy|cle (**rock cycles**) **N-COUNT** SCIENCE The **rock cycle** is the continuous process in which a particular type of rock, such as igneous rock, slowly changes into other types of rock, such as sedimentary or metamorphic rock.

rock|et /rɒkɪt/ (**rockets**)

1 **N-COUNT** SCIENCE A **rocket** is a vehicle that people use to travel into outer space. ❑ *This is the rocket that took them to the moon.*

2 **N-COUNT** A **rocket** is the same as a **missile.** ❑ *There was another rocket attack on the city.* [from Old French]

rock fall (**rock falls**) **N-COUNT** SCIENCE A **rock fall** is the movement of a group of loose rocks down a steep slope such as the side of a mountain.

rocky /rɒki/ (**rockier, rockiest**) **ADJ** A **rocky** place has a lot of rocks in it. ❑ *The paths are very rocky.* [from Old English]

rod /rɒd/ (**rods**)

1 **N-COUNT** A **rod** is a long, thin metal or wooden bar. ❑ *The roof was supported with steel rods.*

2 **N-COUNT** SCIENCE **Rods** are cells in the retina of the eye that help you to see in dim light. Compare with **cone.** [from Old English]

rode /roʊd/ **Rode** is the past tense of **ride.**

ro|dent /roʊdᵊnt/ (**rodents**) **N-COUNT** **Rodents** are small animals such as mice, with sharp front teeth. [from Latin]

ro|deo /roʊdioʊ, roʊdeɪoʊ/ (**rodeos**) **N-COUNT** A **rodeo** is an event where you can watch people riding wild horses and catching animals with ropes. [from Spanish]

R

Word Web rock

Rocks are made of **minerals.** Sometimes they may contain only one **element.** Usually they contain

igneous

sedimentary

metamorphic

compounds of several elements. Each type of rock also has a unique **crystal** structure. Rock is always changing. When **lava erupts** from a **volcano**, it forms **igneous** rock. Wind, water, and ice **erode** this type of rock. The resulting **sediment** collects in rivers. Layers of sediment build up and form **sedimentary** rock. When **tectonic plates** move around, they create heat and pressure. This melting and crushing changes sedimentary rock into **metamorphic** rock.

ROI /ɑr ou aɪ/ BUSINESS **ROI** is short for "return on investment."

role /roʊl/ (roles)

■ **N-COUNT** The **role** of someone or something in a situation is what they should do in it. ❑ *We discussed the role of parents in raising their children.*

■ **N-COUNT** ARTS A **role** is the character that an actor plays in a movie or a play. ❑ *Who plays the role of the doctor?* [from French]

→ look at Word Web: **theater**

Word Partnership	Use **role** with :
ADJ	**active** role, **key** role, **parental** role, **positive** role, **significant** role, **traditional** role, **vital** role ■
	bigger/larger role, **leading** role, **major** role ■ ■
	starring role ■
N	**leadership** role, role **reversal** ■
	lead role ■ ■
V	**play** a role, **take on** a role ■ ■

roll /roʊl/ (rolls, rolling, rolled)

■ **V-T/V-I** When something **rolls**, it moves along a surface, turning over many times. ❑ *The pencil rolled off the desk.* ❑ *I rolled a ball to the baby.*

■ **V-I** When vehicles **roll** along, they move along slowly. ❑ *The truck rolled forward.*

■ **V-I** If drops of liquid **roll** down a surface, they move quickly down it. ❑ *Tears rolled down her cheeks.*

■ **N-COUNT** A **roll** of paper, cloth, or wire is a long piece of it that you form into the shape of a ball or a tube. ❑ *There are twelve rolls of cloth here.*

■ **N-COUNT** A **roll** is an official list of the names of the people in a particular group. ❑ *If your name is not on the roll, you will not have a vote.*

■ **N-COUNT** A **roll** is a small piece of bread that is round or long. ❑ *He spread some butter on a roll.* [from Old French]

■ → see also **rock and roll**

→ look at Picture Dictionary: **bread**

▶ **roll up** If you **roll up** something, you form it into the shape of a ball or tube. ❑ *Steve rolled up the paper bag.*

roll|er /roʊlər/ (rollers) **N-COUNT** A **roller** is a cylinder that turns around in a machine or device. [from Old French]

roll|er-skate (roller-skates, roller-skating, roller-skated)

■ **N-COUNT** **Roller-skates** are boots with small wheels on the bottom. ❑ *...a pair of roller-skates.*

■ **V-I** SPORTS If you **roller-skate**, you move over a flat surface wearing roller-skates. ❑ *Gary was roller-skating outside our house.*

Ro|man /roʊmən/ (Romans)

■ **ADJ** SOCIAL STUDIES **Roman** means related to or connected with ancient Rome and its empire. ❑ *...the Roman Empire.*

■ **N-COUNT** SOCIAL STUDIES A **Roman** was a citizen of ancient Rome or its empire. ❑ *The Romans brought this custom to Britain.*

■ **ADJ** SOCIAL STUDIES **Roman** means related to or connected with modern Rome. ❑ *...a Roman hotel room.*

■ **N-COUNT** SOCIAL STUDIES A **Roman** is someone who lives in or comes from Rome. ❑ *...soccer-mad Romans.* [from Middle English]

r

Picture Dictionary		Roman numerals					
I	1	XI	11	XXI	21	XL	40
II	2	XII	12	XXII	22	L	50
III	3	XIII	13	XXIII	23	LX	60
IV	4	XIV	14	XXIV	24	LXX	70
V	5	XV	15	XXV	25	LXXX	80
VI	6	XVI	16	XXVI	26	XC	90
VII	7	XVII	17	XXVII	27	C	100
VIII	8	XVIII	18	XXVIII	28	D	500
IX	9	XIX	19	XXIX	29	M	1000
X	10	XX	20	XXX	30	MMXIII	2013

Ro|man Catho|lic (**Roman Catholics**)

1 **ADJ** The **Roman Catholic** Church is the same as the **Catholic** Church. ❑ *I am a Roman Catholic priest.*

2 **N-COUNT** A **Roman Catholic** is the same as a **Catholic**. ❑ *Maria was a Roman Catholic.*

ro|mance /roʊmæns, roʊmæns/ (**romances**)

1 **N-COUNT** A **romance** is a relationship between two people who love each other but who are not married. ❑ *After a short romance they got married.*

2 **N-NONCOUNT** **Romance** is the affectionate actions and feelings of people who are in love. ❑ *He still finds time for romance by cooking romantic dinners for his girlfriend.*

3 **N-COUNT** LANGUAGE ARTS A **romance** is a book or a movie about a romantic relationship. ❑ *Claire writes romances and young adult fiction.* [from Old French]
→ look at Word Web: **love**

ro|man|tic /roʊmæntɪk/ **ADJ** You use **romantic** when you are talking about love and romance. ❑ *He was not interested in a romantic relationship with me.* ❑ *It is a lovely romantic movie.* [from French]
→ look at Word Web: **love**

ron|do /rɒndoʊ/ (**rondos**) **N-COUNT** MUSIC A **rondo** is a piece of music in which the main theme is repeated several times, with other themes or sections between each repetition. [from Italian]

roof /ruf/ (**roofs**)

> **PRONUNCIATION HELP**
> Pronounce the plural /rufs/ or /ruvz/.

1 **N-COUNT** The **roof** of a building is the top surface that covers it. ❑ *The house has a red roof.*

2 **N-COUNT** The **roof** of a vehicle is the top of it. ❑ *He listened to the rain on the roof of the car.* [from Old English]

roof

Word Partnership	Use **roof** with :
N	roof **of a building/house**, **metal** roof, **rain on a** roof, **slate** roof, **tin** roof **1**
V	roof **collapses**, roof **leaks**, **repair a** roof **1**
ADJ	**retractable** roof **1** **2**

rook /rʊk/ (**rooks**) **N-COUNT** In chess, a **rook** is one of the pieces that stand in the corners of the board at the beginning of a game. Rooks can move forward, backward, or sideways, but not diagonally.

room /rum/ (**rooms**)

1 **N-COUNT** A **room** is a separate area inside a building that has its own walls. ❑ *A minute later he left the room.*

2 **N-NONCOUNT** If there is **room** somewhere, there is enough empty space. ❑ *There is room for 80 guests.* [from Old English]

3 → see also **chat room, dining room, emergency room, living room, restroom**
→ look at Word Web: **hotel**

room|mate /rummeɪt/ (**roommates**) **N-COUNT** Your **roommate** is the person you share a room or an apartment with. ❑ *Dan and I were roommates in college.*

roost /rust/ (**roosts, roosting, roosted**)

1 **N-COUNT** A **roost** is a place where birds or bats rest or sleep.

2 **V-I** When birds or bats **roost** somewhere, they rest or sleep there. ❑ *The birds roost in nearby bushes.* [from Old English]
→ look at Word Web: **bat**

roost|er /rustər/ (**roosters**) **N-COUNT** A **rooster** is an adult male chicken. [from Old English]

root /rut/ (**roots**)

1 **N-COUNT** The **roots** of a plant are the parts of it that grow under the ground. ❑ *She dug a hole near the roots of an apple tree.*

2 **N-PLURAL** Your **roots** are the place or culture that you come from. ❑ *I am proud of my Brazilian roots.*

3 **N-COUNT** The **root of** of a problem or of an unpleasant situation is the cause of it. ❑ *We got to the root of the problem.* [from Old English]

4 → see also **grassroots**
→ look at Picture Dictionary: **flowers**

Word Partnership	Use **root** with :
N	**tree** root **1**
	root **cause of** *something*, root **of a problem** **3**

root ex|trac|tion (**root extractions**) **N-COUNT/N-NONCOUNT** MATH **Root extraction** is a method of using a particular number to find another number which, when it is multiplied by itself a certain number of times, produces the original number.

root hair (root hairs) **N-COUNT** SCIENCE
A plant's **root hairs** are the thin extensions that grow from its roots and take in water and minerals from the soil.

root sys|tem (root systems) **N-COUNT**
SCIENCE A plant's **root system** is the part of the plant that contains the roots. Compare with **shoot system**.

root word (root words) **N-COUNT**
LANGUAGE ARTS A **root word** is a word or a part of a word to which other letters can be added in order to form new words.

rope /roʊp/ (ropes) **N-COUNT/N-NONCOUNT**
A **rope** is a type of very thick string that is made by twisting together several strings or wires. ❑ He tied the rope around his waist. [from Old English]

rose /roʊz/ (roses)
■ **Rose** is the past tense of **rise**.
■ **N-COUNT** A **rose** is a flower with a pleasant smell. It has thorns on its stems. [from Old English]

rot /rɒt/ (rots, rotting, rotted) **V-T/V-I**
When food, wood, or another substance **rots**, or something **rots** it, it gets old and becomes softer, and sometimes smells bad. ❑ The grain will start to rot after the rain. [from Old English]

ro|tate /roʊteɪt/ (rotates, rotating, rotated)
V-T/V-I When something **rotates**, or when you **rotate** it, it turns in a circle around a central line or point. ❑ The Earth rotates every 24 hours. [from Old English]
→ look at Word Web: **moon**

ro|ta|tion /roʊteɪʃ°n/ (rotations)
■ **N-COUNT/N-NONCOUNT** Rotation is circular movement around a central line or point. A **rotation** is the movement of something through one complete circle. ❑ We learned about the daily rotation of the Earth.
■ **N-COUNT/N-NONCOUNT** MATH In geometry, a **rotation** is a transformation in which the coordinate axes are rotated by a fixed angle about the origin. [from Old English]

rot|ten /rɒt°n/
■ **ADJ** If food, wood, or another substance is **rotten**, it has become old and soft, and

sometimes smells bad. ❑ The smell was very strong—like rotten eggs.
■ **ADJ** If something is **rotten**, it is very unpleasant or bad. [INFORMAL] ❑ I think it's a rotten idea. [from Old Norse]

rough /rʌf/ (rougher, roughest)
■ **ADJ** If a surface is **rough**, it is not smooth or even. ❑ His hands were rough.
■ **ADJ** You say that people or their actions are **rough** when they use too much force. ❑ Football's a rough game. ● **rough|ly** **ADV** ❑ They roughly pushed past him.
■ **ADJ** If you say that someone has a **rough** time, you mean that they have some difficult or unpleasant experiences. ❑ Old people have a rough time in our society.
■ **ADJ** A **rough** idea or guess is not exact or complete. ❑ This is a rough guess of how much gas we need. ● **rough|ly** **ADV** ❑ Cancer kills roughly half a million people a year. [from Old English]

round /raʊnd/ (rounder, roundest, rounds, rounding, rounded)
■ **ADJ** Something that is **round** is shaped like a circle or ball. ❑ She has a round face.
■ **N-COUNT** SPORTS In sports, a **round** is one game or a part of a competition. ❑ The team went through to the fifth round of the competition. ❑ On Sundays, he has a round of golf at the club.
■ **V-T** MATH If you **round** an amount **up** or **down**, or if you **round** it **off**, you change it to the nearest whole number ❑ We needed to round up and round down numbers. [from Old French]
▸ **round up** If the police or army **round up** a number of people, they arrest or capture them. ❑ The police rounded up a number of suspects.

round|ed /raʊndɪd/ **ADJ** Something that is **rounded** is curved in shape, without any points or sharp edges. ❑ We came to a low, rounded hill. [from Old French]

round trip (round trips) **N-COUNT** If you make a **round trip**, you travel to a place and then back again. ❑ The train makes the 2,400-mile round trip every week.

route /rut, raʊt/ (routes) **N-COUNT** A **route** is a way from one place to another. ❑ Which is the most direct route to the center of the town? [from Old French]

r

Word Partnership	Use **route** with :
N	**escape** route, **parade** route
ADJ	**main** route, **scenic** route, **alternative** route, **different** route, **direct** route, **shortest** route

rou|tine /rutin/ (routines)

1 **N-COUNT/N-NONCOUNT** Your **routine** is the usual activities that you do every day. ❑ *The players changed their daily routine.*

2 **ADJ** You use **routine** to describe activities that are done as a normal part of a job or a process. ❑ *...a series of routine medical tests.* [from Old French]

Word Partnership	Use **routine** with :
ADJ	**daily** routine, **normal** routine, **regular** routine, **usual** routine **1**
N	**exercise** routine, **morning** routine **1** routine **maintenance**, routine **tests** **2**

row /roʊ/ (rows, rowing, rowed)

1 **N-COUNT** A **row** is a line of things or people. ❑ *They drove past a row of pretty little houses.*

2 **V-T/V-I** SPORTS When you **row**, you make a boat move through the water by using oars. ❑ *We rowed across the lake.* ❑ *The boatman refused to row the boat to the island.*

3 **PHRASE** If something happens several times **in a row**, it happens that number of times without a break. ❑ *They won five championships in a row.* [from Old English]

row|boat /roʊboʊt/ (rowboats) **N-COUNT**
SPORTS A **rowboat** is a small boat that you move through the water by using oars.
→ look at Word Web: **boat**

roy|al /rɔɪəl/ **ADJ** **Royal** means to do with a king or a queen. ❑ *We have an invitation to a royal garden party.* [from Old French]

roy|al|ty /rɔɪəlti/ **N-NONCOUNT** You sometimes use **royalty** when you are talking about the members of royal families. ❑ *He met royalty and government leaders from around the world.* [from Old French]

rub /rʌb/ (rubs, rubbing, rubbed)

1 **V-T/V-I** If you **rub** a part of your body or if you **rub at** it, you move your hand or fingers backward and forward over it. ❑ *He rubbed at his stiff legs.* ❑ *She took off her glasses and rubbed them with a soft cloth.*

2 **V-T** If you **rub** a substance **into** a surface, you spread it over the surface using your hand. ❑ *He rubbed oil into my back.*

3 **V-T/V-I** If you **rub** two things **together**, or they **rub** together, they move backward and forward, and press against each other. ❑ *He rubbed his hands together.* ❑ *His fingers rubbed together.*

4 **V-T/V-I** If an animal **rubs against** a surface, or **rubs** a part of their body **against** a surface, it moves backward and forward against the surface. ❑ *A cat was rubbing against my leg.* [from Low German]

Word Partnership	Use **rub** with :
PREP	rub **offs**, rub **with** **2**
	rub **against** **4**
ADV	rub **together** **3**

rub|ber /rʌbər/ **N-NONCOUNT** **Rubber** is a strong substance used for making tires, boots, and other products. ❑ *I can smell burning rubber.*

rub|ber band (rubber bands) **N-COUNT**
A **rubber band** is a thin circle of rubber that you put around things such as papers in order to keep them together. ❑ *Her blonde hair was tied back with a rubber band.*
→ look at Picture Dictionary: **office**

ru|bric /rubrɪk/ (rubrics)

1 **N-COUNT** A **rubric** is a title or a heading under which something operates or is studied. [FORMAL]

2 **N-COUNT** A **rubric** is a set of rules or instructions, for example the rules at the beginning of an examination paper. [FORMAL] [from Latin]

ruby /rubi/ (rubies) **N-COUNT** A **ruby** is a dark red stone that is used in jewelry. ❑ *I want a ruby ring.* [from Old French]

rude /rud/ (ruder, rudest)

1 **ADJ** When people are **rude**, they are not polite. ❑ *He's so rude to her friends.* ● **rude|ly** **ADV** ❑ *Some hotel guests treat our employees rudely.* ● **rude|ness** **N-NONCOUNT** ❑ *Mom was annoyed at Cathy's rudeness.*

2 **ADJ** **Rude** words and behavior are likely to embarrass or offend people. ❑ *Fred keeps telling rude jokes.* [from Old French]

ru|di|men|ta|ry /rudɪmɛntəri, -tri/

1 **ADJ** **Rudimentary** things are very basic or simple and are therefore unsatisfactory. [FORMAL] ❑ *There was a rudimentary kitchen.*

2 **ADJ** **Rudimentary** knowledge includes only the simplest and most basic facts. [FORMAL] ❑ *He had only a rudimentary knowledge of French.* [from Latin]

rug /rʌg/ (rugs) **N-COUNT** A **rug** is a piece of thick cloth that you put on a small area of a floor. ❏ *There was a beautiful red rug on the floor.* [of Scandinavian origin]

rug|by /rʌgbi/ **N-NONCOUNT** SPORTS **Rugby** or **rugby football** is a game that is played by two teams who try to get a ball past a line at the end of the field.

ruin /ruɪn/ (ruins, ruining, ruined)
1 **V-T** To **ruin** something means to completely harm, damage, or spoil it. ❏ *My wife was ruining her health.*
2 **N-PLURAL** The **ruins** of a building are the parts of it that remain after something destroys the rest. ❏ *Police found two bodies in the ruins of the house.*
3 **PHRASE** If a place is **in ruins**, only parts of it remain. ❏ *The church was in ruins.* [from Old French]

rule /ruːl/ (rules, ruling, ruled)
1 **N-COUNT** **Rules** are instructions that tell you what you must do or must not do. ❏ *I need a book that explains the rules of basketball.*
2 **N-COUNT** LANGUAGE ARTS SCIENCE The **rules of** a language or a science are statements that describe the way that things usually happen in a particular situation. ❏ *...the rules of the language.*
3 **V-T/V-I** SOCIAL STUDIES The person or group that **rules** a country controls its affairs. ❏ *King Hussein ruled for 46 years.* ❏ *For four centuries, foreigners have ruled Angola.*
4 **PHRASE** If you say that something happens **as a rule**, you mean that it usually happens. ❏ *As a rule, I walk to work rather than drive.*
5 If you **rule out** a course of action, an idea, or a solution, you decide that it is impossible or not practical. [from Old French]

Thesaurus	**rule** Also look up :
N	guideline, law, standard **1** **2**
V	command, dictate, govern **3**

Word Partnership	Use **rule** with :
V	**break** a rule, **change** a rule, **follow** a rule **1**
N	**gag** rule **1**
	exception to a rule **1** **2**
PREP	**against** a rule, **under** a rule **1** **2**

rul|er /ruːlər/ (rulers)
1 **N-COUNT** SOCIAL STUDIES The **ruler** of a country is the person who rules it. ❏ *He was the ruler of France at that time.*
2 **N-COUNT** MATH A **ruler** is a long, flat object that you use for measuring things and for drawing straight lines. [from Old French]
→ look at Picture Dictionary: **measurement**

rul|ing /ruːlɪŋ/ (rulings)
1 **ADJ** SOCIAL STUDIES The **ruling** group of people in a country or an organization is the group that controls its affairs. ❏ *...a ruling party politician.*
2 **N-COUNT** SOCIAL STUDIES A **ruling** is an official decision made by a judge or a court. ❏ *He was angry at the court's ruling.* [from Old French]

rum|ble /rʌmbəl/ (rumbles, rumbling, rumbled)
1 **N-COUNT** A **rumble** is a low, continuous noise. ❏ *We could hear the distant rumble of traffic.*
2 **V-I** If something **rumbles**, it makes a low, continuous noise. ❏ *Her stomach was rumbling because she did not eat breakfast.* [from Middle Dutch]

ru|mor /ruːmər/ (rumors)
N-COUNT/N-NONCOUNT A **rumor** is information that people talk about, that may not be true. ❏ *Last year, a rumor circulated that I was ill.* [from Old French]

Word Partnership	Use **rumor** with :
ADJ	**false** rumor
V	**hear** a rumor, **spread** a rumor, **start** a rumor

run
1 VERB USES
2 NOUN USES AND PHRASAL VERBS

1 run /rʌn/ (runs, running, ran, run)

LANGUAGE HELP
The form **run** is used in the present tense and is also the past participle of the verb.

1 **V-T/V-I** SPORTS When you **run**, you move very quickly on your legs. ❏ *It's very dangerous to run across the road.* ❏ *We had to run home.*
2 **N-COUNT** SPORTS **Run** is also a noun. ❏ *After a six-mile run, Jackie went home for breakfast.*
3 **V-I** If a road **runs** in a particular direction, it goes in that direction. ❏ *The road runs east from Highway 6 to Crownpoint.*
4 **V-T** If you **run** your hand **through** something, you move your hand through it. ❏ *He ran his fingers through his hair.*
5 **V-I** SOCIAL STUDIES If someone **runs for** office in an election, they take part as a

candidate. ❑ *He announced that he was running for president.*

6 **V-T** BUSINESS If you **run** a business or an activity, you are in charge of it. ❑ *She runs a restaurant in San Francisco.*

7 **V-I** If you talk about how a system or an organization **is running**, you are saying how well it is operating or progressing. ❑ *The system is now running smoothly.*

8 **V-T/V-I** If you **run** an experiment or other process, or start it **running**, you start it and let it continue. ❑ *The doctor ran some tests and found that I had an infection.*

9 **V-T/V-I** When a machine **is running**, or when you **are running** it, it is switched on and is working. ❑ *Sam waited in the car, with the engine running.*

10 **V-I** When vehicles **run** from one place to another, they take passengers between those two places. ❑ *A bus runs between the station and downtown.*

11 **V-I** If a liquid **runs** in a particular direction, it flows in that direction. ❑ *Tears were running down her cheeks.*

12 **V-I** ARTS If a play or an event **runs** for a particular period of time, it lasts for that period of time. ❑ *The play ran for only three months.*

13 **V-I** If someone or something **is running** late, they have taken more time than was planned. ❑ *I'll call you back later, I'm running late.* [from Old English]

14 → see also **running**

Thesaurus	run	Also look up :
v	dash, jog, sprint **1**	
	follow, go **2**	
	administer, conduct, manage **6**	

❷ **run** /rʌn/ (**runs, running, ran, run**)

LANGUAGE HELP
The form **run** is used in the present tense and is also the past participle of the verb.

1 **N-COUNT** SPORTS A **run** is one point in the game of baseball. ❑ *The Blue Jays have scored 173 runs in their past 24 games.*

2 **PHRASE** You use **in the long run**, to say what you think will happen over a long period of time in the future. ❑ *Spending more on education now will save money in the long run.* [from Old English]

▶ **run away** If you **run away**, you leave a place because you are unhappy or afraid there. ❑ *The girl turned and ran away.*

▶ **run into** **1** If you **run into** someone, you

meet them unexpectedly. ❑ *He ran into William in the supermarket.*

2 If a vehicle **runs into** something, it hits it. ❑ *The driver was going too fast and ran into a tree.*

▶ **run off** If someone **runs off**, they go away from a place when they should stay there. ❑ *Our dog is always running off.* ❑ *The thief ran off with her purse.*

▶ **run out** If you **run out of** something, you have no more of it left. ❑ *We ran out of milk this morning.*

▶ **run over** If a vehicle **runs** someone **over**, it hits them and they fall to the ground. ❑ *A police car ran her over.*

run-down

1 **ADJ** If someone is **run-down**, they are tired or slightly sick. [INFORMAL]

2 **ADJ** A **run-down** building or area is in very bad condition. ❑ *He promised financial help for run-down areas.*

rung /rʌŋ/ (**rungs**)

1 **Rung** is the past participle of **ring**.

2 **N-COUNT** The **rungs** of a ladder are the steps that you climb up. [from Old English]

run|ner /rʌnər/ (**runners**)

1 **N-COUNT** SPORTS A **runner** is a person who runs, or who is running. ❑ *He is the oldest runner in the race.*

2 **N-COUNT** SCIENCE On a plant, **runners** are long shoots that grow from the main stem and put down roots to form a new plant. [from Old English]

→ look at Word Web: **park**

run|ner-up (**runners-up**) **N-COUNT** SPORTS A **runner-up** is the person who is in second place in a race or a competition. ❑ *The runner-up will receive $500.*

run|ning /rʌnɪŋ/

1 **N-NONCOUNT** SPORTS **Running** is the activity or sport of moving very quickly on your legs. ❑ *He goes running every morning.*

2 **ADJ** You use **running** to describe things that continue or keep occurring over a period of time. ❑ *He began a running argument with Dean.*

3 **ADJ** A **running** total is a total that changes because numbers keep being added to it as something progresses. ❑ *He kept a running total of who called him.*

4 **ADV** You can use **running** when indicating that something keeps happening. ❑ *A lack of rain caused crop failure for the second year running.*

5 → see also **run**

6 **PHRASE** If someone is **in the running for** something, they have a good chance of winning or obtaining it. If they are **out of the running for** something, they have no chance of winning or obtaining it. ❑ *Four people are in the running for managing director.* [from Old English]

run|ny /rʌni/ (**runnier, runniest**)

1 **ADJ** Something that is **runny** has more liquid than usual. ❑ *Warm the jelly until it is runny.*

2 **ADJ** If someone has a **runny** nose, a thick liquid flows from their nose. [from Old English]

run|off /rʌnɔf/ **N-NONCOUNT** SCIENCE Runoff is rainwater that forms a stream rather than being absorbed by the ground.

run-through (**run-throughs**) **N-COUNT** ARTS A **run-through** for a show or event is a practice for it.

run|way /rʌnweɪ/ (**runways**) **N-COUNT** A **runway** is a long road that an aircraft travels on before it starts flying. [from Old English]

rup|ture /rʌptʃər/ (**ruptures, rupturing, ruptured**)

1 **N-COUNT** SCIENCE A **rupture** is a severe injury in which an internal part of your body tears or bursts open. ❑ *He died after a rupture in a blood vessel in his head.*

2 **V-T/V-I** If a person or animal **ruptures** a part of their body or if it **ruptures**, it tears or bursts open. ❑ *His stomach might rupture.* ❑ *I ruptured a tendon in my knee.*

3 **N-COUNT** If there is a **rupture** between people, relations between them get much worse or end completely. ❑ *...a rupture in the political relations between countries.*

4 **V-T** If someone or something **ruptures** relations between people, they damage them, causing them to become worse or to end. ❑ *Fights between protesters and police ruptured the city's government.* [from Latin] → look at Word Web: **crash**

ru|ral /rʊərəl/ **ADJ** Rural places are not near cities or large towns. ❑ *The service is ideal for people who live in rural areas.* [from Old French]

rush /rʌʃ/ (**rushes, rushing, rushed**)

1 **V-I** If you **rush** somewhere, you go there quickly. ❑ *Emma rushed into the room.*

2 **V-T** If people **rush to** do something, they do it quickly. ❑ *Foreign banks rushed to buy as many dollars as they could.*

3 **V-T/V-I** If you **rush** something, or **rush into** something, you do it too quickly or too soon. ❑ *Don't rush the decision. Take a day or two to think about it.* ❑ *He will not rush into marriage.*

● **rushed** **ADJ** ❑ *...a rushed job.*

4 **PHRASE** If you do something **in a rush**, you need to do it quickly. ❑ *The men left in a rush.*

5 **V-T** If you **rush** someone to a place, you take them there quickly. ❑ *They rushed him to a hospital.* [from Old French]

Word Partnership	Use **rush** with :
N	**evening** rush, **morning** rush **3**
ADJ	**mad** rush, **sudden** rush **4**

rush hour (**rush hours**)
N-COUNT/N-NONCOUNT The **rush hour** is a period of the day when most people are traveling to or from their job. ❑ *Try to avoid traveling during the evening rush hour.*

rust /rʌst/ (**rusts, rusting, rusted**)

1 **N-NONCOUNT** Rust is a red-brown substance that forms on iron or steel when it is wet. ❑ *The old car was red with rust.*

2 **V-I** When a metal object **rusts**, rust starts to appear on it. ❑ *Iron rusts.* [from Old English]

rus|tle /rʌsəl/ (**rustles, rustling, rustled**)

1 **V-T/V-I** When something thin and dry **rustles**, or when you **rustle** it, it makes soft sounds as it moves. ❑ *The leaves rustled in the wind.*

2 **N-COUNT** Rustle is also a noun. ❑ *We listened to the rustle of leaves outside.* [from Old English]

rusty /rʌsti/ (**rustier, rustiest**) **ADJ** A **rusty** metal object has some rust on it. ❑ *The house has a rusty iron gate.* [from Old English]

rut /rʌt/ (**ruts**)

1 **N-COUNT** If someone is **in a rut**, he or she has a particular way of doing things that is difficult to change. ❑ *I don't like being in a rut.*

2 **N-COUNT** A **rut** is a deep, narrow mark that the wheels of a vehicle make in the ground. ❑ *He drove slowly over the ruts in the road.* [from French]

ruth|less /ruθlɪs/ **ADJ** If someone is **ruthless**, they are so determined to do something that they do not care if their actions harm other people. ❑ *...a ruthless dictator.* [from Middle English]

rye /raɪ/ **N-NONCOUNT** Rye is a grain that you can use to make flour, bread, or other foods. [from Old English]

r

Ss

sack /sæk/ (**sacks**) **N-COUNT** A **sack** is a large bag made of thick paper or rough material. ❑ ...*a sack of potatoes.* [from Old English]

sa|cred /seɪkrɪd/ **ADJ** Something that is **sacred** has a special religious meaning. ❑ *The eagle is sacred to Native Americans.* [from Latin]

sac|ri|fice /sækrɪfaɪs/ (**sacrifices, sacrificing, sacrificed**)
1 **V-T** If you **sacrifice** something that is valuable or important, you give it up in order to get something else for yourself or for other people. ❑ *She sacrificed family life for her career.*
2 **N-COUNT/N-NONCOUNT** **Sacrifice** is also a noun. ❑ *The family made many sacrifices so that they could send the children to a good school.*
3 **V-T** To **sacrifice** an animal or a person means to kill them in a special religious ceremony in order to say thank you to a god. ❑ *The priest sacrificed a chicken.* [from Old French]

sad /sæd/ (**sadder, saddest**)
1 **ADJ** If you are **sad**, you feel unhappy. ❑ *I'm sad that Jason's leaving.* ● **sad|ly** **ADV** ❑ *"My girlfriend is moving away," he said sadly.*
● **sad|ness** **N-NONCOUNT** ❑ *I left with a mixture of sadness and joy.*
2 **ADJ** If something is **sad**, it makes you feel sad. ❑ *It was a sad ending to a great story.* ❑ *I have some sad news for you.*
3 **ADJ** A **sad** event or situation is unfortunate or undesirable. ❑ *The sad truth is that I never opened that present.* [from Old English]
→ look at Word Webs: **cry, emotion**

Thesaurus sad Also look up :

ADJ	depressed, down, gloomy, unhappy; (ant.) cheerful, happy **1**
	miserable, tragic, unhappy **3**

Word Partnership Use sad with :

V	feel sad, look sad, seem sad **1**
N	sad eyes **1**
	sad news, sad story **2**
	sad day, sad fact, sad truth **3**
ADV	kind of sad, a little sad, really sad, so sad, too sad **1**–**3**

sad|dle /sædᵊl/ (**saddles**)
1 **N-COUNT** A **saddle** is a leather seat that you put on the back of an animal. ❑ *He put a saddle on the horse.*
2 **N-COUNT** A **saddle** is a seat on a bicycle or a motorcycle. [from Old English]
→ look at Picture Dictionary: **horse**

saddle

sa|fa|ri /səfɑri/ (**safaris**) **N-COUNT** A **safari** is a trip to look at or hunt wild animals. ❑ *She went on a seven-day African safari.* [from Swahili]

safe /seɪf/ (**safer, safest, safes**)
1 **ADJ** Something that is **safe** is not dangerous. ❑ *We must try to make our roads safer.*
2 **ADJ** If a person or thing is **safe**, they are not in danger. ❑ *Where's Sophie? Is she safe?*
● **safe|ly** **ADV** ❑ *"Drive safely," he said, waving goodbye.*
3 **N-COUNT** A **safe** is a strong metal box with a lock, where you keep money or other valuable things. ❑ *Who has the key to the safe?* [from Old French]

Word Partnership Use safe with :

N	safe **drinking water**, safe **environment**, safe **neighborhood**, safe **operation**, safe **place**, safe **streets** **1**
	children/kids are safe, safe **at home** **2**
ADV	**completely** safe, **perfectly** safe, **reasonably** safe, **relatively** safe **1** **2**

S

safe|guard /seɪfgɑrd/ (**safeguards, safeguarding, safeguarded**)

1 **V-T** To **safeguard** something or someone means to protect them from being harmed, lost, or badly treated. [FORMAL] ❑ *We must act now to safeguard the planet.*

2 **N-COUNT** SOCIAL STUDIES A **safeguard** is a law, a rule, or a measure intended to prevent someone or something from being harmed. ❑ *There are no safeguards to protect people from harm.*

safe|ty /seɪfti/

1 **N-NONCOUNT** **Safety** is the state of not being in danger. ❑ *We need to improve safety on our roads.*

2 **ADJ** **Safety** equipment is intended to make something less dangerous. ❑ *There are child safety locks on all the gates.* [from Old French]

Word Partnership	Use **safety** with :
V	**improve** safety, **provide** safety **1** **ensure** safety **1**
N	**child** safety, **fire** safety, **health and** safety, safety **measures**, safety **regulations**, safety **standards** **1** safety **device**, safety **equipment** **2**

---

sag /sæg/ (**sags, sagging, sagged**) **V-I** When something **sags**, it hangs down loosely or folds in the middle. ❑ *The dress won't sag or lose its shape after washing.* [of Scandinavian origin]

said /sɛd/ **Said** is the past tense and past participle of **say**. [from Old English]

sail /seɪl/ (**sails, sailing, sailed**)

1 **N-COUNT** **Sails** are large pieces of cloth on a boat, that catch the wind and move the boat along.

2 **V-I** A boat **sails** when it moves over water. ❑ *The ferry sails between Seattle and Bremerton.*

sail

3 **V-T/V-I** SPORTS If you **sail** a boat, or if a boat **sails**, you use its sails to move it across water. ❑ *I'd like to buy a big boat and sail around the world.* [from Old English]

→ look at Word Web: **boat**

sail|boat /seɪlboʊt/ (**sailboats**) **N-COUNT** SPORTS A **sailboat** is a boat with sails.

sail|ing /seɪlɪŋ/ **N-NONCOUNT** SPORTS **Sailing** is the activity or sport of sailing boats. ❑ *There was swimming and sailing on the lake.* [from Old English]

sail|or /seɪlər/ (**sailors**) **N-COUNT** A **sailor** is someone who works on a ship or sails a boat. [from Old English]

saint /seɪnt/ (**saints**) **N-COUNT** In certain religions, a **saint** is someone who has died, and whose life was a perfect example of the way people should live. ❑ *Every church here was named after a saint.* [from Old French]

sake /seɪk/

1 **PHRASE** If you do something **for the sake of** something or someone, you do it because of them. ❑ *For the sake of peace, I am willing to forgive them.* ❑ *They stayed together for the sake of the children.*

2 **PHRASE** If you do something **for** something's or someone's **sake**, you do it to help them or because of them. ❑ *For safety's sake, never stand directly behind a horse.* ❑ *Please do a good job, for Stan's sake.* [from Old English]

sal|ad /sæləd/ (**salads**)

N-COUNT/N-NONCOUNT A **salad** is a mixture of foods, especially vegetables, that you usually serve cold. ❑ *She ordered a pasta and a green salad.* [from Old French]

sala|man|der /sæləmændər/ (**salamanders**) **N-COUNT** A **salamander** is an animal that looks rather like a lizard, and that can live both on land and in water. [from Old French]

sala|ry /sæləri/ (**salaries**)

N-COUNT/N-NONCOUNT BUSINESS A **salary** is the money that you earn from your employer. ❑ *The lawyer was paid a huge salary.* [from Latin]

sale /seɪl/ (**sales**)

1 **N-SING** BUSINESS The **sale** of something is the act of selling it for money. ❑ *He made a lot of money from the sale of the business.*

2 **N-COUNT** BUSINESS A **sale** is a time when a store sells things at less than their normal price. ❑ *Did you know the book store was having a sale?*

3 **N-PLURAL** BUSINESS The **sales** of a product are the quantity of it that is sold. ❑ *The newspaper has sales of 1.72 million.*

4 **PHRASE** If something is **for sale**, it is available for people to buy. ❑ *The house had a "For Sale" sign in the yard.*

S

5 **PHRASE** BUSINESS Products that are **on sale** are available for less than their normal price. ❑ *She bought the coat on sale at a department store.*

6 **PHRASE** BUSINESS Products that are **on sale** can be bought. ❑ *Tickets go on sale this week.* [from Old English]

sales clerk (**sales clerks**) also **salesclerk** **N-COUNT** BUSINESS A **sales clerk** is a person who works in a store and sells things to customers.

sales|man /seɪlzmən/ (**salesmen**) **N-COUNT** BUSINESS A **salesman** is a man whose job is to sell things. ❑ *He's an insurance salesman.*

sales|person /seɪlzpɜrsᵊn/ (**salespeople** or **salespersons**) **N-COUNT** BUSINESS A **salesperson** is a person whose job is to sell things. ❑ *Be sure to ask the salesperson for help.*

sales|woman /seɪlzwʊmən/ (**saleswomen**) **N-COUNT** BUSINESS A **saleswoman** is a woman whose job is to sell things. ❑ *She spent three years as a traveling perfume saleswoman.*

sa|lin|ity /səlɪnɪti/ **N-NONCOUNT** SCIENCE The **salinity** of water is the amount of salt it contains. [from Late Latin]

sa|li|va /səlaɪvə/ **N-NONCOUNT** SCIENCE **Saliva** is the liquid in your mouth that helps you to swallow food. [from Latin]

salm|on /sæmən/ (**salmon**) **1** **N-COUNT** A **salmon** is a large fish with silver skin.

2 **N-NONCOUNT** **Salmon** is the pink flesh of this fish that you can eat. ❑ *He gave them a plate of salmon.* [from Old French]

sa|lon /səlɑn/ (**salons**) **N-COUNT** A **salon** is a place where you go to have your hair cut, or to have beauty treatments. ❑ *The club has a beauty salon and two swimming pools.* [from French]

salt /sɔlt/ (**salts**) **1** **N-NONCOUNT** **Salt** is a white substance that you use to improve the flavor of food. ❑ *Now add salt and pepper.*

2 **N-COUNT** SCIENCE **Salts** are substances that are formed when an acid reacts with an alkali. ❑ *The rock is rich in mineral salts.* [from Old English]
→ look at Word Web: **crystal**

salt

sal|ta|tion /sælteɪʃⁿn/ **N-NONCOUNT** SCIENCE **Saltation** is the movement of sand and other particles as a result of being blown by the wind. [from Latin]

salt|water /sɔltwɔtər/ also **salt water** **1** **N-NONCOUNT** **Saltwater** is water, especially from the ocean, that has salt in it.

2 **ADJ** **Saltwater** fish live in water that is salty. **Saltwater** lakes contain salty water. ❑ *...useful information for owners of saltwater fish.*
→ look at Word Web: **ocean**

salty /sɔlti/ (**saltier, saltiest**) **ADJ** Something that is **salty** has salt in it or tastes of salt. ❑ *Ham and bacon are salty foods.* [from Old English]
→ look at Word Web: **taste**

sa|lute /səlut/ (**salutes, saluting, saluted**) **1** **V-T/V-I** If you **salute** someone, you make a special sign to show your respect for them. Soldiers usually do this by raising their right hand to their head. ❑ *I saluted as the captain entered the room.* ❑ *I stood to attention and saluted my senior officer.*

2 **N-COUNT** **Salute** is also a noun. ❑ *He gave his salute and left.* [from Latin]

sal|vage /sælvɪdʒ/ (**salvages, salvaging, salvaged**) **1** **V-T** If something **is salvaged**, someone manages to save it, for example from a ship that has sunk, or from a building that has been damaged. ❑ *The team had to decide what equipment could be salvaged.*

2 **N-NONCOUNT** **Salvage** is the act of salvaging things from somewhere such as a damaged ship or building. ❑ *The salvage operation went on.*

3 **N-NONCOUNT** The **salvage** from somewhere such as a damaged ship or building is the things that are saved from it. ❑ *They climbed up the hill with their salvage.*

4 **V-T** If you manage to **salvage** a difficult situation, you manage to get something useful from it so that it is not a complete failure. ❑ *We tried hard to salvage the situation.* [from Old French]

sal|va|tion /sælveɪʃⁿn/ **1** **N-NONCOUNT** In Christianity, **salvation** is the fact that Christ has saved a person from evil. ❑ *The church's message of salvation has changed many lives.*

2 **N-NONCOUNT** The **salvation** of someone or something is the act of saving them from harm, destruction, or an unpleasant

S

situation. ❏ *She felt that writing was her salvation.* [from Old French]

same /seɪm/

1 **ADJ** If one thing is **the same** thing **as** another, they are very similar to each other in some way. ❏ *All these people have the same experience in the job.*

2 **PRON** Same is also a pronoun. ❏ *The houses are all the same.*

3 **ADJ** You use **same** to show that you are talking about only one thing, and not two different ones. ❏ *Jayden works at the same office as Gabrielle.* ❏ *He gets up at the same time every day.*

4 **ADJ** Something that is still **the same** has not changed in any way. ❏ *If prices rise and your income stays the same, you have to buy less.*

5 **PRON** You use **the same** to refer to something that has previously been mentioned or suggested. ❏ *I breathed deeply and watched Terry do the same.* [from Old Norse]

Thesaurus	same	Also look up :
ADJ	alike, equal, identical; *(ant.)* different **1**	

sam|ple /sæmpəl/ (**samples**) **N-COUNT**
A **sample** is a small amount of something that shows you what the rest of it is like. ❏ *We're giving away 2,000 free samples.* ❏ *The doctor took a blood sample.* [from Old French]
→ look at Word Web: **laboratory**

sanc|tion /sæŋkʃən/ (**sanctions, sanctioning, sanctioned**)

1 **V-T** If someone in authority **sanctions** an action or a practice, they officially approve of it and allow it to be done. ❏ *He may now sanction the use of force.*

2 **N-NONCOUNT** Sanction is also a noun. ❏ *The newspaper is run by citizens without the sanction of the government.*

3 **N-PLURAL** SOCIAL STUDIES **Sanctions** are measures taken by countries to restrict trade and official contact with a country that has broken international law. ❏ *Unfortunately, they have no power to impose sanctions on countries that break the rules.* [from Latin]

Word Partnership	Use sanction with :
PREP	**without** sanction **1**
	sanction **against** **2**
ADJ	**legal** sanction, **official** sanction, **proposed** sanction **1** **2**
V	**impose a** sanction, **lift a** sanction **2**

sanc|tu|ary /sæŋktʃuɛri/ (**sanctuaries**)

1 **N-COUNT/N-NONCOUNT** A **sanctuary** is a place where people who are in danger from other people can go to be safe. ❏ *His church became a sanctuary for homeless people.*

2 **N-COUNT** A **sanctuary** is a place where birds or animals are protected and allowed to live freely. ❏ *...a bird sanctuary.* [from Old French]

sand /sænd/ **N-NONCOUNT** SCIENCE **Sand** is a powder made of very small pieces of stone. Some deserts and most beaches are made of sand. ❏ *They walked across the sand to the water's edge.* [from Old English]

sand

→ look at Picture Dictionary: **desert**
→ look at Word Webs: **beach, erosion, glass**

san|dal /sændəl/ (**sandals**) **N-COUNT** Sandals are light shoes that you wear in warm weather. ❏ *He put on a pair of old sandals.* [from Medieval Latin]
→ look at Picture Dictionary: **shoe**

sand dune (**sand dunes**) **N-COUNT** GEOGRAPHY A **sand dune** is a hill of sand near the sea or in a sand desert.

sand|wich /sænwɪtʃ, sænd-/ (**sandwiches**) **N-COUNT** A **sandwich** is two slices of bread with another food such as cheese or meat between them. ❏ *She ordered a ham sandwich.*
→ look at Word Web: **meal**

sandy /sændi/ (**sandier, sandiest**) **ADJ** A **sandy** area is covered with sand. ❏ *The island has long, sandy beaches.* [from Old English]

sane /seɪn/ (**saner, sanest**) **ADJ** Someone who is **sane** can think and behave normally and reasonably, and is not mad. ❏ *He seemed perfectly sane.* [from Latin]

sang /sæŋ/ **Sang** is the past tense of **sing**.

sank /sæŋk/ **Sank** is the past tense of **sink**. [from Old English]

sar|casm /sɑrkæzəm/ **N-NONCOUNT** If you say something with **sarcasm**, you say the opposite of what you mean in order to be rude to someone. ❏ *"How nice of you to join us,"* he said with heavy sarcasm. [from Late Latin]

sar|cas|tic /sɑrkæstɪk/ **ADJ** If you say something in a **sarcastic** way, you say the opposite of what you really mean in order to be rude to someone. ❑ *He made some very sarcastic comments.* [from Late Latin]

sar|dine /sɑrdin/ (**sardines**) **N-COUNT** Sardines are small sea fish that you can eat. ❑ *They opened a can of sardines.* [from Old French]

sar|gas|sum /sɑrgæsəm/ **N-NONCOUNT** SCIENCE **Sargassum** is seaweed and other plant material that has formed into a large floating mass. [from New Latin]

sat /sæt/ **Sat** is the past tense and past participle of **sit**. [from Old English]

sat|el|lite /sæt³laɪt/ (**satellites**)
1 **N-COUNT** TECHNOLOGY A **satellite** is a piece of electronic equipment that is sent into space in order to receive and send back information. ❑ *The rocket carried two communications satellites.*
2 **ADJ** TECHNOLOGY **Satellite navigation** is a system that uses information from a satellite to help you to find your way. ❑ *Many of the boats have satellite navigation.* [from Latin]
→ look at Word Webs: **satellite, astronomer, forecast, navigation, radio, television**

sat|el|lite dish (**satellite dishes**) **N-COUNT** TECHNOLOGY A **satellite dish** is a piece of equipment that people put on their house in order to receive television signals from a satellite.

sat|el|lite tele|vi|sion **N-NONCOUNT** TECHNOLOGY **Satellite television** is a system of broadcasting television programs that are sent to your television from a satellite. ❑ *We have access to 49 satellite television channels.*

sat|in /sæt³n/ **N-NONCOUNT** **Satin** is a smooth, shiny type of cloth. ❑ *She's wearing a satin dress.* [from Old French]

sat|ire /sætaɪər/ (**satires**)
1 **N-NONCOUNT** **Satire** is the use of humor to criticize people's behavior or ideas. ❑ *He loved the book's humor and satire.*
2 **N-COUNT** LANGUAGE ARTS A **satire** is a play, a movie, or a piece of writing that uses humor to criticize people's behavior or ideas. ❑ *The movie is a satire on American politics.* [from Latin]

sat|is|fac|tion /sætɪsfækʃ³n/ **N-NONCOUNT** If you feel **satisfaction**, you feel pleased to do or get something. ❑ *It gives me a real sense of satisfaction when I help someone.* [from French]

sat|is|fac|tory /sætɪsfæktəri/ **ADJ** Something that is **satisfactory** is good enough for a particular purpose. ❑ *I never got a satisfactory answer.* [from French]

sat|is|fied /sætɪsfaɪd/ **ADJ** If you are **satisfied with** something, you are happy because you have what you wanted. ❑ *Doctors are satisfied with his condition.* [from Old French]

Word Link	sat, satis ≈ enough : dis*satis*fied, *satis*fy, un*satis*factory

sat|is|fy /sætɪsfaɪ/ (**satisfies, satisfying, satisfied**)
1 **V-T** If someone or something **satisfies** you, they give you enough of what you want or need. ❑ *Milk alone should satisfy your baby's hunger.*
2 **V-T** If you **satisfy** the requirements for something, you are good enough or have the right qualities. ❑ *Private companies have to satisfy the needs of their workers.* [from Old French]

sat|is|fy|ing /sætɪsfaɪɪŋ/ **ADJ** Something that is **satisfying** makes you feel happy because it is what you want. ❑ *Taking care of children can be very satisfying.* [from Old French]

Word Web satellite

The **moon** is the earth's best-known **satellite**. In 1957 humans began **launching** objects into **space**. Today, hundreds of satellites **orbit** the **planet**. The largest satellite is the International **Space Station**. Others, such as the Hubble Telescope, help us learn more about **outer space**. The NOAA 12 measures the earth's climate. TV weather forecasts often use feature pictures taken from satellites.

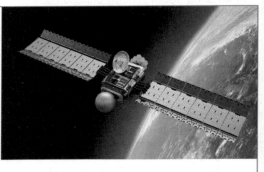

satu|rat|ed /sǽtʃəreɪtɪd/ **ADJ** Saturated fats are types of fat that are found in some foods, especially meat, eggs, butter, and cheese. ❑ ...foods that are rich in cholesterol and saturated fats. [from Latin]

satu|rat|ed hydro|car|bon (**saturated hydrocarbons**) **N-COUNT** SCIENCE A **saturated hydrocarbon** is a compound of hydrogen and carbon which contains the maximum number of hydrogen atoms.

satu|rat|ed so|lu|tion (**saturated solutions**) **N-COUNT** SCIENCE A **saturated solution** is a liquid that contains so much of a dissolved substance that it is unable to contain any more of it.

Sat|ur|day /sǽtərdeɪ, -di/ (**Saturdays**) **N-COUNT/N-NONCOUNT** Saturday is the day after Friday and before Sunday. ❑ He called her on Saturday morning. ❑ Every Saturday, Dad made soup. [from Old English]

Sat|urn /sǽtərn/ **N-PROPER** SCIENCE Saturn is the sixth planet from the sun. It is surrounded by rings made of ice and dust. [from Latin]

sauce /sɔs/ (**sauces**) **N-COUNT/N-NONCOUNT** A **sauce** is a thick liquid that you eat with other food. ❑ The pasta is cooked in a garlic and tomato sauce. [from Old French]
→ look at Word Web: **ketchup**

sauce|pan /sɔspæn/ (**saucepans**) **N-COUNT** A **saucepan** is a deep metal cooking pot, usually with a long handle and a lid. ❑ Place the potatoes in a saucepan and boil them. → look at Word Web: **pan**

sau|cer /sɔsər/ (**saucers**) **N-COUNT** A **saucer** is a small curved plate that you put under a cup. [from Old French]
→ look at Picture Dictionary: **dish**

sau|na /sɔnə/ (**saunas**) **N-COUNT** A **sauna** is a very hot room where people relax. ❑ The hotel has a sauna and a swimming pool. [from Finnish]

sau|sage /sɔsɪdʒ/ (**sausages**) **N-COUNT/N-NONCOUNT** A **sausage** is a mixture of very small pieces of meat, spices, and other foods, inside a long thin skin. ❑ They ate sausages for breakfast. [from Old Norman French]

sav|age /sǽvɪdʒ/ **ADJ** Someone or something that is **savage** is very cruel or violent. ❑ This was a savage attack on a young girl. [from Old French]

sa|van|na /səvǽnə/ (**savannas**) also **savannah** **N-COUNT/N-NONCOUNT** GEOGRAPHY A **savanna** is a large area of flat, grassy land, usually in Africa. [from Spanish]

save /seɪv/ (**saves, saving, saved**)

1 **V-T** If you **save** someone or something, you help them to escape from a dangerous or bad situation. ❑ We must save these children from disease and death.

2 **V-T/V-I** If you **save**, you gradually collect money by spending less than you get. ❑ Tim and Barbara are now saving for a house. ❑ I was saving money to go to college.

3 **Save up** means the same as **save**. ❑ Taylor was saving up for something special.

4 **V-T/V-I** If you **save** time or money, you use less of it. ❑ Going through the city by bike saves time. ❑ Families move in together to save on rent.

5 **V-T** If you **save** something, you keep it because you will need it later. ❑ Save the vegetable water for making the sauce.

6 **V-T/V-I** TECHNOLOGY If you **save** information in a computer, you give the computer an instruction to store the information. ❑ It's important to save frequently when you are working on a document. ❑ Save your work regularly.

7 **N-COUNT** SPORTS In a sports game, if you make a **save**, you stop someone from scoring a goal. ❑ The goalkeeper made some great saves. [from Old French]

sav|ings /seɪvɪŋz/ **N-PLURAL** Your **savings** are the money that you have saved, especially in a bank. ❑ Her savings were in the First National Bank. [from Old French]

sa|vory /seɪvəri/ **ADJ** Savory food has a salty flavor rather than a sweet one. ❑ We had all sorts of sweet and savory breads. [from Old French]

saw /sɔ/ (**saws, sawing, sawed, sawed** or **sawn**)

1 **Saw** is the past tense of **see**.

2 **N-COUNT** A **saw** is a metal tool for cutting wood.

3 **V-T/V-I** If you **saw** something, you cut it with a saw. ❑ He escaped by sawing through the bars of his jail cell. ❑ I sawed the dead branches off the tree. [from Old English]
→ look at Picture Dictionaries: **cut, tool**

saxo|phone /sǽksəfoʊn/ (**saxophones**) **N-COUNT/N-NONCOUNT** MUSIC A **saxophone** is a musical instrument made of metal that you play by blowing into it.

S

say /seɪ/ (**says** /sɛz/, **saying, said** /sɛd/)
■ **V-T** When you **say** something, you speak words. ❑ *She said that they were very pleased.*
❑ *I packed and said goodbye to Charlie.*
■ **V-T** If a piece of writing **says** something, that is the information contained in it.
❑ *Our report says six people were injured.*
■ **V-T** If you **say** something **to yourself**, you think it. ❑ *"I'm still dreaming," I said to myself.*
■ **V-T** You use **say** to show that you are expressing an opinion or stating a fact.
❑ *I would say this is probably illegal.*
■ **N-SING** If you have **a say in** something, you have the right to give your opinion.
❑ *He has the right to have a say in the decisions that affect his life.*
■ **V-T** If a map or a clock **says** something, it gives information in writing, numbers, or signs. ❑ *The clock said four minutes past eleven.*
■ **PHRASE** If something **goes without saying**, it is obvious. ❑ *It goes without saying that the spices must be fresh.* [from Old English]

say|ing /seɪɪŋ/ (**sayings**) **N-COUNT** A **saying** is something that people often say, that gives advice about life. ❑ *Remember that old saying: "Forgive and forget."* [from Old English]

scaf|fold|ing /skæfəldɪŋ/ **N-NONCOUNT** **Scaffolding** is a frame of metal bars that people can stand on when they are working on the outside of a building. ❑ *Builders have put up scaffolding around the tower.* [from Old French]

scal|abil|i|ty /skeɪləbɪlɪti/ **N-NONCOUNT** TECHNOLOGY **Scalability** is the ability of a system, especially a computer system, to adapt to increased demand. ❑ *We chose a database system that has scalability and flexibility.*

sca|lar ma|trix /skeɪlər meɪtrɪks/ (**scalar matrices**) **N-COUNT** SCIENCE A **scalar matrix** is a mathematical arrangement of numbers, symbols, or letters in which all of the diagonal elements are equal.

scald /skɔld/ (**scalds, scalding, scalded**) **V-T** If you **scald yourself**, you burn yourself with very hot liquid or steam. ❑ *A patient scalded herself in the bath.* [from Old Norman French]

Word Link	scal, scala ≈ ladder, stairs : escalate, escalator, scale

scale /skeɪl/ (**scales**)
■ **N-COUNT** A **scale** is a machine that you use for weighing people or things. ❑ *He weighed himself on a bathroom scale.*
■ **N-SING** The **scale** of something is the size

or level of it. ❑ *He doesn't realize the scale of the problem.*
■ **N-COUNT** SCIENCE A **scale** is a set of levels or numbers that you use to measure things. ❑ *The earthquake measured 5.5 on the Richter scale.*
■ **N-COUNT** GEOGRAPHY The **scale** of a map is the relationship between the size of something on the map and its size in the real world. ❑ *The map is on a scale of 1:10,000.*
■ **N-COUNT** SCIENCE **Scales** are small, flat pieces of hard skin that cover the body of animals like fish and snakes.
■ **N-COUNT** MUSIC A **scale** is a set of musical notes that are played in a fixed order.
❑ *...the scale of F major.* ❑ *Celia was practicing her scales on the piano.* [Sense 1 from Old Norse. Senses 2, 3, 4, and 6 from Italian. Sense 5 from Old French.]
■ → see also **large-scale, small-scale**
→ look at Picture Dictionaries: **fish, shellfish, kitchen utensils**
→ look at Word Webs: **graph, thermometer**

scal|lion /skælyən/ (**scallions**) **N-COUNT** A **scallion** is a small onion with long green leaves. [from Latin]

scal|lop /skɒləp, skæl-/ (**scallops**) **N-COUNT** **Scallops** are large shellfish with two flat fan-shaped shells. Scallops can be eaten. [from Old French]
→ look at Picture Dictionary: **shellfish**

scalp /skælp/ (**scalps**) **N-COUNT** SCIENCE Your **scalp** is the skin under the hair on your head. ❑ *Try this treatment for beautiful thick hair and a healthy scalp.* [of Scandinavian origin]

scan /skæn/ (**scans, scanning, scanned**)
■ **V-T/V-I** When you **scan** a piece of writing, you look through it quickly to find important or interesting information.
❑ *She scanned the front page of the newspaper.*
❑ *I don't know the details of the article, as I quickly scanned through it.*
■ **V-T** TECHNOLOGY If you **scan** a picture or a document, you make an electronic copy of it using a special piece of equipment called a scanner. ❑ *She scanned the images into her computer.*
■ **V-T** When luggage **is scanned**, a machine is used to show the things that are inside it.
❑ *Every bag is scanned with an X-ray machine.*
■ **N-COUNT** A **scan** is a medical test in which a machine takes pictures of the inside of your body. ❑ *A brain scan showed a strange shadow.* [from Late Latin]

scan|dal /skǽndᵊl/ (**scandals**) **N-COUNT**
A **scandal** is a situation or an event that people think is shocking. ❑ *It was a financial scandal.* [from Late Latin]

scan|ner /skǽnər/ (**scanners**)
1 **N-COUNT** TECHNOLOGY A **scanner** is a machine that you use to make an electronic copy of something, such as a picture or a document. ❑ *Scan your photos using any desktop scanner.*
2 **N-COUNT** TECHNOLOGY A **scanner** is a machine that gives a picture of the inside of something. ❑ *His bag was passed through the airport X-ray scanner.* [from Late Latin]
→ look at Word Web: **laser**

scar /skɑr/ (**scars, scarring, scarred**)
1 **N-COUNT** A **scar** is a mark that is left on the skin by an old wound. ❑ *He had a scar on his forehead.*
2 **V-T** If your skin **is scarred**, it is badly marked because of an old wound. ❑ *He was scarred for life during a fight.* [from Late Latin]

scarce /skɛərs/ (**scarcer, scarcest**) **ADJ** If something is **scarce**, there is not enough of it. ❑ *Food was scarce and expensive.* ❑ *Jobs are becoming scarce.* [from Old Norman French]

scarce|ly /skɛərsli/ **ADV** You use **scarcely** to emphasize that something is only just true. ❑ *He could scarcely breathe.* [from Old Norman French]

scare /skɛər/ (**scares, scaring, scared**)
1 **V-T** If something **scares** you, it frightens or worries you. ❑ *The thought of failure scares me.*
2 **N-SING** If a sudden, unpleasant experience gives you a **scare**, it frightens you. ❑ *You gave us a terrible scare!*
3 **N-COUNT** A **scare** is a situation where many people are afraid or worried about something. ❑ *The new drug was the subject of a recent health scare.* [from Old Norse]

scared /skɛərd/
1 **ADJ** If you are **scared of** someone or something, you are frightened of them. ❑ *I'm not scared of him.*
2 **ADJ** If you are **scared that** something unpleasant might happen, you are worried because you think that it might happen. ❑ *I was scared that I might be sick.* [from Old Norse]

scarf /skɑrf/ (**scarfs** or **scarves**) **N-COUNT**
A **scarf** is a piece of cloth that you wear

around your neck or head. ❑ *He loosened the scarf around his neck.*

scary /skɛəri/ (**scarier, scariest**) **ADJ**
Something that is **scary** is frightening.
[INFORMAL] ❑ *The movie is too scary for children.* [from Late Latin]

scat|ter /skǽtər/ (**scatters, scattering, scattered**)
1 **V-T** If you **scatter** things over an area, you throw or drop them so that they spread over it. ❑ *She scattered the flowers over the grave.*
2 **V-T/V-I** If a group of people **scatter**, they suddenly move in different directions. ❑ *After dinner, everyone scattered.*

scat|tered /skǽtərd/
1 **ADJ** **Scattered** things are spread over an area in a messy or irregular way. ❑ *He picked up the scattered toys.* ❑ *Tomorrow there will be a few scattered showers.*
2 **ADJ** If something is **scattered with** a lot of small things, they are spread all over it. ❑ *Every surface is scattered with photographs.*

scat|ter|ing /skǽtərɪŋ/ (**scatterings**)
1 **N-COUNT** A **scattering of** things or people is a small number of them spread over an area. ❑ *There's a scattering of houses east of the village.*
2 **N-NONCOUNT** SCIENCE In physics, **scattering** is a process in which light waves are spread out in a disorganized way as a result of hitting a surface or hitting particles in the atmosphere.

scat|ter|plot /skǽtərplɒt/ (**scatterplots**)
N-COUNT SCIENCE A **scatterplot** is a type of graph used in statistics to compare two sets of data.

scav|en|ger /skǽvɪndʒər/ (**scavengers**)
N-COUNT SCIENCE A **scavenger** is an animal that feeds on the bodies of dead animals. ❑ *...scavengers such as rats.* [from Old Norman French]

scene /sin/ (**scenes**)
1 **N-COUNT** LANGUAGE ARTS A **scene** is a part of a play, a movie, or a book that happens in the same place. ❑ *This is the opening scene of "Tom Sawyer."*
2 **N-COUNT** You can call a place a **scene** when you are describing what is there. ❑ *The photographs show scenes of everyday life in the village.* ❑ *It's a scene of complete horror.*
3 **N-COUNT** The **scene of** an event is the place where it happened. ❑ *Firefighters rushed*

S

to the scene of the car accident. [from Latin]
→ look at Word Web: **animation**

scen|ery /sɪnəri/

1 **N-NONCOUNT** The **scenery** in a country area is the land, water, or plants that you can see around you. ❑ *Most visitors come for the island's beautiful scenery.*

2 **N-NONCOUNT** **ARTS** In a theater, the **scenery** is the objects or the backgrounds that show where the action in the play is happening. ❑ *The actors will move the scenery themselves.* [from Italian]

sce|nic /sinɪk/ **ADJ** A **scenic** place has attractive scenery. ❑ *This is an extremely scenic part of America.* [from Latin]

scent /sɛnt/ (**scents**)

1 **N-COUNT** The **scent** of something is the pleasant smell that it has. ❑ *This perfume gives off a heavy scent of roses.* ● **scent|ed** **ADJ** ❑ *...scented soap.*

2 **N-NONCOUNT** **Scent** is a liquid that women put on their necks and wrists to make themselves smell nice. ❑ *She opened her bottle of scent.*

3 **N-COUNT/N-NONCOUNT** The **scent** of a person or an animal is the smell that they leave and that other people sometimes follow when looking for them. ❑ *A police dog picked up the murderer's scent.* [from Old French]

sched|ule /skɛdʒul, -uəl/ (**schedules, scheduling, scheduled**)

1 **N-COUNT** A **schedule** is a plan that gives a list of the times when things will happen. ❑ *For best results, plan a training schedule.* *...the student's class schedule for next semester.*

2 **N-NONCOUNT** If something happens **behind schedule**, it happens after the planned time. ❑ *The project is about three months behind schedule.*

3 **N-NONCOUNT** If something happens **on schedule**, it happens at the planned time. ❑ *The next meeting is scheduled for tomorrow morning.*

4 **N-COUNT** A **schedule** is a list of all the times when trains, buses, or planes are supposed to arrive at or leave a particular place. ❑ *...a bus schedule.*

5 **V-T** If something **is scheduled** to happen at a particular time, arrangements are made for it to happen at that time. ❑ *The next meeting is scheduled for tomorrow morning.* [from Old French]

Word Partnership   Use **schedule** with :

N	**change of** schedule, schedule **of events,** **payment** schedule, **playoff** schedule, **work** schedule **1** **bus** schedule, **train** schedule **4**
ADJ	**busy** schedule, **hectic** schedule **1** **regular** schedule **1** **4**

scheme /skim/ (**schemes, scheming, schemed**)

1 **N-COUNT** A **scheme** is a plan for achieving something, especially something that will bring you some benefit. ❑ *...a quick money-making scheme.*

2 **V-T/V-I** If people **are scheming**, they are making secret plans to do something. ❑ *The family was scheming to stop the wedding.* ❑ *Everyone's always scheming.* [from Latin]

schol|ar /skɒlər/ (**scholars**) **N-COUNT** A **scholar** is a person who studies an academic subject and knows a lot about it. [FORMAL] ❑ *The library is full of scholars and researchers.* [from Old French]
→ look at Word Web: **history**

schol|ar|ship /skɒlərʃɪp/ (**scholarships**) **N-COUNT** If you win a **scholarship**, you receive money to help you to continue studying. ❑ *He got a scholarship to the Pratt Institute of Art.* [from Old French]

school /skul/ (**schools**)

1 **N-COUNT/N-NONCOUNT** A **school** is a place where people go to learn. ❑ *The school was built in the 1960s.*

2 **N-NONCOUNT** You can use **school** to talk about your time in school or college. ❑ *Parents want their kids to do well in school.* ❑ *I graduated from school last spring.*

3 **N-COUNT** A **school** is a college. ❑ *What school did you go to?*

4 **N-COUNT** A **school** is a place where a particular skill or subject is taught. ❑ *He owns a riding school.* [from Old English]

5 → see also **high school, public school**

school|teacher /skultitʃər/ (**schoolteachers**) **N-COUNT** A **schoolteacher** is a teacher in a school.

Word Link   *sci ≈ knowing : conscience, conscious, science*

sci|ence /saɪəns/ (**sciences**)

1 **N-NONCOUNT** **SCIENCE** **Science** is the study of natural things. ❑ *He studied plant science in college.*

Word Web   science

Science is the study of physical laws. These laws govern the natural world. Science uses **research** and **experiments** to explain various **phenomena**. Scientists follow the **scientific method** which begins with **observation** and measurement. Then they state a **hypothesis**, which is a possible explanation for the observations and measurements. Next, scientists make a **prediction**, which is a logical **deduction** based on the hypothesis. The last step is to conduct experiments which **prove** or **disprove** the hypothesis. Scientists construct and modify **theories** based on **empirical findings**. **Pure** science deals with theories only. When people use science to do something, that is **applied** science.

2 **N-COUNT** SCIENCE A **science** is a particular branch of science such as physics, chemistry, or biology. ❑ *He taught music as if it were a science.* [from Old French]
→ look at Word Web: **science**

sci|ence fic|tion **N-NONCOUNT**
LANGUAGE ARTS **Science fiction** is stories in books, magazines, and movies about things that happen in the future or in other parts of the universe.

sci|en|tif|ic /saɪəntɪfɪk/ **ADJ** SCIENCE **Scientific** means to do with science. ❑ *He spends a lot of time conducting scientific research.* [from Old French]
→ look at Word Webs: **experiment, science**

sci|en|tif|ic meth|od **N-SING** SCIENCE The **scientific method** is the set of rules and procedures followed by scientists, especially the use of experiments to test hypotheses.

sci|en|tif|ic no|ta|tion (**scientific notations**) **N-COUNT/N-NONCOUNT** SCIENCE **Scientific notation** is a method of writing very large or very small numbers by expressing them as numbers multiplied by a power of ten.

sci|en|tist /saɪəntɪst/ (**scientists**) **N-COUNT** SCIENCE A **scientist** is someone whose job is to teach or do research in science. ❑ *Scientists have discovered a new gene.* [from Old French]
→ look at Word Webs: **evolution, experiment**

sci-fi /saɪ faɪ/ **N-NONCOUNT** **Sci-fi** is short for **science fiction**. [INFORMAL] ❑ *It's a two hour sci-fi movie.*

scis|sors /sɪzərz/ **N-PLURAL** **Scissors** are a small tool for cutting with two sharp parts that are joined together. ❑ *Cut the card using scissors.* [from Old French]

→ look at Picture Dictionary: **office**

scold /skoʊld/ (**scolds, scolding, scolded**)
V-T If you **scold** a person or an animal, you speak to them in an angry way because they have done something wrong. [FORMAL] ❑ *I could hear Barbara scolding the puppies outside.* ❑ *I scolded myself for talking so much.* [from Old Norse]

scoop /skup/ (**scoops, scooping, scooped**)
1 **V-T** If you **scoop** something from a container, you remove it with your hand or with a spoon. ❑ *He was scooping dog food out of a can.*
2 **N-COUNT** A **scoop** is an object like a spoon that is used for taking ice cream or flour from a container. ❑ *Here, use the ice-cream scoop.* [from Middle Dutch]
▸ **scoop up** If you **scoop** something **up**, you put your hands under it and lift it. ❑ *Use both hands to scoop up the leaves.*

scoot|er /skutər/ (**scooters**)
1 **N-COUNT** A **scooter** is a small light motorcycle with a low seat.
2 **N-COUNT** A **scooter** is a child's vehicle with a long handle and two wheels joined by a long board. [of Scandinavian origin]

scorch /skɔrtʃ/ (**scorches, scorching, scorched**) **V-T** To **scorch** something means to burn it slightly. ❑ *Many of my plants were scorched by the sun.* [from Old Norse]

scorch|ing /skɔrtʃɪŋ/ **ADJ** **Scorching** or **scorching hot** weather or temperatures are very hot indeed. [INFORMAL] ❑ *That race took place in scorching weather.* [from Old Norse]

score /skɔr/ (**scores, scoring, scored**)
1 **V-T/V-I** SPORTS In a sport or a game, if a player **scores** a goal or a point, they get a

goal or a point. ❑ *Patten scored his second goal of the game.* ❑ *He scored late in the third quarter.*

2 **V-T/V-I** If you **score** a particular number or amount, for example, as a mark on a test, you achieve that number or amount. ❑ *Kelly scored 88 on the test.* ❑ *Congress scores low in public opinion polls.*

3 **N-COUNT** Someone's **score** in a game or on a test is the number of points they have won. ❑ *Hogan won, with a score of 287.*

4 **N-COUNT** SPORTS The **score** in a game is the result. ❑ *The final score was 4–1.* [from Old English]

→ look at Word Web: **music**

scorn /skɔrn/ **N-NONCOUNT** If you treat someone or something **with scorn**, you show that you do not like or respect them. ❑ *Her words attracted scorn and anger.* [from Old French]

scorn|ful /skɔrnfəl/ **ADJ** If you are **scornful of** someone or something, you show that you do not like or respect them. ❑ *He is deeply scornful of politicians.* ● **scorn|ful|ly** **ADV** ❑ *They laughed scornfully.* [from Old French]

scout /skaʊt/ (**scouts, scouting, scouted**) **V-T/V-I** If you **scout** somewhere **for** something, you go around that area in order to search for it. ❑ *She's scouting for locations to open a restaurant.* ❑ *The girls scouted the site for materials people had left behind.* [from Old French]

scowl /skaʊl/ (**scowls, scowling, scowled**) **1** **V-I** If you **scowl**, you make an angry face. ❑ *He scowled, and slammed the door.*

2 **N-COUNT** Scowl is also a noun. ❑ *Daniel answered with a scowl.* [of Scandinavian origin]

scram|ble /skræmbəl/ (**scrambles, scrambling, scrambled**) **1** **V-I** If you **scramble** over rocks or up a hill, you move quickly over them or up it, using your hands to help you. ❑ *Tourists were scrambling over the rocks to the beach.*

2 **V-T** If you **scramble** eggs, you break them, mix them together, and then cook them. ❑ *Make the toast and scramble the eggs.*

● **scram|bled** **ADJ** ❑ *We're having scrambled eggs on toast.*

→ look at Picture Dictionary: **egg**

scrap /skræp/ (**scraps, scrapping, scrapped**) **1** **N-COUNT** A **scrap of** something is a very

small piece or amount of it. ❑ *A scrap of red paper was found in her handbag.*

2 **V-T** If you **scrap** something, you get rid of it or cancel it. ❑ *The government has scrapped plans to build a new airport.* [from Old Norse]

scrape /skreɪp/ (**scrapes, scraping, scraped**) **1** **V-T** If you **scrape** a part of your body, you accidentally rub it against something hard and rough, and damage it slightly. ❑ *She fell, scraping her hands and knees.*

2 **V-T** If you **scrape** something from a surface, you remove it by moving a sharp object over the surface. ❑ *She scraped the frost off the car windows.* [from Old English]

scratch /skrætʃ/ (**scratches, scratching, scratched**) **1** **V-T/V-I** If you **scratch**, or **scratch** part of your body, you rub your fingernails against your skin. ❑ *He scratched his head thoughtfully.* ❑ *He scratched underneath his arm.*

2 **V-T** If a sharp object **scratches** someone or something, it makes small cuts on their skin or on its surface. ❑ *The branches scratched my face.*

3 **N-COUNT** Scratches on someone or something are small cuts made by a sharp object. ❑ *He had scratches on his face and neck.*

4 **V-I** If an animal **scratches**, or **scratches at** a surface, it rubs the surface with its claws. ❑ *She was awakened by the dogs whining and scratching at the door.* [from Old French]

scream /skrim/ (**screams, screaming, screamed**) **1** **V-I** When you **scream**, you give a loud, high cry because you are hurt or frightened. ❑ *Women were screaming in the houses nearest the fire.*

2 **N-COUNT** Scream is also a noun. ❑ *Rose gave a loud scream.*

3 **V-T** If you **scream** something, you shout it in a loud, high-pitched voice. ❑ *"Barbara!" she screamed.* [from Germanic]

screech /skritʃ/ (**screeches, screeching, screeched**) **V-I** If a vehicle **screeches**, its tires make an unpleasant high sound on the road. ❑ *Two police cars screeched into the parking lot.*

screen /skrin/ (**screens**) **1** **N-COUNT** TECHNOLOGY A **screen** is a flat surface on a piece of electronic equipment, such as a television or a computer, where you see pictures or words.

2 → see also **widescreen**

S

3 **N-COUNT** A **screen** is the flat area on the wall of a movie theater, where you see the movie. ❑ *The theater has 20 screens.*

4 **N-COUNT** A **screen** is a net of thin wires that you put behind a window or a door to keep out insects. ❑ *...window screens.* [from Old French]
→ look at Word Web: **television**

screen|saver /skrˈinseɪvər/ (**screensavers**) **N-COUNT** TECHNOLOGY A **screensaver** is a moving picture that appears on a computer screen when the computer is not being used.

screen|shot /skrˈinʃɒt/ (**screenshots**) **N-COUNT** TECHNOLOGY A **screenshot** is an image that you create by copying part or all of the display on a computer screen at a particular moment.

screw /skrˈu/ (**screws, screwing, screwed**)
1 **N-COUNT** A **screw** is a small metal object with a sharp end, that you use to join things together. ❑ *Each shelf is attached to the wall with screws.*
2 **V-T/V-I** If you **screw** something somewhere, or if it **screws** somewhere, you join it to another thing using a screw. ❑ *I screwed the shelf on the wall myself.* ❑ *The table was screwed to the floor.*
3 **V-T/V-I** If you **screw** something somewhere, or if it **screws** somewhere, you fix it in place by twisting it around and around. ❑ *Screw down the lid tightly.* [from French]

screw|driver /skrˈudraɪvər/ (**screwdrivers**) **N-COUNT** A **screwdriver** is a tool that you use for turning screws.
→ look at Picture Dictionary: **tools**

scrib|ble /skrˈibəl/ (**scribbles, scribbling, scribbled**) **V-T/V-I** If you **scribble** something, you write or draw it quickly and roughly. ❑ *She scribbled a note to Mom.* ❑ *She was sitting scribbling on her book.* [from Medieval Latin]

script /skrˈipt/ (**scripts**) **N-COUNT** LANGUAGE ARTS A **script** is the written words that actors speak in a play, a movie, or a television program. ❑ *Jenny's writing a movie script.* [from Latin]
→ look at Word Web: **animation**

scroll /skrˈoʊl/ (**scrolls, scrolling, scrolled**) **V-I** TECHNOLOGY If you **scroll** through text on a computer screen, you move the text up or down to find the information that you need.

❑ *I scrolled down to find "United States of America."* [from Old French]

scro|tum /skrˈoʊtəm/ (**scrotums**) **N-COUNT** SCIENCE A man's **scrotum** is the bag of skin that contains his testicles. [from Latin]

scrub /skrˈʌb/ (**scrubs, scrubbing, scrubbed**) **V-T** If you **scrub** something, you rub it hard in order to clean it. ❑ *Surgeons must scrub their hands and arms with soap and water.* [from Middle Low German]

scrub|ber /skrˈʌbər/ (**scrubbers**) **N-COUNT** SCIENCE A **scrubber** is a device that removes pollution from gases that are released into the atmosphere, for example from a factory furnace.

scruffy /skrˈʌfi/ (**scruffier, scruffiest**) **ADJ** Someone or something that is **scruffy** is dirty and messy. ❑ *The man was pale, scruffy and unshaven.*

scru|pu|lous /skrˈupyələs/
1 **ADJ** Someone who is **scrupulous** takes great care to do what is fair, honest, or morally right. ❑ *You are always more scrupulous than other people.* ❑ *The officials are scrupulous about protecting all students.* ● **scru|pu|lous|ly** **ADV** ❑ *He is scrupulously fair.*
2 **ADJ** **Scrupulous** means thorough, exact, and careful about details. ❑ *They admire Knutson's scrupulous attention to detail.*
● **scru|pu|lous|ly** **ADV** ❑ *The streets were scrupulously clean.* [from Latin]

scru|ti|nize /skrˈutᵊnaɪz/ (**scrutinizes, scrutinizing, scrutinized**) **V-T** If you **scrutinize** something, you examine it very carefully. ❑ *She scrutinized his face to see if he was an honest man.* [from Late Latin]

scru|ti|ny /skrˈutᵊni/ **N-NONCOUNT** If a person or thing is under **scrutiny**, they are being studied or observed very carefully. ❑ *His private life came under public scrutiny.* [from Late Latin]

sculp|tor /skˈʌlptər/ (**sculptors**) **N-COUNT** ARTS A **sculptor** is an artist who makes solid works of art out of stone, metal, or wood. ❑ *The sculptor carved the swan from a solid block of ice.*

sculp|ture /skˈʌlptʃər/ (**sculptures**)
1 **N-COUNT/N-NONCOUNT** ARTS A **sculpture** is a piece of art that is made into a shape from a material like stone or wood. ❑ *There were stone sculptures of different animals.*

S

2 N-NONCOUNT ARTS Sculpture is the art of creating sculptures from a substance like stone or wood. ❑ *Both of them studied sculpture.* [from Latin]

sea /siː/ (**seas**) **N-COUNT GEOGRAPHY** A **sea** is a large area of salty water that is part of an ocean or is surrounded by land. ❑ *They swam in the warm Caribbean Sea.* [from Old English]

Word Partnership	Use sea with :
PREP	**above the** sea, **across the** sea, **below the** sea, **by** sea, **from the** sea, **into the** sea, **over the** sea
N	sea **air**, sea **coast**, **land and** sea, sea **voyage**
ADJ	**calm** sea, **deep** sea

sea-floor spread|ing N-NONCOUNT SCIENCE Sea-floor spreading is the expansion of the ocean floor that occurs when two tectonic plates move apart and new rock is formed.

sea|food /siːfuːd/ **N-NONCOUNT Seafood** is fish and other small animals from the ocean that you can eat. ❑ *Let's find a seafood restaurant.*

sea|gull /siːɡʌl/ (**seagulls**) **N-COUNT** A **seagull** is a common type of bird with white or gray feathers that lives near the ocean.

sea|horse /siːhɔrs/ (**seahorses**) also **sea horse N-COUNT** A **seahorse** is a type of small fish that appears to swim in a vertical position and whose head looks a little like the head of a horse.

seal /siːl/ (**seals, sealing, sealed**)
1 V-T When you **seal** an envelope, you close it by folding part of it and sticking it down. ❑ *He sealed the envelope and put on a stamp.*
2 V-T If you **seal** a container or an opening, you cover it with something in order to prevent air, liquid, or other material from getting in or out. ❑ *She filled the containers, sealed them, and stuck on labels.*
3 N-COUNT A **seal** is a large animal with a rounded body and short fur that eats fish and lives near the ocean. [Senses 1 and 2 from Old French. Sense 3 from Old English.]

seam /siːm/ (**seams**) **N-COUNT** A **seam** is a line where two pieces of cloth are joined together. [from Old English]

sea|man /siːmən/ (**seamen**) **N-COUNT** A **seaman** is a sailor, especially one who is not an officer. ❑ *The men all work as seamen.*

sea|mount /siːmaʊnt/ (**seamounts**)
N-COUNT SCIENCE A **seamount** is a mountain that lies beneath the surface of the ocean.

search /sɜrtʃ/ (**searches, searching, searched**)
1 V-I If you **search for** something or someone, you look carefully for them. ❑ *Police are already searching for the men.*
2 V-T/V-I If you **search** a place, you look carefully for something or someone there. ❑ *The police are searching the town for the missing men.* ❑ *She searched for the papers but couldn't find them.*
3 N-COUNT A **search** is an attempt to find something or someone by looking for them carefully. ❑ *The search was stopped because of the heavy snow.*
4 V-T If a police officer **searches** you, they look carefully to see whether you have hidden something under your clothes. ❑ *Of course the police searched her.*
5 V-T If you **search** the Web, you use your computer to find information on the Internet. ❑ *She has searched the Web for the perfect bikini.*
6 N-COUNT Search is also a noun. ❑ *I did a search and found an old boyfriend's e-mail address.* [from Old French]

Word Partnership	Use search with :
N	search **for clues**, **police** search **1**–**4** search **for information 1 3** **investigators** search **1 2 4** search **for a job**, search **for the truth 1 3** search **an area 2** **talent** search **3** search **suspects 4**
V	**conduct a** search **3**

search en|gine (**search engines**) **N-COUNT TECHNOLOGY** A **search engine** is a computer program that you use to search for information on the Internet.

sea|son /siːzən/ (**seasons, seasoning, seasoned**)
1 N-COUNT The **seasons** are the four parts of a year that have their own typical weather conditions. ❑ *Fall is my favorite season.*
2 N-COUNT You can use **season** to talk about a time each year when something happens. ❑ *The baseball season begins again soon.*
3 V-T If you **season** food with spices, you add them to it in order to improve its flavor. ❑ *Season the meat with salt and pepper.* [from Old French]

Word Web   seasons

The ancient Mayans* built a pyramid at Chichen Itzá*. One use of this structure was to predict the **seasons** of the **year**. As the sun shone on the pyramid, it created distinct shadows. These shadows moved during the year. Trained leaders observed these changing patterns of **light** throughout the year. The shadows fell in specific places at the time of the solstices and equinoxes. They showed the leaders the best times to plant and harvest crops. The shadows also told them when to hold special religious ceremonies. Thousands of tourists visit Chichen Itzá each spring to observe the arrival of the vernal* equinox.

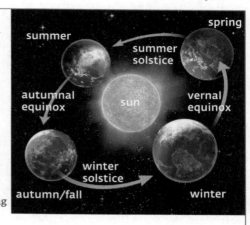

Mayans (250–900 AD): Indians who lived in Mexico and Central America.
Chichen Itzá(700–900 AD): a Mayan city in Mexico.
vernal: spring

sea|son|al /síːzənªl/ **ADJ** A **seasonal** factor, event, or change occurs during one particular time of the year. ❑ *The seasonal workers will return from Mexico in the next few months.*
● **sea|son|al|ly** **ADV** ❑ *Restaurant menus change seasonally here.* [from Old French]

sea star (**sea stars**) also **seastar** **N-COUNT** A **sea star** is a flat, star-shaped creature, usually with five arms, that lives in the sea.

seat /síːt/ (**seats, seating, seated**)
1 **N-COUNT** A **seat** is something that you can sit on. ❑ *We had front-row seats at the concert.* ❑ *The car has comfortable leather seats.*
2 **V-T** If you are **seated** somewhere, you are sitting down. [WRITTEN] ❑ *He was comfortably seated in his favorite armchair in front of a roaring fire.*
3 **V-T** A building or a vehicle that **seats** a particular number of people has enough seats for that number. ❑ *The theater seats 570 people.*
4 **PHRASE** If you **take a seat**, you sit down. [FORMAL] ❑ *"Take a seat," he said.* [from Old English]

Word Partnership	Use **seat** with :		
ADJ	**back** seat, **empty** seat, **front** seat **1**		
	vacant seat, **vacated** seat **1**		
N	**car** seat, **child** seat, **driver's** seat,		
	passenger seat, seat **at a table**, **theater** seat **1**		

seat belt (**seat belts**) **N-COUNT** A **seat belt** is a long thin belt that you fasten around your body in a vehicle to keep you safe. ❑ *Please fasten your seat belts.*
→ look at Word Web: **car**

sea|weed /síːwiːd/ **N-NONCOUNT** Seaweed is a plant that grows in the ocean. ❑ *Seaweed is washed up on the beach.*

sec|ond /sέkənd/ (**seconds**)
1 **N-COUNT** MATH A **second** is a measurement of time. There are sixty seconds in one minute. ❑ *For a few seconds, nobody spoke.*
2 **ADJ** The **second** thing in a series is the one that you count as number two. ❑ *It was the second day of his visit to Florida.*
3 **ADV** **Second** is also an adverb. ❑ *Emma came second in the race.*
4 **PRON** **Second** is also a pronoun. ❑ *The first attempt was less successful than the second.* [from Old French]
→ look at Picture Dictionary: **time**

sec|ond|ary /sέkəndɛri/
1 **ADJ** If something is **secondary**, it is less important than something else. ❑ *Money is of secondary importance to them.*
2 **ADJ** **Secondary** education is given to students between the ages of 11 and 18. ❑ *They take examinations after five years of secondary education.* [from Old French]

sec|ond|ary col|or (**secondary colors**)
N-COUNT ARTS **Secondary colors** are colors such as orange and violet that are a mixture of two primary colors.
→ look at Picture Dictionary: **color**

S

sec|ond|ary pol|lu|tant (secondary pollutants) **N-COUNT** SCIENCE Secondary pollutants are pollutants that are created by chemical reactions in the atmosphere. Compare with **primary pollutant**.

sec|ond-hand
1 **ADJ** Second-hand things are not new and have been used by another person. ❑ *They could just afford a second-hand car.*
2 **ADV** Second-hand is also an adverb. ❑ *They bought the furniture second-hand.*

sec|ond|ly /sɛkəndli/ **ADV** You say **secondly** when you want to talk about a second thing, or give a second reason for something. ❑ *Firstly, involve your children in planning the break, and secondly, ask your travel agent for family-friendly suggestions.* [from Old French]

se|cre|cy /sikrəsi/ **N-NONCOUNT** Secrecy is a situation in which you do not tell anyone about something. ❑ *They met in complete secrecy.* [from Old French]

se|cret /sikrɪt/ (secrets)
1 **ADJ** If something is **secret**, only a small number of people know about it, and they do not tell anyone else. ❑ *They tried to keep their marriage secret.* ● **se|cret|ly** **ADV** ❑ *He wore a microphone to secretly record conversations.*
2 **N-COUNT** A **secret** is something that only a small number of people know, and they do not tell anyone else. ❑ *Can you keep a secret?*
3 **N-SING** If a particular way of doing things is **the secret of** achieving something, it is the best way to achieve it. ❑ *The secret of success is honesty.*
4 **PHRASE** If you do something **in secret**, you do it without anyone else knowing. ❑ *Dan found out that we were meeting in secret.* [from Old French]

Thesaurus secret Also look up :
ADJ   hidden, private, unknown; (ant.) known **1**

sec|re|tar|ial /sɛkrɪtɛəriəl/ **ADJ** Secretarial work is typing letters, answering the telephone, and other work that is done in an office. ❑ *I was doing temporary secretarial work.* [from Medieval Latin]

sec|re|tary /sɛkrɪtɛri/ (secretaries)
1 **N-COUNT** BUSINESS A **secretary** is a person whose job is to type letters, answer the telephone, and do other office work.
2 **N-COUNT** SOCIAL STUDIES A **secretary** is a

person with an important position in the government. ❑ *The defense secretary will meet with the president tomorrow.* [from Medieval Latin]

Sec|re|tary of State (Secretaries of State) **N-COUNT** SOCIAL STUDIES In the United States, **the Secretary of State** is the head of the government department that deals with foreign affairs.

se|crete /sikrit/ (secretes, secreting, secreted) **V-T** SCIENCE If part of a plant, an animal, or a human **secretes** a liquid, it produces it. ❑ *The skin begins to secrete an oily substance.*

se|cre|tion /sɪkriʃⁿn/ **N-NONCOUNT** SCIENCE Secretion is the process by which certain liquid substances are produced by parts of plants or from the bodies of people or animals. ❑ *The amount of natural oil secretion begins to decrease.*

se|cre|tive /sikrətɪv, sɪkrit-/ **ADJ** If you are **secretive**, you do not like to share your knowledge, feelings, or intentions. ❑ *She's very secretive about how much money she has.*

Word Link sect ≈ cutting : bisect, dissect, section

sec|tion /sɛkʃⁿn/ (sections) **N-COUNT** A **section** of something is a particular part of it. ❑ *It is wrong to blame one section of society for all these problems.* ❑ *He works in the Georgetown section of Washington, D.C.* [from Latin]

Word Partnership Use section with :
ADJ   **main** section, **new** section, **special** section, **thin** section
N   section **of a city**, section **of a coast**, **rhythm** section, **sports** section

se|cure /sɪkyʊər/ (secures, securing, secured)
1 **ADJ** A **secure** place is well protected, so that people cannot enter it or leave it if you do not want them to. ❑ *We'll make our home as secure as possible.* ● **se|cure|ly** **ADV** ❑ *He locked the heavy door securely.*
2 **ADJ** If an object is **secure**, it is properly fixed in position. ❑ *The farmer made sure that the fence was always secure.* ● **se|cure|ly** **ADV** ❑ *He fastened his belt securely.*
3 **V-T** If you **secure** an object, you fasten it firmly to another object. ❑ *He secured the rope to the front of the boat.*
4 **ADJ** If a job is **secure**, it will not end soon.

❑ *For the moment, his job is secure.*
5 **ADJ** If you feel **secure**, you feel safe and happy, and you are not worried about life. ❑ *She felt secure when she was with him.* [from Latin]

Thesaurus secure Also look up :
v	catch, get, obtain; *(ant.)* lose **1**
	attach, fasten **4**
ADJ	safe, sheltered **3**
	locked, tight **5**

se|cu|rity /sɪkyʊərɪti/ (**securities**)
1 **N-NONCOUNT** Security is everything that you do to protect a place. ❑ *They are improving airport security.*
2 **N-NONCOUNT** A feeling of **security** is a feeling of being safe and free from worry. ❑ *He loves the security of a happy home life.*
3 **N-PLURAL** BUSINESS **Securities** are stocks, shares, bonds, or other certificates that you buy in order to earn regular interest from them or to sell them later for a profit. ❑ *National banks can package their own mortgages and underwrite them as securities.* [from Latin]
4 → see also **Social Security**

sedi|ment /sɛdɪmənt/ (**sediments**)
N-COUNT/N-NONCOUNT SCIENCE **Sediment** is solid material that settles at the bottom of a liquid. ❑ *At the bottom of the ocean, over time, the sediment forms into rock.* [from Latin]
→ look at Word Web: **rock**

sedi|men|tary /sɛdɪmɛntəri/ **ADJ** SCIENCE **Sedimentary** rocks are formed from sediment left by water, ice, or wind. [from Latin]

se|duce /sɪdus/ (**seduces, seducing, seduced**) **V-T** If something **seduces** you, it is so attractive that it makes you do something that you would not otherwise do. ❑ *The fabulous view always seduces visitors.*
● **se|duc|tion** /sɪdʌkʃ°n/ (**seductions**) **N-COUNT/N-NONCOUNT** ❑ *...the seduction of words.* [from Latin]

see
① VERB USES
② PHRASES AND PHRASAL VERB

① see /si/ (**sees, seeing, saw, seen**)
1 **V-T/V-I** When you **see** something, you notice it using your eyes. ❑ *The fog was so thick that we couldn't see.* ❑ *Have you seen my keys?* ❑ *She can see, hear, touch, smell, and taste.*
2 **V-T** If you **see** someone, you visit or meet them. ❑ *I saw him yesterday.*
3 **V-T** If you **see** a play, a movie, or a sports game, you watch it. ❑ *Let's go see a movie tonight.*
4 **V-T/V-I** If you **see** that something is true, you realize by observing it that it is true. ❑ *I could see she was lonely.*
5 **V-T** If you **see** something, you understand it. ❑ *Oh, I see what you're saying.*
6 **V-T** If you **see** something, you find out information or a fact. ❑ *She looked around to see if anyone was listening.*
7 **V-T** If a person **sees** a particular event, they experience it. ❑ *I have seen many changes here over the past decade.*
8 **V-T** If you **see** someone or something **as** a certain thing, you have the opinion that they are that thing. ❑ *He saw it as an opportunity.* [from Old English]
9 → see also **saw**
→ look at Usage note at **look**

Thesaurus see Also look up :
| v | glimpse, look, observe, watch **1** |
| | grasp, observe, understand **5** |

② see /si/ (**sees, seeing, saw, seen**)
1 People say **I'll see** or **We'll see** to show that they will decide something later. ❑ *"Can we go swimming tomorrow?"—"We'll see. Maybe."*
2 People say **Let's see** when they are trying to remember something. ❑ *Let's see. Where did I leave my purse?*
3 **See you** and **See you later** are ways of saying goodbye to someone. [INFORMAL, SPOKEN] ❑ *"Talk to you later."—"All right. See you."* [from Old English]
▶ **see off** When you **see** someone **off**, you go with someone who is leaving to the station or airport, to say goodbye to them. ❑ *Ben saw Jackie off on her plane.*

seed /sid/ (**seeds**) **N-COUNT/N-NONCOUNT** SCIENCE A **seed** is the small, hard part of a plant from which a new plant grows. ❑ *Plant the seeds in small plastic pots.* [from Old English]
→ look at Picture Dictionary: **fruit**
→ look at Word Webs: **herbivore, rice**

seed fern (**seed ferns**) **N-COUNT** SCIENCE A **seed fern** was a plant, with leaves resembling those of a fern, that is now extinct.

seed|less /sidlɪs/ **ADJ** A **seedless** fruit has no seeds in it. ❑ ...*seedless grapes*. [from Old English]

seed|ling /sidlɪŋ/ (**seedlings**) **N-COUNT** A **seedling** is a young plant that has been grown from a seed. [from Old English]

seek /sik/ (**seeks, seeking, sought**) **V-T** If you **seek** something, you try to find it or get it. [FORMAL] ❑ *They are seeking work in hotels and bars*. [from Old English]

Word Partnership	Use **seek** with :
N	seek **advice**, seek **approval**, seek **assistance/help**, seek **asylum**, seek **counseling**, seek **election**, seek **employment**, seek **justice**, seek **permission**, seek **protection**, seek **revenge**, seek **shelter**, seek **support**

seem /sim/ (**seems, seeming, seemed**)
1 **V-LINK** If someone or something **seems** a particular way, they give that impression. ❑ *The thunder seemed quite close.* ❑ *They seemed a perfect couple to everyone who knew them.* ❑ *It seems that the attack was carefully planned.* ❑ *It seems as if she's never coming back.*
2 **V-LINK** You use **seem** to make your statement less forceful when you are describing your thoughts or feelings. ❑ *I seem to have lost all my self-confidence.* [from Old Norse]

seen /sin/ **Seen** is the past participle of **see**. [from Old English]

seg|ment /sɛgmənt/ (**segments**)
1 **N-COUNT** A **segment of** something is one part of it. ❑ *These people come from the poorer segments of society.*
2 **N-COUNT** SCIENCE The **segments** of an animal's body are its different sections, especially the sections between two joints. [from Latin]
→ look at Picture Dictionary: **fruit**

seg|re|ga|tion /sɛgrɪgeɪʃⁿn/ **N-NONCOUNT** SOCIAL STUDIES **Segregation** is the official practice of separating people, especially based on race or religion. ❑ *The report criticized the racial segregation of students in the school.*

seis|mic /saɪzmɪk/
1 **ADJ** SCIENCE **Seismic** means caused by or relating to an earthquake. ❑ *Earthquakes produce two types of seismic waves.*
2 **ADJ** A **seismic** shift or change is a very sudden or dramatic change. ❑ *I have never*

seen such a seismic shift in public opinion in such a short period of time. [from Greek]
→ look at Word Web: **earthquake**

seis|mic gap (**seismic gaps**) **N-COUNT** SCIENCE A **seismic gap** is a section of a geological fault where there has not been an earthquake for a relatively long time.

seis|mo|gram /saɪzməgræm/ (**seismograms**) **N-COUNT** SCIENCE A **seismogram** is a graph produced by a seismograph that shows the strength of an earthquake.

Word Link	*graph ≈ writing : auto*graph, bio*graphy*, seismo*graph*

seis|mo|graph /saɪzməgræf/ (**seismographs**) **N-COUNT** SCIENCE A **seismograph** is an instrument for recording and measuring the strength of earthquakes.
→ look at Word Webs: **earthquake, tsunami**

seis|mol|ogy /saɪzmɒlədʒi/ **N-NONCOUNT** SCIENCE **Seismology** is the scientific study of earthquakes.

seize /siz/ (**seizes, seizing, seized**)
1 **V-T** If you **seize** something, you take hold of it quickly and firmly. ❑ *He seized my arm and pulled me closer.*
2 **V-T** When you **seize** an opportunity, you use it and do something that you want to do. ❑ *They seized the opportunity to study his pictures during their visits.* [from Old French]

sel|dom /sɛldəm/ **ADV** If something **seldom** happens, it does not happen very often. ❑ *They seldom speak to each other.* ❑ *I've seldom felt so happy.* [from Old English]

se|lect /sɪlɛkt/ (**selects, selecting, selected**) **V-T** If you **select** something, you choose it from a group of similar things. ❑ *Only three players were selected for the Olympic team.* ❑ *Select "Save" from the File menu.* [from Latin]

Thesaurus	select	Also look up :
V	choose, pick out, take	

se|lec|tion /sɪlɛkʃⁿn/ (**selections**) **N-COUNT** A **selection** is a set of people or things that someone has chosen, or that you can choose from. ❑ *The singer will perform a selection of his favorite songs.* ❑ *Choose from our selection of fine wines.* [from Latin]

se|lec|tive /sɪlɛktɪv/
1 **ADJ** A **selective** process applies only to a few things or people. ❑ *They put together a selective list of people to invite to the party.*

● **se|lec|tive|ly** ADV ❑ *Within the project, trees are selectively cut down.*

2 ADJ When someone is **selective**, they choose things carefully, for example the things that they buy or do. ❑ *Sales still happen, but buyers are more selective.* ● **se|lec|tive|ly** ADV ❑ *People on small incomes want to shop selectively.* [from Latin]

se|lec|tive breed|ing N-NONCOUNT SCIENCE **Selective breeding** is the process of breeding certain characteristics in animals in preference to others.

self /sɛlf/ (**selves**) N-COUNT Your **self** is your own personality or nature. ❑ *You're looking like your usual self again.* [from Old English]

self-con|fi|dent ADJ Someone who is **self-confident** behaves confidently because they feel sure of their abilities or value. ❑ *...self-confident young woman.* ● **self-con|fi|dence** N-NONCOUNT ❑ *I lost all my self-confidence.*

self-con|scious ADJ Someone who is **self-conscious** is easily embarrassed because they feel that everyone is judging them. ❑ *I felt a bit self-conscious in my bikini.*

self-con|trol N-NONCOUNT **Self-control** is the ability to control yourself and your feelings. ❑ *She was told to learn self-control.*

self-de|fense N-NONCOUNT **Self-defense** is the use of force to protect yourself against someone who is attacking you. ❑ *Use your weapon only in self-defense.*

self-em|ployed ADJ BUSINESS If you are **self-employed**, you work for yourself, rather than for someone else. ❑ *If you are self-employed, it is easy to leave work early.*

self-es|teem N-NONCOUNT Your **self-esteem** is how you feel about yourself and whether you have a good opinion of yourself. ❑ *Harry was a man of low self-esteem.*

selfie /sɛlfiː/ (**selfies**) N-COUNT A **selfie** is a photograph that you take of yourself, especially using a smartphone. [INFORMAL] ❑ *He took a selfie in front of the Taj Mahal.*

self|ish /sɛlfɪʃ/ ADJ Someone who is **selfish** cares only about themselves, and not about other people. ❑ *I think I've been very selfish.* ● **self|ish|ly** ADV ❑ *He selfishly emptied the cookie jar.* ● **self|ish|ness** N-NONCOUNT ❑ *Julie's selfishness shocked us.* [from Old English]

self-pol|li|nat|ing ADJ SCIENCE If a plant is **self-pollinating**, the female part of the plant is fertilized by pollen from the male part of the same plant.

self-re|spect N-NONCOUNT If you have **self-respect** you feel confident about your own ability and value. ❑ *They have lost their jobs, their homes, and their self-respect.*

self-study N-NONCOUNT **Self-study** is study that you do on your own, without a teacher. ❑ *She's started a self-study course.*

sell /sɛl/ (**sells, selling, sold**)
1 V-T/V-I BUSINESS If you **sell** something that you own, you let someone have it in return for money. ❑ *Emily sold the paintings to an art gallery.* ❑ *The directors sold the business for $14.8 million.* ❑ *When is the best time to sell?*
2 V-T BUSINESS If a store **sells** a particular thing, it is available for people to buy there. ❑ *The store sells newspapers and candy bars.*
3 V-I BUSINESS If something **sells for** a particular price, that price is paid for it. ❑ *The candy usually sells for $5.*
4 V-I BUSINESS If something **sells**, it is bought by the public, usually in large quantities. ❑ *Even if this album doesn't sell, we won't change our style.* [from Old English]
▶ **sell out** **1** BUSINESS If a store **sells out** of something, it sells all of its supply of it. ❑ *The supermarket sold out of milk in a single day.*
2 If a performance, a sports event, or another entertainment **sells out**, all the tickets for it are sold. ❑ *Football games often sell out fast.*

Word Link	*ar, er* ≈ *one who acts as* : *buyer, liar, seller*

sell|er /sɛlər/ (**sellers**)
1 N-COUNT BUSINESS A **seller** of a type of thing is a person or a company that sells that type of thing. ❑ *She's a flower seller.*
2 N-COUNT BUSINESS In a business deal, the **seller** is the person who is selling something to someone else. ❑ *The seller is responsible for collecting the tax.*
3 N-COUNT BUSINESS If you describe a product as, for example, a big **seller**, you mean that large numbers of it are being sold. ❑ *I think our new phone is going to be a big seller.* [from Old English]

selves /sɛlvz/ **Selves** is the plural of **self**. [from Old English]

se|men /siːmən/ N-NONCOUNT SCIENCE **Semen** is the liquid containing sperm that is produced by the sex organs of men and male animals. [from Latin]

se|mes|ter /sɪmɛstər/ (**semesters**) **N-COUNT** A **semester** is half of a school or college year. ❑ *February 22nd is when most of their students begin their spring semester.* [from German]

| Word Link | semi ≈ half: *semicircle, semicolon, semifinal* |

semi|cir|cle /sɛmɪsɜrkəl, sɛmaɪ-/ (**semicircles**) **N-COUNT** MATH A **semicircle** is one half of a circle. ❑ *They sit in a semicircle and share stories.* [from Latin]

semi|co|lon /sɛmikoʊlən/ (**semicolons**) **N-COUNT** LANGUAGE ARTS A **semicolon** is the mark ; that you use in writing to separate different parts of a sentence. [from Latin] → look at Picture Dictionary: **punctuation**

semi|fi|nal /sɛmɪfaɪnəl, sɛmaɪ-/ (**semifinals**) **N-COUNT** SPORTS A **semifinal** is one of the two games in a competition that are played to decide who will play in the final part. ❑ *The basketball team lost in their semifinal yesterday.* [from Latin]

semi|nar /sɛmɪnɑr/ (**seminars**) **N-COUNT** A **seminar** is a class at a college or a university in which the teacher and a small group of students discuss a topic. ❑ *Students are asked to prepare material for the weekly seminars.* [from German]

semi|nif|er|ous tu|bule /sɛmɪnɪfərəs tubyul/ (**seminiferous tubules**) **N-COUNT** SCIENCE **Seminiferous tubules** are tubes inside the testes of male animals where sperm is produced.

semi|tone /sɛmitoʊn, sɛmaɪ-/ (**semitones**) **N-COUNT** MUSIC In Western music, a **semitone** is the smallest interval between two musical notes.

Sen|ate /sɛnɪt/ (**Senates**) **N-PROPER** SOCIAL STUDIES The **Senate** is the smaller and more important of the two parts of the legislature in some U.S. states and in some countries, for example the United States and Australia. ❑ *That year the Republicans gained two Senate seats.*

sena|tor /sɛnɪtər/ (**senators**) **N-COUNT** SOCIAL STUDIES A **senator** is a member of a Senate, for example in the United States or Australia. [from Latin]

send /sɛnd/ (**sends, sending, sent**) **1** **V-T** When you **send** someone a message or a package, you make it go to them. ❑ *I sent her an email this morning.* ❑ *Hannah sent me a letter last week.* **2** **V-T** If you **send** someone somewhere, you make them go there. ❑ *His parents sent him to the grocery store.* [from Old English]

▶ **send for** If you **send for** someone, you send them a message asking them to come and see you. ❑ *When he arrived in Portland, he sent for his wife and children.*

▶ **send off** When you **send off** a letter or package, you send it somewhere by mail. ❑ *He sent off copies to various people.*

sen|ior /sinyər/ (**seniors**) **1** **ADJ** The **senior** people in an organization or a profession have the most important jobs. ❑ *He was a senior official in the Israeli government.* **2** **N-COUNT** **Seniors** are students in a high school, a university, or a college who are in their final year of study. ❑ *How many high school seniors go on to college?* [from Latin]

sen|ior citi|zen (**senior citizens**) **N-COUNT** A **senior citizen** is an older person, especially someone over 65. ❑ *We want to improve healthcare services for senior citizens.* → look at Picture Dictionary: **age**

| Word Link | sens ≈ feeling : *sensation, sensible, sensitive* |

sen|sa|tion /sɛnseɪʃən/ (**sensations**) **1** **N-COUNT** A **sensation** is a physical feeling. ❑ *Floating can be a pleasant sensation.* **2** **N-NONCOUNT** **Sensation** is your ability to feel things physically. ❑ *The pain was so bad that she lost all sensation.* **3** **N-COUNT** If a person, an event, or a situation is a **sensation**, it causes great excitement or interest. ❑ *The movie was an overnight sensation.* [from Medieval Latin] → look at Word Web: **taste**

sen|sa|tion|al /sɛnseɪʃənəl/ **ADJ** A **sensational** result, event, or situation causes great excitement and interest. ❑ *...a sensational victory.* [from Medieval Latin]

sense /sɛns/ (**senses, sensing, sensed**) **1** **N-COUNT** SCIENCE Your **senses** are your physical ability to see, smell, hear, touch, and taste. ❑ *Foxes have a strong sense of smell.* **2** **V-T** If you **sense** something, you become aware of it, although it is not very obvious. ❑ *She probably sensed that I wasn't telling the truth.* **3** **N-SING** If you have a **sense of** something, you feel it. ❑ *She felt a sense of relief as she crossed the finish line.*

S

4 **N-NONCOUNT** Sense is the ability to think carefully about something and do the right thing. ❑ *Now that he's older, he has a bit more sense.*

5 → see also **common sense**

6 **N-COUNT** LANGUAGE ARTS A **sense** of a word is one of its possible meanings. ❑ *This noun has four senses.*

7 **PHRASE** If something **makes sense**, you can understand it. ❑ *Do these figures make sense to you?* [from Latin]

→ look at Word Web: **smell**

sense memo|ry (sense memories) **N-COUNT/N-NONCOUNT** ARTS **Sense memory** is the memory of physical sensations such as sounds and smells, that actors sometimes use in order to gain a better understanding of the character they are playing.

sense of hu|mor **N-SING** Someone who has a **sense of humor** often finds things funny, and is not serious all the time. ❑ *She has a good sense of humor.*

sen|sible /sɛnsɪbᵊl/ **ADJ** Sensible actions or decisions are good because they are based on reasons rather than emotions. ❑ *It might be sensible to get a lawyer.* ❑ *The sensible thing is to leave them alone.* ● **sen|sibly** /sɛnsɪbli/ **ADV** ❑ *He sensibly decided to hide for a while.* [from Old French]

sen|si|tive /sɛnsɪtɪv/

1 **ADJ** A person or thing that is **sensitive to** something is easily affected by it. ❑ *This chemical is sensitive to light.* ❑ *He is very sensitive to the cold.*

2 **ADJ** If you are **sensitive to** other people, you show that you understand their feelings. ❑ *The classroom teacher must be sensitive to a child's needs.*

3 **ADJ** If you are **sensitive about** something, you are easily worried and offended when people talk about it. ❑ *Young people are sensitive about their appearance.*

4 **ADJ** A **sensitive** subject is a subject that people need to deal with carefully, because it might make people upset. ❑ *Employment is a very sensitive issue.* [from Medieval Latin]

Word Partnership	Use sensitive with :
ADV	overly sensitive, so sensitive, too sensitive **1**–**3**
	highly sensitive, very sensitive **1**–**4**
	politically sensitive **3**
N	sensitive areas, sensitive information, sensitive issue, sensitive material **4**

sen|so|ry neu|ron /sɛnsəri nʊərɒn/ (sensory neurons) **N-COUNT** SCIENCE Sensory neurons are nerve cells that respond to stimuli such as light or sound and send the information to the central nervous system. → look at Word Web: **nervous system**

sent /sɛnt/ **Sent** is the past tense and past participle of **send**.

sen|tence /sɛntəns/ (sentences, sentencing, sentenced)

1 **N-COUNT** LANGUAGE ARTS A **sentence** is a group of words that tells you something or asks a question. When a sentence is written, it begins with a capital letter and ends with a period. ❑ *After I've written each sentence, I read it aloud.*

2 **N-COUNT/N-NONCOUNT** SOCIAL STUDIES In a law court, a **sentence** is the punishment that a person receives. ❑ *He was given a four-year sentence.*

3 **V-T** SOCIAL STUDIES When a judge **sentences** someone, he or she tells the court what their punishment will be. ❑ *The court sentenced him to five years in prison.* [from Old French]

→ look at Word Web: **trial**

sen|ti|ment /sɛntɪmənt/ (sentiments)

1 **N-COUNT/N-NONCOUNT** A **sentiment** is an attitude, a feeling, or an opinion. ❑ *Public sentiment was turning against him.*

2 **N-NONCOUNT** **Sentiment** is feelings such as pity or love, especially for things in the past, and may be considered exaggerated and foolish. ❑ *Laura kept that letter out of sentiment.* [from Medieval Latin]

sen|ti|men|tal /sɛntɪmɛntᵊl/

1 **ADJ** Someone or something that is **sentimental** feels or shows too much pity or love. ❑ *I'm trying not to be sentimental about the past.*

2 **ADJ** **Sentimental** means relating to or connected with your feelings. ❑ *Our photographs are of sentimental value.* [from Medieval Latin]

se|pal /sipəl/ (sepals) **N-COUNT** SCIENCE Sepals are a part of the outer structure of a flower, that resemble leaves and protect the bud while it is growing. [from New Latin]

sepa|rate (separates, separating, separated)

PRONUNCIATION HELP
Pronounce the adjective /sɛpərɪt/. Pronounce the verb /sɛpəreɪt/.

S

1 **ADJ** If one thing is **separate from** another, the two things are apart and are not connected. ❑ *Use separate surfaces for cutting raw meats and cooked meats.* ❑ *Men and women have separate exercise rooms.* ❑ *North Carolina and South Carolina are separate states.* ● **sepa|rate|ly** /sɛpərɪtli/ **ADV** ❑ *Cook each vegetable separately.*
2 **V-T/V-I** If you **separate** people or things, or if they **separate**, you move them or they move apart. ❑ *The police tried to separate the two groups.* ❑ *They separated and the boy went home.*
3 **V-T/V-I** If a couple who are married or living together **separate**, they decide to live apart. ❑ *Her parents separated when she was very young.* ● **sepa|rat|ed** /sɛpəreɪtɪd/ **ADJ** ❑ *Rachel's parents are separated.*
4 **V-T** If something **separates** two people, groups, or things, it exists between them. ❑ *The white fence separated the yard from the field.* [from Latin]

Thesaurus	separate Also look up :
ADJ	disconnected, divided **1**
V	divide, split **2** **5** **4**

Sep|tem|ber /sɛptɛmbər/ (**Septembers**) **N-COUNT/N-NONCOUNT** September is the ninth month of the year. ❑ *Her son was born in September.* [from Old English]

sep|tic tank (**septic tanks**) **N-COUNT** A septic tank is an underground tank where feces, urine, and other waste matter are made harmless using bacteria.

Word Link	sequ ≈ following : consequence, sequel, sequence

se|quel /sikwᵊl/ (**sequels**) **N-COUNT** A book or movie that is a **sequel to** an earlier one continues the story of the earlier one. ❑ *She is writing a sequel to Daphne du Maurier's "Rebecca."* [from Late Latin]

se|quence /sikwəns/ (**sequences**) **N-COUNT** A **sequence of** events or things is a number of them that come one after another. ❑ *This is the sequence of events that led to the murder.* [from Medieval Latin]

ser|geant /sɑrdʒᵊnt/ (**sergeants**) **N-COUNT** A **sergeant** is an officer in the army or the police. ❑ *A police sergeant patrolling the area noticed the fire.* [from Old French]

se|rial /sɪəriəl/ (**serials**) **N-COUNT** LANGUAGE ARTS A **serial** is a story that is told in a number of parts on television or radio, or in a magazine or a newspaper. ❑ *The book*

was filmed as a six-part TV serial. [from New Latin]

se|rial mu|sic **N-NONCOUNT** MUSIC **Serial music** is a type of music that uses a particular set of notes, usually twelve, and organizes them in a particular way.

se|ries /sɪəriz/ (**series**)
1 **N-COUNT** A **series of** things or events is a number of them that come one after another. ❑ *There will be a series of meetings with political leaders.*
2 **N-COUNT** A radio or television **series** is a set of programs. ❑ *The long-running TV series is filmed in Los Angeles.* [from Latin]

se|ries cir|cuit (**series circuits**) **N-COUNT** SCIENCE A **series circuit** is an electrical circuit in which there is only one possible path that the electricity can follow.

se|ri|ous /sɪəriəs/
1 **ADJ** **Serious** problems or situations are very bad, and they make people worried or afraid. ❑ *Crime is a serious problem in our society.* ● **se|ri|ous|ness** **N-NONCOUNT** ❑ *They don't realize the seriousness of the crisis.*
2 **ADJ** **Serious** matters are important, and people need to think about them carefully. ❑ *This is a very serious matter.*
3 **ADJ** If you are **serious about** something, you are not joking, and you really mean what you say. ❑ *You really are serious about this, aren't you?*
4 **ADJ** **Serious** people are thoughtful and quiet, and do not laugh very often. ❑ *...a serious person.* [from Late Latin]

se|ri|ous|ly /sɪəriəsli/
1 **PHRASE** If you **take** someone or something **seriously**, you believe that they are important and deserve attention. ❑ *The company takes all complaints seriously.*
2 **ADV** **Seriously** means in a way that is very bad, and that makes you worried or afraid. ❑ *This law could seriously damage my business.*
3 **ADV** You use **seriously** to ask someone whether they are joking, or to show that you really mean what you say. ❑ *"I followed him home."—"Seriously?"* ❑ *I do want to come with you. Seriously.* [from Late Latin]

ser|mon /sɜrmən/ (**sermons**) **N-COUNT** A **sermon** is a talk that a religious leader gives as part of a religious service. ❑ *Cardinal Murphy will deliver the sermon on Sunday.* [from Old French]

S

serv|ant /sɜ́rvᵊnt/ (**servants**)

1 **N-COUNT** A **servant** is someone who works at another person's home, doing work like cooking or cleaning. ❑ *The family employed several servants.* [from Old French]

2 → see also **civil servant**

serve /sɜ́rv/ (**serves, serving, served**)

1 **V-T/V-I** When you **serve** food and drinks, you give people food and drinks. ❑ *The restaurant serves breakfast, lunch, and dinner.* ❑ *Refrigerate the cake until ready to serve.*

2 **V-T/V-I** Someone who **serves** customers in a store or a bar helps them and provides them with what they want to buy. ❑ *Noah served me coffee and pie.* ❑ *Eve was serving in the restaurant yesterday.*

3 **V-T** If you **serve** your country, an organization, or a person, you do useful work for them. ❑ *He spoke of the fine character of those who serve their country.*

4 **V-T/V-I** If something **serves as** something or **serves** a purpose, it performs a function. ❑ *She showed me into the front room, which served as her office.* ❑ *I do not think an investigation would serve any useful purpose.*

5 **V-T** If something **serves** people or an area, it provides them with something that they need. ❑ *There are thousands of small businesses that serve the community.*

6 **V-T** If you **serve** a period of time, you spend a period of time in prison. ❑ *Mills was serving two years for robbery.* [from Old French]

serv|er /sɜ́rvər/ (**servers**)

1 **N-COUNT** TECHNOLOGY A **server** is a computer that stores information and supplies it to a number of computers on a network. ❑ *They couldn't send any emails because the mail server was down.*

2 **N-COUNT** A **server** is a person who works in a restaurant, serving people with food and drink. ❑ *A server came by with a tray of coffee cups.* [from Old French]
→ look at Word Web: **Internet**

ser|vice /sɜ́rvɪs/ (**services**)

1 **N-COUNT** A **service** is something that the public needs, such as transportation or energy supplies. ❑ *There is a regular local bus service to Yorkdale.*

2 **N-NONCOUNT** **Service** is the help that people in a restaurant, a hotel, or a store give you. ❑ *We always receive good service in that restaurant.*

3 **N-NONCOUNT** **Service** is the time that you spend working for someone else. ❑ *Most employees had long service with the company.*

4 **N-COUNT** A **service** is a religious ceremony. ❑ *After the service, his body was taken to a cemetery.*

5 **N-COUNT** If a vehicle or a machine has a **service**, it is examined, repaired, and cleaned so that it will keep working efficiently and safely. ❑ *The car needs a service.* [from Old French]

6 → see also **civil service**
→ look at Word Web: **industry**

ser|vice|man /sɜ́rvɪsmən/ (**servicemen**)

N-COUNT A **serviceman** is a man who is in the army, navy, air force, or marines. ❑ *He was an American serviceman in Vietnam.*

ses|sion /sɛ́ʃᵊn/ (**sessions**) **N-COUNT**

A **session** of a particular activity is a period of that activity. ❑ *The two leaders arrived for a photo session.* [from Latin]

┌─────────────────────────────┐
│   **set**   │
│ ❶ NOUN USES   │
│ ❷ VERB AND ADJECTIVE USES   │
│ ❸ PHRASES AND PHRASAL   │
│   VERBS   │
└─────────────────────────────┘

❶ set /sɛ́t/ (**sets**)

1 **N-COUNT** A **set of** things is a number of things that belong together. ❑ *The table and chairs are normally bought as a set.* ❑ *I got a chess set for my birthday.*

2 **N-COUNT** ARTS The **set** for a movie is the place where it is made. ❑ *The place looked like the set of a James Bond movie.*

3 **N-COUNT** A television **set** is a television. ❑ *Children spend too much time in front of the television set.* [from Old French]
→ look at Picture Dictionary: **drama**
→ look at Word Web: **theater**

❷ set /sɛ́t/ (**sets, setting**)

┌─────────────────────────────────────┐
│ **LANGUAGE HELP**   │
│ The form **set** is used in the present tense │
│ and is the past tense and past participle of │
│ the verb.   │
└─────────────────────────────────────┘

1 **V-T** If you **set** something somewhere, you put it there carefully. ❑ *She set the vase down gently on the table.*

2 **V-T** When you **set** a clock or a device, you change the time or controls on it so that it is ready to start operating. ❑ *I set my alarm clock for seven o'clock every morning.*

3 **V-T** If you **set** a date or a price, you decide what it will be. ❑ *They have finally set the date of their wedding.*

S

4 **v-t** If you **set** a record or an example, you do something that people will want to achieve. ❑ *The new world record was set by Stephen Jones of Great Britain.*

5 **v-i** When the sun **sets**, it goes down in the sky until you can no longer see it. ❑ *They watched the sun set behind the hills.*

6 **v-t** When someone **sets** the table, they prepare it for a meal by putting plates, glasses, knives, forks, and spoons on it.

7 **v-i** When jelly, glue, or cement **sets**, it becomes firm or hard. ❑ *You can add fruit to these desserts as they begin to set.*

8 **ADJ** A **set** time is fixed and cannot be changed. ❑ *The kids have to be home at a set time every evening.*

9 **ADJ** If a movie or a story is **set** in a particular place or time, the events in it happen in that place or at that time. ❑ *The play is set in a small Midwestern town.* [from Old French]

10 → see also **setting**

→ look at Usage note at **sit**

❸ set /sɛt/ (**sets, setting**)

> **LANGUAGE HELP**
> The form **set** is used in the present tense and is the past tense and past participle of the verb.

1 **PHRASE** If you **set fire to** something or **set** something **on fire**, you make it burn. ❑ *Angry protestors threw stones and set cars on fire.*

2 **PHRASE** If you **set** someone **free**, you cause them to be free. ❑ *They agreed to set the prisoners free.* [from Old French]

▶ **set off** When you **set off**, you start going somewhere. ❑ *Nick set off for his farmhouse in Connecticut.*

▶ **set out** **1** If you **set out to** do something, you start trying to do it. ❑ *He did what he set out to do.*

2 When you **set out**, you start a trip. ❑ *When setting out on a long walk, always wear comfortable shoes.*

▶ **set up** If you **set** something **up**, you start or arrange it. ❑ *He plans to set up his own business.*

set|back /sɛtbæk/ (**setbacks**) **N-COUNT** A **setback** is an event that delays your progress or reverses some of the progress that you have made. ❑ *He suffered a serious setback in his career.*

set|ting /sɛtɪŋ/ (**settings**)

1 **N-COUNT** A particular **setting** is a

particular place or type of surroundings where something is or takes place. ❑ *Rome is the perfect setting for romance.*

2 **N-COUNT** A **setting** is one of the positions to which the controls of a device such as a stove or a heater can be adjusted. ❑ *Bake the fish on a high setting.* [from Old English]

3 → see also **set**

set|tle /sɛt³l/ (**settles, settling, settled**)

1 **v-t** If people **settle** an argument or a problem, they decide what to do by talking about it. ❑ *They agreed to try again to settle the dispute.*

2 **v-t** If something **is settled**, it has all been decided and arranged. ❑ *We feel the matter is now settled.*

3 **v-t/v-i** If you **settle** a debt, you pay the amount that you owe. ❑ *I settled the bill for my coffee and left.* ❑ *All my debts are settled.*

4 **v-i** When people **settle** in a place, they start living there permanently. ❑ *He visited Paris and eventually settled there.*

5 **v-t/v-i** If you **settle** somewhere, you sit down and make yourself comfortable. ❑ *Brandon settled in front of the television.*

6 **v-i** If something **settles**, it sinks slowly down and becomes still. ❑ *The fog blows over the mountains and settles in the valley.* [from Old English]

▶ **settle down** **1** If a person **settles down**, they become calm after being excited. ❑ *Come on, kids. Time to settle down and go to sleep now.*

2 When someone **settles down**, they start living a quiet life in one place. ❑ *One day I'll settle down and have a family.*

▶ **settle in** If you **settle in**, you become used to living in a new place, doing a new job, or going to a new school. ❑ *I enjoyed school once I settled in.*

▶ **settle on** If you **settle on** a particular thing, you choose it after considering other choices. ❑ *I finally settled on a Mercedes.*

▶ **settle up** When you **settle up**, you pay a bill or a debt. ❑ *I'll have to settle up before I leave.*

Word Partnership	Use settle with :
N	settle **differences**, settle **things** **1**
	settle **a dispute**, settle **a matter** **1** **2**
V	**agree to** settle, **decide to** settle **1** **2**

set|tled /sɛt³ld/

1 **ADJ** If you have a **settled** way of life, you stay in one place, in one job, or with one person, rather than moving around or

changing. ❏ *He decided to lead a more settled life.*
2 ADJ A **settled** situation or system stays the same all the time. ❏ *The weather will be more settled tomorrow.* [from Old English]

set|tle|ment /sɛt°lmənt/ (**settlements**)
1 N-COUNT SOCIAL STUDIES A **settlement** is an official agreement between two people or groups after they have disagreed about something. ❏ *Officials are hoping for a peaceful settlement of the crisis.*
2 N-COUNT SOCIAL STUDIES A **settlement** is a place where people have come to live and have built homes. ❏ *The village is a settlement of just fifty houses.* [from Old English]

set|tler /sɛtlər, sɛt°l-/ (**settlers**) **N-COUNT** SOCIAL STUDIES **Settlers** are people who go to live in a place where not many people live, and start a new life there. ❏ *He was one of the early settlers in North America.* [from Old English]

set|up /sɛtʌp/ (**setups**) also **set-up N-COUNT** A particular **setup** is a particular system or way of organizing something. [INFORMAL] ❏ *It appears to be the ideal domestic setup.*

sev|en /sɛv°n/ **NUM** MATH **Seven** is the number 7. [from Old English]

> **Word Link** teen ≈ plus ten, from 13-19 : eighteen, seventeen, teenager

sev|en|teen /sɛv°ntin/ **NUM** MATH **Seventeen** is the number 17. [from Old English]

sev|en|teenth /sɛv°ntinθ/ **ADJ/ADV** MATH The **seventeenth** item in a series is the one that you count as number seventeen. ❏ *She got the job just after her seventeenth birthday.* [from Old English]

sev|enth /sɛv°nθ/ (**sevenths**)
1 ADJ/ADV MATH The **seventh** item in a series is the one that you count as number seven. ❏ *I was the seventh child in the family.*
2 N-COUNT MATH A **seventh** is one of seven equal parts of something (⅐). [from Old English]

sev|en|ti|eth /sɛv°ntiəθ/ **ADJ/ADV** MATH The **seventieth** item in a series is the one that you count as number seventy. ❏ *It was my grandmother's seventieth birthday last week.* [from Old English]

sev|en|ty /sɛv°nti/
1 NUM MATH **Seventy** is the number 70.
2 N-PLURAL The **seventies** are the years

between 1970 and 1979. ❏ *In the early Seventies, he wanted to direct.*
3 N-PLURAL When you talk about the **seventies**, you mean the numbers between 70 and 79. For example, if you are in your **seventies**, you are aged between 70 and 79. ❏ *The temperature outside was in the seventies.* [from Old English]

sev|er|al /sɛvrəl/
1 DET You use **several** to talk about a number of people or things that is not large but is greater than two. ❏ *I spent several years in France.* ❏ *There were several blue boxes on the table.*
2 PRON **Several** is also a pronoun. ❏ *The cakes were delicious, and we ate several.* [from Medieval Latin]

se|vere /sɪvɪ̱ər/ (**severer, severest**)
1 ADJ You use **severe** to show that something is very bad. ❏ *The business is having severe financial problems.* ● **se|vere|ly ADV** ❏ *An aircraft crashed on the runway and was severely damaged.*
2 ADJ **Severe** punishments or criticisms are very strong. ❏ *A severe sentence is necessary for this type of crime.* ● **se|vere|ly ADV** ❏ *They want to punish dangerous drivers more severely.* [from Latin]

> **Thesaurus** severe Also look up :
> ADJ critical, extreme, intense, tough **1 2**

> **Word Partnership** Use **severe** with :
> N severe **consequences**, severe **depression**, severe **disease/illness**, severe **drought**, severe **flooding**, severe **injuries**, severe **pain**, severe **problem**, severe **symptoms**, severe **weather 1** severe **penalty**, severe **punishment 2**
> ADV less/more/most severe, **very** severe **1 2**

sew /so̱ʊ/ (**sews, sewing, sewed, sewn**) **V-T/V-I** When you **sew** pieces of cloth together, you join them using a needle and thread. ❏ *She sewed the dresses on the sewing machine.* ❏ *Anyone can sew on a button.* ● **sew|ing N-NONCOUNT** ❏ *She lists her hobbies as cooking, sewing, and going to the movies.* [from Old English]
→ look at Word Web: **quilt**

sew|age /su̱ɪdʒ/ **N-NONCOUNT Sewage** is waste matter such as feces or dirty water from homes and factories, which flows

S

away through sewers. ❏ *...treatment of raw sewage.*

→ look at Word Web: **pollution**

sew|age treat|ment plant (**sewage treatment plants**) **N-COUNT** A **sewage treatment plant** is a factory that removes waste materials from water that comes from sewers and drains.

sew|er /suər/ (**sewers**) **N-COUNT** A **sewer** is a large pipe under the ground that carries waste and rain water away. ❏ *The rain water drains into the city's sewer system.* [from Old French]

sewn /soʊn/ **Sewn** is the past participle of **sew**. [from Old English]

sex /sɛks/ (**sexes**)
1 **N-COUNT** The two **sexes** are the two groups, male and female, into which you can divide people and animals. ❏ *This movie appeals to both sexes.*
2 **N-COUNT** **SCIENCE** The **sex** of a person or an animal is their characteristic of being either male or female. ❏ *We can identify the sex of your unborn baby.*
3 **N-NONCOUNT** **Sex** is the physical activity by which people can produce children. ❏ *He was very open in his attitudes about sex.*
4 **PHRASE** If two people **have sex**, they perform the act of sex. [from Latin]

sex cell (**sex cells**) **N-COUNT** **SCIENCE** **Sex cells** are the two types of male and female cells that join together to make a new creature.

sex chro|mo|some (**sex chromosomes**) **N-COUNT** **SCIENCE** **Sex chromosomes** are the chromosomes that carry the genes that determine whether an individual will be male or female.

sex|ual /sɛkʃuəl/
1 **ADJ** **Sexual** means connected with sex. ❏ *The clinic can provide information about sexual health.*
2 **ADJ** **Sexual** means relating to the differences between male and female people. ❏ *There are laws against sexual discrimination.*
3 **ADJ** **SCIENCE** **Sexual** means relating to the biological process by which people and animals produce young. ❏ *Girls usually reach sexual maturity earlier than boys.* ● **sex|ual|ly** **ADV** ❏ *These organisms can reproduce sexually.* [from Late Latin]

sexu|al|ity /sɛkʃuælɪti/
1 **N-NONCOUNT** A person's **sexuality** is their sexual feelings. ❏ *The program focuses on the scientific aspects of sexuality.*
2 **N-NONCOUNT** You can refer to a person's **sexuality** when you are talking about whether they are sexually attracted to people of the same sex or a different sex. ❏ *...information about sexuality, reproduction, and the human body.* [from Late Latin]

sex|ual|ly trans|mit|ted dis|ease (**sexually transmitted diseases**) **N-COUNT** **SCIENCE** A **sexually transmitted disease** is a disease that can be passed from one person to another as a result of sexual activity. The short form **STD** is also used.

sex|ual re|pro|duc|tion **N-NONCOUNT** **SCIENCE** **Sexual reproduction** is the creation of new people, animals, or plants as a result of sexual activity.

sexy /sɛksi/ (**sexier, sexiest**) **ADJ** **Sexy** describes people and things that you think are sexually attractive. ❏ *She is the sexiest woman I have ever seen.* [from Latin]

shab|by /ʃæbi/ (**shabbier, shabbiest**) **ADJ** **Shabby** things or places look old and in bad condition. ❏ *His clothes were old and shabby.* [from Old English]

shade /ʃeɪd/ (**shades, shading, shaded**)
1 **N-COUNT** A **shade of** a particular color is one of its different forms. ❏ *The walls were painted in two shades of green.*
2 **N-NONCOUNT** **Shade** is an area where direct sunlight does not reach. ❏ *Alexis was reading in the shade of a tree.*
3 **V-T** If a place or an object **is shaded** by something, that thing prevents light from falling on it. ❏ *The beach was shaded by palm trees.*
4 **N-COUNT** A **shade** is a piece of material that you can pull down over a window. ❏ *Nancy left the shades down.*
5 **N-COUNT** A **shade** is color with black added to it. [from Old English]

shad|ow /ʃædoʊ/ (**shadows**) **N-COUNT** A **shadow** is a dark shape on a surface that is made when something blocks the light. ❏ *The long shadows of the trees fell across their path.* [from Old English]

shadow

shad|ow zone (shadow zones) **N-COUNT** SCIENCE A **shadow zone** is an area on the Earth's surface where seismic waves from an earthquake cannot be detected because they are unable to pass through the Earth's core.

shady /ʃeɪdi/ (shadier, shadiest) **ADJ** A **shady** place is not in bright sunlight. ❏ *We stopped in a shady place under some trees.* [from Old English]

shaft /ʃæft/ (shafts)
1 **N-COUNT** A **shaft** is a long vertical passage, for example for an elevator. ❏ *The fire began in an elevator shaft.*
2 **N-COUNT** SCIENCE In a machine, a **shaft** is a rod that turns around continually in order to transfer movement in the machine. ❏ *...a drive shaft.*
3 **N-COUNT** A **shaft of** light is a beam of light, for example sunlight shining through an opening. ❏ *A shaft of sunlight fell through the doorway.* [from Old English]

shake /ʃeɪk/ (shakes, shaking, shook, shaken)
1 **V-T** If someone or something **shakes**, they move quickly backward and forward or up and down. ❏ *My whole body was shaking with fear.*
2 **V-T** If you **shake** something or someone, you hold them and move them quickly backward and forward or up and down. ❏ *Always shake the bottle before you pour out the medicine.*
3 **N-COUNT** **Shake** is also a noun. ❏ *We gave the children a gentle shake to wake them.*
4 **V-T** If you **shake** your **head**, you move it from side to side to say "no." ❏ *"Did you see Crystal?" Kathryn shook her head.*
5 **PHRASE** If you **shake hands with** someone, you say hello or goodbye to them by holding their right hand in your own right hand and moving it up and down. You can also say that two people **shake hands**. ❏ *Michael shook hands with Burke.* [from Old English]

shaky /ʃeɪki/ (shakier, shakiest)
1 **ADJ** If a situation is **shaky**, it seems unlikely to be successful. ❏ *The couple's marriage is shaky.*
2 **ADJ** If your body or your voice is **shaky**, you cannot control it properly because you are sick or nervous. ❏ *Her voice was shaky and she was close to tears.* ● **shak|ily** **ADV** ❏ *"I don't feel well," she said shakily.* [from Old English]

shall /ʃəl, STRONG ʃæl/
1 **MODAL** You use **shall** with "I" and "we" in questions to make offers or suggestions. ❏ *Shall I get the keys?* ❏ *Well, shall we go?*
2 **MODAL** You use **shall**, usually with "I" and "we," when you are talking about something that will happen to you in the future. [FORMAL] ❏ *We shall be landing in Paris in sixteen minutes.* ❏ *I shall know more tomorrow.* [from Old English]

Usage	shall and will

Shall is mainly used in the most formal writing and speech; in everyday English, use *will*. *We shall overcome all obstacles to achieve victory. We will be home later.*

shal|low /ʃæloʊ/ (shallower, shallowest)
1 **ADJ** If something is **shallow**, it is not deep. ❏ *The river is very shallow here.*
2 **ADJ** If you describe a person or an idea as **shallow**, you disapprove of them because they do not show serious thought. ❏ *I think he is shallow and dishonest.* [from Old English]

shame /ʃeɪm/
1 **N-NONCOUNT** **Shame** is the very uncomfortable feeling that you have when you have done something wrong or stupid. ❏ *I was filled with shame.*
2 **N-SING** If you say that something is a **shame**, you feel sad or disappointed about it. ❏ *It was a shame about the weather, but the party was still a great success.* [from Old English]
→ look at Word Web: **emotion**

Word Partnership	Use **shame** with :
V	**experience** shame, **feel** shame **1**
N	**feelings of** shame, **sense of** shame **1**

shame|ful /ʃeɪmfəl/ **ADJ** If someone's behavior is **shameful**, it is very bad. ❏ *The government's treatment of the refugees was shameful.* [from Old English]

sham|poo /ʃæmpu/ (shampoos, shampooing, shampooed)
1 **N-COUNT/N-NONCOUNT** **Shampoo** is a liquid soap that you use for washing your hair. ❏ *Don't forget to pack a towel, soap, and shampoo.*
2 **V-T** If you **shampoo** your hair, you wash it using shampoo. ❏ *I shampooed my hair and dried it, then I got dressed.* [from Hindi]

shan't /ʃænt/ **Shan't** is short for "shall not."

shape /ʃeɪp/ (shapes, shaping, shaped)
1 **N-COUNT** The **shape of** something is its

S

Picture Dictionary · shapes

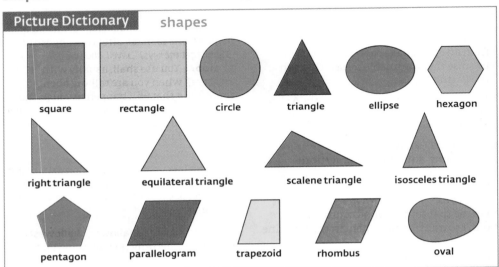

square · rectangle · circle · triangle · ellipse · hexagon

right triangle · equilateral triangle · scalene triangle · isosceles triangle

pentagon · parallelogram · trapezoid · rhombus · oval

form or the appearance of its outside edges or surfaces. ❑ *Pasta comes in all different shapes and sizes.*

2 N-COUNT MATH A **shape** is the form of something, for example a circle, a square, or a triangle. ❑ *Draw a heart shape.*

3 V-T If you **shape** something, you give it a particular shape. ❑ *Shape the dough into a ball and place it in the bowl.*

4 V-T Someone or something that **shapes** a situation has a great influence on the way it develops. ❑ *Our families shape our lives.*

5 PHRASE If someone or something is **in shape**, or **in good shape**, they are in a good state of health or in a good condition. ❑ *He's 76 and still in good shape.*

6 PHRASE If someone or something is **in bad shape**, they are in a bad state of health or in a bad condition. ❑ *The company is in bad shape.*

7 PHRASE If you are **out of shape**, you are unhealthy and you are not able to do a lot of physical activity. ❑ *I weighed 245 pounds and I was out of shape.* [from Old English]

→ look at Picture Dictionary: **shapes**
→ look at Word Webs: **circle, mathematics**

Word Partnership   Use shape with :

V	**change** shape **1**
	change the shape **of something 3**
	get in shape **5**
ADJ	**dark** shape **2**
	(pretty) bad/good/great shape, **better/worse** shape, **terrible** shape **5 6**

shaped /ʃeɪpt/ **ADJ** Something that is **shaped** like a particular object or in a particular way has the shape of that object or a shape of that type. ❑ *The perfume was in a bottle shaped like a flower.* ❑ *...large heart-shaped leaves.* [from Old English]

share /ʃɛər/ (**shares, sharing, shared**)

1 V-T/V-I If you **share** something **with** another person, you both have it or use it. ❑ *Jose shares an apartment with six other students.* ❑ *Maria and I shared a dessert.*

2 N-COUNT Your **share** of something is the part of it that you do or have. ❑ *I do my share of the housework.* ❑ *I need my share of the money now.*

3 N-COUNT BUSINESS A company's **shares** are the equal parts that its value is divided into. People can buy shares, so that they own a part of the company and have a part of its profit. ❑ *I've bought shares in my brother's new company.* [from Old English]

share|crop|per /ʃɛərkrɒpər/ (**sharecroppers**) **N-COUNT** SOCIAL STUDIES A **sharecropper** is a farmer who pays for his land with some of the crops that he produces. ● **share|crop|ping N-NONCOUNT** ❑ *Sharecropping is a contract between a land owner and a farm worker.*

share|holder /ʃɛərhoʊldər/ (**shareholders**) **N-COUNT** BUSINESS A **shareholder** is a person who owns shares.

shark /ʃɑrk/ (**sharks**) **N-COUNT** A **shark** is a very large fish. Some sharks have very sharp teeth and may attack people.

Word Web   shark

Sharks are different from other **fish**. The **skeleton** of a shark is made of **cartilage,** not bone. The flexibility of cartilage allows this **predator** to maneuver around its **prey** easily. Sharks also have several gill **slits** with no flap covering them. Its **scales** are also much smaller and harder than fish scales. And its teeth are special, too. Sharks grow new teeth when they lose old ones. It's almost impossible to escape from a shark. Some of them can swim up to 44 miles per hour. But sharks only kill 50 to 75 people each year worldwide.

→ look at Word Web: **shark**

sharp /ʃɑrp/ (**sharper, sharpest**)
1 **ADJ** A **sharp** point or edge is very thin and can cut through things very easily. ❏ *Cut the skin off the mango using a sharp knife.* ❏ *You'll need a sharp pencil and an eraser.*
2 **ADJ** A **sharp** bend or turn changes direction suddenly. ❏ *I came to a sharp bend in the road and had to brake quickly.* ● **sharp|ly ADV** ❏ *After a mile, the road turns sharply to the right.*
3 **ADV Sharp** is also an adverb. ❏ *Do not cross the bridge but turn sharp left instead.*
4 **ADJ** If you are **sharp,** you are good at noticing and understanding things. ❏ *Dan's very sharp, and a quick thinker.*
5 **ADJ** If you say something in a **sharp** way, you say it suddenly and angrily. ❏ *His sharp reply surprised me.* ● **sharp|ly ADV** ❏ *"Why didn't you tell me?" she asked sharply.*
6 **ADJ** A **sharp** change or feeling happens suddenly and is very big or strong. ❏ *There's been a sharp rise in oil prices.* ❏ *I felt a sharp pain in my right leg.* ● **sharp|ly ADV** ❏ *Unemployment rose sharply last year.*
7 **ADJ** A **sharp** image is very clear and easy to see. ❏ *Digital TV offers sharper images than analog TV.*
8 **ADV** If something will happen at a particular time **sharp,** it will happen at that time exactly. ❏ *Be in my office tomorrow morning at eight o'clock sharp.*
9 **ADJ** MUSIC An F **sharp** or a G **sharp,** for example, is a note that is slightly higher than F or G. Compare with **flat.** [from Old English]

Word Partnership   Use sharp with :

N	sharp **edge,** sharp **point,** sharp **teeth** 1
	sharp **eyes,** sharp **mind** 3
	sharp **criticism** 4
	sharp **decline,** sharp **increase,** sharp **pain** 5
ADV	**very** sharp 1–6

sharp|en /ʃɑrpən/ (**sharpens, sharpening, sharpened**) **V-T** If you **sharpen** something, you make its edge very thin or you make its end pointed. ❏ *What's the best way to sharpen a knife?* ❏ *Mike had to sharpen the pencils every morning.* [from Old English]

shat|ter /ʃætər/ (**shatters, shattering, shattered**) **V-T/V-I** If something **shatters,** or is **shattered,** it breaks into small pieces. ❏ *Megan dropped the glass, and it shattered on the floor.*
→ look at Word Webs: **crash, glass**

shat|tered /ʃætərd/ **ADJ** If you are **shattered,** you are extremely shocked and upset. ❏ *I was shattered to hear the news.*

shave /ʃeɪv/ (**shaves, shaving, shaved**)
1 **V-T/V-I** If you **shave,** you remove hair from your face or body by cutting it off using a razor or a shaver. ❏ *Samuel took a bath and shaved.* ❏ *Many women shave their legs.*
2 **N-COUNT Shave** is also a noun. ❏ *I need a shave.* [from Old English]

shav|er /ʃeɪvər/ (**shavers**) **N-COUNT** A **shaver** is an electric piece of equipment that you use for shaving hair from your face and body. ❏ *In 1937 the company introduced the world's first electric shaver.* [from Old English]

shawl /ʃɔl/ (**shawls**) **N-COUNT** A **shawl** is a large piece of cloth that a woman wears over her shoulders or head. [from Persian]
→ look at Picture Dictionary: **clothing**

she /ʃi, STRONG ʃi/

LANGUAGE HELP

She is a third person singular pronoun.
She is used as the subject of a verb.

PRON You use **she** to talk about a female person or animal when they are the subject of a sentence. ❏ *She's seventeen years old.* [from Old English]

S

shed /ʃɛd/ (sheds, shedding, shed)

> **LANGUAGE HELP**
>
> The form **shed** is used in the present tense and is the past tense and past participle of the verb.

1 N-COUNT A **shed** is a small building where you store things. ❑ *The house has a large shed in the backyard.*

2 V-T When a tree **sheds** its leaves, its leaves fall off in the autumn. ❑ *Some of the trees were already beginning to shed their leaves.*

3 V-T When an animal **sheds** hair or skin, some of its hair or skin falls off. ❑ *The snake sheds it skin periodically so it can grow.*

4 V-T If you **shed** tears, you cry. [FORMAL] ❑ *They will shed a few tears at their daughter's wedding.* [from Old English]
→ look at Word Web: **cry**

she'd /ʃid, ʃɪd/

1 **She'd** is short for "she had." ❑ *She'd been all over the world.*

2 **She'd** is short for "she would." ❑ *She'd do anything for a bit of money.*

sheep /ʃip/ (sheep) N-COUNT A **sheep** is a

farm animal with thick hair called wool. Farmers keep sheep for their wool or for their meat. [from Old English]
→ look at Word Web: **meat**

sheer /ʃɪər/ (sheerer, sheerest)

1 ADJ You can use **sheer** to emphasize that a state or situation is complete and does not involve or is not mixed with anything else. ❑ *His music is sheer delight.* ❑ *By sheer chance he was there.*

2 ADJ A **sheer** cliff or drop is extremely steep or completely vertical. ❑ *There was a sheer drop just outside my window.*

3 ADJ **Sheer** material is very thin, light, and delicate. ❑ *She wore sheer black stockings.* [from Old English]

> **Word Partnership** Use **sheer** with :
>
> N   sheer **delight**, sheer **force**, sheer **luck**, sheer **number**, sheer **pleasure**, sheer **power**, sheer **size**, sheer **strength**, sheer **terror**, sheer **volume** **1**

sheet /ʃit/ (sheets)

1 N-COUNT A **sheet** is a large piece of cloth that you sleep on or cover yourself with in bed. ❑ *Once a week, we change the sheets.*

2 N-COUNT A **sheet of** paper is a piece of

paper. ❑ *Sean folded the sheets of paper and put them in his briefcase.*

3 N-COUNT A **sheet of** glass, metal, or wood is a large, flat, thin piece of it. ❑ *The cranes were lifting giant sheets of steel.* [from Old English]
→ look at Picture Dictionary: **bed**
→ look at Word Web: **paper**

sheikh /ʃik, ʃeɪk/ (sheikhs) also sheik

N-COUNT SOCIAL STUDIES A **sheikh** is a male Arab chief or ruler. ❑ *...Sheikh Khalifa.* [from Arabic]

shelf /ʃɛlf/ (shelves) N-COUNT A **shelf** is a

long flat piece of wood on a wall or in a cabinet that you can keep things on. ❑ *Dad took a book from the shelf.* [from Old English]

shell /ʃɛl/ (shells)

1 N-COUNT The **shell** of something is the hard part that surrounds it and protects it. ❑ *They cracked the nuts and removed their shells.*

2 N-COUNT The **shell** of an animal such as a snail is the hard part that covers its back and protects it.

3 N-COUNT **Shells** are hard outer parts of small sea creatures that you find on beaches. ❑ *I have gathered shells since I was a child.* [from Old English]
→ look at Picture Dictionary: **shellfish**

she'll /ʃil, ʃɪl/ **She'll** is short for "she will."

❑ *Sharon was wonderful. I know she'll be greatly missed.*

shell|fish /ʃɛlfɪʃ/ (shellfish)

N-COUNT/N-NONCOUNT **Shellfish** are small creatures that live in the ocean and have a shell. ❑ *The restaurant serves local fish and shellfish.*
→ look at Picture Dictionary: **shellfish**

shel|ter /ʃɛltər/ (shelters, sheltering, sheltered)

1 N-COUNT A **shelter** is a place that protects you from bad weather or danger. ❑ *...a bus shelter.*

2 N-NONCOUNT **Shelter** is protection from bad weather or danger. ❑ *They took shelter under a tree.*

3 V-T If a place or thing **is sheltered** by something, it is protected by that thing from wind and rain. ❑ *The house was sheltered from the sun by huge trees.*
→ look at Word Web: **habitat**

S

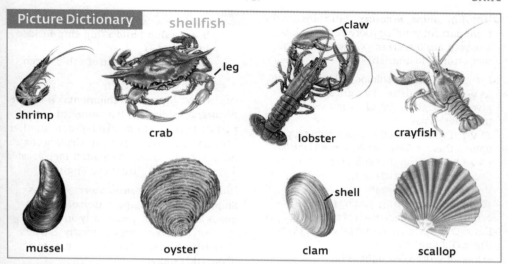

Picture Dictionary shellfish

shrimp

crab

leg

claw

lobster

crayfish

mussel

oyster

shell

clam

scallop

Word Partnership   Use **shelter** with :

N	**bomb** shelter ▮
	emergency shelter ▮ ▯
	shelter **and clothing, food and** shelter ▯
ADJ	**temporary** shelter ▮ ▯
V	**find** shelter, **provide** shelter, **seek** shelter ▯

shel|tered /ʃɛltərd/

1 **ADJ** A **sheltered** place is protected from wind and rain. ❏ *The beach is next to a sheltered bay.*

2 **ADJ** If you say that someone has led a **sheltered** life, you mean that they have been protected from difficult or unpleasant experiences. ❏ *Perhaps I've just led a really sheltered life.*

shep|herd /ʃɛpərd/ (**shepherds, shepherding, shepherded**)

1 **N-COUNT** A **shepherd** is a person, especially a man, whose job is to take care of sheep.

2 **V-T** If you **are shepherded** somewhere, someone takes you there to make sure that you arrive at the right place safely. ❏ *She was shepherded up the steps of the aircraft.* [from Old English]

sher|bet /ʃɜrbɪt/ **N-NONCOUNT** Sherbet is a frozen dessert made with fruit juice, sugar, and water. ❏ *...lemon sherbet.* [from Turkish]

sher|iff /ʃɛrɪf/ (**sheriffs**) **N-COUNT** SOCIAL STUDIES In the United States, a **sheriff** is a law enforcement officer (= a person who makes sure that people obey the law).

A sheriff is usually responsible for a county. ❏ *Her father was the town sheriff.* [from Old English]

she's /ʃiz, ʃɪz/

1 **She's** is short for "she is." ❏ *She's a really good cook.*

2 **She's** is short for "she has." ❏ *She's been married for seven years.*

shield /ʃild/ (**shields, shielding, shielded**)

1 **V-T** If something or someone **shields** you **from** danger or injury, they protect you from it. ❏ *I shielded my eyes from the sun with my hands.*

2 **N-COUNT** A **shield** is a large piece of metal or leather that soldiers carried in the past to protect their bodies. [from Old English] → look at Word Web: **army**

shield vol|ca|no (**shield volcanoes**)

N-COUNT SCIENCE A **shield volcano** is a broad volcano with low, sloping sides that is formed from lava that has erupted and become solid.

shift /ʃɪft/ (**shifts, shifting, shifted**)

1 **V-T/V-I** If you **shift** something, or if it **shifts**, it moves from one place to another. ❏ *Please would you help me shift the table over to the window?* ❏ *He shifted from foot to foot.*

2 **N-COUNT** A **shift** is one of the fixed periods of work in a factory or a hospital. ❏ *Nick works night shifts at the hospital.*

3 **V-T/V-I** If your opinion, a situation, or a policy **shifts**, it changes slightly. ❏ *Attitudes to mental illness have shifted in recent years.*

4 **N-COUNT** Shift is also a noun. ❏ *There's been a shift in government policy.* [from Old English]

S

shin /ʃɪn/ (shins) **N-COUNT** Your **shins** are the front parts of your legs between your knees and your ankles. ❑ *Ken suffered a bruised left shin.* [from Old English]

shine /ʃaɪn/ (shines, shining, shined or shone)
1 V-I When the sun or a light **shines**, it gives out bright light. ❑ *Today it's warm and the sun is shining.*
2 V-T If you **shine** a light somewhere, you point it there. ❑ *The guard shone a light in his face.*
3 V-I Something that **shines** is very bright because it is reflecting light. ❑ *The ocean shone in the silver moonlight.*
4 N-SING Something that has a **shine** is bright and clear because it is reflecting light. ❑ *This gel gives a beautiful shine to the hair.* [from Old English]
→ look at Word Web: **light bulb**

shin pad (shin pads) **N-COUNT** SPORTS A **shin pad** is a thick piece of material that you wear inside your socks to protect the lower part of your leg when you are playing a game such as soccer or football.
→ look at Picture Dictionary: **soccer**

shiny /ʃaɪni/ (shinier, shiniest) **ADJ** If a surface is **shiny**, it is bright and it reflects light. ❑ *Her blonde hair was shiny and clean.* [from Old English]
→ look at Word Web: **metal**

ship /ʃɪp/ (ships, shipping, shipped)
1 N-COUNT A **ship** is a large boat that carries people or goods. ❑ *The ship was ready to sail.*
2 V-T If goods **are shipped** somewhere, they are sent there. ❑ *Our company ships orders worldwide.* [from Old English]
→ look at Word Web: **ship**

ship|ment /ʃɪpmənt/ (shipments) **N-COUNT** BUSINESS A **shipment** is an amount of a particular kind of cargo that is sent to another country on a ship, a train, an airplane, or other vehicle. ❑ *Food shipments to the port could begin in a few weeks.* [from Old English]

ship|ping /ʃɪpɪŋ/ **N-NONCOUNT** BUSINESS **Shipping** is the transportation of cargo or goods as a business, especially on ships. ❑ *...the international shipping industry.* ❑ *Here's a coupon for free shipping of your catalog order.* [from Old English]

shirt /ʃɜrt/ (shirts)
1 N-COUNT A **shirt** is a piece of clothing with a collar and buttons, that you wear on the top part of your body. [from Old English]
2 → see also **T-shirt**
→ look at Picture Dictionary: **clothing**

shiv|er /ʃɪvər/ (shivers, shivering, shivered)
1 V-I If you **shiver**, your body shakes because you are cold, frightened, or sick. ❑ *She shivered with cold and fear.*
2 N-COUNT **Shiver** is also a noun. ❑ *She gave a small shiver.* [from Old English]

Large **ocean-going vessels** are an important way of carrying people and **cargo**. **Oil tankers** and **container ships** are common in many **ports**. **Ocean liners** and **cruise ships** carry tourists and give them a place to stay. Some of these **ships** are several stories tall. **Aircraft carriers** include a **flight deck** where planes can take off and land. **Ferries, barges**, fishing **craft**, and research **boats** are also an important part of the **marine** industry.

Picture Dictionary

shoe

sneaker

shoe

pump

hiking boot

slingback

sandal

flip flop

work boot

clog

dress shoe

boot

Word Partnership   Use shiver with :

v   **feel a** shiver, shiver **goes/runs down** your spine, *something* **makes you** shiver, *something* **sends a** shiver **down your** spine

shock /ʃɒk/ (shocks, shocking, shocked)
■ **N-COUNT** If you have a **shock**, you suddenly feel very upset because something unpleasant has happened. ❑ *William never recovered from the shock of his brother's death.*
■ **V-T** If something **shocks** you, it suddenly makes you feel very upset because it is so unpleasant. ❑ *After forty years as a police officer, nothing shocks me.* ● **shocked** **ADJ** ❑ *She was deeply shocked when she heard the news.*
■ **N-COUNT** A **shock** is the same as an **electric shock**. [from Old French]

Word Partnership   Use shock with :

N   **in a state of** shock, shock **value** ■
V   **come as a** shock, **express** shock, **feel** shock ■
   send a shock ■

shock|ing /ʃɒkɪŋ/ **ADJ** If something is **shocking**, it makes you feel very upset and surprised because you think that it is very bad or morally wrong. ❑ *Everyone found the photos shocking.* [from Old French]

shoe /ʃu/ (shoes) **N-COUNT** Shoes are things that you wear on your feet. ❑ *I need a new pair of shoes.* ❑ *I don't usually wear high-heeled shoes.* [from Old English]
→ look at Picture Dictionaries: **shoe, clothing**

shone /ʃoʊn/ **Shone** is the past tense and past participle of **shine**. [from Old English]

shook /ʃʊk/ **Shook** is the past tense of **shake**. [from Old English]

shoot /ʃut/ (shoots, shooting, shot)
■ **V-T** If someone **shoots** a person or an animal, they kill them or injure them by firing a gun at them. ❑ *The gunmen shot two policemen before they escaped.* ❑ *A man was shot dead during the robbery.*
■ **V-I** If someone **shoots**, they fire a bullet from a weapon. ❑ *He raised his arms above his head and shouted, "Don't shoot!"*
■ **V-I** If someone or something **shoots** in a particular direction, they move in that direction quickly and suddenly. ❑ *A car shot out of the driveway and crashed into them.*
■ **V-T** When people **shoot** a movie, they make a movie. ❑ *Tim wants to shoot his new movie in Mexico.*
■ **N-COUNT** **Shoots** are new parts that are growing from a plant or a tree. ❑ *It was spring, and new shoots began to appear.*
■ **V-I** SPORTS In soccer or basketball, when you **shoot**, you kick or throw the ball toward the goal or net. ❑ *Brennan shot and missed.* [from Old English]
■ → see also **shot**

shoot sys|tem (shoot systems) **N-COUNT** SCIENCE A plant's **shoot system** is the part of the plant that is above the ground, including the stem and leaves. Compare with **root system**.

S

shop /ʃɒp/ (**shops, shopping, shopped**)

1 **N-COUNT** A **shop** is a small store that sells a particular type of thing. ❑ *Paul and his wife run a flower shop.*

2 **V-I** When you **shop**, you go to stores or shops and buy things. ❑ *He always shops on Saturday mornings.* ● **shop|per** (**shoppers**) **N-COUNT** ❑ *The streets were filled with crowds of shoppers.* [from Old English]

Word Partnership	Use **shop** with :
N	**antique** shop, **pet** shop, **souvenir** shop **1** **auto** shop, **barber** shop, **beauty** shop, **repair** shop **1** **2** shop **owner** **1**

shop|ping /ʃɒpɪŋ/ **N-NONCOUNT** When you do **the shopping**, you go to stores or shops and buy things. ❑ *I'll do the shopping this afternoon.* [from Old English]

Word Partnership	Use **shopping** with :
N	shopping **bag**, shopping **district**, **food** shopping, **holiday** shopping, shopping **spree** **1**

shop|ping cart (**shopping carts**) **N-COUNT** A **shopping cart** is a large metal or plastic basket on wheels that you put your shopping in while you are in a store.

shop|ping mall (**shopping malls**) **N-COUNT** A **shopping mall** is a large building with lots of stores and restaurants inside it.

shore /ʃɔr/ (**shores**) **N-COUNT** GEOGRAPHY The **shore** of an ocean or a lake is the land along the edge of it. ❑ *They walked slowly down to the shore.* [from Middle Low German]

shore|line /ʃɔrlaɪn/ (**shorelines**) **N-COUNT** GEOGRAPHY A **shoreline** is the edge of an ocean, a lake, or a wide river. ❑ *We sat on rocks along the shoreline.*

short /ʃɔrt/ (**shorter, shortest, shorts**)

1 **ADJ** If something is **short**, it does not last very long. ❑ *Last year we all went to Miami Beach for a short vacation.*

2 **ADJ** Someone who is **short** is not tall. ❑ *She's a short woman with gray hair.*

3 **ADJ** Something that is **short** measures only a small amount from one end to the other. ❑ *The restaurant is only a short distance away.* ❑ *She has short, curly hair.*

4 **ADJ** If you are **short of** something, you do not have enough of it. ❑ *His family is very short of money.*

5 **ADJ** A word that is **short for** another word is a shorter way of saying it. ❑ *Her name's Jo— it's short for Josephine.*

6 **N-PLURAL** **Shorts** are pants with very short legs. ❑ *She was wearing pink shorts and a black t-shirt.* [from Old English]

→ look at Picture Dictionary: **hair**

Thesaurus	short	Also look up :
ADJ	brief, quick; (ant.) long **1** petite, slight, small; (ant.) tall **2**	

short|age /ʃɔrtɪdʒ/ (**shortages**) **N-COUNT/N-NONCOUNT** If there is a **shortage** of something, there is not enough of it. ❑ *In this town there is a great shortage of cheap housing.* [from Old English]

short|en /ʃɔrtən/ (**shortens, shortening, shortened**) **V-T/V-I** If you **shorten** something, you make it shorter. ❑ *The treatment shortens the length of the illness.* ❑ *The days shorten in winter.* [from Old English]

short|ly /ʃɔrtli/ **ADV** If something is going to happen **shortly**, it is going to happen soon. ❑ *"Please take a seat. Dr. Garcia will see you shortly."* [from Old English]

short-term **ADJ** **Short-term** things last only for a short time, or have an effect soon rather than far in the future. ❑ *This is only a short-term solution.*

shot /ʃɒt/ (**shots**)

1 **Shot** is the past tense and past participle of **shoot**.

2 **N-COUNT** A **shot** is an act of firing a gun. ❑ *The man was killed with a single shot.*

3 **N-COUNT** SPORTS A **shot** is an act of kicking, hitting, or throwing the ball, to try to score a point. ❑ *Grant missed two shots at the goal.*

4 **N-COUNT** A **shot** is a photograph. ❑ *The photographer got some great shots of the bride.*

5 **N-COUNT** A **shot of** a drug is an injection of it. ❑ *The doctor gave me a shot.* [from Old English]

→ look at Word Web: **photography**

Word Partnership	Use **shot** with :
V	**fire a** shot, **hear a** shot **2** **miss a** shot **2** **3** **block a** shot, **hit a** shot **3** **take a** shot **2** **3** **get a** shot, **give** *someone* **a** shot **5**
ADJ	**single** shot, **warning** shot **2** **good** shot **2**–**4** **winning** shot **3**

S

should /ʃəd, STRONG ʃʊd/

■ **MODAL** You use **should** when you are saying what is the right thing to do. ❑ *I should exercise more.* ❑ *You shouldn't stay up so late.*

■ **MODAL** You use **should** when you are saying that something is probably true or will probably happen. ❑ *The doctor said I should be fine by next week.* ❑ *You should have no problems with this exercise.*

■ **MODAL** You use **should** in questions when you are asking someone for advice. ❑ *Should I ask for more help?* ❑ *What should I do?* [from Old English]

shoul|der /ʃoʊldər/ (shoulders) **N-COUNT** Your **shoulders** are the two parts of your body between your neck and the tops of your arms. ❑ *She put her arm round his shoulders.* [from Old English]

→ look at Picture Dictionaries: **body, horse**

Word Partnership	Use **shoulder** with :
ADJ	**bare** shoulder, **broken** shoulder, **dislocated** shoulder
V	**look over** *your* shoulder, **tap** *someone* **on the** shoulder
N	**head on** *someone's* shoulder

shouldn't /ʃʊdᵊnt/ **Shouldn't** is short for "should not."

should've /ʃʊdəv/ **Should've** is short for "should have."

shout /ʃaʊt/ (shouts, shouting, shouted)

■ **V-T/V-I** If you **shout**, you say something very loudly. ❑ *"She's alive!" he shouted.* ❑ *Andrew ran out of the house, shouting for help.*

■ **N-COUNT Shout** is also a noun. ❑ *There were angry shouts from the crowd.* [from Old Norse]

shove /ʃʌv/ (shoves, shoving, shoved)

■ **V-T/V-I** If you **shove** someone or something, you push them roughly. ❑ *The woman shoved the other customers out of the way.* ❑ *He was shoved by his brother.*

■ **N-COUNT Shove** is also a noun. ❑ *She gave Carrie a shove toward the house.* [from Old English]

shov|el /ʃʌvᵊl/ (shovels, shoveling, shoveled)

■ **N-COUNT** A **shovel** is a flat tool with a handle that is used for lifting and moving earth or snow. ❑ *I'll need the coal shovel.*

■ **V-T** If you **shovel** earth or snow, you lift it and move it with a shovel. ❑ *He had to shovel the snow away from the door.* [from Old English]

→ look at Picture Dictionary: **garden**

show
❶ VERB USES
❷ NOUN USES
❸ PHRASAL VERBS

❶ **show** /ʃoʊ/ (shows, showing, showed, shown)

■ **V-T** If information or a fact **shows that** a situation exists, it proves it. ❑ *Research shows that certain foods can help prevent headaches.*

■ **V-T** If a picture, a movie, or a piece of writing **shows** something, it represents it or gives information about it. ❑ *This map shows all the subway lines in NYC.*

■ **V-T** If you **show** someone something, you let them see it. ❑ *She showed me her engagement ring.*

■ **V-T** If you **show** someone how to do something, you teach them how to do it. ❑ *Claire showed us how to make pasta.*

■ **V-T/V-I** If something **shows** or if you **show** it, it is visible or noticeable. ❑ *When I feel angry, it shows.* ❑ *He smiled and showed a row of strong white teeth.* [from Old English]

❷ **show** /ʃoʊ/ (shows)

■ **N-COUNT** A television or radio **show** is a program. ❑ *I never missed his TV show when I was a kid.*

■ **N-COUNT** ARTS A **show** in a theater is a performance. ❑ *How about going to see a show tomorrow?*

■ **N-COUNT** A **show** is a public exhibition of things. ❑ *About 30 fashion shows are planned for this fall.* [from Old English]

→ look at Word Webs: **concert, laser**

❸ **show** /ʃoʊ/ (shows, showing, showed, shown)

▶ **show off** ■ If someone **is showing off**, they are trying to make people admire them. ❑ *He spent the entire evening showing off.*

■ If you **show off** something, you show it to a lot of people because you are proud of it. ❑ *Naomi was showing off her engagement ring.*

▶ **show up** If a person **shows up**, they arrive at the place where you agreed to meet them. ❑ *We waited until five, but he didn't show up.*

show busi|ness N-NONCOUNT ARTS BUSINESS **Show business** is the entertainment industry of movies, theater, and television. ❑ *His show business career lasted more than 45 years.*

S

show|er /ʃaʊər/ (**showers, showering, showered**)

1 **N-COUNT** A **shower** is a thing that you stand under, that covers you with water so you can wash yourself. ❑ *I was in the shower when the phone rang.*

2 **N-COUNT** If you take a **shower**, you wash yourself by standing under the water that comes from a shower. ❑ *I think I'll take a shower.*

3 **V-I** If you **shower**, you wash yourself by standing under the water that comes from a shower. ❑ *I was late and there wasn't time to shower.*

4 **N-COUNT** A **shower** is a short period of rain. ❑ *A few showers are expected in the Ohio Valley Saturday.*

5 **N-COUNT** A **shower** is a party for a woman who is getting married or having a baby. ❑ *Kelly's baby shower is on Thursday night.* [from Old English]
→ look at Picture Dictionary: **bathroom**
→ look at Word Webs: **soap, wedding**

shown /ʃoʊn/ **Shown** is the past participle of **show**. [from Old English]

shrank /ʃræŋk/ **Shrank** is a past tense of **shrink**. [from Old English]

shred /ʃrɛd/ (**shreds, shredding, shredded**)

1 **V-T** If you **shred** something such as food or paper, you cut it or tear it into very small, narrow pieces. ❑ *They are shredding documents.*

2 **N-COUNT** If you cut or tear food or paper **into shreds**, you cut or tear it into small, narrow pieces. ❑ *Cut the cabbage into long shreds.* [from Old English]

shriek /ʃrik/ (**shrieks, shrieking, shrieked**)

1 **V-I** If you **shriek**, you make a short, very loud cry. ❑ *Gwen shrieked with excitement when she heard the news.*

2 **N-COUNT** **Shriek** is also a noun. ❑ *The boy let out a shriek of pain.* [from Old Norse]

shrimp /ʃrɪmp/ (**shrimp** or **shrimps**)

N-COUNT **Shrimp** are small pink or gray sea animals, with long tails and many legs, that you can eat. ❑ *Add the shrimp and cook for 30 seconds.* [from Germanic]
→ look at Picture Dictionary: **shellfish**

shrine /ʃraɪn/ (**shrines**) **N-COUNT** A **shrine** is a religious place where people go to remember a holy person or event. ❑ *They visited the holy shrine of Mecca.* [from Old English]

shrink /ʃrɪŋk/ (**shrinks, shrinking, shrank** or **shrunk**) **V-I** If something **shrinks**, it becomes smaller in size. ❑ *Dad's pants shrank after just one wash.* [from Old English]

shrub /ʃrʌb/ (**shrubs**) **N-COUNT** A **shrub** is a small bush. ❑ *This books tells you how to choose shrubs for your backyard.* [from Old English]
→ look at Picture Dictionaries: **garden, plant**

shrug /ʃrʌg/ (**shrugs, shrugging, shrugged**)

1 **V-I** If you **shrug**, you move your shoulders up to show that you do not know or care about something. ❑ *Melissa just shrugged and replied, "I don't know."*

2 **N-COUNT** **Shrug** is also a noun. ❑ *"Who cares?" said Anna with a shrug.*

shrunk /ʃrʌŋk/ **Shrunk** is a past tense and the past participle of **shrink**. [from Old English]

shud|der /ʃʌdər/ (**shudders, shuddering, shuddered**)

1 **V-I** If you **shudder**, your body shakes because you are frightened or cold, or because you feel disgust. ❑ *Some people shudder at the idea of injections.*

2 **N-COUNT** **Shudder** is also a noun. ❑ *"It was terrifying," she says with a shudder.* [from Middle Low German]

shuf|fle /ʃʌfəl/ (**shuffles, shuffling, shuffled**)

1 **V-I** If you **shuffle**, you walk without lifting your feet off the ground. ❑ *Moira shuffled across the kitchen.*

2 **V-T** If you **shuffle** playing cards, you mix them up before you begin a game. ❑ *Aunt Mary shuffled the cards.* [from Low German]

shut /ʃʌt/ (**shuts, shutting, shut**)

> **LANGUAGE HELP**
> The form **shut** is used in the present tense and is the past tense and past participle.

1 **V-T/V-I** If you **shut** something, you close it. ❑ *Please shut the gate.* ❑ *Lucy's eyes shut and she fell asleep at once.*

2 **ADJ** **Shut** is also an adjective. ❑ *The police have told us to keep our doors and windows shut.* ❑ *Her eyes were shut and she seemed to be asleep.* [from Old English]

▶ **shut down** If a factory or a business **shuts down**, it closes and work there stops. ❑ *The factory was shut down last month and all the workers lost their jobs.*

▶ **shut in** If you **shut** a person or an animal **in** a room, you close the door so that they cannot leave the room. ❑ *We shut the animals in the shelter in bad weather.*

S

▶ **shut off** If you **shut off** an engine or an electrical appliance, you turn it off to stop it from working. ❑ *He shut off the car engine.*

▶ **shut out** If you **shut** something or someone **out**, you prevent them from getting into a place. ❑ *"I shut him out of the house," said Maureen.*

▶ **shut up** If you say **Shut up** to someone, you are asking them, in a rude way, to stop talking. ❑ *Just shut up, will you?*

Word Partnership	Use **shut** with :
N	shut **a door**, shut **a gate**, shut **a window**
V	**force** *something* shut, **pull** *something* shut, **push** *something* shut, **slam** *something* shut
ADV	shut **tight/tightly**, shut **temporarily**

shut|ter /ˈʃʌtər/ (**shutters**) **N-COUNT** **Shutters** are wooden or metal covers on the outside of a window. ❑ *She opened the shutters and looked out of the window.* [from Old English]

shut|tle /ˈʃʌtəl/ (**shuttles**)
1 **N-COUNT** SCIENCE A **shuttle** is the same as a **space shuttle**.
2 **N-COUNT** A **shuttle** is a plane, a bus, or a train that makes regular trips between two places. ❑ *There is a free shuttle between the airport terminals.* [from Old English]

shuttle|cock /ˈʃʌtəlkɒk/ (**shuttlecocks**)
N-COUNT SPORTS A **shuttlecock** is the small object that you hit over the net in a game of badminton.

shy /ʃaɪ/ (**shyer, shyest**) **ADJ** If you are **shy**, you are nervous and embarrassed about talking to people that you do not know well. ❑ *She was a shy, quiet girl.* ❑ *I was too shy to say anything.*
● **shy|ly** **ADV** ❑ *The children smiled shyly.*
● **shy|ness** **N-NONCOUNT** ❑ *His shyness made it difficult for him to make friends.* [from Old English]

Thesaurus	shy Also look up :
ADJ	nervous, quiet, sheepish, uncomfortable

Si|berian ti|ger /saɪbɪəriən taɪɡər/
(**Siberian tigers**) **N-COUNT** A **Siberian tiger** is a species of large tiger that lives in parts of Russia.

sib|ling /ˈsɪblɪŋ/ (**siblings**) **N-COUNT** Your **siblings** are your brothers and sisters. [FORMAL] ❑ *I often had to take care of my five younger siblings.* [from Old English]

sick /sɪk/ (**sicker, sickest**)
1 **ADJ** If you are **sick**, you are not well.

❑ *He's very sick. He needs a doctor.*
2 **ADJ** If you are **sick**, the food that you have eaten comes up from your stomach and out of your mouth. ❑ *I think I'm going to be sick.*
3 **ADJ** If you are **sick of** something that has been happening for a long time, you are very annoyed by it and want it to stop happening. [INFORMAL] ❑ *I am sick of all your complaints!*
4 **PHRASE** If you are **out sick**, you are not at work because you are sick. ❑ *Tom is out sick today.* [from Old English]

Word Partnership	Use **sick** with :
V	**care for** the sick ❶ **become** sick, **feel** sick, **get** sick ❶ ❷
N	sick **children**, sick **mother**, sick **patients**, sick **people**, sick **person** ❶
ADV	**really** sick, **very** sick ❶ ❷

sick|ness /ˈsɪknɪs/ **N-NONCOUNT** **Sickness** is the state of being unwell or unhealthy. ❑ *Grandpa had only one week of sickness in fifty-two years.* [from Old English]

━━━ **side** ━━━
❶ A SURFACE, POSITION, OR PLACE
❷ ONE ASPECT OR ONE POINT OF VIEW
❸ PHRASES

❶ **side** /saɪd/ (**sides**)
1 **N-COUNT** The **side of** something is a position to the left or right of it. ❑ *On the left side of the door there's a door bell.*
2 **N-COUNT** The **side** of an object is any part of it that is not its front, back, top, or bottom. ❑ *He took me along the side of the house and into the yard.*
3 **N-COUNT** The **side of** something is its edge. ❑ *We parked on the side of the road.*
4 **N-COUNT** The **side of** something is one of its flat surfaces. ❑ *You should write on both sides of the paper.*
5 **N-COUNT** Your **sides** are the parts of your body from under your arms to the tops of your legs. ❑ *Hold your arms by your sides and bend your knees.* [from Old English]

❷ **side** /saɪd/ (**sides, siding, sided**)
1 **N-COUNT** The different **sides** in a war or a game are the groups of people who are fighting or playing against each other. ❑ *Both sides want the war to end.*
2 **V-I** If one person or country **sides with** another, they support them in an argument. ❑ *Kentucky eventually sided with the Union.*

S

3 **N-COUNT** A particular **side** of a situation or someone's character is one part of it. ❑ *He showed a kind, gentle side of his character.* [from Old English]

❸ side /saɪd/

1 **PHRASE** If something moves **from side to side**, it moves to the left and to the right. ❑ *She shook her head from side to side.*

2 **PHRASE** If you are **on** someone's **side**, or **taking** their **side**, you are supporting them in an argument. ❑ *Whose side are you on?*

3 **PHRASE** If two people or things are **side by side**, they are next to each other. ❑ *The children were sitting side by side on the sofa.* [from Old English]

side|burns /saɪdbɜrnz/ **N-PLURAL** If a man has **sideburns**, he has a strip of hair growing down the side of each cheek. ❑ *...a young man with long sideburns.*
→ look at Picture Dictionary: **hair**

side ef|fect (**side effects**) also **side-effect** **N-COUNT** SCIENCE The **side effects** of a drug are the effects, usually bad ones, that the drug has on you in addition to its function of curing illness or pain. ❑ *The main side effect of the drug is tiredness.*

side|line /saɪdlaɪn/ (**sidelines**) **N-PLURAL** SPORTS The **sidelines** are the lines marking the long sides of the playing area, for example, on a football field or a tennis court.
→ look at Picture Dictionaries: **basketball**, **soccer**

side|walk /saɪdwɔk/ (**sidewalks**) **N-COUNT** A **sidewalk** is a path with a hard surface by the side of a road. ❑ *She was walking down the sidewalk toward him.*

side|ways /saɪdweɪz/

1 **ADV** If you do something **sideways**, you do it from or toward the side. ❑ *Pete looked sideways at her.*

2 **ADJ** **Sideways** is also an adjective. ❑ *Alfred gave him a sideways look.*

siege /sidʒ/ (**sieges**) **N-COUNT** A **siege** is when soldiers or police officers surround a place in order to force the people there to come out. ❑ *The siege has been going on for three days.* [from Old French]

Word Partnership	Use siege with :
PREP	**after** a siege, **during** a siege, **under** siege
V	**end** a siege, **lift** a siege

sieve /sɪv/ (**sieves, sieving, sieved**)

1 **N-COUNT** A **sieve** is a tool with a fine metal net, that you use for separating solids from liquids. ❑ *Press the soup through a sieve into a bowl.*

2 **V-T** When you **sieve** a substance, you put it through a sieve. ❑ *Sieve the flour into a bowl.* [from Old English]

sigh /saɪ/ (**sighs, sighing, sighed**)

1 **V-I** If you **sigh**, you let out a deep breath because you are disappointed, tired, or pleased. ❑ *Roberta sighed with relief.*

2 **N-COUNT** **Sigh** is also a noun. ❑ *Maria kicked off her shoes and sat down with a sigh.* [from Old English]

Word Partnership	Use sigh with :
ADJ	**collective** sigh, **deep** sigh, **long** sigh
V	**breathe** a sigh, **give** a sigh, **hear** a sigh, **heave** a sigh, **let out** a sigh

sight /saɪt/ (**sights**)

1 **N-NONCOUNT** Your **sight** is your ability to see. ❑ *Grandpa has lost the sight in his right eye.*

2 **N-SING** The **sight of** something is the act of seeing it. ❑ *Liz can't bear the sight of blood.*

3 **N-PLURAL** The **sights** are the places that are interesting to see and that tourists often visit. ❑ *We saw the sights of Paris.*

4 **PHRASE** If you **catch sight of** someone or something, you suddenly see them for a short period of time. ❑ *He caught sight of Helen in the crowd.*

5 **PHRASE** If something is **in sight**, you can see it. If it is **out of sight**, you cannot see it. ❑ *At last the town was in sight.*

6 **PHRASE** If you **lose sight of** someone or something, you can no longer see them. ❑ *The man ran off and I lost sight of him.* [from Old English]

Word Partnership	Use sight with :
V	**catch** sight of *someone/something* **4**
	come into sight, **keep** *someone/something* **in** sight **5**
N	**the end is in** sight **5**

sight|see|ing /saɪtsiɪŋ/ **N-NONCOUNT** If you go **sightseeing** or do some **sightseeing**, you travel around visiting the interesting places that tourists usually visit. ❑ *During our vacation, we had a day's sightseeing in Venice.*
→ look at Word Web: **city**

sight word (**sight words**) **N-COUNT** LANGUAGE ARTS A **sight word** is a word that

S

most readers of a language can recognize immediately without needing to analyze its separate parts.

sign /saɪn/ (**signs, signing, signed**)

■ **N-COUNT** A **sign** is a mark, a shape, or a movement that has a particular meaning. ❑ *In math, + is a plus sign and = is an equals sign.* ❑ *They gave me a sign to show that everything was OK.*

■ **N-COUNT** A **sign** is a piece of wood, metal, or plastic with words or pictures on it that warn you about something or give you information or an instruction. ❑ *The road signs here are in both English and French.* ❑ *The sign said, "Welcome to Hebron."*

■ **N-COUNT/N-NONCOUNT** If there is a **sign of** something, there is something that shows that it exists or is happening. ❑ *Matthew showed no sign of fear.*

■ **V-T** When you **sign** a document, you write your name on it. ❑ *World leaders have signed an agreement to protect the environment.* [from Old French]

▶ **sign up** If you **sign up** for an organization or an activity, you sign a form saying that you will do a job or an activity. ❑ *He signed up as a flight attendant with American Airlines.*

sig|nal /sɪgnəl/ (**signals, signaling, signaled**)

■ **N-COUNT** A **signal** is a movement, a light, or a sound that gives a particular message to the person who sees or hears it. ❑ *The captain gave the signal for the soldiers to attack.*

■ **V-T/V-I** If you **signal to** someone, you make a movement or sound to give them a particular message. ❑ *Mandy signaled to Jesse to follow her.* ❑ *She signaled that she was leaving.*

■ **N-COUNT** SCIENCE A **signal** is a series of radio waves, light waves, or electrical waves that may carry information. ❑ *...high-frequency radio signals.* [from Old French]

→ look at Word Webs: **cellphone, television**

Word Partnership	Use signal with :
V	**give a** signal ■
	send a signal ■ ■
ADJ	**clear** signal, **strong** signal, **wrong** signal ■ ■

sig|na|ture /sɪgnətʃər, -tʃʊər/ (**signatures**) **N-COUNT** Your **signature** is your name, written in your own special way. ❑ *I put my signature at the bottom of the page.* [from Old French]

sig|nifi|cance /sɪgnɪfɪkəns/ **N-NONCOUNT** The **significance** of something is its

importance or meaning. ❑ *What do you think is the significance of this event?* [from Latin]

Word Partnership	Use significance with :
ADJ	**cultural** significance, **great** significance, **historic** significance, **political** significance, **religious** significance
V	**downplay the** significance **of** *something*, **explain the** significance **of** *something*, **understand the** significance **of** *something*

sig|nifi|cant /sɪgnɪfɪkənt/ **ADJ** If something is **significant**, it is important or large. ❑ *There has been a significant increase in the price of oil.*

● **sig|nifi|cant|ly ADV** ❑ *The temperature dropped significantly.* [from Latin]

Thesaurus	significant Also look up :
ADJ	big, important, large; (ant.) insignificant, minor, small

sig|ni|fy /sɪgnɪfaɪ/ (**signifies, signifying, signified**) **V-T** If an event, a sign, or a symbol **signifies** something, it is a sign of that thing or represents that thing. ❑ *These changes signify the end of childhood.* [from Old French]

sign lan|guage (**sign languages**) **N-COUNT/ N-NONCOUNT** **Sign language** is movements of your hands and arms used to communicate. ❑ *Her son used sign language to tell her what happened.*

→ look at Picture Dictionary: **sign language**

Sikh /siːk/ (**Sikhs**) **N-COUNT** A **Sikh** is a person who follows the Indian religion called **Sikhism**. ❑ *Rebecca's husband is a Sikh.* ❑ *...a Sikh temple.* [from Hindi]

si|lence /saɪləns/ (**silences**) **N-COUNT/N-NONCOUNT** If there is **silence**, no one is speaking. ❑ *They stood in silence.* ❑ *There was a long silence before Sarah replied.* [from Old French]

Word Partnership	Use silence with :
ADJ	**awkward** silence, **complete** silence, **long** silence, **sudden** silence, **total** silence
V	silence **falls, listen in** silence, **observe a** silence, **sit in** silence, **watch** *something* **in** silence

si|lent /saɪlənt/

■ **ADJ** If you are **silent**, you are not speaking. ❑ *Jessica was silent because she did not know what*

S

The American Manual Alphabet

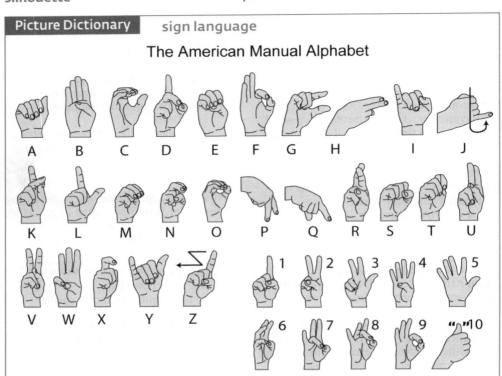

to say. ● **si|lent|ly** **ADV** ❏ *She and Ned sat silently, enjoying the peace.*

2 **ADJ** If something is **silent**, it is completely quiet, with no sound at all. ❏ *The room was silent except for the TV.* ● **si|lent|ly** **ADV** ❏ *The thief moved silently across the room.* [from Latin]

Word Partnership	Use silent with :	
V	go silent, keep silent, remain silent, sit silent **1**	
N	silent prayer, silent reading **1** silent auction **2**	

sil|hou|ette /sɪluɛt/ (**silhouettes**) **N-COUNT** A **silhouette** is the dark shape that you see when someone or something has a bright light behind them. ❏ *He could see the distant silhouette of a castle.* [from French]

sili|ca /sɪlɪkə/ **N-NONCOUNT** **SCIENCE** **Silica** is silicon dioxide, a compound of silicon that is found in sand and quartz, and that is used to make glass. [from New Latin]

sili|cate min|er|al /sɪlɪkɪt mɪnərəl/ (**silicate minerals**) **N-COUNT** **SCIENCE** **Silicate minerals** are minerals that are made mostly of a substance called silica.

sili|con /sɪlɪkən, -kɒn/ **N-NONCOUNT** **SCIENCE** **Silicon** is an element that is found in sand and in minerals such as quartz. Silicon is used to make parts of computers and other electronic equipment. ❏ *...a silicon chip.*

silk /sɪlk/ (**silks**) **N-COUNT/N-NONCOUNT** **Silk** is a smooth, shiny cloth that is made from very thin threads. ❏ *Pauline was wearing a beautiful silk dress.* [from Old English]

silky /sɪlki/ (**silkier, silkiest**) **ADJ** If something is **silky**, it is smooth, soft, and shiny, like silk. ❏ *This shampoo makes your hair beautifully silky.* [from Old English]

sil|ly /sɪli/ (**sillier, silliest**) **ADJ** If you are **silly**, you do not behave in a sensible or serious way. ❏ *"Don't be so silly, darling!"* ❏ *I know it's silly to feel nervous but I can't help it.* [from Old English]

sil|ver /sɪlvər/

1 **N-NONCOUNT** **Silver** is a valuable pale gray metal that is used for making jewelry.

2 **ADJ** Something that is **silver** is shiny and pale gray in color. ❏ *He had thick silver hair.*

3 **N-NONCOUNT** **Silver** is also a noun. ❏ *The car is also available in silver.* [from Old English]

→ look at Word Webs: **mineral, money**

Word Web silverware

dinner knife · soup spoon · dinner fork · dessert spoon · dessert fork · salad fork

Experts say that the first knives were simple cutting tools. They were made from flint and were first used about two million years ago. The first modern knife with a metal **blade** and wooden **handle** was made about 1000 years BC. During the Middle Ages, people carried their own eating knives with them because no one provided knives for guests. The earliest **spoons** were made from scooped-out bones or shells tied to the end of sticks. Later the Romans made bronze and **silver** spoons. The first **forks** had only two tines and were used only for carving and serving meat.

sil|ver med|al (silver medals) **N-COUNT**
A **silver medal** is an award made of silver metal that you get as second prize in a competition.

silver|ware /sɪlvərwɛər/ **N-NONCOUNT**
Silverware is all the things in a house that are made of silver, especially the flatware and dishes.
→ look at Word Web: **silverware**

sil|very /sɪlvəri/ **ADJ** **Silvery** things look like silver or are the color of silver. ❑ *My father is a small man with silvery hair.* [from Old English]

SIM card /sɪm kɑrd/ (SIM cards) **N-COUNT**
TECHNOLOGY A **SIM card** is a small electronic piece of equipment in a cellphone that connects it to a particular phone network.

simi|lar /sɪmɪlər/
1 **ADJ** If one thing is **similar to** another, or if two things are **similar**, they are the same in some ways but not in every way. ❑ *This cake tastes similar to carrot cake.* ❑ *Nowadays, cars all look very similar.*
2 **ADJ** MATH In geometry, two figures, such as triangles, are **similar** if they have the same shape, although they may not be the same size. [from Old French]

simi|lar|ity /sɪmɪlærɪti/ (similarities)
1 **N-COUNT** **Similarities** are things that are the same about two people or things. ❑ *There are many similarities between the two country's cultures.*
2 **N-NONCOUNT** If there is a **similarity between** two or more things, they are similar to each other. ❑ *I was amazed at the similarity between the brothers.*
3 **N-NONCOUNT** MATH In geometry,

similarity is the relationship between two figures such as triangles that have the same shape, although they may not be the same size. [from Old French]

simi|lar|ly /sɪmɪlərli/
1 **ADV** You use **similarly** to say that something is similar to something else. ❑ *Most of the men were similarly dressed.*
2 **ADV** You use **similarly** when mentioning a fact or situation that is similar to the one you have just mentioned. ❑ *Young babies prefer faces to other shapes. Similarly, they prefer familiar faces to ones they don't know.* [from Old French]

simi|le /sɪmɪli/ (similes) **N-COUNT**
LANGUAGE ARTS A **simile** is an expression that describes a person or a thing by comparing it with another person or thing, using the words "like" or "as." An example of a simile is "She swims like a fish." [from Latin]

sim|mer /sɪmər/ (simmers, simmering, simmered) **V-T/V-I** If food **simmers**, or if you **simmer** it, it cooks gently in water that is just boiling. ❑ *Let the soup simmer for 15-20 minutes.* [from German]

sim|ple /sɪmpᵊl/ (simpler, simplest)
1 **ADJ** If something is **simple**, it is easy to understand. ❑ *The recipes in the book are simple and easy to follow.* ❑ *Just follow the simple instructions below.*
2 **ADJ** If something is **simple**, it has all the basic things it needs, but nothing more. ❑ *He ate a simple dinner of rice and beans.* ❑ *Amanda was wearing a simple black silk dress.* [from Old French]

S

sim|ple ma|chine (**simple machines**)
N-COUNT SCIENCE A **simple machine** is a
device such as a lever, a wheel, or a screw
that forms a part of other, more complex
machines. Compare with **compound
machine**.

sim|plic|ity /sɪmplɪsɪti/ **N-NONCOUNT**
Simplicity is the quality of being simple.
❏ I love the simplicity of his designs. [from
Old French]

sim|pli|fy /sɪmplɪfaɪ/ (**simplifies,
simplifying, simplified**) **V-T** If you **simplify**
something, you make it easier to
understand or to do. ❏ This program simplifies
the task of searching for information.
● **sim|pli|fied** **ADJ** ❏ We read a simplified version
of Shakespeare's "Hamlet." [from French]

simp|ly /sɪmpli/
1 ADV You use **simply** to emphasize what
you are saying. ❏ Your behavior is simply
unacceptable.
2 ADV You use **simply** to emphasize that
something consists of only one thing,
happens for only one reason, or is done in
only one way. ❏ The table is simply a circle of
wood.
3 ADV If you do something **simply**, you
do it in a way that is easy to understand.
❏ He explained his views simply and clearly.
4 ADV **Simply** means in a plain or basic
way. ❏ Her house is decorated simply. [from
Old French]

sim|ul|ta|neous /saɪməlteɪniəs/ **ADJ**
Things that are **simultaneous** happen or
exist at the same time. ❏ ...the simultaneous
release of the final three novels.
● **sim|ul|ta|neous|ly** **ADV** ❏ They began to
speak simultaneously. [from Latin]

sin /sɪn/ (**sins, sinning, sinned**)
1 N-COUNT/N-NONCOUNT A **sin** is an action
or a type of behavior that breaks a religious
law. ❏ They believe that lying is a sin.
2 V-I If you **sin**, you do something that
breaks a religious law. ❏ The Bible says that we
have all sinned. ● **sin|ner** /sɪnər/ (**sinners**)
N-COUNT ❏ Is she a sinner or a saint? [from Old
English]

since /sɪns/
1 PREP You use **since** when you are
talking about a time or an event that started
in the past, and that has continued from
then until now. ❏ My uncle has lived in India
since 1995.
2 ADV **Since** is also an adverb. ❏ They worked
together in the 1980s, and have been friends ever
since.
3 CONJ **Since** is also a conjunction. ❏ I've
lived here since I was six years old.
4 CONJ **Since** means "because." ❏ I'm always
on a diet, since I put on weight easily. [from Old
English]

sin|cere /sɪnsɪər/ **ADJ** If you are **sincere**,
you are honest and you really mean what
you say. ❏ Do you think Ryan's being sincere?
[from Latin]

sin|cere|ly /sɪnsɪərli/
1 ADV If you say or feel something
sincerely, you really mean or feel it. ❏ "Well
done!" he said sincerely.
2 PHRASE You write **Sincerely yours** or
Sincerely before your signature at the end of
a formal letter when you have addressed it
to someone by name. ❏ Sincerely yours, Robbie
Weinz. [from Latin]

sine /saɪn/ (**sines**) **N-COUNT** MATH A **sine** is a
mathematical calculation that is used
especially in the study of triangles. In a
right triangle, the sine is the ratio between
the hypotenuse and the side opposite a
particular angle. The abbreviation **sin** is also
used. [from Latin]

si|necure /saɪnɪkyʊər, sɪn-/ (**sinecures**)
N-COUNT A **sinecure** is a job for which you
receive payment but that does not involve
much work or responsibility. ❏ She found him

a sinecure as a Fellow of the Library of Congress. [from Medieval Latin]

sing /sɪŋ/ (sings, singing, sang, sung)
V-T/V-I MUSIC When you **sing**, you make music with your voice. ❑ I love singing. ❑ My brother and I used to sing this song. [from Old English]

Word Partnership	Use **sing** with :
V	**begin to** sing, **can/can't** sing, **dance and** sing, **hear** *someone* sing, **like to** sing
N	**birds** sing, sing *someone's* **praises**, sing **a song**

sing|er /sɪŋər/ (singers) **N-COUNT** MUSIC A **singer** is a person who sings, especially as a job. ❑ My mother was a singer in a band. [from Old English]
→ look at Word Web: **concert**

sin|gle /sɪŋɡ³l/
1 ADJ You use **single** to show that you are talking about only one thing. ❑ She hasn't said a single word about what happened. ❑ We sold over two hundred pizzas in a single day.
2 ADJ If you are **single**, you are not married. ❑ Joseph is a single man in his early twenties.
3 ADJ A **single** room or bed is for one person only. ❑ Would you like to reserve a single or a double room? [from Old French]

sin|gle-re|place|ment re|ac|tion (single-replacement reactions) **N-COUNT** SCIENCE A **single-replacement reaction** is a chemical reaction between an element and a compound in which the atoms of the element switch places with some of the atoms of the compound. Compare with **double-replacement reaction**.

sin|gu|lar /sɪŋɡyələr/
1 ADJ LANGUAGE ARTS The **singular** form of a word is the form that you use when you are talking about one person or thing. ❑ The singular form of "mice" is "mouse."
2 N-SING LANGUAGE ARTS The **singular** of a noun is the form of it that you use when you are talking about one person or thing. ❑ What is the singular of "geese?" [from Latin]

sin|is|ter /sɪnɪstər/ **ADJ** Something that is **sinister** seems evil or harmful. ❑ There was something sinister about him. [from Latin]

sink /sɪŋk/ (sinks, sinking, sank, sunk)
1 N-COUNT A **sink** is a large fixed container in a kitchen or a bathroom that you can fill with water. ❑ The sink was filled with dirty dishes.

❑ The bathroom has a toilet, a shower, and a sink.
2 V-T/V-I If a boat or an object **sinks**, it goes below the surface of water. ❑ The boat hit the rocks and began to sink. ❑ A torpedo from a submarine sank the ship.
3 V-I If something **sinks**, it moves slowly down, to a lower level. ❑ The sun was sinking in the west. [from Old English]
→ look at Picture Dictionary: **bathroom**

Word Partnership	Use **sink** with :
N	**bathroom** sink, **dishes in a** sink, **kitchen** sink **1**
	sink **a ship 2**

sip /sɪp/ (sips, sipping, sipped)
1 V-T/V-I If you **sip** a drink, or **sip** at it, you drink it slowly, taking a small amount at a time. ❑ Jessica sipped her drink slowly. ❑ The girls sipped at their lemonade.
2 N-COUNT A **sip** is a small amount of drink that you take into your mouth. ❑ Harry took a sip of tea. [from Low German]

sir /sɜr/
1 **Sir** is a polite way of talking to a man. ❑ Excuse me, sir, is this your car?
2 PHRASE You write **Dear Sir** at the beginning of a formal letter or a business letter when you are writing to a man. ❑ Dear Sir, Thank you for your letter.

si|ren /saɪrən/ (sirens) **N-COUNT** A **siren** is a piece of equipment that makes a long, loud noise to warn people about something. Fire engines and police cars have sirens. ❑ In the distance I could hear a siren. [from Old French]

sis|ter /sɪstər/ (sisters) **N-COUNT** Your **sister** is a girl or woman who has the same parents as you. ❑ This is my sister Sarah. [from Old English]
→ look at Picture Dictionary: **family**

sis|ter-in-law (sisters-in-law) **N-COUNT** Someone's **sister-in-law** is the sister of their husband or wife, or the woman who is married to their brother.
→ look at Picture Dictionary: **family**

sit /sɪt/ (sits, sitting, sat)
1 V-I If you **are sitting** in a chair, your bottom is resting on the chair and the upper part of your body is straight. ❑ Mother was sitting in her chair in the kitchen. ❑ They sat watching television all evening.
2 V-I When you **sit** or **sit down** somewhere,

S

you move your body down until you are sitting on something. ❑ *Kelly sat on the bed and took off her shoes.* ❑ *Mom sat down beside me.* [from Old English]

▶ **sit up** If you **sit up**, you change the position of your body, so that you are sitting instead of lying down. ❑ *She felt dizzy when she sat up.*

Usage sit and set

Be careful not to confuse the verbs *sit* and *set*. *Sit* means "to be seated," and is generally used intransitively. *Sit down and let's get started. Set* means "to place something down somewhere," and is generally used transitively: *Terence took off his glasses and set them on the table.*

Word Partnership Use sit with :

ADV	sit **alone**, sit **back**, sit **comfortably**, sit **quietly**, sit **still** ◼
PREP	sit **in a circle**, sit **on the porch**, sit **on the sidelines** ◼
	sit **on a bench**, sit **in a chair**, sit **down to dinner**, sit **on the floor**, sit **on** *someone's* **lap**, sit **around/at a table** ◼ ◼
V	sit **and eat**, sit **and enjoy**, sit **and listen**, sit **and talk**, sit **and wait**, sit **and watch** (or sit **watching**) ◼
	sit **down to eat**, sit **down and relax** ◼ ◼

site /saɪt/ (**sites**)

◼ **N-COUNT** A **site** is a place where a particular thing happens. ❑ *Dad works on a building site.* ❑ *This city was the site of a terrible earthquake.*

◼ **N-COUNT** TECHNOLOGY A **site** is the same as a **website**. ❑ *The site contains advice for new teachers.* [from Latin]

site map (**site maps**) **N-COUNT** TECHNOLOGY A **site map** is a plan of a website that provides links to the different sections.

situ|at|ed /sɪtʃueɪtɪd/ **ADJ** If something is **situated** in a particular place, it is in that place. ❑ *The hotel is situated in the center of Berlin.* [from Late Latin]

Word Link *site, situ ≈ position, location : camp*site, *situation, web*site

situa|tion /sɪtʃueɪʃ°n/ (**situations**) **N-COUNT** The **situation** is what is happening in a particular place at a particular time. ❑ *Army officers said the situation was under control.* [from Late Latin]

Word Partnership Use situation with :

ADJ	**bad** situation, **complicated** situation, **current** situation, **dangerous** situation, **difficult** situation, **economic** situation, **financial** situation, **political** situation, **present** situation, **same** situation, **tense** situation, **terrible** situation, **unique** situation, **unusual** situation, **whole** situation
V	**describe a** situation, **discuss a** situation, **handle a** situation, **improve a** situation, **understand a** situation

six /sɪks/ **NUM** MATH **Six** is the number 6. [from Old English]

six king|doms **N-PLURAL** SCIENCE The **six kingdoms** are the six general types of organism that make up all living things: Animalia, Plantae, Fungi, Protista, Archaebacteria and Eubacteria.

six|teen /sɪkstin/ **NUM** MATH **Sixteen** is the number 16. [from Old English]

six|teenth /sɪkstinθ/ (**sixteenths**)

◼ **ADJ/ADV** MATH The **sixteenth** item in a series is the one that you count as number sixteen. ❑ *...the sixteenth century AD.*

◼ **N-COUNT** MATH A **sixteenth** is one of sixteen equal parts of something. ❑ *...a sixteenth of a second.* [from Old English]

sixth /sɪksθ/ (**sixths**)

◼ **ADJ/ADV** MATH The **sixth** item in a series is the one that you count as number six. ❑ *The sixth round of the competition begins tomorrow.* ❑ *Brad came sixth in the swimming race.*

◼ **N-COUNT** MATH A **sixth** is one of six equal parts of something (⅙). [from Old English]

six|ti|eth /sɪkstiəθ/ **ADJ/ADV** MATH The **sixtieth** item in a series is the one that you count as number sixty. ❑ *...his sixtieth birthday.* [from Old English]

six|ty /sɪksti/ (**sixties**)

◼ **NUM** MATH **Sixty** is the number 60.

◼ **N-PLURAL** The **sixties** are the years between 1960 and 1969. ❑ *He came to Chicago in the sixties to work as a doctor.*

◼ **N-PLURAL** When you talk about the **sixties**, you mean the numbers between 60 and 69. For example, if you are in your **sixties**, you are aged between 60 and 69. ❑ *...a woman in her late sixties.* [from Old English]

S

size /saɪz/ (**sizes**)

◻ **N-COUNT/N-NONCOUNT** The **size of** something is how big or small it is. ❑ *The size of the room is about 10 feet by 15 feet.* ❑ *The shelves contain books of various sizes.* ● **-sized** ❑ *I work for a medium-sized company in Chicago.*

◻ **N-COUNT** A **size** is one of a series of particular measurements for clothes and shoes. ❑ *My sister is a size 12.* ❑ *What size are your feet?* ❑ *Do you have these shoes in a size nine?* [from Old French]

Word Partnership	Use **size** with :
ADJ	**average** size, **full** size ◻ size **large/medium/small**, **mid** size, **right** size ◻
N	**bite** size, **class** size, **family** size, **life** size, **pocket** size ◻ size **chart**, **king/queen** size ◻
V	**double in** size, **increase in** size, **vary in** size ◻ a size **fits** ◻

skate /skeɪt/ (**skates, skating, skated**)

◻ **N-COUNT** **SPORTS** **Skates** (or **ice-skates**) are boots that have a long, sharp piece of metal on the bottom of them, so that you can move quickly and smoothly on ice when you are wearing them.

skate

◻ **N-COUNT** **SPORTS** **Skates** (or **roller-skates**) are boots that have wheels on the bottom of them, so that you can move quickly on the ground.

◻ **V-I** **SPORTS** If you **skate**, you move around wearing skates. ❑ *When the pond froze, we skated on it.* ● **skating** **N-NONCOUNT** ❑ *They all went skating together in the winter.* ● **skater** **N-COUNT** ❑ *The ice-rink was full of skaters.* [from Dutch]

skate|board /skeɪtbɔrd/ (**skateboards**)
N-COUNT **SPORTS** A **skateboard** is a narrow board with wheels at each end that you can stand on and ride.

skate|park /skeɪtpɑrk/ (**skateparks**)
N-COUNT **SPORTS** A **skatepark** is an area in which people can practice riding skateboards.

skel|etal mus|cle /skɛlɪtᵊl mʌsᵊl/ (**skeletal muscles**) **N-COUNT/N-NONCOUNT** **SCIENCE** **Skeletal muscle** is muscle that is attached to a bone and can therefore move parts of your body.
→ look at Word Web: **muscle**

skel|eton /skɛlɪtᵊn/ (**skeletons**) **N-COUNT** **SCIENCE** A **skeleton** is all the bones in a person's or an animal's body. ❑ *...a human skeleton.* [from New Latin]
→ look at Word Web: **shark**

skep|ti|cal /skɛptɪkᵊl/ **ADJ** If you are **skeptical about** something, you have doubts about it. ❑ *We are skeptical about whether he has made the right decision.* [from Latin]

sketch /skɛtʃ/ (**sketches, sketching, sketched**)

◻ **N-COUNT** **ARTS** A **sketch** is a drawing that you do quickly, without a lot of details. ❑ *He did a quick sketch of the building.*

◻ **V-T/V-I** **ARTS** If you **sketch** something, you make a quick drawing of it. ❑ *She started sketching designs when she was six years old.* ❑ *I always sketch with a pen.* [from Dutch]
→ look at Picture Dictionary: **draw**
→ look at Word Web: **animation**

sketchy /skɛtʃi/ (**sketchier, sketchiest**) **ADJ** **Sketchy** information about something does not include many details and is therefore incomplete or inadequate. ❑ *Details of what actually happened are sketchy.* [from Dutch]

ski /ski/ (**skis, skiing, skied**)

◻ **N-COUNT** **SPORTS** **Skis** are long, flat, narrow pieces of wood, metal, or plastic that you fasten to your boots so that you can move easily on snow or water.

◻ **V-I** **SPORTS** When you **ski**, you move over snow or water on skis. ❑ *They*

ski

tried to ski down Mount Everest. ● **ski|er** /skiər/ (**skiers**) **N-COUNT** ❑ *My dad's a very good skier.* ● **ski|ing** **N-NONCOUNT** ❑ *My hobbies are skiing and swimming.* [from Norwegian]

skid /skɪd/ (**skids, skidding, skidded**) **V-I** If a vehicle **skids**, it slides sideways or forward when you try to stop it suddenly. ❑ *The car skidded on the icy road.* [of Scandinavian origin]

skill /skɪl/ (**skills**)

1 **N-COUNT** A **skill** is a job or an activity that needs special training and practice. ❑ *You're never too old to learn new skills.*

2 **N-NONCOUNT** **Skill** is your ability to do something well. ❑ *He shows great skill on the football field.* [from Old Norse]

Thesaurus	skill Also look up :
N	ability, proficiency, talent **1** **2**

skilled /skɪld/ **ADJ** If you are **skilled**, you have the knowledge and ability to do something well. ❑ *We need more skilled workers.* [from Old Norse]

skill|ful /skɪlfəl/ **ADJ** If you are **skillful** at something, you do it very well. ❑ *He was a highly skillful football player.* ● **skill|ful|ly** **ADV** ❑ *The story is skillfully written.* [from Old Norse]

skim /skɪm/ (**skims, skimming, skimmed**)

1 **V-T/V-I** If something **skims** a surface, it moves quickly just above it. ❑ *We watched seagulls skimming the waves.* ❑ *We threw stones, making them skim across the water.*

2 **ADJ** **Skim** milk is milk that has the fat removed from it. ❑ *You'll need half a cup of skim milk, one cup of yogurt, and some fruit.*

skin /skɪn/ (**skins**)

1 **N-COUNT/N-NONCOUNT** SCIENCE **Skin** is the substance that covers the outside of a person's or an animal's body. ❑ *His skin is pale and smooth.* ❑ *...a crocodile skin handbag.*

2 **N-COUNT/N-NONCOUNT** The **skin** of a fruit or a vegetable is the outer part that covers it. ❑ *...a banana skin.* [from Old English]

→ look at Picture Dictionary: **fruit**

→ look at Word Web: **skin**

Word Partnership	Use skin with :
N	skin **and bones**, skin **cancer**, skin **cells**, skin **color** (or color of *someone's* skin), skin **cream**, skin **problems**, skin **type** **1**
ADJ	**dark** skin, **dry** skin, **fair** skin, **oily** skin, **pale** skin, **sensitive** skin, **smooth** skin, **soft** skin **1**

skin|ny /skɪni/ (**skinnier, skinniest**) **ADJ** Someone who is **skinny** is extremely thin or too thin. [INFORMAL] ❑ *He was a skinny little boy.* [from Old English]

skip /skɪp/ (**skips, skipping, skipped**)

1 **V-I** If you **skip** along, you move forward quickly, jumping from one foot to the other. ❑ *We skipped down the street, talking and laughing.*

2 **N-COUNT** **Skip** is also a noun. ❑ *Joshua gave a little skip as he left the room.*

3 **V-T** If you **skip** something that you usually do, you decide not to do it. ❑ *Don't skip breakfast.* [of Scandinavian origin]

skip|per /skɪpər/ (**skippers**) **N-COUNT** You can use **skipper** to refer to the captain of a ship or a boat. ❑ *...the skipper of a fishing boat.* [from Middle Low German]

skip rope (**skip ropes**) **N-COUNT** A **skip rope** is a piece of rope with handles at each end. You turn it and jump over it.

skirt /skɜrt/ (**skirts**) **N-COUNT** A **skirt** is a piece of clothing for women and girls. It hangs down from the waist and covers part of the legs. [from Old Norse]

→ look at Picture Dictionary: **clothing**

skull /skʌl/ (**skulls**) **N-COUNT** SCIENCE A person's or an animal's **skull** is the bones of their head. ❑ *After the accident, they X-rayed his skull.* [of Scandinavian origin]

sky /skaɪ/ (**skies**) **N-COUNT/N-NONCOUNT** The

Word Web   skin

What is the best thing you can do for your **skin**? Stay out of the sun. When skin **cells** grow normally, the skin remains smooth and firm. However, the sun's **ultraviolet** rays sometimes cause damage. This can lead to **sunburn**, **wrinkles**, and skin cancer. The damage may not show for several years. However, doctors have discovered that even a light **suntan** can be dangerous. **Sunlight** makes the **melanin** in skin turn dark. This is the body's attempt to protect itself from the ultraviolet radiation. **Dermatologists** recommend limiting exposure to the sun and always using a **sunscreen**.

sky is the space above the Earth that you can see when you stand outside and look upward. ❑ *The sun was shining in the sky.* ❑ *Today we have clear blue skies.* [from Old Norse]
→ look at Word Web: **star**

Word Partnership	Use **sky** with :
ADV	sky **above, the** sky **overhead, up in the** sky
ADJ	**black** sky, **blue** sky, **bright** sky, **clear** sky, **cloudless** sky, **dark** sky, **empty** sky, **high in the** sky

sky|scraper /skaɪskreɪpər/ (**skyscrapers**)
N-COUNT A **skyscraper** is a very tall building in a city.
→ look at Word Web: **city**

slab /slæb/ (**slabs**) **N-COUNT** A **slab of** something is a thick, flat piece of it.
❑ *...slabs of stone.*

slack /slæk/ (**slacker, slackest**)
1 **ADJ** If something is **slack**, it is loose.
❑ *Suddenly, the rope went slack.*
2 **ADJ** If a business has a **slack** period, it is not busy. ❑ *The store has busy times and slack periods.* [from Old English]

slam /slæm/ (**slams, slamming, slammed**)
1 **V-T/V-I** If you **slam** a door or a window or if it **slams**, it shuts noisily and with great force. ❑ *She slammed the door behind her.* ❑ *I heard the front door slam.*
2 **V-T** If you **slam** something **down**, you put it there quickly and roughly. ❑ *Lauren slammed the phone down angrily.*
3 **V-T/V-I** If one thing **slams**, or **slams** into or against another, it crashes into it with great force. ❑ *The car slammed into a tree.* ❑ *I heard the front door slam.* [of Scandinavian origin]

Word Partnership	Use **slam** with :
N	slam **a door** **1**
V	**hear** *something* slam **1**
ADJ	slam *(something)* **shut** **1**

slan|der /slændər/ (**slanders, slandering, slandered**)
1 **N-COUNT/N-NONCOUNT Slander** is an untrue spoken statement about someone that is intended to damage their reputation. Compare with **libel**. ❑ *Dr. Bach is suing the company for slander.*
2 **V-T** To **slander** someone means to say untrue things about them in order to damage their reputation. ❑ *He accused me of*

slandering him. [from Old French]

slang /slæŋ/ **N-NONCOUNT Slang** is informal words that you can use when you are talking to people you know very well. ❑ *...a dictionary of American slang.*

slant /slænt/ (**slants, slanting, slanted**) **V-I** If something **slants**, it has one side higher than the other. ❑ *The roof of the house slants sharply.* [of Scandinavian origin]

slap /slæp/ (**slaps, slapping, slapped**)
1 **V-T** If you **slap** someone, you hit them with the flat inside part of your hand.
❑ *I slapped him hard across the face.*
2 **N-COUNT Slap** is also a noun. ❑ *She gave him a slap on the face.* [from Low German]

Word Partnership	Use **slap** with :
N	a slap **on the back**, a slap **on the wrist**, a slap **in the face**

slash /slæʃ/ (**slashes, slashing, slashed**)
1 **V-T** If you **slash** something, you make a long, deep cut in it. ❑ *Someone slashed my car tires in the night.*
2 **V-T** To **slash** costs or jobs means to reduce them by a large amount. ❑ *Car makers are slashing prices.*
3 **N-COUNT** LANGUAGE ARTS A **slash** is the punctuation mark / that separates numbers, letters, or words in writing. [from Old French]

slate /sleɪt/ (**slates**)
1 **N-NONCOUNT Slate** is a dark gray rock that can be easily split into thin layers. Slate is often used for covering roofs. ❑ *They lived in a cottage with a traditional slate roof.*
2 **N-COUNT** A **slate** is one of the small flat pieces of slate that are used for covering roofs. ❑ *Thieves also stole the slates from the roof.* [from Old French]

slaugh|ter /slɔtər/ (**slaughters, slaughtering, slaughtered**)
1 **V-T** If people **are slaughtered**, a very large number of them are killed violently.
❑ *So many innocent people have been slaughtered.*
2 **N-NONCOUNT Slaughter** is also a noun.
❑ *The slaughter of women and children was common.*
3 **V-T** To **slaughter** animals means to kill them for their meat. ❑ *The farmers here slaughter their own cows.*
4 **N-NONCOUNT Slaughter** is also a noun. ❑ *The sheep were taken away for slaughter.* [from Old English]

S

slave /sleɪv/ (**slaves, slaving, slaved**)
1 **N-COUNT** A **slave** is a person who belongs to another person and who works for them without being paid.
2 **V-T** If you **slave**, you work very hard. ❑ *He was slaving away in the hot kitchen.* [from Old French]

slav|ery /sleɪvəri, sleɪvri/ **N-NONCOUNT**
SOCIAL STUDIES **Slavery** is when people belong to other people as slaves. ❑ *The United States abolished slavery in 1865.* [from Old French]

slave trade **N-SING** SOCIAL STUDIES The **slave trade** was the business of buying and selling slaves. ❑ *Many people made money from the slave trade.*

sled /slɛd/ (**sleds**) **N-COUNT** A **sled** is an object that you sit on in order to travel over snow. ❑ *We pulled the children across the snow on a sled.* [from Middle Dutch]

sleep /slip/ (**sleeps, sleeping, slept**)
1 **N-NONCOUNT** **Sleep** is a person's or an animal's natural state of rest when their eyes are closed, and their body is not active. ❑ *You should try to get as much sleep as possible.*
2 **V-I** When you **are sleeping**, your eyes are closed and your mind and body are not active. ❑ *I didn't sleep well last night—it was too hot.*
3 **N-COUNT** A **sleep** is a period of sleeping. ❑ *Good morning, Pete. Did you have a good sleep?*
4 **PHRASE** When you **go to sleep,** you start sleeping. ❑ *Be quiet and go to sleep!* [from Old English]
→ look at Word Web: **sleep**

Thesaurus sleep Also look up :	
N	nap, rest, slumber
V	doze, rest; (ant.) awaken, wake

Word Partnership	Use sleep with :	
N	sleep **deprivation**, sleep **disorder, hours of** sleep, **lack of** sleep **1**	
	sleep **on the floor**, sleep **nights** **2**	
V	**drift off to** sleep, **get enough** sleep, **get some** sleep, **get some** sleep, **go to** sleep, **need** sleep **1**	
	can't/couldn't sleep **2**	
ADJ	**deep** sleep **1**	
	good sleep **3**	

sleep|ing bag (**sleeping bags**) **N-COUNT** A **sleeping bag** is a large warm bag for sleeping in when you go camping.

sleep|less /sliplɪs/ **ADJ** A **sleepless** night is one during which you do not sleep. ❑ *I have sleepless nights worrying about her.* [from Old English]

sleepy /slipi/ (**sleepier, sleepiest**) **ADJ** If you are **sleepy**, you are very tired and are almost asleep. ❑ *The pills made me sleepy.* [from Old English]

sleet /slit/ **N-NONCOUNT** **Sleet** is a mixture of snow and rain. ❑ *The snow and sleet will continue overnight.* [from Germanic]
→ look at Word Webs: **precipitation, water**

sleeve /sliv/ (**sleeves**) **N-COUNT** The **sleeves** of a piece of clothing are the parts that cover your arms. ❑ *Rachel wore a blue dress with long sleeves.* [from Old English]

sleigh /sleɪ/ (**sleighs**) **N-COUNT** A **sleigh** is a vehicle with two pieces of wood or metal on the bottom, that you sit in to travel over snow. Sleighs are usually pulled by horses. [from Dutch]

slept /slɛpt/ **Slept** is the past tense and past participle of **sleep**. [from Old English]

slice /slaɪs/ (**slices, slicing, sliced**)
1 **N-COUNT** A **slice of** something is a thin piece that you cut from a larger piece.

Word Web   sleep

Do you ever go to **bed** and then discover you can't **fall asleep?** You **yawn.** You feel **tired.** But your body isn't ready for **rest.** You **toss** and **turn** and pound the **pillow** for hours. After a while you may **doze,** but then a few minutes later you're **wide awake.** The scientific name for this condition is **insomnia.** There are many causes for **sleeplessness.** If you **nap** too late in the day it may change your normal sleep cycle. Worrying can also affect sleep patterns.

S

❑ *Would you like a slice of bread?*
❑ *Nicole had a cup of coffee and a large slice of chocolate cake.*

2 V-T If you **slice** food, you cut it into thin pieces.   slice
❑ *I blew out the candles and Mom sliced the cake.* [from Old French]
→ look at Picture Dictionaries: **bread, cut**

Word Partnership	Use **slice** with :
ADJ	**small** slice, **thin** slice **1**
N	slice **of bread**, slice **of pie**, slice **of pizza 1**
	slice **a cake 2**
PREP	slice **into**, slice **off**, slice **through 2**

slick /slɪk/ (**slicker, slickest**) **ADJ** A **slick** action is quick and smooth, and is done without any obvious effort. ❑ *We loved the slick way he passed the ball.* [of Scandinavian origin]

slide /slaɪd/ (**slides, sliding, slid**)
1 V-T/V-I When someone or something **slides**, they move quickly and smoothly over a surface. ❑ *She slid across the ice on her stomach.* ❑ *I slid the cellphone into my pocket.*
2 V-I If someone **slides** somewhere, they move there smoothly and quietly. ❑ *He slid into the car.*
3 N-COUNT A **slide** is a large metal frame that children can play on. They climb the steps at one side, and move down a smooth slope on their bottom.
4 N-COUNT A **slide** is a small piece of film with a picture on it that you can view on a screen. ❑ *...a slide show.*
5 N-COUNT SCIENCE A glass **slide** is a piece of glass on which you put something that you want to examine through a microscope. [from Old English]
→ look at Word Web: **laboratory**

slight /slaɪt/ **ADJ** Something that is **slight** is small and not important or serious. ❑ *The sun was shining and there was a slight breeze.* ❑ *The company has announced a slight increase in sales.* [from Old Norse]

slight|ly /slaɪtli/ **ADV** **Slightly** means just a little. ❑ *We've moved to a slightly larger house.* ❑ *Each person learns in a slightly different way.* [from Old Norse]

slim /slɪm/ (**slimmer, slimmest, slims, slimming, slimmed**) **ADJ** If you are **slim**, your body is thin in an attractive way. ❑ *The young woman was tall and slim.* [from Dutch]
▶ **slim down** If you **slim down**, you lose weight and become thinner. ❑ *I've slimmed down a size or two.*

Word Partnership	Use **slim** with :
ADV	**pretty** slim, **very** slim
ADJ	**tall and** slim

slime /slaɪm/ **N-NONCOUNT** **Slime** is a thick, wet substance that looks or smells unpleasant. ❑ *The rocks are slippery with mud and slime.* [from Old English]

sling /slɪŋ/ (**slings**) **N-COUNT** A **sling** is a piece of cloth that you wear around your neck and arm, to hold up your arm when it is broken or injured. ❑ *Emily had her arm in a sling.* [of Scandinavian origin]

slip /slɪp/ (**slips, slipping, slipped**)
1 V-I If you **slip**, you accidentally slide and fall. ❑ *He slipped on the wet grass.*
2 V-I If something **slips**, it slides out of position. ❑ *Grandpa's glasses slipped down his nose.*
3 V-I If you **slip** somewhere, you go there quickly and quietly. ❑ *In the morning she quietly slipped out of the house.*
4 V-T If you **slip** something somewhere, you put it there quickly and quietly.
❑ *I slipped the letter into my pocket.*
5 N-COUNT A **slip** is a small mistake.
❑ *Even a tiny slip could ruin everything.*
6 N-COUNT A **slip of** paper is a small piece of paper. ❑ *He wrote our names on slips of paper.* [from Middle Low German]
▶ **slip up** If you **slip up**, you make a mistake. ❑ *We slipped up a few times, but no one noticed.*

Thesaurus	slip	Also look up :
V	fall, slide, trip **1**	
N	blunder, failure, flub, mistake **5**	
	leaf, page, paper, sheet **6**	

Word Partnership	Use **slip** with :
ADJ	slip **resistant 1**
N	slip **of paper**, **sales** slip **6**

slip|per /slɪpər/ (**slippers**) **N-COUNT** **Slippers** are loose, soft shoes that you wear indoors. ❑ *She put on a pair of slippers and went downstairs.* [from Middle Low German]

slip|pery /slɪpəri/ **ADJ** If something is **slippery**, it is smooth or wet, and is difficult to walk on or to hold. ❑ *Be careful—the floor is slippery.* [from German]

S

slit /slɪt/ (**slits, slitting, slit**)

> **LANGUAGE HELP**
> The form **slit** is used in the present tense and is the past tense and past participle.

1 **V-T** If you **slit** something, you make a long narrow cut in it. ❑ *He slit open the envelope.*

2 **N-COUNT** A **slit** is a long narrow cut or opening in something. ❑ *Make a slit about half an inch long.* [from Old English]
→ look at Word Web: **shark**

slith|er /slɪðər/ (**slithers, slithering, slithered**) **V-I** If you **slither**, you move along the ground, sliding from side to side, like a snake. ❑ *Robert slithered down into the water.* [from Old English]

sliv|er /slɪvər/ (**slivers**) **N-COUNT** A **sliver of** something is a small thin piece of it. ❑ *A sliver of glass cut my foot.*

slo|gan /sloʊgən/ (**slogans**) **N-COUNT** A **slogan** is a short phrase that you can remember easily. Slogans are used in advertisements and by political parties. ❑ *His campaign slogan was "Time for Action."* [from Gaelic]

slope /sloʊp/ (**slopes, sloping, sloped**)

1 **N-COUNT** GEOGRAPHY A **slope** is the side of a mountain, a hill, or a valley. ❑ *A steep slope leads to the beach.*

2 **V-I** If a surface **slopes**, one end of it is higher than the other. ❑ *The land sloped down sharply to the river.* ● **slop|ing** **ADJ** ❑ *Our house has a sloping roof.*

3 **V-I** If something **slopes**, it leans to the right or to the left rather than being straight. ❑ *John's writing slopes backwards.* [from Old English]

slop|py /slɒpi/ (**sloppier, sloppiest**) **ADJ** If something is **sloppy**, it has been done in a careless and lazy way. ❑ *All teachers hate sloppy work from their students.* [from Old English]

slot /slɒt/ (**slots**) **N-COUNT** A **slot** is a long, narrow hole in something. ❑ *He dropped a coin into the slot and dialed the number.* ❑ *Please place your credit card in the slot.* [from Old French]

slow /sloʊ/ (**slower, slowest, slows, slowing, slowed**)

1 **ADJ** If something is **slow**, it does not move or happen quickly. ❑ *His bike was heavy and slow.* ❑ *The investigation was a long and slow*

process. ❑ *They danced to the slow rhythm of the music.* ● **slow|ly** **ADV** ❑ *He spoke slowly and clearly.*

2 **ADJ** If a clock or a watch is **slow**, it shows a time that is earlier than the correct time. ❑ *The clock is five minutes slow.* [from Old English]

▸ **slow down** If something or someone **slows down** or if something **slows** them **down**, they start to move or happen more slowly. ❑ *The bus slowed down for the next stop.*

Word Partnership	Use **slow** with :	
ADJ	slow **acting**, slow **moving** **1**	
N	slow **death**, slow **growth**, slow **movements**, slow **pace**, slow **process**, slow **progress**, slow **recovery**, slow **response**, slow **speed**, slow **start**, slow **stop**, slow **traffic** **1**	

slow mo|tion also **slow-motion**
N-NONCOUNT When film or television pictures are shown **in slow motion**, they are shown much more slowly than normal. ❑ *They played it again in slow motion.*

slug /slʌg/ (**slugs**) **N-COUNT** A **slug** is a small animal with a long soft body and no legs that moves very slowly. [of Scandinavian origin]

slum /slʌm/ (**slums**) **N-COUNT** SOCIAL STUDIES A **slum** is an area of a city where the buildings are in a bad condition and the people are very poor. ❑ *More than 2.4 million people live in the city's slums.*

slump /slʌmp/ (**slumps, slumping, slumped**)

1 **V-I** If the value of something **slumps**, it falls suddenly and by a large amount. ❑ *The company's profits slumped by 41% in a single year.*

2 **N-COUNT** **Slump** is also a noun. ❑ *There has been a slump in house prices.*

3 **V-I** If you **slump** somewhere, you fall or sit down suddenly and heavily. ❑ *She slumped into a chair and burst into tears.* [of Scandinavian origin]

slur /slɜr/ (**slurs, slurring, slurred**) **V-T/V-I** If you **slur**, or **slur** your words, you do not say each word clearly, because you are drunk, sick, or very tired. ❑ *He was slurring his words and I couldn't understand what he was saying.* ● **slurred** **ADJ** ❑ *Her speech was slurred and she was very pale.* [from Middle Low German]

S

sly /slaɪ/ **ADJ** A **sly** look, expression, or remark shows that you know something that other people do not know or that was meant to be a secret. ❑ *He gave a sly smile.* ●**sly|ly ADV** ❑ *Anna grinned slyly.* [from Old Norse]

smack /smæk/ (**smacks, smacking, smacked**)
■ **V-T** If you **smack** someone, you hit them with your hand. ❑ *She smacked me on the side of the head.*
◻ **N-COUNT** **Smack** is also a noun. ❑ *She gave him a smack.* [from Middle Low German]

small /smɔl/ (**smaller, smallest**)
■ **ADJ** If something is **small**, it is not large in size or amount. ❑ *My daughter is small for her age.* ❑ *Fry the onions in a small amount of butter.*
◻ **ADJ** A **small** child is a young child. ❑ *I have two small children.*
◻ **ADJ** If something is **small**, it is not very serious or important. ❑ *It's a small problem, and we can easily solve it.* [from Old English]

> **Thesaurus**   **small**   Also look up :
>
> ADJ   little, petite, slight; (*ant.*) big, large ■
> young ◻
> insignificant, minor; (*ant.*) important, major, significant ◼

small-scale ADJ A **small-scale** activity or organization is small in size and scale. ❑ *Most of the world's coffee beans are grown by small-scale farmers.*

smart /smɑrt/ (**smarter, smartest**) **ADJ** If you are **smart**, you are clever or intelligent. ❑ *He's a very smart, intelligent player.* [from Old English]

smart|phone /smɑrtfoʊn/ (**smartphones**) **N-COUNT** TECHNOLOGY A **smartphone** is a type of cellphone that can do many of the things that a computer does.

smash /smæʃ/ (**smashes, smashing, smashed**)
■ **V-T/V-I** If you **smash** something, it breaks into many pieces. ❑ *The gang started smashing windows in the street.* ❑ *I dropped the bottle and it smashed on the floor.*
◻ **N-COUNT** **Smash** is also a noun. ❑ *I heard the smash of glass and I shouted, "Get down!"*
◼ **V-T/V-I** If something **is smashed** against something, it moves against it very fast and with great force. ❑ *He smashed his fist down on the table.*

smear /smɪər/ (**smears, smearing, smeared**)
■ **V-T** If you **smear** a sticky substance on a surface, you spread the substance all over it. ❑ *My little sister smeared jam all over her face.*
●**smeared ADJ** ❑ *The child's clothes were smeared with dirt.*
◻ **N-COUNT** A **smear** is a dirty mark on something. ❑ *There were smears of oil on his face.* [from Old English]

smell /smɛl/ (**smells, smelling, smelled**)
■ **N-COUNT** The **smell** of something is the quality of it that you notice when you breathe in through your nose. ❑ *I just love the smell of freshly baked bread.* ❑ *There was a horrible smell in the refrigerator.*
◻ **N-NONCOUNT** Your sense of **smell** is the ability that your nose has to notice things. ❑ *She has lost her sense of smell.*
◼ **V-LINK** If something **smells** a particular way, it has a quality that you notice by breathing in through your nose. ❑ *The room smelled of lemons.* ❑ *The soup smells delicious!*
◼ **V-I** If something **smells**, it smells unpleasant. ❑ *My girlfriend says my feet smell.*
◼ **V-T** If you **smell** something, you notice it when you breathe in through your nose. ❑ *As soon as we opened the front door, we could smell smoke.* [from Middle Dutch]
→ look at Word Webs: **smell, taste**

S

Word Web   smell

Scientists say that the average person can recognize about 10,000 different **odors**. Until recently we did not understand the **sense** of **smell**. Now we know that most substances send odor molecules into the air. They enter the body through the **nose**. When they reach the **nasal cavity**, they attach to **sensory** cells. The olfactory **nerve** carries the information to the brain. The brain identifies the smell. The eyes, mouth, and throat also contain receptors that add to the olfactory experience. Interestingly, our sense of smell is better later in the day than in the morning.

Thesaurus smell Also look up :

N	aroma, fragrance, odor, scent **1**
V	reek, stink **4**
	breathe, inhale, sniff **5**

smelly /smɛli/ (**smellier, smelliest**) **ADJ**
If something is **smelly**, it has an unpleasant smell. ❏ ...smelly socks. [from Middle Dutch]

smile /smaɪl/ (**smiles, smiling, smiled**)
1 **V-I** If you **smile**, the corners of your mouth curve up because you are happy or you think that something is funny. ❏ When he saw me, he smiled. ❏ The children were all smiling at her.

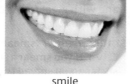
smile

2 **N-COUNT** A **smile** is the expression that you have on your face when you smile. ❏ She gave a little smile. [of Scandinavian origin]

Word Partnership Use smile with :

V	smile **and laugh, make** someone smile, smile **and nod, see** someone smile, **try to** smile **1**
	smile **fades, flash a** smile, **give** someone **a** smile **2**
ADJ	**big/little/small** smile, **broad** smile, **friendly** smile, **half** smile, **sad** smile, **shy** smile, **warm** smile, **wide** smile, **wry** smile **2**

smog /smɒg/ **N-NONCOUNT** Smog is pollution in the air that is a mixture of fog and gases or smoke. ❏ Winter smog was caused by people burning coal in their homes. ❏ A yellow smog hangs over the city on a hot Friday afternoon.

smoke /smoʊk/ (**smokes, smoking, smoked**)
1 **N-NONCOUNT** Smoke is the black or white clouds of gas that you see in the air when something burns. ❏ Thick black smoke blew over the city.
2 **V-T/V-I** If you **smoke** a cigarette, you suck the smoke from it into your mouth and blow it out again. If you **smoke**, you regularly smoke cigarettes. ❏ He smokes 20 cigarettes a day. ❏ You must quit smoking.
● **smok|er** (**smokers**) **N-COUNT** ❏ Smokers have a much higher risk of developing this disease.
● **smok|ing** **N-NONCOUNT** ❏ Smoking is banned in many restaurants.
3 **V-I** If something **is smoking**, smoke is coming from it. ❏ The chimney was smoking. Someone was at home. [from Old English]

→ look at Word Web: **fire**

smoky /smoʊki/ (**smokier, smokiest**) also **smokey** **ADJ** If a place is **smoky**, there is a lot of smoke in the air. ❏ The bar was dark, noisy, and smoky. [from Old English]

smooth /smuð/ (**smoother, smoothest**)
1 **ADJ** If a surface is **smooth**, it is flat and has no rough parts, lumps, or holes. ❏ The baby's skin was soft and smooth. ❏ The surface of the water is as smooth as glass.
2 **ADJ** If a liquid is **smooth**, it has no lumps. ❏ Stir the mixture until it is smooth.
3 **ADJ** A **smooth** movement has no sudden changes in direction or speed. ❏ The pilot made a very smooth landing.
● **smooth|ly** **ADV** ❏ The boat was traveling smoothly through the water.
4 **ADJ** If a process is **smooth**, it goes well and has no problems. ❏ We hope for a smooth move to our new home. ● **smooth|ly** **ADV** ❏ I hope your trip goes smoothly. [from Old English]
→ look at Word Web: **muscle**

smooth mus|cle (**smooth muscles**)
N-COUNT/N-NONCOUNT SCIENCE Smooth muscle is muscle that is mainly found inside the organs of your body and that cannot be controlled voluntarily.

smoth|er /smʌðər/ (**smothers, smothering, smothered**)
1 **V-T** If you **smother** a fire, you cover it with something in order to stop it burning. ❏ She tried to smother the flames with a blanket.
2 **V-T** If you **smother** someone, you kill them by covering their face with something so that they cannot breathe. ❏ She tried to smother him with a pillow. [from Old English]

smudge /smʌdʒ/ (**smudges, smudging, smudged**)
1 **N-COUNT** A **smudge** is a dirty mark. ❏ There was a dark smudge on his forehead.
2 **V-T** If you **smudge** something, you make it dirty or messy by touching it. ❏ Jennifer rubbed her eyes, smudging her makeup.

smug /smʌg/ **ADJ** If you are **smug**, you are very pleased with yourself, in a way that other people find annoying. ❏ "I have everything I need," he said with a smug little smile.
● **smug|ly** **ADV** ❏ Sue smiled smugly and sat down. [from Germanic]

smug|gle /smʌgəl/ (**smuggles, smuggling, smuggled**) **V-T** If you **smuggle** things or people into a place or out of it, you take

S

them there illegally or secretly. ❑ *They smuggled goods into the country.* ●**smug|gler** (**smugglers**) **N-COUNT** ❑ *The police arrested the diamond smugglers yesterday.* ●**smug|gling** **N-NONCOUNT** ❑ *A pilot was arrested and charged with smuggling.* [from Low German]

snack /snǽk/ (**snacks, snacking, snacked**)
1 **N-COUNT** A **snack** is a simple meal that is quick to prepare and to eat. ❑ *The kids have a snack when they come in from school.*
2 **V-I** If you **snack**, you eat a small amount of food between meals. ❑ *During the day, I snack on fruit and drink lots of water.* [from Middle Dutch]
→ look at Word Web: **peanut**

snag /snǽg/ (**snags**) **N-COUNT** A **snag** is a small problem or difficulty. ❑ *There is one possible snag in his plans.* [of Scandinavian origin]

snail /sneɪl/ (**snails**)
N-COUNT A **snail** is a small animal with a long, soft body, no legs, and a round shell on its back. [from Old English]

snail

snake /sneɪk/ (**snakes**) **N-COUNT** A **snake** is a long, thin animal with no legs, that slides along the ground. [from Old English]
→ look at Picture Dictionary: **desert**

snap /snǽp/ (**snaps, snapping, snapped**)
1 **V-T/V-I** If something **snaps**, it breaks with a short, loud noise. ❑ *Angrily, Matthew snapped the plastic pen in two.* ❑ *A twig snapped.*
2 **N-SING** **Snap** is also a noun. ❑ *I heard a snap and a crash as the tree fell.*
3 **V-T/V-I** If you **snap at** someone, you speak to them in a sharp, angry way. ❑ *Sorry, I didn't mean to snap at you.* ❑ *"Of course I don't know,"* Roger snapped.
4 **V-I** If a dog **snaps at** you, it tries to bite you. ❑ *The dog snapped at my ankle.* [from Middle Low German]

snarl /snɑrl/ (**snarls, snarling, snarled**)
1 **V-I** If an animal **snarls**, it makes an angry sound in its throat while it shows its teeth. ❑ *The dog ran after them, barking and snarling.*
2 **N-COUNT** **Snarl** is also a noun. ❑ *With a snarl, the dog bit his leg.* [of Germanic origin]

snatch /snǽtʃ/ (**snatches, snatching, snatched**) **V-T/V-I** If you **snatch** something, you take it away quickly and roughly.

❑ *Michael snatched the cards from Archie's hand.* ❑ *He snatched up the telephone.* [from Middle Dutch]

sneak /snik/ (**sneaks, sneaking, sneaked** or **snuck**)

1 **V-I** If you **sneak** somewhere, you go there very quietly. ❑ *He sneaked out of his house late at night.*
2 **V-T** If you **sneak** something somewhere, you take it there secretly. ❑ *He smuggled papers out, photocopied them, and snuck them back.*
3 **V-T** If you **sneak** a look at something, you secretly have a quick look at it. ❑ *She sneaked a look at her watch.* [from Old English]

sneak|er /snikər/ (**sneakers**) **N-COUNT** **Sneakers** are shoes that people wear especially for sports. ❑ *...a pair of sneakers.* [from Old English]
→ look at Picture Dictionaries: **clothing, shoe**

sneer /snɪər/ (**sneers, sneering, sneered**)
V-T/V-I If you **sneer**, or **sneer at** someone or something, your face shows that you do not like them. ❑ *"I don't need any help from you,"* he sneered. ❑ *Critics have sneered at the movie, saying it is boring.* [from Low Dutch]

sneeze /sniz/ (**sneezes, sneezing, sneezed**)
1 **V-I** When you **sneeze**, you suddenly take in your breath and then blow it down your nose noisily, for example because you have a cold. ❑ *Cover your nose and mouth when you sneeze.*
2 **N-COUNT** **Sneeze** is also a noun. ❑ *The disease is passed from person to person by a sneeze.* [from Old English]

sniff /snɪf/ (**sniffs, sniffing, sniffed**)
1 **V-I** When you **sniff**, you suddenly and quickly breathe in air through your nose. ❑ *She dried her eyes and sniffed.*
2 **N-COUNT** **Sniff** is also a noun. ❑ *I could hear quiet sobs and sniffs.*
3 **V-T/V-I** If you **sniff** something or **sniff at** it, you smell it by sniffing. ❑ *Suddenly, he stopped and sniffed the air.*

snig|ger /snɪgər/ (**sniggers, sniggering, sniggered**)
1 **V-I** If someone **sniggers**, they laugh quietly in an unpleasant way. ❑ *Three kids started sniggering.*

S

2 **N-COUNT** **Snigger** is also a noun. ❑ *I heard a snigger, and looked around.*

snip /snɪp/ (**snips, snipping, snipped**) **V-T/V-I** If you **snip** something, or if you **snip at** or **through** it, you cut it quickly using sharp scissors. ❑ *Snip off the dead flowers with a pair of scissors.* [from Low German]

snob /snɒb/ (**snobs**) **N-COUNT** A **snob** is someone who feels that they are better than other people because of their behavior or social class. ❑ *Her parents did not like him because they were snobs.*

snook|er /snʊkər/ **N-NONCOUNT** **SPORTS** **Snooker** is a game involving balls on a large table. The players use a long stick to hit a white ball, and score points by knocking colored balls into the pockets at the sides of the table. ❑ *...a game of snooker.*

snore /snɔr/ (**snores, snoring, snored**)
1 **V-I** When someone **snores**, they make a loud noise each time they breathe when they are asleep. ❑ *His mouth was open, and he was snoring.*
2 **N-COUNT** **Snore** is also a noun. ❑ *We heard loud snores coming from the next room.* [from Middle Low German]

snor|kel /snɔrkəl/ (**snorkels, snorkeling, snorkeled**)
1 **N-COUNT** A **snorkel** is a tube that a person swimming just under the surface of the ocean can breathe through.
2 **V-I** When someone **snorkels**, they swim under water using a snorkel. ❑ *You can snorkel off the side of the boat.* [from German]

snort /snɔrt/ (**snorts, snorting, snorted**)
1 **V-I** When people or animals **snort**, they breathe air noisily out through their noses. ❑ *Harrell snorted with laughter.*
2 **N-COUNT** **Snort** is also a noun. ❑ *Yana gave a snort of laughter.*

snow /snoʊ/ (**snows, snowing, snowed**)
1 **N-NONCOUNT** **Snow** is soft white frozen water that falls from the sky. ❑ *Six inches of snow fell.*
2 **V-I** When **it snows**, snow falls from the sky. ❑ *It snowed all night.* [from Old English]
→ look at Word Webs: **snow, precipitation, storm, water**

snow|ball /snoʊbɔl/ (**snowballs**) **N-COUNT** A **snowball** is a ball of snow.

snow|board|ing /snoʊbɔrdɪŋ/ **N-NONCOUNT** **SPORTS** **Snowboarding** is the sport of traveling down slopes that are covered with snow, with both your feet fastened to a board. ❑ *He loves skiing and snowboarding.* ● **snow|board|er** (**snowboarders**) **N-COUNT** ❑ *He's one of the world's top snowboarders.*

snow|flake /snoʊfleɪk/ (**snowflakes**) **N-COUNT** A **snowflake** is one of the soft, white pieces of frozen water that fall as snow.
→ look at Word Webs: **precipitation, snow**

snow|plow /snoʊplaʊ/ (**snowplows**) **N-COUNT** A **snowplow** is a vehicle that is used for pushing snow off roads or railroad tracks.

snowy /snoʊi/ (**snowier, snowiest**) **ADJ** **Snowy** means covered with snow. ❑ *...snowy mountains.* [from Old English]

snuck /snʌk/ **Snuck** is a past tense and past participle of **sneak**. [INFORMAL] [from Old English]

snug|gle /snʌgəl/ (**snuggles, snuggling, snuggled**) **V-I** If you **snuggle** or **snuggle up** somewhere, you get into a warm, comfortable position, especially by moving closer to another person. ❑ *Jane snuggled up against his shoulder.*

S

Word Web   snow

Some people love winter. They like to watch **snowflakes** falling softly from the sky. The **snow** forms beautiful **drifts** on the ground and trees. A house with **icicles** hanging from the roof and **frost** on the windows looks warm and cozy. But winter has a dangerous side as well. **Ice** and snow on streets and roads cause many accidents. And a **blizzard** can leave behind large amounts of snow in a single day. In the mountains, heavy snowfall can cause **avalanches**. They usually happen when light, new snow falls on top of older, heavy snow.

so

PRONUNCIATION HELP

Pronounce meanings **2**, **6**, **7**, **8**, and **9** /soʊ/. Pronounce meanings **1**, **3**, **4**, and **5** /soʊ/.

1 **ADV** You use **so** to talk about something that has just been mentioned. ❑ *"Do you think they will stay together?"—"I hope so."* ❑ *If you don't like it, then say so.*

2 **ADV** You use **so** when you are saying that something is also true. ❑ *I enjoy Ann's company and so does Martin.* ❑ *They had a wonderful time and so did I.*

3 **CONJ** You use **so** to introduce the result of a situation. ❑ *I am shy and so I find it hard to talk to people.*

4 **CONJ** You use **so** and **so that** to introduce the reason for doing something. ❑ *Come to dinner so we can talk about what happened.* ❑ *They moved to the corner of the room so that nobody would hear them.*

5 **ADV** You can use **so** in conversations to introduce a new subject. ❑ *So how was your day?*

6 **INTERJ** You say **So?** and **So what?** to show that you think something that someone has said is not important. [INFORMAL] ❑ *"I don't like it."—"So?"*

7 **ADV** You can use **so** in front of adjectives and adverbs to make them stronger. ❑ *I'm surprised they're married—they seemed so different.*

8 **PHRASE** You use **and so on** or **and so forth** at the end of a list if there are other items that you could mention. ❑ *...important issues such as health, education, and so on.*

9 **PHRASE** You use **or so** when you are giving an approximate amount. ❑ *A ticket will cost you $20 or so.* [from Old English]

soak /soʊk/ (**soaks, soaking, soaked**)
1 **V-T/V-I** If you **soak** something, or leave it **to soak**, you put it into a liquid and leave it there. ❑ *Soak the beans overnight.* ❑ *I left the sheets to soak for two hours.*
2 **V-T** If a liquid **soaks** something, it makes that thing very wet. ❑ *The water soaked his jacket.* ● **soaked** /soʊkt/ **ADJ** ❑ *The tent got completely soaked in the storm.* ● **soak|ing** **ADJ** ❑ *My raincoat was soaking wet.*
3 **V-I** If a liquid **soaks through** something, it passes through it. ❑ *Blood soaked through the bandages.* [from Old English]
▶ **soak up** If a soft or dry material **soaks up** a liquid, the liquid goes into it. ❑ *Use a towel to soak up the water.*

soap /soʊp/ **N-NONCOUNT** Soap is a substance that you use with water for washing yourself or for washing clothes. ❑ *...a bar of soap.* [from Old English]
→ look at Word Web: **soap**

soap op|era (**soap operas**) **N-COUNT** A soap opera is a popular television series about the daily lives and problems of a group of people who live in a particular place.

soar /sɔr/ (**soars, soaring, soared**)
1 **V-I** If the amount, the value, or the level of something **soars**, it quickly increases. ❑ *Prices soared in the first half of the year.*
2 **V-I** If a bird or an aircraft **soars** into the air, it goes quickly upward. [LITERARY] ❑ *A golden eagle soared overhead.* [from Old French]

sob /sɒb/ (**sobs, sobbing, sobbed**)
1 **V-I** When someone **sobs**, they cry in a noisy way. ❑ *She began to sob.*
2 **N-COUNT** A **sob** is a noise that you make when you are crying. ❑ *She heard quiet sobs from the next room.* [from Low German]

so|ber /soʊbər/
1 **ADJ** A **sober** person is not drunk. ❑ *He was completely sober.*
2 **ADJ** Sober colors and clothes are plain and not bright. ❑ *He dresses in sober gray suits.* [from Old French]

so-called also **so called**
1 **ADJ** You use **so-called** to show that you think a word or an expression is in fact wrong.

Word Web   soap

Soap is important in everyday life. We **wash** our hands before we eat. We **lather** up with a **bar** of soap in the **shower** or tub. We use liquid **detergent** to **clean** our dishes. We use **laundry** detergent to get our clothes clean. Soap attracts dirt and grease. It makes a **bubble** around the dirt, and **water** washes it all away.

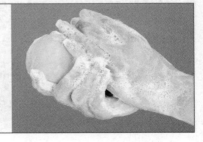

S

❏ *This so-called miracle never actually happened.*
2 ADJ You use **so-called** to show that something generally has the name that you are about to use. ❏ *...the world's eight largest economies, the so-called G-8.*

soc|cer /sɒkər/ **N-NONCOUNT** SPORTS Soccer is a game played by two teams of eleven players using a round ball. Players kick the ball to each other and try to score goals by kicking the ball into a large net. Outside the United States, this game is also called **football**. ❏ *She plays soccer.*
→ look at Picture Dictionary: **soccer**

so|cia|ble /soʊʃəbəl/ **ADJ** Sociable people are friendly and enjoy talking to other people. ❏ *She was extremely sociable.* [from French]

| Word Link | *soci ≈ companion : associate, social, sociology* |

so|cial /soʊʃəl/
1 ADJ Social means relating to society. ❏ *He sings about social problems like poverty.*
● **so|cial|ly ADV** ❏ *It wasn't socially acceptable to eat in the street.*
2 ADJ Social means relating to enjoyable activities that involve meeting other people. ❏ *We organize social events.* ● **so|cial|ly ADV** ❏ *We knew each other socially.* [from Latin]
→ look at Word Web: **myth**

so|cial be|hav|ior N-NONCOUNT SCIENCE Social behavior is the interaction between animals of the same species or between people.

so|cial|ism /soʊʃəlɪzəm/ **N-NONCOUNT** SOCIAL STUDIES Socialism is a set of political principles whose general aim is to create a system in which everyone has equal chances to gain wealth and to own the country's main industries. [from Latin]

so|cial|ist /soʊʃəlɪst/ (**socialists**)
1 ADJ SOCIAL STUDIES Socialist means based on socialism or relating to socialism.

❏ *He's a member of the Socialist Party.*
2 N-COUNT SOCIAL STUDIES A **socialist** is a person who believes in socialism. ❏ *His grandparents were socialists.* [from Latin]

so|cial|ize /soʊʃəlaɪz/ (**socializes, socializing, socialized**) **V-I** If you **socialize**, you meet other people socially, for example at parties. ❏ *I like socializing and making new friends.* [from Latin]

so|cial life (**social lives**) **N-COUNT** Your **social life** is the time you spend with your friends. ❏ *I was popular and had a busy social life.*

so|cial me|dia

> **LANGUAGE HELP**
> Social media can take the singular or plural form of the verb.

N-NONCOUNT TECHNOLOGY Social media refers to websites that people use for communicating with friends and other people who share their interests. ❏ *Politicians often use social media to get their message across.*

so|cial net|work|ing N-NONCOUNT TECHNOLOGY Social networking is the activity of contacting friends, sharing information, and making new friends using links on particular websites. ❏ *Have you used a social networking site such as MySpace or Facebook?*

So|cial Se|cu|rity N-NONCOUNT SOCIAL STUDIES Social Security is a system by which workers and employers in the U.S. have to pay money to the government. The government can then give money to people who are old, or who cannot work.

so|cial ser|vices N-PLURAL SOCIAL STUDIES Social services in a district are the services provided by the local authority or government to help people who have serious family problems or financial problems. ❏ *Social services are trying to help these children.*

so|cial stud|ies N-NONCOUNT SOCIAL STUDIES Social studies is a school subject that

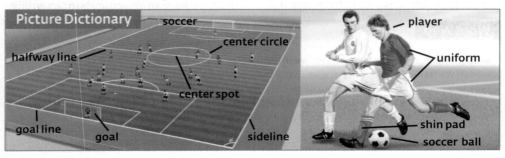

Picture Dictionary
halfway line
center circle
center spot
goal line
goal
sideline
soccer
player
uniform
shin pad
soccer ball

includes history, geography, politics, and economics.

so|cial work|er (social workers) N-COUNT A **social worker** is a person whose job is to help people who have social problems.

so|ci|ety /səsaɪɪti/ (societies)
■ N-COUNT/N-NONCOUNT **Society** consists of all the people in a country, when you think about their general behavior or problems. ❑ *These are common problems in today's society.* ❑ *We live in an unequal society.*
◻ N-COUNT A **society** is an organization for people who have the same interest or aim. ❑ *He's a member of the American Historical Society.* [from Old French]
→ look at Word Web: **culture**

so|ci|ol|ogy /soʊsiɒlədʒi/ N-NONCOUNT SOCIAL STUDIES **Sociology** is the study of society or of the way society is organized. ● **so|cio|logi|cal** /soʊsiəlɒdʒɪkᵊl/ ADJ ❑ *...a sociological study on the importance of the family.* ● **so|ci|olo|gist** (sociologists) N-COUNT ❑ *As a sociologist she is interested in the role of women.* [from French]

sock /sɒk/ (socks) N-COUNT **Socks** are pieces of clothing that cover your foot and ankle and are worn inside shoes. ❑ *...a pair of red socks.* [from Old English]
→ look at Picture Dictionary: **clothing**

sock|et /sɒkɪt/ (sockets) N-COUNT A **socket** is a hole that something fits into to make a connection. ❑ *He took the light bulb out of the socket.* ❑ *There's an electric socket by every seat on the train.* [from Anglo-Norman]

soda /soʊdə/ (sodas)
■ N-NONCOUNT **Soda** is a sweet drink that contains bubbles. ❑ *...a glass of soda.*
◻ N-COUNT A **soda** is a bottle of soda. ❑ *We bought sodas for the children.* [from Medieval Latin]

so|dium /soʊdiəm/ N-NONCOUNT SCIENCE **Sodium** is a silvery white chemical element that combines with other chemicals. Salt is a sodium compound. [from New Latin]

sofa /soʊfə/ (sofas) N-COUNT A **sofa** is a long, comfortable seat with a back, and usually with arms, that two or three people can sit on. [from Arabic]

soft /sɒft/ (softer, softest)
■ ADJ Something that is **soft** is pleasant to touch, and not rough or hard. ❑ *Body lotion*

will keep your skin soft. ❑ *She wiped the baby's face with a soft cloth.*
◻ ADJ Something that is **soft** changes shape easily when you press it. ❑ *Add milk to form a soft dough.*
◼ ADJ A **soft** sound or light is very gentle. ❑ *There was a soft tapping on my door.* ● **soft|ly** ADV ❑ *She walked into the softly lit room.*
◻ ADJ If you are **soft on** someone, you do not treat them as strictly as you should. ❑ *The law is too soft on criminals.* [from Old English]

Thesaurus	soft Also look up :
ADJ	silky; (ant.) firm, hard, rough ■ faint, gentle, light, low; (ant.) clear, strong ◼

soft drink (soft drinks) N-COUNT A **soft drink** is the same as a **soda**. ❑ *Can I get you some tea or coffee, or a soft drink?*

sof|ten /sɒfᵊn/ (softens, softening, softened)
■ V-T/V-I If you **soften** something, or if it **softens**, you make it, or it becomes, less hard. ❑ *Soften the butter in a small saucepan.*
◻ V-T If one thing **softens** the unpleasant effect of another thing, it makes the effect less severe. ❑ *He wanted to soften the impact of the new tax on the poor.* [from Old English]

Word Link	ware ≈ merchandise : hard*ware*, soft*ware*, ware*house*

soft|ware /sɒftwɛər/ N-NONCOUNT TECHNOLOGY Computer programs are called **software**. Compare with **hardware**. ❑ *He writes computer software.*

sog|gy /sɒgi/ (soggier, soggiest) ADJ Something that is **soggy** is unpleasantly wet. ❑ *The cheese and tomato sandwiches were soggy.*

soil /sɔɪl/ (soils) N-COUNT/N-NONCOUNT SCIENCE **Soil** is the substance on the surface of the Earth in which plants grow. ❑ *The soil here is good for growing vegetables.* [from Anglo-Norman]
→ look at Word Webs: **erosion, farm, photosynthesis**

so|lar /soʊlər/ ADJ SCIENCE **Solar** power is obtained from the sun's light and heat. [from Latin]
→ look at Word Webs: **solar, energy, greenhouse effect, photosynthesis**

so|lar col|lec|tor (solar collectors) N-COUNT TECHNOLOGY A **solar collector** is a piece of

Word Web — solar

photovoltaic cells

Sources of **fossil fuel energy** are becoming scarce and expensive. They also cause environmental **pollution**. Scientists are studying alternative sources of energy such as **solar power**. There are two ways to use the **sun's energy**. **Thermal** systems produce heat. Photovoltaic systems generate electricity.

solar collector

Thermal systems use a **solar collector**. This is an insulated box with a clear cover. It stores the sun's energy for use in household air or water heating systems. Photovoltaic systems have thin layers of **semiconductor** materials to change the sun's heat into electricity. They are often used in calculators and solar-powered watches.

equipment that makes electricity from the heat from the sun. ❑ *Large homes should have solar collectors.*

so|lar eclipse (solar eclipses) **N-COUNT** SCIENCE A **solar eclipse** is an occasion when the moon is between the Earth and the sun, so that for a short time you cannot see part or all of the sun. Compare with **lunar eclipse**.
→ look at Word Web: **eclipse**

so|lar neb|ula (solar nebulae or solar nebulas) **N-COUNT** SCIENCE The **solar nebula** is the cloud of gas from which our solar system is believed to have developed.

so|lar sys|tem (solar systems) **N-COUNT** SCIENCE The **solar system** is the sun and all the planets that go around it. ❑ *Saturn is the second biggest planet in the solar system.*
→ look at Picture Dictionary: **solar system**
→ look at Word Webs: **solar system**

sold /soʊld/ **Sold** is the past tense and past participle of **sell**. [from Old English]

sol|dier /soʊldʒər/ (soldiers) **N-COUNT** A **soldier** is a member of an army. [from Old French]

sole /soʊl/ (soles)
1 **ADJ** The **sole** thing or person of a

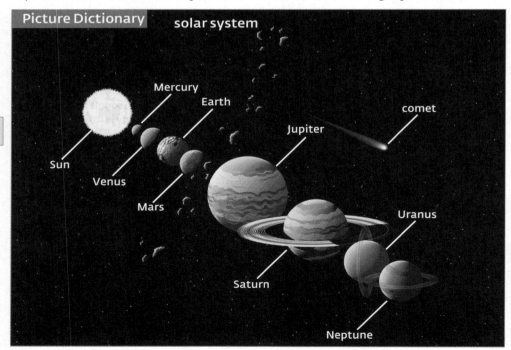

Picture Dictionary — solar system

Sun · Mercury · Venus · Earth · Mars · Jupiter · Saturn · Uranus · Neptune · comet

S

Word Web   solar system

The **sun** formed when a **nebula** turned into a star almost 5 billion years ago. All the **planets**, **comets**, and **asteroids** in our **solar system** came from this nebula. Today they all **orbit** the sun. The four planets closest to the sun are small and rocky. The next four consist mostly of **gases**. Many of the planets have **moons** orbiting them. Most asteroids have irregular shapes and covered with **craters**. Only about 200 asteroids have diameters of more than 100 kilometers.

particular type is the only one of that type. ❑ *Their sole aim is to win.* ● **sole|ly ADV** ❑ *The money you earn belongs solely to you.*

2 N-COUNT The **sole** of your foot or of a shoe or a sock is the underneath surface of it. ❑ *Wear shoes with thick soles.* [from Old French] → look at Picture Dictionary: **foot**

sol|emn /sɒləm/
1 ADJ Someone or something that is **solemn** is very serious rather than cheerful or amusing. ❑ *His face looked solemn.* ● **sol|emn|ly ADV** ❑ *Her listeners nodded solemnly.*
2 ADJ A **solemn** agreement is one that you make in a very formal, sincere way. ❑ *She made a solemn promise not to tell anyone.* [from Old French]

sol|fege /sɒlfɛʒ, soʊl-/ **N-NONCOUNT** MUSIC
Solfege is a system used in the teaching of music and singing, in which the steps of the musical scale are given the names Do, Re, Me, Fa, Sol, La, Ti, and Do. [from French]

so|lici|tor /səlɪsɪtər/ (**solicitors**) **N-COUNT**
SOCIAL STUDIES In the United States, a **solicitor** is the chief lawyer in a government or city department. [from Old French]

sol|id /sɒlɪd/ (**solids**)
1 ADJ A **solid** substance or object stays the same shape whether it is in a container or not. ❑ *The walls are made from solid concrete blocks.*
2 N-COUNT SCIENCE A **solid** is a hard substance. ❑ *Solids turn to liquids at certain temperatures.*
3 ADJ A substance that is **solid** is very hard or firm. ❑ *The lake was frozen solid.*
4 ADJ A **solid** object has no space inside it. ❑ *They had to cut through 50 feet of solid rock.*
5 ADJ A structure that is **solid** is strong and is not likely to fall over. ❑ *Only the most solid buildings were still standing after the earthquake.*
6 ADJ You use **solid** to describe advice or information that is reliable and useful. ❑ *We don't have any solid information on where he is.* [from Old French]
→ look at Picture Dictionary: **solids**
→ look at Word Web: **matter**

soli|dar|ity /sɒlɪdærɪti/ **N-NONCOUNT** If a group of people show **solidarity**, they show support for each other or for another group, especially in political or international

S

Picture Dictionary   solids

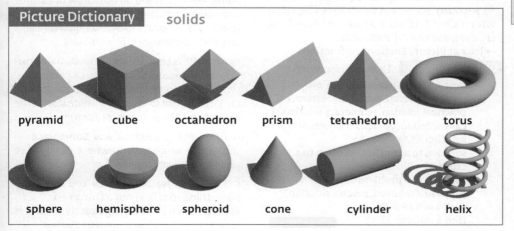

pyramid   cube   octahedron   prism   tetrahedron   torus

sphere   hemisphere   spheroid   cone   cylinder   helix

affairs. ❑ *People marched to show solidarity with their leaders.* [from French]

soli|tary /sɒlɪtɛri/
■ **ADJ** A **solitary** person or animal spends a lot of time alone. ❑ *Paul was a shy, solitary man.*
■ **ADJ** A **solitary** activity is one that you do alone. ❑ *He spent his evenings in solitary reading.* [from Latin]

solo /soʊloʊ/ (**solos**)
■ **ADJ** You use **solo** when someone does something alone rather than with other people. ❑ *He has just recorded his first solo album.*
■ **ADV** Solo is also an adverb. ❑ *Lindbergh flew solo across the Atlantic.*
■ **N-COUNT** ARTS MUSIC A **solo** is a piece of music or a dance performed by one person. ❑ *The music teacher asked me to sing a solo.* [from Italian]

sol|ubil|ity /sɒlyəbɪlɪti/ **N-NONCOUNT**
SCIENCE A substance's **solubility** is its ability to dissolve in another substance or the amount of it that will dissolve in another substance. [from Late Latin]

sol|uble /sɒlyəbᵊl/ **ADJ** SCIENCE A substance that is **soluble** will dissolve in a liquid. ❑ *The red dye is soluble in hot water.* [from Late Latin]

so|lute /sɒlyut, soʊlut/ (**solutes**) **N-COUNT**
SCIENCE A **solute** is any substance that dissolves in another substance. [from Latin]

so|lu|tion /səluʃᵊn/ (**solutions**)
■ **N-COUNT** A **solution to** a problem is a way of dealing with it. ❑ *They both want to find a peaceful solution.*
■ **N-COUNT** The **solution to** a puzzle is the answer to it. ❑ *We asked readers who completed the puzzle to send in their solutions.*
■ **N-COUNT** SCIENCE A **solution** is a liquid in which a solid substance has been dissolved. ❑ *...a soapy solution.* [from Latin]
→ look at Picture Dictionary: **fractions**

Word Partnership	Use **solution** with :
ADJ	**best** solution, **peaceful** solution, **perfect** solution, **possible** solution, **practical** solution, **temporary** solution ■ **easy** solution, **obvious** solution, **simple** solution ■ ■
PREP	solution **to a conflict**, solution **to a crisis** ■ solution **to a problem** ■ ■
V	**propose a** solution, **reach a** solution, **seek a** solution ■ **find a** solution ■ ■

solve /sɒlv/ (**solves, solving, solved**)
■ **V-T** If you **solve** a problem or a question, you find an answer to it. ❑ *They have not solved the problem of unemployment.*
■ **V-T** MATH If you **solve** a problem in math, you work out the answer. [from Latin]

Word Partnership	Use **solve** with :
N	**ability to** solve *something*, solve **a crisis**, solve **a problem**, solve **a puzzle**, **way to** solve *something* ■ ■
V	**attempt/try to** solve *something*, **help** solve *something* ■ ■

some /səm, STRONG sʌm/
■ **DET** You use **some** to talk about an amount of something. ❑ *Would you like some orange juice?*
■ **PRON** Some is also a pronoun. ❑ *When the chicken is cooked, I'll freeze some.* ❑ *Put some of the sauce onto a plate.*
■ **DET** You use **some** to talk about a number of people or things. ❑ *He went to buy some books.*
■ **PRON** Some is also a pronoun. ❑ *The apples are ripe, and we picked some today.* ❑ *Some of the workers will lose their jobs.*
■ **DET** You use **some** to show that a quantity is fairly large. ❑ *We have discussed this in some detail.*
■ **DET** If you talk about **some** person or thing, you mean that you do not know exactly which person or thing. ❑ *She wanted to talk to him about some problem she was having.* [from Old English]

some|body /sʌmbɑdi, -bʌdi/ **PRON**
Somebody means the same as **someone**.

some|how /sʌmhaʊ/ **ADV** You use **somehow** when you do not know or cannot say how something was done or will be done. ❑ *We'll manage somehow, I know we will.* ❑ *I somehow managed to finish the race.*

some|one /sʌmwʌn/ or **somebody** **PRON**
You use **someone** to talk about a person without saying exactly who you mean. ❑ *I got a call from someone who wanted to rent the apartment.* ❑ *I need someone to help me.*

some|place /sʌmpleɪs/ **ADV** Someplace means the same as **somewhere**. ❑ *Maybe we could go someplace together.*

some|thing /sʌmθɪŋ/ **PRON** You use **something** to talk about a thing or a situation, without saying exactly what it is. ❑ *He knew that there was something wrong.*

S

❏ *Was there something you wanted to ask me?* ❏ *I need a knife or something.*

some|time /sʌmtaɪm/ **ADV** You use **sometime** to talk about a time in the future or the past that is not known. ❏ *We will finish sometime next month.* ❏ *Why don't you come and see me sometime?*

Usage   sometime, sometimes, and some time

Sometime, sometimes, and *some time* are easy to confuse. *Sometime* means "at some unknown time"; *sometimes* means "occasionally, from time to time"; *some time* means "some amount of time": *Sometimes Ilya enjoys spending some time catching up on his favorite soap operas; the last time he did that was sometime in August.*

---

some|times /sʌmtaɪmz/ **ADV Sometimes** means on some occasions rather than all the time. ❏ *I sometimes sit out in the garden and read.* ❏ *Sometimes he's a little rude.*

some|what /sʌmwʌt, -wɒt/ **ADV Somewhat** means "a little." [FORMAL] ❏ *She behaved somewhat differently when he was there.*

some|where /sʌmwɛər/
1 **ADV** You use **somewhere** to talk about a place without saying exactly where you mean. ❏ *I've seen him before somewhere.* ❏ *I needed somewhere to live.*
2 **ADV** You use **somewhere** when you are giving an approximate amount or time. ❏ *The house is worth somewhere between $7 million and $10 million.*

son /sʌn/ (**sons**) **N-COUNT** Someone's **son** is their male child. ❏ *Sam is the seven-year-old son of Eric Davies.* [from Old English]
→ look at Word Web: **child**

so|na|ta-al|le|gro form /sənɑtə əlɛgroʊ fɔrm/ (**sonata-allegro forms**) or **sonata form** **N-COUNT/N-NONCOUNT** MUSIC A **sonata-allegro form** is a piece of classical music that consists of three main sections in which musical themes are introduced, developed, and then repeated.

song /sɔŋ/ (**songs**)
1 **N-COUNT** MUSIC A **song** is words and music sung together. ❏ *She sang a Spanish song.*
2 **N-COUNT** A bird's **song** is the pleasant musical sounds that it makes. ❏ *It's lovely to hear a blackbird's song in the evening.* [from Old English]

→ look at Word Webs: **concert, music**

Word Partnership	Use **song** with :
ADJ	**beautiful** song, **favorite** song, **old** song, **popular** song **1**
V	**hear a** song, **play a** song, **record a** song, **sing a** song **1**
N	**hit** song, **love** song, song **lyrics**, song **music**, **pop** song, song **title**, **theme** song, **words of a** song **1**
	bird's song **2**

---

song form (**song forms**)
N-COUNT/N-NONCOUNT MUSIC **Song form** is a way of describing the structure of a song in which different sections of the song are represented by different letters of the alphabet.

son|ic /sɒnɪk/ **ADJ** SCIENCE **Sonic** is used to describe things related to sound. ❏ *...the sonic and visual effects in the show.* [from Latin]
→ look at Word Web: **sound**

son-in-law (**sons-in-law**) **N-COUNT** Someone's **son-in-law** is the husband of their daughter.

soon /sun/ (**sooner, soonest**)
1 **ADV** If something happens **soon**, it happens after a short time. ❏ *I'll call you soon.* ❏ *He arrived sooner than I expected.*
2 **PHRASE** If something happens **as soon as** something else happens, it happens immediately after the other thing. ❏ *As soon as the weather improves we will go.* [from Old English]

soothe /suð/ (**soothes, soothing, soothed**)
1 **V-T** If you **soothe** someone who is angry or upset, you make them feel calmer. ❏ *He sang to her to soothe her.* ● **sooth|ing ADJ** ❏ *Put on some nice soothing music.*
2 **V-T** Something that **soothes** a painful part of your body makes it feel better. ❏ *Use this lotion to soothe dry skin.* ● **sooth|ing ADJ** ❏ *Cold tea is very soothing for burns.* [from Old English]

so|phis|ti|cat|ed /səfɪstɪkeɪtɪd/
1 **ADJ** A **sophisticated** machine or system is complicated and highly developed. ❏ *Bees use a very sophisticated communication system.*
2 **ADJ** Someone who is **sophisticated** knows about things like culture and fashion. ❏ *Claude was a charming, sophisticated man.* [from Medieval Latin]

S

Thesaurus   **sophisticated** Also look up :

ADJ   advanced, complex, elaborate, intricate **1**
cultured, experienced, refined, worldly; (*ant.*) backward, crude **2**

---

sopho|more /sɒfəmɔr/ (**sophomores**)
N-COUNT A **sophomore** is a student in the second year of college or high school.

so|pra|no /səprænoʊ, -prɑn-/ (**sopranos**)
N-COUNT MUSIC A **soprano** is a woman, a girl, or a boy with a high singing voice. ❑ *She was the main soprano at the theater.* [from Italian]

sore /sɔr/ (**sorer, sorest, sores**)
1 **ADJ** If part of your body is **sore**, it is painful and uncomfortable. ❑ *I had a sore throat and a cough.*
2 **N-COUNT** A **sore** is a painful place on the body where the skin is infected. ❑ *Our hands were covered with sores from the ropes.* [from Old English]

sor|row /sɒroʊ/ **N-NONCOUNT** Sorrow is a feeling of deep sadness. ❑ *Words cannot express my sorrow.* [from Old English]

sor|ry /sɒri/ (**sorrier, sorriest**)
1 **INTERJ** You say **Sorry** or **I'm sorry** to apologize for something that you have done. ❑ *"You're making too much noise."—"Sorry."* ❑ *Sorry I took so long.*
2 **ADJ** If you are **sorry** about a situation, you feel regret, sadness, or disappointment about it. ❑ *I'm sorry he's gone.*
3 **INTERJ** You say **I'm sorry** to express your regret and sadness when you hear sad or unpleasant news. ❑ *"Robert's sick today."—"I'm sorry to hear that."*
4 **INTERJ** You use **I'm sorry** or **Sorry** as a polite way of saying "no" or telling someone that you disagree with them. ❑ *I'm sorry but I refuse to pay.*
5 **ADJ** If you feel **sorry for** someone, you feel sadness for them. ❑ *I felt sorry for him because nobody listened to him.* [from Old English]

sort /sɔrt/ (**sorts, sorting, sorted**)
1 **N-COUNT** A particular **sort of** thing is a type of thing that belongs to a larger group. ❑ *What sort of school did you go to?* ❑ *You can buy many different sorts of mushrooms.*
2 **V-T/V-I** If you **sort** things, you separate them into different groups. ❑ *He sorted the materials into their folders.* ❑ *He opened the box*

and sorted through the papers.
3 **PHRASE** You use **sort of** when your description of something is not very accurate. [INFORMAL] ❑ *"What's a sub?"—"Well, it's sort of a sandwich."* [from Old French]
▶ **sort out** **1** If you **sort out** a group of things, you separate them into different groups. ❑ *Sort out all your bills as quickly as possible.*
2 If you **sort out** a problem, you deal with it successfully. ❑ *The two countries have sorted out their disagreement.*

sought /sɔt/ **Sought** is the past tense and past participle of **seek**. [from Old English]

soul /soʊl/ (**souls**)
1 **N-COUNT** Your **soul** is the part of you that consists of your mind, character, thoughts, and feelings. Many people believe that your soul continues existing after your body is dead. ❑ *She prayed for the soul of her dead husband.*
2 **N-NONCOUNT** MUSIC **Soul** is the same as **soul music**. ❑ *The show stars American soul singer Anita Baker.* [from Old English]

soul music **N-NONCOUNT** MUSIC **Soul music** is a type of pop music performed mainly by African-American musicians. It often expresses deep emotions.

---

sound
❶ NOUN AND VERB USES
❷ ADJECTIVE AND ADVERB USES

---

❶ sound /saʊnd/ (**sounds, sounding, sounded**)
1 **N-COUNT** A **sound** is something that you hear. ❑ *Peter heard the sound of a car engine outside.*
2 **V-T/V-I** If a bell **sounds**, or if you **sound** a bell, it makes a noise. ❑ *The fire alarm sounded at about 3:20 a.m.*
3 **V-LINK** When you are describing a noise, you can talk about the way it **sounds**. ❑ *They heard what sounded like a huge explosion.*
4 **V-LINK** The way someone **sounds** is how they seem when they speak. ❑ *She sounds very angry.*
5 **V-LINK** When you are describing your opinion of something, you can talk about the way it **sounds**. ❑ *It sounds like a wonderful idea to me.*
6 **N-SING** You can describe your impression of something you have heard or read about

Word Web · sound

Sound is the only form of energy we can hear. The energy makes molecules in the air **vibrate**. Fast vibrations called high **frequencies** produce high-pitched sounds. Slower vibrations produce lower frequencies. Sound vibrations travel in waves, just like **waves** in water. Each wave has a **crest** and a **trough**. **Amplitude** measures the size of a **wave**. It is the vertical distance between the middle of a wave and its crest. When a **sound wave** bounces off something, it creates an **echo**.

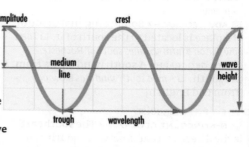

by talking about **the sound of** it. ❑ *I like the sound of this idea.* [from Old French]
→ look at Word Webs: **sound, concert, ear, echo**

❷ **sound** /saʊnd/ (**sounder, soundest**)
 ■ **ADJ** If something is **sound**, it is in good condition. ❑ *The building is perfectly sound.*
 ❷ **ADJ Sound** advice is sensible, and can be trusted. ❑ *Our experts will give you sound advice.*
 ❸ **ADV** If someone is **sound** asleep, they are in a deep sleep. ❑ *He was lying in bed, sound asleep.* [from Old English]

sound en|er|gy N-NONCOUNT SCIENCE
Sound energy is energy in the form of sound waves.

sound|ly /saʊndli/ **ADV** If you sleep **soundly**, you sleep deeply and do not wake during your sleep. ❑ *How can he sleep soundly at night?* [from Old French]

sound|track /saʊndtræk/ (**soundtracks**) also **sound track N-COUNT** MUSIC The **soundtrack** of a movie is its sound, speech, and especially its music. ❑ *...the soundtrack to a movie called "Casino Royale."*

sound wave (**sound waves**) also **soundwave**
N-COUNT SCIENCE **Sound waves** are the waves of energy that we hear as sound.

soup /sup/ **N-NONCOUNT** Soup is liquid food made by boiling meat, fish, or vegetables in water. ❑ *...homemade chicken soup.* [from Old French]

sour /saʊər/
 ■ **ADJ** Something that is **sour** has a sharp,

unpleasant taste like the taste of a lemon. ❑ *The stewed apple was sour.*
 ❷ **ADJ Sour** milk is milk that has an unpleasant taste because it is no longer fresh. ❑ *I can smell sour milk.* [from Old English]
→ look at Word Web: **taste**

source /sɔrs/ (**sources**)
 ■ **N-COUNT** The **source of** something is the person, place, or thing that it comes from. ❑ *Many adults use television as their major source of information.* ❑ *We are developing new sources of energy.*
 ❷ **N-COUNT** GEOGRAPHY The **source** of a river or a stream is the place where it begins. ❑ *...the source of the Tiber.*
 ❸ **N-COUNT** A **source** is a person or a book that provides information for a news story or for a piece of research. ❑ *Military sources say the boat was heading south.* [from Old French]
→ look at Word Web: **diary**

source code (**source codes**)
N-COUNT/N-NONCOUNT TECHNOLOGY **Source code** is the original form of a computer program as it is written by a programmer. ❑ *The source code can be licensed and downloaded for evaluation.*

south /saʊθ/ also **South**
 ■ **N-NONCOUNT** GEOGRAPHY The **south** is the direction that is on your right when you are looking at the sun in the morning. ❑ *It's warmer in the south.* ❑ *The town lies ten miles to the south.*
 ❷ **ADJ** GEOGRAPHY **South** is also an adjective. ❑ *...the south coast of Long Island.* ❑ *...South America.*
 ❸ **N-SING** GEOGRAPHY The **south of** a place or a country is the part that is in the south. ❑ *We organize vacations in the south of Mexico.*

S

4 ADV GEOGRAPHY If you go **south**, you travel toward the south. ❑ *I drove south on Highway 9.*

5 ADV GEOGRAPHY Something that is **south of** a place is located to the south of it. ❑ *They now live on a farm 50 miles south of Rochester.*

6 ADJ GEOGRAPHY A **south** wind blows from the south. ❑ *A mild south wind was blowing.* [from Old English]

south|east /saʊθist/
1 N-NONCOUNT GEOGRAPHY The **southeast** is the direction that is between south and east. ❑ *The train left Colombo for Galle, 70 miles to the southeast.*
2 ADJ GEOGRAPHY **Southeast** is also an adjective. ❑ *I grew up in rural southeast Kansas.* ❑ *...Southeast Asia.*
3 ADV GEOGRAPHY If you go **southeast**, you travel toward the southeast. ❑ *I know we have to go southeast, more or less.*
4 ADV GEOGRAPHY Something that is **southeast of** a place is located to the southeast of it. ❑ *The ship sank 500 miles southeast of Nova Scotia.*

south|eastern /saʊθistərn/ ADJ GEOGRAPHY **Southeastern** means in or from the southeast part of a place. ❑ *The city is on the southeastern edge of the United States.*

south|er|ly /sʌðərli/
1 ADJ GEOGRAPHY **Southerly** means to the south or toward the south. ❑ *We traveled in a southerly direction toward Arkansas.*
2 ADJ A **southerly** wind blows from the south. ❑ *...a strong southerly wind.* [from Old English]

south|ern /sʌðərn/ also **Southern** ADJ GEOGRAPHY **Southern** means in or from the south of a place. ❑ *The Everglades National Park stretches across southern Florida.* [from Old English]

south|west /saʊθwɛst/
1 N-NONCOUNT GEOGRAPHY The **southwest** is the direction that is between south and west. ❑ *He lives about 500 miles to the southwest of Johannesburg.*
2 ADJ GEOGRAPHY **Southwest** is also an adjective. ❑ *Her family comes from southwest Louisiana.*
3 ADV GEOGRAPHY If you go **southwest**, you travel toward the southwest. ❑ *We took a plane southwest to Cappadocia.*
4 ADV GEOGRAPHY Something that is **southwest of** a place is located to the

southwest of it. ❑ *It's about 65 miles southwest of Houston.*

south|western /saʊθwɛstərn/ ADJ GEOGRAPHY **Southwestern** means in or from the southwest part of a place. ❑ *They come from a small town in the southwestern part of the country.*

sou|venir /suvənɪər/ (**souvenirs**) N-COUNT A **souvenir** is something that you buy or keep to remind you of a place or an event. ❑ *Vacation photos are the best souvenir of any trip.* [from French]

sov|er|eign /sɒvrɪn/ (**sovereigns**)
1 ADJ SOCIAL STUDIES A **sovereign** state or country is independent and not under the authority of any other country. ❑ *They are now independent sovereign states.*
2 ADJ SOCIAL STUDIES **Sovereign** is used to describe the person or institution that has the highest power in a country. ❑ *Every organized society needs a sovereign power.*
3 N-COUNT SOCIAL STUDIES A **sovereign** is a king, a queen, or other royal ruler of a country. ❑ *In March 1889, she became the first British sovereign to travel to Spain.* [from Old French]

sov|er|eign|ty /sɒvrɪnti/ N-NONCOUNT SOCIAL STUDIES **Sovereignty** is the power that a country has to govern itself or another country. ❑ *It is important to protect our national sovereignty.* [from Old French]

sow /soʊ/ (**sows, sowing, sowed, sown**) V-T If you **sow** seeds, you plant them in the ground. ❑ *Sow the seed in a warm place in early March.* [from Old English]

soy /sɔɪ/ N-NONCOUNT **Soy** flour, butter, or other food is made from soybeans. [from Japanese]

soy|bean /sɔɪbin/ (**soybeans**) also **soy bean** N-COUNT **Soybeans** are beans that can be eaten, or used for making flour, oil, or sauce.

spa /spɑ/ (**spas**)
1 N-COUNT A **spa** is a place where water comes out of the ground. ❑ *Buxton is a spa town that is famous for its water.*
2 N-COUNT A health **spa** is a place where people go to exercise and have special treatments in order to improve their health. ❑ *Hotel guests may use the health spa.*
→ look at Word Web: **hotel**

space /speɪs/ (**spaces, spacing, spaced**)
1 N-COUNT/N-NONCOUNT You use **space** to

S

talk about an area that is empty. ❏ *They cut down trees to make space for houses.* ❏ *The space under the bed could be used as a storage area.*

2 **N-SING** A **space of** time is a period of time. ❏ *They've come a long way in a short space of time.*

3 **N-NONCOUNT** SCIENCE **Space** is the area beyond the Earth's atmosphere, where the stars and planets are. ❏ *The six astronauts will spend ten days in space.*

4 **V-T** If you **space** a series of things, you separate them so that they are not all together. ❏ *Write the words down, spacing them evenly.*

5 **Space out** means the same as **space**. ❏ *He talks quite slowly and spaces his words out.*

6 **N-COUNT/N-NONCOUNT** ARTS In dance, **space** refers to the immediate space around the body in all directions. **Space** is also the place where a dance takes place. [from Old French]

→ look at Word Webs: **moon, satellite**

space|craft /speɪskræft/ (**spacecraft**) **N-COUNT** SCIENCE A **spacecraft** is a vehicle that can travel in space. ❏ *This is the world's largest and most expensive spacecraft.*

space probe (**space probes**) **N-COUNT** SCIENCE A **space probe** is a spacecraft with no people in it that is sent into space in order to study the planets and send information about them back to Earth.

space|ship /speɪsʃɪp/ (**spaceships**) **N-COUNT** SCIENCE A **spaceship** is the same as a **spacecraft**. [from Old French]

space shut|tle (**space shuttles**) **N-COUNT** SCIENCE A **space shuttle** is a vehicle that is designed to travel into space and back to Earth several times.

space sta|tion (**space stations**) **N-COUNT** A **space station** is a place built for astronauts to live and work in, which is sent into space and then keeps going around the Earth.

→ look at Word Web: **satellite**

space suit (**space suits**) also **space-suit** **N-COUNT** SCIENCE A **space suit** is a special protective suit that is worn by astronauts in space.

spa|cious /speɪʃəs/ **ADJ** A **spacious** place is large, so that you can move around easily in it. ❏ *The house has a spacious kitchen and dining area.* [from Latin]

spade /speɪd/ (**spades**)

1 **N-COUNT** A **spade** is a tool that is used for

digging. ❏ *...a garden spade.*

2 **N-NONCOUNT Spades** is one of the four suits in a deck of playing cards. Each card in the suit is marked with one or more black symbols: ♠. ❏ *...the ace of spades.*

3 **N-COUNT** A **spade** is a playing card of this suit. ❏ *He should play a spade now.* [Sense 1 from Old English. Senses 2 and 3 from Italian.]

spa|ghet|ti /spəgɛti/ **N-NONCOUNT** **Spaghetti** is a type of pasta that looks like long pieces of string. [from Italian]

spam /spæm/ (**spams**)

N-COUNT/N-NONCOUNT TECHNOLOGY **Spam** is advertising messages that are sent automatically by email to large numbers of people. ❏ *Spam is becoming a major problem for many Internet users.*

span /spæn/ (**spans, spanning, spanned**)

1 **N-COUNT** A **span** is a period of time. ❏ *The batteries had a life span of six hours.*

2 **V-T** If something **spans** a long period of time, it lasts for that period of time. ❏ *His professional career spanned 16 years.*

3 **N-COUNT** The **span** of something is the total width of it from one side to the other. ❏ *The butterfly has a 2-inch wing span.*

4 **V-T** A bridge or other structure that **spans** a river or a road stretches right across it. ❏ *There is a footbridge that spans the little stream.* [from Old English]

→ look at Word Web: **bridge**

spank /spæŋk/ (**spanks, spanking, spanked**) **V-T** If someone **spanks** a child, they punish them by hitting them on the bottom with their hand. ❏ *When we were kids, our mom never spanked us.*

spare /spɛər/ (**spares, sparing, spared**)

1 **ADJ Spare** things are extra things that you keep in case you need them. ❏ *It's useful to have a spare pair of glasses.* ❏ *I'll give you the spare key.*

2 **V-T** If you **spare** time or money, you make it available. ❏ *I can only spare 35 minutes for this meeting.*

3 **V-T** If you **spare** someone an unpleasant experience, you prevent them from suffering it. ❏ *I wanted to spare her the embarrassment of talking about it.* [from Old English]

Thesaurus	spare Also look up :
ADJ	additional, backup, emergency, extra, reserve **1**

S

Word Partnership	Use spare with :
N	spare **change**, spare **equipment** ❶ **a moment to** spare, **time to** spare ❷

spare time N-NONCOUNT Your **spare time** is the time when you do not have to work. ❑ *In her spare time she read books on cooking.*

spark /spɑrk/ (**sparks**)

❶ N-COUNT A **spark** is a very small piece of burning material that comes out of something that is burning. ❑ *Sparks flew out of the fire in all directions.*

spark

❷ N-COUNT A **spark** is a flash of light caused by electricity. ❑ *I saw a spark when I connected the wires.* [from Old English]

→ look at Word Web: **fire**

Word Partnership	Use spark with :
PREP	spark **from a fire** ❶
V	**ignite** a spark, **provide** a spark ❷

spar|kle /spɑrkᵊl/ (**sparkles, sparkling, sparkled**) V-I If something **sparkles**, it is clear and bright, and it shines with a lot of very small points of light. ❑ *The jewels on her fingers sparkled.* ❑ *His bright eyes sparkled.*

spar|row /spærou/ (**sparrows**) N-COUNT A **sparrow** is a small brown bird that is very common in the United States. [from Old English]

sparse /spɑrs/ (**sparser, sparsest**) ADJ If something is **sparse**, there is not much of it and it is spread out over an area. ❑ *He was a fat little man in his fifties, with sparse hair.* ● **sparse|ly** ADV ❑ *This is a sparsely populated mountain region.* [from Latin]

speak /spik/ (**speaks, speaking, spoke, spoken**)

❶ V-I When you **speak**, you use your voice in order to say something. ❑ *He opened his mouth to speak.* ❑ *I called the hotel and spoke to Louie.* ❑ *He often speaks about his mother.* ❑ *I need to speak with him.*

❷ V-I When someone **speaks**, they make a speech. ❑ *He will speak at the Democratic Convention.*

❸ V-T If you **speak** a foreign language, you know the language and are able to have a conversation in it. ❑ *He speaks English.* [from Old English]

❹ → see also **spoke, spoken**

▶ **speak up** If you ask someone to **speak up**, you are asking them to speak more loudly. ❑ *I'm quite deaf—you'll have to speak up.*

Thesaurus	speak	Also look up :
V	articulate, communicate, declare, talk ❶	

Word Partnership	Use speak with :
ADV	speak **clearly**, speak **directly**, speak **louder** ❶ speak **freely**, speak **publicly** ❶ ❷
N	**chance to** speak, **opportunity to** speak, speak **the truth** ❶ ❷ speak **English/French/Spanish**, speak **a (foreign) language** ❸

speak|er /spikər/ (**speakers**)

❶ N-COUNT TECHNOLOGY A **speaker** is a piece of electrical equipment that sound comes out of. ❑ *I bought a pair of speakers for my computer.*

❷ N-COUNT A **speaker** is someone who is saying something. ❑ *You can understand a lot from the speaker's tone of voice.*

❸ N-COUNT A **speaker** is someone who makes a speech. ❑ *Bruce Wyatt will be the guest speaker at next month's meeting.* [from Old English]

speak|er|phone /spikərfoʊn/ (**speakerphones**)

❶ N-COUNT TECHNOLOGY A **speakerphone** is a telephone that allows you to hear the other person without holding the phone to your ear. ❑ *...a cordless speakerphone.*

❷ N-NONCOUNT TECHNOLOGY **Speakerphone** is the feature on some telephones that allows you to hear the other person without holding the phone to your ear. ❑ *I put him on speakerphone and we could all hear him talking.*

spear /spɪər/ (**spears**) N-COUNT A **spear** is a weapon consisting of a long pole with a sharp metal point at the end. [from Old English]

→ look at Word Web: **army**

spe|cial /spɛʃᵊl/

❶ ADJ Someone or something that is **special** is better or more important than other people or things. ❑ *You're very special to me.* ❑ *My special guest will be Zac Efron.*

❷ ADJ **Special** means different from normal. ❑ *In special cases, a child can be educated at home.*

S

3 **ADJ** You use **special** to describe something that relates to one particular person, group, or place. ❑ *Every person has his or her own special problems.* [from Old French]

> **Thesaurus** special Also look up :
> ADJ distinctive, exceptional, unique; *(ant.)* ordinary **1** **2**

spe|cial|ist /spɛʃəlɪst/ (**specialists**) **N-COUNT** A **specialist** is a person who knows a lot about a particular subject. ❑ *Peckham is a cancer specialist.* [from Old French]

spe|cial|ize /spɛʃəlaɪz/ (**specializes, specializing, specialized**) **V-I** If you **specialize in** a subject, you concentrate a lot of your time and energy on it. ❑ *He's a professor who specializes in Russian history.* [from Old French]

spe|cial|ized /spɛʃəlaɪzd/ **ADJ** Someone or something that is **specialized** is trained or developed for a particular purpose or area of knowledge. ❑ *Children with learning difficulties need specialized support.* [from Old French]

spe|cial|ly /spɛʃəli/
1 **ADV** If something is **specially for** a particular person, it is only for that person. ❑ *This soap is specially designed for sensitive skin.*
2 **ADV** **Specially** means more than usual. [INFORMAL] ❑ *On his birthday I got up specially early.* [from Old French]

spe|cial|ty /spɛʃ°lti/ (**specialties**)
1 **N-COUNT** Someone's **specialty** is a particular type of work that they do, or a subject that they know a lot about. ❑ *His specialty is international law.*
2 **N-COUNT** A **specialty** of a particular place is a special food or product that is always very good there. ❑ *Catfish is a Southern specialty.* [from Old French]

spe|cia|tion /spiʃieɪʃ°n/ **N-NONCOUNT** SCIENCE **Speciation** is the development of new species of animals or plants that occurs when two populations of the same species develop in different ways.

spe|cies /spiʃiz/ (**species**) **N-COUNT** SCIENCE A **species** is a related group of plants or animals. ❑ *Many species could disappear from our Earth.* [from Latin]
→ look at Word Webs: **evolution, zoo**

spe|cif|ic /spɪsɪfɪk/
1 **ADJ** You use **specific** to talk about a particular subject. ❑ *Do you have pain in any specific part of your body?* ❑ *There are several*

specific problems.
2 **ADJ** If someone is **specific**, they give a description that is exact and clear. ❑ *She refused to be more specific about her plans.* [from Medieval Latin]

spe|cifi|cal|ly /spɪsɪfɪkli/
1 **ADV** You use **specifically** to show that something is being considered separately. ❑ *The show is specifically for children.*
2 **ADV** You use **specifically** to add something more exact to what you have already said. ❑ *Death frightens me, specifically my own death.* [from Medieval Latin]

spe|cif|ic grav|ity (**specific gravities**) **N-COUNT/N-NONCOUNT** SCIENCE The **specific gravity** of a substance is a measure of its weight, compared to the weight of an equal amount of water.

spe|cif|ic heat ca|pac|ity (**specific heat capacities**) **N-COUNT/N-NONCOUNT** SCIENCE The **specific heat capacity** of a substance is the amount of heat that is needed in order to change the temperature of the substance by one degree Celsius.

speci|fy /spɛsɪfaɪ/ (**specifies, specifying, specified**) **V-T** If you **specify** something, you explain it in an exact and detailed way. ❑ *Does the recipe specify the size of egg to be used?* [from Medieval Latin]

speci|men /spɛsɪmɪn/ (**specimens**) **N-COUNT** SCIENCE A **specimen of** something is an example or a small amount of it. ❑ *Job applicants have to give a specimen of handwriting.* [from Latin]

speck /spɛk/ (**specks**) **N-COUNT** A **speck** is a very small mark or piece of something. ❑ *There was a speck of dirt on his collar.* [from Old English]

> **Word Link** spect ≈ looking : spectacle, spectacular, spectator

spec|ta|cle /spɛktək°l/ (**spectacles**) **N-COUNT** A **spectacle** is a big, wonderful sight or event. ❑ *The fireworks were an amazing spectacle.* [from Old French]

spec|tacu|lar /spɛktækyələr/ **ADJ** Something that is **spectacular** is big and dramatic. ❑ *We had spectacular views of Sugar Loaf Mountain.* ● **spec|tacu|lar|ly** **ADV** ❑ *Our sales increased spectacularly.* [from Old French]

spec|ta|tor /spɛkteɪtər/ (**spectators**) **N-COUNT** SPORTS A **spectator** is someone who watches a sports event. ❑ *Thirty thousand spectators watched the game.* [from Latin]

spec|trum /spɛktrəm/ (**spectra** or **spectrums**)
1 **N-SING** SCIENCE **The spectrum** is the range of different colors that is produced when light passes through a glass prism or through a drop of water.
2 **N-COUNT** A **spectrum** is a range of a particular type of thing. ❑ *His moods covered the entire emotional spectrum.* ❑ *Politicians across the political spectrum have criticized her.* [from Latin]

specu|late /spɛkyəleɪt/ (**speculates, speculating, speculated**) **V-T/V-I** If you **speculate** about something, you make guesses about it. ❑ *Everyone has been speculating about why she left.* ❑ *Doctors speculate that his death was caused by a blow on the head.*
● **specu|la|tion** /spɛkyəleɪʃ°n/ (**speculations**) **N-COUNT/N-NONCOUNT** ❑ *There has been a lot of speculation about the future of the band.* [from Latin]

sped /spɛd/ **Sped** is a past tense and past participle of **speed.**

speech /spitʃ/ (**speeches**)
1 **N-NONCOUNT** **Speech** is the ability to speak or the act of speaking. ❑ *We are studying the development of speech in children.* ❑ *The medicine can affect speech.*
2 **N-SING** Your **speech** is the way in which you speak. ❑ *His speech became slow and unclear.*
3 **N-COUNT** A **speech** is a formal talk that someone gives to a group of people. ❑ *The president gave a speech to the nation.* [from Old English]
→ look at Word Web: **election**

	Word Partnership Use **speech** with :
ADJ	**slurred** speech **2**
	famous speech, **major** speech, **political** speech, **recent** speech **3**
N	**acceptance** speech, **campaign** speech, **keynote** speech, speech **writing 3**
V	**deliver** a speech, **give** a speech, **make** a speech, **prepare** a speech **3**

speech marks **N-PLURAL** LANGUAGE ARTS **Speech marks** are the same as **quotation marks.**

speed /spid/ (**speeds, speeding, sped** or **speeded**)

LANGUAGE HELP
Use **sped** in meaning **3**. Use **speeded** for the phrasal verb.

1 **N-COUNT/N-NONCOUNT** SCIENCE The **speed** of something is how fast it moves or is done. ❑ *He drove off at high speed.* ❑ *He invented a way to measure wind speeds.*
2 **N-NONCOUNT** **Speed** is very fast movement or travel. ❑ *Speed is essential for all athletes.*
3 **V-I** If you **speed** somewhere, you move or travel there quickly, usually in a vehicle. ❑ *Trains speed through the tunnel at 186 mph.*
4 **V-I** Someone who **is speeding** is driving a vehicle faster than the legal speed limit. ❑ *Police stopped him because he was speeding.*
● **speed|ing** **N-NONCOUNT** ❑ *He was fined for speeding.* [from Old English]
▶ **speed up** When something **speeds up**, it happens more quickly than before. ❑ *My breathing speeded up a bit.* ❑ *We need to speed up a solution to the problem.*

speedy /spidi/ (**speedier, speediest**) **ADJ** Something that is **speedy** happens or is done very quickly. ❑ *We wish Bill a speedy recovery.* [from Old English]

spell /spɛl/ (**spells, spelling, spelled**)
1 **V-T** LANGUAGE ARTS When you **spell** a word, you write or speak each letter in the correct order. ❑ *He spelled his name.* ❑ *How do you spell "potato?"*
2 **V-T/V-I** LANGUAGE ARTS Someone who can **spell** knows the correct order of letters in words. ❑ *Many of the students can't spell.* ❑ *He could spell his own name when he was three.*
3 **N-COUNT** A **spell** is a set of magic words. ❑ *They say a witch cast a spell on her.*
4 **N-COUNT** A **spell of** a particular condition or a particular activity is a short period of time during which this condition or activity occurs. ❑ *There has been a long spell of dry weather.* [Senses 1 and 2 from Old French. Senses 3 and 4 from Old English.]

	Word Partnership Use **spell** with :
N	spell **a name**, spell **a word 1**
	spell **the end of** *something*
V	**can/can't** spell *something* **2**
	break a spell, **cast** a spell **3**

spell|ing /spɛlɪŋ/ (**spellings**)
1 **N-COUNT** LANGUAGE ARTS A **spelling** is the correct order of the letters in a word. ❑ *I'm not sure about the spelling of his name.*
2 **N-NONCOUNT** LANGUAGE ARTS **Spelling** is the ability to spell words in the correct way. ❑ *His spelling is very bad.* [from Old French]

spend /spɛnd/ (**spends, spending, spent**)

1 **v-t** When you **spend** money, you pay money for things that you want or need. ❑ *I have spent all my money.*

2 **v-t** If you **spend** time doing something, you use your time doing it. ❑ *She spends hours working on her garden.*

3 **v-t** If you **spend** a period of time in a place, you stay there for a period of time. ❑ *We spent the night in a hotel.* [from Old English]

Word Partnership	Use **spend** with :
N	spend **billions/millions, companies** spend, **consumers** spend, spend **money** **1**
	spend **an amount** **1** **2**
	spend **energy**, spend **time** **2**
	spend **a day**, spend **hours/minutes**, spend **months**, spend **a night**, spend **a weekend** **3**
V	**afford to** spend, **expect to** spend, **going to** spend, **plan to** spend **1**–**3**

spent /spɛnt/ **Spent** is the past tense and past participle of **spend**. [from Old English]

sperm /spɜrm/ (**sperms** or **sperm**)

1 **N-COUNT** SCIENCE A **sperm** is a cell that is produced in the sex organs of a male animal and can enter a female animal's egg and fertilize it. ❑ *A baby is conceived when a sperm joins with an egg.*

2 **N-NONCOUNT** SCIENCE **Sperm** is used to refer to the liquid that contains sperm when it is produced. ❑ *...a test tube of sperm.* [from Late Latin]
→ look at Word Web: **reproduction**

sphere /sfɪər/ (**spheres**) **N-COUNT** A **sphere** is an object that is completely round in shape, like a ball. ❑ *A tennis ball is a regular sphere shape.* [from Late Latin]
→ look at Picture Dictionaries: **solids, volume**

spice /spaɪs/ (**spices**) **N-COUNT/N-NONCOUNT** A **spice** is a part of a plant that you put in food to give it flavor. ❑ *...herbs and spices.* [from Old French]
→ look at Word Web: **spice**

spicy /spaɪsi/ (**spicier, spiciest**) **ADJ** Spicy food is strongly flavored with spices. ❑ *Thai food is hot and spicy.* [from Old French]
→ look at Word Web: **spice**

spi|der /spaɪdər/ (**spiders**) **N-COUNT** A **spider** is a small animal with eight legs. [from Old English]

spike /spaɪk/ (**spikes**) **N-COUNT** A **spike** is a long piece of metal with a sharp point. ❑ *There was a high wall around the building with iron spikes at the top.* [from Old English]

spill /spɪl/ (**spills, spilling, spilled** or **spilt**) **v-t/v-i** If you **spill** a liquid, you accidentally make it flow over the edge of a container. ❑ *He always spilled the drinks.* ❑ *Oil spilled into the sea.* [from Old English]

spill

spin /spɪn/ (**spins, spinning, spun**)

1 **v-t/v-i** If something **spins**, or if you **spin** it, it turns quickly around a central point. ❑ *The disk spins 3,600 times a minute.* ❑ *He spun the steering wheel and turned the car around.*

2 **v-t/v-i** When people **spin**, they make

S

Word Web	spice

While studying the use of **spices** in cooking, scientists found that many spices can help prevent disease. Bacteria can grow quickly on food and cause serious illnesses in humans. The researchers found that many spices kill bacteria. For example, **garlic, onion**, allspice, and oregano kill almost all common **germs. Cinnamon,** tarragon, cumin, and **chili peppers** also stop about 75% of bacteria. And even common, everyday **black pepper** kills about 25% of all germs. The scientists also found that food is connected to climate. **Spicy** food is common in hot climates. **Bland** food is common in cold climates.

garlic

onion

chili pepper

ginger

black pepper

cinnamon

cloves

thread by twisting together pieces of wool or cotton. ❑ *It's a machine for spinning wool.* ❑ *She never learned how to spin.* [from Old English]

spin|ach /spɪnɪtʃ/ **N-NONCOUNT** Spinach is a vegetable with large dark green leaves. [from Old French]
→ look at Picture Dictionary: **vegetables**

spi|nal cord (spinal cords) **N-COUNT** SCIENCE Your **spinal cord** is a thick cord of nerves inside your spine that connects your brain to nerves in all parts of your body.

spine /spaɪn/ (spines) **N-COUNT** SCIENCE Your **spine** is the row of bones down your back. ❑ *He suffered injuries to his spine.* [from Old French]

spi|ral /spaɪrəl/ (spirals, spiraling, spiraled)
1 **N-COUNT** A **spiral** is a shape that winds around and around, with each curve above or outside the one before.
2 **ADJ** Spiral is also an adjective. ❑ *...a spiral staircase.*
3 **V-I** If something **spirals** somewhere, it grows or moves in a spiral curve. ❑ *Gray smoke spiraled up into the sky.*
4 **V-I** If an amount **spirals**, it rises quickly. ❑ *Prices began to spiral.* [from French]
→ look at Word Web: **circle**

spi|ral gal|axy (spiral galaxies) **N-COUNT** SCIENCE A **spiral galaxy** is a galaxy consisting of a flat disk at the center and spiral arms that contain many young stars.

spir|it /spɪrɪt/ (spirits)
1 **N-SING** Your **spirit** is the part of you that is not physical and that consists of your character and feelings. ❑ *The human spirit is hard to destroy.*
2 **N-COUNT** A person's **spirit** is the part of them that some people believe remains alive after their death. ❑ *He is gone, but his spirit is still with us.*
3 **N-PLURAL** Your **spirits** are your feelings at a particular time, especially feelings of happiness or unhappiness. ❑ *At supper, everyone was in high spirits.*
4 **N-NONCOUNT** Spirit is the courage and determination that helps people to survive in difficult times. ❑ *She was very brave and everyone admired her spirit.*
5 **N-SING** The **spirit** in which you do something is the attitude you have when you are doing it. ❑ *She took part in the game*

in a spirit of fun. [from Old French]

spir|itu|al /spɪrɪtʃuəl/
1 **ADJ** Spiritual means relating to people's thoughts and beliefs, rather than to their bodies. ❑ *She is a very spiritual person.*
2 **ADJ** Spiritual means relating to people's religious beliefs. ❑ *He is the spiritual leader of the world's Catholics.* [from Old French]
→ look at Word Web: **myth**

spit /spɪt/ (spits, spitting, spit or spat) **V-T** If you **spit** liquid or food somewhere, you force a small amount of it out of your mouth. ❑ *Spit out that gum.* [from Old English]

spite /spaɪt/
1 **PHRASE** You use **in spite of** to introduce a fact that makes the rest of what you are saying seem surprising. ❑ *He hired her in spite of her lack of experience.*
2 **N-NONCOUNT** If you do something out of **spite**, you do it because you want to hurt or upset someone. ❑ *I didn't help him, out of spite I suppose.*

spite|ful /spaɪtfəl/ **ADJ** Someone who is **spiteful** does cruel things to hurt people. ❑ *He could be extremely spiteful sometimes.* ❑ *...a series of spiteful telephone calls.*
● **spite|ful|ly** **ADV** ❑ *We crept into our little sister's bedroom and spitefully destroyed her posters.* [from Old French]

splash /splæʃ/ (splashes, splashing, splashed)
1 **V-I** If you **splash** in water, you hit the water in a noisy way. ❑ *People were splashing around in the water.*
2 **V-T/V-I** If a liquid **splashes**, or if you **splash** it, some of it hits someone or something. ❑ *A little wave splashed in my face.*
3 **N-SING** A **splash** is the sound of something hitting water. ❑ *There was a splash as something fell into the water.*
4 **N-COUNT** A **splash** is a small quantity of a liquid that falls on something. ❑ *There were splashes on the tablecloth.*

splen|did /splɛndɪd/ **ADJ** If something is **splendid**, it is very good. ❑ *The book includes some splendid photographs.* [from Latin]

splin|ter /splɪntər/ (splinters) **N-COUNT** A **splinter** is a thin, sharp piece of wood or glass that has broken off from a larger piece. ❑ *We found splinters of the glass in our clothes.* [from Middle Dutch]

S

split /splɪt/ (splits, splitting, split)

> **LANGUAGE HELP**
> The form **split** is used in the present tense and is the past tense and past participle of the verb.

1 **V-T/V-I** If something **splits**, it breaks into two or more parts. ❑ *The ship split in two during a storm.* ❑ *Split the chicken in half.*

2 **V-T/V-I** If you **split** something, you divide it into two or more parts. ❑ *Split the chicken in half.*

3 **V-T/V-I** If an organization **splits**, or **is split**, one group disagrees strongly with the other members. ❑ *The party could split over this.*

4 **N-SING** Split is also a noun. ❑ *There are rumors of a split in the party.*

5 **V-T/V-I** If wood or a piece of clothing **splits**, a long crack or tear appears in it. ❑ *My pants split while I was climbing over the wall.* ❑ *He split the log with an ax.*

6 **V-T** If two or more people **split** something, they share it between them. ❑ *Let's split the bill.* [from Middle Dutch]

▶ **split up** **1** If two people **split up**, they end their relationship. ❑ *His parents split up when he was ten.* ❑ *I thought that nothing could ever split us up, but I was wrong.*

2 If you **split** something **up**, you divide it into separate sections. ❑ *We are not planning to split up the company.*

Thesaurus	split	Also look up :
V	break, divide, part, separate; (ant.) combine **1** **4**	

Word Partnership	Use **split** with :
PREP	split **into** **1**
	split **over** *something* **3**
	split **between** **5**
N	split **shares**, split **wood** **2**
ADV	split **apart** **1** **2**

spoil /spɔɪl/ (spoils, spoiling, spoiled or spoilt)

1 **V-T** If you **spoil** something, you prevent it from being successful. ❑ *Don't let mistakes spoil your life.*

2 **V-T** If you **spoil** children, you give them everything they want or ask for. ❑ *Grandparents often like to spoil their grandchildren.*

3 **V-I** If food **spoils**, it is not fresh anymore and you cannot eat it. ❑ *Milk spoils easily in hot weather.* [from Old French]

spoke /spoʊk/ (spokes)

1 Spoke is the past tense of **speak**.

2 **N-COUNT** The **spokes** of a wheel are the bars that connect the outer ring to the center. [from Old English]

→ look at Word Webs: **bicycle**, **wheel**

spo|ken /spoʊkən/

1 Spoken is the past participle of **speak**.

2 **ADJ** LANGUAGE ARTS **Spoken** language is language that you speak and not language that you write. ❑ *They took tests in written and spoken English.* [from Old English]

spokes|man /spoʊksmən/ (spokesmen)

N-COUNT A **spokesman** is a man who speaks as the representative of a group or an organization. ❑ *A spokesman said that food is on its way.*

spokes|person /spoʊkspɜrsən/ (spokespersons or spokespeople) **N-COUNT**

A **spokesperson** is a person who speaks as the representative of a group or an organization. ❑ *...a White House spokesperson.*

spokes|woman /spoʊkswʊmən/ (spokeswomen) **N-COUNT** A **spokeswoman** is a woman who speaks as the representative of a group or an organization. ❑ *A hospital spokeswoman said he was recovering well.*

sponge /spʌndʒ/ (sponges)

1 **N-COUNT** A **sponge** is a piece of a very light soft material with lots of little holes in it, that you use for washing yourself or for cleaning things. ❑ *He wiped the table with a sponge.*

2 **N-COUNT** A **sponge** is a sea animal with a soft round body made of natural sponge. [from Old English]

spon|gy bone /spʌndʒi boʊn/ **N-NONCOUNT**

SCIENCE **Spongy bone** is a type of bone that consists of many small pieces with spaces between them. It forms the interior of other bones.

spon|sor /spɒnsər/ (sponsors, sponsoring, sponsored)

1 **V-T** If an organization or a person **sponsors** an event, they pay for it. ❑ *A local bank is sponsoring the race.*

2 **V-T** If you **sponsor** someone who is doing something to raise money, you agree to give them money if they succeed in doing it. ❑ *The children asked friends and family to sponsor them.*

3 **N-COUNT** A **sponsor** is a person or an organization that pays for an event.

S

❏ *Our company is proud to be the sponsor of this event.* [from Latin]

spon|sor|ship /sppnsərʃɪp/ **N-NONCOUNT**
Sponsorship is financial support given by a sponsor. ❏ *Athletes can make a lot of money out of sponsorship.* [from Latin]

spon|ta|neous /sppnteɪniəs/ **ADJ**
Spontaneous acts are done because someone suddenly wants to do them. ❏ *He gave her a spontaneous hug.*
● **spon|ta|neous|ly ADV** ❏ *People spontaneously stood up and cheered.* [from Late Latin]

spooky /spuki/ (**spookier, spookiest**) **ADJ**
A place that is **spooky** seems frightening.
[INFORMAL] ❏ *The house has a slightly spooky atmosphere.* [from Dutch]

spoon /spun/ (**spoons, spooning, spooned**)
1 **N-COUNT** A **spoon** is a long object with a round end that is used for eating, serving, or mixing food. ❏ *He stirred his coffee with a spoon.*
2 **V-T** If you **spoon** food into something, you put it there with a spoon. ❏ *He spooned sugar into the mug.* [from Old English]
→ look at Picture Dictionary: **kitchen utensils**
→ look at Word Web: **silverware**

spo|rad|ic /spərædɪk/ **ADJ Sporadic**
occurrences of something happen at irregular intervals. ❏ *There was sporadic fighting near the border.* ● **spo|radi|cal|ly ADV**
❏ *The thunder continued sporadically.* [from Medieval Latin]

spore /spɔr/ (**spores**) **N-COUNT** SCIENCE
Spores are cells produced by bacteria and fungi that can develop into new bacteria or fungi. [from New Latin]

spo|ro|phyte /spɔrəfaɪt/ (**sporophytes**)
N-COUNT SCIENCE The **sporophyte** is the stage in the life of a plant when it produces spores.

sport /spɔrt/ (**sports**) **N-COUNT/N-NONCOUNT**
SPORTS **Sports** are games and other activities that need physical effort and skill.
❏ *Golf is my favorite sport.* ❏ *He is good at sports.*

sport|ing /spɔrtɪŋ/ **ADJ** SPORTS **Sporting**
means relating to sports or used for sports.
❏ *...major sporting events, such as the U.S. Open.*

sports|man /spɔrtsmən/ (**sportsmen**)
N-COUNT SPORTS A **sportsman** is a man who takes part in sports.

sports|wom|an /spɔrtswʊmən/
(**sportswomen**) **N-COUNT** SPORTS
A **sportswoman** is a woman who takes part in sports.

spot /spɒt/ (**spots, spotting, spotted**)
1 **N-COUNT** **Spots** are small, round, colored areas on a surface. ❏ *The leaves are yellow with orange spots.*
2 **N-COUNT** A particular place can be called a **spot**. ❏ *This is one of the country's top tourist spots.*
3 **V-T** If you **spot** something or someone, you notice them. ❏ *I didn't spot the mistake in his essay.*
4 **PHRASE** If you do something **on the spot**, you do it immediately. ❏ *They offered him the job on the spot.* [from German]

Word Partnership	Use **spot** with :
ADJ	**good** spot, **perfect** spot, **popular** spot, **quiet** spot, **the** spot **2**
N	**parking** spot, **vacation** spot **2**

spot|light /spɒtlaɪt/ (**spotlights**) **N-COUNT**
A **spotlight** is a powerful light that can be directed so that it lights up a small area.
→ look at Word Web: **concert**

spouse /spaʊs/ (**spouses**) **N-COUNT**
Someone's **spouse** is their husband or wife.
❏ *You and your spouse must both sign the contract.*
[from Old French]
→ look at Word Web: **love**

spout /spaʊt/ (**spouts**) **N-COUNT** A **spout** is a long, hollow part of a container through which liquids can be poured out easily. ❏ *Hot tea came out of the spout.* [from Middle Dutch]

sprang /spræŋ/ **Sprang** is the past tense of **spring**. [from Old English]

spray /spreɪ/ (**sprays, spraying, sprayed**)
1 **N-COUNT/N-NONCOUNT** **Spray** is a lot of small drops of water that are thrown into the air. ❏ *We were hit by spray from the waterfall.*
2 **N-COUNT/N-NONCOUNT** A **spray** is a liquid that comes out of a can or other container in very small drops when you press a button.
❏ *...hair spray.*
3 **V-T/V-I** If you **spray** a liquid somewhere, or if it **sprays**, drops of the liquid cover a place. ❏ *Firefighters sprayed water on the fire.*
[from Middle Dutch]

Word Partnership	Use **spray** with :
N	spray **bottle, bug** spray, spray **can, hair** spray, **pepper** spray **2**
PREP	spray **with water 3**

S

spread /sprɛd/ (**spreads, spreading, spread**)

1 **v-t** If you **spread** something somewhere, you open it out over a surface. ❑ *She spread a towel on the sand and lay on it.*

2 **Spread out** means the same as **spread**. ❑ *He spread the papers out on a table.*

3 **v-t** If you **spread** parts of your body, you stretch them out until they are far apart. ❑ *Sitting on the floor, spread your legs.*

4 **Spread out** means the same as **spread**. ❑ *David spread out his hands.*

5 **v-t** If you **spread** a substance on a surface, you put it all over the surface. ❑ *She was spreading butter on the bread.*

6 **v-t/v-i** If something **spreads**, or is **spread**, it gradually reaches a larger area. ❑ *Information technology has spread across the world.*

7 **N-SING** **Spread** is also a noun. ❑ *We closed schools to stop the spread of the disease.* [from Old English]

▶ **spread out** **1** If people **spread out**, they move apart from each other. ❑ *They spread out to search the area.*

2 → look up **spread** **2** **4**

Word Partnership	Use spread with :
ADV	spread **evenly** **1** **3**
	spread **quickly**, spread **rapidly**, spread **widely** **1** **4**
PREP	spread **of an epidemic**, spread **of technology** **4**
N	spread **fear**, **fires** spread, spread **an infection**, spread **a message**, spread **news**, spread **rumors** **4**
V	**continue to** spread, **prevent/stop the** spread **of** *something* **4** **6**

spread|sheet /sprɛdʃit/ (**spreadsheets**) **N-COUNT** TECHNOLOGY A **spreadsheet** is a computer program that deals with numbers. Spreadsheets are mainly used for financial planning.

spring /sprɪŋ/ (**springs, springing, sprang, sprung**)

1 **N-COUNT/N-NONCOUNT** **Spring** is the season between winter and summer when the weather becomes warmer and plants start to grow again. ❑ *They are getting married next spring.* ❑ *We'll come visit you in the spring.*

2 **N-COUNT** A **spring** is a long piece of metal that goes round and round. It goes back to the same shape after you pull it. ❑ *The springs in the bed were old and soft.*

3 **N-COUNT** A **spring** is a place where water

comes up through the ground. ❑ *The town is famous for its hot springs.*

4 **v-i** When a person or an animal **springs** up or forward, they jump suddenly or quickly. ❑ *He sprang to his feet.* [from Old English]

→ look at Picture Dictionary: **river**

▶ **spring up** If something **springs up**, it suddenly appears or begins to exist. ❑ *New theaters sprang up all over the country.*

Word Partnership	Use spring with :
ADJ	**early** spring, **last** spring, **late** spring, **next** spring **1**
	cold spring, **hot** spring, **warm** spring **1** **3**
N	spring **day**, spring **flowers**, spring **rains**, spring **semester**, spring **training**, spring **weather** **1** spring **water** **3**

spring tide (**spring tides**) **N-COUNT** SCIENCE A **spring tide** is an unusually high tide that happens at the time of a new moon or a full moon.

sprin|kle /sprɪŋkəl/ (**sprinkles, sprinkling, sprinkled**) **v-t** If you **sprinkle** something **with** a liquid or a powder, you drop a little of it over the surface. ❑ *Sprinkle the meat with salt before you cook it.* [from Middle Dutch]

sprin|kler /sprɪŋklər/ (**sprinklers**) **N-COUNT** A **sprinkler** is a device used to spray water. Sprinklers are used to water plants or grass, or to put out fires in buildings. [from Middle Dutch]

→ look at Picture Dictionary: **garden**

sprint /sprɪnt/ (**sprints, sprinting, sprinted**)

1 **N-SING** SPORTS The **sprint** is a short, fast race. ❑ *Rob Harmeling won the sprint.*

2 **v-i** If you **sprint**, you run as fast as you can over a short distance. ❑ *Sergeant Adams sprinted to the car.* [of Scandinavian origin]

sprout /spraʊt/ (**sprouts, sprouting, sprouted**)

1 **v-i** When plants, vegetables, or seeds **sprout**, they start to grow. ❑ *It only takes a few days for beans to sprout.*

2 **N-COUNT** **Sprouts** are small round green vegetables. They are also called **Brussels sprouts**. [from Old English]

→ look at Word Web: **tree**

sprung /sprʌŋ/ **Sprung** is the past participle of **spring**. [from Old English]

S

spun /spʌn/ **Spun** is the past tense and past participle of **spin**. [from Old English]

spur /spɜr/ (**spurs, spurring, spurred**)

■ **V-T** If one thing **spurs** you **to** do another, it encourages you to do it. ❑ *Money spurs these men to risk their lives.*

■ **Spur on** means the same as **spur**. ❑ *The applause seemed to spur him on.*

■ **V-T** If something **spurs** a change or event, it makes it happen faster or sooner. ❑ *Our aim is to spur economic growth.*

■ **N-COUNT** Something that acts as a **spur to** something else encourages a person or organization to do that thing or makes it happen more quickly. ❑ *Financial profit can be a spur to progress.*

■ **PHRASE** If you do something **on the spur of the moment**, you do it suddenly, without planning it beforehand. ❑ *They went to the beach on the spur of the moment.* [from Old English]

Word Partnership	Use spur with :
N	spur **demand**, spur **development**, spur **economic growth**, spur **the economy**, spur **interest**, spur **investment**, spur **sales** ■

spurn /spɜrn/ (**spurns, spurning, spurned**)
V-T If you **spurn** someone or something, you reject them. ❑ *He spurned the advice of his boss.* [from Old English]

spy /spaɪ/ (**spies, spying, spied**)

■ **N-COUNT** A **spy** is a person whose job is to find out secret information about another country or organization. ❑ *He used to be a spy.*

■ **V-I** Someone who **spies** tries to find out secret information about another country or organization. ❑ *The two countries are still spying on one another.*

■ **V-I** If you **spy on** someone, you watch them secretly. ❑ *He spied on her while she was on her way to work.* [from Old French]

spy|ware /spaɪwɛər/ **N-NONCOUNT** TECHNOLOGY **Spyware** is computer software that secretly records personal information about you and the websites that you visit. ❑ *The publishers promise not to use spyware to grab your personal information.*

squad /skwɒd/ (**squads**)

■ **N-COUNT** A **squad** is a section of a police force that is responsible for dealing with a particular type of crime. ❑ *Someone called the bomb squad.*

■ **N-COUNT** SPORTS A **squad** is a group of players from which a sports team will be chosen. ❑ *There have been a lot of injuries in the squad.* [from Old French]

square /skwɛər/ (**squares**)

■ **N-COUNT** MATH A **square** is a shape with four straight sides that are all the same length. ❑ *Cut the cake in squares.*

■ **N-COUNT** In a town or a city, a **square** is an open place with buildings around it. ❑ *The restaurant is in the town square.*

■ **ADJ** MATH Something that is **square** has four straight sides that are all the same length. ❑ *They sat at a square table.*

■ **ADJ** MATH **Square** is used for talking about the area of something. ❑ *The house covers an area of 3,000 square feet.*

■ **N-COUNT** MATH The **square of** a number is the number you get when you multiply that number by itself. ❑ *The square of 4 is 16.* [from Old French]

→ look at Picture Dictionary: **shapes**

square root (**square roots**) **N-COUNT** MATH The **square root of** a number is another number that you multiply by itself to produce the first number. ❑ *The square root of 36 is 6.*

squash /skwɒʃ/ (**squashes, squashing, squashed**)

■ **V-T** If someone or something **is squashed**, they are pushed or pressed hard. ❑ *Robert was squashed against a fence by a car.*

■ **N-NONCOUNT** SPORTS **Squash** is a game in which two players hit a small rubber ball against the walls of a court. ❑ *I play squash once a week.*

■ **N-COUNT/N-NONCOUNT** A **squash** is a large vegetable with a thick skin. [from Old French]

→ look at Picture Dictionary: **vegetables**

squeak /skwik/ (**squeaks, squeaking, squeaked**)

■ **V-I** If something or someone **squeaks**, they make a short, high sound. ❑ *My boots squeaked as I walked.*

■ **N-COUNT** **Squeak** is also a noun. ❑ *I heard a squeak, like a mouse.* [of Scandinavian origin]

squeal /skwil/ (**squeals, squealing, squealed**)

■ **V-I** If someone or something **squeals**, they make a long, high sound. ❑ *Jennifer squealed with pleasure.*

■ **N-COUNT** **Squeal** is also a noun. ❑ *There was a squeal of brakes as the car suddenly stopped.*

squeeze /skwiz/ (**squeezes, squeezing, squeezed**)

1 **v-t** If you **squeeze** something, you press it firmly, usually with your hands. ❑ He squeezed her arm gently.

2 **N-COUNT** **Squeeze** is also a noun. ❑ She took my hand and gave it a squeeze.

3 **v-t** If you **squeeze** a soft substance out of a container, you get it out by pressing. ❑ Joe squeezed some toothpaste out of the tube. [from Middle English]

squid /skwɪd/ (**squids** or **squid**)

1 **N-COUNT** A **squid** is a sea animal that has a long soft body and many soft arms called tentacles.

2 **N-NONCOUNT** **Squid** is pieces of this creature eaten as food. ❑ Cook the squid for 2 minutes.

squir|rel /skwɜrəl/ (**squirrels**) **N-COUNT** A **squirrel** is a small animal with a long thick tail. Squirrels live mainly in trees. [from Old French]

squirt /skwɜrt/ (**squirts, squirting, squirted**)

1 **v-t/v-i** If you **squirt** a liquid somewhere, it comes out of a narrow opening very quickly. ❑ Norman squirted tomato sauce onto his plate.

2 **v-t/v-i** If a liquid **squirts** somewhere, it comes out of a narrow opening very quickly. ❑ The mustard squirted all over the front of my shirt.

3 **N-COUNT** **Squirt** is also a noun. ❑ It needs a little squirt of oil.

stab /stæb/ (**stabs, stabbing, stabbed**) **v-t** If someone **stabs** you, they push a knife or a sharp object into your body. ❑ Someone stabbed him in the stomach. [from Middle English]
→ look at Word Web: **carnivore**

Word Link	stab ≈ steady : establish, instability, stabilize

sta|bi|lize /stéɪbɪlaɪz/ (**stabilizes, stabilizing, stabilized**) **v-t/v-i** If something **stabilizes**, or **is stabilized**, it becomes stable. ❑ Doctors say her condition has stabilized. ● **sta|bi|li|za|tion** /stéɪbɪlɪzeɪʃ°n/ **N-NONCOUNT** ❑ ...the stabilization of house prices. [from Old French]

sta|ble /stéɪbəl/ (**stabler, stablest, stables**)

1 **ADJ** If something is **stable**, it is not likely to change suddenly. ❑ The price of oil has remained stable this month. ● **sta|bil|ity** /stəbɪlɪti/ **N-NONCOUNT** ❑ It was a time of political stability.

2 **ADJ** If an object is **stable**, it is firmly fixed in position. ❑ Make sure the ladder is stable.

3 **N-COUNT** A **stable** or **stables** is a building in which horses are kept. [from Old French]

stack /stæk/ (**stacks, stacking, stacked**)

1 **N-COUNT** A **stack of** things is a pile of them. ❑ There were stacks of books on the floor.

2 **v-t** If you **stack** a number of things, you arrange them in piles. ❑ He asked me to stack the dirty dishes. [from Old Norse]

sta|dium /stéɪdiəm/ (**stadiums**) **N-COUNT** SPORTS A **stadium** is a large sports field with rows of seats all around it. ❑ ...a baseball stadium. [from Latin]

staff /stæf/ (**staffs** or **staves, staffs, staffing, staffed**)

LANGUAGE HELP
Staffs is the plural for meaning **1**. **Staves** is the usual plural for meaning **3**.

1 **N-COUNT/N-NONCOUNT** BUSINESS The **staff** of an organization are the people who work for it. ❑ The hospital staff was very good. ❑ ...staff members.

2 **v-t** BUSINESS If an organization **is staffed** by particular people, they are the people who work for it. ❑ The office is staffed by volunteers.

3 **N-COUNT** MUSIC A **staff** is the five lines that music is written on. [from Old English]

stag /stæg/ (**stags**) **N-COUNT** A **stag** is an adult male deer. **Stags** have horns that look like branches. [from Old English]

stage /stéɪdʒ/ (**stages**)

1 **N-COUNT** A **stage of** an activity or a process is one part of it. ❑ We are completing the first stage of the plan.

2 **N-COUNT** In a theater, the **stage** is the area where people perform. ❑ The band walked onto the stage.

3 **N-COUNT** SCIENCE The **stage** on a microscope is the place where you put the specimen that you want to look at. [from Old French]
→ look at Picture Dictionary: **drama**
→ look at Word Webs: **concert, theater**

Word Partnership	Use **stage** with :	
ADJ	**advanced** stage, **critical** stage, **crucial** stage, **final** stage, **late/later** stage **1**	
N	stage **of development**, stage **of a disease**, stage **of a process 1** actors on stage, **center** stage, **concert** stage, stage **fright**, stage **manager 2**	
V	**reach** a stage **1** **leave the** stage, **take the** stage **2**	

S

stage crew (**stage crews**) **N-COUNT** ARTS
A **stage crew** is a team of workers who move
the scenery about in a play or other
theatrical production.

stage left **ADV** ARTS **Stage left** is the left side
of the stage for an actor who is standing
facing the audience.

stage man|ag|er (**stage managers**)
N-COUNT ARTS At a theater, a **stage manager**
is the person who is responsible for the
scenery and lights and for the way that
actors or other performers move around and
use the stage during a performance.

stage right **ADV** ARTS **Stage right** is the
right side of the stage for an actor who is
standing facing the audience.

stag|ger /stǽgər/ (**staggers, staggering,
staggered**) **V-I** If you **stagger**, you cannot
walk properly, for example because you are
ill. ❑ *He staggered back and fell over.* [from
Old Norse]

stag|nant /stǽgnənt/
1 **ADJ** If something such as a business or a
society is **stagnant**, there is little activity or
change. ❑ *When people do the same job for a long
time, they get stagnant.*
2 **ADJ** **Stagnant** water is not flowing, and
therefore often smells unpleasant and is
dirty. ❑ *...a stagnant pond.* [from Latin]

stain /steɪn/ (**stains, staining, stained**)
1 **N-COUNT** A **stain** is a mark on something
that is difficult to remove. ❑ *How do you
remove tea stains?*
2 **V-T** If a liquid **stains** something, it
becomes colored or marked by the liquid.
❑ *Some foods can stain the teeth.* ● **stained**
ADJ ❑ *His clothing was stained with mud.*
[from Old French]

stain|less steel /steɪnlɪs stil/ **N-NONCOUNT**
Stainless steel is a metal made from steel
and chromium. It does not rust.
❑ *...a stainless steel sink.*
→ look at Word Web: **pan**

stair /steər/ (**stairs**)
1 **N-PLURAL** **Stairs** are a set of steps inside
a building that go from one level to another.
❑ *Nancy began to climb the stairs.* ❑ *We walked up
a flight of stairs.*
2 **N-COUNT** A **stair** is one of the steps in a set
of stairs. ❑ *Terry was sitting on the bottom stair.*
[from Old English]

stair|case
/stéərkeɪs/
(**staircases**)
N-COUNT A **staircase**
is a set of stairs
inside a building.
❑ *They walked down
the staircase together.*
→ look at Picture
Dictionary: **house**

stair|way
/stéərweɪ/
(**stairways**) **N-COUNT**
A **stairway** is a set of
steps, inside or outside a building. ❑ *The back
stairway leads to the top floor.* [from Old English]

staircase

stake /steɪk/ (**stakes**)
1 **PHRASE** If something is **at stake**, it might
be lost if you are not successful. ❑ *There was
so much at stake in this game.*
2 **N-COUNT** A **stake** is a pointed wooden
pole that you push into the ground, for
example in order to support a young tree.
❑ *She hung the clothes on a rope tied between two
wooden stakes.* [Sense 2 from Old English.]

stale /steɪl/ (**staler, stalest**) **ADJ** **Stale** food
or air is no longer fresh. ❑ *....stale bread.*
[from Old French]

stalk /stɔk/ (**stalks**) **N-COUNT** The **stalk** of a
flower, a leaf, or a fruit is the thin part that
joins it to the plant or tree. ❑ *A single flower
grows on each long stalk.* [from Old English]

stall /stɔl/ (**stalls, stalling, stalled**)
1 **V-T/V-I** If a process **stalls**, or if someone or
something **stalls** it, the process stops but
may continue at a later time. ❑ *They're trying
to stall the meeting.* ❑ *The peace process stalled.*
2 **V-I** If you **stall**, you try to avoid doing
something until later. ❑ *Thomas spent all week
stalling over his decision.*
3 **V-T/V-I** If a vehicle **stalls** or if you
accidentally **stall** it, the engine stops
suddenly. ❑ *The engine stalled.*
4 **N-COUNT** A **stall** is a large table on which
you put goods that you want to sell, or
information that you want to give people.
❑ *...market stalls selling fruit and vegetables.*
5 **N-COUNT** A **stall** is a small enclosed area
in a room that is used for a particular
purpose, for example a shower. ❑ *She went
into the shower stall and turned on the water.*
[from Old English]
→ look at Word Web: **traffic**

S

sta|men /ˈsteɪmən/ (**stamens**) **N-COUNT**
SCIENCE The **stamen** is the male part of a
flower, that produces pollen. Compare with
pistil. [from Latin]
→ look at Picture Dictionary: **flowers**

stam|mer /ˈstæmər/ (**stammers,
stammering, stammered**) **V-T/V-I** If you
stammer, you find it difficult to speak
without repeating words or sounds. ❑ A lot of
children stammer. ❑ "F-f-forgive me," I stammered.
[from Old English]

stamp /stæmp/ (**stamps, stamping, stamped**)
1 **N-COUNT** A **stamp** is a small piece of paper
that you stick on an envelope before you mail
it. ❑ She put a stamp on the corner of the envelope.
2 **N-COUNT** A **stamp** is a small block of wood
or metal with words, numbers, or a pattern
on it. You put ink on it, then press it onto a
piece of paper. ❑ ...a date stamp.
3 **V-T** If you **stamp** a mark or a word on an
object, you press the mark or word onto it
using a stamp. ❑ They stamp a special number on
new cars.
4 **V-T/V-I** If you **stamp** or **stamp** your **foot**,
you put your foot down very hard on the
ground. ❑ I stamped my foot in anger. ❑ His foot
stamped down on my toe. [from Old English]
▶ **stamp out** If you **stamp** something **out**,
you put an end to it. ❑ It's impossible to stamp
out crime completely.

stance /stæns/ (**stances**)
1 **N-COUNT** Your **stance** on a particular
matter is your attitude to it. ❑ What is your
stance on the war?
2 **N-COUNT** Your **stance** is the way that you
are standing. [FORMAL] ❑ Take a wide stance
and bend your knees a little. [from French]

Word Partnership	Use **stance** with :
PREP	stance **against/on/toward** *something* **1**
ADJ	**aggressive** stance, **critical** stance, **hard-line** stance, **tough** stance **1**
V	**adopt** a stance, **take** a stance **1** **2**

stand
❶ VERB USES
❷ NOUN USES
❸ PHRASAL VERBS

❶ stand /stænd/ (**stands, standing, stood**)
1 **V-I** When you **are standing**, you are on
your feet. ❑ She was standing beside my bed.
2 **V-I** When someone **stands**, they move so
that they are on their feet. ❑ Becker stood and

shook hands with Ben.
3 **Stand up** means the same as **stand**.
❑ When I walked in, they all stood up.
4 **V-I** If you **stand aside** or **stand back**, you
move a short distance away. ❑ I stood aside to
let her pass me.
5 **V-I** If something **stands** somewhere, it is
in that place. [WRITTEN] ❑ The house stands
alone on top of a hill.
6 **V-I** If you ask someone **where** or **how** they
stand on an issue, you are asking them what
their attitude or view is. ❑ Where do you stand
on the issue of private schools?
7 **V-I** If a decision, a law, or an offer **stands**,
it still exists and has not been changed.
❑ The rule still stands.
8 **V-I** If something that can be measured
stands at a particular level, it is at that level.
❑ The number of missing people now stands at 30.
9 **V-T** If something can **stand** a situation or
a test, it is good enough or strong enough.
❑ These shoes can stand a lot of use.
10 **V-T** If you cannot **stand** someone or
something, you dislike them very strongly.
[INFORMAL] ❑ I can't stand that awful man.
❑ I can't stand that smell. [from Old English]

❷ stand /stænd/ (**stands**)
1 **N-COUNT** A **stand** is a small structure
where you can buy things like food, drink,
and newspapers. ❑ I bought a magazine from
a newspaper stand.
2 **N-COUNT** A **stand** is a small piece of
furniture that you use to hold a particular
thing. ❑ Take the television set off the stand.
[from Old English]
→ look at Picture Dictionary: **laboratory**

❸ stand /stænd/ (**stands, standing, stood**)
▶ **stand by** **1** If you **are standing by**, you
are ready to help. ❑ Police officers are standing
by in case of trouble.
2 If you **stand by**, you do not do anything
to stop something bad from happening.
❑ I will not stand by and watch people suffering.
▶ **stand down** If someone **stands down**,
they choose to leave an important job or
position, and let someone else take their
place. ❑ After ten years, the leader stood down.
▶ **stand for** **1** Letters that **stand for** a
particular word are a short form of that
word. ❑ U.S. stands for United States.
2 If you will **not stand for** something,
you will not allow it to happen or continue.
❑ We won't stand for this bad behavior anymore.
▶ **stand out** If someone or something

S

stands out, they are very easy to see. ❑ *The black necklace stood out against her white dress.*

▶ **stand up for** If you **stand up for** a person or a belief, you support them. ❑ *Nelson Mandela stood up for his people and his beliefs.*

▶ **stand up to** If you **stand up to** someone who is more powerful than you, you defend yourself against them. ❑ *He was too afraid to stand up to her.*

stand|ard /stǽndərd/ (**standards**)
1 **N-COUNT** A **standard** is a level of quality. ❑ *The standard of his work is very low.*
2 **N-PLURAL** **Standards** are moral principles that guide people's behavior. ❑ *My father always had high moral standards.*
3 **ADJ** **Standard** describes things that are usual and normal. ❑ *It's just a standard size car.* [from Old French]

	Word Partnership Use standard with :
V	**become a** standard, **maintain a** standard, **meet a** standard, **raise a** standard, **set a** standard, **use a** standard **1**
N	standard **of excellence**, **industry** standard **1** standard **English**, standard **equipment**, standard, standard **procedure 3**

stand|ard Ameri|can Eng|lish
N-NONCOUNT LANGUAGE ARTS **Standard American English** is the form of English that is spoken by most people in the United States.

stan|dard de|via|tion (**standard deviations**) **N-COUNT/N-NONCOUNT** MATH The **standard deviation** of a set of data is a measure of how much variation there is in the data.

stand|ard of liv|ing (**standards of living**) **N-COUNT** Your **standard of living** is the level of comfort and the amount of money that you have. ❑ *We're trying to improve our standard of living.*

stand|by /stǽndbaɪ/ (**standbys**) also **stand-by**
1 **N-COUNT** A **standby** is something or someone that is always ready to be used if they are needed. ❑ *Canned vegetables are a good standby.*
2 **PHRASE** If someone or something is **on standby**, they are ready to be used if they are needed. ❑ *Five ambulances are on standby.*

stand|ing wave (**standing waves**) **N-COUNT** SCIENCE A **standing wave** is a wave such as a sound wave that appears not to move, because another wave of the same frequency is traveling in the opposite direction.

stank /stæŋk/ **Stank** is a past tense of **stink.**

sta|ple /stéɪpᵊl/ (**staples, stapling, stapled**)
1 **ADJ** A **staple** food or product is one that is important in people's lives. ❑ *Rice is the staple food of more than half the world's population.*
2 **N-COUNT** A **staple** is a small piece of bent wire that holds sheets of paper together firmly. You put the staples into the paper using a stapler.
3 **V-T** If you **staple** something, you fix it in place using staples. ❑ *Staple some sheets of paper together.* [Sense 1 from Middle Dutch. Senses 2 and 3 from Old English.]

sta|pler /stéɪplər/ (**staplers**) **N-COUNT** A **stapler** is an instrument that is used for fastening sheets of paper together. [from Old English]

star /stɑr/ (**stars, starring, starred**)
1 **N-COUNT** SCIENCE A **star** is a large ball of burning gas in space. Stars look like small points of light in the sky. ❑ *Stars lit the sky.*
2 **N-COUNT** A **star** is a shape that has four, five, or more points sticking out of it in a regular pattern. ❑ *How many stars are there on the American flag?*
3 **N-COUNT** A **star** is a famous actor, musician, or sports player. ❑ *He's one of the stars of the TV series "Friends."*
4 **V-I** ARTS If an actor or an actress **stars in** a play or a movie, he or she has one of the most important parts in it. ❑ *Meryl Streep stars in the movie "The Devil Wears Prada."*
5 **V-T** ARTS If a play or a movie **stars** a famous actor or actress, he or she has one of the most important parts in it. ❑ *The movie stars Brad Pitt.* [from Old English]
→ look at Word Webs: **star, galaxy, navigation**

	Word Partnership Use star with :
ADJ	**bright** star **1** **bronze** star, **gold** star **2** **big** star, **former** star, **rising** star **3**
N	**all-star cast/game, basketball/football/ tennis** star, star, **guest** star, **pop/rap** star, **TV** star **3** star **in a film/movie/show 4**

S

Word Web star

North Star

Astronomy is the oldest science. It is the study of **stars** and other objects in the **night sky**. People sometimes confuse astronomy and **astrology**. Astrology is the belief that the stars affect people's lives. Long ago people named groups of stars after gods, heroes, and imaginary animals. One of the most famous of these **constellations** is the Big Dipper. Its original name meant "the big bear." It is easy to find and it points toward the **North Star***. For centuries sailors have used the North Star to **navigate**. The best-known star in our **galaxy** is the **sun**.

Big Dipper

North Star: the star that the earth's northern axis points toward.

starch /stɑrtʃ/ (**starches**)

1 **N-COUNT/N-NONCOUNT** SCIENCE **Starch** is a substance that is found in foods such as bread, potatoes, pasta, and rice, and that gives you energy. ❏ *You should eat less starch, salt, and fat.*

2 **N-NONCOUNT** **Starch** is a substance that is used for making cloth stiffer. ❏ *He never puts enough starch in my shirts.* [from Old English]
→ look at Word Web: **rice**

stare /stɛər/ (**stares, staring, stared**)

1 **V-I** If you **stare at** someone or something, you look at them for a long time. ❏ *We all spend too much time staring at computer screens.*

2 **N-COUNT** **Stare** is also a noun. ❏ *Harry gave him a long stare.* [from Old English]

Word Partnership Use **stare** with :

ADJ	**blank** stare
V	**continue to** stare, **turn to** stare

star|fish /stɑrfɪʃ/ (**starfish**) **N-COUNT**
A **starfish** is a flat, star-shaped creature, usually with five arms, that lives in the sea.

stark /stɑrk/ (**starker, starkest**)

1 **ADJ** **Stark** choices or statements are harsh and unpleasant. ❏ *Companies face a stark choice if they want to succeed.* ● **stark|ly** **ADV** ❏ *"She never loved you," he said starkly.*

2 **ADJ** If two things are in **stark** contrast to one another, they are very different from each other. ❏ *His opinions were in stark contrast to my own.* [from Old English]

start /stɑrt/ (**starts, starting, started**)

1 **V-T** If you **start doing** something, you do something that you were not doing before. ❏ *Susanna started working in TV in 2005.*

2 **V-T/V-I** When something **starts**, or if someone **starts** it, it takes place from a particular time or place. ❏ *The fire started in an upstairs room.* ❏ *I started the day with a swim.*

3 **N-SING** **Start** is also a noun. ❏ *It was 1918, four years after the start of the Great War.*

4 **V-T** When someone **starts** something, they create it or cause it to begin. ❏ *She has started a child care center in Ohio.*

5 **V-T/V-I** If you **start** an engine, a car, or a machine, you make it begin to work. ❏ *He started the car and drove off.*

6 **PHRASE** You use **for a start** or **to start with** to introduce the first of a number of things. ❏ *For a start, you need her name and address.* [from Old English]

▸ **start off** If you **start off by** doing something, you do it as the first part of an activity. ❏ *She started off by clearing some space on the table.*

▸ **start out** If someone or something **starts out as** a particular thing, they are that thing at the beginning although they change later. ❏ *Daly started out as a salesman.*

▸ **start over** If you **start over**, you begin something again from the beginning. ❏ *I did it all wrong and had to start over.*

Thesaurus start Also look up :

N	beginning, onset **1** **2**
V	begin, commence, originate **1** **2**
	establish, found, launch **3**

star|tle /stɑrtᵊl/ (**startles, startling, startled**) **V-T** If something sudden and unexpected **startles** you, it surprises and frightens you slightly. ❏ *The telephone startled him.* ● **star|tled** **ADJ** ❏ *Martha gave her a startled look.* [from Old English]

S

star|tling /stɑrtᵊlɪŋ/ **ADJ** Something that is **startling** is so different, unexpected, or remarkable that people react to it with surprise. ❑ *Sometimes the results are startling.* [from Old English]

starve /stɑrv/ (**starves, starving, starved**)
1 **V-I** If people **starve**, they suffer greatly from lack of food, and may die. ❑ *A number of the prisoners are starving.* ● **star|va|tion** /stɑrveɪʃᵊn/ **N-NONCOUNT** ❑ *Over three hundred people died of starvation.*
2 **V-T** To **starve** someone means not to give them any food. ❑ *He was starving himself.* [from Old English]

starv|ing /stɑrvɪŋ/ **ADJ** If you are **starving**, you are very hungry. [INFORMAL] ❑ *Does anyone have any food? I'm starving.* [from Old English]

state /steɪt/ (**states, stating, stated**)
1 **N-COUNT** SOCIAL STUDIES You can call countries **states**, particularly when you are talking about politics. ❑ *...a socialist state.*
2 **N-COUNT** Some large countries such as the U.S. are divided into smaller areas called **states**. ❑ *Leaders of the Southern states are meeting in Louisville.*
3 **N-PROPER** Some people say **the States** when they mean the U.S. [INFORMAL] ❑ *She bought it in the States.*
4 **N-SING** SOCIAL STUDIES **The state** is the government of a country. ❑ *In Sweden, child care is provided by the state.*
5 **N-COUNT** When you talk about the **state of** someone or something, you mean the condition they are in. ❑ *After Daniel died, I was in a state of shock.*
6 **V-T** If you **state** something, you say it or write it in a formal or definite way. ❑ *Clearly state your address and telephone number.*
7 → see also **head of state**
8 **PHRASE** SCIENCE **States of matter** are the different physical forms in which substances can exist. The most common states of matter are solid, liquid, and gas. [from Old French]
→ look at Word Webs: **country, matter**

Thesaurus	state	Also look up :
N	government, land, nation, republic, sovereignty **1**	
	attitude, condition, mood, situation **5**	
V	articulate, express, narrate, relate, say, tell **6**	

state|ment /steɪtmənt/ (**statements**)
N-COUNT A **statement** is something that you say or write that gives information in a formal way. ❑ *I was very angry when I made that statement.* [from Old French]

states|man /steɪtsmən/ (**statesmen**)
N-COUNT SOCIAL STUDIES A **statesman** is an important and experienced politician, especially one who is widely known and respected. ❑ *Hamilton is a great statesman and political thinker.*

Word Link	stat ≈ standing : static, station, stationary

stat|ic /stætɪk/
1 **ADJ** Something that is **static** does not move or change. ❑ *House prices were static last month.*
2 **N-NONCOUNT** SCIENCE **Static** or **static electricity** is electricity that collects on things such as your body or metal objects. [from New Latin]

sta|tion /steɪʃᵊn/ (**stations, stationing, stationed**)
1 **N-COUNT** A **station** is a place where trains stop so that people can get on or off. ❑ *Ingrid went with him to the train station.*
2 **N-COUNT** A bus **station** is a place in a town or a city where a lot of buses stop, usually for a while. ❑ *I walked to the bus station and bought a ticket.*
3 **N-COUNT** A radio or television **station** is a company that broadcasts programs. ❑ *...a local radio station.*
4 **V-T** If soldiers or officials **are stationed** in a place, they are sent there for a period of time. ❑ *Troops are stationed on the streets.* [from Old French]
5 → see also **gas station, police station, power station**
→ look at Word Webs: **cellphone, radio, television**

Word Partnership	Use station with :
N	railroad station, subway station **1**
	radio station, television/TV station **3**
ADJ	local station **3**

sta|tion|ary /steɪʃənɛri/ **ADJ** Something that is **stationary** is not moving. ❑ *A bus crashed into the back of a stationary vehicle.* [from Latin]

sta|tion|ery /steɪʃənɛri/ **N-NONCOUNT** **Stationery** is paper, envelopes, and other materials or equipment used for writing and typing. ❑ *...office stationery.* [from Old French]

S

→ look at Picture Dictionary: **office**

sta|tion mod|el (station models) N-COUNT
SCIENCE A **station model** is a weather map containing symbols that represent the weather conditions around a particular weather station.

sta|tis|tic /stətɪstɪk/ (**statistics**) **N-COUNT**
MATH **Statistics** are facts that are expressed in numbers. ❑ *Statistics show that wages are rising.* [from German]

statue /stætʃu/ (**statues**) **N-COUNT** ARTS
A **statue** is a large model of a person or an animal, made of stone or metal.
❑ *She gave me a stone statue of a horse.*
[from Old French]

stat|ure /stætʃər/
1 N-NONCOUNT Someone's **stature** is their height. ❑ *Mother was of very small stature.*
2 N-NONCOUNT The **stature** of a person is the importance and reputation that they have. ❑ *...his stature as the world's greatest opera singer.* [from Old French]

sta|tus /steɪtəs, stæt-/
1 N-NONCOUNT The **status** of someone or something is the importance that people give them. ❑ *Older family members enjoy high status in many societies.*
2 N-NONCOUNT Status is an official description that gives a person, an organization, or a place particular rights or advantages. ❑ *They were proud of their status as guards.* [from Latin]

Word Partnership	Use **status** with :
V	**achieve** status, **maintain/preserve** *one's* status **1**
N	**celebrity** status, **change of** status, **wealth and** status **1** **marital** status, **tax** status **2**
ADJ	**current** status **1 2** **economic** status, **financial** status **3**

sta|tus bar (**status bars**) **N-COUNT**
TECHNOLOGY A **status bar** is a narrow horizontal area at the bottom of a computer screen showing details about the program that is running. ❑ *Look for the small clock symbol in the status bar.*

statu|tory /stætʃʊtɔri/ **ADJ Statutory** means relating to rules or laws which have been formally written down.
[FORMAL] ❑ *...statutory law.* [from Old French]

stay /steɪ/ (**stays, staying, stayed**)
1 V-I If you **stay** where you are, you continue to be there and do not leave. ❑ *"Stay here," Trish said. "I'll bring the car to you."*
2 V-T/V-I If you **stay** somewhere, you live there for a short time. ❑ *Gordon stayed at The Park Hotel, Milan.* ❑ *Can't you stay a few more days?*
3 N-COUNT Stay is also a noun. ❑ *Please contact the hotel reception if you have any problems during your stay.*
4 V-LINK If someone or something **stays** in a particular state or situation, they continue to be in it. ❑ *Exercise is one of the best ways to stay healthy.*
5 V-I If you **stay away from** a place, you do not go there. ❑ *Most workers stayed away from work during the strike.* [from Anglo-French]
▶ **stay in** If you **stay in**, you remain at home and do not go out. ❑ *We decided to stay in and have dinner at home.*
▶ **stay out** If you **stay out** at night, you remain away from home. ❑ *That was the first time Elliot stayed out all night.*
▶ **stay up** If you **stay up**, you do not go to bed at your usual time. ❑ *I used to stay up late with my mom and watch movies.*

steady /stɛdi/ (**steadier, steadiest, steadies, steadying, steadied**)
1 ADJ A **steady** situation continues or develops gradually and is not likely to change quickly. ❑ *Despite these problems there has been steady progress.* ● **steadi|ly** /stɛdɪli/ **ADV** ❑ *Prices have been rising steadily.*
2 ADJ If an object is **steady**, it is firm, and does not move around. ❑ *Hold the camera steady.*
3 V-T/V-I If you **steady** something, or if it **steadies**, it stops moving around. ❑ *Two men were steadying the ladder.* [from Old High German]

Thesaurus	**steady** Also look up :
ADJ	consistent, continuous, uninterrupted **1** constant, fixed, stable **2**

Word Partnership	Use **steady** with :
N	steady **decline/increase**, steady **diet**, steady **growth**, steady **improvement**, steady **income**, steady **progress**, steady **rain**, steady **rate**, steady **supply** **1**
V	**remain** steady **1 2** **hold/keep** *something* steady **2**

S

steak /steɪk/ (**steaks**)

1 **N-COUNT/N-NONCOUNT** A **steak** is a large flat piece of beef without much fat on it. ❑ *There was a steak cooking on the grill.*

2 **N-COUNT** A fish **steak** is a large piece of fish that does not contain many bones. ❑ *...fresh salmon steaks.* [from Old Norse]

steal /stil/ (**steals, stealing, stole, stolen**)

1 **V-T/V-I** If you **steal** something **from** someone, you take it without their permission. ❑ *They said he stole a small boy's bicycle.* ❑ *It's wrong to steal.* [from Old English]

2 → see also **stolen**

steam /stim/ (**steams, steaming, steamed**)

steam

1 **N-NONCOUNT** **Steam** is the hot gas that forms when water boils. ❑ *The heat converts water into steam.*

2 **V-T/V-I** If you **steam** food, you cook it in steam rather than in water. ❑ *Steam the carrots until they are slightly soft.* ❑ *Leave the vegetables to steam over the rice.* [from Old English]

→ look at Picture Dictionary: **cook**

Word Partnership	Use **steam** with :
N	steam **bath**, **clouds of** steam, steam **engine**, steam **pipes**, steam **turbine** **1**
ADJ	steam **powered**, **rising** steam **1**

steel /stil/ **N-NONCOUNT** **Steel** is a very strong metal that is made mainly from iron. ❑ *...steel pipes.* ❑ *...the steel industry.* [from Old English]

→ look at Word Webs: **bridge, train**

steep /stip/ (**steeper, steepest**)

1 **ADJ** A **steep** slope rises at a very sharp angle. ❑ *Some of the hills in San Francisco are very steep.* ● **steep|ly** **ADV** ❑ *The road climbs steeply.*

2 **ADJ** A **steep** rise in prices is a very big rise. ❑ *There have been steep price increases.* ● **steep|ly** **ADV** ❑ *Unemployment is rising steeply.* [from Old English]

steer /stɪər/ (**steers, steering, steered**)

1 **V-T** When you **steer** a vehicle, you control it so that it goes in the direction that you want. ❑ *What is it like to steer a big ship?*

2 **V-T** If you **steer** someone in a particular direction, you guide them there. ❑ *Nick steered them into the nearest seats.*

3 **PHRASE** If you **steer clear of** someone or something, you deliberately avoid them. ❑ *We steered clear of the subject of politics.* [from Old English]

steer|ing wheel (**steering wheels**) **N-COUNT** In a car or other vehicle, the **steering wheel** is the wheel that the driver holds when he or she is driving.

stem /stɛm/ (**stems, stemming, stemmed**)

1 **N-COUNT** The **stem** of a plant is the long, thin part that the flowers and leaves grow on. ❑ *He cut the stem and gave her the flower.*

2 **V-I** If a condition or a problem **stems from** something, it was caused originally by that thing. ❑ *All my problems stem from my childhood.* [from Old English]

→ look at Picture Dictionary: **flowers**

step /stɛp/ (**steps, stepping, stepped**)

1 **N-COUNT** If you take a **step**, you lift your foot and put it down in a different place. ❑ *I took a step toward him.* ❑ *She walked back a few steps.*

2 **V-I** If you **step on** something, you put your foot on it. ❑ *Neil Armstrong was the first man to step on the Moon.*

3 **N-COUNT** A **step** is a raised flat surface, that you put your feet on in order to walk up or down to a different level. ❑ *We went down some steps into the yard.* ❑ *A girl was sitting on the bottom step.*

4 → see also **doorstep**

5 **N-COUNT** A **step** is one of a series of actions that you take in a process. ❑ *We have taken the first step toward peace.*

6 **PHRASE** If you do something **step by step**, you do it by progressing gradually from one stage to the next. ❑ *I am not rushing things. I'm taking it step by step.* [from Old English]

Word Partnership	Use **step** with :
ADV	step **outside** **1**
	step **ahead**, step **backward**, step **closer**, step **1** **4**
ADJ	**big** step, **bold** step, **critical** step, **important** step, **the right** step **4**
N	step **in a process** **4**

step|father /stɛpfaðər/ (**stepfathers**) also **step-father** **N-COUNT** Someone's **stepfather** is the man who has married their mother but who is not their father.

step|mother /stɛpmʌðər/ (**stepmothers**) also **step-mother** **N-COUNT** Someone's **stepmother** is the woman who has married their father but who is not their mother.

ste|reo /stɛrioʊ, stɪər-/ (**stereos**)
1 **ADJ** TECHNOLOGY **Stereo** is used to describe a sound system in which the sound is played through two speakers. Compare with **mono**. ❑ ...equipment that gives stereo sound.
2 **N-COUNT** TECHNOLOGY A **stereo** is a CD player with two speakers.

ste|reo|type /stɛriətaɪp, stɪər-/ (**stereotypes, stereotyping, stereotyped**)
1 **N-COUNT** A **stereotype** is a fixed general image or set of characteristics that a lot of people believe represents a particular type of person or thing. ❑ There's always been a stereotype about successful businessmen.
2 **V-T** If someone **is stereotyped** as something, people form a fixed general idea or image of them, so that it is assumed that they will behave in a particular way. ❑ He was stereotyped by some people as a trouble-maker. [from French]

ster|ile /stɛrəl/
1 **ADJ** Something that is **sterile** is completely clean. ❑ Cover the cut with a sterile bandage.
2 **ADJ** A person or an animal that is **sterile** is unable to produce babies. ❑ The tests showed that George was sterile. [from Latin]

stern /stɜrn/ (**sterner, sternest**)
1 **ADJ** **Stern** words or actions are very severe. ❑ The AFL last night gave players a stern warning about their behavior. ● **stern|ly** **ADV** ❑ "We will punish anyone who breaks the rules," she said sternly.
2 **ADJ** Someone who is **stern** is very serious and not friendly. ❑ Her father was a stern man. [from Old English]

stew /stu/ (**stews, stewing, stewed**)
1 **N-COUNT/N-NONCOUNT** A **stew** is a meal that you make by cooking meat and vegetables in liquid. ❑ She gave him a bowl of hot stew.
2 **V-T** When you **stew** meat, vegetables, or fruit, you cook them slowly in liquid. ❑ Stew the apples for half an hour. [from Old French]

stew|ard /stuərd/ (**stewards**)
1 **N-COUNT** A **steward** is a man who works on a ship, a plane, or a train, taking care of passengers and serving meals to them.
2 **N-COUNT** A **steward** is a man or a woman who helps to organize a race, a march, or other public event. ❑ The steward at the march was talking to a police officer. [from Old English]

---
stick
❶ NOUN USES
❷ VERB USES
❸ PHRASAL VERBS
---

❶ **stick** /stɪk/ (**sticks**)
1 **N-COUNT** A **stick** is a thin branch from a tree. ❑ She put some dry sticks on the fire.
2 **N-COUNT** A **stick** is a long thin piece of wood that is used for a particular purpose. ❑ He picked up his walking stick and walked away.
3 **N-COUNT** A **stick of** something is a long thin piece of it. ❑ ...a stick of celery. [from Old English]

❷ **stick** /stɪk/ (**sticks, sticking, stuck**)
1 **V-T** If you **stick** one thing to another, you join them together using a sticky substance. ❑ Now stick your picture on a piece of paper.
2 **V-T/V-I** If you **stick** a pointed object **into** something, or if it **sticks in** something, it goes into it or through it. ❑ The doctor stuck the needle into Joe's arm.
3 **V-T** If you **stick** something somewhere, you put it there. [INFORMAL] ❑ He folded the papers and stuck them in his desk.
4 **V-I** If one thing **sticks to** another, it becomes joined to it and is difficult to remove. ❑ The paper sometimes sticks to the bottom of the cake. [from Old English]
5 → see also **stuck**

❸ **stick** /stɪk/ (**sticks, sticking, stuck**)
▶ **stick around** If you **stick around**, you stay where you are. [INFORMAL] ❑ Stick around a while and see what happens.
▶ **stick by** If you **stick by** someone, you continue to give them support. ❑ All my friends stuck by me during the difficult times.
▶ **stick out** **1** If something **sticks out**, it continues further than the main part of something. ❑ His two front teeth stick out slightly.
2 If you **stick** something **out**, you push it forward or away from you. ❑ She stuck out her tongue at him.
▶ **stick to** If you **stick to** a promise or a decision, you do not change your mind. ❑ We are waiting to see if he sticks to his promise.
▶ **stick up for** If you **stick up for** someone or something, you support them and say that they are right. ❑ My father always sticks up for me.

S

stick|er /stɪkər/ (**stickers**) **N-COUNT** A **sticker** is a small piece of paper with writing or a picture on one side, that you can stick onto a surface. ❑ *I bought a sticker that said, "I love Florida."* [from Old English]

sticky /stɪki/ (**stickier, stickiest**)

1 **ADJ** Something that is **sticky** sticks to other things. ❑ *The floor was sticky with spilled orange juice.* ❑ *If the mixture is sticky, add more flour.*

2 **ADJ** A **sticky** situation involves problems. [INFORMAL] ❑ *There were some sticky moments.*

stiff /stɪf/ (**stiffer, stiffest**)

1 **ADJ** Something that is **stiff** is firm or does not bend easily. ❑ *His jeans were new and stiff.*

● **stiff|ly** **ADV** ❑ *Moira sat stiffly in her chair.*

2 **ADJ** If you are **stiff**, your muscles or joints hurt when you move. ❑ *A hot bath is good for stiff muscles.*

3 **ADV** If you are bored **stiff** or worried **stiff**, you are extremely bored or worried. [INFORMAL] ❑ *Anna tried to look interested, but she was bored stiff.* [from Old English]

sti|fle /staɪfᵊl/ (**stifles, stifling, stifled**) **V-T** To **stifle** something means to stop it from happening or continuing. ❑ *He stifled a laugh.* [from Old French]

stig|ma /stɪgmə/ (**stigmas**)

1 **N-COUNT/N-NONCOUNT** If something has a **stigma** attached to it, people think it is something to be ashamed of. ❑ *There is still a stigma attached to cancer.*

2 **N-COUNT** SCIENCE The **stigma** of a flower is the top of the center part which takes in pollen. [from Latin]

still
1 ADVERB USES
2 ADJECTIVE USES

1 **still** /stɪl/

1 **ADV** If a situation that existed in the past **still** exists, it has continued and exists now. ❑ *Do you still live in Illinois?* ❑ *Donald is still teaching at the age of 89.*

2 **ADV** If something that has not yet happened could **still** happen, it is possible that it will happen. ❑ *They could still win the game.*

3 **ADV** You use **still** to say that something is true, despite something else. ❑ *She says she still loves him even though he treats her badly.*

4 **ADV** You use **still** to make another word stronger. ❑ *It's good to travel, but it's better still to*

come home. [from Old English]

2 **still** /stɪl/ (**stiller, stillest**)

1 **ADJ** If you are **still**, you are not moving. ❑ *Please stand still and listen to me!*

2 **ADJ** If it is **still**, there is no wind. ❑ *It was a warm, still evening.* [from Old English]

stimu|late /stɪmyəleɪt/ (**stimulates, stimulating, stimulated**)

1 **V-T** To **stimulate** something means to make it more active. ❑ *America is trying to stimulate its economy.*

2 **V-T** If you **are stimulated by** something, it makes you feel full of ideas and enthusiasm. ❑ *Bill was stimulated by the challenge.*

● **stimu|lat|ing** **ADJ** ❑ *It is a stimulating book.*

● **stimu|la|tion** **N-NONCOUNT** ❑ *Children need stimulation, not relaxation.*

3 **V-T** If something **stimulates** a part of your body, it causes it to move or start working. ❑ *Exercise stimulates your body.* [from Latin]

stimu|lus /stɪmyələs/ (**stimuli** /stɪmyəlaɪ/) **N-COUNT/N-NONCOUNT** A **stimulus** is something that encourages activity in people or things. ❑ *What was the stimulus that made you take this job?* [from Latin]

sting /stɪŋ/ (**stings, stinging, stung**)

1 **V-T/V-I** If a plant, an animal, or an insect **stings** you, a pointed part of it is pushed into your skin so that you feel a sharp pain. ❑ *She was stung by a bee.* ❑ *This type of bee rarely stings.*

2 **N-COUNT** If you feel a **sting**, you feel a sharp pain in your skin. ❑ *This won't hurt—you will just feel a little sting.*

3 **V-T/V-I** If a part of your body **stings**, or if a substance **stings** it, you feel a sharp pain there. ❑ *His cheeks were stinging from the cold wind.* [from Old English]

→ look at Picture Dictionary: **insects**

stink /stɪŋk/ (**stinks, stinking, stank, stunk**)

1 **V-I** To **stink** means to smell very bad. ❑ *We all stank and nobody cared.* ❑ *The kitchen stinks of fish.*

2 **N-SING** **Stink** is also a noun. ❑ *He was aware of the stink of onions on his breath.* [from Old English]

stipu|late /stɪpyəleɪt/ (**stipulates, stipulating, stipulated**) **V-T** If you **stipulate** a condition or **stipulate that** something must be done, you say clearly that it must be done. ❑ *He stipulated that $1 million should go to charity.*

● **stipu|la|tion** /stɪpyəleɪʃᵊn/ (**stipulations**) **N-COUNT** ❑ *Clifford's only stipulation is that his clients must obey his advice.* [from Latin]

S

stir /stɜr/ (**stirs, stirring, stirred**)

1 **v-t** If you **stir** a liquid, you mix it in a container using a spoon. ❑ *Stir the soup for a few seconds.*

2 **v-i** If someone who is asleep **stirs**, they move slightly. [WRITTEN] ❑ *Eileen shook him, and he started to stir.*

3 **v-t/v-i** If a memory or emotion **stirs in** you, you begin to think about it or feel it. [WRITTEN] ❑ *Then a memory stirs in you, and you start feeling anxious.* [from Old English]

▶ **stir up** **1** If something **stirs up** dust in the air or mud in water, it causes the dust or mud to move around. ❑ *They saw first a cloud of dust, and then the car that was stirring it up.*

2 If someone **stirs up** a bad mood or situation, they cause it. ❑ *As usual, Harriet is trying to stir up trouble.*

stitch /stɪtʃ/ (**stitches, stitching, stitched**)

1 **v-t/v-i** If you **stitch** cloth, you sew it using a needle and thread. ❑ *Stitch the two pieces of fabric together.* ❑ *We stitched for hours.*

2 **n-count** **Stitches** are the short lines of thread that have been sewn in a piece of cloth. ❑ *Sew a row of straight stitches.*

3 **v-t** When doctors **stitch** a wound, they use a special needle and thread to sew the skin together. ❑ *Jill washed and stitched the wound.*

4 **n-count** A **stitch** is a line of thread that has been used for sewing the skin of a wound together. ❑ *He had six stitches in the cut.* [from Old English]

stock /stɒk/ (**stocks, stocking, stocked**)

1 **n-count** BUSINESS **Stocks** are parts of the value of a business that may be owned by different people. ❑ *She works for a bank, buying and selling stocks.*

2 **v-t** BUSINESS If a store **stocks** particular products, it keeps a supply of them to sell. ❑ *The store stocks everything from pens to TV sets.*

3 **n-noncount** BUSINESS A store's **stock** is the total amount of goods that it has available to sell. ❑ *Most of the stock was destroyed in the fire.*

4 **n-count** A **stock of** things is a supply of them. ❑ *They keep a stock of ready meals in the freezer.*

5 → see also **stocking**

6 **phrase** BUSINESS If goods are **in stock**, a store has them available to sell. If they are **out of stock**, it does not. ❑ *Check that your size is in stock.* [from Old English]

stock char|ac|ter (**stock characters**)

n-count ARTS A **stock character** is a character in a play or other story who represents a particular type of person, for example the mad scientist, rather than a fully-developed individual.

stock ex|change (**stock exchanges**)

n-count BUSINESS A **stock exchange** is a place where people buy and sell stocks in companies. ❑ *...the New York stock exchange.*

stock|holder /stɒkhoʊldər/ (**stockholders**)

n-count BUSINESS A **stockholder** is a person who owns shares in a company. ❑ *He was a stockholder in a hotel corporation.*

stock|ing /stɒkɪŋ/ (**stockings**)

1 **n-count** **Stockings** are pieces of women's clothing that fit closely over their feet and legs. ❑ *...a pair of nylon stockings.*

2 → see also **stock**

stock mar|ket (**stock markets**) **n-count**

BUSINESS The **stock market** is the activity of buying shares. ❑ *This is a practical guide to investing in the stock market.*

stole /stoʊl/ **Stole** is the past tense of **steal**.

sto|len /stoʊlən/

1 **Stolen** is the past participle of **steal**.

2 **adj** A **stolen** object is something that has been taken from someone without their permission. ❑ *We have now found the stolen car.* [from Old English]

sto|ma (**stomata**) **n-count** SCIENCE **Stomata** are small holes on the leaves of plants that allow water and air to enter and leave the plant. [from New Latin]

stom|ach /stʌmək/ (**stomachs**)

1 **n-count** SCIENCE Your **stomach** is the organ inside your body where food goes when you eat it. ❑ *He has stomach problems.*

2 **n-count** Your **stomach** is the front part of your body above your waist. ❑ *The children lay down on their stomachs.* [from Old French]

stone /stoʊn/ (**stones**)

1 **n-count/n-noncount** **Stone** is a hard solid substance that is found in the ground and is often used for building. ❑ *...a stone floor.*

2 **n-count** A **stone** is a small piece of rock that is found on the ground. ❑ *He removed a stone from his shoe.*

3 **n-count** A **stone** is a piece of valuable rock in jewelry. ❑ *He gave her a diamond ring with three stones.* [from Old English]

S

stood /stʊd/ **Stood** is the past tense and past participle of **stand**. [from Old English]

stool /stul/ (**stools**) **N-COUNT** A **stool** is a seat with legs and no support for your arms or back. ❑ *Kate sat on a stool and leaned on the counter.* [from Old English]

stop /stɒp/ (**stops, stopping, stopped**)
1 **V-T/V-I** If you **stop** doing something, you do not do it anymore. ❑ *Stop throwing those stones! ❑ She stopped and then continued eating.*
2 **V-T** If you **stop** something from happening, you prevent it from happening. ❑ *They are trying to find a way to stop the war.*
3 **V-I** If an activity or a process **stops**, it does not happen anymore. ❑ *The rain has stopped.*
4 **V-T/V-I** If a machine **stops**, or **is stopped**, it is no longer working. ❑ *The clock stopped at 11:59 Saturday night.*
5 **V-T/V-I** When you **stop** a moving person or vehicle, or when they **stop**, they do not move anymore. ❑ *The car failed to stop at a stoplight. ❑ He stopped the car and waited for her.*
6 **N-SING** If something that is moving comes **to a stop**, it slows down and no longer moves. ❑ *Do not open the door before the train comes to a stop.*
7 **N-COUNT** A **stop** is a place where buses or trains regularly stop so that people can get on and off. ❑ *The nearest subway stop is Houston Street.*
8 **PHRASE** If you **put a stop to** something, you prevent it from happening or continuing. ❑ *I'm going to put a stop to all this talk.* [from Old English]
▶ **stop off** If you **stop off** somewhere, you stop for a short time in the middle of a trip. ❑ *The president stopped off in Poland on his way to Munich.*

stor|age /stɔrɪdʒ/ **N-NONCOUNT** Storage is keeping something in a special place until it is needed. ❑ *This room is used for storage.* [from Old French]

store /stɔr/ (**stores, storing, stored**)
1 **N-COUNT** A **store** is a place where things are sold. ❑ *She ran to the store to buy some cookies. ❑ ...a grocery store.*
2 **V-T** When you **store** things, you put them somewhere and leave them there until they are needed. ❑ *Store the cookies in a box.* [from Old French]
3 → see also **department store**
→ look at Word Web: **city**

Thesaurus	store	Also look up :
N	business, market, shop **1**	
V	accumulate, keep, save **2**	

stored en|er|gy **N-NONCOUNT** SCIENCE **Stored energy** is the same as **potential energy**.

store|keeper /stɔrkipər/ (**storekeepers**) **N-COUNT** A **storekeeper** is a person who owns or manages a small store.

storm /stɔrm/ (**storms, storming, stormed**)
1 **N-COUNT** A **storm** is very bad weather, with heavy rain and strong winds. ❑ *There will be violent storms along the East Coast.*
2 **V-I** If you **storm into** or **out of** a place, you enter or leave it quickly and noisily, because you are angry. ❑ *After an argument, he stormed out.* [from Old English]
→ look at Word Webs: **storm, disaster, forecast, hurricane, weather**

Word Partnership	Use storm with :
N	storm **clouds**, storm **damage**, **ice/rain/snow** storm, storm **warning**, storm **winds** **1**
	center of a storm, **eye of a** storm **1**
ADJ	**gathering** storm, **heavy** storm, **severe** storm, **tropical** storm **1**
V	**hit by a** storm, **weather the** storm **1**

storm surge (**storm surges**) **N-COUNT** SCIENCE A **storm surge** is an increase in the sea level along a shore that accompanies a hurricane or a storm.

Word Web   **storm**

Here's how to protect yourself and your property when a severe **storm** hits. Listen for warnings from the **weather** service. Strong **wind** may blow trash cans around and **hail** may damage your car. Both should go into the garage. If you are outdoors when a storm strikes, get under cover. If you are in the open, **lightning** could hit you. Heavy **rainfall** can cause **flooding**.
After the **rain** has passed, do not drive on flooded roads. The water may be deeper than you think. Be sure to buy food and batteries before a **blizzard** since **snow** may close the roads.

stormy /stɔrmi/ (**stormier, stormiest**) **ADJ**
If the weather is **stormy**, there are strong
winds and heavy rain. ❑ *Expect a night of
stormy weather, with heavy rain and strong winds.*
[from Old English]

sto|ry /stɔri/ (**stories**)
1 **N-COUNT** LANGUAGE ARTS A **story** is a
description of imaginary people and events,
that is intended to entertain people. ❑ *I'm
going to tell you a story about four little rabbits.*
2 **N-COUNT** A **story** is a description of
something that has happened. ❑ *The parents
all had interesting stories about their children.*
3 **N-COUNT** A **story** of a building is one of its
different levels. ❑ *Our apartment building is 25
stories high.* [Senses 1 and 2 from Anglo-
French. Sense 3 from Anglo-Latin.]
→ look at Word Web: **myth**

Thesaurus	story	Also look up :
N	epic, fable, fairy tale, romance, tale **1** account, report **2**	

Word Partnership	Use story with :
N	character in a story, horror story, story hour, story line, of a story, title of a story, story writer **1** beginning of a story, end of a story **1**-**3** life story **2**
ADJ	classic story, compelling story, familiar story, funny story, good story **1** **2** the full story, untold story, the whole story **2**
V	hear a story, publish a story, read a story, tell a story, write a story **1** **2**

stove /stoʊv/ (**stoves**) **N-COUNT** A **stove** is a
piece of equipment that provides heat, either
for cooking or for heating a room. ❑ *She put
the saucepan on the gas stove.* [from Old English]

straight /streɪt/ (**straighter, straightest**)
1 **ADJ** If something is **straight**, it continues
in one direction and does not bend or curve.
❑ *Keep the boat moving in a straight line.* ❑ *Grace
had long straight hair.*
2 **ADV** **Straight** is also an adverb. ❑ *Stand
straight and hold your arms out to the side.*
3 **ADV** If you go **straight** to a place, you go
there immediately. ❑ *When he arrived, he went
straight to his office.*
4 **ADJ** If you give someone a **straight** answer,
you answer them clearly and honestly.
5 **PHRASE** If you **get** something **straight**,
you make sure that you understand it
properly. [SPOKEN] ❑ *Now, let me get this*

straight: you say that you were here all evening?
[from Old English]
→ look at Picture Dictionary: **hair**

Word Partnership	Use straight with :
V	drive straight, keep going straight, look straight, straight **1**
N	straight line, straight nose **1**

straight|en /streɪtⁿn/ (**straightens,
straightening, straightened**)
1 **V-T** If you **straighten** something, you
make it neat or put it in its proper position.
❑ *She straightened a picture on the wall.*
2 **V-I** If you are standing and you **straighten**,
you make your back or body straight.
❑ *The three men straightened and stood waiting.*
3 **Straighten up** means the same as
straighten. ❑ *He straightened up and took his
hands out of his pockets.*
4 **V-T/V-I** If you **straighten** something, or if
it **straightens**, it becomes straight.
❑ *Straighten both legs.* [from Old English]

strain /streɪn/ (**strains, straining, strained**)
1 **N-COUNT/N-NONCOUNT** If **strain** is put **on**
a person or an organization, they have to do
more than they are able to do. ❑ *She couldn't
cope with the stresses and strains of her career.*
2 **V-T** To **strain** something means to make
it do more than it is able to do. ❑ *The large
number of customers is straining our system.*
3 **N-COUNT/N-NONCOUNT** A **strain** is an injury
to a muscle in your body, caused by using it
too much. ❑ *Avoid muscle strain by taking rests.*
4 **V-T** If you **strain** a muscle, you injure it by
using it too much. ❑ *He strained his back
playing tennis.*
5 **V-T** If you **strain to** do something, you make
a great effort to do it. ❑ *I had to strain to hear her.*
6 **V-T** When you **strain** food, you separate
the liquid part of it from the solid parts.
❑ *Strain the soup and put it back into the pan.*
[from Old French]

Word Partnership	Use strain with :
ADJ	great strain **1**
N	stress and strain **1** muscle strain **3** strain a muscle **4**

strand /strænd/ (**strands, stranding, stranded**)
1 **N-COUNT** A **strand of** something such as
hair, wire, or thread is a thin piece of it.
❑ *She tried to blow a strand of hair from her eyes.*
2 **V-T** If you **are stranded**, you are prevented
from leaving a place, for example because of

S

bad weather. ❑ *The climbers were stranded by a storm.* [Sense 2 from Old English.]

strange /streɪndʒ/ (**stranger, strangest**)
■ **ADJ** Something that is **strange** is unusual or unexpected. ❑ *There was something strange about the way she spoke.* ● **strange|ly ADV** ❑ *She noticed he was acting strangely.*
■ **ADJ** A **strange** place is somewhere you have never been before. ❑ *I was alone in a strange city.* [from Old French]

> **Thesaurus** strange Also look up :
> ADJ   bizarre, different, eccentric, odd, peculiar, unusual, weird; (ant.) ordinary, usual ■
>   exotic, foreign, unfamiliar ■

stran|ger /streɪndʒər/ (**strangers**)
■ **N-COUNT** A **stranger** is someone that you have never met before. ❑ *We don't want a complete stranger staying with us.*
■ **N-PLURAL** If two people are **strangers**, they do not know each other. ❑ *The two women were strangers.* [from Old French]

stran|gle /stræŋgᵊl/ (**strangles, strangling, strangled**) **V-T** To **strangle** someone means to kill them by pressing their throat tightly so that they cannot breathe. ❑ *He tried to strangle a policeman.* [from Old French]

strap /stræp/ (**straps, strapping, strapped**)
■ **N-COUNT** A **strap** is a long, narrow piece of leather or other material. ❑ *Nancy held the strap of her bag.* ❑ *Her shoes had elastic ankle straps.*
■ **V-T** If you **strap** something somewhere, you fasten it there with a strap. ❑ *She strapped the baby seat into the car.*

stra|tegic /strətidʒɪk/
■ **ADJ** **Strategic** means relating to the most important, general aspects of something such as a military operation or political policy. ❑ *We need a strategic plan for reducing crime.* ● **stra|tegi|cal|ly** /strətidʒɪkli/ **ADV** ❑ *...strategically important roads.*
■ **ADJ** **Strategic** weapons are very powerful missiles that can be fired only after a decision to use them has been made by a political leader. ❑ *...strategic nuclear weapons.*
■ **ADJ** If you put something in a **strategic** position, you place it cleverly in a position where it will be most useful or have the most effect. ❑ *Benches are placed at strategic points throughout the gardens.* ● **stra|tegi|cal|ly ADV** ❑ *We hid behind a strategically placed chair.* [from French]

> **Word Partnership** Use **strategic** with :
> N   strategic **decisions**, strategic **forces**, strategic **interests**, strategic **planning**, strategic **targets**, strategic **thinking** ■ strategic **missiles**, strategic **nuclear weapons** ■
>   strategic **location**, strategic **position** ■

strat|egy /strætədʒi/ (**strategies**) **N-COUNT/ N-NONCOUNT** A **strategy** is a general plan or set of plans for the future. ❑ *Do you have a strategy for solving this type of problem?* [from French]

> **Thesaurus** strategy Also look up :
> N   plan, policy, tactic

> **Word Partnership** Use **strategy** with :
> N   **campaign** strategy, **investment** strategy, **marketing** strategy, **part of a** strategy, **pricing** strategy
> V   **adopt a** strategy, **change a** strategy, **develop a** strategy, **plan a** strategy, **use (a)** strategy
> ADJ **aggressive** strategy, **new** strategy, **political** strategy, **successful** strategy, **winning** strategy

strati|fi|ca|tion /strætɪfɪkeɪʃᵊn/ **N-NONCOUNT SCIENCE** In geology, **stratification** is the process by which layers of sediment build up over time to produce separate layers of rock. [from New Latin]

strati|fied drift /strætɪfaɪd drɪft/ **N-NONCOUNT SCIENCE Stratified drift** is layers of sand and gravel that have been deposited by melted ice from a glacier.

strato|sphere /strætəsfɪər/ **N-SING SCIENCE** The **stratosphere** is the layer of the Earth's atmosphere that lies between 7 and 31 miles above the Earth.

stra|tum /streɪtəm, stræt-/ (**strata**)
■ **N-COUNT SOCIAL STUDIES** A **stratum** of society is a group of people in it who are similar in their education, income, or social status. [FORMAL] ❑ *The changes affected every stratum of society.*
■ **N-COUNT SCIENCE Strata** are different layers of rock. [from New Latin]

straw /strɔ/ (**straws**)
■ **N-NONCOUNT Straw** is the dried, yellow stems of crops. ❑ *The floor of the barn was covered with straw.* ❑ *...a straw hat.*
■ **N-COUNT** A **straw** is a thin tube that you

S

use to suck a drink into your mouth. ❑ *I drank from a bottle of soda with a straw in it.*

3 PHRASE If an event is **the last straw**, it is the last in a series of bad events, and it makes you feel that the situation is now impossible. ❑ *Patrick's crying was the last straw for his mother.* [from Old English]
→ look at Word Web: **rice**

straw|berry /strɔbɛri/ (**strawberries**)
N-COUNT A **strawberry** is a small soft red fruit that has a lot of very small seeds on its skin. ❑ *...strawberries and cream.* [from Old English]

stray /streɪ/ (**strays, straying, strayed**)
1 V-I If someone **strays** somewhere, they go away from where they are supposed to be. ❑ *Be careful not to stray into dangerous parts of the city.*
2 ADJ A **stray** dog or cat has gone away from its owner's home. ❑ *A stray dog came up to him.*
3 N-COUNT Stray is also a noun. ❑ *The dog was a stray.*
4 V-I If your mind or your eyes **stray**, you start thinking about or looking at different subjects rather than one particular subject. ❑ *My mind keeps straying when I'm trying to work.* [from Old French]

streak /strik/ (**streaks, streaking, streaked**)
1 N-COUNT A **streak** is a long mark on a surface. ❑ *There are dark streaks on the surface of the moon.*
2 V-T If something **streaks** a surface, it makes long marks on the surface. ❑ *Rain began to streak the windows.*
3 N-COUNT SCIENCE In geology, the **streak** of a mineral is the color of the powder that is produced when the mineral is rubbed against a hard, white surface. [from Old English]

stream /strim/ (**streams, streaming, streamed**)
1 N-COUNT GEOGRAPHY A **stream** is a small narrow river. ❑ *There was a small stream at the end of the garden.*
2 N-COUNT A **stream of** things is a large number of them that come one after another. ❑ *The TV show caused a stream of complaints.*
3 V-I If something **streams** somewhere, it moves there in large amounts. ❑ *Tears streamed down their faces.* ❑ *Sunlight was streaming into the room.* [from Old English]
→ look at Picture Dictionary: **river**

street /strit/ (**streets**) **N-COUNT** A **street** is a road in a city or a town. ❑ *The streets were*

crowded with shoppers. ❑ *He lived at 66 Bingfield Street.* [from Old English]

Thesaurus	street Also look up :
N	avenue, drive, road

street|car /stritkɑr/ (**streetcars**) **N-COUNT**
A **streetcar** is an electric vehicle for carrying people which travels on rails in the streets of a city or a town.
→ look at Word Web: **transportation**

strength /strɛŋkθ, strɛŋθ/ (**strengths**)
1 N-NONCOUNT Your **strength** is how physically strong you are. ❑ *Swimming builds up the strength of your muscles.* ❑ *He threw the ball forward with all his strength.*
2 N-NONCOUNT Someone's **strength** is their confidence or courage. ❑ *He copes with his illness very well. His strength is amazing.*
3 N-COUNT/N-NONCOUNT The **strength** of an object or a material is how strong it is. ❑ *He checked the strength of the rope.*
4 N-COUNT/N-NONCOUNT The **strength** of a person, an organization, or a country is the power or influence that they have. ❑ *...America's military strength.*
5 N-NONCOUNT If you talk about the **strength of** a feeling or a belief, you are talking about how deeply people feel it or believe it. ❑ *He was surprised at the strength of his own feeling.*
6 N-COUNT/N-NONCOUNT Someone's **strengths** are the good qualities and abilities that they have. ❑ *What are your strengths and weaknesses?* [from Old English]
→ look at Word Web: **muscle**

strength|en /strɛŋθən/ (**strengthens, strengthening, strengthened**) **V-T/V-I** If you **strengthen** something, or if it **strengthens**, it becomes stronger. ❑ *Cycling strengthens all the muscles of the body.* [from Old English]

stress /strɛs/ (**stresses, stressing, stressed**)
1 V-T If you **stress** a point in a discussion, you make it clear that it is very important. ❑ *He stressed that the problem was not serious.*
2 N-COUNT/N-NONCOUNT Stress is also a noun. ❑ *Japanese car makers are putting more stress on overseas sales.*
3 N-COUNT/N-NONCOUNT If you feel under **stress**, you are worried because of difficulties in your life. ❑ *I cannot think clearly when I'm under stress.*
4 V-T LANGUAGE ARTS If you **stress** a word or a part of a word when you say it, you say it

S

slightly more loudly. ❏ *She stressed the words "very important."*

5 **N-COUNT/N-NONCOUNT** LANGUAGE ARTS **Stress** is also a noun. ❏ *The stress is on the first part of the word "animal."*

6 **N-COUNT/N-NONCOUNT** SCIENCE **Stresses** are strong physical pressures applied to an object.

→ look at Word Web: **emotion**

Word Partnership	Use **stress** with :
N	stress **the importance of** *something* **1** **anxiety and** stress, **effects of** stress, **job/work-related** stress, stress **management**, stress **reduction**, **response to** stress, **symptoms of** stress, stress **test** **2**
V	**cause** stress, **cope with** stress, **deal with** stress, **induce** stress, **reduce** stress **2**
ADJ	**emotional** stress, **excessive** stress, **high** stress, stress **related**, **severe** stress **2**

stressed /strɛst/ **ADJ** If you are **stressed**, you feel very worried because of difficulties in your life. ❏ *What situations make you feel stressed?*

stress|ful /strɛsfəl/ **ADJ** A **stressful** situation or experience can make you feel worried or upset. ❏ *I've got one of the most stressful jobs there is.*

stretch /strɛtʃ/ (**stretches, stretching, stretched**)

1 **V-I** Something that **stretches** over a distance covers all of it. ❏ *The line of cars stretched for several miles.*

2 **N-COUNT** A **stretch of** road, water, or land is a length or an area of it. ❏ *It's a very dangerous stretch of road.*

3 **V-T/V-I** When you **stretch**, you put your arms or legs out very straight. ❏ *He yawned and stretched.* ❏ *Try stretching your legs and pulling your toes upwards.*

4 **N-COUNT** **Stretch** is also a noun. ❏ *At the end of a workout do some slow stretches.*

5 **V-T/V-I** When something soft **stretches**, or **is stretched**, it becomes longer and thinner. ❏ *Can you feel your leg muscles stretching?* [from Old English]

▶ **stretch out** **1** If you **stretch out**, you lie with your legs and body in a straight line. ❏ *The bathtub was too small to stretch out in.*

2 If you **stretch out** a part of your body, you hold it out straight. ❏ *He stretched out his hand to touch me.*

Word Partnership	Use **stretch** with :
PREP	stretch **across** **1** **3** **along** a stretch **of road**, **down the road** a stretch **2**
N	stretch **of highway/road**, stretch **of a river** **2** stretch *your* **legs** **3**

stretch|er /strɛtʃər/ (**stretchers**) **N-COUNT** A **stretcher** is a long piece of strong material with a pole along each side, that is used for carrying an injured or sick person. ❏ *They put him on a stretcher and put him in the ambulance.* [from Old English]

strict /strɪkt/ (**stricter, strictest**)

1 **ADJ** A **strict** rule or order is very clear and must be obeyed completely. ❏ *She gave them strict instructions not to get out of the car.* ❏ *The school's rules are very strict.*

2 **ADJ** A **strict** person expects rules to be obeyed. ❏ *My parents were very strict.*

3 **ADJ** You use **strict** to describe someone who never does things that are against their beliefs. ❏ *Millions of Americans are now strict vegetarians.* [from Latin]

strict|ly /strɪktli/

1 **ADV** **Strictly** means in a way that is very precise and must be obeyed completely. ❏ *The number of new members each year is strictly controlled.*

2 **ADV** If someone deals with people **strictly**, they expect rules to be obeyed. ❏ *They brought their children up very strictly.*

3 **ADV** You use **strictly** to emphasize that something is of one particular type, or intended for one particular thing or person, rather than any other. ❏ *The trip was strictly business.* [from Latin]

stride /straɪd/ (**strides, striding, strode**)

1 **V-I** If you **stride** somewhere, you walk there with long steps. ❏ *The farmer came striding across the field.*

2 **N-COUNT** A **stride** is a long step that you take when you are walking or running. ❏ *He crossed the street with long, quick strides.*

3 **N-COUNT** If you **make strides** in something that you are doing, you make rapid progress in it. ❏ *The country has made great strides politically.* [from Old English]

Word Partnership	Use **stride** with :
V	**break** *(your)* stride, **lengthen** *your* stride **2**
ADJ	**long** stride **2**

strike /straɪk/ (**strikes, striking, struck**)

■ **v-T** If a person or a moving object **strikes** someone or something, they hit them. [FORMAL] ❑ *She took two steps forward and struck him across the face.* ❑ *His head struck the bottom when he dived into the pool.*

■ **v-T/v-I** Something that **strikes** has a quick and violent effect. ❑ *A storm struck the northeastern United States on Saturday.* ❑ *Lightning struck last night.*

■ **v-T** If an idea **strikes** you, it suddenly comes into your mind. ❑ *A thought struck her. Was she jealous of her mother?*

■ **v-T/v-I** When a clock **strikes**, it makes a sound so that people know what the time is. ❑ *The clock struck nine.* ❑ *Let's wait until the clock strikes.*

■ **v-T** When you **strike** a match, you make it produce a flame by moving it against something rough. ❑ *Robina struck a match and lit the fire.*

■ **N-COUNT** BUSINESS When there is a **strike**, workers stop working for a period of time, usually in order to try to get more money. ❑ *Staff at the hospital went on strike yesterday.*

■ **v-I** BUSINESS **Strike** is also a verb. ❑ *Workers have the right to strike.* [from Old English]

→ look at Word Web: **union**

▶ **strike out** SPORTS In baseball, if a batter **strikes out**, they fail three times to hit the ball and end their turn. ❑ *The third baseman struck out four times.*

strik|er /straɪkər/ (**strikers**) **N-COUNT** SPORTS In soccer and some other team sports, a **striker** is a player who mainly attacks and scores goals, rather than defends. ❑ *The striker scored a great goal.* [from Old English]

strik|ing /straɪkɪŋ/

■ **ADJ** Something that is **striking** is very noticeable or unusual. ❑ *The most striking feature of the garden is the swimming pool.*
● **strik|ing|ly** **ADV** ❑ *The two men were strikingly similar.*

■ **ADJ** Someone who is **striking** is very attractive, in a noticeable way. ❑ *She was a striking woman with long blonde hair.* [from Old English]

string /strɪŋ/ (**strings**)

■ **N-COUNT/N-NONCOUNT** **String** is thin rope that is made of twisted threads. ❑ *He held out a small bag tied with string.*

■ **N-COUNT** A **string of** things is a number of them on a piece of thread. ❑ *She wore a string of pearls around her neck.*

■ **N-COUNT** MUSIC The **strings** on a musical instrument are the thin pieces of wire that are stretched across it and that make sounds when the instrument is played. ❑ *He changed a guitar string.*

■ **N-PLURAL** MUSIC The **strings** are the section of an orchestra that consists of stringed instruments played with a bow. ❑ *The strings play this section of the music.* [from Old English]

→ look at Picture Dictionary: **strings**

→ look at Word Web: **orchestra**

stringed in|stru|ment /strɪŋd ɪnstrəmənt/ (**stringed instruments**) **N-COUNT** MUSIC A **stringed instrument** is any musical instrument that has strings.

strin|gent /strɪndʒ³nt/ **ADJ** **Stringent** laws, rules, or conditions are very severe or are strictly controlled. [FORMAL] ❑ *The tests were subject to stringent controls.* [from Latin]

S

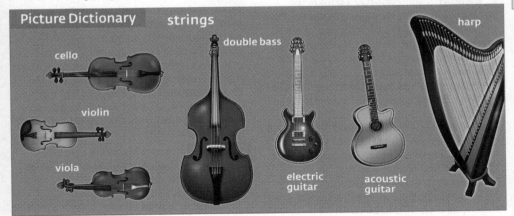

Picture Dictionary   strings

harp

cello

violin

viola

double bass

electric guitar

acoustic guitar

strip /strɪp/ (**strips, stripping, stripped**)

1 **N-COUNT** A **strip of** something is a long, narrow piece of it. ❑ *The rugs are made from strips of fabric.*

2 **N-COUNT** A **strip of** land or water is a long narrow area of it. ❑ *He owns a narrow strip of land along the coast.*

3 **V-I** If you **strip**, you take off your clothes. ❑ *They stripped and jumped into the pool.*

4 **Strip off** means the same as **strip**. ❑ *The children were stripping off and running into the ocean.*

5 **V-T** To **strip** someone **of** their property, rights, or titles means to take those things away from them. ❑ *They stripped us of our passports.* [Senses 1 and 2 from Middle Dutch. Senses 3, 4, and 5 from Old English.]

stripe /straɪp/ (**stripes**) **N-COUNT** A **stripe** is a long line that is a different color from the areas next to it. ❑ *She wore a blue skirt with white stripes.* [from Middle Dutch]

striped /straɪpt/ **ADJ** Something that is **striped** has stripes on it. ❑ *...a striped tie.* [from Middle Dutch]

strive /straɪv/ (**strives, striving, strove** or **strived, striven** or **strived**) **V-I** If you **strive to** do something or **strive for** something, you make a great effort to do it or get it. ❑ *He strives hard to keep himself fit.* [from Old French]

strode /stroʊd/ **Strode** is the past tense and past participle of **stride**. [from Old English]

stroke /stroʊk/ (**strokes, stroking, stroked**)

1 **V-T** If you **stroke** someone or something, you move your hand slowly and gently over them. ❑ *Carla was stroking her cat.*

2 **N-COUNT** If someone has a **stroke**, the blood does not flow through their brain properly, which may kill them or make them unable to move one side of their body. ❑ *He had a stroke last year, and now he can't walk.*

3 **N-COUNT** The **strokes** of a pen or a brush are the movements or marks that you make with it. ❑ *She added a few brush strokes to the painting.*

4 **N-COUNT** SPORTS **Strokes** are the repeated movements that you make with your arms when you are swimming. ❑ *I turned and swam a few strokes further out to sea.*

5 **N-SING** A **stroke of** luck is something lucky that happens. ❑ *It didn't rain, which was a stroke of luck.* [from Old English]

Word Partnership	Use **stroke** with :
v	**die from a** stroke, **have a** stroke, **suffer a** stroke **2**
N	**risk of a** stroke **2** stroke **of a pen 3**

stroll /stroʊl/ (**strolls, strolling, strolled**)

1 **V-I** If you **stroll** somewhere, you walk there in a slow, relaxed way. ❑ *We love strolling along by the river.*

2 **N-COUNT** **Stroll** is also a noun. ❑ *After dinner, I took a stroll around the city.* [from German] → look at Word Web: **park**

stroll|er /stroʊlər/ (**strollers**) **N-COUNT** A **stroller** is a small chair on wheels, that a small child can be pushed around in. [from German]

strong /strɔŋ/ (**stronger** /strɔŋgər/, **strongest** /strɔŋgɪst/)

1 **ADJ** Someone who is **strong** is healthy with good muscles. ❑ *I'm not strong enough to carry him.*

2 **ADJ** Someone who is **strong** is confident and determined. ❑ *You have to be strong and do what you believe is right.*

3 **ADJ** **Strong** objects or materials do not break easily. ❑ *This strong plastic will not crack.* ● **strong|ly** **ADV** ❑ *The wall was very strongly built.*

4 **ADJ** **Strong** means great in degree. ❑ *I have very strong feelings for my family.*

5 **ADJ** **Strong** opinions are very definite opinions that you are willing to express or defend. ❑ *She has strong views on environmental issues.* ● **strong|ly** **ADV** ❑ *Obviously you feel very strongly about this.*

6 **ADJ** Your **strong** points are your best qualities or talents. ❑ *Cooking is not Jeremy's strong point.*

7 **ADJ** A **strong** competitor, candidate, or team is likely to succeed. ❑ *This year we have a very strong team.*

8 **ADJ** A **strong** drink, chemical, or drug contains a lot of the particular substance that makes it effective. ❑ *...a cup of strong coffee.*

9 **ADJ** A **strong** flavor, smell, or light is easily noticed. ❑ *Onions have a strong flavor.* ● **strong|ly** **ADV** ❑ *He smelled strongly of sweat.* [from Old English]

Thesaurus	**strong** Also look up :
ADJ	mighty, powerful, tough; (*ant.*) weak **1** confident, determined; (*ant.*) cowardly **2** solid, sturdy **3**

struck /strʌk/ **Struck** is the past tense and past participle of **strike**. [from Old English]

struc|tur|al /strʌktʃərəl/ **ADJ Structural** means relating to or affecting the structure of something. ❑ *The bomb caused structural damage to the building.* ● **struc|tur|al|ly ADV** ❑ *When we bought the house, it was structurally in very good condition.* [from Latin]

struc|ture /strʌktʃər/ (**structures**)
1 N-COUNT/N-NONCOUNT The **structure of** something is the way in which it is made, built, or organized. ❑ *The typical family structure was two parents and two children.*
2 N-COUNT A **structure** is something that consists of parts that are connected together in an ordered way. ❑ *She had beautiful bone structure and great big eyes.* ❑ *Our experiences can change the structure of the brain.*
3 N-COUNT A **structure** is something that has been built. ❑ *This modern brick and glass structure was built in 1905.* [from Latin]

strug|gle /strʌgəl/ (**struggles, struggling, struggled**)
1 V-I If you **struggle to** do something, you try hard to do it, but you find it very difficult. ❑ *She struggled to find the right words.*
2 N-SING An action or activity that is **a struggle** is very difficult to do. ❑ *Losing weight was a terrible struggle.*
3 N-COUNT/N-NONCOUNT A **struggle** is a long and difficult attempt to achieve something such as freedom. ❑ *The movie is about a young boy's struggle to survive.*
4 V-I If you **struggle** when you are being held, you move violently in order to get free. ❑ *I struggled, but she was too strong for me.*

Word Partnership	Use **struggle** with :
N	struggle **for democracy**, struggle **for equality**, struggle **for freedom/ independence**, struggle **for survival** **1** **2** **power** struggle **2**
ADJ	**bitter** struggle, **internal** struggle, **long** struggle, **political** struggle, **uphill** struggle **2** **locked in a** struggle **3**

strum /strʌm/ (**strums, strumming, strummed**) **V-T** MUSIC If you **strum** a stringed instrument such as a guitar, you play it by moving your fingers backward and forward across the strings. ❑ *One man sat softly strumming a guitar.*

stub|born /stʌbərn/ **ADJ** Someone who is **stubborn** is determined to do what they want. ❑ *I am a very stubborn and determined person.* ● **stub|born|ly ADV** ❑ *He stubbornly refused to tell her the truth.*

stuck /stʌk/
1 Stuck is the past tense and past participle of **stick**.
2 ADJ If something is **stuck** in a particular position, it is unable to move. ❑ *His car got stuck in the snow.*
3 ADJ If you are **stuck** in a place or in a boring or unpleasant situation, you want to get away from it, but are unable to. ❑ *I don't want to get stuck in another job like that.*
4 ADJ If you get **stuck**, you are unable to continue doing something because it is too difficult. ❑ *The teacher will help if you get stuck.* [from Old English]

stu|dent /studᵊnt/ (**students**) **N-COUNT** A **student** is a person who is studying at a school, a college, or a university. ❑ *Warren's eldest son is an art student.* [from Latin]
→ look at Word Web: **graduation**

stu|dio /studiou/ (**studios**)
1 N-COUNT ARTS A **studio** is a room where someone paints, draws, or takes photographs. ❑ *She was in her studio, painting on a large canvas.*
2 N-COUNT ARTS A **studio** is a room where people make radio or television programs, record music, or make movies. ❑ *She's much happier performing in a recording studio.* [from Italian]
→ look at Word Web: **art**

Word Partnership	Use **studio** with :
N	studio **album**, studio **audience**, **music** studio, **recording** studio, **television/TV** studio **2**

study /stʌdi/ (**studies, studying, studied**)
1 V-T/V-I If you **study**, you spend time learning about a particular subject. ❑ *She spends most of her time studying.* ❑ *He studied History and Economics.*
2 N-COUNT/N-NONCOUNT Study is the activity of studying. ❑ *What is the study of earthquakes called?*
3 N-COUNT A **study** of a subject is a piece of research on it. ❑ *Recent studies suggest many new mothers suffer from depression.*
4 N-PLURAL You can talk about education in a particular subject as that type of **studies**.

❑ ...a center for Islamic studies.

5 **V-T** If you **study** something, you look at it or consider it very carefully. ❑ Debbie studied her friend's face.

6 **N-COUNT** A **study** is a room in a house that is used for reading, writing, and studying. ❑ We sat together in his study. [from Old French]
→ look at Word Web: **laboratory**

stuff /stʌf/ (**stuffs, stuffing, stuffed**)
1 **N-NONCOUNT** You can use **stuff** to talk about things in a general way. [INFORMAL] ❑ He pointed to a bag. "That's my stuff." ❑ There is a huge amount of useful stuff on the Internet.
2 **V-T** If you **stuff** something somewhere, you push it there quickly and roughly. ❑ I stuffed the dollar bills into my pocket.
3 **V-T** If you **stuff** food, you put a mixture of another type of food inside it. ❑ Stuff the turkey and put it in the oven for 3 hours. ❑ ...stuffed olives. [from Old French]

Thesaurus	stuff Also look up :
N	belongings, goods, material, substance **1**
V	crowd, fill, jam, squeeze **2** **3**

stuffy /stʌfi/ (**stuffier, stuffiest**) **ADJ** A room that is **stuffy** feels unpleasant because it is warm and there is not enough fresh air. ❑ It was hot and stuffy in the classroom. [from Old French]

stum|ble /stʌmbᵊl/ (**stumbles, stumbling, stumbled**) **V-I** If you **stumble**, you nearly fall down while you are walking or running. ❑ He stumbled and almost fell. [from Norwegian]
▸ **stumble across** or **stumble on** If you **stumble across** something or **stumble on** it, you find it or discover it unexpectedly. ❑ I stumbled across a good way of saving money.

stump /stʌmp/ (**stumps**) **N-COUNT** A **stump** is a small part of something that remains when the rest of it has been removed or broken off. ❑ ...a tree stump. [from Middle Low German]

stun /stʌn/ (**stuns, stunning, stunned**)
1 **V-T** If you **are stunned**, you are extremely shocked or surprised, so that you are unable to speak. ❑ We're stunned by today's news.
2 **V-T** If something **stuns** you, it makes you unconscious for a short time. ❑ The blow to his head stunned him. [from Old French]
3 → see also **stunning**

stung /stʌŋ/ **Stung** is the past tense and past participle of **sting**. [from Old English]

stunk /stʌŋk/ **Stunk** is a past tense and the past participle of **stink**. [from Old English]

stun|ning /stʌnɪŋ/
1 **ADJ** A **stunning** person or thing is extremely beautiful. ❑ She was 55 and still a stunning woman. [from Old French]
2 → see also **stun**

Word Partnership	Use stunning with :
N	stunning **blow**, stunning **defeat/loss**, stunning **images**, stunning **success**, stunning **upset**, stunning **victory**, stunning **views**

stunt /stʌnt/ (**stunts**) **N-COUNT** A **stunt** is a dangerous piece of action in a movie. ❑ Sean Connery did his own stunts.

stu|pid /stupɪd/ (**stupider, stupidest**) **ADJ** If someone or something is **stupid**, they are not at all sensible. ❑ I'll never do anything so stupid again. ❑ I made a stupid mistake.
● **stu|pid|ly** **ADV** ❑ I'm sorry. I behaved stupidly.
● **stu|pid|ity** /stupɪdɪti/ (**stupidities**) **N-COUNT/N-NONCOUNT** ❑ I was surprised by his stupidity. [from French]

Usage	stupid and ignorant

Be careful not to confuse *stupid* and *ignorant*. A *stupid* person isn't intelligent or sensible; an *ignorant* person doesn't know something but can be both intelligent and sensible nevertheless: *When Dayani first came to the United States, she was ignorant about many ordinary things, such as how to have electricity turned on in her apartment; her neighbors thought she was stupid and were very surprised to find out she was studying to be a doctor.*

Word Partnership	Use stupid with :
V	(don't) do anything/ *something* stupid, feel stupid, look stupid, think *something* is stupid
N	stupid idea, stupid man, stupid mistake, stupid question, stupid things

stur|dy /stɜrdi/ (**sturdier, sturdiest**) **ADJ** Someone or something that is **sturdy** looks strong and is unlikely to be easily hurt or damaged. ❑ She was a short, sturdy woman.
● **stur|di|ly** **ADV** ❑ The table was strong and sturdily built. [from Old French]

stut|ter /stʌtər/ (**stutters, stuttering, stuttered**)
1 **V-I** Someone who **stutters** has difficulty speaking because they find it hard to say the first sound of a word. ❑ "I...I'm sorry," he stuttered.

S

2 **N-SING** **Stutter** is also a noun. ❑ *He spoke with a stutter.* [from Middle Low German]

style /staɪl/ (**styles**)

1 **N-COUNT** The **style** of something is the way in which it is done. ❑ *Children have different learning styles.* ❑ *I prefer the Indian style of cooking.*

2 **N-NONCOUNT** If people or places have **style**, they are fashionable and elegant. ❑ *Everything about the club has style.*

3 **N-COUNT/N-NONCOUNT** The **style** of a product is its design. ❑ *These kids want everything in the latest style.*

4 **N-COUNT** ARTS The **style** of a writer, a painter, or other artist is the particular way that their work is constructed and the way that it differs from the work of other artists.

5 **N-COUNT** A **style** is a set of characteristics that defines a culture, a period, or a school of art. [from Latin]

Word Partnership	Use **style** with :
N	**leadership** style, **learning** style, style **of life**, **music** style, **prose** style, **writing** style **1**
	differences in style **1**–**3**
ADJ	**distinctive** style, **particular** style, **personal** style **1** **4**

styl|ish /staɪlɪʃ/ **ADJ** Someone or something that is **stylish** is attractive and fashionable. ❑ *She was an attractive, stylish woman.* [from Latin]

sty|lis|tic nu|ance /staɪlɪstɪk nuɑns/ (**stylistic nuances**) **N-COUNT/N-NONCOUNT** ARTS The **stylistic nuances** of an artistic performance or work are the small details in the way it is performed or constructed that give it a distinctive style.

sub|atom|ic /sʌbətɒmɪk/ **ADJ** SCIENCE A **subatomic** particle is a particle that is part of an atom, for example an electron, a proton, or a neutron.

sub|cul|ture /sʌbkʌltʃər/ (**subcultures**) **N-COUNT** SOCIAL STUDIES A **subculture** is the ideas, art, and way of life of a group of people within a society, which are different from the ideas, art, and way of life of the rest of the society. ❑ *...the latest American subculture.* [from Old French]
→ look at Word Web: **culture**

sub|ject (**subjects**, **subjecting**, **subjected**)

PRONUNCIATION HELP
Pronounce the noun and adjective /sʌbdʒɪkt/. Pronounce the verb /səbdʒɛkt/.

1 **N-COUNT** The **subject** of a conversation or a book is the thing that is being discussed. ❑ *I'd like to hear the president's own views on the subject.*

2 **N-COUNT** A **subject** is an area of knowledge that you study in school or college. ❑ *Math is my favorite subject.*

3 **N-COUNT** LANGUAGE ARTS In grammar, the **subject** is the noun that talks about the person or thing that is doing the action expressed by the verb. For example, in "My cat keeps catching birds," "my cat" is the subject.

4 **N-COUNT** ARTS The **subject** is the person or thing that is shown in a piece of art. ❑ *Spring flowers are a perfect subject for painting.*

5 **ADJ** To be **subject to** something means to be likely to be affected by it. ❑ *Prices may be subject to change.*

6 **V-T** If you **subject** someone **to** something unpleasant, you make them experience it. ❑ *He subjected her to a life of misery.*

7 **N-COUNT** SOCIAL STUDIES The people who live in a country, especially one ruled by a king or a queen, are the **subjects** of that country. ❑ *His subjects thought he was a good king.* [from Latin]

Word Partnership	Use **subject** with :
ADJ	**controversial** subject, **favorite** subject, **touchy** subject **1**
V	**change the** subject **1**
	broach a subject, **study a** subject **1** **2**
N	subject **of a debate**, subject **of an investigation** **1**
	knowledge of a subject **1** **2**
	subject **of a sentence**, subject **of a verb** **3**
PREP	subject **to approval**, subject **to availability**, subject **to laws**, subject **to scrutiny**, subject **to a tax** **5**

sub|jec|tive /səbdʒɛktɪv/ **ADJ** Something that is **subjective** is based on personal opinions and feelings rather than on facts. ❑ *Art is very subjective.* [from Latin]

sub|li|ma|tion /sʌblɪmeɪʃən/ (**sublimations**) **N-COUNT/N-NONCOUNT** SCIENCE **Sublimation** is the change that occurs when a solid substance becomes a gas without first becoming a liquid. [from Latin]

sub|ma|rine /sʌbmərin/ (**submarines**) **N-COUNT** A **submarine** is a type of ship that can travel below the surface of the ocean. ❑ *...a nuclear submarine.* [from Old French]
→ look at Word Web: **tsunami**

S

sub|mit /səbmɪt/ (**submits, submitting, submitted**)

■ **V-T** If you **submit** a proposal, a report, or a request, you formally send it to someone so that they can consider it. ❑ *They submitted their reports yesterday.*

■ **V-I** If you **submit to** something, you do it unwillingly. ❑ *Mrs. Jones submitted to an operation on her knee to relieve the pain.* [from Latin]

sub|scribe /səbskraɪb/ (**subscribes, subscribing, subscribed**)

■ **V-I** If you **subscribe to** an opinion or a belief, you are one of a number of people who have this opinion or belief. ❑ *I don't subscribe to the view that men are better than women.*

■ **V-I** If you **subscribe to** a magazine, a newspaper, or a service, you pay money regularly to receive it. ❑ *Why do you subscribe to "New Scientist?"* ● **sub|scrib|er** (**subscribers**) **N-COUNT** ❑ *I am a subscriber to "Newsweek."* ❑ *China has millions of subscribers to cable television.* [from Latin]

sub|script /sʌbskrɪpt/ (**subscripts**) **N-COUNT** MATH SCIENCE In chemistry and mathematics, a **subscript** is a number or a symbol that is written below another number or symbol and to the right of it, for example the "2" in H_2O.

sub|scrip|tion /səbskrɪpʃən/ (**subscriptions**) **N-COUNT** A **subscription** is an amount of money that you pay regularly in order to belong to an organization or to receive a service. ❑ *Members pay a subscription every year.*

sub|se|quent /sʌbsɪkwənt/ **ADJ** You use **subsequent** to describe something that happened or existed after the time or event that has just been referred to. [FORMAL] ❑ *...the increase of prices in subsequent years.* ● **sub|se|quent|ly** **ADV** ❑ *He subsequently worked in Canada.* [from Latin]

sub|side /səbsaɪd/ (**subsides, subsiding, subsided**)

■ **V-I** If a feeling or a noise **subsides**, it becomes less strong or loud. ❑ *The pain subsided during the night.*

■ **V-I** If the ground or a building **is subsiding**, it is very slowly sinking to a lower level. ❑ *Is the whole house subsiding?* [from Latin]

sub|sidi|ary /səbsɪdiɛri/ (**subsidiaries**)

■ **N-COUNT** BUSINESS A **subsidiary** or a **subsidiary** company is a company that is part of a larger and more important

company. ❑ *WM Financial Services is a subsidiary of Washington Mutual.*

■ **ADJ** If something is **subsidiary**, it is less important than something else with which it is connected. ❑ *The marketing department plays a subsidiary role to the sales department.* [from Latin]

sub|si|dize /sʌbsɪdaɪz/ (**subsidizes, subsidizing, subsidized**) **V-T** If a government or other authority **subsidizes** something, they pay part of the cost of it. ❑ *The government subsidizes farming.* ● **sub|si|dized** **ADJ** ❑ *...subsidized prices for housing, bread, and meat.* [from Latin]

sub|si|dy /sʌbsɪdi/ (**subsidies**) **N-COUNT** A **subsidy** is money that a government pays in order to help an industry or a business. ❑ *...farm subsidies.* [from Latin]

sub|species /sʌbspiʃiz/ (**subspecies**) also **sub-species** **N-COUNT** A **subspecies of** a plant or an animal is one of the types that a particular species is divided into. [from Latin]

sub|stance /sʌbstəns/ (**substances**) **N-COUNT** SCIENCE A **substance** is a solid, a powder, a liquid, or a gas. ❑ *The waste contained several unpleasant substances.* [from Old French]

Word Partnership	Use **substance** with :
ADJ	**banned** substance, **chemical** substance, **natural** substance

sub|stan|tial /səbstænʃəl/ **ADJ** **Substantial** means very large. [FORMAL] ❑ *A substantial number of people disagree with the new plan.* [from Middle English]

Word Partnership	Use **substantial** with :
N	substantial **amount**, substantial **changes**, substantial **evidence**, substantial **increase**, substantial **loss**, substantial **number**, substantial **part**, substantial **savings**, substantial **support**
ADV	**fairly** substantial, **very** substantial

sub|stan|ti|ate /səbstænʃieɪt/ (**substantiates, substantiating, substantiated**) **V-T** To **substantiate** a statement or a story means to supply evidence that proves that it is true. [FORMAL] ❑ *Most research substantiates the idea that the Earth is getting warmer.* [from New Latin]

sub|sti|tute /sʌbstɪtut/ (**substitutes, substituting, substituted**)

1 **V-T/V-I** If you **substitute** one thing **for** another, it takes the place of the other thing. ❑ *You can substitute wholewheat flour for white flour.* ❑ *Will you substitute for me?*

2 **N-COUNT** A **substitute** is something that you use or have instead of something else. ❑ *They are using calculators as a substitute for thinking.*

3 **N-COUNT** SPORTS In team games, a **substitute** is a player who comes into a game to replace another player. ❑ *Jefferson entered as a substitute for the injured player.* [from Latin]

sub|text /sʌbtɛkst/ (**subtexts**)
N-COUNT/N-NONCOUNT The **subtext** of something that is said or written is the message or subject that is suggested but not stated clearly. [from Medieval Latin]

sub|tle /sʌtªl/ (**subtler, subtlest**)

1 **ADJ** Something that is **subtle** is not immediately obvious. ❑ *Subtle changes take place in all living things.* ● **sub|tly** **ADV** ❑ *The truth is subtly different.*

2 **ADJ** **Subtle** smells, tastes, sounds, or colors are pleasant and delicate. ❑ *Brown, gray, or subtle shades of purple are best.* [from Old French]

sub|tract /səbtrækt/ (**subtracts, subtracting, subtracted**) **V-T** MATH If you **subtract** one number **from** another, you take it away from the other number. For example, if you subtract 3 from 5, you get 2. ● **sub|trac|tion** /səbtrækʃ°n/ (**subtractions**) **N-COUNT/N-NONCOUNT** ❑ *She's ready to learn subtraction.* [from Latin]
→ look at Picture Dictionary: **fractions**
→ look at Word Web: **mathematics**

sub|trac|tive sculp|ture /səbtræktɪv skʌlptʃər/ (**subtractive sculptures**) **N-COUNT/ N-NONCOUNT** ARTS **Subtractive sculpture** is sculpture that is created by removing material such as clay or wax until the sculpture is complete. Compare with **additive**.

sub|tropical /sʌbtrɒpɪk°l/ **ADJ** SCIENCE **Subtropical** places have a climate that is warm and wet, and are often near tropical regions. ❑ *...the subtropical region of the Chapare.*

Word Link **urb ≈ city : suburb, suburban, urban**

sub|urb /sʌbɜrb/ (**suburbs**) **N-COUNT**
The **suburbs of** a city are the areas on the edge of it where people live. ❑ *Anna was born in a suburb of Philadelphia.* ❑ *His family lives in the*

suburbs. [from Latin]
→ look at Word Webs: **city, transportation**

sub|ur|ban /səbɜrbən/ **ADJ** **Suburban** means relating to the suburbs. ❑ *They have a comfortable suburban home.* [from Latin]

Word Link **verg, vert ≈ turning : converge, diverge, subvert**

sub|vert /səbvɜrt/ (**subverts, subverting, subverted**) **V-T** To **subvert** something means to destroy its power and influence. [FORMAL] ❑ *...a plan to subvert the state.*

sub|way /sʌbweɪ/ (**subways**) **N-COUNT**
A **subway** is a railroad system that runs under the ground. ❑ *I don't ride the subway late at night.* [from Old English]
→ look at Word Web: **transportation**

suc|ceed /səksid/ (**succeeds, succeeding, succeeded**)

1 **V-I** If you **succeed**, you get the result that you wanted. ❑ *We have already succeeded in starting our own company.* ❑ *Do you think he will succeed?*

2 **V-T** If you **succeed** another person, you are the next person to have their job. ❑ *David Rowland will succeed him as chairman.* [from Latin]

Thesaurus	succeed	Also look up :
V	accomplish, conquer, master; (ant.) fail **1**	
	displace, replace; (ant.) precede **2**	

suc|cess /səksɛs/ (**successes**)

1 **N-NONCOUNT** **Success** is doing well and getting the result that you wanted. ❑ *Hard work is the key to success.* ❑ *We were surprised by the play's success.*

2 **N-COUNT** Someone or something that is a **success** does very well, or is admired very much. ❑ *We hope the movie will be a success.* [from Latin]

Word Partnership	Use success with :
N	success of a business **1** chance for/of success, success or failure, key to success, measure of success **1** **2**
V	achieve success, success depends on something, enjoy success **1** **2**
ADJ	great success, huge success, recent success **1** **2**

suc|cess|ful /səksɛsfəl/ **ADJ** Someone or something that is **successful** does or gets what they wanted. ❑ *How successful will this new treatment be?* ● **suc|cess|ful|ly** **ADV** ❑ *The disease can be successfully treated with drugs.* [from Latin]

suc|ces|sion /səksɛʃ°n/ (**successions**)

1 **N-SING** A **succession of** things of the same kind is a number of them that exist or happen one after the other. ❑ *Adams took a succession of jobs.*

2 **N-NONCOUNT** **Succession** is the act or right of being the next person to have an important job or position. ❑ *He became king in succession to his father.* [from Latin]

suc|ces|sive /səksɛsɪv/ **ADJ** **Successive** means happening or existing one after another without a break. ❑ *Jackson was the winner for a second successive year.* [from Latin]

suc|ces|sor /səksɛsər/ (**successors**)
N-COUNT Someone's **successor** is the person who takes their job after they have left. ❑ *His successor is Dr. John Todd.* [from Latin]

suc|cumb /səkʌm/ (**succumbs, succumbing, succumbed**) **V-I** If you **succumb to** temptation or pressure, you do something that you want to do, or that other people want you to do, although you feel it might be wrong. [FORMAL] ❑ *Don't succumb to the temptation of just one more piece of cake.* [from Latin]

such /sʌtʃ/

> **LANGUAGE HELP**
> When **such** is used as a predeterminer, it is followed by "a" and a count noun in the singular. When it is used as a determiner, it is followed by a count noun in the plural or by an uncountable noun.

1 **DET** **Such** means like this or like that. ❑ *How could you do such a thing?* ❑ *We each have an account. Such individual accounts are held at the local post office.*

2 **DET** You use **such** before a noncount or plural noun to make what you are saying stronger. ❑ *These roads are not designed for such heavy traffic.*

3 **PREDET** You use **such a** or **such an** before a noun to make what you are saying stronger. ❑ *It was such a pleasant surprise.*

4 **DET** You use **such as** to introduce an example. ❑ *Avoid fatty food such as butter and red meat.* [from Old English]

suck /sʌk/ (**sucks, sucking, sucked**)
1 **V-T/V-I** If you **suck** something, you hold it in your mouth for a long time. ❑ *The baby sucked on his bottle of milk.* ❑ *Many young children suck their thumbs.*

2 **V-T/V-I** If you **suck** a liquid, you pull it into your mouth through your lips. ❑ *The baby sucked the milk from his bottle.* ❑ *Are you able to suck quietly?* [from Old English]

suck|er /sʌkər/ (**suckers**)
1 **N-COUNT** If you call someone a **sucker**, you mean that it is very easy to cheat them. [INFORMAL] ❑ *Poor Lionel! What a sucker.*

2 **N-COUNT** If you describe someone as a **sucker for** something, you mean that they find it very difficult to resist it. [INFORMAL] ❑ *I'm such a sucker for romance.*

3 **N-COUNT** SCIENCE The **suckers** on some animals and insects are the parts on the outside of their body that they use in order to stick to a surface. [from Old English]

sud|den /sʌd°n/
1 **ADJ** **Sudden** means happening quickly and unexpectedly. ❑ *He was shocked by the sudden death of his father.* ❑ *It was all very sudden.*
● **sud|den|ly** **ADV** ❑ *Suddenly, she looked ten years older.* ❑ *Her expression suddenly changed.*

2 **PHRASE** If something happens **all of a sudden**, it happens quickly and unexpectedly. ❑ *All of a sudden she didn't look tired anymore.* [from French]

su|do|ku /sudoʊku/ (**sudokus**)
N-COUNT/N-NONCOUNT **Sudoku** is a type of puzzle in which certain numbers must be arranged within a grid. The aim is to avoid repeating any number in the same row or column. [from Japanese]

sue /su/ (**sues, suing, sued**) **V-T/V-I** If you **sue** someone, you start a legal case against them, usually in order to get money from them because they have harmed you. ❑ *The couple are suing the company for $4.4 million.* ❑ *The company could be sued for damages.* [from Old French]

suf|fer /sʌfər/ (**suffers, suffering, suffered**)
1 **V-T/V-I** If you **suffer**, you feel pain, sadness, or worry. ❑ *She was very sick, and suffering great pain.* ❑ *He has suffered terribly the last few days.*

2 **V-I** If you **suffer from** an illness, you are affected by it. ❑ *He was suffering from cancer.*
● **suf|fer|er** (**sufferers**) **N-COUNT** ❑ *...asthma sufferers.*

3 **V-T** If you **suffer** something bad, something bad happens to you. ❑ *They could suffer complete defeat.*

4 **V-I** If you **suffer**, you are badly affected by an event or a situation. ❑ *It is the children who suffer.* [from Old French]

S

suf|fer|ing /sʌfərɪŋ/ (**sufferings**) **N-COUNT/ N-NONCOUNT** Suffering is pain, sadness, or worry that someone feels. ❑ *They began to recover from their pain and suffering.* [from Old French]

suf|fi|cient /səfɪʃ°nt/ **ADJ** If something is **sufficient for** a particular purpose, there is enough of it for the purpose. ❑ *The food we have is sufficient for 12 people.* ●**suf|fi|cient|ly ADV** ❑ *She recovered sufficiently to go on vacation.* [from Latin]

Word Link	fix ≈ fastening : fixture, prefix, suffix

suf|fix /sʌfɪks/ (**suffixes**) **N-COUNT** LANGUAGE ARTS A **suffix** is a letter or a group of letters, for example "-ly" or "-ness," that is added to the end of a word in order to form a different word, often of a different word class. For example, the suffix "-ly" is added to "quick" to form "quickly." Compare with **prefix**. [from New Latin]

suf|fo|cate /sʌfəkeɪt/ (**suffocates, suffocating, suffocated**) **V-T/V-I** If someone **suffocates**, or **is suffocated**, they die because there is no air for them to breathe. ❑ *He either suffocated, or froze to death.* [from Latin]

suf|fra|gist /sʌfrədʒɪst/ (**suffragists**) **N-COUNT** SOCIAL STUDIES A **suffragist** is a person who believes that all adults in a particular country should have the right to vote. Suffragists often fight for women to be allowed to vote. [from Latin]

sug|ar /ʃʊgər/ (**sugars**)
■ **N-NONCOUNT** Sugar is a sweet substance that is used for making food and drinks taste sweet. ❑ *Do you take sugar in your coffee?* ❑ *...a cup of brown sugar.*
■ **N-COUNT** If someone has one **sugar** in

their tea or coffee, they have one small spoon of sugar in it. ❑ *How many sugars do you take?*
■ **N-COUNT** SCIENCE Sugars are substances that occur naturally in food. When you eat them, the body converts them into energy. [from Old French]
→ look at Word Web: **sugar**

sug|gest /səgdʒɛst/ (**suggests, suggesting, suggested**)
■ **V-T** If you **suggest** something, you tell someone what you think they should do. ❑ *I suggest you ask him some questions about his past.* ❑ *I suggested we go for a walk in the park.*
■ **V-T** If you **suggest that** something is true, you say something that you believe is true. ❑ *It is wrong to suggest that there is an easy solution.* [from Latin]

Word Partnership	Use suggest with :
N	**analysts** suggest, **experts** suggest, **researchers** suggest ■ ■

sug|ges|tion /səgdʒɛstʃ°n/ (**suggestions**)
■ **N-COUNT** If you make a **suggestion**, you tell someone what you think they should do. ❑ *Do you have any suggestions for improving the service we provide?*
■ **N-COUNT** A **suggestion** is an opinion that someone gives. ❑ *We reject any suggestion that the law needs changing.* [from Latin]

Word Partnership	Use suggestion with :
V	**follow a** suggestion, **make a** suggestion ■ **reject a** suggestion ■ ■

sui|cide /suɪsaɪd/ (**suicides**) **N-COUNT/N-NONCOUNT** Suicide is the act of killing yourself. ❑ *She tried to commit suicide several times.* ❑ *It was obviously a case of attempted suicide.* [from New Latin]

S

Sugar cane was discovered in prehistoric New Guinea*. As people migrated across the Pacific islands and into India and China, they brought sugar cane with them. At first, people just chewed on the cane. They liked the **sweet taste**. When sugar cane reached the Middle East, people discovered how to **refine** it into **crystals**. **Brown sugar** is created by stopping the refining process earlier. This leaves some of the molasses syrup in the sugar. Today two-fifths of sugar comes from **beets**. Refined sugar is used in many **foods** and **beverages**. Too much sugar can cause health problems, such as **obesity** and **diabetes**.

New Guinea: a large island in the southern Pacific Ocean.

sui|cide bomb|er (suicide bombers)
N-COUNT A **suicide bomber** is a terrorist who carries out a bomb attack, knowing that he or she will be killed in the explosion. ❏ *The blast was caused by a suicide bomber.*

suit /su̱t/ (suits, suiting, suited)
1 **N-COUNT** A **suit** consists of a jacket and pants or a skirt that are made from the same cloth. ❏ *...a dark business suit.*
2 **N-COUNT** A particular type of **suit** is a piece of clothing that you wear for a particular activity. ❏ *The divers wore special rubber suits.*
3 **V-T** If something **suits** you, it makes you look attractive. ❏ *Green suits you.* ❏ *Isabel's soft woolen dress suited her very well.*
4 **V-T** If something **suits** you, it is convenient for you. ❏ *With online shopping, you can do your shopping when it suits you.*
5 **N-COUNT** A **suit** is one of the four types of card in a set of playing cards. These are hearts, diamonds, clubs, and spades. [from Old French]
6 → see also **pantsuit**
→ look at Picture Dictionary: **clothing**

suit|able /su̱təbªl/ **ADJ** Someone or something that is **suitable for** a particular purpose or occasion is right for it. ❏ *This film would be suitable for children 8-13 years.*
● **suit|ably** **ADV** ❏ *He was suitably dressed for the occasion.* [from French]

suit|case /su̱tkeɪs/ (suitcases) **N-COUNT**
A **suitcase** is a case for carrying your clothes when you are traveling. ❏ *It did not take Andrew long to pack a suitcase.*

suite /swi̱t/ (suites)
1 **N-COUNT** A **suite** is a set of rooms in a hotel or other building. ❏ *They stayed in a suite at the Paris Hilton.*
2 **N-COUNT** MUSIC A **suite** is a piece of instrumental music consisting of several short, related sections. [from French]
→ look at Word Web: **hotel**

sul|fur /su̱lfər/ **N-NONCOUNT** SCIENCE Sulfur is a yellow chemical that has a strong smell. ❏ *Burning sulfur creates an unpleasant smell.* [from Old French]
→ look at Word Web: **fireworks**

sulk /su̱lk/ (sulks, sulking, sulked) **V-I** If you **sulk**, you are silent for a while because you are angry about something. ❏ *He turned his back and sulked.* ● **sulk|y** **ADJ** ❏ *I was a sulky, 14-year-old teenager.*

sum /su̱m/ (sums, summing, summed)
1 **N-COUNT** A **sum of** money is an amount of money. ❏ *Large sums of money were lost.*
2 **N-SING** MATH In mathematics, **the sum of** two or more numbers is the number that is obtained when they are added together. ❏ *Fourteen is the sum of eight and six.* [from Old French]
▸ **sum up** If you **sum** something **up**, you describe it as briefly as possible. ❏ *Can you sum up the story in a few words?*

sum|ma|rize /su̱məraɪz/ (summarizes, summarizing, summarized) **V-T/V-I** If you **summarize** something, you give the most important points about it. ❏ *Now summarize the article in three sentences.* ❏ *To summarize, this is a clever solution to the problem.* [from Latin]

sum|mary /su̱məri/ (summaries) **N-COUNT**
LANGUAGE ARTS A **summary of** something is a short description of it, that gives the main points but not the details. ❏ *Here is a short summary of the process.* [from Latin]

sum|mer /su̱mər/ (summers)
N-COUNT/N-NONCOUNT Summer is the season between spring and fall, when the weather is usually warm or hot. ❏ *I flew to Maine this summer.* ❏ *They are getting married in the summer.* [from Old English]

sum|mit /su̱mɪt/ (summits)
1 **N-COUNT** SOCIAL STUDIES A **summit** is a meeting between the leaders of two or more countries. ❏ *The topic will be discussed at next week's Washington summit.*
2 **N-COUNT** GEOGRAPHY The **summit** of a mountain is the top of it. ❏ *He wanted to be the first man to reach the summit of Mount Everest.* [from Old French]
→ look at Picture Dictionary: **mountain**

sum|mon /su̱mən/ (summons, summoning, summoned)
1 **V-T** If you **summon** someone, you order them to come to you. [FORMAL] ❏ *Suddenly we*

were summoned to his office.

2 **v-t** If you **summon** courage or energy, you make a great effort to have it. ❑ *It took her a month to summon the courage to tell her mother.*

3 **Summon up** means the same as **summon**. ❑ *He finally summoned up courage to ask her to a game.* [from Latin]

sun /sʌn/

1 **N-SING** SCIENCE **The sun** is the ball of fire in the sky that gives us heat and light. ❑ *The sun was now high in the sky.* ❑ *Suddenly, the sun came out.*

2 **N-NONCOUNT** **The sun** is the heat and light that comes from the sun. ❑ *They went outside to sit in the sun.* [from Old English]

→ look at Picture Dictionary: **solar system**
→ look at Word Webs: **sun, astronomer, earth, eclipse, navigation, solar, star**

sun|bathe /sʌnbeɪð/ (**sunbathes, sunbathing, sunbathed**) **v-i** When people **sunbathe**, they sit or lie in a place where the sun shines on them, so that their skin becomes browner. ❑ *Frank swam and sunbathed at the pool every morning.* ● **sun|bath|ing** **N-NONCOUNT** ❑ *The beach is perfect for sunbathing.*

sun|burn /sʌnbɜrn/ (**sunburns**) **N-COUNT/ N-NONCOUNT** If someone has **sunburn**, their skin is pink and sore because they have spent too much time in the sun. ❑ *Sunburn can damage your skin.*
→ look at Word Web: **skin**

sun|burned /sʌnbɜrnd/ or **sunburnt** **ADJ** Someone who is **sunburned** has pink, sore skin because they have spent too much time in the sun. ❑ *A sunburned face is extremely painful.*

Sun|day /sʌndeɪ, -di/ (**Sundays**) **N-COUNT/ N-NONCOUNT** **Sunday** is the day after Saturday and before Monday. ❑ *We went for a drive on Sunday.* ❑ *The store is closed Sundays.* [from Old English]

sun|down /sʌndaʊn/ **N-NONCOUNT** **Sundown** is the time when the sun sets. ❑ *We got home about two hours after sundown.*

sun|flower /sʌnflaʊər/ (**sunflowers**) **N-COUNT** A **sunflower** is a very tall plant with large yellow flowers.

sung /sʌŋ/ **Sung** is the past participle of **sing**. [from Old English]

sun|glasses /sʌnglæsɪz/
N-PLURAL **Sunglasses** are dark glasses that you wear to protect your eyes from bright light. ❑ *...a pair of sunglasses.* **sunglasses**

sunk /sʌŋk/ **Sunk** is the past participle of **sink**. [from Old English]

Word Link	light ≈ shining : day**light**, en**light**en, sun**light**

sun|light /sʌnlaɪt/ **N-NONCOUNT** **Sunlight** is the light that comes from the sun. ❑ *Sunlight filled the room.*
→ look at Word Webs: **habitat, photosynthesis, rainbow, skin, sun**

sun|ny /sʌni/ (**sunnier, sunniest**)
1 **ADJ** When it is **sunny**, the sun shines brightly. ❑ *The weather was warm and sunny.*
2 **ADJ** **Sunny** places are brightly lit by the sun. ❑ *...a sunny window seat.* [from Old English]

sun|rise /sʌnraɪz/ (**sunrises**)
1 **N-NONCOUNT** **Sunrise** is the time in the morning when the sun first appears in the sky. ❑ *The rain began before sunrise.*
2 **N-COUNT** A **sunrise** is the colors and light that you see in the sky when the sun first appears. ❑ *There was a beautiful sunrise yesterday morning.*

sun|screen /sʌnskrin/ (**sunscreens**)
N-COUNT/N-NONCOUNT **Sunscreen** is a cream that protects your skin from the sun. ❑ *Use sunscreen when you go outside.*
→ look at Word Web: **skin**

S

Word Web sun

The **sun's** core contains **hydrogen** atoms. These atoms combine to form helium. This process is called **fusion**. It makes the core very hot. The **corona** is a layer of hot, glowing gases surrounding the sun. Large flames also burn on the surface of the sun. They are called solar flares. **Infrared** and **ultraviolet** light are **invisible** parts of **sunlight**.

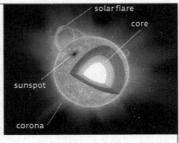

sun|set /sʌnsɛt/ (**sunsets**)

1 **N-NONCOUNT** Sunset is the time in the evening when the sun goes down. ❑ *The party began at sunset.*

2 **N-COUNT** A sunset is the colors and light that you see in the sky when the sun disappears in the evening. ❑ *There was a red sunset over Paris.*

sun|shine /sʌnʃaɪn/ **N-NONCOUNT** Sunshine is the light and heat that comes from the sun. ❑ *She was sitting outside in bright sunshine.*

sun|spot /sʌnspɒt/ (**sunspots**) **N-COUNT** SCIENCE Sunspots are dark cool patches that appear on the surface of the sun and last for about a week.

sun|tan /sʌntæn/ (**suntans**) **N-COUNT** If you have a **suntan**, the sun has made your skin darker. ❑ *They want to go abroad and get a suntan.* → look at Word Web: **skin**

su|per /supər/

1 **ADV** Super shows that someone or something has a lot of a particular quality. ❑ *...Beverly Hills, home of the rich and the super rich.*

2 **ADJ** Super shows that someone or something is larger or better than others. ❑ *My favorite characters were super heroes like Batman and Wonder Woman.* [from Latin]

su|perb /supɜrb/ **ADJ** If something is **superb**, it is very good. ❑ *There is a superb golf course 6 miles away.* ● **su|perb|ly** **ADV** ❑ *The orchestra played superbly.* [from Old French]

super|cell /supərsɛl/ (**supercells**) **N-COUNT** SCIENCE A supercell is a powerful thunderstorm that often produces tornadoes.

Word Link	super ≈ above : super*ficial*, super*natural*, super*power*

super|fi|cial /supərfɪʃ°l/

1 **ADJ** If you describe someone as **superficial**, you disapprove of them because they do not think deeply, and have little understanding of anything serious or important. ❑ *This guy is superficial and stupid.* ● **super|fi|cial|ity** /supərfɪʃiæliti/ **N-NONCOUNT** ❑ *...the superficiality of Hollywood.*

2 **ADJ** If you describe something such as an action, a feeling, or a relationship as **superficial**, you mean that it includes only the simplest and most obvious aspects of that thing, and not those aspects which require more effort to deal with or understand. ❑ *He gave the newspaper a superficial look.* ● **super|fi|cial|ity**

N-NONCOUNT ❑ *...the superficiality of the music business.* ● **super|fi|cial|ly** **ADV** ❑ *The movie deals with these questions, but only superficially.*

3 **ADJ** Superficial injuries are not very serious, and affect only the surface of the body. You can also describe damage to an object as **superficial**. ❑ *He escaped the crash with superficial injuries.*

super|flu|ous /supɜrfluəs/ **ADJ** Something that is **superfluous** is unnecessary or is no longer needed. ❑ *My presence at the meeting was superfluous.*

su|per|food /supərfuːd/ (**superfoods**) **N-COUNT** A superfood is a food that is considered to be very good for your health. ❑ *...superfoods, such as pomegranates and broccoli.*

super|gi|ant /supərdʒaɪənt/ (**supergiants**) **N-COUNT** SCIENCE A supergiant is a very large, bright star.

Word Link	ent ≈ one who does, has : depend*ent*, resid*ent*, superintend*ent*

super|in|ten|dent /supərɪntɛndənt, suprɪn-/ (**superintendents**)

1 **N-COUNT** A superintendent is a person who is responsible for the work of a particular department in an organization. ❑ *He became superintendent of the bank's East African branches.*

2 **N-COUNT** A superintendent is a person whose job is to take care of a large building such as an apartment building. ❑ *The superintendent opened the door with one of his keys.*

su|peri|or /supɪəriər/

1 **ADJ** Someone or something that is **superior** is better than other similar people or things. ❑ *We want to create superior products for our customers.* ❑ *...superior quality coffee.* ● **su|peri|or|ity** /supɪəriɔriti/ **N-NONCOUNT** ❑ *Belonging to a powerful organization gives them a feeling of superiority.*

2 **N-COUNT** BUSINESS Your **superior** at work is a person who has a higher position than you. ❑ *They do not have much communication with their superiors.*

Word Partnership	Use superior with :
ADV	**far** superior, **morally** superior, **vastly** superior **1**
N	superior **performance**, superior **quality**, superior **service** **1**

super|la|tive /supɜrlətɪv/ (**superlatives**)

1 **ADJ** LANGUAGE ARTS In grammar, the

superlative form of an adjective or an adverb is the form that shows that something has more of a quality than anything else in a group. For example, "biggest" is the superlative form of "big." Compare with **comparative**.
2 **N-COUNT** LANGUAGE ARTS **Superlative** is also a noun. ❑ *His writing contains many superlatives.*

super|mar|ket /sˈupərmɑrkɪt/ (**supermarkets**) **N-COUNT** A **supermarket** is a large store that sells all kinds of food and other products for the home. ❑ *Most of us do our food shopping in the supermarket.*

super|natu|ral /sˈupərnˈætʃərəl, -nˈætʃrəl/
1 **ADJ** **Supernatural** creatures, forces, and events are believed by some people to exist or happen, although they are impossible according to scientific laws. ❑ *These evil spirits had supernatural powers.*
2 **N-SING** **The supernatural** is things that are supernatural. ❑ *He writes stories about the supernatural.*

super|no|va /sˈupərnˈouvə/ (**supernovas** or **supernovae** /sˈupərnˈouvi/) **N-COUNT** SCIENCE A **supernova** is an exploding star.

super|pow|er /sˈupərpaʊər/ (**superpowers**) **N-COUNT** SOCIAL STUDIES A **superpower** is a very powerful and influential country, usually one that is rich and has nuclear weapons. ❑ *The United States is a military and economic superpower.*

super|size /sˈupərsaɪz/ (**supersizes, supersizing, supersized**)
1 **ADJ** **Supersize** or **supersized** things are very large. ❑ *...a supersize portion of fries.* ❑ *...a supersized mug of coffee.*
2 **V-T** If a fast-food restaurant **supersizes** a portion of food, it offers the customer a larger portion. ❑ *Fast-food restaurants encourage people to supersize their orders.*

super|sti|tion /sˈupərstˈɪʃᵊn/ (**superstitions**) **N-COUNT/N-NONCOUNT** A **superstition** is a belief that things such as good and bad luck exist, even though they cannot be explained. ❑ *Many people have superstitions about numbers.*

super|sti|tious /sˈupərstˈɪʃəs/ **ADJ** People who are **superstitious** believe in things that cannot be explained. ❑ *Jean was superstitious and believed that the color green brought bad luck.*

super|vise /sˈupərvaɪz/ (**supervises, supervising, supervised**) **V-T** If you **supervise** an activity or a person, you make sure that the activity is done correctly. ❑ *She cooks the supper, supervises the children's homework, and puts them to bed.* ● **super|vi|sion** /sˈupərvˈɪʒᵊn/ **N-NONCOUNT** ❑ *Young children need close supervision.* ● **super|vi|sor** (**supervisors**) **N-COUNT** ❑ *He got a job as a supervisor at a factory.*

sup|per /sˈʌpər/ (**suppers**) **N-COUNT/N-NONCOUNT** **Supper** is a meal that people eat in the evening. ❑ *Would you like to join us for supper?* [from Old French] → look at Word Web: **meal**

sup|plement /sˈʌpləmənt/ (**supplements, supplementing, supplemented**)
1 **V-T** If you **supplement** something, you add something to it in order to improve it. ❑ *Some people do extra jobs to supplement their incomes.*
2 **N-COUNT** **Supplement** is also a noun. ❑ *These classes are a supplement to school study.* [from Latin]

sup|pli|er /səplˈaɪər/ (**suppliers**) **N-COUNT** BUSINESS A **supplier** is a company that sells goods or equipment to customers. ❑ *We are one of the country's biggest food suppliers.* [from Old French]

sup|ply /səplˈaɪ/ (**supplies, supplying, supplied**)
1 **V-T** If you **supply** someone with something, you give them an amount of it. ❑ *The pipeline will supply Greece with Russian natural gas.*
2 **N-COUNT/N-NONCOUNT** A **supply** of something is an amount of it that is available for people to use. ❑ *The brain needs a constant supply of oxygen.*
3 **N-PLURAL** **Supplies** are food, equipment, and other important things that are provided for people. ❑ *What happens when there are no more food supplies?* [from Old French]

Word Partnership	Use **supply** with :
N	supply **electricity**, supply **equipment**, supply **information** **1**
ADJ	**abundant** supply, **large** supply, **limited** supply **2**

sup|port /səpˈɔrt/ (**supports, supporting, supported**)
1 **V-T** If you **support** someone or their ideas, you agree with them, and perhaps help

S

them because you want them to succeed. ❑ *We haven't found any evidence to support that idea.* ● **sup|port|er** (**supporters**) **N-COUNT** ❑ *...the president's supporters.*

2 **N-NONCOUNT** Support is also a noun. ❑ *The president gave his full support to the reforms.*

3 **N-NONCOUNT** If you give **support** to someone, you help them. ❑ *She gave me a lot of support when my husband died.*

4 **V-T** If you **support** someone, you provide them with money or the things that they need. ❑ *I have three children to support.*

5 **V-T** If a fact **supports** a statement or a theory, it helps to show that it is true or correct. ❑ *A lot of research supports this theory.*

6 **N-NONCOUNT** Support is also a noun. ❑ *History offers some support for this view.*

7 **V-T** If something **supports** an object, it is under the object and holding it up. ❑ *Thick wooden posts supported the roof.*

8 **N-COUNT** A **support** is a bar or other object that supports something. ❑ *Each piece of metal was on wooden supports.* [from Old French]

sup|port|ive /səpɔ́rtɪv/ **ADJ** If you are **supportive**, you are kind and helpful to someone at a difficult or unhappy time in their life. ❑ *They were always supportive of each other.* [from Old French]

sup|pose /səpóʊz/ (**supposes, supposing, supposed**)

1 **V-T** You can use **suppose** or **supposing** before suggesting a situation that could happen. ❑ *Suppose someone gave you a check for $6 million. What would you do with it?*

2 **V-T** If you **suppose that** something is true, you imagine that it is probably true. ❑ *I suppose you're in high school, too?*

3 **PHRASE** You can say **I suppose** when you are slightly uncertain about something. [SPOKEN] ❑ *I suppose you're right.* ❑ *"Is that the right way?"—"Yeah. I suppose so."* [from Old French]

sup|posed

> **PRONUNCIATION HELP**
> Pronounce meanings **1** and **2** /səpóʊzd/ or /səpóʊst/. Pronounce meaning **3** /səpóʊzd/.

1 **PHRASE** If you say that something **is supposed to** happen, you mean that it is planned or expected. Sometimes this use suggests that the thing does not really happen in this way. ❑ *This is the girl he is*

supposed to marry. ❑ *He was supposed to go back to Brooklyn on the last bus.*

2 **PHRASE** If you say that something **is supposed to** be true, you mean that people say it is true but you do not know for certain that it is true. ❑ *"The Whipping Block" is supposed to be a really good poem.*

3 **ADJ** You can use **supposed** to suggest that something that people talk about or believe in may not in fact exist, happen, or be as it is described. ❑ *...the supposed cause of the accident.* ● **sup|pos|ed|ly** /səpóʊzɪdli/ **ADV** ❑ *It was supposedly his own work.* [from Old French]

sup|po|si|tion /sʌpəzíʃ°n/ (**suppositions**)

1 **N-COUNT** A **supposition** is an idea or a statement that someone believes to be true, although they may have no evidence for it. [FORMAL] ❑ *There's a popular supposition that we're publicly funded, but most of our money comes from private contracts.*

2 **N-NONCOUNT** You can describe someone's ideas or statements as **supposition** if you disapprove of the fact that they have no evidence to support them. ❑ *The authorities said that most of the report was based on supposition.* [from Old French]

sup|press /səprɛ́s/ (**suppresses, suppressing, suppressed**)

1 **V-T** If someone in authority **suppresses** an activity, they prevent it from continuing, by using force or making it illegal. ❑ *As we know, it's difficult to suppress crime.* ● **sup|pres|sion** /səprɛ́ʃ°n/ **N-NONCOUNT** ❑ *...the suppression of protests.*

2 **V-T** If a natural function or reaction of your body **is suppressed**, it is stopped, for example by drugs or illness. ❑ *The growth of cancer cells can be suppressed by various treatments.* ● **sup|pres|sion** **N-NONCOUNT** ❑ *...suppression of the immune system.*

3 **V-T** If you **suppress** your feelings or reactions, you do not express them, even though you might want to. ❑ *Liz thought of Barry and suppressed a smile.* ● **sup|pres|sion** **N-NONCOUNT** ❑ *A mother's suppression of her own feelings can cause problems.*

4 **V-T** If someone **suppresses** a piece of information, they prevent other people from learning it. ❑ *They did not try to suppress the information.* ● **sup|pres|sion** **N-NONCOUNT** ❑ *...the suppression of official documents.* [from Latin]

su|preme /suprim/
1 **ADJ** **Supreme** is used in the title of a person or an official group to indicate that they are at the highest level in a particular organization or system. ❑ ...the supreme ruler of Eastern Russia. ❑ ...the Supreme Court.
2 **ADJ** You use **supreme** to emphasize that a quality or thing is very great. ❑ Her happiness was of supreme importance.
● **su|preme|ly** **ADV** ❑ She does her job supremely well. [from Latin]

Su|preme Court /suprim kɔrt/
1 **N-PROPER** SOCIAL STUDIES The **Supreme Court** is the highest court of law in the United States.
2 **N-COUNT** SOCIAL STUDIES In each state, the **Supreme Court** is the most important law court in the state.

sure /ʃʊər/ (**surer, surest**)
1 **ADJ** If you are **sure** that something is true, you are certain about it. ❑ He was not sure that he wanted to be a teacher. ❑ I'm not sure where he lives.
2 **ADJ** If someone is **sure of** getting something, they think they will definitely get it. ❑ How can you be sure of getting quality?
3 **PHRASE** If you say that something **is sure to** happen, you believe that it will happen. ❑ With a face like that, she's sure to get a boyfriend.
4 **ADJ** **Sure** is used to say that a sign or a way of doing something is reliable. ❑ There were black clouds in the sky, a sure sign of rain.
5 **INTERJ** **Sure** is an informal way of saying "yes" or "all right." ❑ "Do you know where she lives?"—"Sure."
6 **PHRASE** If something is **for sure**, it is definitely true. ❑ One thing's for sure, women still love Barry Manilow.
7 **PHRASE** If you **make sure that** something is the way that you want it to be, you check that it is that way. ❑ He looked in the bathroom to make sure that he was alone.
8 **PHRASE** If you are **sure of yourself**, you are confident about your own abilities or opinions. ❑ I've never seen him so sure of himself. [from Old French]

sure|ly /ʃʊərli/ **ADV** You use **surely** to show that you think something should be true. ❑ You surely haven't forgotten Dr. Walters? [from Old French]

surf /sɜrf/ (**surfs, surfing, surfed**)
1 **N-NONCOUNT** SCIENCE **Surf** is the mass of white bubbles on the top of waves in the

ocean. ❑ We watched the surf rolling onto the white sandy beach.
2 **V-I** SPORTS If you **surf**, you ride on big waves in the ocean on a special board. ❑ I'm going to buy a board and learn to surf.
● **surf|er** (**surfers**) **N-COUNT** ❑ This small fishing village continues to attract surfers.
● **surf|ing** **N-NONCOUNT** ❑ My favorite sport is surfing.
3 **V-T** TECHNOLOGY If you **surf** the Internet, you spend time looking at different websites on the Internet. ❑ No one knows how many people surf the Net.
→ look at Word Web: **beach**

sur|face /sɜrfɪs/ (**surfaces**)
1 **N-COUNT** The **surface** of something is the flat top part of it or the outside of it. ❑ There were pen marks on the table's surface. ❑ Small waves moved on the surface of the water.
2 **N-SING** The **surface** of a situation is what can be seen easily. ❑ Back home, things appear, on the surface, simpler. [from French]

Word Partnership	Use **surface** with :
N	surface **area**, **Earth's** surface, surface **level**, surface **of the water** **1**
ADJ	**flat** surface, **rough** surface, **smooth** surface **1**
V	**break the** surface **1** **scratch the** surface **1** **2**

sur|face cur|rent (**surface currents**) **N-COUNT** SCIENCE A **surface current** is a current of water that flows at or near the surface of the sea. Compare with **deep current**.

sur|face grav|ity (**surface gravities**) **N-COUNT/N-NONCOUNT** SCIENCE The **surface gravity** of a planet is the gravitational force that exists on the surface of the planet.

sur|face ten|sion (**surface tensions**) **N-COUNT/N-NONCOUNT** SCIENCE **Surface tension** is the force that acts on the surface of a liquid and causes it to form very small drops.

surface-to-volume ra|tio (**surface-to-volume ratios**) **N-COUNT** SCIENCE The **surface-to-volume ratio** of a cell or an organ is the difference between the surface area of the cell or organ and its volume.

sur|face wave (**surface waves**) **N-COUNT** SCIENCE In physics, a **surface wave** is a wave that travels along the boundary between two substances with different densities,

S

such as the sea and the air. In geology, a **surface wave** is a vibration from an earthquake that travels close to the Earth's surface.

surf|board /sɜrfbɔrd/ (**surfboards**) **N-COUNT** SPORTS A **surfboard** is a long narrow board that people use for surfing.

surge /sɜrdʒ/ (**surges, surging, surged**)
1 **N-COUNT** A **surge** is a sudden large increase in something. ❑ ...a surge in prices.
2 **V-I** If a crowd of people **surge** forward, they suddenly move forward together. ❑ The crowd surged forward into the store. [from Latin]

sur|geon /sɜrdʒⁿn/ (**surgeons**) **N-COUNT** A **surgeon** is a doctor who is specially trained to perform operations. ❑ ...a heart surgeon. [from Old French]

Word Link   ery ≈ place where something happens : bakery, cemetery, surgery

sur|gery /sɜrdʒəri/
1 **N-NONCOUNT** Surgery is a process in which a doctor cuts open a patient's body in order to repair, remove, or replace a part that is damaged or affected by disease. ❑ His father just had heart surgery. [from Old French]
2 → see also **plastic surgery**
→ look at Word Webs: **cancer, laser**

sur|gi|cal /sɜrdʒɪkⁱl/ **ADJ** Surgical equipment and clothing are used for doing operations. ❑ ...a collection of surgical instruments. [from Old French]

sur|mise /sərmaɪz/ (**surmises, surmising, surmised**) **V-T** If you **surmise** that something is true, you guess it from the available evidence, although you do not know for certain. [FORMAL] ❑ We can only surmise what happened. [from Old French]

sur|plus /sɜrplʌs, -pləs/ (**surpluses**)
1 **N-COUNT/N-NONCOUNT** If there is a **surplus of** something, there is more than you need. ❑ The world has a surplus of food, but still people are hungry.
2 **ADJ** Surplus describes something that is extra or that is more than you need. ❑ Few people have large sums of surplus cash. [from Old French]

sur|prise /sərpraɪz/ (**surprises, surprising, surprised**)
1 **N-COUNT** A **surprise** is an unexpected event, fact, or piece of news. ❑ I have a surprise for you: We are moving to Switzerland!

2 **ADJ** Surprise is also an adjective. ❑ Baxter arrived this afternoon, on a surprise visit.
3 **N-NONCOUNT** Surprise is the feeling that you have when something that you do not expect happens. ❑ The Pentagon has expressed surprise at his comments.
4 **V-T** If something **surprises** you, it gives you a feeling of surprise. ❑ We'll do the job ourselves and surprise everyone. ❑ It surprised me that he should make such a stupid mistake. [from Old French]

Word Partnership   Use **surprise** with :

ADJ	**big** surprise, **complete** surprise, **great** surprise **1**
N	surprise **announcement**, surprise **attack**, **a bit of a** surprise, surprise **move**, surprise **visit** **1** **element of** surprise **2**

sur|prised /sərpraɪzd/ **ADJ** If you are **surprised** at something, you have a feeling of surprise, because it is not expected. ❑ I was surprised at how easy it was. [from Old French]

sur|pris|ing /sərpraɪzɪŋ/ **ADJ** Something that is **surprising** is not expected and makes you feel surprised. ❑ It is not surprising that children learn to read at different rates.
● **sur|pris|ing|ly ADV** ❑ The party was surprisingly good. [from Old French]

sur|ren|der /sərɛndər/ (**surrenders, surrendering, surrendered**)
1 **V-I** If you **surrender**, you stop fighting because you cannot win. ❑ The army finally surrendered.
2 **N-COUNT/N-NONCOUNT** Surrender is also a noun. ❑ ...the government's surrender to demands made by the people.
3 **V-T** If you **surrender** something you would rather keep, you give it up or let someone else have it. ❑ Nadja had to surrender all rights to her house. [from Old French]

Thesaurus   surrender   Also look up :

V	abandon, give in, give up **1** **2**

sur|round /səraʊnd/ (**surrounds, surrounding, surrounded**)
1 **V-T** If a person or thing **is surrounded** by something, that thing is all around them. ❑ The church was surrounded by a low wall.
2 **V-T** If you **are surrounded** by soldiers or police, they spread out all around you. ❑ When the car stopped it was surrounded by soldiers.

3 **v-т** The circumstances that **surround** something are the circumstances that are closely related to that thing. ❑ *A lot of the facts surrounding the case are unknown.* [from Old French]

sur|round|ings /sərˈaʊndɪŋz/ **N-PLURAL** Your **surroundings** are everything around you or the place where you live. ❑ *He soon felt at home in his new surroundings.* [from Old French]

sur|veil|lance /sərˈveɪləns/ **N-NONCOUNT** **Surveillance** is the careful watching of someone, especially by an organization such as the police or the army. ❑ *They kept him under constant surveillance.* [from French]

sur|vey /sˈɜrveɪ/ (**surveys**) **N-COUNT** If you do a **survey**, you try to find out information about a lot of different people by asking them questions. ❑ *They conducted a survey to see how students study.* [from French]

sur|viv|al /sərˈvaɪvəl/ **N-NONCOUNT** The **survival** of something or someone is the fact that they still exist after a difficult or dangerous time. ❑ *Many of these companies are now struggling for survival.* [from Old French]

Word Link	viv ≈ living : re*viv*al, sur*viv*e, *viv*id

sur|vive /sərˈvaɪv/ (**survives, surviving, survived**)
1 **v-т/v-ɪ** If a person or a living thing **survives** in a dangerous situation, they do not die. ❑ *It's a miracle that anyone survived.* ❑ *He survived heart surgery.* ● **sur|vi|vor** (**survivors**) **N-COUNT** ❑ *There were no survivors of the plane crash.*
2 **v-т/v-ɪ** If you **survive** in difficult circumstances, you manage to live or continue. ❑ *How do people survive the pressure of working all the time?* [from Old French]

sus|pect (**suspects, suspecting, suspected**)

> **PRONUNCIATION HELP**
> Pronounce the verb /səˈspɛkt/. Pronounce the noun /sˈʌspɛkt/.

1 **v-т** If you **suspect** that something is true, you think that it is true but you are not certain. ❑ *He suspected that she was telling lies.*
2 **v-т** If you **suspect** someone **of** doing something bad, you believe that they probably did it. ❑ *The police did not suspect him of anything.*
3 **N-COUNT** A **suspect** is a person who the police think may be guilty of a crime. ❑ *Police have arrested a suspect.* [from Latin]

sus|pend /səˈspɛnd/ (**suspends, suspending, suspended**)
1 **v-т** If you **suspend** something, you delay it or stop it from happening for a period of time. ❑ *The company will suspend production June 1st.*
2 **v-т** If someone **is suspended**, they are forced to leave their job or their school for a period of time. ❑ *Julie was suspended from her job.*
3 **v-т** Something that **is suspended** from a high place is hanging from that place. ❑ *Three television screens were suspended from the ceiling.* [from Latin]

sus|pense /səˈspɛns/ **N-NONCOUNT** **Suspense** is a state of excitement about something that is going to happen very soon. ❑ *The suspense ended when the judges gave their decision.* [from Medieval Latin]

sus|pen|sion /səˈspɛnʃ°n/ (**suspensions**)
1 **N-NONCOUNT** The **suspension** of something is the act of delaying or stopping it for a while or until a decision is made about it. ❑ *There was a suspension of flights out of Miami.*
2 **N-COUNT/N-NONCOUNT** Someone's **suspension** is their removal from a job or position for a period of time or until a decision is made about them. ❑ *No one knows the reason for his suspension.*
3 **N-COUNT/N-NONCOUNT** A vehicle's **suspension** consists of the springs and other devices attached to the wheels, which give a smooth ride over uneven ground. ❑ *There's a problem with the car's suspension.*
4 **N-COUNT** **SCIENCE** In chemistry, a **suspension** is a mixture containing tiny particles floating in a fluid. [from Medieval Latin]
→ look at Word Web: **bridge**

sus|pi|cion /səˈspɪʃ°n/ (**suspicions**) **N-COUNT/ N-NONCOUNT** **Suspicion** is a belief or feeling that someone has done something wrong. ❑ *Don't do anything that might cause suspicion.* [from Old French]

sus|pi|cious /səˈspɪʃəs/
1 **ADJ** If you are **suspicious of** someone or something, you do not trust them. ❑ *He was suspicious of me at first.* ● **sus|pi|cious|ly** **ADJ** ❑ *"What is it you want me to do?" Adams asked suspiciously.*
2 **ADJ** If someone or something is **suspicious**, there is something bad or wrong

S

about them. ❏ *Please contact the police if you see any suspicious person in the area.*

● **sus|pi|cious|ly** **ADV** ❏ *Has anyone been acting suspiciously over the last few days?* [from Old French]

sus|tain /səsteɪn/ (**sustains, sustaining, sustained**)

1 **V-T** If you **sustain** something, you continue it for a period of time. ❏ *He has difficulty sustaining relationships.*

2 **V-T** If you **sustain** a loss or an injury, it happens to you. [FORMAL] ❏ *The aircraft sustained some damage.* [from Old French]

sus|tain|able /səsteɪnəbəl/ **ADJ** You use **sustainable** to talk about using natural products in a way that does not damage the environment. ❏ *The government introduced its program of sustainable development in 2006.*

● **sus|tain|abil|ity** /səsteɪnəbɪlɪti/ **N-NONCOUNT** ❏ *...environmental sustainability.* [from Old French]

swal|low /swɒloʊ/ (**swallows, swallowing, swallowed**)

1 **V-T/V-I** If you **swallow** something, you make it go from your mouth down into your stomach. ❏ *Polly took a bite of the apple and swallowed.* ❏ *I swallowed my coffee.*

2 **N-COUNT** A **swallow** is a type of small bird with pointed wings and a split tail. [from Old English]

swam /swæm/ **Swam** is the past tense of **swim**. [from Old English]

swamp /swɒmp/ (**swamps, swamping, swamped**)

1 **N-COUNT/N-NONCOUNT** A **swamp** is an area of very wet land with wild plants growing in it. ❏ *I spent one night by a swamp listening to frogs.*

2 **V-T** If something **swamps** a place or an object, it fills it with water. ❏ *A big wave swamped the boat.*

3 **V-T** If you **are swamped** by things or people, you have more of them than you can deal with. ❏ *He is swamped with work.* [from Middle Dutch]

swan /swɒn/ (**swans**) **N-COUNT** A **swan** is a large white bird with a very long neck, that lives on rivers and lakes. [from Old English]

swap /swɒp/ (**swaps, swapping, swapped**)

1 **V-T/V-I** If you **swap** something with someone, you give it to them and receive a different thing back from them. ❏ *Next week*

they will swap places.

2 **V-T** If you **swap** one thing **for** another, you remove the first thing and replace it with the second. ❏ *He swapped his overalls for a suit and tie.* ❏ *I swapped my t-shirt for one of Karen's.*

S wave /ɛs weɪv/ (**S waves**) also **S-wave** **N-COUNT** SCIENCE **S waves** are waves of energy that are released in an earthquake, after the release of waves called P waves. **S wave** is short for "secondary wave."

sway /sweɪ/ (**sways, swaying, swayed**)

1 **V-I** When people or things **sway**, they move slowly from one side to the other. ❏ *The people swayed back and forth singing.* ❏ *The tall grass was swaying in the wind.*

2 **V-T** If you **are swayed by** someone or something, you are influenced by them. ❏ *Don't ever be swayed by fashion.* [from Old Norse]

swear /swɛər/ (**swears, swearing, swore, sworn**)

1 **V-I** If someone **swears**, they use language that is considered to be offensive. ❏ *It's wrong to swear and shout.*

2 **V-T** If you **swear to** do something, you promise in a serious way that you will do it. ❏ *I swear to do everything I can to help you.*

3 **V-T/V-I** If you **swear** that something is true, you are saying very firmly that it is true. ❏ *I swear I've told you all I know.* [from Old English]

Word Partnership	Use **swear** with :
N	swear **words** **1**
	swear **allegiance**, swear **an oath** **2**
ADV	**solemnly** swear **3**

sweat /swɛt/ (**sweats, sweating, sweated**)

1 **N-NONCOUNT** **Sweat** is the liquid that comes out of your skin when you are hot, sick, or afraid. ❏ *Both horse and rider were dripping with sweat.*

2 **V-I** When you **sweat**, sweat comes out of your skin. ❏ *It's really hot. I'm sweating.*

3 **N-PLURAL** **Sweats** are loose, warm, comfortable pants, or pants and top, that people wear to relax and do exercise. [INFORMAL] [from Old English]

sweat|er /swɛtər/ (**sweaters**) **N-COUNT** A **sweater** is a warm piece of clothing that covers the upper part of your body and your arms. [from Old English]

→ look at Picture Dictionary: **clothing**

sweat gland (**sweat glands**) **N-COUNT**
SCIENCE Your **sweat glands** are the organs in your skin that release sweat.

sweat|shirt /swɛtʃɜrt/ (**sweatshirts**) also
sweat shirt **N-COUNT** A **sweatshirt** is a loose warm piece of casual clothing that covers the upper part of your body and your arms.
→ look at Picture Dictionary: **clothing**

sweaty /swɛti/ (**sweatier, sweatiest**) **ADJ**
If parts of your body or your clothes are **sweaty**, they are covered with sweat. ·
❑ ...hot, sweaty hands. ❑ ...sweaty socks.
[from Old English]

sweep /swip/ (**sweeps, sweeping, swept**)
1 **V-T/V-I** If you **sweep**, or **sweep** an area, you push dirt off it using a brush with a long handle. ❑ The owner of the store was sweeping his floor. ❑ She was sweeping in the kitchen.
2 **V-T** If you **sweep** things off something, you push them off with a quick smooth movement of your arm. ❑ She swept the cards from the table.
3 **V-T** If wind or another strong force **sweeps** someone or something somewhere, it moves them there quickly. ❑ The flood swept cars into the sea. [from Old English]

sweet /swit/ (**sweeter, sweetest, sweets**)
1 **ADJ** **Sweet** food and drink contains a lot of sugar. ❑ ...a cup of sweet tea. ❑ If the sauce is too sweet, add some salt.
2 **ADJ** A **sweet** smell is a pleasant one.
❑ I recognized the sweet smell of her perfume. ·
3 **ADJ** A **sweet** sound is pleasant, smooth, and gentle. ❑ The young girl's voice was soft and sweet.
4 **ADJ** If someone is **sweet**, they are kind and gentle toward other people. ❑ He was a sweet man. ● **sweet|ly** **ADV** ❑ I just smiled sweetly and said no.
5 **ADJ** If a small person or thing is **sweet**, they are attractive in a simple way.
[INFORMAL] ❑ ...a sweet little baby.
6 **N-PLURAL** **Sweets** are foods that have a lot of sugar. ❑ Eat more fruit and vegetables and less fat and sweets. [from Old English]
→ look at Word Webs: **sugar, taste**

swell /swɛl/ (**swells, swelling, swelled, swollen**)

> **LANGUAGE HELP**
> The forms **swelled** and **swollen** are both used as the past participle.

1 **V-I** If a part of your body **swells**, it becomes larger and thicker than normal.
❑ Do your legs swell at night?
2 **Swell up** means the same as **swell**.
❑ His eye swelled up.
3 **V-T/V-I** If the amount or size of something **swells**, it becomes larger than it was before. ❑ His army swelled to one hundred thousand men.
4 **N-COUNT** **Swells** are large, smooth waves on the surface of the sea that are produced by the wind and can travel long distances.
[from Old English]
5 → see also **swollen**

swept /swɛpt/ **Swept** is the past tense and past participle of **sweep**. [from Old English]

swerve /swɜrv/ (**swerves, swerving, swerved**) **V-T/V-I** If a vehicle or other moving thing **swerves**, or if you **swerve** it, it suddenly changes direction. ❑ Her car swerved off the road. [from Old English]

swift /swɪft/ (**swifter, swiftest**)
1 **ADJ** A **swift** event or process happens very quickly or without delay. ❑ We need to make a swift decision. ● **swift|ly** **ADV** ❑ We have to act as swiftly as we can.
2 **ADJ** Something that is **swift** moves very quickly. ❑ With a swift movement, Matthew sat up. ● **swift|ly** **ADV** ❑ Lenny moved swiftly and silently across the grass. [from Old English]

swim /swɪm/ (**swims, swimming, swam, swum**)
1 **V-T/V-I** SPORTS When you **swim**, you move through water by making movements with your arms and legs. ❑ She learned to swim when she was 10. ❑ I swim a mile a day.
● **swim|mer** (**swimmers**) **N-COUNT** ❑ I'm a good swimmer.
2 **N-SING** SPORTS **Swim** is also a noun.
❑ When can we go for a swim? [from Old English]

swim blad|der (**swim bladders**) **N-COUNT**
SCIENCE A **swim bladder** is an organ in fish that contains air or gas and allows the fish to rise or sink through the water.

swim|ming /swɪmɪŋ/ **N-NONCOUNT** SPORTS
Swimming is the activity of swimming, especially as a sport or for pleasure.
❑ Swimming is a great form of exercise. [from Old English]

swim|ming pool (**swimming pools**)
N-COUNT SPORTS A **swimming pool** is a large hole filled with water that people can swim in.

swim|suit /swɪmsut/ (**swimsuits**) **N-COUNT**
A **swimsuit** is a piece of clothing that you wear for swimming. A swimsuit is also called a **bathing suit**. ❑ *She refused to be photographed in a swimsuit.*

swing /swɪŋ/ (**swings, swinging, swung**)
1 **V-T/V-I** If something **swings**, it moves repeatedly backward and forward or from side to side through the air. ❑ *Amber walked beside him, her arms swinging.* ❑ *She was swinging a bottle of soda in her hand.*
2 **N-COUNT** A **swing** is a seat that hangs by two ropes. You can sit on it and move forward and backward through the air.
❑ *I took the kids to the park to play on the swings.*
3 **V-I** If you **swing at** a person or thing, you try to hit them with your arm or with something that you are holding. ❑ *Blanche swung at her but missed.* [from Old English]

switch /swɪtʃ/ (**switches, switching, switched**)
1 **N-COUNT** A **switch** is a small control for turning electricity on or off. ❑ *She shut the dishwasher and pressed the switch.*
2 **V-T/V-I** If you **switch to** something different, you change to it.
❑ *I'm switching from sweet breakfast cereal to muesli.* ❑ *The law would help companies switch coal for cleaner fuels.*
3 **V-T** If you **switch** two things, you replace one with the other. ❑ *They switched the keys, so Karen had the key to my room and I had the key to hers.* [from Middle Dutch]
▶ **switch off** If you **switch off** an electrical piece of equipment, you stop it from working by operating a switch. ❑ *She switched off the coffee machine.*
▶ **switch on** If you **switch on** an electrical piece of equipment, you make it start working by operating a switch. ❑ *He switched on the lamp.*

switch

	Word Partnership Use **switch** with :
V	**flick a** switch, **flip a** switch, **turn a** switch **1**
N	**ignition** switch, **light** switch, **power** switch **1** switch **sides 3**

swol|len /swoʊlən/
1 **ADJ** If a part of your body is **swollen**, it is larger and thicker than normal, usually as a result of injury or illness. ❑ *My eyes were swollen and I could hardly see.*
2 **Swollen** is the past participle of **swell**. [from Old English]

sword /sɔrd/ (**swords**) **N-COUNT** A **sword** is a weapon with a handle and a long sharp blade. [from Old English]
→ look at Word Web: **army**

swore /swɔr/ **Swore** is the past tense of **swear**. [from Old English]

sworn /swɔrn/ **Sworn** is the past participle of **swear**. [from Old English]

swum /swʌm/ **Swum** is the past participle of **swim**. [from Old English]

swung /swʌŋ/ **Swung** is the past tense and past participle of **swing**. [from Old English]

syl|labi|ca|tion /sɪlæbɪkeɪʃən/ or **syllabification** /sɪlæbɪfɪkeɪʃən/
N-NONCOUNT LANGUAGE ARTS **Syllabication** or **syllabification** is the division of a word into its separate syllables. [from Old French]

syl|la|ble /sɪləbəl/ (**syllables**) **N-COUNT** LANGUAGE ARTS A **syllable** is a part of a word that contains a single vowel sound and that is pronounced as a unit. So, for example, "book" has one syllable, and "reading" has two syllables. [from Old French]

syl|la|bus /sɪləbəs/ (**syllabuses**) **N-COUNT** A **syllabus** is a list of the subjects to be covered in a course. ❑ *The course syllabus consists mainly of novels by American writers.* [from Late Latin]

Word Link	osis ≈ state or condition : hypnosis, metamorphosis, symbiosis

sym|bio|sis /sɪmbioʊsɪs, -baɪ-/
N-NONCOUNT SCIENCE **Symbiosis** is a close relationship between two organisms of different kinds which benefits both organisms. ❑ *...the link between bacteria, symbiosis, and the evolution of plants and animals.* [from New Latin]

sym|bol /sɪmbəl/ (**symbols**)
1 **N-COUNT** LANGUAGE ARTS A **symbol for** something is a number, a letter, or a shape that represents that thing. ❑ *What's the chemical symbol for oxygen?*
2 **N-COUNT** Something that is a **symbol of** an aspect of life seems to represent it

because it is very typical of it. ❑ *For her people, she is a symbol of freedom.* [from Church Latin] → look at Word Web: **myth**

sym|bol|ic /sɪmbɒlɪk/

1 **ADJ** If you describe an event, an action, or a procedure as **symbolic**, you mean that it represents an important change, although it has little practical effect. ❑ *The president's trip is of symbolic importance.* ● **sym|boli|cal|ly** /sɪmbɒlɪkli/ **ADV** ❑ *Museums symbolically remove paintings to remember when particular artists died.*

2 **ADJ** **Symbolic** is used to describe things involving or relating to symbols. ❑ *...the symbolic meaning of names.* ● **sym|bol|ism** /sɪmbəlɪzəm/ **N-NONCOUNT** ❑ *...the writer's use of symbolism.* [from Church Latin]

sym|met|ri|cal /sɪmɛtrɪkəl/ **ADJ** If something is **symmetrical**, it has two halves that are exactly the same. ❑ *The rows of windows were perfectly symmetrical.* [from Latin]

sym|me|try /sɪmɪtri/ (**symmetries**)

1 **N-COUNT/N-NONCOUNT** Something that has **symmetry** is symmetrical in shape, design, or structure. ❑ *...the symmetry of a snowflake.*

2 **N-COUNT/N-NONCOUNT** MATH **Symmetry** is the relationship between two geometric figures that are the same size and shape. [from Latin]

sym|pa|thet|ic /sɪmpəθɛtɪk/

1 **ADJ** A **sympathetic** person is kind and tries to understand other people's feelings. ❑ *Try talking about your problem with a sympathetic teacher.* ● **sym|pa|theti|cal|ly** /sɪmpəθɛtɪkli/ **ADV** ❑ *She nodded sympathetically.*

2 **ADJ** If you are **sympathetic to** a plan or an action, you approve of it and are willing to support it. ❑ *...judges who are more sympathetic to crime control.* [from Latin]

sym|pa|thize /sɪmpəθaɪz/ (**sympathizes, sympathizing, sympathized**) **V-I** If you **sympathize** with someone who is in a bad situation, you show that you are sorry for them. ❑ *It's terrible when a parent dies. I sympathize with you.* [from Latin]

sym|pa|thy /sɪmpəθi/

1 **N-NONCOUNT** If you have **sympathy** for someone who is in a bad situation, you are sorry for them. ❑ *I get no sympathy from my*

family when I'm sick.

2 **N-NONCOUNT** If you have **sympathy** with someone's ideas or opinions, you agree with them. ❑ *I have some sympathy with this point of view.* [from Latin]

Word Partnership	Use **sympathy** with :
ADJ	**deep** sympathy, **great** sympathy, **public** sympathy **1**
V	**express** sympathy, **feel** sympathy, **gain** sympathy, **have** sympathy **1** **2**

sym|pho|ny /sɪmfəni/ (**symphonies**)

1 **N-COUNT** MUSIC A **symphony** is a piece of music that has been written to be played by an orchestra. ❑ *...Beethoven's Ninth Symphony.*

2 **N-COUNT** MUSIC A **symphony** orchestra is a large orchestra that plays classical music. ❑ *...the Boston Symphony Orchestra.* [from Old French] → look at Word Webs: **music, orchestra**

symp|tom /sɪmptəm/ (**symptoms**)

1 **N-COUNT** A **symptom** of an illness is something that is wrong with you that is a sign of the illness. ❑ *All these patients have flu symptoms.*

2 **N-COUNT** A **symptom of** a bad situation is something that happens that is considered to be a sign of this situation. ❑ *The food problem is a symptom of a much deeper crisis in the country.* [from Late Latin] → look at Word Webs: **diagnosis, illness**

syna|gogue /sɪnəgɒg/ (**synagogues**)

N-COUNT A **synagogue** is a building where Jewish people go to pray. [from Old French]

syn|cline /sɪnklaɪn/ (**synclines**) **N-COUNT** SCIENCE A **syncline** is a rock formation in which layers of rock are folded so that they resemble the shape of a letter U. [from Greek]

syn|co|pa|tion /sɪŋkəpeɪʃən/ (**syncopations**) **N-COUNT/N-NONCOUNT** MUSIC **Syncopation** is the quality that music has when the weak beats in a bar are stressed instead of the strong ones. [from Late Latin]

syn|di|cate /sɪndɪkɪt/ (**syndicates**) **N-COUNT** BUSINESS A **syndicate** is an association of people or organizations that is formed for

S

business purposes or in order to carry out a project. ❏ *They formed a syndicate to buy the car.* ❏ *...a syndicate of 152 banks.* [from Old French]

syn|drome /sɪndroʊm/ (**syndromes**)
N-COUNT A **syndrome** is a medical condition. ❏ *No one knows what causes Sudden Infant Death Syndrome.* [from New Latin]

syno|nym /sɪnənɪm/ (**synonyms**) **N-COUNT**
LANGUAGE ARTS A **synonym** is a word or an expression that means the same as another word or expression. ❏ *"Afraid" is a synonym for "frightened."* [from Late Latin]

Word Link	syn ≈ together : syncopation, syndicate, synthesis

syn|the|sis /sɪnθɪsɪs/ (**syntheses** /sɪnθɪsiz/)
N-COUNT A **synthesis of** different ideas or styles is a mixture or combination of these ideas or styles. [FORMAL] ❏ *His novels are a synthesis of history and fiction.* [from Latin]

syn|the|sis re|ac|tion (**synthesis reactions**)
N-COUNT SCIENCE A **synthesis reaction** is a chemical reaction in which two or more substances combine to form a compound.

syn|thet|ic /sɪnθɛtɪk/ **ADJ Synthetic** products are made from chemicals or artificial substances rather than from natural ones. ❏ *...synthetic rubber.* [from New Latin]

sy|ringe /sɪrɪndʒ/ (**syringes**) **N-COUNT**
A **syringe** is a small tube with a thin hollow needle at the end. It is used for putting medicine into a part of the body or for taking blood from your body. [from Late Latin]

syr|up /sɪrəp, sɜr-/ (**syrups**)
N-COUNT/N-NONCOUNT Syrup is a sweet liquid that is made by cooking sugar with water. ❏ *...canned fruit with syrup.* [from Medieval Latin]

sys|tem /sɪstəm/ (**systems**)
1 N-COUNT A **system** is a way of working, organizing, or doing something that follows a plan. ❏ *You need a better system for organizing your DVDs.*
2 N-COUNT A **system** is a set of equipment, parts, or instruments. ❏ *There's something wrong with the computer system.* ❏ *...a heating system.*
3 N-COUNT A **system** is a network of things that are linked together so that people or things can communicate with each other or travel from one place to another. ❏ *...Australia's road and rail system.*
4 N-COUNT A **system** is a particular set of rules that is used to count or measure things. ❏ *...the decimal system of weights and measures.* [from French]
5 → see also **ecosystem, immune system, solar system**

sys|tem|at|ic /sɪstəmætɪk/ **ADJ** Something that is done in a **systematic** way is done according to a fixed plan, in a thorough and efficient way. ❏ *They searched the area in a systematic way.* ● **sys|tem|ati|cal|ly** /sɪstəmætɪkli/ **ADV** ❏ *They have systematically destroyed all our hard work.* [from French]

sys|tem|ic cir|cu|la|tion /sɪstɛmɪk sɜrkyəleɪʃ°n/ **N-NONCOUNT** SCIENCE **Systemic circulation** is the flow of blood between the heart and the rest of the body except for the lungs. Compare with **pulmonary circulation**. → look at Word Web: **cardiovascular system**

S

Tt

tab /tæb/ (**tabs**) **N-COUNT** A **tab** is a small piece of cloth, metal, or paper that is fixed to something, so that you can see it, hold it, or pull it. ❑ *He pushed back the tab on the can with his thumb and drank.*

ta|ble /teɪbªl/ (**tables**)
1 **N-COUNT** A **table** is a piece of furniture with a flat top that you put things on or sit at. ❑ *Mom was sitting at the kitchen table.*
2 **N-COUNT** A **table** is a set of facts or numbers that you arrange in neat rows. ❑ *See the table on page 104.* [from Old French]

tab|leau /tæbloʊ, tæbloʊ/ (**tableaux**)
N-COUNT ARTS A **tableau** is a scene, often from a picture, that consists of a group of people in costumes who do not speak or move. [from French]

table|cloth /teɪbªlklɔθ/ (**tablecloths**)
N-COUNT A **tablecloth** is a cloth that you use to cover a table.

table|spoon /teɪbªlspun/ (**tablespoons**)
N-COUNT A **tablespoon** is a large spoon that you use when you are cooking.

tab|let /tæblɪt/ (**tablets**)
1 **N-COUNT** A **tablet** is a small solid piece of medicine that you swallow. ❑ *...a sleeping tablet.*
2 **N-COUNT** TECHNOLOGY A **tablet** is a small flat computer that you operate by touching the screen. ❑ *...a free guide to the best tablets on the market.* [from Old French]

tab|loid /tæblɔɪd/ (**tabloids**) **N-COUNT** A **tabloid** is a newspaper that has small pages, short articles, and a lot of photographs. ❑ *I sometimes read the tabloids.*

taci|turn /tæsɪtɜrn/ **ADJ** A **taciturn** person does not say much and seems unfriendly. ❑ *He was a taciturn man who replied to questions with one-word answers.* [from Latin]

tack /tæk/ (**tacks, tacking, tacked**)
1 **N-COUNT** A **tack** or a **thumbtack** is a short pin with a broad, flat top that you can push with your thumb, used especially for fastening papers to a bulletin board.
2 **N-COUNT** A **tack** is a short nail with a broad, flat top, especially one that is used for fastening carpets to the floor. ❑ *...a box of carpet tacks.*
3 → see also **thumbtack**
4 **V-T** If you **tack** something to a surface, you pin it there with tacks or thumbtacks. ❑ *He tacked a note to her door.*
5 **N-SING** If you change **tack** or try a different **tack**, you try a different method for dealing with a situation. ❑ *Seeing the puzzled look on his face, she tried a different tack.* [from Middle Low German]
→ look at Picture Dictionary: **office**
▶ **tack on** If you say that something **is tacked on** to something else, you think that it is added in a hurry and in an unsatisfactory way. ❑ *A small kitchen is tacked on to the back of the beautiful stone house.*

tack|le /tækªl/ (**tackles, tackling, tackled**)
1 **V-T** If you **tackle** a problem, you deal with it. ❑ *We discussed the best way to tackle the situation.*
2 **V-T** SPORTS If you **tackle** someone in a sports game, you try to take the ball away from them. ❑ *Foley tackled the quarterback.*
3 **N-COUNT** SPORTS **Tackle** is also a noun. ❑ *A great tackle from Harrison saved the game.* [from Middle Low German]

tact|ful /tæktfəl/ **ADJ** If you are **tactful**, you are very careful not to do or say anything that will upset or embarrass other people. ❑ *Dan obviously overheard our argument but he was too tactful to mention it.* ● **tact|ful|ly** **ADV** ❑ *Tactfully, Jessica changed the subject.* [from Latin]

tac|tic /tæktɪk/ (**tactics**) **N-COUNT** Your **tactics** are the ways that you choose to do something when you are trying to succeed in a particular situation. ❑ *Things weren't going well, so I decided to change my tactics.* [from New Latin]

tac|ti|cal /tæktɪkªl/ **ADJ** A **tactical** action or plan is intended to help someone achieve

t

what they want in the future, rather than immediately. ❑ *His latest offer may simply be a tactical move.* ● **tac|ti|cal|ly** /tæktɪkli/ **ADV** ❑ *Many people voted tactically against the government.* [from New Latin]

tad|pole /tædpoʊl/ (**tadpoles**) **N-COUNT** Tadpoles are small water creatures that look like fish and grow into frogs or toads.
→ look at Word Web: **amphibian**

taf|fy /tæfi/ (**taffies**) **N-COUNT/N-NONCOUNT** Taffy is a sticky candy that you chew. It is made by boiling sugar and butter together with water.

tag /tæg/ (**tags**) **N-COUNT** A **tag** is a small piece of cardboard or cloth that is attached to something. It has information written on it. ❑ *The staff all wear name tags.* ❑ *There's no price tag on this purse.*

tai|ga /taɪgə/ (**taigas**) **N-COUNT/N-NONCOUNT** SCIENCE The **taiga** is an area of thick forest in the far north of Europe, Asia, and North America, situated immediately south of the tundra. [from Russian]

tail /teɪl/ (**tails**)
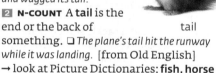
1 **N-COUNT** The **tail** of an animal is the long thin part at the end of its body. ❑ *The dog barked and wagged its tail.*
2 **N-COUNT** A **tail** is the end or the back of something. ❑ *The plane's tail hit the runway while it was landing.* [from Old English]
→ look at Picture Dictionaries: **fish, horse**

tail

tai|lor /teɪlər/ (**tailors**) **N-COUNT** A **tailor** is a person whose job is to make and repair clothes. [from Old French]

---
take
❶ TRANSFER, REMOVE
❷ OTHER VERB USES
❸ PHRASAL VERBS
---

❶ **take** /teɪk/ (**takes, taking, took, taken**)
1 **V-T** If you **take** something, you hold it or remove it. ❑ *Let me take your coat.* ❑ *He took a handkerchief from his pocket.*
2 **V-T** If you **take** something with you, you carry it with you. ❑ *Don't forget to take a map with you when you go somewhere.*
3 **V-T** If you **take** someone somewhere, you go there with them and pay for them. ❑ *He took them to the zoo.*

4 **V-T** If a person or a vehicle **takes** someone somewhere, they transport them there. ❑ *Michael took me to the airport.*
5 **V-T** If you **take** something, you steal it. ❑ *They took my pocketbook.* [from Old English]

❷ **take** /teɪk/ (**takes, taking, took, taken**)
1 **V-T** If something **takes** an amount of time, it needs that time in order to happen. ❑ *The sauce takes 25 minutes to prepare.*
2 **V-T** If you **take** something that someone offers you, you accept it. ❑ *Sylvia has taken a job in Tokyo teaching English.* ❑ *I think you should take my advice.*
3 **V-T** If you **take** a road, you choose to travel along it. ❑ *Take a right at the stop sign.*
4 **V-T** If you **take** a vehicle, you use it to go from one place to another. ❑ *She took the train to New York.*
5 **V-T** You can use **take** to say that someone does something. ❑ *She was too tired to take a bath.* ❑ *Betty took a photograph of us.*
6 **V-T** If you **take** a subject at school, you study it. ❑ *Students can take European history and American history.*
7 **V-T** If you **take** an examination, you do it. ❑ *She took her driving test yesterday and passed.*
8 **V-T** If someone **takes** medicine, they swallow it. ❑ *I try not to take pills of any kind.* [from Old English]
→ look at Word Web: **photography**

❸ **take** /teɪk/ (**takes, taking, took, taken**)
▶ **take after** If you **take after** a member of your family, you look or behave like them. ❑ *Your mom was a smart, brave woman. You take after her.*
▶ **take away** If you **take** something **away**, you remove it. ❑ *The waitress took away the dirty dishes.*
▶ **take back** If you **take** something **back**, you return it. ❑ *If you don't like it, I'll take it back to the store.*
▶ **take down** If you **take down** something, you remove it. ❑ *The Canadian army took down the fences.*
▶ **take off** **1** When an airplane **takes off**, it leaves the ground and starts flying. ❑ *We took off at 11 o'clock.*
2 If you **take** clothes **off**, you remove them. ❑ *Come in and take off your coat.*
3 If you **take** time **off**, you do not go to work for a time. ❑ *My husband was sick and I had to take time off work to look after him.*
▶ **take on** If you **take on** a job or a

responsibility, you accept it. ❑ *No other organization was willing to take on the job.*

▶ **take out** If you **take** someone **out**, you take them somewhere enjoyable. ❑ *Sophia took me out to lunch today.*

▶ **take over** BUSINESS If people **take over** something, they get control of it. ❑ *I'm going to take over this company one day.*

▶ **take up ❶** If you **take up** an activity, you start doing it. ❑ *Peter took up tennis at the age of eight.*
❷ If something **takes up** an amount of time or space, it uses that amount. ❑ *I don't want to take up too much of your time.* ❑ *The round wooden table takes up most of the kitchen.*

tak|en /teɪkən/ **Taken** is the past participle of **take**. [from Old English]

take|off /teɪkɔf/ (**takeoffs**) also **take-off**
N-COUNT/N-NONCOUNT **Takeoff** is the time when an aircraft leaves the ground and starts to fly. ❑ *What time is takeoff?*

take|out /teɪkaʊt/ (**takeouts**)
❶ N-NONCOUNT **Takeout** or **takeout** food is prepared food that you buy from a store or a restaurant and take away to eat somewhere else. ❑ *Let's just get a takeout pizza tonight.*
❷ N-COUNT A **takeout** is a store or a restaurant that sells prepared food that you take away and eat somewhere else. ❑ *We took Kerry to her favorite Chinese takeout for her birthday.*

take|over /teɪkoʊvər/ (**takeovers**)
❶ N-COUNT BUSINESS A **takeover** is the act of gaining control of a company by buying more of its shares than anyone else. ❑ *He lost his job after the takeover.*
❷ N-COUNT SOCIAL STUDIES A **takeover** is the act of taking control of a country, a political party, or a movement by force. ❑ *There was a military takeover.*

tale /teɪl/ (**tales**)
❶ N-COUNT A **tale** is a story. ❑ *It's a tale about the friendship between two boys.* [from Old English]
❷ → see also **fairy tale**

tal|ent /tælənt/ (**talents**)
N-COUNT/N-NONCOUNT **Talent** is your natural ability to do something well. ❑ *Both her children have a talent for music.* ❑ *He's got lots of talent, but he's rather lazy.* [from Old English]

Thesaurus	talent	Also look up :
N	ability, aptitude, gift	

Word Partnership	Use **talent** with :
ADJ	**great** talent, **musical** talent, **natural** talent
V	**have (a)** talent, **have got** talent
N	talent **pool**, talent **search**

tal|ent|ed /tæləntɪd/ ADJ If you are **talented**, you have a natural ability to do something well. ❑ *Howard is a talented pianist.* [from Old English]

talk /tɔk/ (**talks, talking, talked**)
❶ V-I If you **talk**, you say words, or speak to someone about your thoughts, ideas, or feelings. ❑ *After the fight, Mark was too upset to talk.* ❑ *Tom didn't talk until he was three years old.* ❑ *They were all talking about the movie.* ❑ *I talked to him yesterday.*
❷ N-COUNT **Talk** is also a noun. ❑ *I had a long talk with my father.*
❸ N-PLURAL **Talks** are formal discussions between different groups, to try to reach an agreement. ❑ *The government has begun peace talks with the rebels.* [from Old English]

▶ **talk out of** If you **talk** someone **out of** doing something, you persuade them not to do it. ❑ *My mother tried to talk me out of leaving school.*

▶ **talk over** If you **talk over** a problem or a plan, you discuss it. ❑ *He always talked things over with his friends.*

Thesaurus	talk	Also look up :
N	argument, conversation, dialogue, discussion, interview, negotiation; *(ant.)* silence **❶**	
V	chat, discuss, gossip, say, share, speak, tell; *(ant.)* listen **❶**	

Word Link	er ≈ more : *bigger, louder, taller*

tall /tɔl/ (**taller, tallest**)
❶ ADJ If someone or something is **tall**, they are higher than other people or things. ❑ *John is very tall.* ❑ *The lighthouse is a tall square tower.*
❷ ADJ You use **tall** when you are asking or talking about the height of someone or something. ❑ *"How tall are you?"—"I'm six foot five."* [from Old English]

tam|bou|rine /tæmbərin/ (**tambourines**)
N-COUNT MUSIC A **tambourine** is a round musical instrument that you shake or hit with your hand. [from Middle Flemish]

t

tame /teɪm/ (**tamer, tamest, tames, taming, tamed**)

■ **ADJ** If an animal is **tame**, it is not afraid of humans.

■ **V-T** If you **tame** a wild animal, you teach it not to be afraid of humans. [from Old English]

tan /tæn/ (**tans, tanning, tanned**)

■ **N-SING** If you have a **tan**, your skin has become darker because you have spent time in the sun. ❑ *She is tall and blonde, with a tan.*

■ **V-T/V-I** If a part of your body **tans** or if you **tan** it, your skin becomes darker than usual because you spend a lot of time in the sun. ❑ *I have very pale skin that never tans.* ● **tanned** **ADJ** ❑ *Becky's skin was deeply tanned.* [from Old English]

tan|dem /tændəm/ (**tandems**) **N-COUNT** A **tandem** is a bicycle designed for two riders. [from Latin]

→ look at Word Web: **bicycle**

tan|gible /tændʒɪbᵊl/ **ADJ** If something is **tangible**, it is clear enough to be easily seen, felt, or noticed. ❑ *There is tangible evidence that the economy is starting to recover.* [from Late Latin]

tan|gle /tæŋgᵊl/ (**tangles, tangling, tangled**)

■ **N-COUNT** A **tangle of** something is a mass of it that has become twisted together in a messy way. ❑ *A tangle of wires connected the two computers.*

■ **V-T/V-I** If something **is tangled** or **tangles**, it becomes twisted together in a messy way. ❑ *This clip has tangled my hair terribly.* ❑ *Animals get tangled in fishing nets and drown.* [of Scandinavian origin]

tank /tæŋk/ (**tanks**)

■ **N-COUNT** A **tank** is a large container for holding liquid or gas. ❑ *...a fuel tank.*

■ **N-COUNT** A **tank** is a heavy, strong military vehicle, with large guns. It moves on metal tracks that are fixed over the wheels. [from Gujarati]

→ look at Word Web: **aquarium**

tank|er /tæŋkər/ (**tankers**) **N-COUNT** A **tanker** is a large ship or truck that carries large amounts of gas or liquid. ❑ *...an oil tanker.* [from Gujarati]

→ look at Word Webs: **oil, ship**

tan|trum /tæntrəm/ (**tantrums**) **N-COUNT** If someone, especially a child, has a **tantrum**, they suddenly lose their temper in a noisy and uncontrolled way. ❑ *He immediately threw a tantrum, screaming and stomping up and down.*

tap /tæp/ (**taps, tapping, tapped**)

■ **V-T/V-I** If you **tap** something, you hit it or touch it quickly and lightly. ❑ *He tapped the table nervously with his fingers.* ❑ *Karen tapped on the bedroom door and went in.*

■ **N-COUNT** **Tap** is also a noun. ❑ *There was a tap on the door.*

■ **N-COUNT** A **tap** is an object that controls the flow of a liquid or a gas from a pipe. [Senses 1 and 2 from Old French. Sense 3 from Old English.]

→ look at Picture Dictionary: **dance**

tap dance (**tap dances**)

N-COUNT/N-NONCOUNT ARTS A **tap dance** is a dance in which the dancer wears special shoes with pieces of metal on the heels and toes. The shoes make loud sharp sounds when the dancer's feet move.

tape /teɪp/ (**tapes, taping, taped**)

■ **N-NONCOUNT** **Tape** is a sticky strip of plastic used for sticking things together. ❑ *Attach the picture to the cardboard using sticky tape.*

■ **N-NONCOUNT** **Tape** is a long narrow plastic strip that can be used for recording music, sounds, or moving pictures.

tape

■ **V-T/V-I** If you **tape** music, sounds, or moving pictures, you record them on a tape. ❑ *Ms. Pringle secretly taped her conversation with her boss.* ❑ *He shouldn't be taping without the singer's permission.*

■ **V-T** If you **tape** one thing to another, you stick them together using tape. ❑ *I taped the envelope shut.* [from Old English]

■ → see also **videotape**

→ look at Picture Dictionary: **office**

Word Partnership	Use **tape** with :
N	**piece of** tape, **roll of** tape ■
	cassette tape, **music** tape, **reel of** tape, tape **player** ■
	tape **a conversation**, tape **an interview**, tape **a show** ■
V	**listen to** a tape, **make** a tape, **play** a tape, **watch** a tape ■

tape re|cord|er (**tape recorders**) also **tape-recorder** **N-COUNT** A **tape recorder** is a machine some people used to use for recording and playing sound or music.

tape|worm /teɪpwɜrm/ (**tapeworms**)
N-COUNT SCIENCE A **tapeworm** is a long, flat parasite that lives in the stomach and intestines of animals or people.

tap|root /tæprut/ (**taproots**) also **tap root**
N-COUNT SCIENCE Plants that have a **taproot** have one main root that grows straight downward.

tar /tɑr/ **N-NONCOUNT** Tar is a thick, black, sticky substance that is used for making roads. ❑ *It was so hot that the tar melted on the roads.* [from Old English]

tar|get /tɑrgɪt/ (**targets**)
 1 **N-COUNT** A **target** is something that you try to hit with a weapon or another object. ❑ *One of the missiles missed its target.*
 2 **N-COUNT** Your **target** is the result that you are trying to achieve. ❑ *We failed to meet our sales targets last year.* [from Old French]

Word Partnership	Use target with :
V	**attack** a target **1**
	hit a target, **miss** a target **1** **2**
ADJ	**easy** target, **intended** target, **likely** target, **moving** target, **possible** target, **prime** target **1**
N	target **practice** **1**
	target **date** **2**

tar|iff /tærɪf/ (**tariffs**) **N-COUNT** BUSINESS A **tariff** is a tax on goods coming into a country. ❑ *...tariffs on items such as electronics.* [from Italian]

tart /tɑrt/ (**tarts**) **N-COUNT/N-NONCOUNT** A **tart** is a type of food. It is a case made of pastry that you fill with fruit or vegetables and cook in an oven. ❑ *We had apple tarts, served with fresh cream.* [from Old French]

task /tæsk/ (**tasks**) **N-COUNT** A **task** is a piece of work that you have to do. ❑ *I had the task of cleaning the kitchen.* [from Old French]

Thesaurus	task Also look up :
N	assignment, job, responsibility

Word Partnership	Use task with :
V	**accomplish** a task, **assign** *someone* a task, **complete** a task, **face** a task, **give** *someone* a task, **perform** a task
ADJ	**complex** task, **difficult** task, **easy** task, **enormous** task, **important** task, **impossible** task, **main** task, **simple** task

task|bar /tæskbɑr/ (**taskbars**) also **task bar**
N-COUNT TECHNOLOGY The **taskbar** on a computer screen is a narrow strip at the bottom of the screen that shows you which windows are open.

taste /teɪst/ (**tastes, tasting, tasted**)
 1 **N-NONCOUNT** Your sense of **taste** is your ability to recognize the flavor of things with your tongue. ❑ *Over the years my sense of taste has disappeared.*
 2 **N-COUNT** The **taste** of something is the particular quality that it has when you put it in your mouth, for example whether it is sweet or salty. ❑ *I like the taste of chocolate.* ❑ *This medicine has a nasty taste.*
 3 **V-I** If food or drink **tastes of** something, it has that particular flavor. ❑ *The water tasted of metal.* ❑ *The pizza tastes delicious.*
 4 **V-T** If you **taste** some food or drink, you eat or drink a small amount of it in order to see what the flavor is like. ❑ *Don't add salt until you've tasted the food.*
 5 **N-COUNT** Taste is also a noun. ❑ *Have a taste of this pie.*

Word Web taste

What we think of as **taste** is mostly **odor**. The sense of **smell** controls about 80% of the experience. We taste only four **sensations: sweet, salty, sour,** and **bitter.** We experience sweetness and saltiness through **taste buds** near the tip of the **tongue.** We sense sourness at the sides and bitterness at the back of the tongue. Some people have more taste buds than others. Scientists have discovered

some "supertasters" with 425 taste buds per square centimeter. Most of us have about 184 and some "nontasters" have only about 96.

t

6 **V-T** If you can **taste** something that you are eating or drinking, you are aware of its flavor. ❑ *Can you taste the onions in this dish?*
7 **N-NONCOUNT** Your **taste** is your choice in all the things that you like or buy. ❑ *Will's got great taste in clothes.* [from Old French]
→ look at Word Webs: **taste, sugar**

Word Partnership	Use **taste** with :
N	**sense of** taste **1**
ADJ	**bitter/salty/sour/sweet** taste **2**
	taste **bitter/salty/sour/sweet**, taste **good** **3**
	acquired taste, **bad/good/poor** taste **6**
V	**like the** taste of *something* **2**
ADV	taste **like** *something* **4**

taste|ful /teɪstfəl/ **ADJ** If something is **tasteful**, it is attractive, has a good design, and is of good quality. ❑ *Sarah was wearing a purple suit and tasteful jewelry.* ● **taste|ful|ly** **ADV** ❑ *They live in a large and tastefully decorated home.* [from Old French]

taste|less /teɪstlɪs/
1 **ADJ** If something is **tasteless**, it is unattractive, badly designed, and of poor quality. ❑ *Jim's house is full of tasteless furniture.*
2 **ADJ** If a remark or a joke is **tasteless**, it is offensive. ❑ *That was a very tasteless remark.*
3 **ADJ** If food or drink is **tasteless**, it has no flavor. ❑ *The fish was tasteless.* [from Old French]

tasty /teɪsti/ (**tastier, tastiest**) **ADJ** If food is **tasty**, it has a pleasant flavor and is good to eat. ❑ *The food here is tasty and good value.* [from Old French]

tat|too /tætu/ (**tattoos, tattooing, tattooed**)
1 **N-COUNT** A **tattoo** is a design on a person's skin made with a needle and colored ink. ❑ *He has a tattoo of three stars on his arm.*
2 **V-T** If something **is tattooed** on your body, you have a tattoo there. ❑ *She has had a small black cat tattooed on one of her shoulders.* [from Tahitian]

taught /tɔt/ **Taught** is the past tense and past participle of **teach**. [from Old English]

tax /tæks/ (**taxes, taxing, taxed**)
1 **N-COUNT/N-NONCOUNT** BUSINESS **Tax** is an amount of money that you have to pay to the government so that it can pay for public services such as roads and schools. ❑ *No one enjoys paying tax.* ❑ *The government has promised not to raise taxes this year.*
2 **V-T** BUSINESS When a person or company

is taxed, they have to pay a part of their income to the government. ❑ *We are the most heavily taxed people in North America.* [from Old French]
3 → see also **income tax**
→ look at Word Web: **citizenship**

taxa|tion /tækseɪʃ°n/ **N-NONCOUNT** BUSINESS **Taxation** is when a government takes money from people and spends it on things such as education, health, and defense. ❑ *The council wants major changes in taxation.* [from Old French]

taxi /tæksi/ (**taxis**) **N-COUNT** A **taxi** is a car that you can hire, with its driver, to take you where you want to go. ❑ *We took a taxi back to our hotel.*

taxi|cab /tæksikæb/ (**taxicabs**) also **taxi-cab** **N-COUNT** A **taxicab** is the same as a **taxi**.

taxi stand (**taxi stands**) **N-COUNT** A **taxi stand** is a place where taxis wait for passengers, for example at an airport.

tax|ono|my /tæksɒnəmi/ (**taxonomies**) **N-COUNT/N-NONCOUNT** SCIENCE **Taxonomy** is the process of naming and classifying things such as animals and plants into groups within a larger system, according to their similarities and differences. [from French]

tax|payer /tækspeɪər/ (**taxpayers**) **N-COUNT** **Taxpayers** are people who pay tax. ❑ *The government has wasted taxpayers' money.*

tea /ti/ (**teas**)
1 **N-COUNT/N-NONCOUNT** **Tea** is a drink that you make by pouring boiling water on the dry leaves of a plant called the tea bush. ❑ *I made myself a cup of tea and sat down to watch TV.* ❑ *Would you like some tea?*
2 **N-COUNT/N-NONCOUNT** **Tea** is the chopped dried leaves of the plant that tea is made from.
3 **N-COUNT** A **tea** is a type of tea. ❑ *Do they drink the same teas that we drink?* [from Chinese]
→ look at Word Web: **tea**

teach /titʃ/ (**teaches, teaching, taught**)
1 **V-T** If you **teach** someone something, you give them instructions so that they know about it or so that they know how to do it. ❑ *She taught me to read.* ❑ *George taught him how to ride a horse.*
2 **V-T/V-I** If you **teach**, you give lessons in a subject at a school or a college. ❑ *Christine*

Word Web tea

Do you want to **brew** a good cup of **tea?** Don't use a **tea bag**. For the best taste, use fresh **tea leaves**. First, boil water in a **teakettle**. Use some of the water to warm the inside of a china **teapot**. Empty the pot, and add the tea leaves. Pour in more **boiling** water. Let the tea steep for at least five minutes. Serve the tea in thin china **cups**. Add milk and sugar if you wish.

---

teaches biology at Piper High. ❑ Mrs. Garcia has been teaching part-time for 16 years. ● **teach|er** (**teachers**) **N-COUNT** ❑ I was a teacher for 21 years. **3 V-T** To **teach** someone something means to make them think, feel, or act in a new or different way. ❑ We have to teach drivers to respect pedestrians. [from Old English]
→ look at Usage note at **learn**

Word Partnership	Use **teach** with :
ADV	teach *someone* **how** 1
N	teach *someone* **a skill**, teach **students** 1
	teach **children** 1–3
	teach **classes**, teach **courses**, teach **English/history/ reading/science**, teach **school** 2
V	**try to** teach 1–3

teach|ing /tíːtʃɪŋ/ (**teachings**)
1 N-NONCOUNT **Teaching** is the activity or job of giving lessons in a subject at a school or a college. ❑ The quality of teaching in the school is excellent.
2 N-COUNT The **teachings** of a particular person, school of thought, or religion are all the ideas and principles that they teach. ❑ ...the teachings of Jesus. [from Old English]

team /tíːm/ (**teams**)
1 N-COUNT SPORTS A **team** is a group of people who play a particular sport or game against other groups of people. ❑ Kate was on the school basketball team.
2 N-COUNT A **team** is any group of people who work together. ❑ A team of doctors visited the hospital yesterday. [from Old English]

team|mate /tíːmmeɪt/ (**teammates**) also **team-mate N-COUNT** SPORTS In a game or a sport, your **teammates** are the other members of your team. ❑ He was a great example to his teammates.

team|work /tíːmwɜrk/ **N-NONCOUNT** **Teamwork** is the ability that a group of people have to work well together. ❑ She knows the importance of teamwork.

Tea Par|ty N-PROPER SOCIAL STUDIES The **Tea Party** is a right-wing political movement in the U.S.

tea|pot /tíːpɒt/ (**teapots**) also **tea pot N-COUNT** A **teapot** is a container with a lid, a handle, and a spout, used for making and serving tea.
→ look at Word Web: **tea**

--- tear ---
1 CRYING
2 DAMAGING OR MOVING

1 tear /tɪər/ (**tears**)
1 N-COUNT **Tears** are the drops of liquid that come out of your eyes when you are crying. ❑ Her eyes filled with tears.
2 PHRASE If you are **in tears**, you are crying. ❑ By the end of the movie, we were all in tears.
3 PHRASE If you **burst into tears**, you suddenly start crying. ❑ She burst into tears and ran from the kitchen. [from Old English]
→ look at Word Web: **cry**

2 tear /tɛər/ (**tears, tearing, tore, torn**)
1 V-T If you **tear** something, you pull it into pieces or make a hole in it. ❑ I tore my coat on a nail. ❑ She tore the letter into several pieces.
2 N-COUNT **Tear** is also a noun. ❑ I looked through a tear in the curtains. [from Old English]
→ look at Picture Dictionary: **cut**
▶ **tear up** If you **tear up** a piece of paper or cloth, you tear it into small pieces. ❑ He tore up the letter and threw it in the fire.

Usage tear and break
The verbs *tear* and *break* both mean "to damage something," but *tear* is used only for paper, cloth, or other thin, flexible materials that you can pull apart: Philin fell down the stairs; she not only broke her arm, but she also tore a muscle in her leg. When the window broke, a piece of the glass tore Niran's shirt.

tease /tíːz/ (**teases, teasing, teased**) **V-T** If you **tease** someone, you laugh at them or make

t

jokes about them in order to embarrass them or annoy them. ❏ *Amber's brothers are always teasing her.* [from Old English]

Thesaurus	tease	Also look up :
V	aggravate, bother, provoke	

tea|spoon /tíspun/ (**teaspoons**) **N-COUNT**
A **teaspoon** is a small spoon that you use for putting sugar into tea or coffee. ❏ *Use a teaspoon to remove the seeds from the fruit.*

tech|ni|cal /tɛ́knɪkəl/
1 **ADJ** Something that is **technical** involves machines, processes, and materials that are used in science and industry. ❏ *We still have to solve a number of technical problems.*
● **tech|ni|cal|ly** /tɛ́knɪkli/ **ADV** ❏ *It is a very technically advanced car.*
2 **ADJ** You use **technical** to describe the practical skills and methods used to do an activity such as an art, a craft, or a sport. ❏ *Their technical ability is exceptional.* [from French]

Word Partnership	Use technical with :
N	technical **knowledge** **1** technical **assistance**, technical **difficulties**, technical **expertise**, technical **experts**, technical **information**, technical **issues**, technical **problems**, technical **services**, technical **skills**, technical **support**, technical **training** **2**
ADV	**highly** technical **1** **2**

tech|ni|cian /tɛknɪ́ʃən/ (**technicians**)
N-COUNT A **technician** is someone whose job involves skillful use of scientific or medical equipment. ❏ *Joseph works as a laboratory technician at St. Thomas's Hospital.* [from French]

tech|nique /tɛkník/ (**techniques**) **N-COUNT**
A **technique** is a special way of doing something. ❏ *Doctors have recently developed these new techniques.* [from French]

tech|nol|ogy /tɛknɒ́lədʒi/ (**technologies**)
N-COUNT/N-NONCOUNT TECHNOLOGY
Technology is the way that scientific knowledge is used in a practical way.
❏ *Computer technology has developed fast during the last 10 years.* [from Greek]
→ look at Word Web: **technology**

Word Partnership	Use technology with :
ADJ	**advanced** technology, **available** technology, **high** technology, **latest** technology, **medical** technology, **modern** technology, **sophisticated** technology, **wireless** technology
N	**computer** technology, **information** technology

tec|ton|ic plate /tɛktɒ́nɪk pleɪt/ (**tectonic plates**) **N-COUNT** SCIENCE **Tectonic plates** are very large pieces of the Earth's surface or crust.
→ look at Word Webs: **continent, earthquake**

ted|dy bear /tɛ́di bɛər/ (**teddy bears**)
N-COUNT A **teddy bear** is a soft toy that looks like a bear.

te|di|ous /tídiəs/ **ADJ** If something is **tedious**, it continues for too long, and is not interesting. ❏ *The movie was very tedious.* [from Latin]

teen /tín/ (**teens**)
1 **N-PLURAL** If you are in your **teens**, you are between thirteen and nineteen years old. ❏ *I met my husband when I was in my teens.*
2 **N-COUNT** A **teen** is a person who is in his or her teens. [from Old English]

teen|age /tíneɪdʒ/ **ADJ** **Teenage** children are aged between thirteen and nineteen years old. ❏ *Taylor is a typical teenage girl.* [from Old English]

T

Word Web   technology

Innovative technologies affect everything in our lives. In new homes, **state-of-the-art** computer systems control heating, lighting, communication, and entertainment systems. **Gadgets** such as **digital** music players are small and easy to carry. But high technology has a serious side, too. **Biotechnology** may help us cure diseases. It also raises many ethical questions. **Cutting-edge** biometric technology is replacing old-fashioned security systems. Soon your ATM will check your identity by scanning the iris of your eye and your laptop will scan your fingerprint.

| Word Link | *teen* ≈ *plus ten, from 13-19 : eighteen, seventeen, teenager* |

teen|ager /tíneɪdʒər/ (**teenagers**) **N-COUNT**
A **teenager** is someone who is between thirteen and nineteen years old. [from Old English]
→ look at Picture Dictionary: **age**
→ look at Word Web: **child**

teeth /tiθ/ **Teeth** is the plural of **tooth**. [from Old English]
→ look at Picture Dictionary: **face**
→ look at Word Web: **teeth**

tele|com|mu|ni|ca|tions
/tɛlɪkəmyuˌnɪkéɪʃ°nz/ **N-NONCOUNT**
TECHNOLOGY **Telecommunications** is the sending of signals and messages over long distances using electronic equipment.
❑ *Pete has 15 years' experience in the telecommunications industry.*

| Word Link | *gram* ≈ *writing : diagram, program, telegram* |

tele|gram /tɛlɪgræm/ (**telegrams**) **N-COUNT**
A **telegram** is a message that is sent by telegraph and then printed and delivered to someone. ❑ *The president received the news by telegram.*

tele|graph /tɛlɪgræf/ **N-NONCOUNT** **Telegraph** is a system of sending messages over long distances, either by means of electricity or by radio signals. Telegraph was used more often before the invention of telephones.

te|lepa|thy /tɪlɛpəθi/ **N-NONCOUNT** **Telepathy** is the direct communication of thoughts and feelings between people's minds, without the need to use speech or writing.
● **tele|path|ic** /tɛlɪpǽθɪk/ **ADJ** ❑ *They had a telepathic understanding.* [from Greek]

| Word Link | *phon* ≈ *sound : microphone, symphony, telephone* |

| Word Link | *tele* ≈ *distance : telephone, telescope, television* |

tele|phone /tɛlɪfoʊn/ (**telephones, telephoning, telephoned**)
1 **N-COUNT** A **telephone** is the piece of equipment that you use for speaking to someone who is in another place. ❑ *He got up and answered the telephone.*
2 **V-T/V-I** If you **telephone** someone, you speak to them using a telephone.
❑ *I telephoned my boyfriend to say I was sorry.*
❑ *He telephoned for a cab to take him to the airport.*
3 **PHRASE** If you are **on the telephone**, you are speaking to someone by telephone.
❑ *Linda was on the telephone for three hours this evening.*

| Word Link | *scope* ≈ *looking : horoscope, microscope, telescope* |

tele|scope /tɛlɪskoʊp/ (**telescopes**)
N-COUNT A **telescope** is an instrument shaped like a tube. It has special glass inside it that makes things that are far away look bigger and nearer when you look through it. [from Italian]
→ look at Word Web: **telescope**

| Word Link | *vid, vis* ≈ *seeing : television, videotape, visible* |

tele|vi|sion /tɛlɪvɪʒ°n, -vɪʒ-/ (**televisions**)
1 **N-COUNT** A **television** or a **TV** is a piece of electrical equipment with a screen on which you watch moving pictures with sound. ❑ *She turned the television on.*
2 **N-NONCOUNT** **Television** is the moving pictures and sounds that you watch and listen to on a television. ❑ *Michael spends too much time watching television.* ❑ *What's on*

t

Word Web teeth

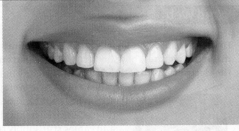

Dentists say **brushing** and **flossing** every day helps prevent **cavities**. Brushing removes food from the surface of the **teeth**. Flossing removes **plaque** from between teeth and **gums**. In many places, the water supply contains **fluoride** which also helps keep teeth healthy. If **tooth decay** does develop, a dentist can use a metal or plastic **filling** to repair the tooth. A badly damaged or broken tooth may require a **crown**. **Braces** straighten crooked teeth. Occasionally, a dentist must remove all of a patient's teeth. Then **dentures** take the place of natural teeth.

Word Web   telescope

Once, there were only two types of **telescopes**.
Refracting telescopes had lenses. **Reflecting**
telescopes had a **concave mirror**. The lenses and the
mirror had the same purpose. They **focused light
rays** and made a clear **image**. Today scientists use
radio telescopes to study the **universe**. These
telescopes can detect **X-rays** and other
types of invisible light **waves**.

television tonight? ❏ My favorite television program
is about to start.
→ look at Word Web: **television**

tell /tɛl/ (**tells, telling, told**)
■ **V-T** If you **tell** someone something, you
give them information. ❏ I told Rachel I got
the job. ❏ I called Anna to tell her how angry I was.
❏ Claire made me promise to tell her the truth.
❏ He told his story to The New York Times.
■ **V-T** If you **tell** someone **to** do something,
you order them to do it. ❏ The police officer told
him to get out of his car.
■ **V-T** If you can **tell** what is happening or
what is true, you are able to judge
correctly what is happening or what is
true. ❏ I could tell that Tom was tired and bored.
[from Old English]
▶ **tell off** If you **tell** someone **off**, you speak
to them angrily or seriously because they
have done something wrong. ❏ He never
listened to us when we told him off. ❏ I'm always
being told off for being so clumsy.

telo|phase /tɛləfeɪz/ (**telophases**) **N-COUNT/
N-NONCOUNT** SCIENCE **Telophase** is the final
stage of cell division, when two completely
separate cells are formed.

tem|per /tɛmpər/ (**tempers**)
■ **N-COUNT/N-NONCOUNT** If you have a
temper, you become angry very easily.
❏ Their mother had a terrible temper.
■ **N-COUNT/N-NONCOUNT** If you are **in** a bad
temper you are likely to become angry very
easily. ❏ I was in a bad temper last night because
I was so tired.
■ **PHRASE** If you **lose** your **temper**, you
suddenly become angry. ❏ Simon lost his
temper and punched me. [from Old English]

Word Partnership	Use **temper** with :
ADJ	**bad** temper, **explosive** temper, **quick** temper, **short** temper, **violent** temper ■
N	temper **tantrum** ■
V	**control your** temper, **have a** temper ■ **lose your** temper ■

tem|per|ate zone /tɛmpərɪt zoʊn, -prɪt/
(**temperate zones**) **N-COUNT** GEOGRAPHY
The Earth's **temperate zones** are the areas
where the climate is never extremely hot or
extremely cold. The northern temperate
zone extends from the Arctic Circle to the
Tropic of Cancer, and the southern
temperate zone extends from the Tropic of
Capricorn to the Antarctic Circle.

Word Web   television

For many years, all **televisions** used **cathode ray tubes**. These tubes
made the picture. They shot a stream of **electrons** at a **screen**. When
the electrons hit the screen, they made a tiny lighted area. This area is
 called a pixel. The average cathode ray TV
screen has about 200,000 pixels. Today, **HDTV**
(high-definition television) is very popular. Ground **stations, satellites**,
and **cables** still supply the TV **signal**. But HDTV uses **digital** information.
It produces the picture on a flat screen. Digital **receivers** can show two
million pixels per square inch, so they produce a much clearer **image**.

tem|pera|ture /tɛmprətʃər, -tʃʊər/ (**temperatures**)

1 N-COUNT/N-NONCOUNT The **temperature** of something is how hot or cold it is. ❑ *At night here, the temperature drops below freezing.*

2 N-NONCOUNT Your **temperature** is the temperature of your body, that shows whether you are healthy or not. ❑ *The baby's temperature continued to rise.*

3 PHRASE If you **have a temperature**, your temperature is higher than it should be.

4 PHRASE If someone **takes** your **temperature**, they use a thermometer to measure the temperature of your body. ❑ *The nurse took my temperature.* [from Latin]

→ look at Word Webs: **calorie, climate, cooking, forecast, greenhouse effect, habitat, thermometer, wind**

Word Partnership	Use **temperature** with :
ADJ	**average** temperature, **high/low** temperature, **normal** temperature **1**
V	**reach a** temperature **1**
N	**changes in/of** temperature, temperature **increase, ocean** temperature, **rise in** temperature, **room** temperature, **surface** temperature, **water** temperature **1**
	body temperature **2**

tem|ple /tɛmpəl/ (**temples**)

N-COUNT/N-NONCOUNT A **temple** is a building where people pray to their god or gods. ❑ *We visited the biggest Sikh temple in India.* [from Old English]

tem|po /tɛmpoʊ/ (**tempos** or **tempi**)

N-COUNT/N-NONCOUNT MUSIC The **tempo** of a piece of music is the speed at which it is played. [from Italian]

Word Link	tempo ≈ time : con**tempo**rary, **tempo**rarily, **tempo**rary

tem|po|rary /tɛmpərɛri/ **ADJ** If something is **temporary**, it lasts for only a certain time. ❑ *His job here is only temporary.*

● **tem|po|rari|ly** /tɛmpərɛərɪli/ **ADV** ❑ *Her website was temporarily shut down yesterday.* [from Latin]

tem|po|rize /tɛmpəraɪz/ (**temporizes, temporizing, temporized**) **V-T/V-I** If you say that someone **is temporizing**, you mean that they are doing unimportant things in order to delay making a decision or stating their opinion. [FORMAL] ❑ *They are still temporizing in*

the face of disaster. ❑ *"Not exactly, sir..." temporized Sloan.* [from French]

tempt /tɛmpt/ (**tempts, tempting, tempted**)

V-T If something **tempts** you, it attracts you and makes you want it, even though it may be wrong or harmful. ❑ *Credit cards can tempt people to buy things they can't afford.* ❑ *I was tempted to lie, but in the end I told the truth.* ● **tempt|ing ADJ** ❑ *The berries look tempting to children, but they're poisonous.* [from Old French]

Word Link	tempt ≈ trying : at**tempt**, **tempt**ation, **tempt**ed

temp|ta|tion /tɛmpteɪʃən/ (**temptations**)

N-COUNT/N-NONCOUNT Temptation is the feeling that you want to do something or to have something, when you know that it is wrong. ❑ *Exercise regularly and resist the temptation to eat snacks.* [from Old French]

tempt|ed /tɛmptɪd/ **ADJ** If you are **tempted to** do something, you would like to do it although it may not be a good idea. ❑ *I was tempted to buy a car, but I paid off my debts instead.* [from Old French]

ten /tɛn/

1 NUM MATH **Ten** is the number 10.

2 N-COUNT A **ten** is a ten-dollar bill. ❑ *Tobias reached into his pocket, pulled out a ten, and gave it to me.* [from Old English]

te|na|cious /tɪneɪʃəs/ **ADJ** A **tenacious** person is very determined and does not give up easily. ❑ *He's a very tenacious guy.*

● **te|na|cious|ly ADV** ❑ *The Dodgers clung tenaciously to their lead.* [from Latin]

ten|ant /tɛnənt/ (**tenants**) **N-COUNT**

A **tenant** is someone who pays money to you for the use of an apartment or an office that you own. ❑ *Each tenant in the apartment pays $200 a week.* [from Old French]

tend /tɛnd/ (**tends, tending, tended**) **V-T** If something **tends to** happen, it usually happens or it often happens. ❑ *Women tend to live longer than men.* [from Old French]

Word Partnership	Use **tend** with :
V	tend **to agree**, tend **to avoid**, tend **to become**, tend **to blame**, tend **to develop**, tend **to feel**, tend **to forget**, tend **to happen**, tend **to lose**, tend **to think**
N	**Americans** tend, **children/men/ women** tend, **people** tend

t

ten|den|cy /tɛndənsi/ (**tendencies**)
N-COUNT A **tendency** is something that usually happens. ❑ *Laura has a tendency to gossip.* [from Medieval Latin]

ten|der /tɛndər/ (**tenderer, tenderest**)
1 ADJ Someone or something that is **tender** is kind and gentle. ❑ *Her voice was tender.*
● **ten|der|ly ADV** ❑ *He kissed her tenderly.*
2 ADJ Meat that is **tender** is easy to cut or bite. ❑ *Cook for about 2 hours, until the meat is tender.*
3 ADJ If part of your body is **tender**, it is painful when you touch it. [from Old French]
→ look at Word Web: **cooking**

ten|nis /tɛnɪs/ **N-NONCOUNT SPORTS** Tennis is a game for two or four players, who use rackets to hit a ball across a net between them. [from Old French]
→ look at Picture Dictionary: **tennis**
→ look at Word Web: **park**

tense /tɛns/ (**tenser, tensest, tenses**)
1 ADJ If you are **tense**, you are anxious and nervous, and you do not feel relaxed. ❑ *The team were very tense before the game.*
2 ADJ If your body is **tense**, your muscles are tight and not relaxed. ❑ *A bath can relax tense muscles.*
3 N-COUNT LANGUAGE ARTS The **tense** of a verb is the form that shows whether something is happening in the past, the present, or the future. [Senses 1 and 2 from Latin. Sense 3 from Old French.]

Word Partnership	Use **tense** with :
N	tense **atmosphere**, tense **moment**, tense **mood**, tense, tense **situation** **1**
V	**feel** tense **1 2**
ADV	**very** tense **1 2**
ADJ	**future/past/perfect/present** tense **3**

ten|sion /tɛnʃ°n/ **N-NONCOUNT** Tension is a feeling of worry and anxiety that makes it impossible for you to feel relaxed. ❑ *Physical exercise can reduce tension.* [from Latin]
→ look at Word Web: **anger**

Word Partnership	Use **tension** with :
V	**ease** tension, tension **grows**, tension, **relieve** tension
N	**source of** tension

tent /tɛnt/ (**tents**) **N-COUNT**
A **tent** is a shelter made of thick cloth that is held up by poles and ropes. You sleep in a tent when you go camping. [from Old French]   tent

ten|ta|tive /tɛntətɪv/
1 ADJ **Tentative** agreements or plans are not definite or certain, but have been made as a first step. ❑ *...a tentative agreement to hold a conference.*
2 ADJ If someone is **tentative**, they are cautious and not very confident because they are uncertain or afraid. ❑ *My first attempts at complaining were tentative.*

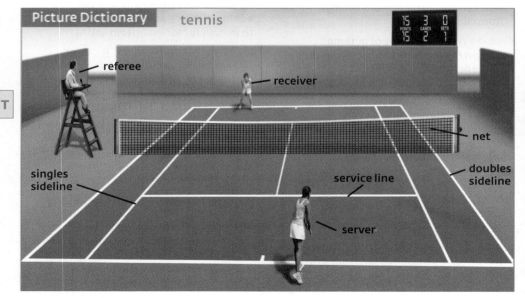

Picture Dictionary   tennis

referee

receiver

net

singles sideline

service line

doubles sideline

server

●**ten|ta|tive|ly** **ADV** ❑ *I tentatively suggested an alternative route.* [from Medieval Latin]

tenth /tɛnθ/ (**tenths**)
1 **ADJ/ADV** MATH The **tenth** item in a series is the one that you count as number ten. ❑ *She's having a party for her tenth birthday.*
2 **N-COUNT** MATH A **tenth** is one of ten equal parts of something (⅒). ❑ *She won the race by a tenth of a second.* [from Old English]

term /tɜrm/ (**terms**)
1 **N-COUNT** A **term** is a special word or expression that is used by experts in a particular subject. ❑ *Sodium chloride is the scientific term for table salt.*
2 **N-COUNT/N-NONCOUNT** A **term** is one of the periods of time that a school, a college, or a university year is divided into. ❑ *The school's Principal, Mrs. Johnson, will retire at the end of the term.*
3 **N-PLURAL** The **terms** of an agreement are the conditions that all of the people involved in it must agree to. ❑ *The terms of the agreement are quite simple.*
4 **PHRASE** If you talk about a subject **in terms of** something, you are saying which aspect of the subject you are considering. ❑ *Our goods compete in terms of quality and price.*
5 **PHRASE** If two people are **on good terms**, they are friendly with each other. ❑ *Madeleine is on good terms with Sarah.*
6 **PHRASE** You use the expressions **in the long term** and **in the short term** to talk about what will happen over a long period of time or over a short period of time. ❑ *In the long term we hope to open an office in Moscow.* [from Old French]

Word Link	**term, termin** ≈ limit, end : de**term**ine, **term**inal, **term**inate

ter|mi|nal /tɜrmɪnᵊl/ (**terminals**) **N-COUNT** A **terminal** is a place where people begin or end a trip by bus, aircraft, or ship. ❑ *Port Authority is the world's busiest bus terminal.* [from Latin]

ter|mi|nal ve|loc|ity (**terminal velocities**) **N-COUNT/N-NONCOUNT** SCIENCE The **terminal velocity** of a falling object is the maximum speed it reaches.

ter|mi|nate /tɜrmɪneɪt/ (**terminates, terminating, terminated**) **V-T/V-I** If you **terminate** something, or when it **terminates**, it ends. [FORMAL] ❑ *His contract was terminated early.* ❑ *She suddenly terminated the conversation.* [from Latin]

ter|race /tɛrɪs/ (**terraces**) **N-COUNT** A **terrace** is a flat area next to a building, where people can sit. ❑ *Our house has a terrace overlooking the ocean.* [from Old French]

ter|rain /təreɪn/ (**terrains**) **N-COUNT/N-NONCOUNT** The **terrain** in an area is the type of land that is there. ❑ *...mountainous terrain.* [from French]

ter|res|trial plan|et /tɪrɛstriəl plænɪt/ (**terrestrial planets**) **N-COUNT** SCIENCE A **terrestrial planet** is a planet with a rocky surface similar to the Earth's. In our solar system the four planets closest to the sun are **terrestrial planets**.

ter|ri|ble /tɛrɪbᵊl/
1 **ADJ** If something is **terrible**, it is extremely bad. ❑ *I have a terrible singing voice.* ●**ter|ri|bly** **ADV** ❑ *Our team played terribly today.*
2 **ADJ** If something is **terrible**, it causes great pain or sadness. ❑ *Thousands of people suffered terrible injuries.* ●**ter|ri|bly** **ADV** ❑ *These people have suffered terribly during 14 years of war.* [from Latin]

ter|rif|ic /tərɪfɪk/ **ADJ** If something is **terrific**, it is very good. [INFORMAL] ❑ *What a terrific idea!* [from Latin]

ter|ri|fy /tɛrɪfaɪ/ (**terrifies, terrifying, terrified**) **V-T** If something **terrifies** you, it makes you feel extremely afraid. ❑ *Flying terrifies him.* ●**ter|ri|fied** **ADJ** ❑ *Jacob is terrified of spiders.* [from Latin]

ter|ri|fy|ing /tɛrɪfaɪɪŋ/ **ADJ** If something is **terrifying**, it makes you very afraid. ❑ *That was a terrifying experience.* [from Latin]

ter|ri|to|rial /tɛrɪtɔriəl/ **ADJ** SOCIAL STUDIES **Territorial** means concerned with the ownership of a particular area of land or water. ❑ *...territorial disputes.* [from Latin]

Word Link	**ory** ≈ place where something happens : dormit**ory**, laborat**ory**, territ**ory**

ter|ri|tory /tɛrətɔri/ (**territories**)
1 **N-COUNT/N-NONCOUNT** SOCIAL STUDIES **Territory** is all the land that a particular country owns. ❑ *The central part of the Chimane forest is now Indian territory.*
2 **N-COUNT/N-NONCOUNT** SCIENCE An animal's **territory** is an area that it regards as its own and that it defends when other animals try to enter it. [from Latin]

t

Word Partnership	Use territory with :
N	**enemy** territory, **part of a** territory **1**
ADJ	**controlled** territory, **disputed** territory **familiar** territory, **vast** territory **1**

ter|ror /tɛrər/ **N-NONCOUNT** Terror is great fear. ❏ *I shook with terror.* [from Old French]

Word Partnership	Use terror with :
N	**acts of** terror, terror **alert**, terror **attack**, terror, **fight against** terror, **reign of** terror, terror **suspects** **2**

ter|ror|ism /tɛrərɪzəm/ **N-NONCOUNT** Terrorism is the use of violence to force a government to do something. ❏ *We need new laws to fight terrorism.*

ter|ror|ist /tɛrərɪst/ (**terrorists**) **N-COUNT** A **terrorist** is a person who uses violence to achieve their aims. ❏ *...terrorist attacks.* [from Old French]

test /tɛst/ (**tests, testing, tested**)
1 **V-T** If you **test** something, you use it or touch it to find out what condition it is in, or how well it works. ❏ *Test the temperature of the water with your wrist before you put your baby in the bath.* ❏ *The drug has only been tested on mice.*
2 **N-COUNT** Test is also a noun. ❏ *The car achieved great results in crash tests.*
3 **V-T** If you **test** someone, you ask them questions to find out how much they know about something. ❏ *The students were tested on grammar, spelling, and punctuation.*
4 **N-COUNT** Test is also a noun. ❏ *Only 15 of the 25 students passed the test.*
5 **N-COUNT** A medical **test** is an examination of a part of someone's body to check that they are healthy. ❏ *...blood tests.* [from Latin]
→ look at Word Web: **experiment**

Word Partnership	Use test with :
N	test **a drug, flight** test, test **a hypothesis 1** **achievement** test, **aptitude** test, **crash** test, test **data/results**, test **items**, **math/reading** test, test **preparation**, test **scores, standardized** test, **stress** test, test **takers 2** **blood** test, **drug** test, **HIV** test, **pregnancy** test **3**
ADJ	**nuclear** test **1** **diagnostic** test **3** **5**
V	**administer** a test, test **drive, fail a** test, **give** *someone* a test, **study for a** test, **take a** test **2**

tes|ti|cle /tɛstɪkəl/ (**testicles**) **N-COUNT** SCIENCE A man's **testicles** are the two reproductive glands that produce sperm. [from Latin]

tes|ti|fy /tɛstɪfaɪ/ (**testifies, testifying, testified**) **V-T/V-I** SOCIAL STUDIES When someone **testifies** in a court of law, they give a statement of what they saw someone do or what they know of a situation, after having promised to tell the truth. ❏ *He testified that he saw the officers hit Milner.* ❏ *Eva testified to seeing Herndon with a gun.* [from Latin]

tes|ti|mo|ny /tɛstɪmoʊni/ (**testimonies**)
1 **N-COUNT/N-NONCOUNT** SOCIAL STUDIES In a court of law, your **testimony** is a formal statement that you make about what you saw someone do or what you know of a situation, after having promised to tell the truth. ❏ *His testimony was an important element of the case.*
2 **N-NONCOUNT/N-SING** If one thing is **testimony to** another, it shows clearly that the second thing has a particular quality. ❏ *The environmental movement is testimony to people's love of nature.* [from Latin]
→ look at Word Web: **trial**

tes|tis /tɛstɪs/ (**testes** /tɛstiz/) **N-COUNT** SCIENCE A man's **testes** are his testicles. [from Latin]

test tube (**test tubes**) **N-COUNT** SCIENCE A **test tube** is a small glass container in the shape of a tube. Test tubes are used in scientific experiments.

text /tɛkst/ (**texts, texting, texted**)
1 **N-NONCOUNT** Text is all the words in a book, a document, a newspaper, or a magazine. ❏ *You can insert text, delete text, or move text around.*
2 **N-COUNT** A **text** is an academic or scientific book or short piece of writing. ❏ *The bookshelves were filled with religious texts.*
3 **N-COUNT** TECHNOLOGY A **text** is a message that you write and send using a cellphone. ❏ *We will send a text to your cellphone when the item is available for collection.*
4 **V-T** TECHNOLOGY If you **text** someone, you send them a text message on a cellphone. ❏ *Mary texted me when she got home.*
5 **N-COUNT** LANGUAGE ARTS The **text** of a speech, a broadcast, or a recording is the written version of it. [from Medieval Latin]
6 → see also **texting**
→ look at Word Web: **diary**

text|book /tɛkstbʊk/ (**textbooks**) also **text book** **N-COUNT** A **textbook** is a book containing facts about a particular subject that is used by people studying that subject. ❑ *Amy was in the library reading a textbook on international law.*

tex|tile /tɛkstaɪl/ (textiles) **N-COUNT**
A **textile** is any type of cloth. ❑ *...the textile industry.* [from Latin]
→ look at Word Webs: **industry, quilt**

text|ing /tɛkstɪŋ/
1 N-NONCOUNT TECHNOLOGY **Texting** is sending messages in writing using a cellphone. ❑ *Texting is more common among 11 to 14-year-olds than making calls.* [from Medieval Latin]
2 → see also **text**

text mes|sage (text messages) **N-COUNT**
TECHNOLOGY A **text message** is the same as a **text**. ❑ *Lauren sent her boyfriend a text message asking him to meet her at the diner at eight.*

text mes|sag|ing **N-NONCOUNT**
TECHNOLOGY **Text messaging** is the same as **texting**. ❑ *...unlimited text messaging for the whole family.*

tex|ture /tɛkstʃər/ (textures)
1 N-COUNT/N-NONCOUNT ARTS The **texture** of something is the way that it feels when you touch it. ❑ *The cheese has a soft, creamy texture.*
2 N-COUNT/N-NONCOUNT MUSIC The **texture** of a piece of music is the way that the different sounds combine to produce an overall effect.
3 N-COUNT/N-NONCOUNT The **texture** of something, especially food or soil, is its structure, for example whether it is light with lots of holes, or very heavy and solid. [from Latin]

than /ðən, STRONG ðæn/
1 PREP You use **than** when you are comparing two people or things. ❑ *Tom is taller than his dad.* ❑ *Children learn faster than adults.* ❑ *They talked on the phone for more than an hour.*
2 CONJ **Than** is also a conjunction. ❑ *He should have helped her more than he did.* [from Old English]

Usage **than** and **then**

Than and *then* are often confused. Use *than* to make a comparison. *The unemployment rate is lower now than it was last year.* *Then* means "at that time" or "next." *There were a lot more unemployed people then. Slice the skin off the fruit and then cut it into quarters.*

thank /θæŋk/ (thanks, thanking, thanked)
1 INTERJ You say **Thank you** or, in more informal English, **Thanks** when you want to show that you are grateful for something that someone has done for you. ❑ *Thank you very much for inviting me to your birthday party.* ❑ *Thanks for the information.* ❑ *"Would you like a cup of coffee?"—"Thank you, I'd love one."* ❑ *"Tea?"— "No thanks."*
2 V-T If you **thank** someone **for** something, you say "thank you" to show that you are grateful to them for it. ❑ *I thanked them for all their kindness to me.*
3 N-PLURAL If you express your **thanks** to someone, you say that you are grateful to them for something. ❑ *I would like to express my thanks and praise to the wonderful hospital staff.*
4 PHRASE If something happens **thanks to** a particular person or thing, it happens because of them. ❑ *Thanks to Sean's courage, his dad survived.* [from Old English]

thank|ful /θæŋkfəl/ **ADJ** If you are **thankful**, you are very grateful and glad that something has happened. ❑ *I'm so thankful that they are all safe.* [from Old English]

thank|ful|ly /θæŋkfəli/ **ADV** You use **thankfully** in order to express approval or happiness about something. ❑ *Thankfully, she was not injured.* [from Old English]

Thanks|giving /θæŋksgɪvɪŋ/ (Thanksgivings) **N-COUNT/N-NONCOUNT**
Thanksgiving or **Thanksgiving Day** is a public holiday in the United States on the fourth Thursday in November, and in Canada on the second Monday in October. At Thanksgiving, families have a special meal together to celebrate all the good things in their lives. ❑ *Dad always managed to be home for Thanksgiving.*

that /ðæt/
1 DET You use **that** to talk about someone or something that is a distance away from you in position or time. ❑ *Look at that guy over there.*
2 PRON **That** is also a pronoun. ❑ *What's that?*
3 PRON You use **that** to talk about something that you have mentioned before. ❑ *They said you wanted to talk to me. Why was that?*
4 PRON You use **that** to show which person or thing you are talking about. ❑ *There's the girl that I told you about.* ❑ *He hates the town that he lives in.*

t

5 **CONJ** You can use **that** to join two parts of a sentence. ❑ *He said that he and his wife were coming to New York.* ❑ *I felt sad that he was leaving.*

6 **CONJ** You use **that** after "so" and "such" to talk about the result of something. ❑ *I shouted so that they could hear me.*

7 **ADV** If something is **not that** bad, it is not as bad as it might be. ❑ *Well, actually, it's not that expensive.*

8 → see also **those**

9 **PHRASE** You can use **That's that** to say that you have finished with a particular subject. [SPOKEN] ❑ *If that's your final decision, I guess that's that.* [from Old English]

that's /ðæts/ **That's** is short for "that is."

thaw /θɔ/ (**thaws, thawing, thawed**) **V-T/V-I** When ice, snow, or something else that is frozen **thaws**, it melts. ❑ *We will leave when the snow thaws.* ❑ *How long does it take to thaw a frozen chicken?* [from Old English]

the

PRONUNCIATION HELP

Pronounce **the** /ði/ before a vowel.
Pronounce **the** /ðə/ before a consonant.

---

1 **DET** You use **the** before a noun when it is clear which person or thing you are talking about. ❑ *The office staff here are all British.* ❑ *It's always hard to think about the future.* ❑ *The doctor's on his way.*

2 **DET** You use **the** before a singular noun to talk about things of that type in general. ❑ *The computer has developed very fast in recent years.*

3 **DET** You use **the** with adjectives and plural nouns to talk about all people of a particular type or nationality. ❑ *...the British and the French.*

4 **DET** You use **the** in front of dates. ❑ *The meeting should take place on the fifth of May.*

5 **DET** You use **the** in front of superlative adjectives and adverbs. ❑ *Daily walks are the best exercise.*

6 **DET** You use **the** in front of each of two comparative adjectives or adverbs when you are describing how one amount or quality changes in relation to another. ❑ *The more you learn, the greater your chances of success.*

7 **DET** When you express rates, prices, and measurements, you can use **the** to say how many units apply to each of the items being measured. ❑ *...cars that get more miles to the gallon.* [from Old English]

thea|ter /θiətər/ (**theaters**)

1 **N-COUNT** ARTS A **theater** is a place where you go to see plays, shows, and movies. ❑ *Last evening, we went to the theater to see a play by Chekhov.* ❑ *A 14-screen movie theater opened in the town last November.*

2 **N-SING** ARTS You can refer to work in the theater such as acting or writing plays as **the theater**. [from Latin]
→ look at Picture Dictionary: **drama**
→ look at Word Webs: **theater, city**

thea|ter of the ab|surd **N-SING** ARTS The **theater of the absurd** is a style of theater that began in the 1950s. It represents life as meaningless or irrational.

the|at|ri|cal /θiætrɪkᵊl/

1 **ADJ** ARTS **Theatrical** means relating to the theater. ❑ *...great theatrical performances.*

2 **ADJ** **Theatrical** behavior is deliberately exaggerated and unnatural. ❑ *...a theatrical gesture.* ● **the|at|ri|cal|ly** /θiætrɪkli/ **ADV** ❑ *He looked theatrically at his watch.* [from Latin]

the|at|ri|cal con|ven|tion (**theatrical conventions**) **N-COUNT/N-NONCOUNT** ARTS

Word Web   theater

It only takes about two hours to watch a **play**. It takes a lot of time, money, and work before the curtain rises on the **stage**. First, a **playwright** writes an interesting story. Then, a **producer** gets the money for the **production** and finds a **theater**. **Actors** **audition** for the play. The **director casts** the actors in the **roles**. **Rehearsals** sometimes go on for months. The **set, lighting,** and **costumes** all have to be designed and made. Special **props** and **makeup** are usually necessary. A **band** or an **orchestra** is needed if the play is a **musical**. It takes a large **crew** to do all these things.

A **theatrical convention** is a part of the style or structure of a play that is traditional and therefore familiar to most audiences.

the|at|ri|cal ex|peri|ence (theatrical experiences) **N-COUNT** ARTS A **theatrical experience** is an occasion when someone attends a play, a musical, or other theatrical production.

the|at|ri|cal game (theatrical games) **N-COUNT** ARTS **Theatrical games** are exercises, such as role-playing, that are designed to develop people's acting skills.

theft /θɛft/ (thefts) **N-COUNT/N-NONCOUNT** **Theft** is the crime of stealing. ❏ *Martinez was arrested for car theft and assault.* [from Old English]
→ look at Picture Dictionary: **crime**

their /ðɛər/

> **LANGUAGE HELP**
> **Their** is the third person plural possessive determiner.

1 **DET** You use **their** to show that something belongs to or relates to the group of people, animals, or things that you are talking about. ❏ *Janis and Kurt have announced their engagement.* ❏ *They took off their coats.*
2 **DET** You use **their** instead of "his or her" to show that something belongs or relates to a person, without saying if that person is a man or a woman. Some people think this use is incorrect. ❏ *Each student works at their own pace.* [from Old Norse]

> **Usage** **their**, **there**, and **they're**
> *Their, there,* and *they're* sound the same but have very different meanings. *Their* is the possessive form of *they: They took off their shoes to avoid getting the floor muddy. There* can be the subject of *be* and can indicate location: *There are two seats here and another two there. They're* is the contraction of *they are: They're wondering what time dinner will be ready.*

theirs /ðɛərz/

> **LANGUAGE HELP**
> **Theirs** is the third person plural possessive pronoun.

PRON You use **theirs** to show that something belongs or relates to the group of people, animals, or things that you are talking about. ❏ *The people at the table next to theirs were talking loudly.* [from Old Norse]

them /ðəm, STRONG ðɛm/

> **LANGUAGE HELP**
> **Them** is a third person plural pronoun. **Them** is used as the object of a verb or preposition.

1 **PRON** You use **them** to talk about more than one person, animal, or thing. ❏ *I've lost my keys. Have you seen them?*
2 **PRON** You can use **them** instead of "him or her" to talk about a person without saying whether that person is a man or a woman. ❏ *If anyone calls, tell them I'm out.* [from Old English]

theme /θim/ (themes)

1 **N-COUNT** LANGUAGE ARTS The **theme** of a piece of writing or a discussion is its most important idea or its subject. ❏ *Progress was the main theme of his speech.*
2 **N-COUNT** ARTS A **theme** in an artist's work or in a work of literature is an idea in it that the artist or writer develops or repeats. [from Latin]
→ look at Word Web: **myth**

> **Word Partnership** Use **theme** with :
>
> | | |
> |---|---|
> | N | theme **of a book/movie/story** **1** |
> | ADJ | **central** theme, **common** theme, **dominant** theme, **main** theme, **major** theme, **new** theme, **recurring** theme **1** |

the|me and vari|ation (themes and variations) **N-COUNT/N-NONCOUNT** MUSIC Music that uses **theme and variation** begins with a particular musical theme and then repeats the theme with small changes.

them|selves /ðəmsɛlvz/

> **LANGUAGE HELP**
> **Themselves** is the third person plural reflexive pronoun.

1 **PRON** You use **themselves** to talk about people, animals, or things that you have just mentioned. ❏ *They all seemed to be enjoying themselves.*
2 **PRON** If some people did something **themselves**, they did it, and not anyone else. ❏ *My parents designed our house themselves.*

then /ðɛn/

1 **ADV** **Then** means at a particular time in the past or in the future. ❏ *I bought this apartment in 2005. Since then, house prices have fallen.*
2 **ADV** You use **then** to say that one thing happens after another. ❏ *Add the onion and then the garlic.*

t

3 **ADV** You can use **then** to start the second part of a sentence that begins with "if." ❑ *If you are not sure about this, then you must say so.*

4 **ADV** You can use **then** to mean "so" or "because." ❑ *I'll get this done right now. Then you won't have to worry about it later.* [from Old English]

→ look at Usage note at **than**

the|ol|o|gy /θiɒlədʒi/ **N-NONCOUNT** **Theology** is the study of religion and the nature of God. ❑ *...questions of theology.*
● theo|logi|cal /θiəlɒdʒɪkəl/ **ADJ** ❑ *...theological books.* [from Late Latin]

theo|reti|cal /θiərɛtɪkəl/ **ADJ** **Theoretical** means based on or using the ideas and abstract principles of a particular subject, rather than its practical aspects. ❑ *...theoretical physics.* [from Late Latin]

theo|reti|cal|ly /θiərɛtɪkli/ **ADV** You use **theoretically** to say that although something is supposed to be true or to happen in the way stated, it may not in fact be true or happen in that way. ❑ *Such an event is theoretically possible but highly unlikely.* [from Late Latin]

theo|ry /θɪəri/ (theories)
N-COUNT/N-NONCOUNT A **theory** is an idea or a set of ideas that tries to explain something. ❑ *The Big Bang Theory explains the beginning of the universe.* [from Late Latin]

→ look at Word Webs: **evolution, experiment, science**

Word Partnership	Use **theory** with :
N	**conspiracy** theory, **evidence for a** theory, theory **and practice, support for a** theory **1**
V	**advance a** theory, **develop a** theory, theory, **test a** theory

thera|pist /θɛrəpɪst/ (therapists) **N-COUNT** A **therapist** is a person who helps people who have emotional or physical problems. ❑ *Scott saw a therapist after his marriage ended in 2004.* [from New Latin]

the|rap|sid /θəræpsɪd/ (therapsids) **N-COUNT SCIENCE** **Therapsids** were animals similar to reptiles that lived in prehistoric times and evolved into mammals. [from New Latin]

thera|py /θɛrəpi/ (therapies)
1 **N-NONCOUNT** **Therapy** is the process of talking to a person with special training

about your problems and your relationships so that you can understand them and then change the way you feel and behave. ❑ *He returned to work, but he was still having therapy.*

2 **N-COUNT/N-NONCOUNT** **Therapy** or a **therapy** is a treatment for a particular illness or condition. ❑ *Scientists are working on a therapy to slow down the aging process.* [from New Latin]

→ look at Word Web: **cancer**

there

> **PRONUNCIATION HELP**
> Pronounce meaning **1** /ðər, STRONG ðɛr/.
> Pronounce meanings **2** to **5** /ðɛər/.

1 **PRON** You use **there** with the verb "be" to say that something exists or is happening. ❑ *There is a swimming pool in the backyard.* ❑ *Are there any cookies left?*

2 **ADV** You use **there** to talk about a place that has already been mentioned. ❑ *I'm going back to California. My family have lived there for many years.*

3 **ADV** You use **there** to talk about a place that you are pointing to or looking at. ❑ *"Where is Mr. Hernandez?"—"He's sitting over there."* ❑ *There she is, at the corner of the street.*

4 **ADV** You use **there** when you are speaking on the telephone, to ask if someone is available to speak to you. ❑ *Hello, is Tony there, please?*

5 **PHRASE** You say **There you are** or **There you go** when you are offering something to someone. [SPOKEN] ❑ *"There you go, Mr. Walters,"* she said, giving him his documents. [from Old English]

→ look at Usage note at **their**

there|after /ðɛəræftər/ **ADV** **Thereafter** means after the event or date mentioned. [FORMAL] ❑ *The plan will help you lose 3–4 pounds the first week, and 1–2 pounds the weeks thereafter.*

there|fore /ðɛərfɔr/ **ADV** You use **therefore** when you are talking about the result of an action or a situation. ❑ *Matthew is injured and therefore will not play in Saturday's game.*

ther|mal /θɜrməl/
1 **ADJ** **Thermal** means relating to or caused by heat. ❑ *...thermal power stations.*
2 **ADJ** **Thermal** clothes are specially designed to keep you warm. ❑ *...thermal underwear.* [from Greek]

→ look at Word Web: **solar**

ther|mal en|er|gy **N-NONCOUNT** SCIENCE
Thermal energy is energy in the form
of heat.

ther|mal equi|lib|rium /θɜrmᵊl
ikwɪlɪbriəm/ **N-NONCOUNT** SCIENCE Two or
more substances that are in **thermal
equilibrium** have the same temperature.

ther|mal ex|pan|sion **N-NONCOUNT**
SCIENCE **Thermal expansion** is the increase
in a substance's size or volume that occurs
when it is heated.

ther|mal im|ag|ing /θɜrmᵊl ɪmɪdʒɪŋ/
N-NONCOUNT TECHNOLOGY **Thermal imaging**
is a way of producing images of people or
things using special equipment that reacts
to the heat that comes from them. ❑ *He was
found by a police helicopter using thermal-imaging
equipment.*

ther|mal pol|lu|tion **N-NONCOUNT** SCIENCE
Thermal pollution is an increase in the
temperature of a river or a lake that is
harmful to the organisms living there.
Thermal pollution often occurs when water
that has been used in industrial processes is
returned to a river or a lake.

ther|mo|cline /θɜrməklaɪn/ (**thermoclines**)
N-COUNT SCIENCE A **thermocline** is a layer of
water in an ocean or a lake that separates
the warmer water on the surface from the
colder water below it.

ther|mo|cou|ple /θɜrməkʌpᵊl/
(**thermocouples**) **N-COUNT** SCIENCE
A **thermocouple** is a kind of thermometer
that uses an electric current to measure
temperature.

ther|mom|eter /θərmɒmɪtər/
(**thermometers**) **N-COUNT** A **thermometer** is
an instrument for measuring how hot or

cold something is.
→ look at Word Web: **thermometer**

ther|mo|sphere /θɜrməsfɪər/
(**thermospheres**) **N-COUNT** SCIENCE The
thermosphere is the highest layer of the
Earth's atmosphere.

these

> **PRONUNCIATION HELP**
> Pronounce the determiner /ðiz/.
> Pronounce the pronoun /ðiz/.

1 **DET** You use **these** to talk about people or
things that are near you, especially when
you touch them or point to them. ❑ *These
scissors are heavy.*
2 **PRON** **These** is also a pronoun. ❑ *Do you
like these?*
3 **DET** You use **these** to talk about someone
or something that you have already
mentioned. ❑ *These people need more support.*
4 **DET** You use **these** to introduce people or
things that you are going to talk about.
❑ *If you're looking for a builder, these phone
numbers will be useful.*
5 **DET** You use **these** in the expression
these days to mean "at the present time."
❑ *These days, people appreciate a chance to relax.*
[from Old English]

they /ðeɪ/

> **LANGUAGE HELP**
> **They** is a third person plural pronoun.
> **They** is used as the subject of a verb.

1 **PRON** You use **they** when you are talking
about more than one person, animal, or thing
that you have already mentioned. ❑ *She said
goodbye to the children as they left for school.*
❑ *"Where are your toys?"—"They're in the garden."*
2 **PRON** You can use **they** instead of "he or
she" when you are talking about a person

t

Word Web   **thermometer**

The first scientist to **measure** heat was Galileo. He invented a simple
water **thermometer** in 1593. But his thermometer did not have a **scale**
to show exact **temperatures**. In 1714, a German named Daniel Fahrenheit
invented a **mercury** thermometer. In 1724, he added the **Fahrenheit scale**
of temperatures with 32°F* as the **freezing** temperature of water. On this
scale, water **boils** at 212°F. In 1742, Anders **Celsius** invented the **centigrade**
scale. Centigrade means "divided into 100 **degrees**." On this scale, water
freezes at 0°C* and boils at 100° C.

32°F = thirty-two degrees Fahrenheit
0°C = zero degrees Celsius or zero degrees centigrade

without saying whether that person is a man or a woman. ❑ *Someone phoned. They said they would call back later.*

■ **PRON** You use **they say** when you are making general statements about what people say, think, or do. ❑ *They say there are plenty of opportunities out there.* [from Old Norse]

they'd /ðeɪd/
■ **They'd** is short for "they had." ❑ *They'd both lived on this road all their lives.*
■ **They'd** is short for "they would." ❑ *He agreed that they'd visit her later.*

they'll /ðeɪl/ **They'll** is short for "they will." ❑ *They'll probably be here Monday.*

they're /ðɛər/ **They're** is short for "they are." ❑ *People eat when they're depressed.*
→ look at Usage note at **their**

they've /ðeɪv/ **They've** is short for "they have," especially when "have" is an auxiliary verb. ❑ *They've gone out.*

thick /θɪk/ (**thicker, thickest**)
■ **ADJ** If something is **thick**, it has a large distance between one side and the other. ❑ *I cut myself a thick slice of bread.*
■ **ADJ** You can use **thick** to say or ask how wide or deep something is. ❑ *The book is two inches thick.* ❑ *How thick are these walls?*
● **thick|ness** (**thicknesses**)
N-COUNT/N-NONCOUNT ❑ *The cooking time depends on the thickness of the steaks.*
■ **ADJ** **Thick** hair consists of a lot of hairs growing closely together. ❑ *Jessica has thick dark curly hair.*
■ **ADJ** **Thick** smoke or cloud is difficult to see through. ❑ *The crash happened in thick fog.*
■ **ADJ** If a liquid is **thick**, it does not flow easily. ❑ *Cook the sauce until it is thick and creamy.* [from Old English]

Word Partnership	Use **thick** with :
N	thick **carpet**, thick **glass**, thick **ice**, thick **layer**, thick **lips**, thick **neck**, thick **slice**, thick **wall** ■
	feet/inches thick ■
	thick **beard**, thick **fur**, thick **grass**, thick **hair** ■
	thick **air**, thick **clouds**, thick **fog**, thick **smoke** ■
ADV	so thick, **too** thick, **very** thick ■-■

thief /θif/ (**thieves** /θivz/) **N-COUNT** A **thief** is a person who steals something from another person. ❑ *The thieves took his camera.* [from Old English]

thigh /θaɪ/ (**thighs**) **N-COUNT** Your **thighs** are the top parts of your legs. ❑ *She's broken her thigh bone.* [from Old English]
→ look at Picture Dictionary: **body**

thin /θɪn/ (**thinner, thinnest**)
■ **ADJ** If something is **thin**, there is a small distance between one side and the other. ❑ *His arms and legs were very thin.* ❑ *The book is printed on very thin paper.*
■ **ADJ** If a person or an animal is **thin**, they have no extra fat on their body. ❑ *Bob was a tall, thin man.*
■ **ADJ** If a liquid is **thin**, it flows easily. ❑ *The soup was thin and tasteless.* [from Old English]

Thesaurus	thin	Also look up :
ADJ		flimsy, transparent; (*ant.*) dense, solid, thick ■
		lean, skinny, slender, slim; (*ant.*) fat, heavy ■
		watery, weak; (*ant.*) thick ■

Word Partnership	Use **thin** with :
N	thin **film**, thin **ice**, thin **layer**, thin **line**, **razor** thin, thin **slice**, thin **smile**, thin **strips** ■
	thin **body**, thin **face**, thin **fingers**, thin **legs**, thin **lips**, thin **mouth** ■ ■
	thin **man/woman** ■
ADJ	**long and** thin ■
	tall and thin ■
ADV	**extremely** thin, **too** thin, **very** thin ■-■

thing /θɪŋ/ (**things**)
■ **N-COUNT** A **thing** is an object. ❑ *What's that thing in the middle of the road?*
■ **N-PLURAL** Your **things** are your possessions. ❑ *She told him to take all his things and not to return.*
■ **N-SING** **Thing** is often used instead of the pronouns "anything," or "everything" in order to emphasize what you are saying. ❑ *Don't you worry about a thing.* ❑ *It isn't going to solve a single thing.*
■ **N-COUNT** A **thing** is something that happens or something that you think or talk about. ❑ *They were driving home when a strange thing happened.* ❑ *We had so many things to talk about.*
■ **N-PLURAL** You can use **things** to talk about life in general. ❑ *How are things with you?* ❑ *Things are a bit busy at the moment.* [from Old English]

think /θɪŋk/ (**thinks, thinking, thought**)
■ **V-T/V-I** If you **think** something, you

believe it or have an opinion about it. ❏ *I think that it will snow tomorrow.* ❏ *What do you think of my idea?*

2 **V-I** When you **think**, you use your mind to consider something. ❏ *She closed her eyes for a moment, trying to think.* ❏ *What are you thinking about?*

3 **V-T** If you **think** something at a particular moment, you have words or ideas in your mind without saying them out loud. ❏ *She must be sick, Tatiana thought.* ❏ *I remember thinking how lovely he looked.*

4 **V-T/V-I** If you **think of** something, it comes into your mind. ❏ *I know who he is but I can't think of his name.* ❏ *I was trying to think what else we could do.*

5 **V-I** If you **are thinking of** or **are thinking about** doing something, you are considering doing it. ❏ *I'm thinking of going to college next year.* ❏ *I was trying to think what else we could do.* [from Old English]

6 → see also **thought**

▶ **think over** If you **think** something **over**, you consider it carefully before you make a decision about it. ❏ *They've offered her the job but she said she needs time to think it over.*

Thesaurus	think	Also look up :
v	believe, consider, feel, judge, understand **1** analyze, evaluate, meditate, reflect, study **2** recall, remember; *(ant.)* forget **4**	

third /θ₃rd/ (**thirds**)

1 **ADJ/ADV** MATH The **third** item in a series is the one that you count as number three. ❏ *My office is the third door on the right.*

2 **N-COUNT** MATH A **third** is one of three equal parts of something (⅓). [from Old English]

Third World **N-PROPER** SOCIAL STUDIES Countries that are poor and do not have much industrial development are sometimes referred to together as **the Third World**. Some people find this term offensive. ❏ *...development in the Third World.*

thirst /θ₃rst/ **N-NONCOUNT/N-SING** Thirst is the feeling that you want to drink something. ❏ *Drink water to satisfy your thirst.* [from Old English]

thirsty /θ₃rsti/ (**thirstier, thirstiest**) **ADJ** If you are **thirsty**, you want to drink something. ❏ *Drink some water whenever you feel thirsty.* [from Old English]

thir|teen /θ₃rtin/ **NUM** MATH **Thirteen** is the number 13. [from Old English]

thir|teenth /θ₃rtinθ/ **ADJ/ADV** MATH The **thirteenth** item in a series is the one that you count as number thirteen. ❏ *...his thirteenth birthday.* [from Old English]

thir|ti|eth /θ₃rtiəθ/ **ADJ/ADV** MATH The **thirtieth** item in a series is the one that you count as number thirty. ❏ *...the thirtieth anniversary of my parents' wedding.* [from Old English]

thir|ty /θ₃rti/

1 **NUM** MATH **Thirty** is the number 30.

2 **N-PLURAL** The **thirties** are the years between 1930 and 1939. ❏ *...Hollywood stars of the thirties.*

3 **N-PLURAL** When you talk about the **thirties**, you mean the numbers between 30 and 39. For example, if you are **in** your **thirties**, you are aged between 30 and 39. ❏ *The temperature was in the low thirties.* [from Old English]

this

PRONUNCIATION HELP
Pronounce the determiner /ðɪs/. Pronounce the pronoun /ðɪs/.

1 **DET** You use **this** to talk about a person or a thing that is near you, especially when you touch them or point to them. ❏ *I like this room much better than the other one.*

2 **PRON** This is also a pronoun. ❏ *"Would you like a different one?"—"No, this is great."*

3 **DET** You use **this** to talk about someone or something that you have already mentioned. ❏ *How can we solve this problem?*

4 **PRON** This is also a pronoun. ❏ *I have seen many movies, but never one like this.*

5 **PRON** You use **this** to introduce someone or something that you are going to talk about. ❏ *This is what I will do. I will telephone Anna and explain.*

6 **PRON** You use **this** when you are talking about a general situation or event that is happening, and that you feel involved in. ❏ *I thought, this is why I traveled thousands of miles.* ❏ *Tim, this is awful.*

7 **DET** You use **this** to talk about the next day, month, or season. ❏ *We have tickets for this Sunday's performance.* ❏ *We're getting married this June.*

8 **PRON** You use **this is** to say who you are when you are speaking on the telephone. ❏ *Hello, this is John Thompson.* [from Old English]

t

thor|ax /ˈθɔːræks/ (**thoraxes** or **thoraces** /ˈθɔːrəsiz/) **N-COUNT** SCIENCE Your **thorax** is the part of your body between your neck and your waist. [from Latin]

thorn /θɔːrn/ (**thorns**) **N-COUNT** **Thorns** are the sharp points on some plants and trees. ❑ *He removed a thorn from his foot.* [from Old English]

thor|ough /ˈθɜːroʊ/ **ADJ** If an action or an activity is **thorough**, it is done completely, and with great attention to detail. ❑ *There will be a thorough investigation into the cause of the crash.* ● **thor|ough|ly** **ADV** ❑ *The food must be thoroughly cooked.* [from Old English]

those

PRONUNCIATION HELP
Pronounce the determiner /ðoʊz/.
Pronounce the pronoun /ðoʊz/.

1 **DET** You use **those** when you are talking about people or things that are a distance away from you in position or time, especially when you point to them. ❑ *What are those buildings?*
2 **PRON** **Those** is also a pronoun. ❑ *Those are nice shoes.*
3 **DET** You use **those** to talk about people or things that have already been mentioned. ❑ *I don't know any of those people you mentioned.* [from Old English]

though /ðoʊ/
1 **CONJ** **Though** means although, or despite the fact that. ❑ *I love him though I do not know him.* ❑ *Ashley plays in adult tennis games even though she is only 15.*
2 **CONJ** **Though** means but. ❑ *I think I left home at about seven thirty, though I could be wrong.* [from Old English]

thought /θɔːt/ (**thoughts**)
1 **Thought** is the past tense and past participle of **think**.
2 **N-COUNT** A **thought** is an idea or an opinion. ❑ *The thought of Nick made her sad.* ❑ *I just had a thought. Why don't you have a party?* ❑ *What are your thoughts about the political situation?*
3 **N-NONCOUNT** **Thought** is the activity of thinking, especially deeply and carefully. ❑ *Alice was deep in thought.* [from Old English]

thought|ful /ˈθɔːtfəl/
1 **ADJ** If you are **thoughtful**, you are quiet and serious because you are thinking about something. ❑ *Nancy paused, looking thoughtful.*

● **thought|ful|ly** **ADV** ❑ *Daniel nodded thoughtfully.*
2 **ADJ** If you are **thoughtful**, you think and care about other people's feelings. ❑ *Ben is a thoughtful and caring boy.* [from Old English]

thought|less /ˈθɔːtlɪs/ **ADJ** If you are **thoughtless**, you do not care or think about other people's feelings. ❑ *It was thoughtless of me to forget your birthday.* [from Old English]

thou|sand /ˈθaʊzᵊnd/ (**thousands**)

LANGUAGE HELP
The plural is **thousand** after a number.

1 **NUM** MATH A **thousand** or one **thousand** is the number 1,000. ❑ *Over five thousand people attended the conference.*
2 **NUM** **Thousands of** things or people means a very large number of them. ❑ *I have been there thousands of times.*
3 **PRON** You can also use **thousands** as a pronoun. ❑ *Thousands lost their homes in the flood.* [from Old English]

thou|sandth /ˈθaʊzᵊnθ/ (**thousandths**)
1 **ADJ/ADV** The **thousandth** item in a series is the one you count as number one thousand. ❑ *She wondered, for the hundredth or thousandth time, what he was thinking.*
2 **N-COUNT** MATH A **thousandth** is one of one thousand equal parts of something. ❑ *The material is only five thousandths of a millimeter thick.* [from Old English]

thread /θrɛd/ (**threads, threading, threaded**)
1 **N-COUNT/N-NONCOUNT** **Thread** or a **thread** is a long, very thin piece of cotton, nylon, or silk, that you use for sewing. ❑ *...a needle and thread.*
2 **V-T** If you **thread** a needle, you put a piece of thread through the hole in the top of the needle so that you can sew with it. ❑ *I threaded a needle and sewed the button on the shirt.* [from Old English]
3 **N-COUNT** TECHNOLOGY A **thread** is a series of messages sent by email or on a website from different people about a particular subject. ❑ *I saw the post but I didn't read the thread below it.*

threat /θrɛt/ (**threats**)
1 **N-COUNT/N-NONCOUNT** If you **make a threat against** someone, you say that something bad will happen to them if they do not do what you want. ❑ *The two boys made death threats against a teacher.*
2 **N-COUNT** A **threat** is something that can

harm someone or something. ❑ *Stress is a threat to people's health.* [from Old English]

threat|en /θrɛtᵊn/ (**threatens, threatening, threatened**)
1 **V-T** If you **threaten** someone, you say that you will hurt them if they do not do what you want. ❑ *Army officers threatened to destroy the town.* ❑ *If you threaten me, I will go to the police.* ● **threat|en|ing** **ADJ** ❑ *He was arrested for using threatening behavior toward police officers.*
2 **V-T** If something **threatens** people or things, it is likely to harm them. ❑ *The fire threatened more than 1,000 homes.* [from Old English]

three /θriː/ **NUM MATH** **Three** is the number 3. ❑ *We waited three months before going back.* [from Old English]

three-di|men|sion|al /θriː dɪmɛnʃənᵊl/
1 **ADJ** ARTS A **three-dimensional** object is solid rather than flat. The short form **3D** is also used. ❑ *We made a three-dimensional model.*
2 **ADJ** ARTS A **three-dimensional** picture looks deep or solid rather than flat. ❑ *The software generates three-dimensional images.*

three-quar|ters **N-PLURAL** **Three-quarters** is an amount that is three out of four equal parts of something. ❑ *Three-quarters of the students are African-American.*

thresh|old /θrɛʃhoʊld/ (**thresholds**)
1 **N-COUNT** The **threshold** of a building or a room is the floor in the doorway, or the doorway itself. ❑ *He stopped at the threshold of the bedroom.*
2 **N-COUNT** A **threshold** is an amount, a level, or a limit on a scale. ❑ *Mathers has a high threshold for pain.*
3 **PHRASE** If you are **on the threshold of** something exciting or new, you are about to experience it. ❑ *We are on the threshold of a new age of discovery.* [from Old English]

threw /θruː/ **Threw** is the past tense of **throw**. [from Old English]

thrill /θrɪl/ (**thrills, thrilling, thrilled**)
1 **N-COUNT** A **thrill** is a sudden feeling of great excitement. ❑ *I can remember the thrill of opening my birthday presents when I was a child.*
2 **V-T** If something **thrills** you, it gives you a feeling of great excitement. ❑ *The Yankees thrilled the crowd with a 7-5 victory.* [from Old English]
3 → see also **thrilling**

thrilled /θrɪld/ **ADJ** If you are **thrilled**, you are very happy and excited about something. ❑ *I was so thrilled to get a good grade on my math exam.* [from Old English]

thrill|er /θrɪlər/ (**thrillers**) **N-COUNT** A **thriller** is an exciting book, movie, or play about a crime. ❑ *The book is a historical thriller.* [from Old English]

thrill|ing /θrɪlɪŋ/
1 **ADJ** If something is **thrilling**, it is very exciting and enjoyable. ❑ *It was a thrilling finish to the tournament.* [from Old English]
2 → see also **thrill**

thrive /θraɪv/ (**thrives, thriving, thrived**) **V-I** If someone or something **thrives**, they do well and they are successful, healthy, or strong. ❑ *Some plants thrive in the shade.* ❑ *Their national film industry is thriving. It produces thousands of films each year.* [from Old Norse]

throat /θroʊt/ (**throats**)
1 **N-COUNT** SCIENCE Your **throat** is the back of your mouth, where you swallow. ❑ *He spent two days at home with a sore throat.*
2 **N-COUNT** Your **throat** is the front part of your neck. ❑ *Mr. Williams grabbed him by the throat.* [from Old English]

throb /θrɒb/ (**throbs, throbbing, throbbed**)
1 **V-I** If something **throbs**, it beats regularly and very strongly, or it makes a regular sound, like your heart. [LITERARY] ❑ *His heart throbbed with excitement.* ❑ *The ship's engines throbbed.*
2 **V-I** If part of your body **throbs**, it beats regularly with pain. ❑ *Kevin's head throbbed.*

throne /θroʊn/ (**thrones**) **N-COUNT** A **throne** is the special chair where a king or a queen sits on important official occasions. [from Old French]

t

through

> **PRONUNCIATION HELP**
> Pronounce the preposition /θru/.
> Pronounce the adverb /θru̲/.

1 PREP If someone or something goes **through** another thing, they go from one side of it to the other side. ❑ *The bullet went through the front windshield.* ❑ *We walked through the crowd.* ❑ *Alice looked through the window.*
2 ADV Through is also an adverb. ❑ *There was a hole in the wall and water was coming through.*
3 PREP Something that happens **through** a period of time happens from the beginning until the end of that period. ❑ *She kept quiet all through breakfast.*
4 PREP If something happens from a period of time **through** another, it starts at the first period and continues until the end of the second period. ❑ *The office is open Monday through Friday from 9 to 5.*
5 PREP Something that happens **through** something else happens because of it. ❑ *I only succeeded through hard work.*
6 PREP Something that happens **through** someone or something else happens because the person or thing helped make it happen. ❑ *We met through a friend when I was 14.* [from Old English]

through|out /θru̲a̲ʊt/

1 PREP If something happens **throughout** a particular period of time, it happens during all of that period. ❑ *It rained heavily throughout the game.*
2 PREP If something happens or exists **throughout** a place, it happens or exists in all parts of that place. ❑ *Thousands of children throughout Africa suffer from the condition.*
3 ADV Throughout is also an adverb. ❑ *The apartment is painted white throughout.*

throw /θro̲ʊ/ (throws, throwing, threw, thrown)

1 V-T If you **throw** an object that you are holding, you move your hand or arm quickly and let go of the object, so that it moves through the air. ❑ *The crowd began throwing stones at the police.*
2 N-COUNT Throw is also a noun. ❑ *That was a good throw.* [from Old English]
▸ **throw away** or **throw out** If you **throw away** or **throw out** something that you do not want, you get rid of it. ❑ *I never throw anything away.* ❑ *I've decided to throw out all the clothes I never wear.*

Word Partnership Use **throw** with :
N   throw **a ball**, throw **a pass**, throw **a pitch**, throw **a rock/stone**, throw **strikes** 2

thrown /θro̲ʊn/ Thrown is the past participle of **throw**. [from Old English]

thrust /θrʌ̲st/ (thrusts, thrusting, thrust)

1 V-T If you **thrust** something or someone somewhere, you push or move them there quickly with a lot of force. ❑ *They thrust him into the back of a car.*
2 N-COUNT Thrust is also a noun. ❑ *...arm thrusts.*
3 N-NONCOUNT Thrust is the power or force that is required to make a vehicle move in a particular direction. [from Old Norse]

thud /θʌ̲d/ (thuds) N-COUNT A thud is the sound that a heavy object makes when it hits the ground. ❑ *She tripped and fell with a thud.* [from Old English]

thumb /θʌ̲m/ (thumbs) N-COUNT Your thumb is the short thick finger on your hand. ❑ *O'Donnell missed the game because of a broken thumb.* [from Old English]
→ look at Picture Dictionary: **hand**

thumb|tack /θʌ̲mtæk/ (thumbtacks) N-COUNT A thumbtack is a short pin with a broad, flat top that you use for fastening papers or pictures to a board or a wall.

thump /θʌ̲mp/ (thumps, thumping, thumped)

1 V-T/V-I If you **thump** something, you hit it hard with your hand. ❑ *Ramon thumped the table with his fist.* ❑ *I heard you thumping on the door.*
2 V-I If your heart **thumps**, it beats strongly and quickly because you are afraid or excited. ❑ *Her heart was thumping loudly in her chest.* [from Icelandic]

thun|der /θʌ̲ndər/ (thunders, thundering, thundered)

1 N-NONCOUNT Thunder is the loud noise that you sometimes hear from the sky during a storm. ❑ *Last night there was thunder and lightning.*
2 V-I When **it thunders**, a loud noise comes from the sky during a storm. ❑ *It will probably thunder later.* [from Old English]

thunder|storm /θʌ̲ndərstɔrm/ (thunderstorms) N-COUNT A thunderstorm is a very noisy storm. ❑ *The tree was hit by lightning during a thunderstorm last night.*
→ look at Word Web: **erosion**

T

Thurs|day /θ<u>ɜ</u>rzdeɪ, -di/ (**Thursdays**)
N-COUNT/N-NONCOUNT Thursday is the day after Wednesday and before Friday. ❑ *On Thursday Barbara invited me to her house for lunch.* ❑ *We go to the supermarket every Thursday morning.* [from Old English]

thus /ð<u>ʌ</u>s/
1 **ADV** You use **thus** to show that what you are about to mention is the result of something else that you have just mentioned. [FORMAL] ❑ *Neither of them turned on the TV. Thus they didn't hear the news.*
2 **ADV** If you say that something is **thus** or happens **thus** you mean that it is, or happens, as you have just described or as you are just about to describe. [FORMAL] ❑ *Joanna was pouring the tea. While she was thus occupied, Charles sat on an armchair.* [from Old English]

thy|mine /θ<u>aɪ</u>min, -mɪn/ (**thymines**)
N-COUNT/N-NONCOUNT SCIENCE Thymine is one of the four basic components of the DNA molecule. It bonds with adenine.

thy|mus /θ<u>aɪ</u>məs/ (**thymuses** /θ<u>aɪ</u>məsɪz/ or **thymi** /θ<u>aɪ</u>maɪ/) **N-COUNT** SCIENCE The **thymus** is an organ in your chest that forms part of the body's immune system. [from New Latin]

tick /t<u>ɪ</u>k/ (**ticks, ticking, ticked**)
1 **V-I** When a clock **ticks**, it makes a regular series of short sounds as it works. ❑ *An alarm clock ticked loudly on the bedside table.* ● **tick|ing** **N-NONCOUNT** ❑ *She could hear the ticking of a clock.*
2 **N-COUNT** Tick is also a noun. ❑ *I could hear the tick of the clock in the hall.* [from Lower German]

tick|et /t<u>ɪ</u>kɪt/ (**tickets**)
1 **N-COUNT** A ticket is a small piece of paper that shows that you have paid to go somewhere or to do something. ❑ *Where are the tickets for tonight's game?* ❑ *He had a first-class plane ticket for London.*

ticket

2 **N-COUNT** A **ticket** is an official piece of paper that orders you to pay a fine or to appear in court because you have parked your car in a way that is illegal. ❑ *Don't park here or you'll get a ticket.* [from Old French]

Word Partnership	Use **ticket** with :
ADJ	free ticket **1**
N	ticket **agent**, ticket **booth**, ticket **counter**, **plane** ticket, ticket **price 1** **parking** ticket, **speeding** ticket **2**
V	**buy/pay for a** ticket **1** **get a** ticket **1** **2**

tick|le /t<u>ɪ</u>kᵊl/ (**tickles, tickling, tickled**) **V-T** If you **tickle** someone, you move your fingers lightly over a part of their body to make them laugh. ❑ *Stephanie was cuddling the baby and tickling her toes.* [from Old English]

tid|al /t<u>aɪ</u>dᵊl/ **ADJ** Tidal means relating to or produced by tides. ❑ *Seabirds flew up from the tidal pools.* [from Old English]

tid|al bore (**tidal bores**) **N-COUNT** SCIENCE A **tidal bore** is a large wave that moves up a river as the tide rises.

tid|al range (**tidal ranges**) **N-COUNT** SCIENCE The **tidal range** is the difference in height between the low tide and the high tide at a particular place.

tide /t<u>aɪ</u>d/ (**tides**) **N-COUNT** SCIENCE The **tide** is the regular change in the level of the ocean on the beach that happens twice a day. ❑ *The tide was going out.* [from Old English]
→ look at Word Webs: **tide, ocean, tsunami**

tidy /t<u>aɪ</u>di/ (**tidier, tidiest, tidies, tidying, tidied**)
1 **ADJ** Someone who is **tidy** likes everything to be in its correct place. ❑ *I'm not a very tidy person.*
2 **ADJ** Something that is **tidy** is neat, and is arranged in an organized way. ❑ *The room was neat and tidy.*
▶ **tidy up** When you **tidy up** a place, you organize it by putting things in their proper places. ❑ *You relax while I tidy up the house.*

tie /t<u>aɪ</u>/ (**ties, tying, tied**)
1 **V-T** If you **tie** something, you fasten it or fix it, using string or a rope. ❑ *He tied the dog to the fence.* ❑ *She tied the ends of the two ropes together.* ❑ *She tied her scarf over her head.* ❑ *His hands were tied with rope.*
2 **Tie up** means the same as **tie**. ❑ *The woman tied up her dog outside the drugstore.*
3 **V-T** If you **tie** two things **together** or **tie** them, you fasten them together with a knot. ❑ *He tied the ends of the plastic bag*

t

The **gravitational** pull of the **moon** on the earth's **oceans** causes **tides**. It moves the water in the earth's oceans. **High tides** occur twice a day at any given point on the earth's surface. Then the water **ebbs** gradually. After six hours, **low tide** occurs. In some places tidal energy powers hydroelectric **plants**.

together. ❏ *I bent down to tie my shoelaces.*
4 **Tie up** means the same as **tie**. ❏ *She tied up the bag and took it outside.*
5 **N-COUNT** A **tie** or a **necktie** is a long narrow piece of cloth that you tie a knot in and wear around your neck with a shirt. ❏ *Jason took off his jacket and loosened his tie.*
6 **N-COUNT** **Ties** are the connections that you have with people or a place. ❏ *Quebec has close ties to France.*
7 **V-T/V-I** SPORTS If two people or teams **tie** in a game, they have the same number of points at the end of the game. ❏ *The teams tied 2-2.*
8 **N-COUNT** SPORTS **Tie** is also a noun. ❏ *The first game ended in a tie.*
[from Old English]
→ look at Picture Dictionary: **clothing**

ti|ger /taɪgər/ (**tigers**)
N-COUNT A **tiger** is a large wild animal of the cat family. Tigers are orange with black stripes. [from Old French]

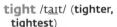
tiger

tight /taɪt/ (**tighter, tightest**)
1 **ADJ** If clothes are **tight**, they are small, and they fit closely to your body. ❏ *Amanda was wearing a tight black dress.* ● **tight|ly** **ADV** ❏ *Her jacket fastened tightly at the waist.*
2 **ADV** If you hold someone or something **tight**, you hold them very firmly. ❏ *Richard put his arms around her and held her tight.* ❏ *Just hold tight to my hand and don't let go.* ● **tight|ly** **ADV** ❏ *My son hugged me tightly.*
3 **ADJ** **Tight** is also an adjective. ❏ *He kept a tight hold of her arm.*
4 **ADJ** **Tight** controls or rules are very strict. ❏ *The rules include tight control of the media.* ❏ *The government is keeping a tight hold on inflation.* ● **tight|ly** **ADV** ❏ *The media was tightly controlled by the government.* [from Old Norse]

tight|en /taɪtən/ (**tightens, tightening, tightened**) **V-T/V-I** If you **tighten** something such as a rope, a chain, or a belt, or if it **tightens**, it is stretched or pulled hard until it is straight. ❏ *She tightened the belt on her robe.* ❏ *He tightened the last screw.* [from Old Norse]

tights /taɪts/ **N-PLURAL** **Tights** are a piece of tight clothing that covers the lower body, worn by women, girls, and dancers. [from Old Norse]

tile /taɪl/ (**tiles**) **N-COUNT/N-NONCOUNT** **Tiles** are flat, square objects that are used for covering floors, walls, or roofs. [from Old English]

till /tɪl/ (**tills**)
1 **PREP** In spoken English and informal written English, **till** is often used instead of **until**. ❏ *They had to wait till Monday to phone the bank.*
2 **CONJ** **Till** is also a conjunction. ❏ *I didn't leave home till I was nineteen.*
3 **N-COUNT** A **till** is the drawer of a cash register, where the money is kept. ❏ *There was money in the till.*
4 **N-NONCOUNT** SCIENCE **Till** or **glacial till** is the same as **glacial drift**. [Senses 1 and 2 from Old English.]

tilt /tɪlt/ (**tilts, tilting, tilted**)
1 **V-T/V-I** If something **tilts**, it has one end higher than the other. ❏ *The boat tilted as Eric leaned over the side.* ❏ *Leonard tilted his chair back and stretched his legs.*
2 **N-NONCOUNT** The **tilt** of something is the fact that it tilts or slopes, or the angle at which it tilts or slopes. [from Old English]

T

tim|ber /tɪmbər/ **N-NONCOUNT** Timber is wood that is used for building and making things. ❑ *There are timber floors throughout the house.* [from Old English]
→ look at Word Web: **forest**

tim|bre /tæmbər/ (timbres) **N-COUNT**
SCIENCE The **timbre** of someone's voice or of a musical instrument is the particular quality of sound that it has. [from French]

---

time
❶ NOUN USES
❷ VERB USE AND PHRASES

---

❶ time /taɪm/ (times)

1 **N-NONCOUNT** Time is something that we measure in minutes, hours, days, and years. ❑ *Time passed, and still Mary did not come back.* ❑ *I've known Mr. Martin for a long time.* ❑ *Listen to me. I haven't got much time.*

2 **N-SING** You use **time** when you are talking about a particular point in the day, that you describe in hours and minutes. ❑ *"What time is it?"—"Eight o'clock."* ❑ *He asked me the time.*

3 **N-COUNT** The **time** is the point in the day when something happens. ❑ *Departure times are 08.15 from Baltimore, and 10.15 from Newark.* ❑ *It's time to go home.*

4 **N-COUNT** You use **time** or **times** to talk about a particular period of time in the past. ❑ *At that time there were no antibiotics.*

5 **N-SING** If you say that something has been happening for **a time**, you mean that it has been happening for a fairly long period of time. ❑ *I lived for a time in Ontario, Canada.*

6 **N-COUNT** You use **time** to talk about an experience that you had. ❑ *Sarah and I had a great time at the party.*

7 **N-COUNT** You use **time** to talk about how often you do something. ❑ *Try to exercise at least three times a week.*

8 **N-PLURAL** You use **times** after numbers when you are showing how much bigger or smaller one thing is than another. ❑ *The sun is 400 times bigger than the moon.*

9 **CONJ** MATH You can use **times** when you are multiplying numbers. Three **times** five is written 3 x 5. ❑ *Four times six is 24.*

10 **N-COUNT** ARTS MUSIC The **time** of a piece of music is the number of beats that the piece has in each bar. The **time** of a dance measures body rhythms such as breath and heartbeat. [from Old English]
→ look at Picture Dictionary: **time**

❷ time /taɪm/ (times, timing, timed)

1 **V-T** If you **time** an activity, you measure how long it lasts. ❑ *Practice your speech and time yourself, so that you don't talk for too long.*

2 → see also **timing**

3 **PHRASE** Something that happens **all the time** happens continually or very often. ❑ *We can't be together all the time.*

4 **PHRASE** If things happen **at a time**, they happen together. ❑ *Patients may have two visitors at a time.*

5 **PHRASE** Something that happens **at times**, happens sometimes. ❑ *Every job is boring at times.*

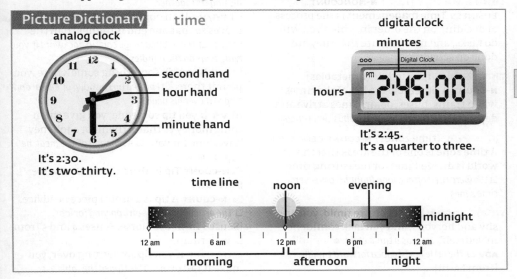

Picture Dictionary   time

analog clock
second hand
hour hand
minute hand
It's 2:30.
It's two-thirty.

digital clock
minutes
Digital Clock
hours
It's 2:45.
It's a quarter to three.

time line
noon
evening
midnight
12 am   6 am   12 pm   6 pm   12 am
morning   afternoon   night

6 **PHRASE** Something that is true **for the time being** is true now, but only for a short time. ❑ *The situation is calm for the time being.*

7 **PHRASE** If you do something **from time to time,** you do it sometimes but not often. ❑ *Her daughters visited her from time to time.*

8 **PHRASE** If you **have time** for something, you are able to spend time doing that thing. ❑ *I don't have time for your games this morning.*

9 **PHRASE** If you are **in time for** something, you are not late. ❑ *I arrived just in time for my flight to Hawaii.*

10 **PHRASE** Something that will happen **in** a week's or a month's **time,** for example, will happen a week or a month from now. ❑ *Presidential elections will be held in ten days' time.*

11 **PHRASE** If **it's time for** something or **it's time to do something,** that thing should happen now. ❑ *It's time for him to go.*

12 **PHRASE** If someone or something is **on time,** they are not late or early. ❑ *The train arrived at the station on time at eleven thirty.*

13 **PHRASE** If you **take** your **time,** you do something slowly. ❑ *"Take your time,"* Ted told him. *"I'm in no hurry."* [from Old English]

time|line /ˈtaɪmlaɪn/ (**timelines**) also time line **N-COUNT** SOCIAL STUDIES A **timeline** is a picture that shows the order of historical events. ❑ *The timeline shows important events from the Earth's creation to the present day.*

time man|age|ment **N-NONCOUNT** BUSINESS **Time management** is the process of deciding on the order in which you will do tasks, and making sure that they are done on schedule.

time|table /ˈtaɪmteɪbəl/ (**timetables**) **N-COUNT** A **timetable** is a list of the times when trains, buses, or airplanes arrive and depart. ❑ *Have you checked the bus timetable?*

time zone (**time zones**) **N-COUNT** GEOGRAPHY A **time zone** is one of the areas that the world is divided into for measuring time. ❑ *We were tired after a long flight across several time zones.*

tim|id /ˈtɪmɪd/ **ADJ** If you are **timid,** you are shy and nervous, and you lack confidence in yourself. ❑ *I was a timid child.* ● **tim|id|ly** **ADV** ❑ *The little boy stepped forward timidly.* [from Latin]

tim|ing /ˈtaɪmɪŋ/

1 **N-NONCOUNT** **Timing** is the skill of judging the right moment to do something. ❑ *"Am I too early?"—"No, your timing is perfect."*

2 **N-NONCOUNT** **Timing** is used to talk about the time at which something happens or is planned to happen, or the length of time that something takes. ❑ *They are worried about the timing of the report.* [from Old English]

3 → see also **time** ❷

tin /tɪn/ (**tins**)

1 **N-NONCOUNT** **Tin** is a type of soft metal. ❑ *...a tin can.*

2 **N-COUNT** A **tin** is a metal container with a lid in which food can be kept. ❑ *Store the cookies in an airtight tin.* [from Old English] → look at Word Web: **pan**

tint /tɪnt/ (**tints, tinting, tinted**)

1 **N-COUNT** A **tint** is a small amount of color. ❑ *Its leaves show a delicate purple tint.*

2 **V-T** If something **is tinted,** it has a small amount of a particular color or dye in it. ❑ *Eyebrows can be tinted with the same dye.*

3 **N-COUNT** ARTS In painting, a **tint** is a color that has had white added to it in order to make it lighter.

tiny /ˈtaɪni/ (**tinier, tiniest**) **ADJ** If something or someone is **tiny,** they are extremely small. ❑ *The living room is tiny.*

tip /tɪp/ (**tips, tipping, tipped**)

1 **N-COUNT** The **tip** of something long and narrow is the end of it. ❑ *He pressed the tips of his fingers together.*

2 **V-T/V-I** If an object **tips,** or if you **tip** it, it moves so that one end is higher than the other. ❑ *The baby carriage can tip backward if you hang bags on the handles.*

3 **V-T** If you **tip** something somewhere, you pour it there. ❑ *I picked up the bowl of cereal and tipped it over his head.*

4 **V-T** If you **tip** someone, you give them some money to thank them for a job they have done for you. ❑ *At the end of the meal, he tipped the waiter.*

5 **N-COUNT** **Tip** is also a noun. ❑ *I gave the barber a tip.*

6 **N-COUNT** A **tip** is a useful piece of advice. ❑ *The article gives tips on applying for jobs.* [Sense 1 from Old Norse. Senses 4 and 5 from Low German.]

▶ **tip over** If you **tip** something **over,** you make it fall over. ❑ *He tipped the table over.*

T

Word Partnership	Use **tip** with :
N	tip **of your finger/nose** 🔳
ADJ	**northern/southern** tip **of an island** 🔳
	anonymous tip 🔳

tipi /típi/ (**tipis**) N-COUNT SOCIAL STUDIES
A **tipi** is a tall round tent made from animal skins, that some Native Americans traditionally lived in. [from Siouan]

tip|toe /típtoʊ/ (**tiptoes, tiptoeing, tiptoed**)
🔳 V-I If you **tiptoe** somewhere, you walk there very quietly on your toes. ❑ *Emma got out of bed and tiptoed to the window.*
🔳 PHRASE If you walk or stand **on tiptoe**, you walk or stand on your toes and you do not put your heels on the ground. ❑ *She stood on tiptoe to look over the wall.*

tire /taɪər/ (**tires, tiring, tired**)
🔳 N-COUNT A **tire** is a thick round piece of rubber that fits around the wheels of cars, buses, and bicycles.
🔳 V-T/V-I If something **tires** you, or you **tire**, you feel that you want to rest or sleep. ❑ *If driving tires you, take the train instead.* [from Old French]
→ look at Word Web: **bicycle**

tired /taɪərd/
🔳 ADJ If you are **tired**, you feel that you want to rest or sleep. ❑ *Michael is tired after his long flight.*
🔳 ADJ If you are **tired of** something, you do not want it to continue because you are bored with it. ❑ *I'm tired of waiting for him.* [from Old English]
→ look at Word Web: **sleep**

Word Partnership	Use **tired** with :
V	**look** tired 🔳
	be tired, **feel** tired, **get** tired, **grow** tired 🔳 🔳
ADV	**a little** tired, **(just) too** tired, **very** tired 🔳 🔳
ADJ	tired **and hungry** 🔳
	sick and tired **of** *something* 🔳

tir|ing /taɪərɪŋ/ ADJ If something is **tiring**, it makes you feel tired so that you want to rest or sleep. ❑ *It was a long and tiring day.* ❑ *Traveling is tiring.* [from Old English]

tis|sue /tíʃu/ (**tissues**)
🔳 N-COUNT/N-NONCOUNT SCIENCE **Tissue** is one of the substances that humans, animals, and plants are made of. ❑ *...brain tissue.*

🔳 N-NONCOUNT **Tissue** or **tissue paper** is thin paper that you use for wrapping things that break easily. ❑ *The package was wrapped in pink tissue paper.*
🔳 N-COUNT A **tissue** is a piece of thin, soft paper that you use to wipe your nose. ❑ *He passed me a box of tissues.* [from Old French]
→ look at Word Web: **cancer**

ti|tle /taɪtəl/ (**titles**)
🔳 N-COUNT LANGUAGE ARTS The **title** of a book, a play, a movie, or a piece of music is its name. ❑ *What is the title of the poem?*
🔳 N-COUNT Someone's **title** is a word such as "Mr." or "Dr." that is used in front of their own name. [from Old French]
→ look at Word Web: **graph**

to

PRONUNCIATION HELP
Pronounce **to** /tə/ before a consonant. Pronounce **to** /tu/ before a vowel.

🔳 PREP You use **to** when you are talking about the position or direction of something. ❑ *Two friends and I drove to Florida.* ❑ *She went to the window and looked out.* ❑ *The bathroom is to the right.*
🔳 PREP When you give something **to** someone, they receive it. ❑ *He picked up the knife and gave it to me.*
🔳 PREP You use **to** when you are talking about how something changes. ❑ *The shouts of the crowd changed to laughter.*
🔳 PREP **To** means the last thing in a range. ❑ *I worked there from 1990 to 1996.* ❑ *I can count from 1 to 100 in Spanish.*
🔳 PREP You use **to** when you are saying how many minutes there are until the next hour. ❑ *At twenty to six I was waiting at the station.*
🔳 You use **to** before the infinitive form of a verb. ❑ *We just want to help.* ❑ *It was time to leave.* [from Old English]
🔳 → see also **according to**
→ look at Usage note at **too**

toad /toʊd/ (**toads**) N-COUNT A **toad** is a small brown or green animal with long legs, that lives in water. [from Old English]

toast /toʊst/ (**toasts, toasting, toasted**)
🔳 N-NONCOUNT **Toast** is slices of bread that you have heated until they are brown. ❑ *For breakfast, he had toast and jam, and a cup of tea.*
🔳 V-T If you **toast** bread, you heat it so that it becomes brown. ❑ *Mom made us some delicious toasted sandwiches.*

t

3 **N-COUNT** If you drink a **toast to** someone, you lift up your glass, wish them happiness, and drink. ❏ *We drank a toast to the bride and groom.*

4 **V-T** Toast is also a verb. ❏ *We all toasted the baby's health.* [from Old French]

→ look at Picture Dictionary: **cook**

toast|er /toʊstər/ (**toasters**) **N-COUNT** A **toaster** is a piece of electrical equipment that you use to heat bread. [from Old French]

to|bac|co /təbækoʊ/ **N-NONCOUNT** Tobacco is the dried leaves of a plant that people smoke in cigarettes. [from Spanish]

to|day /tədeɪ/
1 **ADV** You use **today** when you are talking about the actual day on which you are speaking or writing. ❏ *How are you feeling today?*
2 **N-NONCOUNT** Today is also a noun. ❏ *Today is Friday, September 14th.*
3 → see also **tomorrow, yesterday**
4 **ADV** You can use **today** when you are talking about the present period of history. ❏ *More people have cars today.* [from Old English]

tod|dler /tɒdlər/ (**toddlers**) **N-COUNT** A **toddler** is a young child who has only just learned to walk. ❏ *Toddlers love activities that involve music and singing.*
→ look at Word Web: **child**

toe /toʊ/ (**toes**) **N-COUNT** Your **toes** are the five parts at the end of your foot. ❏ *He is in the hospital with a broken toe.* [from Old English]
→ look at Picture Dictionary: **foot**

toe|nail /toʊneɪl/ (**toenails**) **N-COUNT** Your **toenails** are the hard parts that cover the ends of each of your toes.
→ look at Picture Dictionary: **foot**

to|geth|er /təgɛðər/
1 **ADV** If people do something **together**, they do it with each other. ❏ *We went on long walks together.* ❏ *Richard and I went to school together.*
2 **ADV** If things are joined **together**, they touch each other or make a single object, group, or mixture. ❏ *Beat the butter and sugar together.* ❏ *He joined the two pieces of wood together.* ❏ *We added all the numbers together.*
3 **ADV** If things or people are situated **together**, they are in the same place and are very near to each other. ❏ *The trees grew close together.* ❏ *Carol and Nick live together in Manhattan.*

4 **ADV** If two things happen **together**, they happen at the same time. ❏ *Patrick and Amanda arrived at the party together.* [from Old English]

Word Partnership	Use **together** with :
V	**live** together, **play** together, **work** together **1**
	come together **1**–**4**
	get together **1** **3**
	act together, **go** together **1** **6**
	fit together, **glue** together, **join** together, **lump** together, **mix** together, **string** together, **stuck** together, **tied** together **2**
	gather together, **sit** together, **stand** together **3**
ADJ	**bound** together **2**
	close together **3** **4**

toi|let /tɔɪlɪt/ (**toilets**) **N-COUNT** A **toilet** is a large bowl with a seat that you use when you want to get rid of waste from your body. ❏ *She flushed the toilet and went back into the bedroom.* [from French]
→ look at Picture Dictionary: **bathroom**

toi|let pa|per or **toilet tissue** **N-NONCOUNT** **Toilet paper** is the thin, soft paper that you use to clean yourself after you have gotten rid of waste from your body.
→ look at Picture Dictionary: **bathroom**

toi|let|ries /tɔɪlətriz/ **N-PLURAL** Toiletries are the things that you use when you are washing or taking care of your body, such as soap and toothpaste. [from French]

to|ken /toʊkən/ (**tokens**)
1 **N-COUNT** A **token** is a round, flat piece of metal or plastic that you use in a machine instead of money. ❏ *The machine uses plastic tokens rather than coins.*
2 **N-COUNT** A **token** is a thing or action that is meant to show an intention or feeling. ❏ *Please accept this gift as a token of our thanks.* [from Old English]

told /toʊld/ **Told** is the past tense and past participle of **tell**. [from Old English]

tol|er|ant /tɒlərənt/ **ADJ** If you are **tolerant**, you are happy for other people to say, think, and do what they like even though you do not agree with them. ❏ *We all need to be tolerant of different points of view.* ● **tol|er|ance** **N-NONCOUNT** ❏ *They promote tolerance of all religions.* [from Latin]

tol|er|ate /tɒləreɪt/ (**tolerates, tolerating, tolerated**) **v-T** If you **tolerate** something or someone, you accept them although you do not like them very much. ❏ *The college will not tolerate such behavior.* [from Latin]

toll /toʊl/ (**tolls, tolling, tolled**)
■ **v-I** When a bell **tolls**, it rings slowly and repeatedly, often as a sign that someone has died. ❏ *Church bells tolled as people arrived for the funeral.*
■ **N-COUNT** A **toll** is a sum of money that you have to pay in order to use a particular bridge or road. ❏ *You can pay a toll to drive on Pikes Peak Highway.*
■ **N-COUNT** A **toll** road or **toll** bridge is a road or a bridge that you have to pay to use. ❏ *Most people who drive the toll roads don't use them every day.*
■ **N-COUNT** A **toll** is a total number of deaths, accidents, or disasters that occur in a particular period of time. ❏ *There are fears that the toll of dead and injured may be higher.*
■ **PHRASE** If you say that something **takes its toll** or **takes a heavy toll**, you mean that it has a bad effect or causes a lot of suffering. ❏ *Winter takes its toll on your health.* [from Old English]

toll-free
■ **ADJ** A **toll-free** telephone number is a number that you can dial without having to pay for the call.
■ **ADV** **Toll-free** is also an adverb. ❏ *Call us toll-free 24 hours a day!*

to|ma|to /təmeɪtoʊ/ (**tomatoes**) **N-COUNT/N-NONCOUNT** A **tomato** is a soft, red fruit that you can eat raw in salads or cook like a vegetable. [from Spanish]
→ look at Picture Dictionary: **vegetables**
→ look at Word Web: **ketchup**

tomb /tum/ (**tombs**) **N-COUNT** A **tomb** is a stone grave where the body of a dead person is placed. ❏ *In Xian, we visited the emperor's tomb.* [from Old French]

tomb|stone /tumstoʊn/ (**tombstones**) **N-COUNT** A **tombstone** is a large stone on a person's grave, with words written on it, telling their name and the dates on which they were born and died. [from Old French]

to|mor|row /təmɔroʊ/
■ **ADV** **Tomorrow** is the day after today.
❏ *Bye, see you tomorrow.*
■ **N-NONCOUNT** **Tomorrow** is also a noun.
❏ *What's on your schedule for tomorrow?*
■ **ADV** You can talk about the future as **tomorrow**. ❏ *What is the world going to be like tomorrow?*
■ **N-NONCOUNT** **Tomorrow** is also a noun.
❏ *The children of today are the adults of tomorrow.* [from Old English]

ton /tʌn/ (**tons**) **N-COUNT** MATH A **ton** is a unit for measuring weight. There are 2,000 pounds in a **ton**. ❏ *Hundreds of tons of oil spilled into the ocean.*

to|nal|ity /toʊnælɪti/ (**tonalities**) **N-COUNT/N-NONCOUNT** MUSIC **Tonality** is the presence of a musical key in a piece of music. [from Latin]

tone /toʊn/ (**tones**)
■ **N-COUNT** The **tone** of a sound is its particular quality. ❏ *Lisa has a deep tone to her voice.*
■ **N-COUNT** Someone's **tone** is the quality in their voice that shows what they are feeling or thinking. ❏ *I didn't like his tone of voice; he sounded angry.*
■ **N-COUNT** ARTS In painting, a **tone** is a color that has had gray added to it in order to make it darker. [from Latin]

Word Partnership	Use **tone** with :	
ADJ	**clear** tone, **low** tone ■	
	different tone ■	
	serious tone ■	
V	**change your** tone ■	
N	tone **of voice** ■	

tone poem (**tone poems**) **N-COUNT** MUSIC A **tone poem** is a piece of music for an orchestra that is based upon something such as a novel or a painting.

tongue /tʌŋ/ (**tongues**) **N-COUNT** Your **tongue** is the soft part inside your mouth that moves when you speak or eat. [from Old English]
→ look at Picture Dictionary: **face**
→ look at Word Web: **taste**

to|night /tənaɪt/
■ **ADV** **Tonight** is the evening of today.
❏ *I'm at home tonight.* ❏ *Tonight he showed what a great player he is.*
■ **N-NONCOUNT** **Tonight** is also a noun.
❏ *Tonight is a very important night for him.* [from Old English]

t

ton|sils /tɒnsəlz/

> **LANGUAGE HELP**
> The form **tonsil** is used as a modifier.

N-PLURAL Your **tonsils** are the two small soft lumps in your throat at the back of your mouth. [from Latin]

too /tu/

1 **ADV** **Too** means also. ❑ *I like swimming and tennis too.* ❑ *Can we come too?* ❑ *"I'm excited about the party."—"Me too."*

2 **ADV** You use **too** to mean more than you want or need. ❑ *She talks too much.* ❑ *Sorry, I can't stop. I'm too busy.*

3 **ADV** You use **too** to say that there is a greater amount or degree of something than you would like. ❑ *Jeans that are too big will make you look larger.* ❑ *I'm turning up the heat because it's too cold.*

4 **ADV** You use **too** with a negative to make what you are saying sound less forceful or more polite or cautious. ❑ *I'm not too happy with what I've written.* [from Old English]

> **Usage** **too, two, and to**
> *Too, two,* and *to* are frequently confused. Their meanings and uses are very different, but they sound exactly the same. *Too* means "also" or "excessively"; *two* is the number 2; and *to* has many different uses as a preposition and in the to-infinitive: *Bahati asked Sekou to sit with her on the swing, but it was too small for the two of them, so they went to the movies instead.*

took /tʊk/ **Took** is the past tense of **take**. [from Old English]

tool /tul/ (**tools**) **N-COUNT** A **tool** is anything that you hold in your hands and use to do a particular type of work. ❑ *Do you have the right tools for the job?* [from Old English]
→ look at Picture Dictionary: **tools**

tool|bar /tulbɑr/ (**toolbars**) **N-COUNT** **TECHNOLOGY** A **toolbar** is a narrow strip across a computer screen that contains icons that represent different things that the computer can do.

tooth /tuθ/ (**teeth**)

1 **N-COUNT** Your **teeth** are the hard white objects in your mouth, that you use for biting and eating. ❑ *Brush your teeth at least twice a day.*

2 **N-PLURAL** The **teeth** of a comb are the parts that stick out in a row on its edge. [from Old English]
→ look at Word Web: **teeth**

> **Word Partnership** Use **tooth** with :
> N   tooth **decay**, tooth **enamel** **1**
> V   **lose** a tooth, **pull** a tooth **1**

tooth|brush /tuθbrʌʃ/ (**toothbrushes**) **N-COUNT** A **toothbrush** is a small brush that you use for cleaning your teeth.

tooth|paste /tuθpeɪst/ (**toothpastes**) **N-COUNT/N-NONCOUNT** **Toothpaste** is a thick substance that you put on a toothbrush and use to clean your teeth. ❑ *Don't forget to pack your toothpaste.*

top /tɒp/ (**tops**)

1 **N-COUNT** The **top** of something is its highest point. ❑ *We climbed the path up to the top of the hill.*

2 **ADJ** The **top** thing is the highest one. ❑ *I can't reach the top shelf.*

3 **N-SING** If you are at the **top** of an organization or a career, you are at the highest level in it. ❑ *He joined the company as*

Picture Dictionary · tools

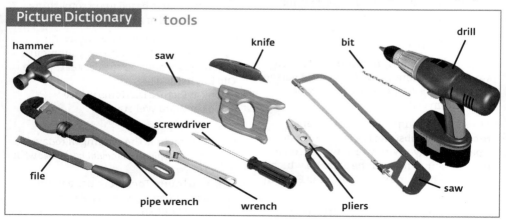

hammer · saw · knife · bit · drill · screwdriver · file · pipe wrench · wrench · pliers · saw

a salesman and worked his way to the top.

4 **ADJ** **Top** is also an adjective. ❑ *...the top people in this company.*

5 **N-COUNT** The **top** of something is its lid. ❑ *He twisted the top off the bottle and handed it to her.*

6 **N-COUNT** A **top** is a piece of clothing that you wear on the upper half of your body. [INFORMAL] ❑ *I was wearing a black skirt and a red top.*

7 **PHRASE** If one thing is **on top** of another, it is placed on its highest part. ❑ *There was a clock on top of the television.* [from Old English]

top|ic /tɒpɪk/ (**topics**) **N-COUNT** A **topic** is a particular subject that you discuss or write about. ❑ *What is the topic of your essay?* [from Latin]

topi|cal /tɒpɪkəl/ **ADJ** **Topical** is used to describe something that concerns or relates to events that are happening at the present time. ❑ *The newscast covers topical events and entertainment.* [from Latin]

top|ic sen|tence (**topic sentences**) **N-COUNT** LANGUAGE ARTS A **topic sentence** is a statement that expresses the main idea in a short piece of writing such as a paragraph.

topo|graph|ic map /tɒpəgræfɪk mæp/ (**topographic maps**) **N-COUNT** GEOGRAPHY A **topographic map** is a map of an area that shows the height of the land by means of contour lines.

top|ple /tɒpəl/ (**topples, toppling, toppled**)
1 **V-I** If someone or something **topples** somewhere, they become unsteady and fall over. ❑ *He toppled slowly backwards.*
2 **Topple over** means the same as **topple**. ❑ *The tree is so badly damaged they are worried it might topple over.*
3 **V-T** SOCIAL STUDIES To **topple** a government or a leader, especially one that is not elected by the people, means to cause them to lose power. ❑ *...the revolution which toppled the government.*

torch /tɔrtʃ/ (**torches**) **N-COUNT** A **torch** is a long stick or object that has a flame at one end. ❑ *Wood carried the Olympic Torch in Sydney in 2002.* [from Old French]

tore /tɔr/ **Tore** is the past tense of **tear**.

tor|ment (**torments, tormenting, tormented**)

PRONUNCIATION HELP
Pronounce the noun /tɔrmɛnt/.
Pronounce the verb /tɔrmɛnt/.

1 **N-COUNT/N-NONCOUNT** **Torment** is extreme suffering, usually mental suffering. ❑ *After years of torment, she is finally at peace.* ❑ *...the torments of being a writer.*
2 **V-T** If something **torments** you, it causes you extreme mental suffering. ❑ *At times the memories returned to torment her.* [from Old French]

torn /tɔrn/ **Torn** is the past participle of **tear**. [from Old English]

tor|na|do /tɔrneɪdoʊ/ (**tornadoes** or **tornados**) **N-COUNT** SCIENCE A **tornado** is a storm with strong winds that spin around very fast and cause a lot of damage. [from Spanish]

tor|pid /tɔrpɪd/ **ADJ** If you are **torpid**, you are feeling lazy or sleepy. [FORMAL] ❑ *He was living the torpid life of a drug addict.* [from Latin]

tor|sion /tɔrʃən/ **N-NONCOUNT** SCIENCE **Torsion** is a twisting effect, especially on a part of the body. ❑ *The torsion cuts off blood supply.* [from Old French]

tor|toise /tɔrtəs/ (**tortoises**) **N-COUNT** A **tortoise** is an animal with a shell on its back. **Tortoises** move very slowly. [from Old French]

tor|ture /tɔrtʃər/ (**tortures, torturing, tortured**)
1 **V-T** If someone **tortures** another person, they deliberately cause that person terrible pain.
2 **N-COUNT/N-NONCOUNT** **Torture** is also a noun. ❑ *The use of torture is prohibited by international law.* [from Late Latin]

toss /tɔs/ (**tosses, tossing, tossed**)
1 **V-T** If you **toss** something, you throw it. ❑ *Kate tossed the ball to Jessica.*
2 **V-T** If something **is tossed about** or **around**, it is made to move up and down, or from side to side, quickly and suddenly. ❑ *The huge waves tossed the boat about.*
3 **V-T** If you decide something by **tossing** a coin, you throw a coin into the air and guess which side of the coin will face upward when it lands. ❑ *We tossed a coin to decide who should go first.* [of Scandinavian origin]

to|tal /toʊtəl/ (**totals**)
1 **N-COUNT** MATH A **total** is the number that you get when you add several numbers together. ❑ *Add all the amounts together, and subtract ten from the total.* ❑ *The three companies have a total of 1,776 employees.*

2 **ADJ** **Total** is also an adjective. ❑ *The total cost of the project was $240 million.*

3 **ADJ** **Total** means complete. ❑ *I felt like a total failure.* ● **to|tal|ly** **ADV** ❑ *I accept that I am totally to blame.* [from Old French]

Word Partnership	Use total with :
N	total **amount**, total **area**, total **cost**, total **expenses**, total **population**, total **sales**, total **savings**, **sum** total, total **value** **2**
ADJ	**grand** total **1** **2**

to|tal eclipse (total eclipses) **N-COUNT**
SCIENCE A **total eclipse of** the sun is an occasion when the moon is between the Earth and the sun, so that for a short time you cannot see any part of the sun. A **total eclipse of** the moon is an occasion when the Earth is between the sun and the moon, so that for a short time you cannot see any part of the moon. Compare with **partial eclipse.**

Word Link	arian ≈ believing in, having : humanit*arian*, totalit*arian*, veget*arian*

to|tali|tar|ian /toʊtælɪtɛəriən/ **ADJ**
SOCIAL STUDIES A **totalitarian** political system is one in which there is only one political party that controls everything.

---
touch
❶ VERB AND NOUN USES
❷ PHRASES
---

❶ touch /tʌtʃ/ (touches, touching, touched)
1 **V-T/V-I** If you **touch** something, you put your hand onto it. ❑ *Her little hands gently touched my face.* ❑ *Don't touch!*

2 **N-COUNT** **Touch** is also a noun. ❑ *She felt the touch of his hand on her arm.*

3 **V-T/V-I** If one thing **touches** another, there is no space between them. ❑ *Their knees were touching.* ❑ *Her feet just touched the floor.*

4 **N-NONCOUNT** Your sense of **touch** is your ability to tell what something is like when you feel it with your hands. ❑ *A baby's sense of touch is fully developed at birth.*

5 **V-I** If you **touch on** a particular subject, you mention it briefly. ❑ *The film only touches on these issues.*

6 **V-T** If something that someone says or does **touches** you, it affects you emotionally. ❑ *Their kindness touched me deeply.* ● **touched** **ADJ** ❑ *He was touched that we came.* ● **touch|ing** **ADJ** ❑ *...the touching story of a husband who nursed the wife he loved.* [from Old French]

❷ touch /tʌtʃ/
1 **PHRASE** If you are **in touch with** someone, you write or speak to them regularly. ❑ *My brother and I keep in touch by phone.*

2 **PHRASE** If you **get in touch with** someone, you write to them or telephone them. ❑ *We'll get in touch with you if we have any news.*

3 **PHRASE** If you **lose touch with** someone, you gradually stop writing or speaking to them. ❑ *When he went to college, I lost touch with him.* [from Old French]

touch|less /tʌtʃləs/ **ADJ** TECHNOLOGY A **touchless** device is controlled by movements and sounds and does not require the user to touch a keypad or screen. ❑ *The phone has a touchless display and is controlled by voice.*

touch|screen /tʌtʃskrin/ (touchscreens) also **touch-screen** **N-COUNT** TECHNOLOGY A **touchscreen** is a computer screen that allows the user to give commands to the computer by touching parts of the screen rather than by using a keyboard or a mouse. ❑ *...touchscreen voting machines.*

touch-sen|si|tive **ADJ** TECHNOLOGY **Touch-sensitive** equipment is operated by the user touching it. ❑ *The touch-sensitive controls are easy to operate.*

tough /tʌf/ (tougher, toughest)
1 **ADJ** If you are **tough**, you are strong and determined. ❑ *Paul has a reputation as a tough businessman.*

2 **ADJ** If a task is **tough**, it is difficult to do. ❑ *We will have to make some tough decisions.*

3 **ADJ** If a substance is **tough**, it is strong, and it is difficult to break or cut. ❑ *... a tough nylon material.* ❑ *The meat was tough and chewy.* [from Old English]

Word Partnership	Use tough with :
N	tough **guy** **1** tough **choices**, tough **competition**, tough **conditions**, tough **decision**, tough **fight**, tough **going**, tough **job**, tough **luck**, tough **question**, tough **sell**, tough **situation**, tough **time** **2**
V	**get** tough, **talk** tough **1** **2** **make the** tough **decisions** **2**

tour /tʊər/ (tours, touring, toured)
1 **V-T/V-I** ARTS When musicians or performers **tour**, they go to several different places, where they perform. ❑ *A few years ago the band toured Europe.* ❑ *The orchestra are touring this month.*

2 **N-COUNT/N-NONCOUNT** ARTS **Tour** is also a noun. ❑ *The band is planning a national tour.* ❑ *Next year, the orchestra will be going on tour.*

3 **N-COUNT** A **tour** is a trip to an interesting place or around several interesting places. ❑ *Michael took me on a tour of the nearby islands.* ❑ *We went on a tour of the new office building.*

4 **V-T** If you **tour** a place, you go on a trip around it. ❑ *Tour the museum with a guide for $5 per person.* [from Old French]

Word Partnership	Use **tour** with :
N	**concert** tour, **farewell** tour **1**
	tour **bus**, tour **guide**, **museum** tour, **walking** tour, **world** tour **2**
V	**begin** a tour, **finish** a tour **1** **2**
	take a tour **2**

tour|ism /tʊ̯ərɪzəm/ **N-NONCOUNT** Tourism is the business of providing hotels, restaurants, trips, and activities for people who are on vacation. ❑ *Tourism is the island's main industry.* [from Old French]
→ look at Word Web: **industry**

tour|ist /tʊ̯ərɪst/ (**tourists**) **N-COUNT** A **tourist** is a person who is visiting a place on vacation. ❑ *About 75,000 tourists visit the town each year.* [from Old French]
→ look at Word Web: **city**

tour|na|ment /tʊ̯ərnəmənt, tɜr-/ (**tournaments**) **N-COUNT** SPORTS A **tournament** is a sports competition. Each player who wins a game plays another game, until just one person or team remains. They win the competition. ❑ *Tiger Woods won the tournament in 2009.* [from Old French]

tow /toʊ/ (**tows, towing, towed**) **V-T** If one vehicle **tows** another vehicle, it pulls it along behind it. ❑ *He uses the truck to tow his trailer.* [from Old English]

to|ward /tɔrd/ or **towards**
1 **PREP** If you move **toward** something or someone, you move in their direction. ❑ *They drove toward Lake Ladoga in silence.*
2 **PREP** If you have a particular attitude **toward** something or someone, that is the way you feel about them. ❑ *How do you feel toward the man who stole your purse?*
3 **PREP** If something happens **toward** a particular time, it happens just before that time. ❑ *We're having another meeting toward the end of the month.*
4 **PREP** If something is **toward** part of a

place, it is near that part. ❑ *...a small island toward the eastern shore.*
5 **PREP** If you give money **toward** something, you give it to help pay for that thing. ❑ *My husband's parents gave us $50,000 toward our first house.* [from Old English]

tow|el /taʊ̯əl/ (**towels**) **N-COUNT** A **towel** is a piece of thick, soft cloth that you use to dry yourself. ❑ *I've put clean towels in the bathroom.* [from Old French]
→ look at Picture Dictionary: **bathroom**

tow|er /taʊ̯ər/ (**towers**) **N-COUNT** A **tower** is a tall, narrow building, or a tall part of another building. ❑ *He looked up at the clock in the church tower. It was ten o'clock.* [from Old French]

town /taʊn/ (**towns**)
1 **N-COUNT** A **town** is a place with many streets, buildings, and stores, where people live and work. ❑ *Larry comes from a small town near the Canadian border.*
2 **N-NONCOUNT** **Town** is the center area of a town where there are stores. ❑ *His sister was getting her hair done in town.* [from Old English]

tox|ic /tɒksɪk/ **ADJ** If a substance is **toxic**, it is poisonous. ❑ *The leaves of the plant are highly toxic.* [from Latin]
→ look at Word Web: **cancer**

toy /tɔɪ/ (**toys**) **N-COUNT** A **toy** is an object that children play with. ❑ *Sophie went to sleep holding her favorite toy.*

trace /treɪs/ (**traces, tracing, traced**)
1 **V-T** If you **trace** someone or something, you find them after looking for them. ❑ *The police quickly traced the owner of the car.*
2 **V-T** If you **trace** a picture, you make a copy of it by covering it with a piece of transparent paper and drawing over the lines below. ❑ *Linda learned to draw by tracing pictures in books.*
3 **N-COUNT** A **trace of** something is a very small amount of it. ❑ *Wash them in cold water to remove all traces of sand.* [from French]
→ look at Picture Dictionary: **draw**

trace gas (**trace gases**) **N-COUNT** SCIENCE **Trace gases** are gases that make up less than one percent of the Earth's atmosphere, such as carbon dioxide and methane.

tra|chea /treɪkiə/ (**tracheas** or **tracheae** /treɪkii/) **N-COUNT** SCIENCE Your **trachea** is the passage from your larynx to your lungs. [from Medieval Latin]

track /træk/ (**tracks, tracking, tracked**)

1 **N-COUNT** A **track** is a rough road or path. ❑ *We walked along a track in the forest.*

2 **N-COUNT** SPORTS A **track** is a piece of ground that is used for races. ❑ *The university's facilities include a 400-meter running track.*

3 **N-COUNT** Railroad **tracks** are the metal lines that trains travel along.

4 **N-COUNT** MUSIC A **track** is one of the songs or pieces of music on an album. ❑ *I only like two of the tracks on their new album.*

5 **N-PLURAL** **Tracks** are the marks that an animal leaves on the ground. ❑ *William found fresh bear tracks in the snow.*

6 **V-T** If you **track** animals or people, you try to find them by following the signs or marks that they leave behind. ❑ *We all got up early to track deer in the woods.*

7 → see also **racetrack, soundtrack**

8 **PHRASE** If you **keep track of** someone or something, you have information about them all the time. ❑ *Keep track of what you spend while you're on vacation.*

9 **PHRASE** If you **lose track of** someone or something, you no longer know where they are or what is happening. ❑ *I'm sorry I'm late. I lost track of time.* [from Old French] → look at Word Webs: **fossil, transportation**

▶ **track down** If you **track down** someone or something, you find them after a difficult or long search. ❑ *She spent years trying to track down her parents.*

trac|tor /træktər/ (**tractors**) **N-COUNT** A **tractor** is a vehicle that a farmer uses to pull farm machinery. [from Late Latin] → look at Picture Dictionary: **barn**

trade /treɪd/ (**trades, trading, traded**)

1 **V-I** BUSINESS If people or countries **trade**, they buy and sell goods. ❑ *We have been trading with this company for over thirty years.*

2 **N-NONCOUNT** BUSINESS **Trade** is also a noun. ❑ *Texas has a long history of trade with Mexico.*

3 **V-I** If you **trade** one thing **for** another, you give someone that thing and get something else from them in exchange. ❑ *He traded his car for a motorcycle.* [from Old Saxon]

trade|mark /treɪdmɑrk/ (**trademarks**) **N-COUNT** BUSINESS A **trademark** is a special name or a symbol that a company owns and uses on its products. ❑ *Kodak is a trademark of Eastman Kodak Company.*

trad|er /treɪdər/ (**traders**) **N-COUNT** BUSINESS A **trader** is a person whose job is to trade in goods or stocks. ❑ *Market traders display a selection of the island's produce.* [from Old Saxon]

trade wind (**trade winds**) also **tradewind** **N-COUNT** SCIENCE The **trade winds** are winds that blow from east to west near the equator.

tra|di|tion /trədɪʃ°n/ (**traditions**) **N-COUNT/ N-NONCOUNT** A **tradition** is a type of behavior or a belief that has existed for a long time. ❑ *Thanksgiving dinner is an American tradition.*

● **tra|di|tion|al** /trədɪʃən°l/ **ADJ** ❑ *The band plays a lot of traditional Scottish music.*

● **tra|di|tion|al|ly** **ADV** ❑ *Christmas is traditionally a time for families.* [from Latin]

traf|fic /træfɪk/

1 **N-NONCOUNT** **Traffic** is all the vehicles that are on a particular road at one time. ❑ *There was heavy traffic on the roads.* ❑ *Yesterday, traffic was light on the freeway.*

2 **N-NONCOUNT** **Traffic** is the movement of ships, trains, or aircraft between one place and another. ❑ *No commercial air traffic was allowed out of the airport.* [from Old French] → look at Word Web: **traffic**

T

traffic

Boston's Southeast Expressway opened in 1959. It was built to handle 75,000 **vehicles** a day. But it wasn't enough and **commuter traffic** crawled. Sometimes it **stalled** completely. The 27 entrance **ramps** and no **breakdown lanes** caused frequent **gridlock**. By the 1990s, **traffic congestion** was even worse. Nearly 200,000 cars were using the **highway** every day and there were constant **traffic jams**. In 1994, a ten-year **road** construction project called the Big Dig began. The project built underground roadways, six-**lane bridges,** and improved **tunnels**. As a result of the project, traffic **flows** more smoothly through the city.

traf|fic jam (traffic jams) **N-COUNT** A **traffic jam** is a long line of vehicles that cannot move forward, or can only move very slowly.

traf|fic light (traffic lights) **N-COUNT** Traffic **lights** are colored lights that control the flow of traffic.

traffic light

trag|edy /trǽdʒɪdi/ (tragedies)
1 N-COUNT/N-NONCOUNT A **tragedy** is an extremely sad event or situation. ❑ They have suffered a terrible personal tragedy.
2 N-COUNT/N-NONCOUNT LANGUAGE ARTS **Tragedy** is a type of serious play, that usually ends with the death of the main character. ❑ ...the tragedies of Shakespeare. [from Old French]

trag|ic /trǽdʒɪk/ **ADJ** A **tragic** event or situation is extremely sad. ❑ It was a tragic accident. ● **tragi|cal|ly** /trǽdʒɪkli/ **ADV** ❑ He died tragically in a car accident. [from Old French]

trail /treɪl/ (trails)
1 N-COUNT A **trail** is a rough path. ❑ He was walking along a trail through the trees.
2 N-COUNT A **trail** is a series of marks that is left by someone or something as they move around. ❑ Everywhere in the house was a sticky trail of orange juice.
3 V-T If you **trail** something, it hangs down loosely behind you as you move along. ❑ She came down the stairs slowly, trailing the coat behind her. [from Old French]

Use **trail** with :	
N	**hiking** trail **1**
V	**follow** a trail **1 2**
	leave a trail, **pick up** a trail **2**

trail|er /treɪlər/ (trailers)
1 N-COUNT A **trailer** is a long narrow house that can be moved to a place where it becomes a permanent home.
2 N-COUNT A **trailer** is a vacation home that is pulled by a car.
3 N-COUNT A **trailer** is a large container on wheels that is pulled by a truck or another vehicle. [from Old French]

train /treɪn/ (trains, training, trained)
1 N-COUNT A **train** is a long vehicle that is pulled by an engine along a railroad. ❑ We caught the early morning train. ❑ He came to New York by train.
2 V-T If you **train to** do something, you learn the skills that you need in order to do it. ❑ Stephen is training to be a teacher. ● **train|ing N-NONCOUNT** ❑ Kennedy had no formal training as an artist.
3 V-T/V-I SPORTS If you **train for** a sports competition, or if someone **trains** you **for** it, you prepare for it. ❑ She spent six hours a day training for the race. ❑ The coach trained the team for the game. ● **train|ing N-NONCOUNT** ❑ He keeps fit through exercise and training. [from Old French]
→ look at Word Webs: **train, transportation**

trait /treɪt/ (traits) **N-COUNT** A **trait** is a particular characteristic, quality, or tendency that someone or something has. ❑ ...personality traits. [from French]
→ look at Word Web: **culture**

trai|tor /treɪtər/ (traitors) **N-COUNT** A **traitor** is someone who harms a group that they belong to by helping its enemies. ❑ There were traitors among us who were sending messages to the enemy. [from Old French]

t

Word Web   train

In sixteenth-century Germany, a **railway** was a horse-drawn **wagon** traveling along wooden **rails**. By the 19th century, **steam locomotives** and **steel rails** had replaced the older system. At first, railroads operated only **freight lines**. Later, they began to run **passenger** trains. Today, Japan's bullet trains carry people at speeds up to 300 miles per hour. This type of train doesn't have an engine or use tracks. Instead, an electromagnetic field allows the **cars** to float just above the ground. This electromagnetic field also pushes the train ahead.

A Japanese Bullet Train.

tram /træm/ (**trams**) **N-COUNT** A **tram** is a public transportation vehicle that travels along rails in the surface of a street. ❑ *You can get to the beach by tram.* [from Low German]
→ look at Word Web: **transportation**

trans|ac|tion /trænzækʃ°n/ (**transactions**) **N-COUNT** BUSINESS A **transaction** is a piece of business, for example an act of buying or selling something. [FORMAL] ❑ *...a cash transaction.* [from Latin]

Word Partnership	Use transaction with :
N	**cash** transaction, transaction **costs**, transaction **fee**
V	**complete** a transaction

Word Link	scend ≈ climbing : ascend, descend, transcend

trans|cend /trænsɛnd/ (**transcends, transcending, transcended**) **V-T** Something that **transcends** normal limits or boundaries goes beyond them, because it is more significant than them. ❑ *...issues that transcend politics.* [from Latin]

trans|con|ti|nen|tal rail|road /trænskɒntɪnɛnt°l reɪlroʊd/ (**transcontinental railroads**) **N-COUNT** SOCIAL STUDIES A **transcontinental railroad** is a railroad that crosses from one side of a continent to the other side. ❑ *The first transcontinental railroad opened in 1869.*

Word Link	script ≈ writing : manuscript, postscript, transcript

tran|script /trænskrɪpt/ (**transcripts**) **N-COUNT** LANGUAGE ARTS A **transcript of** a conversation or speech is a written text of it, based on a recording or notes. ❑ *A transcript of*

this program is available through our website. [from Latin]

Word Link	trans ≈ across : transfer, transition, translate

trans|fer (**transfers, transferring, transferred**)

> PRONUNCIATION HELP
> Pronounce the verb /trænsfɜr/. Pronounce the noun /trænsfɜr/.

◼ **V-T/V-I** If you **transfer** something or someone **from** one place **to** another place, or they **transfer from** one place **to** another, you make them go from the first place to the second place. ❑ *Transfer the meat to a dish.*
◼ **N-COUNT/N-NONCOUNT Transfer** is also a noun. ❑ *Arrange for the transfer of medical records to your new doctor.* [from Latin]

Word Partnership	Use transfer with :
N	**balance** transfer, transfer **funds**, transfer **money**

trans|form /trænsfɔrm/ (**transforms, transforming, transformed**) **V-T** To **transform** someone or something means to change them completely. ❑ *The railroad transformed America.* ❑ *Your body transforms food into energy.* ● **trans|for|ma|tion** /trænsfərmeɪʃ°n/ (**transformations**) **N-COUNT/N-NONCOUNT** ❑ *The TV show follows the transformation of a bedroom into an office.* [from Latin]

trans|form bounda|ry (**transform boundaries**) **N-COUNT** SCIENCE A **transform boundary** is a place on the Earth's surface where two tectonic plates meet and slide past each other. Compare with **plate boundary**.

T

trans|gen|der /trænzdʒɛndər/ **ADJ**
Someone who is **transgender** has a
gender identity which does not fully
correspond to the sex assigned to them
at birth. ❏ ...a three-year-project designed to
overcome prejudice toward gay, lesbian, bisexual,
and transgender people.

tran|sis|tor /trænzɪstər/ (**transistors**)
N-COUNT SCIENCE A **transistor** is a small
electronic part in something, such as a
television or radio, that controls the flow
of electricity.

tran|si|tion /trænzɪʃᵊn/ (**transitions**)
1 **N-COUNT/N-NONCOUNT** Transition is the
process in which something changes from
one state to another. ❏ ...the transition from
dictatorship to democracy. ● **tran|si|tion|al** **ADJ**
❏ ...the transitional stage between the old and new
methods.
2 **N-COUNT** ARTS MUSIC In dance and
music, a **transition** is a part of a dance or a
piece of music where one section ends and
another section begins. [from Latin]

tran|si|tive /trænzɪtɪv/ **ADJ** LANGUAGE ARTS
A **transitive** verb has a direct object. [from
Late Latin]

Word Link   *ator ≈ one who does : cre*ator,
           *narr*ator, *transl*ator

trans|late /trænzleɪt/ (**translates,
translating, translated**) **V-T/V-I** If
something that someone says or writes **is
translated**, it is said or written again in a
different language. ❏ A small number of
Kadare's books have been translated into English.
❏ He translated the speech into Spanish.
● **trans|la|tor** (**translators**) **N-COUNT** ❏ She
works as a translator. [from Latin]

trans|la|tion /trænzleɪʃᵊn/ (**translations**)
1 **N-COUNT** A **translation** is a piece of
writing or speech that has been put into a
different language. ❏ ...a translation of the Bible.
2 **N-COUNT/N-NONCOUNT** MATH In geometry,
translation is the change of position of a
figure such as a triangle in which all the
points of the figure are moved the same
distance and in the same direction.
[from Latin]

trans|lu|cent /trænzlusᵊnt/ **ADJ** If a
material is **translucent**, some light can pass
through it. ❏ The roof is made of translucent
plastic. [from Latin]
→ look at Word Web: **pottery**

trans|mis|sion /trænzmɪʃᵊn/
(**transmissions**)
1 **N-NONCOUNT** The **transmission** of
something is the passing or sending of it
to a different person or place. ❏ ...e-mail and
other forms of electronic data transmission.
2 **N-NONCOUNT** TECHNOLOGY The
transmission of television or radio
programs is the broadcasting of them.
❏ The transmission of the program was canceled.
3 **N-COUNT** A **transmission** is a broadcast.
❏ ...foreign television transmissions.
4 **N-NONCOUNT** SCIENCE Transmission
is the passage of light through matter.
[from Latin]

trans|mit /trænzmɪt/ (**transmits,
transmitting, transmitted**)
1 **V-T/V-I** TECHNOLOGY When radio and
television programs, computer data, or
other electronic messages **are transmitted**,
they are sent using wires, radio waves, or
satellites. ❏ The game was transmitted live.
❏ ...the best way to transmit certain types of
data.
2 **V-T** If one person or animal **transmits** a
disease to another, they have the disease
and cause the other person or animal to
have it. [FORMAL] ❏ ...insects that transmit
disease to humans. [from Latin]

trans|mit|ter /trænzmɪtər/ (**transmitters**)
N-COUNT A **transmitter** is a piece of
equipment that is used for broadcasting
television or radio programs. ❏ ...a homemade
radio transmitter. [from Latin]
→ look at Word Web: **cellphone**

trans|par|ent /trænspɛərənt, -pær-/ **ADJ**
If an object or a substance is **transparent**,
you can see through it. ❏ We used a sheet of
transparent plastic. [from Medieval Latin]
→ look at Word Web: **glass**

tran|spi|ra|tion /trænspɪreɪʃᵊn/
N-NONCOUNT SCIENCE Transpiration is
the process by which plants release water
vapor into the air through their leaves.
[from Medieval Latin]

trans|plant /trænsplænt/ (**transplants**)
N-COUNT/N-NONCOUNT A **transplant** is a
medical operation in which a part of a
person's body is replaced because it is
damaged or has a disease. ❏ ...a heart
transplant.
→ look at Word Webs: **donor, hospital**

t

trans|port /trænspɔrt/ (**transports, transporting, transported**) **v-t** To **transport** people or goods somewhere is to take them from one place to another place in a vehicle. ❑ *Buses transported passengers to the town.* [from Latin]

trans|por|ta|tion /trænspərteɪʃⁿn/
1 **N-NONCOUNT** **Transportation** means any type of vehicle that you can travel in or carry goods in. ❑ *The company will provide transportation.* ❑ *...public transportation.*
2 **N-NONCOUNT** **Transportation** is the activity of taking goods or people from one place to another place in a vehicle. ❑ *...transportation costs.* [from Latin]
→ look at Word Web: **transportation**

trans|sex|ual /trænsɛkʃuəl/ (**transsexuals**) **N-COUNT** A **transsexual** is a person who has decided that they want to live as a person of the opposite sex, and so has changed their name and appearance in order to do this. Transsexuals sometimes have an operation to change their sex.

trans|ver|sal /trænzvɜrsⁿl/ (**transversals**) **N-COUNT** MATH A **transversal** is a straight line that crosses two or more other lines. [from Latin]

trans|verse wave /trænzvɜrs weɪv/ (**transverse waves**) **N-COUNT** SCIENCE **Transverse waves** are waves, such as those in water, in which the material that the waves are passing through moves at right angles to the waves. Compare with **longitudinal wave**.

trap /træp/ (**traps, trapping, trapped**)
1 **N-COUNT** A **trap** is a piece of equipment for catching animals. ❑ *Nathan's dog got caught in a trap.*

2 **v-t** To **trap** animals means to catch them using traps. ❑ *They survived by trapping and killing wild animals.*
3 **N-COUNT** A **trap** is a trick that is intended to catch someone. ❑ *He hesitated, wondering if there was a trap in the question.*
4 **v-t** If someone **traps** you, they trick you so that you do or say something that you do not want to do or say. ❑ *Were you trying to trap her into confessing?*
5 **v-t** If you **are trapped** somewhere, something prevents you from moving. ❑ *The car turned over, trapping both men.* [from Old English]

Word Partnership	Use **trap** with :
v	avoid a trap, caught in a trap, fall into a trap, set a trap **1** **3**

trash /træʃ/ **N-NONCOUNT** **Trash** consists of things that people no longer want. ❑ *The yards are full of trash.*

Thesaurus	**trash** Also look up :
N	debris, garbage, junk, litter

trash can (**trash cans**) **N-COUNT** A **trash can** is a large round container where people put things that they no longer want, or waste from their homes.

trau|ma /traʊmə, trɔ-/ (**traumas**) **N-COUNT/ N-NONCOUNT** **Trauma** is a very severe shock or very upsetting experience, which may cause psychological damage. ❑ *I've been through the trauma of divorce.* [from Greek]

trav|el /trævⁿl/ (**travels, traveling, traveled**)
1 **v-t/v-i** If you **travel**, you go from one place to another, often to a place that is far away. ❑ *I've been traveling for days.* ❑ *People often travel hundreds of miles to get here.*

T

Mass transportation began more than 200 years ago. By 1830, there were horse-drawn **streetcars** in New York City and New Orleans. They ran on **rails** built into the **right of way** of city streets. The first electric **tram** opened in Berlin in 1881. Later, **buses** became more popular because they didn't require **tracks**. Today, **commuter trains** link suburbs to cities everywhere. Many large cities also have a **subway** system below the streets.

2 N-NONCOUNT **Travel** is the activity of traveling. ❑ *He hated air travel.*

3 V-I When light, sound, or information from one place reaches another, you say that it **travels** to the other place. ❑ *The news traveled quickly around the city.* [from Old French]

Thesaurus	travel	Also look up :
V	explore, trek, visit **1** **3**	
N	expedition, journey, trip **2**	

Word Partnership	Use **travel** with :
N	travel **the world** **1**
	air travel, travel **arrangements**, travel **books**, **car** travel, travel **delays**, travel **expenses**, travel **guide**, travel **industry**, travel **insurance**, travel **plans**, travel **reports**, travel **reservations** **2**
ADV	travel **abroad**, travel **overseas** **1** **2**

trav|el|er /trǽvələr/ (**travelers**) also **traveller** N-COUNT A **traveler** is a person who is on a trip or a person who travels a lot. ❑ *...airline travelers.* [from Old French]

tray /treɪ/ (**trays**) N-COUNT A **tray** is a flat piece of wood, plastic, or metal that is used for carrying things, especially food and drinks. [from Old English]

treach|er|ous /trɛtʃərəs/

1 ADJ If you describe someone as **treacherous**, you mean that they are likely to betray you and cannot be trusted. ❑ *He left his political party because of its treacherous leaders.*

2 ADJ If you say that something is **treacherous**, you mean that it is very dangerous and unpredictable. ❑ *The current of the river is fast flowing and treacherous.* [from Old French]

tread /trɛd/ (**treads, treading, trod, trodden**)

1 N-COUNT/N-NONCOUNT The **tread** of a tire or a shoe is the pattern of thin lines cut into its surface that stops it from slipping. ❑ *The tires had a good depth of tread.*

2 V-I If you **tread** in a particular way, you walk that way. [LITERARY] ❑ *There is no safety railing here, so tread carefully.* [from Old English]

treas|ure /trɛʒər/ (**treasures, treasuring, treasured**)

1 N-NONCOUNT In children's stories, **treasure** is a collection of valuable old objects, such as gold coins and jewelry. [LITERARY] ❑ *...buried treasure.*

2 V-T If you **treasure** something that you

have, you keep it or care for it carefully because you think it is very special. ❑ *She treasures her memories of those happy days.*

● **treas|ured** ADJ ❑ *...my most treasured possessions.* [from Old French]

treas|ury /trɛʒəri/ (**treasuries**)

1 N-COUNT SOCIAL STUDIES In the United States and some other countries, **the Treasury** is the government department that deals with the country's finances. ❑ *...a senior official at the Treasury.*

2 N-PLURAL BUSINESS **Treasuries** are financial bonds that are issued by the United States government in order to raise money. ❑ *These people invested in 30-year Treasuries.* [from Old French]

treat /trit/ (**treats, treating, treated**)

1 V-T If you **treat** someone or something in a particular way, you behave toward them in that way. ❑ *Stop treating me like a child.*

2 V-T When a doctor or a nurse **treats** a patient or an illness, he or she tries to make the patient well again. ❑ *The boy was treated for a minor head wound.*

3 V-T If you **treat** someone **to** something special, you buy it or arrange it for them. ❑ *She was always treating him to ice cream.*

4 N-COUNT **Treat** is also a noun. ❑ *Lesley returned from town with a special treat for him.*

5 V-T If something **is treated with** a particular substance, the substance is put onto or into it, for example in order to clean or protect it. ❑ *The fields are treated with insecticide.* [from Old French]

Word Partnership	Use **treat** with :
ADV	treat **differently**, treat **equally**, treat **fairly**, treat **well** **1**
PREP	treat **with contempt/dignity/respect** **1**
N	treat **people**, treat **women** **1** **2**
	treat **AIDS**, treat **cancer**, treat **a disease**, **doctors** treat **2**

treat|ment /trítmənt/ (**treatments**)

1 N-COUNT/N-NONCOUNT **Treatment** is medical attention that is given to a sick or injured person or animal. ❑ *Many patients are not getting the medical treatment they need.*

2 N-NONCOUNT Your **treatment** of someone is the way you behave toward them or deal with them. ❑ *We don't want any special treatment.* [from Old French]

→ look at Word Webs: **cancer, illness**

Word Partnership	Use **treatment** with :
V	**get/receive** treatment, **give** treatment, **undergo** treatment **1**
N	treatment **of addiction**, **AIDS** treatment, **cancer** treatment, treatment **center**, treatment **of an 1** treatment **of prisoners 2**
ADJ	**effective** treatment, **medical** treatment **1** **better** treatment, **equal/unequal** treatment, **fair** treatment, **humane** treatment, **special** treatment **2**

trea|ty /trɪ̱ti/ (**treaties**) **N-COUNT**
SOCIAL STUDIES A **treaty** is a written agreement between countries. ❑ ...*a treaty on global warming.* [from Old French]

tre|ble clef (**treble clefs**) **N-COUNT**
MUSIC A **treble clef** is a symbol that you use when writing music in order to show that the notes on the staff are above middle C.

tree /triː̱/ (**trees**) **N-COUNT** A **tree** is a tall plant that lives for a long time. It has a trunk, branches, and leaves. ❑ ...*apple trees.* [from Old English]
→ look at Picture Dictionaries: **garden, plants**
→ look at Word Webs: **tree, forest**

trek /trɛ̱k/ (**treks, trekking, trekked**)
1 **V-I** If you **trek** somewhere, you go on a journey across difficult country, usually on foot. ❑ *We trekked through the jungle.*
2 **N-COUNT** Trek is also a noun. ❑ *We went on a trek through the desert.* [from Afrikaans]

trem|ble /trɛ̱mbᵊl/ (**trembles, trembling, trembled**)
1 **V-I** If you **tremble**, you shake slightly. [LITERARY] ❑ *Lisa was white and trembling with anger.*
2 **V-I** If something **trembles**, it shakes slightly. ❑ *He felt the earth tremble under him.* [from Old French]

tre|men|dous /trɪmɛ̱ndəs/
1 **ADJ** You use **tremendous** to show how strong a feeling or a quality is, or how large an amount is. ❑ *My students have all made tremendous progress recently.* ● **tre|men|dous|ly** **ADV** ❑ *I thought they played tremendously well, didn't you?*
2 **ADJ** If someone or something is **tremendous**, they are very good. ❑ *I thought her performance was absolutely tremendous.* [from Latin]

trem|or /trɛ̱mər/ (**tremors**)
1 **N-COUNT** SCIENCE A **tremor** is a small earthquake. ❑ *The earthquake sent tremors through the region.*
2 **N-COUNT** A **tremor** is a shaking of your body or voice that you cannot control. ❑ *The old man has a tremor in his hands.* [from Latin]

tremu|lous /trɛ̱myələs/ **ADJ** If your voice, smile, or actions are **tremulous**, they are not steady because you are uncertain, afraid, or upset. [LITERARY] ❑ *She sat down in her chair and took a deep, tremulous breath.* ● **tremu|lous|ly** **ADV** ❑ *"He was so good to me," she said tremulously.* [from Latin]

T

Word Web   **tree**

Trees are one of the oldest living things. They are also the largest **plant**. Some scientists believe that the largest living thing on Earth is a **coniferous** giant **redwood** tree named General Grant. Other scientists think it is a huge **grove** of **deciduous** aspen trees known as Pando. This grove is a single plant because all of the trees grow from the root system of just one tree. Pando covers more than 106 acres. Some aspen trees **germinate** from seeds, but most come from natural cloning. In this process the parent tree sends up new **sprouts** from its root system. Fossil records show tree clones may live up to a million years.

trend /trɛnd/ (**trends**) **N-COUNT** A **trend** is a change or a development toward something different. ❑ *The restaurant is responding to the trend toward healthier eating.* [from Old English]

Word Partnership	Use **trend** with :
V	**continue a** trend, **reverse a** trend, **start a** trend
ADJ	**current** trend, **disturbing** trend, **growing** trend, **latest** trend, **new** trend, **overall** trend, **recent** trend, **upward** trend, **warming** trend

trendy /trɛndi/ (**trendier, trendiest**) **ADJ** If something or someone is **trendy**, they are fashionable and modern. [INFORMAL] ❑ *...a trendy Seattle night club.* [from Old English]

tri|ad /traɪæd/ (**triads**) **N-COUNT** MUSIC A **triad** is a chord consisting of three notes. [from Late Latin]

tri|al /traɪəl/ (**trials**)

1 **N-COUNT/N-NONCOUNT** SOCIAL STUDIES A **trial** is a formal meeting in a law court, at which it is decided whether a person is guilty of a crime. ❑ *New evidence showed the witness lied at the trial.* ❑ *He is on trial for murder.*

2 **N-COUNT/N-NONCOUNT** A **trial** is an experiment in which you test something by using it or doing it for a period of time to see how well it works. ❑ *The drug is being tested in clinical trials.*

3 **PHRASE** If you do something **by trial and error**, you try several different methods of doing it until you find the method that works best. ❑ *Many life-saving drugs were discovered by trial and error.*

→ look at Word Web: **trial**

Word Partnership	Use **trial** with :
V	**await** trial, **bring** *someone* **to** trial, **face** trial, **go on** trial, **put on** trial **1**
ADJ	**civil** trial, **fair** trial, **federal** trial, **speedy** trial, **upcoming** trial **1** **clinical** trial **2**
N	trial **date, jury** trial, **murder** trial, **outcome of a** trial **1** trial **and error 3**

Word Link	tri ≈ three : tri*angle,* tri*llion,* tri*pod*

tri|an|gle /traɪæŋgəl/ (**triangles**) **N-COUNT** MATH A **triangle** is a shape with three straight sides. ❑ *On a piece of paper, draw a triangle like the one below.* ● **tri|an|gu|lar** /traɪæŋgyələr/ **ADJ** ❑ *...a triangular roof.* [from Latin]
→ look at Picture Dictionary: **shapes**
→ look at Word Web: **circle**

tribe /traɪb/ (**tribes**) **N-COUNT** The word **tribe** is sometimes used for talking about a group of people of the same race, language, and culture, especially in a developing country. Some people disapprove of this use. ❑ *...three hundred members of the Xhosa tribe.* ● **trib|al** /traɪbəl/ **ADJ** ❑ *...tribal lands.* [from Latin]

tri|bu|nal /traɪbyunəl/ (**tribunals**) **N-COUNT** SOCIAL STUDIES A **tribunal** is a special court or committee that is appointed to deal with particular problems. ❑ *His case comes before an industrial tribunal in March.* [from Latin]

tribu|tary /trɪbyətɛri/ (**tributaries**) **N-COUNT** GEOGRAPHY A **tributary** is a stream or river that flows into a larger one.

trib|ute /trɪbyut/ (**tributes**) **N-COUNT/N-NONCOUNT** A **tribute** is something that you say, do, or make to

Word Web	trial

Many countries have **trial** by jury. The **judge** begins by explaining the **charges** against the **defendant**. Next the defendant **pleads guilty** or not guilty. Then the **lawyers** for the **plaintiff** and the defendant present **evidence**. Both **attorneys** interview **witnesses**. They can also question each other's **clients**. Sometimes the lawyers **cross-examine** witnesses on their **testimony**. When the lawyers finish, the **jury** meets to **deliberate**. They deliver their **verdict**. If the jury says the defendant is guilty, the judge **pronounces** the **sentence**. Sometimes the defendant may be able to **appeal** the verdict and ask for a new trial.

t

show that you admire and respect someone. ❑ *The song is a tribute to Roy Orbison.* [from Latin]

trick /trɪk/ (**tricks, tricking, tricked**)

1 **V-T** If someone **tricks** you, they do something dishonest in order to make you do something. ❑ *Stephen is going to be very upset when he finds out how you tricked him.* ❑ *They tricked him into signing the contract.*

2 **N-COUNT** Trick is also a noun. ❑ *Andy has a son who loves to play tricks on him.*

3 **N-COUNT** A **trick** is a clever or skillful action that someone does in order to entertain people. ❑ *He showed me some card tricks.* [from Old Northern French]

Word Partnership	Use **trick** with :
ADJ	**cheap** trick **1**
	clever trick, **neat** trick, **old** trick **1** **2**
V	**play** a trick, **try to** trick *someone* **1**
N	**card** trick **2**

trick|le /trɪkᵊl/ (**trickles, trickling, trickled**)

1 **V-T/V-I** When a liquid **trickles**, or when you **trickle** it, a small amount of it flows slowly. ❑ *A tear trickled down the old man's cheek.*

2 **N-COUNT** Trickle is also a noun. ❑ *There was not even a trickle of water.*

tricky /trɪki/ (**trickier, trickiest**) **ADJ** A **tricky** task or problem is difficult to deal with. ❑ *Parking can be tricky downtown.* [from Old Northern French]

trig|ger /trɪgər/ (**triggers, triggering, triggered**)

1 **N-COUNT** The **trigger** of a gun is the part that you pull to make it shoot. ❑ *A man pointed a gun at them and pulled the trigger.*

2 **V-T** If something **triggers** an event or a situation, it causes it to begin to happen or exist. ❑ *...the incident which triggered the outbreak of the war.* [from Dutch]

Word Link	tri ≈ three : triangle, trillion, tripod

tril|lion /trɪlyən/ (**trillions**)

LANGUAGE HELP
The plural is **trillion** after a number.

NUM MATH A **trillion** is 1,000,000,000,000. ❑ *...a 4 trillion dollar debt.* [from French]

trim /trɪm/ (**trims, trimming, trimmed**)

1 **V-T** If you **trim** something, you cut off small amounts of it in order to make it look neater. ❑ *My friend trims my hair every eight weeks.*

2 **N-SING** Trim is also a noun. ❑ *His mustache needed a trim.* [from Old English]

trio /triːoʊ/ (**trios**) **N-COUNT** MUSIC A **trio** is a group of three people, especially musicians or singers. [from Italian]

trip /trɪp/ (**trips, tripping, tripped**)

1 **N-COUNT** A **trip** is a journey that you make to a particular place. ❑ *She has just returned from a week-long trip to Montana.*

2 → see also **round trip**

3 **V-I** If you **trip** when you are walking, you knock your foot against something and fall or nearly fall. ❑ *She tripped and broke her hip.* [from Old French]

Word Partnership	Use **trip** with :
N	**boat** trip, **bus** trip, **business** trip, **camping** trip, **field** trip, trip **home**, **return** trip, **shopping** trip, **train** trip, **vacation** trip **1**
V	**cancel** a trip, **make** a trip, **plan** a trip, **return from** a trip, **take** a trip **1**
ADJ	**free** trip, **last** trip, **long** trip, **next** trip, **recent** trip, **safe** trip, **short** trip **1**

tri|ple /trɪpᵊl/ (**triples, tripling, tripled**)

1 **ADJ** **Triple** means consisting of three things or parts. ❑ *The property includes a triple garage.*

2 **V-T/V-I** Something that **triples** becomes three times as large. ❑ *I got a fantastic new job which tripled my salary.* ❑ *The exhibition has tripled in size from last year.* [from Latin]

tri|ple me|ter (**triple meters**)

N-COUNT/N-NONCOUNT MUSIC Music that is written in **triple meter** has a beat that is repeated in groups of three. Compare with **duple meter**.

tri|plet /trɪplɪt/ (**triplets**) **N-COUNT** **Triplets** are three children that are born at the same time to the same mother.

tri|pod /traɪpɒd/ (**tripods**) **N-COUNT** A **tripod** is a stand with three legs that is used to support something such as a camera or a telescope. [from Latin]

tri|umph /traɪʌmf/ (**triumphs, triumphing, triumphed**)

1 **N-COUNT/N-NONCOUNT** A **triumph** is a great success. ❑ *The championships were a personal triumph for the coach.*

2 **N-NONCOUNT** **Triumph** is a feeling of great satisfaction after a great success. ❑ *She felt a sense of triumph.*

3 **V-I** If someone or something **triumphs**, they win a great victory or succeed in overcoming something. ❑ *The movie is about good triumphing over evil.* [from Old French]

triv|ial /trɪviəl/ **ADJ** Something that is **trivial** is not important or serious. ❑ *I was not interested in the trivial details of his daily life.* [from Latin]

trod /trɒd/ **Trod** is the past tense of **tread**. [from Old English]

trod|den /trɒdᵊn/ **Trodden** is the past participle of **tread**. [from Old English]

trol|ley /trɒli/ (**trolleys**) **N-COUNT** A **trolley** or a **trolley car** is an electric vehicle for carrying people. A trolley travels on rails in the streets of a city. ❑ *He took a northbound trolley on State Street.*

trom|bone /trɒmboʊn/ (**trombones**) **N-COUNT/N-NONCOUNT** MUSIC A **trombone** is a metal musical instrument that you play by blowing into it and sliding part of it backward and forward. ❑ *Her husband plays the trombone.* [from Italian]
→ look at Word Web: **orchestra**

troop /trup/ (**troops**) **N-PLURAL Troops** are soldiers. ❑ *35,000 troops from a dozen countries are already there.* [from French]
→ look at Word Web: **army**

tro|phy /troʊfi/ (**trophies**) **N-COUNT** A **trophy** is a prize that is given to the winner of a competition. ❑ *The special trophy for the best rider went to Chris Read.* [from French]

tropi|cal /trɒpɪkᵊl/ **ADJ** GEOGRAPHY **Tropical** means belonging to or typical of the hot, wet areas of the world. ❑ *...tropical diseases.* [from Late Latin]
→ look at Word Webs: **aquarium, disaster, habitat, hurricane**

tropi|cal de|pres|sion (**tropical depressions**) **N-COUNT** SCIENCE A **tropical depression** is a system of thunderstorms that begins in the tropics and has relatively low wind speeds. It is the second stage in the development of a hurricane.

tropi|cal dis|turb|ance (**tropical disturbances**) **N-COUNT** SCIENCE A **tropical disturbance** is a system of thunderstorms that begins in the tropics and lasts for more than 24 hours. It is the first stage in the development of a hurricane.

tropi|cal storm (**tropical storms**) **N-COUNT** SCIENCE A **tropical storm** is a system of thunderstorms that begins in the tropics and has relatively high wind speeds. It is the third stage in the development of a hurricane.

tropi|cal zone (**tropical zones**) **N-COUNT** GEOGRAPHY The **tropical zone** is the part of the Earth's surface near the equator, where the climate is hot and wet.

Trop|ic of Can|cer /trɒpɪk əv kænsər/ **N-PROPER** GEOGRAPHY The **Tropic of Cancer** is an imaginary line around the Earth 23° 26' north of the equator.

Trop|ic of Cap|ri|corn /trɒpɪk əv kæprɪkɔrn/ **N-PROPER** GEOGRAPHY The **Tropic of Capricorn** is an imaginary line around the Earth 23° 26' south of the equator.

trop|ics /trɒpɪks/ **N-PLURAL** GEOGRAPHY The **tropics** are the hottest parts of the world, where it is hot and wet. [from Late Latin]

tro|pism /troʊpɪzəm/ (**tropisms**) **N-COUNT/N-NONCOUNT** SCIENCE A **tropism** is the movement of a plant or other organism in response to an external stimulus such as heat or light. [from Greek]

tropo|sphere /trɒpəsfɪər, troʊ-/ **N-SING** SCIENCE The **troposphere** is the layer of the Earth's atmosphere that is closest to the Earth's surface.

trot /trɒt/ (**trots, trotting, trotted**)
1 V-I If you **trot** somewhere, you move at a speed between walking and running. ❑ *I trotted down the steps and out to the garden.*
2 V-I When an animal such as a horse **trots**, it moves fairly fast, taking quick small steps. ❑ *My horse was soon trotting around the field.* [from Old French]

trou|ble /trʌbᵊl/ (**troubles, troubling, troubled**)
1 N-COUNT/N-NONCOUNT Trouble is problems or difficulties. ❑ *I had trouble parking.* ❑ *You've caused us a lot of trouble.*
2 N-SING If you say that one thing is **the trouble with** a situation, you mean that it is the thing that is causing problems. ❑ *The trouble is that he's still sick.*
3 N-NONCOUNT If there is **trouble**, people are arguing or fighting. ❑ *Police were sent to the city to prevent trouble.*
4 V-T If something **troubles** you, it makes you feel worried. ❑ *Is anything troubling you?*
5 PHRASE If someone is **in trouble**, they

t

have broken a rule or a law, and they are likely to be punished. ❏ *He was in trouble with his teachers.* [from Old French]

Word Partnership	Use **trouble** with :
DET	**no** trouble **1**
V	**cause** trouble, **have** trouble, **make** trouble, **run into** trouble, **spell** trouble, **start** trouble **1**
	get in/into trouble, **get out of** trouble, **stay out of** trouble **5**
N	**engine** trouble **1**
	sign of trouble **1 3**
ADJ	**financial** trouble **1**
	big trouble, **deep** trouble, **real** trouble, **serious** trouble **1 3**
PREP	trouble **with 1–3**
	in trouble **5**
ADV	trouble **ahead 1 3**

trou|bled /tr⌃bᵊld/ **ADJ Troubled** means worried or full of problems. ❏ *Rose sounded deeply troubled.* ❏ *...this troubled country.* [from Old French]

trouble|maker /tr⌃bᵊlmeɪkər/ (**troublemakers**) **N-COUNT** A **troublemaker** is someone who causes trouble. ❏ *She has always been a troublemaker.*

trough /trɔf/ (**troughs**)
1 N-COUNT A **trough** is a long narrow container from which farm animals drink or eat. ❏ *...the old stone cattle trough.*
2 N-COUNT A **trough** is a low point in a pattern that has regular high and low points. ❏ *The industry's worst trough was in 2001 and 2002.*
3 N-COUNT A **trough** is a low area between two big waves on the sea. [from Old English]
→ look at Word Web: **sound**

trou|sers /traʊzərz/

> **LANGUAGE HELP**
> The form **trouser** is used as a modifier.

N-PLURAL Trousers are a piece of clothing that covers the body from the waist downward, and that covers each leg separately. [FORMAL] ❏ *He was dressed in a shirt, dark trousers, and boots.*

trow|el /traʊəl/ (**trowels**)
1 N-COUNT A **trowel** is a small garden tool which you use for digging small holes or removing weeds.
2 N-COUNT A **trowel** is a small tool with a flat blade that you use for spreading things

such as cement and plaster onto walls and other surfaces.
→ look at Picture Dictionary: **garden**

truce /trus/ (**truces**) **N-COUNT** A **truce** is an agreement between two people or groups of people to stop fighting or arguing for a short time. ❏ *The fighting has given way to an uneasy truce between the two sides.* [from Old English]

truck /tr⌃k/ (**trucks**)
1 N-COUNT A **truck** is a large vehicle that is used for transporting goods by road. ❏ *The fire started on a truck that was carrying paint.* ❏ *My dad is a truck driver.*
2 N-COUNT A **truck** is a vehicle with a large area with low sides in the back for carrying things. ❏ *There are only two seats in the truck.* [from Anglo-Norman]

trucu|lent /tr⌃kyələnt/ **ADJ** If you say that someone is **truculent**, you mean that they are bad-tempered and aggressive. ❏ *He was truculent, offensive, and foul-mouthed.*
● **trucu|lence** /tr⌃kyələns/ **N-NONCOUNT** ❏ *"What do you want?" she asked with her usual truculence.* [from Latin]

true /tru/ (**truer, truest**)
1 ADJ If something is **true**, it is based on facts, and is not invented or imagined. ❏ *Everything she said was true.* ❏ *The movie is based on a true story.*
2 ADJ True means real, genuine, or typical. ❏ *This country claims to be a true democracy.* ❏ *Maybe one day you'll find true love.*
3 PHRASE If a dream or wish **comes true**, it actually happens. ❏ *When I was 13, my dream came true and I got my first horse.* [from Old English]

true-breed|ing ADJ SCIENCE A **true-breeding** plant is a plant that fertilizes itself and therefore produces offspring with exactly the same genetic characteristics as itself.

tru|ly /truli/
1 ADV Truly means really and completely. ❏ *We want a truly democratic system.* ❏ *Believe me, Susan, I am truly sorry.*
2 PHRASE You can write **Yours truly** before your name at the end of a letter to someone you do not know very well. ❏ *Yours truly, Phil Turner.* [from Old English]

trum|pet /tr⌃mpɪt/ (**trumpets**)
N-COUNT/N-NONCOUNT MUSIC A **trumpet** is a metal musical instrument that you blow.

❏ *I played the trumpet in the school orchestra.* [from Old French]
→ look at Word Web: **orchestra**

trunk /trʌŋk/ (**trunks**)

1 **N-COUNT** The **trunk** of a tree is the large main stem from which the branches grow. ❏ *The tree trunk was more than five feet across.*
2 **N-COUNT** The **trunk** of a car is a covered space at the back in which you put bags or other things. ❏ *She opened the trunk of the car and took out a bag of groceries.*
3 **N-COUNT** A **trunk** is a large, strong box that is used for storing things. ❏ *Maloney unlocked his trunk and took out some clothing.*
4 **N-COUNT** An elephant's **trunk** is its long nose. [from Old French]

trust /trʌst/ (**trusts, trusting, trusted**)

1 **V-T** If you **trust** someone, you believe that they are honest and that they will not deliberately do anything to harm you. ❏ *"I trust you completely," he said.*
2 **N-NONCOUNT** **Trust** is also a noun. ❏ *He destroyed my trust in men.* ❏ *There was a shared feeling of trust amongst the members of the team.*
3 **V-T** If you **trust** someone **to** do something, you believe that they will do it. ❏ *I trust you to keep this secret.*
4 **V-T** If you do not **trust** something, you feel that it is not safe. ❏ *She nodded, not trusting her own voice.*
5 **V-T** If you **trust** someone's judgment or advice, you believe that it is good or right. ❏ *Jake has raised two kids and I trust his judgment.* [from Old Norse]

Word Partnership	Use **trust** with :	
V	**build** trust, **create** trust, **learn to** trust, **place** trust in *someone* **1**	
ADJ	**mutual** trust **1**	
N	trust *your instincts*, trust *someone's* judgment **4**	

trus|tee /trʌsti/ (**trustees**) **N-COUNT** BUSINESS A **trustee** is someone with legal control of money or property that is kept or invested for another person, company, or organization. [from Old Norse]

trust|worthy /trʌstwɜrði/ **ADJ** A **trustworthy** person is responsible and can be trusted completely. ❏ *He is a trustworthy leader.*

truth /truθ/ **N-NONCOUNT** The **truth** about something is all the facts about it, rather than things that are imagined or invented. ❏ *There is no truth in this story.* ❏ *Are you telling me*

the truth? [from Old English]

Word Partnership	Use **truth** with :	
V	**accept the** truth, **find the** truth, **know the** truth, **learn the** truth, **search for the** truth, **tell the** truth	
N	**a grain of** truth, **the truth of the matter**	
ADJ	**the awful** truth, **the plain** truth, **the sad** truth, **the simple** truth, **the whole** truth, **absolute** truth	

truth|ful /truθfəl/ **ADJ** A **truthful** person or answer is honest. ❏ *She was always completely truthful with us.* ❏ *The truthful answer is that I don't know.* ● **truth|ful|ly** **ADV** ❏ *I answered all their questions truthfully.* ● **truth|ful|ness** **N-NONCOUNT** ❏ *I can say, with absolute truthfulness, that I did my best.* [from Old English]

try /traɪ/ (**tries, trying, tried**)

1 **V-T/V-I** If you **try** to do something, you make an effort to do it. ❏ *He tried to help her at work.* ❏ *She doesn't seem to try hard enough.* ❏ *I must try and see him.*
2 **N-COUNT** **Try** is also a noun. ❏ *It was a good try.*
3 **V-T** If you **try** something new or different, you use it or do it in order to discover what it is like. ❏ *You could try a little cheese melted on the top.*
4 **N-COUNT** **Try** is also a noun. ❏ *All we're asking is that you give it a try.*
5 **V-T** If you **try** a particular place or person, you go to them because you think that they may be able to give you what you need. ❏ *Have you tried the local music stores?*
6 **V-T** SOCIAL STUDIES When a person is **tried**, they appear in a law court where it is decided if they are guilty of a crime. ❏ *They were arrested and tried for murder.* [from Old French]

▶ **try on** If you **try on** a piece of clothing, you put it on in order to see if it fits you or if it looks nice. ❏ *Try on the shoes to make sure they fit.*
▶ **try out** If you **try** something **out**, you test it in order to find out how useful or effective it is. ❏ *I want to try the boat out next weekend.*
▶ **try out for** ARTS SPORTS If you **try out for** a sports team or an acting role, you perform a test in an attempt to be chosen. ❏ *He should have tried out for the Olympic team.*

T-shirt (**T-shirts**) also **tee-shirt** **N-COUNT** A **T-shirt** is a simple shirt with no collar and short sleeves.
→ look at Picture Dictionary: **clothing**

t

Word Web   tsunami

Ordinary ocean **waves** are mostly the result of wind. The gigantic waves of a **tsunami,** however, are usually the result of an underwater **earthquake.** A **submarine landslide** or **volcano** can also cause a tsunami. Scientists have found ways of predicting when these huge waves will strike. They use **buoys** in the open ocean and **tide gauges** near the shore. They also use **seismographs** to record earthquake activity. A central station **monitors** all this information and produces a tsunami **forecast.**

tsu|na|mi /tsʊnɑmi/ (**tsunamis**) **N-COUNT** SCIENCE A **tsunami** is a very large wave that flows onto the land and can cause a lot of damage. [from Japanese]
→ look at Word Web: **tsunami**

tub /tʌb/ (**tubs**)
■ **N-COUNT** A **tub** is the same as a **bathtub.** ❑ I went into the bathroom to fill the tub.
■ **N-COUNT** A **tub** is a deep container of any size. ❑ We ate four tubs of ice cream between us. [from Middle Dutch]
→ look at Word Web: **soap**

tuba /tubə/ (**tubas**) **N-COUNT/N-NONCOUNT** MUSIC A **tuba** is a large round metal musical instrument with one wide end, that produces very low notes when you blow into it. [from Latin]

tube /tub/ (**tubes**)
■ **N-COUNT** A **tube** is a long hollow object that is usually round, like a pipe. ❑ He is fed by a tube that enters his nose.
■ **N-COUNT** A **tube of** something is a long, thin container that you can press in order to force the substance out. ❑ ...a tube of toothpaste. [from Latin]
→ look at Picture Dictionaries: **containers, laboratory**

tube worm (**tube worms**) also **tubeworm** **N-COUNT** SCIENCE A **tube worm** is a type of worm that lives in the sea and constructs a tube from sand and other material, that it lives in.

tuck /tʌk/ (**tucks, tucking, tucked**) **V-T** If you **tuck** something somewhere, you put it there so that it is safe, comfortable, or neat. ❑ He tucked his shirt inside his pants. [from Old English]

Tues|day /tuzdeɪ, -di/ (**Tuesdays**) **N-COUNT/ N-NONCOUNT** **Tuesday** is the day after Monday and before Wednesday. ❑ He phoned on Tuesday,

just before you arrived. ❑ Work on the project will start next Tuesday. [from Old English]

tug /tʌg/ (**tugs, tugging, tugged**)
■ **V-T/V-I** If you **tug** something, or **tug at** it, you give it a quick, strong pull. ❑ A little boy tugged at his sleeve excitedly.
■ **N-COUNT** Tug is also a noun. ❑ I felt a tug at my sleeve. [from Old English]

tu|lip /tulɪp/ (**tulips**) **N-COUNT** Tulips are flowers that grow in the spring and are shaped like cups. [from New Latin]

tum|ble /tʌmbəl/ (**tumbles, tumbling, tumbled**)
■ **V-I** If someone or something **tumbles,** they fall with a rolling movement. ❑ A small boy tumbled off the step.
■ **N-COUNT** Tumble is also a noun. ❑ He took a tumble down the stairs. [from Old English]

tum|my /tʌmi/ (**tummies**) **N-COUNT** Your **tummy** is your stomach. ❑ Your baby's tummy should feel warm, but not hot.

tu|mor /tumər/ (**tumors**) **N-COUNT** SCIENCE A **tumor** is an unusual lump that has grown in a person's or an animal's body. ❑ ...a brain tumor. [from Latin]
→ look at Word Web: **cancer**

tuna /tunə/ (**tuna** or **tunas**)
■ **N-COUNT/N-NONCOUNT** Tuna or tuna fish are large fish that live in warm seas.
■ **N-NONCOUNT** Tuna or tuna fish is this fish when it is eaten as food. ❑ She opened a can of tuna. [from American Spanish]

tun|dra /tʌndrə/ (**tundras**)
N-COUNT/N-NONCOUNT GEOGRAPHY **Tundra** is one of the large flat areas of land in the north of Europe, Asia, and America. The ground below the top layer of soil is always frozen and no trees grow there. [from Russian]

tune /tun/ (**tunes, tuning, tuned**)

1 **N-COUNT** MUSIC A **tune** is a series of musical notes that is pleasant to listen to. ❑ *She was humming a little tune.*

2 **V-T** MUSIC When someone **tunes** a musical instrument, they adjust it so that it produces the right notes. ❑ *We tune our guitars before we go on stage.*

3 MUSIC **Tune up** means the same as **tune**. ❑ *Others were quietly tuning up their instruments.*

4 **PHRASE** MUSIC A singer or a musical instrument that is **in tune** produces exactly the right notes. A person or a musical instrument that is **out of tune** does not produce exactly the right notes. ❑ *It was just an ordinary voice, but he sang in tune.*

tun|nel /tʌnᵊl/ (**tunnels**) **N-COUNT** A **tunnel** is a long passage that has been made under the ground, usually through a hill or under the sea. [from Old French]
→ look at Word Webs: **tunnel, traffic**

tur|bine /tɜrbɪn, -baɪn/ (**turbines**) **N-COUNT** SCIENCE A **turbine** is a machine or an engine that uses a stream of air, gas, water, or steam to turn a wheel and produce power. ❑ *The ship will be powered by two gas turbines.* [from French]
→ look at Word Webs: **electricity, wheel**

tur|key /tɜrki/ (**turkeys**)

1 **N-COUNT** A **turkey** is a large bird that is kept on a farm for its meat.

2 **N-NONCOUNT** **Turkey** is the meat of this bird when it is eaten as food. [from French]

tur|moil /tɜrmɔɪl/ (**turmoils**) **N-COUNT/ N-NONCOUNT** **Turmoil** is a state of confusion or great anxiety. ❑ *Her feelings were in turmoil.*

turn /tɜrn/ (**turns, turning, turned**)

1 **V-T/V-I** If someone or something **turns**, they move in a different direction or into a different position. ❑ *He turned and walked away.* ❑ *She turned the chair to face the door.*

2 **N-COUNT** **Turn** is also a noun. ❑ *You can't do a right-hand turn here.*

3 **V-T/V-I** When you **turn** in a particular direction, you change the direction in which you are facing. ❑ *He turned away from me.* ❑ *Now turn left to follow West Ferry Road.*

4 **V-T/V-I** When something **turns**, (or when you **turn** it) it moves around in a circle. ❑ *The wheels turned very slowly.* ❑ *Turn the key to the right.*

5 **V-T** If you **turn** a page in a book, you move it so that you can look at the next page. ❑ *He turned the pages of his photo album.*

6 **V-I** If you **turn to** a particular page in a book, you open it and find that page. ❑ *Please turn to page 236.*

7 **V-I** If you **turn to** someone, you ask them for their help. ❑ *She turned to him for support when she lost her job.*

8 **V-T/V-I** If something **turns into** something else, it becomes something different. ❑ *The sky turned pale pink.* ❑ *In the story, the prince turns into a frog.*

9 **V-T** When you **turn** a particular age, you reach that age. ❑ *He made a million dollars before he turned thirty.*

10 **N-COUNT** Your **turn to** do something is the time when you can do it. ❑ *Tonight it's my turn to cook.*

Word Web   tunnel

The Egyptians built the first **tunnels** as entrances to tombs. Later the Babylonians* built a tunnel under the Euphrates River*. It connected the royal palace with the Temple of Jupiter*. The Romans **dug** tunnels when **mining** for gold. By the late 1600s, **explosives** had replaced **digging**. **Gunpowder** was used to build the **underground** section of a canal in France in 1679. The longest continuous tunnel in the world is the Delaware Aqueduct. It carries water from the Catskill Mountains* to New York City and is 105 miles long.

Babylonians: people who lived in the ancient city of Babylon.
Euphrates River: a large river in the Middle East.
Temple of Jupiter: a religious building.
Catskill Mountains: a mountain range in the northeastern U.S.

t

11 PHRASE If two people **take turns**, they do something one after the other several times. ❑ *It's a long way to Washington, so we took turns driving.* [from Old English]

▶ **turn down** **1** If you **turn down** an offer, you refuse it. ❑ *The company offered me a new contract, but I turned it down.*
2 When you **turn down** a piece of equipment, you make it produce less sound or heat. ❑ *Please turn the TV down!* ❑ *I'll turn down the central heating.*

▶ **turn off** When you **turn off** a piece of equipment, you make it stop working. ❑ *The light's a bit bright. Can you turn it off?* ❑ *When the tub was full, she turned off the faucet.*

▶ **turn on** When you **turn on** a piece of equipment, you make it start working. ❑ *I turned on the television.*

▶ **turn out** **1** The way that something **turns out** is the way that it happens. ❑ *I didn't know my life was going to turn out like this.*
2 When you **turn out** a light, you switch it off. ❑ *Turn the lights out when you leave.*

▶ **turn over** If you **turn** something **over**, you move it so that the top part is on the bottom. ❑ *Liz picked up the envelope and turned it over.* ❑ *The car turned over and landed in a river.*

▶ **turn up** **1** If someone **turns up**, they arrive. ❑ *They finally turned up at midnight.*
2 When you **turn up** a piece of equipment, you make it produce more sound or heat. ❑ *I turned the volume up.*

tur|nip /tɜrnɪp/ (**turnips**)
N-COUNT/N-NONCOUNT A **turnip** is a round white vegetable that grows under the ground. [from Latin]

turn|out /tɜrnaʊt/ (**turnouts**) **N-COUNT**
The **turnout** at an event is the number of people who go to it. ❑ *It was a great afternoon with a huge turnout of people.*

turn|over /tɜrnoʊvər/ (**turnovers**)
1 N-COUNT/N-NONCOUNT BUSINESS The **turnover** of a company is the value of the goods or services that are sold during a particular period of time. ❑ *The company had a turnover of $3.8 million.*
2 N-COUNT/N-NONCOUNT BUSINESS The **turnover** of people in an organization is the rate at which people leave and are replaced. ❑ *Staff turnover is high because they don't pay much.*

turn sig|nal (**turn signals**) **N-COUNT** A car's **turn signals** are its lights that flash in order to show that it is going to turn left or right.

❑ *Check the turn signals to make sure they're working.*

tur|quoise /tɜrkwɔɪz/
1 ADJ Something that is **turquoise** is light greenish-blue in color. ❑ *...the clear turquoise ocean.*
2 N-NONCOUNT **Turquoise** is also a noun. ❑ *You look good in turquoise.* [from Old French]

tur|tle /tɜrtəl/ (**turtles**) **N-COUNT** A **turtle** is an animal that has a thick shell around its body, and may live on land or in water. ❑ *Seabirds and sea turtles live on the island.* [from French]

tusk /tʌsk/ (**tusks**) **N-COUNT** **Tusks** are two very long, curved, pointed teeth that grow beside the mouth of an elephant. [from Old English]

tu|tor /tutər/ (**tutors**) **N-COUNT** A **tutor** is someone who gives private lessons to one student or to a very small group of students. ❑ *...a math tutor.* [from Latin]

tux|edo /tʌksidoʊ/
(**tuxedos**) **N-COUNT**
A **tuxedo** is a suit or a jacket, usually black, that some men wear for formal social events. [from New York]

tuxedo

TV /ti vi/ (**TVs**)
N-COUNT/N-NONCOUNT **TV** is the same as **television**. ❑ *The TV was on.* ❑ *What's on TV?* ❑ *They watch too much TV.*

tweet /twit/ (**tweets, tweeting, tweeted**)
V-T/V-I TECHNOLOGY If you **tweet**, or if you **tweet** something, you send a short message on the Twitter® website. ❑ *Thousands of people tweeted their disapproval.*

twelfth /twɛlfθ/ (**twelfths**)
1 ADJ/ADV MATH The **twelfth** item in a series is the one that you count as number twelve. ❑ *They're celebrating the twelfth anniversary of the revolution.*
2 N-COUNT MATH A **twelfth** is one of twelve equal parts of something (1/12). ❑ *She will get a twelfth of her father's money.* [from Old English]

twelve /twɛlv/ **NUM** MATH **Twelve** is the number 12. [from Old English]

twelve-bar blues **N-NONCOUNT** MUSIC
Twelve-bar blues is a form of blues music based on a system of twelve bars to each verse.

twelve-tone **ADJ** MUSIC A **twelve-tone** scale is a musical scale consisting of all twelve notes in an octave. **Twelve-tone** music is music that is composed using a twelve-tone scale.

twen|ti|eth /twɛntiəθ/ (**twentieths**)

■ **ADJ/ADV** MATH The **twentieth** item in a series is the one that you count as number twenty. ❑ ...the twentieth century.
■ **N-COUNT** MATH A **twentieth** is one of twenty equal parts of something. ❑ ...a few twentieths of a gram. [from Old English]

twen|ty /twɛnti/ (**twenties**)

■ **NUM** MATH **Twenty** is the number 20.
■ **N-COUNT** A **twenty** is a twenty-dollar bill. ❑ I reached into my pocket and pulled out a twenty.
■ **N-PLURAL** The **twenties** are the years between 1920 and 1929. ❑ My grandmother was born in the twenties.
■ **N-PLURAL** When you talk about the **twenties**, you mean the numbers between 20 and 29. For example, if you are in your **twenties**, you are aged between 20 and 29. ❑ They got married in their early twenties. [from Old English]

24-7 /twɛntifɔrsɛvⁿn/ also **twenty-four seven**

■ **ADV** If something happens **24-7**, it happens all the time. **24-7** means twenty-four hours a day, seven days a week. [INFORMAL] ❑ I feel like sleeping 24-7.
■ **ADJ** **24-7** is also an adjective. [INFORMAL] ❑ ...a 24-7 radio station.

Word Link	twi ≈ two : twice, twilight, twin

twice /twaɪs/

■ **ADV** If something happens **twice**, it happens two times. ❑ He visited me twice last week. ❑ I phoned twice a day.
■ **ADV** If one thing is **twice as** big **as** another, the first thing is double the size of the second. ❑ Budapest is twice as big as my home town. [from Old English]

twig /twɪg/ (**twigs**) **N-COUNT** A **twig** is a very small thin branch that grows out from a main branch of a tree or a bush. [from Old English]

twi|light /twaɪlaɪt/ **N-NONCOUNT** **Twilight** is the time just before night when the light of the day has almost gone. ❑ They returned at twilight. [from Old English]

twin /twɪn/ (**twins**)

■ **N-COUNT** **Twins** are two people who were born at the same time from the same mother. ❑ Sarah was looking after the twins.
■ **ADJ** **Twin** describes a pair of things that look the same and are close together. ❑ Carter booked a room with twin beds. ❑ The boat's twin engines make the trip fast and safe. [from Old English]
→ look at Word Web: **clone**

twin|kle /twɪŋkəl/ (**twinkles, twinkling, twinkled**) **V-I** If a star or a light **twinkles**, it shines with a light that continuously becomes brighter and then weaker. ❑ Lights twinkled across the valley. [from Old English]

twirl /twɜrl/ (**twirls, twirling, twirled**)

■ **V-T/V-I** If you **twirl** something, or if it **twirls**, you turn it around several times very quickly. ❑ Bonnie twirled her empty glass in her fingers.
■ **V-I** If you **twirl**, you turn around several times quickly. ❑ The dancers twirled around the dance floor.

twist /twɪst/ (**twists, twisting, twisted**)

■ **V-T** If you **twist** something, you turn it to make it into a different shape. ❑ She sat twisting the handles of the bag, and looking worried.
■ **V-T/V-I** If you **twist** part of your body such as your head or your shoulders, or if it **twists**, that part turns while keeping the rest of your body still. ❑ She twisted her head around to look at him.
■ **V-T** If you **twist** a part of your body, you injure it by turning it too suddenly, or in an unusual direction. ❑ He fell and twisted his ankle.
■ **V-T** If you **twist** something, you move it so that it turns. ❑ She was twisting the ring on her finger. [from Old English]

twitch /twɪtʃ/ (**twitches, twitching, twitched**)

■ **V-T/V-I** If a part of your body **twitches**, or if you **twitch** it, it makes a little jumping movement. ❑ Her right eye began to twitch.
■ **N-COUNT** **Twitch** is also a noun. ❑ He had a nervous twitch. [from Old English]

two /tu/ **NUM** MATH **Two** is the number 2. [from Old English]
→ look at Usage note at **too**

two-di|men|sion|al /tu dɪmɛnʃənəl/ **ADJ** ARTS A **two-dimensional** object or figure is flat.

two-point per|spec|tive (**two-point perspectives**) **N-COUNT/N-NONCOUNT** MATH A **two-point perspective** is a method of representing three-dimensional space on a

t

two-dimensional surface by the use of two vanishing points on the horizon.

type /taɪp/ (**types, typing, typed**)

■ **N-COUNT** A **type of** something is a particular kind of it. ❑ *I like most types of music.* ❑ *Have you done this type of work before?*

■ **V-T/V-I** If you **type** something, you write it using a machine such as a computer. ❑ *I can type your essays for you.* ❑ *You should learn to type properly.* [from Latin]

→ look at Word Web: **printing**

type|writ|er /taɪpraɪtər/ (**typewriters**)

N-COUNT A **typewriter** is a machine with keys that you press in order to print writing onto paper.

ty|phoon /taɪfun/ (**typhoons**) **N-COUNT**

SCIENCE A **typhoon** is a very violent tropical storm. [from Chinese]

→ look at Word Web: **disaster**

typi|cal /tɪpɪkəl/

■ **ADJ** A **typical** person or thing is a good example of that type of person or thing. ❑ *Tell me about your typical day.* ❑ *In some ways, Jo is just a typical 12-year old.*

■ **ADJ** If something is **typical of** someone, it shows their usual qualities or characteristics. ❑ *The bear had thick, creamy white fur, typical of polar bears.* [from Medieval Latin]

typi|cal|ly /tɪpɪkli/

■ **ADV** You use **typically** to say that something is a good example of a particular type of person or thing. ❑ *The food is typically American.*

■ **ADV** You can use **typically** when you mean usually. ❑ *The day typically begins with swimming.* [from Medieval Latin]

typ|ist /taɪpɪst/ (**typists**) **N-COUNT** A **typist** is someone who works in an office typing letters and other documents. [from Latin]

ty|rant /taɪrənt/ (**tyrants**) **N-COUNT** A **tyrant** is someone who has a lot of power and treats people in a cruel and unfair way. ❑ *His staff all thought he was a tyrant.* [from Old French]

T

Uu

ugly /ʌgli/ (**uglier, ugliest**)

1 **ADJ** If someone or something is **ugly**, they are very unpleasant to look at. ❏ *He had an ugly scar across the side of his face.*

2 **ADJ** If you refer to an event or a situation as **ugly**, you mean that it is very unpleasant, usually because it involves violence. ❏ *There have been some ugly scenes.* ❏ *The mood turned ugly.* [from Old Norse]

Thesaurus	ugly Also look up :
ADJ	unattractive; *(ant.)* beautiful **1** offensive, unpleasant **2**

Word Link	*ultim ≈ end, last : penultimate, ultimate, ultimatum*

ul|ti|mate /ʌltɪmɪt/

1 **ADJ** You use **ultimate** when you are talking about the final result of a long series of events. ❏ *The ultimate aim is to keep kids in school.*

2 **ADJ** You use **ultimate** to describe the most important or extreme thing of a particular kind. ❏ *This race is the ultimate test of their fitness.* [from Late Latin]

ul|ti|mate|ly /ʌltɪmɪtli/

1 **ADV** **Ultimately** means finally, after a long series of events. ❏ *Who, ultimately, is going to pay?*

2 **ADV** You use **ultimately** to indicate that what you are saying is the most important point in a discussion. ❏ *Ultimately, the judge has the final decision.* [from Late Latin]

ultra|son|ic /ʌltrəsɒnɪk/ **ADJ** SCIENCE **Ultrasonic** sounds have very high frequencies, that human beings cannot hear. [from Latin]

ultra|vio|let /ʌltrəvaɪəlɪt/ **ADJ** SCIENCE **Ultraviolet** light makes your skin become darker in color. ❏ *Although it is invisible, ultraviolet light is extremely powerful.*
→ look at Word Webs: **ozone, skin, sun**

um|bili|cal cord /ʌmbɪlɪkᵊl kɔrd/ (**umbilical cords**) **N-COUNT** SCIENCE The **umbilical cord** is the tube that connects an unborn baby to its mother, through which it receives oxygen and food.

um|brel|la /ʌmbrɛlə/ (**umbrellas**)

1 **N-COUNT** An **umbrella** is a long stick with a cloth or plastic cover that you use to protect yourself from the rain. ❏ *Harry held an umbrella over Denise.*

umbrella

2 **N-SING** An **umbrella** group includes a lot of different organizations. ❏ *...United for Peace and Justice, an umbrella organization for around 700 peace groups.* [from Italian]

um|pire /ʌmpaɪr/ (**umpires, umpiring, umpired**)

1 **N-COUNT** SPORTS An **umpire** is a person whose job is to watch a sports game to make sure that the rules are not broken. ❏ *The umpire's decision is final.*

2 **V-T/V-I** SPORTS To **umpire** means to be the umpire in a sports contest or game. ❏ *He umpired baseball games.* [from Old French]

un|able /ʌneɪbᵊl/ **ADJ** If you are **unable to** do something, you are not able to do it. ❏ *After the car accident, Jacob was unable to walk.* [from Latin]

Word Partnership	Use unable with :
ADV	**physically** unable
V	unable **to afford**, unable **to agree**, unable **to attend**, unable **to control**, unable **to cope**, unable **to decide**, unable **to explain**, unable **to find**, unable **to hold**, unable **to identify**, unable **to make**, unable **to move**, unable **to pay**, unable **to perform**, unable **to reach**, unable **to speak**, unable **to walk**, unable **to work**

un|ac|cep|table /ʌnəksɛptəbᵊl/ **ADJ** If something is **unacceptable**, it is bad or wrong and you cannot accept it or allow it. ❏ *This behavior is unacceptable and will be punished.* [from Latin]

Word Link	*anim ≈ alive, mind : animal, animated, unanimous*

unani|mous /yunænɪməs/ **ADJ** When a group of people are **unanimous**, they all

u

agree about something. ❑ *Their decision was unanimous.* ● **unani|mous|ly** **ADV** ❑ *The board unanimously approved the project last week.* [from Latin]

un|armed /ʌnɑrmd/ **ADJ** An **unarmed** person is not carrying a gun or any weapon. ❑ *The soldiers were unarmed.* [from Old English]

un|at|trac|tive /ʌnətræktɪv/ **ADJ** **Unattractive** people and things are not beautiful or attractive. ❑ *I felt lonely and unattractive.* ❑ *The walls were painted an unattractive orange color.* [from Latin]

un|avail|able /ʌnəveɪləbəl/
1 **ADJ** When people are **unavailable**, you cannot meet them or contact them. ❑ *She was making a film in Canada, and was unavailable for comment.*
2 **ADJ** If something is **unavailable**, you cannot have it or obtain it. ❑ *Figures are unavailable for the period April-June.* [from Old French]

un|avoid|able /ʌnəvɔɪdəbəl/ **ADJ** If something is **unavoidable**, you cannot avoid it or stop it from happening. ❑ *Mr. Earnhardt said that the accident was unavoidable.*

un|aware /ʌnəwɛər/ **ADJ** If you are **unaware** of something, you do not know about it. ❑ *Many people are unaware that they have the disease.* [from Old English]

Word Partnership	Use **unaware** with :
ADV	**apparently** unaware, **blissfully** unaware, **completely** unaware, **totally** unaware

un|bal|anced forces **N-PLURAL** SCIENCE In physics, **unbalanced forces** are forces that are not equal and opposite to each other, so that an object to which the forces are applied moves.

un|bear|able /ʌnbɛərəbəl/ **ADJ** If something is **unbearable**, it is so unpleasant that you cannot deal with it. ❑ *The pain was unbearable.* ● **un|bear|ably** /ʌnbɛərəbli/ **ADV** ❑ *In the afternoon, the sun became unbearably hot.* [from Old English]

un|beat|en /ʌnbitən/ **ADJ** SPORTS In sports, if a person or their performance is **unbeaten**, nobody else has performed well enough to beat them. ❑ *He's unbeaten in 20 fights.*

un|be|liev|able /ʌnbɪlivəbəl/
1 **ADJ** If something is **unbelievable**, it is

very hard to believe. ❑ *The movie was good, but the story was unbelievable.*
2 **ADJ** If something is **unbelievable**, it is very good or bad. ❑ *It's a beautiful island, with unbelievable views.* ● **un|be|liev|ably** /ʌnbɪlivəbli/ **ADV** ❑ *Jarrod is an unbelievably brave guy.* [from Old English]

Thesaurus	unbelievable	Also look up :
ADJ	inconceivable, preposterous, unimaginable **1** astounding, incredible, remarkable **2**

un|bi|ased /ʌnbaɪəst/ also **unbiassed** **ADJ** If you describe someone or something as **unbiased**, you mean they are fair in the way that they treat people or describe a situation. ❑ *There is no clear and unbiased information available for consumers.* [from Old French]

un|born /ʌnbɔrn/ **ADJ** An **unborn** child has not yet been born. ❑ *This is a disease that can harm an unborn child.*

un|cer|tain /ʌnsɜrtən/
1 **ADJ** If you are **uncertain** about something, you are not sure about it. ❑ *If you're uncertain about anything, you must ask.* ● **un|cer|tain|ly** **ADV** ❑ *He entered the room and stood uncertainly.*
2 **ADJ** If something is **uncertain**, it is not known or definite. ❑ *The company's future is uncertain.* ❑ *It's uncertain whether they will accept the plan.* [from Old French]

Word Partnership	Use **uncertain** with :
PREP	uncertain **about** *something* **1**
V	**be** uncertain, **remain** uncertain **1** **2**
ADV	**highly** uncertain, **still** uncertain **1** **2**

un|cer|tain|ty /ʌnsɜrtənti/ (**uncertainties**) **N-COUNT/N-NONCOUNT** **Uncertainty** is a state of doubt about the future or about what is the right thing to do. ❑ *...a time of political uncertainty.*

un|changed /ʌntʃeɪndʒd/ **ADJ** If something is **unchanged**, it has stayed the same for a particular period of time. ❑ *For many years prices have remained unchanged.*

un|cle /ʌŋkəl/ (**uncles**) **N-COUNT** Your **uncle** is the brother of your mother or father, or the husband of your aunt. ❑ *My uncle was the mayor of Memphis.* ❑ *An email from Uncle Fred arrived.* [from Old French]
→ look at Picture Dictionary: **family**

U

un|clear /ʌnklɪ̯ər/
1 **ADJ** If something is **unclear**, it is not known. ❑ *It is unclear who tried to kill the president.*
2 **ADJ** If you are **unclear** about something, you do not understand it well or are not sure about it. ❑ *People are unclear about the present situation.* [from Old French]

un|com|fort|able /ʌnkʌmftəbᵊl, -kʌmfərtə-/
1 **ADJ** If you are **uncomfortable**, you are slightly worried or embarrassed, and not relaxed and confident. ❑ *The request for money made them feel uncomfortable.* ❑ *She was uncomfortable with the situation.*
● **un|com|fort|ably** /ʌnkʌmftəbli, -kʌmfərtə-/ **ADV** ❑ *Sam's face was uncomfortably close.*
2 **ADJ** Something such as a bed or a chair that is **uncomfortable** does not make you feel relaxed when you use it. ❑ *This is an extremely uncomfortable chair.* [from Old French]

Thesaurus	uncomfortable	Also look up :
ADJ	awkward, embarrassed, troubled; (ant.) comfortable **1** irritating, painful **2**	

un|con|di|tion|al /ʌnkəndɪʃənᵊl/ **ADJ** Something that is **unconditional** is done or given freely, without anything being required in return. ❑ *Children need unconditional love from their parents.*
● **un|con|di|tion|al|ly** **ADV** ❑ *They accepted our offer unconditionally.* [from Latin]

un|con|scious /ʌnkɒnʃəs/
1 **ADJ** Someone who is **unconscious** is not awake and not aware of what is happening around them because of illness or a serious injury. ❑ *When the ambulance arrived, he was unconscious.* ● **un|con|scious|ness** **N-NONCOUNT** ❑ *Breathing in this toxic gas can cause unconsciousness and death.*
2 **ADJ** If your feelings or attitudes are **unconscious**, you do not know that you have them, but they show in the way that you behave. ❑ *...my unconscious fear of becoming a mother.* ● **un|con|scious|ly** **ADV** ❑ *We unconsciously form opinions about people we meet.* [from Latin]

un|con|sti|tu|tion|al /ʌnkɒnstɪtuʃənᵊl/ **ADJ** SOCIAL STUDIES If something is **unconstitutional**, it does not follow the rules of a constitution. ❑ *They believe that these laws are unconstitutional.*

un|con|trol|lable /ʌnkəntroʊləbᵊl/ **ADJ** If a feeling or a physical action is **uncontrollable**, you cannot stop yourself from feeling it or doing it. ❑ *She felt an almost uncontrollable excitement.* ● **un|con|trol|lably** /ʌnkəntroʊləbli/ **ADV** ❑ *I started shaking uncontrollably.*

un|con|trolled /ʌnkəntroʊld/ **ADJ** If something such as a feeling or activity is **uncontrolled**, no attempt is made to stop it or to make it less extreme. ❑ *His uncontrolled behavior disturbed the entire class.* ❑ *...uncontrolled immigration.*

un|cov|er /ʌnkʌvər/ (**uncovers, uncovering, uncovered**)
1 **V-T** If you **uncover** something, you take away something that is covering it. ❑ *Uncover the dish and cook the chicken for about 15 minutes.*
2 **V-T** If you **uncover** something secret, you find out about it. ❑ *They want to uncover the truth of what happened that night.* [from Old French]

Word Partnership	Use uncover with :
N	uncover **evidence**, uncover **a plot**, uncover **the truth** **2**
V	**help** uncover *something* **1** **2**

un|de|cid|ed /ʌndɪsaɪdɪd/ **ADJ** If you are **undecided** about something, you have not decided about it. ❑ *Mary is still undecided about her future.* [from Old French]

un|de|ni|able /ʌndɪnaɪəbᵊl/ **ADJ** If you say that something is **undeniable**, you mean that it is definitely true. ❑ *Her charm is undeniable.* ● **un|de|ni|ably** /ʌndɪnaɪəbli/ **ADV** ❑ *Bringing up a baby is undeniably hard work.*

un|der /ʌndər/
1 **PREP** If a person or a thing is **under** something, they are below it. ❑ *There are hundreds of tunnels under the ground.* ❑ *The two girls were sitting under a tree.* ❑ *There was a big splash and she disappeared under the water.*
2 **PREP** If something happens **under** particular circumstances or conditions, it happens when those circumstances or conditions exist. ❑ *Under the circumstances, I think we did well.* ❑ *He was able to work under pressure.*
3 **PREP** If something happens **under** a particular person or government, it happens when that person or government is in power. ❑ *I hope that there will be a change under this government.*

u

4 **PREP** You use **under** to say which section of a list, a book, or a system something is in. ❏ *Look on page 164, under the heading "Top Ten Cities."*

5 **PREP** If something or someone is **under** a particular age or amount, they are less than that age or amount. ❏ *Sarah has three children under ten years of age.*

6 **ADV** Under is also an adverb. ❏ *Children (14 years and under) get in to the show free if accompanied by an adult.* [from Old English]
→ look at Picture Dictionary: **location**

under|cut /ʌndərkʌt/ (**undercuts, undercutting, undercut**)

> **LANGUAGE HELP**
>
> The form **undercut** is used in the present tense and is also the past tense and past participle.

V-T BUSINESS If you **undercut** someone or **undercut** their prices, you sell a product more cheaply than they do. ❏ *...promises to undercut air fares on some routes by 40 percent.*

under|es|ti|mate /ʌndərɛstɪmeɪt/ (**underestimates, underestimating, underestimated**)

1 **V-T** If you **underestimate** something, you do not realize how large or great it is or will be. ❏ *Never underestimate the power of anger.*

2 **V-T** If you **underestimate** someone, you do not realize what they are capable of doing. ❏ *I think a lot of people still underestimate him.*

under|go /ʌndərɡoʊ/ (**undergoes, undergoing, underwent, undergone**) **V-T** If you **undergo** something unpleasant, it happens to you. ❏ *Mia is undergoing treatment for cancer.* [from Old English]

under|gradu|ate /ʌndərɡrædʒuɪt/ (**undergraduates**) **N-COUNT** An **undergraduate** is a student in their first, second, third, or fourth year at a college. ❏ *More than 55 percent of undergraduates are female.*

> **Word Link**   ground ≈ bottom : back**ground**, **ground**water, under**ground**

under|ground

> **PRONUNCIATION HELP**
>
> Pronounce the adverb /ʌndərɡraʊnd/.
> Pronounce the adjective /ʌndərɡraʊnd/.

1 **ADV** Something that is **underground** is below the surface of the ground. ❏ *Much of the White House is built underground.*

2 **ADJ** Underground is also an adjective.

❏ *The new library has an underground parking garage for 143 vehicles.*
→ look at Word Web: **tunnel**

under|line /ʌndərlaɪn/ (**underlines, underlining, underlined**) **V-T** If you **underline** a word or a sentence, you draw a line under it. ❏ *She underlined her name.*
→ look at Picture Dictionary: **answer**

Word Partnership	Use **underline** with :
N	underline **passages**, underline **text**, underline **titles**, underline **words** **2**

un|der|ly|ing /ʌndərlaɪɪŋ/ **ADJ** The **underlying** features of an object, an event, or a situation are not obvious, and it may be difficult to discover or reveal them. ❏ *You have to understand the underlying causes of the problem.*

under|mine /ʌndərmaɪn/ (**undermines, undermining, undermined**) **V-T** If you **undermine** something such as a feeling or a system, you make it less strong or less secure. ❏ *He undermined my position.* [from Middle English]

Word Partnership	Use **undermine** with :
N	undermine **authority**, undermine **government**, undermine **peace**, undermine **security**
V	**threaten to** undermine, **try to** undermine

under|neath /ʌndərniθ/

1 **PREP** If one thing is **underneath** another, it is below or under it. ❏ *The bomb exploded underneath a van.*

2 **ADV** Underneath is also an adverb.
❏ *He was wearing a blue sweater with a white T-shirt underneath.*

3 **ADV** The part of something that is **underneath** is the part that normally touches the ground or faces toward the ground.
❏ *The robin is a brown bird with red underneath.*

4 **N-SING** Underneath is also a noun.
❏ *Now I know what the underneath of a car looks like.*

5 **ADV** You use **underneath** when you are talking about feelings and emotions that people do not show in their behavior.
❏ *He was a kind and sensitive man underneath.*

6 **PREP** Underneath is also a preposition.
❏ *Underneath his friendly behavior Luke was shy.* [from Old English]
→ look at Picture Dictionary: **location**

U

under|pants /ʌndərpænts/ **N-PLURAL**
Underpants are a short piece of underwear that covers the area between your waist and the top of your legs. ❑ *Richard packed a spare shirt, socks, and underpants.*

under|score /ʌndərskɔr/ (**underscores, underscoring, underscored**)
1 **V-T** If something such as an action or an event **underscores** another, it draws attention to the other thing and emphasizes its importance. ❑ *The report underscores a larger problem.*
2 **V-T** If you **underscore** something such as a word or a sentence, you draw a line underneath it in order to make people notice it or give it extra importance. ❑ *He heavily underscored his note to Shelley.*

under|shirt /ʌndərʃɜrt/ (**undershirts**)
N-COUNT You wear an **undershirt** on the top half of your body next to your skin to keep yourself warm. ❑ *Luis put on a pair of shorts and an undershirt.*

under|stand /ʌndərstænd/ (**understands, understanding, understood**)
1 **V-T** If you **understand** someone, or **understand** what they are saying, you know what they mean. ❑ *Toni can speak and understand Russian.* ❑ *Do you understand what I'm telling you, Sean?*
2 **V-T** To **understand** someone means to know how they feel and why they behave in the way that they do. ❑ *I feel she really understands me.*
3 **V-T** You say that you **understand** something when you know why or how it happens. ❑ *They are too young to understand what is going on.* ❑ *I don't understand why you're so afraid of her.*
4 **V-T** If you **understand** that something is true, you believe it is true because you have been given information about it. ❑ *I understand that you're leaving tomorrow.* [from Old English]
→ look at Word Web: **philosophy**

Thesaurus understand Also look up :
v   catch on, comprehend, get, grasp;
     (*ant.*) misunderstand **1**

under|stand|able /ʌndərstændəbəl/ **ADJ** If you describe someone's behavior or feelings as **understandable**, you think that they have reacted to a situation in a natural way or in the way you would expect. ❑ *His unhappiness was understandable.* ● **under|stand|ably**

/ʌndərstændəbli/ **ADV** ❑ *They are understandably upset.* [from Old English]

under|stand|ing /ʌndərstændɪŋ/ (**understandings**)
1 **N-COUNT/N-NONCOUNT** If you have an **understanding of** something, you know how it works or know what it means. ❑ *Children need to have an understanding of right and wrong.*
2 **ADJ** If you are **understanding**, you are kind to other people and you always try to understand their feelings. ❑ *He was very understanding when we told him about our mistake.*
3 **N-COUNT** An **understanding** is an informal agreement about something. ❑ *We have an understanding about the way we work.* ❑ *He was free to come and go as he wished on the understanding that he would not run away.* [from Old English]

Word Partnership	Use **understanding** with :
v	**develop** an understanding, **lack** an understanding **1**
ADJ	**basic** understanding, **clear** understanding, **complete** understanding **1** **deep/deeper** understanding **1** **better** understanding **1** **mutual** understanding **3**

un|der|stood /ʌndərstʊd/ **Understood** is the past tense and past participle of **understand**. [from Old English]

under|take /ʌndərteɪk/ (**undertakes, undertaking, undertook, undertaken**) **V-T** When you **undertake** some work, you start doing it. ❑ *The company has undertaken two large projects in Dubai.* ● **under|tak|ing** /ʌndərteɪkɪŋ/ (**undertakings**) **N-COUNT** ❑ *Organizing the show has been a huge undertaking.*

un|der|took /ʌndərtʊk/ **Undertook** is the past tense of **undertake**.

under|wa|ter /ʌndərwɔtər/
1 **ADV** Something that exists or happens **underwater** exists or happens below the surface of the ocean, a river, or a lake. ❑ *Submarines are able to travel at high speeds underwater.*
2 **ADJ** **Underwater** is also an adjective. ❑ *The divers were using underwater cameras.*

underwater

u

under|way /ʌndərweɪ/ **ADJ** If an activity is **underway**, it has already started. If an activity gets **underway**, it starts. ❑ *Plans are underway to build more homes.* [from Old English]

under|wear /ʌndərwɛər/ **N-NONCOUNT Underwear** is clothes that you wear next to your skin, under your other clothes. ❑ *I bought some new underwear for the children.*

un|der|went /ʌndərwɛnt/ **Underwent** is the past tense of **undergo.** [from Old English]

un|de|sir|able /ʌndɪzaɪərəbᵊl/ **ADJ** If you describe something or someone as **undesirable**, you think they are bad or will have harmful effects. ❑ *...undesirable behavior like fighting.* [from Old French]

un|did /ʌndɪd/ **Undid** is the past tense of **undo.**

Word Link *put ≈ thinking : com**put**er, dis**put**e, undis**put**ed*

un|dis|put|ed /ʌndɪspyutɪd/ **ADJ** If you describe something as **undisputed**, you mean that everyone accepts that it exists or is true. ❑ *...an undisputed fact.* ❑ *Seles was the undisputed world champion.* ❑ *At 78 years of age, he's still undisputed leader of his country.*

undo /ʌndu/ (**undoes, undoing, undid, undone**) **V-T** If you **undo** something that was tied or fastened, you open it or make it loose. ❑ *I managed to undo a corner of the package.* ❑ *I undid the buttons of my shirt.*

un|doubt|ed /ʌndaʊtɪd/ **ADJ** You can use **undoubted** to emphasize that something exists or is true. ❑ *The event was an undoubted success.* ❑ *...a man of your undoubted ability.* ● **un|doubt|ed|ly ADV** ❑ *He was undoubtedly right.*

un|dress /ʌndrɛs/ (**undresses, undressing, undressed**) **V-T/V-I** When you **undress**, you take off your clothes. If you **undress** someone, you take off their clothes. ❑ *Emily undressed, got into bed, and turned off the light.* ❑ *We undressed the baby, then bathed him.* ● **un|dressed ADJ** ❑ *Fifteen minutes later Brandon was undressed and in bed.* [from Old French]

un|due /ʌndu/ **ADJ** If you describe something bad as **undue**, you mean that it is greater or more extreme than you think is reasonable or appropriate. ❑ *I don't want to put any undue pressure on them to win the baseball game.* ● **un|du|ly ADV** ❑ *"But you're not unduly worried about doing this report?"—"No."* [from Old French]

Word Partnership Use **undue** with :

N	undue **attention**, undue **burden**, undue **delay**, undue **emphasis**, undue **hardship**, undue **influence**, undue **interference**, undue **pressure**, undue **risk**

un|easy /ʌnizi/ **ADJ** If you are **uneasy**, you are anxious or afraid about something. ❑ *Madison looked uneasy and refused to answer questions.* ● **un|easi|ly** /ʌnizɪli/ **ADV** ❑ *Meg looked at her watch and moved uneasily on her chair.* [from Old French]

un|em|ployed /ʌnɪmplɔɪd/
1 ADJ If you are **unemployed**, you are able to work but you do not have a job. ❑ *Millions of people are unemployed.* ❑ *This course helps young unemployed people to find work.*
2 N-PLURAL The **unemployed** are people who are unemployed. ❑ *We want to create jobs for the unemployed.*

un|em|ploy|ment /ʌnɪmplɔɪmənt/
1 N-NONCOUNT SOCIAL STUDIES **Unemployment** is when people who want to work cannot work, because there are not enough jobs. ❑ *Robert's family live in an area of high unemployment.*
2 N-NONCOUNT SOCIAL STUDIES **Unemployment** is money that is paid by the government to people who do not have a job. ❑ *She gets $413 a week in unemployment.* [from Old French]

un|even /ʌnivᵊn/ **ADJ** An **uneven** surface is not flat or smooth. ❑ *The ground was uneven and he fell off his bike.* [from Old English]

un|ex|pec|ted /ʌnɪkspɛktɪd/ **ADJ** If something is **unexpected**, it surprises you because you did not think that it was likely to happen. ❑ *Scientists have made an unexpected discovery.* ● **un|ex|pect|ed|ly ADV** ❑ *April was unexpectedly hot.*

un|ex|plained /ʌnɪkspleɪnd/ **ADJ** If something is **unexplained**, the reason for it or cause of it is unclear or is not known. ❑ *Colton suffered a terrifying, unexplained illness.* ❑ *The city's water supply was cut for unexplained reasons.*

U

un|fair /ʌnfɛər/ **ADJ** If something is **unfair**, it does not treat people in an equal way or in the right way. ❑ *It's unfair to expect a child to behave like an adult.* ❑ *They claimed that the test was unfair.* ● **un|fair|ly ADV** ❑ *She feels they treated her unfairly.* ● **un|fair|ness N-NONCOUNT** ❑ *I joined the police to tackle unfairness in society.* [from Old English]

un|fa|mil|iar /ʌnfəmɪlyər/ **ADJ** If something is **unfamiliar to** you, you do not know it, and it is strange to you. ❑ *The woman's voice was unfamiliar to me.* [from Latin]

un|fit /ʌnfɪt/
1 ADJ If someone or something is **unfit** for a particular purpose, they are not good enough for that purpose. ❑ *The water was unfit for drinking.*
2 ADJ If you are **unfit**, your body is not healthy or strong. ❑ *Many children are so unfit they cannot do even basic exercises.* [from Middle Dutch]

un|fold /ʌnfoʊld/ (**unfolds, unfolding, unfolded**)
1 V-I If a situation or story **unfolds**, it develops and becomes known or understood. ❑ *We'll see how the situation unfolds in the next 24 hours.* ❑ *The policeman listened carefully as the story unfolded.*
2 V-T/V-I If someone **unfolds** something that has been folded or if it **unfolds**, it is opened out and becomes flat. ❑ *Mom unfolded the piece of paper.* [from Old English]

un|for|tu|nate /ʌnfɔrtʃənɪt/
1 ADJ If someone is **unfortunate**, something unpleasant or unlucky has happened to them. ❑ *We were very unfortunate to lose the game.*
2 ADJ An **unfortunate** event is one that you did not want to happen. ❑ *We made some unfortunate mistakes in the past.* [from Old French]

un|for|tu|nate|ly /ʌnfɔrtʃənɪtli/ **ADV** You say **unfortunately** when you are sorry about something. ❑ *Unfortunately, I don't have time to stay.* [from Old French]

un|friend|ly /ʌnfrɛndli/ **ADJ** If someone is **unfriendly**, they behave in an unkind or unpleasant way. ❑ *The people he met there were unfriendly and rude.* [from Old English]

un|hap|py /ʌnhæpi/ (**unhappier, unhappiest**)
1 ADJ If you are **unhappy**, you are sad. ❑ *Christopher was a shy, unhappy man.*
● **un|hap|pi|ly ADV** ❑ *Jean shook her head unhappily.* ● **un|hap|pi|ness N-NONCOUNT** ❑ *There was a lot of unhappiness in my childhood.*
2 ADJ If you are **unhappy about** something, you are not satisfied with it. ❑ *Our coach was unhappy with the way we played on Friday.*
● **un|hap|pi|ness N-NONCOUNT** ❑ *She spoke about her unhappiness with her job.*

un|harmed /ʌnhɑrmd/ **ADJ** If someone or something is **unharmed** after an accident or a violent incident, they are not hurt or damaged in any way. ❑ *They both escaped unharmed.*

un|healthy /ʌnhɛlθi/ (**unhealthier, unhealthiest**)
1 ADJ If you are **unhealthy**, you are sick, or not in good physical condition. ❑ *A pale, unhealthy looking man walked into the store.*
2 ADJ Something that is **unhealthy** can make you ill or harm your health. ❑ *Avoid unhealthy foods such as hamburgers and fries.*

un|help|ful /ʌnhɛlpfəl/ **ADJ** If someone or something is **unhelpful**, they do not help you or make things better. ❑ *Josh was rude and unhelpful to Della.* [from Old English]

uni|cel|lu|lar /yunɪsɛlyələr/ **ADJ SCIENCE** **Unicellular** organisms are organisms that consist of a single cell, such as bacteria. Compare with **multicellular**.

un|iden|ti|fied /ʌnaɪdɛntɪfaɪd/ **ADJ** If you describe someone or something as **unidentified**, you mean that nobody knows who or what they are. ❑ *An unidentified woman was in the car.*

uni|fi|ca|tion /yunɪfɪkeɪʃ°n/ **N-NONCOUNT** **SOCIAL STUDIES** **Unification** is the process by which two or more countries join together and become one country. ❑ *...the unification of East and West Germany in 1990.* [from Medieval Latin]

uni|form /yunɪfɔrm/ (**uniforms**)
1 N-COUNT/N-NONCOUNT A **uniform** is the special clothes that are worn by all members of an organization or a team, and that some children wear in school. ❑ *The police wear blue uniforms.*

uniform

u

❑ *Daniel was dressed in his school uniform.*
❑ *...a baseball uniform.*
2 **ADJ** Something that is **uniform** is even and regular. ❑ *Plants do not all grow to uniform size.* [from Latin]
→ look at Picture Dictionaries: **basketball, soccer**

un|im|por|tant /ˌʌnɪmpɔrtᵊnt/ **ADJ** Something or someone that is **unimportant** is not important. ❑ *Abigail always remembers unimportant details.* [from Old Italian]

un|ion /yunyən/ (**unions**)
1 **N-COUNT** BUSINESS A **union** is a workers' organization that tries to improve working conditions. ❑ *Ten new members joined the union.*
2 **N-COUNT** SOCIAL STUDIES A **union** is a group of states or countries that join together. ❑ *The United Kingdom is a union of nations.* [from Church Latin]
→ look at Word Webs: **union, empire, factory**

unique /yunik/ **ADJ** Something that is **unique** is the only one of its kind. ❑ *Each person's signature is unique.* ● **unique|ly** **ADV** ❑ *She's a dog with uniquely colored eyes; one is brown and one is blue.* ● **unique|ness** **N-NONCOUNT** ❑ *I like the uniqueness of flavors in Australian cooking.* [from French]

> **Thesaurus** **unique** Also look up :
> ADJ   different, one-of-a-kind, special;
>   (ant.) common, standard, usual

uni|son /yunɪsən, -zən/
1 **PHRASE** If two or more people do something **in unison**, they do it together at the same time. ❑ *They were singing in unison.*
2 **N-NONCOUNT** ARTS In dance, **unison** is the performance of a series of movements by two or more dancers at the same time. [from Late Latin]

unit /yunɪt/ (**units**)
1 **N-COUNT** A **unit** is a single, complete thing that can belong to something larger. ❑ *The building is divided into twelve units.*
2 **N-COUNT** A **unit** is a group of people who work together at a specific job, often in a particular place. ❑ *...a firefighting unit.*
3 **N-COUNT** MATH A **unit** is a measurement. ❑ *An inch is a unit of measurement.*
→ look at Word Web: **graph**

unite /yunaɪt/ (**unites, uniting, united**)
V-T/V-I If different people or things **unite**, they join together and act as a group. ❑ *The world must unite to fight this disease.* ❑ *Only the president can unite the people.* [from Late Latin]

unit|ed /yunaɪtɪd/
1 **ADJ** When people are **united** about something, they agree about it and act together. ❑ *They were united by their love of music.*
2 **ADJ** SOCIAL STUDIES **United** is used to describe a country that has been formed from two or more states or countries. ❑ *...a united Germany.* [from Late Latin]

Unit|ed Na|tions **N-PROPER** SOCIAL STUDIES **The United Nations** is an organization that most countries belong to. Its role is to encourage international peace, cooperation, and friendship.

unit frac|tion (**unit fractions**) **N-COUNT** MATH A **unit fraction** is a fraction in which the top part of the fraction is always the number one, for example ½ or ¼.

uni|ty /yunɪti/
1 **N-NONCOUNT** SOCIAL STUDIES **Unity** is the state of different areas or groups being joined together to form a single country or

---

Word Web union

In some places, **laborers** work long hours with little chance for a **raise** in **wages**. **Workdays** of 10 to 12 hours are common. Some people work seven days a week. Conditions like this lead to unhappiness among **workers**. At that point, **organizers** can encourage them to join a **union**. Union leaders practice **collective bargaining** with business owners. They may ask for a shorter workday or better working conditions. If the **employees** are not satisfied with the results, they may **strike**. In Sweden, around 70% of laborers and **white-collar** employees belong to unions.

organization. ❑ *...the unity of Eastern and Western Europe.*

2 **N-NONCOUNT** When there is **unity**, people are in agreement and act together for a particular purpose. ❑ *The president called for unity between the United States and Europe.*

3 **N-NONCOUNT** ARTS The **unity** of a work of art such as a painting or a piece of music is the impression it gives that it is complete and that all the different parts belong together. [from Old French]

uni|ver|sal /yunɪvɜrsəl/ **ADJ** Something that is **universal** includes or affects everyone. ❑ *Love is a universal emotion.* ● **uni|ver|sal|ly** /yunɪvɜrsəli/ **ADV** ❑ *Reading is universally accepted as being good for kids.* [from French]

uni|ver|sal gravi|ta|tion /yunɪvɜrsəl grævɪteɪʃ°n/ **N-SING** SCIENCE The **law of universal gravitation** is a principle in physics that states that all objects in the universe attract one another because of the force of gravity.

uni|verse /yunɪvɜrs/ (**universes**) **N-COUNT** SCIENCE The **universe** is everything, including the Earth, the sun, the moon, the planets, and the stars, that exists in space. ❑ *Can you tell us how the universe began?* [from French]
→ look at Word Webs: **biosphere, galaxy, telescope**

uni|ver|sity /yunɪvɜrsiti/ (**universities**) **N-COUNT/N-NONCOUNT** A **university** is a place where you can study after high school. ❑ *Maria goes to Duke University.* ❑ *Robert's mother is a university professor.* [from Old French]

un|just /ʌndʒʌst/ **ADJ** If something is **unjust**, it is not fair or right. ❑ *He was an unjust ruler, responsible for the deaths of thousands of people.* ● **un|just|ly** **ADV** ❑ *Megan was unjustly accused of stealing money.* [from Latin]

un|kind /ʌnkaɪnd/ (**unkinder, unkindest**) **ADJ** If you are **unkind**, you behave in an unpleasant and unfriendly way. ❑ *Tyler was unkind to his sister all evening.* [from Old English]

Thesaurus	unkind Also look up :
ADJ	harsh, mean, unfriendly; *(ant.)* kind **1**

un|known /ʌnnoʊn/ (**unknowns**)
1 **ADJ** If something is **unknown** to you, you do not know it. ❑ *The child's age is unknown.*
2 **ADJ** An **unknown** person is not famous.

❑ *Ten years ago he was an unknown writer but now he is a celebrity.*

3 **N-COUNT** **Unknown** is also a noun. ❑ *...a group of complete unknowns.*

4 **N-SING** The **unknown** refers generally to things or places that people do not know about or understand. ❑ *...fear of the unknown.*

un|leash /ʌnliʃ/ (**unleashes, unleashing, unleashed**) **V-T** If someone or something **unleashes** a powerful force, feeling, activity, or group, they suddenly release it. ❑ *She unleashed her anger on him during the meeting.*

un|less /ʌnlɛs/ **CONJ** **Unless** means "if the thing mentioned does not happen." ❑ *Ryan says he won't go to the party, unless I go too.* [from French]

Word Link	like ≈ similar : *alike, childlike, unlike*

un|like /ʌnlaɪk/
1 **PREP** If one thing is **unlike** another thing, the two things are different. ❑ *You're so unlike your father!*
2 **PREP** You can use **unlike** to contrast two people, things, or situations, and show how they are different. ❑ *Unlike most meetings, this one was a lot of fun.*
3 **PREP** If something that someone has done is **unlike** them, it is not typical of their normal behavior. ❑ *It was unlike him to say something like that.* [from Old English]

un|like|ly /ʌnlaɪkli/ (**unlikelier, unlikeliest**) **ADJ** If something is **unlikely**, it will probably not happen. ❑ *The boys are unlikely to arrive before nine o'clock.* [from Old Norse]

Word Partnership	Use **unlikely** with :
N	unlikely **event**
ADV	**extremely** unlikely, **highly** unlikely, **most** unlikely
V	unlikely **to change**, unlikely **to happen**, **seem** unlikely

un|load /ʌnloʊd/ (**unloads, unloading, unloaded**)
1 **V-T** If you **unload** goods from a ship or a vehicle, you remove them from it. ❑ *We unloaded everything from the car.*
2 **V-T** If you **unload** a ship or a vehicle, you remove things from it. ❑ *The men started unloading the truck.* [from Old English]

un|lock /ʌnlɒk/ (**unlocks, unlocking, unlocked**) **V-T** If you **unlock** something, you open it using a key. ❑ *Taylor unlocked the car*

u

and threw the coat on to the back seat. [from Old English]

un|lucky /ʌnlʌki/ (**unluckier, unluckiest**)
■ **ADJ** If someone is **unlucky**, something bad has happened to them, and it is not their fault. ❑ *Michael was very unlucky not to be chosen for the team.*
■ **ADJ** If something is **unlucky**, it will bring bad luck. ❑ *Four is an unlucky number in the Far East.*

un|mis|tak|able /ʌnmɪsteɪkəbəl/ also **unmistakeable ADJ** If something is **unmistakable**, it is so obvious that it is easy to recognize. ❑ *A few minutes later, we heard Sherrie's unmistakable voice.*

un|natu|ral /ʌnnætʃərəl/ **ADJ** Something that is **unnatural** is different from what you usually expect. ❑ *His eyes were an unnatural shade of blue.* [from Old French]

un|nec|es|sary /ʌnnɛsəsɛri/ **ADJ** If something is **unnecessary**, it is not needed or does not have to be done. ❑ *It is unnecessary to spend huge amounts of money on Christmas presents.* [from Latin]

un|of|fi|cial /ʌnəfɪʃəl/ **ADJ** Something that is **unofficial** is not organized or approved by an official person or group. ❑ *Unofficial reports say at least one police officer was killed.*

un|pack /ʌnpæk/ (**unpacks, unpacking, unpacked**) **v-T/v-I** When you **unpack** a suitcase or a box, you take things out of it. ❑ *He unpacked his bag.* ❑ *Bill helped his daughter to unpack.* [from Middle Low German]

un|paid /ʌnpeɪd/
■ **ADJ** If you do **unpaid** work, you do a job without receiving any money for it. ❑ *Most of the work I do is unpaid.*
■ **ADJ** **Unpaid** taxes or bills have not been paid yet.

un|pal|at|able /ʌnpælɪtəbəl/ **ADJ** If you describe an idea as **unpalatable**, you mean that you find it unpleasant and difficult to accept. ❑ *I began to learn the unpalatable truth about John.* [from Latin]

un|pleas|ant /ʌnplɛzənt/
■ **ADJ** If something is **unpleasant**, it gives you a bad feeling because it makes you feel upset or uncomfortable. ❑ *The plant has an unpleasant smell.* ● **un|pleas|ant|ly ADV** ❑ *She stayed in the bathtub until the water became unpleasantly cold.*

■ **ADJ** An **unpleasant** person is very unfriendly and rude. ❑ *He is such an unpleasant man!* [from Old French]

un|plug /ʌnplʌg/ (**unplugs, unplugging, unplugged**) **v-T** If you **unplug** electrical equipment, you take it from its electrical supply, so that it stops working. ❑ *Whenever there's a storm, I unplug my computer.* [from Middle Dutch]

Word Link	popul ≈ people : popular, population, unpopular

un|popu|lar /ʌnpɒpyələr/ **ADJ** If something or someone is **unpopular**, most people do not like them. ❑ *It was an unpopular decision.* ❑ *I was very unpopular in high school.* [from Latin]

un|prec|edent|ed /ʌnprɛsɪdɛntɪd/
■ **ADJ** If something is **unprecedented**, it has never happened before. ❑ *Such an action is rare, but not unprecedented.*
■ **ADJ** If you describe something as **unprecedented**, you are emphasizing that it is very great in quality or amount. ❑ *...an unprecedented success.*

un|pre|dict|able /ʌnprɪdɪktəbəl/ **ADJ** If someone or something is **unpredictable**, you never know what they are going to do. ❑ *Karen is completely unpredictable.* [from Latin]

un|pre|pared /ʌnprɪpɛərd/ **ADJ** If you are **unprepared for** something, you are not ready for it. ❑ *I was totally unprepared for the news.* [from Latin]

un|rav|el /ʌnrævəl/ (**unravels, unraveling, unraveled**)
■ **v-T/v-I** If you **unravel** something that is knotted or knitted, or if it **unravels**, it becomes one straight piece again or separates into different threads. ❑ *He could unravel knots others couldn't.*
■ **v-T/v-I** If you **unravel** a mystery or puzzle, or it **unravels**, it gradually becomes clearer until you can work out the answer to it. ❑ *Carter was still trying to unravel the truth of the woman's story.*

Word Link	un ≈ not : unfair, unreasonable, unsafe

un|rea|son|able /ʌnriːzənəbəl/ **ADJ** If someone is **unreasonable**, they behave in a way that is not fair or sensible. ❑ *It's unreasonable to expect a child to behave well all the time.* [from Old French]

un|re|li|able /ʌnrɪlaɪəbəl/ **ADJ** If someone or something is **unreliable**, you cannot trust them. ❑ My old car is very slow and unreliable. ❑ The law protects people from unreliable builders. [from Old French]

un|re|pent|ant /ʌnrɪpɛntənt/ **ADJ** If you are **unrepentant**, you are not ashamed of your beliefs or actions. ❑ Pamela was unrepentant about her strong language.

un|rest /ʌnrɛst/ **N-NONCOUNT** SOCIAL STUDIES If there is **unrest** in a particular place or society, people are expressing anger, often by demonstrating or rioting. ❑ There is growing unrest among students in several major cities. [from Old English]

un|ru|ly /ʌnruli/ **ADJ** If people are **unruly**, they are difficult to control. ❑ He was arrested for unruly behavior.

un|safe /ʌnseɪf/ **ADJ** If something is **unsafe**, it is dangerous. ❑ The building is unsafe and beyond repair. ❑ The water here is unsafe to drink. [from Old French]

Word Link	sat, satis ≈ enough : dissatisfied, satisfy, unsatisfactory

un|sat|is|fac|tory /ʌnsætɪsfæktəri/ **ADJ** If something is **unsatisfactory**, it is not good enough. ❑ I found his answer unsatisfactory. [from French]

un|satu|rat|ed hydro|car|bon /ʌnsætʃə reɪtɪd haɪdrəkɑrbən/ (**unsaturated hydrocarbons**) **N-COUNT/N-NONCOUNT** SCIENCE An **unsaturated hydrocarbon** is a chemical compound consisting of carbon and hydrogen in which there is less than the maximum amount of hydrogen.

un|steady /ʌnstɛdi/ **ADJ** If you are **unsteady**, you are likely to fall. ❑ My grandma is unsteady on her feet. [from Old High German]

un|suc|cess|ful /ʌnsəksɛsfəl/
1 **ADJ** If you are **unsuccessful**, or if something you try to do is **unsuccessful**, you do not manage to do what you want to do. ❑ They tried to save the man's life, but they were unsuccessful. ❑ ...an unsuccessful attempt to set a new world record. ● **un|suc|cess|ful|ly ADV** ❑ He tried unsuccessfully to sell the business.
2 **ADJ** Someone who is **unsuccessful** does not achieve what they intended to achieve, especially in their career. ❑ As a young man, Glover appeared unsuccessful and unsure of himself. [from Latin]

un|suit|able /ʌnsutəbəl/ **ADJ** A person or thing that is **unsuitable** is not right for someone or something. ❑ This movie is unsuitable for children. [from French]

un|sure /ʌnʃʊər/ **ADJ** If you are **unsure about** something, you are not certain about it. ❑ Police are unsure exactly when the items were stolen. [from Old French]

un|sym|pa|thet|ic /ʌnsɪmpəθɛtɪk/ **ADJ** An **unsympathetic** person is not kind or helpful to someone who is having problems. ❑ Jane's husband was unsympathetic and she felt she had no one to talk to.

un|til /ʌntɪl/
1 **PREP** If something happens **until** a particular time, it happens before that time and stops at that time. ❑ Until 2004, Julie lived in Canada.
2 **CONJ** Until is also a conjunction. ❑ I waited until it got dark.
3 **PREP** If something does not happen **until** a particular time, it does not happen before that time and only starts happening at that time. ❑ I won't arrive in New York until Saturday.
4 **CONJ** Until is also a conjunction. ❑ They won't be safe until they get out of the country. [from Old High German]

un|true /ʌntru/ **ADJ** Something that is **untrue** is not true or correct. ❑ Bryant said the story was untrue. [from Old English]

Word Link	un ≈ reversal : unusual, unwrap, unzip

un|usual /ʌnyuʒuəl/ **ADJ** If something is **unusual**, it does not happen very often or you do not see it or hear it very often. ❑ It's unusual for our teacher to make a mistake. ● **un|usu|al|ly** /ʌnyuʒuəli/ **ADV** ❑ It was an unusually cold winter. [from Late Latin]

Thesaurus	unusual Also look up :
ADJ	abnormal, different, interesting, strange, uncommon, unconventional; (ant.) common, conventional, normal, usual

un|veil /ʌnveɪl/ (**unveils, unveiling, unveiled**)
1 **V-T** If someone formally **unveils** something such as a new statue or painting, they open the curtain that is covering it. ❑ There is a plan to unveil a statue in front of the building.

u

2 V-T If you **unveil** a plan, a new product, or some other thing that has been kept secret, you introduce it to the public. ❑ *The company unveiled plans to open 100 new stores.* [from Norman French]

un|want|ed /ʌnwɒntɪd/

1 ADJ If something or someone is **unwanted**, you do not want them. ❑ *Every day I have to delete unwanted emails from my computer.*
2 ADJ If something or someone is **unwanted**, nobody wants them. ❑ *Emily felt unwanted and unloved.*

un|war|rant|ed /ʌnwɔrəntɪd/ **ADJ** If you describe something as **unwarranted**, you are critical of it because there is no need or reason for it. [FORMAL] ❑ *...unwarranted use of force.*

un|wel|come /ʌnwɛlkəm/ **ADJ** If someone or something is **unwelcome**, you do not want to see them or have them. ❑ *We were clearly unwelcome guests.* [from Old English]

un|well /ʌnwɛl/ **ADJ** If you are **unwell**, you are sick. ❑ *Grandpa was feeling unwell and had to stay at home.* [from Old English]

un|will|ing /ʌnwɪlɪŋ/ **ADJ** If you are **unwilling** to do something, you do not want to do it. ❑ *Many people are unwilling to change their email addresses.* ● **un|will|ing|ly ADV** ❑ *He accepted his orders very unwillingly.*
● **un|will|ing|ness N-NONCOUNT** ❑ *...their unwillingness to listen to good advice.*

un|wind /ʌnwaɪnd/ (**unwinds, unwinding, unwound**)
1 V-T/V-I If you **unwind** something that is wrapped around something else, you make it loose and straight. You can also say that it **unwinds**. ❑ *She unwound the scarf from her neck.*
2 V-I When you **unwind**, you do something relaxing after you have been working hard or worrying about something. ❑ *Dad needs to unwind after a busy day at work.* [from Old English]

un|wise /ʌnwaɪz/ **ADJ** Something that is **unwise** is not sensible. ❑ *It would be unwise of me to comment.* ● **un|wise|ly ADV** ❑ *She understands that she acted unwisely.* [from Old English]

> **Word Link** *un ≈ reversal : unusual, unwrap, unzip*

un|wrap /ʌnræp/ (**unwraps, unwrapping, unwrapped**) **V-T** When you **unwrap** something, you take off the paper or plastic that is around it. ❑ *I undid the ribbon and unwrapped the small box.*

un|zip /ʌnzɪp/ (**unzips, unzipping, unzipped**)
1 V-T TECHNOLOGY
If you **unzip** a computer file, you make it go back to its original size after it has been zipped.
❑ *Use the "Unzip" command to unzip the file.*
2 V-T/V-I If you **unzip**, or **unzip** clothing, you undo the zipper that is fastening it. ❑ *Pete unzipped his leather jacket and sat down.*

unzip

---

up
① PREPOSITION, ADVERB, AND ADJECTIVE USES
② PHRASES

① up

> **PRONUNCIATION HELP**
> Pronounce the preposition /ʌp/.
> Pronounce the adverb and adjective /ʌp/.

1 PREP Up means toward a higher place. ❑ *They were climbing up a mountain road.* ❑ *I ran up the stairs.*
2 ADV Up is also an adverb. ❑ *Keep your head up.*
3 ADV If someone stands **up**, they move from sitting or lying down, so that they are standing. ❑ *He stood up and went to the window.*
4 PREP If you go **up** a road or a river, you go along it. ❑ *A dark blue truck came up the road.*
5 ADV If you go **up** to something or someone, you move to the place where they are. ❑ *He came up to me and gave me a big hug.*
6 ADV If something goes **up**, it increases. ❑ *Gasoline prices went up in June.* ❑ *Employment is up; income is up.*
7 ADJ If you are **up**, you are not in bed. ❑ *They were up very early to get to the airport on time.*
8 ADJ A period of time is **up** when it comes to an end. ❑ *When the half-hour was up, Brian left.* [from Old English]

② up /ʌp/

1 PHRASE If you move **up and down**, you move first in one direction and then in the opposite direction. ❑ *I used to jump up and down to keep warm.* ❑ *I walked up and down before calling a taxi.*
2 PHRASE If you feel **up to** doing something, you are well enough to do it.

❏ *Do you feel up to seeing visitors?* ❏ *They were not up to running the business without him.*
3 **PHRASE** If it is **up to** someone to do something, it is their responsibility to do it. ❏ *It's up to you to solve your own problems.*
4 **PHRASE** **Up until** or **up to** are used to talk about the latest time at which something can happen. ❏ *Please feel free to call me any time up until 9:30 at night.*
5 **PHRASE** You use **up to** to say how large something can be or what level it has reached. ❏ *...buildings up to thirty stories high.*
6 **PHRASE** If someone or something is **up for** election, review, or discussion, they are about to be considered. ❏ *A third of the Senate is up for election every two years.*
7 **PHRASE** If you are **up against** something, you have a difficult situation to deal with. ❏ *They were up against a good team, but did very well.*
8 **PHRASE** **What's up?** is an informal way of saying "Hello" or "How are you?" ❏ *Hey, guys, what's up?* [from Old English]

up|bring|ing /ʌpbrɪŋɪŋ/ **N-NONCOUNT** Your **upbringing** is the way that your parents treat you and the things that they teach you when you are growing up. ❏ *I had a strict upbringing.*

up|date (**updates, updating, updated**)

> **PRONUNCIATION HELP**
> Pronounce the verb /ʌpdeɪt/. Pronounce the noun /ʌpdeɪt/.

1 **V-T/V-I** If you **update**, or **update** something, you make it more modern or add new information to it. ❏ *We update our news reports regularly.*
2 **N-COUNT** An **update** is when someone provides the most recent information about a particular situation. ❏ *Now here's a weather update.*

up|draft /ʌpdræft/ (**updrafts**) **N-COUNT** SCIENCE An **updraft** is a rising current of air, which often produces a cumulus cloud.

up|grade /ʌpgreɪd, -greɪd/ (**upgrades, upgrading, upgraded**)
1 **V-T** If you **upgrade** something, you improve it or replace it with a better one. ❏ *The road into town is being upgraded.* ❏ *I recently upgraded my computer.*
2 **N-COUNT** **Upgrade** is also a noun. ❏ *...a software upgrade.*
→ look at Word Web: **hotel**

up|hill /ʌphɪl/
1 **ADV** If something or someone is moving

uphill, they are going up a slope. ❏ *He ran uphill a long way.*
2 **ADJ** **Uphill** is also an adjective. ❏ *It was a long, uphill journey.*

up|hold /ʌphoʊld/ (**upholds, upholding, upheld**) **V-T** If you **uphold** something such as a law, a principle, or a decision, you support and maintain it. ❏ *Our policy is to uphold the law.*

up|load /ʌploʊd/ (**uploads, uploading, uploaded**) **V-T** TECHNOLOGY If you **upload** a document or a program, you move it from your computer to another one, using the Internet. ❏ *Next, upload the files on to your website.* [from Old English]

upon /əpɒn/
1 **PREP** **Upon** means on. [LITERARY] ❏ *He put the tray upon the table.* ❏ *The decision was based upon science and fact.*
2 **PREP** If an event is **upon** you, it is just about to happen. [LITERARY] ❏ *The storm was upon us.*

up|per /ʌpər/
1 **ADJ** You use **upper** to describe something that is above something else. ❏ *There is a good restaurant on the upper floor.*
2 **ADJ** The **upper** part of something is the higher part of it. ❏ *The soldier was shot in the upper back.*
3 **PHRASE** If you have **the upper hand** in a situation, you have an advantage over other people involved. ❏ *The home team had the upper hand.* [from Old English]

up|per case /ʌpərkeɪs/ **N-NONCOUNT** LANGUAGE ARTS **Upper case** is the form that you use to write or type the larger letters at the beginning of sentences or people's names. Examples of upper case letters are "A," "D," and "M." These are also called "capital letters." Compare with **lower case**. ❏ *Typing an email using upper case letters is like shouting at someone.*

up|per class (**upper classes**) also **upper-class**
1 **N-COUNT** SOCIAL STUDIES The **upper class** or the **upper classes** are the group of people in a society who own the most property and have the highest social status. ❏ *...members of the upper class.*
2 **ADJ** SOCIAL STUDIES **Upper-class** is also an adjective. ❏ *All of them came from wealthy, upper-class families.*

u

up|per man|tle **N-SING** SCIENCE The upper mantle is the part of the Earth's interior that lies immediately beneath the crust.

up|right /ʌpraɪt/ **ADJ** If someone or something is standing **upright**, they are standing up straight. ❑ *John offered Andrew a seat, but he remained upright.*

up|ris|ing /ʌpraɪzɪŋ/ (**uprisings**) **N-COUNT** SOCIAL STUDIES When there is an **uprising**, a group of people start fighting against the people who are in power in their country, because they want to bring about a political change. ❑ *...an uprising against the government.*

up|roar /ʌprɔr/
1 **N-NONCOUNT/N-SING** If there is **uproar**, there is a lot of shouting and noise because people are very angry or upset about something. ❑ *The uproar was loud and immediate.*
2 **N-NONCOUNT/N-SING** You can also use **uproar** to refer to a lot of public criticism and debate about something that has made people angry. ❑ *The town is in an uproar over the decision.*

up|set /ʌpsɛt/ (**upsets, upsetting, upset**)
1 **ADJ** If you are **upset**, you are unhappy because something bad has happened. ❑ *After Grandma died, I was very, very upset.* ❑ *Marta looked upset.*
2 **V-T** If something **upsets** you, it makes you feel worried or unhappy. ❑ *What you said in your letter really upset me.*
3 **V-T** If something **upsets** your plans, it makes them go wrong. ❑ *Heavy rain upset our plans for a barbecue on the beach.*
4 **ADJ** An **upset** stomach is a slight sickness in your stomach. ❑ *Paul was sick last night with an upset stomach.* [from Middle High German]
→ look at Word Web: **anger**

Thesaurus	**upset** Also look up :
ADJ	disappointed, hurt, unhappy; (*ant.*) happy **1**
	ill, sick, unsettled **4**

Word Partnership	Use **upset** with :
PREP	upset **about/by/over** *something* **1**
V	**become** upset, **feel** upset, **get** upset **1**
ADV	**so** upset, **very** upset, **visibly** upset **1** **really** upset **1** **2**
N	**stomach** upset (*or* upset **stomach**) **4**

up|set|ting /ʌpsɛtɪŋ/ **ADJ** Something that is **upsetting** makes you feel unhappy or worried. ❑ *The death of a family pet is always upsetting.*

up|side down
/ʌpsaɪd daʊn/
1 **ADV** If something is **upside down**, the part that is usually at the bottom is at the top. ❑ *The painting was hanging upside down.*
2 **ADJ** **Upside-down** is also an adjective. ❑ *Paul drew an upside-down triangle and colored it in.*

upside down

up|stage /ʌpsteɪdʒ/ (**upstages, upstaging, upstaged**)
1 **V-T** If someone **upstages** you, they draw attention away from you by being more attractive or interesting. ❑ *He had a younger brother who always upstaged him.*
2 **ADV** ARTS When actors are **upstage** or move **upstage**, they are positioned toward the back of the stage or they move toward the back of the stage.
3 **ADJ** ARTS **Upstage** is also an adjective. ❑ *...the large upstage box that Noble used for his production of King Lear.*

up|stairs /ʌpstɛərz/
1 **ADV** If you go **upstairs** in a building, you walk up the stairs to a higher floor. ❑ *He went upstairs and changed his clothes.*
2 **ADV** If something or someone is **upstairs** in a building, they are on a higher floor. ❑ *The restaurant is upstairs.*
3 **ADJ** An **upstairs** room or object is on a floor of a building that is higher than the ground floor. ❑ *Mark lived in the upstairs apartment.*
4 **N-SING** The **upstairs** of a building is the floor or floors that are higher than the ground floor. ❑ *The upstairs had only two bedrooms.*

up-to-date also **up to date**
1 **ADJ** If something is **up-to-date**, it is the most recent thing of its kind. ❑ *We need some up-to-date weather information.*
2 **ADJ** If you are **up-to-date** on something, you have the latest information about it. ❑ *We'll keep you up to date with any news.*

U

up|ward /ˈʌpwərd/

1 **ADJ** An **upward** movement or look is directed towards a higher place or a higher level. ❑ *She started on the upward climb.*

2 **ADV** If someone moves or looks **upward**, they move or look up toward a higher place. ❑ *She turned her face upward.* [from Old English]

up|wel|ling /ˈʌpwɛlɪŋ/ (upwellings)

N-COUNT SCIENCE An **upwelling** is a process in which cold water from deep in the ocean rises to the surface near a shoreline, bringing nutrients with it.

ura|nium /yʊˈreɪniəm/ **N-NONCOUNT**

SCIENCE **Uranium** is a radioactive metal that is used to produce nuclear energy and weapons. [from New Latin]

Ura|nus /ˈyʊərənəs, yʊˈreɪ-/ **N-PROPER**

SCIENCE **Uranus** is the seventh planet from the sun. [from Latin]

Word Link　urb ≈ city : suburb, suburban, urban

ur|ban /ˈɜrbən/ **ADJ** Urban means relating to

a city or a town. ❑ *Mission High School is situated in an urban neighborhood of San Francisco.* [from Latin]
→ look at Word Web: **city**

ure|thra /yʊˈriːθrə/ (urethras) **N-COUNT**

SCIENCE The **urethra** is the narrow tube inside a man's penis that carries urine and semen out of the body. [from Late Latin]

urge /ˈɜrdʒ/ (urges, urging, urged)

1 **V-T** If you **urge** someone **to** do something, you try hard to persuade them to do it. ❑ *Doctors urged my uncle to change his diet.*

2 **N-COUNT** An **urge** is a strong feeling that you want to do or have something. ❑ *He felt a sudden urge to call Mary.* [from Latin]

Word Partnership	Use **urge** with :
N	**leaders/officials** urge, urge **people,** urge **voters** **1**
ADV	**strongly** urge **1**
V	**feel an** urge, **fight an** urge, **get an** urge, **2**

ur|gent /ˈɜrdʒ°nt/ **ADJ** If something is

urgent, it needs attention as soon as possible. ❑ *The refugees have an urgent need for food and water.* ● **ur|gen|cy** **N-NONCOUNT** ❑ *...the urgency of the problem.* ● **ur|gent|ly** **ADV**

❑ *These people urgently need medical supplies.* [from French]

Word Partnership	Use **urgent** with :
N	urgent **action**, urgent **business**, urgent **care**, urgent **matter**, urgent **meeting**, urgent **mission**, urgent **need**, urgent **problem**, urgent **appeal**, urgent **message**

urine /ˈyʊərɪn/ **N-NONCOUNT** Urine is the liquid

that you get rid of from your body when you go to the toilet. ❑ *The doctor took a urine sample and a blood sample.* [from Old French]

URL /ˈyu ɑr ɛl/ (URLs) **N-COUNT** TECHNOLOGY

A **URL** is an address that shows where you can find a particular page on the World Wide Web. **URL** is short for "Uniform Resource Locator." ❑ *The URL for Collins Dictionaries is http://www.collinslanguage.com.*

us /əs, STRONG ʌs/

1 **PRON** You use **us** to talk about yourself and the person or people with you. ❑ *William's girlfriend has invited us for lunch.*

2 **PRON** You use **us** to talk about yourself and another person or other people who are not with you. ❑ *Heather went to the kitchen to get drinks for us.* [from Old English]

USB /ˈyu ɛs bi/ (USBs) **N-COUNT** TECHNOLOGY

A **USB** or **USB port** on a computer is a part where you can attach another piece of equipment. **USB** is short for "Universal Serial Bus." ❑ *The printer plugs into the computer's USB port.*

USB drive (USB drives) **N-COUNT**

TECHNOLOGY A **USB drive** is the same as a **flash drive**.

use
❶ VERB USES
❷ NOUN USES

❶ use /ˈyuz/ (uses, using, used)

1 **V-T** If you **use** something, you do something with it. ❑ *They wouldn't let him use the phone.* ❑ *She used the money to help her family.*

2 **V-T** If you **use** something, you finish it so that none of it is left. ❑ *She used all the shampoo.*

3 **Use up** means the same as **use.** ❑ *If you use up the milk, please buy some more.*

4 **V-T** If you **use** a particular word or

expression, you say or write it. ❑ *He used the word "sorry" six times.*

5 **V-T** If someone **uses** you, they make you do things for them in order to gain an advantage from it. ❑ *I felt he was using me.* [from Old French]

② use /yus/ (**uses**)

1 **N-NONCOUNT** The **use** of something is the action of using it. ❑ *We encourage the use of computers in the classroom.*

2 **N-COUNT/N-NONCOUNT** The **uses** of something are the ways in which you can use it. ❑ *Bamboo has many uses.*

3 **N-NONCOUNT** If you have the **use of** something, you are able to use it. ❑ *My sister has the use of Mom's car one night a week.*

4 **PHRASE** If a technique, a building, or a machine is **in use**, it is used regularly by people. If it has gone **out of use**, it is no longer used regularly by people. ❑ *...the number of homes with televisions in use.*

5 **PHRASE** If you **make use of** something, you do something with it in order to achieve a particular result. [WRITTEN] ❑ *We made use of the extra time we had.*

6 **PHRASE** You say **It's no use** when you stop doing something because you believe that it is impossible to succeed. ❑ *"It's no use asking him what happened," said Kate. "He won't tell us."* [from Old French]

---
used
① MODAL USES AND PHRASES
② ADJECTIVE USE
---

① used /yust/

1 **PHRASE** You use **used to** to talk about something that was true in the past but is not true now. ❑ *I used to live in Los Angeles.* ❑ *He used to be one of my teachers.*

2 **PHRASE** If you **are used to** something, you are familiar with it because you have done it many times before. ❑ *I'm used to hard work.*

3 **PHRASE** If you **get used to** something, you become familiar with it. ❑ *This is how we do things here. You'll get used to it.* [from Old French]

Usage **used to**

Used to is often confused with *be/get used to.* *Used to* refers to something in the past: *We used to live in an apartment, but we now live in a house.* *Be/get used to* means "be or become accustomed to": *We're used to living in an apartment, but we're getting used to our new house.*

② used /yuzd/

1 **ADJ** A **used** object is dirty or spoiled because it has been used. ❑ *...a used coffee cup.*

2 **ADJ** **Used** objects are not new. ❑ *If you are buying a used car, you will need to check it carefully.* [from Old French]

use|ful /yusfəl/ **ADJ** If something is **useful**, it helps you in some way. ❑ *The book is full of useful advice about growing fruit and vegetables.*
● **use|ful|ly** **ADV** ❑ *The students used their extra time usefully, doing homework or playing sports.*
● **use|ful|ness** **N-NONCOUNT** ❑ *...the usefulness of his work.* [from Old French]

Word Partnership Use **useful** with :

| ADV | also useful, **especially** useful, **extremely** useful, **less/more** useful, **particularly** useful, **very** useful |
| N | useful **information**, useful **knowledge**, useful **life**, useful **purpose**, useful **strategy**, useful **tool** |
---

use|less /yuslɪs/

1 **ADJ** If something is **useless**, it has no use. ❑ *My leather jacket is useless in the rain.*

2 **ADJ** If an action is **useless**, it does not have the result you would like. ❑ *Christina knew it was useless to argue with the police officer.*

3 **ADJ** If you say that someone or something is **useless**, you mean that they are not good at all. ❑ *He was useless at any game with a ball.* [from Old French]

user /yuzər/ (**users**) **N-COUNT** A **user** is a person who uses something. ❑ *Some young Internet users spend up to 70 hours a week online.* ❑ *I'm a regular user of the subway.* [from Old French]

user-friend|ly **ADJ** If a piece of equipment or a system is **user-friendly**, it is well designed and easy to use. ❑ *This is a well designed and user-friendly website.*

user|name /yuzərneɪm/ (**usernames**) **N-COUNT** TECHNOLOGY Your **username** is the name that you type onto your screen each time you open a particular computer program or website. ❑ *You have to log in with a username and a password.*
→ look at Word Web: **Internet**

U-shaped val|ley (**U-shaped valleys**) **N-COUNT** SCIENCE A **U-shaped valley** is a valley with steep sides that forms when a glacier is eroded.

U

usu|al /yuʒuəl/

1 **ADJ** Usual describes what happens most often. ❏ It is a large city with the usual problems. ❏ February was warmer than usual.

2 **PHRASE** You use as usual to describe something that normally happens or that is normally true. ❏ As usual, there will be the local and regional elections on June twelfth.

3 **PHRASE** If something happens as usual, it happens in the way that it normally does. ❏ Dad's late, as usual. [from Late Latin]

Word Partnership	Use usual with :
ADV	less/more than usual, longer than usual **1**
N	usual place, usual routine, usual self, usual stuff, usual suspects, usual way **1**

usu|al|ly /yuʒuəli/ **ADV** If something usually happens, it is the thing that most often happens. ❏ We usually eat in the kitchen. [from Late Latin]

usurp /yusɜrp, -zɜrp/ (usurps, usurping, usurped) **V-T** If you say that someone usurps a job, a role, a title, or a position, they take it from someone when they have no right to do this. [FORMAL] ❏ Did she usurp his place in his mother's heart? [from Old French]

uten|sil /yutɛnsəl/ (utensils) **N-COUNT** Utensils are tools or objects that you use when you are preparing or eating food. ❏ Always wash cooking utensils after handling raw meat. [from Old French]
→ look at Picture Dictionary: **kitchen utensils**

uter|us /yutərəs/ (uteruses) **N-COUNT** SCIENCE The uterus is the part of the female body where babies grow. [from Latin]

util|ity /yutɪlɪti/ (utilities) **N-COUNT** A utility is an important service such as water, electricity, or gas that is provided for everyone, and that everyone pays for. ❏ ...public utilities such as gas and electricity. [from Old French]

uti|lize /yutɪlaɪz/ (utilizes, utilizing, utilized) **V-T** If you utilize something, you use it. [FORMAL] ❏ ...how to utilize the knowledge and talent of everyone in the company. ● **uti|li|za|tion** /yutɪlɪzeɪʃ°n/ **N-NONCOUNT** ❏ ...the best utilization of space. [from Old French]

ut|ter /ʌtər/ (utters, uttering, uttered)

1 **V-T** If you utter sounds or words, you say them. [LITERARY] ❏ He finally uttered the words, "I'm sorry."

2 **ADJ** Utter means complete. ❏ This is utter nonsense. [Sense 1 from Middle Dutch. Sense 2 from Old English.]

ut|ter|ly /ʌtərli/ **ADV** Utterly means completely or very. ❏ Their behavior was utterly stupid. ❏ Patrick felt completely and utterly alone. [from Old English]

u

Vv

v. v. is short for **versus**.

va|can|cy /ve͟ɪkənsi/ (**vacancies**)
 1 N-COUNT If there are **vacancies** at a hotel, some of the rooms are empty. ❑ *The hotel still has a few vacancies.*
 2 N-COUNT A **vacancy** is a job that has not been filled. ❑ *We have a vacancy for an assistant.* [from Latin]

va|cant /ve͟ɪkənt/ **ADJ** If something is **vacant**, it is not being used by anyone. ❑ *They saw two vacant seats in the center.* [from Latin]

va|ca|tion /veɪke͟ɪʃ⁰n/ (**vacations**)
 1 N-COUNT A **vacation** is a period of time when you relax and enjoy yourself, often away from home. ❑ *They planned a vacation in Europe.*
 2 N-COUNT A **vacation** is a period of the year when schools, universities, and colleges are officially closed. ❑ *During his summer vacation he visited Russia.* [from Latin]

vac|ci|nate /væ͟ksɪneɪt/ (**vaccinates, vaccinating, vaccinated**) **V-T** If a person or an animal **is vaccinated**, they are given a substance to prevent them from getting a disease. ❑ *Has your child been vaccinated against measles?* ● **vac|ci|na|tion** /væ͟ksɪne͟ɪʃ⁰n/ (**vaccinations**) **N-COUNT/N-NONCOUNT** ❑ *I got my flu vaccination last week.* [from New Latin]

vac|cine /væ͟ksin/ (**vaccines**)
 N-COUNT/N-NONCOUNT A **vaccine** is a substance containing a harmless form of a particular disease. It is given to people to prevent them from getting that disease. ❑ *The flu vaccine is free for those aged 65 years and over.* [from New Latin]
 → look at Word Web: **hospital**

vacu|ole /væ͟kyuoʊl/ (**vacuoles**) **N-COUNT** SCIENCE A **vacuole** is a space within a plant cell that contains water, waste products, or other substances. [from French]

vac|u|um /væ͟kyum, -yuəm/ (**vacuums, vacuuming, vacuumed**)
 1 V-T When you **vacuum** a room or a surface, you clean it using a vacuum cleaner.
 2 N-COUNT SCIENCE A **vacuum** is a space that does not contain any air or other gas. ❑ *...a vacuum caused by hot air rising.* [from Latin]

vacuum clean|er (**vacuum cleaners**)
 N-COUNT A **vacuum cleaner** or a **vacuum** is an electric machine that cleans surfaces by sucking up dust and dirt.

vacuum cleaner

va|gi|na /vədʒa͟ɪnə/ (**vaginas**) **N-COUNT** SCIENCE A woman's or girl's **vagina** is the passage that leads from the outside of the body to the uterus. [from Latin]

vague /ve͟ɪg/ (**vaguer, vaguest**)
 1 ADJ If something written or spoken is **vague**, it does not explain things clearly. ❑ *The description was pretty vague.*
 2 ADJ If you have a **vague** memory or idea of something, the memory or idea is not clear. ❑ *They have only a vague idea of how much money is left.*
 3 ADJ A **vague** shape is not clear and is therefore not easy to see. ❑ *The bus was a vague shape in the distance.* [from French]

vague|ly /ve͟ɪgli/ **ADV Vaguely** means to a small degree. ❑ *The voice on the phone was vaguely familiar.* [from French]

vain /ve͟ɪn/ (**vainer, vainest**)
 1 ADJ A **vain** attempt does not achieve what was intended.
 2 ADJ If someone is **vain**, they are too proud of the way they look. ❑ *He was so vain he spent hours in front of the mirror.*
 3 PHRASE If you do something **in vain**, you do not succeed in doing what you want. ❑ *She tried in vain to open the door.* [from Old French]

va|lence elec|tron /ve͟ɪləns ɪle͟ktrɒn/ (**valence electrons**) **N-COUNT** SCIENCE **Valence electrons** are the outermost electrons in an atom, which combine with other atoms to form molecules.

val|id /vǽlɪd/
1 **ADJ** A **valid** argument or comment is based on sensible reasoning. ❏ *They gave several valid reasons for not signing the contract.*
2 **ADJ** If a ticket is **valid**, it can be used and will be accepted. ❏ *All tickets are valid for two months.* [from Latin]

val|ley /vǽli/ (**valleys**) **N-COUNT** GEOGRAPHY
A **valley** is a low area of land between hills. ❏ *...a steep mountain valley.* [from Old French]
→ look at Picture Dictionaries: **landforms, river**

valu|able /vǽlyuəbᵊl/
1 **ADJ** If something is **valuable**, it is very useful. ❏ *Television can be a valuable tool in the classroom.*
2 **ADJ** **Valuable** objects are worth a lot of money. ❏ *Do not leave any valuable items in your hotel room.* [from Old French]

Thesaurus	valuable	Also look up :
ADJ	helpful, important, useful; (ant.) useless **1** costly, expensive, priceless; (ant.) worthless **2**	

Word Partnership	Use **valuable** with :
V	**learn a** valuable **lesson 1**
N	valuable **experience**, valuable **information**, valuable **lesson, time is** valuable **1** valuable **asset**, valuable **resource 1 2** valuable **property 2**
ADV	**extremely** valuable, **less** valuable, **very** valuable **1 2**

value /vǽlyu/ (**values, valuing, valued**)
1 **N-NONCOUNT** The **value** of something is its importance or usefulness. ❏ *They didn't recognize the value of language learning.*
2 **V-T** If you **value** something or someone, you think that they are important. ❏ *I value my husband's opinion.*
3 **N-COUNT/N-NONCOUNT** The **value** of something is how much money it is worth. ❏ *The value of the house rose by $50,000 in a year.*
4 **V-T** When experts **value** something, they decide how much money it is worth. ❏ *He valued the property at $130,000.*
5 **N-PLURAL** The **values** of a person or a group are their moral principles and beliefs. ❏ *The countries of South Asia share many common values.*

6 **N-COUNT/N-NONCOUNT** ARTS In painting, the **value** of a color is how light or dark it is. White is the lightest value and black is the darkest value. [from Old French]

Thesaurus	value	Also look up :
N	importance, merit, usefulness **1** cost, price, worth **3**
V	admire, honor, respect **2** appraise, estimate, price **4**

Word Partnership	Use **value** with :
ADJ	**artistic** value **1** **actual** value, **equal** value, **great** value **1 3** **estimated** value **3**
V	**decline in** value, **increase in** value, **lose** value **1 3**
N	**cash** value, **dollar** value, value **of an investment**, value **3**

value scale (**value scales**) **N-COUNT** ARTS
A **value scale** is an arrangement of all the different colors used in painting, organized according to their lightness or darkness.

valve /vǽlv/ (**valves**) **N-COUNT** A **valve** is an object that controls the flow of air or liquid through a tube. [from Latin]
→ look at Word Web: **engine**

vam|pire /vǽmpaɪər/ (**vampires**) **N-COUNT**
In stories, **vampires** are monsters that come out at night and suck the blood of living people. [from French]

van /vǽn/ (**vans**)
N-COUNT A **van** is a vehicle with space for carrying things in the back.
→ look at Word Web: **car**

van

van|dal /vǽndᵊl/ (**vandals**) **N-COUNT**
A **vandal** is someone who deliberately damages property. ❏ *The street lights were broken by vandals.* [from Latin]

van|dal|ism /vǽndᵊlɪzəm/ **N-NONCOUNT**
Vandalism is the act of deliberately damaging property. ❏ *What can be done to stop school vandalism?* [from Latin]

Word Link	ize : **legal**ize, **modern**ize, **vandal**ize

van|dal|ize /vǽndᵊlaɪz/ (**vandalizes, vandalizing, vandalized**) **V-T** If something **is vandalized** by someone, it is damaged on purpose. ❏ *The walls were vandalized with spray paint.* [from Latin]

V

va|nil|la /vənɪlə/ **N-NONCOUNT** Vanilla is a flavor used in sweet food. [from New Latin]

van|ish /vænɪʃ/ (**vanishes, vanishing, vanished**) **v-ı** If someone or something **vanishes**, they go away suddenly or in a way that cannot be explained. ❑ *He vanished ten years ago.* [from Old French]

van|ish|ing point (**vanishing points**)
N-COUNT SCIENCE The **vanishing point** is the point in the distance where parallel lines seem to meet.

van|ity /vænɪti/ **N-NONCOUNT** If you refer to someone's **vanity**, you are critical of them because they are too proud of their appearance or abilities. ❑ *Do you want to lose weight for your health, or out of vanity?* [from Old French]

vape /veɪp/ (**vapes, vaping, vaped**) **v-ı** If you **vape**, you inhale vapor from an e-cigarette.

va|por /veɪpər/ (**vapors**)
N-COUNT/N-NONCOUNT SCIENCE **Vapor** consists of tiny drops of water or other liquids in the air. ❑ *Water vapor rises from Earth and falls again as rain.* [from Latin]
→ look at Word Webs: **greenhouse effect, precipitation, water**

va|por|ize /veɪpəraɪz/ (**vaporizes, vaporizing, vaporized**) **v-т/v-ı** If a liquid or a solid **vaporizes** or if you **vaporize** it, it changes into vapor or gas. ● **va|pori|za|tion** /veɪpərɪzeɪʃᵊn/ **N-NONCOUNT** ❑ *...the energy required to cause vaporization of water.* [from Latin]

vari|able /vɛəriəbᵊl/ (**variables**)
1 **ADJ** Something that is **variable** changes quite often. ❑ *The quality of his work is very variable.*
2 **N-COUNT** MATH A **variable** is a quantity that can have any one of a set of values. [from Latin]
→ look at Word Web: **experiment**

vari|ation /vɛərieɪʃᵊn/ (**variations**)
1 **N-COUNT** A **variation on** something is the same thing presented in a slightly different form. ❑ *This is a delicious variation on an omelet.*
2 **N-COUNT/N-NONCOUNT** A **variation** is a change or difference in a level or an amount. ❑ *Can you explain the wide variation in your prices?* [from Latin]

var|ied /vɛərid/
1 **ADJ** Something that is **varied** consists of different types of things. ❑ *Your diet should be varied.* [from Latin]

2 → see also **vary**

va|ri|ety /vəraɪɪti/
1 **N-NONCOUNT** If something has **variety**, it consists of things that are different from each other. ❑ *Susan wanted variety in her lifestyle.*
2 **N-COUNT** A **variety** of something is a type of it. ❑ *They make 20 varieties of bread every day.*
3 **N-NONCOUNT** ARTS **Variety** is the quality that something such as a painting or a dance has when it consists of different parts that are combined in an interesting way, for example because some parts contrast with other parts or change them. [from Latin]

Word Partnership	Use **variety** with :
N	variety **of activities**, variety **of colors**, variety **of foods**, variety **of issues**, variety **of problems**, variety **of products**, variety **of reasons**, variety **of sizes**, variety **of styles**, variety **of ways** **2**
V	**choose a** variety, **offer a** variety, **provide a** variety **2**

vari|ous /vɛəriəs/ **ADJ** If you talk about **various** things, you mean many different things of the type mentioned. ❑ *He spent the day doing various jobs in the house.* [from Latin]

var|nish /vɑrnɪʃ/ (**varnishes**)
N-COUNT/N-NONCOUNT **Varnish** is a thick, clear liquid that is painted onto things to give them a shiny surface. [from Old French]

var|si|ty /vɑrsɪti/ (**varsities**) **N-COUNT** SPORTS The **varsity** or the **varsity** team is the main team that plays a particular sport for a school or a university. ❑ *He plays for the varsity basketball team.*

vary /vɛəri/ (**varies, varying, varied**)
1 **v-ı** If things **vary**, they are different from each other. ❑ *The bowls are handmade, so they vary slightly.*
2 **v-т/v-ı** If something **varies** or if you **vary** it, it becomes different or changed. ❑ *Be sure to vary the topics you write about.* [from Latin]
3 → see also **varied**

Word Partnership	Use **vary** with :
N	**prices** vary, **rates** vary, **styles** vary **1** vary **by location**, vary **by size**, vary **by state**, vary **by store** **1** **2**
ADV	vary **considerably**, vary **greatly**, vary **slightly**, vary **widely** **1** **2**

V

vas|cu|lar plant /vǽskyələr plǽnt/ (**vascular plants**) **N-COUNT** SCIENCE Vascular plants are plants that have tissues that can carry water and other fluids through the body of the plant.

vas de|fe|rens /vǽs dɛ́fərɛnz/ (**vasa deferentia** /vɛ́ɪzə dɛ́fərɛnʃiə, -ʃə/) **N-COUNT** SCIENCE The **vas deferens** is the pair of narrow tubes in a man's body that carries sperm from his testicles toward his penis. [from New Latin]

vase /vɛ́ɪs, vɑ́z/ (**vases**) **N-COUNT** A **vase** is a container that is used for holding flowers. ❑ *There was a small vase of flowers on the table.* [from French]
→ look at Word Web: **glass**

vast /vǽst/ (**vaster, vastest**) **ADJ** Something that is **vast** is extremely large. ❑ *Australia is a vast continent.* ❑ *Suddenly they have a vast amount of cash.* [from Latin]

Word Partnership	Use **vast** with :
N	vast **amounts**, vast **distance**, vast **expanse**, vast **knowledge**, vast **majority**, vast **quantities**

vault /vɔ́lt/ (**vaults, vaulting, vaulted**)
1 N-COUNT A **vault** is a room where money and other valuable things can be kept safely. ❑ *The jewels were kept in a bank vault.*

2 V-T/V-I If you **vault** something or **vault over** it, you jump quickly over it. ❑ *He could easily vault the wall.* [from Old French]

vec|tor /vɛ́ktər/ (**vectors**) **N-COUNT** SCIENCE A **vector** is a variable quantity, such as force, that has size and direction. [from Latin]

veg|eta|ble /vɛ́dʒtəbᵊl, vɛ́dʒɪ-/ (**vegetables**) **N-COUNT** Vegetables are plants that you can cook and eat. [from Late Latin]
→ look at Picture Dictionary: **vegetables**
→ look at Word Web: **vegetarian**

Word Link	*arian ≈ believing in, having :*
	humanit*arian*, totalit*arian*, veget*arian*

veg|etar|ian /vɛ́dʒɪtɛ́əriən/ (**vegetarians**)
1 ADJ Vegetarian food does not contain meat or fish. ❑ *They did not keep a strict vegetarian diet.* ❑ *...a vegetarian dish.*
2 N-COUNT A **vegetarian** is someone who never eats meat or fish. ❑ *When did you decide to become a vegetarian?* [from Late Latin]
→ look at Word Web: **vegetarian**

veg|eta|tion /vɛ́dʒɪtɛ́ɪʃᵊn/ **N-NONCOUNT** Plants, trees, and flowers can be called **vegetation**. [FORMAL] ❑ *...tropical vegetation.* [from Late Latin]
→ look at Word Webs: **erosion, habitat, herbivore**

Picture Dictionary

vegetables

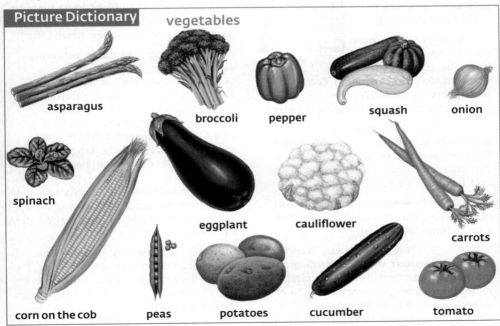

asparagus

broccoli   pepper   squash   onion

spinach

eggplant   cauliflower

carrots

corn on the cob   peas   potatoes   cucumber   tomato

The Greek philosopher Pythagoras was a **vegetarian**. He believed that if humans killed animals, they would also kill each other. So he did not eat **meat**. Vegetarians eat many kinds of food, not just **vegetables**. They eat fruits, grains, oils, fats, and sugar. **Vegans** are vegetarians who don't eat eggs or dairy products. Some people choose this **diet** for health reasons. A well-balanced **veggie** diet can be healthy. Some people choose this diet for religious reasons. Others want to make the world's **food** supply go further. It takes fifteen pounds of **grain** to produce one pound of meat.

veg|eta|tive re|pro|duc|tion /vɛdʒɪteɪtɪv riprədʌkʃən/ or **vegetative propagation** **N-NONCOUNT** SCIENCE **Vegetative reproduction** is a process by which new plants are produced without using seeds, for example by using cuttings instead.

ve|hi|cle /viɪkəl/ (**vehicles**) **N-COUNT** A **vehicle** is a machine that carries people or things from one place to another. ❑ *There are too many vehicles on the road.* ❑ *The car hit another vehicle that was parked nearby.* [from Latin] → look at Word Webs: **car, traffic**

veil /veɪl/ (**veils**) **N-COUNT** A **veil** is a piece of thin soft cloth that women sometimes wear over their heads to cover their faces. ❑ *She wore a veil over her face.* [from Norman French]

veil

vein /veɪn/ (**veins**) **N-COUNT** SCIENCE Your **veins** are the thin tubes in your body that your blood flows through. Compare with **artery**. [from Old French] → look at Word Web: **cardiovascular system**

ve|loc|ity /vəlɒsɪti/ (**velocities**) **N-COUNT/N-NONCOUNT** SCIENCE **Velocity** is the speed at which something moves in a particular direction. ❑ *His velocity was a little lower than usual.* [from Latin]

vel|vet /vɛlvɪt/ **N-NONCOUNT Velvet** is soft cloth that is thick on one side. ❑ *...red velvet drapes.* [from Old French]

Venn dia|gram /vɛn daɪəgræm/ (**Venn diagrams**) **N-COUNT** MATH A **Venn diagram** is a diagram that uses overlapping circles to represent features that are common to, or unique to, two or more sets of data. [after John Venn (1834-1923), an English logician]

vent /vɛnt/ (**vents, venting, vented**)
1 **N-COUNT** A **vent** is a hole that allows clean air to come in, and smoke or gas to go out. ❑ *Vents in the walls allow fresh air to enter the house.*
2 **V-T** If you **vent** your feelings, you express them strongly. ❑ *She telephoned her best friend to vent her anger.*
3 **N-COUNT** GEOGRAPHY A **vent** is a crack in the Earth's surface through which lava and gas are released. [from Old French]

ven|ti|late /vɛntəleɪt/ (**ventilates, ventilating, ventilated**) **V-T** If you **ventilate** a room, you allow fresh air to get into it. ❑ *You must ventilate the room well when painting.*
● **ven|ti|la|tion** /vɛntəleɪʃən/ **N-NONCOUNT** ❑ *The only ventilation came from one small window.* [from Latin]

ven|tri|cle /vɛntrɪkəl/ (**ventricles**) **N-COUNT** SCIENCE A **ventricle** is a part of the heart that pumps blood to the arteries. [from Latin]

ven|ture /vɛntʃər/ (**ventures, venturing, ventured**)
1 **N-COUNT** A **venture** is a project or an activity that is new, exciting, and difficult because it involves the risk of failure. ❑ *...a joint venture between two schools.*
2 **V-I** If you **venture** somewhere, you go somewhere that might be dangerous. [LITERARY] ❑ *People are afraid to venture out at night.*
3 **V-I** If you **venture into** an activity, you do something that involves the risk of failure because it is new and different. ❑ *He ventured into business but had no success.*

ven|ue /vɛnyu/ (**venues**) **N-COUNT** The **venue** for an event or an activity is the place where it will happen. ❑ *Fenway Park will be used as a venue for the rock concert.* [from Old French] → look at Word Web: **concert**

V

Ve|nus /vínəs/ **N-PROPER** SCIENCE **Venus** is the second planet from the sun, between Mercury and the Earth. [from Latin]

ve|rac|ity /vəræsɪti/ **N-NONCOUNT Veracity** is truth or honesty. [FORMAL] ❑ *We have total confidence in the veracity of our research.* [from Medieval Latin]

verb /vɜrb/ (**verbs**)
1 **N-COUNT** LANGUAGE ARTS A **verb** is a word such as "sing," "feel," or "eat" that is used for saying what someone or something does. [from Latin]
2 → see also **phrasal verb**

ver|bal /vɜrbəl/
1 **ADJ** You use **verbal** to show that something is expressed in speech. ❑ *We will not tolerate verbal abuse.* ● **ver|bal|ly** **ADV** ❑ *We complained both verbally and in writing.*
2 **ADJ** LANGUAGE ARTS You use **verbal** to show that something is connected with words and the use of words. ❑ *...verbal skills.* [from Latin]

ver|bal|ize /vɜrbəlaɪz/ (**verbalizes, verbalizing, verbalized**) **V-T** If you **verbalize** your feelings, thoughts, or ideas, you express them in words. [FORMAL] ❑ *...his inability to verbalize his feelings.* [from Latin]

Word Link *ver ≈ truth : verdict, verify, version*

ver|dict /vɜrdɪkt/ (**verdicts**) **N-COUNT** SOCIAL STUDIES The **verdict** is the decision that is given in a court of law. ❑ *The jury delivered a verdict of "not guilty."* [from Medieval Latin]
→ look at Word Web: **trial**

verge /vɜrdʒ/ (**verges, verging, verged**)
PHRASE If you are **on the verge of** something, you are going to do it very soon. ❑ *Carole was on the verge of tears (= she was nearly crying).* [from Old French]
▶ **verge on** If someone or something **verges on** a particular state, they are almost the same as that state. ❑ *Her anger verged on madness.*

veri|fy /vɛrɪfaɪ/ (**verifies, verifying, verified**) **V-T** If you **verify** something, you check that it is true. [FORMAL] ❑ *We haven't yet verified his information.* [from Old French]

ver|sa|tile /vɜrsətəl/
1 **ADJ** A **versatile** person has many different skills. ❑ *He was one of our most versatile athletes.*
2 **ADJ** A tool, a machine, or a material that is **versatile** can be used for many different

purposes. ❑ *Computers today are so versatile.* [from Latin]

verse /vɜrs/ (**verses**)
1 **N-NONCOUNT** LANGUAGE ARTS **Verse** is poetry. ❑ *The story was written in verse.*
2 **N-COUNT** LANGUAGE ARTS A **verse** is one of the parts into which a poem or a song is divided. [from Old English]

ver|sion /vɜrʒ³n/ (**versions**)
1 **N-COUNT** A **version of** something is a particular form of it. ❑ *He is bringing out a new version of his book.*
2 **N-COUNT** Someone's **version of** an event is their own description of it. ❑ *Her version of the story was different from Jack's.* [from Medieval Latin]

ver|sus /vɜrsəs/
1 **PREP** SPORTS **Versus** is used for showing that two teams or people are on different sides in a sports event. The short forms **vs.** and **v.** are also used. ❑ *It will be the U.S. versus Belgium in tomorrow's game.*
2 **PREP** You use **versus** to show that two ideas or choices are being compared to each other. ❑ *They discussed getting a job after graduation versus going to college.* [from Latin]

ver|te|brate /vɜrtɪbrɪt/ (**vertebrates**)
1 **N-COUNT** SCIENCE A **vertebrate** is an animal that has a spine. Compare with **invertebrate**.
2 **ADJ** SCIENCE **Vertebrate** is also an adjective. ❑ *...a vertebrate animal.* [from Latin]

ver|ti|cal /vɜrtɪkəl/ **ADJ** Something that is **vertical** stands or points straight up. ❑ *The climber moved up a vertical wall of rock.* [from Late Latin]
→ look at Word Web: **graph**

verve /vɜrv/ **N-NONCOUNT Verve** is lively and forceful enthusiasm. [WRITTEN] ❑ *She read aloud with a great deal of dramatic verve.* [from Old French]

very /vɛri/
1 **ADV Very** is used before an adjective to make it stronger. ❑ *The answer is very simple.* ❑ *I'm very sorry.*
2 **PHRASE Not very** is used with an adjective or an adverb to say that something is not at all true, or that it is true only to a small degree. ❑ *She's not very impressed with them.*
3 **ADJ** You use **very** with certain nouns to refer to an extreme point. ❑ *I turned to the very end of the book.* [from Old French]

V

vesi|cle /vɛsɪkəl/ (vesicles) N-COUNT SCIENCE
A **vesicle** is a compartment within a living
cell in which substances are carried or
stored. [from Latin]

ves|sel /vɛsəl/ (vessels)
1 N-COUNT A **vessel** is a ship or a large boat.
[FORMAL] ❏ *The vessel sank in 10 meters of water.*
[from Old French]
2 → see also **blood vessel**
→ look at Word Web: **ship**

vest /vɛst/ (vests) N-COUNT A **vest** is a piece
of clothing without sleeves that people
usually wear over a shirt. [from Old French]

ves|tig|ial struc|ture /vɛstɪdʒiəl strʌktʃər,
-stɪdʒəl/ (vestigial structures) or vestigial
organ N-COUNT SCIENCE A **vestigial**
structure or **vestigial organ** is a part of the
body of an animal, such as the appendix in
humans, that was useful at an earlier stage
of the animal's evolution but no longer has
any function.

vet /vɛt/ (vets) N-COUNT A **vet** is a person
whose job is to treat sick or injured animals.
Vet is short for **veterinarian**. [INFORMAL]

vet|er|an /vɛtərən/ (veterans)
1 N-COUNT A **veteran** is someone who has
fought for their country during a war.
❏ *He's a veteran of the Vietnam War.*
2 N-COUNT You use **veteran** to talk about
someone who has been doing a particular
activity for a long time. ❏ *...a veteran teacher.*
[from Latin]

vet|eri|nar|ian /vɛtərɪnɛəriən/
(veterinarians) N-COUNT A **veterinarian** is a
person whose job is to treat sick or injured
animals. [from Latin]

veto /vitoʊ/ (vetoes, vetoing, vetoed)
1 V-T SOCIAL STUDIES If someone **vetoes**
something, they stop it from happening.
❏ *The president vetoed the proposal.*
2 N-NONCOUNT SOCIAL STUDIES **Veto** is the
power that someone has to stop something
from happening. ❏ *The president has power of*
veto over the matter. [from Latin]

via /vaɪə, viə/
1 PREP If you go somewhere **via** a
particular place, you go through that place
on the way. ❏ *I'm flying to Sweden via New York.*

2 PREP If you do something **via** a particular
thing or person, you do it by making use of
that thing or person. ❏ *We can continue the*
discussion via email. [from Latin]

vi|able /vaɪəbəl/ ADJ Something that is
viable is capable of doing what it is intended
to do. ❏ *The business in its current state is not*
viable. ● **vi|abil|ity** /vaɪəbɪlɪti/ N-NONCOUNT
❏ *...worries about the company's long-term viability.*
[from French]

vi|brant /vaɪbrənt/
1 ADJ Someone or something that is
vibrant is full of life, energy, and
enthusiasm. ❏ *...her vibrant personality.*
● **vi|bran|cy** /vaɪbrənsi/ N-NONCOUNT ❏ *She*
was a woman with extraordinary vibrancy.
2 ADJ **Vibrant** colors are very bright and
clear. ❏ *The grass was a vibrant green.*
● **vi|brant|ly** ADV ❏ *...vibrantly colored fabrics.*
[from Latin]

vi|brate /vaɪbreɪt/ (vibrates, vibrating,
vibrated) V-T/V-I If something **vibrates**, or if
you **vibrate** it, it shakes with repeated small,
quick movements. ❏ *There was a loud bang and*
the ground seemed to vibrate. ● **vi|bra|tion**
/vaɪbreɪʃən/ (vibrations) N-COUNT/
N-NONCOUNT ❏ *Vibrations from the train made*
the house shake. [from Latin]
→ look at Word Webs: **ear, sound**

vice /vaɪs/ (vices)
1 N-NONCOUNT **Vice** is criminal activity
connected with sex and drugs.
2 N-COUNT A **vice** is a habit that is seen as a
weakness. ❏ *My only vice is that I spend too much*
on clothes. [from Old French]

vice ver|sa /vaɪsə vɜrsə, vaɪs-/ PHRASE **Vice**
versa shows the opposite of what you have
said. ❏ *The government exists to serve us, and not*
vice versa. [from Latin]

vi|cious /vɪʃəs/
1 ADJ A **vicious** person is violent and cruel.
❏ *He was a cruel and vicious man.*
2 ADJ A **vicious** remark is cruel and intended
to upset someone. ❏ *That wasn't true; it was*
just a vicious rumour. [from Old French]

vic|tim /vɪktəm/ (victims) N-COUNT A **victim**
is someone who has been hurt or killed.
❏ *The driver apologized to the victim's family.*
[from Latin]

V

vic|tim|ize /vɪktəmaɪz/ (**victimizes, victimizing, victimized**) **v-t** If someone **is victimized**, they are deliberately treated unfairly. ❑ *The students were victimized because they opposed the government.* ● **vic|timi|za|tion** /vɪktəmɪzeɪʃˁn/ **N-NONCOUNT** ❑ *...society's victimization of women.* [from Latin]

vic|tor /vɪktər/ (**victors**) **N-COUNT** The **victor** in a battle or a contest is the person who wins. [from Latin] [LITERARY]

Vic|to|rian /vɪktɔriən/ (**Victorians**)
1 **ADJ** SOCIAL STUDIES **Victorian** means belonging to, connected with, or typical of Britain in the middle and last parts of the 19th century, when Victoria was Queen. ❑ *...a lovely old Victorian house.*
2 **ADJ** You can use **Victorian** to describe people who have old-fashioned attitudes, especially about good behavior and morals. ❑ *Victorian attitudes have no place in modern society.*
3 **N-COUNT** SOCIAL STUDIES The **Victorians** were the British people who lived in the time of Queen Victoria.

vic|to|ri|ous /vɪktɔriəs/ **ADJ** **Victorious** describes someone who has won in a war or a competition. ❑ *The Canadian team was victorious in all four games.* [from Old French]

Word Link	*vict, vinc ≈ conquering : con*vict*, con*vince*,* victory

vic|to|ry /vɪktəri, vɪktri/ (**victories**)
N-COUNT/N-NONCOUNT A **victory** is a success in a war or a competition. ❑ *The Democrats are celebrating their victory.* [from Old French]

Thesaurus	victory	Also look up :
N	conquest, success, win; (ant.) defeat	

vid|eo /vɪdioʊ/ (**videos**)
1 **N-COUNT** A **video** is an event that has been recorded. ❑ *We watched a video of my first birthday party.*
2 **N-COUNT** A **video** is a movie that you can watch at home. ❑ *You can rent a video for two dollars and watch it at home.*
3 **N-NONCOUNT** TECHNOLOGY **Video** is the system of recording movies and events in this way. ❑ *She has watched the show on video.* [from Latin]

vid|eo game (**video games**) **N-COUNT** TECHNOLOGY A **video game** is an electronic game that you play on your television or on a computer screen.

Word Link	*vid, vis ≈ seeing : tele*vis*ion,* video*tape,* vis*ible*

video|tape /vɪdioʊteɪp/ (**videotapes**) also **video tape** **N-COUNT/N-NONCOUNT** TECHNOLOGY **Videotape** is magnetic tape that was used to record moving pictures and sounds to be shown on television. ❑ *...the use of videotape in court cases.*

view /vyu/ (**views, viewing, viewed**)
1 **N-COUNT** Your **views** are the opinions that you have about something. ❑ *We have similar views on politics.*
2 **N-COUNT** The **view** from a window or a high place is everything that you can see from there. ❑ *From our hotel room we had a great view of the ocean.*
3 **N-SING** If you have a **view of** something, you can see it. ❑ *He stood up to get a better view of the blackboard.*
4 **V-T** If you **view** something, you look at it for a particular purpose. [FORMAL] ❑ *They came to view the house again.*
5 **V-T** If you **view** something in a particular way, you think of it in that way. ❑ *Immigrants viewed the United States as a land of opportunity.* ❑ *Linda views her daughter's talent with pride.*
6 **PHRASE** If a painting is **on view**, it is in a public place for people to look at. ❑ *Her paintings are on view at the Portland Gallery.* [from Old French]

view|er /vyuər/ (**viewers**) **N-COUNT** **Viewers** are people who are watching a particular program on television. ❑ *Twelve million viewers watch the show every week.* [from Old French]

view|point /vyupɔɪnt/ (**viewpoints**)
N-COUNT Someone's **viewpoint** is the way that they think about things in general, or the way they think about a particular thing. ❑ *The book is written from the girl's viewpoint.*

vig|or|ous /vɪgərəs/ **ADJ** **Vigorous** physical actions involve using a lot of energy. ❑ *You should have an hour of vigorous exercise three times a week.* ● **vig|or|ous|ly** **ADV** ❑ *He shook his head vigorously.* [from Old French]

vil|la /vɪlə/ (**villas**) **N-COUNT** A **villa** is a fairly large house, especially one in a hot country or a resort. [from Italian]

vil|lage /vɪlɪdʒ/ (**villages**) **N-COUNT** GEOGRAPHY A **village** is a small town in the countryside. [from Old French]

vil|lag|er /vɪlɪdʒər/ (**villagers**) **N-COUNT** You refer to the people who live in a village,

V

especially the people who have lived there for most or all of their lives, as the **villagers**. [from Old French]

vil|lain /vɪlən/ (**villains**) **N-COUNT** A villain is someone who deliberately harms other people or breaks the law. ❑ *They called him a villain and a murderer.* [from Old French]

vin|di|cate /vɪndɪkeɪt/ (**vindicates, vindicating, vindicated**) **V-T** If a person or their decisions, actions, or ideas **are vindicated**, they are proved to be correct, after people have said that they were wrong. [FORMAL] ❑ *The court's decision vindicated her claims.* ● **vin|di|ca|tion** /vɪndɪkeɪʃⁿn/ **N-NONCOUNT/N-SING** ❑ *He said their success was a vindication of his party's policy.* [from Latin]

vine /vaɪn/ (**vines**) **N-COUNT/N-NONCOUNT** A vine is a plant that grows up or over things. ❑ *...a grape vine.* [from Old French]

vine

vin|egar /vɪnɪgər/ (**vinegars**) **N-COUNT/N-NONCOUNT** Vinegar is a sour, sharp-tasting liquid that is used in cooking. [from Old French]

vine|yard /vɪnyərd/ (**vineyards**) **N-COUNT** A vineyard is an area of land where grape vines are grown in order to produce wine. [from Old English]

vi|nyl /vaɪnɪl/ **N-NONCOUNT** Vinyl is a strong plastic that is used for making things like floor coverings and furniture. ❑ *...vinyl floor covering.*

vio|la /vioʊlə/ (**violas**) **N-COUNT/N-NONCOUNT** MUSIC A viola is a musical instrument with four strings that produces low notes. You hold it under your chin, and play it by moving a bow across the strings. ❑ *She plays the viola in several different orchestras.* [from Italian]

vio|late /vaɪəleɪt/ (**violates, violating, violated**) **V-T** If someone **violates** an agreement or a law, they break it. [FORMAL] ❑ *The company has violated international law.* ● **vio|la|tion** /vaɪəleɪʃⁿn/ (**violations**) **N-COUNT/N-NONCOUNT** ❑ *This is a violation of state law.* [from Latin]

vio|lence /vaɪələns/ **1 N-NONCOUNT** Violence is behavior that is intended to hurt or kill people. ❑ *Twenty people died in the violence.* **2 N-NONCOUNT** If you do or say something with **violence**, you use a lot of force and energy in doing or saying it. [LITERARY] ❑ *The violence of her reaction shocked him.* [from Old French]

vio|lent /vaɪələnt/ **1 ADJ** If someone is **violent**, or if they do something that is **violent**, they use physical force to hurt or kill other people. ❑ *These men have committed violent crimes.* ● **vio|lent|ly ADV** ❑ *The woman was violently attacked while out walking.* **2 ADJ** A **violent** event happens suddenly and with great force. ❑ *A violent explosion shook the city.* **3 ADJ** If you describe something as **violent**, you mean that it is said, done, or felt very strongly. ❑ *He had violent stomach pains.* [from Latin]

vio|let /vaɪəlɪt/ (**violets**) **1 N-COUNT** A violet is a small plant that has purple or white flowers in the spring. **2 ADJ** Something that is **violet** is blue-purple in color. ❑ *...a violet dress.* **3 N-NONCOUNT** Violet is also a noun. ❑ *She chose cushions in violet and blue.* [from Old French]
→ look at Picture Dictionary: **color**
→ look at Word Web: **rainbow**

vio|lin /vaɪəlɪn/ (**violins**) **N-COUNT/N-NONCOUNT** MUSIC A violin is a musical instrument made of wood with four strings. You hold it under your chin, and play it by moving a bow across the strings. ❑ *Lizzie plays the violin.* [from Italian]
→ look at Picture Dictionary: **strings**
→ look at Word Web: **orchestra**

VIP /vi aɪ pi/ (**VIPs**) **N-COUNT** A VIP is someone who is given better treatment than ordinary people because they are famous or important. **VIP** is short for "very important person." ❑ *Five hundred celebrities and VIPs attended the concert.*

vir|gin /vɜrdʒɪn/ (**virgins**) **1 N-COUNT** A virgin is someone who has never had sex. ● **vir|gin|ity** /vərdʒɪnɪti/ **N-NONCOUNT** ❑ *At American weddings, brides often wear white, the color of purity and virginity.* **2 ADJ** You use **virgin** to describe something such as land that has never been used or spoiled. ❑ ...*virgin forest*. [from Old French]

vir|tual /vɜrtʃuəl/

1 **ADJ** You can use **virtual** to show that something is nearly true. ❑ *He was a virtual prisoner in his own home.* ● **vir|tu|al|ly** /vɜrtʃuəli/ **ADV** ❑ *She does virtually all the cooking.*

2 **ADJ** TECHNOLOGY **Virtual** objects and activities are made by a computer to seem like real objects and activities. ❑ *The virtual world sometimes seems more attractive than the real one.* [from Medieval Latin]

vir|tual re|al|ity N-NONCOUNT TECHNOLOGY

Virtual reality is an environment that is produced by a computer to seem very like it is real to the person experiencing it. ❑ ...*a virtual reality game.*

vir|tue /vɜrtʃu/ (virtues)

1 **N-NONCOUNT Virtue** is thinking good thoughts and doing what is right. ❑ *The priests talked to us about virtue.*

2 **N-COUNT** A **virtue** is a good quality or way of acting. ❑ *His greatest virtue is patience.*

3 **N-COUNT** The **virtue** of something is a benefit that it has. ❑ *The virtue of doing it this way is it's very quick and easy.* [from Old French]

vi|rus /vaɪrəs/ (viruses)

1 **N-COUNT** SCIENCE A **virus** is a very small living thing that can enter your body and cause you to be sick. ❑ *There are thousands of different types of virus, and they change all the time.*

2 **N-COUNT** TECHNOLOGY In computer technology, a **virus** is a program that enters a system and changes or destroys the information held there. ❑ *You should protect your computer against viruses.* [from Latin] → look at Word Web: **illness**

visa /viːzə/ (visas) N-COUNT A **visa** is an official document or a stamp put in your passport, that allows you to enter a particular country. [from French]

vis|cos|ity /vɪskɒsɪti/ N-NONCOUNT SCIENCE

Viscosity is the quality that some liquids have of being thick and sticky. [from Late Latin]

vis|ibil|ity /vɪzɪbɪlɪti/ N-NONCOUNT Visibility means how far or how clearly you can see in particular weather conditions. ❑ *Visibility was poor.* [from Latin]

Word Link	**vid, vis ≈ seeing : tele***vis***ion,** ***vid***eotape,** ***vis***ible**

vis|ible /vɪzɪbᵊl/ ADJ If something is **visible**, it can be seen. ❑ *The warning lights were clearly visible.* [from Latin]

Word Partnership	Use **visible** with :
N	visible **to the naked eye**
ADV	**barely** visible, **clearly** visible, **highly** visible, **less** visible, **more** visible, **still** visible, **very** visible
V	**become** visible

vi|sion /vɪʒᵊn/ (visions)

1 **N-COUNT** Your **vision of** a future situation or society is what you imagine or hope it will be like. ❑ *I have a vision of world peace.*

2 **N-NONCOUNT** Your **vision** is your ability to see clearly with your eyes. ❑ *He's suffering from loss of vision.* [from Latin]

Word Partnership	Use **vision** with :
V	**have a** vision, **share a** vision **1**
N	vision **of the future,** vision **of peace,** vision **of reality 1** color vision, **field of** vision **2**
ADJ	**clear** vision **1 2** **blurred** vision **2**

vis|it /vɪzɪt/ (visits, visiting, visited)

1 **V-T/V-I** If you **visit** someone, you go to see them in order to spend time with them. ❑ *He wanted to visit his brother.* ❑ *In the evenings, friends often visit.*

2 **N-COUNT Visit** is also a noun. ❑ *I recently had a visit from an English relative.*

3 **V-T/V-I** If you **visit** a place, you go there for a short time. ❑ *He'll be visiting four cities on his trip.* ❑ *The family were visiting from Texas.*

4 **N-COUNT Visit** is also a noun. ❑ ...*the Queen's visit to Canada.* [from Latin]

Thesaurus	visit	Also look up :
V	call on, go, see, stop by **1**

Word Partnership	Use **visit** with :
N	visit **family/relatives,** visit **friends,** visit *your* **mother 1** **weekend** visit **1 2** visit **a museum,** visit **a restaurant 2**
V	**come to** visit, **go to** visit, **invite** *someone* **to** visit, **plan to** visit **1 2**
ADJ	**brief** visit, **last** visit, **next** visit, **recent** visit, **short** visit, **surprise** visit **1 2** **foreign** visit, **official** visit **2**

visi|tor /vɪzɪtər/ (**visitors**) **N-COUNT** A **visitor** is someone who is visiting a person or a place. ❑ *We had some visitors from Milwaukee.* [from Latin]

vis|ual /vɪʒuəl/ **ADJ Visual** means relating to sight, or to things that you can see. ❑ *The movie's visual effects are amazing.* [from Late Latin]

Word Partnership	Use visual with :
N	visual **arts**, visual **effects**, visual **information**, visual **memory**, visual **perception**

vis|ual lit|era|cy **N-NONCOUNT** ARTS **Visual literacy** is the ability to understand and interpret visual images.

vis|ual meta|phor (**visual metaphors**) **N-COUNT/N-NONCOUNT** LANGUAGE ARTS A **visual metaphor** is a way of describing something by referring to another thing that shares similar visual qualities to the thing being described. For example, a family tree is a visual metaphor for the history of a family.

vi|tal /vaɪtəl/ **ADJ** If something is **vital**, it is very important. ❑ *It is vital that children attend school regularly.* [from Old French]

Thesaurus	vital Also look up :
ADJ	crucial, essential, necessary; (ant.) unimportant

Word Partnership	Use vital with :
ADV	**absolutely** vital
N	vital **importance**, vital **information**, vital **interests**, vital **link**, vital **organs**, vital **part**, vital **role**

vita|min /vaɪtəmɪn/ (**vitamins**) **N-COUNT** **Vitamins** are substances in food that you need in order to stay healthy. ❑ *These problems are caused by lack of vitamin D.* [from Latin]

Word Link	viv ≈ living : revival, survive, vivid

viv|id /vɪvɪd/
1 **ADJ Vivid** memories and descriptions are very clear and detailed. ❑ *I had a very vivid dream last night.* ● **viv|id|ly** **ADV** ❑ *I can vividly remember the first time I saw him.*
2 **ADJ** Something that is **vivid** is very bright in color. ❑ *She was dressed in a vivid pink jacket.* [from Latin]

vo|cabu|lary /voʊkæbyəlɛri/ (**vocabularies**)
1 **N-COUNT/N-NONCOUNT** LANGUAGE ARTS

Your **vocabulary** is all the words you know in a particular language. ❑ *He has a very large vocabulary.*
2 **N-SING** LANGUAGE ARTS The **vocabulary** of a language is all the words in it. ❑ *English has the biggest vocabulary of any language.* [from Medieval Latin]
→ look at Word Web: **English**

Word Partnership	Use vocabulary with :
N	**part of** *someone's* vocabulary **1** vocabulary **development 1 2**
V	**learn** vocabulary **2**

vo|cal /voʊkəl/
1 **ADJ** Someone who is **vocal** gives their opinion very strongly. ❑ *Local people were very vocal about the problem.*
2 **ADJ Vocal** means using the human voice, especially in singing. ❑ *She has an interesting vocal style.* [from Latin]

vo|cal pro|jec|tion **N-NONCOUNT** **Vocal projection** is the same as **projection**.

vo|cal qual|ity (**vocal qualities**) **N-COUNT/ N-NONCOUNT** A person's **vocal quality** is the way their voice sounds, for example whether it is deep or loud or high-pitched.

vogue /voʊg/
1 **N-SING** If there is a **vogue for** something, it is very popular and fashionable. ❑ *...a vogue for herbal teas.*
2 **PHRASE** If something is **in vogue**, it is very popular and fashionable. If it comes **into vogue**, it becomes very popular and fashionable. ❑ *Pale colors are in vogue.* [from French]

voice /vɔɪs/ (**voices**)
1 **N-COUNT** Someone's **voice** is the sound that comes from their mouth when they speak or sing. ❑ *She spoke in a soft voice.* ❑ *Lucinda sings in the choir and has a beautiful voice.*
2 **N-SING** LANGUAGE ARTS In grammar, if a verb is in **the active voice**, the person who performs the action is the subject of the verb. If a verb is in **the passive voice**, the thing or person affected by the action is the subject of the verb. [from Old French]

void /vɔɪd/ (**voids**) **N-COUNT** A **void** is an empty feeling. ❑ *His death left a void in her life.* [from Old French]

vola|tile /vɒlətəl/
1 **ADJ** A situation that is **volatile** is likely to change suddenly and unexpectedly. ❑ *There*

Word Web volcano

The most famous **volcano** in the world is Mount Vesuvius, near Naples, Italy. This mountain sits in the middle of the much older **volcanic cone** of Mount Somma. In 79 AD the sleeping volcano **erupted**, and **magma** rose to the surface. The people of the nearby city of Pompeii were terrified. Huge black clouds of **ash** and pumice came rushing toward them. The clouds blocked out the sun and smothered thousands of people. Pompeii was buried under hot ash and **molten lava**. Centuries later the remains of the people and town were found. The discovery made this active volcano famous.

have been riots and the situation is volatile.
2 ADJ If someone is **volatile**, their mood often changes quickly. ❏ *...a volatile, passionate man.* [from Latin]

vol|can|ic /vɒlkǽnɪk/ **ADJ** SCIENCE **Volcanic** means coming from or created by volcanoes. ❏ *Over 200 people have been killed by volcanic eruptions.* [from Italian]
→ look at Word Web: **volcano**

vol|ca|no /vɒlkéɪnoʊ/ (**volcanoes**) **N-COUNT** SCIENCE A **volcano** is a mountain that throws out hot, liquid rock and fire. ❏ *The volcano erupted last year.* [from Italian]
→ look at Word Webs: **volcano, rock, tsunami**

volley|ball /vɒ́libɔl/ **N-NONCOUNT** SPORTS **Volleyball** is a game in which two teams hit a large ball over a high net with their arms or hands.

volt /voʊlt/ (**volts**) **N-COUNT** SCIENCE A **volt** is a unit for measuring electricity. [after Count Alessandro Volta (1745-1827), an Italian physicist]

volt|age /voʊltɪdʒ/ (**voltages**) **N-COUNT/N-NONCOUNT** SCIENCE The **voltage** of an electrical current is its force measured in volts. ❏ *...high-voltage power lines.* [from Italian]

vol|ume /vɒ́lyum/ (**volumes**)
1 N-COUNT MATH The **volume** of an object is the amount of space that it contains. ❏ *What is the volume of a cube with sides of length 3 inches?*
2 N-COUNT A **volume** is one book in a series

Picture Dictionary volume

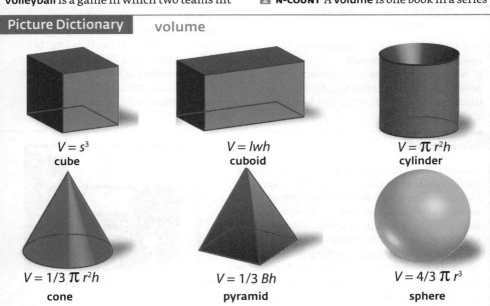

$V = s^3$
cube

$V = lwh$
cuboid

$V = \pi r^2 h$
cylinder

$V = 1/3\, \pi r^2 h$
cone

$V = 1/3\, Bh$
pyramid

$V = 4/3\, \pi r^3$
sphere

V

of books. ❑ *We read the first volume of his autobiography.*

3 **N-NONCOUNT** The **volume** of a sound is how loud or quiet it is. ❑ *He turned down the volume.*

4 **N-COUNT** The **volume of** something is the amount of it that there is. ❑ *The volume of sales has increased.* [from Old French]
→ look at Picture Dictionary: **volume**

vol|un|tary /vɒləntɛri/

1 **ADJ** **Voluntary** actions or activities are done because someone wants to do them and not because they must. ❑ *Participation is completely voluntary.* ● **vol|un|tar|ily** /vɒləntɛərɪli/ **ADV** ❑ *I would never leave here voluntarily.*

2 **ADJ** **Voluntary** work is done by people who are not paid for it, but who do it because they want to do it. ❑ *I do voluntary work with handicapped children.*

3 **ADJ** **Voluntary** movements are movements of your body that you make because you choose to, rather than because they are automatic. [from Latin]
→ look at Word Web: **muscle**

Word Partnership	Use **voluntary** with :
N	voluntary **action**, voluntary **basis**, voluntary **compliance**, voluntary **contributions**, voluntary **program**, voluntary **retirement**, voluntary **test** **1** voluntary **organizations** **2**

Word Link	*eer* ≈ *one who does* : engin**eer**, mountain**eer**, volunt**eer**

vol|un|teer /vɒləntɪər/ (**volunteers, volunteering, volunteered**)

1 **N-COUNT** A **volunteer** is someone who does work without being paid for it, because they want to do it. ❑ *She helps in a local school as a volunteer.*

2 **V-I** If you **volunteer** to do something, you offer to do it without being forced to do it. ❑ *Mary volunteered to clean up the kitchen.* [from French]

Word Partnership	Use **volunteer** with :
N	**community** volunteer, volunteer **organization**, volunteer **program**, **Red Cross** volunteer, volunteer **work** **1** volunteer **for service**, volunteer **for the army** **2**
V	**need a** volunteer **1** **2** volunteer **to help**, volunteer **to work** **2**

vo|lup|tu|ous /vəlʌptʃuəs/ **ADJ** If you describe a woman as **voluptuous**, you mean that she has a large, curved body, and is considered attractive in a sexual way. ❑ *...a voluptuous, well-rounded lady with glossy black hair.* [from Latin]

vom|it /vɒmɪt/ (**vomits, vomiting, vomited**)

1 **V-I** If you **vomit**, food and drink comes back up from your stomach and out through your mouth. ❑ *Milk made him vomit.*

2 **N-NONCOUNT** **Vomit** is partly digested food and drink that comes out of your mouth when you vomit. [from Latin]

vote /voʊt/ (**votes, voting, voted**)

1 **N-COUNT** SOCIAL STUDIES A **vote** is a choice made by a particular person or group in a meeting or an election. ❑ *Mr. Reynolds won the election by 102 votes to 60.*

2 **V-T/V-I** SOCIAL STUDIES When you **vote**, you show your choice officially at a meeting or in an election. ❑ *The workers voted to strike.* ❑ *Nearly everyone voted for Buchanan.* ● **vot|er** (**voters**) **N-COUNT** ❑ *The state has 2.1 million registered voters.* [from Latin]
→ look at Word Webs: **vote, citizenship, election**

Word Web   vote

Today in almost all **democracies** any adult can **vote** for the **candidate** of his or her choice. But years ago women could not vote. Not until the suffrage movement revolutionized voting rights did women have the right to vote. In 1893, New Zealand became the first country to give women full voting rights. Women could finally enter a **polling place** and **cast** a **ballot.** Many countries soon followed. They included Canada, Finland, Germany, Sweden, and the U.S. However, China, France, India, Italy, and Japan didn't grant suffrage until the mid-1900s.

vouch|er /vaʊtʃər/ (**vouchers**) **N-COUNT**
A **voucher** is a ticket or a piece of paper that can be used instead of money to pay for something. ❏ ...a voucher for two movie tickets. [from Old French]

vow /vaʊ/ (**vows, vowing, vowed**)
■ **V-T** If you **vow** to do something, you make a serious promise or decision that you will do it. ❏ She vowed to continue the fight. ❏ I vowed that someday I would go back to Europe.
■ **N-COUNT** A **vow** is a serious promise or decision to do a particular thing. ❏ I made a vow to be more careful in the future. [from Old French]

vow|el /vaʊəl/ (**vowels**) **N-COUNT**
LANGUAGE ARTS A **vowel** is a sound such as the ones written as "a," "e," "i," "o," and "u," and sometimes "y." [from Old French]

voy|age /vɔɪɪdʒ/ (**voyages**) **N-COUNT**
A **voyage** is a long trip on a ship or in a spacecraft. ❏ They began the long voyage down the river. [from Old French]

vs. SPORTS **vs.** is short for **versus**. ❏ We were watching the Yankees vs. the Red Sox.

vul|ner|able /vʌlnərəbəl/ **ADJ** Someone who is **vulnerable** is weak and without protection. ❏ Older people are particularly vulnerable to colds and flu in cold weather. [from Late Latin]

Word Partnership	Use **vulnerable** with :
N	vulnerable **children/people/women**
V	**feel** vulnerable, **become** vulnerable, **remain** vulnerable ■ ■
ADV	**especially** vulnerable, **extremely** vulnerable, **particularly** vulnerable, **too** vulnerable, **very** vulnerable

V

Ww

wade /weɪd/ (wades, wading, waded) **v-ı**
If you **wade** through water, you walk
through it with difficulty. ❑ *I waded across
the river to reach them.* [from Old English]

waf|fle /wɒfᵊl/ (waffles) **n-count** A **waffle** is
a flat, sweet cake with a pattern of squares
on it that is usually eaten warm with syrup
for breakfast. [from Dutch]

wag /wæg/ (wags, wagging, wagged) **v-т**
When a dog **wags** its tail, it moves its tail
from side to side. [from Old English]

wage /weɪdʒ/ (wages) **n-count** BUSINESS
Someone's **wages** are the amount of money
that is paid to them for the work that they
do. ❑ *His wages have gone up.* [from Old
Northern French]
→ look at Word Webs: **factory, union**

Thesaurus	wage	Also look up :
N	earnings, pay, salary **1**	

Word Partnership	Use wage with :
ADJ	**average** wage, **high/higher** wage, **hourly** wage, **low/lower** wage
V	**offer a** wage, **pay a** wage, **raise a** wage
N	wage **cuts**, wage **earners**, wage **increases**, wage **rates**

wag|on /wægən/ (wagons) **n-count** A **wagon**
is a strong vehicle with four wheels, usually
pulled by animals. [from Dutch]
→ look at Word Web: **train**

waist /weɪst/ (waists)
1 **n-count** Your **waist** is the middle part of
your body. ❑ *Ricky put his arm around her waist.*
2 **n-count** The **waist** of a pair of pants is
the part of it that goes around the middle
part of your body. ❑ *The waist of these pants is a
little tight.* [from Old English]
→ look at Picture Dictionary: **body**

wait /weɪt/ (waits, waiting, waited)
1 **v-т/v-ı** When you **wait** for something or
someone, you spend time doing very little
before something happens. ❑ *I walked to the
street corner and waited for the school bus.*

❑ *I waited to hear what she said.* ❑ *We had to wait
a week before we got the results.*
2 **n-count** A **wait** is a period of time in which
you do very little, before something happens.
❑ *There was a four-hour wait at the airport.*
3 **v-т/v-ı** If something **is waiting for** you, it
is ready for you to use, have, or do. ❑ *There'll
be a car waiting when we leave the restaurant.*
❑ *When we came home we had a meal waiting for us.*
4 **v-ı** If you say that something can **wait**,
you mean that it is not very important, so
you will do it later. ❑ *I want to talk to you, but it
can wait.*
5 **v-т** People say **Wait a minute, Wait a
second**, and **Wait a moment** to interrupt
someone when they are speaking. [SPOKEN]
❑ *"Wait a minute!" he interrupted. "This isn't fair!"*
6 **PHRASE** If you **can't wait** to do something,
you are very excited about it. [SPOKEN]
❑ *We can't wait to get started.* [from Old French]

Thesaurus	wait	Also look up :
V	anticipate, expect, hold on, stand by; (ant.) carry out, go ahead **1**	
N	delay, halt, holdup, pause **2**	

Word Partnership	Use wait with :
ADV	wait **forever**, wait **here**, **just** wait, wait **outside**, wait **patiently** **1**
N	wait **for an answer**, wait **days/hours**, wait **a long time**, wait **your turn** **1** wait **a minute**, wait **until tomorrow** **1** **4**
V	**(can't) afford to** wait **1** **can/can't/couldn't** wait, **have to** wait, wait **1** **4** wait **to hear**, wait **to say** **1** **4** **can't** wait, **can hardly** wait **6**
ADJ	**worth the** wait **2**

wait|er /weɪtər/ (waiters) **n-count** A **waiter**
is a man whose job is to serve food in a
restaurant. [from Old French]

wait|ing room (waiting rooms) **n-count**
A **waiting room** is a room where people can
sit down while they wait. ❑ *She sat for half
an hour in the dentist's waiting room.*

wait|ress /weɪtrɪs/ (**waitresses**) **N-COUNT**
A **waitress** is a woman whose job is to serve
food in a restaurant. [from Old French]

wake /weɪk/ (**wakes, waking, woke, woken**)
1 **V-T/V-I** When you **wake**, you stop
sleeping. ❑ It was cold and dark when I woke at
6:30. ❑ She went upstairs to wake Milton.
2 **V-T/V-I** When someone or something
wakes you, they make you stop sleeping.
❑ Betty woke me when she left.
3 **Wake up** means the same as **wake**.
❑ We woke up early to a perfect summer morning.
4 **PHRASE** If one thing follows **in the wake
of** another, it happens after the other thing.
❑ There are a lot of police on the streets in the wake
of last week's attack. [from Old English]

Word Partnership	Use **wake** with :
PREP	wake **up during the night**, wake **up in the middle of**, wake **up in the morning** 1
ADV	wake (*someone*) **up** 2

walk /wɔk/ (**walks, walking, walked**)
1 **V-T/V-I** When you **walk**, you move
forward by putting one foot in front of the
other. ❑ She walked two miles to school every day.
❑ We walked into the hall. ❑ I walked a few steps
toward the fence.
2 **N-COUNT** A **walk** is a trip that you make
by walking, usually for pleasure. ❑ I went for
a walk after lunch.
3 **N-SING** A **walk** is the action of walking
rather than running. ❑ She slowed to a
steady walk.
4 **V-T** If you **walk** someone somewhere, you
walk there with them. ❑ She walked me to my
car. [from Old English]
▶ **walk out** If you **walk out of** a situation,
you leave it suddenly, to show that you are
angry or bored. ❑ Several people walked out of
the meeting in protest.

Thesaurus	walk Also look up :
V	amble, hike, stroll 1
N	hike, march, parade, stroll 1 2

Word Partnership	Use **walk** with :
ADV	walk **alone**, walk **away**, walk **back**, walk **home**, walk **slowly** 1
V	**begin to** walk, **start to** walk 1 **go for a** walk, **take a** walk 2 3
ADJ	**(un)able to** walk 1 **brisk** walk, **long** walk, **short** walk 2–4

wall /wɔl/ (**walls**)

wall

1 **N-COUNT** A **wall** is
one of the sides of a
building or a room.
❑ His bedroom walls
are covered with
pictures of cars.
2 **N-COUNT** A **wall** is a long narrow
structure made of stone or brick that divides
an area of land. ❑ He sat on the wall in the sun.
[from Old English]

Word Partnership	Use **wall** with :
PREP	**against a** wall, **along a** wall, **behind a** wall, **on a** wall 1 2
N	**back to the** wall, **brick** wall, **concrete** wall, **glass** wall 1 2
V	**build a** wall, **climb a** wall, **lean against/on a** wall 1 2

wall cloud (**wall clouds**) **N-COUNT** SCIENCE
A **wall cloud** is an area of cloud that extends
beneath a thunderstorm and sometimes
develops into a tornado.

wal|let /wɒlɪt/ (**wallets**) **N-COUNT** A **wallet** is
a small case in which you can keep money
and cards. [from Germanic]

wall|paper /wɔlpeɪpər/ (**wallpapers,
wallpapering, wallpapered**)
1 **N-COUNT/N-NONCOUNT** Wallpaper is paper
that is used for decorating the walls of rooms.
2 **V-T** If someone **wallpapers** a room, they
cover the walls with wallpaper.
3 **N-NONCOUNT** TECHNOLOGY **Wallpaper** is
the background on a computer screen.

wal|nut /wɔlnʌt, -nət/ (**walnuts**) **N-COUNT/
N-NONCOUNT** Walnuts are nuts that are
hard and round, with a rough texture.
[from Old English]

wan|der /wɒndər/ (**wanders, wandering,
wandered**)
1 **V-T/V-I** If you **wander**, you walk around,
often without intending to go in any
particular direction. ❑ When he got bored he
wandered around the park. ❑ People wandered the
streets.
2 **V-I** If your mind **wanders**, you stop
concentrating on something and start
thinking about other things. ❑ His mind was
starting to wander. [from Old English]

wane /weɪn/ (**wanes, waning, waned**) **V-I**
If something **wanes**, it becomes gradually
weaker or less, often so that it eventually

w

disappears. ❑ *His interest in these sports began to wane.* [from Old English]

want /wɒnt/ (**wants, wanting, wanted**)

■ **V-T** If you **want** something, you feel a need for it. ❑ *I want a drink.* ❑ *People wanted to know who she was.* ❑ *They wanted their father to be the same as other dads.*

■ **V-T** If someone **is wanted** by the police, the police are searching for them because they are thought to have committed a crime. ❑ *He was wanted for the murder of a judge.* ● **want|ed** **ADJ** ❑ *He is one of the most wanted criminals in Europe.* [from Old Norse]

Thesaurus	want Also look up :
v	covet, desire, long, need, require, wish ■

wan|ton /wɒntən/ **ADJ** A **wanton** act deliberately causes harm, damage, or waste with any reason. ❑ *...this unnecessary and wanton destruction of our environment.* [from Old English]

war /wɔr/ (**wars**) **N-COUNT/N-NONCOUNT** A **war** is a period of fighting between countries or groups. ❑ *He spent part of the war in France.* [from Old Northern French] → look at Word Webs: **army, history**

ward /wɔrd/ (**wards**) **N-COUNT** A **ward** is a room in a hospital that has beds for many people. ❑ *They took her to the children's ward.* [from Old English]

ward|robe /wɔrdroʊb/ (**wardrobes**) **N-COUNT** Someone's **wardrobe** is the clothes that they have. ❑ *Ingrid bought a new wardrobe for the trip.* [from Old Northern French]

Word Link	ware ≈ merchandise : hardware, software, warehouse

ware|house /wɛərhaʊs/ (**warehouses**) **N-COUNT** BUSINESS A **warehouse** is a large building where goods are stored before they are sold.

war|fare /wɔrfɛər/ **N-NONCOUNT** **Warfare** is the activity of fighting a war. ❑ *His men were trained in desert warfare.*

warm /wɔrm/ (**warmer, warmest, warms, warming, warmed**)

■ **ADJ** Something that is **warm** has some heat, but is not hot. ❑ *On warm summer days, she would sit outside.* ❑ *Because it was warm, David wore only a white cotton shirt.*

■ **ADJ** **Warm** clothes and blankets are made of a material that protects you from the cold.

● **warm|ly** **ADV** ❑ *Remember to dress warmly on cold days.*

■ **ADJ** A **warm** person is friendly. ❑ *She was a warm and loving mother.* ● **warm|ly** **ADV** ❑ *We warmly welcome new members.*

■ **ADJ** **Warm** colors have red, orange, or yellow in them rather than blue, green, or violet.

■ **V-T** If you **warm** a part of your body or if something hot **warms** it, it stops feeling cold and starts to feel hotter. ❑ *The sun warmed his back.* [from Old English]

▶ **warm up** ■ If you **warm** something **up**, you make it less cold. ❑ *He blew on his hands to warm them up.*

■ SPORTS If you **warm up** for an event such as a race, you prepare yourself for it by doing exercises just before it starts. ❑ *In an hour the runners will be warming up for the main event.*

Word Partnership	Use warm with :
N	warm **air**, warm **bath**, warm **breeze**, warm **hands**, warm **water**, warm **weather** ■
	warm **clothes** ■
	warm **smile**, warm **welcome** ■
ADJ	warm **and sunny** ■
	warm **and cozy**, warm **and dry** ■ ■
	soft and warm ■
	warm **and friendly** ■

warm-blood|ed **ADJ** SCIENCE A **warm-blooded** animal, such as a bird or a mammal, has a fairly high body temperature that does not change much and is not affected by the surrounding temperature. → look at Word Web: **mammal**

warmth /wɔrmθ/

■ **N-NONCOUNT** The **warmth** of something is the heat that it produces. ❑ *Feel the warmth of the sun on your skin.*

■ **N-NONCOUNT** **Warmth** is friendly behavior toward other people. ❑ *They treated us with warmth and kindness.* [from Old English]

warm-up (**warm-ups**) **N-COUNT** SPORTS A **warm-up** is a period of gentle exercise that you do to prepare yourself for a particular sport or activity. ❑ *Training consists of a 20-minute warm-up, followed by ball practice.*

warn /wɔrn/ (**warns, warning, warned**)

■ **V-T/V-I** If you **warn** someone about a possible danger, you tell them about it. ❑ *They warned of the dangers of sailing alone.* ❑ *The doctor warned her that too much sugar was bad for her health.*

2 **V-T/V-I** If you **warn** someone not to do something, you advise them not to do it so that they can avoid possible danger or punishment. ❑ *Joe warned me not to interfere.* ❑ *The public were warned of the impending storms and advised to stay indoors.* [from Old English]

Thesaurus warn Also look up :
V   alert, caution, notify **1** **2**

Word Link *war ≈ watchful : aware, beware, warning*

warn|ing /wɔrnɪŋ/ (**warnings**)
N-COUNT/N-NONCOUNT A **warning** is something that tells people of a possible danger. ❑ *It was a warning that we should be careful.* ❑ *Suddenly and without warning, a car crash changed her life.* [from Old English]

Word Partnership Use warning with :
ADJ   **advance** warning, **early** warning, **stern** warning
N   warning **of danger**, **hurricane** warning, warning **labels**, warning **signs**, **storm** warning
V   **give (a)** warning, **ignore a** warning, **receive (a)** warning, **send a** warning

war|rant /wɔrənt/ (**warrants**) **N-COUNT** A **warrant** is a legal document that allows someone to do something. ❑ *Police issued a warrant for his arrest.* [from Old French]

war|ran|ty /wɔrənti/ (**warranties**) **N-COUNT** BUSINESS A **warranty** is a promise by a company that if you buy something that does not work, they will repair or replace it. ❑ *The TV comes with a twelve-month warranty.* [from Old French]

war|ri|or /wɔriər/ (**warriors**) **N-COUNT** SOCIAL STUDIES A **warrior** is a fighter or a soldier, especially one in former times who was very brave and experienced in fighting. ❑ *...the great warriors of the past.* [from Old Northern French]

war|time /wɔrtaɪm/ **N-NONCOUNT** SOCIAL STUDIES **Wartime** is a period of time when a war is being fought. ❑ *He served his country during wartime.*

wary /wɛəri/ (**warier, wariest**) **ADJ** If you are **wary of** something or someone, you are careful because you do not know much about them and you think they may be dangerous. ❑ *People teach their children to be wary of strangers.*

was /wəz, STRONG wʌz, wɒz/ **Was** is the first and third person singular of the past tense of **be**. [from Old English]

wash /wɒʃ/ (**washes, washing, washed**)
1 **V-T** If you **wash** something, you clean it using water and soap. ❑ *She finished her dinner and washed the dishes.* ❑ *It took a long time to wash the dirt out of his hair.*
2 **V-T/V-I** If you **wash**, or if you **wash** part of your body, you clean your body using soap and water. ❑ *I haven't washed for days.* ❑ *She washed her face with cold water.*
3 **PHRASE** If an item of clothing **is in the wash**, it is being washed. [INFORMAL] ❑ *Your jeans are in the wash.* [from Old English]
→ look at Word Web: **soap**
▶ **wash down** If you **wash** food **down**, you drink something with it. ❑ *...a sandwich washed down with a bottle of lemonade.*
▶ **wash up** If you **wash up**, you clean part of your body with soap and water, especially your hands and face. ❑ *He went to the bathroom to wash up.*

Thesaurus wash Also look up :
V   clean, rinse, scrub **1**
         bathe, clean, soap **2**

Word Partnership Use wash with :
N   wash **a car**, wash **clothes**, wash **dishes** **1**
        wash *your* **face/hair/hands** **2**

wash|cloth /wɒʃklɔθ/ (**washcloths**)
N-COUNT A **washcloth** is a small cloth that you use for washing yourself.
→ look at Picture Dictionary: **bathroom**

wash|ing ma|chine /wɒʃɪŋ məʃiːn/ (**washing machines**)
N-COUNT A **washing machine** is a machine that you use to wash clothes in. ❑ *Dan put his shirts in the washing machine.*

wasn't /wʌzᵊnt, wɒz-/ **Wasn't** is short for "was not."

wasp /wɒsp/ (**wasps**) **N-COUNT** A **wasp** is an insect with wings and yellow and black stripes across its body. Wasps can sting people. [from Old English]

waste /weɪst/ (**wastes, wasting, wasted**)
1 **V-T** If you **waste** time, money, or energy, you use too much of it doing something that is not important. ❑ *She didn't want to waste time looking at old cars.* ❑ *I decided not to waste money on a hotel.*

W

2 **N-SING** **Waste** is also a noun. ❏ *It is a waste of time complaining about it.*

3 **N-NONCOUNT** **Waste** is material that is no longer wanted because the valuable or useful part of it has been taken out. ❏ *Waste materials such as paper and aluminum cans can be recycled.*

4 **V-T** If you **waste** an opportunity, you do not take advantage of it. ❏ *Let's not waste this opportunity.* [from Latin]

→ look at Word Web: **dump**

Thesaurus	waste Also look up :
V	misuse, squander **1**
N	garbage, junk, trash **2**

Word Partnership	Use waste with :
N	waste **energy**, waste **money**, waste **time**, waste **water** **1**
V	**reduce** waste **1** **2** **recycle** waste **2**
ADJ	**hazardous** waste, **human** waste, **industrial** waste, waste, **toxic** waste **2**

waste|basket /we͟ɪstbæskɪt/
(**wastebaskets**) **N-COUNT** A **wastebasket** is a container for things that you no longer want, especially paper. ❏ *He emptied the wastebasket and found her letter.*

watch /wɒtʃ/ (**watches, watching, watched**)

1 **V-T/V-I** If you **watch** someone or something, you look at them for a period of time. ❏ *He watched as the Yankees rallied for a comeback victory.* ❏ *I stayed up late to watch the movie.*

watch

2 **V-T** If you **watch** someone or something, you take care of them for a period of time. ❏ *Could you watch my bags? I need to go to the bathroom.*

3 **V-T/V-I** If you **watch** a situation or an event, you pay attention to it. ❏ *Human rights groups are closely watching the situation.* ❏ *He watched as nine people were swept into the crevasse.*

4 **N-COUNT** A **watch** is a small clock that you wear on your wrist. ❏ *Dan gave me a watch for my birthday.*

5 **PHRASE** If someone **keeps watch**, they keep looking and listening so that they can warn other people of danger. ❏ *Josh climbed a tree to keep watch.*

6 **PHRASE** You say **Watch it** in order to warn someone to be careful. ❏ *"Now watch it, Patsy," said John.*

7 **N-COUNT** A hurricane **watch** or a storm **watch** is an official announcement that severe weather conditions may soon develop in a particular area. [from Old English]

→ look at Picture Dictionary: **jewelry**

→ look at Usage note at **look**

▶ **watch for** or **watch out for** If you **watch for** something or **watch out for** it, you pay attention so that you will notice it if it happens. ❏ *You should watch carefully for signs of the illness.*

▶ **watch out** If you tell someone to **watch out**, you are warning them to be careful. ❏ *Police warned shoppers to watch out for thieves.*

Word Partnership	Use watch with :
ADV	watch **carefully**, watch **closely** **1** **3**
N	watch **a DVD**, watch **a film/movie**, watch **fireworks**, watch **a game**, watch **the news**, watch **people**, watch **a video** **1** watch **children** **2**
V	**check** *your* watch, **glance at** *your* watch, **look at** *your* watch **2**

wa|ter /wɔ͟tər/ (**waters, watering, watered**)

1 **N-NONCOUNT** **Water** is a clear thin liquid that has no color or taste. It falls from clouds as rain. ❏ *Get me a glass of water, please.*

2 **V-T** If you **water** plants, you pour water over them in order to help them to grow.

3 **V-I** If your eyes **water**, tears form in them because they are hurting, or because you are upset.

4 **V-I** If you say that your mouth **is watering**, you mean that you can smell or see some nice food that makes you want to eat it. ❏ *...cookies to make your mouth water.* [from Old English]

→ look at Word Webs: **water, biosphere, erosion, glacier, greenhouse effect, habitat, lake, ocean, photosynthesis, precipitation, rainbow**

water|color /wɔ͟tərkʌlər/ (**watercolors**)

1 **N-COUNT/N-NONCOUNT** **ARTS** **Watercolors** are colored paints that are mixed with water and used for painting pictures. ❏ *Campbell painted with watercolors.*

2 **N-COUNT** **ARTS** A **watercolor** is a picture that has been painted with watercolors. ❏ *...a watercolor by Andrew Wyeth.*

wa|ter cy|cle (**water cycles**) **N-COUNT** **SCIENCE** The **water cycle** is the continuous process in which water from the surface of the Earth evaporates to form clouds

Word Web   water

Water changes its form in the **hydrologic cycle**. The sun warms oceans, lakes, and rivers. Some water **evaporates**. Evaporation creates a gas called **water vapor**. Plants also give off water vapor through transpiration. Water vapor rises into the **atmosphere**. It hits cooler air and **condenses** into drops of water. These drops form **clouds**. When these drops get heavy enough, they begin to fall. They form different types of precipitation. Rain forms in warm air. Cold air creates **freezing rain**, **sleet**, and **snow**.

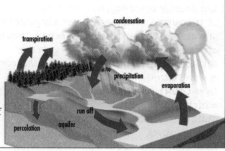

and then returns to the surface as rain or snow.

water|fall /wɔtərfɔl/ (**waterfalls**) **N-COUNT** **SCIENCE** A **waterfall** is a place where water flows over the edge of a steep part of hills or mountains, and falls into a pool below.

water|melon /wɔtərmɛlən/ (**watermelons**) **N-COUNT/N-NONCOUNT** A **watermelon** is a large, heavy fruit with green skin, pink flesh, and black seeds.
→ look at Picture Dictionary: **fruit**

wa|ter pow|er also **waterpower** **N-NONCOUNT** **SCIENCE** **Water power** is the same as **hydropower**.

water|proof /wɔtərpruf/ **ADJ** Something that is **waterproof** does not let water pass through it. ❑ *You'll need to take waterproof clothing when you go camping.*

water|spout /wɔtərspaʊt/ (**waterspouts**) **N-COUNT** **SCIENCE** A **waterspout** is a small tornado that occurs over water.

wa|ter ta|ble (**water tables**) **N-COUNT** **SCIENCE** The **water table** is the level below the surface of the ground where water can be found.

wa|ter va|por **N-NONCOUNT** **SCIENCE** **Water vapor** is water in the form of gas in the air.

wa|ter vas|cu|lar sys|tem /wɔtər væskyələr sɪstəm/ (**water vascular systems**) **N-COUNT** **SCIENCE** The **water vascular system** is a network of water-filled tubes and pumps in the bodies of animals such as starfish, that helps them to move, eat, and breathe.

wa|ter wave (**water waves**) **N-COUNT** **SCIENCE** A **water wave** is a wave that occurs in water, especially in the sea.

watt /wɒt/ (**watts**) **N-COUNT** **SCIENCE** A **watt** is a unit for measuring electrical power. ❑ *The lamp takes a 60 watt lightbulb.* [after James Watt (1736-1819), a Scottish engineer and inventor]

wave /weɪv/ (**waves, waving, waved**)
1 **V-T/V-I** If you **wave** or **wave** your hand, you hold your hand up and move it from side to side, usually in order to say hello or goodbye to someone. ❑ *Jessica saw Lois and waved to her.* ❑ *He smiled, waved his hand, and said, "Hi!"*
2 **N-COUNT** **Wave** is also a noun. ❑ *Steve stopped him with a wave of the hand.*

Word Web   wave

THE ELECTROMAGNETIC SPECTRUM

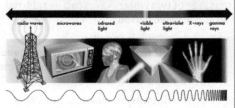

As **wind** blows across water, it makes **waves**. It does this by giving energy to the water. If the waves hit an object, they bounce off it. Light also moves in waves and acts the same way. We can see an object only if light waves bounce off it. Light waves have different **frequencies**. Wave frequency is usually the measure of the number of waves per second. **Radio waves** and **microwaves** are examples of low-frequency light waves. **Visible light** has medium-frequency light waves. **Ultraviolet radiation** and **X-rays** are high-frequency light waves.

w

3 **V-T** If you **wave** something, you hold it up and move it from side to side. ❏ *More than 4,000 people waved flags and sang songs.*

4 **N-COUNT** SCIENCE A **wave** is a higher part of water on the surface of the ocean. **Waves** are caused by the wind blowing on the surface of the water. ❏ *I fell asleep to the sound of waves hitting the rocks.*

5 **N-COUNT** SCIENCE **Waves** are the form in which things such as sound, light, and radio signals travel. ❏ *...sound waves.* ❏ *...radio waves.*

6 **N-COUNT** A **wave of** a particular emotion is a sudden strong feeling of that emotion. ❏ *She felt a wave of panic.*

7 **N-COUNT** A **wave** of something is a sudden increase in a particular activity or type of behavior ❏ *...the current wave of violence.* [from Old English]
→ look at Word Webs: **wave, beach, ear, earthquake, echo, ocean, radio, sound, tsunami**

wave height (**wave heights**)
N-COUNT/N-NONCOUNT SCIENCE The difference in height between the highest point of a water wave and the lowest point of the following wave can be referred to as the **wave height**.

wave|length /weɪvlɛŋθ/ (**wavelengths**)
1 **N-COUNT** SCIENCE A **wavelength** is the size of a radio wave that a particular radio station uses to broadcast its programs. ❏ *She found the station's wavelength on her radio.*

2 **PHRASE** If two people are **on the same wavelength**, they find it easy to understand each other because they share similar interests or opinions. ❏ *We often finished each other's sentences—we were on the same wavelength.*

wave pe|ri|od (**wave periods**) **N-COUNT** SCIENCE The time difference between the passage of two water waves can be referred to as the **wave period**.

wave speed (**wave speeds**)
N-COUNT/N-NONCOUNT SCIENCE Wave speed is the speed at which a wave such as a sound wave or a water wave is traveling.

wavy /weɪvi/ (**wavier, waviest**) **ADJ** Wavy hair is not straight or curly, but curves slightly. ❏ *She had short, wavy brown hair.* [from Old English]
→ look at Picture Dictionary: **hair**

wax /wæks/ **N-NONCOUNT** Wax is a solid, slightly shiny substance that is used for making candles and polish for furniture. ❏ *The candle wax melted in the heat.* [from Old English]

---
way
❶ NOUN AND ADVERB USES
❷ PHRASES
---

❶ way /weɪ/ (**ways**)
1 **N-COUNT** A **way** of doing something is the action that you take to do it. ❏ *One way of making friends is to go to an evening class.* ❏ *She smiled in a friendly way.*

2 **N-COUNT** The **way** to a place is the route that you take in order to get there. ❏ *Do you know the way to the post office?*

3 **N-SING** If you go a particular **way**, you go in that direction. ❏ *Which way do we go now—left or right?*

4 **N-SING** A long **way** is a long distance. ❏ *It's a long way from New York to Nashville.*

5 **N-PLURAL** The **ways** of a particular person or group of people are their habits or their usual behavior. ❏ *I'm too old to change my ways.*

6 **N-SING** Expressions such as **the right way up** and **the other way around** are used for talking about one of two or more positions that something can have. ❏ *Hold that bottle the right way up!*

7 **ADV** **Way** is used for emphasizing distance, level, or amount. ❏ *The town of Freiburg is way down in the valley.* ❏ *You've waited way too long.* [from Old English]

8 → see also **underway**

❷ way /weɪ/ (**ways**)
1 **PHRASE** You say **by the way** when you are going to talk about something different. [SPOKEN] ❏ *By the way, how is your back?*

2 **PHRASE** If someone says that you **can't have it both ways**, they are telling you that you have to choose between two things and cannot do or have both things. ❏ *You can't have it both ways: you're either in charge or you're not.*

3 **PHRASE** If you **get** your **way** or **have** your **way**, nobody stops you from doing what you want to do. ❏ *He likes to get his own way.*

4 **PHRASE** If an object that is supporting something **gives way**, it breaks or falls down. ❏ *He fell when the floor gave way beneath him.*

5 **PHRASE** If something is true **in a way**, it is not completely true. You use **in a way** to

W

reduce the force of a statement. ❑ *In a way, I guess I'm frightened of failing.*

6 **PHRASE** If someone **is in the way**, they are in the same place as you, and so they stop you from doing something. ❑ *Please can you move? You're in the way.*

7 **PHRASE** If one person or thing **makes way for** another, the first is replaced by the second. ❑ *He said he was happy to make way for younger people.*

8 **PHRASE** If someone **gets out of the way**, they are no longer stopping another person from doing something. ❑ *Get out of the way of the ambulance!* [from Old English]

way of life (ways of life) **N-COUNT** A **way of life** is the behavior and habits that are typical of a particular person or group, or that are chosen by them. ❑ *They're teaching me a lot about their way of life.*

we /wɪ, STRONG wi/ **PRON** A speaker or a writer uses **we** to talk about both himself or herself and about one or more other people as a group. ❑ *We said we would be friends for ever.* ❑ *We bought a bottle of lemonade.* [from Old English]

weak /wik/ (weaker, weakest)

1 **ADJ** If someone is **weak**, they are not healthy, or they do not have strong muscles. ❑ *I was too weak to move.* ● **weak|ly** **ADV** ❑ *"I'm all right," Max said weakly.*

2 **ADJ** If an argument is **weak**, there is little evidence to support it. ❑ *The argument against him was weak.*

3 **ADJ** If an organ in your body or a sense is **weak**, it is not very strong. ❑ *She had a weak heart.*

4 **ADJ** A **weak** drink, chemical, or drug contains very little of a particular substance. ❑ *We sat at the table drinking weak coffee.*

5 **ADJ** A **weak** person does not have much determination, and it is easy to influence them. ❑ *He was weak, but he was not a bad man.* [from Old English]

→ look at Word Web: **muscle**

Thesaurus	**weak** Also look up :
ADJ	feeble, frail; (*ant.*) strong **1**
	cowardly, insecure; (*ant.*) strong **5**

Word Partnership	Use **weak** with :
ADV	**relatively** weak, **still** weak, **too** weak, **very** weak **1**–**5**

weak|en /wikən/ (weakens, weakening, weakened) **V-T/V-I** If you **weaken** something, or it **weakens**, it becomes less strong. ❑ *The economy weakened in early 2001.* [from Old English]

weak|ness /wiknıs/ (weaknesses)

1 **N-COUNT** If you have a **weakness for** something, you like it very much. ❑ *Stephen had a weakness for chocolate.*

2 **N-NONCOUNT** **Weakness** is the fact of not being healthy, or not having strong muscles. ❑ *Symptoms of the disease include weakness in the arms.*

3 **N-NONCOUNT** If someone shows **weakness**, they do not have much determination, and it is easy to influence them. ❑ *Some people think that crying is a sign of weakness.* [from Old English]

wealth /wɛlθ/

1 **N-NONCOUNT** **Wealth** is a large amount of money, property, or other valuable things. ❑ *He used his wealth to help others.*

2 **N-SING** A **wealth of** something is a large quantity of it. [FORMAL] ❑ *The city has a wealth of beautiful churches.*

Thesaurus	**wealth** Also look up :
N	affluence, funds, money; (*ant.*) poverty **1**

wealthy /wɛlθi/ (wealthier, wealthiest)

1 **ADJ** Someone who is **wealthy** has a large amount of money, property, or valuable possessions. ❑ *She's going to be a very wealthy woman someday.*

2 **N-PLURAL** The **wealthy** are people who are wealthy. ❑ *Good education should be available to everyone, not just the wealthy.*

weap|on /wɛpən/ (weapons) **N-COUNT** A **weapon** is an object such as a gun, that is used for killing or hurting people. ❑ *He was charged with carrying a dangerous weapon.* [from Old English]

→ look at Word Web: **army**

wear /wɛər/ (wears, wearing, wore, worn)

1 **V-T** When you **wear** clothes, shoes, or jewelry, you have them on your body. ❑ *He was wearing a brown shirt.*

2 **V-T** If you **wear** your hair in a particular way, you have it in that style. ❑ *She wore her hair in a long ponytail.*

3 **N-NONCOUNT** You use **wear** to talk about clothes that are suitable for a certain time or place. ❑ *Jeans are perfect for everyday wear.*

4 **V-I** If something **wears**, it becomes

W

weaker because it is being used a lot. ❑ *The stone steps are beginning to wear.*

5 **N-NONCOUNT** **Wear** is the damage or change that is caused by something being used a lot. ❑ *The suit showed signs of wear.* [from Old English]

6 → see also **worn**

→ look at Word Web: **makeup**

▶ **wear down** If something **wears down**, it becomes flatter or smoother because it has been rubbing against something. ❑ *The heels on my shoes have worn down.*

▶ **wear off** If a sensation or a feeling **wears off**, it disappears slowly. ❑ *The excitement of having a new job soon wore off.*

▶ **wear out** **1** When something **wears out** or when you **wear** it **out**, it is used so much that it becomes thin or weak. ❑ *The batteries of her watch were wearing out.* ❑ *He wore out his shoes wandering around Mexico City.*

2 If something **wears** you **out**, it makes you feel extremely tired. [INFORMAL] ❑ *The kids wore themselves out playing soccer.*

	Word Partnership Use **wear** with :
N	wear **black/red/white**, wear **clothes**, wear **contact lenses**, wear **glasses**, wear **gloves**, wear **a hat/helmet**, wear **a jacket**, wear **jeans**, wear **makeup**, wear **a mask**, wear **a suit**, wear **a uniform** **1**
ADJ	**casual** wear, **day** wear, **evening** wear **3**

wear|able /wɛ̱ərəbəl/ **ADJ** TECHNOLOGY
A **wearable** electronic device is designed to be worn on the body.. ❑ *...wearable technology.*

wea|ry /wɪ̱əri/ (**wearier**, **weariest**)
1 **ADJ** If you are **weary**, you are very tired.

❑ *Rachel looked pale and weary.*

2 **ADJ** If you are **weary of** something, you have become tired of it. ❑ *They were all growing a bit weary of the game.* [from Old English]

weath|er /wɛ̱ðər/ **N-NONCOUNT** SCIENCE
The **weather** is the temperature and conditions outside, for example if it is raining, hot, or windy. ❑ *The weather was bad.* ❑ *I like cold weather.* [from Old English]

→ look at Word Webs: **weather, forecast, storm**

Usage	weather and whether

Weather and *whether* sound exactly alike, but are very different. *Weather* refers to the conditions out of doors—hot or cold, wet or dry, cloudy or clear; *whether* refers to alternative situations: *Umar doesn't care whether it's rainy or sunny outside—he likes running through the park in all kinds of weather.*

Word Partnership	Use **weather** with :		
ADJ	**bad** weather, **clear** weather, **cold** weather, **cool** weather, **dry** weather, **fair** weather, **good** weather, **hot** weather, **inclement** weather, **mild** weather, **nice** weather, **rainy** weather, **rough** weather, **severe** weather, **stormy** weather, **sunny** weather, **warm** weather, **wet** weather		
N	weather **conditions**, weather **prediction**, weather **report**, weather **service**		
V	weather **permitting**		

weath|er fore|cast (**weather forecasts**)
N-COUNT A **weather forecast** is a statement saying what the weather will be like the next day or for the next few days.

weath|er|ing /wɛ̱ðərɪŋ/
1 **N-NONCOUNT** SCIENCE **Weathering** is a

Word Web weather

Researchers believe the **weather** affects our bodies and minds. The **barometric pressure** drops before a **storm**. The difference in pressure may change the blood flow in the brain. Some people get migraine headaches. In **damp**, **humid** weather people have problems with arthritis. A sudden **heat wave** can produce heatstroke. People get seasonal affective disorder or SAD in the winter. They feel depressed during the short, **gloomy** days. As the word "sad" suggests, people with this condition feel depressed. The bitter cold of a **blizzard** can cause frostbite. The **hot, dry** Santa Ana winds* in southern California create confusion and depression in some people.

Santa Ana winds: strong, hot, dry winds that blow in southern California in autumn and early spring.

process in which rocks near the Earth's surface are broken into smaller pieces as a result of exposure to rain, wind, and ice. [from Old English]

2 → see also **chemical weathering, mechanical weathering**

weath|er map (**weather maps**) **N-COUNT** A **weather map** is a chart that shows what the weather is like or what it will be like.

weave /wiːv/ (**weaves, weaving, wove, woven**) **V-T/V-I** If you **weave** cloth, you make it by crossing threads over and under each other. ❑ *We gathered wool and learned how to weave it into cloth.* ❑ *We women were weaving in the corner.* ● **weav|er** (**weavers**) **N-COUNT** ❑ *...a carpet weaver.* ● **weav|ing** **N-NONCOUNT** ❑ *I studied weaving.* [from Old English]
→ look at Word Web: **industry**

web /wɛb/ (**webs**)
1 **N-PROPER** TECHNOLOGY The **Web** is a computer system that helps you find information. You can use it anywhere in the world. It is also called the **World Wide Web**. ❑ *The handbook is available on the Web.*
2 **N-COUNT** A **web** is the thin net made by a spider from a string that comes out of its body. ❑ *...a spider's web.* [from Old English]
→ look at Word Web: **blog**

Web 2.0 /wɛb tu pɔɪnt oʊ/ **N-NONCOUNT** TECHNOLOGY **Web 2.0** is the Internet viewed as an interactive experience rather than simply a place to access information.

web|cam /wɛbkæm/ (**webcams**) **N-COUNT** TECHNOLOGY A **webcam** is a camera on a computer that produces images that can be seen on a website.

web|cast /wɛbkæst/ (**webcasts**) also Webcast **N-COUNT** TECHNOLOGY A **webcast** is an event such as a musical performance that you can listen to or watch on the Internet.

web|i|nar /wɛbɪnɑr/ (**webinars**) **N-COUNT** TECHNOLOGY A **webinar** is an interactive seminar conducted over the Internet.

web|master /wɛbmæstər/ (**webmasters**) **N-COUNT** TECHNOLOGY A **webmaster** is someone who is in charge of a website, especially if they do that as their job.
→ look at Word Web: **Internet**

web page (**web pages**) **N-COUNT** TECHNOLOGY A **web page** is a set of information that you can see on a computer screen as part of a website.
→ look at Word Web: **Internet**

> **Word Link** site, situ ≈ position, location :
> campsite, situation, website

web|site /wɛbsaɪt/ (**websites**) also web site **N-COUNT** TECHNOLOGY A **website** is a set of information about a particular subject that is available on the Internet.
→ look at Word Webs: **blog, Internet**

wed|ding /wɛdɪŋ/ (**weddings**) **N-COUNT** A **wedding** is a marriage ceremony and the party that often takes place after the ceremony. ❑ *Many couples want a big wedding.* [from Old English]
→ look at Word Web: **wedding**

wedge /wɛdʒ/ (**wedges, wedging, wedged**)
1 **V-T** If you **wedge** something, you force it to remain in a particular position by holding it there tightly or by putting something next to it to prevent it from moving. ❑ *I shut the door and wedged it with a piece of wood.*
2 **V-T** If you **wedge** something somewhere, you fit it there tightly. ❑ *Wedge the plug into the hole.*
3 **N-COUNT** A **wedge** of something such as fruit or cheese is a piece of it that has a thick triangular shape. ❑ *...a wedge of lemon.*

> **Word Web** wedding
>
> Some **weddings** are fancy events. Most ceremonies include a group of attendants. The **maid of honor** or **matron of honor** helps the **bride** get ready for the ceremony. She also signs the **marriage certificate** as a legal **witness**. The **bridesmaids** plan the bride's wedding **shower**. The **best man** arranges for the **bachelor party** before the wedding. He also helps the groom dress for the wedding. After the **ceremony,** the guests gather for a **reception**. When the party is over, many couples leave on a **honeymoon** trip.

4 **N-COUNT** A **wedge** is an object with one pointed edge and one thick edge, that you put under a door to keep it firmly in position.

5 **N-COUNT** A **wedge** is a piece of metal with a pointed edge that is used for splitting a material such as stone or wood, by being hammered into a crack in the material. [from Old English]

Wednes|day /wɛnzdeɪ, -di/ (**Wednesdays**) **N-COUNT/N-NONCOUNT** Wednesday is the day after Tuesday and before Thursday. ❑ *Come and have supper with us on Wednesday.* ❑ *They go to the movies every Wednesday evening.* [from Old English]

weed /wid/ (**weeds, weeding, weeded**)
1 **N-COUNT** A **weed** is a plant that grows where you do not want it. ❑ *The garden was full of weeds.*
2 **V-T/V-I** If you **weed** an area, you remove the weeds from it. ❑ *Try not to walk on the flowerbeds while you are weeding.* ❑ *Charles weeded the wrong plants.* [from Old English]
→ look at Picture Dictionary: **plants**

week /wik/ (**weeks**)
1 **N-COUNT** A **week** is a period of seven days. ❑ *I thought about it all week.*
2 **N-COUNT** Your working **week** is the hours that you spend at work during a week. ❑ *I work a 40-hour week.*
3 **N-SING** The **week** is the part of the week that does not include Saturday and Sunday. ❑ *Anna looked after the children during the week.* [from Old English]
→ look at Word Web: **year**

week|day /wikdeɪ/ (**weekdays**) **N-COUNT** A **weekday** is any of the days of the week except Saturday and Sunday.

week|end /wikɛnd/ (**weekends**) **N-COUNT** The **weekend** is Saturday and Sunday. ❑ *I had dinner with Tim last weekend.*

week|ly /wikli/
1 **ADJ** A **weekly** event happens once a week or every week. ❑ *We do the weekly shopping every Thursday.*
2 **ADV** **Weekly** is also an adverb. ❑ *The group meets weekly.* [from Old English]

weep /wip/ (**weeps, weeping, wept**) **V-T/V-I** If someone **weeps**, they cry. [LITERARY] ❑ *She wept tears of joy.* ❑ *He sat and wept.* [from Old English]
→ look at Word Web: **cry**

weigh /weɪ/ (**weighs, weighing, weighed**)
1 **V-T** If someone or something **weighs** a particular amount, this amount is how heavy they are. ❑ *She weighs nearly 120 pounds.*
2 **V-T** If you **weigh** something or someone, you measure how heavy they are. ❑ *Lisa weighed the boxes for postage.*
3 **V-T** If you **weigh** the facts when you are considering a situation, you think about the good and bad aspects before you make a decision. ❑ *She weighed her options.* [from Old English]
▶ **weigh down** If something heavy that you are carrying **weighs** you **down**, it stops you moving easily. ❑ *I was weighed down by my backpack.*

Word Partnership	Use **weigh** with :
ADV	weigh **less**, weigh **more** **1**
	weigh **carefully** **2** **3**
N	weigh **10 pounds** **1**
	weigh **alternatives**, weigh **benefits**, weigh **costs**, weigh **the evidence**, weigh **risks** **3**

weight /weɪt/ (**weights**)
1 **N-COUNT/N-NONCOUNT** The **weight** of a person or a thing is how heavy they are. ❑ *What is your height and weight?*
2 **N-COUNT** **Weights** are objects that people lift as a form of exercise. ❑ *I was in the gym lifting weights.*
3 **PHRASE** If someone **loses weight**, they become thinner. If they **gain weight** or **put on weight**, they become fatter. ❑ *I'm lucky because I never put on weight.*
4 **N-NONCOUNT** SCIENCE The **weight** of something is the vertical force exerted on it as a result of gravitation. Weight is measured in units called "newtons." [from Old English]
→ look at Word Web: **diet**

Word Partnership	Use **weight** with :
V	**add** weight, **gain/lose** weight, **put on** weight **1**
N	**body** weight, weight **gain/loss**, **height and** weight **1**
	weight **training** **2**
ADJ	**excess** weight, **healthy** weight, **ideal** weight **1**
	heavy weight, **light** weight **2**

weird /wɪərd/ (**weirder, weirdest**) **ADJ** If something or someone is **weird**, they are strange. [INFORMAL] ❑ *He's a very weird guy.* [from Old English]

wel|come /wɛlkəm/ (**welcomes, welcoming, welcomed**)

1 V-T/V-I If you **welcome** someone, you act in a friendly way when they arrive somewhere. ❑ *She was there to welcome him home.* ❑ *They were welcomed warmly.*

2 N-COUNT Welcome is also a noun. ❑ *They gave him a warm welcome.*

3 INTERJ You use **welcome** to be friendly to someone who has just arrived somewhere. ❑ *Welcome to Washington.* ❑ *Welcome home.*

4 V-T If you **welcome** an action or a decision, you are pleased that it has occurred. ❑ *She welcomed the decision but said that the changes didn't go far enough.*

5 ADJ If you describe something as **welcome**, you mean that people wanted it and they are happy that it has occurred. ❑ *"Any improvement is welcome," he said.*

6 ADJ If you say that someone is **welcome** in a particular place, you are encouraging them to go there by telling them that they will be liked and accepted. ❑ *New members are always welcome.*

7 ADJ If you tell someone that they are **welcome** to do something, you are encouraging them to do it by telling them that they are allowed to do it. ❑ *You are welcome to visit the hospital at any time.*

8 PHRASE You say **You're welcome** to someone who has thanked you for something. ❑ *"Thank you for dinner."—"You're welcome."* [from Old English]

Word Partnership	Use **welcome** with :
ADJ	**warm** welcome **1**
N	welcome **guests**, welcome **visitors 1 5**
ADV	welcome **home 2**
	always welcome **4**–**6**

wel|fare /wɛlfɛər/

1 N-NONCOUNT The **welfare** of a person or a group is their health and happiness. ❑ *I don't believe he is thinking of Emma's welfare.*

2 N-NONCOUNT Welfare is money that the government pays to people who are poor or sick. ❑ *Some states are making cuts in welfare.* [from Old Norse]

Word Partnership	Use **welfare** with :
ADJ	**public** welfare, **social** welfare **1**
N	**animal** welfare, **child** welfare, **health and** welfare **1**
	welfare **programs**, welfare **reform**, welfare **system 2**
	welfare **benefits**, welfare **checks 2**

well
1 INTRODUCING STATEMENTS
2 ADVERB USES
3 PHRASES
4 ADJECTIVE USE
5 NOUN USE

1 well /wɛl/

1 INTERJ You often say **well** before you begin to speak, or when you are surprised about something. ❑ *Well, it's a pleasure to meet you.* ❑ *Well, I didn't expect to see you here!*

2 INTERJ You say **well** when you pause in order to give yourself time to think about what you are going to say. ❑ *I'm sorry I woke you, and, well, I just wanted to tell you I was all right.*

3 INTERJ You say **well** when you are correcting something that you have just said. ❑ *There was a note. Well, a letter really.*

4 INTERJ You say **Oh well** to show that you accept a situation, even though you are not very happy about it. ❑ *Oh well, I guess it could be worse.* [from Old English]

2 well /wɛl/ (**better, best**)

1 ADV If you do something **well**, you do it in an effective way. ❑ *The team played well last week.* ❑ *He speaks English well.* ❑ *Did you sleep well last night?*

2 ADV If you do something **well**, you do it in a complete way. ❑ *Mix the butter and sugar well.* ❑ *Do you know him well?*

3 ADV You use **well** to ask or talk about the extent or standard of something. ❑ *How well do you remember your mother?*

4 PHRASE If you **do well**, you are successful. ❑ *If she does well in her exams, she will go to college.*

5 PHRASE You say **Well done** to someone when they have done something good. ❑ *This is excellent work. Well done!* [from Old English]

3 well /wɛl/

1 PHRASE As well means also. ❑ *Everywhere he went, I went as well.*

2 PHRASE As well as means and also. ❑ *Adults as well as children will enjoy the movie.*

3 PHRASE If you say that you **may as well** do something, you mean that you will do it because there is nothing better to do. ❑ *Anyway, you're here now—you may as well stay.* [from Old English]

4 well /wɛl/ **ADJ** If you are **well**, you are healthy. ❑ *"How are you?"—"I'm very well, thank you."* ❑ *He said he wasn't feeling well.* [from Old English]

W

❺ well /wɛl/ (**wells**) **N-COUNT** A **well** is a deep hole in the ground from which people take water or oil. ❑ *The women and children were carrying water from the well.* [from Old English]
→ look at Word Web: **oil**

well-being **N-NONCOUNT** Someone's **well-being** is their health and happiness. ❑ *Singing can create a sense of well-being.*

well done
  1 Something that is **well done** is properly done, with good results. ❑ *Many thanks for a job well done.*
  2 **ADJ** If meat is **well done**, it has been cooked thoroughly. ❑ *I like lamb well done.*

well-known **ADJ** A **well-known** person or thing is famous. ❑ *She was a very well-known author.*

well-off **ADJ** Someone who is **well-off** is rich. [INFORMAL]

went /wɛnt/ **Went** is the past tense of **go**. [from Old English]

wept /wɛpt/ **Wept** is the past tense and past participle of **weep**. [from Old English]

were /wər, STRONG wɜr/
  1 **Were** is the plural and second person singular of the past tense of **be**.
  2 **Were** is sometimes used instead of "was" in conditional sentences or after the verb "wish." [FORMAL] ❑ *Jerry wished he were back in Washington.* [from Old English]

weren't /wɜrnt, wɜrənt/ **Weren't** is short for "were not."

west /wɛst/ also **West**
  1 **N-NONCOUNT** GEOGRAPHY The **west** is the direction that is behind you when you look at the sun in the morning. ❑ *I drove to Flagstaff, a hundred miles to the west.* ❑ *The sun was slowly setting in the west.*
  2 **ADJ** GEOGRAPHY **West** is also an adjective. ❑ *...the west coast.*
  3 **N-SING** GEOGRAPHY The **west of** a place or country is the part that is in the west. ❑ *They live in a small town in the west of Canada.*
  4 **ADV** GEOGRAPHY If you go **west**, you travel toward the west. ❑ *We are going west to California.*
  5 **ADV** GEOGRAPHY Something that is **west of** a place is located to the west of it. ❑ *Their farm is about ten miles west of town.*
  6 **ADJ** A **west** wind blows from the west.

  7 **N-SING** GEOGRAPHY The **West** is the United States, Canada, and the countries of Western Europe. ❑ *...relations between Japan and the West.* [from Old English]

west|er|ly /wɛstərli/
  1 **ADJ** GEOGRAPHY **Westerly** means to the west or toward the west. ❑ *They walked in a westerly direction along the riverbank.*
  2 **ADJ** A **westerly** wind blows from the west. ❑ *...a strong westerly wind.*
  3 **N-COUNT** A **westerly** is a wind that blows from the west. [from Old English]

west|ern /wɛstərn/ (**westerns**) also **Western**
  1 **ADJ** GEOGRAPHY **Western** means in or from the west of a place. ❑ *...Western Europe.*
  2 **ADJ** SOCIAL STUDIES **Western** describes things, people, or ideas that come from the United States, Canada, and the countries of Western Europe. ❑ *They need billions of dollars from Western governments.*
  3 **N-COUNT** A **western** is a movie about life in the western United States in the past. [from Old English]

wet /wɛt/ (**wetter, wettest, wets, wetting, wet** or **wetted**)
  1 **ADJ** If something is **wet**, it is covered in liquid. ❑ *He dried his wet hair with a towel.*
  2 **V-T** To **wet** something means to put water or some other liquid over it. ❑ *She wet a cloth and wiped the child's face.*
  3 **ADJ** If the weather is **wet**, it is raining. ❑ *It's cold and wet outside.*
  4 **ADJ** If paint, ink, or cement is **wet**, it is not yet dry or solid. [from Old English]

Word Partnership	Use **wet** with :
V	**get** wet **1**
N	wet **clothes**, wet **feet**, wet **grass**, wet **hair**, wet **sand 1**
	wet **snow**, wet **weather 3**
ADJ	**soaking** wet **1**
	cold and wet **1 3**

wet|land /wɛtlænd/ (**wetlands**) **N-COUNT/ N-NONCOUNT** GEOGRAPHY A **wetland** is an area of very wet, muddy land with wild plants growing in it. You can also refer to an area like this as **wetlands**. ❑ *...a plan to protect the wetlands.*

we've /wɪv, STRONG wiv/ **We've** is short for "we have." ❑ *We've never been to the cinema together.*

Word Web whale

Whales are part of a group of animals called cetaceans. This group also includes **dolphins** and porpoises. Whales live in the water, but they are **mammals**. They breathe air and are **warm-blooded**. Whales are adapted to life in the **ocean**. They have a 2-inch thick layer of **blubber** just under their skin. This insulates them from the cold ocean water. They sing beautiful songs that can be heard miles away. Blue whales are the largest animals in the world. They can become almost 100 feet long and weigh up to 145 tons.

whale /weɪl/ (**whales**) **N-COUNT** Whales are very large mammals that live in the ocean. [from Old English]
→ look at Word Web: **whale**

wharf /wɔrf/ (**wharves** or **wharfs**) **N-COUNT** A **wharf** is a platform by a river or the sea where ships can be tied up. [from Old English]

what /wʌt, wɒt/
1 PRON You use **what** in questions when you ask for information. ❑ *What do you want?* ❑ *"Has something happened?"—"Yes."—"What?"*
2 DET What is also a determiner. ❑ *What time is it?*
3 CONJ What means "the thing that." ❑ *I want to know what happened to Norman.*
4 PREDET You use **what a** or **what an** in exclamations to make an opinion or a reaction stronger. ❑ *What a horrible thing to do!*
5 DET What is also a determiner. ❑ *What pretty hair she has!*
6 INTERJ You say **What?** when you ask someone to repeat something that they have just said. "What?" is more informal than expressions such as "Pardon?" and "Excuse me?" [SPOKEN] ❑ *"We could buy this place," she said. "What?" he asked.*
7 INTERJ You say **What?** to express surprise. ❑ *"I love you."—"What?"*
8 PHRASE You use **what about** when you make a suggestion, an offer, or a request. ❑ *What about going to see a movie?*
9 PHRASE You say **what if...** at the beginning of a question when you ask about something that might happen. ❑ *What if this doesn't work?* [from Old English]

what|ev|er /wʌtɛvər, wɒt-/
1 CONJ You use **whatever** to talk about anything or everything of a particular type. ❑ *Frank was free to do whatever he wanted.*
2 DET Whatever is also a determiner. ❑ *He has to accept whatever punishment they give him.*

3 CONJ You use **whatever** to say that something is the case in all situations. ❑ *I will always love you, whatever happens.*
4 CONJ You use **whatever** when you are saying that you do not know the exact meaning of the thing just mentioned. ❑ *I thought that my childhood was "normal," whatever that is.*

what's /wʌts, wɒts/ **What's** is short for "what is" or "what has." ❑ *What's that?* ❑ *What's happened?*

what|so|ev|er /wʌtsoʊɛvər, wɒt-/ **ADV** You use **whatsoever** to emphasize something negative. ❑ *James did nothing whatsoever to help.* ❑ *It made no sense to me whatsoever.*

wheat /wit/ **N-NONCOUNT** Wheat is a crop that is grown for food. It is made into flour and used for making bread. [from Old English]
→ look at Picture Dictionary: **bread**
→ look at Word Web: **grain**

wheel /wil/ (**wheels, wheeling, wheeled**)
1 N-COUNT The **wheels** of a vehicle are the round objects under it that allow it to move along the ground. ❑ *The car's wheels slipped on the wet road.*
2 N-COUNT The **wheel** of a vehicle is the round object that you turn to make the vehicle go in different directions. ❑ *He sat down behind the wheel and started the engine.*
3 V-T If you **wheel** an object somewhere, you push it along on its wheels. ❑ *He wheeled his bike into the alley.* [from Old English]
4 → see also **steering wheel**
→ look at Picture Dictionary: **color**
→ look at Word Webs: **wheel, bicycle**

Word Partnership	Use wheel with :
N	wheel **of a car/truck/vehicle** **1** **2**
V	**grip the** wheel, **slide behind the** wheel, **spin the** wheel, **turn the** wheel **2**

W

> ### Word Web | **wheel**
>
> In about 5000 BC the **wheel** was invented in Mesopotamia, part of modern-day Iraq. That's when someone first **spun** a potter's wheel to make a clay jar. About 1,500 years later, people put wheels on an **axle** and created the **chariot**. These first wheels were solid wood and were very heavy. However, in about 2000 BC the Egyptians invented much lighter wheels with **spokes**. The wheel has driven the development of all kinds of modern technology. The **water wheel, spinning wheel,** and **turbine** were important to the Industrial Revolution. Even the **propeller** and jet engine are based on the wheel.

wheel|chair /wiltʃɛər/ (**wheelchairs**)
N-COUNT A **wheelchair** is a chair with wheels that you use if you cannot walk very well.
→ look at Word Web: **disability**

when /wɛn/
1 **PRON** You use **when** to ask questions about the time at which things happen. ❏ *When are you going home?* ❏ *When did you get married?*
2 **CONJ** You use **when** to talk about something that happens during a situation. ❏ *When I met Jill, I was living on my own.*
3 **CONJ** You use **when** to introduce the part of the sentence where you mention the time at which something happens. ❏ *I asked him when he was coming back.* ❏ *When he brought Jane her drink she gave him a smile.* [from Old English]

when|ever /wɛnɛvər/ **CONJ** You use **whenever** to talk about any time or every time that something happens. ❏ *Whenever I talked to him, he seemed quite nice.* ❏ *You can stay at my house whenever you like.*

where /wɛər/
1 **PRON** You use **where** to ask questions about the place someone or something is in. ❏ *Where did you meet him?* ❏ *Where's Anna?*
2 **CONJ** You use **where** to talk about the place in which something happens. ❏ *People were looking to see where the noise was coming from.* ❏ *He knew where Henry was.*
3 **PRON** **Where** is also a pronoun. ❏ *This is the room where I work.*
4 **ADV** You use **where** when you are talking about a stage in a process. ❏ *Where will it all end?*
5 **PRON** **Where** is also a pronoun. ❏ *I've got to the point where I'll talk to almost anyone.* [from Old English]

wher|ever /wɛrɛvər/
1 **CONJ** You use **wherever** to say that

something happens in any place or situation. ❏ *Some people enjoy themselves wherever they are.*
2 **CONJ** You use **wherever** when you say that you do not know where a person or a place is. ❏ *I'd like to be with my children, wherever they are.*

wheth|er /wɛðər/
1 **CONJ** You use **whether** when you are talking about a choice between two or more things. ❏ *They now have two weeks to decide whether or not to buy the house.*
2 **CONJ** You use **whether** to say that something is true in any of the situations that you mention. ❏ *You are part of this family whether you like it or not.* [from Old English]
→ look at Usage note at **weather**

> ### Usage | **whether** and **if**
>
> *Whether* and *if* are often interchangeable: *Jorge wondered whether/if Sania really liked the cake—he wasn't sure whether/if she was being sincere or just polite.* Only *whether* can be used after a preposition: *Sania didn't like the cake, but she wanted Jorge to like her—she was uncertain about whether to be honest.*

which /wɪtʃ/
1 **DET** You use **which** to talk about a choice between two or more possible people or things. ❏ *I want to know which school you went to.* ❏ *"You go down that road."—"Which one?"* ❏ *Which teacher do you like best?*
2 **PRON** You use **which** when you want to show the exact thing that you are talking about. ❏ *Police stopped a car which didn't stop at a red light.*
3 **PRON** You use **which** to talk about something that you have just said. ❏ *She spoke extremely good English, which was not surprising.*
4 **DET** **Which** is also a determiner. ❏ *She may*

be ill, in which case she needs to see a doctor. [from Old English]

which|ever /wɪtʃˈɛvər/

1 DET Whichever means any person or thing. ❏ *Whichever way we do this, it isn't going to work.*
2 CONJ Whichever is also a conjunction. ❏ *You can order by phone or from our website—whichever you prefer.*

while /waɪl/

1 CONJ If one thing happens **while** another thing is happening, the two things are happening at the same time. ❏ *His wife got up while he was in bed asleep.*
2 CONJ You use **while** before you introduce some contrasting information. ❏ *The first two services are free, while the third costs $35.* ❏ *While the weather is good today, it may be bad tomorrow.*
3 N-SING A **while** is a period of time. ❏ *They walked on in silence for a while.* [from Old English]

> **Usage**   **while**
> *While is used to join two verb phrases. I listen to music while I exercise.*

whine /waɪn/ (whines, whining, whined)

1 V-I If something or someone **whines**, they make a long high noise that sounds sad or unpleasant. ❏ *He could hear the dog barking and whining in the background.*
2 V-T/V-I If someone **whines**, they complain in an annoying way about something unimportant. ❏ *People were complaining and whining.* ❏ *...children who whine that they are bored.* [from Old English]

whip /wɪp/ (whips, whipping, whipped)

1 N-COUNT A **whip** is a long thin piece of material attached to a handle. It is used for hitting people or animals.
2 V-T If someone **whips** a person or an animal, they hit them with a whip. ❏ *Mr. Melton whipped the horse several times.*
3 V-T If someone **whips** something out or **whips** something off, they take it out or take it off very quickly and suddenly. ❏ *Bob whipped out his notebook.* ❏ *She whipped off her skis and ran up the hill.*
4 V-T When you **whip** cream or egg, you stir it very fast until it is thick or stiff. ❏ *Whip the cream until it is thick.* [from Middle Dutch]

whirl /wɜrl/ (whirls, whirling, whirled)

V-T/V-I If something or someone **whirls**, they turn around very quickly. ❏ *She whirled around to look at him.* ❏ *He was whirling Anne around the floor.* [from Old Norse]

whisk /wɪsk/ (whisks, whisking, whisked)

1 V-T If you **whisk** someone or something somewhere, you take them or move them there quickly. ❏ *He whisked her across the dance floor.*
2 V-T If you **whisk** eggs or cream, you stir them very fast.
3 N-COUNT A **whisk** is a kitchen tool used for whisking eggs or cream. [from Old Norse]
→ look at Picture Dictionary: **kitchen utensils**

whisk|er /wɪskər/ (whiskers) N-COUNT

The **whiskers** of an animal such as a cat or a mouse are the long stiff hairs that grow near its mouth. [from Scottish Gaelic]

whis|key /wɪski/ (whiskeys)

1 N-COUNT/N-NONCOUNT Whiskey is a strong alcoholic drink made, especially in the United States and Ireland, from grain such as rye.
2 N-COUNT A **whiskey** is a glass of whiskey. ❏ *Beattie took two whiskeys from a tray.* [from Scottish Gaelic]

whis|ky /wɪski/ (whiskies)

1 N-COUNT/N-NONCOUNT Whisky is whiskey that is made in Scotland and Canada.
2 N-COUNT A **whisky** is a glass of whisky. [from Scottish Gaelic]

whis|per /wɪspər/ (whispers, whispering, whispered)

1 V-T/V-I When you **whisper**, you say something very quietly. ❏ *"Be quiet," I whispered.* ❏ *He whispered in her ear.*
2 N-COUNT Whisper is also a noun. ❏ *People were talking in whispers.* [from Old English]

whis|tle /wɪsəl/ (whistles, whistling, whistled)

1 V-T/V-I When you **whistle**, or when you **whistle** a tune, you make musical sounds by blowing your breath out between your lips. ❏ *He was whistling softly to himself.*
2 N-COUNT A **whistle** is a small tube that you blow in order to produce a loud sound. ❏ *The guard blew his whistle and the train started to move.* [from Old English]

white /waɪt/ (whiter, whitest, whites)

1 ADJ Something that is **white** is the color of snow or milk. ❏ *He had nice white teeth.*
2 N-NONCOUNT White is also a noun. ❏ *He was dressed in white from head to toe.*
3 ADJ A **white** person has a pale skin. ❏ *A family of white people moved into a house up the street.*
4 N-COUNT White people are sometimes

w

called **whites**, especially when comparing different groups of people. ❑ *The school has brought blacks and whites together.*
5 **ADJ** **White** wine is light yellow in color.
6 **N-COUNT/N-NONCOUNT** The **white** of an egg is the liquid that surrounds the yellow part called the yolk. [from Old English]
→ look at Picture Dictionary: **color**

white blood cell (white blood cells)
N-COUNT SCIENCE **White blood cells** are the cells in your blood which your body uses to fight infection. Compare with **red blood cell**.

white|board /waɪtbɔrd/ (whiteboards)
N-COUNT A **whiteboard** is a shiny white board that you can draw or write on, using special pens. Teachers often use whiteboards.

white|cap /waɪtkæp/ (whitecaps) N-COUNT
SCIENCE A **whitecap** is a wave in the ocean that is blown by the wind so that the top of the wave appears white.

white dwarf (white dwarfs or white dwarves) N-COUNT SCIENCE A **white dwarf** is a very small, dense star that has collapsed.

White House N-PROPER SOCIAL STUDIES
The White House is the official home in Washington DC of the president of the United States. You can also use **the White House** to talk about the president of the United States and his or her officials. ❑ *He drove to the White House.* ❑ *The White House welcomed the decision.*

whiz /wɪz/ (whizzes, whizzing, whizzed) also
whizz **V-I** If something **whizzes** somewhere, it moves there very fast. [INFORMAL]
❑ *Stewart felt a bottle whiz past his head.*

who

1 **PRON** You use **who** in questions when you ask about the name of a person or a group of people. ❑ *Who's there?* ❑ *Who is the strongest man around here?* ❑ *"You remind me of someone."—"Who?"*
2 **CONJ** You use **who** in the part of a sentence before you talk about a person or a group of people. ❑ *Police have not found out who did it.*

3 **PRON** You use **who** to be specific about the person or group of people you are talking about, or to give more information about them. ❑ *...a woman who is 23 years old and has two children.* [from Old English]

who'd /huːd, hud/
1 **Who'd** is short for "who had." ❑ *I met someone who'd been waiting for three hours.*
2 **Who'd** is short for "who would." ❑ *Who'd like a coffee?*

who|ever /huɛvər/
1 **CONJ** You use **whoever** to talk about someone when you do not know who they are. ❑ *Whoever wins the prize is going to be famous for life.*
2 **CONJ** You use **whoever** to talk about any person. ❑ *You can have whoever you like visit you.*

whole /hoʊl/
1 **ADJ** You use **whole** when you are talking about all of something. ❑ *We spent the whole summer in Italy that year.*
2 **ADJ** If something is **whole**, it is in one piece and is not broken. ❑ *He took an ice cube from the glass and swallowed it whole.*
3 **PHRASE** **On the whole** means in general. ❑ *On the whole I agree with him.*
4 **PHRASE** If you refer to something **as a whole**, you are talking about it as a single thing, and not looking at its individual parts. ❑ *He said it was a victory for the people of South Africa as a whole.*
5 **PHRASE** The **whole of** something is all of it. ❑ *This is a problem for the whole of society.* [from Old English]

whole num|ber (whole numbers) N-COUNT
MATH A **whole number** is an exact number such as 1, 7, and 24, as opposed to a number with fractions or decimals.

whole|sale /hoʊlseɪl/
1 **N-NONCOUNT** BUSINESS **Wholesale** is the activity of buying and selling goods in large quantities and therefore at cheaper prices, usually to stores who then sell them to the public. Compare with **retail**. ❑ *Members can buy goods at wholesale prices.*
2 **ADV** BUSINESS If something is sold **wholesale**, it is sold in large quantities and at cheaper prices, usually to stores. ❑ *The goods are sold wholesale.*
3 **ADJ** You use **wholesale** to describe the destruction, removal, or changing of something when it affects a very large number of things or people. ❑ *...the company's*

wholesale reorganization.

who'll /hʊl, hul/ **Who'll** is short for "who will" or "who shall." ❑ *I need to talk to someone who'll listen.*

whol|ly /hoʊlli/ **ADV Wholly** means completely. ❑ *This is a wholly new approach.* [from Old English]

whom /hum/ **PRON Whom** is used in formal or written English instead of "who" when it is the object of a verb or a preposition. ❑ *The book is about her husband, Denis, whom she married in 1951.* ❑ *To whom am I speaking?* [from Old English]

whoop|ing crane /hupɪŋ kreɪn/ (**whooping cranes**) **N-COUNT** A **whooping crane** is a rare bird belonging to the crane family that lives only in North America.

who's /huz, huz/ **Who's** is short for "who is" or "who has." ❑ *Who's going to argue with that?* ❑ *Who's been using my cup?*

whose

> **PRONUNCIATION HELP**
> Pronounce meanings **1** and **2** /huz/.
> Pronounce meaning **3** /huz/.

1 PRON You use **whose** in questions to ask about the person that something belongs to. ❑ *"Whose is this?"—"It's mine."*

2 DET Whose is also a determiner. ❑ *Whose daughter is she?* ❑ *I can't remember whose idea it was.*

3 PRON You use **whose** when you mention something that belongs to the person or thing mentioned before. ❑ *That's the driver whose car was blocking the street.* [from Old English]

> **Usage** whose and who's
> *Whose* and *who's* are often confused. *Whose* expresses possession: *Are you the one whose cell phone kept ringing during class today? Who's* means *who is* or *who has*: *Who's calling you at this hour? Who's been calling you all night?*

who've /huv, huv/ **Who've** is short for "who have." ❑ *These are people who've never used a computer before.*

why

> **PRONUNCIATION HELP**
> Pronounce meanings **1** and **2** /waɪ/.
> Pronounce meanings **3** to **5** /waɪ/.

1 PRON You use **why** in questions when you ask about the reasons for something. ❑ *Why is she here?* ❑ *Why are you laughing?*

2 CONJ You use **why** at the beginning of a statement in which you talk about the reasons for something. ❑ *He wondered why she was late.*

3 ADV Why is also an adverb. ❑ *I liked him—I don't know why.*

4 ADV You use **why** with "not" in questions in order to introduce a suggestion. ❑ *Why not give Jenny a call?*

5 PHRASE You say **Why not?** in order to agree with a suggestion. ❑ *"Would you like to spend the afternoon with me?"—"Why not?"* [from Old English]

wick|ed /wɪkɪd/ **ADJ** If something or someone is **wicked**, they are very bad. ❑ *That's a wicked lie!* [from Old English]

wide /waɪd/ (**wider, widest**)

1 ADJ Something that is **wide** is a large distance from one side to the other. ❑ *The bed is too wide for this room.*

2 ADV If you open something **wide**, you open it as far as possible. ❑ *"It was huge,"* he announced, spreading his arms wide.

3 ADJ You use **wide** to talk or ask about how much something measures from one side to the other. ❑ *The lake was over a mile wide.*

4 ADJ You use **wide** to describe something that includes many different things or people. ❑ *The brochure offers a wide choice of hotels.* ● **wide|ly ADV** ❑ *...the most widely read newspaper in Hungary.* [from Old English]

Thesaurus	wide Also look up :
ADJ	broad, large; *(ant.)* narrow **1 3 4**

Word Partnership	Use **wide** with :
N	wide **grin/smile**, wide **margin**, wide **shoulders 1** arms/eyes/mouth open wide **2** wide **array**, wide **audience**, wide **selection**, wide **variety 4**

wid|en /waɪdən/ (**widens, widening, widened**)

1 V-T/V-I If you **widen** something, or if it **widens**, it grows bigger from one side or edge to the other. ❑ *They are planning to widen the road.*

2 V-T/V-I If you **widen** something, or if it **widens**, it becomes greater in range or it affects a larger number of people or things. ❑ *The search for the missing boy widened.* [from Old English]

w

wide|screen /waɪdskrin/ **ADJ** A **widescreen** television or computer has a screen that is wide in relation to its height.

wide|spread /waɪdsprɛd/ **ADJ** Something that is **widespread** happens over a large area, or to a great extent. ❏ *Food shortages are widespread.*

wid|ow /wɪdoʊ/ (**widows**) **N-COUNT** A **widow** is a woman whose husband has died. ❏ *She became a widow a year ago.* [from Old English]

wid|ow|er /wɪdoʊər/ (**widowers**) **N-COUNT** A **widower** is a man whose wife has died. [from Old English]

width /wɪdθ, wɪtθ/ (**widths**) **N-COUNT/N-NONCOUNT** The **width** of something is the distance from one side of it to the other. ❏ *Measure the full width of the window.*

wife /waɪf/ (**wives**) **N-COUNT** A man's **wife** is the woman he is married to. ❏ *He married his wife, Jane, 37 years ago.* [from Old English]
→ look at Picture Dictionary: **family**
→ look at Word Web: **love**

Wi-Fi /waɪfaɪ/
1 **N-NONCOUNT** TECHNOLOGY **Wi-Fi** is a system of using the Internet without being connected with a wire. ❏ *...products and services focused on linking Wi-Fi and mobile networks.*
2 **ADJ** TECHNOLOGY **Wi-Fi** is also an adjective. ❏ *Wi-Fi networks are becoming common in workplaces.*

wig /wɪg/ (**wigs**) **N-COUNT** A **wig** is a covering of artificial hair that you wear on your head.

wig|gle /wɪgʲl/ (**wiggles, wiggling, wiggled**) **V-T/V-I** If you **wiggle** something, or if it **wiggles**, it moves up and down or from side to side in small quick movements. ❏ *She wiggled her finger.* [from Middle Low German]

wi|ki /wɪki, -i-/ (**wikis**) **N-COUNT** TECHNOLOGY A **wiki** is a website that allows anyone visiting it to change or add to the material in it. ❏ *...wiki technology.* ❏ *Most wikis are collaborative websites.* [from Hawaiian]

wild /waɪld/ (**wilder, wildest**)
1 **ADJ** **Wild** animals or plants live or grow in nature, and people do not take care of them. ❏ *We could hear the calls of wild animals in the jungle.*
2 **ADJ** **Wild** land is natural and is not used

by people. ❏ *...a wild area of woods and lakes.*
3 **ADJ** **Wild** behavior is uncontrolled or excited. ❏ *The crowds went wild when they saw him.*
4 **ADJ** A **wild** idea is unusual or extreme. A **wild** guess is one that you make without much thought. ❏ *Go on, take a wild guess.* [from Old English]
→ look at Word Web: **carnivore**

Thesaurus	**wild** Also look up :
ADJ	desolate, natural, overgrown **2**
	excited, rowdy, uncontrolled **3**

Word Partnership	Use **wild** with :
N	wild **animal**, wild **beasts/creatures**, wild **game**, wild **horse**, wild **mushrooms 1**
	wild **pitch**, wild **swing 4**
V	**go** wild, **run** wild **3**

wil|der|ness /wɪldərnɛs/ (**wildernesses**) **N-COUNT** A **wilderness** is a desert or other area of natural land that is not used by people. ❏ *There will be no wilderness left on the planet within 30 years.* [from Old English]

wild|life /waɪldlaɪf/ **N-NONCOUNT** You can use **wildlife** to talk about the animals and other living things that live in nature. ❏ *The area is rich in wildlife.*
→ look at Word Web: **zoo**

wild|ly /waɪldli/
1 **ADV** If you do something **wildly**, you do it in an uncontrolled or excited way. ❏ *As she finished each song, the crowd clapped wildly.*
2 **ADV** If you guess **wildly**, you make a guess without much thought. ❏ *"Thirteen?" he guessed wildly.*
3 **ADV** You use **wildly** to emphasize the degree, amount, or intensity of something. ❏ *Milk costs twice what it should and meat is also wildly over-priced.* [from Old English]

will
1 MODAL VERB USES
2 NOUN USES

1 will /wɪl/

LANGUAGE HELP
When you are speaking, you can use the short forms **I'll** for **I will** and **won't** for **will not**.

1 **MODAL** You use **will** to talk about things that are going to happen in the future. ❏ *I'm sure things will get better.* ❏ *The concert will finish* *at about 10:30 p.m.* ❑ *One day I will come to visit you in Toronto.*

2 **MODAL** You use **will** when you are asking someone to do something. ❑ *Please will you be quiet?*

3 **MODAL** You use **will** when you offer to do something. ❑ *No, don't call a cab. I'll drive you home.* [from Old English]

→ look at Usage note at **shall**

❷ will /wɪl/ (**wills**)

1 **N-COUNT/N-NONCOUNT** Your **will** is the ability that you have to decide to do something difficult. ❑ *I have a strong will and I'm sure I'll succeed.*

2 **N-SING** If something is **the will of** a person or a group of people, they want it to happen. ❑ *This government seems to have ignored the will of the people.*

3 **N-COUNT** A **will** is a legal document that says who will receive your money when you die. ❑ *He left $8 million in his will to the University of Alabama.* [from Old English]

will|ing /wɪlɪŋ/

1 **ADJ** If someone is **willing**, they are happy about doing something. ❑ *She's willing to answer questions.* ● **will|ing|ly** **ADV** ❑ *Bryant talked willingly to the police.* ● **will|ing|ness** **N-NONCOUNT** ❑ *She showed her willingness to work hard.*

2 **ADJ** **Willing** describes someone who does something because they want to do it rather than because they are forced to do it. ❑ *He was a natural and willing learner.* [from Old English]

wilt /wɪlt/ (**wilts, wilting, wilted**) **V-I** If a plant **wilts**, it gradually bends downward and becomes weak because it needs more water or is dying. [from Middle Dutch]

win /wɪn/ (**wins, winning, won**)

1 **V-T/V-I** SPORTS If you **win** a competition, a fight, or an argument, you do better than

everyone else involved. ❑ *He does not have a chance of winning the fight.* ❑ *The four local teams all won their games.*

2 **N-COUNT** SPORTS **Win** is also a noun. ❑ *They played eight games without a win.*

3 **V-T** If you **win** a prize, you get it because you have done better than everyone else. ❑ *The first correct entry wins the prize.* [from Old English]

▶ **win over** If you **win** someone **over**, you persuade them to support you or agree with you. ❑ *Not everyone agrees but I am winning them over.*

Thesaurus	win	Also look up :
V	conquer, succeed, triumph; *(ant.)* lose **1**	
N	conquest, success, victory; *(ant.)* defeat **1**	

wind
❶ AIR
❷ TURNING

❶ wind /wɪnd/ (**winds**)

1 **N-COUNT/N-NONCOUNT** SCIENCE **Wind** is air that moves. ❑ *A strong wind was blowing from the north.*

2 **N-NONCOUNT** SCIENCE **Wind** energy or **wind** power is energy or power that is obtained from the wind.

→ look at Word Webs: **wind, beach, electricity, erosion, hurricane, storm**

Word Partnership	Use **wind** with :
ADJ	**cold** wind, **hot** wind, **howling** wind, **icy** wind, **warm** wind **❶ 1**
N	**desert** wind, **gust of** wind, **wind** power, **winter** wind **❶ 1**
V	wind **blows, blown/driven by the** wind, wind **whips ❶ 1**

❷ wind /waɪnd/ (**winds, winding, wound**)

1 **V-I** If a road **winds**, it has a lot of bends in it. ❑ *From here, the river winds through attractive countryside.*

Word Web   **wind**

The earth's surface **temperature** isn't the same everywhere. This temperature difference causes **air** to move from one area to another. We call this airflow **wind**. As warm air expands and rises, air pressure goes down. Then denser cool air **blows** in. The amount of difference in air pressure determines how strong the wind will be. It can be anything from a **breeze** to a **gale**. The earth's geography creates prevailing **winds**. For example, air in the warmer areas near the Equator is always rising, and cooler air from polar regions is always flowing in to take its place.

2 **v-t** When you **wind** something long around something else, you wrap it around it several times. ❑ *She wound the rope around her waist.*

3 **v-t** When you **wind** a clock or a watch, you turn part of it several times in order to make it work. ❑ *Did you remember to wind the clock?* [from Old English]

4 → see also **wound**

▶ **wind down** If someone **winds down** an activity, they start to reduce the amount of work that is done before stopping it completely. ❑ *Aid workers have begun winding down their operation.*

Thesaurus	**wind** Also look up :
N	air, current, gust **1** **1**
V	bend, loop, twist; *(ant.)* straighten **2** **2**

wind in|stru|ment /wɪnd ɪnstrəmənt/ (**wind instruments**) **N-COUNT** MUSIC A **wind instrument** is any musical instrument that you blow into to produce sounds.

wind|mill /wɪndmɪl/ (**windmills**) **N-COUNT** A **windmill** is a building with long flat parts on the outside that turn as the wind blows to make machinery move inside. **Windmills** are used for grinding grain or to pump water.

win|dow /wɪndoʊ/ (**windows**)

1 **N-COUNT** A **window** is a space in the wall of a building or in the side of a vehicle that has glass in it. ❑ *He looked out of the window.*

window

2 **N-COUNT** TECHNOLOGY On a computer screen, a **window** is one of the work areas that the screen can be divided into. ❑ *Open the document in a new window.* [from Old Norse]

Word Partnership	Use **window** with :
N	**car** window, window **curtains**, window **display**, window **screen**, **shop** window **1**
ADJ	**broken** window, **dark** window, **large/small** window, **narrow** window **1** **open** window **1** **2**
V	**look in/out** a window, **peer in/into/out/through a** window, **watch through a** window **1** **close/open a** window **1** **2**

wind|pipe /wɪndpaɪp/ (**windpipes**) **N-COUNT** SCIENCE Your **windpipe** is the tube in your body that carries air into your lungs when you breathe.

wind|shield /wɪndʃild/ (**windshields**) **N-COUNT** The **windshield** of a vehicle is the glass window at the front.

wind|shield wip|er /wɪndʃild waɪpər/ (**windshield wipers**) **N-COUNT** A **windshield wiper** is a part that wipes rain from a vehicle's front window.

wind|sock /wɪndsɒk/ (**windsocks**) also **wind sock** **N-COUNT** A **windsock** is a device, consisting of a tube of cloth mounted on a pole, that is used at airports and airfields to indicate the direction and force of the wind.

wind|surf|ing /wɪndsɜrfɪŋ/ **N-NONCOUNT** SPORTS **Windsurfing** is a sport in which you move across water on a long narrow board with a sail on it.

wind vane (**wind vanes**) **N-COUNT** A **wind vane** is a metal object on the roof of a building that turns around as the wind blows. It is used to show the direction of the wind.

windy /wɪndi/ (**windier, windiest**) **ADJ** If it is **windy**, the wind is blowing a lot. ❑ *It was a wet and windy day.* [from Old English]

wine /waɪn/ (**wines**) **N-COUNT/N-NONCOUNT** **Wine** is an alcoholic drink made from grapes. ❑ *...a bottle of white wine.* [from Old English]

wing /wɪŋ/ (**wings**)

1 **N-COUNT** The **wings** of a bird or an insect are the two parts of its body that it uses for flying. ❑ *The bird flapped its wings.*

2 **N-COUNT** The **wings** of an airplane are the long flat parts at the side that support it while it is flying.

3 **N-COUNT** A **wing** of a building is a part of it that sticks out from the main part. ❑ *Her office was in the west wing of the building.*

4 **N-PLURAL** ARTS In a theater, the **wings** are the parts to the left and right of the stage that the audience cannot see. ❑ *I watched the start of the play from the wings.* [of Scandinavian origin]

5 → see also **left-wing, right-wing**

→ look at Picture Dictionary: **insects**

→ look at Word Web: **bird**

wink /wɪŋk/ (**winks, winking, winked**)
1 **V-I** When you **wink at** someone, you look at them and close one eye quickly, usually as a sign that something is a joke or a secret.
2 **N-COUNT** Wink is also a noun. ❑ *I gave her a wink.* [from Old English]

win|ner /wɪnər/ (**winners**) **N-COUNT** The **winner** of a prize, a race, or a competition is the one that wins it. ❑ *She will present the prizes to the winners.* [from Old English]

win|ter /wɪntər/ (**winters**)
N-COUNT/N-NONCOUNT Winter is the season between fall and spring, when the weather is usually cold. ❑ *In winter the nights are long and cold.* ❑ *We had a lot of snow last winter.* [from Old English]

wipe /waɪp/ (**wipes, wiping, wiped**)
1 **V-T** If you **wipe** something, you rub its surface with a cloth to remove dirt or liquid from it. ❑ *I'll just wipe my hands.*
2 **N-COUNT** Wipe is also a noun. ❑ *The table's dirty—could you give it a wipe, please?*
3 **V-T** If you **wipe** dirt or liquid from something, you remove it by using a cloth or your hand. ❑ *Gary wiped the sweat from his face.* [from Old English]
▶ **wipe out** To **wipe out** something means to destroy it completely. ❑ *The disease wiped out thousands of birds.*

Word Partnership	Use wipe with :
ADJ	wipe *something* **clean** 1
N	wipe **blood**, wipe *your* **eyes**, wipe *someone's* **face**, wipe **tears** 2

wire /waɪər/ (**wires**) **N-COUNT/N-NONCOUNT** A **wire** is a long thin piece of metal. ❑ *Eleven birds were sitting on a telephone wire.* ❑ *...a wire fence.* [from Old English]
→ look at Word Web: **metal**

Word Link	less ≈ without : end*less*, hope*less*, wire*less*

wire|less /waɪərlɪs/ **ADJ** TECHNOLOGY **Wireless** equipment uses radio waves instead of wires. ❑ *I have a wireless Internet connection for my laptop.* [from Old English]
→ look at Word Web: **cellphone**

Word Link	dom ≈ state of being : bore*dom*, free*dom*, wis*dom*

wis|dom /wɪzdəm/ **N-NONCOUNT** Wisdom is the ability to use your experience and knowledge to make sensible decisions or judgments. ❑ *He has the wisdom that comes from old age.* [from Old English]

wise /waɪz/ (**wiser, wisest**) **ADJ** A **wise** person is able to use their experience and knowledge to make sensible decisions and judgments. ❑ *She's a wise woman.* ● **wise|ly** **ADV** ❑ *They spent their money wisely.* [from Old English]

wish /wɪʃ/ (**wishes, wishing, wished**)
1 **N-COUNT** If something is your **wish**, you would like it. ❑ *Her wish is to become a doctor.*
2 **V-T/V-I** If you **wish** to do something, you want to do it. [FORMAL] ❑ *I wish to leave a message.* ❑ *We can do as we wish now.*
3 **V-T** If you **wish** something were true, you would like it to be true, even though you know that it is impossible or unlikely. ❑ *I wish I could do that.*
4 **V-I** If you **wish for** something, you say in your mind that you want that thing, and then hope that it will happen. ❑ *Every birthday I closed my eyes and wished for a guitar.*
5 **N-COUNT** Wish is also a noun. ❑ *Did you make a wish?*
6 **V-T** If you **wish** someone luck or happiness, you express the hope that they will be lucky or happy. ❑ *I wish you both a good trip.*
7 **N-PLURAL** If you express your good **wishes** toward someone, you are politely expressing your friendly feelings toward them and your hope that they will be successful or happy. ❑ *Please give him my best wishes.* [from Old English]

Word Partnership	Use wish with :
V	wish **come true**, **get your** wish, **grant a** wish, **have a** wish, wish 1 4
N	wish *someone* **the best**, wish *someone* **luck** 5

wit /wɪt/
1 **N-NONCOUNT** Wit is the ability to use words or ideas in an amusing and clever way. ❑ *He writes with great wit.*
2 **N-PLURAL** Your **wits** are your ability to think quickly in a difficult situation. ❑ *She has used her wits to get to where she is today.* [from Old English]

witch /wɪtʃ/ (**witches**) **N-COUNT** In children's stories, a **witch** is a woman who has magic powers that she uses to do bad things. [from Old English]

W

witch-hunt (**witch-hunts**) **N-COUNT**
SOCIAL STUDIES When people organize a
witch-hunt, they try to find and punish
people that they think have a bad influence
on everyone else.

with /wɪð, wɪθ/
◼ **PREP** If one person is **with** another, they
are together in one place. ❑ *Her son and
daughter were with her.*
◻ **PREP** If you discuss something **with**
someone, or if you fight or argue **with**
someone, you are both involved in a
discussion, a fight, or an argument.
❑ *We didn't discuss it with each other.* ❑ *About a
thousand students fought with police.*
◻ **PREP** If you do something **with** a
particular tool, object, or substance, you do
it using that tool, object, or substance.
❑ *Turn the meat over with a fork.* ❑ *I don't allow my
children to eat with their fingers.*
◻ **PREP** If someone stands or goes somewhere
with something, they are carrying it.
❑ *A woman came in with a cup of coffee.*
◻ **PREP** Someone or something **with** a
particular feature or possession has that
feature or possession. ❑ *He was tall, with
blue eyes.*
◻ **PREP** If something is covered **with** a
substance, it has that substance on it.
❑ *His legs were covered with dirt.*
◻ **PREP** You use **with** when you are talking
about the way that something is done.
❑ *He listened with great care.*
◻ **PREP** You use **with** to talk about the
feeling that makes someone have a
particular appearance or type of behavior.
❑ *Gil was shaking with anger.*
◻ **PREP** You use **with** to indicate what a
particular state involves. ❑ *He has a problem
with money.* [from Old English]

with|draw /wɪðdrɔ, wɪθ-/ (**withdraws,
withdrawing, withdrew, withdrawn**)
◼ **V-T** If you **withdraw** something from a
place, you remove it or take it away.
[FORMAL] ❑ *He reached into his pocket and
withdrew a sheet of paper.*
◻ **V-T/V-I** When groups of people such as
troops **withdraw**, or when someone
withdraws them, they leave the place where
they are fighting and return nearer home.
❑ *The army will withdraw as soon as the war ends.*
◻ **V-T** If you **withdraw** money from a bank
account, you take it out of that account.
❑ *He withdrew $750 from his account.*

◻ **V-I** If you **withdraw from** an activity or an
organization, you stop taking part in it.
❑ *She's the second tennis player to withdraw from
the games.*

Word Partnership	Use **withdraw** with :
N.	withdraw **an offer**, withdraw
	support ◻
	decision to withdraw ◼–◻
	deadline to withdraw, **forces/troops**
	withdraw ◻
	withdraw **money** ◻

with|draw|al /wɪðdrɔəl, wɪθ-/
(**withdrawals**)
◼ **N-COUNT/N-NONCOUNT** The **withdrawal** of
something is the act or process of removing
it or ending it. [FORMAL] ❑ *...the withdrawal of
food and medical treatment.*
◻ **N-NONCOUNT** Someone's **withdrawal
from** an activity or an organization is their
decision to stop taking part in it. ❑ *...his
withdrawal from government in 1946.*
◻ **N-COUNT** A **withdrawal** is an amount of
money that you take from your bank
account. ❑ *I went to the cash machine to make a
withdrawal.*

with|drawn /wɪðdrɔn, wɪθ-/ **Withdrawn** is
the past participle of **withdraw**.

with|drew /wɪðdru, wɪθ-/ **Withdrew** is the
past tense of **withdraw**.

with|er /wɪðər/ (**withers, withering,
withered**)
◼ **V-I** If someone or something **withers**,
they become very weak. ❑ *Her right arm began
to wither as a result of the disease.*
◻ **V-I** If a flower or a plant **withers**, it dries
up and dies. ❑ *The tree withered all the way down
to its roots.* [from German]

with|hold /wɪðhoʊld, wɪθ-/ (**withholds,
withholding, withheld** /wɪðhɛld, wɪθ-/) **V-T**
If you **withhold** something that someone
wants, you do not let them have it. [FORMAL]
❑ *Police withheld the man's name until they could
tell his family about the accident.*

with|in /wɪðɪn, wɪθ-/
◼ **PREP** If something is **within** a place, an
area, or an object, it is inside it or
surrounded by it. [FORMAL] ❑ *The sports fields
must be within the city.*
◻ **PREP** Something that happens or exists
within an organization or a system happens
or exists inside it. ❑ *He is working within a*

W

system that doesn't allow him to make many changes. **3** **ADV** Within is also an adverb. ❑ *The real dangers came from within.*
4 **PREP** If you are **within** a particular distance of a place, you are less than that distance from it. ❑ *The man was within a few feet of him.*
5 **PREP** **Within** a particular length of time means before the end of it. ❑ *Within twenty-four hours I had the money.*

with|out /wɪðˈaʊt, wɪθ-/
1 **PREP** You use **without** to show that someone or something does not have or use the thing mentioned. ❑ *I prefer tea without milk.* ❑ *You shouldn't drive without a seat belt.*
2 **PREP** If one thing happens **without** another thing, the second thing does not happen. ❑ *He left without speaking to me.* ❑ *They worked without stopping.*
3 **PREP** If you do something **without** someone else, they are not in the same place as you are, or they are not involved in the same action as you. ❑ *I told Frank to start dinner without me.*

with|stand /wɪðˈstænd, wɪθ-/ (**withstands, withstanding, withstood**) **V-T** If something or someone **withstands** a force or an action, they survive it or do not give in to it. [FORMAL] ❑ *The building should withstand an earthquake.*

wit|ness /ˈwɪtnɪs/ (**witnesses, witnessing, witnessed**)
1 **N-COUNT** A **witness** is a person who saw a particular event such as an accident or a crime. ❑ *Witnesses say they saw an explosion.*
2 **V-T** If you **witness** something, you see it happen. ❑ *Anyone who witnessed the attack should call the police.*
3 **N-COUNT** SOCIAL STUDIES A **witness** is someone who appears in a court of law to say what they know about a crime or other event. ❑ *Eleven witnesses appeared in court.* [from Old English]
→ look at Word Webs: **trial, wedding**

wit|ti|cism /ˈwɪtɪsɪzəm/ (**witticisms**) **N-COUNT** A **witticism** is a witty remark or joke. [FORMAL] ❑ *They joked a great deal, and exchanged clever witticisms.*

wit|ty /ˈwɪti/ (**wittier, wittiest**) **ADJ** Someone or something that is **witty** is amusing in a clever way. ❑ *His books were very witty.* [from Old English]

wives /waɪvz/ **Wives** is the plural of **wife**. [from Old English]

wiz|ard /ˈwɪzərd/ (**wizards**) **N-COUNT** In children's stories, a **wizard** is a man who has magic powers.
→ look at Word Web: **fantasy**

wob|bly /ˈwɒbli/ **ADJ** Something that is **wobbly** is not steady and moves from side to side. ❑ *He sat on a wobbly plastic chair.* [from Low German]

woke /woʊk/ **Woke** is the past tense of **wake**. [from Old English]

wok|en /ˈwoʊkən/ **Woken** is the past aprticiple of **wake**. [from Old English]

wolf /wʊlf/ (**wolves**) **N-COUNT** A **wolf** is a wild animal that looks like a large dog. [from Old English]
→ look at Word Web: **carnivore**

> **Word Link** man ≈ human being : humane, mankind, woman

wom|an /ˈwʊmən/ (**women**) **N-COUNT** A **woman** is an adult female human being. ❑ *My favorite woman is my mother.* [from Old English]
→ look at Picture Dictionary: **age**
→ look at Usage note at **female**

womb /wum/ (**wombs**) **N-COUNT** SCIENCE A woman's **womb** is the part inside her body where a baby grows before it is born. ❑ *...an unborn child in the womb.* [from Old English]

wom|en /ˈwɪmɪn/ **Women** is the plural of **woman**. [from Old English]

wom|en's room (**women's rooms**) **N-COUNT** The **women's room** is a bathroom for women in a public building.

won /wʌn/ **Won** is the past tense and past participle of **win**.
→ look at Word Web: **election**

won|der /ˈwʌndər/ (**wonders, wondering, wondered**)
1 **V-T/V-I** If you **wonder** about something, you think about it, and try to guess or understand more about it. ❑ *I wondered what the noise was.* ❑ *"We've been wondering about him,"* said Max.
2 **N-SING** If it is a **wonder that** something happened, it is very surprising and unexpected. ❑ *It's a wonder that we're still friends.*
3 **N-NONCOUNT** **Wonder** is a feeling of great surprise and pleasure. ❑ *My eyes opened wide in wonder at the view.*

w

4 **N-COUNT** A **wonder** is something that causes people to feel great surprise or admiration. ❑ *He loved to read about the wonders of nature.*

5 **PHRASE** If you say **No wonder**, you mean that something is not surprising. ❑ *No wonder my brother wasn't feeling well.* [from Old English]

won|der|ful /wʌndərfəl/ **ADJ** If something or someone is **wonderful**, they are extremely good. ❑ *The cold air felt wonderful on his face.* ❑ *It's wonderful to see you.* [from Old English]

won't /wount/ **Won't** is short for "will not." ❑ *I won't hurt you.*

woo /wu/ (**woos, wooing, wooed**) **V-T** If you **woo** people, you try to encourage them to help you, support you, or vote for you, for example by promising them things that they would like. ❑ *They wooed customers with low prices.* [from Old English]
→ look at Word Web: **love**

wood /wʊd/ (**woods**)
1 **N-COUNT/N-NONCOUNT** **Wood** is the hard material that trees are made of. ❑ *Some houses are made of wood.*
2 **N-COUNT** A **wood** or **woods** is a large area of trees growing near each other. ❑ *We went for a walk in the woods.* [from Old English]
→ look at Word Webs: **energy, fire, forest**

wood|en /wʊdən/ **ADJ** **Wooden** objects are made of wood. ❑ *She sat in a wooden chair.* [from Old English]

wood|land /wʊdlənd/ (**woodlands**)
N-COUNT/N-NONCOUNT **Woodland** is land with a lot of trees. ❑ *...an area of dense woodland.*

wood|wind /wʊdwɪnd/ **N-NONCOUNT** MUSIC **Woodwind** instruments are the group of musical instruments that are mainly made of wood, that you play by blowing into them.

wool /wʊl/ (**wools**)
1 **N-NONCOUNT** **Wool** is the hair that grows on sheep and on some other animals.
2 **N-COUNT/N-NONCOUNT** **Wool** is a material made from animal's wool that is used for making things such as clothes. ❑ *The socks are made of wool.* [from Old English]

word /wɜrd/ (**words, wording, worded**)
1 **N-COUNT** LANGUAGE ARTS A **word** is a unit of language with meaning. ❑ *The Italian word for "love" is "amore."*

2 **N-SING** If you have **a word** with someone, you have a short conversation with them. [SPOKEN] ❑ *Could I have a word with you in my office, please?*
3 **N-SING** A **word** is something that you say. ❑ *John didn't say a word all the way home.*
4 **N-SING** If someone does **not** hear, understand, or say **a word**, they do not hear, understand, or say anything at all. ❑ *I can't understand a word she says.*
5 **V-T** To **word** something in a particular way means to use particular words to express it. ❑ *He worded his letter carefully.*
● **-worded** ❑ *...a strongly-worded speech.*
6 **PHRASE** You say **in other words** before you repeat something in a different way. ❑ *Ray is in charge of the office. In other words, he's my boss.*
7 **PHRASE** If you repeat something **word for word**, you say it using exactly the same words. ❑ *I learned the song word for word.* [from Old English]
→ look at Word Web: **English**

word rec|og|ni|tion **N-NONCOUNT** LANGUAGE ARTS **Word recognition** is the ability to recognize a written word and to know how it is pronounced and what it means.

wore /wɔr/ **Wore** is the past tense of **wear**. [from Old English]

work /wɜrk/ (**works, working, worked**)
1 **V-T/V-I** People who **work** have a job and earn money for it. ❑ *He worked as a teacher for 40 years.* ❑ *I can't talk to you right now—I'm working.* ❑ *They work forty hours a week.*
2 **V-I** If you **work**, you do an activity that uses a lot of your time or effort. ❑ *You should work harder at school.*
3 **V-I** If a machine **works**, it operates correctly. ❑ *My cellphone isn't working.*
4 **V-I** If a way of doing something **works**, it is successful. ❑ *Our plan worked perfectly.*
5 **V-T** If you **work** a machine, you use or control it. ❑ *Do you know how to work the DVD player?*
6 **N-NONCOUNT** Your **work** is the job that you do to earn money. ❑ *I start work at 8:30 a.m. and finish at 7 p.m.*
7 **N-NONCOUNT** **Work** is the place where you do your job. ❑ *I'm lucky. I can walk to work.*
8 **N-NONCOUNT** **Work** is any activity that uses a lot of your time or effort. ❑ *I did some work in the backyard this weekend.*
9 **N-COUNT** A **work** is a painting, a book,

W

or a piece of music that someone has produced. ❑ *My uncle bought me the complete works of William Shakespeare for Christmas.* ❑ *...a work of art.*

10 **N-NONCOUNT** SCIENCE In physics, **work** is the energy that is transferred to a moving object as the result of a force acting upon the object. [from Old English]

11 → see also **working**

→ look at Word Web: **factory**

▶ **work out** **1** If you **work out** a solution to a problem, you discover the solution by thinking. ❑ *It took me some time to work out the answer.*

2 If something **works out** at a particular amount, it is calculated to be that amount. ❑ *The price per pound works out to be $3.20.*

3 If a situation **works out**, it develops in a way that is good for you. ❑ *I hope everything works out for you in Australia.*

4 SPORTS If you **work out**, you do physical exercises in order to make your body healthy. ❑ *I work out at a gym twice a week.*

5 → see also **workout**

▶ **work up** **1** If you **work** yourself **up**, you make yourself feel very upset or angry about something. ❑ *She worked herself up into a rage.*
● **worked up** **ADJ** ❑ *Steve shouted at her. He was really worked up now.*

2 If you **work up** the enthusiasm or courage to do something, you succeed in making yourself feel it. ❑ *We could go for a swim, if you can work up the energy.*

Thesaurus	**work** Also look up :
V	labor **1** **2**
	function, go, operate, perform, run **3** **4**
N	business, craft, job, occupation, profession, trade, vocation; *(ant.)* entertainment, fun, pastime **6**

work|er /wɜrkər/ (**workers**)

1 **N-COUNT** **Workers** are people who work, who are below the level of a manager. ❑ *His parents were factory workers.*

2 **N-COUNT** You can use **worker** to say how well or badly someone works. ❑ *He is a hard worker.* [from Old English]

3 → see also **social worker**

→ look at Word Webs: **factory, union**

Thesaurus	**worker** Also look up :
N	employee, help, laborer **1**

work|force /wɜrkfɔrs/ (**workforces**)

1 **N-COUNT** BUSINESS The **workforce** is the

total number of people in a country or a region who are able to do a job and who are available for work. ❑ *Half the workforce is unemployed.*

2 **N-COUNT** BUSINESS The **workforce** is the total number of people who are employed by a particular company. ❑ *The company employs a very large workforce.*

work|ing /wɜrkɪŋ/ (**workings**)

1 **ADJ** **Working** people have jobs that they are paid to do. ❑ *Working women and men come to the evening classes.*

2 **ADJ** Your **working** life is the period of your life in which you have a job or are the right age to have a job. ❑ *He started his working life as a truck driver.*

3 **N-PLURAL** The **workings of** a piece of equipment, an organization, or a system are the ways in which it operates and the processes that are involved in it. ❑ *...computer systems which copy the workings of the brain.* [from Old English]

4 → see also **work**

work|ing class (**working classes**)

1 **N-COUNT** SOCIAL STUDIES The **working class** or **the working classes** are the group of people in a society who do not own much property, who have low social status, and who often do jobs that involve using physical skills.

2 **ADJ** **Working class** is also an adjective. ❑ *...a man from a working class background.*

work in|put (**work inputs**)

N-COUNT/N-NONCOUNT SCIENCE In physics, **work input** is the amount of effort that is applied to a machine in order to do work. Compare with **work output**.

work|out /wɜrkaʊt/ (**workouts**) **N-COUNT** SPORTS A **workout** is a period of physical exercise or training. ❑ *She does a 35-minute workout every day.*

→ look at Word Web: **muscle**

work out|put (**work outputs**)

N-COUNT/N-NONCOUNT SCIENCE In physics, **work output** is the amount of work that is done by a machine. Compare with **work input**.

work|place /wɜrkpleɪs/ (**workplaces**) also **work place** **N-COUNT** BUSINESS Your **workplace** is the place where you work. ❑ *This new law will make the workplace safer for everyone.*

W

work|shop /wɜrkʃɒp/ (**workshops**)

■ **N-COUNT** A **workshop** is a time when people share their knowledge or experience on a particular subject. ❑ *A music workshop for beginners will be held in the town hall.*

■ **N-COUNT** A **workshop** is a place where people make or repair things. ❑ *He works as a mechanic in the workshop.*

work|station /wɜrksteɪʃ°n/ (**workstations**) also **work station**

■ **N-COUNT** Your **workstation** is the desk and computer that you sit at when you are at work.

■ **N-COUNT** A **workstation** is a screen and keyboard that are part of an office computer system.

world /wɜrld/ (**worlds**)

■ **N-SING** GEOGRAPHY **The world** is the planet that we live on. ❑ *Scotland is a beautiful part of the world.*

■ **N-COUNT** Someone's **world** is their everyday life and experiences. ❑ *His world was very different from mine.*

■ **N-SING** A particular type of **world** is a particular field of activity and the people involved in it. ❑ *...the latest news from the movie world.*

■ → see also **Third World**

■ **PHRASE** If someone has **the best of both worlds,** they have the benefits of two things and none of the problems. ❑ *I have a lot of friends but I also have my career, so I have the best of both worlds.* [from Old English]

Word Partnership	Use world with :
PREP	**all over the** world, **anywhere in the** world, **around the** world ■
V	**travel the** world ■
N	world **history,** world **peace,** world **premiere** ■ world **of something** ■

world|wide /wɜrldwaɪd/

■ **ADV** If something exists or happens **worldwide,** it exists or happens throughout the world. ❑ *His books have sold more than 20 million copies worldwide.*

■ **ADJ** **Worldwide** is also an adjective. ❑ *They made $20 billion in worldwide sales last year.*

World Wide Web **N-PROPER** TECHNOLOGY **The World Wide Web** is a computer system that allows you to see information from all over the world on your computer. The short forms **WWW** and the **Web** are often used.

→ look at Word Web: **Internet**

worm /wɜrm/ (**worms**) **N-COUNT** A **worm** is a small animal with a long thin body, no bones, and no legs. [from Old English]

worn /wɔrn/

■ **Worn** is the past participle of **wear.**

■ **ADJ** **Worn** describes something that is damaged or thin because it is old and you have used it a lot. ❑ *There was a worn blue carpet on the floor.* [from Old English]

wor|ry /wɜri, wʌri/ (**worries, worrying, worried**)

■ **V-T/V-I** If you **worry,** you keep thinking about problems that you have or about unpleasant things that might happen. ❑ *Don't worry, I'm sure he'll be fine.* ❑ *I worry about her all the time.* ❑ *They worry that he works too hard.* ● **wor|ried** **ADJ** ❑ *He seemed very worried.*

■ **V-T** If someone or something **worries** you, they make you anxious because you keep thinking about problems or unpleasant things that might be connected with them. ❑ *"Why didn't you tell us?"—"I didn't want to worry you."*

■ **N-NONCOUNT** **Worry** is the state or feeling of anxiety and unhappiness caused by the problems that you have or by thinking about unpleasant things that might happen. ❑ *Modern life is full of worry.*

■ **N-COUNT** A **worry** is a problem that you keep thinking about and that makes you unhappy. ❑ *My parents had a lot of worries.* [from Old English]

Word Partnership	Use worry with :
N	**analysts** worry, **experts** worry, **people** worry ■
V	**begin to** worry, **don't** worry, **have things/nothing to** worry **about, not going to** worry ■

worse /wɜrs/

■ **Worse** is the comparative of **bad.**

■ **Worse** is the comparative of **badly.**

■ **PHRASE** If a situation changes **for the worse,** it becomes more unpleasant or more difficult. ❑ *My luck changed for the worse.* [from Old English]

→ look at Usage note at **worst**

wors|en /wɜrsən/ (**worsens, worsening, worsened**) **V-T/V-I** If a bad situation **worsens** or if something **worsens** it, it becomes more difficult, unpleasant, or unacceptable. ❑ *The weather was worsening.* [from Old English]

wor|ship /wɜ́rʃɪp/ (**worships, worshiping, worshiped**)

■ **V-T/V-I** If you **worship**, you show your respect to God or a god, for example by saying prayers. ❑ *He likes to worship in his own home.* ❑ *We talked about different ways of worshiping God.*

■ **N-NONCOUNT Worship** is also a noun. ❑ *This was his family's place of worship.*

■ **V-T** If you **worship** someone or something, you love them or admire them very much. ❑ *She worshiped him for many years.* [from Old English]

worst /wɜ́rst/

■ **Worst** is the superlative of **bad**.

■ **Worst** is the superlative of **badly**.

■ **N-SING The worst** is the most unpleasant thing that could happen or does happen. ❑ *Many people still fear the worst.* [from Old English]

> **Usage**   worst and worse
>
> *Worst* and *worse* sound very similar. You should avoid substituting one for the other in various expressions: *Emily's condition has changed for the worse; at the worst, she'll have to go to the hospital.*

worth /wɜ́rθ/

■ **ADJ** If something is **worth** a particular amount of money, you can sell it for that amount or you think that it has that value. ❑ *The picture is worth $500.*

■ **N-NONCOUNT** If you talk about a particular amount of money**'s worth of** something, you mean how much of it that you can buy for that amount of money. ❑ *I went and bought six dollars' worth of potato chips.*

■ **ADJ** If something is **worth** having, it is pleasant or useful, and a good thing to have. ❑ *He decided to see if the house was worth buying.*

■ **ADJ** If something is **worth** a visit, a look, or a try, or if it is **worth** doing, there is a good reason to do it. ❑ *This restaurant is well worth a visit.* [from Old English]

> **Word Partnership**   Use **worth** with :
>
> | N | worth **five dollars**, worth **a fortune**, worth **money**, worth **the price** ■
worth **the effort**, worth **the risk**, worth **the trouble**, worth **a try** ■ |
> | V | worth **buying**, worth **having** ■
worth **fighting for**, worth **remembering**, worth **saving**, worth **watching** ■ |

worth|less /wɜ́rθlɪs/ **ADJ** Something that is **worthless** has no value or use. ❑ *He had*

nothing but a worthless piece of paper. [from Old English]

worth|while /wɜ́rθwaɪl/ **ADJ** If something is **worthwhile**, it is enjoyable or useful, and worth the time, money, or effort that you spend on it. ❑ *The president's trip was worthwhile.*

> **Thesaurus**   worthwhile   Also look up :
>
> | ADJ | beneficial, helpful, useful;
(ant.) worthless |

wor|thy /wɜ́rði/ (**worthier, worthiest**) **ADJ** If a person or thing is **worthy of** something, they deserve it because they have the qualities or abilities required. [FORMAL] ❑ *She was a worthy winner.* [from Old English]

would /wəd, STRONG wʊd/

■ **MODAL** You use **would**, usually in questions with "like," when you are making a polite offer or invitation. ❑ *Would you like a drink?*

■ **MODAL** You use **would** with "if" clauses. ❑ *If I had more money, I would go traveling.* ❑ *Would it be all right if I opened a window?*

■ **MODAL** You use **would** when you are saying what someone believed, hoped, or expected to happen. ❑ *We all hoped you would come.*

■ **MODAL** You use **would** when you are talking about the result or effect of a possible situation. ❑ *It would be fun to learn to ski.*

■ **MODAL** You use **would** to say that someone was willing to do something. You use **would not** to say that they refused to do something. ❑ *He said he would help her.* ❑ *She wouldn't say where she bought her shoes.*

■ **MODAL** You use **would**, especially with "like," "love," and "wish," when saying that someone wants to do or have something. ❑ *She asked me what I would like to do.* ❑ *I'd love to have another baby.*

■ **MODAL** You use **would** to talk about something that someone often did in the past. ❑ *He would sit by the window, watching people go by.*

■ **MODAL** You use **would** or **would have** to express your opinion about something that you think is true. ❑ *I think you'd agree he's a very good singer.* ❑ *I would have thought he was too old to do that job.* [from Old English]

wouldn't /wʊ́dənt/ **Wouldn't** is short for "would not." ❑ *My parents wouldn't allow me to stay up late.*

W

would've /wʊdəv/ **Would've** is short for "would have." ❑ *I would've loved to go to the concert.*

wound (**wounds, wounding, wounded**)

> **PRONUNCIATION HELP**
>
> Pronounce meaning **1** /waʊnd/.
> Pronounce meanings **2** to **4** /wund/.

1 **Wound** is the past tense and past participle of **wind**.
2 **N-COUNT** A **wound** is damage to part of your body caused by a gun or something sharp like a knife. ❑ *The wound is healing nicely.*
3 **V-T** If a weapon or something sharp **wounds** you, it damages your body. ❑ *He killed one man with a knife and wounded five other people.*
4 **V-T** If you **are wounded** by what someone says or does, your feelings are deeply hurt. ❑ *He was deeply wounded by his son's comments.* [from Old English]

> | Word Partnership | Use **wound** with : |
> |---|---|
> | N | **bullet** wound, **chest** wound, **gunshot** wound, **head** wound **2** |
> | V | **die from a** wound, wound **heals**, **inflict a** wound **2** |
> | ADJ | **fatal** wound, **open** wound **2** |

wow /waʊ/ **INTERJ** You can say **Wow** when you think something is very good or surprising. [INFORMAL] ❑ *I thought, "Wow, what a good idea."* [of Scottish origin]

wrap /ræp/ (**wraps, wrapping, wrapped**)
1 **V-T** When you **wrap** something, you fold paper or cloth tightly around it to cover it.
2 **Wrap up** means the same as **wrap**. ❑ *Diana is wrapping up the presents.*
3 **V-T** When you **wrap** a piece of paper or cloth around another thing, you put it around it. ❑ *She wrapped a cloth around her hand.*
▶ **wrap up** **1** If you **wrap up**, you put warm clothes on. ❑ *She wrapped up in her warmest clothes.* ❑ *It'll be cold, so wrap up well.*
2 → see also **wrap** **2**

wrap|per /ræpər/ (**wrappers**) **N-COUNT** A **wrapper** is a piece of paper or plastic that covers something that you buy, especially food. ❑ *There were candy wrappers on the floor.*

wreck /rɛk/ (**wrecks, wrecking, wrecked**)
1 **V-T** To **wreck** something means to completely destroy or ruin it. ❑ *The storm wrecked the garden.*
2 **N-COUNT** A **wreck** is a ship, a car, a plane, or a building that has been destroyed, usually in an accident. ❑ *They discovered the wreck of a sailing ship.* [of Scandinavian origin]

wrench /rɛntʃ/ (**wrenches**) **N-COUNT** A **wrench** is a metal tool that you use for turning small metal nuts to make them tighter. [from Old English]
→ look at Picture Dictionary: **tools**

wres|tle /rɛsᵊl/ (**wrestles, wrestling, wrestled**) **V-I** SPORTS If you **wrestle** with someone, you fight them by trying to throw them to the ground. Some people wrestle as a sport. ❑ *My father taught me to wrestle.* [from Old English]

wrin|kle /rɪŋkᵊl/ (**wrinkles, wrinkling, wrinkled**)
1 **N-COUNT** **Wrinkles** are lines that form on your face as you grow old.
2 **V-T/V-I** If cloth **wrinkles**, or if someone or something **wrinkles** it, it gets folds or lines in it ❑ *Her stockings wrinkled at the ankles.*
● **wrin|kled** **ADJ** ❑ *His suit was wrinkled and he looked very tired.* [from Old English]
→ look at Word Web: **skin**

wrist /rɪst/ (**wrists**) **N-COUNT** Your **wrist** is the joint between your hand and your arm that bends when you move your hand. ❑ *She fell over and broke her wrist.* [from Old English]
→ look at Picture Dictionaries: **body, hand**

write /raɪt/ (**writes, writing, wrote, written**)
1 **V-T/V-I** When you **write**, you use a pen or a pencil to produce words, letters, or numbers. ❑ *Write your name and address on a postcard and send it to us.* ❑ *I'm teaching her to read and write.*
2 **V-T** LANGUAGE ARTS If you **write** a book, a poem, or a piece of music, you create it. ❑ *She wrote articles for French newspapers.*
3 **V-T/V-I** When you **write to** someone you give them information, ask them something, or express your feelings in a letter or an email. ❑ *She wrote to her aunt asking for help.* ❑ *I wrote a letter to the manager.* [from Old English]
4 → see also **written**
▶ **write down** When you **write** something **down**, you record it on a piece of paper using a pen or a pencil. ❑ *I wrote down what I thought was good about the program.*
▶ **write up** If you **write up** something that has happened, you write a report about it

using your notes. ❏ *He wrote up his visit in a report.*

| Word Link | *er, or ≈ one who does, that which does : astronomer, author, writer* |

writ|er /rˈaɪtər/ (**writers**)

1 **N-COUNT** LANGUAGE ARTS A **writer** is a person whose job is to write books, stories, or articles. ❏ *She enjoys reading detective stories by American writers.*

2 **N-COUNT** LANGUAGE ARTS The **writer** of a particular article, report, letter, or story is the person who wrote it. ❏ *J. K. Rowling is the writer of "Harry Potter."* [from Old English]

writ|ing /rˈaɪtɪŋ/

1 **N-NONCOUNT** **Writing** is something that has been written or printed. ❏ *Joe tried to read the writing on the next page.*

2 **N-NONCOUNT** LANGUAGE ARTS You can call any piece of written work **writing**, especially when you are considering the style of language used in it. ❏ *The writing is very funny.*

3 **N-NONCOUNT** LANGUAGE ARTS **Writing** is the activity of writing, especially of writing books for money. ❏ *She was bored with novel writing.*

4 **N-NONCOUNT** Your **writing** is the way that you write with a pen or a pencil. ❏ *It's difficult to read your writing.*

writ|ten /rˈɪtᵊn/

1 **Written** is the past participle of **write**.

2 **ADJ** A **written** piece of work involves writing something down. ❏ *...a short written test.* [from Old English]

wrong /rˈɔŋ/

1 **ADJ** If there is something **wrong**, there is something that is not as it should be. ❏ *Pain is the body's way of telling us that something is wrong.* ❏ *What's wrong with him?*

2 **ADJ** If you choose the **wrong** thing, person, or method, you make a mistake and do not choose the one that you really want. ❏ *He went to the wrong house.*

3 **ADJ** If a decision is **the wrong** one, it is not the best or most suitable one. ❏ *I made the wrong decision.*

4 **ADJ** If something is **wrong**, it is not correct. ❏ *I did not know if Mark's answer was right or wrong.*

5 **ADV** **Wrong** is also an adverb. ❏ *I must have added it up wrong.* ● **wrong|ly** **ADV** ❏ *He is an innocent man who was wrongly accused of stealing.*

6 **ADJ** If you are **wrong** about something, what you say or think about it is not correct. ❏ *I was wrong about the time of the meeting.*

7 **ADJ** If you say that something someone does is **wrong**, you mean that it is bad. ❏ *She was wrong to leave her child alone.*

8 **N-NONCOUNT** **Wrong** describes activities or actions that are considered to be morally bad. ❏ *He can't tell the difference between right and wrong.*

9 **PHRASE** If a situation **goes wrong**, it stops progressing in the way that you expected or intended, and becomes much worse. ❏ *We will do everything to make sure that nothing goes wrong.* [from Old English]

Thesaurus	**wrong** Also look up :
ADJ	incorrect; (*ant.*) right **4**
	corrupt, immoral, unjust **6**
N	abuse, offense, sin **7**

wrote /rˈoʊt/ **Wrote** is the past tense of **write**. [from Old English]

WWW /dˈʌbᵊlyu dˈʌbᵊlyu dˈʌbᵊlyu/ TECHNOLOGY **WWW** is short for **World Wide Web**. It appears at the beginning of website addresses in the form **www**. ❏ *Check our website at www.collinslanguage.com.*

W

xeno|pho|bia /zɛnəfoʊbiə/ **N-NONCOUNT**
Xenophobia is strong and unreasonable
dislike or fear of people from other countries.
[FORMAL] ❑ ...a tolerant society which rejects
xenophobia and racism. ● **xeno|pho|bic ADJ** ❑ The
man was obsessively xenophobic. [from Greek]

X-ray (**X-rays, X-raying, X-rayed**) also **x-ray**
1 **N-COUNT** SCIENCE **X-rays** are a type of
radiation that can pass through most solid
materials. X-rays are used by doctors to
examine the bones or organs inside your
body and are also used at airports to see
inside people's bags.
2 **N-COUNT** SCIENCE An **X-ray** is a picture
that is made by sending X-rays through
something, usually someone's body.
❑ She had a chest X-ray at the hospital.
3 **V-T** SCIENCE If someone or something **is
X-rayed**, an X-ray picture is taken of them.
❑ All hand baggage must be x-rayed. [from
German]
→ look at Word Web: **telescope**

xy|lem /zaɪləm, -lɛm/ (**xylems**)
N-COUNT/N-NONCOUNT SCIENCE **Xylem** is the
layer of material in plants that carries water
and nutrients from the roots to the leaves.
Compare with **phloem**. [from Greek]

xy|lo|phone /zaɪləfoʊn/ (**xylophones**)
N-COUNT MUSIC A **xylophone** is a musical
instrument with a row of wooden bars of
different lengths that you play with special
hammers. [from Greek]

Yy

yacht /yɒt/ (**yachts**) **N-COUNT** A **yacht** is a large boat with sails or a motor, used for racing or for pleasure trips. [from Dutch]

yam /yæm/ (**yams**) **N-COUNT/N-NONCOUNT** A **yam** is a vegetable that is similar to a sweet potato. ❑ *Peel and boil the yams, and then mash them.* [from Portuguese]

yank /yæŋk/ (**yanks, yanking, yanked**)
1 **V-T/V-I** If you **yank at**, or **yank**, someone or something, you pull them or it hard. ❑ *She yanked open the drawer.* ❑ *She yanked at the door.*
2 **N-COUNT** Yank is also a noun. ❑ *Shirley grabbed the rope and gave it a yank.*

Yan|kee /yæŋki/ (**Yankees**)
1 **N-COUNT** A **Yankee** is a person from the north or northeast of the United States.
2 **N-COUNT** Sometimes people use **Yankee** to talk about anyone from the United States of America. [from Dutch]

yard /yɑrd/ (**yards**)
1 **N-COUNT** MATH A **yard** is a unit for measuring length. There are 91.4 centimeters or 36 inches in a yard. ❑ *The bomb exploded 500 yards from where he was standing.*
2 **N-COUNT** A **yard** is a piece of land next to a house, with grass and plants growing in it.
3 **N-COUNT** A **yard** is a large open area where a particular type of work is done. ❑ *...a rail yard.* [from Old English]
→ look at Picture Dictionary: **measurements**

yard|stick /yɑrdstɪk/ (**yardsticks**) **N-COUNT** A **yardstick** is a stick that is one yard long, that is used for measuring things.

yarn /yɑrn/ (**yarns**) **N-COUNT/N-NONCOUNT** Yarn is thick cotton or wool thread. ❑ *She brought me a bag of yarn and some knitting needles.* [from Old English]

yarn

yawn /yɔn/ (**yawns, yawning, yawned**)
1 **V-I** If you **yawn**, you open your mouth very wide and breathe in more air than usual because you are tired. ❑ *She yawned, and stretched lazily.*
2 **N-COUNT** Yawn is also a noun. ❑ *Sophia woke and gave a huge yawn.* [from Old English]
→ look at Word Web: **sleep**

yeah /yɛə/ **INTERJ** Yeah means yes. [INFORMAL, SPOKEN] ❑ *"Don't forget your library book."—"Oh, yeah."* ❑ *"Anybody want my ice cream?"—"Um, yeah, sure."*

year /yɪər/ (**years**)
1 **N-COUNT** A **year** is a period of twelve months, beginning on the first of January and ending on the thirty-first of December. ❑ *The year was 1840.* ❑ *We had an election last year.*
2 **N-COUNT** A **year** is any period of twelve months. ❑ *Graceland has more than 650,000 visitors a year.*
3 **N-COUNT** A school **year** or academic **year** is the period of time in each twelve months when schools or colleges are open. The school

---

Word Web   year

The earth takes a **year** to orbit the sun. It is about 365 **days**. The exact time is 365.242199 days. To make years come out even, every four years there is a **leap year**. It has 366 days. The **months** on a **calendar** are based on the phases of the moon. The Greeks had a 10-month calendar. About 60 days were left over. So the Romans added two months. The idea of seven-day **weeks** came from the Bible. The Romans named the days. We still use three of these names: Sunday (sun day), Monday (moon day), and Saturday (Saturn day).

December

January

y

year starts in August or September.

4 **N-COUNT** BUSINESS A financial or business **year** is an exact period of twelve months that businesses use as a basis for organizing their finances.

5 **N-PLURAL** You use **years** to talk about a long time. ❏ *I lived here years ago.*

6 **PHRASE** If something happens **all year round** or **year round**, it happens for the whole year. ❏ *The hotel is open all year round.* [from Old English]

→ look at Word Web: **year**

year|ly /yɪərli/

1 **ADJ** A **yearly** event happens once a year or every year. ❏ *The company dinner is a yearly event.*

2 **ADV** **Yearly** is also an adverb. ❏ *Students may pay fees yearly or by semester.* [from Old English]

yeast /yist/ (**yeasts**) **N-COUNT/N-NONCOUNT** **Yeast** is the substance that makes bread rise. ❏ *Add the yeast to the flour in the bowl.* [from Old English]

→ look at Word Web: **fungus**

yell /yɛl/ (**yells, yelling, yelled**)

1 **V-T/V-I** If you **yell**, you shout loudly. ❏ *"Eva!" he yelled.* ❏ *I'm sorry I yelled at you last night.*

2 **N-COUNT** A **yell** is a loud shout. ❏ *I heard a yell and the sound of something falling.* [from Old English]

Thesaurus	**yell**	Also look up :

v   cry, scream, shout; *(ant.)* whisper **1**

yel|low /yɛloʊ/

1 **ADJ** Something that is **yellow** is the color of lemons or butter. ❏ *She was wearing a yellow dress.*

2 **N-NONCOUNT** **Yellow** is also a noun. ❏ *Her favorite color is yellow.* [from Old English]

→ look at Picture Dictionary: **color**

→ look at Word Web: **rainbow**

yel|low|ish /yɛloʊɪʃ/ **ADJ** Something that is **yellowish** is slightly yellow in color. ❏ *...a small yellowish cauliflower.*

yen /yɛn/ (**yen**) **N-COUNT** The **yen** (¥) is the unit of money used in Japan. ❏ *...2,000 yen.* [from Japanese]

yes /yɛs/

LANGUAGE HELP
In informal English, **yes** is often pronounced in a casual way that is usually written as **yeah**.

1 **INTERJ** You use **Yes** to give a positive answer to a question. ❏ *"Are you a friend of Nick's?"—"Yes."*

2 **INTERJ** You use **Yes** to accept an offer or a request, or to give permission. ❏ *"More coffee?"—"Yes, please."*

3 **INTERJ** You use **Yes** to tell someone that what they have said is correct. ❏ *"Well I suppose it's based on fact, isn't it?"—"Yes, that's right."*

4 **INTERJ** You use **Yes** to say that someone's negative statement or question is wrong or untrue. ❏ *"That is not possible," she said. "Oh, yes, it is!" Mrs. Gruen insisted.* [from Old English]

yes|ter|day /yɛstərdeɪ, -di/

1 **ADV** You use **yesterday** to talk about the day before today. ❏ *She left yesterday.*

2 **N-NONCOUNT** **Yesterday** is also a noun. ❏ *In yesterday's game, the Cowboys were the winners.*

3 **N-NONCOUNT** You can refer to the past, especially the recent past, as **yesterday**. ❏ *The worker of today is different from the worker of yesterday.* [from Old English]

yet /yɛt/

1 **ADV** You use **yet** when something has not happened up to the present time, although it probably will happen. ❏ *They haven't finished yet.* ❏ *They haven't yet set a date for their wedding.*

2 **ADV** You can use **yet** in questions to ask if something has happened before the present time. ❏ *Have they finished yet?*

3 **ADV** If something should not or cannot be done **yet**, it should not or cannot be done now, although it will have to be done at a later time. ❏ *Don't get up yet.* ❏ *You can't go home just yet.*

4 **ADV** You can use **yet** to say that there is still a possibility that something will happen. ❏ *This story may yet have a happy ending.*

5 **ADV** You can use **yet** when you want to say how much longer a situation will continue for. ❏ *Unemployment will go on rising for some time yet.*

6 **ADV** If you have **yet to** do something, you have never done it. ❏ *She has yet to spend a Christmas with her husband.*

7 **CONJ** You can use **yet** to add a fact that is surprising. ❏ *He's a champion tennis player yet he is very modest.*

8 **ADV** You can use **yet** when something is more extreme than previous things of its kind.

❏ *I saw yet another doctor.* [from Old English]
→ look at Usage note at **but**

yield /yi_ld/ (**yields, yielding, yielded**)

1 **v-t** If fields, trees, or plants **yield** crops, fruit, or vegetables, they produce them. ❏ *Each tree yields about 40 pounds of apples.*

2 **v-i** If you **yield**, you finally agree to do what someone wants you to do. ❏ *Finally, he yielded to his parents' demands.*

3 **v-i** If a driver **yields**, they slow down or stop in order to allow people or other vehicles to pass in front of them. ❏ *Drivers must yield to buses.* [from Old English]

Word Partnership	Use **yield** with :
ADJ	**annual** yield, **expected** yield, **high/ higher** yield **1**
N	yield **to pressure**, yield **to temptation** **2**
V	**refuse to** yield **2** **3**

yoga /yougə/ **N-NONCOUNT** SPORTS **Yoga** is a type of exercise in which you move your body into various positions in order to become more fit, and to relax your body and your mind. ❏ *I do yoga twice a week.* [from Sanskrit]

yogurt /yougərt/ (**yogurts**) also **yoghurt** **N-COUNT/N-NONCOUNT** **Yogurt** is a thick liquid food that is made from milk. ❏ *Frozen yogurt is $2 per cup.* [from Turkish]

yolk /youk/ (**yolks**)
N-COUNT/N-NONCOUNT
The **yolk** of an egg is the yellow part in the middle.
❏ *Only the yolk contains cholesterol.* [from Old English]

yolk

you /yu/

LANGUAGE HELP
You is the second person pronoun. **You** can refer to one or more people and is used as the subject of a verb or the object of a verb or a preposition.

1 **PRON** A speaker or writer uses **you** when they mean the person or people that they are talking to or writing to. ❏ *Hurry up! You are really late.* ❏ *I'll call you tonight.*

2 **PRON** In spoken English and informal written English, **you** can sometimes mean people in general. ❏ *Getting good results gives you confidence.* ❏ *In those days you did what you were told.* [from Old English]
→ look at Usage note at **one**

you'd /yud, STRONG yud/
1 **You'd** is short for "you had." ❏ *I think you'd*

better tell us what you want.
2 **You'd** is short for "you would." ❏ *You'd look good in red.*

you'll /yʊl, STRONG yul/ **You'll** is short for "you will." ❏ *Promise me you'll take care of yourself.*

young /yʌŋ/ (**younger** /yʌŋgər/, **youngest** /yʌŋgɪst/)

1 **ADJ** A **young** person, animal, or plant has not lived for very long. ❏ *There is plenty of information on this for young people.* ❏ *...a field of young corn.*

2 **N-PLURAL** The **young** are people who are young. ❏ *Everyone from the young to the elderly can enjoy yoga.*

3 **N-PLURAL** An animal's **young** are its babies. ❏ *You can watch birds feed their young with this wireless camera.* [from Old English]
→ look at Picture Dictionary: **age**
→ look at Word Web: **mammal**

Thesaurus	**young** Also look up :
ADJ	childish, immature, youthful; (ant.) mature, old **1**
N	family, litter **2**

youngster /yʌŋstər/ (**youngsters**) **N-COUNT** **Youngsters** are young people, especially children. ❏ *The children's club will keep the youngsters occupied.* [from Old English]

your /yɔr, yʊər/

LANGUAGE HELP
Your is the second person possessive determiner. **Your** can refer to one or more people.

1 **DET** You use **your** to show that something belongs or relates to the person or people that you are talking or writing to. ❏ *Are you taller than your brother?* ❏ *I left your newspaper on your desk.*

2 **DET** You can use **your** to show that something belongs or relates to people in general. ❏ *You should always wash your hands after touching raw meat.* [from Old English]

Usage	**your** and **you're**

Be careful not to confuse *your* and *you're*, which are pronounced the same. *Your* is the possessive form of *you*, while *you're* is the contraction of *you are: Be careful! You're going to spill your coffee!*

you're /yɔr, yʊər/ **You're** is short for "you are." ❏ *Tell him you're sorry.*

Y

yours /yɔrz, yʊərz/

> **LANGUAGE HELP**
> **Yours** is the second person possessive pronoun. **Yours** can refer to one or more people.

1 PRON You use **yours** when you mean something that belongs or relates to the person or people that you are talking to. ❑ *I believe Paul is a friend of yours.*

2 PHRASE People write **yours, yours sincerely,** or **yours truly** at the end of a letter before they sign their name. ❑ *I hope to see you soon. Yours truly, George.* [from Old English]

your|self /yɔrsɛlf, yʊər-, yər-/ (**yourselves**)

> **LANGUAGE HELP**
> **Yourself** is the second person reflexive pronoun.

1 PRON A speaker or writer uses **yourself** to mean the person that they are talking or writing to. ❑ *Be careful with that knife—you might cut yourself.*

2 PRON You use **yourself** to stress that you mean the person you are talking or writing to and not anyone else. ❑ *You don't know anything about it—you said so yourself.*

3 PRON If you do something **yourself** or **by yourself**, you, and not anyone else, does it.

❑ *Don't do all of that yourself—let me help you.*

youth /yuθ/ (**youths** /yuðz/)
1 N-NONCOUNT Someone's **youth** is the period of their life when they are a child, before they become an adult. ❑ *In my youth, my ambition was to be a dancer.*
2 N-NONCOUNT **Youth** is the quality or state of being young. ❑ *Youth is not an excuse for bad behavior.*
3 N-COUNT A **youth** is a young man. ❑ *A 17-year-old youth was arrested yesterday.*
4 N-PLURAL The **youth** are young people when they are considered as a group. ❑ *The youth of today are just as caring as we were.* [from Old English]

> **Word Partnership** Use **youth** with :
> N   youth **center**, youth **culture**, youth **groups**, youth **organizations**, youth **programs**, youth **services 4**

you've /yuv/ **You've** is short for "you have."
❑ *You've got to see it to believe it.*

yo-yo /yoʊ yoʊ/ (**yo-yos**) **N-COUNT** A **yo-yo** is a round wooden or plastic toy that you hold in your hand. You make it go up and down on a piece of string. [from Filipino]

yup /yʌp/ **INTERJ** **Yup** is a very informal word for yes. ❑ *"Are you ready to leave?"—"Yup!"*

Zz

zeb|ra /zĭbrə/ (**zebras** or **zebra**) **N-COUNT**
A **zebra** is a wild horse with black and white stripes that lives in Africa. [from Italian]

zen|ith /zĭnɪθ/ **N-SING** The **zenith** of a period of activity is the time when it is most successful or powerful. ❏ *His career is now at its zenith.* [from French]

zero /zĭərou/ (**zeros** or **zeroes**)
1 **NUM** MATH **Zero** is the number 0.
2 **N-NONCOUNT** SCIENCE **Zero** is a temperature of 0° C, at which water freezes. ❏ *...a few degrees above zero.*
3 **ADJ** You can use **zero** to say that there is not any of the thing mentioned. ❏ *He has zero personality.* [from Italian]
→ look at Word Web: **zero**

Thesaurus	zero	Also look up :
NUM	none, nothing **1** **3**	

zeros of a func|tion also **zeroes of a function** **N-PLURAL** MATH The **zeros of a function** are the points on a graph or in an algebraic expression at which the value of a mathematical function is zero.

zig|zag /zĭgzæg/ (**zigzags**) also **zig-zag**
N-COUNT A **zigzag** is a line that has angles in it like a series of Ws. [from French]

zinc /zĭŋk/ **N-NONCOUNT** SCIENCE **Zinc** is a blue-white metal. [from German]

zip /zĭp/ (**zips, zipping, zipped**) **V-T**
TECHNOLOGY When you **zip** a computer file, you use a special program to reduce its size so that it is easier to send it to someone using the Internet. ❏ *This is how to zip files so that you can send them via email.*
▶ **zip up** If you **zip up** a piece of clothing, you fasten it using its zipper. ❏ *He zipped up his jeans.*

zip code (**zip codes**) **N-COUNT** Your **zip code** is a short series of numbers at the end of your address that helps the post office to sort the mail.

zip|per /zĭpər/ (**zippers**)
N-COUNT
A **zipper** is a part of a piece of clothing or a bag that has two rows of metal or plastic teeth with a small part that you use to open and close it.
→ look at Picture Dictionary: **button**

zipper

zone /zoʊn/ (**zones, zoning, zoned**) **N-COUNT**
A **zone** is an area where something particular happens. ❏ *The area is a disaster zone.* [from Latin]
▶ **zone out** If you **zone out**, you stop being aware of what is happening around you, either because you are relaxed or because you are bored. ❏ *When I'm on the train, I put on my headphones and zone out.*

Thesaurus	zone	Also look up :
N	area, region, section	

Word Web   zero

The **number zero** developed after the other numbers. At first, ancient peoples used numbers for real objects. They **counted** two children or four sheep. Over time they moved from "four sheep" to "four things" to the concept of "four." The idea of a **place** holder like zero came from the Babylonians*. Originally, they wrote numbers like 23 and 203 the same way. The reader had to figure out the difference based on the context. Later, they used zero to represent the idea of null value. It shows that there is no amount of something. For example, the number 203 shows that there are 2 hundreds, no tens, and 3 ones.

Babylonians: people who lived in the ancient city of Babylon.

Word Web   zoo

In **zoos** people enjoy looking at animals. But zoos are important for another reason, too. More and more **species** are becoming **extinct**. **Zoos** help preserve **biological diversity**. They do this through educational programs, **breeding** programs, and **research** studies. One example is the Smithsonian National Zoological Park in Washington, DC. It trains **wildlife** managers from over 80 countries. The Wolong Reserve in China had a breeding program which produced over 35 **pandas** between 1991 and 2008. And the Tama Zoo in Hino, Japan, does research. It studies **chimpanzee** behavior. One **chimp** has even learned to use a vending machine.

zoo /zu/ (**zoos**) **N-COUNT** A **zoo** is a park where animals are kept and people can go to look at them. ❏ *He took his son to the zoo.* [from Greek]
→ look at Word Webs: **zoo, park**

zo|ol|ogy /zoʊɒlədʒi/ **N-NONCOUNT** SCIENCE **Zoology** is the scientific study of animals. ● **zoo|logi|cal** /zoʊəlɒdʒɪkəl/ **ADJ** ❏ *...zoological specimens.* ● **zo|olo|gist** /zoʊɒlədʒɪst/ (**zoologists**) **N-COUNT** ❏ *...a famous zoologist and writer.* [from Modern Latin]

zoom /zum/ (**zooms, zooming, zoomed**) **V-I** If you **zoom** somewhere, you go there very quickly. [INFORMAL] ❏ *Trucks zoomed past at 70 miles per hour.*
▶ **zoom in** ARTS If a camera **zooms in on**

something, it makes the thing seem closer. ❏ *The television cameras zoomed in on me.*

zoo|plank|ton /zoʊəplæŋktən/ **N-NONCOUNT** SCIENCE **Zooplankton** are tiny animals that live in water and are found in plankton. Compare with **phytoplankton**.

zuc|chi|ni /zukini/ (**zucchini** or **zucchinis**) **N-COUNT/N-NONCOUNT** **Zucchini** are long thin vegetables with a dark green skin. [from Italian]

zy|gote /zaɪgoʊt/ (**zygotes**) **N-COUNT** SCIENCE A **zygote** is an egg that has been fertilized by sperm and that could develop into an embryo. [from Greek]
→ look at Word Web: **reproduction**

Z

Contents

Brief grammar reference

SIMPLE PRESENT TENSE

A. With states, feelings, and perceptions

The simple present tense describes states, feelings, and perceptions that are true at the moment of speaking.

- The box *contains* six cans.   (state)
- Jenny *feels* tired.   (feeling)
- I *see* three stars in the sky.   (perception)

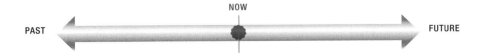

B. With situations that extend before and after the present moment

The simple present tense can also describe ongoing activities, or things that happen all the time.

- Tina *works* for a large corporation.
- She *lives* in California.
- Jim *goes* to San Francisco State University.

The simple present tense can also describe repeated activities that occur at regular intervals, including people's habits or customs.

- I *exercise* every morning.
- Peter usually *walks* to work.
- Anna often *cooks* dinner.

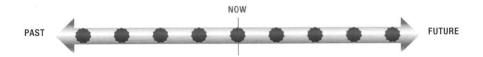

NOTE: Notice the adverbs of frequency *every morning*, *usually*, and *often* in these sentences. Other adverbs of frequency used this way include *always*, *sometimes*, *rarely*, and *never*.

C. With general facts

The simple present tense describes things that are always true.

- The Empire State Building *is* in New York City.
- The heart *pumps* blood throughout the body.
- Water *boils* at 100° Celsius.

D. With future activities

The simple present tense is sometimes used to talk about scheduled events in the future.

- The train *arrives* at 8:00 tonight.
- We *leave* at 10:00 tomorrow morning.
- The new semester *begins* in September.

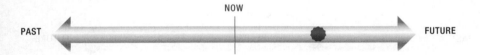

Present continuous tense

A. For actions that are happening right now

The present continuous tense describes an action that is happening at the moment of speaking. These activities started a short time before and will probably end in the near future.

- Ali *is watching* television right now.
- Frank and Lisa *are doing* homework in the library.
- It *is raining*.

B. For ongoing activities that aren't necessarily happening at this moment

The present continuous tense can describe a continuing action that started in the past and will probably continue into the future. However, the action may not be taking place at the exact moment of speaking.

- Mr. Chong *is teaching* a Chinese cooking course.
- We *are practicing* for the soccer championships.
- My sister *is making* a quilt.

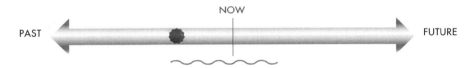

C. With situations that will happen in the future

The present continuous tense can also describe planned activities that will happen in the future.

- I *am studying* French next semester.
- We *are having* a party Friday night.
- Raquel *is taking* her driver's test on Thursday.

NOTE: The use of expressions like *next semester*, *Friday night*, and *on Thursday* help make it clear that the activity is planned and is not happening at the present moment, but will happen in the future.

SIMPLE PAST AND PAST CONTINUOUS

A. Simple past for one-time and repeated activities that happened in the past
The simple past tense can describe single or repeated occurrences in the past.
- I *saw* Linda at the post office yesterday.
- Alex *visited* Paris last year.
- We *played* tennis every day last summer. (repeated activity)

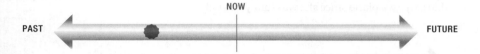

B. Past continuous for continuous actions in the past
The past continuous tense can describe ongoing activities that went on for a period of time in the past.
- Anna *was living* in Mexico.
- The baby *was sleeping*.
- Snow *was falling*.

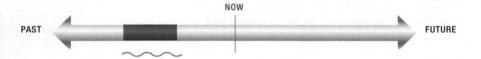

C. Simple past and past continuous to show a past action that was interrupted
The simple past tense can describe an action that interrupted an ongoing (past continuous) activity.
- I *met* Alice while I *was living* in New York.
- I *dropped* my purse while I *was crossing* the street.
- The phone *rang* while I *was studying*.

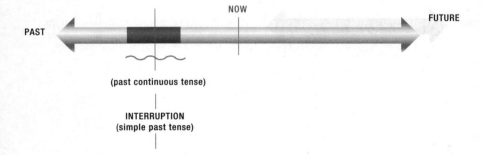

PRESENT PERFECT AND PRESENT PERFECT CONTINUOUS

A. Present perfect for actions or situations that started in the past and continue in the present and possibly the future

The present perfect tense describes an action that started in the past, continues up to the present, and may continue into the future.

- Lee *has collected* stamps for ten years.
- Carmen *has lived* in this country since 2009.
- Yukio *has played* piano since she was four years old.

B. Present perfect for experience in general, without mentioning when something occurred

The present perfect tense can show that something happened in the past and the results can be seen in the present.

- We *have caught* several big fish. (they are on the table/in the boat)
- Larry *has met* my family. (they know each other)
- I *have seen* that movie twice. (I can tell you the plot)

C. Present perfect continuous for ongoing actions that started in the past and continue in the present

The present perfect continuous tense describes an ongoing activity that went on for a period of time in the past and is still going on.

- It *has been raining* for three days. (it's raining now)
- The baby *has been crying* for ten minutes. (she is still crying)
- We *have been waiting* for the bus since 9:00. (we're still waiting)

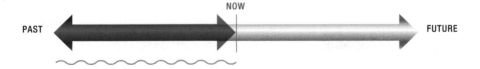

SIMPLE PAST VS. PRESENT PERFECT

A. **Simple past for situations that started and ended in the past vs. present perfect for things that started in the past but continue in the moment**
   The simple past tense describes an action that started and ended in the past, while the present perfect tense describes situations that started in the past but continue up to the present and maybe into the future.
   Past: John *worked* as a waiter for two years when he was in college.
   Present perfect: Carol *has worked* as an engineer since 2011.

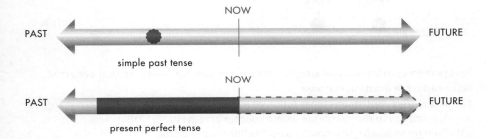

B. **Simple past to emphasize when something happened vs. present perfect to emphasize that something happened, without indicating when**
   The simple past emphasizes when something happened, and the present perfect emphasizes its impact on the present.
   Past: Peter *graduated* from college in 2011. (at a known point in the past: 2011)
   Present perfect: Alice *has graduated* from college, and is working in the city. (exactly when is unknown)

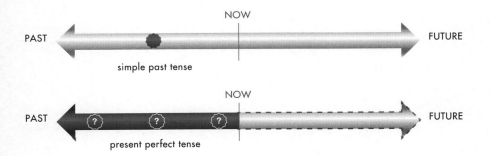

SIMPLE PAST, PAST PERFECT, AND PAST PERFECT CONTINUOUS

A. Past tenses with an activity that occurred before another activity in the past

Two simple past tenses are used to show a sequence of events in the past.

Simple past + simple past: Ali *said* goodbye before he *left*.

I *closed* the door and then *locked* it.

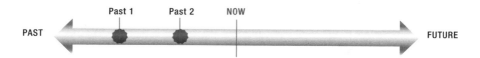

B. Past perfect continuous and simple past for a continuous activity that occurred before another event in the past

The past perfect continuous tense followed by the simple past tense shows that an ongoing activity in the past came before another past event.

- We *had been waiting* for two hours when the bus finally *arrived*.
- I *had been thinking* about the problem for days when the answer suddenly *occurred* to me.
- Terry *had been hoping* for the answer that he *got*.

FUTURE WITH *will* AND *going to*

A. Will or *going to* **for simple facts**
Either *will* or *going to* can be used to give information about the future. *Will* is used to give definite information.
   • Class *will start* in ten minutes.
   • The class *is going* to use a new textbook.
   • Your teacher *will be* Mr. Ellis.
   • There *is going to* be a final exam.

B. Will or *going to* **for prediction**
Either *will* or *going to* can be used to describe things that are likely to happen in the future. *Will* is used when there is evidence that things are likely to happen.
   • It *will rain* this afternoon.
   • You *are going to love* that movie!
   • They *are going to study* a lot the night before the final.
   • They *will* probably *stay up* all night.

C. Will **for promises**
Will is used to give a guarantee concerning a future action.
   • I *will be there* on time.
   • Your father and I *will pay for* your college education.
   • I *won't tell* anyone.
   • I *will save* you a seat.

D. Will **for decisions made at the time of speaking**
Will is used for decisions made at the time of speaking.
   • I *will help* you with your homework.
   • We're out of milk. I*'ll go* to the store on my way home.
   • I can't talk right now, but I*'ll call* you later.
   • Danny *will be* happy to wash your car.

MODALS *can*, *should/ought to*, *must*, AND *have to*

A. *Can* and *can't* for ability, permission, and requests
   Can and *can't* are used to:
   • make statements about things people are and are not able to do.
   • describe what people are allowed or not allowed to do.
   • make requests.

Can/can't for ability:	Alan *can swim* very well.
	I *can't run* very fast.
Can/can't for permission:	You *can leave* whenever you want.
	We *can't use* our dictionaries during the test.
Can/can't for requests:	*Can* I borrow your laptop?
	Can't you turn down the TV?

B. *Should* and *ought to* for advice and warnings
   Should and *ought to* are used to tell people what to do or what to avoid doing.

Should/shouldn't for advice/warnings:	What *should* I *do*?
	You *should ask* questions in class.
	You *shouldn't drive* so fast.
Ought to for advice/warnings:	You *ought to save* more money.
	He *ought to buy* some new clothes.

NOTE: *Ought to* is almost never used in questions or negative statements.
~~Ought I to go?~~   ~~You ought not see that movie.~~

C. *Must* and *mustn't* for rules and laws
   Must and *mustn't* are used in formal situations to show that something is necessary or prohibited.

Must for necessity:	My doctor told me that I *must lose* weight.
Must for obligation:	Swimmers *must shower* before entering the pool.
Mustn't for prohibition:	You *mustn't be* late to class.

Must and *mustn't* are not always opposites. *Needn't (need not)* expresses a lack of obligation to do something, whereas *mustn't* expresses an obligation not to do something.

D. *Have to* and *don't have to* for personal obligations
   Have to and *don't have to* are used in informal or personal situations to show that something is necessary or not necessary.

Have to for necessity:	I *have to call* my mother tonight.
	We *have to remember* to buy Jimmy a birthday present.
Don't/doesn't have to for lack of necessity:	
	You *don't have to return* the pen. You can keep it.
	Grandpa *doesn't have to comb* his hair. He doesn't have any.

MODALS *may*, *might*, *could*, AND *would*

A. *May* and *might* to discuss possibility and permission

May and *might* are used to describe future possibilities. *May* is used to give permission in formal situations.

May for possibility: We're not sure yet, but we *may leave* tomorrow.
                          The weather *may not be* good this weekend.

Might for possibility: I *might fly* to Florida this weekend, but I probably won't.
                          We both *might get* 100 on the test.

NOTE: Sentences with *might* are less definite than sentences with *may*.

May for permission: *May I call* you Jimmy?
                          You *may turn in* your paper Monday if it's not ready today.
                          No, you *may not have* my cell number.

Might for permission: I wonder if I *might leave* early.
                          When *might I need* to see the doctor again?

NOTE: *Can* also works in these sentences, but *may* is more polite and formal. Sentences with *might* are often indirect questions.

B. *Could* to show possibility, past ability, and to make requests

Could is used to indicate future possibilities, past abilities, and to ask for things.

Could for future possibilities: The dog *could have* six or seven puppies.
                                    The movie *could make* a million dollars if it's really popular.

Could for past ability: When I was six, I *could* already *speak* two languages.
                                    Tina *could walk* when she was only eight months old.

Could for requests: *Could* you *give* me the remote control?
                                    Could I *have* another cookie?

C. *Would* to ask permission and to make requests

Would is used to request permission and to ask for things.

Would to ask permission: *Would* you *mind* if I asked your age?
                                    Would he *mind* if I borrowed his book?

Would to make requests: *Would* you *give* me a ride home?
                                    · I *would like* two tickets for the 7:00 show.

Used to

A. *Used to* **for statements and questions about past habits or customs**
Used to shows that something that was true in the past is no longer true.

- Years ago, children *used to be* more polite.
- I *used to hate* broccoli, but now I like it.
- Children *didn't use to have* TVs in their bedrooms.
- Did girls *use to play* on high school football teams?

NOTE: When using the negative and question forms with *used to*, drop the past tense *-d* from the word *used*.

B. *Used to* **for repeated past events**
Used to also shows that something that happened regularly in the past no longer does.

- We *used to go* to the movies every Friday night.
- Taylor *used to visit* his grandmother every Sunday.
- I didn't *use to sleep* late on Saturday, but now I do.
- Did you *use to walk* home every day?

C. *Be used to* **for statements and questions about things people have become accustomed to**
Be used to statements and questions discuss how strange or normal something feels.

- Gail has lived in Chicago and New York. She *is used to living* in big cities.
- I have six brothers and sisters. I *am used to sharing* everything with them.
- Pete *isn't used to doing* homework every night.
- *Are* you *used to* drinking black coffee yet?

NOTE: When using the negative and question forms with *be used to*, don't drop the past tense *-d* from the word *used*.

D. *Get used to* **for statements and questions about becoming accustomed to something new**
Get used to statements and questions focus on the process of becoming accustomed to something.

- After three weeks, I *got used to* the noise outside my apartment.
- I *am getting used to* living with three roommates.

NOTE: The negative form of *get used to* usually employs the modal *can't* or *couldn't*.
    I *can't get used to* getting up at 6:00 a.m.
    Ellen *couldn't get used to* the cold weather in Chicago.

CONDITIONALS

A. Unreal conditions in the present

To describe a conditional situation that is unlikely to happen, use a past form in the conditional clause and the modal *would* or *could* in the main clause.

Conditional clause	Main clause
If I *had* enough money,	I *would buy* a boat.
If we *went* to Paris,	we *could visit* the Eiffel Tower.
If the traffic *got* any worse,	I *wouldn't drive* my car every day.
If Shelia *knew* the answer,	she *would tell* us.

B. Possible conditions in the future

To describe a conditional situation that is likely to happen, use a present form in the conditional clause and the future with *will* or the modal *can* in the main clause.

Conditional clause	Main clause
If I *have* enough money,	I *will buy* a boat.
If we *go* to Paris,	we *can visit* the Eiffel Tower.
If the traffic *gets* any worse,	I *won't drive* my car every day.
If Shelia *knows* the answer,	she *will tell* us.

C. Unreal conditions in the past

To describe a situation from a future point of view, use the past perfect in the conditional clause and *would have* + the past participle in the main clause.

Conditional clause	Main clause
If we *had known* it was raining,	we *would have taken* our umbrellas.
If Roberto *had been* home,	he *would have answered* the doorbell.
If you *had known* my grandmother,	you *would have loved* her.
If the movie *hadn't been* boring,	I *wouldn't have fallen* asleep.

D. Unreal conditions in the present

When discussing unreal conditions, the *if* clause is sometimes not stated; it is implied.

Conditional statement or question	Implied statement
I *would* never *borrow* money from a friend.	(if I had the opportunity)
Would you *want* to visit the moon?	(if you had the chance)
That *wouldn't work*.	(if you tried it)
Would he *borrow* your car without telling you?	(if he had the opportunity)

Passive voice

A. **Passive statements and questions with** *be* + **past participle**
The passive voice is used when it is not important (or we don't know) who performs the action. The passive can be used with any tense as well as with modals.

Sentence with passive voice	Verb form
The winner *was chosen* last night.	past tense
New cures *are being discovered* every day.	present continuous
Will the renovations *be finished* by next week?	future
Aspirin *should be taken* with a full glass of water.	modal *should*

B. **Passives with an agent**
To put the emphasis on the subject of the sentence and also tell who performed the action, use *by* followed by the agent at the end of the sentence.

- The missing girl was finally found *by her older brother*.
- The theory of relativity was discovered *by Albert Einstein*.
- The modern movie camera was invented *by Thomas Edison*.

C. **Passives with** *get*
In everyday speech, *get* instead of *be* is often used to form the passive. The verb *do* (instead of the verb *be*) is used for questions and negatives with the *get* passive.

- Most hourly workers *get paid* on Thursday or Friday.
- I *got caught* going 40 miles per hour in a 25 mile per hour zone.
- *Did* anyone *get killed* in the accident?
- Roger *didn't get hired* for the job.

REPORTED SPEECH

A. Shifting verb tenses in reported speech

When reporting someone's exact words, the verb in the noun clause usually moves back one tense. Only the past perfect tense remains the same in reported speech.

Exact quote	Reported speech	Change in verb tense
I *am* tired.	He said that he *was* tired.	Simple present to simple past
We *are waiting*.	They told me that they *were waiting*.	Present continuous to past continuous
I *finished* the book last night.	She said that she *had finished* the book the night before.	Simple past to past perfect
We *were enjoying* the good weather.	They reported that they *had been enjoying* the good weather.	Past continuous to past perfect continuous
I *have lived* here for two years.	He added that he *had lived* there for two years.	Present perfect to past perfect
We *had eaten* breakfast before we left the house.	They said that they *had eaten* breakfast before they left the house.	Past perfect remains the same

B. Shifting modals in reported speech

Many modals change form in reported speech.

Exact quote	Reported speech	Change in modal form
I *can speak* French.	She said that she *could speak* French.	*Can* to *could*
We *may need* help.	They said that they *might need* help.	*May* (for possibility) to *might*
You *may use* my pencil.	She said that I *could use* her pencil.	*May* (for permission) to *could*
I *must make* a phone call.	He said that he *had to make* a phone call.	*Must* to *had to*
We *will help* you.	They said that they *would help* me.	*Will* to *would*
I *should stop* smoking.	He said that he *should stop* smoking.	*Should* (no change)
We *should have left* at 9:00.	They said that they *should have left* at 9:00.	*Should have* (no change)
I *could have saved* money with a coupon.	She said that she *could have saved* money with a coupon.	*Could have* (no change)
She *must have gone* to bed early.	He said that she *must have gone* to bed early.	*Must have* (no change)

C. *Say* vs. *tell* **in reported speech**

The passive voice is used when it is not important (or we don't know) who performs the action. The passive can be used with any tense as well as with modals.

- When using *say* with reported speech, an object is not required. (Other verbs that work this way are *add*, *answer*, *explain*, and *reply*.)
- When using *tell* with reported speech, there is always a direct object. (Other verbs that work this way are *inform*, *notify*, *remind*, and *promise*.)

Exact quote	Reported speech	Direct object
It is raining.	He *said* that it was raining.	No
I was late to class.	She *explained* that she had been late to class.	No
I bought a camera at the mall.	He *told me* that he had bought a camera at the mall.	Yes
There is a test on Friday.	She *informed the students* that there would be a test on Friday.	Yes

COMPARATIVES AND SUPERLATIVES

Comparatives and superlatives have several different forms.

A. **With one-syllable adjectives and adverbs**

Add *-er* or *-est*.

Adjective / Adverb	Comparative / superlative form	Example
cold	colder	December is *colder* than November.
hard	harder	The wind blows *harder* in winter than in summer.
short	shortest	December 21 is *the shortest* day of the year.
fast	fastest	Summer passes *the fastest* of any season.

B. **With two-syllable adjectives ending in** *-y*

Change the *-y* to *-i* and add *-er* or *-est*.

Adjective / Adverb	Comparative / superlative form	Example
easy	easier	Yesterday's assignment was *easier* than today's.
busy	busiest	This is the *busiest* shopping day of the year.

C. With most adjectives of two or more syllables not ending in -y

Use *more* + adjective for comparatives and *the most* + adjective for superlatives.

Adjective / Adverb	Comparative / superlative form	Example
famous	more famous	Amy's Pizza is *more famous* than Bennie's Pizza.
frequent	most frequent	Amy's has *the most frequent* specials of any pizzeria.
expensive	more expensive	Bennie's Pizza is *more expensive* than Amy's.
delicious	most delicious	Bennie's makes *the most delicious* pizza in town.

D. Irregular comparatives and superlatives

Some adjectives and superlatives have irregular forms.

Adjective / Adverb	Comparative / superlative form	Example
bad	worse, worst	SUVs have *worse* safety records than sedans.
good	better, best	Sedans drive *better* than SUVs.
much	more, most	An SUV can carry *the most* people.
far	farther, farthest	A sedan can go *the farthest* on a tank of gas.

E. Comparisons with *as...as*

Use *as ... as* + adjective or adverb to describe things that are equal, and *not as ... as* + adjective or adverb to describe inequalities.

Adjective	Algebra was *as difficult as* geometry for me.
Adjective with negative	However, geometry was*n't as interesting as* algebra.
Adverb	I worked *as hard as* anyone else, but I got a C in algebra.
Adverb with negative	I did*n't* do *as well as* many other students.

INFINITIVES AND GERUNDS

A verb (or sometimes an adjective) near the beginning of a sentence determines whether a second verb form should be an infinitive or a gerund. Below are lists of some common main verbs (and adjectives) and the type of verb form that follows each.

NOTE: Each list contains several high-frequency items, but the lists are not comprehensive.

A. **Verb + infinitive**
   These verbs are followed by an infinitive, not a gerund: *ask, attempt, begin, decide, expect, hope, like, plan, promise, start*.
   I *attempted* <u>to start</u> the car.
   They *decided* <u>to stay</u> home last night.
   We *hope* <u>to save</u> at least $1000 by the end of the year.

   WRONG: She plans ~~giving~~ a party this weekend.

B. **Causatives + infinitives**
   When a person causes something to happen, the causative verb is followed by a direct object plus an infinitive, not a gerund. These causative verbs are followed by an infinitive: *allow, convince, encourage, get, force, persuade, require*.
   We *convinced* the teacher <u>to postpone</u> the test until Monday.
   The teacher *encouraged* us <u>to study</u> over the weekend.
   I *got* my brother <u>to help</u> me with the grammar.

   WRONG: The teacher required us ~~leaving~~ our dictionaries at home.

C. **Verb + gerund**
   These verbs are followed by a gerund, not an infinitive: *avoid, discuss, dislike, enjoy, finish, imagine, practice, quit, recommend, suggest*.
   The couple *discussed* <u>having</u> another child.
   The children *enjoy* <u>going</u> to the park.
   The couple *can't imagine* <u>having</u> four children.

   WRONG: They avoided ~~to talk~~ about it for a few days.

D. **Preposition + infinitive and preposition + gerund**
   An infinitive is the preposition *to* and the base of a verb: *to speak*. Gerunds can be used with other prepositions such as *about, at, for, in, of,* and *on*.
   I want *to go* on vacation in August.
   I never even think *about* <u>swimming</u> in the winter.
   This organization plans *on* <u>having</u> a fundraising drive.

   WRONG: They are responsible for ~~help~~ thousands of animals.
          The guests are sorry to ~~leaving~~ the party so early.

Writer's handbook

PUNCTUATION

Apostrophe
- The apostrophe + s is used with singular and plural nouns to show possession.

  Jim's computer my boss's file the children's toys

  the Smiths' house Peter Bridges' car [Only the apostrophe is needed when there is difficulty in pronouncing the word with 's]

- The apostrophe + s is used to show ownership.

  Pedro and Ana's CDs [The 's on the second name shows they own the CDs together.]

  Pedro's and Ana's hats [The 's on both names shows they each own different hats.]

- The apostrophe is used in contractions.

  I'm (= I am) they'll (= they will)

Brackets
- Brackets are used to add your own information in quoted material.

  Jason said, "This is a good time [meaning today] for us to start looking for a new apartment."

- Brackets with three dots are used when you omit words from a quotation.

  Jason said, "This is a good time [. . .] for a new apartment."

Colon
- The colon is used with clock time.

  11:30   9:45

- The colon is used to introduce a list.

  Jean enjoys all kinds of physical activity: hiking, playing tennis, and even cleaning house.

- The colon is used in the salutation of a business letter.

  Dear Ms. Mansfield:

Comma
- Commas are used with dates and addresses.

  Monday, December 1, 1964 16 Terhune Street, Teaneck, NJ 07666

- Commas are used after introductory phrases or clauses.

  After finishing school, she joined the Navy.

- Commas are used to set off items in a series.

  They served pizza, pasta, lasagna, and salad at the party.

- Commas are used to set off added information in nonrestrictive phrases or clauses.

  Mr. Karas, my sister's teacher, comes from Greece.

  Rita, who almost never misses class, is absent today.

- Commas are used in the salutation in informal correspondence and at the close of a letter.

  Dear Grace,   Sincerely yours,

Dash

- Dashes are used instead of commas when the added information contains commas. The school offers several math courses—algebra, geometry, and trigonometry—as well as a wide variety of science classes.

Exclamation Point

- An exclamation point is used after a word or group of words to show strong feeling. Stop! Don't run over that cat!

Hyphen

- Hyphens appear in compound words or numbers.
    mother-in-law   twenty-one
- Hyphens are used to divide words at the end of a line.
    After Mrs. Leander finished exploring all her options, she de-
    cided the best plan was to return home and start out tomorrow.

Parentheses

- Parentheses are used with nonessential information and with numbers and letters in lists.
    We left the party (which started at 7:00 P.M.) sometime after midnight.
    My requirements are (1) a room with a view and (2) a working air conditioner.

Period

- A period is used at the end of any sentence that is not a question or an exclamation.
    Rutgers University offers a wide variety of social science courses.

- A period is used after many abbreviations.
    Mr.   etc.   P.M.   Jr.   i.e.

Question Mark

- A question mark is used after a word or sentence that asks a question.
    What?   Did you say you don't have a ride home?

Quotation Marks

- Quotation marks are used to set off a direct quotation but not an indirect quotation.
    Smithers said, "Homer, you must go home now."
    Smithers said Homer must go home.

- Quotation marks are used with the titles of short written material such as poems, short stories, chapters in books, songs, and magazine articles.
    My favorite poem is "A Spider Sewed at Night" by Emily Dickinson.

Semicolon

- The semicolon is used to link independent clauses when there is no coordinating conjunction (such as *and, but, or, nor,* or *for*) between them.
    Some people like country music; some people don't.

- The semicolon is also used to link independent clauses before a conjunctive adverb (such as *however, furthermore*).

  Some people like country music; however, other people dislike it intensely.

Slash

- The slash separates alternatives.

  and/or
- The slash divides numbers in dates, and divides numerators and denominators in fractions.

  the memorable date 9/11/01   Ten and 50/100 dollars
- The slash is used when quoting lines of poetry to show where each line ends.

  My favorite lines from this poem are, "She slept beneath a tree / remembered but by me."

CAPITALIZATION

Capitalize proper nouns and proper adjectives.

- Main words in titles: Gone with the Wind
- People: John Lennon, Pelé
- Cities, nations, states, nationalities, and languages: Istanbul, Turkey, California, Brazil, American, Spanish
- Geographical items: Mekong River, Mount Olympus, Central Park
- Companies and organizations: Ford Motor Company, Harvard University, National Organization for Women
- Departments and government offices: English Department, Internal Revenue Service
- Buildings: the Empire State Building
- Trademarked products: Kleenex tissue, Scotch tape
- Days, months, and holidays: Tuesday, January, Ramadan
- Some abbreviations without periods: **USA, UN, YMCA**
- Religions and related words: Hindu, Bible, Muslim
- Historical periods, events, and documents: Civil War, Declaration of Independence
- Titles of people: Professor Jones, President Lincoln, Ms. Tanaka, Dr. Lee
- Titles of printed matter: COBUILD *Learner's Illustrated Dictionary of American English*

ITALICIZATION

In handwritten or typed copy, italics are shown by underlining.

Use italics for the following types of material.

- Words or phrases you wish to emphasize.

  Is this *really* your first time in an airplane?

  She feeds her dog *T-bone steak*. [It's best not to use italics for emphasis very often.]

- A publication that is not part of a larger publication.
  The Daily News (newspaper)
  The Sun Also Rises (book)
  Newsweek (magazine)
  Titanic (movie)

- Foreign words in an English sentence.
  The first four numbers in Turkish are *bir, iki, üc, dört.*
  The French have a saying: *Plus ça change . . .*

- Letters used in algebraic equations.
  $E = mc^2$

SPELLING

Frequently Misspelled Words

People sometimes confuse the spelling of the following words:

accept, except	conscience, conscious	lay, lie
access, excess	council, counsel	lead, led
advice, advise	diary, dairy	lessen, lesson
affect, effect	decent, descent, dissent	lightning, lightening
aisles, isles	desert, dessert	lose, loose
alley, ally	device, devise	marital, martial
already, all ready	discreet, discrete	maybe, may be
altar, alter	dyeing, dying	miner, minor
altogether, all together	elicit, illicit	moral, morale
always, all ways	emigrate, immigrate	of, off
amoral, immoral	envelop, envelope	passed, past
angel, angle	fair, fare	patience, patients
ask, ax	faze, phase	peace, piece
assistance, assistants	fine, find	personal, personnel
baring, barring, bearing	formerly, formally	plain, plane
began, begin	forth, fourth	pray, prey
believe, belief	forward, foreword	precede, proceed
board, bored	gorilla, guerrilla	presence, presents
break, brake	have, of	principle, principal
breath, breathe	hear, here	prophecy, prophesy
buy, by, bye	heard, herd	purpose, propose
capital, capitol	heroin, heroine	quiet, quit, quite
censor, censure, sensor	hole, whole	raise, rise
choose, chose	holy, wholly	respectfully, respectively
cite, site, sight	horse, hoarse	right, rite, write
clothes, cloths	human, humane	road, rode
coarse, course	its, it's	sat, set
complement, compliment	later, latter	sense, since

shown, shone	throne, thrown	were, wear, where, we're
stationary, stationery	to, too, two	which, witch
straight, strait	tract, track	who's, whose
than, then	waist, waste	your, you're
their, there, they're, there're	weak, week	
threw, through, thorough	weather, whether	

NOTE: The following summary will answer many spelling questions. However, there are many more rules and also many exceptions. Always check your dictionary if in doubt.

Ei **and** *ie*

There is an old saying that says: "I before *e*, except after *c*, or when pronounced like *ay* as in *neighbor* and *weigh*."

- I before *e*: br**ie**f, n**ie**ce, f**ie**rce
- E before *i* after the letter *c*: rec**ei**ve, conc**ei**t, c**ei**ling
- E before *i* when pronounced like *ay*: **ei**ght, w**ei**ght, th**ei**r

Prefixes

A prefix changes the meaning of a word but no letters are added or dropped.

- usual, **un**usual
- interested, **dis**interested
- use, **re**use

Suffixes

- Drop the final *e* on the base word when a suffix beginning with a vowel is added.
  drive, driv**ing**   combine, combin**ation**
- Keep the silent *e* on the base word when a suffix beginning with a consonant is added.
  live, live**ly**   safe, safe**ly** [Exceptions: truly, ninth]
- If the base word (1) ends in a final consonant, (2) is a one-syllable word or a stressed syllable, and (3) the final consonant is preceded by a vowel, double the final consonant.
  hit, hi**tt**ing   drop, dro**pp**ing
- Change a final *y* on a base word to *i* when adding any suffix except *-ing*.
  day, da**i**ly   try, tr**i**ed   BUT: deny, deny**ing**

GRAMMAR

Conjunctions

Conjunctions are words that connect words, phrases, or clauses.

Coordinating Conjunctions

The coordinating conjunctions are: *and, but, for, nor, or, so, yet*

- Sarah **and** Michael
- on vacation **for** three weeks
- You can borrow the book from a library **or** you can buy it at a bookstore.

Correlative Conjunctions

Correlative conjunctions are used in pairs.

The correlative conjunctions are: *both . . . and, either . . . or, neither . . . nor, not only . . . but also, whether . . . or*

- **Neither** Sam **nor** Madeleine could attend the party.
- The singer was **both** out of tune **and** too loud.
- Oscar **not only** ate too much, **but also** fell asleep at the table.

Subordinating Conjunctions

Subordinating conjunctions are used to connect a subordinate clause to a main clause.

- Antonia sighed loudly **as if** she were really exhausted.
- Uri arrived late **because** his car broke down.

Here is a list of subordinating conjunctions:

after	before	no matter how	than	where
although	even if	now that	though	wherever
as far as	even though	once	till	whether
as if	how	provided that	unless	while
as soon as	if	since	until	why
as though	in as much as	so that	when	
because	in case	supposing that	whenever	

Conjunctive Adverbs

Two independent clauses can be connected using a semicolon, plus a conjunctive adverb and a comma. The conjunctive adverb often comes right after the semicolon.

- Kham wanted to buy a car; **however,** he hadn't saved up enough money.
- Larry didn't go right home; **instead,** he stopped at the health club.

Some conjunctive adverbs can appear in different positions in the second clause.

- Kham wanted to buy a car; he hadn't, **however,** saved up enough money.
- Larry didn't go right home; he stopped at the health club **instead.**

Here is a list of conjunctive adverbs:

also	finally	indeed	nevertheless	then
anyhow	furthermore	instead	next	therefore
anyway	hence	likewise	otherwise	thus
besides	however	meanwhile	similarly	
consequently	incidentally	moreover	still	

Transitional Phrases

If all the sentences in a passage begin with subject + verb, the effect can be boring. To add variety, use a transitional phrase, followed by a comma, at the beginning of some sentences.

- Rita needed to study for the test. **On the other hand,** she didn't want to miss the party.
- Yuki stayed up all night studying. **As a result,** he overslept and missed the test.

Here is a list of transitional phrases:

after all	for example
as a result	in addition
at any rate	in fact
at the same time	in other words
by the way	on the contrary
even so	on the other hand

Common Prepositions

A preposition describes a relationship to another part of speech; it is usually used before a noun or pronoun.

- Sancho was waiting **outside** the club.
- I gave the money **to** him.

Here is a list of common prepositions:

about	by	out
above	concerning	outside
across	despite	over
after	during	past
against	down	regarding
among	except	round
around	for	since
as	from	through
at	in	to
before	inside	toward
behind	into	under
below	lie	unlike
beneath	near	until
beside	of	up
between	off	upon
beyond	on	with

Phrasal Prepositions

Here is a list of phrasal prepositions:

according to	by way of	in spite of
along with	due to	instead of
apart from	except for	on account of
as for	in addition to	out of
as regards	in case of	up to
as to	in front of	with reference to
because of	in lieu of	with regard to
by means of	in place of	with respect to
by reason of	in regard to	with the exception of

DOCUMENTATION

College instructors usually require one of three formats (APA, Chicago, or MLA) to document the information you use in research papers and essays. The following pages compare and contrast the highlights of these three styles.

APA Style (American Psychological Association style)

1. General Endnote Format

   Title the page "References." Double-space the page and arrange the names alphabetically by authors' last names, the date in parentheses, followed by the rest of the information about the publication.

2. Citation for a Single Author

   Moore, (1992). *The care of the soul*. New York: HarperPerennial.

3. Citation for Multiple Authors

   List the last names first followed by initials and use the "&" sign before the last author.

   Spinosa, C., Flores, F., & Dreyfus, H.L. (1997). *Disclosing new worlds: Entrepreneurship, democratic action, and the cultivation of solidarity*. Cambridge, MA: MIT Press.

4. Citation for an Editor as Author

   Wellwood, J. (Ed.). (1992). *Ordinary magic: Everyday life as a spiritual path*. Boston: Shambhala Publications.

5. Citation for an Article in a Periodical

   List the author, last name first, the year and month (and day if applicable) of the publication. Then list the title of the article (not underlined), the name of the publication (followed by the volume number if there is one) and the page number or numbers.

   Gibson, S. (2001, November). Hanging wallpaper. *This Old House*, 77.

6. Citation of Online Materials

   Provide enough information so that readers can find the information you refer to.
   Try to include the date on the posting, the title, the original print source (if any), a
   description of where you found the information, and the date you found the material.

   Arnold, W. (April 26, 2002). "State senate announces new tax relief." *Seattle Post-
   Intelligencer*. Retrieved May 1, 2002, from http://seattle.pi.nwsource.com/printer2/
   index.asp?ploc=b

7. General In-text Citation Format

   Include two pieces of information: the last name of the author or authors of the work
   cited in the References and the year of publication.
   (Moore, 1992).

Chicago Style (from *The Chicago Manual of Style*)

1. General Endnote Format

   Title the page "Notes." Double-space the page. Number and indent the first line of
   each entry. Use full authors' names, not initials. Include page references at the end of
   the entry.

2. Citation for a Single Author

   Thomas Moore, *The Care of the Soul* (New York: HarperPerennial, 1992), 7–9.

3. Citation for Multiple Authors

   Charles Spinosa, Ferdinand Flores, and Hubert L. Dreyfus, *Disclosing New Worlds:
   Entrepreneurship, Democratic Action, and the Cultivation of Solidarity* (Cambridge: MIT Press,
   1997), 66.

4. Citation for an Editor as Author

   John Wellwood, ed. 1992. *Ordinary Magic: Everyday Life as Spiritual Path* (Boston:
   Shambhala Publications).

5. Citation for an Article in a Periodical

   List the author, last name first. Then put the title of the article in quotation marks,
   the name of the publication, the volume number (if one is given), the year and the
   page number or numbers.

   Gibson, Stephen, "Hanging Wallpaper," *This Old House* 53 (2001): 77.

6. Citation of Online Materials

   Number and indent each entry and provide enough information so that readers can
   find the information you refer to. Try to include the author (first name first), the
   date on the posting (in parentheses), the title, the original print source (if any), a
   description of where you found the information, the URL, and the date you found the
   material (in parentheses).

1. William Arnold, "State Senate Announces New Tax Relief," *Seattle Post-Intelligencer*, April 26, 2002, http://seattle.pi.nwsource.com/printer2/index.asp?ploc=b

7. General In-text Citation Format

Number all in-text notes. The first time you cite a work within the text, use all the information as shown in 2. above. When citing the same work again, include only the last name of the author or authors and the page or pages you refer to.

(Moore, 8)

MLA Style (Modern Language Association style)

1. General Endnote Format

Title the page "Works Cited." Double-space the page and arrange the names alphabetically by authors' last names, followed by the rest of the information about the publication as shown below.

2. Citation for a Single Author

Moore, Thomas. *The Care of the Soul*. New York: HarperPerennial, 1992.

3. Citation for Multiple Authors

List the authors' names in the same order as on the title page. List only the first author's last name first.

Spinosa, Charles, Ferdinand Flores, and Hubert L. Dreyfus. *Disclosing New Worlds: Entrepreneurship, Democratic Action, and the Cultivation of Solidarity*. Cambridge: MIT, 1997.

4. Citation for an Editor as Author

Wellwood, John, ed. *Ordinary Magic: Everyday Life as Spiritual Path*. Boston; Shambhala, 1992.

5. Citation for an Article in a Periodical

List the author (last name first), the title of the article (using quotation marks), the title of the magazine (with no period), the volume number, the date (followed by a colon), and the page number.

Gibson, Stephen. "Hanging Wallpaper." *This Old House* 53 (2001): 77.

6. Citation of Online Materials

Provide enough information so that readers can find the information you refer to. Try to include the date on the information, the title, the original print source (if any), the date you found the material, and the URL (if possible).

1. Arnold, William. "State Senate Announces New Tax Relief." *Seattle Post-Intelligencer* 26 Apr. 2002 http://seattle.pi.nwsource.com/printer2/index.asp?ploc=b

7. General In-text Citation Format

Do not number entries. When citing a work listed in the "Works Cited" section, include only the last name of the author or authors and the page or pages you refer to. (Moore 7-8)

BLOCK LETTER FORMAT

Using the block letter format, there are no indented lines.

Return address	77 Lincoln Avenue Wellesley, MA 02480
Date	May 10, 2015
Inside address	Dr. Rita Bennett Midland Hospital Senior Care Center 5000 Poe Avenue Dayton, OH 45414
Salutation	Dear Dr. Bennett:
Body of the letter	I am responding to your advertisement for a dietitian in the May 5 edition of the *New York Times*. I graduated from Boston University two years ago. Since graduation, I have been working at Brigham and Women's Hospital and have also earned additional certificates in nutritional support and diabetes education. I am interested in locating to the Midwest and will be happy to arrange for an interview at your convenience.
Complimentary close	Sincerely,
Signature	*Daniel Chin*
Typed name	Daniel Chin

INDENTED LETTER FORMAT

Using the indented format, the return address, the date, and the closing appear at the far right side of the paper. The first line of each paragraph is also indented.

Return address	77 Lincoln Avenue Wellesley, MA 02480
Date	May 15, 2015
Inside address	Dr. Rita Bennett Senior Care Center 5000 Poe Avenue Dayton, OH 45414
Salutation	Dear Dr. Bennett:
Body of the letter	It was a pleasure to meet you and learn more about the programs offered at the Senior Care Center. I appreciate your taking time out to show me around and introduce me to the staff. I am excited about the possibility of working at the Senior Care Center and I look forward to talking with you again soon.
Complimentary close	Sincerely,
Signature	*Daniel Chin*
Typed name	Daniel Chin

RESUMES

Successful resume strategies

- **Length:** One page
- **Honesty:** Never say something that is untrue
- **Inclusiveness:** Include information about your experience and qualifications. You do not have to include your age, religion, marital status, race, or citizenship. It is not necessary to include a photo.

Heading
Include name, address, e-mail, and phone number.

Objective
Include your goals or skills or both.

Skills
Include any skills that you have that may be helpful in the job that you are applying for.

Experience
Describe the jobs you've held. Include your accomplishments and awards. Use positive, action-oriented words with strong verbs. Use present-tense verbs for your current job and past-tense verbs for jobs you've had in the past. Include the job titles that you've held.

Education
Include schools attended. If you are a college graduate, don't include high school. List degrees with most recent first.

Interests
This is not required, but can help a potential employer see you as a well-rounded person.

Sample Resume
There are several different acceptable resume formats. Here is one example.

Maria Gonzales
9166 Main Street, Apartment 3G
Los Angeles, CA 93001
gonzales@email.com
213-555-9878

OBJECTIVE: Experienced manager seeks a management position in retail sales

EXPERIENCE:

Assistant Director of Retail

2011 – Present	Shopmart, Los Angeles, CA
	Manage relationships with vendors to complete orders, create accounts, and resolve issues. Maintain inventory and generate monthly inventory reports. Plan weekly promotions. Communicate with all retail employees to improve product knowledge and selling techniques. Implemented new customer service procedures.

Server

2011 – Present	Chuy's Grill, Santa Monica, CA
	Greet and seat guests. Bus tables. Answer phones and take and prepare in-house, phone, or fax orders. Train new and existing employees. Awarded Employee of the Month five times for exceeding company expectations for quality and service.

Store Supervisor

2005 – 2011	Impact Photography Systems, Waco, TX
	Oversaw daily operations, including customer and employee relations, counter sales, inventory management, maintaining store appearance, banking transactions, and equipment maintenance. Managed, trained, and scheduled staff of 35.

SKILLS: Fluent in English and Spanish. Expert in MS Word and Excel.

EDUCATION:

Associate of Arts Degree

2002 – 2006	Los Angeles Community College, Los Angeles, CA
	Coursework in business management, marketing, studio art, communication, psychology, and sociology.

Study Abroad

2004 – 2005	University of Valencia, Valencia, Spain
	Coursework in Spanish and international business.

INTERESTS: Backpacking, playing softball, and volunteering as a tutor for Literacy First.

PROOFREADING MARKS

Teachers often use the following correction abbreviations and symbols on students' papers.

Problem area	Symbol	Example
agreement	**agr**	He **go** to work at 8:00.
capital letters	**cap**	the United ṣtates
word division or hyphenation	**div** **hy**	disorientati -on
sentence fragment	**frag**	**Where she found the book.**
grammar	**gr**	It's the **bigger** house on the street.
need italics	**ital**	I read it in **The Daily News.**
need lower case	**lc**	I don't like Peanut Butter.
punctuation error	**p**	Where did you find that coat.
plural needed	**pl**	I bought the **grocery** on my way home.
spelling error	**sp**	Did you recieve my letter yet?
wrong tense	**t**	I **see** her yesterday.
wrong word	**ww**	My family used to **rise** corn and wheat.
need an apostrophe	⌵	I **don**⌵**t** know her name.
need a comma	⌄	However⌄we will probably arrive on time.
delete something	ℓ	We had the most best meal of our lives.
start a new paragraph	¶	... since last Friday. ¶ Oh, by the way ...
transpose words	⌢	They live on the floor first.

Speaker's handbook

1. GREETINGS, INTRODUCTIONS, AND LEAVE-TAKING

Greeting someone you know

Hello.

Hi.

Hey.

Morning.

How's it going?   [Informal]

What's up?   [Informal]

Greeting someone you haven't seen for a while

It's good to see you again.

It's been a long time.

How long has it been?

Long time no see!   [Informal]

You look great!   [Informal]

So what have you been up to?   [Informal]

Greeting someone you don't know

Hello.

Good morning.

Good afternoon.

Good evening.

Hi, there!   [Informal]

Saying goodbye

Goodbye.

Bye.

Bye-bye.

See you.

See you later.

Have a good day.

Take care.

Good night. [Only when saying goodbye]

Introducing yourself

Hi, I'm Tom.

Hello, my name is Tom.

Excuse me.

We haven't met.

My name is Tom.   [Formal]

I saw you in (science) class.

I met you at Jane's party.

Introducing other people

Have you two met?

Have you met Maria?

I'd like you to meet Maria.

There's someone I'd like you to meet.

Let me introduce you to Maria.

> **You:** This is my friend Maria.
> **Ali:** Glad to meet you, Maria.
> **You:** Maria, this is Ali.
> **Maria:** Nice to meet you, Ali.

I've been wanting to meet you.

Tom has told me a lot about you.

Greeting guests

Welcome.

Oh, hi.

How are you?

Please come in.

Glad you could make it.

Did you have any trouble finding us?

Can I take your coat?

Have a seat.

Please make yourself at home.

> **You:** Can I get you something to drink?
> **Guest:** Yes, please.
> **You:** What would you like?
> **Guest:** I'll have some orange juice.

What can I get you to drink?

Would you like some . . . ?

Saying goodbye to guests

Thanks for coming.

Thanks for joining us.

I'm so glad you could come.

It wouldn't have been the same without you.

Let me get your things.

Stop by anytime.

2. HAVING A CONVERSATION

Starting a conversation
Nice weather, huh?
Aren't you a friend of Jim's?
Did you see last night's game?
What's your favorite TV show?
So, what do you think about (the situation in Europe)?
So how do you like (your new car)?
Guess what I did last night.

Showing that you are listening
Uh-huh.
Right.
Exactly.
Yeah.
OK . . .
I know what you mean.

Giving yourself time to think
Well . . .
Um . . .
Uh . . .
Let me think.
Just a minute.

> **Other:** We should ride our bikes.
> **You:** It's too far. And, I mean . . . ,
> it's raining and we're already
> late.

Checking for comprehension
Do you see what I mean?
Are you with me?
Does that make sense?

Checking for agreement
Don't you agree?
So what do you think?
We have to (act fast), you know?

Expressing agreement
You're right.
I couldn't agree with you more.
Good thinking! [Informal]
Yeah! [Informal]
You're absolutely right.
Absolutely! [Informal]

Expressing disagreement
I'm afraid I disagree.
I'm not sure I agree.
Yeah, but . . .
I see your point, but . . .
That's not true.
You must be kidding! [Informal]
No way! [Informal]

Asking someone to repeat something
Excuse me?
Sorry?
I didn't quite get that.
Could you repeat that?
Could you say that again?
Say again? [Informal]

Interrupting someone
Excuse me.
Yes, but (we don't have enough time).
I know, but (that will take hours).
Wait a minute. [Informal]
Just hold it right there! [Impolite]

Changing the topic
By the way, what do you think about (the new teacher)?
Before I forget, (are you free later?).
Whatever . . . (Did you see David's new car?) [Impolite]
Enough about me. Let's talk about you.

Ending a conversation
It was nice talking with you.
Good seeing you.
Sorry, I have to go now.

3. USING THE PHONE

Making personal calls
Hi, this is David.
Hi, Alice, it's David.
Is this Alice?
Is Alice there?
May I speak with Alice, please?   [Formal]
We're in the same science class.
Could you tell her I called?
Would you ask her to call me?

Answering personal calls
Hello?
Who's calling, please?
Oh, hi David. How are you?
I can't hear you.
Sorry, we got cut off.
Can I call you back?
What's your number again?
It was nice talking to you.

Using a cellphone
Did you get my text?
Text me later.
I was in class so I had my phone switched off.
Sorry, I had my phone on silent.
The connection's not very good.

Voicemail or answering machine greetings
You've reached 212-555-6701.
Please leave a message after the beep.
Hi, this is Carlos.
I can't take your call right now.
Sorry I missed your call.
Please leave your name and number.
I'll call you back as soon as I can.

Voicemail or answering machine greetings
This is Magda. Call me back when you
   get a chance.   [Informal]
Call me back on my cell.
I'll call you back later.
If you get this message before 11:00, please
   call me back.

Making business calls
Hello. This is Andy Larson.
I'm calling about . . .
Is this an OK time?

Answering business calls
Apex Electronics. Rosa Baker speaking.
   [Formal]
Hello, Rosa Baker.
May I help you?
Who's calling, please?

| Caller: | May I speak with Mr. Hafner, please? |
| Businessperson: | This is he. |

| Caller: | Mr. Hafner, please. |
| Businessperson: | Speaking. |

Talking to an office assistant
Extension 716, please.
Customer Service, please.
May I speak with Sheila Spink, please?
She's expecting my call.
I'm returning her call.
I'd like to leave a message for Ms. Spink.

Making appointments on the phone

You:	I'd like to make an appointment to see Ms. Spink.
Assistant:	How's 11:00 on Wednesday?
You:	Wednesday is really bad for me.
Assistant:	Can you make it Thursday at 9:00?
You:	That would be perfect!
Assistant:	OK. I have you down for Thursday at 9:00.

Special explanations
I'm sorry. She's not available.
Is there something I can help you with?
Can I put you on hold?
I'll transfer you to that extension.
If you'll leave your number, I'll have Ms. Spink
   call you back.
I'll tell her you called.

4. INTERVIEWING FOR A JOB

Small talk by the interviewer
Thanks for coming in today.
Did you have any trouble finding us?
How was the drive?
Would you like a cup of coffee?
Do you happen to know (Terry Mendham)?

Small talk by the candidate
What a great view!
Thanks for arranging to see me.
I've been looking forward to meeting you.
I spent some time exploring the company's
   website.
My friend, Dale, has worked here for
   several years.

Getting serious
OK, let's get started.
So, anyway . . .
Let's get down to business.

General questions for a candidate
Tell me a little about yourself.
How did you get into this line of work?
How long have you been in this country?
How did you learn about the opening?
What do you know about this company?
Why are you interested in working for us?

General answers to an interviewer
I've always been interested in (finance).
I enjoy (working with numbers).
My (uncle) was (an accountant) and
   encouraged me to try it.
I saw your ad in the paper.
This company has a great reputation in
   the field.

Job-related questions for a candidate
What are you qualifications for this job?
Describe your work experience.
What were your responsibilities on your
   last job?
I'd like to hear more about (your supervisory
   experience).

Interviewer:	Have you taken any courses in (bookkeeping)?
You:	Yes, I took two courses in business school and another online course last year.

What interests you about this particular
   job?
Why do you think it's a good fit?
Why did you leave your last job?
Do you have any experience with (HTML)?
Would you be willing to (travel eight weeks
   a year)?
What sort of salary are you looking for?

**Describing job qualifications to an
interviewer**
In (2010), I started working for (Booker's)
   as a (sales rep).
After (two years), I was promoted to (sales
   manager).
You'll notice on my resumé that (I
   supervised six people).
I was responsible for (three territories).
I was in charge of (planning sales
   meetings).
I have experience in all areas of (sales).
I helped implement (online sales reports).
I had to (contact my reps) on a daily basis.
I speak (Spanish) fluently.
I think my strong points are (organization
   and punctuality).

Ending the interview
I'm impressed with your experience.
I'd like to arrange a second interview.
When would you be able to start?
You'll hear from us by (next Wednesday).
We'll be in touch.

5. Presentations

Introducing yourself
Hello, everyone. I'd like to thank you all for coming.
Let me tell you a little bit about myself.
My name is (Rita Nazario).
I am president of (Catco International).
Hi. I'm (Ivan Wolf) from (Peekskill Incorporated).
Two years ago (I started out as a salesperson at Peekskill).
Today (I supervise the West Coast sales team).

Introducing someone else
This is (Tina Gorman), a (woman) who needs no introduction.
(Tina) is one of America's best-known (lawyers).
(She) is going to talk to us about (car insurance).
Let's give (her) a warm welcome.
We are lucky to have with us today (Barry Rogers).
As you know, (he) is (the president of Ranger Incorporated).
It gives me great pleasure to present (Barry Rogers).
And so without further ado, I'd like to present (Barry Rogers).

Stating the purpose
Today I'd like to talk to you about (managing your money).
Today I'm going to show you how to (save a lot of money).
I'll begin by (outlining the basics).
Then I'll (go into more detail).
I'll tell you (everything you need to know about savings accounts).
I'll provide an overview of (different types of investments).
I also hope to interest you in (some safe investments).
I'll list (the three biggest mistakes people make).
By the end, you'll (feel like an expert).

Relating to the audience
Can everyone hear me?
Raise your hand if you need me to repeat anything.
Please stop me at any point if you have a question.
How many people here (plan to continue their education)?
If you're like me, (you haven't saved up enough money).
We all know what that's like, don't we?
Does this ring a bell?
Don't you hate it when (people tell you what you should do)?

Citing sources
According to the *New York Times*, . . .
A study conducted by Harvard University showed that . . .
Recent research shows that . . .
Medical researchers have discovered that . . .
Peter Butler said, and I quote, " . . . "
I read somewhere that . . .
(The federal government) released a report stating that . . .

Making transitions
I'd like to expand on that before we move on.
The next thing I'd like to talk about is . . .
Now let's take a look at . . .
Moving right along . . .
To sum up what I've said so far, . . .
Now let's move on to the question of . . .
Now that you have an overview, let's look at some of the specifics.
Recapping the main points, . . .
I'm afraid we have to move on.

Emphasizing important points
I'd like to emphasize that . . .
Never forget that . . .
This is a key concept.
The bottom line is . . .
If you remember only one thing I've said today, . . .
I can't stress enough the importance of . . .

Using visuals
Take a look at (the chart on the screen).
I'd like to draw your attention to (the poster over there).
You'll notice that . . .
Pay special attention to the . . .
If you look closely, you'll see that . . .
So what does this tell us?

Closing
And in conclusion, . . .
Let's open the floor to questions.
It's been a pleasure being with you today.

6. AGREEING AND DISAGREEING

Agreeing
Yeah, that's right.
I know it.
I agree with you.
You're right.
That's true.
I think so, too.
That's what I think.
Me, too.
Me neither.

Agreeing strongly
You're absolutely right!
Definitely!
Certainly!
Exactly!
Absolutely!
Of course!
I couldn't agree more.
You're telling me!   [Informal]
Totally   [Informal]

Agreeing weakly
I suppose so.
Yeah, I guess so.
It would seem that way.

Remaining neutral
I see your point.
You have a point there.
I understand what you're saying.
I see what you mean.
I'd have to think about that.
I've never thought about it that way before.
Maybe yes, maybe no.
Could be.

Disagreeing
No, I don't think so.
I agree up to a point.
I really don't see it that way.
That's not what I think.
I agree that (going by car is faster), but . . .
But what about (the expense involved)?
Yes, but . . .
I know, but . . .
No, it wasn't. / No, they don't. / etc.

Other person:	We could save a lot of money by taking the bus.
You:	<u>Not really</u>. It would cost almost the same as driving.

Disagreeing strongly
I disagree completely.
That's not true.
That is not an option.
Definitely not!
Absolutely not!
You've made your point, but . . .
No way!   [Informal]
You can't be serious.   [Informal]
You've got to be kidding!   [Informal]
Where did you get that idea?   [Impolite]
Are you out of your mind!   [Impolite]

Disagreeing politely
I'm afraid I have to disagree with you.
I'm not so sure.
I'm not sure that's such a good idea.
I see what you're saying, but . . .
I'm sure many people feel that way, but . . .
But don't you think we should consider (other alternatives)?

7. INTERRUPTING, CLARIFYING, CHECKING FOR UNDERSTANDING

Informal interruptions
Ummm.
Sir? / Ma'am?
Just a minute.
Can I stop you for a minute?
Wait a minute!   [Impolite]
Hold it right there!   [Impolite]

Formal interruptions
Excuse me, sir / ma'am.
Excuse me for interrupting.
Forgive me for interrupting you, but ...
I'm sorry to break in like this, but ...
Could I interrupt you for a minute?
Could I ask a question, please?

Asking for clarification—Informal
What did you say?
I didn't catch that.
Sorry, I didn't get that.
I missed that.
Could you repeat that?
Could you say that again?
Say again?
I'm lost.
Could you run that by me one more time?
Did you say ...?
Do you mean ...?

Asking for clarification—Formal
I beg your pardon?
I'm not sure I understand what you're
  saying.
I can't make sense of what you just said.
Could you explain that in different words?
Could you please repeat that?
Could you go over that again?

Giving clarification—Informal
I'll go over it again.
I'll take it step by step.
I'll take a different tack this time.
Stop me if you get lost.
OK, here's a recap.
Maybe this will clarify things.
To put it another way, ...
In other words, ...

Giving clarification—Formal
Let me put it another way.
Let me give you some examples.
Here are the main points again.
I'm afraid you didn't understand what I
  said.
I'm afraid you've missed the point.
What I meant was ...
I hope you didn't think that ...
I didn't mean to imply that ...
I hope that clears things up.

Checking for understanding
Do you understand now?
Is it clearer now?
Do you see what I'm getting at?
Does that help?
Is there anything that still isn't clear?
What other questions do you have?

> **Speaker:** What else?
> **Listener:** I'm still not clear on the
> difference between a
> preposition and a
> conjunction.

Now explain it to me in your own words.

8. APOLOGIZING

Apologizing for a small accident or mistake

Sorry.

I'm sorry.

Excuse me.

It was an accident.

Pardon me.   [Formal]

Oops!   [Informal]

My mistake.   [Informal]

I'm terrible with (names).

I've never been good with (numbers).

I can't believe I (did) that.

Apologizing for a serious accident or mistake

I'm so sorry.

I am really sorry that I (damaged your car).

I am so sorry about (damaging your car).

I feel terrible about (the accident).

I'm really sorry but (I was being very careful).

I'm sorry for (causing you a problem).

Please accept my apologies for . . .   [Formal]

I sincerely apologize for . . .   [Formal]

Apologizing for upsetting someone

I'm sorry I upset you.

I didn't mean to make you feel bad.

Please forgive me.   [Formal]

I just wasn't thinking straight.

That's not what I meant to say.

I didn't mean it personally.

I'm sorry. I'm having a rough day.

Apologizing for having to say *no*

I'm sorry. I can't.

Sorry, I never (lend anyone my car).

I wish I could say *yes*.

I'm going to have to say *no*.

I can't. I have to (work that evening).

Maybe some other time.

Responding to an apology

Don't worry about it.

Oh, that's OK.

Think nothing of it.   [Formal]

Don't mention it.   [Formal]

Other person: I'm afraid I lost the pen you lent me.

You: No big deal.

It doesn't matter.

It's not important.

Never mind.

No problem.

It happens.

Forget it.

Don't sweat it.   [Informal]

Apology accepted.   [Formal]

Showing regret

I feel really bad.

It won't happen again.

I wish I could go back and start all over again.

I don't know what came over me.

I don't know what to say.

Now I know better.

Too bad I didn't . . .

It was inexcusable of me.   [Formal]

It's not like me to . . .

I hope I can make it up to you.

That didn't come out right.

I didn't mean to take it out on you.

Sympathizing

This must be very difficult for you.

I know what you mean.

I know how you're feeling.

I know how upset you must be.

I can imagine how difficult this is for you.

9. Suggestions, Advice, Insistence

Making informal suggestions
Here's what I suggest.
I know what you should do.
Why don't you (go to the movies with Jane)?
What about (having lunch with Bob)?
Try (the French fries next time).
Have you thought about (riding your bike to work)?

Accepting suggestions
Thanks, I'll do that.
Good idea!
That's a great idea.
Sounds good to me.
That's a plan.
I'll give it a try.
Guess it's worth a try.

Refusing suggestions
No. I don't like (French fries).
That's not for me.
I don't think so.
That might work for some people, but . . .
Nawww. [Informal]
I don't feel like it. [Impolite]

Giving serious advice—Informal
Listen!
Here's the plan.
Take my advice.
Take it from somebody who knows.
Take it from someone who's been there.
Here's what I think you should do.
Hey! Here's an idea.
How about (waiting until you're 30 to get married)?
Don't (settle down too quickly).
Why don't you (see the world while you're young)?
You can always (settle down later).
Don't forget—(you only live once).

Giving serious advice—formal
Have you ever thought about (becoming a doctor)?
Maybe it would be a good idea if you (went back to school).
It looks to me like (Harvard) would be your best choice.
If I were you, I'd study (medicine).
In my opinion, you should (consider it seriously).
Be sure to (get your application in early).
I always advise people to (check that it was received).
The best idea is (to study hard).
If you're really smart, you'll (start right away).

Accepting advice
You're right.
Thanks for the advice.
That makes a lot of sense.
I see what you mean.
That sounds like good advice.
I'll give it a try.
I'll do my best.
You've given me something to think about.
I'll try it and get back to you.

Refusing advice
I don't think that would work for me.
That doesn't make sense to me.
I'm not sure that would be such a good idea.
I could never (become a doctor).
Thanks for the input.
Thanks, but no thanks. [Informal]
You don't know what you're talking about. [Impolite]
I think I know what's best for myself. [Impolite]
Back off! [Impolite]

Insisting
You have to (become a doctor).
Try to see it my way.
I know what I'm talking about.
If you don't (go to medical school), I won't (pay for college).
I don't care what you think. [Impolite]

10. DESCRIBING FEELINGS

Happiness
I'm doing great.
This is the best day of my life.
I've never been so happy in my life.
I'm so pleased for you.
Aren't you thrilled?
What could be better?
Life is good.

Sadness
Are you OK?
Why the long face?
I'm not doing so well.
I feel awful.
I'm devastated.
I'm depressed.
I'm feeling kind of blue.
I just want to crawl in a hole.
Oh, what's the use?

Fear
I'm worried about (money).
He dreads (going to the dentist).
I'm afraid to (drive over bridges).
She can't stand (snakes).
This anxiety is killing me.
He's scared of (big dogs).
How will I ever (pass Friday's test)?
I have a phobia about (germs).

Anger
I'm really mad at (you).
They resent (such high taxes).
How could she (do) that?
I'm annoyed with (the neighbors).
(The noise of car alarms) infuriates her.
He was furious with (the children).

Boredom
I'm so bored.
There's nothing to do around here.
What a bore!
Nothing ever happens.
She was bored to tears.
They were bored to death.
I was bored stiff.
It was such a monotonous (movie).
(That TV show) was so dull.

Disgust
That's disgusting.
Eeew! Yuck!   [Informal]
I hate (raw fish).
How can you stand it?
I almost vomited.
I thought I'd puke.   [Impolite]
I don't even like to think about it.
How can you say something like that?
I wouldn't be caught dead (wearing that
    dirty old coat).

Compassion
I'm sorry.
I understand what you're going through.
Tell me about it.
How can I help?
Is there anything I can do?
She is concerned about him.
He worries about the children.
He cares for her deeply.
My heart goes out to them.
    [Old-fashioned]

Guilt
I feel terrible that I (lost your mother's
    necklace).
I never should have (borrowed it).
I feel so guilty!
It's all my fault.
I blame myself.
I make a mess of everything.
I'll never forgive myself.

Irregular verbs

Infinitive	Past Tense	Past Participle
arise	arose	arisen
be	was, were	been
beat	beat	beaten
become	became	become
begin	began	begun
bend	bent	bent
bet	bet	bet
bind	bound	bound
bite	bit	bitten
bleed	bled	bled
blow	blew	blown
break	broke	broken
bring	brought	brought
build	built	built
burn	burned *or* burnt	burned *or* burnt
burst	burst	burst
buy	bought	bought
can	could	–
cast	cast	cast
catch	caught	caught
choose	chose	chosen
cling	clung	clung
come	came	come
cost	cost *or* costed	cost *or* costed
creep	crept	crept
cut	cut	cut
deal	dealt	dealt
dig	dug	dug
dive	dived *or* dove	dived
do	did	done
draw	drew	drawn
dream	dreamed *or* dreamt	dreamed *or* dreamt
drink	drank	drunk
drive	drove	driven
eat	ate	eaten
fall	fell	fallen
feed	fed	fed
feel	felt	felt
fight	fought	fought
find	found	found
fly	flew	flown
forbid	forbade	forbidden
forget	forgot	forgotten

Irregular verbs

Infinitive	Past Tense	Past Participle
freeze	froze	frozen
get	got	gotten, got
give	gave	given
go	went	gone
grind	ground	ground
grow	grew	grown
hang	hung *or* hanged	hung *or* hanged
have	had	had
hear	heard	heard
hide	hid	hidden
hit	hit	hit
hold	held	held
hurt	hurt	hurt
keep	kept	kept
kneel	kneeled *or* knelt	kneeled *or* knelt
know	knew	known
lay	laid	laid
lead	led	led
lean	leaned	leaned
leap	leaped *or* leapt	leaped *or* leapt
learn	learned	learned
leave	left	left
lend	lent	lent
let	let	let
lie	lay	lain
light	lit *or* lighted	lit *or* lighted
lose	lost	lost
make	made	made
may	might	–
mean	meant	meant
meet	met	met
pay	paid	paid
put	put	put
quit	quit	quit
read	read	read
rid	rid	rid
ride	rode	ridden
ring	rang	rung
rise	rose	risen
run	ran	run
say	said	said
see	saw	seen
seek	sought	sought
sell	sold	sold
send	sent	sent
set	set	set

Infinitive	Past Tense	Past Participle
shake	shook	shaken
shed	shed	shed
shine	shined *or* shone	shined *or* shone
shoe	shod	shod
shoot	shot	shot
show	showed	shown
shrink	shrank	shrunk
shut	shut	shut
sing	sang	sung
sink	sank	sunk
sit	sat	sat
sleep	slept	slept
slide	slid	slid
smell	smelled	smelled
speak	spoke	spoken
speed	sped *or* speeded	sped *or* speeded
spell	spelled *or* spelt	spelled *or* spelt
spend	spent	spent
spill	spilled *or* spilt	spilled *or* spilt
spit	spit *or* spat	spit, *or* spat
spoil	spoiled *or* spoilt	spoiled *or* spoilt
spread	spread	spread
spring	sprang	sprung
stand	stood	stood
steal	stole	stolen
stick	stuck	stuck
sting	stung	stung
stink	stank	stunk
strike	struck	struck *or* stricken
swear	swore	sworn
sweep	swept	swept
swell	swelled	swollen
swim	swam	swum
swing	swung	swung
take	took	taken
teach	taught	taught
tear	tore	torn
tell	told	told
think	thought	thought
throw	threw	thrown
wake	woke *or* waked	woken *or* waked
wear	wore	worn
weep	wept	wept
win	won	won
wind	wound	wound
write	wrote	written

Prefixes and suffixes

Suffixes are word endings that can be added to words, usually to make a new word with a similar meaning but different part of speech. In this dictionary some words have a black circle in front of them and have an example but no definition. These words are formed by adding a suffix.

The list of suffixes is followed by a list of the most frequent prefixes. Prefixes are beginnings of words.

Suffixes

-ability and **-ibility** replace *-able* and *-ible* at the end of adjectives to form nouns that refer to a particular state or quality. For example, *reliability* is the state or quality of being reliable.

-able forms adjectives that indicate what someone or something can have done to them. For example, if something is *movable*, it is possible to move it.

-al forms adjectives that indicate what something is connected with. For example, *environmental* problems are problems connected with the environment.

-ally is added to adjectives ending in *-ic* to form adverbs that indicate how something is done or what something relates to. For example, if something is done *enthusiastically*, it is done in an enthusiastic way.

-ance and **-ence** form nouns that refer to a particular action, state, or quality. For example, *brilliance* is the state or quality of being brilliant, and *appearance* is the action of appearing.

-ation, **-ication**, **-sion**, and **-tion** form nouns that refer to a state or process, or to an instance of that process. For example, the *protection* of something is the process of protecting it.

-cy forms nouns that refer to a particular state or quality. For example, *accuracy* is the state or quality of being accurate.

-ed is added to verbs to make the past tense and past participle. Past participles formed are often used as adjectives that indicate that something has been affected in some way. For example, *cooked* food is food that has been cooked.

-ence see **-ance**

-er and **-or** form nouns that refer to a person who performs a particular action, often because it is their job. For example, a *teacher* is someone who teaches.

-er and **-or** also form nouns which refer to tools and machines that perform a particular action. For example, a *scanner* is a machine that scans things.

-ful forms nouns that refer to the amount of a substance that something contains or can contain. For example, a *handful* of sand is the amount of sand that you can hold in your hand.

-ibility see **-ability**

-ic forms adjectives that indicate that something or someone is connected with a particular thing. For example, *photographic* equipment is equipment connected with photography.

-ication see **-ation**

-ing is added to verbs to make the *-ing* form, or present participle. Present participle forms are often used as adjectives describing a person or thing who is doing something. For example, a *sleeping* baby is a baby that is sleeping and an *amusing* joke is a joke that amuses people. Present participle forms are also used as nouns that refer to activities. For example, if you say you like *dancing*, you mean that you like to dance.

-ish forms adjectives that indicate that someone or something has a quality to a small extent. For example, something that is *yellowish* is slightly yellow in color.

-ish also forms words that indicate that a particular time or age mentioned is approximate. For example, if someone is *fortyish*, they are about forty years old.

-ism forms nouns that refer to particular beliefs, or to behavior based on these beliefs. For example, *professionalism* is behavior that is professional and *racism* is the beliefs and behavior of a racist.

-ist forms nouns that refer to people who do a particular kind of work. For example, a *scientist* is someone whose work is connected with science.

-ist also forms nouns that refer to people who play a particular musical instrument, often as their job. For example, a *guitarist* is someone who plays the guitar.

-ity forms nouns that refer to a particular state or quality. For example, *simplicity* is the quality of being simple.

-less forms adjectives that indicate that someone or something does not have a particular thing. For example, someone who is *jobless* does not have a job.

-ly forms adverbs that indicate how something is done. For example, if someone speaks *cheerfully*, they speak in a cheerful way.

-ment forms nouns that refer to the process of making or doing something, or to the result of this process. For example, *replacement* is the process of replacing something or the thing that replaces it.

-ness forms nouns that refer to a particular state or quality. For example, *gentleness* is the state or quality of being gentle.

-or see **-er**

-ous forms adjectives that indicate that someone or something has a particular quality. For example, a person who is *humorous* has a lot of humor.

-sion, **-tion** see **-ation**

-y forms adjectives that indicate that something is full of something else or covered in it. For example, if something is *dirty*, it is covered with dirt.

-y also forms adjectives that mean that something is like something else. For example, if something looks *silky*, it looks like silk, although it is not actually silk.

Prefixes

anti- forms nouns and adjectives that refer to some sort of opposition. For example, *anti-virus* software protects a computer from attack by viruses.

auto- forms words that refer to someone doing something to, for, or about themselves. For example, your *autobiography* is an account of your life, which you write yourself.

bi- forms nouns and adjectives that have *two* as part of their meaning. For example, if someone is *bilingual*, they speak two languages.

co- forms verbs and nouns that refer to people sharing things or doing things together. For example, if two people *co-write* a book, they write it together. The *co-author* of a book is one of the people who have written it.

counter- forms words that refer to actions or activities that oppose another action or activity. For example, a *counter-measure* is an action you take to weaken the effect of another action or situation.

de- is added to some verbs to make verbs that mean the opposite. For example, if something *degenerates*, it becomes weaker.

dis- can be added to some words to form words that have the opposite meaning. For example, if someone is *dishonest*, they are not honest.

eco- forms nouns and adjectives that refer to something related to the environment. For example, *eco-friendly* products do not harm the environment.

ex- forms words that refer to people who are no longer a particular thing. For example, an *ex-police officer* is someone who is no longer a police officer.

extra- forms adjectives that refer to something being outside or beyond something else. For example, something that is *extraordinary* is more than ordinary, that is, very special.

extra- also forms adjectives that refer to something having a large amount of a particular quality. For example, if something is *extra-strong*, it is very strong.

hyper- forms adjectives that refer to people or things that have a large amount of, or too much, of a particular quality. For example, someone who is *hypersensitive* becomes annoyed or offended very easily.

il-, **im-**, **in-**, and **ir-** can be added to some words to form words that have the opposite meaning. For example, if an activity is *illegal*, it is not legal. If someone is *impatient*, they are not patient.

inter- forms adjectives that refer to things that move, exist, or happen between two or more people or things. For example, *inter-city* trains travel between cities.

ir- see **il**

kilo- forms words that refer to things that have a thousand parts. For example, a *kilometer* is a thousand meters.

mal- forms words that refer to things that are bad or unpleasant, or that are unsuccessful or imperfect. For example, *malware* is a type of computer program that damages a computer.

mega- forms words that refer to units which are a million times bigger. For example, a *megabyte* is a million bytes.

micro- forms nouns that have *small* as part of their meaning. For example, a *micro-organism* is a very small living thing that you cannot see with your eyes alone.

mid- forms nouns and adjectives that refer to the middle part of a particular period of time, or the middle part of a particular place. For example, *mid-June* is the middle of June.

milli- forms nouns that refer to units that are a thousand times smaller. For example, a *millimeter* is a thousandth of a meter.

mini- forms nouns that refer to things that are a smaller version of something else. For example, a *minibus* is a small bus.

mis- forms verbs and nouns that refer to something being done badly or wrongly. For example, *misbehavior* is bad behavior.

mono- forms nouns and adjectives that have *one* or *single* as part of their meaning. For example, a *monochromatic* picture uses only one color.

multi- forms adjectives that refer to something that consists of many things of a particular kind. For example, a *multi-colored* object has many different colors.

neo- forms nouns and adjectives that refer to modern versions of styles and particular groups of the past. For example, *neo-classical* architecture is based on ancient Greek or Roman architecture.

non- forms nouns and adjectives that refer to people or things that do not have a particular quality or characteristic. For example, a *non-fatal* accident is not fatal.

non- also forms nouns that refer to situations where a particular action has not taken place. For example, someone's *non-attendance* at a meeting is the fact that they did not go to the meeting.

over- forms words that refer to a quality of action that exists or is done to too great an extent. For example, if someone is being *over-cautious*, they are being too cautious.

part- forms words that refer to something that is partly but not completely a particular thing. For example, *partly-baked bread* is only partly baked.

poly- forms nouns and adjectives that have *many* as part of their meaning. For example, *polygamy* is the custom in some societies of being married to more than one person at the same time.

post- forms words that refer to something that takes place after a particular date, period, or event. For example, a *postscript* (PS) to a letter is extra information that you write at the end, after you have signed it.

pre- forms words that refer to something that takes place before a particular date, period, or event. For example, *prehistoric* people and things existed at a time before information was written down.

pro- forms adjectives that refer to people who strongly support a particular person or thing. For example, if you are *pro-democracy*, you support democracy.

pseudo- forms nouns and adjectives that refer to something that is not really what it seems or claims to be. For example, a *pseudo-science* is something that claims to be a science, but is not.

re- forms verbs and nouns that refer to an action or process being repeated. For example, if you *re-read* something, you read it again.

semi- forms nouns and adjectives that refer to people and things that are partly, but not completely, in a particular state. For example, if you are *semiconscious*, you are partly, but not wholly, conscious.

sub- forms nouns that refer to things that are part of a larger thing. For example, a *subculture* is the culture of a group of people within a society.

super- forms nouns and adjectives that refer to people and things that are larger, better, or more advanced than others. For example, a *super-fit* athlete is extremely fit.

ultra- forms adjectives that refer to people and things that possess a quality to a very large degree. For example, an *ultra-light* fabric is extremely light.

un- can be added to some words to form words that have the opposite meaning. For example, if something is *unacceptable*, it is not acceptable.

under- forms words that refer to an amount or value being too low or not enough. For example, if someone is *underweight*, their weight is lower than it should be.

Key words

Here is a list of the most common and useful words you need to know:

a	adjust	all	anything	assess
abandon	administration	allegation	anyway	asset
ability	admire	alliance	anywhere	assist
able	admit	allied	apart	assistance
abortion	adopt	allow	apartment	assistant
about	adult	all right	apparent	associate
above	advance	ally	apparently	association
abroad	advanced	almost	appeal	assume
absence	advantage	alone	appear	assumption
absolute	advertise	along	appearance	assured
absolutely	advice	alongside	apple	at
abuse	advise	already	application	athlete
academic	adviser	also	apply	atmosphere
accept	advocate	alter	appoint	attach
acceptable	affair	alternative	appointment	attack
accepted	affect	although	appreciate	attempt
access	afford	altogether	approach	attend
accident	afraid	always	appropriate	attention
accompany	after	amateur	approval	attitude
accord	afternoon	amazing	approve	attorney
according to	afterward	ambassador	April	attract
account	again	ambition	area	attractive
accurate	against	amendment	aren't	auction
accuse	age	among	argue	audience
achieve	agency	amount	argument	audio
achievement	agenda	analysis	arise	August
acid	agent	analyst	arm	aunt
acknowledge	aggressive	ancient	armed	author
acquire	ago	and	armed forces	authority
acquisition	agree	anger	army	automatic
acre	agreement	angle	around	autumn
across	agriculture	angry	arrange	available
act	ahead	animal	arrangement	avenue
action	ahead of	anniversary	arrest	average
active	aid	announce	arrival	avoid
activist	aim	announcement	arrive	await
activity	air	annual	art	award
actor	aircraft	another	article	aware
actress	air force	answer	artist	away
actual	airline	antique	as	awful
actually	airport	anxiety	Asian	
ad	alarm	anxious	aside	baby
add	album	any	ask	back
addition	alcohol	anybody	aspect	background
address	alert	anymore	assault	backing
adequate	alive	anyone	assembly	bad

badly	behave	bone	burst	cat
bag	behavior	book	bury	catch
bake	behind	boom	bus	category
balance	being	boost	business	Catholic
ball	belief	boot	businessman	cause
ballot	believe	border	busy	cautious
ban	bell	bore	but	cave
band	belong	born	butter	cease
bank	below	borrow	button	ceasefire
banker	belt	boss	buy	celebrate
banking	bend	both	by	cell
bar	beneath	bother	bye	center
bare	benefit	bottle		central
barely	beside	bottom	cabinet	century
bargain	besides	bound	cable	ceremony
barrel	best	bowl	cake	certain
barrier	bet	box	call	certainly
base	better	boy	calm	chain
baseball	between	brain	camera	chair
basic	beyond	branch	camp	chairman
basically	bid	brand	campaign	challenge
basis	big	brave	can	chamber
basketball	bike	bread	cancel	champion
bass	bill	break	cancer	championship
bat	billion	breakfast	candidate	chance
bath	bird	breast	cap	chancellor
bathroom	birth	breath	capable	change
battle	birthday	breathe	capacity	channel
bay	bit	breed	capital	chaos
be	bite	bridge	captain	chapter
beach	bitter	brief	caption	character
bean	black	bright	capture	characteristic
bear	blame	brilliant	car	charge
bearing	blast	bring	carbon	charity
beat	blind	broad	card	chart
beautiful	block	broadcast	care	charter
beauty	blood	broker	career	chase
because	bloody	brother	careful	chat
become	blow	brown	caring	cheap
bed	blue	brush	carrier	check
bedroom	board	budget	carry	cheer
beer	boat	build	case	cheese
before	body	building	cash	chemical
begin	boil	bunch	cast	chest
beginning	bomb	burden	castle	chicken
behalf	bond	burn	casualty	chief

child	cold	complete	contain	county
childhood	collapse	complex	contemporary	coup
chip	colleague	complicated	content	couple
chocolate	collect	component	contest	courage
choice	collection	comprehensive	context	course
choose	collective	compromise	continent	court
chop	college	computer	continue	cousin
Christian	colonel	concede	contract	cover
Christmas	color	concentrate	contrast	coverage
church	colored	concentration	contribute	cow
cigarette	column	concept	contribution	crack
cinema	combat	concern	control	craft
circle	combination	concert	controversial	crash
circuit	combine	concession	controversy	crazy
circumstance	come	conclude	convention	cream
cite	comedy	conclusion	conventional	create
citizen	comfort	concrete	conversation	creative
city	comfortable	condemn	convert	credit
civil	coming	condition	convict	crew
civilian	command	conduct	conviction	cricket
civil war	commander	conference	convince	crime
claim	comment	confidence	cook	criminal
clash	commentator	confident	cooking	crisis
class	commerce	confirm	cool	critic
classic	commercial	conflict	cooperate	critical
classical	commission	confront	cope	criticism
clean	commissioner	confrontation	copy	criticize
clear	commit	Congress	core	crop
clever	commitment	connection	corner	cross
client	committee	conscious	corporate	crowd
climate	common	consciousness	corporation	crown
climb	communicate	consequence	correct	crucial
clinic	communication	conservative	correspondent	cruise
clock	communism	consider	corruption	cry
close	community	considerable	cost	crystal
clothes	company	consideration	cottage	cue
clothing	compare	considering	cotton	cultural
cloud	compared	consist	cough	culture
club	comparison	consistent	could	cup
coach	compensation	constant	council	cure
coal	compete	constitution	counsel	curious
coalition	competition	construction	count	currency
coast	competitive	consult	counter	current
coat	competitor	consultant	counterpart	curtain
code	complain	consumer	country	customer
coffee	complaint	contact	countryside	cut

cutting
cycle

dad
daily
damage
dance
danger
dangerous
dare
dark
data
date
daughter
day
dead
deadline
deal
dear
death
debate
debt
debut
decade
December
decide
decision
deck
declaration
declare
decline
decorate
deep
defeat
defend
defense
deficit
define
definitely
definition
degree
delay
delegate
delegation
deliberate
delight

delighted
deliver
delivery
demand
democracy
democrat
democratic
demonstrate
deny
department
departure
depend
deposit
depression
depth
deputy
describe
description
desert
deserve
design
designer
desire
desk
desperate
despite
destroy
detail
detailed
detective
determine
determined
develop
development
device
dialogue
diary
didn't
die
diet
difference
different
difficult
difficulty
dig
digital

dinner
diplomat
diplomatic
direct
direction
director
dirty
disappear
disappointed
disaster
discipline
discount
discover
discovery
discuss
discussion
disease
dish
dismiss
display
dispute
distance
distribution
district
divide
dividend
division
divorce
do
doctor
document
doesn't
dog
dollar
domestic
dominate
done
door
double
doubt
down
downtown
dozen
draft
drag
drain

drama
dramatic
draw
dream
dress
dressed
drift
drink
drive
driver
drop
drug
drum
dry
due
dump
during
dust
duty

each
eager
ear
earlier
early
earn
earnings
earth
ease
easily
east
eastern
easy
eat
echo
economic
economics
economist
economy
edge
edit
edition
editor
editorial
education
effect

effective
efficient
effort
egg
eight
eighteen
eighteenth
eighth
eightieth
eighty
either
elderly
elect
election
electoral
electric
electricity
electronic
elegant
element
eleven
eleventh
eliminate
else
elsewhere
embassy
emerge
emergency
emotion
emotional
emphasis
emphasize
empire
employ
employee
employer
employment
empty
enable
encounter
encourage
end
enemy
energy
engage
engine

engineer	evil	extra	feeling	flood
engineering	exact	extraordinary	fellow	floor
English	exactly	extreme	female	flow
enhance	examination	eye	fence	flower
enjoy	examine		festival	fly
enormous	example	fabric	few	focus
enough	excellent	face	field	fold
ensure	except	facility	fierce	folk
enter	exception	fact	fifteen	follow
enterprise	excerpt	faction	fifteenth	following
entertain	excess	factor	fifth	food
entertainment	exchange	factory	fiftieth	fool
enthusiasm	exchange rate	fade	fifty	foot
entire	exciting	fail	fight	football
entirely	excuse	failure	fighter	for
entitle	execute	fair	figure	force
entrance	executive	fairly	file	forecast
entry	exercise	faith	fill	foreign
environment	exhaust	fall	film	foreigner
equal	exhibition	false	final	forest
equally	exile	familiar	finally	forget
equipment	exist	family	finance	form
equivalent	existence	famous	financial	form
era	existing	fan	find	formal
error	expand	fancy	fine	former
escape	expect	fantasy	finger	formula
especially	expectation	far	finish	forth
essential	expense	fare	fire	fortieth
essentially	expensive	farm	firm	fortune
establish	experience	farmer	first	forty
establishment	experiment	fashion	fiscal	forward
estate	expert	fast	fish	found
estimate	explain	fat	fishing	foundation
ethnic	explanation	fate	fit	founder
European	explode	father	five	four
even	exploit	fault	fix	fourteen
evening	explore	favor	fixed	fourteenth
event	explosion	favorite	flag	fourth
eventually	export	fear	flash	frame
ever	expose	feature	flat	fraud
every	exposure	February	flavor	free
everybody	express	federal	flee	freedom
everyone	expression	federation	fleet	freeze
everything	extend	fee	flexible	frequent
everywhere	extensive	feed	flight	fresh
evidence	extent	feel	float	Friday

Key words

friend	gift	guilty	hide	hundred
friendly	girl	guitar	high	hundredth
friendship	give	gun	highlight	hunt
from	give	guy	highly	hunter
front	given		high school	hurt
fruit	glad	habit	highway	husband
frustrate	glance	hair	hill	
fry	glass	half	him	I
fuel	global	hall	himself	ice
fulfil	go	halt	hint	idea
full	goal	hand	hip	ideal
fully	god	handle	hire	identify
fun	going	hang	his	identity
function	gold	happen	historic	if
fund	golden	happy	historical	ignore
fundamental	golf	harbor	history	ill
funding	gone	hard	hit	illegal
funny	good	hardly	hold	illness
furniture	goods	harm	holder	illustrate
further	got	hat	hole	image
future	govern	hate	holiday	imagination
	government	have	holy	imagine
gain	governor	he	home	immediate
gallery	grab	head	homeless	immediately
game	grade	headline	homosexual	immigrant
gang	graduate	headquarters	honest	immigration
gap	grain	heal	honor	immune
garden	grand	health	hook	impact
gas	grant	health care	hope	implement
gate	grass	healthy	horror	implication
gather	grave	hear	horse	imply
gay	gray	hearing	hospital	import
gear	great	heart	host	important
gene	green	heat	hostage	impose
general	grip	heaven	hot	impossible
general election	gross	heavy	hotel	impress
generally	ground	height	hour	impression
generate	group	helicopter	house	impressive
generation	grow	hell	household	improve
generous	growth	hello	housing	in
gentle	guarantee	help	how	inch
gentleman	guard	her	however	incident
genuine	guerrilla	here	huge	include
gesture	guess	hero	human	including
get	guest	herself	human rights	income
giant	guide	hi	humor	increase

increasingly	interest	judge	later	life
incredible	interested	judgment	latest	lift
indeed	interesting	juice	latter	light
independent	interim	July	laugh	like
index	interior	jump	laughter	likely
indicate	internal	June	launch	limit
indication	international	junior	law	limited
individual	Internet	jury	lawsuit	line
industrial	interview	just	lawyer	link
industry	into	justice	lay	lip
inevitable	introduce	justify	layer	list
infect	invasion		lead	listen
infection	invest	keen	leader	literary
inflation	investigate	keep	leadership	literature
influence	investment	key	leading	little
inform	invitation	kick	leaf	live
information	invite	kid	league	living
ingredient	involve	kill	leak	load
initial	involved	killer	lean	loan
initially	involvement	kilometer	leap	lobby
initiative	iron	kind	learn	local
injured	Islam	king	lease	location
injury	island	kiss	least	lock
inner	issue	kitchen	leather	long
innocent	it	knee	leave	long-time
inquiry	item	knife	lecture	look
inside	its	knock	left	loose
insist	itself	know	leg	lord
inspect		know-how	legal	lose
inspector	jacket	knowledge	legislation	loss
install	jail		lend	lost
instance	January	label	length	lot
instant	jazz	labor	lens	loud
instead	jersey	laboratory	lesbian	love
institute	Jesus	lack	less	lovely
institution	jet	lady	lesson	lover
instruction	Jew	lake	let	low
instrument	Jewish	land	let's	lower
insurance	job	landscape	letter	luck
integrate	join	lane	level	lucky
intellectual	joint	language	liberal	lunch
intelligence	joke	lap	liberate	luxury
intelligent	journal	large	liberty	
intend	journalist	largely	library	machine
intense	journey	last	license	mad
intention	joy	late	lie	magazine

magic	meaning	minute	murder	newly
mail	means	mirror	muscle	news
main	meanwhile	miss	museum	news agency
mainly	measure	missile	music	newscaster
maintain	meat	missing	musical	newspaper
major	mechanism	mission	musician	next
majority	medal	mistake	Muslim	nice
make	media	mix	must	night
maker	medical	mixed	mutual	nightmare
makeup	medicine	mixture	my	nine
male	medium	mobile	myself	nineteen
man	meet	model	mystery	nineteenth
manage	meeting	moderate	myth	ninetieth
management	member	modern		ninth
manager	membership	modest	name	ninety
manner	memory	mom	narrow	no
manufacture	mental	moment	nation	nobody
manufacturer	mention	Monday	national	nod
many	merchant	monetary	nationalist	noise
map	mere	money	native	none
march	merely	monitor	natural	no one
March	merger	month	naturally	nor
margin	mess	monthly	nature	normal
marine	message	mood	naval	normally
mark	metal	moon	navy	north
marked	method	moral	near	northeast
market	middle	more	nearby	northern
marriage	middle class	moreover	nearly	nose
married	Middle East	morning	neat	not
marry	midnight	mortgage	necessarily	note
mask	might	most	necessary	noted
mass	mild	mostly	neck	nothing
massive	mile	mother	need	notice
master	militant	motion	negative	notion
match	military	motivate	negotiate	novel
mate	milk	motor	negotiation	November
material	mill	mount	neighbor	now
matter	million	mountain	neighborhood	nowhere
maximum	millionth	mouth	neither	nuclear
may	mind	move	nerve	number
May	mine	movement	nervous	numerous
maybe	minimum	movie	net	nurse
mayor	minister	Mr.	network	
me	ministry	Mrs.	never	object
meal	minor	Ms.	nevertheless	objective
mean	minority	much	new	observe

observer
obtain
obvious
obviously
occasion
occasional
occupation
occupy
occur
ocean
o'clock
October
odd
of
of course
off
offense
offensive
offer
offering
office
officer
official
often
oh
oil
okay
old
Olympic
on
once
one
one's
online
only
onto
open
opening
opera
operate
operation
operator
opinion
opponent
opportunity
oppose

opposed
opposite
opposition
opt
optimistic
option
or
orange
order
ordinary
organization
organize
organized
origin
original
other
otherwise
ought
our
ourselves
out
outcome
outline
output
outside
outstanding
over
overall
overcome
overnight
overseas
overwhelming
owe
own
owner
ownership

pace
pack
package
pact
page
pain
painful
paint
painting

pair
palace
pale
pan
panel
panic
paper
parent
park
parliament
parliamentary
part
participate
particular
particularly
partly
partner
partnership
party
pass
passage
passenger
passion
past
path
patient
pattern
pause
pay
payment
peace
peaceful
peak
peer
peg
pen
penalty
penny
pension
people
pepper
per
percentage
perfect
perform
performance

perhaps
period
permanent
permission
permit
person
personal
personality
personally
personnel
perspective
persuade
pet
phase
philosophy
phone
photo
photograph
photographer
phrase
physical
pick
picture
piece
pile
pill
pilot
pin
pink
pipe
pit
pitch
place
plain
plan
plane
planet
planning
plant
plastic
plate
platform
play
player
playoff
pleasant

please
pleased
pleasure
pledge
plenty
plot
plunge
plus
pocket
poem
poet
poetry
point
point of view
pole
police
policeman
police officer
policy
political
politician
politics
poll
pollution
pool
poor
pop
popular
population
port
portrait
pose
position
positive
possibility
possible
possibly
post
pot
potato
potential
pound
pour
poverty
power
powerful

practical
practice
praise
precisely
predict
prefer
pregnant
premier
premium
preparation
prepare
prepared
presence
present
preserve
presidency
president
presidential
press
pressure
presumably
pretty
prevent
previous
previously
price
pride
priest
primary
prime
prime minister
prince
princess
principal
principle
print
prior
priority
prison
prisoner
private
privatize
prize
probably
problem
procedure

proceed
process
produce
product
production
profession
professional
professor
profile
profit
program
progress
project
prominent
promise
promote
prompt
proof
proper
property
proportion
proposal
propose
prosecution
prospect
protect
protection
protein
protest
proud
prove
provide
province
provision
provoke
psychological
public
publication
publicity
publish
publisher
publishing
pull
pump
punch
pupil

purchase
pure
purple
purpose
pursue
push
put

qualified
qualify
quality
quantity
quarter
quarterback
queen
question
quick
quiet
quite
quote

race
racial
racing
radical
radio
rage
raid
rail
railway
rain
raise
rally
range
rank
rape
rapid
rare
rarely
rate
rather
rating
raw
ray
reach
react

reaction
read
reader
reading
ready
real
real estate
reality
realize
really
rear
reason
reasonable
rebel
recall
receive
recent
recently
recession
reckon
recognition
recognize
recommend
record
recording
recover
recovery
recruit
red
reduce
reduction
reel
refer
reference
referendum
reflect
reform
refugee
refuse
regard
regime
region
register
regret
regular
regulation

regulator
reject
relate
related
relation
relationship
relative
relax
release
reliable
relief
religion
religious
reluctant
rely
remain
remaining
remark
remarkable
remember
remind
remote
remove
renew
rent
repair
repeat
replace
replacement
reply
report
reporter
reporting
represent
representative
republic
republican
reputation
request
require
requirement
rescue
research
reserve
resident
resign

resignation
resist
resistance
resolution
resolve
resort
resource
respect
respond
response
responsibility
responsible
rest
restaurant
restore
result
resume
retail
retain
retire
retirement
retreat
return
reveal
revenue
reverse
review
revolution
revolutionary
reward
rhythm
rice
rich
rid
ride
rider
right
right wing
ring
riot
rise
risk
rival
river
road
rock

rocket
role
roll
Roman
romantic
roof
room
root
rose
rough
round
route
routine
row
royal
rugby
ruin
rule
ruling
rumor
run
runner
running
rural
rush

sack
sacrifice
sad
safe
safety
sail
saint
sake
salary
sale
salt
same
sample
sanction
sand
satellite
satisfied
Saturday
sauce
save

savings
say
scale
scandal
scene
schedule
scheme
school
science
scientific
scientist
score
scream
screen
script
sea
seal
search
season
seat
second
secret
secretary
Secretary of
   State
section
sector
secure
security
see
seed
seek
seem
segment
seize
select
selection
self
sell
Senate
senator
send
senior
sense
sensible
sensitive

sentence
separate
September
series
serious
seriously
servant
serve
service
session
set
settle
settlement
setup
seven
seventeen
seventeenth
seventh
seventieth
seventy
several
severe
sex
sexual
shade
shadow
shake
shall
shame
shape
shaped
share
shareholder
sharp
she
shed
sheet
shell
shelter
shift
ship
shirt
shock
shoe
shoot
shop

shopping
shore
short
shortage
shortly
short-term
shot
should
shoulder
shout
show
shut
sick
side
sigh
sight
sign
signal
significant
silence
silent
silver
similar
simple
simply
since
sing
singer
single
sink
sir
sister
sit
site
situation
six
sixteen
sixteenth
sixth
sixtieth
sixty
size
ski
skill
skin
sky

sleep	sound	stand	strip	surgery
slice	source	standard	stroke	surplus
slide	south	star	strong	surprise
slight	southeast	stare	structure	surprised
slightly	southern	start	struggle	surprising
slim	southwest	state	student	surrender
slip	space	statement	studio	surround
slow	spare	station	study	survey
small	spark	statistic	stuff	survival
smart	speak	status	stupid	survive
smash	speaker	stay	style	suspect
smell	special	steady	subject	suspend
smile	specialist	steal	subsequent	suspicion
smoke	specialize	steam	subsidy	sustain
smooth	species	steel	substance	sweep
snap	specific	stem	substantial	sweet
snow	specifically	step	substitute	swim
so	spectacular	sterling	succeed	swing
so-called	speculate	stick	success	switch
soccer	speech	still	successful	symbol
social	speed	stimulate	such	sympathy
socialist	spell	stir	sudden	symptom
society	spend	stock	suffer	system
soft	spin	stock exchange	sufficient	
software	spirit	stock market	sugar	table
soil	spiritual	stomach	suggest	tackle
soldier	spite	stone	suggestion	tactic
solicitor	split	stop	suicide	tail
solid	spokesman	store	suit	take
solution	spokeswoman	storm	suitable	takeover
solve	sponsor	story	sum	tale
some	sport	straight	summer	talent
somebody	spot	strain	summit	talk
somehow	spray	strange	sun	tall
someone	spread	strategic	Sunday	tank
something	spring	strategy	super	tap
sometimes	spur	stream	superb	tape
somewhat	squad	street	superior	target
somewhere	square	strength	supply	task
son	squeeze	strengthen	support	taste
song	stable	stress	suppose	tax
soon	stadium	stretch	supposed	tea
sophisticated	staff	strict	supreme	teach
sorry	stage	strike	sure	teaching
sort	stake	striking	surely	team
soul	stamp	string	surface	tear

technical	thirteen	tour	tunnel	upper
technique	thirteenth	tourist	turn	upset
technology	thirtieth	tournament	TV	urban
teenager	thirty	toward	twelfth	urge
telephone	this	tower	twelve	urgent
television	thorough	town	twentieth	us
tell	those	toy	twenty	use
temperature	though	trace	twice	used
temple	thought	track	twin	useful
temporary	thousand	trade	twist	user
ten	threat	trader	two	usual
tend	threaten	tradition	type	usually
tendency	three	traffic	typical	
tennis	throat	tragedy		valley
tension	through	trail	ultimate	valuable
tenth	throughout	train	ultimately	value
term	throw	transaction	unable	van
terrible	Thursday	transfer	uncle	variety
territory	thus	transform	under	various
terror	ticket	transition	underground	vary
terrorist	tide	transport	undermine	vast
test	tie	trap	understand	vegetable
text	tight	travel	understanding	vehicle
than	till	traveler	unemployment	venture
thank	time	treat	unexpected	venue
that	tiny	treatment	unfair	verdict
the	tip	treaty	unfortunately	version
theater	tired	tree	unhappy	very
their	tissue	tremendous	unidentified	vessel
them	title	trend	uniform	veteran
theme	titled	trial	union	via
themselves	to	trick	unique	vice
then	today	trigger	unit	victim
theory	together	trip	united	victimize
therapy	tomorrow	triumph	United Nations	victory
there	ton	troop	unity	video
therefore	tone	trouble	universe	view
these	tonight	truck	university	village
they	too	true	unknown	violate
thick	tool	truly	unless	violence
thin	tooth	trust	unlike	violent
thing	top	truth	unlikely	virus
think	torture	try	until	visible
thinking	total	tube	unusual	vision
third	touch	Tuesday	up	visit
Third World	tough	tune	upon	visitor

vital	weaken	whereas	wipe	wrap
vitamin	wealth	whether	wire	write
voice	weapon	which	wireless	writer
volume	wear	while	wise	writing
voluntary	weather	whip	wish	written
volunteer	web	whisper	with	wrong
vote	website	white	withdraw	
vulnerable	wedding	White House	withdrawal	yard
	Wednesday	who	within	yeah
wage	week	whole	without	year
wait	weekend	whom	witness	yellow
wake	weekly	whose	woman	yen
walk	weigh	why	wonder	yes
wall	weight	wide	wonderful	yesterday
want	welcome	widespread	wood	yet
war	welfare	wife	wooden	yield
warm	well	wild	word	you
warn	well-known	will	work	young
warning	west	willing	worker	youngster
wash	western	win	working	your
waste	wet	wind	world	yours
watch	what	window	world war	yourself
water	whatever	wine	worldwide	youth
wave	wheel	wing	worry	
way	when	winner	worth	zone
we	whenever	winning	would	
weak	where	winter	wound	

Academic word list

This list contains the headwords of the families in the Academic word list. The numbers indicate the sublist of the Academic word list, with Sublist 1 containing the most frequent words, Sublist 2 the next most frequent and so on. For example, *abandon* and its family members are in Sublist 8 of the Academic word list. The Academic word list was created by Averil Coxhead and you can find out more about it here: www.victoria.ac.nz/lals/resources/academicwordlist

abandon	8	arbitrary	8	classic	7
abstract	6	area	1	clause	5
academy	5	aspect	2	code	4
access	4	assemble	10	coherent	9
accommodate	9	assess	1	coincide	9
accompany	8	assign	6	collapse	10
accumulate	8	assist	2	colleague	10
accurate	6	assume	1	commence	9
achieve	2	assure	9	comment	3
acknowledge	6	attach	6	commission	2
acquire	2	attain	9	commit	4
adapt	7	attitude	4	commodity	8
adequate	4	attribute	4	communicate	4
adjacent	10	author	6	community	2
adjust	5	authority	1	compatible	9
administrate	2	automate	8	compensate	3
adult	7	available	1	compile	10
advocate	7	aware	5	complement	8
affect	2	behalf	9	complex	2
aggregate	6	benefit	1	component	3
aid	7	bias	8	compound	5
albeit	10	bond	6	comprehensive	7
allocate	6	brief	6	comprise	7
alter	5	bulk	9	compute	2
alternative	3	capable	6	conceive	10
ambiguous	8	capacity	5	concentrate	4
amend	5	category	2	concept	1
analogy	9	cease	9	conclude	2
analyze	1	challenge	5	concurrent	9
annual	4	channel	7	conduct	2
anticipate	9	chapter	2	confer	4
apparent	4	chart	8	confine	9
append	8	chemical	7	confirm	7
appreciate	8	circumstance	3	conflict	5
approach	1	cite	6	conform	8
appropriate	2	civil	4	consent	3
approximate	4	clarify	8	consequent	2

considerable	3	denote	8	enormous	10
consist	1	deny	7	ensure	3
constant	3	depress	10	entity	5
constitute	1	derive	1	environment	1
constrain	3	design	2	equate	2
construct	2	despite	4	equip	7
consult	5	detect	8	equivalent	5
consume	2	deviate	8	erode	9
contact	5	device	9	error	4
contemporary	8	devote	9	establish	1
context	1	differentiate	7	estate	6
contract	1	dimension	4	estimate	1
contradict	8	diminish	9	ethic	9
contrary	7	discrete	5	ethnic	4
contrast	4	discriminate	6	evaluate	2
contribute	3	displace	8	eventual	8
controversy	9	display	6	evident	1
convene	3	dispose	7	evolve	5
converse	9	distinct	2	exceed	6
convert	7	distort	9	exclude	3
convince	10	distribute	1	exhibit	8
cooperate	6	diverse	6	expand	5
coordinate	3	document	3	expert	6
core	3	domain	6	explicit	6
corporate	3	domestic	4	exploit	8
correspond	3	dominate	3	export	1
couple	7	draft	5	expose	5
create	1	drama	8	external	5
credit	2	duration	9	extract	7
criteria	3	dynamic	7	facilitate	5
crucial	8	economy	1	factor	1
culture	2	edit	6	feature	2
currency	8	element	2	federal	6
cycle	4	eliminate	7	fee	6
data	1	emerge	4	file	7
debate	4	emphasis	3	final	2
decade	7	empirical	7	finance	1
decline	5	enable	5	finite	7
deduce	3	encounter	10	flexible	6
define	1	energy	5	fluctuate	8
definite	7	enforce	5	focus	2
demonstrate	3	enhance	6	format	9

formula	1	individual	1	layer	3
forthcoming	10	induce	8	lecture	6
foundation	7	inevitable	8	legal	1
found	9	infer	7	legislate	1
framework	3	infrastructure	8	levy	10
function	1	inherent	9	liberal	5
fund	3	inhibit	6	license	5
fundamental	5	initial	3	likewise	10
furthermore	6	initiate	6	link	3
gender	6	injure	2	locate	3
generate	5	innovate	7	logic	5
generation	5	input	6	maintain	2
globe	7	insert	7	major	1
goal	4	insight	9	manipulate	8
grade	7	inspect	8	manual	9
grant	4	instance	3	margin	5
guarantee	7	institute	2	mature	9
guideline	8	instruct	6	maximize	3
hence	4	integral	9	mechanism	4
hierarchy	7	integrate	4	media	7
highlight	8	integrity	10	mediate	9
hypothesis	4	intelligence	6	medical	5
identical	7	intense	8	medium	9
identify	1	interact	3	mental	5
ideology	7	intermediate	9	method	1
ignorance	6	internal	4	migrate	6
illustrate	3	interpret	1	military	9
image	5	interval	6	minimal	9
immigrate	3	intervene	7	minimize	8
impact	2	intrinsic	10	minimum	6
implement	4	invest	2	ministry	6
implicate	4	investigate	4	minor	3
implicit	8	invoke	10	mode	7
imply	3	involve	1	modify	5
impose	4	isolate	7	monitor	5
incentive	6	issue	1	motive	6
incidence	6	item	2	mutual	9
incline	10	job	4	negate	3
income	1	journal	2	network	5
incorporate	6	justify	3	neutral	6
index	6	label	4	nevertheless	6
indicate	1	labor	1	nonetheless	10

norm	9	potential	2	regulate	2
normal	2	practitioner	8	reinforce	8
notion	5	precede	6	reject	5
notwithstanding	10	precise	5	relax	9
nuclear	8	predict	4	release	7
objective	5	predominant	8	relevant	2
obtain	2	preliminary	9	reluctance	10
obvious	4	presume	6	rely	3
occupy	4	previous	2	remove	3
occur	1	primary	2	require	1
odd	10	prime	5	research	1
offset	8	principal	4	reside	2
ongoing	10	principle	1	resolve	4
option	4	prior	4	resource	2
orient	5	priority	7	respond	1
outcome	3	proceed	1	restore	8
output	4	process	1	restrain	9
overall	4	professional	4	restrict	2
overlap	9	prohibit	7	retain	4
overseas	6	project	4	reveal	6
panel	10	promote	4	revenue	5
paradigm	7	proportion	3	reverse	7
paragraph	8	prospect	8	revise	8
parallel	4	protocol	9	revolution	9
parameter	4	psychology	5	rigid	9
participate	2	publication	7	role	1
partner	3	publish	3	route	9
passive	9	purchase	2	scenario	9
perceive	2	pursue	5	schedule	8
percent	1	qualitative	9	scheme	3
period	1	quote	7	scope	6
persist	10	radical	8	section	1
perspective	5	random	8	sector	1
phase	4	range	2	secure	2
phenomenon	7	ratio	5	seek	2
philosophy	3	rational	6	select	2
physical	3	react	3	sequence	3
plus	8	recover	6	series	4
policy	1	refine	9	sex	3
portion	9	regime	4	shift	3
pose	10	region	2	significant	1
positive	2	register	3	similar	1

simulate	7	survey	2	transport	6
site	2	survive	7	trend	5
so-called	10	suspend	9	trigger	9
sole	7	sustain	5	ultimate	7
somewhat	7	symbol	5	undergo	10
source	1	tape	6	underlie	6
specific	1	target	5	undertake	4
specify	3	task	3	uniform	8
sphere	9	team	9	unify	9
stable	5	technical	3	unique	7
statistic	4	technique	3	utilize	6
status	4	technology	3	valid	3
straightforward	10	temporary	9	vary	1
strategy	2	tense	8	vehicle	8
stress	4	terminate	8	version	5
structure	1	text	2	via	8
style	5	theme	8	violate	9
submit	7	theory	1	virtual	8
subordinate	9	thereby	8	visible	7
subsequent	4	thesis	7	vision	9
subsidy	6	topic	7	visual	8
substitute	5	trace	6	volume	3
successor	7	tradition	2	voluntary	7
sufficient	3	transfer	2	welfare	5
sum	4	transform	6	whereas	5
summary	4	transit	5	whereby	10
supplement	9	transmit	7	widespread	8

Subject vocabulary

Arts

abstract
acrylic
act
acting
acting area
actor
actor's position
actress
additive
aerial perspective
aesthetic
aesthetic criteria
aesthetics
analogous
animation
arbitrary color
art
art element
articulation
artist
assemblage
background
balance
ballet
blocking
body position
canvas
carve
center stage
ceramic
chalk
charcoal
classic
clay
cold reading
collage
color relationship
color theory
commedia dell'arte
complementary
composition
contour drawing
costume
creative drama
crisis
culture
dance
dance form
dance phrase
dancer
dance sequence
dance structure
dance study
denouement
denouement design
design
designer

director
downstage
drama
dramatic play
dramatic structure
dramaturg
draw
drawing
dress rehearsal
dynamic
easel
elements of art
Elizabethan theater
enact
epic theater
exhibit
exhibition
festival
figurative
film
fine art
focal point
folk
foreground
formal theater
gallery
genre
gesture drawing
graphics
Greek theater
ground
installation art
interpretation
isolation
jazz dance
Kabuki
labanotation
landscape
lead
level
linear perspective
line direction
line quality
maquette
marble
masterpiece
media
medium
mime
minstrel show
mixed media
mode
model
modern dance
monochromatic
monologue
mosaic
multimedia

museum
musicality
musical theater
negative
Noh
nonobjective
nude
oil painting
one-point
    perspective
organic
paint
painter
painting
pantomime
pastel
pattern
pencil
performance art
perspective
photograph
photography
picture
play
point of view
portfolio
positive
postmodern dance
pottery
prewriting
primary color
principle
printmaking
production values
projection
prop
proportion
proscenium
puppetry
reader's theater
rehearsal
rehearse
relief
repetition
retrograde
revival
rhythm
rising action
role
run
run-through
scenery
sculptor
sculpture
secondary color
sense memory
set
show

show business
sketch
social dance
solo
space
stage crew
stage left
stage manager
stage right
star
statue
stock character
studio
style
stylistic nuance
subject
subtractive sculpture
tableau
tap dance
texture
theater
theater of the absurd
theatrical
theatrical
    convention
theatrical experience
theatrical game
theme
three-dimensional
time
tint
tone
tour
transition
try
two-dimensional
unison
unity
upstage
value
value scale
variety
visual literacy
watercolor
wing
zoom

Business

account
acquisition
agency
agent
annuity
asset
bail
bankrupt
bankruptcy
book

broker
budget
capital
cartel
cc
client
collective
concession
consortium
contractor
corporate
corporation
crash
customer service
deal
depreciate
devalue
development
director
distribute
dividend
downturn
enterprise
entrepreneur
equal opportunity
equity
fiscal
foreclosure
foreign exchange
franchise
Inc.
income
income tax
inflation
inject
injection
interest
lay
liability
lose
management
manufacture
market
mass-produce
merger
monetary
monopoly
network
niche
online
operation
operator
partner
patent
people skills
pharmaceutical
premium
private

privatize
productivity
public sector
rate
real estate
receipt
refund
retail
retailer
revenue
ROI
run
salary
sale
sales clerk
salesman
salesperson
saleswoman
secretary
security
self-employed
sell
seller
share
shareholder
shipment
shipping
show business
staff
stock
stock exchange
stockholder
stock market
strike
subsidiary
superior
supplier
syndicate
take
takeover
tariff
tax
taxation
time management
trade
trademark
trader
transaction
treasury
trustee
turnover
undercut
union
wage
warehouse
warranty
wholesale
workforce

workplace
year

Geography
alluvial fan
alluvium
altitude
atlas
azimuthal projection
bay
canal
capital
catchment area
channel
coast
coastline
compass
continent
contour interval
contour line
country
delta
desert
divide
east
easterly
eastern
equator
equatorial
focus
fold
forest
front
funnel
geography
glacial
glacial drift
glacier
globe
gulf
gully
hemisphere
hill
island
lake
land
landform
landslide
latitude
load
longitude
map
mountain
mouth
north
northeast
northeastern
northerly

northern
northwest
northwestern
oasis
ocean
peninsula
plateau
polar
pole
port
prairie
promontory
rainforest
range
region
relief
reservoir
ridge
river
sand dune
savanna
scale
sea
shore
shoreline
slope
source
south
southeast
southeastern
southerly
southern
southwest
southwestern
stream
summit
temperate zone
time zone
topographic map
tributary
tropical
tropical zone
Tropic of Cancer
Tropic of Capricorn
tropics
tundra
valley
vent
village
west
westerly
western
wetland
world

Language Arts
abbreviation
accent

acknowledgment
active
active voice
acute accent
adjective
adverb
affix
alliteration
alphabet
alphabetic principle
anecdotal scripting
annotated
  bibliography
antagonist
antecedent
antonym
apostrophe
appendix
appositive
archetypal criticism
art criticism
article
author
autobiography
auxiliary
base word
bibliography
biography
blend
book
boundary
bracket
capital
chapter
character
clause
colloquial
colon
comedy
comma
comparative
complement
compound
conclusion
conditional
conjunction
consonant
consonant doubling
context clue
continuous
contraction
count
count noun
dash
decoding
definite article
definition
determiner

dialogue
dictionary
digraph
draft
drama
emphasis
English
epic
epilogue
essay
etymology
exclaim
exclamation point
exposition
expressive content
expressive writing
fable
fairy tale
feminine
fiction
figurative
folklore
foreword
form
future tense
gender
glossary
grammar
grammatical
hero
heroine
high-frequency word
homograph
homophone
hyperbole
hyphen
idiom
imperative
indefinite article
index
indirect object
infinitive
initial consonant
interrogative
intransitive
introduction
ironic
irony
irregular
journal
language
legend
legendary
letter
literal
literary analysis
literary criticism
literature

lower case
lyric
main clause
main idea
manuscript
masculine
metaphor
modal
moral
morphology
mystery
myth
narrate
narrative
negative
noncount noun
nonfiction
nonsense syllable
noun
novel
novelist
object
onomatopoeia
orthography
pacing
paragraph
parallelism
parody
participle
part of speech
passage
passive
past participle
past tense
perfect tense
period
person
phoneme
phonemic awareness
phonics
phonogram
phrasal verb
phrase
phrasing
playwright
plot
plural
poem
poet
poetry
possessive
preface
prefix
preposition
present continuous
present participle
present perfect
present tense

principal parts
prologue
pronoun
pronunciation
proper noun
prose
punctuation
punctuation mark
question mark
quotation
quotation mark
quote
r-controlled sound
read
reader
reading
recite
refer
reflexive pronoun
reflexive verb
regular
rewrite
rhetorical strategy
rhyme
romance
root word
rule
satire
scene
science fiction
script
semicolon
sense
sentence
serial
sight word
simile
singular
slash
speech marks
spell
spelling
spoken
standard American
  English
story
stress
subject
suffix
summary
superlative
syllabication
syllable
symbol
synonym
tense
text
theme

title
topic sentence
tragedy
transcript
transitive
upper case
verb
verbal
verse
visual metaphor
vocabulary
voice
vowel
word
word recognition
write
writer
writing

Math
absolute value
acute angle
add
addition
algebra
algebraic
algorithm
angle
area
arithmetic
arithmetic sequence
asymmetrical
asymptote
atomic number
average
axis
billion
binomial
binomial
   distribution
binomial theorem
calculate
calculation
centimeter
circle
circumference
complex number
compute
cone
congruent
cosine
cube
cubic
cylinder
decimal
decimal point
degree
diagonal

diameter
digit
dilation
dimension
divide
division
eight
eighteen
eighteenth
eighth
eightieth
eighty
eleven
eleventh
ellipse
equal
equal sign
equation
even
exponent
exponential function
factor
fifteen
fifteenth
fifth
fiftieth
fifty
figure
five
foot
formula
fortieth
forty
four
fourteen
fourteenth
fourth
fraction
gallon
geometric
geometric sequence
geometry
geothermal energy
gestation period
gram
graph
half
hemisphere
hexagon
hundred
hundredth
hypotenuse
inch
inclined plane
inequality
integer
irrational number
kg

kilo
kilogram
kilometer
km
lb.
linear equation
linear expression
liter
logarithm
math
mathematical
mathematics
mean
median
meter
metric
metric system
mg
mile
milligram
milliliter
millimeter
million
millionth
minus
ml
mm
mode
monomial
mph
multiply
negative
nine
nineteen
nineteenth
ninetieth
ninety
ninth
notation
number
oblong
odd
one
ounce
oval
oz.
parallel
pentagon
percent
percentage
perimeter
pie chart
pint
plus
polynomial
positive
pound
power

prime
prime number
probability
pyramid
qt.
quadratic function
quart
quarter
radius
range
ratio
rational number
real number
reciprocal
rectangle
rectilinear
right angle
rigid motion
root extraction
rotation
round
ruler
second
semicircle
seven
seventeen
seventeenth
seventh
seventieth
seventy
shape
similar
similarity
sine
six
sixteen
sixteenth
sixth
sixtieth
sixty
solve
square
square root
standard deviation
statistic
subscript
subtract
sum
symmetry
ten
tenth
third
thirteen
thirteenth
thirtieth
thirty
thousand
thousandth

three
time
ton
total
translation
transversal
triangle
trillion
twelfth
twelve
twentieth
twenty
two
two-point
  perspective
unit
unit fraction
variable
Venn diagram
volume
whole number
yard
zero
zeros of a function

Music
AB
ABA
accompany
accordion
aerophone
atonal
augmented interval
band
bar
bass
bass clef
bassoon
baton
beat
blue
bow
brass
canon
carol
cello
chimes
choir
chord
chordophone
chorus
clarinet
classical
clef
compose
composer
compound meter
concert

concerto
conduct
conductor
cymbal
descant
diminished interval
double bass
drum
duet
duo
duple meter
dynamic marking
elements of music
embellishment
ensemble
flat
flute
folk music
French horn
fugue
gong
gospel
guitar
guitarist
harmonic
  progression
harmony
harp
hip-hop
horn
hymn
idiophone
instrument
instrumental
interval
jazz
key
keyboard
lyric
major
major key
melody
meter
minor
minor key
mixed meter
mode
mouthpiece
music
musical
musical instrument
musician
notation
note
oboe
octave
opera
opus

orchestra
organ
ostinato
pentatonic scale
percussion
phrase
pianist
piano
piccolo
play
player
quartet
rap
read
record
recorder
reed
reggae
rhythm
rock
rock and roll
rondo
saxophone
scale
semitone
serial music
sharp
sing
singer
solfege
solo
sonata-allegro form
song
song form
soprano
soul
soul music
soundtrack
staff
string
stringed instrument
strum
suite
symphony
syncopation
tambourine
tempo
texture
theme and variation
time
tonality
tone poem
track
transition
treble clef
triad
trio
triple meter

trombone
trumpet
tuba
tune
twelve-bar blues
twelve-tone
viola
violin
wind instrument
woodwind
xylophone

Science
abdomen
abiotic
absolute dating
absolute magnitude
absolute zero
absorb
abyssal plain
acceleration
acid
acoustic
action
activation energy
active solar heating
active transport
adenine
air
air mass
air pollution
air pressure
air sac
algae
alien
alkali
alkali metal
alkaline
alkaline-earth metal
allele
alloy
alpha particle
altricial
alveolus
amnion
amoeba
amphibian
amplitude
amu
anaerobic
anaphase
anatomy
anemometer
angiosperm
animal
Animalia
annual ring
annular eclipse

antenna
anterior
anther
anticline
anus
aphelion
apparent magnitude
appendix
aqueous
aquifer
arachnid
Archaebacteria
Archimedes' principle
arête
artery
artesian spring
asexual reproduction
asteroid
asteroid belt
asthenosphere
astronaut
astronomical unit
astronomy
asymmetry
atmosphere
atmospheric perspective
atmospheric pressure
atom
atomic
atomic mass
atomic mass unit
ATP
atrium
attract
attraction
AU
avalanche
average speed
axial movement
axis
axon
backbone
bacteria
balance
balanced forces
bark
barometer
basalt
base
basket sponge
beach
beaker
beam
behavior
benign

benthic environment
benthos
Bernoulli's principle
beta particle
biceps
big bang theory
bilateral symmetry
bimetallic strip
binary fission
binomial nomenclature
biochemical
biogenetics
biological
biomass
biome
biosphere
biotechnology
biotic
black hole
bladder
blood
blood vessel
boiling point
bone
botany
bowel
box plot
Boyle's law
brain
breaker zone
breast
breathe
breed
bronchi
brooding
bud
budding
bulb
buoyant force
burn
calcium
caldera
calorie
calorimeter
canyon
cape
carbohydrate
carbon
carbon dioxide
carbon monoxide
cardiac muscle
cardio-
cardiovascular system
carnivore
carrying capacity
cartilage

cave
cell
cell cycle
cell division
cell membrane
cell theory
cellular
cellular respiration
cell wall
Celsius
Cenozoic era
central nervous system
centrifugal force
centripetal acceleration
centromere
cephalothorax
cerebellum
cerebrum
change
characteristic property
charge
Charles's law
chemical
chemical bond
chemical bonding
chemical change
chemical energy
chemical equation
chemical formula
chemical property
chemical reaction
chemical weathering
chemist
chemistry
chlorophyll
chloroplast
cholesterol
chromatid
chromosome
chromosphere
chrysalis
cilia
cinder cone
circadian rhythm
circuit
circulation
cleavage
cliff
climate
closed circulatory system
closed system
coarse adjustment
cochlea
cocoon

coefficient
coelom
coevolution
collarbone
colloid
colon
combustion
comet
command module
commensalism
community
compact bone
compacted
composite volcano
compound
compound eye
compound light microscope
concave lens
concentration
condensation
condensation point
conduct
conduction
conductor
cone
conic projection
conifer
connective tissue
conservation
conservation of energy
conservation of mass
consumer
continental drift
continental margin
continental rise
continental shelf
continental slope
contour
contour feather
control
controlled experiment
convection
convection current
convective zone
convergent boundary
convex lens
coordinate system
copper wire
core
Coriolis effect
corona
correlational design
cosmic background radiation
cosmology

cotyledon
covalent bond
covalent compound
crater
creep
crossing over
crystal
crystal lattice
cumulonimbus
cumulus
current
current electricity
curvature
cuticle
cyanobacteria
cycle
cyclone
cytokinesis
cytoplasm
cytosine
data table
daughter cell
deciduous
decompose
decomposer
decomposition
    reaction
deep current
deep ocean basin
deep-water zone
deflation
deformation
degree
dendrite
dense
density
dental
deposition
dermis
desalination
descriptive design
dew point
diaphragm
diatonic scale
dichotomous key
digest
dilute
dimensional analysis
dinoflagellate
discharge
dissect
dissolve
divergent boundary
DNA
DNA fingerprinting
DNA sequencing
dominant
double helix

double-replacement
    reaction
downdraft
down feather
drag
drainage basin
drug
ductility
dune
dwarf planet
dynamic
dysentery
dysfunction
dyspepsia
eardrum
earth
earthquake
echo
eclipse
ecological succession
ecology
ecosystem
ectotherm
effort force
egg
elastic rebound
electric
electrical charge
electrical energy
electric force
electricity
electromagnet
electromagnetic
electromagnetic
    spectrum
electromagnetic
    wave
electron
electron cloud
electron microscope
electrostatic
    discharge
element
elliptical galaxy
El Niño
embryo
emission
endangered species
endocrine
endocytosis
endoplasmic
    reticulum
endoskeleton
endotherm
endothermic
energy
energy conversion
energy efficiency

energy pyramid
energy resource
energy source
environment
environmentalist
enzyme
epidermis
epididymis
epithelial tissue
erupt
esophagus
estivation
Eubacteria
eugenics
euglena
eukaryotic cell
evaporate
evergreen
evolution
evolve
exocytosis
exoskeleton
exosphere
exothermic
expanded form
experiment
experimental design
extensor
external combustion
    engine
external fertilization
external fuel tank
extinct
extrusive
eyeball
eyepiece
Fahrenheit
fallopian tube
family
fault
fault block
fault-block
    mountain
feldspar
felsic
female
fertile
fertilize
fetus
fibrous root
filter
fin
fine adjustment
fir
fission
flagella
flash flood
flexor

flood plain
flow chart
folded mountain
foliated
follicle
food chain
food web
footwall
force
formation
formula
fossil
fossil fuel
fossil record
fracking
fragmentation
free fall
freeze
freezing
freezing point
frequency
friction
fulcrum
fungus
funnel
fusion
galaxy
gametophyte
gamma rays
ganglion
gap hypothesis
gas
gas exchange
gas giant
gene
generation time
genetic
genetically modified
genetic engineering
genetic
    fingerprinting
genetics
genome
genotype
genus
geological time scale
geology
geostationary
gill
gland
global warming
globular cluster
Golgi complex
gram
gravitation
gravitational
gravitational
    potential energy

gravitropism
gravity
Great Red Spot
greenhouse effect
greenhouse gas
green plant
groundwater
group
guanine
guard cell
gum
gut
gymnosperm
habitat
hail
half-life
Halley's comet
halophile
hanging valley
hanging wall
heart
heartbeat
heartworm
heat engine
hedgehog cactus
helium
herbivore
Hertzsprung-Russell
   diagram
heterogeneous
   mixture
hibernate
hibernation
high power lens
histogram
homeopathy
homeostasis
homogeneous
   mixture
homologous
hormone
horn
host
hot spot
H-R diagram
human being
Human Genome
   Project
humus
hurricane
hybrid
hydrocarbon
hydroelectric
hydroelectricity
hydrogen
hydropower
hypersensitive
hypertension

Ice Age
iceberg
ice wedging
ideal machine
igneous
immune system
imperial
implant
incisor
index contour
induction
inertia
infrared
inhibitor
inner core
input force
insulate
integumentary
   system
interference
internal combustion
   engine
internal fertilization
intrusive
invertebrate
ion
ionic bond
ionic compound
iris
irregular galaxy
irrigate
isotope
jaw
jet stream
joint
joule
Jupiter
kangaroo rat
karst topography
kg
kHz
kidney
kilo
kilocalorie
kilogram
kilohertz
kilowatt
kinesthetic
kinetic energy
Kuiper belt
kW
lab
lab apron
labor
laboratory
larynx
laser
lateral line system

launch pad
launch vehicle
lava
law
learned behavior
lens
life cycle
life science
light
light energy
light minute
lightning
light source
limiting factor
line graph
lipid
liquid
liter
lithosphere
littoral zone
live
liver
load
loam
lobotomy
locomotor
loess
loggerhead turtle
longitudinal wave
longshore current
lower mantle
low tide
lunar eclipse
lunar module
lung
lymph
lymphatic system
lymphatic vessel
lymph capillary
lymph node
lymphocyte
lysosome
mafic
magnet
magnetic
magnetic declination
magnetic field
magnetic pole
magnetic reversal
magnetism
main-sequence star
male
malleable
mammal
mammary
mammary glands
mandible
mantle

Mars
marsh
marsupial
mass
mass extinction
mass movement
mass number
mate
matter
mechanical
   advantage
mechanical energy
mechanical
   weathering
medulla
medusa
meiosis
melanin
melting point
membrane
membranophone
meniscus
Mercator projection
mercury
Mercury
mesosphere
Mesozoic era
metallic bond
metalloid
metamorphic
metaphase
meteor
meteoroid
meteorology
meter
methane
methanogen
metric
metric system
metric ton
mg
microbe
microclimate
microorganism
microscope
microscopic
microsecond
mid-ocean ridge
milk
milligram
mineral
mitochondrion
mitosis
mix
ml
Moho
molecular
molecule

molting
momentum
monocline
monotreme
monsoon
moon
moraine
motor neuron
mountain gorilla
mouth
movable pulley
movement pattern
mudflow
multicellular
multiple sclerosis
muscle
muscle tissue
muscular dystrophy
muscular system
musculoskeletal
mutagen
mutualism
natural gas
natural resources
natural selection
nature
neap tide
nebula
negative acceleration
nekton
Neptune
nerve
nervous
nervous tissue
net force
neurology
neuron
neutron
neutron star
newton
niche
nitrate
nitrogen
noble gas
nocturnal
nonfoliated
nonliving
nonmetal
nonpoint-source
   pollution
nonrenewable
nonsilicate mineral
nonstandard unit
nonvascular plant
normal fault
nostril
nuclear
nuclear energy

nuclear reactor
nucleic acid
nucleotide
nucleus
nutrient
objective lens
oceanography
ocean trench
omnivore
omnivorous
Oort cloud
open circulatory
   system
open cluster
open-water zone
opossum
optic
optic nerve
orbit
order
organ
organelle
organic
organic compound
organism
organ system
outer core
output force
ovary
ovule
oxygen
ozone
ozone layer
paleontology
Paleozoic era
Pangaea
parallax
parallel circuit
paramecium
parasite
parasitism
parent cell
partial eclipse
pascal
Pascal's principle
passive solar heating
passive transport
pathological
pathology
pelagic environment
pelvis
penis
perihelion
period
periodic law
periodic table
peripheral nervous
   system

permafrost
perpetual motion
   machine
Petri dish
petroleum
pH
pharynx
phase
phenotype
pheromone
phloem
phospholipid
photocell
photoreceptor
photosphere
photosynthesis
phototropism
photovoltaic
phylum
physical change
physical property
physical science
physics
phytoplankton
pie chart
pistil
placenta
placental mammal
planet
planetesimal
plankton
plant
Plantae
plasma
plate
plate boundary
platelet
plate tectonics
Pluto
point-source
   pollution
polar coordinate
polar easterlies
polar equation
polar zone
polio
pollen
pollinate
pollutant
polyp
porosity
positive acceleration
potential difference
potential energy
pouch
power
Precambrian
precipitation

precocial
predator
preen
pressure
prey
primary pollutant
prime meridian
prism
process
producer
product
prograde rotation
projectile motion
prokaryotic cell
prophase
prosimian
protist
Protista
proton
protozoan
pseudopod
psychology
psychrometer
pulmonary
   circulation
pulsar
pulse
Punnett square
P wave
pyroclastic material
quagga
quasar
radar
radial symmetry
radiation
radiative zone
radioactive
radioactive symbol
radio telescope
radio wave
rain
rainbow
rainfall
random variable
rarefaction
ray
react
reactant
reaction
reactor
read
reading
receptor
recessive
recombinant DNA
red blood cell
red giant
reef

reference point
refine
reflect
reflection
refract
refracting telescope
relationship
relative dating
relative humidity
remote sensing
reproduce
reproductive
resistance
resonance
resource recovery
respiration
respiratory system
response
resultant velocity
retina
retrograde orbit
retrograde rotation
reverse fault
revolution
rhizoid
rhizome
rib
rib cage
ribosome
rift
rift valley
RNA
rock
rock cycle
rocket
rock fall
rod
root hair
root system
rule
runner
runoff
rupture
salinity
saliva
salt
saltation
sand
sargassum
saturated
  hydrocarbon
saturated solution
Saturn
scalar matrix
scale
scalp
scattering
scatterplot

scavenger
science
scientific
scientific method
scientific notation
scientist
scrotum
scrubber
sea-floor spreading
seamount
secondary pollutant
secrete
secretion
sediment
sedimentary
seed
seed fern
segment
seismic
seismic gap
seismogram
seismograph
seismology
selective breeding
self-pollinating
semen
seminiferous tubule
sense
sensory neuron
sepal
series circuit
sex
sex cell
sex chromosome
sexual
sexually transmitted
  disease
sexual reproduction
shadow zone
shaft
shield volcano
shoot system
shuttle
side effect
signal
silica
silicate mineral
silicon
simple machine
single-replacement
  reaction
six kingdoms
skeletal muscle
skeleton
skin
skull
slide
smooth muscle

social behavior
sodium
soil
solar
solar eclipse
solar nebula
solar system
solid
solubility
soluble
solute
solution
sonic
sound energy
sound wave
space
spacecraft
space probe
spaceship
space shuttle
space suit
speciation
species
specific gravity
specific heat capacity
specimen
spectrum
speed
sperm
spinal cord
spine
spiral galaxy
spongy bone
spore
sporophyte
spring tide
stage
stamen
standing wave
star
starch
state
static
station model
stigma
stoma
stomach
stored energy
storm surge
stratification
stratified drift
stratosphere
stratum
streak
stress
subatomic
sublimation
subscript

substance
subtropical
sucker
sugar
sulfur
sun
sunspot
supercell
supergiant
supernova
surf
surface current
surface gravity
surface tension
surface-to-volume
  ratio
surface wave
suspension
S wave
sweat gland
swim bladder
symbiosis
syncline
synthesis reaction
systemic circulation
taiga
tapeworm
taproot
taxonomy
tectonic plate
telophase
terminal velocity
terrestrial planet
territory
testicle
testis
test tube
therapsid
thermal energy
thermal equilibrium
thermal expansion
thermal pollution
thermocline
thermocouple
thermosphere
thorax
throat
thymine
thymus
tidal bore
tidal range
tide
till
timbre
tissue
tornado
torsion
total eclipse

trace gas
trachea
trade wind
transform boundary
transistor
transmission
transpiration
transverse wave
tremor
tropical depression
tropical disturbance
tropical storm
tropism
troposphere
true-breeding
tsunami
tube worm
tumor
turbine
typhoon
ultrasonic
ultraviolet
umbilical cord
unbalanced forces
unicellular
universal gravitation
universe
unsaturated
 hydrocarbon
updraft
upper mantle
upwelling
uranium
Uranus
urethra
U-shaped valley
uterus
vacuole
vacuum
vagina
valence electron
vanishing point
vapor
vascular plant
vas deferens
vector
vegetative
 reproduction
vein
velocity
ventricle
Venus
vertebrate
vesicle
vestigial structure
virus
viscosity
volcanic

volcano
volt
voltage
wall cloud
warm-blooded
water cycle
waterfall
water power
waterspout
water table
water vapor
water vascular
 system
water wave
watt
wave
wave height
wavelength
wave period
wave speed
weather
weathering
weight
white blood cell
whitecap
white dwarf
wind
windpipe
womb
work
work input
work output
X-ray
xylem
zero
zinc
zoology
zooplankton
zygote

Social Studies
abolitionist
absentee
act
AD
African-American
allied
amendment
American
amnesty
ancestor
apartheid
archeology
artifact
assassinate
asylum
Australopithecine
autonomy

BC
big government
bill
Bill of Rights
bloc
border
boycott
budget
cabinet
capitalism
capitalist
capitol
carpetbagger
caste
cavalry
ceasefire
census
centralize
chamber
chancellor
charter
circumnavigate
citizen
civilization
civil rights
civil war
classic
coalition
Cold War
colonel
colonial
colonist
colonize
colony
commander
common ancestor
commonwealth
communism
communist
confederation
Congress
congressman
congresswoman
conquer
conservative
consortium
constituency
constituent
constitution
councilor
counterterrorism
country
coup
Cro-Magnon
cross-party
crown
culture
currency

Declaration of
 Independence
decree
defect
defendant
delegate
delegation
democracy
democrat
democratic
deploy
deport
depression
descendant
developing
dictator
dictatorship
discriminate
discrimination
dissident
doctrine
eastern
economics
economist
economy
elect
election
Electoral College
electoral vote
electorate
emancipate
embargo
emperor
empire
enact
envoy
espionage
ethnic
European
executive branch
exile
export
extremist
fascist
federal
federal government
federalism
federation
feminism
feminist
First Lady
folk
franchise
frontier
front line
general election
global economy
globalization

govern
government
governor
gross national
product
head of state
Hispanic
historian
history
holocaust
homeland
hominid
house
humanitarian
human rights
immigrant
impeach
imperial
imperialism
import
inaugurate
incumbent
indentured servant
independence
Indian
indigenous
industrial
industry
judicial
judicial branch
judiciary
king
kingdom
knight
labor
landslide
Latin American
law
left
left-wing
legacy
legislation
legislative
legislative branch
legislature
libel
macroeconomics
manifesto
map key
Marxism
Marxist
mayor
medieval
Member of
Parliament
microeconomics
Middle Ages
middle class

Middle East
migrant
migrate
militia
ministerial
Minuteman
monarch
monarchy
monopoly
monument
municipal
mythology
nation
nationalism
nationalist
nationality
Native American
naturalization
Neanderthal
neutral
noble
operative
oral history
oratorio
overpopulation
overthrow
overturn
pact
pardon
parish
parliament
parliamentary
pass
patriot
pentagon
petition
pilgrim
pioneer
policy
political
political party
politics
population
prehistoric
prejudice
president
primary
prime minister
progressive
prohibition
propaganda
prosecution
proslavery
public office
Puritan
queen
racism
rally

rank
ratify
rebel
rebellion
recession
Reconstruction
recuse
reelect
referendum
reform
refugee
regulate
rehabilitate
reign
relief
religious freedom
repel
represent
representation
representative
representative
government
republic
Republican
resolution
resource
revenue
revoke
revolt
revolution
revolutionary
right
right-wing
riot
Roman
rule
ruler
ruling
run
safeguard
sanction
secretary
Secretary of State
segregation
Senate
senator
sentence
settlement
settler
sharecropper
sheikh
sheriff
slavery
slave trade
slum
socialism
socialist
Social Security

social services
social studies
sociology
solicitor
sovereign
sovereignty
state
statesman
stratum
subculture
subject
suffragist
summit
superpower
Supreme Court
takeover
Tea Party
territorial
territory
testify
testimony
Third World
timeline
tipi
topple
totalitarian
transcontinental
railroad
treasury
treaty
trial
tribunal
try
unconstitutional
unemployment
unification
union
united
United Nations
unity
unrest
upper class
uprising
verdict
veto
Victorian
vote
warrior
wartime
western
White House
witch-hunt
witness
working class

Sports
ace
aerobics

athlete
athletics
backstroke
badminton
ball
ball game
ballpark
base
baseball
basket
basketball
bat
baton
batter
beat
bicycle
bike
box
boxing
breaststroke
captain
catch
catcher
champion
championship
cheerleader
climber
climbing
coach
course
court
crawl
cricket
cross
cross-country
cycle
cyclist
dart
defend
defender
defense
defensive
discus
dive
diving board
exercise
field
fighter
final
fish
fishing
fishing rod
football
for
foul
game
goal
goalkeeper

goalless
goalpost
golf
golf club
golf course
gym
gymnasium
gymnastics
halftime
heavyweight
high jump
hockey
hockey stick
horseback riding
horse racing
hurdle
ice hockey
in
javelin
jockey
jog
judo
karate
lane
lap
league
lightweight
long jump
major leagues
marathon
match
meet
mountain bike
net
Olympic
opponent
paddle
penalty
physical education
Pilates
pitcher
play
player
pro
push-up
quarterback
quarterfinal
race
racetrack
racing
racket
record
referee
relay
ride
rider
riding
ring

rink
roller-skate
round
row
rowboat
rugby
run
runner
runner-up
running
sail
sailboat
sailing
save
score
semifinal
shin pad
shoot
shot
shuttlecock
sideline
skate
skateboard
skatepark
ski
snooker
snowboarding
soccer
spectator
sport
sporting
sportsman
sportswoman
sprint
squad
squash
stadium
strike
striker
stroke
substitute
surf
surfboard
swim
swimming
swimming pool
tackle
team
teammate
tennis
tie
tournament
track
train
try
umpire
unbeaten
varsity

versus
volleyball
vs.
warm
warm-up
win
windsurfing
work
workout
wrestle
yoga

Technology
account
address
address book
analog
anti-virus
app
application
artificial intelligence
attachment
avatar
back
backup
big data
bit
blog
blogosphere
blogpost
bookmark
boot
broadband
browse
browser
bug
bulletin board
byte
camera phone
captcha
CD
CD burner
CD player
CD-ROM
cellphone
chat
chat room
click
cloud computing
code
command
compact disc
computer
corrupt
crash
crowdfunding
cursor
cut and paste

cyberbullying
cyberspace
data
database
delete
desktop
dialog box
dial-up
digital
disk
disk drive
document
domain name
double-click
down
download
downloadable
drag and drop
drop-down menu
DVD
DVD burner
DVD player
early adopter
e-book
e-card
electronic media
email
emoji
e-reader
exit
FAQ
feedback control
file
filename
file-sharing
flash drive
folder
format
forward slash
game console
gigabyte
graphics
hack
hands-free
hard disk
hard drive
hardware
HDTV
high-tech
home page
HTML
hybrid

hyperlink
icon
IM
inbox
infect
information
  technology
instant messaging
intelligent
Internet
intranet
ISP
I.T.
KB
key
keyboard
keyword
kilobyte
laptop
laser printer
link
liveblog
log
magnetic
mailbox
malware
megabyte
megapixel
meme
memory
memory card
memory stick
menu
message
message board
microchip
modem
mouse
mouse pad
MP3
MP3 player
navigate
net
netbook
network
newsgroup
notebook
offline
online
open
open-source
operating system

outlet
output
password
patch
paywall
PC
PDF
personal computer
phishing
pixel
plasma screen
podcast
pop-up
post
process
program
QR code
RAM
reboot
receiver
reconfigure
record
recording
relay
remote control
retweet
ringtone
satellite
satellite dish
satellite television
save
scalability
scan
scanner
screen
screensaver
screenshot
scroll
search engine
server
SIM card
site
site map
smartphone
social media
social networking
software
solar collector
source code
spam
speaker
speakerphone

spreadsheet
spyware
status bar
stereo
surf
tablet
taskbar
technology
telecommunications
text
texting
text message
text messaging
thermal imaging
thread
toolbar
touchless
touchscreen
touch-sensitive
transmission
transmit
tweet
unzip
upload
URL
USB
USB drive
username
video
video game
videotape
virtual
virtual reality
virus
wallpaper
wearable
web
Web 2.0
webcam
webcast
webinar
webmaster
web page
website
Wi-Fi
wiki
window
wireless
World Wide Web
WWW
zip

SUBJECT VOCABULARY

Visual thesaurus

This Visual thesaurus focuses on the 50 most over-used words in English and gives alternatives to help you develop fluency and creativity in your use of English.

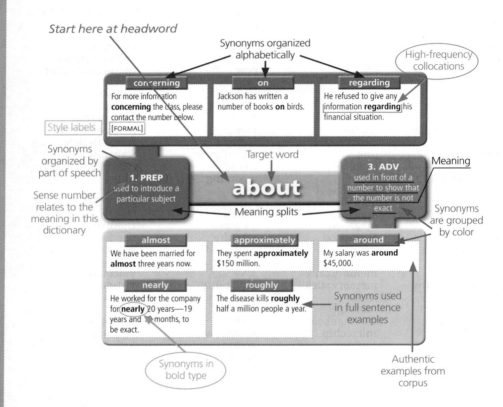

Start here at headword

Synonyms organized
alphabetically

High-frequency
collocations

concerning

For more information **concerning** the class, please contact the number below.
[FORMAL]

on

Jackson has written a number of books **on** birds.

regarding

He refused to give any information **regarding** his financial situation.

Style labels

Synonyms organized by part of speech

Sense number relates to the meaning in this dictionary

1. PREP
used to introduce a particular subject

Target word

about

Meaning splits

3. ADV
used in front of a number to show that the number is not exact

Meaning

Synonyms are grouped by color

almost

We have been married for **almost** three years now.

approximately

They spent **approximately** $150 million.

around

My salary was **around** $45,000.

nearly

He worked for the company for **nearly** 20 years—19 years and 19 months, to be exact.

roughly

The disease kills **roughly** half a million people a year.

Synonyms used in full sentence examples

Synonyms in bold type

Authentic examples from corpus

concerning	on	regarding
For more information **concerning** the class, please contact the number below. [FORMAL]	Jackson has written a number of books **on** birds.	He refused to give any information **regarding** his financial situation.

1. PREP
used to introduce a particular subject

about

3. ADV
used in front of a number to show that the number is not exact

almost	approximately	around
We have been married for **almost** three years now.	They spent **approximately** $150 million.	My salary was **around** $45,000.

nearly	roughly
He worked for the company for **nearly** 20 years—19 years and 10 months, to be exact.	The disease kills **roughly** half a million people a year.

bad

1. ADJ
not good or pleasant, or having harmful effects

damaging
Everyone knows that smoking is **damaging** to health.

nasty
I got a huge phone bill last month, which was a **nasty** surprise.

unhealthy
Try to avoid **unhealthy** foods with a lot of fat or sugar, such as hamburgers, fries and cookies.

unpleasant
There was a very **unpleasant** smell—like old milk or cheese—coming from the refrigerator.

2. ADJ
not of good quality

defective
The company promises to repair or replace any **defective** equipment.

faulty
The cause of the accident was **faulty** brakes.

inferior
She paid less but she got an **inferior** product.

poor
We were disappointed by the **poor** quality of the food.

7. ADJ
used for describing a pain, an injury or an illness that is extreme

acute
He was in **acute** pain and needed immediate treatment.

intense
The pain was so **intense**, I nearly fainted.

painful
Her toe was swollen and **painful** where she hit it.

serious
She suffered a **serious** head injury in the accident and was in the hospital for many months.

severe
From time to time, I get **severe** headaches that no painkiller can treat.

terrible
For months after the accident I had a **terrible** backache and couldn't walk.

8. ADJ
Bad language contains words that a lot of people find unpleasant and insulting.

obscene
I read some advice on how to deal with **obscene** phone calls.

offensive
They found his remarks extremely **offensive** and asked for an apology.

rude
The boys were telling **rude** jokes and laughing loudly.

poorly
Mendez accepted that his team played **poorly** and apologized to the fans.

terribly
She didn't study at all so she did **terribly** on her exams.

1. ADV
in a way that is not successful or effective

badly

2. ADV
If someone or something is **badly** hurt or **badly** affected, they are hurt or affected in an extreme way.

deeply
She liked him very much and was **deeply** saddened to hear the news of his sudden death.

desperately
With no friends or family near him, he was **desperately** lonely.

greatly
He will be **greatly** missed by all who knew and loved him. [FORMAL]

seriously
Carlos suffered a few cuts, but luckily, no one was **seriously** injured in the accident.

severely
A fire has **severely** damaged the school and parts of it will need to be rebuilt.

exceptional
Most of my teachers were pretty good but Peter Johnson was **exceptional**.

finest
Some consider him the **finest** actor alive today.

greatest
He was possibly the **greatest** player that ever lived.

leading
She is one of the **leading** artists of her generation.

outstanding
There is no one else like her—she is in every way an **outstanding** athlete.

3. ADJ
If one thing is **best**, it is better than all the others.

best

more desirable
People consider this a **more desirable** neighborhood so they pay more for houses here.

nicer
This is a much **nicer** restaurant than the one on Gresham Street.

preferable
For me, a trip to the supermarket will always be **preferable** to buying food on the Internet.

superior
If you want **superior** quality coffee, you have to pay a little more for it.

1. ADJ
a form of the adjective *good*, meaning "of a higher quality"

better

4. ADJ
if you are **better** after an illness or injury, you are not now ill or injured

healthy again
When you're **healthy again**, you'll be able to walk for longer.

recovered
Is Dan **recovered** from the flu?

well again
Get plenty of rest and you'll soon be **well again**!

enormous
She has an **enormous** house with eight or nine bedrooms.

giant
They have a **giant** TV screen that takes up most of one wall.

gigantic
The waves there are **gigantic** and great for surfing.

huge
Emily was wearing a **huge** hat that hid most of her face.

large
Can I have a **large** coffee and a chocolate muffin, please?

vast
Australia is a **vast** continent.

1. ADJ
large in size

big

2. ADJ
important or serious

crucial
This is a **crucial** decision and we have to get it right.

grave
These weapons are a **grave** danger to the world.
[FORMAL]

great
The **great** advantage of plastic is that it is strong.

major
Thousands of people are now without homes so this is a **major** problem.

urgent
They have an **urgent** need for food and water and will die without them.

crack
The plate **cracked** when I dropped it but I can still use it.

crumble
The wall was **crumbling** away in places and bits of stone lay on the ground.

demolish
They brought in machines to **demolish** the old houses and built new ones in their place.

smash
The gang used sticks and stones to **smash** windows.

snap
Matthew was so angry he **snapped** his pen in two.

split
The paper bag suddenly **split** and all the groceries fell onto the sidewalk.

1. VERB
When an object **breaks**, it becomes damaged or separates into pieces.

break

cry

"See you soon!" she **cried**, as she walked up the street.

cry out

"You're wrong, you're all wrong!" Henry **cried out**.

scream

Someone was **screaming**, "Help me!" at the top of their voice.

shout

He **shouted**, "Don't shoot!"

yell

"Eva, come back!" he **yelled**.

call back

I'm busy now—can I **call** you **back** later?

call up

When I'm in Pittsburgh, I'll **call** him **up**.

contact

Here's my cellphone number if you need to **contact** me for any reason.

phone

He **phoned** Laura to see if she was better.

1 5. VERB
If you **call** something, you say it in a loud voice.

1 6. VERB
If you **call** someone, you telephone them.

call

1 7. VERB
If you **call** somewhere, you make a short visit there.

call on

I thought I might **call on** Jane while I'm in town.

drop by

I'll **drop by** on my way home from work and give you the book.

drop in

If you're in the neighborhood, why not **drop in** for a cup of coffee?

visit

I thought I'd **visit** my brother for a day or two while I was in New York.

close

adjacent
We had **adjacent** rooms in the hotel so we went down to breakfast together.

handy
Make sure you have a pencil and paper **handy** so you can write down the number.

nearby
He was sitting at a **nearby** table and I could hear what he was saying.

on hand
There are experts **on hand** to give you all the help you need.

2 1. ADJ
Something that is **close to** something else is near to it.

2 2. ADJ
People who are **close** like each other very much and know each other well.

attached
Lena is very **attached** to her family and wouldn't want to leave them.

devoted
He was **devoted** to his wife and her death was a terrible shock to him.

friends
I still want to be **friends** with Alison, even though we disagree about this.

intimate
I told my plans to my **intimate** friends but I didn't tell my colleagues.

loving
My parents had a very **loving** relationship—it was a good marriage.

cry

break down
She **broke down** in tears when she heard the news.

sob
She heard the sound of someone **sobbing** in the next room.

weep
People **wept** openly as the princess's coffin was wheeled past them.

1. VERB
When you **cry**, tears come from your eyes.

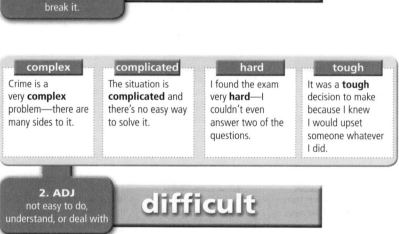

carve
He **carved** the whole statue from one piece of stone.

chop
Chop the pepper into small pieces.

pierce
Pierce the chicken with a sharp knife to check that it is cooked.

slice
Mom **sliced** the cake into ten even pieces.

split
Split the chicken in half, using a sharp knife.

1. VERB
If you **cut** something, you use something sharp to remove part of it, or to break it.

cut

complex
Crime is a very **complex** problem—there are many sides to it.

complicated
The situation is **complicated** and there's no easy way to solve it.

hard
I found the exam very **hard**—I couldn't even answer two of the questions.

tough
It was a **tough** decision to make because I knew I would upset someone whatever I did.

2. ADJ
not easy to do, understand, or deal with

difficult

eat

VERB
When you **eat** something, you put it into your mouth and swallow it.

chew
I couldn't answer him for a moment because I was **chewing** a mouthful of food.

consume
As a nation, we **consume** far too much fat and sugar. [FORMAL]

nibble
She **nibbled** at a piece of bread but was obviously not hungry.

snack
I don't eat lunch but I do **snack** on fruit throughout the day.

swallow
Polly took a bite of the apple and **swallowed** it.

end

1. NOUN
The **end of** a period of time or a story is the final point in it.

4. VERB
When an activity **ends**, or when you end an activity, it reaches its final point and stops.

climax
The evening reached a **climax** with a marvelous performance from the Spanish opera star.

conclusion
The Lakers won their last game 118-107 in an impressive **conclusion** to the season. [FORMAL]

ending
The film has a happy **ending** with the couple getting married.

finish
There was an exciting **finish** to the women's 800-meter race.

cease
Will the fighting never **cease**? [FORMAL]

complete
We hope to **complete** the project by January.

conclude
After a four-course dinner, the evening **concluded** with a speech from the president. [FORMAL]

give up
She had to **give up** her job in order to look after her husband.

quit
Quit talking now and do some work! [INFORMAL]

adore
I **adore** reading—it's the thing that I like doing most.

appreciate
Everyone can **appreciate** this sort of art—that's what's great about it.

be fond of
He's always **been** very **fond of** music.

like
Do you **like** swimming?

love
I really **love** cooking—it's my passion.

1. VERB
If you **enjoy** something, you take pleasure in doing it.

enjoy

dramatic
We watched **dramatic** scenes of the rescue on TV.

exhilarating
I find it **exhilarating** to cycle really fast.

sensational
This was a **sensational** victory for the young tennis player.

thrilling
It was a **thrilling** finish to the tournament and the fans went wild.

ADJ
making you feel very happy and enthusiastic

exciting

fat

1. ADJ weighing too much

chubby
A **chubby** little boy with round cheeks walked into the shop. [INFORMAL]

obese
Obese people often have health problems because they are carrying so much extra weight.

overweight
His doctor warned him that he was **overweight** and should go on a diet.

plump
Maria was small, **plump** and pretty.

funny

1. ADJ making you smile or laugh

2. ADJ strange and surprising

amusing
Dina told an **amusing** story about her last boss that made us all laugh.

comical
James looked very **comical** in his hat and I really had to stop myself from laughing.

hilarious
It was a **hilarious** film—I've never laughed so much in my life.

witty
I think you will enjoy Guy's company—he's very **witty**.

mysterious
A **mysterious** illness kept making him sick and his doctor didn't know what it was.

odd
His behavior was a little **odd** and it was worrying his parents.

peculiar
He has a rather **peculiar** sense of humor and some people don't understand it.

unusual
It's **unusual** for it to be this hot so early in the year.

weird
The other kids thought I was **weird** because I dressed differently.

acquire

The school has recently **acquired** some new sports equipment. [FORMAL]

earn

She **earns** $37,000 a year in her present job.

gain

Students can **gain** valuable experience by working during their vacations.

get hold of

It is hard to **get hold of** medicines in some areas of the country.

win

The first correct entry **wins** the prize.

2 **1. VERB**
If you **get** something, you buy it or obtain it.

get

2 **3. VERB**
If you **get** someone or something, you go and bring them to a particular place.

bring back

When you've finished with my books, could you **bring** them **back** from the office, please?

collect

We all walked around the forest **collecting** wood for the fire.

fetch

Sylvia **fetched** a towel from the bathroom and gave it to me.

pick up

If it's raining I'll **pick** you **up** in the car.

deliver

Only 90% of first-class mail is **delivered** on time.

donate

He **donates** large amounts of money to charity.

hand in

Our teacher told us to **hand in** our homework today but I haven't finished it yet.

provide

The company's website **provides** lots of useful information.

supply

The pipeline will **supply** Greece with natural gas.

1 **1. VERB**
If you **give** someone something, you let them have it.

give

1 **1. VERB**
If you **give** someone an object, you put it in their hand, so that they can take it.

hand

He **handed** me a piece of paper in the meeting.

hand out

My job was to **hand out** the prizes to the children.

pass

Could you **pass** me the book that's behind you, please?

present

The mayor **presented** him with a gold medal.

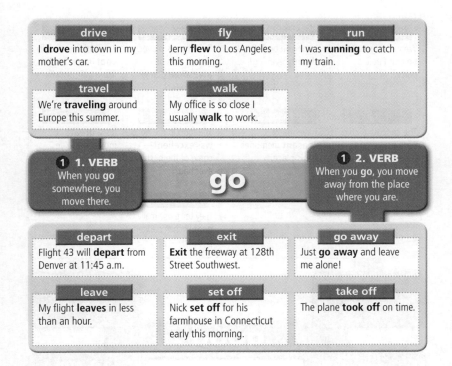

drive
I **drove** into town in my mother's car.

fly
Jerry **flew** to Los Angeles this morning.

run
I was **running** to catch my train.

travel
We're **traveling** around Europe this summer.

walk
My office is so close I usually **walk** to work.

1. VERB
When you **go** somewhere, you move there.

go

2. VERB
When you **go**, you move away from the place where you are.

depart
Flight 43 will **depart** from Denver at 11:45 a.m.

exit
Exit the freeway at 128th Street Southwest.

go away
Just **go away** and leave me alone!

leave
My flight **leaves** in less than an hour.

set off
Nick **set off** for his farmhouse in Connecticut early this morning.

take off
The plane **took off** on time.

VISUAL THESAURUS

great
We had a **great** time at Paolo's party.

lovely
Thank you both for a **lovely** evening!

nice
The chocolate-chip cookies were really **nice**.

pleasant
I have many **pleasant** memories of this place.

awesome
Both teams played well. It was an **awesome** game.
[INFORMAL]

cool
She had some really **cool** boots and I'd like a pair myself.
[INFORMAL]

excellent
The food in the hotel was **excellent**— some of the best I've ever had.

great
It's a **great** movie—you've really got to see it.

neat
They sell these really **neat** kitchen gadgets.
[INFORMAL]

1 1. ADJ enjoyable

1 2. ADJ of a high quality

good

2 1. ADJ A **good** place or time for something is a place or time that is acceptable or right for you.

2 3. ADJ If you are **good at** something, you can do it very well.

convenient
Would it be more **convenient** for you to meet closer to your office?

handy
It's very **handy** having a grocery store so close to the apartment.

suitable
What would be a **suitable** time to meet next week?

capable
She's a very **capable** teacher—I'm sure she'll be able to manage a couple of difficult kids.

competent
A **competent** driver should be able to deal with situations like these.

skillful
He was probably the most **skillful** player we've ever had on the team.

skilled
Of course an employer has to pay more for **skilled** workers.

talented
Both children are **talented** musicians.

great

1. ADJ
Great describes something that is very large.

big	enormous
They have a great **big** house on the East Coast.	It's an **enormous** apartment for one man!

gigantic	huge
There are **gigantic** rocks along the roadside.	A **huge** crowd of people gathered in the square.

massive	vast
It's only when you get near an elephant that you realize how **massive** it is.	We waste a **vast** quantity of food in this country.

2. ADJ
large in amount or degree

excessive	huge
It wasn't an **excessive** amount to spend on a coat.	She made a **huge** effort to come and see us, traveling five hundred miles or more.

immense	incredible
We still need to do an **immense** amount of work to get the job done.	He works an **incredible** number of hours—fifty or more a week.

massive	tremendous
She spends a **massive** amount of money on her appearance.	The students have all made **tremendous** progress and I'm really pleased with them.

3. ADJ
very important

major	serious
With so many people in this city, traffic is a **major** problem.	It's not a **serious** problem—we can easily fix it.

significant	
There has been a **significant** improvement in his work this semester.	

4. ADJ
very good

awesome	excellent
We had an **awesome** evening with you—thank you very much! [INFORMAL]	The food was **excellent**—I've never had better.

fantastic	superb
Sarah has a **fantastic** social life—she's out all the time. [INFORMAL]	There is a **superb** golf course 6 miles away.

terrific	wonderful
What a **terrific** idea! Let's do that.	It was **wonderful** to see them after all these years.

VISUAL THESAURUS

1061

happy

1. ADJ feeling good and satisfied

4. ADJ If you are **happy to** do something, you are willing to do it.

cheerful
Derek was always smiling and **cheerful**—nothing seemed to get him down.

content
She seems quite **content** with her life and doesn't want to change anything.

glad
I'm so **glad** you came!

pleased
I'm really **pleased** that we solved the problem.

content
Most days the old lady seemed **content** to sit and look out of the window.

pleased
I'd be **pleased** to take you there myself.

prepared
If you are **prepared** to wait, she will be able to see you in an hour.

ready
My parents have said they're **ready** to help if we need them.

high

3. ADJ being a long way above the ground

5. ADJ great in amount or strength

tall
It's a very **tall** building.

acute
You could see by his face that he was in **acute** pain.

excessive
Her spending on clothes was **excessive** and used up most of her money.

extreme
These people live in **extreme** poverty and don't even have enough to eat.

great
There is **great** pressure on these children to succeed.

intense
The **intense** heat of the midday sun made him sweat.

bang

Lucy **banged** on the table with her fist.

beat

They **beat** him, and left him on the ground.

knock

She went to Jonathan's apartment and **knocked** on the door.

punch

They claim that the singer **punched** the photographer after he took a photo of him.

slap

She **slapped** him hard across the face.

thump

Ramon **thumped** the table with his fist.

1. VERB
If you **hit** someone or something, you touch them with a lot of force.

hit

2. VERB
When one thing **hits** another, it touches it with a lot of force.

bump

She **bumped** her head on a shelf as she was getting up.

collide

The two cars **collided** at an intersection.

crash

The truck suddenly stopped and the car behind **crashed** into it.

knock

He **knocked** his leg against the corner of the table as he was walking past.

absorbing

It was such an **absorbing** book I couldn't put it down.

entertaining

I'd prefer to see something **entertaining** like a musical.

fascinating

Madagascar is such a **fascinating** place with all its wildlife.

intriguing

The situation sounds **intriguing**—I want to find out more about it.

ADJ
If something is **interesting**, you want to know more about it.

interesting

be aware	grasp	realize	see
I don't think his parents **are aware** of the problem.	The concepts are difficult to **grasp**.	People just don't **realize** how serious the situation is.	Oh, now I **see** what you're saying.

3. VERB
If you **know** something, you understand it.

know

chuckle	giggle	snigger
She **chuckled** to herself as she read the letter.	The girls were **giggling** in the back of the car.	I saw them **sniggering** as she walked past.

1. VERB
When you **laugh**, you make a sound while smiling because you find something funny.

laugh

barely

I was so tired, I could **barely** walk.

hardly ever

We **hardly ever** ate meat because it was so expensive.

not much

My husband was away on business most of the time so I did**n't** see him very **much**.

occasionally

Occasionally he behaves badly but most of the time, he's a very good little boy.

scarcely

There was so much smoke in the room, he could **scarcely** breathe.

seldom

Living so far apart, we **seldom** see each other.

1 **3. ADV**
not often or not much

little

2 **1. ADJ**
small in size

2 **2. ADJ**
not lasting long in time or distance

miniature

The toy house was filled with **miniature** chairs and tables.

minute

You only need a **minute** amount of glue.

short

My mother was very **short** but my father was quite tall.

tiny

She was holding a **tiny** baby who looked days old.

brief

It was just a **brief** visit because I had to be home at six o'clock.

hasty

Think it over. Don't make a **hasty** decision that you might regret.

quick

We had a **quick** lunch and got back to work.

short

If the restaurant is only a **short** distance away we can walk there.

swift

We need to make a **swift** decision because they are waiting for an answer.

endless	lengthy	prolonged
She was a very boring teacher and her classes seemed **endless**.	We had a lot to discuss so it was a fairly **lengthy** meeting.	We had a very **prolonged** period of wet weather— two or three weeks of non-stop rain.

1 1. ADJ
continuing for a lot of time

long

gaze

The young couple on the table next to us were **gazing** into each other's eyes.

glance

He **glanced** at his watch when she wasn't looking.

peer

He found her **peering** at a computer print-out, with a worried look on her face.

scan

She **scanned** the front page of the newspaper, looking for his name.

stare

We all spend too much time **staring** at computer screens.

watch

I **watched** her as she walked along the path.

hunt

Police are still **hunting** for clues at the victim's apartment.

search

Police have been **searching** for the men all night.

seek

They **seek** work in hotels and bars. [FORMAL]

1. VERB
If you look in a particular direction, you turn your eyes so that you can see what is there.

5. VERB
If you look for something or someone, you try to find them.

look

11. VERB
If you look a particular way, you have that appearance.

appear

He was lying on the sofa and **appeared** to be asleep.

seem

Yuko **seemed** happy enough when we met.

VISUAL THESAURUS

assemble

He works in a factory, **assembling** airplanes.

build

They're **building** a hotel next to the church.

construct

His company **constructed** an office building in Denver.

create

I've just **created** a new file.

manufacture

The company **manufactures** plastics.

produce

Together, these companies **produce** about 2.3 million tons of steel a year.

1 1. VERB
If you **make** something, you produce it, build it, or create it.

make

numerous

I called her **numerous** times but she never answered.

several

We've met on **several** occasions but he still can't remember my name.

various

I spent the day doing **various** jobs around the house.

1. DET
You use **many** to talk about a large number of people or things.

many

2. PRON
You use **many of** for talking about a large number of people or things.

a lot of

A lot of these houses have been built in the last ten years.

lots of

Lots of my friends have left town.

masses of

There were **masses of** people at the concert. [INFORMAL]

plenty of

She has **plenty of** clothes.

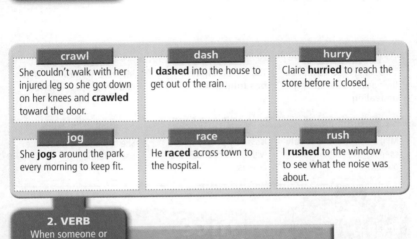

mark

1. NOUN
a small area of dirt or damage on something

bruise
I had a **bruise** on my cheek where the bar hit me.

patch
His hair was dark but there was a small **patch** of gray on one side.

scar
He had a **scar** on his hand where he cut himself a few years back.

scratch
He had **scratches** on his arm where the cat got him.

spot
There were a few **spots** of paint on the floor.

stain
I washed this shirt but I can't seem to remove these blood **stains**.

move

2. VERB
When someone or something **moves**, they change their position or go to a different place.

crawl
She couldn't walk with her injured leg so she got down on her knees and **crawled** toward the door.

dash
I **dashed** into the house to get out of the rain.

hurry
Claire **hurried** to reach the store before it closed.

jog
She **jogs** around the park every morning to keep fit.

race
He **raced** across town to the hospital.

rush
I **rushed** to the window to see what the noise was about.

VISUAL THESAURUS

brand-new
There was a **brand-new** car in the driveway.

fresh
The next morning she saw **fresh** tire tracks in the snow.

latest
These stores only sell the **latest** fashions.

recent
It's a pretty **recent** movie— it's been out three or four months.

up-to-date
Their problem is they don't have **up-to-date** technology.

1. ADJ
made or invented a very short time ago

new

appealing
These long beaches with their golden sand are very **appealing**.

beautiful
This is probably the most **beautiful** town I've ever seen.

charming
My father was a very **charming** man—everyone liked him.

lovely
Mia, thank you for a **lovely** evening! We really enjoyed ourselves.

pretty
It's a very **pretty** village with all its cottages and flowers.

sweet
She had a very **sweet** little baby with her.

1. ADJ
attractive, pleasant, or enjoyable

nice

ancient
Parts of this city go back thousands of years to **ancient** times.

elderly
They were an **elderly** couple in their seventies.

1. ADJ
Someone who is **old** has lived for a long time.

old

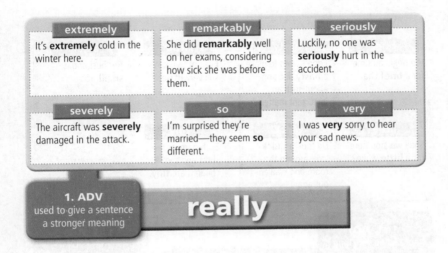

extremely
It's **extremely** cold in the winter here.

remarkably
She did **remarkably** well on her exams, considering how sick she was before them.

seriously
Luckily, no one was **seriously** hurt in the accident.

severely
The aircraft was **severely** damaged in the attack.

so
I'm surprised they're married—they seem **so** different.

very
I was **very** sorry to hear your sad news.

1. ADV
used to give a sentence a stronger meaning

really

VISUAL THESAURUS

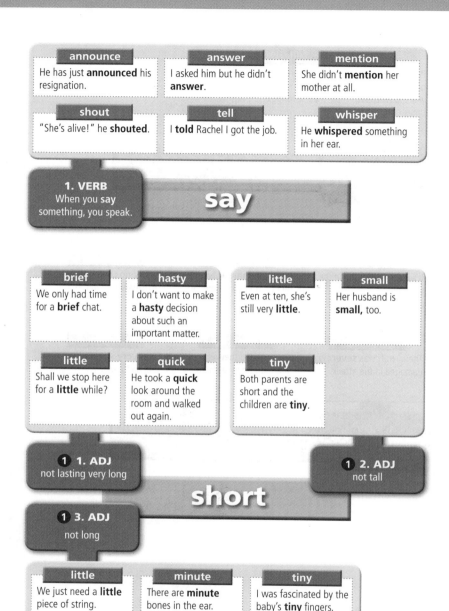

announce
He has just **announced** his resignation.

answer
I asked him but he didn't **answer**.

mention
She didn't **mention** her mother at all.

shout
"She's alive!" he **shouted**.

tell
I **told** Rachel I got the job.

whisper
He **whispered** something in her ear.

1. VERB
When you **say** something, you speak.

say

brief
We only had time for a **brief** chat.

hasty
I don't want to make a **hasty** decision about such an important matter.

little
Even at ten, she's still very **little**.

small
Her husband is **small,** too.

little
Shall we stop here for a **little** while?

quick
He took a **quick** look around the room and walked out again.

tiny
Both parents are short and the children are **tiny**.

1 1. ADJ
not lasting very long

1 2. ADJ
not tall

short

1 3. ADJ
not long

little
We just need a **little** piece of string.

minute
There are **minute** bones in the ear.

tiny
I was fascinated by the baby's **tiny** fingers.

VISUAL THESAURUS

little	minute	tiny
She bought a nice **little** cottage in the country.	You only need a **minute** amount of glue.	I bought a **tiny** sweater for the baby.

1. ADJ not large	**small**	**3. ADJ** not very serious or important

minor	slight	trivial	insignificant
We just made one or two **minor** changes to the document.	There has been a **slight** increase in sales but not as much as we hoped.	It's a very **trivial** matter and I can't understand why they are so upset about it.	In 1949, it was a small, **insignificant** city where nothing much happened.

frequently	now and then	occasionally	often
Here is a list of **frequently** asked questions.	I see her **now and then** when she's in town but it's usually only once or twice a year.	We **occasionally** go to the movies but not as much as we used to.	I **often** see Tom on my way into work.

ADV on some occasions but not all the time	**sometimes**

athletic
He comes from an **athletic** family—they're all runners.

broad
He has very **broad** shoulders.

bold
You have to be **bold** and ask your boss for more money.

determined
He is **determined** to win gold at the Olympics.

firm
Al has a very **firm** handshake.

muscular
Jordan was tall and **muscular** and a great athlete.

firm
She was **firm** with him. "I don't want to see you again."

tough
You have to be **tough** in business to get what you want.

powerful
She noticed the **powerful** muscles in his legs as he ran.

1. ADJ
Someone who is **strong** healthy with good muscles.

2. ADJ
Someone who is **strong** is confident and determined.

strong

3. ADJ
Strong objects or materials do not break easily.

8. ADJ
A **strong** drink, chemical, or drug contains a lot of the substance that makes it work.

durable
Metal is a very **durable** material and it won't bend easily.

solid
The walls are made from **solid** concrete blocks.

effective
These new drugs are very **effective** against this disease.

tough
The meat was **tough** and I couldn't cut it.

powerful
This is a very **powerful** substance and it should be used in small quantities.

sure

1. ADJ certain

confident
We are doing really well and I am **confident** that we will succeed.

definite
They thought he was guilty but they didn't have any **definite** proof.

convinced
She was **convinced** she was right and nothing would make her change her mind.

positive
"Are you sure she said eight o'clock?"— "**Positive**."

thin

1. ADJ having a small distance between one side and the other

2. ADJ A **thin** person or an animal has no extra fat on their body.

fine
He noticed the **fine** hairs on her arms.

narrow
The streets were too **narrow** to drive along.

transparent
The scarf was made of an almost **transparent** material.

slim
She was an attractive woman—tall and **slim**.

skinny
It's nice to be slim but you don't want to be **skinny**. [INFORMAL]

light
I'd like to be a few pounds **lighter**.

slender
She was tall and **slender**, like a dancer.

slight
She was small and **slight**—a delicate little girl.

very

1. ADV
used before an adjective to make it stronger

extremely
I'm **extremely** fond of her and I would hate to see her go.

really
It's a **really** good movie—you must see it.

remarkably
The book was **remarkably** successful, selling thousands of copies in its first week.

so
He's **so** tall—I can't believe how much he's grown!

truly
This is a **truly** great achievement.

walk

1. VERB
When you **walk**, you move forward by putting one foot in front of the other.

creep
He **crept** softly up the stairs, hoping she wouldn't hear him.

hike
We **hiked** through the Fish River Canyon.

march
Soldiers were **marching** down the street.

pace
As they waited, Kravis **paced** the room nervously.

stride
The farmer came **striding** across the field, with an angry look on his face.

wander
I **wandered** around the town, with no clear purpose.

broad	extensive	thick
He looks strong with those **broad** shoulders.	The ad described it as "a four-bedroom house with **extensive** gardens."	She cut two **thick** slices of bread.

1. ADJ
measuring a large distance from one side to the other

wide

Credits

Illustrations:

Higgins Bond: pp. 176, 323, 329, 352, 388, 407, 435, 462, 494, 610, 757, 911: © Higgins Bond/Anita Grien

Richard Carbajal: pp. 32, 150, 155, 262, 301, 323, 516, 550, 766, 825, 919 (bottom): ©Richard Carbajal/ illustrationOnLine.com

Ron Carboni: pp. 112, 134, 166, 253, 340, 520, 759, 784 (bottom), 865: ©Ron Carboni/Anita Grien

Todd Daman: pp. 20, 75: ©Todd Daman/illustrationOnLine.com

Dick Gage: pp. 84, 98, 265: ©Dick Gage/illustrationOnLine.com

Patrick Gnan: pp. 29, 279, 452, 546, 576, 579, 624, 719, 870: ©Patrick Gnan/illustrationOnLine.com

Sharon and Joel Harris: pp. 91 (top and bottom), 203, 228, 333, 383, 561, 709: ©Sharon and Joel Harris/ illustrationOnLine.com

Philip Howe: pp. 116, 302, 553, 601, 737, 941: ©Philip Howe/illustrationOnLine.com

Robert Kayganich: pp. 67, 70, 84, 99, 225, 266 (top), 271, 400, 468, 527, 741, 805, 827, 953: ©Robert Kayganich/illustrationOnLine.com

Robert Kemp: pp. 178, 275, 371, 466: ©Robert Kemp/illustrationOnLine.com

Stephen Peringer: pp. 182, 223, 259, 268, 332, 355: ©Stephen Peringer/illustrationOnLine.com

Alan Reingold: pp. 195, 254, 381: ©Alan Reingold /Anita Grien

Mark Ryan: pp. 754, 785 (bottom) 919 (top): ©Mark Ryan/illustrationOnLine.com

Simon Shaw: pp. 81, 88, 272, 486, 617, 680: ©Simon Shaw/illustrationOnLine.com

Daniel M. Short: pp. 280: ©Daniel M. Short

Gerard Taylor: pp. 18, 73, 307, 441, 789, 927, 927 (top and bottom): ©Gerard Taylor/illustrationOnLine.com

Ralph Voltz: pp. 45, 69, 308, 365, 409, 517, 522, 588, 782, 850: ©Ralph Voltz/illustrationOnLine.com

Cam Wilson: pp. 184, 239, 263, 278, 330, 339, 373, 459, 509, 615, 785 (top), 817, 886: ©Cam Wilson/ illustrationOnLine.com

Photos:

120: AlfvanBeem/Wikimedia CC0 1.0
121: Dick Gage/Wikimedia
264: Yamaguchi/Wikimedia CC by-SA 3.0
396: The Yorck Project/Wikimedia
656: *The Graphic*, June 30, 1877, p617/Wikimedia
878: paukrus/Wikimedia CC by-SA 2.0
881: Comstock/Getty
920: Library of Congress/Wikimedia

5: Evgeny Murtola/Shutterstock
21: (top) Michael G Smith/Shutterstock
21: (bottom) Brian Senic/Shutterstock
23: Elmarie Dreyer/Shutterstock
30: Stephen Coburn/Shutterstock
31: (top) chaoss/Shutterstock
31: (bottom) g-stockstudio/Shutterstock
35: Labanmax/Shutterstock
41: Andrei Zveaghintev/Shutterstock
42: Jonas Jensen/Shutterstock
43: (left) Fabio Mancino Photography/Shutterstock
43: (middle) Nadezda Zavitaeva/Shutterstock
43: (bottom) saiko3p/Shutterstock
46: (left) Noel Powell/Shutterstock
46: (right) Oleg Golovnev/Shutterstock
52: UniqueLight/Shutterstock
63: aleksandr hunta/Shutterstock
64: OHishiapply/Shutterstock
67: Dja65/Shutterstock
70: jakit17/Shutterstock
73: Ekaterina Lin/Shutterstock
73: CLFProductions/Shutterstock
77: Madeleine Openshaw/Shutterstock
78: Karkas/Shutterstock
78: TRINACRIA PHOTO/Shutterstock
86: oatfeelgood/Shutterstock
91: marekusz/Shutterstock
92: Steven Coling/Shutterstock
93: Rodionov/Shutterstock
96: yingthun/Shutterstock
101: Pal Teravagimov/Shutterstock
104: DenisNata/Shutterstock
105: vnlit/Shutterstock
111: svetlovskiy/Shutterstock
117: Monkey Business Images/Shutterstock
118: Joel Blit/Shutterstock
120: Paul Brennan/Shutterstock.com
122: Eric Isselee/Shutterstock
125: guillermo77/Shutterstock

125: Eric Isselee/Shutterstock
128: Alexey Boldin/Shutterstock
137: vvoe/Shutterstock
138: Aman Ahmed Khan/Shutterstock
138: sonya etchison/Shutterstock
140: elnavegante/Shutterstock
142: abramsdesign/Shutterstock
143: Kritchanut/Shutterstock
143: bikeriderlondon/Shutterstock
143: John Gomez/Shutterstock
143: Songquan Deng/Shutterstock
143: Natursports/Shutterstock.com
143: Rena Schild/Shutterstock.com
145: Tikta Alik/Shutterstock
147: Matteo Chinellato/Shutterstock.com
150: Yelena Panyukova/Shutterstock
167: Pavel L Photo and Video/Shutterstock
183: stockcreations/Shutterstock
189: ekler/Shutterstock
192: Skalapendra/Shutterstock
196: Lipsky/Shutterstock
197: James Steidl/Shutterstock
198: Zurijeta/Shutterstock
199: Whiteaster/Shutterstock
200: Cynthia Farmer/Shutterstock
200: catalin eremia/Shutterstock
205: Wasan Srisawat/Shutterstock
206: nicolasdecorte/Shutterstock
206: Lorraine Swanson/Shutterstock
206: Daxiao Productions/Shutterstock
206: Igor Bulgarin/Shutterstock.com
206: dfo28/Shutterstock.com
206: Emena/Shutterstock.com
206: Anky/Shutterstock.com
230: Nordroden/Shutterstock
231: Ljupco Smokovski/Shutterstock
232: Scott Richardson/Shutterstock
235: Jeroen van den Broek/Shutterstock
236: mTaira/Shutterstock.com
247: (left) Ariel Bravy/Shutterstock
247: (right) Sparkling Moments Photography/
  Shutterstock
248: (top) Studio 37/Shutterstock
248: (bottom) David Eby/Shutterstock
249: Matej Kastelic/Shutterstock
254: Galushko Sergey/Shutterstock
256: pics721/Shutterstock
266: BelleMedia/Shutterstock

Credits

Credits

Words to remember

Word:

Definition:

Sentence:

Word:

Definition:

Sentence:

Word:

Definition:

Sentence:

Words to remember

Word:

Definition:

Sentence:

Word:

Definition:

Sentence:

Word:

Definition:

Sentence:

Words to remember

Word:

Definition:

Sentence:

Word:

Definition:

Sentence:

Word:

Definition:

Sentence:

Words to remember

Word:

Definition:

Sentence:

Word:

Definition:

Sentence:

Word:

Definition:

Sentence:

Words to remember

Word:

Definition:

Sentence:

Word:

Definition:

Sentence:

Word:

Definition:

Sentence:

Words to remember

Word:

Definition:

Sentence:

Word:

Definition:

Sentence:

Word:

Definition:

Sentence: